W9-BSR-801

RAND McNALLY

WORLD ATLAS

RAND McNALLY

CONTENTS

USING THE ATLAS .... **I·3 – I·4**

WORLD PATTERNS .... **I·5 – I·16**
World Terrain .... I·6 – I·7
World Climate .... I·8 – I·9
World Vegetation .... I·10 – I·11
World Population .... I·12 – I·13
World Environments .... I·14 – I·15
World Time Zones .... I·16

REFERENCE MAPS .... **1 – 128**
Map Symbols and Index Map 1
World .... 2 – 3

Europe .... **4 – 5**
Scandinavia 6
British Isles 7
Central Europe .... 8 – 9
France and the Alps .... 10 – 11
Spain and Portugal .... 12 – 13
Italy .... 14 – 15
Southeastern Europe .... 16 – 17
Baltic and Moscow Regions .... 18 – 19

Asia .... **20 – 21**
Northwest Asia .... 22 – 23
Northeast Asia .... 24 – 25
China, Japan, and Korea .... 26 – 27
Eastern and Southeastern China .... 28 – 29
Japan .... 30 – 31
Southeastern Asia .... 32 – 33
Myanmar, Thailand, and Indochina 34 – 35
India and Pakistan 36
Southern India and Sri Lanka 37
Northern India and Pakistan .... 38 – 39
Eastern Mediterranean Lands 40

Africa **41**
Northern Africa .... 42 – 43
Southern Africa .... 44 – 45
Eastern Africa and Middle East 46

Antarctica **47**

Pacific Ocean .... **48 – 49**

Australia .... **50 – 51**
New Zealand 52

South America **53**
Northern South America .... 54 – 55
Southern South America 56
Southeastern Brazil 57
Colombia, Ecuador, Venezuela, and Guyana .... 58 – 59

Atlantic Ocean **60**

North America **61**
Mexico .... 62 – 63
Central America and the Caribbean .... 64 – 65

Canada .... ***66 – 67***
Alberta 68
British Columbia 69
Manitoba 70
New Brunswick, Nova Scotia, and Prince Edward Island 71
Newfoundland 72
Ontario 73
Quebec 74
Saskatchewan 75

United States of America .... ***76 – 77***
Alabama 78
Alaska 79
Arizona 80
Arkansas 81
California 82
Colorado 83
Connecticut 84
Delaware 85
Florida 86
Georgia 87
Hawaii 88
Idaho 89
Illinois 90
Indiana 91
Iowa 92
Kansas 93
Kentucky 94
Louisiana 95
Maine 96
Maryland 97
Massachusetts 98
Michigan 99
Minnesota 100
Mississippi 101
Missouri 102
Montana 103
Nebraska 104
Nevada 105
New Hampshire 106
New Jersey 107
New Mexico 108
New York 109
North Carolina 110
North Dakota 111
Ohio 112
Oklahoma 113
Oregon 114
Pennsylvania 115
Rhode Island 116
South Carolina 117
South Dakota 118
Tennessee 119
Texas 120
Utah 121
Vermont 122
Virginia 123
Washington 124
West Virginia 125
Wisconsin 126
Wyoming 127

North Polar Regions **128**

INDEX TO REFERENCE MAPS .... **129 – 192**

WORLD GEOGRAPHICAL TABLES .... **193 – 215**
World Political Information .... 193 – 196
General Information 197
Principal Mountains 198
World Oceans, Seas, Gulfs, Lakes, Rivers, and Islands 199
World Populations .... 200 – 215

UNITED STATES GEOGRAPHICAL TABLES .... **216 – 240**
United States General Information 216

United States Populations and Zip Codes .... **217 – 240**
Latest 1990 Census Information

Library of Congress Catalog Card Number: 96-68366

USING THE ATLAS

Maps and Atlases

Satellite images of the world (figure 1) constantly give us views of the shape and size of the earth. It is hard, therefore, to imagine how difficult it once was to ascertain the look of our planet. Yet from early history we have evidence of humans trying to work out what the world actually looked like.

Twenty-five hundred years ago, on a tiny clay tablet the size of a hand, the Babylonians inscribed the earth as a flat disk (figure 2) with Babylon at the center. The section of the Cantino map of 1502 (figure 3) is an example of a *portolan* chart used to chart the newly discovered Americas. The maps in this atlas show the detail and accuracy that cartographers are now able to achieve.

In 1589 Gerardus Mercator used the word "atlas" to describe a collection of maps. Atlases now bring together not only a variety of maps, but an assortment of tables and other reference material as well. They have become a unique and indispensable reference for graphically defining the world and answering the question, "Where?" With them, routes between places can be traced, trips planned, distances measured, places imagined, and our earth visualized.

FIGURE 1

FIGURE 2

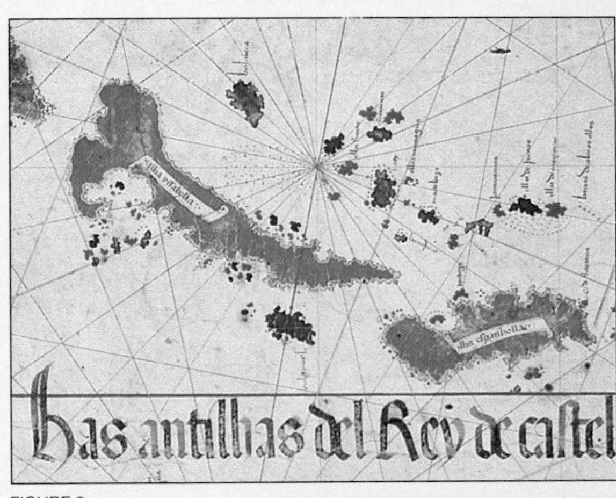

FIGURE 3

Sequence of the Maps

The world is made up of seven major landmasses: the continents of Europe, Asia, Africa, Antarctica, Australia, South America, and North America. The maps in this atlas follow this continental sequence. To allow for the inclusion of detail, each continent is broken down into a series of maps, and this grouping is arranged so that as consecutive pages are turned, a successive part of the continent is shown. Larger-scale maps are used for regions of greater detail or for areas of global significance.

Getting the Information

To realize the potential of an atlas the user must be able to:

1. Find places on the maps
2. Measure distances
3. Determine directions
4. Understand map symbols

Finding Places

One of the most common and important tasks facilitated by an atlas is finding the location of a place in the world. A river's name in a book, a city mentioned in the news, or a vacation spot may prompt your need to know where the place is located. The illustrations and text below explain how to find Yangon (Rangoon), Myanmar (Burma).

Yanohong, China	B9	28
Yandoon, Mya.	F3	34
Yangjiang, China	G9	26
Yangon (Rangoon), Mya.	B2	32
Yangquan, China	D9	26
Yangtze see Chang, stm., China	E10	26
Yangzhou, China	C8	28

FIGURE 4

1. Look up the place-name in the index at the back of the atlas. Yangon, Myanmar can be found on the map on page 32, and it can be located on the map by the letter-number key *B2* (figure 4). If you know the general area in which a place is found, you may turn directly to the appropriate map and use the special marginal index.

2. Turn to the map of Southeastern Asia found on page 32. Note that the letters *A* through *H* and the numbers *1* through *11* appear in the margins of the map.

3. To find Yangon on the map, place your left index finger on *B* and your right index finger on *2*. Move your left finger across the map and your right finger down the map. Your fingers will meet in the area in which Yangon is located (figure 5).

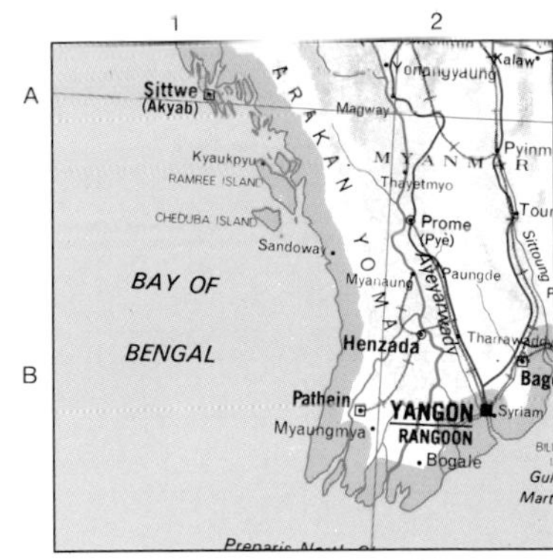

FIGURE 5

Measuring Distances

When planning trips, determining the distance between two places is essential, and an atlas can help in travel preparation. For instance, to determine the approximate distance between Paris and Rouen, France, follow these three steps:

1. Lay a slip of paper on the map on page 10 so that its edge touches the two cities. Adjust the paper so one corner touches Rouen. Mark the paper directly at the spot where Paris is located (figure 6).

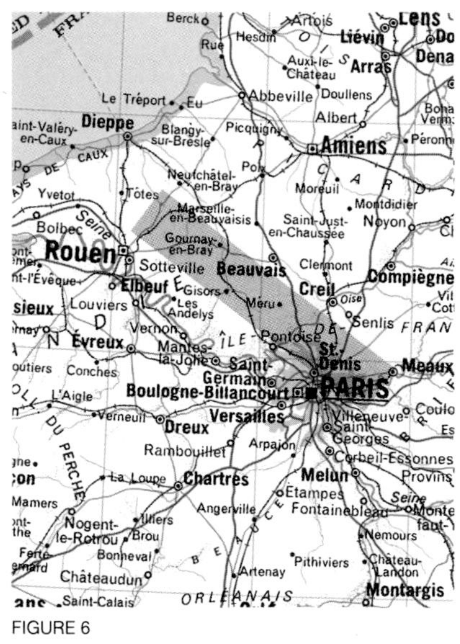

FIGURE 6

2. Place the paper along the scale of miles beneath the map. Position the corner at 0 and line up the edge of the paper along the scale. The pencil mark on the paper indicates Rouen is between 50 and 100 miles from Paris (figure 7).

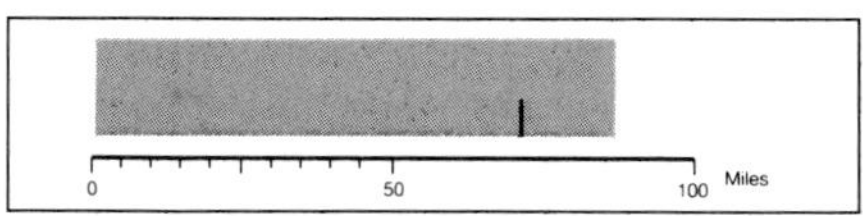

FIGURE 7

3. To find the exact distance, move the paper to the left so that the pencil mark is at 100 on the scale. The corner of the paper stands on the fourth 5-mile unit on the scale. This means that the two towns are 50 plus 20, or 70 miles apart (figure 8).

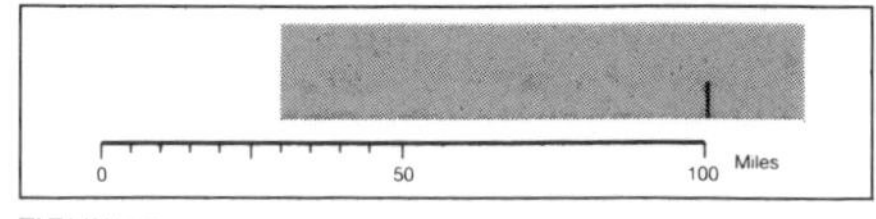

FIGURE 8

Determining Directions

Most of the maps in the atlas are drawn so that when oriented for normal reading, north is at the top of the map, south is at the bottom, west is at the left, and east is at the right. Most maps have a series of lines drawn across them—the lines of *latitude* and *longitude*. Lines of latitude, or *parallels* of latitude, are drawn east and west. Lines of longitude, or *meridians* of longitude, are drawn north and south (figure 9).

Parallels and meridians appear as either curved or straight lines. For example, in the section of the map of Europe (figure 10) the parallels of latitude appear as curved lines. The meridians of longitude are straight lines that come together toward the top of the map. Latitude and longitude lines help locate places on maps. Parallels of latitude are numbered in degrees north and south of the *Equator*. Meridians of longitude are numbered in degrees east and west of a line called the *Prime Meridian*, running through Greenwich, England, near London. Any place on earth can be located by the latitude and longitude lines running through it.

To determine directions or locations on the map, you must use the parallels and meridians. For example, suppose you want to know which is farther north, Bergen, Norway, or Norrköping, Sweden. The map (figure 10) shows that Norrköping is south of the 60° parallel of latitude and Bergen is north of it. Bergen is farther north than Norrköping. By looking at the meridians of longitude, you can determine which city is farther east. Bergen is approximately 5° east of the 0° meridian (Prime Meridian), and Norrköping is more than 15° east of it. Norrköping is farther east than Bergen.

FIGURE 10

Understanding Map Symbols

In a very real sense, the whole map is a symbol, representing the world or a part of it. It is a reduced representation of the earth; each of the world's features—cities, rivers, etc.—is represented on the map by a symbol. Map symbols may take the form of points, such as dots or squares (often used for cities, capital cities, or points of interest), or lines (roads, railroads, rivers). Symbols may also occupy an area, showing extent of coverage (terrain, forests, deserts). They seldom look like the feature they represent and therefore must be identified and interpreted. For instance, the maps in this atlas define political units by a colored line depicting their boundaries. Neither the colors nor the boundary lines are actually found on the surface of the earth, but because countries and states are such important political components of the world, strong symbols are used to represent them. The Map Symbols page in this atlas identifies the symbols used on the maps.

FIGURE 9

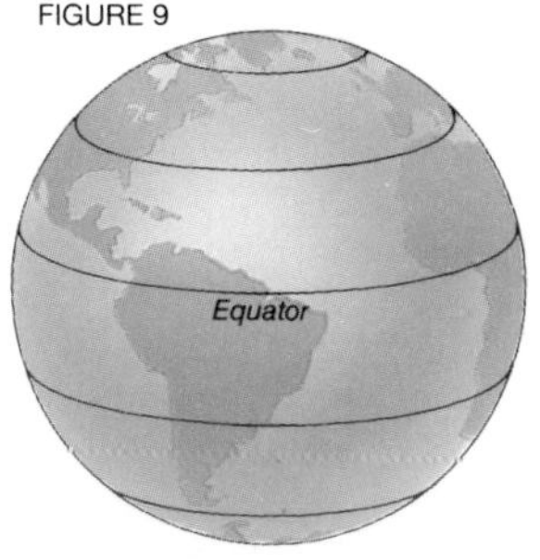

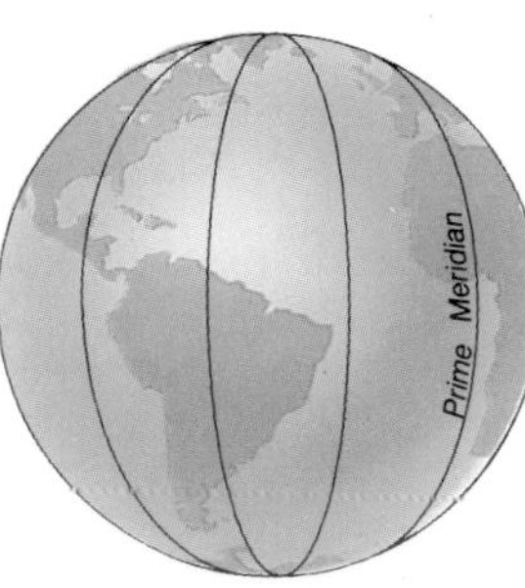

WORLD PATTERNS

The five world maps in this section portray the distribution of major natural and human elements that describe the world's fundamental geographic character. The lines and colors show basic patterns caused by the movement and interaction of land, air, water, and human activity.

The world terrain map on pages I·6 and I·7 portrays the surface of the uppermost layer of the earth's crust. The crust, broken into six gigantic and several smaller plates, floats on denser rock. Constant movement of the plates in the geologic past helped create the terrain features we see today. Motion of the plates along with the erosive force of water, wind, and human development continues to reshape the earth's terrain.

The earth's oceans are in constant motion. Water near the surface and in the deeps flows in well established currents that are like rivers within the ocean. The earth's atmosphere is an ocean of gases with currents that span the globe. The sun drives these moving currents of water and air. The average of the widely varying weather phenomena caused by these movements establishes the patterns of global climate shown on pages I·8 and I·9.

Climate is the single most important factor determining where plants can grow. And vegetation is the major factor determining where animals–including humans–can live. The map on pages I·10 and I·11 shows the distribution of vegetation types that might exist if humans did not intervene. Notice how similar the patterns of vegetation and climate are. Tundra vegetation is associated with polar climates. The rain forests of South America, Africa, and Asia grow in hot, wet climates near the Equator. The steppes of Central Asia and the short-grass prairies of North America grow in cool climates with dry summers. The evergreen forests of northern Eurasia and North America coincide with moist climates with cold winters and cool summers.

The population density map on pages I·12 and I·13 indicates that almost all areas of the earth are inhabited by humankind, from the Poles to the Equator. Humanity's densest settlement has been in the most fertile regions of the earth. These areas combine adequate rainfall and growing season with terrain that is neither too rough nor mountainous. A comparison of the terrain and climate maps with the population map shows this relationship. Abundant mineral deposits as well as people's ability to develop natural resources also explain settlement preferences. Densely settled areas in Southwest Asia, Southeast Asia, and China are rural-agricultural populations. In western Europe, the northeastern United States, and parts of Japan, high-density regions are urban-industrial in character.

The environment map on pages I·14 and I·15 indicates how human habitation has impacted our planet. Compare this map with the vegetation map that shows what the world might be like if humankind had played a less dominant role. Millions of square miles of land that were once forests or grasslands are now plowed fields and pastures. Much of North America, Europe, and Southeast Asia has been almost completely remade by farmers. Though the urban areas occupy a small percentage of the land area in the world, their impact on the environment is extensive.

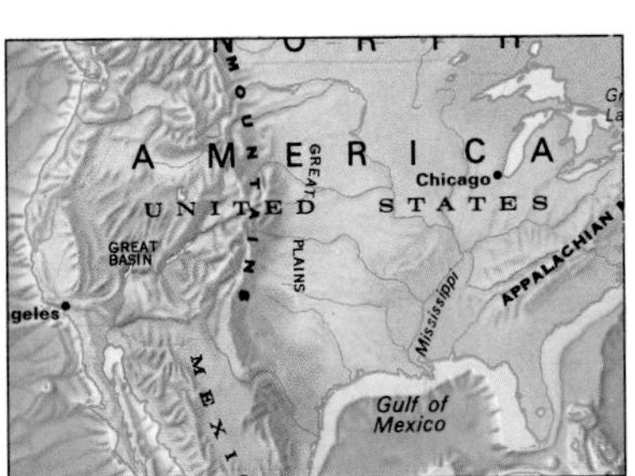

Terrain

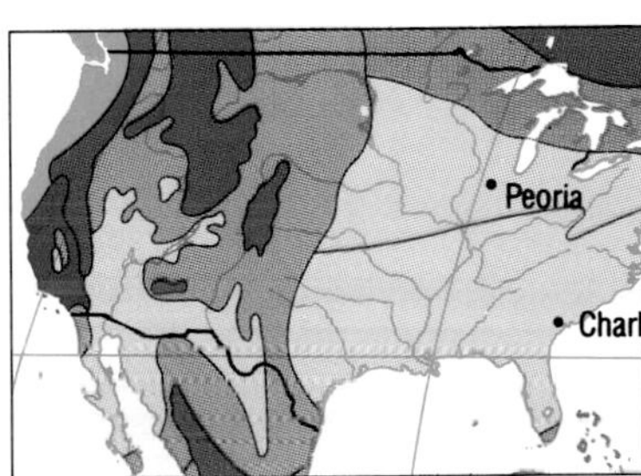

Climate

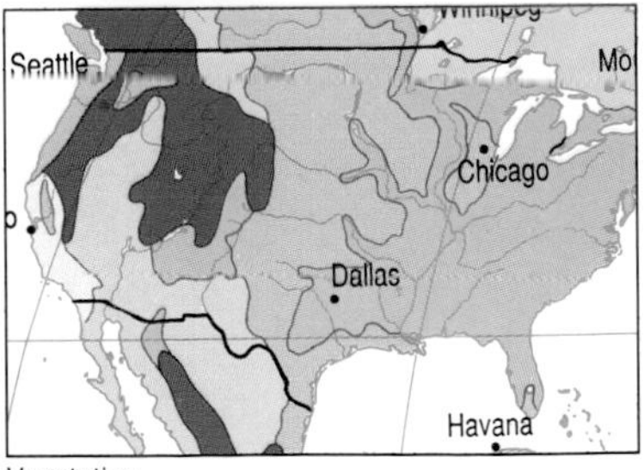

Vegetation

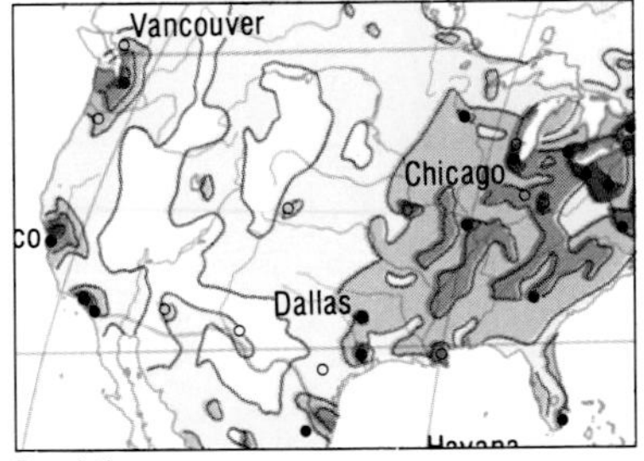

Population

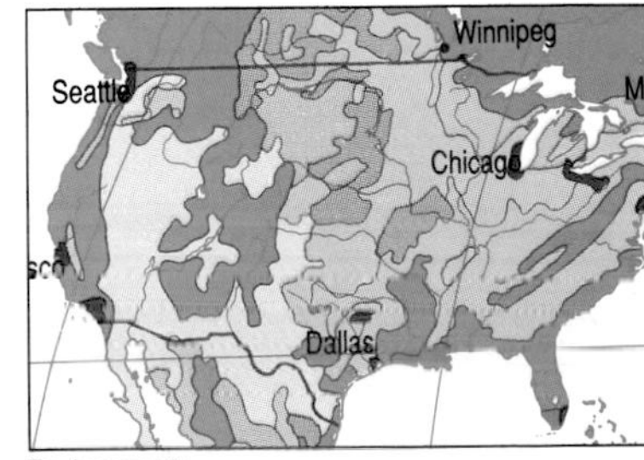

Environments

The distribution, relationship, and interaction of the major elements shown on the maps establish fundamental world patterns that distinguish one area from another. Upon the differences and similarities indicated by these patterns the world builds its intriguing variety of cultures and histories.

WORLD TERRAIN

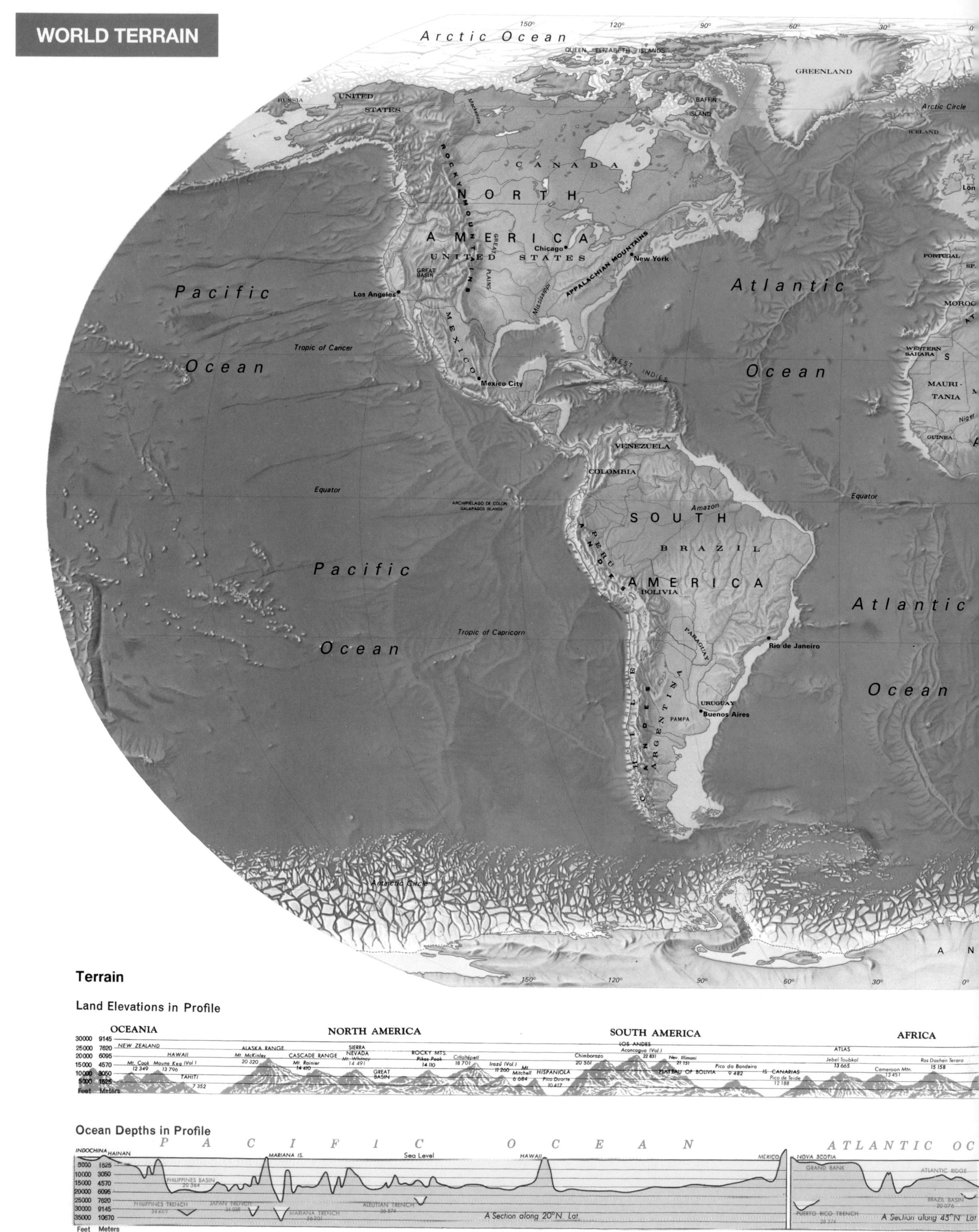

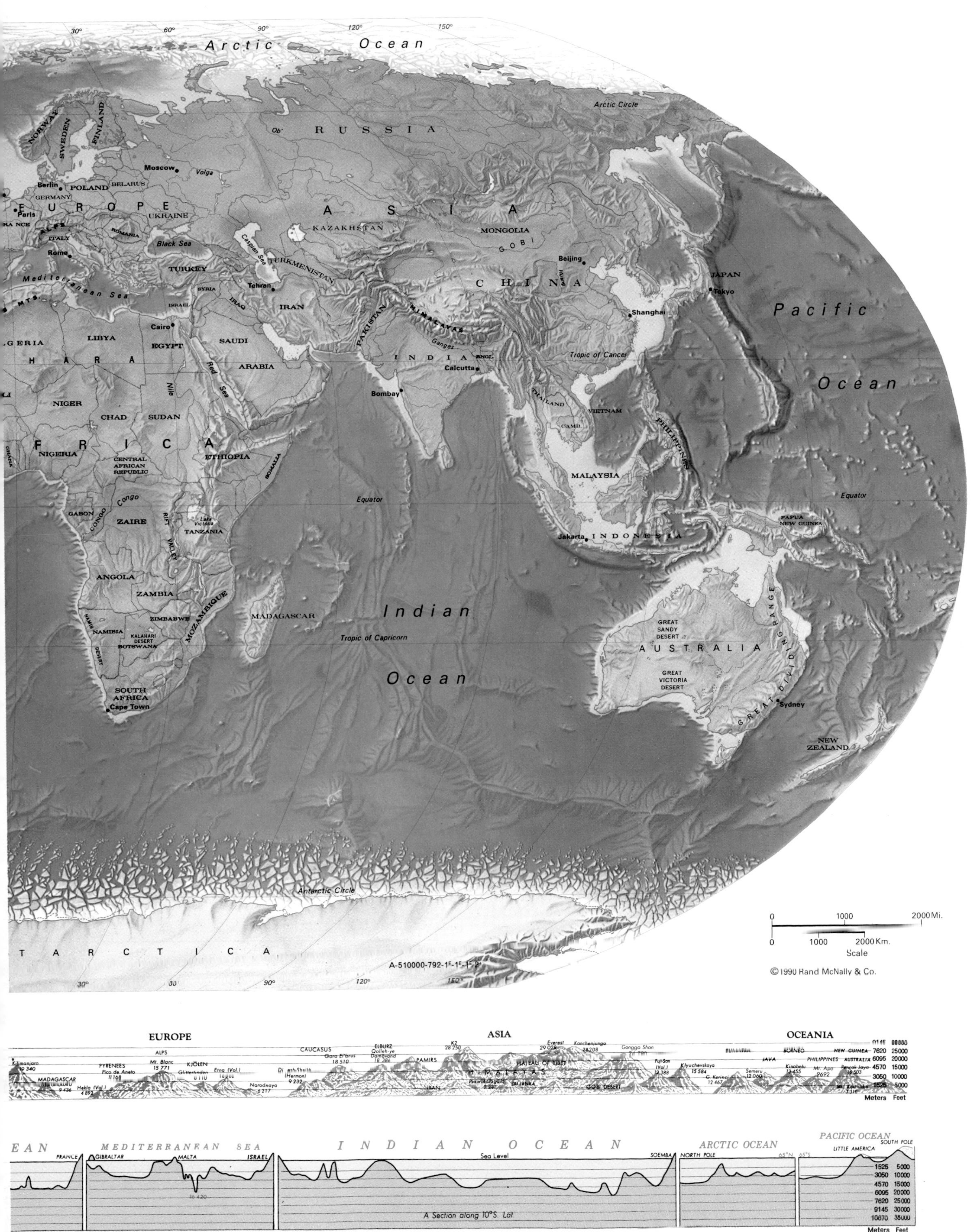

are given in feet

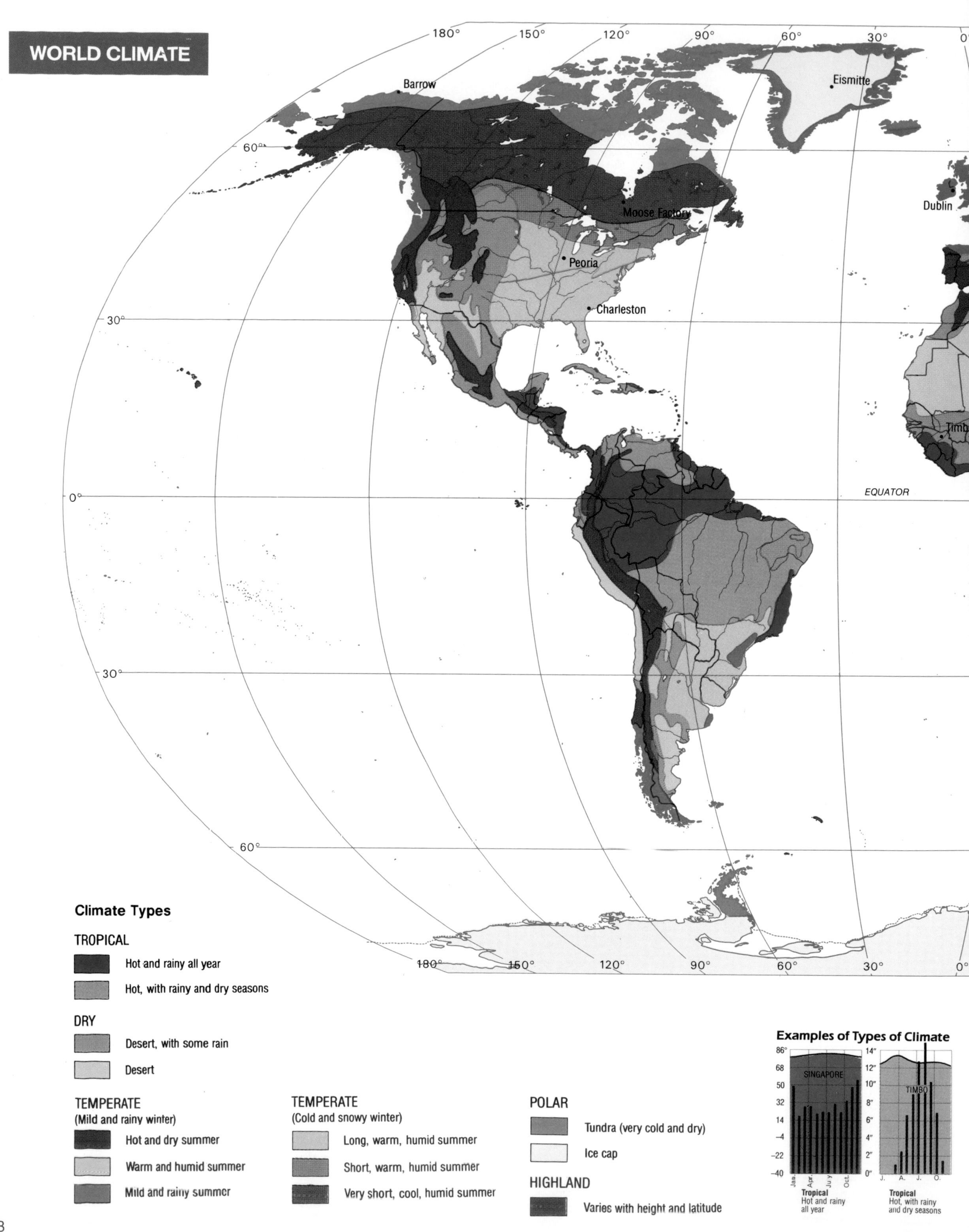
WORLD CLIMATE
180°
150°
120°
90°
60°
30°
0°
60°
30°
0°
30°
60°
Barrow
Eismitte
Dublin
Moose Factory
Peoria
Charleston
Timbo
EQUATOR
Climate Types
TROPICAL
Hot and rainy all year
Hot, with rainy and dry seasons
DRY
Desert, with some rain
Desert
TEMPERATE
(Mild and rainy winter)
Hot and dry summer
Warm and humid summer
Mild and rainy summer
TEMPERATE
(Cold and snowy winter)
Long, warm, humid summer
Short, warm, humid summer
Very short, cool, humid summer
POLAR
Tundra (very cold and dry)
Ice cap
HIGHLAND
Varies with height and latitude
Examples of Types of Climate
86°
68
50
32
14
−4
−22
−40
SINGAPORE
Jan.
Apr.
July
Oct.
Tropical
Hot and rainy all year
14″
12″
10″
8″
6″
4″
2″
0″
TIMBO
J.
A.
J.
O.
Tropical
Hot, with rainy and dry seasons

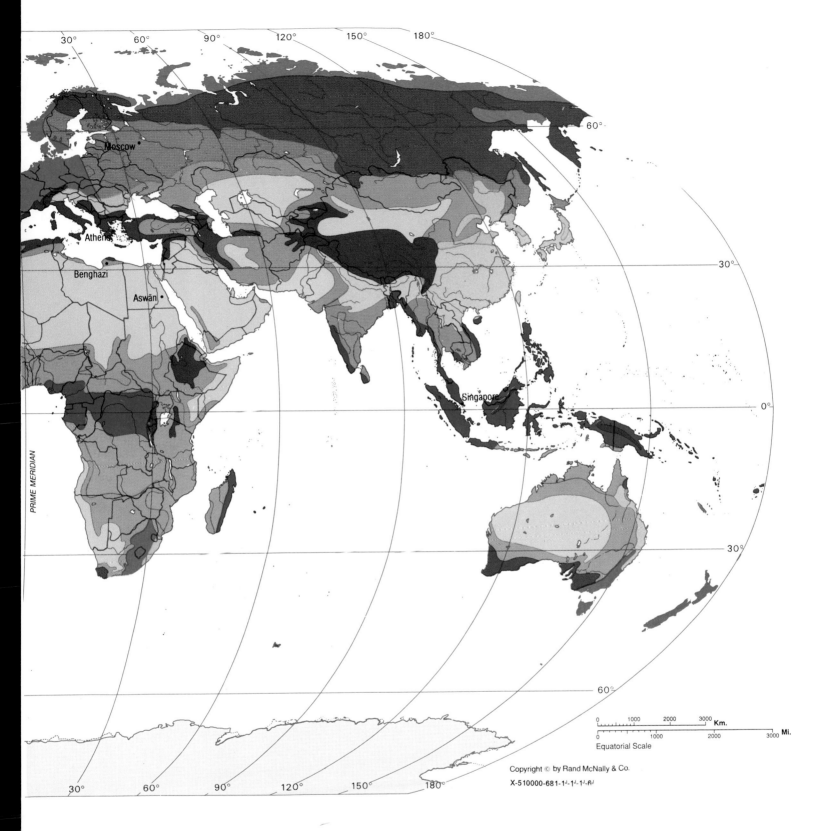

Moscow
Athens
Benghazi
Aswân
Singapore
PRIME MERIDIAN

0 1000 2000 3000 Km.
0 1000 2000 3000 Mi.
Equatorial Scale

X-510000-681-1-1-1-6

The curved lines on the graphs below show fahrenheit temperatures. The vertical bars show rainfall in inches.

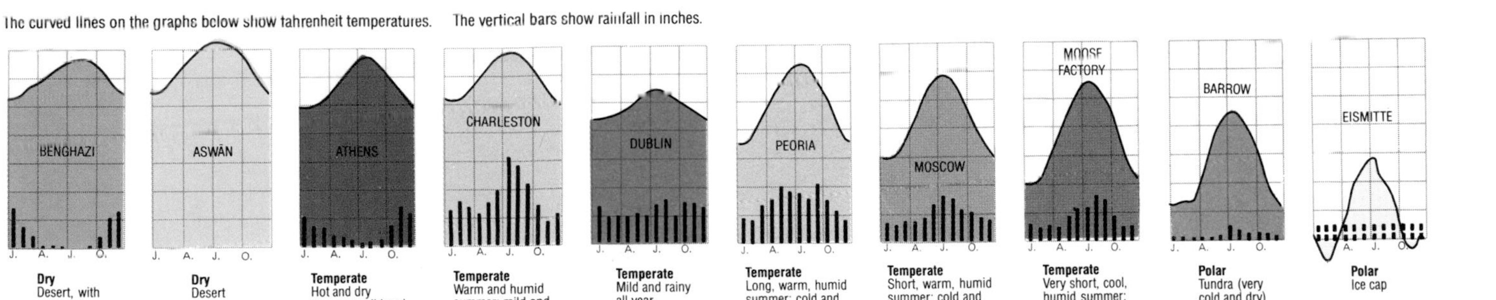

Dry Desert, with some rain

Dry Desert

Temperate Hot and dry summer; mild and rainy winter

Temperate Warm and humid summer; mild and rainy winter

Temperate Mild and rainy all year

Temperate Long, warm, humid summer; cold and snowy winter

Temperate Short, warm, humid summer; cold and snowy winter

Temperate Very short, cool, humid summer; very cold and snowy winter

Polar Tundra (very cold and dry)

Polar Ice cap

WORLD VEGETATION

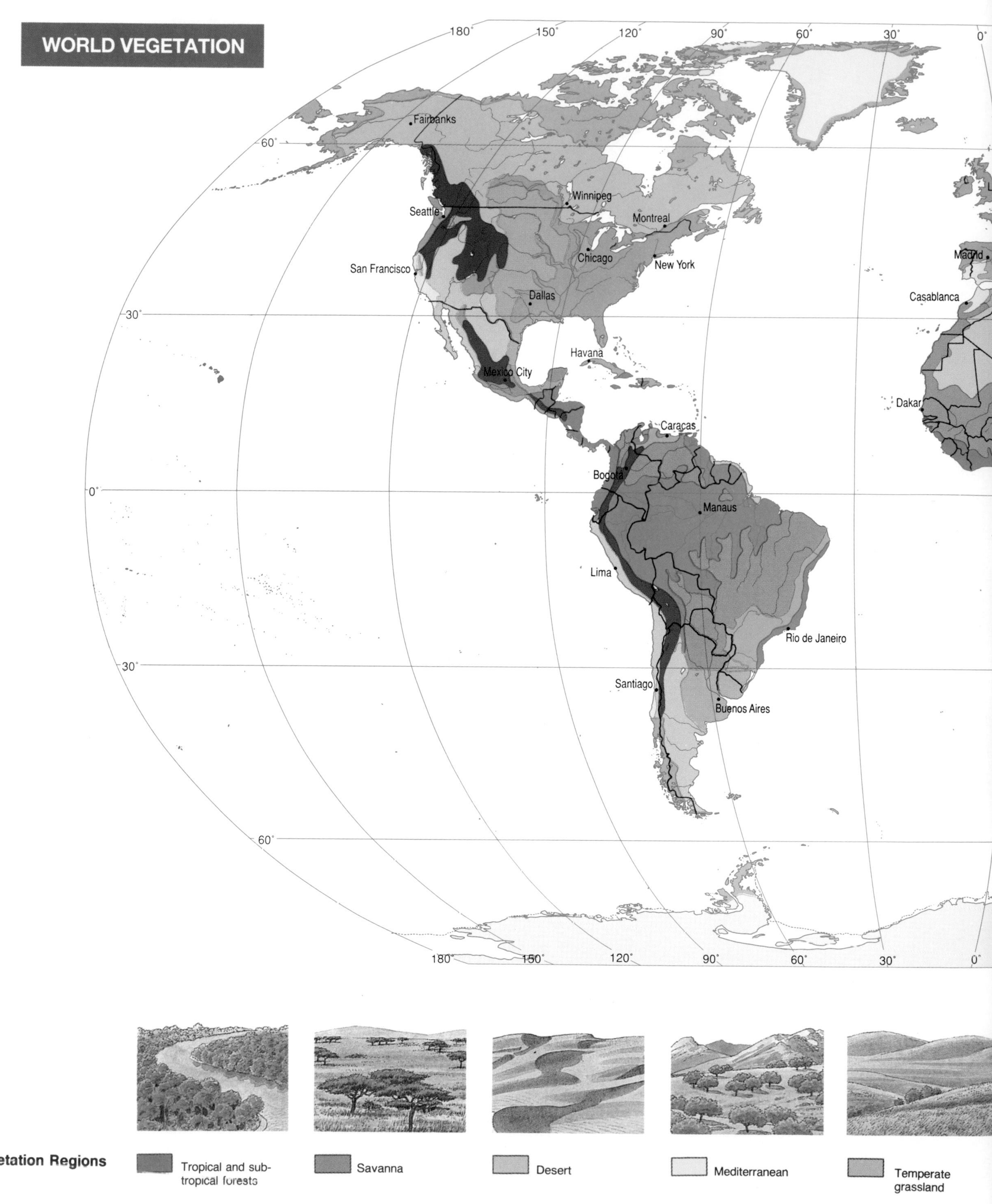
180°
150°
120°
90°
60°
30°
0°
60°
30°
0°
30°
60°
Fairbanks
Winnipeg
Seattle
Montreal
Chicago
New York
San Francisco
Dallas
Casablanca
Madrid
Havana
Mexico City
Dakar
Caracas
Bogotá
Manaus
Lima
Rio de Janeiro
Santiago
Buenos Aires
Vegetation Regions
Tropical and sub-tropical forests
Savanna
Desert
Mediterranean
Temperate grassland

Stockholm
Moscow
Novosibirsk
Berlin
Volgograd
Tashkent
Beijing
Rome
Damascus
Tehrān
Tōkyō
Cairo
New Delhi
Shanghai
Chongqing
Calcutta
Hong Kong
Bombay
Khartoum
Bangkok
Lagos
Nairobi
Kinshasa
Jakarta
Darwin
Johannesburg
Perth
Sydney
Cape Town
30°
60°
90°
120°
150°
180°
0°
Km.
Mi.
Equatorial Scale
Copyright © 1991 by Rand McNally & Co.
Temperate forest
Taiga (northern forests)
Tundra (lichen and moss)
Mountain
Polar and high mountain

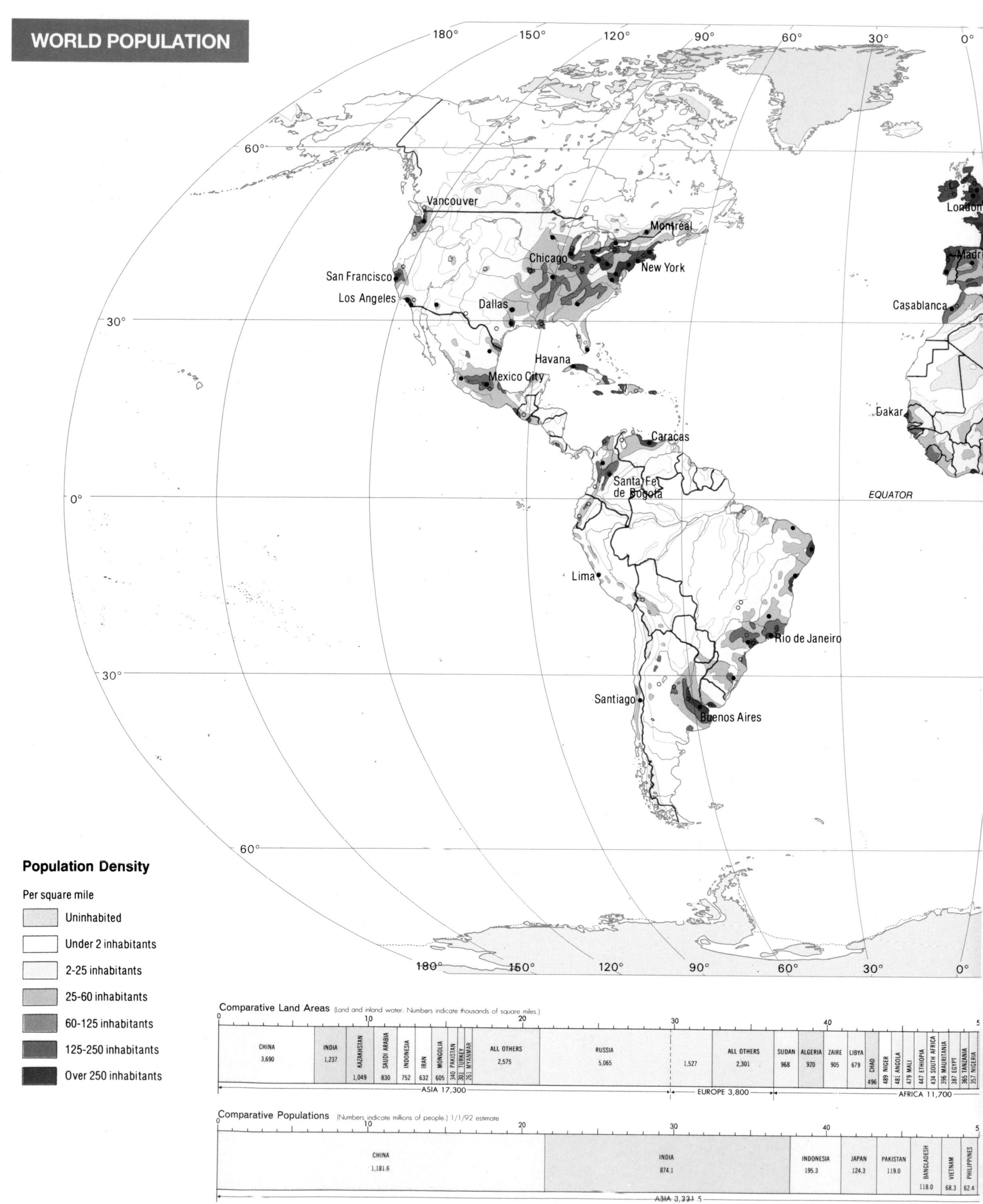

WORLD POPULATION
180°
150°
120°
90°
60°
30°
0°
60°
30°
0°
EQUATOR
Vancouver
Montréal
Chicago
New York
San Francisco
Los Angeles
Dallas
Havana
Mexico City
Caracas
Santa Fe de Bogotá
Lima
Rio de Janeiro
Santiago
Buenos Aires
London
Madrid
Casablanca
Dakar
Population Density
Per square mile
Uninhabited
Under 2 inhabitants
2-25 inhabitants
25-60 inhabitants
60-125 inhabitants
125-250 inhabitants
Over 250 inhabitants
Comparative Land Areas (Land and inland water. Numbers indicate thousands of square miles.)
0
10
20
30
40
5
CHINA 3,690
INDIA 1,237
KAZAKHSTAN 1,049
SAUDI ARABIA 830
INDONESIA 752
IRAN 632
MONGOLIA 605
340 PAKISTAN
301 TURKEY
261 MYANMAR
ALL OTHERS 2,575
RUSSIA 5,065
1,527
ALL OTHERS 2,301
SUDAN 968
ALGERIA 920
ZAIRE 905
LIBYA 679
CHAD 496
489 NIGER
481 ANGOLA
479 MALI
447 ETHIOPIA
434 SOUTH AFRICA
396 MAURITANIA
387 EGYPT
365 TANZANIA
357 NIGERIA
ASIA 17,300
EUROPE 3,800
AFRICA 11,700
Comparative Populations (Numbers indicate millions of people.) 1/1/92 estimate
0
10
20
30
40
5
CHINA 1,181.6
INDIA 874.1
INDONESIA 195.3
JAPAN 124.3
PAKISTAN 119.0
BANGLADESH 118.0
VIETNAM 68.3
PHILIPPINES 62.4
ASIA 3,331.5

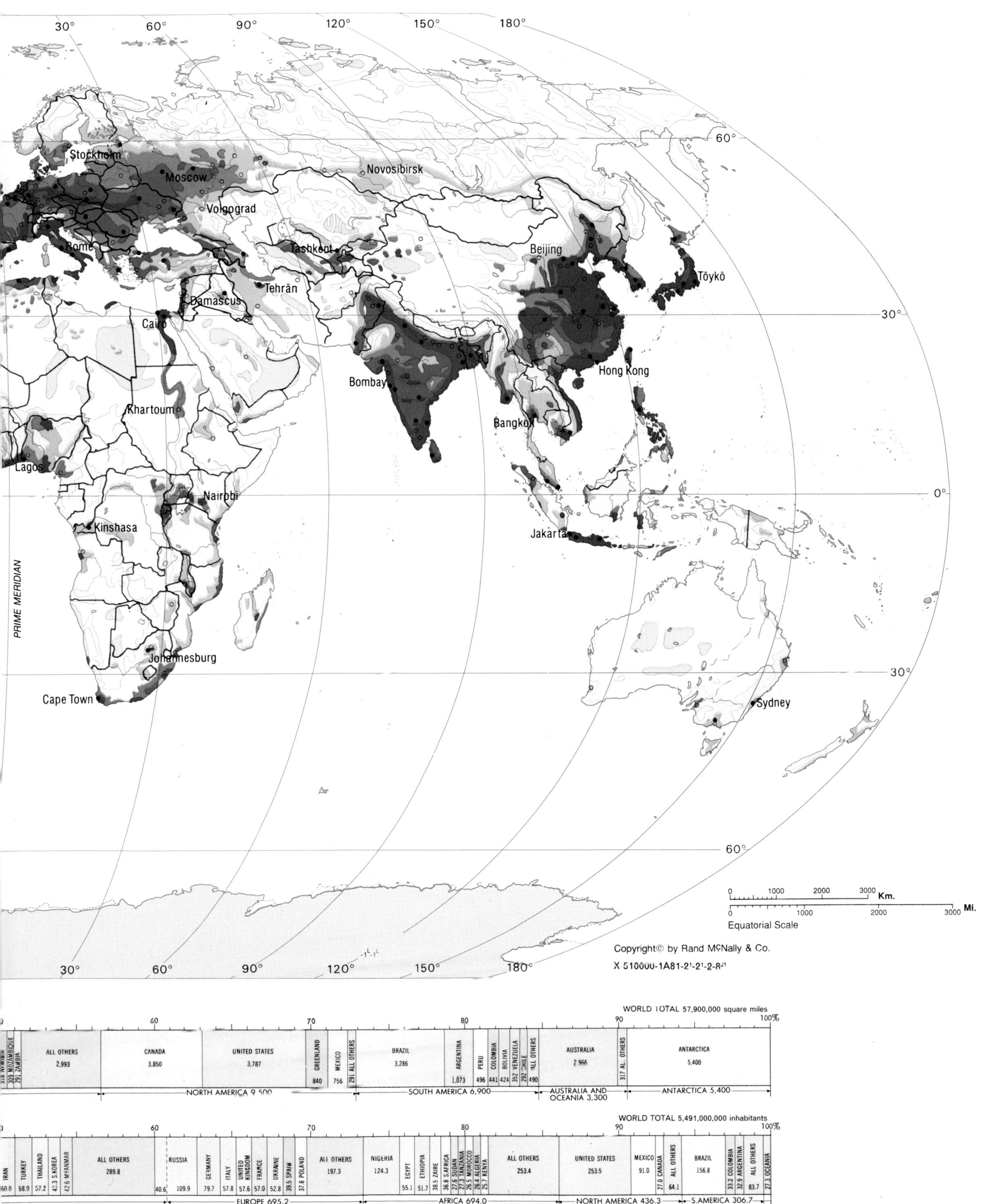

X 510000-1A81-2[1]-2[1]-2-8[J1]

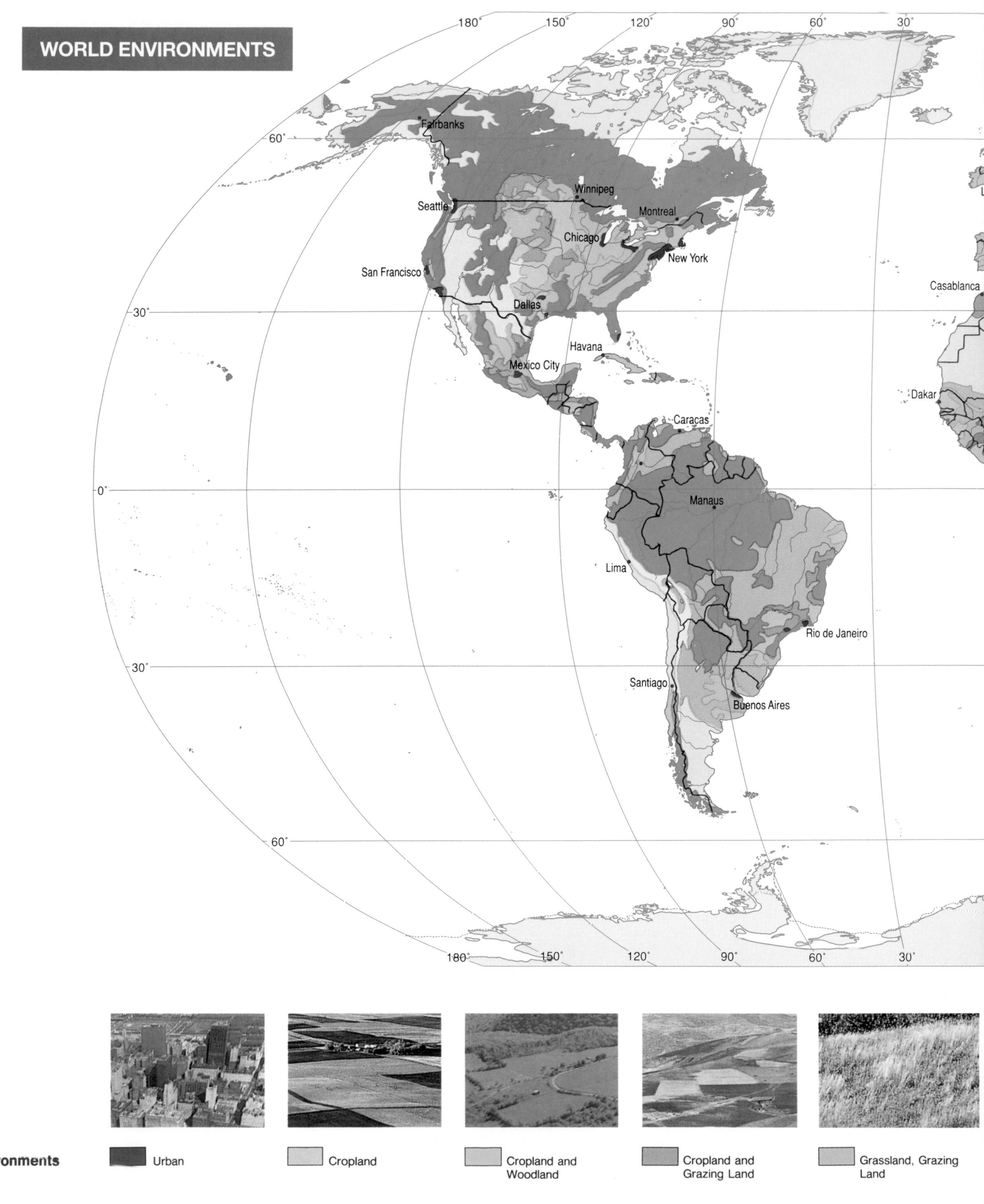
WORLD ENVIRONMENTS
180°
150°
120°
90°
60°
30°
60°
30°
0°
Fairbanks
Seattle
Winnipeg
Montreal
Chicago
New York
San Francisco
Dallas
Havana
Mexico City
Caracas
Manaus
Lima
Rio de Janeiro
Santiago
Buenos Aires
Casablanca
Dakar
Environments
Urban
Cropland
Cropland and Woodland
Cropland and Grazing Land
Grassland, Grazing Land

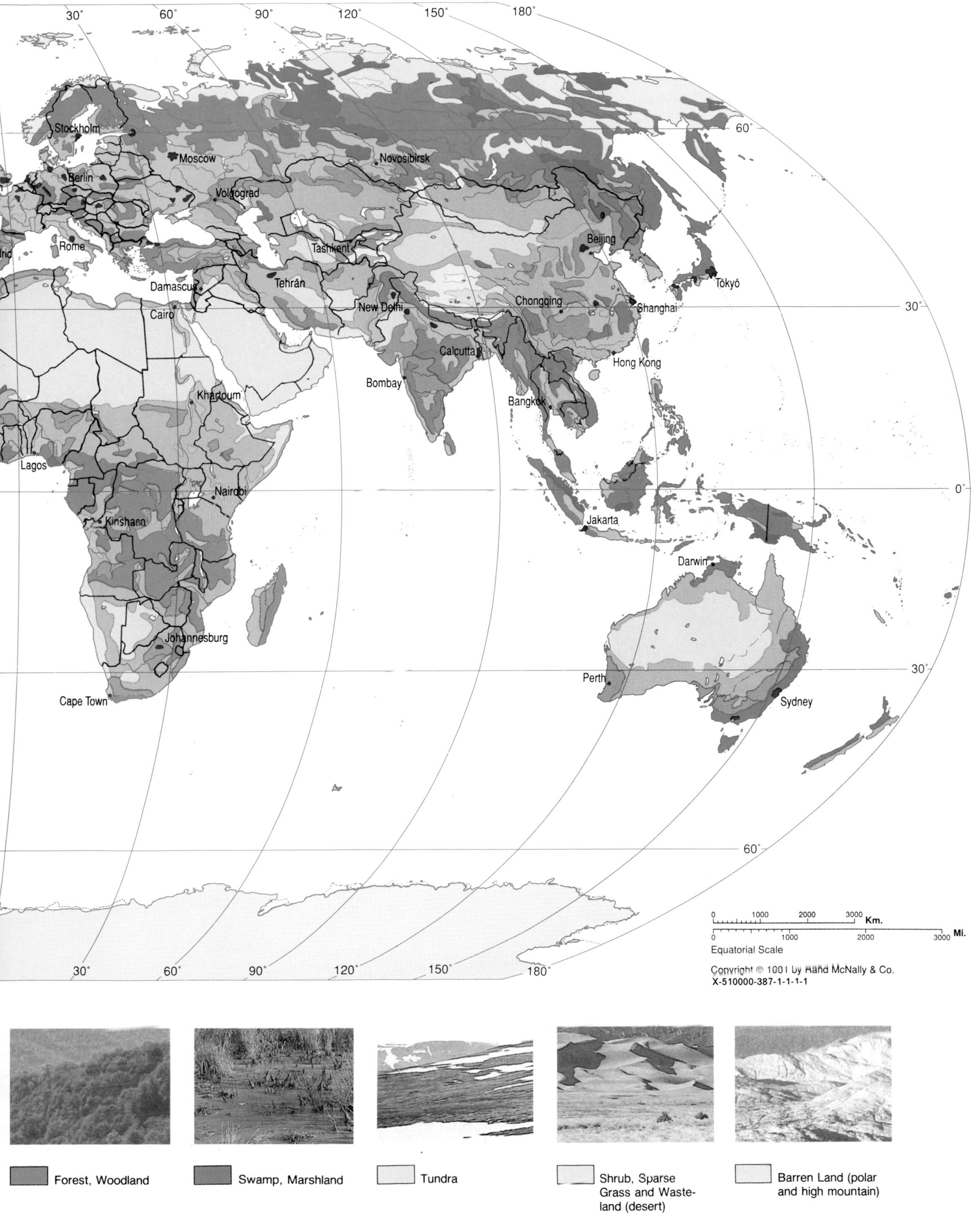
30°
60°
90°
120°
150°
180°
60°
30°
0°
30°
60°
Stockholm
Moscow
Novosibirsk
Berlin
Volgograd
Rome
Tashkent
Beijing
Tōkyō
Damascus
Tehrān
Cairo
New Delhi
Chongqing
Shanghai
Calcutta
Hong Kong
Bombay
Khartoum
Bangkok
Lagos
Nairobi
Kinshasa
Jakarta
Darwin
Johannesburg
Perth
Sydney
Cape Town
0 1000 2000 3000 Km.
0 1000 2000 3000 Mi.
Equatorial Scale
Copyright © 1991 by Rand McNally & Co.
X-510000-387-1-1-1-1
Forest, Woodland
Swamp, Marshland
Tundra
Shrub, Sparse Grass and Wasteland (desert)
Barren Land (polar and high mountain)

WORLD TIME ZONES

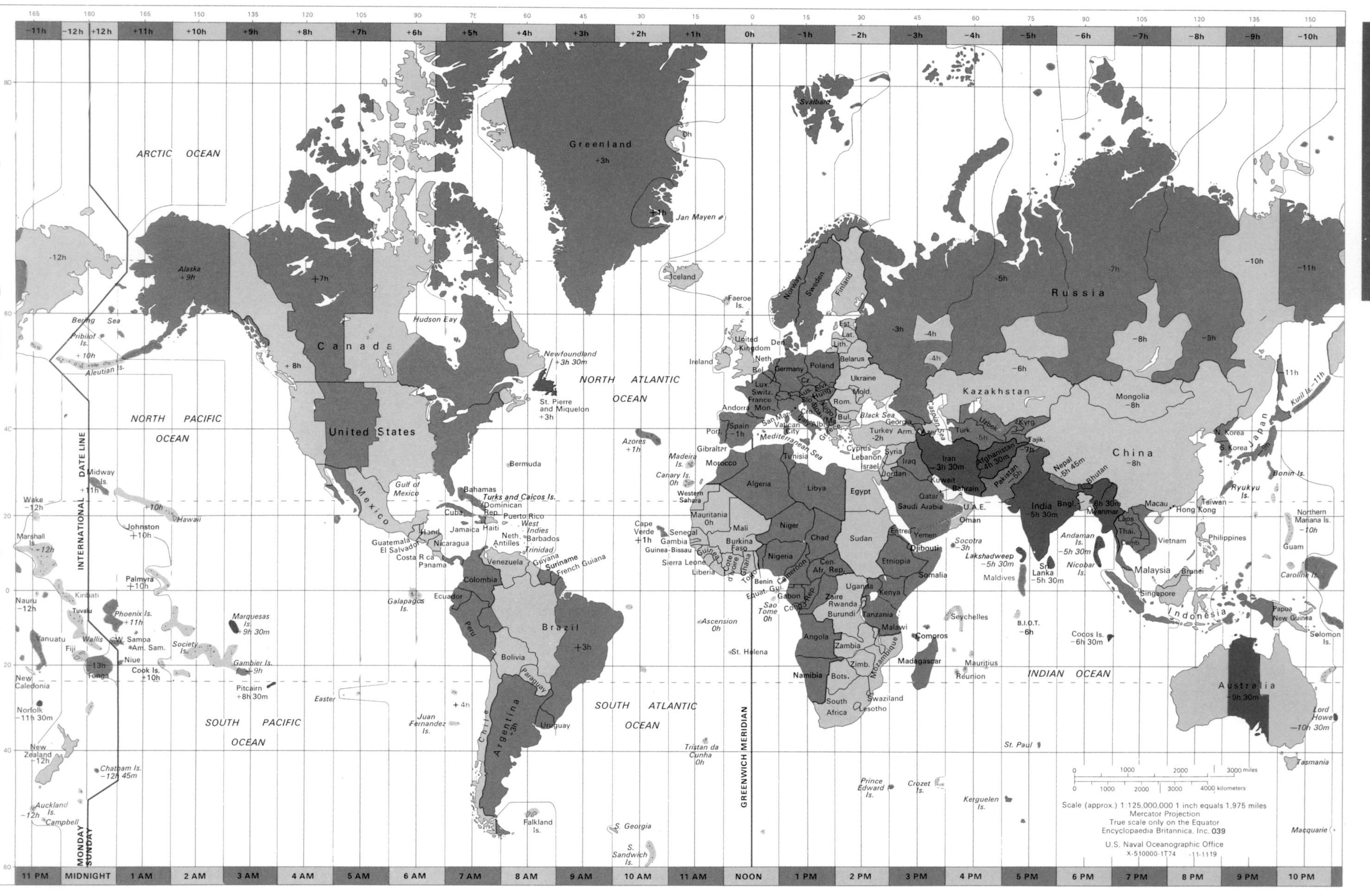

Time Zones

- Standard time zone of even-numbered hours from Greenwich time
- Standard time zone of odd-numbered hours from Greenwich time
- Time varies from the standard time zone by half an hour
- Time varies from the standard time zone by other than half an hour

h m hours, minutes

The standard time zone system, fixed by international agreement and by law in each country, is based on a theoretical division of the globe into 24 zones of 15° longitude each. The mid-meridian of each zone fixes the hour for the entire zone. The zero time zone extends 7½° east and 7½° west of the Greenwich meridian, 0° longitude. Since the earth rotates toward the east, time zones to the west of Greenwich are earlier, to the east, later.

Plus and minus hours at the top of the map are added to or subtracted from local time to find Greenwich time. Local standard time can be determined for any area in the world by adding one hour for each time zone counted in an easterly direction from one's own, or by subtracting one hour for each zone counted in a westerly direction. To separate one day from the next, the 180th meridian has been designated as the international date line. On both sides of the line the time of day is the same, but west of the line it is one day later than it is to the east.

Countries that adhere to the international zone system adopt the zone applicable to their location. Some countries, however, establish time zones based on political boundaries, or adopt the time zone of a neighboring unit. For all or part of the year some countries also advance their time by one hour, thereby utilizing more daylight hours each day.

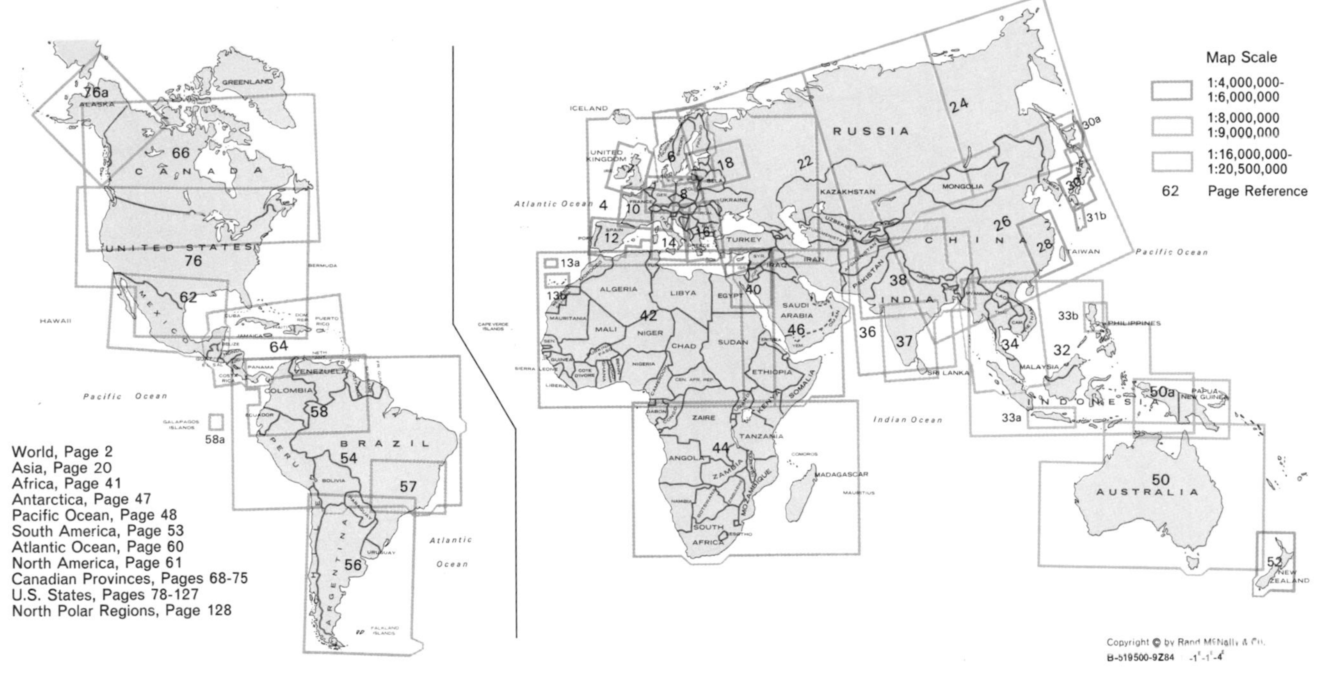

World Maps Symbols

Inhabited Localities

The size of type indicates the relative economic and political importance of the locality

Écommoy　Lisieux　**Rouen**

Trouville　**Orléans**　**PARIS**

Bi'r Safājah ° Oasis

Alternate Names

MOSKVA
MOSCOW

Basel
Bâle

English or second official language names are shown in reduced size lettering

Volgograd
(Stalingrad)

Historical or other alternates in the local language are shown in parentheses

Urban Area (Area of continuous industrial, commercial, and residential development)

Capitals of Political Units

BUDAPEST Independent Nation

Cayenne Dependency (Colony, protectorate, etc.)

Recife State, Province, County, Oblast, etc.

Political Boundaries

International (First-order political unit)

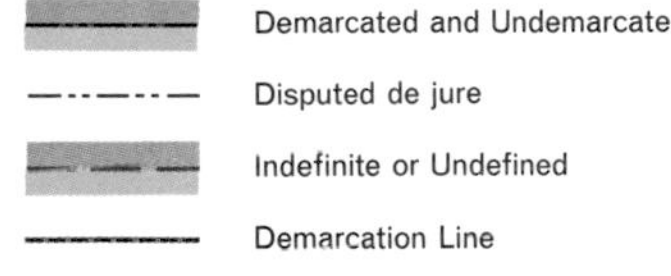

Demarcated and Undemarcated

Disputed de jure

Indefinite or Undefined

Demarcation Line

Internal

State, Province, etc. (Second-order political unit)

MURCIA Historical Region (No boundaries indicated)

GALAPAGOS (Ecuador) Administering Country

Transportation

Primary Road

Secondary Road

Minor Road, Trail

Railway

Canal du Midi Navigable Canal

Bridge

Tunnel

TO MALMÖ Ferry

Hydrographic Features

Shoreline

Undefined or Fluctuating Shoreline

Amur River, Stream

Intermittent Stream

Rapids, Falls

Irrigation or Drainage Canal

Reef

The Everglades Swamp

RIMO GLACIER Glacier

L. Victoria Lake, Reservoir

Tuz Gölü Salt Lake

Intermittent Lake, Reservoir

Dry Lake Bed

(395) Lake Surface Elevation

Topographic Features

Matterhorn △ 4470 Elevation Above Sea Level

76 ▽ Elevation Below Sea Level

Mount Cook ▲ 3764 Highest Elevation in Country

133 ▼ Lowest Elevation in Country

Khyber Pass 1067 Mountain Pass

Elevations are given in meters.
The highest and lowest elevations in a continent are underlined

Sand Area

Lava

Salt Flat

State, Province Maps Symbols

Capital

County Seat

Military Installation

Point of Interest

Mountain Peak

International Boundary

State, Province Boundary

County Boundary

Railroad

Road

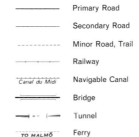

Urban Area

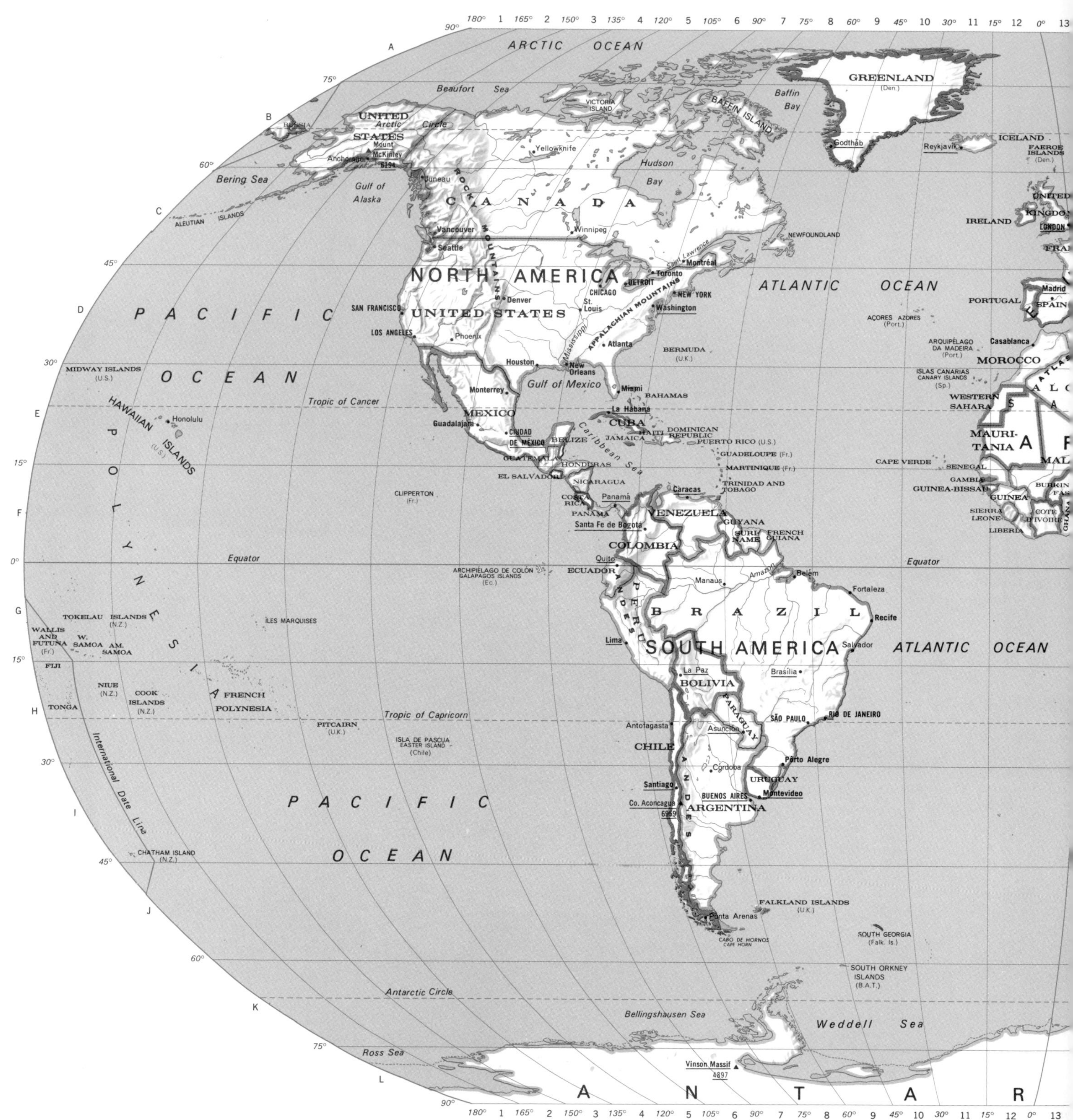
ARCTIC OCEAN
Beaufort Sea
VICTORIA ISLAND
BAFFIN ISLAND
Baffin Bay
GREENLAND
(Den.)
Godthåb
ICELAND
Reykjavík
FAEROE ISLANDS
(Den.)
UNITED STATES
Arctic Circle
Mount McKinley
6194
Anchorage
Yellowknife
Hudson Bay
Bering Sea
Gulf of Alaska
Juneau
ROCKY MOUNTAINS
CANADA
ALEUTIAN ISLANDS
Vancouver
Seattle
Winnipeg
NEWFOUNDLAND
IRELAND
UNITED KINGDOM
LONDON
Saint Lawrence
Montréal
Toronto
NORTH AMERICA
DETROIT
CHICAGO
APPALACHIAN MOUNTAINS
NEW YORK
Washington
ATLANTIC OCEAN
PORTUGAL
Madrid
SPAIN
SAN FRANCISCO
Denver
St. Louis
UNITED STATES
LOS ANGELES
Phoenix
Mississippi
Atlanta
AÇORES AZORES
(Port.)
ARQUIPÉLAGO DA MADEIRA
(Port.)
Casablanca
MOROCCO
PACIFIC OCEAN
MIDWAY ISLANDS
(U.S.)
Houston
New Orleans
BERMUDA
(U.K.)
ISLAS CANARIAS
CANARY ISLANDS
(Sp.)
Monterrey
Gulf of Mexico
Miami
BAHAMAS
WESTERN SAHARA
Tropic of Cancer
HAWAIIAN ISLANDS
(U.S.)
Honolulu
MEXICO
La Habana
CUBA
Guadalajara
CIUDAD DE MÉXICO
BELIZE
JAMAICA
HAITI
DOMINICAN REPUBLIC
PUERTO RICO (U.S.)
Caribbean Sea
GUADELOUPE (Fr.)
MAURITANIA
CAPE VERDE
SENEGAL
GUATEMALA
HONDURAS
MARTINIQUE (Fr.)
GAMBIA
GUINEA-BISSAU
EL SALVADOR
NICARAGUA
TRINIDAD AND TOBAGO
CLIPPERTON
(Fr.)
COSTA RICA
Panamá
PANAMÁ
Caracas
VENEZUELA
GUYANA
GUINEA
SIERRA LEONE
LIBERIA
CÔTE D'IVOIRE
POLYNESIA
Santa Fe de Bogotá
SURINAME
FRENCH GUIANA
COLOMBIA
Equator
Quito
ECUADOR
ARCHIPIÉLAGO DE COLÓN
GALAPAGOS ISLANDS
(Ec.)
Amazon
Belém
Manaus
Fortaleza
ANDES
PERU
BRAZIL
Recife
TOKELAU ISLANDS
(N.Z.)
ÎLES MARQUISES
WALLIS AND FUTUNA
(Fr.)
W. SAMOA
AM. SAMOA
Lima
SOUTH AMERICA
Salvador
ATLANTIC OCEAN
FIJI
La Paz
BOLIVIA
Brasília
NIUE
(N.Z.)
COOK ISLANDS
(N.Z.)
FRENCH POLYNESIA
TONGA
Tropic of Capricorn
PARAGUAY
SÃO PAULO
RIO DE JANEIRO
PITCAIRN
(U.K.)
Antofagasta
Asunción
ISLA DE PASCUA
EASTER ISLAND
(Chile)
CHILE
International Date Line
Córdoba
Pôrto Alegre
Santiago
URUGUAY
Co. Aconcagua
6959
BUENOS AIRES
Montevideo
ARGENTINA
CHATHAM ISLAND
(N.Z.)
FALKLAND ISLANDS
(U.K.)
Punta Arenas
SOUTH GEORGIA
(Falk. Is.)
CABO DE HORNOS
CAPE HORN
SOUTH ORKNEY ISLANDS
(B.A.T.)
Antarctic Circle
Bellingshausen Sea
Weddell Sea
Ross Sea
Vinson Massif
4897
ANTAR

ARCTIC OCEAN
Barents Sea
Karskoje More
More Laptevych
NOVOSIBIRSKIJE OSTROVA
SVALBARD (Nor.)
ZEML'A FRANCA-IOSIFA
NOVAJA ZEML'A
Noril'sk
Jenisej
Arctic Circle
Anadyr
Lena
Jakutsk
Archangel'sk
Ob'
URAL'SKIJE GORY
R U S S I A
NORWAY
SWEDEN
FINLAND
Helsinki
Oslo
Stockholm
SANKT-PETERBURG
MOSKVA
Nižnij Novgorod
Jekaterinburg
Novosibirsk
Sea of Okhotsk
Bering Sea
ALEUTIAN IS. (U.S.)
Petropavlovsk-Kamčatskij
OSTROV SACHALIN
GERMANY
POLAND
Kyyiv
UKRAINE
Ozero Bajkal
Karaganda
K A Z A K H S T A N
A S I A
MONGOLIA
Harbin
Volga
Caspian Sea
Black Sea
Gora El'brus 5633
ROM.
BUL.
Roma
ITALY
GREECE
Istanbul
TURKEY
Taškent
GOBI
BEIJING (PEKING)
Sea of Japan
KOREA
SOUL
JAPAN
ŌSAKA
TŌKYŌ
International Date Line
Mediterranean Sea
Alger
MALTA
SYRIA
IRAQ
Tehrān
IRAN
AFGHANISTAN
ISRAEL
JORDAN
KUWAIT
C H I N A
HIMALAYAS
Xi'an
Wuhan
Yellow Sea
SHANGHAI
Chongqing
LIBYA
AL-QĀHIRAH (CAIRO)
EGYPT
PAKISTAN
DELHI
NEPAL
Mount Everest 8848
BHU.
Karāchi
Tropic of Cancer
CALCUTTA
BNGL.
QATAR
UNITED ARAB EMIRATES
SAUDI ARABIA
OMAN
INDIA
MYANMAR (BURMA)
Guangzhou
HONG KONG (U.K.)
TAIWAN
P A C I F I C
O C E A N
Philippine Sea
WAKE ISLAND (U.S.)
NIGER
CHAD
Nile
Red Sea
Al-Kharṭūm
SUDAN
ERITREA
YEMEN
Adan
DJIBOUTI
BOMBAY
Bay of Bengal
Arabian Sea
Madras
THAILAND
Krung Thep (Bangkok)
LAOS
CAMB.
VIETNAM
South China Sea
MANILA
PHILIPPINES
GUAM (U.S.)
M I C R O N E S I A
NIGERIA
Lagos
CAMEROON
CEN. AFR. REP.
ETHIOPIA
SOMALIA
SRI LANKA
Colombo
BRUNEI
MALAYSIA
Singapore
SUMATERA
BORNEO
SULAWESI
EQUATORIAL GUINEA
GABON
CONGO
UGANDA
KENYA
Muqdisho
MALDIVES
Equator
KIRIBATI
ZAIRE
Kinshasa
RWANDA
BURUNDI
Nairobi
Kilimanjaro 5895
TANZANIA
SEYCHELLES
CHAGOS ARCHIPELAGO (B.I.O.T.)
JAKARTA
INDONESIA
JAWA
IRIAN JAYA
PAPUA NEW GUINEA
NEW GUINEA
SOLOMON ISLANDS
TUVALU
Luanda
ANGOLA
ZAMBIA
MALAWI
MOZAMBIQUE
Mozambique Channel
I N D I A N
O C E A N
TIMOR
Port Moresby
CHRISTMAS ISLAND (Austl.)
M E L A N E S I A
VANUATU
ZIMBABWE
NAMIBIA
BOTSWANA
MADAGASCAR
MAURITIUS
REUNION (Fr.)
Tropic of Capricorn
Cairns
Coral Sea
NEW CALEDONIA (Fr.)
FIJI
Johannesburg
SWAZILAND
LESOTHO
Durban
SOUTH AFRICA
Cape Town
CAPE OF GOOD HOPE
A U S T R A L I A
Brisbane
Perth
Sydney
Mount Kosciusko 2230
Melbourne
Tasman Sea
NEW ZEALAND
Wellington
TASMANIA
ÎLES KERGUELEN (F.S.A.T.)
Antarctic Circle
ENDERBY LAND
WILKES LAND
C T I C A
Copyright © by Rand McNally & Co.
Map prepared by Rand McNally & Co.
C-510000-264
Kilometers 0 1000 2000 3000 Km.
Miles 0 1000 2000 3000 Mi.
Robinson Projection

Europe

ALBANIA G11
Amsterdam, 6,965,000 ('89) (1,860,000★) .... E 8
ANDORRA .... G 8
Antwerpen, 497,748 ('87) (1,100,000★) .... E 8
Athínai (Athens), 885,737 ('81) (3,027,331★) ... H12
AUSTRIA F10
Barcelona, 1,714,355 ('88) (4,040,000★) .... G 8
BELARUS E13
Belfast, 303,800 ('87) (685,000★) .... E 6
BELGIUM .... E 8
Beograd (Belgrade), 1,130,000 ('87) (1,400,000★) G12
Berlin, 3,352,848 ('89) (3,825,000★) E10
Bern, 134,393 ('90) (298,800★) .... F 9
Birmingham, 1,013,995 ('81) (2,675,000★) .... E 7
Bonn, 282,190 ('89) (570,000★) .... E 9
BOSNIA AND HERZEGOVINA G11
Bratislava, 444,482 ('91) F11
Bremen, 535,058 ('89) (800,000★) .... E 9
Bruxelles, 136,920 ('87) (2,385,000★) .... E 8
București, 1,989,823 ('86) (2,275,000★) G13
Budapest, 2,016,132 ('90) (2,565,000★) F11
BULGARIA G12
Cardiff, 262,313 ('81) (625,000★) .... E 7
CROATIA F11
CZECH REPUBLIC F11
DENMARK .... D 9
Dnipropetrovsk, 1,179,000 ('89) (1,600,000★) F14
Donets'k, 1,110,000 ('89) (2,200,000★) F15
Dresden, 518,057 ('89) (670,000★) E10
Dublin, 502,749 ('86) (1,140,000★) .... E 6
Düsseldorf, 569,641 ('89) (1,190,000★) .... E 9
Edinburgh, 433,200 ('89) (630,000★) .... D 7
Essen, 620,594 ('89) (4,950,000★) .... E 9
ESTONIA D12
FAEROE ISLANDS ...... C 6
FINLAND C13
Firenze, 425,835 ('87) (640,000★) G10
FRANCE .... F 8
Frankfurt, 625,258 ('89) (1,855,000★) .... E 9
Gdańsk, 461,500 ('89) (909,000★) E11
Genève (Geneva), 165,404 ('90) (460,000★) .... F 9
Genova, 727,427 ('87) (805,000★) .... G 9
GERMANY E10
Gibraltar, 30,077 ('88). H 6
Glasgow, 695,630 ('89) (1,800,000★) .... D 7
GREECE H12
GUERNSEY .... F 7
Hamburg, 1,603,070 ('89) (2,225,000★) .... E 9
Helsinki, 490,034 ('88) (1,040,000★) C12
HUNGARY F11
ICELAND .... B 4
IRELAND .... E 6
ISLE OF MAN .... E 7
İstanbul, 6,748,435 ('90) (7,000,000★) G13
ITALY G10
JERSEY .... F 7
Katowice, 365,800 ('89) (2,778,000★) E11
Kazan', 1,094,000 ('89) (1,140,000★) D17
Kharkiv, 1,611,000 ('89) (1,940,000★) F15
København, 466,723 ('90) (1,685,000★) D10
Köln, 937,482 ('89) (1,760,000★) .... E 9
Kraków, 743,700 ('89) (828,000★) E11
Kyyiv (Kiev), 2,587,000 ('89) (2,900,000★) ... E14
LATVIA D12
Leipzig, 545,307 ('89) (700,000★) E10
Leningrad *see* Sankt-Peterburg D14
LIECHTENSTEIN .... F 9
Ljubljana, 233,200 ('87) (316,607▲) F10
Lisboa, 807,167 ('81) (2,250,000★) .... H 6

★ Population of metropolitan area, including suburbs.

1 : 16 000 000

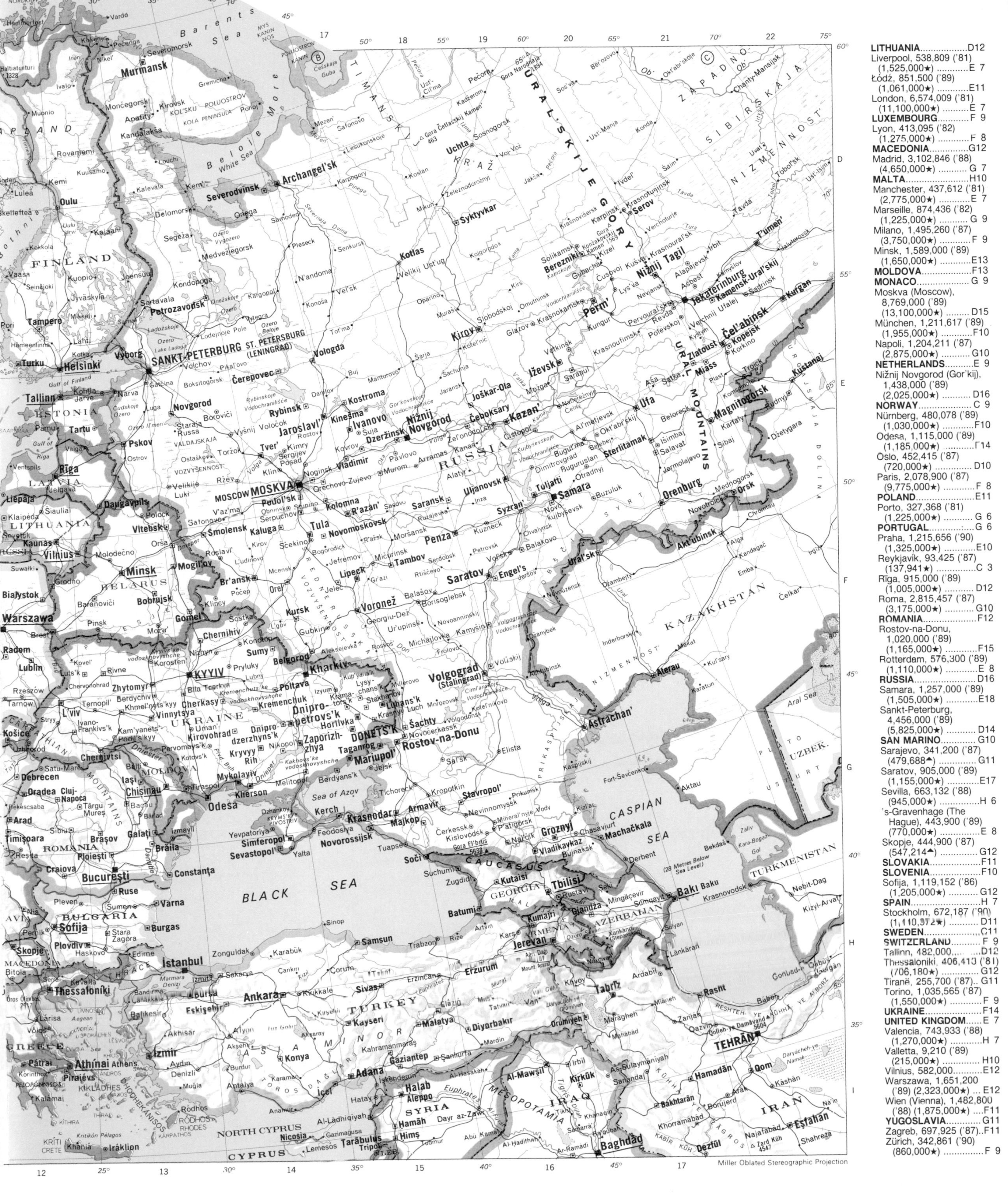

LITHUANIA..................D12
Liverpool, 538,809 ('81) (1,525,000★) ....E 7
Łódź, 851,500 ('89) (1,061,000★) E11
London, 6,574,009 ('81) (11,100,000★) ....E 7
LUXEMBOURG............F 9
Lyon, 413,095 ('82) (1,275,000★) ....F 8
MACEDONIA..............G12
Madrid, 3,102,846 ('88) (4,650,000★) .... G 7
MALTA.......................H10
Manchester, 437,612 ('81) (2,775,000★) ....E 7
Marseille, 874,436 ('82) (1,225,000★) .... G 9
Milano, 1,495,260 ('87) (3,750,000★) ....F 9
Minsk, 1,589,000 ('89) (1,650,000★) E13
MOLDOVA...................F13
MONACO................... G 9
Moskva (Moscow), 8,769,000 ('89) (13,100,000★) D15
München, 1,211,617 ('89) (1,955,000★) F10
Napoli, 1,204,211 ('87) (2,875,000★) G10
NETHERLANDS...........E 9
Nižnij Novgorod (Gor'kij), 1,438,000 ('89) (2,025,000★) D16
NORWAY................... C 9
Nürnberg, 480,078 ('89) (1,030,000★) F10
Odesa, 1,115,000 ('89) (1,185,000★) F14
Oslo, 452,415 ('87) (720,000★) D10
Paris, 2,078,900 ('87) (9,775,000★) ....F 8
POLAND......................E11
Porto, 327,368 ('81) (1,225,000★) .... G 6
PORTUGAL..................G 6
Praha, 1,215,656 ('90) (1,325,000★) E10
Reykjavík, 93,425 ('87) (137,941★) ....C 3
Rīga, 915,000 ('89) (1,005,000★) D12
Roma, 2,815,457 ('87) (3,175,000★) G10
ROMANIA....................F12
Rostov-na-Donu, 1,020,000 ('89) (1,165,000★) F15
Rotterdam, 576,300 ('89) (1,110,000★) ....E 8
RUSSIA........................D16
Samara, 1,257,000 ('89) (1,505,000★) E18
Sankt-Peterburg, 4,456,000 ('89) (5,825,000★) D14
SAN MARINO............ G10
Sarajevo, 341,200 ('87) (479,688▲) G11
Saratov, 905,000 ('89) (1,155,000★) E17
Sevilla, 663,132 ('88) (945,000★) ....H 6
's-Gravenhage (The Hague), 443,900 ('89) (770,000★) ....E 8
Skopje, 444,900 ('87) (547,214▲) G12
SLOVAKIA...................F11
SLOVENIA...................F10
Sofija, 1,119,152 ('86) (1,205,000★) G12
SPAIN..........................H 7
Stockholm, 672,187 ('90) (1,110,972★) D11
SWEDEN.....................C11
SWITZERLAND.......... F 9
Tallinn, 482,000..........D12
Thessaloniki, 406,413 ('81) (706,180★) G12
Tiranë, 255,700 ('87).. G11
Torino, 1,035,565 ('87) (1,550,000★) ....F 9
UKRAINE.....................F14
UNITED KINGDOM......E 7
Valencia, 743,933 ('88) (1,270,000★) ....H 7
Valletta, 9,210 ('89) (215,000★) H10
Vilnius, 582,000...........E12
Warszawa, 1,651,200 ('89) (2,323,000★) ... E12
Wien (Vienna), 1,482,800 ('88) (1,875,000★) F11
YUGOSLAVIA............ G11
Zagreb, 697,925 ('87)..F11
Zürich, 342,861 ('90) (860,000★) ....F 9

Scandinavia

Denmark

1990 ESTIMATE

Ålborg, 114,000 (155,019▲)........H 7
Århus, 202,300 (261,437▲)........H 8
Copenhagen *see* København........I 9
København (Copenhagen), 466,723 (1,685,000★)......I 9
Odense, 140,100 (176,133▲)........I 8

Finland

1988 ESTIMATE

Helsinki (Helsingfors), 490,034 (1,040,000★)......F15
Lahti, 74,300 (108,000★)........F15
Oulu, 98,582 (121,000★)........D15
Tampere, 170,533 (241,000★)........F14
Turku (Åbo), 160,456 (228,000★)........F14

Norway

1987 ESTIMATE

Bergen, 209,320 (239,000★)........F 5
Hammerfest, 7,208('83)........A14
Oslo, 452,415 (720,000★)...... G 8
Stavanger, 94,200 (132,000★)('85)....G 5
Trondheim, 135,010..E 8

Sweden

1990 ESTIMATE

Göteborg (Gothenburg), 431,840 (710,894★) H 8
Helsingborg, 108,359 H 9
Jönköping, 110,860..H10
Linköping, 120,562..G10
Malmö, 232,908 (445,000★)........I 9
Norrköping, 119,921 G11
Örebro, 120,353....G10
Stockholm, 672,187 (1,449,972★)......G12
Uppsala, 164,754....G11
Västerås, 118,386..G11

★ Population of metropolitan area, including suburbs.
▲ Population of entire district, including rural area.

Kilometers 0 100 200 300 Km.
Miles 0 100 200 300 Mi.

1:8 000 000

British Isles

Ireland

1986 CENSUS

Cork, 133,271 (173,694★) . . . . . . J 4
Dublin (Baile Átha Cliath), 502,749 (1,140,000★) . . . . H 6
Galway, 47,104 . . . . H 3
Limerick, 56,279 (76,557★) . . . . I 4
Waterford, 39,529 (41,054★) . . . . I 5

Isle of Man

1986 CENSUS

Douglas, 20,368 (28,500★) . . . . . . G 8

United Kingdom

England

1981 CENSUS

Birmingham, 1,013,995 (2,675,000★) I11
Blackpool, 146,297 (280,000★) . . . . . . H 9
Bournemouth, 142,829 (315,000★) K11
Bradford, 293,336 . . H11
Brighton, 134,581 (420,000★) K12
Bristol, 413,861 (630,000★) J10
Coventry, 318,718 (645,000★) I11
Derby, 218,026 (275,000★) I11
Kingston upon Hull, 322,144 (350,000★) H12
Leeds, 445,242 (1,540,000★) H11
Leicester, 324,394 (495,000★) I11
Liverpool, 538,809 (1,525,000★) H10
London, 6,574,009 (11,100,000★) J12
Manchester, 437,612 (2,775,000★) H10
Newcastle upon Tyne, 199,064 (1,300,000★) G11
Nottingham, 273,300 (655,000★) I11
Oxford, 113,847 (230,000★) J11
Plymouth, 238,583 (290,000★) . . . . . . K 8
Portsmouth, 174,218 (485,000★) K11
Preston, 166,675 (250,000★) H10
Reading, 194,727 (200,000★) J12
Sheffield, 470,685 (710,000★) H11
Southampton, 211,321 (415,000★) K11
Southend-on-Sea, 155,720 . . . . J13
Stoke-on-Trent, 272,446 (440,000★) H10
Sunderland, 195,064 G11
Teesside, 158,516 (580,000★) G11
Wolverhampton, 263,501 . . . . I10

Northern Ireland

1987 ESTIMATE

Bangor, 70,700 . . . . G 7
Belfast, 303,800 (685,000★) . . . . . . G 7
Londonderry, 97,500 (97,200★) . . . . . . G 5
Newtownabbey, 72,300 . . . . G 7

Scotland

1989 ESTIMATE

Aberdeen, 210,700 . . D10
Dundee, 172,540 . . . . E 9
Edinburgh, 433,200 (630,000★) . . . . . . F 9
Glasgow, 695,630 (1,800,000★) . . . . . . F 8
Greenock, 58,436 (101,000★)('81) . . F 8
Inverness, 38,204('81) D 8
Paisley, 84,330('81) . . F 8

Wales

1981 CENSUS

Cardiff, 262,313 (625,000★) . . . . . . J 9
Newport, 115,896 (310,000★) . . . . . . J 9
Swansea, 172,433 (275,000★) . . . . . . J 9

★ Population of metropolitan area, including suburbs.

Conic Projection, Two Standard Parallels

Kilometers 0 50 100 150 Km.
Miles 0 50 100 150 Mi.
1:5 000 000

Central Europe

Austria
1981 CENSUS
Graz, 243,166 (325,000★) H15
Innsbruck, 117,287 (185,000★) H11
Linz, 199,910 (335,000★) G14
Salzburg, 139,426 (220,000★) H13
Vienna *see* Wien G16
Villach, 52,692 (65,000★) I13
Wien (Vienna), 1,482,800 (1,875,000★)('88) . . G16

Belgium
1987 ESTIMATE
Antwerpen (Antwerp), 479,748 (1,100,000★) . . . . . D 4
Brugge, 117,755 (223,000★) . . . . D 3
Bruxelles (Brussel), 136,920 (2,385,000★) . . . . . E 4
Charleroi, 209,395 (480,000★) . . . . E 4
Gent (Gand), 233,856 (465,000★) . . . . D 3
Hasselt, 65,563 (290,000★) . . . . E 5
Liège, 200,891 (750,000★) . . . . E 5
Mons, 89,697 (242,000★) . . . . E 3

Czech Republic
1990 ESTIMATE
Brno, 392,285 (450,000★) F16
Hradec Králové, 101,302 (113,000★) E15
Liberec, 104,256 (175,000★) E15
Olomouc, 107,044 (126,000★) F17
Ostrava, 331,557 (760,000★) F18
Plzeň, 175,038 (210,000★) F13
Praha (Prague), 1,215,656 (1,325,000★) E14
Ústí nad Labem, 106,499 (115,000★) E14

Germany
1989 ESTIMATE
Aachen, 233,255 (535,000★) . . . . E 6
Augsburg, 247,731 (405,000★) G10
Berlin, 3,352,848 (3,825,000★) C13
Bielefeld, 311,946 (515,000★) . . . . C 8
Bochum, 389,087 . . . D 7
Bonn, 282,190 (570,000★) . . . . E 7
Braunschweig, 253,794 (330,000★) C10
Bremen, 535,058 (800,000★) . . . . B 8
Bremerhaven, 126,934 (190,000★) . . . . B 8
Chemnitz, 311,765 (450,000★) E12
Cologne *see* Köln . . . . E 6
Dortmund, 587,328 . . D 7
Dresden, 518,057 (670,000★) D13
Duisburg, 527,447 . . D 6
Düsseldorf, 569,641 (1,190,000★) . . . . . D 6
Erfurt, 220,016 . . . . . . E11
Essen, 620,594 (4,950,000★) . . . . . . D 7
Frankfurt am Main, 625,258 (1,855,000★) . . . . . . E 8
Gelsenkirchen, 287,255 . . . . D 7
Hagen, 210,640 . . . . D 7
Halle, 236,044 (475,000★) D11
Hamburg, 1,603,070 (2,225,000★) . . . . . . B 9
Hannover, 498,495 (1,000,000★) . . . . . . C 9
Karlsruhe, 265,100 (485,000★) . . . . F 8
Kiel, 240,675 (335,000★) A10
Köln (Cologne), 937,482 (1,760,000★) . . . . . . E 6
Leipzig, 545,307 (700,000★) D12
Lübeck, 210,681 (260,000★) B10
Magdeburg, 290,579 (400,000★) C11

★ Population of metropolitan area, including suburbs.

Mannheim, 300,468
(1,400,000★) . . . . . . F 8
Mönchengladbach,
252,910 (410,000★) D 6
München (Munich),
1,211,617
(1,955,000★) G11
Münster, 248,919 . . . . D 7
Nürnberg, 480,078
(1,030,000★) F11
Potsdam, 142,862 . . C13
Rostock, 253,990 . . . . A12
Saarbrücken, 188,467
(385,000★) . . . . F 6
Stuttgart, 562,658
(1,925,000★) . . . . . . G 9
Wiesbaden, 254,209
(795,000★) . . . . E 8
Wuppertal, 371,283
(830,000★) . . . . D 7

Hungary
1990 ESTIMATE

Budapest, 2,016,132
(2,565,000★) H19
Debrecen, 212,247 . . H21
Miskolc, 196,449 . . . . G20
Pécs, 170,119 . . . . . . I18
Szeged, 175,338 . . . . I20
Szombathely, 85,418 H16

Liechtenstein
1990 ESTIMATE

Vaduz, 4,874 . . . . . . H 9

Luxembourg
1985 ESTIMATE

Luxembourg, 76,130
(136,000★) . . . . F 6

Netherlands
1989 ESTIMATE

Amsterdam, 6,965,000
(1,860,000★) . . . . . . C 4
Eindhoven, 190,700
(379,377★) . . . . D 5
Groningen, 167,800
(206,781★) . . . . B 6
Rotterdam, 576,300
(1,110,000★) . . . . . . D 4
's-Gravenhage (The
Hague), 443,900
(770,000★) . . . . C 4
Tilburg, 155,100
(224,934★) . . . . D 5
Utrecht, 230,700
(518,779★) . . . . C 5

Poland
1989 ESTIMATE

Białystok, 263,900 . . B23
Bydgoszcz, 377,900 B18
Gdańsk (Danzig), 461,500
(909,000★) A18
Gdynia, 250,200 . . . . A18
Katowice, 365,800
(2,778,000★) E19
Kielce, 211,100 . . . . . . E20
Kraków, 743,700
(828,000★) E19
Łódź, 851,500
(1,061,000★) D19
Lublin, 309,500
(389,000★) D22
Poznań, 586,500
(672,000★) C16
Radom, 223,600 . . . . D21
Szczecin (Stettin), 409,500
(449,000★) B14
Toruń, 199,600 . . . . . . B18
Wałbrzych (Waldenburg),
141,400 (207,000★) E16
Warszawa (Warsaw),
1,651,200
(2,323,000★) C21
Wrocław (Breslau),
637,400 . . . . D17

Slovakia
1990 ESTIMATE

Bratislava, 442,999 . . G17
Košice, 237,099 . . . . G21

France

1982 CENSUS

Aix-en-Provence, 121,327 (126,552★) I12
Alès, 43,268 (70,180★) H11
Amiens, 131,332 (154,498★) .... C 9
Angers, 136,038 (195,859★) .... E 6
Angoulême, 46,197 (103,552★) ...... G 7
Bayonne, 41,381 (127,477★) .... I 5
Belfort, 51,206 (76,221★) E13
Besançon, 113,283 (120,772★) E13
Béziers, 76,647 (81,347★) I10
Bordeaux, 208,159 (640,012★) .... H 6
Boulogne-Billancourt, 102,582 .... D 9
Boulogne-sur-Mer, 47,653 (98,566★) .... B 8
Brest, 156,060 (201,145★) .... D 2
Brive-la-Gaillarde, 51,511 (64,301★) .... G 8
Caen, 114,068 (183,526★) .... C 6
Calais, 76,527 (100,823★) .... B 8
Cannes, 72,259 (295,525★) I14
Chalon-sur-Saône, 56,194 (78,064★) F11
Chambéry, 53,427 (96,163★) G12
Cherbourg, 28,442 (85,485★) .... C 5
Cholet, 55,524 ...... E 6
Clermont-Ferrand, 147,361 (256,189★) G10
Compiègne, 40,384 (62,778★) .... C 9
Creil, 34,709 (82,505★) .... C 9
Dieppe, 35,957 (41,812★) .... C 8
Dijon, 140,942 (215,865★) E12
Douai, 42,576 (202,366★) B10
Dunkerque, 73,120 (195,705★) .... A 9
Fontainebleau, 15,679 (35,629★) .... D 9
Grenoble, 156,637 (392,021★) G12
La Rochelle, 75,840 (102,143★) .... F 5
Laval, 50,360 (55,984★) .... D 6
Le Havre, 199,388 (254,595★) .... C 7
Le Mans, 147,697 (191,080★) .... D 7
Lens, 38,244 (327,383★) .... B 9
Lille, 168,424 (1,020,000★) B10
Limoges, 140,400 (171,689★) ...... G 8
Lorient, 62,554 (104,025★) .... E 3
Lourdes, 17,425 ...... I 6
Lyon, 413,095 (1,275,000★) G11
Mâcon, 38,404 (47,274★) F11
Marseille, 874,436 (1,225,000★) J12
Maubeuge, 36,061 (105,714★) B10
Meaux, 45,005 (55,797★) .... D 9
Melun, 35,005 (82,479★) .... D 9
Metz, 114,232 (186,437★) C13
Montbéliard, 31,836 (128,194★) E13
Montluçon, 49,912 (67,963★) .... F 9
Montpellier, 197,231 (221,307★) I10
Mulhouse, 112,157 (220,613★) E14
Nancy, 96,317 (306,982★) D13
Nantes, 240,539 (464,857★) .... E 5
Nevers, 43,013 (59,274★) E10
Nice, 337,085 (449,496★) I14
Nîmes, 124,220 (132,343★) I11
Niort, 58,203 (61,959★) .... F 6

Orléans, 102,710 (220,478★)........E 8
Paris, 2,078,900 (9,775,000★)('87)..D 9
Pau, 83,790 (131,265★)........I 6
Perpignan, 111,669 (137,915★)........J 9
Poitiers, 79,350 (103,204★)........F 7
Quimper, 56,907....D 2
Reims, 194,656 (199,388★)........C11
Rennes, 117,234 (234,418★)........D 5
Roanne, 48,705 (81,786★)........F11
Roubaix, 101,602....B10
Rouen, 101,945 (379,879★)........C 8
Saint-Brieuc, 48,563 (83,900★)........D 4
Saint-Denis, 90,829..D 9
Saint-Étienne, 204,955 (317,228★)........G11
Saint-Germain, 38,499 D 9
Saint-Malo, 46,347..D 4
Saint-Nazaire, 68,348 (130,271★)........E 4
Saint-Quentin, 63,567 (71,887★)........C10
Saint-Tropez, 4,961 (6,213▲)........I13
Sedan, 23,477 (30,871★)........C11
Strasbourg, 248,712 (400,000★)........D14
Toulon, 179,423 (410,393★)........I12
Toulouse, 347,995 (541,271★)........I 8
Tourcoing, 96,908..B10
Tours, 132,209 (262,786★)........E 7
Troyes, 63,581 (125,240★)........D11
Valence, 66,356 (106,041★)........H11
Valenciennes, 40,275 (349,505★)........B10
Verdun, 21,516 (26,944★)........C12
Versailles, 91,494....D 9
Vichy, 30,527 (63,501★)........F10
Villeurbanne, 115,960 G11

Guernsey

1986 CENSUS

Saint Peter Port, 16,085 (36,000★)........C 4

Jersey

1986 CENSUS

Saint Helier, 27,083 (46,500★)........C 4

Liechtenstein

1990 ESTIMATE

Vaduz, 4,874........E16

Luxembourg

1985 ESTIMATE

Luxembourg, 76,130 (136,000★)........C13

Monaco

1982 CENSUS

Monaco, 27,063 (87,000★)........I14

Switzerland

1990 ESTIMATE

Basel (Bâle), 169,587 (575,000★)........F14
Bern (Berne), 134,393 (298,800★)........F14
Fribourg (Freiburg), 33,962 (56,800★)........F14
Genève, 165,404 (460,000★)........F13
Lausanne, 122,600 (259,900★)........F13
Luzern, 59,115 (159,500★)........E15
Neuchâtel, 32,509 (65,900★)........F13
Sankt Gallen, 73,191 (125,000★)........E16
Sankt Moritz, 5,335('87)........F16
Schaffhausen, 33,956 (53,000★)........E15
Thun, 37,707 (77,200★)........F14
Winterthur, 85,174 (107,400★)........E15
Zürich, 342,861 (860,000★)........E15

★ Population of metropolitan area, including suburbs.
▲ Population of entire district, including rural area.

Lambert Conformal Conic Projection

Spain and Portugal

Andorra

1986 CENSUS

Andorra, 18,463 .... C13

Gibraltar

1988 ESTIMATE

Gibraltar, 30,077 .... I 6

Portugal

1981 CENSUS

Almada, 42,607 .... G 2
Barreiro, 50,863 .... G 2
Beja, 19,643 .... G 4
Braga, 63,033 ...... D 3
Coimbra, 74,616 .... E 3
Covilhã, 21,807 ...... E 4
Évora, 34,851 ...... G 4
Faro, 27,974 .... H 4
Funchal, 44,111 .... m21
Guimarães, 21,947 .. D 3
Lisboa (Lisbon), 807,167 (2,250,000★)...... G 2
Montijo, 23,017...... G 3
Porto, 327,368 (1,225,000★)...... D 3
Póvoa de Varzim, 23,729 .... D 3
Santarém, 19,761.... F 3
Setúbal, 77,885 .... G 3
Vila do Conde, 20,613 D 3
Vila Nova de Gaia, 62,469 .... D 3

Spain

1988 ESTIMATE

Albacete, 125,997 .. G10
Alcalá de Guadaira, 50,935 .... H 6
Alcalá de Henares, 150,021 .... E 8
Alcantarilla, 28,279 .. H10
Alcázar de San Juan, 26,258 .... F 8
Alcira, 40,575 ...... F11
Alcoy, 66,074 ...... G11
Algeciras, 99,528 .... I 6
Alicante, 261,051.... G11
Almendralejo, 25,352 G 5
Almería, 157,644 .... I 9
Andújar, 32,300 (37,020▲)........ G 7
Antequera, 32,200 (41,284▲)........ H 7
Aranjuez, 37,694 .... E 8
Arcos de la Frontera, 19,600 (27,311▲) .. I 6
Arrecife, 36,297...... p27
Ávila, 45,092........ E 7
Avilés, 87,811 (131,000★)........ B 6
Badajoz, 106,400 (122,407▲) ...... G 5
Badalona, 225,229 .. D14
Barcelona, 1,714,355 (4,040,000★)........ D14
Baza, 20,910 ...... H 9
Bilbao, 384,733 (985,000★)........ B 9
Burgos, 160,561 .... C 8
Burjasot, 35,011 .... F11
Cáceres, 71,598 .... F 5
Cádiz, 156,591 (240,000★)........ I 5
Cartagena, 70,000 (172,710▲)........ H11
Castellón de la Plana, 131,809 .... F11
Chiclana de la Frontera, 43,157 .... I 5
Ciudad Real, 56,300 G 8
Córdoba, 302,301 .. H 7
Coria del Río, 21,844 H 5
Cuenca, 42,222...... E 9
Don Benito, 24,500 (29,324▲) .... G 6
Durango, 27,425 .... B 9
Écija, 30,900 (35,836▲) .... H 6
Éibar, 34,355 ...... B 9
Elche, 158,300 (180,256▲) G11
Elda, 56,756 .... G11
El Ferrol del Caudillo, 86,503 (129,000★) B 3
El Puerto de Santa María, 49,900 (62,285▲) .. I 5
Gandía, 46,100 (52,646▲) G11
Gavá, 34,613 ...... D14
Gerona, 30,900 (68,902▲) D14
Getafe, 135,367 .... E 8
Gijón, 262,156 ...... B 6
Granada, 263,334.... H 8
Granollers, 49,045 .. D14
Guadalajara, 61,309 .. E 8
Hospitalet, 278,449 .. D14
Huelva, 137,826 .... H 5
Huesca, 41,841 .... C11
Irún, 54,886 .... B10
Jaén, 106,435 ...... H 8

★ Population of metropolitan area, including suburbs.
▲ Population of entire district, including rural area.

Játiva, 23,755 ...... G11
Jerez de la Frontera, 156,200 (183,007▲) I 5
La Coruña, 248,862 .. B 3
La Línea, 60,956 .... I 6
Las Palmas de Gran Canaria, 319,000 (366,347▲)........p25
León, 136,558 (159,000★)........C 6
Lérida, 91,500 (109,795▲)........D12
Linares, 58,622......G 8
Logroño, 119,038....C 9
Lorca, 26,700 (66,437▲) H10
Los Palacios y Villafranca, 28,798 .... H 6
Lugo, 68,700 (78,795▲) .... B 4
Madrid, 3,102,846 (4,650,000★)......E 8
Málaga, 574,456 .... I 7
Manresa, 65,607 .... D13
Mataró, 100,817 .... D14
Mérida, 52,368......G 5
Miranda de Ebro, 36,201 .... C 9
Morón de la Frontera, 29,048 .... H 6
Motril, 38,600 (45,901▲) .... I 8
Murcia, 149,800 (314,124▲)........H10
Onteniente, 29,591 .. G11
Orense, 106,042 .... C 4
Oviedo, 168,900 (190,073▲)........B 6
Palencia, 76,692 .... C 7
Palma [de Mallorca], 249,000 (314,608▲) F14
Pamplona, 180,598 .. C10
Plasencia, 33,613....E 5
Ponferrada, 33,900 (59,868▲) .... C 5
Pontevedra, 40,500 (68,223▲) .... C 3
Portugalete, 57,813 .. B 8
Prat de Llobregat, 64,193 .... D14
Puertollano, 52,284 .. G 7
Reus, 83,800 ...... D13
Sabadell, 189,489....D14
Sagunto, 19,600 (56,551▲) F11
Salamanca, 159,342..E 6
San Fernando, 81,975 I 5
Sanlúcar de Barrameda, 38,100 (54,690▲) .. I 5
San Sebastián, 177,622 (285,000★)........B10
Santa Cruz de Tenerife, 215,228 .... p24
Santander, 166,800 (190,795▲)........B 8
Santiago de Compostela, 68,800 (88,110▲)..C 3
San Vicente de Baracaldo, 113,502..........B 9
Segovia, 54,402 .... E 7
Sevilla, 663,132 (945,000★)........H 6
Soria, 31,926 ...... D 9
Sueca, 24,667 ...... F11
Talavera de la Reina, 68,158 .... F 7
Tarragona, 63,500 (109,586▲)........D13
Tarrasa, 161,410 .... D14
Teruel, 28,029 ...... E10
Toledo, 59,551 ...... F 7
Tomelloso, 28,386 .. F 9
Torrelavega, 28,900 (59,601▲) .... B 7
Torrente, 55,751 .... F11
Tudela, 26,618 ...... C10
Úbeda, 31,179 ...... G 8
Utrera, 36,300 (41,002▲) .... H 6
Valdepeñas, 25,568 .. G 8
Valencia, 743,933 (1,270,000★) F11
Valladolid, 331,461 .. D 7
Vall de Uxó, 27,853 .. F11
Vélez-Málaga, 32,200 (51,132▲) .... I 7
Vich, 28,873 .... D14
Vigo, 179,500 (271,128▲)........C 3
Villanueva y Geltrú, 46,364 .... D13
Vitoria, 204,264 .... C 9
Zamora, 62,047 .... D 6
Zaragoza, 582,239 .. D11

Spanish North Africa

1988 ESTIMATE

Ceuta, 67,188 ...... J 6
Melilla, 55,717 ...... J 9

Bosnia and Herzegovina

1987 ESTIMATE

- Banja Luka, 130,900 (193,890▲) E12
- Mostar, 47,606('71) F12
- Sarajevo, 341,200 (479,688▲) F13
- Tuzla, 67,300 (129,967▲) E13
- Zenica, 67,500 (144,869▲) E12

Croatia

1987 ESTIMATE

- Osijek, 106,800 (162,490▲)('87) D13
- Rijeka, 166,400 (199,282▲)('87) .... D 9
- Sisak, 38,421('71) D11
- Split, 191,074('87) F11
- Zadar, 43,187('71) E10
- Zagreb, 697,925('87) .. D10

Italy

1987 ESTIMATE

- Acireale, 46,997 ...... L10
- Agrigento, 41,200 (54,600▲) .... L 8
- Alcamo, 43,072 ...... L 7
- Alessandria, 75,100 (96,014▲) .... E 3
- Altamura, 54,784 ...... I11
- Ancona, 104,409 ...... F 8
- Andria, 88,348 .... H11
- Anzio, 30,806 .... H 7
- Arezzo, 74,200 (91,681▲) .... F 6
- Asti, 63,600 (75,459▲) E 3
- Avellino, 56,407 .... I 9
- Bagheria, 43,725 ...... K 8
- Bari, 362,524 (475,000★) H11
- Barletta, 86,954 ...... H11
- Benevento, 54,400 (65,661▲) .... H 9
- Bergamo, 118,959 (345,000★) .... D 4
- Bisceglie, 47,771 ...... H11
- Bologna, 432,406 (525,000★) .... E 6
- Bolzano (Bozen), 101,515 .... C 6
- Brescia, 199,286 ...... D 5
- Brindisi, 92,280 .... I12
- Busto Arsizio, 78,056 .. D 3
- Cagliari, 220,574 (305,000★) .... J 4
- Caltanissetta, 62,352 .. L 9
- Carrara, 69,229 ...... E 5
- Caserta, 65,974 ...... H 9
- Castellammare [di Stabia], 68,491 .... I 9
- Catania, 372,486 (550,000★) L10
- Catanzaro, 102,558 ... K11
- Cerignola, 53,463 .... H10
- Cesena, 72,600 (90,012▲) .... E 7
- Civitavecchia, 50,806 .. G 6
- Como, 91,738 (165,000★) .... D 4
- Cosenza, 106,026 (150,000★) J11
- Cremona, 76,979 ...... D 5
- Ferrara, 113,300 (143,950▲) .... E 6
- Firenze (Florence), 425,835 (640,000★) .... F 6
- Foggia, 155,051 ...... H10
- Forlì, 91,200 (110,482▲) E 7
- Gela, 79,378 .... L 9
- Genova (Genoa), 727,427 (805,000★) .... E 3
- Grosseto, 56,400 (70,592▲) .... G 6
- Iesi, 40,855 .... F 8
- Imola, 48,200 (61,587▲) E 6
- Imperia, 41,481 ...... F 3
- La Spezia, 108,937 (185,000★) .... E 4

★ Population of metropolitan area, including suburbs. ▲ Population of entire district, including rural area.

Latina, 67,800 (98,479▲) . . . . H 7
Lecce, 100,981 . . . . I13
Livorno (Leghorn), 174,065 . . . . F 5
Lucca, 88,024 . . . . F 5
Manfredonia, 57,707 . . H10
Marsala, 80,468 . . . . . . L 7
Massa, 66,872 (145,000★) . . . . E 5
Messina, 268,896 . . . . K10
Mestre, 189,700 . . . . . . D 7
Milano (Milan), 1,495,260 (3,750,000★) . . . . D 4
Modena, 176,330 . . . E 5
Molfetta, 64,519 . . . . . . H11
Monza, 122,064 . . . . . D 4
Napoli (Naples), 1,204,211 (2,875,000★) . . . . . . I 9
Novara, 102,742 . . . . D 3
Padova, 225,769 (270,000★) . . . . D 6
Palermo, 723,732 . . . . K 8
Parma, 175,842 . . . . . . E 5
Pavia, 82,065 . . . . D 4
Perugia, 106,700 (146,713▲) . . . . F 7
Pesaro, 78,700 (90,336▲) . . . . F 7
Pescara, 131,027 . . . . G 9
Piacenza, 105,626 . . . . D 4
Pisa, 104,384 . . . . F 5
Pistoia, 76,800 (90,689▲) . . . . F 5
Pozzuoli, 65,000 . . . . . . I 9
Prato, 164,595 (215,000★) . . . . F 6
Ragusa, 67,748 . . . . . . M 9
Ravenna, 86,500 (136,016▲) . . . . E 7
Reggio di Calabria, 178,821 . . . . K10
Reggio nell'Emilia, 107,300 (130,086▲) . . E 5
Rimini, 114,600 (130,698▲) . . . . E 7
Roma (Rome), 2,815,457 (3,175,000★) . . . . . . H 7
Salerno, 154,848 (250,000★) . . . . I 9
San Remo, 60,797 . . . . F 2
Sassari, 120,152 . . . . . . I 3
Siracusa, 122,857 . . . . L10
Taranto, 244,997 . . . . . . I12
Terni, 94,500 (111,157▲) . . . . G 7
Torino (Turin), 1,035,565 (1,550,000★) . . . . . . D 2
Trento, 81,500 (100,202▲) . . . . C 6
Treviso, 85,083 . . . . . . D 7
Trieste, 239,031 . . . . . . D 8
Udine, 100,211 (126,000★) . . . . C 8
Varese, 88,353 . . . . . . D 3
Venezia (Venice), 88,700 (420,000★) . . . . D 7
Verona, 259,151 . . . . . . D 6
Vicenza, 110,449 . . . . . . D 6

Malta

1989 ESTIMATE

Valletta, 9,210 (215,000★) . . . . N 9

San Marino

1988 ESTIMATE

San Marino, 2,777 . . . . F 7

Slovenia

1987 ESTIMATE

Ljubljana, 233,200 (316,607▲)('87) . . . . C 9
Maribor, 107,400 (187,651▲)('87) C10

Vatican City

1988 ESTIMATE

Vatican City, 766 . . . . . . H 7

Southeastern Europe

Albania
1987 ESTIMATE

- Berat, 40,500 . . . . I 3
- Durrës, 78,700 . . . . . . H 3
- Elbasan, 78,300 . . . . . . H 4
- Fier, 40,300('83) . . . . . . I 3
- Korçë, 61,500 . . . . I 4
- Shkodër, 76,300 . . . . G 3
- Tiranë, 255,700 . . . . . . H 3
- Vlorë, 67,700 . . . . I 3

Bosnia and Herzegovina
1987 ESTIMATE

- Sarajevo, 341,200 (479,688▲) . . . . F 2
- Zenica, 67,500 (144,869▲) . . . . E 1

Bulgaria
1986 ESTIMATE

- Burgas, 186,369 . . . . G11
- Dobrič, 110,471 . . . . . F11
- Gabrovo, 81,688 . . . . G 9
- Haskovo, 89,273 . . . . H 9
- Jambol, 92,321 . . . . . . G10
- Pernik, 96,277 . . . . . . G 7
- Pleven, 132,206 . . . . . . F 8
- Plovdiv, 349,148 . . . . G 8
- Ruse, 186,428 . . . . F 9
- Sliven, 104,345 . . . . . . G10
- Sofia *see* Sofija . . . . . . G 7
- Sofija (Sofia), 1,119,152 (1,205,000★) . . . . . . G 7
- Stara Zagora, 153,538 G 9
- Šumen, 102,886 . . . . . . F10
- Varna, 303,071 . . . . . . F11
- Veliko Târnovo, 70,610 F 9
- Vidin, 63,813 . . . . F 6
- Vraca, 77,934 . . . . F 7

Greece
1981 CENSUS

- Agrínion, 35,774 (45,087★) . . . . K 5
- Athínai (Athens), 885,737 (3,027,331★) . . . . . . L 7
- Iráklion, 102,398 (110,958★) . . . . N 9
- Kalámai, 42,075 (43,235★) . . . . L 6
- Kavála, 56,375 . . . . . . I 8
- Kérkira (Corfu), 33,561 J 3
- Khaniá, 47,451 (61,976★) . . . . N 8
- Lárisa, 102,048 . . . . . . J 6
- Pátrai, 142,163 (154,596★) . . . . K 5
- Piraiévs (Piraeus), 196,389 . . . . L 7
- Ródhos (Rhodes), 40,392 . . . . M12
- Thessaloníki (Salonika), 406,413 (706,180★) . . I 6
- Vólos, 71,378 (107,407★) . . . . J 6

Macedonia
1987 ESTIMATE

- Skopje, 444,900 (547,214▲) . . . . H 5

Moldova
1989 CENSUS

- Bălți, 159,000 . . . . . . B11
- Chișinău, 665,000 . . . . B12
- Râbnița, 58,000('87) . . B13
- Tighina, 130,000 . . . . C13
- Tiraspol, 182,000 . . . . C13

Romania
1986 ESTIMATE

- Arad, 187,744 . . . . . . C 5
- Bacău, 179,877 . . . . . . C10
- Baia Mare, 139,704 . . B 7
- Brăila, 235,620 . . . . . . D11
- Brașov, 351,493 . . . . D 9

★ Population of metropolitan area, including suburbs. ▲ Population of entire district, including rural area.

Kilometers 0 50 100 150 Km.
Miles 0 50 100 150 Mi.
1:4 000 000

Bucureşti (Bucharest), 1,989,823 (2,275,000★) E10
Buzău, 136,080 . . . . . . D10
Cluj-Napoca, 310,017 . . C 7
Constanţa, 327,676 . . E12
Craiova, 281,044 . . . . E 7
Galaţi, 295,372 . . . . . . D12
Iaşi, 313,060 . . . . B11
Oradea, 213,846 . . . . B 5
Ploieşti, 234,886 (310,000★) E10
Satu Mare, 130 082 . . B 6
Sibiu, 177,511 . . . . . . D 8
Târgu Mureş, 158,998 C 8
Timişoara, 325,272 . . . D 5

Turkey

1990 CENSUS

Bursa, 838,323 . . . . . . I13
Denizli, 203,130 . . . . . L13
İstanbul, 6,748,435 (7,000,000★) H12
İzmir, 2,553,209 (1,620,000★) K11
Manisa, 158,283 . . . . K11
Ödemiş, 511,110 . . . . K11

Yugoslavia

1987 ESTIMATE

Beograd (Belgrade), 1,130,000 (1,400,000★) . . . . . . E 4
Niš, 168,400 (240,219▲) F 5
Novi Sad, 176,000 (266,772▲) . . . . D 3
Pančevo, 62,700 . . . . E 4
Podgorica, 82,500 (145,163▲) . . . . G 3
Priština, 125,400 (244,830▲) . . . . G 5
Subotica, 100,500 (153,306▲) . . . . C 3
Zrenjanin, 65,400 (140,009▲) . . . . D 4

Baltic and Moscow Regions

Belarus

1989 CENSUS

Baranoviči, 159,000 .. H 9
Bobrujsk, 223,000 .. H12
Borisov, 144,000 .... G11
Brest, 258,000 ...... I 6
Gomel', 500,000 ...... I14
Grodno, 270,000 .... H 6
Lida, 81,000('87) .... H 8
Minsk, 1,589,000 (1,650,000★) H10
Mogil'ov, 356,000 .... H13
Molodečno, 87,000('87) ...... G 9
Novopolock, 90,000('87) F11
Orša, 123,000 ...... G13
Pinsk, 119,000 ...... I 9
Polock, 80,000('87) .. F11
Rečica, 71,000('87) .. I13
Sluck, 55,000('87) .. H10
Svetlogorsk, 68,000('87) ...... G 3
Vitebsk, 350,000 .... F13
Žlobin, 52,000('87) I13

Estonia

1989 CENSUS

Kohtla-Järve, 78,000('87) B10
Narva, 81,000('87) .. B11
Pärnu, 53,000('87) .. C 7
Tallinn, 482,000 .... B 7
Tartu, 114,000 ...... C 9

Latvia

1989 CENSUS

Daugavpils, 127,000 .. F 9
Jelgava, 72,000('87) .. E 6
Jūrmala, 65,000('87) .. E 6
Liepāja, 114,000 .... E 4
Rēzekne, 35,620('79) E10
Rīga, 915,000 (1,005,000★) ...... E 7
Ventspils, 52,000('87) D 4

Lithuania

1989 CENSUS

Kaunas, 423,000 .... G 6
Klaipėda (Memel), 204,000 .... F 4
Panevėžys, 126,000 .. F 7
Šiauliai, 145,000 .... F 6
Vilnius, 582,000 .... G 8

Russia

1989 CENSUS

Aleksandrov, 66,000('87) E21
Aleksin, 72,000('87) .. G20
Balachna, 35,359('79) E26
Balašicha, 136,000 .. F20
Bežeck, 30,711('79) .. D19
Bor, 65,000('87) E27
Boroviči, 64,000('87) C16
Br'ansk, 452,000 .... H17
Čechov, 57,000('87) .. F20
Čerepovec, 310,000 .. B20
Čern'achovsk, 36,361('79) ...... G 4
Chimki, 133,000 .... F20
Dmitrov, 64,000('87) .. E20
Domodedovo, 51,000('87) F20
Dubna, 64,000('87) .. E20
Dzeržinsk, 285,000 .. E26
Elektrostal', 153,000 .. F21
Furmanov, 44,430('79) D24
Gatčina, 81,000('87) .. B13
Gorki *see* Nižnij Novgorod E27
Gr'azi, 41,082('79) I22
Gus'-Chrustal'nyj, 75,000('87) F23
Ivanovo, 481,000 .... D23
Jarcevo, 40,908('79) .. F15
Jaroslavl', 633,000 .. D22
Jefremov, 58,000('87) I21
Jegorjevsk, 73,000('87) F22

★ Population of metropolitan area, including suburbs.

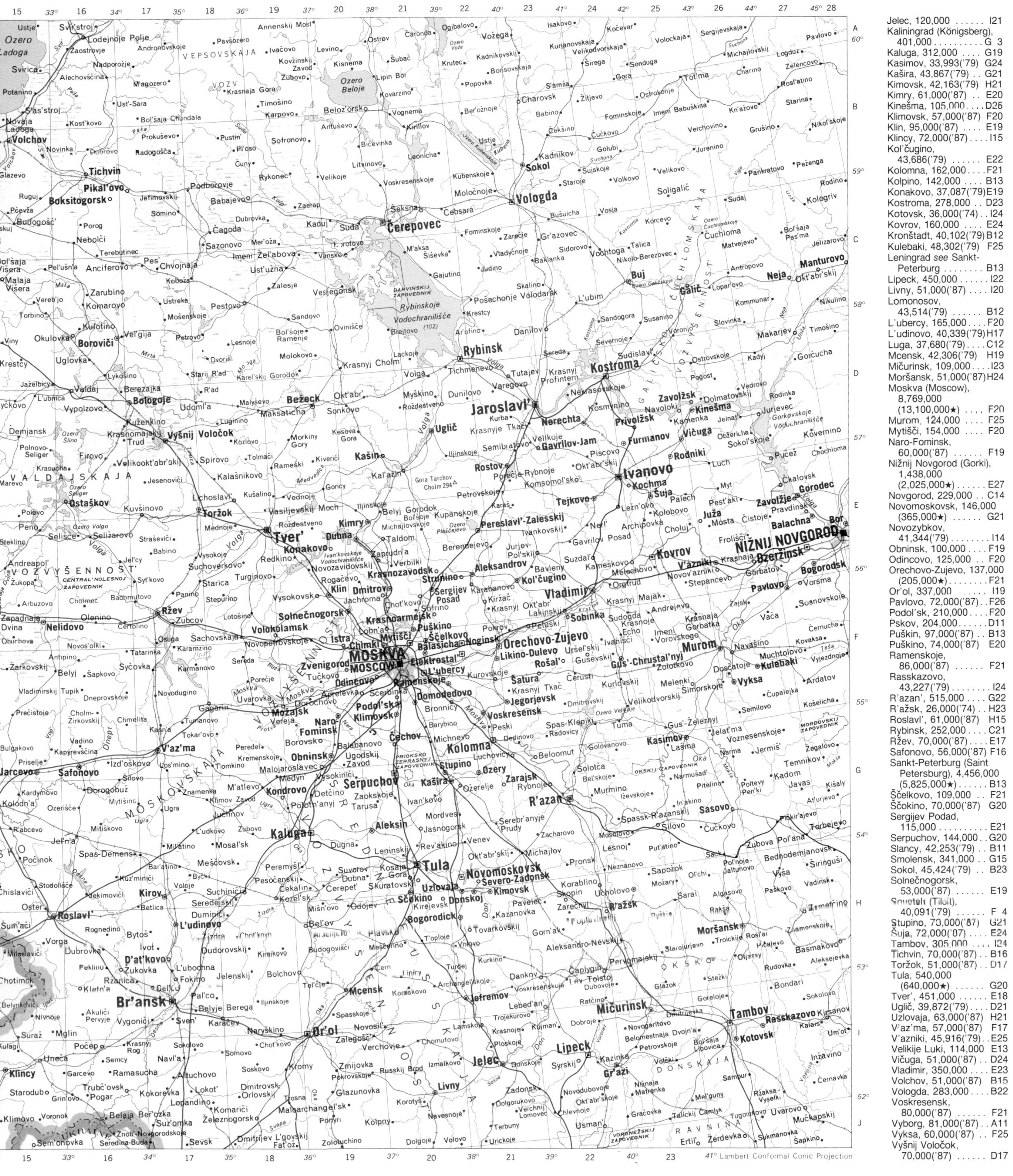

Ozero Ladoga
Tichvin
Boksitogorsk
Pikal'ovo
Volchov
Borovi či
Okulovka
Valdaj
Bologoje
Vyšnij Voloček
Ostaškov
Toržok
Tver'
Konakovo
Kimry
Dubna
Ržev
Nelidovo
Vologda
Čerepovec
Sokol
Rybinsk
Rybinskoje Vodochranilišče
Jaroslavl'
Kostroma
Kinešma
Ivanovo
Vladimir
Kovrov
Murom
Nižnij Novgorod
Dzeržinsk
Bor
Balachna
Gorodec
Uglič
Rostov
Pereslavl'-Zalesskij
Sergijev Posad
Klin
Dmitrov
Moskva
Moscow
Mytišči
Ščelkovo
Noginsk
Elektrostal'
Orechovo-Zujevo
L'ubercy
Ramenskoje
Podol'sk
Klimovsk
Domodedovo
Voskresensk
Kolomna
Serpuchov
Stupino
Kašira
Ozery
R'azan'
Kasimov
Vyksa
Kulebaki
Obninsk
Naro-Fominsk
Možajsk
Zvenigorod
Odincovo
Istra
Volokolamsk
Solnečnogorsk
V'az'ma
Safonovo
Jarcevo
Roslavl'
Kirov
L'udinovo
Kaluga
Aleksin
Tula
Novomoskovsk
Ščokino
Kimovsk
Uzlovaja
Bogorodick
Efremov
Mcensk
Or'ol
Br'ansk
Klincy
Livny
Jelec
Lipeck
Mičurinsk
Tambov
Rasskazovo
Kotovsk
Moršansk
Sasovo
R'ažsk
Lambert Conformal Conic Projection

Jelec, 120,000 ...... I21
Kaliningrad (Königsberg), 401,000 .... G 3
Kaluga, 312,000 .... G19
Kasimov, 33,993('79) G24
Kašira, 43,867('79) .. G21
Kimovsk, 42,163('79) H21
Kimry, 61,000('87) .. E20
Kinešma, 105,000 .... D25
Klimovsk, 57,000('87) F20
Klin, 95,000('87) E19
Klincy, 72,000('87) I15
Kol'čugino, 43,686('79) E22
Kolomna, 162,000 .... F21
Kolpino, 142,000 .... B13
Konakovo, 37,087('79) E19
Kostroma, 278,000 .. D23
Kotovsk, 36,000('74) .. I24
Kovrov, 160,000 .... E24
Kronštadt, 40,102('79) B12
Kulebaki, 48,302('79) F25
Leningrad *see* Sankt-Peterburg B13
Lipeck, 450,000 ...... I22
Livny, 51,000('87) I20
Lomonosov, 43,514('79) B12
L'ubercy, 165,000 .... F20
L'udinovo, 40,339('79) H17
Luga, 37,680('79) C12
Mcensk, 42,306('79) H19
Mičurinsk, 109,000 .... I23
Moršansk, 51,000('87) H24
Moskva (Moscow), 8,769,000 (13,100,000★) F20
Murom, 124,000 .... F25
Mytišči, 154,000 .... F20
Naro-Fominsk, 60,000('87) F19
Nižnij Novgorod (Gorki), 1,438,000 (2,025,000★) E27
Novgorod, 229,000 .. C14
Novomoskovsk, 146,000 (365,000★) G21
Novozybkov, 41,344('79) I14
Obninsk, 100,000 .... F19
Odincovo, 125,000 .. F20
Orechovo-Zujevo, 137,000 (205,000★) F21
Or'ol, 337,000 ...... I19
Pavlovo, 72,000('87) .. F26
Podol'sk, 210,000 .... F20
Pskov, 204,000 ...... D11
Puškin, 97,000('87) .. B13
Puškino, 74,000('87) E20
Ramenskoje, 86,000('87) F21
Rasskazovo, 43,227('79) I24
R'azan', 515,000 .... G22
R'ažsk, 26,000('74) .. H23
Roslavl', 61,000('87) H15
Rybinsk, 252,000 .... C21
Ržev, 70,000('87) E17
Safonovo, 56,000('87) F16
Sankt-Peterburg (Saint Petersburg), 4,456,000 (5,825,000★) B13
Ščelkovo, 109,000 .. F21
Ščokino, 70,000('87) G20
Sergijev Podad, 115,000 .... E21
Serpuchov, 144,000 .. G20
Slancy, 42,253('79) .. B11
Smolensk, 341,000 .. G15
Sokol, 45,424('79) .. B23
Solnečnogorsk, 53,000('87) E19
Sovetsk (Tilsit), 40,091('79) ...... F 4
Stupino, 73,000('87) G21
Šuja, 72,000('87) E24
Tambov, 305,000 .... I24
Tichvin, 70,000('87) .. B16
Toržok, 51,000('87) .. D17
Tula, 540,000 (640,000★) G20
Tver', 451,000 ...... E18
Uglič, 39,872('79) D21
Uzlovaja, 63,000('87) H21
V'az'ma, 57,000('87) F17
V'azniki, 45,916('79) .. E25
Velikije Luki, 114,000 E13
Vičuga, 51,000('87) .. D24
Vladimir, 350,000 .... E23
Volchov, 51,000('87) B15
Vologda, 283,000 .... B22
Voskresensk, 80,000('87) F21
Vyborg, 81,000('87) .. A11
Vyksa, 60,000('87) .. F25
Vyšnij Voloček, 70,000('87) D17

Asia

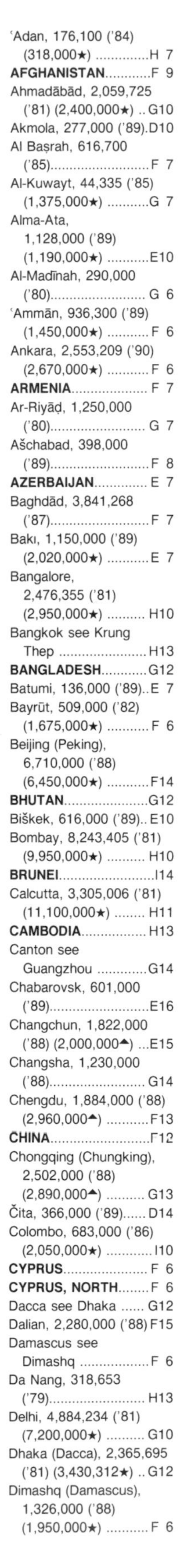

ʻAdan, 176,100 ('84)
(318,000★) ....H 7
AFGHANISTAN...........F 9
Ahmadābād, 2,059,725
('81) (2,400,000★) .. G10
Akmola, 277,000 ('89).D10
Al Baṣrah, 616,700
('85).........................F 7
Al-Kuwayt, 44,335 ('85)
(1,375,000★) ....G 7
Alma-Ata,
1,128,000 ('89)
(1,190,000★) E10
Al-Madīnah, 290,000
('80)........................ G 6
ʻAmmān, 936,300 ('89)
(1,450,000★) .... F 6
Ankara, 2,553,209 ('90)
(2,670,000★) .... F 6
ARMENIA.................... F 7
Ar-Riyāḍ, 1,250,000
('80)......................... G 7
Aščhabad, 398,000
('89).........................F 8
AZERBAIJAN............. E 7
Baghdād, 3,841,268
('87)..........................F 7
Bakı, 1,150,000 ('89)
(2,020,000★) ....E 7
Bangalore,
2,476,355 ('81)
(2,950,000★) H10
Bangkok see Krung
Thep H13
BANGLADESH...........G12
Batumi, 136,000 ('89)..E 7
Bayrūt, 509,000 ('82)
(1,675,000★) .... F 6
Beijing (Peking),
6,710,000 ('88)
(6,450,000★) F14
BHUTAN.....................G12
Biškek, 616,000 ('89).. E10
Bombay, 8,243,405 ('81)
(9,950,000★) H10
BRUNEI........................I14
Calcutta, 3,305,006 ('81)
(11,100,000★) H11
CAMBODIA................ H13
Canton see
Guangzhou G14
Chabarovsk, 601,000
('89).........................E16
Changchun, 1,822,000
('88) (2,000,000▲) ...E15
Changsha, 1,230,000
('88)........................ G14
Chengdu, 1,884,000 ('88)
(2,960,000▲) F13
CHINA.........................F12
Chongqing (Chungking),
2,502,000 ('88)
(2,890,000▲) G13
Čita, 366,000 ('89)...... D14
Colombo, 683,000 ('86)
(2,050,000★) I10
CYPRUS..................... F 6
CYPRUS, NORTH........ F 6
Dacca see Dhaka G12
Dalian, 2,280,000 ('88) F15
Damascus see
Dimashq .... F 6
Da Nang, 318,653
('79)......................... H13
Delhi, 4,884,234 ('81)
(7,200,000★) G10
Dhaka (Dacca), 2,365,695
('81) (3,430,312★) .. G12
Dimashq (Damascus),
1,326,000 ('88)
(1,950,000★) .... F 6

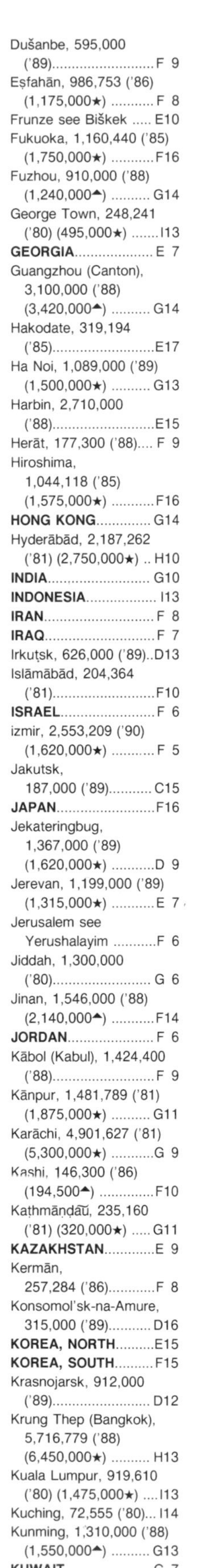

Dušanbe, 595,000
('89)......................... F 9
Eṣfahān, 986,753 ('86)
(1,175,000★) .... F 8
Frunze see Biškek E10
Fukuoka, 1,160,440 ('85)
(1,750,000★) F16
Fuzhou, 910,000 ('88)
(1,240,000▲) G14
George Town, 248,241
('80) (495,000★) I13
GEORGIA................... E 7
Guangzhou (Canton),
3,100,000 ('88)
(3,420,000▲) G14
Hakodate, 319,194
('85).........................E17
Ha Noi, 1,089,000 ('89)
(1,500,000★) G13
Harbin, 2,710,000
('88).........................E15
Herāt, 177,300 ('88).... F 9
Hiroshima,
1,044,118 ('85)
(1,575,000★) F16
HONG KONG............. G14
Hyderābād, 2,187,262
('81) (2,750,000★) .. H10
INDIA......................... G10
INDONESIA.................. I13
IRAN........................... F 8
IRAQ........................... F 7
Irkuṭsk, 626,000 ('89)..D13
Islāmābād, 204,364
('81).........................F10
ISRAEL........................ F 6
izmir, 2,553,209 ('90)
(1,620,000★) .... F 5
Jakutsk,
187,000 ('89).......... C15
JAPAN.........................F16
Jekateringbug,
1,367,000 ('89)
(1,620,000★) ....D 9
Jerevan, 1,199,000 ('89)
(1,315,000★) .... E 7
Jerusalem see
Yerushalayim ....F 6
Jiddah, 1,300,000
('80)......................... G 6
Jinan, 1,546,000 ('88)
(2,140,000▲) F14
JORDAN...................... F 6
Kābol (Kabul), 1,424,400
('88)......................... F 9
Kānpur, 1,481,789 ('81)
(1,875,000★) G11
Karāchi, 4,901,627 ('81)
(5,300,000★) ....G 9
Kashi, 146,300 ('86)
(194,500▲) F10
Kaṭhmāṇḍāū, 235,160
('81) (320,000★) G11
KAZAKHSTAN.............E 9
Kermān,
257,284 ('86)...........F 8
Konsomol'sk-na-Amure,
315,000 ('89).......... D16
KOREA, NORTH..........E15
KOREA, SOUTH..........F15
Krasnojarsk, 912,000
('89)......................... D12
Krung Thep (Bangkok),
5,716,779 ('88)
(6,450,000★) H13
Kuala Lumpur, 919,610
('80) (1,475,000★) I13
Kuching, 72,555 ('80)... I14
Kunming, 1,310,000 ('88)
(1,550,000▲) G13
KUWAIT...................... G 7

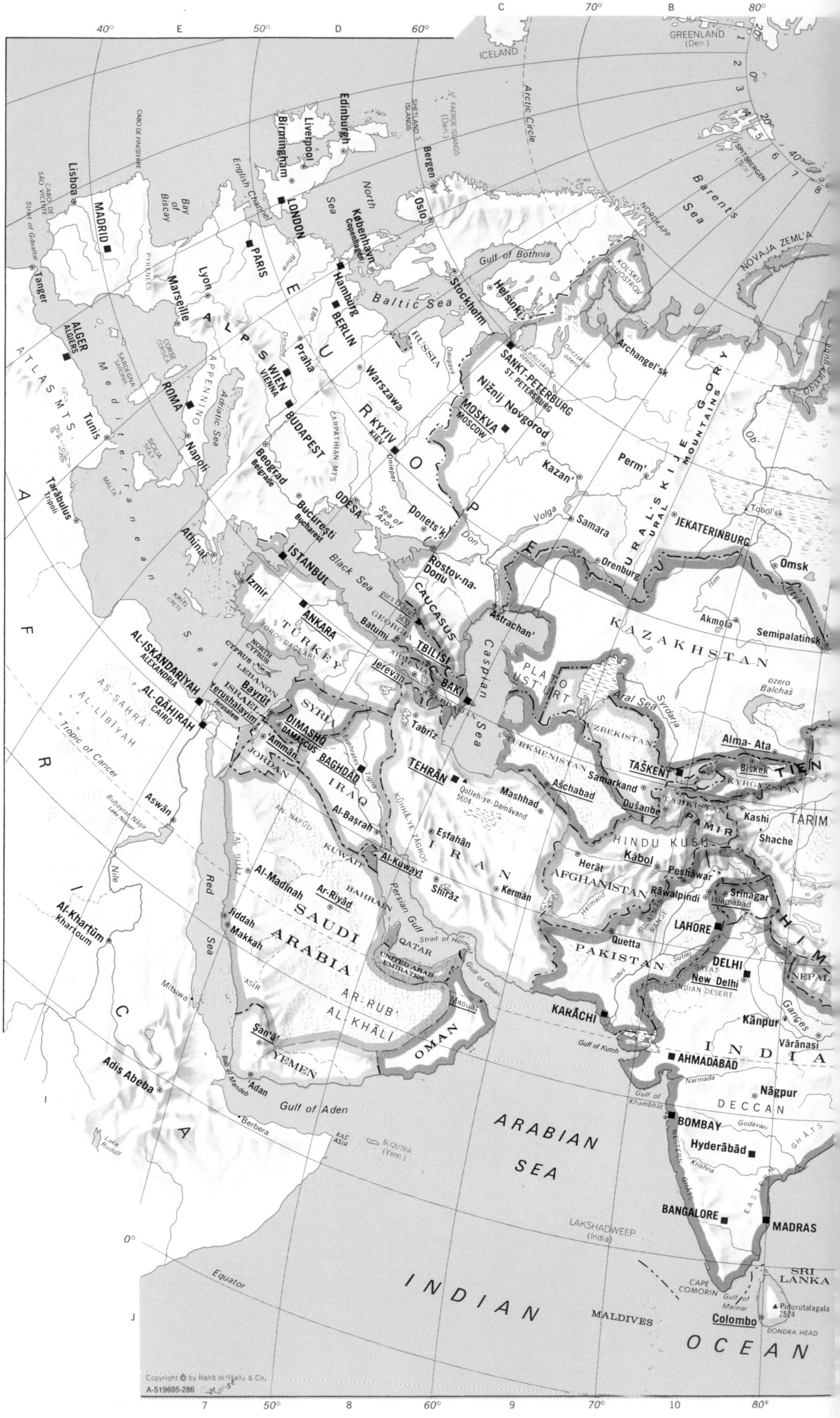

Kyōto,
1,479,218 ('85)........F16
KYRGYZSTAN........... E10
Kyzyl, 80,000 ('87)......D12
Lahore, 2,707,215 ('81)
(3,025,000★) F10
Lanzhou, 1,297,000 ('88)
(1,420,000▲) F13
LAOS........................ H13
LEBANON...................F 6
Lhasa, 84,400 ('86)
(107,700▲) G12
MACAU...................... G14
Madras, 3,276,622 ('81)
(4,475,000★) H11
Makkah,
550,000 ('80).......... G 6
MALAYSIA.................. I13
MALDIVES...................I10
Mandalay, 532,949
('83)........................ G12
Manila, 1,587,000 ('90)
(6,800,000★) H15
Mashhad, 1,463,508
('86)......................... F 8
Masqaṭ, 50,000 ('81)...G 8
Mawlamyine, 219,961
('83)......................... H12
MONGOLIA................ E13
MYANMAR..................G12
Nāgpur, 1,219,461 ('81)
(1,302,066★) G10
Nanjing, 2,390,000
('88).........................F14
NEPAL....................... G11
New Delhi, 273,036
('81)......................... G10
Novosibirsk, 1,436,000
('89) (1,600,000★) .. D11
Ochotsk, 9,000.......... D17
OMAN......................... G 8
Omsk, 1,148,000 ('89)
(1,175,000★) D10
Ōsaka, 2,636,249 ('85)
(1,645,000★) F16
PAKISTAN..................G 9
Patna, 776,371 ('81)
(1,025,000★) G11
Peking see Beijing F14
Peshāwar, 506,896 ('81)
(566,248★) F10
Petropavlovsk-Kamčatskij,
269,000 ('89).......... D18
PHILIPPINES...............H15
Phnum Penh, 700,000
('86)......................... H13
Pyŏngyang, 1,283,000
('81) (1,600,000★) ...F15
QATAR.......................G 8
Qingdao (Tsingtao),
1,300,000 ('88)........F15
Quetta, 244,842 ('81)
(285,719★) .... F 9
Quezon City, 1,632,000
('90)......................... H15
Rangoon see
Yangon H12
Rāwalpindi, 457,091 ('81)
(1,040,000★) F10
RUSSIA......................D10
Saigon see Thanh Pho Ho
Chi Minh H13
Samarkand, 366,000
('89)......................... F 9
Ṣan'ā', 427,150 ('86)...H 7
SAUDI ARABIA.......... G 7
Semipalatinsk, 334,000
('89)......................... D11
Sendai, 700,254 ('85)
(1,175,000★) F17

Shanghai,
7,220,000 ('88)
(9,300,000★) F15
Shenyang (Mukden),
3,910,000 ('88)
(4,370,000▲) E15
Shīrāz, 848,289 ('86)...G 8
SINGAPORE.................I13
Sŏul, 10,522,000 ('89)
(15,850,000★) F15
SRI LANKA...................I11
Srīnagar, 594,775 ('81)
(606,002★) F10
SYRIA..........................F 6
Tabrīz, 971,482 ('86)... F 7
T'aipei, 2,637,100 ('88)
(6,130,000★) G15
TAIWAN......................G15
Taiyuan, 1,700,000 ('88)
(1,980,000▲) F14
TAJIKISTAN................F10
Taškent, 2,073,000 ('89)
(2,325,000★) ....E 9
Tbilisi, 1,260,000 ('89)
(1,460,000★) ....E 7
Tehrān, 6,042,584 ('86)
(7,500,000★) ....F 8
THAILAND.................. H13
Thanh Pho Ho Chi Minh
(Saigon), 3,169,000 ('89)
(3,100,000★) H13
Tianjin (Tientsin),
4,950,000 ('88)
(5,540,000▲) F14
Tobol'sk,
82,000 ('87)............ D 9
Tōkyō, 8,354,615 ('85)
(27,700,000★) F16
Tomsk, 502,000 ('89)..D11
TURKEY.......................F 6
TURKMENISTAN.......... F 9
Ulaanbaatar, 548,400
('89)..........................E13
UNITED ARAB EMIRATES............. G 8
Ürümqi, 1,060,000
('88)..........................E11
UZBEKISTAN............. E 9
Vārānasi, 708,647 ('81)
(925,000★) G11
Verchojansk, 1,400..... C16
Viangchan, 377,409
('85)......................... H13
VIETNAM................... H13
Vladivostok, 648,000
('89)..........................E16
Wuhan, 3,570,000
('88)..........................F14
Xiamen, 343,700 ('86)
(546,400▲) G14
Xi'an, 2,210,000 ('88)
(2,580,000▲) F13
Yangon (Rangoon),
2,705,039 ('83)
(2,800,000★) H12
YEMEN.......................H 7
Yerevan see Jerevan ..E 7
Yerushalayim (Jerusalem),
493,500 ('89)
(530,000★) ....F 6
Yokohama, 2,992,926
('85)..........................F16
Zhangjiakou,
500,000 ('88)
(640,000▲) E14

★ Population of metropolitan area, including suburbs
▲ Population of entire district, including rural area.

Northwest Asia

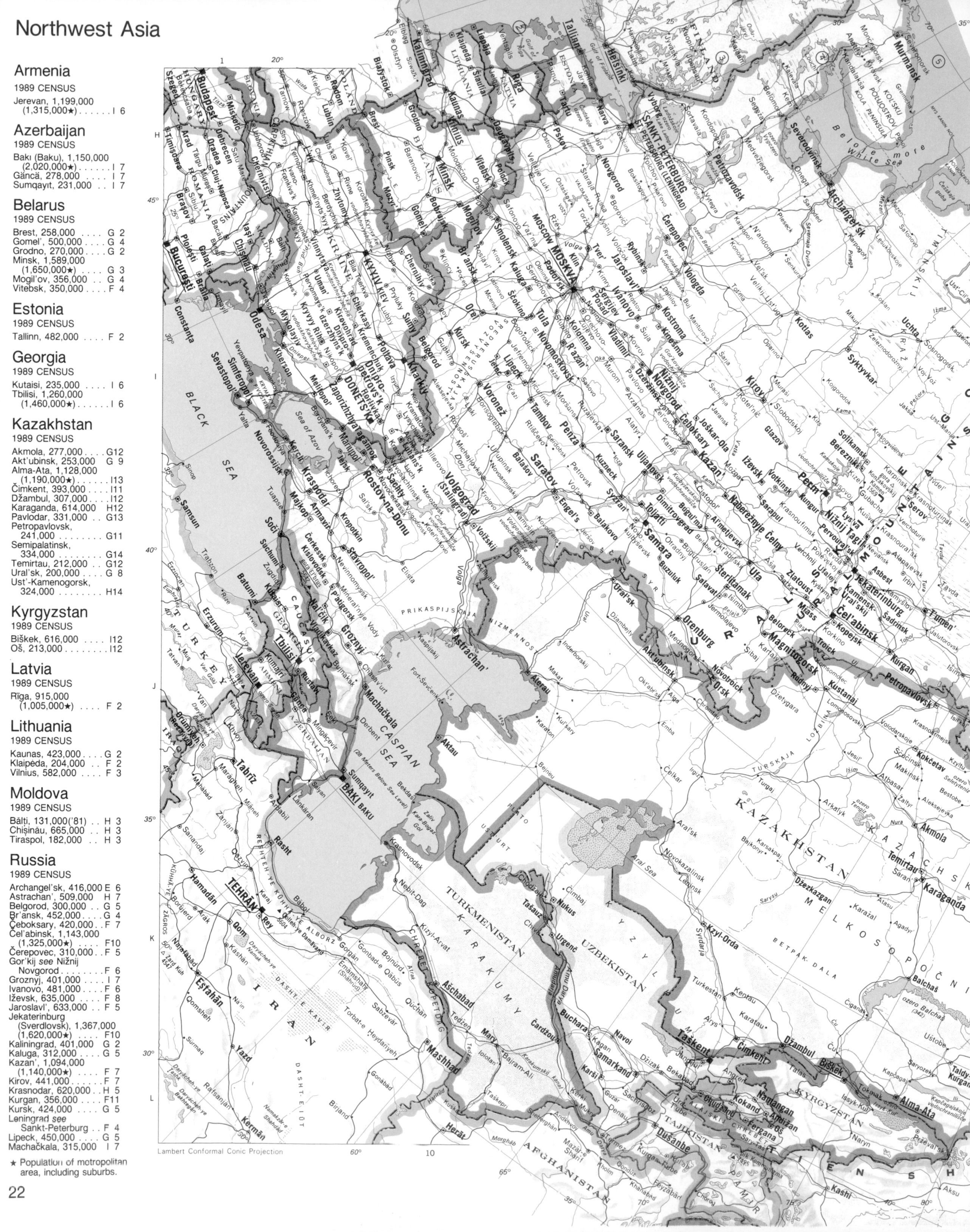

Armenia
1989 CENSUS

Jerevan, 1,199,000 (1,315,000★) . . . . . . I 6

Azerbaijan
1989 CENSUS

Bakı (Baku), 1,150,000 (2,020,000★) . . . . . . I 7
Gäncä, 278,000 . . . . I 7
Sumqayıt, 231,000 . . I 7

Belarus
1989 CENSUS

Brest, 258,000 . . . . G 2
Gomel', 500,000 . . . . G 4
Grodno, 270,000 . . . . G 2
Minsk, 1,589,000 (1,650,000★) . . . . G 3
Mogil'ov, 356,000 . . G 4
Vitebsk, 350,000 . . . . F 4

Estonia
1989 CENSUS

Tallinn, 482,000 . . . . F 2

Georgia
1989 CENSUS

Kutaisi, 235,000 . . . . I 6
Tbilisi, 1,260,000 (1,460,000★) . . . . . . I 6

Kazakhstan
1989 CENSUS

Akmola, 277,000 . . . . G12
Akt'ubinsk, 253,000 G 9
Alma-Ata, 1,128,000 (1,190,000★) I13
Čimkent, 393,000 . . . . I11
Džambul, 307,000 . . . . I12
Karaganda, 614,000 H12
Pavlodar, 331,000 . . G13
Petropavlovsk, 241,000 . . . . G11
Semipalatinsk, 334,000 . . . . G14
Temirtau, 212,000 . . G12
Ural'sk, 200,000 . . . . G 8
Ust'-Kamenogorsk, 324,000 . . . . H14

Kyrgyzstan
1989 CENSUS

Biškek, 616,000 . . . . I12
Oš, 213,000 . . . . I12

Latvia
1989 CENSUS

Rīga, 915,000 (1,005,000★) . . . . F 2

Lithuania
1989 CENSUS

Kaunas, 423,000 . . . . G 2
Klaipėda, 204,000 . . F 2
Vilnius, 582,000 . . . . F 3

Moldova
1989 CENSUS

Bălți, 131,000('81) . . H 3
Chișinău, 665,000 . . H 3
Tiraspol, 182,000 . . H 3

Russia
1989 CENSUS

Archangel'sk, 416,000 E 6
Astrachan', 509,000 H 7
Belgorod, 300,000 . . G 5
Br'ansk, 452,000 . . . . G 4
Čeboksary, 420,000 . . F 7
Čel'abinsk, 1,143,000 (1,325,000★) F10
Čerepovec, 310,000 . . F 5
Gor'kij *see* Nižnij Novgorod . . . . F 6
Groznyj, 401,000 . . . . I 7
Ivanovo, 481,000 . . . . F 6
Iževsk, 635,000 . . . . F 8
Jaroslavl', 633,000 . . F 5
Jekaterinburg (Sverdlovsk), 1,367,000 (1,620,000★) F10
Kaliningrad, 401,000 G 2
Kaluga, 312,000 . . . . G 5
Kazan', 1,094,000 (1,140,000★) . . . . F 7
Kirov, 441,000 . . . . . . F 7
Krasnodar, 620,000 . . H 5
Kurgan, 356,000 . . . . F11
Kursk, 424,000 . . . . G 5
Leningrad *see* Sankt-Peterburg . . F 4
Lipeck, 450,000 . . . . G 5
Machačkala, 315,000 I 7

★ Population of metropolitan area, including suburbs.

Magnitogorsk, 440,000 .... G 9
Moskva (Moscow), 8,769,000 (13,100,000★) .... F 5
Murmansk, 468,000 .. D 4
Naberežnyje Čelny, 501,000 .... F 8
Nižnij Novgorod (Gor'kij), 1,438,000 (2,025,000★) .... F 6
Nižnij Tagil, 440,000 F 9
Orel, 337,000 ...... G 5
Orenburg, 547,000 .. G 9
Orsk, 271,000 ..... G 9
Penza, 543,000 .... G 7
Perm', 1,091,000 (1,160,000★) .... F 9
Petrozavodsk, 270,000 .... E 4
R'azan', 515,000 .... G 5
Rostov-na-Donu, 1,020,000 (1,165,000★) .... H 5
Samara, 1,257,000 (1,505,000★) .... G 8
Sankt-Peterburg (St. Petersburg), 4,456,000 (5,825,000★) .... F 4
Saransk, 312,000 .. G 7
Saratov, 905,000 (1,155,000★) .... G 7
Smolensk, 341,000 .. G 4
Soči, 337,000 ...... I 5
Stalingrad *see* Volgograd ...... H 6
Stavropol', 318,000 .. H 6
Sverdlovsk *see* Jekaterinburg F10
Syktyvkar, 233,000 .. E 8
Taganrog, 291,000 .. H 5
Tambov, 305,000 .. G 6
Toljatti, 630,000 .... G 7
Tula, 540,000 (640,000★) ...... G 5
Tver' (Kalinin), 451,000 .... F 5
Ufa, 1,083,000 (1,100,000★) .... G 9
Uljanovsk, 625,000 .. G 7
Vladikavkaz, 300,000 I 6
Vladimir, 350,000 .... F 6
Volgograd (Stalingrad), 999,000 (1,360,000★) .... H 6
Vologda, 283,000 .. F 5
Volžskij, 269,000 .... H 6
Voronež, 887,000 .. G 5

Tajikistan

1989 CENSUS

Dušanbe, 595,000 .. J11

Turkmenistan

1989 CENSUS

Aščhabad, 398,000 .. J 9

Ukraine

1989 CENSUS

Cherkasy, 290,000 .. H 4
Chernihiv, 296,000 .. G 4
Dniprodzerzhynsk, 282,000 .... H 4
Dnipropetrovsk, 1,179,000 (1,600,000★) .... H 4
Donets'k, 1,110,000 (2,200,000★) .... H 5
Horlivka, 337,000 (710,000★) ...... H 5
Kharkiv, 1,611,000 (1,940,000★) .... G 5
Kherson, 355,000 .. H 4
Kryvyy Rih, 713,000 H 4
Kyyiv (Kiev), 2,587,000 (2,900,000★) .... G 4
Luhansk, 497,000 .. H 5
L'viv, 790,000 ...... H 2
Mariupol' (Ždanov), 517,000 ...... H 5
Mykolayiv, 503,000 H 4
Odesa, 1,115,000 (1,185,000★) .... H 4
Poltava, 315,000 .... H 4
Sevastopol', 356,000 I 4
Simferopol', 344,000 .. I 4
Sumy, 291,000 .... G 4
Vinnytsya, 374,000 .. H 3
Yalta, 89,000('87) .... I 4
Zaporizhzhya, 884,000 .... H 5
Zhytomyr, 292,000 .. G 3

Uzbekistan

1989 CENSUS

Andižan, 293,000 .... I12
Buchara, 224,000 .... J10
Fergana, 200,000 .... I12
Namangan, 308,000 .. I12
Samarkand, 366,000 J11
Taškent, 2,073,000 (2,325,000★) I11

Northeast Asia

Russia

1989 CENSUS

Abakan, 154,000 .... G12
Ačinsk, 122,000 .... F12
Alapajevsk, 51,000('87) ...... F 6
Aldan, 20,000('74) .. F19
Alejsk, 31,390('79) .. G10
Aleksandrovsk-Sachalinskij, 20,000('74) G22
Angarsk, 266,000 .... G14
Anžero-Sudžensk, 108,000 .... F11
Arsenjev, 67,000('87) .. I20
Art'om, 73,000('87) .. I20
Art'omovsk, 17,000('79) G12
Asbest, 83,000('87) .. F 6
Asino, 31,329('79) ... F11
Balej, 25,000('79) G17
Barabinsk, 35,035('79) F 9
Barnaul, 602,000 (665,000★) G10
Belogorsk, 71,000('87) G19
Belovo, 118,000('87) G11
Berdsk, 77,000('87) .. G10
Berezniki, 201,000 .. F 5
Bijsk, 233,000 ...... G11
Bikin, 18,000('79) H20
Birobidžan, 82,000('87) H20
Blagoveščensk, 206,000 .... G19
Bogotol, 29,000('79) .. F11
Bolotnoje, 20,000('79) F10
Bratsk, 255,000 .... F14
Čel'abinsk, 1,143,000 (1,325,000★) ...... F 6
Čeremchovo, 73,000('87) G14
Černogorsk, 80,000('87) G12
Chabarovsk, 601,000 H21
Chanty-Mansijsk, 27,961('79) ...... E 7
Čholmsk, 50,000('87) H22
Čita, 366,000 ...... G16
Čusovoj, 59,000('87) F 5
Dudinka, 23,000('74) D11
Gorno-Altajsk, 39,917('79) G11
Gubacha, 32,461('79) F 5
Gusinoozersk, 18,000('79) G15
Igarka, 16,918('79) .. D11
Inta, 58,000('87) .... D 6
Irbit, 53,000('87) .... F 6
Irkutsk, 626,000 .... G14
Iskitim, 69,000('87) .. G10
Issyk-Kul', 64,000('87) I 9
Jakutsk, 187,000 .... E19
Jekaterinburg, 1,367,000 (1,620,000★) ...... F 6
Jenisejsk, 22,000('79) F12
Jurga, 92,000('87) .. F10
Južno-Sachalinsk, 157,000 .... H22
Kamen'-na-Obi, 40,684('79) G10
Kamensk-Ural'skij, 209,000 .... F 6
Kansk, 110,000 ...... F13
Karpinsk, 36,569('79) F 6
Kemerovo, 520,000 .. F11
Kirensk, 16,000('74) .. F15
Kisel'ovsk, 128,000 .. G11
Kizel, 40,157('79) .... F 5
Kolpaševo, 27,000('79) F10
Komsomol'sk-na-Amure, 315,000 .... G21
Kopejsk, 99,000('87) F 6
Korkino, 63,000('81) G 6
Korsakov, 43,348('79) H22
Krasnojarsk, 912,000 F12

★ Population of metropolitan area, including suburbs.

Kilometers 0 200 400 600 Km.
Miles 0 200 400 600 Mi.

1:16 000 000

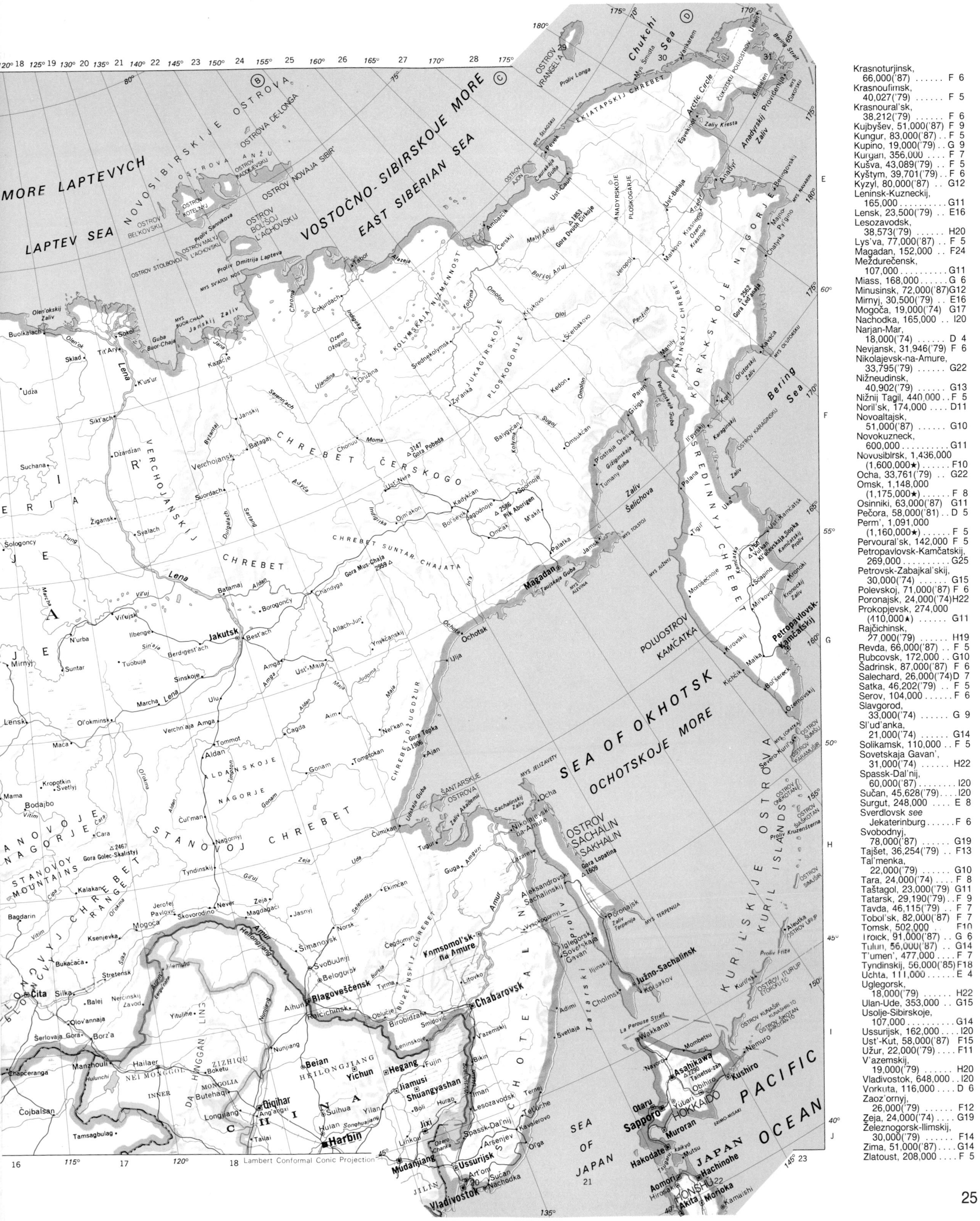

Krasnoturjinsk, 66,000('87) . . . . . . F 6
Krasnoufimsk, 40,027('79) . . . . . . F 5
Krasnoural'sk, 38,212('79) . . . . . . F 6
Kujbyšev, 51,000('87) F 9
Kungur, 83,000('87) . . F 5
Kupino, 19,000('79) . . G 9
Kurgan, 356,000 . . . . F 7
Kušva, 43,089('79) . . F 5
Kyštym, 39,701('79) . . F 6
Kyzyl, 80,000('87) . . G12
Leninsk-Kuzneckij, 165,000 . . . . G11
Lensk, 23,500('79) . . E16
Lesozavodsk, 38,573('79) H20
Lys'va, 77,000('87) . . F 5
Magadan, 152,000 . . F24
Meždurečensk, 107,000 . . . . G11
Miass, 168,000 . . . . . . G 6
Minusinsk, 72,000('87)G12
Mirnyj, 30,500('79) . . E16
Mogoča, 19,000('74) G17
Nachodka, 165,000 . . I20
Narjan-Mar, 18,000('74) . . . . . . D 4
Nevjansk, 31,946('79) F 6
Nikolajevsk-na-Amure, 33,795('79) G22
Nižneudinsk, 40,902('79) G13
Nižnij Tagil, 440,000 . . F 5
Noril'sk, 174,000 . . . . D11
Novoaltajsk, 51,000('87) G10
Novokuzneck, 600,000 . . . . G11
Novosibirsk, 1,436,000 (1,600,000★) F10
Ocha, 33,761('79) . . G22
Omsk, 1,148,000 (1,175,000★) . . . . . . F 8
Osinniki, 63,000('87) G11
Pečora, 58,000('81) . . D 5
Perm', 1,091,000 (1,160,000★) . . . . . . F 5
Pervoural'sk, 142,000 F 5
Petropavlovsk-Kamčatskij, 269,000 . . . . G25
Petrovsk-Zabajkal'skij, 30,000('74) G15
Polevskoj, 71,000('87) F 6
Poronajsk, 24,000('74)H22
Prokopjevsk, 274,000 (410,000★) G11
Rajčichinsk, 27,000('79) H19
Revda, 66,000('87) . . F 5
Rubcovsk, 172,000 . . G10
Šadrinsk, 87,000('87) F 6
Salechard, 26,000('74)D 7
Satka, 46,202('79) . . F 5
Serov, 104,000 . . . . . . F 6
Slavgorod, 33,000('74) . . . . . . G 9
Sl'ud'anka, 21,000('74) G14
Solikamsk, 110,000 . . F 5
Sovetskaja Gavan', 31,000('74) H22
Spassk-Dal'nij, 60,000('87) I20
Sučan, 45,628('79) I20
Surgut, 248,000 . . . . E 8
Sverdlovsk see Jekaterinburg . . . . . . F 6
Svobodnyj, 78,000('87) G19
Tajšet, 36,254('79) . . F13
Tal'menka, 22,000('79) G10
Tara, 24,000('74) . . . . F 8
Taštagol, 23,000('79) G11
Tatarsk, 29,190('79) . . F 9
Tavda, 46,115('79) . . F 7
Tobol'sk, 82,000('87) F 7
Tomsk, 502,000 . . . F10
Troick, 91,000('87) . . G 6
Tulun, 56,000('87) . . G14
T'umen', 477,000 . . . . F 7
Tyndinskij, 56,000('85) F18
Uchta, 111,000 . . . . . . E 4
Uglegorsk, 18,000('79) H22
Ulan-Ude, 353,000 . . G15
Usolje-Sibirskoje, 107,000 . . . . G14
Ussurijsk, 162,000 . . . . I20
Ust'-Kut, 58,000('87) F15
Užur, 22,000('79) F11
V'azemskij, 19,000('79) H20
Vladivostok, 648,000 . . I20
Vorkuta, 116,000 . . . . D 6
Zaoz'ornyj, 26,000('79) F12
Zeja, 24,000('74) G19
Železnogorsk-Ilimskij, 30,000('79) F14
Zima, 51,000('87) G14
Zlatoust, 208,000 . . . . F 5

China, Japan, and Korea

Bhutan

1982 ESTIMATE

Thimphu, 12,000 .... F 4

China

1988 ESTIMATE

Andong, 579,800('86) C11
Anshan, 1,330,000 .. C11
Bangbu, 403,900 (612,600▲)('86) E10
Baoding, 423,200 (535,100▲)('86) D10
Baotou, 1,130,000 .. C 8
Beijing (Peking), 6,710,000 (6,450,000★) D10
Benxi, 860,000 ...... C11
Canton *see* Guangzhou ...... G 9
Changchun, 1,822,000 (2,000,000▲) C12
Changsha, 1,230,000 F 9
Changzhou, 522,700('86) E10
Chengdu, 1,884,000 (2,960,000▲) ...... E 7
Chongqing, 2,502,000 (2,890,000▲) ...... F 8
Dalian, 2,280,000 .... D11
Datong, 810,000 (1,040,000▲) ...... C 9
Fushun, 1,290,000 .. C11
Fuzhou, 910,000 (1,240,000▲) F10
Guangzhou (Canton), 3,100,000 (3,420,000▲) ...... G 9
Guiyang, 1,030,000 (1,430,000▲) ...... F 8
Handan, 870,000 (1,030,000▲) ...... D 9
Hanzhou, 1,290,000 E 11
Harbin, 2,710,000 .... B12
Hefei, 740,000 (930,000▲) E10
Hegang, 588,300('86) B13
Hengyang, 419,200 (601,300▲)('86) .... F 9
Hohhot, 670,000 (830,000▲) .... C 9
Huainan, 700,000 (1,110,000▲) E10
Huangshi, 451,900('86) E10
Jilin, 1,200,000 ...... C12
Jinan (Tsinan), 1,546,000 (2,140,000▲) D10
Jinzhou, 710,000 (810,000▲) C11
Jixi, 700,000 (820,000▲) B13
Kaifeng, 458,800 (629,100▲)('86) .... E 9
Kunming, 1,310,000 (1,550,000▲) ...... F 7
Lanzhou, 1,297,000 (1,420,000▲) ...... D 7
Lasa (Lhasa), 84,400 (107,700▲)('86) .... F 5
Liuzhou, 680,000 .... G 8
Luoyang, 760,000 (1,090,000▲) ...... E 9
Mudanjiang, 650,000 C12
Nanchang, 1,090,000 (1,260,000▲) F10
Nanjing, 2,390,000 .. E10
Nanning, 720,000 (1,000,000▲) ...... G 8
Ningbo, 570,000 (1,050,000▲) F11
Peking *see* Beijing .. D10
Qingdao (Tsingtao), 1,300,000 .... D11
Shanghai, 7,220,000 (9,300,000★) E11
Shantou (Swatow), 560,000 (790,000▲) G10
Shenyang (Mukden), 3,910,000 (4,370,000▲) C11
Shijiazhuang, 1,220,000 .... D 9
Suzhou, 740,000 .... E11
Taiyuan, 1,700,000 (1,980,000▲) ...... D 9
Tangshan, 1,080,000 (1,440,000▲) D10
Tianjin (Tientsin), 4,950,000 (5,540,000▲) D10
Ürümqi, 1,060,000 .. C 4
Wenzhou, 372,200 (530,600▲)('86) F11
Wuhan, 3,570,000 .. E 9
Wuhu, 396,000 (502,200▲)('86) E10
Wuxi, 880,000 ...... E11
Xi'an (Sian), 2,210,000 (2,580,000▲) ...... E 8
Xining, 620,000 ...... D 7
Xuzhou, 860,000 .... E10
Zhangjiakou (Kalgan), 500,000 (640,000▲) C 9

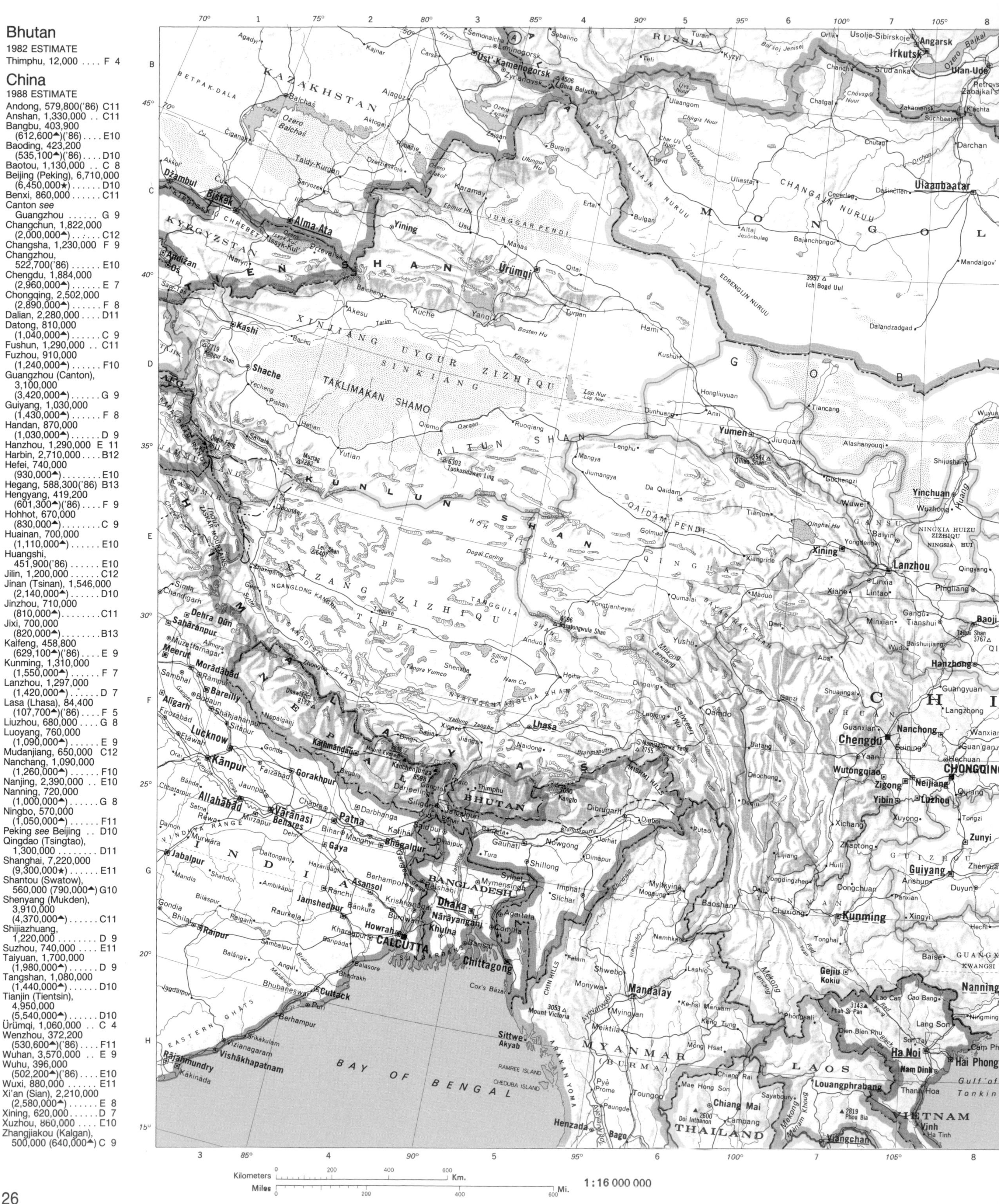

Zhengzhou, 1,150,000 (1,580,000▲) ...... E 9
Zibo, 840,000 (2,370,000▲) D10

Hong Kong
1986 CENSUS

Kowloon (Jiulong), 774,781 .... G 9
Victoria (Xianggang), 1,175,860 (4,770,000★) ...... G 9

Japan
1985 CENSUS

Asahikawa, 363,631 .. C15
Chiba, 788,930 ...... D15
Fukuoka, 1,160,440 (1,750,000★) E13
Hakodate, 319,194 .. C15
Hamamatsu, 514,118 E14
Himeji, 452,917 (660,000★) E13
Hiroshima, 1,044,118 (1,575,000★) E13
Kagoshima, 530,502 .. E13
Kanazawa, 430,481 .. D14
Kitakyūshū, 1,056,402 (1,525,000★) E13
Kōbe, 1,410,834 .... E14
Kumamoto, 555,719 .. E13
Kurashiki, 413,632 .. E13
Kyōto, 1,479,218 .... D14
Matsuyama, 426,658 E13
Nagasaki, 449,382 .. E12
Nagoya, 2,116,381 (4,800,000★) D14
Niigata, 475,630 .... D14
Okayama, 572,479 .. E13
Ōsaka, 2,636,249 (16,450,000★) E14
Sapporo, 1,542,979 (1,900,000★) C15
Sendai, 700,254 (1,175,000★) D15
Shizuoka, 468,362 (975,000★) E14
Tōkyō, 8,354,615 (27,700,000★) D14
Utsunomiya, 405,375 D14
Yokohama, 2,992,926 D14

Korea, North
1981 ESTIMATE

Ch'ŏngjin, 490,000 .. C12
Kaesŏng, 259,000 .. D12
Namp'o, 241,000 .... D12
P'yŏngyang, 1,283,000 (1,600,000★) D12
Sinŭiju, 305,000 .... C11
Wŏnsan, 398,000 .... D12

Korea, South
1989 ESTIMATE

Chŏnju, 426,473('85) D12
Inch'ŏn, 1,628,000 .. D12
Kwangju, 1,165,000 .. D12
Masan, 448,746 (625,000★)('85) D12
Pusan, 3,773,000 (3,800,000★) D12
Soŭl (Seoul), 10,522,000 (15,850,000★) D12
Taegu, 2,207,000 .... D12
Taejŏn, 1,041,000 .. D12

Macau
1987 ESTIMATE

Macau (Aomen), 429,000 .... G 9

Mongolia
1989 ESTIMATE

Ulaanbaatar (Ulan Bator), 548,400 .... B 8

Nepal
1981 CENSUS

Kāṭhmāṇḍau (Kathmandu), 235,160 (320,000★) .... F 4

Taiwan
1988 ESTIMATE

Kaohsiung, 1,342,797 (1,845,000★) G11
T'aichung, 715,107 .. G11
T'ainan, 656,927 .... G11
T'aipei, 2,637,100 (6,130,000★) F11

★ Population of metropolitan area, including suburbs.
▲ Population of entire district, including rural area.

Eastern and Southeastern China

China

1986 ESTIMATE

Anlu, 35,199('85) . . . . . D 2
Anqing, 213,200 (433,900▲) . . . . E 6
Baoying, 50,479('85) . . B 8
Bengbu, 403,900 (612,600▲) . . . . C 6
Binhai (Dongkan), 37,565('85) . . . . A 8
Boxian, 63,222('85) . . . . B 4
Canton *see* Guangzhou L 2
Changsha, 1,230,000('88) . . . . . G 1
Changshu, 281,300 (998,000▲) . . . . D 9
Changzhou (Changchow), 522,700 . . . . D 8
Chaoan, 265,400 (1,214,500▲) . . . . L 5
Chaoxian, 116,800 (739,500▲) . . . . D 6
Chezhou, 143,500 (191,900▲) . . . . J 1
Chuxian, 113,300 (365,000▲) . . . . C 7
Dinghai, 50,161('85) . . E11
Dingshan, 46,373('85) . . D 8
Dongguan, 254,900 (1,208,500▲) . . . . L 2
Echeng, 217,400 (938,000▲) . . . . E 3
Foshan, 243,500 (312,700▲) . . . . L 2
Fuyang, 143,400 (195,200▲) . . . . C 4
Fuzhou, 106,700 (171,800▲) . . . . G 5
Fuzhou (Foochow), 910,000 (1,240,000▲)('88) . . . . I 8
Ganzhou, 191,600 (346,000▲) . . . . J 3
Gaoyou, 57,844('85) . . C 8
Guangzhou (Canton), 3,100,000 (3,420,000▲)('88) . . . L 2
Hangzhou (Hangchow), 1,290,000('88) . . . . . E 9
Hefei, 740,000 (930,000▲)('88) . . . . D 6
Huainan, 700,000 (1,110,000▲)('88) . . . . C 6
Huaiyin, 201,700 (382,500▲) . . . . B 8
Huanggang, 65,961('82) E 3
Huangshi, 451,900 . . . . E 4
Huiyang (Huizhou), 117,000 (182,100▲) . . . . L 3
Huzhou, 208,500 (964,400▲) . . . . E 9
Jian, 132,200 (184,300▲) . . . . H 3
Jiangmen, 168,800 (231,700▲) . . . . M 2
Jiangyin, 66,476('85) . . D 9
Jiaxing, 210,200 (686,500▲) . . . . E 9
Jieyang, 98,531('85) . . L 5
Jingdezhen (Kingtechen), 304,000 (569,700▲) . . F 6
Jinhua, 147,800 (799,900▲) . . . . F 8
Jiujiang, 248,500 (382,300▲) . . . . F 4
Lanxi, 70,500 (606,800▲) . . . . F 8
Lechang, 56,913 . . . . . . J 2
Liling, 107,100 (856,300▲) . . . . H 2
Linhai, 52,653('85) G10
Liuan, 122,600 (163,400▲) . . . . D 5
Longyan, 114,500 (378,500▲) . . . . J 6
Luohe, 102,300 (159,100▲) . . . . B 3
Maanshan, 258,900 (367,000▲) . . . . D 7
Meixian, 169,100 (740,600▲) . . . . K 5
Nanchang, 1,090,000 (1,260,000)('88) . . . . G 4
Nanjing (Nanking), 2,390,000('88) . . . . . . C 7

★ Population of metropolitan area, including suburbs. ▲ Population of entire district, including rural area.

Nanping, 157,100 (420,800▲) .... I 7
Nantong, 308,800 (411,000▲) .... C 9
Nanyang, 199,400 (294,800▲) .... B 1
Ningbo, 570,000 (1,050,000▲)('88) F10
Pingxiang, 368,700 (1,286,700▲) ...... H 2
Quanzhou, 157,000 (436,000▲) .... K 7
Shanghai, 7,220,000 (9,300,000★('88) D10
Shantou (Swatow), 560,000 (790,000▲)('88) .... L 5
Shaoguan, 363,100 (344,892▲) .... K 2
Shaoxing, 167,100 (250,900▲) .... E 9
Suixian, 187,700 (1,281,600▲) ...... D 2
Suzhou (Soochow), 740,000('88) .... D 9
Tongling, 182,900 (216,400▲) .... E 6
Wenzhou, 372,200 (530,600▲) .... G 9
Wuhan, 3,570,000('88) E 3
Wuhu, 396,000 (502,200▲) .... D 7
Wusong, 64,017('82) .. D10
Wuxi (Wuhsi), 880,000('88) .... D 9
Xiamen (Amoy), 343,700 (546,400▲) .... K 7
Xiangcheng, 363,200 (819,900▲) .... B 2
Xiangtan, 389,500 (511,100▲) .... H 1
Xinyang, 169,100 (234,200▲) .... C 3
Xuchang, 167,800 (247,200▲) .... A 2
Xuzhou (Süchow), 860,000('88) .... A 6
Yancheng, 258,400 (1,251,400▲) ...... B 9
Yangzhou, 321,500 (417,300▲) .... C 8
Yanling, 52,679('82) .. C 8
Yueyang, 239,500 (411,300▲) .... F 2
Yuyao, 169,700 (772,700▲) E10
Zhangzhou (Longxi), 159,400 (310,400▲) K 6
Zhenjiang, 412,400 .... C 8
Zhongshan, 238,700 (1,059,700▲) ...... M 2
Zhuzhou, 344,800 (499,600▲) .... H 2

Hong Kong

1986 CENSUS

Kowloon (Jiulong), 774,781 .... M 3
Victoria (Xianggang), 1,175,860 (4,770,000★) ...... M 3

Macau

1987 ESTIMATE

Macau (Aomen), 429,000 .... M 2

Taiwan

1988 ESTIMATE

Changhua, 158,400 (206,603▲) .... K 9
Chiai, 254,875 .... L 9
Chilung, 348,541 ...... J10
Hsinchu, 309,899 .... K 9
Kaohsiung, 1,342,797 (1,845,000★) ...... M 9
Kaohsiungnsien, 276,259 .... M 9
P'ingtung, 167,600 (204,990▲) .... M 9
T'ainan, 656,927 ...... L 9
T'aipei, 2,637,100 (6,130,000★) J10
T'aipeihsien, 506,220 .. J10

Japan

1985 CENSUS

Aizu-wakamatsu, 118,140 . . . . E12
Akashi, 263,363 . . . . . . H 7
Akita, 296,400 . . . . C13
Amagasaki, 509,115 . . H 8
Aomori, 294,045 . . . . . . B13
Asahikawa, 363,631 . . p20
Ashikaga, 167,656 . . . . F12
Beppu, 134,775 . . . . . . I 4
Chiba, 788,930 . . . . . . G13
Chigasaki, 185,030 . . . . G12
Chōshi, 87,883 . . . . . . G13
Fuji, 214,448 (370,000★) G11
Fujinomiya, 112,642 . . G11
Fujisawa, 328,387 . . . . G12
Fukui, 250,261 . . . . F 9
Fukuoka, 1,160,440 (1,750,000★) . . . . I 3
Fukushima, 270,762 . . E13
Fukuyama, 360,261 . . H 6
Funabashi, 506,966 . . G13
Gifu, 411,743 . . . . G 9
Hachinohe, 241,430 . . B14
Hachiōji, 426,654 . . . . G12
Hakodate, 319,194 . . . . r18
Hamamatsu, 514,118 . . H10
Handa, 92,883 . . . . H 9
Higashiōsaka, 522,805 H 8
Hikone, 94,204 . . . . . . G 9
Himeji, 452,917 (660,000★) . . . . H 7
Hiratsuka, 229,990 . . . . G12
Hirosaki, 134,800 (176,082▲) B13
Hiroshima, 1,044,118 (1,575,000★) . . . . . . H 5
Hitachi, 206,074 . . . . . . F13
Hōfu, 118,067 . . . . H 4
Ichinomiya, 257,388 . . G 9
Iizuka, 81,868 (110,000★) . . . . I 3
Imabari, 125,115 . . . . . . H 6
Ise, 105,455 . . . . H 9
Isesaki, 112,459 . . . . . . F12
Ishinomaki, 122,674 . . D14
Iwaki (Taira), 350,569 . . E13
Iwakuni, 111,833 . . . . . . H 5
Kagoshima, 530,502 . . K 3
Kakogawa, 227,311 . . H 7
Kamaishi, 60,007 . . . . . . C14
Kamakura, 175,495 . . . . G12
Kanazawa, 430,481 . . . . F 9
Kariya, 112,403 . . . . . . H 9
Kashiwa, 273,128 . . . . G12
Kasugai, 256,990 . . . . G 9
Kawagoe, 285,437 . . . . G12
Kawaguchi, 403,015 . . G12
Kawasaki, 1,088,624 . . G12
Kiryū, 131,267 . . . . F12
Kishiwada, 185,731 . . . . H 8
Kitakyūshū, 1,056,402 (1,525,000★) . . . . I 3
Kitami, 107,281 . . . . . . p21
Kōbe, 1,410,834 . . . . . . H 8
Kōchi, 312,241 . . . . I 6
Kōfu, 202,405 . . . . G11
Komatsu, 106,041 . . . . F 9
Kōriyama, 301,673 . . . . E13
Kumagaya, 143,496 . . F12
Kumamoto, 555,719 . . J 3
Kurashiki, 413,632 . . . . H 6
Kure, 226,488 . . . . H 5
Kurume, 222,847 . . . . . . I 3
Kushiro, 214,541 . . . . . . q22
Kyōto, 1,479,218 . . . . . . G 8
Maebashi, 277,319 . . . . F12
Maizuru, 98,775 . . . . . . G 8
Matsudo, 427,473 . . . . G12
Matsue, 140,005 . . . . . . G 6
Matsumoto, 197,340 . . F10
Matsusaka, 116,886 . . H 9
Matsuyama, 426,658 . . I 5
Mito, 228,985 . . . . F13
Miyazaki, 279,114 . . . . K 4
Morioka, 235,469 . . . . C14
Muroran, 136,208 (195,000★) q18
Nagahama, 55,531 . . . . G 9
Nagano, 336,973 . . . . . . F11
Nagaoka, 183,756 . . . . E11
Nagasaki, 449,382 . . . . J 2

★ Population of metropolitan area, including suburbs. ▲ Population of entire district, including rural area.

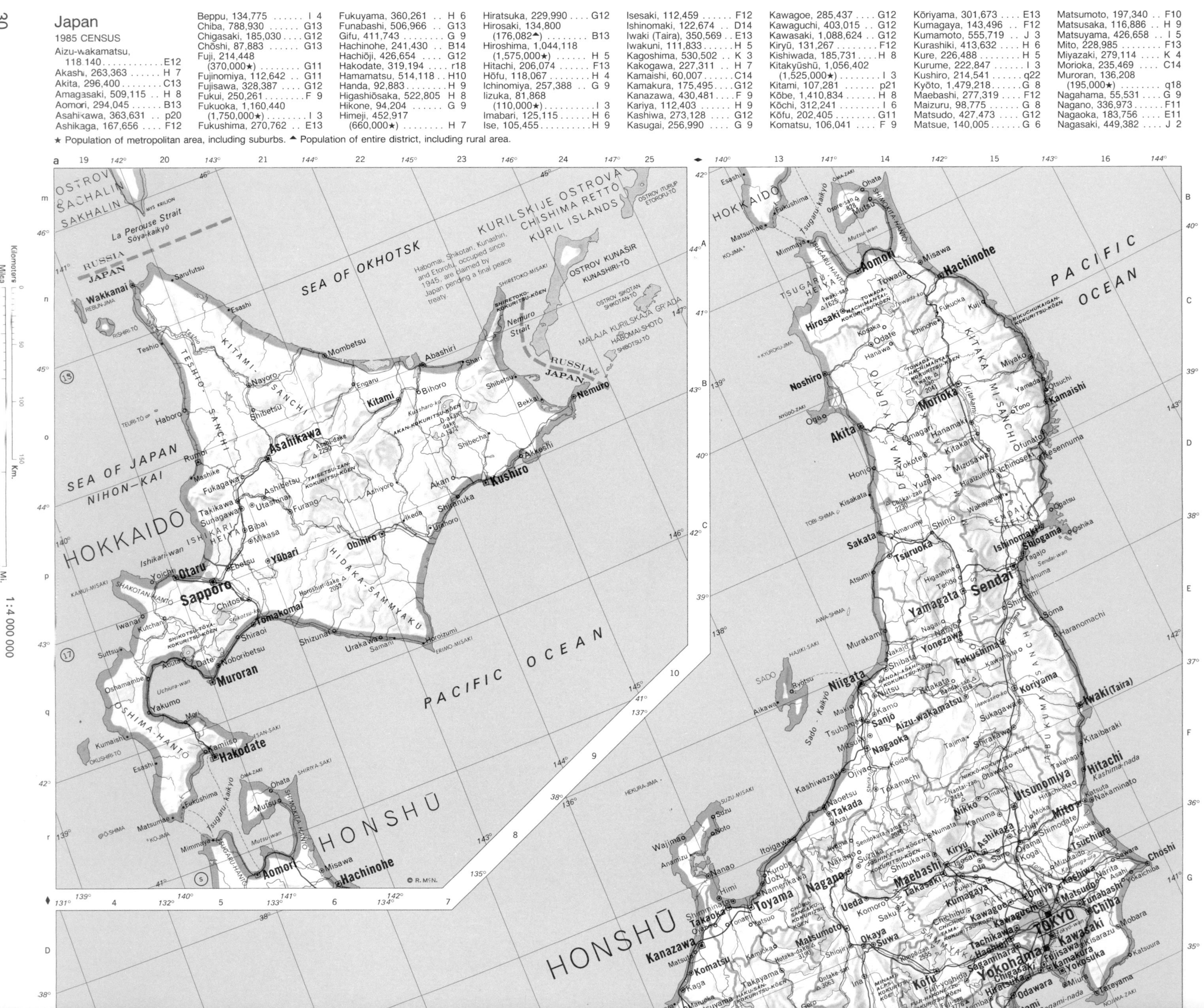

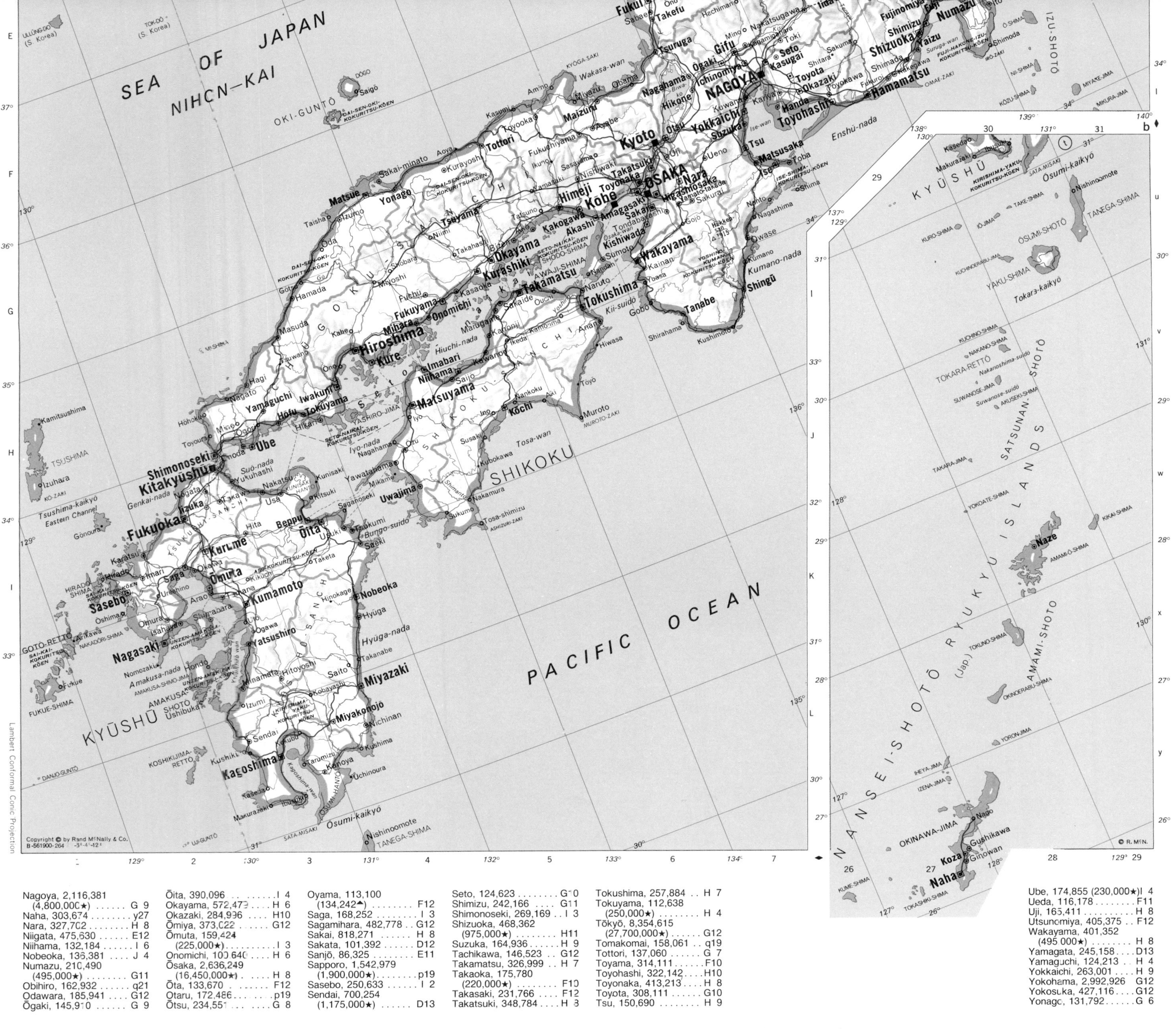

Nagoya, 2,116,381 (4,800,000★) ...... G 9
Naha, 303,674 .... y27
Nara, 327,702 .... H 8
Niigata, 475,630 ...... E12
Niihama, 132,184 ...... I 6
Nobeoka, 136,381 .... J 4
Numazu, 210,490 (495,000★) G11
Obihiro, 162,932 ...... q21
Odawara, 185,941 .... G12
Ōgaki, 145,910 ...... G 9
Ōita, 390,096 .... I 4
Okayama, 572,479 .... H 6
Okazaki, 284,996 .... H10
Ōmiya, 373,022 ...... G12
Ōmuta, 159,424 (225,000★) .... I 3
Onomichi, 100,640 .... H 6
Ōsaka, 2,636,249 (16,450,000★) ...... H 8
Ōta, 133,670 .... F12
Otaru, 172,486 .... p19
Ōtsu, 234,551 .... G 8
Oyama, 113,100 (134,242▲) F12
Saga, 168,252 .... I 3
Sagamihara, 482,778 .. G12
Sakai, 818,271 .... H 8
Sakata, 101,392 ...... D12
Sanjō, 86,325 .... E11
Sapporo, 1,542,979 (1,900,000★) p19
Sasebo, 250,633 ...... I 2
Sendai, 700,254 (1,175,000★) D13
Seto, 124,623 .... G10
Shimizu, 242,166 .... G11
Shimonoseki, 269,169 .. I 3
Shizuoka, 468,362 (975,000★) H11
Suzuka, 164,936 ...... H 9
Tachikawa, 146,523 .. G12
Takamatsu, 326,999 .. H 7
Takaoka, 175,780 (220,000★) F10
Takasaki, 231,766 .... F12
Takatsuki, 348,784 .... H 8
Tokushima, 257,884 .. H 7
Tokuyama, 112,638 (250,000★) .... H 4
Tōkyō, 8,354,615 (27,700,000★) G12
Tomakomai, 158,061 .. q19
Tottori, 137,060 ...... G 7
Toyama, 314,111 ...... F10
Toyohashi, 322,142 .... H10
Toyonaka, 413,213 .... H 8
Toyota, 308,111 ...... G10
Tsu, 150,690 .... H 9
Ube, 174,855 (230,000★) I 4
Ueda, 116,178 .... F11
Uji, 165,411 .... H 8
Utsunomiya, 405,375 .. F12
Wakayama, 401,352 (495,000★) .... H 8
Yamagata, 245,158 .... D13
Yamaguchi, 124,213 .. H 4
Yokkaichi, 263,001 .... H 9
Yokohama, 2,992,926 G12
Yokosuka, 427,116 .... G12
Yonago, 131,792 ...... G 6

Southeastern Asia

Brunei
1981 CENSUS
Bandar Seri Begawan, 22,777 (64,000★) . . E 5

Cambodia
1986 ESTIMATE
Phnum Pénh, 700,000 C 3

Indonesia
1980 CENSUS
Ambon, 111,914 (207,702▲) . . . . F 8
Balikpapan, 208,040 (279,852▲) . . . . F 6
Bandung, 1,633,000 (1,800,000★)('85) . . m13
Banjarmasin, 424,000('83) . . . . . . F 5
Banjuwangi, 90,378 . . n17
Blitar, 78,503 (100,000★) n16
Bogor, 246,946 (560,000★) m13
Cilacap, 127,017 . . . . m14
Cirebon, 223,504 (275,000★) m14
Denpasar, 159,233 . . G 6
Dili, 6,890 (67,039▲) G 8
Garut, 145,624 . . . . . . m13
Jakarta, 9,200,000 (10,000,000★)('89) m13
Jambi, 155,761 (230,046▲) . . . . F 3
Jember, 171,284 . . . . n16
Kediri, 176,261 (221,830▲) m16
Kudus, 154,478 . . . . m15
Kupang, 84,587 . . . . H 7
Madiun, 150,562 (180,000★) m15
Magelang, 123,358 (160,000★) m15
Malang, 547,000('83) m16
Manado, 217,091 . . . . E 7
Medan, 2,110,000('85) E 2
Padang, 405,600 (657,000▲)('83) . . . . F 3
Pakanbaru, 186,199 . . E 3
Palembang, 874,000('83) . . . . . . F 3
Pangkalpinang, 90,078 F 4
Pasuruan, 95,864 (125,000★) m16
Pekalongan, 132,413 (260,000★) m14
Pemalang, 72,663 . . m14
Pematangsiantar, 150,296 (175,000★) . . . . E 2
Pontianak, 343,000('83) . . . . . . F 4
Probolinggo, 100,296 m16
Purwokerto, 143,787 m14
Salatiga, 85,740 . . . . m15
Samarinda, 182,473 (264,012▲) . . . . F 6
Semarang, 1,206,000('83) m15
Sukabumi, 109,898 (225,000★) m13
Surabaya, 2,345,000('85) m16
Surakarta, 491,000 (575,000★)('83) m15
Tanjungkarang-Telukbetung, 284,167 (375,000★) k12
Tasikmalaya, 192,267 m14
Tegal, 131,440 (340,000★) m14
Tual, 7,833 . . . . G 9
Tulungagung, 91,585 n15
Ujungpandang, 841,000('83) . . . . . . G 6
Yogyakarta, 421,000 (510,000★)('83) m15

Laos
1975 ESTIMATE
Louangphrabang, 46,000 . . . . B 3
Paksé, 47,000 . . . . . . B 4
Savannakhet, 53,000 B 3
Viangchan, 377,409('85) . . . . . . B 3

Malaysia
1980 CENSUS
Alor Setar, 69,435 . . D 3
George Town (Pinang), 248,241 (495,000★) D 3
Ipoh, 293,849 . . . . . . E 3
Johor Baharu, 246,395 . . . . E 3
Kelang, 192,080 . . . . E 3
Kota Baharu, 167,872 D 3
Kuala Lumpur, 919,610 (1,475,000★) . . . . . . E 3
Kuala Terengganu, 180,296 . . . . D 3
Kuantan, 131,547 . . . . E 3

Kuching, 72,555 .... E 5
Melaka, 87,494 ...... E 3
Sandakan, 70,420 .. D 6
Seremban, 132,911 .. E 3
Sibu, 85,231 .... E 5

Myanmar

1983 CENSUS

Bago, 150,528 ..... B 2
Henzada, 82,005 .... B 2
Mandalay, 532,949 .. A 2
Mawlamyine, 219,961 B 2
Monywa, 106,843 .... A 2
Pathein, 144,096 .... B 1
Pyè (Prome), 83,332 .. B 2
Sittwe (Akyab), 107,621 .... A 1
Yangon (Rangoon), 2,705,039 (2,800,000★) ...... B 2

Philippines

1990 CENSUS

Angeles, 236,000 .... q19
Bacolod, 364,000 .... C 7
Baguio, 183,000 .... p19
Batangas, 31,600 (184,000▲) r19
Cabanatuan, 75,700 (173,000▲) q19
Cavite, 92,000 (175,000★) q19
Cebu, 610,000 (720,000★) .... C 7
Cotabato, 127,000 .. D 7
Dagupan, 122,000 .. p19
Davao, 569,300 (850,000▲) .... D 8
Dumaguete, 80,000 .. D 7
Iloilo, 311,000 ...... C 7
Legaspi, 63,000 (121,000▲) r20
Lipa, 30,000 (160,000▲) r19
Lucena, 151,000 .... r19
Malalos, 95,699('80) .. q19
Manila, 1,587,000 (6,800,000★) q19
Naga, 115,000 ...... r20
Pasig, 318,853('84) .. q19
Puerto Princesa, 52,000 (92,000▲) .... D 6
Quezon City, 1,632,000 .... q19
San Fernando, 110,891('80) q19
San Pablo, 83,900 (161,000▲) q19
Tarlac, 38,205 (175,691▲)('80) q19
Zamboanga, 107,000 (444,000▲) .... D 7

Singapore

1989 ESTIMATE

Singapore, 2,685,400 (3,025,000★) ...... E 3

Thailand

1988 ESTIMATE

Bangkok *see* Krung Thep .... C 3
Chiang Mai, 164,030 B 2
Hat Yai, 138,046 .... D 3
Khon Kaen, 131,340 B 3
Krung Thep (Bangkok), 5,716,779 (6,450,000★) ...... C 3
Nakhon Ratchasima, 204,982 .... C 3
Nakhon Sawan, 105,220 .... B 3
Nakhon Si Thammarat, 72,407 .... D 2
Phitsanulok, 77,675 .. B 3
Songkhla, 84,433 .... D 3
Ubon Ratchathani, 100,374 .... B 3
Udon Thani, 81,202 .. B 3

Vietnam

1979 CENSUS

Can Tho, 182,856 .. C 4
Da Nang, 318,653 .. B 4
Hai Phong, 456,000 (1,279,067▲)('89) .. A 4
Ha Noi, 1,089,000 (1,500,000★)('89) .. A 4
Hue, 165,710 ...... B 4
My Tho, 101,493 .... C 4
Nam Dinh, 160,179 .. A 4
Nha Trang, 172,663 .. C 4
Phan Thiet, 75,241 .. C 4
Qui Nhon, 127,211 .. C 4
Rach Gia, 81,075 .... C 4
Saigon *see* Thanh Pho Ho Chi Minh .... C 4
Thanh Pho Ho Chi Minh (Saigon), 3,169,000 (3,300,000★)('89) .. C 4
Vinh, 159,753 ...... B 4

★ Population of metropolitan area, including suburbs.
▲ Population of entire district, including rural area.

Myanmar, Thailand, and Indochina

Cambodia
1986 ESTIMATE
Bătdâmbâng, 38,780('62) . . . . H 7
Kâmpóng Cham, 35,000('71) . . . . H 8
Kâmpóng Saôm, 53,000('81) . . . . I 7
Phnum Pénh (Phnom Penh), 700,000 . . . . I 8

Indonesia
1980 CENSUS
Banda Aceh, 71,868 . . L 3
Binjai, 71,444 . . . . M 5
Bukittinggi, 55,577 (70,691▲) . . . . O 6
Medan, 2,110,000('85) M 5
Padang, 405,600 (657,000▲)('83) . . . . O 6
Padangsidempuan, 56,984 . . . . N 5
Payakumbuh, 24,567 (78,789▲) . . . . O 6
Pekanbaru, 186,199 . . N 6
Pematangsiantar, 150,296 (175,000★) . . . . M 5
Rantauprapat, 25,043 M 5
Sibolga, 59,466 . . . . . . N 5
Singkawang, 58,693 . . N10
Tanjungpinang, 36,999 N 8
Tarutung, 5,522 . . . . . . M 5
Tebingtinggi, 69,569 (92,068▲) . . . . M 5

Laos
1975 ESTIMATE
Louangphrabang, 46,000 . . . . E 7
Pakxé, 47,000 . . . . G 8
Savannakhet, 53,000 . . F 8
Viangchan, 377,409('85) F 7

Malaysia
1980 CENSUS
Batu Pahat, 64,727 . . . . N 7
Butterworth, 77,982 . . L 6
George Town (Pinang), 248,241 (495,000★) . . L 6
Ipoh, 293,849 . . . . L 6
Johor Baharu, 246,395 N 7
Kelang, 192,080 . . . . . . M 6
Kota Baharu, 167,872 . . K 7
Kuala Lumpur, 919,610 (1,475,000★) . . . . . . M 6
Kuala Terengganu, 180,296 . . . . L 7
Kuantan, 131,547 . . . . M 7
Kuching, 72,555 . . . . . . N11
Melaka, 87,494 . . . . . . M 7
Muar, 65,151 . . . . M 7
Seremban, 132,911 . . M 6
Taiping, 146,000 . . . . . . L 6

Myanmar
1983 CENSUS
Bago, 150,528 . . . . F 4
Chauk, 51,437 . . . . D 3
Dawei, 69,882 . . . . G 5
Henzada, 82,005 . . . . . . F 3
Mandalay, 532,949 . . . . C 4
Mawlamyine (Moulmein), 219,961 . . . . F 4
Maymyo, 63,782 . . . . . . C 4
Meiktila, 96,496 . . . . . . D 3
Mergui (Myeik), 88,600 H 5
Monywa, 106,843 . . . . C 3
Myingyan, 77,060 . . . . D 3
Myitkyinā, 56,427 . . . . B 4
Pakokku, 71,860 . . . . . . D 3
Pathein, 144,096 . . . . . . F 3
Pyè (Prome), 83,332 . . E 3
Rangoon *see* Yangon . . F 4
Sittwe (Akyab), 107,621 D 2
Thaton, 61,790 . . . . F 4
Toungoo, 65,861 . . . . . . E 4
Yangon (Rangoon), 2,705,039 (2,800,000★) . . . . F 4
Yenangyaung, 62,582 . . D 3

★ Population of metropolitan area, including suburbs. ▲ Population of entire district, including rural area.

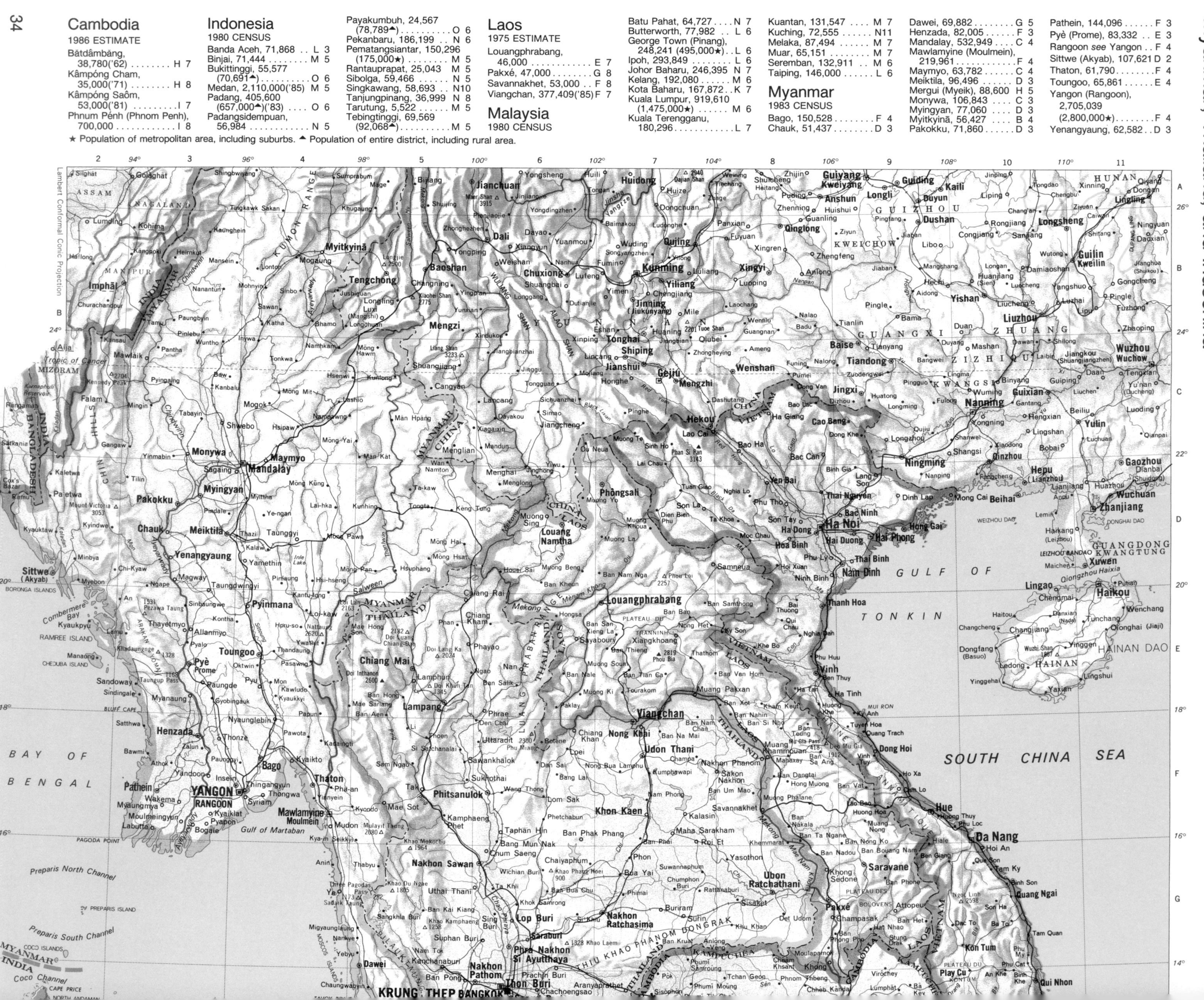

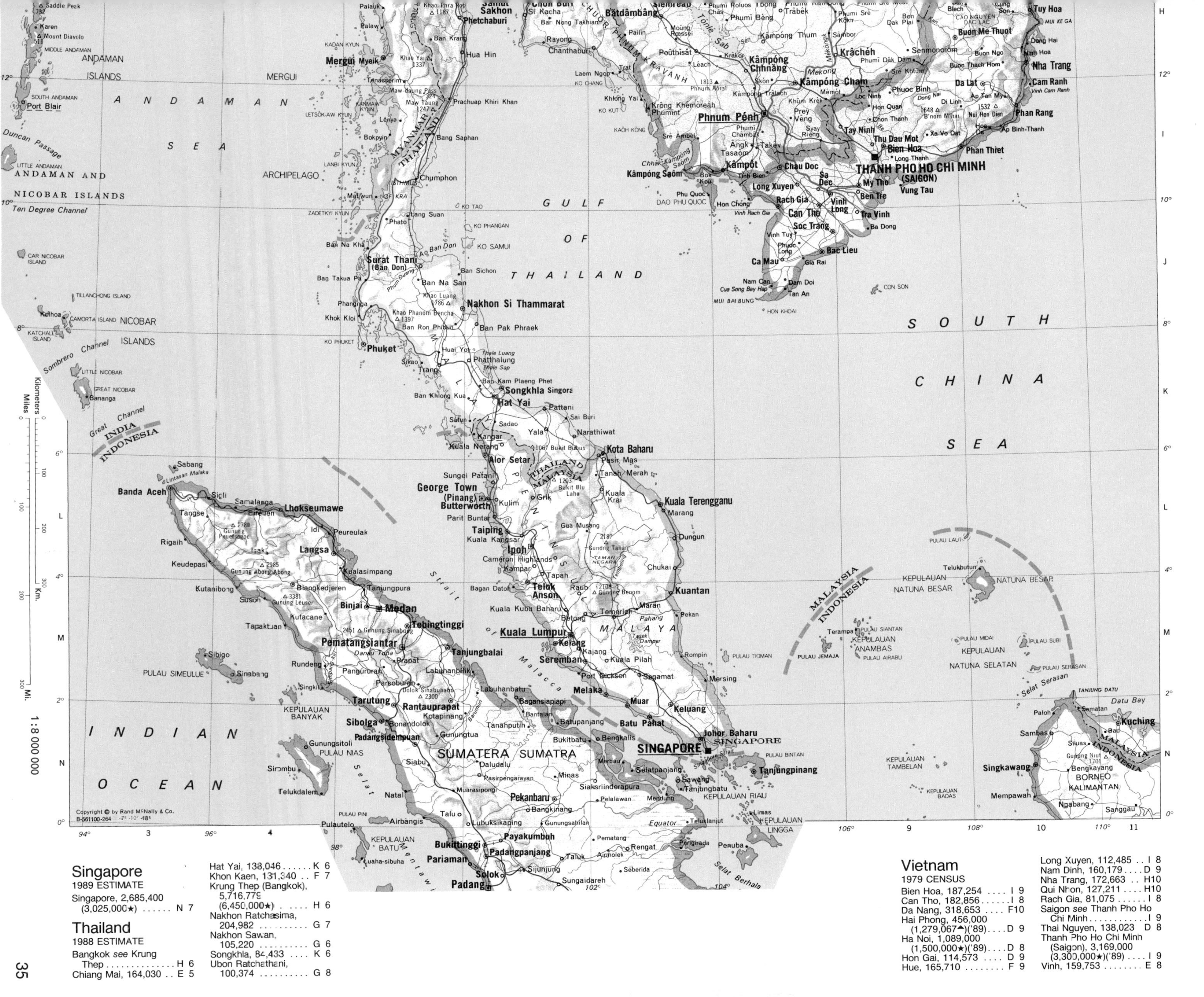

Singapore

1989 ESTIMATE

Singapore, 2,685,400 (3,025,000★) . . . . . . N 7

Thailand

1988 ESTIMATE

Bangkok *see* Krung Thep . . . . H 6
Chiang Mai, 164,030 . . E 5
Hat Yai, 138,046 . . . . . . K 6
Khon Kaen, 131,340 . . F 7
Krung Thep (Bangkok), 5,716,779 (6,450,000★) . . . . . H 6
Nakhon Ratchasima, 204,982 . . . . G 7
Nakhon Sawan, 105,220 . . . . G 6
Songkhla, 84,433 . . . . K 6
Ubon Ratchathani, 100,374 . . . . G 8

Vietnam

1979 CENSUS

Bien Hoa, 187,254 . . . . I 9
Can Tho, 182,856 . . . . . . I 8
Da Nang, 318,653 . . . . F10
Hai Phong, 456,000 (1,279,067▲)('89) . . . . D 9
Ha Noi, 1,089,000 (1,500,000★)('89) . . . . D 8
Hon Gai, 114,573 . . . . D 9
Hue, 165,710 . . . . F 9
Long Xuyen, 112,485 . . I 8
Nam Dinh, 160,179 . . . . D 9
Nha Trang, 172,663 . . H10
Qui Nhon, 127,211 . . . . H10
Rach Gia, 81,075 . . . . . . I 8
Saigon *see* Thanh Pho Ho Chi Minh . . . . I 9
Thai Nguyen, 138,023 D 8
Thanh Pho Ho Chi Minh (Saigon), 3,169,000 (3,300,000★)('89) . . . . I 9
Vinh, 159,753 . . . . E 8

India and Pakistan

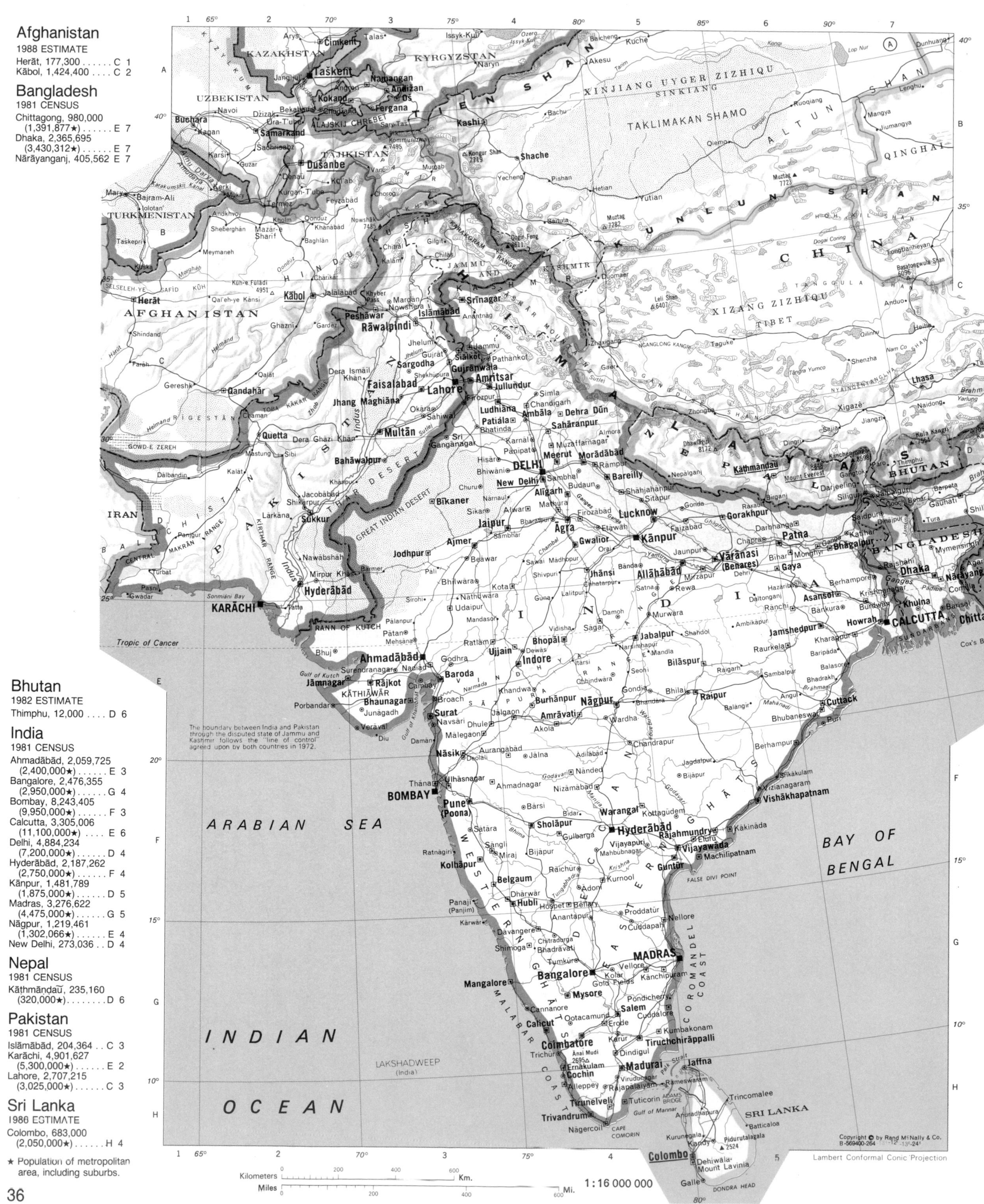

Afghanistan
1988 ESTIMATE
Herāt, 177,300 . . . . . . C 1
Kābol, 1,424,400 . . . . C 2

Bangladesh
1981 CENSUS
Chittagong, 980,000 (1,391,877★) . . . . . . E 7
Dhaka, 2,365,695 (3,430,312★) . . . . . . E 7
Nārāyanganj, 405,562 E 7

Bhutan
1982 ESTIMATE
Thimphu, 12,000 . . . . D 6

India
1981 CENSUS
Ahmadābād, 2,059,725 (2,400,000★) . . . . . . E 3
Bangalore, 2,476,355 (2,950,000★) . . . . . . G 4
Bombay, 8,243,405 (9,950,000★) . . . . . . F 3
Calcutta, 3,305,006 (11,100,000★) . . . . E 6
Delhi, 4,884,234 (7,200,000★) . . . . . . D 4
Hyderābād, 2,187,262 (2,750,000★) . . . . . . F 4
Kānpur, 1,481,789 (1,875,000★) . . . . . . D 5
Madras, 3,276,622 (4,475,000★) . . . . . . G 5
Nāgpur, 1,219,461 (1,302,066★) . . . . . . E 4
New Delhi, 273,036 . . D 4

Nepal
1981 CENSUS
Kāthmāndau, 235,160 (320,000★) . . . . D 6

Pakistan
1981 CENSUS
Islāmābād, 204,364 . . C 3
Karāchi, 4,901,627 (5,300,000★) . . . . . . E 2
Lahore, 2,707,215 (3,025,000★) . . . . . . C 3

Sri Lanka
1986 ESTIMATE
Colombo, 683,000 (2,050,000★) . . . . . . H 4

★ Population of metropolitan area, including suburbs.

India

1981 CENSUS

Akola, 225,412 .... B 4
Amrāvati, 261,404 .. B 4
Aurangābād, 284,607 (316,421★) .... C 3
Bangalore, 2,476,355 (2,950,000★) ...... F 4
Baroda, 734,473 (744,881★) .... A 2
Belgaum, 274,430 (300,372★) .... E 3
Bhāvnagar, 307,121 (308,642★) .... B 2
Bhilai, 290,090 (490,214★) .... B 6
Bhubaneswar, 219,211 .... B 8
Bombay, 8,243,405 (9,950,000★) ...... C 2
Calicut, 394,447 (546,058★) ...... G 3
Cochin, 513,249 (685,836★) .... H 4
Coimbatore, 704,514 (965,000★) ...... G 4
Cuttack, 269,950 (327,412★) .... B 8
Dhule, 210,759 ...... B 3
Gulbarga, 221,325 .. D 4
Guntūr, 367,699 .... D 6
Hubli, 527,108 ...... E 3
Hyderābād, 2,187,262 (2,750,000★) ...... D 5
Indore, 829,327 (850,000★) .... A 3
Kolhāpur, 340,625 (351,392★) .... D 3
Madras, 3,276,622 (4,475,000★) ...... F 6
Madurai, 820,891 (960,000★) .... H 5
Mālegaon, 245,883 .. B 3
Mysore, 441,754 (479,081★) .... F 4
Nāgpur, 1,219,461 (1,302,066★) ...... B 5
Nāsik, 262,428 (429,034★) .... C 2
Nellore, 237,065 .... E 5
Pondicherry, 162,636 (251,420★) ...... G 5
Pune (Poona), 1,203,351 (1,775,000★) ...... C 2
Raipur, 338,245 .... B 6
Salem, 361,394 (518,615★) ...... G 5
Sholāpur, 511,103 (514,860★) .... D 3
Surat, 776,583 (913,806★) .... B 2
Thāna, 309,897 .... C 2
Tiruchchirāppalli, 362,045 (609,548★) ...... G 5
Trivandrum, 483,086 (520,125★) .... H 4
Ulhāsnagar, 273,668 C 2
Vijayawāda, 454,577 (543,008★) .... D 6
Vishākhapatnam, 565,321 (603,630★) .... D 7
Warangal, 335,150 .. C 5

Sri Lanka

1986 ESTIMATE

Colombo, 683,000 (2,050,000★) ...... I 5
Dehiwala-Mount Lavinia, 191,000 .... I 5
Kandy, 130,000 ...... I 6
Kotte, 104,000 ...... I 5

★ Population of metropolitan area, including suburbs.

Northern India and Pakistan

Afghanistan
1981 ESTIMATE
Baghlān, 41,000('82) B 3
Ghaznī, 31,196 . . . . . . D 3
Jalālābād, 58,000('82) C 4
Kābol, 1,424,400('88) C 3
Khānābād, 27,482 . . B 3
Kholm, 28,788 . . . . . . B 2
Mazār-e Sharīf,
 130,600('88) . . . . . . B 2
Meymaneh, 39,218 . . C 1
Qandahār,
 225,500('88) . . . . . . E 1
Sheberghān, 19,475 . . B 1

Bangladesh
1981 CENSUS
Barisāl, 172,905 . . . . . . I14
Brāhmanbāria, 87,570 I14
Chittagong, 980,000
 (1,391,877★) I14
Comilla, 184,132 . . . . I14
Dhaka, 2,365,695
 (3,430,312★) I14
Jessore, 148,927 . . . . I13
Khulna, 648,359 . . . . . . I13
Mymensingh, 190,991 H14
Nārāyanganj, 405,562 I14
Pābna, 109,065 . . . . H13
Rājshāhi, 253,740 . . . . H13
Rangpur, 153,174 . . . . H13
Saidpur, 126,608 . . . . H13
Sirājganj, 106,774 . . . . H13
Sylhet, 168,371 . . . . H14

Bhutan
1982 ESTIMATE
Thimphu, 12,000 . . . . G13

India
1981 CENSUS
Āgra, 694,191
 (747,318★) . . . . . . G 8
Ahmadābād, 2,059,725
 (2,400,000★) . . . . . . I 5
Ajmer, 375,593 . . . . . . G 6
Alīgarh, 320,861 . . . . G 8
Allāhābād, 616,051
 (650,070★) . . . . H 9
Alwar, 145,795 . . . . . . G 7
Amritsar, 594,844 . . . . E 6
Asansol, 183,375
 (1,050,000★) I12
Bareilly, 386,734
 (449,425★) . . . . F 8
Baroda, 734,473
 (744,881★) . . . . I 5
Bhāgalpur, 225,062 . . H12
Bhātpāra, 260,761 . . . . I13
Bhāvnagar, 307,121
 (308,642★) . . . . J 5
Bhilai, 290,090
 (490,214★) . . . . J 9
Bhopāl, 671,018 . . . . . . I 7
Bhubaneswar, 219,211J11
Bīkaner, 253,174
 (287,712★) . . . . F 5
Calcutta, 3,305,006
 (11,100,000★) I13
Chandīgarh, 373,789
 (422,841★) . . . . E 7
Cuttack, 269,950
 (327,412★) J11
Dehra Dūn, 211,416
 (293,010★) . . . . E 8
Delhi, 4,884,234
 (7,200,000★) . . . . F 7
Durgāpur, 311,798 . . . . I12
Gaya, 247,075 . . . . . . H11
Ghāziābād, 271,730
 (287,170★) . . . . F 7
Gorakhpur, 290,814
 (307,501★) G10
Gwalior, 539,015
 (555,862★) . . . . . . G 8
Howrah, 744,429 . . . . I13
Indore, 829,327
 (850,000★) . . . . I 6
Jabalpur, 614,162
 (757,303★) . . . . I 8
Jaipur, 977,165
 (1,025,000★) . . . . . . G 6
Jammu, 206,135
 (223,361★) . . . . D 6
Jāmnagar, 277,615
 (317,362★) . . . . I 4
Jamshedpur, 438,385
 (669,580★) I12
Jhānsi, 246,172
 (284,141★) . . . . H 8
Jodhpur, 506,345 . . . . G 5
Jullundur, 408,186
 (441,552★) . . . . E 6
Kānpur, 1,481,789
 (1,875,000★) . . . . . . G 9
Kota, 358,241 . . . . . . H 6
Lucknow, 895,721
 (1,060,000★) . . . . . . G 9
Ludhiāna, 607,052 . . E 6
Mathura, 147,493
 (160,995★) . . . . . . G 7

★ Population of metropolitan area, including suburbs.

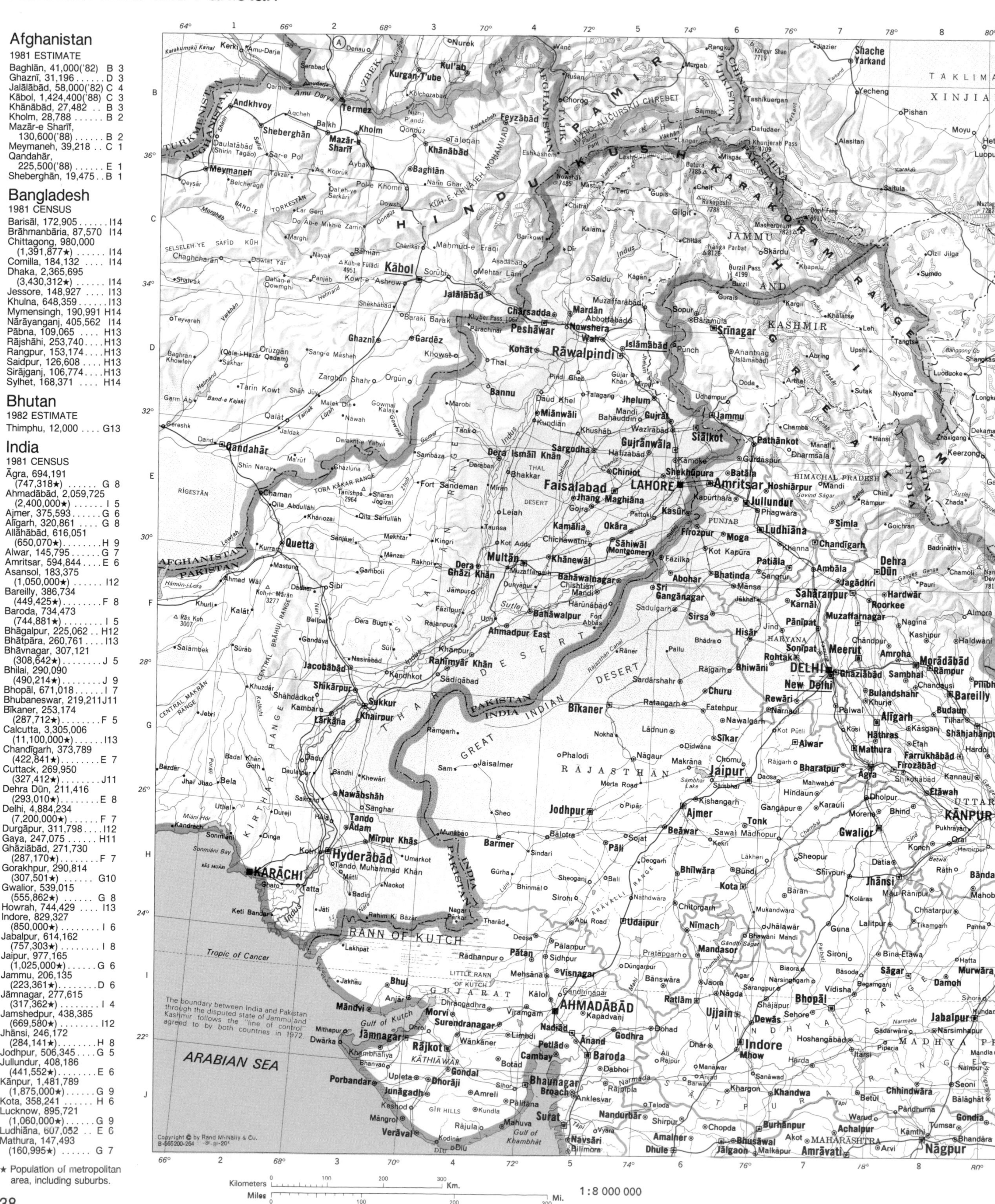

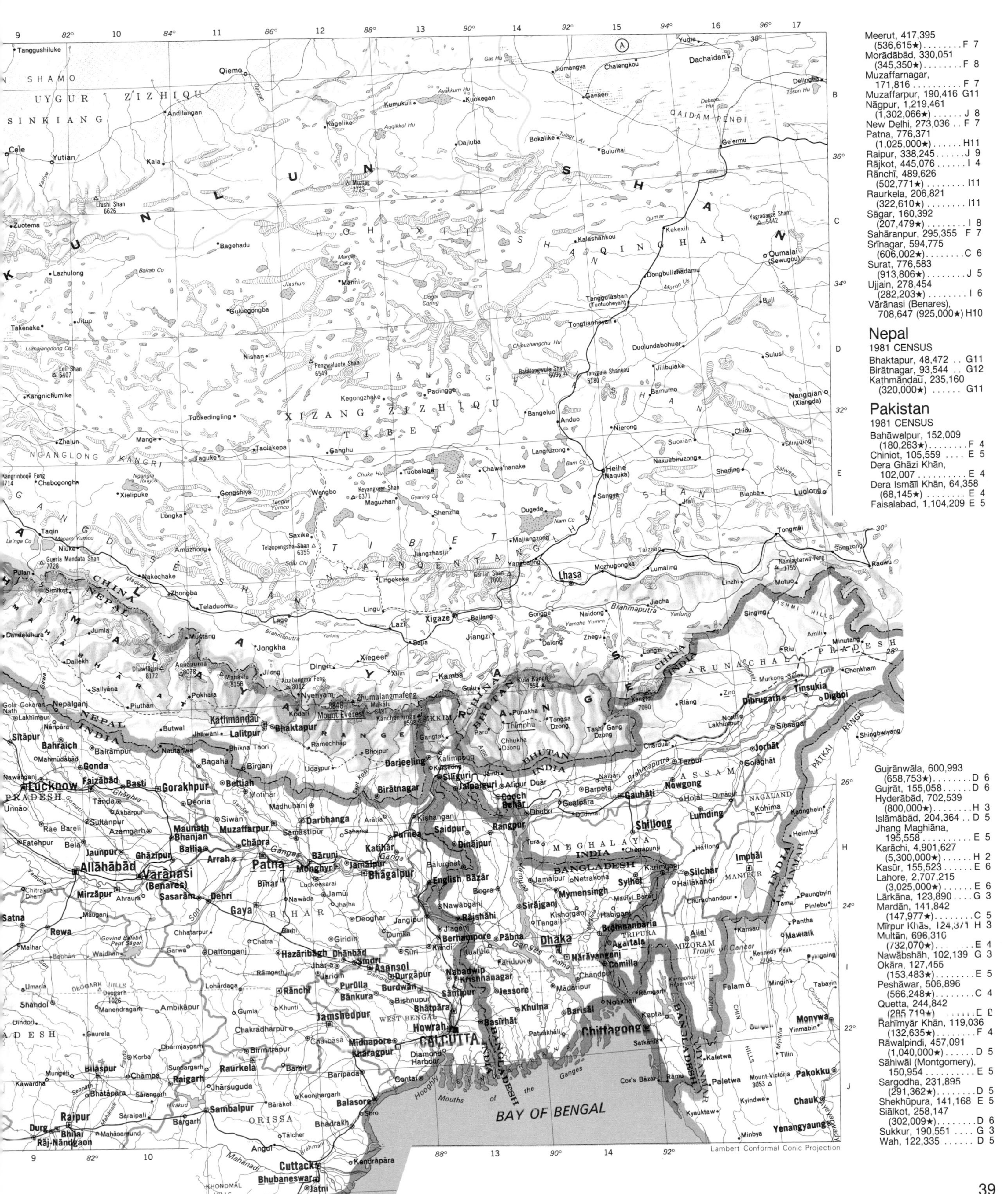

Meerut, 417,395 (536,615★)........F 7
Morādābād, 330,051 (345,350★)........F 8
Muzaffarnagar, 171,816..........F 7
Muzaffarpur, 190,416 G11
Nāgpur, 1,219,461 (1,302,066★)......J 8
New Delhi, 273,036 .. F 7
Patna, 776,371 (1,025,000★)......H11
Raipur, 338,245......J 9
Rājkot, 445,076......I 4
Rānchī, 489,626 (502,771★)........I11
Raurkela, 206,821 (322,610★)........I11
Sāgar, 160,392 (207,479★)........I 8
Sahāranpur, 295,355 F 7
Srīnagar, 594,775 (606,002★)........C 6
Surat, 776,583 (913,806★)........J 5
Ujjain, 278,454 (282,203★)........I 6
Vārānasi (Benares), 708,647 (925,000★) H10

Nepal

1981 CENSUS

Bhaktapur, 48,472 .. G11
Birātnagar, 93,544 .. G12
Kathmāndau, 235,160 (320,000★) G11

Pakistan

1981 CENSUS

Bahāwalpur, 152,009 (180,263★)........F 4
Chiniot, 105,559 .... E 5
Dera Ghāzi Khān, 102,007..........E 4
Dera Ismāīl Khān, 64,358 (68,145★)........E 4
Faisalabad, 1,104,209 E 5
Gujrānwāla, 600,993 (658,753★)........D 6
Gujrāt, 155,058......D 6
Hyderābād, 702,539 (800,000★)........H 3
Islāmābād, 204,364 .. D 5
Jhang Maghiāna, 195,558..........E 5
Karāchi, 4,901,627 (5,300,000★)......H 2
Kasūr, 155,523........E 6
Lahore, 2,707,215 (3,025,000★)........E 6
Lārkāna, 123,890....G 3
Mardān, 141,842 (147,977★)..........C 5
Mīrpur Khās, 124,371 H 3
Multān, 696,316 (732,070★)..........E 4
Nawābshāh, 102,139 G 3
Okāra, 127,455 (153,483★)..........E 5
Peshāwar, 506,896 (566,248★)..........C 4
Quetta, 244,842 (285,719★)........[illegible]
Rahīmyār Khān, 119,036 (132,635★)..........F 4
Rāwalpindi, 457,091 (1,040,000★)........D 5
Sāhiwāl (Montgomery), 150,954............E 5
Sargodha, 231,895 (291,362★)..........D 5
Shekhūpura, 141,168 E 5
Siālkot, 258,147 (302,009★)..........D 6
Sukkur, 190,551 .... G 3
Wah, 122,335 ...... D 5

Eastern Mediterranean Lands

Cyprus
1982 CENSUS

Lemesós (Limassol), 74,782 (107,161★) B 3
Nicosia, 48,221 (185,000★) . . . . . . B 3

Cyprus, North
1985 ESTIMATE

Nicosia, 37,400 . . . . B 3

Egypt
1986 CENSUS

Al-Iskandarīyah (Alexandria), 2,917,327 (3,350,000★) . . . . D 1
Al-Ismā'īlīyah (Ismailia), 212,567 (235,000★) . . . . . . D 3
Al-Jīzah (Giza), 1,870,508 . . . . . . D 2
Al-Qāhirah (Cairo), 6,052,836 (9,300,000★) . . . . D 2
As-Suways (Suez), 326,820 . . . . E 3
Asyūt, 273,191 . . . . F 2
Būr Sa'īd (Port Said), 399,793 . . . . D 3
Cairo *see* Al-Qāhirah D 2
Ţanţā, 334,505 . . . . D 2

Israel
1989 ESTIMATE

Be'er Sheva', 113,200 D 4
Ḥefa (Haifa), 222,600 (435,000★) . . . . . . C 4
Jerusalem *see* Yerushalayim . . . . D 4
Nābulus, 64,000 . . . . C 4
Tel Aviv-Yafo, 317,800 (1,735,000★) . . . . C 4
Yerushalayim (Jerusalem), 493,500 (530,000★) D 4

Jordan
1989 ESTIMATE

'Ammān, 936,300 (1,450,000★) . . . . D 4
Az-Zarqā', 318,055 . . C 5
Irbid, 167,785 . . . . . . C 4

Lebanon
1982 ESTIMATE

Bayrūt (Beirut), 509,000 (1,675,000★) . . . . C 4
Ţarābulus (Tripoli), 198,000 . . . . B 4

Saudi Arabia
1980 ESTIMATE

Al-Madīnah (Medina), 290,000 . . . . G 6

Syria
1988 ESTIMATE

Al-Lādhiqīyah (Latakia), 249,000 . . . . B 4
Al-Qāmishlī, 126,236 A 7
Dayr az-Zawr, 112,000 . . . . B 7
Dimashq (Damascus), 1,326,000 (1,950,000★) . . . . C 5
Halab (Aleppo), 1,261,000 (1,275,000★) . . . . A 5
Hamāh, 222,000 . . . . B 5
Ḥimṣ (Homs), 447,000 B 5

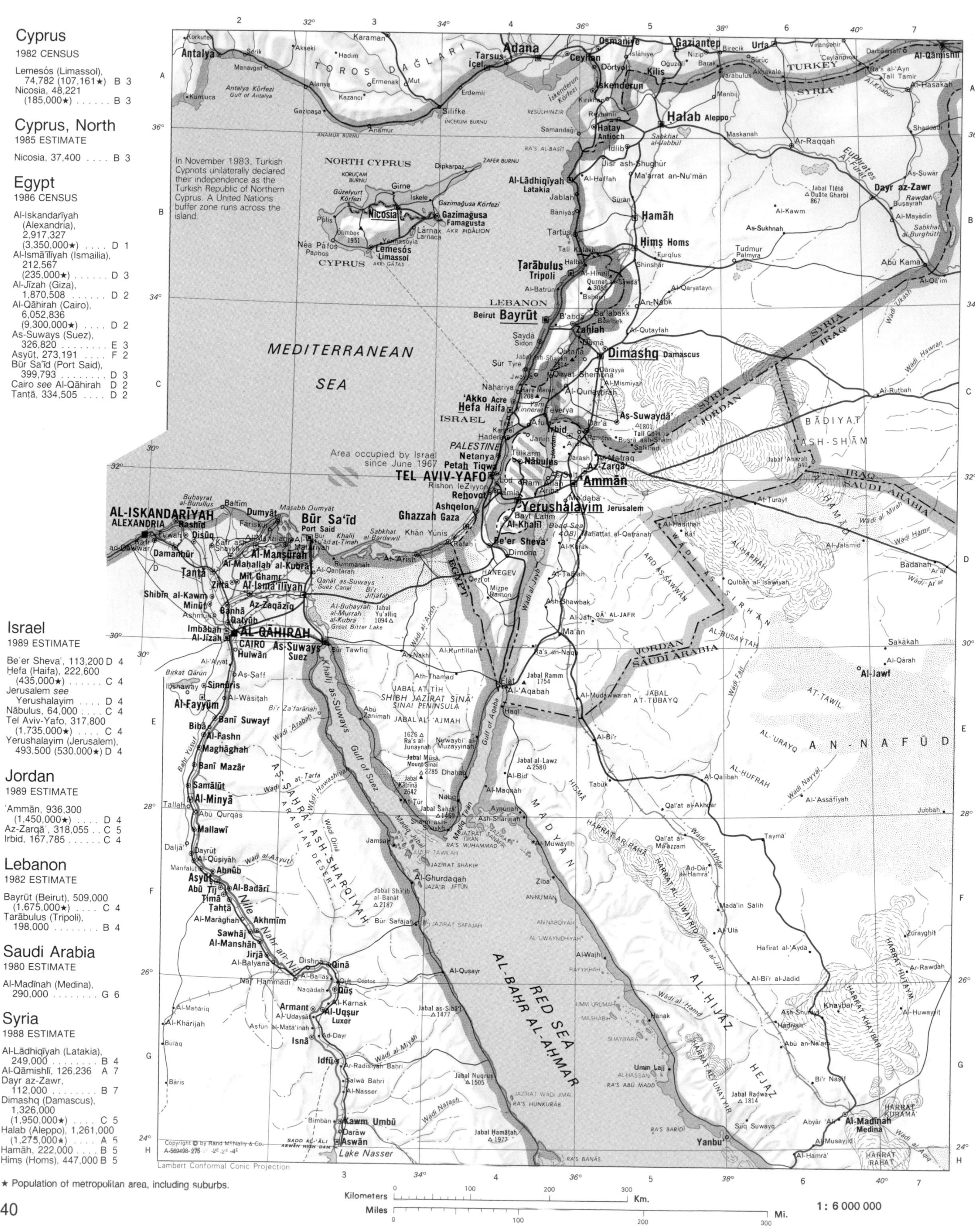

★ Population of metropolitan area, including suburbs.

Kilometers 0 100 200 300 Km.
Miles 0 100 200 300 Mi.
1 : 6 000 000

Abidjan, 1,950,000 ('83)....E 3
Accra, 859,640 ('84) (1,250,000★)....E 3
Adis Abeba (Addis Ababa), 1,686,300 ('88) (1,500,000★)....E 7
Alger (Algiers), 1,507,241 ('87) (2,547,983★)...B 4
ALGERIA....C 4
Al-Iskandarīyah (Alexandria), 2,917,327 ('86) (3,350,000★)....B 6
Al-Khartūm (Khartoum), 476,218 ('83) (1,450,000★)....D 7
Al-Qāhirah (Cairo), 6,052,836 ('86) (9,300,000★)....B 7
ANGOLA....G 5
BENIN....E 4
BOTSWANA....H 6
Brazzaville, 585,812 ('84)....F 5
BURKINA FASO....D 3
BURUNDI....F 6
CAMEROON....E 5
Cape Town, 776,617 ('85) (1,790,000★)....I 5
Casablanca, 2,139,204 ('82) (2,475,000★)...B 3
CENTRAL AFRICAN REPUBLIC....E 5
CHAD....D 5
COMOROS....G 8
CONGO....F 5
COTE D'IVOIRE....E 3
Dakar, 1,447,642 ('88) D 2
Dar es Salaam, 1,300,000 ('84)....F 7
DJIBOUTI....D 8
EGYPT....C 6
EQUATORIAL GUINEA....E 4
ERITREA....D 7
ETHIOPIA....E 7
GABON....F 5
GAMBIA....D 2
GHANA....E 3
GUINEA....D 2
GUINEA-BISSAU....D 2
Johannesburg, 632,369 ('85) (3,650,000★)....H 6
Kampala, 1,008,707 ('90)....E 7
KENYA....E 7
Kinshasa (Léopoldville), 3,000,000 ('86)....F 5
Lagos, 1,213,000 ('87) (3,800,000★)....E 4
LESOTHO....H 6
LIBERIA....E 3
LIBYA....C 5
MADAGASCAR....G 8
MALAWI....G 7
MALI....D 3
Maputo (Lourenço Marques), 1,069,727 ('89)....H 7
MAURITANIA....D 2
MOROCCO....B 3
MOZAMBIQUE....G 7
Nairobi, 1,505,000 ('90)....F 7
NAMIBIA....H 5
NIGER....D 4
NIGERIA....E 4
RWANDA....F 6
SAO TOME AND PRINCIPE....E 4
SENEGAL....D 2
SIERRA LEONE....E 2
SOMALIA....E 8
SOUTH AFRICA....I 6
SUDAN....D 6
SWAZILAND....H 7
TANZANIA....F 7
Tarābulus (Tripoli), 990,697 ('84)....B 5
TOGO....E 4
Tunis, 596,654 ('84) (1,225,000★)....B 5
TUNISIA....B 4
UGANDA....E 7
WESTERN SAHARA...C 2
ZAIRE....F 6
ZAMBIA....G 6
ZIMBABWE....G 6

★ Population of metropolitan area, including suburbs.

Northern Africa

Algeria
1987 CENSUS
Alger (Algiers), 1,507,241 (2,547,983★) . . . . . A 6
Annaba (Bône), 305,526 . . . . A 7
Batna, 181,601 . . . . . A 7
Blida, 170,935 . . . . . A 6
Constantine (Qacentina), 440,842 . . . . A 7
Oran (Wahran), 628,558 . . . . A 5
Sidi bel Abbès, 152,778 . . . . A 5
Skikda, 128,747 . . . . A 7

Benin
1984 ESTIMATE
Cotonou, 478,000 . . G 6
Porto-Novo, 164,000 G 6

Burkina Faso
1985 ESTIMATE
Bobo Dioulasso, 228,668 . . . . F 5
Ouagadougou, 441,514 . . . . F 5

Cameroon
1986 ESTIMATE
Douala, 1,029,731 . . H 7
Yaoundé, 653,670 . . H 8

Central African Republic
1984 ESTIMATE
Bangui, 473,817 . . . . H 9

Chad
1979 ESTIMATE
N'Djamena (Fort-Lamy), 303,000 . . . . F 9

Cote d'Ivoire
1983 ESTIMATE
Abidjan, 1,950,000 . . G 5
Bouaké, 275,000 . . . . G 4
Yamoussoukro, 80,000 . . . . G 4

Egypt
1986 CENSUS
Al-Fayyūm, 212,523 . . C12
Al-Iskandarīyah (Alexandria), 2,917,327 (3,350,000★) B11
Al-Manṣūrah, 316,870 (375,000★) B12
Al-Qāhirah (Cairo), 6,052,836 (9,300,000★) B12
Al-Uqṣur (Luxor), 125,404 . . . . C12
As-Suways (Suez), 326,820 . . . . C12
Aswān, 191,461 . . . . D12
Asyūt, 273,191 . . . . . C12
Banī Suwayf, 151,813 C12
Būr Sa'īd (Port Said), 399,793 . . . . B12
Cairo *see* Al-Qāhirah B12
Qinā, 119,794 . . . . . C12
Ṭanṭā, 334,505 . . . . . B12

Equatorial Guinea
1983 CENSUS
Malabo, 31,630 . . . . . H 7

Gambia
1983 CENSUS
Banjul, 44,536 (95,000★) . . . . F 2

Ghana
1984 CENSUS
Accra, 859,640 (1,250,000★) . . . . . G 5
Cape Coast, 86,620 . . G 5
Kumasi, 348,880 (600,000★) . . . . . . G 5
Sekondi-Takoradi, 93,882 . . . . H 5
Tamale, 136,828 (168,091★) . . . . . . G 5

Guinea
1986 ESTIMATE
Conakry, 800,000 . . . G 3
Kankan, 100,000 . . . . F 4

Guinea-Bissau
1988 ESTIMATE
Bissau, 125,000 . . . . F 2

★ Population of metropolitan area, including suburbs.

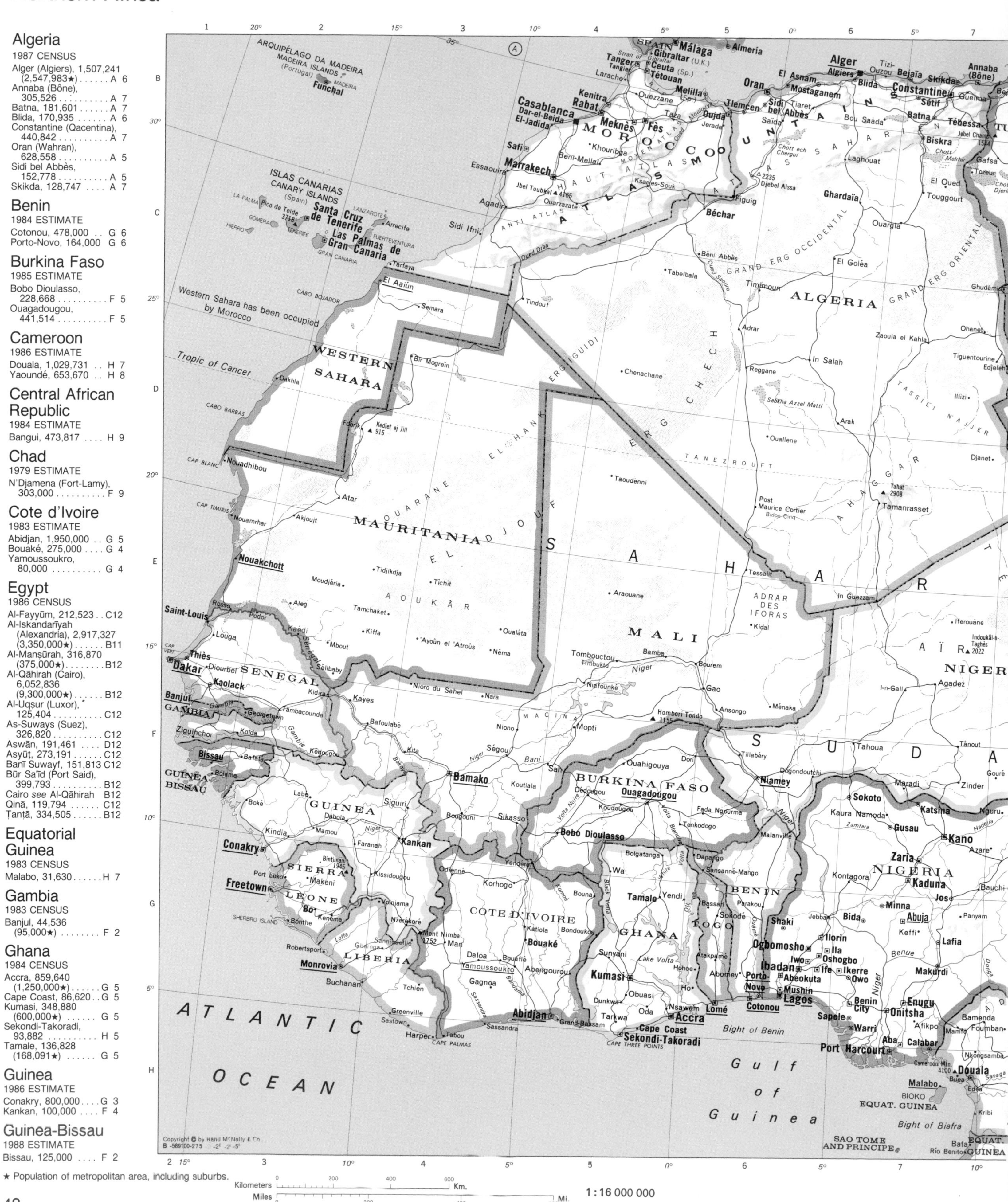

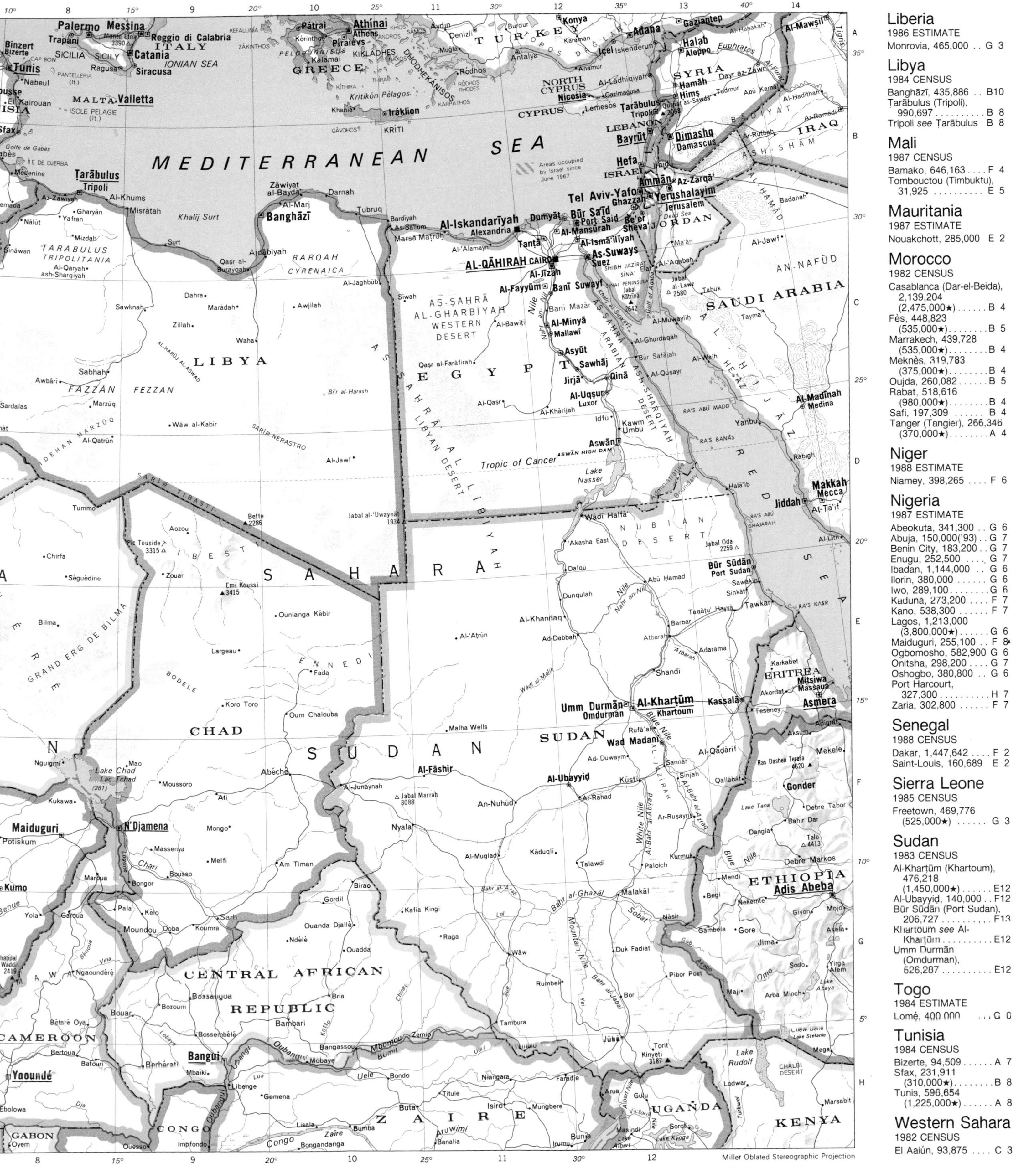

Liberia
1986 ESTIMATE
Monrovia, 465,000 .. G 3

Libya
1984 CENSUS
Banghāzī, 435,886 .. B10
Ṭarābulus (Tripoli), 990,697 .... B 8
Tripoli *see* Ṭarābulus B 8

Mali
1987 CENSUS
Bamako, 646,163 .... F 4
Tombouctou (Timbuktu), 31,925 .... E 5

Mauritania
1987 ESTIMATE
Nouakchott, 285,000 E 2

Morocco
1982 CENSUS
Casablanca (Dar-el-Beida), 2,139,204 (2,475,000★) ...... B 4
Fès, 448,823 (535,000★) .... B 5
Marrakech, 439,728 (535,000★) .... B 4
Meknès, 319,783 (375,000★) .... B 4
Oujda, 260,082 ...... B 5
Rabat, 518,616 (980,000★) .... B 4
Safi, 197,309 ...... B 4
Tanger (Tangier), 266,346 (370,000★) .... A 4

Niger
1988 ESTIMATE
Niamey, 398,265 .... F 6

Nigeria
1987 ESTIMATE
Abeokuta, 341,300 .. G 6
Abuja, 150,000('93) .. G 7
Benin City, 183,200 .. G 7
Enugu, 252,500 .... G 7
Ibadan, 1,144,000 .. G 6
Ilorin, 380,000 ...... G 6
Iwo, 289,100 .... G 6
Kaduna, 273,200 .... F 7
Kano, 538,300 ...... F 7
Lagos, 1,213,000 (3,800,000★) ..... G 6
Maiduguri, 255,100 .. F 8
Ogbomosho, 582,900 G 6
Onitsha, 298,200 .... G 7
Oshogbo, 380,800 .. G 6
Port Harcourt, 327,300 .... H 7
Zaria, 302,800 ...... F 7

Senegal
1988 CENSUS
Dakar, 1,447,642 .... F 2
Saint-Louis, 160,689 E 2

Sierra Leone
1985 CENSUS
Freetown, 469,776 (525,000★) ...... G 3

Sudan
1983 CENSUS
Al-Kharṭūm (Khartoum), 476,218 (1,450,000★) E12
Al-Ubayyiḍ, 140,000 .. F12
Būr Sūdān (Port Sudan), 206,727 .... F13
Khartoum *see* Al-Kharṭūm E12
Umm Durmān (Omdurman), 526,287 .... E12

Togo
1984 ESTIMATE
Lomé, 400,000 ...... G 0

Tunisia
1984 CENSUS
Bizerte, 94,509 ...... A 7
Sfax, 231,911 (310,000★) .... B 8
Tunis, 596,654 (1,225,000★) ...... A 8

Western Sahara
1982 CENSUS
El Aaiún, 93,875 .... C 3

Southern Africa

Angola
1983 ESTIMATE
Benguela, 155,000 .. D 2
Huambo, 203,000 .. D 3
Lobito, 150,000 .... D 2
Luanda, 1,459,900('89) .... C 2
Namibe, 100,000('81) E 2

Botswana
1987 ESTIMATE
Gaborone, 107,677 .. F 5

Burundi
1986 ESTIMATE
Bujumbura, 273,000 B 5

Comoros
1990 ESTIMATE
Moroni, 23,432 .... D 8

Congo
1984 CENSUS
Brazzaville, 585,812 B 3
Pointe-Noire, 294,203 B 2

Gabon
1985 ESTIMATE
Libreville, 235,700 .. A 1
Port-Gentil, 124,400..B 1

Kenya
1990 ESTIMATE
Mombasa, 537,000 .. B 7
Nairobi, 1,505,000 .. B 7
Nakuru, 101,700('84) B 7

Lesotho
1986 CENSUS
Maseru, 109,382....G 5

Madagascar
1984 ESTIMATE
Antananarivo, 663,000('85) .... E 9
Antsiranana, 100,000 D 9
Fianarantsoa, 130,000 F 9
Mahajanga, 85,000 .. E 9
Toamasina, 100,000 E 9

Malawi
1987 CENSUS
Blantyre, 331,588 .. E 7
Lilongwe, 233,973 .. D 6
Zomba, 42,878 .... E 7

Mauritius
1987 ESTIMATE
Port Louis, 139,730 (420,000★) F11

Mayotte
1985 ESTIMATE
Dzaoudzi, 5,865 (6,979★) .... D 9

Mozambique
1989 ESTIMATE
Beira, 291,604......E 6
Maputo (Lourenço Marques), 1,069,727 ...... G 6
Xai-Xai, 51,620('86)..G 6

Namibia
1988 ESTIMATE
Windhoek, 114,500 .. F 3

Reunion
1982 CENSUS
Saint-Denis, 84,400 (109,072▲) F11

Rwanda
1983 ESTIMATE
Kigali, 181,600 .... B 6

Sao Tome and Principe
1970 CENSUS
São Tomé, 17,380 .. A 1

Seychelles
1984 ESTIMATE
Victoria, 23,000 .... B11

★ Population of metropolitan area, including suburbs.
▲ Population of entire district, including rural area.

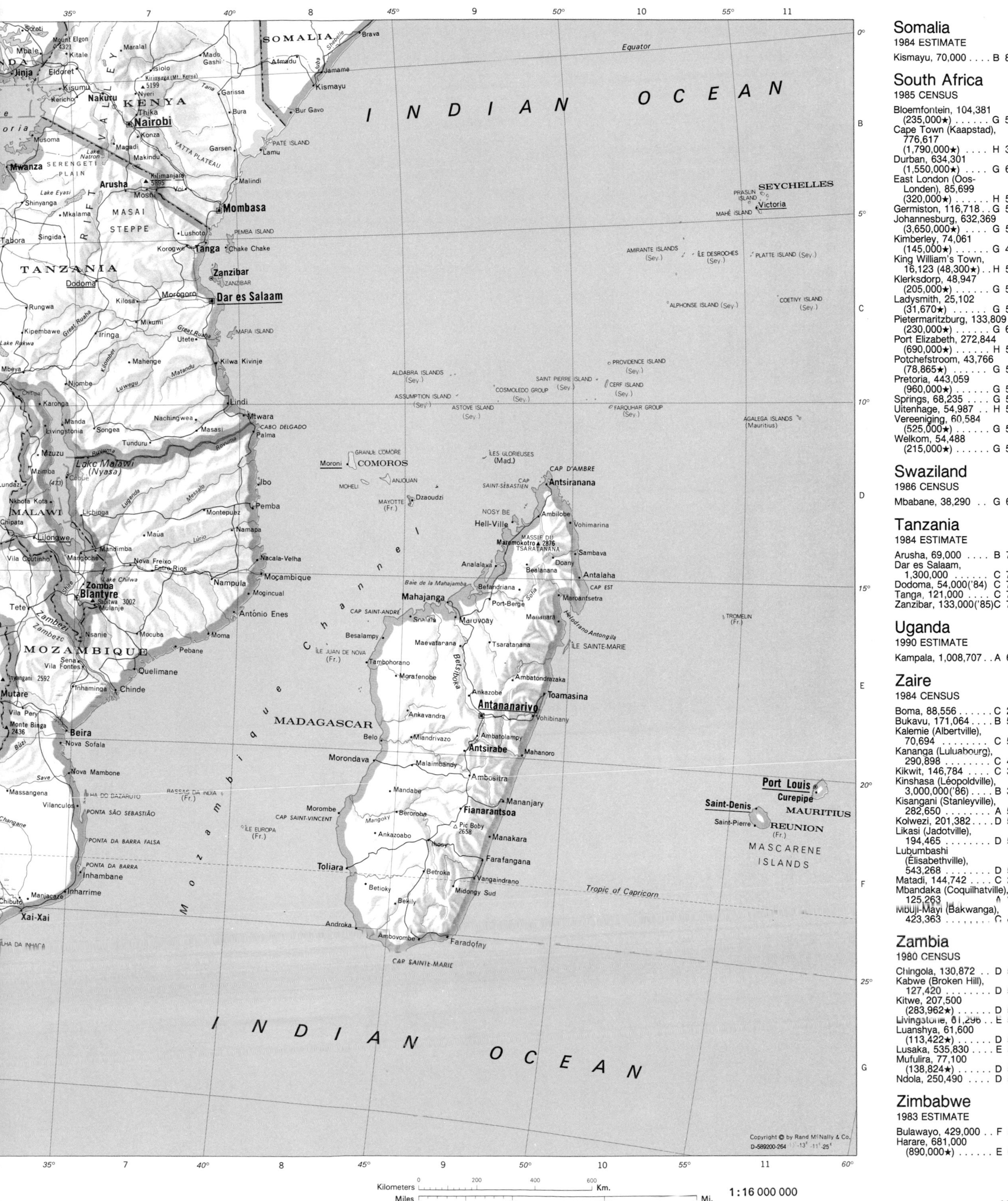

Somalia
1984 ESTIMATE

Kismayu, 70,000 . . . . B 8

South Africa
1985 CENSUS

Bloemfontein, 104,381 (235,000★) . . . . . . G 5
Cape Town (Kaapstad), 776,617 (1,790,000★) . . . . H 3
Durban, 634,301 (1,550,000★) . . . . G 6
East London (Oos-Londen), 85,699 (320,000★) . . . . . . H 5
Germiston, 116,718 . . G 5
Johannesburg, 632,369 (3,650,000★) . . . . G 5
Kimberley, 74,061 (145,000★) . . . . . . G 4
King William's Town, 16,123 (48,300★) . . H 5
Klerksdorp, 48,947 (205,000★) . . . . . . G 5
Ladysmith, 25,102 (31,670★) . . . . . . G 5
Pietermaritzburg, 133,809 (230,000★) . . . . . . G 6
Port Elizabeth, 272,844 (690,000★) . . . . . . H 5
Potchefstroom, 43,766 (78,865★) . . . . . . G 5
Pretoria, 443,059 (960,000★) . . . . . . G 5
Springs, 68,235 . . . . G 5
Uitenhage, 54,987 . . H 5
Vereeniging, 60,584 (525,000★) . . . . . . G 5
Welkom, 54,488 (215,000★) . . . . . . G 5

Swaziland
1986 CENSUS

Mbabane, 38,290 . . G 6

Tanzania
1984 ESTIMATE

Arusha, 69,000 . . . . B 7
Dar es Salaam, 1,300,000 . . . . . . C 7
Dodoma, 54,000('84) C 7
Tanga, 121,000 . . . . C 7
Zanzibar, 133,000('85)C 7

Uganda
1990 ESTIMATE

Kampala, 1,008,707 . . A 6

Zaire
1984 CENSUS

Boma, 88,556 . . . . . . C 2
Bukavu, 171,064 . . . . B 5
Kalemie (Albertville), 70,694 . . . . C 5
Kananga (Luluabourg), 290,898 . . . . C 4
Kikwit, 146,784 . . . . C 3
Kinshasa (Léopoldville), 3,000,000('86) . . . . B 3
Kisangani (Stanleyville), 282,650 . . . . A 5
Kolwezi, 201,382 . . . D 5
Likasi (Jadotville), 194,465 . . . . D 5
Lubumbashi (Élisabethville), 543,268 . . . . D 5
Matadi, 144,742 . . . . C 2
Mbandaka (Coquilhatville), 125,263 . . . . A 3
Mbuji-Mayi (Bakwanga), 423,363 . . . . C 4

Zambia
1980 CENSUS

Chingola, 130,872 . . D 5
Kabwe (Broken Hill), 127,420 . . . . D 5
Kitwe, 207,500 (283,962★) . . . . . . D 5
Livingstone, 61,296 . . E 5
Luanshya, 61,600 (113,422★) . . . . . . D 5
Lusaka, 535,830 . . . . E 5
Mufulira, 77,100 (138,824★) . . . . . . D 5
Ndola, 250,490 . . . . D 5

Zimbabwe
1983 ESTIMATE

Bulawayo, 429,000 . . F 5
Harare, 681,000 (890,000★) . . . . . . E 6

Eastern Africa and Middle East

Bahrain
1981 CENSUS
Al-Manāmah, 115,054 (224,643★) . . . . . C 5

Djibouti
1976 ESTIMATE
Djibouti, 120,000 . . . . . F 3

Eritrea
1988 ESTIMATE
Asmara, 319,353 . . . . . E 2

Ethiopia
1988 ESTIMATE
Adis Abeba, 1,686,300 (1,500,000★) . . . . . G 2
Asmera, 319,353 . . . . . E 2

Iran
1986 CENSUS
Esfahān, 986,753 (1,175,000★) . . . . . B 5
Shīrāz, 848,289 . . . . . C 5

Iraq
1985 ESTIMATE
Al-Basrah, 616,700 . . . . . B 4
Baghdād, 3,841,268('87) . . . . . B 3

Kuwait
1985 CENSUS
Al-Kuwayt, 44,335 (1,375,000★) . . . . . C 4

Oman
1981 ESTIMATE
Masqat (Muscat), 50,000 . . . . . D 6

Qatar
1986 CENSUS
Ad-Dawhah (Doha), 217,294 (310,000★) C 5

Saudi Arabia
1980 ESTIMATE
Al-Madīnah (Medina), 290,000 . . . . . D 2
Ar-Riyāḍ (Riyadh), 1,250,000 . . . . . D 4
Jiddah, 1,300,000 . . . . . D 2
Makkah (Mecca), 550,000 . . . . . D 2

Somalia
1984 ESTIMATE
Muqdisho, 600,000 . . . . . H 4

United Arab Emirates
1980 CENSUS
Abū Ẓaby, 242,975 . . . . . D 5
Dubayy (Dubai), 265,702 . . . . . C 6

Yemen
1984 ESTIMATE
'Adan (Aden), 176,100 (318,000★) . . . . . F 4
San'ā', 427,150('86) . . . . . E 3

★ Population of metropolitan area, including suburbs

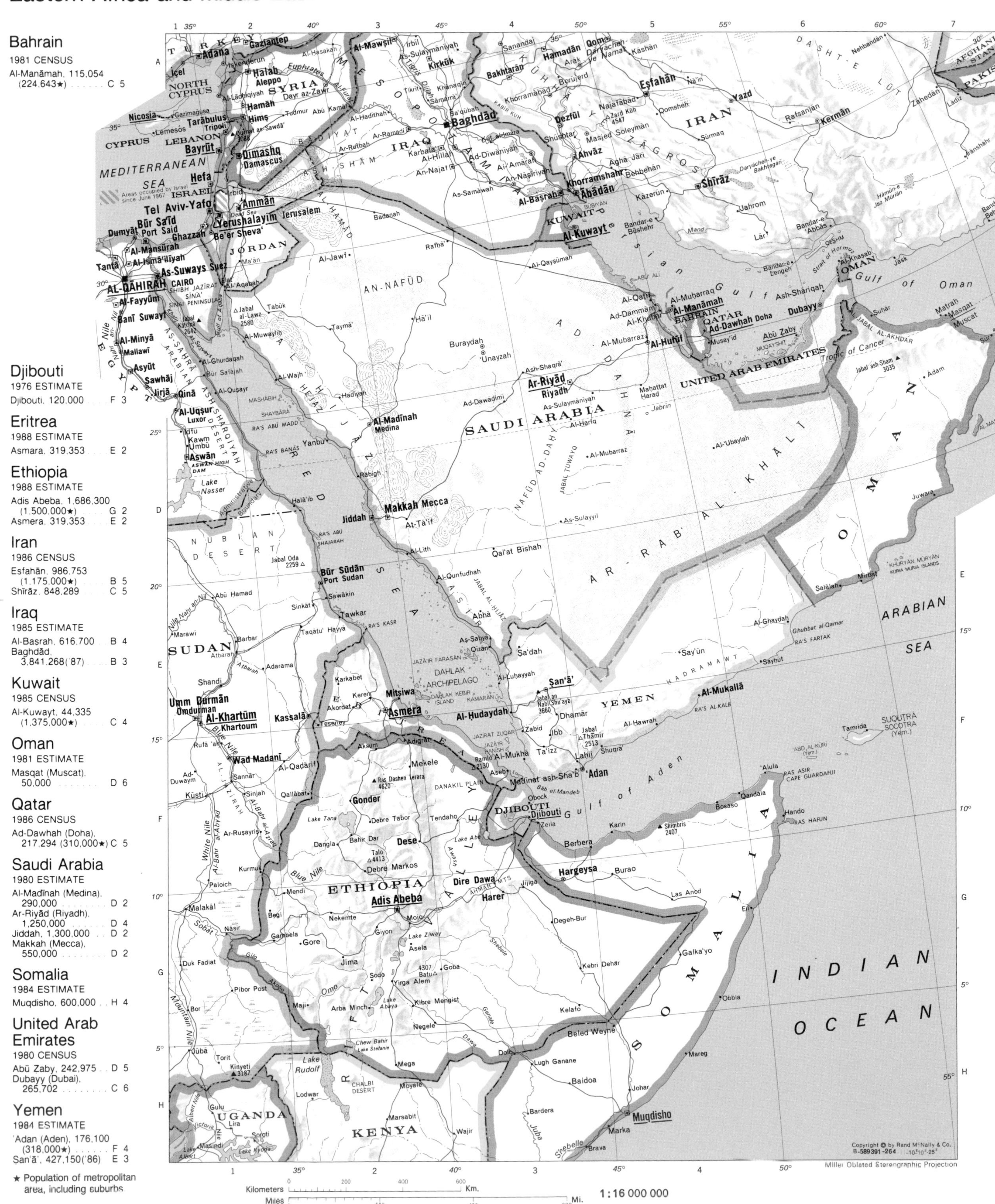

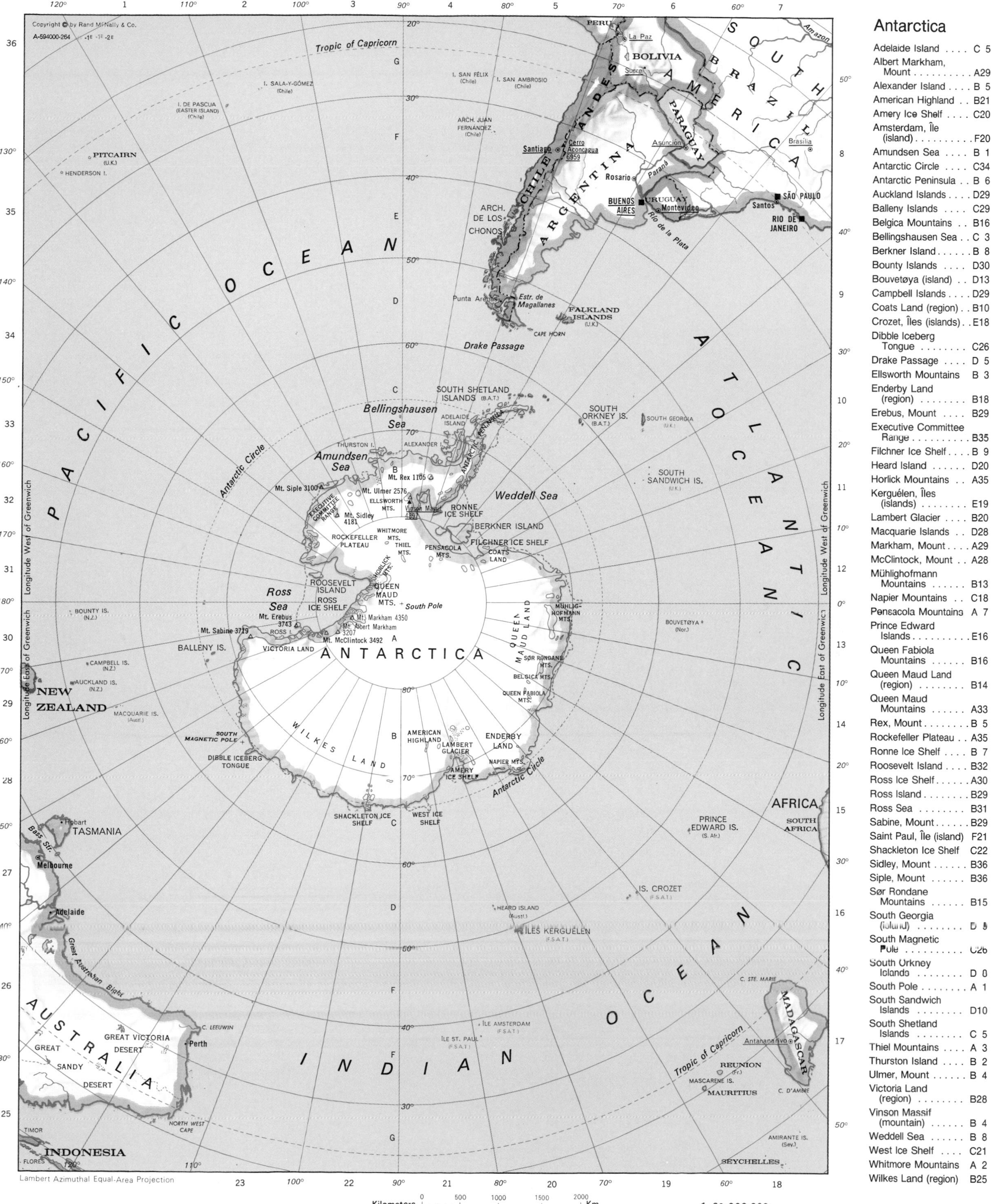

Copyright © by Rand McNally & Co.
A-594000-264
Tropic of Capricorn
I. SALA-Y-GÓMEZ (Chile)
I. SAN FÉLIX (Chile)
I. SAN AMBROSIO (Chile)
I. DE PASCUA (EASTER ISLAND) (Chile)
ARCH. JUAN FERNÁNDEZ (Chile)
PITCAIRN (U.K.)
HENDERSON I.
PERU
La Paz
BOLIVIA
Sucre
SOUTH AMERICA
BRAZIL
Amazon
PARAGUAY
Asunción
Brasília
ANDES
CHILE
ARGENTINA
Santiago
Cerro Aconcagua 6959
Rosario
Paraná
BUENOS AIRES
URUGUAY
Montevideo
Río de la Plata
SÃO PAULO
Santos
RIO DE JANEIRO
ARCH. DE LOS CHONOS
PACIFIC OCEAN
ATLANTIC OCEAN
Punta Arenas
Estr. de Magallanes
FALKLAND ISLANDS (U.K.)
CAPE HORN
Drake Passage
SOUTH SHETLAND ISLANDS (B.A.T.)
SOUTH ORKNEY IS. (B.A.T.)
SOUTH GEORGIA (U.K.)
Bellingshausen Sea
ADELAIDE ISLAND
ANTARCTIC PENINSULA
THURSTON I.
ALEXANDER I.
Amundsen Sea
Antarctic Circle
Mt. Siple 3100
Mt. Rex 1105
Mt. Ulmer 2576
ELLSWORTH MTS.
Vinson Massif 4897
EXECUTIVE COMMITTEE RANGE
Mt. Sidley 4181
RONNE ICE SHELF
Weddell Sea
SOUTH SANDWICH IS. (U.K.)
BERKNER ISLAND
FILCHNER ICE SHELF
COATS LAND
WHITMORE MTS.
ROCKEFELLER PLATEAU
THIEL MTS.
PENSACOLA MTS.
HORLICK MTS.
ROOSEVELT ISLAND
QUEEN MAUD MTS.
South Pole
Ross Sea
ROSS ICE SHELF
Mt. Erebus 3743
ROSS I.
Mt. Markham 4350
Mt. Albert Markham 3207
Mt. McClintock 3492
Mt. Sabine 3719
BALLENY IS.
VICTORIA LAND
ANTARCTICA
QUEEN MAUD LAND
MÜHLIG-HOFMANN MTS.
BOUVETØYA (Nor.)
SØR RONDANE MTS.
BELGICA MTS.
QUEEN FABIOLA MTS.
BOUNTY IS. (N.Z.)
CAMPBELL IS. (N.Z.)
AUCKLAND IS. (N.Z.)
NEW ZEALAND
MACQUARIE IS. (Austl.)
SOUTH MAGNETIC POLE
DIBBLE ICEBERG TONGUE
WILKES LAND
AMERICAN HIGHLAND
LAMBERT GLACIER
ENDERBY LAND
NAPIER MTS.
AMERY ICE SHELF
SHACKLETON ICE SHELF
WEST ICE SHELF
AFRICA
SOUTH AFRICA
PRINCE EDWARD IS. (S. Afr.)
Hobart
TASMANIA
Bass Str.
Melbourne
Adelaide
IS. CROZET (F.S.A.T.)
HEARD ISLAND (Austl.)
ÎLES KERGUELEN (F.S.A.T.)
Great Australian Bight
AUSTRALIA
C. LEEUWIN
Perth
GREAT VICTORIA DESERT
GREAT SANDY DESERT
ÎLE AMSTERDAM (F.S.A.T.)
ÎLE ST. PAUL (F.S.A.T.)
INDIAN OCEAN
C. STE. MARIE
MADAGASCAR
Antananarivo
Tropic of Capricorn
REUNION (Fr.)
MASCARENE IS.
MAURITIUS
C. D'AMBRE
NORTH WEST CAPE
TIMOR
INDONESIA
FLORES
AMIRANTE IS. (Sey.)
SEYCHELLES
Longitude West of Greenwich
Longitude East of Greenwich
Lambert Azimuthal Equal-Area Projection
Kilometers 0 500 1000 1500 2000 Km.
Miles 0 500 1000 1500 2000 Mi.
1:60 000 000

Antarctica

Pacific Ocean

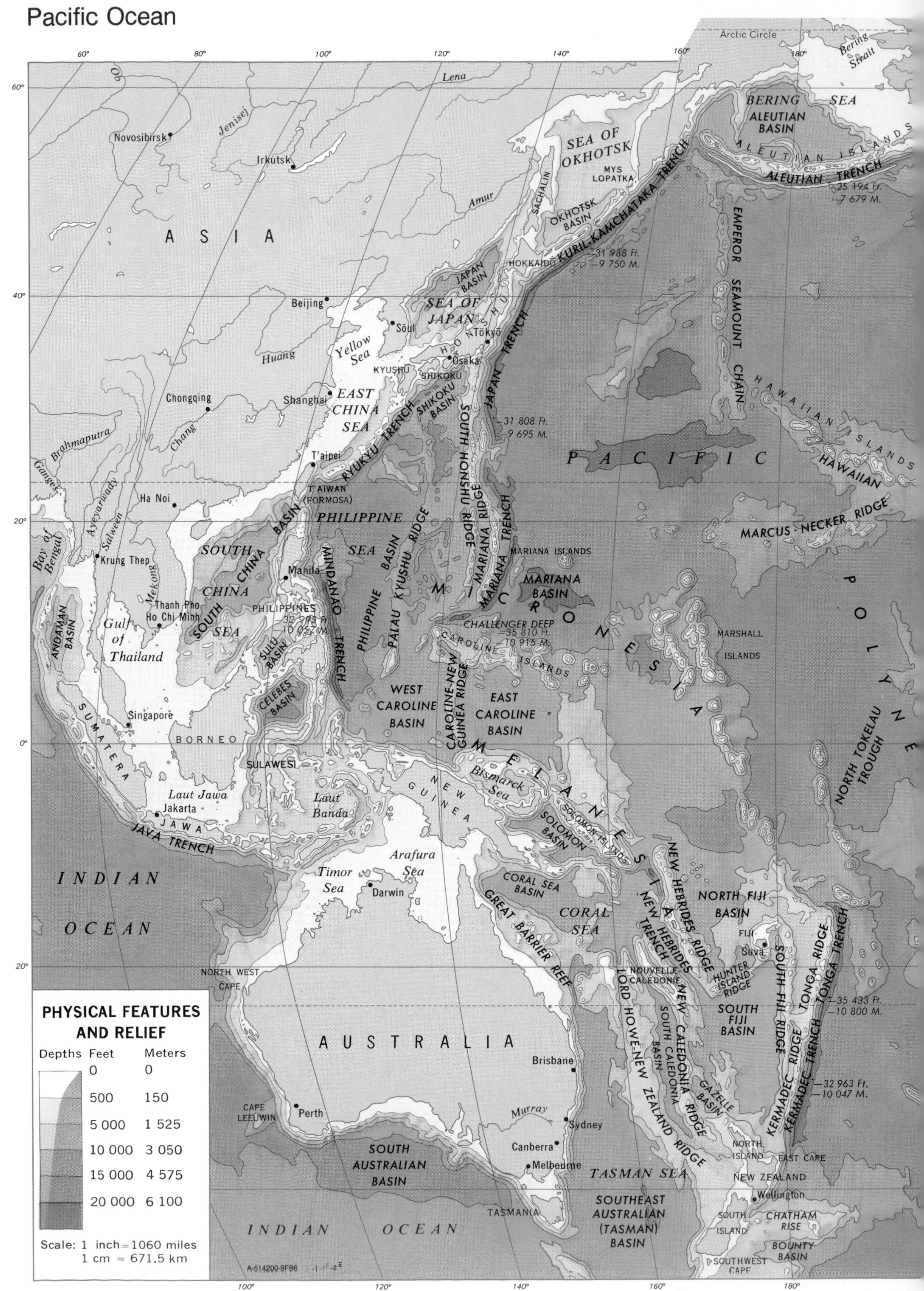

PHYSICAL FEATURES AND RELIEF
Depths Feet Meters
0 0
500 150
5 000 1 525
10 000 3 050
15 000 4 575
20 000 6 100
Scale: 1 inch=1060 miles
1 cm = 671.5 km
A S I A
P A C I F I C
A U S T R A L I A
I N D I A N O C E A N
SEA OF OKHOTSK
BERING SEA
ALEUTIAN BASIN
ALEUTIAN TRENCH
KURIL-KAMCHATKA TRENCH
EMPEROR SEAMOUNT CHAIN
HAWAIIAN ISLANDS
SEA OF JAPAN
JAPAN TRENCH
Yellow Sea
EAST CHINA SEA
PHILIPPINE SEA
SOUTH CHINA SEA
MARIANA TRENCH
CHALLENGER DEEP
MARCUS-NECKER RIDGE
M I C R O N E S I A
M E L A N E S I A
P O L Y N E S I A
WEST CAROLINE BASIN
EAST CAROLINE BASIN
Bismarck Sea
Arafura Sea
Timor Sea
CORAL SEA
GREAT BARRIER REEF
NORTH FIJI BASIN
SOUTH FIJI BASIN
TONGA TRENCH
KERMADEC TRENCH
TASMAN SEA
SOUTH AUSTRALIAN BASIN
SOUTHEAST AUSTRALIAN (TASMAN) BASIN
NEW ZEALAND
CHATHAM RISE
Beijing
Shanghai
Tōkyō
Manila
Singapore
Jakarta
Darwin
Perth
Brisbane
Sydney
Canberra
Melbourne
Wellington
Suva

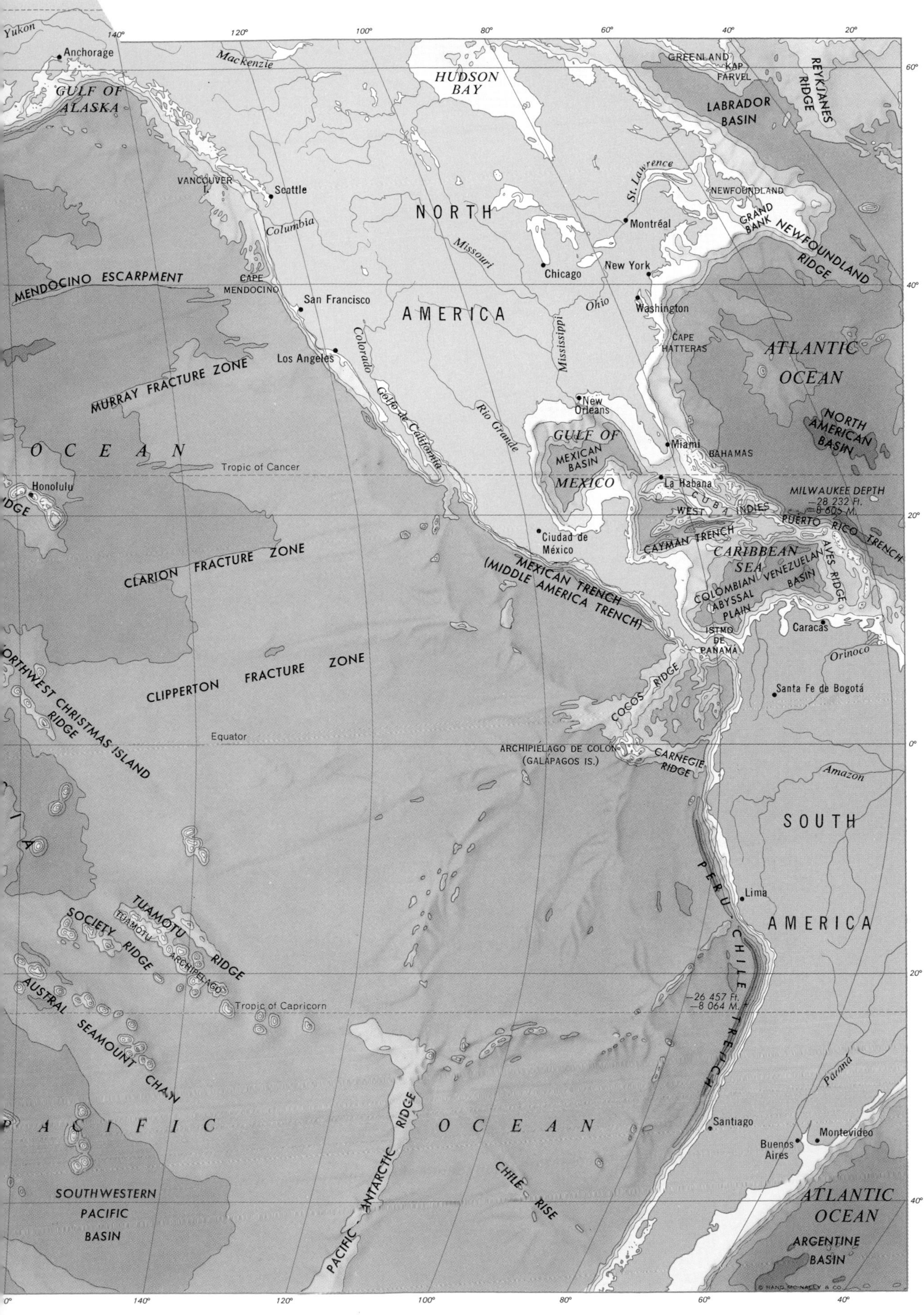

NORTH
AMERICA
HUDSON BAY
GULF OF ALASKA
LABRADOR BASIN
REYKJANES RIDGE
GREENLAND
KAP FARVEL
NEWFOUNDLAND
GRAND BANK
NEWFOUNDLAND RIDGE
Anchorage
Seattle
VANCOUVER I.
Montréal
Chicago
New York
Washington
San Francisco
Los Angeles
CAPE MENDOCINO
MENDOCINO ESCARPMENT
MURRAY FRACTURE ZONE
CAPE HATTERAS
ATLANTIC OCEAN
NORTH AMERICAN BASIN
New Orleans
GULF OF MEXICO
MEXICAN BASIN
Miami
BAHAMAS
La Habana
CUBA
WEST INDIES
MILWAUKEE DEPTH
−28 232 Ft.
−8 605 M.
PUERTO RICO TRENCH
CAYMAN TRENCH
CARIBBEAN SEA
COLOMBIAN ABYSSAL PLAIN
VENEZUELAN BASIN
AVES RIDGE
Ciudad de México
MEXICAN TRENCH (MIDDLE AMERICA TRENCH)
ISTMO DE PANAMA
Caracas
Santa Fe de Bogotá
COCOS RIDGE
ARCHIPIÉLAGO DE COLON (GALÁPAGOS IS.)
CARNEGIE RIDGE
Tropic of Cancer
Honolulu
OCEAN
CLARION FRACTURE ZONE
CLIPPERTON FRACTURE ZONE
NORTHWEST CHRISTMAS ISLAND RIDGE
Equator
SOUTH AMERICA
Lima
PERU CHILE TRENCH
−26 457 Ft.
−8 064 M.
TUAMOTU RIDGE
TUAMOTU ARCHIPELAGO
SOCIETY RIDGE
AUSTRAL SEAMOUNT CHAIN
Tropic of Capricorn
PACIFIC OCEAN
PACIFIC - ANTARCTIC RIDGE
CHILE RISE
Santiago
Buenos Aires
Montevideo
SOUTHWESTERN PACIFIC BASIN
ATLANTIC OCEAN
ARGENTINE BASIN
Yukon
Mackenzie
Columbia
Missouri
St. Lawrence
Ohio
Mississippi
Colorado
Golfo de California
Rio Grande
Orinoco
Amazon
Paraná
60°
40°
20°
0°
140°
120°
100°
80°
© RAND McNALLY & CO.

Australia

1989 ESTIMATE

Adelaide, 12,340 (1,036,747★) . . . . . . F 7
Albany, 14,958 . . . . . . G 3
Albury, 40,730 (66,530★) . . . . G 9
Alice Springs, 23,600 . . . . D 6
Ararat, 8,015('86) . . . . G 8
Armidale, 21,600 . . . . F10
Augusta, 933('86) . . . . F 3
Ballarat, 36,680 (80,090★) . . . . G 8
Barcaldine, 1,427('86) . . . . D 9
Bendigo, 32,050 (67,920★) . . . . G 8
Blackall, 1,497('86) . . D 9
Bombala, 1,458('86) . . G 9
Bordertown, 2,318('86) . . . . G 8
Bourke, 3,018('86) . . F 9
Bowen, 7,705('86) . . C 9
Brisbane, 744,828 (1,273,511★) E10
Broken Hill, 22,550 . . F 8
Broome, 5,778('86) . . C 4
Bunbury, 26,398 . . . . F 3
Bundaberg, 33,024 (45,161★) D10
Burketown, 232('86) . . . . C 7
Burnie, 20,665('86) . . H 9
Busselton, 7,784('86) . . . . F 3
Cairns, 42,839 (80,875★) . . . . C 9
Camooweal, 315('86) . . . . C 7
Canberra, 247,194 (271,362★)('86) . . . . G 9
Carnarvon, 6,847('86) . . . . D 2
Ceduna, 2,877('86) . . F 6
Cessnock, 43,870 . . . . F10
Charleville, 3,588('86) . . . . E 9
Charters Towers, 7,208('86) . . . . D 9
Cloncurry, 2,297('86) . . . . D 8
Coffs Harbour, 47,890 . . . . F10
Cooktown, 964('86) . . C 9
Coolgardie, 989('86) . . F 4
Cooma, 7,406('86) . . G 9
Croydon, 229('86) . . C 8
Cunnamulla, 1,697('86) . . . . E 9
Dampier, 2,201('86) . . D 3
Darwin, 63,900 (72,937★) . . . . B 6
Derby, 3,258('86) . . . . C 4
Devonport, 25,370 . . H 9
Dongara, 1,496('86) . . E 2
Dubbo, 32,230 . . . . . . F 9
Elizabeth, 29,998 . . . . F 7
Emerald, 5,982('86) . . D 9
Esperance, 6,440('86) . . . . F 4
Geelong, 13,190 (148,980★) . . . . . . G 8
Geraldton, 20,968 . . . . E 2
Gladstone, 22,033('86) D10
Glen Innes, 5,971('86) E10
Goondiwindi, 4,103('86) E10
Goulburn, 21,580 . . . . F 9
Grafton, 15,890 . . . . . E10
Griffith, 13,630('86) . . F 9
Gympie, 10,772('86) . . E10
Halls Creek, 1,182('86) . . . . C 5
Hay, 2,961('86) . . . . . . F 8
Hobart, 47,280 (181,210★) . . . . H 9
Home Hill, 3,286('86) . . . . C 9
Horsham, 12,850 . . . . G 8
Hughenden, 1,791('86) . . . . D 8
Ingham, 5,202('86) . . C 9
Inverell, 9,693('86) . . E10
Ipswich, 75,283 . . . . . . E10
Kalgoorlie, 26,813 . . . . F 4
Kingaroy, 6,362('86) . . E10
Launceston, 32,150 (92,350★) . . . . H 9
Leonora, 1,004('86) . . E 4
Lismore, 39,450 . . . . E10
Longreach, 3,159('86) . . . . D 8
Mackay, 22,583 (50,885★) . . . . D 9
Maitland, 47,280 . . . . F10
Marble Bar, 332('86) D 3
Mareeba, 6,614('86) . . C 9
Marree, 300('76) . . . . E 7
Meekatharra, 1,018('86) . . . . E 3

★ Population of metropolitan area, including suburbs.

Melbourne, 55,300
(3,039,100★) . . . . . . G 8
Mildura, 20,512('86) . . F 8
Mitchell, 1,212('86) . . E 9
Moora, 1,469('86) . . . . F 3
Moree, 10,215('86) . . E 9
Morwell, 16,880 . . . . G 9
Mount Gambier, 22,194
(27,228★) . . . . G 8
Mount Isa, 24,023 . . D 7
Mount Magnet,
1,000('86) . . . . E 3
Mullewa, 758('86) . . . . E 3
Murwillumbah,
7,678('86) E10
Nambour, 9,579('86) E10
Naracoorte,
4,636('86) . . . . G 8
Newcastle, 130,940
(425,610★) F10
New Norfolk,
6,152('86) . . . . H 9
Normanton,
1,109('86) . . . . C 8
Norseman,
1,775('86) . . . . F 4
Northam, 6,377('86) . . F 3
Nyngan, 2,502('86) . . F 9
Onslow, 750('86) . . . . D 3
Oodnadatta, 200('76) E 7
Orange, 32,980 . . . . . . F 9
Pemberton, 802('86) . . F 3
Perth, 82,413
(1,158,387★) . . . . . . F 3
Peterborough,
2,239('86) . . . . F 7
Port Augusta,
15,752 . . . . F 7
Port Hedland,
13,069('86) . . . . . . D 3
Port Lincoln, 12,941 . . F 7
Port Macquarie,
22,884('86) F10
Port Pirie, 15,210 . . . . F 7
Quilpie, 780('86) . . . . E 8
Ravensthorpe,
299('86) . . . . F 3
Richmond, 704('86) . . D 8
Rockhampton, 58,890
(61,694★) D10
Roebourne,
1,269('86) . . . . D 3
Roma, 6,069('86) . . . . E 9
Saint George,
2,323('86) . . . . E 9
Sale, 13,800 . . . . G 9
Shepparton, 26,420
(39,700★) . . . . G 9
Smithton, 3,414('86) . . H 9
Southern Cross,
898('86) . . . . F 3
Swan Hill,
8,831('86) . . . . G 8
Sydney, 9,800
(3,623,550★) F10
Tamworth, 34,430 . . F10
Taree, 38,760 . . . . . . F10
Tennant Creek,
3,503('86) . . . . C 6
Tenterfield,
3,370('86) E10
Theodore, 576('86) . . D10
Toowoomba,
81,071 . . . . E10
Townsville, 83,339
(111,972★) . . . . C 9
Wagga Wagga,
52,180 . . . . G 9
Walgett, 2,151('86) . . E 9
Wangaratta, 16,320 . . G 9
Warrnambool,
24,480 . . . . G 8
Weipa, 2,406('86) . . . . B 8
Whyalla, 26,706 . . . . F 7
Wilcannia, 1,048('86) F 8
Wiluna, 279('86) . . . . E 4
Winton, 1,281('86) . . D 8
Wollongong, 174,770
(236,690★) F10
Woomera,
1,805('86) . . . . F 7
Wyndham,
1,329('86) . . . . C 5

Indonesia

1980 CENSUS

Jayapura, 60,641 . . . . k15
Kupang, 84,587 . . . . D 4
Sorong, 52,041 . . . . . . k13

Papua New Guinea

1987 ESTIMATE

Lae, 79,600 . . . . m16
Madang, 24,700 . . . . m16
Port Moresby,
152,100 . . . . m16
Rabaul, 14,954('80) . . k17
Wewak, 23,200 . . . . . . k15

New Zealand

New Zealand

1986 CENSUS

Alexandra, 4,842 . . . . F 2
Ashburton, 14,030 . . E 3
Auckland, 149,046 (850,000★) . . . . . . B 5
Blenheim, 18,308 (22,681★) . . . . . . D 4
Bluff, 2,537 . . . . G 2
Cambridge, 10,145 . . B 5
Christchurch, 168,200 (320,000★) . . . . . . E 4
Dannevirke, 5,873 . . D 6
Dargaville, 4,859 . . . . A 4
Devonport, 10,543 . . B 5
Dunedin, 76,964 (109,000★) . . . . . . F 3
Gisborne, 30,020 (32,238★) . . . . . . C 7
Gore, 8,594 (11,249★) G 2
Greymouth, 7,624 (11,261★) . . . . . . E 3
Hamilton, 94,511 (101,814★) . . . . . . B 5
Hastings, 37,658 . . . . C 6
Hawera, 4,151 (11,375★) . . . . . . C 5
Hokitika, 3,427 . . . . E 3
Huntly, 6,750 . . . . . . B 5
Invercargill, 48,197 (52,807★) . . . . . . G 2
Kaiapoi, 5,234 . . . . . . E 4
Kaikoura, 2,209 . . . . E 4
Levin, 15,368 (18,962★) . . . . . . D 5
Lower Hutt, 63,862 . . D 5
Masterton, 18,511 (20,145★) . . . . . . D 5
Milton, 2,154 . . . . . . G 2
Morrinsville, 5,281 . . B 5
Motueka, 5,052 . . . . D 4
Murapara, 2,566 . . . . C 6
Napier, 49,428 (107,060★) . . . . . . C 6
Nelson, 34,274 (44,593★) . . . . . . D 4
New Plymouth, 36,865 (47,384★) . . . . . . C 5
Oamaru, 12,652 (14,247★) . . . . F 3
Opotiki, 3,719 . . . . . . C 6
Otaki, 4,407 . . . . . . D 5
Palmerston North, 60,503 (67,405★) . . . . . . D 5
Picton, 4,129 . . . . . . D 5
Port Chalmers, 2,871 F 3
Pukekohe, 9,398 (13,823★) . . . . . . B 5
Queenstown, 3,659 . . F 2
Richmond, 7,204 . . . . D 4
Rotorua, 40,597 (52,001★) . . . . . . C 6
Stratford, 5,528 . . . . C 5
Taihape, 2,472 . . . . C 5
Takapuna, 69,419 . . B 5
Taumarunui, 6,387 . . C 5
Taupo, 15,873 . . . . C 6
Tauranga, 41,611 (59,435★) . . . . . . B 6
Te Awamutu, 8,096 . . C 5
Te Kuiti, 4,787 . . . . C 5
Thames, 6,461 . . . . B 5
Timaru, 27,757 (28,621★) . . . . F 3
Tokoroa, 17,628 (18,193★) . . . . . . C 5
Waihi, 3,679 . . . . . . B 5
Waimate, 3,250 . . . . F 3
Waipukurau, 3,862 . . D 6
Wairoa, 5,094 . . . . . . C 6
Waitara, 6,482 . . . . C 5
Waiuku, 4,357 . . . . . . B 5
Wanaka, 1,710 . . . . F 2
Wanganui, 38,084 (40,758★) . . . . . . C 5
Wellington, 137,495 (350,000★) . . . . . . D 5
Wellsford, 1,627 . . . . B 5
Westport, 4,660 . . . . D 3
Whakatane, 12,800 (15,954★) . . . . . . B 6
Whangarei, 40,179 (44,043★) . . . . . . A 5
Winton, 2,082 . . . . . . G 2

★ Population of metropolitan area, including suburbs.

Antofagasta, 185,486 ('82) .... F 3
Arequipa, 108,023 ('81) (446,942★) .... E 3
ARGENTINA .... G 4
Asunción, 477,100 ('85) (700,000★) .... F 5
Barranquilla, 899,781 ('85) (1,140,000★) .... B 3
Belém, 1,116,578 ('85) (1,200,000★) .... D 6
Belo Horizonte, 2,114,429 ('85) (2,950,000★) ... E 6
Bogotá *see* Santa Fe de Bogotá .... C 3
BOLIVIA .... E 4
Brasília, 1,567,709 ('85) .... E 6
BRAZIL .... E 5
Buenos Aires, 2,922,829 ('80) (10,750,000★) G 5
Caracas, 1,816,901 ('81) (3,600,000★) .... B 4
Cartagena, 531,426 ('85) .... B 3
Cayenne, 38,091 ('82). C 5
Chiclayo, 213,095 ('81) (279,527★) .... D 3
CHILE .... G 3
Ciudad Bolívar, 182,941 ('81) .... C 4
COLOMBIA .... C 3
Concepción, 267,891 ('82) (675,000★) .... G 3
Cuzco, 89,563 ('81) (184,550★) .... E 3
ECUADOR .... D 3
FALKLAND ISLANDS ... I 5
Fortaleza, 1,582,414 ('85) (1,825,000★) .... D 7
FRENCH GUIANA .... C 5
Georgetown, 78,500 ('83) (188,000★) .... C 5
Guayaquil, 1,572,615 ('87) (1,580,000★) .... D 3
GUYANA .... C 5
Iquitos, 178,738 ('81).. D 3
João Pessoa, 348,500 ('85) (550,000★) ..... D 7
La Paz, 992,592 ('85).. E 4
La Plata, 477,175 ('80) .... G 5
Lima, 371,122 ('81) (4,608,010★) .... E 3
Maceió, 482,195 ('85). D 7
Manaus, 809,914 ('85) D 5
Maracaibo, 890,643 ('81) .... B 3
Medellín, 1,468,089 ('85) (2,095,000★) .... C 3
Mendoza, 119,088 ('80) (650,000★) .... G 4
Montevideo, 1,251,647 ('85) (1,550,000★) .. G 5
Natal, 510,106 ('85)..... D 7
PARAGUAY .... F 5
Paramaribo, 241,000 ('88) (296,000★) .... C 5
PERU .... E 3
Porto Alegre, 1,272,121 ('85) (2,600,000★) .. G 5
Quito, 1,137,705 ('87) (1,300,000★) .... D 3
Recife, 1,287,623 ('85) (2,625,000★) .... D 7
Rio Branco, 109,800 ('85) (145,486▲) .... D 4
Rio de Janeiro, 5,603,388 ('85) (10,150,000★) . F 6
Rosario, 938,120 ('80) (1,045,000★) .... G 4
Salta, 260,744 ('80)..... F 4
Salvador, 1,804,438 ('85) (2,050,000★) .... E 7
San Miguel de Tucumán, 392,888 ('80) (525,000★) .... F 4
Santa Fe, 292,165 ('80) .... G 4
Santa Fe de Bogotá, 3,002,941 ('85) (4,260,000★) .... C 3
Santiago, 232,667 ('82) (4,100,000★) .... G 3
Santos, 460,100 ('85) (1,065,000★) .... F 6
São Luís, 227,900 ('85) (600,000★) .... D 6
São Paulo, 10,063,110 ('85) (15,175,000★) . F 6
Stanley, 1,200 ('86)....... I 5
Sucre, 86,609 ('85)...... E 4
SURINAME .... C 5
Teresina, 425,300 ('85) (525,000★) .... D 6
Trujillo, 202,469 ('81) (354,301★) .... D 3
URUGUAY .... G 5
Valparaíso, 265,355 ('82) (675,000★) .... G 3
VENEZUELA .... C 4
Vitória, 201,500 ('85) (735,000★) .... F 6

★ Population of metropolitan area, including suburbs.
▲ Population of entire district, including rural area.

Miles 0 200 400 600 800 1000 Mi.
Kilometers 0 400 800 1200 1600 Km.
1:40 000 000

Northern South America

Bolivia

1985 ESTIMATE

Cochabamba, 317,251 G 5
La Paz, 992,592 .... G 5
Oruro, 178,393 ...... G 5
Potosí, 113,380 .... G 5
Santa Cruz, 441,717 G 6
Sucre, 86,609 ...... G 5

Brazil

1985 ESTIMATE

Anápolis, 225,840 .. G 9
Aracaju, 360,013 .... F11
Araçatuba, 129,304 .. H 8
Bauru, 220,105 ...... H 9
Belém, 1,116,578 (1,200,000★) ...... D 9
Belo Horizonte, 2,114,429 (2,950,000★) G10
Brasília, 1,567,709 .. G 9
Campina Grande, 279,929 .... E11
Campinas, 841,016 (1,125,000★) ...... H 9
Campo Grande, 384,398 .... H 8
Campos, 187,900 (366,716▲) H10
Caruaru, 152,100 (190,794▲) E11
Cuiabá, 220,400 (279,651▲) ...... G 7
Feira de Santana, 278,600 (355,201▲) F11
Fortaleza, 1,582,414 (1,825,000★) D11
Goiânia, 923,333 (990,000★) ...... G 9
Governador Valadares, 192,300 (216,957▲) G10
João Pessoa, 348,500 (550,000★) E12
Juàzeiro do Norte, 159,806 .... E11
Juiz de Fora, 349,720 H10
Jundiaí, 268,900 (313,652▲) .... H 9
Maceió, 482,195 .... E11
Manaus, 809,914 .... D 6
Montes Claros, 183,500 (214,472▲) G10
Natal, 510,106 ...... E11
Niterói, 441,684 .... H10
Petrolina, 92,100 (225,000★) E10
Petrópolis, 170,300 .. H10
Piracicaba, 211,000 (252,079▲) .... H 9
Porto Velho, 152,700 (202,011▲) .... E 6
Presidente Prudente, 155,883 .... H 8
Recife, 1,287,623 (2,625,000★) E12
Ribeirão Prêto, 383,125 .... H 9
Rio de Janeiro, 5,603,388 (10,150,000★) H10
Salvador, 1,804,438 (2,050,000★) F11
Santarém, 120,800 (226,618▲) .... D 8
Santos, 460,100 (1,065,000★) ...... H 9
São Carlos, 140,383 H 9
São José do Rio Prêto, 229,221 .... H 9
São Luís, 227,900 (600,000★) D10
São Paulo, 10,063,110 (15,175,000★) .... H 9
Sorocaba, 327,468 .. H 9
Teresina, 425,300 (525,000★) E10
Uberaba, 244,875 .... G 9
Uberlândia, 312,024 .. G 9
Vitória, 201,500 (735,000★) H10
Vitória da Conquista, 145,800 (198,150▲) F10
Volta Redonda, 219,267 (375,000★) H10

Colombia

1985 CENSUS

Armenia, 187,130 .... C 3
Barrancabermeja, 137,406 .... B 4
Barranquilla, 899,781 (1,140,000★) ...... A 4
Bogotá *see* Santa Fe de Bogotá .... C 4
Bucaramanga, 352,326 (550,000★) .... B 4
Buenaventura, 160,342 .... C 3
Buga, 82,992 ...... C 3
Cali, 1,350,565 (1,400,000★) ...... C 3
Cartagena, 531,426 .. A 3
Cúcuta, 379,478 (445,000★) .... B 4

Ibagué, 292,965 . . . . C 3
Manizales, 299,352 (330,000★). . . . . . . B 3
Medellín, 1,468,089 (2,095,000★) . . . . . . B 3
Montería, 157,466 . . B 3
Neiva, 194,556 . . . . . . C 3
Palmira, 175,186 . . . . C 3
Pasto, 197,407 . . . . . . C 3
Pereira, 233,271 (390,000★). . . . . C 3
Popayán, 141,964 . . C 3
Santa Fe de Bogotá, 3,982,941 (4,260,000★) . . . . . . C 4
Santa Marta, 177,922 A 4
Tuluá, 99,721 . . . . . . C 3
Valledupar, 142,771 . . A 4
Villavicencio, 178,685 C 4

Ecuador
1987 ESTIMATE

Ambato, 126,067 . . . . D 3
Cuenca, 201,490 . . . . D 3
Guayaquil, 1,572,615 (1,580,000★) . . . . . . D 3
Machala, 144,396 . . . . D 3
Manta, 135,990 . . . . D 2
Portoviejo, 141,568 . . D 2
Quito, 1,137,705 (1,300,000★) . . . . . . D 3

French Guiana
1982 CENSUS

Cayenne, 38,091 . . . . C 8

Guyana
1983 ESTIMATE

Georgetown, 78,500 (188,000★) . . . . B 7

Peru
1981 CENSUS

Arequipa, 108,023 (446,942★) . . . . . . G 4
Ayacucho, 57,432 (69,533★) . . . . F 4
Cajamarca, 62,259 . . E 3
Callao, 264,133 . . . . . . F 3
Cerro de Pasco, 55,597 (66,373★) . . . . F 3
Chiclayo, 213,095 (279,527★). . . . . E 3
Chimbote, 223,341 . . E 3
Cuzco, 89,563 (184,550★). . . . . F 4
Huancayo, 84,845 (164,954★). . . . . F 3
Huánuco, 61,812 . . . . E 3
Ica, 114,786 . . . . F 3
Iquitos, 178,738 . . . . D 4
Lima, 371,122 (4,608,010★) . . . . . . F 3
Piura, 144,609 (207,934★). . . . . E 2
Sullana, 89,037 . . . . . . D 2
Tacna, 97,173 . . . . . . G 4
Trujillo, 202,469 (354,301★). . . . . E 3
Tumbes, 47,936 . . . . D 2
Vitarte, 145,504 . . . . F 3

Suriname
1988 ESTIMATE

Paramaribo, 241,000 (296,000★). . . . . B 7

Venezuela
1981 CENSUS

Acarigua, 91,662 . . . . B 5
Barinas, 110,462 . . . . B 4
Barquisimeto, 497,635 A 5
Cabimas, 140,435 . . A 4
Calabozo, 61,995 . . . . B 5
Caracas, 1,816,901 (3,600,000★) . . . . . . A 5
Ciudad Bolívar, 182,941 . . . . B 6
Ciudad Guayana, 314,497 . . . . B 6
Ciudad Ojeda, 83,565 . A 4
Cumaná, 179,814 . . . . A 6
El Tigre, 73,595 . . . . B 6
Maracaibo, 890,643 . . A 4
Maracay, 322,560 . . . . A 5
Maturín, 154,976 . . . . B 6
Mérida, 143,209 . . . . B 4
Puerto Cabello, 71,759 . . . . A 5
Punto Fijo, 71,114 . . A 4
San Cristóbal, 198,793 . . . . B 4
Valencia, 616,224 . . . . A 5
Valera, 102,068 . . . . B 4

★ Population of metropolitan area, including suburbs.
▲ Population of entire district, including rural area.

Southern South America

Argentina
1980 CENSUS

Avellaneda, 334,145 . . C 5
Bahía Blanca, 223,818 D 4
Buenos Aires, 2,922,829 (10,750,000★) . . . . C 5
Catamarca, 78,799 (90,000★) . . . . B 3
Comodoro Rivadavia, 96,817 . . . . F 3
Concordia, 94,222 . . C 5
Córdoba, 993,055 (1,070,000★) . . . . . . C 4
Corrientes, 180,612 . . B 5
La Plata, 477,175 . . . . C 5
Mar del Plata, 414,696 . . . . D 5
Mendoza, 119,088 (650,000★) . . . . C 3
Paraná, 161,638 . . . . C 4
Posadas, 143,889 . . . . B 5
Río Cuarto, 110,254 . . C 4
Rosario, 938,120 (1,045,000★) . . . . . . C 4
Salta, 260,744 . . . . . . A 3
San Isidro, 289,170 . . C 5
San Juan, 118,046 (300,000★) . . . . C 3
San Miguel de Tucumán, 392,888 (525,000★) B 3
Santa Fe, 292,165 . . C 4
Santiago del Estero, 148,758 (200,000★) B 4

Brazil
1985 ESTIMATE

Bauru, 220,105 . . . . . . A 7
Blumenau, 192,074 . . B 7
Campinas, 841,016 (1,125,000★) . . . . . . A 7
Caxias do Sul, 266,809 . . . . B 6
Curitiba, 1,279,205 (1,700,000★) . . . . . . B 7
Florianópolis, 178,400 (365,000★) . . . . B 7
Joinvile, 302,877 . . . . B 7
Jundiaí, 268,900 (313,652▲) . . . . A 7
Londrina, 296,400 (346,676▲) . . . . A 6
Maringá, 196,871 . . . . A 6
Pelotas, 210,300 (277,730▲) . . . . C 6
Piracicaba, 211,000 (252,079▲) . . . . A 7
Ponta Grossa, 223,154 . . . . B 6
Porto Alegre, 1,272,121 (2,600,000★) . . . . . . C 6
Presidente Prudente, 155,883 . . . . A 6
Ribeirão Prêto, 383,125 . . . . A 7
Rio Grande, 164,221 C 6
Santa Maria, 163,900 (196,827▲) . . . . B 6
Santos, 460,100 (1,065,000★) . . . . . . A 7
São Carlos, 140,383 A 7
São Paulo, 10,063,110 (15,175,000★) . . . . A 7
Sorocaba, 327,468 . . A 7

Chile
1982 CENSUS

Antofagasta, 185,486 A 2
Chillán, 118,163 . . . . D 2
Concepción, 267,891 (675,000★) . . . . D 2
Osorno, 95,286 . . . . . . E 2
Punta Arenas, 95,332 G 2
Rancagua, 139,925 . . C 2
Santiago, 232,667 (4,100,000★) . . . . . . C 2
Talca, 128,544 . . . . . . D 2
Talcahuano, 202,368 D 2
Temuco, 157,297 . . . D 2
Valdivia, 100,046 . . . . D 2
Valparaíso, 265,355 (675,000★) . . . . C 2
Viña del Mar, 244,899 C 2

Falkland Islands
1986 ESTIMATE

Stanley, 1,200 . . . . . . G 5

Paraguay
1985 ESTIMATE

Asunción, 477,100 (700,000★) . . . . B 5

Uruguay
1985 CENSUS

Montevideo, 1,251,647 (1,550,000★) . . . . C 5
Paysandú, 76,191 . . . . C 5
Salto, 80,823 . . . . . . C 5

★ Population of metropolitan area, including suburbs.
▲ Population of entire district, including rural area.

Kilometers 0 200 400 600 Km.
Miles 0 200 400 600 Mi.

1:16 000 000

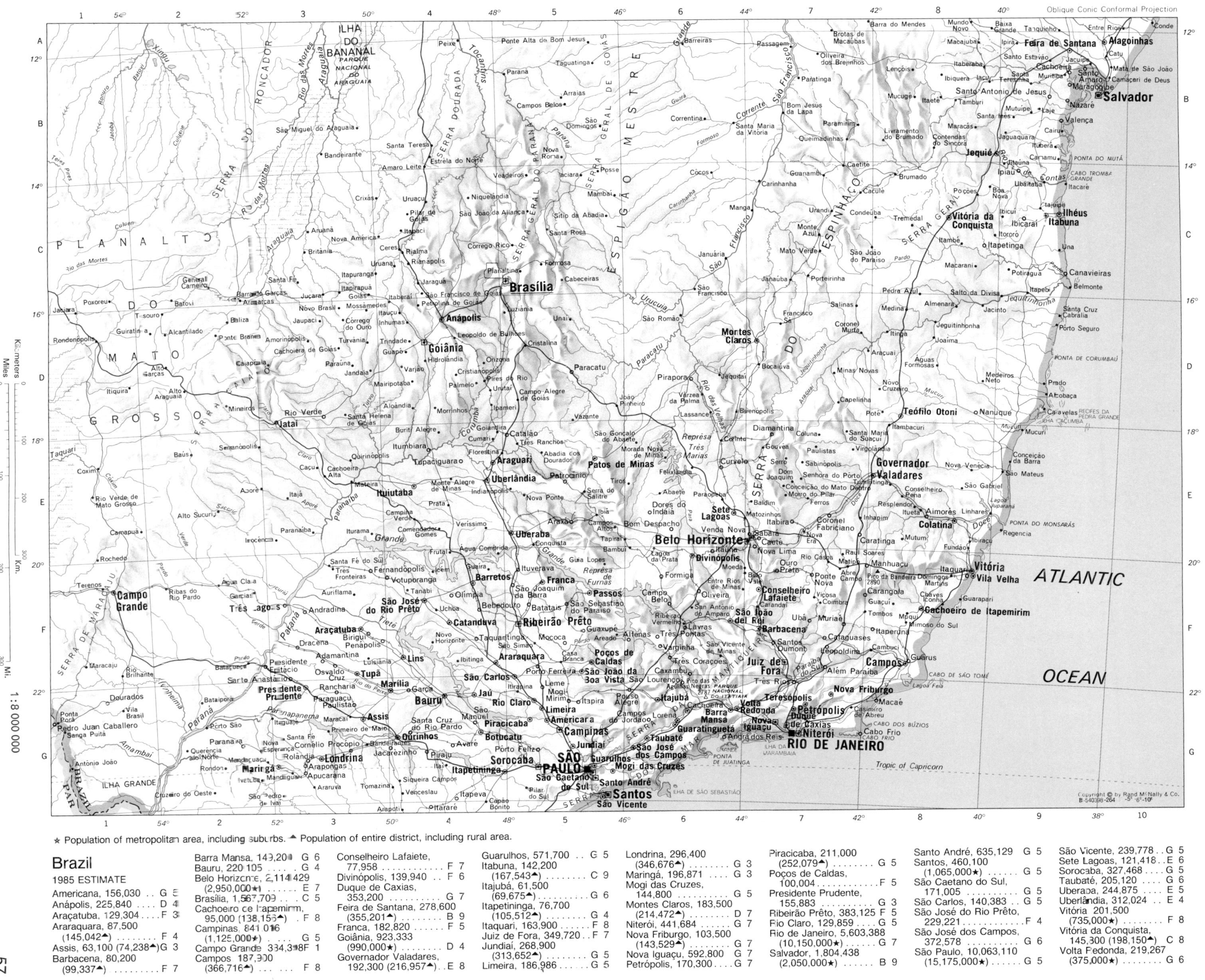

★ Population of metropolitan area, including suburbs. ▲ Population of entire district, including rural area.

Brazil

1985 ESTIMATE

Americana, 156,030 .. G 5
Anápolis, 225,840 .... D 4
Araçatuba, 129,304 .... F 3
Araraquara, 87,500 (145,042▲) .... F 4
Assis, 63,100 (74,238▲) G 3
Barbacena, 80,200 (99,337▲) .... F 7
Barra Mansa, 149,200 G 6
Bauru, 220,105 ..... G 4
Belo Horizonte, 2,114,429 (2,950,000★) .... E 7
Brasília, 1,567,709 .. C 5
Cachoeiro de Itapemirim, 95,000 (138,156▲) . F 8
Campinas, 841,016 (1,125,000★) ..... G 5
Campo Grande, 334,398 F 1
Campos, 187,900 (366,716▲) ...... F 8
Conselheiro Lafaiete, 77,958 .... F 7
Divinópolis, 139,940 .. F 6
Duque de Caxias, 353,200 .... G 7
Feira de Santana, 278,600 (355,201▲) .... B 9
Franca, 182,820 ...... F 5
Goiânia, 923,333 (990,000★) .... D 4
Governador Valadares, 192,300 (216,957▲) .. E 8
Guarulhos, 571,700 .. G 5
Itabuna, 142,200 (167,543▲) .... C 9
Itajubá, 61,500 (69,675▲) .... G 6
Itapetininga, 76,700 (105,512▲) .... G 4
Itaquari, 163,900 ...... F 8
Juiz de Fora, 349,720 .. F 7
Jundiaí, 268,900 (313,652▲) .... G 5
Limeira, 186,986 ...... G 5
Londrina, 296,400 (346,676▲) .... G 3
Maringá, 196,871 .... G 3
Mogi das Cruzes, 144,800 .... G 5
Montes Claros, 183,500 (214,472▲) .... D 7
Niterói, 441,684 ...... G 7
Nova Friburgo, 103,500 (143,529▲) .... G 7
Nova Iguaçu, 592,800 G 7
Petrópolis, 170,300 .... G 7
Piracicaba, 211,000 (252,079▲) .... G 5
Poços de Caldas, 100,004 .... F 5
Presidente Prudente, 155,883 .... G 3
Ribeirão Prêto, 383,125 F 5
Rio Claro, 129,859 .... G 5
Rio de Janeiro, 5,603,388 (10,150,000★) ...... G 7
Salvador, 1,804,438 (2,050,000★) ...... B 9
Santo André, 635,129 G 5
Santos, 460,100 (1,065,000★) ...... G 5
São Caetano do Sul, 171,005 .... G 5
São Carlos, 140,383 .. G 5
São José do Rio Prêto, 229,221 .... F 4
São José dos Campos, 372,578 .... G 6
São Paulo, 10,063,110 (15,175,000★) ...... G 5
São Vicente, 239,778 .. G 5
Sete Lagoas, 121,418 .. E 6
Sorocaba, 327,468 .... G 5
Taubaté, 205,120 .... G 6
Uberaba, 244,875 .... E 5
Uberlândia, 312,024 .. E 4
Vitória, 201,500 (735,000★) .... F 8
Vitória da Conquista, 145,300 (198,150▲) C 8
Volta Redonda, 219,267 (375,000★) .... G 6

Colombia, Ecuador, Venezuela, and Guyana

Aruba
1987 ESTIMATE
Oranjestad, 19,800 . . A 7

Colombia
1985 CENSUS
Armenia, 187,130 . . . . E 5
Barrancabermeja, 137,406 . . . . D 6
Barranquilla, 899,781 (1,140,000★) . . . . . . B 5
Bello, 212,861 . . . . . . D 5
Bogotá *see* Santa Fe de Bogotá . . . . E 5
Bucaramanga, 352,326 (550,000★) . . . . D 6
Buenaventura, 160,342 . . . . F 4
Buga, 82,992 . . . . F 4
Cali, 1,350,565 (1,400,000★) . . . . . . F 4
Cartagena, 531,426 . . B 5
Cartago, 97,791 . . . . E 5
Ciénaga, 56,860 . . . . B 5
Cúcuta, 379,478 (445,000★) . . . . D 6
Duitama, 56,390 . . . . E 6
Envigado, 91,391 . . . . D 5
Espinal, 37,563 . . . . . . E 5
Facatativá, 44,331 . . E 5
Florencia, 66,430 . . . . G 5
Florida, 30,040 . . . . . . F 4
Floridablanca, 143,824 . . . . D 6
Girardot, 70,078 . . . . E 5
Ibagué, 292,965 . . . . E 5
Ipiales, 45,419 . . . . . . G 4
Itagüí, 137,623 . . . . . . D 5
La Dorada, 48,572 . . E 5
Magangué, 49,160 . . C 5
Manizales, 299,352 (330,000★) . . . . E 5
Medellín, 1,468,089 (2,095,000★) . . . . . . D 5
Montería, 157,466 . . C 5
Neiva, 194,556 . . . . . . F 5
Ocaña, 51,443 . . . . . . C 6
Palmira, 175,186 . . . . F 4
Pamplona, 34,213 . . D 6
Pasto, 197,407 . . . . . . G 4
Pereira, 233,271 (390,000★) . . . . E 5
Planeta Rica, 24,238 C 5
Popayán, 141,964 . . . . F 4
Puerto Berrío, 21,414 D 5
Quibdó, 47,950 . . . . . . E 4
Ríohacha, 46,667 . . . . B 6
Santa Fe de Bogotá, 3,982,941 (4,260,000★) . . . . . . E 5
Santa Marta, 177,922 . . . . B 5
Santa Rosa de Cabal, 37,112 . . . . E 5
Sincelejo, 120,537 . . C 5
Sogamoso, 64,437 . . E 6
Soledad, 165,791 . . . . B 5
Tuluá, 99,721 . . . . . . E 4
Tumaco, 45,456 . . . . G 3
Tunja, 93,792 . . . . . . E 6
Valledupar, 142,771 . . B 6
Villavicencio, 178,685 E 6
Zipaquirá, 45,676 . . . . E 5

Ecuador
1987 ESTIMATE
Alfaro, 51,023('82) . . . . I 3
Ambato, 126,067 . . . . H 3
Babahoyo, 42,266('82) . . . . . . H 3
Chone, 33,839('82) . . H 2
Cuenca, 201,490 . . . . . . I 3
Esmeraldas, 120,387 G 3
Guayaquil, 1,572,615 (1,580,000★) . . . . . . I 3
Ibarra, 53,428('82) . . G 3
Jipijapa, 27,146('82) . . H 2
Latacunga, 28,764('82) . . . . . . H 3
Loja, 71,652('82) . . . . J 3
Machala, 144,396 . . . . I 3
Manta, 135,990 . . . . H 2
Milagro, 102,884 . . . . I 3
Portoviejo, 141,568 . . H 2
Quevedo, 67,023('82) . . . . . . H 3
Quito, 1,137,705 (1,300,000★) . . . . . . H 3
Riobamba, 75,455('82) . . . . . . H 3
Santo Domingo de los Colorados, 104,059 H 3
Tulcán, 30,985('82) . . G 4

Guyana
1983 ESTIMATE
Georgetown, 78,500 (188,000★) D13
New Amsterdam, 20,000('82) D14

★ Population of metropolitan area, including suburbs.

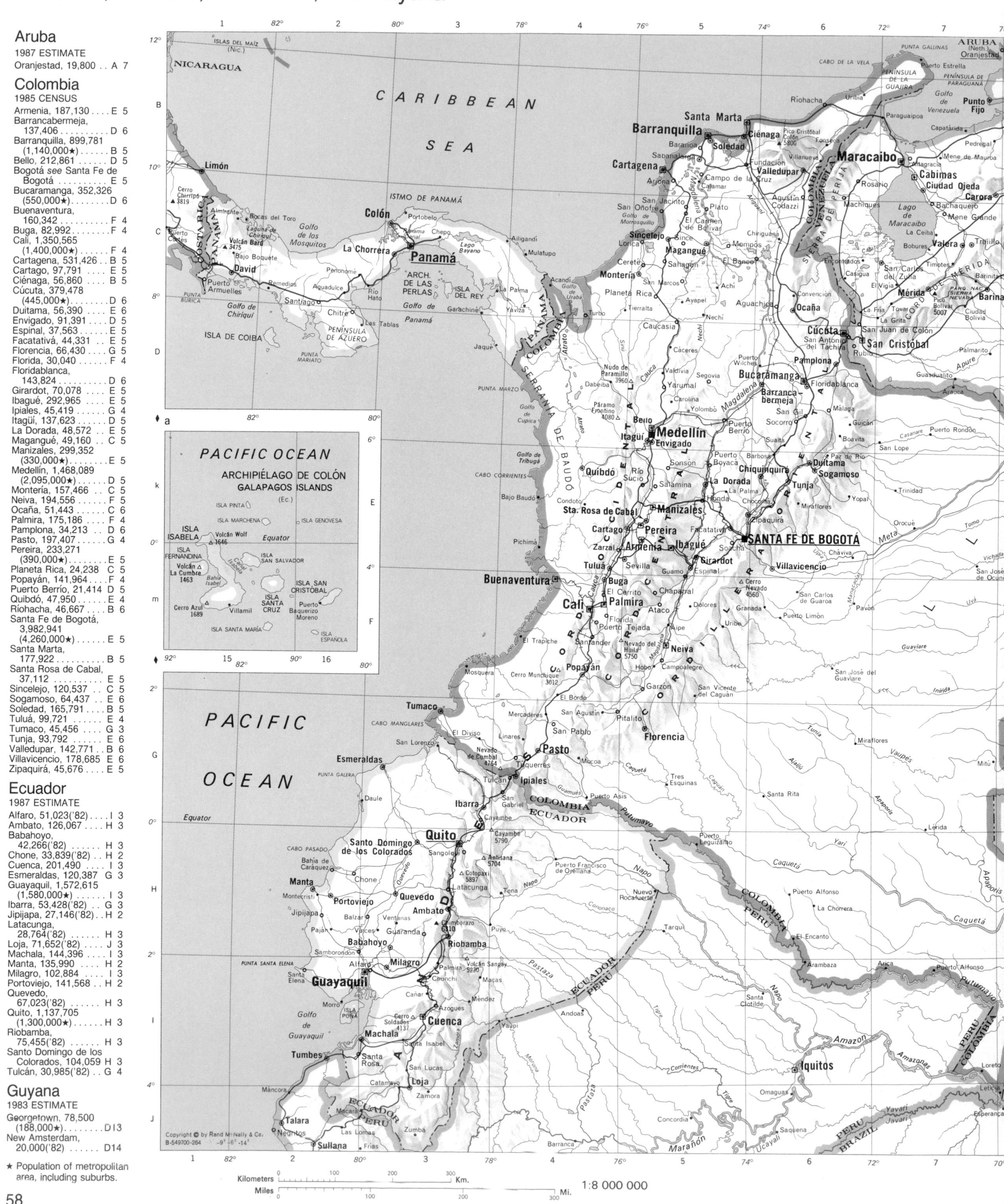

Netherlands Antilles
1981 CENSUS

Willemstad, 31,883 (130,000★) . . . . A 8

Panama
1990 CENSUS

Colón, 54,469 (96,000★) . . . . C 3
David, 65,635 . . . . . . C 1
La Chorrera, 44,110 . . C 3
Panamá, 411,549 (770,000★) . . . . C 3
Puerto Armuelles, 12,562('80) . . . . . . C 1
Santiago, 43,678 . . . . C 2

Trinidad and Tobago
1990 CENSUS

Arima, 29,695 . . . . . . B12
Point Fortin, 6,538('80) B12
Port of Spain, 50,878 (370,000★) B12
San Fernando, 30,092 (75,000★) B12
Scarborough, 6,089('80) B12

Venezuela
1981 CENSUS

Acarigua, 91,662 . . . . C 8
Altagracia de Orituco, 31,582 . . . . C 9
Anaco, 43,607 . . . . . . C10
Araure, 41,747 . . . . . . C 8
Barcelona, 156,461 . . B10
Barinas, 110,462 . . . . C 7
Barquisimeto, 497,635 . . . . B 8
Cabimas, 140,435 . . B 7
Calabozo, 61,995 . . . . C 9
Cantaura, 21,236 . . . . C10
Caracas, 1,816,901 (3,600,000★) . . . . . . B 9
Caripito, 18,172 . . . . B11
Carora, 58,694 . . . . . . B 7
Carúpano, 64,579 . . . . B11
Ciudad Bolívar, 182,941 . . . . C11
Ciudad Guayana, 314,497 . . . . C11
Ciudad Ojeda (Lagunillas), 83,565 . . . . B 7
Coro, 96,339 . . . . B 8
Cumaná, 179,814 . . . . B10
El Tigre, 73,595 . . . . C10
El Tocuyo, 22,854 . . C 8
Guanare, 64,025 . . . . C 8
La Guaira, 21,815 . . . . B 9
Los Teques, 112,857 B 9
Machiques, 27,242 . . B 6
Maiquetía, 66,056 . . . . B 9
Maracaibo, 890,643 . . B 7
Maracay, 322,560 . . . . B 9
Maturín, 154,976 . . . . C11
Mérida, 143,209 . . . . C 7
Ocumare del Tuy, 40,666 . . . . B 9
Porlamar, 51,079 . . . . B11
Puerto Ayacucho, 28,248 . . . . E 9
Puerto Cabello, 71,759 . . . . B 8
Puerto la Cruz, 53,881 . . . . B10
Punto Fijo, 71,114 . . B 7
Rosario, 23,914 . . . . . B 6
San Carlos, 37,892 . . C 8
San Carlos del Zulia, 31,437 . . . . C 7
San Cristóbal, 198,793 . . . . D 6
San Felipe, 57,526 . . B 8
San Fernando de Apure, 57,308 . . . . D 9
San José de Guanipa, 35,689 . . . . C10
San Juan de Colón, 23,447 . . . . C 6
San Juan de los Morros, 57,219 . . . . C 9
Tinaquillo, 28,168 . . . . C 8
Trujillo, 31,774 . . . . . . C 7
Tucupita, 27,299 . . . . C11
Upata, 33,238 . . . . . . C11
Valencia, 616,224 . . . . C 8
Valera, 102,068 . . . . C 7
Valle de la Pascua, 55,761 . . . . C 9
Yaritagua, 31,936 . . . . B 8
Zaraza, 24,562 . . . . . . C10

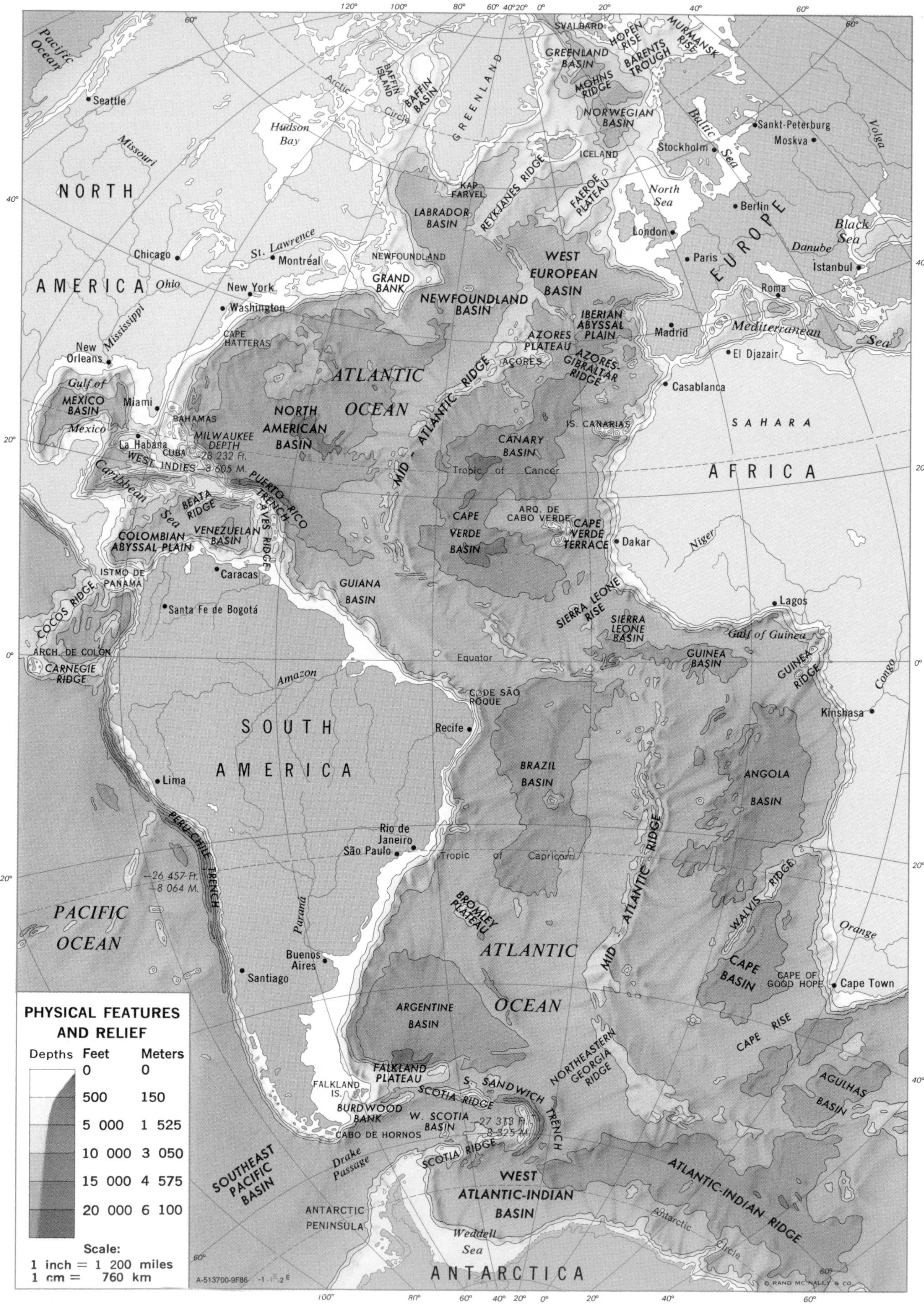

PHYSICAL FEATURES AND RELIEF
Depths Feet Meters
0 0
500 150
5 000 1 525
10 000 3 050
15 000 4 575
20 000 6 100
Scale:
1 inch = 1 200 miles
1 cm = 760 km
NORTH AMERICA
SOUTH AMERICA
EUROPE
AFRICA
ANTARCTICA
ATLANTIC OCEAN
PACIFIC OCEAN
MID ATLANTIC RIDGE
NORTH AMERICAN BASIN
WEST EUROPEAN BASIN
NEWFOUNDLAND BASIN
LABRADOR BASIN
CANARY BASIN
CAPE VERDE BASIN
GUIANA BASIN
BRAZIL BASIN
ANGOLA BASIN
ARGENTINE BASIN
CAPE BASIN
AGULHAS BASIN
WEST ATLANTIC-INDIAN BASIN
ATLANTIC-INDIAN RIDGE
WALVIS RIDGE
CAPE RISE
SIERRA LEONE RISE
SIERRA LEONE BASIN
GUINEA BASIN
PUERTO RICO TRENCH
PERU-CHILE TRENCH
S. SANDWICH TRENCH
MILWAUKEE DEPTH 28 232 Ft. 8 605 M.

Atlanta, 394,017 ('90)..F12
BAHAMAS.................. G13
Baltimore, 736,014 ('90)..........................F13
BARBADOS................ H14
BELIZE........................H12
Boston, 574,283 ('90). E13
Calgary, 636,104 ('86) (671,326★) ....D 9
CANADA..................... D11
Chicago, 2,783,726 ('90)..........................E12
Ciudad de México (Mexico City), 8,831,079 ('80) (14,100,000★) H11
COSTA RICA............. H12
CUBA........................ G13
Dallas, 1,006,877 ('90) F11
Denver, 467,610 ('90)..F10
Detroit, 1,027,974 ('90)..........................E12
DOMINICAN REPUBLIC.............. H13
EL SALVADOR........... H12
GREENLAND............... B16
Guadalajara, 1,626,152 ('80) (2,325,000★) .. H10
GUATEMALA.............. H11
HAITI.......................... H13
HONDURAS................. H12
Houston, 1,630,553 ('90).......................... G11
JAMAICA.................... H13
Kansas City, 435,146 ('90)..........................F11
La Habana (Havana), 2,036,800 ('87) (2,125,000★) G12
Los Angeles, 3,485,398 ('90)..........................F 9
Memphis, 610,337 ('90)..........................F11
MEXICO...................... G10
Miami, 358,548 ('90)... G12
Milwaukee, 628,088 ('90)..........................E12
Minneapolis, 368,383 ('90)..........................E11
Montréal, 1,015,420 ('86) (2,921,357★) E13
New Orleans, 496,938 ('90).......................... G11
New York, 7,322,564 ('90)..........................E13
NICARAGUA............... H12
Ottawa, 300,763 ('86) (819,263★) E13
PANAMA....................... I13
Philadelphia, 1,585,577 ('90)..........................F13
Phoenix, 900,013 ('90) F 9
PUERTO RICO............ H14
San Antonio, 935,933 ('90).......................... G11
San Francisco, 723,959 ('90).......................... F 8
Santo Domingo, 1,313,172 ('81).......................... H13
Seattle, 516,259 ('90)..E 8
Toronto, 612,289 ('86) (3,427,168★) E13
TRINIDAD AND TOBAGO................. H14
UNITED STATES.........F11
Washington, 606,900 ('90)..........................F13

★ Population of metropolitan area, including suburbs.

Miles 0 200 400 600 800 1000 Mi.
Kilometers 0 400 800 1200 1600 Km.
1:40 000 000

Mexico

1980 CENSUS

Acámbaro, 38,224 . . G 9
Acapulco [de Juárez], 301,902 . . . . I10
Aguascalientes, 293,152 . . . . G 8
Ameca, 25,946 . . . . G 7
Apatzingán [de la Constitución], 55,522 . . . . H 8
Apizaco, 30,498 . . . . H10
Caborca, 33,696 . . . . B 3
Campeche, 128,434 H14
Celaya, 141,675 . . . . G 9
Chihuahua, 385,603 C 6
Chilpancingo [de los Bravos], 67,498 . . . . I10
Ciudad Acuña, 38,898 C 9
Ciudad Chetumal, 56,709 . . . . H15
Ciudad del Carmen, 72,489 . . . . H14
Ciudad de México (Mexico City), 8,831,079 (14,100,000★) H10
Ciudad de Valles, 65,609 . . . . G10
Ciudad Guzmán, 60,938 . . . . H 8
Ciudad Hidalgo, 32,311 . . . . H 9
Ciudad Juárez, 544,496 . . . . B 6
Ciudad Madero, 132,444 . . . . F11
Ciudad Mante, 70,647 F10
Ciudad Obregón, 165,572 . . . . D 5
Ciudad Victoria, 140,161 . . . . F10
Coatzacoalcos, 127,170 . . . . H12
Colima, 86,044 . . . . H 8
Córdoba, 99,972 . . . . H11
Cuernavaca, 192,770 H10
Culiacán, 304,826 . . E 6
Delicias, 65,504 . . . . C 7
Durango, 257,915 . . E 7
Empalme, 31,555 . . D 4
Ensenada, 120,483 . . B 1
Fresnillo, 56,066 . . . . F 8
Gómez Palacio, 116,967 . . . . E 8
Guadalajara, 1,626,152 (2,325,000★) . . . . G 8
Guadalupe, 370,524 . . E 9
Guanajuato, 48,981 . . G 9
Guaymas, 54,826 . . D 4
Hermosillo, 297,175 . . C 4
Hidalgo del Parral, 75,590 . . . . D 7
Iguala, 66,005 . . . . . . H10
Irapuato, 170,138 . . G 9
Jalapa Enríquez, 204,594 . . . . H11
Juchitán [de Zaragoza], 38,801 . . . . I12
La Barca, 20,889 . . G 8
Lagos de Moreno, 44,223 . . . . G 9
La Paz, 91,453 . . . . E 4
La Piedad [Cavadas], 47,441 . . . . G 8
León [de los Aldamas], 593,002 . . . . G 9
Los Mochis, 122,531 E 5
Manzanillo, 39,088 . . H 7
Matamoros, 188,745 E11
Matehuala, 41,550 . . F 9
Mazatlán, 199,830 . . F 6
Mérida, 400,142 . . . . G15
Mexicali, 341,559 (365,000★) . . . . . . A 2
Mexico City *see* Ciudad de México H10
Minatitlán, 106,765 . . I12
Monclova, 115,786 . . D 9
Montemorelos, 28,342 E10
Monterrey, 1,090,009 (2,015,000★) . . . . E 9
Morelia, 297,544 . . . . H 9
Navojoa, 62,901 . . . . D 5
Nogales, 65,603 . . . . B 4
Nueva Casas Grandes, 28,514 . . . . B 6
Nueva Rosita, 33,121 D 9
Nuevo Laredo, 201,731 . . . . D10
Oaxaca [de Juárez], 154,223 . . . . I11
Ocotlán, 48,931 . . . . G 8
Orizaba, 114,848 (215,000★) H11
Pachuca [de Soto], 110,351 . . . . G10
Papantla [de Olarte], 43,935 . . . . G11
Pátzcuaro, 32,902 . . H 9
Piedras Negras, 67,455 . . . . C 9
Poza Rica de Hidalgo, 166,799 . . . . G11

★ Population of metropolitan area, including suburbs.

GULF
OF
MEXICO
Bahía de Campeche
Golfo de Tehuantepec
Tropic of Cancer
TEXAS
LOUISIANA
MISSISSIPPI
ALABAMA
EDWARDS PLATEAU
SIERRA MADRE ORIENTAL
SIERRA MADRE DEL SUR
YUCATAN PENINSULA
GUATEMALA
BELIZE
HONDURAS
Houston
Dallas
San Antonio
New Orleans
Monterrey
CIUDAD DE MÉXICO
MEXICO CITY
Tampico
Veracruz
Lambert Conformal Conic Projection

Progreso, 24,257 .. G15
Puebla [de Zaragoza], 835,759 (1,055,000★) H10
Puerto Vallarta, 38,645 .... G 7
Querétaro, 215,976 .. G 9
Reynosa, 194,693 .. D10
Sabinas, 27,413 .... D 9
Sabinas Hidalgo, 23,187 .... D 9
Sahuayo, 43,258 .... G 8
Salamanca, 96,703 .. G 9
Salina Cruz, 40,010 .. I12
Saltillo, 284,937 ..... E 9
Salvatierra, 28,878 .. G 9
San Andrés Tuxtla, 40,412 .... H12
San Cristóbal las Casas, 42,026 .... I13
San Francisco del Rincón, 40,943 .... G 9
San Luis Potosí, 362,371 (470,000★) ...... F 9
San Luis Río Colorado, 76,684 ....A 2
San Pedro de las Colonias, 35,879 .. E 8
Santa Bárbara, 14,894D 7
Tampico, 267,957 (435,000★) F11
Tapachula, 85,766 .. J13
Tecomán, 46,371 .. H 8
Tehuacán, 79,547 .. H11
Tehuantepec, 22,019 I12
Teocaltiche, 16,559 . G 8
Tepatitlán [de Morelos], 41,813 .... G 8
Tepic, 145,741 .... G 7
Ticul, 18,255 .... G15
Tierra Blanca, 31,653 H11
Tijuana, 429,500 .... A 1
Tizimín, 26,305 .... G15
Toluca [de Lerdo], 199,778 .... H10
Torreón, 328,086 (575,000★) .... E 8
Tulancingo, 53,400 .. G10
Tuxpan de Rodríguez Cano, 56,037 .... G11
Tuxtla Gutiérrez, 131,096 .... I13
Uruapan [del Progreso], 122,828 .... H 8
Valle de Santiago, 37,645 .... G 9
Valle Hermoso, 27,966E11
Veracruz [Llave], 284,822 (385,000★) H11
Villa Frontera, 32,568 D 9
Villahermosa, 158,216 I13
Zacapu, 39,570 .... H 9
Zacatecas, 80,088 .. F 8
Zamora de Hidalgo, 86,998 .... H 8
Zitácuaro, 47,520 .. H 9

Central America and the Caribbean

Antigua and Barbuda
1977 ESTIMATE
Saint Johns, 24,359 . . F17

Bahamas
1982 ESTIMATE
Nassau, 135,000 . . . . B 9

Barbados
1980 CENSUS
Bridgetown, 7,466
(115,000★) H18

Belize
1985 ESTIMATE
Belize City, 47,000 . . F 3
Belmopan, 4,500 . . . . F 3

Cayman Islands
1988 ESTIMATE
Georgetown, 13,700 E 7

Costa Rica
1988 ESTIMATE
Limón, 40,400
(62,600▲) . . . . I 6
San José, 278,600
(670,000★) . . . . . . J 5

Cuba
1987 ESTIMATE
Camagüey, 265,588 D 9
Guantánamo, 179,091 D10
Havana *see* La Habana . . . . C 6
Holguín, 199,861 . . . D 9
La Habana (Havana), 2,036,800
(2,125,000★) . . . . C 6
Santa Clara, 182,349 C 8
Santiago de Cuba, 364,554 . . . . D10

Dominican Republic
1981 CENSUS
Santiago, 278,638 . . E 12
Santo Domingo, 1,313,172 . . . . . . E 13

El Salvador
1985 ESTIMATE
San Salvador, 462,652
(920,000★) . . . . . . H 3
Santa Ana, 137,879 . . H 3

Guadeloupe
1982 CENSUS
Basse-Terre, 13,656
(26,600★) F17

Guatemala
1989 ESTIMATE
Guatemala, 1,057,210
(1,400,000★) . . . . G 2

★ Population of metropolitan area, including suburbs.

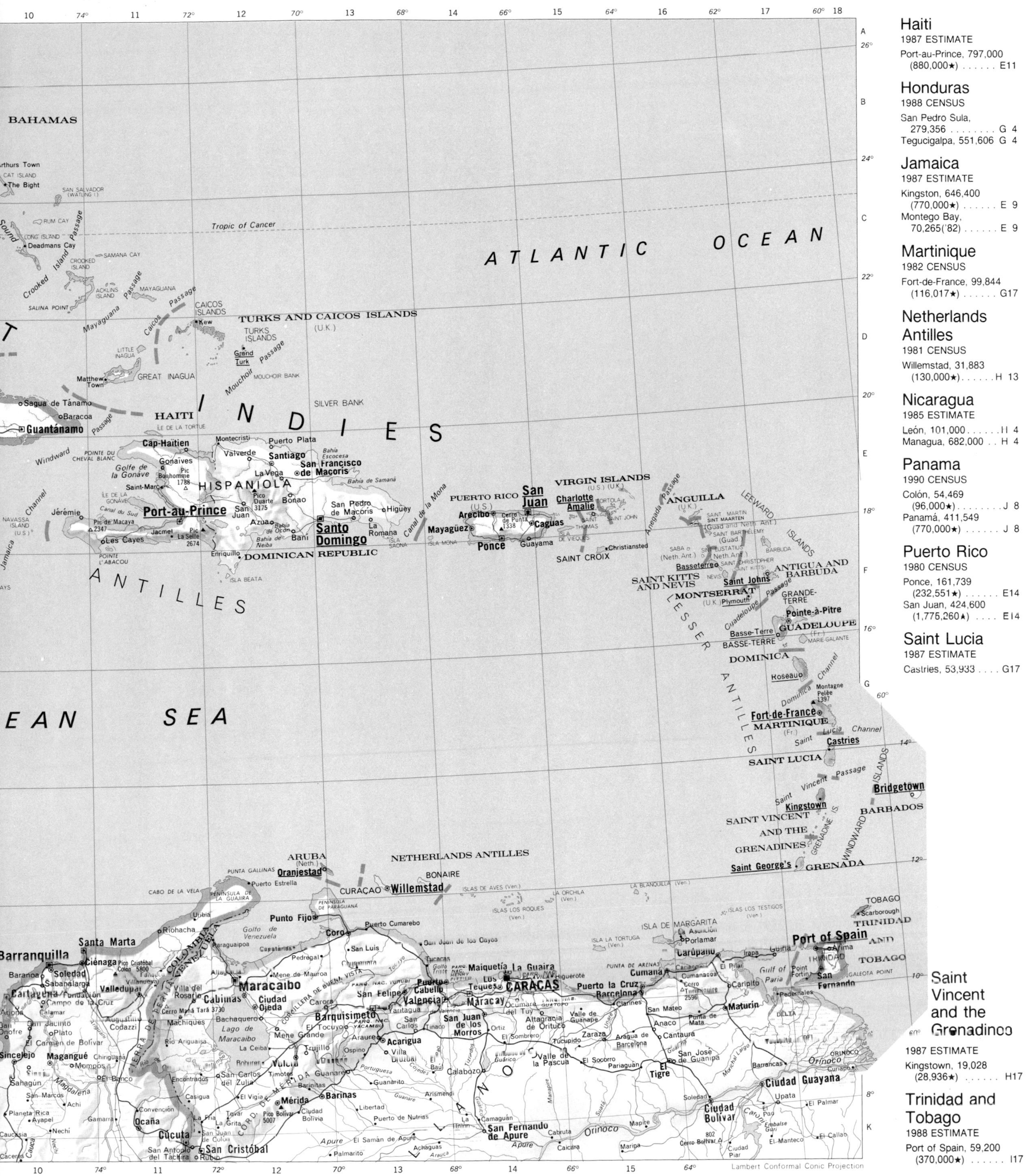

Haiti
1987 ESTIMATE

Port-au-Prince, 797,000 (880,000★) E11

Honduras
1988 CENSUS

San Pedro Sula, 279,356 . . . . G 4

Tegucigalpa, 551,606 G 4

Jamaica
1987 ESTIMATE

Kingston, 646,400 (770,000★) . . . . . . E 9

Montego Bay, 70,265('82) . . . . . . E 9

Martinique
1982 CENSUS

Fort-de-France, 99,844 (116,017★) G17

Netherlands Antilles
1981 CENSUS

Willemstad, 31,883 (130,000★). . . . . .H 13

Nicaragua
1985 ESTIMATE

León, 101,000 . . . . . .I 4

Managua, 682,000 . . H 4

Panama
1990 CENSUS

Colón, 54,469 (96,000★) . . . . J 8

Panamá, 411,549 (770,000★) . . . . . . J 8

Puerto Rico
1980 CENSUS

Ponce, 161,739 (232,551★) E14

San Juan, 424,600 (1,775,260▲) E14

Saint Lucia
1987 ESTIMATE

Castries, 53,933 . . . . G17

Saint Vincent and the Grenadines
1987 ESTIMATE

Kingstown, 19,028 (28,936★) H17

Trinidad and Tobago
1988 ESTIMATE

Port of Spain, 59,200 (370,000★) I17

ALBERTA F10
Alma, 25,923 ('86)
(29,977★) G18
Baie-Comeau, 26,244 ('86)
(33,047★) G19
Banff, 4,208 ('81).........F 9
Barrie, 48,287 ('86)
(67,703★) H17
Bathurst, 14,683 ('86)
(34,895★) G19
Belleville, 36,041 ('86)
(87,530★) H17
Brandon, 38,708 ('86). G13
BRITISH COLUMBIA... F 8
Brockville, 20,880 ('86)
(37,115★) H17
Calgary, 636,104 ('86)
(671,326★) F10
Cambridge, 79,920
('86)......................... H16
Campbell River, 15,370
('81)..........................F 7
Campbellton, 9,077 ('86)
(17,418★) G19
CANADA.................... D13
Charlottetown, 15,776
('86) (53,868★) G20
Chatham, 42,211 ('86) H16
Chicoutimi, 61,083 ('86)
(158,468★) G18
Chilliwack, 41,337 ('86)
(50,288★) .... G 8
Churchill, 1,186 ('81)... E14
Corner Brook, 22,719
('86) (33,730★) G21
Cornwall, 46,425 ('86)
(51,719★) G18
Dartmouth, 65,243
('86)......................... H20
Dawson Creek, 10,544
('86)..........................E 8
Dolbeau, 8,554 ('86)
(15,288★) G18
Drummondville, 36,020
('86) (56,283★) G18
Edmonton, 573,982 ('86)
(785,465★) F10
Edmundston, 11,497 ('86)
(22,614★) G19
Eskimo Point, 1,189
('86)......................... D14
Flin Flon, 7,591 ('86)
(9,211★) F12
Fort McMurray, 34,949
('86) (48,497★) E10
Fort Saint John, 13,355
('86)..........................E 8
Fredericton, 44,352 ('86)
(65,768★) G19
Gander, 10,207 ('86)
(10,899★) G22
Gaspé, 17,350 ('86).... G20
Granby, 38,508 ('86)
(51,176★) G18
Grande-Prairie, 26,471
('86)..........................E 9
Grand Falls, 9,121 ('86)
(25,612★) G21
Guelph, 78,235 ('86)
(85,962★) H16
Halifax, 113,577 ('86)
(295,990★) H20
Hamilton, 306,728 ('86)
(557,029★) H17
Happy Valley-Goose Bay,
7,248 ('86)................ F20
Hull, 58,722 ('86)........ G17
Inuvik, 3,389 ('86)....... C 6
Jasper, 3,269 ('81).......F 9
Joliette, 16,845 ('86)
(34,897★) G18
Jonquière, 58,467
('86)......................... G18
Kamloops, 61,773
('86)..........................F 8
Kelowna, 61,213 ('86)
(89,730★) .... G 9
Kenora, 9,621 ('86)
(15,456★) G14
Kirkland Lake, 11,604
('86)......................... G16
Kitchener, 150,604 ('86)
(311,195★) H16
Kitimat, 11,196 ('86).... F 7
Labrador City, 8,664 ('86)
(11,301★) F19
La Tuque, 10,723 ('86)
(13,468★) G18
Laval, 284,164 ('86).... G18
Lethbridge, 58,841
('86)......................... G10
Lloydminster, 17,356
('86)..........................F11
London, 269,140 ('86)
(342,302★) H16
MANITOBA..................F13
Matane, 13,243 ('86)
(15,361★) G19
Medicine Hat, 41,804 ('86)
(50,734★) F10
Midland, 12,092 ('86)
(35,003★) H17
Moncton, 55,468 ('86)
(102,084★) G20

★ Population of metropolitan area, including suburbs.

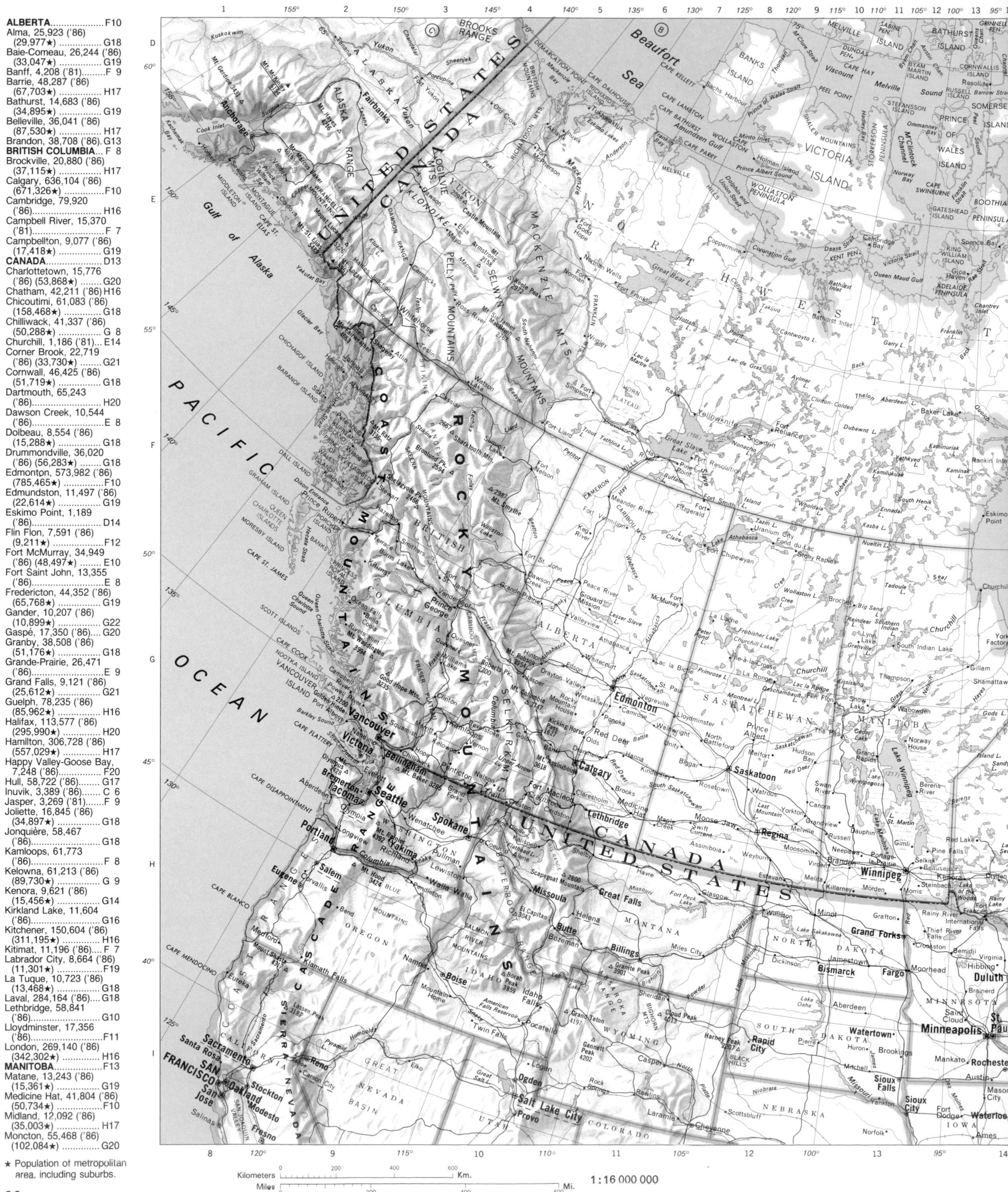

Baffin Bay
Davis Strait
GREENLAND (Denmark)
Labrador Sea
ATLANTIC OCEAN
Hudson Bay
James Bay
Ungava Bay
Hudson Strait
Foxe Basin
Gulf of St. Lawrence
BAFFIN ISLAND
PÉNINSULE D'UNGAVA
LABRADOR
NEWFOUNDLAND
QUÉBEC
ONTARIO
NEW BRUNSWICK
NOVA SCOTIA
PRINCE EDWARD ISLAND
ST. PIERRE AND MIQUELON (Fr.)
APPALACHIAN MTS.
NOTRE DAME MTS.
All islands within Hudson Bay, James Bay, and Ungava Bay lie within Northwest Territories
MONTRÉAL
Ottawa
Québec
TORONTO
Halifax
St. John's
BOSTON
NEW YORK
PHILADELPHIA
CHICAGO
DETROIT
Copyright © by Rand McNally & Co.
Lambert Conformal Conic Projection

Montréal, 1,015,420 ('86) (2,921,357★) G18
Moose Jaw, 35,073 ('86) (37,219★) F11
Nanaimo, 49,029 ('86) (60,420★) .... G 8
NEW BRUNSWICK..... G19
NEWFOUNDLAND.......F21
New Glasgow, 10,022 ('86) (38,737★) G20
Niagara Falls, 72,107 ('86)......................... H17
North Bay, 50,623 ('86) (57,422★) G17
NORTHWEST TERRITORIES.......... C13
NOVA SCOTIA........... G20
ONTARIO.................... G16
Orillia, 24,077 ('86) (31,252★) H17
Oshawa, 123,651 ('86) (203,543★) H17
Ottawa, 300,763 ('86) (819,263★) G17
Owen Sound, 19,804 ('86) (27,364★) H16
Pembroke, 14,131 ('86) (22,560★) G17
Penticton, 23,588 ('86) (38,966★) .... G 9
Peterborough, 61,049 ('86) (87,083★) H17
Portage-la-Prairie, 13,198 ('86)........................ G13
Port Alberni, 18,241 ('86)......................... G 8
Prince Albert, 33,686 ('86) (40,841★) F11
PRINCE EDWARD ISLAND.................. G20
Prince George, 67,621 ('86)..........................F 8
Prince Rupert, 15,755 ('86) (17,581★) ....F 6
QUÉBEC......................F18
Québec, 164,580 ('86) (603,267★) G18
Rankin Inlet, 1,374 ('86)......................... D14
Red Deer, 54,425 ('86)F10
Regina, 175,064 ('86) (186,521★) F12
Saint-Hyacinthe, 38,603 ('86) (48,303★) G18
Saint-Jérôme, 23,316 ('86) (44,048★) G18
Saint John, 76,831 ('86) (121,265★) G19
Saint John's, 96,216 ('86) (161,901★) G22
Sarnia, 49,033 ('86) (85,700★) H16
SASKATCHEWAN.......F11
Saskatoon, 177,641 ('86) (200,665★) F11
Sault Sainte Marie, 80,905 ('86) (84,617★) G16
Selkirk, 10,013 ('86).... F13
Sept-Îles (Seven Islands), 25,637 ('86) (28,050★) F19
Shawinigan, 21,470 ('86) (61,965★) G18
Sherbrooke, 74,438 ('86) (129,960★) G18
Sorel, 19,522 ('86) (46,096★) G18
Sudbury, 88,717 ('86) (148,877★) G16
Summerside, 8,020 ('86) (15,614★) G20
Swift Current, 15,666 ('86)..........................F11
Sydney Mines, 8,063 ('86)......................... G20
Thetford Mines, 18,561 ('86) (31,940★) G18
Thunder Bay, 112,272 ('86) (122,217★) G15
Timmins, 46,657 ('86). G16
Toronto, 612,289 ('86) (3,427,168★) H17
Trail, 7,948 ('86) (20,257★) .... G 9
Trois-Rivières, 50,122 ('86) (128,888★) G18
Truro, 12,124 ('86) (41,516★) G20
Val-d'Or, 22,252 ('86) (27,170★) G17
Vancouver, 431,147 ('86) (1,380,729★) .... G 8
Victoria, 66,303 ('86) (255,547★) .... G 8
Whitehorse, 15,199 ('86)......................... D 5
Windsor, 193,111 ('86) (253,988★) H16
Winnipeg, 594,551 ('86) (625,304★) G13
Yellowknife, 11,753 ('86)......................... D10
YUKON.......................D 5

Alberta

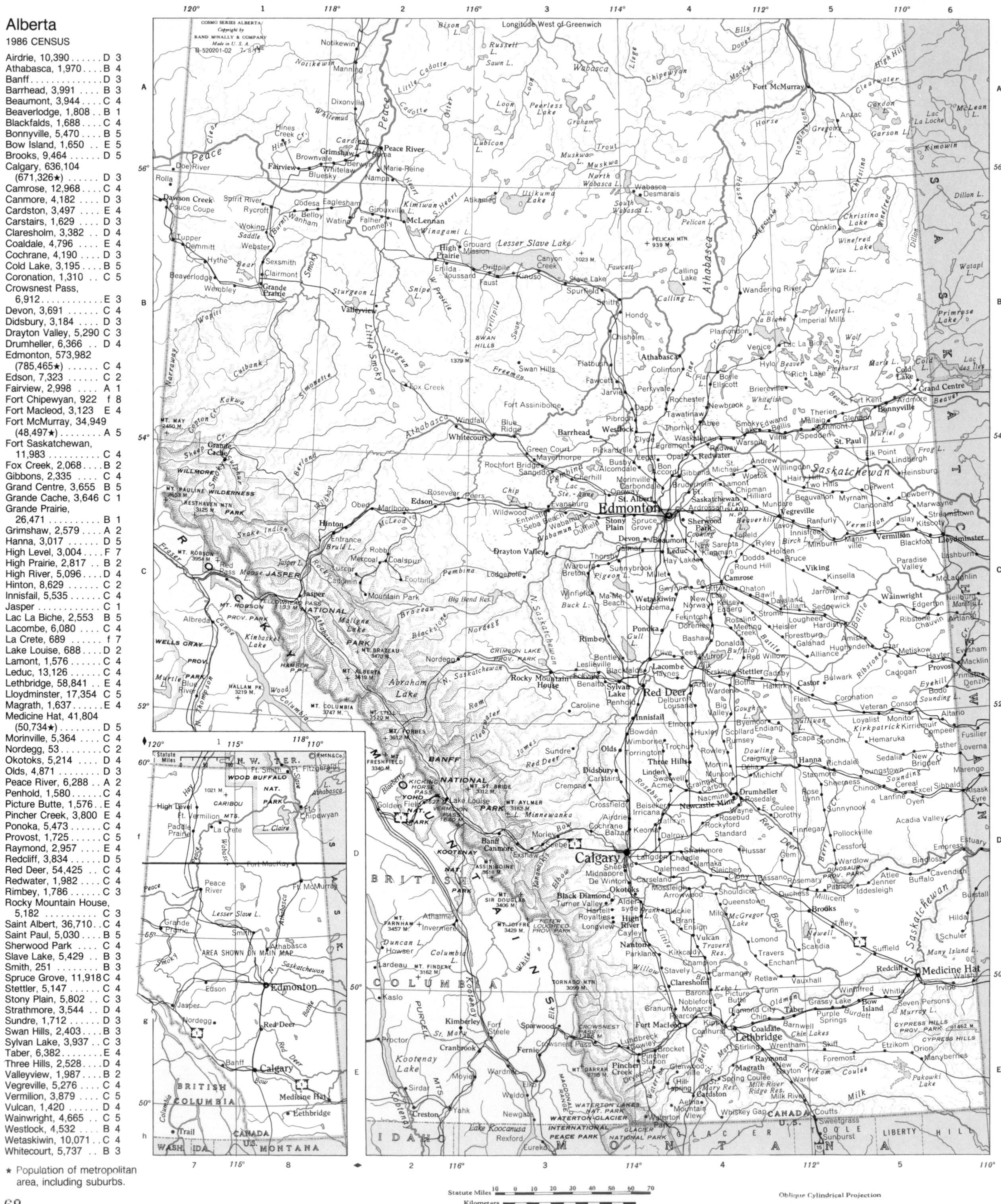

Alberta

1986 CENSUS

- Airdrie, 10,390 . . . . . D 3
- Athabasca, 1,970 . . . B 4
- Banff . . . . D 3
- Barrhead, 3,991 . . . . B 3
- Beaumont, 3,944 . . . C 4
- Beaverlodge, 1,808 . . B 1
- Blackfalds, 1,688 . . . C 4
- Bonnyville, 5,470 . . . . B 5
- Bow Island, 1,650 . . . E 5
- Brooks, 9,464 . . . . . . D 5
- Calgary, 636,104 (671,326★) . . . . . . D 3
- Camrose, 12,968 . . . C 4
- Canmore, 4,182 . . . . D 3
- Cardston, 3,497 . . . . E 4
- Carstairs, 1,629 . . . . D 3
- Claresholm, 3,382 . . D 4
- Coaldale, 4,796 . . . . E 4
- Cochrane, 4,190 . . . . D 3
- Cold Lake, 3,195 . . . . B 5
- Coronation, 1,310 . . C 5
- Crowsnest Pass, 6,912 . . . . E 3
- Devon, 3,691 . . . . . . C 4
- Didsbury, 3,184 . . . . D 3
- Drayton Valley, 5,290 C 3
- Drumheller, 6,366 . . D 4
- Edmonton, 573,982 (785,465★) . . . . . . C 4
- Edson, 7,323 . . . . . . C 2
- Fairview, 2,998 . . . . . A 1
- Fort Chipewyan, 922 f 8
- Fort Macleod, 3,123 E 4
- Fort McMurray, 34,949 (48,497★) . . . . A 5
- Fort Saskatchewan, 11,983 . . . . C 4
- Fox Creek, 2,068 . . . B 2
- Gibbons, 2,335 . . . . C 4
- Grand Centre, 3,655 B 5
- Grande Cache, 3,646 C 1
- Grande Prairie, 26,471 . . . . B 1
- Grimshaw, 2,579 . . . . A 2
- Hanna, 3,017 . . . . . . D 5
- High Level, 3,004 . . . F 7
- High Prairie, 2,817 . . B 2
- High River, 5,096 . . . D 4
- Hinton, 8,629 . . . . . . C 2
- Innisfail, 5,535 . . . . . C 4
- Jasper . . . . C 1
- Lac La Biche, 2,553 B 5
- Lacombe, 6,080 . . . . C 4
- La Crete, 689 . . . . . . f 7
- Lake Louise, 688 . . . D 2
- Lamont, 1,576 . . . . . C 4
- Leduc, 13,126 . . . . . C 4
- Lethbridge, 58,841 . . E 4
- Lloydminster, 17,354 C 5
- Magrath, 1,637 . . . . . E 4
- Medicine Hat, 41,804 (50,734★) . . . . D 5
- Morinville, 5,364 . . . . C 4
- Nordegg, 53 . . . . C 2
- Okotoks, 5,214 . . . . . D 4
- Olds, 4,871 . . . . D 3
- Peace River, 6,288 . . A 2
- Penhold, 1,580 . . . . . C 4
- Picture Butte, 1,576 . . E 4
- Pincher Creek, 3,800 E 4
- Ponoka, 5,473 . . . . . C 4
- Provost, 1,725 . . . . . C 5
- Raymond, 2,957 . . . E 4
- Redcliff, 3,834 . . . . . D 5
- Red Deer, 54,425 . . C 4
- Redwater, 1,982 . . . . C 4
- Rimbey, 1,786 . . . . . C 3
- Rocky Mountain House, 5,182 . . . . C 3
- Saint Albert, 36,710 . . C 4
- Saint Paul, 5,030 . . . . B 5
- Sherwood Park . . . . C 4
- Slave Lake, 5,429 . . B 3
- Smith, 251 . . . . B 3
- Spruce Grove, 11,918 C 4
- Stettler, 5,147 . . . . . C 4
- Stony Plain, 5,802 . . C 3
- Strathmore, 3,544 . . D 4
- Sundre, 1,712 . . . . . . D 3
- Swan Hills, 2,403 . . . B 3
- Sylvan Lake, 3,937 . . C 3
- Taber, 6,382 . . . . E 4
- Three Hills, 2,528 . . . D 4
- Valleyview, 1,987 . . . B 2
- Vegreville, 5,276 . . . . C 4
- Vermilion, 3,879 . . . . C 5
- Vulcan, 1,420 . . . . . . D 4
- Wainwright, 4,665 . . C 5
- Westlock, 4,532 . . . . B 4
- Wetaskiwin, 10,071 . . C 4
- Whitecourt, 5,737 . . B 3

★ Population of metropolitan area, including suburbs.

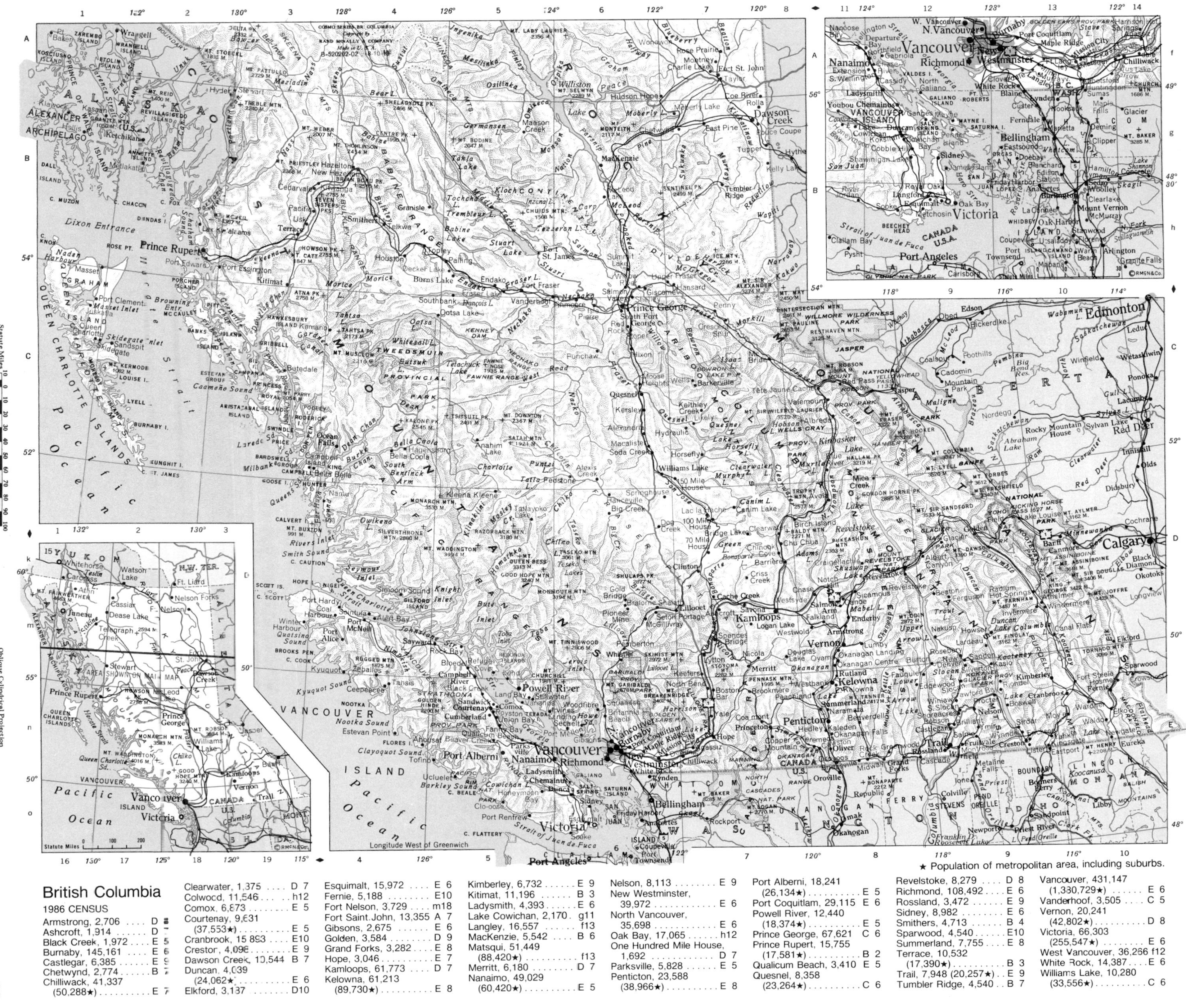

British Columbia

1986 CENSUS

Armstrong, 2,706 .... D 8
Ashcroft, 1,914 ...... D 7
Black Creek, 1,972 .... E 5
Burnaby, 145,161 .... E 6
Castlegar, 6,385 ...... E 9
Chetwynd, 2,774 ...... B 7
Chilliwack, 41,337 (50,288★) .... E 7
Clearwater, 1,375 .... D 7
Colwood, 11,546 ..... h12
Comox, 6,873 .... E 5
Courtenay, 9,631 (37,553★) .... E 5
Cranbrook, 15,893 .... E10
Creston, 4,098 .... E 9
Dawson Creek, 10,544 B 7
Duncan, 4,039 (24,062★) .... E 6
Elkford, 3,137 .... D10
Esquimalt, 15,972 .... E 6
Fernie, 5,188 .... E10
Fort Nelson, 3,729 .... m18
Fort Saint John, 13,355 A 7
Gibsons, 2,675 .... E 6
Golden, 3,584 .... D 9
Grand Forks, 3,282 .... E 8
Hope, 3,046 .... E 7
Kamloops, 61,773 .... D 7
Kelowna, 61,213 (89,730★) .... E 8
Kimberley, 6,732 ...... E 9
Kitimat, 11,196 ...... B 3
Ladysmith, 4,393 ...... E 6
Lake Cowichan, 2,170 . g11
Langley, 16,557 ...... f13
MacKenzie, 5,542 .... B 6
Matsqui, 51,449 (88,420★) f13
Merritt, 6,180 .... D 7
Nanaimo, 49,029 (60,420★) .... E 5
Nelson, 8,113 .... E 9
New Westminster, 39,972 .... E 6
North Vancouver, 35,698 .... E 6
Oak Bay, 17,065 ...... h12
One Hundred Mile House, 1,692 .... D 7
Parksville, 5,828 ...... E 5
Penticton, 23,588 (38,966★) .... E 8
Port Alberni, 18,241 (26,134★) .... E 5
Port Coquitlam, 29,115 E 6
Powell River, 12,440 (18,374★) .... E 5
Prince George, 67,621 C 6
Prince Rupert, 15,755 (17,581★) .... B 2
Qualicum Beach, 3,410 E 5
Quesnel, 8,358 (23,264★) .... C 6
Revelstoke, 8,279 .... D 8
Richmond, 108,492 .... E 6
Rossland, 3,472 .... E 9
Sidney, 8,982 .... E 6
Smithers, 4,713 ...... B 4
Sparwood, 4,540 ...... E10
Summerland, 7,755 .... E 8
Terrace, 10,532 (17,390★) .... B 3
Trail, 7,948 (20,257★) .. E 9
Tumbler Ridge, 4,540 .. B 7
Vancouver, 431,147 (1,330,729★) ...... E 6
Vanderhoof, 3,505 .... C 5
Vernon, 20,241 (42,802★) .... D 8
Victoria, 66,303 (255,547★) .... E 6
West Vancouver, 36,266 f12
White Rock, 14,387 .... E 6
Williams Lake, 10,280 (33,556★) .... C 6

★ Population of metropolitan area, including suburbs.

Manitoba

Manitoba

1986 CENSUS

Altona, 2,958 . . . . . . E 3
Arborg, 1,018 . . . . . . D 3
Ashern, 620 . . . . D 2
Beausejour, 2,535 . . D 3
Birch River, 509 . . . . C 1
Birtle, 850 . . . . .D 1
Boissevain, 1,572 . . . E 1
Brandon, 38,708 . . . . E 2
Camperville, 588 . . . . D 1
Carberry, 1,544 . . . . E 2
Carman, 2,500 . . . . . . E 2
Churchill, 1,109 . . . . . . f 9
Cranberry Portage, 849 . . . . B 1
Cross Lake, 580 . . . . B 3
Crystal City, 487 . . . . E 2
Dauphin, 8,875 . . . . D 1
Deloraine, 1,134 . . . . E 1
Duck Bay, 559 . . . . . C 1
Easterville, 675 . . . . C 2
East Selkirk, 572 . . . . D 3
Elkhorn, 534 . . . . E 1
Emerson, 725 . . . . . . E 3
Erickson, 565 . . . . . . D 2
Flin Flon, 7,591 (9,211★) . . . . B 1
Gilbert Plains, 816 . . D 1
Gillam, 1,909 . . . . . . A 4
Gimli, 1,681 . . . . D 3
Gladstone, 951 . . . . D 2
Glenboro, 719 . . . . . . E 2
Grandview, 941 . . . . D 1
Gretna, 503 . . . . E 3
Grunthal, 639 . . . . . . E 3
Hamiota, 815 . . . . . . D 1
Hartney, 523 . . . . . . E 1
Killarney, 2,318 . . . . . E 2
Lac du Bonnet, 1,021 D 3
Leaf Rapids, 1,950 . . A 1
Lorette, 1,169 . . . . . . E 3
Lundar, 562 . . . . D 2
MacGregor, 854 . . . . E 2
Manitou, 856 . . . . . . E 2
McCreary, 578 . . . . . . D 2
Melita, 1,239 . . . . . . E 1
Minitonas, 559 . . . . . . C 1
Minnedosa, 2,520 . . D 2
Moose Lake, 541 . . . . C 1
Morden, 5,004 . . . . . . E 2
Morris, 1,613 . . . . . . E 3
Neepawa, 3,314 . . . . D 2
Niverville, 1,452 . . . . E 3
Norway House, 633 . . C 3
Notre Dame de Lourdes, 628 . . . . E 2
Pilot Mound, 819 . . . . E 2
Pine Falls, 831 . . . . . . D 3
Plum Coulee, 677 . . E 3
Portage la Prairie, 13,198 . . . . E 2
Powerview, 724 . . . . D 3
Reston, 616 . . . . E 1
Rivers, 1,157 . . . . . . D 1
Riverton, 635 . . . . . . D 3
Roblin, 1,913 . . . . . . D 1
Rossburn, 664 . . . . . . D 1
Russell, 1,669 . . . . . . D 1
Saint Adolphe, 1,059 E 3
Sainte Anne-des-Chênes, 1,402 . . . . E 3
Saint Claude, 610 . . . E 2
Saint Jean Baptiste, 571 . . . . E 3
Saint Malo, 742 . . . . E 3
Saint Pierre-Jolys, 912 . . . . E 3
Sainte Rose du Lac, 1,030 . . . . D 2
Selkirk, 10,013 . . . . . D 3
Shoal Lake, 832 . . . . D 1
Snow Lake, 1,837 . . B 1
Somerset, 534 . . . . . . E 2
Souris, 1,751 . . . . . . E 1
South Indian Lake, 743 . . . . A 2
Steinbach, 7,473 . . . . E 3
Stonewall, 2,349 . . . . D 3
Swan River, 3,946 . . C 1
Teulon, 953 . . . . D 3
The Pas, 6,283 . . . . C 1
Thompson, 14,701 . . B 3
Treherne, 762 . . . . . . E 2
Virden, 3,054 . . . . . . E 1
Wabowden, 571 . . . . . B 2
Wawanesa, 502 . . . . E 2
Winkler, 5,926 . . . . . . E 3
Winnipeg, 594,551 (625,304★) . . . . . E 3
Winnipeg Beach, 548 D 3
Winnipegosis, 832 . . D 2

★ Population of metropolitan area, including suburbs.

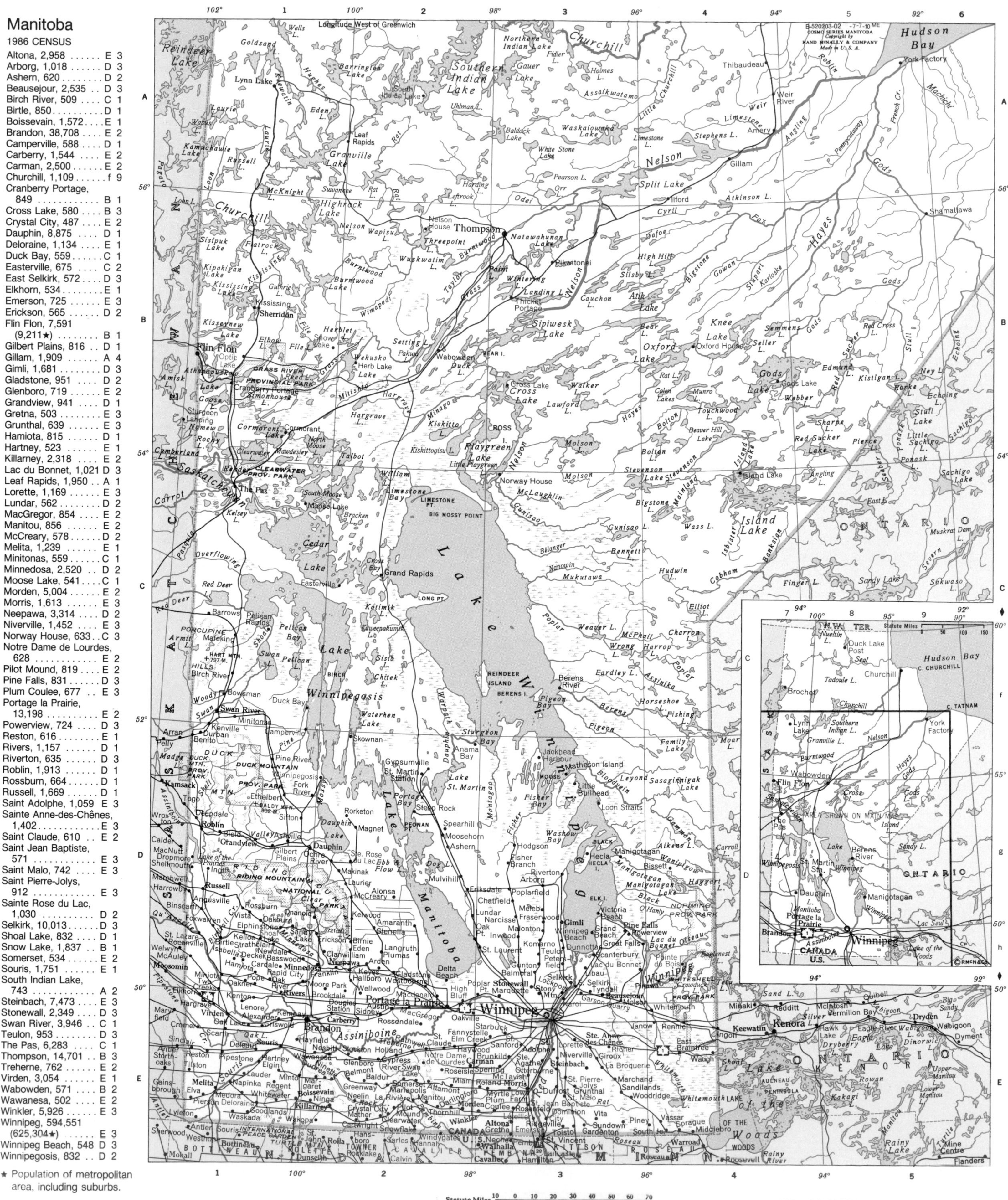

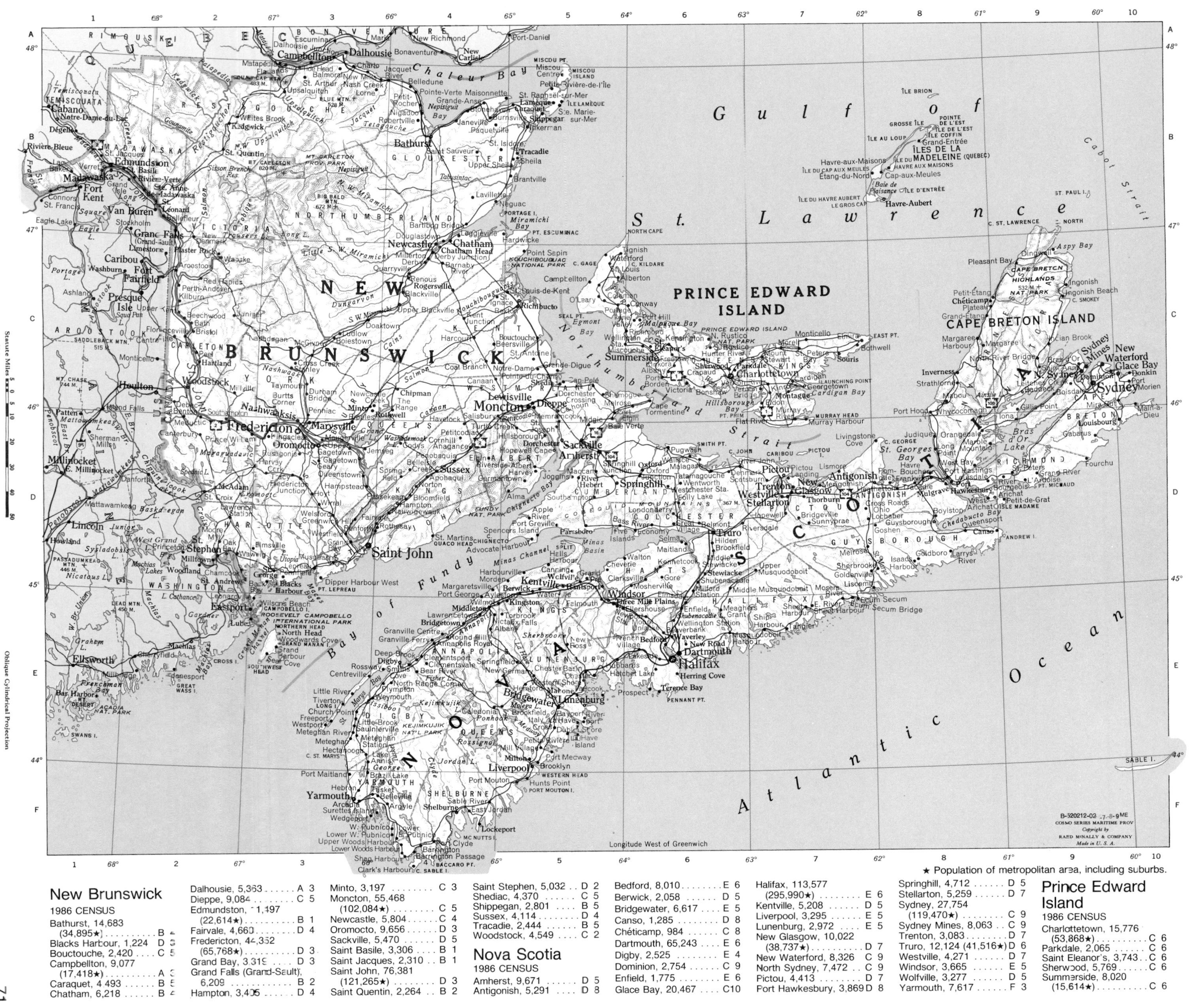

★ Population of metropolitan area, including suburbs.

New Brunswick

1986 CENSUS

Place	Grid
Bathurst, 14,683 (34,895★)	B 4
Blacks Harbour, 1,224	D 3
Bouctouche, 2,420	C 5
Campbellton, 9,077 (17,418★)	A 3
Caraquet, 4,493	B 5
Chatham, 6,218	B 4
Dalhousie, 5,363	A 3
Dieppe, 9,084	C 5
Edmundston, 11,197 (22,614★)	B 1
Fairvale, 4,660	D 4
Fredericton, 44,352 (65,768★)	D 3
Grand Bay, 3,319	D 3
Grand Falls (Grand-Sault), 6,209	B 2
Hampton, 3,405	D 4
Minto, 3,197	C 3
Moncton, 55,468 (102,084★)	C 5
Newcastle, 5,804	C 4
Oromocto, 9,656	D 3
Sackville, 5,470	D 5
Saint Basile, 3,306	B 1
Saint Jacques, 2,310	B 1
Saint John, 76,381 (121,265★)	D 3
Saint Quentin, 2,264	B 2
Saint Stephen, 5,032	D 2
Shediac, 4,370	C 5
Shippegan, 2,801	B 5
Sussex, 4,114	D 4
Tracadie, 2,444	B 5
Woodstock, 4,549	C 2

Nova Scotia

1986 CENSUS

Place	Grid
Amherst, 9,671	D 5
Antigonish, 5,291	D 8
Bedford, 8,010	E 6
Berwick, 2,058	D 5
Bridgewater, 6,617	E 5
Canso, 1,285	D 8
Chéticamp, 984	C 8
Dartmouth, 65,243	E 6
Digby, 2,525	E 4
Dominion, 2,754	C 9
Enfield, 1,775	E 6
Glace Bay, 20,467	C 10
Halifax, 113,577 (295,990★)	E 6
Kentville, 5,208	D 5
Liverpool, 3,295	E 5
Lunenburg, 2,972	E 5
New Glasgow, 10,022 (38,737★)	D 7
New Waterford, 8,326	C 9
North Sydney, 7,472	C 9
Pictou, 4,413	D 7
Port Hawkesbury, 3,869	D 8
Springhill, 4,712	D 5
Stellarton, 5,259	D 7
Sydney, 27,754 (119,470★)	C 9
Sydney Mines, 8,063	C 9
Trenton, 3,083	D 7
Truro, 12,124 (41,516★)	D 6
Westville, 4,271	D 7
Windsor, 3,665	E 5
Wolfville, 3,277	D 5
Yarmouth, 7,617	F 3

Prince Edward Island

1986 CENSUS

Place	Grid
Charlottetown, 15,776 (53,868★)	C 6
Parkdale, 2,065	C 6
Saint Eleanor's, 3,743	C 6
Sherwood, 5,769	C 6
Summerside, 8,020 (15,614★)	C 6

Newfoundland and Labrador

1986 CENSUS

Arnold's Cove, 1,117 E 4
Badger, 1,151 ...... D 3
Baie Verte, 2,049 .... D 3
Bay Bulls, 1,114 .... E 5
Bay Roberts, 4,446 .. E 5
Bishop's Falls, 4,213 D 4
Bonavista, 4,605 .... D 5
Botwood, 3,916 .... D 4
Buchans, 1,281 .... D 3
Burgeo, 2,582 ...... E 3
Burin, 2,892 .... E 4
Burnt Islands, 1,042 E 2
Carbonear, 5,337 (13,082★) .... E 5
Carmanville, 987 .... D 4
Cartwright, 674 .... B 3
Catalina, 1,211 .... D 5
Channel-Port-aux-Basques, 5,901 .. E 2
Clarenville, 2,967 .... D 4
Conception Bay South, 15,531 .... E 5
Corner Brook, 22,719 (33,730★) .... D 3
Cox's Cove, 999 .... D 2
Deer Lake, 4,233 .... D 3
Dunville, 1,833 ...... E 5
Durrell, 1,060 ...... D 4
Englee, 1,012 ...... C 3
Fogo, 1,153 .... D 4
Fortune, 2,370 ...... E 4
Gambo, 2,723 .... D 4
Gander, 10,207 .... D 4
Glenwood, 1,038 .... D 4
Glovertown, 2,184 .. D 4
Grand Bank, 3,732 .. E 4
Grand Falls, 9,121 (25,612★) .... D 4
Hampden, 875 ...... D 3
Happy Valley-Goose Bay, 7,248 .... B 1
Harbour Breton, 2,432 .... E 4
Harbour Grace, 3,053 E 5
Hare Bay, 1,436 .... D 4
Hermitage, 831 ..... E 4
Isle-aux-Morts, 1,203 E 2
Joe Batt's Arm [-Barr'd Islands-Shoal Bay], 1,232 .... D 4
King's Point, 923 .... D 3
Labrador City, 8,664 (11,301★) .... h 8
Lark Harbour, 829 .. D 2
La Scie, 1,429 ...... D 4
Lawn, 1,015 .... E 4
Lewisporte, 3,978 .. D 4
Lourdes, 937 .... D 2
Marystown, 6,660 .. E 4
Milltown [-Head of Bay d'Espoir], 1,276 .. E 4
Mount Pearl, 20,293 E 5
Musgrave Harbour, 1,527 .... D 5
Nain, 1,018 .... g 9
New Harbour, 957 .. E 5
Norris Arm, 1,127 .. D 4
Norris Point, 1,010 .. D 3
Pasadena, 3,268 .... D 3
Placentia, 2,016 ..... E 5
Point Leamington, 850 .... D 4
Port au Port [West-Aguathuna-Felix Cove], 842 .... D 2
Pouch Cove, 1,576 .. E 5
Ramea, 1,380 .... E 3
Robert's Arm, 1,111 D 4
Rocky Harbour, 1,268 D 3
Roddickton, 1,223 .. C 3
Rose-Blanche [-Harbour le Cou], 967 .... E 2
Saint Alban's, 1,780 E 4
Saint Anthony, 3,182 C 4
Saint George's, 1,852 D 2
Saint John's, 96,216 (161,901★) ...... E 5
Saint Lawrence, 1,841 .... E 4
Shoal Harbour, 1,049 D 4
Spaniard's Bay, 2,190 E 5
Springdale, 3,555 .... D 3
Stephenville, 7,994 .. D 2
Stephenville Crossing, 2,252 .... D 2
Summerford, 1,169 .. D 4
Torbay, 3,730 .... E 5
Trepassey, 1,460 .... E 5
Twillingate, 1,506 .... D 4
Upper Island Cove, 2,055 .... E 5
Victoria, 1,895 ...... E 5
Wabana (Bell Island), 4,057 .... E 5
Wabush, 2,637 .... h 8
Wesleyville, 1,208 .. D 5
Whitbourne, 1,151 .. E 5
Windsor, 5,545 ...... D 4
Witless Bay, 1,022 .. E 5

★ Population of metropolitan area, including suburbs.

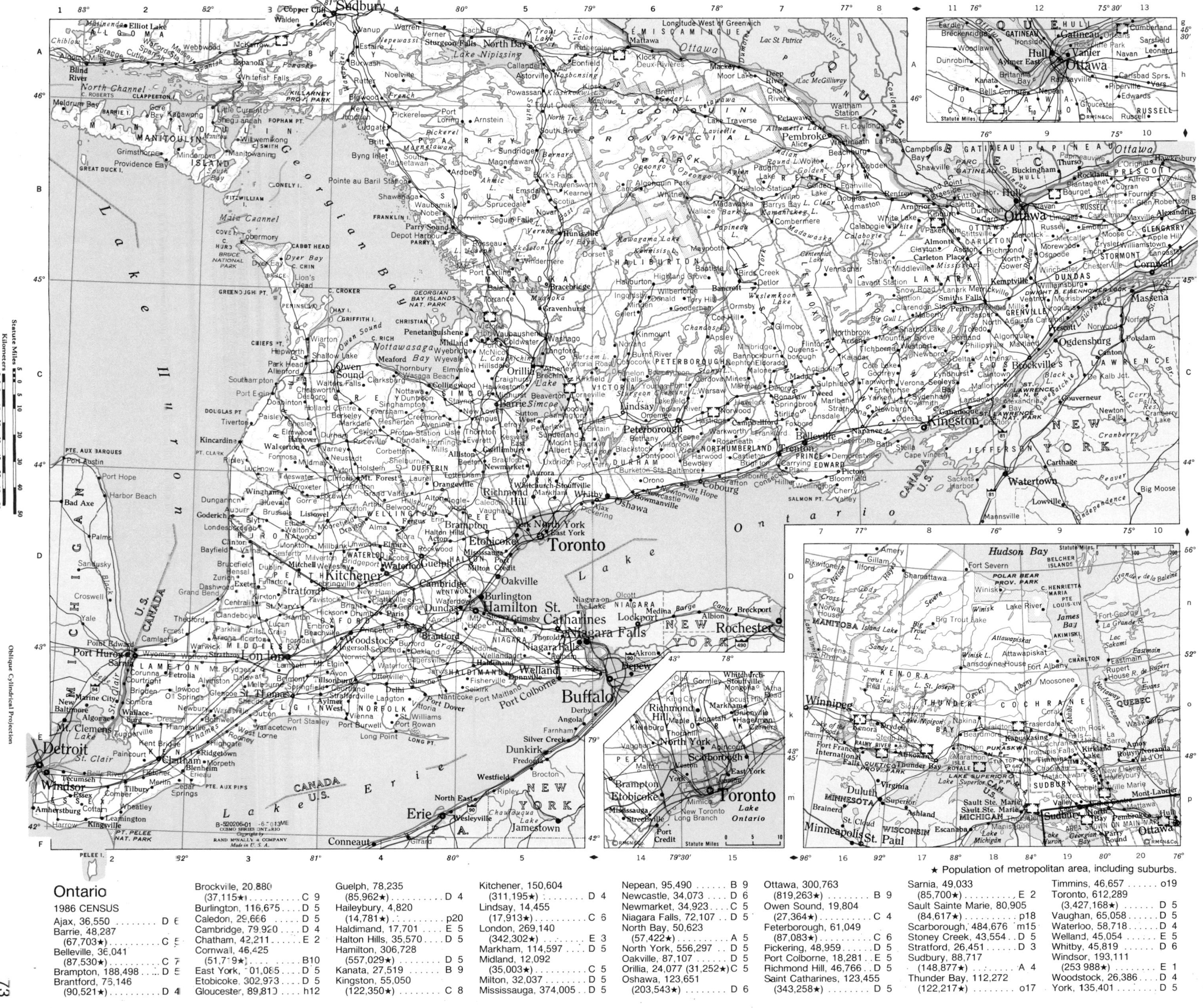

Ontario

1986 CENSUS

Ajax, 36,550 . . . . D 6
Barrie, 48,287 (67,703★) . . . . C 5
Belleville, 36,041 (87,530★) . . . . C 7
Brampton, 188,498 . . . . D 5
Brantford, 76,146 (90,521★) . . . . D 4
Brockville, 20,880 (37,115★) . . . . C 9
Burlington, 116,675 . . . . D 5
Caledon, 29,666 . . . . . D 5
Cambridge, 79,920 . . . . D 4
Chatham, 42,211 . . . . . . E 2
Cornwall, 46,425 (51,719★) B10
East York, 101,085 . . . . D 5
Etobicoke, 302,973 . . . . D 5
Gloucester, 89,810 . . . . h12
Guelph, 78,235 (85,962★) . . . . D 4
Haileybury, 4,820 (14,781★) p20
Haldimand, 17,701 . . . . E 5
Halton Hills, 35,570 . . . . D 5
Hamilton, 306,728 (557,029★) . . . . D 5
Kanata, 27,519 . . . . . . B 9
Kingston, 55,050 (122,350★) . . . . C 8
Kitchener, 150,604 (311,195★) . . . . D 4
Lindsay, 14,455 (17,913★) . . . . C 6
London, 269,140 (342,302★) . . . . E 3
Markham, 114,597 . . . . D 5
Midland, 12,092 (35,003★) . . . . C 5
Milton, 32,037 . . . . D 5
Mississauga, 374,005 . . D 5
Nepean, 95,490 . . . . . . B 9
Newcastle, 34,073 . . . . D 6
Newmarket, 34,923 . . . . C 5
Niagara Falls, 72,107 . . D 5
North Bay, 50,623 (57,422★) . . . . A 5
North York, 556,297 . . D 5
Oakville, 87,107 . . . . . . D 5
Orillia, 24,077 (31,252★) C 5
Oshawa, 123,651 (203,543★) . . . . D 6
Ottawa, 300,763 (819,263★) . . . . B 9
Owen Sound, 19,804 (27,364★) . . . . C 4
Peterborough, 61,049 (87,083★) . . . . C 6
Pickering, 48,959 . . . . . . D 5
Port Colborne, 18,281 . . E 5
Richmond Hill, 46,766 . . D 5
Saint Catharines, 123,455 (343,258★) . . . . D 5
Sarnia, 49,033 (85,700★) . . . . E 2
Sault Sainte Marie, 80,905 (84,617★) p18
Scarborough, 484,676 m15
Stoney Creek, 43,554 . . D 5
Stratford, 26,451 . . . . . . D 3
Sudbury, 88,717 (148,877★) . . . . A 4
Thunder Bay, 112,272 (122,217★) o17
Timmins, 46,657 . . . . . . o19
Toronto, 612,289 (3,427,168★) . . . . . . D 5
Vaughan, 65,058 . . . . . . D 5
Waterloo, 58,718 . . . . . . D 4
Welland, 45,054 . . . . . . E 5
Whitby, 45,819 . . . . . . D 6
Windsor, 193,111 (253,988★) . . . . E 1
Woodstock, 26,386 . . . . D 4
York, 135,401 . . . . D 5

★ Population of metropolitan area, including suburbs.

Quebec

1986 CENSUS

Alma, 25,923 (29,977★) A 6
Ancienne-Lorette, 13,747 . . . . C 6
Anjou, 36,916 . . . . p19
Aylmer East, 28,976 . . D 2
Baie-Comeau, 26,244 (33,047★) k13
Beaconsfield, 19,301 . . q19
Beauport, 62,869 . . . . . . n17
Boucherville, 31,116 . . D 4
Brossard, 57,441 . . . . . . q20
Cap-de-la-Madeleine, 32,800 . . . . C 5
Charlesbourg, 68,996 . . n17
Châteauguay, 37,865 . . D 4
Chicoutimi, 61,083 (158,468★) . . . . A 6
Drummondville, 36,020 (56,283★) . . . . D 5
Gaspé, 17,350 . . . . k14
Gatineau, 81,244 . . . . . . D 2
Granby, 38,508 (51,176★) . . . . D 5
Grand-Mère, 14,582 . . C 5
Hull, 58,722 . . . . D 2
Joliette, 16,845 (34,897★) . . . . C 4
Jonquière, 58,467 . . . . A 6
Lachine, 34,906 . . . . . . D 4
Lachute, 11,586 . . . . . . D 3
LaSalle, 75,621 . . . . . . q19
La Tuque, 10,723 (13,468★) . . . . B 5
Laval, 284,164 . . . . D 4
Lévis, 18,310 . . . . C 6
Longueuil, 125,441 . . . . D 4
Magog, 13,530 (18,738★) . . . . D 5
Mascouche, 21,285 . . . . D 4
Matane, 13,243 (15,361★) k13
Montréal, 1,015,420 (2,921,357★) . . . . . . D 4
Montréal-Nord, 90,303 . . p19
Outremont, 23,080 . . . . p19
Pierrefonds, 39,605 . . . . q19
Pointe-Claire, 26,026 . . D 4
Québec, 164,580 (603,267★) . . . . C 6
Repentigny, 40,778 . . . . D 4
Rimouski, 29,672 (46,210★) . . . . A 9
Rivière-du-Loup, 13,321 (22,471★) . . . . B 8
Rouyn, 17,319 (36,495★) k11
Saint-Eustache, 32,226 . D 4
Sainte-Foy, 69,615 . . . . n17
Saint-Hubert, 66,218 . . q20
Saint-Hyacinthe, 38,603 (48,303★) . . . . D 5
Saint-Jean-sur-Richelieu, 34,745 (59,958★) . . . D 4
Saint-Jérôme, 23,316 (44,048★) . . . . D 3
Saint-Laurent, 67,002 . . p19
Salaberry-de-Valleyfield, 27,942 (38,797★) . . . D 3
Sept-Îles (Seven Islands), 25,637 (28,050★) h13
Shawinigan, 21,412 (61,965★) . . . . C 5
Sherbrooke, 74,438 (129,960★) . . . . D 6
Sorel, 19,522 (46,096★) C 4
Terrebonne, 31,310 . . . . D 4
Thetford Mines, 18,561 (31,940★) . . . . C 6
Trois-Rivières, 50,122 (128,888★) . . . . C 5
Verdun, 60,246 . . . . . . q19
Victoriaville, 21,587 (38,003★) . . . . C 6
Ville Saint-Georges, 11,723 (21,022★) . . . . C 7

★ Population of metropolitan area, including suburbs.

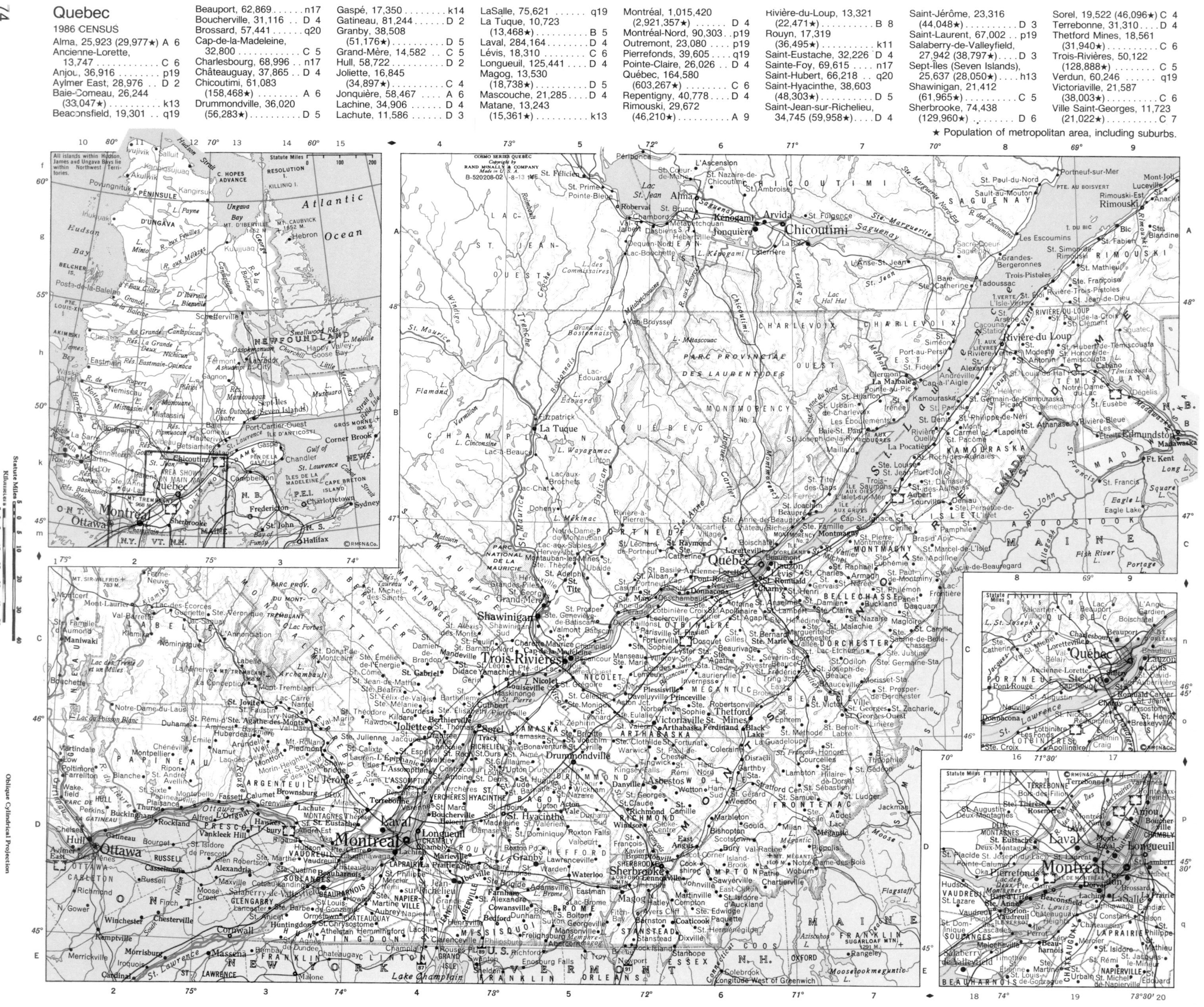

Statute Miles 5 0 5 10 20 30 40

Kilometers 5 0 5 15 25 35 45 55

Oblique Cylindrical Projection

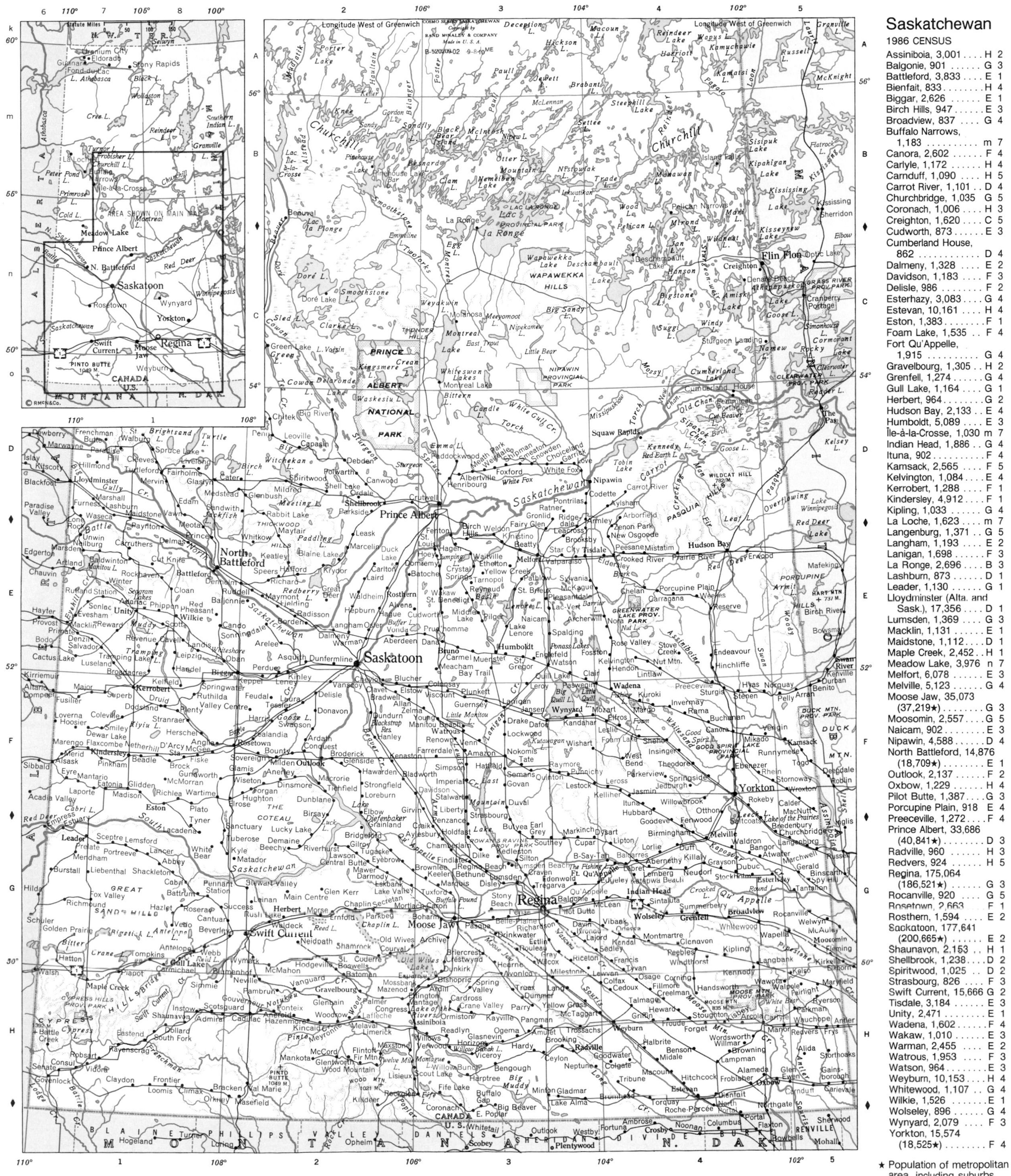

Saskatchewan

1986 CENSUS

Assiniboia, 3,001 . . . . H 2
Balgonie, 901 . . . . . . G 3
Battleford, 3,833 . . . . E 1
Bienfait, 833 . . . . H 4
Biggar, 2,626 . . . . . . E 1
Birch Hills, 947 . . . . . . E 3
Broadview, 837 . . . . G 4
Buffalo Narrows, 1,183 . . . . m 7
Canora, 2,602 . . . . . . F 4
Carlyle, 1,172 . . . . . . H 4
Carnduff, 1,090 . . . . H 5
Carrot River, 1,101 . . D 4
Churchbridge, 1,035 G 5
Coronach, 1,006 . . . . H 3
Creighton, 1,620 . . . . C 5
Cudworth, 873 . . . . . . E 3
Cumberland House, 862 . . . . D 4
Dalmeny, 1,328 . . . . E 2
Davidson, 1,183 . . . . F 3
Delisle, 986 . . . . F 2
Esterhazy, 3,083 . . . . G 4
Estevan, 10,161 . . . . H 4
Eston, 1,383 . . . . F 1
Foam Lake, 1,535 . . F 4
Fort Qu'Appelle, 1,915 . . . . G 4
Gravelbourg, 1,305 . . H 2
Grenfell, 1,274 . . . . . . G 4
Gull Lake, 1,164 . . . . G 1
Herbert, 964 . . . . G 2
Hudson Bay, 2,133 . . E 4
Humboldt, 5,089 . . . . E 3
Île-à-la-Crosse, 1,030 m 7
Indian Head, 1,886 . . G 4
Ituna, 902 . . . . F 4
Kamsack, 2,565 . . . . F 5
Kelvington, 1,084 . . . . E 4
Kerrobert, 1,288 . . . . F 1
Kindersley, 4,912 . . . . F 1
Kipling, 1,033 . . . . . . G 4
La Loche, 1,623 . . . . m 7
Langenburg, 1,371 . . G 5
Langham, 1,193 . . . . E 2
Lanigan, 1,698 . . . . . . F 3
La Ronge, 2,696 . . . . B 3
Lashburn, 873 . . . . . . D 1
Leader, 1,130 . . . . . . G 1
Lloydminster (Alta. and Sask.), 17,356 . . . . D 1
Lumsden, 1,369 . . . . G 3
Macklin, 1,131 . . . . . . E 1
Maidstone, 1,112 . . . . D 1
Maple Creek, 2,452 . . H 1
Meadow Lake, 3,976 n 7
Melfort, 6,078 . . . . . . E 3
Melville, 5,123 . . . . . . G 4
Moose Jaw, 35,073 (37,219★) . . . . G 3
Moosomin, 2,557 . . . . G 5
Naicam, 902 . . . . E 3
Nipawin, 4,588 . . . . . . D 4
North Battleford, 14,876 (18,709★) . . . . E 1
Outlook, 2,137 . . . . . . F 2
Oxbow, 1,229 . . . . . . H 4
Pilot Butte, 1,387 . . . . G 3
Porcupine Plain, 918 E 4
Preeceville, 1,272 . . . . F 4
Prince Albert, 33,686 (40,841★) . . . . D 3
Radville, 960 . . . . . . H 3
Redvers, 924 . . . . . . H 5
Regina, 175,064 (186,521★) . . . . . . G 3
Rocanville, 920 . . . . G 5
Rosetown, 2,663 . . . . . F 1
Rosthern, 1,594 . . . . E 2
Saskatoon, 177,641 (200,665★) . . . . . . E 2
Shaunavon, 2,153 . . H 1
Shellbrook, 1,238 . . . . D 2
Spiritwood, 1,025 . . D 2
Strasbourg, 826 . . . . F 3
Swift Current, 15,666 G 2
Tisdale, 3,184 . . . . . . E 3
Unity, 2,471 . . . . E 1
Wadena, 1,602 . . . . . . F 4
Wakaw, 1,010 . . . . E 3
Warman, 2,455 . . . . E 2
Watrous, 1,953 . . . . F 3
Watson, 964 . . . . E 3
Weyburn, 10,153 . . . . H 4
Whitewood, 1,107 . . G 4
Wilkie, 1,526 . . . . E 1
Wolseley, 896 . . . . . . G 4
Wynyard, 2,079 . . . . F 3
Yorkton, 15,574 (18,525★) . . . . F 4

★ Population of metropolitan area, including suburbs.

United States of America

Akron, 223,019 ('90)... C10
ALABAMA.................. E 9
ALASKA.................... M19
Albany, 101,082 ('90).. C12
Albuquerque, 384,736 ('90)......................... D 5
Amarillo, 157,615 ('90) D 6
Anchorage, 226,338 ('90)........................... M20
Annapolis, 33,187 ('90)........................... D11
ARIZONA.................... E 4
ARKANSAS................. E 8
Atlanta, 394,017 ('90).. E10
Augusta, 21,325 ('90). C13
Austin, 465,622 ('90)... E 7
Baltimore, 736,014 ('90)........................... D11
Baton Rouge, 219,531 ('90)........................... E 8
Billings, 81,151 ('90).... B 5
Birmingham, 265,968 ('90)........................... E 9
Bismarck, 49,256 ('90) B 6
Boise, 125,738 ('90).... C 3
Boston, 574,283 ('90). C12
Buffalo, 328,123 ('90). C11
CALIFORNIA.............. D 2
Carson City, 40,443 ('90)........................... D 3
Charleston, 57,287 ('90)........................... D10
Charleston, 80,414 ('90)........................... E11
Charlotte, 395,934 ('90)........................... D10
Chattanooga, 152,466 ('90)........................... D 9
Cheyenne, 50,008 ('90)........................... C 6
Chicago, 2,783,726 ('90)........................... C 9
Cincinnati, 364,040 ('90)........................... D10
Cleveland, 505,616 ('90)........................... C10
COLORADO................ D 5
Colorado Springs, 281,140 ('90)........................... D 6
Columbia, 98,052 ('90) E10
Columbus, 178,681 ('90)........................... E10
Columbus, 632,910 ('90)........................... D10
Concord, 36,006 ('90). C12
CONNECTICUT.......... C12
Dallas, 1,006,877 ('90) E 7
DELAWARE............... D11
Denver, 467,610 ('90). D 6
Des Moines, 193,187 ('90)........................... C 8
Detroit, 1,027,974 ('90)........................... C10
Dover, 27,630 ('90)..... D11
El Paso, 515,342 ('90). E 5
FLORIDA.................... F10
Fort Wayne, 173,072 ('90)........................... C 9
Fort Worth, 447,619 ('90)........................... E 7
Frankfort, 25,968 ('90) D10
Fresno, 354,202 ('90).. D 3
GEORGIA................... E10
Grand Rapids, 189,126 ('90)........................... C 9
Harrisburg, 52,376 ('90)........................... C11
Hartford, 139,739 ('90)........................... C12
Helena, 24,569 ('90).... B 4
Houston, 1,630,553 ('90)........................... F 7
IDAHO....................... C 4
ILLINOIS.................... C 9
INDIANA..................... C 9
Indianapolis, 731,327 ('90)........................... D 9
IOWA.......................... C 8
Jackson, 196,637 ('90) E 8
Jacksonville, 635,230 ('90)........................... E10
Jefferson City, 35,481 ('90)........................... D 8
Juneau, 26,751 ('90)... N21
KANSAS..................... D 7
Kansas City, 435,146 ('90)........................... D 8
KENTUCKY................. D 9
Knoxville, 165,121 ('90)........................... D10
Las Vegas, 258,295 ('90)........................... D 3
Lincoln, 191,972 ('90).. C 7
Little Rock, 175,795 ('90)........................... E 8
Los Angeles, 3,485,398 ('90)........................... E 3
LOUISIANA................. E 8
Louisville, 269,063 ('90)........................... D 9
Madison, 191,262 ('90)........................... C 9
MAINE........................ B13
MARYLAND................ D11

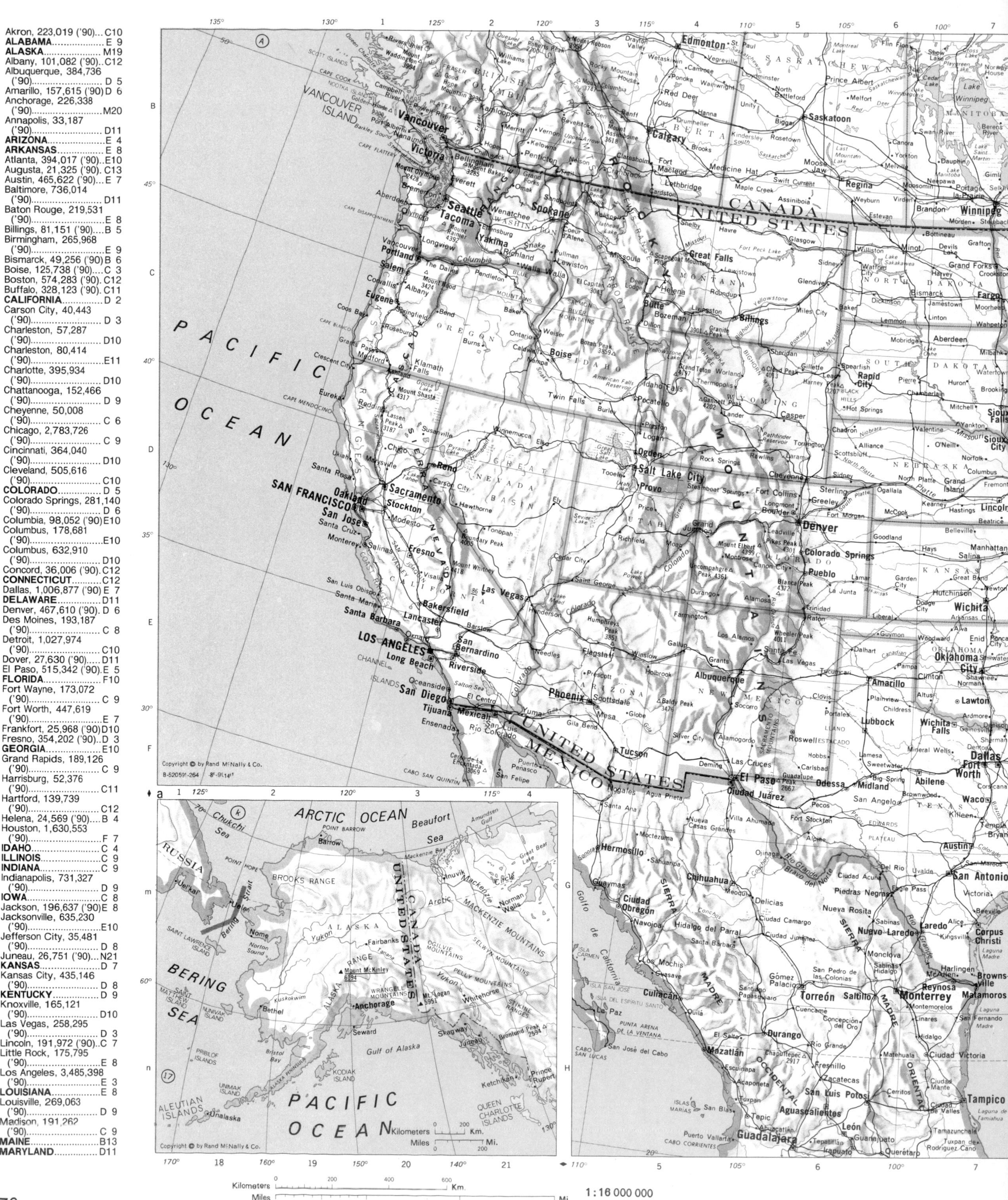

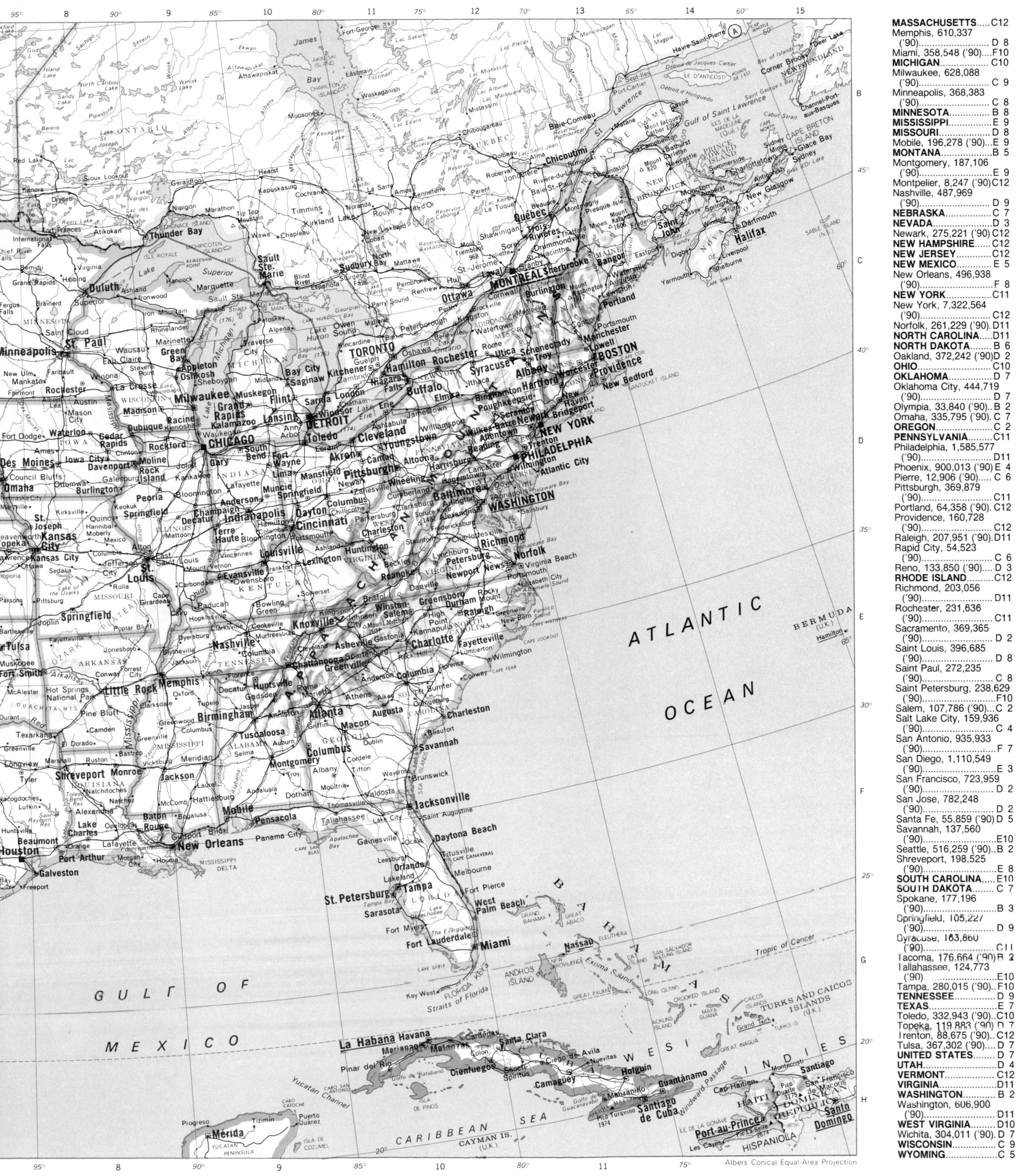

MASSACHUSETTS.....C12
Memphis, 610,337 ('90).......................... D 8
Miami, 358,548 ('90)....F10
MICHIGAN................. C10
Milwaukee, 628,088 ('90).......................... C 9
Minneapolis, 368,383 ('90).......................... C 8
MINNESOTA.............. B 8
MISSISSIPPI................E 9
MISSOURI.................. D 8
Mobile, 196,278 ('90)...E 9
MONTANA..................B 5
Montgomery, 187,106 ('90)..........................E 9
Montpelier, 8,247 ('90) C12
Nashville, 487,969 ('90).......................... D 9
NEBRASKA................C 7
NEVADA.....................D 3
Newark, 275,221 ('90) C12
NEW HAMPSHIRE......C12
NEW JERSEY.............C12
NEW MEXICO............ E 5
New Orleans, 496,938 ('90)..........................F 8
NEW YORK................C11
New York, 7,322,564 ('90).......................... C12
Norfolk, 261,229 ('90). D11
NORTH CAROLINA.....D11
NORTH DAKOTA........ B 6
Oakland, 372,242 ('90) D 2
OHIO.......................... C10
OKLAHOMA............... D 7
Oklahoma City, 444,719 ('90).......................... D 7
Olympia, 33,840 ('90).. B 2
Omaha, 335,795 ('90). C 7
OREGON....................C 2
PENNSYLVANIA.........C11
Philadelphia, 1,585,577 ('90).......................... D11
Phoenix, 900,013 ('90) E 4
Pierre, 12,906 ('90)..... C 6
Pittsburgh, 369,879 ('90).......................... C11
Portland, 64,358 ('90). C12
Providence, 160,728 ('90).......................... C12
Raleigh, 207,951 ('90). D11
Rapid City, 54,523 ('90).......................... C 6
Reno, 133,850 ('90).... D 3
RHODE ISLAND..........C12
Richmond, 203,056 ('90).......................... D11
Rochester, 231,636 ('90).......................... C11
Sacramento, 369,365 ('90).......................... D 2
Saint Louis, 396,685 ('90).......................... D 8
Saint Paul, 272,235 ('90).......................... C 8
Saint Petersburg, 238,629 ('90)..........................F10
Salem, 107,786 ('90)...C 2
Salt Lake City, 159,936 ('90).......................... C 4
San Antonio, 935,933 ('90)..........................F 7
San Diego, 1,110,549 ('90)..........................E 3
San Francisco, 723,959 ('90).......................... D 2
San Jose, 782,248 ('90).......................... D 2
Santa Fe, 55,859 ('90) D 5
Savannah, 137,560 ('90)..........................E10
Seattle, 516,259 ('90)..B 2
Shreveport, 198,525 ('90)..........................E 8
SOUTH CAROLINA.....E10
SOUTH DAKOTA........ C 7
Spokane, 177,196 ('90)..........................B 3
Springfield, 105,227 ('90).......................... D 9
Syracuse, 163,860 ('90).......................... C11
Tacoma, 176,664 ('90) B 2
Tallahassee, 124,773 ('90)..........................E10
Tampa, 280,015 ('90)..F10
TENNESSEE.............. D 9
TEXAS..........................E 7
Toledo, 332,943 ('90)..C10
Topeka, 119,883 ('90) D 7
Trenton, 88,675 ('90).. C12
Tulsa, 367,302 ('90).... D 7
UNITED STATES........ D 7
UTAH..........................D 4
VERMONT.................. C12
VIRGINIA.....................D11
WASHINGTON........... B 2
Washington, 606,900 ('90).......................... D11
WEST VIRGINIA.........D10
Wichita, 304,011 ('90). D 7
WISCONSIN............... C 9
WYOMING....................C 5

Alabama

1990 CENSUS

Alabaster, 14,732 .. B 3
Albertville, 14,507 .. A 3
Alexander City, 14,917 .... C 4
Andalusia, 9,269 .... D 3
Anniston, 26,623 .... B 4
Arab, 6,321 .... A 3
Athens, 16,901 .... A 3
Atmore, 8,046 ...... D 2
Attalla, 6,859 ...... A 3
Auburn, 33,830 .... C 4
Bay Minette, 7,168 .. E 2
Bessemer, 33,497 .. B 3
Birmingham, 265,968 B 3
Bluff Park, 8,000('85) g 7
Boaz, 6,928 .... A 3
Brewton, 5,885 .... D 2
Center Point, 22,000('85) ...... f 7
Chickasaw, 6,649 .. E 1
Childersburg, 4,579 .. B 3
Clanton, 7,669 ...... C 3
Cullman, 13,367 .... A 3
Decatur, 48,761 .... A 3
Demopolis, 7,512 ... C 2
Dothan, 53,589 .... D 4
Enterprise, 20,123 .. D 4
Eufaula, 13,220 .... D 4
Fairfield, 12,200 .... B 3
Fairhope, 8,485 .... E 2
Fayette, 4,909 ...... B 2
Florence, 36,426 .... A 2
Fort Payne, 11,838 .. A 4
Frisco City, 1,581 .. D 2
Fultondale, 6,400 .... f 7
Gadsden, 42,523 .... A 3
Gardendale, 9,251 .. B 3
Geneva, 4,681 ...... D 4
Greenville, 7,492 .... D 3
Guntersville, 7,038 .. A 3
Haleyville, 4,452 .... A 2
Hamilton, 5,787 .... A 2
Hartselle, 10,795 .... A 3
Homewood, 22,922 .. g 7
Hueytown, 15,280 .. g 6
Huntsville, 159,789 .. A 3
Irondale, 9,454 ...... f 7
Jackson, 5,819 .... D 2
Jacksonville, 10,283 B 4
Jasper, 13,553 ...... B 2
Lanett, 8,985 ...... C 4
Leeds, 9,946 ...... B 3
Millbrook, 6,050 .... C 3
Mobile, 196,278 .... E 1
Monroeville, 6,993 .. D 2
Montgomery, 187,106 C 3
Moundville, 1,348 ... C 2
Mountain Brook, 19,810 .... g 7
Muscle Shoals, 9,611 A 2
Northport, 17,366 .. B 2
Oneonta, 4,844 .... B 3
Opelika, 22,122 .... C 4
Opp, 6,985 .... D 3
Oxford, 9,362 ...... B 4
Ozark, 12,922 ...... D 4
Pelham, 9,765 ...... B 3
Pell City, 8,118 .... B 3
Phenix City, 25,312 .. C 4
Piedmont, 5,288 .... B 4
Pleasant Grove, 8,458 g 7
Prattville, 19,587 .... C 3
Prichard, 34,311 .... E 1
Rainbow City, 7,673 A 3
Roanoke, 6,362 .... B 4
Russellville, 7,812 ... A 2
Saraland, 11,751 .... E 1
Scottsboro, 13,786 .. A 3
Selma, 23,755 ...... C 2
Sheffield, 10,380 .... A 2
Spanish Fort, 3,415('80) .... E 2
Sylacauga, 12,520 .. B 3
Talladega, 18,175 .. B 3
Tallassee, 5,112 .... C 4
Tarrant, 8,046 ...... B 3
Theodore, 6,392('80) E 1
Tillmans Corner, 5,000('85) .... E 1
Troy, 13,051 ...... D 4
Tuscaloosa, 77,759 .. B 2
Tuscumbia, 8,413 .... A 2
Tuskegee, 12,257 .. C 4
Vestavia Hills, 19,749 g 7
Warrior, 3,280 ...... B 3
Wetumpka, 4,670 .. C 3

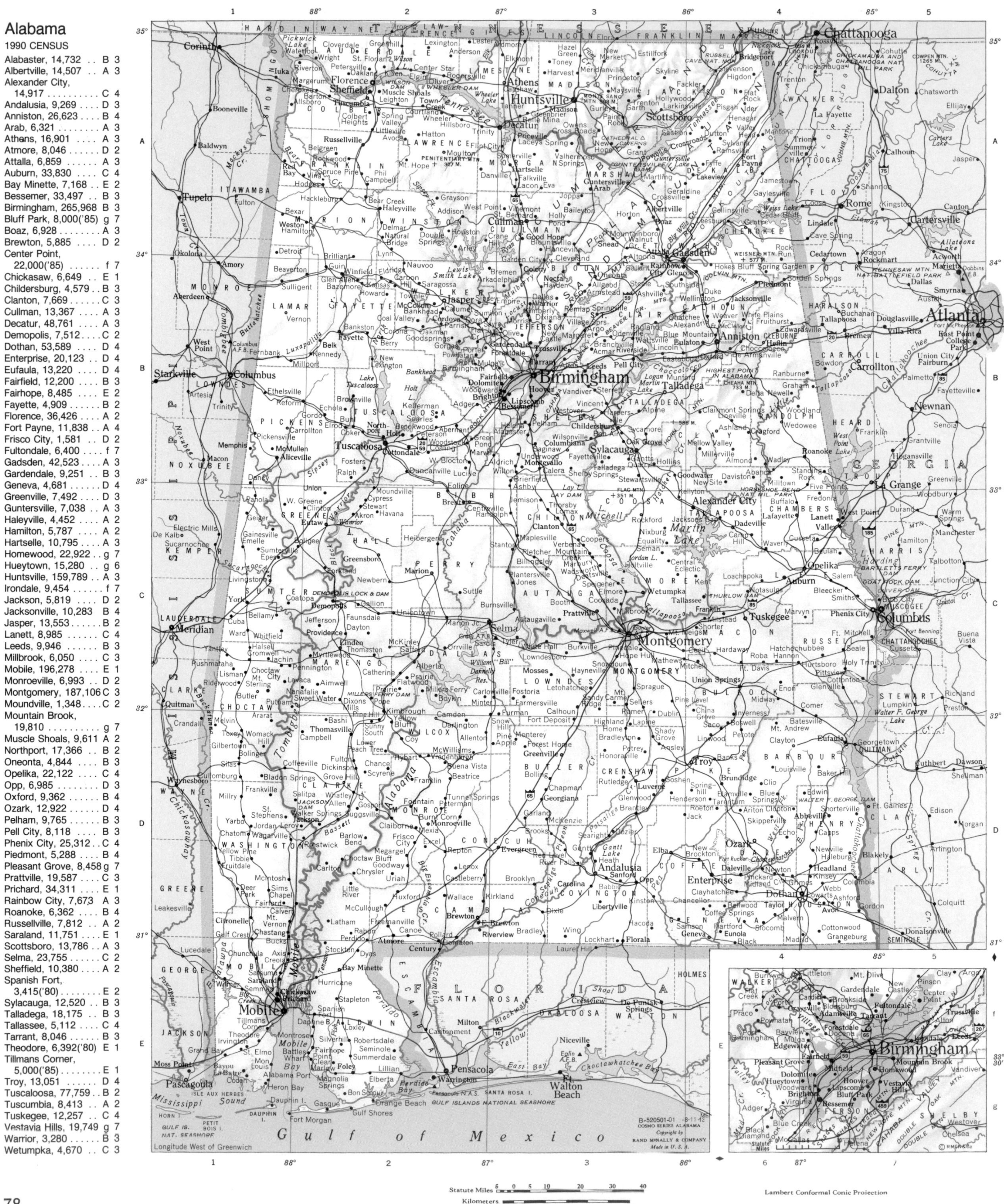

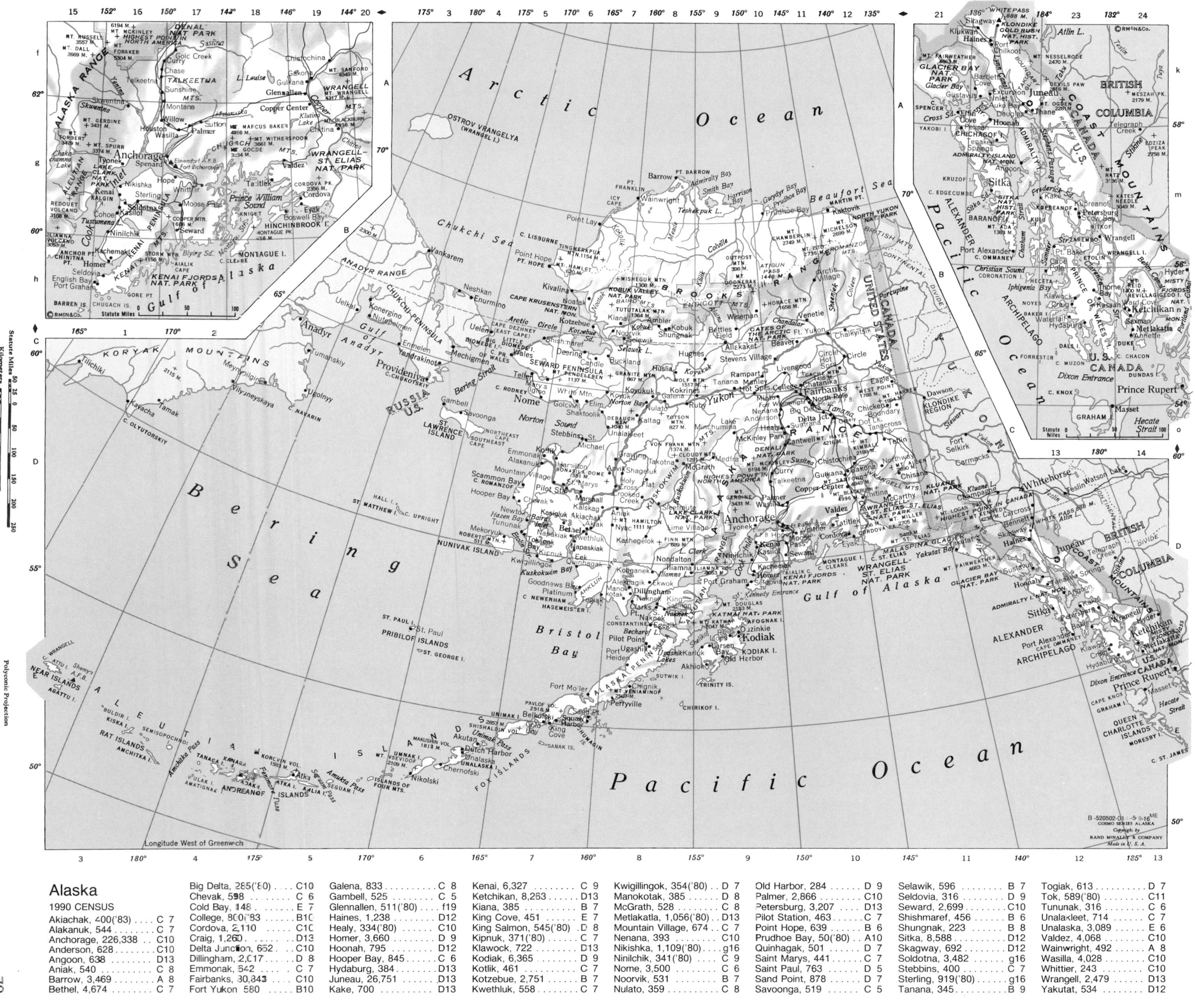

Alaska

1990 CENSUS

Akiachak, 400('83) .... C 7
Alakanuk, 544 .... C 7
Anchorage, 226,338 .. C10
Anderson, 628 .... C10
Angoon, 638 .... D13
Aniak, 540 .... C 8
Barrow, 3,469 .... A 8
Bethel, 4,674 .... C 7
Big Delta, 285('80) C10
Chevak, 598 .... C 6
Cold Bay, 148 .... E 7
College, 8C0('83 ...... B10
Cordova, 2,110 ..... C10
Craig, 1,260 .... D13
Delta Junction, 652 ... C10
Dillingham, 2,017 ...... D 8
Emmonak, 642 ..... C 7
Fairbanks, 30,843 .... C10
Fort Yukon 580 ..... B10
Galena, 833 .... C 8
Gambell, 525 .... C 5
Glennallen, 511('80) f19
Haines, 1,238 .... D12
Healy, 334('80) C10
Homer, 3,660 .... D 9
Hoonah, 795 .... D12
Hooper Bay, 845 ...... C 6
Hydaburg, 384 .... D13
Juneau, 26,751 ...... D13
Kake, 700 .... D13
Kenai, 6,327 .... C 9
Ketchikan, 8,263 ...... D13
Kiana, 385 .... B 7
King Cove, 451 ...... E 7
King Salmon, 545('80) . D 8
Kipnuk, 371('80) ...... C 7
Klawock, 722 .... D13
Kodiak, 6,365 .... D 9
Kotlik, 461 .... C 7
Kotzebue, 2,751 ...... B 7
Kwethluk, 558 .... C 7
Kwigillingok, 354('80) .. D 7
Manokotak, 385 ...... D 8
McGrath, 528 .... C 8
Metlakatla, 1,056('80) .. D13
Mountain Village, 674 .. C 7
Nenana, 393 .... C10
Nikishka, 1,109('80) g16
Ninilchik, 341('80) .... C 9
Nome, 3,500 .... C 6
Noorvik, 531 .... B 7
Nulato, 359 .... C 8
Old Harbor, 284 ...... D 9
Palmer, 2,866 .... C10
Petersburg, 3,207 .... D13
Pilot Station, 463 ...... C 7
Point Hope, 639 ...... B 6
Prudhoe Bay, 50('80) .. A10
Quinhagak, 501 ...... D 7
Saint Marys, 441 ...... C 7
Saint Paul, 763 ...... D 5
Sand Point, 878 ...... D 7
Savoonga, 519 ...... C 5
Selawik, 596 .... B 7
Seldovia, 316 .... D 9
Seward, 2,699 .... C10
Shishmaref, 456 ...... B 6
Shungnak, 223 ...... B 8
Sitka, 8,588 .... D12
Skagway, 692 .... D12
Soldotna, 3,482 ...... g16
Stebbins, 400 .... C 7
Sterling, 919('80) g16
Tanana, 345 .... B 9
Togiak, 613 .... D 7
Tok, 589('80) C11
Tununak, 316 .... C 6
Unalakleet, 714 ...... C 7
Unalaska, 3,089 ...... E 6
Valdez, 4,068 .... C10
Wainwright, 492 ...... A 8
Wasilla, 4,028 .... C10
Whittier, 243 .... C10
Wrangell, 2,479 ...... D13
Yakutat, 534 .... D12

Arizona

1990 CENSUS

Ajo, 5,189('80) . . . . . E 3
Apache Junction, 18,100 . . . . m 9
Avondale, 16,169 . . . D 3
Bagdad, 2,331('80) . . C 2
Benson, 3,824 . . . . . . F 5
Bisbee, 6,288 . . . . . . F 6
Black Canyon City, 850('86) . . . . C 3
Buckeye, 5,038 . . . . D 3
Bullhead City, 21,951 B 1
Camp Verde, 6,243 . . C 4
Casa Grande, 19,082 E 4
Casas Adobes, 12,155('86) . . . . . . E 5
Cashion, 3,014('80) . . m 8
Cave Creek, 2,925 . . D 4
Chandler, 90,533 . . . D 4
Chinle, 2,815('80) . . . A 6
Chino Valley, 4,837 . . C 3
Claypool, 2,362('80) D 5
Clifton, 2,840 . . . . . . D 6
Coolidge, 6,927 . . . . E 4
Cottonwood, 5,918 . . C 3
Crane, 2,650('86) . . . . E 1
Douglas, 12,822 . . . . F 6
Eagar, 4,025 . . . . . . C 6
El Mirage, 5,001 . . . . k 8
Eloy, 7,211 . . . . E 4
Flagstaff, 45,857 . . . . B 4
Florence, 7,510 . . . . D 4
Fort Defiance, 3,431('80) . . . . B 6
Ganado, 3,400('86) . . B 6
Gila Bend, 1,747 . . . . E 3
Gilbert, 29,188 . . . . . . D 4
Glendale, 148,134 . . D 3
Globe, 6,062 . . . . D 5
Goodyear, 6,258 . . . . D 3
Grand Canyon, 1,348('80) . . . . A 3
Green Valley, 7,999('80) . . . . F 5
Guadalupe, 5,458 . . . m 9
Holbrook, 4,686 . . . . C 5
Huachuca City, 1,782 F 5
Kayenta, 3,343('80) . . A 5
Kearny, 2,262 . . . . . . D 5
Kingman, 12,722 . . . . B 1
Lake Havasu City, 24,363 . . . . C 1
Litchfield Park, 3,303 m 8
Mammoth, 1,845 . . . . E 5
Mesa, 288,091 . . . . . . D 4
Miami, 2,018 . . . . D 5
Nogales, 19,489 . . . . F 5
Oracle, 2,484('80) . . E 5
Page, 6,598 . . . . A 4
Paradise Valley, 11,671 . . . . k 9
Parker, 2,897 . . . . . . C 1
Payson, 8,377 . . . . . . C 4
Peoria, 50,618 . . . . . . D 3
Phoenix, 900,013 . . . . D 3
Pinetop-Lakeside, 2,422 . . . . C 6
Prescott, 26,455 . . . . C 3
Sacaton, 1,951('80) . . D 4
Safford, 7,359 . . . . . . E 6
Saint Johns, 3,294 . . C 6
San Carlos, 2,668('80) . . . . D 5
San Luis, 70('86) . . . . E 3
San Manuel, 5,443('80) . . . . E 5
Scottsdale, 130,069 D 4
Sedona, 7,720 . . . . . . C 4
Sells, 1,864('80) . . . . . F 4
Show Low, 5,019 . . . C 5
Sierra Vista, 32,983 . . F 5
Snowflake, 3,679 . . . . C 5
Somerton, 5,282 . . . . . E 1
South Tucson, 5,093 E 5
Sun City, 57,000 . . . . k 8
Superior, 3,468 . . . . D 4
Surprise, 7,122 . . . . . . k 8
Taylor, 2,418 . . . . . . C 5
Tempe, 141,865 . . . . D 4
Thatcher, 3,763 . . . . E 6
Tolleson, 4,434 . . . . m 8
Tombstone, 1,220 . . . F 5
Tuba City, 5,045('80) A 4
Tucson, 405,390 . . . . E 5
Twin Knolls, 5,210('86) . . . . m 9
Wickenburg, 4,515 . . D 3
Willcox, 3,122 . . . . . . E 6
Williams, 2,532 . . . . . . B 3
Window Rock, 2,230('80) . . . . B 6
Winslow, 8,190 . . . . C 5
Youngtown, 2,542 . . . k 8
Yuma, 54,923 . . . . . . E 1

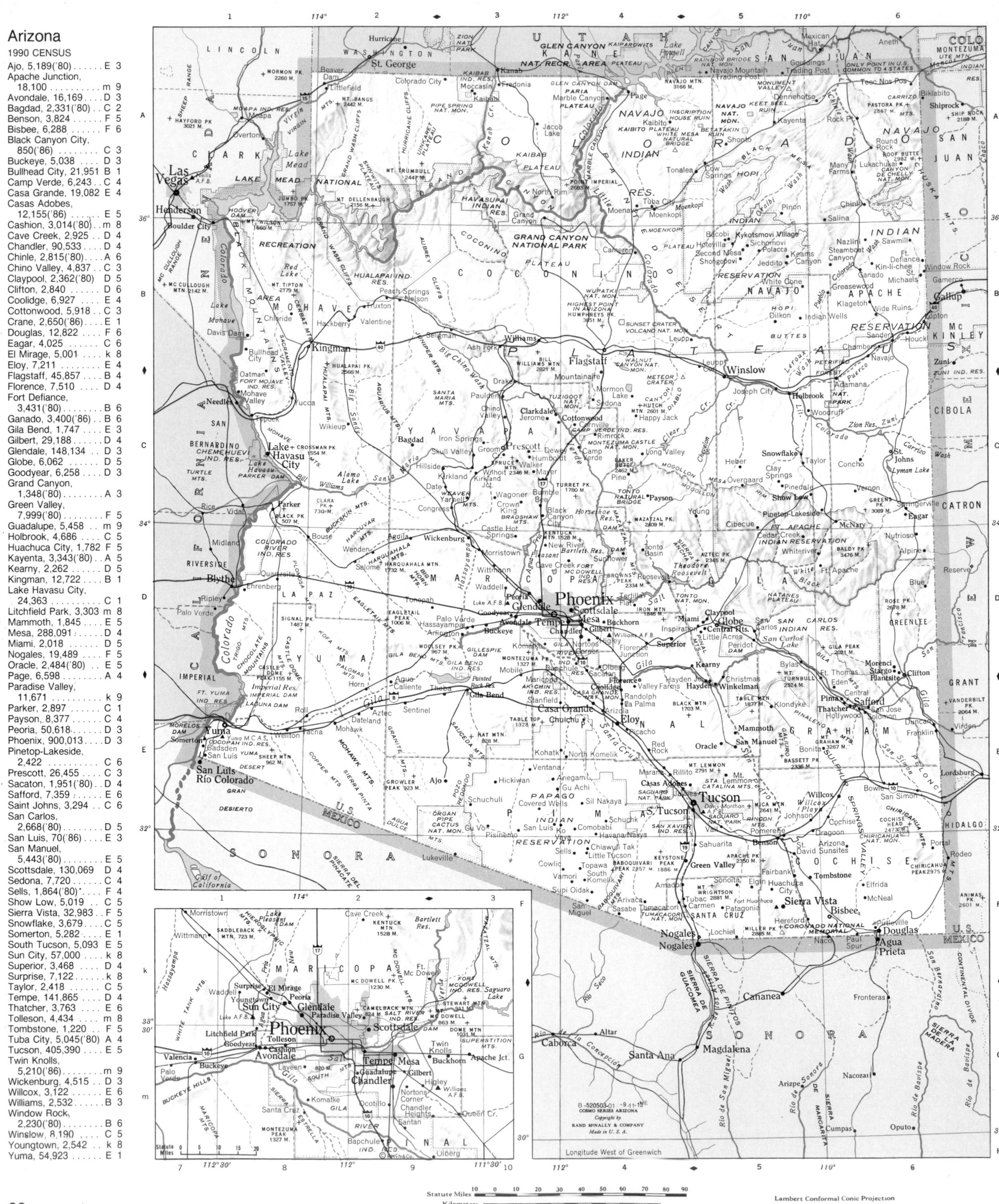

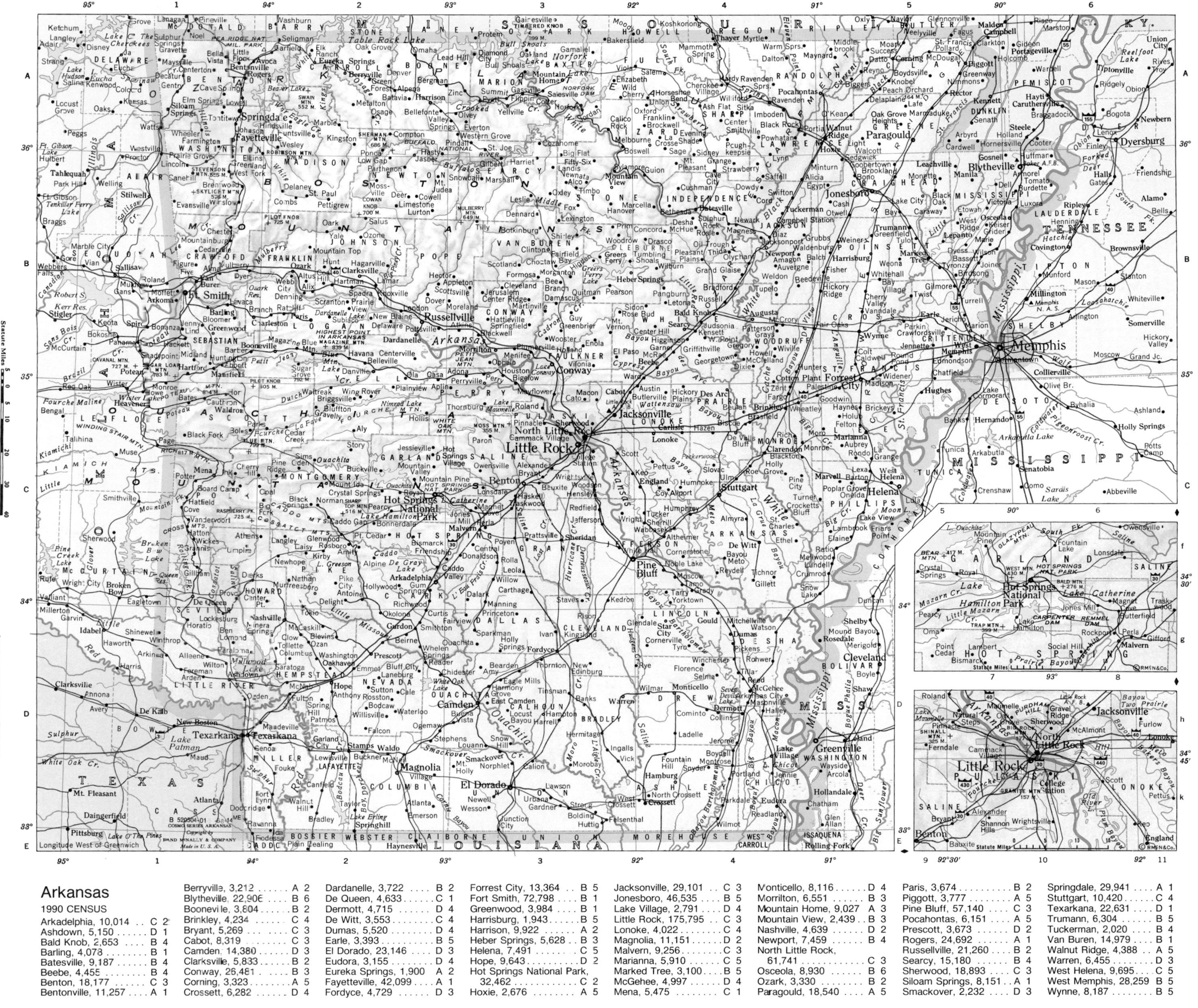

Arkansas

1990 CENSUS

Arkadelphia, 10,014 .. C 2
Ashdown, 5,150 ...... D 1
Bald Knob, 2,653 .... B 4
Barling, 4,078 .... B 1
Batesville, 9,187 ..... B 4
Beebe, 4,455 .... B 4
Benton, 18,177 ...... C 3
Bentonville, 11,257 .... A 1
Berryville, 3,212 ...... A 2
Blytheville, 22,906 .... B 6
Booneville, 3,804 ..... B 1
Brinkley, 4,234 ...... C 4
Bryant, 5,269 .... C 3
Cabot, 8,319 .... C 3
Camden, 14,380 ...... D 3
Clarksville, 5,833 ..... B 2
Conway, 26,481 ..... B 3
Corning, 3,323 .... A 5
Crossett, 6,282 ...... D 4
Dardanelle, 3,722 .... B 2
De Queen, 4,633 ...... C 1
Dermott, 4,715 ...... D 4
De Witt, 3,553 .... C 4
Dumas, 5,520 .... D 4
Earle, 3,393 .... B 5
El Dorado, 23,146 .... D 3
Eudora, 3,155 .... D 4
Eureka Springs, 1,900 A 2
Fayetteville, 42,099 .... A 1
Fordyce, 4,729 .... D 3
Forrest City, 13,364 .. B 5
Fort Smith, 72,798 .... B 1
Greenwood, 3,984 .... B 1
Harrisburg, 1,943 ..... B 5
Harrison, 9,922 .... A 2
Heber Springs, 5,628 .. B 3
Helena, 7,491 .... C 5
Hope, 9,643 .... D 2
Hot Springs National Park,
32,462 .... C 2
Hoxie, 2,676 .... A 5
Jacksonville, 29,101 .. C 3
Jonesboro, 46,535 .... B 5
Lake Village, 2,791 .... D 4
Little Rock, 175,795 .. C 3
Lonoke, 4,022 .... C 4
Magnolia, 11,151 ...... D 2
Malvern, 9,256 .... C 3
Marianna, 5,910 ...... C 5
Marked Tree, 3,100.... B 5
McGehee, 4,997 ...... D 4
Mena, 5,475 .... C 1
Monticello, 8,116 ...... D 4
Morrilton, 6,551 .... B 3
Mountain Home, 9,027 A 3
Mountain View, 2,439 .. B 3
Nashville, 4,639 .... D 2
Newport, 7,459 .... B 4
North Little Rock,
61,741 .... C 3
Osceola, 8,930 .... B 6
Ozark, 3,330 .... B 2
Paragould, 18,540 .... A 5
Paris, 3,674 .... B 2
Piggott, 3,777 .... A 5
Pine Bluff, 57,140 .... C 3
Pocahontas, 6,151 .... A 5
Prescott, 3,673 .... D 2
Rogers, 24,692 .... A 1
Russellville, 21,260 .... B 2
Searcy, 15,180 .... B 4
Sherwood, 18,893 .... C 3
Siloam Springs, 8,151 .. A 1
Smackover, 2,232 .... D 3
Springdale, 29,941 .... A 1
Stuttgart, 10,420 ...... C 4
Texarkana, 22,631 .... D 1
Trumann, 6,304 ...... B 5
Tuckerman, 2,020 .... B 4
Van Buren, 14,979 .... B 1
Walnut Ridge, 4,388 .. A 5
Warren, 6,455 .... D 3
West Helena, 9,695 ... C 5
West Memphis, 28,259 B 5
Wynne, 8,187 .... B 5

California

1990 CENSUS

Alameda, 76,459 .... h 8
Alhambra, 82,106 .. m12
Anaheim, 266,406 .. F 5
Antioch, 62,195 .... h 9
Bakersfield, 174,820 E 4
Berkeley, 102,724 .. D 2
Beverly Hills, 31,971 m12
Burbank, 93,643 .... E 4
Calexico, 18,633 .... F 6
Chico, 40,079 ...... C 3
Chula Vista, 135,163 F 5
Compton, 90,454 .... n12
Concord, 111,348 .. h 8
Costa Mesa, 96,357 .. n13
Daly City, 92,311 .... h 8
Davis, 46,209 ...... C 3
Downey, 91,444 .... n12
East Los Angeles, 126,379 .... m12
El Cajon, 88,693 .... F 5
El Centro, 31,384 .... F 6
Escondido, 108,635 .. F 5
Eureka, 27,025 .... B 1
Fairfield, 77,211 .... C 2
Fremont, 173,339 .. D 2
Fresno, 354,202 .... D 4
Fullerton, 114,144 .. n13
Garden Grove, 143,050 .... n13
Glendale, 180,038 .. m12
Hayward, 111,498 .. h 8
Huntington Beach, 181,519 .... F 4
Indio, 36,793 ...... F 5
Inglewood, 109,602 .. n12
Irvine, 110,330 ...... n13
Lancaster, 97,291 .. E 4
Lompoc, 37,649 .... E 3
Long Beach, 429,433 F 4
Los Angeles, 3,485,398 .... E 4
Marysville, 12,324 .. C 3
Menlo Park, 28,040 .. k 8
Merced, 56,216 .... D 3
Modesto, 164,730 .. D 3
Monterey, 31,954 .. D 3
Napa, 61,842 ...... C 2
Newport Beach, 66,643 .... n13
Norwalk, 94,279 .... n12
Oakland, 372,242 .. D 2
Oceanside, 128,398 .. F 5
Ontario, 133,179 .... E 5
Orange, 110,658 .... n13
Oxnard, 142,216 .... E 4
Palm Springs, 40,181 F 5
Palo Alto, 55,900 .... D 2
Pasadena, 131,591 .. E 4
Pomona, 131,723 .... E 5
Redding, 66,462 .... B 2
Redwood City, 66,072 .... D 2
Richmond, 87,425 .. D 2
Riverside, 226,505 .. F 5
Sacramento, 369,365 C 3
Salinas, 108,777 .... D 3
San Bernardino, 164,164 .... E 5
San Clemente, 41,100 F 5
San Diego, 1,110,549 F 5
San Francisco, 723,959 .... D 2
San Jose, 782,248 .. D 3
San Juan Capistrano, 26,183 .... F 5
San Luis Obispo, 41,958 .... E 3
San Mateo, 85,486 .. D 2
Santa Ana, 293,742 .. F 5
Santa Barbara, 85,571 .... E 4
Santa Clara, 93,613 D 2
Santa Cruz, 49,040 .. D 2
Santa Maria, 61,284 E 3
Santa Monica, 86,905 m12
Santa Rosa, 113,313 C 2
Simi Valley, 100,217 E 4
South Gate, 86,284 .. n12
South Lake Tahoe, 21,586 .... C 4
Stockton, 210,943 .. D 3
Sunnyvale, 117,229 .. k 8
Torrance, 133,107 .. n12
Tulare, 33,249 ...... D 4
Turlock, 42,198 .... D 3
Vallejo, 109,199 .... C 2
Ventura (San Buenaventura), 92,575 .... E 4
Visalia, 75,636 ...... D 4
West Covina, 96,086 m13
Westminster, 78,118 n12
Whittier, 77,671 .... F 4
Yuba City, 27,437 .. C 3

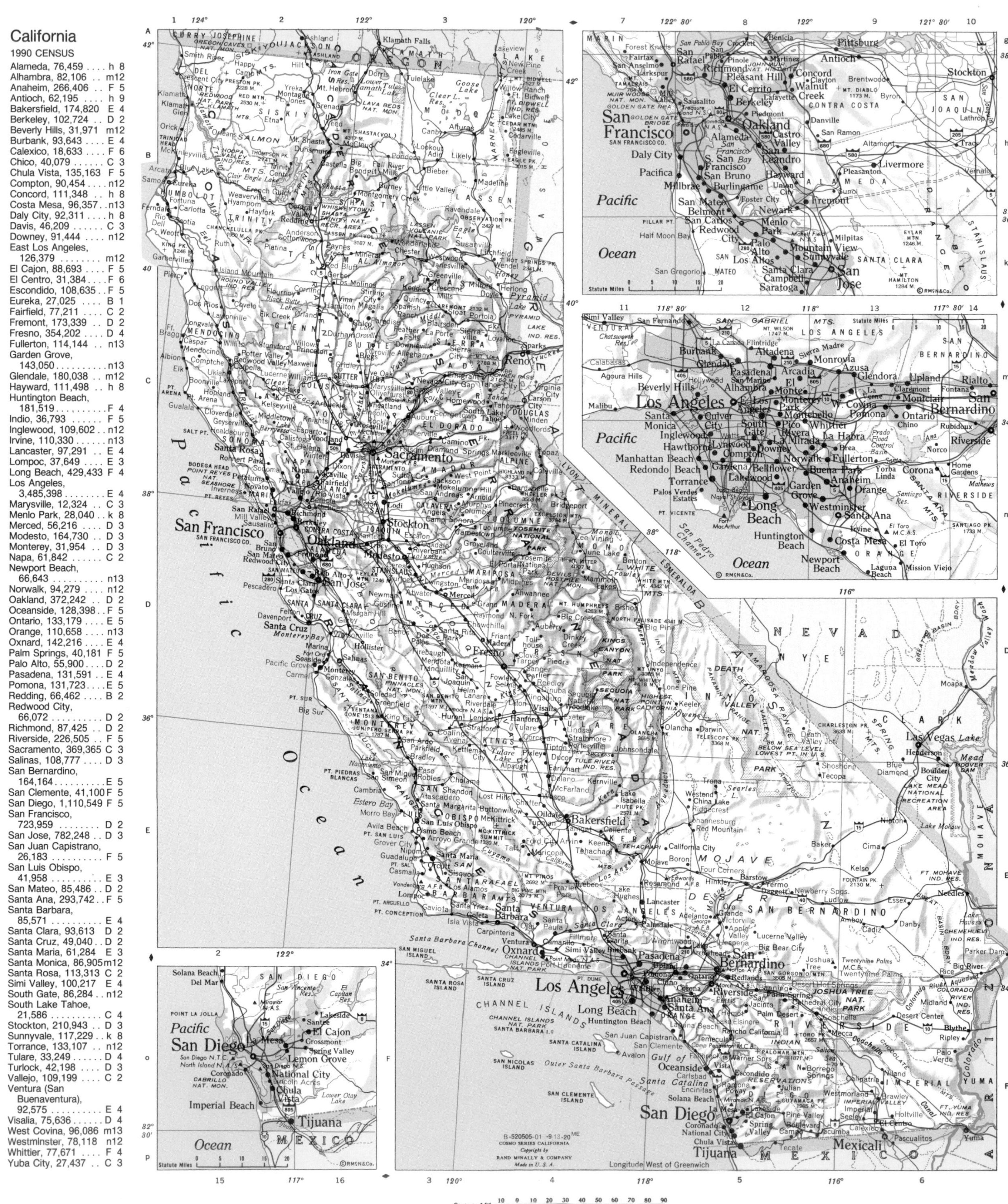

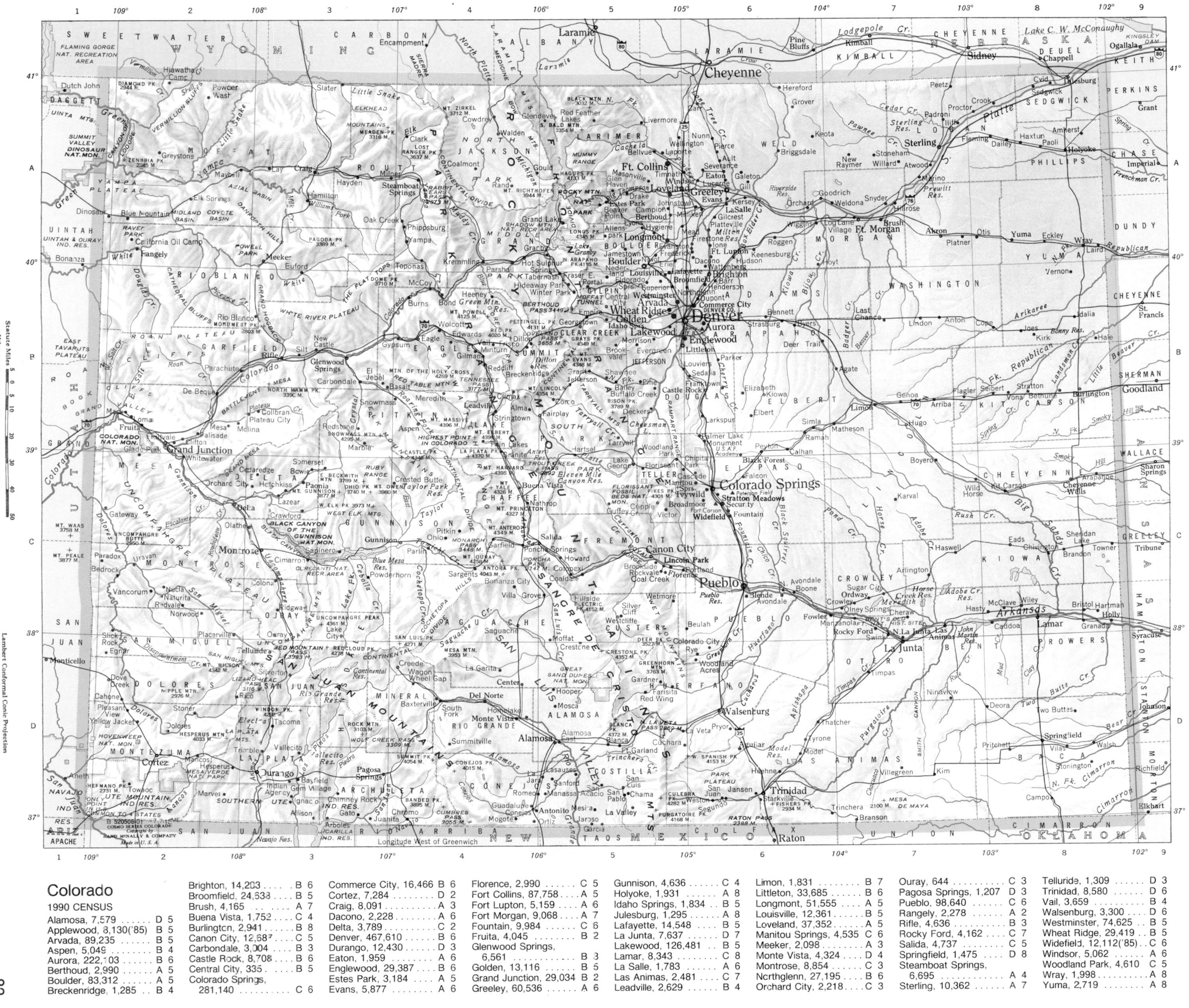

Colorado

1990 CENSUS

Place	Grid
Alamosa, 7,579	D 5
Applewood, 8,130('85)	B 5
Arvada, 89,235	B 5
Aspen, 5,049	B 4
Aurora, 222,103	B 6
Berthoud, 2,990	A 5
Boulder, 83,312	A 5
Breckenridge, 1,285	B 4
Brighton, 14,203	B 6
Broomfield, 24,638	B 5
Brush, 4,165	A 7
Buena Vista, 1,752	C 4
Burlington, 2,941	B 8
Canon City, 12,687	C 5
Carbondale, 3,004	B 3
Castle Rock, 8,708	B 6
Central City, 335	B 5
Colorado Springs, 281,140	C 6
Commerce City, 16,466	B 6
Cortez, 7,284	D 2
Craig, 8,091	A 3
Dacono, 2,228	A 6
Delta, 3,789	C 2
Denver, 467,610	B 6
Durango, 12,430	D 3
Eaton, 1,959	A 6
Englewood, 29,387	B 6
Estes Park, 3,184	A 5
Evans, 5,877	A 6
Florence, 2,990	C 5
Fort Collins, 87,758	A 5
Fort Lupton, 5,159	A 6
Fort Morgan, 9,068	A 7
Fountain, 9,984	C 6
Fruita, 4,045	B 2
Glenwood Springs, 6,561	B 3
Golden, 13,116	B 5
Grand Junction, 29,034	B 2
Greeley, 60,536	A 6
Gunnison, 4,636	C 4
Holyoke, 1,931	A 8
Idaho Springs, 1,834	B 5
Julesburg, 1,295	A 8
Lafayette, 14,548	B 5
La Junta, 7,637	D 7
Lakewood, 126,481	B 5
Lamar, 8,343	C 8
La Salle, 1,783	A 6
Las Animas, 2,481	C 7
Leadville, 2,629	B 4
Limon, 1,831	B 7
Littleton, 33,685	B 6
Longmont, 51,555	A 5
Louisville, 12,361	B 5
Loveland, 37,352	A 5
Manitou Springs, 4,535	C 6
Meeker, 2,098	A 3
Monte Vista, 4,324	D 4
Montrose, 8,854	C 3
Northglenn, 27,195	B 6
Orchard City, 2,218	C 3
Ouray, 644	C 3
Pagosa Springs, 1,207	D 3
Pueblo, 98,640	C 6
Rangely, 2,278	A 2
Rifle, 4,636	B 3
Rocky Ford, 4,162	C 7
Salida, 4,737	C 5
Springfield, 1,475	D 8
Steamboat Springs, 6,695	A 4
Sterling, 10,362	A 7
Telluride, 1,309	D 3
Trinidad, 8,580	D 6
Vail, 3,659	B 4
Walsenburg, 3,300	D 6
Westminster, 74,625	B 5
Wheat Ridge, 29,419	B 5
Widefield, 12,112('85)	C 6
Windsor, 5,062	A 6
Woodland Park, 4,610	C 5
Wray, 1,998	A 8
Yuma, 2,719	A 8

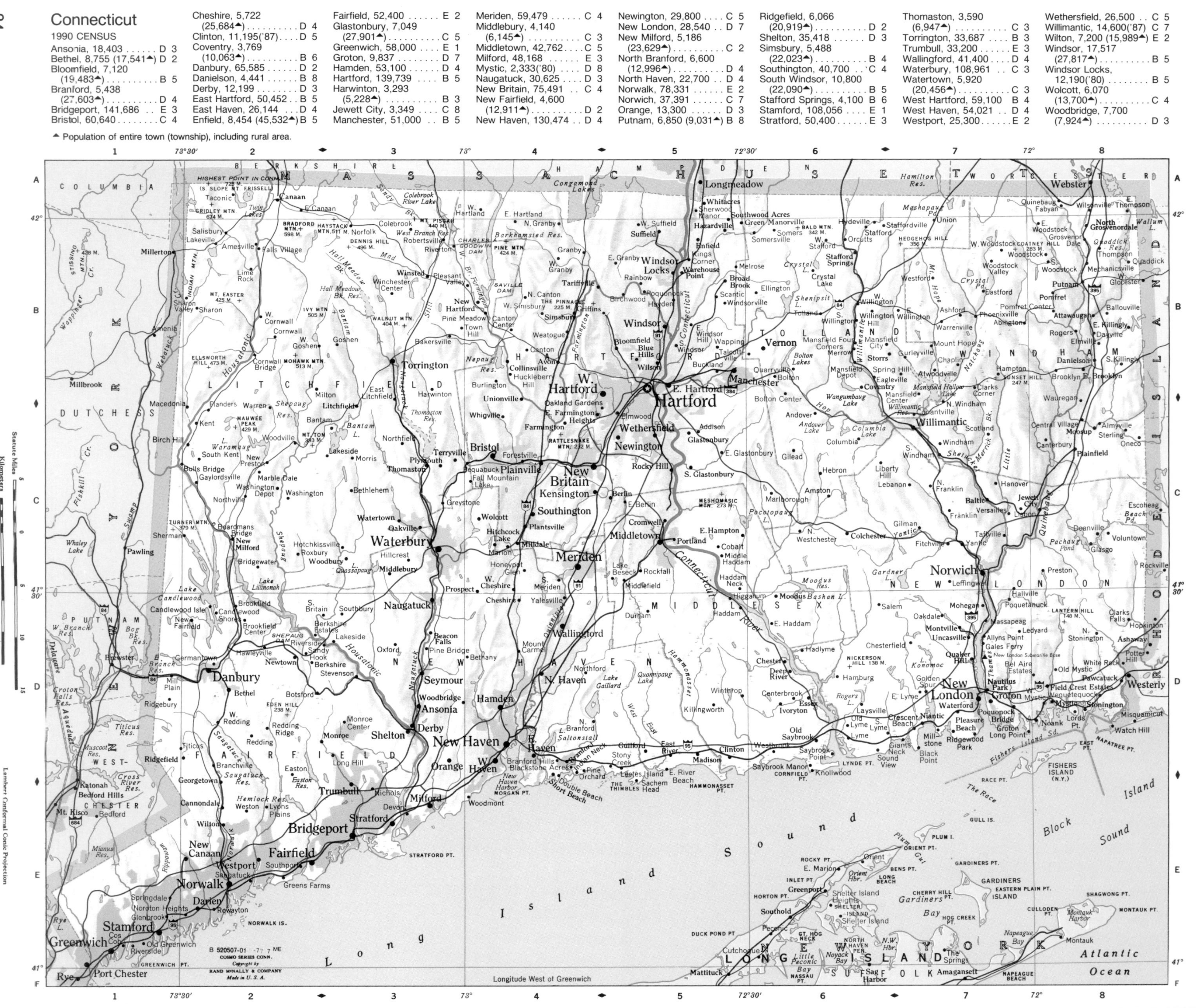

Connecticut
1990 CENSUS
Ansonia, 18,403 . . . . . . D 3
Bethel, 8,755 (17,541▲) D 2
Bloomfield, 7,120 (19,483▲) . . . . B 5
Branford, 5,438 (27,603▲) . . . . D 4
Bridgeport, 141,686 . . E 3
Bristol, 60,640 . . . . C 4
Cheshire, 5,722 (25,684▲) . . . . D 4
Clinton, 11,195('87) . . . D 5
Coventry, 3,769 (10,063▲) . . . . B 6
Danbury, 65,585 . . . . . . D 2
Danielson, 4,441 . . . . . . B 8
Derby, 12,199 . . . . D 3
East Hartford, 50,452 . . B 5
East Haven, 26,144 . . . D 4
Enfield, 8,454 (45,532▲) B 5
Fairfield, 52,400 . . . . . . E 2
Glastonbury, 7,049 (27,901▲) . . . . C 5
Greenwich, 58,000 . . . . E 1
Groton, 9,837 . . . . D 7
Hamden, 53,100 . . . . . . D 4
Hartford, 139,739 . . . . B 5
Harwinton, 3,293 (5,228▲) . . . . B 3
Jewett City, 3,349 . . . . C 8
Manchester, 51,000 . . B 5
Meriden, 59,479 . . . . . . C 4
Middlebury, 4,140 (6,145▲) . . . . C 3
Middletown, 42,762 . . . C 5
Milford, 48,168 . . . . . . E 3
Mystic, 2,333('80) . . . . D 8
Naugatuck, 30,625 . . . . D 3
New Britain, 75,491 . . . C 4
New Fairfield, 4,600 (12,911▲) . . . . D 2
New Haven, 130,474 . . D 4
Newington, 29,800 . . . . C 5
New London, 28,540 . . D 7
New Milford, 5,186 (23,629▲) . . . . C 2
North Branford, 6,600 (12,996▲) . . . . D 4
North Haven, 22,700 . . D 4
Norwalk, 78,331 . . . . . . E 2
Norwich, 37,391 . . . . . . C 7
Orange, 13,300 . . . . . . D 3
Putnam, 6,850 (9,031▲) B 8
Ridgefield, 6,066 (20,919▲) . . . . D 2
Shelton, 35,418 . . . . . . D 3
Simsbury, 5,488 (22,023▲) . . . . B 4
Southington, 40,700 . . C 4
South Windsor, 10,800 (22,090▲) . . . . B 5
Stafford Springs, 4,100 B 6
Stamford, 108,056 . . . . E 1
Stratford, 50,400 . . . . . E 3
Thomaston, 3,590 (6,947▲) . . . . C 3
Torrington, 33,687 . . . . B 3
Trumbull, 33,200 . . . . . E 3
Wallingford, 41,400 . . . D 4
Waterbury, 108,961 . . C 3
Watertown, 5,920 (20,456▲) . . . . C 3
West Hartford, 59,100 B 4
West Haven, 54,021 . . D 4
Westport, 25,300 . . . . . E 2
Wethersfield, 26,500 . . C 5
Willimantic, 14,600('87) C 7
Wilton, 7,200 (15,989▲) E 2
Windsor, 17,517 (27,817▲) . . . . B 5
Windsor Locks, 12,190('80) . . . . B 5
Wolcott, 6,070 (13,700▲) . . . . C 4
Woodbridge, 7,700 (7,924▲) . . . . D 3
▲ Population of entire town (township), including rural area.
Longitude West of Greenwich
Statute Miles
Kilometers
Lambert Conformal Conic Projection
B 520507-01 -7 7 ME
COSMO SERIES CONN.
Copyright by
RAND McNALLY & COMPANY
Made in U. S. A.

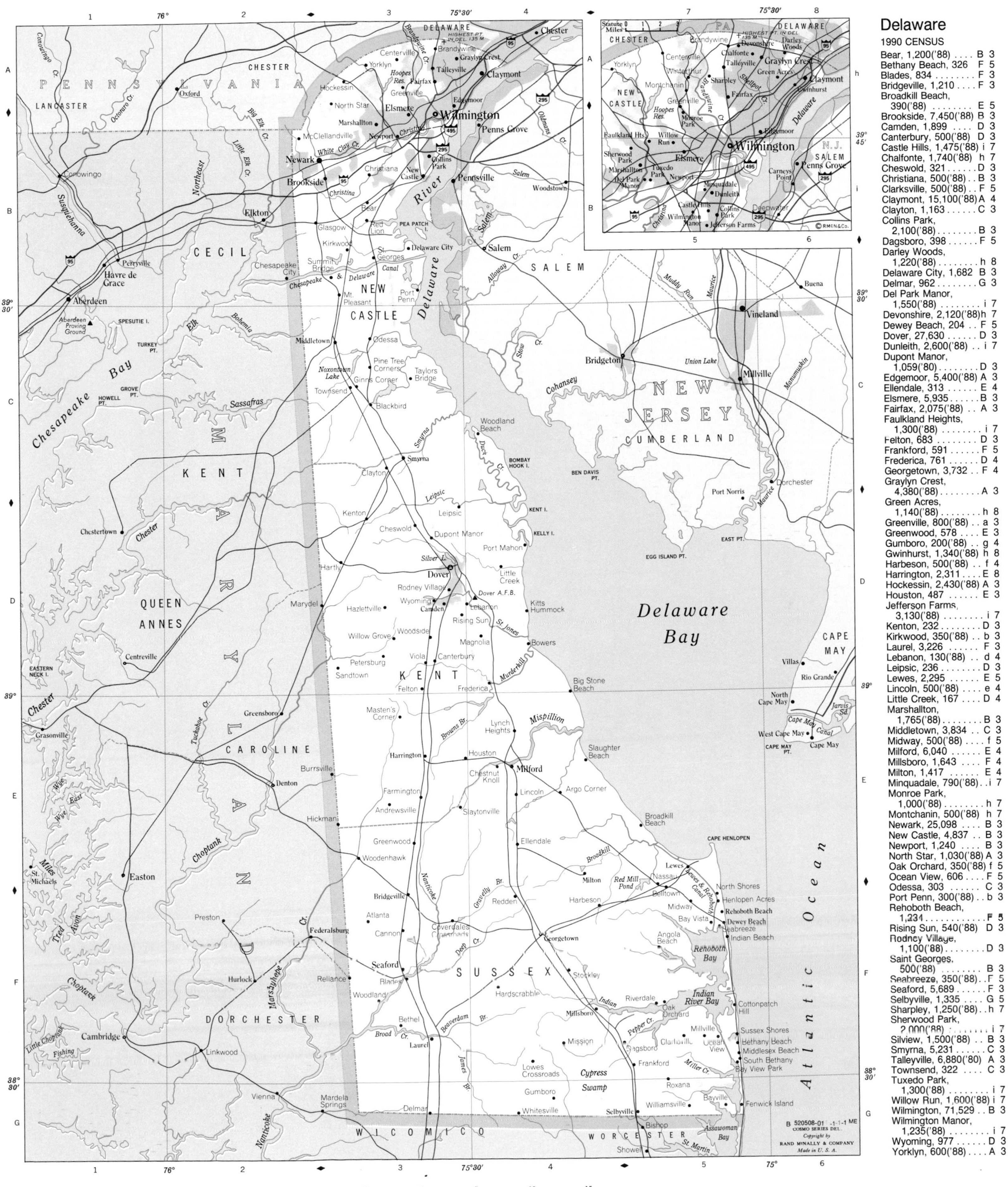

Delaware

1990 CENSUS

Bear, 1,200('88) .... B 3
Bethany Beach, 326 F 5
Blades, 834 .... F 3
Bridgeville, 1,210 .... F 3
Broadkill Beach, 390('88) .... E 5
Brookside, 7,450('88) B 3
Camden, 1,899 .... D 3
Canterbury, 500('88) D 3
Castle Hills, 1,475('88) i 7
Chalfonte, 1,740('88) h 7
Cheswold, 321 ...... D 3
Christiana, 500('88) .. B 3
Clarksville, 500('88) .. F 5
Claymont, 15,100('88) A 4
Clayton, 1,163 ...... C 3
Collins Park, 2,100('88) .... B 3
Dagsboro, 398 ...... F 5
Darley Woods, 1,220('88) .... h 8
Delaware City, 1,682 B 3
Delmar, 962 .... G 3
Del Park Manor, 1,550('88) .... i 7
Devonshire, 2,120('88) h 7
Dewey Beach, 204 .. F 5
Dover, 27,630 ...... D 3
Dunleith, 2,600('88) .. i 7
Dupont Manor, 1,059('80) .... D 3
Edgemoor, 5,400('88) A 3
Ellendale, 313 ...... E 4
Elsmere, 5,935 ...... B 3
Fairfax, 2,075('88) .. A 3
Faulkland Heights, 1,300('88) .... i 7
Felton, 683 .... D 3
Frankford, 591 ...... F 5
Frederica, 761 ...... D 4
Georgetown, 3,732 .. F 4
Graylyn Crest, 4,380('88) .... A 3
Green Acres, 1,140('88) .... h 8
Greenville, 800('88) .. a 3
Greenwood, 578 .... E 3
Gumboro, 200('88) .. g 4
Gwinhurst, 1,340('88) h 8
Harbeson, 500('88) .. f 4
Harrington, 2,311 .... E 8
Hockessin, 2,430('88) A 3
Houston, 487 ...... E 3
Jefferson Farms, 3,130('88) .... i 7
Kenton, 232 .... D 3
Kirkwood, 350('88) .. b 3
Laurel, 3,226 ...... F 3
Lebanon, 130('88) .. d 4
Leipsic, 236 .... D 3
Lewes, 2,295 ...... E 5
Lincoln, 500('88) .... e 4
Little Creek, 167 .... D 4
Marshallton, 1,765('88) .... B 3
Middletown, 3,834 .. C 3
Midway, 500('88) .... f 5
Milford, 6,040 ...... E 4
Millsboro, 1,643 .... F 4
Milton, 1,417 ...... E 4
Minquadale, 790('88) .. i 7
Monroe Park, 1,000('88) .... h 7
Montchanin, 500('88) h 7
Newark, 25,098 .... B 3
New Castle, 4,837 .. B 3
Newport, 1,240 .... B 3
North Star, 1,030('88) A 3
Oak Orchard, 350('88) f 5
Ocean View, 606 .... F 5
Odessa, 303 ...... C 3
Port Penn, 300('88) .. b 3
Rehoboth Beach, 1,234 .... F 5
Rising Sun, 540('88) D 3
Rodney Village, 1,100('88) .... D 3
Saint Georges, 500('88) .... B 3
Seabreeze, 350('88) .. F 5
Seaford, 5,689 ...... F 3
Selbyville, 1,335 .... G 5
Sharpley, 1,250('88) .. h 7
Sherwood Park, 2,000('88) .... i 7
Silview, 1,500('88) .. B 3
Smyrna, 5,231 ...... C 3
Talleyville, 6,880('80) A 3
Townsend, 322 .... C 3
Tuxedo Park, 1,300('88) .... i 7
Willow Run, 1,600('88) i 7
Wilmington, 71,529 .. B 3
Wilmington Manor, 1,235('88) .... i 7
Wyoming, 977 ...... D 3
Yorklyn, 600('88) .... A 3

Florida

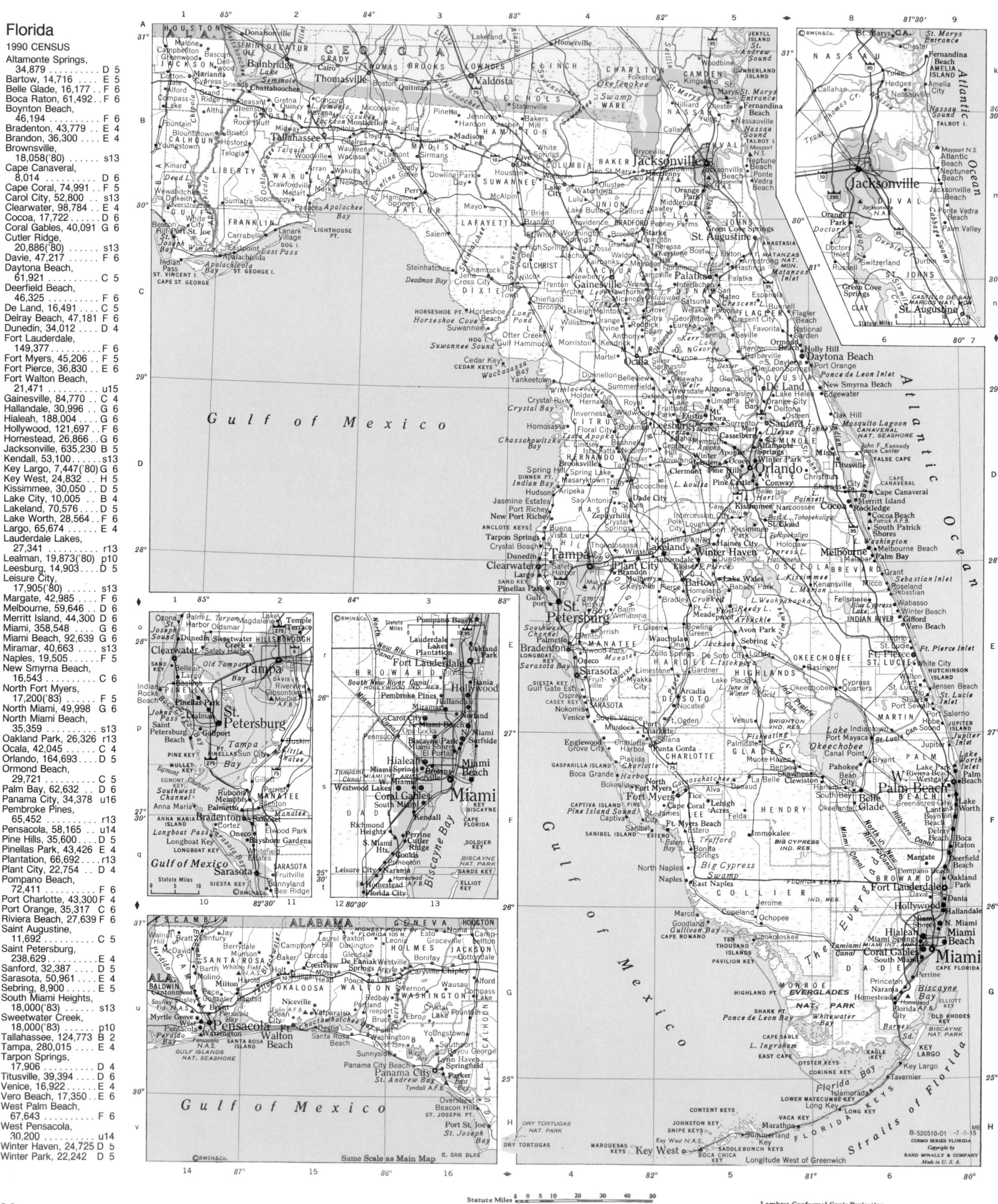

Florida

1990 CENSUS

Altamonte Springs, 34,879 .... D 5
Bartow, 14,716 .... E 5
Belle Glade, 16,177 .. F 6
Boca Raton, 61,492 .. F 6
Boynton Beach, 46,194 .... F 6
Bradenton, 43,779 .. E 4
Brandon, 36,300 .... E 4
Brownsville, 18,058('80) s13
Cape Canaveral, 8,014 .... D 6
Cape Coral, 74,991 .. F 5
Carol City, 52,800 .. s13
Clearwater, 98,784 .. E 4
Cocoa, 17,722 .... D 6
Coral Gables, 40,091 G 6
Cutler Ridge, 20,886('80) s13
Davie, 47,217 ...... F 6
Daytona Beach, 61,921 .... C 5
Deerfield Beach, 46,325 .... F 6
De Land, 16,491 .... C 5
Delray Beach, 47,181 F 6
Dunedin, 34,012 .... D 4
Fort Lauderdale, 149,377 .... F 6
Fort Myers, 45,206 .. F 5
Fort Pierce, 36,830 .. E 6
Fort Walton Beach, 21,471 .... u15
Gainesville, 84,770 .. C 4
Hallandale, 30,996 .. G 6
Hialeah, 188,004 .... G 6
Hollywood, 121,697 .. F 6
Homestead, 26,866 .. G 6
Jacksonville, 635,230 B 5
Kendall, 53,100 ...... s13
Key Largo, 7,447('80) G 6
Key West, 24,832 .. H 5
Kissimmee, 30,050 .. D 5
Lake City, 10,005 .. B 4
Lakeland, 70,576 .... D 5
Lake Worth, 28,564 .. F 6
Largo, 65,674 ...... E 4
Lauderdale Lakes, 27,341 .... r13
Lealman, 19,873('80) p10
Leesburg, 14,903 .... D 5
Leisure City, 17,905('80) s13
Margate, 42,985 .... F 6
Melbourne, 59,646 .. D 6
Merritt Island, 44,300 D 6
Miami, 358,548 ..... G 6
Miami Beach, 92,639 G 6
Miramar, 40,663 .... s13
Naples, 19,505 ...... F 5
New Smyrna Beach, 16,543 .... C 6
North Fort Myers, 17,200('83) ...... F 5
North Miami, 49,998 G 6
North Miami Beach, 35,359 .... s13
Oakland Park, 26,326 r13
Ocala, 42,045 ...... C 4
Orlando, 164,693 .... D 5
Ormond Beach, 29,721 .... C 5
Palm Bay, 62,632 .. D 6
Panama City, 34,378 u16
Pembroke Pines, 65,452 .... r13
Pensacola, 58,165 .. u14
Pine Hills, 35,600 .... D 5
Pinellas Park, 43,426 E 4
Plantation, 66,692 .... r13
Plant City, 22,754 .. D 4
Pompano Beach, 72,411 .... F 6
Port Charlotte, 43,300 F 4
Port Orange, 35,317 C 6
Riviera Beach, 27,639 F 6
Saint Augustine, 11,692 .... C 5
Saint Petersburg, 238,629 .... E 4
Sanford, 32,387 .... D 5
Sarasota, 50,961 .... E 4
Sebring, 8,900 ...... E 5
South Miami Heights, 18,000('83) s13
Sweetwater Creek, 18,000('83) p10
Tallahassee, 124,773 B 2
Tampa, 280,015 .... E 4
Tarpon Springs, 17,906 .... D 4
Titusville, 39,394 .... D 6
Venice, 16,922 ...... E 4
Vero Beach, 17,350 .. E 6
West Palm Beach, 67,643 .... F 6
West Pensacola, 30,200 .... u14
Winter Haven, 24,725 D 5
Winter Park, 22,242 D 5

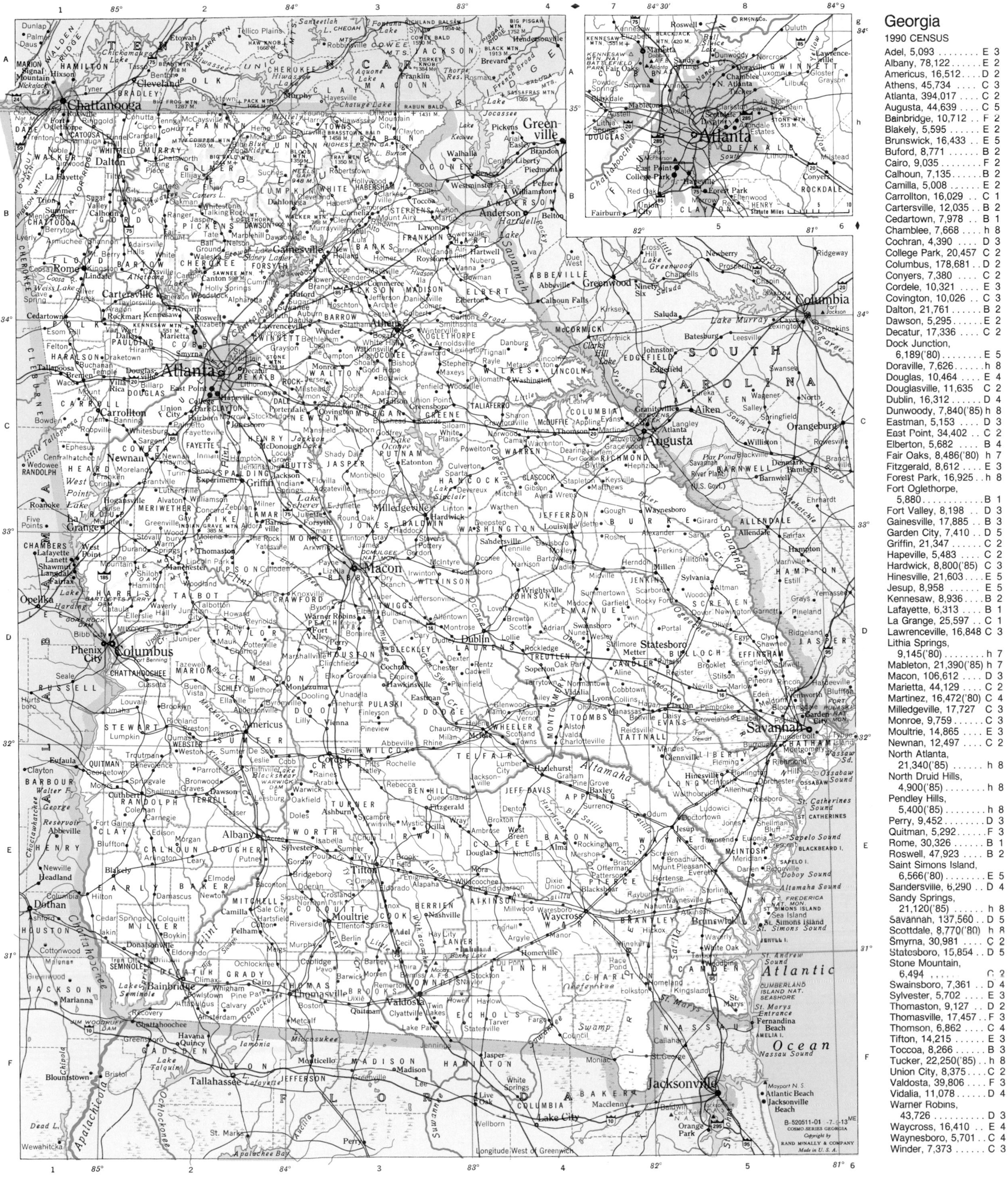

Georgia

1990 CENSUS

Adel, 5,093 . . . . E 3
Albany, 78,122 . . . . . . E 2
Americus, 16,512 . . . . D 2
Athens, 45,734 . . . . C 3
Atlanta, 394,017 . . . . C 2
Augusta, 44,639 . . . . C 5
Bainbridge, 10,712 . . F 2
Blakely, 5,595 . . . . . . E 2
Brunswick, 16,433 . . E 5
Buford, 8,771 . . . . . . B 2
Cairo, 9,035 . . . . F 2
Calhoun, 7,135 . . . . . . B 2
Camilla, 5,008 . . . . . . E 2
Carrollton, 16,029 . . C 1
Cartersville, 12,035 . . B 2
Cedartown, 7,978 . . B 1
Chamblee, 7,668 . . . . h 8
Cochran, 4,390 . . . . D 3
College Park, 20,457 C 2
Columbus, 178,681 . . D 2
Conyers, 7,380 . . . . C 2
Cordele, 10,321 . . . . E 3
Covington, 10,026 . . C 3
Dalton, 21,761 . . . . . . B 2
Dawson, 5,295 . . . . . . E 2
Decatur, 17,336 . . . . C 2
Dock Junction, 6,189('80) . . . . E 5
Doraville, 7,626 . . . . . . h 8
Douglas, 10,464 . . . . E 4
Douglasville, 11,635 C 2
Dublin, 16,312 . . . . . . D 4
Dunwoody, 7,840('85) h 8
Eastman, 5,153 . . . . D 3
East Point, 34,402 . . C 2
Elberton, 5,682 . . . . B 4
Fair Oaks, 8,486('80) h 7
Fitzgerald, 8,612 . . . . E 3
Forest Park, 16,925 . . h 8
Fort Oglethorpe, 5,880 . . . . B 1
Fort Valley, 8,198 . . D 3
Gainesville, 17,885 . . B 3
Garden City, 7,410 . . D 5
Griffin, 21,347 . . . . . . C 2
Hapeville, 5,483 . . . . C 2
Hardwick, 8,800('85) C 3
Hinesville, 21,603 . . . . E 5
Jesup, 8,958 . . . . . . E 5
Kennesaw, 8,936 . . . . B 2
Lafayette, 6,313 . . . . B 1
La Grange, 25,597 . . C 1
Lawrenceville, 16,848 C 3
Lithia Springs, 9,145('80) . . . . h 7
Mableton, 21,390('85) h 7
Macon, 106,612 . . . . D 3
Marietta, 44,129 . . . . C 2
Martinez, 16,472('80) C 4
Milledgeville, 17,727 C 3
Monroe, 9,759 . . . . . . C 3
Moultrie, 14,865 . . . . E 3
Newnan, 12,497 . . . . C 2
North Atlanta, 21,340('85) . . . . . . h 8
North Druid Hills, 4,900('85) . . . . h 8
Pendley Hills, 5,400('85) . . . . h 8
Perry, 9,452 . . . . D 3
Quitman, 5,292 . . . . . . F 3
Rome, 30,326 . . . . . . B 1
Roswell, 47,923 . . . . B 2
Saint Simons Island, 6,566('80) . . . . E 5
Sandersville, 6,290 . . D 4
Sandy Springs, 21,120('85) . . . . . . h 8
Savannah, 137,560 . . D 5
Scottdale, 8,770('80) h 8
Smyrna, 30,981 . . . . C 2
Statesboro, 15,854 . . D 5
Stone Mountain, 6,494 . . . . . . C 2
Swainsboro, 7,361 . . D 4
Sylvester, 5,702 . . . . E 3
Thomaston, 9,127 . . D 2
Thomasville, 17,457 . . F 3
Thomson, 6,862 . . . . C 4
Tifton, 14,215 . . . . . . E 3
Toccoa, 8,266 . . . . . . B 3
Tucker, 22,250('85) . . h 8
Union City, 8,375 . . . . C 2
Valdosta, 39,806 . . . . F 3
Vidalia, 11,078 . . . . . . D 4
Warner Robins, 43,726 . . . . D 3
Waycross, 16,410 . . E 4
Waynesboro, 5,701 . . C 4
Winder, 7,373 . . . . . . C 3

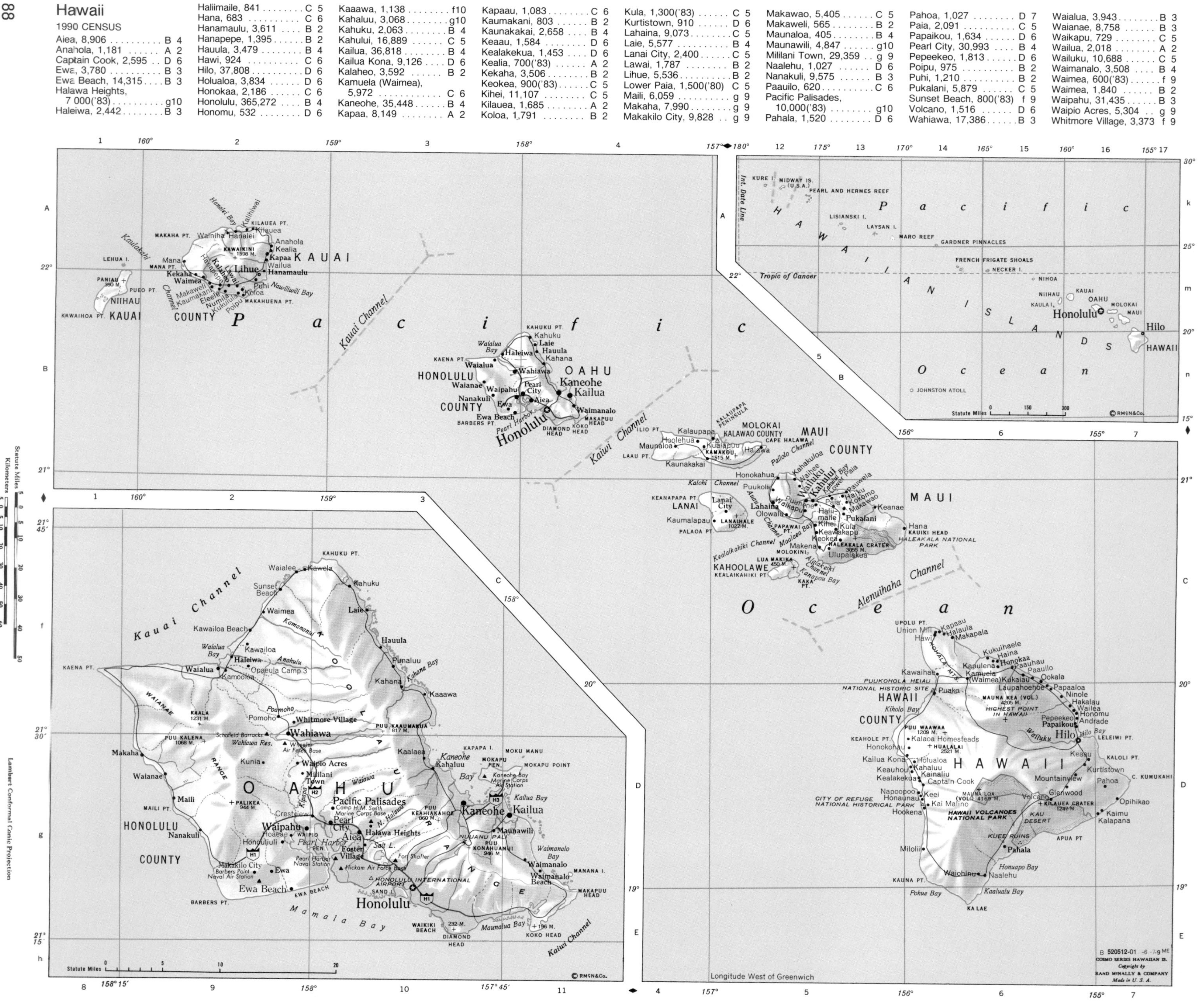
Hawaii
1990 CENSUS
Aiea, 8,906 . . . . B 4
Anahola, 1,181 . . . . . . A 2
Captain Cook, 2,595 . . D 6
Ewa, 3,780 . . . . B 3
Ewa Beach, 14,315 . . . . B 3
Halawa Heights, 7 000('83) g10
Haleiwa, 2,442 . . . . B 3
Haliimaile, 841 . . . . C 5
Hana, 683 . . . . C 6
Hanamaulu, 3,611 . . . . B 2
Hanapepe, 1,395 . . . . . . B 2
Hauula, 3,479 . . . . B 4
Hawi, 924 . . . . C 6
Hilo, 37,808 . . . . D 6
Holualoa, 3,834 . . . . . . D 6
Honokaa, 2,186 . . . . . . C 6
Honolulu, 365,272 . . . . B 4
Honomu, 532 . . . . D 6
Kaaawa, 1,138 . . . . f10
Kahaluu, 3,068 . . . . g10
Kahuku, 2,063 . . . . B 4
Kahului, 16,889 . . . . . . C 5
Kailua, 36,818 . . . . B 4
Kailua Kona, 9,126 . . . . D 6
Kalaheo, 3,592 . . . . . . B 2
Kamuela (Waimea), 5,972 . . . . C 6
Kaneohe, 35,448 . . . . . . B 4
Kapaa, 8,149 . . . . A 2
Kapaau, 1,083 . . . . C 6
Kaumakani, 803 . . . . . . B 2
Kaunakakai, 2,658 . . . . B 4
Keaau, 1,584 . . . . D 6
Kealakekua, 1,453 . . . . D 6
Kealia, 700('83) . . . . . . A 2
Kekaha, 3,506 . . . . B 2
Keokea, 900('83) . . . . . . C 5
Kihei, 11,107 . . . . C 5
Kilauea, 1,685 . . . . A 2
Koloa, 1,791 . . . . B 2
Kula, 1,300('83) . . . . . . C 5
Kurtistown, 910 . . . . . . D 6
Lahaina, 9,073 . . . . C 5
Laie, 5,577 . . . . B 4
Lanai City, 2,400 . . . . . . C 5
Lawai, 1,787 . . . . B 2
Lihue, 5,536 . . . . B 2
Lower Paia, 1,500('80) C 5
Maili, 6,059 . . . . g 9
Makaha, 7,990 . . . . g 9
Makakilo City, 9,828 . . g 9
Makawao, 5,405 . . . . . . C 5
Makaweli, 565 . . . . B 2
Maunaloa, 405 . . . . B 4
Maunawili, 4,847 . . . . g10
Mililani Town, 29,359 . . . g 9
Naalehu, 1,027 . . . . . . D 6
Nanakuli, 9,575 . . . . . . B 3
Paauilo, 620 . . . . C 6
Pacific Palisades, 10,000('83) g10
Pahala, 1,520 . . . . D 6
Pahoa, 1,027 . . . . D 7
Paia, 2,091 . . . . C 5
Papaikou, 1,634 . . . . . . D 6
Pearl City, 30,993 . . . . B 4
Pepeekeo, 1,813 . . . . . . D 6
Poipu, 975 . . . . B 2
Puhi, 1,210 . . . . B 2
Pukalani, 5,879 . . . . . . C 5
Sunset Beach, 800('83) f 9
Volcano, 1,516 . . . . . . D 6
Wahiawa, 17,386 . . . . . . B 3
Waialua, 3,943 . . . . B 3
Waianae, 8,758 . . . . . . B 3
Waikapu, 729 . . . . C 5
Wailua, 2,018 . . . . A 2
Wailuku, 10,688 . . . . . . C 5
Waimanalo, 3,508 . . . . B 4
Waimea, 600('83) . . . . . . f 9
Waimea, 1,840 . . . . . . B 2
Waipahu, 31,435 . . . . . . B 3
Waipio Acres, 5,304 . . g 9
Whitmore Village, 3,373 f 9
KAUAI
NIIHAU
KAUAI COUNTY
Kauai Channel
Kaulakahi Channel
HONOLULU COUNTY
OAHU
Kaiwi Channel
MOLOKAI
KALAWAO COUNTY
MAUI COUNTY
LANAI
KAHOOLAWE
MAUI
Alenuihaha Channel
HAWAII
HAWAII COUNTY
Pacific Ocean
HAWAIIAN ISLANDS
Tropic of Cancer
Int. Date Line
JOHNSTON ATOLL
Mamala Bay
Honolulu
Kaneohe
Kailua
Pearl Harbor
Hilo
Longitude West of Greenwich
Statute Miles
Kilometers
Lambert Conformal Conic Projection
B 520512-01 -6 -7-9 ME
COSMO SERIES HAWAIIAN IS.
Copyright by RAND McNALLY & COMPANY
Made in U. S. A.

Idaho

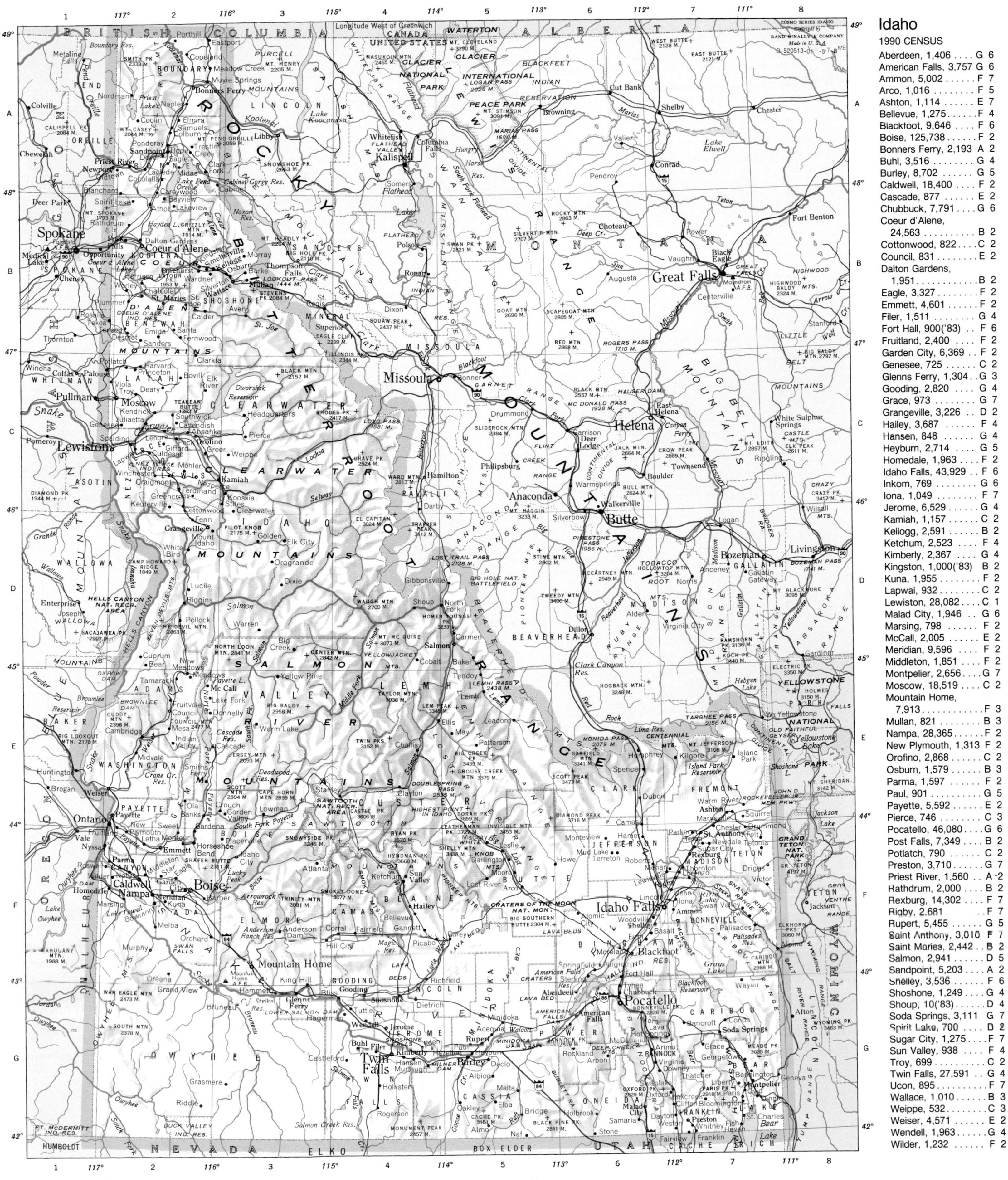

Idaho

1990 CENSUS

Aberdeen, 1,406 . . . . G 6
American Falls, 3,757 G 6
Ammon, 5,002 . . . . . . F 7
Arco, 1,016 . . . . F 5
Ashton, 1,114 . . . . . . E 7
Bellevue, 1,275 . . . . . F 4
Blackfoot, 9,646 . . . . F 6
Boise, 125,738 . . . . . F 2
Bonners Ferry, 2,193 A 2
Buhl, 3,516 . . . . G 4
Burley, 8,702 . . . . . . G 5
Caldwell, 18,400 . . . . F 2
Cascade, 877 . . . . . . E 2
Chubbuck, 7,791 . . . . G 6
Coeur d'Alene, 24,563 . . . . B 2
Cottonwood, 822 . . . . C 2
Council, 831 . . . . E 2
Dalton Gardens, 1,951 . . . . B 2
Eagle, 3,327 . . . . F 2
Emmett, 4,601 . . . . . . F 2
Filer, 1,511 . . . . G 4
Fort Hall, 900('83) . . . F 6
Fruitland, 2,400 . . . . F 2
Garden City, 6,369 . . F 2
Genesee, 725 . . . . . . C 2
Glenns Ferry, 1,304 . . G 3
Gooding, 2,820 . . . . G 4
Grace, 973 . . . . G 7
Grangeville, 3,226 . . D 2
Hailey, 3,687 . . . . . . F 4
Hansen, 848 . . . . . . G 4
Heyburn, 2,714 . . . . G 5
Homedale, 1,963 . . . . F 2
Idaho Falls, 43,929 . . F 6
Inkom, 769 . . . . G 6
Iona, 1,049 . . . . F 7
Jerome, 6,529 . . . . . . G 4
Kamiah, 1,157 . . . . . . C 2
Kellogg, 2,591 . . . . . . B 2
Ketchum, 2,523 . . . . F 4
Kimberly, 2,367 . . . . G 4
Kingston, 1,000('83) B 2
Kuna, 1,955 . . . . F 2
Lapwai, 932 . . . . C 2
Lewiston, 28,082 . . . . C 1
Malad City, 1,946 . . G 6
Marsing, 798 . . . . . . F 2
McCall, 2,005 . . . . . . E 2
Meridian, 9,596 . . . . F 2
Middleton, 1,851 . . . . . F 2
Montpelier, 2,656 . . . . G 7
Moscow, 18,519 . . . . C 2
Mountain Home, 7,913 . . . . F 3
Mullan, 821 . . . . B 3
Nampa, 28,365 . . . . . . F 2
New Plymouth, 1,313 F 2
Orofino, 2,868 . . . . . . C 2
Osburn, 1,579 . . . . . . B 3
Parma, 1,597 . . . . . . F 2
Paul, 901 . . . . G 5
Payette, 5,592 . . . . . . E 2
Pierce, 746 . . . . C 3
Pocatello, 46,080 . . . . G 6
Post Falls, 7,349 . . . . B 2
Potlatch, 790 . . . . . . C 2
Preston, 3,710 . . . . . . G 7
Priest River, 1,560 . . A 2
Rathdrum, 2,000 . . . . B 2
Rexburg, 14,302 . . . . F 7
Rigby, 2,681 . . . . F 7
Rupert, 5,455 . . . . . . G 5
Saint Anthony, 3,010 F 7
Saint Maries, 2,442 . . B 2
Salmon, 2,941 . . . . . . D 5
Sandpoint, 5,203 . . . . A 2
Shelley, 3,536 . . . . . . F 6
Shoshone, 1,249 . . . . G 4
Shoup, 10('83) . . . . . . D 4
Soda Springs, 3,111 G 7
Spirit Lake, 700 . . . . D 2
Sugar City, 1,275 . . . . F 7
Sun Valley, 938 . . . . F 4
Troy, 699 . . . . C 2
Twin Falls, 27,591 . . G 4
Ucon, 895 . . . . F 7
Wallace, 1,010 . . . . . . B 3
Weippe, 532 . . . . C 3
Weiser, 4,571 . . . . . . E 2
Wendell, 1,963 . . . . . G 4
Wilder, 1,232 . . . . . . F 2

Illinois

Illinois

1990 CENSUS

Addison, 32,058 .... k 8
Alton, 32,905 ...... E 3
Arlington Heights,
75,460 .... A 5
Aurora, 99,581 ..... B 5
Belleville, 42,785 .... E 4
Berwyn, 45,426 .... k 9
Bloomington, 51,972 C 4
Bolingbrook, 40,843 . k 8
Bourbonnais, 13,934 B 6
Brookfield, 18,876 .. k 9
Burbank, 27,600 .... k 9
Cahokia, 17,550 .... E 3
Cairo, 4,846 .... F 4
Calumet City, 37,840 B 6
Canton, 13,922 .... C 3
Carbondale, 27,033 .. F 4
Centralia, 14,274 .... E 4
Champaign, 63,502 .. C 5
Charleston, 20,398 .. D 5
Chicago, 2,783,726 .. B 6
Chicago Heights,
33,072 .... B 6
Cicero, 67,436 ..... B 6
Danville, 33,828 .... C 6
Decatur, 83,885 .... D 5
De Kalb, 34,925 .... B 5
Des Plaines, 53,223 .. A 6
Dixon, 15,144 ...... B 4
Downers Grove,
46,858 .... B 5
East Saint Louis,
40,944 .... E 3
Elgin, 77,010 ...... A 5
Elk Grove Village,
33,429 .... h 9
Elmhurst, 42,029 .... B 6
Evanston, 73,233 .... A 6
Freeport, 25,840 .... A 4
Galena, 3,647 ...... A 3
Galesburg, 33,530 .. C 3
Glenview, 37,093 .... h 9
Granite City, 32,862 .. E 3
Gurnee, 13,701 .... h 9
Hanover Park, 32,895 k 8
Harvey, 29,771 .... B 6
Highland Park, 30,575 A 6
Hoffman Estates,
46,561 .... h 8
Jacksonville, 19,324 D 3
Joliet, 76,836 ...... B 5
Kankakee, 27,575 .. B 6
Kewanee, 12,969 .... B 4
Lake Forest, 17,836 A 6
Lansing, 28,086 .... B 6
La Salle, 9,717 ..... B 4
Lincoln, 15,418 .... C 4
Lombard, 39,408 .... k 8
Macomb, 19,952 .... C 3
Marion, 14,545 ..... F 5
Mattoon, 18,441 .... D 5
Moline, 43,202 ..... B 3
Monmouth, 9,489 .. C 3
Mount Prospect,
53,170 .... A 6
Mount Vernon, 16,988 E 5
Naperville, 85,351 .. B 5
Nauvoo, 1,108 ...... C 2
Niles, 28,284 .... h 9
Normal, 40,023 .... C 5
Northbrook, 32,308 .. h 9
North Chicago,
34,978 .... A 6
Oak Lawn, 56,182 .. B 6
Oak Park, 53,648 .. B 6
Ottawa, 17,451 .... B 5
Palatine, 39,253 .... A 5
Park Ridge, 36,175 .. B 6
Pekin, 32,254 ...... C 4
Peoria, 113,504 .... C 4
Peru, 9,302 .... B 4
Pontiac, 11,428 .... C 5
Quincy, 39,681 ...... D 2
Rockford, 139,426 .. A 4
Rock Island, 40,552 .. B 3
Salem, 7,470 ...... E 5
Schaumburg, 68,586 h 8
Skokie, 59,432 ...... A 6
Springfield, 105,227 .. D 4
Sterling, 15,132 .... B 4
Streator, 14,121 .... B 5
Taylorville, 11,133 .. D 4
Tinley Park, 37,121 .. k 9
Urbana, 36,344 .... C 5
Vandalia, 6,114 .... E 4
Waukegan, 69,392 .. A 6
Wheaton, 51,464 .... B 5
Zion, 19,775 .... A 6

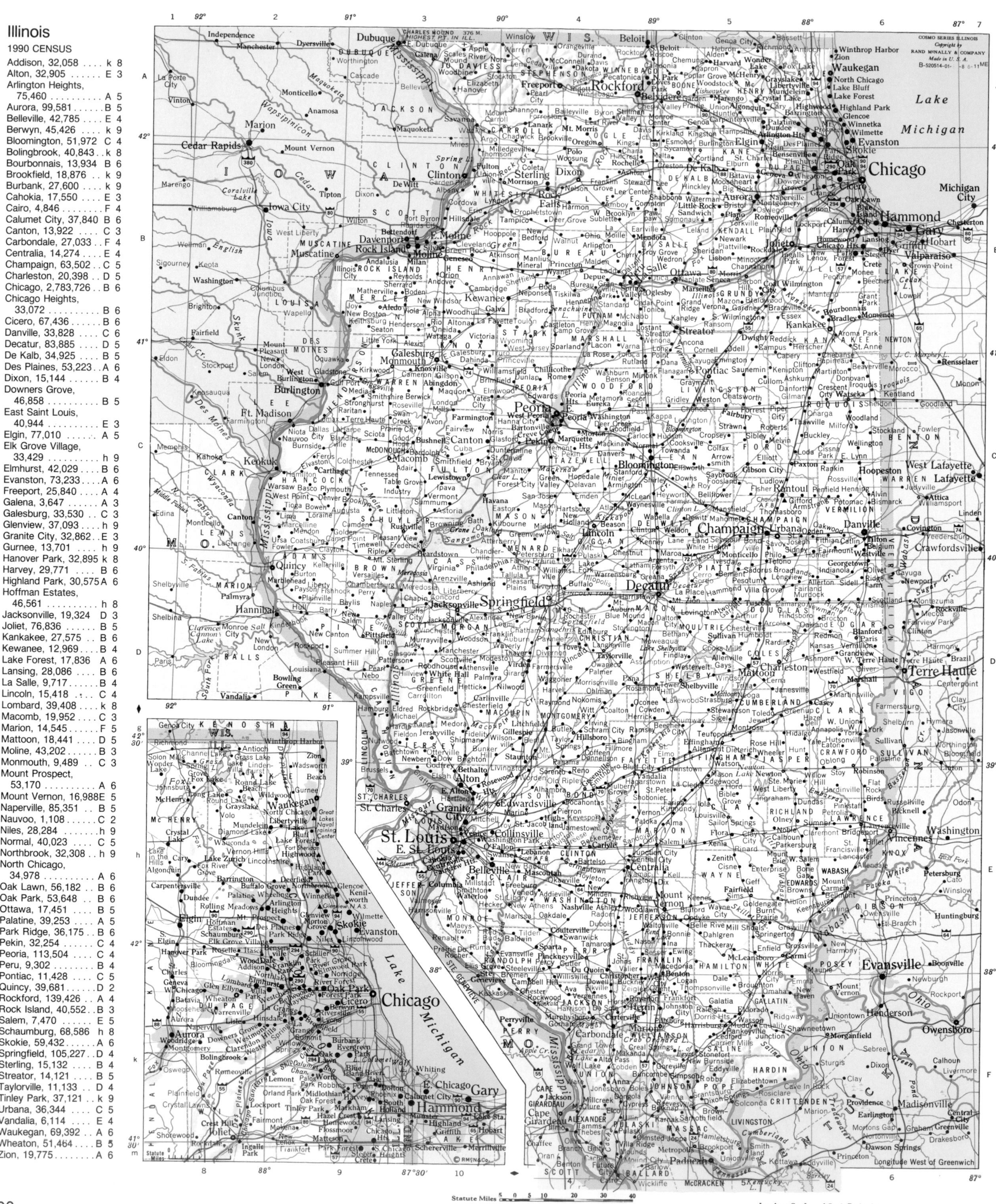

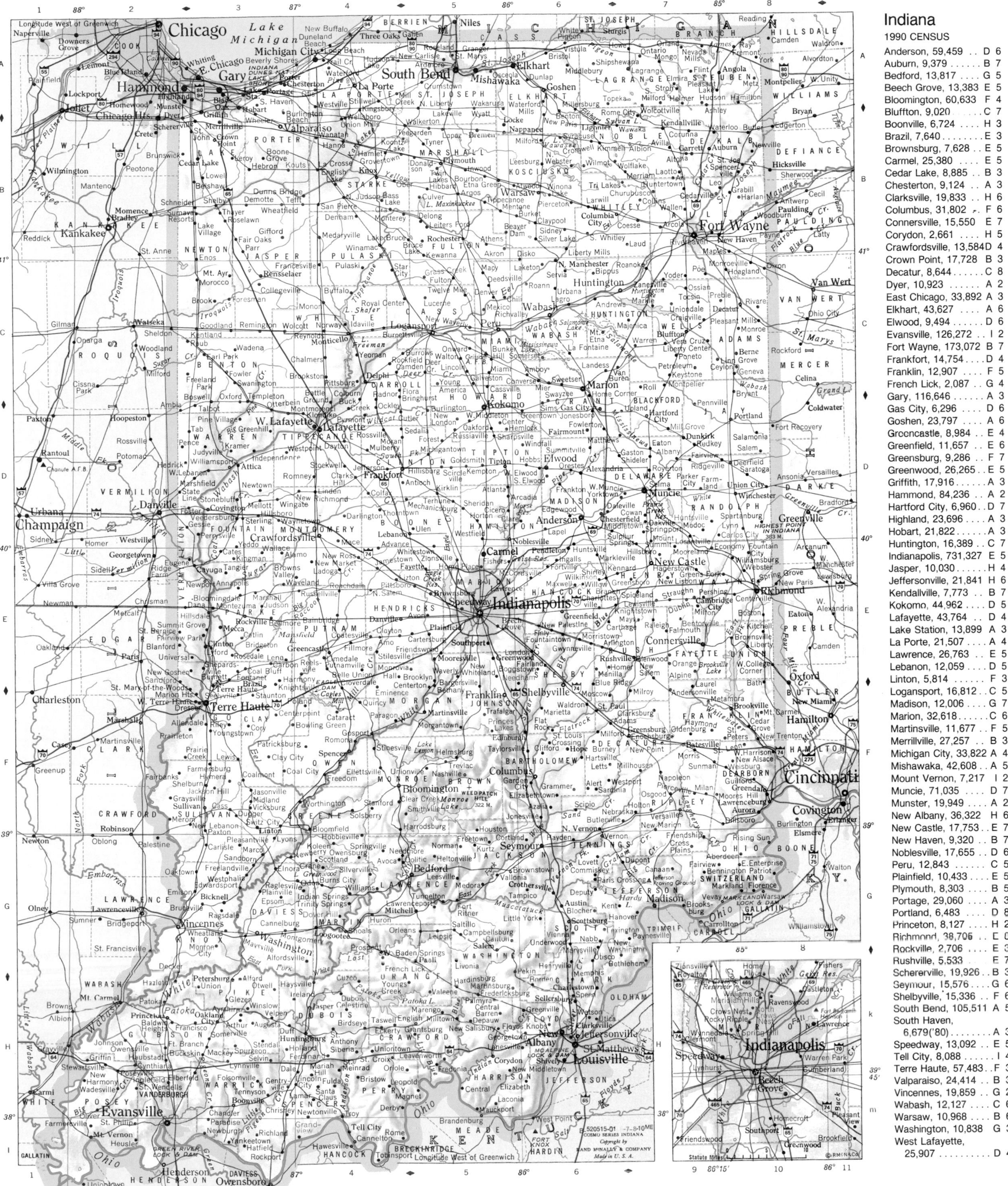

Indiana

1990 CENSUS

Anderson, 59,459 .. D 6
Auburn, 9,379 ...... B 7
Bedford, 13,817 .... G 5
Beech Grove, 13,383 E 5
Bloomington, 60,633 F 4
Bluffton, 9,020 ..... C 7
Boonville, 6,724 ..... H 3
Brazil, 7,640 .... E 3
Brownsburg, 7,628 .. E 5
Carmel, 25,380 ...... E 5
Cedar Lake, 8,885 .. B 3
Chesterton, 9,124 .. A 3
Clarksville, 19,833 .. H 6
Columbus, 31,802 .. F 6
Connersville, 15,550 E 7
Corydon, 2,661 .... H 5
Crawfordsville, 13,584D 4
Crown Point, 17,728 B 3
Decatur, 8,644 ...... C 8
Dyer, 10,923 .... A 2
East Chicago, 33,892 A 3
Elkhart, 43,627 .... A 6
Elwood, 9,494 ...... D 6
Evansville, 126,272 .. I 2
Fort Wayne, 173,072 B 7
Frankfort, 14,754 .... D 4
Franklin, 12,907 .... F 5
French Lick, 2,087 .. G 4
Gary, 116,646 ...... A 3
Gas City, 6,296 .... D 6
Goshen, 23,797 .... A 6
Greencastle, 8,984 .. E 4
Greenfield, 11,657 .. E 6
Greensburg, 9,286 .. F 7
Greenwood, 26,265 .. E 5
Griffith, 17,916 ...... A 3
Hammond, 84,236 .. A 2
Hartford City, 6,960 .. D 7
Highland, 23,696 .... A 3
Hobart, 21,822 ...... A 3
Huntington, 16,389 .. C 7
Indianapolis, 731,327 E 5
Jasper, 10,030 ...... H 4
Jeffersonville, 21,841 H 6
Kendallville, 7,773 .. B 7
Kokomo, 44,962 .... D 5
Lafayette, 43,764 .. D 4
Lake Station, 13,899 A 3
La Porte, 21,507 .... A 4
Lawrence, 26,763 .. E 5
Lebanon, 12,059 .... D 5
Linton, 5,814 .... F 3
Logansport, 16,812 .. C 5
Madison, 12,006 .... G 7
Marion, 32,618 ...... C 6
Martinsville, 11,677 .. F 5
Merrillville, 27,257 .. B 3
Michigan City, 33,822 A 4
Mishawaka, 42,608 .. A 5
Mount Vernon, 7,217 I 2
Muncie, 71,035 .... D 7
Munster, 19,949 .... A 2
New Albany, 36,322 H 6
New Castle, 17,753 .. E 7
New Haven, 9,320 .. B 7
Noblesville, 17,655 .. D 6
Peru, 12,843 ...... C 5
Plainfield, 10,433 .... E 5
Plymouth, 8,303 .... B 5
Portage, 29,060 .... A 3
Portland, 6,483 .... D 8
Princeton, 8,127 .... H 2
Richmond, 38,705 .... E 8
Rockville, 2,706 .... E 3
Rushville, 5,533 .... E 7
Schererville, 19,926 .. B 3
Seymour, 15,576 .... G 6
Shelbyville, 15,336 .. F 6
South Bend, 105,511 A 5
South Haven, 6,679('80) .... A 3
Speedway, 13,092 .. E 5
Tell City, 8,088 ...... I 4
Terre Haute, 57,483 .. F 3
Valparaiso, 24,414 .. B 3
Vincennes, 19,859 .. G 2
Wabash, 12,127 .... C 6
Warsaw, 10,968 .... B 6
Washington, 10,838 G 3
West Lafayette, 25,907 .... D 4

Iowa

1990 CENSUS

- Algona, 6,015 . . . . A 3
- Altoona, 7,191 . . . . . . C 4
- Amana, 540('87) . . . . . C 6
- Ames, 47,198 . . . . B 4
- Anamosa, 5,100 . . . . . B 6
- Ankeny, 18,482 . . . . . C 4
- Atlantic, 7,432 . . . . . . C 2
- Bettendorf, 28,132 . . . . C 7
- Boone, 12,392 . . . . B 4
- Burlington, 27,208 . . . . D 6
- Camanche, 4,436 . . . . C 7
- Carroll, 9,579 . . . . B 3
- Cedar Falls, 34,298 . . . B 5
- Cedar Rapids, 108,751 C 6
- Centerville, 5,936 . . . . . D 5
- Chariton, 4,616 . . . . . . C 4
- Charles City, 7,878 . . . A 5
- Cherokee, 6,026 . . . . . B 2
- Clarinda, 5,104 . . . . . D 2
- Clear Lake, 8,183 . . . . A 4
- Clinton, 29,201 . . . . . . C 7
- Clive, 7,462 . . . . e 8
- Coralville, 10,347 . . . . . C 6
- Council Bluffs, 54,315 . . C 2
- Creston, 7,911 . . . . C 3
- Davenport, 95,333 . . . . C 7
- Decorah, 8,063 . . . . . . A 6
- Denison, 6,604 . . . . . . B 2
- Des Moines, 193,187 . . C 4
- Dubuque, 57,546 . . . . . B 7
- Estherville, 6,720 . . . . . . A 3
- Evansdale, 4,638 . . . . . B 5
- Fairfield, 9,768 . . . . C 6
- Forest City, 4,430 . . . . A 4
- Fort Dodge, 25,894 . . . B 3
- Fort Madison, 11,618 . . D 6
- Glenwood, 4,571 . . . . . . C 2
- Grinnell, 8,902 . . . . C 5
- Hampton, 4,133 . . . . . . B 4
- Harlan, 5,148 . . . . C 2
- Hiawatha, 4,986 . . . . . . B 6
- Humboldt, 4,438 . . . . . . B 3
- Independence, 5,972 . . B 6
- Indianola, 11,340 . . . . . C 4
- Iowa City, 59,738 . . . . . C 6
- Iowa Falls, 5,424 . . . . . B 4
- Jefferson, 4,292 . . . . . . B 3
- Keokuk, 12,451 . . . . . . D 6
- Knoxville, 8,232 . . . . . . C 4
- Le Mars, 8,454 . . . . B 1
- Manchester, 5,137 . . . . B 6
- Maquoketa, 6,111 . . . . B 7
- Marion, 20,403 . . . . . . B 6
- Marshalltown, 25,178 . . B 5
- Mason City, 29,040 . . . . A 4
- Mount Pleasant, 8,027 D 6
- Muscatine, 22,881 . . . . C 6
- Nevada, 6,009 . . . . B 4
- New Hampton, 3,660 . . A 5
- Newton, 14,789 . . . . . . C 4
- Oelwein, 6,493 . . . . B 6
- Orange City, 4,940 . . . . B 1
- Oskaloosa, 10,632 . . . . C 5
- Ottumwa, 24,488 . . . . C 5
- Pella, 9,270 . . . . C 5
- Perry, 6,652 . . . . C 3
- Red Oak, 6,264 . . . . . . D 2
- Sheldon, 4,937 . . . . . . A 2
- Shenandoah, 5,572 . . . D 2
- Sioux Center, 5,074 . . . A 1
- Sioux City, 80,505 . . . . B 1
- Spencer, 11,066 . . . . . . A 2
- Spirit Lake, 3,871 . . . . A 2
- Storm Lake, 8,769 . . . . B 2
- Urbandale, 23,500 . . . . C 4
- Vinton, 5,103 . . . . B 5
- Washington, 7,074 . . . . C 6
- Waterloo, 66,467 . . . . . B 5
- Waukon, 4,019 . . . . . . A 6
- Waverly, 8,539 . . . . . . B 5
- Webster City, 7,894 . . B 4
- West Branch, 1,908 . . C 6
- West Des Moines, 31,702 . . . . C 4
- Windsor Heights, 5,190 e 8

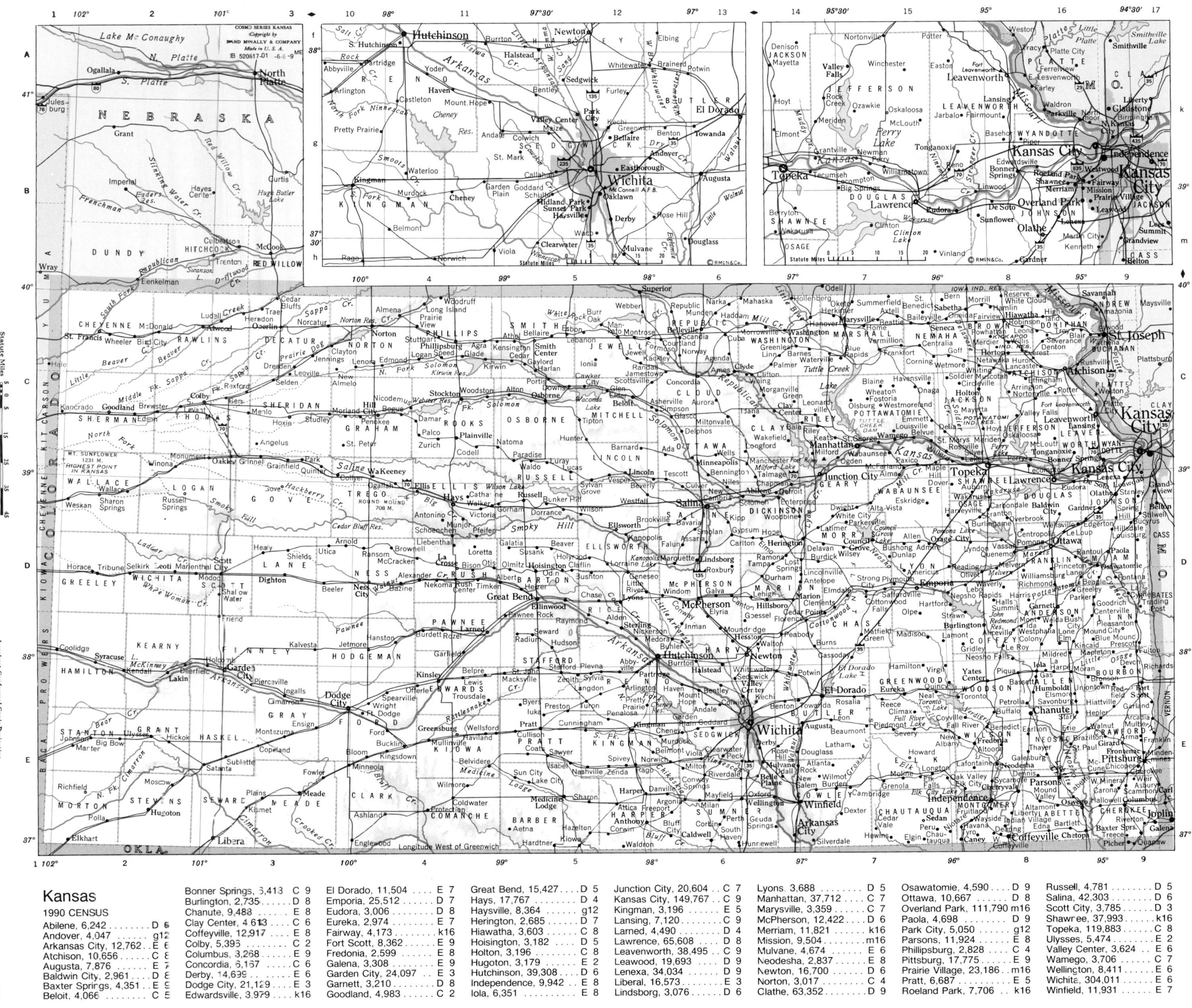

Kansas

1990 CENSUS

Place	Grid
Abilene, 6,242	D 6
Andover, 4,047	g12
Arkansas City, 12,762	E 6
Atchison, 10,656	C 8
Augusta, 7,876	E 7
Baldwin City, 2,961	D 8
Baxter Springs, 4,351	E 9
Beloit, 4,066	C 5
Bonner Springs, 3,413	C 9
Burlington, 2,735	D 8
Chanute, 9,488	E 8
Clay Center, 4,613	C 6
Coffeyville, 12,917	E 8
Colby, 5,396	C 2
Columbus, 3,268	E 9
Concordia, 6,167	C 6
Derby, 14,699	E 6
Dodge City, 21,129	E 3
Edwardsville, 3,979	k16
El Dorado, 11,504	E 7
Emporia, 25,512	D 7
Eudora, 3,006	D 8
Eureka, 2,974	E 7
Fairway, 4,173	k16
Fort Scott, 8,362	E 9
Fredonia, 2,599	E 8
Galena, 3,308	E 9
Garden City, 24,097	E 3
Garnett, 3,210	D 8
Goodland, 4,983	C 2
Great Bend, 15,427	D 5
Hays, 17,767	D 4
Haysville, 8,364	g12
Herington, 2,685	D 7
Hiawatha, 3,603	C 8
Hoisington, 3,182	D 5
Holton, 3,196	C 8
Hugoton, 3,179	E 2
Hutchinson, 39,308	D 6
Independence, 9,942	E 8
Iola, 6,351	E 8
Junction City, 20,604	C 7
Kansas City, 149,767	C 9
Kingman, 3,196	E 5
Lansing, 7,120	C 9
Larned, 4,490	D 4
Lawrence, 65,608	D 8
Leavenworth, 38,495	C 9
Leawood, 19,693	D 9
Lenexa, 34,034	D 9
Liberal, 16,573	E 3
Lindsborg, 3,076	D 6
Lyons, 3,688	D 5
Manhattan, 37,712	C 7
Marysville, 3,359	C 7
McPherson, 12,422	D 6
Merriam, 11,821	k16
Mission, 9,504	m16
Mulvane, 4,674	E 6
Neodesha, 2,837	E 8
Newton, 16,700	D 6
Norton, 3,017	C 4
Olathe, 63,352	D 9
Osawatomie, 4,590	D 9
Ottawa, 10,667	D 8
Overland Park, 111,790	m16
Paola, 4,698	D 9
Park City, 5,050	g12
Parsons, 11,924	E 8
Phillipsburg, 2,828	C 4
Pittsburg, 17,775	E 9
Prairie Village, 23,186	m16
Pratt, 6,687	E 5
Roeland Park, 7,706	k16
Russell, 4,781	D 5
Salina, 42,303	D 6
Scott City, 3,785	D 3
Shawnee, 37,993	k16
Topeka, 119,883	C 8
Ulysses, 5,474	E 2
Valley Center, 3,624	E 6
Wamego, 3,706	C 7
Wellington, 8,411	E 6
Wichita, 304,011	E 6
Winfield, 11,931	E 7

Kentucky

1990 CENSUS

Alexandria, 5,592 .... B 5
Ashland, 23,622 ...... B 7
Barbourville, 3,658 .... D 6
Bardstown, 6,801 ...... C 4
Bellevue, 6,997 ...... h13
Benton, 3,899 .... f 9
Berea, 9,126 .... C 5
Bowling Green, 40,641 D 3
Campbellsville, 9,577 .. C 4
Carrollton, 3,715 ...... B 4
Cave City, 1,953 ...... C 4
Central City, 4,979 .... C 2
Columbia, 3,845 ...... C 4
Corbin, 7,419 .... D 5
Covington, 43,264 ..... A 5
Cumberland, 3,112 .... D 7
Cynthiana, 6,497 ...... B 5
Danville, 12,420 ...... C 5
Dayton, 6,576 .... h14
Edgewood, 8,143 ...... h13
Elizabethtown, 18,167 C 4
Elsmere, 6,847 ...... B 5
Erlanger, 15,979 ...... A 5
Flatwoods, 7,799 ...... B 7
Florence, 18,624 ...... A 5
Fort Mitchell, 7,438 .... h13
Fort Thomas, 16,032 .. h14
Fort Wright, 6,570 .... h13
Frankfort, 25,968 ...... B 5
Franklin, 7,607 .... D 3
Georgetown, 11,414 .. B 5
Glasgow, 12,351 ...... C 4
Greenville, 4,689 ...... C 2
Harrodsburg, 7,335 .... C 5
Hazard, 5,416 .... C 6
Henderson, 25,945 .... C 2
Hopkinsville, 29,809 ... D 2
Independence, 10,444 . B 5
Jeffersontown, 23,221 B 4
Lawrenceburg, 5,911 .. B 5
Lebanon, 5,695 ...... C 4
Leitchfield, 4,965 ...... C 3
Lexington, 225,366 .... B 5
London, 5,757 .... C 5
Louisville, 269,063 .... B 4
Ludlow, 4,736 .... h13
Madisonville, 16,200 ... C 2
Mayfield, 9,935 .... f 9
Maysville, 7,169 ...... B 6
Middlesboro, 11,328 .. D 6
Monticello, 5,357 ...... D 5
Morehead, 8,357 ...... B 6
Morganfield, 3,776 .... C 2
Mount Sterling, 5,362 .. B 6
Mount Washington, 5,226 .... B 4
Murray, 14,439 .... f 9
Newport, 18,871 ...... A 5
Nicholasville, 13,603 .. C 5
Owensboro, 53,549 .. C 2
Paducah, 27,256 ...... e 9
Paintsville, 4,354 ...... C 7
Paris, 8,730 .... B 5
Pikeville, 6,324 ...... C 7
Prestonsburg, 3,558 ... C 7
Princeton, 6,940 ...... C 2
Providence, 4,123 .... C 2
Radcliff, 19,772 ...... C 4
Richmond, 21,155 .... C 5
Russell, 4,014 .... B 7
Russellville, 7,454 .... D 3
Saint Matthews, 15,800 B 4
Scottsville, 4,278 ...... D 3
Shelbyville, 6,238 ...... B 4
Shepherdsville, 4,805 .. C 4
Shively, 15,535 ...... B 4
Somerset, 10,733 .... C 5
Taylor Mill, 5,530 ...... k14
Tompkinsville, 2,861 .. D 4
Valley Station, 20,000('84) g11
Versailles, 7,269 ...... B 5
Williamsburg, 5,493 .. D 5
Wilmore, 4,215 .... C 5
Winchester, 15,799 .... C 5

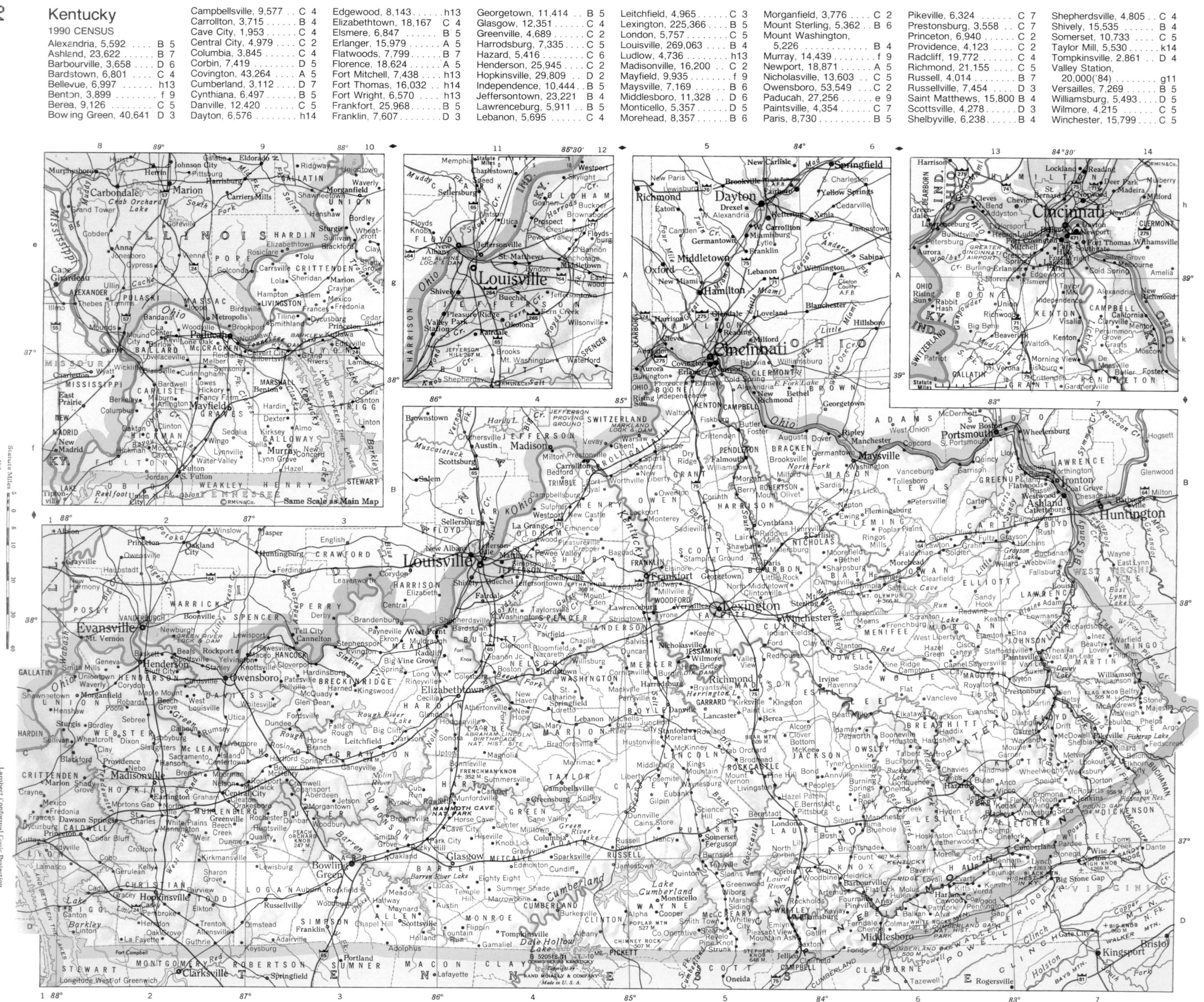

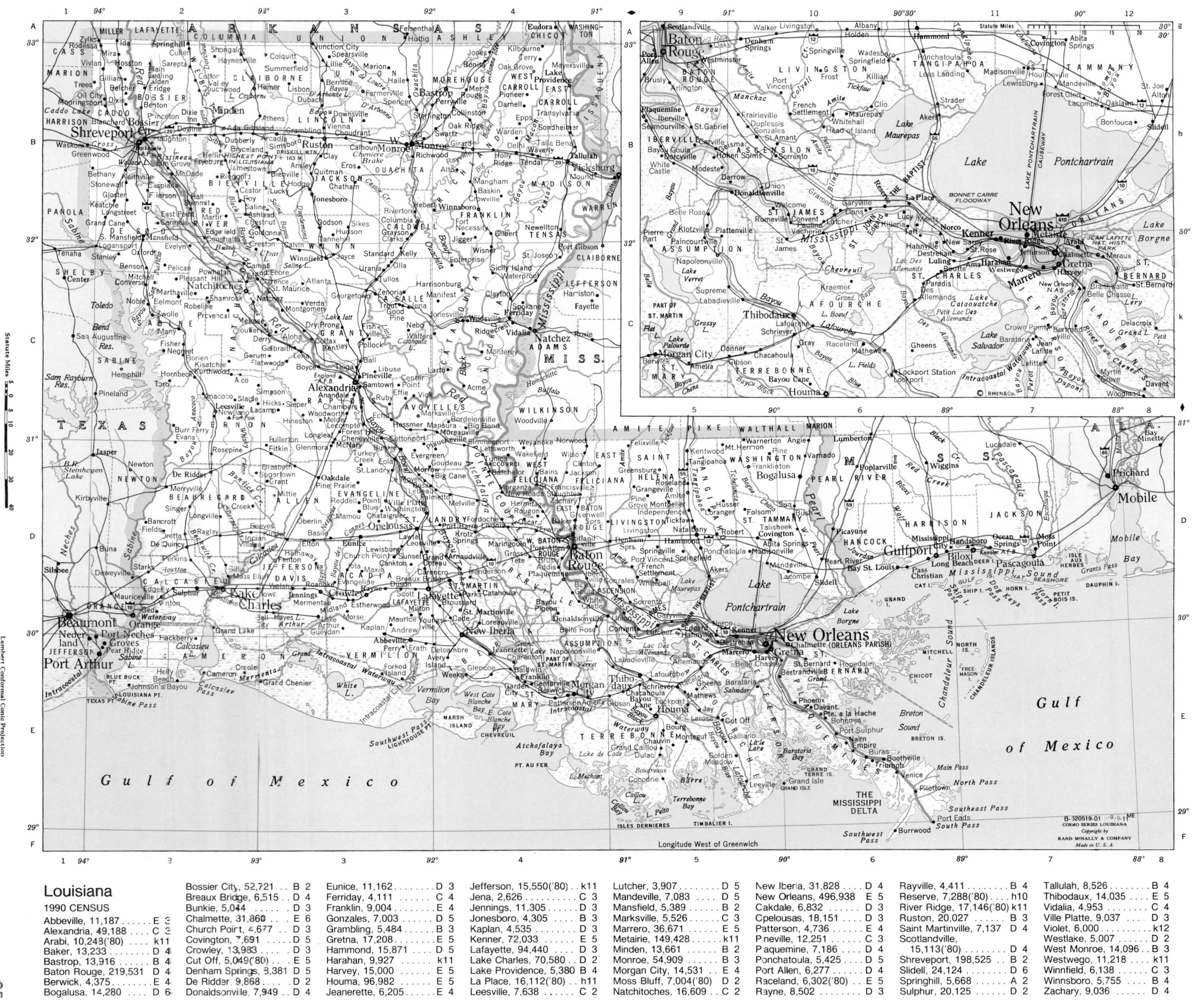

Louisiana

1990 CENSUS

Abbeville, 11,187 . . . . . E 3
Alexandria, 49,188 . . . . C 3
Arabi, 10,248('80) k11
Baker, 13,233 . . . . D 4
Bastrop, 13,916 . . . . . . B 4
Baton Rouge, 219,531 D 4
Berwick, 4,375 . . . . E 4
Bogalusa, 14,280 . . . . D 6
Bossier City, 52,721 . . B 2
Breaux Bridge, 6,515 . . D 4
Bunkie, 5,044 . . . . D 3
Chalmette, 31,860 . . . . E 6
Church Point, 4,677 . . D 3
Covington, 7,691 . . . . . D 5
Crowley, 13,983 . . . . . D 3
Cut Off, 5,049('80) . . . E 5
Denham Springs, 8,381 D 5
De Ridder, 9,868 . . . . . D 2
Donaldsonville, 7,949 . . D 4
Eunice, 11,162 . . . . D 3
Ferriday, 4,111 . . . . . . C 4
Franklin, 9,004 . . . . E 4
Gonzales, 7,003 . . . . . . D 5
Grambling, 5,484 . . . . . . B 3
Gretna, 17,208 . . . . E 5
Hammond, 15,871 . . . . . D 5
Harahan, 9,927 . . . . . . k11
Harvey, 15,000 . . . . . . E 5
Houma, 96,982 . . . . . . E 5
Jeanerette, 6,205 . . . . . E 4
Jefferson, 15,550('80) . . k11
Jena, 2,626 . . . . C 3
Jennings, 11,305 . . . . . D 3
Jonesboro, 4,305 . . . . . B 3
Kaplan, 4,535 . . . . D 3
Kenner, 72,033 . . . . E 5
Lafayette, 94,440 . . . . D 3
Lake Charles, 70,580 . . D 2
Lake Providence, 5,380 B 4
La Place, 16,112('80) . . h11
Leesville, 7,638 . . . . . . C 2
Lutcher, 3,907 . . . . D 5
Mandeville, 7,083 . . . . D 5
Mansfield, 5,389 . . . . . . B 2
Marksville, 5,526 . . . . . C 3
Marrero, 36,671 . . . . . . E 5
Metairie, 149,428 . . . . . k11
Minden, 13,661 . . . . . . B 2
Monroe, 54,909 . . . . . . B 3
Morgan City, 14,531 . . E 4
Moss Bluff, 7,004('80) D 2
Natchitoches, 16,609 . . C 2
New Iberia, 31,828 . . . . D 4
New Orleans, 496,938 E 5
Oakdale, 6,832 . . . . . . D 3
Opelousas, 18,151 . . . . D 3
Patterson, 4,736 . . . . . . E 4
Pineville, 12,251 . . . . . C 3
Plaquemine, 7,186 . . . . D 4
Ponchatoula, 5,425 . . . D 5
Port Allen, 6,277 . . . . . D 4
Raceland, 6,302('80) . . E 5
Rayne, 8,502 . . . . D 3
Rayville, 4,411 . . . . B 4
Reserve, 7,288('80) h10
River Ridge, 17,146('80) k11
Ruston, 20,027 . . . . . . B 3
Saint Martinville, 7,137 D 4
Scotlandville, 15,113('80) . . . . D 4
Shreveport, 198,525 . . B 2
Slidell, 24,124 . . . . D 6
Springhill, 5,668 . . . . . . A 2
Sulphur, 20,125 . . . . . . D 2
Tallulah, 8,526 . . . . B 4
Thibodaux, 14,035 . . . . E 5
Vidalia, 4,953 . . . . C 4
Ville Platte, 9,037 . . . . D 3
Violet, 6,000 . . . . k12
Westlake, 5,007 . . . . . . D 2
West Monroe, 14,096 . . B 3
Westwego, 11,218 . . . . k11
Winnfield, 6,138 . . . . . . C 3
Winnsboro, 5,755 . . . . . B 4
Zachary, 9,036 . . . . D 4

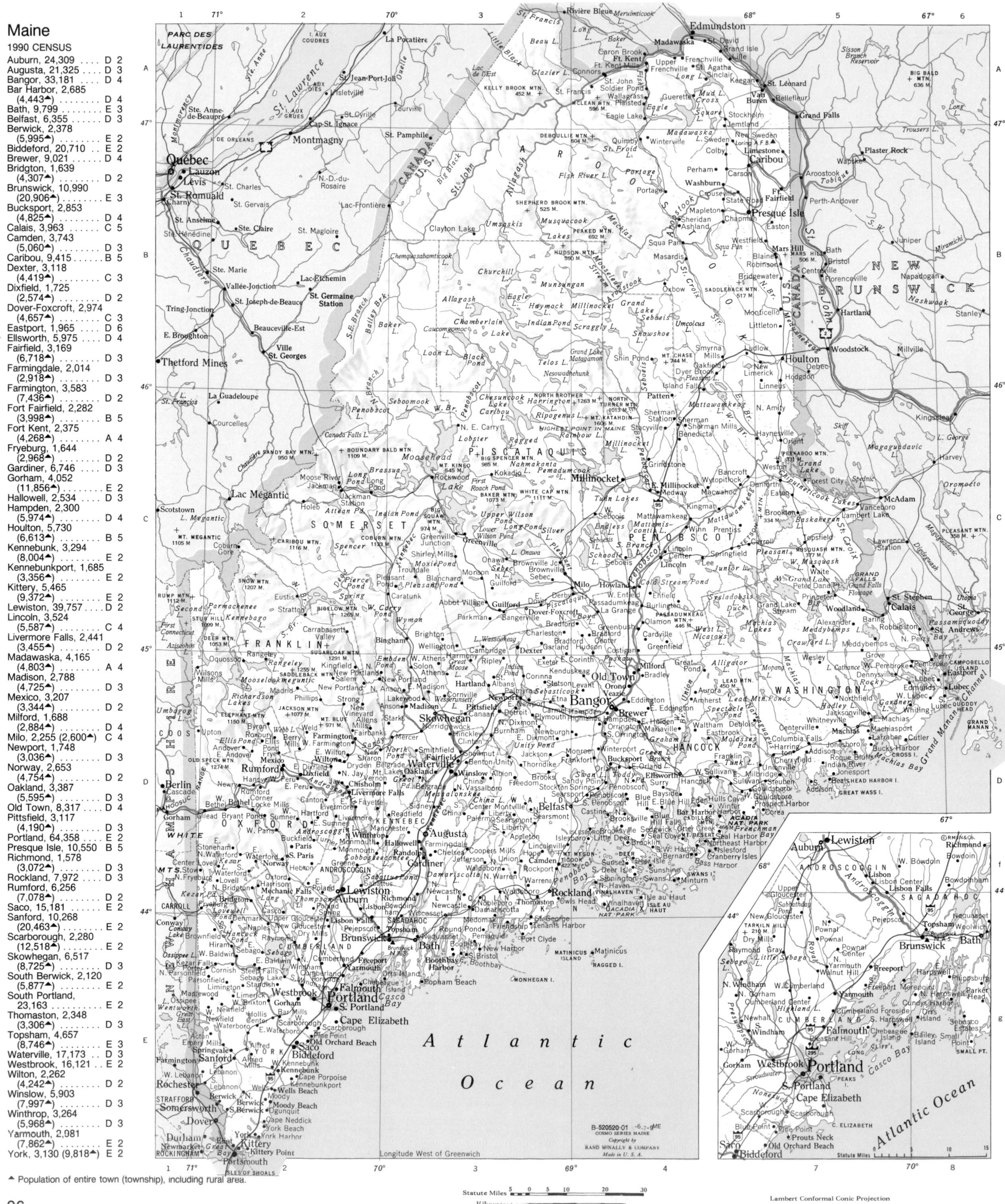

Maine

1990 CENSUS

Auburn, 24,309 .... D 2
Augusta, 21,325 .... D 3
Bangor, 33,181 .... D 4
Bar Harbor, 2,685 (4,443▲) .... D 4
Bath, 9,799 .... E 3
Belfast, 6,355 ...... D 3
Berwick, 2,378 (5,995▲) .... E 2
Biddeford, 20,710 .. E 2
Brewer, 9,021 ...... D 4
Bridgton, 1,639 (4,307▲) .... D 2
Brunswick, 10,990 (20,906▲) .... E 3
Bucksport, 2,853 (4,825▲) .... D 4
Calais, 3,963 ...... C 5
Camden, 3,743 (5,060▲) .... D 3
Caribou, 9,415 ...... B 5
Dexter, 3,118 (4,419▲) .... C 3
Dixfield, 1,725 (2,574▲) .... D 2
Dover-Foxcroft, 2,974 (4,657▲) .... C 3
Eastport, 1,965 .... D 6
Ellsworth, 5,975 .... D 4
Fairfield, 3,169 (6,718▲) .... D 3
Farmingdale, 2,014 (2,918▲) .... D 3
Farmington, 3,583 (7,436▲) .... D 2
Fort Fairfield, 2,282 (3,998▲) .... B 5
Fort Kent, 2,375 (4,268▲) .... A 4
Fryeburg, 1,644 (2,968▲) .... D 2
Gardiner, 6,746 .... D 3
Gorham, 4,052 (11,856▲) .... E 2
Hallowell, 2,534 .... D 3
Hampden, 2,300 (5,974▲) .... D 4
Houlton, 5,730 (6,613▲) .... B 5
Kennebunk, 3,294 (8,004▲) .... E 2
Kennebunkport, 1,685 (3,356▲) .... E 2
Kittery, 5,465 (9,372▲) .... E 2
Lewiston, 39,757 .... D 2
Lincoln, 3,524 (5,587▲) .... C 4
Livermore Falls, 2,441 (3,455▲) .... D 2
Madawaska, 4,165 (4,803▲) .... A 4
Madison, 2,788 (4,725▲) .... D 3
Mexico, 3,207 (3,344▲) .... D 2
Milford, 1,688 (2,884▲) .... D 4
Milo, 2,255 (2,600▲) C 4
Newport, 1,748 (3,036▲) .... D 3
Norway, 2,653 (4,754▲) .... D 2
Oakland, 3,387 (5,595▲) .... D 3
Old Town, 8,317 .... D 4
Pittsfield, 3,117 (4,190▲) .... D 3
Portland, 64,358 .... E 2
Presque Isle, 10,550 B 5
Richmond, 1,578 (3,072▲) .... D 3
Rockland, 7,972 .... D 3
Rumford, 6,256 (7,078▲) .... D 2
Saco, 15,181 ...... E 2
Sanford, 10,268 (20,463▲) .... E 2
Scarborough, 2,280 (12,518▲) .... E 2
Skowhegan, 6,517 (8,725▲) .... D 3
South Berwick, 2,120 (5,877▲) .... E 2
South Portland, 23,163 .... E 2
Thomaston, 2,348 (3,306▲) .... D 3
Topsham, 4,657 (8,746▲) .... E 3
Waterville, 17,173 .. D 3
Westbrook, 16,121 .. E 2
Wilton, 2,262 (4,242▲) .... D 2
Winslow, 5,903 (7,997▲) .... D 3
Winthrop, 3,264 (5,968▲) .... D 3
Yarmouth, 2,981 (7,862▲) .... E 2
York, 3,130 (9,818▲) E 2

▲ Population of entire town (township), including rural area.

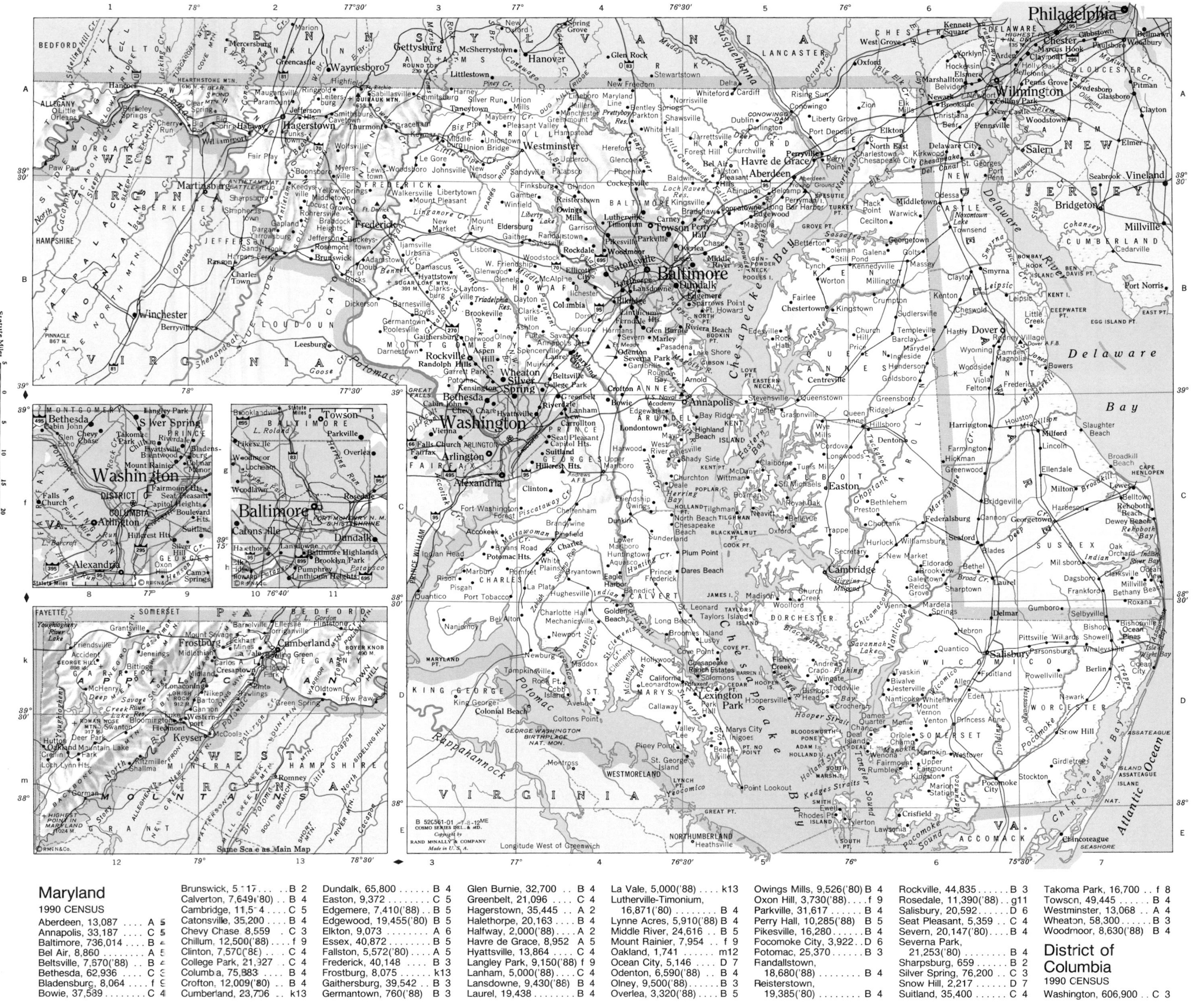

Maryland

1990 CENSUS

Aberdeen, 13,087 .... A 5
Annapolis, 33,187 .... C 5
Baltimore, 736,014 .... B 4
Bel Air, 8,860 .... A 5
Beltsville, 7,670('88) .. B 4
Bethesda, 62,936 .... C 3
Bladensburg, 8,064 .... f 9
Bowie, 37,589 .... C 4
Brunswick, 5,117 ..... B 2
Calverton, 7,649('80) .. B 4
Cambridge, 11,514 .... C 5
Catonsville, 35,200 .... B 4
Chevy Chase, 8,559 .. C 3
Chillum, 12,500('88) .... f 9
Clinton, 7,570('88) .... C 4
College Park, 21,927 .. C 4
Columbia, 75,883 .... B 4
Crofton, 12,009('80) .. B 4
Cumberland, 23,706 .. k13
Dundalk, 65,800 ...... B 4
Easton, 9,372 .... C 5
Edgemere, 7,410('88) .. B 5
Edgewood, 19,455('80) B 5
Elkton, 9,073 .... A 6
Essex, 40,872 .... B 5
Fallston, 5,572('80) .... A 5
Frederick, 40,148 .... B 3
Frostburg, 8,075 ...... k13
Gaithersburg, 39,542 .. B 3
Germantown, 760('88) B 3
Glen Burnie, 32,700 .. B 4
Greenbelt, 21,096 .... C 4
Hagerstown, 35,445 .. A 2
Halethorpe, 20,163 .... B 4
Halfway, 2,000('88).... A 2
Havre de Grace, 8,952 A 5
Hyattsville, 13,864 .... C 4
Langley Park, 9,150('88) f 9
Lanham, 5,000('88).... C 4
Lansdowne, 9,430('88) B 4
Laurel, 19,438 .... B 4
La Vale, 5,000('88) k13
Lutherville-Timonium,
16,871('80) .... B 4
Lynne Acres, 5,910('88) B 4
Middle River, 24,616 .. B 5
Mount Rainier, 7,954 .. f 9
Oakland, 1,741 ...... m12
Ocean City, 5,146 .... D 7
Odenton, 6,590('88) .. B 4
Olney, 9,500('88)...... B 3
Overlea, 3,320('88) .... B 5
Owings Mills, 9,526('80) B 4
Oxon Hill, 3,730('88).... f 9
Parkville, 31,617 ...... B 4
Perry Hall, 10,285('88) B 5
Pikesville, 16,280...... B 4
Pocomoke City, 3,922.. D 6
Potomac, 25,370...... B 3
Randallstown,
18,680('88) .... B 4
Reisterstown,
19,385('80) .... B 4
Rockville, 44,835...... B 3
Rosedale, 11,390('88).. g11
Salisbury, 20,592...... D 6
Seat Pleasant, 5,359 .. C 4
Severn, 20,147('80).... B 4
Severna Park,
21,253('80) .... B 4
Sharpsburg, 659 ...... B 2
Silver Spring, 76,200 .. C 3
Snow Hill, 2,217 ...... D 7
Suitland, 35,400 ...... C 4
Takoma Park, 16,700 .. f 8
Towson, 49,445 ...... B 4
Westminster, 13,068 .. A 4
Wheaton, 58,300...... B 3
Woodmoor, 8,630('88) B 4

District of Columbia

1990 CENSUS

Washington, 606,900 .. C 3

Massachusetts

1990 CENSUS

Amherst, 17,773 (35,228▲) . . . . B 2
Arlington, 44,630 . . . . . B 5
Attleboro, 38,383 . . . . . C 5
Belmont, 24,720 . . . . . . g11
Beverly, 38,195 . . . . . . A 6
Boston, 574,283 . . . . . B 5
Braintree, 33,836 . . . . . B 5
Brockton, 92,788 . . . . . . B 5
Brookline, 54,718 . . . . . B 5
Burlington, 23,302 . . . . f11
Cambridge, 95,802 . . . . B 5
Chelmsford, 32,383 . . . . A 5
Chelsea, 28,710 . . . . . . B 5
Chicopee, 56,632 . . . . B 2
Concord, 4,680 (17,076▲) . . . . B 5
Danvers, 24,174 . . . . . . A 6
Dedham, 23,782 . . . . . . B 5
Everett, 35,701 . . . . . . g11
Fall River, 92,703 . . . . C 5
Fitchburg, 41,194 . . . . . A 4
Framingham, 64,989 . . B 5
Gardner, 20,125 . . . . . . A 4
Gloucester, 28,716 . . . . A 6
Greenfield, 14,198 (18,666▲) . . . . A 2
Haverhill, 51,418 . . . . . . A 5
Holyoke, 43,704 . . . . . . B 2
Hyannis, 9,900 . . . . . . C 7
Lawrence, 70,207 . . . . A 5
Leominster, 38,145 . . . . A 4
Lexington, 28,974 . . . . B 5
Lowell, 103,439 . . . . . . A 5
Lynn, 81,245 . . . . B 6
Malden, 53,884 . . . . . . B 5
Marblehead, 20,126('80) B 6
Marlborough, 31,813 . . B 4
Medford, 57,407 . . . . . . B 5
Melrose, 28,150 . . . . . . B 5
Methuen, 40,300 . . . . . . A 5
Milford, 25,200 . . . . . . B 4
Milton, 25,725 . . . . B 5
Nantucket, 3,229 (6,012▲) . . . . D 7
Natick, 30,100 . . . . B 5
Needham, 27,557 . . . . g11
New Bedford, 99,922 . . C 6
Newburyport, 16,317 . . A 6
Newton, 82,585 . . . . . . B 5
North Adams, 16,797 . . A 1
Northampton, 29,289 . . B 2
North Andover, 20,129('87) . . . . A 5
North Attleboro, 24,200 C 5
Norwood, 28,700 . . . . . B 5
Peabody, 47,039 . . . . . . A 6
Pittsfield, 48,622 . . . . . . B 1
Plymouth, 7,232 (45,608▲) . . . . C 6
Quincy, 84,985 . . . . . . B 5
Randolph, 30,093 . . . . B 5
Reading, 22,539 . . . . . . A 5
Revere, 42,786 . . . . . . g11
Salem, 38,091 . . . . A 6
Saugus, 25,549 . . . . . . B 5
Shrewsbury, 23,400 . . . B 4
Somerville, 76,210 . . . . B 5
Springfield, 156,983 . . B 2
Stoneham, 22,203 . . . . g11
Stoughton, 27,800 . . . . B 5
Taunton, 49,832 . . . . . . C 5
Vineyard Haven, 1,704('80) . . . . D 6
Wakefield, 24,825 . . . . B 5
Waltham, 57,878 . . . . . . B 5
Watertown, 33,284 . . . . g11
Wellesley, 26,615 . . . . . B 5
Westfield, 38,372 . . . . . B 2
West Springfield, 27,537 B 2
Weymouth, 54,063 . . . . B 6
Winchester, 20,701('80) g11
Winthrop, 19,294('80) . . B 6
Woburn, 35,943 . . . . . . B 5
Worcester, 169,759 . . . . B 4

▲ Population of entire town (township), including rural area.

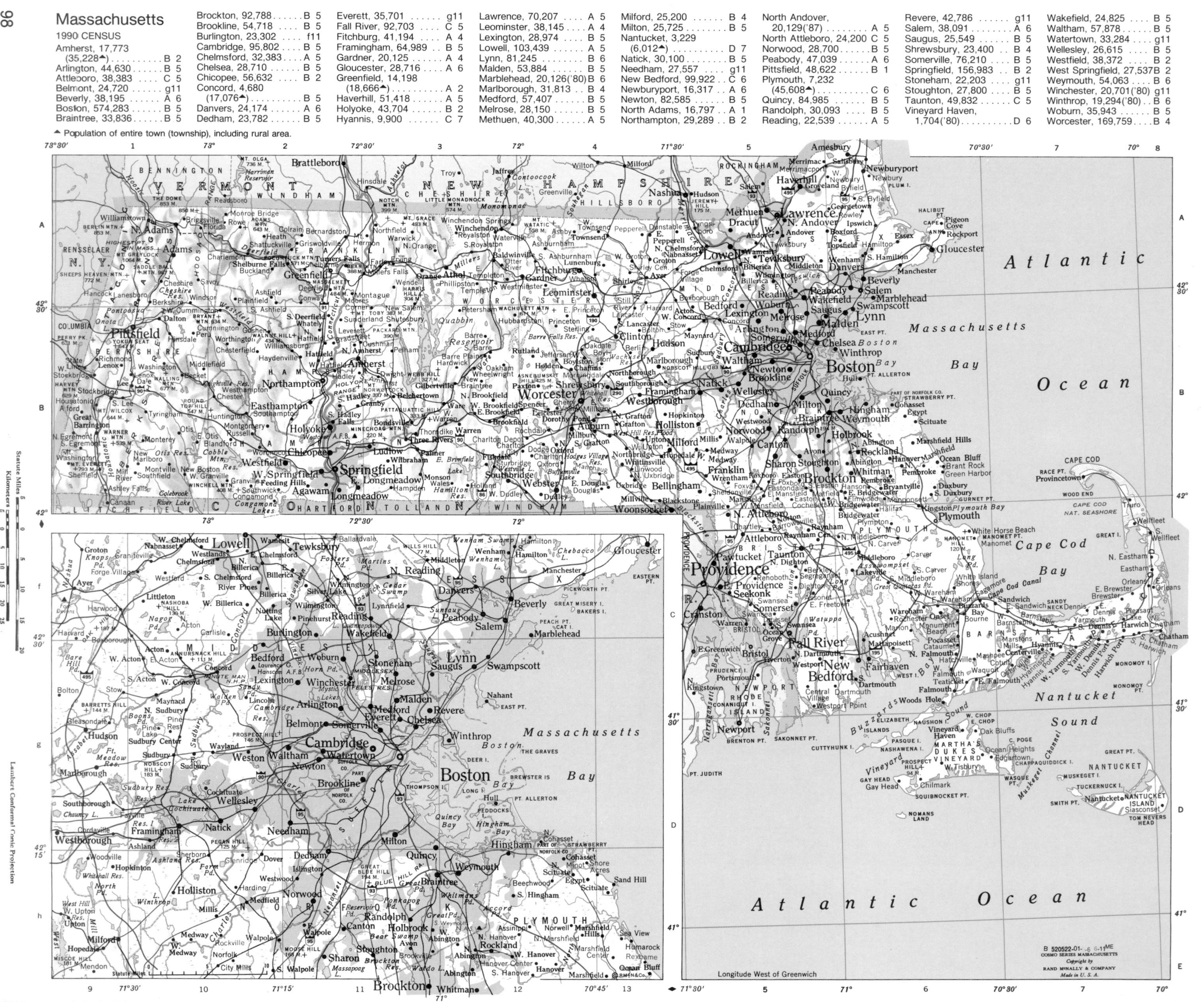

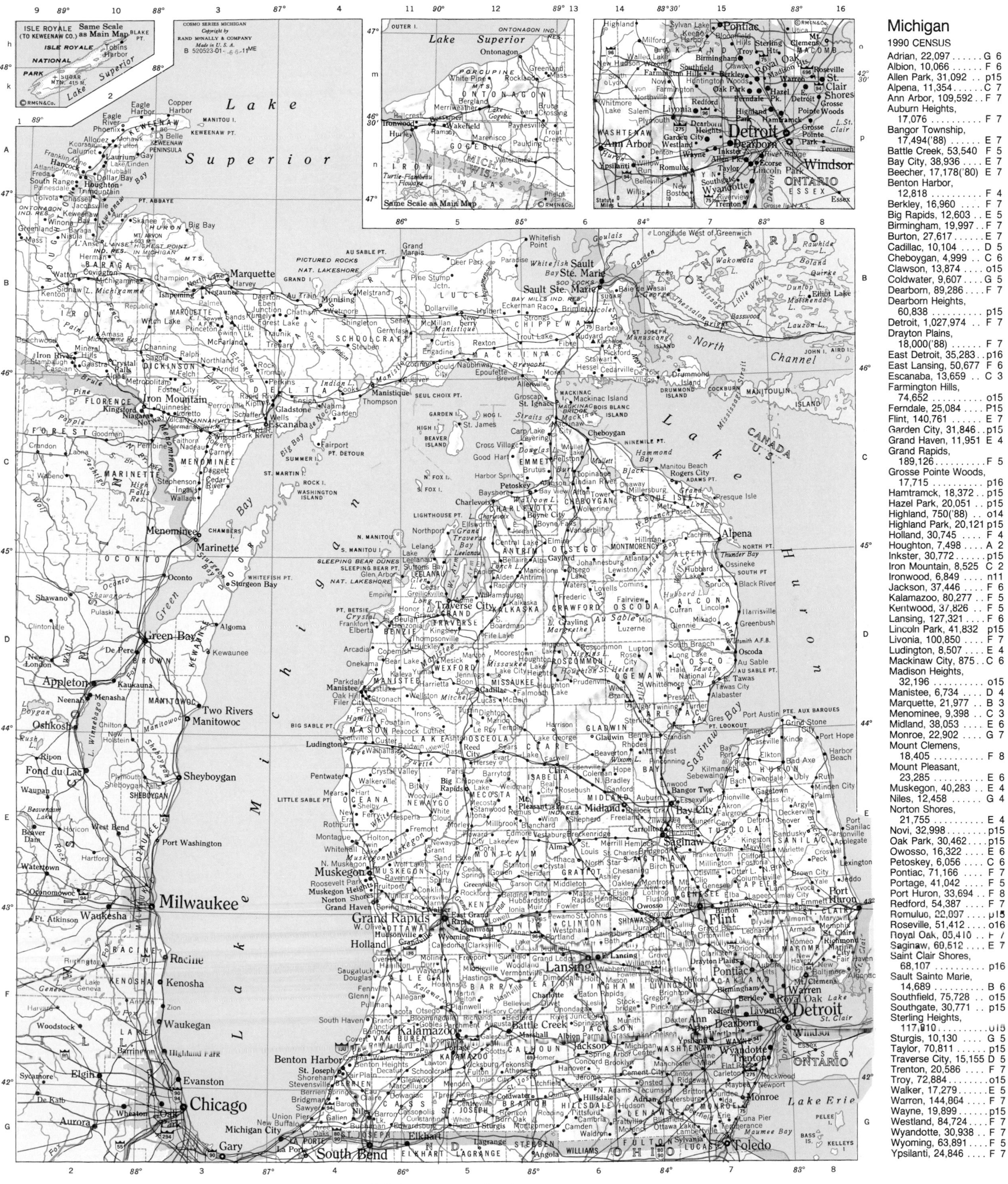

Michigan

1990 CENSUS

Adrian, 22,097 . . . . . . G 6
Albion, 10,066 . . . . . . F 6
Allen Park, 31,092 . . p15
Alpena, 11,354 . . . . . . C 7
Ann Arbor, 109,592 . . F 7
Auburn Heights, 17,076 . . . . F 7
Bangor Township, 17,494('88) . . . . . . E 7
Battle Creek, 53,540 F 5
Bay City, 38,936 . . . . E 7
Beecher, 17,178('80) E 7
Benton Harbor, 12,818 . . . . F 4
Berkley, 16,960 . . . . F 7
Big Rapids, 12,603 . . E 5
Birmingham, 19,997 . . F 7
Burton, 27,617 . . . . . . E 7
Cadillac, 10,104 . . . . D 5
Cheboygan, 4,999 . . C 6
Clawson, 13,874 . . . . o15
Coldwater, 9,607 . . . . G 5
Dearborn, 89,286 . . . . F 7
Dearborn Heights, 60,838 . . . . p15
Detroit, 1,027,974 . . F 7
Drayton Plains, 18,000('88) . . . . . . F 7
East Detroit, 35,283 . . p16
East Lansing, 50,677 F 6
Escanaba, 13,659 . . C 3
Farmington Hills, 74,652 . . . . o15
Ferndale, 25,084 . . . . P15
Flint, 140,761 . . . . . . E 7
Garden City, 31,846 . . p15
Grand Haven, 11,951 E 4
Grand Rapids, 189,126 . . . . F 5
Grosse Pointe Woods, 17,715 . . . . p16
Hamtramck, 18,372 . . p15
Hazel Park, 20,051 . . p15
Highland, 750('88) . . o14
Highland Park, 20,121 p15
Holland, 30,745 . . . . F 4
Houghton, 7,498 . . . . A 2
Inkster, 30,772 . . . . . . p15
Iron Mountain, 8,525 C 2
Ironwood, 6,849 . . . . n11
Jackson, 37,446 . . . . F 6
Kalamazoo, 80,277 . . F 5
Kentwood, 37,826 . . F 5
Lansing, 127,321 . . . . F 6
Lincoln Park, 41,832 p15
Livonia, 100,850 . . . . F 7
Ludington, 8,507 . . . . E 4
Mackinaw City, 875 . . C 6
Madison Heights, 32,196 . . . . o15
Manistee, 6,734 . . . . D 4
Marquette, 21,977 . . B 3
Menominee, 9,398 . . C 3
Midland, 38,053 . . . . E 6
Monroe, 22,902 . . . . G 7
Mount Clemens, 18,405 . . . . F 8
Mount Pleasant, 23,285 . . . . E 6
Muskegon, 40,283 . . E 4
Niles, 12,458 . . . . . . G 4
Norton Shores, 21,755 . . . . E 4
Novi, 32,998 . . . . p15
Oak Park, 30,462 . . . . p15
Owosso, 16,322 . . . . E 6
Petoskey, 6,056 . . . . C 6
Pontiac, 71,166 . . . . F 7
Portage, 41,042 . . . . F 5
Port Huron, 33,694 . . F 8
Redford, 54,387 . . . . F 7
Romulus, 22,897 . . . . p15
Roseville, 51,412 . . . . o16
Royal Oak, 65,410 . . F 7
Saginaw, 69,512 . . . . E 7
Saint Clair Shores, 68,107 . . . . p16
Sault Sainte Marie, 14,689 . . . . B 6
Southfield, 75,728 . . o15
Southgate, 30,771 . . p15
Sterling Heights, 117,810 . . . . o15
Sturgis, 10,130 . . . . G 5
Taylor, 70,811 . . . . . . p15
Traverse City, 15,155 D 5
Trenton, 20,586 . . . . F 7
Troy, 72,884 . . . . o15
Walker, 17,279 . . . . . . E 5
Warren, 144,864 . . . . F 7
Wayne, 19,899 . . . . . . p15
Westland, 84,724 . . . . F 7
Wyandotte, 30,938 . . F 7
Wyoming, 63,891 . . . . F 5
Ypsilanti, 24,846 . . . . F 7

Minnesota

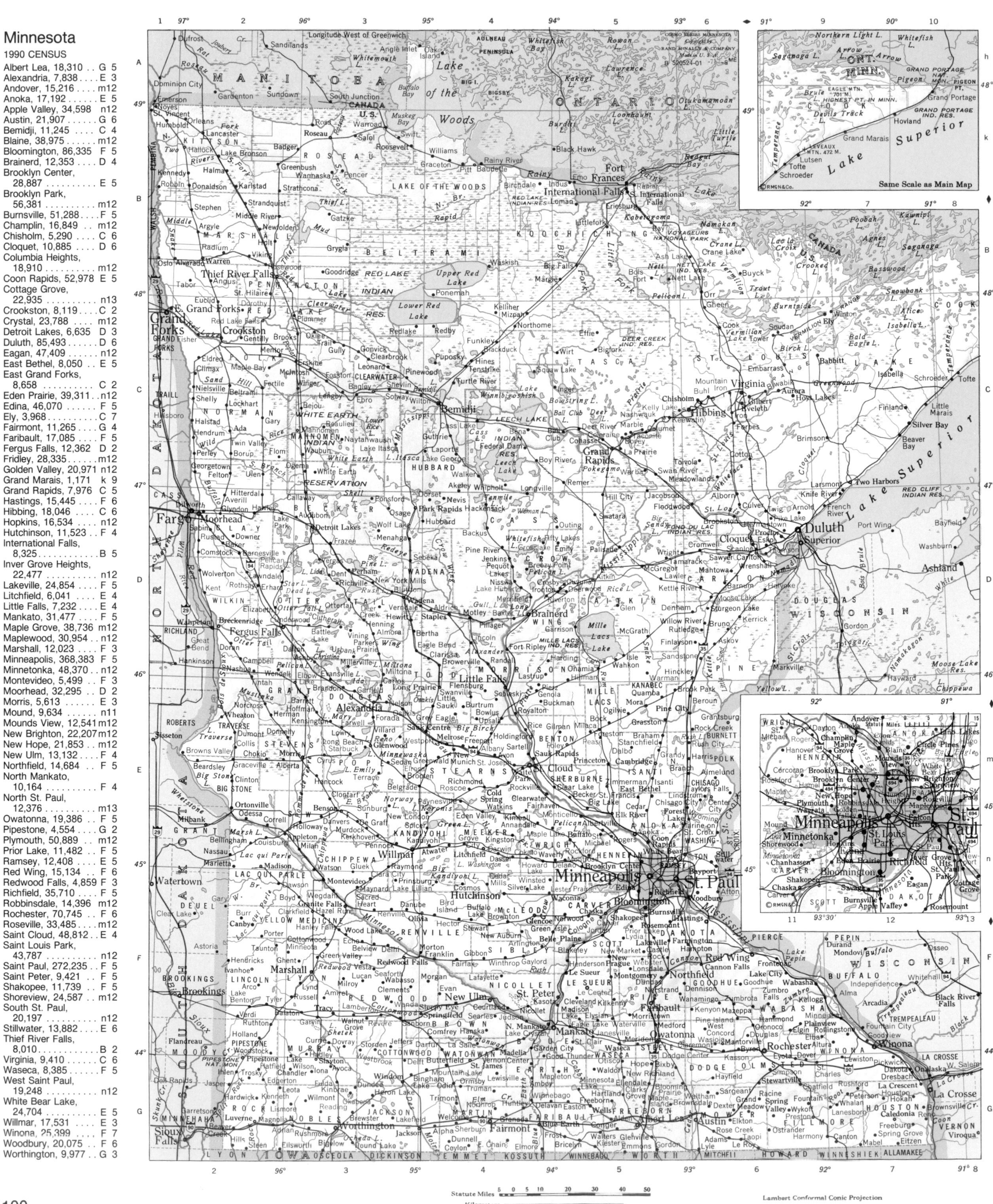

Minnesota

1990 CENSUS

- Albert Lea, 18,310 .. G 5
- Alexandria, 7,838 .... E 3
- Andover, 15,216 .... m12
- Anoka, 17,192 ...... E 5
- Apple Valley, 34,598 n12
- Austin, 21,907 ...... G 6
- Bemidji, 11,245 .... C 4
- Blaine, 38,975 ...... m12
- Bloomington, 86,335 F 5
- Brainerd, 12,353 .... D 4
- Brooklyn Center, 28,887 .... E 5
- Brooklyn Park, 56,381 .... m12
- Burnsville, 51,288.... F 5
- Champlin, 16,849 ... m12
- Chisholm, 5,290 .... C 6
- Cloquet, 10,885 .... D 6
- Columbia Heights, 18,910 .... m12
- Coon Rapids, 52,978 E 5
- Cottage Grove, 22,935 .... n13
- Crookston, 8,119.... C 2
- Crystal, 23,788 .... m12
- Detroit Lakes, 6,635 D 3
- Duluth, 85,493 ...... D 6
- Eagan, 47,409 ...... n12
- East Bethel, 8,050 .. E 5
- East Grand Forks, 8,658 .... C 2
- Eden Prairie, 39,311.. n12
- Edina, 46,070 ...... F 5
- Ely, 3,968.......... C 7
- Fairmont, 11,265.... G 4
- Faribault, 17,085 .... F 5
- Fergus Falls, 12,362 D 2
- Fridley, 28,335...... m12
- Golden Valley, 20,971 n12
- Grand Marais, 1,171 k 9
- Grand Rapids, 7,976 C 5
- Hastings, 15,445 .... F 6
- Hibbing, 18,046 .... C 6
- Hopkins, 16,534 .... n12
- Hutchinson, 11,523 .. F 4
- International Falls, 8,325............ B 5
- Inver Grove Heights, 22,477 .... n12
- Lakeville, 24,854 .... F 5
- Litchfield, 6,041 .... E 4
- Little Falls, 7,232.... E 4
- Mankato, 31,477 .... F 5
- Maple Grove, 38,736 m12
- Maplewood, 30,954 .. n12
- Marshall, 12,023 .... F 3
- Minneapolis, 368,383 F 5
- Minnetonka, 48,370 .. n12
- Montevideo, 5,499 .. F 3
- Moorhead, 32,295 .. D 2
- Morris, 5,613 ...... E 3
- Mound, 9,634 ...... n11
- Mounds View, 12,541m12
- New Brighton, 22,207m12
- New Hope, 21,853 .. m12
- New Ulm, 13,132.... F 4
- Northfield, 14,684 .. F 5
- North Mankato, 10,164 .... F 4
- North St. Paul, 12,376 .... m13
- Owatonna, 19,386 .. F 5
- Pipestone, 4,554.... G 2
- Plymouth, 50,889 .. m12
- Prior Lake, 11,482 .. F 5
- Ramsey, 12,408 .... E 5
- Red Wing, 15,134 .. F 6
- Redwood Falls, 4,859 F 3
- Richfield, 35,710 .... F 5
- Robbinsdale, 14,396 m12
- Rochester, 70,745 .. F 6
- Roseville, 33,485.... m12
- Saint Cloud, 48,812.. E 4
- Saint Louis Park, 43,787 .... n12
- Saint Paul, 272,235.. F 5
- Saint Peter, 9,421 .. F 5
- Shakopee, 11,739 .. F 5
- Shoreview, 24,587 .. m12
- South St. Paul, 20,197 .... n12
- Stillwater, 13,882.... E 6
- Thief River Falls, 8,010............B 2
- Virginia, 9,410...... C 6
- Waseca, 8,385...... F 5
- West Saint Paul, 19,248 .... n12
- White Bear Lake, 24,704 .... E 5
- Willmar, 17,531 .... E 3
- Winona, 25,399 .... F 7
- Woodbury, 20,075 .. F 6
- Worthington, 9,977 .. G 3

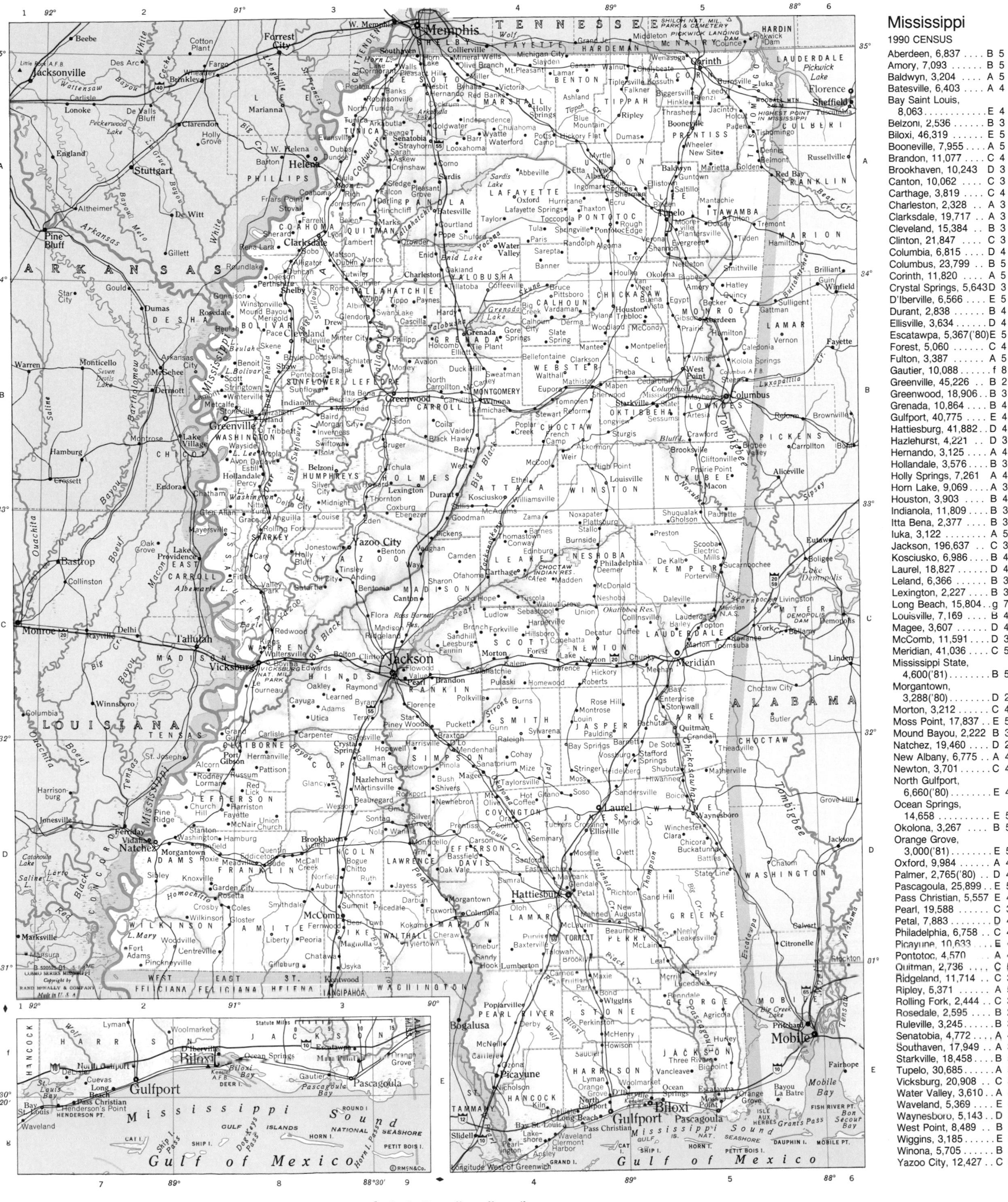

Mississippi

1990 CENSUS

- Aberdeen, 6,837 .... B 5
- Amory, 7,093 ...... B 5
- Baldwyn, 3,204 ..... A 5
- Batesville, 6,403 .... A 4
- Bay Saint Louis, 8,063 .... E 4
- Belzoni, 2,536 ...... B 3
- Biloxi, 46,319 ...... E 5
- Booneville, 7,955 .... A 5
- Brandon, 11,077 .... C 4
- Brookhaven, 10,243 D 3
- Canton, 10,062 .... C 3
- Carthage, 3,819 ..... C 4
- Charleston, 2,328 .. A 3
- Clarksdale, 19,717 .. A 3
- Cleveland, 15,384 .. B 3
- Clinton, 21,847 .... C 3
- Columbia, 6,815 .... D 4
- Columbus, 23,799 .. B 5
- Corinth, 11,820 .... A 5
- Crystal Springs, 5,643 D 3
- D'Iberville, 6,566 ..... E 5
- Durant, 2,838 ...... B 4
- Ellisville, 3,634 ...... D 4
- Escatawpa, 5,367('80) E 5
- Forest, 5,060 ...... C 4
- Fulton, 3,387 ...... A 5
- Gautier, 10,088 ...... f 8
- Greenville, 45,226 .. B 2
- Greenwood, 18,906 .. B 3
- Grenada, 10,864 .... B 4
- Gulfport, 40,775 .... E 4
- Hattiesburg, 41,882 .. D 4
- Hazlehurst, 4,221 ... D 3
- Hernando, 3,125 .... A 4
- Hollandale, 3,576 .... B 3
- Holly Springs, 7,261 A 4
- Horn Lake, 9,069 .... A 3
- Houston, 3,903 .... B 4
- Indianola, 11,809 .... B 3
- Itta Bena, 2,377 .... B 3
- Iuka, 3,122 .... A 5
- Jackson, 196,637 .. C 3
- Kosciusko, 6,986 .... B 4
- Laurel, 18,827 ...... D 4
- Leland, 6,366 ...... B 3
- Lexington, 2,227 .... B 3
- Long Beach, 15,804 .. g 7
- Louisville, 7,169 .... B 4
- Magee, 3,607 ...... D 4
- McComb, 11,591 .... D 3
- Meridian, 41,036 .... C 5
- Mississippi State, 4,600('81) .... B 5
- Morgantown, 3,288('80) .... D 2
- Morton, 3,212 ...... C 4
- Moss Point, 17,837 .. E 5
- Mound Bayou, 2,222 B 3
- Natchez, 19,460 .... D 2
- New Albany, 6,775 .. A 4
- Newton, 3,701 ...... C 4
- North Gulfport, 6,660('80) .... E 4
- Ocean Springs, 14,658 .... E 5
- Okolona, 3,267 .... B 5
- Orange Grove, 3,000('81) .... E 5
- Oxford, 9,984 ...... A 4
- Palmer, 2,765('80) .. D 4
- Pascagoula, 25,899 .. E 5
- Pass Christian, 5,557 E 4
- Pearl, 19,588 ...... C 3
- Petal, 7,883 .... D 4
- Philadelphia, 6,758 .. C 4
- Picayune, 10,633 ..... E 4
- Pontotoc, 4,570 ..... A 4
- Quitman, 2,736 ..... C 5
- Ridgeland, 11,714 ... C 3
- Ripley, 5,371 ...... A 5
- Rolling Fork, 2,444 .. C 3
- Rosedale, 2,595 .... B 2
- Ruleville, 3,245 ...... B 3
- Senatobia, 4,772 ..... A 4
- Southaven, 17,949 .. A 3
- Starkville, 18,458 .... B 5
- Tupelo, 30,685 ...... A 5
- Vicksburg, 20,908 ... C 3
- Water Valley, 3,610 .. A 4
- Waveland, 5,369 .... E 4
- Waynesboro, 5,143 .. D 5
- West Point, 8,489 .. B 5
- Wiggins, 3,185 ...... E 4
- Winona, 5,705 ...... B 4
- Yazoo City, 12,427 .. C 3

Missouri

1990 CENSUS

Arrold, 18,828 . . . . C 7
Aurora, 6,459 . . . . E 4
Ballwin, 21,816 . . . . f12
Belton, 18,150 . . . . C 3
Berkeley, 12,450 . . . . . . f13
Blue Springs, 40,153 . . h11
Bolivar, 6,845 . . . . D 4
Boonville, 7,095 . . . . . . C 5
Brentwood, 8,150 . . . . . . f13
Bridgeton, 17,779 . . . . C 7
Brookfield, 4,888 . . . . . . B 4
Cape Girardeau, 34,438 D 8
Carthage, 10,747 . . . . D 3
Caruthersville, 7,389 . . E 8
Charleston, 5,085 . . . . E 8
Chillicothe, 8,804 . . . . . B 4
Clayton, 13,874 . . . . . . C 7
Clinton, 8,703 . . . . C 4
Columbia, 69,101 . . . . C 5
De Soto, 5,993 . . . . . . C 7
Des Peres, 8,395 . . . . . . f13
Dexter, 7,559 . . . . E 8
Ellisville, 7,545 . . . . f12
Eureka, 4,683 . . . . f12
Excelsior Springs,
10,354 . . . . B 3
Farmington, 11,598 . . . . D 7
Ferguson, 22,286 . . . . . C 7
Festus, 8,105 . . . . C 7
Florissant, 51,206 . . . . . . f13
Fulton, 10,033 . . . . C 6
Gladstone, 26,243 . . . . h10
Grandview, 24,967 . . . . C 3
Hannibal, 18,004 . . . . . . B 6
Harrisonville, 7,683 . . . . C 3
Independence, 112,301 B 3
Jackson, 9,256 . . . . . . D 8
Jefferson City, 35,481 C 5
Jennings, 15,905 . . . . . f13
Joplin, 40,961 . . . . D 3
Kansas City, 435,146 . . B 3
Kennett, 10,941 . . . . . . E 7
Kirksville, 17,152 . . . . . . A 5
Kirkwood, 27,291 . . . . . . f13
Lebanon, 9,983 . . . . D 5
Lees Summit, 46,418 . . C 3
Liberty, 20,459 . . . . . . B 3
Macon, 5,571 . . . . B 5
Malden, 5,123 . . . . E 8
Manchester, 6,542 . . . . f12
Maplewood, 9,962 . . . . f13
Marshall, 12,711 . . . . . . B 4
Maryland Heights,
25,407 . . . . f13
Maryville, 10,663 . . . . . . A 3
Mexico, 11,290 . . . . B 6
Moberly, 12,839 . . . . . . B 5
Monett, 6,529 . . . . E 4
Neosho, 9,254 . . . . E 3
Nevada, 8,597 . . . . D 3
O'Fallon, 18,698 . . . . . . f12
Overland, 17,987 . . . . . . f13
Perryville, 6,933 . . . . . . D 8
Pine Lawn, 5,092 . . . . . . f13
Poplar Bluff, 16,996 . . E 7
Raytown, 30,601 . . . . . . h11
Richmond Heights,
10,448 . . . . f13
Rolla, 14,090 . . . . D 6
Saint Charles, 54,555 . . C 7
Sainte Genevieve, 4,411 D 7
Saint Joseph, 71,852 . . B 3
Saint Louis, 396,685 . . C 7
Saint Peters, 45,779 . . C 7
Sedalia, 19,800 . . . . C 4
Sikeston, 17,641 . . . . . . E 8
Springfield, 140,494 . . D 4
Sullivan, 5,661 . . . . C 6
Trenton, 6,129 . . . . A 4
University City, 40,087 C 7
Warrensburg, 15,244 . . C 4
Washington, 10,704 . . C 6
Webb City, 7,449 . . . . D 3
Webster Groves, 22,987 f13
West Plains, 8,913 . . . . E 6

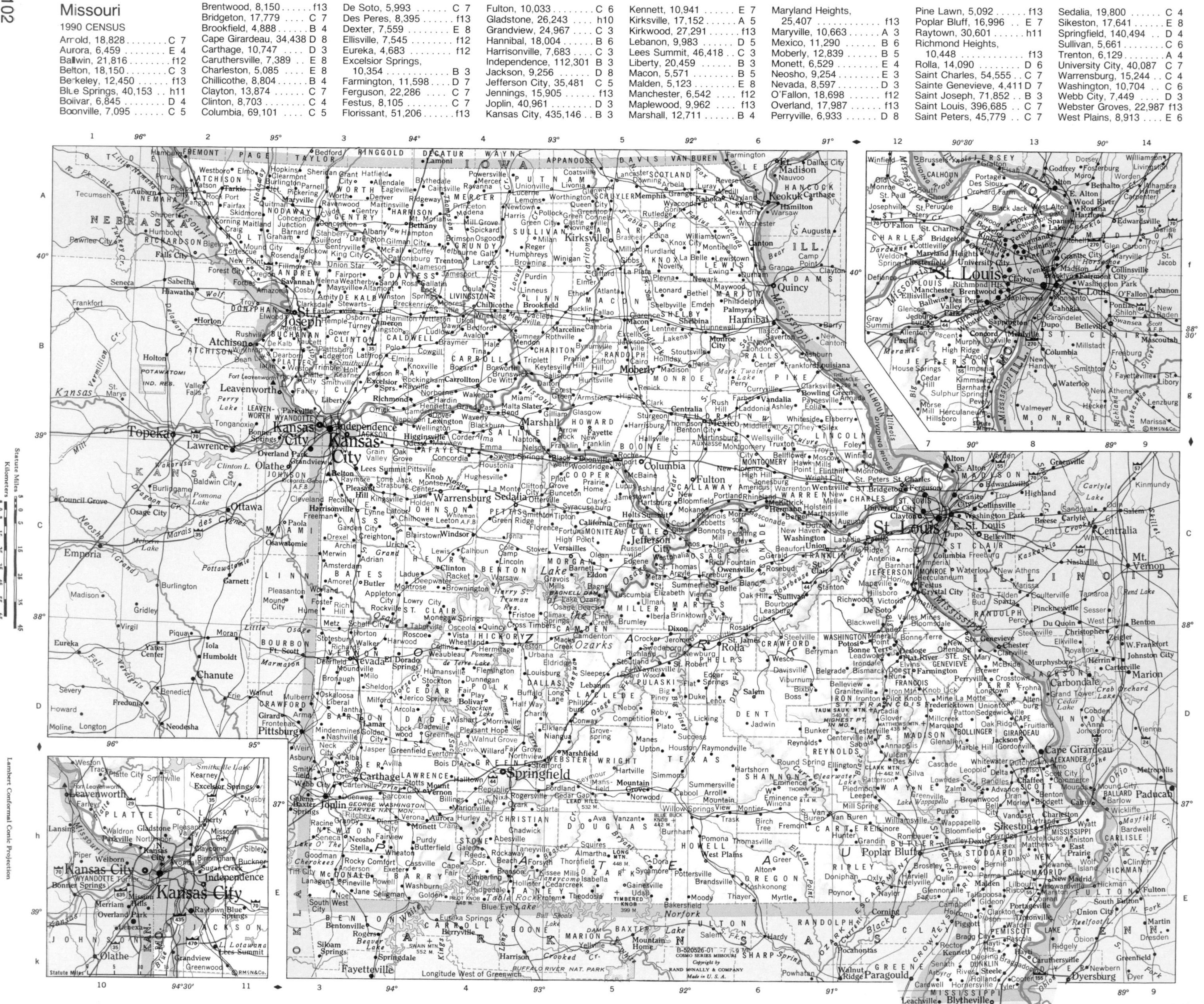

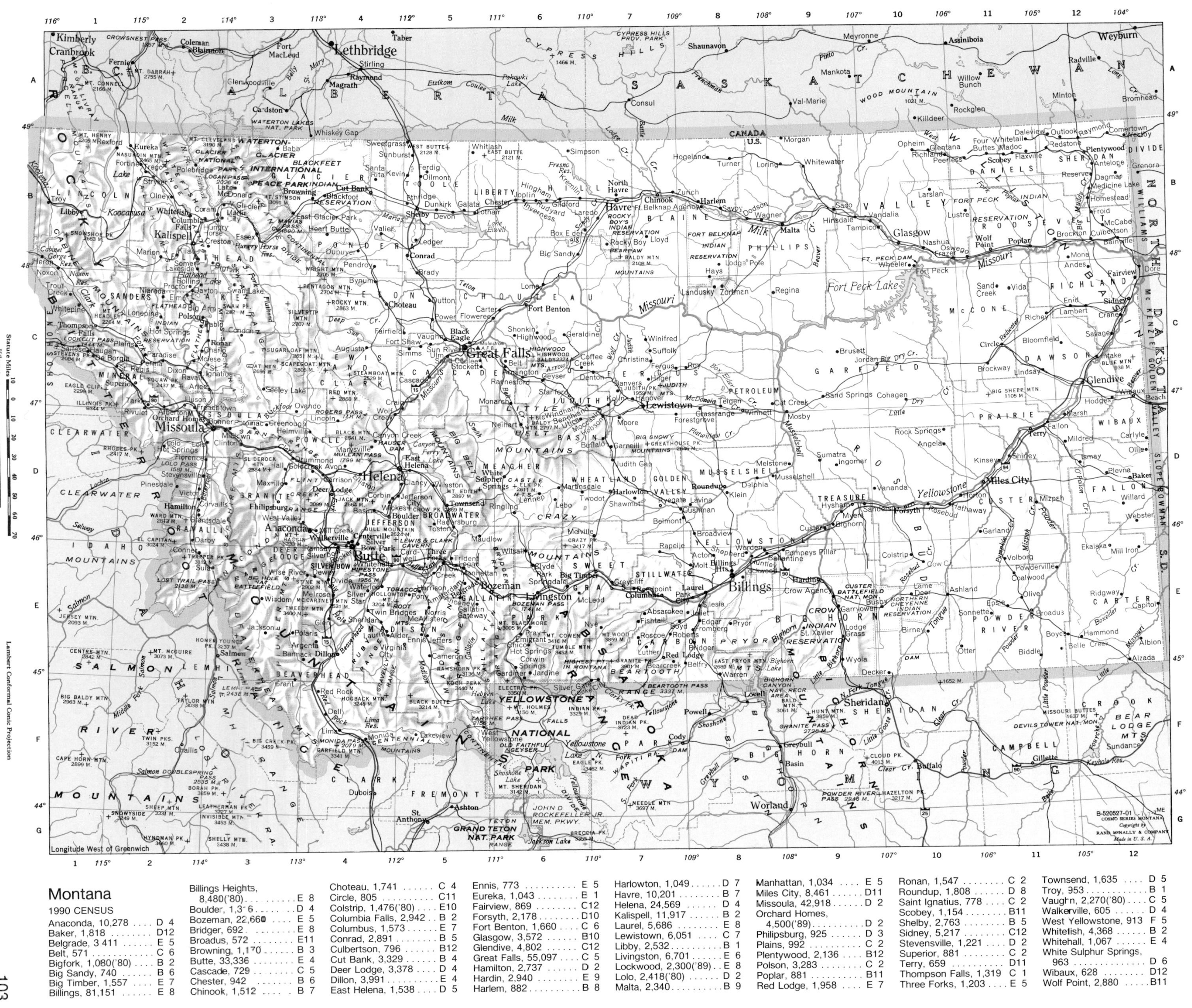

Montana

1990 CENSUS

Anaconda, 10,278 .... D 4
Baker, 1,818 .... D12
Belgrade, 3 411 .... E 5
Belt, 571 .... C 6
Bigfork, 1,080('80) .... B 2
Big Sandy, 740 .... B 6
Big Timber, 1,557 .... E 7
Billings, 81,151 .... E 8
Billings Heights, 8,480('80) .... E 8
Boulder, 1,3‑6 .... D 4
Bozeman, 22,660 .... E 5
Bridger, 692 .... E 8
Broadus, 572 .... E11
Browning, 1,170 .... B 3
Butte, 33,336 .... E 4
Cascade, 729 .... C 5
Chester, 942 .... B 6
Chinook, 1,512 .... B 7
Choteau, 1,741 .... C 4
Circle, 805 .... C11
Colstrip, 1,476('80) E10
Columbia Falls, 2,942 .... B 2
Columbus, 1,573 .... E 7
Conrad, 2,891 .... B 5
Culbertson, 796 .... B12
Cut Bank, 3,329 .... B 4
Deer Lodge, 3,378 .... D 4
Dillon, 3,991 .... E 4
East Helena, 1,538 .... D 5
Ennis, 773 .... E 5
Eureka, 1,043 .... B 1
Fairview, 869 .... C12
Forsyth, 2,178 .... D10
Fort Benton, 1,660 .... C 6
Glasgow, 3,572 .... B10
Glendive, 4,802 .... C12
Great Falls, 55,097 .... C 5
Hamilton, 2,737 .... D 2
Hardin, 2,940 .... E 9
Harlem, 882 .... B 8
Harlowton, 1,049 .... D 7
Havre, 10,201 .... B 7
Helena, 24,569 .... D 4
Kalispell, 11,917 .... B 2
Laurel, 5,686 .... E 8
Lewistown, 6,051 .... C 7
Libby, 2,532 .... B 1
Livingston, 6,701 .... E 6
Lockwood, 2,300('89) .... E 8
Lolo, 2,418('80) .... D 2
Malta, 2,340 .... B 9
Manhattan, 1,034 .... E 5
Miles City, 8,461 .... D11
Missoula, 42,918 .... D 2
Orchard Homes, 4,500('89) .... D 2
Philipsburg, 925 .... D 3
Plains, 992 .... C 2
Plentywood, 2,136 .... B12
Polson, 3,283 .... C 2
Poplar, 881 .... B11
Red Lodge, 1,958 .... E 7
Ronan, 1,547 .... C 2
Roundup, 1,808 .... D 8
Saint Ignatius, 778 .... C 2
Scobey, 1,154 .... B11
Shelby, 2,763 .... B 5
Sidney, 5,217 .... C12
Stevensville, 1,221 .... D 2
Superior, 881 .... C 2
Terry, 659 .... D11
Thompson Falls, 1,319 .... C 1
Three Forks, 1,203 .... E 5
Townsend, 1,635 .... D 5
Troy, 953 .... B 1
Vaughn, 2,270('80) .... C 5
Walkerville, 605 .... D 4
West Yellowstone, 913 .... F 5
Whitefish, 4,368 .... B 2
Whitehall, 1,067 .... E 4
White Sulphur Springs, 963 .... D 6
Wibaux, 628 .... D12
Wolf Point, 2,880 .... B11

Nebraska

1990 CENSUS

Ainsworth, 1,870 . . . . . . B 6
Albion, 1,916 . . . . C 7
Alliance, 9,765 . . . . B 3
Alma, 1,226 . . . . D 6
Ashland, 2,136 . . . . C 9
Atkinson, 1,380 . . . . . . B 7
Auburn, 3,443 . . . . D10
Aurora, 3,810 . . . . D 7
Bayard, 1,196 . . . . C 2
Beatrice, 12,354 . . . . . . D 9
Bellevue, 30,982 . . . . . . C10
Blair, 6,860 . . . . C 9
Bridgeport, 1,581 . . . . C 2
Broken Bow, 3,778 . . . . C 6
Central City, 2,868 . . . . C 7
Chadron, 5,588 . . . . . . B 3
Columbus, 19,480 . . . . C 8
Cozad, 3,823 . . . . D 6
Creighton, 1,223 . . . . . B 8
Crete, 4,841 . . . . D 9
Dakota City, 1,470 . . . . B 9
David City, 2,522 . . . . . . C 8
Elkhorn, 1,398 . . . . g12
Fairbury, 4,335 . . . . . . D 8
Falls City, 4,769 . . . . . . D10
Fremont, 23,680 . . . . . . C 9
Fullerton, 1,452 . . . . . . C 8
Geneva, 2,310 . . . . D 8
Gering, 7,946 . . . . C 2
Gibbon, 1,525 . . . . D 7
Gordon, 1,803 . . . . B 3
Gothenburg, 3,232 . . . . D 5
Grand Island, 39,386 . . D 7
Gretna, 2,249 . . . . C 9
Hartington, 1,583 . . . . . B 8
Hastings, 22,837 . . . . . D 7
Hebron, 1,765 . . . . D 8
Holdrege, 5,671 . . . . . . D 6
Imperial, 2,007 . . . . D 4
Kearney, 24,396 . . . . . . D 6
Kimball, 2,574 . . . . C 2
La Vista, 9,840 . . . . . . g12
Lexington, 6,601 . . . . . . D 6
Lincoln, 191,972 . . . . . . D 9
Loup City, 1,104 . . . . . . C 7
Madison, 2,135 . . . . . . C 8
McCook, 8,112 . . . . D 5
Milford, 1,886 . . . . D 8
Minden, 2,749 . . . . D 7
Mitchell, 1,743 . . . . C 2
Nebraska City, 6,547 . . D10
Neligh, 1,742 . . . . B 7
Norfolk, 21,476 . . . . . . B 8
North Bend, 1,249 . . . . C 9
North Platte, 22,605 . . . C 5
Ogallala, 5,095 . . . . . . C 4
Omaha, 335,795 . . . . . . C10
O'Neill, 3,852 . . . . B 7
Ord, 2,481 . . . . C 7
Papillion, 10,372 . . . . . C 9
Pierce, 1,615 . . . . B 8
Plainview, 1,333 . . . . . . B 8
Plattsmouth, 6,412 . . . . D10
Ralston, 6,236 . . . . g12
Saint Paul, 2,009 . . . . . . C 7
Schuyler, 4,052 . . . . C 8
Scottsbluff, 13,711 . . . . C 2
Seward, 5,634 . . . . D 8
Sidney, 5,959 . . . . C 3
South Sioux City, 9,677 B 9
Stanton, 1,549 . . . . C 8
Superior, 2,397 . . . . . . D 7
Sutton, 1,353 . . . . D 8
Syracuse, 1,646 . . . . . . D 9
Tecumseh, 1,702 . . . . . D 9
Tekamah, 1,852 . . . . . . C 9
Valentine, 2,826 . . . . . . B 5
Valley, 1,775 . . . . C 9
Wahoo, 3,681 . . . . C 9
Waverly, 1,869 . . . . D 9
Wayne, 5,142 . . . . B 8
West Point, 3,250 . . . . C 9
Wilber, 1,527 . . . . D 9
Wymore, 1,611 . . . . D 9
York, 7,884 . . . . D 8

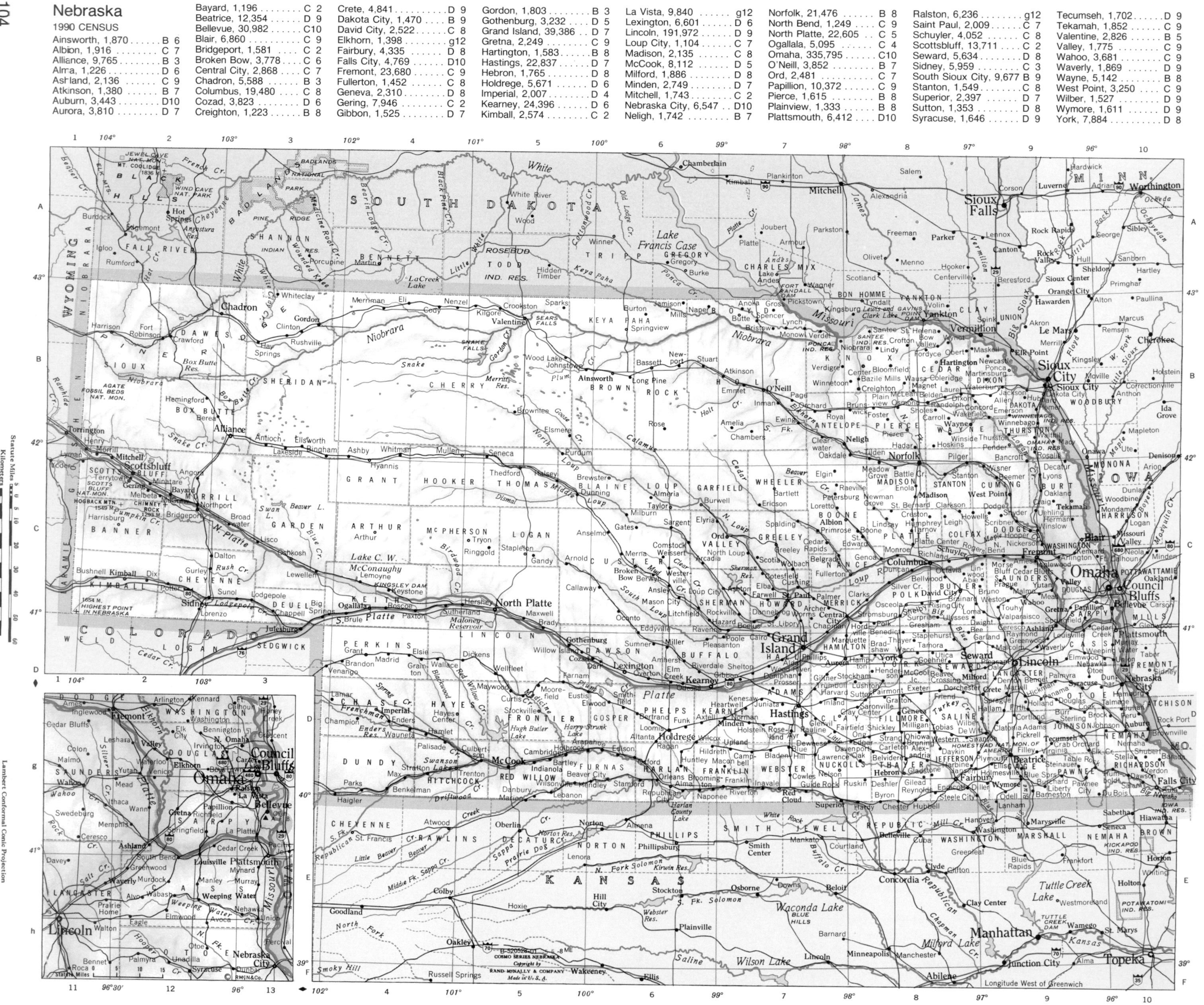

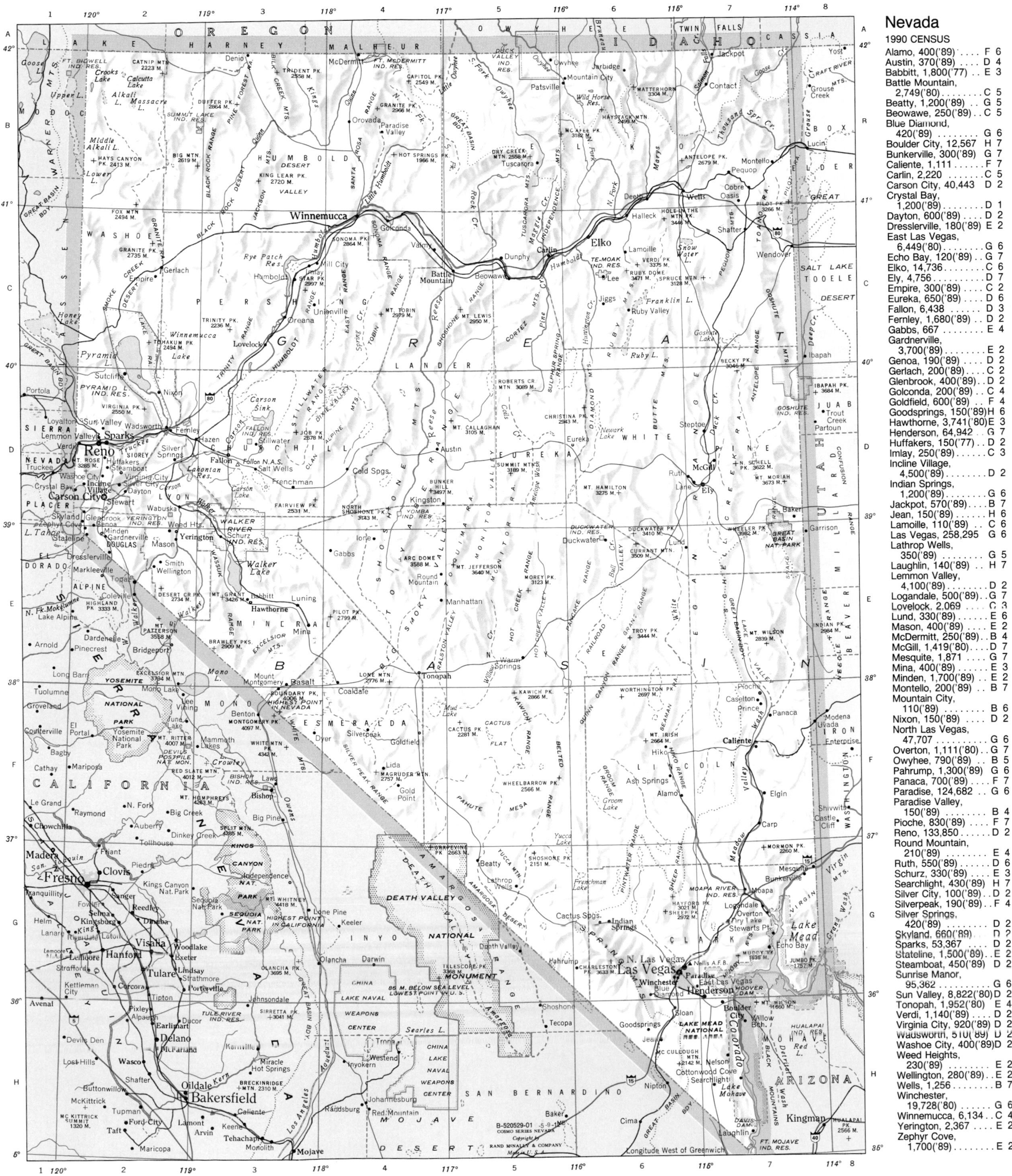

Nevada

1990 CENSUS

Alamo, 400('89) .... F 6
Austin, 370('89) .... D 4
Babbitt, 1,800('77) .. E 3
Battle Mountain, 2,749('80) .... C 5
Beatty, 1,200('89) .. G 5
Beowawe, 250('89) .. C 5
Blue Diamond, 420('89) .... G 6
Boulder City, 12,567 H 7
Bunkerville, 300('89) G 7
Caliente, 1,111 ...... F 7
Carlin, 2,220 .... C 5
Carson City, 40,443 D 2
Crystal Bay, 1,200('89) .... D 1
Dayton, 600('89) .... D 2
Dresslerville, 180('89) E 2
East Las Vegas, 6,449('80) .... G 6
Echo Bay, 120('89) .. G 7
Elko, 14,736 .... C 6
Ely, 4,756 .... D 7
Empire, 300('89) ..... C 2
Eureka, 650('89) ..... D 6
Fallon, 6,438 ...... D 3
Fernley, 1,680('89) .. D 2
Gabbs, 667 .... E 4
Gardnerville, 3,700('89) .... E 2
Genoa, 190('89) .... D 2
Gerlach, 200('89) .... C 2
Glenbrook, 400('89) .. D 2
Golconda, 200('89) .. C 4
Goldfield, 600('89) .. F 4
Goodsprings, 150('89) H 6
Hawthorne, 3,741('80) E 3
Henderson, 64,942 .. G 7
Huffakers, 150('77) .. D 2
Imlay, 250('89) ...... C 3
Incline Village, 4,500('89) .... D 2
Indian Springs, 1,200('89) .... G 6
Jackpot, 570('89) .... B 7
Jean, 150('89) ...... H 6
Lamoille, 110('89) .. C 6
Las Vegas, 258,295 G 6
Lathrop Wells, 350('89) .... G 5
Laughlin, 140('89) .. H 7
Lemmon Valley, 4,100('89) .... D 2
Logandale, 500('89) .. G 7
Lovelock, 2,069 .... C 3
Lund, 330('89) ...... E 6
Mason, 400('89) ...... E 2
McDermitt, 250('89) .. B 4
McGill, 1,419('80) .... D 7
Mesquite, 1,871 .... G 7
Mina, 400('89) ...... E 3
Minden, 1,700('89) .. E 2
Montello, 200('89) .. B 7
Mountain City, 110('89) .... B 6
Nixon, 150('89) .... D 2
North Las Vegas, 47,707 .... G 6
Overton, 1,111('80) .. G 7
Owyhee, 790('89) .. B 5
Pahrump, 1,300('89) G 6
Panaca, 700('89) .... F 7
Paradise, 124,682 .. G 6
Paradise Valley, 150('89) .... B 4
Pioche, 830('89) .... F 7
Reno, 133,850 ...... D 2
Round Mountain, 210('89) .... E 4
Ruth, 550('89) ...... D 6
Schurz, 330('89) .... E 3
Searchlight, 430('89) H 7
Silver City, 100('89) .. D 2
Silverpeak, 190('89) .. F 4
Silver Springs, 420('89) .... D 2
Skyland, 660('89) .... D 2
Sparks, 53,367 .... D 2
Stateline, 1,500('89) .. E 2
Steamboat, 450('89) D 2
Sunrise Manor, 95,362 .... G 6
Sun Valley, 8,822('80) D 2
Tonopah, 1,952('80) E 4
Verdi, 1,140('89) .... D 2
Virginia City, 920('89) D 2
Wadsworth, 510('89) D 2
Washoe City, 400('89) D 2
Weed Heights, 230('89) .... E 2
Wellington, 280('89) .. E 2
Wells, 1,256 .... B 7
Winchester, 19,728('80) .... G 6
Winnemucca, 6,134 .. C 4
Yerington, 2,367 .... E 2
Zephyr Cove, 1,700('89) .... E 2

New Hampshire

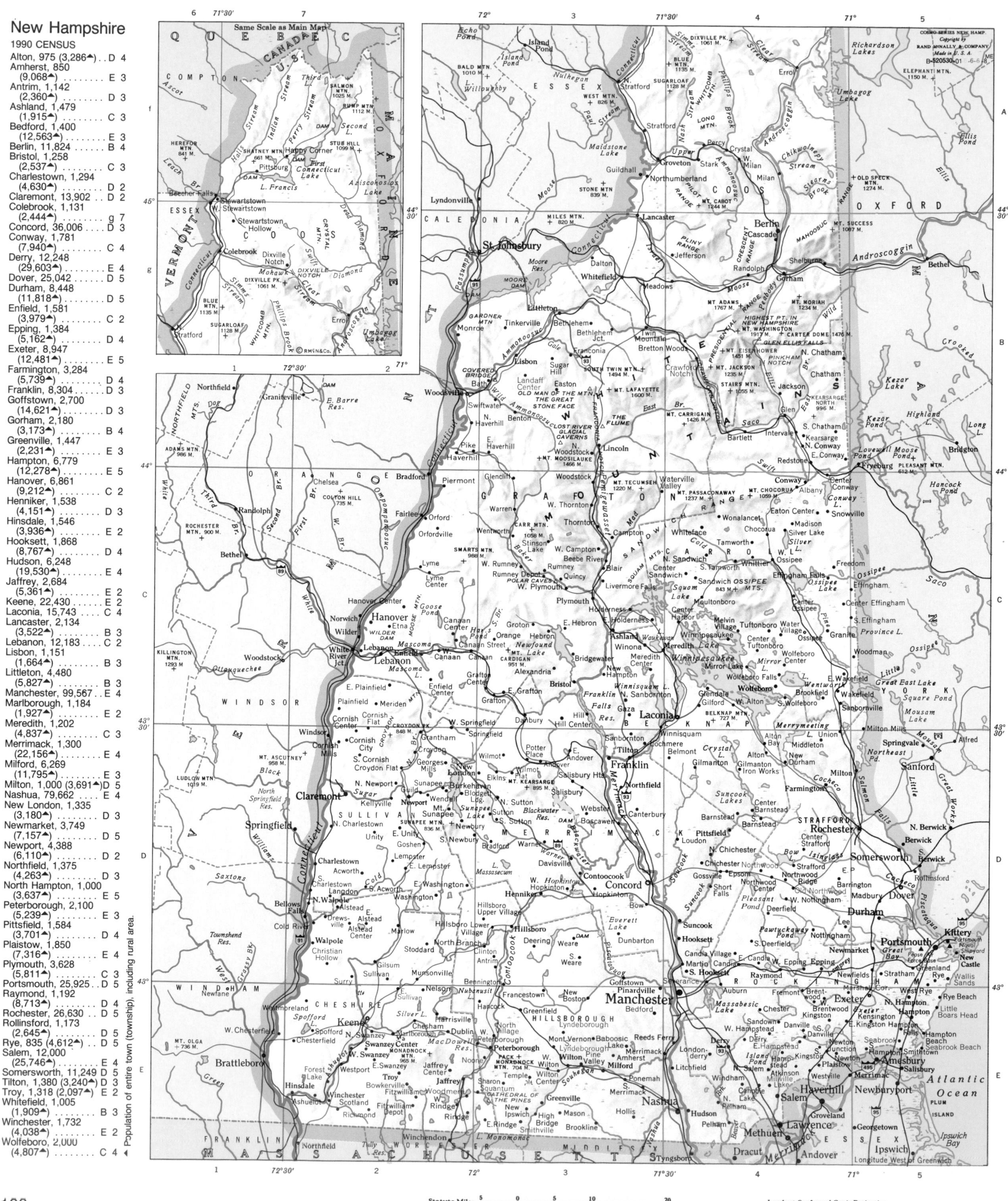

New Hampshire

1990 CENSUS

Alton, 975 (3,286▲) . . D 4
Amherst, 850 (9,068▲) . . . . E 3
Antrim, 1,142 (2,360▲) . . . . D 3
Ashland, 1,479 (1,915▲) . . . . C 3
Bedford, 1,400 (12,563▲) . . . . E 3
Berlin, 11,824 . . . . . . B 4
Bristol, 1,258 (2,537▲) . . . . C 3
Charlestown, 1,294 (4,630▲) . . . . D 2
Claremont, 13,902 . . D 2
Colebrook, 1,131 (2,444▲) . . . . g 7
Concord, 36,006 . . . . D 3
Conway, 1,781 (7,940▲) . . . . C 4
Derry, 12,248 (29,603▲) . . . . E 4
Dover, 25,042 . . . . . . D 5
Durham, 8,448 (11,818▲) . . . . D 5
Enfield, 1,581 (3,979▲) . . . . C 2
Epping, 1,384 (5,162▲) . . . . D 4
Exeter, 8,947 (12,481▲) . . . . E 5
Farmington, 3,284 (5,739▲) . . . . D 4
Franklin, 8,304 . . . . . D 3
Goffstown, 2,700 (14,621▲) . . . . D 3
Gorham, 2,180 (3,173▲) . . . . B 4
Greenville, 1,447 (2,231▲) . . . . E 3
Hampton, 6,779 (12,278▲) . . . . E 5
Hanover, 6,861 (9,212▲) . . . . C 2
Henniker, 1,538 (4,151▲) . . . . D 3
Hinsdale, 1,546 (3,936▲) . . . . E 2
Hooksett, 1,868 (8,767▲) . . . . D 4
Hudson, 6,248 (19,530▲) . . . . E 4
Jaffrey, 2,684 (5,361▲) . . . . E 2
Keene, 22,430 . . . . . . E 2
Laconia, 15,743 . . . . C 4
Lancaster, 2,134 (3,522▲) . . . . B 3
Lebanon, 12,183 . . . . C 2
Lisbon, 1,151 (1,664▲) . . . . B 3
Littleton, 4,480 (5,827▲) . . . . B 3
Manchester, 99,567 . . E 4
Marlborough, 1,184 (1,927▲) . . . . E 2
Meredith, 1,202 (4,837▲) . . . . C 3
Merrimack, 1,300 (22,156▲) . . . . E 4
Milford, 6,269 (11,795▲) . . . . E 3
Milton, 1,000 (3,691▲) D 5
Nashua, 79,662 . . . . E 4
New London, 1,335 (3,180▲) . . . . D 3
Newmarket, 3,749 (7,157▲) . . . . D 5
Newport, 4,388 (6,110▲) . . . . D 2
Northfield, 1,375 (4,263▲) . . . . D 3
North Hampton, 1,000 (3,637▲) . . . . E 5
Peterborough, 2,100 (5,239▲) . . . . E 3
Pittsfield, 1,584 (3,701▲) . . . . D 4
Plaistow, 1,850 (7,316▲) . . . . E 4
Plymouth, 3,628 (5,811▲) . . . . C 3
Portsmouth, 25,925 . . D 5
Raymond, 1,192 (8,713▲) . . . . D 4
Rochester, 26,630 . . D 5
Rollinsford, 1,173 (2,645▲) . . . . D 5
Rye, 835 (4,612▲) . . D 5
Salem, 12,000 (25,746▲) . . . . E 4
Somersworth, 11,249 D 5
Tilton, 1,380 (3,240▲) D 3
Troy, 1,318 (2,097▲) E 2
Whitefield, 1,005 (1,909▲) . . . . B 3
Winchester, 1,732 (4,038▲) . . . . E 2
Wolfeboro, 2,000 (4,807▲) . . . . C 4

▲ Population of entire town (township), including rural area.

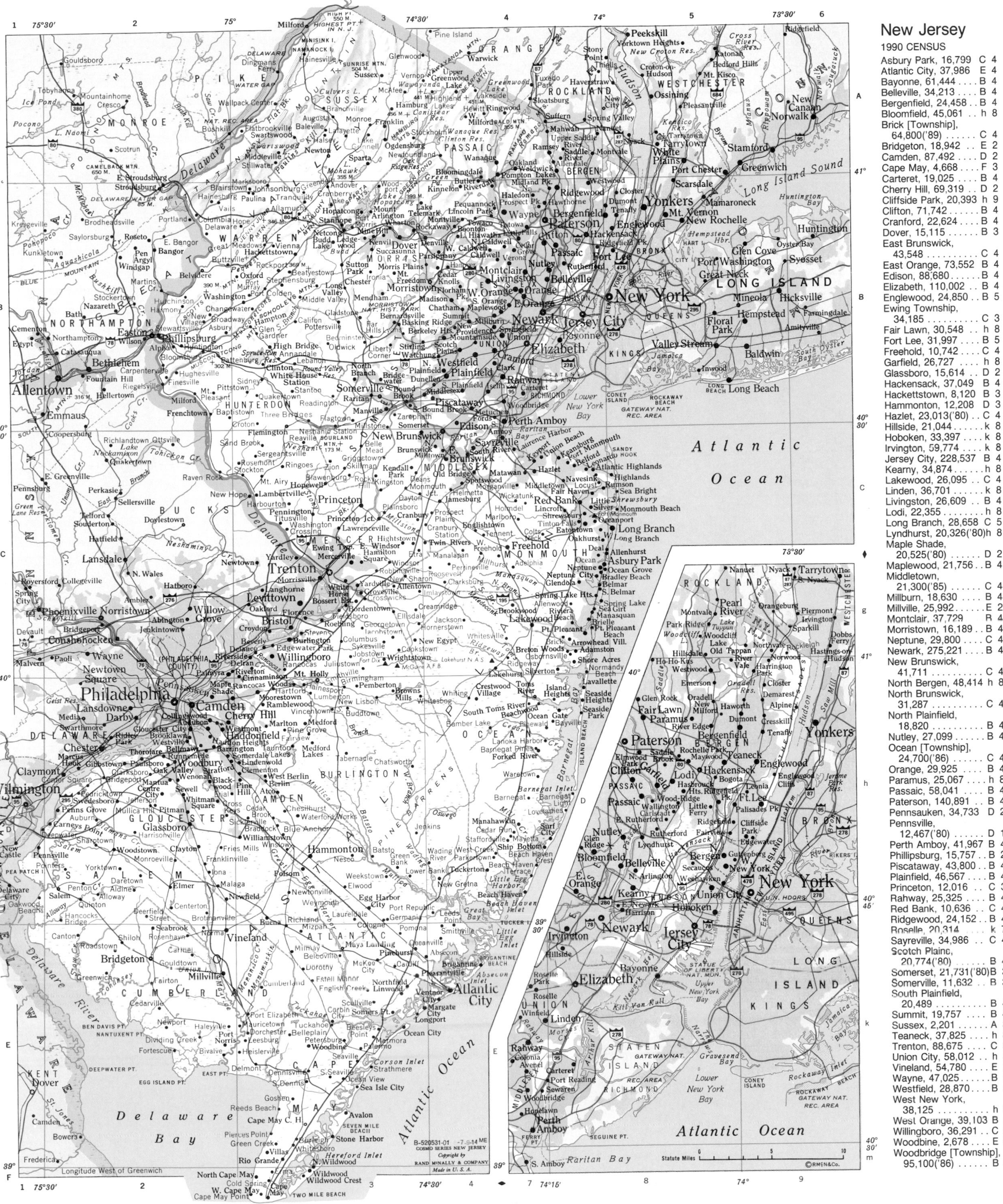
New Jersey
1990 CENSUS
Asbury Park, 16,799 C 4
Atlantic City, 37,986 E 4
Bayonne, 61,444 . . . . B 4
Belleville, 34,213 . . . . B 4
Bergenfield, 24,458 . . B 4
Bloomfield, 45,061 . . . h 8
Brick [Township], 64,800('89) . . . . . . C 4
Bridgeton, 18,942 . . E 2
Camden, 87,492 . . . . D 2
Cape May, 4,668 . . . . F 3
Carteret, 19,025 . . . . B 4
Cherry Hill, 69,319 . . D 2
Cliffside Park, 20,393 h 9
Clifton, 71,742 . . . . . . B 4
Cranford, 22,624 . . . . B 4
Dover, 15,115 . . . . . . B 3
East Brunswick, 43,548 . . . . C 4
East Orange, 73,552 B 4
Edison, 88,680 . . . . . . B 4
Elizabeth, 110,002 . . B 4
Englewood, 24,850 . . B 5
Ewing Township, 34,185 . . . . C 3
Fair Lawn, 30,548 . . . h 8
Fort Lee, 31,997 . . . . B 5
Freehold, 10,742 . . . . C 4
Garfield, 26,727 . . . . . h 8
Glassboro, 15,614 . . D 2
Hackensack, 37,049 B 4
Hackettstown, 8,120 B 3
Hammonton, 12,208 D 3
Hazlet, 23,013('80) . . C 4
Hillside, 21,044 . . . . . k 8
Hoboken, 33,397 . . . . k 8
Irvington, 59,774 . . . . k 8
Jersey City, 228,537 B 4
Kearny, 34,874 . . . . . . h 8
Lakewood, 26,095 . . C 4
Linden, 36,701 . . . . . . k 8
Livingston, 26,609 . . B 4
Lodi, 22,355 . . . . h 8
Long Branch, 28,658 C 5
Lyndhurst, 20,326('80)h 8
Maple Shade, 20,525('80) . . . . . . D 2
Maplewood, 21,756 . . B 4
Middletown, 21,300('85) . . . . . . C 4
Millburn, 18,630 . . . . B 4
Millville, 25,992 . . . . . . E 2
Montclair, 37,729 B 4
Morristown, 16,189 . . B 4
Neptune, 29,800 . . . . C 4
Newark, 275,221 . . . . B 4
New Brunswick, 41,711 . . . . C 4
North Bergen, 48,414 h 8
North Brunswick, 31,287 . . . . C 4
North Plainfield, 18,820 . . . . B 4
Nutley, 27,099 . . . . . . B 4
Ocean [Township], 24,700('86) . . . . . . C 4
Orange, 29,925 . . . . B 4
Paramus, 25,067 . . . . h 8
Passaic, 58,041 . . . . B 4
Paterson, 140,891 . . B 4
Pennsauken, 34,733 D 2
Pennsville, 12,467('80) . . . . . . D 1
Perth Amboy, 41,967 B 4
Phillipsburg, 15,757 . . B 2
Piscataway, 43,800 . . B 4
Plainfield, 46,567 . . . . B 4
Princeton, 12,016 . . C 3
Rahway, 25,325 . . . . B 4
Red Bank, 10,636 . . C 4
Ridgewood, 24,152 . . B 4
Roselle, 20,314 . . . . . . k 7
Sayreville, 34,986 . . C 4
Scotch Plains, 20,774('80) . . . . . . B 4
Somerset, 21,731('80)B 3
Somerville, 11,632 . . B 3
South Plainfield, 20,489 . . . . B 4
Summit, 19,757 . . . . . B 4
Sussex, 2,201 . . . . . . A 3
Teaneck, 37,825 . . . . h 8
Trenton, 88,675 . . . . C 3
Union City, 58,012 . . h 8
Vineland, 54,780 . . . . E 2
Wayne, 47,025 . . . . . B 4
Westfield, 28,870 . . . . B 4
West New York, 38,125 . . . . h 8
West Orange, 39,103 B 4
Willingboro, 36,291 . . C 3
Woodbine, 2,678 . . . . E 3
Woodbridge [Township], 95,100('86) . . . . . . B 4
Atlantic Ocean
Delaware Bay
Longitude West of Greenwich
B-520531-01 -7-9-14 ME
COSMO SERIES NEW JERSEY
Copyright by RAND MCNALLY & COMPANY
Made in U. S. A.
Statute Miles
Kilometers
Lambert Conformal Conic Projection

New Mexico

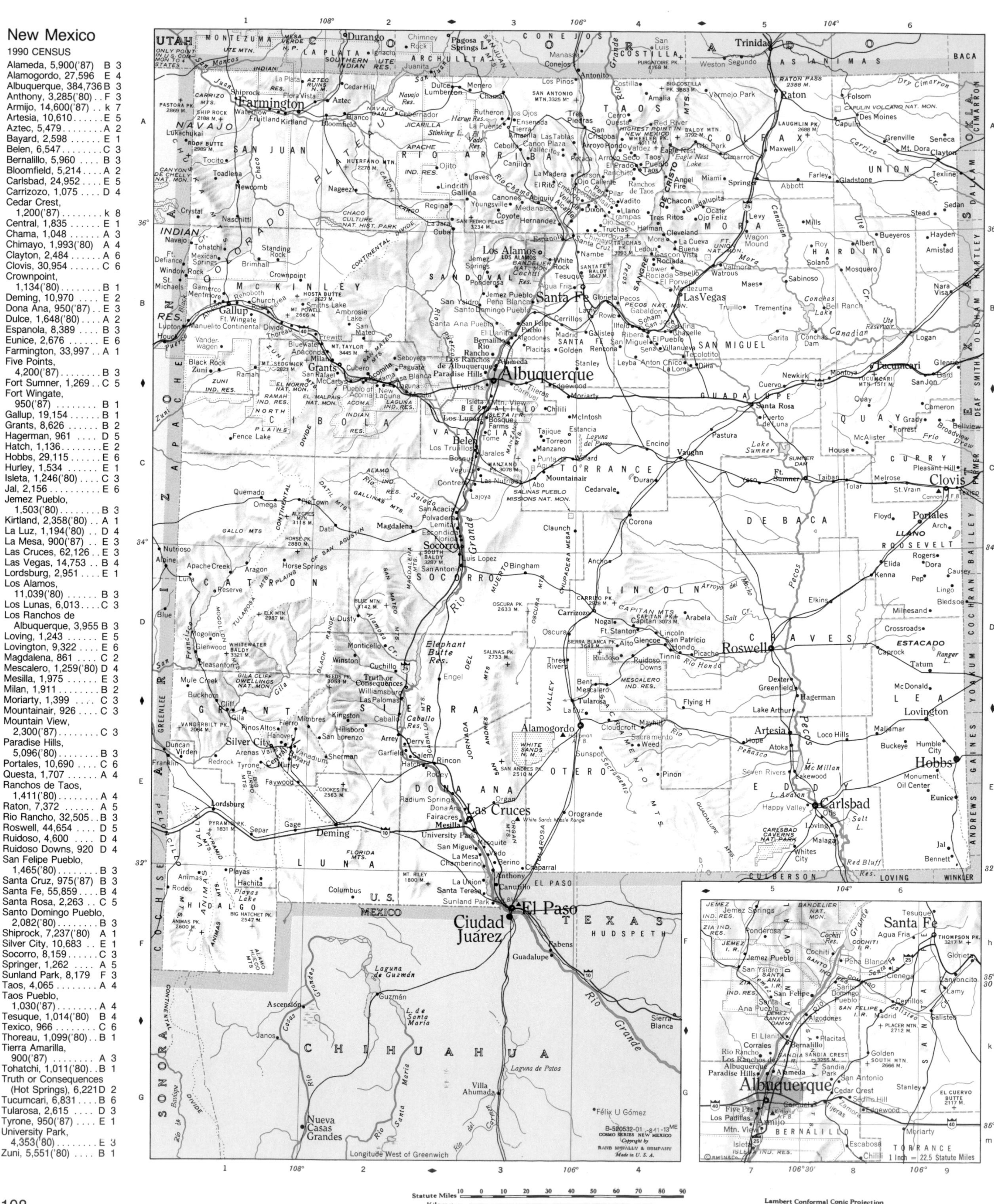

New Mexico

1990 CENSUS

Alameda, 5,900('87) B 3
Alamogordo, 27,596 E 4
Albuquerque, 384,736 B 3
Anthony, 3,285('80) .. F 3
Armijo, 14,600('87) .. k 7
Artesia, 10,610 ...... E 5
Aztec, 5,479 .... A 2
Bayard, 2,598 ...... E 1
Belen, 6,547 .... C 3
Bernalillo, 5,960 .... B 3
Bloomfield, 5,214 .... A 2
Carlsbad, 24,952 .... E 5
Carrizozo, 1,075 .... D 4
Cedar Crest, 1,200('87) .... k 8
Central, 1,835 .... E 1
Chama, 1,048 .... A 3
Chimayo, 1,993('80) A 4
Clayton, 2,484 ...... A 6
Clovis, 30,954 ...... C 6
Crownpoint, 1,134('80) .... B 1
Deming, 10,970 .... E 2
Dona Ana, 950('87) .. E 3
Dulce, 1,648('80) .... A 2
Espanola, 8,389 .... B 3
Eunice, 2,676 ...... E 6
Farmington, 33,997 .. A 1
Five Points, 4,200('87) .... B 3
Fort Sumner, 1,269 .. C 5
Fort Wingate, 950('87) .... B 1
Gallup, 19,154 ...... B 1
Grants, 8,626 .... B 2
Hagerman, 961 .... D 5
Hatch, 1,136 .... E 2
Hobbs, 29,115 ...... E 6
Hurley, 1,534 ...... E 1
Isleta, 1,246('80) .... C 3
Jal, 2,156 .... E 6
Jemez Pueblo, 1,503('80) .... B 3
Kirtland, 2,358('80) .. A 1
La Luz, 1,194('80) .. D 4
La Mesa, 900('87) .. E 3
Las Cruces, 62,126 .. E 3
Las Vegas, 14,753 .. B 4
Lordsburg, 2,951 .... E 1
Los Alamos, 11,039('80) ...... B 3
Los Lunas, 6,013 .... C 3
Los Ranchos de Albuquerque, 3,955 B 3
Loving, 1,243 ...... E 5
Lovington, 9,322 .... E 6
Magdalena, 861 .... C 2
Mescalero, 1,259('80) D 4
Mesilla, 1,975 ...... E 3
Milan, 1,911 .... B 2
Moriarty, 1,399 .... C 3
Mountainair, 926 .... C 3
Mountain View, 2,300('87) .... C 3
Paradise Hills, 5,096('80) .... B 3
Portales, 10,690 .... C 6
Questa, 1,707 ...... A 4
Ranchos de Taos, 1,411('80) .... A 4
Raton, 7,372 ...... A 5
Rio Rancho, 32,505 .. B 3
Roswell, 44,654 .... D 5
Ruidoso, 4,600 ...... D 4
Ruidoso Downs, 920 D 4
San Felipe Pueblo, 1,465('80) .... B 3
Santa Cruz, 975('87) B 3
Santa Fe, 55,859 .... B 4
Santa Rosa, 2,263 .. C 5
Santo Domingo Pueblo, 2,082('80) .... B 3
Shiprock, 7,237('80) A 1
Silver City, 10,683 .. E 1
Socorro, 8,159 .... C 3
Springer, 1,262 .... A 5
Sunland Park, 8,179 F 3
Taos, 4,065 .... A 4
Taos Pueblo, 1,030('87) .... A 4
Tesuque, 1,014('80) B 4
Texico, 966 .... C 6
Thoreau, 1,099('80) .. B 1
Tierra Amarilla, 900('87) .... A 3
Tohatchi, 1,011('80) .. B 1
Truth or Consequences (Hot Springs), 6,221 D 2
Tucumcari, 6,831 .... B 6
Tularosa, 2,615 ...... D 3
Tyrone, 950('87) .... E 1
University Park, 4,353('80) .... E 3
Zuni, 5,551('80) .... B 1

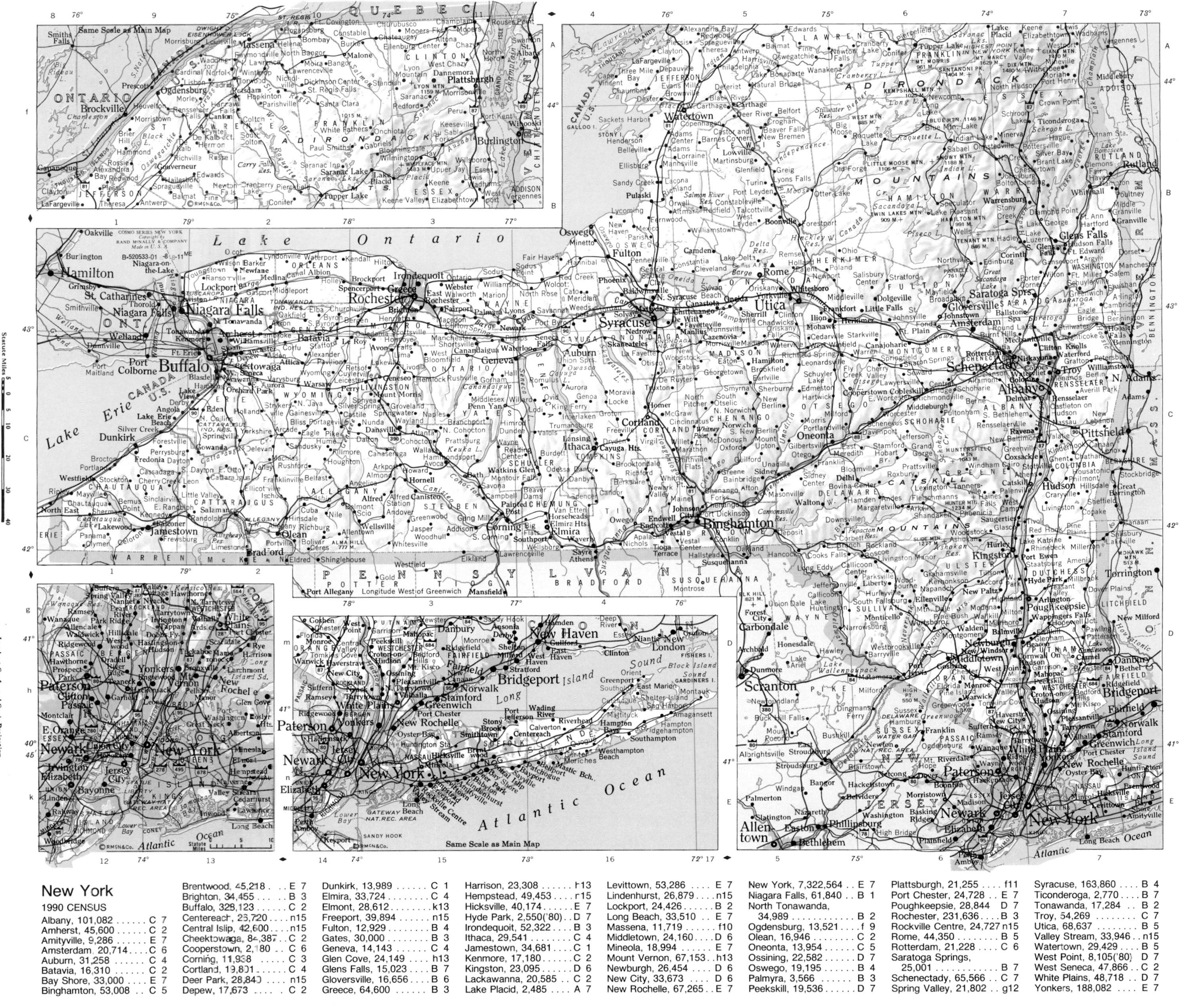

New York

1990 CENSUS

Albany, 101,082 . . . . . . C 7
Amherst, 45,600 . . . . . . C 2
Amityville, 9,286 . . . . . . E 7
Amsterdam, 20,714 . . . C 6
Auburn, 31,258 . . . . . . C 4
Batavia, 16,310 . . . . . . C 2
Bay Shore, 33,000 . . . . E 7
Binghamton, 53,008 . . C 5
Brentwood, 45,218 . . . E 7
Brighton, 34,455 . . . . . B 3
Buffalo, 328,123 . . . . . . C 2
Centereach, 23,720 . . . . n15
Central Islip, 42,600 . . . . n15
Cheektowaga, 84,387 . . C 2
Cooperstown, 2,180 . . C 6
Corning, 11,938 . . . . . . C 3
Cortland, 19,801 . . . . . C 4
Deer Park, 28,840 . . . . n15
Depew, 17,673 . . . . . . C 2
Dunkirk, 13,989 . . . . . . C 1
Elmira, 33,724 . . . . C 4
Elmont, 28,612 . . . . k13
Freeport, 39,894 . . . . . . n15
Fulton, 12,929 . . . . B 4
Gates, 30,000 . . . . B 3
Geneva, 14,143 . . . . . . C 4
Glen Cove, 24,149 . . . . . h13
Glens Falls, 15,023 . . . . B 7
Gloversville, 16,656 . . . . B 6
Greece, 64,600 . . . . B 3
Harrison, 23,308 . . . . . . h13
Hempstead, 49,453 . . . . n15
Hicksville, 40,174 . . . . . . E 7
Hyde Park, 2,550('80) . . D 7
Irondequoit, 52,322 . . . . B 3
Ithaca, 29,541 . . . . C 4
Jamestown, 34,681 . . . . C 1
Kenmore, 17,180 . . . . . . C 2
Kingston, 23,095 . . . . . . D 6
Lackawanna, 20,585 . . . C 2
Lake Placid, 2,485 . . . . . A 7
Levittown, 53,286 . . . . . E 7
Lindenhurst, 26,879 . . . . n15
Lockport, 24,426 . . . . . . B 2
Long Beach, 33,510 . . . E 7
Massena, 11,719 . . . . . . f10
Middletown, 24,160 . . . . D 6
Mineola, 18,994 . . . . . . E 7
Mount Vernon, 67,153 . . h13
Newburgh, 26,454 . . . . D 6
New City, 33,673 . . . . . D 6
New Rochelle, 67,265 . . E 7
New York, 7,322,564 . . E 7
Niagara Falls, 61,840 . . B 1
North Tonawanda,
34,989 . . . . B 2
Ogdensburg, 13,521 . . . . f 9
Olean, 16,946 . . . . C 2
Oneonta, 13,954 . . . . . . C 5
Ossining, 22,582 . . . . . . D 7
Oswego, 19,195 . . . . B 4
Palmyra, 3,566 . . . . B 3
Peekskill, 19,536 . . . . . . D 7
Plattsburgh, 21,255 . . . . f11
Port Chester, 24,728 . . E 7
Poughkeepsie, 28,844 D 7
Rochester, 231,636 . . . . B 3
Rockville Centre, 24,727 n15
Rome, 44,350 . . . . B 5
Rotterdam, 21,228 . . . . C 6
Saratoga Springs,
25,001 . . . . B 7
Schenectady, 65,566 . . C 7
Spring Valley, 21,802 . . g12
Syracuse, 163,860 . . . . B 4
Ticonderoga, 2,770 . . . . B 7
Tonawanda, 17,284 . . B 2
Troy, 54,269 . . . . C 7
Utica, 68,637 . . . . B 5
Valley Stream, 33,946 . . n15
Watertown, 29,429 . . . . B 5
West Point, 8,105('80) D 7
West Seneca, 47,866 . . C 2
White Plains, 48,718 . . D 7
Yonkers, 188,082 . . . . E 7

North Carolina

1990 CENSUS

Ahoskie, 4,391 . . . . A 6
Albemarle, 14,939 . . . . B 2
Archdale, 6,913 . . . . . . B 3
Asheboro, 16,362 . . . . B 3
Asheville, 61,607 . . . . . . f10
Bessemer City, 4,698 . . B 1
Boone, 12,915 . . . . A 1
Brevard, 5,388 . . . . f10
Burlington, 39,498 . . . . A 3
Carrboro, 11,553 . . . . . . B 3
Cary, 43,858 . . . . B 4
Chapel Hill, 38,719 . . . . B 3
Charlotte, 395,934 . . . . B 2
Cherryville, 4,756 . . . . . . B 1
Clemmons, 6,020 . . . . A 2
Clinton, 8,204 . . . . C 4
Concord, 27,347 . . . . . . B 2
Dunn, 8,336 . . . . B 4
Durham, 136,611 . . . . . . B 4
Eden, 15,238 . . . . A 3
Edenton, 5,268 . . . . . . A 6
Elizabeth City, 14,292 . . A 6
Farmville, 4,392 . . . . . . B 5
Fayetteville, 75,695 . . . . B 4
Forest City, 7,475 . . . . B 1
Garner, 14,967 . . . . . . B 4
Gastonia, 54,732 . . . . . . B 1
Goldsboro, 40,709 . . . . B 5
Graham, 10,426 . . . . . . A 3
Greensboro, 183,521 . . A 3
Greenville, 44,972 . . . . B 5
Hamlet, 6,196 . . . . C 3
Havelock, 20,268 . . . . C 6
Henderson, 15,655 . . . . A 4
Hendersonville, 7,284 . . f10
Hickory, 28,301 . . . . . . B 1
High Point, 69,496 . . . . B 2
Hope Mills, 8,184 . . . . C 4
Jacksonville, 30,013 . . . C 5
Kannapolis, 29,696 . . . . B 2
Kernersville, 10,836 . . . . A 2
Kings Mountain, 8,763 B 1
Kinston, 25,295 . . . . . . B 5
Laurinburg, 11,643 . . . . C 3
Lenoir, 14,192 . . . . B 1
Lexington, 16,581 . . . . B 2
Lincolnton, 6,847 . . . . . . B 1
Lumberton, 18,601 . . . . C 3
Matthews, 13,651 . . . . B 2
Mint Hill, 11,567 . . . . . . B 2
Monroe, 16,127 . . . . . . C 2
Mooresville, 9,317 . . . . B 2
Morehead City, 6,046 . . C 6
Morganton, 15,085 . . . . B 1
Mount Airy, 7,156 . . . . A 2
Mount Olive, 4,582 . . . . B 4
Nags Head, 1,838 . . . . B 7
New Bern, 17,363 . . . . B 5
Newton, 9,304 . . . . B 1
Oxford, 7,913 . . . . A 4
Plymouth, 4,328 . . . . . . B 6
Raleigh, 207,951 . . . . . . B 4
Reidsville, 12,183 . . . . A 3
Roanoke Rapids, 15,722 . . . . A 5
Rockingham, 9,399 . . . . C 3
Rocky Mount, 48,997 . . B 5
Roxboro, 7,332 . . . . . . A 4
Salisbury, 23,087 . . . . . . B 2
Sanford, 14,475 . . . . . . B 3
• Selma, 4,600 . . . . B 4
Shelby, 14,669 . . . . . . B 1
Smithfield, 7,540 . . . . . . B 4
Southern Pines, 9,129 . . B 3
Spring Lake, 7,524 . . . . B 4
Statesville, 17,567 . . . . B 2
Tarboro, 11,037 . . . . . . B 5
Thomasville, 15,915 . . B 2
Washington, 9,075 . . B 5
Waynesville, 6,758 . . . . f10
Whiteville, 5,078 . . . . . . C 4
Williamston, 5,503 . . . . B 5
Wilmington, 55,530 . . . C 5
Wilson, 36,930 . . . . B 5
Winston-Salem, 143,485 A 2

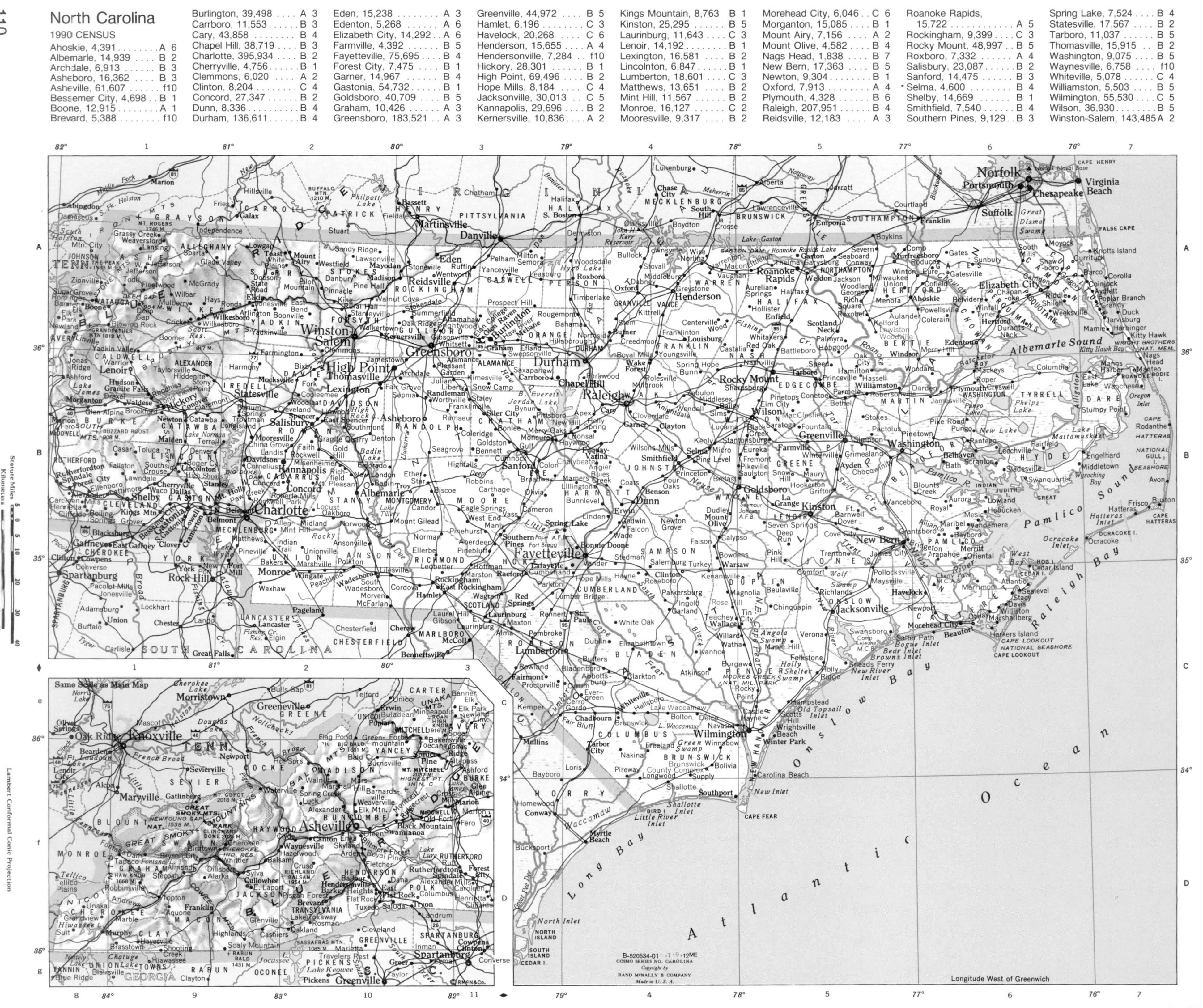

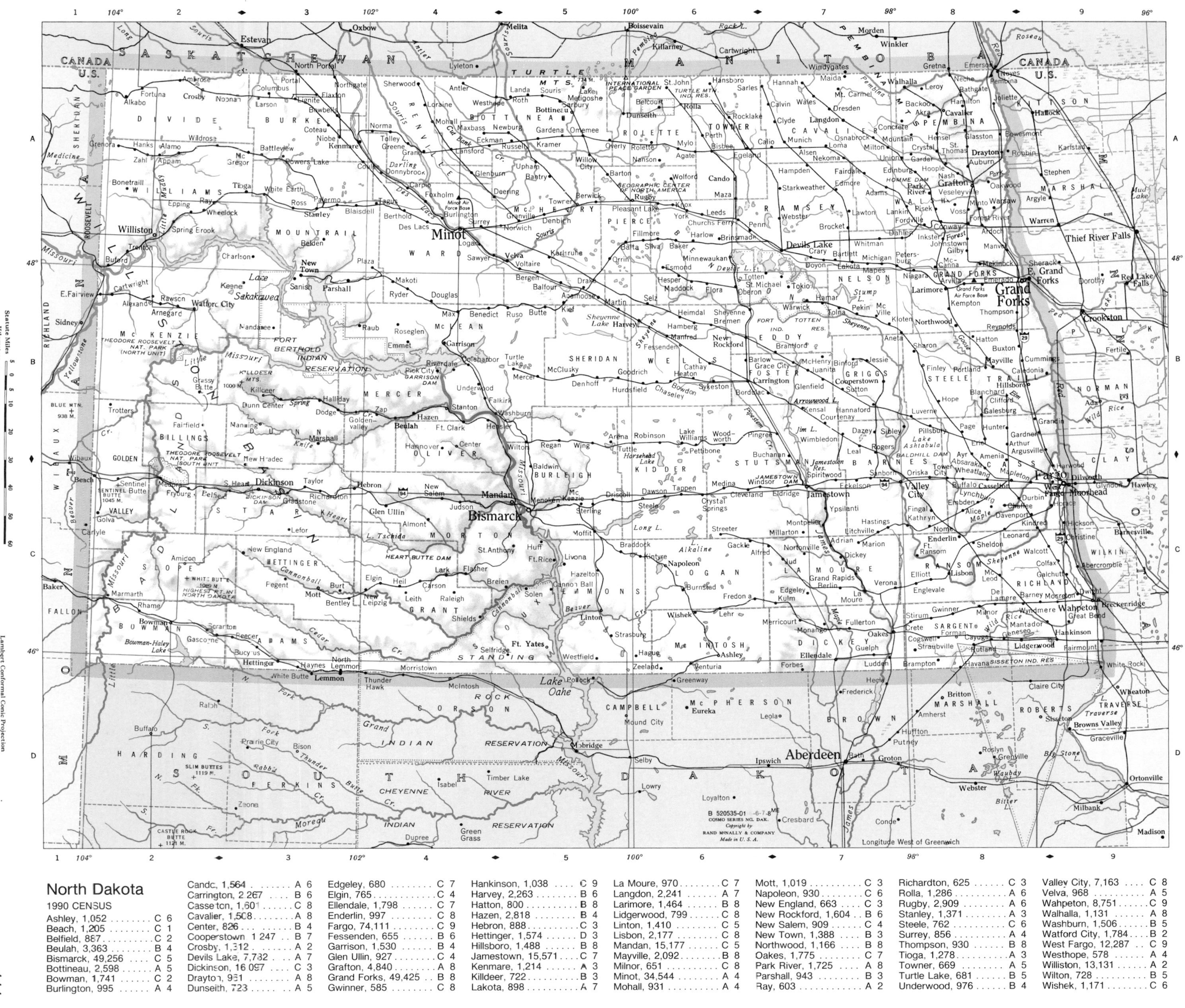

North Dakota

1990 CENSUS

- Ashley, 1,052 .... C 6
- Beach, 1,205 .... C 1
- Belfield, 887 .... C 2
- Beulah, 3,363 .... B 4
- Bismarck, 49,256 .... C 5
- Bottineau, 2,598 ..... A 5
- Bowman, 1,741 ...... C 2
- Burlington, 995 ...... A 4
- Cando, 1,564 .... A 6
- Carrington, 2,267 .... B 6
- Casselton, 1,601 ..... C 8
- Cavalier, 1,508 .... A 8
- Center, 826 .... B 4
- Cooperstown 1,247 .. B 7
- Crosby, 1,312 .... A 2
- Devils Lake, 7,782 .... A 7
- Dickinson, 16,097 ..... C 3
- Drayton, 961 .... A 8
- Dunseith, 723 .... A 5
- Edgeley, 680 .... C 7
- Elgin, 765 .... C 4
- Ellendale, 1,798 ...... C 7
- Enderlin, 997 .... C 8
- Fargo, 74,111 .... C 9
- Fessenden, 655 ...... B 6
- Garrison, 1,530 ...... B 4
- Glen Ullin, 927 .... C 4
- Grafton, 4,840 .... A 8
- Grand Forks, 49,425 .. B 8
- Gwinner, 585 .... C 8
- Hankinson, 1,038 .... C 9
- Harvey, 2,263 .... B 6
- Hatton, 800 .... B 8
- Hazen, 2,818 .... B 4
- Hebron, 888 .... C 3
- Hettinger, 1,574 ...... D 3
- Hillsboro, 1,488 ...... B 8
- Jamestown, 15,571 ... C 7
- Kenmare, 1,214 ...... A 3
- Killdeer, 722 .... B 3
- Lakota, 898 .... A 7
- La Moure, 970 .... C 7
- Langdon, 2,241 .... A 7
- Larimore, 1,464 ...... B 8
- Lidgerwood, 799 ...... C 8
- Linton, 1,410 .... C 5
- Lisbon, 2,177 .... C 8
- Mandan, 15,177 ...... C 5
- Mayville, 2,092 .... B 8
- Milnor, 651 .... C 8
- Minot, 34,544 .... A 4
- Mohall, 931 .... A 4
- Mott, 1,019 .... C 3
- Napoleon, 930 .... C 6
- New England, 663 .... C 3
- New Rockford, 1,604 .. B 6
- New Salem, 909 ...... C 4
- New Town, 1,388 ..... B 3
- Northwood, 1,166 .... B 8
- Oakes, 1,775 .... C 7
- Park River, 1,725 .... A 8
- Parshall, 943 .... B 3
- Ray, 603 .... A 2
- Richardton, 625 ...... C 3
- Rolla, 1,286 .... A 6
- Rugby, 2,909 .... A 6
- Stanley, 1,371 .... A 3
- Steele, 762 .... C 6
- Surrey, 856 .... A 4
- Thompson, 930 .... B 8
- Tioga, 1,278 .... A 3
- Towner, 669 .... A 5
- Turtle Lake, 681 ...... B 5
- Underwood, 976 ...... B 4
- Valley City, 7,163 .... C 8
- Velva, 968 .... A 5
- Wahpeton, 8,751 ...... C 9
- Walhalla, 1,131 .... A 8
- Washburn, 1,506 ...... B 5
- Watford City, 1,784 ... B 2
- West Fargo, 12,287 .. C 9
- Westhope, 578 .... A 4
- Williston, 13,131 ...... A 2
- Wilton, 728 .... B 5
- Wishek, 1,171 .... C 6

Ohio

1990 CENSUS

Akron, 223,019 . . . . . . A 4
Alliance, 23,376 . . . . . . B 4
Ashland, 20,079 . . . . . . B 3
Ashtabula, 21,633 . . . . A 5
Athens, 21,265 . . . . . . C 3
Austintown, 23,300 . . . A 5
Barberton, 27,623 . . . . A 4
Beavercreek, 33,626 . . C 1
Bellefontaine, 12,142 . . B 2
Boardman, 38,596 . . . . A 5
Bowling Green, 28,176 A 2
Brook Park, 22,865 . . . h 9
Brunswick, 28,230 . . . . A 4
Canton, 84,161 . . . . . . B 4
Chillicothe, 21,923 . . . . C 3
Cincinnati, 364,040 . . . . C 1
Cleveland, 505,616 . . . . A 4
Cleveland Heights, 54,052 . . . . A 4
Columbus, 632,910 . . . . C 2
Cuyahoga Falls, 48,950 A 4
Dayton, 182,044 . . . . . . C 1
Defiance, 16,768 . . . . . . A 1
Delaware, 20,030 . . . . B 2
East Cleveland, 33,096 g 9
Eastlake, 21,161 . . . . . A 4
East Liverpool, 13,654 B 5
Elyria, 56,746 . . . . A 3
Euclid, 54,875 . . . . A 4
Fairborn, 31,300 . . . . . . C 1
Fairfield, 39,729 . . . . . . n12
Findlay, 35,703 . . . . . . A 2
Fostoria, 14,983 . . . . . . A 2
Fremont, 17,648 . . . . . . A 2
Garfield Heights, 31,739 h 9
Greenville, 12,863 . . . . . B 1
Hamilton, 61,368 . . . . . C 1
Ironton, 12,751 . . . . . . D 3
Kent, 28,835 . . . . A 4
Kettering, 60,569 . . . . . C 1
Lakewood, 59,718 . . . . A 4
Lancaster, 34,507 . . . . C 3
Lima, 45,549 . . . . B 1
Lorain, 71,245 . . . . A 3
Mansfield, 50,627 . . . . . B 3
Maple Heights, 27,089 . . h 9
Marietta, 15,026 . . . . . . C 4
Marion, 34,075 . . . . . . B 2
Massillon, 31,007 . . . . B 4
Medina, 19,231 . . . . . . A 4
Mentor, 47,358 . . . . . . A 4
Middletown, 46,022 . . . . C 1
Mount Vernon, 14,550 B 3
Newark, 44,389 . . . . . . B 3
New Philadelphia, 15,698 . . . . B 4
Niles, 21,128 . . . . A 5
North Olmsted, 34,204 h 9
Norwalk, 14,731 . . . . . . A 3
Norwood, 23,674 . . . . . . o13
Oxford, 18,937 . . . . . . C 1
Parma, 87,876 . . . . A 4
Parma Heights, 21,448 h 9
Piqua, 20,612 . . . . B 1
Portsmouth, 22,676 . . D 3
Reynoldsburg, 25,748 . . C 3
Salem, 12,233 . . . . B 5
Sandusky, 29,764 . . . . . A 3
Shaker Heights, 30,831 A 4
South Euclid, 23,866 . . g 9
Springfield, 70,487 . . . . C 2
Steubenville, 22,125 . . . B 5
Stow, 27,702 . . . . A 4
Strongsville, 35,308 . . . A 4
Tiffin, 18,604 . . . . A 2
Toledo, 332,943 . . . . . . A 2
Upper Arlington, 34,128 B 2
Urbana, 11,353 . . . . . . B 2
Warren, 50,793 . . . . . . A 5
Westerville, 30,269 . . . B 3
Whitehall, 20,572 . . . . m11
Wooster, 22,191 . . . . . . B 4
Xenia, 24,664 . . . . C 2
Youngstown, 95,732 . . A 5
Zanesville, 26,778 . . . . C 4

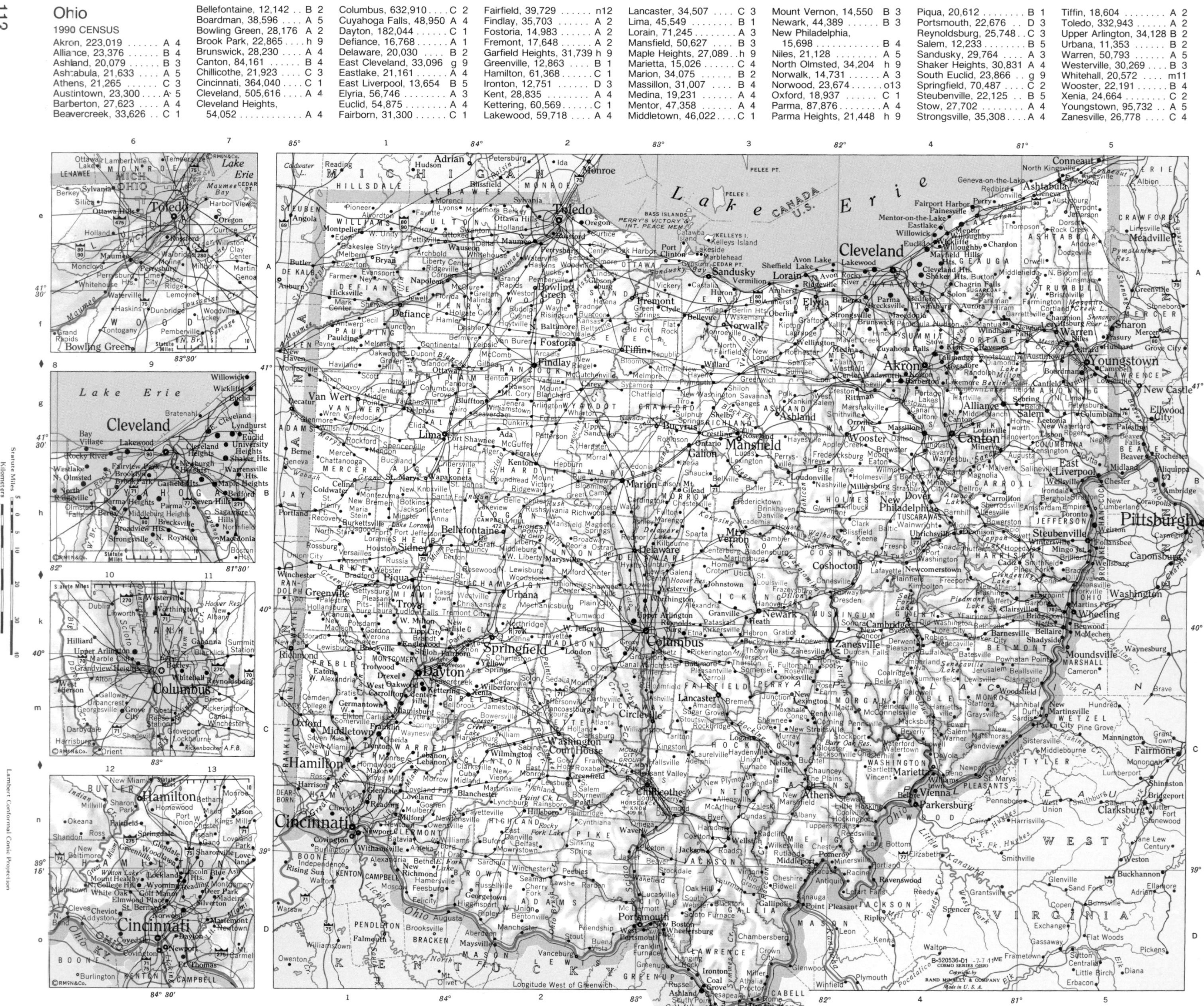

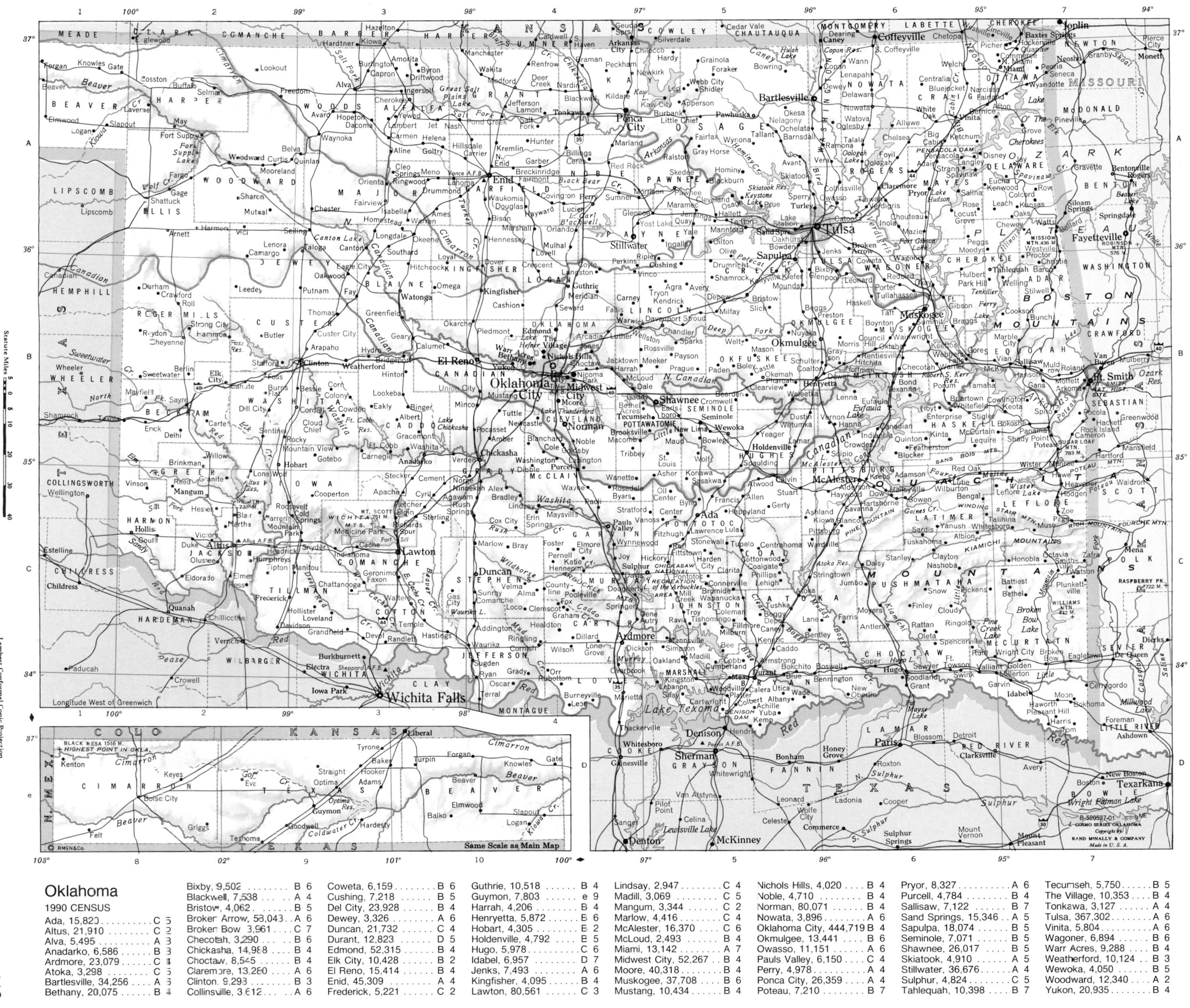

Oklahoma

1990 CENSUS

Ada, 15,820 ... C 5	Bixby, 9,502 ... B 6	Coweta, 6,159 ... B 6	Guthrie, 10,518 ... B 4	Lindsay, 2,947 ... C 4	Nichols Hills, 4,020 ... B 4	Pryor, 8,327 ... A 6	Tecumseh, 5,750 ... B 5
Altus, 21,910 ... C 2	Blackwell, 7,538 ... A 4	Cushing, 7,218 ... B 5	Guymon, 7,803 ... e 9	Madill, 3,069 ... C 5	Noble, 4,710 ... B 4	Purcell, 4,784 ... B 4	The Village, 10,353 ... B 4
Alva, 5,495 ... A 3	Bristow, 4,062 ... B 5	Del City, 23,928 ... B 4	Harrah, 4,206 ... B 4	Mangum, 3,344 ... C 2	Norman, 80,071 ... B 4	Sallisaw, 7,122 ... B 7	Tonkawa, 3,127 ... A 4
Anadarko, 6,586 ... B 3	Broken Arrow, 58,043 ... A 6	Dewey, 3,326 ... A 6	Henryetta, 5,872 ... B 6	Marlow, 4,416 ... C 4	Nowata, 3,896 ... A 6	Sand Springs, 15,346 ... A 5	Tulsa, 367,302 ... A 6
Ardmore, 23,079 ... C 4	Broken Bow, 3,961 ... C 7	Duncan, 21,732 ... C 4	Hobart, 4,305 ... B 2	McAlester, 16,370 ... C 6	Oklahoma City, 444,719 B 4	Sapulpa, 18,074 ... B 5	Vinita, 5,804 ... A 6
Atoka, 3,298 ... C 5	Checotah, 3,290 ... B 6	Durant, 12,823 ... D 5	Holdenville, 4,792 ... B 5	McLoud, 2,493 ... B 4	Okmulgee, 13,441 ... B 6	Seminole, 7,071 ... B 5	Wagoner, 6,894 ... B 6
Bartlesville, 34,256 ... A 5	Chickasha, 14,988 ... B 4	Edmond, 52,315 ... B 4	Hugo, 5,978 ... C 6	Miami, 13,142 ... A 7	Owasso, 11,151 ... A 6	Shawnee, 26,017 ... B 5	Warr Acres, 9,288 ... B 4
Bethany, 20,075 ... B 4	Choctaw, 8,545 ... B 4	Elk City, 10,428 ... B 2	Idabel, 6,957 ... D 7	Midwest City, 52,267 ... B 4	Pauls Valley, 6,150 ... C 4	Skiatook, 4,910 ... A 5	Weatherford, 10,124 ... B 3
	Claremore, 13,280 ... A 6	El Reno, 15,414 ... B 4	Jenks, 7,493 ... A 6	Moore, 40,318 ... B 4	Perry, 4,978 ... A 4	Stillwater, 36,676 ... A 4	Wewoka, 4,050 ... B 5
	Clinton, 9,298 ... B 3	Enid, 45,309 ... A 4	Kingfisher, 4,095 ... B 4	Muskogee, 37,708 ... B 6	Ponca City, 26,359 ... A 4	Sulphur, 4,824 ... C 5	Woodward, 12,340 ... A 2
	Collinsville, 3,612 ... A 6	Frederick, 5,221 ... C 2	Lawton, 80,561 ... C 3	Mustang, 10,434 ... B 4	Poteau, 7,210 ... B 7	Tahlequah, 10,398 ... B 7	Yukon, 20,935 ... B 4

Oregon

1990 CENSUS

Albany, 29,462 . . . . . . C 3
Aloha, 10,000('82) h12
Altamont, 19,805('80) . . E 5
Ashland, 16,234 . . . . . . E 4
Astoria, 10,069 . . . . . . A 3
Baker, 9,140 . . . . C 9
Beaverton, 53,310 . . . . B 4
Bend, 20,469 . . . . C 5
Brookings, 4,400 . . . . . . E 2
Burns, 2,913 . . . . D 7
Canby, 8,983 . . . . B 4
Central Point, 7,509 . . . E 4
Coos Bay, 15,076 . . . . D 2
Coquille, 4,121 . . . . D 2
Cornelius, 6,148 . . . . . . g11
Corvallis, 44,757 . . . . . . C 3
Cottage Grove, 7,402 . . D 3
Dallas, 9,422 . . . . C 3
Eugene, 112,669 . . . . . . C 3
Florence, 5,162 . . . . . . D 2
Forest Grove, 13,559 . . B 3
Gladstone, 10,152 . . . . B 4
Grants Pass, 17,488 . . . E 3
Green, 3,897('80) . . . . D 3
Gresham, 68,235 . . . . . B 4
Hermiston, 10,040 . . . . B 7
Hillsboro, 37,520 . . . . . B 4
Hood River, 4,632 . . . . B 5
Independence, 4,425 . . . C 3
John Day, 1,836 . . . . . . C 8
Junction City, 3,670 . . . C 3
Keizer, 21,884 . . . . C 3
Klamath Falls, 17,737 . . E 5
La Grande, 11,766 . . . . B 8
Lake Oswego, 30,576 . . B 4
Lakeview, 2,526 . . . . . . E 6
Lebanon, 10,950 . . . . . . C 4
Lincoln City, 5,892 . . . . C 3
McMinnville, 17,894 . . . . B 3
Medford, 46,951 . . . . . . E 4
Metzger, 5,544('80) h12
Milton-Freewater, 5,533 B 8
Milwaukie, 18,692 . . . . B 4
Molalla, 3,651 . . . . B 4
Monmouth, 6,288 . . . . . C 3
Mount Angel, 2,778 . . . . B 4
Myrtle Creek, 3,063 . . . D 3
Myrtle Point, 2,712 . . . . D 2
Newberg, 13,086 . . . . . . B 4
Newport, 8,437 . . . . . . C 2
North Albany, 4,499('80) k11
North Bend, 9,614 . . . . D 2
Nyssa, 2,629 . . . . D 9
Oak Grove, 11,640('80) B 4
Oakridge, 3,063 . . . . . . D 4
Ontario, 9,392 . . . . C10
Oregon City, 14,698 . . . B 4
Parkrose, 21,108('80) . . B 4
Pendleton, 15,126 . . . . B 8
Portland, 437,319 . . . . B 4
Prineville, 5,355 . . . . . . C 6
Redmond, 7,163 . . . . . . C 5
Reedsport, 4,796 . . . . D 2
River Road, 10,370('80) C 3
Roseburg, 17,032 . . . . D 3
Saint Helens, 7,535 . . . B 4
Salem, 107,786 . . . . . . C 4
Sandy, 4,152 . . . . B 4
Scappoose, 3,529 . . . . B 4
Seaside, 5,359 . . . . B 3
Silverton, 5,635 . . . . . . C 4
Springfield, 44,683 . . . . C 4
Stayton, 5,011 . . . . C 4
Sutherlin, 5,020 . . . . . . D 3
Sweet Home, 6,850 . . C 4
The Dalles, 11,060 . . . . B 5
Tigard, 29,344 . . . . h12
Tillamook, 4,001 . . . . . B 3
Toledo, 3,174 . . . . C 3
Tri City, 3,439('80) . . . E 3
Umatilla, 3,046 . . . . B 7
West Linn, 16,367 . . . . B 4
Wilsonville, 7,106 . . . . . h12
Winston, 3,773 . . . . . . D 3
Woodburn, 13,404 . . . . B 4

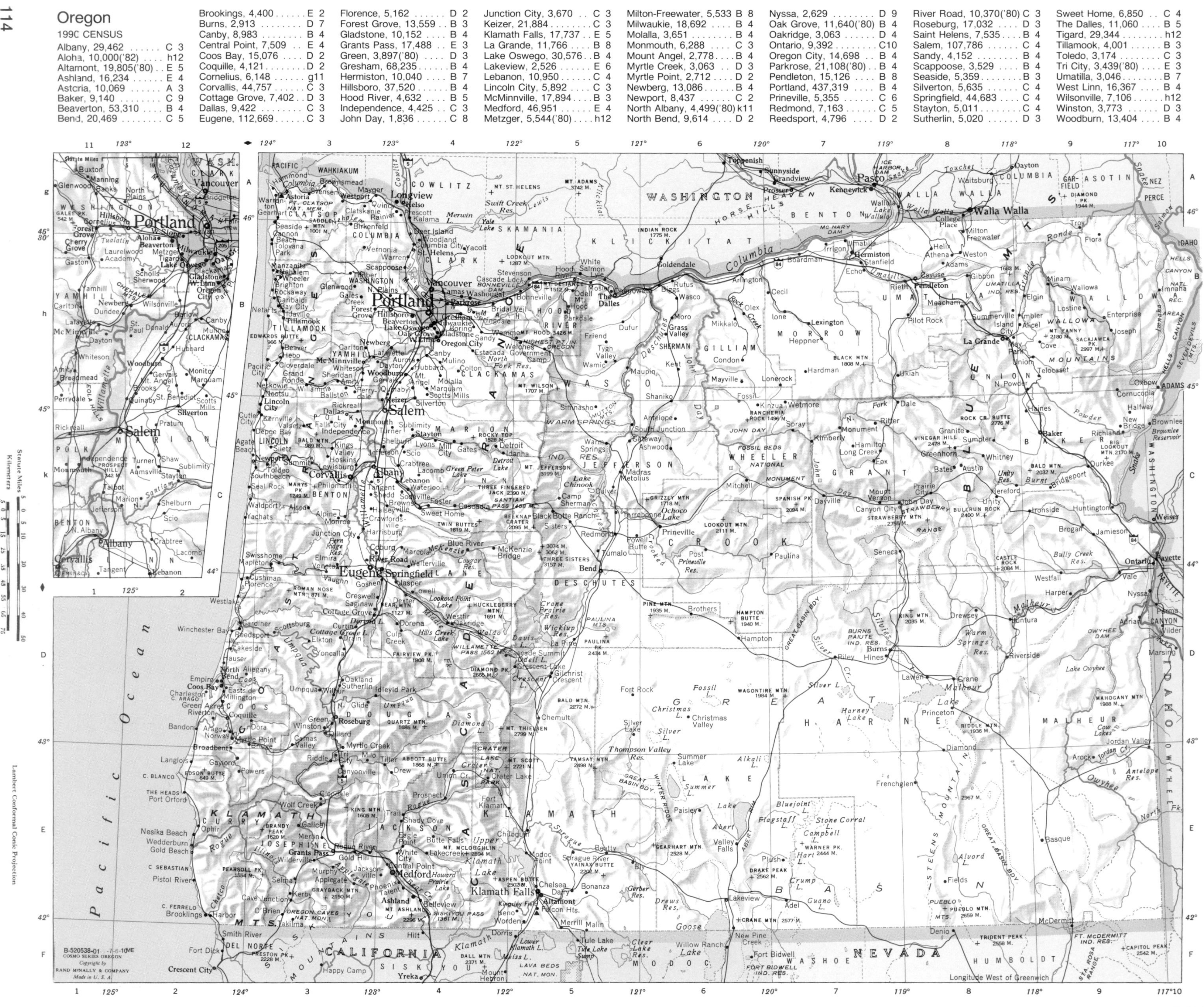

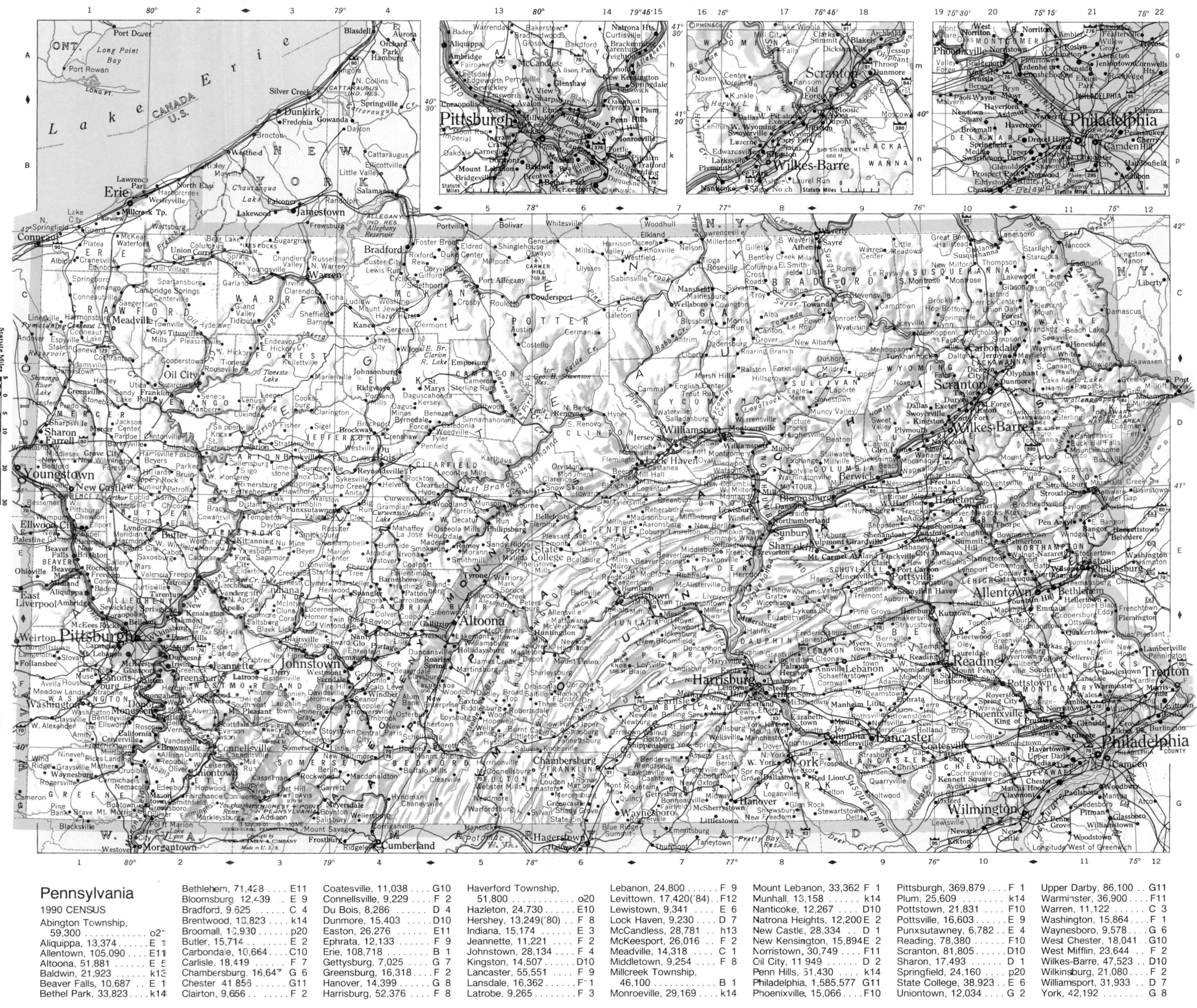

Statute Miles 5 0 5 10 20 30
Kilometers 5 0 5 15 25 35 45

Lambert Conformal Conic Projection

Pennsylvania

1990 CENSUS

Abington Township, 59,300 . . . . . o2[illegible]
Aliquippa, 13,374 . . . . E 1
Allentown, 105,090 . . . . E11
Altoona, 51,881 . . . . E 5
Baldwin, 21,923 . . . . k13
Beaver Falls, 10,687 . . E 1
Bethel Park, 33,823 . . . k14
Bethlehem, 71,428 . . . . E11
Bloomsburg, 12,439 . . . E 9
Bradford, 9,625 . . . . . C 4
Brentwood, 10,823 . . . . k14
Broomall, 10,930 . . . . . p20
Butler, 15,714 . . . . . . E 2
Carbondale, 10,664 . . . C10
Carlisle, 18,419 . . . . . F 7
Chambersburg, 16,647 G 6
Chester, 41,856 . . . . . G11
Clairton, 9,656 . . . . . F 2
Coatesville, 11,038 . . . . G10
Connellsville, 9,229 . . . . F 2
Du Bois, 8,286 . . . . . . D 4
Dunmore, 15,403 . . . . . D10
Easton, 26,276 . . . . . . E11
Ephrata, 12,133 . . . . . F 9
Erie, 108,718 . . . . B 1
Gettysburg, 7,025 . . . . G 7
Greensburg, 16,318 . . . F 2
Hanover, 14,399 . . . . . G 8
Harrisburg, 52,376 . . . . F 8
Haverford Township, 51,800 . . . . o20
Hazleton, 24,730 . . . . . E10
Hershey, 13,249('80) . . F 8
Indiana, 15,174 . . . . . . E 3
Jeannette, 11,221 . . . . F 2
Johnstown, 28,134 . . . . F 4
Kingston, 14,507 . . . . . D10
Lancaster, 55,551 . . . . F 9
Lansdale, 16,362 . . . . . F 1
Latrobe, 9,265 . . . . F 3
Lebanon, 24,800 . . . . . . F 9
Levittown, 17,420('84) . . F12
Lewistown, 9,341 . . . . . E 6
Lock Haven, 9,230 . . . . D 7
McCandless, 28,781 . . . h13
McKeesport, 26,016 . . . F 2
Meadville, 14,318 . . . . C 1
Middletown, 9,254 . . . . F 8
Millcreek Township, 46,100 . . . . B 1
Monroeville, 29,169 . . . . k14
Mount Lebanon, 33,362 F 1
Munhall, 13,158 . . . . . . k14
Nanticoke, 12,267 . . . . . D10
Natrona Heights, 12,200 E 2
New Castle, 28,334 . . . D 1
New Kensington, 15,894 E 2
Norristown, 30,749 . . . . F11
Oil City, 11,949 . . . . . . D 2
Penn Hills, 51,430 . . . . k14
Philadelphia, 1,585,577 G11
Phoenixville, 15,066 . . . . F10
Pittsburgh, 369,879 . . . . F 1
Plum, 25,609 . . . . k14
Pottstown, 21,831 . . . . F10
Pottsville, 16,603 . . . . . E 9
Punxsutawney, 6,782 . . E 4
Reading, 78,380 . . . . . . F10
Scranton, 81,805 . . . . . D10
Sharon, 17,493 . . . . . . D 1
Springfield, 24,160 . . . . p20
State College, 38,923 . . E 6
Uniontown, 12,034 . . . . G 2
Upper Darby, 86,100 . . G11
Warminster, 36,900 . . . . F11
Warren, 11,122 . . . . . . C 3
Washington, 15,864 . . . . F 1
Waynesboro, 9,578 . . . . G 6
West Chester, 18,041 . . G10
West Mifflin, 23,644 . . . F 2
Wilkes-Barre, 47,523 . . D10
Wilkinsburg, 21,080 . . . F 2
Williamsport, 31,933 . . D 7
York, 42,192 . . . . G 8

Rhode Island

1990 CENSUS

Abbott Run Valley, 1,050('87) . . . . B 4
Adamsville, 600('87) E 6
Albion, 1,600('87) . . B 4
Allenton, 600('87) . . . . E 4
Anthony, 2,980('87) . . D 3
Arnold Mills, 600('87) B 4
Ashton, 820('87) . . . . B 4
Barrington, 16,174('80) . . . . . . D 5
Berkeley, 830('87) . . B 4
Block Island, 620('87) h 7
Branch Village, 400('87) . . . . B 3
Bristol, 20,128('80) . . D 5
Burdickville, 500('87) F 2
Carolina, 650('87) . . . . F 2
Central Falls, 17,637 B 4
Charlestown, 1,500 (6,478▲) . . . . F 2
Chepachet, 900('87) B 2
Common Fence Point, 860('87) . . . . D 6
Coventry, 6,980 (31,083▲) . . . . D 3
Cranston, 76,060 . . . . C 4
Davisville, 500('87) . . E 4
Diamond Hill, 810('87) B 4
East Greenwich, 10,211('87) . . . . . . D 4
East Matunuck, 500('87) . . . . F 3
East Providence, 50,380 . . . . C 4
Esmond, 4,320('87) . . B 4
Forestdale, 530('87) B 3
Glendale, 700('87) . . B 2
Greenville, 7,576('80) C 3
Harmony, 820('87) . . B 3
Harris, 1,050('87) . . . . D 3
Hope, 270('87) . . . . . . D 3
Hopkinton, 550 (6,873▲) . . . . F 1
Island Park, 1,240('87) . . . . E 6
Jamestown, 4,040('87) . . . . F 5
Johnston, 26,800 . . . . C 4
Kenyon, 400('87) . . . . F 2
Kingston, 5,479('80) . . F 3
La Fayette, 640('87) E 4
Little Compton, 500 (3,339▲) . . . . E 6
Lonsdale, 3,850('87) B 4
Manville, 3,030('87) . . B 4
Mapleville, 1,300('87) B 2
Matunuck, 550('87) . . G 3
Middletown, 3,350 (19,460▲) . . . . E 5
Mount View, 610('87) D 4
Narragansett, 3,342 (14,985▲) . . . . F 4
Newport, 28,227 . . . . F 5
North Kingstown, 2,750 (23,786▲) . . . . E 4
North Providence, 32,090 . . . . C 4
Oakland, 600('87) . . B 2
Pascoag, 3,807('80) B 2
Pawtucket, 72,644 . . C 4
Peace Dale, 3,100('87) . . . . F 3
Plum Beach, 400('87) E 4
Portsmouth, 3,540 (16,857▲) . . . . E 6
Primrose, 500('87) . . B 3
Providence, 160,728 C 4
Quidnessett, 3,300('87) . . . . E 4
Quidnick, 2,300('87) D 3
Quonochontaug, 1,500('87) . . . . G 2
Saunderstown, 400('87) . . . . E 4
Saylesville, 3,510('87) B 4
Shannock, 950('87) . . F 2
Shores Acres, 410('87) . . . . E 4
Slatersville, 2,330('87) A 3
South Hopkinton, 900('87) . . . . F 1
Tiverton, 7,653 (14,312▲) . . . . D 6
Union Village, 2,150('87) . . . . B 3
Usquepaug, 400('87) F 3
Valley Falls, 10,892('80) . . . . . . B 4
Wakefield, 3,450('87) F 3
Warren, 10,640('87) . . D 5
Warwick, 85,427 . . . . D 4
Westerly, 16,477 (21,605▲) . . . . F 1
West Kingston, 1,150('87) . . . . F 3
West Warwick, 29,268 . . . . D 3
Woonsocket, 43,877 A 3
Yorktown Manor, 2,520('87) . . . . C 3

▲ Population of entire town (township), including rural area

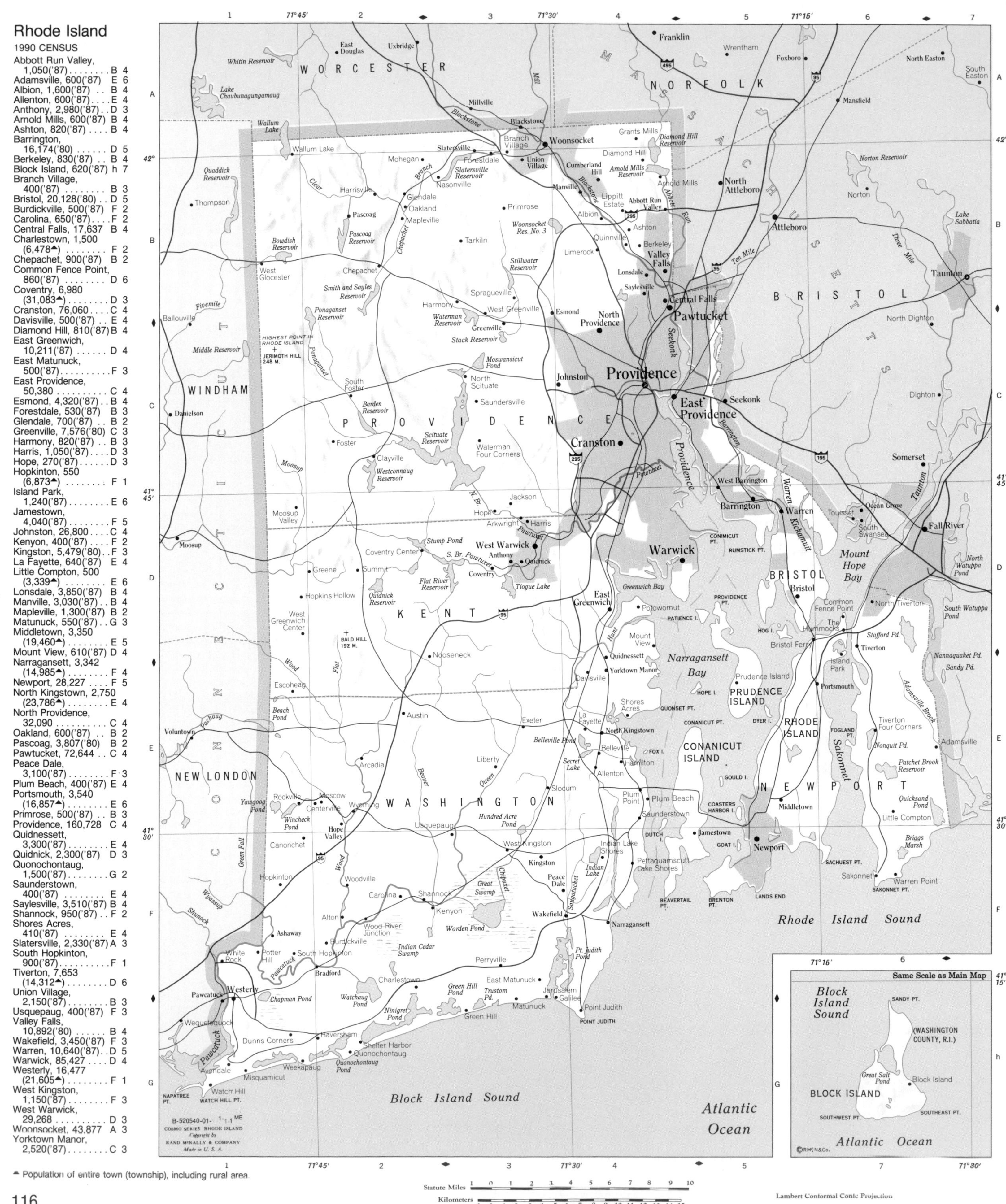

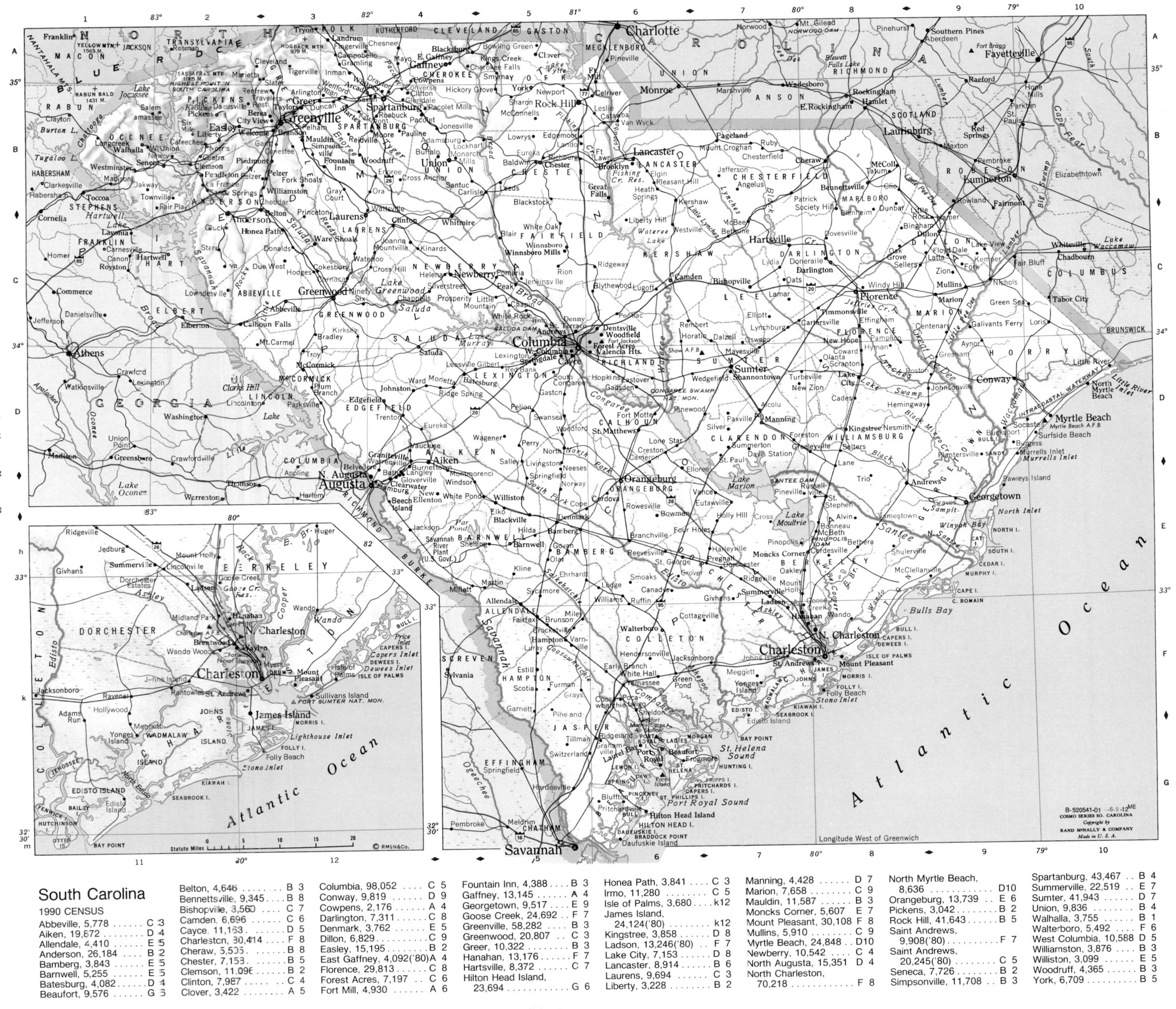

South Carolina

1990 CENSUS

Abbeville, 5,778 . . . . . . C 3
Aiken, 19,872 . . . . D 4
Allendale, 4,410 . . . . . . E 5
Anderson, 26,184 . . . . B 2
Bamberg, 3,843 . . . . . . E 5
Barnwell, 5,255 . . . . . . E 5
Batesburg, 4,082. . . . . .D 4
Beaufort, 9,576 . . . . . . G 5
Belton, 4,646 . . . . B 3
Bennettsville, 9,345 . . . B 8
Bishopville, 3,560 . . . . . C 7
Camden, 6,696 . . . . C 6
Cayce, 11,163. . . . . D 5
Charleston, 80,414 . . . . F 8
Cheraw, 5,505. . . . . . . .B 8
Chester, 7,153. . . . . . . B 5
Clemson, 11,096 . . . . . . B 2
Clinton, 7,987 . . . . C 4
Clover, 3,422 . . . . A 5
Columbia, 98,052 . . . . C 5
Conway, 9,819 . . . . . . D 9
Cowpens, 2,176 . . . . . . A 4
Darlington, 7,311. . . . . .C 8
Denmark, 3,762 . . . . . . E 5
Dillon, 6,829. . . . . .C 9
Easley, 15,195. . . . . . . .B 2
East Gaffney, 4,092('80)A 4
Florence, 29,813 . . . . . . C 8
Forest Acres, 7,197 . . . C 6
Fort Mill, 4,930 . . . . . . A 6
Fountain Inn, 4,388 . . . B 3
Gaffney, 13,145 . . . . . . A 4
Georgetown, 9,517 . . . . E 9
Goose Creek, 24,692 . . F 7
Greenville, 58,282 . . . . B 3
Greenwood, 20,807 . . . C 3
Greer, 10,322 . . . . B 3
Hanahan, 13,176 . . . . . . F 7
Hartsville, 8,372 . . . . . . C 7
Hilton Head Island,
23,694 . . . . G 6
Honea Path, 3,841 . . . . C 3
Irmo, 11,280 . . . . C 5
Isle of Palms, 3,680. . . . k12
James Island,
24,124('80) k12
Kingstree, 3,858 . . . . . . D 8
Ladson, 13,246('80) . . F 7
Lake City, 7,153 . . . . . . D 8
Lancaster, 8,914 . . . . . . B 6
Laurens, 9,694 . . . . . . C 3
Liberty, 3,228 . . . . B 2
Manning, 4,428 . . . . . . D 7
Marion, 7,658 . . . . C 9
Mauldin, 11,587 . . . . B 3
Moncks Corner, 5,607 E 7
Mount Pleasant, 30,108 F 8
Mullins, 5,910 . . . . C 9
Myrtle Beach, 24,848 . . D10
Newberry, 10,542 . . . . C 4
North Augusta, 15,351 D 4
North Charleston,
70,218 . . . . F 8
North Myrtle Beach,
8,636 . . . . D10
Orangeburg, 13,739 . . E 6
Pickens, 3,042 . . . . B 2
Rock Hill, 41,643 . . . . . . B 5
Saint Andrews,
9,908('80) . . . . F 7
Saint Andrews,
20,245('80) . . . . C 5
Seneca, 7,726 . . . . B 2
Simpsonville, 11,708 . . B 3
Spartanburg, 43,467 . . B 4
Summerville, 22,519 . . E 7
Sumter, 41,943 . . . . . . D 7
Union, 9,836 . . . . B 4
Walhalla, 3,755 . . . . B 1
Walterboro, 5,492 . . . . F 6
West Columbia, 10,588 D 5
Williamston, 3,876 . . . . B 3
Williston, 3,099 . . . . . . E 5
Woodruff, 4,365 . . . . . . B 3
York, 6,709 . . . . B 5

South Dakota

1990 CENSUS

Place	Grid
Aberdeen, 24,927	B 7
Alcester, 843	D 9
Arlington, 908	C 8
Armour, 854	D 7
Belle Fourche, 4,335	C 2
Beresford, 1,849	D 9
Box Elder, 2,680	C 2
Brandon, 3,543	D 9
Britton, 1,394	B 8
Brookings, 16,270	C 9
Burke, 756	D 6
Canton, 2,787	D 9
Centerville, 887	D 9
Chamberlain, 2,347	D 6
Clark, 1,292	C 8
Clear Lake, 1,247	C 9
Custer, 1,741	D 2
Deadwood, 1,830	C 2
Dell Rapids, 2,484	D 9
De Smet, 1,172	C 8
Edgemont, 906	D 2
Elk Point, 1,423	E 9
Eureka, 1,197	B 6
Faulkton, 809	B 6
Flandreau, 2,311	C 9
Fort Pierre, 1,854	C 5
Freeman, 1,293	D 8
Garretson, 924	D 9
Gettysburg, 1,510	C 6
Gregory, 1,384	D 6
Groton, 1,196	B 7
Hartford, 1,262	D 9
Highmore, 835	C 6
Hot Springs, 4,325	D 2
Howard, 1,156	C 8
Huron, 12,448	C 7
Ipswich, 965	B 6
Kadoka, 736	D 4
Lake Andes, 846	D 7
Lake Preston, 663	C 8
Lead, 3,632	C 2
Lemmon, 1,614	B 3
Lennox, 1,767	D 9
Madison, 6,257	C 8
Marion, 831	D 8
Martin, 1,151	D 4
McLaughlin, 780	B 5
Menno, 768	D 8
Milbank, 3,879	B 9
Miller, 1,678	C 7
Mitchell, 13,798	D 7
Mobridge, 3,768	B 5
North Sioux City, 2,019	E 9
Onida, 761	C 5
Parker, 984	D 8
Parkston, 1,572	D 8
Philip, 1,077	C 4
Pierre, 12,906	C 5
Platte, 1,311	D 7
Presho, 654	D 5
Rapid City, 54,523	C 2
Redfield, 2,770	C 7
Saint Francis, 815	D 5
Salem, 1,289	D 8
Scotland, 968	D 8
Selby, 707	B 5
Sioux Falls, 100,814	D 9
Sisseton, 2,181	B 8
Spearfish, 6,966	C 2
Springfield, 834	E 8
Sturgis, 5,330	C 2
Tyndall, 1,201	E 8
Valley Springs, 739	D 9
Vermillion, 10,034	E 9
Volga, 1,263	C 9
Wagner, 1,462	D 7
Wall, 834	D 3
Watertown, 17,592	C 8
Webster, 2,017	B 8
Wessington Springs, 1,083	C 7
Whitewood, 891	C 2
Winner, 3,354	D 6
Woonsocket, 766	C 7
Yankton, 12,703	E 8

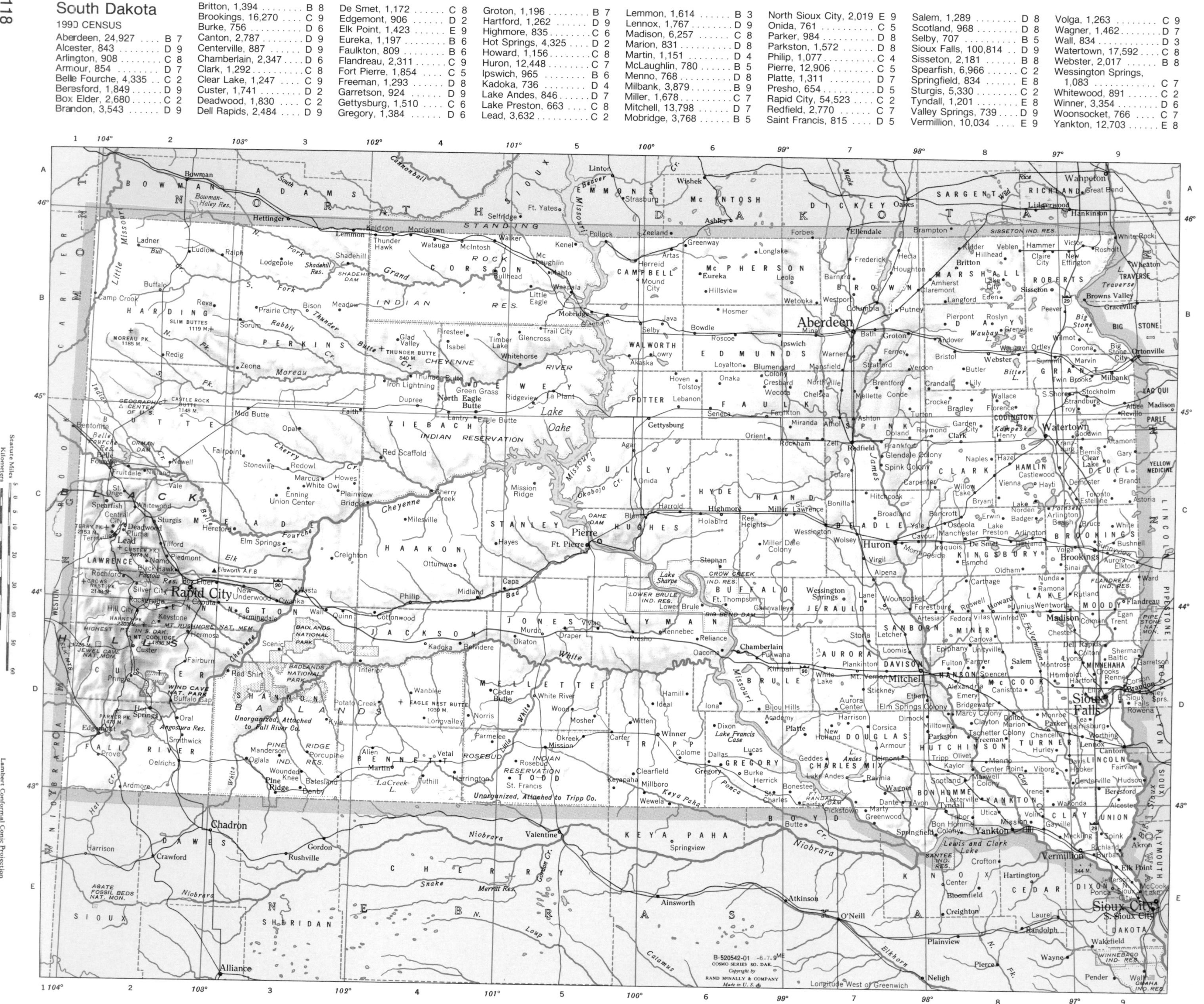

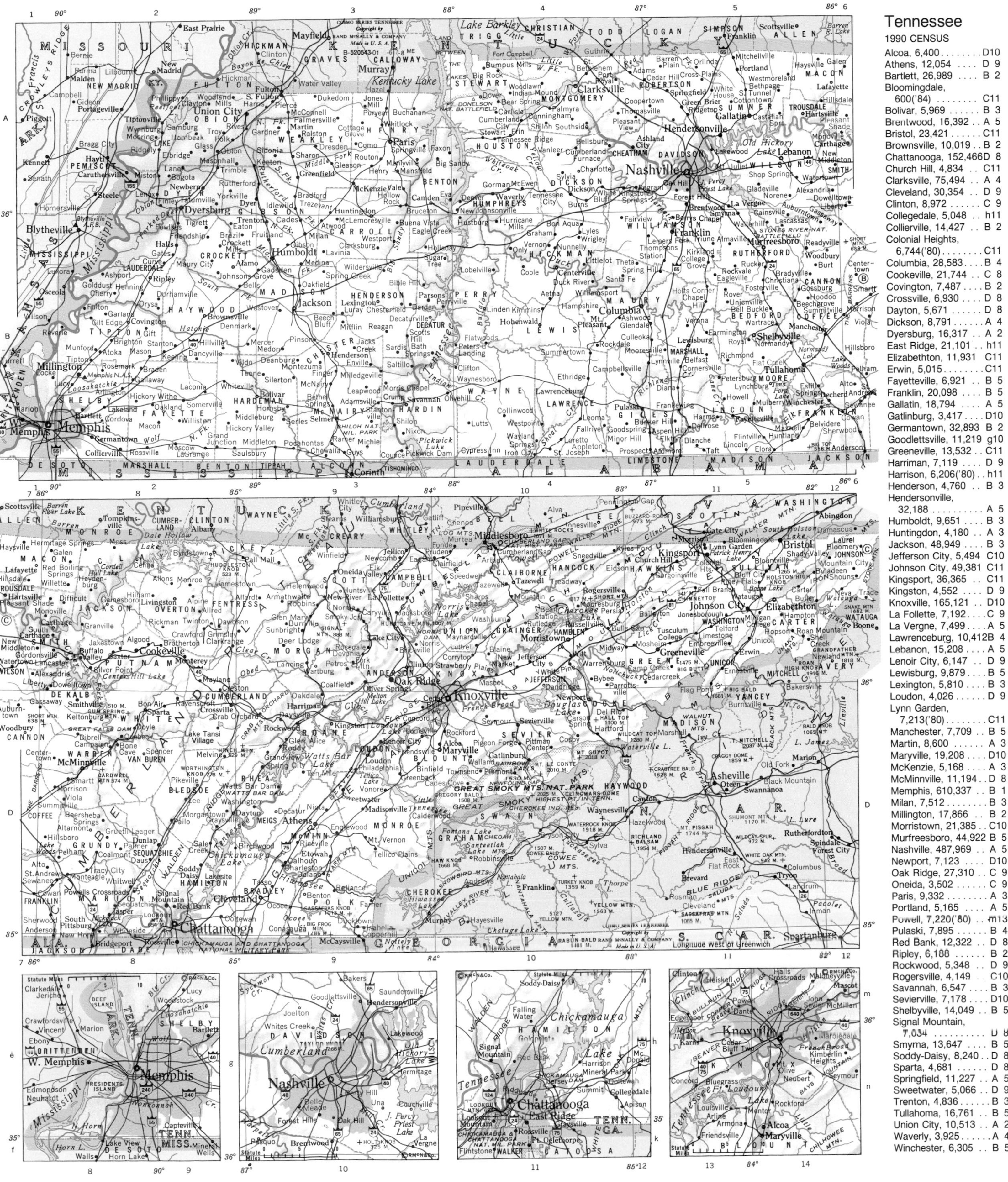

Tennessee

1990 CENSUS

Alcoa, 6,400 . . . . D10
Athens, 12,054 . . . . D 9
Bartlett, 26,989 . . . . B 2
Bloomingdale, 600('84) C11
Bolivar, 5,969 . . . . . . B 3
Brentwood, 16,392 . . A 5
Bristol, 23,421 . . . . . . C11
Brownsville, 10,019 . . B 2
Chattanooga, 152,466D 8
Church Hill, 4,834 . . C11
Clarksville, 75,494 . . A 4
Cleveland, 30,354 . . D 9
Clinton, 8,972 . . . . . . C 9
Collegedale, 5,048 . . h11
Collierville, 14,427 . . B 2
Colonial Heights, 6,744('80) C11
Columbia, 28,583 . . . . B 4
Cookeville, 21,744 . . C 8
Covington, 7,487 . . . . B 2
Crossville, 6,930 . . . . D 8
Dayton, 5,671 . . . . . . D 8
Dickson, 8,791 . . . . . . A 4
Dyersburg, 16,317 . . . A 2
East Ridge, 21,101 . . h11
Elizabethton, 11,931 C11
Erwin, 5,015 . . . . C11
Fayetteville, 6,921 . . B 5
Franklin, 20,098 . . . . B 5
Gallatin, 18,794 . . . . A 5
Gatlinburg, 3,417 . . . . D10
Germantown, 32,893 B 2
Goodlettsville, 11,219 g10
Greeneville, 13,532 . . C11
Harriman, 7,119 . . . . D 9
Harrison, 6,206('80) . . h11
Henderson, 4,760 . . B 3
Hendersonville, 32,188 . . . . A 5
Humboldt, 9,651 . . . . B 3
Huntingdon, 4,180 . . A 3
Jackson, 48,949 . . . . B 3
Jefferson City, 5,494 C10
Johnson City, 49,381 C11
Kingsport, 36,365 . . C11
Kingston, 4,552 . . . . D 9
Knoxville, 165,121 . . D10
La Follette, 7,192 . . . . C 9
La Vergne, 7,499 . . . . A 5
Lawrenceburg, 10,412B 4
Lebanon, 15,208 . . . . A 5
Lenoir City, 6,147 . . . D 9
Lewisburg, 9,879 . . . . B 5
Lexington, 5,810 . . . . B 3
Loudon, 4,026 . . . . . . D 9
Lynn Garden, 7,213('80) C11
Manchester, 7,709 . . B 5
Martin, 8,600 . . . . . . A 3
Maryville, 19,208 . . . . D10
McKenzie, 5,168 . . . . A 3
McMinnville, 11,194 . . D 8
Memphis, 610,337 . . B 1
Milan, 7,512 . . . . B 3
Millington, 17,866 . . B 2
Morristown, 21,385 . . C10
Murfreesboro, 44,922 B 5
Nashville, 487,969 . . A 5
Newport, 7,123 . . . . D10
Oak Ridge, 27,310 . . C 9
Oneida, 3,502 . . . . . . C 9
Paris, 9,332 . . . . A 3
Portland, 5,165 . . . . A 5
Powell, 7,220('80) . . m13
Pulaski, 7,895 . . . . . . B 4
Red Bank, 12,322 . . D 8
Ripley, 6,188 . . . . . . B 2
Rockwood, 5,348 . . D 9
Rogersville, 4,149 . . C10
Savannah, 6,547 . . . . B 3
Sevierville, 7,178 . . . . D10
Shelbyville, 14,049 . . B 5
Signal Mountain, 7,034 . . . . D 8
Smyrna, 13,647 . . . . B 5
Soddy-Daisy, 8,240 . . D 8
Sparta, 4,681 . . . . . . D 8
Springfield, 11,227 . . A 5
Sweetwater, 5,066 . . D 9
Trenton, 4,836 . . . . . . B 3
Tullahoma, 16,761 . . B 5
Union City, 10,513 . . A 2
Waverly, 3,925 . . . . . . A 4
Winchester, 6,305 . . B 5

Lambert Conformal Conic Projection

Texas

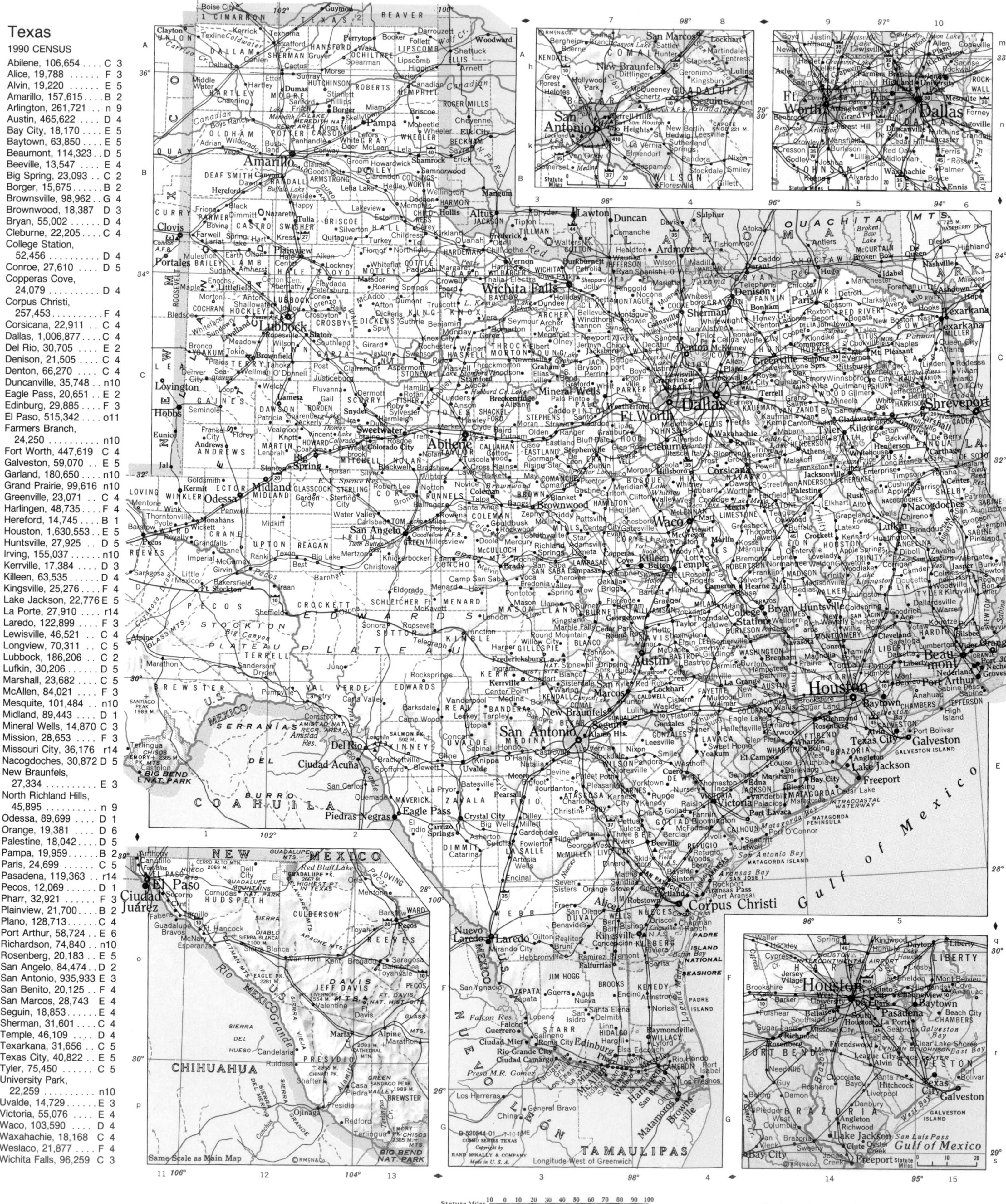

Texas

1990 CENSUS

Abilene, 106,654 . . . . C 3
Alice, 19,788 . . . . . . F 3
Alvin, 19,220 . . . . . . E 5
Amarillo, 157,615 . . . . B 2
Arlington, 261,721 . . . n 9
Austin, 465,622 . . . . . D 4
Bay City, 18,170 . . . . . E 5
Baytown, 63,850 . . . . E 5
Beaumont, 114,323 . . D 5
Beeville, 13,547 . . . . E 4
Big Spring, 23,093 . . C 2
Borger, 15,675 . . . . . . B 2
Brownsville, 98,962 . . G 4
Brownwood, 18,387 D 3
Bryan, 55,002 . . . . . . D 4
Cleburne, 22,205 . . . . C 4
College Station, 52,456 . . . . D 4
Conroe, 27,610 . . . . . D 5
Copperas Cove, 24,079 . . . . D 4
Corpus Christi, 257,453 . . . . F 4
Corsicana, 22,911 . . C 4
Dallas, 1,006,877 . . . C 4
Del Rio, 30,705 . . . . E 2
Denison, 21,505 . . . . C 4
Denton, 66,270 . . . . C 4
Duncanville, 35,748 . . n10
Eagle Pass, 20,651 . . E 2
Edinburg, 29,885 . . . . F 3
El Paso, 515,342 . . . . o11
Farmers Branch, 24,250 . . . . n10
Fort Worth, 447,619 C 4
Galveston, 59,070 . . E 5
Garland, 180,650 . . . . n10
Grand Prairie, 99,616 n10
Greenville, 23,071 . . C 4
Harlingen, 48,735 . . . . F 4
Hereford, 14,745 . . . . B 1
Houston, 1,630,553 . . E 5
Huntsville, 27,925 . . D 5
Irving, 155,037 . . . . . . n10
Kerrville, 17,384 . . . . D 3
Killeen, 63,535 . . . . . D 4
Kingsville, 25,276 . . . . F 4
Lake Jackson, 22,776 E 5
La Porte, 27,910 . . . . r14
Laredo, 122,899 . . . . F 3
Lewisville, 46,521 . . C 4
Longview, 70,311 . . C 5
Lubbock, 186,206 . . C 2
Lufkin, 30,206 . . . . . . D 5
Marshall, 23,682 . . . . C 5
McAllen, 84,021 . . . . F 3
Mesquite, 101,484 . . n10
Midland, 89,443 . . . . D 1
Mineral Wells, 14,870 C 3
Mission, 28,653 . . . . . F 3
Missouri City, 36,176 r14
Nacogdoches, 30,872 D 5
New Braunfels, 27,334 . . . . E 3
North Richland Hills, 45,895 . . . . n 9
Odessa, 89,699 . . . . D 1
Orange, 19,381 . . . . D 6
Palestine, 18,042 . . . . D 5
Pampa, 19,959 . . . . . B 2
Paris, 24,699 . . . . . . C 5
Pasadena, 119,363 . . r14
Pecos, 12,069 . . . . . . D 1
Pharr, 32,921 . . . . . . F 3
Plainview, 21,700 . . . . B 2
Plano, 128,713 . . . . . . C 4
Port Arthur, 58,724 . . E 6
Richardson, 74,840 . . n10
Rosenberg, 20,183 . . E 5
San Angelo, 84,474 . . D 2
San Antonio, 935,933 E 3
San Benito, 20,125 . . F 4
San Marcos, 28,743 E 4
Seguin, 18,853 . . . . . E 4
Sherman, 31,601 . . . C 4
Temple, 46,109 . . . . D 4
Texarkana, 31,656 . . C 5
Texas City, 40,822 . . E 5
Tyler, 75,450 . . . . . . C 5
University Park, 22,259 . . . . n10
Uvalde, 14,729 . . . . . E 3
Victoria, 55,076 . . . . . E 4
Waco, 103,590 . . . . D 4
Waxahachie, 18,168 C 4
Weslaco, 21,877 . . . . . F 4
Wichita Falls, 96,259 C 3

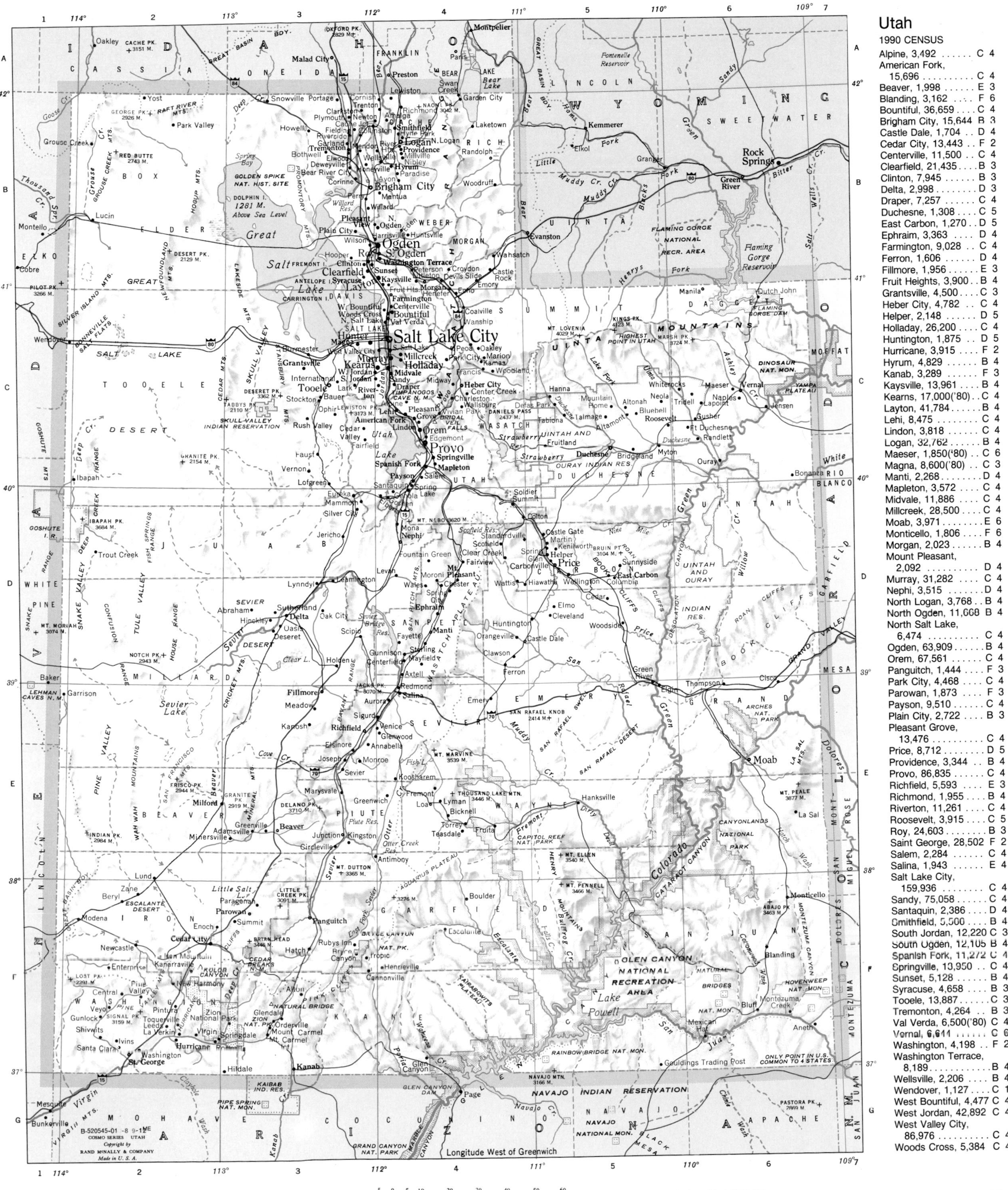

Utah

1990 CENSUS

Alpine, 3,492 ...... C 4
American Fork, 15,696 .... C 4
Beaver, 1,998 ...... E 3
Blanding, 3,162 ..... F 6
Bountiful, 36,659 .... C 4
Brigham City, 15,644 B 3
Castle Dale, 1,704 .. D 4
Cedar City, 13,443 .. F 2
Centerville, 11,500 .. C 4
Clearfield, 21,435 .... B 3
Clinton, 7,945 .... B 3
Delta, 2,998 .... D 3
Draper, 7,257 .... C 4
Duchesne, 1,308 .... C 5
East Carbon, 1,270 .. D 5
Ephraim, 3,363 ..... D 4
Farmington, 9,028 ... C 4
Ferron, 1,606 ...... D 4
Fillmore, 1,956 ...... E 3
Fruit Heights, 3,900 .. B 4
Grantsville, 4,500 .... C 3
Heber City, 4,782 ... C 4
Helper, 2,148 ...... D 5
Holladay, 26,200 .... C 4
Huntington, 1,875 ... D 5
Hurricane, 3,915 .... F 2
Hyrum, 4,829 ...... B 4
Kanab, 3,289 ...... F 3
Kaysville, 13,961 .... B 4
Kearns, 17,000('80) .. C 4
Layton, 41,784 ...... B 4
Lehi, 8,475 .... C 4
Lindon, 3,818 ...... C 4
Logan, 32,762 ...... B 4
Maeser, 1,850('80) .. C 6
Magna, 8,600('80) .. C 3
Manti, 2,268 .... D 4
Mapleton, 3,572 .... C 4
Midvale, 11,886 .... C 4
Millcreek, 28,500 .... C 4
Moab, 3,971 .... E 6
Monticello, 1,806 .... F 6
Morgan, 2,023 ...... B 4
Mount Pleasant, 2,092 .... D 4
Murray, 31,282 .... C 4
Nephi, 3,515 .... D 4
North Logan, 3,768 .. B 4
North Ogden, 11,668 B 4
North Salt Lake, 6,474 .... C 4
Ogden, 63,909 ...... B 4
Orem, 67,561 ...... C 4
Panguitch, 1,444 .... F 3
Park City, 4,468 .... C 4
Parowan, 1,873 .... F 3
Payson, 9,510 ...... C 4
Plain City, 2,722 .... B 3
Pleasant Grove, 13,476 .... C 4
Price, 8,712 .... D 5
Providence, 3,344 .. B 4
Provo, 86,835 ...... C 4
Richfield, 5,593 .... E 3
Richmond, 1,955 .... B 4
Riverton, 11,261 .... C 4
Roosevelt, 3,915 .... C 5
Roy, 24,603 .... B 3
Saint George, 28,502 F 2
Salem, 2,284 ...... C 4
Salina, 1,943 ...... E 4
Salt Lake City, 159,936 .... C 4
Sandy, 75,058 .... C 4
Santaquin, 2,386 .... D 4
Smithfield, 5,500 .... B 4
South Jordan, 12,220 C 3
South Ogden, 12,105 B 4
Spanish Fork, 11,272 C 4
Springville, 13,950 .. C 4
Sunset, 5,128 .... B 4
Syracuse, 4,658 .... B 3
Tooele, 13,887 ...... C 3
Tremonton, 4,264 .. B 3
Val Verda, 6,500('80) C 4
Vernal, 6,644 .... C 6
Washington, 4,198 .. F 2
Washington Terrace, 8,189 .... B 4
Wellsville, 2,206 .... B 4
Wendover, 1,127 .... C 1
West Bountiful, 4,477 C 4
West Jordan, 42,892 C 4
West Valley City, 86,976 .... C 4
Woods Cross, 5,384 C 4

Vermont

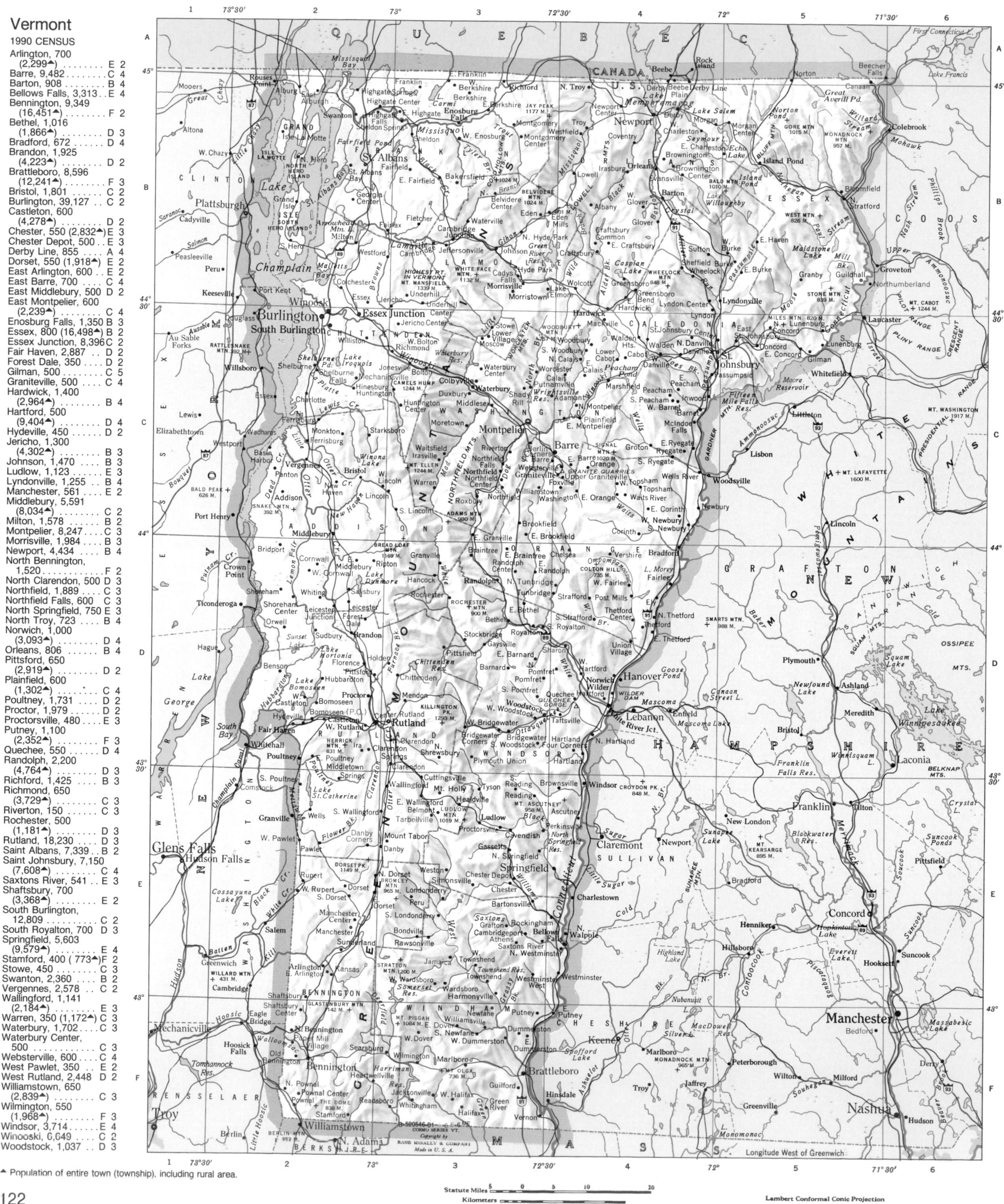

Vermont

1990 CENSUS

Arlington, 700 (2,299▲) .... E 2
Barre, 9,482 .... C 4
Barton, 908 .... B 4
Bellows Falls, 3,313 .. E 4
Bennington, 9,349 (16,451▲) .... F 2
Bethel, 1,016 (1,866▲) .... D 3
Bradford, 672 ...... D 4
Brandon, 1,925 (4,223▲) .... D 2
Brattleboro, 8,596 (12,241▲) .... F 3
Bristol, 1,801 ...... C 2
Burlington, 39,127 .. C 2
Castleton, 600 (4,278▲) .... D 2
Chester, 550 (2,832▲) E 3
Chester Depot, 500 .. E 3
Derby Line, 855 .... A 4
Dorset, 550 (1,918▲) E 2
East Arlington, 600 .. E 2
East Barre, 700 .... C 4
East Middlebury, 500 D 2
East Montpelier, 600 (2,239▲) .... C 4
Enosburg Falls, 1,350 B 3
Essex, 800 (16,498▲) B 2
Essex Junction, 8,396 C 2
Fair Haven, 2,887 .. D 2
Forest Dale, 350 .... D 2
Gilman, 500 .... C 5
Graniteville, 500 .... C 4
Hardwick, 1,400 (2,964▲) .... B 4
Hartford, 500 (9,404▲) .... D 4
Hydeville, 450 ...... D 2
Jericho, 1,300 (4,302▲) .... B 3
Johnson, 1,470 .... B 3
Ludlow, 1,123 ...... E 3
Lyndonville, 1,255 .. B 4
Manchester, 561 .... E 2
Middlebury, 5,591 (8,034▲) .... C 2
Milton, 1,578 ...... B 2
Montpelier, 8,247 .... C 3
Morrisville, 1,984 .... B 3
Newport, 4,434 .... B 4
North Bennington, 1,520 .... F 2
North Clarendon, 500 D 3
Northfield, 1,889 .... C 3
Northfield Falls, 600 C 3
North Springfield, 750 E 3
North Troy, 723 .... B 4
Norwich, 1,000 (3,093▲) .... D 4
Orleans, 806 ...... B 4
Pittsford, 650 (2,919▲) .... D 2
Plainfield, 600 (1,302▲) .... C 4
Poultney, 1,731 .... D 2
Proctor, 1,979 ...... D 2
Proctorsville, 480 .... E 3
Putney, 1,100 (2,352▲) .... F 3
Quechee, 550 ...... D 4
Randolph, 2,200 (4,764▲) .... D 3
Richford, 1,425 .... B 3
Richmond, 650 (3,729▲) .... C 3
Riverton, 150 ...... C 3
Rochester, 500 (1,181▲) .... D 3
Rutland, 18,230 .... D 3
Saint Albans, 7,339 .. B 2
Saint Johnsbury, 7,150 (7,608▲) .... C 4
Saxtons River, 541 .. E 3
Shaftsbury, 700 (3,368▲) .... E 2
South Burlington, 12,809 .... C 2
South Royalton, 700 D 3
Springfield, 5,603 (9,579▲) .... E 4
Stamford, 400 (773▲) F 2
Stowe, 450 .... C 3
Swanton, 2,360 .... B 2
Vergennes, 2,578 .. C 2
Wallingford, 1,141 (2,184▲) .... E 3
Warren, 350 (1,172▲) C 3
Waterbury, 1,702 .... C 3
Waterbury Center, 500 .... C 3
Websterville, 600 .... C 4
West Pawlet, 350 .. E 2
West Rutland, 2,448 D 2
Williamstown, 650 (2,839▲) .... C 3
Wilmington, 550 (1,968▲) .... F 3
Windsor, 3,714 ...... E 4
Winooski, 6,649 ...... C 2
Woodstock, 1,037 .. D 3

▲ Population of entire town (township), including rural area.

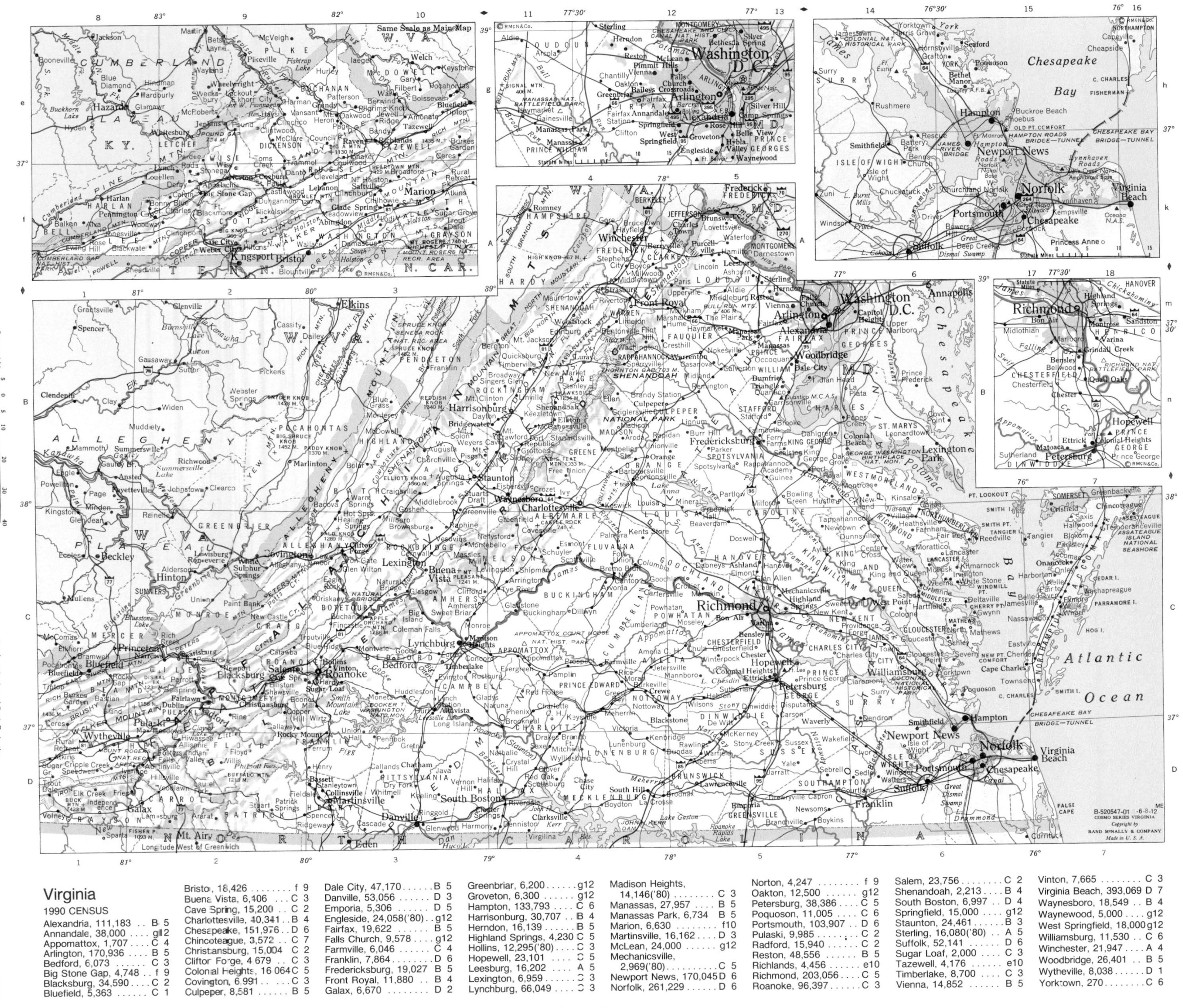

Virginia

1990 CENSUS

Alexandria, 111,183 .. B 5
Annandale, 38,000 .... g12
Appomattox, 1,707 .... C 4
Arlington, 170,936 ..... B 5
Bedford, 6,073 .... C 3
Big Stone Gap, 4,748 .. f 9
Blacksburg, 34,590 .... C 2
Bluefield, 5,363 .... C 1
Bristol, 18,426 .... f 9
Buena Vista, 6,406 .... C 3
Cave Spring, 15,200 .. C 2
Charlottesville, 40,341 . B 4
Chesapeake, 151,976 . D 6
Chincoteague, 3,572 .. C 7
Christiansburg, 15,004 C 2
Clifton Forge, 4,679 .. C 3
Colonial Heights, 16,064 C 5
Covington, 6,991 ...... C 3
Culpeper, 8,581 .... B 5
Dale City, 47,170 ...... B 5
Danville, 53,056 .... D 3
Emporia, 5,306 .... D 5
Engleside, 24,058('80) . g12
Fairfax, 19,622 .... B 5
Falls Church, 9,578 .... g12
Farmville, 6,046 .... C 4
Franklin, 7,864 .... D 6
Fredericksburg, 19,027 B 5
Front Royal, 11,880 .. B 4
Galax, 6,670 .... D 2
Greenbriar, 6,200 ...... g12
Groveton, 6,300 ...... g12
Hampton, 133,793 .... C 6
Harrisonburg, 30,707 .. B 4
Herndon, 16,139 ...... B 5
Highland Springs, 4,230 C 5
Hollins, 12,295('80) ... C 3
Hopewell, 23,101 .... C 5
Leesburg, 16,202 ..... A 5
Lexington, 6,959 ...... C 3
Lynchburg, 66,049 .... C 3
Madison Heights, 14,146('80) .... C 3
Manassas, 27,957 .... B 5
Manassas Park, 6,734 B 5
Marion, 6,630 .... f10
Martinsville, 16,162 .... D 3
McLean, 24,000 .... g12
Mechanicsville, 2,969('80) .... C 5
Newport News, 170,045 D 6
Norfolk, 261,229 ...... D 6
Norton, 4,247 .... f 9
Oakton, 12,500 ...... g12
Petersburg, 38,386 .... C 5
Poquoson, 11,005 .... C 6
Portsmouth, 103,907 .. D 6
Pulaski, 9,985 .... C 2
Radford, 15,940 ...... C 2
Reston, 48,556 ...... B 5
Richlands, 4,456 ...... e10
Richmond, 203,056 .... C 5
Roanoke, 96,397 ...... C 3
Salem, 23,756 .... C 2
Shenandoah, 2,213 .... B 4
South Boston, 6,997 .. D 4
Springfield, 15,000 .... g12
Staunton, 24,461 ...... B 3
Sterling, 16,080('80) .. A 5
Suffolk, 52,141 .... D 6
Sugar Loaf, 2,000 .... C 3
Tazewell, 4,176 .... e10
Timberlake, 8,700 .... C 3
Vienna, 14,852 .... B 5
Vinton, 7,665 .... C 3
Virginia Beach, 393,069 D 7
Waynesboro, 18,549 .. B 4
Waynewood, 5,000 .... g12
West Springfield, 18,000 g12
Williamsburg, 11,530 .. C 6
Winchester, 21,947 .... A 4
Woodbridge, 26,401 .. B 5
Wytheville, 8,038 ...... D 1
Yorktown, 270 .... C 6

Washington

1990 CENSUS

Aberdeen, 16,565 . . . . C 2
Anacortes, 11,451 . . . . A 3
Auburn, 33,102 . . . . . B 3
Bellevue, 86,874 . . . . . e11
Bellingham, 52,179 . . . . A 3
Bonney Lake, 7,494 . . B 3
Bothell, 12,345 . . . . . . B 3
Bremerton, 38,142 . . . . . B 3
Camas, 6,442 . . . . D 3
Centralia, 12,101 . . . . . . C 3
Chehalis, 6,527 . . . . . . C 3
Cheney, 7,723 . . . . B 8
Clarkston, 6,753 . . . . . . C 8
College Place, 6,308 . . C 7
Colville, 4,360 . . . . A 8
Coulee Dam, 1,087 . . . B 7
Des Moines, 17,283 . . B 3
Edmonds, 30,744 . . . . B 3
Ellensburg, 12,361 . . . . C 5
Enumclaw, 7,227 . . . . . B 4
Ephrata, 5,349 . . . . B 6
Everett, 69,961 . . . . . . B 3
Ferndale, 5,398 . . . . . . A 3
Fircrest, 5,258 . . . . f10
Goldendale, 3,319 . . . . D 5
Grandview, 7,169 . . . . C 6
Hoquiam, 8,972 . . . . . . C 2
Issaquah, 7,786 . . . . . . B 3
Kelso, 11,820 . . . . C 3
Kennewick, 42,155 . . . . C 6
Kent, 37,960 . . . . B 3
Kirkland, 40,052 . . . . . . B 3
Lacey, 19,279 . . . . B 3
Lakewood Center, 62,000 . . . . B 3
Longview, 31,499 . . . . . C 3
Lynden, 5,709 . . . . A 3
Lynnwood, 28,695 . . . . . B 3
Marysville, 10,328 . . . . A 3
Medical Lake, 3,664 . . B 8
Mercer Island, 20,816 . . B 3
Montesano, 3,064 . . . . C 2
Moses Lake, 11,235 . . B 6
Mount Vernon, 17,647 . . A 3
Oak Harbor, 17,176 . . A 3
Olympia, 33,840 . . . . . . B 3
Omak, 4,117 . . . . A 6
Othello, 4,638 . . . . C 6
Parkland, 27,300 . . . . . . f11
Parkwater, 4,300('91) . . g14
Pasco, 20,337 . . . . C 6
Port Angeles, 17,710 . . A 2
Port Orchard, 4,984 . . B 3
Port Townsend, 7,001 . A 3
Prosser, 4,476 . . . . C 6
Pullman, 23,478 . . . . . . C 8
Puyallup, 23,875 . . . . . B 3
Quincy, 3,738 . . . . B 6
Redmond, 35,800 . . . . e11
Renton, 41,688 . . . . . . B 3
Richland, 32,315 . . . . . . C 6
Richmond Beach, 6,700('91) . . . . B 3
Richmond Highlands, 27,900 . . . . B 3
Riverton Heights, 14,182 f11
Seattle, 516,259 . . . . . . B 3
Sedro Woolley, 6,031 . . A 3
Selah, 5,113 . . . . C 5
Shelton, 7,241 . . . . B 2
Snohomish, 6,499 . . . . . B 3
Spokane, 177,196 . . . . B 8
Steilacoom, 5,728 . . . . . f10
Sumner, 6,281 . . . . B 3
Sunnyside, 11,238 . . . . C 5
Tacoma, 176,664 . . . . . B 3
Toppenish, 7,419 . . . . . C 5
Tukwila, 11,874 . . . . f11
Tumwater, 9,976 . . . . . . B 3
Vancouver, 46,380 . . . . D 3
Walla Walla, 26,478 . . C 7
Wenatchee, 21,756 . . . . B 5
White Center, 18,000('91) e11
Yakima, 54,827 . . . . C 5

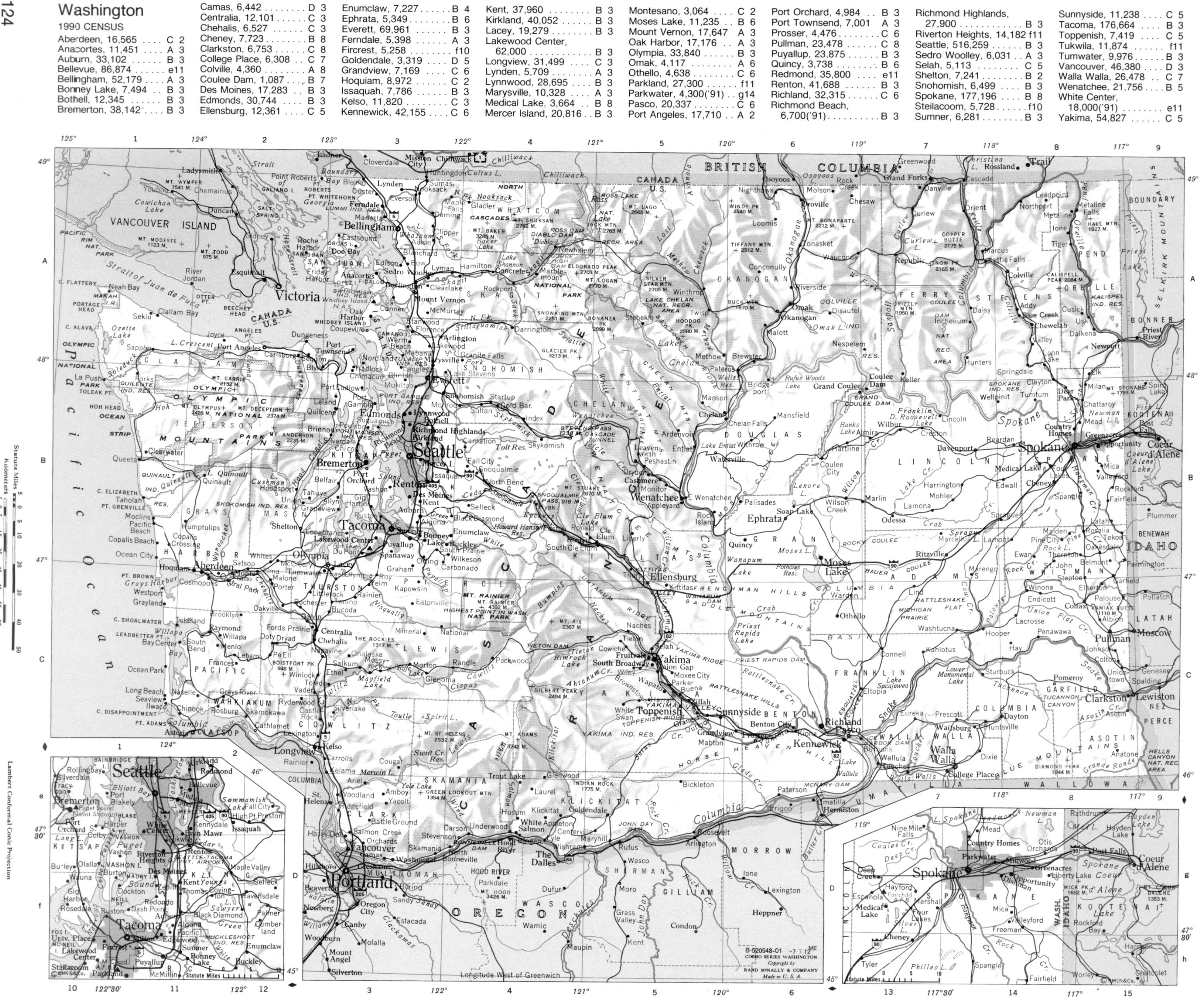

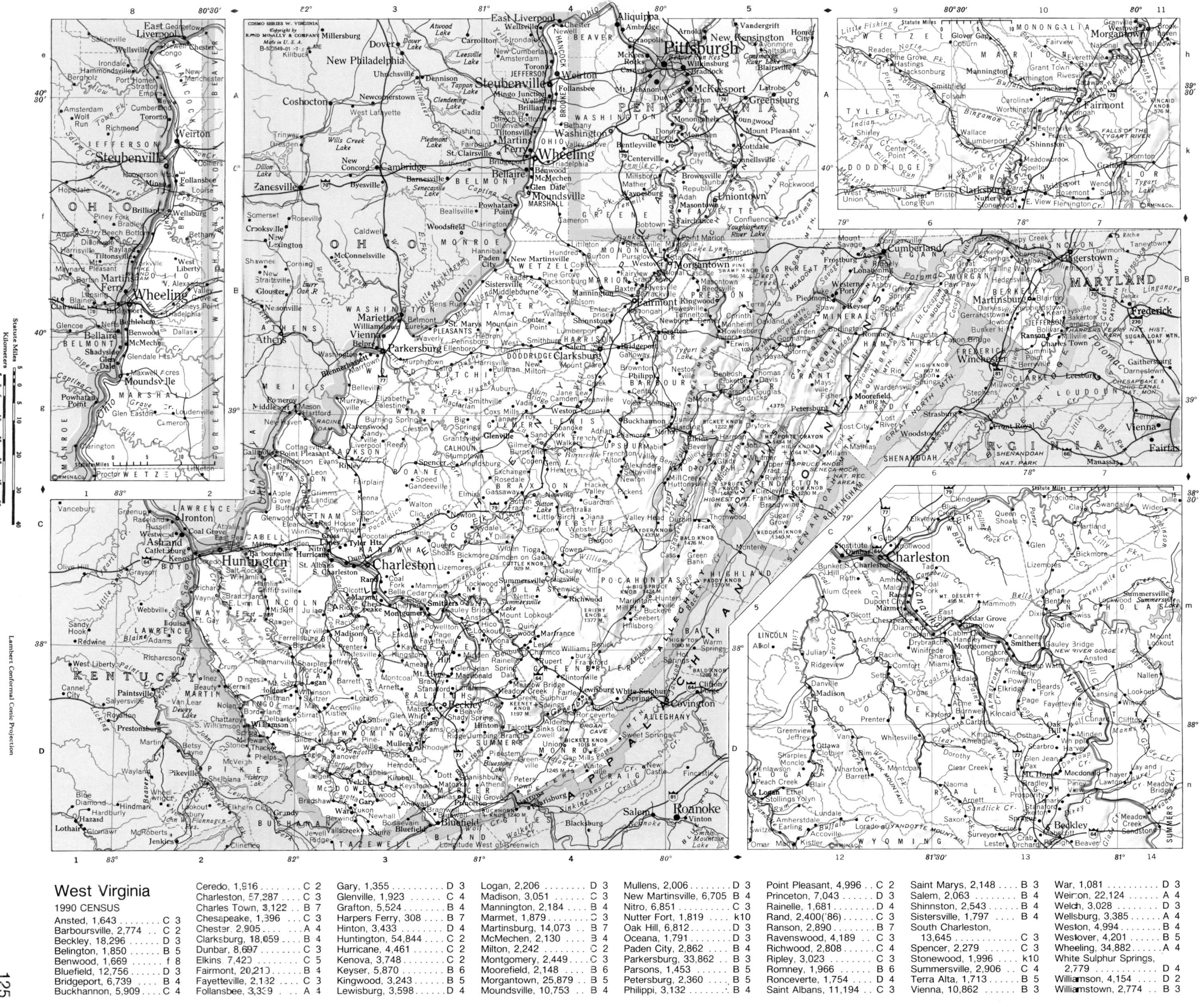

West Virginia

1990 CENSUS

Place	Key
Ansted, 1,643	C 3
Barboursville, 2,774	C 2
Beckley, 18,296	D 3
Belington, 1,850	B 5
Benwood, 1,669	f 8
Bluefield, 12,756	D 3
Bridgeport, 6,739	B 4
Buckhannon, 5,909	C 4
Ceredo, 1,916	C 2
Charleston, 57,287	C 3
Charles Town, 3,122	B 7
Chesapeake, 1,396	C 3
Chester, 2,905	A 4
Clarksburg, 18,059	B 4
Dunbar, 8,697	C 3
Elkins, 7,420	C 5
Fairmont, 20,210	B 4
Fayetteville, 2,182	C 3
Follansbee, 3,339	A 4
Gary, 1,355	D 3
Glenville, 1,923	C 4
Grafton, 5,524	B 4
Harpers Ferry, 308	B 7
Hinton, 3,433	D 4
Huntington, 54,844	C 2
Hurricane, 4,461	C 2
Kenova, 3,748	C 2
Keyser, 5,870	B 6
Kingwood, 3,243	B 5
Lewisburg, 3,598	D 4
Logan, 2,206	D 3
Madison, 3,051	C 3
Mannington, 2,184	B 4
Marmet, 1,879	C 3
Martinsburg, 14,073	B 7
McMechen, 2,130	B 4
Milton, 2,242	C 2
Montgomery, 2,449	C 3
Moorefield, 2,148	B 6
Morgantown, 25,879	B 5
Moundsville, 10,753	B 4
Mullens, 2,006	D 3
New Martinsville, 6,705	B 4
Nitro, 6,851	C 3
Nutter Fort, 1,819	k10
Oak Hill, 6,812	D 3
Oceana, 1,791	D 3
Paden City, 2,862	B 4
Parkersburg, 33,862	B 3
Parsons, 1,453	B 5
Petersburg, 2,360	B 5
Philippi, 3,132	B 4
Point Pleasant, 4,996	C 2
Princeton, 7,043	D 3
Rainelle, 1,681	D 4
Rand, 2,400('86)	C 3
Ranson, 2,890	B 7
Ravenswood, 4,189	C 3
Richwood, 2,808	C 4
Ripley, 3,023	C 3
Romney, 1,966	B 6
Ronceverte, 1,754	D 4
Saint Albans, 11,194	C 3
Saint Marys, 2,148	B 3
Salem, 2,063	B 4
Shinnston, 2,543	B 4
Sistersville, 1,797	B 4
South Charleston, 13,645	C 3
Spencer, 2,279	C 3
Stonewood, 1,996	k10
Summersville, 2,906	C 4
Terra Alta, 1,713	B 5
Vienna, 10,862	B 3
War, 1,081	D 3
Weirton, 22,124	A 4
Welch, 3,028	D 3
Wellsburg, 3,385	A 4
Weston, 4,994	B 4
Westover, 4,201	B 5
Wheeling, 34,882	A 4
White Sulphur Springs, 2,779	D 4
Williamson, 4,154	D 2
Williamstown, 2,774	B 3

Wisconsin

Wisconsin

1990 CENSUS

Allouez, 14,431 .... h 9
Antigo, 8,276 ...... C 4
Appleton, 65,695 .... D 5
Ashland, 8,695 ...... B 3
Ashwaubenon, 16,376D 5
Baraboo, 9,203 .... E 4
Beaver Dam, 14,196 E 5
Beloit, 35,573 ...... F 4
Brookfield, 35,184 .. m11
Brown Deer, 12,236 m12
Burlington, 8,855 .... F 5
Cedarburg, 9,895 .... E 6
Chippewa Falls, 12,727 .... D 2
Cudahy, 18,659 .... F 6
De Pere, 16,569 .... D 5
Eau Claire, 56,856 .. D 2
Fond du Lac, 37,757 E 5
Fort Atkinson, 10,227 F 5
Franklin, 21,855 .... n11
Germantown, 13,658 E 5
Glendale, 14,088 .... m12
Grafton, 9,340 ...... E 6
Green Bay, 96,466 .. D 6
Greendale, 15,128 .. F 6
Greenfield, 33,403 .. n11
Hayward, 1,897 .... B 2
Howard, 9,874 ...... D 5
Hudson, 6,378 ...... D 1
Janesville, 52,133 .... F 4
Kaukauna, 11,982 .. D 5
Kenosha, 80,352 .... F 6
La Crosse, 51,003 .. E 2
Lake Geneva, 5,979 .. F 5
Little Chute, 9,207 .. D 5
Madison, 191,262 .. E 4
Manitowoc, 32,520 .. D 6
Marinette, 11,843 .. C 6
Marshfield, 19,291 .. D 3
Menasha, 14,711 .... D 5
Menomonee Falls, 26,840 .... E 5
Menomonie, 13,547 .. D 2
Mequon, 18,885 .... E 6
Merrill, 9,860 ...... C 4
Middleton, 13,289 .. E 4
Milwaukee, 628,088 .. E 6
Monona, 8,637 ...... E 4
Monroe, 10,241 .... F 4
Muskego, 16,813 .... F 5
Neenah, 23,219 .... D 5
New Berlin, 33,592 .. n11
New London, 6,658 .. D 5
Oak Creek, 19,513 .. n12
Oconomowoc, 10,993 E 5
Oconto, 4,474 ...... D 6
Onalaska, 11,284 .... E 2
Oshkosh, 55,006 .... D 5
Park Falls, 3,104 .... C 3
Platteville, 9,708 .... F 3
Portage, 8,640 ...... E 4
Port Washington, 9,338 .... E 6
Prairie du Chien, 5,659 .... E 2
Racine, 84,298 ...... F 6
Reedsburg, 5,834 .. E 3
Rhinelander, 7,427 .. C 4
Rice Lake, 7,998 .... C 2
River Falls, 10,610 .. D 1
Saint Francis, 9,245 .. n12
Shawano, 7,598 .... D 5
Sheboygan, 49,676 .. E 6
Shorewood, 14,116 .. E 6
South Milwaukee, 20,958 .... F 6
Stevens Point, 23,006 D 4
Stoughton, 8,786 .... F 4
Sturgeon Bay, 9,176 D 6
Sun Prairie, 15,333 .. E 4
Superior, 27,134 .... B 1
Tomah, 7,570 ...... E 3
Two Rivers, 13,030 .. D 6
Watertown, 19,142 .. E 5
Waukesha, 56,958 .. F 5
Waupun, 8,207 ...... E 5
Wausau, 37,060 .... D 4
Wauwatosa, 49,366 m12
West Allis, 63,221 .. m11
West Bend, 23,916 .. E 5
Weston, 8,775('80) .. D 4
Whitefish Bay, 14,272 m12
Whitewater, 12,636 .. F 5
Wisconsin Dells, 2,393 .... E 4
Wisconsin Rapids, 18,245 .... D 4

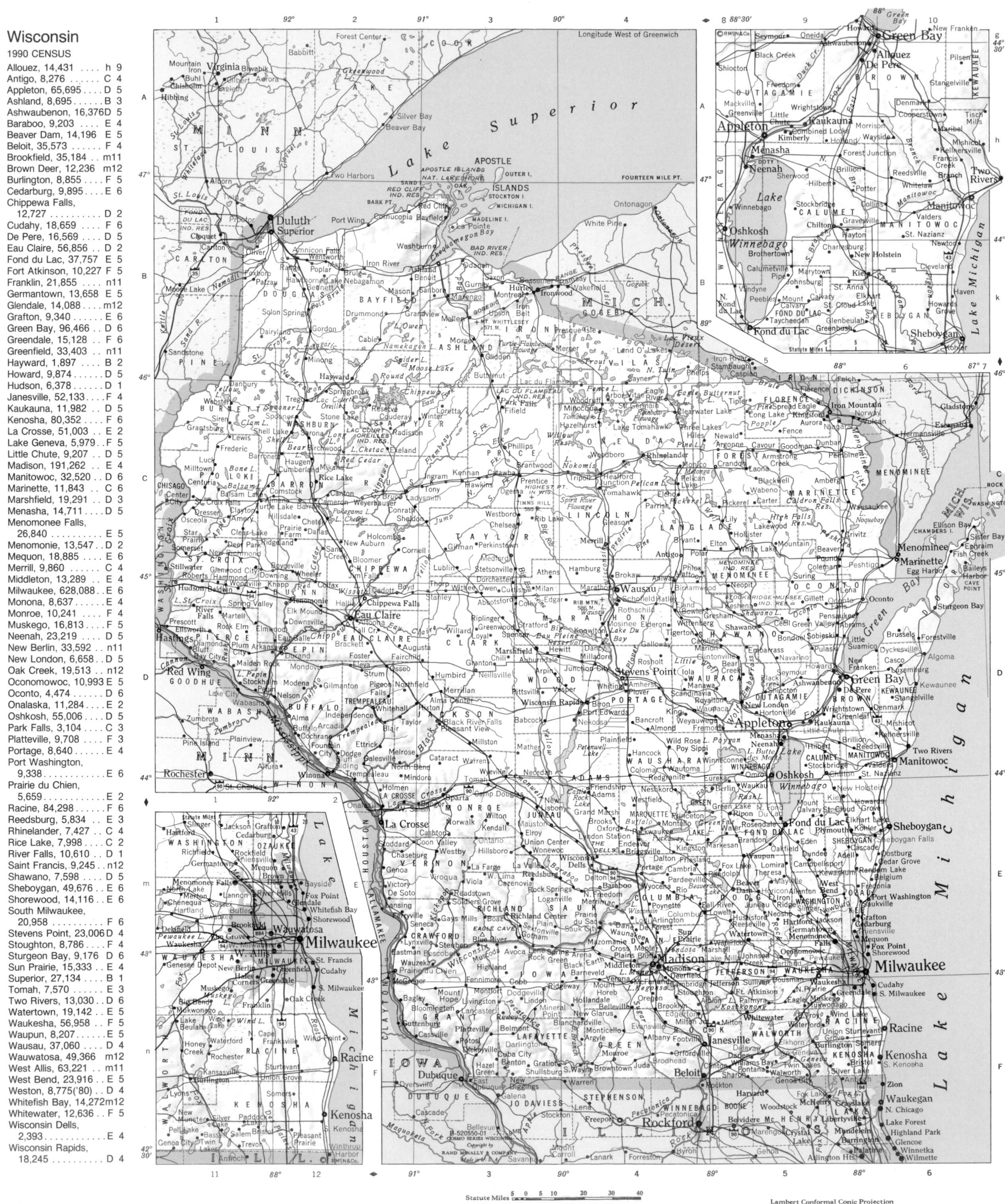

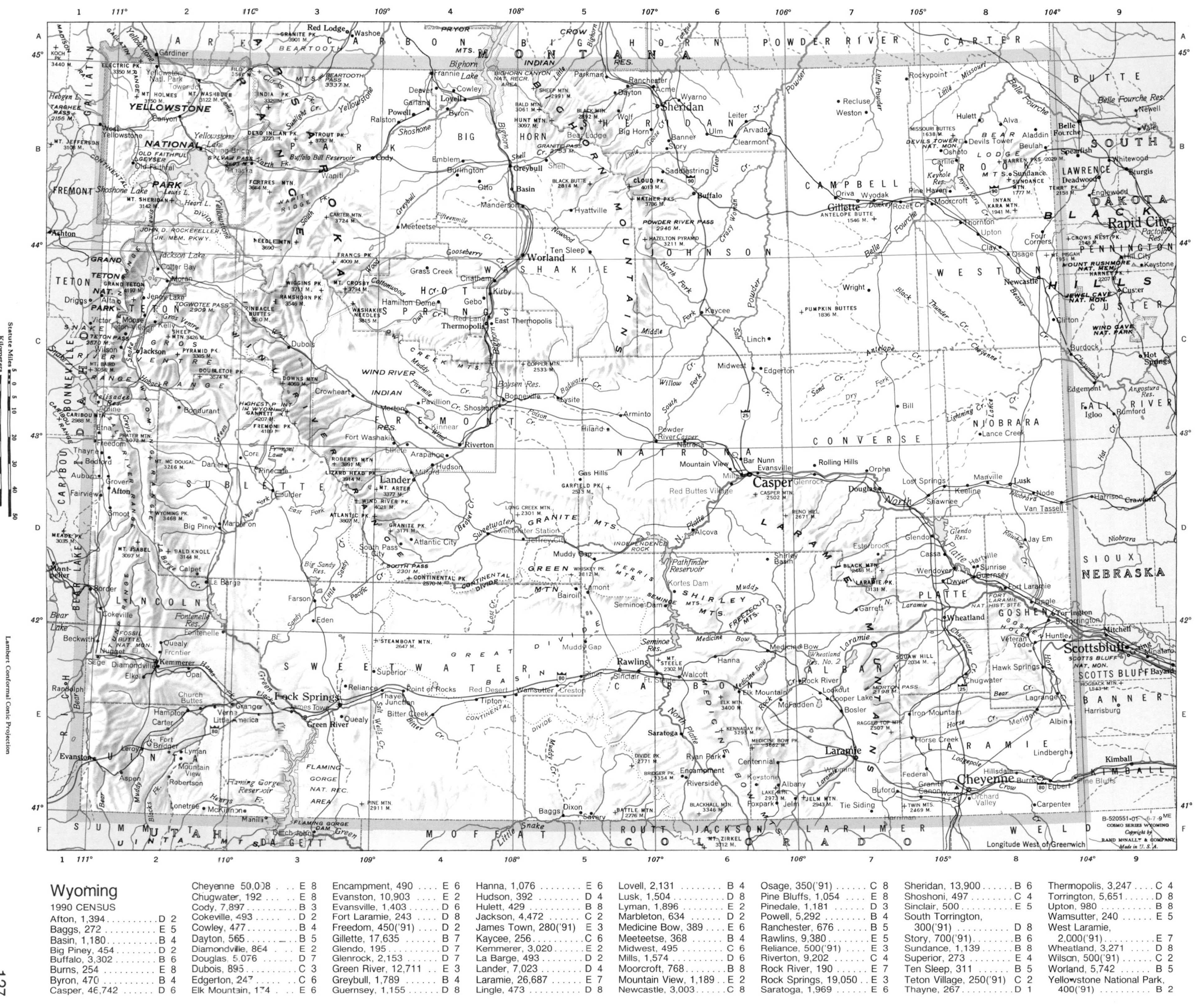

Wyoming

1990 CENSUS

- Afton, 1,394 . . . D 2
- Baggs, 272 . . . E 5
- Basin, 1,180 . . . B 4
- Big Piney, 454 . . . D 2
- Buffalo, 3,302 . . . B 6
- Burns, 254 . . . E 8
- Byron, 470 . . . B 4
- Casper, 46,742 . . . D 6
- Cheyenne 50,008 . . . E 8
- Chugwater, 192 . . . E 8
- Cody, 7,897 . . . B 3
- Cokeville, 493 . . . D 2
- Cowley, 477 . . . B 4
- Dayton, 565 . . . B 5
- Diamondville, 864 . . . E 2
- Douglas, 5,076 . . . D 7
- Dubois, 895 . . . C 3
- Edgerton, 247 . . . C 6
- Elk Mountain, 174 . . . E 6
- Encampment, 490 . . . E 6
- Evanston, 10,903 . . . E 2
- Evansville, 1,403 . . . D 6
- Fort Laramie, 243 . . . D 8
- Freedom, 450('91) . . . D 2
- Gillette, 17,635 . . . B 7
- Glendo, 195 . . . D 7
- Glenrock, 2,153 . . . D 7
- Green River, 12,711 . . . E 3
- Greybull, 1,789 . . . B 4
- Guernsey, 1,155 . . . D 8
- Hanna, 1,076 . . . E 6
- Hudson, 392 . . . D 4
- Hulett, 429 . . . B 8
- Jackson, 4,472 . . . C 2
- James Town, 280('91) . . . E 3
- Kaycee, 256 . . . C 6
- Kemmerer, 3,020 . . . E 2
- La Barge, 493 . . . D 2
- Lander, 7,023 . . . D 4
- Laramie, 26,687 . . . E 7
- Lingle, 473 . . . D 8
- Lovell, 2,131 . . . B 4
- Lusk, 1,504 . . . D 8
- Lyman, 1,896 . . . E 2
- Marbleton, 634 . . . D 2
- Medicine Bow, 389 . . . E 6
- Meeteetse, 368 . . . B 4
- Midwest, 495 . . . C 6
- Mills, 1,574 . . . D 6
- Moorcroft, 768 . . . B 8
- Mountain View, 1,189 . . E 2
- Newcastle, 3,003 . . . C 8
- Osage, 350('91) . . . C 8
- Pine Bluffs, 1,054 . . . E 8
- Pinedale, 1,181 . . . D 3
- Powell, 5,292 . . . B 4
- Ranchester, 676 . . . B 5
- Rawlins, 9,380 . . . E 5
- Reliance, 500('91) . . . E 3
- Riverton, 9,202 . . . C 4
- Rock River, 190 . . . E 7
- Rock Springs, 19,050 . . E 3
- Saratoga, 1,969 . . . E 6
- Sheridan, 13,900 . . . B 6
- Shoshoni, 497 . . . C 4
- Sinclair, 500 . . . E 5
- South Torrington, 300('91) . . . D 8
- Story, 700('91) . . . B 6
- Sundance, 1,139 . . . B 8
- Superior, 273 . . . E 4
- Ten Sleep, 311 . . . B 5
- Teton Village, 250('91) C 2
- Thayne, 267 . . . D 1
- Thermopolis, 3,247 . . . C 4
- Torrington, 5,651 . . . D 8
- Upton, 980 . . . B 8
- Wamsutter, 240 . . . E 5
- West Laramie, 2,000('91) . . . E 7
- Wheatland, 3,271 . . . D 8
- Wilson, 500('91) . . . C 2
- Worland, 5,742 . . . B 5
- Yellowstone National Park, 400('91) . . . B 2

North Polar Regions

Anchorage, 226,338 ('90)........................C27
Archangel'sk, 416,000 ('89)........................C 8
BELGIUM...................D12
Berlin, 3,352,848 ('89) (3,825,000★) D11
CANADA.....................D22
Chicago, 2,783,726 ('90)........................E21
CHINA........................F 2
Churchill, 1,186 ('81)...D22
DENMARK.................D11
Dublin, 502,749 ('86) (1,140,000★) D13
Dutch Harbor, 20 ('81)D29
Edmonton, 573,982 ('86) (785,465★) D24
ESTONIA....................C10
FAEROE ISLANDS.....C13
Fairbanks, 30,843 ('90)........................C27
FINLAND....................C10
FRANCE......................E12
Gander, 10,207 ('86) (10,899★) E18
GERMANY..................D11
Godthåb, 12,217 ('90).C18
GREENLAND.............B17
Hammerfest, 7,208 ('83)........................B10
Happy Valley-Goose Bay, 7,248 ('86)..............D19
Helsinki, 490,034 ('88) (1,040,000★) C10
ICELAND.....................C14
Igarka, 16,918 ('79).....C 4
IRELAND....................D13
JAPAN........................F35
Jekaterinburg, 1,367,000 ('89) (1,620,000★) .. D 6
Juneau, 26,751 ('90)...D26
Kijev (Kiev), 2,587,000 ('89) (2,900,000★) .. D 9
KOREA, NORTH..........E36
KOREA, SOUTH..........F36
LATVIA.......................C10
LITHUANIA..................C10
Leningrad, 4,456,000 ('89) (5,825,000★) ....D 9
LUXEMBOURG...........E12
Magadan, 152,000 ('89)........................D33
MONGOLIA................ E 2
Moskva (Moscow), 8,769,000 ('89) (13,100,000★) ....D 9
Murmansk, 468,000 ('89)........................C 9
NETHERLANDS..........D12
New York, 7,322,564 ('90)........................E20
Nižnij Novgorod (Gorky), 1,438,000 ('89) (2,025,000★) ....D 8
Nome, 3,500 ('90).......C29
Noril'sk, 174,000 ('89).C 4
NORWAY....................C12
Novosibirsk, 1,436,000 ('89) (1,600,000★) .. D 4
Ōsaka, 2,636,249 ('85) (16,450,000★) F35
Oslo, 452,415 ('87) (720,000★) D11
Ottawa, 300,763 ('86) (819,263★) E20
Paris, 2,078,900 ('87) (9,775,000★) E12
POLAND.....................D11
Québec, 164,580 ('86) (603,267★) E20
Reykjavík, 93,425 ('87) (137,941★) C15
RUSSIA....................... C 4
Saint John's, 96,216 ('86) (161,901★) E18
Sankt-Peterburg, 4,456,000 ('89) (5,825,000★) ....D 9
Seattle, 516,259 ('90)..E25
Shenyang (Mukden), 3,910,000 ('88) (4,370,000▲) E36
Sŏul (Seoul), 10,522,000 ('89) (15,850,000★) .F36
Stockholm, 672,187 ('90) (1,449,972★) D11
SWEDEN.....................C11
Thule, 551 ('90)...........B19
Tōkyō, 8,354,615 ('85) (27,700,000★) F35
UKRAINE.....................E 9
Ulaanbaatar (Ulan Bator), 548,400 ('89)...........E 2
UNITED KINGDOM..... D13
UNITED STATES.........F22
Vancouver, 431,147 ('86) (1,380,729★) E25
Vladivostok, 648,000 ('89)........................E35
Vorkuta, 116,000 ('89) C 6
Warszawa, 1,651,200 ('89) (2,323,000★) .. D10
Winnipeg, 594,551 ('86) (625,304★) E22

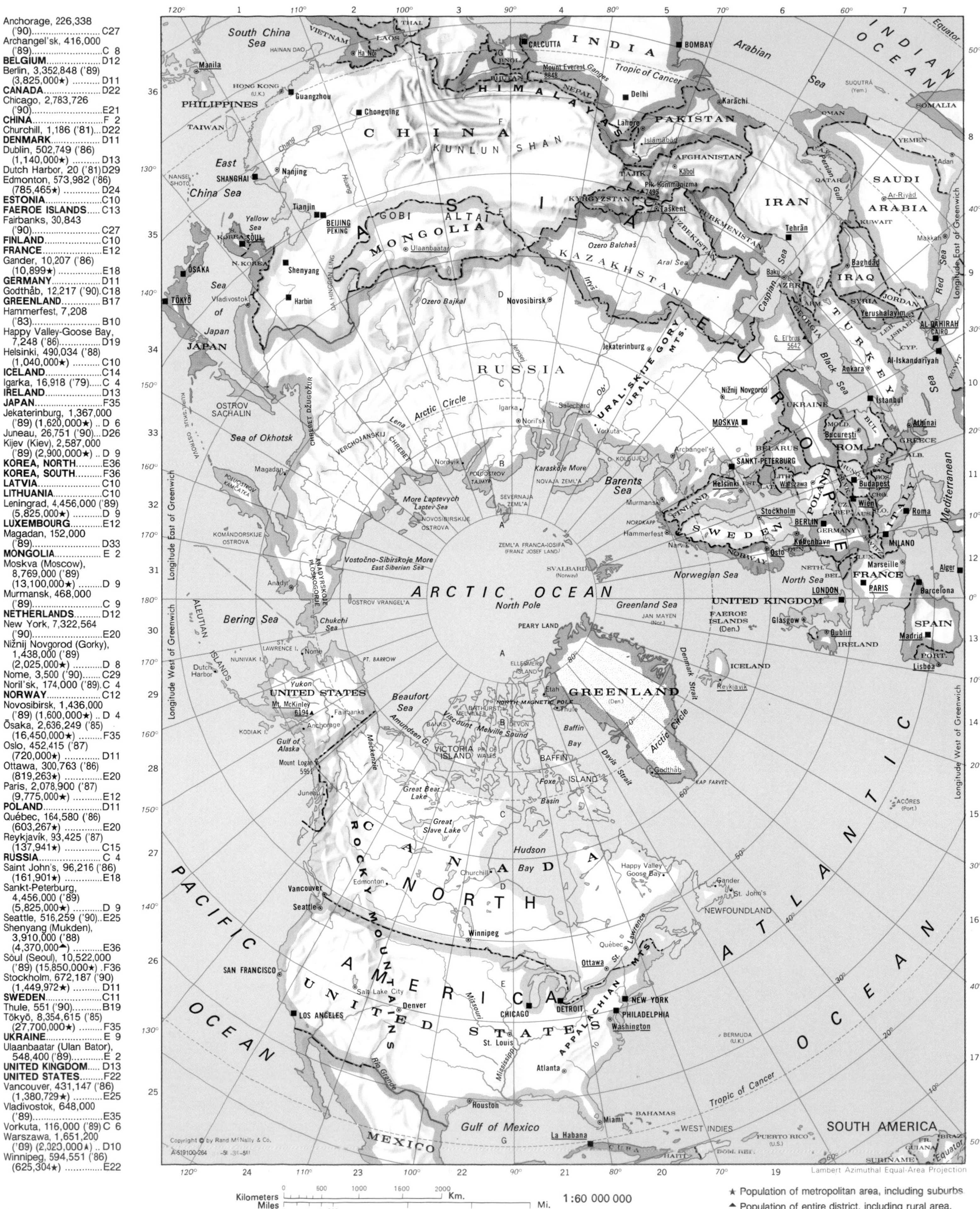

Index to World Reference Maps

Introduction to the Index

This universal index includes in a single alphabetical list approximately 38,000 names of features that appear on the reference maps. Each name is followed by the name of the country or continent in which it is located, a map-reference key and a page reference.

Names The names of cities appear in the index in regular type. The names of all other features appear in *italics*, followed by descriptive terms (hill, mtn., state) to indicate their nature.

Names that appear in shortened versions on the maps due to space limitations are spelled out in full in the index. The portions of these names omitted from the maps are enclosed in brackets — for example, Acapulco [de Juárez].

Abbreviations of names on the maps have been standardized as much as possible. Names that are abbreviated on the maps are generally spelled out in full in the index.

Country names and names of features that extend beyond the boundaries of one country are followed by the name of the continent in which each is located. Country designations follow the names of all other places in the index. The locations of places in the United States, Canada, and the United Kingdom are further defined by abbreviations that indicate the state, province, or political division in which each is located.

All abbreviations used in the index are defined in the List of Abbreviations below.

Alphabetization Names are alphabetized in the order of the letters of the English alphabet. Spanish *ll* and *ch*, for example, are not treated as distinct letters. Furthermore, diacritical marks are disregarded in alphabetization — German or Scandinavian *ä* or *ö* are treated as *a* or *o*.

The names of physical features may appear inverted, since they are always alphabetized under the proper, not the generic, part of the name, thus: 'Gibraltar, Strait of'. Otherwise every entry, whether consisting of one word or more, is alphabetized as a single continuous entity. 'Lakeland', for example, appears after 'La Crosse' and before 'La Salle'. Names beginning with articles (Le Havre, Den Helder, Al Manşūrah) are not inverted. Names beginning 'St.', 'Ste.' and 'Sainte' are alphabetized as though spelled 'Saint'.

In the case of identical names, towns are listed first, then political divisions, then physical features. Entries that are completely identical are listed alphabetically by country name.

Map-Reference Keys and Page References The map-reference keys and page references are found in the last two columns of each entry.

Each map-reference key consists of a letter and number. The letters appear along the sides of the maps. Lowercase letters indicate reference to inset maps. Numbers appear across the tops and bottoms of the maps.

Map reference keys for point features, such as cities and mountain peaks, indicate the locations of the symbols. For extensive areal features, such as countries or mountain ranges, locations are given for the approximate centers of the features. Those for linear features, such as canals and rivers, are given for the locations of the names.

Names of some important places or features that are omitted from the maps due to space limitations are included in the index. Each of these places is identified by an asterisk (*) preceding the map-reference key.

The page number generally refers to the main map for the country in which the feature is located. Page references to two-page maps always refer to the left-hand page.

List of Abbreviations

Afg.	Afghanistan
Afr.	Africa
Ak., U.S.	Alaska, U.S.
Al., U.S.	Alabama, U.S.
Alb.	Albania
Alg.	Algeria
Alta., Can.	Alberta, Can.
Am. Sam.	American Samoa
anch.	anchorage
And.	Andorra
Ang.	Angola
Ant.	Antarctica
Antig.	Antigua and Barbuda
Ar., U.S.	Arkansas, U.S.
Arg.	Argentina
Arm.	Armenia
Aus.	Austria
Austl.	Australia
Az., U.S.	Arizona, U.S.
Azer.	Azerbaijan
b.	bay, gulf, inlet, lagoon
Bah.	Bahamas
Bahr.	Bahrain
Barb.	Barbados
B.A.T.	British Antarctic Territory
B.C., Can.	British Columbia, Can.
Bdi.	Burundi
Bel.	Belgium
Bela.	Belarus
Ber.	Bermuda
Bhu.	Bhutan
B.I.O.T.	British Indian Ocean Territory
Bngl.	Bangladesh
Bol.	Bolivia
Bos.	Bosnia and Herzegovina
Bots.	Botswana
Braz.	Brazil
Bru.	Brunei
Br. Vir. Is.	British Virgin Islands
Bul.	Bulgaria
Burkina	Burkina Faso
c.	cape, point
Ca., U.S.	California, U.S.
Cam.	Cameroon
Camb.	Cambodia
Can.	Canada
Cay. Is.	Cayman Islands
Cen. Afr. Rep.	Central African Republic
Christ. I.	Christmas Island
C. Iv.	Cote d'Ivoire
clf.	cliff, escarpment
co.	county, parish
Co., U.S.	Colorado, U.S.
Col.	Colombia
Com.	Comoros
cont.	continent
C.R.	Costa Rica
crat.	crater
Cro.	Croatia
Ct., U.S.	Connecticut, U.S.
ctry.	country
C.V.	Cape Verde
Cyp.	Cyprus
Czech.	Czech Republic
D.C., U.S.	District of Columbia, U.S.
De., U.S.	Delaware, U.S.
Den.	Denmark
dep.	dependency, colony
depr.	depression
dept.	department, district
des.	desert
Dji.	Djibouti
Dom.	Dominica
Dom. Rep.	Dominican Republic
Ec.	Ecuador
El Sal.	El Salvador
Eng., U.K.	England, U.K.
Eq. Gui.	Equatorial Guinea
Erit.	Eritrea
est.	estuary
Est.	Estonia
Eth.	Ethiopia
Eur.	Europe
Faer. Is.	Faeroe Islands
Falk. Is.	Falkland Islands
Fin.	Finland
Fl., U.S.	Florida, U.S.
for.	forest, moor
Fr.	France
Fr. Gu.	French Guiana
Fr. Poly.	French Polynesia
F.S.A.T.	French Southern and Antarctic Territory
Ga., U.S.	Georgia, U.S.
Gam.	Gambia
Geor.	Georgia
Ger.	Germany
Gib.	Gibraltar
Golan Hts.	Golan Heights
Grc.	Greece
Gren.	Grenada
Grnld.	Greenland
Guad.	Guadeloupe
Guat.	Guatemala
Gui.	Guinea
Gui.-B.	Guinea-Bissau
Guy.	Guyana
Hi., U.S.	Hawaii, U.S.
hist.	historic site, ruins
hist. reg.	historic region
H.K.	Hong Kong
Hond.	Honduras
Hung.	Hungary
i.	island
Ia., U.S.	Iowa, U.S.
Ice.	Iceland
ice	ice feature, glacier
Id., U.S.	Idaho, U.S.
Il., U.S.	Illinois, U.S.
In., U.S.	Indiana, U.S.
Indon.	Indonesia
I. of Man	Isle of Man
Ire.	Ireland
is.	islands
Isr.	Israel
Jam.	Jamaica
Jord.	Jordan
Kaz.	Kazakhstan
Kir.	Kiribati
Ks., U.S.	Kansas, U.S.
Kuw.	Kuwait
Ky., U.S.	Kentucky, U.S.
Kyrg.	Kyrgyzstan
l.	lake, pond
La., U.S.	Louisiana, U.S.
Lat.	Latvia
Leb.	Lebanon
Leso.	Lesotho
Lib.	Liberia
Liech.	Liechtenstein
Lith.	Lithuania
Lux.	Luxembourg
Ma., U.S.	Massachusetts, U.S.
Mac.	Macedonia
Madag.	Madagascar
Malay.	Malaysia
Mald.	Maldives
Man., Can.	Manitoba, Can.
Marsh. Is.	Marshall Islands
Mart.	Martinique
Maur.	Mauritania
May.	Mayotte
Md., U.S.	Maryland, U.S.
Me., U.S.	Maine, U.S.
Mex.	Mexico
Mi., U.S.	Michigan, U.S.
Micron.	Federated States of Micronesia
Mid. Is.	Midway Islands
mil.	military installation
Mn., U.S.	Minnesota, U.S.
Mo., U.S.	Missouri, U.S.
Mol.	Moldova
Mon.	Monaco
Mong.	Mongolia
Monts.	Montserrat
Mor.	Morocco
Moz.	Mozambique
Mrts.	Mauritius
Ms., U.S.	Mississippi, U.S.
Mt., U.S.	Montana, U.S.
mth.	river mouth or channel
mtn.	mountain
mts.	mountains
Mwi.	Malawi
Mya.	Myanmar
N.A.	North America
N.B., Can.	New Brunswick, Can.
N.C., U.S.	North Carolina, U.S.
N. Cal.	New Caledonia
N. Cyp.	North Cyprus
N.D., U.S.	North Dakota, U.S.
Ne., U.S.	Nebraska, U.S.
Neth.	Netherlands
Neth. Ant.	Netherlands Antilles
Newf., Can.	Newfoundland, Can.
N.H., U.S.	New Hampshire, U.S.
Nic.	Nicaragua
Nig.	Nigeria
N. Ire., U.K.	Northern Ireland, U.K.
N.J., U.S.	New Jersey, U.S.
N. Kor.	North Korea
N.M., U.S.	New Mexico, U.S.
N. Mar. Is.	Northern Mariana Islands
Nmb.	Namibia
Nor.	Norway
Norf. I.	Norfolk Island
N.S., Can.	Nova Scotia, Can.
Nv., U.S.	Nevada, U.S.
N.W. Ter., Can.	Northwest Territories, Can.
N.Y., U.S.	New York, U.S.
N.Z.	New Zealand
Oc.	Oceania
Oh., U.S.	Ohio, U.S.
Ok., U.S.	Oklahoma, U.S.
Ont., Can.	Ontario, Can.
Or., U.S.	Oregon, U.S.
Pa., U.S.	Pennsylvania, U.S.
Pak.	Pakistan
Pan.	Panama
Pap. N. Gui.	Papua New Guinea
Para.	Paraguay
P.E.I., Can.	Prince Edward Island, Can.
pen.	peninsula
Phil.	Philippines
Pit.	Pitcairn
pl.	plain, flat
plat.	plateau, highland
Pol.	Poland
Port.	Portugal
P.R.	Puerto Rico
prov.	province, region
Que., Can.	Quebec, Can.
reg.	physical region
res.	reservoir
Reu.	Reunion
rf.	reef, shoal
R.I., U.S.	Rhode Island, U.S.
Rom.	Romania
Rw.	Rwanda
S.A.	South America
S. Afr.	South Africa
Sask., Can.	Saskatchewan, Can.
Sau. Ar.	Saudi Arabia
S.C., U.S.	South Carolina, U.S.
sci.	scientific station
Scot., U.K.	Scotland, U.K.
S.D., U.S.	South Dakota, U.S.
Sen.	Senegal
Sey.	Seychelles
Sing.	Singapore
S. Kor.	South Korea
S.L.	Sierra Leone
Slo.	Slovenia
Slov.	Slovakia
S. Mar.	San Marino
Sol. Is.	Solomon Islands
Som.	Somalia
Sp. N. Afr.	Spanish North Africa
Sri L.	Sri Lanka
state	state, republic, canton
St. Hel.	St. Helena
St. K./N	St. Kitts and Nevis
St. Luc.	St. Lucia
stm.	stream (river, creek)
S. Tom./P.	Sao Tome and Principe
St. P./M.	St. Pierre and Miquelon
strt.	strait, channel, sound
St. Vin.	St. Vincent and the Grenadines
Sud.	Sudan
Sur.	Suriname
sw.	swamp, marsh
Swaz.	Swaziland
Swe.	Sweden
Switz.	Switzerland
Tai.	Taiwan
Taj.	Tajikistan
Tan.	Tanzania
T./C. Is.	Turks and Caicos Islands
ter.	territory
Thai.	Thailand
Tn., U.S.	Tennessee, U.S.
Tok.	Tokelau
Trin.	Trinidad and Tobago
Tun.	Tunisia
Tur.	Turkey
Turk.	Turkmenistan
Tx., U.S.	Texas, U.S.
U.A.E.	United Arab Emirates
Ug.	Uganda
U.K.	United Kingdom
Ukr.	Ukraine
Ur.	Uruguay
U.S.	United States
Ut., U.S.	Utah, U.S.
Uzb.	Uzbekistan
Va., U.S.	Virginia, U.S.
val.	valley, watercourse
Vat.	Vatican City
Ven.	Venezuela
Viet.	Vietnam
V.I.U.S.	Virgin Islands (U.S.)
vol.	volcano
Vt., U.S.	Vermont, U.S.
Wa., U.S.	Washington, U.S.
Wal./F.	Wallis and Futuna
W. Bank	West Bank
Wi., U.S.	Wisconsin, U.S.
W. Sah.	Western Sahara
W. Sam.	Western Samoa
wtfl.	waterfall
W.V., U.S.	West Virginia, U.S.
Wy., U.S.	Wyoming, U.S.
Yugo.	Yugoslavia
Yukon, Can.	Yukon Territory, Can.
Zam.	Zambia
Zimb.	Zimbabwe

Index

A

Name	Map Ref	Page
Aachen, Ger.	E6	8
Aalen, Ger.	G10	8
Aalst, Bel.	E4	8
Äänekoski, Fin.	E15	6
Aarau, Switz.	E15	10
Aarschot, Bel.	E4	8
Aba, China	E7	26
Aba, Nig.	G7	42
Ābādān, Iran	B4	46
Abaeté, Braz.	E6	57
Abajo Peak, mtn., Ut., U.S.	F6	121
Abakan, Russia	G12	24
Abancay, Peru	F4	54
Abashiri, Japan	o22	30a
Abasolo, Mex.	E7	62
Abaya, Lake, l., Eth.	G2	46
Abaza, Russia	G12	24
Abbadia San Salvatore, Italy	G6	14
Abbaye, Point, c., Mi., U.S.	B2	99
Abbeville, Fr.	B8	10
Abbeville, Al., U.S.	D4	78
Abbeville, Ga., U.S.	E3	87
Abbeville, La., U.S.	E3	95
Abbeville, S.C., U.S.	C3	117
Abbeville, co., S.C., U.S.	C2	117
Abbotsford, Wi., U.S.	D3	126
Abbottābād, Pak.	C5	38
Abbott Butte, mtn., Or., U.S.	E4	114
Abbott Run, stm., U.S.	B4	116
Abbott Run Valley, R.I., U.S.	B4	116
'Abd al-Kūrī, i., Yemen	F5	46
Abe, Lake, l., Afr.	F3	46
Abéché, Chad	F10	42
Abéjar, Spain	D9	12
Abengourou, C. Iv.	G5	42
Abeokuta, Nig.	G6	42
Aberayron, Wales, U.K.	I8	7
Aberdeen, Scot., U.K.	D10	7
Aberdeen, Id., U.S.	G6	89
Aberdeen, Md., U.S.	A5	97
Aberdeen, Ms., U.S.	B5	101
Aberdeen, N.C., U.S.	B3	110
Aberdeen, Oh., U.S.	D2	112
Aberdeen, S.D., U.S.	B7	118
Aberdeen, Wa., U.S.	C2	124
Aberdeen Lake, l., N.W. Ter., Can.	D13	66
Aberdeen Proving Ground, mil., Md., U.S.	A5	97
Abernathy, Tx., U.S.	C2	120
Abert, Lake, l., Or., U.S.	E6	114
Abert Rim, clf, Or., U.S.	E6	114
Aberystwyth, Wales, U.K.	I8	7
Abhā, Sau. Ar.	E3	46
Abidjan, C. Iv.	G5	42
Abilene, Ks., U.S.	D6	93
Abilene, Tx., U.S.	C3	120
Abingdon, Il., U.S.	C3	90
Abingdon, Md., U.S.	B5	97
Abingdon, Va., U.S.	f10	123
Abington, Ma., U.S.	B6	98
Abington [Township], Pa., U.S.	o21	115
Abisko, Swe.	B12	6
Abita Springs, La., U.S.	D5	95
Abitibi, stm., Ont., Can.	o19	73
Abitibi, Lake, l., Can.	G17	66
Abohar, India	E6	38
Abomey, Benin	G6	42
Aborigen, Pik, mtn., Russia	E23	24
Abraham Lake, res., Alta., Can.	C2	68
Abraham Lincoln Birthplace National Historic Site, hist., Ky., U.S.	C4	94
Abrantes, Port.	F3	12
Absaroka Range, mts., U.S.	F7	127
Absarokee, Mt., U.S.	E7	103
Absecon, N.J., U.S.	E4	107
Absecon Inlet, b., N.J., U.S.	E4	107
Abū 'Alī, i., Sau. Ar.	C4	46
Abu Dhabi see Abū Ẓaby, U.A.E.	D5	46
Abū Hamad, Sudan	E12	42
Abuja, Nig.	G7	42
Abū Kamāl, Syria	B7	40
Abukuma-sanchi, mts., Japan	E13	30
Abū Madd, Ra's, c., Sau. Ar.	D2	46
Abunā, Braz.	E5	54
Abū Shajarah, Ra's, c., Sudan	D13	42
Abū Ẓaby, U.A.E.	D5	46
Academia, Oh., U.S.	B3	112
Acadia, co., La., U.S.	D3	95
Acadia National Park, Me., U.S.	D4	96
Acajutla, El Sal.	H3	64
Acámbaro, Mex.	G9	62
Acaponeta, Mex.	F7	62
Acapulco [de Juárez], Mex.	I10	62
Acarai Mountains, mts., S.A.	C7	54
Acaraú, Braz.	D10	54
Acarigua, Ven.	C8	58
Acatlán [de Osorio], Mex.	H10	62
Acayucan, Mex.	I12	62
Accomack, co., Va., U.S.	C7	123
Accoville, W.V., U.S.	D3	125
Accra, Ghana	G5	42
Acerra, Italy	I9	14
Achaguas, Ven.	D8	58
Achalpur, India	B4	37
Acheng, China	B12	26
Achí, Col.	C5	58
Achill Island, i., Ire.	H2	7
Achtubinsk, Russia	H7	22
Ačinsk, Russia	F12	24
Acireale, Italy	L10	14
Ackerman, Ms., U.S.	B4	101
Ackley, Ia., U.S.	B4	92
Acklins Island, i., Bah.	C10	64
Acoma Indian Reservation, N.M., U.S.	C2	108
Aconcagua, Cerro, mtn., Arg.	C2	56
Açores (Azores), is., Port.	D11	2
Acquapendente, Italy	G6	14
Acqui Terme, Italy	E3	14
Acre, stm., S.A.	E5	54
Acri, Italy	J11	14
Acton, Ma., U.S.	B5	98
Acton Vale, Que., Can.	D5	74
Acushnet, Ma., U.S.	C6	98
Acworth, Ga., U.S.	B2	87
Ada, Mn., U.S.	C2	100
Ada, Oh., U.S.	B2	112
Ada, Ok., U.S.	C5	113
Ada, co., Id., U.S.	F2	89
Ada, Mount, mtn., Ak., U.S.	m22	79
Adair, Ia., U.S.	C3	92
Adair, Ok., U.S.	A6	113
Adair, co., Ia., U.S.	C3	92
Adair, co., Ky., U.S.	C4	94
Adair, co., Mo., U.S.	A5	102
Adair, co., Ok., U.S.	B7	113
Adair, Cape, c., N.W. Ter., Can.	B18	66
Adairsville, Ga., U.S.	B2	87
Adairville, Ky., U.S.	D3	94
Adak Island, i., Ak., U.S.	E4	79
Adak Naval Station, mil., Ak., U.S.	E4	79
Ādam, Oman	D6	46
Adamantina, Braz.	F3	57
Adamawa, mts., Afr.	G8	42
Adam Island, i., Md., U.S.	D5	97
Adams, Ma., U.S.	A1	98
Adams, Mn., U.S.	G6	100
Adams, N.Y., U.S.	B4	109
Adams, Wi., U.S.	E4	126
Adams, co., Co., U.S.	B6	83
Adams, co., Id., U.S.	E2	89
Adams, co., Il., U.S.	D2	90
Adams, co., In., U.S.	C8	91
Adams, co., Ia., U.S.	C3	92
Adams, co., Ms., U.S.	D2	101
Adams, co., Ne., U.S.	D7	104
Adams, co., N.D., U.S.	C3	111
Adams, co., Oh., U.S.	D2	112
Adams, co., Pa., U.S.	G7	115
Adams, co., Wa., U.S.	B7	124
Adams, co., Wi., U.S.	D4	126
Adams, Mount, mtn., N.H., U.S.	B4	106
Adams, Mount, mtn., Wa., U.S.	C4	124
Adams Bridge, rf., Asia	H5	37
Adams Point, c., Mi., U.S.	C7	99
Adams Run, S.C., U.S.	k11	117
Adamstown, Pa., U.S.	F9	115
Adamsville, Al., U.S.	f7	78
Adamsville, R.I., U.S.	E6	116
Adamsville, Tn., U.S.	B3	119
Adamsville Brook, stm., R.I., U.S.	E6	116
'Adan (Aden), Yemen	F4	46
Adana, Tur.	H15	4
Adarama, Sudan	E12	42
Ad-Dabbah, Sudan	E12	42
Ad-Dahnā, des., Sau. Ar.	D4	46
Ad-Dammām, Sau. Ar.	C5	46
Ad-Dawādimī, Sau. Ar.	D3	46
Ad-Dawhah (Doha), Qatar	C5	46
Addis, La., U.S.	D4	95
Addis Ababa see Adis Abeba, Eth.	G2	46
Addison, Al., U.S.	A2	78
Addison, Ct., U.S.	C5	84
Addison, Il., U.S.	k8	90
Addison, N.Y., U.S.	C3	109
Addison, co., Vt., U.S.	C2	122
Ad-Dīwānīyah, Iraq	B3	46
Ad-Duwaym, Sudan	F12	42
Addyston, Oh., U.S.	o12	112
Adel, Ga., U.S.	E3	87
Adel, Ia., U.S.	C3	92
Adelaide, Austl.	F7	50
Adelaide Peninsula, pen., N.W. Ter., Can.	C13	66
Adelanto, Ca., U.S.	E5	82
Aden, Gulf of, b.	F4	46
Aden see 'Adan, Yemen	F4	46
Adieu, Cape, c., Austl.	F6	50
Adige, stm., Italy	D7	14
Adigrat, Eth.	F2	46
Ādilābād, India	C5	37
Adimi, Russia	H21	24
Adirondack Mountains, mts., N.Y., U.S.	A6	109
Adis Abeba, Eth.	G2	46
Admiralty Bay, b., Ak., U.S.	A9	79
Admiralty Inlet, b., N.W. Ter., Can.	B15	66
Admiralty Island, i., Ak., U.S.	m22	79
Admiralty Islands, is., Pap. N. Gui.	k16	50a
Adobe Acres, N.M., U.S.	*B3	108
Adobe Creek Reservoir, res., Co., U.S.	C7	83
Adolfo López Mateos, Presa, res., Mex.	E6	62
Ādoni, India	E4	37
Adour, stm., Fr.	I7	10
Adra, Spain	I8	12
Adrano, Italy	L9	14
Adrar, Alg.	C5	42
Adria, Italy	D7	14
Adrian, Ga., U.S.	D4	87
Adrian, Mi., U.S.	G6	99
Adrian, Mn., U.S.	G3	100
Adrian, Mo., U.S.	C3	102
Adriatic Sea, Eur.	G11	4
Advance, Mo., U.S.	D8	102
Adyča, stm., Russia	D21	24
Aegean Sea	J8	16
Afars and Issas see Djibouti, ctry., Afr.	F3	46
Afghanistan, ctry., Asia	C1	36
Afikpo, Nig.	G7	42
Åfjord, Nor.	E8	6
Afmadu, Som.	A8	44
Afognak Island, i., Ak., U.S.	D9	79
Africa	D6	41
Afton, Ia., U.S.	C3	92
Afton, Mn., U.S.	F6	100
Afton, Ok., U.S.	A7	113
Afton, Wy., U.S.	D2	127
'Afula, Isr.	C4	40
Afyon, Tur.	H14	4
Agadez, Niger	E7	42
Agadir, Mor.	B4	42
Agaloga Islands, is., Mrts.	D11	44
Agalta, Cordillera de, mts., Hond.	G5	64
Agapa, Russia	C11	24
Agartala, India	I14	38
Agate Fossil Beds National Monument, Ne., U.S.	B2	104
Agattu Island, i., Ak., U.S.	E2	79
Agawam, Ma., U.S.	B2	98
Agen, Fr.	H7	10
Agency, Ia., U.S.	D5	92
Agency, Mo., U.S.	B3	102
Āghā Jārī, Iran	B4	46
Agira, Italy	L9	14
Agnone, Italy	H9	14
Agoura Hills, Ca., U.S.	m11	82
Āgra, India	G8	38
Ágreda, Spain	D10	12
Ağrı Dağı (Mount Ararat), mtn., Tur.	H16	4
Agrigento, Italy	L8	14
Agrínion, Grc.	K5	16
Agropoli, Italy	I9	14
Agua Caliente, Mex.	F7	62
Agua Caliente Grande, Mex.	D5	62
Aguachica, Col.	C6	58
Água Clara, Braz.	F2	57
Agua Fria, N.M., U.S.	B3	108
Agua Fria, stm., Az., U.S.	D3	80
Agua Prieta, Mex.	B5	62
Aguascalientes, Mex.	G8	62
Águas Formosas, Braz.	D8	57
Águeda, Port.	E3	12
Aguila, Az., U.S.	D2	80
Aguilar, Spain	H7	12
Águilas, Spain	H10	12
Agulhas, Cape, c., S. Afr.	H3	44
Agustín Codazzi, Col.	B6	58
Agustín Codazzi, Col.	I11	64
Ahaggar, mts., Alg.	D7	42
Ahipara Bay, b., N.Z.	A4	52
Ahklun Mountains, mts., Ak., U.S.	D7	79
Ahlen, Ger.	D7	8
Ahmadābād, India	I5	38
Ahmadnagar, India	C3	37
Ahmadpur East, Pak.	F4	38
Ahmar Mountains, mts., Eth.	G3	46
Ahoskie, N.C., U.S.	A6	110
Ahtanum Creek, stm., Wa., U.S.	C5	124
Ahu, China	A7	28
Ahuacatlán, Mex.	G7	62
Ahvāz, Iran	B4	46
Ahvenanmaa (Åland), is., Fin.	F12	6
Aialik, Cape, c., Ak., U.S.	D10	79
Aichach, Ger.	G11	8
Aiea, Hi., U.S.	B4	88
Aihun, China	A12	26
Aijal, India	I15	38
Aiken, S.C., U.S.	D4	117
Aiken, co., S.C., U.S.	D4	117
Ailsa Craig, Ont., Can.	D3	73
Aim, Russia	F20	24
Aimorés, Braz.	E8	57
Ainslie Lake, l., N.S., Can.	C8	71
Ainsworth, Ne., U.S.	B6	104
Aipe, Col.	F5	58
Aïr, mts., Niger	E7	42
Airdrie, Alta., Can.	D3	68
Aire-sur-l'Adour, Fr.	I6	10
Air Force Island, i., N.W. Ter., Can.	C18	66
Air Park West, Ne., U.S.	*D9	104
Aisne, stm., Fr.	C10	10
Aïssa, Djebel, mtn., Alg.	B5	42
Aitape, Pap. N. Gui.	k15	50a
Aitkin, Mn., U.S.	D5	100
Aitkin, co., Mn., U.S.	D5	100
Aix, Mount, mtn., Wa., U.S.	C4	124
Aix-en-Provence, Fr.	I12	10
Aix-la-Chapelle see Aachen, Ger.	E6	8
Aix-les-Bains, Fr.	G12	10
Aizu-wakamatsu, Japan	E12	30
Ajaccio, Fr.	n23	11a
Ajaguz, Kaz.	H10	24
Ajan, Russia	F21	24
Ajan, stm., Russia	C13	24
Ajax, Ont., Can.	D6	73
Ajdābiyah, Libya	B10	42
Ajjer, Tassili n', plat., Alg.	C7	42
'Ajlūn, Jord.	C4	40
Ajmer, India	G6	38
Ajo, Az., U.S.	E3	80
Ajo, Cabo de, c., Spain	B8	12
Ajon, Ostrov, i., Russia	D27	24
Ajtos, Bul.	G11	16
Akademii, Zaliv, b., Russia	G21	24
Akaltara, India	A7	37
Akan, Japan	p22	30a
'Akasha East, Sudan	D12	42
Akashi, Japan	H7	30
Akçakale, Tur.	A6	40
Ak-Chin Indian Reservation, Az., U.S.	E3	80
Akesu, China	C3	26
Akharnai, Grc.	K7	16
Akhisar, Tur.	H13	4
Akiachak, Ak., U.S.	C7	79
Akimiski Island, i., N.W. Ter., Can.	F16	66
Akita, Japan	C13	30
Akjoujt, Maur.	E3	42
'Akko (Acre), Isr.	C4	40
Aklavik, N.W. Ter., Can.	C6	66
Akmola, Kaz.	G8	24
Akō, Japan	H7	30
Akobo, stm., Afr.	G12	42
Akola, India	B4	37
Akordat, Erit.	E2	46
Akot, India	B4	37
Akpatok Island, i., N.W. Ter., Can.	D19	66
Akron, Co., U.S.	A7	83
Akron, In., U.S.	B5	91
Akron, Ia., U.S.	B1	92
Akron, N.Y., U.S.	B2	109
Akron, Oh., U.S.	A4	112
Akron, Pa., U.S.	F9	115
Aksaray, Tur.	H14	4
Akşehir, Tur.	H14	4
Aksum, Eth.	F2	46
Aktau, Kaz.	I8	22
Akt'ubinsk, Kaz.	G9	22
Akureyri, Ice.	B4	4
Ål, Nor.	F7	6
Alabama, state, U.S.	C3	78
Alabama, stm., Al., U.S.	D2	78
Alabaster, Al., U.S.	B3	78
Alachua, Fl., U.S.	C4	86
Alachua, co., Fl., U.S.	C4	86
Alagoinhas, Braz.	B9	57
Alagón, Spain	D10	12
Alajuela, C.R.	I5	64
Alakanuk, Ak., U.S.	C7	79
Alalakeiki Channel, strt., Hi., U.S.	C5	88
Al-'Alamayn, Egypt	B11	42
Alamance, co., N.C., U.S.	B3	110
Al-'Amārah, Iraq	B4	46
Alameda, Ca., U.S.	h8	82
Alameda, N.M., U.S.	B3	108
Alameda, co., Ca., U.S.	D3	82
Alameda Naval Air Station, mil., Ca., U.S.	h8	82
Alamito Creek, stm., Tx., U.S.	p12	120
Alamo, Ga., U.S.	D4	87
Alamo, Nv., U.S.	F6	105
Alamo, Tn., U.S.	B2	119
Alamo, Tx., U.S.	F3	120
Alamogordo, N.M., U.S.	E4	108
Alamo Heights, Tx., U.S.	E3	120
Alamo Hueco Mountains, mts., N.M., U.S.	F1	108
Alamo Indian Reservation, N.M., U.S.	C2	108
Alamo Lake, res., Az., U.S.	C2	80
Alamosa, Co., U.S.	D5	83
Alamosa, co., Co., U.S.	D5	83
Alamosa, stm., Co., U.S.	D4	83
Alamosa Creek, stm., N.M., U.S.	D2	108
Alamosa East, Co., U.S.	D5	83
Alanäs, Swe.	D10	6
Alanya, Tur.	A3	40
Alapaha, Ga., U.S.	E3	87
Alapaha, stm., U.S.	E3	87
Al-'Aqabah, Jord.	E4	40
Alaşehir, Tur.	K12	16
Alashanyouqi, China	C7	26
Alaska, state, U.S.	C9	79
Alaska, Gulf of, b., Ak., U.S.	D10	79
Alaska Peninsula, pen., Ak., U.S.	D8	79
Alaska Range, mts., Ak., U.S.	C9	79
Alassio, Italy	E3	14
Alatna, stm., Ak., U.S.	B9	79
Al-'Aṭrūn, Sudan	E11	42
Alava, Cape, c., Wa., U.S.	A1	124
Alazeja, stm., Russia	C24	24
Alba, Italy	E3	14
Albacete, Spain	G10	12
Alba de Tormes, Spain	E6	12
Albaida, Spain	G11	12
Albanel, Lac, l., Que., Can.	F18	66
Albania, ctry., Eur.	G11	4
Albano Laziale, Italy	H7	14
Albany, Austl.	G3	50
Albany, Ga., U.S.	E2	87
Albany, Il., U.S.	B3	90
Albany, In., U.S.	D7	91
Albany, Ky., U.S.	D4	94
Albany, La., U.S.	g10	95
Albany, Mn., U.S.	E4	100
Albany, Mo., U.S.	A3	102
Albany, N.Y., U.S.	C7	109
Albany, Or., U.S.	C3	114
Albany, Tx., U.S.	C3	120
Albany, Wi., U.S.	F4	126
Albany, co., N.Y., U.S.	C6	109
Albany, co., Wy., U.S.	E7	127
Albany, stm., Ont., Can.	o18	73
Al-Baṣrah, Iraq	B4	46
Albatross Bay, b., Austl.	B8	50
Al-Batrūn, Leb.	B4	40
Al-Bawīṭī, Egypt	C11	42
Albemarle, N.C., U.S.	B2	110
Albemarle, co., Va., U.S.	C4	123
Albemarle Lake, l., Ms., U.S.	C2	101
Albemarle Sound, strt., N.C., U.S.	A6	110
Albenga, Italy	E3	14
Albergaria-a-Velha, Port.	E3	12
Albert, Fr.	B9	10
Albert, Lake, l., Afr.	A6	44
Alberta, prov., Can.	C4	68
Alberta, Mount, mtn., Alta., Can.	C2	68
Albert City, Ia., U.S.	B3	92
Albert Lea, Mn., U.S.	G5	100
Albert Nile, stm., Ug.	H12	42
Alberton, P.E.I., Can.	C5	71
Albertson, N.Y., U.S.	k13	109
Albertville, Fr.	G13	10
Albertville, Al., U.S.	A3	78
Albertville, Mn., U.S.	E5	100
Albertville see Kalemie, Zaire	C5	44
Albi, Fr.	I9	10
Albia, Ia., U.S.	C5	92
Albino, Italy	D4	14
Albion, Il., U.S.	E5	90
Albion, In., U.S.	B7	91
Albion, Mi., U.S.	F6	99
Albion, Ne., U.S.	C7	104
Albion, N.Y., U.S.	B2	109
Albion, Pa., U.S.	C1	115
Albion, R.I., U.S.	B4	116
Albion, Wa., U.S.	C8	124
Alborán, Isla de, i., Spain	J8	12
Ålborg, Den.	H7	6
Alborz, Reshteh-ye Kūhhā-ye, mts., Iran	J8	22
Albufeira, Port.	H3	12
Albuñol, Spain	I8	12
Albuquerque, N.M., U.S.	B3	108
Alburquerque, Spain	F4	12
Alburtis, Pa., U.S.	F10	115
Albury, Austl.	G9	50
Alcácer do Sal, Port.	G3	12
Alcalá de Guadaira, Spain	H6	12
Alcalá de Henares, Spain	E8	12
Alcalá la Real, Spain	H8	12
Alcalde, N.M., U.S.	A3	108
Alcamo, Italy	L7	14
Alcañices, Spain	D5	12
Alcañiz, Spain	D11	12
Alcântara, Braz.	D10	54
Alcántara, Spain	F5	12
Alcantarilla, Spain	H10	12
Alcaraz, Spain	G9	12
Alcázar de San Juan, Spain	F8	12
Alcester, S.D., U.S.	D9	118
Alcira, Spain	F11	12
Alcoa, Tn., U.S.	D10	119
Alcobaça, Braz.	D9	57
Alcobaça, Port.	F3	12
Alcolu, S.C., U.S.	D7	117
Alcona, co., Mi., U.S.	D7	99
Alconchel, Spain	G4	12
Alcorn, co., Ms., U.S.	A5	101
Alcoy, Spain	G11	12
Aldabra Islands, atoll, Sey.	C9	44
Aldan, Russia	F19	24
Aldan, stm., Russia	E20	24
Aldanskoje Nagorje, plat., Russia	F19	24
Alden, Ia., U.S.	B4	92
Alden, Mn., U.S.	G5	100
Alden, N.Y., U.S.	C2	109
Alder Brook, stm., Vt., U.S.	B4	122
Aldershot, Eng., U.K.	J12	7
Alderson, W.V., U.S.	D4	125
Aldrich, Al., U.S.	B3	78
Aledo, Il., U.S.	B3	90
Aleg, Maur.	E3	42
Alegres Mountain, mtn., N.M., U.S.	C2	108
Alegrete, Braz.	B5	56
Alejsk, Russia	G10	24
Aleksandrov, Russia	E21	18
Aleksandrovsk-Sachalinskij, Russia	G22	24
Aleksejevsk, Russia	F15	24
Aleksin, Russia	G20	18
Além Paraíba, Braz.	F7	57
Alençon, Fr.	D7	10
Alenuihaha Channel, strt., Hi., U.S.	C5	88
Aleppo see Ḥalab, Syria	A5	40
Alert Bay, B.C., Can.	D4	69
Alès, Fr.	H11	10
Alessandria, Italy	E3	14
Alessano, Italy	J13	14
Ålesund, Nor.	E6	6
Aleutian Islands, is., Ak., U.S.	E3	79
Aleutian Range, mts., Ak., U.S.	D9	79
Aleutka, Russia	H24	24
Alevina, Mys, c., Russia	F24	24
Alex, Ok., U.S.	C4	113
Alexander, co., Il., U.S.	F4	90
Alexander, co., N.C., U.S.	B1	110
Alexander, Lake, l., Mn., U.S.	D4	100
Alexander Archipelago, is., Ak., U.S.	D12	79
Alexander Bay, S. Afr.	G3	44
Alexander City, Al., U.S.	C4	78
Alexander Island, i., Ant.	B6	47
Alexandra, N.Z.	F2	52
Alexandretta, Gulf of see İskenderun Körfezi, b., Tur.	A4	40
Alexandria, Ont., Can.	B10	73
Alexandria, In., U.S.	D6	91
Alexandria, Ky., U.S.	B5	94
Alexandria, La., U.S.	C3	95
Alexandria, Mn., U.S.	E3	100
Alexandria, Tn., U.S.	A5	119
Alexandria, Va., U.S.	B5	123
Alexandria see Al-Iskandarīyah, Egypt	B11	42
Alexandroúpolis, Grc.	I9	16
Alexis, Il., U.S.	B3	90
Alfalfa, co., Ok., U.S.	A3	113
Alfaro, Ec.	I3	58
Alfaro, Spain	C10	12
Alfarrás, Spain	D12	12
Al-Fāshir, Sudan	F11	42
Al-Fayyūm, Egypt	C12	42
Alfeld, Ger.	D9	8
Alfenas, Braz.	F6	57
Alfred, Ont., Can.	B10	73
Alfred, N.Y., U.S.	C3	109
Algarve, hist. reg., Port.	H3	12
Algeciras, Spain	I6	12
Algemesí, Spain	F11	12
Alger (Algiers), Alg.	A6	42
Alger, Oh., U.S.	B2	112
Alger, co., Mi., U.S.	B4	99
Algeria, ctry., Afr.	C6	42
Al-Ghayḍah, Yemen	E5	46
Alghero, Italy	I3	14
Al-Ghurdaqah, Egypt	C12	42
Algiers see Alger, Alg.	A6	42
Algoma, Wi., U.S.	D6	126
Algona, Ia., U.S.	A3	92
Algona, Wa., U.S.	B3	124
Algonac, Mi., U.S.	F8	99
Algonquin, Il., U.S.	A5	90
Algonquin Provincial Park, Ont., Can.	B6	73
Algood, Tn., U.S.	C8	119
Algorta, Ur.	C5	56
Al-Ḥadīthah, Iraq	B3	46
Al-Haffah, Syria	B5	40
Al-Hamād, pl., Sau. Ar.	B2	46
Alhama de Granada, Spain	H8	12
Alhambra, Ca., U.S.	m12	82
Al-Ḥarīq, Sau. Ar.	D4	46
Al-Harūj al-Aswad, hills, Libya	C9	42
Al-Ḥasakah, Syria	A7	40
Alhaurín el Grande, Spain	I7	12
Al-Ḥawrah, Yemen	F4	46
Al-Ḥijāz (Hejaz), reg., Sau. Ar.	C2	46
Al-Ḥillah, Iraq	B3	46
Al-Hirmil, Leb.	B5	40
Al-Hudaydah, Yemen	F3	46
Al-Hufūf, Sau. Ar.	C4	46
Aliaga, Spain	E11	12
Alicante, Spain	G11	12
Alice, Tx., U.S.	F3	120
Alice Lake, l., Mn., U.S.	C7	100
Alice Springs, Austl.	D6	50
Aliceville, Al., U.S.	B1	78
Alīgarh, India	G8	38
Alijos, Escollos, Mex.	E2	62
Alingsås, Swe.	H9	6
Alīpur Duār, India	G13	38
Aliquippa, Pa., U.S.	E1	115
Al-Iskandarīyah (Alexandria), Egypt	B11	42
Al-Ismā'īlīyah, Egypt	B12	42
Aliwal North, S. Afr.	H5	44
Alix, Alta., Can.	C4	68
Al-Jabal al-Akhḍar, mts., Oman	D6	46
Al-Jafr, Jord.	D5	40
Al-Jaghbūb, Libya	C10	42

Name	Map Ref	Page
Al-Jawf, Libya	D10	42
Al-Jawf, Sau. Ar.	C2	46
Al-Jazīrah, reg., Sudan	F12	42
Aljezur, Port.	H3	12
Al-Jīzah, Egypt	B12	42
Al-Junaynah, Sudan	F10	42
Aljustrel, Port.	H3	12
Alkali Lake, l., Nv., U.S.	B2	105
Alkali Lake, l., Or., U.S.	E6	114
Alkaline Lake, l., N.D., U.S.	C6	111
Al-Karak, Jord.	D4	40
Al-Kawm, Syria	B6	40
Al-Khābūr, stm., Syria	A7	40
Al-Khalīl, W. Bank	D4	40
Al-Khandaq, Sudan	E12	42
Al-Khārijah, Egypt	C12	42
Al-Kharṭūm (Khartoum), Sudan	E12	42
Al-Khaṣab, Oman	C6	46
Al-Khubar, Sau. Ar.	C5	46
Al-Khums, Libya	B8	42
Alkmaar, Neth.	C4	8
Al-Kuwayt, Kuw.	C4	46
Allach-Jun', Russia	E21	24
Al-Lādhiqīyah (Latakia), Syria	B4	40
Allagash, stm., Me., U.S.	B3	96
Allagash Lake, l., Me., U.S.	B3	96
Allāhābād, India	H9	38
Allamakee, co., Ia., U.S.	A6	92
Allan, Sask., Can.	F2	75
Allanche, Fr.	G9	10
Allanmyo, Mya.	E3	34
Allardt, Tn., U.S.	C9	119
Allatoona Lake, res., Ga., U.S.	B2	87
Allegan, Mi., U.S.	F5	99
Allegan, co., Mi., U.S.	F5	99
Allegany, N.Y., U.S.	C2	109
Allegany, co., Md., U.S.	k13	97
Allegany, co., N.Y., U.S.	C2	109
Allegany Indian Reservation, N.Y., U.S.	C2	109
Alleghany, co., N.C., U.S.	A1	110
Alleghany, co., Va., U.S.	C2	123
Allegheny, co., Pa., U.S.	E2	115
Allegheny, stm., U.S.	E2	115
Allegheny Reservoir, res., U.S.	B4	115
Allemands, Lac Des, l., La., U.S.	E5	95
Allen, Ok., U.S.	C5	113
Allen, co., In., U.S.	B7	91
Allen, co., Ks., U.S.	E8	93
Allen, co., Ky., U.S.	D3	94
Allen, co., La., U.S.	D3	95
Allen, co., Oh., U.S.	B1	112
Allen, Mount, mtn., Ak., U.S.	C11	79
Allendale, N.J., U.S.	A4	107
Allendale, S.C., U.S.	E5	117
Allendale, co., S.C., U.S.	F5	117
Allen Park, Mi., U.S.	p15	99
Allenton, R.I., U.S.	E4	116
Allenton, Wi., U.S.	E5	126
Allentown, Pa., U.S.	E11	115
Allentsteig, Aus.	G15	8
Alleppey, India	H4	37
Aller, stm., Ger.	C9	8
Allerton, Point, c., Ma., U.S.	B6	98
Allgäuer Alpen, mts., Eur.	H10	8
Alliance, Ne., U.S.	B3	104
Alliance, Oh., U.S.	B4	112
Alligator, stm., N.C., U.S.	B6	110
Alligator Lake, l., Me., U.S.	D4	96
Allison, Ia., U.S.	B5	92
Allison, Pa., U.S.	G2	115
Allison Park, Pa., U.S.	h14	115
Alliston [Beeton Tecumseth and Tottenham], Ont., Can.	C5	73
Al-Līth, Sau. Ar.	D3	46
Allouez, Wi., U.S.	h9	126
Alloway Creek, stm., N.J., U.S.	D2	107
Al-Luḥayyah, Yemen	E3	46
Allumette Lake, l., Can.	B7	73
Allyn, Wa., U.S.	B3	124
Alma, Que., Can.	A6	74
Alma, Ar., U.S.	B1	81
Alma, Ga., U.S.	E4	87
Alma, Ks., U.S.	C7	93
Alma, Mi., U.S.	E6	99
Alma, Ne., U.S.	D6	104
Alma, Wi., U.S.	D2	126
Alma-Ata, Kaz.	I9	24
Almada, Port.	G2	12
Al-Madīnah (Medina), Sau. Ar.	D2	46
Al-Mafraq, Jord.	C5	40
Almagro, Spain	G8	12
Al-Manāmah, Bahr.	C5	46
Almanor, Lake, l., Ca., U.S.	B3	82
Almansa, Spain	G10	12
Al-Manṣūrah, Egypt	B12	42
Al-Marj, Libya	B10	42
Almas, Pico das, mtn., Braz.	F10	54
Al-Maṣīrah, i., Oman	D6	46
Al-Mawṣil, Iraq	A3	46
Al-Mayādīn, Syria	B7	40
Almazán, Spain	D9	12
Almelo, Neth.	C6	8
Almenara, Braz.	D8	57
Almendralejo, Spain	G5	12
Almería, Spain	I9	12
Al'metjevsk, Russia	G8	22
Al-Minyā, Egypt	C12	42
Almirante, Pan.	J6	64
Al-Mismīyah, Syria	C5	40
Almodôvar, Port.	H3	12
Almodóvar del Campo, Spain	G7	12
Almont, Mi., U.S.	F7	99
Almonte, Ont., Can.	B8	73
Almonte, Spain	H5	12
Almora, India	F8	38
Al-Mubarraz, Sau. Ar.	C4	46
Al-Mubarraz, Sau. Ar.	D4	46
Al-Muglad, Sudan	F11	42
Al-Muḥarraq, Bahr.	C5	46
Al-Mukallā, Yemen	F4	46
Al-Mukhā, Yemen	F3	46
Al-Muwayliḥ, Sau. Ar.	C2	46
Alnwick, Eng., U.K.	F11	7
Aloândia, Braz.	D4	57
Aloha, Or., U.S.	h12	114
Alor, Pulau, i., Indon.	G7	32
Álora, Spain	I7	12
Alor Setar, Malay.	K6	34
Aloysius, Mount, mtn., Austl.	E5	50
Alpena, Mi., U.S.	C7	99
Alpena, co., Mi., U.S.	D7	99
Alpharetta, Ga., U.S.	B2	87
Alphonse Island, i., Sey.	C10	44
Alpiarça, Port.	F3	12
Alpine, Az., U.S.	D6	80
Alpine, Tx., U.S.	D1	120
Alpine, Ut., U.S.	C4	121
Alpine, co., Ca., U.S.	C4	82
Alps, mts., Eur.	F9	4
Al-Qaḍārif, Sudan	F13	42
Al-Qāhirah (Cairo), Egypt	B12	42
Al-Qāmishlī, Syria	A7	40
Al-Qaryah ash-Sharqīyah, Libya	B8	42
Al-Qaryatayn, Syria	B5	40
Al-Qaṣr, Egypt	C11	42
Al-Qaṭīf, Sau. Ar.	C4	46
Al-Qaṭrūn, Libya	D8	42
Al-Qayṣūmah, Sau. Ar.	C4	46
Al-Qunayṭirah, Golan Hts.	C4	40
Al-Qunfudhah, Sau. Ar.	E3	46
Al-Quṣayr, Egypt	C12	42
Al-Quṭayfah, Syria	C5	40
Alsace, hist. reg., Fr.	E14	10
Alsasua, Spain	C9	12
Alsfeld, Ger.	E9	8
Alta, Nor.	B14	6
Alta, Ia., U.S.	B2	92
Altadena, Ca., U.S.	m12	82
Altagracia, Ven.	B7	58
Altagracia de Orituco, Ven.	C9	58
Altai, mts., Asia	B4	26
Altaj (Jesönbulag), Mong.	B6	26
Altamaha, stm., Ga., U.S.	E4	87
Altamira, Braz.	D8	54
Altamont, Il., U.S.	D5	90
Altamont, Ks., U.S.	E8	93
Altamont, Or., U.S.	E5	114
Altamont, Tn., U.S.	D8	119
Altamonte Springs, Fl., U.S.	D5	86
Altamura, Italy	I11	14
Altar, Mex.	B4	62
Altar, Desierto de, des., Mex.	B3	62
Altata, Mex.	E6	62
Altavista, Va., U.S.	C3	123
Altdorf, Switz.	F15	10
Altenburg, Ger.	E12	8
Altheimer, Ar., U.S.	C4	81
Altiplano, plat., S.A.	G5	54
Alto, Ga., U.S.	B3	87
Alto, N.M., U.S.	D4	108
Alto Araguaia, Braz.	D2	57
Alton, Il., U.S.	E3	90
Alton, Ia., U.S.	B2	92
Alton, Mo., U.S.	E6	102
Alton, N.H., U.S.	D4	106
Altona, Man., Can.	E3	70
Alton Bay, N.H., U.S.	D4	106
Altoona, Al., U.S.	A3	78
Altoona, Fl., U.S.	D5	86
Altoona, Ia., U.S.	C4	92
Altoona, Pa., U.S.	E5	115
Altoona, Wi., U.S.	D2	126
Alto Parnaíba, Braz.	E9	54
Altötting, Ger.	G12	8
Altun Shan, mts., China	D4	26
Alturas, Ca., U.S.	B3	82
Altus, Ok., U.S.	C2	113
Altus Air Force Base, mil., Ok., U.S.	C2	113
Altus Reservoir, res., Ok., U.S.	C2	113
Al-'Ubaylah, Sau. Ar.	D5	46
Al-Ubayyiḍ, Sudan	F12	42
'Alula, Som.	F5	46
Alum Bank, Pa., U.S.	F4	115
Alum Creek, stm., Oh., U.S.	k11	112
Al-Uqṣur (Luxor), Egypt	C12	42
Alva, Fl., U.S.	F5	86
Alva, Ok., U.S.	A3	113
Alvarado, Mex.	H12	62
Alvarado, Tx., U.S.	C4	120
Álvaro Obregón, Presa, res., Mex.	D5	62
Älvdalen, Swe.	F10	6
Alvin, Tx., U.S.	E5	120
Alvinston, Ont., Can.	E3	73
Älvkarleby, Swe.	F11	6
Alvord Lake, l., Or., U.S.	E8	114
Älvsbyn, Swe.	D13	6
Al-Wajh, Sau. Ar.	C2	46
Alwar, India	G7	38
Alzamaj, Russia	F13	24
Ama, La., U.S.	k11	95
Amadeus, Lake, l., Austl.	D6	50
Amadjuak Lake, l., N.W. Ter., Can.	C18	66
Amador, co., Ca., U.S.	C3	82
Amagansett, N.Y., U.S.	n16	109
Amagasaki, Japan	H8	30
Amakusa-nada, Japan	J2	30
Amakusa-shotō, is., Japan	J3	30
Åmål, Swe.	G9	6
Amalāpuram, India	D7	37
Amalfi, Italy	I9	14
Amalner, India	J6	38
Amambaí, stm., Braz.	G1	57
Amambaí, Serra de, mts., S.A.	H7	54
Amami-Ō-shima, i., Japan	w29	31b
Amami-shotō, is., Japan	x29	31b
Amana, Ia., U.S.	C6	92
Amantea, Italy	J11	14
Amares, Port.	D3	12
Amargosa, stm., U.S.	D5	82
Amargosa Desert, des., U.S.	G5	105
Amargosa Range, mts., U.S.	G5	105
Amarillo, Tx., U.S.	B2	120
Amatignak Island, i., Ak., U.S.	E4	79
Amazon (Solimões) (Amazonas), stm., S.A.	D7	54
Ambāla, India	E7	38
Ambarčik, Russia	D26	24
Ambāsamudram, India	H4	37
Ambato, Ec.	H3	58
Ambatolampy, Madag.	E9	44
Ambatondrazaka, Madag.	E9	44
Amberg, Ger.	F11	8
Ambérieu-en-Bugey, Fr.	G1	10
Ambert, Fr.	G10	10
Ambikāpur, India	I10	38
Ambilobe, Madag.	D9	44
Amble, Eng., U.K.	F11	7
Ambler, Pa., U.S.	F11	115
Amboise, Fr.	E7	10
Ambon, Indon.	F8	32
Ambositra, Madag.	F9	44
Ambovombe, Madag.	G9	44
Amboy, Il., U.S.	B4	90
Ambre, Cap d', c., Madag.	D9	44
Ambridge, Pa., U.S.	E1	115
Ambrières, Fr.	D6	10
Ambriz, Ang.	C2	44
Āmbūr, India	F5	37
Amchitka Island, i., Ak., U.S.	E3	79
Amchitka Pass, strt., Ak., U.S.	E4	79
Ameca, Mex.	G7	62
Amecameca [de Juárez], Mex.	H10	62
Amelia, La., U.S.	E4	95
Amelia, Oh., U.S.	C1	112
Amelia, co., Va., U.S.	C4	123
Amelia Court House, Va., U.S.	C5	123
Amelia Island, i., Fl., U.S.	k9	86
American, stm., Ca., U.S.	C3	82
Americana, Braz.	G5	57
American Falls, Id., U.S.	G6	89
American Falls Dam, Id., U.S.	G6	89
American Falls Reservoir, res., Id., U.S.	F5	89
American Fork, Ut., U.S.	C4	121
American Highland, plat., Ant.	B20	47
American Samoa, dep., Oc.	G1	2
Americus, Ga., U.S.	D2	87
Americus, Ks., U.S.	D7	93
Amersfoort, Neth.	C5	8
Amery, Wi., U.S.	C1	126
Ames, Ia., U.S.	B4	92
Amesbury, Ma., U.S.	A6	98
Amfilokhía, Grc.	K5	16
Ámfissa, Grc.	K6	16
Amga, Russia	E20	24
Amga, stm., Russia	E20	24
Amgun', stm., Russia	G21	24
Amherst, Ma., U.S.	B2	98
Amherst, N.H., U.S.	E3	106
Amherst, N.Y., U.S.	C2	109
Amherst, Oh., U.S.	A3	112
Amherst, Va., U.S.	C3	123
Amherst, Wi., U.S.	D4	126
Amherst, co., Va., U.S.	C3	123
Amherstburg, Ont., Can.	E1	73
Amherstdale, W.V., U.S.	n12	125
Amiens, Fr.	C9	10
Amīndīvi Islands, is., India	G2	37
Amirante Islands, is., Sey.	C10	44
Amisk Lake, l., Sask., Can.	C4	75
Amistad National Recreation Area, Tx., U.S.	E2	120
Amistad Reservoir, res., N.A.	C9	62
Amite, La., U.S.	D5	95
Amite, co., Ms., U.S.	D3	101
Amite, stm., La., U.S.	D5	95
Amity, Or., U.S.	B3	114
Amityville, N.Y., U.S.	E7	109
Amlia Island, i., Ak., U.S.	E5	79
'Ammān, Jord.	D4	40
Ämmänsaari, Fin.	D17	6
Ammon, Id., U.S.	F7	89
Ammonoosuc, stm., N.H., U.S.	B3	106
Amo, stm., Asia	G13	38
Amory, Ms., U.S.	B5	101
Amos, Que., Can.	k11	74
Åmot, Nor.	G6	6
Amoy see Xiamen, China	K7	28
Amposta, Spain	E12	12
Amrāvati, India	B4	37
Amreli, India	J4	38
Amritsar, India	E6	38
Amroha, India	F8	38
Amsterdam, Neth.	C4	8
Amsterdam, N.Y., U.S.	C6	109
Amstetten, Aus.	G14	8
Am Timan, Chad	F10	42
Amu Darya (Amudarja), stm., Asia	I10	22
Amukta Pass, strt., Ak., U.S.	E5	79
Amundsen Gulf, b., N.W. Ter., Can.	B8	66
Amundsen Sea, Ant.	B1	47
Amuntai, Indon.	F6	32
Amur (Heilongjiang), stm., Asia	G21	24
An, Mya.	E3	34
Anabar, stm., Russia	C16	24
Anaco, Ven.	C10	58
Anacoco, La., U.S.	C2	95
Anaconda, Mt., U.S.	D4	103
Anaconda Range, mts., Mt., U.S.	E3	103
Anacortes, Wa., U.S.	A3	124
Anacostia, stm., U.S.	C4	97
Anacostia, Northwest Branch, stm., Md., U.S.	B3	97
Anadarko, Ok., U.S.	B3	113
Anadyr', Russia	E29	24
Anadyr', stm., Russia	E29	24
Anadyrskij Zaliv, b., Russia	E30	24
Anagni, Italy	H8	14
Anaheim, Ca., U.S.	F5	82
Anahola, Hi., U.S.	A2	88
Anahuac, Tx., U.S.	E5	120
Ānai Mudi, mtn., India	G4	37
Anakāpalle, India	D7	37
Analalava, Madag.	D9	44
Ana María, Golfo de, b., Cuba	D8	64
Anambas, Kepulauan, is., Indon.	M9	34
Anamosa, Ia., U.S.	B6	92
Anamur, Tur.	H14	4
Anamur Burnu, c., Tur.	A3	40
Anan, Japan	I7	30
Ānand, India	I5	38
Anantapur, India	E4	37
Anantnāg (Islāmābād), India	D6	38
Anápolis, Braz.	D4	57
Anastasia Island, i., Fl., U.S.	C5	86
Añatuya, Arg.	B4	56
'Anazah, Jabal, mtn., Asia	C6	40
Ancaster, Ont., Can.	D4	73
Ancha, Sierra, mts., Az., U.S.	D4	80
Anchang, China	E9	28
Anchorage, Ak., U.S.	C10	79
Anchorage, Ky., U.S.	g11	94
Anchor Point, Ak., U.S.	D9	79
Anchor Point, c., Ak., U.S.	h15	79
Ancienne-Lorette, Que., Can.	C6	74
Anclote Keys, is., Fl., U.S.	D4	86
Ancona, Italy	F8	14
Ancud, Chile	E2	56
Ancud, Golfo de, b., Chile	E2	56
Andalucía, hist. reg., Spain	H7	12
Andalusia, Al., U.S.	D3	78
Andalusia, Il., U.S.	B3	90
Andaman Islands, is., India	H2	34
Andaman Sea, Asia	I3	34
Andermatt, Switz.	F15	10
Andernach, Ger.	E7	8
Anderson, Ak., U.S.	C10	79
Anderson, Ca., U.S.	B2	82
Anderson, In., U.S.	D6	91
Anderson, Mo., U.S.	E3	102
Anderson, S.C., U.S.	B2	117
Anderson, co., Ks., U.S.	D8	93
Anderson, co., Ky., U.S.	C4	94
Anderson, co., S.C., U.S.	B2	117
Anderson, co., Tn., U.S.	C9	119
Anderson, co., Tx., U.S.	D5	120
Anderson, stm., N.W. Ter., Can.	C7	66
Anderson, stm., In., U.S.	H4	91
Anderson, Mount, mtn., Wa., U.S.	B2	124
Anderson Ranch Reservoir, res., Id., U.S.	F3	89
Andes, mts., S.A.	F4	53
Andes, Lake, l., S.D., U.S.	D7	118
Andhra Pradesh, state, India	D5	37
Andižan, Uzb.	I12	22
Andkhvoy, Afg.	B1	38
Andong, China	C11	26
Andong, S. Kor.	D12	26
Andorra, And.	C13	12
Andorra, ctry., Eur.	G8	4
Andover, Ks., U.S.	g12	93
Andover, Ma., U.S.	A5	98
Andover, Mn., U.S.	m12	100
Andover, Oh., U.S.	A5	112
Andover Lake, res., Ct., U.S.	C6	84
Andradina, Braz.	F3	57
Andreanof Islands, is., Ak., U.S.	E4	79
Andrew, co., Mo., U.S.	B3	102
Andrew Island, i., N.S., Can.	D9	71
Andrews, In., U.S.	C6	91
Andrews, N.C., U.S.	f9	110
Andrews, S.C., U.S.	E8	117
Andrews, Tx., U.S.	C1	120
Andrews, co., Tx., U.S.	C1	120
Andrews Air Force Base, mil., Md., U.S.	C4	97
Andria, Italy	H11	14
Androka, Madag.	G8	44
Ándros, i., Grc.	L8	16
Androscoggin, co., Me., U.S.	D2	96
Androscoggin, stm., Me., U.S.	D2	96
Androscoggin Lake, l., Me., U.S.	D2	96
Andros Island, i., Bah.	B8	64
Andros Town, Bah.	B9	64
Andújar, Spain	G7	12
Anduo, China	D14	38
Anegada Passage, strt., N.A.	E16	64
Anfeng, China	C9	28
Anfu, China	H3	28
Ang'angxi, China	B11	26
Angara, stm., Russia	F13	24
Angarsk, Russia	G14	24
Ånge, Swe.	E10	6
Ángel, Salto (Angel Falls), wtfl, Ven.	E11	58
Ángel de la Guarda, Isla, i., Mex.	C3	62
Angeles, Phil.	q19	32
Angeles Point, c., Wa., U.S.	A2	124
Angel Falls see Ángel, Salto, wtfl, Ven.	E11	58
Ängelholm, Swe.	H9	6
Angelina, co., Tx., U.S.	D5	120
Angels Camp, Ca., U.S.	C3	82
Angermünde, Ger.	B13	8
Angers, Fr.	E6	10
Angerville, Fr.	D8	10
Angicos, Braz.	E11	54
Angier, N.C., U.S.	B4	110
Ângk Tasaôm, Camb.	I8	34
Angleton, Tx., U.S.	E5	120
Angmagssalik, Grnld.	C25	66
Angol, Chile	D2	56
Angola, In., U.S.	A8	91
Angola, N.Y., U.S.	C1	109
Angola, ctry., Afr.	D3	44
Angola Swamp, sw., N.C., U.S.	C5	110
Angoon, Ak., U.S.	D13	79
Angostura Reservoir, res., S.D., U.S.	D2	118
Angoulême, Fr.	G7	10
Angra dos Reis, Braz.	G6	57
Anguilla, Ms., U.S.	C3	101
Anguilla, dep., N.A.	E16	64
Anguille, Cape, c., Newf., Can.	E2	72
Angul, India	J11	38
Anhai, China	K7	28
Anhui, prov., China	E10	26
Aniak, Ak., U.S.	C8	79
Animas, stm., U.S.	D3	83
Animas Mountains, mts., N.M., U.S.	F1	108
Animas Peak, mtn., N.M., U.S.	F2	108
Animas Valley, val., N.M., U.S.	F1	108
Anita, Ia., U.S.	C3	92
Anjār, India	I4	38
Anji, China	E8	28
Anjiang, China	F9	26
Anjou, Que., Can.	p19	74
Anjouan, i., Com.	D8	44
Ankang, China	E8	26
Ankara, Tur.	H14	4
Ankavandra, Madag.	E9	44
Ankazoabo, Madag.	F8	44
Ankazobe, Madag.	E9	44
Ankeny, Ia., U.S.	C4	92
Anklesvar, India	B2	37
Anlong, China	B8	34
Anlu, China	D2	28
Ann, Cape, c., Ma., U.S.	A6	98
Anna, Il., U.S.	F4	90
Anna, Oh., U.S.	B1	112
Anna, Lake, res., Va., U.S.	B5	123
Annaba (Bône), Alg.	A7	42
Annaberg-Buchholz, Ger.	E12	8
An-Nabk, Syria	B5	40
An-Nafūd, des., Sau. Ar.	C3	46
An-Najaf, Iraq	B3	46
Anna Maria, Fl., U.S.	p10	86
Anna Maria Island, i., Fl., U.S.	q10	86
Annandale, Mn., U.S.	E4	100
Annandale, Va., U.S.	g12	123
Annapolis, Md., U.S.	C5	97
Annapolis, stm., N.S., Can.	E4	71
Annapolis Junction, Md., U.S.	B4	97
Annapolis Royal, N.S., Can.	E4	71
Annapurna, mtn., Nepal	F10	38
Ann Arbor, Mi., U.S.	F7	99
Anna Regina, Guy.	D13	58
An-Nāṣirīyah, Iraq	B4	46
Annawan, Il., U.S.	B4	90
Anne Arundel, co., Md., U.S.	B4	97
Annecy, Fr.	G13	10
Annemasse, Fr.	F13	10
Annette, Ak., U.S.	n24	79
Anniston, Al., U.S.	B4	78
Annobón, i., Eq. Gui.	B1	44
Annonay, Fr.	G11	10
An-Nuhūd, Sudan	F11	42
Annville, Pa., U.S.	F8	115
Anoka, Mn., U.S.	E5	100
Anoka, co., Mn., U.S.	E5	100
Anqing, China	E6	28
Anren, China	I2	28
Ansbach, Ger.	F10	8
Anshan, China	C11	26
Anshun, China	A8	34
Anson, Me., U.S.	D3	96
Anson, Tx., U.S.	C3	120
Anson, co., N.C., U.S.	B2	110
Ansonia, Ct., U.S.	D3	84
Ansonia, Oh., U.S.	B1	112
Ansted, W.V., U.S.	C3	125
Antalaha, Madag.	D10	44
Antalya, Tur.	H14	4
Antalya, Gulf of see Antalya Körfezi, b., Tur.	A2	40
Antalya Körfezi, b., Tur.	A2	40
Antananarivo, Madag.	E9	44
Antarctica	A18	47
Antarctic Peninsula, pen., Ant.	C6	47
Antelope, co., Ne., U.S.	B7	104
Antelope Creek, stm., Wy., U.S.	C7	127
Antelope Island, i., Ut., U.S.	B3	121
Antelope Peak, mtn., Nv., U.S.	B7	105
Antelope Range, mts., Nv., U.S.	D7	105
Antelope Reservoir, res., Or., U.S.	E9	114
Antelope Wash, val., Nv., U.S.	D5	105
Antequera, Spain	H7	12
Antero, Mount, mtn., Co., U.S.	C4	83
Antero Reservoir, res., Co., U.S.	C5	83
Anthon, Ia., U.S.	B2	92
Anthony, Fl., U.S.	C4	86
Anthony, Ks., U.S.	E5	93
Anthony, N.M., U.S.	F3	108
Anthony, R.I., U.S.	D3	116
Anthony, Tx., U.S.	o11	120
Anthony Creek, stm., W.V., U.S.	D4	125
Anti Atlas, mts., Mor.	B4	42
Antibes, Fr.	I14	10
Anticosti, Île d', i., Que., Can.	k14	74
Antietam National Battlefield, hist., Md., U.S.	B2	97
Antigo, Wi., U.S.	C4	126
Antigua and Barbuda, ctry., N.A.	F17	64
Antioch, Ca., U.S.	h9	82
Antioch, Il., U.S.	A5	90
Antioch see Hatay, Tur.	A5	40
Antisana, vol., Ec.	H3	58
Antlers, Ok., U.S.	C6	113
Antofagasta, Chile	A2	56
Antofalla, Salar de, pl., Arg.	B3	56
Anton, Tx., U.S.	C1	120
Antongila, Helodrano, b., Madag.	E9	44
António Enes, Moz.	E7	44
Antônio João, Braz.	G1	57
Antonito, Co., U.S.	D5	83
Antora Peak, mtn., Co., U.S.	C4	83
Antrim, N.H., U.S.	D3	106
Antrim, co., Mi., U.S.	C5	99
Antrodoco, Italy	G8	14
Antsirabe, Madag.	E9	44
Antsiranana, Madag.	D9	44
Antwerp, Oh., U.S.	A1	112
Antwerp see Antwerpen, Bel.	D4	8
Antwerpen (Antwerp), Bel.	D4	8
Anuradhapura, Sri L.	H6	37
Anxi, China	C6	26
Anxi, China	J7	28
Anyang, China	D9	26
Anyi, China	G4	28
Anyuan, China	H3	26
Anyuan, China	J4	28
Anžero-Sudžensk, Russia	F11	24
Anzio, Italy	H7	14
Anžu, Ostrova, is., Russia	B23	24
Aoíz, Spain	C10	12
Aomori, Japan	B13	30
Aóös (Vijosë), stm., Eur.	J4	16
Aôral, Phnum, mtn., Camb.	H8	34
Aosta, Italy	D2	14
Aoukâr, reg., Maur.	F4	42
Aozou, Chad	D9	42
Apache, Ok., U.S.	C3	113
Apache, co., Az., U.S.	B6	80
Apache Junction, Az., U.S.	m9	80
Apache Peak, mtn., Az., U.S.	F5	80
Apalachee Bay, b., Fl., U.S.	B2	86
Apalachicola, Fl., U.S.	C2	86
Apalachicola, stm., Fl., U.S.	B1	86
Apalachicola Bay, b., Fl., U.S.	C2	86
Apaporis, stm., S.A.	H7	58
Aparri, Phil.	B7	32
Apatzingán [de la Constitución], Mex.	H8	62
Apeldoorn, Neth.	C5	8
Apennines see Appennino, mts., Italy	F7	14
Apex, N.C., U.S.	B4	110

Name	Map Ref	Page
Apishapa, stm., Co., U.S.	D6	83
Apizaco, Mex.	H10	62
Aplington, Ia., U.S.	B5	92
Apo, Mount, mtn., Phil.	D8	32
Apolda, Ger.	D11	8
Apollo, Pa., U.S.	E2	115
Apopka, Fl., U.S.	D5	86
Apopka, Lake, l., Fl., U.S.	D5	86
Aporé, Braz.	E2	57
Apostle Islands, is., Wi., U.S.	A3	126
Apostle Islands National Lakeshore, Wi., U.S.	A3	126
Appalachia, Va., U.S.	f9	123
Appalachian Mountains, mts., N.A.	D10	76
Appanoose, co., Ia., U.S.	D5	92
Appennino (Apennines), mts., Italy	F7	14
Appiano, Italy	C6	14
Apple, stm., Wi., U.S.	C1	126
Apple Creek, Oh., U.S.	B4	112
Applegate, Or., U.S.	E3	114
Applegate, stm., Or., U.S.	E3	114
Appleton, Mn., U.S.	E2	100
Appleton, Wi., U.S.	D5	126
Appleton City, Mo., U.S.	C3	102
Apple Valley, Ca., U.S.	E5	82
Apple Valley, Mn., U.S.	n12	100
Applewood, Co., U.S.	*B5	83
Appleyard, Wa., U.S.	B5	124
Appling, co., Ga., U.S.	E4	87
Appomattox, Va., U.S.	C4	123
Appomattox, co., Va., U.S.	C4	123
Appomattox, stm., Va., U.S.	C4	123
Appomattox Court House National Historical Park, Va., U.S.	C4	123
Apua Point, c., Hi., U.S.	D6	88
Apucarana, Braz.	G3	57
Apure, stm., Ven.	D9	58
Apurímac, stm., Peru	F4	54
Aqaba, Gulf of, b.	E4	40
Āqcheh, Afg.	B2	38
Āq Koprūk, Afg.	B2	38
Aquarius Mountains, mts., Az., U.S.	C2	80
Aquidauana, Braz.	H7	54
Arab, Al., U.S.	A3	78
'Arab, Bahr al-, stm., Sudan	G11	42
Arabelo, Ven.	E10	58
Arabi, La., U.S.	k11	95
Arabian Desert see Sharqīyah, Aṣ-Ṣaḥrā' al-, des., Egypt	C12	42
Arabian Sea	E17	2
Aracaju, Braz.	F11	54
Aracati, Braz.	D11	54
Araçatuba, Braz.	F3	57
Aracena, Spain	H5	12
Araçuaí, Braz.	D7	57
Arad, Rom.	C5	16
Arafura Sea	G9	32
Arago, Cape, c., Or., U.S.	D2	114
Aragon, Ga., U.S.	B1	87
Aragón, hist. reg., Spain	D11	12
Araguacema, Braz.	E9	54
Aragua de Barcelona, Ven.	C10	58
Araguari, Braz.	E4	57
Arak, Alg.	C6	42
Arāk, Iran	B4	46
Arakan Yoma, mts., Mya.	E3	34
Aral Sea, Asia	H10	22
Arambaza, Col.	I6	58
Aranda de Duero, Spain	D8	12
Arandas, Mex.	G8	62
Ārani, India	F5	37
Aran Island, i., Ire.	G4	7
Aran Islands, is., Ire.	H3	7
Aranjuez, Spain	E8	12
Aransas, co., Tx., U.S.	E4	120
Aransas Bay, b., Tx., U.S.	E4	120
Aransas Pass, Tx., U.S.	F4	120
Aranyaprathet, Thai.	H7	34
Arao, Japan	I3	30
Arapaho, Ok., U.S.	B3	113
Arapahoe, Ne., U.S.	D6	104
Arapahoe, co., Co., U.S.	B6	83
Arapiraca, Braz.	E11	54
Arapongas, Braz.	G3	57
Araraquara, Braz.	F4	57
Ararat, Austl.	G8	50
Ararat, Mount see Ağrı Dağı, mtn., Tur.	H16	4
Arauca, Col.	D7	58
Araure, Ven.	C8	58
Arāvalli Range, mts., India	H5	38
Araxá, Braz.	E5	57
Araya, Punta de, c., Ven.	B10	58
Arba Minch, Eth.	G2	46
Arbois, Fr.	F12	10
Arbon, Switz.	E16	10
Arborg, Man., Can.	D3	70
Arbroath, Scot., U.K.	E10	7
Arbuckle, Lake, l., Fl., U.S.	E5	86
Arbuckle Mountains, mts., Ok., U.S.	C4	113
Arbuckles, Lake of the, res., Ok., U.S.	C5	113
Arcachon, Fr.	H5	10
Arcade, Ca., U.S.	*C3	82
Arcade, Ga., U.S.	B3	87
Arcade, N.Y., U.S.	C2	109
Arcadia, Ca., U.S.	m12	82
Arcadia, Fl., U.S.	E5	86
Arcadia, In., U.S.	D5	91
Arcadia, La., U.S.	B3	95
Arcadia, Mo., U.S.	D7	102
Arcadia, S.C., U.S.	B4	117
Arcadia, Wi., U.S.	D2	126
Arcanum, Oh., U.S.	C1	112
Arcata, Ca., U.S.	B1	82
Arc Dome, mtn., Nv., U.S.	E4	105
Archangel'sk, Russia	E6	22
Archbald, Pa., U.S.	m18	115
Archbold, Oh., U.S.	A1	112
Archdale, N.C., U.S.	B3	110
Archer, Fl., U.S.	C4	86
Archer, co., Tx., U.S.	C3	120
Archer City, Tx., U.S.	C3	120
Arches National Park, Ut., U.S.	E6	121
Archidona, Spain	H7	12
Archie, Mo., U.S.	C3	102
Archuleta, co., Co., U.S.	D3	83
Arcis-sur-Aube, Fr.	D11	10
Arco, Id., U.S.	F5	89
Arco de Baúlhe, Port.	D4	12
Arcola, Il., U.S.	D5	90
Arcos de la Frontera, Spain	I6	12
Arctic Bay, N.W. Ter., Can.	B15	66
Arctic Ocean	A32	128
Arda, stm., Eur.	H9	16
Ardabīl, Iran	J7	22
Årdalstangen, Nor.	F6	6
Ardennes, reg., Eur.	E5	8
Ardlussa, Scot., U.K.	E7	7
Ardmore, Al., U.S.	A3	78
Ardmore, In., U.S.	A5	91
Ardmore, Ok., U.S.	C4	113
Ardmore, Tn., U.S.	B5	119
Ardsley, N.Y., U.S.	g13	109
Åre, Swe.	E9	6
Arecibo, P.R.	E14	64
Arena, Point, c., Ca., U.S.	C2	82
Arena, Punta, c., Mex.	F5	62
Arenac, co., Mi., U.S.	D7	99
Arenas de San Pedro, Spain	E6	12
Arendal, Nor.	G7	6
Arequipa, Peru	G4	54
Arès, Fr.	H5	10
Arévalo, Spain	D7	12
Arezzo, Italy	F6	14
Arganda, Spain	E8	12
Arga-Sala, stm., Russia	D15	24
Argelès-Gazost, Fr.	I7	10
Argenta, Italy	E6	14
Argenta, Il., U.S.	D5	90
Argentan, Fr.	D6	10
Argentat, Fr.	G8	10
Argentera, mtn., Italy	E2	14
Argentina, ctry., S.A.	C4	56
Argentino, Lago, l., Arg.	G2	56
Argenton-sur-Creuse, Fr.	F8	10
Argonne, reg., Fr.	C12	10
Árgos, Grc.	L6	16
Argos, In., U.S.	B5	91
Argostólion, Grc.	K4	16
Argun' (Ergun), stm., Asia	A11	26
Argyle, Mn., U.S.	B2	100
Argyle, Wi., U.S.	F4	126
Århus, Den.	H8	6
Ariano Irpino, Italy	H10	14
Arica, Chile	G4	54
Arica, Col.	I7	58
Arichat, N.S., Can.	D8	71
Arid, Cape, c., Austl.	F4	50
Arīḥā (Jericho), W. Bank	D4	40
Arikaree, stm., U.S.	B8	83
Arima, Trin.	I17	64
Arinos, stm., Braz.	F7	54
Aripuanã, stm., Braz.	E7	54
Ariquemes, Braz.	E6	54
Arismendi, Ven.	C8	58
Aristazabal Island, i., B.C., Can.	C3	69
Ariton, Al., U.S.	D4	78
Arizona, state, U.S.	C4	80
Arizona Sunsites, Az., U.S.	F6	80
Arjay, Ky., U.S.	D6	94
Arjeplog, Swe.	C11	6
Arjona, Col.	B5	58
Arkabutla Lake, res., Ms., U.S.	A4	101
Arkadelphia, Ar., U.S.	C2	81
Arkansas, co., Ar., U.S.	C4	81
Arkansas, state, U.S.	C3	81
Arkansas, stm., U.S.	D8	76
Arkansas City, Ks., U.S.	E6	93
Arklow, Ire.	I6	7
Arkoma, Ok., U.S.	B7	113
Arkonam, India	F5	37
Arktičeskogo Instituta, Ostrova, is., Russia	B10	24
Arles, Fr.	I11	10
Arlington, Ga., U.S.	E2	87
Arlington, Ma., U.S.	B5	98
Arlington, Mn., U.S.	F4	100
Arlington, Ne., U.S.	C9	104
Arlington, N.Y., U.S.	D7	109
Arlington, N.C., U.S.	A2	110
Arlington, Oh., U.S.	B2	112
Arlington, S.C., U.S.	B3	117
Arlington, S.D., U.S.	C8	118
Arlington, Tn., U.S.	B2	119
Arlington, Tx., U.S.	n9	120
Arlington, Vt., U.S.	E2	122
Arlington, Va., U.S.	B5	123
Arlington, Wa., U.S.	A3	124
Arlington, co., Va., U.S.	g12	123
Arlington, Lake, res., Tx., U.S.	n9	120
Arlington Heights, Il., U.S.	A5	90
Arma, Ks., U.S.	E9	93
Armada, Mi., U.S.	F8	99
Armagh, Que., Can.	C7	74
Armavir, Russia	H6	22
Armenia, Col.	E5	58
Armenia, ctry., Asia	I6	22
Armentières, Fr.	B9	10
Armidale, Austl.	F10	50
Armijo, N.M., U.S.	k7	108
Armour, S.D., U.S.	D7	118
Armstrong, B.C., Can.	D8	69
Armstrong, Ia., U.S.	A3	92
Armstrong, co., Pa., U.S.	E2	115
Armstrong, co., Tx., U.S.	B2	120
Armstrong, Mount, mtn., Yukon, Can.	D6	66
Armstrong Creek, stm., W.V., U.S.	m13	125
Arnaudville, La., U.S.	D4	95
Arnedo, Spain	C9	12
Arnett, W.V., U.S.	D3	125
Arnhem, Neth.	D5	8
Arnhem, Cape, c., Austl.	B7	50
Arnhem Land, reg., Austl.	B6	50
Árnissa, Grc.	I5	16
Arno, stm., Italy	F5	14
Arnold, Mn., U.S.	D6	100
Arnold, Mo., U.S.	C7	102
Arnold, Ne., U.S.	C5	104
Arnold, Pa., U.S.	h14	115
Arnold Mills, R.I., U.S.	B4	116
Arnold Mills Reservoir, res., R.I., U.S.	B4	116
Arnold's Cove, Newf., Can.	E4	72
Arnolds Park, Ia., U.S.	A2	92
Arnprior, Ont., Can.	B8	73
Arnsberg, Ger.	D8	8
Arnstadt, Ger.	E10	8
Arona, Italy	D3	14
Aroostook, co., Me., U.S.	B4	96
Arpajon, Fr.	D9	10
Ar-Rab' al-Khālī, des., Asia	D5	46
Arrah, India	H11	38
Ar-Rahad, Sudan	F12	42
Ar-Ramadi, Iraq	B3	46
Ar-Ramthā, Jord.	C4	40
Arran, Island of, i., Scot., U.K.	F7	7
Ar-Raqqah, Syria	B6	40
Arras, Fr.	B9	10
Arrecife, Spain	C3	42
Arriaga, Mex.	I13	62
Ar-Riyāḍ (Riyadh), Sau. Ar.	D4	46
Arronches, Port.	F4	12
Arrowhead Mountain Lake, res., Vt., U.S.	B2	122
Arrowrock Reservoir, res., Id., U.S.	F3	89
Arrowwood Lake, res., N.D., U.S.	B7	111
Arroyo de la Luz, Spain	F5	12
Arroyo Grande, Ca., U.S.	E3	82
Ar-Ruṣayriṣ, Sudan	F12	42
Ar-Ruṭbah, Iraq	C7	40
Arsenjev, Russia	I20	24
Árta, Grc.	J4	16
Artá, Spain	F15	12
Artemisa, Cuba	C6	64
Artemus, Ky., U.S.	D6	94
Artenay, Fr.	D8	10
Arter, Mount, mtn., Wy., U.S.	D4	127
Artesia, N.M., U.S.	E5	108
Arthabaska, Que., Can.	C6	74
Arthur, Ont., Can.	D4	73
Arthur, Il., U.S.	D5	90
Arthur, co., Ne., U.S.	C4	104
Arthur, Lake, l., La., U.S.	D3	95
Arthur, Lake, res., Pa., U.S.	E1	115
Arthur Kill, stm., N.J., U.S.	k8	107
Arthurs Town, Bah.	B10	64
Artigas, Ur.	C5	56
Art'om, Russia	I20	24
Art'omovsk, Russia	G12	24
Artvin, Tur.	G16	4
Aru, Kepulauan, is., Indon.	G9	32
Arua, Ug.	H12	42
Aruanã, Braz.	C3	57
Aruba, dep., N.A.	H13	64
Arunachal Pradesh, ter., India	F16	38
Aruppukkottai, India	H5	37
Arusha, Tan.	B7	44
Aruwimi, stm., Zaire	A5	44
Arvada, Co., U.S.	B5	83
Arvi, India	B5	37
Arvidsjaur, Swe.	D12	6
Arvika, Swe.	G9	6
Arvin, Ca., U.S.	E4	82
Arvon, Mount, mtn., Mi., U.S.	B2	99
Arvonia, Va., U.S.	C4	123
Arzachena, Italy	H4	14
Arzignano, Italy	D6	14
Arzúa, Spain	C3	12
Asadābād, Afg.	C4	38
Asahi-dake, mtn., Japan	p20	30a
Asahikawa, Japan	p20	30a
Asansol, India	I12	38
Asbestos, Que., Can.	D6	74
Asbury Park, N.J., U.S.	C4	107
Ascensión, Mex.	E10	62
Ascension, co., La., U.S.	D5	95
Ascensión, Bahía de la, b., Mex.	H16	62
Aščhabad, Turk.	J9	22
Aschaffenburg, Ger.	F9	8
Aschersleben, Ger.	D11	8
Asciano, Italy	F6	14
Ascoli Piceno, Italy	G8	14
Ascoli Satriano, Italy	H10	14
Aseb, Erit.	F3	46
Āsela, Eth.	G2	46
Åsele, Swe.	D11	6
Åsen, Nor.	E8	6
Asenovgrad, Bul.	G8	16
Ashaway, R.I., U.S.	F1	116
Ashburn, Ga., U.S.	E3	87
Ashburton, N.Z.	E3	52
Ashcroft, B.C., Can.	D7	69
Ashdown, Ar., U.S.	D1	81
Ashe, co., N.C., U.S.	A1	110
Asheboro, N.C., U.S.	B3	110
Ashepoo, stm., S.C., U.S.	F6	117
Ashern, Man., Can.	D2	70
Asherton, Tx., U.S.	E3	120
Asheville, N.C., U.S.	f10	110
Ash Flat, Ar., U.S.	A4	81
Ashford, Eng., U.K.	J13	7
Ashford, Al., U.S.	D4	78
Ashford, W.V., U.S.	m12	125
Ash Grove, Mo., U.S.	D4	102
Ashibetsu, Japan	p20	30a
Ashikaga, Japan	F12	30
Ashizuri-zaki, c., Japan	J6	30
Ashkhabad see Aščhabad, Turk.	J9	22
Ashland, Al., U.S.	B4	78
Ashland, Il., U.S.	D3	90
Ashland, Ks., U.S.	E4	93
Ashland, Ky., U.S.	B7	94
Ashland, Me., U.S.	B4	96
Ashland, Ma., U.S.	g10	98
Ashland, Mo., U.S.	C5	102
Ashland, Ne., U.S.	C9	104
Ashland, N.H., U.S.	C3	106
Ashland, Oh., U.S.	B3	112
Ashland, Or., U.S.	E4	114
Ashland, Pa., U.S.	E9	115
Ashland, Va., U.S.	C5	123
Ashland, Wi., U.S.	B3	126
Ashland, co., Oh., U.S.	B3	112
Ashland, co., Wi., U.S.	B3	126
Ashland, Mount, mtn., Or., U.S.	E4	114
Ashland City, Tn., U.S.	A4	119
Ashland Reservoir, res., Ma., U.S.	h10	98
Ashley, In., U.S.	A7	91
Ashley, N.D., U.S.	C6	111
Ashley, Oh., U.S.	B3	112
Ashley, Pa., U.S.	n17	115
Ashley, co., Ar., U.S.	D4	81
Ashley, stm., S.C., U.S.	F7	117
Ashley Creek, stm., Ut., U.S.	C6	121
Ashmore, Il., U.S.	D5	90
Ashokan Reservoir, res., N.Y., U.S.	D6	109
Ashqelon, Isr.	D4	40
Ash-Shaqrā', Sau. Ar.	C4	46
Ash-Shāriqah, U.A.E.	C6	46
Ash-Shawbak, Jord.	D4	40
Ashtabula, Oh., U.S.	A5	112
Ashtabula, co., Oh., U.S.	A5	112
Ashtabula, Lake, res., N.D., U.S.	B8	111
Ashton, Id., U.S.	E7	89
Ashton, Il., U.S.	B4	90
Ashton, Md., U.S.	B3	97
Ashton, R.I., U.S.	B4	116
Ashuanipi Lake, l., Newf., Can.	h8	72
Ashuelot, stm., N.H., U.S.	E2	106
Ashville, Al., U.S.	B3	78
Ashville, Oh., U.S.	C3	112
Ashwaubenon, Wi., U.S.	D5	126
Asia	D12	20
Asia, Kepulauan, is., Indon.	E9	32
Asia Minor, reg., Tur.	H14	4
Asino, Russia	F11	24
'Asīr, reg., Sau. Ar.	E3	46
Asir, Ras, c., Som.	F5	46
Askham, S. Afr.	G4	44
Askvoll, Nor.	F5	6
Asmara see Asmera, Erit.	E2	46
Asmera, Erit.	E2	46
Asotin, Wa., U.S.	C8	124
Asotin, co., Wa., U.S.	C8	124
Asotin Creek, stm., Wa., U.S.	C8	124
Aspang Markt, Aus.	H16	8
Aspen, Co., U.S.	B4	83
Aspen Butte, mtn., Or., U.S.	E4	114
Aspermont, Tx., U.S.	C2	120
Aspinwall, Pa., U.S.	k14	115
Aspiring, Mount, mtn., N.Z.	F2	52
Aspres-sur-Buëch, Fr.	H12	10
Aspy Bay, b., N.S., Can.	C9	71
Assabet, stm., Ma., U.S.	g9	98
Aṣ-Ṣabyā, Sau. Ar.	E3	46
As-Sallūm, Egypt	B11	42
As-Salṭ, Jord.	C4	40
Assam, state, India	G15	38
As-Samāwah, Iraq	B4	46
Assateague Island, i., U.S.	D7	97
Assateague Island National Seashore, U.S.	D7	97
Assawoman Bay, b., Md., U.S.	D7	97
Assen, Neth.	C6	8
Assiniboine, stm., Can.	E2	70
Assiniboine, Mount, mtn., Can.	D3	68
Assis, Braz.	G3	57
Assisi, Italy	F7	14
As-Sulaymānīyah, Iraq	A4	46
As-Sulaymānīyah, Sau. Ar.	D4	46
As-Sulayyil, Sau. Ar.	D4	46
Assumption, Il., U.S.	D4	90
Assumption, co., La., U.S.	E4	95
Assumption Island, i., Sey.	C9	44
Aṣ-Ṣuwār, Syria	B7	40
As-Suwaydā', Syria	C5	40
As-Suways (Suez), Egypt	C12	42
Asti, Italy	E3	14
Astorga, Spain	C5	12
Astoria, Il., U.S.	C3	90
Astoria, Or., U.S.	A3	114
Astove Island, i., Sey.	D9	44
Astrachan', Russia	H7	22
Astrakhan see Astrachan', Russia	H7	22
Astudillo, Spain	C7	12
Asunción, Para.	B5	56
Aswān, Egypt	D12	42
Aswān High Dam, Egypt	D12	42
Asyūṭ, Egypt	C12	42
Atacama, Desierto de, des., Chile	A3	56
Atacama, Puna de, plat., S.A.	A3	56
Atacama, Salar de, pl., Chile	A3	56
Ataco, Col.	F5	58
Atakpamé, Togo	G6	42
Atami, Japan	G12	30
Atar, Maur.	D3	42
Atascadero, Ca., U.S.	E3	82
Atascosa, co., Tx., U.S.	E3	120
'Aṭbarah, Sudan	E12	42
'Aṭbarah (Atbara), stm., Afr.	E12	42
Atchafalaya, stm., La., U.S.	D4	95
Atchafalaya Bay, b., La., U.S.	E4	95
Atchison, Ks., U.S.	C8	93
Atchison, co., Ks., U.S.	C8	93
Atchison, co., Mo., U.S.	A2	102
Ateca, Spain	D10	12
Aterau, Kaz.	H8	22
Athabasca, Alta., Can.	B4	68
Athabasca, stm., Alta., Can.	f8	68
Athabasca, Lake, l., Can.	m7	75
Athena, Or., U.S.	B8	114
Athenry, Ire.	H4	7
Athens, Ont., Can.	C9	73
Athens, Al., U.S.	A3	78
Athens, Ga., U.S.	C3	87
Athens, Il., U.S.	D4	90
Athens, Mi., U.S.	F5	99
Athens, N.Y., U.S.	C7	109
Athens, Oh., U.S.	C3	112
Athens, Pa., U.S.	C8	115
Athens, Tn., U.S.	D9	119
Athens, Tx., U.S.	C5	120
Athens, W.V., U.S.	D3	125
Athens, Wi., U.S.	C3	126
Athens, co., Oh., U.S.	C3	112
Athens see Athínai, Grc.	L7	16
Athínai (Athens), Grc.	L7	16
Athlone, Ire.	H5	7
Athol, Ma., U.S.	A3	98
Ati, Chad	F9	42
Atienza, Spain	D9	12
Atik Lake, l., Man., Can.	B4	70
Atikonak Lake, l., Newf., Can.	h8	72
Atka Island, i., Ak., U.S.	E5	79
Atkins, Ar., U.S.	B3	81
Atkins, Va., U.S.	D1	123
Atkinson, Il., U.S.	B3	90
Atkinson, Ne., U.S.	B7	104
Atkinson, N.H., U.S.	E4	106
Atkinson, co., Ga., U.S.	E4	87
Atlanta, Ga., U.S.	C2	87
Atlanta, Il., U.S.	C4	90
Atlanta, In., U.S.	D5	91
Atlanta, Mi., U.S.	C6	99
Atlanta, Tx., U.S.	C5	120
Atlantic, Ia., U.S.	C2	92
Atlantic, N.C., U.S.	C6	110
Atlantic, co., N.J., U.S.	E3	107
Atlantic Beach, Fl., U.S.	m9	86
Atlantic City, N.J., U.S.	E4	107
Atlantic Highlands, N.J., U.S.	C4	107
Atlantic Ocean	G11	2
Atlantic Peak, mtn., Wy., U.S.	D3	127
Atlas Mountains, mts., Afr.	B5	42
Atlas Saharien, mts., Alg.	B6	42
Atmore, Al., U.S.	D2	78
Atna Peak, mtn., B.C., Can.	C3	69
Atoka, Ok., U.S.	C5	113
Atoka, Tn., U.S.	B2	119
Atoka, co., Ok., U.S.	C5	113
Atoka Reservoir, res., Ok., U.S.	C5	113
Atotonilco el Alto, Mex.	G8	62
Atrato, stm., Col.	D4	58
Aṭ-Ṭafīlah, Jord.	D4	40
Aṭ-Ṭā'if, Sau. Ar.	D3	46
Attala, co., Ms., U.S.	B4	101
Attalla, Al., U.S.	A3	78
Attawapiskat, stm., Ont., Can.	n18	73
Attica, In., U.S.	D3	91
Attica, Ks., U.S.	E5	93
Attica, N.Y., U.S.	C2	109
Attica, Oh., U.S.	A3	112
Attleboro, Ma., U.S.	C5	98
Attopeu, Laos	G9	34
Attow, Ben, mtn., Scot., U.K.	D7	7
Attu Island, i., Ak., U.S.	E2	79
Aṭṭūr, India	G5	37
Atwater, Ca., U.S.	D3	82
Atwater, Mn., U.S.	E4	100
Atwood, Ont., Can.	D3	73
Atwood, Il., U.S.	D5	90
Atwood, Ks., U.S.	C2	93
Atwood, Tn., U.S.	B3	119
Atwood Lake, res., Oh., U.S.	B4	112
Auau Channel, strt., Hi., U.S.	C5	88
Aubagne, Fr.	I12	10
Aube, stm., Fr.	D11	10
Auberry, Ca., U.S.	D4	82
Aubigny-sur-Nère, Fr.	E9	10
Aubin, Fr.	H9	10
Auburn, Al., U.S.	C4	78
Auburn, Ca., U.S.	C3	82
Auburn, Ga., U.S.	B3	87
Auburn, Il., U.S.	D4	90
Auburn, In., U.S.	B7	91
Auburn, Ks., U.S.	D8	93
Auburn, Ky., U.S.	D3	94
Auburn, Me., U.S.	D2	96
Auburn, Ma., U.S.	B4	98
Auburn, Mi., U.S.	E6	99
Auburn, Ne., U.S.	D10	104
Auburn, N.Y., U.S.	C4	109
Auburn, Wa., U.S.	B3	124
Auburndale, Fl., U.S.	D5	86
Auburn Heights, Mi., U.S.	F7	99
Aubusson, Fr.	G9	10
Auch, Fr.	I7	10
Aucilla, stm., Fl., U.S.	B3	86
Auckland, N.Z.	B5	52
Audincourt, Fr.	E13	10
Audrain, co., Mo., U.S.	B6	102
Audubon, Ia., U.S.	C3	92
Audubon, N.J., U.S.	D2	107
Audubon, co., Ia., U.S.	C2	92
Aue, Ger.	E12	8
Auglaize, co., Oh., U.S.	B1	112
Auglaize, stm., Oh., U.S.	A1	112
Au Gres, Mi., U.S.	D7	99
Augsburg, Ger.	G10	8
Augusta, Italy	L10	14
Augusta, Ar., U.S.	B4	81
Augusta, Ga., U.S.	C5	87
Augusta, Ks., U.S.	E7	93
Augusta, Ky., U.S.	B6	94
Augusta, Me., U.S.	D3	96
Augusta, Mi., U.S.	F5	99
Augusta, Wi., U.S.	D2	126
Augusta, co., Va., U.S.	B3	123
Augustus, Mount, mtn., Austl.	D3	50
Aulander, N.C., U.S.	A5	110
Auld, Lake, l., Austl.	D4	50
Aulneau Peninsula, pen., Ont., Can.	E4	70
Ault, Co., U.S.	A6	83
Aumont-Aubrac, Fr.	H10	10
Aumsville, Or., U.S.	k12	114
Aurangābād, India	C3	37
Auray, Fr.	E4	10
Aurelia, Ia., U.S.	B2	92
Aurich, Ger.	B7	8
Auriflama, Braz.	F3	57
Aurillac, Fr.	H9	10
Aurora, Ont., Can.	C5	73
Aurora, Co., U.S.	B6	83
Aurora, Il., U.S.	B5	90
Aurora, In., U.S.	F8	91
Aurora, Mn., U.S.	C6	100
Aurora, Mo., U.S.	E4	102
Aurora, Ne., U.S.	D7	104
Aurora, Oh., U.S.	A4	112
Aurora, S.D., U.S.	C9	118
Aurora, Ut., U.S.	E4	121
Aurora, co., S.D., U.S.	D7	118
Aus, Nmb.	G3	44
Au Sable, Mi., U.S.	D7	99
Au Sable, stm., Mi., U.S.	D6	99
Ausable, stm., N.Y., U.S.	f11	109
Au Sable Forks, N.Y., U.S.	f11	109
Au Sable Point, c., Mi., U.S.	D7	99
Au Sable Point, c., Mi., U.S.	B4	99
Auschwitz see Oświęcim, Pol.	E19	8
Austell, Ga., U.S.	h7	87
Austin, In., U.S.	G6	91
Austin, Mn., U.S.	G6	100

Name — Map Ref — Page
Austin, Nv., U.S. D4 105
Austin, Tx., U.S. D4 120
Austin, co., Tx., U.S. E4 120
Austin, Lake, l., Austl. E3 50
Austin Channel, strt., N.W. Ter., Can. A12 66
Austintown, Oh., U.S. A5 112
Austinville, Va., U.S. D2 123
Australia, ctry., Oc. D6 50
Australian Capital Territory, ter., Austl. G9 50
Austria, ctry., Eur. F10 4
Autauga, co., Al., U.S. C3 78
Autaugaville, Al., U.S. C3 78
Autlán de Navarro, Mex. H7 62
Autun, Fr. F11 10
Auxerre, Fr. E10 10
Auxier, Ky., U.S. C7 94
Auxi-le-Château, Fr. B9 10
Auxonne, Fr. E12 10
Auxvasse, Mo., U.S. B6 102
Auyán Tepuy, mtn., Ven. E11 58
Auzances, Fr. F9 10
Ava, Mo., U.S. E5 102
Avallon, Fr. E10 10
Avalon, Ca., U.S. F4 82
Avalon, Pa., U.S. h13 115
Avalon, Lake, res., N.M., U.S. E5 108
Avalon Peninsula, pen., Newf., Can. E5 72
Avaré, Braz. G4 57
Aveiro, Port. E3 12
Avella, Pa., U.S. F1 115
Avellaneda, Arg. C5 56
Avellino, Italy I9 14
Avenal, Ca., U.S. E3 82
Avery, co., N.C., U.S. e11 110
Aves, Islas de, is., Ven. A9 58
Avesnes, Fr. B10 10
Avesta, Swe. F11 6
Avezzano, Italy G8 14
Aviemore, Scot., U.K. D9 7
Avignon, Fr. I11 10
Ávila, Spain E7 12
Avilés, Spain B6 12
Avilla, In., U.S. B7 91
Avis, Pa., U.S. D7 115
Avispa, Cerro, mtn., Ven. G10 58
Aviston, Il., U.S. E4 90
Aviz, Port. F4 12
Avoca, Ia., U.S. C2 92
Avoca, Pa., U.S. m18 115
Avola, Italy M10 14
Avon, Ct., U.S. B4 84
Avon, Il., U.S. C3 90
Avon, Ma., U.S. B5 98
Avon, Mn., U.S. E4 100
Avon, N.Y., U.S. C3 109
Avon, Oh., U.S. A3 112
Avondale, Az., U.S. D3 80
Avondale, Co., U.S. C6 83
Avondale, Pa., U.S. G10 115
Avondale Estates, Ga., U.S. h8 87
Avon Lake, Ia., U.S. e8 92
Avon Lake, Oh., U.S. A3 112
Avonmore, Pa., U.S. E3 115
Avon Park, Fl., U.S. E5 86
Avoyelles, co., La., U.S. C3 95
Avranches, Fr. D5 10
Awaji-shima, i., Japan H7 30
Awash, stm., Eth. F3 46
Awbārī, Libya C8 42
Awe, Loch, l., Scot., U.K. E7 7
Awjilah, Libya C10 42
Axiós (Vardar), stm., Eur. I6 16
Axis, Al., U.S. E1 78
Axtell, Ne., U.S. D6 104
Ayabe, Japan G8 30
Ayacucho, Peru F4 54
Ayamonte, Spain H4 12
Ayapel, Col. C5 58
Ayaviri, Peru F4 54
Āybak, Afg. B3 38
Ayden, N.C., U.S. B5 110
Aydın, Tur. H13 4
Ayer, Ma., U.S. A4 98
Ayers Cliff, Que., Can. D5 74
Ayeyarwady (Irrawaddy), stm., Mya. G3 34
Áyion Óros, pen., Grc. I8 16
Áyios Nikólaos, Grc. N9 16
Aylesbury, Eng., U.K. J12 7
Aylesford, N.S., Can. D5 71
Aylmer, Mount, mtn., Alta., Can. D3 68
Aylmer East, Que., Can. D2 74
Aylmer Lake, l., N.W. Ter., Can. D11 66
Aylmer West, Ont., Can. E4 73
Ayora, Spain F10 12
'Ayoûn el 'Atroûs, Maur. E4 42
Ayr, Scot., U.K. F8 7
Ayre, Point of, c., I. of Man G8 7
Ayu, Kepulauan, is., Indon. E9 32
Ayvalık, Tur. J10 16
Azambuja, Port. F3 12
Azamgarh, India G10 38
Azare, Nig. F8 42
Azerbaijan, ctry., Asia I7 22
Aziscohos Lake, l., Me., U.S. C1 96
Azle, Tx., U.S. n9 120
Azogues, Ec. I3 58
Azores see Açores, is., Port. D11 2
Azov, Sea of, Eur. H5 22
Aztec, N.M., U.S. A2 108
Aztec Peak, mtn., Az., U.S. D5 80
Aztec Ruins National Monument, N.M., U.S. A1 108
Azua, Dom. Rep. E12 64
Azuaga, Spain G6 12
Azuero, Península de, pen., Pan. K7 64
Azul, Arg. D5 56
Azur, Côte d', Fr. I14 10
Azusa, Ca., U.S. m13 82
Az-Zaqāzīq, Egypt D2 40
Az-Zarqā', Jord. C5 40
Az-Zāwiyah, Libya B8 42
Azzel Matti, Sebkha, pl., Alg. C6 42

B

Ba, stm., Viet. H10 34
Babaeski, Tur. H11 16
Babahoyo, Ec. H3 58
Babar, Kepulauan, is., Indon. G8 32
Babb Creek, stm., Pa., U.S. C7 115
Babbitt, Mn., U.S. C7 100
Babbitt, Nv., U.S. E3 105
B'abdā, Leb. C4 40
Bāb el-Mandeb see Mandeb, Bāb el-, strt. F3 46
Babine, stm., B.C., Can. B4 69
Babine Lake, l., B.C., Can. B5 69
Babine Range, mts., B.C., Can. B4 69
Bābol, Iran J8 22
Baboquivari Mountains, mts., Az., U.S. F4 80
Baboquivari Peak, mtn., Az., U.S. F4 80
Babuyan Islands, is., Phil. B7 32
Babylon, N.Y., U.S. n15 109
Baca, co., Co., U.S. D8 83
Bacabal, Braz. D10 54
Bacan, Pulau, i., Indon. F8 32
Bacău, Rom. C10 16
Bac Can, Viet. C8 34
Bacerac, Mex. B5 62
Bachaquero, Ven. C7 58
Bachta, Russia E11 24
Bachu, China D2 26
Back, stm., N.W. Ter., Can. C13 66
Back, stm., S.C., U.S. h12 117
Backbone Mountain, mtn., U.S. m12 97
Backnang, Ger. G9 8
Bac Lieu, Viet. J8 34
Bac Ninh, Viet. D9 34
Bacolod, Phil. C7 32
Bacon, co., Ga., U.S. E4 87
Baconton, Ga., U.S. E2 87
Bacoor, Phil. q19 33b
Bad, stm., S.D., U.S. C5 118
Bad, stm., Wi., U.S. B3 126
Badagara, India G3 37
Badajia, China B9 28
Badajoz, Spain G5 12
Badalona, Spain D14 12
Badanah, Sau. Ar. B3 46
Bad Aussee, Aus. H13 8
Bad Axe, Mi., U.S. E8 99
Baddeck, N.S., Can. C9 71
Bad Doberan, Ger. A11 8
Bad Ems, Ger. E7 8
Baden, Aus. G16 8
Baden, Ont., Can. D4 73
Baden, Switz. E15 10
Baden, Pa., U.S. E1 115
Baden-Baden, Ger. G8 8
Badgastein, Aus. H13 8
Badger, Newf., Can. D3 72
Bad Hersfeld, Ger. E9 8
Bad Homburg [vor der Höhe], Ger. E8 8
Bad Honnef, Ger. E7 8
Badin, N.C., U.S. B2 110
Badin Lake, res., N.C., U.S. B2 110
Bad Ischl, Aus. H13 8
Bad Kissingen, Ger. E10 8
Bad Kreuznach, Ger. F7 8
Badlands, hills, S.D., U.S. D3 118
Badlands, reg., U.S. C2 111
Badlands National Park, S.D., U.S. D3 118
Bad Lauterberg, Ger. D10 8
Bad Nauheim, Ger. E8 8
Bad Neustadt an der Saale, Ger. E10 8
Bad Oldesloe, Ger. B10 8
Bad Reichenhall, Ger. H12 8
Bad River Indian Reservation, Wi., U.S. B3 126
Bad Salzungen, Ger. E10 8
Bad Schwartau, Ger. B10 8
Bad Segeberg, Ger. B10 8
Bad Tölz, Ger. H11 8
Badulla, Sri L. I6 37
Badwater Creek, stm., Wy., U.S. C5 127
Bad Wildungen, Ger. D9 8
Bad Wörishofen, Ger. G10 8
Baena, Spain H7 12
Baeza, Spain H8 12
Bafatá, Gui.-B. F3 42
Baffin Bay, b., N.A. B14 61
Baffin Bay, b., Tx., U.S. E4 120
Baffin Island, i., N.W. Ter., Can. C18 66
Bafwasende, Zaire A5 44
Bagaha, India G11 38
Bāgalkot, India D3 37
Bagansiapiapi, Indon. M6 34
Bağarası, Tur. L11 16
Bagdad, Az., U.S. C2 80
Bagdad, Fl., U.S. u14 86
Bagdad see Baghdād, Iraq B3 46
Bagdarin, Russia G16 24
Bagé, Braz. C6 56
Baggs, Wy., U.S. E5 127
Baghdād, Iraq B3 46
Bagheria, Italy K8 14
Baghlān, Afg. B3 38
Baghrān Khowleh, Afg. D1 38
Bagley, Mn., U.S. C3 100
Bagnères-de-Bigorre, Fr. I7 10
Bagnères-de-Luchon, Fr. J7 10
Bagnols-sur-Cèze, Fr. H11 10
Bago, Mya. F4 34
Baguio, Phil. p19 32
Bahamas, ctry., N.A. B9 64
Bahāwalnagar, Pak. F5 38
Bahāwalpur, Pak. F4 38
Bahía, Islas de la, is., Hond. F4 64
Bahía Blanca, Arg. D4 56
Bahía de Caráquez, Ec. H2 58
Bahía Kino, Mex. C4 62
Bahir Dar, Eth. F2 46
Bahraich, India G9 38
Bahrain, ctry., Asia C5 46
Baia-Mare, Rom. B7 16
Bai Bung, Muy, c., Viet. J8 34
Baicheng, China B11 26
Baicheng, China C3 26
Baidoa, Som. H3 46
Baie-Comeau, Que., Can. k13 74
Baie-d'Urfé, Que., Can. q19 74
Baie-Saint-Paul, Que., Can. B7 74
Baie Verte, Newf., Can. D3 72
Baigneux-les-Juifs, Fr. E11 10
Baiju, China B9 28
Bailén, Spain G8 12
Bailey, co., Tx., U.S. B1 120
Bailey Island, Me., U.S. g8 96
Bailey Island, i., S.C., U.S. k11 117
Baileys Crossroads, Va., U.S. g12 123
Bainbridge, Ga., U.S. F2 87
Bainbridge, In., U.S. E4 91
Bainbridge, Oh., U.S. C2 112
Bainbridge Island, i., Wa., U.S. e10 124
Bain-de-Bretagne, Fr. E5 10
Baing, Indon. H7 32
Baird, Tx., U.S. C3 120
Bairdford, Pa., U.S. h14 115
Baird Inlet, b., Ak., U.S. C7 79
Baird Mountains, mts., Ak., U.S. B7 79
Bais, Fr. D6 10
Baise, China C9 34
Baishuijiang, China E8 26
Baiyin, China D7 26
Baiyunebo, China C9 26
Baja, Hung. I18 8
Baja, Punta, c., Mex. C4 62
Baja California, pen., Mex. D3 62
Bajanchongor, Mong. B7 26
Bajkal, Ozero (Lake Baykal), l., Russia G15 24
Bajkal'skoje, Russia F15 24
Bajkit, Russia E13 24
Bajkonyr, Kaz. H11 22
Bajo Baudó, Col. E4 58
Baker, La., U.S. D4 95
Baker, Mt., U.S. D12 103
Baker, Or., U.S. C9 114
Baker, co., Fl., U.S. B4 86
Baker, co., Ga., U.S. E2 87
Baker, co., Or., U.S. C9 114
Baker, stm., N.H., U.S. C3 106
Baker, Mount, mtn., Wa., U.S. A4 124
Baker Air Force Base, mil., Ar., U.S. B6 81
Baker Butte, mtn., Az., U.S. C4 80
Baker Island, i., Ak., U.S. n22 79
Baker Lake, N.W. Ter., Can. D13 66
Baker Lake, l., Me., U.S. B3 96
Baker Lake, res., Wa., U.S. A4 124
Bakersfield, Ca., U.S. E4 82
Bakers Island, i., Ma., U.S. f12 98
Bakerstown, Pa., U.S. h14 115
Bakhtarān, Iran B4 46
Bakhtegān, Daryācheh-ye, l., Iran C5 46
Bakı (Baku), Azer. I7 22
Bakır, stm., Tur. J11 16
Bakoye, stm., Afr. F4 42
Baku see Bakı, Azer. I7 22
Balabac Island, i., Phil. D6 32
Balabac Strait, strt., Asia D6 32
Baʿlabakk (Baalbek), Leb. B5 40
Balachna, Russia E26 18
Bālāghāt, India J9 38
Bālāghāt Range, mts., India C4 37
Balaguer, Spain D12 12
Balakovo, Russia G7 22
Balallan, Scot., U.K. C6 7
Balāngīr, India B7 37
Balašicha, Russia F20 18
Balasore, India J12 38
Balašov, Russia G6 22
Balaton, Mn., U.S. F3 100
Balaton, l., Hung. I17 8
Balbriggan, Ire. H6 7
Balcarres, Sask., Can. G4 75
Balchaš, Ozero, l., Kaz. H9 24
Bald Eagle Lake, l., Mn., U.S. m12 100
Bald Eagle Lake, l., Mn., U.S. C7 100
Baldhill Dam, N.D., U.S. B7 111
Bald Knob, Ar., U.S. B4 81
Bald Knoll, mtn., Wy., U.S. D2 127
Bald Mountain, mtn., Or., U.S. D5 114
Bald Mountain, mtn., Or., U.S. C9 114
Bald Mountain, mtn., Wy., U.S. B5 127
Bald Mountains, mts., N.C., U.S. f10 110
Baldwin, Fl., U.S. B5 86
Baldwin, Ga., U.S. B3 87
Baldwin, La., U.S. E4 95
Baldwin, Mi., U.S. E5 99
Baldwin, Pa., U.S. k14 115
Baldwin, S.C., U.S. B5 117
Baldwin, Wi., U.S. D1 126
Baldwin, co., Al., U.S. E2 78
Baldwin, co., Ga., U.S. C3 87
Baldwin City, Ks., U.S. D8 93
Baldwinsville, N.Y., U.S. B4 109
Baldwinville, Ma., U.S. A3 98
Baldwyn, Ms., U.S. A5 101
Baldy Mountain, mtn., B.C., Can. D7 69
Baldy Mountain, mtn., Man., Can. D1 70
Baldy Mountain, mtn., Mt., U.S. B7 103
Baldy Mountain, mtn., N.M., U.S. A4 108
Baldy Peak, mtn., Az., U.S. D6 80
Baleares, Islas (Balearic Islands), is., Spain F14 12
Balearic Islands see Baleares, Islas, is., Spain E15 12
Baleine, Rivière à la, stm., Que., Can. g13 74
Balej, Russia G17 24
Balfate, Hond. G4 64
Balfour, N.C., U.S. f10 110
Bali, i., Indon. G5 32
Bali, Laut (Bali Sea), Indon. G6 32
Balıkesir, Tur. H13 4
Balikpapan, Indon. F6 32
Balimo, Pap. N. Gui. G11 32
Balingen, Ger. G8 8
Balintang Channel, strt., Phil. B7 32
Baliza, Braz. D2 57
Balkan Mountains see Stara Planina, mts., Eur. G8 16
Balkh, Afg. B2 38
Balkhash, Lake see Balchaš, Ozero, l., Kaz. H9 24
Ball, La., U.S. C3 95
Ballachulish, Scot., U.K. E7 7
Ballālpur, India C5 37
Ballarat, Austl. G8 50
Ballard, co., Ky., U.S. e8 94
Ball Club Lake, l., Mn., U.S. C5 100
Ballenas, Canal de, strt., Mex. C3 62
Ball Ground, Ga., U.S. B2 87
Ballia, India H11 38
Ballina, Ire. G3 7
Ballinger, Tx., U.S. D3 120
Ballinrobe, Ire. H3 7
Ball Mountain Lake, res., Vt., U.S. E3 122
Ballston Spa, N.Y., U.S. B7 109
Ballwin, Mo., U.S. f12 102
Bally, Pa., U.S. F10 115
Ballycastle, N. Ire., U.K. F6 7
Ballymena, N. Ire., U.K. G6 7
Ballyshannon, Ire. G4 7
Balmoral, N.B., Can. B3 71
Balmoral, Scot., U.K. D9 7
Balmville, N.Y., U.S. D6 109
Balovale, Zam. D4 44
Balrāmpur, India G10 38
Balsam Lake, Wi., U.S. C1 126
Balsam Lake, l., Wi., U.S. C1 126
Balsas, Braz. E9 54
Baltasar Brum, Ur. C5 56
Baltic, Ct., U.S. C7 84
Baltic, S.D., U.S. D9 118
Baltic Sea, Eur. H12 6
Baltijsk, Russia G2 18
Baltijskaja Kosa, spit, Eur. A19 8
Baltimore, Ire. J3 7
Baltimore, Md., U.S. B4 97
Baltimore, Oh., U.S. C3 112
Baltimore, co., Md., U.S. B4 97
Baltimore Highlands, Md., U.S. h11 97
Baluchistan, hist. reg., Asia D1 36
Bālurghāt, India H13 38
Balygyčan, Russia E24 24
Balzar, Ec. H3 58
Bamako, Mali F4 42
Bambana, stm., Nic. H6 64
Bambari, Cen. Afr. Rep. G10 42
Bamberg, Ger. F10 8
Bamberg, S.C., U.S. E5 117
Bamberg, co., S.C., U.S. E5 117
Bamenda, Cam. G8 42
Bāmīān, Afg. C2 38
Banalia, Zaire A5 44
Banana, Zaire C2 44
Bananal, Ilha do, i., Braz. F8 54
Banana River, b., Fl., U.S. D6 86
Banās, Ra's, c., Egypt D13 42
Banbridge, N. Ire., U.K. G6 7
Banbury, Eng., U.K. I11 7
Bancroft, Ont., Can. B7 73
Bancroft, Ia., U.S. A3 92
Bānda, India H9 38
Banda, Kepulauan, is., Indon. F8 32
Banda, Laut (Banda Sea), Indon. G8 32
Banda Aceh, Indon. D2 32
Bandama, stm., C. Iv. G4 42
Bandar Beheshtī, Iran C7 46
Bandar-e ʿAbbās, Iran C6 46
Bandar-e Būshehr, Iran C5 46
Bandar-e Lengeh, Iran C5 46
Bandar Seri Begawan, Bru. E5 32
Banded Peak, mtn., Co., U.S. D4 83
Bandeira, Pico da, mtn., Braz. F8 57
Bandelier National Monument, N.M., U.S. B3 108
Bandera, co., Tx., U.S. E3 120
Banderas, Bahía de, b., Mex. G7 62
Bandırma, Tur. G13 4
Bandon, Ire. J4 7
Bandon, Or., U.S. D2 114
Bandundu, Zaire B3 44
Bandung, Indon. m13 32
Banes, Cuba D10 64
Banff, Scot., U.K. D10 7
Banff National Park, Alta., Can. D2 68
Bangalore, India F4 37
Bangassou, Cen. Afr. Rep. H10 42
Banggai, Kepulauan, is., Indon. F7 32
Banggi, Pulau, i., Malay. D6 32
Banghāzī, Libya B10 42
Bangil, Indon. m16 33a
Bangka, i., Indon. F4 32
Bangkalan, Indon. m16 33a
Bangkinang, Indon. N6 34
Bangkok see Krung Thep, Thai. H6 34
Bangladesh, ctry., Asia E6 36
Bangor, N. Ire., U.K. G7 7
Bangor, Wales, U.K. H8 7
Bangor, Me., U.S. D4 96
Bangor, Mi., U.S. F4 99
Bangor, Pa., U.S. E11 115
Bangor, Wi., U.S. E3 126
Bangor Township, Mi., U.S. E7 99
Bangs, Tx., U.S. D3 120
Bangs, Mount, mtn., Az., U.S. A2 80
Bangui, Cen. Afr. Rep. H9 42
Bangweulu, Lake, l., Zam. D5 44
Baní, Dom. Rep. E12 64
Banī Mazār, Egypt C12 42
Banister, stm., Va., U.S. D4 123
Banī Suwayf, Egypt C12 42
Bāniyās, Syria B4 40
Banja Luka, Bos. E12 14
Banjarmasin, Indon. F5 32
Banjul, Gam. F2 42
Bankhead Lake, res., Al., U.S. B2 78
Banks, co., Ga., U.S. B3 87
Banks Island, i., B.C., Can. C2 69
Banks Island, i., N.W. Ter., Can. B8 66
Banks Lake, res., Wa., U.S. B6 124
Banks Strait, strt., Austl. H9 50
Bānkura, India I12 38
Bann, stm., N. Ire., U.K. G6 7
Banner, co., Ne., U.S. C2 104
Banner Elk, N.C., U.S. A1 110
Banning, Ca., U.S. F5 82
Bannock, co., Id., U.S. G6 89
Bannock Peak, mtn., Id., U.S. F6 89
Bannock Range, mts., Id., U.S. G6 89
Bannu, Pak. D4 38
Baños de Cerrato, Spain D7 12
Ban Pak Phraek, Thai. J6 34
Ban Phak Phang, Thai. F6 34
Ban Pong, Thai. H5 34
Banská Bystrica, Slov. G19 8
Bānswāra, India I6 38
Bantam, stm., Ct., U.S. B3 84
Bantam Lake, l., Ct., U.S. C3 84
Bantry, Ire. J3 7
Banyak, Kepulauan, is., Indon. M4 34
Banyuwangi, Indon. n17 33a
Baoding, China D10 26
Baofeng, China B2 28
Bao Ha, Viet. C8 34
Baoji, China E8 26
Baoshan, China B5 34
Baotou, China C8 26
Baoying, China B8 28
Ba'qūbah, Iraq B3 46
Baquedano, Chile A3 56
Baraboo, Wi., U.S. E4 126
Baraboo, stm., Wi., U.S. E3 126
Baracoa, Cuba D10 64
Baraga, Mi., U.S. B2 99
Baraga, co., Mi., U.S. B2 99
Barakī Barak, Afg. D3 38
Baram, stm., Malay. E5 32
Bārāmati, India C3 37
Bāramūla, India C6 38
Bārān, India H7 38
Baranagar, India I13 38
Baranoa, Col. B5 58
Baranof Island, i., Ak., U.S. m22 79
Baranoviči, Bela. H9 18
Barataria, La., U.S. E5 95
Barataria Bay, b., La., U.S. E6 95
Barat Daya, Kepulauan, is., Indon. G8 32
Barbacena, Braz. F7 57
Barbados, ctry., N.A. H18 64
Barbar, Sudan E12 42
Barbas, Cabo, c., W. Sah. D2 42
Barbastro, Spain C12 12
Barbate de Franco, Spain I6 12
Barber, co., Ks., U.S. E5 93
Barbers Point, c., Hi., U.S. B3 88
Barbers Point Naval Air Station, mil., Hi., U.S. g9 88
Barberton, Oh., U.S. A4 112
Barbezieux, Fr. G6 10
Barbosa, Col. E6 58
Barbour, co., Al., U.S. D4 78
Barbour, co., W.V., U.S. B4 125
Barboursville, W.V., U.S. C2 125
Barbourville, Ky., U.S. D6 94
Barbuda, i., Antig. F17 64
Barcaldine, Austl. D9 50
Barcellona Pozzo di Gotto, Italy K10 14
Barcelona, Spain D14 12
Barcelona, Ven. B10 58
Barcelos, Braz. D6 54
Barcelos, Port. D3 12
Barcroft, Lake, res., Va., U.S. g12 123
Barden Reservoir, res., R.I., U.S. C2 116
Bardera, Som. H3 46
Bardīyah, Libya B11 42
Bardstown, Ky., U.S. C4 94
Bardufoss, Nor. B12 6
Bardwell, Ky., U.S. f9 94
Bardwell Lake, res., Tx., U.S. C4 120
Bareilly, India F8 38
Barents Sea, Eur. B8 128
Barfleur, Fr. C5 10
Bargersville, In., U.S. E5 91
Bar Harbor, Me., U.S. D4 96
Bari, Italy H11 14
Barīkowṭ, Afg. C4 38
Barillas, Guat. G2 64
Barinas, Ven. C7 58
Barinitas, Ven. C7 58
Baripāda, India J12 38
Barisāl, Bngl. I14 38
Barisan, Pegunungan, mts., Indon. F3 32
Barito, stm., Indon. F5 32
Barker Heights, N.C., U.S. f10 110
Barkhamsted Reservoir, res., Ct., U.S. B3 84
Barkley, Lake, res., U.S. f10 94
Barkley Sound, strt., B.C., Can. E5 69
Barkly Tableland, plat., Austl. C7 50
Bark Point, c., Wi., U.S. B2 126
Barksdale Air Force Base, mil., La., U.S. B2 95
Bar-le-Duc, Fr. D12 10
Barlee, Lake, l., Austl. E3 50
Barletta, Italy H11 14
Barling, Ar., U.S. B1 81
Barlow, Ky., U.S. e8 94
Barmer, India H4 38
Barmouth, Wales, U.K. I8 7
Barnaul, Russia G10 24
Barnegat Bay, b., N.J., U.S. D4 107
Barnegat Inlet, b., N.J., U.S. D4 107
Barnes, co., N.D., U.S. B7 111
Barnesboro, Pa., U.S. E4 115
Barnes Sound, strt., Fl., U.S. G6 86
Barnesville, Ga., U.S. C2 87
Barnesville, Mn., U.S. D2 100
Barnesville, Oh., U.S. C4 112
Barneville-Carteret, Fr. C5 10
Barnhart, Mo., U.S. C7 102
Barnsdall, Ok., U.S. A5 113
Barnsley, Eng., U.K. H11 7
Barnstable, Ma., U.S. C7 98
Barnstable, co., Ma., U.S. C7 98
Barnstaple, Eng., U.K. J8 7
Barnwell, S.C., U.S. E5 117
Barnwell, co., S.C., U.S. E5 117
Baroda, India I5 38
Barpeta, India G14 38
Barqah (Cyrenaica), reg., Libya B10 42
Barques, Pointe aux, c., Mi., U.S. D8 99
Barquisimeto, Ven. B8 58
Barra, Braz. F10 54
Barra, Ponta da, c., Moz. F7 44
Barrackville, W.V., U.S. B4 125
Barra do Corda, Braz. E9 54
Barra Falsa, Ponta da, c., Moz. F7 44
Barra Mansa, Braz. G6 57

Index

Name — Map Ref — Page

Barrancabermeja, Col. D6 58
Barranca del Cobre, Parque Nacional, Mex. D6 62
Barrancas, Ven. C11 58
Barrancos, Port. G5 12
Barranquilla, Col. B5 58
Barras, Braz. D10 54
Barrax, Spain F9 12
Barre, Vt., U.S. C4 122
Barre, Lake, l., La., U.S. E5 95
Barre Falls Reservoir, res., Ma., U.S. B4 98
Barreiras, Braz. B6 57
Barreiro, Port. G2 12
Barreiros, Braz. E11 54
Barrême, Fr. I13 10
Barren, co., Ky., U.S. D4 94
Barren, stm., Ky., U.S. C3 94
Barren Island, i., Md., U.S. D5 97
Barren Islands, is., Ak., U.S. h15 79
Barren River Lake, res., Ky., U.S. D3 94
Barretos, Braz. F4 57
Barrett, W.V., U.S. D3 125
Barrhead, Alta., Can. B3 68
Barrie, Ont., Can. C5 73
Barrie Island, i., Ont., Can. B2 73
Barrière, B.C., Can. D7 69
Barrington, Il., U.S. A5 90
Barrington, N.J., U.S. D2 107
Barrington, R.I., U.S. D5 116
Barrington, stm., R.I., U.S. C5 116
Barron, Wi., U.S. C2 126
Barron, co., Wi., U.S. C2 126
Barron Lake, Mi., U.S. G4 99
Barrow, Ak., U.S. A8 79
Barrow, co., Ga., U.S. B3 87
Barrow, Point, c., Ak., U.S. A8 79
Barrow Creek, Austl. D6 50
Barrow-in-Furness, Eng., U.K. G9 7
Barrow Island, i., Austl. D3 50
Barrow Strait, strt., N.W. Ter., Can. B14 66
Barry, Il., U.S. D2 90
Barry, co., Mi., U.S. F5 99
Barry, co., Mo., U.S. E4 102
Barrys Bay, Ont., Can. B7 73
Bārsi, India C3 37
Barstow, Ca., U.S. E5 82
Bar-sur-Aube, Fr. D11 10
Barth, Ger. A12 8
Bartholomew, co., In., U.S. F6 91
Bartholomew, Bayou, stm., U.S. D4 81
Bartica, Guy. D13 58
Bartlesville, Ok., U.S. A6 113
Bartlett, N.H., U.S. B4 106
Bartlett, Tn., U.S. B2 119
Bartlett, Tx., U.S. D4 120
Bartlett Reservoir, res., Az., U.S. D4 80
Bartletts Ferry Dam, U.S. C4 78
Barton, Oh., U.S. B5 112
Barton, Vt., U.S. B4 122
Barton, co., Ks., U.S. D5 93
Barton, co., Mo., U.S. D3 102
Barton, stm., Vt., U.S. B4 122
Bartonville, Il., U.S. C4 90
Bartow, Fl., U.S. E5 86
Bartow, co., Ga., U.S. B2 87
Barú, Volcán, vol., Pan. J6 64
Bāruni, India H11 38
Baruun Urt, Mong. B9 26
Barvas, Scot., U.K. C6 7
Basalt, Co., U.S. B3 83
Basankusu, Zaire A3 44
Basatongwula Shan, mtn., China D14 38
Bascuñán, Cabo, c., Chile B2 56
Basehor, Ks., U.S. k16 93
Basel (Bâle), Switz. E14 10
Bashan Lake, l., Ct., U.S. D6 84
Bashaw, Alta., Can. C4 68
Bashi Channel, strt., Asia G11 26
Basilan Island, i., Phil. D7 32
Basildon, Eng., U.K. J13 7
Basile, La., U.S. D3 95
Basin, Wy., U.S. B4 127
Basingstoke, Eng., U.K. J11 7
Basīrhāt, India I13 38
Basīt, Ra's al-, c., Syria B4 40
Baskahegan Lake, l., Me., U.S. C5 96
Baskatong, Réservoir, res., Que., Can. G17 66
Basking Ridge, N.J., U.S. B3 107
Basoko, Zaire A4 44
Basra see Al-Baṣrah, Iraq B4 46
Bassano, Alta., Can. D4 68
Bassano del Grappa, Italy D6 14
Bassari, Togo G6 42
Bassas da India, rf., Reu. F7 44
Basse-Terre, Guad. F17 64
Basseterre, St. K./N. F16 64
Basse-Terre, i., Guad. F17 64
Bassett, Ne., U.S. B6 104
Bassett, Va., U.S. D3 123
Bassett Peak, mtn., Az., U.S. E5 80
Bass Islands, is., Oh., U.S. A3 112
Bass Lake, In., U.S. B4 91
Bass Strait, strt., Austl. G9 50
Basswood Lake, l., Mn., U.S. B7 100
Basti, India G10 38
Bastogne, Bel. E5 8
Bastrop, La., U.S. B4 95
Bastrop, Tx., U.S. D4 120
Bastrop, co., Tx., U.S. D4 120
Bastuträsk, Swe. D13 6
Bata, Eq. Gui. H7 42
Bataan Peninsula, pen., Phil. q19 33b
Batabanó, Golfo de, b., Cuba C6 64
Batagaj, Russia D20 24
Bataguaçu, Braz. F2 57
Bataiporã, Braz. G2 57
Batāla, India E6 38
Batalha, Port. F3 12
Batamaj, Russia E19 24
Batang, China E6 26
Batangas, Phil. r19 33b
Batan Islands, is., Phil. A7 32
Batanta, Pulau, i., Indon. F9 32
Batatais, Braz. F5 57
Batavia, Il., U.S. B5 90
Batavia, N.Y., U.S. C2 109
Batavia, Oh., U.S. C1 112
Batchelor Bay, b., N.C., U.S. B6 110
Bătdâmbâng, Camb. H7 34
Batepito, Mex. B5 62
Bates, co., Mo., U.S. C3 102
Batesburg, S.C., U.S. D4 117
Batesville, Ar., U.S. B4 81
Batesville, In., U.S. F7 91
Batesville, Ms., U.S. A4 101
Bath, N.B., Can. C2 71
Bath, Ont., Can. C8 73
Bath, Eng., U.K. J10 7
Bath, Me., U.S. E3 96
Bath, N.Y., U.S. C3 109
Bath, Pa., U.S. E11 115
Bath, S.C., U.S. D4 117
Bath, co., Ky., U.S. B6 94
Bath, co., Va., U.S. B3 123
Bathurst, N.B., Can. B4 71
Bathurst, Cape, c., N.W. Ter., Can. B7 66
Bathurst Inlet, N.W. Ter., Can. C11 66
Bathurst Inlet, b., N.W. Ter., Can. C11 66
Bathurst Island, i., Austl. B6 50
Bathurst Island, i., N.W. Ter., Can. A12 66
Batiscan, stm., Que., Can. B5 74
Batna, Alg. A7 42
Baton Rouge, La., U.S. D4 95
Batouri, Cam. H8 42
Batsto, stm., N.J., U.S. D3 107
Batten Kill, stm., U.S. E2 122
Batticaloa, Sri L. I6 37
Battle, stm., Can. F10 66
Battle Creek, Ia., U.S. B2 92
Battle Creek, Mi., U.S. F5 99
Battle Creek, Ne., U.S. C8 104
Battle Ground, In., U.S. C4 91
Battle Ground, Wa., U.S. D3 124
Battle Lake, Mn., U.S. D3 100
Battle Mountain, Nv., U.S. C5 105
Battle Mountain, mtn., Wy., U.S. E5 127
Batu, mtn., Eth. G2 46
Batu, Kepulauan, is., Indon. O5 34
Batumi, Geor. I6 22
Batu Pahat, Malay. N7 34
Baturité, Braz. D11 54
Baubau, Indon. G7 32
Bauchi, Nig. F7 42
Baud, Fr. E3 10
Baudette, Mn., U.S. B4 100
Bauld, Cape, c., Newf., Can. C4 72
Baume-les-Dames, Fr. E13 10
Baunei, Italy I4 14
Bauru, Braz. G4 57
Baús, Braz. E2 57
Bautzen, Ger. D14 8
Bawean, Pulau, i., Indon. G5 32
Baxley, Ga., U.S. E4 87
Baxter, Ia., U.S. C4 92
Baxter, Mn., U.S. D4 100
Baxter, Tn., U.S. C8 119
Baxter, co., Ar., U.S. A3 81
Baxter Springs, Ks., U.S. E9 93
Bay, Ar., U.S. B5 81
Bay, co., Fl., U.S. u16 86
Bay, co., Mi., U.S. E6 99
Bay, Laguna de, l., Phil. q19 33b
Bayamo, Cuba D9 64
Bayan Har Shan, mts., China E6 26
Bayard, Ne., U.S. C2 104
Bayard, N.M., U.S. E1 108
Bayberry, N.Y., U.S. *B4 109
Bayboro, N.C., U.S. B6 110
Bay Bulls, Newf., Can. E5 72
Bay City, Mi., U.S. E7 99
Bay City, Or., U.S. B3 114
Bay City, Tx., U.S. E5 120
Bay de Verde, Newf., Can. D5 72
Bayerische Alpen, mts., Eur. H11 8
Bayeux, Fr. C6 10
Bayfield, Ont., Can. D3 73
Bayfield, Co., U.S. D3 83
Bayfield, Wi., U.S. B3 126
Bayfield, co., Wi., U.S. B2 126
Bayındır, Tur. K11 16
Baykonur see Bajkonyr, Kaz. H11 22
Baylor, co., Tx., U.S. C3 120
Bay Mills Indian Reservation, Mi., U.S. B6 99
Bay Minette, Al., U.S. E2 78
Bayo, Spain B3 12
Bayona, Spain C3 12
Bayonne, Fr. I5 10
Bayonne, N.J., U.S. B4 107
Bayou Bodcau Reservoir, res., La., U.S. B2 95
Bayou D'Arbonne Lake, res., La., U.S. B3 95
Bayou George, Fl., U.S. u16 86
Bayou Goula, La., U.S. D4 95
Bayou La Batre, Al., U.S. E1 78
Bay Point, c., S.C., U.S. G7 117
Bayport, Mn., U.S. E6 100
Bayport, N.Y., U.S. n15 109
Bayramiç, Tur. J10 16
Bayreuth, Ger. F11 8
Bay Ridge, Md., U.S. C5 97
Bay Roberts, Newf., Can. E5 72
Bayrūt (Beirut), Leb. C4 40
Bays, Lake of, l., Ont., Can. B5 73
Bay Saint Louis, Ms., U.S. E4 101
Bay Shore, N.Y., U.S. E7 109
Bayshore Gardens, Fl., U.S. q10 86
Bayside, Wi., U.S. m12 126
Bay Springs, Ms., U.S. D4 101
Bayt Lahm, W. Bank D4 40
Baytown, Tx., U.S. E5 120
Bayview, Al., U.S. f7 78
Bay Village, Oh., U.S. h9 112
Baza, Spain H9 12
Bazaruto, Ilha do, i., Moz. F7 44
Bazas, Fr. H6 10
Be, Nosy, i., Madag. D9 44
Beach, Il., U.S. h9 90
Beach, N.D., U.S. C1 111
Beachburg, Ont., Can. B8 73
Beach City, Oh., U.S. B4 112
Beach Haven Inlet, b., N.J., U.S. D4 107
Beach Pond, res., U.S. C8 84
Beachville, Ont., Can. D4 73
Beachwood, N.J., U.S. D4 107
Beachy Head, c., Eng., U.K. K13 7
Beacon, N.Y., U.S. D7 109
Beacon Falls, Ct., U.S. D3 84
Beaconsfield, Que., Can. q19 74
Beadle, co., S.D., U.S. C7 118
Beagle Gulf, b., Austl. B6 50
Bealanana, Madag. D9 44
Beale, Cape, c., B.C., Can. E5 69
Beale Air Force Base, mil., Ca., U.S. C3 82
Bear, De., U.S. B3 85
Bear, stm., U.S. B3 121
Bear Creek, Al., U.S. A2 78
Bear Creek, stm., U.S. E2 93
Bear Creek, stm., Or., U.S. E4 114
Bear Creek, stm., Wy., U.S. E8 127
Bearden, Ar., U.S. D3 81
Beardstown, Il., U.S. C3 90
Bear Inlet, b., N.C., U.S. C5 110
Bear Lake, co., Id., U.S. G7 89
Bear Lake, l., U.S. A4 121
Bear Lake, l., Wi., U.S. C2 126
Bear Lodge Mountains, mts., Wy., U.S. B8 127
Bear Mountain, mtn., Or., U.S. D4 114
Bearpaw Mountains, mts., Mt., U.S. B7 103
Bear River, N.S., Can. E4 71
Bear River City, Ut., U.S. B3 121
Beartooth Pass, Wy., U.S. B3 127
Beartooth Range, mts., U.S. E7 103
Bear Town, Ms., U.S. D3 101
Beasain, Spain B9 12
Beas de Segura, Spain G9 12
Beata, Isla, i., Dom. Rep. F12 64
Beatrice, Ne., U.S. D9 104
Beatton, stm., B.C., Can. E8 66
Beatty, Nv., U.S. G5 105
Beattyville, Ky., U.S. C6 94
Beaucaire, Fr. I11 10
Beaufort, N.C., U.S. C6 110
Beaufort, S.C., U.S. G6 117
Beaufort, co., N.C., U.S. B5 110
Beaufort, co., S.C., U.S. G6 117
Beaufort Marine Corps Air Station, mil., S.C., U.S. F6 117
Beaufort Sea, N.A. B7 61
Beaufort West, S. Afr. H4 44
Beaugency, Fr. E8 10
Beauharnois, Que., Can. D4 74
Beau Lake, l., Me., U.S. A3 96
Beauly, Scot., U.K. D8 7
Beaumont, Alta., Can. C4 68
Beaumont, Ms., U.S. D5 101
Beaumont, Tx., U.S. D5 120
Beaumont-sur-Sarthe, Fr. D7 10
Beaune, Fr. E11 10
Beauport, Que., Can. n17 74
Beaupré, Que., Can. B7 74
Beaupréau, Fr. E5 10
Beauregard, co., La., U.S. D2 95
Beausejour, Man., Can. D3 70
Beauvais, Fr. C9 10
Beauval, Sask., Can. B2 75
Beauvoir-sur-Niort, Fr. F6 10
Beaver, Ok., U.S. A1 113
Beaver, Pa., U.S. E1 115
Beaver, Ut., U.S. E3 121
Beaver, W.V., U.S. D3 125
Beaver, co., Ok., U.S. e10 113
Beaver, co., Pa., U.S. E1 115
Beaver, co., Ut., U.S. E2 121
Beaver, stm., Can. D7 66
Beaver, stm., Can. B2 75
Beaver, stm., U.S. A2 113
Beaver, stm., N.Y., U.S. B6 109
Beaver, stm., R.I., U.S. E2 116
Beaver, stm., Ut., U.S. E2 121
Beaverbank, N.S., Can. E6 71
Beaver Brook, stm., U.S. E4 106
Beaver City, Ne., U.S. D6 104
Beavercreek, Oh., U.S. C1 112
Beaver Creek, stm., U.S. E4 104
Beaver Creek, stm., U.S. C8 127
Beaver Creek, stm., N.D., U.S. C5 111
Beaver Creek, stm., N.D., U.S. C1 111
Beaver Creek, stm., Ok., U.S. C3 113
Beaver Creek, stm., Tn., U.S. m13 119
Beaver Creek, stm., Wy., U.S. D4 127
Beaverdale, Pa., U.S. F4 115
Beaver Dam, Ky., U.S. C3 94
Beaver Dam, Wi., U.S. E5 126
Beaverdam Branch, stm., De., U.S. F3 85
Beaverdam Lake, res., Wi., U.S. E5 126
Beaver Falls, Pa., U.S. E1 115
Beaverhead, co., Mt., U.S. E3 103
Beaverhead, stm., Mt., U.S. E4 103
Beaverhead Mountains, mts., U.S. D5 89
Beaverhill Lake, l., Alta., Can. C4 68
Beaver Island, i., Mi., U.S. C5 99
Beaver Lake, res., Ar., U.S. A2 81
Beaverlodge, Alta., Can. B1 68
Beaver Meadows, Pa., U.S. E10 115
Beaver Run Reservoir, res., Pa., U.S. F2 115
Beavertail Point, c., R.I., U.S. F4 116
Beaverton, Mi., U.S. E6 99
Beaverton, Or., U.S. B4 114
Beāwar, India G6 38
Bebedouro, Braz. F4 57
Bécancour, Que., Can. C5 74
Bečej, Yugo. D4 16
Becerreá, Spain C4 12
Béchar, Alg. B5 42
Becharof Lake, l., Ak., U.S. D8 79
Beckemeyer, Il., U.S. E4 90
Becker, Mn., U.S. E5 100
Becker, co., Mn., U.S. D3 100
Beckham, co., Ok., U.S. B2 113
Beckley, W.V., U.S. D3 125
Beckum, Ger. D8 8
Becky Peak, mtn., Nv., U.S. D7 105
Bédarieux, Fr. I10 10
Bedford, Que., Can. D5 74
Bedford, Eng., U.K. I12 7
Bedford, In., U.S. G5 91
Bedford, Ia., U.S. D3 92
Bedford, Ky., U.S. B4 94
Bedford, Ma., U.S. B5 98
Bedford, N.H., U.S. E3 106
Bedford, Oh., U.S. A4 112
Bedford, Pa., U.S. F4 115
Bedford, Va., U.S. C3 123
Bedford, co., Pa., U.S. G4 115
Bedford, co., Tn., U.S. B5 119
Bedford, co., Va., U.S. C3 123
Bedford Hills, N.Y., U.S. D7 109
Bee, co., Tx., U.S. E4 120
Beebe, Que., Can. D5 74
Beebe, Ar., U.S. B4 81
Beecher, Il., U.S. B6 90
Beecher, Mi., U.S. *E7 99
Beech Fork, stm., Ky., U.S. C4 94
Beech Grove, In., U.S. E5 91
Beech Island, S.C., U.S. E4 117
Beemer, Ne., U.S. C9 104
Bee Ridge, Fl., U.S. q11 86
Beersheba see Be'er Sheva', Isr. D4 40
Be'er Sheva', Isr. D4 40
Beeton (part of Alliston Beeton Tecumseth and Tottenham), Ont., Can. C5 73
Beeville, Tx., U.S. E4 120
Befale, Zaire A4 44
Befandriana, Madag. E9 44
Beggs, Ok., U.S. B5 113
Begī, Eth. G1 46
Behbehān, Iran B5 46
Behm Canal, strt., Ak., U.S. n24 79
Bei, stm., China G9 26
Bei'an, China B12 26
Beihai, China D10 34
Beijing (Peking), China D10 26
Beijing Shih, China C10 26
Beipiao, China C11 26
Beira, Moz. E6 44
Beirut see Bayrūt, Leb. C4 40
Beja, Port. G4 12
Béja, Tun. M4 14
Bejaïa, Alg. A7 42
Béjar, Spain E6 12
Békéscsaba, Hung. I21 8
Bekily, Madag. F9 44
Bela, India H9 38
Bel Air, Md., U.S. A5 97
Belalcázar, Spain G6 12
Bel Alton, Md., U.S. D4 97
Belampalli, India C5 37
Belarus, ctry., Eur. G3 22
Belau see Palau, ctry., Oc. D9 32
Bela Vista, Braz. A5 56
Belcamp, Md., U.S. B5 97
Belcherāgh, Afg. C1 38
Belcher Islands, is., N.W. Ter., Can. E17 66
Belchertown, Ma., U.S. B3 98
Belchite, Spain D11 12
Belcourt, N.D., U.S. A6 111
Belden, Ms., U.S. A5 101
Belding, Mi., U.S. E5 99
Beled Weyne, Som. H4 46
Belém, Braz. D9 54
Belén, Para. A5 56
Belen, N.M., U.S. C3 108
Belfair, Wa., U.S. B3 124
Belfast, N. Ire., U.K. G7 7
Belfast, Me., U.S. D3 96
Belfield, N.D., U.S. C2 111
Belford, N.J., U.S. C4 107
Belfort, Fr. E13 10
Belfry, Ky., U.S. C7 94
Belgaum, India E3 37
Belgium, Wi., U.S. E6 126
Belgium, ctry., Eur. E8 4
Belgorod, Russia G5 22
Belgrade, Mn., U.S. E3 100
Belgrade, Mt., U.S. E5 103
Belgrade see Beograd, Yugo. E4 16
Belhaven, N.C., U.S. B6 110
Belin, Fr. H6 10
Belington, W.V., U.S. B5 125
Belitung, i., Indon. F4 32
Belize, ctry., N.A. F3 64
Belize City, Belize F3 64
Belknap, co., N.H., U.S. C3 106
Belknap Crater, crat., Or., U.S. C5 114
Bell, co., Ky., U.S. D6 94
Bell, co., Tx., U.S. D4 120
Bellac, Fr. F8 10
Bella Coola, stm., B.C., Can. C4 69
Bellaire, Ks., U.S. g12 93
Bellaire, Mi., U.S. D5 99
Bellaire, Oh., U.S. C5 112
Bellaire, Tx., U.S. r14 120
Bellamy, Al., U.S. C1 78
Bellary, India E4 37
Bellavista, Peru E3 54
Bella Vista, Ar., U.S. A1 81
Bellbrook, Oh., U.S. C1 112
Belle, Mo., U.S. C6 102
Belle, W.V., U.S. C3 125
Belle, stm., La., U.S. k9 95
Belleair, Fl., U.S. p10 86
Belle Bay, b., Newf., Can. E4 72
Belle Chasse, La., U.S. E5 95
Bellefontaine, Oh., U.S. B2 112
Bellefonte, Pa., U.S. E6 115
Belle Fourche, S.D., U.S. C2 118
Belle Fourche, stm., U.S. C3 118
Belle Fourche Reservoir, res., S.D., U.S. C2 118
Bellegarde, Fr. F12 10
Belle Glade, Fl., U.S. F6 86
Belle Isle, Fl., U.S. D5 86
Belle Isle, i., Newf., Can. C4 72
Belle Isle, Strait of, strt., Newf., Can. C3 72
Belle Meade, Tn., U.S. g10 119
Belle Plaine, Ia., U.S. C5 92
Belle Plaine, Ks., U.S. E6 93
Belle Plaine, Mn., U.S. F5 100
Belle River, Ont., Can. E2 73
Belle Rose, La., U.S. D4 95
Belle Vernon, Pa., U.S. F2 115
Belleview, Fl., U.S. C4 86
Belle View, Va., U.S. g12 123
Belleville, Ont., Can. C7 73
Belleville, Il., U.S. E4 90
Belleville, Ks., U.S. C6 93
Belleville, Mi., U.S. p15 99
Belleville, N.J., U.S. B4 107
Belleville, Pa., U.S. E6 115
Belleville, Wi., U.S. F4 126
Belleville Pond, l., R.I., U.S. E4 116
Bellevue, Id., U.S. F4 89
Bellevue, Ia., U.S. B7 92
Bellevue, Ky., U.S. h13 94
Bellevue, Mi., U.S. F5 99
Bellevue, Ne., U.S. C10 104
Bellevue, Oh., U.S. A3 112
Bellevue, Pa., U.S. F1 115
Bellevue, Wa., U.S. e11 124
Belley, Fr. G12 10
Bellflower, Ca., U.S. n12 82
Bellingham, Ma., U.S. B5 98
Bellingham, Wa., U.S. A3 124
Bellingshausen Sea, Ant. B4 47
Bellinzona, Switz. F16 10
Bell Island, i., Newf., Can. C4 72
Bellmawr, N.J., U.S. D2 107
Bello, Col. D5 58
Bellows Falls, Vt., U.S. E4 122
Bell Peninsula, pen., N.W. Ter., Can. D16 66
Bellport, N.Y., U.S. n16 109
Bells, Tn., U.S. B2 119
Bells Creek, stm., W.V., U.S. m13 125
Belluno, Italy C7 14
Bell Ville, Arg. C4 56
Bellville, Oh., U.S. B3 112
Bellville, Tx., U.S. E4 120
Bellwood, Il., U.S. k9 90
Bellwood, Pa., U.S. E5 115
Bellwood, Va., U.S. n18 123
Belmar, N.J., U.S. C4 107
Belmond, Ia., U.S. B4 92
Belmont, Ont., Can. E3 73
Belmont, Ca., U.S. h8 82
Belmont, Ma., U.S. g11 98
Belmont, Ms., U.S. A5 101
Belmont, N.H., U.S. D4 106
Belmont, N.C., U.S. B1 110
Belmont, W.V., U.S. B3 125
Belmont, Wi., U.S. F3 126
Belmont, co., Oh., U.S. C4 112
Belmonte, Braz. C9 57
Belmonte, Port. E4 12
Belmonte, Spain B5 12
Belmonte, Spain F9 12
Belmopan, Belize F3 64
Belmullet, Ire. G2 7
Bel-Nor, Mo., U.S. f13 102
Belo, Madag. E8 44
Beloeil, Que., Can. D4 74
Belogorsk, Russia G19 24
Belo Horizonte, Braz. E7 57
Beloit, Ks., U.S. C5 93
Beloit, Oh., U.S. B5 112
Beloit, Wi., U.S. F4 126
Beloit North, Wi., U.S. *F4 126
Beloje, Ozero, l., Russia A20 18
Beloje more (White Sea), Russia D5 22
Belorado, Spain C8 12
Beloreck, Russia G9 22
Belorussia see Belarus, ctry., Eur. G3 22
Belovo, Russia G11 24
Belpre, Oh., U.S. C4 112
Belt, Mt., U.S. C6 103
Belted Range, mts., Nv., U.S. F5 105
Belton, Mo., U.S. C3 102
Belton, S.C., U.S. B3 117
Belton, Tx., U.S. D4 120
Belton Lake, res., Tx., U.S. D4 120
Beltrami, co., Mn., U.S. B3 100
Beltsville, Md., U.S. B4 97
Belucha, Gora, mtn., Asia H11 24
Belvedere, S.C., U.S. D4 117
Belvedere Marittimo, Italy J10 14
Belvidere, Il., U.S. A5 90
Belvidere, N.J., U.S. B2 107
Belyj, Ostrov, i., Russia C8 24
Belyj Jar, Russia F11 24
Belzoni, Ms., U.S. B3 101
Bement, Il., U.S. D5 90
Bemidji, Mn., U.S. C4 100
Bemidji, Lake, l., Mn., U.S. C4 100
Benabarre, Spain C12 12
Bena-Dibele, Zaire B4 44
Benavente, Port. G3 12
Benavente, Spain C6 12
Benavides, Tx., U.S. F3 120
Benbrook Lake, res., Tx., U.S. n9 120
Bend, Or., U.S. C5 114
Ben Davis Point, c., N.J., U.S. E2 107
Bendeleben, Mount, mtn., Ak., U.S. B7 79
Bendigo, Austl. G8 50
Benedict, Md., U.S. C4 97
Benedito Leite, Braz. E10 54
Benevento, Italy H9 14
Benewah, co., Id., U.S. B2 89
Bengal, Bay of, b., Asia F6 36
Bengbu, China C6 28
Benghazi see Banghāzī, Libya B10 42
Bengkalis, Indon. N7 34
Bengkulu, Indon. F3 32
Benguela, Ang. D2 44
Benham, Ky., U.S. D7 94
Ben Hill, co., Ga., U.S. E3 87
Beni, stm., Bol. F5 54
Béni Abbès, Alg. B5 42
Benicarló, Spain E12 12
Benicia, Ca., U.S. C2 82
Beni-Mellal, Mor. B4 42
Benin, ctry., Afr. G6 42
Benin, Bight of, Afr. G6 42
Benin City, Nig. G7 42
Benisa, Spain G12 12
Benito Juárez, Presa, res., Mex. I12 62
Benjamin Constant, Braz. D4 54

Name — Map Ref — Page

Benjamín Hill, Mex. **B4** 62
Benkelman, Ne., U.S. **D4** 104
Benld, Il., U.S. **D4** 90
Bennett, Co., U.S. **B6** 83
Bennett, co., S.D., U.S. **D4** 118
Bennettsville, S.C., U.S. **B8** 117
Bennington, Ne., U.S. **g12** 104
Bennington, N.H., U.S. **D3** 106
Bennington, Vt., U.S. **F2** 122
Bennington, co., Vt., U.S. **E2** 122
Benoit, Ms., U.S. **B2** 101
Bénoué (Benue), stm., Afr. **G8** 42
Bensenville, Il., U.S. **B6** 90
Bensheim, Ger. **F8** 8
Bensley, Va., U.S. **C5** 123
Benson, Az., U.S. **F5** 80
Benson, Mn., U.S. **E3** 100
Benson, N.C., U.S. **B4** 110
Benson, co., N.D., U.S. **A6** 111
Bent, co., Co., U.S. **D7** 83
Bentley, Alta., Can. **C3** 68
Bentleyville, Pa., U.S. **F1** 115
Benton, Ar., U.S. **C3** 81
Benton, Il., U.S. **E5** 90
Benton, Ks., U.S. **E6** 93
Benton, Ky., U.S. **f9** 94
Benton, La., U.S. **B2** 95
Benton, Pa., U.S. **D9** 115
Benton, Tn., U.S. **B7** 119
Benton, Wi., U.S. **F3** 126
Benton, co., Ar., U.S. **A1** 81
Benton, co., In., U.S. **C3** 91
Benton, co., Ia., U.S. **B5** 92
Benton, co., Mn., U.S. **E4** 100
Benton, co., Ms., U.S. **A4** 101
Benton, co., Mo., U.S. **C4** 102
Benton, co., Or., U.S. **C3** 114
Benton, co., Tn., U.S. **A3** 119
Benton, co., Wa., U.S. **C6** 124
Benton City, Wa., U.S. **C6** 124
Benton Harbor, Mi., U.S. **F4** 99
Benton Heights, Mi., U.S. **F4** 99
Bentonville, Ar., U.S. **A1** 81
Ben Treang, Viet. **I9** 34
Bent's Old Fort National Historic Site, hist., Co., U.S. **C7** 83
Benue (Bénoué), stm., Afr. **G7** 42
Benwood, W.V., U.S. **f8** 125
Benxi, China **C11** 26
Benzie, co., Mi., U.S. **D4** 99
Beograd (Belgrade), Yugo. **E4** 16
Beowawe, Nv., U.S. **C5** 105
Beppu, Japan **I4** 30
Berau, Teluk, b., Indon. **F9** 32
Berbera, Som. **F4** 46
Berbérati, Cen. Afr. Rep. **H9** 42
Berchtesgaden, Ger. **H13** 8
Berck, Fr. **B8** 10
Berdigest'ach, Russia **E19** 24
Berdsk, Russia **G10** 24
Berea, Ky., U.S. **C5** 94
Berea, Oh., U.S. **A4** 112
Berea, S.C., U.S. **B3** 117
Berens, stm., Can. **F13** 66
Berens, stm., Can. **C3** 70
Beresford, S.D., U.S. **D9** 118
Berg, Nor. **B11** 6
Berga, Spain **C13** 12
Bergama, Tur. **J11** 16
Bergamo, Italy **D4** 14
Bergen, Nor. **F5** 6
Bergen, co., N.J., U.S. **A4** 107
Bergen [auf Rügen], Ger. **A13** 8
Bergenfield, N.J., U.S. **B4** 107
Bergen op Zoom, Neth. **D4** 8
Bergerac, Fr. **H7** 10
Bergland, Mi., U.S. **m12** 99
Bergstrom Air Force Base, mil., Tx., U.S. **D4** 120
Berhampore, India **H13** 38
Berhampur, India **C8** 37
Beringovskij, Russia **E29** 24
Bering Sea **D30** 128
Bering Strait, strt. **m18** 76a
Berja, Spain **I9** 12
Berkåk, Nor. **E7** 6
Berkeley, Ca., U.S. **D2** 82
Berkeley, Mo., U.S. **f13** 102
Berkeley, R.I., U.S. **B4** 116
Berkeley, co., S.C., U.S. **E8** 117
Berkeley, co., W.V., U.S. **B6** 125
Berkeley Heights, N.J., U.S. **B4** 107
Berkeley Springs, W.V., U.S. **B6** 125
Berkley, Mi., U.S. **F7** 99
Berkner Island, i., Ant. **B8** 47
Berks, co., Pa., U.S. **F9** 115
Berkshire, co., Ma., U.S. **B1** 98
Berkshire Hills, hills, Ma., U.S. **B1** 98
Berlin, Ger. **C13** 8
Berlin, Ct., U.S. **C5** 84
Berlin, Md., U.S. **D7** 97
Berlin, N.H., U.S. **B4** 106
Berlin, N.J., U.S. **D3** 107
Berlin, Pa., U.S. **G4** 115
Berlin, Wi., U.S. **E5** 126
Berlin Lake, res., Oh., U.S. **A4** 112
Bermeo, Spain **B9** 12
Bermuda, dep., N.A. **E14** 76
Bern (Berne), Switz. **F14** 10
Bernalillo, N.M., U.S. **B3** 108
Bernalillo, co., N.M., U.S. **C3** 108
Bernardsville, N.J., U.S. **B3** 107
Bernasconi, Arg. **D4** 56
Bernau bei Berlin, Ger. **C13** 8
Bernay, Fr. **C7** 10
Bernburg, Ger. **D11** 8
Berne, In., U.S. **C8** 91
Bernice, La., U.S. **B3** 95
Bernie, Mo., U.S. **E8** 102
Bernier Island, i., Austl. **D2** 50
Bernina, Piz, mtn., Eur. **F16** 10
Beroroha, Madag. **F9** 44
Berre, Étang de, b., Fr. **I12** 10
Berrien, co., Ga., U.S. **E3** 87
Berrien, co., Mi., U.S. **F4** 99
Berrien Springs, Mi., U.S. **G4** 99
Berry, Al., U.S. **B2** 78
Berryessa, Lake, res., Ca., U.S. **C2** 82
Berry Hill, Tn., U.S. **g10** 119
Berry Islands, is., Bah. **B9** 64
Berryville, Ar., U.S. **A2** 81
Berryville, Va., U.S. **A5** 123
Berthierville, Que., Can. **C4** 74
Berthoud, Co., U.S. **A5** 83
Berthoud Pass, Co., U.S. **B5** 83
Bertie, co., N.C., U.S. **A5** 110
Bertoua, Cam. **H8** 42
Bertrand, Mo., U.S. **E8** 102
Bertrand, Ne., U.S. **D6** 104
Berwick, Ia., U.S. **e8** 92
Berwick, La., U.S. **E4** 95
Berwick, Me., U.S. **E2** 96
Berwick, Pa., U.S. **D9** 115
Berwick-upon-Tweed, Eng., U.K. **F10** 7
Berwyn, Alta., Can. **A2** 68
Berwyn, Il., U.S. **k9** 90
Berwyn, Pa., U.S. **o20** 115
Besalampy, Madag. **E8** 44
Besançon, Fr. **E13** 10
Beskid Mountains, mts., Eur. **F19** 8
Bessemer, Al., U.S. **B3** 78
Bessemer, Mi., U.S. **n11** 99
Bessemer, Pa., U.S. **E1** 115
Bessemer City, N.C., U.S. **B1** 110
Best'ach, Russia **E19** 24
Betanzos, Spain **B3** 12
Bétaré Oya, Cam. **G8** 42
Betatakin Ruin, hist., Az., U.S. **A5** 80
Bethalto, Il., U.S. **E3** 90
Bethany, Ct., U.S. **D4** 84
Bethany, Il., U.S. **D5** 90
Bethany, Mo., U.S. **A3** 102
Bethany, Ok., U.S. **B4** 113
Bethany, W.V., U.S. **A4** 125
Bethany Beach, De., U.S. **F5** 85
Bethel, Ak., U.S. **C7** 79
Bethel, Ct., U.S. **D2** 84
Bethel, Me., U.S. **D2** 96
Bethel, N.C., U.S. **B5** 110
Bethel, Oh., U.S. **D1** 112
Bethel, Vt., U.S. **D3** 122
Bethel Park, Pa., U.S. **k14** 115
Bethel Springs, Tn., U.S. **B3** 119
Bethesda, Md., U.S. **C3** 97
Bethesda, Oh., U.S. **B4** 112
Bethlehem, S. Afr. **G5** 44
Bethlehem, Ct., U.S. **C3** 84
Bethlehem, N.H., U.S. **B3** 106
Bethlehem, Pa., U.S. **E11** 115
Bethlehem see Bayt Lahm, W. Bank **D4** 40
Béthune, Fr. **B9** 10
Beticos, Sistemas, mts., Spain **H9** 12
Betioky, Madag. **F8** 44
Betong, Malay. **M6** 34
Betroka, Madag. **F9** 44
Betsiboka, stm., Madag. **E9** 44
Betsie, Point, c., Mi., U.S. **D4** 99
Betsy Layne, Ky., U.S. **C7** 94
Bette, mtn., Libya **D9** 42
Bettendorf, Ia., U.S. **C7** 92
Bettiah, India **G11** 38
Betūl, India **B4** 37
Betzdorf, Ger. **E7** 8
Beulah, Co., U.S. **C6** 83
Beulah, N.D., U.S. **B4** 111
Beulah, Lake, l., Ms., U.S. **B3** 101
Beulaville, N.C., U.S. **C5** 110
B. Everett Jordan Lake, res., N.C., U.S. **B3** 110
Beverley, Austl. **F3** 50
Beverley, Eng., U.K. **H12** 7
Beverley Head, c., Newf., Can. **D2** 72
Beverly, Ma., U.S. **A6** 98
Beverly, N.J., U.S. **C3** 107
Beverly, Oh., U.S. **C4** 112
Beverly, W.V., U.S. **C5** 125
Beverly Hills, Ca., U.S. **m12** 82
Beverly Shores, In., U.S. **A4** 91
Bexar, co., Tx., U.S. **E3** 120
Bexley, Oh., U.S. **m11** 112
Beypore, India **G3** 37
Bežeck, Russia **D19** 18
Béziers, Fr. **I10** 10
Bhadrakh, India **J12** 38
Bhadrāvati, India **F3** 37
Bhāgalpur, India **H12** 38
Bhakkar, Pak. **E4** 38
Bhaktapur, Nepal **G11** 38
Bhandāra, India **B5** 37
Bharatpur, India **G7** 38
Bhatinda, India **E6** 38
Bhātpāra, India **I13** 38
Bhāvnagar, India **J5** 38
Bhilai, India **B6** 37
Bhīlwāra, India **H6** 38
Bhīma, stm., India **D4** 37
Bhīmavaram, India **D6** 37
Bhind, India **G8** 38
Bhiwandi, India **C2** 37
Bhiwāni, India **F7** 38
Bhopāl, India **I7** 38
Bhubaneswar, India **J11** 38
Bhuj, India **I3** 38
Bhusāwal, India **B3** 37
Bhutan, ctry., Asia **D7** 36
Bia, Phou, mtn., Laos **E7** 34
Biafra, Bight of, Afr. **H7** 42
Biak, i., Indon. **F10** 32
Biała Podlaska, Pol. **C23** 8
Białystok, Pol. **B23** 8
Biarritz, Fr. **I5** 10
Biasca, Switz. **F15** 10
Bibai, Japan **p19** 30a
Bibb, co., Al., U.S. **C2** 78
Bibb, co., Ga., U.S. **D3** 87
Biberach an der Riss, Ger. **G9** 8
Bic, Que., Can. **A9** 74
Bic, Île du, i., Que., Can. **A9** 74
Biche, Lac la, l., Alta., Can. **B4** 68
Bicknell, In., U.S. **G3** 91
Bida, Nig. **G7** 42
Bīdar, India **D4** 37
Biddeford, Me., U.S. **E2** 96
Bideford, Eng., U.K. **J8** 7
Bidwell, Mount, mtn., Ca., U.S. **B3** 82
Biel [Bienne], Switz. **E14** 10
Bielefeld, Ger. **C8** 8
Bieler Lake, l., N.W. Ter., Can. **B18** 66
Bielersee, l., Switz. **E14** 10
Biella, Italy **D3** 14
Bielsko-Biała, Pol. **F19** 8
Bien Hoa, Viet. **I9** 34
Bienville, co., La., U.S. **B2** 95
Bienville, Lac, l., Que., Can. **g12** 74
Big, stm., Mo., U.S. **c7** 102
Biga, Tur. **I11** 16
Bigadiç, Tur. **J12** 16
Big Bald, mtn., Ga., U.S. **B2** 87
Big Bald Mountain, mtn., N.B., Can. **B3** 71
Big Baldy, mtn., Id., U.S. **E3** 89
Big Baldy Mountain, mtn., Mt., U.S. **D6** 103
Big Bay De Noc, b., Mi., U.S. **C4** 99
Big Bear City, Ca., U.S. **E5** 82
Big Belt Mountains, mts., Mt., U.S. **D5** 103
Big Bend, Wi., U.S. **n11** 126
Big Bend Dam, S.D., U.S. **C6** 118
Big Bend National Park, Tx., U.S. **E1** 120
Big Birch Lake, l., Mn., U.S. **E4** 100
Big Black, stm., Me., U.S. **B3** 96
Big Black, stm., Ms., U.S. **C3** 101
Big Blue, stm., In., U.S. **E6** 91
Big Burro Mountains, mts., N.M., U.S. **E1** 108
Big Cabin Creek, stm., Ok., U.S. **A6** 113
Big Coal, stm., W.V., U.S. **C3** 125
Big Costilla Peak, mtn., N.M., U.S. **A4** 108
Big Creek, stm., Tn., U.S. **e8** 119
Big Creek Lake, res., Al., U.S. **E1** 78
Big Creek Peak, mtn., Id., U.S. **E5** 89
Big Cypress Indian Reservation, Fl., U.S. **F5** 86
Big Cypress Swamp, sw., Fl., U.S. **F5** 86
Big Darby Creek, stm., Oh., U.S. **C2** 112
Big Delta, Ak., U.S. **C10** 79
Big Duke Dam, N.C., U.S. **B2** 110
Big Eau Pleine, stm., Wi., U.S. **D3** 126
Big Eau Pleine Reservoir, res., Wi., U.S. **D4** 126
Big Escambia Creek, stm., U.S. **D2** 78
Big Flats, N.Y., U.S. **C4** 109
Bigfork, Mt., U.S. **B2** 103
Big Fork, stm., Mn., U.S. **B5** 100
Biggs, Ca., U.S. **C3** 82
Big Hatchet Peak, mtn., N.M., U.S. **F1** 108
Big Hole, stm., Mt., U.S. **E4** 103
Big Hole National Battlefield, hist., Mt., U.S. **E3** 103
Big Horn, co., Mt., U.S. **E9** 103
Big Horn, co., Wy., U.S. **B4** 127
Bighorn Canyon National Recreation Area, U.S. **F8** 103
Bighorn Lake, res., U.S. **E8** 103
Bighorn Mountains, mts., U.S. **B5** 127
Big Horn Mountains, mts., Az., U.S. **D2** 80
Big Kandiyohi Lake, l., Mn., U.S. **F4** 100
Big Lake, Mn., U.S. **E5** 100
Big Lake, Tx., U.S. **D2** 120
Big Lake, l., Me., U.S. **C5** 96
Biglerville, Pa., U.S. **G7** 115
Big Lookout Mountain, mtn., Or., U.S. **C9** 114
Big Lost, stm., Id., U.S. **F5** 89
Big Mossy Point, c., Man., Can. **C2** 70
Big Mountain, mtn., Nv., U.S. **B2** 105
Big Muddy, stm., Il., U.S. **F4** 90
Big Nemaha, stm., Ne., U.S. **D10** 104
Big Otter, stm., Va., U.S. **C3** 123
Big Pine Lake, l., Mn., U.S. **D3** 100
Big Pine Mountain, mtn., Ca., U.S. **E4** 82
Big Piney, Wy., U.S. **D2** 127
Big Piney, stm., Mo., U.S. **D5** 102
Bigpoint, Ms., U.S. **E5** 101
Big Rapids, Mi., U.S. **E5** 99
Big Rib, stm., Wi., U.S. **C3** 126
Big River, Sask., Can. **D2** 75
Big Sable Point, c., Mi., U.S. **D4** 99
Big Sandy, Mt., U.S. **B6** 103
Big Sandy, Tx., U.S. **C5** 120
Big Sandy, stm., U.S. **C2** 125
Big Sandy, stm., Az., U.S. **C2** 80
Big Sandy, stm., Tn., U.S. **B3** 119
Big Sandy, stm., Wy., U.S. **D3** 127
Big Sandy Creek, stm., W.V., U.S. **C3** 125
Big Sandy Lake, l., Mn., U.S. **D5** 100
Big Sandy Reservoir, res., Wy., U.S. **D3** 127
Big Sheep Mountain, mtn., Mt., U.S. **C11** 103
Big Sioux, stm., U.S. **E9** 118
Big Smoky Valley, val., Nv., U.S. **E4** 105
Big Snowy Mountains, mts., Mt., U.S. **D7** 103
Big Southern Butte, mtn., Id., U.S. **F5** 89
Big South Fork, stm., Ky., U.S. **k13** 94
Big Spring, Tx., U.S. **C2** 120
Big Stone, co., Mn., U.S. **E2** 100
Big Stone City, S.D., U.S. **B9** 118
Big Stone Gap, Va., U.S. **f9** 123
Big Stone Lake, l., U.S. **E2** 100
Big Sunflower, stm., Ms., U.S. **B3** 101
Big Thompson, stm., Co., U.S. **A5** 83
Big Timber, Mt., U.S. **E7** 103
Big Trout Lake, l., Ont., Can. **n17** 73
Big Walnut Creek, stm., Oh., U.S. **m11** 112
Big Wood, stm., Id., U.S. **F4** 89
Bihać, Bos. **E10** 14
Bihār, India **H11** 38
Bihār, state, India **H11** 38
Biharamulo, Tan. **B6** 44
Bihoro, Japan **p22** 30a
Bija, stm., Russia **G11** 24
Bijāpur, India **C6** 37
Bījāpur, India **D3** 37
Bijsk, Russia **G11** 24
Bīkaner, India **F5** 38
Bikin, Russia **H20** 24
Bikoro, Zaire **B3** 44
Bilāspur, India **I10** 38
Bila Tserkva, Ukr. **H4** 22
Bilauktaung Range, mts., Asia **G5** 34
Bilbao, Spain **B9** 12
Bilimora, India **B2** 37
Bilk Creek Mountains, mts., Nv., U.S. **B3** 105
Billerica, Ma., U.S. **A5** 98
Billings, Mo., U.S. **D4** 102
Billings, Mt., U.S. **E8** 103
Billings, co., N.D., U.S. **B2** 111
Billings Heights, Mt., U.S. **E8** 103
Bill Williams, stm., Az., U.S. **C1** 80
Bill Williams Mountain, mtn., Az., U.S. **B3** 80
Bilma, Niger **E8** 42
Biloxi, Ms., U.S. **E5** 101
Biloxi, stm., Ms., U.S. **E4** 101
Biloxi Bay, b., Ms., U.S. **f8** 101
Biltmore Forest, N.C., U.S. **f10** 110
Bimini Islands, is., Bah. **B8** 64
Bīna-Etāwa, India **H8** 38
Bindura, Zimb. **E6** 44
Binéfar, Spain **D12** 12
Binga, Monte, mtn., Afr. **E6** 44
Bingamon Creek, stm., W.V., U.S. **k10** 125
Bingen, Ger. **F7** 8
Bingen, Wa., U.S. **D4** 124
Binger, Ok., U.S. **B3** 113
Bingham, Me., U.S. **C3** 96
Bingham, co., Id., U.S. **F6** 89
Binghamton, N.Y., U.S. **C5** 109
Binhai (Dongkan), China **A8** 28
Binjai, Indon. **M5** 34
Bintimani, mtn., S.L. **G3** 42
Biograd, Cro. **F10** 14
Bioko, i., Eq. Gui. **H7** 42
Bīr, India **C3** 37
Birao, Cen. Afr. Rep. **F10** 42
Birātnagar, Nepal **G12** 38
Birch, stm., W.V., U.S. **C4** 125
Birch Island, i., Man., Can. **C2** 70
Birch Lake, l., Mn., U.S. **C7** 100
Birch River, Man., Can. **C1** 70
Birch Run, Mi., U.S. **E7** 99
Birchwood City, Md., U.S. ***f9** 97
Birchy Bay, Newf., Can. **D4** 72
Bird Creek, stm., Ok., U.S. **A6** 113
Bird Island, Mn., U.S. **F4** 100
Bird Island, i., N.C., U.S. **D4** 110
Birdsboro, Pa., U.S. **F10** 115
Birdum, Austl. **C6** 50
Birecik, Tur. **A5** 40
Bīrganj, Nepal **G11** 38
Birigui, Braz. **F3** 57
Biril'ussy, Russia **F12** 24
Bīrjand, Iran **K9** 22
Birkenfeld, Ger. **F7** 8
Birkenhead, Eng., U.K. **H9** 7
Bîrlad, Rom. **C11** 16
Birmingham, Eng., U.K. **I11** 7
Birmingham, Al., U.S. **B3** 78
Birmingham, Mi., U.S. **F7** 99
Birmitrapur, India **I11** 38
Bir Mogreïn, Maur. **C3** 42
Birobidžan, Russia **H20** 24
Biron, Wi., U.S. **D4** 126
Birr, Ire. **H5** 7
Bi'r Safājah, Egypt **C12** 42
Birtle, Man., Can. **D1** 70
Bisbee, Az., U.S. **F6** 80
Biscarrosse, Fr. **H5** 10
Biscay, Bay of, b., Eur. **G7** 4
Biscayne, Key, i., Fl., U.S. **s13** 86
Biscayne Bay, b., Fl., U.S. **G6** 86
Biscayne National Monument, Fl., U.S. **G6** 86
Biscayne Park, Fl., U.S. **s13** 86
Bisceglie, Italy **H11** 14
Bischofshofen, Aus. **H13** 8
Biscoe, N.C., U.S. **B3** 110
Bishnupur, India **I12** 38
Bishop, Ca., U.S. **D4** 82
Bishop, Tx., U.S. **F4** 120
Bishop Auckland, Eng., U.K. **G11** 7
Bishop's Falls, Newf., Can. **D4** 72
Bishopville, S.C., U.S. **C7** 117
Biškek (Bishkek), Kyrg. **I12** 22
Biskra, Alg. **B7** 42
Bismarck, Il., U.S. **C6** 90
Bismarck, Mo., U.S. **D7** 102
Bismarck, N.D., U.S. **C5** 111
Bismarck Archipelago, is., Pap. N. Gui. **m16** 50a
Bismarck Range, mts., Pap. N. Gui. **m15** 50a
Bison Peak, mtn., Co., U.S. **B5** 83
Bissau, Gui.-B. **F2** 42
Bistineau, Lake, res., La., U.S. **B2** 95
Bistrița, Rom. **B8** 16
Bitola, Mac. **H5** 16
Bitonto, Italy **H11** 14
Bitter Creek, stm., Wy., U.S. **E4** 127
Bitterfeld, Ger. **D12** 8
Bitterfontein, S. Afr. **H3** 44
Bitter Lake, l., S.D., U.S. **B8** 118
Bitterroot, stm., Mt., U.S. **D2** 103
Bitterroot Range, mts., U.S. **B3** 89
Bitti, Italy **I4** 14
Biwabik, Mn., U.S. **C6** 100
Biwa-ko, l., Japan **G9** 30
Bixby, Ok., U.S. **B6** 113
Biyang, China **C2** 28
Bizen, Japan **H7** 30
Bizerte, Tun. **L4** 14
Bjelovar, Cro. **D11** 14
Black (Lixian) (Da), stm., Asia **D8** 34
Black, stm., Az., U.S. **D5** 80
Black, stm., Ar., U.S. **B4** 81
Black, stm., La., U.S. **C4** 95
Black, stm., Mi., U.S. **E8** 99
Black, stm., N.Y., U.S. **B4** 109
Black, stm., N.C., U.S. **C4** 110
Black, stm., S.C., U.S. **D8** 117
Black, stm., Vt., U.S. **B4** 122
Black, stm., Vt., U.S. **E3** 122
Black, stm., Wi., U.S. **D3** 126
Blackall, Austl. **D9** 50
Black Bear Creek, stm., Ok., U.S. **A4** 113
Blackbeard Island, i., Ga., U.S. **E5** 87
Blackburn, Eng., U.K. **H10** 7
Blackburn, Mount, mtn., Ak., U.S. **C11** 79
Black Butte, mtn., Mt., U.S. **F5** 103
Black Butte Lake, res., Ca., U.S. **C2** 82
Black Canyon, val., Co., U.S. **C3** 83
Black Canyon City, Az., U.S. **C3** 80
Black Canyon of the Gunnison National Monument, Co., U.S. **C3** 83
Black Creek, B.C., Can. **E5** 69
Black Creek, Wi., U.S. **D5** 126
Black Creek, stm., U.S. **B1** 108
Black Creek, stm., S.C., U.S. **B7** 117
Black Diamond, Alta., Can. **D3** 68
Black Diamond, Wa., U.S. **B4** 124
Blackduck, Mn., U.S. **C4** 100
Black Eagle, Mt., U.S. **C5** 103
Black Earth, Wi., U.S. **E4** 126
Blackfalds, Alta., Can. **C4** 68
Blackfeet Indian Reservation, Mt., U.S. **B4** 103
Blackfoot, Id., U.S. **F6** 89
Blackfoot, stm., Mt., U.S. **C3** 103
Blackfoot Mountains, mts., Id., U.S. **F7** 89
Blackfoot Reservoir, res., Id., U.S. **G7** 89
Blackford, co., In., U.S. **D7** 91
Black Forest, Co., U.S. **C6** 83
Black Forest see Schwarzwald, mts., Ger. **G8** 8
Blackhall Mountain, mtn., Wy., U.S. **E6** 127
Black Hawk, S.D., U.S. **C2** 118
Black Hawk, co., Ia., U.S. **B5** 92
Black Hills, mts., U.S. **C2** 118
Blackjack Mountain, mtn., Ga., U.S. **h8** 87
Black Lake, Que., Can. **C6** 74
Black Lake, l., Mi., U.S. **C6** 99
Black Lake, l., N.Y., U.S. **f9** 109
Black Lick, Pa., U.S. **F3** 115
Blacklick Estates, Oh., U.S. ***m11** 112
Black Mesa, mtn., Ok., U.S. **e8** 113
Black Mingo Creek, stm., S.C., U.S. **D9** 117
Blackmore, Mount, mtn., Mt., U.S. **E6** 103
Black Mountain, N.C., U.S. **f10** 110
Black Mountain, mtn., U.S. **D7** 94
Black Mountain, mtn., Az., U.S. **E4** 80
Black Mountain, mtn., Co., U.S. **A5** 83
Black Mountain, mtn., Id., U.S. **C3** 89
Black Mountain, mtn., Mt., U.S. **D4** 103
Black Mountain, mtn., Or., U.S. **B7** 114
Black Mountain, mtn., Wy., U.S. **B5** 127
Black Mountains, mts., Az., U.S. **B1** 80
Black Peak, mtn., Az., U.S. **C1** 80
Black Pine Peak, mtn., Id., U.S. **G5** 89
Blackpool, Eng., U.K. **H9** 7
Black Range, mts., N.M., U.S. **D2** 108
Black River Falls, Wi., U.S. **D3** 126
Black Rock, Ar., U.S. **A4** 81
Black Rock, N.M., U.S. **B1** 108
Black Rock Desert, des., Nv., U.S. **B3** 105
Black Rock Range, mts., Nv., U.S. **B3** 105
Blacksburg, S.C., U.S. **A4** 117
Blacksburg, Va., U.S. **C2** 123
Black Sea **G14** 4
Blacks Fork, stm., U.S. **E3** 127
Blacks Harbour, N.B., Can. **D3** 71
Blackshear, Ga., U.S. **E4** 87
Blackstone, Ma., U.S. **B4** 98
Blackstone, Va., U.S. **C5** 123
Blackstone, stm., R.I., U.S. **B4** 116
Black Thunder Creek, stm., Wy., U.S. **C8** 127
Blackville, N.B., Can. **C4** 71
Blackville, S.C., U.S. **E5** 117
Black Volta (Volta Noire), stm., Afr. **G5** 42
Blackwalnut Point, c., Md., U.S. **C5** 97
Black Warrior, stm., Al., U.S. **C2** 78
Blackwater, stm., Fl., U.S. **u15** 86
Blackwater, stm., Md., U.S. **D5** 97
Blackwater, stm., N.H., U.S. **D3** 106
Blackwater, stm., Va., U.S. **D6** 123
Blackwater Reservoir, res., N.H., U.S. **D3** 106
Blackwell, Ok., U.S. **A4** 113
Blackwood, N.J., U.S. **D2** 107
Bladen, co., N.C., U.S. **C4** 110
Bladenboro, N.C., U.S. **C4** 110
Bladensburg, Md., U.S. **f9** 97
Blades, De., U.S. **F3** 85
Blagoevgrad, Bul. **G7** 16
Blagoveščensk, Russia **G19** 24
Blaine, Me., U.S. **B5** 96
Blaine, Mn., U.S. **m12** 100
Blaine, Tn., U.S. **C10** 119
Blaine, Wa., U.S. **A3** 124
Blaine, co., Id., U.S. **F4** 89
Blaine, co., Mt., U.S. **B7** 103
Blaine, co., Ne., U.S. **C6** 104
Blaine, co., Ok., U.S. **B3** 113
Blaine Lake, Sask., Can. **E2** 75
Blair, Ne., U.S. **C9** 104
Blair, Ok., U.S. **C2** 113
Blair, W.V., U.S. **n12** 125
Blair, Wi., U.S. **D2** 126
Blair, co., Pa., U.S. **E5** 115
Blair Athol, Austl. **D9** 50
Blairstown, Ia., U.S. **C5** 92
Blairsville, Pa., U.S. **F3** 115
Blake Island, i., Wa., U.S. **e11** 124
Blakely, Ga., U.S. **E2** 87
Blakely, Pa., U.S. **m18** 115
Blake Point, c., Mi., U.S. **h10** 99
Blanc, Cap, c., Afr. **D2** 42
Blanc, Mont (Monte Bianco), mtn., Eur. **G13** 10
Blanca Peak, mtn., Co., U.S. **D5** 83
Blanchard, La., U.S. **B2** 95
Blanchard, Ok., U.S. **B4** 113
Blanchard, stm., Oh., U.S. **A1** 112
Blanchardville, Wi., U.S. **F4** 126
Blanchester, Oh., U.S. **C2** 112

Index

Name — Map Ref — Page

Blanco, Tx., U.S. D3 120
Blanco, co., Tx., U.S. D3 120
Blanco, Cape, c., Or., U.S. E2 114
Bland, Mo., U.S. C6 102
Bland, co., Va., U.S. C1 123
Blanding, Ut., U.S. F6 121
Blandinsville, Il., U.S. C3 90
Blanes, Spain D14 12
Blangkedjeren, Indon. M4 34
Blangy-sur-Bresle, Fr. C8 10
Blanquilla, Isla, i., Ven. B10 58
Blantyre, Mwi. E7 44
Blasdell, N.Y., U.S. C2 109
Blawnox, Pa., U.S. k14 115
Blaye-et-Sainte-Luce, Fr. G6 10
Bleckley, co., Ga., U.S. D3 87
Bled, Slo. C9 14
Bledsoe, co., Tn., U.S. D8 119
Blende, Co., U.S. C6 83
Blenheim, Ont., Can. E3 73
Blenheim, N.Z. D4 52
Blennerhassett, W.V., U.S. B3 125
Bléré, Fr. E7 10
Blida, Alg. A6 42
Blind, stm., La., U.S. h10 95
Blind River, Ont., Can. A2 73
Blissfield, Mi., U.S. G7 99
Blitar, Indon. n16 32
Block Island, R.I., U.S. h7 116
Block Island, i., R.I., U.S. h7 116
Block Island Sound, strt., U.S. G2 116
Bloemfontein, S. Afr. G5 44
Bloemhof, S. Afr. G5 44
Blois, Fr. E8 10
Blood Mountain, mtn., Ga., U.S. B3 87
Bloodsworth Island, i., Md., U.S. D5 97
Bloodvein, stm., Can. D3 70
Bloody Foreland, c., Ire. F4 7
Bloomer, Wi., U.S. C2 126
Bloomfield, Ont., Can. D7 73
Bloomfield, Ct., U.S. B5 84
Bloomfield, In., U.S. F4 91
Bloomfield, Ia., U.S. D5 92
Bloomfield, Ky., U.S. C4 94
Bloomfield, Mo., U.S. E8 102
Bloomfield, Ne., U.S. B8 104
Bloomfield, N.J., U.S. h8 107
Bloomfield, N.M., U.S. A2 108
Bloomfield Hills, Mi., U.S. o15 99
Bloomingdale, Ga., U.S. D5 87
Bloomingdale, Il., U.S. k8 90
Bloomingdale, N.J., U.S. A4 107
Bloomingdale, Tn., U.S. C11 119
Blooming Prairie, Mn., U.S. G5 100
Bloomington, Il., U.S. C4 90
Bloomington, In., U.S. F4 91
Bloomington, Mn., U.S. F5 100
Bloomington, Tx., U.S. E4 120
Bloomington, Wi., U.S. F3 126
Bloomington, Lake, res., Il., U.S. C5 90
Bloomsburg, Pa., U.S. E9 115
Bloomville, Oh., U.S. A2 112
Blora, Indon. m15 33a
Blossburg, Pa., U.S. C7 115
Blossom, Tx., U.S. C5 120
Blount, co., Al., U.S. B3 78
Blount, co., Tn., U.S. D10 119
Blountstown, Fl., U.S. B1 86
Blountsville, Al., U.S. A3 78
Blountville, Tn., U.S. C11 119
Blowing Rock, N.C., U.S. A1 110
Bludenz, Aus. H9 8
Blue, stm., Co., U.S. B4 83
Blue, stm., In., U.S. H5 91
Blue, stm., Mo., U.S. k10 102
Blue, stm., Ok., U.S. C5 113
Blue Ash, Oh., U.S. o13 112
Blue Buck Point, c., La., U.S. E2 95
Blue Creek, W.V., U.S. m13 125
Blue Creek, stm., W.V., U.S. m13 125
Blue Cypress Lake, l., Fl., U.S. E6 86
Blue Diamond, Nv., U.S. G6 105
Blue Earth, Mn., U.S. G4 100
Blue Earth, co., Mn., U.S. G4 100
Blue Earth, stm., Mn., U.S. G4 100
Bluefield, Va., U.S. C1 123
Bluefield, W.V., U.S. D3 125
Bluefields, Nic. H6 64
Blue Grass, Ia., U.S. C7 92
Blue Hill, Me., U.S. D4 96
Blue Hill, Ne., U.S. D7 104
Blue Hill Range, hills, Ma., U.S. h11 98
Blue Hills, Ct., U.S. B5 84
Blue Island, Il., U.S. B6 90
Bluejoint Lake, l., Or., U.S. E7 114
Blue Lake, Ca., U.S. B2 82
Blue Mesa Reservoir, res., Co., U.S. C3 83
Blue Mound, Il., U.S. D4 90
Blue Mountain, Ms., U.S. A4 101
Blue Mountain, mtn., Mt., U.S. C12 103
Blue Mountain, mtn., N.M., U.S. D2 108
Blue Mountain, mtn., Pa., U.S. F6 115
Blue Mountain Lake, res., Ar., U.S. B2 81
Blue Mountain Peak, mtn., Jam. E9 64
Blue Nile (Al-Bahr al-Azraq), stm., Afr. F12 42
Blue Point, Me., U.S. g7 96
Blue Rapids, Ks., U.S. C7 93
Blue Ridge, Ga., U.S. B2 87
Blue Ridge, Va., U.S. C3 123
Blue Ridge, mtn., U.S. E10 76
Blue Ridge Summit, Pa., U.S. G7 115
Blue Springs, Mo., U.S. h11 102
Bluestone, stm., W.V., U.S. D3 125
Bluestone Lake, res., U.S. D4 125
Bluewell, W.V., U.S. D3 125
Bluff City, Tn., U.S. C11 119
Bluff Creek, stm., Ok., U.S. A4 113
Bluff Lake, res., Ms., U.S. B5 101
Bluff Park, Al., U.S. g7 78
Bluffs, Il., U.S. D3 90
Bluffton, In., U.S. C7 91
Bluffton, Oh., U.S. B2 112
Bluffton, S.C., U.S. G6 117
Blumenau, Braz. B7 56
Bly, Or., U.S. E5 114
Blying Sound, strt., Ak., U.S. h17 79
Blyth, Ont., Can. D3 73
Blyth, Eng., U.K. F11 7
Blythe, Ca., U.S. F6 82
Blytheville, Ar., U.S. B6 81
Bø, Nor. B10 6
Bø, Nor. G7 6
Bo, S.L. G3 42
Boaco, Nic. H5 64
Boalsburg, Pa., U.S. E6 115
Boa Nova, Braz. C8 57
Boardman, Oh., U.S. A5 112
Boardman, Or., U.S. B7 114
Boa Vista, Braz. C6 54
Boavita, Col. D6 58
Boaz, Al., U.S. A3 78
Bobbili, India C7 37
Bobbio, Italy E4 14
Bobcaygeon, Ont., Can. C6 73
Böblingen, Ger. G9 8
Bobo Dioulasso, Burkina F5 42
Bobrujsk, Bela. H12 18
Bobtown, Pa., U.S. G2 115
Bobures, Ven. C7 58
Boby, Pic, mtn., Madag. F9 44
Boca Chica Key, i., Fl., U.S. H5 86
Boca Ciega Bay, b., Fl., U.S. p10 86
Bôca do Acre, Braz. E5 54
Boca Grande, Fl., U.S. F4 86
Boca Raton, Fl., U.S. F6 86
Bocas del Toro, Pan. J6 64
Bocholt, Ger. D6 8
Bochum, Ger. D7 8
Bodajbo, Russia F16 24
Bodega Head, c., Ca., U.S. C2 82
Bodele, reg., Chad E9 42
Boden, Swe. D13 6
Bodensee, l., Eur. H9 8
Bodhan, India C4 37
Bodie Island, i., N.C., U.S. B7 110
Bodināyakkanūr, India G4 37
Bodkin Point, c., Md., U.S. B5 97
Bodø, Nor. C10 6
Boende, Zaire B4 44
Boën-sur-Lignon, Fr. G10 10
Boerne, Tx., U.S. E3 120
Boeuf, stm., La., U.S. C4 95
Boeuf, Lake, l., La., U.S. k10 95
Bogale, Mya. F3 34
Bogalusa, La., U.S. D6 95
Bogart, Ga., U.S. C3 87
Bogata, Tx., U.S. C5 120
Bogenfels, Nmb. G3 44
Boger City, N.C., U.S. B1 110
Bognes, Nor. B10 6
Bogor, Indon. m13 32
Bogorodick, Russia H21 18
Bogorodsk, Russia E26 18
Bogota, N.J., U.S. h8 107
Bogotá see Santa Fe de Bogotá, Col. E5 58
Bogotol, Russia F11 24
Bogra, Bngl. H13 38
Bogučany, Russia F13 24
Bogue Chitto, Ms., U.S. D3 101
Bogue Chitto, stm., U.S. D5 95
Bogue Inlet, b., N.C., U.S. C5 110
Bogue Phalia, stm., Ms., U.S. B3 101
Bo Hai, b., China D10 26
Bohain-en-Vermandois, Fr. C10 10
Bohemia see Čechy, hist. reg., Czech. F14 8
Bohemian Forest, mts., Eur. F12 8
Bohol, i., Phil. D7 32
Boiano, Italy H9 14
Boigu, i., Austl. A8 50
Boiling Springs, N.C., U.S. B1 110
Boiling Springs, Pa., U.S. F7 115
Bois Blanc Island, i., Mi., U.S. C6 99
Bois Brule, stm., Wi., U.S. B2 126
Boischâtel, Que., Can. C6 74
Bois-des-Filion, Que., Can. p19 74
Bois de Sioux, stm., Mn., U.S. E2 100
Boise, Id., U.S. F2 89
Boise, co., Id., U.S. F3 89
Boise City, Ok., U.S. e8 113
Boissevain, Man., Can. E1 70
Boissevain, Va., U.S. e10 123
Boistfort Peak, mtn., Wa., U.S. C2 124
Boizenburg, Ger. B10 8
Bojador, Cabo, c., W. Sah. C3 42
Bojeador, Cape, c., Phil. B7 32
Bojnūrd, Iran J9 22
Bojonegoro, Indon. m15 33a
Boké, Gui. F3 42
Boketu, China B11 26
Boknafjorden, Nor. G5 6
Boksitogorsk, Russia B16 18
Bokungu, Zaire B4 44
Bolama, Gui.-B. F2 42
Bolbec, Fr. C7 10
Bolesławiec, Pol. D15 8
Boley, Ok., U.S. B5 113
Bolgatanga, Ghana F5 42
Boli, China B13 26
Bolingbrook, Il., U.S. k8 90
Bolívar, Arg. D4 56
Bolivar, Mo., U.S. D4 102
Bolivar, Oh., U.S. B4 112
Bolivar, Tn., U.S. B3 119
Bolivar, W.V., U.S. B7 125
Bolivar, co., Ms., U.S. B3 101
Bolívar, Cerro, mtn., Ven. D11 58
Bolivar, Lake, l., Ms., U.S. B3 101
Bolívar, Pico, mtn., Ven. C7 58
Bolivia, ctry., S.A. G5 54
Bollène, Fr. H11 10
Bollinger, co., Mo., U.S. D7 102
Bollnäs, Swe. F11 6
Bollullos par del Condado, Spain H5 12
Bolobo, Zaire B3 44
Bologna, Italy E6 14
Bologoje, Russia D17 18
Bolotnoje, Russia F10 24
Bolsena, Italy G6 14
Bol'šereck, Russia G25 24
Bol'ševik, Russia E23 24
Bol'ševik, Ostrov, i., Russia B14 24
Bol'šoj An'uj, stm., Russia D26 24
Bol'šoj Begičev, Ostrov, i., Russia C16 24
Bol'šoj L'achovskij, Ostrov, i., Russia C22 24
Bolton, Eng., U.K. H10 7
Bolton, Ms., U.S. C3 101
Bolton Lakes, l., Ct., U.S. B6 84
Bolton Landing, N.Y., U.S. B7 109
Bolzano (Bozen), Italy C6 14
Boma, Zaire C2 44
Bombala, Austl. G9 50
Bombarral, Port. F2 12
Bombay, India C2 37
Bombay Hook Island, i., De., U.S. C4 85
Bom Despacho, Braz. E6 57
Bom Jesus da Lapa, Braz. B7 57
Bomoseen, Lake, l., Vt., U.S. D2 122
Bomu (Mbomou), stm., Afr. H10 42
Bon, Cap, c., Tun. A8 42
Bon Accord, Alta., Can. C4 68
Bon Air, Va., U.S. C5 123
Bonaire, Ga., U.S. D3 87
Bonaire, i., Neth. Ant. H13 64
Bonanza Peak, mtn., Wa., U.S. A5 124
Bonao, Dom. Rep. E12 64
Bonaparte, Mount, mtn., Wa., U.S. A6 124
Bonaparte Archipelago, is., Austl. B5 50
Bonarbridge, Scot., U.K. D8 7
Bonasila Dome, mtn., Ak., U.S. C7 79
Bonaventure, Que., Can. A4 71
Bonavista, Newf., Can. D5 72
Bonavista, Cape, c., Newf., Can. D5 72
Bonavista Bay, b., Newf., Can. G22 66
Bonavista Bay, b., Newf., Can. D5 72
Bond, co., Il., U.S. E4 90
Bondeno, Italy E6 14
Bondo, Zaire H10 42
Bondoukou, C. Iv. G5 42
Bondowoso, Indon. m16 33a
Bondsville, Ma., U.S. B3 98
Bonduel, Wi., U.S. D5 126
Bondurant, Ia., U.S. C4 92
Bone, Teluk, b., Indon. F7 32
Bone Lake, l., Wi., U.S. C1 126
Bongandanga, Zaire A4 44
Bongor, Chad F9 42
Bonham, Tx., U.S. C4 120
Bon Homme, co., S.D., U.S. D8 118
Bonifati, Capo, c., Italy J10 14
Bonifay, Fl., U.S. u16 86
Bonita Springs, Fl., U.S. F5 86
Bonn, Ger. E7 8
Bonneauville, Pa., U.S. G7 115
Bonne Bay, b., Newf., Can. D3 72
Bonner, co., Id., U.S. A2 89
Bonners Ferry, Id., U.S. A2 89
Bonner Springs, Ks., U.S. C9 93
Bonnet Carre Floodway, La., U.S. h11 95
Bonne Terre, Mo., U.S. D7 102
Bonneval, Fr. D8 10
Bonneville, Fr. F13 10
Bonneville, co., Id., U.S. F7 89
Bonneville Dam, U.S. B4 114
Bonneville Peak, mtn., Id., U.S. F6 89
Bonneville Salt Flats, pl., Ut., U.S. C2 121
Bonney Lake, Wa., U.S. B3 124
Bonnie Doone, N.C., U.S. B4 110
Bonny Reservoir, res., Co., U.S. B8 83
Bonnyville, Alta., Can. B5 68
Bono, Ar., U.S. B5 81
Bonorva, Italy I3 14
Bon Secour, Al., U.S. E2 78
Bonthe, S.L. G3 42
Booker, Tx., U.S. A2 120
Booker T. Washington National Monument, Va., U.S. C3 123
Boomer, W.V., U.S. C3 125
Boone, Ia., U.S. B4 92
Boone, N.C., U.S. A1 110
Boone, co., Ar., U.S. A2 81
Boone, co., Il., U.S. A5 90
Boone, co., In., U.S. D4 91
Boone, co., Ia., U.S. B3 92
Boone, co., Ky., U.S. B5 94
Boone, co., Mo., U.S. B5 102
Boone, co., Ne., U.S. C7 104
Boone, co., W.V., U.S. C3 125
Boone, stm., Ia., U.S. B4 92
Boone Lake, res., Tn., U.S. C11 119
Booneville, Ar., U.S. B2 81
Booneville, Ms., U.S. A5 101
Boonsboro, Md., U.S. A2 97
Boonton, N.J., U.S. B4 107
Boonville, In., U.S. H3 91
Boonville, Mo., U.S. C5 102
Boonville, N.Y., U.S. B5 109
Boonville, N.C., U.S. A2 110
Boothbay Harbor, Me., U.S. E3 96
Boothia, Gulf of, b., N.W. Ter., Can. B14 66
Boothia Peninsula, pen., N.W. Ter., Can. B14 66
Booths Creek, stm., W.V., U.S. h11 125
Boothville, La., U.S. E6 95
Booué, Gabon B2 44
Boquete, Pan. J6 64
Boquillas del Carmen, Mex. C8 62
Bor, Russia E27 18
Bor, Sudan G12 42
Boraha, Nosy, i., Madag. E9 44
Borah Peak, mtn., Id., U.S. E5 89
Borås, Swe. H9 6
Bordeaux, Fr. H6 10
Borden, co., Tx., U.S. C2 120
Borden Peninsula, pen., N.W. Ter., Can. B16 66
Bordentown, N.J., U.S. C3 107
Bordertown, Austl. G8 50
Borgå (Porvoo), Fin. F15 6
Borgarnes, Ice. C3 4
Borger, Tx., U.S. B2 120
Borgne, Lake, b., La., U.S. D6 95
Borgo, Italy C6 14
Borgo San Dalmazzo, Italy E2 14
Borgosesia, Italy D3 14
Borgo Val di Taro, Italy E4 14
Borisov, Bela. G11 18
Borja, Spain D10 12
Borjas Blancas, Spain D12 12
Borken, Ger. D6 8
Borlänge, Swe. F10 6
Borlu, Tur. K12 16
Borneo (Kalimantan), i., Asia E5 32
Bornholm, i., Den. I10 6
Bornova, Tur. K11 16
Borogoncy, Russia E20 24
Boron, Ca., U.S. E5 82
Boronga Islands, is., Mya. E2 34
Boroviči, Russia C16 18
Borrego Springs, Ca., U.S. F5 82
Bort-les-Orgues, Fr. G9 10
Borūjerd, Iran B4 46
Borz'a, Russia G17 24
Bosa, Italy I3 14
Bosanska Gradiška, Bos. D12 14
Bosanska Krupa, Bos. E11 14
Bosanski Novi, Bos. D11 14
Bosanski Petrovac, Bos. E11 14
Bosaso, Som. F4 46
Boscobel, Wi., U.S. E3 126
Boshan, China D10 26
Bosnia and Herzegovina, ctry., Eur. E12 14
Bosporus see İstanbul Boğazı, strt., Tur. H13 16
Bosque, co., Tx., U.S. D4 120
Bossangoa, Cen. Afr. Rep. G9 42
Bossembélé, Cen. Afr. Rep. G9 42
Bossier, co., La., U.S. B2 95
Bossier City, La., U.S. B2 95
Bosten Hu, l., China C4 26
Boston, Eng., U.K. I12 7
Boston, Ga., U.S. F3 87
Boston, Ma., U.S. B5 98
Boston Bay, b., Ma., U.S. B6 98
Boston Mountains, mts., Ar., U.S. B2 81
Boswell, In., U.S. C3 91
Boswell, Ok., U.S. C6 113
Boswell, Pa., U.S. F3 115
Botād, India I4 38
Boteti, stm., Bots. F4 44
Botetourt, co., Va., U.S. C3 123
Bothell, Wa., U.S. B3 124
Bothnia, Gulf of, b., Eur. E12 6
Bothwell, Ont., Can. E3 73
Botkins, Oh., U.S. B1 112
Botoșani, Rom. B10 16
Botswana, ctry., Afr. F4 44
Bottenhavet (Selkämeri), b., Eur. F12 6
Bottenviken (Perämeri), b., Eur. D14 6
Bottineau, N.D., U.S. A5 111
Bottineau, co., N.D., U.S. A4 111
Botucatu, Braz. G4 57
Botwood, Newf., Can. D4 72
Bouaflé, C. Iv. G4 42
Bouaké, C. Iv. G4 42
Bouar, Cen. Afr. Rep. G9 42
Bou Arada, Tun. M4 14
Boucherville, Que., Can. D4 74
Bouctouche, N.B., Can. C5 71
Boudreaux, Lake, l., La., U.S. E5 95
Bou Ficha, Tun. M5 14
Bougainville Reef, rf., Austl. C9 50
Bougouni, Mali F4 42
Bouillon, Bel. F5 8
Boulder, Co., U.S. A5 83
Boulder, Mt., U.S. D4 103
Boulder, co., Co., U.S. A5 83
Boulder City, Nv., U.S. H7 105
Boulevard Heights, Md., U.S. f9 97
Boulogne-Billancourt, Fr. D9 10
Boulogne-sur-Gesse, Fr. I7 10
Boulogne-sur-Mer, Fr. B8 10
Bouna, C. Iv. G5 42
Boundary, co., Id., U.S. A2 89
Boundary Bay, b., Wa., U.S. A3 124
Boundary Peak, mtn., Nv., U.S. F3 105
Bound Brook, N.J., U.S. B3 107
Bountiful, Ut., U.S. C4 121
Bourbeuse, stm., Mo., U.S. C6 102
Bourbon, In., U.S. B5 91
Bourbon, Mo., U.S. C6 102
Bourbon, co., Ks., U.S. E9 93
Bourbon, co., Ky., U.S. B5 94
Bourbonnais, Il., U.S. B6 90
Bourbonnais, hist. reg., Fr. F9 10
Bourbonne-les-Bains, Fr. E12 10
Bourem, Mali E5 42
Bourg, La., U.S. E5 95
Bourganeuf, Fr. G8 10
Bourg-en-Bresse, Fr. F12 10
Bourges, Fr. E9 10
Bourg-Lastic, Fr. G9 10
Bourgogne, hist. reg., Fr. E11 10
Bourgoin, Fr. G12 10
Bourg-Saint-Andéol, Fr. H11 10
Bourg-Saint-Maurice, Fr. G13 10
Bourke, Austl. F9 50
Bournemouth, Eng., U.K. K11 7
Bou Saâda, Alg. A6 42
Bouse, Az., U.S. D2 80
Boussac, Fr. F9 10
Bousso, Chad F9 42
Boutte, La., U.S. k11 95
Bøvågen, Nor. F5 6
Bovalino Marina, Italy K11 14
Bovec, Slo. C8 14
Bøverdal, Nor. F7 6
Bovey, Mn., U.S. C5 100
Bovina, Tx., U.S. B1 120
Bow, N.H., U.S. D3 106
Bow, stm., Alta., Can. D4 68
Bowden, Alta., Can. D4 68
Bowdish Reservoir, res., R.I., U.S. B1 116
Bowdon, Ga., U.S. C1 87
Bowen, Austl. C9 50
Bowie, Az., U.S. E6 80
Bowie, Md., U.S. C4 97
Bowie, Tx., U.S. C4 120
Bowie, co., Tx., U.S. C5 120
Bow Island, Alta., Can. E5 68
Bow Lake, l., N.H., U.S. D4 106
Bowling Green, Fl., U.S. E5 86
Bowling Green, Ky., U.S. D3 94
Bowling Green, Mo., U.S. B6 102
Bowling Green, Oh., U.S. A2 112
Bowling Green, S.C., U.S. A5 117
Bowling Green, Va., U.S. B5 123
Bowman, Ga., U.S. B3 87
Bowman, N.D., U.S. C2 111
Bowman, S.C., U.S. E6 117
Bowman, co., N.D., U.S. C2 111
Bowman Creek, stm., Pa., U.S. m16 115
Bowman-Haley Lake, res., N.D., U.S. C2 111
Bowron, stm., B.C., Can. C7 69
Bowstring Lake, l., Mn., U.S. C5 100
Box Butte, co., Ne., U.S. B2 104
Box Butte Reservoir, res., Ne., U.S. B2 104
Box Elder, S.D., U.S. C2 118
Box Elder, co., Ut., U.S. B2 121
Boxford, Ma., U.S. A6 98
Boxian, China B4 28
Boyce, La., U.S. C3 95
Boyceville, Wi., U.S. C1 126
Boyd, Tx., U.S. C4 120
Boyd, co., Ky., U.S. B7 94
Boyd, co., Ne., U.S. B7 104
Boyden, Ia., U.S. A2 92
Boyd Lake, l., Me., U.S. C4 96
Boyer, stm., Ia., U.S. C2 92
Boyertown, Pa., U.S. F10 115
Boykins, Va., U.S. D5 123
Boyle, Alta., Can. B4 68
Boyle, Ire. H4 7
Boyle, Ms., U.S. B3 101
Boyle, co., Ky., U.S. C5 94
Boyne City, Mi., U.S. C6 99
Boynton Beach, Fl., U.S. F6 86
Boysen Reservoir, res., Wy., U.S. C4 127
Boys Town, Ne., U.S. g12 104
Bozburun, Tur. M12 16
Boz Dağ, mtn., Tur. L13 16
Bozeman, Mt., U.S. E5 103
Bozeman Pass, Mt., U.S. E6 103
Bozoum, Cen. Afr. Rep. G9 42
Bra, Italy E2 14
Bracciano, Italy G7 14
Bracebridge, Ont., Can. B5 73
Bräcke, Swe. E10 6
Bracken, co., Ky., U.S. B5 94
Brackenridge, Pa., U.S. h15 115
Brackettville, Tx., U.S. E2 120
Braddock, Pa., U.S. k14 115
Braddock Heights, Md., U.S. B2 97
Braddock Point, c., S.C., U.S. G6 117
Bradenton, Fl., U.S. E4 86
Bradenville, Pa., U.S. F3 115
Bradford, Eng., U.K. H11 7
Bradford, Ar., U.S. B4 81
Bradford, Oh., U.S. B1 112
Bradford, Pa., U.S. C4 115
Bradford, R.I., U.S. F2 116
Bradford, Tn., U.S. A3 119
Bradford, Vt., U.S. D4 122
Bradford, co., Fl., U.S. C4 86
Bradford, co., Pa., U.S. C8 115
Bradford [West Gwillimbury], Ont., Can. C5 73
Bradfordwoods, Pa., U.S. h13 115
Bradley, Il., U.S. B6 90
Bradley, Me., U.S. D4 96
Bradley, W.V., U.S. D3 125
Bradley, co., Ar., U.S. D3 81
Bradley, co., Tn., U.S. D9 119
Bradley Beach, N.J., U.S. C4 107
Bradner, Oh., U.S. A2 112
Bradshaw, Md., U.S. B5 97
Bradshaw Mountains, mts., Az., U.S. C3 80
Brady, Tx., U.S. D3 120
Braga, Port. D3 12
Bragado, Arg. D4 56
Bragança, Port. D5 12
Braham, Mn., U.S. E5 100
Brāhmanbāria, Bngl. I14 38
Brāhmani, stm., India J11 38
Brahmaputra (Yarlung), stm., Asia G15 38
Braich y Pwll, c., Wales, U.K. I8 7
Braidwood, Il., U.S. B5 90
Brăila, Rom. D11 16
Brainerd, Mn., U.S. D4 100
Braintree, Ma., U.S. B5 98
Brake, Ger. B8 8
Brampton, Ont., Can. D5 73
Bramsche, Ger. C7 8
Bramwell, W.V., U.S. D3 125
Branch, co., Mi., U.S. G5 99
Branch, stm., R.I., U.S. B3 116
Branch, stm., Wi., U.S. h10 126
Branch Lake, l., Me., U.S. D4 96
Branch Village, R.I., U.S. B3 116
Branchville, S.C., U.S. E6 117
Branco, stm., Braz. C6 54
Brandberg, mtn., Nmb. F2 44
Brandbu, Nor. F8 6
Brandenburg, Ger. C12 8
Brandenburg, Ky., U.S. C3 94
Brandon, Man., Can. E2 70
Brandon, Fl., U.S. E4 86
Brandon, Ms., U.S. C4 101
Brandon, S.C., U.S. B3 117
Brandon, S.D., U.S. D9 118
Brandon, Vt., U.S. D2 122
Brandon, Wi., U.S. E5 126
Brandvlei, S. Afr. H4 44
Brandy Peak, mtn., Or., U.S. E3 114
Brandywine, Md., U.S. C4 97
Brandywine Creek, stm., U.S. A3 85
Branford, Ct., U.S. D4 84
Branford Hills, Ct., U.S. D4 84
Br'ansk, Russia H17 18
Branson, Mo., U.S. E4 102
Brantford, Ont., Can. D4 73
Brantley, Al., U.S. D3 78
Brantley, co., Ga., U.S. E4 87
Brantôme, Fr. G7 10
Brant Rock, Ma., U.S. B6 98
Brantville, N.B., Can. B5 71
Bras d'Or Lake, l., N.S., Can. D9 71
Brasília, Braz. C5 57
Brașov, Rom. D9 16
Brasstown Bald, mtn., Ga., U.S. B3 87
Brassua Lake, res., Me., U.S. C3 96

Name	Map Ref	Page
Bratenahl, Oh., U.S.	g9	112
Bratislava, Slov.	G17	8
Bratsk, Russia	F14	24
Bratskoje Vodochranilišče, res., Russia	F14	24
Brattleboro, Vt., U.S.	F3	122
Braunau [am Inn], Aus.	G13	8
Braunschweig, Ger.	C10	8
Brava, Som.	H3	46
Brava, Costa, Spain	D15	12
Bravo del Norte (Rio Grande), stm., N.A.	F6	76
Brawley, Ca., U.S.	F6	82
Brawley Peaks, mts., Nv., U.S.	E3	105
Braxton, co., W.V., U.S.	C4	125
Bray, Ire.	H6	7
Bray, Ok., U.S.	C4	113
Bray Island, i., N.W. Ter., Can.	C17	66
Braymer, Mo., U.S.	B4	102
Brazeau, stm., Alta., Can.	C2	68
Brazil, In., U.S.	E3	91
Brazil, ctry., S.A.	E7	54
Brazoria, Tx., U.S.	r14	120
Brazoria, co., Tx., U.S.	E5	120
Brazos, co., Tx., U.S.	D4	120
Brazos, stm., Tx., U.S.	D4	120
Brazzaville, Congo	B3	44
Brčko, Bos.	E2	16
Brea, Ca., U.S.	n13	82
Breakenridge, Mount, mtn., B.C., Can.	E7	69
Breathitt, co., Ky., U.S.	C6	94
Breaux Bridge, La., U.S.	D4	95
Brebes, Indon.	m14	33a
Breckenridge, Co., U.S.	B4	83
Breckenridge, Mi., U.S.	E6	99
Breckenridge, Mn., U.S.	D2	100
Breckenridge, Tx., U.S.	C3	120
Breckinridge, co., Ky., U.S.	C3	94
Brecksville, Oh., U.S.	A4	112
Brecon Beacons National Park, Wales, U.K.	J9	7
Breda, Neth.	D4	8
Bredstedt, Ger.	A8	8
Breese, Il., U.S.	E4	90
Bréhal, Fr.	D5	10
Brekstad, Nor.	E7	6
Bremen, Ger.	B8	8
Bremen, Ga., U.S.	C1	87
Bremen, In., U.S.	B5	91
Bremen, Oh., U.S.	C3	112
Bremer, co., Ia., U.S.	B5	92
Bremerhaven, Ger.	B8	8
Bremerton, Wa., U.S.	B3	124
Bremond, Tx., U.S.	D4	120
Brenham, Tx., U.S.	D4	120
Brenner Pass, Eur.	B6	14
Breno, Italy	D5	14
Brent, Al., U.S.	C2	78
Brent, Fl., U.S.	u14	86
Brenton Point, c., R.I., U.S.	F5	116
Brentwood, Ca., U.S.	h9	82
Brentwood, Md., U.S.	f9	97
Brentwood, Mo., U.S.	f13	102
Brentwood, N.Y., U.S.	E7	109
Brentwood, Pa., U.S.	k14	115
Brentwood, S.C., U.S.	k11	117
Brentwood, Tn., U.S.	A5	119
Brescia, Italy	D5	14
Breslau see Wrocław, Pol.	D17	8
Bressanone, Italy	C6	14
Bressuire, Fr.	F6	10
Brest, Bela.	I6	18
Brest, Fr.	D2	10
Bretagne, hist. reg., Fr.	D3	10
Breton Islands, is., La., U.S.	E6	95
Breton Sound, strt., La., U.S.	E6	95
Brevard, N.C., U.S.	f10	110
Brevard, co., Fl., U.S.	E6	86
Brevoort Lake, l., Mi., U.S.	B6	99
Brewer, Me., U.S.	D4	96
Brewster, Ma., U.S.	C7	98
Brewster, N.Y., U.S.	D7	109
Brewster, Oh., U.S.	B4	112
Brewster, Wa., U.S.	A6	124
Brewster, co., Tx., U.S.	E1	120
Brewster Islands, is., Ma., U.S.	g12	98
Brewton, Al., U.S.	D2	78
Brežice, Slo.	D10	14
Bria, Cen. Afr. Rep.	G10	42
Brian Boru Peak, mtn., B.C., Can.	B4	69
Briançon, Fr.	H13	10
Brian Head, mtn., Ut., U.S.	F3	121
Briare, Fr.	E9	10
Briceville, Tn., U.S.	C9	119
Brick [Township], N.J., U.S.	C4	107
Bricquebec, Fr.	C5	10
Bridal Veil Falls, wtfl, Ut., U.S.	C4	121
Bridgehampton, N.Y., U.S.	n16	109
Bridgeport, Al., U.S.	A4	78
Bridgeport, Ct., U.S.	E3	84
Bridgeport, Il., U.S.	E6	90
Bridgeport, Mi., U.S.	E7	99
Bridgeport, Ne., U.S.	C2	104
Bridgeport, Oh., U.S.	B5	112
Bridgeport, Pa., U.S.	o20	115
Bridgeport, Tx., U.S.	C4	120
Bridgeport, Wa., U.S.	B6	124
Bridgeport, W.V., U.S.	B4	125
Bridger, Mt., U.S.	E8	103
Bridger Peak, mtn., Wy., U.S.	E5	127
Bridger Range, mts., Mt., U.S.	E6	103
Bridgeton, Mo., U.S.	C7	102
Bridgeton, N.J., U.S.	E2	107
Bridgetown, Barb.	H18	64
Bridgetown, N.S., Can.	E4	71
Bridgeville, De., U.S.	F3	85
Bridgeville, Pa., U.S.	k13	115
Bridgewater, Ma., U.S.	C6	98
Bridgewater, N.J., U.S.	B3	107
Bridgewater, Va., U.S.	B4	123
Bridgman, Mi., U.S.	G4	99
Bridgton, Me., U.S.	D2	96
Bridgwater, Eng., U.K.	J9	7
Bridlington, Eng., U.K.	G12	7
Briec, Fr.	D2	10
Brielle, N.J., U.S.	C4	107
Brienne-le-Château, Fr.	D11	10
Brienz, Switz.	F15	10
Brig, Switz.	F14	10
Brigantine, N.J., U.S.	E4	107
Brigantine Beach, N.J., U.S.	E4	107
Brigden, Ont., Can.	E2	73
Briggs Marsh, sw., R.I., U.S.	F6	116
Brigham City, Ut., U.S.	B3	121
Brighton, Ont., Can.	C7	73
Brighton, Eng., U.K.	K12	7
Brighton, Al., U.S.	B3	78
Brighton, Co., U.S.	B6	83
Brighton, Il., U.S.	D3	90
Brighton, Ia., U.S.	C6	92
Brighton, Mi., U.S.	F7	99
Brighton, N.Y., U.S.	B3	109
Brighton, Tn., U.S.	B2	119
Brighton Indian Reservation, Fl., U.S.	E5	86
Brihuega, Spain	E9	12
Brilliant, Al., U.S.	A2	78
Brilliant, Oh., U.S.	B5	112
Brillion, Wi., U.S.	D5	126
Brilon, Ger.	D8	8
Brimfield, Il., U.S.	C4	90
Brindisi, Italy	I12	14
Brinkley, Ar., U.S.	C4	81
Brinnon, Wa., U.S.	B3	124
Brioude, Fr.	G10	10
Brisbane, Austl.	E10	50
Briscoe, co., Tx., U.S.	B2	120
Bristol, N.B., Can.	C2	71
Bristol, Eng., U.K.	J10	7
Bristol, Ct., U.S.	C4	84
Bristol, In., U.S.	A6	91
Bristol, N.H., U.S.	C3	106
Bristol, R.I., U.S.	D5	116
Bristol, Tn., U.S.	C11	119
Bristol, Vt., U.S.	C2	122
Bristol, Va., U.S.	f9	123
Bristol, co., Ma., U.S.	C5	98
Bristol, co., R.I., U.S.	D5	116
Bristol Bay, b., Ak., U.S.	D7	79
Bristol Channel, strt., U.K.	J8	7
Bristol [Township], Pa., U.S.	F12	115
Bristow, Ok., U.S.	B5	113
British Columbia, prov., Can.	C6	69
British Honduras see Belize, ctry., N.A.	F3	64
British Indian Ocean Territory, dep., Afr.	G17	2
British Mountains, mts., N.A.	C5	66
British Solomon Islands see Solomon Islands, ctry., Oc.	G23	2
Britstown, S. Afr.	H4	44
Britt, Ia., U.S.	A4	92
Brittany see Bretagne, hist. reg., Fr.	D3	10
Britton, S.D., U.S.	B8	118
Brive-la-Gaillarde, Fr.	G8	10
Briviesca, Spain	C8	12
Brno, Czech.	F16	8
Broach, India	B2	37
Broad, stm., S.C., U.S.	C5	117
Broad Brook, Ct., U.S.	B5	84
Broadford, Scot., U.K.	D7	7
Broadkill, stm., De., U.S.	E4	85
Broadkill Beach, De., U.S.	E5	85
Broad Law, mtn., Scot., U.K.	F9	7
Broad Run, stm., Va., U.S.	g11	123
Broadus, Mt., U.S.	E11	103
Broadview Heights, Oh., U.S.	h9	112
Broadwater, co., Mt., U.S.	D5	103
Broadway, N.C., U.S.	B3	110
Broadway, Va., U.S.	B4	123
Brockport, N.Y., U.S.	B3	109
Brockton, Ma., U.S.	B5	98
Brockton Reservoir, res., Ma., U.S.	h11	98
Brockville, Ont., Can.	C9	73
Brockway, Pa., U.S.	D4	115
Brodeur Peninsula, pen., N.W. Ter., Can.	B15	66
Brodhead, Ky., U.S.	C5	94
Brodhead, Wi., U.S.	F4	126
Brodheadsville, Pa., U.S.	E11	115
Broken Arrow, Ok., U.S.	A6	113
Broken Bow, Ne., U.S.	C6	104
Broken Bow, Ok., U.S.	C7	113
Broken Bow Lake, res., Ok., U.S.	C7	113
Broken Hill, Austl.	F8	50
Brokopondo, Sur.	B8	54
Brome, Lac, l., Que., Can.	D5	74
Bromptonville, Que., Can.	D6	74
Bromsgrove, Eng., U.K.	I10	7
Bronlund Peak, mtn., B.C., Can.	E7	66
Brønnøysund, Nor.	D9	6
Bronson, Mi., U.S.	G5	99
Bronte, Italy	L9	14
Bronx, co., N.Y., U.S.	E7	109
Bronxville, N.Y., U.S.	h13	109
Brook, In., U.S.	C3	91
Brooke, co., W.V., U.S.	A4	125
Brookfield, N.S., Can.	D6	71
Brookfield, Ct., U.S.	D2	84
Brookfield, Il., U.S.	k9	90
Brookfield, Mo., U.S.	B4	102
Brookfield, Va., U.S.	*B5	123
Brookfield, Wi., U.S.	m11	126
Brookfield Center, Ct., U.S.	D2	84
Brookhaven, Ms., U.S.	D3	101
Brookhaven, W.V., U.S.	h11	125
Brookings, Or., U.S.	E2	114
Brookings, S.D., U.S.	C9	118
Brookings, co., S.D., U.S.	C9	118
Brookland, Ar., U.S.	B5	81
Brooklandville, Md., U.S.	g10	97
Brooklet, Ga., U.S.	D5	87
Brookline, Ma., U.S.	B5	98
Brooklyn, N.S., Can.	E5	71
Brooklyn, Ct., U.S.	B8	84
Brooklyn, In., U.S.	E5	91
Brooklyn, Ia., U.S.	C5	92
Brooklyn, Mi., U.S.	F6	99
Brooklyn, Ms., U.S.	D4	101
Brooklyn, Oh., U.S.	h9	112
Brooklyn, S.C., U.S.	B6	117
Brooklyn, Wi., U.S.	F4	126
Brooklyn Center, Mn., U.S.	E5	100
Brooklyn Park, Md., U.S.	h11	97
Brooklyn Park, Mn., U.S.	m12	100
Brookneal, Va., U.S.	C4	123
Brook Park, Oh., U.S.	h9	112
Brookport, Il., U.S.	F5	90
Brooks, Alta., Can.	D5	68
Brooks, Ky., U.S.	g11	94
Brooks, co., Ga., U.S.	F3	87
Brooks, co., Tx., U.S.	F3	120
Brooks Air Force Base, mil., Tx., U.S.	k7	120
Brookshire, Tx., U.S.	E5	120
Brookside, Al., U.S.	f7	78
Brookside, De., U.S.	B3	85
Brooks Range, mts., Ak., U.S.	B9	79
Brookston, In., U.S.	C4	91
Brooksville, Fl., U.S.	D4	86
Brooksville, Ky., U.S.	B5	94
Brooksville, Ms., U.S.	B5	101
Brookville, In., U.S.	F8	91
Brookville, Oh., U.S.	C1	112
Brookville, Pa., U.S.	D3	115
Brookville Lake, res., In., U.S.	E7	91
Brookwood, Al., U.S.	B2	78
Brookwood, N.J., U.S.	C4	107
Broomall, Pa., U.S.	p20	115
Broome, Austl.	C4	50
Broome, co., N.Y., U.S.	C5	109
Broomfield, Co., U.S.	B5	83
Broons, Fr.	D4	10
Brossard, Que., Can.	q20	74
Brou, Fr.	D8	10
Broussard, La., U.S.	D4	95
Broward, co., Fl., U.S.	F6	86
Browerville, Mn., U.S.	D4	100
Brown, co., Il., U.S.	D3	90
Brown, co., In., U.S.	F5	91
Brown, co., Ks., U.S.	C8	93
Brown, co., Mn., U.S.	F4	100
Brown, co., Ne., U.S.	B6	104
Brown, co., Oh., U.S.	D2	112
Brown, co., S.D., U.S.	B7	118
Brown, co., Tx., U.S.	D3	120
Brown, co., Wi., U.S.	D6	126
Brown, Point, c., Wa., U.S.	C1	124
Brown City, Mi., U.S.	E8	99
Brown Deer, Wi., U.S.	m12	126
Brownfield, Tx., U.S.	C1	120
Browning, Mt., U.S.	B3	103
Brownlee Dam, U.S.	E2	89
Brownlee Reservoir, res., U.S.	C10	114
Browns, stm., Vt., U.S.	B2	122
Browns Branch, stm., De., U.S.	E3	85
Brownsburg, Que., Can.	D3	74
Brownsburg, In., U.S.	E5	91
Brownsdale, Mn., U.S.	G6	100
Browns Inlet, b., N.C., U.S.	C5	110
Browns Mills, N.J., U.S.	D3	107
Browns Peak, mtn., Az., U.S.	D4	80
Brownstown, In., U.S.	G5	91
Browns Valley, Mn., U.S.	E2	100
Brownsville, Fl., U.S.	s13	86
Brownsville, Ky., U.S.	C3	94
Brownsville, Or., U.S.	C4	114
Brownsville, Pa., U.S.	F2	115
Brownsville, Tn., U.S.	B2	119
Brownsville, Tx., U.S.	G4	120
Brownton, Mn., U.S.	F4	100
Brownville Junction, Me., U.S.	C3	96
Brownwood, Tx., U.S.	D3	120
Brownwood, Lake, res., Tx., U.S.	D3	120
Broxton, Ga., U.S.	E4	87
Bruay-en-Artois, Fr.	B9	10
Bruce, Ms., U.S.	B4	101
Bruce, Wi., U.S.	C2	126
Bruce, Mount, mtn., Austl.	D3	50
Bruce National Park, Ont., Can.	B3	73
Bruce Peninsula, pen., Ont., Can.	B3	73
Bruceton, Tn., U.S.	A3	119
Bruchsal, Ger.	F8	8
Bruck an der Leitha, Aus.	H16	8
Bruck an der Mur, Aus.	H15	8
Bruderheim, Alta., Can.	C4	68
Brugge, Bel.	D3	8
Bruin Point, mtn., Ut., U.S.	D5	121
Brule, co., S.D., U.S.	D6	118
Brule, stm., U.S.	C5	126
Brule Lake, l., Mn., U.S.	k9	100
Brundidge, Al., U.S.	D4	78
Bruneau, stm., U.S.	G3	89
Brunei, ctry., Asia	E5	32
Brunico, Italy	C6	14
Brunkeberg, Nor.	G7	6
Bruno, Sask., Can.	E3	75
Brunsbüttel, Ger.	B9	8
Brunswick, Ga., U.S.	E5	87
Brunswick, Me., U.S.	E3	96
Brunswick, Md., U.S.	B2	97
Brunswick, Mo., U.S.	B4	102
Brunswick, Oh., U.S.	A4	112
Brunswick, co., N.C., U.S.	C4	110
Brunswick, co., Va., U.S.	D5	123
Brunswick Naval Air Station, mil., Me., U.S.	E3	96
Brush, Co., U.S.	A7	83
Brushy Mountains, mts., N.C., U.S.	B1	110
Brus Laguna, Hond.	G5	64
Brusly, La., U.S.	D4	95
Brussels, Ont., Can.	D3	73
Brussels see Bruxelles, Bel.	E4	8
Bruxelles (Brussel), Bel.	E4	8
Bryan, Oh., U.S.	A1	112
Bryan, Tx., U.S.	D4	120
Bryan, co., Ga., U.S.	D5	87
Bryan, co., Ok., U.S.	D5	113
Bryans Road, Md., U.S.	C3	97
Bryant, Ar., U.S.	C3	81
Bryantville, Ma., U.S.	B6	98
Bryce Canyon National Park, Ut., U.S.	F3	121
Bryn Mawr, Wa., U.S.	e11	124
Bryson City, N.C., U.S.	f9	110
Brzeg, Pol.	E17	8
Bsharrī, Leb.	B5	40
Būbiyān, i., Kuw.	C4	46
Bucaramanga, Col.	D6	58
Buccaneer Archipelago, is., Austl.	C4	50
Buchanan, Lib.	G3	42
Buchanan, Ga., U.S.	C1	87
Buchanan, Mi., U.S.	G4	99
Buchanan, Va., U.S.	C3	123
Buchanan, co., Ia., U.S.	B6	92
Buchanan, co., Mo., U.S.	B3	102
Buchanan, co., Va., U.S.	e9	123
Buchan Gulf, b., N.W. Ter., Can.	B18	66
Buchans, Newf., Can.	D3	72
Buchara, Uzb.	J10	22
Bucharest see București, Rom.	E10	16
Buchholz, Ger.	B9	8
Buckatunna, Ms., U.S.	D5	101
Bückeburg, Ger.	C9	8
Buckeye, Az., U.S.	D3	80
Buckeye Lake, Oh., U.S.	C3	112
Buckhannon, W.V., U.S.	C4	125
Buck Hill Falls, Pa., U.S.	D11	115
Buckhorn Lake, res., Ky., U.S.	C6	94
Buckingham, Que., Can.	D2	74
Buckingham, co., Va., U.S.	C4	123
Buckley, Wa., U.S.	B3	124
Bucklin, Ks., U.S.	E4	93
Bucklin, Mo., U.S.	B5	102
Buck Mountain, mtn., Wa., U.S.	A6	124
Buckner, Mo., U.S.	h11	102
Bucks, co., Pa., U.S.	F11	115
Buckskin Mountains, mts., Az., U.S.	C2	80
Bucksport, Me., U.S.	D4	96
Bucksport, S.C., U.S.	D9	117
București (Bucharest), Rom.	E10	16
Bucyrus, Oh., U.S.	B3	112
Buda, Tx., U.S.	D4	120
Budapest, Hung.	H19	8
Budaun, India	F8	38
Budd Lake, l., N.J., U.S.	B3	107
Buddusò, Italy	I4	14
Bude, Eng., U.K.	K8	7
Bude, Ms., U.S.	D3	101
Buea, Cam.	H7	42
Buechel, Ky., U.S.	B4	94
Buena, N.J., U.S.	D3	107
Buena, Wa., U.S.	C5	124
Buena Park, Ca., U.S.	n12	82
Buena Vista, Bol.	G6	54
Buena Vista, Co., U.S.	C4	83
Buena Vista, Fl., U.S.	D4	86
Buena Vista, Ga., U.S.	D2	87
Buena Vista, Va., U.S.	C3	123
Buena Vista, co., Ia., U.S.	B2	92
Buenópolis, Braz.	D6	57
Buenos Aires, Arg.	C5	56
Buffalo, Ia., U.S.	C7	92
Buffalo, Mn., U.S.	E5	100
Buffalo, Mo., U.S.	D4	102
Buffalo, N.Y., U.S.	C2	109
Buffalo, Ok., U.S.	A2	113
Buffalo, S.C., U.S.	B4	117
Buffalo, Tx., U.S.	D5	120
Buffalo, W.V., U.S.	C3	125
Buffalo, Wi., U.S.	D2	126
Buffalo, Wy., U.S.	B6	127
Buffalo, co., Ne., U.S.	D6	104
Buffalo, co., S.D., U.S.	C6	118
Buffalo, co., Wi., U.S.	D2	126
Buffalo, stm., Ar., U.S.	B3	81
Buffalo, stm., Mn., U.S.	D2	100
Buffalo, stm., Tn., U.S.	B4	119
Buffalo, stm., Wi., U.S.	D2	126
Buffalo Bill Reservoir, res., Wy., U.S.	B3	127
Buffalo Center, Ia., U.S.	A4	92
Buffalo Creek, stm., U.S.	f8	125
Buffalo Creek, stm., W.V., U.S.	h10	125
Buffalo Creek, stm., W.V., U.S.	n12	125
Buffalo Grove, Il., U.S.	h9	90
Buffalo Lake, Mn., U.S.	F4	100
Buffalo Lake, l., Alta., Can.	C4	68
Buffalo Lake, l., N.W. Ter., Can.	D9	66
Buffalo Lake, res., Tx., U.S.	B1	120
Buffalo Lake, res., Wi., U.S.	E4	126
Buffumville Lake, res., Ma., U.S.	B4	98
Buford, Ga., U.S.	B2	87
Bug, stm., Eur.	E12	4
Buga, Col.	F4	58
Bugøynes, Nor.	B17	6
Bugsuk Island, i., Phil.	D6	32
Bugul'ma, Russia	G8	22
Buhl, Id., U.S.	G4	89
Buhl, Mn., U.S.	C6	100
Buhler, Ks., U.S.	D6	93
Buies Creek, N.C., U.S.	B4	110
Buj, Russia	C24	18
Bujalance, Spain	H7	12
Bujaraloz, Spain	D11	12
Bujumbura, Bdi.	B5	44
Bukačača, Russia	G17	24
Bukama, Zaire	C5	44
Bukavu, Zaire	B5	44
Bukittinggi, Indon.	F3	32
Bukoba, Tan.	B6	44
Bukovina, hist. reg., Eur.	B9	16
Bula, Indon.	F9	32
Bulan, Ky., U.S.	C6	94
Bulandshahr, India	F7	38
Bulawayo, Zimb.	F5	44
Buldan, Tur.	K12	16
Buldāna, India	B4	37
Bulgan, Mong.	B5	26
Bulgaria, ctry., Eur.	G12	4
Bulkley, stm., B.C., Can.	B4	69
Bull Creek, stm., S.D., U.S.	B2	118
Bulle, Switz.	F14	10
Bullfinch, Austl.	F3	50
Bullfrog Creek, stm., Ut., U.S.	F5	121
Bullhead City, Az., U.S.	B1	80
Bull Island, i., S.C., U.S.	G6	117
Bull Island, i., S.C., U.S.	D9	117
Bull Island, i., S.C., U.S.	F8	117
Bullitt, co., Ky., U.S.	C4	94
Bull Mountain, mtn., Mt., U.S.	D4	103
Bulloch, co., Ga., U.S.	D5	87
Bullock, co., Al., U.S.	C4	78
Bullock Creek, Mi., U.S.	E6	99
Bull Run, stm., Va., U.S.	g11	123
Bullrun Rock, mtn., Or., U.S.	C8	114
Bulls Bay, b., S.C., U.S.	F8	117
Bulls Gap, Tn., U.S.	C10	119
Bull Shoals, Ar., U.S.	A3	81
Bull Shoals Lake, res., U.S.	A3	81
Bully Creek Reservoir, res., Or., U.S.	C9	114
Bulsār, India	B2	37
Bulukumba, Indon.	G7	32
Bumba, Zaire	A4	44
Bumping, stm., Wa., U.S.	C4	124
Buna, Tx., U.S.	D6	120
Bunbury, Austl.	F3	50
Buncombe, co., N.C., U.S.	f10	110
Buncrana, Ire.	F5	7
Bundaberg, Austl.	D10	50
Būndi, India	H6	38
Bundoran, Ire.	G4	7
Bungo-suidō, strt., Japan	I5	30
Bunia, Zaire	A6	44
Bunker Hill, Il., U.S.	D4	90
Bunker Hill, In., U.S.	C5	91
Bunker Hill, W.V., U.S.	B6	125
Bunker Hill, W.V., U.S.	m12	125
Bunker Hill, mtn., Nv., U.S.	D4	105
Bunkerville, Nv., U.S.	G7	105
Bunkie, La., U.S.	D3	95
Bunnell, Fl., U.S.	C5	86
Buñol, Spain	F11	12
Buntok, Indon.	F5	32
Buolkalach, Russia	C17	24
Buon Me Thuot, Viet.	H10	34
Buor-Chaja, Guba, b., Russia	C20	24
Buor-Chaja, Mys, c., Russia	C20	24
Bura, Kenya	B7	44
Burao, Som.	G4	46
Buras, La., U.S.	E6	95
Buraydah, Sau. Ar.	C3	46
Burbank, Ca., U.S.	E4	82
Burbank, Il., U.S.	k9	90
Burbank, Wa., U.S.	C7	124
Burdickville, R.I., U.S.	F2	116
Burdur, Tur.	H14	4
Burdwān, India	I12	38
Bureau, co., Il., U.S.	B4	90
Bureinskij Chrebet, mts., Russia	G20	24
Bureja, stm., Russia	G20	24
Burfjord, Nor.	B13	6
Burgas, Bul.	G11	16
Bur Gavo, Som.	B8	44
Burgaw, N.C., U.S.	C5	110
Burg [bei Magdeburg], Ger.	C11	8
Burgdorf, Switz.	E14	10
Burgeo, Newf., Can.	E3	72
Burgettstown, Pa., U.S.	F1	115
Burghausen, Ger.	G12	8
Burghūth, Sabkhat al-, l., Syria	B7	40
Burgin, China	B4	26
Burgin, Ky., U.S.	C5	94
Burglengenfeld, Ger.	F12	8
Burgos, Spain	C8	12
Burgsteinfurt, Ger.	C7	8
Burgundy see Bourgogne, hist. reg., Fr.	E11	10
Burhaniye, Tur.	J10	16
Burhānpur, India	B4	37
Burica, Punta, c., N.A.	J6	64
Burin, Newf., Can.	E4	72
Burin Peninsula, pen., Newf., Can.	E4	72
Buriram, Thai.	G7	34
Burjasot, Spain	F11	12
Burkburnett, Tx., U.S.	B3	120
Burke, S.D., U.S.	D6	118
Burke, co., Ga., U.S.	C4	87
Burke, co., N.C., U.S.	B1	110
Burke, co., N.D., U.S.	A3	111
Burke Channel, strt., B.C., Can.	C4	69
Burkesville, Ky., U.S.	D4	94
Burketown, Austl.	C7	50
Burkina Faso, ctry., Afr.	F5	42
Burk's Falls, Ont., Can.	B5	73
Burleigh, co., N.D., U.S.	C5	111
Burleson, Tx., U.S.	n9	120
Burleson, co., Tx., U.S.	D4	120
Burley, Id., U.S.	G5	89
Burlingame, Ca., U.S.	h8	82
Burlingame, Ks., U.S.	D8	93
Burlington, Ont., Can.	D5	73
Burlington, Co., U.S.	B8	83
Burlington, Ia., U.S.	D6	92
Burlington, Ks., U.S.	D8	93
Burlington, Ky., U.S.	A5	94
Burlington, Ma., U.S.	f11	98
Burlington, N.J., U.S.	C3	107
Burlington, N.C., U.S.	A3	110
Burlington, N.D., U.S.	A4	111
Burlington, Vt., U.S.	C2	122
Burlington, Wa., U.S.	A3	124
Burlington, Wi., U.S.	F5	126
Burlington, co., N.J., U.S.	D3	107
Burlington Beach, In., U.S.	B3	91
Burlington Junction, Mo., U.S.	A2	102
Burma, ctry., Asia	A2	32
Burnaby, B.C., Can.	E6	69
Burnet, Tx., U.S.	D3	120
Burnet, co., Tx., U.S.	D3	120
Burnett, co., Wi., U.S.	C1	126
Burney, Ca., U.S.	B3	82
Burnham, Pa., U.S.	E6	115
Burnie, Austl.	H9	50
Burns, Or., U.S.	D7	114
Burns, Tn., U.S.	A4	119
Burns, Wy., U.S.	E8	127
Burns Flat, Ok., U.S.	B2	113
Burnside, Ky., U.S.	D5	94
Burns Lake, B.C., Can.	B5	69
Burns Paiute Indian Reservation, Or., U.S.	D7	114
Burnsville, Mn., U.S.	F5	100
Burnsville, Ms., U.S.	A5	101
Burnsville, N.C., U.S.	f10	110
Burnsville Lake, res., W.V., U.S.	C4	125
Burnt Islands, Newf., Can.	E2	72
Burnt Mills, Lake, l., Va., U.S.	k14	123
Burntside Lake, l., Mn., U.S.	C6	100
Burntwood, stm., Man., Can.	B2	70
Burravoe, Scot., U.K.	A11	7
Burr Oak, Mi., U.S.	G5	99
Burr Oak Reservoir, res., Oh., U.S.	C3	112
Burrton, Ks., U.S.	D6	93
Bursa, Tur.	G13	4

Name — Map Ref — Page

Būr Sa'īd (Port Said), Egypt B12 42
Būr Sūdān (Port Sudan), Sudan E13 42
Burt, co., Ne., U.S. C9 104
Burt Lake, l., Mi., U.S. C6 99
Burton, Mi., U.S. F7 99
Burton, Oh., U.S. A4 112
Burton upon Trent, Eng., U.K. I11 7
Burtts Corner, N.B., Can. C3 71
Buru, i., Indon. F8 32
Burundi, ctry., Afr. B5 44
Burwell, Ne., U.S. C6 104
Burwick, Scot., U.K. C10 7
Bury Saint Edmunds, Eng., U.K. I13 7
Busalla, Italy E3 14
Buşayrah, Syria B7 40
Bushnell, Fl., U.S. D4 86
Bushnell, Il., U.S. C3 90
Bush River, b., Md., U.S. B5 97
Buşrá ash-Shām, Syria C5 40
Busselton, Austl. F3 50
Busto Arsizio, Italy D3 14
Busuanga Island, i., Phil. C7 32
Buta, Zaire H10 42
Butare, Rw. B5 44
Butehaqi, China B11 26
Bute Inlet, b., B.C., Can. D5 69
Butler, Al., U.S. C1 78
Butler, Ga., U.S. D2 87
Butler, In., U.S. B8 91
Butler, Ky., U.S. B5 94
Butler, Mo., U.S. C3 102
Butler, N.J., U.S. B4 107
Butler, Oh., U.S. B3 112
Butler, Pa., U.S. E2 115
Butler, Wi., U.S. m11 126
Butler, co., Al., U.S. D3 78
Butler, co., Ia., U.S. B5 92
Butler, co., Ks., U.S. E7 93
Butler, co., Ky., U.S. C3 94
Butler, co., Mo., U.S. E7 102
Butler, co., Ne., U.S. C8 104
Butler, co., Oh., U.S. C1 112
Butler, co., Pa., U.S. E2 115
Butner, N.C., U.S. A4 110
Buttahatchee, stm., U.S. B5 101
Butte, Mt., U.S. E4 103
Butte, co., Ca., U.S. C3 82
Butte, co., Id., U.S. F5 89
Butte, co., S.D., U.S. C2 118
Butte des Morts, Lake, l., Wi., U.S. D5 126
Butte Mountains, mts., Nv., U.S. D6 105
Butternut Lake, l., Wi., U.S. C5 126
Butterworth, Malay. L6 34
Butt of Lewis, c., Scot., U.K. C6 7
Buttonwillow, Ca., U.S. E4 82
Butts, co., Ga., U.S. C3 87
Butuan, Phil. D8 32
Butung, Pulau, i., Indon. F7 32
Bützow, Ger. B11 8
Buxtehude, Ger. B9 8
Buxton, N.C., U.S. B7 110
Büyükmenderes, stm., Tur. L11 16
Buzançais, Fr. F8 10
Buzău, Rom. D10 16
Búzi, stm., Moz. F6 44
Buzuluk, Russia G8 22
Buzzards Bay, Ma., U.S. C6 98
Buzzards Bay, b., Ma., U.S. C6 98
Byam Channel, strt., N.W. Ter., Can. A11 66
Byam Martin Island, i., N.W. Ter., Can. A12 66
Bydgoszcz, Pol. B18 8
Byers, Co., U.S. B6 83
Byesville, Oh., U.S. C4 112
Byhalia, Ms., U.S. A4 101
Bylas, Az., U.S. D5 80
Bylot Island, i., N.W. Ter., Can. B17 66
Byng, Ok., U.S. C5 113
Byrdstown, Tn., U.S. C8 119
Byron, Ga., U.S. D3 87
Byron, Il., U.S. A4 90
Byron, Mn., U.S. F6 100
Byron, Wy., U.S. B4 127
Byrranga, Gory, mts., Russia B14 24
Bytantaj, stm., Russia D20 24
Bytom (Beuthen), Pol. E18 8
Byxelkrok, Swe. H11 6

C

Caacupé, Para. B5 56
Cabaiguán, Cuba C8 64
Caballo Mountains, mts., N.M., U.S. E2 108
Caballo Reservoir, res., N.M., U.S. E2 108
Cabanatuan, Phil. q19 32
Cabano, Que., Can. B9 74
Cabarrus, co., N.C., U.S. B2 110
Cabbage Swamp, sw., Fl., U.S. m9 86
Cabell, co., W.V., U.S. C2 125
Cabeza del Buey, Spain G6 12
Cabimas, Ven. B7 58
Cabin Creek, W.V., U.S. m13 125
Cabin Creek, stm., W.V., U.S. m13 125
Cabinda, Ang. C2 44
Cabinda, dept., Ang. C2 44
Cabinet Gorge Reservoir, res., U.S. B1 103
Cabinet Mountains, mts., Mt., U.S. B1 103
Cabin John, Md., U.S. C3 97
Cabo Frio, Braz. G7 57
Cabonga, Réservoir, res., Que., Can. k11 74
Cabool, Mo., U.S. D5 102
Caborca, Mex. B3 62
Cabot, Ar., U.S. C3 81
Cabot, Mount, mtn., N.H., U.S. A4 106
Cabot Head, c., Ont., Can. B3 73
Cabot Strait, strt., Can. G21 66
Cabra, Spain H7 12
Cabri, Sask., Can. G1 75
Cabrillo National Monument, Ca., U.S. o15 82
Cabrobó, Braz. E11 54
Cabruta, Ven. D9 58
Çaçador, Braz. B6 56
Čačak, Yugo. F4 16
Cacapon, stm., W.V., U.S. B6 125
Cáceres, Braz. G7 54
Cáceres, Col. D5 58
Cáceres, Spain F5 12
Cache, Ok., U.S. C3 113
Cache, co., Ut., U.S. B4 121
Cache, stm., Ar., U.S. C4 81
Cache, stm., Il., U.S. F4 90
Cache Bay, Ont., Can. A5 73
Cache Creek, B.C., Can. D7 69
Cache la Poudre, stm., Co., U.S. A5 83
Cache Mountain, mtn., Ak., U.S. B10 79
Cache Peak, mtn., Id., U.S. G5 89
Cachimbo, Serra do, mts., Braz. E7 54
Cachoeira, Braz. B9 57
Cachoeira do Sul, Braz. C6 56
Cachoeiro de Itapemirim, Braz. F8 57
Cacólo, Ang. D3 44
Caconda, Ang. D3 44
Cactus Flat, pl., Nv., U.S. F5 105
Cactus Peak, mtn., Nv., U.S. F5 105
Caddo, Ok., U.S. C5 113
Caddo, co., La., U.S. B2 95
Caddo, co., Ok., U.S. B3 113
Caddo, stm., Ar., U.S. C2 81
Caddo Creek, stm., Ok., U.S. C4 113
Caddo Lake, res., U.S. B2 95
Cader Idris, mtn., Wales, U.K. I9 7
Cadillac, Fr. H6 10
Cadillac, Mi., U.S. D5 99
Cadillac Mountain, mtn., Me., U.S. D4 96
Cádiz, Spain I5 12
Cadiz, Ky., U.S. D2 94
Cadiz, Oh., U.S. B4 112
Cádiz, Golfo de, b., Eur. I4 12
Cadott, Wi., U.S. D2 126
Caen, Fr. C6 10
Caernarvon, Wales, U.K. H8 7
Caesar Creek Lake, res., Oh., U.S. C2 112
Caeté, Braz. E7 57
Cagayan de Oro, Phil. D7 32
Cagayan Islands, is., Phil. D7 32
Čagda, Russia F20 24
Cagles Mill Lake, res., In., U.S. F4 91
Cagli, Italy F7 14
Cagliari, Italy J4 14
Caguas, P.R. E14 64
Cahaba, stm., Al., U.S. C2 78
Caha Mountains, mts., Ire. J3 7
Cahirciveen, Ire. J2 7
Cahokia, Il., U.S. E3 90
Cahore Point, c., Ire. I6 7
Cahors, Fr. H8 10
Caiapó, Serra, mts., Braz. D2 57
Caibarién, Cuba C8 64
Caicara, Ven. D9 58
Caicos Islands, is., T./C. Is. D12 64
Caicos Passage, strt., N.A. C11 64
Caillou Bay, b., La., U.S. E5 95
Caillou Lake, l., La., U.S. E5 95
Cairnbrook, Pa., U.S. F4 115
Cairngorm Mountains, mts., Scot., U.K. D9 7
Cairns, Austl. C9 50
Cairo, Ga., U.S. F2 87
Cairo, Il., U.S. F4 90
Cairo, Ne., U.S. D7 104
Cairo see Al-Qāhirah, Egypt B12 42
Caiundo, Ang. E3 44
Cajamarca, Peru E3 54
Cajàzeiras, Braz. E11 54
Čakovec, Cro. C11 14
Calabar, Nig. H7 42
Calabozo, Ven. C9 58
Calahorra, Spain C10 12
Calais, Fr. B8 10
Calais, Me., U.S. C5 96
Calais, Pas de (Strait of Dover), strt., Eur. K14 7
Calamar, Col. B5 58
Calamian Group, is., Phil. C6 32
Calamocha, Spain E10 12
Calamus, stm., Ne., U.S. B6 104
Calanda, Spain E11 12
Calapan, Phil. r19 33b
Călăraşi, Rom. E11 16
Calatayud, Spain D10 12
Calaveras, co., Ca., U.S. C3 82
Calcasieu, co., La., U.S. D2 95
Calcasieu, stm., La., U.S. D2 95
Calcasieu Lake, l., La., U.S. E2 95
Calcasieu Pass, strt., La., U.S. E2 95
Calçoene, Braz. C8 54
Calcutta, India I13 38
Calcutta, Oh., U.S. B5 112
Calcutta Lake, l., Nv., U.S. B2 105
Caldas da Rainha, Port. F2 12
Calderwood, Tn., U.S. D10 119
Caldron Falls Reservoir, res., Wi., U.S. C5 126
Caldwell, Id., U.S. F2 89
Caldwell, Ks., U.S. E6 93
Caldwell, N.J., U.S. B4 107
Caldwell, Oh., U.S. C4 112
Caldwell, Tx., U.S. D4 120
Caldwell, co., Ky., U.S. C2 94
Caldwell, co., La., U.S. B3 95
Caldwell, co., Mo., U.S. B3 102
Caldwell, co., N.C., U.S. B1 110
Caldwell, co., Tx., U.S. E4 120
Caledon, Ont., Can. D5 73
Caledonia, Mi., U.S. F5 99
Caledonia, Mn., U.S. G7 100
Caledonia, Ms., U.S. B5 101
Caledonia, N.Y., U.S. C3 109
Caledonia, co., Vt., U.S. C4 122
Calera, Al., U.S. B3 78
Calera, Ok., U.S. D5 113
Calexico, Ca., U.S. F6 82
Calgary, Alta., Can. D3 68
Calhoun, Ga., U.S. B2 87
Calhoun, Ky., U.S. C2 94
Calhoun, co., Al., U.S. B4 78
Calhoun, co., Ar., U.S. D3 81
Calhoun, co., Fl., U.S. B1 86
Calhoun, co., Ga., U.S. E2 87
Calhoun, co., Il., U.S. D3 90
Calhoun, co., Ia., U.S. B3 92
Calhoun, co., Mi., U.S. F5 99
Calhoun, co., Ms., U.S. B4 101
Calhoun, co., S.C., U.S. D6 117
Calhoun, co., Tx., U.S. E4 120
Calhoun, co., W.V., U.S. C3 125
Calhoun City, Ms., U.S. B4 101
Calhoun Falls, S.C., U.S. C2 117
Cali, Col. F4 58
Calico Rock, Ar., U.S. A3 81
Calicut, India G3 37
Caliente, Nv., U.S. F7 105
California, Mo., U.S. C5 102
California, Pa., U.S. F2 115
California, state, U.S. D4 82
California, Golfo de, b., Mex. D4 62
California Aqueduct, Ca., U.S. E4 82
Calimere, Point, c., India G5 37
Calipatria, Ca., U.S. F6 82
Calispell Peak, mtn., Wa., U.S. A8 124
Calistoga, Ca., U.S. C2 82
Calitri, Italy I10 14
Callac, Fr. D3 10
Callaghan, Mount, mtn., Nv., U.S. D5 105
Callahan, co., Tx., U.S. C3 120
Callao, Peru F3 54
Callaway, co., Mo., U.S. C6 102
Calling Lake, l., Alta., Can. B4 68
Callosa de Ensarriá, Spain G11 12
Calloway, co., Ky., U.S. f9 94
Calmar, Alta., Can. C4 68
Calmar, Ia., U.S. A6 92
Caloosahatchee, stm., Fl., U.S. F5 86
Caltagirone, Italy L9 14
Caltanissetta, Italy L9 14
Calumet, Que., Can. D3 74
Calumet, Mi., U.S. A2 99
Calumet, co., Wi., U.S. D5 126
Calumet, Lake, l., Il., U.S. k9 90
Calumet City, Il., U.S. B6 90
Calunda, Ang. D4 44
Calvert, Tx., U.S. D4 120
Calvert, co., Md., U.S. C4 97
Calvert City, Ky., U.S. e9 94
Calverton, Md., U.S. *B4 97
Calverton Park, Mo., U.S. f13 102
Calvinia, S. Afr. H3 44
Camacho, Mex. E8 62
Camacupa, Ang. D3 44
Camaguán, Ven. C9 58
Camagüey, Cuba D9 64
Camaná, Peru G4 54
Camanche, Ia., U.S. C7 92
Camano Island, i., Wa., U.S. A3 124
Camapuã, Braz. E1 57
Camaquã, Braz. C6 56
Camas, Spain H5 12
Camas, Wa., U.S. D3 124
Camas, co., Id., U.S. F4 89
Ca Mau, Viet. J8 34
Cambados, Spain C3 12
Cambay, India I5 38
Cambodia (Kampuchea), ctry., Asia C3 32
Cambrai, Fr. B10 10
Cambria, Ca., U.S. E3 82
Cambria, Wi., U.S. E4 126
Cambria, co., Pa., U.S. E4 115
Cambrian Mountains, mts., Wales, U.K. I9 7
Cambridge, Ont., Can. D4 73
Cambridge, Eng., U.K. I13 7
Cambridge, Il., U.S. B3 90
Cambridge, Ia., U.S. C4 92
Cambridge, Md., U.S. C5 97
Cambridge, Ma., U.S. B5 98
Cambridge, Mn., U.S. E5 100
Cambridge, Ne., U.S. D5 104
Cambridge, N.Y., U.S. B7 109
Cambridge, Oh., U.S. B4 112
Cambridge, Wi., U.S. F4 126
Cambridge Bay, N.W. Ter., Can. C11 66
Cambridge City, In., U.S. E7 91
Cambridge Reservoir, res., Ma., U.S. g10 98
Cambridge Springs, Pa., U.S. C1 115
Cambuci, Braz. F8 57
Camden, Al., U.S. D2 78
Camden, Ar., U.S. D3 81
Camden, De., U.S. D3 85
Camden, In., U.S. C4 91
Camden, Me., U.S. D3 96
Camden, N.J., U.S. D2 107
Camden, N.Y., U.S. B5 109
Camden, Oh., U.S. C1 112
Camden, S.C., U.S. C6 117
Camden, Tn., U.S. A3 119
Camden, co., Ga., U.S. F5 87
Camden, co., Mo., U.S. C5 102
Camden, co., N.J., U.S. D3 107
Camden, co., N.C., U.S. A6 110
Camdenton, Mo., U.S. D5 102
Camelback Mountain, mtn., Az., U.S. k9 80
Cameron, Az., U.S. B4 80
Cameron, La., U.S. E2 95
Cameron, Mo., U.S. B3 102
Cameron, Tx., U.S. D4 120
Cameron, W.V., U.S. B4 125
Cameron, Wi., U.S. C2 126
Cameron, co., La., U.S. E2 95
Cameron, co., Pa., U.S. D5 115
Cameron, co., Tx., U.S. F4 120
Cameron Highlands, Malay. L6 34
Cameron Hills, hills, Can. E9 66
Cameroon, ctry., Afr. G8 42
Cameroon Mountain, mtn., Cam. H7 42
Cametá, Braz. D9 54
Camilla, Ga., U.S. E2 87
Camino, Ca., U.S. C3 82
Camiranga, Braz. D9 54
Camissombo, Ang. C4 44
Cam Lo, Viet. F9 34
Cammack Village, Ar., U.S. C3 81
Camooweal, Austl. C7 50
Camorta Island, i., India J2 34
Camp, co., Tx., U.S. C5 120
Campana, Isla, i., Chile F1 56
Campanero, Cerro, mtn., Ven. E10 58
Campbell, Ca., U.S. k8 82
Campbell, Fl., U.S. D5 86
Campbell, Mo., U.S. E7 102
Campbell, Oh., U.S. A5 112
Campbell, co., Ky., U.S. B5 94
Campbell, co., S.D., U.S. B5 118
Campbell, co., Tn., U.S. C9 119
Campbell, co., Va., U.S. C3 123
Campbell, co., Wy., U.S. B7 127
Campbellford, Ont., Can. C7 73
Campbell Hill, hill, Oh., U.S. B2 112
Campbell Lake, l., Or., U.S. E7 114
Campbellsburg, In., U.S. G5 91
Campbellsburg, Ky., U.S. B4 94
Campbells Creek, stm., W.V., U.S. m13 125
Campbellsport, Wi., U.S. E5 126
Campbellsville, Ky., U.S. C4 94
Campbellton, N.B., Can. A3 71
Campbellton, Newf., Can. D4 72
Campbeltown, Scot., U.K. F7 7
Campeche, Mex. H14 62
Campeche, Bahía de, b., Mex. H13 62
Camperville, Man., Can. D1 70
Camp Hill, Al., U.S. C4 78
Camp Hill, Pa., U.S. F8 115
Camp H. M. Smith Marine Corps Base, mil., Hi., U.S. g10 88
Camp Howard Ridge, mtn., Id., U.S. D2 89
Campina Grande, Braz. E11 54
Campinas, Braz. G5 57
Camp Lejeune Marine Corps Base, mil., N.C., U.S. C5 110
Campoalegre, Col. F5 58
Campo Alegre de Goiás, Braz. D5 57
Campobasso, Italy H9 14
Campobello Island, i., N.B., Can. E3 71
Campo Belo, Braz. F6 57
Campo de Criptana, Spain F8 12
Campo de la Cruz, Col. B5 58
Campo Grande, Braz. F1 57
Campo Maior, Braz. D10 54
Campos, Braz. F8 57
Campos do Jordão, Braz. G6 57
Camp Pendleton Marine Corps Base, mil., Ca., U.S. F5 82
Camp Point, Il., U.S. C2 90
Camp Springs, Md., U.S. f9 97
Campti, La., U.S. C2 95
Campton, N.H., U.S. C3 106
Camp Verde, Az., U.S. C4 80
Camp Verde Indian Reservation, Az., U.S. C4 80
Cam Ranh, Viet. I10 34
Camrose, Alta., Can. C4 68
Canaan, Ct., U.S. A2 84
Canaan, N.H., U.S. C2 106
Canaan, stm., N.B., Can. C4 71
Canada, ctry., N.A. D14 66
Canada Bay, b., Newf., Can. C3 72
Canada Falls Lake, res., Me., U.S. C2 96
Canadensis, Pa., U.S. D11 115
Canadian, Tx., U.S. B2 120
Canadian, co., Ok., U.S. B3 113
Canadian, stm., U.S. D6 76
Canajoharie, N.Y., U.S. C6 109
Çanakkale, Tur. G13 4
Çanakkale Boğazı (Dardanelles), strt., Tur. I10 16
Canal Flats, B.C., Can. D10 69
Canal Fulton, Oh., U.S. B4 112
Canal Winchester, Oh., U.S. C3 112
Canandaigua, N.Y., U.S. C3 109
Canandaigua Lake, l., N.Y., U.S. C3 109
Cananea, Mex. B4 62
Cañar, Ec. I3 58
Canarias, Islas (Canary Islands), is., Spain p24 136
Canary Islands see Canarias, Islas, is., Spain p24 136
Cañas, C.R. I5 64
Canastota, N.Y., U.S. B5 109
Canaveral, Cape, c., Fl., U.S. D6 86
Canaveral National Seashore, Fl., U.S. D6 86
Canavieiras, Braz. C9 57
Canberra, Austl. G9 50
Canby, Mn., U.S. F2 100
Canby, Or., U.S. B4 114
Cancale, Fr. D5 10
Cancon, Fr. H7 10
Cancún, Mex. G16 62
Candeleda, Spain E6 12
Candiac, Que., Can. q19 74
Candle Lake, l., Sask., Can. D3 75
Candler, co., Ga., U.S. D4 87
Candlewood, Lake, l., Ct., U.S. D1 84
Candlewood Isle, Ct., U.S. D2 84
Candlewood Shores, Ct., U.S. D2 84
Cando, N.D., U.S. A6 111
Candor, N.C., U.S. B3 110
Cane, stm., La., U.S. C2 95
Cañete, Spain E10 12
Caney, Ks., U.S. E8 93
Caney, stm., Ok., U.S. A5 113
Caney Creek, stm., Tx., U.S. r14 120
Caney Fork, stm., Tn., U.S. C8 119
Canfield, Oh., U.S. A5 112
Canfranc, Spain C11 12
Cangas de Onís, Spain B6 12
Cangombe, Ang. D3 44
Canguçu, Braz. C6 56
Cangzhou, China D10 26
Caniapiscau, stm., Que., Can. g13 74
Caniapiscau, Lac, l., Que., Can. F19 66
Canicattì, Italy L8 14
Canistear Reservoir, res., N.J., U.S. A4 107
Canisteo, N.Y., U.S. C3 109
Canisteo, stm., N.Y., U.S. C3 109
Canistota, S.D., U.S. D8 118
Cañitas, Mex. F8 62
Çankırı, Tur. G14 4
Canmore, Alta., Can. D3 68
Cannanore, India G3 37
Cannelton, In., U.S. I4 91
Cannes, Fr. I14 10
Canning, N.S., Can. D5 71
Cannon, co., Tn., U.S. B5 119
Cannon, stm., Mn., U.S. F5 100
Cannon Air Force Base, mil., N.M., U.S. C6 108
Cannonball, stm., N.D., U.S. C5 111
Cannon Beach, Or., U.S. B3 114
Cannondale, Ct., U.S. E2 84
Cannon Falls, Mn., U.S. F6 100
Cannonsburg, Ky., U.S. B7 94
Cannonsville Reservoir, res., N.Y., U.S. C5 109
Canon, Ga., U.S. B3 87
Canon City, Co., U.S. C5 83
Canonsburg, Pa., U.S. F1 115
Canosa [di Puglia], Italy H11 14
Cantábrica, Cordillera, mts., Spain B7 12
Cantalejo, Spain D8 12
Cantanhede, Port. E3 12
Cantaura, Ven. C10 58
Canterbury, Eng., U.K. J14 7
Canterbury, De., U.S. D3 85
Canterbury Bight, N.Z. F3 52
Can Tho, Viet. I8 34
Canton, Ct., U.S. B4 84
Canton, Ga., U.S. B2 87
Canton, Il., U.S. C3 90
Canton, Ks., U.S. D6 93
Canton, Ma., U.S. B5 98
Canton, Ms., U.S. C3 101
Canton, Mo., U.S. A6 102
Canton, N.Y., U.S. f9 109
Canton, N.C., U.S. f10 110
Canton, Oh., U.S. B4 112
Canton, Ok., U.S. A3 113
Canton, Pa., U.S. C8 115
Canton, S.D., U.S. D9 118
Canton, Tx., U.S. C5 120
Canton see Guangzhou, China L2 28
Canton Lake, res., Ok., U.S. A3 113
Cantonment, Fl., U.S. u14 86
Cantù, Italy D4 14
Canutillo, Tx., U.S. o11 120
Canyon, Tx., U.S. B2 120
Canyon, co., Id., U.S. F2 89
Canyon City, Or., U.S. C8 114
Canyon de Chelly National Monument, Az., U.S. A6 80
Canyon Ferry Lake, res., Mt., U.S. D5 103
Canyon Lake, Tx., U.S. E3 120
Canyon Lake, res., Tx., U.S. E3 120
Canyonlands National Park, Ut., U.S. E6 121
Canyonville, Or., U.S. E3 114
Cao Bang, Viet. C9 34
Capac, Mi., U.S. F8 99
Cap-à-l'Aigle, Que., Can. B7 74
Cap-aux-Meules, Que., Can. B8 71
Cap-de-la-Madeleine, Que., Can. C5 74
Cape Breton Highlands National Park, N.S., Can. C9 71
Cape Breton Island, i., N.S., Can. C9 71
Cape Broyle, Newf., Can. E5 72
Cape Canaveral, Fl., U.S. D6 86
Cape Charles, Va., U.S. C6 123
Cape Coast, Ghana G5 42
Cape Cod Bay, b., Ma., U.S. C7 98
Cape Cod Canal, Ma., U.S. C6 98
Cape Cod National Seashore, Ma., U.S. C7 98
Cape Coral, Fl., U.S. F5 86
Cape Dorset, N.W. Ter., Can. D17 66
Cape Elizabeth, Me., U.S. E2 96
Cape Fear, stm., N.C., U.S. C4 110
Cape Girardeau, Mo., U.S. D8 102
Cape Girardeau, co., Mo., U.S. D8 102
Cape Hatteras National Seashore, N.C., U.S. B7 110
Cape Horn Mountain, mtn., Id., U.S. E3 89
Cape Island, i., S.C., U.S. E9 117
Cape Lookout National Seashore, N.C., U.S. C6 110
Cape May, N.J., U.S. F3 107
Cape May, co., N.J., U.S. E3 107
Cape May Court House, N.J., U.S. E3 107
Capers Inlet, b., S.C., U.S. k12 117
Capers Island, i., S.C., U.S. G6 117
Capers Island, i., S.C., U.S. F8 117
Cape Sable Island, i., N.S., Can. F4 71
Cape Town (Kaapstad), S. Afr. H3 44
Cape Verde, ctry., Afr. E11 2
Cape York Peninsula, pen., Austl. B8 50
Cap-Haïtien, Haiti E11 64
Capim, stm., Braz. D9 54
Capitan, N.M., U.S. D4 108
Capitan Mountains, mts., N.M., U.S. D4 108
Capitan Peak, mtn., N.M., U.S. D4 108
Capitol Heights, Ia., U.S. e8 92
Capitol Heights, Md., U.S. C4 97
Capitol Peak, mtn., Nv., U.S. B4 105
Capitol Reef National Park, Ut., U.S. E4 121
Čapljina, Bos. F12 14
Cap-Pelé, N.B., Can. C5 71
Capreol, Ont., Can. p19 73
Capri, Italy I9 14
Caprivi Strip, hist. reg., Nmb. E4 44
Cap-Rouge, Que., Can. n17 74
Cap-Saint-Ignace, Que., Can. B7 74
Captain Cook, Hi., U.S. D6 88
Captieux, Fr. H6 10
Captiva, Fl., U.S. F4 86
Captiva Island, i., Fl., U.S. F4 86
Capua, Italy H9 14
Capulin Volcano National Monument, N.M., U.S. A6 108
Caquetá (Japurá), stm., S.A. D5 54
Čara, Russia F17 24
Čara, stm., Russia F17 24
Caracaraí, Braz. C6 54
Caracas, Ven. B9 58
Carajás, Serra dos, mts., Braz. E8 54

Name | Map Ref | Page

Carangola, Braz. F7 57
Caraquet, N.B., Can. B5 71
Caratasca, Laguna de, b., Hond. G6 64
Caratinga, Braz. E7 57
Carauari, Braz. D5 54
Caravaca, Spain G10 12
Caravelas, Braz. D9 57
Caraway, Ar., U.S. B5 81
Carballo, Spain B3 12
Carberry, Man., Can. E2 70
Carbon, co., Mt., U.S. E7 103
Carbon, co., Pa., U.S. E10 115
Carbon, co., Ut., U.S. D5 121
Carbon, co., Wy., U.S. E5 127
Carbondale, Co., U.S. B3 83
Carbondale, Il., U.S. F4 90
Carbondale, Ks., U.S. D8 93
Carbondale, Pa., U.S. C10 115
Carbonear, Newf., Can. E5 72
Carboneras de Guadazaon, Spain F10 12
Carbon Hill, Al., U.S. B2 78
Carbonia, Italy J3 14
Carcagente, Spain F11 12
Carcassonne, Fr. I9 10
Carcross, Yukon, Can. D6 66
Cárdenas, Cuba C7 64
Cárdenas, Mex. F10 62
Cardiff, Wales, U.K. J9 7
Cardigan, Wales, U.K. I8 7
Cardigan Bay, b., P.E.I., Can. C7 71
Cardigan Bay, b., Wales, U.K. I8 7
Cardinal, Ont., Can. C9 73
Cardington, Oh., U.S. B3 112
Cardston, Alta., Can. E4 68
Cardwell, Mo., U.S. E7 102
Čardžou, Turk. J10 22
Carencro, La., U.S. D3 95
Carentan, Fr. C5 10
Caretta, W.V., U.S. D3 125
Carey, Id., U.S. F5 89
Carey, Oh., U.S. B2 112
Carey, Lake, l., Austl. E4 50
Caribbean Sea G10 64
Cariboo Mountains, mts., B.C., Can. C7 69
Caribou, Me., U.S. B5 96
Caribou, co., Id., U.S. G7 89
Caribou Island, i., N.S., Can. D7 71
Caribou Lake, l., Me., U.S. C3 96
Caribou Mountain, mtn., Id., U.S. F7 89
Caribou Mountains, mts., Alta., Can. f7 68
Caribou Range, mts., Id., U.S. F7 89
Carignan, Fr. C12 10
Cariñena, Spain D10 12
Carinhanha, Braz. C7 57
Carini, Italy K8 14
Caripito, Ven. B11 58
Carl Blackwell, Lake, res., Ok., U.S. A4 113
Carleton, Mi., U.S. F7 99
Carleton, Mount, mtn., N.B., Can. B3 71
Carleton Place, Ont., Can. B8 73
Carlin, Nv., U.S. C5 105
Carlinville, Il., U.S. D4 90
Carlisle, Eng., U.K. G10 7
Carlisle, Ar., U.S. C4 81
Carlisle, In., U.S. G3 91
Carlisle, Ia., U.S. C4 92
Carlisle, Ky., U.S. B5 94
Carlisle, Oh., U.S. C1 112
Carlisle, Pa., U.S. F7 115
Carlisle, co., Ky., U.S. f8 94
Carl Junction, Mo., U.S. D3 102
Carlow, Ire. I6 7
Carlsbad, Ca., U.S. F5 82
Carlsbad, N.M., U.S. E5 108
Carlsbad Caverns National Park, N.M., U.S. E5 108
Carlstadt, N.J., U.S. h8 107
Carlton, Mn., U.S. D6 100
Carlton, Or., U.S. B3 114
Carlton, co., Mn., U.S. D6 100
Carlyle, Il., U.S. E4 90
Carlyle Lake, res., Il., U.S. E4 90
Carmacks, Yukon, Can. D5 66
Carmagnola, Italy E2 14
Carman, Man., Can. E2 70
Carmanville, Newf., Can. D4 72
Carmarthen, Wales, U.K. J8 7
Carmaux, Fr. H9 10
Carmel, Ca., U.S. D3 82
Carmel, In., U.S. E5 91
Carmel, N.Y., U.S. D7 109
Carmel Head, c., Wales, U.K. H8 7
Carmen, Isla, i., Mex. E4 62
Carmen, Isla del, i., Mex. H14 62
Carmen de Patagones, Arg. E4 56
Carmi, Il., U.S. E5 90
Carmi, Lake, l., Vt., U.S. B3 122
Carmona, Spain H6 12
Carnarvon, Austl. D2 50
Carnarvon, S. Afr. H4 44
Carnation, Wa., U.S. B4 124
Carndonagh, Ire. F5 7
Carnegie, Ok., U.S. B3 113
Carnegie, Pa., U.S. F1 115
Carnegie, Lake, l., Austl. E4 50
Carneys Point, N.J., U.S. D2 107
Carniche, Alpi, mts., Eur. C8 14
Car Nicobar Island, i., India J2 34
Carnsore Point, c., Ire. I6 7
Caro, Mi., U.S. E7 99
Carol City, Fl., U.S. s13 86
Caroleen, N.C., U.S. B1 110
Carolina, Braz. E9 54
Carolina, Col. D5 58
Carolina, R.I., U.S. F2 116
Carolina, W.V., U.S. k10 125
Carolina Beach, N.C., U.S. C5 110
Caroline, co., Md., U.S. C6 97
Caroline, co., Va., U.S. C5 123
Caroní, stm., Ven. D11 58
Carora, Ven. B7 58
Carpathian Mountains, mts., Eur. F12 4
Carpații Meridionali, mts., Rom. D8 16
Carpentaria, Gulf of, b., Austl. B7 50
Carpenter Dam, Ar., U.S. g7 81
Carpentersville, Il., U.S. A5 90
Carpentras, Fr. H12 10
Carpi, Italy E5 14
Carpinteria, Ca., U.S. E4 82
Carquefou, Fr. E5 10
Carrabelle, Fl., U.S. C2 86
Carrara, Italy E5 14
Carrauntoohill, mtn., Ire. I3 7
Carrboro, N.C., U.S. B3 110
Carreta, Punta, c., Peru F3 54
Carrickfergus, N. Ire., U.K. G7 7
Carrickmacross, Ire. H6 7
Carrie, Mount, mtn., Wa., U.S. B2 124
Carriere, Ms., U.S. E4 101
Carrier Mills, Il., U.S. F5 90
Carrillo, Mex. D8 62
Carrington, N.D., U.S. B6 111
Carrington Island, i., Ut., U.S. C3 121
Carrión de los Condes, Spain C7 12
Carrizo Creek, stm., U.S. A1 120
Carrizo Mountain, mtn., N.M., U.S. D4 108
Carrizo Mountains, mts., U.S. A6 80
Carrizo Springs, Tx., U.S. *E3 120
Carrizozo, N.M., U.S. D4 108
Carroll, Ia., U.S. B3 92
Carroll, co., Ar., U.S. A2 81
Carroll, co., Ga., U.S. C1 87
Carroll, co., Il., U.S. A4 90
Carroll, co., In., U.S. C4 91
Carroll, co., Ia., U.S. B3 92
Carroll, co., Ky., U.S. B4 94
Carroll, co., Md., U.S. A3 97
Carroll, co., Ms., U.S. B4 101
Carroll, co., Mo., U.S. B4 102
Carroll, co., N.H., U.S. C4 106
Carroll, co., Oh., U.S. B4 112
Carroll, co., Tn., U.S. B3 119
Carroll, co., Va., U.S. D2 123
Carrollton, Al., U.S. B1 78
Carrollton, Ga., U.S. C1 87
Carrollton, Il., U.S. D3 90
Carrollton, Ky., U.S. B4 94
Carrollton, Mi., U.S. E7 99
Carrollton, Mo., U.S. B4 102
Carrollton, Oh., U.S. B4 112
Carrolltown, Pa., U.S. E4 115
Carrot, stm., Can. D4 75
Carry Falls Reservoir, res., N.Y., U.S. f10 109
Čarsk, Kaz. H10 24
Carson, Ia., U.S. C2 92
Carson, Wa., U.S. D4 124
Carson, co., Tx., U.S. B2 120
Carson, stm., Nv., U.S. D2 105
Carson City, Mi., U.S. E6 99
Carson City, Nv., U.S. D2 105
Carson Lake, l., Nv., U.S. D3 105
Carson Sink, l., Nv., U.S. D3 105
Carson Spring, Tn., U.S. D10 119
Carstairs, Alta., Can. D3 68
Carswell Air Force Base, mil., Tx., U.S. n9 120
Cartagena, Col. B5 58
Cartagena, Spain H11 12
Cartago, Col. E5 58
Cartago, C.R. J6 64
Carter, co., Ky., U.S. B6 94
Carter, co., Mo., U.S. E7 102
Carter, co., Mt., U.S. E12 103
Carter, co., Ok., U.S. C4 113
Carter, co., Tn., U.S. C11 119
Carteret, N.J., U.S. B4 107
Carteret, co., N.C., U.S. C6 110
Carter Lake, Ia., U.S. C2 92
Carter Mountain, mtn., Wy., U.S. B3 127
Carters Lake, res., Ga., U.S. B2 87
Cartersville, Ga., U.S. B2 87
Carterville, Il., U.S. F4 90
Carterville, Mo., U.S. D3 102
Carthage, Il., U.S. C2 90
Carthage, In., U.S. E6 91
Carthage, Ms., U.S. C4 101
Carthage, Mo., U.S. D3 102
Carthage, N.Y., U.S. B5 109
Carthage, N.C., U.S. B3 110
Carthage, Tn., U.S. C8 119
Carthage, Tx., U.S. C5 120
Cartier Island, i., Austl. B4 50
Cartwright, Newf., Can. B3 72
Cartwright, Ok., U.S. D5 113
Caruaru, Braz. E11 54
Carúpano, Ven. B11 58
Caruthersville, Mo., U.S. E8 102
Carver, Ma., U.S. C6 98
Carver, Mn., U.S. F5 100
Carver, co., Mn., U.S. F5 100
Carville, La., U.S. h9 95
Cary, Il., U.S. A5 90
Cary, N.C., U.S. B4 110
Caryville, Tn., U.S. C9 119
Casablanca (Dar-el-Beida), Mor. B4 42
Casacalenda, Italy H9 14
Casa Grande, Az., U.S. E4 80
Casa Grande National Monument, Az., U.S. E4 80
Casale Monferrato, Italy D3 14
Casarano, Italy I13 14
Casas Adobes, Az., U.S. E5 80
Casas Ibáñez, Spain F10 12
Cascade, Co., U.S. C6 83
Cascade, Id., U.S. E2 89
Cascade, Ia., U.S. B6 92
Cascade, Mt., U.S. C5 103
Cascade, co., Mt., U.S. C5 103
Cascade Locks, Or., U.S. B5 114
Cascade Range, mts., N.A. C2 76
Cascade Reservoir, res., Id., U.S. E3 89
Cascade Tunnel, Wa., U.S. B4 124
Cascais, Port. G2 12
Cascina, Italy F5 14
Casco Bay, b., Me., U.S. E3 96
Caserta, Italy H9 14
Caseville, Mi., U.S. E7 99
Casey, Il., U.S. D6 90
Casey, co., Ky., U.S. C5 94
Casey, Mount, mtn., Id., U.S. A2 89
Casey Key, i., Fl., U.S. E4 86
Cashion, Az., U.S. m8 80
Cashmere, Wa., U.S. B5 124
Cashton, Wi., U.S. E3 126
Casigua, Ven. C6 58
Caspe, Spain D11 12
Casper, Wy., U.S. D6 127
Casper Mountain, mtn., Wy., U.S. D6 127
Caspian, Mi., U.S. B2 99
Caspian Lake, l., Vt., U.S. B4 122
Caspian Sea G17 4
Cass, co., Il., U.S. D3 90
Cass, co., In., U.S. C5 91
Cass, co., Ia., U.S. C3 92
Cass, co., Mi., U.S. G4 99
Cass, co., Mn., U.S. D4 100
Cass, co., Mo., U.S. C3 102
Cass, co., Ne., U.S. D9 104
Cass, co., N.D., U.S. C8 111
Cass, co., Tx., U.S. C5 120
Cass, stm., Mi., U.S. E7 99
Cassai (Kasai), stm., Afr. C4 44
Cassano allo Ionio, Italy J11 14
Cass City, Mi., U.S. E7 99
Casselberry, Fl., U.S. D5 86
Casselman, Ont., Can. B9 73
Casselman, stm., U.S. k12 97
Casselton, N.D., U.S. C8 111
Cassia, co., Id., U.S. G5 89
Cassiar, B.C., Can. m17 69
Cassinga, Ang. E3 44
Cassino, Italy H8 14
Cass Lake, Mn., U.S. C4 100
Cass Lake, l., Mn., U.S. C4 100
Cassopolis, Mi., U.S. G4 99
Cassville, Ga., U.S. B2 87
Cassville, Mo., U.S. E4 102
Cassville, Wi., U.S. F3 126
Castalia, Oh., U.S. A3 112
Castanea, Pa., U.S. D7 115
Castanheira de Pêra, Port. E3 12
Castel del Piano, Italy G6 14
Castelfranco Veneto, Italy D6 14
Castellamare del Golfo, Italy K7 14
Castellammare [di Stabia], Italy I9 14
Castellane, Fr. I13 10
Castellón de la Plana, Spain F11 12
Castelnaudary, Fr. I8 10
Castelo Branco, Port. F4 12
Castelsarrasin, Fr. H8 10
Castelvetrano, Italy L7 14
Castets, Fr. I5 10
Castiglione del Lago, Italy F7 14
Castilla, Peru E2 54
Castilla la Nueva, hist. reg., Spain F8 12
Castillo de San Marcos National Monument, Fl., U.S. n9 86
Castine, Me., U.S. D4 96
Castle Air Force Base, mil., Ca., U.S. D3 82
Castlebar, Ire. H3 7
Castleberry, Al., U.S. D2 78
Castle Dale, Ut., U.S. D4 121
Castle Dome Mountains, mts., Az., U.S. D1 80
Castle Dome Peak, mtn., Az., U.S. D1 80
Castlegar, B.C., Can. E9 69
Castle Hayne, N.C., U.S. C5 110
Castle Hills, De., U.S. i7 85
Castle Mountain, mtn., Yukon, Can. D5 66
Castle Mountains, mts., Mt., U.S. D6 103
Castle Peak, mtn., Co., U.S. B4 83
Castle Peak, mtn., Id., U.S. E4 89
Castle Point, Mo., U.S. f13 102
Castle Rock, Co., U.S. B6 83
Castle Rock, Wa., U.S. C3 124
Castle Rock, mtn., Or., U.S. C8 114
Castle Rock Lake, res., Wi., U.S. E4 126
Castleton, Vt., U.S. D2 122
Castletown, I. of Man G8 7
Castletown Berehaven, Ire. J3 7
Castlewood, Va., U.S. f9 123
Castor, Alta., Can. C5 68
Castor, stm., Mo., U.S. D7 102
Castres, Fr. I9 10
Castries, St. Luc. G17 64
Castro, co., Tx., U.S. B1 120
Castro Daire, Port. E4 12
Castro del Río, Spain H7 12
Castropol, Spain B4 12
Castro Valley, Ca., U.S. h8 82
Castrovillari, Italy J11 14
Castroville, Tx., U.S. E3 120
Castuera, Spain G6 12
Caswell, co., N.C., U.S. A3 110
Catacamas, Hond. G5 64
Cataguases, Braz. F7 57
Catahoula, co., La., U.S. C4 95
Catahoula Lake, l., La., U.S. C3 95
Catalão, Braz. E5 57
Catalina, Newf., Can. D5 72
Catalina, Chile B3 56
Catamarca, Arg. B3 56
Catamayo, Ec. I3 58
Catanduanes Island, i., Phil. C7 32
Catanduva, Braz. F4 57
Catania, Italy L10 14
Catanzaro, Italy K11 14
Cataouatche, Lake, l., La., U.S. k11 95
Catarman, Phil. C7 32
Catasauqua, Pa., U.S. E11 115
Catastrophe, Cape, c., Austl. F7 50
Cataumet, Ma., U.S. C6 98
Catawba, co., N.C., U.S. B1 110
Catawba, stm., S.C., U.S. B6 117
Catawba, South Fork, stm., N.C., U.S. B1 110
Catawissa, Pa., U.S. E9 115
Catete, Ang. C2 44
Cathance, Lake, l., Me., U.S. D5 96
Cathcart, S. Afr. H5 44
Cathedral City, Ca., U.S. F5 82
Cathedral of the Pines, N.H., U.S. E3 106
Catherine, Lake, res., Ar., U.S. C3 81
Cat Island, i., Bah. B10 64
Cat Island, i., Ma., U.S. f12 98
Cat Island, i., Ms., U.S. E4 101
Cat Island, i., S.C., U.S. E9 117
Catlettsburg, Ky., U.S. B7 94
Catlin, Il., U.S. C6 90
Catnip Mountain, mtn., Nv., U.S. B2 105
Catoche, Cabo, c., Mex. G16 62
Cato Island, i., Austl. D11 50
Catonsville, Md., U.S. B4 97
Catoosa, Ok., U.S. A6 113
Catoosa, co., Ga., U.S. B1 87
Catorce, Mex. F9 62
Catron, co., N.M., U.S. D1 108
Catskill, N.Y., U.S. C7 109
Catskill Mountains, mts., N.Y., U.S. C6 109
Catt, Mount, mtn., B.C., Can. B3 69
Cattaraugus, co., N.Y., U.S. C2 109
Cattaraugus Creek, stm., N.Y., U.S. C2 109
Cattaraugus Indian Reservation, N.Y., U.S. C2 109
Cattolica, Italy F7 14
Catus, Fr. H8 10
Caubvick, Mount (Mont d'Iberville), mtn., Can. f9 72
Cauca, stm., Col. D5 58
Caucasia, Col. C5 58
Caucasus, mts., Eur. I6 22
Caucomgomoc Lake, l., Me., U.S. B3 96
Caudry, Fr. B10 10
Caulonia, Italy K11 14
Caúngula, Ang. C3 44
Čaunskaja Guba, b., Russia D27 24
Cauquenes, Chile D2 56
Caura, stm., Ven. D10 58
Caussade, Fr. H8 10
Cauvery, stm., India G5 37
Cavalaire-sur-Mer, Fr. I13 10
Cavalier, N.D., U.S. A8 111
Cavalier, co., N.D., U.S. A7 111
Cavan, Ire. G5 7
Cave City, Ar., U.S. B4 81
Cave City, Ky., U.S. C4 94
Cave Creek, Az., U.S. D4 80
Cave Junction, Or., U.S. E3 114
Cave Point, c., Wi., U.S. D6 126
Cave Run Lake, res., Ky., U.S. B6 94
Cave Spring, Ga., U.S. B1 87
Cave Spring, Va., U.S. C2 123
Cavetown, Md., U.S. A2 97
Caviana, Ilha, i., Braz. C8 54
Cavite, Phil. q19 33b
Cawood, Ky., U.S. D6 94
Cawston, B.C., Can. E8 69
Caxambu, Braz. F6 57
Caxias, Braz. D10 54
Caxias do Sul, Braz. B6 56
Caxito, Ang. C2 44
Cayambe, Ec. G3 58
Cayambe, vol., Ec. H4 58
Cayce, S.C., U.S. D5 117
Cayenne, Fr. Gu. C8 54
Cayman Brac, i., Cay. Is. E8 64
Cayman Islands, dep., N.A. E7 64
Cayuga, In., U.S. E3 91
Cayuga, co., N.Y., U.S. C4 109
Cayuga Heights, N.Y., U.S. C4 109
Cayuga Lake, l., N.Y., U.S. C4 109
Cazenovia, N.Y., U.S. C5 109
Cazères, Fr. I8 10
Cazin, Bos. E10 14
Cazorla, Spain H8 12
Čeboksary, Russia F7 22
Cebollar, Arg. B3 56
Cebreros, Spain E7 12
Cebu, Phil. C7 32
Cebu, i., Phil. C7 32
Čecerleg, Mong. B7 26
Čechov, Russia F20 18
Čechy, hist. reg., Czech. F14 8
Cecil, co., Md., U.S. A6 97
Cecil Field Naval Air Station, mil., Fl., U.S. B5 86
Cecilia, Ky., U.S. C4 94
Cecina, Italy F5 14
Cedar, co., Ia., U.S. C6 92
Cedar, co., Mo., U.S. D4 102
Cedar, co., Ne., U.S. B8 104
Cedar, stm., U.S. C6 92
Cedar, stm., Ne., U.S. B7 104
Cedar, stm., Wa., U.S. B4 124
Cedar Bluff, Al., U.S. A4 78
Cedar Bluff Reservoir, res., Ks., U.S. D4 93
Cedar Bluff Two, Tn., U.S. D9 119
Cedar Breaks National Monument, Ut., U.S. F3 121
Cedarburg, Wi., U.S. E6 126
Cedar City, Ut., U.S. F2 121
Cedar Creek, stm., N.J., U.S. D4 107
Cedar Creek, stm., N.D., U.S. C3 111
Cedar Creek, stm., Oh., U.S. e7 112
Cedar Creek Lake, res., Tx., U.S. C4 120
Cedar Crest, N.M., U.S. k8 108
Cedaredge, Co., U.S. C3 83
Cedar Falls, Ia., U.S. B5 92
Cedar Grove, N.J., U.S. B4 107
Cedar Grove, W.V., U.S. C3 125
Cedar Grove, Wi., U.S. E6 126
Cedar Hill, Mo., U.S. g12 102
Cedar Hill, Tx., U.S. n10 120
Cedarhurst, N.Y., U.S. k13 109
Cedar Island, i., N.C., U.S. C6 110
Cedar Island, i., S.C., U.S. E9 117
Cedar Island, i., Va., U.S. C7 123
Cedar Key, Fl., U.S. C3 86
Cedar Keys, is., Fl., U.S. C3 86
Cedar Lake, In., U.S. B3 91
Cedar Lake, res., Man., Can. C1 70
Cedar Lake, res., Il., U.S. F4 90
Cedar Mountain, mtn., Ca., U.S. B3 82
Cedar Point, c., Md., U.S. D5 97
Cedar Point, c., Oh., U.S. A3 112
Cedar Point, c., Oh., U.S. e7 112
Cedar Rapids, Ia., U.S. C6 92
Cedar Springs, Mi., U.S. E5 99
Cedartown, Ga., U.S. B1 87
Cedar Vale, Ks., U.S. E7 93
Cedarville, Oh., U.S. C2 112
Cedros, Isla, i., Mex. C2 62
Ceduna, Austl. F6 50
Cefalù, Italy K9 14
Čegdomyn, Russia G20 24
Cegléd, Hung. H19 8
Cehegín, Spain G10 12
Cela, Ang. D3 44
Čel'abinsk, Russia F10 22
Celano, Italy G8 14
Celanova, Spain C4 12
Celaya, Mex. G9 62
Cele, China B9 38
Celebes Sea, Asia E7 32
Celebes see Sulawesi, i., Indon. F7 32
Celina, Oh., U.S. B1 112
Celina, Tn., U.S. C8 119
Celina, Tx., U.S. C4 120
Celje, Slo. C10 14
Celle, Ger. C10 8
Cement, Ok., U.S. C3 113
Cementon, Pa., U.S. E10 115
Centennial Mountains, mts., Id., U.S. E7 89
Center, Co., U.S. D4 83
Center, N.D., U.S. B4 111
Center, Tx., U.S. D5 120
Centerbrook, Ct., U.S. D6 84
Centerburg, Oh., U.S. B3 112
Centereach, N.Y., U.S. n15 109
Centerfield, Ut., U.S. D4 121
Center Hill Lake, res., Tn., U.S. C8 119
Center Moriches, N.Y., U.S. n16 109
Center Mountain, mtn., Id., U.S. D3 89
Center Point, Al., U.S. f7 78
Center Point, Ia., U.S. B6 92
Centerville, In., U.S. E8 91
Centerville, Ia., U.S. D5 92
Centerville, La., U.S. E4 95
Centerville, Ma., U.S. C7 98
Centerville, Oh., U.S. C1 112
Centerville, Pa., U.S. F2 115
Centerville, S.D., U.S. D9 118
Centerville, Tn., U.S. B4 119
Centerville, Ut., U.S. C4 121
Cento, Italy E6 14
Central, N.M., U.S. E1 108
Central, S.C., U.S. B2 117
Central, Cordillera, mts., Bol. G6 54
Central, Cordillera, mts., Col. E5 58
Central, Cordillera, mts., Peru E3 54
Central, Massif, mts., Fr. G10 10
Central, Planalto, plat., Braz. G9 54
Central, Sistema, mts., Spain E6 12
Central African Republic, ctry., Afr. G10 42
Central City, Co., U.S. B5 83
Central City, Il., U.S. E4 90
Central City, Ia., U.S. B6 92
Central City, Ky., U.S. C2 94
Central City, Ne., U.S. C7 104
Central City, Pa., U.S. F4 115
Central Falls, R.I., U.S. B4 116
Central Heights, Az., U.S. D5 80
Centralia, Il., U.S. E4 90
Centralia, Mo., U.S. B5 102
Centralia, Wa., U.S. C3 124
Central Islip, N.Y., U.S. n15 109
Central Lake, Mi., U.S. C5 99
Central Makrān Range, mts., Pak. D1 36
Central Park, Wa., U.S. C2 124
Central Point, Or., U.S. E4 114
Central Square, N.Y., U.S. B4 109
Central Valley, Ca., U.S. B2 82
Central Valley, N.Y., U.S. D6 109
Central Village, Ct., U.S. C8 84
Centre, Al., U.S. A4 78
Centre, co., Pa., U.S. E6 115
Centre Hall, Pa., U.S. E6 115
Centreville, Al., U.S. C2 78
Centreville, Il., U.S. E3 90
Centreville, Md., U.S. B5 97
Centreville, Mi., U.S. G5 99
Centreville, Ms., U.S. D2 101
Centuria, Wi., U.S. C1 126
Century, Fl., U.S. u14 86
Cepu, Indon. m15 33a
Ceram Sea see Seram, Laut, Indon. F8 32
Cerbat Mountains, mts., Az., U.S. B1 80
Ceredo, W.V., U.S. C2 125
Čeremchovo, Russia G14 24
Čerepovec, Russia B20 18
Ceres, Ca., U.S. D3 82
Ceresco, Ne., U.S. C9 104
Céret, Fr. J9 10
Cereté, Col. C5 58
Cerf Island, i., Sey. C10 44
Cerignola, Italy H10 14
Cérilly, Fr. F9 10
Čerkassy, Ukr. H4 22
Čerkessk, Russia I6 22
Čern'achovsk, Russia G4 18
Černigov, Ukr. G4 22
Černogorsk, Russia G12 24
Černyševskij, Russia E16 24
Cerralvo, Isla, i., Mex. E5 62
Cerritos, Mex. F9 62
Cerro de Pasco, Peru F3 54
Cerro Gordo, Il., U.S. D5 90
Cerro Gordo, co., Ia., U.S. A4 92
Čerskij, Russia D26 24
Čerskogo, Chrebet, mts., Russia E23 24
Cervera del Río Alhama, Spain C10 12
Cervera de Pisuerga, Spain C7 12
Cervia, Italy E7 14
Cesena, Italy E7 14
Cesenatico, Italy E7 14
České Budějovice, Czech. G14 8
Cessnock, Austl. F10 50
Ceuta, Sp. N. Afr. A4 42
Ceyhan, Tur. A4 40
Ceylânpınar, Tur. A7 40
Ceylon see Sri Lanka, ctry., Asia H5 36
Chabanais, Fr. G7 10
Chabarovsk, Russia H21 24
Chachoengsao, Thai. H6 34
Chaco, stm., N.M., U.S. A1 108
Chaco Culture National Historic Park, N.M., U.S. A2 108
Chacon, Cape, c., Ak., U.S. n24 79

Name | Map Ref | Page

Chad, ctry., Afr. E9 42
Chad, Lake (Lac Tchad), l., Afr. F8 42
Chadbourn, N.C., U.S. C4 110
Chadds Ford, Pa., U.S. G10 115
Chadileuvú, stm., Arg. D3 56
Chadron, Ne., U.S. B3 104
Chadwicks, N.Y., U.S. B5 109
Chaffee, Mo., U.S. D8 102
Chaffee, co., Co., U.S. C4 83
Chaffin, Ma., U.S. B4 98
Chaghcharān, Afg. C1 38
Chagny, Fr. F11 10
Chagos Archipelago, is., B.I.O.T. G17 2
Chagrin Falls, Oh., U.S. A4 112
Chaibāsā, India I11 38
Chaîne Annamitique, mts., Asia F9 34
Chakachamna Lake, l., Ak., U.S. g15 79
Chake Chake, Tan. C7 44
Chalais, Fr. G7 10
Chalbi Desert, des., Kenya H2 46
Chalcuapa, El Sal. H3 64
Chaleur Bay, b., Can. B4 71
Chalfonte, De., U.S. h7 85
Chālisgaon, India B3 37
Chalk River, Ont., Can. A7 73
Challans, Fr. F5 10
Challis, Id., U.S. E4 89
Chalmette, La., U.S. E6 95
Chalonnes-sur-Loire, Fr. E6 10
Châlons-sur-Marne, Fr. D11 10
Chalon-sur-Saône, Fr. F11 10
Châlus, Fr. G7 10
Cham, Ger. F12 8
Chama, N.M., U.S. A3 108
Chama, Rio, stm., N.M., U.S. A3 108
Chaman, Pak. E2 38
Chambal, stm., India G7 38
Chamberlain, S.D., U.S. D6 118
Chamberlain Lake, l., Me., U.S. B3 96
Chamberlin, Mount, mtn., Ak., U.S. B10 79
Chambers, co., Al., U.S. C4 78
Chambers, co., Tx., U.S. E5 120
Chambersburg, Pa., U.S. G6 115
Chambers Island, i., Wi., U.S. C6 126
Chambéry, Fr. G12 10
Chambi, Jebel, mtn., Tun. A7 42
Chamblee, Ga., U.S. h8 87
Chambly, Que., Can. D4 74
Chambon-sur-Voueize, Fr. F9 10
Chamisal, N.M., U.S. A4 108
Chamonix-Mont-Blanc, Fr. G13 10
Champagne, hist. reg., Fr. D11 10
Champagnole, Fr. F12 10
Champaign, Il., U.S. C5 90
Champaign, co., Il., U.S. C5 90
Champaign, co., Oh., U.S. B2 112
Champassak, Laos G8 34
Champion, Oh., U.S. A5 112
Champlain, Lake, l., N.A. C12 76
Champlin, Mn., U.S. m12 100
Chāmrājnagar Rāmasamudram, India G4 37
Chañaral, Chile B2 56
Chance, Md., U.S. D6 97
Chanch, Mong. A7 26
Chanchelulla Peak, mtn., Ca., U.S. B2 82
Chandalar, stm., Ak., U.S. B10 79
Chandausi, India F8 38
Chandeleur Islands, is., La., U.S. E7 95
Chandeleur Sound, strt., La., U.S. E6 95
Chandīgarh, India E7 38
Chandler, Que., Can. k14 74
Chandler, Az., U.S. D4 80
Chandler, In., U.S. H3 91
Chandler, Ok., U.S. B5 113
Chandler, Tx., U.S. C5 120
Chandler Heights, Az., U.S. m9 80
Chāndpur, Bngl. I14 38
Chāndpur, India F8 38
Chandrapur, India C5 37
Chandyga, Russia E21 24
Chang (Yangtze), stm., China E10 26
Changajn Nuruu, mts., Mong. B6 26
Changchun, China C12 26
Changde, China F9 26
Changhua, Tai. K9 28
Changjiang, China J5 28
Changli, China D10 26
Changsha, China G1 28
Changshu, China D9 28
Changzhi, China D9 26
Changzhou (Changchow), China D8 28
Chanhassen, Mn., U.S. n11 100
Chanka, Ozero (Xingkathu), l., Asia I20 24
Channahon, Il., U.S. B5 90
Channapatna, India F4 37
Channel Islands, is., Eur. C4 10
Channel Islands National Park, Ca., U.S. F4 82
Channel Lake, Il., U.S. H8 90
Channel-Port-aux-Basques, Newf., Can. E2 72
Channelview, Tx., U.S. r14 120
Chantada, Spain C4 12
Chantajskoje, Ozero, l., Russia D12 24
Chanthaburi, Thai. H7 34
Chantilly, Va., U.S. g12 123
Chantrey Inlet, b., N.W. Ter., Can. C13 66
Chanute, Ks., U.S. E8 93
Chanute Air Force Base, mil., Il., U.S. C5 90
Chaoan, China L5 28
Chao Phraya, stm., Thai. G6 34
Chapala, Lago de, l., Mex. G8 62
Chaparral, Col. F5 58
Chapčeranga, Russia H16 24
Chapel Hill, N.C., U.S. B3 110
Chapel Hill, Tn., U.S. B5 119
Chaplin, stm., Ky., U.S. C4 94
Chaplin Lake, l., Sask., Can. G2 75
Chapman, Ks., U.S. D6 93
Chapman Pond, l., R.I., U.S. F1 116
Chapmanville, W.V., U.S. D2 125
Chappaquiddick Island, i., Ma., U.S. D7 98
Chappell, Ne., U.S. C3 104
Chāpra, India H11 38
Chapultepec, mtn., Mex. F8 62
Charadai, Arg. B5 56
Charcas, Mex. F9 62
Chardon, Oh., U.S. A4 112
Chardzhou see Čardžou, Turk. J10 22
Charenton, La., U.S. E4 95
Chari, stm., Afr. F9 42
Chārīkār, Afg. C3 38
Chariton, Ia., U.S. C4 92
Chariton, co., Mo., U.S. B4 102
Chariton, stm., U.S. A5 102
Charity, Guy. D13 58
Charleroi, Bel. E4 8
Charleroi, Pa., U.S. F2 115
Charles, co., Md., U.S. C3 97
Charles, stm., Ma., U.S. B5 98
Charles, Cape, c., Va., U.S. C6 123
Charles A. Goodwin Dam, Ct., U.S. B3 84
Charlesbourg, Que., Can. n17 74
Charles City, Ia., U.S. A5 92
Charles City, co., Va., U.S. C5 123
Charles Island, i., N.W. Ter., Can. D18 66
Charles Mill Lake, res., Oh., U.S. B3 112
Charles Mix, co., S.D., U.S. D7 118
Charles Mound, hill, Il., U.S. A3 90
Charleston, Ar., U.S. B1 81
Charleston, Il., U.S. D5 90
Charleston, Ms., U.S. A3 101
Charleston, Mo., U.S. E8 102
Charleston, Or., U.S. D2 114
Charleston, S.C., U.S. F8 117
Charleston, Tn., U.S. D9 119
Charleston, W.V., U.S. C3 125
Charleston, co., S.C., U.S. F8 117
Charleston Air Force Base, mil., S.C., U.S. k11 117
Charleston Naval Shipyard, mil., S.C., U.S. k12 117
Charleston Peak, mtn., Nv., U.S. G6 105
Charlestown, In., U.S. H6 91
Charlestown, N.H., U.S. D2 106
Charlestown, R.I., U.S. F2 116
Charles Town, W.V., U.S. B7 125
Charleville, Austl. E9 50
Charleville-Mézières, Fr. C11 10
Charlevoix, Mi., U.S. C5 99
Charlevoix, co., Mi., U.S. C5 99
Charlevoix, Lake, l., Mi., U.S. C5 99
Charlo, N.B., Can. B3 71
Charlotte, Mi., U.S. F6 99
Charlotte, N.C., U.S. B2 110
Charlotte, Tn., U.S. A4 119
Charlotte, Tx., U.S. E3 120
Charlotte, co., Fl., U.S. F5 86
Charlotte, co., Va., U.S. C4 123
Charlotte Amalie, V.I.U.S. E15 64
Charlotte Hall, Md., U.S. D4 97
Charlotte Harbor, Fl., U.S. F4 86
Charlotte Harbor, b., Fl., U.S. F4 86
Charlottenberg, Swe. G9 6
Charlottesville, Va., U.S. B4 123
Charlottetown, P.E.I., Can. C6 71
Charlton, co., Ga., U.S. F4 87
Charmco, W.V., U.S. C4 125
Charmes, Fr. D13 10
Charny, Que., Can. C6 74
Charolles, Fr. F11 10
Chārsadda, Pak. C4 38
Charters Towers, Austl. D9 50
Chartres, Fr. D8 10
Char Us Nuur, l., Mong. B5 26
Chascomús, Arg. D5 56
Chase, B.C., Can. D8 69
Chase, Md., U.S. B5 97
Chase, co., Ks., U.S. D7 93
Chase, co., Ne., U.S. D4 104
Chase City, Va., U.S. D4 123
Chase Field Naval Air Station, mil., Tx., U.S. E4 120
Chaska, Mn., U.S. F5 100
Chassahowitzka Bay, b., Fl., U.S. D4 86
Chassell, Mi., U.S. B2 99
Chatanbulag, Mong. C8 26
Chatanga, Russia C14 24
Chatanga, stm., Russia C14 24
Chatangskij Zaliv, b., Russia C15 24
Châteaubriant, Fr. E5 10
Château-du-Loir, Fr. E7 10
Châteaudun, Fr. D8 10
Château-Gontier, Fr. E6 10
Châteauguay, Que., Can. D4 74
Château-Landon, Fr. D9 10
Châteaulin, Fr. D2 10
Châteaumeillant, Fr. F9 10
Châteauneuf-sur-Charente, Fr. G6 10
Châteauneuf-sur-Loire, Fr. E9 10
Château-Renault, Fr. E7 10
Château-Richer, Que., Can. C6 74
Châteauroux, Fr. F8 10
Château-Thierry, Fr. C10 10
Châtellerault, Fr. F7 10
Chatfield, Mn., U.S. G6 100
Chatgal, Mong. A7 26
Chatham, N.B., Can. B4 71
Chatham, Ont., Can. E2 73
Chatham, Eng., U.K. J13 7
Chatham, Il., U.S. D4 90
Chatham, La., U.S. B3 95
Chatham, Ma., U.S. C8 98
Chatham, N.J., U.S. B4 107
Chatham, N.Y., U.S. C7 109
Chatham, Va., U.S. D3 123
Chatham, co., Ga., U.S. E5 87
Chatham, co., N.C., U.S. B3 110
Chatham Strait, strt., Ak., U.S. m22 79
Châtillon, Italy D2 14
Châtillon-Coligny, Fr. E9 10
Châtillon-sur-Indre, Fr. F8 10
Châtillon-sur-Seine, Fr. E11 10
Chatom, Al., U.S. D1 78
Chatsworth, Ga., U.S. B2 87
Chatsworth, Il., U.S. C5 90
Chatsworth Reservoir, res., Ca., U.S. m11 82
Chattahoochee, Fl., U.S. B2 86
Chattahoochee, co., Ga., U.S. D2 87
Chattahoochee, stm., U.S. E1 87
Chattanooga, Tn., U.S. D8 119
Chattaroy, W.V., U.S. D2 125
Chattooga, co., Ga., U.S. B1 87
Chattooga, stm., U.S. B1 117
Chatuge Lake, res., U.S. g9 110
Chatyrka, Russia E29 24
Chaudière, stm., Que., Can. C7 74
Chau Doc, Viet. I8 34
Chauk, Mya. D3 34
Chaumont, Fr. D12 10
Chauncey, Oh., U.S. C3 112
Chauny, Fr. C10 10
Chautauqua, co., Ks., U.S. E7 93
Chautauqua, co., N.Y., U.S. C1 109
Chautauqua Lake, l., N.Y., U.S. C1 109
Chauvigny, Fr. F7 10
Chauvin, La., U.S. E5 95
Chavakkad, India G4 37
Chaves, Port. D4 12
Chaves, co., N.M., U.S. D5 108
Cháviva, Col. E6 58
Chbukha Dzong, Bhu. G13 38
Cheaha Mountain, mtn., Al., U.S. B4 78
Cheat, Shavers Fork, stm., W.V., U.S. B5 125
Cheatham, co., Tn., U.S. A4 119
Chebanse, Il., U.S. C6 90
Cheboygan, Mi., U.S. C6 99
Cheboygan, co., Mi., U.S. C6 99
Chech, Erg, des., Afr. C5 42
Checotah, Ok., U.S. B6 113
Chedabucto Bay, b., N.S., Can. D8 71
Cheduba Island, i., Mya. E2 34
Cheektowaga, N.Y., U.S. C2 109
Cheeseman Lake, res., Co., U.S. B5 83
Chehalem Mountains, mts., Or., U.S. h12 114
Chehalis, Wa., U.S. C3 124
Chehalis, stm., Wa., U.S. C2 124
Cheju-do, i., S. Kor. E12 26
Chelan, Wa., U.S. B5 124
Chelan, co., Wa., U.S. B4 124
Chelan, Lake, l., Wa., U.S. A5 124
Chelan Mountains, mts., Wa., U.S. A5 124
Chełm, Pol. D23 8
Chełmno, Pol. B18 8
Chelmsford, Eng., U.K. J13 7
Chelmsford, Ma., U.S. A5 98
Chelsea, Que., Can. D2 74
Chelsea, Al., U.S. g7 78
Chelsea, Ma., U.S. B5 98
Chelsea, Mi., U.S. F6 99
Chelsea, Ok., U.S. A6 113
Cheltenham, Eng., U.K. J10 7
Cheltenham, Md., U.S. C4 97
Chelva, Spain F11 12
Chelyabinsk see Čel'abinsk, Russia F10 22
Chelyan, W.V., U.S. C3 125
Chemehuevi Indian Reservation, Ca., U.S. E6 82
Chemnitz, Ger. E12 8
Chemquasabamticook Lake (Ross Lake), l., Me., U.S. B3 96
Chemung, co., N.Y., U.S. C4 109
Chemung, stm., Pa., U.S. C8 115
Chemung Lake, l., Ont., Can. C6 73
Chenāb, stm., Asia E5 38
Chenachane, Alg. C6 42
Chenango, co., N.Y., U.S. C5 109
Chenango, stm., N.Y., U.S. C5 109
Chenango Bridge, N.Y., U.S. C5 109
Chenes, River Aux, b., La., U.S. k12 95
Chénéville, Que., Can. D2 74
Cheney, Ks., U.S. E6 93
Cheney, Wa., U.S. B8 124
Cheney Reservoir, res., Ks., U.S. E6 93
Cheneyville, La., U.S. C3 95
Chengde, China C10 26
Chengdu, China E7 26
Chengutu, Zimb. E6 44
Chenoa, Il., U.S. C5 90
Chenoweth, Or., U.S. B5 114
Chepachet, R.I., U.S. B2 116
Chepachet, stm., R.I., U.S. B2 116
Chepo, Pan. J8 64
Chequamegon Bay, b., Wi., U.S. B3 126
Cheraw, S.C., U.S. B8 117
Cherbourg, Fr. C5 10
Chergui, Chott ech, l., Alg. B6 42
Cherkasy, Ukr. H4 22
Chernihiv, Ukr. G4 22
Chernivtsi, Ukr. H3 22
Cherokee, Al., U.S. A2 78
Cherokee, Ia., U.S. B2 92
Cherokee, Ks., U.S. E9 93
Cherokee, Ok., U.S. A3 113
Cherokee, co., Al., U.S. A4 78
Cherokee, co., Ga., U.S. B2 87
Cherokee, co., Ia., U.S. B2 92
Cherokee, co., Ks., U.S. E9 93
Cherokee, co., N.C., U.S. f8 110
Cherokee, co., Ok., U.S. B6 113
Cherokee, co., S.C., U.S. A4 117
Cherokee, co., Tx., U.S. D5 120
Cherokee Indian Reservation, N.C., U.S. f9 110
Cherokee Lake, res., Tn., U.S. C10 119
Cherokees, Lake O' The, res., Ok., U.S. A7 113
Cherokee Village, Ar., U.S. A4 81
Cherry, co., Ne., U.S. B4 104
Cherry Creek, stm., S.D., U.S. C3 118
Cherry Hill, N.J., U.S. D2 107
Cherry Point, c., Va., U.S. C6 123
Cherry Point Marine Corps Air Station, mil., N.C., U.S. C6 110
Cherryvale, Ks., U.S. E8 93
Cherry Valley, Ar., U.S. B5 81
Cherry Valley, Il., U.S. A5 90
Cherryville, N.C., U.S. B1 110
Chesaning, Mi., U.S. E6 99
Chesapeake, Oh., U.S. D3 112
Chesapeake, Va., U.S. D6 123
Chesapeake, W.V., U.S. C3 125
Chesapeake and Delaware Canal, U.S. B3 85
Chesapeake Bay, b., U.S. D11 76
Chesapeake Bay Bridge-Tunnel, Va., U.S. D7 123
Chesapeake Beach, Md., U.S. C4 97
Chesapeake City, Md., U.S. A6 97
Chesdin, Lake, res., Va., U.S. C5 123
Cheshire, Ct., U.S. D4 84
Cheshire, co., N.H., U.S. E2 106
Cheshire Reservoir, res., Ma., U.S. A1 98
Chesley, Ont., Can. C3 73
Chesnee, S.C., U.S. A4 117
Chester, Eng., U.K. H10 7
Chester, Ca., U.S. B3 82
Chester, Ct., U.S. D6 84
Chester, Ga., U.S. D3 87
Chester, Il., U.S. F4 90
Chester, Md., U.S. C5 97
Chester, Mt., U.S. B6 103
Chester, N.H., U.S. E4 106
Chester, N.Y., U.S. D6 109
Chester, Pa., U.S. G11 115
Chester, S.C., U.S. B5 117
Chester, Vt., U.S. E3 122
Chester, Va., U.S. C5 123
Chester, W.V., U.S. A4 125
Chester, co., Pa., U.S. G10 115
Chester, co., S.C., U.S. B5 117
Chester, co., Tn., U.S. B3 119
Chester, stm., Md., U.S. B5 97
Chester Basin, N.S., Can. E5 71
Chester Depot, Vt., U.S. E3 122
Chesterfield, In., U.S. D6 91
Chesterfield, S.C., U.S. B7 117
Chesterfield, co., S.C., U.S. B7 117
Chesterfield, co., Va., U.S. C5 123
Chesterfield, Îles, is., N. Cal. C11 50
Chesterfield Inlet, N.W. Ter., Can. D14 66
Chesterfield Inlet, b., N.W. Ter., Can. D14 66
Chesterton, In., U.S. A3 91
Chestertown, Md., U.S. B5 97
Chesterville, Ont., Can. B9 73
Chesuncook Lake, l., Me., U.S. C3 96
Cheswick, Pa., U.S. h14 115
Cheswold, De., U.S. D3 85
Cheta, stm., Russia C13 24
Chetac, Lake, l., Wi., U.S. C2 126
Chetco, stm., Or., U.S. E2 114
Chetek, Wi., U.S. C2 126
Chetek, Lake, l., Wi., U.S. C2 126
Chetopa, Ks., U.S. E8 93
Chetumal Bay, b., N.A. H15 62
Chetwynd, B.C., Can. B7 69
Chevak, Ak., U.S. C6 79
Cheval Blanc, Pointe du, c., Haiti E11 64
Cheviot, Oh., U.S. C1 112
Chevreuil, Point, c., La., U.S. E4 95
Chevy Chase, Md., U.S. C3 97
Chewack, stm., Wa., U.S. A5 124
Chew Bahir (Lake Stefanie), l., Afr. H2 46
Chewelah, Wa., U.S. A8 124
Cheyenne, Ok., U.S. B2 113
Cheyenne, Wy., U.S. E8 127
Cheyenne, co., Co., U.S. C8 83
Cheyenne, co., Ks., U.S. C2 93
Cheyenne, co., Ne., U.S. C2 104
Cheyenne, stm., U.S. C4 118
Cheyenne, Dry Fork, stm., Wy., U.S. C7 127
Cheyenne River Indian Reservation, S.D., U.S. B4 118
Cheyenne Wells, Co., U.S. C8 83
Chezhou, China J1 28
Chhatarpur, India H8 38
Chhindwāra, India I8 38
Chi, stm., Thai. G8 34
Chiai, Tai. L9 28
Chiali, Tai. L9 28
Chiang Khan, Thai. F6 34
Chiang Mai, Thai. E5 34
Chiang Rai, Thai. E5 34
Chiari, Italy D4 14
Chiavari, Italy E4 14
Chiavenna, Italy C4 14
Chiba, Japan G13 30
Chiblow Lake, l., Ont., Can. A1 73
Chibougamau, Que., Can. k12 74
Chibuto, Moz. F6 44
Chicago, Il., U.S. B6 90
Chicago Heights, Il., U.S. B6 90
Chicago Sanitary and Ship Canal, Il., U.S. k8 90
Chicamacomico, stm., Md., U.S. D6 97
Chicapa, stm., Afr. C4 44
Chichagof Island, i., Ak., U.S. m22 79
Chīchāwatni, Pak. E5 38
Chichén Itzá, Mex. G15 62
Chichibu, Japan G12 30
Chickahominy, stm., Va., U.S. C5 123
Chickamauga, Ga., U.S. B1 87
Chickamauga and Chattanooga National Military Park, U.S. k11 119
Chickamauga Dam, Tn., U.S. h11 119
Chickamauga Lake, res., Tn., U.S. D8 119
Chickasaw, Al., U.S. E1 78
Chickasaw, co., Ia., U.S. A5 92
Chickasaw, co., Ms., U.S. B5 101
Chickasawhay, stm., Ms., U.S. D5 101
Chickasaw National Recreation Area, Ok., U.S. C5 113
Chickasha, Ok., U.S. B4 113
Chickasha, Lake, res., Ok., U.S. B3 113
Chickwolnepy Stream, stm., N.H., U.S. A4 106
Chiclana de la Frontera, Spain I5 12
Chiclayo, Peru E3 54
Chico, Ca., U.S. C3 82
Chicoa, Moz. E6 44
Chicopee, Ga., U.S. B3 87
Chicopee, Ma., U.S. B2 98
Chicora, Pa., U.S. E2 115
Chicot, Lake, l., Ar., U.S. D4 81
Chicot Island, i., La., U.S. E6 95
Chicoutimi, Que., Can. A6 74
Chicoutimi, stm., Que., Can. A6 74
Chidambaram, India G5 37
Chidley, Cape, c., Can. D20 66
Chiefland, Fl., U.S. C4 86
Chieri, Italy D2 14
Chieti, Italy G9 14
Chifeng, China C10 26
Chigasaki, Japan G12 30
Chignecto, Cape, c., N.S., Can. D5 71
Chignecto Bay, b., Can. D5 71
Ch'ihu, Tai. L9 28
Chihuahua, Mex. C6 62
Chikaskia, stm., U.S. A4 113
Chik Ballāpur, India F4 37
Chikmagalūr, India F3 37
Chilakalūrupet, India D6 37
Chilapa de Alvarez, Mex. I10 62
Chilās, Pak. C6 38
Childersburg, Al., U.S. B3 78
Childress, Tx., U.S. B2 120
Childress, co., Tx., U.S. B2 120
Chile, ctry., S.A. C2 56
Chilete, Peru E3 54
Chilhowie, Va., U.S. f10 123
Chililabombwe (Bancroft), Zam. D5 44
Chilka Lake, l., India C8 37
Chilko, stm., B.C., Can. D6 69
Chilko Lake, l., B.C., Can. D5 69
Chillán, Chile D2 56
Chillicothe, Il., U.S. C4 90
Chillicothe, Mo., U.S. B4 102
Chillicothe, Oh., U.S. C3 112
Chilliwack, B.C., Can. E7 69
Chillum, Md., U.S. f9 97
Chiloé, Isla de, i., Chile E2 56
Chilok, Russia G16 24
Chiloquin, Or., U.S. E5 114
Chilpancingo [de los Bravos], Mex. I10 62
Chilton, Wi., U.S. D5 126
Chilton, co., Al., U.S. C3 78
Chilung, Tai. J10 28
Chilwa, Lake, l., Afr. E7 44
Chimacum, Wa., U.S. A3 124
Chimayo, N.M., U.S. A4 108
Chimborazo, vol., Ec. H3 58
Chimbote, Peru E3 54
Chimkent see Čimkent, Kaz. I11 22
Chimki, Russia F20 18
Chimney Rock, mtn., Ne., U.S. C2 104
China, ctry., Asia D7 26
China Grove, N.C., U.S. B2 110
China Lake, l., Me., U.S. D3 96
Chinandega, Nic. H4 64
Chincha Alta, Peru F3 54
Chincilla de Monte Aragón, Spain G10 12
Chincoteague, Va., U.S. C7 123
Chincoteague Bay, b., U.S. D7 97
Chinde, Moz. E7 44
Chindwinn, stm., Mya. C3 34
Chingleput, India F5 37
Chingola, Zam. D5 44
Ch'ingshui, Tai. K9 28
Chin Hills, hills, Mya. D2 34
Chinhoyi, Zimb. E6 44
Chiniot, Pak. E5 38
Chinitna Point, c., Ak., U.S. h15 79
Chinju, S. Kor. D12 26
Chinko, stm., Cen. Afr. Rep. G10 42
Chinkuashih, Tai. J10 28
Chinle, Az., U.S. A6 80
Chinmen Tao, i., Tai. K7 28
Chino, Ca., U.S. F5 82
Chinon, Fr. E7 10
Chinook, Mt., U.S. B7 103
Chinook, Wa., U.S. C2 124
Chinook, Lake, res., Or., U.S. C5 114
Chino Valley, Az., U.S. C3 80
Chinshan, Tai. J10 28
Chioggia, Italy D7 14
Chipata, Zam. D6 44
Chipita Park, Co., U.S. C6 83
Chipley, Fl., U.S. u16 86
Chipman, N.B., Can. C4 71
Chipola, stm., Fl., U.S. B1 86
Chippewa, co., Mi., U.S. B6 99
Chippewa, co., Mn., U.S. E3 100
Chippewa, co., Wi., U.S. C2 126
Chippewa, stm., Mn., U.S. E3 100
Chippewa, stm., Wi., U.S. D2 126
Chippewa, Lake, l., Wi., U.S. C2 126
Chippewa Falls, Wi., U.S. D2 126
Chipuxet, stm., R.I., U.S. F3 116
Chiquimula, Guat. G3 64
Chiquinquirá, Col. E6 58
Chīrāla, India E6 37
Chirfa, Niger D8 42
Chirgis Nuur, l., Mong. B5 26
Chiricahua Mountains, mts., Az., U.S. E6 80
Chiricahua National Monument, Az., U.S. F6 80
Chiricahua Peak, mtn., Az., U.S. F6 80
Chiriguaná, Col. C6 58
Chirikof Island, i., Ak., U.S. D8 79
Chiriquí, Golfo, b., Pan. K6 64
Chiriquí, Laguna de, b., Pan. J7 64
Chirripó, Cerro, mtn., C.R. J6 64
Chisago, co., Mn., U.S. E6 100
Chisago City, Mn., U.S. E6 100
Chisholm, Me., U.S. D2 96
Chisholm, Mn., U.S. C6 100
Chishtiān Mandi, Pak. F5 38
Chişinău, Mol. H3 22
Chisos Mountains, mts., Tx., U.S. E1 120
Chitato, Ang. C4 44
Chitembo, Ang. D3 44
Chitina, stm., Ak., U.S. g19 79
Chitipa, Mwi. C6 44
Chitorgarh, India H6 38
Chitose, Japan q19 30a
Chitradurga, India E4 37
Chitrāl, Pak. C4 38
Chitré, Pan. K7 64
Chittagong, Bngl. I14 38
Chittenango, N.Y., U.S. B5 109
Chittenden, co., Vt., U.S. C2 122
Chittenden Reservoir, res., Vt., U.S. D3 122
Chittoor, India F5 37

Name — Map Ref — Page

Chiusi, Italy F6 14
Chivasso, Italy D2 14
Choapan, Mex. I12 62
Chocolate Mountains, mts., U.S. F6 82
Chocontá, Col. E6 58
Choctaw, Ok., U.S. B4 113
Choctaw, co., Al., U.S. C1 78
Choctaw, co., Ms., U.S. B4 101
Choctaw, co., Ok., U.S. C6 113
Choctawhatchee Bay, b., Fl., U.S. u15 86
Choctaw Indian Reservation, Ms., U.S. C4 101
Choele Choel, Arg. D3 56
Cholet, Fr. E6 10
Cholmsk, Russia H22 24
Choluteca, Hond. H4 64
Choma, Zam. E5 44
Chomutov, Czech. E13 8
Chon Buri, Thai. H6 34
Chone, Ec. H2 58
Ch'ŏngjin, N. Kor. C12 26
Ch'ŏngju, S. Kor. D12 26
Chongmingdao, i., China D10 28
Chongqing, China F8 26
Chŏnju, S. Kor. D12 26
Chonos, Archipiélago de los, is., Chile F2 56
Chonuu, Russia D22 24
Choptank, stm., Md., U.S. C6 97
Chōshi, Japan G13 30
Chos Malal, Arg. D2 56
Choteau, Mt., U.S. C4 103
Chouteau, Ok., U.S. A6 113
Chouteau, co., Mt., U.S. C6 103
Chovd, Mong. B5 26
Chövsgöl Nuur, l., Mong. A7 26
Chowan, co., N.C., U.S. A6 110
Chowan, stm., N.C., U.S. A6 110
Chowchilla, Ca., U.S. D3 82
Chrisman, Il., U.S. D6 90
Christanshåb, Grnld. C22 66
Christchurch, N.Z. E4 52
Christian, co., Il., U.S. D4 90
Christian, co., Ky., U.S. D2 94
Christian, co., Mo., U.S. E4 102
Christian, Cape, c., N.W. Ter., Can. B19 66
Christiana, De., U.S. B3 85
Christiana, Pa., U.S. G9 115
Christiansburg, Va., U.S. C2 123
Christian Sound, strt., Ak., U.S. n22 79
Christiansted, V.I.U.S. F15 64
Christina, stm., Alta., Can. A5 68
Christina, stm., De., U.S. B3 85
Christina, Lake, l., Mn., U.S. D3 100
Christina Peak, mtn., Nv., U.S. D6 105
Christmas, Fl., U.S. D5 86
Christmas Island, dep., Oc. H4 32
Christmas Lake, l., Or., U.S. D6 114
Christopher, Il., U.S. F4 90
Chroma, stm., Russia C22 24
Chrzanów, Pol. E19 8
Chubbuck, Id., U.S. G6 89
Chugach Islands, is., Ak., U.S. h16 79
Chugach Mountains, mts., Ak., U.S. g18 79
Chūgoku-sanchi, mts., Japan H5 30
Chugwater, Wy., U.S. E8 127
Chugwater Creek, stm., Wy., U.S. E8 127
Chukai, Malay. L7 34
Chukchi Sea C30 128
Chula Vista, Ca., U.S. F5 82
Chulucanas, Peru E2 54
Chumphon, Thai. I5 34
Chum Saeng, Thai. G6 34
Chunchi, Ec. I3 58
Ch'unch'ŏn, S. Kor. D12 26
Chunchula, Al., U.S. E1 78
Ch'ungju, S. Kor. D12 26
Chungking see Chongqing, China F8 26
Chungli, Tai. K10 28
Chungyang Shanmo, mts., Tai. L10 28
Chuŏr Phnum Krâvanh, mts., Asia H7 34
Chupadera Mesa, mtn., N.M., U.S. D3 108
Chupaderos, Mex. F8 62
Chuquicamata, Chile A3 56
Chur, Switz. F16 10
Church Hill, Tn., U.S. C11 119
Churchill, Man., Can. f9 70
Churchill, co., Nv., U.S. D3 105
Churchill, stm., Can. E13 66
Churchill, stm., Newf., Can. h9 72
Churchill, Cape, c., Man., Can. f9 70
Churchill, Mount, mtn., B.C., Can. E6 69
Churchill Falls, wtfl, Newf., Can. h8 72
Churchill Lake, l., Sask., Can. m7 75
Churchill Lake, l., Me., U.S. B3 96
Church Point, La., U.S. D3 95
Church Rock, N.M., U.S. B1 108
Churchton, Md., U.S. C4 97
Churchville, N.Y., U.S. B3 109
Churu, India F6 38
Churubusco, In., U.S. B7 91
Churuguara, Ven. B8 58
Chuska Mountains, mts., Az., U.S. A6 80
Chutag, Mong. B7 26
Chuxian, China C7 28
Chuxiong, China B6 34
Chužir, Russia G13 24
Cianjur, Indon. G4 32
Cibecue, Az., U.S. C5 80
Cibinong, Indon. m13 33a
Cibola, co., N.M., U.S. C1 108
Cibolo Creek, stm., Tx., U.S. h7 120
Cicero, Il., U.S. B6 90
Cicero, In., U.S. D5 91
Ciechanów, Pol. C20 8
Ciego de Avila, Cuba D8 64
Ciempozuelos, Spain E8 12
Ciénaga, Col. B5 58
Cienfuegos, Cuba C7 64
Cieszyn, Pol. F18 8
Cieza, Spain G10 12
Cifuentes, Spain E9 12
Cikampek, Indon. m13 33a
Cilacap, Indon. m14 33a
Cilleruelo de Bezana, Spain C8 12
Cimarron, Ks., U.S. E3 93
Cimarron, N.M., U.S. A5 108
Cimarron, co., Ok., U.S. e8 113
Čimkent, Kaz. I11 22
Çınarcık, Tur. I13 16
Cincinnati, Oh., U.S. C1 112
Çine, Tur. L12 16
Ciney, Bel. E5 8
Cinnaminson, N.J., U.S. D3 107
Cipa, stm., Russia F17 24
Cipolletti, Arg. D3 56
Circle, Ak., U.S. B11 79
Circle, Mt., U.S. C11 103
Circle Pines, Mn., U.S. m12 100
Circleville, Oh., U.S. C3 112
Cirebon, Indon. m14 32
Cirencester, Eng., U.K. J11 7
Ciriè, Italy D2 14
Cirò Marina, Italy J12 14
Cisco, Tx., U.S. C3 120
Cispus, stm., Wa., U.S. C4 124
Cissna Park, Il., U.S. C6 90
Çistierna, Spain C6 12
Čita, Russia G16 24
Citra, Fl., U.S. C4 86
Citronelle, Al., U.S. D1 78
Citrus, co., Fl., U.S. D4 86
Città di Castello, Italy F7 14
City of Refuge National Historical Park, Hi., U.S. D5 88
City View, S.C., U.S. B3 117
Ciudad, Mex. F7 62
Ciudad Acuña, Mex. C9 62
Ciudad Altamirano, Mex. H9 62
Ciudad Bolívar, Ven. C11 58
Ciudad Bolivia, Ven. C7 58
Ciudad Camargo, Mex. D7 62
Ciudad Chetumal, Mex. H15 62
Ciudad del Carmen, Mex. H14 62
Ciudad del Maíz, Mex. F10 62
Ciudad de México (Mexico City), Mex. H10 62
Ciudad de Nutrias, Ven. C8 58
Ciudad de Valles, Mex. G10 62
Ciudadela, Spain E15 12
Ciudad Guayana, Ven. C11 58
Ciudad Guzmán, Mex. H8 62
Ciudad Hidalgo, Mex. H9 62
Ciudad Ixtepec, Mex. I12 62
Ciudad Jiménez, Mex. D7 62
Ciudad Juárez, Mex. B6 62
Ciudad Madero, Mex. F11 62
Ciudad Mante, Mex. F10 62
Ciudad Melchor Múzquiz, Mex. D9 62
Ciudad Obregón, Mex. D5 62
Ciudad Ojeda (Lagunillas), Ven. B7 58
Ciudad Piar, Ven. D11 58
Ciudad Real, Spain G8 12
Ciudad Rodrigo, Spain E5 12
Ciudad Victoria, Mex. F10 62
Civita Castellana, Italy G7 14
Civitanova Marche, Italy F8 14
Civitavecchia, Italy G6 14
Civray, Fr. F7 10
C.J. Strike Reservoir, res., Id., U.S. G3 89
Clackamas, Or., U.S. h12 114
Clackamas, co., Or., U.S. B4 114
Clacton-on-Sea, Eng., U.K. J14 7
Claflin, Ks., U.S. D5 93
Claiborne, co., La., U.S. B2 95
Claiborne, co., Ms., U.S. D3 101
Claiborne, co., Tn., U.S. C10 119
Claiborne, Lake, res., La., U.S. B3 95
Clair, N.B., Can. B1 71
Claire, Lake, l., Alta., Can. f8 68
Clair Engle Lake, res., Ca., U.S. B2 82
Clairton, Pa., U.S. F2 115
Clallam, co., Wa., U.S. B1 124
Clallam Bay, Wa., U.S. A1 124
Clamecy, Fr. E10 10
Clam Lake, l., Wi., U.S. C1 126
Clan Alpine Mountains, mts., Nv., U.S. D4 105
Clanton, Al., U.S. C3 78
Clanwilliam, S. Afr. H3 44
Clara City, Mn., U.S. F3 100
Clara Peak, mtn., Az., U.S. C2 80
Clare, Mi., U.S. E6 99
Clare, co., Mi., U.S. E6 99
Claremont, Ca., U.S. m13 82
Claremont, N.H., U.S. D2 106
Claremont, N.C., U.S. B1 110
Claremont, mtn., Ca., U.S. C3 82
Claremore, Ok., U.S. A6 113
Claremorris, Ire. H3 7
Clarence, Ia., U.S. C6 92
Clarence, Mo., U.S. B5 102
Clarence Strait, strt., Ak., U.S. n23 79
Clarendon, Ar., U.S. C4 81
Clarendon, Tx., U.S. B2 120
Clarendon, co., S.C., U.S. D7 117
Clarendon, stm., Vt., U.S. E2 122
Clarendon Hills, Il., U.S. k9 90
Clarenville, Newf., Can. D4 72
Claresholm, Alta., Can. D4 68
Claridge, Pa., U.S. F2 115
Clarinda, Ia., U.S. D2 92
Clarines, Ven. C10 58
Clarion, Ia., U.S. B4 92
Clarion, Pa., U.S. D3 115
Clarion, co., Pa., U.S. D3 115
Clarion, stm., Pa., U.S. D3 115
Clarión, Isla, i., Mex. H2 62
Clarissa, Mn., U.S. D4 100
Clark, N.J., U.S. B4 107
Clark, S.D., U.S. C8 118
Clark, co., Ar., U.S. C2 81
Clark, co., Id., U.S. E6 89
Clark, co., Il., U.S. D6 90
Clark, co., In., U.S. H6 91
Clark, co., Ks., U.S. E4 93
Clark, co., Ky., U.S. C5 94
Clark, co., Mo., U.S. A6 102
Clark, co., Nv., U.S. G6 105
Clark, co., Oh., U.S. C2 112
Clark, co., S.D., U.S. C8 118
Clark, co., Wa., U.S. D3 124
Clark, co., Wi., U.S. D3 126
Clark, Lake, l., Ak., U.S. C9 79
Clark, Point, c., Ont., Can. C3 73
Clarkdale, Az., U.S. C3 80
Clarkdale, Ga., U.S. h7 87
Clarke, co., Al., U.S. D2 78
Clarke, co., Ga., U.S. C3 87
Clarke, co., Ia., U.S. D4 92
Clarke, co., Ms., U.S. C5 101
Clarke, co., Va., U.S. A4 123
Clarkesville, Ga., U.S. B3 87
Clarkfield, Mn., U.S. F3 100
Clark Fork, stm., U.S. C1 103
Clarks, La., U.S. B3 95
Clarks, stm., Ky., U.S. f9 94
Clarksburg, Md., U.S. B3 97
Clarksburg, W.V., U.S. B4 125
Clarksdale, Ms., U.S. A3 101
Clarks Grove, Mn., U.S. G5 100
Clark's Harbour, N.S., Can. F4 71
Clarks Hill, In., U.S. D4 91
Clarkson, Ky., U.S. C3 94
Clarkson, Ne., U.S. C8 104
Clarks Summit, Pa., U.S. m18 115
Clarkston, Ga., U.S. h8 87
Clarkston, Mi., U.S. F7 99
Clarkston, Ut., U.S. B3 121
Clarkston, Wa., U.S. C8 124
Clarksville, Ar., U.S. B2 81
Clarksville, De., U.S. F5 85
Clarksville, In., U.S. H6 91
Clarksville, Ia., U.S. B5 92
Clarksville, Tn., U.S. A4 119
Clarksville, Tx., U.S. C5 120
Clarksville, Va., U.S. D4 123
Clarkton, Mo., U.S. E8 102
Clarkton, N.C., U.S. C4 110
Clatskanie, Or., U.S. A3 114
Clatsop, co., Or., U.S. A3 114
Claude, Tx., U.S. B2 120
Clausthal-Zellerfeld, Ger. D10 8
Clawson, Mi., U.S. o15 99
Claxton, Ga., U.S. D5 87
Clay, Ky., U.S. C2 94
Clay, co., Al., U.S. B4 78
Clay, co., Ar., U.S. A5 81
Clay, co., Fl., U.S. B5 86
Clay, co., Ga., U.S. E2 87
Clay, co., Il., U.S. E5 90
Clay, co., In., U.S. F3 91
Clay, co., Ia., U.S. A2 92
Clay, co., Ks., U.S. C6 93
Clay, co., Ky., U.S. C6 94
Clay, co., Mn., U.S. D2 100
Clay, co., Ms., U.S. B5 101
Clay, co., Mo., U.S. B3 102
Clay, co., Ne., U.S. D7 104
Clay, co., N.C., U.S. f9 110
Clay, co., S.D., U.S. E8 118
Clay, co., Tn., U.S. C8 119
Clay, co., Tx., U.S. C3 120
Clay, co., W.V., U.S. C3 125
Clay Center, Ks., U.S. C6 93
Clay Center, Ne., U.S. D7 104
Clay City, Il., U.S. E5 90
Clay City, In., U.S. F3 91
Clay City, Ky., U.S. C6 94
Clay Creek, stm., S.D., U.S. D8 118
Claymont, De., U.S. A4 85
Clayoquot Sound, strt., B.C., Can. E4 69
Claypool, Az., U.S. D5 80
Claysburg, Pa., U.S. F5 115
Claysville, Pa., U.S. F1 115
Clayton, Al., U.S. D4 78
Clayton, De., U.S. C3 85
Clayton, Ga., U.S. B3 87
Clayton, In., U.S. E4 91
Clayton, La., U.S. C4 95
Clayton, Mo., U.S. f13 102
Clayton, N.J., U.S. D2 107
Clayton, N.M., U.S. A6 108
Clayton, N.Y., U.S. A4 109
Clayton, N.C., U.S. B4 110
Clayton, Ok., U.S. C6 113
Clayton, co., Ga., U.S. C2 87
Clayton, co., Ia., U.S. B6 92
Clayton Lake, res., Va., U.S. C2 123
Clear, stm., R.I., U.S. B2 116
Clear Boggy Creek, stm., Ok., U.S. C5 113
Clear Creek, co., Co., U.S. B5 83
Clear Creek, stm., Tn., U.S. C9 119
Clear Creek, stm., Wy., U.S. B6 127
Cleare, Cape, c., Ak., U.S. D10 79
Clearfield, Ky., U.S. B6 94
Clearfield, Pa., U.S. D5 115
Clearfield, Ut., U.S. B3 121
Clearfield, co., Pa., U.S. D5 115
Clear Fork, stm., W.V., U.S. D3 125
Clear Fork, stm., W.V., U.S. n13 125
Clearlake, Ca., U.S. C2 82
Clear Lake, Ia., U.S. A4 92
Clear Lake, S.D., U.S. C9 118
Clearlake, Wa., U.S. A3 124
Clear Lake, Wi., U.S. C1 126
Clear Lake, l., Ia., U.S. A4 92
Clear Lake, l., Ut., U.S. D3 121
Clear Lake, res., Ca., U.S. C2 82
Clear Lake Reservoir, res., Ca., U.S. B3 82
Clear Lake Shores, Tx., U.S. r15 120
Clear Stream, stm., N.H., U.S. g7 106
Clearwater, B.C., Can. D7 69
Clearwater, Fl., U.S. E4 86
Clearwater, Ks., U.S. E6 93
Clearwater, S.C., U.S. E4 117
Clearwater, co., Id., U.S. C3 89
Clearwater, co., Mn., U.S. C3 100
Clearwater, stm., Can. A5 68
Clearwater, stm., Id., U.S. C2 89
Clearwater, stm., Mn., U.S. C3 100
Clearwater Lake, res., Mo., U.S. D7 102
Clearwater Mountains, mts., Id., U.S. C2 89
Cleburne, Tx., U.S. C4 120
Cleburne, co., Al., U.S. B4 78
Cleburne, co., Ar., U.S. B3 81
Cle Elum, Wa., U.S. B5 124
Cle Elum, stm., Wa., U.S. B4 124
Cle Elum Lake, res., Wa., U.S. B4 124
Clementon, N.J., U.S. D3 107
Clemmons, N.C., U.S. A2 110
Clemson, S.C., U.S. B2 117
Clendenin, W.V., U.S. C3 125
Clendening Lake, res., Oh., U.S. B4 112
Cleona, Pa., U.S. F9 115
Clermont, Que., Can. B7 74
Clermont, Fr. C9 10
Clermont, Fl., U.S. D5 86
Clermont, co., Oh., U.S. C1 112
Clermont-Ferrand, Fr. G10 10
Cles, Italy C6 14
Cleveland, Al., U.S. A3 78
Cleveland, Ga., U.S. B3 87
Cleveland, Mn., U.S. F5 100
Cleveland, Ms., U.S. B3 101
Cleveland, N.C., U.S. B2 110
Cleveland, Oh., U.S. A4 112
Cleveland, Ok., U.S. A5 113
Cleveland, Tn., U.S. D9 119
Cleveland, Tx., U.S. D5 120
Cleveland, Wi., U.S. k10 126
Cleveland, co., Ar., U.S. D3 81
Cleveland, co., N.C., U.S. B1 110
Cleveland, co., Ok., U.S. B4 113
Cleveland, Mount, mtn., Mt., U.S. B3 103
Cleveland Heights, Oh., U.S. A4 112
Cleves, Oh., U.S. o12 112
Clewiston, Fl., U.S. F6 86
Clifden, Ire. H2 7
Cliff Island, i., Me., U.S. g7 96
Clifford, Ont., Can. D4 73
Cliffside, N.C., U.S. B1 110
Cliffside Park, N.J., U.S. h9 107
Clifton, Az., U.S. D6 80
Clifton, Co., U.S. B2 83
Clifton, Il., U.S. C6 90
Clifton, N.J., U.S. B4 107
Clifton, S.C., U.S. B4 117
Clifton, Tn., U.S. B4 119
Clifton, Tx., U.S. D4 120
Clifton Forge, Va., U.S. C3 123
Clifton Knolls, N.Y., U.S. C7 109
Clifton Springs, N.Y., U.S. C3 109
Clinch, co., Ga., U.S. F4 87
Clinch, stm., U.S. D9 119
Clinchco, Va., U.S. e9 123
Clinch Mountain, mtn., U.S. C10 119
Clingmans Dome, mtn., U.S. D10 119
Clinton, B.C., Can. D7 69
Clinton, Ont., Can. D3 73
Clinton, Ar., U.S. B3 81
Clinton, Ct., U.S. D5 84
Clinton, Il., U.S. C5 90
Clinton, In., U.S. E3 91
Clinton, Ia., U.S. C7 92
Clinton, Ky., U.S. f9 94
Clinton, La., U.S. D4 95
Clinton, Me., U.S. D3 96
Clinton, Md., U.S. C4 97
Clinton, Ma., U.S. B4 98
Clinton, Mi., U.S. F7 99
Clinton, Ms., U.S. C3 101
Clinton, Mo., U.S. C4 102
Clinton, N.Y., U.S. B5 109
Clinton, N.C., U.S. C4 110
Clinton, Ok., U.S. B3 113
Clinton, S.C., U.S. C4 117
Clinton, Tn., U.S. C9 119
Clinton, Ut., U.S. B3 121
Clinton, Wa., U.S. B3 124
Clinton, Wi., U.S. F5 126
Clinton, co., Il., U.S. E4 90
Clinton, co., In., U.S. D4 91
Clinton, co., Ia., U.S. C7 92
Clinton, co., Ky., U.S. D4 94
Clinton, co., Mi., U.S. F6 99
Clinton, co., Mo., U.S. B3 102
Clinton, co., N.Y., U.S. f11 109
Clinton, co., Oh., U.S. C2 112
Clinton, co., Pa., U.S. D6 115
Clinton Lake, res., Il., U.S. C5 90
Clinton-Colden Lake, l., N.W. Ter., Can. D11 66
Clinton Lake, res., Ks., U.S. m15 93
Clinton Reservoir, res., N.J., U.S. A4 107
Clintonville, Wi., U.S. D5 126
Clintwood, Va., U.S. e9 123
Clio, Al., U.S. D4 78
Clio, Mi., U.S. E7 99
Clio, S.C., U.S. B8 117
Clive, Ia., U.S. e8 92
Clogher Head, c., Ire. H6 7
Cloncurry, Austl. D8 50
Clonmel, Ire. I5 7
Cloppenburg, Ger. C8 8
Cloquet, Mn., U.S. D6 100
Cloquet, stm., Mn., U.S. C6 100
Closter, N.J., U.S. B5 107
Clothier, W.V., U.S. n12 125
Cloud, co., Ks., U.S. C6 93
Cloudcroft, N.M., U.S. E4 108
Cloud Peak, mtn., Wy., U.S. B5 127
Clover, S.C., U.S. A5 117
Cloverdale, Al., U.S. A2 78
Cloverdale, Ca., U.S. C2 82
Cloverdale, In., U.S. E4 91
Cloverport, Ky., U.S. C3 94
Clovis, Ca., U.S. D4 82
Clovis, N.M., U.S. C6 108
Cluj-Napoca, Rom. C7 16
Cluny, Fr. F11 10
Cluses, Fr. F13 10
Clusone, Italy D4 14
Clute, Tx., U.S. r14 120
Clutha, stm., N.Z. G2 52
Clyde, N.W. Ter., Can. B19 66
Clyde, Ks., U.S. C6 93
Clyde, N.Y., U.S. B4 109
Clyde, N.C., U.S. f10 110
Clyde, Oh., U.S. A3 112
Clyde, Tx., U.S. C3 120
Clyde, stm., Scot., U.K. F9 7
Clyde, Firth of, est., Scot., U.K. F7 7
Clymer, Pa., U.S. E3 115
Coachella, Ca., U.S. F5 82
Coachella Canal, Ca., U.S. F6 82
Coacoyole, Mex. E6 62
Coahoma, Tx., U.S. C2 120
Coahoma, co., Ms., U.S. A3 101
Coal, co., Ok., U.S. C5 113
Coal, stm., W.V., U.S. C3 125
Coal Branch, N.B., Can. C4 71
Coal City, Il., U.S. B5 90
Coalcomán de Matamoros, Mex. H8 62
Coal Creek, stm., Ok., U.S. B6 113
Coaldale, Alta., Can. E4 68
Coal Fork, W.V., U.S. C3 125
Coal Fork, stm., W.V., U.S. m13 125
Coalgate, Ok., U.S. C5 113
Coal Grove, Oh., U.S. D3 112
Coal Hill, Ar., U.S. B2 81
Coalhurst, Alta., Can. E4 68
Coalinga, Ca., U.S. D3 82
Coalmont, Tn., U.S. D8 119
Coalville, Ut., U.S. C4 121
Coalwood, W.V., U.S. D3 125
Coari, Braz. D6 54
Coasters Harbor Island, i., R.I., U.S. E5 116
Coast Mountains, mts., N.A. E6 66
Coast Ranges, mts., U.S. C2 76
Coatepeque, Guat. G2 64
Coatesville, Pa., U.S. G10 115
Coaticook, Que., Can. D6 74
Coats, N.C., U.S. B4 110
Coats Island, i., N.W. Ter., Can. D16 66
Coats Land, reg., Ant. B10 47
Coatzacoalcos, Mex. H12 62
Cobalt, Ont., Can. p19 73
Cobb, co., Ga., U.S. C2 87
Cobb, stm., Mn., U.S. G5 100
Cobble Mountain Reservoir, res., Ma., U.S. B2 98
Cobbosseecontee Lake, l., Me., U.S. D3 96
Cobden, Ont., Can. B8 73
Cobden, Il., U.S. F4 90
Cobequid Mountains, mts., N.S., Can. D5 71
Cobham, stm., Can. C4 70
Cobija, Bol. F5 54
Cobleskill, N.Y., U.S. C6 109
Cobourg, Ont., Can. D6 73
Cóbuè, Moz. D6 44
Cobun Creek, stm., W.V., U.S. h11 125
Coburg, Ger. E10 8
Coburg, Or., U.S. C3 114
Coburg Island, i., N.W. Ter., Can. A17 66
Cochabamba, Bol. G5 54
Cocheco, stm., N.H., U.S. D5 106
Cochin, India H4 37
Cochise, co., Az., U.S. F5 80
Cochise Head, mtn., Az., U.S. E6 80
Cochiti Indian Reservation, N.M., U.S. h8 108
Cochiti Reservoir, res., N.M., U.S. B3 108
Cochituate, Ma., U.S. g10 98
Cochituate, Lake, l., Ma., U.S. g10 98
Cochran, Ga., U.S. D3 87
Cochran, co., Tx., U.S. C1 120
Cochrane, Alta., Can. D3 68
Cochrane, Ont., Can. o19 73
Cochranton, Pa., U.S. C1 115
Cocke, co., Tn., U.S. D10 119
Cockeysville, Md., U.S. B4 97
Cockrell Hill, Tx., U.S. n10 120
Coco, stm., N.A. G6 64
Coco, Isla del, i., C.R. B1 54
Cocoa, Fl., U.S. D6 86
Cocoa Beach, Fl., U.S. D6 86
Coco Channel, strt., Asia H2 34
Coco Islands, is., Mya. G2 34
Coconino, co., Az., U.S. B3 80
Cocopah Indian Reservation, Az., U.S. E1 80
Côcos, Braz. C6 57
Cocula, Mex. G8 62
Cod, Cape, c., Ma., U.S. C7 98
Codajás, Braz. D6 54
Coden, Al., U.S. E1 78
Codigoro, Italy E7 14
Codington, co., S.D., U.S. C8 118
Codogno, Italy D4 14
Codroipo, Italy D7 14
Cody, Wy., U.S. B3 127
Coeburn, Va., U.S. f9 123
Coen, Austl. B8 50
Coetivy Island, i., Sey. C11 44
Coeur d'Alene, Id., U.S. B2 89
Coeur d'Alene, stm., Id., U.S. B2 89
Coeur d'Alene Indian Reservation, Id., U.S. B2 89
Coeur d'Alene Lake, res., Id., U.S. B2 89
Coeur d'Alene Mountains, mts., Id., U.S. B2 89
Coffee, co., Al., U.S. D3 78
Coffee, co., Ga., U.S. E4 87
Coffee, co., Tn., U.S. B5 119
Coffeeville, Ms., U.S. B4 101
Coffey, co., Ks., U.S. D8 93
Coffeyville, Ks., U.S. E8 93
Coffs Harbour, Austl. F10 50
Coggon, Ia., U.S. B6 92
Cognac, Fr. G6 10
Cohansey, stm., N.J., U.S. E2 107
Cohasset, Ma., U.S. B6 98
Cohasset, Mn., U.S. C5 100
Cohocton, stm., N.Y., U.S. C3 109
Cohoes, N.Y., U.S. C7 109
Cohoon, Lake, res., Va., U.S. k14 123
Cohutta Mountain, mtn., Ga., U.S. B2 87
Coiba, Isla de, i., Pan. K7 64
Coimbatore, India G4 37
Coimbra, Braz. F7 57
Coimbra, Port. E3 12
Çoín, Spain I7 12
Čojbalsan, Mong. B9 26
Cokato, Mn., U.S. E4 100
Coke, co., Tx., U.S. D2 120
Çokeville, Wy., U.S. D2 127
Čokurdach, Russia C23 24
Colatina, Braz. E8 57
Colbert, Ok., U.S. D5 113
Colbert, co., Al., U.S. A2 78

Name	Map Ref	Page
Colborne, Ont., Can.	C7	73
Colby, Ks., U.S.	C2	93
Colby, Wi., U.S.	D3	126
Colchester, Eng., U.K.	J13	7
Colchester, Ct., U.S.	C6	84
Colchester, Il., U.S.	C3	90
Colcord, Ok., U.S.	A7	113
Cold, stm., N.H., U.S.	C4	106
Cold, stm., N.H., U.S.	D2	106
Cold Bay, Ak., U.S.	E7	79
Cold Lake, Alta., Can.	B5	68
Cold Spring, Ky., U.S.	A5	94
Cold Spring, Mn., U.S.	E4	100
Coldwater, Ont., Can.	C5	73
Coldwater, Ks., U.S.	E4	93
Coldwater, Mi., U.S.	G5	99
Coldwater, Ms., U.S.	A4	101
Coldwater, Oh., U.S.	B1	112
Coldwater, stm., Ms., U.S.	A3	101
Coldwater Creek, stm., U.S.	e9	113
Cole, co., Mo., U.S.	C5	102
Colebrook, N.H., U.S.	g7	106
Colebrook River Lake, res., Ct., U.S.	A3	84
Cole Camp, Mo., U.S.	C4	102
Coleen, stm., Ak., U.S.	B11	79
Coleman, Mi., U.S.	E6	99
Coleman, Tx., U.S.	D3	120
Coleman, Wi., U.S.	C5	126
Coleman, co., Tx., U.S.	D3	120
Coleraine, N. Ire., U.K.	F6	7
Coleraine, Mn., U.S.	C5	100
Coles, co., Il., U.S.	D5	90
Colesberg, S. Afr.	H5	44
Colfax, Ca., U.S.	C3	82
Colfax, Il., U.S.	C5	90
Colfax, In., U.S.	D4	91
Colfax, Ia., U.S.	C4	92
Colfax, La., U.S.	C3	95
Colfax, Wa., U.S.	C8	124
Colfax, Wi., U.S.	D2	126
Colfax, co., Ne., U.S.	C8	104
Colfax, co., N.M., U.S.	A5	108
Colhué Huapi, Lago, l., Arg.	F3	56
Colima, Mex.	H8	62
Colima, Nevado de, mtn., Mex.	H8	62
Colinas, Braz.	E10	54
Coll, i., Scot., U.K.	E6	7
College, Ak., U.S.	B10	79
Collegedale, Tn., U.S.	h11	119
College Park, Ga., U.S.	C2	87
College Park, Md., U.S.	C4	97
College Place, Wa., U.S.	C7	124
College Station, Ar., U.S.	C3	81
College Station, Tx., U.S.	D4	120
Collegeville, In., U.S.	C3	91
Collegeville, Pa., U.S.	F11	115
Colleton, co., S.C., U.S.	F6	117
Collier, co., Fl., U.S.	F5	86
Collier Bay, b., Austl.	C4	50
Colliers, W.V., U.S.	f8	125
Collierville, Tn., U.S.	B2	119
Collin, co., Tx., U.S.	C4	120
Collingdale, Pa., U.S.	p20	115
Collingswood, N.J., U.S.	D2	107
Collingsworth, co., Tx., U.S.	B2	120
Collingwood, Ont., Can.	C4	73
Collins, Ms., U.S.	D4	101
Collins Park, De., U.S.	B3	85
Collinsville, Al., U.S.	A4	78
Collinsville, Ct., U.S.	B4	84
Collinsville, Il., U.S.	E4	90
Collinsville, Ms., U.S.	C5	101
Collinsville, Ok., U.S.	A6	113
Collinsville, Va., U.S.	D3	123
Collinwood, Tn., U.S.	B4	119
Collooney, Ire.	G4	7
Colmar, Fr.	D14	10
Colmar Manor, Md., U.S.	f9	97
Colmenar, Spain	I7	12
Colmenar de Oreja, Spain	E8	12
Colmenar Viejo, Spain	E8	12
Colo, Ia., U.S.	B4	92
Cologne see Köln, Ger.	E6	8
Coloma, Mi., U.S.	F4	99
Colomb-Béchar see Béchar, Alg.	B5	42
Colombia, ctry., S.A.	C4	54
Colombo, Sri L.	I5	37
Colón, Cuba	C7	64
Colón, Pan.	J8	64
Colon, Mi., U.S.	G5	99
Colon, Archipiélago de (Galapagos Islands), is., Ec.	m15	58a
Colonia Dora, Arg.	B4	56
Colonia Las Heras, Arg.	F3	56
Colonial Beach, Va., U.S.	B6	123
Colonial Heights, Tn., U.S.	C11	119
Colonial Heights, Va., U.S.	C5	123
Colonial National Historical Park, Va., U.S.	C6	123
Colonia Vicente Guerrero, Mex.	B1	62
Colonie, N.Y., U.S.	C7	109
Coloradas, Lomas, hills, Arg.	E3	56
Colorado, co., Tx., U.S.	E4	120
Colorado, state, U.S.	B5	83
Colorado, stm., Arg.	D4	56
Colorado, stm., N.A.	E4	76
Colorado, stm., Tx., U.S.	D3	120
Colorado City, Az., U.S.	A3	80
Colorado City, Co., U.S.	D6	83
Colorado City, Tx., U.S.	C2	120
Colorado City, Lake, res., Tx., U.S.	C2	120
Colorado National Monument, Co., U.S.	B2	83
Colorado River Aqueduct, Ca., U.S.	F6	82
Colorado River Indian Reservation, U.S.	D1	80
Colorado Springs, Co., U.S.	C6	83
Colotlán, Mex.	F8	62
Colquitt, Ga., U.S.	E2	87
Colquitt, co., Ga., U.S.	E3	87
Colstrip, Mt., U.S.	E10	103
Colton, S.D., U.S.	D9	118
Coltons Point, Md., U.S.	D4	97
Columbia, Al., U.S.	D4	78
Columbia, Il., U.S.	E3	90
Columbia, Ky., U.S.	C4	94
Columbia, Md., U.S.	B4	97
Columbia, Ms., U.S.	D4	101
Columbia, Mo., U.S.	C5	102
Columbia, N.C., U.S.	B6	110
Columbia, Pa., U.S.	F9	115
Columbia, S.C., U.S.	C5	117
Columbia, Tn., U.S.	B4	119
Columbia, co., Ar., U.S.	D2	81
Columbia, co., Fl., U.S.	B4	86
Columbia, co., Ga., U.S.	C4	87
Columbia, co., N.Y., U.S.	C7	109
Columbia, co., Or., U.S.	B3	114
Columbia, co., Pa., U.S.	D9	115
Columbia, co., Wa., U.S.	C7	124
Columbia, co., Wi., U.S.	E4	126
Columbia, stm., N.A.	G8	66
Columbia, Mount, mtn., Can.	C2	68
Columbia City, In., U.S.	B7	91
Columbia City, Or., U.S.	B4	114
Columbia Falls, Mt., U.S.	B2	103
Columbia Heights, Mn., U.S.	m12	100
Columbia Lake, res., Ct., U.S.	C6	84
Columbia Mountains, mts., B.C., Can.	C7	69
Columbiana, Al., U.S.	B3	78
Columbiana, Oh., U.S.	B5	112
Columbiana, co., Oh., U.S.	B5	112
Columbiaville, Mi., U.S.	E7	99
Columbus, Ga., U.S.	D2	87
Columbus, In., U.S.	F6	91
Columbus, Ks., U.S.	E9	93
Columbus, Ms., U.S.	B5	101
Columbus, Mt., U.S.	E7	103
Columbus, Ne., U.S.	C8	104
Columbus, N.M., U.S.	F2	108
Columbus, N.C., U.S.	f10	110
Columbus, Oh., U.S.	C2	112
Columbus, Tx., U.S.	E4	120
Columbus, Wi., U.S.	E4	126
Columbus, co., N.C., U.S.	C4	110
Columbus Air Force Base, mil., Ms., U.S.	B5	101
Columbus Grove, Oh., U.S.	B1	112
Columbus Junction, Ia., U.S.	C6	92
Columbus Lake, res., Ms., U.S.	B5	101
Colusa, Ca., U.S.	C2	82
Colusa, co., Ca., U.S.	C2	82
Colver, Pa., U.S.	E4	115
Colville, Wa., U.S.	A8	124
Colville, stm., Ak., U.S.	B9	79
Colville, stm., Wa., U.S.	A8	124
Colville Indian Reservation, Wa., U.S.	A6	124
Colvos Passage, strt., Wa., U.S.	f10	124
Colwich, Ks., U.S.	E6	93
Colwood, B.C., Can.	h12	69
Comacchio, Italy	E7	14
Comal, co., Tx., U.S.	E3	120
Comanche, Ok., U.S.	C4	113
Comanche, Tx., U.S.	D3	120
Comanche, co., Ks., U.S.	E4	93
Comanche, co., Ok., U.S.	C3	113
Comanche, co., Tx., U.S.	D3	120
Comandante Fontana, Arg.	B5	56
Comayagua, Hond.	G4	64
Combahee, stm., S.C., U.S.	F6	117
Combarbalá, Chile	C2	56
Combeaufontaine, Fr.	E12	10
Comber, Ont., Can.	E2	73
Combermere Bay, b., Mya.	E2	34
Combined Locks, Wi., U.S.	h9	126
Combourg, Fr.	D5	10
Combs, Ky., U.S.	C6	94
Comer, Ga., U.S.	B3	87
Comfort, Tx., U.S.	E3	120
Comilla, Bngl.	I14	38
Comitán [de Domínguez], Mex.	I13	62
Comite, stm., La., U.S.	D4	95
Commentry, Fr.	F9	10
Commerce, Ga., U.S.	B3	87
Commerce, Ok., U.S.	A7	113
Commerce, Tx., U.S.	C5	120
Commerce City, Co., U.S.	B6	83
Committee Bay, b., N.W. Ter., Can.	C15	66
Common Fence Point, R.I., U.S.	D6	116
Como, Italy	D4	14
Como, Ms., U.S.	A4	101
Como, Lago di, l., Italy	C4	14
Comodoro Rivadavia, Arg.	F3	56
Comorin, Cape, c., India	H4	37
Comoros, ctry., Afr.	D8	44
Comox, B.C., Can.	E5	69
Compiègne, Fr.	C9	10
Compton, Que., Can.	D6	74
Compton, Ca., U.S.	n12	82
Comstock, Mi., U.S.	F5	99
Çon, stm., Viet.	E8	34
Cona, stm., Russia	E16	24
Conakry, Gui.	G3	42
Conanicut Island, i., R.I., U.S.	E5	116
Conanicut Point, c., R.I., U.S.	E5	116
Concarneau, Fr.	E3	10
Conceição do Araguaia, Braz.	E9	54
Concepción, Arg.	B3	56
Concepción, Bol.	G6	54
Concepción, Chile	D2	56
Concepción, Para.	A5	56
Concepción, Laguna, l., Bol.	G6	54
Concepción, Volcán, vol., Nic.	I5	64
Concepcion del Oro, Mex.	E9	62
Concepción del Uruguay, Arg.	C5	56
Conception, Point, c., Ca., U.S.	E3	82
Conception Bay, b., Newf., Can.	E5	72
Conception Bay South, Newf., Can.	E5	72
Conchas Lake, res., N.M., U.S.	B5	108
Conches, Fr.	D7	10
Concho, co., Tx., U.S.	D3	120
Concho, stm., Tx., U.S.	D2	120
Conchos, stm., Mex.	C7	62
Concord, Ca., U.S.	h8	82
Concord, Ma., U.S.	B5	98
Concord, Mi., U.S.	F6	99
Concord, Mo., U.S.	g13	102
Concord, N.H., U.S.	D3	106
Concord, N.C., U.S.	B2	110
Concord, stm., Ma., U.S.	A5	98
Concordia, Arg.	C5	56
Concordia, Mex.	F6	62
Concordia, Ks., U.S.	C6	93
Concordia, Mo., U.S.	C4	102
Concordia, co., La., U.S.	C4	95
Concrete, Wa., U.S.	A4	124
Condé, Fr.	D6	10
Condom, Fr.	I7	10
Condon, Or., U.S.	B6	114
Condoto, Col.	E4	58
Conecuh, co., Al., U.S.	D2	78
Conecuh, stm., U.S.	D3	78
Conegliano, Italy	D7	14
Conejos, co., Co., U.S.	D4	83
Conejos, stm., Co., U.S.	D4	83
Conejos Peak, mtn., Co., U.S.	D4	83
Conemaugh, Pa., U.S.	F4	115
Conemaugh River Lake, res., Pa., U.S.	F3	115
Confolens, Fr.	F7	10
Congamond Lakes, l., U.S.	A4	84
Congaree, stm., S.C., U.S.	D6	117
Congaree Swamp National Monument, S.C., U.S.	D6	117
Congo, ctry., Afr.	B2	44
Congo (Zaire), stm., Afr.	C2	44
Congress, Az., U.S.	C3	80
Conimicut Point, c., R.I., U.S.	D5	116
Conitaca, Mex.	E6	62
Conklin, N.Y., U.S.	C5	109
Conn, Lough, l., Ire.	G3	7
Connaught, hist. reg., Ire.	H3	7
Conneaut, Oh., U.S.	A5	112
Conneaut Creek, stm., Oh., U.S.	A5	112
Conneaut Lake, l., Pa., U.S.	C1	115
Connecticut, state, U.S.	C5	84
Connecticut, stm., U.S.	C12	76
Connell, Wa., U.S.	C7	124
Connellsville, Pa., U.S.	F2	115
Connemara, reg., Ire.	H3	7
Connersville, In., U.S.	E7	91
Conover, N.C., U.S.	B1	110
Conowingo, Md., U.S.	A5	97
Conrad, Ia., U.S.	B5	92
Conrad, Mt., U.S.	B5	103
Conroe, Tx., U.S.	D5	120
Conselheiro Lafaiete, Braz.	F7	57
Conshohocken, Pa., U.S.	F11	115
Con Son, is., Viet.	J9	34
Consort, Alta., Can.	C5	68
Constance, Lake see Bodensee, l., Eur.	H9	8
Constanța, Rom.	E12	16
Constantina, Spain	H6	12
Constantine (Qacentina), Alg.	A7	42
Constantine, Mi., U.S.	G5	99
Constantine, Cape, c., Ak., U.S.	D8	79
Consuegra, Spain	F8	12
Contai, India	J12	38
Contas, Rio de, stm., Braz.	C9	57
Content Keys, is., Fl., U.S.	H5	86
Continental, Oh., U.S.	A1	112
Continental Peak, mtn., Wy., U.S.	D4	127
Continental Reservoir, res., Co., U.S.	D3	83
Contoocook, N.H., U.S.	D3	106
Contoocook, stm., N.H., U.S.	D3	106
Contra Costa, co., Ca., U.S.	D3	82
Contrecoeur, Que., Can.	D4	74
Contres, Fr.	E8	10
Contwoyto Lake, l., N.W. Ter., Can.	C10	66
Convención, Col.	C6	58
Conversano, Italy	I12	14
Converse, In., U.S.	C6	91
Converse, S.C., U.S.	B4	117
Converse, co., Wy., U.S.	C7	127
Convoy, Oh., U.S.	B1	112
Conway, Ar., U.S.	B3	81
Conway, Fl., U.S.	D5	86
Conway, Mo., U.S.	D5	102
Conway, N.H., U.S.	C4	106
Conway, N.C., U.S.	A5	110
Conway, Pa., U.S.	E1	115
Conway, S.C., U.S.	D9	117
Conway, co., Ar., U.S.	B3	81
Conway, Lake, res., Ar., U.S.	B3	81
Conway Lake, l., N.H., U.S.	C4	106
Conway Springs, Ks., U.S.	E6	93
Conyers, Ga., U.S.	C2	87
Cooch Behār, India	G13	38
Cook, Mn., U.S.	C6	100
Cook, co., Ga., U.S.	E3	87
Cook, co., Il., U.S.	B6	90
Cook, co., Mn., U.S.	k9	100
Cook, Cape, c., B.C., Can.	D4	69
Cook, Mount, mtn., N.Z.	E3	52
Cooke, co., Tx., U.S.	C4	120
Cookes Peak, mtn., N.M., U.S.	E2	108
Cookeville, Tn., U.S.	C8	119
Cook Inlet, b., Ak., U.S.	D9	79
Cook Islands, dep., Oc.	H2	2
Cook Point, c., Md., U.S.	C5	97
Cookshire, Que., Can.	D6	74
Cookson, Ok., U.S.	B7	113
Cookstown, N. Ire., U.K.	G6	7
Cook Strait, strt., N.Z.	D5	52
Cooktown, Austl.	C9	50
Cooleemee, N.C., U.S.	B2	110
Coolgardie, Austl.	F4	50
Coolidge, Az., U.S.	E4	80
Coolidge, Ga., U.S.	E3	87
Cooma, Austl.	G9	50
Coonoor, India	G4	37
Coon Rapids, Ia., U.S.	C3	92
Coon Rapids, Mn., U.S.	E5	100
Coon Valley, Wi., U.S.	E2	126
Cooper, Tx., U.S.	C5	120
Cooper, co., Mo., U.S.	C5	102
Cooper, stm., S.C., U.S.	F8	117
Cooper Mountain, mtn., Ak., U.S.	g17	79
Coopersburg, Pa., U.S.	F11	115
Cooperstown, N.Y., U.S.	C6	109
Cooperstown, N.D., U.S.	B7	111
Coopersville, Mi., U.S.	E5	99
Coos, co., N.H., U.S.	A4	106
Coos, co., Or., U.S.	D2	114
Coos, stm., Or., U.S.	D2	114
Coosa, co., Al., U.S.	C3	78
Coosa, stm., U.S.	C3	78
Coosada, Al., U.S.	C3	78
Coosawhatchie, stm., S.C., U.S.	F5	117
Coos Bay, Or., U.S.	D2	114
Copalis Beach, Wa., U.S.	B1	124
Copan, Ok., U.S.	A6	113
Copan Reservoir, res., Ok., U.S.	A6	113
Copenhagen see København, Den.	I9	6
Copiah, co., Ms., U.S.	D3	101
Copiapó, Chile	B2	56
Coplay, Pa., U.S.	E10	115
Copparo, Italy	E6	14
Copper, stm., Ak., U.S.	C11	79
Copperas Cove, Tx., U.S.	D4	120
Copper Butte, mtn., Wa., U.S.	A7	124
Coppermine, N.W. Ter., Can.	C9	66
Coppermine, stm., N.W. Ter., Can.	C10	66
Copper Mountain, mtn., Wy., U.S.	C5	127
Copper Mountains, mts., Az., U.S.	E2	80
Coquille, Or., U.S.	D2	114
Coquimbo, Chile	B2	56
Coral Gables, Fl., U.S.	G6	86
Coral Harbour, N.W. Ter., Can.	D16	66
Coral Sea, Oc.	B10	50
Coralville, Ia., U.S.	C6	92
Coralville Lake, res., Ia., U.S.	C5	92
Corantijn (Corentyne), stm., S.A.	E14	58
Coraopolis, Pa., U.S.	E1	115
Corato, Italy	H11	14
Corbeil-Essonnes, Fr.	D9	10
Corbigny, Fr.	E10	10
Corbin, Ky., U.S.	D5	94
Corcoran, Ca., U.S.	D4	82
Corcoran, Mn., U.S.	m11	100
Corcovado, Golfo, b., Chile	E2	56
Corcovado, Volcán, vol., Chile	E2	56
Corcubión, Spain	C2	12
Cordele, Ga., U.S.	E3	87
Cordell, Ok., U.S.	B3	113
Cordell Hull Lake, res., Tn., U.S.	C8	119
Cordes, Fr.	H8	10
Córdoba, Arg.	C4	56
Córdoba, Mex.	H11	62
Córdoba, Spain	H7	12
Cordova, Al., U.S.	B2	78
Cordova, Ak., U.S.	C10	79
Cordova, N.M., U.S.	A4	108
Cordova, N.C., U.S.	C3	110
Cordova Peak, mtn., Ak., U.S.	C10	79
Corentyne (Corantijn), stm., S.A.	E14	58
Corfu see Kérkira, Grc.	J3	16
Coria, Spain	F5	12
Coria del Río, Spain	H5	12
Corigliano Calabro, Italy	J11	14
Coringa Islets, is., Austl.	C9	50
Corinna, Me., U.S.	D3	96
Corinne, Ut., U.S.	B3	121
Corinne Key, i., Fl., U.S.	G6	86
Corinth, Ms., U.S.	A5	101
Corinth, N.Y., U.S.	B7	109
Corinth see Kórinthos, Grc.	L6	16
Corinto, Braz.	E6	57
Cork, Ire.	J4	7
Corlay, Fr.	D3	10
Corleone, Italy	L8	14
Corleto Perticara, Italy	I11	14
Çorlu, Tur.	H11	16
Cormorant Lake, l., Man., Can.	B1	70
Cornelia, Ga., U.S.	B3	87
Cornélio Procópio, Braz.	G3	57
Cornelius, N.C., U.S.	B2	110
Cornelius, Or., U.S.	g11	114
Cornell, Wi., U.S.	C2	126
Corner Brook, Newf., Can.	D3	72
Cornersville, Tn., U.S.	B5	119
Cornfield Point, c., Ct., U.S.	D6	84
Cornie Bayou, stm., U.S.	D3	81
Corning, Ar., U.S.	A5	81
Corning, Ca., U.S.	C2	82
Corning, Ia., U.S.	D3	92
Corning, N.Y., U.S.	C3	109
Cornish, Me., U.S.	E2	96
Corn Islands, is., Nic.	H6	64
Corno Grande, mtn., Italy	G8	14
Cornville, Az., U.S.	C4	80
Cornwall, Ont., Can.	B10	73
Cornwall, Pa., U.S.	F9	115
Cornwallis Island, i., N.W. Ter., Can.	A14	66
Cornwall on Hudson, N.Y., U.S.	D6	109
Coro, Ven.	B8	58
Corocoro, Bol.	G5	54
Coroico, Bol.	G5	54
Coromandel Coast, India	F6	37
Coromandel Peninsula, pen., N.Z.	B5	52
Corona, Ca., U.S.	F5	82
Coronado, Ca., U.S.	F5	82
Coronado National Memorial, Az., U.S.	F5	80
Coronation, Alta., Can.	C5	68
Coronation Gulf, b., N.W. Ter., Can.	C10	66
Coronation Island, i., Ak., U.S.	n22	79
Coronel Dorrego, Arg.	D4	56
Coronel Fabriciano, Braz.	E7	57
Coronel Pringles, Arg.	D4	56
Coronel Suárez, Arg.	D4	56
Coropuna, Nevado, mtn., Peru	G4	54
Corpus Christi, Tx., U.S.	F4	120
Corpus Christi Naval Air Station, mil., Tx., U.S.	F4	120
Corral de Almaguer, Spain	F8	12
Correctionville, Ia., U.S.	B2	92
Correggio, Italy	E5	14
Corrente, stm., Braz.	B7	57
Corrib, Lough, l., Ire.	H3	7
Corrientes, Arg.	B5	56
Corrientes, Cabo, c., Col.	E4	58
Corrientes, Cabo, c., Cuba	D5	64
Corrientes, Cabo, c., Mex.	G7	62
Corrigan, Tx., U.S.	D5	120
Corriganville, Md., U.S.	k13	97
Corry, Pa., U.S.	C2	115
Corse (Corsica), i., Fr.	m19	11a
Corsica, S.D., U.S.	D7	118
Corsica see Corse, i., Fr.	m19	11a
Corsicana, Tx., U.S.	C4	120
Corson, co., S.D., U.S.	B4	118
Corson Inlet, b., N.J., U.S.	E3	107
Cortemilia, Italy	E3	14
Cortez, Co., U.S.	D2	83
Cortez, Fl., U.S.	q10	86
Cortez Mountains, mts., Nv., U.S.	C5	105
Cortina d'Ampezzo, Italy	C7	14
Cortland, Il., U.S.	B5	90
Cortland, N.Y., U.S.	C4	109
Cortland, Oh., U.S.	A5	112
Cortland, co., N.Y., U.S.	C4	109
Çorum, Tur.	G14	4
Corumbá, Braz.	G7	54
Corumbá, stm., Braz.	E4	57
Corunna, Mi., U.S.	F6	99
Corvallis, Or., U.S.	C3	114
Corydon, In., U.S.	H5	91
Corydon, Ia., U.S.	D4	92
Corydon, Ky., U.S.	C2	94
Coryell, co., Tx., U.S.	D4	120
Cosamaloapan [de Carpio], Mex.	H12	62
Cosenza, Italy	J11	14
Coshocton, Oh., U.S.	B4	112
Coshocton, co., Oh., U.S.	B4	112
Cosmoledo Group, is., Sey.	C9	44
Cosmopolis, Wa., U.S.	C2	124
Cosmos, Mn., U.S.	F4	100
Cosne-sur-Loire, Fr.	E9	10
Cossatot, stm., Ar., U.S.	C1	81
Costa Mesa, Ca., U.S.	n13	82
Costa Rica, Mex.	C4	62
Costa Rica, ctry., N.A.	I5	64
Costilla, co., Co., U.S.	D5	83
Cotabato, Phil.	D7	32
Coteau-Landing, Que., Can.	D3	74
Cotentin, pen., Fr.	C5	10
Cotonou, Benin	G6	42
Cotopaxi, vol., Ec.	H3	58
Cottage Grove, Mn., U.S.	n13	100
Cottage Grove, Or., U.S.	D3	114
Cottage Grove Reservoir, res., Or., U.S.	D3	114
Cottam, Ont., Can.	E2	73
Cottbus, Ger.	D14	8
Cotter, Ar., U.S.	A3	81
Cottiennes, Alpes (Alpi Cozie), mts., Eur.	H13	10
Cottle, co., Tx., U.S.	B2	120
Cottleville, Mo., U.S.	f12	102
Cotton, co., Ok., U.S.	C3	113
Cottondale, Al., U.S.	B2	78
Cotton Plant, Ar., U.S.	B4	81
Cottonport, La., U.S.	C3	95
Cotton Valley, La., U.S.	B2	95
Cottonwood, Al., U.S.	D4	78
Cottonwood, Az., U.S.	C3	80
Cottonwood, Ca., U.S.	B2	82
Cottonwood, Id., U.S.	C2	89
Cottonwood, Mn., U.S.	F3	100
Cottonwood, co., Mn., U.S.	F3	100
Cottonwood, stm., Ks., U.S.	D7	93
Cottonwood, stm., Mn., U.S.	F3	100
Cottonwood Creek, stm., Wy., U.S.	C4	127
Cottonwood Falls, Ks., U.S.	D7	93
Cotuit, Ma., U.S.	C7	98
Cotulla, Tx., U.S.	E3	120
Coudersport, Pa., U.S.	C5	115
Cougar Reservoir, res., Or., U.S.	C4	114
Couhé, Fr.	F7	10
Coulee Creek, stm., Wa., U.S.	g13	124
Coulee Dam, Wa., U.S.	B7	124
Coulee Dam National Recreation Area, Wa., U.S.	A7	124
Coulommiers, Fr.	D10	10
Coulterville, Il., U.S.	E4	90
Counce, Tn., U.S.	B3	119
Council, Id., U.S.	E2	89
Council Bluffs, Ia., U.S.	C2	92
Council Grove, Ks., U.S.	D7	93
Council Grove Lake, res., Ks., U.S.	D7	93
Council Mountain, mtn., Id., U.S.	E2	89
Country Homes, Wa., U.S.	B8	124
Coupeville, Wa., U.S.	A3	124
Courtenay, B.C., Can.	E5	69
Courte Oreilles, Lac, l., Wi., U.S.	C2	126
Courtland, Ont., Can.	E4	73
Courtland, Al., U.S.	A2	78
Courtland, Va., U.S.	D5	123
Coushatta, La., U.S.	B2	95
Coutances, Fr.	C5	10
Coutras, Fr.	G6	10
Cove Creek, stm., Ut., U.S.	E3	121
Covedale, Oh., U.S.	o12	112
Coventry, Eng., U.K.	I11	7
Coventry, Ct., U.S.	B6	84
Coventry, R.I., U.S.	D3	116
Cove Point, c., Md., U.S.	D5	97
Covilhã, Port.	E4	12
Covina, Ca., U.S.	m13	82
Covington, Ga., U.S.	C3	87
Covington, In., U.S.	D3	91
Covington, Ky., U.S.	A5	94
Covington, La., U.S.	D5	95
Covington, Oh., U.S.	B1	112
Covington, Tn., U.S.	B2	119
Covington, Va., U.S.	C3	123
Covington, co., Al., U.S.	D3	78
Covington, co., Ms., U.S.	D4	101
Cowan, Tn., U.S.	B5	119
Cowan, Lake, l., Austl.	F4	50
Cowansville, Que., Can.	D5	74
Cowarts, Al., U.S.	D4	78
Cow Creek, stm., Wa., U.S.	C7	124
Cowee Mountains, mts., N.C., U.S.	f9	110
Cowen, Mount, mtn., Mt., U.S.	E6	103
Coweta, Ok., U.S.	B6	113
Coweta, co., Ga., U.S.	C2	87
Cow Head, Newf., Can.	D3	72
Cowichan Bay, B.C., Can.	g12	69
Cow Lakes, l., Or., U.S.	D9	114
Cowley, Wy., U.S.	B4	127
Cowley, co., Ks., U.S.	E7	93
Cowlington, Ok., U.S.	B7	113
Cowlitz, co., Wa., U.S.	C2	124

Name Map Ref Page

Cowlitz, stm., Wa., U.S. C3 124
Cowpasture, stm., Va., U.S. B3 123
Cowpen Mountain, mtn., Ga., U.S. B2 87
Cowpens, S.C., U.S. A4 117
Coxim, Braz. E1 57
Coxsackie, N.Y., U.S. C7 109
Cox's Bāzār, Bngl. J14 38
Cox's Cove, Newf., Can. D2 72
Coyhaique, Chile F2 56
Cozad, Ne., U.S. D6 104
Cozumel, Isla de, i., Mex. G16 62
Crab Creek, stm., Wa., U.S. C6 124
Crab Creek, stm., Wa., U.S. B7 124
Crab Orchard, Ky., U.S. C5 94
Crab Orchard, Tn., U.S. D9 119
Crab Orchard, W.V., U.S. n13 125
Crab Orchard Lake, res., Il., U.S. F4 90
Crabtree, Pa., U.S. F3 115
Crabtree Mills, Que., Can. D4 74
Cradock, S. Afr. H5 44
Crafton, Pa., U.S. k13 115
Craig, Ak., U.S. D13 79
Craig, Co., U.S. A3 83
Craig, co., Ok., U.S. A6 113
Craig, co., Va., U.S. C2 123
Craig Air Force Base, mil., Al., U.S. C3 78
Craig Creek, stm., Va., U.S. C2 123
Craighead, co., Ar., U.S. B5 81
Craigsville, Va., U.S. B3 123
Craigsville, W.V., U.S. C4 125
Crailsheim, Ger. F10 8
Craiova, Rom. E7 16
Cramerton, N.C., U.S. B1 110
Cranberry Lake, l., N.Y., U.S. A6 109
Cranberry Portage, Man., Can. B1 70
Cranbrook, B.C., Can. E10 69
Crandall, Tx., U.S. n10 120
Crandon, Wi., U.S. C5 126
Crane, Az., U.S. *E1 80
Crane, Mo., U.S. E4 102
Crane, Tx., U.S. D1 120
Crane, co., Tx., U.S. D1 120
Crane Creek, stm., Oh., U.S. e7 112
Crane Creek Reservoir, res., Id., U.S. E2 89
Crane Lake, l., Il., U.S. C3 90
Crane Lake, l., Mn., U.S. B6 100
Crane Mountain, mtn., Or., U.S. E6 114
Crane Prairie Reservoir, res., Or., U.S. D5 114
Cranford, N.J., U.S. B4 107
Cranston, R.I., U.S. C4 116
Craon, Fr. E6 10
Craponne, Fr. G10 10
Crater Lake, l., Or., U.S. E4 114
Crater Lake National Park, Or., U.S. E4 114
Craters of the Moon National Monument, Id., U.S. F5 89
Cratéus, Braz. E10 54
Crato, Braz. E11 54
Crauford, Cape, c., N.W. Ter., Can. B16 66
Craven, co., N.C., U.S. B5 110
Crawford, Ga., U.S. C3 87
Crawford, Ms., U.S. B5 101
Crawford, Ne., U.S. B2 104
Crawford, co., Ar., U.S. B1 81
Crawford, co., Ga., U.S. D3 87
Crawford, co., Il., U.S. D6 90
Crawford, co., In., U.S. H4 91
Crawford, co., Ia., U.S. B2 92
Crawford, co., Ks., U.S. E9 93
Crawford, co., Mi., U.S. D6 99
Crawford, co., Mo., U.S. D6 102
Crawford, co., Oh., U.S. B3 112
Crawford, co., Pa., U.S. C1 115
Crawford, co., Wi., U.S. E3 126
Crawford Lake, l., Me., U.S. C5 96
Crawford Notch State Park, N.H., U.S. B4 106
Crawfordsville, Ar., U.S. B5 81
Crawfordsville, In., U.S. D4 91
Crawfordville, Fl., U.S. B2 86
Crazy Mountains, mts., Mt., U.S. D6 103
Crazy Peak, mtn., Mt., U.S. D6 103
Crazy Woman Creek, stm., Wy., U.S. B6 127
Creal Springs, Il., U.S. F5 90
Cree, stm., Sask., Can. E11 66
Creedmoor, N.C., U.S. A4 110
Creek, co., Ok., U.S. B5 113
Cree Lake, l., Sask., Can. m7 75
Creemore, Ont., Can. C4 73
Creighton, Ne., U.S. B8 104
Creighton, Pa., U.S. h14 115
Creil, Fr. C9 10
Crema, Italy B1 14
Cremona, Italy D5 14
Crenshaw, Ms., U.S. A3 101
Crenshaw, co., Al., U.S. D3 78
Creola, Al., U.S. E1 78
Cres, Cro. E9 14
Cresaptown, Md., U.S. k13 97
Crescent, Ok., U.S. B4 113
Crescent, Or., U.S. D5 114
Crescent, Lake, l., Wa., U.S. A2 124
Crescent City, Ca., U.S. B1 82
Crescent City, Fl., U.S. C5 86
Crescent Lake, l., Fl., U.S. C5 86
Crescent Lake, l., Or., U.S. D5 114
Crescent Springs, Ky., U.S. h13 94
Cresco, Ia., U.S. A5 92
Cresskill, N.J., U.S. h9 107
Cresson, Pa., U.S. F4 115
Cressona, Pa., U.S. E9 115
Crest, Fr. H12 10
Crested Butte, Co., U.S. C4 83
Crest Hill, Il., U.S. k8 90
Crestline, Oh., U.S. B3 112
Creston, B.C., Can. E9 69
Creston, Ia., U.S. C3 92
Creston, Oh., U.S. B4 112
Crestone Peak, mtn., Co., U.S. D5 83
Crestview, Fl., U.S. u15 86
Crestview, Hi., U.S. g10 88
Crestwood, Ky., U.S. B4 94
Crestwood Village, N.J., U.S. D4 107
Creswell, Or., U.S. D3 114
Crete, Il., U.S. B6 90
Crete, Ne., U.S. D9 104
Crete see Kríti, i., Grc. N8 16
Creve Coeur, Il., U.S. C4 90
Crevillente, Spain G11 12
Crewe, Eng., U.K. H10 7
Crewe, Va., U.S. C4 123
Criciúma, Braz. B7 56
Cricket, N.C., U.S. A1 110
Cridersville, Oh., U.S. B1 112
Crikvenica, Cro. D9 14
Crimea see Kryms'kyy pivostriv, pen., Ukr. H4 22
Crimmitschau, Ger. E12 8
Crisfield, Md., U.S. E6 97
Crisp, co., Ga., U.S. E3 87
Cristalândia, Braz. F9 54
Cristalina, Braz. D5 57
Cristianópolis, Braz. D4 57
Cristóbal Colón, Pico, mtn., Col. B6 58
Crittenden, Ky., U.S. B5 94
Crittenden, co., Ar., U.S. B5 81
Crittenden, co., Ky., U.S. e9 94
Crivitz, Wi., U.S. C6 126
Črnomelj, Slo. D10 14
Croatia, ctry., Eur. D10 14
Crocker, Mo., U.S. D5 102
Crockett, Ca., U.S. g8 82
Crockett, Tx., U.S. D5 120
Crockett, co., Tn., U.S. B2 119
Crockett, co., Tx., U.S. D2 120
Crofton, Ky., U.S. C2 94
Crofton, Md., U.S. B4 97
Crofton, Ne., U.S. B8 104
Croix, Lac la, l., Mn., U.S. B6 100
Croker, Cape, c., Ont., Can. C4 73
Croker Island, i., Austl. B6 50
Cromarty, Scot., U.K. D8 7
Cromona, Ky., U.S. C7 94
Cromwell, Ct., U.S. C5 84
Crook, co., Or., U.S. C6 114
Crook, co., Wy., U.S. B8 127
Crooked, stm., Or., U.S. C6 114
Crooked Creek, stm., U.S. E3 93
Crooked Creek, stm., Pa., U.S. C7 115
Crooked Creek Lake, res., Pa., U.S. E3 115
Crooked Island, i., Bah. C10 64
Crooked Island Passage, strt., Bah. C10 64
Crooked Lake, l., Fl., U.S. E5 86
Crooked Lake, l., Mn., U.S. B7 100
Crooks, S.D., U.S. D9 118
Crooks Lake, l., Nv., U.S. B2 105
Crookston, Mn., U.S. C2 100
Crooksville, Oh., U.S. C3 112
Crosby, Mn., U.S. D5 100
Crosby, N.D., U.S. A2 111
Crosby, Tx., U.S. r14 120
Crosby, co., Tx., U.S. C2 120
Crosby, Mount, mtn., Wy., U.S. C3 127
Crosbyton, Tx., U.S. C2 120
Cross, co., Ar., U.S. B5 81
Cross Bay, b., Man., Can. C2 70
Cross City, Fl., U.S. C3 86
Cross Creek, stm., W.V., U.S. f8 125
Crossett, Ar., U.S. D4 81
Crossfield, Alta., Can. D3 68
Cross Island, i., Me., U.S. D5 96
Cross Lake, Man., Can. B3 70
Crosslake, Mn., U.S. D4 100
Cross Lake, l., Me., U.S. A4 96
Cross Lake, res., La., U.S. B2 95
Cross Lanes, W.V., U.S. C3 125
Crossman Peak, mtn., Az., U.S. C1 80
Cross Plains, Tn., U.S. A5 119
Cross Plains, Tx., U.S. C3 120
Cross Plains, Wi., U.S. E4 126
Cross Sound, strt., Ak., U.S. k21 79
Crossville, Al., U.S. A4 78
Crossville, Il., U.S. E5 90
Crossville, Tn., U.S. D8 119
Croswell, Mi., U.S. E8 99
Crothersville, In., U.S. G6 91
Crotone, Italy J12 14
Croton-on-Hudson, N.Y., U.S. D7 109
Crouse, N.C., U.S. B1 110
Crow, stm., Mn., U.S. F4 100
Crow Agency, Mt., U.S. E9 103
Crow Creek, stm., U.S. A6 83
Crow Creek Indian Reservation, S.D., U.S. C6 118
Crowder, Ms., U.S. A3 101
Crowell, Tx., U.S. C3 120
Crow Indian Reservation, Mt., U.S. E9 103
Crowley, La., U.S. D3 95
Crowley, Tx., U.S. n9 120
Crowley, co., Co., U.S. C7 83
Crowley, Lake, res., Ca., U.S. D4 82
Crowleys Ridge, mtn., U.S. B5 81
Crown Point, In., U.S. B3 91
Crown Point, La., U.S. k11 95
Crownpoint, N.M., U.S. B1 108
Crown Prince Frederick Island, i., N.W. Ter., Can. B15 66
Crow Peak, mtn., Mt., U.S. D5 103
Crowsnest Pass, Alta., Can. E3 68
Crowsnest Pass, Can. E3 68
Crow Wing, co., Mn., U.S. D4 100
Crow Wing, stm., Mn., U.S. D4 100
Croydon, Austl. C8 50
Crozet, Va., U.S. B4 123
Crozon, Fr. D2 10
Cruces, Cuba C7 64
Crump Lake, l., Or., U.S. E7 114
Cruz Alta, Braz. B6 56
Cruz del Eje, Arg. C4 56
Cruzeiro do Sul, Braz. E4 54
Crystal, Mn., U.S. m12 100
Crystal, stm., Co., U.S. B3 83
Crystal Bay, Nv., U.S. D1 105
Crystal Bay, b., Fl., U.S. D4 86
Crystal Beach, Fl., U.S. D4 86
Crystal City, Man., Can. E2 70
Crystal City, Mo., U.S. C7 102
Crystal City, Tx., U.S. E3 120
Crystal Falls, Mi., U.S. B2 99
Crystal Lake, Ct., U.S. B6 84
Crystal Lake, Fl., U.S. u16 86
Crystal Lake, Il., U.S. A5 90
Crystal Lake, l., Ct., U.S. B6 84
Crystal Lake, l., Mi., U.S. D4 99
Crystal Lake, l., N.H., U.S. D4 106
Crystal Lake, l., Vt., U.S. B4 122
Crystal Lawns, Il., U.S. k8 90
Crystal Pond, res., Ct., U.S. B7 84
Crystal River, Fl., U.S. D4 86
Crystal Springs, Ms., U.S. D3 101
Cuando (Kwando), stm., Afr. E4 44
Cuangar, Ang. E3 44
Cuango, Ang. C3 44
Cuango (Kwango), stm., Afr. C3 44
Cuanza, stm., Ang. C3 44
Cuauhtémoc, Mex. C6 62
Cuautla, Mex. H10 62
Cuba, Port. G4 12
Cuba, Il., U.S. C3 90
Cuba, Mo., U.S. C6 102
Cuba, N.M., U.S. A3 108
Cuba, N.Y., U.S. C2 109
Cuba, ctry., N.A. D8 64
Cuba City, Wi., U.S. F3 126
Cubango (Okavango), stm., Afr. E3 44
Cubero, N.M., U.S. B2 108
Cucharas, Mex. F7 62
Cucharas, stm., Co., U.S. D6 83
Cudahy, Wi., U.S. F6 126
Cuddalore, India G5 37
Cuddapah, India E5 37
Cuddy Mountain, mtn., Id., U.S. E2 89
Čudskoje Ozero (Peipsi Järv), l., Eur. C10 18
Cuéllar, Spain D7 12
Cuenca, Ec. I3 58
Cuenca, Spain E9 12
Cuencamé [de Ceniceros], Mex. E8 62
Cuernavaca, Mex. H10 62
Cuero, Tx., U.S. E4 120
Cuers, Fr. I13 10
Cuervos, Mex. A2 62
Cuevas del Almanzora, Spain H10 12
Cuglieri, Italy I3 14
Cuiabá, Braz. G7 54
Cuiseaux, Fr. F12 10
Cuíto, stm., Ang. E3 44
Cuíto-Cuanavale, Ang. E3 44
Cuivre, West Fork, stm., Mo., U.S. B6 102
Čukotskij, Mys, c., Russia E31 24
Čukotskij Poluostrov, pen., Russia D30 24
Culberson, co., Tx., U.S. o12 120
Culbertson, Mt., U.S. B12 103
Culbertson, Ne., U.S. D5 104
Culebra Peak, mtn., Co., U.S. D5 83
Culiacán, Mex. E6 62
Cullen, La., U.S. B2 95
Cullman, Al., U.S. A3 78
Cullman, co., Al., U.S. A3 78
Culloden, W.V., U.S. C2 125
Cullowhee, N.C., U.S. f9 110
Čul'man, Russia F18 24
Culpeper, Va., U.S. B4 123
Culpeper, co., Va., U.S. B5 123
Culver, In., U.S. B5 91
Culver City, Ca., U.S. m12 82
Culvers Lake, l., N.J., U.S. A3 107
Čulym, Russia F10 24
Cumalı, Tur. M11 16
Cumaná, Ven. B10 58
Cumanacoa, Ven. B11 58
Cumbal, Nevado de, mtn., Col. G4 58
Cumberland, B.C., Can. E5 69
Cumberland, Ky., U.S. D7 94
Cumberland, Md., U.S. k13 97
Cumberland, Wi., U.S. C2 126
Cumberland, co., Il., U.S. D5 90
Cumberland, co., Ky., U.S. D4 94
Cumberland, co., Me., U.S. E2 96
Cumberland, co., N.J., U.S. E2 107
Cumberland, co., N.C., U.S. C4 110
Cumberland, co., Pa., U.S. F7 115
Cumberland, co., Tn., U.S. D8 119
Cumberland, co., Va., U.S. C4 123
Cumberland, stm., U.S. D4 94
Cumberland, Lake, res., Ky., U.S. D5 94
Cumberland Center, Me., U.S. g7 96
Cumberland Foreside, Me., U.S. E2 96
Cumberland Gap, U.S. D6 94
Cumberland Gap National Historical Park, U.S. D6 94
Cumberland Hill, R.I., U.S. B4 116
Cumberland Island National Seashore, Ga., U.S. F5 87
Cumberland Islands, is., Austl. D9 50
Cumberland Lake, l., Sask., Can. C4 75
Cumberland Peninsula, pen., N.W. Ter., Can. C19 66
Cumberland Sound, strt., N.W. Ter., Can. C19 66
Cumbres Pass, Co., U.S. D4 83
Cumikan, Russia G21 24
Cuming, co., Ne., U.S. C9 104
Cumming, Ga., U.S. B2 87
Cumnock, Scot., U.K. F8 7
Čuna, stm., Russia F13 24
Čun'a, stm., Russia E13 24
Cunani, Braz. C8 54
Cunene, stm., Afr. E2 44
Cuneo, Italy E2 14
Cunnamulla, Austl. E9 50
Cunningham, Ky., U.S. f9 94
Cupar, Sask., Can. G3 75
Curaçao, i., Neth. Ant. H13 64
Curecanti National Recreation Area, Co., U.S. C3 83
Curepipe, Mrts. F11 44
Curiapo, Ven. C12 58
Curicó, Chile C2 56
Curitiba, Braz. B7 56
Curlew Creek, stm., Wa., U.S. A7 124
Curlew Lake, l., Wa., U.S. A7 124
Curralinho, Braz. D9 54
Currant Mountain, mtn., Nv., U.S. E6 105
Current, stm., U.S. A5 81
Currituck, co., N.C., U.S. A6 110
Curry, co., N.M., U.S. C6 108
Curry, co., Or., U.S. E2 114
Curtis, Ne., U.S. D5 104
Curtisville, Pa., U.S. E2 115
Curvelo, Braz. E6 57
Curwensville, Pa., U.S. E4 115
Curwensville Lake, res., Pa., U.S. E4 115
Curwood, Mount, mtn., Mi., U.S. B2 99
Cushing, Ok., U.S. B5 113
Cushman, Lake, res., Wa., U.S. B2 124
Cusseta, Ga., U.S. D2 87
Custer, S.D., U.S. D2 118
Custer, co., Co., U.S. C5 83
Custer, co., Id., U.S. E4 89
Custer, co., Mt., U.S. D11 103
Custer, co., Ne., U.S. C6 104
Custer, co., Ok., U.S. B2 113
Custer, co., S.D., U.S. D2 118
Custer Battlefield National Monument, Mt., U.S. E9 103
Cut Bank, Mt., U.S. B4 103
Cut Bank Creek, stm., N.D., U.S. A4 111
Cutchogue, N.Y., U.S. m16 109
Cuthbert, Ga., U.S. E2 87
Cutler Ridge, Fl., U.S. s13 86
Cut Off, La., U.S. E5 95
Cutro, Italy J11 14
Cuttack, India J11 38
Cuttyhunk Island, i., Ma., U.S. D6 98
Cuxhaven, Ger. B8 8
Cuyahoga, co., Oh., U.S. A4 112
Cuyahoga, stm., Oh., U.S. A4 112
Cuyahoga Falls, Oh., U.S. A4 112
Cuyama, stm., Ca., U.S. E4 82
Cuyamaca Peak, mtn., Ca., U.S. F5 82
Cuyo Islands, is., Phil. C7 32
Cuyuni, stm., S.A. D13 58
Cuzco, Peru F4 54
C.W. McConaughy, Lake, res., Ne., U.S. C4 104
Cyclades see Kikládhes, is., Grc. L8 16
Cynthiana, In., U.S. H2 91
Cynthiana, Ky., U.S. B5 94
Cypress Creek, stm., Tx., U.S. r14 120
Cypress Hills Provincial Park, Sask., Can. H1 75
Cypress Lake, l., Fl., U.S. D5 86
Cypress Quarters, Fl., U.S. E6 86
Cypress Swamp, sw., U.S. F4 85
Cyprus, ctry., Asia B3 40
Cyril, Ok., U.S. C3 113
Czech Republic, ctry., Eur. F11 4
Częstochowa, Pol. E19 8

D

Dabeiba, Col. D4 58
Dabhoi, India I5 38
Dabie Shan, mts., China D4 28
Dabola, Gui. F3 42
Dacca see Dhaka, Bngl. I14 38
Dachaidan, China B16 38
Dachau, Ger. G11 8
Dacono, Co., U.S. A6 83
Dacula, Ga., U.S. C3 87
Dadanawa, Guy. F13 58
Dade, co., Fl., U.S. G6 86
Dade, co., Ga., U.S. B1 87
Dade, co., Mo., U.S. D4 102
Dade City, Fl., U.S. D4 86
Dadeville, Al., U.S. C4 78
Dādra and Nagar Haveli, ter., India B2 37
Dādu, Pak. G2 38
Daet, Phil. q20 33b
Daggett, co., Ut., U.S. C6 121
Dagsboro, De., U.S. F5 85
Dagupan, Phil. p19 33b
Dahan-e Qowmghī, Afg. C2 38
Da Hinggan Ling, mts., China C11 26
Dahlak Archipelago, is., Erit. E3 46
Dahlak Kebir Island, i., Erit. E3 46
Dahlonega, Ga., U.S. B3 87
Dahomey see Benin, ctry., Afr. G6 42
Dahra, Libya C9 42
Dahy, Nafūd ad-, des., Sau. Ar. D4 46
Daimiel, Spain F8 12
Daingerfield, Tx., U.S. C5 120
Dairen see Dalian, China D11 26
Dakar, Sen. F2 42
Dakhla, W. Sah. D2 42
Dakota, co., Mn., U.S. F5 100
Dakota, co., Ne., U.S. B9 104
Dakota City, Ia., U.S. B3 92
Dakota City, Ne., U.S. B9 104
Dalandzadgad, Mong. C7 26
Da Lat, Viet. I10 34
Dālbandin, Pak. D1 36
Dalby, Austl. E10 50
Dale, In., U.S. H4 91
Dale, co., Al., U.S. D4 78
Dale City, Va., U.S. B5 123
Dale Hollow Lake, res., U.S. C8 119
Daleville, Al., U.S. D4 78
Daleville, In., U.S. D6 91
Dalhart, Tx., U.S. A1 120
Dalhousie, N.B., Can. A3 71
Dalhousie, Cape, c., N.W. Ter., Can. B7 66
Dali, China B6 34
Dalian, China D11 26
Dall, Mount, mtn., Ak., U.S. f15 79
Dallam, co., Tx., U.S. A1 120
Dallas, Ga., U.S. C2 87
Dallas (part of Melcher), Ia., U.S. C4 92
Dallas, N.C., U.S. B1 110
Dallas, Or., U.S. C3 114
Dallas, Pa., U.S. D10 115
Dallas, Tx., U.S. C4 120
Dallas, co., Al., U.S. C2 78
Dallas, co., Ar., U.S. D3 81
Dallas, co., Ia., U.S. C3 92
Dallas, co., Mo., U.S. D4 102
Dallas, co., Tx., U.S. C4 120
Dallas Center, Ia., U.S. C4 92
Dallas City, Il., U.S. C2 90
Dallas Naval Air Station, mil., Tx., U.S. n9 120
Dallastown, Pa., U.S. G8 115
Dall Island, i., Ak., U.S. n23 79
Dalmacija, hist. reg., Eur. F11 14
Dalmatia see Dalmacija, hist. reg., Eur. F11 14
Daloa, C. Iv. G4 42
Dalqū, Sudan D12 42
Dalton, Ga., U.S. B2 87
Dalton, Ma., U.S. B1 98
Dalton, Oh., U.S. B4 112
Dalton, Pa., U.S. C10 115
Daltonganj, India H11 38
Dalton Gardens, Id., U.S. B2 89
Dalwallinu, Austl. F3 50
Daly City, Ca., U.S. h8 82
Damān, India B2 37
Damān, ter., India B2 37
Damar, Pulau, i., Indon. G8 32
Damariscotta, Me., U.S. D3 96
Damariscotta Lake, l., Me., U.S. D3 96
Damascus, Md., U.S. B3 97
Damascus, Va., U.S. f10 123
Damascus see Dimashq, Syria C5 40
Damāvand, Qolleh-ye, mtn., Iran J8 22
Damba, Ang. C3 44
Damoh, India I8 38
Dampar, Tasek, l., Malay. M7 34
Dampier, Austl. D3 50
Dampier, Selat, strt., Indon. F9 32
Dampier Archipelago, is., Austl. D3 50
Dan, stm., U.S. D3 123
Dana, In., U.S. E3 91
Danakil Plain, pl., Erit. F3 46
Da Nang, Viet. F10 34
Danbury, Ct., U.S. D2 84
Danbury, Tx., U.S. r14 120
Dand, Afg. E1 38
Dandridge, Tn., U.S. C10 119
Dane, co., Wi., U.S. E4 126
Dangla, Eth. F2 46
Dania, Fl., U.S. F6 86
Daniels, co., Mt., U.S. B11 103
Danielson, Ct., U.S. B8 84
Daniels Pass, Ut., U.S. C4 121
Danilov, Russia C23 18
Danlí, Hond. G4 64
Dannemora, N.Y., U.S. f11 109
Dansville, N.Y., U.S. C3 109
Dante, Va., U.S. f9 123
Danube, stm., Eur. G13 4
Danube, Mouths of the, mth., Eur. D13 16
Danvers, Il., U.S. C4 90
Danvers, Ma., U.S. A6 98
Danville, Que., Can. D5 74
Danville, Ar., U.S. B2 81
Danville, Ca., U.S. h9 82
Danville, Il., U.S. C6 90
Danville, In., U.S. E4 91
Danville, Ia., U.S. D6 92
Danville, Ky., U.S. C5 94
Danville, Oh., U.S. B3 112
Danville, Pa., U.S. E8 115
Danville, Va., U.S. D3 123
Danyang, China C8 28
Danzig, Gulf of, b., Eur. A19 8
Danzig see Gdańsk, Pol. A18 8
Daocheng, China F7 26
Dapango, Togo F6 42
Daphne, Al., U.S. E2 78
Dar'ā, Syria C5 40
Darakht-e Yahyá, Afg. E3 38
Dārayyā, Syria C5 40
Darbāsīyah, Syria A7 40
Darbhanga, India G11 38
Darby, Mt., U.S. D2 103
Darby, Pa., U.S. G11 115
Darchan, Mong. B8 26
Dardanelle, Ar., U.S. B2 81
Dardanelle Lake, res., Ar., U.S. B2 81
Dardanelles see Çanakkale Boğazı, strt., Tur. I10 16
Dare, co., N.C., U.S. B7 110
Dar es Salaam, Tan. C7 44
Dargaville, N.Z. A4 52
Dari, China E6 26
Darien, Ct., U.S. E2 84
Darien, Ga., U.S. E5 87
Darien, Wi., U.S. F5 126
Dariganga, Mong. B9 26
Darjeeling, India G13 38
Darke, co., Oh., U.S. B1 112
Darley Woods, De., U.S. h8 85
Darling, stm., Austl. F9 50
Darling, Lake, res., N.D., U.S. A4 111
Darling Range, mts., Austl. F3 50
Darlington, Eng., U.K. G11 7
Darlington, In., U.S. D4 91
Darlington, Md., U.S. A5 97
Darlington, S.C., U.S. C8 117
Darlington, Wi., U.S. F3 126
Darlington, co., S.C., U.S. C8 117
Darmstadt, Ger. F8 8
Darnah, Libya B10 42
Daroca, Spain D10 12
Darrah, Mount, mtn., Can. E3 68
Darrington, Wa., U.S. A4 124
Dartmoor National Park, Eng., U.K. K9 7
Dartmouth, Eng., U.K. K9 7
Daru, Pap. N. Gui. G11 32
Darwin, Austl. B6 50
Dašinčilen, Mong. B7 26
Dassel, Mn., U.S. E4 100
Datia, India H8 38
Datil Mountains, mts., N.M., U.S. C2 108
D'at'kovo, Russia H17 18
Datong, China C9 26
Datu, Tanjung, c., Asia M10 34
Dāūd Khel, Pak. D4 38
Daufuskie Island, i., S.C., U.S. G6 117
Daugavpils, Lat. F9 18
Daulatābād (Shirin Tagāo), Afg. B1 38
Daule, Ec. G2 58
Dauphin, Man., Can. D1 70
Dauphin, co., Pa., U.S. F8 115
Dauphin, stm., Man., Can. D2 70

Name — Map Ref — Page

Dauphin Island, Al., U.S. E1 78
Dauphin Island, i., Al., U.S. E1 78
Dauphin Lake, l., Man., Can. D2 70
Dāvangere, India E3 37
Davao, Phil. D8 32
Davao Gulf, b., Phil. D8 32
Daveluyville, Que., Can. C5 74
Davenport, Fl., U.S. D5 86
Davenport, Ia., U.S. C7 92
Davenport, Ok., U.S. B5 113
Davenport, Wa., U.S. B7 124
David, Pan. J6 64
David City, Ne., U.S. C8 104
Davidson, N.C., U.S. B2 110
Davidson, co., N.C., U.S. B2 110
Davidson, co., Tn., U.S. A5 119
Davidsville, Pa., U.S. F4 115
Davie, Fl., U.S. F6 86
Davie, co., N.C., U.S. B2 110
Daviess, co., In., U.S. G3 91
Daviess, co., Ky., U.S. C2 94
Daviess, co., Mo., U.S. B3 102
Davis, Ca., U.S. C3 82
Davis, Ok., U.S. C4 113
Davis, W.V., U.S. B5 125
Davis, co., Ia., U.S. D5 92
Davis, co., Ut., U.S. C3 121
Davis, Mount, mtn., Pa., U.S. G3 115
Davis Creek, stm., W.V., U.S. m12 125
Davis Dam, U.S. H7 105
Davis Islands, is., Fl., U.S. p11 86
Davis Lake, l., Or., U.S. E5 114
Davis-Monthan Air Force Base, mil., Az., U.S. E5 80
Davison, Mi., U.S. E7 99
Davison, co., S.D., U.S. D7 118
Davis Strait, strt., N.A. C21 66
Davisville, R.I., U.S. E4 116
Davos, Switz. F16 10
Dawa (Daua), stm., Afr. H3 46
Dawei, Mya. G5 34
Dawes, co., Ne., U.S. B2 104
Daws Island, i., S.C., U.S. G6 117
Dawson, Ga., U.S. E2 87
Dawson, Mn., U.S. F2 100
Dawson, co., Ga., U.S. B2 87
Dawson, co., Mt., U.S. C11 103
Dawson, co., Ne., U.S. D6 104
Dawson, co., Tx., U.S. C1 120
Dawson, Mount, mtn., B.C., Can. D9 69
Dawson Creek, B.C., Can. B7 69
Dawson Springs, Ky., U.S. C2 94
Dax, Fr. I5 10
Day, co., S.D., U.S. B8 118
Dayr az-Zawr, Syria B7 40
Daysland, Alta., Can. C4 68
Dayton, In., U.S. D4 91
Dayton, Ia., U.S. B3 92
Dayton, Ky., U.S. h14 94
Dayton, Md., U.S. B4 97
Dayton, Mn., U.S. m12 100
Dayton, Nv., U.S. D2 105
Dayton, Oh., U.S. C1 112
Dayton, Or., U.S. B3 114
Dayton, Tn., U.S. D8 119
Dayton, Tx., U.S. D5 120
Dayton, Va., U.S. B4 123
Dayton, Wa., U.S. C8 124
Dayton, Wy., U.S. B5 127
Daytona Beach, Fl., U.S. C5 86
Da Yunhe, China E10 26
Dayville, Ct., U.S. B8 84
De Aar, S. Afr. H4 44
Dead, North Branch, stm., Me., U.S. C2 96
Dead, South Branch, stm., Me., U.S. C2 96
Dead Creek, stm., Vt., U.S. C2 122
Dead Diamond, stm., N.H., U.S. g7 106
Dead Indian Peak, mtn., Wy., U.S. B3 127
Dead Lake, l., Mn., U.S. D3 100
Dead Lakes, l., Fl., U.S. B1 86
Deadman Bay, b., Fl., U.S. C3 86
Deadman Creek, stm., Wa., U.S. g14 124
Deadmans Cay, Bah. C10 64
Dead Sea, l., Asia D4 40
Deadwood, S.D., U.S. C2 118
Deadwood Reservoir, res., Id., U.S. E3 89
Deaf Smith, co., Tx., U.S. B1 120
Deale, Md., U.S. C4 97
Deal Island, Md., U.S. D6 97
Deal Island, i., Md., U.S. D6 97
Dean, stm., B.C., Can. C4 69
Dean Channel, strt., B.C., Can. C4 69
Deán Funes, Arg. C4 56
Dearborn, Mi., U.S. F7 99
Dearborn, co., In., U.S. F7 91
Dearborn Heights, Mi., U.S. p15 99
Dearg, Beinn, mtn., Scot., U.K. D8 7
Dease Strait, strt., N.W. Ter., Can. C11 66
Death Valley, val., Ca., U.S. D5 82
Death Valley National Park, U.S. D5 82
Deauville, Fr. C7 10
De Baca, co., N.M., U.S. C5 108
De Bary, Fl., U.S. D5 86
Debauch Mountain, mtn., Ak., U.S. C8 79
Dębica, Pol. E21 8
Debrecen, Hung. H21 8
Debre Markos, Eth. F2 46
Debre Tabor, Eth. F2 46
De Cade, Lake, l., La., U.S. E5 95
Decatur, Al., U.S. A3 78
Decatur, Ar., U.S. A1 81
Decatur, Ga., U.S. C2 87
Decatur, Il., U.S. D5 90
Decatur, In., U.S. C8 91
Decatur, Mi., U.S. F5 99
Decatur, Ms., U.S. C4 101
Decatur, Ne., U.S. B9 104
Decatur, Tn., U.S. D9 119
Decatur, Tx., U.S. C4 120
Decatur, co., Ga., U.S. F2 87
Decatur, co., In., U.S. F6 91
Decatur, co., Ia., U.S. D4 92
Decatur, co., Ks., U.S. C3 93
Decatur, co., Tn., U.S. B3 119
Decatur, Lake, res., Il., U.S. D5 90
Decaturville, Tn., U.S. B3 119
Decazeville, Fr. H9 10
Deccan, plat., India E4 37
Deception, Mount, mtn., Wa., U.S. B2 124
Decherd, Tn., U.S. B5 119
Děčín, Czech. E14 8
Decize, Fr. F10 10
Deckerville, Mi., U.S. E8 99
Decorah, Ia., U.S. A6 92
Dedham, Ma., U.S. B5 98
Dédougou, Burkina F5 42
Dedovsk, Russia F20 18
Deep, stm., N.C., U.S. B3 110
Deep Creek, stm., Ut., U.S. C2 121
Deep Creek, stm., Ut., U.S. B3 121
Deep Creek, stm., Ut., U.S. F3 121
Deep Creek, stm., Wa., U.S. g13 124
Deep Creek Lake, res., Md., U.S. K12 97
Deep Creek Mountains, mts., Id., U.S. G6 89
Deep Fork, stm., Ok., U.S. B5 113
Deep Inlet, b., Newf., Can. g10 72
Deep Red Creek, stm., Ok., U.S. C3 113
Deep River, Ont., Can. A7 73
Deep River, Ct., U.S. D6 84
Deer Creek, stm., Oh., U.S. C2 112
Deer Creek Indian Reservation, Mn., U.S. C5 100
Deerfield, Il., U.S. h9 90
Deerfield, Ks., U.S. E2 93
Deerfield, Ma., U.S. A2 98
Deerfield, Mi., U.S. G7 99
Deerfield, Wi., U.S. E4 126
Deerfield, stm., U.S. A2 98
Deerfield Beach, Fl., U.S. F6 86
Deer Island, pen., Ma., U.S. g12 98
Deer Island, i., Ms., U.S. f8 101
Deer Isle, i., Me., U.S. D4 96
Deer Lake, Newf., Can. D3 72
Deer Lake, l., Newf., Can. D3 72
Deer Lake, l., Mn., U.S. C5 100
Deer Lodge, Mt., U.S. D4 103
Deer Lodge, co., Mt., U.S. E3 103
Deer Park, N.Y., U.S. n15 109
Deer Park, Oh., U.S. o13 112
Deer Park, Wa., U.S. B8 124
Deer Peak, mtn., Co., U.S. C5 83
Deer River, Mn., U.S. C5 100
Deesa, India H5 38
Defiance, Oh., U.S. A1 112
Defiance, co., Oh., U.S. A1 112
Defiance, Mount, mtn., Or., U.S. B5 114
De Forest, Wi., U.S. E4 126
De Funiak Springs, Fl., U.S. u15 86
Degeh-Bur, Eth. G3 46
Dégelis, Que., Can. B9 74
Deggendorf, Ger. G12 8
De Graff, Oh., U.S. B2 112
De Gray Lake, res., Ar., U.S. C2 81
Dehiwala-Mount Lavinia, Sri L. I5 37
Dehra Dūn, India E8 38
Dehri, India H11 38
Dehu, India C2 37
Dehui, China C12 26
Dej, Rom. B7 16
Deje, Swe. G9 6
De Kalb, Il., U.S. B5 90
De Kalb, Ms., U.S. C5 101
De Kalb, Tx., U.S. C5 120
De Kalb, co., Al., U.S. A4 78
De Kalb, co., Ga., U.S. C2 87
De Kalb, co., Il., U.S. B5 90
De Kalb, co., In., U.S. B7 91
De Kalb, co., Mo., U.S. B3 102
De Kalb, co., Tn., U.S. D8 119
Dekese, Zaire B4 44
Delafield, Wi., U.S. m11 126
Delanco, N.J., U.S. C3 107
De Land, Fl., U.S. C5 86
Delano, Ca., U.S. E4 82
Delano, Mn., U.S. E5 100
Delano Peak, mtn., Ut., U.S. E3 121
Delaronde Lake, l., Sask., Can. C2 75
Delavan, Il., U.S. C4 90
Delavan, Wi., U.S. F5 126
Delaware, Oh., U.S. B2 112
Delaware, co., In., U.S. D7 91
Delaware, co., Ia., U.S. B6 92
Delaware, co., N.Y., U.S. C5 109
Delaware, co., Oh., U.S. B2 112
Delaware, co., Ok., U.S. A7 113
Delaware, co., Pa., U.S. G11 115
Delaware, state, U.S. D3 85
Delaware, stm., U.S. G11 115
Delaware, stm., Ks., U.S. C8 93
Delaware, East Branch, stm., N.Y., U.S. C5 109
Delaware Bay, b., U.S. D11 76
Delaware City, De., U.S. B3 85
Delaware Lake, res., Oh., U.S. B3 112
Delaware Water Gap, N.J., U.S. B2 107
Delaware Water Gap National Recreation Area, U.S. B2 107
Delbarton, W.V., U.S. D2 125
Delcambre, La., U.S. E4 95
Del City, Ok., U.S. B4 113
Delémont, Switz. E14 10
De Leon, Tx., U.S. C3 120
De Leon Springs, Fl., U.S. C5 86
Delft, Neth. C4 8
Delfzijl, Neth. B6 8
Delgado, Cabo, c., Moz. D8 44
Delhi, India F7 38
Delhi, La., U.S. B4 95
Delhi, N.Y., U.S. C6 109
Delicias, Mex. C7 62
De Lisle, Ms., U.S. E4 101
Delitzsch, Ger. D12 8
Dellenbaugh, Mount, mtn., Az., U.S. A2 80
Dell Rapids, S.D., U.S. D9 118
Del Mar, Ca., U.S. o15 82
Delmar, De., U.S. G3 85
Delmar, Md., U.S. D6 97
Delmar, N.Y., U.S. C7 109
Delmenhorst, Ger. B8 8
Delnice, Cro. D9 14
Del Norte, Co., U.S. D4 83
Del Norte, co., Ca., U.S. B2 82
De-Longa, Ostrova, is., Russia B23 24
Deloraine, Man., Can. E1 70
Del Park Manor, De., U.S. i7 85
Delphi, In., U.S. C4 91
Delphos, Oh., U.S. B1 112
Delran, N.J., U.S. C3 107
Delray Beach, Fl., U.S. F6 86
Del Rio, Tx., U.S. E2 120
Delson, Que., Can. q19 74
Delta, Co., U.S. C2 83
Delta, Oh., U.S. A2 112
Delta, Ut., U.S. D3 121
Delta, co., Co., U.S. C3 83
Delta, co., Mi., U.S. C3 99
Delta, co., Tx., U.S. C5 120
Delta, reg., Ms., U.S. B3 101
Delta Junction, Ak., U.S. C10 79
Delta Peak, mtn., B.C., Can. A3 69
Delta Reservoir, res., N.Y., U.S. B5 109
Deltaville, Va., U.S. C6 123
Deltona, Fl., U.S. D5 86
Demarest, N.J., U.S. h9 107
Deming, N.M., U.S. E2 108
Demirci, Tur. J12 16
Demirköy, Tur. H11 16
Demmin, Ger. B13 8
Demopolis, Al., U.S. C2 78
Demorest, Ga., U.S. B3 87
Demotte, In., U.S. B3 91
Denain, Fr. B10 10
Denali National Park, Ak., U.S. C9 79
Denare Beach, Sask., Can. C4 75
Denham Springs, La., U.S. D5 95
Den Helder, Neth. C4 8
Denia, Spain G12 12
Denison, Ia., U.S. B2 92
Denison, Tx., U.S. C4 120
Denison Dam, U.S. D5 113
Denizli, Tur. H13 4
Denmark, S.C., U.S. E5 117
Denmark, Wi., U.S. D6 126
Denmark, ctry., Eur. D9 4
Denmark Strait, strt. C15 128
Dennehotso, Az., U.S. A6 80
Dennis, Ma., U.S. C7 98
Dennison, Oh., U.S. B4 112
Dennis Port, Ma., U.S. C7 98
Denny Terrace, S.C., U.S. C5 117
Denpasar, Indon. G6 32
Dent, co., Mo., U.S. D6 102
Denton, Md., U.S. C6 97
Denton, N.C., U.S. B2 110
Denton, Tx., U.S. C4 120
Denton, co., Tx., U.S. C4 120
D'Entrecasteaux Islands, is., Pap. N. Gui. m17 50a
Dentsville, S.C., U.S. C6 117
Denver, Co., U.S. B6 83
Denver, Ia., U.S. B5 92
Denver, Pa., U.S. F9 115
Denver, co., Co., U.S. B6 83
Denver City, Tx., U.S. C1 120
Denville, N.J., U.S. B4 107
Deoghar, India H12 38
Deolāli, India C2 37
Deoria, India G10 38
De Pere, Wi., U.S. D5 126
Depew, N.Y., U.S. C2 109
Depoe Bay, Or., U.S. C2 114
Depok, Indon. m13 33a
Deposit, N.Y., U.S. C5 109
Depue, Il., U.S. B4 90
Deqin, China F6 26
De Queen, Ar., U.S. C1 81
De Queen Reservoir, res., Ar., U.S. C1 81
De Quincy, La., U.S. D2 95
Dera Ghāzi Khān, Pak. E4 38
Dera Ismāīl Khān, Pak. E4 38
Derby, Austl. C4 50
Derby, Eng., U.K. I11 7
Derby, Ct., U.S. D3 84
Derby, Ks., U.S. E6 93
Derby, Vt., U.S. B4 122
Derby Line, Vt., U.S. A4 122
Derg, Lough, l., Ire. I4 7
De Ridder, La., U.S. D2 95
Derma, Ms., U.S. B4 101
Dermott, Ar., U.S. D4 81
Dernieres, Isles, is., La., U.S. E5 95
Derry, N.H., U.S. E4 106
Derry, Pa., U.S. F3 115
Derval, Fr. E5 10
Derventa, Bos. E12 14
Derwood, Md., U.S. B3 97
Desaguadero, stm., Arg. C3 56
Des Allemands, La., U.S. E5 95
Des Arc, Ar., U.S. C4 81
Desbiens, Que., Can. A6 74
Descartes, Fr. F7 10
Deschaillons [-sur-Saint-Laurent], Que., Can. C5 74
Deschambault, Que., Can. C6 74
Deschambault Lake, l., Sask., Can. C4 75
Deschutes, co., Or., U.S. D5 114
Deschutes, stm., Or., U.S. B6 114
Dese, Eth. F2 46
Deseado, stm., Arg. F3 56
Deseret Peak, mtn., Ut., U.S. C3 121
Deseronto, Ont., Can. C7 73
Desert Creek Peak, mtn., Nv., U.S. E2 105
Desert Hot Springs, Ca., U.S. F5 82
Desert Peak, mtn., Ut., U.S. B2 121
Desert Valley, val., Nv., U.S. B3 105
Desha, Ar., U.S. B4 81
Desha, co., Ar., U.S. D4 81
Deshler, Ne., U.S. D8 104
Deshler, Oh., U.S. A2 112
Des Lacs, stm., N.D., U.S. A4 111
Desloge, Mo., U.S. D7 102
De Smet, S.D., U.S. C8 118
Des Moines, Ia., U.S. C4 92
Des Moines, Wa., U.S. B3 124
Des Moines, co., Ia., U.S. D6 92
Des Moines, stm., U.S. D5 92
Desolación, Isla, i., Chile G2 56
De Soto, Il., U.S. F4 90
De Soto, Ia., U.S. C3 92
De Soto, Ks., U.S. D9 93
De Soto, Mo., U.S. C7 102
De Soto, co., Fl., U.S. E5 86
De Soto, co., La., U.S. B2 95
De Soto, co., Ms., U.S. A3 101
Despard, W.V., U.S. k10 125
Des Peres, Mo., U.S. f13 102
Des Plaines, Il., U.S. A6 90
Des Plaines, stm., U.S. k8 90
Desroches, Île, i., Sey. C10 44
Dessau, Ger. D12 8
Destin, Fl., U.S. u15 86
Destrehan, La., U.S. E5 95
Desvres, Fr. B8 10
Detmold, Ger. D8 8
Detour, Point, c., Mi., U.S. C4 99
Detroit, Mi., U.S. F7 99
Detroit Lake, res., Or., U.S. C4 114
Detroit Lakes, Mn., U.S. D3 100
Deuel, co., Ne., U.S. C3 104
Deuel, co., S.D., U.S. C9 118
Deutsche Bucht, b., Ger. A7 8
Deutschlandsberg, Aus. I15 8
Deux-Montagnes, Que., Can. p19 74
Deux Montagnes, Lac des, l., Que., Can. q19 74
Deva, Rom. D6 16
Devakottai, India H5 37
De Valls Bluff, Ar., U.S. C4 81
Deventer, Neth. C6 8
DeView, Bayou, stm., Ar., U.S. B4 81
Devil's Island see Diable, Île du, i., Fr. Gu. B8 54
Devils Lake, N.D., U.S. A7 111
Devils Lake, l., N.D., U.S. A6 111
Devils Paw, mtn., Ak., U.S. k23 79
Devils Postpile National Monument, Ca., U.S. D4 82
Devils Tower National Monument, Wy., U.S. B8 127
Devil Track Lake, l., Mn., U.S. k9 100
Devine, Tx., U.S. E3 120
DeVola, Oh., U.S. C4 112
Devon, Alta., Can. C4 68
Devon Island, i., N.W. Ter., Can. A15 66
Devonport, Austl. H9 50
Devonport, N.Z. B5 52
Devonshire, De., U.S. h7 85
Dewa-kyūryō, hills, Japan C13 30
Dewar, Ok., U.S. B6 113
Dewās, India I7 38
Dewees Inlet, b., S.C., U.S. k12 117
Dewees Island, i., S.C., U.S. F8 117
Dewey, Az., U.S. C3 80
Dewey, Ok., U.S. A6 113
Dewey, co., Ok., U.S. B2 113
Dewey, co., S.D., U.S. B4 118
Dewey Beach, De., U.S. F5 85
Dewey Lake, res., Ky., U.S. C7 94
Deweyville, Tx., U.S. D6 120
De Witt, Ar., U.S. C4 81
De Witt, Ia., U.S. C7 92
De Witt, Mi., U.S. F6 99
De Witt, N.Y., U.S. B4 109
De Witt, co., Il., U.S. C4 90
De Witt, co., Tx., U.S. E4 120
Dexter, Ia., U.S. C3 92
Dexter, Me., U.S. C3 96
Dexter, Mi., U.S. F7 99
Dexter, Mo., U.S. E8 102
Dexter, N.M., U.S. D5 108
Dexter, Lake, l., Fl., U.S. C5 86
Dezfūl, Iran B4 46
Dezhou, China D10 26
Dhaka, Bngl. I14 38
Dhamār, Yemen F3 46
Dhamtari, India B6 37
Dhānbād, India I12 38
Dhār, India I6 38
Dharmapuri, India F5 37
Dharmavaram, India E4 37
Dhārwār, India E3 37
Dhawlāgiri, mtn., Nepal F10 38
Dhodhekánisos (Dodecanese), is., Grc. M10 16
Dholpur, India G7 38
Dhorāji, India J4 38
Dhrol, India I4 38
Dhubri, India G13 38
Dhule, India B3 37
Diable, Île du, i., Fr. Gu. B8 54
Diablo, Canyon, val., Az., U.S. C4 80
Diablo, Mount, mtn., Ca., U.S. h9 82
Diablo Dam, Wa., U.S. A4 124
Diablo Lake, res., Wa., U.S. A4 124
Diablo Range, mts., Ca., U.S. D3 82
Diamante, Arg. C4 56
Diamantina, Braz. E7 57
Diamantino, Braz. F7 54
Diamond Head, crat., Hi., U.S. B4 88
Diamond Hill, R.I., U.S. B4 116
Diamond Hill Reservoir, res., R.I., U.S. A4 116
Diamond Lake, Il., U.S. h9 90
Diamond Lake, l., Or., U.S. D4 114
Diamond Mountains, mts., Nv., U.S. D6 105
Diamond Peak, mtn., Co., U.S. A2 83
Diamond Peak, mtn., Id., U.S. E5 89
Diamond Peak, mtn., Or., U.S. D4 114
Diamond Peak, mtn., Wa., U.S. C8 124
Diamondville, Wy., U.S. E2 127
Diaz, Ar., U.S. B4 81
Dibaya, Zaire C4 44
D'Iberville, Ms., U.S. E5 101
Diboll, Tx., U.S. D5 120
Dibrugarh, India G16 38
Dickens, co., Tx., U.S. C2 120
Dickenson, co., Va., U.S. e9 123
Dickerson, Md., U.S. B3 97
Dickey, co., N.D., U.S. C7 111
Dickeyville, Wi., U.S. F3 126
Dickinson, N.D., U.S. C3 111
Dickinson, co., Ia., U.S. A2 92
Dickinson, co., Ks., U.S. D6 93
Dickinson, co., Mi., U.S. B3 99
Dickinson Dam, N.D., U.S. C3 111
Dickson, Ok., U.S. C5 113
Dickson, Tn., U.S. A4 119
Dickson, co., Tn., U.S. A4 119
Dickson City, Pa., U.S. D10 115
Didsbury, Alta., Can. D3 68
Die, Fr. H12 10
Dieburg, Ger. F8 8
Dieciocho de Marzo, Mex. E11 62
Diefenbaker, Lake, res., Sask., Can. F2 75
Diégo-Suarez see Antsiranana, Madag. D9 44
Dien Bien Phu, Viet. D7 34
Diepholz, Ger. C8 8
Dieppe, N.B., Can. C5 71
Dieppe, Fr. C8 10
Dierks, Ar., U.S. C1 81
Dieuze, Fr. D13 10
Digboi, India G16 38
Dighton, Ks., U.S. D3 93
Digne, Fr. H13 10
Digoin, Fr. F10 10
Dijon, Fr. E12 10
Dike, Ia., U.S. B5 92
Dikson, Russia C10 24
Dili, Indon. G8 32
Dillard, Or., U.S. D3 114
Dill City, Ok., U.S. B2 113
Dilley, Tx., U.S. E3 120
Dillingen [an der Donau], Ger. G10 8
Dillingham, Ak., U.S. D8 79
Dillon, Mt., U.S. E4 103
Dillon, S.C., U.S. C9 117
Dillon, co., S.C., U.S. C9 117
Dillon Lake, res., Oh., U.S. B3 112
Dillon Reservoir, res., Co., U.S. B4 83
Dillonvale, Oh., U.S. B5 112
Dillsboro, In., U.S. F7 91
Dillsburg, Pa., U.S. F7 115
Dilolo, Zaire D4 44
Dilworth, Mn., U.S. D2 100
Dimāpur, India H15 38
Dimashq (Damascus), Syria C5 40
Dimitrovgrad, Bul. G9 16
Dimitrovgrad, Russia G7 22
Dimmit, co., Tx., U.S. E3 120
Dimmitt, Tx., U.S. B1 120
Dimona, Isr. D4 40
Dimondale, Mi., U.S. F6 99
Dinagat Island, i., Phil. C8 32
Dinājpur, Bngl. H13 38
Dinan, Fr. D4 10
Dinant, Bel. E4 8
Dinara, mts., Eur. F11 14
Dinard, Fr. D4 10
Dinaric Alps see Dinara, mts., Eur. F11 14
Dindigul, India G4 37
Dinghai, China E11 28
Dingle, Ire. I2 7
Dingmans Ferry, Pa., U.S. D12 115
Dingolfing, Ger. G12 8
Dingqing, China E16 38
Dingri, China F12 38
Dingshan, China D8 28
Dingwall, Scot., U.K. D8 7
Dinh Lap, Viet. D9 34
Dinner Point, c., Fl., U.S. D4 86
Dinosaur National Monument, U.S. C6 121
Dinuba, Ca., U.S. D4 82
Dinwiddie, co., Va., U.S. C5 123
Diourbel, Sen. F2 42
Dipkarpaz, N. Cyp. B4 40
Dipolog, Phil. D7 32
Dire Dawa, Eth. G3 46
Diriamba, Nic. I4 64
Dirico, Ang. E4 44
Dirk Hartog Island, i., Austl. E2 50
Dirty Devil, stm., Ut., U.S. E5 121
Disappointment, Cape, c., Falk. Is. G9 56
Disappointment, Cape, c., Wa., U.S. C1 124
Disappointment, Lake, l., Austl. D4 50
Disentis, Switz. F15 10
Dishman, Wa., U.S. g14 124
Disko, i., Grnld. C22 66
Disko Bugt, b., Grnld. C22 66
Dismal, stm., Ne., U.S. C5 104
Disraëli, Que., Can. D6 74
District of Columbia, dept., U.S. f8 97
Diu, India J4 38
Diu, ter., India J4 38
Divernon, Il., U.S. D4 90
Divide, co., N.D., U.S. A2 111
Divide Peak, mtn., Wy., U.S. E5 127
Divinópolis, Braz. F6 57
Divisor, Serra do, plat., S.A. E4 54
Dix, stm., Ky., U.S. C5 94
Dixfield, Me., U.S. D2 96
Dixie, co., Fl., U.S. C3 86
Dixie Valley, val., Nv., U.S. D4 105
Dixon, Ca., U.S. C3 82
Dixon, Il., U.S. B4 90
Dixon, Mo., U.S. D5 102
Dixon, N.M., U.S. A4 108
Dixon, co., Ne., U.S. B9 104
Dixon Entrance, strt., N.A. F6 66
Dixonville, Pa., U.S. E3 115
Diyarbakır, Tur. H16 4
Dja, stm., Afr. H8 42
Djakarta see Jakarta, Indon. m13 32
Djambala, Congo B2 44
Djanet, Alg. D7 42
Djebel Abiod, Tun. M4 14
Djebibina, Tun. M5 14
Djemmal, Tun. N5 14
Djerba, Île de, i., Tun. B8 42
Djerid, Chott, sw., Tun. B7 42
Djibouti, Dji. F3 46
Djibouti, ctry., Afr. F3 46
Dmitrija Lapteva, Proliv, strt., Russia C22 24
Dmitrov, Russia E20 18
Dnieper, stm., Eur. H4 22
Dniester, stm., Eur. H3 22
Dniprodzerzhyns'k, Ukr. H4 22

Name	Map Ref	Page
Dnipropetrovs'k, Ukr.	H4	22
Dno, Russia	D12	18
Do Āb-e Mīkh-e Zarrīn, Afg.	C2	38
Doaktown, N.B., Can.	C3	71
Doany, Madag.	D9	44
Doba, Chad	E9	42
Dobbiaco, Italy	C7	14
Dobbs Ferry, N.Y., U.S.	g13	109
Döbeln, Ger.	D13	8
Doberai, Jazirah, pen., Indon.	F9	32
Dobo, Indon.	G9	32
Doboj, Bos.	E2	16
Dobrič, Bul.	F11	16
Dobruš, Bela.	I14	18
Dobson, N.C., U.S.	A2	110
Doce, stm., Braz.	E8	57
Docena, Al., U.S.	f7	78
Dock Junction, Ga., U.S.	*E5	87
Doctors Lake, l., Fl., U.S.	m8	86
Doddridge, co., W.V., U.S.	B4	125
Dodecanese see Dhodhekánisos, is., Grc.	M10	16
Dodge, Ne., U.S.	C9	104
Dodge, co., Ga., U.S.	D3	87
Dodge, co., Mn., U.S.	G6	100
Dodge, co., Ne., U.S.	C9	104
Dodge, co., Wi., U.S.	E5	126
Dodge Center, Mn., U.S.	F6	100
Dodge City, Ks., U.S.	E3	93
Dodgeville, Wi., U.S.	F3	126
Dodoma, Tan.	C7	44
Doerun, Ga., U.S.	E3	87
Doe Run, Mo., U.S.	D7	102
Doetinchem, Neth.	D6	8
Dog, stm., Vt., U.S.	C3	122
Dogai Coring, l., China	C13	38
Dog Island, i., Fl., U.S.	C2	86
Dog Keys Pass, strt., Ms., U.S.	g8	101
Dog Lake, l., Man., Can.	D2	70
Dogondoutchi, Niger	F6	42
Doha see Ad-Dawḥah, Qatar	C5	46
Dohad, India	I6	38
Doiran, Lake, l., Eur.	H6	16
Dokka, Nor.	F8	6
Dokkum, Neth.	B5	8
Dolak, Pulau, i., Indon.	G10	32
Dolbeau, Que., Can.	k12	74
Dol-de-Bretagne, Fr.	D5	10
Dolgeville, N.Y., U.S.	B6	109
Dolianova, Italy	J4	14
Dolisie, Congo	B2	44
Dollar Bay, Mi., U.S.	A2	99
Dolo, Som.	H3	46
Dolomite, Al., U.S.	B3	78
Dolomites see Dolomiti, mts., Italy	C6	14
Dolomiti, mts., Italy	C6	14
Dolores, Arg.	D5	56
Dolores, Col.	F5	58
Dolores, Co., U.S.	D2	83
Dolores, co., Co., U.S.	D2	83
Dolores, stm., U.S.	E7	121
Dolores Hidalgo, Mex.	G9	62
Dolphin and Union Strait, strt., N.W. Ter., Can.	C9	66
Dolphin Island, i., Ut., U.S.	B3	121
Dolton, Il., U.S.	k9	90
Dombås, Nor.	E7	6
Dome Mountain, mtn., Az., U.S.	k9	80
Dome Peak, mtn., Co., U.S.	B3	83
Domeyko, Chile	B2	56
Domeyko, Cordillera, mts., Chile	A3	56
Domfront, Fr.	D6	10
Dominica, ctry., N.A.	G17	64
Dominica Channel, strt., N.A.	G17	64
Dominican Republic, ctry., N.A.	E12	64
Dominion, Cape, c., N.W. Ter., Can.	C18	66
Domodedovo, Russia	F20	18
Domodossola, Italy	C3	14
Domžale, Slo.	C9	14
Don, stm., Russia	H6	22
Dona Ana, N.M., U.S.	E3	108
Dona Ana, co., N.M., U.S.	E2	108
Donaldsonville, La., U.S.	D4	95
Donalsonville, Ga., U.S.	E2	87
Donaueschingen, Ger.	H8	8
Donauwörth, Ger.	G10	8
Don Benito, Spain	G6	12
Doncaster, Eng., U.K.	H11	7
Dondo, Ang.	C2	44
Dondra Head, c., Sri L.	J6	37
Donegal Bay, b., Ire.	G4	7
Doneraile, S.C., U.S.	C8	117
Donetsk, Ukr.	H5	22
Donga, stm., Nig.	G8	42
Dongara, Austl.	E2	50
Dongchuan, China	A7	34
Dongfang, China	H8	26
Dongfang (Basuo), China	E10	34
Dongguan, China	L2	28
Donghai Dao, i., China	D11	34
Dong Hoi, Viet.	F9	34
Dongshan, China	L6	28
Dongtai, China	C9	28
Dongting Hu, l., China	F1	28
Doniphan, Mo., U.S.	E7	102
Doniphan, Ne., U.S.	D7	104
Doniphan, co., Ks., U.S.	C8	93
Donkey Creek, stm., Wy., U.S.	B7	127
Donkin, N.S., Can.	C10	71
Donley, co., Tx., U.S.	B2	120
Donna, Tx., U.S.	F3	120
Donnacona, Que., Can.	C6	74
Donnellson, Ia., U.S.	D6	92
Donner Pass, Ca., U.S.	C3	82
Donora, Pa., U.S.	F2	115
Donskoj, Russia	H21	18
Dooly, co., Ga., U.S.	D3	87
Doonerak, Mount, mtn., Ak., U.S.	B9	79
Door, co., Wi., U.S.	D6	126
Dora, Al., U.S.	B2	78
Doraville, Ga., U.S.	h8	87
Dorcheat, Bayou, stm., U.S.	B2	95
Dorchester, N.B., Can.	D5	71
Dorchester, Eng., U.K.	K10	7
Dorchester, Ne., U.S.	D8	104
Dorchester, co., Md., U.S.	D5	97
Dorchester, co., S.C., U.S.	E7	117
Dorchester, Cape, c., N.W. Ter., Can.	C17	66
Dordogne, stm., Fr.	H8	10
Dordrecht, Neth.	D4	8
Doré Lake, l., Sask., Can.	C2	75
Dorena Lake, res., Or., U.S.	D3	114
Dores do Indaiá, Braz.	E6	57
Dorgali, Italy	I4	14
Dori, Burkina	F5	42
Dorion-Vaudreuil, Que., Can.	q18	74
Dormont, Pa., U.S.	k13	115
Dornbirn, Aus.	H9	8
Dorothy Pond, Ma., U.S.	B4	98
Dorr, Mi., U.S.	F5	99
Dorset, Vt., U.S.	E2	122
Dorsey, Md., U.S.	B4	97
Dortmund, Ger.	D7	8
Dorton, Ky., U.S.	C7	94
Dorval, Que., Can.	q19	74
Dos Bahías, Cabo, c., Arg.	E3	56
Dothan, Al., U.S.	D4	78
Douai, Fr.	B10	10
Douala, Cam.	H7	42
Douarnenez, Fr.	D2	10
Double Beach, Ct., U.S.	D4	84
Doublespring Pass, Id., U.S.	E5	89
Double Springs, Al., U.S.	A2	78
Doubletop Peak, mtn., Wy., U.S.	C2	127
Doubs, stm., Eur.	E12	10
Dougherty, co., Ga., U.S.	E2	87
Douglas, I. of Man	G8	7
Douglas, Az., U.S.	F6	80
Douglas, Ga., U.S.	E4	87
Douglas, Mi., U.S.	F4	99
Douglas, Wy., U.S.	D7	127
Douglas, co., Co., U.S.	B6	83
Douglas, co., Ga., U.S.	C2	87
Douglas, co., Il., U.S.	D5	90
Douglas, co., Ks., U.S.	D8	93
Douglas, co., Mn., U.S.	E3	100
Douglas, co., Mo., U.S.	E5	102
Douglas, co., Ne., U.S.	C9	104
Douglas, co., Nv., U.S.	E2	105
Douglas, co., Or., U.S.	D3	114
Douglas, co., S.D., U.S.	D7	118
Douglas, co., Wa., U.S.	B6	124
Douglas, co., Wi., U.S.	B2	126
Douglas, Mount, mtn., Ak., U.S.	D9	79
Douglas Channel, strt., B.C., Can.	C3	69
Douglas Lake, l., Mi., U.S.	C6	99
Douglas Lake, res., Tn., U.S.	D10	119
Douglass, Ks., U.S.	E7	93
Douglastown, N.B., Can.	B4	71
Douglasville, Ga., U.S.	C2	87
Dourada, Serra, plat., Braz.	B4	57
Dourados, Braz.	G1	57
Douro (Duero), stm., Eur.	D4	12
Dousman, Wi., U.S.	E5	126
Dove Creek, Co., U.S.	D2	83
Dover, Eng., U.K.	J14	7
Dover, Ar., U.S.	B2	81
Dover, De., U.S.	D3	85
Dover, Fl., U.S.	D4	86
Dover, Ma., U.S.	h10	98
Dover, N.H., U.S.	D5	106
Dover, N.J., U.S.	B3	107
Dover, Oh., U.S.	B4	112
Dover, Pa., U.S.	F8	115
Dover, Tn., U.S.	A4	119
Dover, Strait of (Pas de Calais), strt., Eur.	J14	7
Dover Air Force Base, mil., De., U.S.	D4	85
Dover-Foxcroft, Me., U.S.	C3	96
Dover Plains, N.Y., U.S.	D7	109
Dowagiac, Mi., U.S.	G4	99
Dowlat Yār, Afg.	C1	38
Downers Grove, Il., U.S.	B5	90
Downey, Ca., U.S.	n12	82
Downey, Id., U.S.	G6	89
Downingtown, Pa., U.S.	F10	115
Downpatrick, N. Ire., U.K.	G7	7
Downpatrick Head, c., Ire.	G3	7
Downs, Ks., U.S.	C5	93
Downs Mountain, mtn., Wy., U.S.	C3	127
Downton, Mount, mtn., B.C., Can.	C5	69
Dows, Ia., U.S.	B4	92
Dowshī, Afg.	C3	38
Doylestown, Oh., U.S.	B4	112
Doylestown, Pa., U.S.	F11	115
Doyline, La., U.S.	B2	95
Drâa, Oued, val., Afr.	C4	42
Dracena, Braz.	F3	57
Drachten, Neth.	B6	8
Dracut, Ma., U.S.	A5	98
Draguignan, Fr.	I13	10
Drain, Or., U.S.	D3	114
Drake Passage, strt.	D6	47
Drake Peak, mtn., Or., U.S.	E6	114
Dráma, Grc.	H8	16
Drammen, Nor.	G8	6
Draper, Ut., U.S.	C4	121
Drau (Drava), stm., Eur.	C8	14
Drava (Drau), stm., Eur.	D13	14
Drayton, Ont., Can.	D4	73
Drayton, N.D., U.S.	A8	111
Drayton, S.C., U.S.	B4	117
Drayton Plains, Mi., U.S.	F7	99
Drayton Valley, Alta., Can.	C3	68
Dresden, Ont., Can.	E2	73
Dresden, Ger.	D13	8
Dresden, Oh., U.S.	B3	112
Dresden, Tn., U.S.	A3	119
Dresslerville, Nv., U.S.	E2	105
Dreux, Fr.	D8	10
Drew, Ms., U.S.	B3	101
Drew, co., Ar., U.S.	D4	81
Drews Reservoir, res., Or., U.S.	E6	114
Drexel, Mo., U.S.	C3	102
Drexel, N.C., U.S.	B1	110
Drexel, Oh., U.S.	C1	112
Drift, Ky., U.S.	C7	94
Driggs, Id., U.S.	F7	89
Driskill Mountain, hill, La., U.S.	B3	95
Drogheda, Ire.	H6	7
Drumheller, Alta., Can.	D4	68
Drum Island, i., S.C., U.S.	k12	117
Drummond, Lake, l., Va., U.S.	D6	123
Drummond Island, i., Mi., U.S.	C7	99
Drummondville, Que., Can.	D5	74
Drumright, Ok., U.S.	B5	113
Družina, Russia	D23	24
Drybranch, W.V., U.S.	m13	125
Dry Cimarron, stm., U.S.	A6	108
Dry Creek Mountain, mtn., Nv., U.S.	B5	105
Dryden, Ont., Can.	o16	73
Dryden, N.Y., U.S.	C4	109
Dry Fork, stm., Mo., U.S.	D6	102
Dry Fork, stm., W.V., U.S.	D3	125
Dry Fork, stm., W.V., U.S.	B5	125
Dry Ridge, Ky., U.S.	B5	94
Dry Tortugas, is., Fl., U.S.	H5	86
Dry Tortugas National Park, Fl., U.S.	H4	86
Duarte, Pico, mtn., Dom. Rep.	E12	64
Dubach, La., U.S.	B3	95
Dubai see Dubayy, U.A.E.	C6	46
Dubawnt, stm., N.W. Ter., Can.	D12	66
Dubawnt Lake, l., N.W. Ter., Can.	D12	66
Du Bay, Lake, res., Wi., U.S.	D4	126
Dubayy (Dubai), U.A.E.	C6	46
Dubbo, Austl.	F9	50
Dublin (Baile Átha Cliath), Ire.	H6	7
Dublin, Ga., U.S.	D4	87
Dublin, In., U.S.	E7	91
Dublin, N.H., U.S.	E2	106
Dublin, Oh., U.S.	k10	112
Dublin, Pa., U.S.	F11	115
Dublin, Tx., U.S.	C3	120
Dublin, Va., U.S.	C2	123
Dubna, Russia	E20	18
Dubois, In., U.S.	H4	91
Du Bois, Pa., U.S.	D4	115
Dubois, Wy., U.S.	C3	127
Dubois, co., In., U.S.	H4	91
Duboistown, Pa., U.S.	D7	115
Dubrovnik, Cro.	G13	14
Dubuque, Ia., U.S.	B7	92
Dubuque, co., Ia., U.S.	B7	92
Duchesne, Ut., U.S.	C5	121
Duchesne, co., Ut., U.S.	C5	121
Duchesne, stm., Ut., U.S.	C5	121
Duchess, Austl.	D7	50
Duck, stm., Tn., U.S.	B4	119
Duck Bay, Man., Can.	C1	70
Duck Creek, stm., Oh., U.S.	C4	112
Duck Creek, stm., Wi., U.S.	h9	126
Duck Lake, Sask., Can.	E2	75
Duck Lake, l., Me., U.S.	C4	96
Duck Mountain Provincial Park, Sask., Can.	F5	75
Duck Valley Indian Reservation, U.S.	B5	105
Duckwater Indian Reservation, Nv., U.S.	E6	105
Duckwater Peak, mtn., Nv., U.S.	E6	105
Dudelange, Lux.	F6	8
Dudinka, Russia	D11	24
Dudley, Ma., U.S.	B4	98
Duenweg, Mo., U.S.	D3	102
Duero (Douro), stm., Eur.	D5	12
Due West, S.C., U.S.	C3	117
Duffer Peak, mtn., Nv., U.S.	B3	105
Dufour Spitze, mtn., Eur.	G14	10
Duga Resa, Cro.	D10	14
Dugdemona, stm., La., U.S.	B3	95
Dugger, In., U.S.	F3	91
Duida, Cerro, mtn., Ven.	F10	58
Duifken Point, c., Austl.	B8	50
Duisburg, Ger.	D6	8
Duke Island, i., Ak., U.S.	n24	79
Dukes, co., Ma., U.S.	D6	98
Duk Fadiat, Sudan	G12	42
Dulce, N.M., U.S.	A2	108
Dulgalach, stm., Russia	D20	24
Duluth, Ga., U.S.	B2	87
Duluth, Mn., U.S.	D6	100
Dūmā, Syria	C5	40
Dumaguete, Phil.	D7	32
Dumaran Island, i., Phil.	C6	32
Dumaring, Indon.	E6	32
Dumas, Ar., U.S.	D4	81
Dumas, Tx., U.S.	B2	120
Dumbarton, Scot., U.K.	F8	7
Dumfries, Scot., U.K.	F9	7
Dumfries, Va., U.S.	B5	123
Dumont, Ia., U.S.	B5	92
Dumont, N.J., U.S.	B5	107
Dumyāṭ, Egypt	B12	42
Dunaújváros, Hung.	I18	8
Dunbar, Pa., U.S.	G2	115
Dunbar, W.V., U.S.	C3	125
Duncan, B.C., Can.	E6	69
Duncan, Az., U.S.	E6	80
Duncan, Ok., U.S.	C4	113
Duncan, S.C., U.S.	B3	117
Duncan Falls, Oh., U.S.	C4	112
Duncan Lake, res., B.C., Can.	D9	69
Duncannon, Pa., U.S.	F7	115
Duncansville, Pa., U.S.	F5	115
Duncanville, Tx., U.S.	n10	120
Dundalk, Ont., Can.	C4	73
Dundalk, Ire.	G6	7
Dundalk, Md., U.S.	B4	97
Dundas, Ont., Can.	D5	73
Dundas Peninsula, pen., N.W. Ter., Can.	B10	66
Dundee, S. Afr.	G6	44
Dundee, Scot., U.K.	E9	7
Dundee, Fl., U.S.	D5	86
Dundee, Il., U.S.	A5	90
Dundee, Mi., U.S.	G7	99
Dundee, N.Y., U.S.	C4	109
Dundee, Or., U.S.	h11	114
Dundy, co., Ne., U.S.	D4	104
Dunedin, N.Z.	F3	52
Dunedin, Fl., U.S.	D4	86
Dunellen, N.J., U.S.	B4	107
Dunfermline, Scot., U.K.	E9	7
Dungarvan, Ire.	I5	7
Dungeness, stm., Wa., U.S.	A2	124
Dungun, Malay.	L7	34
Dunham, Que., Can.	D5	74
Dunhua, China	C12	26
Dunhuang, China	C5	26
Dunkard Creek, stm., U.S.	B4	125
Dunkerque, Fr.	A9	10
Dunkerton, Ia., U.S.	B5	92
Dunkirk, In., U.S.	D7	91
Dunkirk, N.Y., U.S.	C1	109
Dunkirk, Oh., U.S.	B2	112
Dunklin, co., Mo., U.S.	E7	102
Dunkwa, Ghana	G5	42
Dún Laoghaire, Ire.	H6	7
Dunlap, Il., U.S.	C4	90
Dunlap, In., U.S.	A6	91
Dunlap, Ia., U.S.	C2	92
Dunlap, Tn., U.S.	D8	119
Dunleith, De., U.S.	i7	85
Dunloup Creek, stm., W.V., U.S.	n13	125
Dunmore, Pa., U.S.	D10	115
Dunmore, Lake, l., Vt., U.S.	D2	122
Dunn, N.C., U.S.	B4	110
Dunn, co., N.D., U.S.	B3	111
Dunn, co., Wi., U.S.	D2	126
Dunnellon, Fl., U.S.	C4	86
Dunnville, Ont., Can.	E5	73
Dunqulah, Sudan	E12	42
Duns, Scot., U.K.	F10	7
Dunseith, N.D., U.S.	A5	111
Dunsmuir, Ca., U.S.	B2	82
Duntou, China	F8	28
Dunville, Newf., Can.	E5	72
Dunwoody, Ga., U.S.	h8	87
Duomaer, China	E2	26
Du Page, co., Il., U.S.	B5	90
Du Page, stm., Il., U.S.	k8	90
Duplin, co., N.C., U.S.	C5	110
Dupnica, Bul	G7	16
Dupont, Co., U.S.	B6	83
Dupont, Pa., U.S.	n18	115
Dupont City, W.V., U.S.	m12	125
Dupont Manor, De., U.S.	B1	41
Dupont Manor, De., U.S.	D3	85
Duque de Caxias, Braz.	G7	57
Duque de York, Isla, i., Chile	G1	56
Duquesne, Pa., U.S.	F2	115
Du Quoin, Il., U.S.	E4	90
Durand, Il., U.S.	A4	90
Durand, Mi., U.S.	F6	99
Durand, Wi., U.S.	D2	126
Durango, Mex.	E7	62
Durango, Spain	B9	12
Durango, Co., U.S.	D3	83
Durant, Ia., U.S.	C7	92
Durant, Ms., U.S.	B4	101
Durant, Ok., U.S.	D5	113
Durazno, Ur.	C5	56
Durban, S. Afr.	G6	44
Đurđevac, Cro.	C12	14
Düren, Ger.	E6	8
Durg, India	B6	37
Durgāpur, India	I12	38
Durham, Ont., Can.	C4	73
Durham, Eng., U.K.	G11	7
Durham, Ca., U.S.	C3	82
Durham, Ct., U.S.	D5	84
Durham, N.H., U.S.	D5	106
Durham, N.C., U.S.	B4	110
Durham, co., N.C., U.S.	A4	110
Durness, Scot., U.K.	C8	7
Durrell, Newf., Can.	D4	72
Durrës, Alb.	H3	16
Dursunbey, Tur.	J12	16
D'Urville, Tanjung, c., Indon.	F10	32
Duryea, Pa., U.S.	D10	115
Dušanbe, Taj.	J11	22
Dušekan, Russia	E15	24
Dushan, China	B9	34
Dushanbe see Dušanbe, Taj.	J11	22
Duson, La., U.S.	D3	95
Düsseldorf, Ger.	D6	8
Dutchess, co., N.Y., U.S.	D7	109
Dutch Island, i., R.I., U.S.	F4	116
Dutton, Ont., Can.	E3	73
Dutton, Mount, mtn., Ut., U.S.	E3	121
Duval, co., Fl., U.S.	B5	86
Duval, co., Tx., U.S.	F3	120
Duxbury, Ma., U.S.	B6	98
Duyun, China	A9	34
Dwight, Il., U.S.	B5	90
Dwight D. Eisenhower Lock, N.Y., U.S.	f9	109
Dworshak Reservoir, res., Id., U.S.	C3	89
Dyer, In., U.S.	A2	91
Dyer, Tn., U.S.	A3	119
Dyer, co., Tn., U.S.	A2	119
Dyer, Cape, c., N.W. Ter., Can.	C20	66
Dyer Island, i., R.I., U.S.	E5	116
Dyersburg, Tn., U.S.	A2	119
Dyersville, Ia., U.S.	B6	92
Dyess Air Force Base, mil., Tx., U.S.	C3	120
Dysart, Ia., U.S.	B5	92
Džalinda, Russia	G18	24
Džambul, Kaz.	I12	22
Dzaoudzi, May.	D9	44
Džardžan, Russia	D18	24
Dzavchan, stm., Mong.	B5	26
Dzeržinsk, Russia	E26	18
Dzeržinskoje, Kaz.	H10	24
Džezkazgan, Kaz.	H11	22
Dzhambul see Džambul, Kaz.	I12	22
Dzierżoniów (Reichenbach), Pol.	E16	8
Džugdžur, Chrebet, mts., Russia	F21	24

E

Name	Map Ref	Page
Eads, Co., U.S.	C8	83
Eagan, Mn., U.S.	n12	100
Eagar, Az., U.S.	C6	80
Eagle, Co., U.S.	B4	83
Eagle, Id., U.S.	F2	89
Eagle, Ne., U.S.	h12	104
Eagle, Wi., U.S.	F5	126
Eagle, co., Co., U.S.	B4	83
Eagle, stm., Newf., Can.	B2	72
Eagle Creek Reservoir, res., In., U.S.	E5	91
Eagle Grove, Ia., U.S.	B4	92
Eagle Key, i., Fl., U.S.	G6	86
Eagle Lake, Me., U.S.	A4	96
Eagle Lake, Mn., U.S.	F5	100
Eagle Lake, Tx., U.S.	E4	120
Eagle Lake, l., Ca., U.S.	B3	82
Eagle Lake, l., Me., U.S.	A4	96
Eagle Lake, l., Me., U.S.	B3	96
Eagle Lake, l., Ms., U.S.	C3	101
Eagle Lake, l., Wi., U.S.	C4	126
Eagle Mountain, mtn., Mn., U.S.	k9	100
Eagle Mountain Lake, res., Tx., U.S.	m9	120
Eagle Nest Lake, l., N.M., U.S.	A4	108
Eagle Pass, Tx., U.S.	E2	120
Eagle Peak, mtn., Ca., U.S.	B3	82
Eagle Point, Or., U.S.	E4	114
Eagle River, Wi., U.S.	C4	126
Eagletail Mountains, mts., Az., U.S.	D2	80
Eagletail Peak, mtn., Az., U.S.	D2	80
Eagletown, Ok., U.S.	C7	113
Earle, Ar., U.S.	B5	81
Earlham, Ia., U.S.	C3	92
Earlimart, Ca., U.S.	E4	82
Earlington, Ky., U.S.	C2	94
Earlville, Il., U.S.	B5	90
Earlville, Ia., U.S.	B6	92
Early, Ia., U.S.	B2	92
Early, co., Ga., U.S.	E2	87
Earth, Tx., U.S.	B1	120
Easley, S.C., U.S.	B2	117
East, stm., Ct., U.S.	D5	84
East, stm., N.Y., U.S.	k13	109
East, stm., Wi., U.S.	h9	126
East Alton, Il., U.S.	E3	90
East Angus, Que., Can.	D6	74
East Arlington, Vt., U.S.	E2	122
East Aurora, N.Y., U.S.	C2	109
East Bangor, Pa., U.S.	E11	115
East Bank, W.V., U.S.	m13	125
East Barre, Vt., U.S.	C4	122
East Baton Rouge, co., La., U.S.	D4	95
East Bay, b., Fl., U.S.	u16	86
East Bay, b., Tx., U.S.	R15	120
East Beckwith Mountain, mtn., Co., U.S.	C3	83
East Berlin, Ct., U.S.	C5	84
East Berlin, Pa., U.S.	G8	115
East Bernard, Tx., U.S.	E4	120
East Bernstadt, Ky., U.S.	C5	94
East Bethel, Mn., U.S.	E5	100
East Billerica, Ma., U.S.	f11	98
Eastborough, Ks., U.S.	g12	93
Eastbourne, Eng., U.K.	K13	7
East Brady, Pa., U.S.	E2	115
East Branch Clarion River Lake, res., Pa., U.S.	C4	115
East Brewton, Al., U.S.	D2	78
East Bridgewater, Ma., U.S.	B6	98
East Brimfield Lake, res., Ma., U.S.	B3	98
East Brooklyn, Ct., U.S.	B8	84
East Broughton, Que., Can.	C6	74
East Brunswick, N.J., U.S.	C4	107
East Butte, mtn., Mt., U.S.	B5	103
East Cache Creek, stm., Ok., U.S.	C3	113
East Cape, c., Fl., U.S.	G5	86
East Carbon, Ut., U.S.	D5	121
East Carroll, co., La., U.S.	B4	95
East Chicago, In., U.S.	A3	91
East China Sea, Asia	E12	26
East Chop, c., Ma., U.S.	D6	98
East Cleveland, Oh., U.S.	g9	112
East Cote Blanche Bay, b., La., U.S.	E4	95
East Dennis, Ma., U.S.	C7	98
East Derry, N.H., U.S.	E4	106
East Detroit, Mi., U.S.	p16	99
East Douglas, Ma., U.S.	B4	98
East Dubuque, Il., U.S.	A3	90
Eastend, Sask., Can.	H1	75
Easter Island see Pascua, Isla de, i., Chile	H5	2
Eastern Bay, b., Md., U.S.	C5	97
Eastern Channel see Tsushima-kaikyō, strt., Japan	I2	30
Eastern Ghāts, mts., India	F5	37
Eastern Neck Island, i., Md., U.S.	B5	97
Eastern Point, c., Ma., U.S.	f13	98
Easterville, Man., Can.	C2	70
East Falkland, i., Falk. Is.	G5	56
East Falmouth, Ma., U.S.	C6	98
East Feliciana, co., La., U.S.	D4	95
East Flat Rock, N.C., U.S.	f10	110
East Fork, stm., Wy., U.S.	D3	127
East Fork Lake, res., Oh., U.S.	C1	112
East Gaffney, S.C., U.S.	A4	117
East Galesburg, Il., U.S.	C3	90
East Granby, Ct., U.S.	B5	84
East Grand Forks, Mn., U.S.	C2	100
East Grand Rapids, Mi., U.S.	F5	99
East Greenville, Pa., U.S.	F10	115
East Greenwich, R.I., U.S.	D4	116
East Gwillimbury, Ont., Can.	C5	73
East Hampstead, N.H., U.S.	E4	106
East Hampton, Ct., U.S.	C5	84
Easthampton, Ma., U.S.	B2	98
East Hanover, N.J., U.S.	*B4	107
East Hartford, Ct., U.S.	B5	84
East Hartland, Ct., U.S.	B4	84
East Haven, Ct., U.S.	D4	84
East Helena, Mt., U.S.	D5	103
East Jordan, Mi., U.S.	C5	99
Eastlake, Oh., U.S.	A4	112
East Lake Tohopekaliga, l., Fl., U.S.	D5	86
Eastland, Tx., U.S.	C3	120
Eastland, co., Tx., U.S.	C3	120
East Lansing, Mi., U.S.	F6	99
East Las Vegas, Nv., U.S.	G6	105
East Liverpool, Oh., U.S.	B5	112
East London (Oos-Londen), S. Afr.	H5	44
East Longmeadow, Ma., U.S.	B2	98
East Los Angeles, Ca., U.S.	m12	82
East Lyme, Ct., U.S.	D7	84
East Lynn Lake, res., W.V., U.S.	C2	125
Eastmain, stm., Que., Can.	F17	66
Eastmain-Opinaca, Réservoir, res., Que., Can.	h11	74

Name	Map Ref	Page
Eastman, Que., Can.	D5	74
Eastman, Ga., U.S.	D3	87
East Matunuck, R.I., U.S.	F3	116
East Middlebury, Vt., U.S.	D2	122
East Millinocket, Me., U.S.	C4	96
East Moline, Il., U.S.	B3	90
East Montpelier, Vt., U.S.	C4	122
East Naples, Fl., U.S.	F5	86
East Newnan, Ga., U.S.	C2	87
East Nishnabotna, stm., Ia., U.S.	C2	92
East Norriton, Pa., U.S.	o20	115
East Olympia, Wa., U.S.	C3	124
Easton, Md., U.S.	C5	97
Easton, Pa., U.S.	E11	115
Easton Reservoir, res., Ct., U.S.	E2	84
East Orange, N.J., U.S.	B4	107
East Orleans, Ma., U.S.	C8	98
Eastover, S.C., U.S.	D6	117
East Palatka, Fl., U.S.	C5	86
East Palestine, Oh., U.S.	B5	112
East Pass, strt., Fl., U.S.	C2	86
East Pea Ridge, W.V., U.S.	C2	125
East Peoria, Il., U.S.	C4	90
East Pepperell, Ma., U.S.	A4	98
East Petersburg, Pa., U.S.	F9	115
East Pittsburgh, Pa., U.S.	k14	115
Eastpoint, Fl., U.S.	C2	86
East Point, Ga., U.S.	C2	87
East Point, c., P.E.I., Can.	C8	71
East Point, c., Ma., U.S.	B6	98
East Point, c., N.J., U.S.	E2	107
Eastport, Newf., Can.	D5	72
Eastport, Me., U.S.	D6	96
East Prairie, Mo., U.S.	E8	102
East Providence, R.I., U.S.	C4	116
East Pryor Mountain, mtn., Mt., U.S.	E8	103
East Quogue, N.Y., U.S.	n16	109
East Range, mts., Nv., U.S.	C4	105
East Ridge, Tn., U.S.	h11	119
East River, Ct., U.S.	D5	84
East Rochester, N.Y., U.S.	B3	109
East Rockingham, N.C., U.S.	C3	110
East Rutherford, N.J., U.S.	h8	107
East Saint Louis, Il., U.S.	E3	90
East Selkirk, Man., Can.	D3	70
Eastsound, Wa., U.S.	A3	124
East Spencer, N.C., U.S.	B2	110
East Stroudsburg, Pa., U.S.	D11	115
East Tawas, Mi., U.S.	D7	99
East Troy, Wi., U.S.	F5	126
East Vestal, N.Y., U.S.	C4	109
East View, W.V., U.S.	k10	125
East Walker, stm., U.S.	E2	105
East Walpole, Ma., U.S.	h11	98
East Wareham, Ma., U.S.	C6	98
East Washington, Pa., U.S.	F1	115
East Wenatchee, Wa., U.S.	B5	124
East Windsor, N.J., U.S.	C3	107
East York, Ont., Can.	D5	73
Eaton, Co., U.S.	A6	83
Eaton, In., U.S.	D7	91
Eaton, Oh., U.S.	C1	112
Eaton, co., Mi., U.S.	F6	99
Eaton Rapids, Mi., U.S.	F6	99
Eatonton, Ga., U.S.	C3	87
Eatontown, N.J., U.S.	C4	107
Eatonville, Wa., U.S.	C3	124
Eau Claire, Wi., U.S.	D2	126
Eau Claire, co., Wi., U.S.	D2	126
Eau Claire, stm., Wi., U.S.	D2	126
Eau Claire, Lac à l', l., Que., Can.	g11	74
Eauze, Fr.	I7	10
Ebano, Mex.	F10	62
Ebba Ksour, Tun.	N3	14
Ebbw Vale, Wales, U.K.	J9	7
Ebensburg, Pa., U.S.	F4	115
Eberndorf, Aus.	I14	8
Eberswalde, Ger.	C13	8
Ebetsu, Japan	p19	30a
Ebingen, Ger.	G9	8
Ebinur Hu, l., China	B3	26
Eboli, Italy	I10	14
Ebolowa, Cam.	H8	42
Ebro, stm., Spain	E12	12
Ebro, Delta del, Spain	E12	12
Eccles, W.V., U.S.	n13	125
Echo Bay, Nv., U.S.	G7	105
Echo Lake, l., Me., U.S.	D3	96
Echo Lake, l., Vt., U.S.	B5	122
Echols, co., Ga., U.S.	F4	87
Écija, Spain	H6	12
Eckernförde, Ger.	A9	8
Eckhart Mines, Md., U.S.	k13	97
Eckville, Alta., Can.	C3	68
Eclectic, Al., U.S.	C3	78
Eclipse Sound, strt., N.W. Ter., Can.	B17	66
Écommoy, Fr.	E7	10
Econfina, stm., Fl., U.S.	B3	86
Economy, Pa., U.S.	*h13	115
Écorces, Rivière aux, stm., Que., Can.	A6	74
Ecorse, Mi., U.S.	p15	99
Ecru, Ms., U.S.	A4	101
Ector, co., Tx., U.S.	D1	120
Ecuador, ctry., S.A.	D3	54
Ed, Swe.	G8	6
Edcouch, Tx., U.S.	F4	120
Eddy, co., N.M., U.S.	E5	108
Eddy, co., N.D., U.S.	B7	111
Eddystone, Pa., U.S.	p20	115
Eddyville, Ia., U.S.	C5	92
Eddyville, Ky., U.S.	e9	94
Ede, Neth.	C5	8
Edéa, Cam.	H8	42
Eden, Ga., U.S.	D5	87
Eden, Md., U.S.	D6	97
Eden, N.Y., U.S.	C2	109
Eden, N.C., U.S.	A3	110
Eden, Tx., U.S.	D3	120
Edenderry, Ire.	H5	7
Eden Prairie, Mn., U.S.	n12	100
Edenton, N.C., U.S.	A6	110
Eden Valley, Mn., U.S.	E4	100
Edgar, Ne., U.S.	D8	104
Edgar, Wi., U.S.	D4	126
Edgar, co., Il., U.S.	D6	90
Edgard, La., U.S.	D5	95
Edgartown, Ma., U.S.	D6	98
Edgecombe, co., N.C., U.S.	B5	110
Edgecumbe, Cape, c., Ak., U.S.	m21	79
Edgefield, S.C., U.S.	D4	117
Edgefield, co., S.C., U.S.	D4	117
Edgeley, N.D., U.S.	C7	111
Edgemere, Md., U.S.	B5	97
Edgemont, S.D., U.S.	D2	118
Edgemoor, De., U.S.	A3	85
Edgerton, Ks., U.S.	D8	93
Edgerton, Mn., U.S.	G2	100
Edgerton, Oh., U.S.	A1	112
Edgerton, Wi., U.S.	F4	126
Edgerton, Wy., U.S.	C6	127
Edgewater, Al., U.S.	f7	78
Edgewater, Fl., U.S.	D6	86
Edgewater, Md., U.S.	C4	97
Edgewater, N.J., U.S.	h9	107
Edgewater Park, N.J., U.S.	C3	107
Edgewood, In., U.S.	D6	91
Edgewood, Ia., U.S.	B6	92
Edgewood, Ky., U.S.	h13	94
Edgewood, Md., U.S.	B5	97
Edgewood, N.M., U.S.	B3	108
Edgewood, Oh., U.S.	A5	112
Edgewood, Pa., U.S.	k14	115
Edgewood, Wa., U.S.	f11	124
Edgeworth, Pa., U.S.	h13	115
Edina, Mn., U.S.	F5	100
Edina, Mo., U.S.	A5	102
Edinboro, Pa., U.S.	C1	115
Edinburg, Il., U.S.	D4	90
Edinburg, Tx., U.S.	F3	120
Edinburg, Va., U.S.	B4	123
Edinburgh, Scot., U.K.	F9	7
Edinburgh, In., U.S.	F6	91
Edirne, Tur.	G13	4
Edison, Ga., U.S.	E2	87
Edison, N.J., U.S.	B4	107
Edisto, stm., S.C., U.S.	E6	117
Edisto Island, i., S.C., U.S.	F7	117
Edith, Mount, mtn., Mt., U.S.	D5	103
Edjeleh, Alg.	C7	42
Edmond, Ok., U.S.	B4	113
Edmonds, Wa., U.S.	B3	124
Edmondson Heights, Md., U.S.	*g10	97
Edmonson, co., Ky., U.S.	C3	94
Edmonton, Alta., Can.	C4	68
Edmonton, Ky., U.S.	D4	94
Edmore, Mi., U.S.	E5	99
Edmunds, co., S.D., U.S.	B6	118
Edmundston, N.B., Can.	B1	71
Edna, Tx., U.S.	E4	120
Edon, Oh., U.S.	A1	112
Édouard, Lac, l., Que., Can.	B5	74
Edremit, Tur.	J11	16
Edrengijn Nuruu, mts., Mong.	C6	26
Edsbyn, Swe.	F10	6
Edson, Alta., Can.	C2	68
Edson Butte, mtn., Or., U.S.	E2	114
Eduardo Castex, Arg.	D4	56
Edward, Lake, l., Afr.	B5	44
Edwards, Ms., U.S.	C3	101
Edwards, co., Il., U.S.	E5	90
Edwards, co., Ks., U.S.	E4	93
Edwards, co., Tx., U.S.	E2	120
Edwards Air Force Base, mil., Ca., U.S.	E5	82
Edwardsburg, Mi., U.S.	G4	99
Edwards Butte, mtn., Or., U.S.	B3	114
Edwardsville, Il., U.S.	E4	90
Edwardsville, Ks., U.S.	k16	93
Edwardsville, Pa., U.S.	n17	115
Eel, stm., Ca., U.S.	B2	82
Eel, stm., In., U.S.	F3	91
Eel, stm., In., U.S.	C6	91
Effigy Mounds National Monument, Ia., U.S.	A6	92
Effingham, Il., U.S.	D5	90
Effingham, co., Ga., U.S.	D5	87
Effingham, co., Il., U.S.	D5	90
Efland, N.C., U.S.	A3	110
Egan Range, mts., Nv., U.S.	E7	105
Eganville, Ont., Can.	B7	73
Egede og Rothes Fjord, Grnld.	C25	66
Egedesminde, Grnld.	C22	66
Eger, Hung.	H20	8
Egersund, Nor.	G5	6
Eggenfelden, Ger.	G12	8
Egg Harbor City, N.J., U.S.	D3	107
Egg Island Point, c., N.J., U.S.	E2	107
Égletons, Fr.	G9	10
Eglin Air Force Base, mil., Fl., U.S.	u15	86
Egmont, Mount, mtn., N.Z.	C5	52
Egmont Bay, b., P.E.I., Can.	C5	71
Egmont Channel, strt., Fl., U.S.	p10	86
Egmont Key, i., Fl., U.S.	p10	86
Egvekinot, Russia	D29	24
Egypt, ctry., Afr.	C11	42
Egypt, Lake of, res., Il., U.S.	F5	90
Ehingen, Ger.	G9	8
Ehrenberg, Az., U.S.	D1	80
Eibar, Spain	B9	12
Eichstätt, Ger.	G11	8
Eidsvoll, Nor.	F8	6
Eielson Air Force Base, mil., Ak., U.S.	C10	79
Eifel, mts., Ger.	E6	8
Eighty Mile Beach, Austl.	C4	50
Eil, Som.	G4	46
Eilenburg, Ger.	D12	8
Eindhoven, Neth.	D5	8
Einsiedeln, Switz.	E15	10
Eirunepé, Braz.	E5	54
Eisenach, Ger.	E10	8
Eisenberg, Ger.	E11	8
Eisenerz, Aus.	H14	8
Eisenhower, Mount, mtn., N.H., U.S.	B4	106
Eisenhüttenstadt, Ger.	C14	8
Eisenstadt, Aus.	H16	8
Eisleben, Ger.	D11	8
Ejea de los Caballeros, Spain	C10	12
Ekiatapskij Chrebet, mts., Russia	D29	24
Ekimčan, Russia	G20	24
Ekwan, stm., Ont., Can.	F16	66
El Aaiún, W. Sah.	C3	42
Elaine, Ar., U.S.	C5	81
El Asnam, Alg.	A6	42
Elat, Isr.	E4	40
El Avión, Mex.	E6	62
Elâzığ, Tur.	H15	4
Elba, Al., U.S.	D3	78
Elba, Isola d', i., Italy	G5	14
El Banco, Col.	C6	58
El Barco de Valdeorras, Spain	C5	12
Elbasan, Alb.	H4	16
El Baúl, Ven.	C8	58
Elbe (Labe), stm., Eur.	B9	8
Elberfeld, In., U.S.	H3	91
Elbert, co., Co., U.S.	B6	83
Elbert, co., Ga., U.S.	B4	87
Elbert, Mount, mtn., Co., U.S.	B4	83
Elberta, Ga., U.S.	D3	87
Elberton, Ga., U.S.	B4	87
Elbeuf, Fr.	C8	10
Elbląg (Elbing), Pol.	A19	8
El Bonillo, Spain	G9	12
El Bordo, Col.	F4	58
Elbow, stm., Alta., Can.	D3	68
Elbow Lake, Mn., U.S.	E3	100
El'brus, gora (Mount Elbrus), mtn., Russia	I6	22
El Burgo de Osma, Spain	D8	12
Elburn, Il., U.S.	B5	90
Elburz Mountains see Alborz, Reshteh-ye Kūhhā-ye, mts., Iran	J8	22
El Cajon, Ca., U.S.	F5	82
El Callao, Ven.	D12	58
El Campo, Tx., U.S.	E4	120
El Capitan, mtn., Mt., U.S.	D2	103
El Capitan Reservoir, res., Ca., U.S.	o16	82
El Carmen, Arg.	A3	56
El Carmen de Bolívar, Col.	C5	58
El Centro, Ca., U.S.	F6	82
El Cerrito, Col.	F4	58
El Cerrito, Ca., U.S.	h8	82
Elche, Spain	G11	12
Elche de la Sierra, Spain	G9	12
El Cozón, Mex.	B3	62
El Cuervo Butte, mtn., N.M., U.S.	k9	108
Elda, Spain	G11	12
El Desemboque, Mex.	C3	62
El Diviso, Col.	G3	58
El Djouf, des., Afr.	D4	42
Eldon, Ia., U.S.	D5	92
Eldon, Mo., U.S.	C5	102
Eldora, Ia., U.S.	B4	92
Eldorado, Mex.	E6	62
El Dorado, Ar., U.S.	D3	81
Eldorado, Il., U.S.	F5	90
El Dorado, Ks., U.S.	E7	93
Eldorado, Tx., U.S.	D2	120
El Dorado, co., Ca., U.S.	C3	82
Eldorado Peak, mtn., Wa., U.S.	A4	124
Eldorado Springs, Co., U.S.	B5	83
El Dorado Springs, Mo., U.S.	D3	102
Eldoret, Kenya	A7	44
Eldridge, Ia., U.S.	C7	92
Eleanor, W.V., U.S.	C3	125
Electra, Tx., U.S.	C3	120
Electra Lake, res., Co., U.S.	D3	83
Electric Peak, mtn., Co., U.S.	C5	83
Electric Peak, mtn., Mt., U.S.	E6	103
Elektrostal', Russia	F21	18
El Encanto, Col.	H6	58
Elephant Butte Reservoir, res., N.M., U.S.	D2	108
El Estor, Guat.	G3	64
Eleuthera, i., Bah.	B9	64
Eleven Mile Canyon Reservoir, res., Co., U.S.	C5	83
Eleven Point, stm., U.S.	A4	81
Elevsís, Grc.	K7	16
El Fahs, Tun.	M4	14
El Ferrol del Caudillo, Spain	B3	12
El Galpón, Arg.	B4	56
Elgin, Scot., U.K.	D9	7
Elgin, Il., U.S.	A5	90
Elgin, Ia., U.S.	B6	92
Elgin, Mn., U.S.	F6	100
Elgin, Ne., U.S.	C7	104
Elgin, N.D., U.S.	C4	111
Elgin, Ok., U.S.	C3	113
Elgin, Or., U.S.	B9	114
Elgin, S.C., U.S.	B6	117
Elgin, Tx., U.S.	D4	120
El Goléa, Alg.	B6	42
El Golfo de Santa Clara, Mex.	B2	62
Elgon, Mount, mtn., Afr.	A6	44
El Hank, clf, Afr.	D4	42
El Haouaria, Tun.	L6	14
Elida, Oh., U.S.	B1	112
Élisabethville see Lubumbashi, Zaire	D5	44
Elizabeth, Austl.	F7	50
Elizabeth, Co., U.S.	B6	83
Elizabeth, N.J., U.S.	B4	107
Elizabeth, W.V., U.S.	B3	125
Elizabeth, Cape, c., Wa., U.S.	B1	124
Elizabeth City, N.C., U.S.	A6	110
Elizabeth Islands, is., Ma., U.S.	D6	98
Elizabeth Reef, atoll, Austl.	E11	50
Elizabethton, Tn., U.S.	C11	119
Elizabethtown, Ky., U.S.	C4	94
Elizabethtown, N.C., U.S.	C4	110
Elizabethtown, Pa., U.S.	F8	115
Elizabethville, Pa., U.S.	E8	115
El-Jadida, Mor.	B4	42
El Jebel, Co., U.S.	B3	83
Ełk, Pol.	B22	8
Elk, co., Ks., U.S.	E7	93
Elk, co., Pa., U.S.	D4	115
Elk, stm., U.S.	A2	78
Elk, stm., Co., U.S.	A4	83
Elk, stm., Ks., U.S.	E7	93
Elk, stm., W.V., U.S.	C3	125
Elk, stm., Wi., U.S.	C3	126
Elkader, Ia., U.S.	B6	92
El Kairouan, Tun.	N5	14
Elk City, Id., U.S.	D3	89
Elk City, Ok., U.S.	B2	113
Elk City Lake, res., Ks., U.S.	E7	93
Elk Creek, stm., Ok., U.S.	B2	113
Elk Creek, stm., S.D., U.S.	C3	118
El Kef, Tun.	M3	14
Elkford, B.C., Can.	D10	69
Elk Grove, Ca., U.S.	C3	82
Elk Grove Village, Il., U.S.	h9	90
Elkhart, In., U.S.	A6	91
Elkhart, Ks., U.S.	E2	93
Elkhart, Tx., U.S.	D5	120
Elkhart, co., In., U.S.	A6	91
Elkhart, stm., In., U.S.	B6	91
Elkhart Lake, Wi., U.S.	E5	126
Elkhead Mountains, mts., Co., U.S.	A3	83
Elkhorn, Man., Can.	E1	70
Elk Horn, Ia., U.S.	C2	92
Elkhorn, Ne., U.S.	g12	104
Elkhorn, Wi., U.S.	F5	126
Elkhorn, stm., Ne., U.S.	B7	104
Elkhorn City, Ky., U.S.	C7	94
Elkhorn Peaks, mts., Id., U.S.	F7	89
Elkin, N.C., U.S.	A2	110
Elkins, Ar., U.S.	A1	81
Elkins, W.V., U.S.	C5	125
Elkland, Pa., U.S.	C7	115
Elk Mills, Md., U.S.	A6	97
Elk Mound, Wi., U.S.	D2	126
Elk Mountain, Wy., U.S.	E6	127
Elk Mountain, mtn., N.M., U.S.	D1	108
Elk Mountain, mtn., Wy., U.S.	E6	127
Elk Mountains, mts., U.S.	D1	118
Elk Mountains, mts., Co., U.S.	B3	83
Elko, Nv., U.S.	C6	105
Elko, co., Nv., U.S.	B6	105
Elk Peak, mtn., Mt., U.S.	D6	103
Elk Point, Alta., Can.	C5	68
Elk Point, S.D., U.S.	E9	118
Elk Rapids, Mi., U.S.	D5	99
El Krib, Tun.	M4	14
Elkridge, Md., U.S.	B4	97
Elk River, Mn., U.S.	E5	100
Elkton, Ky., U.S.	D2	94
Elkton, Md., U.S.	A6	97
Elkton, Mi., U.S.	E7	99
Elkton, S.D., U.S.	C9	118
Elkton, Va., U.S.	B4	123
Elkview, W.V., U.S.	m13	125
Elkville, Il., U.S.	F4	90
Ellaville, Ga., U.S.	D2	87
Ellen, Mount, mtn., Ut., U.S.	E5	121
Ellendale, De., U.S.	E4	85
Ellendale, N.D., U.S.	C7	111
Ellensburg, Wa., U.S.	C5	124
Ellenton, Fl., U.S.	E4	86
Ellenville, N.Y., U.S.	D6	109
Ellerbe, N.C., U.S.	B3	110
Ellerslie, Md., U.S.	k13	97
Ellesmere Island, i., N.W. Ter., Can.	A21	128
Ellettsville, In., U.S.	F4	91
Ellice Islands see Tuvalu, ctry., Oc.	G24	2
Ellicott City, Md., U.S.	B4	97
Ellijay, Ga., U.S.	B2	87
Ellington, Ct., U.S.	B6	84
Ellington, Mo., U.S.	D7	102
Ellinwood, Ks., U.S.	D5	93
Elliot Lake, Ont., Can.	A2	73
Elliott, Ms., U.S.	B4	101
Elliott, co., Ky., U.S.	B6	94
Elliott Bay, b., Wa., U.S.	e11	124
Elliott Key, i., Fl., U.S.	G6	86
Ellis, Ks., U.S.	D4	93
Ellis, co., Ks., U.S.	D4	93
Ellis, co., Ok., U.S.	A2	113
Ellis, co., Tx., U.S.	C4	120
Ellis, stm., N.H., U.S.	B4	106
Elliston, Va., U.S.	C2	123
Ellisville, Ms., U.S.	D4	101
Ellisville, Mo., U.S.	f12	102
Ellon, Scot., U.K.	D10	7
Elloree, S.C., U.S.	D6	117
Ellport, Pa., U.S.	E1	115
Ellsworth, Ks., U.S.	D5	93
Ellsworth, Me., U.S.	D4	96
Ellsworth, Pa., U.S.	F1	115
Ellsworth, Wi., U.S.	D1	126
Ellsworth, co., Ks., U.S.	D5	93
Ellsworth Air Force Base, mil., S.D., U.S.	C2	118
Ellwangen, Ger.	G10	8
Ellwood City, Pa., U.S.	E1	115
Elm, stm., N.D., U.S.	B8	111
Elma, Ia., U.S.	A5	92
Elma, Wa., U.S.	C2	124
El Mahdia, Tun.	N6	14
El Manteco, Ven.	D11	58
Elm City, N.C., U.S.	B5	110
Elm Creek, Ne., U.S.	D6	104
El Médano, Mex.	E4	62
Elmendorf Air Force Base, mil., Ak., U.S.	C10	79
Elm Grove, Wi., U.S.	m11	126
Elmhurst, Il., U.S.	B6	90
Elmhurst, Pa., U.S.	D10	115
Elmira, N.Y., U.S.	C4	109
El Mirage, Az., U.S.	k8	80
Elmira Heights, N.Y., U.S.	C4	109
El Mokrine, Tun.	N5	14
Elmont, N.Y., U.S.	k13	109
Elmora, Pa., U.S.	E4	115
Elmore, Mn., U.S.	G4	100
Elmore, Oh., U.S.	A2	112
Elmore, co., Al., U.S.	C3	78
Elmore, co., Id., U.S.	F3	89
El Morro National Monument, N.M., U.S.	B1	108
Elmsdale, N.S., Can.	E6	71
Elmshorn, Ger.	B9	8
Elm Springs, Ar., U.S.	A1	81
Elmvale, Ont., Can.	C5	73
Elmwood, Il., U.S.	C3	90
Elmwood, Wi., U.S.	D1	126
Elmwood Park, Il., U.S.	k9	90
Elmwood Park, N.J., U.S.	h8	107
Elmwood Place, Oh., U.S.	o13	112
Elne, Fr.	J9	10
Elnora, In., U.S.	G3	91
Eloise, Fl., U.S.	E5	86
Elon College, N.C., U.S.	A3	110
Elora, Ont., Can.	D4	73
Elorza, Ven.	D8	58
El Oued, Alg.	B7	42
Eloy, Az., U.S.	E4	80
El Palmar, Ven.	D12	58
El Paso, Il., U.S.	C4	90
El Paso, Tx., U.S.	o11	120
El Paso, co., Co., U.S.	C6	83
El Paso, co., Tx., U.S.	o11	120
El Pilar, Ven.	B11	58
El Pital, Cerro, mtn., N.A.	G3	64
El Portal, Fl., U.S.	s13	86
El Prado, N.M., U.S.	A4	108
El Progreso, Hond.	G4	64
El Puente del Arzobispo, Spain	F6	12
El Puerto de Santa María, Spain	I5	12
El Quelite, Mex.	F6	62
El Reno, Ok., U.S.	B4	113
Elrose, Sask., Can.	F1	75
Elroy, Wi., U.S.	E3	126
Elsa, Yukon, Can.	D5	66
Elsa, Tx., U.S.	F3	120
Elsah, Il., U.S.	E3	90
El Salto, Mex.	F7	62
El Salvador, ctry., N.A.	H3	64
El Sauce, Nic.	H4	64
El Sauzal, Mex.	B1	62
Elsberry, Mo., U.S.	B7	102
Elsie, Mi., U.S.	E6	99
Elsinore, Ut., U.S.	E3	121
Elsmere, De., U.S.	B3	85
Elsmere, Ky., U.S.	B5	94
El Socorro, Ven.	C10	58
El Sombrero, Ven.	C9	58
Elspe, Ger.	D8	8
Elsterwerda, Ger.	D13	8
El Tigre, Col.	F8	58
El Tigre, Ven.	C10	58
El Tocuyo, Ven.	C8	58
Elton, La., U.S.	D3	95
El Toro Marine Corps Air Station, mil., Ca., U.S.	n13	82
El Trapiche, Col.	F4	58
El Triunfo, Mex.	F4	62
El Turbio, Arg.	G2	56
Elūru, India	D6	37
El Vado Reservoir, res., N.M., U.S.	A3	108
Elvas, Port.	G4	12
Elverum, Nor.	F8	6
El Vigía, Ven.	C7	58
Elvins, Mo., U.S.	D7	102
Elwell, Lake, res., Mt., U.S.	B5	103
Elwha, stm., Wa., U.S.	A2	124
Elwood, In., U.S.	D6	91
Elwood, Ks., U.S.	C9	93
Elwood, Ne., U.S.	D6	104
Ely, Eng., U.K.	I13	7
Ely, Mn., U.S.	C7	100
Ely, Nv., U.S.	D7	105
Elyria, Oh., U.S.	A3	112
Elysburg, Pa., U.S.	E8	115
Emanuel, co., Ga., U.S.	D4	87
Embarcación, Arg.	A4	56
Embarras, stm., Il., U.S.	E6	90
Embarrass, stm., Wi., U.S.	D5	126
Embro, Ont., Can.	D4	73
Embrun, Fr.	H13	10
Emden, Ger.	B7	8
Emerald, Austl.	D9	50
Emerson, Man., Can.	E3	70
Emerson, Ga., U.S.	B2	87
Emerson, Ne., U.S.	B9	104
Emerson, N.J., U.S.	h8	107
Emery, co., Ut., U.S.	E5	121
Emet, Tur.	J13	16
Emily, Mn., U.S.	D5	100
Emily, Lake, l., Mn., U.S.	E3	100
Eminence, Ky., U.S.	B4	94
Emmaus, Pa., U.S.	E11	115
Emmen, Neth.	C6	8
Emmendingen, Ger.	G7	8
Emmet, co., Ia., U.S.	A3	92
Emmet, co., Mi., U.S.	C6	99
Emmetsburg, Ia., U.S.	A3	92
Emmett, Id., U.S.	F2	89
Emmiganūru, India	E4	37
Emmitsburg, Md., U.S.	A3	97
Emmonak, Ak., U.S.	C7	79
Emmons, co., N.D., U.S.	C5	111
Emory Peak, mtn., Tx., U.S.	E1	120
Empalme, Mex.	D4	62
Empangeni, S. Afr.	G6	44
Empedrado, Arg.	B5	56
Empire, La., U.S.	E6	95
Empire, Nv., U.S.	C2	105
Empoli, Italy	F5	14
Emporia, Ks., U.S.	D7	93
Emporia, Va., U.S.	D5	123
Emporium, Pa., U.S.	D5	115
Empty Quarter see Ar-Rab' al-Khālī, des., Asia	D5	46
Emsdetten, Ger.	C7	8
Emsworth, Pa., U.S.	h13	115
Encampment, Wy., U.S.	E6	127
Encarnación, Para.	B5	56
Encinitas, Ca., U.S.	F5	82
Encontrados, Ven.	C6	58
Ende, Indon.	G7	32
Enderby, B.C., Can.	D8	69
Enderby Land, reg., Ant.	C18	47
Enderlin, N.D., U.S.	C8	111
Enders Reservoir, res., Ne., U.S.	D4	104
Endicott, N.Y., U.S.	C4	109
Endicott Mountains, mts., Ak., U.S.	B9	79
Endless Lake, l., Me., U.S.	C4	96
Endwell, N.Y., U.S.	C4	109
Enfida, Tun.	M5	14
Enfield (Thompsonville), Ct., U.S.	B5	84
Enfield, N.H., U.S.	C2	106
Enfield, N.C., U.S.	A5	110
Engel's, Russia	G7	22
Enggano, Pulau, i., Indon.	G3	32
England, Ar., U.S.	C4	81
England, ter., U.K.	I11	7
England Air Force Base, mil., La., U.S.	C3	95

Name	Map Ref	Page
Englee, Newf., Can.	C3	72
Engleside, Va., U.S.	g12	123
Englewood, Co., U.S.	B6	83
Englewood, Fl., U.S.	F4	86
Englewood, N.J., U.S.	B5	107
Englewood, Oh., U.S.	C1	112
Englewood, Tn., U.S.	D9	119
Englewood Cliffs, N.J., U.S.	h9	107
English, In., U.S.	H5	91
English Bāzār, India	H13	38
English Channel (La Manche), strt., Eur.	B5	10
Enguera, Spain	G11	12
Enid, Ok., U.S.	A4	113
Enid Lake, res., Ms., U.S.	A4	101
Enigma, Ga., U.S.	E3	87
Enka, N.C., U.S.	f10	110
Enkhuizen, Neth.	C5	8
Enköping, Swe.	G11	6
Enmelen, Russia	D30	24
Enna, Italy	L9	14
Ennadai Lake, l., N.W. Ter., Can.	D12	66
Ennedi, plat., Chad	E10	42
Ennis, Ire.	I4	7
Ennis, Mt., U.S.	E5	103
Ennis, Tx., U.S.	C4	120
Enniskillen, N. Ire., U.K.	G5	7
Enoch, Ut., U.S.	F2	121
Enola, Pa., U.S.	F8	115
Enon, Oh., U.S.	*C2	112
Enoree, S.C., U.S.	B4	117
Enoree, stm., S.C., U.S.	B3	117
Enosburg Falls, Vt., U.S.	B3	122
Enriquillo, Dom. Rep.	F12	64
Enschede, Neth.	C6	8
Ensenada, Mex.	B1	62
Enshi, China	E8	26
Enshū-nada, Japan	H10	30
Ensley, Fl., U.S.	u14	86
Entebbe, Ug.	A6	44
Enterprise, Al., U.S.	D4	78
Enterprise, Ks., U.S.	D6	93
Enterprise, Or., U.S.	B9	114
Enterprise, Ut., U.S.	F2	121
Enterprise, W.V., U.S.	B4	125
Entiat, stm., Wa., U.S.	B5	124
Entiat, Lake, l., Wa., U.S.	B5	124
Entiat Mountains, mts., Wa., U.S.	B5	124
Entraygues, Fr.	H9	10
Entre-Rios, Moz.	D7	44
Enugu, Nig.	G7	42
Enumclaw, Wa., U.S.	B4	124
Envigado, Col.	D5	58
Eola Hills, hills, Or., U.S.	h11	114
Épernay, Fr.	C10	10
Ephraim, Ut., U.S.	D4	121
Ephrata, Pa., U.S.	F9	115
Ephrata, Wa., U.S.	B6	124
Épila, Spain	D10	12
Épinal, Fr.	D13	10
Epping, N.H., U.S.	D4	106
Epworth, Ia., U.S.	B7	92
Equatorial Guinea, ctry., Afr.	H7	42
Eraclea, Italy	D7	14
Erath, La., U.S.	E3	95
Erath, co., Tx., U.S.	C3	120
Erdek, Tur.	I11	16
Erdemli, Tur.	A4	40
Erebus, Mount, mtn., Ant.	B29	47
Erechim, Braz.	B6	56
Erfurt, Ger.	E11	8
Erichsen Lake, l., N.W. Ter., Can.	B16	66
Erick, Ok., U.S.	B2	113
Erickson, Man., Can.	D2	70
Erie, Co., U.S.	A5	83
Erie, Il., U.S.	B3	90
Erie, Ks., U.S.	E8	93
Erie, Mi., U.S.	G7	99
Erie, Pa., U.S.	B1	115
Erie, co., N.Y., U.S.	C2	109
Erie, co., Oh., U.S.	A3	112
Erie, co., Pa., U.S.	C1	115
Erie, Lake, l., N.A.	C10	76
Erie Canal, N.Y., U.S.	B5	109
Erimo-misaki, c., Japan	r21	30a
Erin, Ont., Can.	D4	73
Erin, Tn., U.S.	A4	119
Eritrea, ctry., Afr.	E2	46
Erlangen, Ger.	F11	8
Erlanger, Ky., U.S.	A5	94
Erlian, China	C9	26
Erling, Lake, res., Ar., U.S.	D2	81
Ermelo, S. Afr.	G5	44
Ermenak, Tur.	A3	40
Ernākulam, India	H4	37
Erne, Lower Lough, l., N. Ire., U.K.	G5	7
Ernée, Fr.	D6	10
Erode, India	G4	37
Errigal, mtn., Ire.	F4	7
Ertai, China	B5	26
Erwin, N.C., U.S.	B4	110
Erwin, Tn., U.S.	C11	119
Erzgebirge (Krušné hory), mts., Eur.	E12	8
Erzincan, Tur.	H15	4
Erzurum, Tur.	H16	4
Esashi, Japan	A13	30
Esbjerg, Den.	I7	6
Escalante, Ut., U.S.	F4	121
Escalante, stm., Ut., U.S.	F4	121
Escalón, Mex.	D7	62
Escalon, Ca., U.S.	D3	82
Escambia, co., Al., U.S.	D2	78
Escambia, co., Fl., U.S.	u14	86
Escambia, stm., Fl., U.S.	u14	86
Escanaba, Mi., U.S.	C3	99
Escanaba, stm., Mi., U.S.	B3	99
Escarpada Point, c., Phil.	B7	32
Escatawpa, Ms., U.S.	E5	101
Escatawpa, stm., U.S.	D5	101
Esch-sur-Alzette, Lux.	F5	8
Eschwege, Ger.	D10	8
Escondido, Ca., U.S.	F5	82
Escoumins, Rivière des, stm., Que., Can.	A8	74
Escuinapa [de Hidalgo], Mex.	F7	62
Escuintla, Guat.	G2	64
Escuintla, Mex.	J13	62
Escuminac, Point, c., N.B., Can.	B5	71
Eşfahān, Iran	B5	46
Eshkāshem, Afg.	B4	38
Eskilstuna, Swe.	G11	6
Eskimo Lakes, l., N.W. Ter., Can.	C6	66
Eskimo Point, N.W. Ter., Can.	D14	66
Eskişehir, Tur.	H14	4
Eşme, Tur.	K12	16
Esmeralda, co., Nv., U.S.	F4	105
Esmeraldas, Ec.	G3	58
Esmond, R.I., U.S.	B4	116
Espalion, Fr.	H9	10
Espanola, Ont., Can.	A3	73
Espanola, N.M., U.S.	B3	108
Esparto, Ca., U.S.	C2	82
Espelkamp, Ger.	C8	8
Esperance, Austl.	F4	50
Espinal, Col.	E5	58
Espinhaço, Serra do, mts., Braz.	C7	57
Espinho, Port.	D3	12
Espíritu Santo, Bahía del, b., Mex.	H16	62
Espíritu Santo, Isla del, i., Mex.	E4	62
Espoo (Esbo), Fin.	F15	6
Espy, Pa., U.S.	D9	115
Esquel, Arg.	E2	56
Esquimalt, B.C., Can.	E6	69
Esquina, Arg.	B5	56
Essaouira, Mor.	B4	42
Essen, Ger.	D7	8
Essendon, Mount, mtn., Austl.	D4	50
Essequibo, stm., Guy.	E13	58
Es Sers, Tun.	M4	14
Essex, Ont., Can.	E2	73
Essex, Ct., U.S.	D6	84
Essex, Ia., U.S.	D2	92
Essex, Md., U.S.	B5	97
Essex, Ma., U.S.	A6	98
Essex, Vt., U.S.	B2	122
Essex, co., Ma., U.S.	A5	98
Essex, co., N.J., U.S.	B4	107
Essex, co., N.Y., U.S.	B7	109
Essex, co., Vt., U.S.	B5	122
Essex, co., Va., U.S.	C6	123
Essex Junction, Vt., U.S.	C2	122
Essexville, Mi., U.S.	E7	99
Esslingen, Ger.	G9	8
Es Smala es Souassi, Tun.	N5	14
Est, Cap, c., Madag.	E10	44
Est, Pointe de l', c., Que., Can.	G20	66
Estacada, Or., U.S.	B4	114
Estaca de Bares, Punta de la, c., Spain	B4	12
Estacado, Llano, pl., U.S.	C1	120
Estados, Isla de los, i., Arg.	G4	56
Estancia, N.M., U.S.	C3	108
Estcourt, S. Afr.	G5	44
Este, Italy	D6	14
Estelí, Nic.	H4	64
Estella, Spain	C9	12
Estelline, S.D., U.S.	C9	118
Estepona, Spain	I6	12
Esternay, Fr.	D10	10
Estero Bay, b., Ca., U.S.	E3	82
Estero Bay, b., Fl., U.S.	F5	86
Estero Island, i., Fl., U.S.	F5	86
Estes Park, Co., U.S.	A5	83
Estherville, Ia., U.S.	A3	92
Estherwood, La., U.S.	D3	95
Estill, S.C., U.S.	F5	117
Estill, co., Ky., U.S.	C6	94
Estill Springs, Tn., U.S.	B5	119
Estonia, ctry., Eur.	C9	18
Estremoz, Port.	G4	12
Esztergom, Hung.	H18	8
Etah, Grnld.	B20	128
Etah, India	G8	38
Étampes, Fr.	D9	10
Étang-du-Nord, Que., Can.	B8	71
Étaples, Fr.	B8	10
Etāwah, India	G8	38
Ethel, W.V., U.S.	n12	125
Ethiopia, ctry., Afr.	G2	46
Etna, Pa., U.S.	k14	115
Etna, Monte, vol., Italy	L9	14
Etobicoke, Ont., Can.	D5	73
Etolin Island, i., Ak., U.S.	m23	79
Etolin Strait, strt., Ak., U.S.	C6	79
Etoshapan, pl., Nmb.	E3	44
Etowah, Tn., U.S.	D9	119
Etowah, co., Al., U.S.	A3	78
Etowah, stm., Ga., U.S.	B2	87
Ettelbruck, Lux.	F6	8
Ettlingen, Ger.	G8	8
Ettrick, Va., U.S.	C5	123
Eu, Fr.	B8	10
Eucla, Austl.	F5	50
Euclid, Oh., U.S.	A4	112
Eudora, Ar., U.S.	D4	81
Eudora, Ks., U.S.	D8	93
Eufaula, Al., U.S.	D4	78
Eufaula, Ok., U.S.	B6	113
Eufaula Lake, res., Ok., U.S.	B6	113
Eugene, Or., U.S.	C3	114
Eugenia, Punta, c., Mex.	D2	62
Eunice, La., U.S.	D3	95
Eunice, N.M., U.S.	E6	100
Euphrates (Al-Furāt), stm., Asia	A2	46
Eupora, Ms., U.S.	B4	101
Eureka, Ca., U.S.	B1	82
Eureka, Il., U.S.	C4	90
Eureka, Ks., U.S.	E7	93
Eureka, Mo., U.S.	f12	102
Eureka, Mt., U.S.	B1	103
Eureka, Nv., U.S.	D6	105
Eureka, S.C., U.S.	B5	117
Eureka, S.D., U.S.	B6	118
Eureka, co., Nv., U.S.	D5	105
Eureka Springs, Ar., U.S.	A2	81
Europa, Île, i., Reu.	F8	44
Europa Point, c., Gib.	I6	12
Europe	E11	4
Euskirchen, Ger.	E6	8
Eustis, Fl., U.S.	D5	86
Eutaw, Al., U.S.	C2	78
Eutin, Ger.	A10	8
Eutsuk Lake, l., B.C., Can.	C4	69
Evangeline, co., La., U.S.	D3	95
Evans, Co., U.S.	A6	83
Evans, Ga., U.S.	C4	87
Evans, W.V., U.S.	C3	125
Evans, co., Ga., U.S.	D5	87
Evans, Lac, l., Que., Can.	F17	66
Evans, Mount, mtn., Co., U.S.	B5	83
Evansburg, Alta., Can.	C3	68
Evans City, Pa., U.S.	E1	115
Evansdale, Ia., U.S.	B5	92
Evans Strait, strt., N.W. Ter., Can.	D16	66
Evanston, Il., U.S.	A6	90
Evanston, Wy., U.S.	E2	127
Evansville, Il., U.S.	E4	90
Evansville, In., U.S.	I2	91
Evansville, Wi., U.S.	F4	126
Evansville, Wy., U.S.	D6	127
Evart, Mi., U.S.	E5	99
Evarts, Ky., U.S.	D6	94
Eveleth, Mn., U.S.	C6	100
Everard, Lake, l., Austl.	F7	50
Everest, Mount, mtn., Asia	G12	38
Everett, Ma., U.S.	g11	98
Everett, Pa., U.S.	F5	115
Everett, Wa., U.S.	B3	124
Everett Lake, res., N.H., U.S.	D3	106
Everglades National Park, Fl., U.S.	G5	86
Evergreen, Al., U.S.	D3	78
Evergreen, Co., U.S.	B5	83
Evergreen Park, Il., U.S.	k9	90
Everly, Ia., U.S.	A2	92
Everson, Wa., U.S.	A3	124
Evesham, Eng., U.K.	I11	7
Evje, Nor.	G6	6
Évora, Port.	G4	12
Évreux, Fr.	C8	10
Évros (Marica) (Meriç), stm., Eur.	H10	16
E.V. Spence Reservoir, res., Tx., U.S.	D2	120
Évvoia, i., Grc.	K7	16
Ewa, Hi., U.S.	B3	88
Ewa Beach, Hi., U.S.	B3	88
Ewa Beach, Hi., U.S.	g9	88
Ewing Township, N.J., U.S.	C3	107
Ewo, Congo	B2	44
Excelsior Mountain, mtn., Ca., U.S.	C4	82
Excelsior Mountains, mts., Nv., U.S.	E3	105
Excelsior Springs, Mo., U.S.	B3	102
Executive Committee Range, mts., Ant.	B36	47
Exeter, Ont., Can.	D3	73
Exeter, Eng., U.K.	K9	7
Exeter, Ca., U.S.	D4	82
Exeter, Ne., U.S.	D8	104
Exeter, N.H., U.S.	E5	106
Exeter, Pa., U.S.	D10	115
Exeter, stm., N.H., U.S.	E5	106
Exeter Sound, strt., N.W. Ter., Can.	C20	66
Exira, Ia., U.S.	C3	92
Exmore, Va., U.S.	C7	123
Exmouth, Eng., U.K.	K9	7
Exmouth Gulf, b., Austl.	D2	50
Experiment, Ga., U.S.	C2	87
Exploits, stm., Newf., Can.	D3	72
Exploits, Bay of, b., Newf., Can.	D4	72
Export, Pa., U.S.	F2	115
Exuma Sound, strt., Bah.	B9	64
Eyasi, Lake, l., Tan.	B6	44
Eylar Mountain, mtn., Ca., U.S.	D3	82
Eymoutiers, Fr.	G8	10
Eyota, Mn., U.S.	G6	100
Eyre (North), Lake, l., Austl.	E7	50
Eyre (South), Lake, l., Austl.	E7	50
Eyre Peninsula, pen., Austl.	F7	50

F

Name	Map Ref	Page
Fabens, Tx., U.S.	o11	120
Fabius, stm., Mo., U.S.	A6	102
Fabriano, Italy	F7	14
Facatativá, Col.	E5	58
Factoryville, Pa., U.S.	C10	115
Fada, Chad	E10	42
Fada Ngourma, Burkina	F6	42
Faddejevskij, Ostrov, i., Russia	B22	24
Faenza, Italy	E6	14
Faeroe Islands, dep., Eur.	C6	4
Fagernes, Nor.	F7	6
Fagersta, Swe.	F10	6
Fairacres, N.M., U.S.	E3	108
Fairbank, Ia., U.S.	B5	92
Fairbanks, Ak., U.S.	C10	79
Fair Bluff, N.C., U.S.	C3	110
Fairborn, Oh., U.S.	C1	112
Fairburn, Ga., U.S.	C2	87
Fairbury, Il., U.S.	C5	90
Fairbury, Ne., U.S.	D8	104
Fairchance, Pa., U.S.	G2	115
Fairchild Air Force Base, mil., Wa., U.S.	g13	124
Fairdale, Ky., U.S.	B4	94
Fairfax, Ca., U.S.	C2	82
Fairfax, De., U.S.	A3	85
Fairfax, Ia., U.S.	C6	92
Fairfax, Mn., U.S.	F4	100
Fairfax, Mo., U.S.	A2	102
Fairfax, Ok., U.S.	A5	113
Fairfax, S.C., U.S.	F5	117
Fairfax, Va., U.S.	B5	123
Fairfax, co., Va., U.S.	B5	123
Fairfield, Al., U.S.	B3	78
Fairfield, Ca., U.S.	C2	82
Fairfield, Ct., U.S.	E2	84
Fairfield, Il., U.S.	E5	90
Fairfield, Ia., U.S.	C6	92
Fairfield, Me., U.S.	D3	96
Fairfield, Mt., U.S.	C5	103
Fairfield, Oh., U.S.	n12	112
Fairfield, Tx., U.S.	D4	120
Fairfield, co., Ct., U.S.	D2	84
Fairfield, co., Oh., U.S.	C3	112
Fairfield, co., S.C., U.S.	C5	117
Fairfield Bay, Ar., U.S.	B3	81
Fairfield Pond, l., Vt., U.S.	B3	122
Fair Grove, Mo., U.S.	D4	102
Fair Grove, N.C., U.S.	B2	110
Fairhaven, Ma., U.S.	C6	98
Fair Haven, Mi., U.S.	F8	99
Fair Haven, N.J., U.S.	C4	107
Fair Haven, Vt., U.S.	D2	122
Fairhope, Al., U.S.	E2	78
Fair Isle, i., Scot., U.K.	B11	7
Fairland, In., U.S.	E6	91
Fairland, Ok., U.S.	A7	113
Fair Lawn, N.J., U.S.	h8	107
Fairlawn, Va., U.S.	C2	123
Fairlea, W.V., U.S.	D4	125
Fairmont, Il., U.S.	C6	90
Fairmont, Mn., U.S.	G4	100
Fairmont, Ne., U.S.	D8	104
Fairmont, N.C., U.S.	C3	110
Fairmont, W.V., U.S.	B4	125
Fairmount, Ga., U.S.	B2	87
Fairmount, In., U.S.	D6	91
Fairmount Heights, Md., U.S.	f9	97
Fair Oaks, Ga., U.S.	h7	87
Fairoaks, Pa., U.S.	h13	115
Fair Plain, Mi., U.S.	F4	99
Fairport, N.Y., U.S.	B3	109
Fairport Harbor, Oh., U.S.	A4	112
Fairvale, N.B., Can.	D4	71
Fairview, Alta., Can.	A1	68
Fairview, Mt., U.S.	C12	103
Fairview, N.J., U.S.	h8	107
Fairview, Ok., U.S.	A3	113
Fairview, Pa., U.S.	B1	115
Fairview, Tn., U.S.	B4	119
Fairview, Ut., U.S.	D4	121
Fairview Heights, Il., U.S.	E3	90
Fairview Park, In., U.S.	E3	91
Fairview Park, Oh., U.S.	g9	112
Fairview Peak, mtn., Nv., U.S.	D3	105
Fairview Peak, mtn., Or., U.S.	D4	114
Fairway, Ks., U.S.	k16	93
Fairweather, Mount, mtn., N.A.	E5	66
Faisalabad, Pak.	E5	38
Faison, N.C., U.S.	B4	110
Faizābād, India	G10	38
Fakenham, Eng., U.K.	I13	7
Fakfak, Indon.	F9	32
Falaise, Fr.	D6	10
Falam, Mya.	C2	34
Falconer, N.Y., U.S.	C1	109
Falcon Heights, Mn., U.S.	n12	100
Falcon Heights, Or., U.S.	E5	114
Falcon Reservoir, res., N.A.	D10	62
Falfurrias, Tx., U.S.	F3	120
Falher, Alta., Can.	B2	68
Falkenberg, Swe.	H9	6
Falkensee, Ger.	C13	8
Falkenstein, Ger.	E12	8
Falkland Islands (Islas Malvinas), dep., S.A.	G5	56
Falköping, Swe.	G9	6
Falkville, Al., U.S.	A3	78
Fall, stm., Ks., U.S.	E7	93
Fall Branch, Tn., U.S.	C11	119
Fallbrook, Ca., U.S.	F5	82
Fall City, Wa., U.S.	B4	124
Fall Creek, Wi., U.S.	D2	126
Falling Creek, stm., Va., U.S.	n17	123
Falling Rock Creek, stm., W.V., U.S.	m13	125
Fall Mountain Lake, Ct., U.S.	C4	84
Fallon, Nv., U.S.	D3	105
Fallon, co., Mt., U.S.	D12	103
Fallon Indian Reservation, Nv., U.S.	D3	105
Fallon Naval Air Station, mil., Nv., U.S.	D3	105
Fall River, Ma., U.S.	C5	98
Fall River, Wi., U.S.	E4	126
Fall River, co., S.D., U.S.	D2	118
Fall River Lake, res., Ks., U.S.	E7	93
Falls, co., Tx., U.S.	D4	120
Falls Church, Va., U.S.	g12	123
Falls City, Ne., U.S.	D10	104
Falls City, Or., U.S.	C3	114
Falls Creek, Pa., U.S.	D4	115
Fallston, Md., U.S.	A5	97
Falmouth, N.S., Can.	E5	71
Falmouth, Eng., U.K.	K7	7
Falmouth, Ky., U.S.	B5	94
Falmouth, Me., U.S.	E2	96
Falmouth, Ma., U.S.	C6	98
Falmouth, Va., U.S.	B5	123
False Cape, c., Fl., U.S.	D6	86
False Cape, c., Va., U.S.	D7	123
False Divi Point, c., India	E6	37
Falset, Spain	D12	12
Falun, Swe.	F10	6
Famagusta see Gazimağusa, N. Cyp.	B3	40
Famatina, Nevado de, mts., Arg.	B3	56
Fancy Farm, Ky., U.S.	f9	94
Fangcheng, China	B1	[illegible]
Fannin, co., Ga., U.S.	B2	87
Fannin, co., Tx., U.S.	C4	120
Fanny, Mount, mtn., Or., U.S.	B9	114
Fano, Italy	F8	14
Faradje, Zaire	H11	42
Faradofay, Madag.	G9	44
Farafangana, Madag.	F9	44
Farāh, Afg.	C1	36
Faranah, Gui.	F3	42
Farasān, Jazā'ir, is., Sau. Ar.	E3	46
Farewell, Cape, c., N.Z.	D4	52
Fargo, Ga., U.S.	F4	87
Fargo, N.D., U.S.	C9	111
Faribault, Mn., U.S.	F5	100
Faribault, co., Mn., U.S.	G4	100
Farīdpur, Bngl.	I13	38
Färjestaden, Swe.	H11	6
Farley, Ia., U.S.	B6	92
Farmer City, Il., U.S.	C5	90
Farmers Branch, Tx., U.S.	n10	120
Farmersburg, In., U.S.	F3	91
Farmerville, La., U.S.	B3	95
Farmingdale, Me., U.S.	D3	96
Farmington, Ar., U.S.	A1	81
Farmington, Ct., U.S.	C4	84
Farmington, Il., U.S.	C3	90
Farmington, Ia., U.S.	D6	92
Farmington, Me., U.S.	D2	96
Farmington, Mi., U.S.	p15	99
Farmington, Mn., U.S.	F5	100
Farmington, Mo., U.S.	D7	102
Farmington, N.H., U.S.	D4	106
Farmington, N.M., U.S.	A1	108
Farmington, Ut., U.S.	C4	121
Farmington, stm., Ct., U.S.	B4	84
Farmington Hills, Mi., U.S.	o15	99
Farmland, In., U.S.	D7	91
Farmville, N.C., U.S.	B5	110
Farmville, Va., U.S.	C4	123
Farnham, Que., Can.	D5	74
Faro, Braz.	D7	54
Faro, Port.	H4	12
Faro, Punta del, c., Italy	K10	14
Fårösund, Swe.	H12	6
Farquhar Group, is., Sey.	D10	44
Farrell, Pa., U.S.	D1	115
Farrukhābād, India	G8	38
Fartak, Ra's, c., Yemen	E5	46
Farvel, Kap, c., Grnld.	E24	66
Farwell, Mi., U.S.	E6	99
Farwell, Tx., U.S.	B1	120
Fasano, Italy	I12	14
Fatehpur, India	H9	38
Fatehpur, India	G6	38
Faulk, co., S.D., U.S.	B6	118
Faulkland Heights, De., U.S.	i7	85
Faulkner, co., Ar., U.S.	B3	81
Faulkton, S.D., U.S.	B6	118
Fauquier, co., Va., U.S.	B5	123
Fauske, Nor.	C10	6
Favara, Italy	L8	14
Faverges, Fr.	G13	10
Fawnie Nose, mtn., B.C., Can.	C5	69
Fayette, Al., U.S.	B2	78
Fayette, Ia., U.S.	B6	92
Fayette, Ms., U.S.	D2	101
Fayette, Mo., U.S.	B5	102
Fayette, Oh., U.S.	A1	112
Fayette, co., Al., U.S.	B3	78
Fayette, co., Ga., U.S.	C2	87
Fayette, co., Il., U.S.	D5	90
Fayette, co., In., U.S.	E7	91
Fayette, co., Ia., U.S.	B6	92
Fayette, co., Ky., U.S.	B5	94
Fayette, co., Oh., U.S.	C2	112
Fayette, co., Pa., U.S.	G2	115
Fayette, co., Tn., U.S.	B2	119
Fayette, co., Tx., U.S.	E4	120
Fayette, co., W.V., U.S.	C3	125
Fayetteville, Ar., U.S.	A1	81
Fayetteville, Ga., U.S.	C2	87
Fayetteville, N.C., U.S.	B4	110
Fayetteville, Pa., U.S.	G6	115
Fayetteville, Tn., U.S.	B5	119
Fayetteville, W.V., U.S.	C3	125
Fāzilka, India	E6	38
Fazzān (Fezzan), reg., Libya	C8	42
Fdérik, Maur.	D3	42
Fear, Cape, c., N.C., U.S.	D5	110
Feather, stm., Ca., U.S.	C3	82
Fécamp, Fr.	C7	10
Federalsburg, Md., U.S.	C6	97
Feeding Hills, Ma., U.S.	B2	98
Fehmarn Belt, strt., Eur.	A11	8
Feijó, Braz.	E4	54
Feira de Santana, Braz.	B9	57
Felanitx, Spain	F15	12
Feldbach, Aus.	I15	8
Feldkirch, Aus.	H9	8
Feldkirchen in Kärnten, Aus.	I14	8
Félix Gómez, Mex.	C4	62
Felletin, Fr.	G9	10
Fellsmere, Fl., U.S.	E6	86
Felton, Ca., U.S.	D2	82
Felton, De., U.S.	D3	85
Feltre, Italy	C6	14
Femundsenden, Nor.	F8	6
Fence, stm., Mi., U.S.	B2	99
Fence Lake, l., Wi., U.S.	C4	126
Fenelon Falls, Ont., Can.	C6	73
Fengcheng, China	G4	28
Fengzhen, China	C9	26
Fenimore Pass, strt., Ak., U.S.	E4	79
Fennimore, Wi., U.S.	F3	126
Fennville, Mi., U.S.	F4	99
Fenton, Mi., U.S.	F7	99
Fentress, co., Tn., U.S.	C9	119
Fenwick Island, i., S.C., U.S.	k11	117
Fenyang, China	D9	26
Feodosiya, Ukr.	H5	22
Fer, Point au, c., La., U.S.	E4	95
Ferdinand, In., U.S.	H4	91
Fergana, Uzb.	I12	22
Fergus, Ont., Can.	D4	73
Fergus, co., Mt., U.S.	C7	103
Fergus Falls, Mn., U.S.	D2	100
Ferguson, Ky., U.S.	C5	94
Ferguson, Mo., U.S.	C7	102
Ferme-Neuve, Que., Can.	C2	74
Fermo, Italy	F8	14
Fermont, Que., Can.	h13	74
Fermoy, Ire.	I4	7
Fernandina Beach, Fl., U.S.	B5	86
Fernando de Noronha, Ilha, i., Braz.	D12	54
Fernandópolis, Braz.	F3	57
Fernando Póo see Bioko, i., Eq. Gui.	H7	42
Fernán-Núñez, Spain	H7	12
Fern Creek, Ky., U.S.	g11	94
Ferndale, Ca., U.S.	B1	82
Ferndale, Md., U.S.	B4	97
Ferndale, Mi., U.S.	P15	99
Ferndale, Pa., U.S.	F4	115
Ferndale, Wa., U.S.	A3	124
Fernie, B.C., Can.	E10	69
Fernley, Nv., U.S.	D2	105
Fern Ridge Lake, res., Or., U.S.	C3	114
Fernwood, Id., U.S.	B2	89
Fernwood, Ms., U.S.	D3	101
Ferrara, Italy	E6	14
Ferreira do Alentejo, Port.	G3	12
Ferrelo, Cape, c., Or., U.S.	E2	114
Ferriday, La., U.S.	C4	95
Ferris, Tx., U.S.	C4	120

Name	Map Ref	Page
Ferris Mountains, mts., Wy., U.S.	D5	127
Ferron, Ut., U.S.	D4	121
Ferrum, Va., U.S.	D2	123
Ferry, co., Wa., U.S.	A7	124
Ferry Farms, Va., U.S.	B5	123
Ferryland, Newf., Can.	E5	72
Ferry Point, c., N.J., U.S.	k7	107
Fertile, Mn., U.S.	C2	100
Fès, Mor.	B5	42
Feshi, Zaire	C3	44
Fessenden, N.D., U.S.	B6	111
Festus, Mo., U.S.	C7	102
Fethiye, Tur.	M13	16
Feuilles, Rivière aux, stm., Que., Can.	g12	74
Feurs, Fr.	G11	10
Feyzābād, Afg.	B4	38
Fez see Fès, Mor.	B5	42
Fianarantsoa, Madag.	F9	44
Ficksburg, S. Afr.	G5	44
Fidalgo Island, i., Wa., U.S.	A3	124
Fidenza, Italy	E5	14
Fieldale, Va., U.S.	D3	123
Fields, Lake, l., Fl., U.S.	B3	86
Fields, Lake, l., La., U.S.	k10	95
Fier, Alb.	I3	16
Fifteenmile Creek, stm., Wy., U.S.	B4	127
Fifteen Mile Falls Reservoir, res., U.S.	C5	122
Figeac, Fr.	H9	10
Figueira da Foz, Port.	E3	12
Figueras, Spain	C14	12
Figuig, Mor.	B5	42
Fiji, ctry., Oc.	H1	2
Filchner Ice Shelf, Ant.	B9	47
Filer, Id., U.S.	G4	89
Fillmore, Ca., U.S.	E4	82
Fillmore, Ut., U.S.	E3	121
Fillmore, co., Mn., U.S.	G6	100
Fillmore, co., Ne., U.S.	D8	104
Finale Ligure, Italy	E3	14
Findlay, Il., U.S.	D5	90
Findlay, Oh., U.S.	A2	112
Finisterre, Cabo de, c., Spain	C2	12
Finland, ctry., Eur.	C13	4
Finland, Gulf of, b., Eur.	G16	6
Finlay, stm., B.C., Can.	E7	66
Finley, Tn., U.S.	A2	119
Finney, co., Ks., U.S.	D3	93
Finn Mountain, mtn., Ak., U.S.	C8	79
Finse, Nor.	F6	6
Finspång, Swe.	G10	6
Finsterwalde, Ger.	D13	8
Fiorenzuola d'Arda, Italy	E4	14
Fircrest, Wa., U.S.	f10	124
Firebaugh, Ca., U.S.	D3	82
Firenze (Florence), Italy	F6	14
Firenzuola, Italy	E6	14
Firestone, Co., U.S.	A6	83
Firminy, Fr.	G11	10
Fīrozābād, India	G8	38
Fīrozpur, India	E6	38
First Connecticut Lake, l., N.H., U.S.	f7	106
Fish, stm., Al., U.S.	E2	78
Fish, stm., Me., U.S.	A4	96
Fish Creek, stm., W.V., U.S.	g8	125
Fisher, Il., U.S.	C5	90
Fisher, co., Tx., U.S.	C2	120
Fisher Bay, b., Man., Can.	D3	70
Fishermans Island, i., Va., U.S.	h15	123
Fishers, In., U.S.	E5	91
Fishers Island, i., N.Y., U.S.	m16	109
Fishers Peak, mtn., Co., U.S.	D6	83
Fisher Strait, strt., N.W. Ter., Can.	D16	66
Fishersville, Va., U.S.	B4	123
Fishing Bay, b., Md., U.S.	D5	97
Fishing Creek, Md., U.S.	D5	97
Fishing Creek, stm., N.C., U.S.	A5	110
Fishing Creek, stm., S.C., U.S.	B5	117
Fishing Creek, stm., W.V., U.S.	B4	125
Fishing Creek Reservoir, res., S.C., U.S.	B6	117
Fishkill, N.Y., U.S.	D7	109
Fish Lake, l., Ut., U.S.	E4	121
Fish River Lake, l., Me., U.S.	B4	96
Fishtrap Lake, res., Ky., U.S.	C7	94
Fiskdale, Ma., U.S.	B3	98
Fitchburg, Ma., U.S.	A4	98
Fitzgerald, Ga., U.S.	E3	87
Fitz Roy, Arg.	F3	56
Fitzroy, stm., Austl.	C4	50
Fitzroy, Monte (Cerro Chaltel), mtn., S.A.	F2	56
Fitzroy Crossing, Austl.	C5	50
Fitzwilliam, N.H., U.S.	E2	106
Fitzwilliam Island, i., Ont., Can.	B3	73
Five Island Lake, l., Ia., U.S.	A3	92
Fivemile Creek, stm., Wy., U.S.	C4	127
Five Points, N.M., U.S.	B3	108
Flagler, co., Fl., U.S.	C5	86
Flagler Beach, Fl., U.S.	C5	86
Flagstaff, Az., U.S.	B4	80
Flagstaff Lake, l., Or., U.S.	E7	114
Flambeau, stm., Wi., U.S.	C3	126
Flamborough Head, c., Eng., U.K.	G12	7
Flaming Gorge Dam, Ut., U.S.	C6	121
Flaming Gorge National Recreation Area, U.S.	E3	127
Flaming Gorge Reservoir, res., U.S.	E3	127
Flanagan, Il., U.S.	C5	90
Flandreau, S.D., U.S.	C9	118
Flandreau Indian Reservation, S.D., U.S.	C9	118
Flat, stm., Mi., U.S.	E5	99
Flat, stm., N.C., U.S.	A4	110
Flat, stm., R.I., U.S.	E2	116
Flat Brook, stm., N.J., U.S.	A3	107
Flathead, co., Mt., U.S.	B2	103
Flathead, South Fork, stm., Mt., U.S.	C3	103
Flathead Indian Reservation, Mt., U.S.	C2	103
Flathead Lake, l., Mt., U.S.	C2	103
Flathead Valley, val., Mt., U.S.	C2	103
Flat Lake, l., La., U.S.	k9	95
Flat Lick, Ky., U.S.	D6	94
Flatonia, Tx., U.S.	E4	120
Flat River, Mo., U.S.	D7	102
Flat River Reservoir, res., R.I., U.S.	D3	116
Flat Rock, Mi., U.S.	F7	99
Flat Rock, N.C., U.S.	f10	110
Flatrock, stm., In., U.S.	F6	91
Flattery, Cape, c., Wa., U.S.	A1	124
Flatwoods, Ky., U.S.	B7	94
Fleetwood, Eng., U.K.	H9	7
Fleetwood, Pa., U.S.	F10	115
Flekkefjord, Nor.	G6	6
Fleming, co., Ky., U.S.	B6	94
Fleming-Neon, Ky., U.S.	C7	94
Flemingsburg, Ky., U.S.	B6	94
Flemington, N.J., U.S.	B3	107
Flemington, Pa., U.S.	D7	115
Flensburg, Ger.	A9	8
Flers, Fr.	D6	10
Fletcher, N.C., U.S.	f10	110
Fletcher, Ok., U.S.	C3	113
Fleurance, Fr.	I7	10
Flinders, stm., Austl.	C8	50
Flinders Island, i., Austl.	G9	50
Flin Flon, Man., Can.	B1	70
Flint, Wales, U.K.	H9	7
Flint, Mi., U.S.	E7	99
Flint, stm., Ga., U.S.	E2	87
Flint City, Al., U.S.	A3	78
Flint Creek Range, mts., Mt., U.S.	D3	103
Flint Run, stm., W.V., U.S.	k9	125
Flippin, Ar., U.S.	A3	81
Flomaton, Al., U.S.	D2	78
Flora, Il., U.S.	E5	90
Flora, In., U.S.	C4	91
Flora, Ms., U.S.	C3	101
Florac, Fr.	H10	10
Florala, Al., U.S.	D3	78
Floral City, Fl., U.S.	D4	86
Florence, Al., U.S.	A2	78
Florence, Az., U.S.	D4	80
Florence, Co., U.S.	C5	83
Florence, Ks., U.S.	D7	93
Florence, Ky., U.S.	A5	94
Florence, Ms., U.S.	C3	101
Florence, N.J., U.S.	C3	107
Florence, Or., U.S.	D2	114
Florence, S.C., U.S.	C8	117
Florence, co., S.C., U.S.	C8	117
Florence, co., Wi., U.S.	C5	126
Florence see Firenze, Italy	F6	14
Florenceville, N.B., Can.	C2	71
Florencia, Col.	G5	58
Flores, i., Indon.	G7	32
Flores, Laut (Flores Sea), Indon.	G6	32
Floresville, Tx., U.S.	E3	120
Florham Park, N.J., U.S.	B4	107
Floriano, Braz.	E10	54
Florianópolis, Braz.	B7	56
Florida, Col.	F4	58
Florida, Cuba	D8	64
Florida, N.Y., U.S.	D6	109
Florida, state, U.S.	E5	86
Florida, Cape, c., Fl., U.S.	G6	86
Florida, Straits of, strt., N.A.	B7	64
Florida Bay, b., Fl., U.S.	H6	86
Floridablanca, Col.	D6	58
Florida City, Fl., U.S.	G6	86
Florida Keys, is., Fl., U.S.	H6	86
Florida Mountains, mts., N.M., U.S.	E2	108
Florida State Indian Reservation, Fl., U.S.	F5	86
Florien, La., U.S.	C2	95
Florissant, Mo., U.S.	f13	102
Florissant Fossil Beds National Monument, Co., U.S.	C5	83
Florø, Nor.	F5	6
Flossmoor, Il., U.S.	k9	90
Flovilla, Ga., U.S.	C3	87
Flower Brook, stm., Vt., U.S.	E2	122
Flowery Branch, Ga., U.S.	B3	87
Flowood, Ms., U.S.	C3	101
Floyd, co., Ga., U.S.	B1	87
Floyd, co., In., U.S.	H6	91
Floyd, co., Ia., U.S.	A5	92
Floyd, co., Ky., U.S.	C7	94
Floyd, co., Tx., U.S.	B2	120
Floyd, co., Va., U.S.	D2	123
Floyd, stm., Ia., U.S.	B1	92
Floydada, Tx., U.S.	C2	120
Floyds Fork, stm., Ky., U.S.	B4	94
Floyds Knobs, In., U.S.	H6	91
Flushing, Mi., U.S.	E7	99
Flushing, Oh., U.S.	B4	112
Flushing see Vlissingen, Neth.	D3	8
Fluvanna, co., Va., U.S.	C4	123
Fly, stm.	m15	50a
Foard, co., Tx., U.S.	B3	120
Foça, Tur.	K10	16
Focșani, Rom.	D11	16
Fogang (Shijiao), China	L2	28
Foggia, Italy	H10	14
Fogland Point, c., R.I., U.S.	E6	116
Fogo, Newf., Can.	D4	72
Fogo, Cape, c., Newf., Can.	D5	72
Fogo Island, i., Newf., Can.	D4	72
Fohnsdorf, Aus.	H14	8
Foix, Fr.	J8	10
Foley, Al., U.S.	E2	78
Foley, Mn., U.S.	E5	100
Foley Island, i., N.W. Ter., Can.	C17	66
Foligno, Italy	G7	14
Folkestone, Eng., U.K.	J14	7
Folkston, Ga., U.S.	F4	87
Follansbee, W.V., U.S.	A4	125
Follonica, Italy	G5	14
Folly Beach, S.C., U.S.	F8	117
Folly Island, i., S.C., U.S.	F8	117
Folsom, Ca., U.S.	C3	82
Fonda, Ia., U.S.	B3	92
Fond du Lac, Wi., U.S.	E5	126
Fond du Lac, co., Wi., U.S.	E5	126
Fond du Lac Indian Reservation, Mn., U.S.	D6	100
Fondi, Italy	H8	14
Fondouk el Aouareb, Tun.	N4	14
Fonni, Italy	I4	14
Fonseca, Col.	B6	58
Fonseca, Golfo de, b., N.A.	H4	64
Fontainebleau, Fr.	D9	10
Fontana, Ca., U.S.	m14	82
Fontana, Wi., U.S.	F5	126
Fontana Lake, res., N.C., U.S.	f9	110
Fontanelle, Ia., U.S.	C3	92
Fonte Boa, Braz.	D5	54
Fontenay-le-Comte, Fr.	F6	10
Fontenelle Reservoir, res., Wy., U.S.	D2	127
Fontur, c., Ice.	B5	4
Foochow see Fuzhou, China	I8	28
Footville, Wi., U.S.	F4	126
Foraker, Mount, mtn., Ak., U.S.	f16	79
Forbach, Fr.	C13	10
Forbach, Ger.	G8	8
Forbes, Mount, mtn., Alta., Can.	D2	68
Forcalquier, Fr.	I12	10
Forchheim, Ger.	F11	8
Ford, co., Il., U.S.	C5	90
Ford, co., Ks., U.S.	E4	93
Ford, stm., Mi., U.S.	C3	99
Ford City, Ca., U.S.	E4	82
Ford City, Pa., U.S.	E2	115
Førde, Nor.	F5	6
Fordoche, La., U.S.	D4	95
Fords Prairie, Wa., U.S.	C2	124
Fordyce, Ar., U.S.	D3	81
Forel, Mont, mtn., Grnld.	C25	66
Foreman, Ar., U.S.	D1	81
Forest, Ont., Can.	D2	73
Forest, Ms., U.S.	C4	101
Forest, Oh., U.S.	B2	112
Forest, co., Pa., U.S.	C3	115
Forest, co., Wi., U.S.	C5	126
Forest, stm., N.D., U.S.	A8	111
Forest Acres, S.C., U.S.	C6	117
Forestburg, Alta., Can.	C4	68
Forest City, Ia., U.S.	A4	92
Forest City, N.C., U.S.	B1	110
Forest City, Pa., U.S.	C11	115
Forestdale, R.I., U.S.	B3	116
Forest Dale, Vt., U.S.	D2	122
Forest Glen, La., U.S.	h12	95
Forest Grove, Or., U.S.	B3	114
Forest Hill, Md., U.S.	A5	97
Forest Hills, Pa., U.S.	k14	115
Forest Knolls, Ca., U.S.	g7	82
Forest Lake, Mn., U.S.	E6	100
Forest Park, Ga., U.S.	h8	87
Forest Park, Il., U.S.	k9	90
Forest Park, La., U.S.	*B3	95
Forest Park, Oh., U.S.	*n12	112
Forfar, Scot., U.K.	E10	7
Forillon, Parc National de, Que., Can.	k14	74
Fork Creek, stm., W.V., U.S.	m12	125
Forked Deer, stm., Tn., U.S.	B2	119
Forkland, Al., U.S.	C2	78
Forks, Wa., U.S.	B1	124
Forlì, Italy	E7	14
Formia, Italy	H8	14
Formiga, Braz.	F6	57
Formosa, Arg.	B5	56
Formosa, Braz.	C5	57
Formosa, Serra, plat., Braz.	F8	54
Formosa see Taiwan, i., Asia	L9	28
Forney, Tx., U.S.	C4	120
Fornovo di Taro, Italy	E5	14
Forrest, Austl.	F5	50
Forrest, Il., U.S.	C5	90
Forrest, co., Ms., U.S.	D4	101
Forrest City, Ar., U.S.	B5	81
Forrester Island, i., Ak., U.S.	n23	79
Forreston, Il., U.S.	A4	90
Forsayth, Austl.	C8	50
Forst, Ger.	D14	8
Forsyth, Ga., U.S.	C3	87
Forsyth, Il., U.S.	D5	90
Forsyth, Mo., U.S.	E4	102
Forsyth, Mt., U.S.	D10	103
Forsyth, co., Ga., U.S.	B2	87
Forsyth, co., N.C., U.S.	A2	110
Fortaleza, Braz.	D11	54
Fort Apache Indian Reservation, Az., U.S.	D5	80
Fort-Archambault see Sarh, Chad	G9	42
Fort Ashby, W.V., U.S.	B6	125
Fort Atkinson, Wi., U.S.	F5	126
Fort Augustus, Scot., U.K.	D8	7
Fort Beaufort, S. Afr.	H5	44
Fort Belknap Indian Reservation, Mt., U.S.	B8	103
Fort Belvoir, mil., Va., U.S.	g12	123
Fort Bend, co., Tx., U.S.	E5	120
Fort Benjamin Harrison, mil., In., U.S.	k10	91
Fort Benning, mil., Ga., U.S.	D2	87
Fort Benton, Mt., U.S.	C6	103
Fort Berthold Indian Reservation, N.D., U.S.	B3	111
Fort Bidwell Indian Reservation, Ca., U.S.	B3	82
Fort Bliss, mil., Tx., U.S.	o11	120
Fort Bragg, Ca., U.S.	C2	82
Fort Bragg, mil., N.C., U.S.	B3	110
Fort Branch, In., U.S.	H2	91
Fort Calhoun, Ne., U.S.	C9	104
Fort Campbell, mil., U.S.	A4	119
Fort Carson, mil., Co., U.S.	C6	83
Fort Chipewyan, Alta., Can.	f8	68
Fort Clatsop National Memorial, hist., Or., U.S.	A3	114
Fort Cobb, Ok., U.S.	B3	113
Fort Cobb Reservoir, res., Ok., U.S.	B3	113
Fort Collins, Co., U.S.	A5	83
Fort Coulonge, Que., Can.	B8	73
Fort Davis, Tx., U.S.	o13	120
Fort Davis National Historic Site, hist., Tx., U.S.	o13	120
Fort Defiance, Az., U.S.	B6	80
Fort-de-France, Mart.	G17	64
Fort Deposit, Al., U.S.	D3	78
Fort Detrick, mil., Md., U.S.	B3	97
Fort Devens, mil., Ma., U.S.	f9	98
Fort Dix, mil., N.J., U.S.	C3	107
Fort Dodge, Ia., U.S.	B3	92
Fort Donelson National Battlefield, Tn., U.S.	A4	119
Fort Edward, N.Y., U.S.	B7	109
Fort Erie, Ont., Can.	E6	73
Fortescue, stm., Austl.	D3	50
Fort Eustis, mil., Va., U.S.	h14	123
Fort Fairfield, Me., U.S.	B5	96
Fort Frances, Ont., Can.	o16	73
Fort Franklin, N.W. Ter., Can.	C8	66
Fort Gaines, Ga., U.S.	E1	87
Fort Gay, W.V., U.S.	C2	125
Fort Gibson, Ok., U.S.	B6	113
Fort Gibson Lake, res., Ok., U.S.	A6	113
Fort Good Hope, N.W. Ter., Can.	C7	66
Fort Gordon, mil., Ga., U.S.	C4	87
Fort Greely, mil., Ak., U.S.	C10	79
Forth, Firth of, est., Scot., U.K.	E10	7
Fort Hall, Id., U.S.	F6	89
Fort Hall Indian Reservation, Id., U.S.	F6	89
Fort Hood, mil., Tx., U.S.	D4	120
Fort Howard, Md., U.S.	B5	97
Fort Huachuca, mil., Az., U.S.	F5	80
Fortín Coronel Eugenio Garay, Para.	H6	54
Fort Jackson, mil., S.C., U.S.	C6	117
Fort Kent, Me., U.S.	A4	96
Fort Knox, mil., Ky., U.S.	B4	94
Fort-Lamy see N'Djamena, Chad	F9	42
Fort Laramie, Wy., U.S.	D8	127
Fort Laramie National Historic Site, hist., Wy., U.S.	D8	127
Fort Lauderdale, Fl., U.S.	F6	86
Fort Lawn, S.C., U.S.	B6	117
Fort Leavenworth, mil., Ks., U.S.	C9	93
Fort Lee, N.J., U.S.	B5	107
Fort Lee, mil., Va., U.S.	C5	123
Fort Leonard Wood, mil., Mo., U.S.	D5	102
Fort Lewis, mil., Wa., U.S.	B3	124
Fort Liard, N.W. Ter., Can.	D8	66
Fort Loramie, Oh., U.S.	B1	112
Fort Loudon, Pa., U.S.	G6	115
Fort Loudoun Lake, res., Tn., U.S.	D9	119
Fort Lupton, Co., U.S.	A6	83
Fort MacArthur, mil., Ca., U.S.	n12	82
Fort Macleod, Alta., Can.	E4	68
Fort Madison, Ia., U.S.	D6	92
Fort Matanzas National Monument, Fl., U.S.	C5	86
Fort McClellan, mil., Al., U.S.	B4	78
Fort McDermitt Indian Reservation, U.S.	B4	105
Fort McDowell Indian Reservation, Az., U.S.	D4	80
Fort McHenry National Monument And Historic Shrine, Md., U.S.	g11	97
Fort McMurray, Alta., Can.	A5	68
Fort Meade, Fl., U.S.	E5	86
Fort Meade, mil., Md., U.S.	B4	97
Fort Meadow Reservoir, res., Ma., U.S.	g9	98
Fort Mill, S.C., U.S.	A6	117
Fort Mitchell, Al., U.S.	C4	78
Fort Mitchell, Ky., U.S.	h13	94
Fort Mojave Indian Reservation, U.S.	C1	80
Fort Monmouth, mil., N.J., U.S.	C4	107
Fort Monroe, mil., Va., U.S.	h15	123
Fort Morgan, Co., U.S.	A7	83
Fort Myer, mil., Va., U.S.	g12	123
Fort Myers, Fl., U.S.	F5	86
Fort Myers Beach, Fl., U.S.	F5	86
Fort Nelson, B.C., Can.	m18	69
Fort Norman, N.W. Ter., Can.	D7	66
Fort Oglethorpe, Ga., U.S.	B1	87
Fort Ord, mil., Ca., U.S.	D3	82
Fort Payne, Al., U.S.	A4	78
Fort Peck Indian Reservation, Mt., U.S.	B11	103
Fort Peck Lake, res., Mt., U.S.	C9	103
Fort Pierce, Fl., U.S.	E6	86
Fort Pierce Inlet, b., Fl., U.S.	E6	86
Fort Pierre, S.D., U.S.	C5	118
Fort Plain, N.Y., U.S.	C6	109
Fort Polk, mil., La., U.S.	C2	95
Fort Portal, Ug.	A6	44
Fort Providence, N.W. Ter., Can.	D9	66
Fort Randall Dam, S.D., U.S.	D7	118
Fort Recovery, Oh., U.S.	B1	112
Fort Reliance, N.W. Ter., Can.	D11	66
Fort Resolution, N.W. Ter., Can.	D10	66
Fortress Mountain, mtn., Wy., U.S.	B3	127
Fort Richardson, mil., Ak., U.S.	C10	79
Fort Riley, mil., Ks., U.S.	C7	93
Fort Ritchie, mil., Md., U.S.	A3	97
Fort Rucker, mil., Al., U.S.	D4	78
Fort Saint James, B.C., Can.	B5	69
Fort Saint John, B.C., Can.	A7	69
Fort Sam Houston, mil., Tx., U.S.	k7	120
Fort Sandeman, Pak.	E3	38
Fort Saskatchewan, Alta., Can.	C4	68
Fort Scott, Ks., U.S.	E9	93
Fort Shafter, mil., Hi., U.S.	g10	88
Fort Shawnee, Oh., U.S.	B1	112
Fort Sheridan, mil., Il., U.S.	h9	90
Fort Sill, mil., Ok., U.S.	C3	113
Fort Simpson, N.W. Ter., Can.	D8	66
Fort Smith, N.W. Ter., Can.	D10	66
Fort Smith, Ar., U.S.	B1	81
Fort Stewart, mil., Ga., U.S.	D5	87
Fort Stockton, Tx., U.S.	D1	120
Fort Sumner, N.M., U.S.	C5	108
Fort Sumter National Monument, S.C., U.S.	k12	117
Fort Supply Lake, res., Ok., U.S.	A2	113
Fort Thomas, Ky., U.S.	h14	94
Fort Totten, N.D., U.S.	B7	111
Fort Totten Indian Reservation, N.D., U.S.	B7	111
Fortuna, Ca., U.S.	B1	82
Fortune, Newf., Can.	E4	72
Fortune Bay, b., Newf., Can.	E4	72
Fort Union National Monument, N.M., U.S.	B5	108
Fort Valley, Ga., U.S.	D3	87
Fort Vermilion, Alta., Can.	f7	68
Fortville, In., U.S.	E6	91
Fort Wainwright, mil., Ak., U.S.	C10	79
Fort Walton Beach, Fl., U.S.	u15	86
Fort Washington Forest, Md., U.S.	C4	97
Fort Wayne, In., U.S.	B7	91
Fort William, Scot., U.K.	E7	7
Fort Wingate, N.M., U.S.	B1	108
Fort Worth, Tx., U.S.	C4	120
Fort Wright, Ky., U.S.	h13	94
Forty Fort, Pa., U.S.	D10	115
Fort Yukon, Ak., U.S.	B10	79
Fort Yuma Indian Reservation, Ca., U.S.	F6	82
Foshan, China	L2	28
Fossano, Italy	E2	14
Fossil Butte National Monument, Wy., U.S.	E2	127
Fossil Lake, l., Or., U.S.	D6	114
Fossombrone, Italy	F7	14
Foss Reservoir, res., Ok., U.S.	B2	113
Fosston, Mn., U.S.	C3	100
Foster, Or., U.S.	C4	114
Foster, co., N.D., U.S.	B6	111
Foster Village, Hi., U.S.	g10	88
Fostoria, Oh., U.S.	A2	112
Fougamou, Gabon	B2	44
Fougères, Fr.	D5	10
Fouke, Ar., U.S.	D2	81
Foula, i., Scot., U.K.	A10	7
Foumban, Cam.	G8	42
Fountain, Co., U.S.	C6	83
Fountain, co., In., U.S.	D3	91
Fountain City, In., U.S.	E8	91
Fountain City, Wi., U.S.	D2	126
Fountain Hill, Pa., U.S.	E11	115
Fountain Inn, S.C., U.S.	B3	117
Fountain Peak, mtn., Ca., U.S.	E6	82
Fountain Place, La., U.S.	*D4	95
Fourche LaFave, stm., Ar., U.S.	C2	81
Fourche Maline, stm., Ok., U.S.	C6	113
Fourmies, Fr.	B11	10
Four Mountains, Islands of, is., Ak., U.S.	E6	79
Four Oaks, N.C., U.S.	B4	110
Fowler, Ca., U.S.	D4	82
Fowler, Co., U.S.	C6	83
Fowler, In., U.S.	C3	91
Fowler, Mi., U.S.	E6	99
Fowlerville, Mi., U.S.	F6	99
Fox, stm., Man., Can.	B4	70
Fox, stm., U.S.	B5	90
Fox, stm., U.S.	A6	102
Fox, stm., Mi., U.S.	B4	99
Fox, stm., Wi., U.S.	D5	126
Foxboro, Ont., Can.	C7	73
Foxboro, Ma., U.S.	B5	98
Fox Creek, Alta., Can.	B2	68
Foxe Basin, b., N.W. Ter., Can.	C17	66
Foxe Channel, strt., N.W. Ter., Can.	D16	66
Foxe Peninsula, pen., N.W. Ter., Can.	D17	66
Fox Island, i., R.I., U.S.	E4	116
Fox Island, i., Wa., U.S.	f10	124
Fox Islands, is., Ak., U.S.	E6	79
Fox Lake, Il., U.S.	A5	90
Fox Lake, Wi., U.S.	E5	126
Fox Lake, l., Il., U.S.	h8	90
Fox Mountain, mtn., Nv., U.S.	B2	105
Fox Point, Wi., U.S.	E6	126
Fox River Grove, Il., U.S.	h8	90
Foxworth, Ms., U.S.	D4	101
Foz do Cunene, Ang.	E2	44
Foz do Iguaçu, Braz.	B6	56
Frackville, Pa., U.S.	E9	115
Fraga, Spain	D12	12
Framingham, Ma., U.S.	B5	98
Franca, Braz.	F5	57
Francavilla Fontana, Italy	I12	14
France, ctry., Eur.	F8	4
Francesville, In., U.S.	C4	91
Franceville, Gabon	B2	44
Francis, Lake, l., N.H., U.S.	f7	106
Francis Case, Lake, res., S.D., U.S.	D6	118
Francistown, Bots.	F5	44
Francofonte, Italy	L9	14
Franconia, N.H., U.S.	B3	106
Franconia Notch, N.H., U.S.	B3	106
Francs Peak, mtn., Wy., U.S.	C3	127
Frankenberg, Ger.	E13	8
Frankenberg-Eder, Ger.	D8	8
Frankenmuth, Mi., U.S.	E7	99
Frankford, Ont., Can.	C7	73
Frankford, De., U.S.	F5	85
Frankfort, Il., U.S.	m9	90
Frankfort, In., U.S.	D4	91
Frankfort, Ks., U.S.	C7	93
Frankfort, Ky., U.S.	B5	94
Frankfort, Mi., U.S.	D4	99
Frankfort, N.Y., U.S.	B5	109
Frankfort, Oh., U.S.	C2	112
Frankfurt am Main, Ger.	E8	8
Frankfurt an der Oder, Ger.	C14	8
Franklin, Ga., U.S.	C1	87
Franklin, In., U.S.	F5	91
Franklin, Ky., U.S.	D3	94
Franklin, La., U.S.	E4	95
Franklin, Ma., U.S.	B5	98
Franklin, Ne., U.S.	D7	104
Franklin, N.H., U.S.	D3	106
Franklin, N.J., U.S.	A3	107
Franklin, N.C., U.S.	f9	110
Franklin, Oh., U.S.	C1	112
Franklin, Pa., U.S.	D2	115
Franklin, Tn., U.S.	B5	119
Franklin, Tx., U.S.	D4	120
Franklin, Va., U.S.	D6	123
Franklin, W.V., U.S.	C5	125
Franklin, Wi., U.S.	n11	126
Franklin, co., Al., U.S.	A2	78
Franklin, co., Ar., U.S.	B2	81
Franklin, co., Fl., U.S.	C2	86
Franklin, co., Ga., U.S.	B3	87
Franklin, co., Id., U.S.	G7	89
Franklin, co., Il., U.S.	E4	90
Franklin, co., In., U.S.	F7	91
Franklin, co., Ia., U.S.	B4	92
Franklin, co., Ks., U.S.	D8	93

Name — Map Ref — Page

Franklin, co., Ky., U.S. B5 94
Franklin, co., La., U.S. B4 95
Franklin, co., Me., U.S. C2 96
Franklin, co., Ma., U.S. A2 98
Franklin, co., Ms., U.S. D3 101
Franklin, co., Mo., U.S. C6 102
Franklin, co., Ne., U.S. D7 104
Franklin, co., N.Y., U.S. f10 109
Franklin, co., N.C., U.S. A4 110
Franklin, co., Oh., U.S. B2 112
Franklin, co., Pa., U.S. G6 115
Franklin, co., Tn., U.S. B5 119
Franklin, co., Tx., U.S. C5 120
Franklin, co., Vt., U.S. B2 122
Franklin, co., Va., U.S. D3 123
Franklin, co., Wa., U.S. C6 124
Franklin, Point, c., Ak., U.S. A8 79
Franklin Bay, b., N.W. Ter., Can. C7 66
Franklin D. Roosevelt Lake, res., Wa., U.S. B7 124
Franklin Falls Reservoir, res., N.H., U.S. C3 106
Franklin Grove, Il., U.S. B4 90
Franklin Lake, l., N.W. Ter., Can. C13 66
Franklin Lake, l., Nv., U.S. C6 105
Franklin Mountains, mts., N.W. Ter., Can. D8 66
Franklin Park, Il., U.S. k9 90
Franklin Park, Pa., U.S. *h13 115
Franklin Strait, strt., N.W. Ter., Can. B13 66
Franklinton, La., U.S. D5 95
Franklinton, N.C., U.S. A4 110
Franklinville, N.Y., U.S. C2 109
Frankston, Tx., U.S. C5 120
Frankton, In., U.S. D6 91
Frascati, Italy H7 14
Fraser, stm., B.C., Can. E7 69
Fraser, stm., Newf., Can. g9 72
Fraser, Mount, mtn., Can. C8 69
Fraserburgh, Scot., U.K. D10 7
Fraser Lake, B.C., Can. B5 69
Fraser Plateau, plat., B.C., Can. D6 69
Frauenfeld, Switz. E15 10
Frazee, Mn., U.S. D3 100
Frazeysburg, Oh., U.S. B3 112
Frazier Park, Ca., U.S. E4 82
Fr'azino, Russia F21 18
Frederic, Wi., U.S. C1 126
Frederica, De., U.S. D4 85
Fredericia, Den. I7 6
Frederick, Co., U.S. A6 83
Frederick, Md., U.S. B3 97
Frederick, Ok., U.S. C2 113
Frederick, co., Md., U.S. B3 97
Frederick, co., Va., U.S. A4 123
Fredericksburg, Ia., U.S. B5 92
Fredericksburg, Tx., U.S. D3 120
Fredericksburg, Va., U.S. B5 123
Frederick Sound, strt., Ak., U.S. m23 79
Fredericktown, Mo., U.S. D7 102
Fredericktown, Oh., U.S. B3 112
Fredericktown, Pa., U.S. F1 115
Fredericton, N.B., Can. D3 71
Fredericton Junction, N.B., Can. D3 71
Frederikshåb, Grnld. D23 66
Frederikshavn, Den. H8 6
Fredonia, Az., U.S. A3 80
Fredonia, Ks., U.S. E8 93
Fredonia, N.Y., U.S. C1 109
Fredonia, Wi., U.S. E6 126
Fredrikstad, Nor. G8 6
Freeborn, co., Mn., U.S. G5 100
Freeburg, Il., U.S. E4 90
Freedom, Pa., U.S. E1 115
Freedom, Wy., U.S. D2 127
Freehold, N.J., U.S. C4 107
Freeland, Mi., U.S. E6 99
Freeland, Pa., U.S. D10 115
Freelandville, In., U.S. G3 91
Freel Peak, mtn., Ca., U.S. C4 82
Freels, Cape, c., Newf., Can. D5 72
Freels, Cape, c., Newf., Can. E5 72
Freeman, S.D., U.S. D8 118
Freeman, Lake, l., In., U.S. C4 91
Freemansburg, Pa., U.S. E11 115
Freemason Island, i., La., U.S. E7 95
Freeport, Bah. A8 64
Freeport, Il., U.S. A4 90
Freeport, Me., U.S. E2 96
Freeport, N.Y., U.S. n15 109
Freeport, Pa., U.S. E2 115
Freeport, Tx., U.S. E5 120
Freer, Tx., U.S. F3 120
Freestone, co., Tx., U.S. D4 120
Freetown, S.L. G3 42
Freetown, In., U.S. G5 91
Freezeout Mountains, mts., Wy., U.S. D6 127
Fregenal de la Sierra, Spain G5 12
Freiberg, Ger. E13 8
Freiburg [im Breisgau], Ger. H7 8
Freising, Ger. G11 8
Freistadt, Aus. G14 8
Freital, Ger. D13 8
Fréjus, Fr. I13 10
Fremont, Ca., U.S. D2 82
Fremont, In., U.S. A8 91
Fremont, Ia., U.S. C5 92
Fremont, Mi., U.S. E5 99
Fremont, Ne., U.S. C9 104
Fremont, N.C., U.S. B5 110
Fremont, Oh., U.S. A2 112
Fremont, co., Co., U.S. C5 83
Fremont, co., Id., U.S. E7 89
Fremont, co., Ia., U.S. D2 92
Fremont, co., Wy., U.S. C4 127
Fremont, stm., Ut., U.S. E4 121
Fremont Island, i., Ut., U.S. B3 121
Fremont Lake, l., Wy., U.S. D3 127
Fremont Peak, mtn., Wy., U.S. C3 127
French Broad, stm., U.S. D10 119
Frenchburg, Ky., U.S. C6 94
French Creek, stm., Pa., U.S. C2 115
French Frigate Shoals, rf., Hi., U.S. m14 88
French Guiana, dep., S.A. C8 54
French Lick, In., U.S. G4 91
Frenchman Bay, b., Me., U.S. D4 96
Frenchman Creek, stm., U.S. D4 104
Frenchman Hills, hills, Wa., U.S. C6 124
Frenchman Lake, l., Nv., U.S. G6 105
French Polynesia, dep., Oc. G3 2
French Settlement, La., U.S. D5 95
Freshfield, Mount, mtn., Can. D2 68
Fresnillo, Mex. F8 62
Fresno, Ca., U.S. D4 82
Fresno, co., Ca., U.S. D4 82
Fresno Reservoir, res., Mt., U.S. B6 103
Freudenstadt, Ger. G8 8
Frewsburg, N.Y., U.S. C1 109
Fria, Cape, c., Nmb. E2 44
Friars Point, Ms., U.S. A3 101
Frías, Arg. B3 56
Fribourg (Freiburg), Switz. F14 10
Friday Harbor, Wa., U.S. A2 124
Fridley, Mn., U.S. m12 100
Friedberg, Aus. H16 8
Friedrichshafen, Ger. H9 8
Friend, Ne., U.S. D8 104
Friendsville, Tn., U.S. D9 119
Fries, Va., U.S. D2 123
Friesland, hist. reg., Neth. B5 8
Frio, co., Tx., U.S. E3 120
Frio, stm., Tx., U.S. E3 120
Frio, Cabo, c., Braz. G7 57
Friona, Tx., U.S. B1 120
Fripps Island, i., S.C., U.S. G7 117
Frisco, Co., U.S. B4 83
Frisco City, Al., U.S. D2 78
Frisco Peak, mtn., Ut., U.S. E2 121
Frissell, Mount, mtn., U.S. A2 84
Fritch, Tx., U.S. B2 120
Fritzlar, Ger. D9 8
Friza, Proliv, strt., Russia H23 24
Frobisher Bay, b., N.W. Ter., Can. D19 66
Frobisher Lake, l., Sask., Can. m7 75
Frohnleiten, Aus. H15 8
Frontenac, Ks., U.S. E9 93
Frontier, co., Ne., U.S. D5 104
Front Range, mts., Co., U.S. A5 83
Front Royal, Va., U.S. B4 123
Frosinone, Italy H8 14
Frostburg, Md., U.S. k13 97
Frostproof, Fl., U.S. E5 86
Fruita, Co., U.S. B2 83
Fruit Heights, Ut., U.S. B4 121
Fruitland, Id., U.S. F2 89
Fruitland, Md., U.S. D6 97
Fruitland, N.M., U.S. A1 108
Fruitland Park, Fl., U.S. D5 86
Fruitport, Mi., U.S. E4 99
Fruitvale, B.C., Can. E9 69
Fruitvale, Co., U.S. B2 83
Fruitvale, Wa., U.S. C5 124
Fruitville, Fl., U.S. E4 86
Frunze see Biškek, Kyrg. I12 22
Frutigen, Switz. F14 10
Fryeburg, Me., U.S. D2 96
Fuchū, Japan H6 30
Fuencaliente, Spain G7 12
Fuente de Cantos, Spain G5 12
Fuente-obejuna, Spain G6 12
Fuerteventura, i., Spain p27 13b
Fuji, Japan G11 30
Fuji, Mount see Fuji-san, vol., Japan G11 30
Fujian, prov., China F10 26
Fujin, China B13 26
Fujinomiya, Japan G11 30
Fuji-san (Fujiyama), vol., Japan G11 30
Fujisawa, Japan G12 30
Fujiyama see Fuji-san, vol., Japan G11 30
Fuji-yoshida, Japan G11 30
Fukagawa, Japan p20 30a
Fukaya, Japan F12 30
Fukuchiyama, Japan G8 30
Fukue, Japan J1 30
Fukui, Japan F9 30
Fukuoka, Japan I3 30
Fukushima, Japan E13 30
Fukushima, Japan r18 30a
Fukuyama, Japan H6 30
Fūlādī, Kūh-e, mtn., Afg. C2 38
Fulda, Ger. E9 8
Fulda, Mn., U.S. G3 100
Fullerton, Ca., U.S. n13 82
Fullerton, Ne., U.S. C8 104
Fulton, Il., U.S. B3 90
Fulton, Ky., U.S. f9 94
Fulton, Md., U.S. B4 97
Fulton, Ms., U.S. A5 101
Fulton, Mo., U.S. C6 102
Fulton, N.Y., U.S. B4 109
Fulton, co., Ar., U.S. A4 81
Fulton, co., Ga., U.S. C2 87
Fulton, co., Il., U.S. C3 90
Fulton, co., In., U.S. B5 91
Fulton, co., Ky., U.S. f8 94
Fulton, co., N.Y., U.S. B6 109
Fulton, co., Oh., U.S. A1 112
Fulton, co., Pa., U.S. G5 115
Fultondale, Al., U.S. f7 78
Funabashi, Japan G13 30
Funchal, Port. n21 13a
Fundación, Col. B5 58
Fundy, Bay of, b., Can. D4 71
Fundy National Park, N.B., Can. D4 71
Funkstown, Md., U.S. A2 97
Fuquay-Varina, N.C., U.S. B4 110
Furano, Japan p20 30a
Furmanov, Russia D24 18
Furnace Brook, stm., Vt., U.S. D3 122
Furnas, co., Ne., U.S. D6 104
Furnas, Represa de, res., Braz. F5 57
Furneaux Group, is., Austl. H9 50
Furqlus, Syria B5 40
Fürstenfeld, Aus. H16 8
Fürstenfeldbruck, Ger. G11 8
Fürstenwalde, Ger. C14 8
Fürth, Ger. F10 8
Furth im Wald, Ger. F12 8
Furudal, Swe. F10 6
Fushun, China C11 26
Füssen, Ger. H10 8
Fuxian, China D11 26
Fuxian, China D8 26
Fuxinshi, China C11 26
Fuyang, China C4 28
Fuzhou, China G5 28
Fuzhou (Foochow), China I8 28
Fyffe, Al., U.S. A4 78

G

Gabbs, Nv., U.S. E4 105
Gabès, Tun. B8 42
Gabès, Golfe de, b., Tun. B8 42
Gabon, ctry., Afr. B2 44
Gaborone, Bots. F5 44
Gabriel Strait, strt., N.W. Ter., Can. D19 66
Gabriola, B.C., Can. f12 69
Gabrovo, Bul. G9 16
Gadag, India E3 37
Gäddede, Swe. D10 6
Gadsden, Al., U.S. A3 78
Gadsden, co., Fl., U.S. B2 86
Gaeta, Italy H8 14
Gaffney, S.C., U.S. A4 117
Gafsa, Tun. B7 42
Gage, co., Ne., U.S. D9 104
Gagetown, N.B., Can. D3 71
Gagliano del Capo, Italy J13 14
Gagnoa, C. Iv. G4 42
Gahanna, Oh., U.S. k11 112
Gaillac, Fr. I8 10
Gaillard, Lake, l., Ct., U.S. D5 84
Gaines, co., Tx., U.S. C1 120
Gainesboro, Tn., U.S. C8 119
Gaines Creek, stm., Ok., U.S. C6 113
Gainesville, Fl., U.S. C4 86
Gainesville, Ga., U.S. B3 87
Gainesville, Mo., U.S. E5 102
Gainesville, Tx., U.S. C4 120
Gainesville, Va., U.S. g11 123
Gairdner, Lake, l., Austl. F7 50
Gaithersburg, Md., U.S. B3 97
Galán, Cerro, mtn., Arg. B3 56
Galapagos Islands see Colón, Archipiélago de, is., Ec. m15 58a
Galashiels, Scot., U.K. F10 7
Galați, Rom. D12 16
Galatia, Il., U.S. F5 90
Galatina, Italy I13 14
Galax, Va., U.S. D2 123
Galdhøpiggen, mtn., Nor. F7 6
Galena, Ak., U.S. C8 79
Galena, Il., U.S. A3 90
Galena, Ks., U.S. E9 93
Galeota Point, c., Trin. I17 64
Galera, Punta, c., Chile D2 56
Galera, Punta, c., Ec. G2 58
Galesburg, Il., U.S. C3 90
Galesburg, Mi., U.S. F5 99
Gales Ferry, Ct., U.S. D7 84
Galesville, Md., U.S. C4 97
Galesville, Wi., U.S. D2 126
Galeton, Pa., U.S. C6 115
Galič, Russia C25 18
Galicia, hist. reg., Eur. F21 8
Galicia, hist. reg., Spain B3 12
Galilee, Sea of see Kinneret, Yam, l., Isr. C4 40
Galion, Oh., U.S. B3 112
Galisteo Creek, stm., N.M., U.S. k8 108
Galiuro Mountains, mts., Az., U.S. E5 80
Galka'yo, Som. G4 46
Gallant, Al., U.S. B3 78
Gallarate, Italy D3 14
Gallatin, Mo., U.S. B4 102
Gallatin, Tn., U.S. A5 119
Gallatin, co., Il., U.S. F5 90
Gallatin, co., Ky., U.S. B5 94
Gallatin, co., Mt., U.S. E5 103
Gallatin, stm., Mt., U.S. E5 103
Gallatin Range, mts., Mt., U.S. E5 103
Gallaway, Tn., U.S. B2 119
Galle, Sri L. I6 37
Gallia, co., Oh., U.S. D3 112
Galliano, La., U.S. E5 95
Gallinas, Punta, c., Col. A7 58
Gallinas Mountains, mts., N.M., U.S. C2 108
Gallipoli, Italy I12 14
Gallipoli see Gelibolu, Tur. I10 16
Gallipolis, Oh., U.S. D3 112
Gallitzin, Pa., U.S. F4 115
Gällivare, Swe. C13 6
Gallo Mountains, mts., N.M., U.S. C1 108
Galloo Island, i., N.Y., U.S. B4 109
Galloway, Mull of, c., Scot., U.K. G8 7
Gallup, N.M., U.S. B1 108
Galt, Ca., U.S. C3 82
Galtür, Aus. I10 8
Galty Mountains, mts., Ire. I4 7
Galva, Il., U.S. B3 90
Galva, Ks., U.S. D6 93
Galveston, In., U.S. C5 91
Galveston, Tx., U.S. E5 120
Galveston, co., Tx., U.S. E5 120
Galveston Bay, b., Tx., U.S. E5 120
Galveston Island, i., Tx., U.S. E5 120
Gálvez, Arg. C4 56
Galway, Ire. H3 7
Gambela, Eth. G1 46
Gambell, Ak., U.S. C5 79
Gambia, ctry., Afr. F2 42
Gambia (Gambie), stm., Afr. F2 42
Gambier, Oh., U.S. B3 112
Gambo, Newf., Can. D4 72
Gambrills, Md., U.S. B4 97
Gamleby, Swe. H11 6
Ganado, Az., U.S. B6 80
Ganado, Tx., U.S. E4 120
Gananoque, Ont., Can. C8 73
Gäncä, Azer. I7 22
Ganda, Ang. D2 44
Gandak, stm., Asia G11 38
Gander, Newf., Can. D4 72
Gander, stm., Newf., Can. D4 72
Ganderkesee, Ger. B8 8
Gander Lake, l., Newf., Can. D4 72
Gandesa, Spain D12 12
Gāndhinagar, India I5 38
Gāndhi Sāgar, res., India H6 38
Gandía, Spain G11 12
Gangāpur, India G7 38
Gangāwati, India E4 37
Gangdisê Shan, mts., China E10 38
Ganges, B.C., Can. g12 69
Ganges (Ganga) (Padma), stm., Asia I13 38
Ganges, Mouths of the, mth., Asia J13 38
Gang Mills, N.Y., U.S. C3 109
Gangtok, India G13 38
Gangu, China E8 26
Gannat, Fr. F10 10
Gannett Peak, mtn., Wy., U.S. C3 127
Gansu, prov., China D7 26
Gantt, S.C., U.S. B3 117
Gantt Lake, res., Al., U.S. D3 78
Ganzhou, China J3 28
Ganzi, China E7 26
Gao, Mali E5 42
Gaokeng, China H2 28
Gaoyou, China C8 28
Gaozhou, China D11 34
Gap, Fr. H13 10
Gap, Pa., U.S. G9 115
Gar, China E9 38
Garanhuns, Braz. E11 54
Garber, Ok., U.S. A4 113
Garberville, Ca., U.S. B2 82
Garça, Braz. G4 57
Garda, Lago di, l., Italy D5 14
Gardelegen, Ger. C11 8
Garden, co., Ne., U.S. C3 104
Gardena, Ca., U.S. n12 82
Garden City, Ga., U.S. D5 87
Garden City, Id., U.S. F2 89
Garden City, Ks., U.S. E3 93
Garden City, Mi., U.S. p15 99
Garden City, Mo., U.S. C3 102
Gardendale, Al., U.S. B3 78
Garden Grove, Ca., U.S. n13 82
Garden Island, i., Mi., U.S. C5 99
Garden Plain, Ks., U.S. E6 93
Garden Reach, India I13 38
Gardēz, Afg. D3 38
Gardiner, Me., U.S. D3 96
Gardiner, Mt., U.S. E6 103
Gardiner, Or., U.S. D2 114
Gardiners Island, i., N.Y., U.S. m16 109
Gardner, Il., U.S. B5 90
Gardner, Ks., U.S. D9 93
Gardner, Ma., U.S. A4 98
Gardner Canal, strt., B.C., Can. C3 69
Gardner Lake, l., Ct., U.S. C6 84
Gardner Lake, l., Me., U.S. D5 96
Gardner Pinnacles, Hi., U.S. k14 88
Gardnerville, Nv., U.S. E2 105
Gardone Val Trompia, Italy D5 14
Garfield, N.J., U.S. h8 107
Garfield, co., Co., U.S. B2 83
Garfield, co., Mt., U.S. C9 103
Garfield, co., Ne., U.S. C6 104
Garfield, co., Ok., U.S. A4 113
Garfield, co., Ut., U.S. F4 121
Garfield, co., Wa., U.S. C8 124
Garfield Heights, Oh., U.S. h9 112
Garfield Mountain, mtn., Mt., U.S. F4 103
Garfield Peak, mtn., Wy., U.S. D5 127
Garibaldi, Or., U.S. B3 114
Garibaldi, Mount, mtn., B.C., Can. E6 69
Garies, S. Afr. H3 44
Garissa, Kenya B7 44
Garland, N.C., U.S. C4 110
Garland, Tx., U.S. n10 120
Garland, Ut., U.S. B3 121
Garland, co., Ar., U.S. C2 81
Garlin, Fr. I6 10
Garm Āb, Afg. D1 38
Garmisch-Partenkirchen, Ger. H11 8
Garnavillo, Ia., U.S. B6 92
Garner, Ia., U.S. A4 92
Garner, N.C., U.S. B4 110
Garnet Range, mts., Mt., U.S. D3 103
Garnett, Ks., U.S. D8 93
Garnish, Newf., Can. E4 72
Garonne, stm., Eur. H6 10
Garoua, Cam. G8 42
Garrard, co., Ky., U.S. C5 94
Garretson, S.D., U.S. D9 118
Garrett, In., U.S. B7 91
Garrett, co., Md., U.S. k12 97
Garrett Park, Md., U.S. B3 97
Garrettsville, Oh., U.S. A4 112
Garrison, Ky., U.S. B6 94
Garrison, Md., U.S. B4 97
Garrison, N.D., U.S. B4 111
Garrison Dam, N.D., U.S. B4 111
Garrovillas, Spain F5 12
Garry Lake, l., N.W. Ter., Can. C12 66
Garsen, Kenya B8 44
Garut, Indon. m13 33a
Garvin, co., Ok., U.S. C4 113
Gary, In., U.S. A3 91
Gary, W.V., U.S. D3 125
Garysburg, N.C., U.S. A5 110
Garyville, La., U.S. D5 95
Garza, co., Tx., U.S. C2 120
Garza-Little Elm Reservoir, res., Tx., U.S. C4 120
Garzón, Col. F5 58
Gas City, In., U.S. D6 91
Gasconade, co., Mo., U.S. C6 102
Gasconade, stm., Mo., U.S. C6 102
Gascoyne, stm., Austl. E3 50
Gasparilla Island, i., Fl., U.S. F4 86
Gaspé, Que., Can. k14 74
Gaspésie, Péninsule de la, pen., Que., Can. k13 74
Gassaway, W.V., U.S. C4 125
Gassville, Ar., U.S. A3 81
Gaston, In., U.S. D7 91
Gaston, N.C., U.S. A5 110
Gaston, S.C., U.S. D5 117
Gaston, co., N.C., U.S. B1 110
Gaston, Lake, res., U.S. A5 110
Gaston Dam, N.C., U.S. A5 110
Gastonia, N.C., U.S. B1 110
Gátas, Akrotírion, c., Cyp. B3 40
Gatčina, Russia B13 18
Gate City, Va., U.S. f9 123
Gates, N.Y., U.S. *B3 109
Gates, Tn., U.S. B2 119
Gates, co., N.C., U.S. A6 110
Gateshead, Eng., U.K. G11 7
Gateshead Island, i., N.W. Ter., Can. B12 66
Gates of the Arctic National Park, Ak., U.S. B9 79
Gatesville, Tx., U.S. D4 120
Gatineau, Que., Can. D2 74
Gatineau, stm., Que., Can. D2 74
Gatineau, Parc de la, Que., Can. D2 74
Gatlinburg, Tn., U.S. D10 119
Gaucín, Spain I6 12
Gauhāti, India G14 38
Gauley, stm., W.V., U.S. C3 125
Gauley Bridge, W.V., U.S. C3 125
Gautier, Ms., U.S. f8 101
Gauting, Ger. G11 8
Gavá, Spain D14 12
Gavins Point Dam, U.S. B8 104
Gävle, Swe. F11 6
Gavrilov-Jam, Russia D22 18
Gawler Ranges, mts., Austl. F7 50
Gaya, India H11 38
Gay Head, c., Ma., U.S. D6 98
Gaylord, Mi., U.S. C6 99
Gaylord, Mn., U.S. F4 100
Gayndah, Austl. E10 50
Gaza see Ghazzah, Gaza Strip D4 40
Gaziantep, Tur. H15 4
Gazimağusa, N. Cyp. B3 40
Gazimağusa Körfezi, b., N. Cyp. B4 40
Gbarnga, Lib. G4 42
Gdańsk (Danzig), Pol. A18 8
Gdynia, Pol. A18 8
Gearhart, Or., U.S. A3 114
Gearhart Mountain, mtn., Or., U.S. E6 114
Geary, N.B., Can. D3 71
Geary, Ok., U.S. B3 113
Geary, co., Ks., U.S. D7 93
Geauga, co., Oh., U.S. A4 112
Gebze, Tur. I13 16
Gediz, stm., Tur. K11 16
Geel, Bel. D4 8
Geelong, Austl. G8 50
Ge'ermu, China B16 38
Geesthacht, Ger. B10 8
Geilo, Nor. F7 6
Geislingen, Ger. G9 8
Geistown, Pa., U.S. F4 115
Geist Reservoir, res., In., U.S. E6 91
Gejiu (Kokiu), China C7 34
Gela, Italy L9 14
Gelibolu, Tur. I10 16
Gelibolu Yarımadası (Gallipoli Peninsula), pen., Tur. I10 16
Gelsenkirchen, Ger. D7 8
Gem, co., Id., U.S. E2 89
Gembloux, Bel. E4 8
Gemena, Zaire H9 42
Gemlik, Tur. I13 16
Gemona del Friuli, Italy C8 14
Genale (Juba), stm., Afr. G3 46
General Alvear, Arg. C3 56
General Bravo, Mex. E10 62
General Carneiro, Braz. C2 57
General Levalle, Arg. C4 56
General Pico, Arg. D4 56
General Pinedo, Arg. B4 56
General Roca, Arg. D3 56
General Villegas, Arg. D4 56
Genesee, Id., U.S. C2 89
Genesee, Mi., U.S. E7 99
Genesee, co., Mi., U.S. E7 99
Genesee, co., N.Y., U.S. B2 109
Genesee, stm., N.Y., U.S. C2 109
Geneseo, Il., U.S. B3 90
Geneseo, N.Y., U.S. C3 109
Geneva, Al., U.S. D4 78
Geneva, Il., U.S. B5 90
Geneva, In., U.S. C8 91
Geneva, Ne., U.S. D8 104
Geneva, N.Y., U.S. C4 109
Geneva, Oh., U.S. A5 112
Geneva, co., Al., U.S. D4 78
Geneva, Lake, l., Eur. F13 10
Geneva, Lake, l., Wi., U.S. F5 126
Geneva see Genève, Switz. F13 10
Geneva-on-the-Lake, Oh., U.S. A5 112
Genève, Switz. F13 10
Genk, Bel. E5 8
Genkai-nada, Japan I3 30
Genoa, Il., U.S. A5 90
Genoa, Ne., U.S. C8 104
Genoa, Nv., U.S. D2 105
Genoa, Oh., U.S. A2 112
Genoa City, Wi., U.S. F5 126
Genoa see Genova, Italy E3 14
Genola, Ut., U.S. D4 121
Genova (Genoa), Italy E3 14
Genova, Golfo di, b., Italy E3 14
Gent (Gand), Bel. D3 8
Genteng, Indon. n17 33a
Genthin, Ger. C12 8
Gentry, Ar., U.S. A1 81
Gentry, co., Mo., U.S. A3 102
Geographe Bay, b., Austl. F3 50
George, S. Afr. H4 44
George, Ia., U.S. A2 92
George, co., Ms., U.S. E5 101
George, stm., Que., Can. g13 74
George, Cape, c., N.S., Can. D8 71
George, Lake, l., Ug. B6 44
George, Lake, l., Fl., U.S. C5 86
George, Lake, l., N.Y., U.S. B7 109
George Air Force Base, mil., Ca., U.S. E5 82
George B. Stevenson Reservoir, res., Pa., U.S. D6 115
George Peak, mtn., Ut., U.S. B2 121
Georgetown, P.E.I., Can. C7 71
Georgetown, Cay. Is. E7 64

Name — Map Ref — Page

Georgetown, Gam. F3 42
Georgetown, Guy. D13 58
George Town (Pinang), Malay. L6 34
Georgetown, Ca., U.S. C3 82
Georgetown, Co., U.S. B5 83
Georgetown, Ct., U.S. D2 84
Georgetown, De., U.S. F4 85
Georgetown, Ga., U.S. E1 87
Georgetown, Il., U.S. D6 90
Georgetown, In., U.S. H6 91
Georgetown, Ky., U.S. B5 94
Georgetown, Ma., U.S. A6 98
Georgetown, Oh., U.S. D2 112
Georgetown, S.C., U.S. E9 117
Georgetown, Tx., U.S. D4 120
Georgetown, co., S.C., U.S. E9 117
George Washington Birthplace National Monument, Va., U.S. B6 123
George Washington Carver National Monument, Mo., U.S. E3 102
George West, Tx., U.S. E3 120
Georgia, ctry., Asia I6 22
Georgia, state, U.S. D3 87
Georgia, Strait of, strt., N.A. B2 76
Georgiana, Al., U.S. D3 78
Georgian Bay, b., Ont., Can. B3 73
Georgina, stm., Austl. D7 50
Gera, Ger. E12 8
Gerald, Mo., U.S. C6 102
Geraldine, Al., U.S. A4 78
Geral do Paranã, Serra, hills, Braz. C5 57
Geraldton, Austl. E2 50
Geraldton, Ont., Can. o18 73
Gérardmer, Fr. D13 10
Gerber Reservoir, res., Or., U.S. E5 114
Gerdine, Mount, mtn., Ak., U.S. C9 79
Gereshk, Afg. E1 38
Gérgal, Spain H9 12
Gering, Ne., U.S. C2 104
Gerlach, Nv., U.S. C2 105
Germantown, Il., U.S. E4 90
Germantown, Md., U.S. B3 97
Germantown, Oh., U.S. C1 112
Germantown, Tn., U.S. B2 119
Germantown, Wi., U.S. E5 126
Germany, ctry., Eur. E10 4
Germiston, S. Afr. G5 44
Gerona, Spain D14 12
Geronimo, Ok., U.S. C3 113
Gervais, Or., U.S. B4 114
Geseke, Ger. D8 8
Getafe, Spain E8 12
Gettysburg, Pa., U.S. G7 115
Gettysburg, S.D., U.S. C6 118
Ghāghra, stm., Asia G10 38
Ghana, ctry., Afr. G5 42
Ghanzi, Bots. F4 44
Gharbīyah, Aṣ-Ṣaḥrā' al- (Western Desert), des., Egypt C11 42
Ghardaïa, Alg. B6 42
Gharyān, Libya B8 42
Ghāt, Libya D8 42
Għawdex, i., Malta M9 14
Ghazāl, Bahr al-, stm., Sudan G12 42
Ghāziābād, India F7 38
Ghāzīpur, India H10 38
Ghaznī, Afg. D3 38
Ghazzah (Gaza), Gaza Strip D4 40
Ghedi, Italy D5 14
Gheen, Mn., U.S. C6 100
Ghent see Gent, Bel. D3 8
Ghīn, Tall, mtn., Syria C5 40
Ghudāmis, Libya B7 42
Giants Neck, Ct., U.S. D7 84
Gibbon, Mn., U.S. F4 100
Gibbon, Ne., U.S. D7 104
Gibbons, Alta., Can. C4 68
Gibbstown, N.J., U.S. D2 107
Gibeon, Nmb. G3 44
Gibraltar, Gib. I6 12
Gibraltar, dep., Eur. H6 4
Gibraltar, Strait of (Estrecho de Gibraltar), strt. J6 12
Gibraltar Point, c., Eng., U.K. H13 7
Gibsland, La., U.S. B2 95
Gibson, Ga., U.S. C4 87
Gibson, co., In., U.S. H2 91
Gibson, co., Tn., U.S. A3 119
Gibsonburg, Oh., U.S. A2 112
Gibson City, Il., U.S. C5 90
Gibson Desert, des., Austl. D4 50
Gibsonia, Pa., U.S. h14 115
Gibson Island, i., Md., U.S. B5 97
Gibsons, B.C., Can. E6 69
Gibsonton, Fl., U.S. p11 86
Gibsonville, N.C., U.S. A3 110
Giddings, Tx., U.S. D4 120
Gideon, Mo., U.S. E8 102
Gien, Fr. E9 10
Giessen, Ger. E8 8
Gifford, Fl., U.S. E6 86
Gifford, Il., U.S. C5 90
Gifu, Japan G9 30
Gig Harbor, Wa., U.S. B3 124
Gihon, stm., Vt., U.S. B3 122
Gijón, Spain B6 12
Gila, co., Az., U.S. D5 80
Gila, stm., U.S. E4 76
Gila Bend, Az., U.S. E3 80
Gila Bend Indian Reservation, Az., U.S. D3 80
Gila Bend Mountains, mts., Az., U.S. D2 80
Gila Cliff Dwellings National Monument, N.M., U.S. D1 108
Gila Mountains, mts., Az., U.S. D6 80
Gila Peak, mtn., Az., U.S. D6 80
Gila River Indian Reservation, Az., U.S. D4 80
Gilbert, Az., U.S. D4 80
Gilbert, Ia., U.S. B4 92
Gilbert, La., U.S. B4 95
Gilbert, Mn., U.S. C6 100
Gilbert Islands see Kiribati, ctry., Oc. G24 2
Gilbert Peak, mtn., Wa., U.S. C4 124
Gilbert Plains, Man., Can. D1 70
Gilbertsville, Ky., U.S. f9 94
Gilbertsville, Pa., U.S. F10 115
Gilbertville, Ia., U.S. B5 92
Gilbués, Braz. E9 54
Gilchrist, Or., U.S. D5 114
Gilchrist, co., Fl., U.S. C4 86
Gilcrest, Co., U.S. A6 83
Giles, co., Tn., U.S. B4 119
Giles, co., Va., U.S. C2 123
Gilford Island, i., B.C., Can. D4 69
Gilgit, Pak. C6 38
Gillam, Man., Can. A4 70
Gillespie, Il., U.S. D4 90
Gillespie, co., Tx., U.S. D3 120
Gillespie Dam, Az., U.S. D3 80
Gillett, Ar., U.S. C4 81
Gillett, Wi., U.S. D5 126
Gillette, Wy., U.S. B7 127
Gilliam, co., Or., U.S. B6 114
Gilman, Il., U.S. C5 90
Gilman, Vt., U.S. C5 122
Gilmanton, N.H., U.S. D4 106
Gilmer, Tx., U.S. C5 120
Gilmer, co., Ga., U.S. B2 87
Gilmer, co., W.V., U.S. C4 125
Gilo, stm., Eth. G1 46
Gilpin, co., Co., U.S. B5 83
Gilroy, Ca., U.S. D3 82
Gil'uj, stm., Russia G19 24
Giluwe, Mount, mtn., Pap. N. Gui. m15 50a
Gimli, Man., Can. D3 70
Ginosa, Italy I11 14
Ginowan, Japan y27 31b
Gioia del Colle, Italy I11 14
Gioia Tauro, Italy K10 14
Girard, Il., U.S. D4 90
Girard, Ks., U.S. E9 93
Girard, Oh., U.S. A5 112
Girard, Pa., U.S. B1 115
Girardot, Col. E5 58
Girardville, Pa., U.S. E9 115
Girīdih, India H12 38
Girifalco, Italy K11 14
Girne, N. Cyp. B3 40
Girwa, stm., Asia F9 38
Gisborne, N.Z. C7 52
Gisenyi, Rw. B5 44
Gisors, Fr. C8 10
Giugliano [in Campania], Italy I9 14
Giulianova, Italy G8 14
Giurgiu, Rom. F9 16
Givet, Fr. B11 10
Givors, Fr. G11 10
Giyon, Eth. G2 46
Giza see Al-Jīzah, Egypt B12 42
Gižiga, Russia E26 24
Gižiginskaja Guba, b., Russia E25 24
Gjirokastër, Alb. I4 16
Gjoa Haven, N.W. Ter., Can. C13 66
Glacier, co., Mt., U.S. B3 103
Glacier Bay, b., Ak., U.S. k21 79
Glacier Bay National Park, Ak., U.S. D12 79
Glacier National Park, B.C., Can. D9 69
Glacier National Park, Mt., U.S. B2 103
Glacier Peak, mtn., Wa., U.S. A4 124
Gladbrook, Ia., U.S. B5 92
Glade Creek, stm., Wa., U.S. C6 124
Glade Creek, stm., W.V., U.S. n13 125
Glade Creek, stm., W.V., U.S. n14 125
Glades, co., Fl., U.S. F5 86
Glade Spring, Va., U.S. f10 123
Gladewater, Tx., U.S. C5 120
Gladstone, Austl. D10 50
Gladstone, Man., Can. D2 70
Gladstone, Mi., U.S. C4 99
Gladstone, Mo., U.S. h10 102
Gladstone, Or., U.S. B4 114
Gladwin, Mi., U.S. E6 99
Gladwin, co., Mi., U.S. D6 99
Glåma, stm., Nor. F8 6
Glarner Alpen, mts., Switz. F15 10
Glarus, Switz. E16 10
Glascock, co., Ga., U.S. C4 87
Glasford, Il., U.S. C4 90
Glasgow, Scot., U.K. F8 7
Glasgow, Ky., U.S. C4 94
Glasgow, Mo., U.S. B5 102
Glasgow, Mt., U.S. B10 103
Glasgow, Va., U.S. C3 123
Glasgow, W.V., U.S. m13 125
Glassboro, N.J., U.S. D2 107
Glasscock, co., Tx., U.S. D2 120
Glassport, Pa., U.S. F2 115
Glastonbury, Ct., U.S. C5 84
Glauchau, Ger. E12 8
Glazier Lake, l., Me., U.S. A3 96
Glazov, Russia F8 22
Gleason, Tn., U.S. A3 119
Gleisdorf, Aus. H15 8
Glen Allan, Ms., U.S. B2 101
Glen Allen, Va., U.S. C5 123
Glenboro, Man., Can. E2 70
Glenbrook, Nv., U.S. D2 105
Glen Burnie, Md., U.S. B4 97
Glen Canyon Dam, Az., U.S. A4 80
Glen Canyon National Recreation Area, U.S. F5 121
Glencoe, Ont., Can. E3 73
Glencoe, Al., U.S. B4 78
Glencoe, Il., U.S. A6 90
Glencoe, Mn., U.S. F4 100
Glen Cove, N.Y., U.S. h13 109
Glendale, Az., U.S. D3 80
Glendale, Ca., U.S. m12 82
Glendale, Ms., U.S. D4 101
Glendale, Oh., U.S. C1 112
Glendale, Or., U.S. E3 114
Glendale, R.I., U.S. B2 116
Glendale, S.C., U.S. B4 117
Glen Dale, W.V., U.S. B4 125
Glendale, Wi., U.S. m12 126
Glendale Heights, W.V., U.S. g8 125
Glendive, Mt., U.S. C12 103
Glendo, Wy., U.S. D7 127
Glendora, Ca., U.S. m13 82
Glendo Reservoir, res., Wy., U.S. D8 127
Glenelg, Md., U.S. B4 97
Glen Ellis Falls, wtfl, N.H., U.S. B4 106
Glen Ellyn, Il., U.S. k8 90
Glenham, N.Y., U.S. D7 109
Glen Innes, Austl. E10 50
Glen Jean, W.V., U.S. D3 125
Glen Lake, l., Mi., U.S. D5 99
Glen Lyon, Pa., U.S. D9 115
Glenmora, La., U.S. D3 95
Glenn, co., Ca., U.S. C2 82
Glennallen, Ak., U.S. f19 79
Glenns Ferry, Id., U.S. G3 89
Glennville, Ga., U.S. E5 87
Glenolden, Pa., U.S. p20 115
Glenpool, Ok., U.S. B5 113
Glen Raven, N.C., U.S. A3 110
Glen Ridge, N.J., U.S. h8 107
Glen Rock, N.J., U.S. h8 107
Glen Rock, Pa., U.S. G8 115
Glenrock, Wy., U.S. D7 127
Glen Rose, Tx., U.S. C4 120
Glens Falls, N.Y., U.S. B7 109
Glen Ullin, N.D., U.S. C4 111
Glenview, Il., U.S. h9 90
Glenview Naval Air Station, mil., Il., U.S. h9 90
Glenville, Mn., U.S. G5 100
Glenville, W.V., U.S. C4 125
Glenwood, Newf., Can. D4 72
Glenwood, Ar., U.S. C2 81
Glenwood, Ga., U.S. D4 87
Glenwood, Ia., U.S. C2 92
Glenwood, Mn., U.S. E3 100
Glenwood, Va., U.S. D3 123
Glenwood City, Wi., U.S. C1 126
Glenwood Springs, Co., U.S. B3 83
Glidden, Ia., U.S. B3 92
Glide, Or., U.S. D3 114
Glina, Cro. D11 14
Gliwice (Gleiwitz), Pol. E18 8
Globe, Az., U.S. D5 80
Gloggnitz, Aus. H15 8
Gloster, Ms., U.S. D2 101
Gloucester, Ont., Can. h12 73
Gloucester, Eng., U.K. J10 7
Gloucester, Ma., U.S. A6 98
Gloucester, Va., U.S. C6 123
Gloucester, co., N.J., U.S. D2 107
Gloucester, co., Va., U.S. C6 123
Gloucester City, N.J., U.S. D2 107
Gloucester Point, Va., U.S. C6 123
Glouster, Oh., U.S. C3 112
Glover Island, i., Newf., Can. D3 72
Gloversville, N.Y., U.S. B6 109
Glovertown, Newf., Can. D4 72
Gloverville, S.C., U.S. E4 117
Gluck, S.C., U.S. C2 117
Glücksburg, Ger. A9 8
Glückstadt, Ger. B9 8
Glyndon, Md., U.S. B4 97
Glyndon, Mn., U.S. D2 100
Glynn, co., Ga., U.S. E5 87
Gmünd, Aus. G14 8
Gmunden, Aus. H13 8
Gnadenhutten, Oh., U.S. B4 112
Gnarp, Swe. E11 6
Gniezno, Pol. C17 8
Gnjilane, Yugo. G5 16
Gō, stm., Japan H5 30
Goa, ter., India E2 37
Goat Island, i., R.I., U.S. F5 116
Goat Mountain, mtn., Mt., U.S. C3 103
Goat Rock Dam, U.S. C4 78
Goba, Eth. G3 46
Gobabis, Nmb. F3 44
Gobi, des., Asia C7 26
Gobles, Mi., U.S. F5 99
Godāvari, stm., India D6 37
Goddard, Ks., U.S. E6 93
Goderich, Ont., Can. D3 73
Godfrey, Il., U.S. E3 90
Godhavn, Grnld. C22 66
Godhra, India I5 38
Godoy Cruz, Arg. C3 56
Gods, stm., Man., Can. A5 70
Gods Lake, l., Man., Can. B4 70
Godthåb, Grnld. D22 66
Godwin Austen see K2, mtn., Asia C7 38
Goéland, Lac au, l., Que., Can. G17 66
Goélands, Lac aux, l., Que., Can. E20 66
Goff Creek, stm., Ok., U.S. e9 113
Goffstown, N.H., U.S. D3 106
Gogebic, co., Mi., U.S. n12 99
Gogebic, Lake, l., Mi., U.S. m12 99
Goiana, Braz. G9 54
Goiânia, Braz. D4 57
Goiás, Braz. C3 57
Gojra, Pak. E5 38
Gokāk, India D3 37
Gökçeada, i., Tur. I9 16
Gol'čicha, Russia C10 24
Golconda, Il., U.S. F5 90
Golconda, Nv., U.S. C4 105
Gold Bar, Wa., U.S. B4 124
Gold Beach, Or., U.S. E2 114
Golden, B.C., Can. D9 69
Golden, Co., U.S. B5 83
Golden City, Mo., U.S. D3 102
Goldendale, Wa., U.S. D5 124
Golden Gate Bridge, Ca., U.S. h7 82
Golden Gate National Recreation Area, Ca., U.S. h7 82
Golden Hinde, mtn., B.C., Can. E5 69
Golden Meadow, La., U.S. E5 95
Golden Spike National Historic Site, hist., Ut., U.S. B3 121
Golden Valley, Mn., U.S. n12 100
Golden Valley, co., Mt., U.S. D7 103
Golden Valley, co., N.D., U.S. B2 111
Goldfield, Ia., U.S. B4 92
Goldfield, Nv., U.S. F4 105
Gold Hill, Or., U.S. E3 114
Goldsboro, N.C., U.S. B5 110
Goldsby, Ok., U.S. B4 113
Goldthwaite, Tx., U.S. D3 120
Goleta, Ca., U.S. E4 82
Golf Manor, Oh., U.S. o13 112
Goliad, Tx., U.S. E4 120
Goliad, co., Tx., U.S. E4 120
Golspie, Scot., U.K. D9 7
Gomati, stm., India G9 38
Gombe, stm., Tan. B6 44
Gomel', Bela. I14 18
Gomera, i., Spain C2 42
Gómez Palacio, Mex. E8 62
Gonābād, Iran K9 22
Gonaïves, Haiti E11 64
Gonam, Russia F20 24
Gonam, stm., Russia F28 24
Gonâve, Golfe de la, b., Haiti E11 64
Gonâve, Île de la, i., Haiti E11 64
Gonda, India G9 38
Gondal, India J4 38
Gonder, Eth. F2 46
Gondia, India B6 37
Gondomar, Port. D3 12
Gondrecourt-le-Château, Fr. D12 10
Gönen, Tur. I11 16
Gōnoura, Japan I2 30
Gonzales, Ca., U.S. D3 82
Gonzales, La., U.S. D5 95
Gonzales, Tx., U.S. E4 120
Gonzales, co., Tx., U.S. E4 120
Gonzalez, Fl., U.S. u14 86
Goochland, co., Va., U.S. C5 123
Goode, Mount, mtn., Ak., U.S. g18 79
Goodfellow Air Force Base, mil., Tx., U.S. D2 120
Good Hope, Cape of, c., S. Afr. H3 44
Good Hope Mountain, mtn., B.C., Can. D5 69
Goodhue, co., Mn., U.S. F6 100
Gooding, Id., U.S. G4 89
Gooding, co., Id., U.S. F4 89
Goodland, In., U.S. C3 91
Goodland, Ks., U.S. C2 93
Goodlettsville, Tn., U.S. g10 119
Goodman, Ms., U.S. C4 101
Goodman, Mo., U.S. E3 102
Good Pine, La., U.S. C3 95
Goodsprings, Nv., U.S. H6 105
Goodview, Mn., U.S. F7 100
Goodwater, Al., U.S. B3 78
Goodwell, Ok., U.S. e9 113
Goodyear, Az., U.S. D3 80
Goole, Eng., U.K. H12 7
Goondiwindi, Austl. E10 50
Goose, stm., N.D., U.S. B8 111
Goose Bay, b., Newf., Can. B1 72
Gooseberry Creek, stm., Wy., U.S. B4 127
Goose Creek, S.C., U.S. F7 117
Goose Creek, stm., U.S. G5 89
Goose Creek, stm., Va., U.S. C3 123
Goose Creek Reservoir, res., S.C., U.S. k11 117
Goose Lake, l., U.S. B3 82
Goose Pond, l., N.H., U.S. C2 106
Göppingen, Ger. G9 8
Gorakhpur, India G10 38
Gorda, Punta, c., Cuba C6 64
Gordil, Cen. Afr. Rep. G10 42
Gordo, Al., U.S. B2 78
Gordon, Ga., U.S. D3 87
Gordon, Ne., U.S. B3 104
Gordon, co., Ga., U.S. B2 87
Gordonsville, Tn., U.S. C8 119
Gordonsville, Va., U.S. B4 123
Gore, Eth. G2 46
Gore, N.Z. G2 52
Gore, Ok., U.S. B6 113
Gore Bay, Ont., Can. B2 73
Gore Point, c., Ak., U.S. h16 79
Gore Range, mts., Co., U.S. B4 83
Goreville, Il., U.S. F5 90
Gorey, Ire. I6 7
Gorgān, Iran J8 22
Gorge High Dam, Wa., U.S. A4 124
Gorham, Me., U.S. E2 96
Gorham, N.H., U.S. B4 106
Gorinchem, Neth. D4 8
Gorizia, Italy D8 14
Gorki, Bela. G13 18
Gorki see Nižnij Novgorod, Russia E27 18
Gorkovskoje Vodochranilišče, res., Russia D26 18
Görlitz, Ger. B13 8
Gorman, Tx., U.S. C3 120
Gornja Radgona, Slo. C10 14
Gorno-Altajsk, Russia G11 24
Gorodec, Russia E26 18
Gorontalo, Indon. E7 32
Gort, Ire. H4 7
Gorzów Wielkopolski (Landsberg an der Warthe), Pol. C15 8
Goshen, In., U.S. A6 91
Goshen, N.Y., U.S. D6 109
Goshen, Oh., U.S. C1 112
Goshen, co., Wy., U.S. D8 127
Goshute Indian Reservation, U.S. D7 105
Goshute Lake, l., Nv., U.S. C7 105
Goshute Mountains, mts., Nv., U.S. C7 105
Goslar, Ger. D10 8
Gosper, co., Ne., U.S. D6 104
Gosport, In., U.S. F4 91
Göteborg (Gothenburg), Swe. H8 6
Gotemba, Japan G11 30
Gotha, Ger. E10 8
Gothenburg, Ne., U.S. D5 104
Gothenburg see Göteborg, Swe. H8 6
Gotland, i., Swe. H12 6
Gotō-rettō, is., Japan J1 30
Göttingen, Ger. D9 8
Gouda, Neth. C4 8
Gouin, Réservoir, res., Que., Can. k12 74
Goulburn, Austl. F9 50
Goulburn Islands, is., Austl. B6 50
Gould, Ar., U.S. D4 81
Goulding, Fl., U.S. u14 86
Gould Island, i., R.I., U.S. E5 116
Goulds, Fl., U.S. s13 86
Gourdon, Fr. H8 10
Gouré, Niger F8 42
Gourin, Fr. D3 10
Gournay-en-Bray, Fr. C8 10
Gouverneur, N.Y., U.S. f9 109
Gove, co., Ks., U.S. D3 93
Governador Valadares, Braz. E8 57
Governors Harbour, Bah. B9 64
Govind Balabh Pant Sāgar, res., India H10 38
Govind Sāgar, res., India E7 38
Gowanda, N.Y., U.S. C2 109
Gower, Mo., U.S. B3 102
Gowmal (Gumal), stm., Asia D3 38
Gowmal Kalay, Afg. D3 38
Gowrie, Ia., U.S. B3 92
Goya, Arg. B5 56
Gozo see Għawdex, i., Malta M9 14
Graaff-Reinet, S. Afr. H4 44
Grabill, In., U.S. B8 91
Grace, Id., U.S. G7 89
Graceville, Fl., U.S. u16 86
Graceville, Mn., U.S. E2 100
Gracewood, Ga., U.S. C4 87
Gracias a Dios, Cabo, c., N.A. G6 64
Gradaús, Braz. E8 54
Gradaús, Serra dos, plat., Braz. E8 54
Grado, Italy D8 14
Grady, co., Ga., U.S. F2 87
Grady, co., Ok., U.S. C4 113
Graettinger, Ia., U.S. A3 92
Grafton, Austl. E10 50
Grafton, Il., U.S. E3 90
Grafton, Ma., U.S. B4 98
Grafton, N.D., U.S. A8 111
Grafton, Oh., U.S. A3 112
Grafton, Va., U.S. h15 123
Grafton, W.V., U.S. B4 125
Grafton, Wi., U.S. E6 126
Grafton, co., N.H., U.S. C3 106
Grafton, Cape, c., Austl. C9 50
Graham, N.C., U.S. A3 110
Graham, Tx., U.S. C3 120
Graham, co., Az., U.S. E5 80
Graham, co., Ks., U.S. C4 93
Graham, co., N.C., U.S. f9 110
Graham, Lake, res., Tx., U.S. C3 120
Graham, Mount, mtn., Az., U.S. E6 80
Graham Island, i., B.C., Can. C1 69
Graham Lake, l., Me., U.S. D4 96
Graham Moore, Cape, c., N.W. Ter., Can. B17 66
Grahamstown, S. Afr. H5 44
Grahn, Ky., U.S. B6 94
Grainger, co., Tn., U.S. C10 119
Grain Valley, Mo., U.S. B3 102
Grajaú, Braz. E9 54
Gramat, Fr. H8 10
Grambling, La., U.S. B3 95
Gramercy, La., U.S. h10 95
Grammichele, Italy L9 14
Grampian Mountains, mts., Scot., U.K. E8 7
Granada, Col. F6 58
Granada, Nic. I5 64
Granada, Spain H8 12
Granard, Ire. H5 7
Granbury, Tx., U.S. C4 120
Granby, Que., Can. D5 74
Granby, Co., U.S. A5 83
Granby, Ct., U.S. B4 84
Granby, Mo., U.S. E3 102
Granby, Lake, res., Co., U.S. A5 83
Gran Canaria, i., Spain p25 13a
Gran Chaco, pl., S.A. A4 56
Grand, co., Co., U.S. A4 83
Grand, co., Ut., U.S. E6 121
Grand, stm., Ont., Can. D4 73
Grand, stm., Mi., U.S. E5 99
Grand, stm., Mo., U.S. A3 102
Grand, stm., Oh., U.S. A4 112
Grand, stm., S.D., U.S. B4 118
Grandas, Spain B5 12
Grand Bahama, i., Bah. A8 64
Grand Bank, Newf., Can. E4 72
Grand-Bassam, C. Iv. G5 42
Grand Bay, N.B., Can. D3 71
Grand Bay, Al., U.S. E1 78
Grand Bend, Ont., Can. D3 73
Grand Blanc, Mi., U.S. F7 99
Grand Caillou, La., U.S. E5 95
Grand Canal, Ire. H5 7
Grand Canal see Da Yunhe, China E10 26
Grand Canyon, Az., U.S. A3 80
Grand Canyon, val., Az., U.S. A3 80
Grand Canyon National Park, Az., U.S. B3 80
Grand Cayman, i., Cay. Is. E7 64
Grand Centre, Alta., Can. B5 68
Grand Coteau, La., U.S. D3 95
Grand Coulee, Wa., U.S. B6 124
Grand Coulee Dam, Wa., U.S. B6 124
Grande, stm., Bol. G6 54
Grande, stm., Braz. E3 57
Grande, Bahía, b., Arg. G3 56
Grande, Boca, mth., Ven. C12 58
Grande, Ilha, i., Braz. G6 57
Grande, Ilha, i., Braz. G1 57
Grande, Rio (Bravo del Norte), stm., N.A. F7 76
Grande-Anse, N.B., Can. B4 71
Grande Cache, Alta., Can. C1 68
Grande Comore, i., Com. D8 44
Grande de Matagalpa, stm., Nic. H5 64
Grande de Santiago, Río, stm., Mex. G7 62
Grande do Gurupá, Ilha, i., Braz. D8 54
Grand-Entrée, Que., Can. B8 71
Grande Prairie, Alta., Can. B1 68
Grand Erg de Bilma, des., Niger E8 42
Grand Erg Occidental, des., Alg. B6 42
Grand Erg Oriental, des., Alg. B7 42
Grande rivière de la Baleine, stm., Que., Can. g11 74
Grande Ronde, stm., U.S. C8 124
Grandes, Salinas, pl., Arg. B4 56
Grandes-Bergeronnes, Que., Can. A8 74
Grande-Terre, i., Guad. F17 64
Grand Falls (Grand-Sault), N.B., Can. B2 71
Grand Falls, wtfl, Me., U.S. C5 96
Grand Falls [-Windsor], Newf., Can. D4 72

Name — Map Ref — Page

Grandfather Mountain, mtn., N.C., U.S. A1 110
Grandfield, Ok., U.S. C3 113
Grand Forks, B.C., Can. E8 69
Grand Forks, N.D., U.S. B8 111
Grand Forks, co., N.D., U.S. B8 111
Grand Forks Air Force Base, mil., N.D., U.S. B8 111
Grand-Fougeray, Fr. E5 10
Grand Harbour, N.B., Can. E3 71
Grand Haven, Mi., U.S. E4 99
Grand Island, Ne., U.S. D7 104
Grand Island, i., La., U.S. D6 95
Grand Island, i., Mi., U.S. B4 99
Grand Isle, La., U.S. E6 95
Grand Isle, co., Vt., U.S. B2 122
Grand Isle, i., La., U.S. E6 95
Grand Junction, Co., U.S. B2 83
Grand Junction, Ia., U.S. B3 92
Grand Lake, l., N.B., Can. D3 71
Grand Lake, l., Newf., Can. D3 72
Grand Lake, l., La., U.S. E6 95
Grand Lake, l., La., U.S. E3 95
Grand Lake, l., Mi., U.S. C7 99
Grand Lake, l., Oh., U.S. B1 112
Grand Lake Matagamon, l., Me., U.S. B4 96
Grand Lake Seboeis, l., Me., U.S. B4 96
Grand Ledge, Mi., U.S. F6 99
Grand Manan Island, i., N.B., Can. E3 71
Grand Marais, Mn., U.S. k9 100
Grand Meadow, Mn., U.S. G6 100
Grand-Mère, Que., Can. C5 74
Grand Mound, Ia., U.S. C7 92
Grand Portage Indian Reservation, Mn., U.S. k10 100
Grand Portage National Monument, Mn., U.S. h10 100
Grand Prairie, Tx., U.S. n10 120
Grand Rapids, Mi., U.S. F5 99
Grand Rapids, Mn., U.S. C5 100
Grand Rapids, Oh., U.S. f6 112
Grand Rivière de la Baleine, stm., Que., Can. E17 66
Grand-Saint-Bernard, Tunnel du, Eur. G14 10
Grand Saline, Tx., U.S. C5 120
Grand Terre Islands, is., La., U.S. E6 95
Grand Teton, mtn., Wy., U.S. C2 127
Grand Teton National Park, Wy., U.S. C2 127
Grand Tower, Il., U.S. F4 90
Grand Traverse, co., Mi., U.S. D5 99
Grand Traverse Bay, b., Mi., U.S. C5 99
Grand Turk, T./C. Is. D12 64
Grand Valley, Ont., Can. D4 73
Grandview, Man., Can. D1 70
Grandview, In., U.S. I4 91
Grandview, Mo., U.S. C3 102
Grandview, Wa., U.S. C6 124
Grandview Heights, Oh., U.S. m10 112
Grandville, Mi., U.S. F5 99
Grandy, N.C., U.S. A7 110
Granger, In., U.S. A5 91
Granger, Ia., U.S. C4 92
Granger, Tx., U.S. D4 120
Granger, Wa., U.S. C5 124
Grangeville, Id., U.S. D2 89
Granisle, B.C., Can. B4 69
Granite, Ok., U.S. C2 113
Granite, co., Mt., U.S. D3 103
Granite City, Il., U.S. E3 90
Granite Falls, Mn., U.S. F3 100
Granite Falls, N.C., U.S. B1 110
Granite Falls, Wa., U.S. A4 124
Granite Lake, res., Newf., Can. D3 72
Granite Mountain, mtn., Ak., U.S. B7 79
Granite Mountains, mts., Az., U.S. E2 80
Granite Mountains, mts., Wy., U.S. D5 127
Granite Pass, Wy., U.S. B5 127
Granite Peak, mtn., Mt., U.S. E7 103
Granite Peak, mtn., Nv., U.S. C2 105
Granite Peak, mtn., Nv., U.S. B4 105
Granite Peak, mtn., Ut., U.S. C2 121
Granite Peak, mtn., Ut., U.S. E3 121
Granite Peak, mtn., Wy., U.S. D4 127
Granite Quarry, N.C., U.S. B2 110
Granite Range, mts., Nv., U.S. C2 105
Graniteville, S.C., U.S. D4 117
Graniteville, Vt., U.S. C4 122
Granollers, Spain D14 12
Grant, Al., U.S. A3 78
Grant, Mi., U.S. E5 99
Grant, Ne., U.S. D4 104
Grant, co., Ar., U.S. C3 81
Grant, co., In., U.S. D6 91
Grant, co., Ks., U.S. E2 93
Grant, co., Ky., U.S. B5 94
Grant, co., La., U.S. C3 95
Grant, co., Mn., U.S. E2 100
Grant, co., Ne., U.S. C4 104
Grant, co., N.M., U.S. E1 108
Grant, co., N.D., U.S. C4 111
Grant, co., Ok., U.S. A4 113
Grant, co., Or., U.S. C7 114
Grant, co., S.D., U.S. B8 118
Grant, co., Wa., U.S. B6 124
Grant, co., W.V., U.S. B5 125
Grant, co., Wi., U.S. F3 126
Grant, Mount, mtn., Nv., U.S. E3 105
Grant City, Mo., U.S. A3 102
Grantham, Eng., U.K. I12 7
Grant Park, Il., U.S. B6 90
Grant Range, mts., Nv., U.S. E6 105
Grants, N.M., U.S. B2 108
Grantsburg, Wi., U.S. C1 126
Grants Pass, Or., U.S. E3 114
Grantsville, Ut., U.S. C3 121
Grantsville, W.V., U.S. C3 125
Grant Town, W.V., U.S. B4 125
Grantville, Ga., U.S. C2 87
Granville, Fr. D5 10
Granville, Il., U.S. B4 90
Granville, N.Y., U.S. B7 109
Granville, Oh., U.S. B3 112
Granville, W.V., U.S. h11 125
Granville, co., N.C., U.S. A4 110
Granville Lake, l., Man., Can. A1 70
Granvin, Nor. F6 6
Grapeland, Tx., U.S. D5 120
Grapeview, Wa., U.S. B3 124
Grapevine, Tx., U.S. C4 120
Grapevine Lake, res., Tx., U.S. n9 120
Grapevine Peak, mtn., Nv., U.S. G4 105
Gras, Lac de, l., N.W. Ter., Can. D10 66
Grasonville, Md., U.S. C5 97
Grass, stm., Man., Can. B2 70
Grass, stm., N.Y., U.S. f9 109
Grasse, Fr. I13 10
Grass Lake, Il., U.S. h8 90
Grass Lake, Mi., U.S. F6 99
Grass Lake, l., Il., U.S. h8 90
Grass Valley, Ca., U.S. C3 82
Grassy Brook, stm., Vt., U.S. E3 122
Grassy Lake, l., La., U.S. k9 95
Grates Point, c., Newf., Can. D5 72
Gratiot, co., Mi., U.S. E6 99
Gratis, Oh., U.S. C1 112
Grave Creek, stm., W.V., U.S. g8 125
Gravelly Branch, stm., De., U.S. F4 85
Gravelly Range, mts., Mt., U.S. E4 103
Gravenhurst, Ont., Can. C5 73
Grave Peak, mtn., Id., U.S. C4 89
Graves, co., Ky., U.S. f9 94
Gravette, Ar., U.S. A1 81
Gravina in Puglia, Italy I11 14
Gray, Fr. E12 10
Gray, Ga., U.S. C3 87
Gray, Ky., U.S. D5 94
Gray, La., U.S. k10 95
Gray, Me., U.S. g7 96
Gray, co., Ks., U.S. E3 93
Gray, co., Tx., U.S. B2 120
Grayback Mountain, mtn., Or., U.S. E3 114
Gray Court, S.C., U.S. B3 117
Grayland, Wa., U.S. C1 124
Grayling, Mi., U.S. D6 99
Graylyn Crest, De., U.S. A3 85
Grays Harbor, co., Wa., U.S. B2 124
Grays Harbor, b., Wa., U.S. C1 124
Grayslake, Il., U.S. A5 90
Grays Lake, sw., Id., U.S. F7 89
Grayson, Ky., U.S. B7 94
Grayson, co., Ky., U.S. C3 94
Grayson, co., Tx., U.S. C4 120
Grayson, co., Va., U.S. D1 123
Grayson Lake, res., Ky., U.S. B7 94
Grays Peak, mtn., Co., U.S. B5 83
Gray Summit, Mo., U.S. g12 102
Graysville, Al., U.S. f7 78
Graysville, Tn., U.S. D8 119
Grayville, Il., U.S. E5 90
Graz, Aus. H15 8
Gr'azi, Russia I22 18
Great Abaco, i., Bah. A9 64
Great Artesian Basin, Austl. D8 50
Great Australian Bight, Austl. F5 50
Great Averill Pond, l., Vt., U.S. B5 122
Great Barrier Reef, rf., Austl. C9 50
Great Barrington, Ma., U.S. B1 98
Great Basin National Park, Nv., U.S. E7 105
Great Bay, b., N.H., U.S. D5 106
Great Bay, b., N.J., U.S. D4 107
Great Bear Lake, l., N.W. Ter., Can. C9 66
Great Bend, Ks., U.S. D5 93
Great Captain Island, i., Ct., U.S. F1 84
Great Channel, strt., Asia K3 34
Great Dismal Swamp, sw., U.S. D6 123
Great Divide Basin, Wy., U.S. E4 127
Great Dividing Range, mts., Austl. D9 50
Great East Lake, l., U.S. C5 106
Great Egg Harbor, stm., N.J., U.S. D3 107
Greater Antilles, is., N.A. D10 64
Greater Sunda Islands, is., Asia F4 32
Great Exuma, i., Bah. C10 64
Great Falls, Mt., U.S. C5 103
Great Falls, S.C., U.S. B6 117
Great Falls, wtfl, Md., U.S. B3 97
Great Falls Dam, Tn., U.S. D6 119
Great Guana Cay, i., Bah. B9 64
Great Himalaya Range, mts., Asia F10 38
Greathouse Peak, mtn., Mt., U.S. D7 103
Great Inagua, i., Bah. D11 64
Great Indian Desert (Thar Desert), des., Asia G4 38
Great Island, spit, Ma., U.S. C7 98
Great Island, i., N.C., U.S. B6 110
Great Karroo, plat., S. Afr. H4 44
Great Lakes Naval Training Center, mil., Il., U.S. h9 90
Great Miami, stm., U.S. C1 112
Great Misery Island, i., Ma., U.S. f12 98
Great Moose Lake, l., Me., U.S. D3 96
Great Neck, N.Y., U.S. h13 109
Great Nicobar, i., India K2 34
Great Pee Dee, stm., U.S. D9 117
Great Plain of the Koukdjuak, pl., N.W. Ter., Can. C18 66
Great Plains, pl., N.A. E10 61
Great Point, c., Ma., U.S. D7 98
Great Ruaha, stm., Tan. C7 44
Great Sacandaga Lake, l., N.Y., U.S. C6 109
Great Salt Lake, l., Ut., U.S. B3 121
Great Salt Lake Desert, des., Ut., U.S. C2 121
Great Salt Plains Lake, res., Ok., U.S. A3 113
Great Salt Pond, b., R.I., U.S. h7 116
Great Sand Dunes National Monument, Co., U.S. D5 83
Great Sandy Desert, des., Austl. D4 50
Great Slave Lake, l., N.W. Ter., Can. D10 66
Great Smoky Mountains, mts., U.S. B8 119
Great Smoky Mountains National Park, U.S. B8 119
Great Swamp, sw., R.I., U.S. F3 116
Great Victoria Desert, des., Austl. E5 50
Great Village, N.S., Can. D6 71
Great Wass Island, i., Me., U.S. D5 96
Great Yarmouth, Eng., U.K. I14 7
Greece, N.Y., U.S. B3 109
Greece, ctry., Eur. H12 4
Greeley, Co., U.S. A6 83
Greeley, Pa., U.S. D12 115
Greeley, co., Ks., U.S. D2 93
Greeley, co., Ne., U.S. C7 104
Green, Or., U.S. D3 114
Green, co., Ky., U.S. C4 94
Green, co., Wi., U.S. F4 126
Green, stm., U.S. D5 76
Green, stm., U.S. A1 83
Green, stm., U.S. F3 122
Green, stm., Il., U.S. B4 90
Green, stm., Ky., U.S. C2 94
Green, stm., Wa., U.S. B3 124
Green Acres, De., U.S. h8 85
Greenacres, Wa., U.S. B8 124
Greenacres City, Fl., U.S. F6 86
Greenback, Tn., U.S. D9 119
Green Bay, Wi., U.S. D6 126
Green Bay, b., U.S. D3 99
Greenbelt, Md., U.S. C4 97
Greenbriar, Va., U.S. g12 123
Greenbrier, Ar., U.S. B3 81
Green Brier, Tn., U.S. A5 119
Greenbrier, co., W.V., U.S. D4 125
Greenbrier, stm., W.V., U.S. D4 125
Greenbush, Mn., U.S. B2 100
Greencastle, In., U.S. E4 91
Greencastle, Pa., U.S. G6 115
Green City, Mo., U.S. A5 102
Green Cove Springs, Fl., U.S. C5 86
Greendale, In., U.S. F8 91
Greendale, Wi., U.S. F6 126
Greene, Ia., U.S. B5 92
Greene, N.Y., U.S. C5 109
Greene, co., Al., U.S. C1 78
Greene, co., Ar., U.S. A5 81
Greene, co., Ga., U.S. C3 87
Greene, co., Il., U.S. D3 90
Greene, co., In., U.S. F4 91
Greene, co., Ia., U.S. B3 92
Greene, co., Ms., U.S. D5 101
Greene, co., Mo., U.S. D4 102
Greene, co., N.Y., U.S. C6 109
Greene, co., N.C., U.S. B5 110
Greene, co., Oh., U.S. C2 112
Greene, co., Pa., U.S. G1 115
Greene, co., Tn., U.S. C11 119
Greene, co., Va., U.S. B4 123
Greeneville, Tn., U.S. C11 119
Green Fall, stm., U.S. F1 116
Greenfield, Ca., U.S. D3 82
Greenfield, Il., U.S. D3 90
Greenfield, In., U.S. E6 91
Greenfield, Ia., U.S. C3 92
Greenfield, Ma., U.S. A2 98
Greenfield, Mo., U.S. D4 102
Greenfield, N.H., U.S. E3 106
Greenfield, Oh., U.S. C2 112
Greenfield, Tn., U.S. A3 119
Greenfield, Wi., U.S. n12 126
Greenfield Plaza, Ia., U.S. e8 92
Green Forest, Ar., U.S. A2 81
Green Harbor, Ma., U.S. B6 98
Green Hill Pond, l., R.I., U.S. G3 116
Greenhills, Oh., U.S. n12 112
Green Lake, Wi., U.S. E5 126
Green Lake, co., Wi., U.S. E4 126
Green Lake, l., Me., U.S. D4 96
Green Lake, l., Wi., U.S. E5 126
Greenland, Ar., U.S. B1 81
Greenland, N.H., U.S. D5 106
Greenland, dep., N.A. B16 61
Greenland Sea B13 128
Greenlee, co., Az., U.S. D6 80
Green Lookout Mountain, mtn., Wa., U.S. D3 124
Green Mountain, mtn., Wy., U.S. D5 127
Green Mountain Reservoir, res., Co., U.S. B4 83
Green Mountains, mts., Vt., U.S. F2 122
Greenock, Scot., U.K. F8 7
Greenock, Pa., U.S. F2 115
Green Peter Lake, res., Or., U.S. C4 114
Green Pond, Al., U.S. B2 78
Green Pond, l., N.J., U.S. A4 107
Greenport, N.Y., U.S. m16 109
Green River, Ut., U.S. E5 121
Green River, Wy., U.S. E3 127
Green River Lake, res., Ky., U.S. C4 94
Green River Lock and Dam, U.S. I2 91
Green River Reservoir, res., Vt., U.S. B3 122
Green Rock, Il., U.S. B3 90
Greensboro, Al., U.S. C2 78
Greensboro, Ga., U.S. C3 87
Greensboro, Md., U.S. C6 97
Greensboro, N.C., U.S. A3 110
Greensburg, In., U.S. F7 91
Greensburg, Ks., U.S. E4 93
Greensburg, Ky., U.S. C4 94
Greensburg, Pa., U.S. F2 115
Greens Peak, mtn., Az., U.S. C6 80
Green Springs, Oh., U.S. A2 112
Greensville, co., Va., U.S. D5 123
Green Swamp, sw., N.C., U.S. C4 110
Greentown, In., U.S. D6 91
Greenup, Il., U.S. D5 90
Greenup, Ky., U.S. B7 94
Greenup, co., Ky., U.S. B7 94
Green Valley, Az., U.S. F5 80
Greenview, Il., U.S. C4 90
Greenville, Lib. G4 42
Greenville, Al., U.S. D3 78
Greenville, Ca., U.S. B3 82
Greenville, De., U.S. A3 85
Greenville, Ga., U.S. C2 87
Greenville, Il., U.S. E4 90
Greenville, Ky., U.S. C2 94
Greenville, Me., U.S. C3 96
Greenville, Mi., U.S. E5 99
Greenville, Ms., U.S. B2 101
Greenville, N.H., U.S. E3 106
Greenville, N.C., U.S. B5 110
Greenville, Oh., U.S. B1 112
Greenville, Pa., U.S. D1 115
Greenville, R.I., U.S. C3 116
Greenville, S.C., U.S. B3 117
Greenville, Tx., U.S. C4 120
Greenville, co., S.C., U.S. B3 117
Greenville Creek, stm., Oh., U.S. B1 112
Greenville Junction, Me., U.S. C3 96
Greenwich, Ct., U.S. E1 84
Greenwich, N.Y., U.S. B7 109
Greenwich, Oh., U.S. A3 112
Greenwich Bay, b., R.I., U.S. D4 116
Greenwich Point, c., Ct., U.S. E1 84
Greenwood, B.C., Can. E8 69
Greenwood, Ar., U.S. B1 81
Greenwood, De., U.S. E3 85
Greenwood, In., U.S. E5 91
Greenwood, La., U.S. B2 95
Greenwood, Ms., U.S. B3 101
Greenwood, Mo., U.S. k11 102
Greenwood, Pa., U.S. E5 115
Greenwood, S.C., U.S. C3 117
Greenwood, Wi., U.S. D3 126
Greenwood, co., Ks., U.S. E7 93
Greenwood, co., S.C., U.S. C3 117
Greenwood, Lake, res., In., U.S. G4 91
Greenwood, Lake, res., S.C., U.S. C4 117
Greenwood Lake, N.Y., U.S. D6 109
Greenwood Lake, l., U.S. A4 107
Greenwood Lake, l., Mn., U.S. C7 100
Greer, S.C., U.S. B3 117
Greer, co., Ok., U.S. C2 113
Greers Ferry Lake, res., Ar., U.S. B3 81
Greeson, Lake, res., Ar., U.S. C2 81
Gregg, co., Tx., U.S. C5 120
Gregory, S.D., U.S. D6 118
Gregory, co., S.D., U.S. D6 118
Greifswald, Ger. A13 8
Greilickville, Mi., U.S. D5 99
Greiz, Ger. E12 8
Grenada, Ms., U.S. B4 101
Grenada, co., Ms., U.S. B4 101
Grenada, ctry., N.A. H17 64
Grenada Lake, res., Ms., U.S. B4 101
Grenadine Islands, is., N.A. H17 64
Grenchen, Switz. E14 10
Grenoble, Fr. G12 10
Grenville, Que., Can. D3 74
Grenville, Cape, c., Austl. B8 50
Grenville, Point, c., Wa., U.S. B1 124
Gresham, Or., U.S. B4 114
Gresik, Indon. m16 33a
Gretna, Man., Can. E3 70
Gretna, Fl., U.S. B2 86
Gretna, La., U.S. E5 95
Gretna, Ne., U.S. C9 104
Gretna, Va., U.S. D3 123
Greven, Ger. C7 8
Grevená, Grc. I5 16
Grevesmühlen, Ger. B11 8
Grey, stm., Newf., Can. E3 72
Greybull, Wy., U.S. B4 127
Greybull, stm., Wy., U.S. B4 127
Greylock, Mount, mtn., Ma., U.S. A1 98
Greymouth, N.Z. E3 52
Greys, stm., Wy., U.S. C2 127
Gridley, Ca., U.S. C3 82
Gridley, Il., U.S. C5 90
Griffin, Ga., U.S. C2 87
Griffiss Air Force Base, mil., N.Y., U.S. B5 109
Griffith, Austl. F9 50
Griffith, In., U.S. A3 91
Grifton, N.C., U.S. B5 110
Griggs, co., N.D., U.S. B7 111
Griggsville, Il., U.S. D3 90
Grik, Malay. L6 34
Grimes, Ia., U.S. C4 92
Grimes, co., Tx., U.S. D4 120
Grimmen, Ger. A13 8
Grimsby, Ont., Can. D5 73
Grimsby, Eng., U.K. H12 7
Grimselpass, Switz. F15 10
Grimshaw, Alta., Can. A2 68
Grimsley, Tn., U.S. C9 119
Grimstad, Nor. G7 6
Grindall Creek, Va., U.S. n18 123
Grinnell, Ia., U.S. C5 92
Grinnell Peninsula, pen., N.W. Ter., Can. A14 66
Gris-Nez, Cap, c., Fr. B8 10
Grissom Air Force Base, mil., In., U.S. C5 91
Griswold, Ia., U.S. C2 92
Grizzly Mountain, mtn., Id., U.S. B2 89
Grizzly Mountain, mtn., Or., U.S. C6 114
Grizzly Mountain, mtn., Wa., U.S. A7 124
Groais Island, i., Newf., Can. C4 72
Grodno, Bela. H6 18
Groesbeck, Tx., U.S. D4 120
Grombalia, Tun. M5 14
Gronau, Ger. C6 8
Grong, Nor. D9 6
Groningen, Neth. B6 8
Groom Lake, l., Nv., U.S. F6 105
Groom Range, mts., Nv., U.S. F6 105
Groote Eylandt, i., Austl. B7 50
Grootfontein, Nmb. E3 44
Gros Morne National Park, Newf., Can. D3 72
Grosse Isle Naval Air Station, mil., Mi., U.S. p15 99
Grossenhain, Ger. D13 8
Grosse Pointe, Mi., U.S. *p16 99
Grosse Pointe Park, Mi., U.S. p16 99
Grosse Pointe Woods, Mi., U.S. p16 99
Grosseto, Italy G6 14
Grossglockner, mtn., Aus. H12 8
Grossmont, Ca., U.S. o16 82
Gros Ventre, stm., Wy., U.S. C2 127
Gros Ventre Range, mts., Wy., U.S. C2 127
Groswater Bay, b., Newf., Can. F21 66
Groton, Ct., U.S. D7 84
Groton, N.Y., U.S. C4 109
Groton, S.D., U.S. B7 118
Groton Long Point, Ct., U.S. D7 84
Grottaglie, Italy I12 14
Grottaminarda, Italy H10 14
Grottoes, Va., U.S. B4 123
Grouse Creek, stm., Ut., U.S. B2 121
Grouse Creek Mountain, mtn., Id., U.S. E5 89
Grove, Ok., U.S. A7 113
Grove City, Fl., U.S. F4 86
Grove City, Oh., U.S. C2 112
Grove City, Pa., U.S. D1 115
Grove Hill, Al., U.S. D2 78
Groveland, Fl., U.S. D5 86
Groveland, Ma., U.S. A5 98
Grove Point, c., Md., U.S. B5 97
Groveport, Oh., U.S. C3 112
Grover City, Ca., U.S. E3 82
Groves, Tx., U.S. E6 120
Groveton, N.H., U.S. A3 106
Groveton, Tx., U.S. D5 120
Groveton, Va., U.S. g12 123
Groveton Gardens, Va., U.S. *B5 123
Grovetown, Ga., U.S. C4 87
Groveville, N.J., U.S. C3 107
Growler Peak, mtn., Az., U.S. E2 80
Groznyj, Russia I7 22
Grudziądz, Pol. B18 8
Gruetli-Laager, Tn., U.S. D8 119
Grulla, Tx., U.S. F3 120
Grundy, Va., U.S. e9 123
Grundy, co., Il., U.S. B5 90
Grundy, co., Ia., U.S. B5 92
Grundy, co., Mo., U.S. A4 102
Grundy, co., Tn., U.S. D8 119
Grundy Center, Ia., U.S. B5 92
Grunthal, Man., Can. E3 70
Gruver, Tx., U.S. A2 120
Guacanayabo, Golfo de, b., Cuba D9 64
Guachochic, Mex. D6 62
Guadalajara, Mex. G8 62
Guadalajara, Spain E8 12
Guadalcanal, i., Sol.Is. A11 50
Guadalquivir, stm., Spain H6 12
Guadalupe, Mex. E9 62
Guadalupe, Az., U.S. m9 80
Guadalupe, Ca., U.S. E3 82
Guadalupe, co., N.M., U.S. C5 108
Guadalupe, co., Tx., U.S. E4 120
Guadalupe Garzarón, Mex. E9 62
Guadalupe Mountains, mts., U.S. E5 108
Guadalupe Mountains National Park, Tx., U.S. o12 120
Guadalupe Peak, mtn., Tx., U.S. o12 120
Guadeloupe, dep., N.A. F17 64
Guadeloupe Passage, strt., N.A. F17 64
Guadiana, stm., Eur. H4 12
Guadix, Spain H8 12
Guafo, Isla, i., Chile E2 56
Guajará Mirim, Braz. F5 54
Gualeguaychú, Arg. C5 56
Gualicho, Salina, pl., Arg. E3 56
Guam, dep., Oc. F22 2
Guaminí, Arg. D4 56
Guamo, Col. E5 58
Guampí, Sierra de, mts., Ven. B5 54
Guanaja, Isla de, i., Hond. F5 64
Guanajuato, Mex. G9 62
Guanambi, Braz. C7 57
Guanare, Ven. C8 58
Guanarito, Ven. C8 58
Guanay, Cerro, mtn., Ven. E9 58
Guane, Cuba C5 64
Guang'an, China E8 26
Guangdong, prov., China G9 26
Guanghua, China E9 26
Guangxi Zhuang Zizhiqu, prov., China G8 26
Guangyuan, China E8 26
Guangzhou (Canton), China L2 28
Guano Lake, l., Or., U.S. E7 114
Guantánamo, Cuba D10 64
Guanxian, China E7 26
Guápiles, C.R. I6 64
Guaporé (Iténez), stm., S.A. F6 54
Guaqui, Bol. G5 54
Guarabira, Braz. E11 54
Guaranda, Ec. H3 58
Guarapuava, Braz. B6 56
Guaratinguetá, Braz. G6 57
Guarda, Port. E4 12
Guardo, Spain C7 12
Guárico, Embalse del, res., Ven. C9 58
Guarulhos, Braz. G5 57
Guarus, Braz. F8 57
Guasave, Mex. E5 62
Guasdualito, Ven. D7 58
Guatemala, Guat. G2 64
Guatemala, ctry., N.A. G2 64
Guaviare, stm., Col. F8 58
Guaxupé, Braz. F5 57
Guayama, P.R. F14 64
Guayaquil, Ec. I3 58
Guayaquil, Golfo de, b., S.A. I2 58
Guaymallén, Arg. C3 56
Guaymas, Mex. D4 62
Gubbio, Italy F7 14
Guben, Ger. D14 8
Guchengzi, China D7 26
Gūdalūr, India G4 37
Gudiyāttam, India F5 37
Gūdūr, India E5 37
Guebwiller, Fr. E14 10
Guelma, Alg. A7 42
Guelph, Ont., Can. D4 73
Guérande, Fr. E4 10
Guéret, Fr. F8 10
Guernsey, Wy., U.S. D8 127
Guernsey, co., Oh., U.S. B4 112
Guernsey, dep., Eur. C4 10
Gueydan, La., U.S. D3 95
Guga, Russia G21 24
Guibes, Nmb. G3 44
Güicán, Col. D6 58
Guichen, Fr. E5 10
Guiding, China A9 34
Guijuelo, Spain E6 12
Guilford, Ct., U.S. D5 84
Guilford, Me., U.S. C3 96
Guilford, co., N.C., U.S. A3 110
Guilin (Kweilin), China B11 34
Guillaumes, Fr. H13 10
Guimarães, Port. D3 12
Guin, Al., U.S. B2 78
Guinea, ctry., Afr. F3 42

Name — Map Ref — Page

Guinea, Gulf of, b., Afr. H6 42
Guinea-Bissau, ctry., Afr. F2 42
Güines, Cuba C6 64
Guingamp, Fr. D3 10
Güira de Melena, Cuba C6 64
Guiratinga, Braz. G8 54
Güiria, Ven. B11 58
Guixian, China C10 34
Guiyang (Kweiyang), China A9 34
Guizhou, prov., China F8 26
Gujarat, state, India I4 38
Gūjar Khān, Pak. D5 38
Gujrānwāla, Pak. D6 38
Gujrāt, Pak. D6 38
Gulbarga, India D4 37
Guledagudda, India D3 37
Gulf, co., Fl., U.S. C1 86
Gulf Gate Estates, Fl., U.S. E4 86
Gulf Islands National Seashore, U.S. E5 101
Gulfport, Fl., U.S. E4 86
Gulfport, Ms., U.S. E4 101
Gulf Shores, Al., U.S. E2 78
Gull Island, i., N.C., U.S. B7 110
Gullivan Bay, b., Fl., U.S. G5 86
Gull Lake, l., Alta., Can. C4 68
Gull Lake, l., Mn., U.S. D4 100
Güllük, Tur. L11 16
Gülpınar, Tur. J10 16
Gulu, Ug. H12 42
Gumal (Gowmal), stm., Asia D3 38
Gumboro, De., U.S. G4 85
Gummersbach, Ger. D7 8
Guna, India H7 38
Gunisao, stm., Man., Can. C3 70
Gunnarn, Swe. D11 6
Gunnison, Co., U.S. C4 83
Gunnison, Ms., U.S. B3 101
Gunnison, Ut., U.S. D4 121
Gunnison, co., Co., U.S. C3 83
Gunnison, stm., Co., U.S. C2 83
Gunnison, Mount, mtn., Co., U.S. C3 83
Gunpowder Neck, c., Md., U.S. B5 97
Gunpowder River, b., Md., U.S. B5 97
Guntakal, India E4 37
Gunter Air Force Base, mil., Al., U.S. C3 78
Guntersville, Al., U.S. A3 78
Guntersville Lake, res., Al., U.S. A3 78
Guntown, Ms., U.S. A5 101
Guntūr, India D6 37
Gunungsitoli, Indon. N4 34
Günzburg, Ger. G10 8
Gunzenhausen, Ger. F10 8
Gurdāspur, India D6 38
Gurdon, Ar., U.S. D2 81
Guri, Embalse, res., Ven. D11 58
Gurley, Al., U.S. A3 78
Gurnee, Il., U.S. h9 90
Gurnet Point, c., Ma., U.S. B6 98
Gurupi, Braz. F9 54
Gurupi, stm., Braz. D9 54
Gusau, Nig. F7 42
Gus'-Chrustal'nyj, Russia F23 18
Gusev, Russia G5 18
Gushi, China C4 28
Gushikawa, Japan y27 31b
Gusinoozersk, Russia G15 24
Guspini, Italy J3 14
Gustav Holm, Kap, c., Grnld. C26 66
Gustine, Ca., U.S. D3 82
Güstrow, Ger. B12 8
Gütersloh, Ger. D8 8
Guthrie, Ky., U.S. D2 94
Guthrie, Ok., U.S. B4 113
Guthrie, W.V., U.S. m12 125
Guthrie, co., Ia., U.S. C3 92
Guthrie Center, Ia., U.S. C3 92
Guttenberg, Ia., U.S. B6 92
Guttenberg, N.J., U.S. h8 107
Guyana, ctry., S.A. B7 54
Guyandotte, stm., W.V., U.S. C2 125
Guymon, Ok., U.S. e9 113
Guysborough, N.S., Can. D8 71
Guyton, Ga., U.S. D5 87
Güzelyurt Körfezi, b., N. Cyp. B3 40
Gwādar, Pak. D1 36
Gwai, Zimb. E5 44
Gwalior, India G8 38
Gwanda, Zimb. F5 44
Gweru, Zimb. E5 44
Gwinhurst, De., U.S. h8 85
Gwinn, Mi., U.S. B3 99
Gwinner, N.D., U.S. C8 111
Gwinnett, co., Ga., U.S. C2 87
Gwydyr Bay, b., Ak., U.S. A10 79
Gwynns Falls, stm., Md., U.S. g10 97
Gympie, Austl. E10 50
Gyöngyös, Hung. H19 8
Győr, Hung. H17 8
Gypsum, Co., U.S. B4 83

H

Haakon, co., S.D., U.S. C4 118
Haapajärvi, Fin. E15 6
Haapamäki, Fin. E15 6
Haar, Ger. G11 8
Haarlem, Neth. C4 8
Haast, N.Z. E2 52
Habersham, co., Ga., U.S. B3 87
Habiganj, Bngl. H14 38
Hachijō-jima, i., Japan E14 26
Hachinohe, Japan B14 30
Hachiōji, Japan G12 30
Hackberry, La., U.S. E2 95
Hackensack, N.J., U.S. B4 107
Hackensack, stm., N.J., U.S. h8 107
Hackettstown, N.J., U.S. B3 107
Hackleburg, Al., U.S. A2 78
Hadd, Ra's al-, c., Oman D6 46
Haddam, Ct., U.S. D5 84
Haddock, Ga., U.S. C3 87
Haddonfield, N.J., U.S. D2 107
Haddon Heights, N.J., U.S. D2 107
Hadejia, stm., Nig. F8 42
Hadera, Isr. C4 40
Haderslev, Den. I7 6
Hadīyah, Sau. Ar. C2 46
Hadjeb el Aïoun, Tun. N4 14
Hadley Bay, b., N.W. Ter., Can. B11 66
Hadley Lake, l., Me., U.S. D5 96
Hadlock, Wa., U.S. A3 124
Ha Dong, Viet. D8 34
Hadramawt, reg., Yemen E4 46
Haeju, N. Kor. D12 26
Hāfizābād, Pak. D5 38
Hafun, Ras, c., Som. F5 46
Hagan, Ga., U.S. D5 87
Hagemeister Island, i., Ak., U.S. D7 79
Hagen, Ger. D7 8
Hagerman, Id., U.S. G4 89
Hagerman, N.M., U.S. D5 108
Hagerstown, In., U.S. E7 91
Hagerstown, Md., U.S. A2 97
Hagfors, Swe. F9 6
Haggin, Mount, mtn., Mt., U.S. D3 103
Hagi, Japan H4 30
Ha Giang, Viet. C8 34
Hague, Sask., Can. E2 75
Hague, Cap de la, c., Fr. C5 10
Haguenau, Fr. D14 10
Hagues Peak, mtn., Co., U.S. A5 83
Ha Ha, Baie des, b., Que., Can. C2 72
Hahira, Ga., U.S. F3 87
Hahnville, La., U.S. E5 95
Haian, China C9 28
Haicheng, China C11 26
Hai Duong, Viet. D9 34
Haifa see Hefa, Isr. C4 40
Haikou, China D11 34
Haiku, Hi., U.S. C5 88
Hā'il, Sau. Ar. C3 46
Hailaer, China B10 26
Hailey, Id., U.S. F4 89
Haileybury, Ont., Can. p20 73
Haileyville, Ok., U.S. C6 113
Haimen, China G10 28
Haimen, China L5 28
Hainan, China H8 26
Hainan Dao, i., China E10 34
Haines, Ak., U.S. D12 79
Haines City, Fl., U.S. D5 86
Haines Junction, Yukon, Can. D5 66
Hainfeld, Aus. G15 8
Haining, China E9 28
Hai Phong, Viet. D9 34
Haiti (Haïti), ctry., N.A. E11 64
Haizhou, China A8 28
Hakodate, Japan r18 30a
Hāla, Pak. H3 38
Halab (Aleppo), Syria A5 40
Halā'ib, Sudan D13 42
Halawa, Cape, c., Hi., U.S. B5 88
Halawa Heights, Hi., U.S. g10 88
Halbā, Leb. B5 40
Halberstadt, Ger. D11 8
Halden, Nor. G8 6
Haldensleben, Ger. C11 8
Haldimand, Ont., Can. E5 73
Haldwāni, India F8 38
Hale, co., Al., U.S. C2 78
Hale, co., Tx., U.S. B2 120
Haleakala Crater, crat., Hi., U.S. C5 88
Haleakala National Park, Hi., U.S. C6 88
Hale Center, Tx., U.S. B2 120
Haleiwa, Hi., U.S. B3 88
Hales Corners, Wi., U.S. n11 126
Halethorpe, Md., U.S. B4 97
Haleyville, Al., U.S. A2 78
Half Moon Bay, Ca., U.S. k8 82
Halfway, Md., U.S. A2 97
Haliburton, Ont., Can. B6 73
Halibut Point, c., Ma., U.S. A6 98
Halifax, N.S., Can. E6 71
Halifax, Va., U.S. D4 123
Halifax, co., N.C., U.S. A5 110
Halifax, co., Va., U.S. D4 123
Halifax Bay, b., Austl. C9 50
Haliimaile, Hi., U.S. C5 88
Halkirk, Scot., U.K. C9 7
Hall, co., Ga., U.S. B3 87
Hall, co., Ne., U.S. D7 104
Hall, co., Tx., U.S. B2 120
Hallam Peak, mtn., B.C., Can. C8 69
Hallandale, Fl., U.S. G6 86
Halla-san, mtn., S. Kor. E12 26
Halle, Ger. D11 8
Hällefors, Swe. G10 6
Hallein, Aus. H13 8
Hallettsville, Tx., U.S. E4 120
Hallie, Wi., U.S. D2 126
Hall Island, i., Ak., U.S. C5 79
Hall Meadow Brook Reservoir, res., Ct., U.S. B3 84
Hall Mountain, mtn., Wa., U.S. A8 124
Hällnäs, Swe. D12 6
Hallock, Mn., U.S. B2 100
Hallowell, Me., U.S. D3 96
Hall Peninsula, pen., N.W. Ter., Can. D19 66
Halls, Tn., U.S. B2 119
Hallsberg, Swe. G10 6
Halls Creek, Austl. C5 50
Halls Creek, stm., Ut., U.S. F5 121
Halls Crossroads, Tn., U.S. m14 119
Halls Stream, stm., N.H., U.S. f7 106
Hallstavik, Swe. F12 6
Hallstead, Pa., U.S. C10 115
Hallsville, Mo., U.S. B5 102
Hallsville, Tx., U.S. C5 120
Halmahera, i., Indon. E8 32
Halmahera, Laut, Indon. F8 32
Halmstad, Swe. H9 6
Halsey, Or., U.S. C3 114
Hälsingborg see Helsingborg, Swe. H9 6
Halstad, Mn., U.S. C2 100
Halstead, Ks., U.S. E6 93
Haltern, Ger. D7 8
Haltiatunturi, mtn., Eur. B13 6
Halton Hills, Ont., Can. D5 73
Hamada, Japan H5 30
Hamadān, Iran B4 46
Hamāh, Syria B5 40
Hamamatsu, Japan H10 30
Hamar, Nor. F8 6
Hamblen, co., Tn., U.S. C10 119
Hamburg, Ger. B9 8
Hamburg, Ar., U.S. D4 81
Hamburg, Ia., U.S. D2 92
Hamburg, N.Y., U.S. C2 109
Hamburg, Pa., U.S. E10 115
Hamden, Ct., U.S. D4 84
Hamden, Oh., U.S. C3 112
Hämeenlinna, Fin. F15 6
Hamel, Mn., U.S. m11 100
Hameln, Ger. C9 8
Hamersley Range, mts., Austl. D3 50
Hamhŭng, N. Kor. D12 26
Hami, China C5 26
Hamilton, Ber. E14 76
Hamilton, Ont., Can. D5 73
Hamilton, N.Z. B5 52
Hamilton, Scot., U.K. F8 7
Hamilton, Al., U.S. A2 78
Hamilton, Il., U.S. C2 90
Hamilton, In., U.S. A8 91
Hamilton, Mi., U.S. F4 99
Hamilton, Ms., U.S. B5 101
Hamilton, Mo., U.S. B3 102
Hamilton, Mt., U.S. D2 103
Hamilton, N.Y., U.S. C5 109
Hamilton, Oh., U.S. C1 112
Hamilton, Tx., U.S. D3 120
Hamilton, Va., U.S. A5 123
Hamilton, co., Fl., U.S. B3 86
Hamilton, co., Il., U.S. E5 90
Hamilton, co., In., U.S. D5 91
Hamilton, co., Ia., U.S. B4 92
Hamilton, co., Ks., U.S. E2 93
Hamilton, co., Ne., U.S. D7 104
Hamilton, co., N.Y., U.S. B6 109
Hamilton, co., Oh., U.S. C1 112
Hamilton, co., Tn., U.S. D8 119
Hamilton, co., Tx., U.S. D3 120
Hamilton, Lake, res., Ar., U.S. C2 81
Hamilton, Mount, mtn., Ak., U.S. C8 79
Hamilton, Mount, mtn., Ca., U.S. k9 82
Hamilton, Mount, mtn., Nv., U.S. D6 105
Hamilton Inlet, b., Newf., Can. A2 72
Hamilton Reservoir, res., Ma., U.S. B3 98
Hamilton Sound, strt., Newf., Can. D4 72
Hamilton Square, N.J., U.S. C3 107
Hamiota, Man., Can. D1 70
Hamlet, In., U.S. B4 91
Hamlet, N.C., U.S. C3 110
Hamlet, Mount, mtn., Ak., U.S. B6 79
Hamlin, Pa., U.S. D11 115
Hamlin, Tx., U.S. C2 120
Hamlin, W.V., U.S. C2 125
Hamlin, co., S.D., U.S. C8 118
Hamlin Lake, l., Mi., U.S. D4 99
Hamm, Ger. D7 8
Hammamet, Tun. M5 14
Hammam Lif, Tun. M5 14
Hammerdal, Swe. E10 6
Hammon, Ok., U.S. B2 113
Hammonasset, stm., Ct., U.S. D5 84
Hammonasset Point, c., Ct., U.S. E5 84
Hammond, In., U.S. A2 91
Hammond, La., U.S. D5 95
Hammond, Wi., U.S. D1 126
Hammond Bay, b., Mi., U.S. C6 99
Hammonton, N.J., U.S. D3 107
Hampden, Newf., Can. D3 72
Hampden, Me., U.S. D4 96
Hampden, co., Ma., U.S. B2 98
Hampden Highlands, Me., U.S. D4 96
Hampshire, Il., U.S. A5 90
Hampshire, co., Ma., U.S. B2 98
Hampshire, co., W.V., U.S. B6 125
Hampstead, Md., U.S. A4 97
Hampstead, N.C., U.S. C5 110
Hampton, N.B., Can. D4 71
Hampton, Ar., U.S. D3 81
Hampton, Ga., U.S. C2 87
Hampton, Ia., U.S. B4 92
Hampton, N.H., U.S. E5 106
Hampton, S.C., U.S. F5 117
Hampton, Tn., U.S. C11 119
Hampton, Va., U.S. C6 123
Hampton, co., S.C., U.S. F5 117
Hampton Bays, N.Y., U.S. n16 109
Hampton Beach, N.H., U.S. E5 106
Hampton Butte, mtn., Or., U.S. D6 114
Hampton Roads, Va., U.S. k15 123
Hampton Roads Bridge-Tunnel, Va., U.S. k15 123
Hams Fork, stm., Wy., U.S. E2 127
Hamtramck, Mi., U.S. p15 99
Hana, Hi., U.S. C6 88
Hanahan, S.C., U.S. F7 117
Hanalei Bay, b., Hi., U.S. A2 88
Hanamaki, Japan C14 30
Hanamaulu, Hi., U.S. B2 88
Hanapepe, Hi., U.S. B2 88
Hanau, Ger. E8 8
Hanceville, Al., U.S. A3 78
Hancock, Md., U.S. A1 97
Hancock, Mi., U.S. A2 99
Hancock, Mn., U.S. E3 100
Hancock, co., Ga., U.S. C3 87
Hancock, co., Il., U.S. C2 90
Hancock, co., In., U.S. E6 91
Hancock, co., Ia., U.S. A4 92
Hancock, co., Ky., U.S. C3 94
Hancock, co., Me., U.S. D4 96
Hancock, co., Ms., U.S. E4 101
Hancock, co., Oh., U.S. A2 112
Hancock, co., Tn., U.S. C10 119
Hancock, co., W.V., U.S. A4 125
Hand, co., S.D., U.S. C6 118
Handa, Japan H9 30
Handan, China D9 26
Hando, Som. F5 46
HaNegev, reg., Isr. D4 40
Hanford, Ca., U.S. D4 82
Hangchow see Hangzhou, China E9 28
Hangman Creek, stm., Wa., U.S. B8 124
Hangö (Hanko), Fin. G14 6
Hangzhou (Hangchow), China E9 28
Hangzhou Wan, b., China E9 28
Hanish, Jazā'ir, is., Yemen F3 46
Hanjiang, China J8 28
Hankinson, N.D., U.S. C9 111
Hanna, Alta., Can. D5 68
Hanna, Wy., U.S. E6 127
Hanna City, Il., U.S. C4 90
Hannahville Indian Reservation, Mi., U.S. C3 99
Hannibal, Mo., U.S. B6 102
Hannover, Ger. C9 8
Ha Noi, Viet. D8 34
Hanover, Ont., Can. C3 73
Hanover, Il., U.S. A3 90
Hanover, In., U.S. G7 91
Hanover, Ks., U.S. C7 93
Hanover, Ma., U.S. B6 98
Hanover, Mn., U.S. m11 100
Hanover, N.H., U.S. C2 106
Hanover, Pa., U.S. G8 115
Hanover, co., Va., U.S. C5 123
Hanover Park, Il., U.S. k8 90
Hansen, Id., U.S. G4 89
Hansford, co., Tx., U.S. A2 120
Hanson, Ma., U.S. B6 98
Hanson, co., S.D., U.S. D8 118
Hantsport, N.S., Can. D5 71
Hanzhong, China E8 26
Haparanda, Swe. D15 6
Hapeville, Ga., U.S. C2 87
Happy Valley, N.M., U.S. E5 108
Happy Valley-Goose Bay, Newf., Can. B1 72
Harahan, La., U.S. k11 95
Haralson, co., Ga., U.S. C1 87
Harare, Zimb. E6 44
Harash, Bi'r al-, well, Libya C10 42
Harbeson, De., U.S. F4 85
Harbin, China B12 26
Harbor, Or., U.S. E2 114
Harbor Beach, Mi., U.S. E8 99
Harborcreek, Pa., U.S. B2 115
Harbor Springs, Mi., U.S. C6 99
Harbour Breton, Newf., Can. E4 72
Harbour Grace, Newf., Can. E5 72
Harcuvar Mountains, mts., Az., U.S. D2 80
Harda, India I7 38
Hardangerfjorden, Nor. F5 6
Hardee, co., Fl., U.S. E5 86
Hardeeville, S.C., U.S. G5 117
Hardeman, co., Tn., U.S. B2 119
Hardeman, co., Tx., U.S. B3 120
Hardin, Il., U.S. D3 90
Hardin, Mt., U.S. E9 103
Hardin, co., Il., U.S. F5 90
Hardin, co., Ia., U.S. B4 92
Hardin, co., Ky., U.S. C4 94
Hardin, co., Oh., U.S. B2 112
Hardin, co., Tn., U.S. B3 119
Hardin, co., Tx., U.S. D5 120
Harding, co., N.M., U.S. B5 108
Harding, co., S.D., U.S. B2 118
Harding, Lake, res., U.S. C4 78
Hardinsburg, Ky., U.S. C3 94
Hardisty, Alta., Can. C5 68
Hardwār, India F8 38
Hardwick, Ga., U.S. C3 87
Hardwick, Vt., U.S. B4 122
Hardwood Ridge, mtn., Pa., U.S. D11 115
Hardy, co., W.V., U.S. B6 125
Hardy Lake, res., In., U.S. G6 91
Hare Bay, Newf., Can. D4 72
Hare Bay, b., Newf., Can. C4 72
Harer, Eth. G3 46
Harford, co., Md., U.S. A5 97
Hargeysa, Som. G3 46
Harihar, India E3 37
Harīrūd (Tedžen), stm., Asia J10 22
Harkers Island, N.C., U.S. C6 110
Harlan, In., U.S. B8 91
Harlan, Ia., U.S. C2 92
Harlan, Ky., U.S. D6 94
Harlan, co., Ky., U.S. D6 94
Harlan, co., Ne., U.S. D6 104
Harlan County Lake, res., Ne., U.S. E6 104
Harlem, Fl., U.S. F6 86
Harlem, Ga., U.S. C4 87
Harlem, Mt., U.S. B8 103
Harleyville, S.C., U.S. E7 117
Harlingen, Neth. B5 8
Harlingen, Tx., U.S. F4 120
Harlow, Eng., U.K. J13 7
Harlowton, Mt., U.S. D7 103
Harmon, co., Ok., U.S. C2 113
Harmon Creek, stm., W.V., U.S. f8 125
Harmony, In., U.S. E3 91
Harmony, Mn., U.S. G6 100
Harmony, Pa., U.S. E1 115
Harmony, R.I., U.S. B3 116
Harnett, co., N.C., U.S. B4 110
Harney, co., Or., U.S. D7 114
Harney, Lake, l., Fl., U.S. D5 86
Harney Lake, l., Or., U.S. D7 114
Harney Peak, mtn., S.D., U.S. D2 118
Härnösand, Swe. E11 6
Haro, Spain C9 12
Haro Strait, strt., Wa., U.S. A2 124
Harper, Lib. H4 42
Harper, Ks., U.S. E5 93
Harper, co., Ks., U.S. E5 93
Harper, co., Ok., U.S. A2 113
Harper, Mount, mtn., Ak., U.S. C11 79
Harpers Ferry, W.V., U.S. B7 125
Harpers Ferry National Historical Park, W.V., U.S. B7 125
Harpersville, Al., U.S. B3 78
Harpeth, stm., Tn., U.S. A5 119
Harquahala Mountain, mtn., Az., U.S. D2 80
Harquahala Mountains, mts., Az., U.S. D2 80
Harrah, Ok., U.S. B4 113
Harricana, stm., Can. F17 66
Harriman, Tn., U.S. D9 119
Harriman Reservoir, res., Vt., U.S. F3 122
Harrington, De., U.S. E3 85
Harrington Park, N.J., U.S. h9 107
Harris, Mn., U.S. E6 100
Harris, R.I., U.S. D3 116
Harris, co., Ga., U.S. D2 87
Harris, co., Tx., U.S. E5 120
Harris, Lake, l., Fl., U.S. D5 86
Harrisburg, Ar., U.S. B5 81
Harrisburg, Il., U.S. F5 90
Harrisburg, Or., U.S. C3 114
Harrisburg, Pa., U.S. F8 115
Harrisburg, S.D., U.S. D9 118
Harrison, Ar., U.S. A2 81
Harrison, Mi., U.S. D6 99
Harrison, N.J., U.S. k8 107
Harrison, N.Y., U.S. h13 109
Harrison, Oh., U.S. C1 112
Harrison, Tn., U.S. h11 119
Harrison, co., In., U.S. H5 91
Harrison, co., Ia., U.S. C2 92
Harrison, co., Ky., U.S. B5 94
Harrison, co., Ms., U.S. E4 101
Harrison, co., Mo., U.S. A3 102
Harrison, co., Oh., U.S. B4 112
Harrison, co., Tx., U.S. C5 120
Harrison, co., W.V., U.S. B4 125
Harrison, Cape, c., Newf., Can. g10 72
Harrison Bay, b., Ak., U.S. A9 79
Harrisonburg, Va., U.S. B4 123
Harrison Hot Springs, B.C., Can. f14 69
Harrison Lake, l., B.C., Can. E7 69
Harrisonville, Mo., U.S. C3 102
Harriston, Ont., Can. D4 73
Harristown, Il., U.S. D4 90
Harrisville, R.I., U.S. B2 116
Harrisville, Ut., U.S. B4 121
Harrisville, W.V., U.S. B3 125
Harrodsburg, Ky., U.S. C5 94
Harrogate, Eng., U.K. G11 7
Harrow, Ont., Can. E2 73
Harry S. Truman Reservoir, res., Mo., U.S. C4 102
Harry Strunk Lake, res., Ne., U.S. D5 104
Harstad, Nor. B11 6
Hart, Mi., U.S. E4 99
Hart, Tx., U.S. B1 120
Hart, co., Ga., U.S. B4 87
Hart, co., Ky., U.S. C4 94
Hart, Lake, l., Fl., U.S. D5 86
Hartford, Al., U.S. D4 78
Hartford, Ar., U.S. B1 81
Hartford, Ct., U.S. B5 84
Hartford, Il., U.S. E3 90
Hartford, Ia., U.S. C4 92
Hartford, Ky., U.S. C3 94
Hartford, Mi., U.S. F4 99
Hartford, S.D., U.S. D9 118
Hartford, Vt., U.S. D4 122
Hartford, Wi., U.S. E5 126
Hartford, co., Ct., U.S. B4 84
Hartford City, In., U.S. D7 91
Hartington, Ne., U.S. B8 104
Hart Lake, l., Or., U.S. E7 114
Hartland, N.B., Can. C2 71
Hartland, Me., U.S. D3 96
Hartland, Wi., U.S. E5 126
Hartland Point, c., Eng., U.K. J8 7
Hartlepool, Eng., U.K. G11 7
Hartley, Ia., U.S. A2 92
Hartley, co., Tx., U.S. B1 120
Hartney, Man., Can. E1 70
Hartselle, Al., U.S. A3 78
Hartshorne, Ok., U.S. C6 113
Hartsville, S.C., U.S. C7 117
Hartsville, Tn., U.S. A5 119
Hartville, Oh., U.S. B4 112
Hartwell, Ga., U.S. B4 87
Hartwell Lake, res., U.S. B1 117
Hārūnābād, Pak. F5 38
Hārūt, stm., Afg. C1 36
Harvard, Il., U.S. A5 90
Harvard, Ne., U.S. D7 104
Harvard, Mount, mtn., Co., U.S. C4 83
Harvey, Il., U.S. B6 90
Harvey, La., U.S. E5 95
Harvey, Mi., U.S. B3 99
Harvey, N.D., U.S. B6 111
Harvey, co., Ks., U.S. D6 93
Harvey Lake, res., Pa., U.S. m16 115
Harveys Creek, stm., Pa., U.S. n16 115
Harwich, Eng., U.K. J14 7
Harwich Port, Ma., U.S. C7 98
Harwinton, Ct., U.S. B3 84
Haryana, state, India F7 38
Harz, mts., Ger. D10 8
Hasbrouck Heights, N.J., U.S. h8 107
Haskell, Ar., U.S. C3 81
Haskell, Ok., U.S. B6 113
Haskell, Tx., U.S. C3 120
Haskell, co., Ks., U.S. E3 93
Haskell, co., Ok., U.S. B6 113
Haskell, co., Tx., U.S. C3 120
Haskovo, Bul. H9 16
Hassan, India F4 37
Hassayampa, stm., Az., U.S. D3 80
Hasselt, Bel. E5 8
Hassfurt, Ger. E10 8
Hässleholm, Swe. H9 6
Hastings, Ont., Can. C7 73
Hastings, N.Z. C6 52
Hastings, Eng., U.K. K13 7
Hastings, Mi., U.S. F5 99
Hastings, Mn., U.S. F6 100
Hastings, Ne., U.S. D7 104
Hastings, Pa., U.S. E4 115
Hastings-on-Hudson, N.Y., U.S. h13 109
Hatay (Antioch), Tur. A5 40
Hatch, N.M., U.S. E2 108
Hatchet Lake, N.S., Can. E6 71
Hatchie, stm., Tn., U.S. B2 119
Hatchineha, Lake, l., Fl., U.S. D5 86
Hat Creek, stm., S.D., U.S. E2 118
Hatfield, In., U.S. I3 91
Hatfield, Pa., U.S. F11 115
Hāthras, India G8 38
Ha Tinh, Viet. E8 34
Hat Mountain, mtn., Az., U.S. E3 80
Hatteras, N.C., U.S. B7 110
Hatteras, Cape, c., N.C., U.S. B7 110

Name	Map Ref	Page
Hatteras Inlet, b., N.C., U.S.	B7	110
Hattiesburg, Ms., U.S.	D4	101
Hatton, N.D., U.S.	B8	111
Hat Yai, Thai.	K6	34
Haubstadt, In., U.S.	H2	91
Haugesund, Nor.	G5	6
Haughton, La., U.S.	B2	95
Haukivuori, Fin.	E16	6
Hauser, Or., U.S.	D2	114
Haut, Isle au, i., Me., U.S.	D4	96
Haut Atlas, mts., Mor.	B4	42
Hauula, Hi., U.S.	B4	88
Havana, Fl., U.S.	B2	86
Havana, Il., U.S.	C3	90
Havana see La Habana, Cuba	C6	64
Havant, Eng., U.K.	K12	7
Havasu, Lake, res., U.S.	C1	80
Havasupai Indian Reservation, Az., U.S.	A3	80
Havelberg, Ger.	C12	8
Havelock, Ont., Can.	C7	73
Havelock, N.C., U.S.	C6	110
Haven, Ks., U.S.	E6	93
Haverford [Township], Pa., U.S.	o20	115
Haverhill, Ma., U.S.	A5	98
Hāveri, India	E3	37
Haverstraw, N.Y., U.S.	D7	109
Haviland, Ks., U.S.	E4	93
Havířov, Czech.	F18	8
Havre, Mt., U.S.	B7	103
Havre de Grace, Md., U.S.	A5	97
Havre North, Mt., U.S.	B7	103
Haw, stm., N.C., U.S.	B3	110
Hawaii, co., Hi., U.S.	D6	88
Hawaii, state, U.S.	C5	88
Hawaii, i., Hi., U.S.	D6	88
Hawaiian Islands, is., Hi., U.S.	m14	88
Hawaii Volcanoes National Park, Hi., U.S.	D6	88
Hawarden, Ia., U.S.	A1	92
Hawesville, Ky., U.S.	C3	94
Hawi, Hi., U.S.	C6	88
Hawick, Scot., U.K.	F10	7
Hawke Bay, b., N.Z.	C6	52
Hawkesbury, Ont., Can.	B10	73
Hawkesbury Island, i., B.C., Can.	C3	69
Hawkins, co., Tn., U.S.	C11	119
Hawkinsville, Ga., U.S.	D3	87
Hawley, Mn., U.S.	D2	100
Hawley, Pa., U.S.	D11	115
Haworth, N.J., U.S.	h9	107
Haw River, N.C., U.S.	A3	110
Hawthorne, Ca., U.S.	n12	82
Hawthorne, Fl., U.S.	C4	86
Hawthorne, Nv., U.S.	E3	105
Hawthorne, N.J., U.S.	B4	107
Hawthorne, N.Y., U.S.	g13	109
Haxtun, Co., U.S.	A8	83
Hay, Austl.	F8	50
Hay, stm., Austl.	D7	50
Hay, stm., Can.	E9	66
Hay, Cape, c., N.W. Ter., Can.	B10	66
Hayange, Fr.	C13	10
Hayden, Az., U.S.	E5	80
Hayden, Co., U.S.	A3	83
Hayden Lake, l., Id., U.S.	B2	89
Hayes, La., U.S.	D3	95
Hayes, co., Ne., U.S.	D4	104
Hayes, stm., Man., Can.	B5	70
Hayes, Mount, mtn., Ak., U.S.	C10	79
Hayfield, Mn., U.S.	G6	100
Hayford Peak, mtn., Nv., U.S.	G6	105
Haymock Lake, l., Me., U.S.	B3	96
Haynesville, La., U.S.	B2	95
Hayneville, Al., U.S.	C3	78
Hayrabolu, Tur.	H11	16
Hay River, N.W. Ter., Can.	D9	66
Hays, Ks., U.S.	D4	93
Hays, N.C., U.S.	A1	110
Hays, co., Tx., U.S.	D3	120
Hays Canyon Peak, mtn., Nv., U.S.	B2	105
Hay Springs, Ne., U.S.	B3	104
Haystack Mountain, mtn., Nv., U.S.	B6	105
Haysville, Ks., U.S.	g12	93
Hayti, Mo., U.S.	E8	102
Hayti Heights, Mo., U.S.	E8	102
Hayward, Ca., U.S.	h8	82
Hayward, Wi., U.S.	B2	126
Haywood, co., N.C., U.S.	f9	110
Haywood, co., Tn., U.S.	B2	119
Hazard, Ky., U.S.	C6	94
Hazardville, Ct., U.S.	B5	84
Hazāribāgh, India	I11	38
Hazel Crest, Il., U.S.	k9	90
Hazel Dell, Wa., U.S.	D3	124
Hazel Green, Al., U.S.	A3	78
Hazel Green, Wi., U.S.	F3	126
Hazel Park, Mi., U.S.	p15	99
Hazelton Pyramid, mtn., Wy., U.S.	B5	127
Hazelwood, N.C., U.S.	f10	110
Hazen, Ar., U.S.	C4	81
Hazen, N.D., U.S.	B4	111
Hazen Bay, b., Ak., U.S.	C6	79
Hazlehurst, Ga., U.S.	E4	87
Hazlehurst, Ms., U.S.	D3	101
Hazlet, N.J., U.S.	C4	107
Hazleton, Ia., U.S.	B6	92
Hazleton, Pa., U.S.	E10	115
Head Harbor Island, i., Me., U.S.	D5	96
Headland, Al., U.S.	D4	78
Headley, Mount, mtn., Mt., U.S.	C1	103
Healdsburg, Ca., U.S.	C2	82
Healdton, Ok., U.S.	C4	113
Healy, Ak., U.S.	C10	79
Heard, co., Ga., U.S.	C1	87
Hearne, Tx., U.S.	D4	120
Hearst, Ont., Can.	o19	73
Heart, stm., N.D., U.S.	C3	111
Heart Butte Dam, N.D., U.S.	C4	111
Heart Lake, l., Wy., U.S.	B2	127
Heart's Content, Newf., Can.	E5	72
Heath, Oh., U.S.	B3	112
Heath Springs, S.C., U.S.	B6	117
Heavener, Ok., U.S.	C7	113
Hebbronville, Tx., U.S.	F3	120
Hebei, prov., China	D10	26
Heber, Az., U.S.	C5	80
Heber City, Ut., U.S.	C4	121
Heber Springs, Ar., U.S.	B3	81
Hébertville, Que., Can.	A6	74
Hebgen Lake, res., Mt., U.S.	F5	103
Hebrides, is., Scot., U.K.	D6	4
Hebron, N.S., Can.	F3	71
Hebron, Il., U.S.	A5	90
Hebron, In., U.S.	B3	91
Hebron, Ky., U.S.	h13	94
Hebron, Md., U.S.	D6	97
Hebron, Ne., U.S.	D8	104
Hebron, N.D., U.S.	C3	111
Hebron, Oh., U.S.	C3	112
Hebron see Al-Khalīl, Jord.	D4	40
Hecate Strait, strt., B.C., Can.	C2	69
Heceta Island, i., Ak., U.S.	n23	79
Hechi, China	B9	34
Hechingen, Ger.	G8	8
Hechuan, China	E8	26
Hecla Island, i., Man., Can.	D3	70
Hector, Mn., U.S.	F4	100
Hedemora, Swe.	F10	6
He Devil, mtn., Id., U.S.	D2	89
Hedrick, Ia., U.S.	C5	92
Heerenveen, Neth.	C5	8
Heerlen, Neth.	E5	8
Ḥefa (Haifa), Isr.	C4	40
Hefei, China	D6	28
Heflin, Al., U.S.	B4	78
Hefner, Lake, res., Ok., U.S.	B4	113
Hegang, China	B13	26
Hegins, Pa., U.S.	E9	115
Heide, Ger.	A9	8
Heidelberg, Ger.	F8	8
Heidelberg, Ms., U.S.	D5	101
Heidenheim, Ger.	F10	8
Heidenreichstein, Aus.	G15	8
Heidrick, Ky., U.S.	D6	94
Heihe (Naquka), China	E14	38
Heilbron, S. Afr.	G5	44
Heilbronn, Ger.	F9	8
Heiligenstadt, Ger.	D10	8
Heilongjiang, prov., China	B12	26
Heilongjiang (Amur), stm., Asia	G19	24
Heinola, Fin.	F16	6
Hejaz see Al-Ḥijāz, reg., Sau. Ar.	C2	46
Hekla, vol., Ice.	C4	4
Hekou, China	C7	34
Helena, Al., U.S.	B3	78
Helena, Ar., U.S.	C5	81
Helena, Ga., U.S.	D4	87
Helena, Mt., U.S.	D4	103
Helena, Ok., U.S.	A3	113
Helensburgh, Scot., U.K.	E8	7
Helgoland, i., Ger.	A7	8
Helgoländer Bucht, b., Ger.	A8	8
Hellam, Pa., U.S.	G8	115
Hellertown, Pa., U.S.	E11	115
Hellesylt, Nor.	E6	6
Hellín, Spain	G10	12
Hells Canyon, val., U.S.	B10	114
Hells Canyon National Recreation Area, U.S.	B10	114
Hell-Ville, Madag.	D9	44
Helmand, stm., Asia	C2	36
Helmond, Neth.	D5	8
Helmsdale, Scot., U.K.	C9	7
Helmstedt, Ger.	C10	8
Helotes, Tx., U.S.	h7	120
Helper, Ut., U.S.	D5	121
Helsingborg, Swe.	H9	6
Helsingfors see Helsinki, Fin.	F15	6
Helsingør (Elsinore), Den.	H9	6
Helsinki (Helsingfors), Fin.	F15	6
Hematite, Mo., U.S.	C7	102
Hemet, Ca., U.S.	F5	82
Hemingford, Ne., U.S.	B2	104
Hemingway, S.C., U.S.	D9	117
Hemlock, Mi., U.S.	E6	99
Hemlock Reservoir, res., Ct., U.S.	E2	84
Hemmingford, Que., Can.	D4	74
Hemphill, Tx., U.S.	D6	120
Hemphill, co., Tx., U.S.	B2	120
Hempstead, N.Y., U.S.	n15	109
Hempstead, Tx., U.S.	D4	120
Hempstead, co., Ar., U.S.	D2	81
Hemse, Swe.	H12	6
Henagar, Al., U.S.	A4	78
Henan, prov., China	E9	26
Henderson, Ky., U.S.	C2	94
Henderson, La., U.S.	D4	95
Henderson, Mn., U.S.	F5	100
Henderson, Ne., U.S.	D8	104
Henderson, Nv., U.S.	G7	105
Henderson, N.C., U.S.	A4	110
Henderson, Tn., U.S.	B3	119
Henderson, Tx., U.S.	C5	120
Henderson, co., Il., U.S.	C3	90
Henderson, co., Ky., U.S.	C2	94
Henderson, co., N.C., U.S.	f10	110
Henderson, co., Tn., U.S.	B3	119
Henderson, co., Tx., U.S.	C5	120
Henderson's Point, Ms., U.S.	g7	101
Hendersonville, N.C., U.S.	f10	110
Hendersonville, Tn., U.S.	A5	119
Hendricks, Mn., U.S.	F2	100
Hendricks, co., In., U.S.	E4	91
Hendry, co., Fl., U.S.	F5	86
Hengelo, Neth.	C6	8
Hengshan, China	H1	28
Hengyang, China	F9	26
Henlawson, W.V., U.S.	n12	125
Henlopen, Cape, c., De., U.S.	E5	85
Hennef, Ger.	E7	8
Hennepin, co., Mn., U.S.	E5	100
Hennessey, Ok., U.S.	A4	113
Henniker, N.H., U.S.	D3	106
Henning, Mn., U.S.	D3	100
Henning, Tn., U.S.	B2	119
Henrico, co., Va., U.S.	C5	123
Henrietta, N.C., U.S.	B1	110
Henrietta, Tx., U.S.	C3	120
Henrietta Maria, Cape, c., Ont., Can.	n19	73
Henry, Il., U.S.	B4	90
Henry, co., Al., U.S.	D4	78
Henry, co., Ga., U.S.	C2	87
Henry, co., Il., U.S.	B3	90
Henry, co., In., U.S.	E7	91
Henry, co., Ia., U.S.	C6	92
Henry, co., Ky., U.S.	B4	94
Henry, co., Mo., U.S.	C4	102
Henry, co., Oh., U.S.	A1	112
Henry, co., Tn., U.S.	A3	119
Henry, co., Va., U.S.	D3	123
Henry, Mount, mtn., Mt., U.S.	B1	103
Henryetta, Ok., U.S.	B6	113
Henry Kater, Cape, c., N.W. Ter., Can.	C19	66
Henrys Fork, stm., U.S.	E2	127
Henryville, Que., Can.	D4	74
Henryville, In., U.S.	G6	91
Hensall, Ont., Can.	D3	73
Henzada, Mya.	F3	34
Hephzibah, Ga., U.S.	C4	87
Heppner, Or., U.S.	B7	114
Hepu (Lianzhou), China	D10	34
Herāt, Afg.	C1	36
Herbes, Isle aux, i., Al., U.S.	E1	78
Herbignac, Fr.	E4	10
Herculaneum, Mo., U.S.	C7	102
Hereford, Eng., U.K.	I10	7
Hereford, Md., U.S.	A4	97
Hereford, Tx., U.S.	B1	120
Hereford Inlet, b., N.J., U.S.	E3	107
Herford, Ger.	C8	8
Herington, Ks., U.S.	D7	93
Herkimer, N.Y., U.S.	B6	109
Herkimer, co., N.Y., U.S.	B5	109
Hermann, Mo., U.S.	C6	102
Hermano Peak, mtn., Co., U.S.	D2	83
Hermantown, Mn., U.S.	D6	100
Hermanus, S. Afr.	H3	44
Herminie, Pa., U.S.	F2	115
Hermiston, Or., U.S.	B7	114
Hermitage, Newf., Can.	E4	72
Hermitage, Ar., U.S.	D3	81
Hermitage Bay, b., Newf., Can.	E3	72
Hermosillo, Mex.	C4	62
Hernando, Fl., U.S.	D4	86
Hernando, Ms., U.S.	A4	101
Hernando, co., Fl., U.S.	D4	86
Herndon, Va., U.S.	B5	123
Herning, Den.	H7	6
Heron Lake, Mn., U.S.	G3	100
Herrera del Duque, Spain	F6	12
Herrera de Pisuerga, Spain	C7	12
Herrin, Il., U.S.	F4	90
Herring Bay, b., Md., U.S.	C4	97
Herring Cove, N.S., Can.	E6	71
Herrington Lake, res., Ky., U.S.	C5	94
Herscher, Il., U.S.	B5	90
Hershey, Pa., U.S.	F8	115
Hertford, N.C., U.S.	A6	110
Hertford, co., N.C., U.S.	A5	110
Hervás, Spain	E6	12
Hesdin, Fr.	B9	10
Hesperia, Ca., U.S.	E5	82
Hesperia, Mi., U.S.	E4	99
Hesperus Mountain, mtn., Co., U.S.	D2	83
Hesston, Ks., U.S.	D6	93
Hetian, China	B8	38
Hettinger, N.D., U.S.	D3	111
Hettinger, co., N.D., U.S.	C3	111
Heyburn, Id., U.S.	G5	89
Heyworth, Il., U.S.	C5	90
Hialeah, Fl., U.S.	G6	86
Hiawatha, Ia., U.S.	B6	92
Hiawatha, Ks., U.S.	C8	93
Hibbing, Mn., U.S.	C6	100
Hickam Air Force Base, mil., Hi., U.S.	g10	88
Hickman, Ky., U.S.	f8	94
Hickman, Ne., U.S.	D9	104
Hickman, co., Ky., U.S.	f8	94
Hickman, co., Tn., U.S.	B4	119
Hickory, N.C., U.S.	B1	110
Hickory, co., Mo., U.S.	D4	102
Hicksville, N.Y., U.S.	E7	109
Hicksville, Oh., U.S.	A1	112
Hico, Tx., U.S.	D3	120
Hico, W.V., U.S.	C3	125
Hidaka-sammyaku, mts., Japan	q20	30a
Hidalgo, Mex.	E10	62
Hidalgo, Tx., U.S.	F3	120
Hidalgo, co., N.M., U.S.	F1	108
Hidalgo, co., Tx., U.S.	F3	120
Hidalgo del Parral, Mex.	D7	62
Hiddenite, N.C., U.S.	B1	110
Hieroglyphic Mountains, mts., Az., U.S.	k8	80
Hierro, i., Spain	C2	42
Higashiōsaka, Japan	H8	30
Higbee, Mo., U.S.	B5	102
Higganum, Ct., U.S.	D5	84
Higgins Lake, l., Mi., U.S.	D6	99
Higgins Millpond, res., Md., U.S.	C6	97
Higginsville, Mo., U.S.	B4	102
High Bridge, N.J., U.S.	B3	107
High Falls Reservoir, res., Wi., U.S.	C5	126
High Island, i., Mi., U.S.	C5	99
Highland, Il., U.S.	E4	90
Highland, In., U.S.	A3	91
Highland, Ks., U.S.	C8	93
Highland, Mi., U.S.	o14	99
Highland, N.Y., U.S.	D7	109
Highland, Wi., U.S.	E3	126
Highland, co., Oh., U.S.	C2	112
Highland, co., Va., U.S.	B3	123
Highland Lake, l., Me., U.S.	g7	96
Highland Lakes, N.J., U.S.	A4	107
Highland Park, Il., U.S.	A6	90
Highland Park, Mi., U.S.	p15	99
Highland Park, Tx., U.S.	n10	120
Highland Peak, mtn., Ca., U.S.	C4	82
Highland Point, c., Fl., U.S.	G5	86
Highlands, N.J., U.S.	C5	107
Highlands, N.C., U.S.	f9	110
Highlands, Tx., U.S.	r14	120
Highlands, co., Fl., U.S.	E5	86
Highland Springs, Va., U.S.	C5	123
High Level, Alta., Can.	F7	68
Highmore, S.D., U.S.	C6	118
High Point, N.C., U.S.	B2	110
High Prairie, Alta., Can.	B2	68
High Ridge, Mo., U.S.	g12	102
High River, Alta., Can.	D4	68
Highrock Lake, l., Man., Can.	B1	70
High Rock Lake, res., N.C., U.S.	B2	110
High Spire, Pa., U.S.	F8	115
High Springs, Fl., U.S.	C4	86
Hightstown, N.J., U.S.	C3	107
Highwood, Il., U.S.	A6	90
Highwood Baldy, mtn., Mt., U.S.	C6	103
Highwood Mountains, mts., Mt., U.S.	C6	103
Higuerote, Ven.	B9	58
Higüey, Dom. Rep.	E13	64
Híjar, Spain	D11	12
Hikari, Japan	I4	30
Hikone, Japan	G9	30
Hiko Range, mts., Nv., U.S.	F6	105
Hilbert, Wi., U.S.	D5	126
Hildale, Ut., U.S.	F3	121
Hilden, N.S., Can.	D6	71
Hildesheim, Ger.	C9	8
Hill, co., Mt., U.S.	B6	103
Hill, co., Tx., U.S.	D4	120
Hill City, Ks., U.S.	C4	93
Hill City, S.D., U.S.	D2	118
Hillcrest, Il., U.S.	B4	90
Hillcrest Heights, Md., U.S.	C4	97
Hilliard, Fl., U.S.	B5	86
Hilliard, Oh., U.S.	k10	112
Hill Island Lake, l., N.W. Ter., Can.	D11	66
Hill Lake, l., Ar., U.S.	h10	81
Hills, Ia., U.S.	C6	92
Hills, Mn., U.S.	G2	100
Hillsboro, Il., U.S.	D4	90
Hillsboro, Ks., U.S.	D6	93
Hillsboro, Mo., U.S.	C7	102
Hillsboro, N.H., U.S.	D3	106
Hillsboro, N.D., U.S.	B8	111
Hillsboro, Oh., U.S.	C2	112
Hillsboro, Or., U.S.	B4	114
Hillsboro, Tx., U.S.	C4	120
Hillsboro, Wi., U.S.	E3	126
Hillsboro Canal, Fl., U.S.	F6	86
Hillsborough, N.B., Can.	D5	71
Hillsborough, N.C., U.S.	A3	110
Hillsborough, co., Fl., U.S.	E4	86
Hillsborough, co., N.H., U.S.	E3	106
Hillsborough Bay, b., P.E.I., Can.	C6	71
Hillsburgh, Ont., Can.	D4	73
Hills Creek Lake, res., Or., U.S.	D4	114
Hillsdale, Mi., U.S.	G6	99
Hillsdale, N.J., U.S.	g8	107
Hillsdale, co., Mi., U.S.	G6	99
Hillside, N.J., U.S.	k8	107
Hillsville, Pa., U.S.	D1	115
Hillsville, Va., U.S.	D2	123
Hilo, Hi., U.S.	D6	88
Hilo Bay, b., Hi., U.S.	D6	88
Hilton, N.Y., U.S.	B3	109
Hilton Head Island, S.C., U.S.	G6	117
Hilton Head Island, i., S.C., U.S.	G6	117
Hilversum, Neth.	C5	8
Himachal Pradesh, ter., India	E7	38
Himalayas, mts., Asia	F10	38
Himeji, Japan	H7	30
Himi, Japan	F9	30
Ḥimṣ (Homs), Syria	B5	40
Hinchinbrook Island, i., Austl.	C9	50
Hinchinbrook Island, i., Ak., U.S.	g18	79
Hinckley, Il., U.S.	B5	90
Hinckley, Mn., U.S.	D6	100
Hinckley, Ut., U.S.	D3	121
Hinckley Reservoir, res., N.Y., U.S.	B5	109
Hindaun, India	G7	38
Hindman, Ky., U.S.	C7	94
Hinds, co., Ms., U.S.	C3	101
Hindu Kush, mts., Asia	B4	38
Hindupur, India	F4	37
Hines, Or., U.S.	D7	114
Hinesville, Ga., U.S.	E5	87
Hinganghāt, India	B5	37
Hingham, Ma., U.S.	B6	98
Hingham Bay, b., Ma., U.S.	g12	98
Hingoli, India	C4	37
Hinojosa del Duque, Spain	G6	12
Hinsdale, Il., U.S.	k9	90
Hinsdale, N.H., U.S.	E2	106
Hinsdale, co., Co., U.S.	D3	83
Hinton, Alta., Can.	C2	68
Hinton, Ia., U.S.	B1	92
Hinton, Ok., U.S.	B3	113
Hinton, W.V., U.S.	D4	125
Hirado, Japan	I2	30
Hīrākud, res., India	J10	38
Hiram, Ga., U.S.	C2	87
Hiram, Oh., U.S.	A4	112
Hirara, Japan	G12	26
Hiratsuka, Japan	G12	30
Hirosaki, Japan	B13	30
Hiroshima, Japan	H5	30
Hirson, Fr.	C11	10
Hisār, India	F6	38
Hispaniola, i., N.A.	E12	64
Hita, Japan	I3	30
Hitachi, Japan	F13	30
Hitchcock, Tx., U.S.	r14	120
Hitchcock, co., Ne., U.S.	D4	104
Hitchcock Lake, Ct., U.S.	C4	84
Hitoyoshi, Japan	J3	30
Hitra, i., Nor.	E7	6
Hiwassee, stm., Tn., U.S.	D9	119
Hiwassee Lake, res., N.C., U.S.	f8	110
Hjørring, Den.	H7	6
Ho, Ghana	G6	42
Hoa Binh, Viet.	D8	34
Hoagland, In., U.S.	C8	91
Hoback, stm., Wy., U.S.	C2	127
Hobart, Austl.	H9	50
Hobart, In., U.S.	A3	91
Hobart, Ok., U.S.	B2	113
Hobbs, N.M., U.S.	E6	108
Hobe Sound, Fl., U.S.	E6	86
Hobo, Col.	F5	58
Hoboken, N.J., U.S.	k8	107
Höchstadt an der Aisch, Ger.	F10	8
Hockessin, De., U.S.	A3	85
Hocking, co., Oh., U.S.	C3	112
Hocking, stm., Oh., U.S.	C3	112
Hockley, co., Tx., U.S.	C1	120
Hodgeman, co., Ks., U.S.	D4	93
Hodgenville, Ky., U.S.	C4	94
Hodges Village Reservoir, res., Ma., U.S.	B4	98
Hódmezővásárhely, Hung.	I20	8
Hodna, Chott el, l., Alg.	J16	12
Hodonín, Czech.	G17	8
Hof, Ger.	E11	8
Hoffman Estates, Il., U.S.	h8	90
Hofgeismar, Ger.	D9	8
Hofheim in Unterfranken, Ger.	E10	8
Hofors, Swe.	F11	6
Hōfu, Japan	H4	30
Hogansville, Ga., U.S.	C2	87
Hogback Mountain, mtn., Mt., U.S.	F4	103
Hog Island, i., Fl., U.S.	C3	86
Hog Island, i., Mi., U.S.	C5	99
Hog Island, i., N.C., U.S.	B6	110
Hog Island, i., R.I., U.S.	D5	116
Hog Island, i., Va., U.S.	C7	123
Hoh, stm., Wa., U.S.	B1	124
Hohenau an der March, Aus.	G16	8
Hohenwald, Tn., U.S.	B4	119
Hohe Tauern, mts., Aus.	H12	8
Hoh Head, c., Wa., U.S.	B1	124
Hohhot, China	C9	26
Hohoe, Ghana	G5	42
Hōhoku, Japan	H3	30
Ho-Ho-Kus, N.J., U.S.	h8	107
Hoh Xil Shan, mts., China	C13	38
Hoi An, Viet.	G10	34
Hoisington, Ks., U.S.	D5	93
Hokah, Mn., U.S.	G7	100
Hoke, co., N.C., U.S.	B3	110
Hokes Bluff, Al., U.S.	B4	78
Hokitika, N.Z.	E3	52
Hokkaidō, i., Japan	p20	30a
Holbrook, Az., U.S.	C5	80
Holbrook, Ma., U.S.	B5	98
Holcomb, Ks., U.S.	E3	93
Holden, Ma., U.S.	B4	98
Holden, Mo., U.S.	C4	102
Holden, W.V., U.S.	D2	125
Holdenville, Ok., U.S.	B5	113
Holdrege, Ne., U.S.	D6	104
Hole in the Mountain Peak, mtn., Nv., U.S.	C6	105
Holgate, Oh., U.S.	A1	112
Holguín, Cuba	D9	64
Höljes, Swe.	F9	6
Hollabrunn, Aus.	G16	8
Holladay, Ut., U.S.	C4	121
Holland, In., U.S.	H3	91
Holland, Mi., U.S.	F4	99
Holland, Oh., U.S.	A2	112
Holland, Tx., U.S.	D4	120
Hollandale, Ms., U.S.	B3	101
Holland Island, i., Md., U.S.	D5	97
Holland see Netherlands, ctry., Eur.	E9	4
Holland Point, c., Md., U.S.	C4	97
Holland Straits, strt., Md., U.S.	D5	97
Holley, N.Y., U.S.	B2	109
Holliday, Tx., U.S.	C3	120
Hollidaysburg, Pa., U.S.	F5	115
Hollins, Va., U.S.	C3	123
Hollis, Ok., U.S.	C2	113
Hollister, Ca., U.S.	D3	82
Hollister, Mo., U.S.	E4	102
Holliston, Ma., U.S.	B5	98
Holloman Air Force Base, mil., N.M., U.S.	E3	108
Hollow Rock, Tn., U.S.	A3	119
Hollowtop Mountain, mtn., Mt., U.S.	E4	103
Holly, Co., U.S.	C8	83
Holly, Mi., U.S.	F7	99
Holly Grove, Ar., U.S.	C4	81
Holly Hill, Fl., U.S.	C5	86
Holly Hill, S.C., U.S.	E7	117
Holly Pond, Al., U.S.	A3	78
Holly Ridge, N.C., U.S.	C5	110
Holly Shelter Swamp, sw., N.C., U.S.	C5	110
Holly Springs, Ga., U.S.	B2	87
Holly Springs, Ms., U.S.	A4	101
Holly Springs, N.C., U.S.	B4	110
Hollywood, Al., U.S.	A4	78
Hollywood, Fl., U.S.	F6	86
Hollywood, Md., U.S.	D4	97
Hollywood, S.C., U.S.	k11	117
Hollywood Indian Reservation, Fl., U.S.	r3	86
Holman Island, N.W. Ter., Can.	B9	66
Holmen, Wi., U.S.	E2	126
Holmes, co., Fl., U.S.	u16	86
Holmes, co., Ms., U.S.	B3	101
Holmes, co., Oh., U.S.	B4	112
Holmes, Mount, mtn., Wy., U.S.	B2	127
Holmes Reefs, rf., Austl.	C9	50
Holstebro, Den.	H7	6
Holstein, Ia., U.S.	B2	92
Holsteinsborg, Grnld.	C22	66
Holston, stm., Tn., U.S.	C11	119
Holston, Middle Fork, stm., Va., U.S.	f10	123
Holston High Knob, mtn., Tn., U.S.	C11	119
Holsworthy, Eng., U.K.	K8	7
Holt, Al., U.S.	B2	78
Holt, Mi., U.S.	F6	99
Holt, co., Mo., U.S.	A2	102
Holt, co., Ne., U.S.	B7	104
Holt Lake, res., Al., U.S.	B2	78
Holton, Ks., U.S.	C8	93
Holtville, Ca., U.S.	F6	82
Holualoa, Hi., U.S.	D6	88
Holy Cross, Mountain of the, mtn., Co., U.S.	B4	83
Holyhead, Wales, U.K.	H8	7
Holyoke, Co., U.S.	A8	83
Holyoke, Ma., U.S.	B2	98
Holyoke Range, hills, Ma., U.S.	B2	98
Holzminden, Ger.	D9	8

Name | Map Ref | Page
Hombori Tondo, mtn., Mali E5 42
Homburg, Ger. F7 8
Home Bay, b., N.W. Ter., Can. C19 66
Homecroft, In., U.S. m10 91
Homedale, Id., U.S. F2 89
Home Hill, Austl. C9 50
Homeland, Ga., U.S. F4 87
Home Place, In., U.S. E5 91
Homer, Ak., U.S. D9 79
Homer, Ga., U.S. B3 87
Homer, Il., U.S. C6 90
Homer, La., U.S. B2 95
Homer, Mi., U.S. F6 99
Homer, N.Y., U.S. C4 109
Homer City, Pa., U.S. E3 115
Homerville, Ga., U.S. E4 87
Homer Youngs Peak, mtn., Mt., U.S. E3 103
Homestead, Fl., U.S. G6 86
Homestead, Pa., U.S. k14 115
Homestead Air Force Base, mil., Fl., U.S. G6 86
Homestead National Monument of America, Ne., U.S. D9 104
Homewood, Al., U.S. g7 78
Homewood, Il., U.S. B6 90
Homewood, Oh., U.S. C1 112
Hominy, Ok., U.S. A5 113
Hominy Creek, stm., Ok., U.S. A5 113
Homme Dam, N.D., U.S. A8 111
Homochitto, stm., Ms., U.S. D2 101
Homosassa, Fl., U.S. D4 86
Homs see Ḩimṣ, Syria B5 40
Honaker, Va., U.S. e10 123
Honaunau, Hi., U.S. D6 88
Honda, Col. E5 58
Hondo, Japan J3 30
Hondo, Tx., U.S. E3 120
Hondo, stm., N.A. H15 62
Hondo, Rio, stm., N.M., U.S. D4 108
Honduras, ctry., N.A. G4 64
Honduras, Gulf of, b., N.A. F4 64
Honea Path, S.C., U.S. C3 117
Hønefoss, Nor. F8 6
Honeoye Falls, N.Y., U.S. C3 109
Honesdale, Pa., U.S. C11 115
Honey Brook, Pa., U.S. F10 115
Honey Grove, Tx., U.S. C5 120
Honey Lake, l., Ca., U.S. B3 82
Honeypot Glen, Ct., U.S. C4 84
Honeyville, Ut., U.S. B3 121
Hon Gai, Viet. D9 34
Honga River, b., Md., U.S. D5 97
Hongdong, China D9 26
Honghu, China F2 28
Hong Kong, dep., Asia M3 28
Hongliuyuan, China C6 26
Honguedo, Détroit d', strt., Que., Can. G20 66
Hongze Hu, l., China B7 28
Honiara, Sol.Is. A11 50
Honjō, Japan F12 30
Honningsvåg, Nor. A15 6
Honokaa, Hi., U.S. C6 88
Honolulu, Hi., U.S. B4 88
Honolulu, co., Hi., U.S. B3 88
Honolulu International Airport, Hi., U.S. g10 88
Honomu, Hi., U.S. D6 88
Honouliuli, Hi., U.S. g9 88
Honshū, i., Japan F10 30
Honuapo Bay, b., Hi., U.S. D6 88
Hood, co., Tx., U.S. C4 120
Hood, Mount, mtn., Or., U.S. B5 114
Hood Canal, b., Wa., U.S. B2 124
Hoodoo Peak, mtn., Wa., U.S. A5 124
Hood River, Or., U.S. B5 114
Hood River, co., Or., U.S. B5 114
Hoodsport, Wa., U.S. B2 124
Hoogeveen, Neth. C6 8
Hooker, Ok., U.S. e9 113
Hooker, co., Ne., U.S. C4 104
Hook Head, c., Ire. I6 7
Hooksett, N.H., U.S. D4 106
Hoonah, Ak., U.S. D12 79
Hoopa Valley Indian Reservation, Ca., U.S. B2 82
Hooper, Ne., U.S. C9 104
Hooper Bay, Ak., U.S. C6 79
Hooper Islands, is., Md., U.S. D5 97
Hooper Strait, strt., Md., U.S. D5 97
Hoopes Reservoir, res., De., U.S. A3 85
Hoopeston, Il., U.S. C6 90
Hoorn, Neth. C5 8
Hoosac Range, mts., U.S. A1 98
Hoosic, stm., U.S. C7 109
Hoosick Falls, N.Y., U.S. C7 109
Hoover Dam, U.S. G7 105
Hoover Reservoir, res., Oh., U.S. B3 112
Hooverson Heights, W.V., U.S. f8 125
Hopatcong, N.J., U.S. B3 107
Hopatcong, Lake, l., N.J., U.S. A3 107
Hope, B.C., Can. E7 69
Hope, Ar., U.S. D2 81
Hope, In., U.S. F6 91
Hope, R.I., U.S. D3 116
Hope, Ben, mtn., Scot., U.K. C8 7
Hope, Point, c., Ak., U.S. B6 79
Hopedale, Il., U.S. C4 90
Hopedale, Ma., U.S. B4 98
Hope Island, i., R.I., U.S. E5 116
Hope Mills, N.C., U.S. C4 110
Hopes Advance, Cap, c., Que., Can. f13 74
Hopetown, S. Afr. G4 44
Hope Valley, R.I., U.S. E2 116
Hopewell, Va., U.S. C5 123
Hopewell Junction, N.Y., U.S. D7 109
Hopi Indian Reservation, Az., U.S. A5 80
Hopkins, Mn., U.S. n12 100
Hopkins, S.C., U.S. D6 117
Hopkins, co., Ky., U.S. C2 94
Hopkins, co., Tx., U.S. C5 120
Hopkinsville, Ky., U.S. D2 94
Hopkinton, Ia., U.S. B6 92
Hopkinton, Ma., U.S. B4 98
Hopkinton, R.I., U.S. F1 116
Hopkinton Lake, res., N.H., U.S. D3 106
Hopwood, Pa., U.S. G2 115
Hoquiam, Wa., U.S. C2 124
Horace, N.D., U.S. C9 111
Horace Mountain, mtn., Ak., U.S. B10 79
Horatio, Ar., U.S. D1 81
Horgen, Switz. E15 10
Horicon, Wi., U.S. E5 126
Horine, Mo., U.S. C7 102
Horlivka, Ukr. H5 22
Hormuz, Strait of, strt., Asia C6 46
Horn, Aus. G15 8
Horn, Cape see Hornos, Cabo de, c., Chile H3 56
Hornell, N.Y., U.S. C3 109
Hornersville, Mo., U.S. E7 102
Horn Island, i., Ms., U.S. E5 101
Horn Island Pass, strt., Ms., U.S. g8 101
Horn Lake, Ms., U.S. A3 101
Hornos, Cabo de (Cape Horn), c., Chile H3 56
Horn Plateau, plat., N.W. Ter., Can. D9 66
Horqin Youyi Qianqi, China B11 26
Horry, co., S.C., U.S. D10 117
Horse, stm., Ct., U.S. C6 84
Horse Cave, Ky., U.S. C4 94
Horse Creek, stm., U.S. E8 127
Horse Creek Reservoir, res., Co., U.S. C7 83
Horsehead Lake, l., N.D., U.S. B6 111
Horseheads, N.Y., U.S. C4 109
Horse Heaven Hills, hills, Wa., U.S. C6 124
Horsens, Den. I7 6
Horse Peak, mtn., N.M., U.S. D1 108
Horseshoe Bend, Id., U.S. F2 89
Horseshoe Bend National Military Park, Al., U.S. C4 78
Horseshoe Cove, b., Fl., U.S. C3 86
Horseshoe Point, c., Fl., U.S. C3 86
Horseshoe Reservoir, res., Az., U.S. C4 80
Horsham, Austl. G8 50
Horten, Nor. G8 6
Horton, Ks., U.S. C8 93
Hortonia, Lake, l., Vt., U.S. D2 122
Hortonville, Wi., U.S. D5 126
Hoschton, Ga., U.S. B3 87
Hoshangābād, India I7 38
Hoshiārpur, India E6 38
Hospers, Ia., U.S. A2 92
Hospet, India E4 37
Hospitalet, Spain D14 12
Hosta Butte, mtn., N.M., U.S. B1 108
Hoste, Isla, i., Chile H3 56
Hotchkiss, Co., U.S. C3 83
Hot Creek Range, mts., Nv., U.S. E5 105
Hot Creek Valley, val., Nv., U.S. E5 105
Hoting, Swe. D11 6
Hot Spring, co., Ar., U.S. C2 81
Hot Springs, S.D., U.S. D2 118
Hot Springs, co., Wy., U.S. C4 127
Hot Springs National Park, Ar., U.S. C2 81
Hot Springs National Park, Ar., U.S. C2 81
Hot Springs Peak, mtn., Ca., U.S. B3 82
Hot Springs Peak, mtn., Nv., U.S. B4 105
Hottah Lake, l., N.W. Ter., Can. C9 66
Houghton, Mi., U.S. A2 99
Houghton, N.Y., U.S. C2 109
Houghton, co., Mi., U.S. B2 99
Houghton Lake, Mi., U.S. D6 99
Houghton Lake, l., Mi., U.S. D6 99
Houghton Lake Heights, Mi., U.S. D6 99
Houlton, Me., U.S. B5 96
Houma, China D9 26
Houma, La., U.S. E5 95
Housatonic, stm., U.S. D3 84
House Springs, Mo., U.S. g12 102
Houston, De., U.S. E3 85
Houston, Mn., U.S. G7 100
Houston, Ms., U.S. B4 101
Houston, Mo., U.S. D6 102
Houston, Pa., U.S. F1 115
Houston, Tx., U.S. E5 120
Houston, co., Al., U.S. D4 78
Houston, co., Ga., U.S. D3 87
Houston, co., Mn., U.S. G7 100
Houston, co., Tn., U.S. A4 119
Houston, co., Tx., U.S. D5 120
Houston, stm., La., U.S. D2 95
Houston, Lake, res., Tx., U.S. r14 120
Houston Intercontinental Airport, Tx., U.S. r14 120
Houtman Rocks, Austl. E2 50
Houtzdale, Pa., U.S. E5 115
Hovenweep National Monument, Ut., U.S. F6 121
Hovmantorp, Swe. H10 6
Howard, Ks., U.S. E7 93
Howard, S.D., U.S. C8 118
Howard, Wi., U.S. D5 126
Howard, co., Ar., U.S. C2 81
Howard, co., In., U.S. C5 91
Howard, co., Ia., U.S. A5 92
Howard, co., Md., U.S. B4 97
Howard, co., Mo., U.S. B5 102
Howard, co., Ne., U.S. C7 104
Howard, co., Tx., U.S. C2 120
Howard City, Mi., U.S. E5 99
Howard Hanson Reservoir, res., Wa., U.S. B4 124
Howard Lake, Mn., U.S. E4 100
Howard Prairie Lake, res., Or., U.S. E4 114
Howards Grove-Millersville, Wi., U.S. E6 126
Howell, Mi., U.S. F7 99
Howell, co., Mo., U.S. E6 102
Howells, Ne., U.S. C8 104
Howe Sound, strt., B.C., Can. E6 69
Howick, Que., Can. D4 74
Howland, Me., U.S. C4 96
Howrah, India I13 38
Hoxie, Ar., U.S. A5 81
Hoxie, Ks., U.S. C3 93
Höxter, Ger. D9 8
Hoy, i., Scot., U.K. C9 7
Høyanger, Nor. F6 6
Hoyerswerda, Ger. D14 8
Hoyos, Spain E5 12
Hoyt Lakes, Mn., U.S. C6 100
Hradec Králové, Czech. E15 8
Hsilo, Tai. L9 28
Hsinchu, Tai. K9 28
Hsüehchia, Tai. L9 28
Huacho, Peru F3 54
Huachuca City, Az., U.S. F5 80
Hua Hin, Thai. H5 34
Huahua, stm., Nic. G6 64
Huaian, China B8 28
Huainan, China C6 28
Huaiyang, China B3 28
Huaiyin, China B8 28
Huaiyuan, China C6 28
Hualalai, vol., Hi., U.S. D6 88
Hualapai Indian Reservation, Az., U.S. B2 80
Hualapai Mountains, mts., Az., U.S. C2 80
Hualapai Peak, mtn., Az., U.S. B2 80
Hualien, Tai. L10 28
Huallaga, stm., Peru E3 54
Huallanca, Peru E3 54
Huamachuco, Peru E3 54
Huambo, Ang. D3 44
Huancayo, Peru F3 54
Huang (Yellow), stm., China D10 26
Huangchuan, China C4 28
Huangling, China D8 26
Huangshi, China E4 28
Huangyan, China G10 28
Huánuco, Peru E3 54
Huaraz, Peru E3 54
Huascarán, Nevado, mtn., Peru E3 54
Huasco, Chile B2 56
Huatabampo, Mex. D5 62
Huauchinango, Mex. G10 62
Hubbard, Ia., U.S. B4 92
Hubbard, Oh., U.S. A5 112
Hubbard, Or., U.S. B4 114
Hubbard, Tx., U.S. D4 120
Hubbard, co., Mn., U.S. C4 100
Hubbard Creek Lake, res., Tx., U.S. C3 120
Hubbard Lake, l., Mi., U.S. D7 99
Hubbardton, stm., Vt., U.S. D2 122
Hubbell, Mi., U.S. A2 99
Hubei, prov., China E9 26
Hubli, India E3 37
Huckleberry Mountain, mtn., Or., U.S. D4 114
Huddersfield, Eng., U.K. H11 7
Huddinge, Swe. G11 6
Hudiksvall, Swe. F11 6
Hudson, Que., Can. D3 74
Hudson, Co., U.S. A6 83
Hudson, Fl., U.S. D4 86
Hudson, Il., U.S. C5 90
Hudson, Ia., U.S. B5 92
Hudson, Ma., U.S. B4 98
Hudson, Mi., U.S. G6 99
Hudson, N.H., U.S. E4 106
Hudson, N.Y., U.S. C7 109
Hudson, N.C., U.S. B1 110
Hudson, Oh., U.S. A4 112
Hudson, Wi., U.S. D1 126
Hudson, Wy., U.S. D4 127
Hudson, co., N.J., U.S. B4 107
Hudson, stm., U.S. E7 109
Hudson, Lake, res., Ok., U.S. A6 113
Hudson Bay, b., Can. D15 66
Hudson Falls, N.Y., U.S. B7 109
Hudson Hope, B.C., Can. A6 69
Hudson Lake, In., U.S. A4 91
Hudson Strait, strt., Can. D18 66
Hudsonville, Mi., U.S. F5 99
Hudspeth, co., Tx., U.S. o12 120
Hue, Viet. F9 34
Huehuetenango, Guat. G2 64
Huelma, Spain H8 12
Huelva, Spain H5 12
Huércal-Overa, Spain H10 12
Huerfano, co., Co., U.S. D5 83
Huerfano, stm., Co., U.S. D6 83
Huerfano Mountain, mtn., N.M., U.S. A2 108
Huesca, Spain C11 12
Hueytown, Al., U.S. g6 78
Huffakers, Nv., U.S. D2 105
Hugh Butler Lake, res., Ne., U.S. D5 104
Hughenden, Austl. D8 50
Hughes, Ar., U.S. C5 81
Hughes, co., Ok., U.S. B5 113
Hughes, co., S.D., U.S. C5 118
Hughes, North Fork, stm., W.V., U.S. B3 125
Hughes, South Fork, stm., W.V., U.S. B3 125
Hughesville, Md., U.S. C4 97
Hughesville, Pa., U.S. D8 115
Hugo, Co., U.S. B7 83
Hugo, Mn., U.S. m13 100
Hugo, Ok., U.S. C6 113
Hugo Lake, res., Ok., U.S. C6 113
Hugoton, Ks., U.S. E2 93
Huidong, China A7 34
Huila, Nevado del, mtn., Col. F4 58
Huili, China A7 34
Huinan, China C12 26
Huittinen (Lauttakylä), Fin. F14 6
Huitzuco [de los Figueroa], Mex. H10 62
Huixtla, Mex. J13 62
Huiyang (Huizhou), China L3 28
Hulah Lake, res., Ok., U.S. A5 113
Hulan, China B12 26
Hulett, Wy., U.S. B8 127
Hull, Que., Can. D2 74
Hull, Ia., U.S. A1 92
Hull, Ma., U.S. B6 98
Hultsfred, Swe. H10 6
Hulun Nur, l., China B10 26
Humaitá, Braz. E6 54
Humansville, Mo., U.S. D4 102
Humber, stm., Eng., U.K. H12 7
Humble, Tx., U.S. E5 120
Humboldt, Az., U.S. C3 80
Humboldt, Ia., U.S. B3 92
Humboldt, Ks., U.S. E8 93
Humboldt, Ne., U.S. D10 104
Humboldt, Tn., U.S. B3 119
Humboldt, co., Ca., U.S. B2 82
Humboldt, co., Ia., U.S. B3 92
Humboldt, co., Nv., U.S. B3 105
Humboldt, stm., Nv., U.S. C3 105
Humboldt Range, mts., Nv., U.S. C3 105
Hummels Wharf, Pa., U.S. E8 115
Humphrey, Ar., U.S. C4 81
Humphrey, Ne., U.S. C8 104
Humphreys, co., Ms., U.S. B3 101
Humphreys, co., Tn., U.S. A4 119
Humphreys, Mount, mtn., Ca., U.S. D4 82
Humphreys Peak, mtn., Az., U.S. B4 80
Hunan, prov., China F9 26
Hundred Acre Pond, l., R.I., U.S. E3 116
Hunedoara, Rom. D6 16
Hünfeld, Ger. E9 8
Hungary, ctry., Eur. F11 4
Hungf'ou Hsü, i., Tai. M10 28
Hŭngnam, N. Kor. D12 26
Hungry Horse, Mt., U.S. B2 103
Hungry Horse Reservoir, res., Mt., U.S. B3 103
Hunsrück, mts., Ger. F6 8
Hunt, co., Tx., U.S. C4 120
Hunt, stm., R.I., U.S. D4 116
Hunterdon, co., N.J., U.S. B3 107
Hunter Island, i., Austl. H8 50
Hunter Island, i., B.C., Can. D3 69
Huntertown, In., U.S. B7 91
Huntingburg, In., U.S. H4 91
Huntingdon, Que., Can. D3 74
Huntingdon, Pa., U.S. F6 115
Huntingdon, Tn., U.S. A3 119
Huntingdon, co., Pa., U.S. F5 115
Hunting Island, i., S.C., U.S. G7 117
Huntington, Ar., U.S. B1 81
Huntington, In., U.S. C7 91
Huntington, N.Y., U.S. E7 109
Huntington, Tx., U.S. D5 120
Huntington, Ut., U.S. D5 121
Huntington, W.V., U.S. C2 125
Huntington, co., In., U.S. C6 91
Huntington Beach, Ca., U.S. F4 82
Huntington Lake, res., In., U.S. C7 91
Huntington Woods, Mi., U.S. p15 99
Huntingtown, Md., U.S. C4 97
Huntland, Tn., U.S. B5 119
Huntley, Il., U.S. A5 90
Hunt Mountain, mtn., Wy., U.S. B5 127
Huntsville, Ont., Can. B5 73
Huntsville, Al., U.S. A3 78
Huntsville, Ar., U.S. A2 81
Huntsville, Mo., U.S. B5 102
Huntsville, Tn., U.S. C9 119
Huntsville, Tx., U.S. D5 120
Huon Gulf, b., Pap. N. Gui. m16 50a
Hurao, China B13 26
Hurd, Cape, c., Ont., Can. B3 73
Hurley, Ms., U.S. E5 101
Hurley, N.M., U.S. E1 108
Hurley, N.Y., U.S. D6 109
Hurley, Wi., U.S. B3 126
Hurlock, Md., U.S. C6 97
Huron, Oh., U.S. A3 112
Huron, S.D., U.S. C7 118
Huron, co., Mi., U.S. E7 99
Huron, co., Oh., U.S. A3 112
Huron, stm., Mi., U.S. p14 99
Huron, Lake, l., N.A. C10 76
Huron Mountains, hills, Mi., U.S. B3 99
Hurricane, Ut., U.S. F2 121
Hurricane, W.V., U.S. C2 125
Hurst, Il., U.S. F4 90
Hurt, Va., U.S. C3 123
Hurtsboro, Al., U.S. C4 78
Húsavík, Ice. B4 4
Huskvarna, Swe. H10 6
Hustisford, Wi., U.S. E5 126
Husum, Ger. A9 8
Hutchins, Tx., U.S. n10 120
Hutchinson, Ks., U.S. D6 93
Hutchinson, Mn., U.S. F4 100
Hutchinson, co., S.D., U.S. D8 118
Hutchinson, co., Tx., U.S. B2 120
Hutchinson Island, i., Fl., U.S. E6 86
Hutchinson Island, i., S.C., U.S. k11 117
Hutch Mountain, mtn., Az., U.S. C4 80
Hüttental, Ger. E8 8
Huttig, Ar., U.S. D3 81
Huwei, Tai. L9 28
Huxley, Ia., U.S. C4 92
Huy, Bel. E5 8
Huzhou, China E9 28
Hvannadalshnúkur, mtn., Ice. C4 4
Hvar, Cro. F11 14
Hwange, Zimb. E5 44
Hwang Ho see Huang, stm., China D10 26
Hyannis, Ma., U.S. C7 98
Hyannis Port, Ma., U.S. C7 98
Hyattsville, Md., U.S. C4 97
Hybla Valley, Va., U.S. g12 123
Hyco, stm., Va., U.S. D3 123
Hyco Lake, res., N.C., U.S. A3 110
Hydaburg, Ak., U.S. D13 79
Hyde, Pa., U.S. D5 115
Hyde, co., N.C., U.S. B6 110
Hyde, co., S.D., U.S. C6 118
Hyde Park, Guy. D13 58
Hyde Park, N.Y., U.S. D7 109
Hyde Park, Ut., U.S. B4 121
Hyder, Ak., U.S. D13 79
Hyderābād, India D5 37
Hyderābād, Pak. H3 38
Hydeville, Vt., U.S. D2 122
Hydro, Ok., U.S. B3 113
Hyères, Fr. I13 10
Hyesan, N. Kor. C12 26
Hymera, In., U.S. F3 91
Hyndman, Pa., U.S. G4 115
Hyndman Peak, mtn., Id., U.S. F4 89
Hyrum, Ut., U.S. B4 121
Hythe, Alta., Can. B1 68
Hyūga, Japan J4 30
Hyūga-nada, Japan J4 30
Hyvinkää, Fin. F15 6

I

Iamonia, Lake, l., Fl., U.S. B2 86
Iași, Rom. B11 16
Iatt, Lake, res., La., U.S. C3 95
Ibadan, Nig. G6 42
Ibagué, Col. E5 58
Ibapah Peak, mtn., Ut., U.S. D2 121
Ibarra, Ec. G3 58
Ibb, Yemen F3 46
Iberia, Mo., U.S. C5 102
Iberia, co., La., U.S. E4 95
Iberville, Que., Can. D4 74
Iberville, co., La., U.S. D4 95
Iberville, Mont d' (Mount Caubvick), mtn., Can. g14 74
Ibiá, Braz. E5 57
Ibicaraí, Braz. C9 57
Ibiza, Spain G13 12
Ibiza, i., Spain G13 12
Ibo, Moz. D8 44
Ica, Peru F3 54
Içá (Putumayo), stm., S.A. I8 58
Içana, Braz. C5 54
Içana, stm., S.A. C5 54
Ice Harbor Dam, Wa., U.S. C7 124
İçel, Tur. H14 4
Iceland, ctry., Eur. B4 4
Ichalkaranji, India D3 37
Ich Bogd Uul, mts., Mong. C7 26
Ichinomiya, Japan G9 30
Ichinoseki, Japan D14 30
Icicle Creek, stm., Wa., U.S. B5 124
Icó, Braz. E11 54
Icy Cape, c., Ak., U.S. A7 79
Icy Strait, strt., Ak., U.S. k22 79
Ida, Mi., U.S. G7 99
Ida, co., Ia., U.S. B2 92
Ida, Lake, l., Mn., U.S. D3 100
Idabel, Ok., U.S. D7 113
Ida Grove, Ia., U.S. B2 92
Idaho, co., Id., U.S. D3 89
Idaho, state, U.S. E3 89
Idaho Falls, Id., U.S. F6 89
Idaho Springs, Co., U.S. B5 83
Idalou, Tx., U.S. C2 120
Idamay, W.V., U.S. k10 125
Idanha-a-Nova, Port. F4 12
Idappādi, India G4 37
Idar-Oberstein, Ger. F7 8
Idaville, In., U.S. C4 91
Ider, Al., U.S. A4 78
Idfū, Egypt D12 42
Idlib, Syria B5 40
Ídolo, Isla del, i., Mex. G11 62
Ieper, Bel. E2 8
Ierápetra, Grc. N9 16
Iesi, Italy F8 14
Ife, Nig. G6 42
Iferouâne, Niger E7 42
Iforas, Adrar des, mts., Afr. D6 42
Iglesias, Italy J3 14
Igloolik, N.W. Ter., Can. C16 66
Ignacio, Co., U.S. D3 83
Iguaçu, Saltos do (Iguassu Falls), wtfl, S.A. B6 56
Iguala, Mex. H10 62
Igualada, Spain D13 12
Iguape, Braz. A7 56
Iguatu, Braz. E11 54
Iguéla, Gabon B1 44
Iguidi, Erg, dunes, Afr. C4 42
Ihosy, Madag. F9 44
Iida, Japan G10 30
Iisalmi, Fin. E16 6
Iizuka, Japan I3 30
IJmuiden, Neth. C4 8
IJsselmeer (Zuiderzee), Neth. C5 8
Ika, Russia F15 24
Ikela, Zaire B4 44
Ikerre, Nig. G7 42
Ila, Nig. G6 42
Ilagan, Phil. B7 32
Ilan, Tai. K10 28
Ilbenge, Russia E18 24
Île-à-la-Crosse, Lac, l., Sask., Can. B2 75
Ilebo, Zaire B4 44
Île-de-France, hist. reg., Fr. C9 10
Île-Perrot, Que., Can. q19 74
Ilhéus, Braz. C9 57
Ili, stm., Asia I13 22
Iliamna Lake, l., Ak., U.S. D8 79
Iliamna Volcano, vol., Ak., U.S. C9 79
Ilion, N.Y., U.S. B5 109
Ilio Point, c., Hi., U.S. B4 88
Ilirska Bistrica, Slo. D9 14
Iljinskij, Russia H22 24
Ilkal, India E4 37
Illampu, Nevado, mtn., Bol. G5 54
Illapel, Chile C2 56
Illescas, Mex. F8 62
Illiers, Fr. D8 10
Illimani, Nevado, mtn., Bol. G5 54
Illinois, state, U.S. C4 90
Illinois, stm., U.S. A7 113
Illinois, stm., Il., U.S. B5 90
Illinois, stm., Or., U.S. E3 114
Illinois Peak, mtn., Id., U.S. B3 89
Illiopolis, Il., U.S. D4 90
Illizi, Alg. C7 42
Ilmo, Mo., U.S. D8 102
Il'men', Ozero, l., Russia C14 18
Ilo, Peru G4 54
Iloilo, Phil. C7 32
Ilomantsi, Fin. E18 6
Ilorin, Nig. G6 42
Il'pyrskij, Russia F26 24
Ilwaco, Wa., U.S. C1 124
Imabari, Japan H6 30
Iman, Russia H20 24
Imari, Japan I2 30

Name — Map Ref — Page

Imatra, Fin. F17 6
Imboden, Ar., U.S. A4 81
Imlay, Nv., U.S. C3 105
Imlay City, Mi., U.S. E7 99
Immenstadt, Ger. H10 8
Immokalee, Fl., U.S. F5 86
Imnaha, stm., Or., U.S. B10 114
Imola, Italy E6 14
Imperatriz, Braz. E9 54
Imperia, Italy F3 14
Imperial, Ca., U.S. F6 82
Imperial, Mo., U.S. C7 102
Imperial, Ne., U.S. D4 104
Imperial, Pa., U.S. k13 115
Imperial, co., Ca., U.S. F6 82
Imperial Beach, Ca., U.S. o15 82
Imperial Dam, U.S. E1 80
Imperial Reservoir, res., U.S. E1 80
Imperial Valley, val., Ca., U.S. F6 82
Impfondo, Congo A3 44
Imphāl, India H15 38
Imst, Aus. H10 8
Imuris, Mex. B4 62
Ina, Japan G10 30
Inari, Fin. B16 6
Inca, Spain F14 12
İncekum Burnu, c., Tur. A3 40
Inch'ŏn, S. Kor. D12 26
Incline Village, Nv., U.S. D2 105
Independence, Ia., U.S. B6 92
Independence, Ks., U.S. E8 93
Independence, Ky., U.S. B5 94
Independence, La., U.S. D5 95
Independence, Mo., U.S. B3 102
Independence, Or., U.S. C3 114
Independence, Va., U.S. D1 123
Independence, Wi., U.S. D2 126
Independence, co., Ar., U.S. B4 81
Independence, stm., N.Y., U.S. B5 109
Independence Mountains, mts., Nv., U.S. C5 105
Independence National Historical Park, Pa., U.S. p21 115
Independence Rock, mtn., Wy., U.S. D5 127
India, ctry., Asia E4 36
Indian, stm., Ont., Can. B7 73
Indian, stm., De., U.S. F4 85
Indian, stm., Mi., U.S. B4 99
Indian, stm., N.Y., U.S. A5 109
Indiana, Pa., U.S. E3 115
Indiana, co., Pa., U.S. E3 115
Indiana, state, U.S. E5 91
Indiana Dunes National Lakeshore, In., U.S. A3 91
Indianapolis, In., U.S. E5 91
Indian Bay, b., Fl., U.S. D4 86
Indian Cedar Swamp, sw., R.I., U.S. F2 116
Indian Creek, stm., Oh., U.S. C1 112
Indian Creek, stm., S.D., U.S. B2 118
Indian Creek, stm., Tn., U.S. B3 119
Indian Creek, stm., W.V., U.S. k9 125
Indian Creek, stm., W.V., U.S. D4 125
Indian Head, Md., U.S. C3 97
Indian Island, i., N.C., U.S. B6 110
Indian Lake, l., Mi., U.S. C4 99
Indian Lake, l., N.Y., U.S. B6 109
Indian Lake, l., Oh., U.S. B2 112
Indian Lake, l., R.I., U.S. F4 116
Indian Neck, Ct., U.S. D4 84
Indian Ocean G17 2
Indianola, Ia., U.S. C4 92
Indianola, Ms., U.S. B3 101
Indianola, Ne., U.S. D5 104
Indian Peak, mtn., Ut., U.S. E2 121
Indian Peak, mtn., Wy., U.S. B3 127
Indian Prairie Canal, Fl., U.S. E5 86
Indian River, co., Fl., U.S. E6 86
Indian River, b., Fl., U.S. D6 86
Indian River Bay, b., De., U.S. F5 85
Indian Rock, mtn., Wa., U.S. D5 124
Indian Rocks Beach, Fl., U.S. p10 86
Indian Springs, Nv., U.S. G6 105
Indian Stream, stm., N.H., U.S. f7 106
Indiantown, Fl., U.S. E6 86
Indian Trail, N.C., U.S. B2 110
Indigirka, stm., Russia C23 24
Indio, Ca., U.S. F5 82
Indispensable Reefs, rf., Sol.Is. B12 50
Indonesia, ctry., Asia F6 32
Indore, India I6 38
Indoukâl-n-Taghès, mtn., Niger E7 42
Indramayu, Indon. m14 33a
Indrāvati, stm., India C6 37
Indus, stm., Asia H2 38
İnegöl, Tur. I13 16
Infiernillo, Presa del, res., Mex. H9 62
I-n-Gall, Niger E7 42
Ingalls, In., U.S. E6 91
Ingalls Park, Il., U.S. B5 90
Ingersoll, Ont., Can. D4 73
Ingham, Austl. C9 50
Ingham, co., Mi., U.S. F6 99
Ingleside, Tx., U.S. F4 120
Inglewood, Ca., U.S. n12 82
Ingolstadt, Ger. G11 8
Ingraham, Lake, l., Fl., U.S. G5 86
Ingram, Pa., U.S. k13 115
In Guezzam, Alg. E7 42
Inhambane, Moz. F7 44
Inhambupe, Braz. F11 54
Inhaminga, Moz. E6 44
Inharrime, Moz. F7 44
Inírida, stm., Col. F8 58
Inkerman, N.B., Can. B5 71
Inkom, Id., U.S. G6 89
Inkster, Mi., U.S. p15 99
Inland Sea see Seto-naikai, Japan H6 30
Inle Lake, l., Mya. D4 34
Inman, Ks., U.S. D6 93
Inman, S.C., U.S. A3 117
Inn (En), stm., Eur. G13 8
Innamincka, Austl. E8 50
Inner Hebrides, is., Scot., U.K. E6 7
Innisfail, Alta., Can. C4 68
Innsbruck, Aus. H11 8
Inola, Ok., U.S. A6 113
Inongo, Zaire B3 44
Inowrocław, Pol. C18 8
In Salah, Alg. C6 42
Inscription House Ruin, hist., Az., U.S. A5 80
Insein, Mya. F4 34
Institute, W.V., U.S. m12 125
Interlachen, Fl., U.S. C5 86
Interlaken, Switz. F14 10
International Falls, Mn., U.S. B5 100
Inthanon, Doi, mtn., Thai. E5 34
Intiyaco, Arg. B4 56
Intracoastal Waterway, U.S. E4 95
Inukjuak, Que., Can. g11 74
Inveraray, Scot., U.K. E7 7
Invercargill, N.Z. G2 52
Inverell, Austl. E10 50
Inver Grove Heights, Mn., U.S. n12 100
Invermere, B.C., Can. D9 69
Inverness, Scot., U.K. D8 7
Inverness, Ca., U.S. C2 82
Inverness, Fl., U.S. D4 86
Inverness, Ms., U.S. B3 101
Inverurie, Scot., U.K. D10 7
Investigator Group, is., Austl. F6 50
Investigator Strait, strt., Austl. G7 50
Invisible Mountain, mtn., Id., U.S. F5 89
Inwood, Ia., U.S. A1 92
Inwood, N.Y., U.S. k13 109
Inwood, W.V., U.S. B6 125
Inyangani, mtn., Zimb. E6 44
Inyan Kara Creek, stm., Wy., U.S. B8 127
Inyan Kara Mountain, mtn., Wy., U.S. B8 127
Inyo, co., Ca., U.S. D5 82
Inyo, Mount, mtn., Ca., U.S. D5 82
Inyo Mountains, mts., Ca., U.S. D4 82
Ioánnina, Grc. J4 16
Iola, Ks., U.S. E8 93
Iola, Wi., U.S. D4 126
Iona, Id., U.S. F7 89
Ione, Ca., U.S. C3 82
Ionia, Mi., U.S. F5 99
Ionia, co., Mi., U.S. F5 99
Ionian Islands see Iónioi Nísoi, is., Grc. K4 16
Ionian Sea, Eur. H11 4
Iónioi Nísoi, is., Grc. K4 16
Iosco, co., Mi., U.S. D7 99
Iota, La., U.S. D3 95
Iowa, La., U.S. D2 95
Iowa, co., Ia., U.S. C5 92
Iowa, co., Wi., U.S. E3 126
Iowa, state, U.S. C4 92
Iowa, stm., Ia., U.S. C6 92
Iowa, West Branch, stm., Ia., U.S. B4 92
Iowa City, Ia., U.S. C6 92
Iowa Falls, Ia., U.S. B4 92
Iowa Indian Reservation, U.S. C8 93
Iowa Lake, l., U.S. A3 92
Iowa Park, Tx., U.S. C3 120
Ipameri, Braz. D4 57
Iphigenia Bay, b., Ak., U.S. n22 79
Ipiales, Col. G4 58
Ipiaú, Braz. C9 57
Ipoh, Malay. L6 34
Ipswich, Austl. E10 50
Ipswich, Eng., U.K. I14 7
Ipswich, Ma., U.S. A6 98
Ipswich, S.D., U.S. B6 118
Ipswich, stm., Ma., U.S. A5 98
Ipu, Braz. D10 54
Iqaluit, N.W. Ter., Can. D19 66
Iquique, Chile H4 54
Iquitos, Peru D4 54
Iraan, Tx., U.S. D2 120
Iráklion, Grc. N9 16
Iran, ctry., Asia B5 46
Iran Mountains, mts., Asia E5 32
Īrānshahr, Iran C7 46
Irapa, Ven. B11 58
Irapuato, Mex. G9 62
Iraq, ctry., Asia B3 46
Irazú, Volcán, vol., C.R. J6 64
Irbid, Jord. C4 40
Irbīl, Iraq A3 46
Iredell, co., N.C., U.S. B2 110
Ireland, ctry., Eur. E6 4
Iriga, Phil. r20 32
Iringa, Tan. C7 44
Irion, co., Tx., U.S. D2 120
Iriri, stm., Braz. D8 54
Irish, Mount, mtn., Nv., U.S. F6 105
Irish Sea, Eur. H8 7
Irkutsk, Russia G14 24
Irmo, S.C., U.S. C5 117
Iron, co., Mi., U.S. B2 99
Iron, co., Mo., U.S. D7 102
Iron, co., Ut., U.S. F2 121
Iron, co., Wi., U.S. B3 126
Irondale, Al., U.S. f7 78
Irondequoit, N.Y., U.S. B3 109
Iron Gate, val., Eur. E6 16
Iron Gate Reservoir, res., Eur. E5 16
Iron Gate Reservoir, res., Ca., U.S. B2 82
Iron Mountain, Mi., U.S. C2 99
Iron Mountain, mtn., Az., U.S. D4 80
Iron Mountains, mts., U.S. D1 123
Iron Ridge, Wi., U.S. E5 126
Iron River, Mi., U.S. B2 99
Iron River, Wi., U.S. B2 126
Ironton, Mo., U.S. D7 102
Ironton, Oh., U.S. D3 112
Ironwood, Mi., U.S. n11 99
Iroquois, Ont., Can. C9 73
Iroquois, co., Il., U.S. C6 90
Iroquois, stm., U.S. C6 90
Iroquois, Lake, l., Vt., U.S. B2 122
Irrawaddy see Ayeyarwady, stm., Mya. G3 34
Irricana, Alta., Can. D4 68
Irrigon, Or., U.S. B7 114
Irtyš (Ertix), stm., Asia F11 22
Irumu, Zaire A5 44
Irún, Spain B10 12
Irurzun, Spain C10 12
Irú Tepuy, mtn., Ven. E12 58
Irvine, Scot., U.K. F8 7
Irvine, Ca., U.S. n13 82
Irvine, Ky., U.S. C6 94
Irving, Tx., U.S. n10 120
Irvington, Al., U.S. E1 78
Irvington, Il., U.S. E4 90
Irvington, Ky., U.S. C3 94
Irvington, N.J., U.S. k8 107
Irvington, N.Y., U.S. g13 109
Irwin, Pa., U.S. F2 115
Irwin, co., Ga., U.S. E3 87
Irwinton, Ga., U.S. D3 87
Isabel, Mount, mtn., Wy., U.S. D2 127
Isabella, co., Mi., U.S. E6 99
Isabella, Cordillera, mts., Nic. G5 64
Isabella Indian Reservation, Mi., U.S. E6 99
Isabella Lake, l., Mn., U.S. C7 100
Ísafjördur, Ice. B3 4
Isahaya, Japan J3 30
Isanti, Mn., U.S. E5 100
Isanti, co., Mn., U.S. E5 100
Isar, stm., Eur. G11 8
Ischia, Italy I8 14
Ise, Japan H9 30
Isernia, Italy H9 14
Isesaki, Japan F12 30
Ise-wan, b., Japan H9 30
Isherton, Guy. F13 58
Ishikari-wan, b., Japan p18 30a
Ishinomaki, Japan D14 30
Ishpeming, Mi., U.S. B3 99
Isinglass, stm., N.H., U.S. D4 106
Isiolo, Kenya A7 44
Isiro, Zaire H11 42
İskele, N. Cyp. B3 40
İskenderun, Tur. H15 4
İskenderun Körfezi, b., Tur. A4 40
Iskitim, Russia G10 24
İslâhiye, Tur. A5 40
Islāmābād, Pak. D5 38
Islamorada, Fl., U.S. H6 86
Isla Mujeres, Mex. G16 62
Island, co., Wa., U.S. A3 124
Island Beach, N.J., U.S. D4 107
Island City, Or., U.S. B8 114
Island Falls, Me., U.S. B4 96
Island Lake, l., Man., Can. C4 70
Island Park, R.I., U.S. E6 116
Island Park Reservoir, res., Id., U.S. E7 89
Island Pond, Vt., U.S. B5 122
Island Pond, l., N.H., U.S. E4 106
Islands, Bay of, b., Newf., Can. D2 72
Isla Vista, Ca., U.S. E4 82
Islay, i., Scot., U.K. F6 7
Isle-aux-Morts, Newf., Can. E2 72
Isle of Man, dep., Eur. E7 4
Isle of Palms, S.C., U.S. k12 117
Isle of Wight, co., Va., U.S. D6 123
Isle of Wight Bay, b., Md., U.S. D7 97
Isle Royale National Park, Mi., U.S. h9 99
Islesboro Island, i., Me., U.S. D4 96
Isleta, N.M., U.S. C3 108
Isleta Indian Reservation, N.M., U.S. C3 108
Islington, Ma., U.S. h11 98
Isola, Ms., U.S. B3 101
Isola della Scala, Italy D5 14
Ispica, Italy M9 14
Israel (Yisra'el), ctry., Asia D4 40
Israel, stm., N.H., U.S. B3 106
Issano, Guy. E13 58
Issaquah, Wa., U.S. B3 124
Issaquena, co., Ms., U.S. C2 101
Issoire, Fr. G10 10
Issoudun, Fr. F8 10
Is-sur-Tille, Fr. E12 10
Issyk-Kul', Kyrg. I13 22
İstanbul, Tur. G13 4
İstanbul Boğazı (Bosporus), strt., Tur. H13 16
Isto, Mount, mtn., Ak., U.S. B11 79
Istokpoga, Lake, l., Fl., U.S. E5 86
Itabaiana, Braz. F11 54
Itaberaí, Braz. G9 54
Itabira, Braz. E7 57
Itabuna, Braz. C9 57
Itacoatiara, Braz. D7 54
Itagüí, Col. D5 58
Itaituba, Braz. D7 54
Itajaí, Braz. B7 56
Itajubá, Braz. G6 57
Italy, Tx., U.S. C4 120
Italy, ctry., Eur. G10 4
Itaperuna, Braz. F8 57
Itapetinga, Braz. C8 57
Itapetininga, Braz. G4 57
Itapeva, Braz. G4 57
Itapicuru, stm., Braz. D10 54
Itapira, Braz. G5 57
Itaquari, Braz. F8 57
Itararé, Braz. H4 57
Itārsi, India I7 38
Itasca, Il., U.S. k8 90
Itasca, Tx., U.S. C4 120
Itasca, co., Mn., U.S. C5 100
Itasca, Lake, l., Mn., U.S. C3 100
Itawamba, co., Ms., U.S. A5 101
Ithaca, Mi., U.S. E6 99
Ithaca, N.Y., U.S. C4 109
Itō, Japan H12 30
Itta Bena, Ms., U.S. B3 101
Ittiri, Italy I3 14
Ituberá, Braz. B9 57
Ituiutaba, Braz. E4 57
Itumbiara, Braz. E4 57
Ituni, Guy. E13 58
Ituri, stm., Zaire A5 44
Iturup, Ostrov (Etorofu-tō), i., Russia I23 24
Ituverava, Braz. F5 57
Ituxi, stm., Braz. E5 54
Itzehoe, Ger. B9 8
Iuka, Ms., U.S. A5 101
Iva, S.C., U.S. C2 117
Ivalo, Fin. B16 6
Ivanhoe, Mn., U.S. F2 100
Ivanić Grad, Cro. D11 14
Ivano-Frankivs'k, Ukr. H2 22
Ivanovo, Russia D23 18
Ivigtut, Grnld. D23 66
Ivinheima, stm., Braz. G2 57
Ivins, Ut., U.S. F2 121
Ivory Coast, ctry., Afr. G4 42
Ivoryton, Ct., U.S. D6 84
Ivrea, Italy D2 14
Iwaki (Taira), Japan E13 30
Iwakuni, Japan H5 30
Iwanai, Japan q18 30a
Iwanuma, Japan D13 30
Iwo, Nig. G6 42
Ixtacihuatl, vol., Mex. H10 62
Iyo-nada, Japan I5 30
Izabal, Lago de, l., Guat. G3 64
Izard, co., Ar., U.S. A4 81
Izegem, Bel. E3 8
Iževsk, Russia F8 22
İzmir, Tur. H13 4
İzmit, Tur. G13 4
Iznalloz, Spain H8 12
İznik Gölü, l., Tur. I13 16
Izozog, Bañados de, sw., Bol. G6 54
Izúcar de Matamoros, Mex. H10 62
Izuhara, Japan H2 30
Izumo, Japan G5 30
Izu-shotō, is., Japan H12 30
Izvestij CIK, Ostrova, is., Russia B10 24

J

Jabalpur, India I8 38
Jabbūl, Sabkhat al-, l., Syria A5 40
Jablah, Syria B4 40
Jablonec nad Nisou, Czech. E15 8
Jaboatão, Braz. E11 54
Jabrīn, well, Sau. Ar. D4 46
Jaca, Spain C11 12
Jacarèzinho, Braz. G4 57
Jáchal, Arg. C3 56
Jacinto City, Tx., U.S. r14 120
Jack, co., Tx., U.S. C3 120
Jackfish Lake, l., Sask., Can. D1 75
Jackman, Me., U.S. C2 96
Jackman Station, Me., U.S. C2 96
Jack Mountain, mtn., Mt., U.S. D4 103
Jack Mountain, mtn., Wa., U.S. A5 124
Jackpot, Nv., U.S. B7 105
Jacksboro, Tn., U.S. C9 119
Jacksboro, Tx., U.S. C3 120
Jacks Mountain, mtn., Pa., U.S. E6 115
Jackson, Al., U.S. D2 78
Jackson, Ca., U.S. C3 82
Jackson, Ga., U.S. C3 87
Jackson, Ky., U.S. C6 94
Jackson, La., U.S. D4 95
Jackson, Mi., U.S. F6 99
Jackson, Mn., U.S. G4 100
Jackson, Ms., U.S. C3 101
Jackson, Mo., U.S. D8 102
Jackson, Oh., U.S. C3 112
Jackson, S.C., U.S. E4 117
Jackson, Tn., U.S. B3 119
Jackson, Wi., U.S. E5 126
Jackson, Wy., U.S. C2 127
Jackson, co., Al., U.S. A3 78
Jackson, co., Ar., U.S. B4 81
Jackson, co., Co., U.S. A4 83
Jackson, co., Fl., U.S. B1 86
Jackson, co., Ga., U.S. B3 87
Jackson, co., Il., U.S. F4 90
Jackson, co., In., U.S. G5 91
Jackson, co., Ia., U.S. B7 92
Jackson, co., Ks., U.S. C8 93
Jackson, co., Ky., U.S. C5 94
Jackson, co., La., U.S. B3 95
Jackson, co., Mi., U.S. F6 99
Jackson, co., Mn., U.S. G3 100
Jackson, co., Ms., U.S. E5 101
Jackson, co., Mo., U.S. B3 102
Jackson, co., N.C., U.S. f9 110
Jackson, co., Oh., U.S. C3 112
Jackson, co., Ok., U.S. C2 113
Jackson, co., Or., U.S. E4 114
Jackson, co., S.D., U.S. D4 118
Jackson, co., Tn., U.S. C8 119
Jackson, co., Tx., U.S. E4 120
Jackson, co., W.V., U.S. C3 125
Jackson, co., Wi., U.S. D3 126
Jackson, stm., Va., U.S. C3 123
Jackson, Lake, l., Fl., U.S. E5 86
Jackson, Lake, l., Fl., U.S. B2 86
Jackson, Mount, mtn., N.H., U.S. B4 106
Jackson Center, Oh., U.S. B1 112
Jackson Lake, res., Wy., U.S. C2 127
Jackson Mountains, mts., Nv., U.S. B3 105
Jackson's Arm, Newf., Can. D3 72
Jacksons Gap, Al., U.S. C4 78
Jacksonville, Al., U.S. B4 78
Jacksonville, Ar., U.S. C3 81
Jacksonville, Fl., U.S. B5 86
Jacksonville, Il., U.S. D3 90
Jacksonville, N.C., U.S. C5 110
Jacksonville, Or., U.S. E4 114
Jacksonville, Tx., U.S. D5 120
Jacksonville Beach, Fl., U.S. B5 86
Jacksonville Naval Air Station, mil., Fl., U.S. B5 86
Jacks Peak, mtn., Ut., U.S. E3 121
Jacmel, Haiti E11 64
Jacobābād, Pak. F3 38
Jacques-Cartier, stm., Que., Can. B6 74
Jacques-Cartier, Détroit de, strt., Que., Can. h8 72
Jacquet River, N.B., Can. B4 71
Jadraque, Spain E9 12
Jaén, Peru E3 54
Jaén, Spain H8 12
Jaffna, Sri L. H6 37
Jaffrey, N.H., U.S. E2 106
Jafr, Qā' al-, depr., Jord. D5 40
Jagādhri, India E7 38
Jagdalpur, India C7 37
Jagersfontein, S. Afr. G5 44
Jagodnoje, Russia E23 24
Jagtiāl, India C5 37
Jaguarão, Braz. C6 56
Jahrom, Iran C5 46
Jaidak, Afg. E2 38
Jaipur, India G6 38
Jajce, Bos. E12 14
Jakarta, Indon. m13 32
Jakobshavn, Grnld. C22 66
Jakobstad (Pietarsaari), Fin. E14 6
Jakutsk, Russia E19 24
Jal, N.M., U.S. E6 108
Jalālābād, Afg. C4 38
Jalapa, Guat. G3 64
Jalapa Enríquez, Mex. H11 62
Jālgaon, India B3 37
Jālna, India C3 37
Jalostotitlán, Mex. G8 62
Jalpaiguri, India G13 38
Jaltepec, stm., Mex. I12 62
Jamaica, ctry., N.A. E9 64
Jamaica Bay, b., N.Y., U.S. k13 109
Jamaica Channel, strt., N.A. E10 64
Jamālpur, Bngl. H13 38
Jamālpur, India H12 38
Jamame, Som. A8 44
Jambi, Indon. F3 32
Jambol, Bul. G10 16
James, stm., U.S. C7 76
James, stm., Mo., U.S. E4 102
James, stm., Va., U.S. C5 123
James, Lake, l., In., U.S. A7 91
James, Lake, res., N.C., U.S. B1 110
James Bay, b., Can. F16 66
James Branch, stm., De., U.S. F3 85
Jamesburg, N.J., U.S. C4 107
James City, N.C., U.S. B5 110
James City, co., Va., U.S. C6 123
James Island, S.C., U.S. k12 117
James Island, i., Md., U.S. C5 97
James Island, i., S.C., U.S. F8 117
James River Bridge, Va., U.S. k15 123
Jamestown, In., U.S. E4 91
Jamestown, Ky., U.S. D4 94
Jamestown, N.Y., U.S. C1 109
Jamestown, N.C., U.S. B3 110
Jamestown, N.D., U.S. C7 111
Jamestown, Oh., U.S. C2 112
Jamestown, R.I., U.S. F5 116
Jamestown, Tn., U.S. C9 119
James Town, Wy., U.S. E3 127
Jamestown Dam, N.D., U.S. C7 111
Jamestown Reservoir, res., N.D., U.S. C7 111
Jamiltepec, Mex. I11 62
Jamkhandi, India D3 37
Jammu, India D6 38
Jammu and Kashmir, dep., Asia C6 38
Jāmnagar, India I4 38
Jāmpur, Pak. F4 38
Jämsä, Fin. F15 6
Jamshedpur, India I12 38
Jamsk, Russia F24 24
Jamūi, India H12 38
Jamuna, stm., Bngl. H13 38
Jana, stm., Russia C21 24
Janaucu, Ilha, i., Braz. C8 54
Janesville, Ca., U.S. B3 82
Janesville, Ia., U.S. B5 92
Janesville, Mn., U.S. F5 100
Janesville, Wi., U.S. F4 126
Jangipur, India H13 38
Janīn, W. Bank C4 40
Janskij, Russia D20 24
Janskij Zaliv, b., Russia C21 24
Januária, Braz. C6 57
Jaora, India I6 38
Japan, ctry., Asia D14 26
Japan, Sea of, Asia D13 26
Japurá (Caquetá), stm., S.A. D5 54
Jaqué, Pan. K8 64
Jarābulus, Syria A6 40
Jaraiz de la Vera, Spain E6 12
Jarash, Jord. C4 40
Jarcevo, Russia F15 18
Jardines de la Reina, is., Cuba D8 64
Jari, stm., Braz. D8 54
Jaridih, India I12 38
Jaroslavl', Russia D22 18
Jarosław, Pol. E22 8
Jarrettsville, Md., U.S. A5 97
Järvenpää, Fin. F15 6
Järvsö, Swe. F11 6
Jask, Iran C6 46
Jasmine Estates, Fl., U.S. D4 86
Jasnyj, Russia G19 24
Jasonville, In., U.S. F3 91
Jasper, Al., U.S. B2 78
Jasper, Fl., U.S. B4 86
Jasper, Ga., U.S. B2 87
Jasper, In., U.S. H4 91
Jasper, Mo., U.S. D3 102
Jasper, Tn., U.S. D8 119
Jasper, Tx., U.S. D6 120
Jasper, co., Ga., U.S. C3 87
Jasper, co., Il., U.S. D5 90
Jasper, co., In., U.S. B3 91
Jasper, co., Ia., U.S. C4 92
Jasper, co., Ms., U.S. C4 101
Jasper, co., Mo., U.S. D3 102
Jasper, co., S.C., U.S. G5 117
Jasper, co., Tx., U.S. D5 120
Jasper National Park, Alta., Can. C1 68
Jataí, Braz. D3 57
Játiva, Spain G11 12
Jatni, India J11 38
Jaú, Braz. G4 57
Jauaperi, stm., Braz. C6 54
Jauja, Peru F3 54
Jaunpur, India H10 38
Java see Jawa, i., Indon. G4 32
Javari (Yavarí), stm., S.A. D4 54
Java Sea see Jawa, Laut, Indon. G4 32

Name | Map Ref | Page
Jävre, Swe. D13 6
Jawa, i., Indon. G4 32
Jawa, Laut (Java Sea), Indon. G4 32
Jaworzno, Pol. E19 8
Jay, Ok., U.S. A7 113
Jay, co., In., U.S. D7 91
Jaya, Puncak, mtn., Indon. F10 32
Jayapura, Indon. F11 32
Jayb, Wādī al-, val., Asia D4 40
J. B. Thomas, Lake, res., Tx., U.S. C2 120
Jean, Nv., U.S. H6 105
Jeanerette, La., U.S. E4 95
Jean Lafitte National Historical Park, La., U.S. k12 95
Jeannette, Pa., U.S. F2 115
Jebba, Nig. G6 42
Jeddore Lake, res., Newf., Can. D3 72
Jeff Davis, co., Ga., U.S. E4 87
Jeff Davis, co., Tx., U.S. o12 120
Jefferson, Ga., U.S. B3 87
Jefferson, Ia., U.S. B3 92
Jefferson, La., U.S. k11 95
Jefferson, N.C., U.S. A1 110
Jefferson, Oh., U.S. A5 112
Jefferson, Or., U.S. C3 114
Jefferson, S.C., U.S. B7 117
Jefferson, Tx., U.S. C5 120
Jefferson, Wi., U.S. E5 126
Jefferson, co., Al., U.S. B3 78
Jefferson, co., Ar., U.S. C3 81
Jefferson, co., Co., U.S. B5 83
Jefferson, co., Fl., U.S. B3 86
Jefferson, co., Ga., U.S. C4 87
Jefferson, co., Id., U.S. F6 89
Jefferson, co., Il., U.S. E5 90
Jefferson, co., In., U.S. G6 91
Jefferson, co., Ia., U.S. C5 92
Jefferson, co., Ks., U.S. C8 93
Jefferson, co., Ky., U.S. B4 94
Jefferson, co., La., U.S. E5 95
Jefferson, co., Ms., U.S. D2 101
Jefferson, co., Mo., U.S. C7 102
Jefferson, co., Mt., U.S. D4 103
Jefferson, co., Ne., U.S. D8 104
Jefferson, co., N.Y., U.S. A5 109
Jefferson, co., Oh., U.S. B5 112
Jefferson, co., Ok., U.S. C4 113
Jefferson, co., Or., U.S. C5 114
Jefferson, co., Pa., U.S. D3 115
Jefferson, co., Tn., U.S. C10 119
Jefferson, co., Tx., U.S. E5 120
Jefferson, co., Wa., U.S. B1 124
Jefferson, co., W.V., U.S. B7 125
Jefferson, co., Wi., U.S. E5 126
Jefferson, stm., Mt., U.S. E5 103
Jefferson, Mount, mtn., Id., U.S. E7 89
Jefferson, Mount, mtn., Nv., U.S. E5 105
Jefferson, Mount, mtn., Or., U.S. C5 114
Jefferson City, Mo., U.S. C5 102
Jefferson City, Tn., U.S. C10 119
Jefferson Davis, co., La., U.S. D3 95
Jefferson Davis, co., Ms., U.S. D4 101
Jefferson Farms, De., U.S. i7 85
Jefferson Proving Ground, mil., In., U.S. G7 91
Jeffersontown, Ky., U.S. B4 94
Jeffersonville, Ga., U.S. D3 87
Jeffersonville, In., U.S. H6 91
Jeffersonville, Ky., U.S. C6 94
Jeffersonville, Oh., U.S. C2 112
Jeffrey, W.V., U.S. D3 125
Jeffrey City, Wy., U.S. D5 127
Jeffries Creek, stm., S.C., U.S. C8 117
Jefremov, Russia H21 18
Jegorjevsk, Russia F22 18
Jehossee Island, i., S.C., U.S. k11 117
Jejsk, Russia H5 22
Jekaterinburg, Russia F10 22
Jekyll Island, i., Ga., U.S. E5 87
Jelec, Russia I21 18
Jelenia Góra (Hirschberg), Pol. E15 8
Jelgava, Lat. E6 18
Jellico, Tn., U.S. C9 119
Jelm Mountain, mtn., Wy., U.S. E7 127
Jeloguj, stm., Russia E11 24
Jember, Indon. n16 32
Jemez, stm., N.M., U.S. k7 108
Jemez Canyon Dam, N.M., U.S. k7 108
Jemez Indian Reservation, N.M., U.S. h7 108
Jemez Pueblo, N.M., U.S. B3 108
Jemison, Al., U.S. C3 78
Jena, Ger. E11 8
Jena, La., U.S. C3 95
Jenašimskij Polkan, Gora, mtn., Russia F12 24
Jendouba (Souk el Arba), Tun. M3 14
Jenisej, stm., Russia D11 24
Jenisejsk, Russia F12 24
Jenisejskij Zaliv, b., Russia C10 24
Jenkins, Ky., U.S. C7 94
Jenkins, co., Ga., U.S. D5 87
Jenkintown, Pa., U.S. o21 115
Jenks, Ok., U.S. A6 113
Jennings, La., U.S. D3 95
Jennings, Mo., U.S. f13 102
Jennings, co., In., U.S. G6 91
Jensen Beach, Fl., U.S. E6 86
Jepara, Indon. m15 33a
Jequié, Braz. B8 57
Jequitinhonha, stm., Braz. D9 57
Jerada, Mor. B5 42
Jerauld, co., S.D., U.S. C7 118
Jérémie, Haiti E10 64
Jeremoabo, Braz. F11 54
Jerevan, Arm. I6 22
Jerez de García Salinas, Mex. F8 62
Jerez de la Frontera, Spain I5 12
Jerez de los Caballeros, Spain G5 12
Jericho, Vt., U.S. B3 122
Jericho see Arīḥā, W. Bank D4 40
Jerimoth Hill, hill, R.I., U.S. C1 116
Jermyn, Pa., U.S. C10 115
Jerofej Pavlovič, Russia G18 24
Jerome, Id., U.S. G4 89
Jerome, Pa., U.S. F4 115
Jerome, co., Id., U.S. G4 89
Jeropol, Russia D27 24
Jersey, co., Il., U.S. D3 90
Jersey, dep., Eur. C4 10
Jersey City, N.J., U.S. B4 107
Jersey Mountain, mtn., Id., U.S. E3 89
Jersey Shore, Pa., U.S. D7 115
Jerseyville, Il., U.S. D3 90
Jerusalem see Yerushalayim, Isr. D4 40
Jervis Inlet, b., B.C., Can. D6 69
Jesenice, Slo. C9 14
Jessamine, co., Ky., U.S. C5 94
Jessore, Bngl. I13 38
Jessup, Md., U.S. B4 97
Jessup, Pa., U.S. m18 115
Jesup, Ga., U.S. E5 87
Jesup, Ia., U.S. B5 92
Jesup, Lake, l., Fl., U.S. D5 86
Jésus, Île, i., Que., Can. p19 74
Jesús Carranza, Mex. I12 62
Jetmore, Ks., U.S. D4 93
Jeumont, Fr. B11 10
Jever, Ger. B7 8
Jewel Cave National Monument, S.D., U.S. D2 118
Jewell, Ia., U.S. B4 92
Jewell, co., Ks., U.S. C5 93
Jewett City, Ct., U.S. C8 84
Jeypore, India C7 37
Jhang Maghiāna, Pak. E5 38
Jhānsi, India H8 38
Jharia, India I12 38
Jhelum, Pak. D5 38
Jhelum, stm., Asia E5 38
Jiading, China D10 28
Jiaganj, India H13 38
Jiamusi, China B13 26
Jian, China H3 28
Jianchuan, China A5 34
Jiangmen, China M2 28
Jiangsu, prov., China E10 26
Jiangxi, prov., China F10 26
Jiangyin, China D9 28
Jiangzi, China F13 38
Jianou, China H7 28
Jianshui, China C7 34
Jiaoxian, China D10 26
Jiaozuo, China D9 26
Jiashan, China C6 28
Jiawang, China A6 28
Jiaxian, China A2 28
Jiaxing, China E9 28
Jiazi, China M5 28
Jicarilla Apache Indian Reservation, N.M., U.S. A2 108
Jiddah, Sau. Ar. D2 46
Jieshou, China B4 28
Jieyang, China L5 28
Jihlava, Czech. F15 8
Jijiga, Eth. G3 46
Jijona, Spain G11 12
Jilemutu, China A11 26
Jilin, China C12 26
Jilin, prov., China C12 26
Jill, Kediet ej, mtn., Maur. D3 42
Jima, Eth. G2 46
Jimena de la Frontera, Spain I6 12
Jim Hogg, co., Tx., U.S. F3 120
Jim Lake, res., N.D., U.S. B7 111
Jim Thorpe, Pa., U.S. E10 115
Jim Wells, co., Tx., U.S. F3 120
Jinan (Tsinan), China D10 26
Jīnd, India F7 38
Jingdezhen (Kingtechen), China F6 28
Jingjiang, China C9 28
Jingxi, China C9 34
Jinhua, China F8 28
Jining, China C9 26
Jining, China D10 26
Jinja, Ug. A6 44
Jinning (Jiukunyang), China B7 34
Jinotega, Nic. H4 64
Jinshi, China F9 26
Jinxian, China D11 26
Jinzhou, China C11 26
Jiparaná, stm., Braz. E6 54
Jipijapa, Ec. H2 58
Jirjā, Egypt C12 42
Jisr ash-Shughūr, Syria B5 40
Jiujiang, China F4 28
Jiuling Shan, mts., China G3 28
Jiumangya, China B14 38
Jiuquan, China D6 26
Jixi, China B13 26
Joaçaba, Braz. B6 56
Joanna, S.C., U.S. C4 117
João Pessoa, Braz. E12 54
Joaquín V. González, Arg. B4 56
Job Peak, mtn., Nv., U.S. D3 105
Jobson (Vera), Arg. B4 56
Jocassee, Lake, res., U.S. B1 117
Jódar, Spain H8 12
Jo Daviess, co., Il., U.S. A3 90
Jodhpur, India G5 38
Joe Batt's Arm [-Barr'd Islands-Shoal Bay], Newf., Can. D4 72
Joensuu, Fin. E17 6
Joes Brook, stm., Vt., U.S. C4 122
Joes Creek, stm., W.V., U.S. m12 125
Joffre, Mount, mtn., Can. D3 68
Jogjakarta see Yogyakarta, Indon. G5 32
Johannesburg, S. Afr. G5 44
Johar, Som. H4 46
John, Cape, c., N.S., Can. D6 71
John Day, Or., U.S. C8 114
John Day, stm., Or., U.S. B6 114
John Day Dam, U.S. D5 124
John Day Fossil Beds National Monument, Or., U.S. C6 114
John F. Kennedy Space Center, sci., Fl., U.S. D6 86
John H. Kerr Dam, Va., U.S. D4 123
John H. Kerr Reservoir, res., U.S. D4 123
John Martin Reservoir, res., Co., U.S. C7 83
John Muir National Historical Site, hist., Ca., U.S. h8 82
John o' Groats, Scot., U.K. C9 7
John Redmond Reservoir, res., Ks., U.S. D8 93
John Sevier, Tn., U.S. m14 119
Johns Island, i., S.C., U.S. F7 117
Johnson, Ks., U.S. E2 93
Johnson, Vt., U.S. B3 122
Johnson, co., Ar., U.S. B2 81
Johnson, co., Ga., U.S. D4 87
Johnson, co., Il., U.S. F5 90
Johnson, co., In., U.S. F5 91
Johnson, co., Ia., U.S. C6 92
Johnson, co., Ks., U.S. D9 93
Johnson, co., Ky., U.S. C7 94
Johnson, co., Mo., U.S. C4 102
Johnson, co., Ne., U.S. D9 104
Johnson, co., Tn., U.S. C12 119
Johnson, co., Tx., U.S. C4 120
Johnson, co., Wy., U.S. B6 127
Johnsonburg, Pa., U.S. D4 115
Johnson City, N.Y., U.S. C5 109
Johnson City, Tn., U.S. C11 119
Johnson City, Tx., U.S. D3 120
Johnson Creek, Wi., U.S. E5 126
Johnsonville, S.C., U.S. D9 117
Johns Pass, strt., Fl., U.S. p10 86
Johnston, Ia., U.S. e8 92
Johnston, R.I., U.S. C4 116
Johnston, S.C., U.S. D4 117
Johnston, co., N.C., U.S. B4 110
Johnston, co., Ok., U.S. C5 113
Johnston City, Il., U.S. F5 90
Johnston Key, i., Fl., U.S. H5 86
Johnstown, Co., U.S. A6 83
Johnstown, N.Y., U.S. B6 109
Johnstown, Oh., U.S. B3 112
Johnstown, Pa., U.S. F4 115
John W. Flannagan Reservoir, res., Va., U.S. e9 123
Johor Baharu, Malay. N7 34
Joigny, Fr. E10 10
Joiner, Ar., U.S. B5 81
Joinvile, Braz. B7 56
Joinville, Fr. D12 10
Jokkmokk, Swe. C12 6
Joliet, Il., U.S. B5 90
Joliette, Que., Can. C4 74
Jolo Island, i., Phil. D7 32
Jombang, Indon. m16 33a
Jones, Ok., U.S. B4 113
Jones, co., Ga., U.S. C3 87
Jones, co., Ia., U.S. B6 92
Jones, co., Ms., U.S. D4 101
Jones, co., N.C., U.S. B5 110
Jones, co., S.D., U.S. D5 118
Jones, co., Tx., U.S. C3 120
Jonesboro, Ar., U.S. B5 81
Jonesboro, Ga., U.S. C2 87
Jonesboro, Il., U.S. F4 90
Jonesboro, In., U.S. D6 91
Jonesboro, La., U.S. B3 95
Jonesborough, Tn., U.S. C11 119
Jonesburg, Mo., U.S. C6 102
Jones Creek, Tx., U.S. s14 120
Jones Mill, Ar., U.S. C3 81
Jonesport, Me., U.S. D5 96
Jones Sound, strt., N.W. Ter., Can. A15 66
Jonestown, Ms., U.S. A3 101
Jonesville, La., U.S. C4 95
Jonesville, Mi., U.S. G6 99
Jonesville, N.C., U.S. A2 110
Jonesville, S.C., U.S. B4 117
Jonesville, Va., U.S. f8 123
Jongkha, China F11 38
Jönköping, Swe. H10 6
Jonquière, Que., Can. A6 74
Jonzac, Fr. G6 10
Joplin, Mo., U.S. D3 102
Joppatowne, Md., U.S. B5 97
Jordan, Mn., U.S. F5 100
Jordan, ctry., Asia D5 40
Jordan, stm., Asia C4 40
Jordan, stm., Ut., U.S. C4 121
Jordan Creek, stm., U.S. E9 114
Jordan Lake, res., Al., U.S. C3 78
Jorhāt, India G16 38
Jörn, Swe. D13 6
Jornado del Muerto, des., N.M., U.S. D3 108
Jos, Nig. G7 42
José Battle y Ordóñez, Ur. C5 56
Joseph, Or., U.S. B9 114
Joseph, Lac, l., Newf., Can. h8 72
Joseph Bonaparte Gulf, b., Austl. B5 50
Joseph City, Az., U.S. C5 80
Josephine, co., Or., U.S. E3 114
Joshua, Tx., U.S. n9 120
Joshua Tree, Ca., U.S. E5 82
Joshua Tree National Park, Ca., U.S. F6 82
Joškar-Ola, Russia F7 22
Jourdanton, Tx., U.S. E3 120
Joutsijärvi, Fin. C16 6
Jovellanos, Cuba C7 64
J. Percy Priest Lake, res., Tn., U.S. A5 119
Juab, co., Ut., U.S. D2 121
Juan Aldama, Mex. E8 62
Juan de Fuca, Strait of, strt., N.A. G8 66
Juan de Nova, Île, i., Reu. E8 44
Juárez, Arg. D5 56
Juàzeiro, Braz. E10 54
Juàzeiro do Norte, Braz. E11 54
Jūbā, Sudan H12 42
Juba (Genale), stm., Afr. H3 46
Juchitán [de Zaragoza], Mex. I12 62
Judenburg, Aus. H14 8
Judith, stm., Mt., U.S. C7 103
Judith, Point, c., R.I., U.S. G4 85
Judith Basin, co., Mt., U.S. C6 103
Judith Island, i., N.C., U.S. B6 110
Judith Mountains, mts., Mt., U.S. C7 103
Judith Peak, mtn., Mt., U.S. C7 103
Judoma, stm., Russia F21 24
Judsonia, Ar., U.S. B4 81
Juigalpa, Nic. H5 64
Juiz de Fora, Braz. F7 57
Jukagirskoje Ploskogorje, plat., Russia D24 24
Jukte, Russia E15 24
Julesburg, Co., U.S. A8 83
Juliaca, Peru G4 54
Julian, Ca., U.S. F5 82
Julian, W.V., U.S. C3 125
Julian Alps, mts., Eur. C8 14
Juliana Top, mtn., Sur. C7 54
Julianehåb, Grnld. D23 66
Jülich, Ger. E6 8
Jullundur, India E6 38
Jumbo Peak, mtn., Nv., U.S. G7 105
Jumentos Cays, is., Bah. C10 64
Jumet, Bel. E4 8
Jumilla, Spain G10 12
Jump, stm., Wi., U.S. C3 126
Junāgadh, India J4 38
Junction, Tx., U.S. D3 120
Junction City, Ar., U.S. D3 81
Junction City, Ks., U.S. C7 93
Junction City, Ky., U.S. C5 94
Junction City, La., U.S. A3 95
Junction City, Or., U.S. C3 114
Jundiaí, Braz. G5 57
Juneau, Ak., U.S. D13 79
Juneau, Wi., U.S. E5 126
Juneau, co., Wi., U.S. E3 126
June in Winter, Lake, l., Fl., U.S. E5 86
Jungfrau, mtn., Switz. F14 10
Junggar Pendi, China B4 26
Juniata, Ne., U.S. D7 104
Juniata, co., Pa., U.S. F7 115
Juniata, stm., Pa., U.S. F7 115
Junín, Arg. C4 56
Junín, Lago de, l., Peru F3 54
Junín de los Andes, Arg. D2 56
Junior Lake, l., Me., U.S. C4 96
Juniper Mountains, mts., Az., U.S. B2 80
Junipero Serra Peak, mtn., Ca., U.S. D3 82
Junsele, Swe. E11 6
Jupiter, Fl., U.S. F6 86
Jupiter Inlet, b., Fl., U.S. F6 86
Jupiter Island, i., Fl., U.S. E6 86
Jura, mts., Eur. F13 10
Jura, i., Scot., U.K. F7 7
Jurga, Russia F10 24
Jūrmala, Lat. E6 18
Juruá, stm., S.A. D5 54
Juruena, stm., Braz. E7 54
Justin, Tx., U.S. C4 120
Justo Daract, Arg. C3 56
Jutaí, stm., Braz. D5 54
Jüterbog, Ger. D13 8
Jutiapa, Guat. G3 64
Juticalpa, Hond. G4 64
Jutland see Jylland, pen., Den. H7 6
Juventud, Isla de la (Isle of Pines), i., Cuba D6 64
Juwara, Oman E6 46
Juža, Russia E25 18
Južno-Sachalinsk, Russia H22 24
Južnyj, Mys, c., Russia F25 24
Jwayyā, Leb. C4 40
Jylland, pen., Den. H7 6
Jyväskylä, Fin. E15 6

K

K2 (Qogir Feng), mtn., Asia C7 38
Kaaawa, Hi., U.S. f10 88
Kaala, mtn., Hi., U.S. f9 88
Kaala Djerda, Tun. N3 14
Kaalualu Bay, b., Hi., U.S. E6 88
Kaamakua, Puu, mtn., Hi., U.S. f10 88
Kabale, Ug. B5 44
Kabalo, Zaire C5 44
Kabambare, Zaire B5 44
Kåbdalis, Swe. C12 6
Kabetogama Lake, l., Mn., U.S. B5 100
Kabīr Kūh, mts., Iran B4 46
Kābol, Afg. C3 38
Kabompo, stm., Zam. D4 44
Kabongo, Zaire C5 44
Kābul, stm., Asia C4 38
Kabwe (Broken Hill), Zam. D5 44
Kachess Lake, res., Wa., U.S. B4 124
K'achta, Russia G15 24
Kačug, Russia G15 24
Kadan Kyun, i., Mya. H5 34
Kadiri, India E5 37
Kadoka, S.D., U.S. D4 118
Kaduna, Nig. F7 42
Kāduqlī, Sudan F11 42
Kadykčan, Russia E23 24
Kaédi, Maur. E3 42
Kaena Point, c., Hi., U.S. B3 88
Kaesŏng, N. Kor. D12 26
Kafia Kingi, Sudan G10 42
Kafue, stm., Zam. D5 44
Kaga, Japan F9 30
Kagamigahara, Japan G9 30
Kagaznagar, India C5 37
Kagoshima, Japan K3 30
Kahaluu, Hi., U.S. D6 88
Kahaluu, Hi., U.S. g10 88
Kahana Bay, b., Hi., U.S. f10 88
Kahemba, Zaire C3 44
Kahoka, Mo., U.S. A6 102
Kahoolawe, i., Hi., U.S. C5 88
Kahramanmaraş, Tur. H15 4
Kahuku, Hi., U.S. B4 88
Kahuku Point, c., Hi., U.S. B4 88
Kahului, Hi., U.S. C5 88
Kahului Bay, b., Hi., U.S. C5 88
Kai, Kepulauan, is., Indon. G9 32
Kaibab Indian Reservation, Az., U.S. A3 80
Kaieteur Fall, wtfl, Guy. E13 58
Kaifeng, China E9 26
Kaikoura, N.Z. E4 52
Kaili, China A10 34
Kailua, Hi., U.S. B4 88
Kailua Bay, b., Hi., U.S. g11 88
Kailua Kona, Hi., U.S. D6 88
Kaimana, Indon. F9 32
Kaimanawa Mountains, mts., N.Z. C5 52
Kainan, Japan H8 30
Kaiserslautern, Ger. F7 8
Kaitangata, N.Z. G2 52
Kaiwi Channel, strt., Hi., U.S. B4 88
Kajaani, Fin. D16 6
Kajakī, Band-e, res., Afg. D1 38
Kajan, stm., Indon. E6 32
Kajang, Malay. M6 34
Kakamas, S. Afr. G4 44
Kaka Point, c., Hi., U.S. C5 88
Kake, Ak., U.S. D13 79
Kakegawa, Japan H11 30
Kakie, Bots. F4 44
Kākināda, India D7 37
Kakogawa, Japan H7 30
Kaladan, stm., Asia D2 34
Ka Lae, c., Hi., U.S. E6 88
Kalahari Desert, des., Afr. F4 44
Kālahasti, India F5 37
Kalaheo, Hi., U.S. B2 88
Kalajoki, Fin. D14 6
Kalakan, Russia F17 24
Kalām, Pak. C5 38
Kalama, Wa., U.S. C3 124
Kalámai, Grc. L6 16
Kalamazoo, Mi., U.S. F5 99
Kalamazoo, co., Mi., U.S. F5 99
Kalamazoo, stm., Mi., U.S. F5 99
Kalasin, Thai. F7 34
Kalāt, Pak. F2 38
Kalaupapa Peninsula, pen., Hi., U.S. B5 88
Kalawao, co., Hi., U.S. B5 88
Kalb, Ra's al-, c., Yemen F4 46
Kale, Tur. L12 16
Kaleden, B.C., Can. E8 69
Kalemie (Albertville), Zaire C5 44
Kalena, Puu, mtn., Hi., U.S. g9 88
Kalgin Island, i., Ak., U.S. g16 79
Kalgoorlie, Austl. F4 50
Kalima, Zaire B5 44
Kálimnos, Grc. M10 16
Kaliningrad (Königsberg), Russia G3 18
Kalinkoviči, Bela. I12 18
Kalispel Indian Reservation, Wa., U.S. A8 124
Kalispell, Mt., U.S. B2 103
Kalisz, Pol. D18 8
Kalkaska, Mi., U.S. D5 99
Kalkaska, co., Mi., U.S. D5 99
Kalmar, Swe. H11 6
Kalohi Channel, strt., Hi., U.S. C4 88
Kālol, India I5 38
Kaloli Point, c., Hi., U.S. D7 88
Kalona, Ia., U.S. C6 92
Kalone Peak, mtn., B.C., Can. C4 69
Kaluga, Russia G19 18
Kalutara, Sri L. I5 37
Kamaishi, Japan C14 30
Kamakou, mtn., Hi., U.S. B5 88
Kamakura, Japan G12 30
Kamālia, Pak. E5 38
Kamarān, i., Yemen E3 46
Kamas, Ut., U.S. C4 121
Kamba, China F13 38
Kambam, India H4 37
Kambar, Pak. G2 38
Kamčatka, stm., Russia F25 24
Kamčatka, Poluostrov, pen., Russia F25 24
Kamčatskij Zaliv, b., Russia F26 24
Kamen', Gora, mtn., Russia D12 24
Kamen'-na-Obi, Russia G10 24
Kamenz, Ger. D14 8
Kamiah, Id., U.S. C2 89
Kamiak Butte, mtn., Wa., U.S. C8 124
Kamienna Góra, Pol. E16 8
Kamilukuak Lake, l., N.W. Ter., Can. D12 66
Kamina, Zaire C5 44
Kaminak Lake, l., N.W. Ter., Can. D13 66
Kaminuriak Lake, l., N.W. Ter., Can. D13 66
Kamitsushima, Japan H2 30
Kamloops, B.C., Can. D7 69
Kamo, Japan E12 30
Kāmoke, Pak. E6 38
Kampala, Ug. A6 44
Kampar, Malay. L6 34
Kampen, Neth. C5 8
Kampeska, Lake, l., S.D., U.S. C8 118
Kâmpóng Cham, Camb. H8 34
Kâmpóng Chhnăng, Camb. H8 34
Kâmpóng Saôm, Camb. I7 34
Kâmpóng Saôm, Chhâk, b., Camb. I7 34
Kâmpóng Thum, Camb. H8 34
Kâmpôt, Camb. I8 34
Kāmthi, India B5 37
Kamuela (Waimea), Hi., U.S. C6 88
Kamui-misaki, c., Japan p18 30a
Kan, stm., Asia H9 34
Kanab, Ut., U.S. F3 121
Kanab Creek, stm., U.S. A3 80
Kanabec, co., Mn., U.S. E5 100
Kanaga Island, i., Ak., U.S. E4 79
Kanairiktok, stm., Newf., Can. g9 72
Kananga (Luluabourg), Zaire C4 44
Kanapou Bay, b., Hi., U.S. C5 88
Kanata, Ont., Can. B9 73
Kanawha, Ia., U.S. B4 92
Kanawha, co., W.V., U.S. C3 125
Kanawha, stm., W.V., U.S. C3 125
Kanazawa, Japan F9 30
Kanchanaburi, Thai. G5 34

Name	Map Ref	Page
Kānchenjunga, mtn., Asia	G13	38
Kānchipuram, India	F5	37
Kandhkot, Pak.	F3	38
Kāndi, India	I13	38
Kandiyohi, co., Mn., U.S.	E3	100
Kandy, Sri L.	I6	37
Kane, Pa., U.S.	C4	115
Kane, co., Il., U.S.	B5	90
Kane, co., Ut., U.S.	F3	121
Kaneohe, Hi., U.S.	B4	88
Kaneohe Bay, b., Hi., U.S.	g10	88
Kaneohe Bay Marine Corps Air Station, mil., Hi., U.S.	g10	88
Kangar, Malay.	K6	34
Kangaroo Island, i., Austl.	G7	50
Kangean, Kepulauan, is., Indon.	G6	32
Kangnŭng, S. Kor.	D12	26
Kango, Gabon	A2	44
Kangto, mtn., Asia	G15	38
Kaniama, Zaire	C4	44
Kankakee, Il., U.S.	B6	90
Kankakee, co., Il., U.S.	B6	90
Kankakee, stm., U.S.	B5	90
Kankan, Gui.	F4	42
Kanmaw Kyun, i., Mya.	I5	34
Kannapolis, N.C., U.S.	B2	110
Kannauj, India	G8	38
Kannonkoski, Fin.	E15	6
Kannus, Fin.	E14	6
Kano, Nig.	F7	42
Kanonji, Japan	H6	30
Kanopolis, Ks., U.S.	D5	93
Kanopolis Lake, res., Ks., U.S.	D5	93
Kanoya, Japan	K3	30
Kānpur, India	G9	38
Kansas, Il., U.S.	D6	90
Kansas, state, U.S.	D5	93
Kansas, stm., Ks., U.S.	C7	93
Kansas City, Ks., U.S.	C9	93
Kansas City, Mo., U.S.	B3	102
Kansk, Russia	F13	24
Kantō-sammyaku, mts., Japan	F11	30
Kanuma, Japan	F12	30
Kanye, Bots.	F5	44
Kaohsiung, Tai.	M9	28
Kaohsiunghsien, Tai.	M9	28
Kaokoveld, plat., Nmb.	E2	44
Kaolack, Sen.	F2	42
Kapaa, Hi., U.S.	A2	88
Kapaau, Hi., U.S.	C6	88
Kapadvanj, India	I5	38
Kapanga, Zaire	C4	44
Kapapa Island, i., Hi., U.S.	g10	88
Kapfenberg, Aus.	H15	8
Kaplan, La., U.S.	D3	95
Kaposvár, Hung.	I17	8
Kaptai, Bngl.	I15	38
Kapuas, stm., Indon.	F4	32
Kapūrthala, India	E6	38
Kapuskasing, Ont., Can.	o19	73
Karabük, Tur.	G14	4
Karacabey, Tur.	I12	16
Karacaköy, Tur.	H12	16
Karāchi, Pak.	H2	38
Karād, India	D3	37
Karaganda, Kaz.	H8	24
Karaginskij, Ostrov, i., Russia	F26	24
Karaginskij Zaliv, b., Russia	F26	24
Karagoš, Gora, mtn., Russia	G11	24
Kāraikkudi, India	G5	37
Karakelong, Pulau, i., Indon.	E8	32
Karakoram Range, mts., Asia	C7	38
Karakumskij kanal, Turk.	J10	22
Karaman, Tur.	H14	4
Karaman, Tur.	L13	16
Karamay, China	B3	26
Karamürsel, Tur.	I13	16
Kāranja, India	B4	37
Karasburg, Nmb.	G3	44
Karasjok, Nor.	B15	6
Karatsu, Japan	I2	30
Karaul, Russia	C10	24
Karauli, India	G7	38
Karawang, Indon.	m13	33a
Karawanken, mts., Eur.	C9	14
Karbalā', Iraq	B3	46
Kårböle, Swe.	F10	6
Karcag, Hung.	H20	8
Kardeljevo, Cro.	F12	14
Kardhítsa, Grc.	J5	16
Kărdžali, Bul.	H9	16
Kargasok, Russia	F10	24
Karhula, Fin.	F16	6
Kariba, Zimb.	E5	44
Kariba, Lake, res., Afr.	E5	44
Karibib, Nmb.	F3	44
Karigasniemi, Fin.	B15	6
Karimata, Kepulauan, is., Indon.	F4	32
Karimata, Selat (Karimata Strait), strt., Indon.	F4	32
Karīmganj, India	H15	38
Karīmnagar, India	C5	37
Karin, Som.	F4	46
Karis (Karjaa), Fin.	F14	6
Kariya, Japan	H9	30
Karkabet, Erit.	E2	46
Karlovac, Cro.	D10	14
Karlovo, Bul.	G8	16
Karlovy Vary, Czech.	E12	8
Karlshamn, Swe.	H10	6
Karlskoga, Swe.	G10	6
Karlskrona, Swe.	H10	6
Karlsruhe, Ger.	F8	8
Karlstad, Swe.	G9	6
Karlstad, Mn., U.S.	B2	100
Karnāl, India	F7	38
Karnaphuli Reservoir, res., Bngl.	I15	38
Karnataka, state, India	E3	37
Karnes, co., Tx., U.S.	E4	120
Karnes City, Tx., U.S.	E4	120
Karns, Tn., U.S.	n13	119
Karonga, Mwi.	C6	44
Kárpathos, i., Grc.	N11	16
Karpenísion, Grc.	K5	16
Kars, Tur.	G16	4
Kärsämäki, Fin.	E15	6
Karši, Uzb.	J11	22
Kartal, Tur.	I13	16
Karufa, Indon.	F9	32
Karungi, Swe.	C14	6
Karūr, India	G5	37
Karviná, Czech.	F18	8
Kārwār, India	E3	37
Kasai (Cassai), stm., Afr.	B3	44
Kasaji, Zaire	D4	44
Kasama, Zam.	D6	44
Kasanga, Tan.	C6	44
Kasaoka, Japan	H6	30
Kāsaragod, India	F3	37
Kasba Lake, l., N.W. Ter., Can.	D12	66
Kaseda, Japan	K3	30
Kasempa, Zam.	D5	44
Kasenga, Zaire	D5	44
Kasese, Zaire	B5	44
Kāsganj, India	G8	38
Kāshān, Iran	B5	46
Kashi, China	D2	26
Kashima-nada, Japan	F13	30
Kashīpur, India	F8	38
Kashiwa, Japan	G12	30
Kashiwazaki, Japan	E11	30
Kashmir see Jammu and Kashmir, dep., Asia	C6	38
Kasimov, Russia	G24	18
Kašin, Russia	D20	18
Kašira, Russia	G21	18
Kaskaskia, stm., Il., U.S.	D5	90
Kaskö (Kaskinen), Fin.	E13	6
Kaslo, B.C., Can.	E9	69
Kasongo, Zaire	B5	44
Kasota, Mn., U.S.	F5	100
Kasr, Ra's, c., Sudan	E13	42
Kassalā, Sudan	E13	42
Kassel, Ger.	D9	8
Kasson, Mn., U.S.	F6	100
Kastoria, Grc.	I5	16
Kasugai, Japan	G9	30
Kasūr, Pak.	E6	38
Katahdin, Mount, mtn., Me., U.S.	C4	96
Katanga Plateau, plat., Zaire	D5	44
Katchall Island, i., India	K2	34
Kateríni, Grc.	I6	16
Kates Needle, mtn., Ak., U.S.	m24	79
Katherine, Austl.	B6	50
Kāthiāwār, pen., India	I4	38
Kathleen, Fl., U.S.	D4	86
Kāṭhmāṇḍau, Nepal	G11	38
Katihār, India	H12	38
Katiola, C. Iv.	G4	42
Katmai, Mount, mtn., Ak., U.S.	D9	79
Katmai National Park, Ak., U.S.	D9	79
Katmandu see Kāṭhmāṇḍau, Nepal	G11	38
Katowice, Pol.	E19	8
Kātrīnā, Jabal, mtn., Egypt	C12	42
Katrineholm, Swe.	G11	6
Katsina, Nig.	F7	42
Katsuta, Japan	F13	30
Kattegat, strt., Eur.	H8	6
Katy, Tx., U.S.	r14	120
Kauai, co., Hi., U.S.	B1	88
Kauai, i., Hi., U.S.	A2	88
Kauai Channel, strt., Hi., U.S.	B3	88
Kau Desert, des., Hi., U.S.	D6	88
Kaufbeuren, Ger.	H10	8
Kaufman, Tx., U.S.	C4	120
Kaufman, co., Tx., U.S.	C4	120
Kauiki Head, c., Hi., U.S.	C6	88
Kaukauna, Wi., U.S.	D5	126
Kaukauveld, mts., Afr.	F3	44
Kaula Island, i., Hi., U.S.	m15	88
Kaulakahi Channel, strt., Hi., U.S.	A2	88
Kaumakani, Hi., U.S.	B2	88
Kaunakakai, Hi., U.S.	B4	88
Kauna Point, c., Hi., U.S.	D6	88
Kaunas, Lith.	G6	18
Kaura Namoda, Nig.	F7	42
Kaustinen, Fin.	E14	6
Kavača, Russia	E27	24
Kavacık, Tur.	J12	16
Kavalerovo, Russia	I21	24
Kavála, Grc.	I8	16
Kavaratti, India	G2	37
Kavieng, Pap. N. Gui.	k17	50a
Kawagoe, Japan	G12	30
Kawaguchi, Japan	G12	30
Kawaihoa Point, c., Hi., U.S.	B1	88
Kawaikini, mtn., Hi., U.S.	A2	88
Kawambwa, Zam.	C5	44
Kawanoe, Japan	H6	30
Kawasaki, Japan	G12	30
Kawich Peak, mtn., Nv., U.S.	F5	105
Kawich Range, mts., Nv., U.S.	F5	105
Kaw Lake, res., Ok., U.S.	A5	113
Kawm Umbū, Egypt	D12	42
Kay, co., Ok., U.S.	A4	113
Kayankulam, India	H4	37
Kaycee, Wy., U.S.	C6	127
Kayenta, Az., U.S.	A5	80
Kayes, Mali	F3	42
Kayseri, Tur.	H15	4
Kaysville, Ut., U.S.	B4	121
Kažačinskoje, Russia	F12	24
Kazačje, Russia	C21	24
Kazakhstan, ctry., Asia	H11	22
Kazan', Russia	F7	22
Kazanlăk, Bul.	G9	16
Kāzerūn, Iran	C5	46
Keaau, Hi., U.S.	D6	88
Keahiakahoe, Puu, mtn., Hi., U.S.	g10	88
Keahole Point, c., Hi., U.S.	D5	88
Kealaikahiki Channel, strt., Hi., U.S.	C5	88
Kealaikahiki Point, c., Hi., U.S.	C5	88
Kealakekua, Hi., U.S.	D6	88
Kealia, Hi., U.S.	A2	88
Keams Canyon, Az., U.S.	B5	80
Keanapapa Point, c., Hi., U.S.	C4	88
Keansburg, N.J., U.S.	C4	107
Kearney, Mo., U.S.	B3	102
Kearney, Ne., U.S.	D6	104
Kearney, co., Ne., U.S.	D7	104
Kearns, Ut., U.S.	C4	121
Kearny, Az., U.S.	D5	80
Kearny, N.J., U.S.	h8	107
Kearny, co., Ks., U.S.	D2	93
Kebri Dehar, Eth.	G3	46
Kechika, stm., B.C., Can.	E7	66
Kecskemét, Hung.	I19	8
Kedges Straits, strt., Md., U.S.	D5	97
Kedgwick, N.B., Can.	B2	71
Kediri, Indon.	m16	32
Kedon, Russia	E25	24
Kédougou, Sen.	F3	42
Kędzierzyn, Pol.	E18	8
Keego Harbor, Mi., U.S.	o15	99
Keele Peak, mtn., Yukon, Can.	D6	66
Keelung see Chilung, Tai.	J10	28
Keene, N.H., U.S.	E2	106
Keene, Tx., U.S.	n9	120
Keeper Hill, hill, Ire.	I4	7
Keeseville, N.Y., U.S.	f11	109
Keesler Air Force Base, mil., Ms., U.S.	E5	101
Keetmanshoop, Nmb.	G3	44
Keet Seel Ruin, hist., Az., U.S.	A5	80
Keewatin, Ont., Can.	E4	70
Keewatin, Mn., U.S.	C5	100
Kefallinía, i., Grc.	K4	16
Keffi, Nig.	G7	42
Keflavík, Ice.	C3	4
Ke Ga, Mui, c., Viet.	H10	34
Kegonsa, Lake, l., Wi., U.S.	F4	126
Keiser, Ar., U.S.	B5	81
Keith, Scot., U.K.	D10	7
Keith, co., Ne., U.S.	C4	104
Keizer, Or., U.S.	C3	114
Kejimkujik National Park, N.S., Can.	E4	71
Kekaha, Hi., U.S.	B2	88
Kelafo, Eth.	G3	46
Kelang, Malay.	M6	34
Kelheim, Ger.	G11	8
Kelibia, Tun.	M6	14
Keller, Tx., U.S.	n9	120
Kellett, Cape, c., N.W. Ter., Can.	B7	66
Kelleys Island, i., Oh., U.S.	A3	112
Kellogg, Id., U.S.	B2	89
Kellogg, Ia., U.S.	C5	92
Kelloselkä, Fin.	C17	6
Kelly Air Force Base, mil., Tx., U.S.	k7	120
Kelly Island, i., De., U.S.	D4	85
Kellyville, Ok., U.S.	B5	113
Kélo, Chad	G9	42
Kelottijärvi, Fin.	B14	6
Kelowna, B.C., Can.	E8	69
Kelso, Wa., U.S.	C3	124
Keluang, Malay.	M7	34
Kemerovo, Russia	F11	24
Kemi, Fin.	D15	6
Kemijärvi, Fin.	C16	6
Kemijoki, stm., Fin.	C15	6
Kemmerer, Wy., U.S.	E2	127
Kemp, Tx., U.S.	C4	120
Kemp, Lake, res., Tx., U.S.	C3	120
Kemper, co., Ms., U.S.	C5	101
Kemps Bay, Bah.	B9	64
Kempt, Lac, l., Que., Can.	G18	66
Kempten [Allgäu], Ger.	H10	8
Kemptville, Ont., Can.	B9	73
Kemul, Kong, mtn., Indon.	E6	32
Kenai, Ak., U.S.	C9	79
Kenai Fjords National Park, Ak., U.S.	D10	79
Kenai Mountains, mts., Ak., U.S.	h16	79
Kenai Peninsula, pen., Ak., U.S.	h16	79
Kenansville, N.C., U.S.	C5	110
Kenbridge, Va., U.S.	D4	123
Kendall, Fl., U.S.	s13	86
Kendall, co., Il., U.S.	B5	90
Kendall, co., Tx., U.S.	E3	120
Kendall, Cape, c., N.W. Ter., Can.	D15	66
Kendall Park, N.J., U.S.	C3	107
Kendallville, In., U.S.	B7	91
Kendari, Indon.	F7	32
Kenedy, Tx., U.S.	E4	120
Kenedy, co., Tx., U.S.	F4	120
Kenema, S.L.	G3	42
Kenesaw, Ne., U.S.	D7	104
Kēng Tung, Mya.	D5	34
Kenhardt, S. Afr.	G4	44
Kenilworth, Il., U.S.	h9	90
Kenitra, Mor.	B4	42
Kenly, N.C., U.S.	B4	110
Kenmare, N.D., U.S.	A3	111
Kenmore, N.Y., U.S.	C2	109
Kennaday Peak, mtn., Wy., U.S.	E6	127
Kennebago Lake, l., Me., U.S.	C2	96
Kennebec, co., Me., U.S.	D3	96
Kennebec, stm., Me., U.S.	D3	96
Kennebunk, Me., U.S.	E2	96
Kennebunkport, Me., U.S.	E2	96
Kennedy Entrance, strt., Ak., U.S.	D9	79
Kennedy Peak, mtn., Mya.	C2	34
Kenner, La., U.S.	E5	95
Kennesaw, Ga., U.S.	B2	87
Kennesaw Mountain, mtn., Ga., U.S.	C2	87
Kennett, Mo., U.S.	E7	102
Kennett Square, Pa., U.S.	G10	115
Kennewick, Wa., U.S.	C6	124
Kenn Reefs, rf., Austl.	D11	50
Kennydale, Wa., U.S.	e11	124
Keno, Or., U.S.	E5	114
Kénogami, Lac, l., Que., Can.	A6	74
Kenora, Ont., Can.	o16	73
Kenosha, Wi., U.S.	F6	126
Kenosha, co., Wi., U.S.	F5	126
Kenova, W.V., U.S.	C2	125
Kensett, Ar., U.S.	B4	81
Kensico Reservoir, res., N.Y., U.S.	g13	109
Kensington, P.E.I., Can.	C6	71
Kensington, Ct., U.S.	C4	84
Kensington, Md., U.S.	B3	97
Kent, Oh., U.S.	A4	112
Kent, Wa., U.S.	B3	124
Kent, co., De., U.S.	D3	85
Kent, co., Md., U.S.	B5	97
Kent, co., Mi., U.S.	E5	99
Kent, co., R.I., U.S.	D2	116
Kent, co., Tx., U.S.	C2	120
Kent City, Mi., U.S.	E5	99
Kent Island, i., De., U.S.	D4	85
Kent Island, i., Md., U.S.	C5	97
Kentland, In., U.S.	C3	91
Kenton, De., U.S.	D3	85
Kenton, Oh., U.S.	B2	112
Kenton, Tn., U.S.	A2	119
Kenton, co., Ky., U.S.	B5	94
Kent Peninsula, pen., N.W. Ter., Can.	C11	66
Kent Point, c., Md., U.S.	C5	97
Kentucky, state, U.S.	C4	94
Kentucky, stm., Ky., U.S.	B5	94
Kentwood, La., U.S.	D5	95
Kentwood, Mi., U.S.	F5	99
Kenvil, N.J., U.S.	B3	107
Kenvir, Ky., U.S.	D6	94
Kenya, ctry., Afr.	B7	44
Kenya, Mount see Kirinyaga, mtn., Kenya	B7	44
Kenyon, Mn., U.S.	F6	100
Kenyon, R.I., U.S.	F2	116
Keokea, Hi., U.S.	C5	88
Keokuk, Ia., U.S.	D6	92
Keokuk, co., Ia., U.S.	C5	92
Keokuk Lock and Dam, U.S.	D6	92
Keosauqua, Ia., U.S.	D6	92
Keota, Ia., U.S.	C6	92
Keota, Ok., U.S.	B7	113
Keowee, Lake, res., S.C., U.S.	B2	117
Kepi, Indon.	G10	32
Kerala, state, India	G4	37
Kerch, Ukr.	H5	22
Keremeos, B.C., Can.	E8	69
Keren, Erit.	E2	46
Kerens, Tx., U.S.	C4	120
Kerguélen, Îles, is., F.S.A.T.	J17	2
Kerhonkson, N.Y., U.S.	D6	109
Kericho, Kenya	B7	44
Kerinci, Gunung, mtn., Indon.	F3	32
Kerkhoven, Mn., U.S.	E3	100
Kérkira (Corfu), Grc.	J3	16
Kérkira, i., Grc.	J3	16
Kermān, Iran	B6	46
Kerme Körfezi, b., Tur.	M11	16
Kermit, Tx., U.S.	D1	120
Kermode, Mount, mtn., B.C., Can.	C2	69
Kern, co., Ca., U.S.	E4	82
Kern, stm., Ca., U.S.	E4	82
Kernersville, N.C., U.S.	A2	110
Kernville, Ca., U.S.	E4	82
Kerr, co., Tx., U.S.	D3	120
Kerr, Lake, l., Fl., U.S.	C5	86
Kerrville, Tx., U.S.	D3	120
Kerry Head, c., Ire.	I3	7
Kersey, Co., U.S.	A6	83
Kershaw, S.C., U.S.	B6	117
Kershaw, co., S.C., U.S.	C6	117
Kerulen (Cherlen), stm., Asia	B9	26
Kesagami Lake, l., Ont., Can.	F16	66
Keşan, Tur.	I10	16
Kesennuma, Japan	D14	30
Keshena, Wi., U.S.	D5	126
Ket', stm., Russia	F11	24
Keta, Ozero, l., Russia	D11	24
Ketchikan, Ak., U.S.	D13	79
Ketchum, Id., U.S.	F4	89
Kettering, Eng., U.K.	I12	7
Kettering, Oh., U.S.	C1	112
Kettle, stm., Mn., U.S.	D6	100
Kettle Creek, stm., Pa., U.S.	D6	115
Kettle Creek Lake, res., Pa., U.S.	D6	115
Kettle Falls, Wa., U.S.	A7	124
Keuka Lake, l., N.Y., U.S.	C3	109
Kew, T./C. Is.	D11	64
Kewanee, Il., U.S.	B4	90
Kewaskum, Wi., U.S.	E5	126
Kewaunee, Wi., U.S.	D6	126
Kewaunee, co., Wi., U.S.	D6	126
Keweenaw, co., Mi., U.S.	A2	99
Keweenaw Bay, b., Mi., U.S.	B2	99
Keweenaw Peninsula, pen., Mi., U.S.	A3	99
Keweenaw Point, c., Mi., U.S.	A3	99
Keya Paha, co., Ne., U.S.	B6	104
Keya Paha, stm., U.S.	A5	104
Keyhole Reservoir, res., Wy., U.S.	B8	127
Key Largo, Fl., U.S.	G6	86
Keyport, N.J., U.S.	C4	107
Keyser, W.V., U.S.	B6	125
Keystone, W.V., U.S.	D3	125
Keystone Heights, Fl., U.S.	C4	86
Keystone Lake, res., Ok., U.S.	A5	113
Keystone Peak, mtn., Az., U.S.	F4	80
Keysville, Va., U.S.	C4	123
Key West, Fl., U.S.	H5	86
Key West Naval Air Station, mil., Fl., U.S.	H5	86
Kezar Falls, Me., U.S.	E2	96
Kezar Lake, l., Me., U.S.	D2	96
Kežma, Russia	F14	24
Khadki (Kirkee), India	C2	37
Khairpur, Pak.	G3	38
Khalkís, Grc.	K7	16
Khambhāliya, India	I3	38
Khambhāt, Gulf of, b., India	B2	37
Khāmgaon, India	B4	37
Khammam, India	D6	37
Khānābād, Afg.	B3	38
Khānaqīn, Iraq	B4	46
Khandwa, India	B4	37
Khānewāl, Pak.	E4	38
Khaniá, Grc.	N8	16
Khanna, India	E7	38
Khānpur, Pak.	F4	38
Khān Yūnus, Isr. Occ.	D4	40
Kharagpur, India	I12	38
Khargon, India	J6	38
Kharkiv, Ukr.	G5	22
Khartoum see Al-Kharṭūm, Sudan	E12	42
Kherson, Ukr.	H4	22
Khíos, Grc.	K10	16
Kholm, Afg.	B2	38
Khong, Laos	G8	34
Khong Sédone, Laos	G8	34
Khon Kaen, Thai.	F7	34
Khóra Sfakíon, Grc.	N8	16
Khorramābād, Iran	B4	46
Khorramshahr, Iran	B4	46
Khouribga, Mor.	B4	42
Khowst, Afg.	D3	38
Khulna, Bngl.	I13	38
Khunjerab Pass, Asia	B6	38
Khurja, India	F7	38
Khūryān Mūryān (Kuria Muria Isla, is., Oman	E6	46
Khushāb, Pak.	D5	38
Khvājeh Moḥammad, Kūh-e, mts., Afg.	B4	38
Khvoy, Iran	J6	22
Khyber Pass, Asia	C4	38
Kiamichi, stm., Ok., U.S.	C6	113
Kiamika, stm., Que., Can.	C2	74
Kiana, Ak., U.S.	B7	79
Kiawah Island, i., S.C., U.S.	F7	117
Kibangou, Congo	B2	44
Kibombo, Zaire	B5	44
Kibre Mengist, Eth.	G2	46
Kičevo, Mac.	H4	16
Kichčik, Russia	G25	24
Kickamuit, stm., R.I., U.S.	D5	116
Kickapoo, stm., Wi., U.S.	E3	126
Kickapoo, Lake, res., Tx., U.S.	C3	120
Kickapoo Indian Reservation, Ks., U.S.	C8	93
Kicking Horse Pass, Can.	D2	68
Kidal, Mali	E6	42
Kidder, co., N.D., U.S.	C6	111
Kidira, Sen.	F3	42
Kiefer, Ok., U.S.	B5	113
Kiel, Ger.	A10	8
Kiel, Wi., U.S.	E5	126
Kielce, Pol.	E20	8
Kieler Bucht, b., Ger.	A10	8
Kiester, Mn., U.S.	G5	100
Kiev see Kyyiv, Ukr.	G4	22
Kiffa, Maur.	E3	42
Kigali, Rw.	B6	44
Kigoma, Tan.	B5	44
Kihei, Hi., U.S.	C5	88
Kihniö, Fin.	E14	6
Kiholo Bay, b., Hi., U.S.	D5	88
Kii-suidō, strt., Japan	I7	30
Kikinda, Yugo.	D4	16
Kikládhes, is., Grc.	L8	16
Kikwit, Zaire	C3	44
Kilauea, Hi., U.S.	A2	88
Kilauea Crater, crat., Hi., U.S.	D6	88
Kilauea Point, c., Hi., U.S.	A2	88
Kilgore, Tx., U.S.	C5	120
Kilimanjaro, mtn., Tan.	B7	44
Kilis, Tur.	A5	40
Kilkee, Ire.	I3	7
Kilkenny, Ire.	I5	7
Kilkís, Grc.	H6	16
Killala, Ire.	G3	7
Killaloe Station, Ont., Can.	B7	73
Killam, Alta., Can.	C5	68
Killarney, Man., Can.	E2	70
Killarney, Ire.	I3	7
Killarney Provincial Park, Ont., Can.	A3	73
Killdeer, N.D., U.S.	B3	111
Killeen, Tx., U.S.	D4	120
Killen, Al., U.S.	A2	78
Killian, La., U.S.	h10	95
Killik, stm., Ak., U.S.	B9	79
Killona, La., U.S.	h11	95
Killorglin, Ire.	I3	7
Kilmarnock, Scot., U.K.	F8	7
Kilmarnock, Va., U.S.	C6	123
Kilmichael, Ms., U.S.	B4	101
Kiln, Ms., U.S.	E4	101
Kilombero, stm., Tan.	C7	44
Kilosa, Tan.	C7	44
Kilpisjärvi, Fin.	B13	6
Kilwa, Zaire	C5	44
Kilwa Kivinje, Tan.	C7	44
Kimball, Mn., U.S.	E4	100
Kimball, Ne., U.S.	C2	104
Kimball, S.D., U.S.	D7	118
Kimball, co., Ne., U.S.	C2	104
Kimball, Mount, mtn., Ak., U.S.	C11	79
Kimberley, B.C., Can.	E9	69
Kimberley, S. Afr.	G4	44
Kimberley Plateau, plat., Austl.	C5	50
Kimberlin Heights, Tn., U.S.	n14	110
Kimberly, Al., U.S.	B3	78
Kimberly, Id., U.S.	G4	89
Kimberly, W.V., U.S.	m13	125
Kimberly, Wi., U.S.	h9	126
Kimble, co., Tx., U.S.	D3	120
Kimch'aek, N. Kor.	C12	26
Kimovsk, Russia	H21	18
Kimry, Russia	E20	18
Kinabalu, Gunong, mtn., Malay.	D6	32
Kinbasket Lake, res., B.C., Can.	D8	69
Kincaid, Il., U.S.	D4	90
Kincaid, W.V., U.S.	m13	125
Kincaid, Lake, res., Il., U.S.	D4	90
Kincardine, Ont., Can.	C3	73
Kincheloe Air Force Base, mil., Mi., U.S.	B6	99
Kinder, La., U.S.	D3	95
Kindia, Gui.	F3	42
Kindu, Zaire	B5	44
Kinešma, Russia	D25	18
King, N.C., U.S.	A2	110
King, Wi., U.S.	D4	126
King, co., Tx., U.S.	C2	120
King, co., Wa., U.S.	B3	124
King and Queen, co., Va., U.S.	C6	123
Kingaroy, Austl.	E10	50
King City, Ca., U.S.	D3	82
King City, Mo., U.S.	A3	102

Name	Map Ref	Page
King Cove, Ak., U.S.	E7	79
Kingfield, Me., U.S.	D2	96
Kingfisher, Ok., U.S.	B4	113
Kingfisher, co., Ok., U.S.	B3	113
King George, co., Va., U.S.	B5	123
King Island, i., Austl.	G8	50
King Island, i., B.C., Can.	C4	69
King Lear Peak, mtn., Nv., U.S.	B3	105
King Leopold Ranges, mts., Austl.	C5	50
Kingman, Az., U.S.	B1	80
Kingman, Ks., U.S.	E5	93
Kingman, co., Ks., U.S.	E5	93
King Mountain, mtn., Or., U.S.	E3	114
King Mountain, mtn., Or., U.S.	D8	114
King Peak, mtn., Ca., U.S.	B1	82
Kings, Ms., U.S.	C3	101
Kings, co., Ca., U.S.	D4	82
Kings, co., N.Y., U.S.	E7	109
Kings, stm., Ar., U.S.	A2	81
Kings, stm., Ca., U.S.	D4	82
Kings, stm., Nv., U.S.	B3	105
King Salmon, Ak., U.S.	D8	79
Kingsburg, Ca., U.S.	D4	82
Kingsbury, co., S.D., U.S.	C8	118
Kings Canyon National Park, Ca., U.S.	D4	82
Kingsey-Falls, Que., Can.	D5	74
Kingsford, Mi., U.S.	C2	99
Kingsland, Ga., U.S.	F5	87
Kingsland, Tx., U.S.	D3	120
Kingsley, Ia., U.S.	B2	92
Kingsley, Mi., U.S.	D5	99
King's Lynn, Eng., U.K.	I13	7
Kings Mountain, N.C., U.S.	B1	110
King Sound, strt., Austl.	C4	50
Kings Park West, Va., U.S.	*B5	123
Kings Peak, mtn., Ut., U.S.	C5	121
King's Point, Newf., Can.	D3	72
Kingsport, Tn., U.S.	C11	119
Kingston, Ont., Can.	C8	73
Kingston, Jam.	E9	64
Kingston, Ga., U.S.	B2	87
Kingston, Id., U.S.	B2	89
Kingston, Ma., U.S.	C6	98
Kingston, N.H., U.S.	E4	106
Kingston, N.Y., U.S.	D6	109
Kingston, Oh., U.S.	C3	112
Kingston, Ok., U.S.	D5	113
Kingston, Pa., U.S.	D10	115
Kingston, R.I., U.S.	F3	116
Kingston, Tn., U.S.	D9	119
Kingston Springs, Tn., U.S.	A4	119
Kingston upon Hull, Eng., U.K.	H12	7
Kingstown, St. Vin.	H17	64
Kingstown, Md., U.S.	B5	97
Kingstree, S.C., U.S.	D8	117
Kingsville, Ont., Can.	E2	73
Kingsville, Md., U.S.	B5	97
Kingsville (North Kingsville), Oh., U.S.	A5	112
Kingsville, Tx., U.S.	F4	120
Kingsville Naval Air Station, mil., Tx., U.S.	F4	120
King William, co., Va., U.S.	C5	123
King William Island, i., N.W. Ter., Can.	C13	66
King William's Town, S. Afr.	H5	44
Kingwood, W.V., U.S.	B5	125
Kinistino, Sask., Can.	E3	75
Kinkaid Lake, res., Il., U.S.	F4	90
Kinloch, Mo., U.S.	f13	102
Kinmundy, Il., U.S.	E5	90
Kinna, Swe.	H9	6
Kinnairds Head, c., Scot., U.K.	D10	7
Kinnelon, N.J., U.S.	B4	107
Kinneret, Yam, l., Isr.	C4	40
Kinney, co., Tx., U.S.	E2	120
Kinross, Scot., U.K.	E9	7
Kinsale, Ire.	J4	7
Kinsarvik, Nor.	F6	6
Kinsey, Al., U.S.	D4	78
Kinshasa (Léopoldville), Zaire	B3	44
Kinsley, Ks., U.S.	E4	93
Kinston, N.C., U.S.	B5	110
Kintyre, pen., Scot., U.K.	F7	7
Kintyre, Mull of, c., Scot., U.K.	F7	7
Kinyeti, mtn., Sudan	H12	42
Kiowa, Ks., U.S.	E5	93
Kiowa, Ok., U.S.	C6	113
Kiowa, co., Co., U.S.	C8	83
Kiowa, co., Ks., U.S.	E4	93
Kiowa, co., Ok., U.S.	C2	113
Kiowa Creek, stm., Ok., U.S.	A1	113
Kipembawe, Tan.	C6	44
Kipili, Tan.	C6	44
Kipnuk, Ak., U.S.	C7	79
Kipushi, Zaire	D5	44
Kirbyville, Tx., U.S.	D6	120
Kirchdorf an der Krems, Aus.	H14	8
Kirenga, stm., Russia	F15	24
Kirensk, Russia	F15	24
Kirghizia see Kyrgyzstan, state, Asia	I12	22
Kiribati, ctry., Oc.	G24	2
Kırıkhan, Tur.	A5	40
Kırıkkale, Tur.	H14	4
Kirin see Jilin, China	C12	26
Kirinyaga (Mount Kenya), mtn., Kenya	B7	44
Kırkağaç, Tur.	J11	16
Kirkcaldy, Scot., U.K.	E9	7
Kirkcudbright, Scot., U.K.	G8	7
Kirkenes, Nor.	B18	6
Kirkland, Il., U.S.	A5	90
Kirkland, Wa., U.S.	B3	124
Kirkland Lake, Ont., Can.	o19	73
Kırklareli, Tur.	H11	16
Kirklin, In., U.S.	D5	91
Kirksville, Mo., U.S.	A5	102
Kirkūk, Iraq	A3	46
Kirkwall, Scot., U.K.	C10	7
Kirkwood, De., U.S.	B3	85
Kirkwood, Il., U.S.	C3	90
Kirkwood, Mo., U.S.	f13	102
Kirov, Russia	G17	18
Kirov, Russia	F7	22
Kirovohrad, Ukr.	H4	22
Kirovskij, Russia	G25	24
Kırşehir, Tur.	H14	4
Kīrthar Range, mts., Pak.	G2	38
Kirtland, N.M., U.S.	A1	108
Kirtland Air Force Base, mil., N.M., U.S.	k7	108
Kiruna, Swe.	C13	6
Kirwin Reservoir, res., Ks., U.S.	C4	93
Kiryū, Japan	F12	30
Kisa, Swe.	H10	6
Kisangani (Stanleyville), Zaire	A5	44
Kisarazu, Japan	G12	30
K.I. Sawyer Air Force Base, mil., Mi., U.S.	B3	99
Kisel'ovsk, Russia	G11	24
Kishanganj, India	G12	38
Kishangarh, India	G6	38
Kishinev see Chişinău, Mol.	H3	22
Kishiwada, Japan	H8	30
Kishorganj, Bngl.	H14	38
Kishwaukee, stm., Il., U.S.	A5	90
Kiska Island, i., Ak., U.S.	E3	79
Kiskunfélegyháza, Hung.	I19	8
Kiskunhalas, Hung.	I19	8
Kislovodsk, Russia	I6	22
Kismayu, Som.	B8	44
Kissidougou, Gui.	G3	42
Kissimmee, Fl., U.S.	D5	86
Kissimmee, stm., Fl., U.S.	E5	86
Kissimmee, Lake, l., Fl., U.S.	E5	86
Kississing Lake, l., Man., Can.	B1	70
Kistanje, Cro.	F10	14
Kistler, W.V., U.S.	D3	125
Kisumu, Kenya	B6	44
Kitaibaraki, Japan	F13	30
Kitakami, stm., Japan	C14	30
Kitakami-sanchi, mts., Japan	C14	30
Kitakyūshū, Japan	I3	30
Kitale, Kenya	A6	44
Kitami, Japan	p21	30a
Kitami-sanchi, mts., Japan	o20	30a
Kit Carson, co., Co., U.S.	B8	83
Kitchener, Ont., Can.	D4	73
Kíthira, i., Grc.	M6	16
Kitimat, B.C., Can.	B3	69
Kitsap, co., Wa., U.S.	B3	124
Kitscoty, Alta., Can.	C5	68
Kittanning, Pa., U.S.	E2	115
Kittatinny Mountain, mtn., U.S.	B2	107
Kittery, Me., U.S.	E2	96
Kittery Point, Me., U.S.	E2	96
Kittilä, Fin.	C15	6
Kittitas, Wa., U.S.	C5	124
Kittitas, co., Wa., U.S.	B4	124
Kitts, Ky., U.S.	D6	94
Kittson, co., Mn., U.S.	B2	100
Kitty Hawk, N.C., U.S.	A7	110
Kitty Hawk Bay, b., N.C., U.S.	A7	110
Kitwe, Zam.	D5	44
Kitzbühel, Aus.	H12	8
Kitzingen, Ger.	F10	8
Kivu, Lac, l., Afr.	B5	44
Kızıl, stm., Tur.	G14	4
Kjustendil, Bul.	G6	16
Kladno, Czech.	E14	8
Klagenfurt, Aus.	I14	8
Klaipėda (Memel), Lith.	F4	18
Klamath, co., Or., U.S.	E5	114
Klamath, stm., U.S.	B2	82
Klamath Falls, Or., U.S.	E5	114
Klamath Mountains, mts., U.S.	E2	114
Klangenan, Indon.	m14	33a
Klarälven, stm., Eur.	F9	6
Klawock, Ak., U.S.	D13	79
Kleberg, co., Tx., U.S.	F4	120
Klerksdorp, S. Afr.	G5	44
Kleve, Ger.	D6	8
Klickitat, Wa., U.S.	D4	124
Klickitat, co., Wa., U.S.	D4	124
Klickitat, stm., Wa., U.S.	C4	124
Klimovsk, Russia	F20	18
Klin, Russia	E19	18
Klincy, Russia	I15	18
Kłodzko, Pol.	E16	8
Klondike, hist. reg., Yukon, Can.	D5	66
Klondike Gold Rush National Historical Park, Ak., U.S.	k22	79
Klosterneuburg, Aus.	G16	8
Kluane Lake, l., Yukon, Can.	D5	66
Klutina Lake, l., Ak., U.S.	g19	79
Knapp Creek, stm., W.V., U.S.	C5	125
Knee Lake, l., Man., Can.	B4	70
Kneža, Bul.	F8	16
Knife, stm., N.D., U.S.	B3	111
Knightdale, N.C., U.S.	B4	110
Knight Inlet, b., B.C., Can.	D5	69
Knight Island, i., Ak., U.S.	g18	79
Knightstown, In., U.S.	E6	91
Knightsville, In., U.S.	E3	91
Knightville Reservoir, res., Ma., U.S.	B2	98
Knin, Cro.	E11	14
Knittelfeld, Aus.	H14	8
Knob Noster, Mo., U.S.	C4	102
Knokke, Bel.	D3	8
Knollwood, W.V., U.S.	m12	125
Knott, co., Ky., U.S.	C6	94
Knox, In., U.S.	B4	91
Knox, Pa., U.S.	D2	115
Knox, co., Il., U.S.	B3	90
Knox, co., In., U.S.	G3	91
Knox, co., Ky., U.S.	D6	94
Knox, co., Me., U.S.	D4	96
Knox, co., Mo., U.S.	A5	102
Knox, co., Ne., U.S.	B8	104
Knox, co., Oh., U.S.	B3	112
Knox, co., Tn., U.S.	C10	119
Knox, co., Tx., U.S.	C3	120
Knox, Cape, c., B.C., Can.	B1	69
Knox City, Tx., U.S.	C3	120
Knoxville, Il., U.S.	C3	90
Knoxville, Ia., U.S.	C4	92
Knoxville, Tn., U.S.	D10	119
Knysna, S. Afr.	H4	44
Kōbe, Japan	H8	30
København (Copenhagen), Den.	I9	6
Koblenz, Ger.	E7	8
Kobrin, Bela.	I7	18
Kobuk, stm., Ak., U.S.	B8	79
Kobuk Valley National Park, Ak., U.S.	B8	79
Kočani, Mac.	H6	16
Kočevje, Slo.	D9	14
Kōchi, Japan	I6	30
Koch Peak, mtn., Mt., U.S.	E5	103
Kodiak, Ak., U.S.	D9	79
Kodiak Island, i., Ak., U.S.	D9	79
Koes, Nmb.	G3	44
Kofa Mountains, mts., Az., U.S.	D2	80
Köflach, Aus.	H15	8
Kōfu, Japan	G11	30
Koga, Japan	F12	30
Kogaluc, Baie, b., Que., Can.	E17	66
Kogaluk, stm., Newf., Can.	g9	72
Køge Bugt, b., Grnld.	D24	66
Kohala Mountains, mts., Hi., U.S.	C6	88
Kohāt, Pak.	D4	38
Kohīma, India	H16	38
Kohler, Wi., U.S.	E6	126
Kohtla-Järve, Est.	B10	18
Kokand, Uzb.	I12	22
Kokanee Glacier Provincial Park, B.C., Can.	E9	69
Kokemäki, Fin.	F14	6
Kokkola (Gamlakarleby), Fin.	E14	6
Koko Head, c., Hi., U.S.	B4	88
Kokolik, stm., Ak., U.S.	B7	79
Kokomo, In., U.S.	D5	91
Kokonau, Indon.	F10	32
Kokopo, Pap. N. Gui.	k17	50a
Kokosing, stm., Oh., U.S.	B3	112
Koksoak, stm., Que., Can.	E19	66
Kokstad, S. Afr.	H5	44
Kolaka, Indon.	F7	32
Kola Peninsula see Kol'skij poluostrov, pen., Russia	D5	22
Kolār, India	F5	37
Kolār Gold Fields, India	F5	37
Kol'čugino, Russia	E22	18
Kolda, Sen.	F3	42
Kolding, Den.	I7	6
Kolhāpur, India	D3	37
Kolín, Czech.	E15	8
Kollegāl, India	F4	37
Köln (Cologne), Ger.	E6	8
Koloa, Hi., U.S.	B2	88
Kołobrzeg, Pol.	A15	8
Kolomna, Russia	F21	18
Kolpaševo, Russia	F10	24
Kolpino, Russia	B13	18
Kol'skij poluostrov (Kola Peninsula), pen., Russia	D5	22
Kolwezi, Zaire	D5	44
Kolyma, stm., Russia	D25	24
Kolymskaja Nizmennost', pl., Russia	D24	24
Komárno, Slov.	H18	8
Komatsu, Japan	F9	30
Komló, Hung.	I18	8
Kommunizma, pik, mtn., Taj.	J12	22
Komoé, stm., Afr.	G5	42
Komotiní, Grc.	H9	16
Komsomolec, Ostrov, i., Russia	A12	24
Komsomol'sk-na-Amure, Russia	G21	24
Komsomol'skoj Pravdy, Ostrova, is., Russia	B15	24
Konahuanui, Puu, mtn., Hi., U.S.	g10	88
Konakovo, Russia	E19	18
Konawa, Ok., U.S.	C5	113
Konch, India	H8	38
Kondrovo, Russia	G18	18
Kŏng, Kaôh, i., Camb.	I7	34
Kongolo, Zaire	C5	44
Kongsberg, Nor.	G7	6
Kongsvinger, Nor.	F8	6
Kongsvoll, Nor.	E7	6
Kongur Shan, mtn., China	A6	38
Königs Wusterhausen, Ger.	C13	8
Konin, Pol.	C18	8
Konjic, Bos.	F12	14
Konomoc, Lake, res., Ct., U.S.	D7	84
Konqi, stm., China	C4	26
Konstanz, Ger.	H9	8
Kontagora, Nig.	F7	42
Kontiomäki, Fin.	D17	6
Kon Tum, Viet.	G10	34
Konya, Tur.	H14	4
Konza, Kenya	B7	44
Koochiching, co., Mn., U.S.	B4	100
Koolau Range, mts., Hi., U.S.	f10	88
Koontz Lake, In., U.S.	B5	91
Kooskia, Id., U.S.	C3	89
Kootenai, co., Id., U.S.	B2	89
Kootenay Lake, l., B.C., Can.	E9	69
Kootenay National Park, B.C., Can.	D9	69
Kopargaon, India	C3	37
Koper, Slo.	D8	14
Kopetdag, chrebet, mts., Asia	J9	22
Köping, Swe.	G10	6
Koppal, India	E4	37
Koppang, Nor.	F8	6
Koppel, Pa., U.S.	E1	115
Koprivnica, Cro.	C11	14
Kor'akskoje Nagorje, mts., Russia	E27	24
Korba, India	I10	38
Korbach, Ger.	D8	8
Korçë, Alb.	I4	16
Korčula, Cro.	G12	14
Korea, North, ctry., Asia	C12	26
Korea, South, ctry., Asia	D12	26
Korea Bay, b., Asia	D11	26
Korea Strait, strt., Asia	E12	26
Korf, Russia	E27	24
Korhogo, C. Iv.	G4	42
Korinthiakós Kólpos, b., Grc.	K6	16
Kórinthos (Corinth), Grc.	L6	16
Kōriyama, Japan	E13	30
Korliki, Russia	E10	24
Korogwe, Tan.	C7	44
Koronis, Lake, l., Mn., U.S.	E4	100
Koro Toro, Chad	E9	42
Korovin Volcano, vol., Ak., U.S.	E5	79
Korsakov, Russia	H22	24
Korsnäs, Fin.	E13	6
Korso, Fin.	F15	6
Kortrijk (Courtrai), Bel.	E3	8
Koruçam Burnu, c., N. Cyp.	B3	40
Koš-Agač, Russia	G11	24
Kosciusko, Ms., U.S.	B4	101
Kosciusko, co., In., U.S.	B6	91
Kosciusko, Mount, mtn., Austl.	G9	50
Koshkonong, Lake, l., Wi., U.S.	F5	126
Košice, Slov.	G21	8
Kosovska Mitrovica, Yugo.	G4	16
Kossuth, co., Ia., U.S.	A3	92
Kostroma, Russia	D23	18
Koszalin (Köslin), Pol.	A16	8
Kota, India	H6	38
Kota Baharu, Malay.	K7	34
Kotabumi, Indon.	F3	32
Kot Addu, Pak.	E4	38
Kota Kinabalu (Jesselton), Malay.	D6	32
Kotel'nyj, Ostrov, i., Russia	B21	24
Köthen, Ger.	D11	8
Kotka, Fin.	F16	6
Kot Kapūra, India	E6	38
Kotlas, Russia	E7	22
Kotlik, Ak., U.S.	C7	79
Kotor Varoš, Bos.	E12	14
Kotovsk, Russia	I24	18
Kotri, Pak.	H3	38
Kötschach [-Mauthen], Aus.	I12	8
Kottagūdem, India	D6	37
Kottayam, India	H4	37
Kotte, Sri L.	I5	37
Kotto, stm., Cen. Afr. Rep.	G10	42
Kotuj, stm., Russia	C14	24
Kotzebue, Ak., U.S.	B7	79
Kotzebue Sound, strt., Ak., U.S.	B7	79
Kouchibouguac National Park, N.B., Can.	C5	71
Koudougou, Burkina	F5	42
Koula-Moutou, Gabon	B2	44
Koumra, Chad	G9	42
Kountze, Tx., U.S.	D5	120
Koussi, Emi, mtn., Chad	E9	42
Koutiala, Mali	F4	42
Kouts, In., U.S.	B3	91
Kouvola, Fin.	F16	6
Kovrov, Russia	E24	18
Kowkcheh, stm., Afg.	B4	38
Kowloon (Jiulong), H.K.	M3	28
Kowt-e 'Ashrow, Afg.	C3	38
Koyukuk, stm., Ak., U.S.	B8	79
Koza, Japan	y27	31b
Kozáni, Grc.	I5	16
Kra, Isthmus of, Asia	I5	34
Krâchéh, Camb.	H9	34
Kragerø, Nor.	G7	6
Kragujevac, Yugo.	E4	16
Kraków, Pol.	E19	8
Kraljevica, Cro.	D9	14
Kraljevo, Yugo.	F4	16
Kramfors, Swe.	E11	6
Krångede, Swe.	E11	6
Kranj, Slo.	C9	14
Krasneno, Russia	E28	24
Krasnodar, Russia	H5	22
Krasnogorsk, Russia	F20	18
Krasnojarsk, Russia	F12	24
Krasnoje, Ozero, l., Russia	E28	24
Krasnosel'kup, Russia	D10	24
Krasnozavodsk, Russia	E21	18
Krebs, Ok., U.S.	C6	113
Kremenchuk, Ukr.	H4	22
Kremmling, Co., U.S.	A4	83
Krems an der Donau, Aus.	G15	8
Kresta, Zaliv, b., Russia	D30	24
Kribi, Cam.	H7	42
Kričov, Bela.	H14	18
Krishna, stm., India	D5	37
Krishnanagar, India	I13	38
Kristiansand, Nor.	G7	6
Kristianstad, Swe.	H10	6
Kristiansund, Nor.	E6	6
Kristinehamn, Swe.	G10	6
Kríti, i., Grc.	N8	16
Kritikón Pélagos, Grc.	N8	16
Krivoy Rog see Kryvyy Rih, Ukr.	H4	22
Krnov, Czech.	E17	8
Kroken, Nor.	D10	6
Kroměříž, Czech.	F17	8
Kronach, Ger.	E11	8
Kröng Khémôreǎh Phumint, Camb.	I7	34
Kronockij Zaliv, b., Russia	G26	24
Kronoki, Russia	G26	24
Kronštadt, Russia	B12	18
Kroonstad, S. Afr.	G5	44
Kropotkin, Russia	F17	24
Krosno, Pol.	F21	8
Krotz Springs, La., U.S.	D4	95
Krško, Slo.	D10	14
Kr'ukovo, Russia	D25	24
Krung Thep (Bangkok), Thai.	H6	34
Kruševac, Yugo.	F5	16
Krušné hory (Erzgebirge), mts., Eur.	E12	8
Kruzenšterna, Proliv, strt., Russia	H24	24
Kruzof Island, i., Ak., U.S.	m21	79
Krymskyy pivostriv (Crimea), pen., Ukr.	H4	22
Kryvyy Rih, Ukr.	H4	22
Ksenjevka, Russia	G17	24
Ksour Essaf, Tun.	N5	14
Kuala Kangsar, Malay.	L6	34
Kualakapuas, Indon.	F5	32
Kuala Krai, Malay.	L7	34
Kuala Kubu Baharu, Malay.	M6	34
Kuala Lumpur, Malay.	M6	34
Kuala Nerang, Malay.	K6	34
Kuala Pilah, Malay.	M7	34
Kuala Terengganu, Malay.	L7	34
Kuantan, Malay.	M7	34
Kubokawa, Japan	I6	30
Kuche, China	C3	26
Kuching, Malay.	E5	32
Kudat, Malay.	D6	32
Kudus, Indon.	m15	32
Kuee Ruins, hist., Hi., U.S.	D6	88
Kufstein, Aus.	H12	8
Kuhmo, Fin.	D17	6
Kuito, Ang.	D3	44
Kuiu Island, i., Ak., U.S.	m23	79
Kuivaniemi, Fin.	D15	6
Kukawa, Nig.	F8	42
Kula, Tur.	K12	16
Kula, Hi., U.S.	C5	88
Kul'ab, Taj.	B3	38
Kula Kangri, mtn., Bhu.	F14	38
Kulebaki, Russia	F25	18
Kulen Vakuf, Bos.	E11	14
Kulim, Malay.	L6	34
Kulmbach, Ger.	E11	8
Kulpmont, Pa., U.S.	E9	115
Kulunqi, China	C11	26
Kumagaya, Japan	F12	30
Kumajri, Arm.	I6	22
Kumamoto, Japan	J3	30
Kumano, Japan	I9	30
Kumano-nada, Japan	I9	30
Kumanovo, Mac.	G5	16
Kumasi, Ghana	G5	42
Kumbakonam, India	G5	37
Kume-shima, i., Japan	y26	31b
Kumo, Nig.	F8	42
Kumon Range, mts., Mya.	B4	34
Kumukahi, Cape, c., Hi., U.S.	D7	88
Kuna, Id., U.S.	F2	89
Kunašir, Ostrov (Kunashiri-tō), i., Russia	I23	24
Kundiān, Pak.	D4	38
Kundla, India	J4	38
Kunes, Nor.	A16	6
Kunghit Island, i., B.C., Can.	C2	69
Kuningan, Indon.	m14	33a
Kunlun Shan, mts., China	B12	38
Kunming, China	B7	34
Kunsan, S. Kor.	D12	26
Kunshan, China	D9	28
Kuopio, Fin.	E16	6
Kupang, Indon.	H7	32
Kupreanof Island, i., Ak., U.S.	m23	79
Kupres, Bos.	E12	14
Kur, stm., Asia	I7	22
Kurashiki, Japan	H6	30
Kurayoshi, Japan	G6	30
Kure, Japan	H5	30
Kure Island, i., Hi., U.S.	k12	88
Kurejka, stm., Russia	D11	24
Kurenalus, Fin.	D16	6
Kurgan-T'ube, Taj.	B3	38
Kurikka, Fin.	E14	6
Kuril'sk, Russia	H23	24
Kuril'skije Ostrova (Kuril Islands), is., Russia	H23	24
Kurmuk, Sudan	F12	42
Kurnool, India	E5	37
Kurow, N.Z.	F3	52
Kursk, Russia	G5	22
Kurtistown, Hi., U.S.	D6	88
Kuruman, S. Afr.	G4	44
Kurume, Japan	I3	30
Kurumkan, Russia	G16	24
Kurunegala, Sri L.	I6	37
Kuşadası Körfezi, b., Tur.	L11	16
Kuş Gölü, l., Tur.	I11	16
Kushima, Japan	K4	30
Kushiro, Japan	q22	30a
Kushtia, Bngl.	I13	38
Kushui, China	C5	26
Kuskokwim, stm., Ak., U.S.	C8	79
Kuskokwim Bay, b., Ak., U.S.	D7	79
Kuskokwim Mountains, mts., Ak., U.S.	C8	79
Kūstī, Sudan	F12	42
K'us'ur, Russia	C19	24
Kut, Ko, i., Thai.	I7	34
Kutaisi, Geor.	I6	22
Kūt al-Imāra, Iraq	B4	46
Kutch, Gulf of, b., India	I3	38
Kutina, Cro.	D11	14
Kutno, Pol.	C19	8
Kutu, Zaire	B3	44
Kutztown, Pa., U.S.	E10	115
Kuujjuaq, Que., Can.	g13	74
Kuusamo, Fin.	D17	6
Kuusankoski, Fin.	F16	6
Kuvango, Ang.	D3	44
Kuwait, ctry., Asia	C4	46
Kuwait see Al-Kuwayt, Kuw.	C4	46
Kuwana, Japan	G9	30
Kuybyshev see Samara, Russia	G8	22
Kuzneck, Russia	G7	22
Kvikkjokk, Swe.	C11	6
Kwando (Cuando), stm., Afr.	E4	44
Kwangchow see Guangzhou, China	L2	28
Kwangju, S. Kor.	D12	26
Kwango (Cuango), stm., Afr.	B3	44
Kwekwe, Zimb.	E5	44
Kwethluk, Ak., U.S.	C7	79
Kwidzyn, Pol.	B18	8
Kwigillingok, Ak., U.S.	D7	79
Kwilu (Cuilo), stm., Afr.	B3	44
Kyaiklat, Mya.	F3	34
Kyaikto, Mya.	F4	34
Kykotsmovi Village, Az., U.S.	B5	80
Kyle, Tx., U.S.	E4	120
Kyle of Lochalsh, Scot., U.K.	D7	7
Kyoga, Lake, l., Ug.	A6	44
Kyōto, Japan	G8	30
Kyrgyzstan, ctry., Asia	I12	22
Kyuquot Sound, strt., B.C., Can.	E4	69
Kyūshū, i., Japan	I3	30
Kyūshū-sanchi, mts., Japan	J4	30
Kyyiv, Ukr.	G4	22
Kyyjärvi, Fin.	E15	6
Kyzyl, Russia	G12	24

Name	Map Ref	Page
Kzyl-Orda, Kaz.	I11	22

L

Name	Map Ref	Page
Laa an der Thaya, Aus.	G16	8
La Almunia de Doña Godina, Spain	D10	12
La Asunción, Ven.	B11	58
Laau Point, c., Hi., U.S.	B4	88
L'Abacou, Pointe, c., Haiti	E11	64
Labadieville, La., U.S.	E5	95
La Bañeza, Spain	C6	12
La Barca, Mex.	G8	62
La Barge, Wy., U.S.	D2	127
La Barge Creek, stm., Wy., U.S.	D2	127
La Baule, Fr.	E4	10
Labé, Gui.	F3	42
Labe (Elbe), stm., Eur.	E14	8
La Belle, Fl., U.S.	F5	86
La Belle, Mo., U.S.	A6	102
Labette, co., Ks., U.S.	E8	93
Labin, Cro.	D9	14
La Bisbal, Spain	D15	12
Labouheyre, Fr.	H6	10
Labrador, reg., Newf., Can.	g9	72
Labrador City, Newf., Can.	h8	72
Labrador Sea, N.A.	E22	66
Lábrea, Braz.	E6	54
Labutta, Mya.	F3	34
La Canada Flintridge, Ca., U.S.	m12	82
Lacanau, Fr.	H5	10
La Cañiza, Spain	C3	12
La Canourgue, Fr.	H10	10
La Carolina, Spain	G8	12
Lacaune, Fr.	I9	10
Lac-Bouchette, Que., Can.	A5	74
Lac-Brome, Que., Can.	D5	74
Laccadive Sea, Asia	H3	37
Lac-Carré, Que., Can.	C3	74
Lac Courte Oreilles Indian Reservation, Wi., U.S.	C2	126
Lac du Bonnet, Man., Can.	D3	70
Lac du Flambeau, Wi., U.S.	B4	126
Lac du Flambeau Indian Reservation, Wi., U.S.	C3	126
La Ceiba, Hond.	G4	64
La Ceiba, Ven.	C7	58
La Center, Ky., U.S.	e9	94
Lac-Etchemin, Que., Can.	C7	74
Lacey, Wa., U.S.	B3	124
La Charité [-sur-Loire], Fr.	E10	10
La Châtre, Fr.	F8	10
La Chaux-de-Fonds, Switz.	E13	10
Lachine, Que., Can.	D4	74
La Chorrera, Col.	H6	58
La Chorrera, Pan.	J8	64
Lachute, Que., Can.	D3	74
La Ciotat, Fr.	I12	10
Lackawanna, N.Y., U.S.	C2	109
Lackawanna, co., Pa., U.S.	D10	115
Lackland Air Force Base, mil., Tx., U.S.	k7	120
Lac La Biche, Alta., Can.	B5	68
Lac la Hache, B.C., Can.	D7	69
Laclede, co., Mo., U.S.	D5	102
Lac-Mégantic, Que., Can.	D7	74
Lacolle, Que., Can.	D4	74
Lacombe, Alta., Can.	C4	68
Lacombe, La., U.S.	D6	95
Lacon, Il., U.S.	B4	90
Laconia, N.H., U.S.	C4	106
La Conner, Wa., U.S.	A3	124
Lacoochee, Fl., U.S.	D4	86
La Coruña, Spain	B3	12
Lac qui Parle, co., Mn., U.S.	F2	100
Lac qui Parle, stm., Mn., U.S.	F2	100
La Creek Lake, l., S.D., U.S.	D4	118
La Crescent, Mn., U.S.	G7	100
La Crete, Alta., Can.	f7	68
La Crosse, In., U.S.	B4	91
La Crosse, Ks., U.S.	D4	93
La Crosse, Wi., U.S.	E2	126
La Crosse, co., Wi., U.S.	E2	126
La Crosse, stm., Wi., U.S.	E3	126
La Cruz, Nic.	H5	64
La Cygne, Ks., U.S.	D9	93
Ladd, Il., U.S.	B4	90
Ladies Island, i., S.C., U.S.	G6	117
Lādīz, Iran	C7	46
Lādnun, India	G6	38
Ladoga, In., U.S.	E4	91
Ladoga, Lake see Ladožskoje Ozero, l., Russia	F18	6
La Dorada, Col.	E5	58
Ladožskoje Ozero (Lake Ladoga), l., Russia	F18	6
Ladson, S.C., U.S.	F7	117
Lady Lake, Fl., U.S.	D5	86
Lady Laurier, Mount, mtn., B.C., Can.	A6	69
Ladysmith, B.C., Can.	E6	69
Ladysmith, S. Afr.	G5	44
Ladysmith, Wi., U.S.	C2	126
Lae, Pap. N. Gui.	m16	50a
La Encantada, Cerro de, mtn., Mex.	B2	62
La Esmeralda, Ven.	F10	58
La Esperanza, Hond.	G3	64
La Estrada, Spain	C3	12
La Farge, Wi., U.S.	E3	126
Lafayette, Al., U.S.	C4	78
Lafayette, Co., U.S.	B5	83
Lafayette, Ga., U.S.	B1	87
Lafayette, In., U.S.	D4	91
Lafayette, La., U.S.	D3	95
Lafayette, N.C., U.S.	B3	110
Lafayette, Or., U.S.	B3	114
La Fayette, R.I., U.S.	E4	116
Lafayette, Tn., U.S.	A5	119
Lafayette, co., Ar., U.S.	D2	81
Lafayette, co., Fl., U.S.	C3	86
Lafayette, co., La., U.S.	D3	95
Lafayette, co., Ms., U.S.	A4	101
Lafayette, co., Mo., U.S.	B4	102
Lafayette, co., Wi., U.S.	F3	126
Lafayette, Mount, mtn., N.H., U.S.	B3	106
La Feria, Tx., U.S.	F4	120
La Ferté-Bernard, Fr.	D7	10
La Ferté-Macé, Fr.	D6	10
La Ferté-Saint-Aubin, Fr.	E8	10
Lafia, Nig.	G7	42
Lafitte, La., U.S.	k11	95
La Flèche, Fr.	E6	10
La Follette, Tn., U.S.	C9	119
La Fontaine, In., U.S.	C6	91
La Fortuna, C.R.	I5	64
Lafourche, La., U.S.	E5	95
Lafourche, co., La., U.S.	E5	95
La France, S.C., U.S.	B2	117
La Fregeneda, Spain	E5	12
La Fría, Ven.	C6	58
La Fuente de San Esteban, Spain	E5	12
Lågen, stm., Nor.	F8	6
Laghouat, Alg.	B6	42
Lago, Mount, mtn., Wa., U.S.	A5	124
Lagonegro, Italy	I10	14
Lagos, Nig.	G6	42
Lagos de Moreno, Mex.	G9	62
La Goulette, Tun.	M5	14
La Grand'Combe, Fr.	H11	10
La Grande, Or., U.S.	B8	114
La Grande, stm., Que., Can.	h11	74
La Grande Deux, Réservoir, res., Que., Can.	h11	74
La Grange, Austl.	C4	50
La Grange, Ga., U.S.	C1	87
La Grange, Il., U.S.	B6	90
Lagrange, In., U.S.	A7	91
La Grange, Ky., U.S.	B4	94
La Grange, Mo., U.S.	A6	102
La Grange, N.C., U.S.	B5	110
Lagrange, Oh., U.S.	A3	112
La Grange, Tx., U.S.	E4	120
Lagrange, co., In., U.S.	A7	91
La Grange Park, Il., U.S.	k9	90
La Gran Sabana, pl., Ven.	E12	58
La Grita, Ven.	C7	58
La Guadeloupe (Saint-Evariste), Que., Can.	D7	74
La Guaira, Ven.	B9	58
La Guajira, Península de, pen., S.A.	A7	58
Laguardia, Spain	C9	12
La Guardia, Spain	D3	12
La Guerche-de-Bretagne, Fr.	E5	10
La Guerche-sur-l'Aubois, Fr.	F9	10
Laguiole, Fr.	H9	10
Laguna, N.M., U.S.	B2	108
Laguna Beach, Ca., U.S.	F5	82
Laguna Dam, U.S.	E1	80
Laguna Indian Reservation, N.M., U.S.	C2	108
Lagunillas, Bol.	G6	54
La Habana (Havana), Cuba	C6	64
La Habra, Ca., U.S.	n13	82
Lahaina, Hi., U.S.	C5	88
La Harpe, Il., U.S.	C3	90
La Harpe, Ks., U.S.	E8	93
Lahat, Indon.	F3	32
La Have, stm., N.S., Can.	E5	71
La Haye-du-Puits, Fr.	C5	10
Lahij, Yemen	F3	46
Laholm, Swe.	H9	6
Lahoma, Ok., U.S.	A3	113
Lahontan Reservoir, res., Nv., U.S.	D2	105
Lahore, Pak.	E6	38
Lahr, Ger.	G7	8
Lahti, Fin.	F15	6
Laie, Hi., U.S.	B4	88
L'Aigle, Fr.	D7	10
Laignes, Fr.	E11	10
Laihia, Fin.	E14	6
Laingsburg, S. Afr.	H4	44
Laingsburg, Mi., U.S.	F6	99
Lairg, Scot., U.K.	C8	7
Laissac, Fr.	H9	10
Laiyang, China	D11	26
La Jara, Co., U.S.	D5	83
Lajes, Braz.	E11	54
La Jolla, Point, c., Ca., U.S.	o15	82
La Joya, Mex.	A2	62
La Junta, Mex.	C6	62
La Junta, Co., U.S.	D7	83
Lake, co., Ca., U.S.	C2	82
Lake, co., Co., U.S.	B4	83
Lake, co., Fl., U.S.	D5	86
Lake, co., Il., U.S.	A6	90
Lake, co., In., U.S.	B3	91
Lake, co., Mi., U.S.	E5	99
Lake, co., Mn., U.S.	C7	100
Lake, co., Mt., U.S.	C2	103
Lake, co., Oh., U.S.	A4	112
Lake, co., Or., U.S.	E6	114
Lake, co., S.D., U.S.	C8	118
Lake, co., Tn., U.S.	A2	119
Lake Alfred, Fl., U.S.	D5	86
Lake Andes, S.D., U.S.	D7	118
Lake Ariel, Pa., U.S.	D11	115
Lake Arrowhead, Ca., U.S.	E5	82
Lake Arthur, La., U.S.	D3	95
Lake Barcroft, Va., U.S.	*B5	123
Lake Benton, Mn., U.S.	F2	100
Lake Bluff, Il., U.S.	A6	90
Lake Butler, Fl., U.S.	B4	86
Lake Charles, La., U.S.	D2	95
Lake Chelan National Recreation Area, Wa., U.S.	A5	124
Lake City, Ar., U.S.	B5	81
Lake City, Fl., U.S.	B4	86
Lake City, Ia., U.S.	B3	92
Lake City, Mi., U.S.	D5	99
Lake City, Mn., U.S.	F6	100
Lake City, Pa., U.S.	B1	115
Lake City, S.C., U.S.	D8	117
Lake City, Tn., U.S.	C9	119
Lake Clark National Park, Ak., U.S.	C9	79
Lake Cowichan, B.C., Can.	g11	69
Lake Creek, stm., Wa., U.S.	B7	124
Lake Crystal, Mn., U.S.	F4	100
Lake Delta, N.Y., U.S.	B5	109
Lake Delton, Wi., U.S.	E4	126
Lake District National Park, Eng., U.K.	G9	7
Lake Elsinore, Ca., U.S.	F5	82
Lake Erie Beach, N.Y., U.S.	C1	109
Lakefield, Ont., Can.	C6	73
Lakefield, Mn., U.S.	G3	100
Lake Forest, Il., U.S.	A6	90
Lake Fork, stm., Ut., U.S.	C5	121
Lake Geneva, Wi., U.S.	F5	126
Lake Hamilton, Ar., U.S.	g7	81
Lake Harbour, N.W. Ter., Can.	D19	66
Lake Havasu City, Az., U.S.	C1	80
Lake Helen, Fl., U.S.	D5	86
Lakehurst, N.J., U.S.	C4	107
Lakehurst Naval Air Station, mil., N.J., U.S.	C4	107
Lake in the Hills, Il., U.S.	h8	90
Lake Jackson, Tx., U.S.	r14	120
Lake Katrine, N.Y., U.S.	D7	109
Lakeland, Fl., U.S.	D5	86
Lakeland, Ga., U.S.	E3	87
Lake Linden, Mi., U.S.	A2	99
Lake Louise, Alta., Can.	D2	68
Lake Magdalene, Fl., U.S.	o11	86
Lake Mary, Fl., U.S.	D5	86
Lake Mead National Recreation Area, U.S.	H7	105
Lake Meredith National Recreation Area, Tx., U.S.	B2	120
Lake Mills, Ia., U.S.	A4	92
Lake Mills, Wi., U.S.	E5	126
Lakemore, Oh., U.S.	A4	112
Lake Mountain, mtn., Wy., U.S.	E6	127
Lake Nebagamon, Wi., U.S.	B2	126
Lake Odessa, Mi., U.S.	F5	99
Lake of the Woods, co., Mn., U.S.	B4	100
Lake Orion, Mi., U.S.	F7	99
Lake Oswego, Or., U.S.	B4	114
Lake Ozark, Mo., U.S.	C5	102
Lake Park, Fl., U.S.	F6	86
Lake Park, Ia., U.S.	A2	92
Lake Park, Mn., U.S.	D2	100
Lake Placid, Fl., U.S.	E5	86
Lake Placid, N.Y., U.S.	A7	109
Lake Pontchartrain Causeway, La., U.S.	h11	95
Lakeport, Ca., U.S.	C2	82
Lake Preston, S.D., U.S.	C8	118
Lake Providence, La., U.S.	B4	95
Lake Range, mts., Nv., U.S.	C2	105
Lake Ridge, Va., U.S.	*B5	123
Lake Shore, Md., U.S.	B5	97
Lakeshore, Ms., U.S.	E4	101
Lakeside, Ca., U.S.	F5	82
Lakeside, Ct., U.S.	D3	84
Lakeside, Mt., U.S.	B2	103
Lakeside, Oh., U.S.	A3	112
Lakeside, Or., U.S.	D2	114
Lakeside Park, Ky., U.S.	h13	94
Lake Station, In., U.S.	A3	91
Lake Station, Ok., U.S.	A5	113
Lake Stevens, Wa., U.S.	A3	124
Lake Superior Provincial Park, Ont., Can.	p18	73
Lake Swamp, stm., S.C., U.S.	D8	117
Lake Tansi Village, Tn., U.S.	D8	119
Lake Valley, val., Nv., U.S.	E7	105
Lake View, Ia., U.S.	B2	92
Lakeview, Mi., U.S.	E5	99
Lakeview, Oh., U.S.	B2	112
Lakeview, Or., U.S.	E6	114
Lake View, S.C., U.S.	C9	117
Lake Villa, Il., U.S.	h8	90
Lake Village, Ar., U.S.	D4	81
Lake Village, In., U.S.	B3	91
Lakeville, Ct., U.S.	B2	84
Lakeville, In., U.S.	A5	91
Lakeville, Ma., U.S.	C6	98
Lakeville, Mn., U.S.	F5	100
Lake Waccamaw, N.C., U.S.	C4	110
Lake Wales, Fl., U.S.	E5	86
Lakewood, Ca., U.S.	n12	82
Lakewood, Co., U.S.	B5	83
Lakewood, Il., U.S.	D5	90
Lakewood, Ia., U.S.	f8	92
Lakewood, N.J., U.S.	C4	107
Lakewood, N.Y., U.S.	C1	109
Lakewood, Oh., U.S.	A4	112
Lakewood Center, Wa., U.S.	B3	124
Lake Worth, Fl., U.S.	F6	86
Lake Worth Inlet, b., Fl., U.S.	F7	86
Lake Zurich, Il., U.S.	h8	90
Lakhīmpur, India	G9	38
Lakin, Ks., U.S.	E2	93
Lakota, N.D., U.S.	A7	111
Lakselv, Nor.	A15	6
Lakshadweep, state, India	H3	37
Lakshadweep, is., India	H2	37
Lalbenque, Fr.	H8	10
La Libertad, Guat.	F2	64
La Libertad, Mex.	C3	62
Lalinde, Fr.	H7	10
La Línea, Spain	I6	12
Lalitpur, India	H8	38
Lalitpur, Nepal	G11	38
La Loupe, Fr.	D8	10
La Luz, N.M., U.S.	E4	108
Lama, Ozero, l., Russia	D12	24
La Maddalena, Italy	H4	14
La Madrid, Arg.	B3	56
La Malbaie, Que., Can.	B7	74
La Mancha, Mex.	E8	62
La Mancha, reg., Spain	G8	12
Lamar, Ar., U.S.	B2	81
Lamar, Co., U.S.	C8	83
Lamar, Mo., U.S.	D3	102
Lamar, Pa., U.S.	D7	115
Lamar, S.C., U.S.	C7	117
Lamar, co., Al., U.S.	B1	78
Lamar, co., Ga., U.S.	C2	87
Lamar, co., Ms., U.S.	D4	101
Lamar, co., Tx., U.S.	C5	120
Lamar, stm., Wy., U.S.	B2	127
Lamarche, Fr.	D12	10
La Mauricie, Parc National de, Que., Can.	C5	74
Lamb, co., Tx., U.S.	B1	120
Lamballe, Fr.	D4	10
Lambaréné, Gabon	B2	44
Lambert, Ms., U.S.	A3	101
Lambert Glacier, Ant.	B19	47
Lamberton, Mn., U.S.	F3	100
Lambert's Bay, S. Afr.	H3	44
Lambertville, Mi., U.S.	G7	99
Lambertville, N.J., U.S.	C3	107
Lambton, Cape, c., N.W. Ter., Can.	B8	66
Lame Deer, Mt., U.S.	E10	103
Lamego, Port.	D4	12
Lamèque, N.B., Can.	B5	71
Lamèque, Île, i., N.B., Can.	B5	71
La Mesa, Ca., U.S.	F5	82
La Mesa, N.M., U.S.	E3	108
Lamesa, Tx., U.S.	C2	120
Lamía, Grc.	K6	16
Lamoille, Nv., U.S.	C6	105
Lamoille, co., Vt., U.S.	B3	122
Lamoille, stm., Vt., U.S.	B3	122
La Moine, stm., Il., U.S.	C3	90
Lamoni, Ia., U.S.	D4	92
Lamont, Alta., Can.	C4	68
Lamont, Ca., U.S.	E4	82
La Monte, Mo., U.S.	C4	102
La Motte, Isle, i., Vt., U.S.	B2	122
Lamotte-Beuvron, Fr.	E9	10
La Moure, N.D., U.S.	C7	111
La Moure, co., N.D., U.S.	C7	111
Lampang, Thai.	E5	34
Lampasas, Tx., U.S.	D3	120
Lampasas, co., Tx., U.S.	D3	120
Lampedusa, Isola di, i., Italy	N7	14
Lampertheim, Ger.	F8	8
Lampman, Sask., Can.	H4	75
Lamprey, stm., N.H., U.S.	D4	106
Lamu, Kenya	B8	44
La Mure, Fr.	H12	10
Lanai, i., Hi., U.S.	C4	88
Lanai City, Hi., U.S.	C5	88
Lanaihale, mtn., Hi., U.S.	C5	88
Lanark, Ont., Can.	C8	73
Lanark, Il., U.S.	A4	90
Lanark, W.V., U.S.	D3	125
Lanbi Kyun, i., Mya.	I5	34
Lancaster, Ont., Can.	B10	73
Lancaster, Eng., U.K.	G10	7
Lancaster, Ca., U.S.	E4	82
Lancaster, Ky., U.S.	C5	94
Lancaster, Mo., U.S.	A5	102
Lancaster, N.H., U.S.	B3	106
Lancaster, N.Y., U.S.	C2	109
Lancaster, Oh., U.S.	C3	112
Lancaster, Pa., U.S.	F9	115
Lancaster, S.C., U.S.	B6	117
Lancaster, Tx., U.S.	n10	120
Lancaster, Wi., U.S.	F3	126
Lancaster, co., Ne., U.S.	D9	104
Lancaster, co., Pa., U.S.	G9	115
Lancaster, co., S.C., U.S.	B6	117
Lancaster, co., Va., U.S.	C6	123
Lancaster Sound, strt., N.W. Ter., Can.	B16	66
Lance Creek, stm., Wy., U.S.	C8	127
Lanciano, Italy	G9	14
Landau, Ger.	F8	8
Landau an der Isar, Ger.	G12	8
Land Between the Lakes, U.S.	f9	94
Lander, Wy., U.S.	D4	127
Lander, co., Nv., U.S.	C4	105
Landerneau, Fr.	D2	10
Landess, In., U.S.	C6	91
Landete, Spain	F10	12
Landis, N.C., U.S.	B2	110
Lando, S.C., U.S.	B5	117
Landquart, Switz.	F16	10
Landrum, S.C., U.S.	A3	117
Land's End, c., Eng., U.K.	K7	7
Lands End, c., R.I., U.S.	F5	116
Landshut, Ger.	G12	8
Landskrona, Swe.	I9	6
Lane, co., Ks., U.S.	D3	93
Lane, co., Or., U.S.	C4	114
Lanesboro, Mn., U.S.	G7	100
Lanett, Al., U.S.	C4	78
Langar, Afg.	B5	38
Långban, Swe.	G10	6
Langdon, N.D., U.S.	A7	111
Langeac, Fr.	G10	10
Langeais, Fr.	E7	10
Langeloth, Pa., U.S.	F1	115
Langenhagen, Ger.	C9	8
Langenthal, Switz.	E14	10
Langholm, Scot., U.K.	F9	7
Langhorne, Pa., U.S.	F12	115
Langlade, co., Wi., U.S.	C4	126
Langley, B.C., Can.	f13	69
Langley, S.C., U.S.	E4	117
Langley, Wa., U.S.	A3	124
Langley Air Force Base, mil., Va., U.S.	h15	123
Langley Park, Md., U.S.	f9	97
Langnau, Switz.	F14	10
Langogne, Fr.	H10	10
Langon, Fr.	H6	10
Langres, Fr.	E1	10
Langsa, Indon.	E2	32
Lang Son, Viet.	D9	34
Langston, Ok., U.S.	B4	113
Languedoc, hist. reg., Fr.	I9	10
L'Anguille, stm., Ar., U.S.	B5	81
Langzhong, China	E8	26
Lanham, Md., U.S.	C4	97
Lanier, co., Ga., U.S.	E3	87
Lannemezan, Fr.	I7	10
Lannilis, Fr.	D2	10
Lannion, Fr.	D3	10
Lannon, Wi., U.S.	m11	126
L'Annonciation, Que., Can.	C3	74
Lansdale, Pa., U.S.	F11	115
Lansdowne, Md., U.S.	B4	97
L'Anse, Mi., U.S.	B2	99
L'Anse-au-Loup, Newf., Can.	C3	72
L'Anse Indian Reservation, Mi., U.S.	B2	99
Lansford, Pa., U.S.	E10	115
Lansing, Il., U.S.	B6	90
Lansing, Ia., U.S.	A6	92
Lansing, Ks., U.S.	C9	93
Lansing, Mi., U.S.	F6	99
Lantana, Fl., U.S.	F6	86
Lantau Island, i., H.K.	M2	28
Lanusei, Italy	J4	14
Lanxi, China	F8	28
Lanzarote, i., Spain	p27	13b
Lanzhou, China	D7	26
Laoag, Phil.	B7	32
Lao Cai, Viet.	C7	34
Laon, Fr.	C10	10
La Oroya, Peru	F3	54
Laos, ctry., Asia	B3	32
Lapalisse, Fr.	F10	10
La Palma, Col.	E5	58
La Palma, Pan.	J8	64
La Palma, i., Spain	p23	13b
La Paragua, Ven.	D11	58
La Paz, Arg.	C5	56
La Paz, Arg.	C3	56
La Paz, Bol.	G5	54
La Paz, Mex.	E4	62
La Paz, co., Az., U.S.	D2	80
La Paz, Bahía de, b., Mex.	E4	62
Lapeer, Mi., U.S.	E7	99
Lapeer, co., Mi., U.S.	E7	99
Lapel, In., U.S.	D6	91
La Perouse Strait, strt., Asia	B15	26
La Piedad [Cavadas], Mex.	G8	62
La Pine, Or., U.S.	D5	114
Lapinlahti, Fin.	E16	6
La Place, La., U.S.	h11	95
Lapland, reg., Eur.	C14	6
La Plata, Arg.	C5	56
La Plata, Md., U.S.	C4	97
La Plata, Mo., U.S.	A5	102
La Plata, co., Co., U.S.	D3	83
La Plata Mountains, mts., Co., U.S.	D3	83
La Plata Peak, mtn., Co., U.S.	B4	83
La Platte, stm., Vt., U.S.	C2	122
La Pocatière, Que., Can.	B7	74
Laporte, Co., U.S.	A5	83
La Porte, In., U.S.	A4	91
La Porte, Tx., U.S.	r14	120
La Porte, co., In., U.S.	A4	91
La Porte City, Ia., U.S.	B5	92
Lappeenranta, Fin.	F17	6
La Prairie, Que., Can.	D4	74
La Pryor, Tx., U.S.	E3	120
Laptevych, More (Laptev Sea), Russia	B19	24
Lapua, Fin.	E14	6
La Puebla, Spain	F15	12
La Puebla de Montalbán, Spain	F7	12
La Push, Wa., U.S.	B1	124
Lapwai, Id., U.S.	C2	89
La Quiaca, Arg.	A3	56
L'Aquila, Italy	G8	14
Lār, Iran	C5	46
Larache, Mor.	A4	42
Laramie, Wy., U.S.	E7	127
Laramie, co., Wy., U.S.	E8	127
Laramie, stm., U.S.	E7	127
Laramie Mountains, mts., Wy., U.S.	D7	127
Laramie Peak, mtn., Wy., U.S.	D7	127
Larantuka, Indon.	G7	32
L'Arbresle, Fr.	G11	10
Lärbro, Swe.	H12	6
Larche, Col de, Eur.	H13	10
Larchmont, N.Y., U.S.	h13	109
Larchwood, Ia., U.S.	A1	92
Laredo, Tx., U.S.	F3	120
La Réole, Fr.	H6	10
Largeau, Chad	E9	42
L'argentière-la-Bessée, Fr.	H13	10
Lar Gerd, Afg.	C2	38
Largo, Fl., U.S.	E4	86
Largo, Cañon, val., N.M., U.S.	A2	108
Largo, Key, i., Fl., U.S.	G6	86
Largs, Scot., U.K.	F8	7
Larimer, co., Co., U.S.	A5	83
Larimore, N.D., U.S.	B8	111
La Rioja, Arg.	B3	56
Lárisa, Grc.	J6	16
Larjak, Russia	E10	24
Lārkāna, Pak.	G3	38
Lark Harbour, Newf., Can.	D2	72
Larkspur, Ca., U.S.	h7	82
Larksville, Pa., U.S.	n17	115
Lárnax (Larnaca), Cyp.	B3	40
Larne, N. Ire., U.K.	G7	7
Larned, Ks., U.S.	D4	93
La Robla, Spain	C6	12
La Roca de la Sierra, Spain	F5	12
La Rochefoucauld, Fr.	G7	10
La Rochelle, Fr.	F5	10
La Roche-sur-Yon, Fr.	F5	10
La Roda, Spain	F9	12
La Romana, Dom. Rep.	E13	64
Laroquebrou, Fr.	H9	10
Larose, La., U.S.	E5	95
La Rubia, Arg.	C4	56
Larue, co., Ky., U.S.	C4	94
Laruns, Fr.	J6	10
Larvik, Nor.	G7	6
LaSalle, Que., Can.	q19	74
La Salle, Co., U.S.	A6	83
La Salle, Il., U.S.	B4	90
La Salle, co., Il., U.S.	B4	90
La Salle, co., La., U.S.	C3	95
La Salle, co., Tx., U.S.	E3	120
Las Animas, Co., U.S.	C7	83
Las Animas, co., Co., U.S.	D6	83
Las Anod, Som.	G4	46
La Sarre, Que., Can.	k11	74

Name — Map Ref — Page

Las Casitas, Cerro, mtn., Mex. F5 62
Las Choapas, Mex. I12 62
La Scie, Newf., Can. D4 72
Las Colimas, Mex. E10 62
Las Cruces, N.M., U.S. E3 108
Las Delicias, Mex. J14 62
La Selle, Pic, mtn., Haiti E11 64
La Serena, Chile B2 56
Las Escobas, Mex. B2 62
La Seyne, Fr. I12 10
Las Flores, Arg. D5 56
Lashio, Mya. C4 34
Laško, Slo. C10 14
Las Lomitas, Arg. A4 56
Las Minas, Cerro, mtn., Hond. G3 64
La Solana, Spain G8 12
Las Palmas de Gran Canaria, Spain p25 13b
La Spezia, Italy E4 14
Las Piedras, Ur. C5 56
Las Plumas, Arg. E3 56
Lassen, co., Ca., U.S. B3 82
Lassen Peak, vol., Ca., U.S. B3 82
Lassen Volcanic National Park, Ca., U.S. B3 82
L'Assomption, Que., Can. D4 74
Las Termas, Arg. B4 56
Last Mountain Lake, l., Sask., Can. F3 75
Las Tórtolas, Cerro, mtn., S.A. B3 56
Las Varas, Mex. C5 62
Las Vegas, Nv., U.S. G6 105
Las Vegas, N.M., U.S. B4 108
Latacunga, Ec. H3 58
Latah, co., Id., U.S. C2 89
Latakia see Al-Lādhiqīyah, Syria B4 40
La Teste-de-Buch, Fr. H5 10
Lathrop, Mo., U.S. B3 102
Lathrop Wells, Nv., U.S. G5 105
Latimer, co., Ok., U.S. C6 113
Latina, Italy H7 14
Laton, Ca., U.S. D4 82
La Tortuga, Isla, i., Ven. B10 58
Latour Peak, mtn., Id., U.S. B2 89
Latrobe, Pa., U.S. F3 115
Latta, S.C., U.S. C9 117
La Tuque, Que., Can. B5 74
Lātūr, India C4 37
Latvia, ctry., Eur. E7 18
Lauchhammer, Ger. D13 8
Lauderdale, Ms., U.S. C5 101
Lauderdale, co., Al., U.S. A2 78
Lauderdale, co., Ms., U.S. C5 101
Lauderdale, co., Tn., U.S. B2 119
Lauderdale Lakes, Fl., U.S. r13 86
Lauenburg, Ger. B10 8
Laughlin, Nv., U.S. H7 105
Laughlin Air Force Base, mil., Tx., U.S. E2 120
Laughlin Peak, mtn., N.M., U.S. A5 108
Laughlintown, Pa., U.S. F3 115
Launceston, Austl. H9 50
Launceston, Eng., U.K. K8 7
Launching Point, c., P.E.I., Can. C7 71
La Union, El Sal. H4 64
La Unión, Spain H11 12
La Unión, Ven. C9 58
La Urbana, Ven. D9 58
Laurel, De., U.S. F3 85
Laurel, Fl., U.S. E4 86
Laurel, Md., U.S. B4 97
Laurel, Ms., U.S. D4 101
Laurel, Mt., U.S. E8 103
Laurel, Ne., U.S. B8 104
Laurel, Va., U.S. C5 123
Laurel, co., Ky., U.S. C5 94
Laurel, stm., Ky., U.S. D5 94
Laurel Bay, S.C., U.S. G6 117
Laurel Creek, stm., W.V., U.S. n14 125
Laurel Creek, stm., W.V., U.S. m12 125
Laureldale, Pa., U.S. F10 115
Laurel Fork, stm., W.V., U.S. C5 125
Laurel Hill, N.C., U.S. C3 110
Laurel River Lake, res., Ky., U.S. D5 94
Laurence G. Hanscom Air Force Base, mil., Ma., U.S. g10 98
Laurence Harbor, N.J., U.S. C4 107
Laurens, Ia., U.S. B3 92
Laurens, S.C., U.S. C3 117
Laurens, co., Ga., U.S. D4 87
Laurens, co., S.C., U.S. C4 117
Laurentides, Que., Can. D4 74
Laurentides, Parc Provincial des, Que., Can. B6 74
Laurier, Que., Can. C6 74
Laurière, Fr. F8 10
Laurierville, Que., Can. C6 74
Laurinburg, N.C., U.S. C3 110
Laurium, Mi., U.S. A2 99
Lausanne, Switz. F13 10
Laut, Pulau, i., Indon. F6 32
Laut, Pulau, i., Indon. L9 34
Lautaro, Chile D2 56
Lauterbach, Ger. E9 8
Laut Kecil, Kepulauan, is., Indon. F6 32
Lauzon (part of Lévis-Lauzon), Que., Can. C6 74
Lava Beds National Monument, Ca., U.S. B3 82
Lavaca, Ar., U.S. B1 81
Lavaca, co., Tx., U.S. E4 120
Lavagh More, mtn., Ire. G4 7
Laval, Que., Can. D4 74
Laval, Fr. D6 10
La Vale, Md., U.S. k13 97
Lavaltrie, Que., Can. D4 74
Lavapié, Punta, c., Chile D2 56
Laveen, Az., U.S. m8 80
La Vega, Dom. Rep. E12 64
La Vela, Cabo de, c., Col. A6 58
Lavello, Italy H10 14
L'Avenir, Que., Can. D5 74
La Vergne, Tn., U.S. A5 119
La Verkin, Ut., U.S. F2 121
La Verne, Ca., U.S. m13 82
Laverne, Ok., U.S. A2 113
La Veta, Co., U.S. D5 83
Lavia, Fin. F14 6
La Vista, Ga., U.S. *h8 87
La Vista, Ne., U.S. g12 104
Lavonia, Ga., U.S. B3 87
Lavon Lake, res., Tx., U.S. m10 120
La Voulte-sur-Rhône, Fr. H11 10
Lavras, Braz. F6 57
Lawai, Hi., U.S. B2 88
Lawang, Indon. m16 33a
Lawers, Ben, mtn., Scot., U.K. E8 7
Lawn, Newf., Can. E4 72
Lawrence, In., U.S. E5 91
Lawrence, Ks., U.S. D8 93
Lawrence, Ma., U.S. A5 98
Lawrence, Mi., U.S. F4 99
Lawrence, N.Y., U.S. k13 109
Lawrence, co., Al., U.S. A2 78
Lawrence, co., Ar., U.S. A4 81
Lawrence, co., Il., U.S. E6 90
Lawrence, co., In., U.S. G4 91
Lawrence, co., Ky., U.S. B7 94
Lawrence, co., Ms., U.S. D3 101
Lawrence, co., Mo., U.S. D4 102
Lawrence, co., Oh., U.S. D3 112
Lawrence, co., Pa., U.S. E1 115
Lawrence, co., Tn., U.S. B4 119
Lawrenceburg, In., U.S. F8 91
Lawrenceburg, Ky., U.S. B5 94
Lawrenceburg, Tn., U.S. B4 119
Lawrence Park, Pa., U.S. B1 115
Lawrenceville, Ga., U.S. C3 87
Lawrenceville, Il., U.S. E6 90
Lawrenceville, Va., U.S. D5 123
Lawson, Mo., U.S. B3 102
Lawsonia, Md., U.S. E6 97
Lawtell, La., U.S. D3 95
Lawton, Mi., U.S. F5 99
Lawton, Ok., U.S. C3 113
Lawz, Jabal al-, mtn., Sau. Ar. C2 46
Lay Lake, res., Al., U.S. B3 78
Laysan Island, i., Hi., U.S. k13 88
Layton, Ut., U.S. B4 121
La Zarca, Mex. E7 62
Lazarev, Russia G22 24
Lazi, China F12 38
Lea, co., N.M., U.S. D6 108
Leachville, Ar., U.S. B5 81
Lead, S.D., U.S. C2 118
Leadbetter Point, c., Wa., U.S. C1 124
Leadville, Co., U.S. B4 83
Leadwood, Mo., U.S. D7 102
Leaf, stm., Ms., U.S. D5 101
Leaf Rapids, Man., Can. A1 70
Leake, co., Ms., U.S. C4 101
Leakesville, Ms., U.S. D5 101
Lealman, Fl., U.S. p10 86
Leamington, Ont., Can. E2 73
Leary, Ga., U.S. E2 87
Leatherman Peak, mtn., Id., U.S. E5 89
Leavenworth, Ks., U.S. C9 93
Leavenworth, Wa., U.S. B5 124
Leavenworth, co., Ks., U.S. C8 93
Leavittsburg, Oh., U.S. A5 112
Leawood, Ks., U.S. D9 93
Lebanon, De., U.S. D4 85
Lebanon, Il., U.S. E4 90
Lebanon, In., U.S. D5 91
Lebanon, Ky., U.S. C4 94
Lebanon, Mo., U.S. D5 102
Lebanon, N.H., U.S. C2 106
Lebanon, Oh., U.S. C1 112
Lebanon, Or., U.S. C4 114
Lebanon, Pa., U.S. F9 115
Lebanon, Tn., U.S. A5 119
Lebanon, Va., U.S. f9 123
Lebanon, co., Pa., U.S. F8 115
Lebanon, ctry., Asia C4 40
Lebanon Junction, Ky., U.S. C4 94
Le Blanc, Fr. F8 10
Lebo, Ks., U.S. D8 93
Lębork, Pol. A17 8
Lebrija, Spain I5 12
Lecce, Italy I13 14
Lecco, Italy D4 14
Le Center, Mn., U.S. F5 100
Le Cheylard, Fr. H11 10
Le Claire, Ia., U.S. C7 92
Lecompte, La., U.S. C3 95
Lecompton, Ks., U.S. C8 93
Le Creusot, Fr. F11 10
Le Dorat, Fr. F8 10
Leduc, Alta., Can. C4 68
Lee, Ma., U.S. B1 98
Lee, co., Al., U.S. C4 78
Lee, co., Ar., U.S. C5 81
Lee, co., Fl., U.S. F5 86
Lee, co., Ga., U.S. E2 87
Lee, co., Il., U.S. B4 90
Lee, co., Ia., U.S. D6 92
Lee, co., Ky., U.S. C6 94
Lee, co., Ms., U.S. A5 101
Lee, co., N.C., U.S. B3 110
Lee, co., S.C., U.S. C7 117
Lee, co., Tx., U.S. D4 120
Lee, co., Va., U.S. f8 123
Lee, Lake, l., Ms., U.S. B3 101
Leechburg, Pa., U.S. E2 115
Leech Lake, l., Mn., U.S. C4 100
Leech Lake Indian Reservation, Mn., U.S. C4 100
Lee Creek, stm., U.S. B1 81
Leeds, Eng., U.K. H11 7
Leeds, Al., U.S. B3 78
Leelanau, co., Mi., U.S. D5 99
Leelanau, Lake, l., Mi., U.S. C5 99
Lee Park, Pa., U.S. n17 115
Leer, Ger. B7 8
Leesburg, Fl., U.S. D5 86
Leesburg, Ga., U.S. E2 87
Leesburg, Oh., U.S. C2 112
Leesburg, Va., U.S. A5 123
Lees Summit, Mo., U.S. C3 102
Leesville, La., U.S. C2 95
Leesville, S.C., U.S. D4 117
Leesville Lake, res., Va., U.S. C3 123
Leeton, Mo., U.S. C4 102
Leetonia, Oh., U.S. B5 112
Leetsdale, Pa., U.S. h13 115
Leeuwarden, Neth. B5 8
Leeuwin, Cape, c., Austl. F3 50
Leeward Islands, is., N.A. F17 64
Leflore, co., Ms., U.S. B3 101
Le Flore, co., Ok., U.S. C7 113
Legal, Alta., Can. C4 68
Legazpi, Phil. r20 33b
Leghorn see Livorno, Italy F5 14
Legnago, Italy D6 14
Legnano, Italy D3 14
Legnica (Liegnitz), Pol. D16 8
Le Grand, Ca., U.S. D3 82
Le Grand, Ia., U.S. B5 92
Le Havre, Fr. C7 10
Lehi, Ut., U.S. C4 121
Lehigh, co., Pa., U.S. E10 115
Lehigh, stm., Pa., U.S. E10 115
Lehigh Acres, Fl., U.S. F5 86
Lehighton, Pa., U.S. E10 115
Lehua Island, i., Hi., U.S. A1 88
Lehututu, Bots. F4 44
Leiah, Pak. E4 38
Leibnitz, Aus. I15 8
Leicester, Eng., U.K. I11 7
Leicester, Ma., U.S. B4 98
Leichhardt, stm., Austl. C7 50
Leiden, Neth. C4 8
Leighton, Al., U.S. A2 78
Leikanger, Nor. F6 6
Leinster, hist. reg., Ire. H5 7
Leinster, Mount, mtn., Ire. I6 7
Leipsic, De., U.S. D3 85
Leipsic, Oh., U.S. A2 112
Leipsic, stm., De., U.S. C3 85
Leipzig, Ger. D12 8
Leiria, Port. F3 12
Leisler, Mount, mtn., Austl. D5 50
Leisure City, Fl., U.S. s13 86
Leitchfield, Ky., U.S. C3 94
Leitrim, Ire. G4 7
Leiyang, China I1 28
Leizhou Bandao, pen., China D11 34
Leland, Il., U.S. B5 90
Leland, Ms., U.S. B3 101
Leleiwi Point, c., Hi., U.S. D7 88
Leleque, Arg. E2 56
Le Lion-d'Angers, Fr. E6 10
Leli Shan, mtn., China D9 38
Le Locle, Switz. E13 10
Le Lude, Fr. E7 10
Le Maire, Estrecho de, strt., Arg. G4 56
Le Mans, Fr. D7 10
Le Mars, Ia., U.S. B1 92
Leme, Braz. G5 57
Lemesós (Limassol), Cyp. B3 40
Lemgo, Ger. C8 8
Lemhi, co., Id., U.S. E4 89
Lemhi, stm., Id., U.S. E5 89
Lemhi Pass, Id., U.S. E5 89
Lemhi Range, mts., Id., U.S. E5 89
Lemmon, S.D., U.S. B3 118
Lemmon, Mount, mtn., Az., U.S. E5 80
Lemmon Valley, Nv., U.S. D2 105
Lemon, Lake, l., In., U.S. F5 91
Lemon Fair, stm., Vt., U.S. C2 122
Lemon Grove, Ca., U.S. o15 82
Lemon Island, i., S.C., U.S. G6 117
Lemont, Il., U.S. B6 90
Lemont, Pa., U.S. E6 115
Lemonweir, stm., Wi., U.S. D3 126
Lemoore, Ca., U.S. D4 82
Lemoore Naval Air Station, mil., Ca., U.S. D4 82
Lempa, stm., N.A. H3 64
Lem Peak, mtn., Id., U.S. E5 89
Lena, Il., U.S. A4 90
Lena, stm., Russia C19 24
Lenawee, co., Mi., U.S. G6 99
Lencloître, Fr. F7 10
Lenexa, Ks., U.S. D9 93
Lenghu, China D5 26
Leninabad, Taj. I11 22
Leningrad see Sankt-Peterburg, Russia B13 18
Leninogorsk, Kaz. G10 24
Leninsk-Kuzneckij, Russia G11 24
Leninskoje, Russia H20 24
Lennox, S.D., U.S. D9 118
Lennoxville, Que., Can. D6 74
Lenoir, N.C., U.S. B1 110
Lenoir, co., N.C., U.S. B5 110
Lenoir City, Tn., U.S. D9 119
Lenore Lake, l., Sask., Can. E3 75
Lenore Lake, l., Wa., U.S. B6 124
Lenox, Ga., U.S. E3 87
Lenox, Ia., U.S. D3 92
Lenox, Ma., U.S. B1 98
Lens, Fr. B9 10
Lensk, Russia E16 24
Lentini, Italy L10 14
Leo, In., U.S. B7 91
Leoben, Aus. H15 8
Leominster, Eng., U.K. I10 7
Leominster, Ma., U.S. A4 98
León, Nic. H4 64
León, Spain C6 12
Leon, Ia., U.S. D4 92
Leon, Ks., U.S. E7 93
Leon, co., Fl., U.S. B2 86
Leon, co., Tx., U.S. D4 120
Leonard, Tx., U.S. C4 120
Leonardo, N.J., U.S. C4 107
Leonardtown, Md., U.S. D4 97
Leonberg, Ger. G9 8
León [de los Aldamas], Mex. G9 62
Leonia, N.J., U.S. h9 107
Leonora, Austl. E4 50
Leonville, La., U.S. D4 95
Léopold II, Lac see Mai-Ndombe, Lac, l., Zaire B3 44
Leopoldina, Braz. F7 57
Léopoldville see Kinshasa, Zaire B3 44
Leoti, Ks., U.S. D2 93
Le Palais, Fr. E3 10
Lepanto, Ar., U.S. B5 81
Lepe, Spain H4 12
Leping, China G6 28
L'Épiphanie, Que., Can. D4 74
Lepontine, Alpi, mts., Eur. F15 10
Le Puy, Fr. G10 10
Lercara Friddi, Italy L8 14
Lerici, Italy E4 14
Lérida, Col. G7 58
Lérida, Spain D12 12
Lerma, Spain C8 12
Le Roy, Il., U.S. C5 90
Le Roy, Mn., U.S. G6 100
Le Roy, N.Y., U.S. C3 109
Lerwick, Scot., U.K. A11 7
Léry, Que., Can. q19 74
Lery, Lake, l., La., U.S. k12 95
Les Andelys, Fr. C8 10
Lesbos see Lésvos, i., Grc. J10 16
Les Cayes, Haiti E11 64
Les Échelles, Fr. G12 10
Les Herbiers, Fr. F5 10
Leskovac, Yugo. G5 16
Leslie, Mi., U.S. F6 99
Leslie, S.C., U.S. B6 117
Leslie, co., Ky., U.S. C6 94
Lesotho, ctry., Afr. G5 44
Lesozavodsk, Russia H20 24
Les Sables-d'Olonne, Fr. F5 10
Lesser Antilles, is. G17 64
Lesser Slave Lake, l., Alta., Can. B3 68
Lesser Sunda Islands, is., Indon. G6 32
Lester Prairie, Mn., U.S. F4 100
Le Sueur, Mn., U.S. F5 100
Le Sueur, co., Mn., U.S. F5 100
Lésvos (Lesbos), i., Grc. J10 16
Leszno, Pol. D16 8
Letcher, co., Ky., U.S. C7 94
Lethbridge, Alta., Can. E4 68
Lethbridge, Newf., Can. D5 72
Lethem, Guy. F13 58
Le Thillot, Fr. E13 10
Leti, Kepulauan, is., Indon. G8 32
Leticia, Col. J8 58
Le Tréport, Fr. B8 10
Letsôk-Aw Kyun, i., Mya. I5 34
Letterkenny, Ire. G5 7
Leutkirch, Ger. H10 8
Leuven, Bel. E4 8
Levádhia, Grc. K6 16
Levante, Riviera di, Italy E4 14
Levelland, Tx., U.S. C1 120
Leveque, Cape, c., Austl. C4 50
Leverkusen, Ger. D6 8
Le Vigan, Fr. I10 10
Levisa Fork, stm., U.S. C7 94
Lévis [-Lauzon], Que., Can. C6 74
Levittown, N.Y., U.S. E7 109
Levittown, Pa., U.S. F12 115
Levy, co., Fl., U.S. C4 86
Levy Lake, l., Fl., U.S. C4 86
Lewes, Eng., U.K. K13 7
Lewes, De., U.S. E5 85
Lewes and Rehoboth Canal, De., U.S. F5 85
Lewis, co., Id., U.S. C2 89
Lewis, co., Ky., U.S. B6 94
Lewis, co., Mo., U.S. A6 102
Lewis, co., N.Y., U.S. B5 109
Lewis, co., Tn., U.S. B4 119
Lewis, co., Wa., U.S. C3 124
Lewis, co., W.V., U.S. C4 125
Lewis, stm., Wa., U.S. C4 124
Lewis, stm., Wy., U.S. B2 127
Lewis, Isle of, i., Scot., U.K. C6 7
Lewis, Mount, mtn., Nv., U.S. C5 105
Lewis and Clark, co., Mt., U.S. C4 103
Lewis and Clark Cavern, Mt., U.S. D5 103
Lewis and Clark Lake, res., U.S. E8 118
Lewisburg, Ky., U.S. D3 94
Lewisburg, Oh., U.S. C1 112
Lewisburg, Pa., U.S. E8 115
Lewisburg, Tn., U.S. B5 119
Lewisburg, W.V., U.S. D4 125
Lewis Creek, stm., Vt., U.S. C2 122
Lewis Lake, l., Wy., U.S. B2 127
Lewisport, Ky., U.S. C3 94
Lewisporte, Newf., Can. D4 72
Lewis Smith Lake, res., Al., U.S. B2 78
Lewiston, Id., U.S. C1 89
Lewiston, Me., U.S. D2 96
Lewiston, Mn., U.S. G7 100
Lewiston, N.Y., U.S. B1 109
Lewiston, Ut., U.S. B4 121
Lewiston Peak, mtn., Ut., U.S. C3 121
Lewiston Woodville, N.C., U.S. A5 110
Lewistown, Il., U.S. C3 90
Lewistown, Mt., U.S. C7 103
Lewistown, Pa., U.S. E6 115
Lewisville, Ar., U.S. D2 81
Lewisville, Tx., U.S. C4 120
Lewisville Lake, res., Tx., U.S. C4 120
Lexington, Al., U.S. A2 78
Lexington, Il., U.S. C5 90
Lexington, Ky., U.S. B5 94
Lexington, Ma., U.S. B5 98
Lexington, Mi., U.S. E8 99
Lexington, Ms., U.S. B3 101
Lexington, Mo., U.S. B4 102
Lexington, Ne., U.S. D6 104
Lexington, N.C., U.S. B2 110
Lexington, Oh., U.S. B3 112
Lexington, Ok., U.S. B4 113
Lexington, S.C., U.S. D5 117
Lexington, Tn., U.S. B3 119
Lexington, Va., U.S. C3 123
Lexington, co., S.C., U.S. D5 117
Lexington Park, Md., U.S. D5 97
Leyte, i., Phil. C7 32
Leyte Gulf, b., Phil. C8 32
Lhasa, China F14 38
Lhokseumawe, Indon. D2 32
Lianhua Shan, mts., China L4 28
Lianxian, China G9 26
Lianyungang, China E10 26
Liao, stm., China C11 26
Liaocheng, China D10 26
Liaodong Wan, b., China C11 26
Liaoning, prov., China C11 26
Liaotung, Gulf of see Liaodong Wan, b., China C11 26
Liaoyang, China C11 26
Liaoyuan, China C12 26
Liard, stm., Can. E8 66
Libby, Mt., U.S. B1 103
Libenge, Zaire H9 42
Liberal, Ks., U.S. E3 93
Liberal, Mo., U.S. D3 102
Liberec, Czech. E15 8
Liberia, C.R. I5 64
Liberia, ctry., Afr. G4 42
Libertad, Ven. C8 58
Liberty, In., U.S. E8 91
Liberty, Ky., U.S. C5 94
Liberty, Ms., U.S. D3 101
Liberty, Mo., U.S. B3 102
Liberty, N.Y., U.S. D6 109
Liberty, N.C., U.S. B3 110
Liberty, S.C., U.S. B2 117
Liberty, Tx., U.S. D5 120
Liberty, co., Fl., U.S. B2 86
Liberty, co., Ga., U.S. E5 87
Liberty, co., Mt., U.S. B5 103
Liberty, co., Tx., U.S. D5 120
Liberty Center, Oh., U.S. A1 112
Liberty Lake, Wa., U.S. g14 124
Liberty Lake, res., Md., U.S. B4 97
Libertyville, Il., U.S. A6 90
Lībīyah, Aṣ-Ṣaḥrā' al- (Libyan Desert), des., Afr. D11 42
Libourne, Fr. H6 10
Libreville, Gabon A1 44
Libuse, La., U.S. C3 95
Libya, ctry., Afr. C9 42
Libyan Desert see Lībīyah, Aṣ-Ṣaḥrā' al-, des., Afr. D11 42
Licata, Italy L8 14
Lichinga, Moz. D7 44
Lichtenfels, Ger. E11 8
Lick Creek, stm., Tn., U.S. C11 119
Licking, Mo., U.S. D6 102
Licking, co., Oh., U.S. B3 112
Licking, stm., Ky., U.S. B6 94
Lida, Bela. H8 18
Lida, Lake, l., Mn., U.S. D3 100
Lidgerwood, N.D., U.S. C8 111
Lidköping, Swe. G9 6
Lido di Ostia, Italy H7 14
Liechtenstein, ctry., Eur. F9 4
Liège, Bel. E5 8
Lieksa, Fin. E18 6
Lienz, Aus. I12 8
Liepāja, Lat. E4 18
Lier, Bel. D4 8
Liestal, Switz. E14 10
Liévin, Fr. B9 10
Lièvre, Rivière du, stm., Que., Can. D2 74
Liezen, Aus. H14 8
Lifford, Ire. G5 7
Ligao, Phil. r20 33b
Lighthouse Inlet, b., S.C., U.S. k12 117
Lighthouse Point, c., Fl., U.S. C2 86
Lighthouse Point, c., La., U.S. E3 95
Lighthouse Point, c., Mi., U.S. C5 99
Lightning Creek, stm., Wy., U.S. C8 127
Ligny-en-Barrois, Fr. D12 10
Ligonier, In., U.S. B6 91
Ligonier, Pa., U.S. F3 115
Ligurian Sea, Eur. F3 14
Lihou Reefs, rf., Austl. C10 50
Lihue, Hi., U.S. B2 88
Lijiang, China F7 26
Likasi (Jadotville), Zaire D5 44
Likino-Dulevo, Russia F22 18
Liknes, Nor. G6 6
Likouala, stm., Congo B3 44
Lilbourn, Mo., U.S. E8 102
Lilburn, Ga., U.S. h8 87
Liling, China H2 28
Lille, Fr. B10 10
Lillehammer, Nor. F8 6
Lillestrøm, Nor. G8 6
Lillian, Al., U.S. E2 78
Lillington, N.C., U.S. B4 110
Lillinonah, Lake, l., Ct., U.S. C2 84
Lillo, Spain F8 12
Lillooet, B.C., Can. D7 69
Lillooet, stm., B.C., Can. D6 69
Lilly, Pa., U.S. F4 115
Lilly Fork, stm., W.V., U.S. m13 125
Lilly Grove, W.V., U.S. D3 125
Lilongwe, Mwi. D6 44
Lily, Ky., U.S. C5 94
Lima, Peru F3 54
Lima, N.Y., U.S. C3 109
Lima, Oh., U.S. B1 112
Lima Reservoir, res., Mt., U.S. F4 103
Limassol see Lemesós, Cyp. B3 40
Limbdi, India I4 38
Limburg an der Lahn, Ger. E8 8
Limeira, Braz. G5 57
Limerick, Ire. I4 7
Limestone, Me., U.S. B5 96
Limestone, co., Al., U.S. A2 78
Limestone, co., Tx., U.S. D4 120
Limestone Point, pen., Man., Can. C2 70
Liminka, Fin. D15 6
Limmen Bight, Austl. B7 50
Límnos, i., Grc. J9 16
Limoges, Ont., Can. B9 73
Limoges, Fr. G8 10
Limón, C.R. I6 64
Limon, Co., U.S. B7 83
Limousins, Plateau du, plat., Fr. G8 10
Limoux, Fr. I9 10
Limpopo, stm., Afr. F6 44

Name	Map Ref	Page
Linares, Chile	**D2**	56
Linares, Col.	**G4**	58
Linares, Mex.	**E10**	62
Linares, Spain	**G8**	12
Lincoln, Arg.	**C4**	56
Lincoln, Ont., Can.	**D5**	73
Lincoln, Eng., U.K.	**H12**	7
Lincoln, Al., U.S.	**B3**	78
Lincoln, Ar., U.S.	**B1**	81
Lincoln, Ca., U.S.	**C3**	82
Lincoln, De., U.S.	**E4**	85
Lincoln, Id., U.S.	**F6**	89
Lincoln, Il., U.S.	**C4**	90
Lincoln, Ks., U.S.	**C5**	93
Lincoln, Me., U.S.	**C4**	96
Lincoln, Ma., U.S.	**g10**	98
Lincoln, Mo., U.S.	**C4**	102
Lincoln, Ne., U.S.	**D9**	104
Lincoln, N.H., U.S.	**B3**	106
Lincoln, co., Ar., U.S.	**D4**	81
Lincoln, co., Co., U.S.	**C7**	83
Lincoln, co., Ga., U.S.	**C4**	87
Lincoln, co., Id., U.S.	**G4**	89
Lincoln, co., Ks., U.S.	**C5**	93
Lincoln, co., Ky., U.S.	**C5**	94
Lincoln, co., La., U.S.	**B3**	95
Lincoln, co., Me., U.S.	**D3**	96
Lincoln, co., Mn., U.S.	**F2**	100
Lincoln, co., Ms., U.S.	**D3**	101
Lincoln, co., Mo., U.S.	**B7**	102
Lincoln, co., Mt., U.S.	**B1**	103
Lincoln, co., Ne., U.S.	**D5**	104
Lincoln, co., Nv., U.S.	**F6**	105
Lincoln, co., N.M., U.S.	**D4**	108
Lincoln, co., N.C., U.S.	**B1**	110
Lincoln, co., Ok., U.S.	**B5**	113
Lincoln, co., Or., U.S.	**C3**	114
Lincoln, co., S.D., U.S.	**D9**	118
Lincoln, co., Tn., U.S.	**B5**	119
Lincoln, co., Wa., U.S.	**B7**	124
Lincoln, co., W.V., U.S.	**C2**	125
Lincoln, co., Wi., U.S.	**C4**	126
Lincoln, co., Wy., U.S.	**D2**	127
Lincoln, Mount, mtn., Co., U.S.	**B4**	83
Lincoln Acres, Ca., U.S.	**o15**	82
Lincoln City, Or., U.S.	**C3**	114
Lincoln Heights, Oh., U.S.	**o13**	112
Lincoln Park, Co., U.S.	**C5**	83
Lincoln Park, Ga., U.S.	**D2**	87
Lincoln Park, Mi., U.S.	**p15**	99
Lincoln Park, N.J., U.S.	**B4**	107
Lincolnshire, Il., U.S.	**h9**	90
Lincoln Tomb State Memorial, hist., Il., U.S.	**D4**	90
Lincolnton, Ga., U.S.	**C4**	87
Lincolnton, N.C., U.S.	**B1**	110
Lincolnville, S.C., U.S.	**h11**	117
Lincolnwood, Il., U.S.	**h9**	90
Lincroft, N.J., U.S.	**C4**	107
Lindale, Ga., U.S.	**B1**	87
Lindale, Tx., U.S.	**C5**	120
Lindau, Ger.	**H9**	8
Linden, Al., U.S.	**C2**	78
Linden, In., U.S.	**D4**	91
Linden, Mi., U.S.	**F7**	99
Linden, N.J., U.S.	**k8**	107
Linden, Tn., U.S.	**B4**	119
Linden, Tx., U.S.	**C5**	120
Lindenhurst, Il., U.S.	**h8**	90
Lindenhurst, N.Y., U.S.	**n15**	109
Lindenwold, N.J., U.S.	**D3**	107
Lindesnes, c., Nor.	**G6**	6
Lindi, Tan.	**C7**	44
Lindon, Ut., U.S.	**C4**	121
Lindsay, Ont., Can.	**C6**	73
Lindsay, Ca., U.S.	**D4**	82
Lindsay, Ok., U.S.	**C4**	113
Lindsborg, Ks., U.S.	**D6**	93
Lindstrom, Mn., U.S.	**E6**	100
Linesville, Pa., U.S.	**C1**	115
Lineville, Al., U.S.	**B4**	78
Lingao, China	**D10**	34
Lingayen, Phil.	**B7**	32
Lingen, Ger.	**C7**	8
Lingga, Kepulauan, is., Indon.	**F3**	32
Lingle, Wy., U.S.	**D8**	127
Linglestown, Pa., U.S.	**F8**	115
Lingling, China	**A11**	34
Linh, Ngoc, mtn., Viet.	**G9**	34
Linhai, China	**G10**	28
Linière, Que., Can.	**C7**	74
Linjiang, China	**C12**	26
Linköping, Swe.	**G10**	6
Linkou, China	**B13**	26
Linn, Mo., U.S.	**C6**	102
Linn, co., Ia., U.S.	**B6**	92
Linn, co., Ks., U.S.	**D9**	93
Linn, co., Mo., U.S.	**B4**	102
Linn, co., Or., U.S.	**C4**	114
Lino Lakes, Mn., U.S.	**m13**	100
Linqing, China	**D10**	26
Linru, China	**A1**	28
Lins, Braz.	**F4**	57
Lintao, China	**D7**	26
Linthicum Heights, Md., U.S.	**B4**	97
Linton, In., U.S.	**F3**	91
Linton, N.D., U.S.	**C5**	111
Linwood, N.J., U.S.	**E3**	107
Linxi, China	**C10**	26
Linxia, China	**D7**	26
Linyi, China	**D10**	26
Linz, Aus.	**G14**	8
Lion, Golfe du, b., Fr.	**I11**	10
Lipa, Phil.	**r19**	33b
Lipeck, Russia	**I22**	18
Lippstadt, Ger.	**D8**	8
Lipscomb, Al., U.S.	**B3**	78
Lipscomb, co., Tx., U.S.	**A2**	120
Lira, Ug.	**H12**	42
Liria, Spain	**F11**	12
Lisala, Zaire	**A4**	44
Lisboa (Lisbon), Port.	**G2**	12
Lisbon, Ia., U.S.	**C6**	92
Lisbon, Me., U.S.	**D2**	96
Lisbon, Md., U.S.	**B3**	97
Lisbon, N.H., U.S.	**B3**	106
Lisbon, N.D., U.S.	**C8**	111
Lisbon, Oh., U.S.	**B5**	112
Lisbon Center, Me., U.S.	**f7**	96
Lisbon Falls, Me., U.S.	**E2**	96
Lisbon see Lisboa, Port.	**G2**	12
Lisburne, Cape, c., Ak., U.S.	**B6**	79
Lishui, China	**G8**	28
Lisianski Island, i., Hi., U.S.	**k13**	88
Lisieux, Fr.	**C7**	10
Lisle, Il., U.S.	**k8**	90
L'Isle Jourdain, Fr.	**F7**	10
L'Isle-Jourdain, Fr.	**I8**	10
L'Islet-sur-Mer, Que., Can.	**B7**	74
L'Isle-Verte, Que., Can.	**A8**	74
Lismore, Austl.	**E10**	50
Listowel, Ont., Can.	**D4**	73
Listowel, Ire.	**I3**	7
Lit, Swe.	**E10**	6
Litang, China	**G8**	26
Litchfield, Ct., U.S.	**C3**	84
Litchfield, Il., U.S.	**D4**	90
Litchfield, Mi., U.S.	**F6**	99
Litchfield, Mn., U.S.	**E4**	100
Litchfield, co., Ct., U.S.	**B2**	84
Litchfield Park, Az., U.S.	**m8**	80
Lithia Springs, Ga., U.S.	**h7**	87
Lithonia, Ga., U.S.	**C2**	87
Lithuania, ctry., Eur.	**F6**	18
Litija, Slo.	**C9**	14
Lititz, Pa., U.S.	**F9**	115
Litovko, Russia	**H21**	24
Little, stm., U.S.	**B5**	81
Little, stm., U.S.	**D7**	113
Little, stm., Ct., U.S.	**C7**	84
Little, stm., Ky., U.S.	**D2**	94
Little, stm., La., U.S.	**C3**	95
Little, stm., N.C., U.S.	**B3**	110
Little, stm., Ok., U.S.	**B5**	113
Little, stm., S.C., U.S.	**C2**	117
Little, stm., Tn., U.S.	**n14**	119
Little, stm., Vt., U.S.	**C3**	122
Little, stm., Va., U.S.	**D2**	123
Little Abaco Island, i., Bah.	**A9**	64
Little Acres, Az., U.S.	**D5**	80
Little Andaman, i., India	**I2**	34
Little Arkansas, stm., Ks., U.S.	**D6**	93
Little Belt Mountains, mts., Mt., U.S.	**D6**	103
Little Bighorn, stm., U.S.	**E9**	103
Little Black, stm., Me., U.S.	**A3**	96
Little Blue, stm., U.S.	**C6**	93
Little Blue, stm., In., U.S.	**H5**	91
Little Bow, stm., Alta., Can.	**D4**	68
Little Cacapon, stm., W.V., U.S.	**B6**	125
Little Catalina, Newf., Can.	**D5**	72
Little Cayman, i., Cay. Is.	**E7**	64
Little Cedar, stm., Ia., U.S.	**A5**	92
Little Churchill, stm., Man., Can.	**A4**	70
Little Chute, Wi., U.S.	**D5**	126
Little Coal, stm., W.V., U.S.	**C3**	125
Little Colorado, stm., Az., U.S.	**B4**	80
Little Compton, R.I., U.S.	**E6**	116
Little Creek, De., U.S.	**D4**	85
Little Creek Naval Amphibious Base, mil., Va., U.S.	**k15**	123
Little Creek Peak, mtn., Ut., U.S.	**F3**	121
Little Current, Ont., Can.	**B3**	73
Little Diomede Island, i., Ak., U.S.	**B6**	79
Little Egg Harbor, b., N.J., U.S.	**D4**	107
Little Egg Inlet, b., N.J., U.S.	**E4**	107
Little Falls, Mn., U.S.	**E4**	100
Little Falls, N.J., U.S.	**B4**	107
Little Falls, N.Y., U.S.	**B6**	109
Little Ferry, N.J., U.S.	**h8**	107
Littlefield, Tx., U.S.	**C1**	120
Little Fishing Creek, stm., W.V., U.S.	**h9**	125
Littlefork, Mn., U.S.	**B5**	100
Little Fork, stm., Mn., U.S.	**B5**	100
Little Goose Creek, stm., Wy., U.S.	**B6**	127
Little Gunpowder Falls, stm., Md., U.S.	**A4**	97
Little Humboldt, stm., Nv., U.S.	**B4**	105
Little Inagua, i., Bah.	**D11**	64
Little Kanawha, stm., W.V., U.S.	**C4**	125
Little Lake, Mi., U.S.	**B3**	99
Little Lake, l., La., U.S.	**E5**	95
Little Lynches, stm., S.C., U.S.	**C7**	117
Little Manatee, stm., Fl., U.S.	**p11**	86
Little Mecatina, stm., Can.	**h9**	72
Little Miami, stm., Oh., U.S.	**C1**	112
Little Minch, strt., Scot., U.K.	**D6**	7
Little Missouri, stm., U.S.	**B6**	76
Little Missouri, stm., Ar., U.S.	**D2**	81
Little Muddy, stm., Il., U.S.	**E4**	90
Little Muddy, stm., N.D., U.S.	**A2**	111
Little Nicobar, i., India	**K2**	34
Little Osage, stm., U.S.	**E9**	93
Little Otter Creek, stm., Vt., U.S.	**C2**	122
Little Owyhee, stm., U.S.	**B5**	105
Little Pee Dee, stm., S.C., U.S.	**C9**	117
Little Powder, stm., U.S.	**F11**	103
Little Red, stm., Ar., U.S.	**B4**	81
Little River, co., Ar., U.S.	**D1**	81
Little River Inlet, b., S.C., U.S.	**D10**	117
Little Rock, Ar., U.S.	**C3**	81
Little Rock, stm., U.S.	**A1**	92
Little Rock Air Force Base, mil., Ar., U.S.	**C3**	81
Little Sable Point, c., Mi., U.S.	**E4**	99
Little Salt Lake, l., Ut., U.S.	**F3**	121
Little Sandy, stm., Ky., U.S.	**B6**	94
Little Sandy Creek, stm., Wy., U.S.	**D3**	127
Little Sebago Lake, l., Me., U.S.	**g7**	96
Little Silver, N.J., U.S.	**C4**	107
Little Sioux, stm., U.S.	**B2**	92
Little Sioux, West Fork, stm., Ia., U.S.	**B2**	92
Little Smoky, stm., Alta., Can.	**B2**	68
Little Snake, stm., U.S.	**A2**	83
Little Spokane, stm., Wa., U.S.	**B8**	124
Littlestown, Pa., U.S.	**G7**	115
Little Tallapoosa, stm., U.S.	**B4**	78
Little Tenmile Creek, stm., W.V., U.S.	**k10**	125
Little Tennessee, stm., U.S.	**D9**	119
Littleton, Co., U.S.	**B6**	83
Littleton, Me., U.S.	**B5**	96
Littleton, Ma., U.S.	**f10**	98
Littleton, N.H., U.S.	**B3**	106
Littleton, N.C., U.S.	**A5**	110
Littleville, Al., U.S.	**A2**	78
Little Wabash, stm., Il., U.S.	**E5**	90
Little Walnut, stm., Ks., U.S.	**g13**	93
Little White, stm., S.D., U.S.	**D5**	118
Little Wolf, stm., Wi., U.S.	**D4**	126
Little Wood, stm., Id., U.S.	**F4**	89
Liuan, China	**D5**	28
Liuhe, China	**C7**	28
Liuzhou, China	**B10**	34
Live Oak, Ca., U.S.	**C3**	82
Live Oak, Fl., U.S.	**B4**	86
Live Oak, co., Tx., U.S.	**E3**	120
Livermore, Ca., U.S.	**h9**	82
Livermore, Ky., U.S.	**C2**	94
Livermore, Mount, mtn., Tx., U.S.	**o12**	120
Livermore Falls, Me., U.S.	**D2**	96
Liverpool, Eng., U.K.	**H10**	7
Liverpool, Cape, c., N.W. Ter., Can.	**B17**	66
Livingston, Al., U.S.	**C1**	78
Livingston, Ca., U.S.	**D3**	82
Livingston, Il., U.S.	**E4**	90
Livingston, La., U.S.	**D5**	95
Livingston, Mt., U.S.	**E6**	103
Livingston, N.J., U.S.	**B4**	107
Livingston, Tn., U.S.	**C8**	119
Livingston, Tx., U.S.	**D5**	120
Livingston, co., Il., U.S.	**C5**	90
Livingston, co., Ky., U.S.	**e9**	94
Livingston, co., La., U.S.	**D5**	95
Livingston, co., Mi., U.S.	**F7**	99
Livingston, co., Mo., U.S.	**B4**	102
Livingston, co., N.Y., U.S.	**C3**	109
Livingston, Lake, res., Tx., U.S.	**D5**	120
Livingstone, Zam.	**E5**	44
Livingstonia, Mwi.	**D6**	44
Livno, Bos.	**F12**	14
Livny, Russia	**I20**	18
Livonia, La., U.S.	**D4**	95
Livonia, Mi., U.S.	**F7**	99
Livorno (Leghorn), Italy	**F5**	14
Liyang, China	**D8**	28
Lizard Head Pass, Co., U.S.	**D3**	83
Lizard Head Peak, mtn., Wy., U.S.	**D3**	127
Lizard Point, c., Eng., U.K.	**L7**	7
Lizella, Ga., U.S.	**D3**	87
Ljubljana, Slo.	**C9**	14
Ljungby, Swe.	**H9**	6
Ljusdal, Swe.	**F11**	6
Llandudno, Wales, U.K.	**H9**	7
Llanelli, Wales, U.K.	**J8**	7
Llanes, Spain	**B7**	12
Llanidloes, Wales, U.K.	**I9**	7
Llano, Tx., U.S.	**D3**	120
Llano, co., Tx., U.S.	**D3**	120
Llano, stm., Tx., U.S.	**D3**	120
Llanos, pl., S.A.	**E7**	58
Llanwrtyd Wells, Wales, U.K.	**I9**	7
Llera, Mex.	**F10**	62
Llerena, Spain	**G5**	12
Lloyd, Ky., U.S.	**B7**	94
Lloydminster, Alta., Can.	**C5**	68
Lloyds, stm., Newf., Can.	**D3**	72
Llucmayor, Spain	**F14**	12
Llullaillaco, Volcán, vol., S.A.	**A3**	56
Lo, stm., Viet.	**C8**	34
Loami, Il., U.S.	**D4**	90
Loange, stm., Afr.	**C3**	44
Löbau, Ger.	**D14**	8
Lobaye, stm., Cen. Afr. Rep.	**G9**	42
Lobelville, Tn., U.S.	**B4**	119
Lobito, Ang.	**D2**	44
Lobos de Afuera, Islas, is., Peru	**E2**	54
Lobos de Tierra, Isla, i., Peru	**E2**	54
Lobster Lake, l., Me., U.S.	**C3**	96
Locarno, Switz.	**F15**	10
Lochaline, Scot., U.K.	**E7**	7
Lochboisdale, Scot., U.K.	**D5**	7
Loches, Fr.	**E7**	10
Lochgilphead, Scot., U.K.	**E7**	7
Loch Lomond, Va., U.S.	***B5**	123
Loch Raven Reservoir, res., Md., U.S.	**B4**	97
Lochsa, stm., Id., U.S.	**C3**	89
Lockeport, N.S., Can.	**F4**	71
Lockesburg, Ar., U.S.	**D1**	81
Lockhart, Tx., U.S.	**E4**	120
Lock Haven, Pa., U.S.	**D7**	115
Lockland, Oh., U.S.	**o13**	112
Lockney, Tx., U.S.	**B2**	120
Lockport, Il., U.S.	**B5**	90
Lockport, La., U.S.	**E5**	95
Lockport, N.Y., U.S.	**B2**	109
Lockwood, Mo., U.S.	**D4**	102
Lockwood, Mt., U.S.	**E8**	103
Loc Ninh, Viet.	**I9**	34
Locust, N.C., U.S.	**B2**	110
Locust Fork, stm., Al., U.S.	**B3**	78
Locust Grove, Ga., U.S.	**C2**	87
Locust Grove, Ok., U.S.	**A6**	113
Lod, Isr.	**D4**	40
Lodejnoje Pole, Russia	**A16**	18
Lodève, Fr.	**I10**	10
Lodgepole Creek, stm., U.S.	**C3**	104
Lodi, Italy	**D4**	14
Lodi, Ca., U.S.	**C3**	82
Lodi, N.J., U.S.	**h8**	107
Lodi, Oh., U.S.	**A3**	112
Lodi, Wi., U.S.	**E4**	126
Lodja, Zaire	**B4**	44
Lodore, Canyon of, val., Co., U.S.	**A2**	83
Lodwar, Kenya	**H2**	46
Łodź, Pol.	**D19**	8
Loffa, stm., Afr.	**G3**	42
Logan, Ia., U.S.	**C2**	92
Logan, Ks., U.S.	**C4**	93
Logan, N.M., U.S.	**B6**	108
Logan, Oh., U.S.	**C3**	112
Logan, Ut., U.S.	**B4**	121
Logan, W.V., U.S.	**D3**	125
Logan, co., Ar., U.S.	**B2**	81
Logan, co., Co., U.S.	**A7**	83
Logan, co., Il., U.S.	**C4**	90
Logan, co., Ks., U.S.	**D2**	93
Logan, co., Ky., U.S.	**D3**	94
Logan, co., Ne., U.S.	**C5**	104
Logan, co., N.D., U.S.	**C6**	111
Logan, co., Oh., U.S.	**B2**	112
Logan, co., Ok., U.S.	**B4**	113
Logan, co., W.V., U.S.	**D3**	125
Logan, Mount, mtn., Yukon, Can.	**D4**	66
Logan, Mount, mtn., Wa., U.S.	**A5**	124
Logandale, Nv., U.S.	**G7**	105
Logan Lake, B.C., Can.	**D7**	69
Logan Martin Lake, res., Al., U.S.	**B3**	78
Logan Pass, Mt., U.S.	**B2**	103
Logansport, In., U.S.	**C5**	91
Logansport, La., U.S.	**C2**	95
Loganville, Ga., U.S.	**C3**	87
Loganville, Pa., U.S.	**G8**	115
Loggieville, N.B., Can.	**B4**	71
Log Lane Village, Co., U.S.	**A7**	83
Logone, stm., Afr.	**F9**	42
Logroño, Spain	**C9**	12
Logrosán, Spain	**F6**	12
Lohr, Ger.	**E9**	8
Loi-Kaw, Mya.	**E4**	34
Loimaa, Fin.	**F14**	6
Loire, stm., Fr.	**E5**	10
Loja, Ec.	**J3**	58
Loja, Spain	**H7**	12
Lokolama, Zaire	**B3**	44
Lol, stm., Sudan	**G11**	42
Lola, Mount, mtn., Ca., U.S.	**C3**	82
Lolo, Mt., U.S.	**D2**	103
Lolo Pass, U.S.	**C4**	89
Lomami, stm., Zaire	**B4**	44
Lombard, Il., U.S.	**k8**	90
Lomblen, Pulau, i., Indon.	**G7**	32
Lombok, i., Indon.	**G6**	32
Lomé, Togo	**G6**	42
Lomela, Zaire	**B4**	44
Lomela, stm., Zaire	**B4**	44
Lomira, Wi., U.S.	**E5**	126
Lomond, Loch, l., Scot., U.K.	**E8**	7
Lomonosov, Russia	**B12**	18
Lompoc, Ca., U.S.	**E3**	82
Łomża, Pol.	**B22**	8
Lonaconing, Md., U.S.	**k13**	97
Lonāvale, India	**C2**	37
Loncoche, Chile	**D2**	56
London, Ont., Can.	**E3**	73
London, Eng., U.K.	**J12**	7
London, Ar., U.S.	**B2**	81
London, Ky., U.S.	**C5**	94
London, Oh., U.S.	**C2**	112
Londonderry, N. Ire., U.K.	**G5**	7
Londonderry, N.H., U.S.	**E4**	106
Londonderry, Cape, c., Austl.	**B5**	50
Londonderry, Isla, i., Chile	**H2**	56
Londontown, Md., U.S.	**C4**	97
Londrina, Braz.	**G3**	57
Lone Grove, Ok., U.S.	**C4**	113
Lone Mountain, mtn., Nv., U.S.	**E4**	105
Lone Pine, Ca., U.S.	**D4**	82
Lone Tree, Ia., U.S.	**C6**	92
Long, co., Ga., U.S.	**E5**	87
Longa, Proliv, strt., Russia	**C29**	24
Longarone, Italy	**C7**	14
Long Bar Harbor, Md., U.S.	**B5**	97
Long Beach, Ca., U.S.	**F4**	82
Long Beach, In., U.S.	**A4**	91
Long Beach, Md., U.S.	**D5**	97
Long Beach, Ms., U.S.	**g7**	101
Long Beach, N.Y., U.S.	**E7**	109
Long Beach, Wa., U.S.	**C1**	124
Long Beach Naval Shipyard, mil., Ca., U.S.	**n12**	82
Longboat Key, Fl., U.S.	**q10**	86
Longboat Key, i., Fl., U.S.	**E4**	86
Longboat Pass, strt., Fl., U.S.	**q10**	86
Long Branch, N.J., U.S.	**C5**	107
Longbranch, Wa., U.S.	**B3**	124
Long Creek Mountain, mtn., Wy., U.S.	**D5**	127
Longeau, Fr.	**E12**	10
Long Grove, Ia., U.S.	**C7**	92
Long Harbour [-Mount Arlington Heights], Newf., Can.	**E5**	72
Long Island, i., Bah.	**C10**	64
Long Island, i., N.S., Can.	**E3**	71
Long Island, i., Me., U.S.	**g7**	96
Long Island, i., Ma., U.S.	**g12**	98
Long Island, i., N.Y., U.S.	**E7**	109
Long Island Sound, strt., U.S.	**E7**	109
Longjiang, China	**B11**	26
Long Key, i., Fl., U.S.	**H6**	86
Long Lake, Il., U.S.	**h8**	90
Long Lake, l., Me., U.S.	**A4**	96
Long Lake, l., Me., U.S.	**D2**	96
Long Lake, l., Mi., U.S.	**D5**	99
Long Lake, l., Mi., U.S.	**C7**	99
Long Lake, l., Mn., U.S.	**D4**	100
Long Lake, l., N.Y., U.S.	**B6**	109
Long Lake, l., N.D., U.S.	**C6**	111
Long Lake, l., Wa., U.S.	**f10**	124
Long Lake, l., Wi., U.S.	**C2**	126
Longli, China	**A9**	34
Longmeadow, Ma., U.S.	**B2**	98
Longmont, Co., U.S.	**A5**	83
Long Point, c., Man., Can.	**C2**	70
Long Point, pen., Ont., Can.	**E4**	73
Long Pond, res., Fl., U.S.	**C4**	86
Long Prairie, Mn., U.S.	**E4**	100
Long Range Mountains, mts., Newf., Can.	**D3**	72
Longreach, Austl.	**D8**	50
Longsheng, China	**B11**	34
Longs Peak, mtn., Co., U.S.	**A5**	83
Longué, Fr.	**E6**	10
Longueuil, Que., Can.	**D4**	74
Longuyon, Fr.	**C12**	10
Long View, N.C., U.S.	**B1**	110
Longview, Tx., U.S.	**C5**	120
Longview, Wa., U.S.	**C3**	124
Longwy, Fr.	**C12**	10
Long Xuyen, Viet.	**I8**	34
Lonigo, Italy	**D6**	14
Löningen, Ger.	**C7**	8
Lonoke, Ar., U.S.	**C4**	81
Lonoke, co., Ar., U.S.	**C4**	81
Lønsdal, Nor.	**C10**	6
Lonsdale, Mn., U.S.	**F5**	100
Lonsdale, R.I., U.S.	**B4**	116
Lons-le-Saunier, Fr.	**F12**	10
Loogootee, In., U.S.	**G4**	91
Lookout, Ky., U.S.	**C7**	94
Lookout, Cape, c., N.C., U.S.	**C6**	110
Lookout, Point, c., Mi., U.S.	**d7**	99
Lookout Mountain, Tn., U.S.	**h11**	119
Lookout Mountain, mtn., U.S.	**D8**	119
Lookout Mountain, mtn., Or., U.S.	**C6**	114
Lookout Pass, U.S.	**B3**	89
Lookout Point Lake, res., Or., U.S.	**D4**	114
Loon Lake, Wa., U.S.	**A8**	124
Loon Lake, l., Me., U.S.	**B3**	96
Loop Creek, stm., W.V., U.S.	**m13**	125
Loop Head, c., Ire.	**I3**	7
Loosahatchie, stm., Tn., U.S.	**B2**	119
Lopatina, Gora, mtn., Russia	**G22**	24
Lopatka, Mys, c., Russia	**G25**	24
Lop Buri, Thai.	**G6**	34
Lopez, Cap, c., Gabon	**B1**	44
López Collada, Mex.	**B3**	62
Lopez Island, i., Wa., U.S.	**A3**	124
Lop Nur, l., China	**C5**	26
Lora del Río, Spain	**H6**	12
Lorain, Oh., U.S.	**A3**	112
Lorain, co., Oh., U.S.	**A3**	112
Loramie, Lake, res., Oh., U.S.	**B1**	112
Lorca, Spain	**H10**	12
Lord Howe Island, i., Austl.	**F11**	50
Lordsburg, N.M., U.S.	**E1**	108
Loreauville, La., U.S.	**D4**	95
Lorena, Braz.	**G6**	57
Lorenzo, Tx., U.S.	**C2**	120
Loreto, Braz.	**E9**	54
Loreto, Col.	**I7**	58
Loreto, Mex.	**F9**	62
Lorette, Man., Can.	**E3**	70
Loretteville, Que., Can.	**C6**	74
Loretto, Ky., U.S.	**C4**	94
Loretto, Pa., U.S.	**F4**	115
Loretto, Tn., U.S.	**B4**	119
Lorica, Col.	**C5**	58
Lorient, Fr.	**E3**	10
L'Orignal, Ont., Can.	**B10**	73
Loring Air Force Base, mil., Me., U.S.	**B5**	96
Loriol [-du-Comtat], Fr.	**H11**	10
Loris, S.C., U.S.	**C10**	117
Lorne, N.B., Can.	**B3**	71
Lörrach, Ger.	**H7**	8
Lorraine, hist. reg., Fr.	**D13**	10
Los Alamos, N.M., U.S.	**B3**	108
Los Alamos, co., N.M., U.S.	**B3**	108
Los Aldamas, Mex.	**D10**	62
Los Altos, Ca., U.S.	**k8**	82
Los Ángeles, Chile	**D2**	56
Los Angeles, Ca., U.S.	**E4**	82
Los Angeles, co., Ca., U.S.	**E4**	82
Los Angeles Aqueduct, Ca., U.S.	**E4**	82
Los Banos, Ca., U.S.	**D3**	82
Los Blancos, Arg.	**A4**	56
Los Fresnos, Tx., U.S.	**F4**	120
Los Gatos, Ca., U.S.	**D2**	82
Los Lagos, Chile	**D2**	56
Los Lunas, N.M., U.S.	**C3**	108
Los Mochis, Mex.	**E5**	62
Los Palacios y Villafranca, Spain	**H6**	12
Los Pinos, stm., Co., U.S.	**D3**	83
Los Ranchos de Albuquerque, N.M., U.S.	**B3**	108
Los Roques, Islas, is., Ven.	**B9**	58
Lost, stm., In., U.S.	**G4**	91
Lost, stm., Wa., U.S.	**A5**	124
Lost, stm., W.V., U.S.	**B6**	125
Lost Creek, stm., Wy., U.S.	**D4**	127
Los Teques, Ven.	**B9**	58
Los Testigos, Islas, is., Ven.	**B11**	58
Lost Peak, mtn., Ut., U.S.	**F2**	121
Lost Ranger Peak, mtn., Co., U.S.	**A4**	83
Lost River Glacial Caverns, N.H., U.S.	**B3**	106
Lost River Range, mts., Id., U.S.	**E5**	89
Lost Trail Pass, U.S.	**D5**	89
Los Vilos, Chile	**C2**	56
Los Yébenes, Spain	**F8**	12
Lota, Chile	**D2**	56
Lotawana, Lake, res., Mo., U.S.	**k11**	102
Lotbinière, Que., Can.	**C6**	74
Louang Namtha, Laos	**D6**	34
Louangphrabang, Laos	**E7**	34
Loudéac, Fr.	**D4**	10
Loudon, Tn., U.S.	**D9**	119
Loudon, co., Tn., U.S.	**D9**	119
Loudonville, Oh., U.S.	**B3**	112
Loudoun, co., Va., U.S.	**A5**	123
Loudun, Fr.	**E7**	10
Louga, Sen.	**E2**	42
Loughrea, Ire.	**H4**	7
Louhans, Fr.	**F12**	10
Louisa, Ky., U.S.	**B7**	94
Louisa, Va., U.S.	**B4**	123
Louisa, co., Ia., U.S.	**C6**	92
Louisa, co., Va., U.S.	**C5**	123
Louisa, Lake, l., Fl., U.S.	**D5**	86
Louisbourg, N.S., Can.	**D10**	71
Louisburg, Ks., U.S.	**D9**	93
Louisburg, N.C., U.S.	**A4**	110
Louisdale, N.S., Can.	**D8**	71
Louise, Lake, l., Ak., U.S.	**f18**	79
Louise Island, i., B.C., Can.	**C2**	69
Louiseville, Que., Can.	**C5**	74
Louisiade Archipelago, is., Pap. N. Gui.	**B10**	50
Louisiana, Mo., U.S.	**B6**	102

Index

Name — Map Ref — Page

Louisiana, state, U.S. C3 95
Louisiana Point, c., La., U.S. E2 95
Louis Trichardt, S. Afr. F5 44
Louisville, Al., U.S. D4 78
Louisville, Co., U.S. B5 83
Louisville, Ga., U.S. C4 87
Louisville, Il., U.S. E5 90
Louisville, Ky., U.S. B4 94
Louisville, Ms., U.S. B4 101
Louisville, Ne., U.S. D9 104
Louisville, Oh., U.S. B4 112
Louis-XIV, Pointe, c., Que., Can. h11 74
Loulé, Port. H3 12
Loup, co., Ne., U.S. C6 104
Loup, stm., Ne., U.S. C8 104
Loup City, Ne., U.S. C7 104
Lourdes, Newf., Can. D2 72
Lourdes, Fr. I6 10
Lourenço Marques see Maputo, Moz. G6 44
Louth, Eng., U.K. H12 7
Louviers, Fr. C8 10
Louviers, Co., U.S. B6 83
Love, co., Ok., U.S. D4 113
Loveč, Bul. F8 16
Loveland, Co., U.S. A5 83
Loveland, Oh., U.S. n13 112
Loveland Park, Oh., U.S. C1 112
Loveland Pass, Co., U.S. B5 83
Lovell, Wy., U.S. B4 127
Lovelock, Nv., U.S. C3 105
Lovely, Ky., U.S. C7 94
Lovenia, Mount, mtn., Ut., U.S. C5 121
Love Point, c., Md., U.S. B5 97
Lovere, Italy D5 14
Loves Park, Il., U.S. A4 90
Lovettsville, Va., U.S. A5 123
Loving, N.M., U.S. E5 108
Loving, co., Tx., U.S. D1 120
Lovington, Il., U.S. D5 90
Lovington, Ia., U.S. e8 92
Lovington, N.M., U.S. E6 108
Lövstabruk, Swe. F11 6
Low, Cape, c., N.W. Ter., Can. D15 66
Lowden, Ia., U.S. C7 92
Lowell, Ar., U.S. A1 81
Lowell, In., U.S. B3 91
Lowell, Ma., U.S. A5 98
Lowell, Mi., U.S. F5 99
Lowell, N.C., U.S. B1 110
Lowell, Or., U.S. D4 114
Lowell, Lake, res., Id., U.S. F2 89
Lowellville, Oh., U.S. A5 112
Lower Arrow Lake, res., B.C., Can. E8 69
Lower Brule Indian Reservation, S.D., U.S. C6 118
Lower California see Baja California, pen., Mex. D3 62
Lower Hutt, N.Z. D5 52
Lower Klamath Lake, l., Ca., U.S. B3 82
Lower Matecumbe Key, i., Fl., U.S. H6 86
Lower Monumental Lake, res., Wa., U.S. C7 124
Lower New York Bay, b., N.J., U.S. B4 107
Lower Otay Lake, res., Ca., U.S. o16 82
Lower Paia, Hi., U.S. C5 88
Lower Red Lake, l., Mn., U.S. C3 100
Lower Rice Lake, l., Mn., U.S. C3 100
Lower Salmon Dam, Id., U.S. G4 89
Lower West Pubnico, N.S., Can. F4 71
Lowestoft, Eng., U.K. I14 7
Lowndes, co., Al., U.S. C3 78
Lowndes, co., Ga., U.S. F3 87
Lowndes, co., Ms., U.S. B5 101
Lowry Air Force Base, mil., Co., U.S. B6 83
Lowry City, Mo., U.S. C4 102
Lowville, N.Y., U.S. B5 109
Loxley, Al., U.S. E2 78
Loyal, Wi., U.S. D3 126
Loyall, Ky., U.S. D6 94
Loyalsock Creek, stm., Pa., U.S. D8 115
Loznica, Yugo. E3 16
Lozoyuela, Spain E8 12
Lua, stm., Zaire H9 42
Lualaba, stm., Zaire B5 44
Lua Makika, crat., Hi., U.S. C5 88
Luanda, Ang. C2 44
Luang Praban Range, mts., Asia E6 34
Luanguinga, stm., Afr. D4 44
Luangwa, stm., Afr. D6 44
Luanshya, Zam. D5 44
Luarca, Spain B5 12
Luau, Ang. D4 44
Lubang Island, i., Phil. C7 32
Lubango, Ang. D2 44
Lübben, Ger. D13 8
Lübbenau, Ger. D13 8
Lubbock, Tx., U.S. C2 120
Lubbock, co., Tx., U.S. C2 120
Lubec, Me., U.S. D6 96
Lübeck, Ger. B10 8
Lübecker Bucht, b., Ger. A11 8
L'ubercy, Russia F20 18
Lubilash, stm., Zaire C4 44
Lubin, Pol. D16 8
Lublin, Pol. D22 8
Lubudi, Zaire C4 44
Lubuksikaping, Indon. N6 34
Lubumbashi (Élisabethville), Zaire D5 44
Lubutu, Zaire B5 44
Lucama, N.C., U.S. B4 110
Lucan, Ont., Can. D3 73
Lucania, Mount, mtn., Yukon, Can. D4 66
Lucas, co., Ia., U.S. C4 92
Lucas, co., Oh., U.S. A2 112
Lucasville, Oh., U.S. D3 112
Lucca, Italy F5 14
Luce, co., Mi., U.S. B5 99
Luce Bay, b., Scot., U.K. G8 7
Lucedale, Ms., U.S. E5 101
Lucena, Phil. r19 33b
Lucena, Spain H7 12
Lucena del Cid, Spain E11 12
Luc-en-Diois, Fr. H12 10
Lucera, Italy H10 14
Lucerne, Ca., U.S. C2 82
Lucerne see Luzern, Switz. E15 10
Lucernemines, Pa., U.S. E3 115
Lucerne Valley, Ca., U.S. E5 82
Luceville, Que., Can. A9 74
Luchiang, Tai. K9 28
Lüchow, Ger. C11 8
Lucira, Ang. D2 44
Luck, Wi., U.S. C1 126
Luckeesarai, India H12 38
Luckenwalde, Ger. C13 8
Lucknow, Ont., Can. D3 73
Lucknow, India G9 38
Lucky Peak Lake, res., Id., U.S. F3 89
Luçon, Fr. F5 10
Lüderitz, Nmb. G3 44
Ludhiāna, India E6 38
Ludington, Mi., U.S. E4 99
L'udinovo, Russia H17 18
Ludlow, Ky., U.S. h13 94
Ludlow, Ma., U.S. B3 98
Ludlow, Vt., U.S. E3 122
Ludowici, Ga., U.S. E5 87
Ludvika, Swe. F10 6
Ludwigsburg, Ger. G9 8
Ludwigsfelde, Ger. C13 8
Ludwigshafen, Ger. F8 8
Luena, stm., Ang. D4 44
Luene, Ang. D3 44
Lufeng, China M4 28
Lufkin, Tx., U.S. D5 120
Luga, Russia C12 18
Lugano, Switz. F15 10
Lugenda, stm., Moz. D7 44
Lugh Ganane, Som. H3 46
Lugnaquillia Mountain, mtn., Ire. I6 7
Lugo, Italy E6 14
Lugo, Spain B4 12
Lugoff, S.C., U.S. C6 117
Lugoj, Rom. D5 16
Luhans'k, Ukr. H5 22
Luhit, stm., Asia G16 38
Luilaka, stm., Zaire B4 44
Luino, Italy C3 14
Lukachukai, Az., U.S. A6 80
Luke Air Force Base, mil., Az., U.S. D3 80
Lukulu, Zam. D4 44
Lula, Ga., U.S. B3 87
Luleå, Swe. D14 6
Lüleburgaz, Tur. H11 16
Luling, La., U.S. k11 95
Luling, Tx., U.S. E4 120
Lulonga, stm., Zaire A3 44
Lumajang, Indon. n16 33a
Lumber, stm., U.S. C9 117
Lumber City, Ga., U.S. E4 87
Lumberport, W.V., U.S. B4 125
Lumberton, Ms., U.S. D4 101
Lumberton, N.C., U.S. C3 110
Lumbrales, Spain E5 12
Lumby, B.C., Can. D8 69
Lumding, India H15 38
Lummi Indian Reservation, Wa., U.S. A3 124
Lumpkin, Ga., U.S. D2 87
Lumpkin, co., Ga., U.S. B2 87
Lumsden, Newf., Can. D5 72
Luna, co., N.M., U.S. E2 108
Luna Pier, Mi., U.S. G7 99
Lund, Swe. I9 6
Lund, Nv., U.S. E6 105
Lundar, Man., Can. D2 70
Lundazi, Zam. D6 44
Lüneburg, Ger. B10 8
Lüneburger Heide, reg., Ger. B10 8
Lunel, Fr. I11 10
Lunenburg, Ma., U.S. A4 98
Lunenburg, co., Va., U.S. D4 123
Lunéville, Fr. D13 10
Lunga, stm., Zam. D5 44
Luohe, China B3 28
Luolong, China E17 38
Luopu, China B9 38
Luoyang, China E9 26
Lūrah, stm., Afg. D2 38
Luray, Va., U.S. B4 123
Lure, Fr. E13 10
Lure, Lake, res., N.C., U.S. f10 110
Lurgan, N. Ire., U.K. G6 7
Lúrio, stm., Moz. D7 44
Lusaka, Zam. E5 44
Lusambo, Zaire B4 44
Lusby, Md., U.S. D5 97
Luseland, Sask., Can. E1 75
Lushan, China B1 28
Lushnje, Alb. I3 16
Lushoto, Tan. B7 44
Lüshun (Port Arthur), China D11 26
Lusk, Wy., U.S. D8 127
Lussac-les-Châteaux, Fr. F7 10
Lūt, Dasht-e, des., Iran B6 46
Lutcher, La., U.S. D5 95
Luther, Ok., U.S. B4 113
Luthersville, Ga., U.S. C2 87
Lutherville-Timonium, Md., U.S. B4 97
Luton, Eng., U.K. J12 7
Luts'k, Ukr. G3 22
Luttrell, Tn., U.S. C10 119
Lutz, Fl., U.S. D4 86
Luverne, Al., U.S. D3 78
Luverne, Mn., U.S. G2 100
Luwegu, stm., Tan. C7 44
Luxapallila Creek, stm., U.S. B5 101
Luxembourg, Lux. F6 8
Luxembourg, ctry., Eur. F9 4
Luxemburg, Wi., U.S. D6 126
Luxomni, Ga., U.S. h8 87
Luxora, Ar., U.S. B6 81
Luzern, Switz. E15 10
Luzerne, Pa., U.S. n17 115
Luzerne, co., Pa., U.S. D9 115
Luzhou, China F8 26
Luzon, i., Phil. B7 32
Luzon Strait, strt., Asia G11 26
Luzy, Fr. F10 10
L'viv, Ukr. H2 22
Lycksele, Swe. D12 6
Lycoming, co., Pa., U.S. D7 115
Lycoming Creek, stm., Pa., U.S. D7 115
Lydenburg, S. Afr. G6 44
Lyell, Mount, mtn., Can. D2 68
Lyford, Tx., U.S. F4 120
Lykens, Pa., U.S. E8 115
Lyle, Wa., U.S. D4 124
Lyman, S.C., U.S. B3 117
Lyman, Wy., U.S. E2 127
Lyman, co., S.D., U.S. D6 118
Lyman Lake, res., Az., U.S. C6 80
Lynch, Ky., U.S. D7 94
Lynchburg, Oh., U.S. C2 112
Lynchburg, Tn., U.S. B5 119
Lynchburg, Va., U.S. C3 123
Lynches, stm., S.C., U.S. D8 117
Lynden, Wa., U.S. A3 124
Lynde Point, c., Ct., U.S. D6 84
Lyndhurst, N.J., U.S. h8 107
Lyndhurst, Oh., U.S. g9 112
Lyndon, Ks., U.S. D8 93
Lyndon, Ky., U.S. g11 94
Lyndon B. Johnson National Historical Site, hist., Tx., U.S. D3 120
Lyndon B. Johnson Space Center, sci., Tx., U.S. r14 120
Lyndonville, Vt., U.S. B4 122
Lyndora, Pa., U.S. E2 115
Lynher Reef, rf., Austl. C4 50
Lynn, Al., U.S. A2 78
Lynn, In., U.S. D8 91
Lynn, Ma., U.S. B6 98
Lynn, co., Tx., U.S. C2 120
Lynn, Lake, res., W.V., U.S. B5 125
Lynn Canal, b., Ak., U.S. k22 79
Lynne Acres, Md., U.S. *B4 97
Lynnfield, Ma., U.S. f11 98
Lynn Garden, Tn., U.S. C11 119
Lynn Garden, Tn., U.S. A9 119
Lynn Haven, Fl., U.S. u16 86
Lynnhaven Roads, b., Va., U.S. k15 123
Lynnville, In., U.S. H3 91
Lynnwood, Wa., U.S. B3 124
Lynton, Eng., U.K. J9 7
Lynwood, Ca., U.S. n12 82
Lyon, Fr. G11 10
Lyon, co., Ia., U.S. A1 92
Lyon, co., Ks., U.S. D7 93
Lyon, co., Ky., U.S. C1 94
Lyon, co., Mn., U.S. F3 100
Lyon, co., Nv., U.S. D2 105
Lyons, Co., U.S. A5 83
Lyons, Ga., U.S. D4 87
Lyons, Il., U.S. k9 90
Lyons, In., U.S. G3 91
Lyons, Ks., U.S. D5 93
Lyons, Mi., U.S. F6 99
Lyons, Ne., U.S. C9 104
Lyons, N.Y., U.S. B3 109
Lyons, Or., U.S. C4 114
Lyster Station, Que., Can. C6 74
Lysychans'k, Ukr. H5 22
Lytle, Tx., U.S. E3 120

M

Ma, stm., Asia D8 34
Maalaea Bay, b., Hi., U.S. C5 88
Ma'ān, Jord. D4 40
Maanshan, China D7 28
Ma'arrat an-Nu'mān, Syria B5 40
Maas (Meuse), stm., Eur. D5 8
Maastricht, Neth. E5 8
Mabank, Tx., U.S. C4 120
Mabaruma, Guy. C13 58
Mabel, Mn., U.S. G7 100
Maben, Ms., U.S. B4 101
Mableton, Ga., U.S. h7 87
Mabscott, W.V., U.S. D3 125
Mabton, Wa., U.S. C5 124
Mača, Russia F17 24
Macaé, Braz. G8 57
Macão, Port. F3 12
Macao see Macau, dep., Asia M2 28
Macapá, Braz. C8 54
Macará, Ec. J3 58
Macarani, Braz. C8 57
Macas, Ec. I3 58
Macau, Braz. E11 54
Macau (Aomen), Macao M2 28
Macau (Aomen), dep., Asia M2 28
MacClenny, Fl., U.S. B4 86
MacDill Air Force Base, mil., Fl., U.S. E4 86
Macdonnell Ranges, mts., Austl. D6 50
MacDowell Reservoir, res., N.H., U.S. E2 106
Macduff, Scot., U.K. D10 7
Macdui, Ben, mtn., Scot., U.K. D9 7
Macedo de Cavaleiros, Port. D5 12
Macedonia, Oh., U.S. A4 112
Macedonia, hist. reg., Eur. H6 16
Macedonia, ctry., Eur. H5 16
Maceió, Braz. E11 54
Macerata, Italy F8 14
Maces Bay, b., N.B., Can. D3 71
MacGregor, Man., Can. E2 70
Machačkala, Russia I7 22
Machagai, Arg. B4 56
Machala, Ec. I3 58
Machecoul, Fr. E5 10
Machias, Me., U.S. D5 96
Machias, stm., Me., U.S. B4 96
Machias, stm., Me., U.S. D5 96
Machias Bay, b., Me., U.S. D5 96
Machias Lakes, l., Me., U.S. C5 96
Machilīpatnam (Bandar), India D6 37
Machiques, Ven. B6 58
Macho, Arroyo del, val., N.M., U.S. C4 108
Machupicchu, Peru F4 54
Macina, reg., Mali F4 42
Mackay, Austl. D9 50
Mackay, Lake, l., Austl. D5 50
MacKenzie, B.C., Can. B6 69
Mackenzie, stm., N.W. Ter., Can. C6 66
Mackenzie Bay, b., Can. C5 66
Mackenzie Mountains, mts., Can. D7 66
Mackinac, co., Mi., U.S. B5 99
Mackinac, Straits of, strt., Mi., U.S. C6 99
Mackinac Bridge, Mi., U.S. C6 99
Mackinac Island, i., Mi., U.S. C6 99
Mackinaw, Il., U.S. C4 90
Mackinaw, stm., Il., U.S. C4 90
Mackinaw City, Mi., U.S. C6 99
Maclear, S. Afr. H5 44
Macmillan, stm., Yukon, Can. D6 66
Macomb, Il., U.S. C3 90
Macomb, co., Mi., U.S. F8 99
Macomer, Italy I3 14
Mâcon, Fr. F11 10
Macon, Ga., U.S. D3 87
Macon, Il., U.S. D5 90
Macon, Ms., U.S. B5 101
Macon, Mo., U.S. B5 102
Macon, co., Al., U.S. C4 78
Macon, co., Ga., U.S. D2 87
Macon, co., Il., U.S. D4 90
Macon, co., Mo., U.S. B5 102
Macon, co., N.C., U.S. f9 110
Macon, co., Tn., U.S. A5 119
Macon, Bayou, stm., U.S. B4 95
Macoupin, co., Il., U.S. D4 90
MacTier, Ont., Can. B5 73
Macungie, Pa., U.S. E10 115
Mad, stm., Ca., U.S. B2 82
Mad, stm., Ct., U.S. B3 84
Mad, stm., N.H., U.S. C3 106
Mad, stm., Oh., U.S. C2 112
Mad, stm., Vt., U.S. C3 122
Ma'dabā, Jord. D4 40
Madagascar, ctry., Afr. E9 44
Madame, Isle, i., N.S., Can. D9 71
Madanapalle, India F5 37
Madang, Pap. N. Gui. m16 50a
Mādārīpur, Bngl. I14 38
Madawaska, Me., U.S. A4 96
Madawaska, stm., Can. B9 74
Madawaska, stm., Ont., Can. B7 73
Madawaska Lake, l., Me., U.S. A4 96
Maddaloni, Italy H9 14
Madeira, Oh., U.S. o13 112
Madeira, i., Port. B2 42
Madeira, stm., S.A. E6 54
Madeira, Arquipélago da (Madeira Islands), is., Port. m20 13a
Mädelegabel, mtn., Eur. E17 10
Madeleine, Îles de la, is., Que., Can. B8 71
Madelia, Mn., U.S. F4 100
Madeline Island, i., Wi., U.S. B3 126
Madera, Ca., U.S. D3 82
Madera, co., Ca., U.S. D4 82
Madhubani, India G12 38
Madhya Pradesh, state, India I8 38
Madill, Ok., U.S. C5 113
Madīnat ash-Sha'b, Yemen F3 46
Madingou, Congo B2 44
Madison, Al., U.S. A3 78
Madison, Ar., U.S. B5 81
Madison, Ct., U.S. D5 84
Madison, Fl., U.S. B3 86
Madison, Ga., U.S. C3 87
Madison, Il., U.S. E3 90
Madison, In., U.S. G7 91
Madison, Ks., U.S. D7 93
Madison, Me., U.S. D3 96
Madison, Mn., U.S. E2 100
Madison, Ms., U.S. C3 101
Madison, Ne., U.S. C8 104
Madison, N.J., U.S. B4 107
Madison, N.C., U.S. A3 110
Madison, Oh., U.S. A4 112
Madison, S.D., U.S. D8 118
Madison, W.V., U.S. C3 125
Madison, Wi., U.S. E4 126
Madison, co., Al., U.S. A3 78
Madison, co., Ar., U.S. B2 81
Madison, co., Fl., U.S. B3 86
Madison, co., Ga., U.S. B3 87
Madison, co., Id., U.S. F7 89
Madison, co., Il., U.S. E4 90
Madison, co., In., U.S. D6 91
Madison, co., Ia., U.S. C3 92
Madison, co., Ky., U.S. C5 94
Madison, co., La., U.S. B4 95
Madison, co., Ms., U.S. C4 101
Madison, co., Mo., U.S. D7 102
Madison, co., Mt., U.S. E5 103
Madison, co., Ne., U.S. C8 104
Madison, co., N.Y., U.S. C5 109
Madison, co., N.C., U.S. f10 110
Madison, co., Oh., U.S. C2 112
Madison, co., Tn., U.S. B3 119
Madison, co., Tx., U.S. D5 120
Madison, co., Va., U.S. B4 123
Madison, stm., Mt., U.S. E5 103
Madison Heights, Mi., U.S. o15 99
Madison Heights, Va., U.S. C3 123
Madison Lake, Mn., U.S. F5 100
Madison Range, mts., Mt., U.S. E5 103
Madisonville, Ky., U.S. C2 94
Madisonville, La., U.S. D5 95
Madisonville, Tn., U.S. D9 119
Madisonville, Tx., U.S. D5 120
Madiun, Indon. m15 32
Madoc, Ont., Can. C7 73
Mado Gashi, Kenya B7 44
Madras, India F6 37
Madras, Or., U.S. C5 114
Madre, Laguna, b., Mex. E11 62
Madre, Laguna, b., Tx., U.S. F4 120
Madre, Sierra, mts., N.A. J14 62
Madre, Sierra, mts., Phil. B7 32
Madre de Dios, stm., S.A. F5 54
Madre de Dios, Isla, i., Chile G1 56
Madre del Sur, Sierra, mts., Mex. I10 62
Madre Occidental, Sierra, mts., Mex. E6 62
Madre Oriental, Sierra, mts., Mex. F9 62
Madrid, Spain E8 12
Madrid, Ia., U.S. C4 92
Madridejos, Spain F8 12
Maduo, China E6 26
Madura, i., Indon. G5 32
Madurai, India H5 37
Maebashi, Japan F12 30
Mae Hong Son, Thai. E4 34
Maeser, Ut., U.S. C6 121
Mae Sot, Thai. F5 34
Maestra, Sierra, mts., Cuba D9 64
Maevatanana, Madag. E9 44
Mafia Island, i., Tan. C7 44
Mafikeng, S. Afr. G5 44
Mafra, Braz. B7 56
Magadan, Russia F24 24
Magadi, Kenya B7 44
Magallanes, Estrecho de (Strait of Magellan), strt., S.A. G2 56
Magangué, Col. C5 58
Magazine, Ar., U.S. B2 81
Magazine Mountain, mtn., Ar., U.S. B2 81
Magdagači, Russia G19 24
Magdalena, Bol. F6 54
Magdalena, Mex. B4 62
Magdalena, N.M., U.S. C2 108
Magdalena, stm., Col. B5 58
Magdalena, Bahía, b., Mex. E3 62
Magdalena, Isla, i., Chile E2 56
Magdalena Mountains, mts., N.M., U.S. D2 108
Magdeburg, Ger. C11 8
Magee, Ms., U.S. D4 101
Magelang, Indon. m15 33a
Magellan, Strait of see Magallanes, Estrecho de, strt., S.A. G2 56
Magenta, Italy D3 14
Maggie Creek, stm., Nv., U.S. C5 105
Maggiore, Lago, l., Eur. C3 14
Magic Reservoir, res., Id., U.S. F4 89
Magione, Italy F7 14
Magna, Ut., U.S. C3 121
Magnetawan, stm., Ont., Can. B4 73
Magnitogorsk, Russia G9 22
Magnolia, Ar., U.S. D2 81
Magnolia, Ky., U.S. C4 94
Magnolia, Ms., U.S. D3 101
Magnolia, N.C., U.S. C4 110
Magnolia, Oh., U.S. B4 112
Magoffin, co., Ky., U.S. C6 94
Magog, Que., Can. D5 74
Magothy River, b., Md., U.S. B4 97
Magpie, Lac, l., Que., Can. F20 66
Magrath, Alta., Can. E4 68
Magruder Mountain, mtn., Nv., U.S. F4 105
Maguarinho, Cabo, c., Braz. D9 54
Magway, Mya. D3 34
Mahābād, Iran J7 22
Mahābhārat Range, mts., Nepal F10 38
Mahaicony Village, Guy. D14 58
Mahajamba, Baie de la, b., Madag. E9 44
Mahajanga, Madag. E9 44
Mahakam, stm., Indon. E6 32
Mahānadi, stm., India J11 38
Mahanoro, Madag. E9 44
Mahanoy City, Pa., U.S. E9 115
Mahārāshtra, state, India C3 37
Maha Sarakham, Thai. F7 34
Mahaska, co., Ia., U.S. C5 92
Maḥaṭṭat al-Qaṭrānah, Jord. D5 40
Maḥaṭṭat Ḥaraḍ, Sau. Ar. D4 46
Mahbūbnagar, India D4 37
Mahé Island, i., Sey. B11 44
Mahenge, Tan. C7 44
Mahi, stm., India I5 38
Mahmūd-e 'Erāqī, Afg. C3 38
Mahnomen, Mn., U.S. C3 100
Mahnomen, co., Mn., U.S. C3 100
Mahoba, India H8 38
Mahogany Mountain, mtn., Or., U.S. D9 114
Mahomet, Il., U.S. C5 90
Mahón, Spain F16 12
Mahone Bay, N.S., Can. E5 71
Mahoning, co., Oh., U.S. B5 112
Mahoning, stm., U.S. A5 112
Mahopac, N.Y., U.S. D7 109
Mahuva, India J4 38
Mahwah, N.J., U.S. A4 107
Maiden, N.C., U.S. B1 110
Maidstone, Eng., U.K. J13 7
Maidstone Lake, l., Vt., U.S. B5 122
Maiduguri, Nig. F8 42
Maili, Hi., U.S. g9 88
Maili Point, c., Hi., U.S. g9 88
Maillezais, Fr. F6 10
Main, stm., Ger. F9 8
Mainburg, Ger. G11 8
Main Channel, strt., Ont., Can. B3 73
Mai-Ndombe, Lac, l., Zaire B3 44
Maine, state, U.S. C3 96
Mainland, i., Scot., U.K. B9 7
Mainland, i., Scot., U.K. A11 7
Main Pass, strt., La., U.S. E6 95
Mainz, Ger. E8 8
Maipo, Volcán, vol., S.A. C3 56
Maipú, Arg. D5 56
Maiquetía, Ven. B9 58
Maisonnette, N.B., Can. B4 71
Maitland, Austl. F10 50
Maitland, Ont., Can. C9 73
Maize, Ks., U.S. g12 93
Maizuru, Japan G8 30

Name	Map Ref	Page
Maja, stm., Russia	F20	24
Majene, Indon.	F6	32
Maji, Eth.	G2	46
Majkop, Russia	I6	22
Majno-Pyl'gino, Russia	E29	24
Major, co., Ok., U.S.	A3	113
Majorca see Mallorca, i., Spain	F15	12
Makaha, Hi., U.S.	g9	88
Makaha Point, c., Hi., U.S.	A2	88
Makah Indian Reservation, Wa., U.S.	A1	124
Makahuena Point, c., Hi., U.S.	B2	88
Makakilo City, Hi., U.S.	g9	88
Makale, Indon.	F6	32
Makapuu Head, c., Hi., U.S.	B4	88
Makarska, Cro.	F12	14
Makasar, Selat (Makassar Strait), strt., Indon.	F6	32
Makasar see Ujungpandang, Indon.	G6	32
Makawao, Hi., U.S.	C5	88
Makaweli, Hi., U.S.	B2	88
Makeni, S.L.	G3	42
Makgadikgadi Pans, pl., Bots.	F5	44
Makhachkala see Machačkala, Russia	I7	22
Makindu, Kenya	B7	44
M'akit, Russia	E24	24
Makkah (Mecca), Sau. Ar.	D2	46
Maklakovo, Russia	F12	24
Makó, Hung.	I20	8
Makokou, Gabon	A2	44
Makthar, Tun.	N4	14
Makumbi, Zaire	C4	44
Makurazaki, Japan	K3	30
Makurdi, Nig.	G7	42
Makushin Volcano, vol., Ak., U.S.	E6	79
Malabar, Fl., U.S.	D6	86
Malabar Coast, India	G4	37
Malabo, Eq. Gui.	H7	42
Malacca, Strait of, strt., Asia	M6	34
Malad City, Id., U.S.	G6	89
Málaga, Col.	D6	58
Málaga, Spain	I7	12
Malagón, Spain	F8	12
Malaimbandy, Madag.	F9	44
Malaja Kuril'skaja Gr'ada (Habomai-shotō), is., Russia	p24	30a
Malakāl, Sudan	G12	42
Malakoff, Tx., U.S.	C4	120
Malang, Indon.	m16	32
Malanje, Ang.	C3	44
Malanville, Benin	F6	42
Mälaren, l., Swe.	G11	6
Malargüe, Arg.	D3	56
Malartic, Que., Can.	k11	74
Malaspina Glacier, Ak., U.S.	D11	79
Malatya, Tur.	H15	4
Malawi, ctry., Afr.	D6	44
Malaya, reg., Malay.	M7	34
Malay Peninsula, pen., Asia	K6	34
Malaysia, ctry., Asia	E3	32
Malbaie, stm., Que., Can.	B7	74
Malbork, Pol.	A19	8
Malcolm, Austl.	E4	50
Malden, Ma., U.S.	B5	98
Malden, Mo., U.S.	E8	102
Malden, W.V., U.S.	m12	125
Maldives, ctry., Asia	I2	37
Maldonado, Ur.	C6	56
Mālegaon, India	B3	37
Malek Dīn, Afg.	D3	38
Malha Wells, Sudan	E11	42
Malheur, co., Or., U.S.	D9	114
Malheur, stm., Or., U.S.	D9	114
Malheur Lake, l., Or., U.S.	D8	114
Mali, ctry., Afr.	E5	42
Malibu, Ca., U.S.	m11	82
Malik, Wādī al-, val., Sudan	E11	42
Malin, Or., U.S.	E5	114
Malindi, Kenya	B8	44
Malino, Bukit, mtn., Indon.	E7	32
Malka, Russia	G25	24
Malkāpur, India	B4	37
Malkara, Tur.	I10	16
Mallaig, Scot., U.K.	D7	7
Mallawī, Egypt	C12	42
Malletts Bay, b., Vt., U.S.	B2	122
Mallnitz, Aus.	I13	8
Mallorca, i., Spain	F14	12
Mallow, Ire.	I4	7
Malmberget, Swe.	C13	6
Malmédy, Bel.	E6	8
Malmesbury, S. Afr.	H3	44
Malmö, Swe.	I9	6
Malmstrom Air Force Base, mil., Mt., U.S.	C5	103
Malolos, Phil.	q19	33b
Malone, N.Y., U.S.	f10	109
Maloney Reservoir, res., Ne., U.S.	C5	104
Måløy, Nor.	F5	6
Malpaso, Presa de, res., Mex.	I13	62
Malpelo, Isla de, i., Col.	C2	54
Malpeque Bay, b., P.E.I., Can.	C6	71
Malta, Il., U.S.	B5	90
Malta, Mt., U.S.	B9	103
Malta, ctry., Eur.	H10	4
Malta Channel, strt., Eur.	M9	14
Maltahöhe, Nmb.	F3	44
Maluku (Moluccas), is., Indon.	F8	32
Maluku, Laut (Molucca Sea), Indon.	F7	32
Malung, Swe.	F9	6
Malvern, Ar., U.S.	C3	81
Malvern, Ia., U.S.	D2	92
Malvern, Oh., U.S.	B4	112
Malvern, Pa., U.S.	o19	115
Malverne, N.Y., U.S.	k13	109
Malyj An'uj, stm., Russia	D26	24
Malyj Tajmyr, Ostrov, i., Russia	B15	24
Mama, Russia	F16	24
Mamala Bay, b., Hi., U.S.	g10	88
Mamaroneck, N.Y., U.S.	h13	109
Mamberamo, stm., Indon.	F10	32
Mamers, Fr.	D7	10
Mamfe, Cam.	G7	42
Mammoth, Az., U.S.	E5	80
Mammoth Cave National Park, Ky., U.S.	C4	94
Mammoth Lakes, Ca., U.S.	D4	82
Mammoth Spring, Ar., U.S.	A4	81
Mamoré, stm., S.A.	F5	54
Mamou, Gui.	F3	42
Mamou, La., U.S.	D3	95
Man, C. Iv.	G4	42
Man, W.V., U.S.	D3	125
Manacapuru, Braz.	D6	54
Manacor, Spain	F15	12
Manado, Indon.	E7	32
Managua, Nic.	H4	64
Managua, Lago de, l., Nic.	H4	64
Manakara, Madag.	F9	44
Manama see Al-Manāmah, Bahr.	C5	46
Manana Island, i., Hi., U.S.	g11	88
Mananara, Madag.	E9	44
Mananjary, Madag.	F9	44
Manantico Creek, stm., N.J., U.S.	E3	107
Mana Point, c., Hi., U.S.	A2	88
Manas, China	C4	26
Manasquan, N.J., U.S.	C4	107
Manasquan, stm., N.J., U.S.	C4	107
Manassa, Co., U.S.	D5	83
Manassas, Va., U.S.	B5	123
Manassas National Battlefield Park, Va., U.S.	g11	123
Manassas Park, Va., U.S.	B5	123
Manatee, co., Fl., U.S.	E4	86
Manatee, stm., Fl., U.S.	E4	86
Manaus, Braz.	D6	54
Manawa, Wi., U.S.	D5	126
Manbij, Syria	A5	40
Mancelona, Mi., U.S.	D5	99
Mancha Real, Spain	H8	12
Manchester, Eng., U.K.	H10	7
Manchester, Ct., U.S.	B5	84
Manchester, Ga., U.S.	D2	87
Manchester, Ia., U.S.	B6	92
Manchester, Ky., U.S.	C6	94
Manchester, Me., U.S.	D3	96
Manchester, Md., U.S.	A4	97
Manchester, Ma., U.S.	A6	98
Manchester, Mi., U.S.	F6	99
Manchester, Mo., U.S.	f12	102
Manchester, N.H., U.S.	E4	106
Manchester, N.Y., U.S.	C3	109
Manchester, Oh., U.S.	D2	112
Manchester, Pa., U.S.	F8	115
Manchester, Tn., U.S.	B5	119
Manchester, Vt., U.S.	E2	122
Manchester Center, Vt., U.S.	E2	122
Manchuria, reg., China	B12	26
Manciano, Italy	G6	14
Mancos, Co., U.S.	D2	83
Mancos, stm., U.S.	D2	83
Mand, stm., Iran	C5	46
Manda, Tan.	D6	44
Mandal, Nor.	G6	6
Mandalay, Mya.	C4	34
Mandalgov', Mong.	B8	26
Mandan, N.D., U.S.	C5	111
Mandas, Italy	J4	14
Mandasor, India	H6	38
Mandeb, Bāb el-, strt.	F3	46
Mandeville, Ar., U.S.	D2	81
Mandeville, La., U.S.	D5	95
Mandi Bahāuddīn, Pak.	D5	38
Mandimba, Moz.	D7	44
Mandla, India	I9	38
Manduria, Italy	I12	14
Māndvi, India	I3	38
Mandya, India	F4	37
Manerbio, Italy	D5	14
Manfredonia, Italy	H10	14
Mangabeiras, Chapada das, hills, Braz.	F9	54
Mangalore, India	F3	37
Mangkalihat, Tanjung, c., Indon.	E6	32
Manglares, Cabo, c., Col.	G3	58
Mangoche, Mwi.	D7	44
Mangoky, stm., Madag.	F8	44
Mangole, Pulau, i., Indon.	F8	32
Māngrol, India	J4	38
Mangrove Cay, i., Bah.	B9	64
Mangualde, Port.	E4	12
Mangum, Ok., U.S.	C2	113
Mangya, China	D5	26
Manhattan, Ks., U.S.	C7	93
Manhattan, Mt., U.S.	E5	103
Manhattan Beach, Ca., U.S.	n12	82
Manhattan Island, i., N.Y., U.S.	h13	109
Manheim, Pa., U.S.	F9	115
Manhuaçu, Braz.	F7	57
Manicoré, Braz.	E6	54
Manicouagan, stm., Que., Can.	F10	66
Manicouagan, Réservoir, res., Que., Can.	h13	74
Manila, Phil.	q19	32
Manila, Ar., U.S.	B5	81
Manila Bay, b., Phil.	C7	32
Manilla, Ia., U.S.	C2	92
Manipur, ter., India	H15	38
Manisa, Tur.	K11	16
Manistee, Mi., U.S.	D4	99
Manistee, co., Mi., U.S.	D4	99
Manistee, stm., Mi., U.S.	D5	99
Manistique, Mi., U.S.	C4	99
Manistique, stm., Mi., U.S.	B4	99
Manistique Lake, l., Mi., U.S.	B5	99
Manito, Il., U.S.	C4	90
Manitoba, prov., Can.	C3	70
Manitoba, Lake, l., Man., Can.	D2	70
Manitou, Man., Can.	E2	70
Manitou, Lake, l., Ont., Can.	B3	73
Manitou Island, i., Mi., U.S.	A3	99
Manitou Lake, l., Sask., Can.	E1	75
Manitoulin Island, i., Ont., Can.	B2	73
Manitou Springs, Co., U.S.	C6	83
Manitowoc, Wi., U.S.	D6	126
Manitowoc, co., Wi., U.S.	D6	126
Manitowoc, stm., Wi., U.S.	h10	126
Maniwaki, Que., Can.	C2	74
Manizales, Col.	E5	58
Manjacaze, Moz.	F6	44
Mānjra, stm., India	C4	37
Mankato, Ks., U.S.	C5	93
Mankato, Mn., U.S.	F5	100
Mankoya, Zam.	D4	44
Manlius, N.Y., U.S.	C5	109
Manlléu, Spain	C14	12
Manly, Ia., U.S.	A4	92
Manmād, India	B3	37
Mannar, Gulf of, b., Asia	H5	37
Mannārgudi, India	G5	37
Mannar Island, i., Sri L.	H5	37
Mannford, Ok., U.S.	A5	113
Mannheim, Ger.	F8	8
Manning, Alta., Can.	A2	68
Manning, Ia., U.S.	C2	92
Manning, S.C., U.S.	D7	117
Mannington, W.V., U.S.	B4	125
Manns Creek, stm., W.V., U.S.	n14	125
Mannville, Alta., Can.	C5	68
Manokin, stm., Md., U.S.	D6	97
Manokotak, Ak., U.S.	D8	79
Manokwari, Indon.	F9	32
Manomet, Ma., U.S.	C6	98
Manomet Point, c., Ma., U.S.	C6	98
Manono, Zaire	C5	44
Manor, Tx., U.S.	D4	120
Manosque, Fr.	I12	10
Manouane, Lac, l., Que., Can.	h12	74
Manresa, Spain	D13	12
Mānsa, India	F6	38
Mansa, Zam.	D5	44
Manseau, Que., Can.	C5	74
Mansel Island, i., N.W. Ter., Can.	D17	66
Mansfield, Eng., U.K.	H11	7
Mansfield, Ar., U.S.	B1	81
Mansfield, Il., U.S.	C5	90
Mansfield, La., U.S.	B2	95
Mansfield, Ma., U.S.	B5	98
Mansfield, Mo., U.S.	D5	102
Mansfield, Oh., U.S.	B3	112
Mansfield, Pa., U.S.	C7	115
Mansfield, Tx., U.S.	n9	120
Mansfield, Mount, mtn., Vt., U.S.	B3	122
Mansfield Center, Ct., U.S.	B7	84
Mansfield Hollow Lake, res., Ct., U.S.	B7	84
Manson, Ia., U.S.	B3	92
Manson, Wa., U.S.	B5	124
Mansonville, Que., Can.	D5	74
Mansura, La., U.S.	C3	95
Manta, Ec.	H2	58
Mantachie, Ms., U.S.	A5	101
Manteca, Ca., U.S.	D3	82
Manteno, Il., U.S.	B6	90
Manteo, N.C., U.S.	B7	110
Mantes-la-Jolie, Fr.	D8	10
Manti, Ut., U.S.	D4	121
Mantiqueira, Serra da, mts., Braz.	F6	57
Manton, Mi., U.S.	D5	99
Mantorville, Mn., U.S.	F6	100
Mantova, Italy	D5	14
Mantua, Oh., U.S.	A4	112
Mantua, Ut., U.S.	B4	121
Manturovo, Russia	C27	18
Manukau Harbour, b., N.Z.	B5	52
Manumuskin, stm., N.J., U.S.	E3	107
Manus Island, i., Pap. N. Gui.	k16	50a
Manvel, Tx., U.S.	r14	120
Manville, N.J., U.S.	B3	107
Manville, R.I., U.S.	B4	116
Many, La., U.S.	C2	95
Many Farms, Az., U.S.	A6	80
Manzanares, Spain	F8	12
Manzanillo, Cuba	D9	64
Manzanillo, Mex.	H7	62
Manzano Mountains, mts., N.M., U.S.	C3	108
Manzano Peak, mtn., N.M., U.S.	C3	108
Manzhouli, China	B10	26
Mao, Chad	F9	42
Maoke, Pegunungan, mts., Indon.	F10	32
Mapastepec, Mex.	J13	62
Mapi, Indon.	G10	32
Mapia, Kepulauan, is., Indon.	E9	32
Mapimí, Mex.	E8	62
Mapimí, Bolsón de, des., Mex.	D8	62
Mapire, Ven.	D10	58
Maple, stm., U.S.	A7	118
Maple, stm., Ia., U.S.	B2	92
Maple, stm., N.D., U.S.	C8	111
Maple Bluff, Wi., U.S.	E4	126
Maple Grove, Mn., U.S.	m12	100
Maple Heights, Oh., U.S.	h9	112
Maple Lake, Mn., U.S.	E5	100
Maple Plain, Mn., U.S.	m11	100
Maple Shade, N.J., U.S.	D2	107
Maplesville, Al., U.S.	C3	78
Mapleton, Ia., U.S.	B2	92
Mapleton, Mn., U.S.	G5	100
Mapleton, N.D., U.S.	C8	111
Mapleton, Or., U.S.	C3	114
Mapleton, Ut., U.S.	C4	121
Maple Valley, Wa., U.S.	f11	124
Mapleville, R.I., U.S.	B2	116
Maplewood, Mn., U.S.	n12	100
Maplewood, Mo., U.S.	f13	102
Maplewood, N.J., U.S.	B4	107
Mapuera, stm., Braz.	D7	54
Maputo (Lourenço Marques), Moz.	G6	44
Maqueda, Spain	E7	12
Maquela do Zombo, Ang.	C3	44
Maquinchao, Arg.	E3	56
Maquoketa, Ia., U.S.	B7	92
Maquoketa, stm., Ia., U.S.	B6	92
Maquoketa, North Fork, stm., Ia., U.S.	B7	92
Mar, Serra do, clf, Braz.	A7	56
Marabá, Braz.	E9	54
Maracá, Ilha de, i., Braz.	C8	54
Maracaibo, Ven.	B7	58
Maracaibo, Lago de, l., Ven.	C7	58
Maracay, Ven.	B9	58
Marādah, Libya	C9	42
Maradi, Niger	F7	42
Marāgheh, Iran	J7	22
Maragogipe, Braz.	B9	57
Marahuaca, Cerro, mtn., Ven.	F10	58
Marais des Cygnes, stm., U.S.	D8	93
Marajó, Baía de, b., Braz.	D9	54
Marajó, Ilha de, i., Braz.	D9	54
Maralal, Kenya	A7	44
Marambaia, Ilha da, i., Braz.	G7	57
Marana, Az., U.S.	E4	80
Marang, Malay.	L7	34
Marañón, stm., Peru	D3	54
Marans, Fr.	F5	10
Marapanim, Braz.	D9	54
Marathon, Fl., U.S.	H5	86
Marathon, Wi., U.S.	D4	126
Marathon, co., Wi., U.S.	D4	126
Marawī, Sudan	E1	46
Marble, Mn., U.S.	C5	100
Marble, N.C., U.S.	f9	110
Marble Bar, Austl.	D3	50
Marble Canyon, val., Az., U.S.	A4	80
Marble Falls, Tx., U.S.	D3	120
Marblehead, Ma., U.S.	B6	98
Marble Hill, Mo., U.S.	D8	102
Marbleton, Wy., U.S.	D2	127
Marburg an der Lahn, Ger.	E8	8
Marbury, Md., U.S.	C3	97
Marcaria, Italy	D5	14
Marceline, Mo., U.S.	B5	102
Marcellus, Mi., U.S.	F5	99
March (Morava), stm., Eur.	G16	8
Marcha, Russia	E18	24
March Air Force Base, mil., Ca., U.S.	F5	82
Marche-en-Famenne, Bel.	E5	8
Marchena, Spain	H6	12
Mar Chiquita, Laguna, l., Arg.	C4	56
Marco, Fl., U.S.	G5	86
Marcus, Ia., U.S.	B2	92
Marcus Baker, Mount, mtn., Ak., U.S.	g18	79
Marcus Hook, Pa., U.S.	G11	115
Marcy, Mount, mtn., N.Y., U.S.	A7	109
Mardān, Pak.	C5	38
Mar del Plata, Arg.	D5	56
Mardin, Tur.	H16	4
Mareeba, Austl.	C9	50
Mareg, Som.	H4	46
Marengo, Il., U.S.	A5	90
Marengo, In., U.S.	H5	91
Marengo, Ia., U.S.	C5	92
Marengo, co., Al., U.S.	C2	78
Marennes, Fr.	G5	10
Marfa, Tx., U.S.	o12	120
Margaret, Al., U.S.	B3	78
Margarita, Isla de, i., Ven.	B10	58
Margate, Fl., U.S.	F6	86
Margate City, N.J., U.S.	E3	107
Margherita Peak, mtn., Afr.	A5	44
Marghī, Afg.	C2	38
Margrethe, Lake, l., Mi., U.S.	D6	99
María Cleofas, Isla, i., Mex.	G6	62
María Madre, Isla, i., Mex.	G6	62
María Magdalena, Isla, i., Mex.	G6	62
Marian, Lake, l., Fl., U.S.	E5	86
Marianao, Cuba	C6	64
Marianna, Ar., U.S.	C5	81
Marianna, Fl., U.S.	B1	86
Marias, stm., Mt., U.S.	B4	103
Marías, Islas, is., Mex.	G6	62
Marias Pass, Mt., U.S.	B3	103
Mariato, Punta, c., Pan.	K7	64
Mariazell, Aus.	H15	8
Maribor, Slo.	C10	14
Marica (Évros) (Meriç), stm., Eur.	G9	16
Maricopa, Az., U.S.	E3	80
Maricopa, Ca., U.S.	E4	82
Maricopa, co., Az., U.S.	D3	80
Maricopa Mountains, mts., Az., U.S.	m7	80
Marie-Galante, i., Guad.	G17	64
Mariehamn, Fin.	F12	6
Mariemont, Oh., U.S.	o13	112
Mariental, Nmb.	F3	44
Marienville, Pa., U.S.	D3	115
Maries, co., Mo., U.S.	C6	102
Mariestad, Swe.	G9	6
Marietta, Ga., U.S.	C2	87
Marietta, Oh., U.S.	C4	112
Marietta, Ok., U.S.	D4	113
Marietta, S.C., U.S.	A2	117
Marieville, Que., Can.	D4	74
Marília, Braz.	G4	57
Marimba, Ang.	C3	44
Marín, Spain	C3	12
Marin, co., Ca., U.S.	C2	82
Marinduque Island, i., Phil.	C7	32
Marine, Il., U.S.	E4	90
Marine City, Mi., U.S.	F8	99
Marine On St. Croix, Mn., U.S.	E6	100
Marinette, Wi., U.S.	C6	126
Marinette, co., Wi., U.S.	C5	126
Maringá, Braz.	G3	57
Maringouin, La., U.S.	D4	95
Marinha Grande, Port.	F3	12
Marion, Al., U.S.	C2	78
Marion, Ar., U.S.	B5	81
Marion, Il., U.S.	F5	90
Marion, In., U.S.	C6	91
Marion, Ia., U.S.	B6	92
Marion, Ks., U.S.	D6	93
Marion, Ky., U.S.	e9	94
Marion, La., U.S.	B3	95
Marion, Mi., U.S.	D5	99
Marion, Ms., U.S.	C5	101
Marion, N.C., U.S.	B1	110
Marion, Oh., U.S.	B2	112
Marion, Pa., U.S.	G6	115
Marion, S.C., U.S.	C9	117
Marion, S.D., U.S.	D8	118
Marion, Va., U.S.	f10	123
Marion, Wi., U.S.	D5	126
Marion, co., Al., U.S.	A2	78
Marion, co., Ar., U.S.	A3	81
Marion, co., Fl., U.S.	C4	86
Marion, co., Ga., U.S.	D2	87
Marion, co., Il., U.S.	E4	90
Marion, co., In., U.S.	E5	91
Marion, co., Ia., U.S.	C4	92
Marion, co., Ks., U.S.	D6	93
Marion, co., Ky., U.S.	C4	94
Marion, co., Ms., U.S.	D4	101
Marion, co., Mo., U.S.	B6	102
Marion, co., Oh., U.S.	B2	112
Marion, co., Or., U.S.	C4	114
Marion, co., S.C., U.S.	C9	117
Marion, co., Tn., U.S.	D8	119
Marion, co., Tx., U.S.	C5	120
Marion, co., W.V., U.S.	B4	125
Marion, Lake, res., S.C., U.S.	E7	117
Marion Station, Md., U.S.	D6	97
Marionville, Mo., U.S.	D4	102
Maripa, Ven.	D10	58
Mariposa, co., Ca., U.S.	D3	82
Mariscal Estigarribia, Para.	A4	56
Marissa, Il., U.S.	E4	90
Maritime Alps, mts., Eur.	H14	10
Mariupol' (Ždanov), Ukr.	H5	22
Marka, Som.	H3	46
Markaryd, Swe.	H9	6
Markdale, Ont., Can.	C4	73
Marked Tree, Ar., U.S.	B5	81
Markesan, Wi., U.S.	E5	126
Markham, Ont., Can.	D5	73
Markham, Il., U.S.	k9	90
Markham, Tx., U.S.	E4	120
Markham, Mount, mtn., Ant.	A29	47
Markland Lock and Dam, U.S.	B5	94
Markle, In., U.S.	C7	91
Markovo, Russia	E28	24
Marks, Ms., U.S.	A3	101
Marksville, La., U.S.	C3	95
Marktredwitz, Ger.	E12	8
Mark Twain Lake, res., Mo., U.S.	B6	102
Marlboro, N.Y., U.S.	D6	109
Marlboro, Va., U.S.	n17	123
Marlboro, co., S.C., U.S.	B8	117
Marlborough, Ct., U.S.	C6	84
Marlborough, Ma., U.S.	B4	98
Marlborough, N.H., U.S.	E2	106
Marle, Fr.	C10	10
Marlette, Mi., U.S.	E7	99
Marley, Md., U.S.	B4	97
Marlin, Tx., U.S.	D4	120
Marlinton, W.V., U.S.	C4	125
Marlow, Ok., U.S.	C4	113
Marlowe, W.V., U.S.	B7	125
Marlton, N.J., U.S.	D3	107
Marmaduke, Ar., U.S.	A5	81
Marmande, Fr.	H7	10
Marmara Adası, i., Tur.	I11	16
Marmara Denizi (Sea of Marmara), Tur.	I12	16
Marmaris, Tur.	M12	16
Marmet, W.V., U.S.	C3	125
Marmora, Ont., Can.	C7	73
Marne, stm., Fr.	C10	10
Maroa, Il., U.S.	C5	90
Maroa, Ven.	F9	58
Maroantsetra, Madag.	E9	44
Maromokotro, mtn., Madag.	D9	44
Marondera, Zimb.	E6	44
Maros (Mureş), stm., Eur.	C4	16
Maroua, Cam.	F8	42
Marovoay, Madag.	E9	44
Marquesas Keys, is., Fl., U.S.	H4	86
Marquette, Mi., U.S.	B3	99
Marquette, co., Mi., U.S.	B3	99
Marquette, co., Wi., U.S.	E4	126
Marquette Heights, Il., U.S.	C4	90
Marquise, Fr.	B8	10
Marrah, Jabal, mtn., Sudan	F10	42
Marrakech, Mor.	B4	42
Marrero, La., U.S.	E5	95
Mars, Pa., U.S.	E1	115
Marsabit, Kenya	H2	46
Marsala, Italy	L7	14
Marsā Maṭrūḥ, Egypt	B11	42
Marseille, Fr.	J12	10
Marseille-en-Beauvaisis, Fr.	C8	10
Marseilles, Il., U.S.	B5	90
Marshall, Sask., Can.	D1	75
Marshall, Ar., U.S.	B3	81
Marshall, Il., U.S.	D6	90
Marshall, Mi., U.S.	F6	99
Marshall, Mn., U.S.	F3	100
Marshall, Mo., U.S.	B4	102
Marshall, N.C., U.S.	f10	110
Marshall, Tx., U.S.	C5	120
Marshall, Va., U.S.	B5	123
Marshall, Wi., U.S.	E4	126
Marshall, co., Al., U.S.	A3	78
Marshall, co., Il., U.S.	B4	90
Marshall, co., In., U.S.	B5	91
Marshall, co., Ia., U.S.	C4	92
Marshall, co., Ks., U.S.	C7	93
Marshall, co., Ky., U.S.	f9	94
Marshall, co., Mn., U.S.	B2	100
Marshall, co., Ms., U.S.	A4	101
Marshall, co., Ok., U.S.	C5	113
Marshall, co., S.D., U.S.	B8	118
Marshall, co., Tn., U.S.	B5	119
Marshall, co., W.V., U.S.	B4	125
Marshallton, De., U.S.	B3	85
Marshalltown, Ia., U.S.	B5	92
Marshallville, Ga., U.S.	D3	87
Marshes Siding, Ky., U.S.	D5	94
Marshfield, Ma., U.S.	B6	98
Marshfield, Mo., U.S.	D5	102
Marshfield, Wi., U.S.	D3	126
Marshfield Hills, Ma., U.S.	B6	98
Marsh Fork, stm., W.V., U.S.	n13	125
Marsh Harbour, Bah.	A9	64
Mars Hill, Me., U.S.	B5	96
Mars Hill, N.C., U.S.	f10	110
Marsh Island, i., La., U.S.	E4	95
Marsh Lake, res., Mn., U.S.	E2	100
Marsh Peak, mtn., Ut., U.S.	C6	121
Marshville, N.C., U.S.	C2	110

Name	Map Ref	Page
Marsing, Id., U.S.	F2	89
Märsta, Swe.	G11	6
Marston, Mo., U.S.	E8	102
Mart, Tx., U.S.	D4	120
Martaban, Gulf of, b., Mya.	F4	34
Marthasville, Mo., U.S.	C6	102
Martha's Vineyard, i., Ma., U.S.	D6	98
Martigny, Switz.	F14	10
Martigues, Fr.	I12	10
Martin, Slov.	F18	8
Martin, Ky., U.S.	C7	94
Martin, S.D., U.S.	D4	118
Martin, Tn., U.S.	A3	119
Martin, co., Fl., U.S.	E6	86
Martin, co., In., U.S.	G4	91
Martin, co., Ky., U.S.	C7	94
Martin, co., Mn., U.S.	G4	100
Martin, co., N.C., U.S.	B5	110
Martin, co., Tx., U.S.	C2	120
Martina Franca, Italy	I12	14
Martinez, Ca., U.S.	C2	82
Martinez, Ga., U.S.	C4	87
Martínez de la Torre, Mex.	G11	62
Martinique, dep., N.A.	G17	64
Martin Lake, res., Al., U.S.	C4	78
Martin Point, c., Ak., U.S.	A11	79
Martinsberg, Aus.	G15	8
Martinsburg, Pa., U.S.	F5	115
Martinsburg, W.V., U.S.	B7	125
Martins Ferry, Oh., U.S.	B5	112
Martinsville, Il., U.S.	D6	90
Martinsville, In., U.S.	F5	91
Martinsville, Va., U.S.	D3	123
Martos, Spain	H8	12
Martre, Lac la, l., N.W. Ter., Can.	D9	66
Martti, Fin.	C17	6
Marugame, Japan	H6	30
Ma'rūt, Afg.	E2	38
Marvejols, Fr.	H10	10
Marvell, Ar., U.S.	C5	81
Marvine, Mount, mtn., Ut., U.S.	E4	121
Mary, Turk.	J10	22
Mary, Lake, l., Mn., U.S.	E3	100
Mary, Lake, l., Ms., U.S.	D2	101
Maryborough, Austl.	E10	50
Maryland, state, U.S.	B4	97
Maryland City, Md., U.S.	B4	97
Maryland Heights, Mo., U.S.	f13	102
Maryland Point, c., Md., U.S.	D3	97
Maryport, Eng., U.K.	G9	7
Marys, stm., Nv., U.S.	B6	105
Marys Peak, mtn., Or., U.S.	C3	114
Marystown, Newf., Can.	E4	72
Marysville, Ca., U.S.	C3	82
Marysville, Ks., U.S.	C7	93
Marysville, Mi., U.S.	F8	99
Marysville, Oh., U.S.	B2	112
Marysville, Pa., U.S.	F8	115
Marysville, Wa., U.S.	A3	124
Maryville, Mo., U.S.	A3	102
Maryville, Tn., U.S.	D10	119
Marzūq, Libya	C8	42
Marzūq, Idehan, reg., Libya	C8	42
Masai Steppe, plat., Tan.	B7	44
Masaka, Ug.	B6	44
Masan, S. Kor.	D12	26
Masasi, Tan.	D7	44
Masaya, Nic.	I4	64
Masbate Island, i., Phil.	C7	32
Mascarene Islands, is., Afr.	F11	44
Mascoma, stm., N.H., U.S.	C2	106
Mascoma Lake, l., N.H., U.S.	C2	106
Mascot, Tn., U.S.	C10	119
Mascota, Mex.	G7	62
Mascouche, Que., Can.	D4	74
Mascoutah, Il., U.S.	E4	90
Maseru, Leso.	G5	44
Mashābih, i., Sau. Ar.	C2	46
Mashapaug Pond, l., Ct., U.S.	A7	84
Masherbrum, mtn., Pak.	C7	38
Mashhad, Iran	J9	22
Masi Manimba, Zaire	B3	44
Masindi, Ug.	H12	42
Masjed Soleymān, Iran	B4	46
Mask, Lough, l., Ire.	H3	7
Maskanah, Syria	A6	40
Maskinongé, Que., Can.	C4	74
Mason, Mi., U.S.	F6	99
Mason, Nv., U.S.	E2	105
Mason, Oh., U.S.	C1	112
Mason, Tx., U.S.	D3	120
Mason, W.V., U.S.	B2	125
Mason, co., Il., U.S.	C4	90
Mason, co., Ky., U.S.	B6	94
Mason, co., Mi., U.S.	D4	99
Mason, co., Tx., U.S.	D3	120
Mason, co., Wa., U.S.	B2	124
Mason, co., W.V., U.S.	C3	125
Mason City, Il., U.S.	C4	90
Mason City, Ia., U.S.	A4	92
Masontown, Pa., U.S.	G2	115
Masontown, W.V., U.S.	B5	125
Masqaṭ (Muscat), Oman	D6	46
Massa, Italy	E5	14
Massabesic Lake, l., N.H., U.S.	E4	106
Massac, co., Il., U.S.	F5	90
Massachusetts, state, U.S.	B4	98
Massachusetts Bay, b., Ma., U.S.	B6	98
Massacre Lake, l., Nv., U.S.	B2	105
Massafra, Italy	I12	14
Massa Marittima, Italy	F5	14
Massangena, Moz.	F6	44
Massapoag Lake, l., Ma., U.S.	h11	98
Massarosa, Italy	F5	14
Massasecum, Lake, l., N.H., U.S.	D3	106
Massena, N.Y., U.S.	f10	109
Massenya, Chad	F9	42
Masset, B.C., Can.	C1	69
Massey, Ont., Can.	A2	73
Massif Central see Central, Massif, mts., Fr.	G10	10
Massillon, Oh., U.S.	B4	112
Massive, Mount, mtn., Co., U.S.	B4	83
Masterton, N.Z.	D5	52
Mastic Beach, N.Y., U.S.	n16	109
Mastung, Pak.	F2	38
Masuda, Japan	H4	30
Masury, Oh., U.S.	A5	112
Matadi, Zaire	C2	44
Matagalpa, Nic.	H5	64
Matagorda, co., Tx., U.S.	E5	120
Matagorda Bay, b., Tx., U.S.	E4	120
Matagorda Island, i., Tx., U.S.	E4	120
Matagorda Peninsula, pen., Tx., U.S.	E5	120
Matale, Sri L.	I6	37
Matamoras, Pa., U.S.	D12	115
Matamoros, Mex.	E11	62
Matamoros de la Laguna, Mex.	E8	62
Matandu, stm., Tan.	C7	44
Matane, Que., Can.	k13	74
Matanuska, stm., Ak., U.S.	g18	79
Matanzas, Cuba	C7	64
Matanzas Inlet, b., Fl., U.S.	C5	86
Matara, Sri L.	J6	37
Mataró, Spain	D14	12
Matatiele, S. Afr.	H5	44
Matawan, N.J., U.S.	C4	107
Matehuala, Mex.	F9	62
Mateira, Braz.	E3	57
Matelica, Italy	F7	14
Matera, Italy	I11	14
Mateur, Tun.	L4	14
Matewan, W.V., U.S.	D2	125
Mather, Pa., U.S.	G1	115
Mather Air Force Base, mil., Ca., U.S.	C3	82
Mather Peaks, mts., Wy., U.S.	B5	127
Mathews, La., U.S.	E5	95
Mathews, Va., U.S.	C6	123
Mathews, co., Va., U.S.	C6	123
Mathews, Lake, l., Ca., U.S.	n14	82
Mathis, Tx., U.S.	E4	120
Mathiston, Ms., U.S.	B4	101
Mathura, India	G7	38
Matías Romero, Mex.	I12	62
Matinicus Island, i., Me., U.S.	E3	96
Mātli, Pak.	H3	38
Mato, Cerro, mtn., Ven.	D10	58
Matoaca, Va., U.S.	n18	123
Mato Grosso, Braz.	F7	54
Mato Grosso, Planalto do, plat., Braz.	G7	54
Matosinhos, Port.	D3	12
Matou, Tai.	L9	28
Maṭraḥ, Oman	D6	46
Matsqui, B.C., Can.	f13	69
Matsudo, Japan	G12	30
Matsue, Japan	G6	30
Matsumae, Japan	r18	30a
Matsumoto, Japan	F10	30
Matsusaka, Japan	H9	30
Matsu Tao, i., Tai.	I8	28
Matsuyama, Japan	I5	30
Mattagami, stm., Ont., Can.	F16	66
Mattamiscontis Lake, l., Me., U.S.	C4	96
Mattamuskeet, Lake, l., N.C., U.S.	B6	110
Mattāncheri, India	H4	37
Mattapoisett, Ma., U.S.	C6	98
Mattaponi, stm., Va., U.S.	C5	123
Mattawa, Ont., Can.	A6	73
Mattawamkeag, Me., U.S.	C4	96
Mattawamkeag, stm., Me., U.S.	C4	96
Mattawamkeag Lake, l., Me., U.S.	C4	96
Matterhorn, mtn., Eur.	G14	10
Matterhorn, mtn., Nv., U.S.	B6	105
Matteson, Il., U.S.	k9	90
Matthews, Mo., U.S.	E8	102
Matthews, N.C., U.S.	B2	110
Matthews Ridge, Guy.	D12	58
Matthew Town, Bah.	D11	64
Mattighofen, Aus.	G13	8
Mattituck, N.Y., U.S.	n16	109
Mattoon, Il., U.S.	D5	90
Mattoon, Lake, res., Il., U.S.	D5	90
Mattydale, N.Y., U.S.	B4	109
Matunuck, R.I., U.S.	G3	116
Maturín, Ven.	C11	58
Maúa, Moz.	D7	44
Maubeuge, Fr.	B10	10
Maud, Ok., U.S.	B5	113
Maugansville, Md., U.S.	A2	97
Maui, co., Hi., U.S.	B5	88
Maui, i., Hi., U.S.	C6	88
Mauldin, S.C., U.S.	B3	117
Mauléon-Licharre, Fr.	I6	10
Maulvi Bāzār, Bngl.	H14	38
Maumee, Oh., U.S.	A2	112
Maumee, stm., U.S.	A2	112
Maumee Bay, b., U.S.	G7	99
Maumelle, Lake, res., Ar., U.S.	C3	81
Maun, Bots.	E4	44
Mauna Kea, vol., Hi., U.S.	D6	88
Maunaloa, Hi., U.S.	B4	88
Mauna Loa, vol., Hi., U.S.	D6	88
Maunalua Bay, b., Hi., U.S.	g10	88
Maunath Bhanjan, India	H10	38
Maunawili, Hi., U.S.	g10	88
Mau Rānīpur, India	H8	38
Maurepas, Lake, l., La., U.S.	D5	95
Mauriac, Fr.	G9	10
Maurice, Ia., U.S.	B1	92
Maurice, stm., N.J., U.S.	E2	107
Mauritania, ctry., Afr.	D3	42
Mauritius, ctry., Afr.	F11	44
Maurs, Fr.	H9	10
Maury, co., Tn., U.S.	B4	119
Maury City, Tn., U.S.	B2	119
Maury Island, i., Wa., U.S.	f11	124
Mauston, Wi., U.S.	E3	126
Mauterndorf, Aus.	H13	8
Mauthausen, Aus.	G14	8
Maverick, co., Tx., U.S.	E2	120
Maw-Daung Pass, Asia	I5	34
Mawlaik, Mya.	C3	34
Mawlamyine (Moulmein), Mya.	F4	34
Maw Taung, mtn., Asia	I5	34
Maxinkuckee, Lake, l., In., U.S.	B5	91
Max Meadows, Va., U.S.	D2	123
Maxton, N.C., U.S.	C3	110
Maxville, Ont., Can.	B10	73
Maxwell, Ia., U.S.	C4	92
Maxwell Acres, W.V., U.S.	g8	125
Maxwell Air Force Base, mil., Al., U.S.	C3	78
Mayaguana, i., Bah.	C11	64
Mayaguana Passage, strt., Bah.	C11	64
Mayagüez, P.R.	E14	64
Maya Mountains, mts., N.A.	F3	64
Maybole, Scot., U.K.	F8	7
Mayen, Ger.	E7	8
Mayenne, Fr.	D6	10
Mayer, Az., U.S.	C3	80
Mayerthorpe, Alta., Can.	C3	68
Mayes, co., Ok., U.S.	A6	113
Mayesville, S.C., U.S.	D7	117
Mayfield, Ky., U.S.	f9	94
Mayfield, Pa., U.S.	C10	115
Mayfield Heights, Oh., U.S.	A4	112
Mayfield Lake, res., Wa., U.S.	C3	124
Mayflower, Ar., U.S.	C3	81
Mayking, Ky., U.S.	C7	94
Maykop see Majkop, Russia	I6	22
Maymyo, Mya.	C4	34
Maynard, Ma., U.S.	B5	98
Maynardville, Tn., U.S.	C10	119
Mayne, B.C., Can.	g12	69
Mayo, Yukon, Can.	D5	66
Mayo, Md., U.S.	C4	97
Mayo, S.C., U.S.	A4	117
Mayodan, N.C., U.S.	A3	110
Mayotte, ter., Afr.	D9	44
Mayotte, i., May.	D9	44
May Park, Or., U.S.	B8	114
Mayport Naval Station, mil., Fl., U.S.	B5	86
Maysville, Ga., U.S.	B3	87
Maysville, Ky., U.S.	B6	94
Maysville, Mo., U.S.	B3	102
Maysville, N.C., U.S.	C5	110
Maysville, Ok., U.S.	C4	113
Mayumba, Gabon	B2	44
Māyūram, India	G5	37
Mayville, Mi., U.S.	E7	99
Mayville, N.Y., U.S.	C1	109
Mayville, N.D., U.S.	B8	111
Mayville, Wi., U.S.	E5	126
Maywood, Il., U.S.	k9	90
Maywood, N.J., U.S.	h8	107
Maywood Park, Or., U.S.	*B4	114
Mazabuka, Zam.	E5	44
Mazamet, Fr.	I9	10
Mazara del Vallo, Italy	L7	14
Mazār-e Sharīf, Afg.	B2	38
Mazaruni, stm., Guy.	E13	58
Mazatenango, Guat.	G2	64
Mazatlán, Mex.	F6	62
Mazatzal Mountains, mts., Az., U.S.	C4	80
Mazatzal Peak, mtn., Az., U.S.	C4	80
Mazeppa, Mn., U.S.	F6	100
Mazoe, stm., Afr.	E6	44
Mazomanie, Wi., U.S.	E4	126
Mazon, Il., U.S.	B5	90
Mbabane, Swaz.	G6	44
Mbaïki, Cen. Afr. Rep.	H9	42
Mbala, Zam.	C6	44
Mbale, Ug.	A6	44
Mbandaka (Coquilhatville), Zaire	A3	44
Mbanza-Ngungu, Zaire	C2	44
M'banz Congo, Ang.	C2	44
Mbeya, Tan.	C6	44
Mbomou (Bomu), stm., Afr.	H10	42
Mbout, Maur.	E3	42
Mbuji-Mayi (Bakwanga), Zaire	C4	44
McAdam, N.B., Can.	D2	71
McAdoo, Pa., U.S.	E9	115
McAfee Peak, mtn., Nv., U.S.	B6	105
McAlester, Ok., U.S.	C6	113
McAlester, Lake, res., Ok., U.S.	B6	113
McAllen, Tx., U.S.	F3	120
McAlmont, Ar., U.S.	h10	81
McAlpine, Md., U.S.	B4	97
McAlpine Lock and Dam, U.S.	H6	91
McArthur, Oh., U.S.	C3	112
McBee, S.C., U.S.	C7	117
McCall, Id., U.S.	E2	89
McCalla, Al., U.S.	g6	78
McCamey, Tx., U.S.	D1	120
McCammon, Id., U.S.	G6	89
McCandless, Pa., U.S.	h13	115
McCartney Mountain, mtn., Mt., U.S.	E4	103
McCaysville, Ga., U.S.	B2	87
McChord Air Force Base, mil., Wa., U.S.	f11	124
McClain, co., Ok., U.S.	C4	113
McCleary, Wa., U.S.	B2	124
McClellan Air Force Base, mil., Ca., U.S.	C3	82
McClintock, Mount, mtn., Ant.	A28	47
McCloud, Ca., U.S.	B2	82
McClure, Pa., U.S.	E7	115
McColl, S.C., U.S.	B8	117
McComas, W.V., U.S.	D3	125
McComb, Ms., U.S.	D3	101
McComb, Oh., U.S.	A2	112
McCone, co., Mt., U.S.	C11	103
McConnell Air Force Base, mil., Ks., U.S.	g12	93
McConnellsburg, Pa., U.S.	G6	115
McConnelsville, Oh., U.S.	C4	112
McCook, Ne., U.S.	D5	104
McCook, co., S.D., U.S.	D8	118
McCordsville, In., U.S.	E6	91
McCormick, S.C., U.S.	D3	117
McCormick, co., S.C., U.S.	D3	117
McCracken, co., Ky., U.S.	e9	94
McCreary, Man., Can.	D2	70
McCreary, co., Ky., U.S.	D5	94
McCrory, Ar., U.S.	B4	81
McCulloch, co., Tx., U.S.	D3	120
McCullough Mountain, mtn., Nv., U.S.	H6	105
McCurtain, co., Ok., U.S.	C7	113
McDermitt, Nv., U.S.	B4	105
McDonald, co., Mo., U.S.	E3	102
McDonough, Ga., U.S.	C2	87
McDonough, co., Il., U.S.	C3	90
McDougall, Mount, mtn., Wy., U.S.	D2	127
McDowell, Ky., U.S.	C7	94
McDowell, co., N.C., U.S.	f10	110
McDowell, co., W.V., U.S.	D3	125
McDowell Mountains, mts., Az., U.S.	k9	80
McDowell Peak, mtn., Az., U.S.	k9	80
McDuffie, co., Ga., U.S.	C4	87
McElroy Creek, stm., W.V., U.S.	k9	125
Mcensk, Russia	H19	18
McEwen, Tn., U.S.	A4	119
McFarland, Ca., U.S.	E4	82
McFarland, Wi., U.S.	E4	126
McGehee, Ar., U.S.	D4	81
McGill, Nv., U.S.	D7	105
McGrath, Ak., U.S.	C8	79
McGregor, Ia., U.S.	A6	92
McGregor, Tx., U.S.	D4	120
McGregor, stm., B.C., Can.	B7	69
McGregor Lake, l., Alta., Can.	D4	68
McGuire, Mount, mtn., Id., U.S.	D4	89
McGuire Air Force Base, mil., N.J., U.S.	C3	107
McHenry, Il., U.S.	A5	90
McHenry, Md., U.S.	k12	97
McHenry, co., Il., U.S.	A5	90
McHenry, co., N.D., U.S.	A5	111
McIntosh, Mn., U.S.	C3	100
McIntosh, co., Ga., U.S.	E5	87
McIntosh, co., N.D., U.S.	C6	111
McIntosh, co., Ok., U.S.	B6	113
McKean, co., Pa., U.S.	C4	115
McKee, Ky., U.S.	C6	94
McKeesport, Pa., U.S.	F2	115
McKees Rocks, Pa., U.S.	F1	115
McKenzie, Tn., U.S.	A3	119
McKenzie, co., N.D., U.S.	B2	111
McKenzie, stm., Or., U.S.	C4	114
McKinley, co., N.M., U.S.	B1	108
McKinley, Mount, mtn., Ak., U.S.	C9	79
McKinleyville, Ca., U.S.	B1	82
McKinney, Tx., U.S.	C4	120
McKinney, Lake, l., Ks., U.S.	E2	93
McKittrick Summit, mtn., Ca., U.S.	E4	82
McLaughlin, S.D., U.S.	B5	118
McLean, Il., U.S.	C4	90
McLean, Va., U.S.	g12	123
McLean, co., Il., U.S.	C4	90
McLean, co., Ky., U.S.	C2	94
McLean, co., N.D., U.S.	B4	111
McLeansboro, Il., U.S.	E5	90
McLennan, Alta., Can.	B2	68
McLennan, co., Tx., U.S.	D4	120
McLeod, co., Mn., U.S.	F4	100
McLeod, Lake, l., Austl.	D2	50
M'Clintock Channel, strt., N.W. Ter., Can.	B12	66
McLoud, Ok., U.S.	B4	113
McLoughlin, Mount, mtn., Or., U.S.	D4	114
McLouth, Ks., U.S.	C8	93
McMechen, W.V., U.S.	B4	125
McMillan, Lake, res., N.M., U.S.	E5	108
McMinn, co., Tn., U.S.	D9	119
McMinnville, Or., U.S.	B3	114
McMinnville, Tn., U.S.	D8	119
McMullen, co., Tx., U.S.	E3	120
McNairy, co., Tn., U.S.	B3	119
McNary, Az., U.S.	C6	80
McNary Dam, U.S.	B7	114
McNeil, Ar., U.S.	D2	81
McNeil, Mount, mtn., B.C., Can.	B2	69
McNeil Island, i., Wa., U.S.	f10	124
McNeill, Ms., U.S.	E4	101
McPherson, Ks., U.S.	D6	93
McPherson, co., Ks., U.S.	D6	93
McPherson, co., Ne., U.S.	C4	104
McPherson, co., S.D., U.S.	B6	118
McQueeney, Tx., U.S.	h7	120
McRae, Ar., U.S.	B4	81
McRae, Ga., U.S.	D4	87
McRoberts, Ky., U.S.	C7	94
McSherrystown, Pa., U.S.	G7	115
Mead, Wa., U.S.	B8	124
Mead, Lake, res., U.S.	A1	80
Meade, Ks., U.S.	E3	93
Meade, co., Ks., U.S.	E3	93
Meade, co., Ky., U.S.	C3	94
Meade, co., S.D., U.S.	C3	118
Meade, stm., Ak., U.S.	B8	79
Meaden Peak, mtn., Co., U.S.	A3	83
Meade Peak, mtn., Id., U.S.	G7	89
Meadow, stm., W.V., U.S.	C4	125
Meadow Creek, stm., W.V., U.S.	n14	125
Meadow Lands, Pa., U.S.	F1	115
Meadow Valley Wash, val., Nv., U.S.	F7	105
Meadowview, Va., U.S.	f10	123
Meadville, Pa., U.S.	C1	115
Meaford, Ont., Can.	C4	73
Meagher, co., Mt., U.S.	D6	103
Mealhada, Port.	E3	12
Meander Creek Reservoir, res., Oh., U.S.	A5	112
Meath, hist. reg., Ire.	H5	7
Meaux, Fr.	D9	10
Mebane, N.C., U.S.	A3	110
Mecca, Ca., U.S.	F5	82
Mecca see Makkah, Sau. Ar.	D2	46
Mechanic Falls, Me., U.S.	D2	96
Mechanicsburg, Oh., U.S.	B2	112
Mechanicsburg, Pa., U.S.	F7	115
Mechanicsville, Ia., U.S.	C6	92
Mechanicsville, Md., U.S.	D4	97
Mechanicsville, Va., U.S.	C5	123
Mechanicville, N.Y., U.S.	C7	109
Mechant, Lake, l., La., U.S.	E4	95
Mechelen, Bel.	D4	8
Mecklenburg, co., N.C., U.S.	B2	110
Mecklenburg, co., Va., U.S.	D4	123
Mecklenburg, hist. reg., Ger.	B12	8
Mecklenburger Bucht, b., Ger.	A11	8
Mecosta, co., Mi., U.S.	E5	99
Medan, Indon.	E2	32
Medanosa, Punta, c., Arg.	F3	56
Medaryville, In., U.S.	B4	91
Meddybumps Lake, l., Me., U.S.	C5	96
Medeiros Neto, Braz.	D8	57
Medellín, Col.	D5	58
Médenine, Tun.	B8	42
Medfield, Ma., U.S.	h10	98
Medford, Ma., U.S.	B5	98
Medford, Mn., U.S.	F5	100
Medford, Ok., U.S.	A4	113
Medford, Or., U.S.	E4	114
Medford, Wi., U.S.	C3	126
Medford Lakes, N.J., U.S.	D3	107
Medgidia, Rom.	E12	16
Media, Pa., U.S.	G11	115
Mediapolis, Ia., U.S.	C6	92
Mediaș, Rom.	C8	16
Medical Lake, Wa., U.S.	B8	124
Medicine Bow, Wy., U.S.	E6	127
Medicine Bow, stm., Wy., U.S.	E6	127
Medicine Bow Mountains, mts., U.S.	E6	127
Medicine Bow Peak, mtn., Wy., U.S.	E6	127
Medicine Hat, Alta., Can.	D5	68
Medicine Lodge, Ks., U.S.	E5	93
Medicine Lodge, stm., U.S.	E4	93
Medina, N.Y., U.S.	B2	109
Medina, Oh., U.S.	A4	112
Medina, Tn., U.S.	B3	119
Medina, Wa., U.S.	e11	124
Medina, co., Oh., U.S.	A4	112
Medina, co., Tx., U.S.	E3	120
Medina, stm., Tx., U.S.	k7	120
Medina see Al-Madīnah, Sau. Ar.	D2	46
Medinaceli, Spain	D9	12
Medina del Campo, Spain	D7	12
Medina de Ríoseco, Spain	D6	12
Mediterranean Sea	D14	2
Medjez el Bab, Tun.	M4	14
Médoc, reg., Fr.	G5	10
Medora, In., U.S.	G5	91
Médouneu, Gabon	A2	44
Medway, Me., U.S.	C4	96
Medway, Ma., U.S.	B5	98
Medway, stm., N.S., Can.	E5	71
Meekatharra, Austl.	E3	50
Meeker, Co., U.S.	A3	83
Meeker, Ok., U.S.	B5	113
Meeker, co., Mn., U.S.	E4	100
Meelpaeg Lake, res., Newf., Can.	D3	72
Meerut, India	F7	38
Meeteetse, Wy., U.S.	B4	127
Mega, Eth.	H2	46
Mégantic, Lac, l., Que., Can.	D7	74
Mégantic, Mont, mtn., Que., Can.	D6	74
Mégara, Grc.	K7	16
Meggett, S.C., U.S.	F7	117
Meghalaya, state, India	H14	38
Meherrin, stm., U.S.	A4	110
Mehlville, Mo., U.S.	f13	102
Mehsāna, India	I5	38
Mehtar Lām, Afg.	C4	38
Mehun-sur-Yèvre, Fr.	E9	10
Meigs, Ga., U.S.	E2	87
Meigs, co., Oh., U.S.	C3	112
Meigs, co., Tn., U.S.	D9	119
Meiktila, Mya.	D3	34
Meiningen, Ger.	E10	8
Meissen, Ger.	D13	8
Meixian, China	K5	28
Mekambo, Gabon	A2	44
Mekele, Eth.	F2	46
Meknès, Mor.	B4	42
Mekong, stm., Asia	H8	34
Melaka, Malay.	M7	34
Melanesia, is., Oc.	G23	2
Melbourne, Austl.	G8	50
Melbourne, Ar., U.S.	A4	81
Melbourne, Fl., U.S.	D6	86
Melbourne, Ia., U.S.	C4	92
Melbourne, Ky., U.S.	h14	94
Melbourne Beach, Fl., U.S.	D6	86
Melcher, Ia., U.S.	C4	92
Meldorf, Ger.	A9	8
Mélèzes, Rivière aux, stm., Que., Can.	g12	74
Melfi, Chad	F9	42
Melfi, Italy	I10	14
Melgaço, Port.	C3	12
Melhus, Nor.	E8	6
Melilla, Sp. N. Afr.	A5	42
Melita, Man., Can.	E1	70
Melito di Porto Salvo, Italy	L10	14
Melitopol', Ukr.	H5	22
Melk, Aus.	G15	8
Mellansel, Swe.	E12	6
Melle, Fr.	F6	10
Mellen, Wi., U.S.	B3	126
Mellerud, Swe.	G9	6
Mellette, co., S.D., U.S.	D5	118
Mellish Reef, atoll, Austl.	C11	50
Melo, Ur.	C6	56
Melocheville, Que., Can.	q19	74
Melrhir, Chott, l., Alg.	B7	42
Melrose, Fl., U.S.	C4	86
Melrose, Ma., U.S.	B5	98
Melrose, Mn., U.S.	E4	100
Melrose, N.M., U.S.	C6	108
Meltaus, Fin.	C15	6
Melton Hill Lake, res., Tn., U.S.	D9	119
Melton Mowbray, Eng., U.K.	I12	7
Melun, Fr.	D9	10
Melvern Lake, res., Ks., U.S.	D8	93
Melville, La., U.S.	D4	95
Melville, Lake, l., Newf., Can.	B2	72
Melville Hills, hills, N.W. Ter., Can.	C8	66
Melville Island, i., Austl.	B6	50
Melville Island, i., N.W. Ter., Can.	A10	66
Melville Peninsula, pen., N.W. Ter., Can.	C16	66
Melvin, Ky., U.S.	C7	94
Memmingen, Ger.	H10	8

Name — Map Ref — Page

Memphis, Fl., U.S. p10 86
Memphis, Mi., U.S. F8 99
Memphis, Mo., U.S. A5 102
Memphis, Tn., U.S. B1 119
Memphis, Tx., U.S. B2 120
Memphis Naval Air Station, mil., Tn., U.S. B2 119
Mena, Ar., U.S. C1 81
Menahga, Mn., U.S. D3 100
Ménaka, Mali E6 42
Menan, Id., U.S. F7 89
Menands, N.Y., U.S. C7 109
Menard, Tx., U.S. D3 120
Menard, co., Il., U.S. C4 90
Menard, co., Tx., U.S. D3 120
Menasha, Wi., U.S. D5 126
Mendawai, stm., Indon. F5 32
Mende, Fr. H10 10
Mendenhall, Ms., U.S. D4 101
Méndez, Ec. I3 58
Mendham, N.J., U.S. B3 107
Mendi, Eth. G2 46
Mendip Hills, hills, Eng., U.K. J10 7
Mendocino, co., Ca., U.S. C2 82
Mendon, Il., U.S. C2 90
Mendon, Mi., U.S. F5 99
Mendon, Ut., U.S. B4 121
Mendota, Ca., U.S. D3 82
Mendota, Il., U.S. B4 90
Mendota, Lake, l., Wi., U.S. E4 126
Mendoza, Arg. C3 56
Mene de Mauroa, Ven. B7 58
Mene Grande, Ven. C7 58
Menemen, Tur. K11 16
Menfi, Italy L7 14
Mengzhi, China C7 34
Mengzi, China B5 34
Menifee, co., Ky., U.S. C6 94
Menlo Park, Ca., U.S. k8 82
Menno, S.D., U.S. D8 118
Menominee, Mi., U.S. C3 99
Menominee, co., Mi., U.S. C3 99
Menominee, co., Wi., U.S. C5 126
Menominee, stm., U.S. C6 126
Menominee Indian Reservation, Wi., U.S. C5 126
Menomonee, stm., Wi., U.S. m11 126
Menomonee Falls, Wi., U.S. E5 126
Menomonie, Wi., U.S. D2 126
Menongue, Ang. D3 44
Menorca, i., Spain F16 12
Mentawai, Kepulauan, is., Indon. F2 32
Menton, Fr. I14 10
Mentone, In., U.S. B5 91
Mentor, Oh., U.S. A4 112
Mentor-on-the-Lake, Oh., U.S. A4 112
Menzel Bourguiba, Tun. L4 14
Meoqui, Mex. C7 62
Meppel, Neth. C6 8
Meppen, Ger. C7 8
Mequon, Wi., U.S. E6 126
Mer, Fr. E8 10
Meramec, stm., Mo., U.S. C7 102
Merano (Meran), Italy C6 14
Merasheen Island, i., Newf., Can. E4 72
Merauke, Indon. G11 32
Meraux, La., U.S. k12 95
Mercaderes, Col. G4 58
Merced, Ca., U.S. D3 82
Merced, co., Ca., U.S. D3 82
Merced, stm., Ca., U.S. D3 82
Mercedes, Arg. B5 56
Mercedes, Arg. C3 56
Mercedes, Tx., U.S. F4 120
Mercedes, Ur. C5 56
Mercer, Pa., U.S. D1 115
Mercer, Wi., U.S. B3 126
Mercer, co., Il., U.S. B3 90
Mercer, co., Ky., U.S. C5 94
Mercer, co., Mo., U.S. A4 102
Mercer, co., N.J., U.S. C3 107
Mercer, co., N.D., U.S. B4 111
Mercer, co., Oh., U.S. B1 112
Mercer, co., Pa., U.S. D1 115
Mercer, co., W.V., U.S. D3 125
Mercer Island, Wa., U.S. B3 124
Mercer Island, i., Wa., U.S. e11 124
Mercersburg, Pa., U.S. G6 115
Mercerville, N.J., U.S. C3 107
Mercier, Que., Can. D4 74
Meredith, N.H., U.S. C3 106
Meredith, Lake, l., Co., U.S. C7 83
Meredith, Lake, res., Tx., U.S. B2 120
Meredosia, Il., U.S. D3 90
Meredosia Lake, l., Il., U.S. D3 90
Mergui (Myeik), Mya. H5 34
Mergui Archipelago, is., Mya. H4 34
Meriç (Marica) (évros), stm., Eur. H10 16
Mérida, Mex. G15 62
Mérida, Spain G5 12
Mérida, Ven. C7 58
Meriden, Ct., U.S. C4 84
Meriden, Ks., U.S. C8 93
Meridian, Id., U.S. F2 89
Meridian, Ms., U.S. C5 101
Meridian, Pa., U.S. E2 115
Meridian, Tx., U.S. D4 120
Meridian Hills, In., U.S. k10 91
Meridian Naval Air Station, mil., Ms., U.S. C5 101
Meridianville, Al., U.S. A3 78
Mérignac, Fr. H6 10
Merikarvia, Fin. F13 6
Meriwether, co., Ga., U.S. C2 87
Merkel, Tx., U.S. C2 120
Merlin, Ont., Can. E2 73
Mermentau, La., U.S. D3 95
Mermentau, stm., La., U.S. E3 95
Meron, Hare, mtn., Isr. C4 40
Merriam, Ks., U.S. k16 93
Merrick, co., Ne., U.S. C7 104
Merrickville, Ont., Can. C9 73
Merrill, Ia., U.S. B1 92
Merrill, Mi., U.S. E6 99
Merrill, Or., U.S. E5 114
Merrill, Wi., U.S. C4 126
Merrillville, In., U.S. B3 91
Merrimac, Ma., U.S. A5 98
Merrimack, N.H., U.S. E4 106
Merrimack, co., N.H., U.S. D3 106
Merrimack, stm., U.S. A5 98
Merritt, B.C., Can. D7 69
Merritt Island, Fl., U.S. D6 86
Merritt Reservoir, res., Ne., U.S. B5 104
Merrymeeting Lake, l., N.H., U.S. D4 106
Merryville, La., U.S. D2 95
Merseburg, Ger. D11 8
Merthyr Tydfil, Wales, U.K. J9 7
Mértola, Port. H4 12
Merton, Wi., U.S. m11 126
Méru, Fr. C9 10
Merwin Lake, res., Wa., U.S. C3 124
Merzig, Ger. F6 8
Mesa, Az., U.S. D4 80
Mesa, co., Co., U.S. C2 83
Mesabi Range, hills, Mn., U.S. C6 100
Mesagne, Italy I12 14
Mesa Mountain, mtn., Co., U.S. D4 83
Mesa Verde National Park, Co., U.S. D2 83
Mescalero, N.M., U.S. D4 108
Mescalero Indian Reservation, N.M., U.S. D4 108
Mesilla, N.M., U.S. E3 108
Mesolóngion, Grc. K5 16
Mesopotamia, reg., Asia B3 46
Mesquite, Nv., U.S. G7 105
Mesquite, N.M., U.S. E3 108
Mesquite, Tx., U.S. n10 120
Messalo, stm., Moz. D7 44
Messalonskee Lake, l., Me., U.S. D3 96
Messina, Italy K10 14
Messina, S. Afr. F5 44
Messina, Stretto di, strt., Italy K10 14
Mesta (Néstos), stm., Eur. H7 16
Mestre, Italy D7 14
Meta, stm., S.A. D9 58
Métabetchouan, Que., Can. A6 74
Métabetchouane, stm., Que., Can. A5 74
Metairie, La., U.S. k11 95
Metamora, Il., U.S. C4 90
Metán, Arg. B3 56
Metcalfe, Ont., Can. B9 73
Metcalfe, Ms., U.S. B2 101
Metcalfe, co., Ky., U.S. C4 94
Metedeconk, North Branch, stm., N.J., U.S. C4 107
Metedeconk, South Branch, stm., N.J., U.S. C3 107
Meteghan, N.S., Can. E3 71
Meteghan River, N.S., Can. E3 71
Meteor Crater, crat., Az., U.S. C4 80
Methow, stm., Wa., U.S. A5 124
Methuen, Ma., U.S. A5 98
Metković, Cro. F12 14
Metlakatla, Ak., U.S. D13 79
Metlatonoc, Mex. I10 62
Metlika, Slo. D10 14
Metonga, Lake, l., Wi., U.S. C5 126
Metro, Indon. k12 33a
Metropolis, Il., U.S. F5 90
Mettawee, stm., U.S. E2 122
Metter, Ga., U.S. D4 87
Mettūr, India G4 37
Metuchen, N.J., U.S. B4 107
Metz, Fr. C13 10
Metzger, Or., U.S. h12 114
Meuse (Maas), stm., Eur. E5 8
Mexia, Tx., U.S. D4 120
Mexia, Lake, res., Tx., U.S. D4 120
Mexiana, Ilha, i., Braz. D9 54
Mexicali, Mex. A2 62
Mexico, In., U.S. C5 91
Mexico, Me., U.S. D2 96
Mexico, Mo., U.S. B6 102
Mexico (México), ctry., N.A. F8 62
Mexico, Gulf of, b., N.A. F9 76
Mexico City see Ciudad de México, Mex. H10 62
Meximieux, Fr. G12 10
Meycauayan, Phil. q19 33b
Meyersdale, Pa., U.S. G3 115
Meymaneh, Afg. C1 38
Meyrueis, Fr. H10 10
Meždurečensk, Russia G11 24
Mèze, Fr. I10 10
Mezőtúr, Hung. H20 8
Mezquital, Mex. F7 62
Mezzolombardo, Italy C6 14
Mhow, India I6 38
Miami, Az., U.S. D5 80
Miami, Fl., U.S. G6 86
Miami, Ok., U.S. A7 113
Miami, co., In., U.S. C5 91
Miami, co., Ks., U.S. D9 93
Miami, co., Oh., U.S. B1 112
Miami Beach, Fl., U.S. G6 86
Miami Canal, Fl., U.S. F6 86
Miami International Airport, Fl., U.S. G6 86
Miamisburg, Oh., U.S. C1 112
Miami Shores, Fl., U.S. G6 86
Miami Springs, Fl., U.S. G6 86
Miandrivazo, Madag. E9 44
Mianeh, Iran J7 22
Mianus Reservoir, res., U.S. E1 84
Miānwāli, Pak. D4 38
Mica Mountain, mtn., Az., U.S. E5 80
Micco, Fl., U.S. E6 86
Miccosukee, Lake, res., Fl., U.S. B2 86
Michelson, Mount, mtn., Ak., U.S. B11 79
Michie, Tn., U.S. B3 119
Michigamme, Lake, l., Mi., U.S. B2 99
Michigamme Reservoir, res., Mi., U.S. B2 99
Michigan, state, U.S. E6 99
Michigan, stm., Co., U.S. A4 83
Michigan, Lake, l., U.S. C9 76
Michigan Center, Mi., U.S. F6 99
Michigan City, In., U.S. A4 91
Michigan Island, i., Wi., U.S. B3 126
Michikamau Lake, l., Newf., Can. F20 66
Michipicoten Island, i., Ont., Can. G15 66
Micronesia, is., Oc. F23 2
Mičurinsk, Russia I23 18
Middelburg, Neth. D3 8
Middelburg, S. Afr. H4 44
Middelharnis, Neth. D4 8
Middle, stm., Ia., U.S. C3 92
Middle, stm., Mn., U.S. B2 100
Middle Andaman, i., India H2 34
Middleboro (Middleborough Center), Ma., U.S. C6 98
Middlebourne, W.V., U.S. B4 125
Middleburg, Fl., U.S. B5 86
Middleburg, Pa., U.S. E7 115
Middleburg Heights, Oh., U.S. h9 112
Middlebury, Ct., U.S. C3 84
Middlebury, In., U.S. A6 91
Middlebury, Vt., U.S. C2 122
Middlefield, Ct., U.S. C5 84
Middlefield, Oh., U.S. A4 112
Middle Island Creek, stm., W.V., U.S. B3 125
Middle Nodaway, stm., Ia., U.S. C3 92
Middle Park, val., Co., U.S. A4 83
Middle Patuxent, stm., Md., U.S. B4 97
Middleport, N.Y., U.S. B2 109
Middleport, Oh., U.S. C3 112
Middle Raccoon, stm., Ia., U.S. C3 92
Middle River, Md., U.S. B5 97
Middlesboro, Ky., U.S. D6 94
Middlesex, N.J., U.S. B4 107
Middlesex, N.C., U.S. B4 110
Middlesex, co., Ct., U.S. D5 84
Middlesex, co., Ma., U.S. A5 98
Middlesex, co., N.J., U.S. C4 107
Middlesex, co., Va., U.S. C6 123
Middlesex Fells Reservation, Ma., U.S. g11 98
Middleton, N.S., Can. E4 71
Middleton, Id., U.S. F2 89
Middleton, Ma., U.S. A5 98
Middleton, Wi., U.S. E4 126
Middleton Reef, atoll, Austl. E11 50
Middletown, Ca., U.S. C2 82
Middletown, Ct., U.S. C5 84
Middletown, De., U.S. C3 85
Middletown, In., U.S. D6 91
Middletown, Ky., U.S. g11 94
Middletown, Md., U.S. B2 97
Middletown, N.J., U.S. C4 107
Middletown, N.Y., U.S. D6 109
Middletown, Oh., U.S. C1 112
Middletown, Pa., U.S. F8 115
Middletown, R.I., U.S. E5 116
Middletown, Va., U.S. A4 123
Middleville, Mi., U.S. F5 99
Midfield, Al., U.S. g7 78
Midland, Ont., Can. C5 73
Midland, Mi., U.S. E6 99
Midland, N.C., U.S. B2 110
Midland, Pa., U.S. E1 115
Midland, Tx., U.S. D1 120
Midland, co., Mi., U.S. E6 99
Midland, co., Tx., U.S. D1 120
Midland City, Al., U.S. D4 78
Midland Park, Ks., U.S. g12 93
Midland Park, N.J., U.S. B4 107
Midland Park, S.C., U.S. k11 117
Midleton, Ire. J4 7
Midlothian, Il., U.S. k9 90
Midlothian, Tx., U.S. C4 120
Midnapore, India I12 38
Midongy Sud, Madag. F9 44
Midvale, Ut., U.S. C4 121
Midville, Ga., U.S. D4 87
Midway, B.C., Can. E8 69
Midway, De., U.S. F5 85
Midway, Ky., U.S. B5 94
Midway, Pa., U.S. G7 115
Midway, Ut., U.S. C4 121
Midway Islands, dep., Oc. E1 2
Midwest, Wy., U.S. C6 127
Midwest City, Ok., U.S. B4 113
Mielec, Pol. E21 8
Mieres, Spain B6 12
Miesbach, Ger. H11 8
Mifflin, co., Pa., U.S. E6 115
Mifflinburg, Pa., U.S. E7 115
Mifflinville, Pa., U.S. D9 115
Miguel Alemán, Presa, res., Mex. H11 62
Miguel Auza, Mex. E8 62
Mihara, Japan H6 30
Mikasa, Japan p19 30a
Mikkeli, Fin. F16 6
Mikumi, Tan. C7 44
Milaca, Mn., U.S. E5 100
Milagro, Arg. C3 56
Milagro, Ec. I3 58
Milam, co., Tx., U.S. D4 120
Milan, Ga., U.S. D3 87
Milan, Il., U.S. B3 90
Milan, In., U.S. F7 91
Milan, Mi., U.S. F7 99
Milan, Mo., U.S. A4 102
Milan, N.M., U.S. B2 108
Milan, Oh., U.S. A3 112
Milan, Tn., U.S. B3 119
Milan see Milano, Italy D4 14
Milano (Milan), Italy D4 14
Milâs, Tur. L11 16
Milazzo, Italy K10 14
Milbank, S.D., U.S. B9 118
Mildmay, Ont., Can. C3 73
Mildura, Austl. F8 50
Milesburg, Pa., U.S. E6 115
Miles City, Mt., U.S. D11 103
Milestone, Sask., Can. G3 75
Milford, Ct., U.S. E3 84
Milford, De., U.S. E4 85
Milford, Il., U.S. C6 90
Milford, In., U.S. B6 91
Milford, Ia., U.S. A2 92
Milford, Me., U.S. D4 96
Milford, Ma., U.S. B4 98
Milford, Mi., U.S. F7 99
Milford, Ne., U.S. D8 104
Milford, N.H., U.S. E3 106
Milford, Oh., U.S. C1 112
Milford, Pa., U.S. D12 115
Milford, Ut., U.S. E2 121
Milford Haven, Wales, U.K. J7 7
Milford Lake, res., Ks., U.S. C6 93
Milford Station, N.S., Can. D6 71
Mililani Town, Hi., U.S. g9 88
Mil'kovo, Russia G25 24
Milk River, Alta., Can. E4 68
Mill, stm., Ma., U.S. h9 98
Millard, co., Ut., U.S. D2 121
Millau, Fr. H10 10
Millbrae, Ca., U.S. h8 82
Millbrook, Ont., Can. C6 73
Millbrook, Al., U.S. C3 78
Mill Brook, stm., Vt., U.S. B5 122
Millburn, N.J., U.S. B4 107
Millbury, Ma., U.S. B4 98
Millbury, Oh., U.S. e7 112
Mill City, Or., U.S. C4 114
Millcreek, Ut., U.S. C4 121
Mill Creek, W.V., U.S. C5 125
Mill Creek, stm., N.J., U.S. D4 107
Mill Creek, stm., Oh., U.S. B2 112
Mill Creek, stm., Tn., U.S. g10 119
Mill Creek, stm., W.V., U.S. m13 125
Mill Creek, stm., W.V., U.S. C3 125
Millcreek Township, Pa., U.S. B1 115
Milledgeville, Ga., U.S. C3 87
Milledgeville, Il., U.S. B4 90
Mille Îles, Rivière des, stm., Que., Can. p19 74
Mille Lacs, co., Mn., U.S. E5 100
Mille Lacs, Lac des, l., Ont., Can. G14 66
Mille Lacs Indian Reservation, Mn., U.S. D5 100
Mille Lacs Lake, l., Mn., U.S. D5 100
Millen, Ga., U.S. D5 87
Miller, S.D., U.S. C7 118
Miller, co., Ar., U.S. D2 81
Miller, co., Ga., U.S. E2 87
Miller, co., Mo., U.S. C5 102
Miller, Mount, mtn., Ak., U.S. C11 79
Miller Peak, mtn., Az., U.S. F5 80
Miller Run, stm., Vt., U.S. B4 122
Millers, stm., Ma., U.S. A3 98
Millersburg, In., U.S. A6 91
Millersburg, Ky., U.S. B5 94
Millersburg, Oh., U.S. B4 112
Millersburg, Pa., U.S. E8 115
Millersport, Oh., U.S. C3 112
Millersville, Pa., U.S. F9 115
Millet, Alta., Can. C4 68
Mill Hall, Pa., U.S. D7 115
Milliken, Co., U.S. A6 83
Millington, Mi., U.S. E7 99
Millington, Tn., U.S. B2 119
Millinocket, Me., U.S. C4 96
Millinocket Lake, l., Me., U.S. C4 96
Millinocket Lake, l., Me., U.S. B4 96
Millis, Ma., U.S. B5 98
Millport, Al., U.S. B1 78
Millry, Al., U.S. D1 78
Mills, Wy., U.S. D6 127
Mills, co., Ia., U.S. C2 92
Mills, co., Tx., U.S. D3 120
Millsboro, De., U.S. F4 85
Millsboro, Pa., U.S. G1 115
Millstadt, Il., U.S. E3 90
Millstone, stm., N.J., U.S. C4 107
Milltown, In., U.S. H5 91
Milltown, N.J., U.S. C4 107
Milltown, Wi., U.S. C1 126
Milltown [-Head of Bay d'Espoir], Newf., Can. E4 72
Milltown Malbay, Ire. I3 7
Millvale, Pa., U.S. k14 115
Mill Valley, Ca., U.S. D2 82
Millville, Ma., U.S. B4 98
Millville, N.J., U.S. E2 107
Millville, Pa., U.S. D9 115
Millville, Ut., U.S. B4 121
Millville Lake, N.H., U.S. E4 106
Millwood, Wa., U.S. g14 124
Millwood Lake, res., Ar., U.S. D1 81
Milner Dam, Id., U.S. G5 89
Milnor, N.D., U.S. C8 111
Milo, Ia., U.S. C4 92
Milo, Me., U.S. C4 96
Milparinka, Austl. E8 50
Milroy, In., U.S. F7 91
Milroy, Pa., U.S. E6 115
Milstead, Ga., U.S. C3 87
Milton, Ont., Can. D5 73
Milton, De., U.S. E4 85
Milton, Fl., U.S. u14 86
Milton, In., U.S. E7 91
Milton, Ma., U.S. B5 98
Milton, N.H., U.S. D5 106
Milton, Pa., U.S. D8 115
Milton, Vt., U.S. B2 122
Milton, Wa., U.S. f11 124
Milton, W.V., U.S. C2 125
Milton, Wi., U.S. F5 126
Milton, Lake, l., Oh., U.S. A4 112
Miltona, Lake, l., Mn., U.S. D3 100
Milton-Freewater, Or., U.S. B8 114
Milton Reservoir, res., Co., U.S. A6 83
Milverton, Ont., Can. D4 73
Milwaukee, Wi., U.S. E6 126
Milwaukee, co., Wi., U.S. E6 126
Milwaukee, stm., Wi., U.S. m12 126
Milwaukie, Or., U.S. B4 114
Mimizan, Fr. H5 10
Mims, Fl., U.S. D6 86
Min, stm., China I7 28
Mina, Nv., U.S. E3 105
Minahasa, pen., Indon. E7 32
Minamata, Japan J3 30
Minas, Ur. C5 56
Minas, Sierra de las, mts., Guat. G3 64
Minas Basin, b., N.S., Can. D5 71
Minas Channel, strt., N.S., Can. D5 71
Minas de Barroterán, Mex. D9 62
Minas Novas, Braz. D7 57
Minatare, Ne., U.S. C2 104
Minatitlán, Mex. I12 62
Minco, Ok., U.S. B4 113
Mindanao, i., Phil. D7 32
Mindanao, stm., Phil. D7 32
Mindanao Sea, Phil. D7 32
Mindelheim, Ger. G10 8
Minden, Ger. C8 8
Minden, La., U.S. B2 95
Minden, Ne., U.S. D7 104
Minden, Nv., U.S. E2 105
Minden, W.V., U.S. D3 125
Mindoro, i., Phil. C7 32
Mindoro Strait, strt., Phil. C7 32
Mine Hill, N.J., U.S. B3 107
Mineiros, Braz. D2 57
Mineola, N.Y., U.S. E7 109
Mineola, Tx., U.S. C5 120
Miner, Mo., U.S. E8 102
Miner, co., S.D., U.S. D8 118
Mineral, co., Co., U.S. D4 83
Mineral, co., Mt., U.S. C1 103
Mineral, co., Nv., U.S. E3 105
Mineral, co., W.V., U.S. B6 125
Mineral Point, Wi., U.S. F3 126
Mineral Springs, Ar., U.S. D2 81
Mineral Wells, Tx., U.S. C3 120
Minersville, Pa., U.S. E9 115
Minersville, Ut., U.S. E3 121
Minerva, Oh., U.S. B4 112
Minervino Murge, Italy H11 14
Minetto, N.Y., U.S. B4 109
Mingo, co., W.V., U.S. D2 125
Mingo Junction, Oh., U.S. B5 112
Minho (Miño), stm., Eur. D3 12
Minidoka, co., Id., U.S. G5 89
Minidoka Dam, Id., U.S. G5 89
Minier, Il., U.S. C4 90
Minisink Island, i., N.J., U.S. A3 107
Minitonas, Man., Can. C1 70
Minna, Nig. G7 42
Minneapolis, Ks., U.S. C6 93
Minneapolis, Mn., U.S. F5 100
Minnedosa, Man., Can. D2 70
Minnedosa, stm., Man., Can. D1 70
Minnehaha, co., S.D., U.S. D9 118
Minneola, Ks., U.S. E3 93
Minneota, Mn., U.S. F3 100
Minnesota, state, U.S. E4 100
Minnesota, stm., Mn., U.S. F2 100
Minnesota Lake, Mn., U.S. G5 100
Minnetonka, Mn., U.S. n12 100
Minnetonka, Lake, l., Mn., U.S. n11 100
Minnewaska, Lake, l., Mn., U.S. E3 100
Miño (Minho), stm., Eur. D3 12
Minocqua, Wi., U.S. C4 126
Minonk, Il., U.S. C4 90
Minooka, Il., U.S. B5 90
Minot, N.D., U.S. A4 111
Minot Air Force Base, mil., N.D., U.S. A4 111
Minquadale, De., U.S. i7 85
Minsk, Bela. H10 18
Mińsk Mazowiecki, Pol. C21 8
Minster, Oh., U.S. B1 112
Mint Hill, N.C., U.S. B2 110
Minto, N.B., Can. C3 71
Minto Inlet, b., N.W. Ter., Can. B9 66
Minturn, Co., U.S. B4 83
Minturno, Italy H8 14
Minusinsk, Russia G12 24
Minute Man National Historical Park, Ma., U.S. g10 98
Minxian, China E7 26
Mio, Mi., U.S. D6 99
Mira, Italy D7 14
Mirabel, Que., Can. D3 74
Miraflores, Col. E6 58
Miraflores, Col. G6 58
Miraj, India D3 37
Miramar, Fl., U.S. s13 86
Miramar Naval Air Station, mil., Ca., U.S. F5 82
Miramas, Fr. I11 10
Mirambeau, Fr. G6 10
Miramichi Bay, b., N.B., Can. B5 71
Miranda de Ebro, Spain C9 12
Miranda do Douro, Port. D5 12
Mirande, Fr. I7 10
Mirandela, Port. D4 12
Mirandola, Italy E6 14
Mirbāṭ, Oman E5 46
Mirebeau-sur-Bèze, Fr. E12 10
Miri, Malay. E5 32
Mirnyj, Russia C10 24
Mīrpur Khās, Pak. H3 38
Mirror Lake, l., N.H., U.S. C4 100
Mirzāpur, India H10 38
Misawa, Japan B14 30
Miscouche, P.E.I., Can. C6 71
Miscou Island, i., N.B., Can. B5 71
Miscou Point, c., N.B., Can. A5 71
Misenheimer, N.C., U.S. B2 110
Mishawaka, In., U.S. A5 91
Misheguk Mountain, mtn., Ak., U.S. B7 79
Mishicot, Wi., U.S. D6 126
Mishmi Hills, hills, Asia F16 38
Misima Island, i., Pap. N. Gui. B10 50
Miskitos, Cayos, is., Nic. G6 64
Miskolc, Hung. G20 8
Misool, Pulau, i., Indon. F9 32
Mispillion, stm., De., U.S. E4 85
Misrātah, Libya B9 42
Missaukee, co., Mi., U.S. D5 99
Missaukee, Lake, l., Mi., U.S. D5 99
Mission, Ks., U.S. m16 93
Mission, S.D., U.S. D5 118
Mission, Tx., U.S. F3 120
Mission Range, mts., Mt., U.S. C3 103
Mission Viejo, Ca., U.S. n13 82
Missisquoi, stm., Vt., U.S. B3 122
Missisquoi Bay, b., Vt., U.S. A2 122

Index

Name	Map Ref	Page
Mississauga, Ont., Can.	D5	73
Mississinewa, stm., U.S.	D7	91
Mississinewa Lake, res., In., U.S.	C6	91
Mississippi, co., Ar., U.S.	B5	81
Mississippi, co., Mo., U.S.	E8	102
Mississippi, state, U.S.	C4	101
Mississippi, stm., U.S.	E8	76
Mississippi Delta, La., U.S.	E6	95
Mississippi Sound, strt., U.S.	E5	101
Mississippi State, Ms., U.S.	B5	101
Missoula, Mt., U.S.	D2	103
Missoula, co., Mt., U.S.	D2	103
Missouri, state, U.S.	C5	102
Missouri, stm., U.S.	C7	76
Missouri City, Tx., U.S.	r14	120
Missouri Valley, Ia., U.S.	C2	92
Mistassini, Que., Can.	h12	74
Mistassini, Lac, l., Que., Can.	h12	74
Misti, Volcán, vol., Peru	G4	54
Mistretta, Italy	L9	14
Mita, Punta de, c., Mex.	G7	62
Mitchell, Austl.	E9	50
Mitchell, Ont., Can.	D3	73
Mitchell, Il., U.S.	E3	90
Mitchell, In., U.S.	G5	91
Mitchell, Ne., U.S.	C2	104
Mitchell, S.D., U.S.	D7	118
Mitchell, co., Ga., U.S.	E2	87
Mitchell, co., Ia., U.S.	A5	92
Mitchell, co., Ks., U.S.	C5	93
Mitchell, co., N.C., U.S.	e10	110
Mitchell, co., Tx., U.S.	C2	120
Mitchell, stm., Austl.	C8	50
Mitchell, Lake, l., Mi., U.S.	D5	99
Mitchell, Lake, res., Al., U.S.	C3	78
Mitchell, Mount, mtn., N.C., U.S.	f10	110
Mitchell Island, i., La., U.S.	E6	95
Mitchellville, Ia., U.S.	C4	92
Mitilíni, Grc.	J10	16
Mitkof Island, i., Ak., U.S.	m23	79
Mito, Japan	F13	30
Mitsiwa, Erit.	E2	46
Mitsuke, Japan	E11	30
Mittenwald, Ger.	H11	8
Mittweida, Ger.	E12	8
Mitú, Col.	G7	58
Mitumba, Monts, mts., Zaire	C5	44
Mitwaba, Zaire	C5	44
Mitzic, Gabon	A2	44
Miura, Japan	G12	30
Mixian, China	A2	28
Miyako, Japan	C14	30
Miyako-jima, i., Japan	G12	26
Miyakonojō, Japan	K4	30
Miyazaki, Japan	K4	30
Miyoshi, Japan	H5	30
Miyun, China	C10	26
Mizdah, Libya	B8	42
Mizen Head, c., Ire.	J3	7
Mizoram, ter., India	I15	38
Mizpe Ramon, Isr.	D4	40
Mizque, Bol.	G5	54
Mjölby, Swe.	G10	6
Mjøsa, l., Nor.	F8	6
Mkalama, Tan.	B6	44
Mladá Boleslav, Czech.	E14	8
Mława, Pol.	B20	8
Mo, Nor.	C10	6
Moab, Ut., U.S.	E6	121
Moanda, Gabon	B2	44
Moapa River Indian Reservation, Nv., U.S.	G7	105
Moate, Ire.	H5	7
Mobara, Japan	G13	30
Mobaye, Cen. Afr. Rep.	H10	42
Moberly, Mo., U.S.	B5	102
Mobile, Al., U.S.	E1	78
Mobile, co., Al., U.S.	E1	78
Mobile, stm., Al., U.S.	E1	78
Mobile Bay, b., Al., U.S.	E1	83
Mobridge, S.D., U.S.	B5	118
Moçambique, Moz.	E8	44
Mocanaqua, Pa., U.S.	D9	115
Mocha, Isla, i., Chile	D2	56
Mochudi, Bots.	F5	44
Mocksville, N.C., U.S.	B2	110
Moclips, Wa., U.S.	B1	124
Môco, Serra do, mtn., Ang.	D3	44
Mocoa, Col.	G4	58
Mococa, Braz.	F5	57
Moctezuma, Mex.	C5	62
Mocuba, Moz.	E7	44
Modane, Fr.	G13	10
Model Reservoir, res., Co., U.S.	D6	83
Modena, Italy	E5	14
Modesto, Ca., U.S.	D3	82
Modica, Italy	M9	14
Mödling, Aus.	G16	8
Modoc, co., Ca., U.S.	B3	82
Modowi, Indon.	F9	32
Moengo, Sur.	B8	54
Moenkopi, Az., U.S.	A4	80
Moffat, Scot., U.K.	F9	7
Moffat, co., Co., U.S.	A2	83
Moffat Tunnel, Co., U.S.	B5	83
Moffett Field Naval Air Station, mil., Ca., U.S.	k8	82
Moga, India	E6	38
Mogadisho see Muqdisho, Som.	H4	46
Mogadore, Oh., U.S.	A4	112
Mogadouro, Port.	D5	12
Mogaung, Mya.	B4	34
Mogi das Cruzes, Braz.	G5	57
Mogil'ov, Bela.	H13	18
Mogi-Mirim, Braz.	G5	57
Mogincual, Moz.	E8	44
Mogoča, Russia	G17	24
Mogočin, Russia	F10	24
Mogok, Mya.	C4	34
Mogollon Mountains, mts., N.M., U.S.	D1	108
Mogollon Rim, clf, Az., U.S.	C5	80
Mogotón, Pico, mtn., N.A.	H4	64
Mohall, N.D., U.S.	A4	111
Mohave, co., Az., U.S.	B1	80
Mohave, Lake, res., U.S.	H7	105
Mohave Mountains, mts., Az., U.S.	C1	80
Mohave Valley, Az., U.S.	C1	80
Mohawk, N.Y., U.S.	C5	109
Mohawk, stm., N.H., U.S.	g7	106
Mohawk, stm., N.Y., U.S.	C6	109
Mohawk Lake, l., N.J., U.S.	A3	107
Mohawk Mountains, mts., Az., U.S.	E2	80
Moheli, i., Com.	D8	44
Mohican, stm., Oh., U.S.	B3	112
Mohinora, Cerro, mtn., Mex.	D6	62
Mohnton, Pa., U.S.	F10	115
Moi, Nor.	G6	6
Moisie, Que., Can.	h8	72
Moisie, stm., Que., Can.	F19	66
Moissac, Fr.	H8	10
Mojave, Ca., U.S.	E4	82
Mojave, stm., Ca., U.S.	E5	82
Mojave Desert, des., Ca., U.S.	E5	82
Mojjero, stm., Russia	D14	24
Mojo, Eth.	G2	46
Mokapu Peninsula, pen., Hi., U.S.	g10	88
Mokapu Point, c., Hi., U.S.	g11	88
Mokelumne, stm., Ca., U.S.	C3	82
Mokena, Il., U.S.	k9	90
Mokp'o, S. Kor.	E12	26
Moku Manu, i., Hi., U.S.	g11	88
Mol, Bel.	D5	8
Molalla, Or., U.S.	B4	114
Moldau see Vltava, stm., Czech.	F14	8
Moldavia see Moldova, ctry., Eur.	H3	22
Molde, Nor.	E6	6
Moldova, ctry., Eur.	H3	22
Molepolole, Bots.	F5	44
Molfetta, Italy	H11	14
Molina de Aragón, Spain	E10	12
Molina de Segura, Spain	G10	12
Moline, Il., U.S.	B3	90
Moline, Mi., U.S.	F5	99
Molino, Fl., U.S.	u14	86
Molins de Rey, Spain	D14	12
Mollendo, Peru	G4	54
Mölln, Ger.	B10	8
Mölndal, Swe.	H9	6
Molodečno, Bela.	G9	18
Molokai, i., Hi., U.S.	B5	88
Molokini, i., Hi., U.S.	C5	88
Molson Lake, l., Man., Can.	B3	70
Molucca Sea see Maluku, Laut, Indon.	F7	32
Moluccas see Maluku, is., Indon.	F8	32
Moma, Moz.	E7	44
Moma, stm., Russia	D22	24
Mombasa, Kenya	B7	44
Mombetsu, Japan	o21	30a
Momence, Il., U.S.	B6	90
Momotombo, Volcán, vol., Nic.	H4	64
Mon, stm., Mya.	D3	34
Mona, Canal de la, strt., N.A.	E14	64
Mona, Isla, i., P.R.	E14	64
Monaca, Pa., U.S.	E1	115
Monaco, ctry., Eur.	G9	4
Monadhliath Mountains, mts., Scot., U.K.	D8	7
Monadnock, Mount, mtn., N.H., U.S.	E2	106
Monadnock Mountain, mtn., Vt., U.S.	B5	122
Monahans, Tx., U.S.	D1	120
Monarch Mills, S.C., U.S.	B4	117
Monarch Pass, Co., U.S.	C4	83
Monashee Mountains, mts., B.C., Can.	D8	69
Monastir, Tun.	N5	14
Moncalieri, Italy	D2	14
Monção, Braz.	D9	54
Mönchengladbach, Ger.	D6	8
Monchique, Port.	H3	12
Moncks Corner, S.C., U.S.	E7	117
Monclova, Mex.	D9	62
Moncton, N.B., Can.	C5	71
Mondoñedo, Spain	B4	12
Mondovì, Italy	E2	14
Mondovi, Wi., U.S.	D2	126
Mondragone, Italy	H8	14
Monee, Il., U.S.	B6	90
Monessen, Pa., U.S.	F2	115
Monett, Mo., U.S.	E4	102
Monette, Ar., U.S.	B5	81
Monfalcone, Italy	D8	14
Monforte de Lemos, Spain	C4	12
Monfort Heights, Oh., U.S.	*o12	112
Mong Cai, Viet.	D9	34
Möng Hsat, Mya.	D5	34
Monghyr, India	H12	38
Mongo, Chad	F9	42
Mongol Altajn Nuruu, mts., Asia	B5	26
Mongolia, ctry., Asia	B7	26
Mongu, Zam.	E4	44
Monhegan Island, i., Me., U.S.	E3	96
Monida Pass, U.S.	E6	89
Moniteau, co., Mo., U.S.	C5	102
Monitor Range, mts., Nv., U.S.	E5	105
Monitor Valley, val., Nv., U.S.	D5	105
Monmouth, Il., U.S.	C3	90
Monmouth, Or., U.S.	C3	114
Monmouth, co., N.J., U.S.	C4	107
Monmouth Beach, N.J., U.S.	C5	107
Monmouth Mountain, mtn., B.C., Can.	D6	69
Mono, co., Ca., U.S.	D4	82
Monocacy, stm., Md., U.S.	B3	97
Mono Lake, l., Ca., U.S.	D4	82
Monomonac, Lake, l., U.S.	E3	106
Monomoy Island, i., Ma., U.S.	C7	98
Monomoy Point, c., Ma., U.S.	C7	98
Monon, In., U.S.	C4	91
Monona, Ia., U.S.	A6	92
Monona, Wi., U.S.	E4	126
Monona, co., Ia., U.S.	B1	92
Monona, Lake, l., Wi., U.S.	E4	126
Monongah, W.V., U.S.	B4	125
Monongahela, Pa., U.S.	F2	115
Monongahela, stm., U.S.	G2	115
Monongalia, co., W.V., U.S.	B4	125
Monopoli, Italy	I12	14
Monóvar, Spain	G11	12
Monreal del Campo, Spain	E10	12
Monroe, Ga., U.S.	C3	87
Monroe, In., U.S.	C8	91
Monroe, Ia., U.S.	C4	92
Monroe, La., U.S.	B3	95
Monroe, Mi., U.S.	G7	99
Monroe, N.Y., U.S.	D6	109
Monroe, N.C., U.S.	C2	110
Monroe, Oh., U.S.	C1	112
Monroe, Ut., U.S.	E3	121
Monroe, Wa., U.S.	B4	124
Monroe, Wi., U.S.	F4	126
Monroe, co., Al., U.S.	D2	78
Monroe, co., Ar., U.S.	C4	81
Monroe, co., Fl., U.S.	G5	86
Monroe, co., Ga., U.S.	D3	87
Monroe, co., Il., U.S.	E3	90
Monroe, co., In., U.S.	F4	91
Monroe, co., Ia., U.S.	D5	92
Monroe, co., Ky., U.S.	D4	94
Monroe, co., Mi., U.S.	G7	99
Monroe, co., Ms., U.S.	B5	101
Monroe, co., Mo., U.S.	B5	102
Monroe, co., N.Y., U.S.	B3	109
Monroe, co., Oh., U.S.	C4	112
Monroe, co., Pa., U.S.	D11	115
Monroe, co., Tn., U.S.	D9	119
Monroe, co., W.V., U.S.	D4	125
Monroe, co., Wi., U.S.	E3	126
Monroe Center, Ct., U.S.	D3	84
Monroe City, Mo., U.S.	B6	102
Monroe Lake, res., In., U.S.	F5	91
Monroe Park, De., U.S.	h7	85
Monroeville, Al., U.S.	D2	78
Monroeville, In., U.S.	C8	91
Monroeville, Oh., U.S.	A3	112
Monroeville, Pa., U.S.	k14	115
Monrovia, Lib.	G3	42
Monrovia, Ca., U.S.	m13	82
Monrovia, In., U.S.	E5	91
Mons, Bel.	E3	8
Monson, Ma., U.S.	B3	98
Montague, P.E.I., Can.	C7	71
Montague, Ca., U.S.	B2	82
Montague, Mi., U.S.	E4	99
Montague, co., Tx., U.S.	C4	120
Montague, Isla, i., Mex.	B2	62
Montague Island, i., Ak., U.S.	D10	79
Montague Peak, mtn., Ak., U.S.	g18	79
Montague Strait, strt., Ak., U.S.	h18	79
Montaigu, Fr.	F5	10
Montalbán, Spain	E11	12
Montalcino, Italy	F6	14
Montalegre, Port.	D4	12
Mont Alto, Pa., U.S.	G6	115
Montana, Bul.	F7	16
Montana, state, U.S.	D7	103
Montánchez, Spain	F5	12
Montargis, Fr.	D9	10
Montauban, Fr.	H8	10
Montauk, N.Y., U.S.	m17	109
Montbard, Fr.	E11	10
Montbéliard, Fr.	E13	10
Mont Belvieu, Tx., U.S.	E5	120
Montblanch, Spain	D13	12
Montbrison, Fr.	G11	10
Montcalm, co., Mi., U.S.	E5	99
Montchanin, De., U.S.	h7	85
Montclair, Ca., U.S.	m13	82
Montclair, N.J., U.S.	B4	107
Mont Clare, Pa., U.S.	o19	115
Mont-de-Marsan, Fr.	I6	10
Montdidier, Fr.	C9	10
Monteagle, Tn., U.S.	D8	119
Monteagudo, Bol.	G6	54
Monte Azul, Braz.	C7	57
Montebello, Que., Can.	D3	74
Montebello, Ca., U.S.	m12	82
Monte Caseros, Arg.	C5	56
Montecatini Terme, Italy	F5	14
Monte Comán, Arg.	C3	56
Montecristi, Dom. Rep.	E12	64
Montecristi, Ec.	H2	58
Montefiascone, Italy	G7	14
Montego Bay, Jam.	E9	64
Montegut, La., U.S.	E5	95
Montélimar, Fr.	H11	10
Montello, Nv., U.S.	B7	105
Montello, Wi., U.S.	E4	126
Montemorelos, Mex.	E10	62
Montemor-o-Novo, Port.	G3	12
Montendre, Fr.	G6	10
Montenero di Bisaccia, Italy	H9	14
Montepuez, Moz.	D8	44
Montepulciano, Italy	F6	14
Monte Quemado, Arg.	B4	56
Montereau-faut-Yonne, Fr.	D9	10
Monterey, Ca., U.S.	D3	82
Monterey, Tn., U.S.	C8	119
Monterey, co., Ca., U.S.	D3	82
Monterey Bay, b., Ca., U.S.	D2	82
Monterey Park, Ca., U.S.	m12	82
Montería, Col.	C5	58
Monterotondo, Italy	G7	14
Monterrey, Mex.	E9	62
Montesano, Wa., U.S.	C2	124
Monte Sant'Angelo, Italy	H10	14
Montes Claros, Braz.	D7	57
Montevallo, Al., U.S.	B3	78
Montevarchi, Italy	F6	14
Montevideo, Mn., U.S.	F3	100
Montevideo, Ur.	C5	56
Monte Vista, Co., U.S.	D4	83
Montezuma, Ga., U.S.	D2	87
Montezuma, In., U.S.	E3	91
Montezuma, Ia., U.S.	C5	92
Montezuma, Ks., U.S.	E3	93
Montezuma, co., Co., U.S.	D2	83
Montezuma Castle National Monument, Az., U.S.	C4	80
Montezuma Peak, mtn., Az., U.S.	D3	80
Montgomery, Al., U.S.	C3	78
Montgomery, Il., U.S.	B5	90
Montgomery, La., U.S.	C3	95
Montgomery, Mn., U.S.	F5	100
Montgomery, N.Y., U.S.	D6	109
Montgomery, Oh., U.S.	o13	112
Montgomery, Pa., U.S.	D8	115
Montgomery, W.V., U.S.	C3	125
Montgomery, co., Al., U.S.	C3	78
Montgomery, co., Ar., U.S.	C2	81
Montgomery, co., Ga., U.S.	D4	87
Montgomery, co., Il., U.S.	D4	90
Montgomery, co., In., U.S.	D4	91
Montgomery, co., Ia., U.S.	C2	92
Montgomery, co., Ks., U.S.	E8	93
Montgomery, co., Ky., U.S.	B6	94
Montgomery, co., Md., U.S.	B3	97
Montgomery, co., Ms., U.S.	B4	101
Montgomery, co., Mo., U.S.	C6	102
Montgomery, co., N.Y., U.S.	C6	109
Montgomery, co., N.C., U.S.	B3	110
Montgomery, co., Oh., U.S.	C1	112
Montgomery, co., Pa., U.S.	F11	115
Montgomery, co., Tn., U.S.	A4	119
Montgomery, co., Tx., U.S.	D5	120
Montgomery, co., Va., U.S.	C2	123
Montgomery City, Mo., U.S.	C6	102
Monthey, Switz.	F13	10
Monticello, Ar., U.S.	D4	81
Monticello, Fl., U.S.	B3	86
Monticello, Ga., U.S.	C3	87
Monticello, Il., U.S.	C5	90
Monticello, In., U.S.	C4	91
Monticello, Ia., U.S.	B6	92
Monticello, Ky., U.S.	D5	94
Monticello, Mn., U.S.	E5	100
Monticello, Ms., U.S.	D3	101
Monticello, N.Y., U.S.	D6	109
Monticello, Ut., U.S.	F6	121
Monticello, Wi., U.S.	F4	126
Montichiari, Italy	D5	14
Montignac, Fr.	G8	10
Montijo, Port.	G3	12
Montijo, Spain	G5	12
Montilla, Spain	H7	12
Montivilliers, Fr.	C7	10
Mont-Joli, Que., Can.	A9	74
Mont-Laurier, Que., Can.	C2	74
Mont-Louis, Fr.	J9	10
Montluçon, Fr.	F9	10
Montmagny, Que., Can.	C7	74
Montmorenci, S.C., U.S.	D4	117
Montmorency, co., Mi., U.S.	C6	99
Montmorillon, Fr.	F7	10
Montmort, Fr.	D10	10
Montoro, Spain	G7	12
Montour, co., Pa., U.S.	D8	115
Montour Falls, N.Y., U.S.	C4	109
Montoursville, Pa., U.S.	D8	115
Montpelier, Id., U.S.	G7	89
Montpelier, In., U.S.	C7	91
Montpelier, Oh., U.S.	A1	112
Montpelier, Vt., U.S.	C3	122
Montpellier, Fr.	I10	10
Montréal, Que., Can.	D4	74
Montreal, Wi., U.S.	B3	126
Montréal, Île de, i., Que., Can.	q19	74
Montreal Lake, l., Sask., Can.	C3	75
Montréal-Nord, Que., Can.	p19	74
Montreat, N.C., U.S.	f10	110
Montreuil-Bellay, Fr.	E6	10
Montreux, Switz.	F13	10
Mont-Rolland, Que., Can.	D3	74
Montrose, B.C., Can.	E9	69
Montrose, Scot., U.K.	E10	7
Montrose, Al., U.S.	E2	78
Montrose, Co., U.S.	C3	83
Montrose, Ia., U.S.	D6	92
Montrose, Mi., U.S.	E7	99
Montrose, Pa., U.S.	C10	115
Montrose, Va., U.S.	m18	123
Montrose, co., Co., U.S.	C2	83
Mont-Royal, Que., Can.	p19	74
Montserrat, dep., N.A.	F16	64
Mont-Tremblant, Parc Provincial du, Que., Can.	C3	74
Montvale, N.J., U.S.	A4	107
Montville, Ct., U.S.	D7	84
Monument, Co., U.S.	B6	83
Monument Beach, Ma., U.S.	C6	98
Monument Peak, mtn., Co., U.S.	B3	83
Monument Peak, mtn., Id., U.S.	G4	89
Monument Valley, val., Az., U.S.	A5	80
Monywa, Mya.	C3	34
Monza, Italy	D4	14
Monzón, Spain	D12	12
Moodus, Ct., U.S.	D6	84
Moodus Reservoir, res., Ct., U.S.	C6	84
Moody, Tx., U.S.	D4	120
Moody, co., S.D., U.S.	C9	118
Moon Lake, l., Ms., U.S.	A3	101
Moora, Austl.	F3	50
Moorcroft, Wy., U.S.	B8	127
Moore, Ok., U.S.	B4	113
Moore, co., N.C., U.S.	B3	110
Moore, co., Tn., U.S.	B5	119
Moore, co., Tx., U.S.	B2	120
Moore Dam, U.S.	B3	106
Moorefield, W.V., U.S.	B6	125
Moore Haven, Fl., U.S.	F5	86
Mooreland, Ok., U.S.	A2	113
Moore Reservoir, res., U.S.	B3	106
Moores Creek National Military Park, N.C., U.S.	C4	110
Moores Hill, In., U.S.	F7	91
Moorestown, N.J., U.S.	D3	107
Mooresville, In., U.S.	E5	91
Mooresville, N.C., U.S.	B2	110
Moorhead, Mn., U.S.	D2	100
Moorhead, Ms., U.S.	B3	101
Mooringsport, La., U.S.	B2	95
Moose, stm., N.H., U.S.	B4	106
Moose, stm., N.Y., U.S.	B5	109
Moose, stm., Vt., U.S.	B5	122
Moosehead Lake, l., Me., U.S.	C3	96
Moose Jaw, stm., Sask., Can.	G3	75
Moose Lake, Man., Can.	C1	70
Moose Lake, Mn., U.S.	D6	100
Moose Lake, l., Wi., U.S.	B2	126
Mooseleuk Stream, stm., Me., U.S.	B4	96
Mooselookmeguntic Lake, l., Me., U.S.	D2	96
Moose Mountain Creek, stm., Sask., Can.	H4	75
Moose Mountain Provincial Park, Sask., Can.	H4	75
Moosic, Pa., U.S.	m18	115
Moosup, Ct., U.S.	C8	84
Moosup, stm., U.S.	C1	116
Mopang Lake, l., Me., U.S.	D5	96
Mopti, Mali	F5	42
Moquegua, Peru	G4	54
Mora, Port.	G3	12
Mora, Spain	F8	12
Mora, Swe.	F10	6
Mora, Mn., U.S.	E5	100
Mora, N.M., U.S.	B4	108
Mora, co., N.M., U.S.	A5	108
Mora, stm., N.M., U.S.	B5	108
Morādābād, India	F8	38
Morada Nova de Minas, Braz.	E6	57
Morafenobe, Madag.	E8	44
Moraleda, Canal, strt., Chile	E2	56
Morant Cays, is., Jam.	F9	64
Mor'arovskij Zaton, Russia	F10	24
Moratuwa, Sri L.	I5	37
Morava, hist. reg., Czech.	F17	8
Morava (March), stm., Eur.	G16	8
Moravia, Ia., U.S.	D5	92
Moravia see Morava, hist. reg., Czech.	F17	8
Morawhanna, Guy.	C13	58
Moray Firth, est., Scot., U.K.	D9	7
Morden, Man., Can.	E2	70
More, Ben, mtn., Scot., U.K.	E8	7
More Assynt, Ben, mtn., Scot., U.K.	C8	7
Moreau, stm., S.D., U.S.	B3	118
Moreauville, La., U.S.	C4	95
Morecambe, Eng., U.K.	G10	7
Moree, Austl.	E9	50
Morehead, Ky., U.S.	B6	94
Morehead City, N.C., U.S.	C6	110
Morehouse, Mo., U.S.	E8	102
Morehouse, co., La., U.S.	B4	95
Morelia, Mex.	H9	62
Morella, Spain	E11	12
Morena, India	G8	38
Morenci, Az., U.S.	D6	80
Morenci, Mi., U.S.	G6	99
Moresby Island, i., B.C., Can.	C2	69
Moreuil, Fr.	C9	10
Morey, Lake, l., Vt., U.S.	D4	122
Morey Peak, mtn., Nv., U.S.	E5	105
Morgan, Mn., U.S.	F4	100
Morgan, Ut., U.S.	B4	121
Morgan, co., Al., U.S.	A3	78
Morgan, co., Co., U.S.	A7	83
Morgan, co., Ga., U.S.	C3	87
Morgan, co., Il., U.S.	D3	90
Morgan, co., In., U.S.	F5	91
Morgan, co., Ky., U.S.	C6	94
Morgan, co., Mo., U.S.	C5	102
Morgan, co., Oh., U.S.	C4	112
Morgan, co., Tn., U.S.	C9	119
Morgan, co., Ut., U.S.	B4	121
Morgan, co., W.V., U.S.	B6	125
Morgan City, La., U.S.	E4	95
Morganfield, Ky., U.S.	C2	94
Morgan Hill, Ca., U.S.	D3	82
Morgan Island, i., S.C., U.S.	G6	117
Morgan Point, c., Ct., U.S.	E4	84
Morganton, N.C., U.S.	B1	110
Morgantown, In., U.S.	F5	91
Morgantown, Ky., U.S.	C3	94
Morgantown, Ms., U.S.	D2	101
Morgantown, Tn., U.S.	D8	119
Morgantown, W.V., U.S.	B5	125
Morganza, La., U.S.	D4	95
Mori, Japan	q18	30a
Moriah, Mount, mtn., Nv., U.S.	D7	105
Moriarty, N.M., U.S.	C3	108
Morinville, Alta., Can.	C4	68
Morioka, Japan	C14	30
Morkoka, stm., Russia	D16	24
Morlaix, Fr.	D3	10
Morley, Mo., U.S.	D8	102
Mormon Peak, mtn., Nv., U.S.	G7	105
Morning Sun, Ia., U.S.	C6	92
Mornington Island, i., Austl.	C7	50
Morobe, Pap. N. Gui.	m16	50a
Morocco, In., U.S.	C3	91
Morocco, ctry., Afr.	B4	42
Morogoro, Tan.	C7	44
Moro Gulf, b., Phil.	D7	32
Morombe, Madag.	F8	44
Morón, Cuba	C8	64
Morondava, Madag.	F8	44
Morón de la Frontera, Spain	H6	12
Moroni, Com.	D8	44
Moroni, Ut., U.S.	D4	121
Morošečnoje, Russia	F25	24
Morotai, i., Indon.	E8	32
Morrill, Ne., U.S.	C2	104
Morrill, co., Ne., U.S.	C2	104
Morrilton, Ar., U.S.	B3	81
Morrinhos, Braz.	D4	57
Morris, Man., Can.	E3	70
Morris, Al., U.S.	B3	78
Morris, Il., U.S.	B5	90
Morris, Mn., U.S.	E3	100
Morris, Ok., U.S.	B6	113
Morris, co., Ks., U.S.	D7	93
Morris, co., N.J., U.S.	B3	107
Morris, co., Tx., U.S.	C5	120
Morrisburg, Ont., Can.	C9	73
Morris Island, i., S.C., U.S.	F8	117
Morrison, Il., U.S.	B4	90
Morrison, Ok., U.S.	A4	113
Morrison, co., Mn., U.S.	D4	100
Morrison City, Tn., U.S.	C11	119

Name	Map Ref	Page
Morrisonville, Il., U.S.	D4	90
Morrisonville, N.Y., U.S.	f11	109
Morris Plains, N.J., U.S.	B4	107
Morristown, In., U.S.	E6	91
Morristown, Mn., U.S.	F5	100
Morristown, N.J., U.S.	B4	107
Morristown, Tn., U.S.	C10	119
Morristown National Historical Park, N.J., U.S.	B3	107
Morrisville, N.Y., U.S.	C5	109
Morrisville, Pa., U.S.	F12	115
Morrisville, Vt., U.S.	B3	122
Morro, Ec.	I2	58
Morro, Punta, c., Chile	B2	56
Morro Bay, Ca., U.S.	E3	82
Morro do Chapéu, Braz.	F10	54
Morrow, Ga., U.S.	C2	87
Morrow, Oh., U.S.	C1	112
Morrow, co., Oh., U.S.	B3	112
Morrow, co., Or., U.S.	B7	114
Moršansk, Russia	H24	18
Morse, La., U.S.	D3	95
Morse Reservoir, res., In., U.S.	D5	91
Morses Creek, stm., N.J., U.S.	k8	107
Mortagne, Fr.	D7	10
Mortagne-sur-Sèvre, Fr.	E6	10
Mortara, Italy	D3	14
Mortes, Rio das, stm., Braz.	G8	54
Morton, Il., U.S.	C4	90
Morton, Ms., U.S.	C4	101
Morton, Tx., U.S.	C1	120
Morton, Wa., U.S.	C3	124
Morton, co., Ks., U.S.	E2	93
Morton, co., N.D., U.S.	C4	111
Morton Grove, Il., U.S.	h9	90
Morton Pass, Wy., U.S.	E7	127
Mortons Gap, Ky., U.S.	C2	94
Morven, mtn., Scot., U.K.	C9	7
Morvi, India	I4	38
Morwell, Austl.	G9	50
Mosbach, Ger.	F9	8
Moscos Islands, is., Mya.	G4	34
Moscow, Id., U.S.	C2	89
Moscow, Pa., U.S.	m18	115
Moscow Mills, Mo., U.S.	C7	102
Moscow see Moskva, Russia	F20	18
Mosel (Moselle), stm., Eur.	F6	8
Moselle, Ms., U.S.	D4	101
Moselle (Mosel), stm., Eur.	F6	8
Moses Coulee, val., Wa., U.S.	B6	124
Moses Lake, Wa., U.S.	B6	124
Moses Lake, l., Wa., U.S.	B6	124
Mosheim, Tn., U.S.	C11	119
Moshi, Tan.	B7	44
Mosinee, Wi., U.S.	D4	126
Mosjøen, Nor.	D9	6
Moskva (Moscow), Russia	F20	18
Mosquera, Col.	F3	58
Mosquito Creek Lake, res., Oh., U.S.	A5	112
Mosquito Lagoon, b., Fl., U.S.	D6	86
Mosquitos, Golfo de los, b., Pan.	J7	64
Moss, Nor.	G8	6
Mossaka, Congo	B3	44
Moss Bluff, La., U.S.	D2	95
Mosselbaai, S. Afr.	H4	44
Mossendjo, Congo	B2	44
Mossoró, Braz.	E11	54
Moss Point, Ms., U.S.	E5	101
Most, Czech.	E13	8
Mostaganem, Alg.	A6	42
Mostar, Bos.	F12	14
Mostardas, Braz.	C6	56
Møsting, Kap, c., Grnld.	D24	66
Moswansicut Pond, l., R.I., U.S.	C3	116
Mota del Marqués, Spain	D6	12
Motala, Swe.	G10	6
Motherwell, Scot., U.K.	F8	7
Motīhāri, India	G11	38
Motilla del Palancar, Spain	F10	12
Motley, co., Tx., U.S.	B2	120
Motril, Spain	I8	12
Mott, N.D., U.S.	C3	111
Motueka, N.Z.	D4	52
Motul de Felipe Carrillo Puerto, Mex.	G15	62
Motygino, Russia	F12	24
Mouchoir Passage, strt., N.A.	D12	64
Moudjéria, Maur.	E3	42
Mouila, Gabon	B2	44
Moulamein Creek, stm., Austl.	G8	50
Moulins, Fr.	F10	10
Moulmeingyun, Mya.	F3	34
Moulouya, Oued, stm., Mor.	B5	42
Moulton, Al., U.S.	A2	78
Moulton, Ia., U.S.	D5	92
Moultrie, Ga., U.S.	E3	87
Moultrie, co., Il., U.S.	D5	90
Moultrie, Lake, res., S.C., U.S.	E7	117
Mound, Mn., U.S.	n11	100
Mound Bayou, Ms., U.S.	B3	101
Mound City, Il., U.S.	F4	90
Mound City, Ks., U.S.	D9	93
Mound City, Mo., U.S.	A2	102
Mound City Group National Monument, Oh., U.S.	C2	112
Moundou, Chad	G9	42
Moundridge, Ks., U.S.	D6	93
Mounds, Il., U.S.	F4	90
Mounds, Ok., U.S.	B5	113
Mounds View, Mn., U.S.	m12	100
Moundsville, W.V., U.S.	B4	125
Moundville, Al., U.S.	C2	78
Mountainair, N.M., U.S.	C3	108
Mountainaire, Az., U.S.	B4	80
Mountain Brook, Al., U.S.	g7	78
Mountain City, Ga., U.S.	B3	87
Mountain City, Nv., U.S.	B6	105
Mountain City, Tn., U.S.	C12	119
Mountain Fork, stm., U.S.	C7	113
Mountain Grove, Mo., U.S.	D5	102
Mountain Home, Ar., U.S.	A3	81
Mountain Home, Id., U.S.	F3	89
Mountain Home Air Force Base, mil., Id., U.S.	F3	89
Mountain Iron, Mn., U.S.	C6	100
Mountain Lake, Mn., U.S.	G4	100
Mountain Lake Park, Md., U.S.	m12	97
Mountain Nile (Baḥr al-Jabal), stm., Sudan	G12	42
Mountain Pine, Ar., U.S.	C2	81
Mountainside, N.J., U.S.	B4	107
Mountain View, Ar., U.S.	B3	81
Mountain View, Ca., U.S.	k8	82
Mountain View, Mo., U.S.	D6	102
Mountain View, N.M., U.S.	C3	108
Mountain View, Ok., U.S.	B3	113
Mountain View, Wy., U.S.	E2	127
Mountain Village, Ak., U.S.	C7	79
Mount Airy, Md., U.S.	B3	97
Mount Airy, N.C., U.S.	A2	110
Mount Albert, Ont., Can.	C5	73
Mount Angel, Or., U.S.	B4	114
Mount Arlington, N.J., U.S.	B3	107
Mount Ayr, Ia., U.S.	D3	92
Mount Carmel, Il., U.S.	E6	90
Mount Carmel, Oh., U.S.	o13	112
Mount Carmel, Pa., U.S.	E9	115
Mount Carmel [-Mitchell's Brook-Saint Catherine's], Newf., Can.	E5	72
Mount Carroll, Il., U.S.	A4	90
Mount Clare, W.V., U.S.	B4	125
Mount Clemens, Mi., U.S.	F8	99
Mount Desert Island, i., Me., U.S.	D4	96
Mount Dora, Fl., U.S.	D5	86
Mount Forest, Ont., Can.	D4	73
Mount Gambier, Austl.	G8	50
Mount Gay, W.V., U.S.	D2	125
Mount Gilead, N.C., U.S.	B3	110
Mount Gilead, Oh., U.S.	B3	112
Mount Healthy, Oh., U.S.	o12	112
Mount Holly, N.J., U.S.	D3	107
Mount Holly, N.C., U.S.	B1	110
Mount Holly Springs, Pa., U.S.	F7	115
Mount Hope, Austl.	F7	50
Mount Hope, Ks., U.S.	E6	93
Mount Hope, W.V., U.S.	D3	125
Mount Hope, stm., Ct., U.S.	B7	84
Mount Hope Bay, b., U.S.	D6	116
Mount Horeb, Wi., U.S.	E4	126
Mount Ida, Ar., U.S.	C2	81
Mount Isa, Austl.	D7	50
Mount Jackson, Va., U.S.	B4	123
Mount Jewett, Pa., U.S.	C4	115
Mount Joy, Pa., U.S.	F9	115
Mount Juliet, Tn., U.S.	A5	119
Mount Kisco, N.Y., U.S.	D7	109
Mount Lebanon, Pa., U.S.	F1	115
Mount Magnet, Austl.	E3	50
Mount Morris, Il., U.S.	A4	90
Mount Morris, Mi., U.S.	E7	99
Mount Morris, N.Y., U.S.	C3	109
Mount Olive, Al., U.S.	B3	78
Mount Olive, Il., U.S.	D4	90
Mount Olive, Ms., U.S.	D4	101
Mount Olive, N.C., U.S.	B4	110
Mount Olive, Tn., U.S.	n14	119
Mount Orab, Oh., U.S.	C2	112
Mount Pearl, Newf., Can.	E5	72
Mount Penn, Pa., U.S.	F10	115
Mount Pleasant, Ia., U.S.	D6	92
Mount Pleasant, Mi., U.S.	E6	99
Mount Pleasant, N.C., U.S.	B2	110
Mount Pleasant, Pa., U.S.	F2	115
Mount Pleasant, S.C., U.S.	F8	117
Mount Pleasant, Tn., U.S.	B4	119
Mount Pleasant, Tx., U.S.	C5	120
Mount Pleasant, Ut., U.S.	D4	121
Mount Pocono, Pa., U.S.	D11	115
Mount Prospect, Il., U.S.	A6	90
Mount Pulaski, Il., U.S.	C4	90
Mountrail, co., N.D., U.S.	A3	111
Mount Rainier, Md., U.S.	f9	97
Mount Rainier National Park, Wa., U.S.	C4	124
Mount Revelstoke National Park, B.C., Can.	D8	69
Mount Rogers National Recreation Area, Va., U.S.	D1	123
Mount Rushmore National Memorial, hist., S.D., U.S.	D2	118
Mount Savage, Md., U.S.	k13	97
Mount Shasta, Ca., U.S.	B2	82
Mount Sterling, Il., U.S.	D3	90
Mount Sterling, Ky., U.S.	B6	94
Mount Sterling, Oh., U.S.	C2	112
Mount Uniacke, N.S., Can.	E6	71
Mount Union, Pa., U.S.	F6	115
Mount Vernon, Al., U.S.	D1	78
Mount Vernon, Ga., U.S.	D4	87
Mount Vernon, Il., U.S.	E5	90
Mount Vernon, In., U.S.	I2	91
Mount Vernon, Ia., U.S.	C6	92
Mount Vernon, Ky., U.S.	C5	94
Mount Vernon, Mo., U.S.	D4	102
Mount Vernon, N.Y., U.S.	h13	109
Mount Vernon, Oh., U.S.	B3	112
Mount Vernon, Tx., U.S.	C5	120
Mount Vernon, Wa., U.S.	A3	124
Mount View, R.I., U.S.	D4	116
Mount Washington, Ky., U.S.	B4	94
Mount Wolf, Pa., U.S.	F8	115
Mount Zion, Il., U.S.	D5	90
Moura, Braz.	D6	54
Moura, Port.	G4	12
Mourne Mountains, mts., N. Ire., U.K.	G6	7
Moussoro, Chad	F9	42
Moutong, Indon.	E7	32
Moville, Ia., U.S.	B1	92
Moweaqua, Il., U.S.	D4	90
Mower, co., Mn., U.S.	G6	100
Moxee City, Wa., U.S.	C5	124
Moxos, Llanos de, pl., Bol.	G6	54
Moyahua, Mex.	G8	62
Moyale, Kenya	H2	46
Moyen Atlas, mts., Mor.	B5	42
Moyeuvre-Grande, Fr.	C13	10
Moyock, N.C., U.S.	A6	110
Moyu, China	B8	38
Možajsk, Russia	F19	18
Mozambique, ctry., Afr.	E6	44
Mozambique Channel, strt., Afr.	E8	44
Mozyr', Bela.	G3	22
Mpanda, Tan.	C6	44
Mpika, Zam.	D6	44
Mrkonjić Grad, Bos.	E12	14
Msaken, Tun.	N5	14
Mtwara, Tan.	D8	44
Muang Khammouan, Laos	F8	34
Muang Pakxan, Laos	E7	34
Muar, Malay.	M7	34
Muaratewe, Indon.	F5	32
Muāri, Rās, c., Pak.	H2	38
Mücheln, Ger.	D11	8
Muchinga Mountains, mts., Zam.	D6	44
Muckleshoot Indian Reservation, Wa., U.S.	f11	124
Mud, stm., Ky., U.S.	C3	94
Mud, stm., Mn., U.S.	B3	100
Mud, stm., W.V., U.S.	C2	125
Mudanjiang, China	C12	26
Mud Creek, stm., Ok., U.S.	C4	113
Muddy Boggy Creek, stm., Ok., U.S.	C6	113
Muddy Creek, stm., Ut., U.S.	E4	121
Muddy Creek, stm., Wy., U.S.	E2	127
Muddy Creek, stm., Wy., U.S.	E5	127
Muddy Creek, stm., Wy., U.S.	D6	127
Muddy Creek, stm., Wy., U.S.	C4	127
Muddy Mountains, mts., Nv., U.S.	G7	105
Muddy Peak, mtn., Nv., U.S.	G7	105
Mud Lake, l., Me., U.S.	A4	96
Mud Lake, l., Nv., U.S.	F4	105
Mudon, Mya.	F4	34
Muenster, Tx., U.S.	C4	120
Mufulira, Zam.	D5	44
Mu Gia, Deo (Mu Gia Pass), Asia	F8	34
Muğla, Tur.	H13	4
Mühldorf, Ger.	G12	8
Muhlenberg, co., Ky., U.S.	C2	94
Mühlhausen, Ger.	D10	8
Mühlviertel, reg., Aus.	G14	8
Muhola, Fin.	E15	6
Muirkirk, Md., U.S.	B4	97
Muiron Islands, is., Austl.	D2	50
Muir Woods National Monument, Ca., U.S.	h7	82
Mukden see Shenyang, China	C11	26
Mukilteo, Wa., U.S.	B3	124
Mukwonago, Wi., U.S.	F5	126
Mula, Spain	G10	12
Mulanje, Mwi.	E7	44
Mulberry, Ar., U.S.	B1	81
Mulberry, Fl., U.S.	E4	86
Mulberry, In., U.S.	D4	91
Mulberry, N.C., U.S.	A1	110
Mulberry, stm., Ar., U.S.	B1	81
Mulberry Fork, stm., Al., U.S.	B3	78
Muldraugh, Ky., U.S.	C4	94
Muldrow, Ok., U.S.	B7	113
Muleshoe, Tx., U.S.	B1	120
Mulgrave, N.S., Can.	D8	71
Mulhacén, mtn., Spain	H8	12
Mulhouse, Fr.	E14	10
Mull, Island of, i., Scot., U.K.	E6	7
Mullan, Id., U.S.	B3	89
Mullan Pass, Mt., U.S.	D4	103
Mullens, W.V., U.S.	D3	125
Muller, Pegunungan, mts., Indon.	E5	32
Mullet Key, i., Fl., U.S.	p10	86
Mullett Lake, l., Mi., U.S.	C6	99
Mullewa, Austl.	E3	50
Mullica, stm., N.J., U.S.	D3	107
Mullins, S.C., U.S.	C9	117
Multān, Pak.	E4	38
Multnomah, co., Or., U.S.	B4	114
Mulvane, Ks., U.S.	E6	93
Mumbwa, Zam.	D5	44
Mummy Range, mts., Co., U.S.	A5	83
Muna, Pulau, i., Indon.	F7	32
Muncar, Indon.	n17	33a
München (Munich), Ger.	G11	8
Muncie, In., U.S.	D7	91
Muncy, Pa., U.S.	D8	115
Munday, Tx., U.S.	C3	120
Mundelein, Il., U.S.	A5	90
Münden, Ger.	D9	8
Munford, Al., U.S.	B4	78
Munford, Tn., U.S.	B2	119
Munfordville, Ky., U.S.	C4	94
Mungbere, Zaire	H11	42
Munhall, Pa., U.S.	k14	115
Munhango, Ang.	D3	44
Munich see München, Ger.	G11	8
Munising, Mi., U.S.	B4	99
Munster, Ger.	C10	8
Münster, Ger.	D7	8
Munster, In., U.S.	A2	91
Munster, hist. reg., Ire.	I4	7
Munsungan Lake, l., Me., U.S.	B3	96
Munuscong Lake, l., Mi., U.S.	B6	99
Muong Sing, Laos	D6	34
Muqayshiṭ, i., U.A.E.	D5	46
Muqdisho, Som.	H4	46
Mur (Mura), stm., Eur.	I15	8
Mura (Mur), stm., Eur.	I16	8
Murat, Fr.	G9	10
Murat, stm., Tur.	H16	4
Murau, Aus.	H14	8
Muravera, Italy	J4	14
Murča, Port.	D4	12
Murchison, stm., Austl.	E3	50
Murcia, Spain	H10	12
Murderkill, stm., De., U.S.	D4	85
Murdo, S.D., U.S.	D5	118
Mureș (Maros), stm., Eur.	C5	16
Muret, Fr.	I8	10
Murfreesboro, Ar., U.S.	C2	81
Murfreesboro, N.C., U.S.	A5	110
Murfreesboro, Tn., U.S.	B5	119
Mūrīān, Hāmūn-e, l., Iran	C6	46
Murmansk, Russia	D4	22
Murom, Russia	F25	18
Muroran, Japan	q18	30a
Muros, Spain	C2	12
Muroto, Japan	I7	30
Muroto-zaki, c., Japan	I7	30
Murphy, Mo., U.S.	g13	102
Murphy, N.C., U.S.	f8	110
Murphy Island, i., S.C., U.S.	E9	117
Murphysboro, Il., U.S.	F4	90
Murray, Ia., U.S.	C4	92
Murray, Ky., U.S.	f9	94
Murray, Ut., U.S.	C4	121
Murray, co., Ga., U.S.	B2	87
Murray, co., Mn., U.S.	F3	100
Murray, co., Ok., U.S.	C4	113
Murray, stm., Austl.	F7	50
Murray, Lake, res., Ok., U.S.	C4	113
Murray, Lake, res., S.C., U.S.	C5	117
Murray Head, c., P.E.I., Can.	C7	71
Murraysburg, S. Afr.	H4	44
Murrayville, Ga., U.S.	B3	87
Murrells Inlet, S.C., U.S.	D9	117
Murrells Inlet, b., S.C., U.S.	D10	117
Murten, Switz.	F14	10
Murukta, Russia	D14	24
Murwāra, India	I9	38
Murwillumbah, Austl.	E10	50
Mürzzuschlag, Aus.	H15	8
Muş, Tur.	H16	4
Musayʿīd, Qatar	D5	46
Muscat and Oman see Oman, ctry., Asia	D6	46
Muscatatuck, stm., In., U.S.	G5	91
Muscatine, Ia., U.S.	C6	92
Muscatine, co., Ia., U.S.	C6	92
Muscat see Masqaṭ, Oman	D6	46
Mus-Chaja, Gora, mtn., Russia	E22	24
Muscle Shoals, Al., U.S.	A2	78
Musclow, Mount, mtn., B.C., Can.	C4	69
Muscoda, Wi., U.S.	E3	126
Muscogee, co., Ga., U.S.	D2	87
Musconetcong, stm., N.J., U.S.	B4	107
Muscooten Bay, l., Il., U.S.	C3	90
Muse, Pa., U.S.	F1	115
Musgrave, Austl.	B8	50
Musgrave Harbour, Newf., Can.	D5	72
Musgrave Ranges, mts., Austl.	E6	50
Musgravetown, Newf., Can.	D5	72
Mushin, Nig.	G6	42
Muskeg Bay, b., Mn., U.S.	B3	100
Muskeget Island, i., Ma., U.S.	D7	98
Muskego, Wi., U.S.	F5	126
Muskego Lake, l., Wi., U.S.	n11	126
Muskegon, Mi., U.S.	E4	99
Muskegon, co., Mi., U.S.	E4	99
Muskegon, stm., Mi., U.S.	E4	99
Muskegon Heights, Mi., U.S.	E4	99
Muskegon Lake, l., Mi., U.S.	E4	99
Muskingum, co., Oh., U.S.	B4	112
Muskingum, stm., Oh., U.S.	C4	112
Muskogee, Ok., U.S.	B6	113
Muskogee, co., Ok., U.S.	B6	113
Musoma, Tan.	B6	44
Musquacook Lakes, l., Me., U.S.	B3	96
Musquodoboit Harbour, N.S., Can.	E6	71
Musselshell, co., Mt., U.S.	D8	103
Musselshell, stm., Mt., U.S.	D9	103
Mussidan, Fr.	G7	10
Mussuma, Ang.	D4	44
Mustafakemalpaşa, Tur.	I12	16
Mustang, Ok., U.S.	B4	113
Mustinka, stm., Mn., U.S.	E2	100
Mut, Tur.	A3	40
Mutare, Zimb.	E6	44
Mutoraj, Russia	E14	24
Mutsu, Japan	A14	30
Mutsu-wan, b., Japan	A13	30
Mutton Mountains, mts., Or., U.S.	C5	114
Muzaffarābād, Pak.	C5	38
Muzaffarnagar, India	F7	38
Muzaffarpur, India	G11	38
Muzon, Cape, c., Ak., U.S.	n23	79
Muztag, mtn., China	B9	38
Muztag, mtn., China	B12	38
Mvuma, Zimb.	E6	44
Mwanza, Tan.	B6	44
Mweelrea, mtn., Ire.	H3	7
Mweka, Zaire	B4	44
Mwenezi, Zimb.	F6	44
Mweru, Lake, l., Afr.	C5	44
Mwinilunga, Zam.	D4	44
Myakka, stm., Fl., U.S.	E4	86
Myanaung, Mya.	E3	34
Myaungmya, Mya.	F3	34
Myerstown, Pa., U.S.	F9	115
Myingyan, Mya.	D3	34
Myitkyinā, Mya.	B4	34
Mykolayiv, Ukr.	H4	22
Myllymäki, Fin.	E15	6
Mymensingh, Bngl.	I14	38
Mynämäki, Fin.	F13	6
Myrskylä (Mörskom), Fin.	F15	6
Myrtle Beach, S.C., U.S.	D10	117
Myrtle Beach Air Force Base, mil., S.C., U.S.	D10	117
Myrtle Grove, Fl., U.S.	u14	86
Myrtle Point, Or., U.S.	D2	114
Mysen, Nor.	G8	6
Mysore, India	F4	37
Mys Šmidta, Russia	D30	24
Mystic, Ct., U.S.	D8	84
Mystic Lakes, l., Ma., U.S.	g11	98
My Tho, Viet.	I9	34
Mytišči, Russia	F20	18
Mzimba, Mwi.	D6	44
Mzuzu, Mwi.	D6	44

N

Name	Map Ref	Page
Naalehu, Hi., U.S.	D6	88
Naas, Ire.	H6	7
Nabadwīp, India	I13	38
Nabereżnyje Čelny, Russia	F8	22
Nabeul, Tun.	M5	14
Nabī Shuʿayb, Jabal an-, mtn., Yemen	E3	46
Nabnasset, Ma., U.S.	A5	98
Nābulus, W. Bank	C4	40
Nacala-Velha, Moz.	D8	44
Naches, stm., Wa., U.S.	C5	124
Nachingwea, Tan.	D7	44
Nachodka, Russia	I20	24
Nacimiento, Lake, res., Ca., U.S.	E3	82
Naco, Mex.	B5	62
Naco, Az., U.S.	F6	80
Nacogdoches, Tx., U.S.	D5	120
Nacogdoches, co., Tx., U.S.	D5	120
Nadiād, India	I5	38
Nadym, stm., Russia	E8	24
Næstved, Den.	I8	6
Naga, Phil.	r20	32
Nagahama, Japan	G9	30
Nagaland, state, India	H16	38
Nagano, Japan	F11	30
Nagaoka, Japan	E11	30
Nāgappattinam, India	G5	37
Nagasaki, Japan	J2	30
Nāgaur, India	G5	38
Nāgda, India	I6	38
Nāgercoil, India	H4	37
Nago, Japan	y27	31b
Nagornyj, Russia	F18	24
Nagoya, Japan	G9	30
Nāgpur, India	B5	37
Nags Head, N.C., U.S.	B7	110
Nagykanizsa, Hung.	I16	8
Nagykőrös, Hung.	H19	8
Naha, Japan	y27	31b
Nahant, Ma., U.S.	g12	98
Nahariya, Isr.	C4	40
Nahmakanta Lake, l., Me., U.S.	C3	96
Nahunta, Ga., U.S.	E5	87
Naidong, China	F14	38
Nain, Newf., Can.	g9	72
Nāʾīn, Iran	B5	46
Nairn, Scot., U.K.	D9	7
Nairobi, Kenya	B7	44
Najafābād, Iran	B5	46
Nájera, Spain	C9	12
Najin, N. Kor.	C13	26
Nakaminato, Japan	F13	30
Nakatsu, Japan	I4	30
Nakatsugawa, Japan	G10	30
Nakhon Pathom, Thai.	H6	34
Nakhon Phanom, Thai.	F8	34
Nakhon Ratchasima, Thai.	G7	34
Nakhon Sawan, Thai.	G6	34
Nakhon Si Thammarat, Thai.	J5	34
Nakina, Ont., Can.	o18	73
Naknek, Ak., U.S.	D8	79
Naknek Lake, l., Ak., U.S.	D8	79
Nakskov, Den.	I8	6
Nakuru, Kenya	B7	44
Nakusp, B.C., Can.	D9	69
Nalchik see Nal'čik, Russia	I6	22
Nal'čik, Russia	I6	22
Nalgonda, India	D5	37
Nālūt, Libya	B8	42
Namak, Daryācheh-ye, l., Iran	K8	22
Namangan, Uzb.	I12	22
Namanock Island, i., N.J., U.S.	A3	107
Namapa, Moz.	D7	44
Namatanai, Pap. N. Gui.	k17	50a
Nambour, Austl.	E10	50
Namcha Barwa see Namjagbarwa Feng, mtn., China	F16	38
Nam Co, l., China	E14	38
Nam Dinh, Viet.	D9	34
Namekagon, stm., Wi., U.S.	B2	126
Namekagon Lake, l., Wi., U.S.	B2	126
Namhkam, Mya.	C4	34
Namib Desert, des., Nmb.	F2	44
Namibe, Ang.	E2	44
Namibia, ctry., Afr.	F3	44
Namjagbarwa Feng, mtn., China	F16	38
Namlea, Indon.	F8	32
Nampa, Id., U.S.	F2	89
Namp'o, N. Kor.	D12	26
Nampula, Moz.	E7	44
Namsos, Nor.	D8	6
Namur, Bel.	E4	8
Nanaimo, B.C., Can.	E5	69
Nanakuli, Hi., U.S.	B3	88
Nanao, Japan	E9	30
Nance, co., Ne., U.S.	C7	104
Nanchang, China	G4	28
Nanchong, China	E8	26
Nancy, Fr.	D13	10
Nanda Devi, mtn., India	E8	38
Nānded, India	C4	37
Nandurbār, India	B3	37
Nandyāl, India	E5	37
Nānga Parbat, mtn., Pak.	C6	38
Nangqian (Xiangda), China	D17	00
Nanjing (Nanking), China	C7	28
Nanking see Nanjing, China	C7	28
Nankoku, Japan	I6	30
Nankou, China	C10	26
Nan Ling, mts., China	F9	26
Nanning, China	C10	34
Nanping, China	I7	28
Nansei-shotō (Ryukyu Islands), is., Japan	F12	26
Nansemond, stm., Va., U.S.	k14	123
Nantes, Fr.	E5	10
Nanticoke, Ont., Can.	E4	73
Nanticoke, Pa., U.S.	D10	115
Nanticoke, stm., U.S.	D6	97
Nanton, Alta., Can.	D4	68
Nantong, China	C9	28
Nant'ou, Tai.	L9	28
Nantua, Fr.	F12	10
Nantucket, Ma., U.S.	D7	98
Nantucket, co., Ma., U.S.	D7	98
Nantucket Island, i., Ma., U.S.	D7	98
Nantucket Sound, strt., Ma., U.S.	C7	98
Nantuxent Point, c., N.J., U.S.	E2	107
Nanty Glo, Pa., U.S.	F4	115
Nanuet, N.Y., U.S.	g12	109
Nanuque, Braz.	D8	57
Nanxiang, China	D10	28
Nanxiong, China	J3	28

Name — Map Ref — Page

Nanyang, China B1 28
Naoetsu, Japan E11 30
Naoma, W.V., U.S. n13 125
Naomi Peak, mtn., Ut., U.S. B4 121
Náousa, Grc. I6 16
Napa, Ca., U.S. C2 82
Napa, co., Ca., U.S. C2 82
Napanee, Ont., Can. C8 73
Napatree Point, c., R.I., U.S. G1 116
Napavine, Wa., U.S. C3 124
Naperville, Il., U.S. B5 90
Napier, N.Z. C6 52
Napierville, Que., Can. D4 74
Naples, Fl., U.S. F5 86
Naples, Tx., U.S. C5 120
Naples, Ut., U.S. C6 121
Naples see Napoli, Italy I9 14
Napo, stm., S.A. I6 58
Napoleon, N.D., U.S. C6 111
Napoleon, Oh., U.S. A1 112
Napoleonville, La., U.S. E4 95
Napoli (Naples), Italy I9 14
Nappanee, In., U.S. B5 91
Nara, Japan H8 30
Nara, Mali E4 42
Naracoorte, Austl. G8 50
Naramata, B.C., Can. E8 69
Naranja, Fl., U.S. G6 86
Narasapur, India D6 37
Narasaraopet, India D6 37
Narathiwat, Thai. K6 34
Nārāyanganj, Bngl. I14 38
Narberth, Pa., U.S. p20 115
Narbonne, Fr. I9 10
Nardò, Italy I13 14
Narew, stm., Eur. C21 8
Nārīn Ghar, Afg. B3 38
Narita, Japan G13 30
Narmada, stm., India J5 38
Nārnaul, India F7 38
Narni, Italy G7 14
Naro-Fominsk, Russia F19 18
Narragansett, R.I., U.S. F4 116
Narragansett Bay, b., R.I., U.S. E5 116
Narraguagus, stm., Me., U.S. D5 96
Narrows, Va., U.S. C2 123
Narsimhapur, India I8 38
Narssag, Grnld. D23 66
Naruto, Japan H7 30
Narva, Est. B11 18
Narvik, Nor. B11 6
Naselle, Wa., U.S. C2 124
Nash, Tx., U.S. C5 120
Nash, co., N.C., U.S. A4 110
Nashawena Island, i., Ma., U.S. D6 98
Nash Stream, stm., N.H., U.S. A4 106
Nashua, Ia., U.S. B5 92
Nashua, N.H., U.S. E4 106
Nashua, stm., U.S. E3 106
Nashville, Ar., U.S. D2 81
Nashville, Ga., U.S. E3 87
Nashville, Il., U.S. E4 90
Nashville, In., U.S. F5 91
Nashville, Mi., U.S. F5 99
Nashville, N.C., U.S. B5 110
Nashville, Tn., U.S. A5 119
Nashwauk, Mn., U.S. C5 100
Nāsik, India C2 37
Nāsir, Sudan G12 42
Naskaupi, stm., Newf., Can. g9 72
Nassau, Bah. B9 64
Nassau, co., Fl., U.S. B5 86
Nassau, co., N.Y., U.S. E7 109
Nassau, stm., Fl., U.S. k8 86
Nassau Sound, b., Fl., U.S. B5 86
Nasser, Lake, res., Afr. D12 42
Nässjö, Swe. H10 6
Nasukoin Mountain, mtn., Mt., U.S. B2 103
Natal, Braz. E11 54
Natalbany, La., U.S. D5 95
Natalia, Tx., U.S. E3 120
Natashquan, stm., Can. h9 72
Natchaug, stm., Ct., U.S. B7 84
Natchez, Ms., U.S. D2 101
Natchitoches, La., U.S. C2 95
Natchitoches, co., La., U.S. C2 95
Nāthdwāra, India H5 38
Natick, Ma., U.S. B5 98
National City, Ca., U.S. F5 82
Natron, Lake, l., Afr. B7 44
Natrona, co., Wy., U.S. D5 127
Natrona Heights, Pa., U.S. E2 115
Nattaung, mtn., Mya. E4 34
Natuna Besar, i., Indon. M10 34
Natuna Besar, Kepulauan, is., Indon. M10 34
Natuna Selatan, Kepulauan, is., Indon. M10 34
Natural Bridge, Ut., U.S. F3 121
Natural Bridge, Va., U.S. C3 123
Natural Bridges National Monument, Ut., U.S. F6 121
Naturaliste, Cape, c., Austl. F3 50
Nauen, Ger. C12 8
Naugatuck, Ct., U.S. D3 84
Naugatuck, stm., Ct., U.S. D3 84
Naumburg, Ger. D11 8
Naushon Island, i., Ma., U.S. D6 98
Nautilus Park, Ct., U.S. D7 84
Nauvoo, Il., U.S. C2 90
Nava del Rey, Spain D6 12
Navahermosa, Spain F7 12
Navajo, co., Az., U.S. B5 80
Navajo Dam, N.M., U.S. A2 108
Navajo Indian Reservation, U.S. A4 80
Navajo Mountain, mtn., Ut., U.S. F5 121
Navajo National Monument, Az., U.S. A5 80
Navajo Reservoir, res., U.S. A2 108
Navalcarnero, Spain E7 12
Navalmoral de la Mata, Spain F6 12
Navalvillar de Pela, Spain F6 12
Navan, Ont., Can. B9 73
Navan, Ire. H6 7
Navarin, Mys, c., Russia E29 24
Navarino, Isla, i., Chile H3 56
Navarre, Oh., U.S. B4 112
Navarro, co., Tx., U.S. D4 120
Navasota, Tx., U.S. D4 120
Navassa Island, i., N.A. E10 64
Navoi, Uzb. I11 22
Navojoa, Mex. D5 62
Navolato, Mex. E6 62
Navsāri, India B2 37
Nawābganj, Bngl. H13 38
Nawābganj, India G9 38
Nawābshāh, Pak. G3 38
Nāwah, Afg. D2 38
Nawalgarh, India G6 38
Nawiliwili Bay, b., Hi., U.S. B2 88
Náxos, i., Grc. L9 16
Nayak, Afg. C2 38
Naylor, Mo., U.S. E7 102
Nayoro, Japan o20 30a
Nazaré, Braz. B9 57
Nazaré, Port. F2 12
Nazareth, Pa., U.S. E11 115
Nazca, Peru F4 54
Naze, Japan w29 31b
Nazilli, Tur. L12 16
Nazko, stm., B.C., Can. C6 69
Ndélé, Cen. Afr. Rep. G10 42
N'Djamena (Fort-Lamy), Chad F9 42
Ndola, Zam. D5 44
Neagh, Lough, l., N. Ire., U.K. G6 7
Neah Bay, Wa., U.S. A1 124
Néa Páfos (Paphos), Cyp. B3 40
Neápolis, Grc. M7 16
Near Islands, is., Ak., U.S. E2 79
Nebo, Mount, mtn., Ut., U.S. D4 121
Nebraska, state, U.S. C6 104
Nebraska City, Ne., U.S. D10 104
Nechako, stm., B.C., Can. C5 69
Neches, stm., Tx., U.S. D5 120
Nechí, Col. C5 58
Neckar, stm., Ger. F9 8
Necker Island, i., Hi., U.S. m15 88
Necochea, Arg. D5 56
Nederland, Co., U.S. B5 83
Nederland, Tx., U.S. E6 120
Nedrow, N.Y., U.S. C4 109
Needham, Ma., U.S. g11 98
Needle Mountain, mtn., Wy., U.S. B3 127
Needles, Ca., U.S. E6 82
Needville, Tx., U.S. r14 120
Neenah, Wi., U.S. D5 126
Neepawa, Man., Can. D2 70
Neffs, Oh., U.S. B5 112
Neffsville, Pa., U.S. F9 115
Negage, Ang. C3 44
Negaunee, Mi., U.S. B3 99
Negele, Eth. G2 46
Negev Desert see Hanegev, reg., Isr. D4 40
Negley, Oh., U.S. B5 112
Negombo, Sri L. I5 37
Negra, Punta, c., Peru E2 54
Negro, stm., Arg. E4 56
Negro, stm., S.A. H12 58
Negros, i., Phil. C7 32
Neguac, N.B., Can. B4 71
Nehalem, stm., Or., U.S. A3 114
Nehbandān, Iran B7 46
Neheim-Hüsten, Ger. D7 8
Neiba, Bahía de, b., Dom. Rep. E12 64
Neijiang, China F8 26
Neill Point, c., Wa., U.S. f11 124
Neillsville, Wi., U.S. D3 126
Nei Monggol Zizhiqu (Inner Mongolia), prov., China C10 26
Neisse (Nysa Łużycka), stm., Eur. D14 8
Neiva, Col. F5 58
Neja, Russia C26 18
Nekemte, Eth. G2 46
Nekoosa, Wi., U.S. D4 126
Nelidovo, Russia E15 18
Neligh, Ne., U.S. B7 104
Nel'kan, Russia F21 24
Nellikuppam, India G5 37
Nellis Air Force Base, mil., Nv., U.S. G6 105
Nellore, India E5 37
Nelson, B.C., Can. E9 69
Nelson, N.Z. D4 52
Nelson, Ne., U.S. D7 104
Nelson, co., Ky., U.S. C4 94
Nelson, co., N.D., U.S. B7 111
Nelson, co., Va., U.S. C4 123
Nelson, stm., Man., Can. A4 70
Nelsonville, Oh., U.S. C3 112
Néma, Maur. E4 42
Nemacolin, Pa., U.S. G2 115
Nemadji, stm., U.S. B1 126
Nemaha, co., Ks., U.S. C7 93
Nemaha, co., Ne., U.S. D10 104
Nemours, Fr. D9 10
Nemuro, Japan p23 30a
Nemuro Strait, strt., Asia o23 30a
Nenagh, Ire. I4 7
Nenana, Ak., U.S. C10 79
Neodesha, Ks., U.S. E8 93
Neoga, Il., U.S. D5 90
Neola, Ia., U.S. C2 92
Neola, Ut., U.S. C5 121
Neopit, Wi., U.S. D5 126
Neosho, Mo., U.S. E3 102
Neosho, co., Ks., U.S. E8 93
Neosho, stm., Ok., U.S. A6 113
Nepal (Nepāl), ctry., Asia D5 36
Nepālganj, Nepal F9 38
Nepaug Reservoir, res., Ct., U.S. B3 84
Nepean, Ont., Can. h12 73
Nepewassi Lake, l., Ont., Can. A4 73
Nephi, Ut., U.S. D4 121
Nepisiguit, stm., N.B., Can. B3 71
Nepisiguit Bay, b., N.B., Can. B4 71
Neponset, stm., Ma., U.S. h11 98
Neptune, N.J., U.S. C4 107
Neptune Beach, Fl., U.S. B5 86
Neptune City, N.J., U.S. C4 107
Nérac, Fr. H7 10
Nerastro, Sarīr, des., Libya D10 42
Nerčinskij Zavod, Russia G17 24
Nerechta, Russia D23 18
Neriquinha, Ang. E4 44
Nerva, Spain H5 12
Nesbyen, Nor. F7 6
Nescopeck, Pa., U.S. D9 115
Neshanic, stm., N.J., U.S. C3 107
Neshoba, co., Ms., U.S. C4 101
Neskaupstaður, Ice. B5 4
Nesna, Nor. C9 6
Nesowadnehunk, l., Me., U.S. B3 96
Nesquehoning, Pa., U.S. E10 115
Ness, co., Ks., U.S. D4 93
Ness, Loch, l., Scot., U.K. D8 7
Ness City, Ks., U.S. D4 93
Néstos (Mesta), stm., Eur. H8 16
Netanya, Isr. C4 40
Netcong, N.J., U.S. B3 107
Netherlands, ctry., Eur. E9 4
Netherlands Antilles (Nederlandse Antillen), dep., N.A. H13 64
Netrakona, Bngl. H14 38
Nettie, W.V., U.S. C4 125
Nettilling Lake, l., N.W. Ter., Can. C18 66
Nett Lake, l., Mn., U.S. B5 100
Nett Lake Indian Reservation, Mn., U.S. B6 100
Nettleton, Ms., U.S. A5 101
Nettuno, Italy H7 14
Neubrandenburg, Ger. B13 8
Neuburg an der Donau, Ger. G11 8
Neuchâtel, Switz. F13 10
Neuchâtel, Lac de, l., Switz. F13 10
Neufchâteau, Bel. F5 8
Neufchâteau, Fr. D12 10
Neufchâtel-en-Bray, Fr. C8 10
Neuillé-Pont-Pierre, Fr. E7 10
Neumarkt in der Oberpfalz, Ger. F11 8
Neumünster, Ger. A9 8
Neunkirchen, Aus. H16 8
Neunkirchen/Saar, Ger. F7 8
Neuquén, Arg. D3 56
Neuruppin, Ger. C12 8
Neuse, stm., N.C., U.S. B6 110
Neusiedler See, l., Eur. H16 8
Neuss, Ger. D6 8
Neustadt Jan der Aisch—, Ger. F10 8
Neustadt an der Weinstrasse, Ger. F8 8
Neustadt in Holstein, Ger. A10 8
Neustrelitz, Ger. B13 8
Neu-Ulm, Ger. G10 8
Neuville, Que., Can. C6 74
Neuville-de-Poitou, Fr. F7 10
Neuwied, Ger. E7 8
Nevada, Ia., U.S. B4 92
Nevada, Mo., U.S. D3 102
Nevada, co., Ar., U.S. D2 81
Nevada, co., Ca., U.S. C3 82
Nevada, state, U.S. D5 105
Nevada, Sierra, mts., Spain H8 12
Nevada, Sierra, mts., Ca., U.S. D4 82
Nevada City, Ca., U.S. C3 82
Nevado, Cerro, mtn., Arg. D3 56
Nevado, Cerro, mtn., Col. F5 58
Never, Russia G18 24
Nevers, Fr. E10 10
Neversink, stm., N.Y., U.S. D6 109
Nevis, i., St. K./N. F16 64
Nevis, Ben, mtn., Scot., U.K. E7 7
New, stm., U.S. C3 125
New, stm., Az., U.S. k8 80
New, stm., N.C., U.S. C5 110
New Albany, In., U.S. H6 91
New Albany, Ms., U.S. A4 101
New Albany, Oh., U.S. k11 112
New Amsterdam, Guy. D14 58
Newark, Ar., U.S. B4 81
Newark, Ca., U.S. h8 82
Newark, De., U.S. B3 85
Newark, Il., U.S. B5 90
Newark, N.J., U.S. B4 107
Newark, N.Y., U.S. B3 109
Newark, Oh., U.S. B3 112
Newark Bay, b., N.J., U.S. k8 107
Newark Lake, l., Nv., U.S. D6 105
New Athens, Il., U.S. E4 90
New Augusta, Ms., U.S. D4 101
Newaygo, Mi., U.S. E5 99
Newaygo, co., Mi., U.S. E5 99
New Baden, Il., U.S. E4 90
New Baltimore, Mi., U.S. F8 99
New Bedford, Ma., U.S. C6 98
New Bedford, Pa., U.S. D1 115
Newberg, Or., U.S. B4 114
New Berlin, Il., U.S. D4 90
New Berlin, Wi., U.S. n11 126
New Bern, N.C., U.S. B5 110
Newbern, Tn., U.S. A2 119
Newberry, Fl., U.S. C4 86
Newberry, Mi., U.S. B5 99
Newberry, S.C., U.S. C4 117
Newberry, co., S.C., U.S. C4 117
New Bethlehem, Pa., U.S. D3 115
New Bloomfield, Pa., U.S. F7 115
New Boston, Mi., U.S. p15 99
New Boston, Oh., U.S. D3 112
New Boston, Tx., U.S. C5 120
New Braunfels, Tx., U.S. E3 120
New Bremen, Oh., U.S. B1 112
New Brighton, Mn., U.S. m12 100
New Brighton, Pa., U.S. E1 115
New Britain, Ct., U.S. C4 84
New Britain, i., Pap. N. Gui. m16 50a
New Brockton, Al., U.S. D4 78
New Brunswick, N.J., U.S. C4 107
New Brunswick, prov., Can. C3 71
New Buffalo, Mi., U.S. G4 99
Newburg, Wi., U.S. E5 126
Newburgh, Ont., Can. C8 73
Newburgh, In., U.S. I3 91
Newburgh, N.Y., U.S. D6 109
Newburgh Heights, Oh., U.S. h9 112
Newburyport, Ma., U.S. A6 98
New Caledonia, dep., Oc. H24 2
New Canaan, Ct., U.S. E2 84
New Carlisle, In., U.S. A4 91
New Carlisle, Oh., U.S. C1 112
Newcastle, Austl. F10 50
Newcastle, N.B., Can. C4 71
Newcastle, Ont., Can. D6 73
Newcastle, S. Afr. G5 44
Newcastle, N. Ire., U.K. G7 7
New Castle, Al., U.S. B3 78
New Castle, Co., U.S. B3 83
New Castle, De., U.S. B3 85
New Castle, In., U.S. E7 91
New Castle, Ky., U.S. B4 94
Newcastle, Ok., U.S. B4 113
New Castle, Pa., U.S. D1 115
Newcastle, Wy., U.S. C8 127
New Castle, co., De., U.S. B3 85
Newcastle upon Tyne, Eng., U.K. G11 7
Newcastle Waters, Austl. C6 50
New City, N.Y., U.S. D6 109
Newcomerstown, Oh., U.S. B4 112
New Concord, Oh., U.S. C4 112
New Cumberland, Pa., U.S. F8 115
New Cumberland, W.V., U.S. A4 125
Newdegate, Austl. F3 50
New Delhi, India F7 38
Newell, Ia., U.S. B2 92
Newell, S.D., U.S. C2 118
Newell, W.V., U.S. A4 125
New Ellenton, S.C., U.S. E4 117
Newellton, La., U.S. B4 95
New England, N.D., U.S. C3 111
Newenham, Cape, c., Ak., U.S. D7 79
New Fairfield, Ct., U.S. D2 84
Newfane, N.Y., U.S. B2 109
Newfields, N.H., U.S. D5 106
New Florence, Mo., U.S. C6 102
Newfound Gap, U.S. f9 110
Newfound Lake, l., N.H., U.S. C3 106
Newfoundland, prov., Can. D4 72
Newfoundland, i., Newf., Can. D3 72
New Franklin, Mo., U.S. B5 102
New Freedom, Pa., U.S. G8 115
New Georgia, i., Sol.Is. A11 50
New Germany, N.S., Can. E5 71
New Glarus, Wi., U.S. F4 126
New Guinea, i. m14 50a
Newhall, Ia., U.S. C6 92
New Hampshire, state, U.S. C3 106
New Hampton, Ia., U.S. A5 92
New Hanover, co., N.C., U.S. C5 110
New Hanover, i., Pap. N. Gui. k17 50a
New Harbour, Newf., Can. E5 72
New Harmony, In., U.S. H2 91
New Hartford, Ct., U.S. B4 84
New Hartford, Ia., U.S. B5 92
New Haven, Ct., U.S. D4 84
New Haven, In., U.S. B7 91
New Haven, Ky., U.S. C4 94
New Haven, Mi., U.S. F8 99
New Haven, Mo., U.S. C6 102
New Haven, W.V., U.S. C3 125
New Haven, co., Ct., U.S. D4 84
New Haven, stm., Vt., U.S. C2 122
New Haven Harbor, b., Ct., U.S. E4 84
New Hazelton, B.C., Can. B4 69
New Hebrides see Vanuatu, ctry., Oc. H24 2
New Holland, Ga., U.S. B3 87
New Holland, Pa., U.S. F9 115
New Holstein, Wi., U.S. E5 126
New Hope, Al., U.S. A3 78
New Hope, Ky., U.S. C4 94
New Hope, Mn., U.S. m12 100
New Hope, Pa., U.S. F12 115
New Hudson, Mi., U.S. o14 99
New Iberia, La., U.S. D4 95
Newington, Ct., U.S. C5 84
New Inlet, b., N.C., U.S. D5 110
New Ireland, i., Pap. N. Gui. k17 50a
New Jersey, state, U.S. C4 107
New Johnsonville, Tn., U.S. A4 119
New Kensington, Pa., U.S. E2 115
New Kent, co., Va., U.S. C5 123
Newkirk, Ok., U.S. A4 113
New Laguna, N.M., U.S. B2 108
New Lake, l., N.C., U.S. B6 110
New Lenox, Il., U.S. B6 90
New Lexington, Oh., U.S. C3 112
New Lisbon, Wi., U.S. E3 126
New Liskeard, Ont., Can. p20 73
Newllano, La., U.S. C2 95
New London, Ct., U.S. D7 84
New London, Ia., U.S. D6 92
New London, Mn., U.S. E4 100
New London, Mo., U.S. B6 102
New London, N.H., U.S. D3 106
New London, Oh., U.S. A3 112
New London, Wi., U.S. D5 126
New London, co., Ct., U.S. C7 84
New London Submarine Base, mil., Ct., U.S. D7 84
New Madison, Oh., U.S. C1 112
New Madrid, Mo., U.S. E8 102
New Madrid, co., Mo., U.S. E8 102
Newman, Ca., U.S. D3 82
Newman, Il., U.S. D6 90
New Manchester, W.V., U.S. e8 125
Newman Grove, Ne., U.S. C8 104
Newman Lake, l., Wa., U.S. B8 124
Newmanstown, Pa., U.S. F9 115
Newmarket, Ont., Can. C5 73
New Market, Al., U.S. A3 78
New Market, In., U.S. E4 91
Newmarket, N.H., U.S. D5 106
New Market, Tn., U.S. C10 119
New Market, Va., U.S. B4 123
New Martinsville, W.V., U.S. B4 125
New Matamoras, Oh., U.S. C4 112
New Mexico, state, U.S. C3 108
New Miami, Oh., U.S. C1 112
New Milford, Ct., U.S. C2 84
New Milford, N.J., U.S. h8 107
New Milford, Pa., U.S. C10 115
Newnan, Ga., U.S. C2 87
Newnans Lake, l., Fl., U.S. C4 86
New Norfolk, Austl. H9 50
New Orleans, La., U.S. E5 95
New Orleans Naval Air Station, mil., La., U.S. k11 95
New Oxford, Pa., U.S. G7 115
New Palestine, In., U.S. E6 91
New Paltz, N.Y., U.S. D6 109
New Paris, In., U.S. B6 91
New Paris, Oh., U.S. C1 112
New Philadelphia, Oh., U.S. B4 112
New Philadelphia, Pa., U.S. E9 115
New Plymouth, N.Z. C5 52
New Plymouth, Id., U.S. F2 89
New Point Comfort, c., Va., U.S. C6 123
Newport, Eng., U.K. K11 7
Newport, Wales, U.K. J9 7
Newport, Ar., U.S. B4 81
Newport, De., U.S. B3 85
Newport, In., U.S. E3 91
Newport, Ky., U.S. A5 94
Newport, Me., U.S. D3 96
Newport, Mi., U.S. G7 99
Newport, Mn., U.S. n13 100
Newport, N.H., U.S. D2 106
Newport, N.C., U.S. C6 110
Newport, Oh., U.S. C4 112
Newport, Or., U.S. C2 114
Newport, Pa., U.S. F7 115
Newport, R.I., U.S. F5 116
Newport, Tn., U.S. D10 119
Newport, Vt., U.S. B4 122
Newport, Wa., U.S. A8 124
Newport, co., R.I., U.S. E5 116
Newport Beach, Ca., U.S. n13 82
Newport News, Va., U.S. D6 123
New Port Richey, Fl., U.S. D4 86
New Prague, Mn., U.S. F5 100
New Preston, Ct., U.S. C2 84
New Providence, N.J., U.S. B4 107
New Providence, i., Bah. B9 64
Newquay, Eng., U.K. K7 7
New Richland, Mn., U.S. G5 100
New Richmond, Que., Can. A4 71
New Richmond, Oh., U.S. D1 112
New Richmond, Wi., U.S. C1 126
New River Inlet, b., N.C., U.S. C5 110
New Roads, La., U.S. D4 95
New Rochelle, N.Y., U.S. E7 109
New Rockford, N.D., U.S. B6 111
New Ross, Ire. I6 7
Newry, N. Ire., U.K. G6 7
New Salem, N.D., U.S. C4 111
New Sarpy, La., U.S. k11 95
New Sharon, Ia., U.S. C5 92
New Site, Al., U.S. B4 78
New Smyrna Beach, Fl., U.S. C6 86
New South Wales, state, Austl. F9 50
New Straitsville, Oh., U.S. C3 112
New Tazewell, Tn., U.S. C10 119
Newton, Al., U.S. D4 78
Newton, Ga., U.S. E2 87
Newton, Il., U.S. E5 90
Newton, Ia., U.S. C4 92
Newton, Ks., U.S. D6 93
Newton, Ma., U.S. B5 98
Newton, Ms., U.S. C4 101
Newton, N.J., U.S. A3 107
Newton, N.C., U.S. B1 110
Newton, Tx., U.S. D6 120
Newton, Ut., U.S. B4 121
Newton, co., Ar., U.S. B2 81
Newton, co., Ga., U.S. C3 87
Newton, co., In., U.S. B3 91
Newton, co., Ms., U.S. C4 101
Newton, co., Mo., U.S. E3 102
Newton, co., Tx., U.S. D6 120
Newton Falls, Oh., U.S. A5 112
Newton Lake, res., Il., U.S. E5 90
Newton Stewart, Scot., U.K. G8 7
Newtown, Ct., U.S. D2 84
New Town, N.D., U.S. B3 111
Newtown, Oh., U.S. C1 112
Newtownabbey, N. Ire., U.K. G7 7
Newtownards, N. Ire., U.K. G7 7
Newtown Square, Pa., U.S. p20 115
New Ulm, Mn., U.S. F4 100
New Vienna, Oh., U.S. C2 112
Newville, Pa., U.S. F7 115
New Washington, In., U.S. G6 91
New Washington, Oh., U.S. B3 112
New Waterford, Oh., U.S. B5 112
New Westminster, B.C., Can. E6 69
New Whiteland, In., U.S. E5 91
New Wilmington, Pa., U.S. D1 115
New Windsor, Il., U.S. B3 90
New Windsor, Md., U.S. A3 97
New Windsor, N.Y., U.S. D6 109
New World Island, i., Newf., Can. D4 72
New York, N.Y., U.S. E7 109
New York, co., N.Y., U.S. k13 109
New York, state, U.S. C6 109
New York Mills, Mn., U.S. D3 100
New Zealand, ctry., Oc. D4 52
Nez Perce, co., Id., U.S. C2 89
Nez Perce Indian Reservation, Id., U.S. C2 89
Ngami, Lake, l., Bots. F4 44
Nganglong Kangri, mts., China D10 38
Nganjuk, Indon. m15 33a
Ngaoundéré, Cam. G8 42
Nguigmi, Niger F8 42
Nguru, Nig. F8 42
Nha Trang, Viet. H10 34
Niafounké, Mali E5 42
Niagara, Wi., U.S. C6 126
Niagara, co., N.Y., U.S. B2 109
Niagara Falls, Ont., Can. D5 73
Niagara Falls, N.Y., U.S. B1 109
Niagara-on-the-Lake, Ont., Can. D5 73
Niamey, Niger F6 42
Niangara, Zaire H11 42
Niangua, stm., Mo., U.S. D5 102
Niantic, Ct., U.S. D7 84

Name	Map Ref	Page
Nias, Pulau, i., Indon.	N4	34
Nibley, Ut., U.S.	B4	121
Nicaragua, ctry., N.A.	H5	64
Nicaragua, Lago de, l., Nic.	I5	64
Nicastro (Lamezia Terme), Italy	K11	14
Nicatous Lake, l., Me., U.S.	C4	96
Nice, Fr.	I14	10
Niceville, Fl., U.S.	u15	86
Nichinan, Japan	K4	30
Nicholas, co., Ky., U.S.	B6	94
Nicholas, co., W.V., U.S.	C4	125
Nicholas Channel, strt., N.A.	C7	64
Nicholasville, Ky., U.S.	C5	94
Nicholls, Ga., U.S.	E4	87
Nichols Hills, Ok., U.S.	B4	113
Nicholson, Ms., U.S.	E4	101
Nickajack Lake, res., Tn., U.S.	D8	119
Nickel Centre, Ont., Can.	p19	73
Nickerson, Ks., U.S.	D5	93
Nicobar Islands, is., India	J2	34
Nicolet, Que., Can.	C5	74
Nicolet, stm., Que., Can.	C5	74
Nicolet, Lake, l., Mi., U.S.	B6	99
Nicollet, Mn., U.S.	F4	100
Nicollet, co., Mn., U.S.	F4	100
Nicolls Town, Bah.	B8	64
Nicoma Park, Ok., U.S.	B4	113
Nicosia, Cyp.	B3	40
Nicosia, N. Cyp.	B3	40
Nicosia, Italy	L9	14
Nicoya, Golfo de, b., C.R.	J5	64
Nicoya, Península de, pen., C.R.	I5	64
Niebüll, Ger.	A8	8
Nienburg, Ger.	C9	8
Nieuw Nickerie, Sur.	B7	54
Nieves, Mex.	E8	62
Nigadoo, N.B., Can.	B4	71
Niger, ctry., Afr.	E7	42
Niger, stm., Afr.	G7	42
Nigeria, ctry., Afr.	F7	42
Nigríta, Grc.	I7	16
Nihoa, i., Hi., U.S.	m15	88
Niigata, Japan	E12	30
Niihama, Japan	I6	30
Niihau, i., Hi., U.S.	B1	88
Niinisalo, Fin.	F14	6
Niitsu, Japan	E12	30
Níjar, Spain	I9	12
Nijmegen, Neth.	D5	8
Nikishka, Ak., U.S.	g16	79
Nikkō, Japan	F12	30
Nikolajevsk-na-Amure, Russia	G22	24
Nikšić, Yugo.	G2	16
Niland, Ca., U.S.	F6	82
Nile (Nahr an-Nīl), stm., Afr.	C12	42
Niles, Il., U.S.	h9	90
Niles, Mi., U.S.	G4	99
Niles, Oh., U.S.	A5	112
Nileshwar, India	F3	37
Nīmach, India	H6	38
Nimba, Mont, mtn., Afr.	G4	42
Nîmes, Fr.	I11	10
Nimrod Lake, res., Ar., U.S.	C2	81
Nine Degree Channel, strt., India	H2	37
Nine Mile Creek, stm., Ut., U.S.	D5	121
Ninemile Point, c., Mi., U.S.	C6	99
Ninety Six, S.C., U.S.	C3	117
Ningbo, China	F10	28
Ningming, China	C9	34
Ningxia Huizu Zizhiqu, prov., China	D8	26
Ninh Binh, Viet.	D8	34
Ninigret Pond, l., R.I., U.S.	G2	116
Ninilchik, Ak., U.S.	C9	79
Ninnescah, stm., Ks., U.S.	E6	93
Niobrara, co., Wy., U.S.	C8	127
Niobrara, stm., U.S.	B7	104
Niono, Mali	F4	42
Nioro du Sahel, Mali	E4	42
Niort, Fr.	F6	10
Niota, Tn., U.S.	D9	119
Nipāni, India	D3	37
Nipigon, Lake, l., Ont., Can.	o17	73
Nipissing, Lake, l., Ont., Can.	A5	73
Nipomo, Ca., U.S.	E3	82
Nipple Mountain, mtn., Co., U.S.	D2	83
Nirmal, India	C5	37
Niš, Yugo.	F5	16
Nisa, Port.	F4	12
Nishinoomote, Japan	u30	31b
Nishiwaki, Japan	H7	30
Niskayuna, N.Y., U.S.	C7	109
Nisqually, stm., Wa., U.S.	C3	124
Nisswa, Mn., U.S.	D4	100
Niterói, Braz.	G7	57
Nitra, Slov.	G18	8
Nitro, W.V., U.S.	C3	125
Niue, dep., Oc.	H1	2
Nivelles, Bel.	E4	8
Nivorville, Man., Can.	E3	70
Niwot, Co., U.S.	A5	83
Nixa, Mo., U.S.	D4	102
Nixon, Nv., U.S.	D2	105
Nixon, Tx., U.S.	E4	120
Nizāmābād, India	C5	37
Nizip, Tur.	A5	40
Nižn'aja Pojma, Russia	F13	24
Nižn'aja Tunguska, stm., Russia	E12	24
Nižneangarsk, Russia	F15	24
Nižneilimsk, Russia	F14	24
Nižneudinsk, Russia	G13	24
Nižnij Novgorod (Gorki), Russia	E27	18
Nizza Monferrato, Italy	E3	14
Njombe, Tan.	C6	44
Nkhota Kota, Mwi.	D6	44
Nkongsamba, Cam.	H7	42
Noākhāli, Bngl.	I14	38
Noank, Ct., U.S.	D8	84
Noatak, Ak., U.S.	B7	79
Noatak, stm., Ak., U.S.	B7	79
Nobel, Ont., Can.	B4	73
Nobeoka, Japan	J4	30
Noble, Ok., U.S.	B4	113
Noble, co., In., U.S.	B7	91
Noble, co., Oh., U.S.	C4	112
Noble, co., Ok., U.S.	A4	113
Nobles, co., Mn., U.S.	G3	100
Noblesville, In., U.S.	D6	91
Noboribetsu, Japan	q19	30a
Nocatee, Fl., U.S.	E5	86
Nocera [Inferiore], Italy	I9	14
Nochixtlán, Mex.	I11	62
Nocona, Tx., U.S.	C4	120
Nodaway, co., Mo., U.S.	A3	102
Nodaway, stm., U.S.	A2	102
Noel, Mo., U.S.	E3	102
Nogales, Mex.	B4	62
Nogales, Az., U.S.	F5	80
Nōgata, Japan	I3	30
Nogent-le-Rotrou, Fr.	D7	10
Noginsk, Russia	F21	18
Nogoyá, Arg.	C5	56
Noirmoutier, Fr.	E4	10
Nojima-zaki, c., Japan	H12	30
Nokia, Fin.	F14	6
Nokomis, Fl., U.S.	E4	86
Nokomis, Il., U.S.	D4	90
Nokomis, Lake, res., Wi., U.S.	C4	126
Nolan, co., Tx., U.S.	C2	120
Nolichucky, stm., Tn., U.S.	C10	119
Nolin, stm., Ky., U.S.	C3	94
Nolin Lake, res., Ky., U.S.	C3	94
Nomans Land, i., Ma., U.S.	D6	98
Nombre de Dios, Mex.	F7	62
Nome, Ak., U.S.	C6	79
Nominingue, Que., Can.	C2	74
Nonacho Lake, l., N.W. Ter., Can.	D11	66
Nonesuch, stm., Me., U.S.	g7	96
Nong'an, China	C12	26
Nong Khai, Thai.	F7	34
Nonquit Pond, l., R.I., U.S.	E6	116
Nontron, Fr.	G7	10
Nooksack, North Fork, stm., Wa., U.S.	A4	124
Nooksack, South Fork, stm., Wa., U.S.	A3	124
Noordoost Polder, reg., Neth.	C5	8
Noorvik, Ak., U.S.	B7	79
Nootka Island, i., B.C., Can.	G7	66
Nootka Sound, strt., B.C., Can.	E4	69
No Point, Point, c., Md., U.S.	D5	97
Noquebay, Lake, l., Wi., U.S.	C6	126
Noranda (part of Rouyn [-Noranda]), Que., Can.	k11	74
Nora Springs, Ia., U.S.	A5	92
Norborne, Mo., U.S.	B4	102
Norco, La., U.S.	E5	95
Norcross, Ga., U.S.	C2	87
Norden, Ger.	B7	8
Nordenham, Ger.	B8	8
Nordenšel'da, Archipelag, is., Russia	B13	24
Norderney, i., Ger.	B7	8
Nordfjordeid, Nor.	F5	6
Nordfold, Nor.	C10	6
Nordhausen, Ger.	D10	8
Nordhorn, Ger.	C7	8
Nordkapp, c., Nor.	A15	6
Nordkjosbotn, Nor.	B12	6
Nördlingen, Ger.	G10	8
Nordmaling, Swe.	E12	6
Nordreisa, Nor.	B13	6
Nordre Strømfjord, Grnld.	C22	66
Nordvik, Russia	C16	24
Norfolk, Ct., U.S.	B3	84
Norfolk, Ne., U.S.	B8	104
Norfolk, N.Y., U.S.	f9	109
Norfolk, Va., U.S.	D6	123
Norfolk, co., Ma., U.S.	B5	98
Norfolk Naval Base, mil., Va., U.S.	k15	123
Norfolk Naval Shipyard, mil., Va., U.S.	k15	123
Norfork Dam, Ar., U.S.	A3	81
Norfork Lake, res., U.S.	A3	81
Noril'sk, Russia	D11	24
Norland, Fl., U.S.	s13	86
Norlina, N.C., U.S.	A4	110
Normal, Il., U.S.	C5	90
Norman, Ok., U.S.	B4	113
Norman, co., Mn., U.S.	C2	100
Norman, Lake, res., N.C., U.S.	B2	110
Normandie, hist. reg., Fr.	D6	10
Normandy, Mo., U.S.	f13	102
Normandy see Normandie, hist. reg., Fr.	D6	10
Norman Park, Ga., U.S.	E3	87
Normanton, Austl.	C8	50
Norman Wells, N.W. Ter., Can.	C7	66
Norphlet, Ar., U.S.	D3	81
Ñorquincó, Arg.	E2	56
Norridge, Il., U.S.	k9	90
Norridgewock, Me., U.S.	D3	96
Norris, S.C., U.S.	B2	117
Norris, Tn., U.S.	C9	119
Norris Arm, Newf., Can.	D4	72
Norris City, Il., U.S.	F5	90
Norris Dam, Tn., U.S.	C9	119
Norris Lake, res., Tn., U.S.	C10	119
Norris Point, Newf., Can.	D3	72
Norristown, Pa., U.S.	F11	115
Norrköping, Swe.	G11	6
Norrtälje, Swe.	G12	6
Norseman, Austl.	F4	50
Norsk, Russia	G19	24
Norte, Serra do, plat., Braz.	F7	54
North, S.C., U.S.	D5	117
North, stm., Al., U.S.	B2	78
North, stm., Ia., U.S.	f8	92
North, stm., Ma., U.S.	h12	98
North, stm., W.V., U.S.	B6	125
North, Cape, c., N.S., Can.	B9	71
North Adams, Ma., U.S.	A1	98
North Albany, Or., U.S.	k11	114
Northam, Austl.	F3	50
North America	E10	61
North Amherst, Ma., U.S.	B2	98
Northampton, Eng., U.K.	I12	7
Northampton, Ma., U.S.	B2	98
Northampton, Pa., U.S.	E11	115
Northampton, co., N.C., U.S.	A5	110
Northampton, co., Pa., U.S.	E11	115
Northampton, co., Va., U.S.	C7	123
North Andaman, i., India	H2	34
North Andover, Ma., U.S.	A5	98
North Andrews Gardens, Fl., U.S.	*r13	86
North Anna, stm., Va., U.S.	B5	123
North Anson, Me., U.S.	D3	96
North Apollo, Pa., U.S.	E2	115
North Arapaho Peak, mtn., Co., U.S.	A5	83
North Arlington, N.J., U.S.	h8	107
North Atlanta, Ga., U.S.	h8	87
North Attleboro, Ma., U.S.	C5	98
North Augusta, S.C., U.S.	D4	117
North Aurora, Il., U.S.	k8	90
North Baltimore, Oh., U.S.	A2	112
North Bay, Ont., Can.	A5	73
North Beach, Md., U.S.	C4	97
North Belmont, N.C., U.S.	B1	110
North Bend, Ne., U.S.	C9	104
North Bend, Or., U.S.	D2	114
North Bend, Wa., U.S.	B4	124
North Bennington, Vt., U.S.	F2	122
North Bergen, N.J., U.S.	h8	107
North Berwick, Me., U.S.	E2	96
North Billerica, Ma., U.S.	A5	98
Northborough, Ma., U.S.	B4	98
North Branch, Mi., U.S.	E7	99
North Branch, Mn., U.S.	E6	100
North Branch, N.H., U.S.	D3	106
North Branch, N.J., U.S.	B3	107
North Branford, Ct., U.S.	D4	84
Northbridge, Ma., U.S.	B4	98
Northbrook, Il., U.S.	h9	90
North Brookfield, Ma., U.S.	B3	98
North Brunswick, N.J., U.S.	C4	107
North Caldwell, N.J., U.S.	B4	107
North Canadian, stm., Ok., U.S.	A5	113
North Canton, Ga., U.S.	B2	87
North Canton, Oh., U.S.	B4	112
North Cape, c., P.E.I., Can.	B6	71
North Cape May, N.J., U.S.	F3	107
North Cape see Nordkapp, c., Nor.	A15	6
North Caribou Lake, l., Ont., Can.	F14	66
North Carolina, state, U.S.	B3	110
North Cascades National Park, Wa., U.S.	A4	124
North Channel, strt., Ont., Can.	A2	73
North Channel, strt., U.K.	F7	7
North Charleston, S.C., U.S.	F8	117
North Chicago, Il., U.S.	A6	90
North Clarendon, Vt., U.S.	D3	122
North College Hill, Oh., U.S.	o12	112
North Conway, N.H., U.S.	B4	106
North Corbin, Ky., U.S.	D5	94
North Crossett, Ar., U.S.	D4	81
North Cyprus, ctry., Asia	B3	40
North Dakota, state, U.S.	B5	111
North Dartmouth, Ma., U.S.	C6	98
North Druid Hills, Ga., U.S.	*h8	87
North Eagle Butte, S.D., U.S.	B4	118
North East, Md., U.S.	A6	97
North East, Pa., U.S.	B2	115
Northeast, stm., Md., U.S.	A6	97
Northeast Cape, c., Ak., U.S.	C6	79
Northeast Cape Fear, stm., N.C., U.S.	C5	110
Northeast Harbor, Me., U.S.	D4	96
Northeast Henrietta, N.Y., U.S.	*B3	109
North Easton, Ma., U.S.	B5	98
Northeast Pond, l., N.H., U.S.	D5	106
Northeast Providence Channel, strt., Bah.	B9	64
North Edisto, stm., S.C., U.S.	k11	117
Northeim, Ger.	D9	8
North English, Ia., U.S.	C5	92
North English, stm., Ia., U.S.	C5	92
North Enid, Ok., U.S.	A4	113
Northern Cheyenne Indian Reservation, Mt., U.S.	E10	103
Northern Indian Lake, l., Man., Can.	A3	70
Northern Ireland, ter., U.K.	G6	7
Northern Territory, ter., Austl.	C6	50
North Falmouth, Ma., U.S.	C6	98
Northfield, Mn., U.S.	F5	100
Northfield, N.H., U.S.	D3	106
Northfield, N.J., U.S.	E3	107
Northfield, Oh., U.S.	h9	112
Northfield, Vt., U.S.	C3	122
Northfield Falls, Vt., U.S.	C3	122
North Flinders Ranges, mts., Austl.	F7	50
North Fond du Lac, Wi., U.S.	E5	126
Northford, Ct., U.S.	D4	84
North Fork Reservoir, res., Or., U.S.	B4	114
North Fort Myers, Fl., U.S.	F5	86
North Fox Island, i., Mi., U.S.	C5	99
North Frisian Islands, is., Eur.	A8	8
Northglenn, Co., U.S.	B6	83
North Gower, Ont., Can.	B9	73
North Grafton, Ma., U.S.	B4	98
North Grosvenordale, Ct., U.S.	B8	84
North Gulfport, Ms., U.S.	E4	101
North Haledon, N.J., U.S.	B4	107
North Hampton, N.H., U.S.	E5	106
North Hartland Reservoir, res., Vt., U.S.	D4	122
North Hatley, Que., Can.	D6	74
North Haven, Ct., U.S.	D4	84
North Head, N.B., Can.	E3	71
North Hero Island, i., Vt., U.S.	B2	122
North Horn Lake, l., Tn., U.S.	e8	119
North Industry, Oh., U.S.	B4	112
North Inlet, b., S.C., U.S.	E9	117
North Island, i., N.Z.	C5	52
North Island, i., S.C., U.S.	E9	117
North Island Naval Air Station, mil., Ca., U.S.	o15	82
North Islands, is., La., U.S.	E7	95
North Judson, In., U.S.	B4	91
North Kansas City, Mo., U.S.	h10	102
North Kingstown, R.I., U.S.	E4	116
North Kingsville, Oh., U.S.	A5	112
North La Junta, Co., U.S.	C7	83
Northlake, Il., U.S.	k9	90
North Laramie, stm., Wy., U.S.	D7	127
North Las Vegas, Nv., U.S.	G6	105
North La Veta Pass, Co., U.S.	D5	83
North Lewisburg, Oh., U.S.	B2	112
North Liberty, In., U.S.	A5	91
North Liberty, Ia., U.S.	C6	92
North Lima, Oh., U.S.	B5	112
North Little Rock, Ar., U.S.	C3	81
North Logan, Ut., U.S.	B4	121
North Loon Mountain, mtn., Id., U.S.	D3	89
North Magnetic Pole	B22	128
North Mamm Peak, mtn., Co., U.S.	B3	83
North Manchester, In., U.S.	C6	91
North Manitou Island, i., Mi., U.S.	C4	99
North Mankato, Mn., U.S.	F4	100
North Merrydale, La., U.S.	*D4	95
North Miami, Fl., U.S.	G6	86
North Miami Beach, Fl., U.S.	s13	86
North Middletown, Ky., U.S.	B5	94
North Moose Lake, l., Man., Can.	B1	70
North Mountain, mtn., Pa., U.S.	D9	115
North Muskegon, Mi., U.S.	E4	99
North Myrtle Beach, S.C., U.S.	D10	117
North Naples, Fl., U.S.	F5	86
North New River Canal, Fl., U.S.	F6	86
North Ogden, Ut., U.S.	B4	121
North Olmsted, Oh., U.S.	h9	112
North Palisade, mtn., Ca., U.S.	D4	82
North Park, Il., U.S.	A4	90
North Park, val., Co., U.S.	A4	83
North Pass, strt., La., U.S.	E7	95
North Pembroke, Ma., U.S.	B6	98
North Plainfield, N.J., U.S.	B4	107
North Plains, Or., U.S.	B4	114
North Plains, pl., N.M., U.S.	C1	108
North Platte, Ne., U.S.	C5	104
North Platte, stm., U.S.	C6	76
North Point, c., Md., U.S.	B5	97
North Point, c., Mi., U.S.	C7	99
North Pole	A12	128
Northport, Al., U.S.	B2	78
North Prairie, Wi., U.S.	F5	126
North Providence, R.I., U.S.	C4	116
North Raccoon, stm., Ia., U.S.	C3	92
North Reading, Ma., U.S.	f11	98
North Richland Hills, Tx., U.S.	n9	120
Northridge, Oh., U.S.	C2	112
North Ridgeville, Oh., U.S.	A3	112
North Royalton, Oh., U.S.	h9	112
North Rustico, P.E.I., Can.	C6	71
North Salem, N.H., U.S.	E4	106
North Salt Lake, Ut., U.S.	C4	121
North Santee, stm., S.C., U.S.	E9	117
North Saskatchewan, stm., Can.	F10	66
North Schell Peak, mtn., Nv., U.S.	D7	105
North Scituate, Ma., U.S.	h12	98
North Sea, Eur.	D8	4
North Shoshone Peak, mtn., Nv., U.S.	D4	105
North Sioux City, S.D., U.S.	E9	118
North Skunk, stm., Ia., U.S.	C5	92
North Springfield, Vt., U.S.	E3	122
North Springfield Reservoir, res., Vt., U.S.	E4	122
North Star, De., U.S.	A3	85
North St. Paul, Mn., U.S.	m13	100
North Stratford, N.H., U.S.	A3	106
North Sudbury, Ma., U.S.	g10	98
North Swanzey, N.H., U.S.	E2	106
North Syracuse, N.Y., U.S.	B4	109
North Tarrytown, N.Y., U.S.	D7	109
North Terre Haute, In., U.S.	E3	91
North Thompson, stm., B.C., Can.	D8	69
North Tonawanda, N.Y., U.S.	B2	109
North Troy, Vt., U.S.	B4	122
North Tunica, Ms., U.S.	A3	101
North Twin Lake, l., Wi., U.S.	B4	126
Northumberland, Pa., U.S.	E8	115
Northumberland, co., Pa., U.S.	D8	115
Northumberland, co., Va., U.S.	C6	123
Northumberland National Park, Eng., U.K.	F10	7
Northumberland Strait, strt., Can.	C6	71
North Umpqua, stm., Or., U.S.	D3	114
North Uxbridge, Ma., U.S.	B4	98
Northvale, N.J., U.S.	g9	107
North Vancouver, B.C., Can.	E6	69
North Vassalboro, Me., U.S.	D3	96
North Vernon, In., U.S.	F6	91
Northville, Mi., U.S.	p15	99
North Wales, Pa., U.S.	F11	115
North Walpole, N.H., U.S.	D2	106
North Warren, Pa., U.S.	C3	115
North Webster, In., U.S.	B6	91
North West Cape, c., Austl.	D2	50
Northwest Miramichi, stm., N.B., Can.	B3	71
Northwest Providence Channel, strt., Bah.	A8	64
Northwest Territories, prov., Can.	C13	66
North Wildwood, N.J., U.S.	E3	107
North Wilkesboro, N.C., U.S.	A1	110
North Windham, Ct., U.S.	C7	84
North Windham, Me., U.S.	E2	96
Northwood, Ia., U.S.	A4	92
Northwood, N.D., U.S.	B8	111
North Woodstock, N.H., U.S.	B3	106
North York, Ont., Can.	D5	73
North York, Pa., U.S.	G8	115
North York Moors National Park, Eng., U.K.	G12	7
Norton, N.B., Can.	D4	71
Norton, Ks., U.S.	C4	93
Norton, Ma., U.S.	C5	98
Norton, Oh., U.S.	A4	112
Norton, Va., U.S.	f9	123
Norton, co., Ks., U.S.	C4	93
Norton Air Force Base, mil., Ca., U.S.	E5	82
Norton Bay, b., Ak., U.S.	C7	79
Norton Pond, l., Vt., U.S.	B5	122
Norton Reservoir, res., Ks., U.S.	C3	93
Norton Shores, Mi., U.S.	E4	99
Norton Sound, strt., Ak., U.S.	C6	79
Nortonville, Ks., U.S.	C8	93
Nortonville, Ky., U.S.	C2	94
Norwalk, Ca., U.S.	n12	82
Norwalk, Ct., U.S.	E2	84
Norwalk, Ia., U.S.	C4	92
Norwalk, Oh., U.S.	A3	112
Norwalk, stm., Ct., U.S.	E2	84
Norwalk Islands, is., Ct., U.S.	E2	84
Norway, Me., U.S.	D2	96
Norway, Mi., U.S.	C3	99
Norway, ctry., Eur.	C9	4
Norway Bay, b., N.W. Ter., Can.	B12	66
Norway House, Man., Can.	C3	70
Norway Lake, l., Mn., U.S.	E3	100
Norwegian Sea, Eur.	C12	128
Norwich, Eng., U.K.	I14	7
Norwich, Ct., U.S.	C7	84
Norwich, N.Y., U.S.	C5	109
Norwich, Vt., U.S.	D4	122
Norwood, Ont., Can.	C7	73
Norwood, Ma., U.S.	B5	98
Norwood, Mn., U.S.	F5	100
Norwood, N.J., U.S.	h9	107
Norwood, N.Y., U.S.	f10	109
Norwood, N.C., U.S.	B2	110
Norwood, Oh., U.S.	o13	112
Norwood, Pa., U.S.	p20	115
Norwoodville, Ia., U.S.	e8	92
Noshiro, Japan	B13	30
Notasulga, Al., U.S.	C4	78
Notch Peak, mtn., Ut., U.S.	D2	121
Noto, Italy	M10	14
Notodden, Nor.	G7	6
Notre Dame, Monts, mts., Que., Can.	k13	74
Notre Dame Bay, b., Newf., Can.	D4	72
Notre Dame de Lourdes, Man., Can.	E2	70
Notre-Dame-du-Lac, Que., Can.	B9	74
Nottawasaga Bay, b., Ont., Can.	C4	73
Nottaway, stm., Que., Can.	h11	74
Nottingham, Eng., U.K.	I11	7
Nottingham Island, i., N.W. Ter., Can.	D17	66
Nottoway, co., Va., U.S.	C4	123
Nottoway, stm., Va., U.S.	D5	123
Nouadhibou, Maur.	D2	42
Nouakchott, Maur.	E2	42
Nouamrhar, Maur.	E2	42
Noupoort, S. Afr.	H4	44
Nouveau-Québec, Cratère du, crat., Que., Can.	D18	66
Nova América, Braz.	C4	57
Nova Cruz, Braz.	E11	54
Nova Freixo, Moz.	D7	44
Nova Friburgo, Braz.	G7	57
Nova Gaia, Ang.	D3	44
Nova Gradiška, Cro.	D12	14
Nova Iguaçu, Braz.	G7	57
Novaja Sibir', Ostrov, i., Russia	B23	24
Novaja Zeml'a, is., Russia	C5	24
Nova Lima, Braz.	E7	57
Nova Lisboa see Huambo, Ang.	D3	44
Nova Mambone, Moz.	F7	44
Novara, Italy	D3	14
Nova Scotia, prov., Can.	D6	71
Nova Sofala, Moz.	F6	44
Novato, Ca., U.S.	C2	82
Novelda, Spain	G11	12
Nové Zámky, Slov.	H18	8
Novgorod, Russia	C14	18
Novi, Mi., U.S.	p15	99
Novi Ligure, Italy	E3	14
Novi Pazar, Bul.	F11	16
Novi Pazar, Yugo.	F4	16
Novi Sad, Yugo.	D3	16
Novoaltajsk, Russia	G10	24
Novo Aripuanã, Braz.	E6	54
Novogrudok, Bela.	H8	18
Novokuzneck, Russia	G11	24
Novo Mesto, Slo.	D10	14
Novo Redondo, Ang.	D2	44
Novorossijsk, Russia	I5	22
Novorybnoje, Russia	C15	24
Novosibirsk, Russia	D4	128
Novosibirskije Ostrova, is., Russia	B22	24
Novosibirskoje Vodochranilišče, res., Russia	G10	24
Novotroick, Russia	G9	22
Novozybkov, Russia	I14	18
Novska, Cro.	D11	14
Nowa Sól (Neusalz), Pol.	D15	8
Nowata, Ok., U.S.	A6	113
Nowata, co., Ok., U.S.	A6	113
Nowgong, India	G15	00
Nowood, stm., Wy., U.S.	B5	127
Nowshāk, mtn., Asia	B1	38
Nowshera, Pak.	C4	38
Nowy Sącz, Pol.	F20	8
Nowy Targ, Pol.	F20	8
Noxon Reservoir, res., Mt., U.S.	C1	103
Noxontown Lake, res., De., U.S.	C3	85
Noxubee, co., Ms., U.S.	B5	101
Noxubee, stm., U.S.	B5	101
Noyes Island, i., Ak., U.S.	n22	79
Noyon, Fr.	C9	10
Nozay, Fr.	E5	10
Nsanje, Mwi.	E7	44
Nsawam, Ghana	G5	42
Nubanusit Lake, l., N.H., U.S.	E2	106
Nubian Desert, des., Sudan	D12	42
Nuckolls, co., Ne., U.S.	D7	104
Nucla, Co., U.S.	C2	83
Nueces, co., Tx., U.S.	F4	120
Nueces, stm., Tx., U.S.	E3	120
Nueltin Lake, l., Can.	E13	66
Nueva Casas Grandes, Mex.	B6	62
Nueva Rosita, Mex.	D9	62
Nueva San Salvador, El Sal.	H3	64
Nueve de Julio, Arg.	D4	56
Nuevitas, Cuba	D9	64
Nuevo, Golfo, b., Arg.	E4	56
Nuevo Laredo, Mex.	D10	62

Name — Map Ref — Page

Nuevo Rocafuerte, Ec. H5 58
Nuits-Saint-Georges, Fr. E11 10
Nukus, Uzb. I9 22
Nulato, Ak., U.S. C8 79
Nulhegan, stm., Vt., U.S. B5 122
Nullagine, Austl. D4 50
Nullarbor Plain, pl., Austl. F5 50
Numata, Japan F12 30
Numazu, Japan G11 30
Numfoor, Pulau, i., Indon. F9 32
Nun, stm., China A12 26
Nunivak Island, i., Ak., U.S. D6 79
Nunjiang, China B12 26
Nuoro, Italy I4 14
N'urba, Russia E17 24
Nuremberg, Pa., U.S. E9 115
Nuremberg see Nürnberg, Ger. F11 8
Nürnberg, Ger. F11 8
Nurri, Italy J4 14
Nutley, N.J., U.S. B4 107
Nutter Fort, W.V., U.S. k10 125
Nutting Lake, Ma., U.S. f10 98
Nuuanu Pali, Hi., U.S. g10 88
Nyack, N.Y., U.S. D7 109
Nyainqêntanglha Shan, mts., China E13 38
Nyala, Sudan F10 42
Nyanda, Zimb. F6 44
Nyasa, Lake, I., Afr. D6 44
Nyaunglebin, Mya. F4 34
Nybro, Swe. H10 6
Nye, co., Nv., U.S. E5 105
Nyenyam, China F11 38
Nyeri, Kenya B7 44
Nyíregyháza, Hung. H21 8
Nykøbing, Den. I8 6
Nyköping, Swe. G11 6
Nylstroom, S. Afr. F5 44
Nynäshamn, Swe. G11 6
Nyngan, Austl. F9 50
Nyon, Switz. F13 10
Nyons, Fr. H12 10
Nysa, Pol. E17 8
Nysa Łużycka (Neisse) (Nisa), stm., Eur. D14 8
Nyssa, Or., U.S. D9 114
Nzérékoré, Gui. G4 42
N'zeto, Ang. C2 44

O

Oahe, Lake, res., U.S. B6 76
Oahe Dam, S.D., U.S. C5 118
Oahu, i., Hi., U.S. B4 88
Oak Bay, B.C., Can. h12 69
Oak Bluffs, Ma., U.S. D6 98
Oak Creek, Co., U.S. A4 83
Oak Creek, Wi., U.S. n12 126
Oakdale, Ca., U.S. D3 82
Oakdale, Ga., U.S. h8 87
Oakdale, La., U.S. D3 95
Oakdale, Pa., U.S. k13 115
Oakes, N.D., U.S. C7 111
Oakfield, N.Y., U.S. B2 109
Oakfield, Wi., U.S. E5 126
Oak Forest, Il., U.S. k9 90
Oak Grove, Ky., U.S. D2 94
Oak Grove, La., U.S. B4 95
Oak Grove, Or., U.S. B4 114
Oak Harbor, Oh., U.S. A2 112
Oak Harbor, Wa., U.S. A3 124
Oak Hill, Mi., U.S. D4 99
Oak Hill, Oh., U.S. D3 112
Oak Hill, W.V., U.S. D3 125
Oak Hill, mtn., Ma., U.S. f9 98
Oakhurst, Ok., U.S. A5 113
Oak Island, i., Wi., U.S. B3 126
Oak Lake, I., Man., Can. E1 70
Oakland, Ca., U.S. D2 82
Oakland, Il., U.S. D5 90
Oakland, Ia., U.S. C2 92
Oakland, Me., U.S. D3 96
Oakland, Md., U.S. m12 97
Oakland, Ne., U.S. C9 104
Oakland, N.J., U.S. A4 107
Oakland, Ok., U.S. C5 113
Oakland, Or., U.S. D3 114
Oakland, R.I., U.S. B2 116
Oakland, co., Mi., U.S. F7 99
Oakland City, In., U.S. H3 91
Oakland Park, Fl., U.S. r13 86
Oak Lawn, Il., U.S. B6 90
Oaklawn, Ks., U.S. g12 93
Oakley, Id., U.S. G5 89
Oakley, Ks., U.S. C3 93
Oakman, Al., U.S. B2 78
Oakmont, Pa., U.S. E2 115
Oak Mountain, mtn., Ga., U.S. D2 87
Oak Orchard, De., U.S. F5 85
Oak Park, Il., U.S. B6 90
Oak Park, Mi., U.S. p15 99
Oak Ridge, N.C., U.S. A3 110
Oakridge, Or., U.S. D4 114
Oak Ridge, Tn., U.S. C9 119
Oak Ridge Reservoir, res., N.J., U.S. A3 107
Oakton, Va., U.S. g12 123
Oaktown, In., U.S. G3 91
Oak Valley, N.J., U.S. D2 107
Oakville, Ont., Can. D5 73
Oakville, Ct., U.S. C3 84
Oakville, Mo., U.S. g13 102
Oakwood, Ga., U.S. B3 87
Oakwood, Il., U.S. C6 90
Oakwood, Oh., U.S. C1 112
Oamaru, N.Z. F3 52
Oaxaca [de Juárez], Mex. I11 62
Ob', stm., Russia D7 24
Oban, Scot., U.K. E7 7
Obbia, Som. G4 46
Obed, stm., Tn., U.S. C9 119
Oberlin, Ks., U.S. C3 93
Oberlin, La., U.S. D3 95
Oberlin, Oh., U.S. A3 112
Oberwart, Aus. H16 8
Obetz, Oh., U.S. C3 112
Obi, Kepulauan, is., Indon. F8 32
Obi, Pulau, i., Indon. F8 32
Óbidos, Braz. D7 54
Obihiro, Japan q21 30a
Obion, Tn., U.S. A2 119
Obion, co., Tn., U.S. A2 119
Obion, stm., Tn., U.S. A2 119
Oblong, Il., U.S. D6 90
Oblučje, Russia H20 24
Obninsk, Russia F19 18
Obock, Dji. F3 46
O'Brien, co., Ia., U.S. A2 92
Obrovac, Cro. E10 14
Observation Peak, mtn., Ca., U.S. B3 82
Observatoire, Caye de l', i., N. Cal. D11 50
Obuasi, Ghana G5 42
Ocala, Fl., U.S. C4 86
Ocaña, Col. C6 58
Ocaña, Spain F8 12
Occidental, Cordillera, mts., Col. E4 58
Occidental, Cordillera, mts., Peru F4 54
Ocean, co., N.J., U.S. D4 107
Oceana, W.V., U.S. D3 125
Oceana, co., Mi., U.S. E4 99
Oceana Naval Air Station, mil., Va., U.S. k15 123
Ocean Bluff, Ma., U.S. B6 98
Ocean City, Fl., U.S. u15 86
Ocean City, Md., U.S. D7 97
Ocean City, N.J., U.S. E3 107
Ocean Grove, Ma., U.S. C5 98
Ocean Park, Wa., U.S. C1 124
Oceanport, N.J., U.S. C4 107
Oceanside, Ca., U.S. F5 82
Ocean Springs, Ms., U.S. E5 101
Ocean [Township], N.J., U.S. C4 107
Ocean View, De., U.S. F5 85
Ocha, Russia G22 24
Ocheda Lake, I., Mn., U.S. G3 100
Ocheyedan, stm., Ia., U.S. A2 92
Ochiltree, co., Tx., U.S. A2 120
Ochlockonee, stm., Fl., U.S. B2 86
Ochoco Lake, res., Or., U.S. C6 114
Ocho Rios, Jam. E9 64
Ochota, stm., Russia F22 24
Ochotsk, Russia F22 24
Ochsenfurt, Ger. F10 8
Ocilla, Ga., U.S. E3 87
Ockelbo, Swe. F11 6
Ocmulgee, stm., Ga., U.S. D3 87
Ocoee, Fl., U.S. D5 86
Ocoee, Lake, res., Tn., U.S. D9 119
Oconee, co., Ga., U.S. C3 87
Oconee, co., S.C., U.S. B1 117
Oconee, stm., Ga., U.S. C3 87
Oconee, Lake, res., Ga., U.S. C3 87
Oconomowoc, Wi., U.S. E5 126
Oconto, Wi., U.S. D6 126
Oconto, co., Wi., U.S. D5 126
Oconto, stm., Wi., U.S. D5 126
Oconto Falls, Wi., U.S. D5 126
Ocotal, Nic. H4 64
Ocotlán, Mex. G8 62
Ocracoke Inlet, b., N.C., U.S. B6 110
Ocracoke Island, i., N.C., U.S. B7 110
Octoraro Creek, stm., U.S. A5 97
Ocumare del Tuy, Ven. B9 58
Ocussi, Indon. G7 32
Oda, Ghana G5 42
Oda, Jabal, mtn., Sudan D13 42
Ōdate, Japan B13 30
Odawara, Japan G12 30
Odda, Nor. F6 6
Odebolt, Ia., U.S. B2 92
Odell, Il., U.S. B5 90
Odell, Or., U.S. B5 114
Odell Lake, I., Or., U.S. E5 114
Odem, Tx., U.S. F4 120
Odemira, Port. H3 12
Ödemiş, Tur. K11 16
Odense, Den. I8 6
Odenton, Md., U.S. B4 97
Odenville, Al., U.S. B3 78
Oder (Odra), stm., Eur. C14 8
Oderberg, Ger. C14 8
Odesa, Ukr. H4 22
Odessa, Ont., Can. C8 73
Odessa, De., U.S. C3 85
Odessa, Mo., U.S. C4 102
Odessa, Tx., U.S. D1 120
Odessa, Wa., U.S. B7 124
Odienné, C. Iv. G4 42
Odin, Il., U.S. E4 90
Odincovo, Russia F20 18
Odon, In., U.S. G4 91
O'Donnell, Tx., U.S. C2 120
Odra (Oder), stm., Eur. C14 8
Oelsnitz, Ger. E12 8
Oelwein, Ia., U.S. B6 92
O'Fallon, Il., U.S. E4 90
O'Fallon, Mo., U.S. f12 102
Offenbach, Ger. E8 8
Offenburg, Ger. G7 8
Offutt Air Force Base, mil., Ne., U.S. g3 104
Ōfunato, Japan C14 30
Ōgaki, Japan G9 30
Ogallala, Ne., U.S. C4 104
Ogbomosho, Nig. G6 42
Ogden, Ia., U.S. B3 92
Ogden, Ks., U.S. C7 93
Ogden, Ut., U.S. B4 121
Ogden, Mount, mtn., N.A. k23 79
Ogdensburg, N.J., U.S. A3 107
Ogdensburg, N.Y., U.S. f9 109
Ogeechee, stm., Ga., U.S. D5 87
Ogemaw, co., Mi., U.S. D6 99
Ogilvie Mountains, mts., Yukon, Can. D5 66
Ogle, co., Il., U.S. A4 90
Oglesby, Il., U.S. B4 90
Oglethorpe, Ga., U.S. D2 87
Oglethorpe, co., Ga., U.S. C3 87
Oglethorpe, Mount, mtn., Ga., U.S. B2 87
Ogooué, stm., Afr. B2 44
Ogulin, Cro. D10 14
Ogunquit, Me., U.S. E2 96
Oğuzeli, Tur. A5 40
Ohanet, Alg. C7 42
Ōhata, Japan A14 30
Ohatchee, Al., U.S. B3 78
O'Higgins, Lago (Lago San Martín), I., S.A. F2 56
Ohio, co., In., U.S. G7 91
Ohio, co., Ky., U.S. C3 94
Ohio, co., W.V., U.S. A4 125
Ohio, state, U.S. B3 112
Ohio, stm., U.S. D9 76
Ohio Brush Creek, stm., Oh., U.S. D2 112
Ohio City, Oh., U.S. B1 112
Ohio Peak, mtn., Co., U.S. C3 83
Ohioville, Pa., U.S. E1 115
Ohoopee, stm., Ga., U.S. D4 87
Ohrid, Lake, I., Eur. H4 16
Öhringen, Ger. F9 8
Oiapoque, Braz. C8 54
Oil City, La., U.S. B2 95
Oil City, Pa., U.S. D2 115
Oil Creek, stm., Pa., U.S. C2 115
Oildale, Ca., U.S. E4 82
Oil Springs, Ont., Can. E2 73
Oilton, Ok., U.S. A5 113
Ōita, Japan I4 30
Ojai, Ca., U.S. E4 82
Ojinaga, Mex. C7 62
Ojm'akon, Russia E22 24
Ojo de Liebre, Laguna, b., Mex. D2 62
Ojos del Salado, Cerro, mtn., S.A. B3 56
Oka, stm., Russia F25 18
Oka, stm., Russia G14 24
Okaba, Indon. G10 32
Okahandja, Nmb. F3 44
Okaloosa, co., Fl., U.S. u15 86
Okamanpeedan Lake, I., U.S. A3 92
Okanagan Falls, B.C., Can. E8 69
Okanagan Lake, I., B.C., Can. D8 69
Okanagan Landing, B.C., Can. D8 69
Okanogan, Wa., U.S. A6 124
Okanogan, co., Wa., U.S. A5 124
Okāra, Pak. E5 38
Okarche, Ok., U.S. B4 113
Okatibee Reservoir, res., Ms., U.S. C5 101
Okauchee Lake, Wi., U.S. *E5 126
Okavango (Cubango), stm., Afr. E3 44
Okavango Swamp, sw., Bots. E4 44
Ōkawa, Japan I3 30
Okawville, Il., U.S. E4 90
Okaya, Japan F11 30
Okayama, Japan H6 30
Okazaki, Japan H10 30
Okeechobee, Fl., U.S. E6 86
Okeechobee, co., Fl., U.S. E6 86
Okeechobee, Lake, I., Fl., U.S. F6 86
Okeene, Ok., U.S. A3 113
Okefenokee Swamp, sw., U.S. F4 87
Okemah, Ok., U.S. B5 113
Okfuskee, co., Ok., U.S. B5 113
Okhotsk, Sea of (Ochotskoje More), Asia G23 24
Oki-guntō, is., Japan F6 30
Okinawa-jima, i., Japan y27 31b
Okinoerabu-shima, i., Japan x28 31b
Okino-Tori-shima, i., Japan G14 26
Oklahoma, co., Ok., U.S. B4 113
Oklahoma, state, U.S. B4 113
Oklahoma City, Ok., U.S. B4 113
Oklawaha, Fl., U.S. C5 86
Oklawaha, stm., Fl., U.S. C5 86
Oklawaha, Lake, res., Fl., U.S. C5 86
Okmulgee, Ok., U.S. B6 113
Okmulgee, co., Ok., U.S. B5 113
Okoboji, Ia., U.S. A2 92
Okobojo Creek, stm., S.D., U.S. C5 118
Okolona, Ky., U.S. g11 94
Okolona, Ms., U.S. B5 101
Okotoks, Alta., Can. D4 68
Okt'abr'skoj Revol'ucii, Ostrov, i., Russia B13 24
Oktibbeha, co., Ms., U.S. B5 101
Ola, Ar., U.S. B2 81
Olancha Peak, mtn., Ca., U.S. D4 82
Olanchito, Hond. G4 64
Öland, i., Swe. H11 6
Olanta, S.C., U.S. D8 117
Olathe, Co., U.S. C3 83
Olathe, Ks., U.S. D9 93
Olavarría, Arg. D4 56
Olbia, Italy I4 14
Ol'chon, Ostrov, i., Russia G15 24
Olcott, N.Y., U.S. B2 109
Old Bahama Channel, strt., N.A. C8 64
Old Bridge, N.J., U.S. C4 107
Oldenburg, Ger. B8 8
Oldenburg, In., U.S. F7 91
Oldenburg [in Holstein], Ger. A10 8
Old Faithful Geyser, Wy., U.S. B2 127
Old Forge, Pa., U.S. D10 115
Old Fort, N.C., U.S. f10 110
Oldham, co., Ky., U.S. B4 94
Oldham, co., Tx., U.S. B1 120
Old Harbor, Ak., U.S. D9 79
Old Head of Kinsale, c., Ire. J4 7
Old Hickory Lake, res., Tn., U.S. A5 119
Oldman, stm., Alta., Can. E4 68
Old Man of the Mountain, N.H., U.S. B3 106
Oldmans Creek, stm., N.J., U.S. D2 107
Old Orchard Beach, Me., U.S. E2 96
Old Perlican, Newf., Can. D5 72
Old Point Comfort, c., Va., U.S. h15 123
Old Rhodes Key, i., Fl., U.S. G6 86
Old River Lake, I., Ar., U.S. k10 81
Olds, Alta., Can. D3 68
Old Saybrook, Ct., U.S. D6 84
Oldsmar, Fl., U.S. o10 86
Old Tampa Bay, b., Fl., U.S. p10 86
Old Tappan, N.J., U.S. g9 107
Old Topsail Inlet, b., N.C., U.S. C5 110
Old Town, Me., U.S. D4 96
Old Wives Lake, I., Sask., Can. G2 75
Olean, N.Y., U.S. C2 109
O'Leary, P.E.I., Can. C5 71
Ølen, Nor. G5 6
Olenij, Ostrov, i., Russia C9 24
Olen'ok, Russia D16 24
Olen'ok, stm., Russia C18 24
Olen'okskij Zaliv, b., Russia C18 24
Olentangy, stm., Oh., U.S. B3 112
Oleśnica, Pol. D17 8
Ol'ga, Russia I21 24
Olga, Mount, mtn., Austl. E6 50
Olhão, Port. H3 12
Ólimbos, mtn., Cyp. B3 40
Ólimbos, Óros, mtn., Grc. I6 16
Olímpia, Braz. F4 57
Olin, Ia., U.S. B6 92
Olinda, Braz. E12 54
Olite, Spain C10 12
Oliva, Arg. C4 56
Oliva, Spain G11 12
Oliva de la Frontera, Spain G5 12
Olive Branch, Ms., U.S. A4 101
Olive Hill, Ky., U.S. B6 94
Olivehurst, Ca., U.S. C3 82
Oliveira, Braz. F6 57
Olivenza, Spain G4 12
Oliver, B.C., Can. E8 69
Oliver, Pa., U.S. G2 115
Oliver, co., N.D., U.S. B4 111
Oliver Dam, U.S. C5 78
Oliver Springs, Tn., U.S. C9 119
Olivet, Mi., U.S. F6 99
Olivia, Mn., U.S. F4 100
Olla, La., U.S. C3 95
Ollagüe, Chile A3 56
Olmedo, Spain D7 12
Olmito, Tx., U.S. F4 120
Olmos, Peru E3 54
Olmos Park, Tx., U.S. k7 120
Olmsted, co., Mn., U.S. G6 100
Olmsted Falls, Oh., U.S. h9 112
Olney, Il., U.S. E5 90
Olney, Md., U.S. B3 97
Olney, Tx., U.S. C3 120
Oloj, stm., Russia D26 24
Ol'okma, stm., Russia F18 24
Ol'okminsk, Russia E18 24
Olomouc, Czech. F17 8
Olongapo, Phil. q19 33b
Oloron-Sainte-Marie, Fr. I6 10
Olot, Spain C14 12
Olov'annaja, Russia G17 24
Olsztyn (Allenstein), Pol. B20 8
Olten, Switz. E14 10
Olton, Tx., U.S. B1 120
Oluan Pi, c., Tai. N9 28
Olustee, Ok., U.S. C2 113
Ol'utorskij, Mys, c., Russia F28 24
Olympia, Wa., U.S. B3 124
Olympic Mountains, mts., Wa., U.S. B2 124
Olympic National Park, Wa., U.S. B2 124
Olympus, Mount, mtn., Wa., U.S. B2 124
Olympus, Mount see Ólimbos, Óros, mtn., Grc. I6 16
Olyphant, Pa., U.S. D10 115
Omae-zaki, c., Japan H11 30
Omagh, N. Ire., U.K. G5 7
Omaha, Ne., U.S. C10 104
Omaha Indian Reservation, Ne., U.S. B9 104
Omak, Wa., U.S. A6 124
Omak Lake, I., Wa., U.S. A6 124
Oman, ctry., Asia D6 46
Oman, Gulf of, b., Asia D6 46
Omar, W.V., U.S. D3 125
Ōma-zaki, c., Japan A13 30
Omčak, Russia E23 24
Omega, Ga., U.S. E3 87
Omegna, Italy D3 14
Omemee, Ont., Can. C6 73
Omerville, Que., Can. D5 74
Ometepe, Isla de, i., Nic. I5 64
Ometepec, Mex. I10 62
Omineca, stm., B.C., Can. B5 69
Omineca Mountains, mts., B.C., Can. A4 69
Ōmiya, Japan G12 30
Ommaney, Cape, c., Ak., U.S. D12 79
Ommanney Bay, b., N.W. Ter., Can. B12 66
Ommen, Neth. C6 8
Omo, stm., Eth. G2 46
Omolon, stm., Russia D25 24
Ompompanoosuc, stm., Vt., U.S. D4 122
Omro, Wi., U.S. D5 126
Omsk, Russia F8 24
Omsukčan, Russia E25 24
Ōmura, Japan J2 30
Ōmuta, Japan I3 30
Onaga, Ks., U.S. C7 93
Onalaska, Wa., U.S. C3 124
Onalaska, Wi., U.S. E2 126
Onamia, Mn., U.S. D5 100
Onancock, Va., U.S. C7 123
Onarga, Il., U.S. C6 90
Onawa, Ia., U.S. B1 92
Onawa, Lake, I., Me., U.S. C3 96
Onaway, Mi., U.S. C6 99
Onda, Spain F11 12
Ondangua, Nmb. E3 44
Ondjiva, Ang. E3 44
Öndörchaan, Mong. B9 26
Oneco, Fl., U.S. E4 86
Onega, Lake see Onežskoje ozero, I., Russia E5 22
One Hundred Fifty Mile House, B.C., Can. C7 69
One Hundred Mile House, B.C., Can. D7 69
Oneida, Ky., U.S. C6 94
Oneida, N.Y., U.S. B5 109
Oneida, Oh., U.S. C1 112
Oneida, Tn., U.S. C9 119
Oneida, co., Id., U.S. G6 89
Oneida, co., N.Y., U.S. B5 109
Oneida, co., Wi., U.S. C4 126
Oneida Lake, I., N.Y., U.S. B5 109
O'Neill, Ne., U.S. B7 104
Onekotan, Ostrov, i., Russia H24 24
Oneonta, Al., U.S. B3 78
Oneonta, N.Y., U.S. C5 109
Onești, Rom. C10 16
Onežskoje ozero, I., Russia E5 22
Ongole, India E6 37
Onida, S.D., U.S. C5 118
Onitsha, Nig. G7 42
Onoda, Japan I4 30
Onomichi, Japan H6 30
Onondaga, co., N.Y., U.S. C4 109
Onondaga Indian Reservation, N.Y., U.S. C4 109
Onota Lake, I., Ma., U.S. B1 98
Onoway, Alta., Can. C3 68
Onset, Ma., U.S. C6 98
Onslow, Austl. D3 50
Onslow, co., N.C., U.S. C5 110
Onslow Bay, b., N.C., U.S. C5 110
Onsted, Mi., U.S. F6 99
Ontario, Ca., U.S. E5 82
Ontario, Oh., U.S. B3 112
Ontario, Or., U.S. C10 114
Ontario, co., N.Y., U.S. C3 109
Ontario, prov., Can. C6 73
Ontario, Lake, I., N.A. C11 76
Onteniente, Spain G11 12
Ontonagon, Mi., U.S. m12 99
Ontonagon, co., Mi., U.S. m12 99
Ontonagon Indian Reservation, Mi., U.S. B1 99
Onverwacht, Sur. B7 54
Oodnadatta, Austl. E7 50
Ooldea, Austl. F6 50
Oolitic, In., U.S. G4 91
Oologah, Ok., U.S. A6 113
Oologah Lake, res., Ok., U.S. A6 113
Ooltewah, Tn., U.S. D8 119
Oostburg, Wi., U.S. E6 126
Oostende (Ostende), Bel. D2 8
Oosterhout, Neth. D4 8
Ootacamund, India G4 37
Ootsa Lake, I., B.C., Can. C4 69
Opala, Zaire B4 44
Opa-Locka, Fl., U.S. s13 86
Opatija, Cro. D9 14
Opava, Czech. F17 8
Opelika, Al., U.S. C4 78
Opelousas, La., U.S. D3 95
Opequon Creek, stm., W.V., U.S. B6 125
Opiscotéo, Lac, I., Que., Can. F19 66
Opole (Oppeln), Pol. E17 8
Opotiki, N.Z. C6 52
Opp, Al., U.S. D3 78
Oppdal, Nor. E7 6
Oppelo, Ar., U.S. B3 81
Opportunity, Wa., U.S. B8 124
Optima Reservoir, res., Ok., U.S. e9 113
Oquawka, Il., U.S. C3 90
Ora, Italy C6 14
Oracle, Az., U.S. E5 80
Oradea, Rom. B5 16
Oradell, N.J., U.S. h8 107
Oradell Reservoir, res., N.J., U.S. h9 107
Orai, India H8 38
Oran (Wahran), Alg. A5 42
Oran, Mo., U.S. D8 102
Orange, Austl. F9 50
Orange, Fr. H11 10
Orange, Ca., U.S. n13 82
Orange, Ct., U.S. D3 84
Orange, Ma., U.S. A3 98
Orange, N.J., U.S. B4 107
Orange, Tx., U.S. D6 120
Orange, Va., U.S. B4 123
Orange, co., Ca., U.S. F5 82
Orange, co., Fl., U.S. D5 86
Orange, co., In., U.S. G4 91
Orange, co., N.Y., U.S. D6 109
Orange, co., N.C., U.S. A3 110
Orange, co., Tx., U.S. D6 120
Orange, co., Vt., U.S. D3 122
Orange, co., Va., U.S. B4 123
Orange (Oranje), stm., Afr. G3 44
Orange, Cabo, c., Braz. C8 54
Orange Beach, Al., U.S. E2 78
Orangeburg, S.C., U.S. E6 117
Orangeburg, co., S.C., U.S. E6 117
Orange City, Fl., U.S. D5 86
Orange City, Ia., U.S. B1 92
Orange Grove, Ms., U.S. E5 101
Orange Grove, Tx., U.S. F4 120
Orange Lake, I., Fl., U.S. C4 86
Orange Park, Fl., U.S. B5 86
Orangeville, Ont., Can. D4 73
Orangeville, Ut., U.S. D4 121
Orange Walk, Belize E3 64
Orani, Phil. q19 33b
Oranienburg, Ger. C13 8
Oranjestad, Aruba H12 64
Orbetello, Italy G6 14
Orbost, Austl. G9 50
Örbyhus, Swe. F11 6
Orcas Island, i., Wa., U.S. A3 124
Orcera, Spain G9 12
Orchard City, Co., U.S. C3 83
Orchard Homes, Mt., U.S. D2 103
Orchard Park, N.Y., U.S. C2 109
Orchards, Wa., U.S. D3 124
Orchard Valley, Wy., U.S. E8 127
Orchila, Isla, i., Ven. B9 58
Orchon, stm., Mong. B7 26
Orcutt, Ca., U.S. E3 82
Ord, Ne., U.S. C7 104
Ord, Mount, mtn., Austl. C5 50
Ordenes, Spain B3 12
Ordway, Co., U.S. C7 83

Name	Map Ref	Page
Ordzhonikidze see Vladikavkaz, Russia	I6	22
Oreana, Il., U.S.	D5	90
Örebro, Swe.	G10	6
Orechovo-Zujevo, Russia	F21	18
Oregon, Il., U.S.	A4	90
Oregon, Mo., U.S.	B2	102
Oregon, Oh., U.S.	A2	112
Oregon, Wi., U.S.	F4	126
Oregon, co., Mo., U.S.	E6	102
Oregon, state, U.S.	C6	114
Oregon Caves National Monument, Or., U.S.	E2	114
Oregon City, Or., U.S.	B4	114
Oregon Inlet, b., N.C., U.S.	B7	110
Orel, Russia	I19	18
Orem, Ut., U.S.	C4	121
Orenburg, Russia	G9	22
Orense, Spain	C4	12
Orestiás, Grc.	H10	16
Orfordville, Wi., U.S.	F4	126
Organ Mountains, mts., N.M., U.S.	E3	108
Organ Pipe Cactus National Monument, Az., U.S.	E3	80
Orgūn, Afg.	D3	38
Oriental, N.C., U.S.	B6	110
Oriental, Cordillera, mts., Col.	E6	58
Oriental, Cordillera, mts., Peru	F4	54
Orihuela, Spain	G11	12
Orillia, Ont., Can.	C5	73
Orinoco, stm., S.A.	C11	58
Orinoco, Delta del, Ven.	C12	58
Orion, Il., U.S.	B3	90
Oripää, Fin.	F14	6
Orissa, state, India	J11	38
Oristano, Italy	I3	14
Orivesi, Fin.	F15	6
Orizaba, Mex.	H11	62
Orizaba, Pico de (Volcán Citlaltépetl), vol., Mex.	H11	62
Orkney Islands, is., Scot., U.K.	B9	7
Orland, Ca., U.S.	C2	82
Orlando, Fl., U.S.	D5	86
Orland Park, Il., U.S.	k9	90
Orléans, Fr.	E8	10
Orleans, Ma., U.S.	C7	98
Orleans, Vt., U.S.	B4	122
Orleans, co., La., U.S.	E6	95
Orleans, co., N.Y., U.S.	B2	109
Orleans, co., Vt., U.S.	B4	122
Orléans, Île d', i., Que., Can.	C6	74
Orman Dam, S.D., U.S.	C2	118
Ormond Beach, Fl., U.S.	C5	86
Ormož, Slo.	C11	14
Ormstown, Que., Can.	D3	74
Ornans, Fr.	E13	10
Örnsköldsvik, Swe.	E12	6
Orocué, Col.	E7	58
Orofino, Id., U.S.	C2	89
Oromocto, N.B., Can.	D3	71
Oromocto Lake, l., N.B., Can.	D2	71
Orono, Me., U.S.	D4	96
Oronoco, Mn., U.S.	F6	100
Oroville, Ca., U.S.	C3	82
Oroville, Wa., U.S.	A6	124
Oroville, Lake, res., Ca., U.S.	C3	82
Orrick, Mo., U.S.	B3	102
Orrville, Oh., U.S.	B4	112
Orsk, Russia	G9	22
Orta Nova, Italy	H10	14
Ortegal, Cabo, c., Spain	B4	12
Orting, Wa., U.S.	B3	124
Ortiz, Ven.	C9	58
Ortona, Italy	G9	14
Ortonville, Mi., U.S.	F7	99
Ortonville, Mn., U.S.	E2	100
Orūmīyeh (Reẓā'īyeh), Iran	J7	22
Orūmīyeh, Daryācheh-ye, l., Iran	J7	22
Oruro, Bol.	G5	54
Orūzgān (Qala-I-Hazār Qadam), Afg.	D2	38
Orvieto, Italy	G7	14
Orwell, Oh., U.S.	A5	112
Orwigsburg, Pa., U.S.	E9	115
Oš, Kyrg.	I12	22
Osa, Península de, pen., C.R.	J6	64
Osage, Ia., U.S.	A5	92
Osage, Wy., U.S.	C8	127
Osage, co., Ks., U.S.	D8	93
Osage, co., Mo., U.S.	C6	102
Osage, co., Ok., U.S.	A5	113
Osage, stm., Mo., U.S.	C3	102
Osage Beach, Mo., U.S.	C5	102
Osage City, Ks., U.S.	D8	93
Ōsaka, Japan	H8	30
Ōsaka-wan, b., Japan	H8	30
Osakis, Mn., U.S.	E3	100
Osakis, Lake, l., Mn., U.S.	E3	100
Osawatomie, Ks., U.S.	D9	93
Osborne, Ks., U.S.	C5	93
Osborne, co., Ks., U.S.	C5	93
Osburn, Id., U.S.	B3	89
Osceola, Ar., U.S.	B6	81
Osceola, In., U.S.	A5	91
Osceola, Ia., U.S.	C4	92
Osceola, Mo., U.S.	C4	102
Osceola, Ne., U.S.	C8	104
Osceola, Wi., U.S.	C1	126
Osceola, co., Fl., U.S.	E5	86
Osceola, co., Ia., U.S.	A2	92
Osceola, co., Mi., U.S.	E5	99
Osceola Mills, Pa., U.S.	E5	115
Oschersleben, Ger.	C11	8
Oscoda, Mi., U.S.	D7	99
Oscoda, co., Mi., U.S.	D6	99
Oscura Mountains, mts., N.M., U.S.	D3	108
Osen, Nor.	D8	6
Osgood, In., U.S.	F7	91
Oshawa, Ont., Can.	D6	73
Oshima-hantō, pen., Japan	q18	30a
Oshkosh, Ne., U.S.	C3	104
Oshkosh, Wi., U.S.	D5	126
Oshogbo, Nig.	G6	42
Osh see Oš, Kyrg.	I12	22
Oshwe, Zaire	B3	44
Osijek, Cro.	D2	16
Osimo, Italy	F8	14
Osinniki, Russia	G11	24
Osipoviči, Bela.	H11	18
Oskaloosa, Ia., U.S.	C5	92
Oskaloosa, Ks., U.S.	C8	93
Oskarshamn, Swe.	H11	6
Oslo, Nor.	G8	6
Osmānābād, India	C4	37
Osmaniye, Tur.	A5	40
Osmond, Ne., U.S.	B8	104
Osnabrück, Ger.	C8	8
Osorno, Chile	E2	56
Osorno, Spain	C7	12
Osoyoos, B.C., Can.	E8	69
Osoyoos Lake, l., Wa., U.S.	A6	124
Ospino, Ven.	C8	58
Osprey, Fl., U.S.	E4	86
Osprey Reef, rf., Austl.	B9	50
Ossa, Mount, mtn., Austl.	H9	50
Ossabaw Island, i., Ga., U.S.	E5	87
Osseo, Mn., U.S.	m12	100
Osseo, Wi., U.S.	D2	126
Ossian, In., U.S.	C7	91
Ossian, Ia., U.S.	A6	92
Ossining, N.Y., U.S.	D7	109
Ossipee, stm., U.S.	C5	106
Ossipee Lake, l., N.H., U.S.	C4	106
Ostaškov, Russia	D16	18
Osterholz-Scharmbeck, Ger.	B8	8
Osterode, Ger.	D10	8
Östersund, Swe.	E10	6
Osterville, Ma., U.S.	C7	98
Ostrava, Czech.	F18	8
Ostrołęka, Pol.	B21	8
Ostrov, Russia	D11	18
Ostrowiec Świętokrzyski, Pol.	E21	8
Ostrów Wielkopolski, Pol.	D17	8
Ostuni, Italy	I12	14
Ōsumi-kaikyō, strt., Japan	L3	30
Ōsumi-shotō, is., Japan	u30	31b
Osuna, Spain	H6	12
Osvaldo Cruz, Braz.	F3	57
Oswegatchie, stm., N.Y., U.S.	f9	109
Oswego, Il., U.S.	B5	90
Oswego, Ks., U.S.	E8	93
Oswego, N.Y., U.S.	B4	109
Oswego, co., N.Y., U.S.	B4	109
Oswego, stm., N.J., U.S.	D4	107
Oswego, stm., N.Y., U.S.	B4	109
Oswestry, Eng., U.K.	I9	7
Oświęcim, Pol.	E19	8
Ōta, Japan	F12	30
Otaki, N.Z.	D5	52
Otaru, Japan	p18	30a
Otavi, Nmb.	E3	44
Oteen, N.C., U.S.	f10	110
Otero, co., Co., U.S.	D7	83
Otero, co., N.M., U.S.	E3	108
Othello, Wa., U.S.	C6	124
Oti, stm., Afr.	G6	42
Otish, Monts, mts., Que., Can.	F18	66
Otis Orchards, Wa., U.S.	g14	124
Otis Reservoir, res., Ma., U.S.	B1	98
Otisville, Mi., U.S.	E7	99
Otjiwarongo, Nmb.	F3	44
Otočac, Cro.	E10	14
Otoe, co., Ne., U.S.	D9	104
Otranto, Italy	I13	14
Otranto, Strait of, mth., Eur.	I2	16
Otsego, Mi., U.S.	F5	99
Otsego, co., Mi., U.S.	C6	99
Otsego, co., N.Y., U.S.	C5	109
Otsego Lake, l., N.Y., U.S.	C6	109
Ōtsu, Japan	G8	30
Otta, Nor.	F7	6
Ottauquechee, stm., Vt., U.S.	D4	122
Ottawa, Ont., Can.	B9	73
Ottawa, Il., U.S.	B5	90
Ottawa, Ks., U.S.	D8	93
Ottawa, Oh., U.S.	A1	112
Ottawa, co., Ks., U.S.	C6	93
Ottawa, co., Mi., U.S.	F4	99
Ottawa, co., Oh., U.S.	A2	112
Ottawa, co., Ok., U.S.	A7	113
Ottawa, stm., Can.	G17	66
Ottawa, stm., Oh., U.S.	e6	112
Ottawa Hills, Oh., U.S.	e6	112
Ottawa Islands, is., N.W. Ter., Can.	E16	66
Ottenby, Swe.	H11	6
Otterbein, In., U.S.	D3	91
Otter Brook, stm., N.H., U.S.	E2	106
Otter Brook Lake, res., N.H., U.S.	E2	106
Otter Creek, stm., Ut., U.S.	E4	121
Otter Creek, stm., Vt., U.S.	C2	122
Otter Creek Reservoir, res., Ut., U.S.	E4	121
Otter Islands, is., S.C., U.S.	m11	117
Otter Tail, co., Mn., U.S.	D3	100
Otter Tail, stm., Mn., U.S.	D2	100
Otter Tail Lake, l., Mn., U.S.	D3	100
Otterville, Ont., Can.	E4	73
Ottumwa, Ia., U.S.	C5	92
Otwock, Pol.	C21	8
Ötztaler Alpen, mts., Eur.	C5	14
Ouachita, co., Ar., U.S.	D3	81
Ouachita, co., La., U.S.	B3	95
Ouachita, Lake, res., Ar., U.S.	C2	81
Ouachita Mountains, mts., U.S.	E8	76
Ouadda, Cen. Afr. Rep.	G10	42
Ouagadougou, Burkina	F5	42
Ouahigouya, Burkina	F5	42
Oualâta, Maur.	E4	42
Ouallene, Alg.	D6	42
Ouanda Djallé, Cen. Afr. Rep.	G10	42
Ouarane, reg., Maur.	D3	42
Ouargla, Alg.	B7	42
Ouarzazate, Mor.	B4	42
Oubangui, stm., Afr.	A3	44
Oudtshoorn, S. Afr.	H4	44
Oued Meliz, Tun.	M3	14
Oued Zarga, Tun.	M4	14
Ouémé, stm., Benin	G6	42
Ouesso, Congo	A3	44
Ouezzane, Mor.	B4	42
Oujda, Mor.	B5	42
Oulu, Fin.	D15	6
Oulujärvi, l., Fin.	D16	6
Oum Chalouba, Chad	E10	42
Ounianga Kébir, Chad	E10	42
Ouray, Co., U.S.	C3	83
Ouray, co., Co., U.S.	C3	83
Ouray, Mount, mtn., Co., U.S.	C4	83
Ourinhos, Braz.	G4	57
Ourique, Port.	H3	12
Ouro Prêto, Braz.	F7	57
Ōu-sammyaku, mts., Japan	D13	30
Outagamie, co., Wi., U.S.	D5	126
Outardes Quatre, Réservoir, res., Que., Can.	h13	74
Outer Hebrides, is., Scot., U.K.	D5	7
Outer Island, i., Wi., U.S.	A3	126
Outer Santa Barbara Passage, strt., Ca., U.S.	F4	82
Outpost Mountain, mtn., Ak., U.S.	B9	79
Outremont, Que., Can.	p19	74
Ovalle, Chile	C2	56
Ovamboland, hist. reg., Nmb.	E3	44
Ovana, Cerro, mtn., Ven.	E9	58
Ovar, Port.	E3	12
Overbrook, Ks., U.S.	D8	93
Overgaard, Az., U.S.	C5	80
Overland, Mo., U.S.	f13	102
Overland Park, Ks., U.S.	m16	93
Overlea, Md., U.S.	B4	97
Overton, Nv., U.S.	G7	105
Overton, Tx., U.S.	C5	120
Overton, co., Tn., U.S.	C8	119
Övertorneå, Swe.	C14	6
Ovett, Ms., U.S.	D4	101
Ovid, Mi., U.S.	E6	99
Oviedo, Spain	B6	12
Owando, Congo	B3	44
Owasco Lake, l., N.Y., U.S.	C4	109
Owase, Japan	H9	30
Owasso, Ok., U.S.	A6	113
Owatonna, Mn., U.S.	F5	100
Owego, N.Y., U.S.	C4	109
Owen, Wi., U.S.	D3	126
Owen, co., In., U.S.	F4	91
Owen, co., Ky., U.S.	B5	94
Owen, Lake, l., Wi., U.S.	B2	126
Owen, Mount, mtn., Co., U.S.	C3	83
Owens, stm., Ca., U.S.	D4	82
Owensboro, Ky., U.S.	C2	94
Owens Cross Roads, Al., U.S.	A3	78
Owens Lake, l., Ca., U.S.	D5	82
Owen Sound, Ont., Can.	C4	73
Owen Sound, b., Ont., Can.	C4	73
Owen Stanley Range, mts., Pap. N. Gui.	m16	50a
Owensville, In., U.S.	H2	91
Owensville, Mo., U.S.	C6	102
Owensville, Oh., U.S.	C1	112
Owenton, Ky., U.S.	B5	94
Owings Mills, Md., U.S.	B4	97
Owingsville, Ky., U.S.	B6	94
Owl Creek, stm., Wy., U.S.	C4	127
Owl Creek Mountains, mts., Wy., U.S.	C4	127
Owo, Nig.	G7	42
Owosso, Mi., U.S.	E6	99
Owsley, co., Ky., U.S.	C6	94
Owyhee, Nv., U.S.	B5	105
Owyhee, co., Id., U.S.	G2	89
Owyhee, stm., U.S.	E9	114
Owyhee, Lake, res., Or., U.S.	D9	114
Owyhee Dam, Or., U.S.	D9	114
Owyhee Mountains, mts., U.S.	G2	89
Oxbow Dam, U.S.	E2	89
Oxelösund, Swe.	G11	6
Oxford, N.S., Can.	D6	71
Oxford, N.Z.	E4	52
Oxford, Eng., U.K.	J11	7
Oxford, Al., U.S.	B4	78
Oxford, Ct., U.S.	D3	84
Oxford, Ga., U.S.	C3	87
Oxford, In., U.S.	C3	91
Oxford, Ia., U.S.	C6	92
Oxford, Ks., U.S.	E6	93
Oxford, Me., U.S.	D2	96
Oxford, Md., U.S.	C5	97
Oxford, Ma., U.S.	B4	98
Oxford, Mi., U.S.	F7	99
Oxford, Ms., U.S.	A4	101
Oxford, Ne., U.S.	D6	104
Oxford, N.Y., U.S.	C5	109
Oxford, N.C., U.S.	A4	110
Oxford, Oh., U.S.	C1	112
Oxford, Pa., U.S.	G10	115
Oxford, co., Me., U.S.	D2	96
Oxford Lake, l., Man., Can.	B4	70
Oxford Peak, mtn., Id., U.S.	G6	89
Oxnard, Ca., U.S.	E4	82
Oxon Hill, Md., U.S.	f9	97
Oxus see Amu Darya, stm., Asia	I10	22
Oyama, B.C., Can.	D8	69
Oyama, Japan	F12	30
Oyem, Gabon	A2	44
Oyen, Alta., Can.	D5	68
Oyonnax, Fr.	F12	10
Oyster Bay, N.Y., U.S.	E7	109
Oyster Keys, is., Fl., U.S.	G6	86
Ozamiz, Phil.	D7	32
Ozark, Al., U.S.	D4	78
Ozark, Ar., U.S.	B2	81
Ozark, Mo., U.S.	D4	102
Ozark, co., Mo., U.S.	E5	102
Ozark Plateau, plat., U.S.	D8	76
Ozark Reservoir, res., Ar., U.S.	B1	81
Ozarks, Lake of the, res., Mo., U.S.	C5	102
Ozaukee, co., Wi., U.S.	E6	126
Ózd, Hung.	G20	8
Ozernovskij, Russia	G25	24
Ozette Lake, l., Wa., U.S.	A1	124
Ozieri, Italy	I3	14
Ožogino, Ozero, l., Russia	D23	24
Ozona, Fl., U.S.	o10	86
Ozona, Tx., U.S.	D2	120
Ōzu, Japan	I5	30
P		
Paarl, S. Afr.	H3	44
Paauilo, Hi., U.S.	C6	88
Pabianice, Pol.	D19	8
Pābna, Bngl.	H13	38
Pacasmayo, Peru	E3	54
Pace, Fl., U.S.	u14	86
Pachaug Pond, l., Ct., U.S.	C8	84
Pachino, Italy	M10	14
Pachuca [de Soto], Mex.	G10	62
Pacific, Mo., U.S.	C7	102
Pacific, Wa., U.S.	f11	124
Pacific, co., Wa., U.S.	C2	124
Pacifica, Ca., U.S.	h8	82
Pacific Beach, Wa., U.S.	B1	124
Pacific City, Or., U.S.	B3	114
Pacific Creek, stm., Wy., U.S.	D3	127
Pacific Grove, Ca., U.S.	D3	82
Pacific Ocean	F2	2
Pacific Palisades, Hi., U.S.	g10	88
Pacific Ranges, mts., B.C., Can.	D4	69
Pacific Rim National Park, B.C., Can.	E5	69
Pack Monadnock Mountain, mtn., N.H., U.S.	E3	106
Packwood, Wa., U.S.	C4	124
Pacolet, S.C., U.S.	B4	117
Pacolet, stm., S.C., U.S.	A4	117
Pacolet Mills, S.C., U.S.	B4	117
Pactola Reservoir, res., S.D., U.S.	C2	118
Padang, Indon.	F3	32
Padangpanjang, Indon.	O6	34
Padangsidempuan, Indon.	N5	34
Paddock Lake, Wi., U.S.	n11	126
Paden City, W.V., U.S.	B4	125
Paderborn, Ger.	D8	8
Padova, Italy	D6	14
Padre Island, i., Tx., U.S.	F4	120
Padre Island National Seashore, Tx., U.S.	F4	120
Padrón, Spain	C3	12
Padstow, Eng., U.K.	K8	7
Padua see Padova, Italy	D6	14
Paducah, Ky., U.S.	e9	94
Paducah, Tx., U.S.	B2	120
Paektu-san, mtn., Asia	C12	26
Pafúri, Moz.	F6	44
Pag, Cro.	E10	14
Pagai Selatan, Pulau, i., Indon.	F3	32
Page, Az., U.S.	A4	80
Page, W.V., U.S.	C3	125
Page, co., Ia., U.S.	D2	92
Page, co., Va., U.S.	B4	123
Pageland, S.C., U.S.	B7	117
Pagoda Peak, mtn., Co., U.S.	A3	83
Pagoda Point, c., Mya.	G3	34
Pagosa Springs, Co., U.S.	D3	83
Paguate, N.M., U.S.	B2	108
Pahala, Hi., U.S.	D6	88
Pahang, stm., Malay.	M7	34
Pahoa, Hi., U.S.	D7	88
Pahokee, Fl., U.S.	F6	86
Pahrump, Nv., U.S.	G6	105
Pahute Mesa, mtn., Nv., U.S.	F5	105
Paia, Hi., U.S.	C5	88
Päijänne, l., Fin.	F15	6
Pailolo Channel, strt., Hi., U.S.	B5	88
Paimpol, Fr.	D3	10
Paincourtville, La., U.S.	k9	95
Painesville, Oh., U.S.	A4	112
Paint, stm., Mi., U.S.	B2	99
Paint Creek, stm., Oh., U.S.	C2	112
Paint Creek, stm., W.V., U.S.	m13	125
Paint Creek, North Fork, stm., Oh., U.S.	C2	112
Paint Creek Lake, res., Oh., U.S.	C2	112
Painted Desert, des., Az., U.S.	B4	80
Painted Post, N.Y., U.S.	C3	109
Painted Rock Reservoir, res., Az., U.S.	D3	80
Paintsville, Ky., U.S.	C7	94
Paisley, Ont., Can.	C3	73
Paisley, Scot., U.K.	F8	7
Paita, Peru	E2	54
Pajala, Swe.	C14	6
Paján, Ec.	H2	58
Pakanbaru, Indon.	E3	32
Pakaraima Mountains, mts., S.A.	E12	58
Pakistan (Pākistān), ctry., Asia	D2	36
Pakistan, East see Bangladesh, ctry., Asia	E6	36
Pakokku, Mya.	D3	34
Pakowki Lake, l., Alta., Can.	E5	68
P'akupur, stm., Russia	E9	24
Pakxé, Laos	G8	34
Pala, Chad	G9	42
Palacios, Tx., U.S.	E4	120
Palamós, Spain	D15	12
Palana, Russia	F25	24
Pālanpur, India	H5	38
Palaoa Point, c., Hi., U.S.	C4	88
Palapye, Bots.	F5	44
Palatine, Il., U.S.	A5	90
Palatka, Russia	E24	24
Palatka, Fl., U.S.	C5	86
Palau (Belau), ctry, Oc.	D9	32
Palawan, i., Phil.	D6	32
Pālayankottai, India	H4	37
Palembang, Indon.	F3	32
Palencia, Spain	C7	12
Palermo, Italy	K8	14
Palestine, Ar., U.S.	C5	81
Palestine, Il., U.S.	D6	90
Palestine, Tx., U.S.	D5	120
Palestine, ctry., Asia	C4	40
Palestine, Lake, res., Tx., U.S.	C5	120
Paletwa, Mya.	D2	34
Pālghāt, India	G4	37
Pāli, India	H5	38
Palikea, mtn., Hi., U.S.	g9	88
Palisade, Co., U.S.	B2	83
Palisades Park, N.J., U.S.	h8	107
Palisades Reservoir, res., U.S.	F7	89
Pālitāna, India	J4	38
Palk Strait, strt., Asia	H5	37
Pallastunturi, mtn., Fin.	B14	6
Palma, Moz.	D8	44
Palma del Río, Spain	H6	12
Palma [de Mallorca], Spain	F14	12
Palma di Montechiaro, Italy	L8	14
Palmanova, Italy	D8	14
Palmarito, Ven.	D7	58
Palmas, Cape, c., Lib.	H4	42
Palma Soriano, Cuba	D9	64
Palm Bay, Fl., U.S.	D6	86
Palm Beach, Fl., U.S.	F6	86
Palm Beach, co., Fl., U.S.	F6	86
Palm Beach Gardens, Fl., U.S.	*F6	86
Palmdale, Ca., U.S.	E4	82
Palmelo, Braz.	D4	57
Palmer, Ak., U.S.	C10	79
Palmer, Ma., U.S.	B3	98
Palmer, Mi., U.S.	B3	99
Palmer, Ms., U.S.	D4	101
Palmer, Ne., U.S.	C7	104
Palmer, Tn., U.S.	D8	119
Palmer, Tx., U.S.	n10	120
Palmer Lake, Co., U.S.	B6	83
Palmerston, Ont., Can.	D4	73
Palmerston, Cape, c., Austl.	D9	50
Palmerston North, N.Z.	D5	52
Palmerton, Pa., U.S.	E10	115
Palmetto, Fl., U.S.	E4	86
Palmetto, Ga., U.S.	C2	87
Palm Harbor, Fl., U.S.	o10	86
Palmi, Italy	K10	14
Palmira, Col.	F4	58
Palmira, Ec.	I3	58
Palms, Isle of, i., S.C., U.S.	F8	117
Palm Springs, Ca., U.S.	F5	82
Palm Springs, Fl., U.S.	*F6	86
Palmyra, In., U.S.	H5	91
Palmyra, Mo., U.S.	B6	102
Palmyra, N.J., U.S.	C2	107
Palmyra, N.Y., U.S.	B3	109
Palmyra, Pa., U.S.	F8	115
Palmyra, Wi., U.S.	F5	126
Palni, India	G4	37
Palo Alto, Ca., U.S.	D2	82
Palo Alto, co., Ia., U.S.	A3	92
Paloich, Sudan	F12	42
Palomar Mountain, mtn., Ca., U.S.	F5	82
Palomas Mountains, mts., Az., U.S.	D2	80
Palo Pinto, co., Tx., U.S.	C3	120
Palos Park, Il., U.S.	k9	90
Palos Verdes Estates, Ca., U.S.	n12	82
Palourde, Lake, l., La., U.S.	k9	95
Palouse, Wa., U.S.	C8	124
Palouse, stm., Wa., U.S.	C7	124
Palu, Indon.	F6	32
Palwal, India	F7	38
Pamekasan, Indon.	m16	33a
Pamiers, Fr.	I8	10
Pamir, mts., Asia	B3	36
Pamlico, co., N.C., U.S.	B6	110
Pamlico, stm., N.C., U.S.	B6	110
Pamlico Sound, strt., N.C., U.S.	B6	110
Pampa, Tx., U.S.	B2	120
Pampas, reg., Arg.	C4	56
Pamplico, S.C., U.S.	D8	117
Pamplona, Col.	D6	58
Pamplona, Spain	C10	12
Pamunkey, stm., Va., U.S.	C5	123
Pana, Il., U.S.	D4	90
Panaca, Nv., U.S.	F7	105
Panache, Lake, l., Ont., Can.	A3	73
Panaji (Panjim), India	E2	37
Panamá, Pan.	J8	64
Panama, Ok., U.S.	B7	113
Panama, ctry., N.A.	J7	64
Panamá, Gulf of, b., Pan.	J8	64
Panama, Isthmus of, Pan.	J8	64
Panama Canal, Pan.	J8	64
Panama City, Fl., U.S.	u16	86
Panama City Beach, Fl., U.S.	u16	86
Panamint Range, mts., Ca., U.S.	D5	82
Panay, i., Phil.	C7	32
Pancake Range, mts., Nv., U.S.	E6	105
Pandharpur, India	D3	37
Pandora, Oh., U.S.	B2	112
P'andž (Panj), stm., Asia	A4	38
Panevėžys, Lith.	F7	18
Pangala, Congo	B2	44
Pangburn, Ar., U.S.	B4	81
Pangkalanbuun, Indon.	F5	32
Pangkalpinang, Indon.	F4	32
Pangnirtung, N.W. Ter., Can.	C19	66
Panguitch, Ut., U.S.	F3	121
Pangutaran Group, is., Phil.	D7	32
Panhandle, Tx., U.S.	B2	120
Paniau, mtn., Hi., U.S.	B1	88
Pānīpat, India	F7	38
Panj (P'andž), stm., Asia	B4	38
Panjāb, Afg.	C2	38
Panjgūr, Pak.	D1	36
Panola, co., Ms., U.S.	A3	101
Panola, co., Tx., U.S.	C5	120
Panora, Ia., U.S.	C3	92
Pantelleria, Italy	M6	14
Panvel, India	C2	37
Panxian, China	B8	34
Panyam, Nig.	G7	42
Panyu, China	M2	28
Paola, Italy	J11	14
Paola, Ks., U.S.	D9	93
Paoli, In., U.S.	G5	91
Paoli, Pa., U.S.	o20	115
Paonia, Co., U.S.	C3	83
Pápa, Hung.	H17	8
Papago Indian Reservation, Az., U.S.	E3	80
Papaikou, Hi., U.S.	D6	88
Papantla [de Olarte], Mex.	G11	62
Papawai Point, c., Hi., U.S.	C5	88

Name | Map Ref | Page

Papenburg, Ger. B7 8
Papillion, Ne., U.S. C9 104
Papineauville, Que., Can. D2 74
Papua, Gulf of, b., Pap. N. Gui. m15 50a
Papua New Guinea, ctry., Oc. m15 50a
Pará, stm., Braz. D9 54
Paracatu, Braz. D5 57
Paracatu, stm., Braz. D6 57
Paracel Islands, is., Asia B5 32
Parachute, Co., U.S. B2 83
Paradis, La., U.S. k11 95
Paradise, Ca., U.S. C3 82
Paradise, Nv., U.S. G6 105
Paradise, stm., Newf., Can. B3 72
Paradise Hills, N.M., U.S. B3 108
Paradise Valley, Az., U.S. k9 80
Paradise Valley, Nv., U.S. B4 105
Paragould, Ar., U.S. A5 81
Paraguaçu Paulista, Braz. G3 57
Paraguaipoa, Ven. B7 58
Paraguaná, Península de, pen., Ven. B7 58
Paraguarí, Para. B5 56
Paraguay, ctry., S.A. A5 56
Paraguay, stm., S.A. B5 56
Paraíba do Sul, stm., Braz. F7 57
Parakou, Benin G6 42
Paramagudi, India H5 37
Paramaribo, Sur. B7 54
Paramirim, Braz. B7 57
Paramount, Md., U.S. A2 97
Paramus, N.J., U.S. h8 107
Paramušir, Ostrov, i., Russia G25 24
Paraná, Arg. C4 56
Paranã, Braz. B5 57
Paranã, stm., Braz. B5 57
Paraná, stm., S.A. C5 56
Paranaguá, Braz. B7 56
Paranaíba, Braz. E3 57
Paranaíba, stm., Braz. E3 57
Paranapanema, stm., Braz. G3 57
Paranavaí, Braz. G2 57
Parangaba, Braz. D11 54
Paratinga, Braz. B7 57
Paraúna, Braz. D3 57
Paray-le-Monial, Fr. F11 10
Pārbati, stm., India H7 38
Parbhani, India C4 37
Parchim, Ger. B11 8
Parchment, Mi., U.S. F5 99
Pardeeville, Wi., U.S. E4 126
Pardo, stm., Braz. F5 57
Pardubice, Czech. E15 8
Parece Vela see Okino-Tori-shima, i., Japan G14 26
Parecis, Serra dos, mts., Braz. F7 54
Paredes de Nava, Spain C7 12
Paren', Russia E26 24
Parepare, Indon. F6 32
Pargas (Parainen), Fin. F14 6
Paria, stm., U.S. A4 80
Paria, Gulf of, b. I16 64
Pariaguán, Ven. C10 58
Pariaman, Indon. O6 34
Parícutin, vol., Mex. H8 62
Parikkala, Fin. F17 6
Parima, Sierra, mts., S.A. F10 58
Pariñas, Punta, c., Peru D2 54
Parintins, Braz. D7 54
Paris, Ont., Can. D4 73
Paris, Fr. D9 10
Paris, Ar., U.S. B2 81
Paris, Il., U.S. D6 90
Paris, Ky., U.S. B5 94
Paris, Mo., U.S. B5 102
Paris, Tn., U.S. A3 119
Paris, Tx., U.S. C5 120
Paris Peak, mtn., Id., U.S. G7 89
Parit Buntar, Malay. L6 34
Park, co., Co., U.S. B5 83
Park, co., Mt., U.S. E6 103
Park, co., Wy., U.S. B3 127
Park, stm., N.D., U.S. A8 111
Parkano, Fin. E14 6
Park City, Ks., U.S. g12 93
Park City, Ut., U.S. C4 121
Parkdale, P.E.I., Can. C6 71
Parke, co., In., U.S. E3 91
Parker, Az., U.S. C1 80
Parker, Co., U.S. B6 83
Parker, Fl., U.S. u16 86
Parker, S.D., U.S. D8 118
Parker, co., Tx., U.S. C4 120
Parker, Cape, c., N.W. Ter., Can. A17 66
Parker City, In., U.S. D7 91
Parker Dam, U.S. C1 80
Parkersburg, Ia., U.S. B5 92
Parkersburg, W.V., U.S. B3 125
Parkers Prairie, Mn., U.S. D3 100
Parkesburg, Pa., U.S. G10 115
Park Falls, Wi., U.S. C3 126
Park Forest, Il., U.S. B6 90
Park Hall, Md., U.S. D5 97
Parkhill, Ont., Can. D3 73
Park Hills, Ky., U.S. h13 94
Parkin, Ar., U.S. B5 81
Parkland, Wa., U.S. f11 124
Park Layne, Oh., U.S. C1 112
Park Range, mts., Co., U.S. A4 83
Park Rapids, Mn., U.S. D3 100
Park Ridge, Il., U.S. B6 90
Park Ridge, N.J., U.S. g8 107
Park River, N.D., U.S. A8 111
Parkrose, Or., U.S. B4 114
Parksley, Va., U.S. C7 123
Parkston, S.D., U.S. D8 118
Parksville, B.C., Can. E5 69
Parkville, Md., U.S. B4 97
Parkville, Mo., U.S. B3 102
Parkwater, Wa., U.S. g14 124
Parkwood, N.C., U.S. B4 110
Parlākimidi, India C8 37
Parle, Lac qui, l., Mn., U.S. E3 100
Parlier, Ca., U.S. D4 82
Parma, Italy E5 14
Parma, Id., U.S. F2 89
Parma, Mi., U.S. F6 99
Parma, Mo., U.S. E8 102
Parma, Oh., U.S. A4 112
Parmachenee Lake, l., Me., U.S. C2 96
Parma Heights, Oh., U.S. h9 112
Parmer, co., Tx., U.S. B1 120
Parnaíba, Braz. D10 54
Parnaíba, stm., Braz. D10 54
Pärnu, Est. C7 18
Paro, Bhu. G13 38
Parowan, Ut., U.S. F3 121
Par Pond, res., S.C., U.S. D5 117
Parral, Chile D2 56
Parramore Island, i., Va., U.S. C7 123
Parras de la Fuente, Mex. E8 62
Parrish, Al., U.S. B2 78
Parrsboro, N.S., Can. D5 71
Parry, Cape, c., N.W. Ter., Can. B8 66
Parry, Mount, mtn., B.C., Can. C3 69
Parry Bay, b., N.W. Ter., Can. C16 66
Parry Sound, Ont., Can. B4 73
Parshall, N.D., U.S. B3 111
Parsons, Ks., U.S. E8 93
Parsons, Tn., U.S. B3 119
Parsons, W.V., U.S. B5 125
Parsonsburg, Md., U.S. D7 97
Parthenay, Fr. F6 10
Partinico, Italy K8 14
Partridge Point, c., Newf., Can. C3 72
Paru, stm., Braz. D8 54
Pārvatīpuram, India C7 37
Parys, S. Afr. G5 44
Pasadena, Newf., Can. D3 72
Pasadena, Ca., U.S. E4 82
Pasadena, Md., U.S. B4 97
Pasadena, Tx., U.S. r14 120
Pascagoula, Ms., U.S. E5 101
Pascagoula, stm., Ms., U.S. E5 101
Pascagoula Bay, b., Ms., U.S. f8 101
Pasco, Wa., U.S. C6 124
Pasco, co., Fl., U.S. D4 86
Pascoag, R.I., U.S. B2 116
Pascoag Reservoir, res., R.I., U.S. B2 116
Pascua, Isla de (Easter Island), i., Chile H5 2
Pasewalk, Ger. B13 8
Pasig, Phil. q19 33b
P'asina, stm., Russia C11 24
P'asino, Ozero, l., Russia D11 24
P'asinskij Zaliv, b., Russia C10 24
Pasirpengarajan, Indon. N6 34
Pasir Puteh, Malay. L7 34
Pasni, Pak. D1 36
Paso de Indios, Arg. E3 56
Paso de los Libres, Arg. B5 56
Paso Robles, Ca., U.S. E3 82
Pasque Island, i., Ma., U.S. D6 98
Pasquotank, co., N.C., U.S. A6 110
Passagem, Braz. B7 57
Passaic, N.J., U.S. B4 107
Passaic, co., N.J., U.S. A4 107
Passaic, stm., N.J., U.S. h8 107
Passamaquoddy Bay, b., Me., U.S. C6 96
Passau, Ger. G13 8
Pass Christian, Ms., U.S. E4 101
Passo Fundo, Braz. B6 56
Passos, Braz. F5 57
Passumpsic, stm., Vt., U.S. C4 122
Pasto, Col. G4 58
Pastora Peak, mtn., Az., U.S. A6 80
Pastrana, Spain E9 12
Pasuruan, Indon. m16 33a
Patagonia, Az., U.S. F5 80
Patagonia, reg., Arg. E3 56
Pātan, India I5 38
Patapsco, stm., Md., U.S. B4 97
Pataskala, Oh., U.S. C3 112
Patchet Brook Reservoir, res., R.I., U.S. E6 116
Patchogue, N.Y., U.S. n15 109
Pate Island, i., Kenya B8 44
Paternò, Italy L9 14
Paterson, N.J., U.S. B4 107
Pathānkot, India D6 38
Pathein, Mya. F3 34
Pathfinder Reservoir, res., Wy., U.S. D6 127
Pati, Indon. m15 33a
Patiāla, India E7 38
Patience Island, i., R.I., U.S. D5 116
P'atigorsk, Russia I6 22
Pātkai Range, mts., Asia G16 38
Patman, Lake, res., Tx., U.S. C5 120
Patna, India H11 38
Patoka, In., U.S. H2 91
Patoka, stm., In., U.S. H2 91
Patoka Lake, res., In., U.S. H4 91
Patos, Braz. E11 54
Patos, Lagoa dos, b., Braz. C6 56
Patos de Minas, Braz. E5 57
Patquía, Arg. C3 56
Pátrai, Grc. K5 16
Patricio Lynch, Isla, i., Chile F1 56
Patrick, co., Va., U.S. D2 123
Patrick Air Force Base, mil., Fl., U.S. D6 86
Patrocínio, Braz. E5 57
Pattani, Thai. K6 34
Patten, Me., U.S. C4 96
Patterson, Ga., U.S. E4 87
Patterson, La., U.S. E4 95
Patterson Creek, stm., W.V., U.S. B5 125
Pattoki, Pak. E5 38
Patton, Pa., U.S. E4 115
Patuākhāli, Bngl. I14 38
Patuca, stm., Hond. G5 64
Patuxent, stm., Md., U.S. D4 97
Patuxent Naval Air Test Center, mil., Md., U.S. D5 97
Pátzcuaro, Mex. H9 62
Pau, Fr. I6 10
Paul, Id., U.S. G5 89
Paulding, Oh., U.S. A1 112
Paulding, co., Ga., U.S. C2 87
Paulding, co., Oh., U.S. A1 112
Paulina, La., U.S. h10 95
Paulina Mountains, mts., Or., U.S. D5 114
Paulina Peak, mtn., Or., U.S. E5 114
Paulins Kill, stm., N.J., U.S. A3 107
Paulistana, Braz. E10 54
Paulistas, Braz. E7 57
Paullina, Ia., U.S. B2 92
Paulo Afonso, Braz. E11 54
Paulsboro, N.J., U.S. D2 107
Paul Stream, stm., Vt., U.S. B5 122
Pauls Valley, Ok., U.S. C4 113
Paungde, Mya. E3 34
Pavia, Italy D4 14
Pavilion Key, i., Fl., U.S. G5 86
Pavlodar, Kaz. G9 24
Pavlof Volcano, vol., Ak., U.S. D7 79
Pavlovo, Russia F26 18
Pavlovsk, Russia G7 24
Pavlovskij Posad, Russia F21 18
Pavo, Ga., U.S. F3 87
Pavón, Col. F6 58
Pavullo nel Frignano, Italy E5 14
Pawcatuck, Ct., U.S. D8 84
Pawcatuck, stm., R.I., U.S. G1 116
Paw Creek, N.C., U.S. B2 110
Pawhuska, Ok., U.S. A5 113
Pawling, N.Y., U.S. D7 109
Pawnee, Il., U.S. D4 90
Pawnee, Ok., U.S. A5 113
Pawnee, co., Ks., U.S. D4 93
Pawnee, co., Ne., U.S. D9 104
Pawnee, co., Ok., U.S. A5 113
Pawnee, stm., Ks., U.S. D3 93
Pawnee City, Ne., U.S. D9 104
Pawpaw, Il., U.S. B5 90
Paw Paw, Mi., U.S. F5 99
Paw Paw, stm., Mi., U.S. F4 99
Pawpaw Creek, stm., W.V., U.S. h10 125
Pawtuckaway Pond, l., N.H., U.S. D4 106
Pawtucket, R.I., U.S. C4 116
Pawtuxet, stm., R.I., U.S. C4 116
Paxton, Il., U.S. C5 90
Paxton, Ma., U.S. B4 98
Payakumbuh, Indon. O6 34
Payette, Id., U.S. E2 89
Payette, co., Id., U.S. E2 89
Payette, North Fork, stm., Id., U.S. E2 89
Payette, South Fork, stm., Id., U.S. E3 89
Payette Lake, res., Id., U.S. E3 89
Payne, Oh., U.S. A1 112
Payne, co., Ok., U.S. A4 113
Paynesville, Mn., U.S. E4 100
Paysandú, Ur. C5 56
Payson, Az., U.S. C4 80
Payson, Il., U.S. D2 90
Payson, Ut., U.S. C4 121
Pazardžik, Bul. G8 16
Pazarköy, Tur. J11 16
Paz de Río, Col. E6 58
Pazin, Cro. D8 14
Pea, stm., Al., U.S. D3 78
Peabody, Ks., U.S. D6 93
Peabody, Ma., U.S. A6 98
Peabody, stm., N.H., U.S. B4 106
Peace, stm., Can. E9 66
Peace, stm., Fl., U.S. E5 86
Peace Dale, R.I., U.S. F3 116
Peace River, Alta., Can. A2 68
Peach, co., Ga., U.S. D3 87
Peacham Pond, res., Vt., U.S. C4 122
Peach Point, c., Ma., U.S. f12 98
Peach Springs, Az., U.S. B2 80
Peak District National Park, Eng., U.K. H11 7
Peaks Island, i., Me., U.S. g7 96
Peale, Mount, mtn., Ut., U.S. E6 121
Pea Patch Island, i., De., U.S. B3 85
Pea Ridge, Ar., U.S. A1 81
Pea Ridge National Military Park, Ar., U.S. A1 81
Pearisburg, Va., U.S. C2 123
Pearl, Ms., U.S. C3 101
Pearl, stm., U.S. D3 101
Pearland, Tx., U.S. r14 120
Pearl and Hermes Reef, rf., Hi., U.S. k12 88
Pearl City, Hi., U.S. B4 88
Pearl Harbor, b., Hi., U.S. B3 88
Pearl Harbor Naval Station, mil., Hi., U.S. g10 88
Pearlington, Ms., U.S. E4 101
Pearl River, La., U.S. D6 95
Pearl River, N.Y., U.S. g12 109
Pearl River, co., Ms., U.S. E4 101
Pearsall, Tx., U.S. E3 120
Pearsoll Peak, mtn., Or., U.S. E3 114
Pearson, Ga., U.S. E4 87
Peary Land, reg., Grnld. A16 128
Pease, stm., Tx., U.S. B3 120
Pease Air Force Base, mil., N.H., U.S. D5 106
Pebane, Moz. E7 44
Peć, Yugo. G4 16
Pecatonica, Il., U.S. A4 90
Pecatonica, stm., U.S. A4 90
Pecatonica, East Branch, stm., Wi., U.S. F4 126
Peckerwood Lake, res., Ar., U.S. C4 81
Pečora, stm., Russia D5 24
Pecos, N.M., U.S. B4 108
Pecos, Tx., U.S. D1 120
Pecos, co., Tx., U.S. D1 120
Pecos, stm., U.S. E6 76
Pecos National Monument, N.M., U.S. B4 108
Pécs, Hung. I18 8
Peculiar, Mo., U.S. C3 102
Peddocks Island, i., Ma., U.S. g12 98
Pedernales, Ven. C11 58
Pedregal, Ven. B7 58
Pedro, Point, c., Sri L. H6 37
Pedro de Valdivia, Chile A3 56
Pedro Juan Caballero, Para. G1 57
Peebles, Oh., U.S. D2 112
Peekskill, N.Y., U.S. D7 109
Peel, I. of Man G8 7
Peel, stm., Can. C5 66
Peel Point, c., N.W. Ter., Can. B10 66
Peel Sound, strt., N.W. Ter., Can. B13 66
Pegram, Tn., U.S. A4 119
Pehuajó, Arg. D4 56
Peikang, Tai. L9 28
Peine, Ger. C10 8
Pekalongan, Indon. m14 32
Pekin, Il., U.S. C4 90
Pekin, In., U.S. G5 91
Peking see Beijing, China D10 26
Pelagie, Isole, is., Italy N7 14
Pelahatchie, Ms., U.S. C4 101
Pelée, Montagne, mtn., Mart. G17 64
Pelee Island, i., Ont., Can. F2 73
Peleng, Pulau, i., Indon. F7 32
Pelham, Ont., Can. D5 73
Pelham, Al., U.S. B3 78
Pelham, Ga., U.S. E2 87
Pelham, N.H., U.S. E4 106
Pelham Manor, N.Y., U.S. h13 109
Pelican Bay, b., Man., Can. C1 70
Pelican Lake, l., Man., Can. C1 70
Pelican Lake, l., Mn., U.S. D4 100
Pelican Lake, l., Mn., U.S. D3 100
Pelican Lake, l., Mn., U.S. B6 100
Pelican Lake, l., Mn., U.S. E5 100
Pelican Lake, l., Wi., U.S. C4 126
Pelican Mountain, mtn., Alta., Can. B4 68
Pelican Rapids, Mn., U.S. D2 100
Pella, Ia., U.S. C5 92
Pell City, Al., U.S. B3 78
Pell Lake, Wi., U.S. n11 126
Pello, Fin. C14 6
Pelly Mountains, mts., Yukon, Can. D6 66
Pelopónnisos, reg., Grc. L5 16
Pelotas, Braz. C6 56
Pelton, Lake, l., La., U.S. E5 95
Pemadumcook Lake, l., Me., U.S. C3 96
Pemalang, Indon. m14 33a
Pematangsiantar, Indon. E2 32
Pemba, Moz. D8 44
Pemba Island, i., Tan. C7 44
Pemberton, Austl. F3 50
Pemberville, Oh., U.S. A2 112
Pembina, N.D., U.S. A8 111
Pembina, co., N.D., U.S. A8 111
Pembina, stm., Alta., Can. C3 68
Pembroke, Ont., Can. B7 73
Pembroke, Wales, U.K. J8 7
Pembroke, Ga., U.S. D5 87
Pembroke, Ky., U.S. D2 94
Pembroke, Ma., U.S. B6 98
Pembroke, N.C., U.S. C3 110
Pembroke, Va., U.S. C2 123
Pembroke Pines, Fl., U.S. r13 86
Pemigewasset, stm., N.H., U.S. C3 106
Pemiscot, co., Mo., U.S. E8 102
Peñafiel, Spain D7 12
Penápolis, Braz. F3 57
Peñaranda de Bracamonte, Spain E6 12
Pen Argyl, Pa., U.S. E11 115
Peñarroya-Pueblonuevo, Spain G6 12
Penas, Golfo de, b., Chile F1 56
Penasco, N.M., U.S. A4 108
Peñasco, Rio, stm., N.M., U.S. E4 108
Penbrook, Pa., U.S. F8 115
Pender, Ne., U.S. B9 104
Pender, co., N.C., U.S. C4 110
Pendleton, In., U.S. E6 91
Pendleton, Or., U.S. B8 114
Pendleton, S.C., U.S. B2 117
Pendleton, co., Ky., U.S. B5 94
Pendleton, co., W.V., U.S. C5 125
Pendley Hills, Ga., U.S. *h8 87
Pend Oreille, co., Wa., U.S. A8 124
Pend Oreille, Lake, l., Id., U.S. A2 89
Pend Oreille, Mount, mtn., Id., U.S. A2 89
Penetanguishene, Ont., Can. C5 73
P'enghu Liehtao, is., Tai. L8 28
Penglai, China D11 26
Penhold, Alta., Can. C4 68
Peniche, Port. F2 12
Penjamo, Mex. G9 62
Pennant Point, c., N.S., Can. E6 71
Pennask Mountain, mtn., B.C., Can. E7 69
Penne, Italy G8 14
Pennell, Mount, mtn., Ut., U.S. F5 121
Penner, stm., India E5 37
Penn Hills, Pa., U.S. k14 115
Pennines, mts., Eng., U.K. G10 7
Pennines, Alpes, mts., Eur. F14 10
Pennington, co., Mn., U.S. B2 100
Pennington, co., S.D., U.S. D2 118
Pennington Gap, Va., U.S. f8 123
Pennsauken, N.J., U.S. D2 107
Pennsboro, W.V., U.S. B4 125
Pennsburg, Pa., U.S. F11 115
Penns Grove, N.J., U.S. D2 107
Pennsville, N.J., U.S. D1 107
Pennsylvania, state, U.S. E7 115
Pennville, In., U.S. D7 91
Penn Yan, N.Y., U.S. C3 109
Penobscot, co., Me., U.S. C4 96
Penobscot, stm., Me., U.S. C4 96
Penobscot Bay, b., Me., U.S. D3 96
Penobscot Lake, l., Me., U.S. C2 96
Penonomé, Pan. J7 64
Penrith, Eng., U.K. G10 7
Pensacola, Fl., U.S. u14 86
Pensacola Bay, b., Fl., U.S. u14 86
Pensacola Dam, Ok., U.S. A6 113
Pensacola Naval Air Station, mil., Fl., U.S. u14 86
Pentagon Mountain, mtn., Mt., U.S. C3 103
Penticton, B.C., Can. E8 69
Pentland Firth, strt., Scot., U.K. C9 7
Pentwater, Mi., U.S. E4 99
Penyu, Kepulauan, is., Indon. G8 32
Penza, Russia G7 22
Penzance, Eng., U.K. K7 7
Penžina, stm., Russia E27 24
Penžinskaja Guba, b., Russia E26 24
Penžinskij Chrebet, mts., Russia E27 24
Peonan Point, c., Man., Can. D2 70
Peoria, Az., U.S. D3 80
Peoria, Il., U.S. C4 90
Peoria, co., Il., U.S. C4 90
Peoria Heights, Il., U.S. C4 90
Peotone, Il., U.S. B6 90
Pepacton Reservoir, res., N.Y., U.S. C6 109
Pepeekeo, Hi., U.S. D6 88
Pepin, Wi., U.S. D1 126
Pepin, co., Wi., U.S. D2 126
Pepin, Lake, l., U.S. D1 126
Pepperell, Ma., U.S. A4 98
Pequannock, N.J., U.S. B4 107
Pequest, stm., N.J., U.S. B2 107
Pequop Mountains, mts., Nv., U.S. C7 105
Pequot Lakes, Mn., U.S. D4 100
Perabumulih, Indon. F3 32
Percy, Il., U.S. E4 90
Perdido, Al., U.S. D2 78
Perdido, stm., U.S. E2 78
Perdido Bay, b., Al., U.S. E2 78
Pereira, Col. E5 58
Pere Marquette, stm., Mi., U.S. E4 99
Pereslavl'-Zalesskij, Russia E21 18
Pergamino, Arg. C4 56
Pergine Valsugana, Italy C6 14
Perham, Mn., U.S. D3 100
Péribonca, stm., Que., Can. G18 66
Peridot, Az., U.S. D5 80
Périgueux, Fr. G7 10
Perijá, Sierra de, mts., S.A. B6 58
Perkasie, Pa., U.S. F11 115
Perkins, Ok., U.S. B4 113
Perkins, co., Ne., U.S. D4 104
Perkins, co., S.D., U.S. B3 118
Perkinston, Ms., U.S. E4 101
Perlas, Archipiélago de las, is., Pan. J8 64
Perlas, Laguna de, b., Nic. H6 64
Perleberg, Ger. B11 8
Perm', Russia F9 22
Pernik, Bul. G7 16
Péronne, Fr. C9 10
Perpignan, Fr. J9 10
Perquimans, co., N.C., U.S. A6 110
Perrine, Fl., U.S. G6 86
Perris, Ca., U.S. F5 82
Perro, Laguna del, l., N.M., U.S. C4 108
Perros-Guirec, Fr. D3 10
Perrot, Île, i., Que., Can. q19 74
Perry, Fl., U.S. B3 86
Perry, Ga., U.S. D3 87
Perry, Ia., U.S. C3 92
Perry, Ks., U.S. C8 93
Perry, Mi., U.S. F6 99
Perry, Mo., U.S. B6 102
Perry, N.Y., U.S. C2 109
Perry, Oh., U.S. A4 112
Perry, Ok., U.S. A4 113
Perry, Ut., U.S. B3 121
Perry, co., Al., U.S. C2 78
Perry, co., Ar., U.S. C3 81
Perry, co., Il., U.S. E4 90
Perry, co., In., U.S. H4 91
Perry, co., Ky., U.S. C6 94
Perry, co., Ms., U.S. D4 101
Perry, co., Mo., U.S. D8 102
Perry, co., Oh., U.S. C3 112
Perry, co., Pa., U.S. F7 115
Perry, co., Tn., U.S. B4 119
Perry Hall, Md., U.S. B5 97
Perry Lake, res., Ks., U.S. C8 93
Perryman, Md., U.S. B5 97
Perrysburg, Oh., U.S. A2 112
Perry Stream, stm., N.H., U.S. f7 106
Perry's Victory and International Peace Memorial, hist., Oh., U.S. A2 112
Perryton, Tx., U.S. A2 120
Perryville, Ar., U.S. B3 81
Perryville, Ky., U.S. C5 94
Perryville, Md., U.S. A5 97
Perryville, Mo., U.S. D8 102
Pershing, co., Nv., U.S. C3 105
Persia see Iran, ctry., Asia B5 46
Persian Gulf, b., Asia C5 46
Person, co., N.C., U.S. A3 110
Perth, Austl. F3 50
Perth, Ont., Can. C8 73
Perth, Scot., U.K. E9 7
Perth Amboy, N.J., U.S. B4 107
Perth-Andover, N.B., Can. D10 71
Pertuis, Fr. I12 10
Peru, Il., U.S. B4 90
Peru, In., U.S. C5 91
Peru, Ne., U.S. D10 104
Peru, N.Y., U.S. f11 109
Peru (Perú), ctry., S.A. E3 54
Perugia, Italy F7 14
Perušić, Cro. E10 14
Pesaro, Italy F7 14
Pescadores see P'enghu Liehtao, is., Tai. L8 28
Pescara, Italy G9 14
Pescia, Italy F5 14
Peshastin, Wa., U.S. B5 124
Peshāwar, Pak. C4 38
Peshtigo, Wi., U.S. C6 126
Peshtigo, stm., Wi., U.S. C5 126
Pesqueira, Braz. E11 54
Pessac, Fr. H6 10
Petah Tiqwa, Isr. C4 40
Petal, Ms., U.S. D4 101
Petaluma, Ca., U.S. C2 82
Petatlán, Mex. I9 62
Petawawa, Ont., Can. B7 73
Petawawa, stm., Ont., Can. A6 73

Name	Map Ref	Page
Petenwell Lake, res., Wi., U.S.	D4	126
Peterborough, Austl.	F7	50
Peterborough, Ont., Can.	C6	73
Peterborough, Eng., U.K.	I12	7
Peterborough, N.H., U.S.	E3	106
Peterhead, Scot., U.K.	D11	7
Peter Pond Lake, l., Sask., Can.	m7	75
Petersburg, Ak., U.S.	D13	79
Petersburg, Il., U.S.	C4	90
Petersburg, In., U.S.	H3	91
Petersburg, Mi., U.S.	G7	99
Petersburg, Oh., U.S.	B5	112
Petersburg, Tx., U.S.	C2	120
Petersburg, Va., U.S.	C5	123
Petersburg, W.V., U.S.	B5	125
Peters Creek, stm., W.V., U.S.	m14	125
Peterson, Al., U.S.	B2	78
Peterson Field, mil., Co., U.S.	C6	83
Petersville, Al., U.S.	A2	78
Petit Bois Island, i., Ms., U.S.	E5	101
Petitcodiac, N.B., Can.	D4	71
Petitcodiac, stm., N.B., Can.	C5	71
Petite Amite, stm., La., U.S.	h10	95
Petit Jean, stm., Ar., U.S.	B2	81
Petit Lac Des Allemands, l., La., U.S.	k11	95
Petit Lake, l., La., U.S.	k12	95
Petitot, stm., Can.	E8	66
Petit-Rocher, N.B., Can.	B4	71
Petitsikapau Lake, l., Newf., Can.	g8	72
Petlād, India	I5	38
Petone, N.Z.	D5	52
Petoskey, Mi., U.S.	C6	99
Petrified Forest National Park, Az., U.S.	B6	80
Petrila, Rom.	D7	16
Petrinja, Cro.	D11	14
Petroleum, co., Mt., U.S.	C8	103
Petrolia, Ont., Can.	E2	73
Petrolina, Braz.	E10	54
Petropavlovsk-Kamčatskij, Russia	G25	24
Petrópolis, Braz.	G7	57
Petros, Tn., U.S.	C9	119
Petroșani, Rom.	D7	16
Petrovsk-Zabajkal'skij, Russia	G15	24
Petrozavodsk, Russia	E4	22
Pettaquamscutt Lake Shores, R.I., U.S.	F4	116
Pettingell Peak, mtn., Co., U.S.	B5	83
Pettis, co., Mo., U.S.	C4	102
Pevek, Russia	D28	24
Pevely, Mo., U.S.	g13	102
Pewaukee, Wi., U.S.	E5	126
Pewaukee Lake, l., Wi., U.S.	m11	126
Pewee Valley, Ky., U.S.	B4	94
Pézenas, Fr.	I10	10
Pforzheim, Ger.	G8	8
Pfungstadt, Ger.	F8	8
Pha-an, Mya.	F4	34
Phagwāra, India	E6	38
Phalsbourg, Fr.	D14	10
Phaltan, India	D3	37
Phangan, Ko, i., Thai.	J6	34
Phangnga, Thai.	J5	34
Phanom Dongrak, Thiu Khao, mts., Asia	G7	34
Phan Rang, Viet.	I10	34
Phan Si Pan, mtn., Viet.	C7	34
Phan Thiet, Viet.	I10	34
Pharr, Tx., U.S.	F3	120
Phatthalung, Thai.	K6	34
Phayao, Thai.	E5	34
Phelps, Ky., U.S.	C7	94
Phelps, N.Y., U.S.	C3	109
Phelps, Wi., U.S.	B4	126
Phelps, co., Mo., U.S.	D6	102
Phelps, co., Ne., U.S.	D6	104
Phelps Lake, l., N.C., U.S.	B6	110
Phenix City, Al., U.S.	C4	78
Phetchaburi, Thai.	H5	34
Philadelphia, Ms., U.S.	C4	101
Philadelphia, Pa., U.S.	G11	115
Philadelphia, co., Pa., U.S.	G12	115
Philadelphia Naval Shipyard, mil., Pa., U.S.	P21	115
Phil Campbell, Al., U.S.	A2	78
Philip, S.D., U.S.	C4	118
Philippeville, Bel.	E4	8
Philippi, W.V., U.S.	B4	125
Philippines, ctry., Asia	C7	32
Philippine Sea	E21	2
Philipsburg, Mt., U.S.	D3	103
Philipsburg, Pa., U.S.	E5	115
Philleo Lake, l., Wa., U.S.	h14	124
Phillips, Me., U.S.	D2	96
Phillips, Tx., U.S.	B2	120
Phillips, Wi., U.S.	C3	126
Phillips, co., Ar., U.S.	C5	81
Phillips, co., Co., U.S.	A8	83
Phillips, co., Ks., U.S.	C4	93
Phillips, co., Mt., U.S.	B8	103
Phillips Brook, stm., N.H., U.S.	A4	106
Phillipsburg, Ks., U.S.	C4	93
Phillipsburg, N.J., U.S.	B2	107
Philmont, N.Y., U.S.	C7	109
Philo, Il., U.S.	C5	90
Philomath, Or., U.S.	C3	114
Philpots Island, i., N.W. Ter., Can.	B17	66
Philpott Reservoir, res., Va., U.S.	D2	123
Phitsanulok, Thai.	F6	34
Phnom Penh see Phnum Pénh, Camb.	I8	34
Phnum Pénh (Phnom Penh), Camb.	I8	34
Phoenix, Az., U.S.	D3	80
Phoenix, Il., U.S.	k9	90
Phoenix, N.Y., U.S.	B4	109
Phoenix, Or., U.S.	E4	114
Phoenixville, Pa., U.S.	F10	115
Phôngsali, Laos	D7	34
Phrae, Thai.	E6	34
Phra Nakhon Si Ayutthaya, Thai.	G6	34
Phuket, Thai.	K5	34
Phuket, Ko, i., Thai.	K5	34
Phu Ly, Viet.	D8	34
Phumĭ Béng, Camb.	H8	34
Phumĭ Kâmpóng Trâbêk, Camb.	H8	34
Phu Quoc, Dao, i., Viet.	I7	34
Phu Tho, Viet.	D8	34
Piacenza, Italy	D4	14
Piatra-Neamț, Rom.	C10	16
Piatt, co., Il., U.S.	D5	90
Piazza Armerina, Italy	L9	14
Pibor Post, Sudan	G12	42
Picacho, Az., U.S.	E4	80
Picardie, hist. reg., Fr.	C9	10
Picayune, Ms., U.S.	E4	101
Piccadilly, Newf., Can.	D2	72
Pichanal, Arg.	A4	56
Picher, Ok., U.S.	A7	113
Pickaway, co., Oh., U.S.	C2	112
Pickens, Ms., U.S.	C4	101
Pickens, S.C., U.S.	B2	117
Pickens, co., Al., U.S.	B1	78
Pickens, co., Ga., U.S.	B2	87
Pickens, co., S.C., U.S.	B2	117
Pickerel Lake, l., Wi., U.S.	C5	126
Pickering, Ont., Can.	D5	73
Pickerington, Oh., U.S.	C3	112
Pickett, co., Tn., U.S.	C8	119
Pickwick Lake, res., U.S.	A6	101
Pickworth Point, c., Ma., U.S.	f12	98
Pico Rivera, Ca., U.S.	n12	82
Picos, Braz.	E10	54
Picquigny, Fr.	C9	10
Picton, Ont., Can.	D7	73
Pictou Island, i., N.S., Can.	D7	71
Picture Butte, Alta., Can.	E4	68
Pictured Rocks National Lakeshore, Mi., U.S.	B4	99
Pidálion, Akrotírion, c., Cyp.	B4	40
Pidurutalagala, mtn., Sri L.	I6	37
Piedmont, Al., U.S.	B4	78
Piedmont, Ca., U.S.	h8	82
Piedmont, Mo., U.S.	D7	102
Piedmont, Ok., U.S.	B4	113
Piedmont, S.C., U.S.	B3	117
Piedmont, W.V., U.S.	B5	125
Piedmont Lake, res., Oh., U.S.	B4	112
Piedra, stm., Co., U.S.	D3	83
Piedrabuena, Spain	F7	12
Piedrahita, Spain	E6	12
Piedras Blancas, Point, c., Ca., U.S.	E3	82
Piedras Negras, Guat.	F2	64
Piedras Negras, Mex.	C9	62
Pieksämäki, Fin.	E16	6
Pierce, Co., U.S.	A6	83
Pierce, Id., U.S.	C3	89
Pierce, Ne., U.S.	B8	104
Pierce, co., Ga., U.S.	E4	87
Pierce, co., Ne., U.S.	B8	104
Pierce, co., N.D., U.S.	A5	111
Pierce, co., Wa., U.S.	C3	124
Pierce, co., Wi., U.S.	D1	126
Pierce, Lake, l., Fl., U.S.	E5	86
Pierce City, Mo., U.S.	E3	102
Pierceton, In., U.S.	B6	91
Pierre, S.D., U.S.	C5	118
Pierre-Buffière, Fr.	G8	10
Pierrefonds, Que., Can.	q19	74
Pierre Part, La., U.S.	k9	95
Pierreville, Que., Can.	C5	74
Pierson, Fl., U.S.	C5	86
Pierz, Mn., U.S.	E4	100
Pietermaritzburg, S. Afr.	G6	44
Pietersburg, S. Afr.	F5	44
Pietrasanta, Italy	F5	14
Piet Retief, S. Afr.	G6	44
Pigeon, Mi., U.S.	E7	99
Pigeon, stm., U.S.	f9	110
Pigeon, stm., In., U.S.	A6	91
Pigeon, stm., Mn., U.S.	h10	100
Pigeon, stm., Wi., U.S.	k10	126
Pigeon Cove, Ma., U.S.	A6	98
Pigeon Forge, Tn., U.S.	D10	119
Pigeon Point, c., Mn., U.S.	h10	100
Pigg, stm., Va., U.S.	D3	123
Piggott, Ar., U.S.	A5	81
Pihlajavesi, l., Fin.	F17	6
Pihtipudas, Fin.	E15	6
Pijijiapan, Mex.	J13	62
Pikal'ovo, Russia	B17	18
Pike, co., Al., U.S.	D4	78
Pike, co., Ar., U.S.	C2	81
Pike, co., Ga., U.S.	C2	87
Pike, co., Il., U.S.	D2	90
Pike, co., In., U.S.	H3	91
Pike, co., Ky., U.S.	C7	94
Pike, co., Ms., U.S.	D3	101
Pike, co., Mo., U.S.	B6	102
Pike, co., Oh., U.S.	C2	110
Pike, co., Pa., U.S.	D11	115
Pike, stm., Wi., U.S.	C6	126
Pike Island Dam, U.S.	f8	125
Pike Lake, Mn., U.S.	D6	100
Pikes Peak, mtn., Co., U.S.	C5	83
Pikesville, Md., U.S.	B4	97
Piketberg, S. Afr.	H3	44
Piketon, Oh., U.S.	C2	112
Pikeville, Ky., U.S.	C7	94
Pikeville, Tn., U.S.	D8	119
Piła (Schneidemühl), Pol.	B16	8
Pilar do Sul, Braz.	G5	57
Pilcomayo, stm., S.A.	A4	56
Pīlībhīt, India	F8	38
Pillar Point, c., Ca., U.S.	k7	82
Pilot Grove, Mo., U.S.	C5	102
Pilot Knob, Mo., U.S.	D7	102
Pilot Knob, mtn., Id., U.S.	D3	89
Pilot Mound, Man., Can.	E2	70
Pilot Mountain, N.C., U.S.	A2	110
Pilot Peak, mtn., Nv., U.S.	B7	105
Pilot Peak, mtn., Nv., U.S.	E4	105
Pilot Peak, mtn., Wy., U.S.	B3	127
Pilot Point, Tx., U.S.	C4	120
Pilot Range, mts., Nv., U.S.	B7	105
Pilot Rock, Or., U.S.	B8	114
Pilot Station, Ak., U.S.	C7	79
Pima, Az., U.S.	E6	80
Pima, co., Az., U.S.	E3	80
Pimentel, Peru	E3	54
Pimmit Hills, Va., U.S.	g12	123
Pina, Spain	D11	12
Pinal, co., Az., U.S.	E4	80
Pinaleno Mountains, mts., Az., U.S.	E5	80
Pinal Mountains, mts., Az., U.S.	D5	80
Pinang see George Town, Malay.	L6	34
Pinar del Río, Cuba	C6	64
Pinardville, N.H., U.S.	E3	106
Pincher Creek, Alta., Can.	E4	68
Pinckard, Al., U.S.	D4	78
Pinckney, Mi., U.S.	F7	99
Pinckney Island, i., S.C., U.S.	G6	117
Pinckneyville, Il., U.S.	E4	90
Pinconning, Mi., U.S.	E7	99
Píndhos Óros, mts., Grc.	J5	16
Pindi Gheb, Pak.	D5	38
Pindus Mountains see Píndhos Óros, mts., Grc.	J5	16
Pine, Az., U.S.	C4	80
Pine, co., Mn., U.S.	D6	100
Pine, stm., Mi., U.S.	D7	99
Pine, stm., Mi., U.S.	D5	99
Pine, stm., N.H., U.S.	C4	106
Pine, stm., Wi., U.S.	C5	126
Pine, stm., Wi., U.S.	C4	126
Pine Barrens, reg., N.J., U.S.	D3	107
Pine Bluff, Ar., U.S.	C3	81
Pinebluff, N.C., U.S.	B3	110
Pine Bluffs, Wy., U.S.	E8	127
Pine Bridge, Ct., U.S.	D3	84
Pine Castle, Fl., U.S.	D5	86
Pine City, Mn., U.S.	E6	100
Pine Creek, stm., Nv., U.S.	C5	105
Pine Creek, stm., Pa., U.S.	C6	115
Pine Creek, stm., Wa., U.S.	B8	124
Pine Creek Lake, res., Ok., U.S.	C6	113
Pinedale, Wy., U.S.	D3	127
Pine Falls, Man., Can.	D3	70
Pine Forest Range, mts., Nv., U.S.	B3	105
Pine Grove, Pa., U.S.	E9	115
Pine Grove Mills, Pa., U.S.	E6	115
Pine Hill, N.J., U.S.	D3	107
Pine Hills, Fl., U.S.	D5	86
Pinehouse Lake, Sask., Can.	B2	75
Pinehouse Lake, l., Sask., Can.	B2	75
Pinehurst, Ma., U.S.	f11	98
Pinehurst, N.C., U.S.	B3	110
Pine Island, Mn., U.S.	F6	100
Pine Island, i., Fl., U.S.	F4	86
Pine Island Sound, strt., Fl., U.S.	F4	86
Pine Key, i., Fl., U.S.	p10	86
Pine Knot, Ky., U.S.	D5	94
Pine Lake, Ga., U.S.	h8	87
Pine Lake, l., In., U.S.	A4	91
Pine Lake, l., Wi., U.S.	C5	126
Pine Lawn, Mo., U.S.	f13	102
Pine Level, N.C., U.S.	B4	110
Pinellas, co., Fl., U.S.	D4	86
Pinellas, Point, c., Fl., U.S.	p10	86
Pinellas Park, Fl., U.S.	E4	86
Pine Mountain, Ga., U.S.	D2	87
Pine Mountain, mtn., Or., U.S.	D6	114
Pine Mountain, mtn., Wy., U.S.	E3	127
Pine Point, N.W. Ter., Can.	D10	66
Pine Point, Me., U.S.	E2	96
Pine Prairie, La., U.S.	D3	95
Pine Ridge, S.D., U.S.	D3	118
Pine Ridge Indian Reservation, S.D., U.S.	D3	118
Pine River, Mn., U.S.	D4	100
Pinerolo, Italy	E2	14
Pines, Lake O' the, res., Tx., U.S.	C5	120
Pinesdale, Mt., U.S.	D2	103
Pinetop-Lakeside, Az., U.S.	C6	80
Pinetops, N.C., U.S.	B5	110
Pine Valley, val., Ut., U.S.	E2	121
Pineville, Ky., U.S.	D6	94
Pineville, La., U.S.	C3	95
Pineville, N.C., U.S.	B2	110
Pineville, W.V., U.S.	D3	125
Pinewood, S.C., U.S.	D7	117
Piney Creek, stm., W.V., U.S.	n13	125
Piney Fork, stm., W.V., U.S.	h9	125
Piney Point, Md., U.S.	D4	97
Piney View, W.V., U.S.	n13	125
Ping, stm., Thai.	F5	34
Pingdingshan, China	E9	26
Pinghu, China	E10	28
Pingliang, China	D8	26
Pingtan Dao, i., China	J8	28
P'ingtung, Tai.	M9	28
Pingxiang, China	H2	28
Pingyao, China	D9	26
Pinhal, Port.	E4	12
Pinnacles National Monument, Ca., U.S.	D3	82
Pinneberg, Ger.	B9	8
Pinole, Ca., U.S.	h8	82
Pinopolis Dam, S.C., U.S.	E8	117
Pinos, Mount, mtn., Ca., U.S.	E4	82
Pins, Pointe aux, c., Ont., Can.	E3	73
Pinsk, Bela.	I9	18
Pinson, Al., U.S.	f7	78
Pinta, Sierra, mts., Az., U.S.	E2	80
Pintwater Range, mts., Nv., U.S.	G6	105
Pioche, Nv., U.S.	F7	105
Piombino, Italy	G5	14
Pioneer, Oh., U.S.	A1	112
Pioneer Mountains, mts., Id., U.S.	F5	89
Pioneer Mountains, mts., Mt., U.S.	E3	103
Pioner, Ostrov, i., Russia	B12	24
Piotrków Trybunalski, Pol.	D19	8
Pipe Spring National Monument, Az., U.S.	A3	80
Pipestem Creek, stm., N.D., U.S.	B6	111
Pipestone, Mn., U.S.	G2	100
Pipestone, co., Mn., U.S.	F2	100
Pipestone, stm., Ont., Can.	F14	66
Pipestone National Monument, Mn., U.S.	G2	100
Pipestone Pass, Mt., U.S.	E4	103
Pipmuacan, Réservoir, res., Que., Can.	k12	74
Piqua, Oh., U.S.	B1	112
Piracicaba, Braz.	G5	57
Piraeus see Piraiévs, Grc.	L7	16
Piraí do Sul, Braz.	A7	56
Piraiévs (Piraeus), Grc.	L7	16
Piraju, Braz.	G4	57
Piran, Slo.	D8	14
Pirané, Arg.	B5	56
Pirapora, Braz.	D6	57
Pires do Rio, Braz.	D4	57
Pírgos, Grc.	L5	16
Pirmasens, Ger.	F7	8
Pirna, Ger.	E13	8
Pirtleville, Az., U.S.	F6	80
Piru, Indon.	F8	32
Pisa, Italy	F5	14
Pisagua, Chile	G4	54
Piscataqua, stm., N.H., U.S.	D5	106
Piscataquis, co., Me., U.S.	C3	96
Piscataquis, stm., Me., U.S.	C3	96
Piscataquog, stm., N.H., U.S.	D3	106
Piscataway, N.J., U.S.	B4	107
Pisco, Peru	F3	54
Piseco Lake, l., N.Y., U.S.	B6	109
Písek, Czech.	F14	8
Pisgah, Al., U.S.	A4	78
Pisgah, Oh., U.S.	n13	112
Pisgah, Mount, mtn., Wy., U.S.	B8	127
Pisgah Forest, N.C., U.S.	f10	110
Pishan, China	B8	38
Pismo Beach, Ca., U.S.	E3	82
Pisticci, Italy	I11	14
Pistoia, Italy	F5	14
Pistolet Bay, b., Newf., Can.	C4	72
Pit, stm., Ca., U.S.	B3	82
Pitalito, Col.	G4	58
Pitcairn, Pa., U.S.	k14	115
Pitcairn, dep., Oc.	H4	2
Piteå, Swe.	D13	6
Pitești, Rom.	E8	16
Pithāpuram, India	D7	37
Pithiviers, Fr.	D9	10
Pitiquito, Mex.	B3	62
Pitkin, co., Co., U.S.	B4	83
Pitlochry, Scot., U.K.	E9	7
Pitman, N.J., U.S.	D2	107
Pitt, co., N.C., U.S.	B5	110
Pitt Island, i., B.C., Can.	C3	69
Pittsboro, In., U.S.	E5	91
Pittsboro, N.C., U.S.	B3	110
Pittsburg, Ca., U.S.	g9	82
Pittsburg, Ks., U.S.	E9	93
Pittsburg, Ky., U.S.	C5	94
Pittsburg, Tx., U.S.	C5	120
Pittsburg, co., Ok., U.S.	C6	113
Pittsburgh, Pa., U.S.	F1	115
Pittsfield, Il., U.S.	D3	90
Pittsfield, Me., U.S.	D3	96
Pittsfield, Ma., U.S.	B1	98
Pittsfield, N.H., U.S.	D4	106
Pittsford, Vt., U.S.	D2	122
Pittston, Pa., U.S.	D10	115
Pittsville, Md., U.S.	D7	97
Pittsville, Wi., U.S.	D3	126
Pittsylvania, co., Va., U.S.	D3	123
Piu, Cerro, mtn., Nic.	H5	64
Piura, Peru	E2	54
Piute, co., Ut., U.S.	E3	121
Piute Peak, mtn., Ca., U.S.	E4	82
Piute Reservoir, res., Ut., U.S.	E3	121
Pivdennyy Buh, stm., Ukr.	H3	22
Pixley, Ca., U.S.	E4	82
Pizzo, Italy	K11	14
Placentia, Newf., Can.	E5	72
Placentia Bay, b., Newf., Can.	E4	72
Placer, co., Ca., U.S.	C3	82
Placer Mountain, mtn., N.M., U.S.	k8	108
Placerville, Ca., U.S.	C3	82
Placetas, Cuba	C8	64
Placid, Lake, l., Fl., U.S.	E5	86
Placid, Lake, l., N.Y., U.S.	f11	109
Placitas, N.M., U.S.	B3	108
Plain City, Oh., U.S.	B2	112
Plain City, Ut., U.S.	B3	121
Plain Dealing, La., U.S.	B2	95
Plainfield, Ct., U.S.	C8	84
Plainfield, Il., U.S.	B5	90
Plainfield, In., U.S.	E5	91
Plainfield, N.J., U.S.	B4	107
Plainfield, Vt., U.S.	C4	122
Plainfield, Wi., U.S.	D4	126
Plainfield Heights, Mi., U.S.	*E5	99
Plains, Ga., U.S.	D2	87
Plains, Ks., U.S.	E3	93
Plains, Mt., U.S.	C2	103
Plains, Pa., U.S.	n17	115
Plains, Tx., U.S.	C1	120
Plainview, Ar., U.S.	C2	81
Plainview, Mn., U.S.	F6	100
Plainview, Ne., U.S.	B8	104
Plainview, Tx., U.S.	B2	120
Plainville, Ct., U.S.	C4	84
Plainville, Ks., U.S.	C4	93
Plainville, Ma., U.S.	B5	98
Plainwell, Mi., U.S.	F5	99
Plaistow, N.H., U.S.	E4	106
Plankinton, S.D., U.S.	D7	118
Plano, Il., U.S.	B5	90
Plano, Tx., U.S.	C4	120
Plantagenet, Ont., Can.	B9	73
Plantation, Fl., U.S.	r13	86
Plant City, Fl., U.S.	D4	86
Plantersville, Al., U.S.	C3	78
Plantersville, Ms., U.S.	A5	101
Plantsite, Az., U.S.	D6	80
Plantsville, Ct., U.S.	C4	84
Plaquemine, La., U.S.	D4	95
Plaquemines, co., La., U.S.	E6	95
Plasencia, Spain	E5	12
Plaški, Cro.	D10	14
Plaster Rock, N.B., Can.	C2	71
Plata, Río de la, est., S.A.	D5	56
Platte, S.D., U.S.	D7	118
Platte, co., Mo., U.S.	B3	102
Platte, co., Ne., U.S.	C8	104
Platte, co., Wy., U.S.	D7	127
Platte, stm., U.S.	B3	102
Platte, stm., Mn., U.S.	E4	100
Platte, stm., Ne., U.S.	D6	104
Platte City, Mo., U.S.	B3	102
Platte Island, i., Sey.	C11	44
Platteville, Co., U.S.	A6	83
Platteville, Wi., U.S.	F3	126
Plattling, Ger.	G12	8
Plattsburg, Mo., U.S.	B3	102
Plattsburgh, N.Y., U.S.	f11	109
Plattsburgh Air Force Base, mil., N.Y., U.S.	f11	109
Plattsmouth, Ne., U.S.	D10	104
Plau, Ger.	B12	8
Plauen, Ger.	E12	8
Playas Lake, l., N.M., U.S.	F2	108
Play Cu, Viet.	H9	34
Playgreen Lake, l., Man., Can.	B2	70
Pleasant, stm., Me., U.S.	C3	96
Pleasant, Lake, res., Az., U.S.	D3	80
Pleasant Gap, Pa., U.S.	E6	115
Pleasant Garden, N.C., U.S.	B3	110
Pleasant Grove, Al., U.S.	g7	78
Pleasant Grove, Ut., U.S.	C4	121
Pleasant Hill, Ca., U.S.	h8	82
Pleasant Hill, Il., U.S.	D3	90
Pleasant Hill, Ia., U.S.	e8	92
Pleasant Hill, La., U.S.	C2	95
Pleasant Hill, Mo., U.S.	C3	102
Pleasant Hill, Oh., U.S.	B1	112
Pleasant Lake, In., U.S.	A7	91
Pleasant Lake, l., Me., U.S.	C5	96
Pleasant Lake, l., N.H., U.S.	D4	106
Pleasanton, Ca., U.S.	h9	82
Pleasanton, Ks., U.S.	D9	93
Pleasanton, Tx., U.S.	E3	120
Pleasant Prairie, Wi., U.S.	n12	126
Pleasants, co., W.V., U.S.	B3	125
Pleasant Valley, Ia., U.S.	g11	92
Pleasant Valley, Mo., U.S.	h11	102
Pleasant View, Ut., U.S.	B3	121
Pleasantville, Ia., U.S.	C4	92
Pleasantville, N.J., U.S.	E3	107
Pleasantville, N.Y., U.S.	D7	109
Pleasantville, Oh., U.S.	C3	112
Pleasure Beach, Ct., U.S.	D7	84
Pleasure Ridge Park, Ky., U.S.	g11	94
Pleasureville, Ky., U.S.	B4	94
Pleiku see Play Cu, Viet.	H9	34
Pléneuf, Fr.	D4	10
Plenty, Bay of, b., N.Z.	B6	52
Plentywood, Mt., U.S.	B12	103
Plessisville, Que., Can.	C6	74
Pleternica, Cro.	D12	14
Plétipi, Lac, l., Que., Can.	F18	66
Pleven, Bul.	F8	16
Pljevlja, Yugo.	F3	16
Płock, Pol.	C19	8
Ploërmel, Fr.	E4	10
Ploiești, Rom.	E10	16
Plomosa Mountains, mts., Az., U.S.	D1	80
Plonge, Lac la, l., Sask., Can.	B2	75
Plouguenast, Fr.	D4	10
Plovdiv, Bul.	G8	16
Plover, Wi., U.S.	D4	126
Plover, stm., Wi., U.S.	D4	126
Plum, Pa., U.S.	k14	115
Plumas, co., Ca., U.S.	B3	82
Plum Coulee, Man., Can.	E3	70
Plumerville, Ar., U.S.	B3	81
Plum Island, i., Ma., U.S.	A6	98
Plummer, Id., U.S.	B2	89
Plumsteadville, Pa., U.S.	F11	115
Plumtree, Zimb.	F5	44
Plymouth, Monts.	F16	64
Plymouth, Eng., U.K.	K8	7
Plymouth, Ct., U.S.	C3	84
Plymouth, Fl., U.S.	D5	86
Plymouth, In., U.S.	B5	91
Plymouth, Ma., U.S.	C6	98
Plymouth, Mi., U.S.	p15	99
Plymouth, Mn., U.S.	m12	100
Plymouth, N.H., U.S.	C3	106
Plymouth, N.C., U.S.	B6	110
Plymouth, Oh., U.S.	A3	112
Plymouth, Pa., U.S.	D10	115
Plymouth, Wi., U.S.	E6	126
Plymouth, co., Ia., U.S.	B1	92
Plymouth, co., Ma., U.S.	C6	98
Plymouth Bay, b., Ma., U.S.	C6	98
Plzeň, Czech.	F13	8
Po, stm., Italy	E7	14
Po, stm., Va., U.S.	B5	123
Pobeda, Gora, mtn., Russia	D23	24
Pocahontas, Ar., U.S.	A5	81
Pocahontas, Il., U.S.	E4	90
Pocahontas, Ia., U.S.	B3	92
Pocahontas, co., Ia., U.S.	B3	92
Pocahontas, co., W.V., U.S.	C4	126
Pocasset, Ma., U.S.	C6	98
Pocatalico, W.V., U.S.	C3	125
Pocatalico, stm., W.V., U.S.	C3	125
Pocatello, Id., U.S.	G6	89
Počep, Russia	I16	18
Pochutla, Mex.	J11	62
Poções, Braz.	C8	57
Pocola, Ok., U.S.	B7	113
Pocomoke, stm., Md., U.S.	D7	97
Pocomoke City, Md., U.S.	D6	97
Pocomoke Sound, strt., Md., U.S.	E6	97
Pocono Mountains, hills, Pa., U.S.	E11	115
Pocono Pines, Pa., U.S.	D11	115
Poços de Caldas, Braz.	F5	57
Pocotopaug Lake, res., Ct., U.S.	C6	84
Podensac, Fr.	H6	10
Podgorica, Yugo.	G3	16
Podkamennaja Tunguska, Russia	E12	24
Podkamennaja Tunguska, stm., Russia	E13	24
Podol'sk, Russia	F20	18
Podor, Sen.	E3	42
Podravska Slatina, Cro.	D12	14

Name	Map Ref	Page
Pofadder, S. Afr.	G3	44
Poge, Cape, c., Ma., U.S.	D7	98
Poggibonsi, Italy	F6	14
P'ohang, S. Kor.	D12	26
Pohénégamook, Que., Can.	B8	74
Pohue Bay, b., Hi., U.S.	E6	88
Poinsett, co., Ar., U.S.	B5	81
Poinsett, Lake, l., Fl., U.S.	D6	86
Poinsett, Lake, l., S.D., U.S.	C8	118
Point Clear, Al., U.S.	E2	78
Pointe a la Hache, La., U.S.	E6	95
Pointe-à-Pitre, Guad.	F17	64
Pointe-au-Pic, Que., Can.	B7	74
Pointe-Calumet, Que., Can.	p19	74
Pointe-Claire, Que., Can.	D4	74
Pointe Coupee, co., La., U.S.	D4	95
Pointe-des-Cascades, Que., Can.	q19	74
Point Edward, Ont., Can.	D2	73
Pointe-Noire, Congo	B2	44
Pointe-Verte, N.B., Can.	B4	71
Point Fortin, Trin.	I17	64
Point Hope, Ak., U.S.	B6	79
Point Imperial, mtn., Az., U.S.	A4	80
Point Judith Pond, l., R.I., U.S.	F4	116
Point Lake, l., N.W. Ter., Can.	C10	66
Point Leamington, Newf., Can.	D4	72
Point Marion, Pa., U.S.	G2	115
Point Mugu Naval Air Station, mil., Ca., U.S.	E4	82
Point of Rocks, Md., U.S.	B2	97
Point Pelee National Park, Ont., Can.	F2	73
Point Pleasant, N.J., U.S.	C4	107
Point Pleasant, W.V., U.S.	C2	125
Point Pleasant Beach, N.J., U.S.	C4	107
Point Reyes National Seashore, Ca., U.S.	C2	82
Point Roberts, Wa., U.S.	A2	124
Poipu, Hi., U.S.	B2	88
Poison Creek, stm., Wy., U.S.	C5	127
Poisson Blanc, Lac du, res., Que., Can.	C2	74
Poitiers, Fr.	F7	10
Poitou, reg., Fr.	F6	10
Poix, Fr.	C8	10
Pokegama Lake, l., Mn., U.S.	C5	100
Pokegama Lake, l., Wi., U.S.	C2	126
Polacca, Az., U.S.	B5	80
Poland, ctry., Eur.	E11	4
Polar Bear Provincial Park, Ont., Can.	n18	73
Polecat Creek, stm., Ok., U.S.	B5	113
Pol-e Khomrī, Afg.	C3	38
Polesje, reg., Eur.	I10	18
Pólis, Cyp.	B3	40
Polistena, Italy	K11	14
Polk, Pa., U.S.	D2	115
Polk, co., Ar., U.S.	C1	81
Polk, co., Fl., U.S.	E5	86
Polk, co., Ga., U.S.	C1	87
Polk, co., Ia., U.S.	C4	92
Polk, co., Mn., U.S.	C2	100
Polk, co., Mo., U.S.	D4	102
Polk, co., Ne., U.S.	C8	104
Polk, co., N.C., U.S.	f10	110
Polk, co., Or., U.S.	C3	114
Polk, co., Tn., U.S.	D9	119
Polk, co., Tx., U.S.	D5	120
Polk, co., Wi., U.S.	C1	126
Polk City, Fl., U.S.	D5	86
Polk City, Ia., U.S.	C4	92
Pol'kino, Russia	C13	24
Pollāchi, India	G4	37
Polo, Il., U.S.	B4	90
Polock, Bela.	F11	18
Polson, Mt., U.S.	C2	103
Poltava, Ukr.	H4	22
Polynesia, is., Oc.	G2	2
Pomabamba, Peru	E3	54
Pomaro, Mex.	H8	62
Pombal, Port.	F3	12
Pomerania, hist. reg., Pol.	A16	8
Pomeranian Bay, b., Eur.	A14	8
Pomeroy, Ia., U.S.	B3	92
Pomeroy, Oh., U.S.	C3	112
Pomeroy, Wa., U.S.	C8	124
Pomme de Terre, stm., Mn., U.S.	E3	100
Pomme de Terre, stm., Mo., U.S.	D4	102
Pomme de Terre Lake, res., Mo., U.S.	D4	102
Pomona, Ca., U.S.	E5	82
Pomona, Ks., U.S.	D8	93
Pomona Lake, res., Ks., U.S.	D7	93
Pompano Beach, Fl., U.S.	F6	86
Pompton Lakes, N.J., U.S.	A4	107
Ponaganset, stm., R.I., U.S.	C2	116
Ponaganset Reservoir, res., R.I., U.S.	B2	116
Ponca, Ne., U.S.	B9	104
Ponca City, Ok., U.S.	A4	113
Ponca Creek, stm., U.S.	A6	104
Ponca Indian Reservation, Ne., U.S.	B7	104
Ponce, P.R.	E14	64
Ponce de Leon Bay, b., Fl., U.S.	G5	86
Ponce de Leon Inlet, b., Fl., U.S.	C6	86
Poncha Pass, Co., U.S.	C4	83
Ponchatoula, La., U.S.	D5	95
Pond, stm., Ky., U.S.	C2	94
Pond Creek, Ok., U.S.	A3	113
Pondera, co., Mt., U.S.	B4	103
Pond Fork, stm., W.V., U.S.	D3	125
Pondicherry, India	G5	37
Pondicherry, ter., India	G5	37
Pond Inlet, N.W. Ter., Can.	B17	66
Pone Island, i., Md., U.S.	D5	97
Ponferrada, Spain	C5	12
Ponoka, Alta., Can.	C4	68
Ponorogo, Indon.	m15	33a
Pons, Fr.	G6	10
Ponta Grossa, Braz.	B6	56
Pont-à-Mousson, Fr.	D13	10
Ponta Porã, Braz.	G1	57
Pontarlier, Fr.	F13	10
Pontassieve, Italy	F6	14
Pont-Audemer, Fr.	C7	10
Pontchartrain, Lake, l., La., U.S.	D5	95
Pontchâteau, Fr.	E4	10
Pont de Suert, Spain	C12	12
Ponte Branca, Braz.	D2	57
Ponte da Barca, Port.	D3	12
Pontedera, Italy	F5	14
Ponte de Sor, Port.	F3	12
Ponteix, Sask., Can.	H2	75
Ponte Nova, Braz.	F7	57
Pontevedra, Spain	C3	12
Ponte Vedra Beach, Fl., U.S.	B5	86
Pontgibaud, Fr.	F9	10
Pontiac, Il., U.S.	C5	90
Pontiac, Mi., U.S.	F7	99
Pontianak, Indon.	F4	32
Pontivy, Fr.	D4	10
Pont-l'Abbé, Fr.	E2	10
Pontoise, Fr.	C9	10
Pontoosuc Lake, l., Ma., U.S.	B1	98
Pontorson, Fr.	D5	10
Pontotoc, Ms., U.S.	A4	101
Pontotoc, co., Ms., U.S.	A4	101
Pontotoc, co., Ok., U.S.	C5	113
Pont-Rouge, Que., Can.	C6	74
Pontypool, Ont., Can.	C6	73
Pontypool, Wales, U.K.	J9	7
Poole, Eng., U.K.	K11	7
Pooler, Ga., U.S.	D5	87
Pooles Island, i., Md., U.S.	B5	97
Poolesville, Md., U.S.	B3	97
Poopó, Lago de, l., Bol.	G5	54
Popayán, Col.	F4	58
Pope, co., Ar., U.S.	B2	81
Pope, co., Il., U.S.	F5	90
Pope, co., Mn., U.S.	E3	100
Pope Air Force Base, mil., N.C., U.S.	B3	110
Poplar, Mt., U.S.	B11	103
Poplar, stm., Can.	C3	70
Poplar, stm., Mn., U.S.	C2	100
Poplar Bluff, Mo., U.S.	E7	102
Poplar Island, i., Md., U.S.	C5	97
Poplarville, Ms., U.S.	E4	101
Popocatépetl, Volcán, vol., Mex.	H10	62
Popokabaka, Zaire	C3	44
Popomanasiu, Mount, mtn., Sol.Is.	A11	50
Popondetta, Pap. N. Gui.	m16	50a
Popple, stm., Wi., U.S.	C5	126
Poquonock, Ct., U.S.	B5	84
Poquonock Bridge, Ct., U.S.	D7	84
Poquoson, Va., U.S.	C6	123
Porangatu, Braz.	F9	54
Porbandar, India	J3	38
Porcher Island, i., B.C., Can.	C2	69
Porcupine Mountains, mts., Mi., U.S.	m12	99
Pordenone, Italy	D7	14
Poreč, Cro.	D8	14
Pori, Fin.	F13	6
Porkkala, Fin.	G15	6
Porlamar, Ven.	B11	58
Poronajsk, Russia	H22	24
Porsgrunn, Nor.	G7	6
Portadown, N. Ire., U.K.	G6	7
Portage, In., U.S.	A3	91
Portage, Mi., U.S.	F5	99
Portage, Pa., U.S.	F4	115
Portage, Wi., U.S.	E4	126
Portage, co., Oh., U.S.	A4	112
Portage, co., Wi., U.S.	D4	126
Portage, stm., Oh., U.S.	B2	112
Portage Bay, b., Man., Can.	D2	70
Portage Head, c., Wa., U.S.	A1	124
Portage Lake, l., Me., U.S.	B4	96
Portage Lakes, Oh., U.S.	B4	112
Portage la Prairie, Man., Can.	E2	70
Portageville, Mo., U.S.	E8	102
Port Alberni, B.C., Can.	E5	69
Portalegre, Port.	F4	12
Portales, N.M., U.S.	C6	108
Port Alice, B.C., Can.	D4	69
Port Allegany, Pa., U.S.	C5	115
Port Allen, La., U.S.	D4	95
Port Angeles, Wa., U.S.	A2	124
Port Antonio, Jam.	E9	64
Port Aransas, Tx., U.S.	F4	120
Port Arthur, Tx., U.S.	E6	120
Port Arthur see Lüshun, China	D11	26
Port Augusta, Austl.	F7	50
Port au Port Bay, b., Newf., Can.	D2	72
Port au Port [West-Aguathuna-Felix Cove], Newf., Can.	D2	72
Port-au-Prince, Haiti	E11	64
Port au Prince Peninsula, pen., Newf., Can.	D2	72
Port Austin, Mi., U.S.	D7	99
Port Barre, La., U.S.	D4	95
Port-Bergé, Madag.	E9	44
Port Blair, India	I2	34
Port Blandford, Newf., Can.	D4	72
Port Bolivar, Tx., U.S.	E5	120
Port Burwell, Ont., Can.	E4	73
Port Byron, Il., U.S.	B3	90
Port Carbon, Pa., U.S.	E9	115
Port Carling, Ont., Can.	B5	73
Port-Cartier-Ouest, Que., Can.	k13	74
Port Chalmers, N.Z.	F3	52
Port Charlotte, Fl., U.S.	F4	86
Port Chester, N.Y., U.S.	E7	109
Port Clinton, Oh., U.S.	A3	112
Port Colborne, Ont., Can.	E5	73
Port Coquitlam, B.C., Can.	E6	69
Port Deposit, Md., U.S.	A5	97
Port Dickinson, N.Y., U.S.	C5	109
Port Dickson, Malay.	M6	34
Port Edward, B.C., Can.	B2	69
Port Edwards, Wi., U.S.	D4	126
Portel, Braz.	D8	54
Portel, Port.	G4	12
Port Elgin, Ont., Can.	C3	73
Port Elizabeth, S. Afr.	H5	44
Port Ellen, Scot., U.K.	F6	7
Porter, In., U.S.	A3	91
Porter, Tx., U.S.	D5	120
Porter, co., In., U.S.	B3	91
Porter Creek, stm., W.V., U.S.	m13	125
Porterdale, Ga., U.S.	C3	87
Porterville, Ca., U.S.	D4	82
Port Ewen, N.Y., U.S.	D7	109
Port Gamble Indian Reservation, Wa., U.S.	B3	124
Port-Gentil, Gabon	B1	44
Port Gibson, Ms., U.S.	D3	101
Port Harcourt, Nig.	H7	42
Port Hedland, Austl.	D3	50
Port Hood, N.S., Can.	C8	71
Port Hope, Ont., Can.	D6	73
Port Hope Simpson, Newf., Can.	B3	72
Port Hueneme, Ca., U.S.	E4	82
Port Huron, Mi., U.S.	F8	99
Portimão, Port.	H3	12
Port Isabel, Tx., U.S.	F4	120
Port Jefferson, N.Y., U.S.	n15	109
Port Jervis, N.Y., U.S.	D6	109
Portland, Austl.	G8	50
Portland, Ct., U.S.	C5	84
Portland, In., U.S.	D8	91
Portland, Me., U.S.	E2	96
Portland, Mi., U.S.	F6	99
Portland, N.D., U.S.	B8	111
Portland, Or., U.S.	B4	114
Portland, Tn., U.S.	A5	119
Portland, Tx., U.S.	F4	120
Portland, Bill of, c., Eng., U.K.	K10	7
Portland Inlet, b., B.C., Can.	B2	69
Portland Point, c., Jam.	F9	64
Port Lavaca, Tx., U.S.	E4	120
Port Lincoln, Austl.	F7	50
Port Loko, S.L.	G3	42
Port Louis, Mrts.	F11	44
Port Ludlow, Wa., U.S.	B3	124
Port-Lyautey see Kenitra, Mor.	B4	42
Port Macquarie, Austl.	F10	50
Port Madison Indian Reservation, Wa., U.S.	B3	124
Port McNeil, B.C., Can.	D4	69
Port McNicoll, Ont., Can.	C5	73
Port Monmouth, N.J., U.S.	C4	107
Port Moresby, Pap. N. Gui.	m16	50a
Port Morien, N.S., Can.	C10	71
Port Neches, Tx., U.S.	E6	120
Portneuf, Que., Can.	C6	74
Port Nolloth, S. Afr.	G3	44
Porto, Port.	D3	12
Porto Alegre, Braz.	C6	56
Porto Amboim, Ang.	D2	44
Portobelo, Pan.	J8	64
Porto de Moz, Braz.	D8	54
Porto Esperança, Braz.	G7	54
Porto Esperidião, Braz.	G7	54
Pôrto Feliz, Braz.	G5	57
Portoferraio, Italy	G5	14
Pôrto Ferreira, Braz.	F5	57
Port of Spain, Trin.	I17	64
Portogruaro, Italy	D7	14
Portola, Ca., U.S.	C3	82
Porto Murtinho, Braz.	H7	54
Porto Nacional, Braz.	F9	54
Porto-Novo, Benin	G6	42
Port Orange, Fl., U.S.	C6	86
Port Orchard, Wa., U.S.	B3	124
Port Orford, Or., U.S.	E2	114
Porto San Giorgio, Italy	F8	14
Porto Santo Stefano, Italy	G6	14
Pôrto São José, Braz.	G2	57
Pôrto Seguro, Braz.	D9	57
Porto Torres, Italy	I3	14
Pôrto União, Braz.	B6	56
Porto Velho, Braz.	E6	54
Portoviejo, Ec.	H2	58
Port Penn, De., U.S.	B3	85
Port Pirie, Austl.	F7	50
Port Richey, Fl., U.S.	D4	86
Port Rowan, Ont., Can.	E4	73
Port Royal, S.C., U.S.	G6	117
Port Royal Island, i., S.C., U.S.	G6	117
Port Royal Sound, strt., S.C., U.S.	G6	117
Port Said see Būr Sa'īd, Egypt	B12	42
Port-Sainte-Marie, Fr.	H7	10
Port Saint Joe, Fl., U.S.	C1	86
Port Saint Johns, S. Afr.	H5	44
Port Saint Lucie, Fl., U.S.	E6	86
Port Salerno, Fl., U.S.	E6	86
Port Saunders, Newf., Can.	C3	72
Port Shepstone, S. Afr.	H6	44
Portsmouth, Eng., U.K.	K11	7
Portsmouth, N.H., U.S.	D5	106
Portsmouth, Oh., U.S.	D3	112
Portsmouth, R.I., U.S.	E6	116
Portsmouth, Va., U.S.	D6	123
Portsmouth Naval Shipyard, mil., Me., U.S.	D5	106
Port Stanley, Ont., Can.	E3	73
Port Sulphur, La., U.S.	E6	95
Port Talbot, Wales, U.K.	J9	7
Port Townsend, Wa., U.S.	A3	124
Portugal, ctry., Eur.	H6	4
Portugalete, Spain	B8	12
Portuguese Guinea see Guinea-Bissau, ctry., Afr.	F2	42
Portumna, Ire.	H4	7
Port Union, Newf., Can.	D5	72
Port-Vendres, Fr.	J10	10
Port Washington, N.Y., U.S.	h13	109
Port Washington, Wi., U.S.	E6	126
Port Wentworth, Ga., U.S.	D5	87
Porum, Ok., U.S.	B6	113
Porz, Ger.	E7	8
Porzuna, Spain	F7	12
Posadas, Arg.	B5	56
Poschiavo, Switz.	F17	10
Posen, Il., U.S.	k9	90
Posey, co., In., U.S.	H2	91
Poseyville, In., U.S.	H2	91
Poso, Indon.	F7	32
Posse, Braz.	C5	57
Pössneck, Ger.	E11	8
Post, Tx., U.S.	C2	120
Post Falls, Id., U.S.	B2	89
Post Maurice Cortier (Bidon Cinq), Alg.	D6	42
Postojna, Slo.	D9	14
P'ostraja Dresva, Russia	E25	24
Postville, Ia., U.S.	A6	92
Potawatomi Indian Reservation, Ks., U.S.	C8	93
Potchefstroom, S. Afr.	G5	44
Poté, Braz.	D8	57
Poteau, Ok., U.S.	B7	113
Poteau, stm., U.S.	B7	113
Poteet, Tx., U.S.	E3	120
Potenza, Italy	I10	14
Potes, Spain	B7	12
Potgietersrus, S. Afr.	F5	44
Poth, Tx., U.S.	E3	120
Potholes Reservoir, res., Wa., U.S.	B6	124
Potiraguá, Braz.	C9	57
Potiskum, Nig.	F8	42
Potlatch, Id., U.S.	C2	89
Potomac, Md., U.S.	B3	97
Potomac, stm., U.S.	D4	97
Potomac Heights, Md., U.S.	C3	97
Potomac Park, Md., U.S.	k13	97
Potosí, Bol.	G5	54
Potosi, Mo., U.S.	D7	102
Potosí, Cerro, mtn., Mex.	E9	62
Potsdam, Ger.	C13	8
Potsdam, N.Y., U.S.	f10	109
Pottawatomie, co., Ks., U.S.	C7	93
Pottawatomie, co., Ok., U.S.	B4	113
Pottawattamie, co., Ia., U.S.	C2	92
Potter, co., Pa., U.S.	C6	115
Potter, co., S.D., U.S.	B6	118
Potter, co., Tx., U.S.	B2	120
Potter Valley, Ca., U.S.	C2	82
Potts Creek, stm., U.S.	C2	123
Pottstown, Pa., U.S.	F10	115
Pottsville, Ar., U.S.	B2	81
Pottsville, Pa., U.S.	E9	115
P'otzu, Tai.	L9	28
Pouce Coupe, B.C., Can.	B7	69
Pouch Cove, Newf., Can.	E5	72
Poughkeepsie, N.Y., U.S.	D7	109
Poulan, Ga., U.S.	E3	87
Poulsbo, Wa., U.S.	B3	124
Poultney, Vt., U.S.	D2	122
Poultney, stm., Vt., U.S.	D2	122
Pound, Va., U.S.	e9	123
Pound Gap, U.S.	C7	94
Pouso Alegre, Braz.	G6	57
Poŭthĭsăt, Camb.	H7	34
Pouzauges, Fr.	F6	10
Póvoa de Varzim, Port.	D3	12
Povungnituk, Que., Can.	f11	74
Powassan, Ont., Can.	A5	73
Poway, Ca., U.S.	F5	82
Powder, stm., U.S.	B5	76
Powder, stm., Or., U.S.	C9	114
Powder, Middle Fork, stm., Wy., U.S.	C6	127
Powder, North Fork, stm., Wy., U.S.	C6	127
Powder, South Fork, stm., Wy., U.S.	C6	127
Powder River, co., Mt., U.S.	E11	103
Powder River Pass, Wy., U.S.	B5	127
Powder Springs, Ga., U.S.	h8	87
Powell, Oh., U.S.	B2	112
Powell, Tn., U.S.	m13	119
Powell, Wy., U.S.	B4	127
Powell, co., Ky., U.S.	C6	94
Powell, co., Mt., U.S.	D4	103
Powell, stm., U.S.	C10	119
Powell, Lake, res., U.S.	F5	121
Powell, Mount, mtn., Co., U.S.	B4	83
Powell, Mount, mtn., N.M., U.S.	B1	108
Powell Butte, Or., U.S.	C5	114
Powell Park, reg., Co., U.S.	A2	83
Powell River, B.C., Can.	E5	69
Powellton, W.V., U.S.	C3	125
Power, co., Id., U.S.	G5	89
Powers, Or., U.S.	E2	114
Powerview, Man., Can.	D3	70
Poweshiek, co., Ia., U.S.	C5	92
Powhatan, Va., U.S.	C5	123
Powhatan, co., Va., U.S.	C5	123
Powhatan Point, Oh., U.S.	C5	112
Poxoreu, Braz.	C1	57
Poyang, China	G5	28
Poyang Hu, l., China	F5	28
Poygan, Lake, l., Wi., U.S.	D5	126
Poynette, Wi., U.S.	E4	126
Poza Rica de Hidalgo, Mex.	G11	62
Poznań, Pol.	C16	8
Pozo Alcón, Spain	H9	12
Pozoblanco, Spain	G7	12
Pozo Redondo Mountains, mts., Az., U.S.	E3	80
Pozuelo de Alarcón, Spain	E8	12
Pozzuoli, Italy	I9	14
Prachin Buri, Thai.	G6	34
Prachuap Khiri Khan, Thai.	I5	34
Prague, Ok., U.S.	B5	113
Prague see Praha, Czech.	E14	8
Praha (Prague), Czech.	E14	8
Prainha, Braz.	E6	54
Prairie, co., Ar., U.S.	C4	81
Prairie, co., Mt., U.S.	D11	103
Prairie, stm., Mn., U.S.	C5	100
Prairie, stm., Wi., U.S.	C4	126
Prairie City, Ia., U.S.	C4	92
Prairie City, Or., U.S.	C8	114
Prairie Creek Reservoir, res., In., U.S.	D7	91
Prairie Dog Creek, stm., U.S.	C3	93
Prairie du Chien, Wi., U.S.	E2	126
Prairie du Sac, Wi., U.S.	E4	126
Prairie Grove, Ar., U.S.	B1	81
Prairies, Rivière des, stm., Que., Can.	p19	74
Prairie View, Tx., U.S.	D5	120
Prairie Village, Ks., U.S.	m16	93
Praslin Island, i., Sey.	B11	44
Pratas Islands see Tungsha Tao, is., Tai.	G10	26
Prat de Llobregat, Spain	D14	12
Prater Mountain, mtn., Wy., U.S.	C2	127
Prato, Italy	F6	14
Pratt, Ks., U.S.	E5	93
Pratt, co., Ks., U.S.	E5	93
Prattville, Al., U.S.	C3	78
Pravia, Spain	B5	12
Preble, co., Oh., U.S.	C1	112
Predazzo, Italy	C6	14
Predlitz [-Turrach], Aus.	H13	8
Pré-en-Pail, Fr.	D6	10
Preetz, Ger.	A10	8
Premont, Tx., U.S.	F3	120
Prentiss, Ms., U.S.	D4	101
Prentiss, co., Ms., U.S.	A5	101
Prenzlau, Ger.	B13	8
Preparis Island, i., Mya.	G2	34
Preparis North Channel, strt., Mya.	G2	34
Preparis South Channel, strt., Mya.	G2	34
Přerov, Czech.	F17	8
Prescott, Ont., Can.	C9	73
Prescott, Az., U.S.	C3	80
Prescott, Ar., U.S.	D2	81
Prescott, Wi., U.S.	D1	126
Presho, S.D., U.S.	D5	118
Presidencia Roca, Arg.	B5	56
Presidente Epitácio, Braz.	F2	57
Presidente Prudente, Braz.	G3	57
Presidential Range, mts., N.H., U.S.	B4	106
Presidio, Tx., U.S.	p12	120
Presidio, co., Tx., U.S.	o12	120
Presidio of San Francisco, mil., Ca., U.S.	h8	82
Prešov, Slov.	F21	8
Prespa, Lake, l., Eur.	I4	16
Presque Isle, Me., U.S.	B5	96
Presque Isle, co., Mi., U.S.	C6	99
Preston, Eng., U.K.	H10	7
Preston, Id., U.S.	G7	89
Preston, Ia., U.S.	B7	92
Preston, Mn., U.S.	G6	100
Preston, co., W.V., U.S.	B5	125
Preston Peak, mtn., Ca., U.S.	B2	82
Prestonsburg, Ky., U.S.	C7	94
Presumpscot, stm., Me., U.S.	g7	96
Pretoria, S. Afr.	G5	44
Prettyboy Reservoir, res., Md., U.S.	A4	97
Pretty Prairie, Ks., U.S.	E5	93
Préveza, Grc.	K4	16
Prewitt Reservoir, res., Co., U.S.	A7	83
Prey Vêng, Camb.	I8	34
Pribilof Islands, is., Ak., U.S.	D5	79
Příbram, Czech.	F14	8
Price, Ut., U.S.	D5	121
Price, co., Wi., U.S.	C3	126
Price, stm., Ut., U.S.	D5	121
Price Inlet, b., S.C., U.S.	k12	117
Prichard, Al., U.S.	E1	78
Priego, Spain	E9	12
Priego de Córdoba, Spain	H7	12
Prien, Ger.	H12	8
Prieska, S. Afr.	G4	44
Priest Lake, l., Id., U.S.	A2	89
Priest Rapids Dam, Wa., U.S.	C6	124
Priest Rapids Lake, res., Wa., U.S.	C6	124
Priest River, Id., U.S.	A2	89
Prievidza, Slov.	G18	8
Prijedor, Bos.	E11	14
Prilep, Mac.	H5	16
Prim, Point, c., P.E.I., Can.	C6	71
Primghar, Ia., U.S.	A2	92
Primrose, R.I., U.S.	B3	116
Primrose Lake, l., Can.	F11	66
Prince, Lake, res., Va., U.S.	k14	123
Prince Albert National Park, Sask., Can.	C2	75
Prince Albert Sound, strt., N.W. Ter., Can.	B9	66
Prince Charles Island, i., N.W. Ter., Can.	C17	66
Prince-de-Galles, Cap du, c., Que., Can.	D18	66
Prince Edward, co., Va., U.S.	C4	123
Prince Edward Island, prov., Can.	C6	71
Prince Edward Island National Park, P.E.I., Can.	C6	71
Prince Frederick, Md., U.S.	C4	97
Prince George, B.C., Can.	C6	69
Prince George, co., Va., U.S.	C5	123
Prince Georges, co., Md., U.S.	C4	97
Prince of Wales, Cape, c., Ak., U.S.	B6	79
Prince of Wales Island, i., Austl.	B8	50
Prince of Wales Island, i., N.W. Ter., Can.	B13	66
Prince of Wales Island, i., Ak., U.S.	n23	79
Prince of Wales Strait, strt., N.W. Ter., Can.	B9	66
Prince Regent Inlet, b., N.W. Ter., Can.	B14	66
Prince Rupert, B.C., Can.	B2	69
Princes Lakes, In., U.S.	F5	91
Princess Anne, Md., U.S.	D6	97
Princess Royal Channel, strt., B.C., Can.	C3	69
Princess Royal Island, i., B.C., Can.	C3	69
Princeton, B.C., Can.	E7	69
Princeton, Fl., U.S.	G6	86
Princeton, Il., U.S.	B4	90
Princeton, In., U.S.	H2	91
Princeton, Ia., U.S.	C7	92
Princeton, Ky., U.S.	C2	94
Princeton, Me., U.S.	C5	96
Princeton, Mn., U.S.	E5	100
Princeton, Mo., U.S.	A4	102
Princeton, N.J., U.S.	C3	107
Princeton, N.C., U.S.	B4	110

Name / Map Ref / Page

Princeton, W.V., U.S. D3 125
Princeton, Wi., U.S. E4 126
Princeton, Mount, mtn., Co., U.S. C4 83
Princeville, Que., Can. C6 74
Princeville, Il., U.S. C4 90
Princeville, N.C., U.S. B5 110
Prince William, co., Va., U.S. B5 123
Prince William Sound, strt., Ak., U.S. g18 79
Príncipe, i., S. Tom./P. A1 44
Principe Channel, strt., B.C., Can. C3 69
Príncipe da Beira, Braz. F6 54
Prineville, Or., U.S. C6 114
Prineville Reservoir, res., Or., U.S. C6 114
Pringsewu, Indon. k12 33a
Prinzapolca, Nic. H6 64
Prior Lake, Mn., U.S. F5 100
Priština, Yugo. G5 16
Pritchards Island, i., S.C., U.S. G6 117
Pritzwalk, Ger. B12 8
Privas, Fr. H11 10
Privolžsk, Russia D24 18
Probolinggo, Indon. m16 33a
Proctor, Mn., U.S. D6 100
Proctor, Vt., U.S. D2 122
Proctor Lake, res., Tx., U.S. C3 120
Proctorsville, Vt., U.S. E3 122
Proddatūr, India E5 37
Professor Dr. Ir. W.J. van Blommestein Meer, res., Sur. C7 54
Progreso, Mex. G15 62
Prokopjevsk, Russia G11 24
Prokuplje, Yugo. F5 16
Promontory Mountains, mts., Ut., U.S. B3 121
Prophetstown, Il., U.S. B4 90
Propriá, Braz. F11 54
Prospect, Ct., U.S. C4 84
Prospect, Ky., U.S. g11 94
Prospect, Oh., U.S. B2 112
Prospect, Or., U.S. E4 114
Prospect, Pa., U.S. E1 115
Prospect Hill, mtn., Or., U.S. k11 114
Prospect Park, N.J., U.S. B4 107
Prospect Park, Pa., U.S. p20 115
Prosperity, S.C., U.S. C4 117
Prosperity, W.V., U.S. n13 125
Prosser, Wa., U.S. C6 124
Prostějov, Czech. F17 8
Protection, Ks., U.S. E4 93
Protville, Tun. M5 14
Provence, hist. reg., Fr. I13 10
Providence, Ky., U.S. C2 94
Providence, R.I., U.S. C4 116
Providence, Ut., U.S. B4 121
Providence, co., R.I., U.S. C2 116
Providence, stm., R.I., U.S. C5 116
Providence Island, i., Sey. C10 44
Providence Point, c., R.I., U.S. D5 116
Providencia, Isla de, i., Col. H7 64
Providenija, Russia E31 24
Province Lake, l., N.H., U.S. C5 106
Provincetown, Ma., U.S. B7 98
Provins, Fr. D10 10
Provo, Ut., U.S. C4 121
Provo, stm., Ut., U.S. C4 121
Provost, Alta., Can. C5 68
Prowers, co., Co., U.S. D8 83
Prozor, Bos. F12 14
Prudence Island, i., R.I., U.S. E5 116
Prudenville, Mi., U.S. D6 99
Prudhoe Bay, Ak., U.S. A10 79
Prudhoe Bay, b., Ak., U.S. A10 79
Prüm, Ger. E6 8
Pruszków, Pol. C20 8
Prut, stm., Eur. D12 16
Pryor, Mt., U.S. E8 103
Pryor, Ok., U.S. A6 113
Pryor Mountains, mts., Mt., U.S. E8 103
Przemyśl, Pol. F22 8
Pskov, Russia D11 18
Ptolemaís, Grc. I5 16
Ptuj, Slo. C10 14
Pucallpa, Peru E4 54
Pucheng, China H7 28
Puckaway Lake, l., Wi., U.S. E4 126
Pudukkottai, India G5 37
Puebla de Sanabria, Spain C5 12
Puebla de Trives, Spain C4 12
Puebla [de Zaragoza], Mex. H10 62
Pueblo, Co., U.S. C6 83
Pueblo, co., Co., U.S. C6 83
Pueblo Hundido, Chile B2 56
Pueblo Mountain, mtn., Or., U.S. E8 114
Pueblo Mountains, mts., Or., U.S. E8 114
Pueblo Reservoir, res., Co., U.S. C6 83
Puentedeume, Spain B3 12
Puente-Genil, Spain H7 12
Pueo Point, c., Hi., U.S. B1 88
Puerco, stm., U.S. C6 80
Puerco, Rio, stm., N.M., U.S. B2 108
Puerto Aisén, Chile F2 56
Puerto Alfonso, Col. I7 58
Puerto Ángel, Mex. J11 62
Puerto Armuelles, Pan. J6 64
Puerto Asís, Col. G4 58
Puerto Ayacucho, Ven. E9 58
Puerto Barrios, Guat. G3 64
Puerto Berrío, Col. D5 58
Puerto Boyacá, Col. E5 58
Puerto Cabello, Ven. B8 58
Puerto Cabezas, Nic. G6 64
Puerto Carreño, Col. D9 58
Puerto Casado, Para. A5 56
Puerto Chicama, Peru E3 54
Puerto Cortés, C.R. J6 64
Puerto Cortés, Hond. G4 64
Puerto Cumarebo, Ven. B8 58
Puerto de Pollensa, Spain F15 12
Puerto de San José, Guat. H2 64
Puerto Deseado, Arg. F3 56
Puerto Escondido, Mex. J11 62
Puerto Francisco de Orellana, Ec. H4 58
Puerto Inírida, Col. F9 58
Puerto Juárez, Mex. G16 62
Puerto la Cruz, Ven. B10 58
Puerto Leguízamo, Col. H5 58
Puerto Limón, Col. F6 58
Puertollano, Spain G7 12
Puerto Lobos, Arg. E3 56
Puerto Madryn, Arg. E3 56
Puerto Maldonado, Peru F5 54
Puerto Montt, Chile E2 56
Puerto Morelos, Mex. G16 62
Puerto Nariño, Col. E9 58
Puerto Natales, Chile G2 56
Puerto Padre, Cuba D9 64
Puerto Peñasco, Mex. B3 62
Puerto Plata, Dom. Rep. E12 64
Puerto Princesa, Phil. D6 32
Puerto Real, Spain I5 12
Puerto Rico, dep., N.A. E14 64
Puerto Rondón, Col. D7 58
Puerto Suárez, Bol. G7 54
Puerto Tejada, Col. F4 58
Puerto Vallarta, Mex. G7 62
Puerto Wilches, Col. D6 58
Puget Sound, strt., Wa., U.S. B3 124
Puget Sound Naval Shipyard, mil., Wa., U.S. e10 124
Pugwash, N.S., Can. D6 71
Puhi, Hi., U.S. B2 88
Puigcerdá, Spain C13 12
Pukalani, Hi., U.S. C5 88
Pukaskwa National Park, Ont., Can. o18 73
Pukch'ŏng, N. Kor. C12 26
Pukë, Alb. G3 16
Pukeashun Mountain, mtn., B.C., Can. D8 69
Pukekohe, N.Z. B5 52
Pukou, China C7 28
Pula, Cro. E8 14
Pulacayo, Bol. H5 54
Pulaski, N.Y., U.S. B4 109
Pulaski, Tn., U.S. B4 119
Pulaski, Va., U.S. C2 123
Pulaski, Wi., U.S. D5 126
Pulaski, co., Ar., U.S. C3 81
Pulaski, co., Ga., U.S. D3 87
Pulaski, co., Il., U.S. F4 90
Pulaski, co., In., U.S. B4 91
Pulaski, co., Ky., U.S. C5 94
Pulaski, co., Mo., U.S. D5 102
Pulaski, co., Va., U.S. C2 123
Puli, Tai. L9 28
Puliyangudi, India H4 37
Pulkkila, Fin. D15 6
Pullman, Wa., U.S. C8 124
Pulog, Mount, mtn., Phil. B7 32
Pumphrey, Md., U.S. h11 97
Puná, Isla, i., Ec. I2 58
Punakha, Bhu. G13 38
Pūnch, India D6 38
Pune (Poona), India C2 37
Pungo Lake, l., N.C., U.S. B6 110
Punjab, state, India E6 38
Puno, Peru G4 54
Punta, Cerro de, mtn., P.R. E14 64
Punta Alta, Arg. D4 56
Punta Arenas, Chile G2 56
Punta Delgada, Arg. E4 56
Punta de Mata, Ven. C11 58
Punta Gorda, Belize F3 64
Punta Gorda, Nic. I6 64
Punta Gorda, Fl., U.S. F4 86
Puntarenas, C.R. J5 64
Punto Fijo, Ven. B7 58
Punxsutawney, Pa., U.S. E4 115
Puolanka, Fin. D16 6
Purcell, Ok., U.S. B4 113
Purcellville, Va., U.S. A5 123
Purdy, Mo., U.S. E4 102
Purgatoire, stm., Co., U.S. D7 83
Purgatoire Peak, mtn., Co., U.S. D5 83
Puri, India K11 38
Purli, India C4 37
Purnea, India H12 38
Purūlia, India I12 38
Purus (Purús), stm., S.A. D6 54
Purvis, Ms., U.S. D4 101
Purwakarta, Indon. m13 33a
Purwokerto, Indon. m14 32
Purworejo, Indon. m15 33a
Pusan, S. Kor. D12 26
Pushaw Lake, l., Me., U.S. D4 96
Pushmataha, co., Ok., U.S. C6 113
Puškin, Russia B13 18
Puškino, Russia E20 18
Putao, Mya. F6 26
Putian, China J8 28
Puting, Tanjung, c., Indon. F5 32
Putnam, Ct., U.S. B8 84
Putnam, co., Fl., U.S. C5 86
Putnam, co., Ga., U.S. C3 87
Putnam, co., Il., U.S. B4 90
Putnam, co., In., U.S. E4 91
Putnam, co., Mo., U.S. A4 102
Putnam, co., N.Y., U.S. D7 109
Putnam, co., Oh., U.S. B1 112
Putnam, co., Tn., U.S. C8 119
Putnam, co., W.V., U.S. C3 125
Putney, Ga., U.S. E2 87
Putney, Vt., U.S. F3 122
Putorana, Plato, plat., Russia D12 24
Puttalam, Sri L. H5 37
Puttgarden, Ger. A11 8
Putumayo (Içá), stm., S.A. I7 58
Putuo, China F11 28
Puukohola Heiau National Historic Site, hist., Hi., U.S. D6 88
Puxico, Mo., U.S. E7 102
Puyallup, Wa., U.S. B3 124
Puyallup, stm., Wa., U.S. C3 124
Puy de Dôme, mtn., Fr. G9 10
Puy de Sancy, mtn., Fr. G9 10
Puylaurens, Fr. I9 10
Puyo, Ec. H4 58
Pweto, Zaire C5 44
Pwllheli, Wales, U.K. I8 7
Pyapon, Mya. F3 34
Pyatigorsk see P'atigorsk, Russia I6 22
Pyè (Prome), Mya. E3 34
Pyhäjoki, Fin. D15 6
Pyhäselkä, Fin. E17 6
Pyinmana, Mya. E4 34
Pyles Fork, stm., W.V., U.S. h10 125
Pymatuning Reservoir, res., U.S. C1 115
P'yŏngyang, N. Kor. D12 26
Pyramid Lake, l., Nv., U.S. C2 105
Pyramid Lake Indian Reservation, Nv., U.S. D2 105
Pyramid Mountains, mts., N.M., U.S. E1 108
Pyramid Peak, mtn., N.M., U.S. E1 108
Pyramid Peak, mtn., Wy., U.S. C2 127
Pyrenees, mts., Eur. C12 12
Pyskowice, Pol. E18 8
Pyu, Mya. E4 34

Q

Qaidam Pendi, China B16 38
Qalāt, Afg. D2 38
Qal'at Bīshah, Sau. Ar. E3 46
Qal'eh-ye Kānsī, Afg. C2 36
Qal'eh-ye Sarkārī, Afg. C2 38
Qallābāt, Sudan F13 42
Qamar, Ghubbat al-, b., Yemen E5 46
Qamdo, China E6 26
Qandahār, Afg. E1 38
Qandala, Som. F4 46
Qarqan, stm., China B11 38
Qarqīn, Afg. B2 38
Qaṣr al-Burayqah, Libya B9 42
Qaṣr al-Farāfirah, Egypt C11 42
Qaṭanā, Syria C5 40
Qatar, ctry., Asia C5 46
Qazvīn, Iran J8 22
Qeshm, i., Iran C6 46
Qeyṣār, Afg. C1 38
Qeẓi'ot, Isr. D4 40
Qiemo, China A11 38
Qijiang, China F8 26
Qinā, Egypt C12 42
Qingdao (Tsingtao), China D11 26
Qinghai, prov., China D6 26
Qinghai Hu, l., China D7 26
Qingjiang, China G4 28
Qinglong, China B8 34
Qingyang, China D8 26
Qingyuan, China G8 26
Qingyuan, China L2 28
Qinhuangdao, China D10 26
Qin Ling, mts., China E8 26
Qinzhou, China D10 34
Qiongzhou Haixia, strt., China D11 34
Qiqihar, China B11 26
Qiryat Shemona, Isr. C4 40
Qitai, China C4 26
Qīzān, Sau. Ar. E3 46
Qom, Iran B5 46
Qomsheh, Iran B5 46
Qondūz, Afg. B3 38
Qondūz, stm., Afg. C3 38
Quabbin Reservoir, res., Ma., U.S. B3 98
Quaddick Reservoir, res., Ct., U.S. B8 84
Quail Oaks, Va., U.S. n18 123
Quaker Hill, Ct., U.S. D7 84
Quakertown, Pa., U.S. F11 115
Qualicum Beach, B.C., Can. E5 69
Quanah, Tx., U.S. B3 120
Quang Ngai, Viet. G10 34
Quannapowitt, Lake, l., Ma., U.S. f11 98
Quantico, Va., U.S. B5 123
Quantico Marine Corps Air Station, mil., Va., U.S. B5 123
Quanzhou, China K7 28
Quapaw, Ok., U.S. A7 113
Qu'Appelle, Sask., Can. G4 75
Qu'Appelle, stm., Can. G4 75
Quarryville, Pa., U.S. G9 115
Quartu Sant'Elena, Italy J4 14
Quartz Lake, l., N.W. Ter., Can. B16 66
Quartz Mountain, mtn., Or., U.S. D4 114
Quartzsite, Az., U.S. D1 80
Quassapaug, Lake, l., Ct., U.S. C3 84
Quatsino Sound, strt., B.C., Can. D3 69
Quay, co., N.M., U.S. C6 108
Qūchān, Iran J9 22
Québec, Que., Can. C6 74
Québec, prov., Can. C5 74
Quechee, Vt., U.S. D4 122
Quedlinburg, Ger. D11 8
Queen, stm., R.I., U.S. E3 116
Queen Annes, co., Md., U.S. B5 97
Queen Bess, Mount, mtn., B.C., Can. D5 69
Queen Charlotte, B.C., Can. C1 69
Queen Charlotte Islands, is., B.C., Can. C1 69
Queen Charlotte Mountains, mts., B.C., Can. C1 69
Queen Charlotte Sound, strt., B.C., Can. n17 69
Queen Charlotte Strait, strt., B.C., Can. D4 69
Queen City, Mo., U.S. A5 102
Queen City, Tx., U.S. C5 120
Queen Creek, Az., U.S. m9 80
Queen Maud Gulf, b., N.W. Ter., Can. C12 66
Queen Maud Land, reg., Ant. B14 47
Queens, co., N.Y., U.S. E7 109
Queens Channel, strt., N.W. Ter., Can. A13 66
Queensland, state, Austl. D8 50
Queenstown, N.Z. F2 52
Queenstown, S. Afr. H5 44
Quelimane, Moz. E7 44
Quemoy see Chinmen Tao, i., Tai. K7 28
Querétaro, Mex. G9 62
Querobabi, Mex. B4 62
Quesnel, B.C., Can. C6 69
Quesnel, stm., B.C., Can. C6 69
Quesnel Lake, l., B.C., Can. C7 69
Questa, N.M., U.S. A4 108
Questembert, Fr. E4 10
Quetico Provincial Park, Ont., Can. o17 73
Quetta, Pak. E2 38
Quevedo, Ec. H3 58
Quevedo, stm., Ec. H3 58
Quezaltenango, Guat. G2 64
Quezon City, Phil. q19 32
Qufu, China D10 26
Quibdó, Col. E4 58
Quiberon, Fr. E3 10
Quicksand Pond, l., R.I., U.S. E6 116
Quidnessett, R.I., U.S. E4 116
Quidnick, R.I., U.S. D3 116
Quidnick Reservoir, res., R.I., U.S. D2 116
Quilá, Mex. E6 62
Quilcene, Wa., U.S. B3 124
Quileute Indian Reservation, Wa., U.S. B1 124
Quillan, Fr. J9 10
Quilon, India H4 37
Quilpie, Austl. E8 50
Quimilí, Arg. B4 56
Quimper, Fr. D2 10
Quimperlé, Fr. E3 10
Quinault, stm., Wa., U.S. B1 124
Quinault, Lake, l., Wa., U.S. B2 124
Quinault Indian Reservation, Wa., U.S. B1 124
Quincemil, Peru F4 54
Quincy, Ca., U.S. C3 82
Quincy, Fl., U.S. B2 86
Quincy, Il., U.S. D2 90
Quincy, Ma., U.S. B5 98
Quincy, Mi., U.S. G6 99
Quincy, Wa., U.S. B6 124
Quincy Bay, b., Ma., U.S. g12 98
Quinebaug, Ct., U.S. A8 84
Quinebaug, stm., Ct., U.S. C8 84
Quinhagak, Ak., U.S. D7 79
Qui Nhon, Viet. H10 34
Quinlan, Tx., U.S. C4 120
Quinn, stm., Nv., U.S. B3 105
Quinn Canyon Range, mts., Nv., U.S. F6 105
Quinnesec, Mi., U.S. C3 99
Quinnipiac, stm., Ct., U.S. D4 84
Quintanar de la Orden, Spain F8 12
Quinter, Ks., U.S. C3 93
Quinton, Ok., U.S. B6 113
Quiroga, Spain C4 12
Quitman, Ar., U.S. B3 81
Quitman, Ga., U.S. F3 87
Quitman, Ms., U.S. C5 101
Quitman, Tx., U.S. C5 120
Quitman, co., Ga., U.S. E1 87
Quitman, co., Ms., U.S. A3 101
Quito, Ec. H3 58
Quixadá, Braz. D11 54
Qujing, China B7 34
Qumalai (Sewugou), China C16 38
Quoich, stm., N.W. Ter., Can. D14 66
Quonnipaug Lake, l., Ct., U.S. D5 84
Quonochontaug, R.I., U.S. G2 116
Quonochontaug Pond, l., R.I., U.S. G2 116
Quonset Point, c., R.I., U.S. E4 116
Qutdligssat, Grnld. B22 66
Quthing, Leso. H5 44
Quxian, China G7 28

R

Raalte, Neth. C6 8
Rab, Cro. E9 14
Raba, Indon. G6 32
Rába (Raab), stm., Eur. H17 8
Rábade, Spain B4 12
Rabat (Victoria), Malta M9 14
Rabat, Mor. B4 42
Rabaul, Pap. N. Gui. k17 50a
Rabbit Creek, stm., S.D., U.S. B3 118
Rabbit Ears Pass, Co., U.S. A4 83
Rābigh, Sau. Ar. D2 46
Rabun, co., Ga., U.S. B3 87
Rabun Bald, mtn., Ga., U.S. B3 87
Raccoon Creek, stm., Oh., U.S. D3 112
Raccourci Island, i., La., U.S. D4 95
Race, Cape, c., Newf., Can. E5 72
Raceland, Ky., U.S. B7 94
Raceland, La., U.S. E5 95
Race Point, c., Ma., U.S. B7 98
Rach Gia, Viet. I8 34
Racibórz (Ratibor), Pol. E18 8
Racine, W.V., U.S. C3 125
Racine, Wi., U.S. F6 126
Racine, co., Wi., U.S. F5 126
Racine Dam, U.S. C3 125
Radcliff, Ky., U.S. C4 94
Radeberg, Ger. D13 8
Radebeul, Ger. D13 8
Radeče, Slo. C10 14
Radford, Va., U.S. C2 123
Radolfzell, Ger. H8 8
Radom, Pol. D21 8
Radomsko, Pol. D19 8
Rae, N.W. Ter., Can. D9 66
Rāe Bareli, India G9 38
Raeford, N.C., U.S. C3 110
Rae Isthmus, N.W. Ter., Can. C15 66
Rae Strait, strt., N.W. Ter., Can. C13 66
Raetihi, N.Z. C5 52
Rafaela, Arg. C4 56
Rafaḥ, Gaza Strip D4 40
Rafḥā', Sau. Ar. C3 46
Rafsanjān, Iran K9 22
Rafsanjān, Iran B6 46
Raft, stm., Id., U.S. G5 89
Raft River Mountains, mts., Ut., U.S. B2 121
Raga, Sudan G11 42
Ragged Island, i., Me., U.S. E4 96
Ragged Lake, l., Me., U.S. C3 96
Ragged Top Mountain, mtn., Wy., U.S. E7 127
Ragland, Al., U.S. B3 78
Ragusa, Italy M9 14
Ragusa see Dubrovnik, Cro. G13 14
Rahīmyār Khān, Pak. F4 38
Rahway, N.J., U.S. B4 107
Rahway, stm., N.J., U.S. k7 107
Rāichūr, India D4 37
Raigarh, India B7 37
Railroad Valley, val., Nv., U.S. E6 105
Rainbow Bridge National Monument, Ut., U.S. F5 121
Rainbow Falls, wtfl, Tn., U.S. D10 119
Rainbow Flowage, res., Wi., U.S. C4 126
Rainbow Lake, l., Me., U.S. C3 96
Rainelle, W.V., U.S. D4 125
Rainier, Or., U.S. A4 114
Rainier, Wa., U.S. C3 124
Rainier, Mount, mtn., Wa., U.S. C4 124
Rains, co., Tx., U.S. C5 120
Rainsville, Al., U.S. A4 78
Rainy Lake, l., N.A. G14 66
Rainy Lake, l., Mn., U.S. B5 100
Rainy River, Ont., Can. o16 73
Raipur, India B6 37
Rājahmundry, India D6 37
Raja-Jooseppi, Fin. B17 6
Rājapālaiyam, India H4 37
Rājasthān, prov., India G5 38
Rājasthān Canal, India F5 38
Rajčichinsk, Russia H19 24
Rājkot, India I4 38
Rāj-Nāndgaon, India B6 37
Rājpīpla, India J5 38
Rājshāhi, Bngl. H13 38
Rakaposhi, mtn., Pak. B6 38
Rakata, Pulau, i., Indon. m12 33a
Råkvåg, Nor. E8 6
Raleigh, Ms., U.S. C4 101
Raleigh, N.C., U.S. B4 110
Raleigh, W.V., U.S. n13 125
Raleigh, co., W.V., U.S. D3 125
Raleigh Bay, b., N.C., U.S. C6 110
Ralls, Tx., U.S. C2 120
Ralls, co., Mo., U.S. B6 102
Ralston, Ne., U.S. g12 104
Ralston Valley, val., Nv., U.S. E4 105
Rama, Nic. H5 64
Ramah, N.M., U.S. B1 108
Ramah Indian Reservation, N.M., U.S. C1 108
Rām Allāh, W. Bank D4 40
Ramapo, stm., N.J., U.S. A4 107
Ramblewood, N.J., U.S. D3 107
Rambouillet, Fr. D8 10
Ramea, Newf., Can. E3 72
Ramenskoje, Russia F21 18
Rāmeswaram, India H5 37
Rāmgarh, Bngl. I14 38
Ramla, Isr. D4 40
Ramlo, mtn., Erit. F3 46
Ramona, Ca., U.S. F5 82
Rampart Range, mts., Co., U.S. B5 83
Rāmpur, India F8 38
Ramree Island, i., Mya. E2 34
Ramsay, Mi., U.S. n12 99
Ramseur, N.C., U.S. B3 110
Ramsey, I. of Man G8 7
Ramsey, Il., U.S. D4 90
Ramsey, Mn., U.S. *E5 100
Ramsey, N.J., U.S. A4 107
Ramsey, co., Mn., U.S. E5 100
Ramsey, co., N.D., U.S. A7 111
Ramsgate, Eng., U.K. J14 7
Ramshorn Peak, mtn., Mt., U.S. E5 103
Ramshorn Peak, mtn., Wy., U.S. C3 127
Rāmu, Bngl. J15 38
Ramu, stm., Pap. N. Gui. m16 50a
Rancagua, Chile C2 56
Rancharia, Braz. G3 57
Rancheria Rock, mtn., Or., U.S. C6 114
Ranchester, Wy., U.S. B5 127
Rānchī, India I11 38
Rancho Palos Verdes, Ca., U.S. *n12 82
Ranchos de Taos, N.M., U.S. A4 108
Rancocas Creek, stm., N.J., U.S. C3 107
Rand, W.V., U.S. C3 125
Randall, co., Tx., U.S. B2 120
Randallstown, Md., U.S. B4 97
Randazzo, Italy L9 14
Randers, Den. H8 6
Randle, Wa., U.S. C4 124
Randleman, N.C., U.S. B3 110
Randolph, Me., U.S. D3 96
Randolph, Ma., U.S. B5 98
Randolph, Ne., U.S. B8 104
Randolph, Vt., U.S. D3 122
Randolph, Wi., U.S. E5 126
Randolph, co., Al., U.S. B4 78
Randolph, co., Ar., U.S. A4 81
Randolph, co., Ga., U.S. E2 87
Randolph, co., Il., U.S. E4 90
Randolph, co., In., U.S. D7 91
Randolph, co., Mo., U.S. B5 102
Randolph, co., N.C., U.S. B3 110
Randolph, co., W.V., U.S. C5 125
Randolph Air Force Base, mil., Tx., U.S. h7 120
Randolph Hills, Md., U.S. B3 97
Random Island, i., Newf., Can. D5 72
Random Lake, Wi., U.S. E6 126
Rangeley, Me., U.S. D2 96
Rangeley Lake, l., Me., U.S. D2 96
Rangely, Co., U.S. A2 83
Ranger, Tx., U.S. C3 120
Ranger Lake, l., N.M., U.S. D6 108
Rangoon see Yangon, Mya. B2 32
Rangpur, Bngl. H13 38
Rankin, Pa., U.S. k14 115
Rankin, co., Ms., U.S. C4 101
Rankin Inlet, N.W. Ter., Can. D14 66
Rann of Kutch, pl., Asia H3 38
Ransom, co., N.D., U.S. C8 111

Name — Map Ref — Page

Ranson, W.V., U.S. **B7** 125
Rantauprapat, Indon. **E2** 32
Rantekombola, Bulu, mtn., Indon. **F7** 32
Rantoul, Il., U.S. **C5** 90
Raoping, China **L6** 28
Raoul, Ga., U.S. **B3** 87
Rapallo, Italy **E4** 14
Rapid, stm., Mn., U.S. **B4** 100
Rapid City, S.D., U.S. **C2** 118
Rapides, co., La., U.S. **C3** 95
Rapid River, Mi., U.S. **C4** 99
Rapids City, Il., U.S. **B3** 90
Rappahannock, co., Va., U.S. **B4** 123
Rappahannock, stm., Va., U.S. **B5** 123
Raquette, stm., N.Y., U.S. **f10** 109
Raquette Lake, l., N.Y., U.S. **B6** 109
Raritan, N.J., U.S. **B3** 107
Raritan, stm., N.J., U.S. **C4** 107
Raritan Bay, b., N.J., U.S. **C4** 107
Ra's al-'Ayn, Syria **A7** 40
Ra's an-Naqb, Jord. **D4** 40
Ras Dashen, mtn., Eth. **F2** 46
Ras Djebel, Tun. **L5** 14
Rasht, Iran **J7** 22
Rāsipuram, India **G5** 37
Rasskazovo, Russia **I24** 18
Rastatt, Ger. **G8** 8
Ratangarh, India **F6** 38
Rätansbyn, Swe. **E10** 6
Rathbun Lake, res., Ia., U.S. **D5** 92
Rathdrum, Id., U.S. **B2** 89
Rathenow, Ger. **C12** 8
Rathkeale, Ire. **I4** 7
Rathlin Island, i., N. Ire., U.K. **F6** 7
Rat Islands, is., Ak., U.S. **E3** 79
Ratlām, India **I6** 38
Ratnāgiri, India **D2** 37
Ratnapura, Sri L. **I6** 37
Raton, N.M., U.S. **A5** 108
Raton Pass, N.M., U.S. **A5** 108
Rattlesnake Creek, stm., Oh., U.S. **C2** 112
Rattlesnake Creek, stm., Wa., U.S. **C6** 124
Rättvik, Swe. **F10** 6
Ratz, Mount, mtn., B.C., Can. **E6** 66
Ratzeburg, Ger. **B10** 8
Raub, Malay. **M6** 34
Rauch, Arg. **D5** 56
Rauma, Fin. **F13** 6
Raurkela, India **I11** 38
Ravalli, co., Mt., U.S. **D2** 103
Raven, Va., U.S. **e10** 123
Ravena, N.Y., U.S. **C7** 109
Ravenel, S.C., U.S. **k11** 117
Ravenna, Italy **E7** 14
Ravenna, Ky., U.S. **C6** 94
Ravenna, Mi., U.S. **E5** 99
Ravenna, Ne., U.S. **C7** 104
Ravenna, Oh., U.S. **A4** 112
Raven Park, reg., Co., U.S. **A2** 83
Ravensburg, Ger. **H9** 8
Ravenshoe, Austl. **C9** 50
Ravensthorpe, Austl. **F3** 50
Ravenswood, W.V., U.S. **C3** 125
Rāwalpindi, Pak. **D5** 38
Rawdon, Que., Can. **C4** 74
Rawhide Creek, stm., Wy., U.S. **D8** 127
Rawlings, Md., U.S. **k13** 97
Rawlinna, Austl. **F5** 50
Rawlins, Wy., U.S. **E5** 127
Rawlins, co., Ks., U.S. **C2** 93
Rawson, Arg. **E3** 56
Ray, N.D., U.S. **A2** 111
Ray, co., Mo., U.S. **B3** 102
Ray, Cape, c., Newf., Can. **E2** 72
Raya, Bukit, mtn., Indon. **F5** 32
Rāyadrug, India **E4** 37
Ray City, Ga., U.S. **E3** 87
Raymond, Alta., Can. **E4** 68
Raymond, Il., U.S. **D4** 90
Raymond, Mn., U.S. **E3** 100
Raymond, Ms., U.S. **C3** 101
Raymond, N.H., U.S. **D4** 106
Raymond, Wa., U.S. **C2** 124
Raymondville, Tx., U.S. **F4** 120
Raymore, Sask., Can. **F3** 75
Raymore, Mo., U.S. **C3** 102
Rayne, La., U.S. **D3** 95
Raynham, Ma., U.S. **C5** 98
Raynham Center, Ma., U.S. **C5** 98
Raytown, Mo., U.S. **h11** 102
Rayville, La., U.S. **B4** 95
R'azan', Russia **G22** 18
Razgrad, Bul. **F10** 16
R'ažsk, Russia **H23** 18
Reader, W.V., U.S. **B4** 125
Reading, Eng., U.K. **J12** 7
Reading, Ma., U.S. **A5** 98
Reading, Mi., U.S. **G6** 99
Reading, Oh., U.S. **C1** 112
Reading, Pa., U.S. **F10** 115
Readlyn, Ia., U.S. **B5** 92
Reagan, co., Tx., U.S. **D2** 120
Real, co., Tx., U.S. **E3** 120
Realicó, Arg. **D4** 56
Réalmont, Fr. **I9** 10
Reamstown, Pa., U.S. **F9** 115
Recanati, Italy **F8** 14
Recherche, Archipelago of the, is., Austl. **F4** 50
Rečica, Bela. **I13** 18
Recife, Braz. **E12** 54
Recklinghausen, Ger. **D7** 8
Recreo, Arg. **B3** 56
Rector, Ar., U.S. **A5** 81
Red (Hong) (Yuan), stm., Asia **C8** 34
Red, stm., N.A. **B7** 76
Red, stm., U.S. **E8** 76
Red, stm., Ky., U.S. **C6** 94
Red, stm., Tn., U.S. **A4** 119
Red Bank, N.J., U.S. **C4** 107
Red Bank, Tn., U.S. **D8** 119
Red Bay, Al., U.S. **A1** 78
Redberry Lake, l., Sask., Can. **E2** 75
Redbird, Oh., U.S. **A4** 112
Red Bird, stm., Ky., U.S. **C6** 94
Red Bluff, Ca., U.S. **B2** 82
Red Bluff Lake, res., U.S. **o12** 120
Red Boiling Springs, Tn., U.S. **C8** 119
Red Bud, Il., U.S. **E4** 90
Red Butte, mtn., Ut., U.S. **B2** 121
Red Cedar, stm., Wi., U.S. **C2** 126
Red Cedar Lake, l., Wi., U.S. **C2** 126
Redcliff, Alta., Can. **D5** 68
Redcliffe, Mount, mtn., Austl. **E4** 50
Red Cliff Indian Reservation, Wi., U.S. **B2** 126
Red Cloud, Ne., U.S. **D7** 104
Redcloud Peak, mtn., Co., U.S. **D3** 83
Red Deer, Alta., Can. **C4** 68
Red Deer, stm., Can. **D4** 68
Red Deer, stm., Can. **E4** 75
Redding, Ca., U.S. **B2** 82
Redding, Ct., U.S. **D2** 84
Redeye, stm., Mn., U.S. **D3** 100
Redfield, Ar., U.S. **C3** 81
Redfield, Ia., U.S. **C3** 92
Redfield, S.D., U.S. **C7** 118
Redford, Mi., U.S. **F7** 99
Redgranite, Wi., U.S. **D4** 126
Red Hook, N.Y., U.S. **C7** 109
Red Indian Lake, l., Newf., Can. **D3** 72
Red Jacket, W.V., U.S. **D2** 125
Redkey, In., U.S. **D7** 91
Redlake, Mn., U.S. **C3** 100
Red Lake, co., Mn., U.S. **C2** 100
Red Lake, l., Az., U.S. **B1** 80
Red Lake, stm., Mn., U.S. **C2** 100
Red Lake Falls, Mn., U.S. **C2** 100
Red Lake Indian Reservation, Mn., U.S. **B3** 100
Redlands, Ca., U.S. **E5** 82
Red Lion, Pa., U.S. **G8** 115
Red Lodge, Mt., U.S. **E7** 103
Red Mill Pond, l., De., U.S. **E5** 85
Redmond, Or., U.S. **C5** 114
Redmond, Ut., U.S. **E4** 121
Redmond, Wa., U.S. **e11** 124
Red Mountain, mtn., Ca., U.S. **B2** 82
Red Mountain, mtn., Mt., U.S. **C4** 103
Red Mountain Pass, Co., U.S. **D3** 83
Red Oak, Ga., U.S. **h7** 87
Red Oak, Ia., U.S. **D2** 92
Red Oak, Ok., U.S. **C6** 113
Red Oak, Tx., U.S. **n10** 120
Red Oaks, La., U.S. **h9** 95
Redon, Fr. **E4** 10
Redondela, Spain **C3** 12
Redondo, Port. **G4** 12
Redondo, Wa., U.S. **f11** 124
Redondo Beach, Ca., U.S. **n12** 82
Redoubt Volcano, vol., Ak., U.S. **g15** 79
Red Peak, mtn., Co., U.S. **B4** 83
Red River, co., La., U.S. **B2** 95
Red River, co., Tx., U.S. **C5** 120
Red Rock, stm., Mt., U.S. **F4** 103
Red Rock, Lake, res., Ia., U.S. **C4** 92
Red Sea **D2** 46
Red Springs, N.C., U.S. **C3** 110
Red Table Mountain, mts., Co., U.S. **B4** 83
Redwater, Alta., Can. **C4** 68
Redwater, stm., Mt., U.S. **C11** 103
Red Willow, co., Ne., U.S. **D5** 104
Redwillow, stm., Can. **B7** 69
Red Wing, Mn., U.S. **F6** 100
Redwood, co., Mn., U.S. **F3** 100
Redwood, stm., Mn., U.S. **F3** 100
Redwood City, Ca., U.S. **D2** 82
Redwood Falls, Mn., U.S. **F3** 100
Redwood National Park, Ca., U.S. **B2** 82
Redwood Valley, Ca., U.S. **C2** 82
Ree, Lough, l., Ire. **H4** 7
Reed City, Mi., U.S. **E5** 99
Reedley, Ca., U.S. **D4** 82
Reedsburg, Wi., U.S. **E3** 126
Reeds Peak, mtn., N.M., U.S. **D2** 108
Reedsport, Or., U.S. **D2** 114
Reedsville, Pa., U.S. **E6** 115
Reedsville, Wi., U.S. **D6** 126
Reedy, stm., S.C., U.S. **C3** 117
Reedy Lake, l., Fl., U.S. **E5** 86
Reelfoot Lake, l., Tn., U.S. **A2** 119
Reese, Mi., U.S. **E7** 99
Reese, stm., Nv., U.S. **C4** 105
Reese Air Force Base, mil., Tx., U.S. **C1** 120
Reeves, co., Tx., U.S. **o13** 120
Reform, Al., U.S. **B1** 78
Refugio, Tx., U.S. **E4** 120
Refugio, co., Tx., U.S. **E4** 120
Regen, Ger. **G13** 8
Regencia, Braz. **E9** 57
Regensburg, Ger. **F12** 8
Reggane, Alg. **C6** 42
Reggio di Calabria, Italy **K10** 14
Reggio nell'Emilia, Italy **E5** 14
Regina, Sask., Can. **G3** 75
Regina Beach, Sask., Can. **G3** 75
Rehoboth, Nmb. **E3** 44
Rehoboth Bay, b., De., U.S. **F5** 85
Rehoboth Beach, De., U.S. **F5** 85
Reḥovot, Isr. **D4** 40
Reichenbach, Ger. **E12** 8
Reid, Mount, mtn., Ak., U.S. **n24** 79
Reidland, Ky., U.S. **e9** 94
Reidsville, Ga., U.S. **D4** 87
Reidsville, N.C., U.S. **A3** 110
Reims, Fr. **C11** 10
Reina Adelaida, Archipiélago, is., Chile **G2** 56
Reinbeck, Ia., U.S. **B5** 92
Reindeer Island, i., Man., Can. **C3** 70
Reindeer Lake, l., Can. **m8** 75
Reinosa, Spain **B7** 12
Reisterstown, Md., U.S. **B4** 97
Reliance, Wy., U.S. **E3** 127
Remada, Tun. **B8** 42
Remanso, Braz. **E10** 54
Rembang, Indon. **m15** 33a
Remington, In., U.S. **C3** 91
Remiremont, Fr. **D13** 10
Remmel Dam, Ar., U.S. **g8** 81
Remscheid, Ger. **D7** 8
Remsen, Ia., U.S. **B2** 92
Rend Lake, res., Il., U.S. **E5** 90
Rendova, i., Sol.Is. **A11** 50
Rendsburg, Ger. **A9** 8
Renforth, N.B., Can. **D4** 71
Renfrew, Ont., Can. **B8** 73
Rengat, Indon. **O7** 34
Rennell Island, i., Sol.Is. **B12** 50
Rennes, Fr. **D5** 10
Reno, Nv., U.S. **D2** 105
Reno, co., Ks., U.S. **E5** 93
Reno, Lake, l., Mn., U.S. **E3** 100
Reno Hill, mtn., Wy., U.S. **D6** 127
Renovo, Pa., U.S. **D6** 115
Rensselaer, In., U.S. **C3** 91
Rensselaer, N.Y., U.S. **C7** 109
Rensselaer, co., N.Y., U.S. **C7** 109
Renton, Wa., U.S. **B3** 124
Renville, Mn., U.S. **F3** 100
Renville, co., Mn., U.S. **F4** 100
Renville, co., N.D., U.S. **A4** 111
Reo, Indon. **G7** 32
Repentigny, Que., Can. **D4** 74
Republic, Mi., U.S. **B3** 99
Republic, Mo., U.S. **D4** 102
Republic, Pa., U.S. **G2** 115
Republic, Wa., U.S. **A7** 124
Republic, co., Ks., U.S. **C6** 93
Republican, stm., U.S. **C6** 93
Repulse Bay, N.W. Ter., Can. **C15** 66
Repvåg, Nor. **A15** 6
Réquista, Fr. **H9** 10
Reschenpass, Eur. **C5** 14
Reserve, La., U.S. **h10** 95
Resistencia, Arg. **B5** 56
Reșița, Rom. **D5** 16
Resolute, N.W. Ter., Can. **B14** 66
Resolution Island, i., N.W. Ter., Can. **D20** 66
Reston, Man., Can. **E1** 70
Reston, Va., U.S. **B5** 123
Resülhınzır, c., Tur. **A4** 40
Retalhuleu, Guat. **G2** 64
Rethel, Fr. **C11** 10
Réthimnon, Grc. **N8** 16
Reunion (Réunion), dep., Afr. **F11** 44
Reus, Spain **D13** 12
Reutlingen, Ger. **G9** 8
Revelo, Ky., U.S. **D5** 94
Revelstoke, B.C., Can. **D8** 69
Revelstoke, Lake, res., B.C., Can. **D8** 69
Revere, Ma., U.S. **g11** 98
Revillagigedo, Islas de, is., Mex. **H4** 62
Revillagigedo Island, i., Ak., U.S. **n24** 79
Revin, Fr. **C11** 10
Rewa, India **H9** 38
Rewāri, India **F7** 38
Rex, Ga., U.S. **h8** 87
Rexburg, Id., U.S. **F7** 89
Rexton, N.B., Can. **C5** 71
Rey, Iran **J8** 22
Rey, Isla del, i., Pan. **J8** 64
Reyes, Bol. **F5** 54
Reyes, Point, c., Ca., U.S. **C2** 82
Reyhanlı, Tur. **A5** 40
Reykjavík, Ice. **C3** 4
Reynolds, Ga., U.S. **D2** 87
Reynolds, co., Mo., U.S. **D6** 102
Reynoldsburg, Oh., U.S. **C3** 112
Reynoldsville, Pa., U.S. **D4** 115
Reynosa, Mex. **D10** 62
Rēzekne, Lat. **E10** 18
Rhaetian Alps, mts., Eur. **F16** 10
Rhea, co., Tn., U.S. **D9** 119
Rheine, Ger. **C7** 8
Rheydt, Ger. **D6** 8
Rhine (Rhein) (Rhin), stm., Eur. **D6** 8
Rhinebeck, N.Y., U.S. **D7** 109
Rhinelander, Wi., U.S. **C4** 126
Rho, Italy **D4** 14
Rhode Island, state, U.S. **D3** 116
Rhode Island, i., R.I., U.S. **E5** 116
Rhode Island Sound, strt., U.S. **F5** 116
Rhodesia see Zimbabwe, ctry., Afr. **E5** 44
Rhodes Peak, mtn., Id., U.S. **C4** 89
Rhodes see Ródhos, Grc. **M12** 16
Rhodope Mountains, mts., Eur. **H8** 16
Rhondda, Wales, U.K. **J9** 7
Rhône, stm., Eur. **H11** 10
Rialto, Ca., U.S. **m14** 82
Riau, Kepulauan, is., Indon. **N8** 34
Riaza, Spain **D8** 12
Ribadeo, Spain **B4** 12
Ribadesella, Spain **B6** 12
Ribeirão Prêto, Braz. **F5** 57
Ribera, Italy **L8** 14
Riberalta, Bol. **F5** 54
Rib Lake, Wi., U.S. **C3** 126
Ribnitz-Damgarten, Ger. **A12** 8
Riccione, Italy **F7** 14
Rice, Mn., U.S. **E4** 100
Rice, co., Ks., U.S. **D5** 93
Rice, co., Mn., U.S. **F5** 100
Riceboro, Ga., U.S. **E5** 87
Rice Lake, Wi., U.S. **C2** 126
Rice Lake, l., Ont., Can. **C6** 73
Rice Lake, l., Mn., U.S. **D5** 100
Riceville, Ia., U.S. **A5** 92
Rich, co., Ut., U.S. **B4** 121
Rich, Cape, c., Ont., Can. **C4** 73
Richards-Gebaur Air Force Base, mil., Mo., U.S. **C3** 102
Richards Island, i., N.W. Ter., Can. **C6** 66
Richardson, Tx., U.S. **n10** 120
Richardson, co., Ne., U.S. **D10** 104
Richardson Lakes, l., Me., U.S. **D2** 96
Richardson Mountains, mts., Can. **C5** 66
Richardton, N.D., U.S. **C3** 111
Rich Creek, Va., U.S. **C2** 123
Riche, Pointe, c., Newf., Can. **C3** 72
Richfield, Mn., U.S. **F5** 100
Richfield, Ut., U.S. **E3** 121
Richford, Vt., U.S. **B3** 122
Rich Hill, Mo., U.S. **C3** 102
Richibucto, N.B., Can. **C5** 71
Richland, Ga., U.S. **D2** 87
Richland, Mo., U.S. **D5** 102
Richland, Wa., U.S. **C6** 124
Richland, co., Il., U.S. **E5** 90
Richland, co., La., U.S. **B4** 95
Richland, co., Mt., U.S. **C12** 103
Richland, co., N.D., U.S. **C8** 111
Richland, co., Oh., U.S. **B3** 112
Richland, co., S.C., U.S. **D6** 117
Richland, co., Wi., U.S. **E3** 126
Richland Balsam, mtn., N.C., U.S. **f10** 110
Richland Center, Wi., U.S. **E3** 126
Richland Creek, stm., Tn., U.S. **B5** 119
Richlands, N.C., U.S. **C5** 110
Richlands, Va., U.S. **e10** 123
Richlandtown, Pa., U.S. **F11** 115
Richmond, Austl. **D8** 50
Richmond, B.C., Can. **E6** 69
Richmond, Que., Can. **D5** 74
Richmond, Ca., U.S. **D2** 82
Richmond, Il., U.S. **A5** 90
Richmond, In., U.S. **E8** 91
Richmond, Ky., U.S. **C5** 94
Richmond, Me., U.S. **D3** 96
Richmond, Mi., U.S. **F8** 99
Richmond, Mn., U.S. **E4** 100
Richmond, Mo., U.S. **B4** 102
Richmond, Tx., U.S. **E5** 120
Richmond, Ut., U.S. **B4** 121
Richmond, Vt., U.S. **C3** 122
Richmond, Va., U.S. **C5** 123
Richmond, co., Ga., U.S. **C4** 87
Richmond, co., N.Y., U.S. **E6** 109
Richmond, co., N.C., U.S. **B3** 110
Richmond, co., Va., U.S. **C6** 123
Richmond Beach, Wa., U.S. **B3** 124
Richmond Heights, Fl., U.S. **s13** 86
Richmond Heights, Mo., U.S. **f13** 102
Richmond Highlands, Wa., U.S. **B3** 124
Richmond Hill, Ont., Can. **D5** 73
Richmond Hill, Ga., U.S. **E5** 87
Richmond National Battlefield Park, Va., U.S. **n18** 123
Rich Square, N.C., U.S. **A5** 110
Richthofen, Mount, mtn., Co., U.S. **A5** 83
Richton, Ms., U.S. **D5** 101
Richwood, Oh., U.S. **B2** 112
Richwood, W.V., U.S. **C4** 125
Rickenbacker Air Force Base, mil., Oh., U.S. **m11** 112
Rickman, Tn., U.S. **C8** 119
Riddle, Or., U.S. **E3** 114
Riddle Mountain, mtn., Or., U.S. **D8** 114
Rideau, stm., Ont., Can. **B9** 73
Ridgecrest, Ca., U.S. **E5** 82
Ridge Farm, Il., U.S. **D6** 90
Ridgefield, Ct., U.S. **D2** 84
Ridgefield, N.J., U.S. **h8** 107
Ridgefield, Wa., U.S. **D3** 124
Ridgefield Park, N.J., U.S. **B4** 107
Ridgeland, Ms., U.S. **C3** 101
Ridgeland, S.C., U.S. **G6** 117
Ridgeley, W.V., U.S. **B6** 125
Ridgely, Md., U.S. **C6** 97
Ridgely, Tn., U.S. **A2** 119
Ridge Spring, S.C., U.S. **D4** 117
Ridgetop, Tn., U.S. **A5** 119
Ridgetown, Ont., Can. **E3** 73
Ridgeview, W.V., U.S. **C3** 125
Ridgeville, In., U.S. **D7** 91
Ridgeville, S.C., U.S. **E7** 117
Ridgeway, Va., U.S. **D3** 123
Ridgewood, N.J., U.S. **B4** 107
Ridgway, Il., U.S. **F5** 90
Ridgway, Pa., U.S. **D4** 115
Riding Mountain National Park, Man., Can. **D1** 70
Ridley Park, Pa., U.S. **p20** 115
Ried im Innkreis, Aus. **G13** 8
Riesa, Ger. **D13** 8
Riesi, Italy **L9** 14
Rieti, Italy **G7** 14
Rif, mts., Mor. **A5** 42
Riffe Lake, res., Wa., U.S. **C3** 124
Rifle, Co., U.S. **B3** 83
Rifle, stm., Mi., U.S. **D6** 99
Rift Valley, val., Afr. **B5** 44
Rīga, Lat. **E7** 18
Riga, Gulf of, b., Eur. **D6** 18
Rigaud, Que., Can. **D3** 74
Rigby, Id., U.S. **F7** 89
Rīgestān, reg., Afg. **C1** 36
Riihimäki, Fin. **F15** 6
Rijeka, Cro. **D9** 14
Riley, Ks., U.S. **C7** 93
Riley, co., Ks., U.S. **C7** 93
Riley, Mount, mtn., N.M., U.S. **F2** 108
Rimbey, Alta., Can. **C3** 68
Rimersburg, Pa., U.S. **D3** 115
Rimini, Italy **E7** 14
Rimouski, Que., Can. **A9** 74
Rimouski, stm., Que., Can. **A9** 74
Rimouski-Est, Que., Can. **A9** 74
Rimrock Lake, res., Wa., U.S. **C4** 124
Rincon, Ga., U.S. **D5** 87
Rincon Mountains, mts., Az., U.S. **E5** 80
Rindal, Nor. **E7** 6
Ringebu, Nor. **F8** 6
Ringgold, Ga., U.S. **B1** 87
Ringgold, La., U.S. **B2** 95
Ringgold, co., Ia., U.S. **D3** 92
Ringling, Ok., U.S. **C4** 113
Ringwood, N.J., U.S. **A4** 107
Rio, Fl., U.S. **E6** 86
Rio, Wi., U.S. **E4** 126
Rio Arriba, co., N.M., U.S. **A2** 108
Riobamba, Ec. **H3** 58
Río Benito, Eq. Gui. **H7** 42
Rio Blanco, co., Co., U.S. **B2** 83
Rio Branco, Braz. **E5** 54
Rio Claro, Braz. **G5** 57
Río Colorado, Arg. **D4** 56
Río Cuarto, Arg. **C4** 56
Rio de Janeiro, Braz. **G7** 57
Rio Dell, Ca., U.S. **B1** 82
Rio do Sul, Braz. **B7** 56
Río Gallegos, Arg. **G3** 56
Río Grande, Arg. **G3** 56
Rio Grande, Braz. **C6** 56
Río Grande, Mex. **F8** 62
Río Grande, Nic. **H6** 64
Rio Grande, Oh., U.S. **D3** 112
Rio Grande, co., Co., U.S. **D4** 83
Rio Grande City, Tx., U.S. **F3** 120
Rio Grande Reservoir, res., Co., U.S. **D3** 83
Ríohacha, Col. **B6** 58
Rio Hondo, Tx., U.S. **F4** 120
Rioja, Peru **E3** 54
Riom, Fr. **G10** 10
Río Mayo, Arg. **F2** 56
Río Negro, Embalse del, res., Ur. **C5** 56
Rio Negro, Pantanal do, sw., Braz. **G7** 54
Rionero in Vulture, Italy **I10** 14
Rio Pardo, Braz. **B6** 56
Rio Pardo de Minas, Braz. **G10** 54
Rio Rancho, N.M., U.S. **B3** 108
Río Sucio, Col. **E5** 58
Rio Verde, Braz. **D3** 57
Ríoverde, Mex. **G10** 62
Rio Vista, Ca., U.S. **C3** 82
Rioz, Fr. **E13** 10
Ripley, Ms., U.S. **A5** 101
Ripley, Oh., U.S. **D2** 112
Ripley, Tn., U.S. **B2** 119
Ripley, W.V., U.S. **C3** 125
Ripley, co., In., U.S. **F7** 91
Ripley, co., Mo., U.S. **E7** 102
Ripoll, Spain **C14** 12
Ripon, Eng., U.K. **G11** 7
Ripon, Wi., U.S. **E5** 126
Rippowam, stm., Ct., U.S. **E1** 84
Ririe Lake, res., Id., U.S. **F7** 89
Rishon leẔiyyon, Isr. **D4** 40
Rising Sun, De., U.S. **D3** 85
Rising Sun, In., U.S. **G8** 91
Rising Sun, Md., U.S. **A5** 97
Rison, Ar., U.S. **D3** 81
Ritchie, co., W.V., U.S. **B3** 125
Ritter, Mount, mtn., Ca., U.S. **D4** 82
Rittman, Oh., U.S. **B4** 112
Ritzville, Wa., U.S. **B7** 124
Riva, Italy **D5** 14
Rivanna, stm., Va., U.S. **C4** 123
Rivas, Nic. **I5** 64
Rivera, Ur. **C5** 56
Riverbank, Ca., U.S. **D3** 82
River Bourgeois, N.S., Can. **D9** 71
Riverdale, Ca., U.S. **D4** 82
Riverdale, Il., U.S. **k9** 90
Riverdale, Md., U.S. **C4** 97
River Edge, N.J., U.S. **h8** 107
River Falls, Al., U.S. **D3** 78
River Falls, Wi., U.S. **D1** 126
River Forest, Il., U.S. **k9** 90
River Grove, Il., U.S. **k9** 90
Riverhead, N.Y., U.S. **n16** 109
River Hebert, N.S., Can. **D5** 71
River Heights, Ut., U.S. **B4** 121
River Hills, Wi., U.S. **m12** 126
River Pines, Ma., U.S. **f10** 98
River Ridge, La., U.S. **k11** 95
River Road, Or., U.S. **C3** 114
River Rouge, Mi., U.S. **p15** 99
Rivers, Man., Can. **D1** 70
Riverside, Al., U.S. **B3** 78
Riverside, Ca., U.S. **F5** 82
Riverside, Il., U.S. **k9** 90
Riverside, Ia., U.S. **C6** 92
Riverside, N.J., U.S. **C3** 107
Riverside, Pa., U.S. **E8** 115
Riverside, co., Ca., U.S. **F5** 82
Riverside Reservoir, res., Co., U.S. **A6** 83
Riverton, Man., Can. **D3** 70
Riverton, Il., U.S. **D4** 90
Riverton, Ks., U.S. **E9** 93
Riverton, N.J., U.S. **C3** 107
Riverton, Ut., U.S. **C4** 121
Riverton, Vt., U.S. **C3** 122
Riverton, Wy., U.S. **C4** 127
Riverton Heights, Wa., U.S. **f11** 124
River Vale, N.J., U.S. **h8** 107
Riverview, Fl., U.S. **p11** 86
Riverview, Mi., U.S. **p15** 99
Rivesaltes, Fr. **J9** 10
Rivesville, W.V., U.S. **B4** 125
Riviera Beach, Fl., U.S. **F6** 86
Riviera Beach, Md., U.S. **B4** 97
Rivière-du-Loup, Que., Can. **B8** 74
Rivière-Verte, N.B., Can. **B1** 71
Rivne, Ukr. **G3** 22
Rivoli, Italy **D2** 14
Riyadh see Ar-Riyāḍ, Sau. Ar. **D4** 46
Rize, Tur. **G16** 4
Roa, Spain **D8** 12
Roachdale, In., U.S. **E4** 91
Roane, co., Tn., U.S. **D9** 119
Roane, co., W.V., U.S. **C3** 125
Roan Mountain, Tn., U.S. **C11** 119
Roanne, Fr. **F11** 10
Roanoke, Al., U.S. **B4** 78
Roanoke, Il., U.S. **C4** 90
Roanoke, In., U.S. **C7** 91
Roanoke, La., U.S. **D3** 95
Roanoke, Tx., U.S. **m9** 120
Roanoke, Va., U.S. **C3** 123
Roanoke, co., Va., U.S. **C2** 123
Roanoke, stm., U.S. **A5** 110
Roanoke Island, i., N.C., U.S. **B7** 110
Roanoke Rapids, N.C., U.S. **A5** 110
Roanoke Rapids Lake, res., U.S. **A5** 110
Roaring Fork, stm., Co., U.S. **C4** 83

Name — Map Ref — Page

Roaring Spring, Pa., U.S. F5 115
Roatán, Isla de, i., Hond. F4 64
Robbins, Il., U.S. k9 90
Robbins, N.C., U.S. B3 110
Robbinsdale, Mn., U.S. m12 100
Robbinsville, N.C., U.S. f9 110
Röbel, Ger. B12 8
Robersonville, N.C., U.S. B5 110
Roberta, Ga., U.S. D2 87
Robert Lee, Tx., U.S. D2 120
Roberts, Wi., U.S. C1 126
Roberts, co., S.D., U.S. B8 118
Roberts, co., Tx., U.S. B2 120
Roberts, Point, c., Wa., U.S. A2 124
Robert's Arm, Newf., Can. D4 72
Roberts Creek Mountain, mtn., Nv., U.S. D5 105
Robertsdale, Al., U.S. E2 78
Robertsfors, Swe. D13 6
Robert S. Kerr Reservoir, res., Ok., U.S. B6 113
Roberts Mountain, mtn., Ak., U.S. C6 79
Roberts Mountain, mtn., Wy., U.S. D3 127
Robertson, co., Ky., U.S. B5 94
Robertson, co., Tn., U.S. A5 119
Robertson, co., Tx., U.S. D4 120
Robertsonville, Que., Can. C6 74
Roberts Peak, mtn., B.C., Can. F8 66
Robertsport, Lib. G3 42
Robertville, N.B., Can. B4 71
Roberval, Que., Can. A5 74
Robeson, co., N.C., U.S. C3 110
Robins, Ia., U.S. B6 92
Robinson, Il., U.S. D6 90
Robinson Fork, stm., W.V., U.S. m14 125
Robinson Fork, stm., W.V., U.S. k9 125
Roblin, Man., Can. D1 70
Roboré, Bol. G7 54
Robson, Mount, mtn., B.C., Can. C8 69
Robstown, Tx., U.S. F4 120
Roca Partida, Isla, i., Mex. H3 62
Roca Partida, Punta, c., Mex. H12 62
Rocas, Atol das, atoll, Braz. D12 54
Roccastrada, Italy F6 14
Rocha, Ur. C6 56
Rochefort, Fr. G6 10
Rochelle, Ga., U.S. E3 87
Rochelle, Il., U.S. B4 90
Rochelle Park, N.J., U.S. h8 107
Rochester, Il., U.S. D4 90
Rochester, In., U.S. B5 91
Rochester, Mi., U.S. F7 99
Rochester, Mn., U.S. F6 100
Rochester, N.H., U.S. D5 106
Rochester, N.Y., U.S. B3 109
Rochester, Pa., U.S. E1 115
Rochester, Vt., U.S. D3 122
Rochester, Wa., U.S. C2 124
Rochester, Wi., U.S. n11 126
Rock, co., Mn., U.S. G2 100
Rock, co., Ne., U.S. B6 104
Rock, co., Wi., U.S. F4 126
Rock, stm., U.S. B3 90
Rock, stm., U.S. A1 92
Rockall, i., Scot., U.K. D5 4
Rockaway, N.J., U.S. B3 107
Rockaway, Or., U.S. B3 114
Rockbridge, co., Va., U.S. C3 123
Rockcastle, co., Ky., U.S. C5 94
Rockcastle, stm., Ky., U.S. C5 94
Rockcliffe Park, Ont., Can. h12 73
Rock Creek, Mn., U.S. E6 100
Rock Creek, stm., U.S. B3 97
Rock Creek, stm., U.S. h14 124
Rock Creek, stm., Nv., U.S. C5 105
Rock Creek, stm., Or., U.S. B6 114
Rock Creek, stm., Wa., U.S. D5 124
Rock Creek, stm., Wa., U.S. B8 124
Rock Creek, stm., Wy., U.S. E6 127
Rock Creek Butte, mtn., Or., U.S. C8 114
Rockdale, Il., U.S. B5 90
Rockdale, Md., U.S. B4 97
Rockdale, Tx., U.S. D4 120
Rockdale, co., Ga., U.S. C3 87
Rockfall, Ct., U.S. C5 84
Rock Falls, Il., U.S. B4 90
Rockford, Il., U.S. A4 90
Rockford, Ia., U.S. A5 92
Rockford, Mi., U.S. E5 99
Rockford, Mn., U.S. E5 100
Rockford, Oh., U.S. B1 112
Rockford, Tn., U.S. D10 119
Rock Hall, Md., U.S. B5 97
Rockhampton, Austl. D10 50
Rock Hill, S.C., U.S. B5 117
Rockingham, N.C., U.S. C3 110
Rockingham, co., N.H., U.S. D4 106
Rockingham, co., N.C., U.S. A3 110
Rockingham, co., Va., U.S. B4 123
Rock Island, Que., Can. D5 74
Rock Island, Il., U.S. B3 90
Rock Island, co., Il., U.S. B3 90
Rock Island, i., Fl., U.S. C3 86
Rock Island, i., Wi., U.S. C7 126
Rock Lake, l., Wa., U.S. B8 124
Rockland, Ont., Can. B9 73
Rockland, Me., U.S. D3 96
Rockland, Ma., U.S. B6 98
Rockland, co., N.Y., U.S. D6 109
Rockledge, Fl., U.S. D6 86
Rockledge, Pa., U.S. o20 115
Rocklin, Ca., U.S. C3 82
Rockmart, Ga., U.S. B1 87
Rock Mountain, mtn., Co., U.S. D3 83
Rockport, In., U.S. I3 91
Rockport, Me., U.S. D3 96
Rockport, Ma., U.S. A6 98
Rock Port, Mo., U.S. A2 102
Rockport, Tx., U.S. F4 120
Rock Rapids, Ia., U.S. A1 92
Rock River, Wy., U.S. E7 127
Rock Sound, Bah. B9 64
Rocksprings, Tx., U.S. D2 120
Rock Springs, Wy., U.S. E3 127
Rockstone, Guy. E13 58
Rockton, Il., U.S. A4 90
Rock Valley, Ia., U.S. A1 92
Rockville, In., U.S. E3 91
Rockville, Md., U.S. B3 97
Rockville Centre, N.Y., U.S. n15 109
Rockwall, Tx., U.S. C4 120
Rockwall, co., Tx., U.S. C4 120
Rockwell, Ia., U.S. B4 92
Rockwell, N.C., U.S. B2 110
Rockwell City, Ia., U.S. B3 92
Rockwell Park, N.C., U.S. B2 110
Rockwood, Mi., U.S. F7 99
Rockwood, Pa., U.S. G3 115
Rockwood, Tn., U.S. D9 119
Rocky, stm., N.C., U.S. B2 110
Rocky, stm., S.C., U.S. C2 117
Rocky, East Branch, stm., Oh., U.S. h9 112
Rocky, West Branch, stm., Oh., U.S. h9 112
Rocky Boys Indian Reservation, Mt., U.S. B7 103
Rocky Ford, Co., U.S. C7 83
Rocky Fork Lake, l., Oh., U.S. C2 112
Rocky Harbour, Newf., Can. D3 72
Rocky Hill, Ct., U.S. C5 84
Rocky Lake, l., Me., U.S. D5 96
Rocky Mount, N.C., U.S. B5 110
Rocky Mount, Va., U.S. D3 123
Rocky Mountain, mtn., Mt., U.S. C4 103
Rocky Mountain House, Alta., Can. C3 68
Rocky Mountain National Park, Co., U.S. A5 83
Rocky Mountains, mts., N.A. E9 61
Rocky Ripple, In., U.S. k10 91
Rocky River, Oh., U.S. A4 112
Rocky Top, mtn., Or., U.S. C4 114
Roddickton, Newf., Can. C3 72
Roderfield, W.V., U.S. D3 125
Rodez, Fr. H9 10
Ródhos (Rhodes), Grc. M12 16
Ródhos, i., Grc. M11 16
Rodney, Ont., Can. E3 73
Rodney, Cape, c., Ak., U.S. C6 79
Rodney Village, De., U.S. D3 85
Rodniki, Russia D24 18
Roebourne, Austl. D3 50
Roebuck, S.C., U.S. B4 117
Roeland Park, Ks., U.S. k16 93
Roeselare, Bel. E3 8
Roes Welcome Sound, strt., N.W. Ter., Can. D15 66
Roff, Ok., U.S. C5 113
Rogagua, Lago, l., Bol. F5 54
Roger Mills, co., Ok., U.S. B2 113
Rogers, Ar., U.S. A1 81
Rogers, Mn., U.S. E5 100
Rogers, Tx., U.S. D4 120
Rogers, co., Ok., U.S. A6 113
Rogers, Mount, mtn., Va., U.S. f10 123
Rogers City, Mi., U.S. C7 99
Rogers Lake, res., Ct., U.S. D6 84
Rogers Pass, Mt., U.S. C4 103
Rogersville, N.B., Can. C4 71
Rogersville, Al., U.S. A2 78
Rogersville, Mo., U.S. D4 102
Rogersville, Tn., U.S. C10 119
Roggiano Gravina, Italy J11 14
Rogue, stm., Or., U.S. E2 114
Rogue River, Or., U.S. E3 114
Rohtak, India F7 38
Roi Et, Thai. F7 34
Rojo, Cabo, c., Mex. G11 62
Roland, Ia., U.S. B4 92
Roland, Ok., U.S. B7 113
Roland, Lake, res., Md., U.S. g11 97
Rolândia, Braz. G3 57
Røldal, Nor. G6 6
Rolette, N.D., U.S. A6 111
Rolette, co., N.D., U.S. A6 111
Rolfe, Ia., U.S. B3 92
Rolla, Mo., U.S. D6 102
Rolla, N.D., U.S. A6 111
Rollingbay, Wa., U.S. e10 124
Rolling Fork, Ms., U.S. C3 101
Rolling Fork, stm., Ar., U.S. C1 81
Rolling Fork, stm., Ky., U.S. C4 94
Rolling Meadows, Il., U.S. h8 90
Rollingstone, Mn., U.S. F7 100
Rollinsford, N.H., U.S. D5 106
Roma (Rome), Italy H7 14
Roma, Tx., U.S. F3 120
Romain, Cape, c., S.C., U.S. F9 117
Roman, Rom. C10 16
Romania, ctry., Eur. F13 4
Roman Nose Mountain, mtn., Or., U.S. D3 114
Romano, Cape, c., Fl., U.S. G5 86
Romano, Cayo, i., Cuba C8 64
Romans [-sur-Isère], Fr. G12 10
Romanzof, Cape, c., Ak., U.S. C6 79
Romanzof Mountains, mts., Ak., U.S. B11 79
Rome, Ga., U.S. B1 87
Rome, Il., U.S. C4 90
Rome, N.Y., U.S. B5 109
Rome City, In., U.S. B7 91
Romeo, Mi., U.S. F7 99
Romeoville, Il., U.S. k8 90
Rome see Roma, Italy H7 14
Romilly-sur-Seine, Fr. D10 10
Romney, W.V., U.S. B6 125
Romorantin-Lanthenay, Fr. E8 10
Romulus, Mi., U.S. p15 99
Ron, Mui, c., Viet. E9 34
Ronan, Mt., U.S. C2 103
Roncador, Serra do, plat., Braz. F8 54
Roncesvalles, Spain B10 12
Ronceverte, W.V., U.S. D4 125
Ronda, Spain I6 12
Rondônia, Braz. F6 54
Rondonópolis, Braz. D1 57
Ronge, Lac la, l., Sask., Can. B3 75
Rønne, Den. I10 6
Ronneby, Swe. H10 6
Ronne Ice Shelf, Ant. B6 47
Ronse, Bel. E3 8
Roodhouse, Il., U.S. D3 90
Rooks, co., Ks., U.S. C4 93
Roorkee, India F7 38
Roosendaal, Neth. D4 8
Roosevelt, Ut., U.S. C5 121
Roosevelt, co., Mt., U.S. B11 103
Roosevelt, co., N.M., U.S. C6 108
Roosevelt, stm., Braz. E6 54
Roosevelt Park, Mi., U.S. E4 99
Root, stm., Mn., U.S. G7 100
Root, stm., Wi., U.S. n12 126
Roper, N.C., U.S. B6 110
Roquefort, Fr. H6 10
Roraima, Mount, mtn., S.A. E12 58
Røros, Nor. E8 6
Rorschach, Switz. E16 10
Rørvik, Nor. D8 6
Rošal', Russia F22 18
Rosamond, Ca., U.S. E4 82
Rosamorada, Mex. F7 62
Rosario, Arg. C4 56
Rosário, Braz. D10 54
Rosario, Mex. F7 62
Rosario, Mex. B2 62
Rosario, Ven. B6 58
Rosário Oeste, Braz. F7 54
Rosarno, Italy K10 14
Rosas, Golfo de, b., Spain C15 12
Roscoe, Il., U.S. A4 90
Roscoe, Tx., U.S. C2 120
Roscommon, Ire. H4 7
Roscommon, Mi., U.S. D6 99
Roscommon, co., Mi., U.S. D6 99
Roscrea, Ire. I5 7
Rose, Mount, mtn., Nv., U.S. D2 105
Roseau, Dom. G17 64
Roseau, Mn., U.S. B3 100
Roseau, co., Mn., U.S. B3 100
Roseau, South Fork, stm., Mn., U.S. B3 100
Rose-Blanche [-Harbour le Cou], Newf., Can. E2 72
Roseboro, N.C., U.S. C4 110
Rosebud, S.D., U.S. D5 118
Rosebud, Tx., U.S. D4 120
Rosebud, co., Mt., U.S. D10 103
Rosebud Indian Reservation, S.D., U.S. D5 118
Roseburg, Or., U.S. D3 114
Rosedale, In., U.S. E3 91
Rosedale, Md., U.S. g11 97
Rosedale, Ms., U.S. B2 101
Rose Hill, Ks., U.S. E6 93
Rose Hill, N.C., U.S. C4 110
Rose Hill, Va., U.S. f8 123
Roseland, Fl., U.S. E6 86
Roseland, In., U.S. A5 91
Roseland, La., U.S. D5 95
Roseland, Oh., U.S. B3 112
Roselle, Il., U.S. k8 90
Roselle, N.J., U.S. k7 107
Roselle Park, N.J., U.S. k7 107
Rosemère, Que., Can. p19 74
Rosemount, Mn., U.S. F5 100
Rosenberg, Tx., U.S. E5 120
Rosendale, Wi., U.S. E5 126
Rosenheim, Ger. H12 8
Rose Peak, mtn., Az., U.S. D6 80
Rosepine, La., U.S. D2 95
Rose Point, c., B.C., Can. B2 69
Roseto, Pa., U.S. E11 115
Roseville, Ca., U.S. C3 82
Roseville, Il., U.S. C3 90
Roseville, Mi., U.S. o16 99
Roseville, Mn., U.S. m12 100
Roseville, Oh., U.S. C3 112
Rosewood Heights, Il., U.S. E3 90
Rosiclare, Il., U.S. F5 90
Rosignano Marittimo, Italy F5 14
Roskilde, Den. I9 6
Roslags-Näsby, Swe. G12 6
Roslavl', Russia H15 18
Roslyn, Wa., U.S. B4 124
Roslyn Heights, N.Y., U.S. h13 109
Ross, Oh., U.S. C1 112
Ross, co., Oh., U.S. C2 112
Rossano, Italy J11 14
Rossan Point, c., Ire. G4 7
Ross Barnett Reservoir, res., Ms., U.S. C3 101
Rossburn, Man., Can. D1 70
Ross Dam, Wa., U.S. A4 124
Rossel Island, i., Pap. N. Gui. B10 50
Rossford, Oh., U.S. A2 112
Ross Ice Shelf, Ant. A31 47
Rossignol, Lake, l., N.S., Can. E4 71
Ross Island, i., Man., Can. B3 70
Ross Lake National Recreation Area, Wa., U.S. A5 124
Rossland, B.C., Can. E9 69
Rosslare, Ire. I6 7
Rosso, Maur. E2 42
Ross River, Yukon, Can. D6 66
Ross Sea, Ant. B31 47
Rossville, Ga., U.S. B1 87
Rossville, Il., U.S. C6 90
Rossville, In., U.S. D4 91
Rossville, Ks., U.S. C8 93
Rostock, Ger. A12 8
Rostov, Russia D22 18
Rostov-na-Donu, Russia H5 22
Roswell, Ga., U.S. B2 87
Roswell, N.M., U.S. D5 108
Rotan, Tx., U.S. C2 120
Rotenburg, Ger. B9 8
Rothaargebirge, mts., Ger. D8 8
Rothenburg ob der Tauber, Ger. F10 8
Rothesay, N.B., Can. D4 71
Rothschild, Wi., U.S. D4 126
Rothsville, Pa., U.S. F9 115
Roti, Pulau, i., Indon. H7 32
Rotondella, Italy I11 14
Rotorua, N.Z. C6 52
Rotterdam, Neth. D4 8
Rotterdam, N.Y., U.S. C6 109
Rottweil, Ger. G8 8
Roubaix, Fr. B10 10
Rouen, Fr. C8 10
Rouge, stm., Que., Can. D3 74
Rough, stm., Ky., U.S. C3 94
Rough River Lake, res., Ky., U.S. C3 94
Roulette, Pa., U.S. C5 115
Round Island, i., Ms., U.S. g8 101
Round Lake, Il., U.S. h8 90
Round Lake Beach, Il., U.S. h8 90
Round Mountain, Nv., U.S. E4 105
Round Rock, Tx., U.S. D4 120
Roundup, Mt., U.S. D8 103
Round Valley Indian Reservation, Ca., U.S. C2 82
Round Valley Reservoir, res., N.J., U.S. B3 107
Rouses Point, N.Y., U.S. f11 109
Roussillon, hist. reg., Fr. J9 10
Routt, co., Co., U.S. A3 83
Rouyn [-Noranda], Que., Can. k11 74
Rouzerville, Pa., U.S. G6 115
Rovaniemi, Fin. C15 6
Rovato, Italy D4 14
Rovereto, Italy D6 14
Rovigo, Italy D6 14
Rovinj, Cro. D8 14
Rowan, co., Ky., U.S. B6 94
Rowan, co., N.C., U.S. B2 110
Rowland, N.C., U.S. C3 110
Rowlesburg, W.V., U.S. B5 125
Rowley Island, i., N.W. Ter., Can. C17 66
Rowley Shoals, rf., Austl. C3 50
Roxboro, N.C., U.S. A4 110
Roxton Falls, Que., Can. D5 74
Roxton Pond, Que., Can. D5 74
Roy, Ut., U.S. B3 121
Royal, stm., Me., U.S. g7 96
Royal Canal, Ire. H5 7
Royal Center, In., U.S. C4 91
Royale, Isle, i., Mi., U.S. h9 99
Royal Gorge, val., Co., U.S. C5 83
Royal Oak, Mi., U.S. F7 99
Royal Pines, N.C., U.S. f10 110
Royalton, Il., U.S. F4 90
Royalton, Mn., U.S. E4 100
Royan, Fr. G5 10
Royersford, Pa., U.S. F10 115
Royerton, In., U.S. D7 91
Royse City, Tx., U.S. C4 120
Royston, B.C., Can. E5 69
Royston, Ga., U.S. B3 87
Rubbestadneset, Nor. G5 6
Rubcovsk, Russia G10 24
Rubidoux, Ca., U.S. n14 82
Rubio, Ven. D6 58
Ruby Dome, mtn., Nv., U.S. C6 105
Ruby Lake, l., Nv., U.S. C6 105
Ruby Mountains, mts., Nv., U.S. C6 105
Ruby Range, mts., Co., U.S. C3 83
Ruby Range, mts., Mt., U.S. E4 103
Rudolf, Lake, l., Afr. H2 46
Rudolstadt, Ger. E11 8
Rudyard, Mi., U.S. B6 99
Rue, Fr. B8 10
Rufā'ah, Sudan F12 42
Ruffec, Fr. F7 10
Rufino, Arg. C4 56
Rufus Woods Lake, res., Wa., U.S. A6 124
Rugao, China C9 28
Rugby, Eng., U.K. I11 7
Rugby, N.D., U.S. A6 111
Ruian, China H9 28
Ruidoso, N.M., U.S. D4 108
Ruidoso Downs, N.M., U.S. D4 108
Ruijin, China F10 26
Ruijin, China J4 28
Rukwa, Lake, l., Tan. C6 44
Ruleville, Ms., U.S. B3 101
Rum, stm., Mn., U.S. D5 100
Ruma, Yugo. D3 16
Rumbek, Sudan G11 42
Rum Cay, i., Bah. C10 64
Rum Creek, stm., W.V., U.S. n12 125
Rumford, Me., U.S. D2 96
Rumia, Pol. A18 8
Rum Jungle, Austl. B6 50
Rumoi, Japan p19 30a
Rumson, N.J., U.S. C4 107
Rumstick Point, c., R.I., U.S. D5 116
Ru'nan, China B3 28
Runanga, N.Z. E3 52
Runge, Tx., U.S. E4 120
Rungwa, Tan. C6 44
Runnels, co., Tx., U.S. D3 120
Runnemede, N.J., U.S. D2 107
Ruoqiang, China D4 26
Rupert, Id., U.S. G5 89
Rupert, W.V., U.S. D4 125
Rupert, Rivière de, stm., Que., Can. h11 74
Rural Hall, N.C., U.S. A2 110
Rural Retreat, Va., U.S. D1 123
Rusagonis, N.B., Can. D3 71
Ruse, Bul. F9 16
Rush, co., In., U.S. E6 91
Rush, co., Ks., U.S. D4 93
Rush, stm., Mn., U.S. F4 100
Rush, stm., Wi., U.S. D1 126
Rush City, Mn., U.S. E6 100
Rush Creek, stm., Oh., U.S. B2 112
Rush Creek, stm., Ok., U.S. C4 113
Rushford, Mn., U.S. G7 100
Rush Lake, l., Mn., U.S. E5 100
Rush Lake, l., Mn., U.S. D3 100
Rush Lake, l., Wi., U.S. E5 126
Rushmere, Va., U.S. h14 123
Rush Springs, Ok., U.S. C4 113
Rushville, Il., U.S. C3 90
Rushville, In., U.S. E7 91
Rushville, Ne., U.S. B3 104
Rusk, Tx., U.S. D5 120
Rusk, co., Tx., U.S. C5 120
Rusk, co., Wi., U.S. C2 126
Ruskin, Fl., U.S. E4 86
Russas, Braz. D11 54
Russell, Man., Can. D1 70
Russell, Ont., Can. B9 73
Russell, Ks., U.S. D5 93
Russell, Ky., U.S. B7 94
Russell, Pa., U.S. C3 115
Russell, co., Al., U.S. C4 78
Russell, co., Ks., U.S. D5 93
Russell, co., Ky., U.S. D4 94
Russell, co., Va., U.S. f9 123
Russell, Mount, mtn., Ak., U.S. f16 79
Russell Cave National Monument, Al., U.S. A4 78
Russell Fork, stm., U.S. C7 94
Russell Island, i., N.W. Ter., Can. B13 66
Russell Springs, Ky., U.S. C4 94
Russellville, Al., U.S. A2 78
Russellville, Ar., U.S. B2 81
Russellville, Ky., U.S. D3 94
Russellville, Mo., U.S. C5 102
Russellville, Tn., U.S. C10 119
Rüsselsheim, Ger. E8 8
Russia, ctry., Eur. E15 22
Russian, stm., Ca., U.S. C2 82
Russiaville, In., U.S. D5 91
Rustavi, Geor. I7 22
Rustburg, Va., U.S. C3 123
Rustenburg, S. Afr. G5 44
Ruston, La., U.S. B3 95
Ruston, Wa., U.S. B3 124
Ruth, Nv., U.S. D6 105
Rutherford, N.J., U.S. B4 107
Rutherford, Tn., U.S. A3 119
Rutherford, co., N.C., U.S. B1 110
Rutherford, co., Tn., U.S. B5 119
Rutherfordton, N.C., U.S. B1 110
Ruthven, Ia., U.S. A3 92
Rutland, Ma., U.S. B4 98
Rutland, Vt., U.S. D3 122
Rutland, co., Vt., U.S. D2 122
Rutledge, Ga., U.S. C3 87
Rutledge, Tn., U.S. C10 119
Ruukki, Fin. D15 6
Ruvuma (Rovuma), stm., Afr. D7 44
Ružomberok, Slov. F19 8
Rwanda, ctry., Afr. B5 44
Ryan, Ok., U.S. C4 113
Ryan Peak, mtn., Id., U.S. F4 89
Rybinsk, Russia C21 18
Rybinskoje Vodochranilišče, res., Russia C21 18
Rybnik, Pol. E18 8
Rycroft, Alta., Can. B1 68
Ryde, Eng., U.K. K11 7
Rye, N.H., U.S. D5 106
Rye, N.Y., U.S. h13 109
Rye Beach, N.H., U.S. E5 106
Rye Patch Dam, Nv., U.S. C3 105
Rye Patch Reservoir, res., Nv., U.S. C3 105
Ryfoss, Nor. F7 6
Ryōtsu, Japan D11 30
Rysy, mtn., Eur. F20 8
Ryukyu Islands see Nansei-shotō, is., Japan F12 26
Rzeszów, Pol. E21 8
Ržev, Russia E17 18

S

Saalfeld, Ger. E11 8
Saarbrücken, Ger. F6 8
Saaremaa, i., Est. C5 18
Saarijärvi, Fin. E15 6
Saarlouis, Ger. F6 8
Sab, Tônlé, l., Camb. H7 34
Saba, i., Neth. Ant. F16 64
Sabadell, Spain D14 12
Sabae, Japan G9 30
Sabana, Archipiélago de, is., Cuba C8 64
Sabanagrande, Hond. H4 64
Sabanalarga, Col. B5 58
Sabang, Indon. E6 32
Sabanilla, Mex. E9 62
Sabará, Braz. E7 57
Sabattus, Me., U.S. D2 96
Sabetha, Ks., U.S. C8 93
Sabhah, Libya C8 42
Sabi (Save), stm., Afr. F6 44
Sabillasville, Md., U.S. A3 97
Sabina, Oh., U.S. C2 112
Sabinal, Tx., U.S. E3 120
Sabiñánigo, Spain C11 12
Sabinas, Mex. D9 62
Sabinas Hidalgo, Mex. D9 62
Sabine, co., La., U.S. C2 95
Sabine, co., Tx., U.S. D6 120
Sabine, stm., U.S. D6 120
Sabine Lake, l., U.S. E2 95
Sabine Pass, strt., U.S. E2 95
Sable, Cape, c., N.S., Can. H19 66
Sable, Cape, c., Fl., U.S. G5 86
Sable, Îles de, i., N. Cal. C11 50
Sable Island, i., N.S., Can. F10 71
Sabula, Ia., U.S. B7 92
Sabzevār, Iran J9 22
Sac, co., Ia., U.S. B2 92
Sac, stm., Mo., U.S. D4 102
Sacajawea, Lake, res., Wa., U.S. C7 124
Sacajawea Peak, mtn., Or., U.S. B9 114
Sacandaga Lake, l., N.Y., U.S. B6 109
Sac and Fox Indian Reservation, Ia., U.S. C5 92
Sacaton, Az., U.S. D4 80
Sac City, Ia., U.S. B2 92
Sacedón, Spain E9 12
Sachalin, Ostrov (Sakhalin), i., Russia G22 24
Sachalinskij Zaliv, b., Russia G22 24
Sachigo, stm., Ont., Can. F14 66
Sachse, Tx., U.S. n10 120

Name Map Ref Page

Sachs Harbour, N.W. Ter., Can. B8 66
Sachty, Russia H6 22
Sachuest Point, c., R.I., U.S. F6 116
Sackville, N.B., Can. D5 71
Saco, Me., U.S. E2 96
Saco, stm., U.S. E2 96
Saco, East Branch, stm., N.H., U.S. B4 106
Sacramento, Ca., U.S. C3 82
Sacramento, co., Ca., U.S. C3 82
Sacramento, stm., Ca., U.S. C3 82
Sacramento, stm., N.M., U.S. E4 108
Sacramento Mountains, mts., N.M., U.S. E4 108
Sacramento Valley, val., Ca., U.S. C2 82
Sacré-Coeur-Saguenay, Que., Can. A8 74
Sacred Heart, Mn., U.S. F3 100
Sádaba, Spain C10 12
Ṣa'dah, Yemen E3 46
Saddle, stm., N.J., U.S. h8 107
Saddleback Mountain, mtn., Az., U.S. k8 80
Saddle Brook, N.J., U.S. h8 107
Saddlebunch Keys, is., Fl., U.S. H5 86
Saddle Mountain, mtn., Or., U.S. B3 114
Saddle Mountains, mts., Wa., U.S. C5 124
Saddle River, N.J., U.S. A4 107
Sa Dec, Viet. I8 34
Sādiqābad, Pak. F4 38
Sado, i., Japan D11 30
Sado-kaikyō, strt., Japan E11 30
Saegertown, Pa., U.S. C1 115
Safety Harbor, Fl., U.S. E4 86
Säffle, Swe. G9 6
Safford, Az., U.S. E6 80
Safi, Mor. B4 42
Safīd, stm., Afg. B1 38
Safīd Kūh, Selseleh-ye, mts., Afg. C1 36
Safonovo, Russia F16 18
Saga, Japan I3 30
Sagadahoc, co., Me., U.S. E3 96
Sagaing, Mya. D3 34
Sagamihara, Japan G12 30
Sagami-nada, b., Japan G12 30
Sagamore Hills, Oh., U.S. h9 112
Saganaga Lake, l., Mn., U.S. B7 100
Sāgar, India E3 37
Sāgar, India I8 38
Sag Harbor, N.Y., U.S. m16 109
Saginaw, Mi., U.S. E7 99
Saginaw, Tx., U.S. n9 120
Saginaw, co., Mi., U.S. E6 99
Saginaw Bay, b., Mi., U.S. E7 99
Saglek Bay, b., Newf., Can. f9 72
Sagres, Port. H3 12
Saguache, co., Co., U.S. C4 83
Sagua de Tánamo, Cuba D10 64
Sagua la Grande, Cuba C7 64
Saguaro Lake, res., Az., U.S. k10 80
Saguaro National Park, Az., U.S. E5 80
Saguaro National Park (Tucson Mountain Section), Az., U.S. E4 80
Saguenay, stm., Que., Can. A7 74
Sagunto, Spain F11 12
Sahagún, Col. C5 58
Sahagún, Spain C6 12
Sahara, des., Afr. D6 42
Sahāranpur, India F7 38
Sāhīwāl (Montgomery), Pak. E5 38
Sahuaripa, Mex. C5 62
Sahuarita, Az., U.S. F5 80
Sahuayo, Mex. G8 62
Saibai, i., Austl. A8 50
Saïda, Alg. B6 42
Saidpur, Bngl. H13 38
Saidu, Pak. C5 38
Saigō, Japan F6 30
Saigon see Thanh Pho Ho Chi Minh, Viet. I9 34
Saijō, Japan I6 30
Saimaa, l., Fin. F16 6
Saint Abb's Head, c., Scot., U.K. F10 7
Saint Adolphe, Man., Can. E3 70
Saint-Affrique, Fr. I9 10
Sainte-Agathe, Que., Can. C6 74
Sainte-Agathe-des-Monts, Que., Can. C3 74
Saint-Aimé (Massueville), Que., Can. D5 74
Saint-Alban, Que., Can. C5 74
Saint Alban's, Newf., Can. E4 72
Saint Albans, Eng., U.K. J12 7
Saint Albans, Vt., U.S. B2 122
Saint Albans, W.V., U.S. C3 125
Saint Albans Bay, b., Vt., U.S. B2 122
Saint Albert, Alta., Can. C4 68
Saint-Amand-Mont-Rond, Fr. F9 10
Saint-Ambroise, Que., Can. A6 74
Saint-Ambroix, Fr. H11 10
Saint-André, Cap, c., Madag. E8 44
Saint-André-Avellin, Que., Can. D2 74
Saint-André-Est, Que., Can. D3 74
Saint-André-les-Alpes, Fr. I13 10
Saint Andrew Bay, b., Fl., U.S. u16 86
Saint Andrews, N.B., Can. D2 71
Saint Andrews, Scot., U.K. E10 7
Saint Andrews, S.C., U.S. F7 117
Saint Andrews, S.C., U.S. C5 117
Saint Anne, Il., U.S. B6 90
Sainte-Anne-de-Beaupré, Que., Can. B7 74
Sainte-Anne [-de-Bellevue], Que., Can. q19 74
Sainte Anne-de-Madawaska, N.B., Can. B1 71
Sainte-Anne-des-Chênes, Man., Can. E3 70
Saint-Anselme, Que., Can. C7 74
Saint Ansgar, Ia., U.S. A5 92
Saint Anthony, Newf., Can. C4 72
Saint Anthony, Id., U.S. F7 89
Saint Antoine, N.B., Can. C5 71
Saint-Apollinaire, Que., Can. C6 74
Saint Arthur, N.B., Can. B3 71
Saint-Astier, Fr. G7 10
Saint-Aubert, Que., Can. B7 74
Saint Augustin, stm., Can. C2 72
Saint Augustine, Fl., U.S. C5 86
Saint Austell, Eng., U.K. K8 7
Saint-Avold, Fr. C13 10
Saint-Barthélemy, i., Guad. F16 64
Saint Basile, N.B., Can. B1 71
Saint-Basile [-Sud], Que., Can. C6 74
Saint-Benoît-du-Sault, Fr. F8 10
Saint-Bernard, Que., Can. C6 74
Saint Bernard, Al., U.S. A3 78
Saint Bernard, La., U.S. E6 95
Saint Bernard, Oh., U.S. o13 112
Saint Bernard, co., La., U.S. E6 95
Saint Bernice, In., U.S. E2 91
Saint Bride, Mount, mtn., Alta., Can. D3 68
Saint Bride's, Newf., Can. E4 72
Saint-Brieuc, Fr. D4 10
Saint-Bruno, Que., Can. A6 74
Saint-Calais, Fr. E7 10
Saint-Casimir, Que., Can. C5 74
Saint Catharines, Ont., Can. D5 73
Saint Catherine, Lake, l., Vt., U.S. E2 122
Saint Catherines Island, i., Ga., U.S. E5 87
Saint-Célestin (Annaville), Que., Can. C5 74
Saint-Céré, Fr. H8 10
Saint-Césaire, Que., Can. D4 74
Saint-Chamond, Fr. G11 10
Saint-Charles, Que., Can. C7 74
Saint Charles, Il., U.S. B5 90
Saint Charles, Mi., U.S. E6 99
Saint Charles, Mn., U.S. G6 100
Saint Charles, Mo., U.S. C7 102
Saint Charles, co., La., U.S. E5 95
Saint Charles, co., Mo., U.S. C7 102
Saint-Chély-d'Apcher, Fr. H10 10
Saint Christopher (Saint Kitts), i., St. K./N. F16 64
Saint Christopher-Nevis see Saint Kitts and Nevis, ctry., N.A. F16 64
Saint-Chrysostome, Que., Can. D4 74
Saint Clair, Mi., U.S. F8 99
Saint Clair, Mn., U.S. F5 100
Saint Clair, Mo., U.S. C6 102
Saint Clair, Pa., U.S. E9 115
Saint Clair, co., Al., U.S. B3 78
Saint Clair, co., Il., U.S. E3 90
Saint Clair, co., Mi., U.S. F8 99
Saint Clair, co., Mo., U.S. C4 102
Saint Clair Shores, Mi., U.S. p16 99
Saint Clairsville, Oh., U.S. B5 112
Saint Claude, Man., Can. E2 70
Saint-Claude, Fr. F12 10
Saint Cloud, Fl., U.S. D5 86
Saint Cloud, Mn., U.S. E4 100
Saint-Coeur-de-Marie, Que., Can. A6 74
Saint-Constant, Que., Can. q19 74
Sainte-Croix, Que., Can. C6 74
Saint Croix, co., Wi., U.S. C1 126
Saint Croix, i., V.I.U.S. F15 64
Saint Croix, stm., U.S. C1 126
Saint Croix, Lake, l., U.S. D1 126
Saint Croix Falls, Wi., U.S. C1 126
Saint Croix Stream, stm., Me., U.S. B4 96
Saint-Damase, Que., Can. D4 74
Saint David, Az., U.S. F5 80
Saint-David-de-l'Auberivière, Que., Can. n17 74
Saint David's, Wales, U.K. J7 7
Saint-Denis, Que., Can. D4 74
Saint-Denis, Fr. D9 10
Saint-Denis, Reu. F11 44
Saint-Dié, Fr. D13 10
Saint-Dizier, Fr. D11 10
Saint-Dominique, Que., Can. D5 74
Saint Edward, Ne., U.S. C8 104
Saint Eleanor's, P.E.I., Can. C6 71
Saint Elias, Cape, c., Ak., U.S. D11 79
Saint Elmo, Al., U.S. E1 78
Saint Elmo, Il., U.S. D5 90
Saint-Éphrem [-de-Tring], Que., Can. C7 74
Saint Étienne, Fr. G11 10
Saint-Eustache, Que., Can. D4 74
Saint-Félicien, Que., Can. A5 74
Saint-Félix-de-Valois, Que., Can. C4 74
Saint-Ferdinand (Bernierville), Que., Can. C6 74
Saint-Ferréol [-les-Neiges], Que., Can. B7 74
Saint-Flavien, Que., Can. C6 74
Saint-Florentin, Fr. D10 10
Saint-Florent-sur-Cher, Fr. F9 10
Saint-Flour, Fr. G10 10
Sainte-Foy, Que., Can. n17 74
Sainte-Foy-la-Grande, Fr. H7 10
Saint Francis, Ks., U.S. C2 93
Saint Francis, Mn., U.S. E5 100
Saint Francis, S.D., U.S. D5 118
Saint Francis, Wi., U.S. n12 126
Saint Francis, co., Ar., U.S. B5 81
Saint Francis, stm., U.S. A5 81
Saint Francis, Cape, c., Newf., Can. E5 72
Saint Francisville, Il., U.S. E6 90
Saint Francisville, La., U.S. D4 95
Saint Francois, co., Mo., U.S. D7 102
Saint-François, stm., Que., Can. D5 74
Saint-François, Lac, l., Que., Can. D6 74
Saint Francois Mountains, hills, Mo., U.S. D7 102
Saint Froid Lake, l., Me., U.S. B4 96
Saint-Fulgence, Que., Can. A7 74
Saint-Gabriel, Que., Can. C4 74
Saint-Gaudens, Fr. I7 10
Saint-Gédéon, Que., Can. D7 74
Sainte Genevieve, Mo., U.S. D7 102
Sainte Genevieve, co., Mo., U.S. D7 102
Saint George, Austl. E9 50
Saint George, N.B., Can. D3 71
Saint George, Ont., Can. D4 73
Saint George, S.C., U.S. E6 117
Saint George, Ut., U.S. F2 121
Saint George, Cape, c., Newf., Can. D2 72
Saint George, Cape, c., Fl., U.S. C1 86
Saint George Island, i., Ak., U.S. D6 79
Saint George Island, i., Fl., U.S. C2 86
Saint George's, Newf., Can. D2 72
Saint-Georges, Que., Can. C5 74
Saint-Georges, Fr. Gu. C8 54
Saint George's, Gren. H17 64
Saint Georges, De., U.S. B3 85
Saint George's Bay, b., Newf., Can. D2 72
Saint Georges Bay, b., N.S., Can. D8 71
Saint George's Channel, strt., Eur. J6 7
Saint-Georges-Ouest (part of Ville-Saint-Georges), Que., Can. C7 74
Saint-Germain, Fr. D9 10
Saint-Gervais, Que., Can. C7 74
Saint-Gilles, Que., Can. C6 74
Saint-Gilles-Croix-de-Vie, Fr. F5 10
Saint-Girons, Fr. J8 10
Saint-Grégoire (Larochelle), Que., Can. C5 74
Saint-Guénolé, Fr. E2 10
Saint-Guillaume-d'Upton, Que., Can. D5 74
Saint Helen, Lake, l., Mi., U.S. D6 99
Saint Helena, Ca., U.S. C2 82
Saint Helena, co., La., U.S. D5 95
Saint Helena Bay, b., S. Afr. H3 44
Saint Helena Island, i., S.C., U.S. G6 117
Saint Helena Sound, strt., S.C., U.S. G7 117
Saint Helens, Or., U.S. B4 114
Saint Helens, Mount, vol., Wa., U.S. C3 124
Saint Helier, Jersey C4 10
Saint Henry, Oh., U.S. B1 112
Saint-Hippolyte, Fr. E13 10
Saint-Honoré, Que., Can. D7 74
Saint-Hubert, Que., Can. q20 74
Saint-Hubert-de-Témiscouata, Que., Can. B8 74
Saint-Hyacinthe, Que., Can. D5 74
Saint Ignace, Mi., U.S. C6 99
Saint Ignace Island, i., Ont., Can. G15 66
Saint Ignatius, Mt., U.S. C2 103
Saint Isidore de Prescott, Ont., Can. B10 73
Saint Jacobs, Ont., Can. D4 73
Saint Jacques, N.B., Can. B1 71
Saint-Jacques, Que., Can. D4 74
Saint James, Mn., U.S. G4 100
Saint James, Mo., U.S. D6 102
Saint James, co., La., U.S. D5 95
Saint James, Cape, c., B.C., Can. D2 69
Saint James City, Fl., U.S. F4 86
Saint-Jean, stm., Que., Can. A7 74
Saint-Jean, Lac, l., Que., Can. A5 74
Saint Jean Baptiste, Man., Can. E3 70
Saint-Jean-Chrysostome, Que., Can. o17 74
Saint-Jean-d'Angély, Fr. G6 10
Saint-Jean-de-Luz, Fr. I5 10
Saint-Jean-de-Maurienne, Fr. G13 10
Saint-Jean-de-Monts, Fr. F4 10
Saint-Jean-Pied-de-Port, Fr. I5 10
Saint-Jean-sur-Richelieu, Que., Can. D4 74
Saint-Jérôme, Que., Can. D3 74
Saint Jo, Tx., U.S. C4 120
Saint-Joachim, Que., Can. B7 74
Saint Joe, stm., Id., U.S. B3 89
Saint John, N.B., Can. D3 71
Saint John, In., U.S. B3 91
Saint John, Ks., U.S. E5 93
Saint John, i., V.I.U.S. E15 64
Saint John, stm., N.A. G19 66
Saint John, Cape, c., Newf., Can. D4 72
Saint John Bay, b., Newf., Can. C3 72
Saint Johns, Antig. F17 64
Saint John's, Newf., Can. E5 72
Saint Johns, Az., U.S. C6 80
Saint Johns, Mi., U.S. F6 99
Saint Johns, co., Fl., U.S. C5 86
Saint Johns, stm., Fl., U.S. B5 86
Saint Johnsbury, Vt., U.S. C4 122
Saint Johnsville, N.Y., U.S. B6 109
Saint John the Baptist, co., La., U.S. D5 95
Saint Jones, stm., De., U.S. D4 85
Saint Joseph, N.B., Can. D5 71
Saint Joseph, Il., U.S. C5 90
Saint Joseph, La., U.S. C4 95
Saint Joseph, Mi., U.S. F4 99
Saint Joseph, Mn., U.S. E4 100
Saint Joseph, Mo., U.S. B3 102
Saint Joseph, Tn., U.S. B4 119
Saint Joseph, co., In., U.S. A5 91
Saint Joseph, co., Mi., U.S. G5 99
Saint Joseph, stm., U.S. F5 99
Saint-Joseph, Lac, l., Que., Can. n16 74
Saint Joseph, Lake, l., Ont., Can. o17 73
Saint Joseph Bay, b., Fl., U.S. C1 86
Saint-Joseph-de-Beauce, Que., Can. C7 74
Saint Joseph Point, c., Fl., U.S. v16 86
Saint Joseph Sound, strt., Fl., U.S. o10 86
Saint-Jovite, Que., Can. C3 74
Saint-Julien-en-Born, Fr. H5 10
Saint-Junien, Fr. G7 10
Saint-Just-en-Chaussée, Fr. C9 10
Saint Kilda, i., Scot., U.K. D4 7
Saint Kitts-Nevis, ctry., N.A. F16 64
Saint-Lambert, Que., Can. p19 74
Saint Landry, co., La., U.S. D3 95
Saint-Laurent, Que., Can. p19 74
Saint Lawrence, Newf., Can. E4 72
Saint Lawrence, co., N.Y., U.S. A5 109
Saint Lawrence, stm., N.A. G19 66
Saint Lawrence, Cape, c., N.S., Can. B9 71
Saint Lawrence, Gulf of, b., Can. G20 66
Saint Lawrence Island, i., Ak., U.S. C5 79
Saint Lawrence Islands National Park, Ont., Can. C9 73
Saint Léonard, N.B., Can. B2 71
Saint-Léonard [-d'Aston], Que., Can. C5 74
Saint-Liboire, Que., Can. D5 74
Saint-Lô, Fr. C5 10
Saint-Louis, Sen. E2 42
Saint Louis, Mi., U.S. E6 99
Saint Louis, Mo., U.S. C7 102
Saint Louis, co., Mn., U.S. C6 100
Saint Louis, co., Mo., U.S. C7 102
Saint Louis, stm., U.S. D6 100
Saint-Louis, Lac, l., Que., Can. q19 74
Saint Louis Bay, b., Ms., U.S. f7 101
Saint-Louis-de-Gonzague, Que., Can. D3 74
Saint Louis-de-Kent, N.B., Can. C5 71
Saint-Louis-du-Ha! Ha!, Que., Can. B8 74
Saint Louis Park, Mn., U.S. n12 100
Saint-Luc, Que., Can. D4 74
Saint Lucia, ctry., N.A. H17 64
Saint Lucia Channel, strt., N.A. G17 64
Saint Lucie, co., Fl., U.S. E6 86
Saint Lucie Canal, Fl., U.S. F6 86
Saint Lucie Inlet, b., Fl., U.S. E6 86
Sainte-Madeleine, Que., Can. D4 74
Saint Malo, Man., Can. E3 70
Saint-Malo, Fr. D4 10
Saint-Malo, Golfe de, b., Fr. D4 10
Saint-Marc, Haiti E11 64
Saint-Marc [-des-Carrières], Que., Can. C5 74
Saint-Marcellin, Fr. G12 10
Saint Margaret Bay, b., Newf., Can. C3 72
Sainte-Marguerite, stm., Que., Can. A7 74
Sainte-Marie, Que., Can. C6 74
Sainte-Marie, Cap, c., Madag. G9 44
Saint Maries, Id., U.S. B2 89
Sainte-Marthe, Que., Can. D3 74
Saint Martin, co., La., U.S. D4 95
Saint-Martin (Sint Maarten), i., N.A. E16 64
Saint Martin, Lake, l., Man., Can. D2 70
Saint Martin Island, i., Mi., U.S. C4 99
Saint Martinville, La., U.S. D4 95
Saint Mary, co., La., U.S. E4 95
Saint Mary-of-the-Woods, In., U.S. E3 91
Saint Mary Peak, mtn., Austl. F7 50
Saint Marys, Austl. H9 50
Saint Mary's, Newf., Can. E5 72
Saint Mary's, Ont., Can. D3 73
Saint Marys, Ak., U.S. C7 79
Saint Marys, Ga., U.S. F5 87
Saint Marys, In., U.S. A5 91
Saint Marys, Ks., U.S. C7 93
Saint Marys, Oh., U.S. B1 112
Saint Marys, Pa., U.S. D4 115
Saint Marys, W.V., U.S. B3 125
Saint Marys, co., Md., U.S. D4 97
Saint Marys, stm., N.S., Can. D8 71
Saint Marys, stm., U.S. F5 87
Saint Marys, stm., U.S. C8 91
Saint Marys, stm., Md., U.S. D5 97
Saint Mary's, Cape, c., Newf., Can. E4 72
Saint Mary's Bay, b., Newf., Can. E5 72
Saint Marys Bay, b., N.S., Can. E3 71
Saint Marys City, Md., U.S. D5 97
Saint-Mathieu, Pointe de, c., Fr. D2 10
Saint Matthew Island, i., Ak., U.S. C5 79
Saint Matthews, Ky., U.S. B4 94
Saint Matthews, S.C., U.S. D6 117
Sainte-Maure-du-Touraine, Fr. E7 10
Saint-Maurice, stm., Que., Can. C5 74
Sainte-Maxime, Fr. I13 10
Saint-Méen-le-Grand, Fr. D4 10
Sainte-Menehould, Fr. C11 10
Sainte-Mère-Église, Fr. C5 10
Saint Michael, Mn., U.S. E5 100
Saint Michaels, Md., U.S. C5 97
Saint-Michel [-de-Bellechasse], Que., Can. C7 74
Saint-Mihiel, Fr. D12 10
Saint-Moritz see Sankt Moritz, Switz. F16 10
Saint-Nazaire, Fr. E4 10
Saint-Nicolas, Que., Can. o17 74
Saint-Odilon, Que., Can. C7 74
Saint-Omer, Fr. B9 10
Saint-Ours, Que., Can. D4 74
Saint-Pacôme, Que., Can. B8 74
Saint-Pamphile, Que., Can. C8 74
Saint Paris, Oh., U.S. B2 112
Saint-Pascal, Que., Can. B8 74
Saint Paul, Alta., Can. B5 68
Saint Paul, Ak., U.S. D5 79
Saint Paul, In., U.S. F6 91
Saint Paul, Ks., U.S. E8 93
Saint Paul, Mn., U.S. F5 100
Saint Paul, Mo., U.S. f12 102
Saint Paul, Ne., U.S. C7 104
Saint Paul, Va., U.S. f9 123
Saint Paul Island, i., Ak., U.S. D5 79
Saint Paul Park, Mn., U.S. n12 100
Saint Pauls, N.C., U.S. C4 110
Sainte-Perpétue-de-L'Islet, Que., Can. B8 74
Saint Peter, Mn., U.S. F5 100
Saint Peter Port, Guernsey C4 10
Saint Peters, N.S., Can. D9 71
Saint Peters, Mo., U.S. C7 102
Saint Petersburg, Fl., U.S. E4 86
Saint Petersburg Beach, Fl., U.S. p10 86
Saint Petersburg see Sankt-Peterburg, Russia B13 18
Saint Phillips Island, i., S.C., U.S. G6 117
Saint-Pie, Que., Can. D5 74
Saint-Pierre, Reu. F11 44
Saint-Pierre, St. P./M. E3 72
Saint-Pierre, Lac, l., Que., Can. C5 74
Saint Pierre and Miquelon, dep., N.A. G21 66
Saint Pierre Island, i., Sey. C10 44
Saint-Pierre-Jolys, Man., Can. E3 70
Saint-Pierre-le-Moûtier, Fr. F10 10
Saint-Pol-de-Léon, Fr. D3 10
Saint-Pons, Fr. I9 10
Saint-Pourçain-sur-Sioule, Fr. F10 10
Saint-Prime, Que., Can. A5 74
Saint Quentin, N.B., Can. B2 71
Saint-Quentin, Fr. C10 10
Saint-Raphaël, Que., Can. C7 74
Saint-Raphaël, Fr. I13 10
Saint-Raymond, Que., Can. C6 74
Saint-Rédempteur, Que., Can. o17 74
Saint Regis, Mt., U.S. C1 103
Saint Regis, West Branch, stm., N.Y., U.S. f10 109
Saint-Rémi, Que., Can. D4 74
Saint-Romuald, Que., Can. C6 74
Saint Rose, La., U.S. k11 95
Sainte Rose du Lac, Man., Can. D2 70
Saintes, Fr. G6 10
Saint Sauveur, N.B., Can. B4 71
Saint-Sauveur-des-Monts, Que., Can. D3 74
Saint-Sébastien, Cap, c., Madag. D9 44
Saint-Siméon, Que., Can. B8 74
Saint Simons Island, Ga., U.S. E5 87
Saint Simons Island, i., Ga., U.S. E5 87
Saint Stephen, N.B., Can. D2 71
Saint Stephen, S.C., U.S. E8 117
Saint Tammany, co., La., U.S. D5 95
Sainte-Thècle, Que., Can. C5 74
Sainte-Thérèse, Que., Can. D4 74
Saint Thomas, Ont., Can. E3 73
Saint Thomas, i., V.I.U.S. E15 64
Saint Timothée, Que., Can. q18 74
Saint-Tite, Que., Can. C5 74
Saint-Tropez, Fr. I13 10
Saint-Valéry-en-Caux, Fr. C7 10
Saint-Varent, Fr. F6 10
Sainte-Véronique, Que., Can. C3 74
Saint-Victor, Que., Can. C7 74
Saint-Vincent, Cap, c., Madag. F8 44
Saint Vincent, Gulf, b., Austl. F7 50
Saint Vincent and the Grenadines, ctry., N.A. H17 64
Saint Vincent Island, i., Fl., U.S. C1 86
Saint Vincent Passage, strt., N.A. H17 64
Saint Vincent's [-Saint Stephens-Peter's River], Newf., Can. E5 72
Saint-Vith, Bel. E6 8
Saint Walburg, Sask., Can. D1 75
Saint-Zacharie, Que., Can. C7 74
Sairecábur, Cerro, mtn., S.A. A3 56
Saito, Japan J4 30
Saitula, China B8 38
Sajama, Nevado, mtn., Bol. G5 54
Sajia, China F13 38
Sajnšand, Mong. C9 26
Sakai, Japan H8 30
Sakaide, Japan H6 30
Sakai-minato, Japan G6 30
Sakakawea, Lake, res., N.D., U.S. B3 111
Sakami, Lac, l., Que., Can. F17 66
Sakarya, Tur. G14 4
Sakata, Japan D12 30
Sakhalin see Sachalin, Ostrov, i., Russia G22 24
Sākhar, Afg. D1 38
Sakishima-shotō, is., Japan G11 26
Sakon Nakhon, Thai. F8 34
Sakonnet, stm., R.I., U.S. E6 116
Sakonnet Point, c., R.I., U.S. F6 116
Saku, Japan F11 30
Sakurai, Japan H8 30
Sal, Point, c., Ca., U.S. E3 82
Sala, Swe. G11 6
Salaberry-de-Valleyfield, Que., Can. D3 74
Sala Consilina, Italy I10 14
Salado, stm., Arg. C4 56
Salado, Rio, stm., N.M., U.S. C2 108
Ṣalālah, Oman E5 46
Salamanca, Mex. G9 62
Salamanca, Spain E6 12
Salamanca, N.Y., U.S. C2 109
Salamina, Col. E5 58
Salamonie, stm., In., U.S. C6 91
Salamonie Lake, res., In., U.S. C6 91
Salatiga, Indon. m15 33a
Salavat, Russia G9 22
Salawati, i., Indon. F9 32
Saldanha, S. Afr. H3 44
Sale, Austl. G9 50
Sale Creek, Tn., U.S. D8 119
Salem, India G5 37
Salem, Ar., U.S. A4 81
Salem, Il., U.S. E5 90
Salem, In., U.S. G5 91
Salem, Ky., U.S. e9 94
Salem, Ma., U.S. A6 98
Salem, Mo., U.S. D6 102
Salem, N.H., U.S. E4 106
Salem, N.J., U.S. D2 107
Salem, Oh., U.S. B5 112
Salem, Or., U.S. C4 114
Salem, S.D., U.S. D8 118
Salem, Ut., U.S. C4 121
Salem, Va., U.S. C2 123
Salem, W.V., U.S. B4 125
Salem, Wi., U.S. n11 126
Salem, co., N.J., U.S. D2 107
Salem, stm., N.J., U.S. D2 107
Salem Lake, l., Vt., U.S. B4 122
Salemi, Italy L7 14
Sälen, Swe. F9 6
Salerno, Italy I9 14
Salford, Eng., U.K. H10 7
Salgótarján, Hung. G19 8
Sali, Cro. F10 14
Salida, Co., U.S. C5 83

Name Map Ref Page
Salies-de-Béarn, Fr. I6 10
Salihli, Tur. K12 16
Salina, Ks., U.S. D6 93
Salina, Ok., U.S. A6 113
Salina, Ut., U.S. E4 121
Salina Cruz, Mex. I12 62
Salinas, Braz. D7 57
Salinas, Ca., U.S. D3 82
Salinas, stm., Ca., U.S. D3 82
Salinas de Hidalgo, Mex. F9 62
Salinas Peak, mtn., N.M., U.S. D3 108
Salinas Pueblo Missions National Monument, N.M., U.S. C3 108
Saline, Mi., U.S. F7 99
Saline, co., Ar., U.S. C3 81
Saline, co., Il., U.S. F5 90
Saline, co., Ks., U.S. D6 93
Saline, co., Mo., U.S. B4 102
Saline, co., Ne., U.S. D8 104
Saline, stm., Ar., U.S. C1 81
Saline, stm., Ar., U.S. D4 81
Saline, stm., Ks., U.S. C3 93
Saline, North Fork, stm., Il., U.S. F5 90
Saline Lake, res., La., U.S. C3 95
Salineville, Oh., U.S. B5 112
Salisbury, N.B., Can. C4 71
Salisbury, Eng., U.K. J11 7
Salisbury, Ct., U.S. B2 84
Salisbury, Md., U.S. D6 97
Salisbury, Ma., U.S. A6 98
Salisbury, Mo., U.S. B5 102
Salisbury, N.C., U.S. B2 110
Salisbury see Harare, Zimb. E6 44
Salisbury Island, i., N.W. Ter., Can. D17 66
Salisbury Plain, pl., Eng., U.K. J11 7
Salish Mountains, mts., Mt., U.S. B2 103
Salkehatchie, stm., S.C., U.S. E5 117
Ṣalkhad, Syria C5 40
Salles-Curan, Fr. H9 10
Sallisaw, Ok., U.S. B7 113
Salluit, Que., Can. f11 74
Salmo, B.C., Can. E9 69
Salmon, Id., U.S. D5 89
Salmon, stm., N.B., Can. C4 71
Salmon, stm., Id., U.S. D3 89
Salmon Creek, Wa., U.S. D3 124
Salmon Creek Reservoir, res., Id., U.S. G4 89
Salmon Falls, stm., U.S. D5 106
Salmon Falls Creek, stm., U.S. G4 89
Salmon Mountains, mts., Ca., U.S. B2 82
Salmon Point, c., Ont., Can. D7 73
Salmon River Mountains, mts., Id., U.S. E3 89
Salmon River Reservoir, res., N.Y., U.S. B5 109
Salo, Fin. F14 6
Salome, Az., U.S. D2 80
Salon-De-Provence, Fr. I12 10
Salonika see Thessaloníki, Grc. I6 16
Salsomaggiore Terme, Italy E4 14
Salt, stm., Az., U.S. D4 80
Salt, stm., Ky., U.S. C4 94
Salt, stm., Mo., U.S. B6 102
Salta, Arg. A3 56
Salt Creek, stm., N.M., U.S. D5 108
Salt Creek, stm., Oh., U.S. C3 112
Salt Creek, stm., Wy., U.S. C6 127
Salter Path, N.C., U.S. C6 110
Salt Fork Lake, res., Oh., U.S. B4 112
Saltillo, Mex. E9 62
Saltillo, Ms., U.S. A5 101
Salt Lake, co., Ut., U.S. C3 121
Salt Lake, l., Hi., U.S. g10 88
Salt Lake, l., N.M., U.S. E6 108
Salt Lake City, Ut., U.S. C4 121
Salto, Ur. C5 56
Salton Sea, l., Ca., U.S. F5 82
Saltonstall, Lake, l., Ct., U.S. D4 84
Salt Point, c., Ca., U.S. C2 82
Salt River Indian Reservation, Az., U.S. k9 80
Salt River Range, mts., Wy., U.S. D2 127
Saltsburg, Pa., U.S. F3 115
Salt Springs, Fl., U.S. C5 86
Saltville, Va., U.S. f10 123
Salt Wells Creek, stm., Wy., U.S. E4 127
Saluda, S.C., U.S. C4 117
Saluda, co., S.C., U.S. C4 117
Saluda, stm., S.C., U.S. C4 117
Saluda Dam, S.C., U.S. C5 117
Sālūr, India C7 37
Saluzzo, Italy F2 14
Salvador, Braz. B9 57
Salvador, Lake, l., La., U.S. E5 95
Salvatierra, Mex. G9 62
Salween (Nu) (Thanlwin), stm., Asia D5 34
Salyersville, Ky., U.S. C6 94
Salzburg, Aus. H13 8
Salzgitter, Ger. C10 8
Salzwedel, Ger. C11 8
Sama [de Langreo], Spain B6 12
Samaná, Bahía de, b., Dom. Rep. E13 64
Samana Cay, i., Bah. C11 64
Samandağı, Tur. A4 40
Samar, i., Phil. C8 32
Samara, Russia G8 22
Samarai, Pap. N. Gui. n17 50a
Samariapo, Ven. E9 58
Samarinda, Indon. F6 32
Samarkand, Uzb. J11 22
Sāmarrā', Iraq B3 46
Samāstipur, India H11 38
Sambalpur, India J10 38
Sambas, Indon. E4 32
Sambava, Madag. D10 44
Sambhal, India F8 38
Sāmbhar, India G6 38
Samborondón, Ec. H3 58
Sammamish Lake, l., Wa., U.S. e11 124
Samneua, Laos D8 34
Samobor, Cro. D10 14
Sámos, i., Grc. L10 16
Samoset, Fl., U.S. q10 86
Sampit, Indon. F5 32
Sampit, stm., S.C., U.S. E9 117
Sampson, co., N.C., U.S. B4 110
Sam Rayburn Reservoir, res., Tx., U.S. D5 120
Samson, Al., U.S. D3 78
Samsun, Tur. G15 4
Samuels, Id., U.S. A2 89
Samui, Ko, i., Thai. J6 34
Samut Prakan, Thai. H6 34
Samut Sakhon, Thai. H6 34
San, Mali F5 42
San, stm., Eur. E22 8
Şan'ā', Yemen E3 46
Sanaga, stm., Cam. H7 42
San Agustín, Col. G4 58
San Agustin, Cape, c., Phil. D8 32
San Agustin, Plains of, pl., N.M., U.S. C2 108
Sanak Islands, is., Ak., U.S. E7 79
Sanana, Pulau, i., Indon. F8 32
Sanandaj, Iran A4 46
San Andreas, Ca., U.S. C3 82
San Andrés, Isla de, i., Col. H7 64
San Andres Mountains, mts., N.M., U.S. E3 108
San Andres Peak, mtn., N.M., U.S. E3 108
San Andrés Tuxtla, Mex. H12 62
San Angelo, Tx., U.S. D2 120
San Anselmo, Ca., U.S. h7 82
San Antonio, Tx., U.S. E3 120
San Antonio, Cabo, c., Arg. D5 56
San Antonio, Cabo, c., Cuba D5 64
San Antonio Abad, Spain G13 12
San Antonio Bay, b., Tx., U.S. E4 120
San Antonio de Bravo, Mex. B7 62
San Antonio de los Cobres, Arg. A3 56
San Antonio del Táchira, Ven. D6 58
San Antonio Mountain, mtn., N.M., U.S. A3 108
San Antonio Oeste, Arg. E4 56
San Augustine, Tx., U.S. D5 120
San Augustine, co., Tx., U.S. D5 120
San Benedetto del Tronto, Italy G8 14
San Benedicto, Isla, i., Mex. H4 62
San Benito, Guat. F3 64
San Benito, Tx., U.S. F4 120
San Benito, co., Ca., U.S. D3 82
San Benito Mountain, mtn., Ca., U.S. D3 82
San Bernardino, Ca., U.S. E5 82
San Bernardino, co., Ca., U.S. E5 82
San Bernardo, Chile C2 56
San Blas, Mex. G7 62
San Blas, Mex. D5 62
San Blas, Cape, c., Fl., U.S. v16 86
San Borja, Bol. F5 54
Sanborn, Ia., U.S. A2 92
Sanborn, co., S.D., U.S. D7 118
Sanbornville, N.H., U.S. C4 106
San Bruno, Ca., U.S. D2 82
San Carlos, Nic. I5 64
San Carlos, Az., U.S. D5 80
San Carlos, Ca., U.S. k8 82
San Carlos, Ven. C8 58
San Carlos de Bariloche, Arg. E2 56
San Carlos de Guaroa, Col. F6 58
San Carlos de la Rápita, Spain E12 12
San Carlos del Zulia, Ven. C7 58
San Carlos de Río Negro, Ven. G9 58
San Carlos Indian Reservation, Az., U.S. D5 80
San Carlos Lake, res., Az., U.S. D5 80
San Cataldo, Italy L9 14
Sancerre, Fr. E9 10
Sánchez, Mex. D10 62
San Clemente, Ca., U.S. F5 82
San Clemente Island, i., Ca., U.S. F4 82
Sancoins, Fr. F9 10
San Cristóbal, Arg. C4 56
San Cristóbal, Ven. D6 58
San Cristóbal, Volcán, vol., Nic. H4 64
San Cristóbal las Casas, Mex. I13 62
Sancti-Spíritus, Cuba D8 64
Sand, Nor. G6 6
Sandakan, Malay. D6 32
Sanday, i., Scot., U.K. B10 7
Sand Creek, stm., Wy., U.S. C7 127
Sanders, Az., U.S. B6 80
Sanders, co., Mt., U.S. C1 103
Sanderson, Tx., U.S. D1 120
Sandersville, Ga., U.S. D4 87
Sandersville, Ms., U.S. D4 101
Sand Hill, Ma., U.S. h13 98
Sand Hill, stm., Mn., U.S. C2 100
Sandia, Peru F5 54
Sandia Crest, mtn., N.M., U.S. k8 108
Sandia Indian Reservation, N.M., U.S. k7 108
Sandia Mountains, mts., N.M., U.S. k8 108
San Diego, Ca., U.S. F5 82
San Diego, Tx., U.S. F3 120
San Diego, co., Ca., U.S. F5 82
San Diego, stm., Ca., U.S. o15 82
San Diego Naval Station, mil., Ca., U.S. o15 82
San Diego Naval Training Center, mil., Ca., U.S. o15 82
Sand Island, i., Hi., U.S. g10 88
Sand Island, i., Wi., U.S. B3 126
Sand Key, i., Fl., U.S. E4 86
Sandlick Creek, stm., W.V., U.S. n13 125
Sandnes, Nor. G5 6
Sandoa, Zaire C4 44
San Donà di Piave, Italy D7 14
Sandoval, Il., U.S. E4 90
Sandoval, co., N.M., U.S. B2 108
Sandoway, Mya. E3 34
Sand Point, Ak., U.S. D7 79
Sandpoint, Id., U.S. A2 89
Sands Key, i., Fl., U.S. s3 86
Sand Springs, Ok., U.S. A5 113
Sandston, Va., U.S. m18 123
Sandstone, Austl. E3 50
Sandstone, Mn., U.S. D6 100
Sandusky, Mi., U.S. E8 99
Sandusky, Oh., U.S. A3 112
Sandusky, co., Oh., U.S. A2 112
Sandusky, stm., Oh., U.S. B2 112
Sandviken, Swe. F11 6
Sandwich, Il., U.S. B5 90
Sandwich, Ma., U.S. C7 98
Sandwich Bay, b., Newf., Can. B3 72
Sandy, Or., U.S. B4 114
Sandy, Ut., U.S. C4 121
Sandy, stm., Me., U.S. D2 96
Sandy Creek, stm., Oh., U.S. B4 112
Sandy Creek, stm., Ok., U.S. C2 113
Sandy Hook, Ct., U.S. D2 84
Sandy Hook, spit, N.J., U.S. C5 107
Sandy Island, i., S.C., U.S. D9 117
Sandy Lake, l., Newf., Can. D3 72
Sandy Lake, l., Ont., Can. n16 73
Sandy Neck, pen., Ma., U.S. C7 98
Sandy Point, c., R.I., U.S. h7 116
Sandy Springs, Ga., U.S. h8 87
Sandy Springs, S.C., U.S. B2 117
Sandyville, Md., U.S. A4 97
San Felipe, Ven. B8 58
San Felipe Indian Reservation, N.M., U.S. k8 108
San Felipe Pueblo, N.M., U.S. B3 108
San Feliu de Guixols, Spain D15 12
San Fernando, Chile C2 56
San Fernando, Mex. E10 62
San Fernando, Phil. B7 32
San Fernando, Phil. q19 32
San Fernando, Spain I5 12
San Fernando, Trin. I17 64
San Fernando, Ca., U.S. m12 82
San Fernando de Apure, Ven. D9 58
San Fernando de Atabapo, Ven. E9 58
Sanford, Co., U.S. D5 83
Sanford, Fl., U.S. D5 86
Sanford, Me., U.S. E2 96
Sanford, Mi., U.S. E6 99
Sanford, N.C., U.S. B3 110
Sanford, Mount, mtn., Ak., U.S. C11 79
San Francisco, Arg. C4 56
San Francisco, Ca., U.S. D2 82
San Francisco, co., Ca., U.S. D2 82
San Francisco, stm., U.S. D6 80
San Francisco Bay, b., Ca., U.S. h8 82
San Francisco de Borja, Mex. D6 62
San Francisco del Oro, Mex. D7 62
San Francisco del Rincón, Mex. G9 62
San Francisco de Macorís, Dom. Rep. E12 64
San Fratello, Italy K9 14
San Gabriel, Ec. G4 58
San Gabriel, Ca., U.S. *m12 82
San Gabriel Mountains, mts., Ca., U.S. m12 82
Sangamner, India C3 37
Sangamon, co., Il., U.S. D4 90
Sangamon, stm., Il., U.S. C3 90
San Gavino Monreale, Italy J3 14
Sangay, Volcán, vol., Ec. H3 58
Sang-e Māsheh, Afg. D2 38
Sanger, Ca., U.S. D4 82
Sanger, Tx., U.S. C4 120
Sangerhausen, Ger. D11 8
Sangha, stm., Afr. B3 44
Sanghar, Pak. G3 38
Sangihe, Kepulauan, is., Indon. E8 32
Sangihe, Pulau, i., Indon. E8 32
San Gil, Col. D6 58
San Giovanni in Fiore, Italy J11 14
San Giovanni in Persiceto, Italy E6 14
San Giovanni Valdarno, Italy F6 14
Sāngli, India D3 37
Sangolquí, Ec. H3 58
San Gorgonio Mountain, mtn., Ca., U.S. E5 82
San Gregorio, Ur. C5 56
Sangrūr, India E6 38
Sangüesa, Spain C10 12
Sanibel, Fl., U.S. F4 86
Sanibel Island, i., Fl., U.S. F4 86
San Ignacio, Arg. B5 56
San Ignacio, Hond. G4 64
Sanilac, co., Mi., U.S. E8 99
San Isidro, Arg. C5 56
San Isidro, C.R. J6 64
San Jacinto, Col. C5 58
San Jacinto, Ca., U.S. F5 82
San Jacinto, co., Tx., U.S. D5 120
San Jacinto, stm., Tx., U.S. r14 120
Sanjō, Japan E11 30
San Joaquin, co., Ca., U.S. D3 82
San Joaquin, stm., Ca., U.S. D3 82
San Joaquin Valley, val., Ca., U.S. D3 82
San Jorge, Golfo, b., Arg. F3 56
San Jorge, Golfo de, b., Spain E12 12
San José, C.R. J5 64
San Jose, Ca., U.S. D3 82
San José, Isla, i., Mex. E4 62
San José de Chiquitos, Bol. G6 54
San José de Guanipa, Ven. C10 58
San José del Cabo, Mex. F5 62
San José del Guaviare, Col. F6 58
San José de Mayo, Ur. C5 56
San José de Ocuné, Col. E7 58
San José de Raíces, Mex. E9 62
San Jose Island, i., Tx., U.S. E4 120
San Juan, Arg. C3 56
San Juan, Mex. D8 62
San Juan, P.R. E14 64
San Juan, Tx., U.S. F3 120
San Juan, co., Co., U.S. D3 83
San Juan, co., N.M., U.S. A1 108
San Juan, co., Ut., U.S. F5 121
San Juan, co., Wa., U.S. A2 124
San Juan, stm., N.A. I6 64
San Juan Capistrano, Ca., U.S. F5 82
San Juan de Colón, Ven. C6 58
San Juan [de la Maguana], Dom. Rep. E12 64
San Juan del Norte, Nic. I6 64
San Juan de los Cayos, Ven. B8 58
San Juan de los Morros, Ven. C9 58
San Juan del Río, Mex. G9 62
San Juan del Sur, Nic. I5 64
San Juan Island, i., Wa., U.S. A2 124
San Juan Mountains, mts., Co., U.S. D3 83
San Julián, Arg. F3 56
San Justo, Arg. C4 56
Sankt Gallen, Aus. H14 8
Sankt Gallen, Switz. E16 10
Sankt Johann im Pongau, Aus. H13 8
Sankt Moritz, Switz. F16 10
Sankt Peter, Ger. A8 8
Sankt-Peterburg (Saint Petersburg), Russia B13 18
Sankt Pölten, Aus. G15 8
Sankt Veit an der Glan, Aus. I14 8
Sankt Wendel, Ger. F7 8
Sankuru, stm., Zaire B4 44
San Lázaro, Cabo, c., Mex. E3 62
San Leandro, Ca., U.S. h8 82
Şanlıurfa, Tur. H15 4
San Lope, Col. D7 58
San Lorenzo, Arg. C4 56
San Lorenzo, Ec. G3 58
San Lorenzo, Isla, i., Peru F3 54
San Lorenzo de El Escorial, Spain E7 12
San Lorenzo de la Parrilla, Spain F9 12
Sanlúcar de Barrameda, Spain I5 12
San Lucas, Ec. I3 58
San Lucas, Cabo, c., Mex. F5 62
San Luis, Arg. C3 56
San Luis, Cuba D10 64
San Luis, Guat. F3 64
San Luis, Az., U.S. E1 80
San Luis, Co., U.S. D5 83
San Luis, Ven. B8 58
San Luis, Lago de, l., Bol. F6 54
San Luis, Point, c., Ca., U.S. E3 82
San Luis de la Paz, Mex. G9 62
San Luis Obispo, Ca., U.S. E3 82
San Luis Obispo, co., Ca., U.S. E3 82
San Luis Pass, strt., Tx., U.S. r14 120
San Luis Peak, mtn., Co., U.S. D4 83
San Luis Potosí, Mex. F9 62
San Luis Río Colorado, Mex. A2 62
San Luis Valley, val., Co., U.S. D4 83
San Manuel, Az., U.S. E5 80
San Marcos, Col. C5 58
San Marcos, Mex. D8 62
San Marcos, Mex. I10 62
San Marcos, Tx., U.S. E4 120
San Marcos, stm., Tx., U.S. h8 120
San Marino, Ca., U.S. m12 82
San Marino, ctry., Eur. G10 4
San Martín de Valdeiglesias, Spain E7 12
San Mateo, Spain E12 12
San Mateo, Ca., U.S. D2 82
San Mateo, co., Ca., U.S. D2 82
San Mateo Mountains, mts., N.M., U.S. B2 108
San Mateo Mountains, mts., N.M., U.S. D2 108
San Matías, Golfo, b., Arg. E4 56
San Miguel, El Sal. H3 64
San Miguel, co., Co., U.S. D2 83
San Miguel, co., N.M., U.S. B5 108
San Miguel, stm., Bol. F6 54
San Miguel, stm., Co., U.S. C2 83
San Miguel de Allende, Mex. G9 62
San Miguel del Monte, Arg. D5 56
San Miguel de Tucumán, Arg. B3 56
San Miguel el Alto, Mex. G8 62
San Miguel Island, i., Ca., U.S. E3 82
San Miguel Mountains, mts., Co., U.S. D2 83
Sannār, Sudan F12 42
Sannicandro Garganico, Italy H10 14
San Nicolas, Phil. o19 33b
San Nicolás de los Arroyos, Arg. C4 56
San Nicolas Island, i., Ca., U.S. F4 82
Sannikova, Proliv, strt., Russia C21 24
Sanniquellie, Lib. G4 42
Sano, Japan F12 30
Sanok, Pol. F22 8
San Onofre, Col. C5 58
San Pablo, Col. G4 58
San Pablo, Phil. q19 32
San Pablo Balleza, Mex. D6 62
San Pablo Bay, b., Ca., U.S. g8 82
San Patricio, co., Tx., U.S. E4 120
San Pedro, stm., Az., U.S. E5 80
San Pedro, Punta, c., Chile B2 56
San Pedro, Volcán, vol., Chile A3 56
San Pedro Bay, b., Ca., U.S. n12 82
San Pedro Carchá, Guat. G2 64
San Pedro de las Colonias, Mex. E8 62
San Pedro de Macorís, Dom. Rep. E13 64
San Pedro Mártir, Sierra, mts., Mex. B2 62
San Pedro Peaks, mts., N.M., U.S. A3 108
San Pedro Sula, Hond. G4 64
Sanpete, co., Ut., U.S. D4 121
Sanpoil, stm., Wa., U.S. A7 124
San Quintín, Cabo, c., Mex. B1 62
San Rafael, Arg. C3 56
San Rafael, Mex. E9 62
San Rafael, Ca., U.S. D2 82
San Rafael, N.M., U.S. B2 108
San Rafael, stm., Ut., U.S. D5 121
San Rafael Knob, mtn., Ut., U.S. E5 121
San Rafael Mountains, mts., Ca., U.S. E4 82
San Ramón, Nic. G5 64
San Ramon, Ca., U.S. h9 82
San Remo, Italy F2 14
San Saba, Tx., U.S. D3 120
San Saba, co., Tx., U.S. D3 120
San Salvador, El Sal. H3 64
San Salvador (Watling Island), i., Bah. B10 64
San Salvador de Jujuy, Arg. A3 56
Sansanné-Mango, Togo F6 42
San Sebastián, Spain B10 12
Sansepolcro, Italy F7 14
San Severo, Italy H10 14
San Simon, stm., Az., U.S. E6 80
Sanski Most, Bos. E11 14
Santa Ana, Bol. G5 54
Santa Ana, Bol. F5 54
Santa Ana, El Sal. H3 64
Santa Ana, Mex. E9 62
Santa Ana, Mex. B4 62
Santa Ana, Ca., U.S. F5 82
Santa Ana, stm., Ca., U.S. n13 82
Santa Ana Indian Reservation, N.M., U.S. h7 108
Santa Ana Mountains, mts., Ca., U.S. n13 82
Santa Anna, Tx., U.S. D3 120
Santa Bárbara, Mex. D7 62
Santa Barbara, Ca., U.S. E4 82
Santa Barbara, co., Ca., U.S. E3 82
Santa Barbara Channel, strt., Ca., U.S. E3 82
Santa Barbara Island, i., Ca., U.S. F4 82
Santa Catalina, Gulf of, b., Ca., U.S. F5 82
Santa Catalina Island, i., Ca., U.S. F4 82
Santa Catalina Mountains, mts., Az., U.S. E5 80
Santa Catarina, Ilha de, i., Braz. B7 56
Santa Clara, Cuba C8 64
Santa Clara, Ca., U.S. D2 82
Santa Clara, Ut., U.S. F2 121
Santa Clara, co., Ca., U.S. D3 82
Santa Clara, stm., Ca., U.S. E4 82
Santa Claus, In., U.S. H4 91
Santa Coloma de Farnés, Spain D14 12
Santa Comba Dão, Port. E3 12
Santa Cruz, Arg. F3 56
Santa Cruz, Bol. G6 54
Santa Cruz, C.R. I5 64
Santa Cruz, Phil. q19 33b
Santa Cruz, Ca., U.S. D2 82
Santa Cruz, N.M., U.S. B3 108
Santa Cruz, co., Az., U.S. F5 80
Santa Cruz, co., Ca., U.S. D2 82
Santa Cruz, stm., Az., U.S. E4 80
Santa Cruz del Quiché, Guat. G2 64
Santa Cruz de Tenerife, Spain p24 13b
Santa Cruz do Rio Pardo, Braz. G4 57
Santa Cruz Island, i., Ca., U.S. F4 82
Santa Elena, Ec. I2 58
Santa Elena, Punta, c., Ec. I2 58
Santa Eugenia, Spain C2 12
Santa Eulalia, Spain E10 12
Santa Eulalia del Río, Spain G13 12
Santa Fe, Arg. C4 56
Santa Fé, Braz. C3 57
Santa Fé, Cuba D6 64
Santa Fe, Spain H8 12
Santa Fe, N.M., U.S. B4 108
Santa Fe, Tx., U.S. r14 120
Santa Fe, co., N.M., U.S. B3 108
Santa Fe, stm., N.M., U.S. h8 108
Santa Fe Baldy, mtn., N.M., U.S. B4 108
Santa Fe de Bogotá, Col. E5 58
Santa Inés, Isla, i., Chile G2 56
Santa Isabel, Ec. I3 58
Santa Isabel, i., Sol.Is. A11 50
Santa Isabel see Malabo, Eq. Gui. H7 42
Santa Lucia Range, mts., Ca., U.S. E3 82
Santa Magdalena, Isla, i., Mex. E3 62
Santa Margarita, Ca., U.S. E3 82
Santa Margarita, Isla de, i., Mex. E4 62
Santa Maria, Braz. B6 56
Santa Maria, Ca., U.S. E3 82
Santa Maria, stm., Az., U.S. C2 80
Santa Maria, Cabo de, c., Ang. D2 44
Santa Maria do Suaçuí, Braz. E7 57
Santa Maria Mountains, mts., Az., U.S. C3 80
Santa Marta, Col. B5 58
Santa Monica, Ca., U.S. m12 82
Santana do Livramento, Braz. C5 56
Santander, Col. F4 58
Santander, Spain B8 12
Sant' Antioco, Italy J3 14
Santa Paula, Ca., U.S. E4 82
Santaquin, Ut., U.S. D4 121
Sant'Arcangelo, Italy I11 14
Santarém, Braz. D8 54
Santarém, Port. F3 12
Santa Rita, Col. G6 58
Santa Rita, Hond. G4 64
Santa Rosa, Arg. D4 56
Santa Rosa, Arg. C3 56
Santa Rosa, Ec. I3 58
Santa Rosa, Ca., U.S. C2 82
Santa Rosa, N.M., U.S. C5 108
Santa Rosa, co., Fl., U.S. u14 86
Santa Rosa de Cabal, Col. E5 58
Santa Rosa [de Copán], Hond. G3 64
Santa Rosa Island, i., Ca., U.S. F3 82
Santa Rosa Island, i., Fl., U.S. u14 86
Santa Rosa Range, mts., Nv., U.S. B4 105
Šantarskije Ostrova, is., Russia F21 24
Santa Teresa Gallura, Italy H4 14
Santa Vitória do Palmar, Braz. C6 56
Santa Ynez, Ca., U.S. E3 82
Santee, Ca., U.S. o16 82
Santee, stm., S.C., U.S. E8 117
Santee Dam, S.C., U.S. E7 117
Santee Indian Reservation, Ne., U.S. B8 104
Santhià, Italy D3 14
Santiago, Chile C2 56
Santiago, Dom. Rep. E12 64
Santiago, Pan. J7 64
Santiago de Compostela, Spain C3 12
Santiago de Cuba, Cuba D10 64
Santiago del Estero, Arg. B4 56

Name — Map Ref — Page
Santiago do Cacém, Port. G3 12
Santiago Ixcuintla, Mex. G7 62
Santiago Papasquiaro, Mex. E7 62
Santiago Peak, mtn., Ca., U.S. n13 82
Santiago Reservoir, res., Ca., U.S. n13 82
Santiaguillo, Laguna de, l., Mex. E7 62
Santiam Pass, Or., U.S. C4 114
Sāntipur, India I13 38
Santisteban del Puerto, Spain G8 12
Santo Amaro, Braz. B9 57
Santo Anastácio, Braz. F3 57
Santo André, Braz. G5 57
Santo Ângelo, Braz. B6 56
Santo Antônio de Jesus, Braz. B9 57
Santo Antônio do Içá, Braz. D5 54
Santo Domingo, Dom. Rep. E13 64
Santo Domingo, Nic. H5 64
Santo Domingo de la Calzada, Spain C9 12
Santo Domingo de los Colorados, Ec. H3 58
Santo Domingo Indian Reservation, N.M., U.S. h8 108
Santo Domingo Pueblo, N.M., U.S. B3 108
Santoña, Spain B8 12
Santos, Braz. G5 57
Santos Dumont, Braz. F7 57
Santo Tomás, Mex. B1 62
Santo Tomé, Arg. B5 56
San Valentín, Monte, mtn., Chile F2 56
San Vicente, El Sal. H3 64
San Vicente, Mex. B1 62
San Vicente de Baracaldo, Spain B9 12
San Vicente de la Barquera, Spain B7 12
San Vicente del Caguán, Col. F5 58
San Vicente Reservoir, res., Ca., U.S. o16 82
San Xavier Indian Reservation, Az., U.S. E4 80
Sanzao Dao, i., China M2 28
Sanza Pombo, Ang. C3 44
São Bento, Braz. D10 54
São Borja, Braz. B5 56
São Caetano do Sul, Braz. G5 57
São Carlos, Braz. G5 57
São Domingos, Braz. B5 57
São Francisco, stm., Braz. E11 54
São Francisco do Sul, Braz. B7 56
São Gabriel, Braz. E8 57
São João da Boa Vista, Braz. F5 57
São João da Madeira, Port. E3 12
São João del Rei, Braz. F6 57
São Joaquim da Barra, Braz. F5 57
São José do Rio Prêto, Braz. F4 57
São José dos Campos, Braz. G6 57
São Leopoldo, Braz. B6 56
São Lourenço, Braz. G6 57
São Lourenço, Pantanal de, sw., Braz. G7 54
São Luís, Braz. D10 54
São Manuel, Braz. G4 57
São Mateus, Braz. E9 57
Saona, Isla, i., Dom. Rep. E13 64
Saône, stm., Fr. F11 10
São Paulo, Braz. G5 57
São Pedro do Ivaí, Braz. G3 57
São Pedro do Sul, Port. E3 12
São Romão, Braz. D6 57
São Roque, Cabo de, c., Braz. E11 54
São Sebastião, Ponta, c., Moz. F7 44
São Sebastião do Paraíso, Braz. F5 57
São Tomé, S. Tom./P. A1 44
São Tomé, i., S. Tom./P. A1 44
São Tomé, Cabo de, c., Braz. F8 57
Sao Tome and Principe, ctry., Afr. A1 44
São Vicente, Braz. G5 57
São Vicente, Cabo de, c., Port. H2 12
Sapé, Braz. E11 54
Sapele, Nig. G7 42
Sapelo Island, i., Ga., U.S. E5 87
Sapitwa, mtn., Mwi. E7 44
Sappa Creek, stm., U.S. E5 104
Sapphire Mountains, mts., Mt., U.S. D3 103
Sappington, Mo., U.S. f13 102
Sapporo, Japan p19 30a
Sapri, Italy I10 14
Sapulpa, Ok., U.S. B5 113
Sara Buri, Thai. G6 34
Sarajevo, Bos. F2 16
Saraland, Al., U.S. E1 78
Saranac, Mi., U.S. F5 99
Saranac, stm., N.Y., U.S. F11 109
Saranac Lake, N.Y., U.S. f10 109
Saranac Lakes, l., N.Y., U.S. f10 109
Sarangani Islands, is., Phil. D8 32
Saransk, Russia G7 22
Sarapul, Russia F8 22
Sarasota, Fl., U.S. E4 86
Sarasota, co., Fl., U.S. E4 86
Sarasota Bay, b., Fl., U.S. E4 86
Saratoga, Ca., U.S. k8 82
Saratoga, Tx., U.S. D5 120
Saratoga, Wy., U.S. E6 127
Saratoga, co., N.Y., U.S. B7 109
Saratoga Lake, l., N.Y., U.S. C7 109
Saratoga National Historical Park, N.Y., U.S. B7 109
Saratoga Springs, N.Y., U.S. B7 109
Saratov, Russia G7 22
Saravane, Laos G9 34
Sarcoxie, Mo., U.S. D3 102
Sardalas, Libya C8 42
Sardārshahr, India F6 38
Sardegna, i., Italy I3 14
Sardinia see Sardegna, i., Italy I3 14
Sardis, Ga., U.S. D5 87
Sardis, Ms., U.S. A4 101
Sardis Lake, res., Ms., U.S. A4 101
Sar-e Pol, Afg. B1 38
Sarepta, La., U.S. B2 95
Sarera, Teluk, b., Indon. F10 32
Sargent, Ga., U.S. C2 87
Sargent, Ne., U.S. C6 104
Sargent, co., N.D., U.S. C8 111
Sargodha, Pak. D5 38
Sarh, Chad G9 42
Sariñena, Spain D11 12
Şarköy, Tur. I11 16
Sarlat-la-Canéda, Fr. H8 10
Sarmi, Indon. F10 32
Sarmiento, Arg. F3 56
Särna, Swe. F9 6
Sarnia, Ont., Can. E2 73
Sarpy, co., Ne., U.S. C9 104
Sarralbe, Fr. C14 10
Sarrebourg, Fr. D14 10
Sarreguemines, Fr. C14 10
Sarria, Spain C4 12
Sartang, stm., Russia D20 24
Sartell, Mn., U.S. E4 100
Sarthe, stm., Fr. E6 10
Sarufutsu, Japan n20 30a
Sarzeau, Fr. E4 10
Sasarām, India H11 38
Sasebo, Japan I2 30
Saskatchewan, prov., Can. E3 75
Saskatchewan, stm., Can. F12 66
Saskylach, Russia C16 24
Sasovo, Russia G24 18
Sassafras, stm., Md., U.S. B5 97
Sassafras Mountain, mtn., U.S. A2 117
Sassandra, C. Iv. H4 42
Sassandra, stm., C. Iv. G4 42
Sassari, Italy I3 14
Sassnitz, Ger. A13 8
Sassuolo, Italy E5 14
Sastown, Lib. H4 42
Satah Mountain, mtn., B.C., Can. C5 69
Sata-misaki, c., Japan L3 30
Satanta, Ks., U.S. E3 93
Sātāra, India D2 37
Satilla, stm., Ga., U.S. E5 87
Satkānia, Bngl. I15 38
Satna, India H9 38
Sātpura Range, mts., India B4 37
Satsuma, Al., U.S. E1 78
Satsunan-shotō, is., Japan v29 31b
Satu Mare, Rom. B6 16
Šatura, Russia F22 18
Satus Creek, stm., Wa., U.S. C5 124
Sauceda Mountains, mts., Az., U.S. E3 80
Sauda, Nor. G6 6
Saudi Arabia, ctry., Asia D4 46
Saufley Field Naval Air Station, mil., Fl., U.S. u14 86
Saugatuck, Mi., U.S. F4 99
Saugatuck, stm., Ct., U.S. D2 84
Saugatucket, stm., R.I., U.S. F4 116
Saugatuck Reservoir, res., Ct., U.S. D2 84
Saugerties, N.Y., U.S. C7 109
Saugus, Ma., U.S. B5 98
Saugus, stm., Ma., U.S. g11 98
Sauk, co., Wi., U.S. E4 126
Sauk, stm., Mn., U.S. E4 100
Sauk, stm., Wa., U.S. A4 124
Sauk Centre, Mn., U.S. E4 100
Sauk City, Wi., U.S. E4 126
Sauk Rapids, Mn., U.S. E4 100
Saukville, Wi., U.S. E6 126
Saulgau, Ger. G9 8
Saulnierville, N.S., Can. E3 71
Sault-au-Mouton, Que., Can. A8 74
Sault Sainte Marie, Ont., Can. p18 73
Sault Sainte Marie, Mi., U.S. B6 99
Saumarez Reef, rf., Austl. D10 50
Saumur, Fr. E6 10
Saunders, co., Ne., U.S. C9 104
Saunderstown, R.I., U.S. E4 116
Saurimo, Ang. C4 44
Sausalito, Ca., U.S. D2 82
Sava, Italy I12 14
Sava, stm., Eur. E3 16
Savage, Md., U.S. B4 97
Savage, stm., Md., U.S. k12 97
Savage River Reservoir, res., Md., U.S. k12 97
Savanna, Il., U.S. A3 90
Savanna, Ok., U.S. C6 113
Savannah, Ga., U.S. D5 87
Savannah, Mo., U.S. B3 102
Savannah, Tn., U.S. B3 119
Savannah, stm., U.S. F5 117
Savannah River Plant, sci., S.C., U.S. E4 117
Savannakhet, Laos F8 34
Savanna Lake, l., Md., U.S. D6 97
Savanna-la-Mar, Jam. E8 64
Savaştepe, Tur. J11 16
Save (Sabi), stm., Afr. F6 44
Savenay, Fr. E5 10
Saverdun, Fr. I8 10
Saverne, Fr. D14 10
Savigliano, Italy E2 14
Saville Dam, Ct., U.S. B4 84
Savona, Italy E3 14
Savonlinna, Fin. F17 6
Savonranta, Fin. E17 6
Savoonga, Ak., U.S. C5 79
Savoy, Il., U.S. C5 90
Savu Sea see Sawu, Laut, Indon. G7 32
Sawai Mādhopur, India G7 38
Sawākin, Sudan E13 42
Sawang, Indon. N7 34
Sawatch Range, mts., Co., U.S. B4 83
Sawdā', Qurnat as-, mtn., Leb. B5 40
Sawel Mountain, mtn., N. Ire., U.K. G5 7
Sawhāj, Egypt C12 42
Sawknah, Libya C9 42
Sawnee Mountain, mtn., Ga., U.S. B2 87
Sawtooth Mountains, mts., Id., U.S. F4 89
Sawtooth National Recreation Area, Id., U.S. E3 89
Sawu, Laut (Savu Sea), Indon. G7 32
Sawu, Pulau, i., Indon. H7 32
Şawwān, Arḑ aş-, pl., Jord. D5 40
Sawyer, co., Wi., U.S. C2 126
Sawyerville, Que., Can. D6 74
Saxmundham, Eng., U.K. I14 7
Saxonburg, Pa., U.S. E2 115
Saxtons, stm., Vt., U.S. E3 122
Saxtons River, Vt., U.S. E3 122
Sayaboury, Laos E6 34
Sayan Mountains (Sajany), mts., Asia G12 24
Sayaxché, Guat. F2 64
Saybrook, Il., U.S. C5 90
Saybrook Manor, Ct., U.S. D6 84
Şaydā (Sidon), Leb. C4 40
Saydel, Ia., U.S. e8 92
Sayhūt, Yemen E5 46
Saylesville, R.I., U.S. B4 116
Saylorsburg, Pa., U.S. E11 115
Saylorville, Ia., U.S. e8 92
Saylorville Lake, res., Ia., U.S. C4 92
Sayre, Al., U.S. B3 78
Sayre, Ok., U.S. B2 113
Sayre, Pa., U.S. C8 115
Sayreville, N.J., U.S. C4 107
Sayula, Mex. H8 62
Say'ūn, Yemen E4 46
Sayville, N.Y., U.S. n15 109
Scafell Pikes, mtn., Eng., U.K. G9 7
Scalp Level, Pa., U.S. F4 115
Scanlon, Mn., U.S. D6 100
Scapegoat Mountain, mtn., Mt., U.S. C3 103
Ščapino, Russia F25 24
Scappoose, Or., U.S. B4 114
Scarborough, Ont., Can. m15 73
Scarborough, Trin. I17 64
Scarborough, Me., U.S. E2 96
Scarbro, W.V., U.S. n13 125
Scarsdale, N.Y., U.S. h13 109
Ščelkovo, Russia F21 18
Ščerbakovo, Russia D26 24
Schaefferstown, Pa., U.S. F9 115
Schaffhausen, Switz. E15 10
Schaller, Ia., U.S. B2 92
Schaumburg, Il., U.S. h8 90
Schell Creek Range, mts., Nv., U.S. D7 105
Schenectady, N.Y., U.S. C7 109
Schenectady, co., N.Y., U.S. C6 109
Schererville, In., U.S. B3 91
Schertz, Tx., U.S. h7 120
Schiller Park, Il., U.S. k9 90
Schio, Italy D6 14
Schladming, Aus. H13 8
Schleicher, co., Tx., U.S. D2 120
Schleiden, Ger. E6 8
Schleswig, Ger. A9 8
Schleswig, Ia., U.S. B2 92
Schley, co., Ga., U.S. D2 87
Schneverdingen, Ger. B9 8
Schofield, Wi., U.S. D4 126
Schofield Barracks, mil., Hi., U.S. g9 88
Schoharie, co., N.Y., U.S. C6 109
Schoharie Creek, stm., N.Y., U.S. C6 109
Schönebeck, Ger. B13 8
Schongau, Ger. H10 8
Schoodic Lake, l., Me., U.S. C4 96
Schoolcraft, Mi., U.S. F5 99
Schoolcraft, co., Mi., U.S. B4 99
Schramberg, Ger. G8 8
Schrobenhausen, Ger. G11 8
Schroon Lake, l., N.Y., U.S. B7 109
Schulenburg, Tx., U.S. E4 120
Schulter, Ok., U.S. B6 113
Schurz, Nv., U.S. E3 105
Schuyler, Ne., U.S. C8 104
Schuyler, co., Il., U.S. C3 90
Schuyler, co., Mo., U.S. A5 102
Schuyler, co., N.Y., U.S. C4 109
Schuylkill, co., Pa., U.S. E9 115
Schuylkill, stm., Pa., U.S. F10 115
Schuylkill Haven, Pa., U.S. E9 115
Schwabach, Ger. F11 8
Schwaben, hist. reg., Ger. G10 8
Schwäbische Alb, mts., Ger. G9 8
Schwäbisch Gmünd, Ger. G9 8
Schwäbisch Hall, Ger. F9 8
Schwandorf in Bayern, Ger. F12 8
Schwaner, Pegunungan, mts., Indon. F5 32
Schwarzwald, mts., Ger. G8 8
Schwaz, Aus. H11 8
Schwechat, Aus. G16 8
Schwedt, Ger. B14 8
Schweinfurt, Ger. E10 8
Schwerin, Ger. B11 8
Schwyz, Switz. E15 10
Sciacca, Italy L8 14
Scicli, Italy M9 14
Science Hill, Ky., U.S. C5 94
Scilly, Isles of, is., Eng., U.K. L6 7
Scio, Or., U.S. C4 114
Scioto, co., Oh., U.S. D3 112
Scioto, stm., Oh., U.S. B2 112
Scituate, Ma., U.S. B6 98
Scituate Reservoir, res., R.I., U.S. C3 116
Scobey, Mt., U.S. B11 103
Scofield Reservoir, res., Ut., U.S. D4 121
Ščokino, Russia G20 18
Scotch Plains, N.J., U.S. B4 107
Scotia, Ca., U.S. B1 82
Scotia, N.Y., U.S. C7 109
Scotland, Ont., Can. D4 73
Scotland, S.D., U.S. D8 118
Scotland, co., Mo., U.S. A5 102
Scotland, co., N.C., U.S. C3 110
Scotland, ter., U.K. D8 7
Scotland Neck, N.C., U.S. A5 110
Scotlandville, La., U.S. D4 95
Scotrun, Pa., U.S. D11 115
Scotstown, Que., Can. D6 74
Scott, La., U.S. D3 95
Scott, co., Ar., U.S. C1 81
Scott, co., Il., U.S. D3 90
Scott, co., In., U.S. G6 91
Scott, co., Ia., U.S. C7 92
Scott, co., Ks., U.S. D3 93
Scott, co., Ky., U.S. B5 94
Scott, co., Mn., U.S. F5 100
Scott, co., Ms., U.S. C4 101
Scott, co., Mo., U.S. D8 102
Scott, co., Tn., U.S. C9 119
Scott, co., Va., U.S. f9 123
Scott, Cape, c., B.C., Can. D3 69
Scott, Mount, mtn., Or., U.S. E4 114
Scott Air Force Base, mil., Il., U.S. E4 90
Scott City, Ks., U.S. D3 93
Scott City, Mo., U.S. D8 102
Scottdale, Ga., U.S. h8 87
Scottdale, Pa., U.S. F2 115
Scott Islands, is., B.C., Can. F7 66
Scott Mountain, mtn., Id., U.S. E3 89
Scott Peak, mtn., Id., U.S. E6 89
Scott Reef, rf., Austl. B4 50
Scott Reservoir, res., N.C., U.S. A1 110
Scottsbluff, Ne., U.S. C2 104
Scotts Bluff, co., Ne., U.S. C2 104
Scotts Bluff National Monument, Ne., U.S. C2 104
Scottsboro, Al., U.S. A3 78
Scottsburg, In., U.S. G6 91
Scottsdale, Austl. H9 50
Scottsdale, Az., U.S. D4 80
Scottsville, Ky., U.S. D3 94
Scottsville, N.Y., U.S. B3 109
Scottville, Mi., U.S. E4 99
Scourie, Scot., U.K. C7 7
Scraggly Lake, l., Me., U.S. B4 96
Scranton, Ks., U.S. D8 93
Scranton, Pa., U.S. D10 115
Scranton, S.C., U.S. D8 117
Screven, Ga., U.S. E4 87
Screven, co., Ga., U.S. D5 87
Scribner, Ne., U.S. C9 104
Scugog, Lake, l., Ont., Can. C6 73
Scurry, co., Tx., U.S. C2 120
Scutari, Lake, l., Eur. G3 16
Seaboard, N.C., U.S. A5 110
Seabreeze, De., U.S. F5 85
Seabrook, N.H., U.S. E5 106
Seabrook, Tx., U.S. r14 120
Seabrook Island, i., S.C., U.S. F7 117
Seadrift, Tx., U.S. E4 120
Seaford, De., U.S. F3 85
Seaford, Va., U.S. h15 123
Seaforth, Ont., Can. D3 73
Seagoville, Tx., U.S. n10 120
Seagraves, Tx., U.S. C1 120
Seaham, Eng., U.K. G11 7
Sea Isle City, N.J., U.S. E3 107
Seal, stm., Man., Can. E13 66
Seal Cove, Newf., Can. D3 72
Seal Point, c., P.E.I., Can. C5 71
Seal Rock, Or., U.S. C2 114
Sealy, Tx., U.S. E4 120
Seaman, Oh., U.S. D2 112
Seaman Range, mts., Nv., U.S. F6 105
Searchlight, Nv., U.S. H7 105
Searcy, Ar., U.S. B4 81
Searcy, co., Ar., U.S. B3 81
Searles Lake, l., Ca., U.S. E5 82
Searsport, Me., U.S. D4 96
Seaside, Or., U.S. B3 114
Seat Pleasant, Md., U.S. C4 97
Seattle, Wa., U.S. B3 124
Seattle-Tacoma International Airport, Wa., U.S. f11 124
Seaview, Wa., U.S. C1 124
Sebago Lake, Me., U.S. E2 96
Šebalino, Russia G11 24
Sebastian, Fl., U.S. E6 86
Sebastian, co., Ar., U.S. B1 81
Sebastian, Cape, c., Or., U.S. E2 114
Sebastian Inlet, b., Fl., U.S. E6 86
Sebastián Vizcaíno, Bahía, b., Mex. C2 62
Sebasticook Lake, l., Me., U.S. D3 96
Sebec Lake, l., Me., U.S. C3 96
Sebeka, Mn., U.S. D3 100
Sebewaing, Mi., U.S. E7 99
Seboeis, stm., Me., U.S. B4 96
Seboeis Lake, l., Me., U.S. C4 96
Seboomook Lake, l., Me., U.S. C3 96
Sebree, Ky., U.S. C2 94
Sebring, Fl., U.S. E5 86
Sebring, Oh., U.S. B4 112
Secaucus, N.J., U.S. h8 107
Sechelt, B.C., Can. E6 69
Second Lake, l., N.H., U.S. f7 106
Second Mesa, Az., U.S. B5 80
Secret Lake, l., R.I., U.S. E4 116
Section, Al., U.S. A4 78
Security, Co., U.S. C6 83
Sedalia, Mo., U.S. C4 102
Sedan, Fr. C11 10
Sedan, Ks., U.S. E7 93
Sedano, Spain C8 12
Sedgewick, Alta., Can. C5 68
Sedgwick, Mount, mtn., N.M., U.S. B1 108
Sedgwick, Ks., U.S. E6 93
Sedgwick, co., Co., U.S. A8 83
Sedgwick, co., Ks., U.S. E6 93
Sedley, Va., U.S. D6 123
Sedona, Az., U.S. C4 80
Sedro Woolley, Wa., U.S. A3 124
Seeheim, Nmb. G3 44
Seekonk, Ma., U.S. C5 98
Seekonk, stm., R.I., U.S. C4 116
Seeley, Ca., U.S. F6 82
Seeley Lake, Mt., U.S. C3 103
Seelyville, In., U.S. F3 91
Sées, Fr. D7 10
Segamat, Malay. M7 34
Ségou, Mali F4 42
Segovia, Col. D5 58
Segovia, Spain E7 12
Segré, Fr. E6 10
Seguam Island, i., Ak., U.S. E5 79
Seguam Pass, strt., Ak., U.S. E5 79
Séguédine, Niger D8 42
Seguin, Tx., U.S. E4 120
Sehore, India I7 38
Seia, Port. E4 12
Seiling, Ok., U.S. A3 113
Seinäjoki, Fin. E14 6
Seine, stm., Fr. C7 10
Seki, Tur. M13 16
Sekiu, Wa., U.S. A1 124
Sekondi-Takoradi, Ghana H5 42
Šelagskij, Mys, c., Russia C28 24
Selah, Wa., U.S. C5 124
Selaru, Pulau, i., Indon. G9 32
Selatan, Tanjung, c., Indon. F5 32
Selawik, Ak., U.S. B7 79
Selawik Lake, l., Ak., U.S. B7 79
Selayar, Pulau, i., Indon. G7 32
Selb, Ger. E12 8
Selby, S.D., U.S. B5 118
Selbyville, De., U.S. G5 85
Selçuk, Tur. L11 16
Seldovia, Ak., U.S. D9 79
Selemdža, stm., Russia G20 24
Selenn'ach, stm., Russia D21 24
Sélestat, Fr. D14 10
Sélibaby, Maur. E3 42
Šelichova, Zaliv, b., Russia E25 24
Seligman, Az., U.S. B3 80
Selinsgrove, Pa., U.S. E8 115
Selkirk, Man., Can. D3 70
Selkirk, Scot., U.K. F10 7
Selkirk Mountains, mts., N.A. F9 66
Sellersburg, In., U.S. H6 91
Sellersville, Pa., U.S. F11 115
Selles-sur-Cher, Fr. E8 10
Sells, Az., U.S. F4 80
Selma, Al., U.S. C2 78
Selma, Ca., U.S. D4 82
Selma, In., U.S. D7 91
Selma, N.C., U.S. B4 110
Selmer, Tn., U.S. B3 119
Selva, Arg. B4 56
Selvas, for., Braz. E6 54
Selway, stm., Id., U.S. C3 89
Selwyn Mountains, mts., Can. D6 66
Semara, W. Sah. C3 42
Semarang, Indon. m15 32
Semeru, Gunung, vol., Indon. n16 33a
Seminoe Mountains, mts., Wy., U.S. D6 127
Seminoe Reservoir, res., Wy., U.S. D6 127
Seminole, Ok., U.S. B5 113
Seminole, Tx., U.S. C1 120
Seminole, co., Fl., U.S. D5 86
Seminole, co., Ga., U.S. F2 87
Seminole, co., Ok., U.S. B5 113
Seminole, Lake, res., U.S. F2 87
Semipalatinsk, Kaz. G10 24
Semisopochnoi Island, i., Ak., U.S. E3 79
Semmes, Al., U.S. E1 78
Šemonaicha, Kaz. G10 24
Semur-en-Auxois, Fr. E11 10
Sên, stm., Camb. H8 34
Sena, Moz. E6 44
Senachwine Lake, l., Il., U.S. B4 90
Senador Pompeu, Braz. E11 54
Sena Madureira, Braz. E5 54
Senanga, Zam. E4 44
Senath, Mo., U.S. E7 102
Senatobia, Ms., U.S. A4 101
Sendai, Japan K3 30
Sendai, Japan D13 30
Seneca, Il., U.S. B5 90
Seneca, Ks., U.S. C7 93
Seneca, Mo., U.S. E3 102
Seneca, Pa., U.S. D2 115
Seneca, S.C., U.S. B2 117
Seneca, co., N.Y., U.S. C4 109
Seneca, co., Oh., U.S. A2 112
Seneca Falls, N.Y., U.S. C4 109
Seneca Lake, l., N.Y., U.S. C4 109
Senecaville Lake, res., Oh., U.S. C4 112
Senegal (Sénégal), ctry., Afr. F3 42
Sénégal, stm., Afr. E3 42
Senekal, S. Afr. G5 44
Senftenberg, Ger. D13 8
Senigallia, Italy F8 14
Senise, Italy I11 14
Senmonorom, Camb. H9 34
Senneterre, Que., Can. k11 74
Sennori, Italy I3 14
Senoia, Ga., U.S. C2 87
Sens, Fr. D10 10
Senta, Yugo. D4 16
Sentinel, Ok., U.S. B2 113
Seo de Urgel, Spain C13 12
Seoni, India I8 38
Seoul see Sŏul, S. Kor. D12 26
Sept-Îles (Seven Islands), Que., Can. h13 74
Sepulga, stm., Al., U.S. D3 78
Sepúlveda, Spain D8 12
Sequatchie, co., Tn., U.S. D8 119
Sequatchie, stm., Tn., U.S. D8 119
Sequim, Wa., U.S. A2 124
Sequoia National Park, Ca., U.S. D4 82
Sequoyah, co., Ok., U.S. B7 113
Seraing, Bel. E5 8
Seram, i., Indon. F8 32
Seram, Laut (Ceram Sea), Indon. F8 32
Serang, Indon. m13 33a
Seremban, Malay. M6 34
Serengeti Plain, pl., Tan. B6 44
Serenje, Zam. D6 44
Sergeant Bluff, Ia., U.S. B1 92
Sergeja Kirova, Ostrova, is., Russia B11 24
Sergijev Posad, Russia E21 18
Serowe, Bots. F5 44
Serpa, Port. H4 12
Serpuchov, Russia G20 18
Sérrai, Grc. H7 16
Serra San Bruno, Italy K11 14
Serra Talhada, Braz. E11 54
Serres, Fr. H12 10
Serrezuela, Arg. C3 56

Name — Map Ref — Page

Serri, Italy J4 14
Serrinha, Braz. F11 54
Sertã, Port. F3 12
Sesfontein, Nmb. E2 44
Sesheke, Zam. E4 44
Sessa Aurunca, Italy H8 14
Sesser, Il., U.S. E4 90
Sestri Levante, Italy E4 14
Sète, Fr. I10 10
Sete Lagoas, Braz. E6 57
Seth, W.V., U.S. C3 125
Sétif, Alg. A7 42
Seto, Japan G10 30
Seto-naikai, Japan H6 30
Setúbal, Port. G3 12
Seul, Lac, l., Ont., Can. o16 73
Seul Choix Point, c., Mi., U.S. C5 99
Sevan, ozero, l., Arm. I7 22
Sevastopol', Ukr. I4 22
Seven Devils Lake, res., Ar., U.S. D4 81
Seven Devils Mountains, mts., Id., U.S. D2 89
Seven Hills, Oh., U.S. h9 112
Seven Mile Beach, N.J., U.S. E3 107
Sévérac-le-Château, Fr. H10 10
Severn, Md., U.S. B4 97
Severn, stm., Ont., Can. n17 73
Severn, stm., Eng., U.K. J10 7
Severnaja Dvina, stm., Russia E6 22
Severnaja Zemľa, is., Russia B13 24
Severna Park, Md., U.S. B4 97
Severn River, b., Md., U.S. B4 97
Severodvinsk, Russia E5 22
Severo-Kuril'sk, Russia G25 24
Severo-Sibirskaja Nizmennosť, pl., Russia C13 24
Severo-Zadonsk, Russia G21 18
Sevettijärvi, Fin. B17 6
Sevier, co., Ar., U.S. D1 81
Sevier, co., Tn., U.S. D10 119
Sevier, co., Ut., U.S. E4 121
Sevier, stm., Ut., U.S. D3 121
Sevier Bridge Reservoir, res., Ut., U.S. D4 121
Sevier Lake, l., Ut., U.S. E2 121
Sevierville, Tn., U.S. D10 119
Sevilla, Col. E5 58
Sevilla, Spain H6 12
Seville, Oh., U.S. A4 112
Seville see Sevilla, Spain H6 12
Sewanee, Tn., U.S. D8 119
Seward, Ak., U.S. C10 79
Seward, Ne., U.S. D8 104
Seward, co., Ks., U.S. E3 93
Seward, co., Ne., U.S. D8 104
Seward Peninsula, pen., Ak., U.S. B7 79
Sewickley, Pa., U.S. E1 115
Sexsmith, Alta., Can. B1 68
Seychelles, ctry., Afr. B11 44
Seydisfjördur, Ice. B5 4
Seymour, Ct., U.S. D3 84
Seymour, In., U.S. G6 91
Seymour, Ia., U.S. D4 92
Seymour, Mo., U.S. D5 102
Seymour, Tx., U.S. C3 120
Seymour, Wi., U.S. D5 126
Seymour Inlet, b., B.C., Can. D4 69
Seymour Johnson Air Force Base, mil., N.C., U.S. B5 110
Seymour Lake, l., Vt., U.S. B4 122
Seymourville, La., U.S. h9 95
Seyne, Fr. H13 10
Seyssel, Fr. G12 10
Sézanne, Fr. D10 10
Sezze, Italy H8 14
Sfax, Tun. B8 42
's-Gravenhage (The Hague), Neth. C4 8
Shabbona, Il., U.S. B5 90
Shache, China A7 38
Shackelford, co., Tx., U.S. C3 120
Shackleton Ice Shelf, Ant. C22 47
Shaddādī, Syria A7 40
Shadehill Dam, S.D., U.S. B3 118
Shadehill Reservoir, res., S.D., U.S. B3 118
Shadow Mountain National Recreation Area, Co., U.S. A4 83
Shady Cove, Or., U.S. E4 114
Shady Side, Md., U.S. C4 97
Shadyside, Oh., U.S. C5 112
Shady Spring, W.V., U.S. D3 125
Shafer, Lake, l., In., U.S. C4 91
Shafer Butte, mtn., Id., U.S. F2 80
Shafter, Ca., U.S. E4 82
Shaftsbury, Vt., U.S. E2 122
Shāhdādkot, Pak. G2 38
Shahdol, India I9 38
Shāhjahānpur, India G8 38
Shāh Juy, Afg. D2 38
Shahrak, Afg. C1 38
Shājāpur, India I7 38
Shakawe, Bots. E4 44
Shaker Heights, Oh., U.S. A4 112
Shakhty see Šachty, Russia H6 22
Shaki, Nig. G6 42
Shakopee, Mn., U.S. F5 100
Shaler Mountains, mts., N.W. Ter., Can. B10 66
Shallotte, N.C., U.S. D4 110
Shallotte Inlet, b., N.C., U.S. D4 110
Shallowater, Tx., U.S. C2 120
Shām, Bādiyat ash-, des., Asia C6 40
Shām, Jabal ash-, mtn., Oman D6 46
Shamokin, Pa., U.S. E8 115
Shamokin Dam, Pa., U.S. E8 115
Shamrock, Tx., U.S. B2 120
Shandī, Sudan E12 42
Shandong, prov., China D10 26
Shandong Bandao, pen., China D11 26
Shanghai, China D11 26
Shanghai Shih, China E11 26
Shangqiu, China A4 28
Shangrao, China G6 28
Shangshui, China B3 28
Shangzhi, China B12 26
Shannock, R.I., U.S. F2 116
Shannon, Ga., U.S. B1 87
Shannon, Il., U.S. A4 90
Shannon, Ms., U.S. A5 101
Shannon, co., Mo., U.S. D6 102
Shannon, co., S.D., U.S. D3 118
Shannon, stm., Ire. I3 7
Shannon, Lake, l., Wa., U.S. A4 124
Shannontown, S.C., U.S. D7 117
Shantou (Swatow), China L5 28
Shantung Peninsula see Shandong Bandao, pen., China D11 26
Shănxī, prov., China D8 26
Shānxī, prov., China D9 26
Shanyin, China D9 26
Shaoguan, China K2 28
Shaowu, China H6 28
Shaoxing, China E9 28
Shaoyang, China F9 26
Shark Bay, b., Austl. E2 50
Sharkey, co., Ms., U.S. C3 101
Shark Point, c., Fl., U.S. H5 86
Sharktooth Mountain, mtn., B.C., Can. E7 66
Sharon, Ct., U.S. B2 84
Sharon, Ma., U.S. B5 98
Sharon, Pa., U.S. D1 115
Sharon, Tn., U.S. A3 119
Sharon, Wi., U.S. F5 126
Sharon Hill, Pa., U.S. p20 115
Sharon Park, Oh., U.S. n12 112
Sharon Springs, Ks., U.S. D2 93
Sharonville, Oh., U.S. n13 112
Sharp, co., Ar., U.S. A4 81
Sharpe, Lake, res., S.D., U.S. C6 118
Sharpes, Fl., U.S. D6 86
Sharpley, De., U.S. h7 85
Sharpsburg, Md., U.S. B2 97
Sharpsburg, N.C., U.S. B5 110
Sharpsburg, Pa., U.S. k14 115
Sharpsville, In., U.S. D5 91
Sharpsville, Pa., U.S. D1 115
Sharptown, Md., U.S. C6 97
Sharqīyah, Aş-Şahrā' ash- (Arabian Desert), des., Egypt C12 42
Shashi, China E9 26
Shashi, stm., Afr. F5 44
Shasta, co., Ca., U.S. B3 82
Shasta, Mount, vol., Ca., U.S. B2 82
Shasta Lake, res., Ca., U.S. B2 82
Shattuck, Ok., U.S. A2 113
Shaw, Ms., U.S. B3 101
Shaw Air Force Base, mil., S.C., U.S. D7 117
Shawano, Wi., U.S. D5 126
Shawano, co., Wi., U.S. D5 126
Shawano Lake, l., Wi., U.S. D5 126
Shawinigan, Que., Can. C5 74
Shawinigan-Sud, Que., Can. C5 74
Shawnee, Ks., U.S. k16 93
Shawnee, Ok., U.S. B5 113
Shawnee, co., Ks., U.S. D8 93
Shawneetown, Il., U.S. F5 90
Shawsheen, stm., Ma., U.S. f11 98
Shaybārā, i., Sau. Ar. C2 46
Shaykh, Jabal ash-, mtn., Asia C4 40
Shebele (Shebelle), stm., Afr. G3 46
Sheberghān, Afg. B1 38
Sheboygan, Wi., U.S. E6 126
Sheboygan, co., Wi., U.S. E6 126
Sheboygan, stm., Wi., U.S. k10 126
Sheboygan Falls, Wi., U.S. E6 126
Shediac, N.B., Can. C5 71
Sheenjek, stm., Ak., U.S. B11 79
Sheep Mountain, mtn., Az., U.S. E1 80
Sheep Mountain, mtn., Wy., U.S. B5 127
Sheep Mountain, mtn., Wy., U.S. C2 127
Sheep Peak, mtn., Nv., U.S. G6 105
Sheep Range, mts., Nv., U.S. G6 105
Sheet Harbour, N.S., Can. E7 71
Sheffield, Eng., U.K. H11 7
Sheffield, Al., U.S. A2 78
Sheffield, Il., U.S. B4 90
Sheffield, Ia., U.S. B4 92
Sheffield, Pa., U.S. C3 115
Sheffield Lake, Oh., U.S. A3 112
Sheila, N.B., Can. B5 71
Shekhābād, Afg. C3 38
Shekhūpura, Pak. E5 38
Shelagyote Peak, mtn., B.C., Can. B4 69
Shelbiana, Ky., U.S. C7 94
Shelbina, Mo., U.S. B5 102
Shelburn, In., U.S. F3 91
Shelburne, Ont., Can. C4 73
Shelburne Falls, Ma., U.S. A2 98
Shelburne Pond, l., Vt., U.S. C2 122
Shelby, Al., U.S. B3 78
Shelby, In., U.S. B3 91
Shelby, Ia., U.S. C2 92
Shelby, Mi., U.S. E4 99
Shelby, Ms., U.S. B3 101
Shelby, Mt., U.S. B5 103
Shelby, Ne., U.S. C8 104
Shelby, N.C., U.S. B1 110
Shelby, Oh., U.S. B3 112
Shelby, co., Al., U.S. B3 78
Shelby, co., Il., U.S. D5 90
Shelby, co., In., U.S. E6 91
Shelby, co., Ia., U.S. C2 92
Shelby, co., Ky., U.S. B4 94
Shelby, co., Mo., U.S. B5 102
Shelby, co., Oh., U.S. B1 112
Shelby, co., Tn., U.S. B2 119
Shelby, co., Tx., U.S. D5 120
Shelbyville, Il., U.S. D5 90
Shelbyville, In., U.S. F6 91
Shelbyville, Ky., U.S. B4 94
Shelbyville, Tn., U.S. B5 119
Shelbyville, Lake, res., Il., U.S. D5 90
Sheldon, Il., U.S. C6 90
Sheldon, Ia., U.S. A2 92
Sheldon, Tx., U.S. r14 120
Shelikof Strait, strt., Ak., U.S. D9 79
Shell Creek, stm., U.S. A2 83
Shell Creek, stm., Wy., U.S. B5 127
Shelley, Id., U.S. F6 89
Shell Lake, Wi., U.S. C2 126
Shell Lake, l., Mn., U.S. D3 100
Shell Lake, l., Wi., U.S. C2 126
Shellman, Ga., U.S. E2 87
Shell Rock, Ia., U.S. B5 92
Shell Rock, stm., Ia., U.S. B5 92
Shellsburg, Ia., U.S. B6 92
Shelly Mountain, mtn., Id., U.S. F5 89
Shelter Island, N.Y., U.S. m16 109
Shelton, Ct., U.S. D3 84
Shelton, Ne., U.S. D7 104
Shelton, Wa., U.S. B2 124
Shemya Air Force Base, mil., Ak., U.S. E2 79
Shenandoah, Ia., U.S. D2 92
Shenandoah, Pa., U.S. E9 115
Shenandoah, Va., U.S. B4 123
Shenandoah, co., Va., U.S. B4 123
Shenandoah, stm., U.S. A5 123
Shenandoah, North Fork, stm., Va., U.S. B4 123
Shenandoah, South Fork, stm., Va., U.S. B4 123
Shenandoah Mountain, mtn., U.S. B3 123
Shenandoah National Park, Va., U.S. B4 123
Shenango River Lake, res., U.S. D1 115
Shengfang, China D10 26
Shengze, China E9 28
Shenipsit Lake, l., Ct., U.S. B6 84
Shenyang (Mukden), China C11 26
Shenzha, China E13 38
Shepaug, stm., Ct., U.S. C2 84
Shepaug Dam, Ct., U.S. D2 84
Shepaug Reservoir, res., Ct., U.S. C2 84
Shepherd, Mi., U.S. E6 99
Shepherd, Tx., U.S. D5 120
Shepherdstown, W.V., U.S. B7 125
Shepherdsville, Ky., U.S. C4 94
Sheppard Air Force Base, mil., Tx., U.S. C3 120
Shepparton, Austl. G9 50
Sherborn, Ma., U.S. h10 98
Sherbro Island, i., S.L. G3 42
Sherbrooke, Que., Can. D6 74
Sherburn, Mn., U.S. G4 100
Sherburne, co., Mn., U.S. E5 100
Sheridan, Ar., U.S. C3 81
Sheridan, Il., U.S. B5 90
Sheridan, In., U.S. D5 91
Sheridan, Mi., U.S. E5 99
Sheridan, Mt., U.S. E4 103
Sheridan, Or., U.S. B3 114
Sheridan, Wy., U.S. B6 127
Sheridan, co., Ks., U.S. C3 93
Sheridan, co., Mt., U.S. B12 103
Sheridan, co., Ne., U.S. B3 104
Sheridan, co., N.D., U.S. B5 111
Sheridan, co., Wy., U.S. B5 127
Sheridan, Mount, mtn., Wy., U.S. B2 127
Sheringham Cromer, Eng., U.K. I14 7
Sherman, Tx., U.S. C4 120
Sherman, co., Ks., U.S. C2 93
Sherman, co., Ne., U.S. C6 104
Sherman, co., Or., U.S. B6 114
Sherman, co., Tx., U.S. A2 120
Sherman Reservoir, res., Ne., U.S. C7 104
Sherrelwood, Co., U.S. *B6 83
Sherrill, N.Y., U.S. B5 109
's-Hertogenbosch, Neth. D5 8
Sherwood, P.E.I., Can. C6 71
Sherwood, Ar., U.S. C3 81
Sherwood, Or., U.S. h12 114
Sherwood, Wi., U.S. h9 126
Sherwood Manor, Ct., U.S. A5 84
Sherwood Park, De., U.S. i7 85
Shetek, Lake, l., Mn., U.S. G3 100
Shetland Islands, is., Scot., U.K. A11 7
Shetucket, stm., Ct., U.S. C7 84
Sheyenne, stm., N.D., U.S. C8 111
Sheyenne Lake, res., N.D., U.S. B5 111
Shiawassee, co., Mi., U.S. F6 99
Shibata, Japan E12 30
Shibetsu, Japan p23 30a
Shibukawa, Japan F11 30
Shickshinny, Pa., U.S. D9 115
Shijiazhuang, China D9 26
Shijushan, China D8 26
Shikārpur, Pak. G3 38
Shikohābād, India G8 38
Shikoku, i., Japan I6 30
Shikoku-sanchi, mts., Japan I6 30
Shikotsu-ko, l., Japan q19 30a
Shillington, Pa., U.S. F10 115
Shillong, India H14 38
Shiloh National Military Park, Tn., U.S. B3 119
Shilong, China L2 28
Shimabara, Japan J3 30
Shimada, Japan H11 30
Shimbiris, mtn., Som. F4 46
Shimizu, Japan G11 30
Shimminato, Japan F10 30
Shimodate, Japan F12 30
Shimoga, India F3 37
Shimonoseki, Japan I3 30
Shinano, stm., Japan E11 30
Shīndand, Afg. C1 36
Shiner, Tx., U.S. E4 120
Shinglehouse, Pa., U.S. C5 115
Shingū, Japan I8 30
Shinjō, Japan D13 30
Shinnston, W.V., U.S. B4 125
Shinshār, Syria B5 40
Shinyanga, Tan. B6 44
Shiocton, Wi., U.S. D5 126
Shiogama, Japan D14 30
Shiojiri, Japan F10 30
Shiping, China C7 34
Ship Island, i., Ms., U.S. E5 101
Ship Island Pass, strt., Ms., U.S. g7 101
Shippegan, N.B., Can. B5 71
Shippensburg, Pa., U.S. F6 115
Shiprock, N.M., U.S. A1 108
Ship Rock, mtn., N.M., U.S. A1 108
Shirakawa, Japan E13 30
Shīrāz, Iran C5 46
Shire, stm., Afr. E6 44
Shiretoko-misaki, c., Japan o23 30a
Shirley, In., U.S. E6 91
Shirley, Ma., U.S. A4 98
Shirley Mountains, mts., Wy., U.S. D6 127
Shirpur, India B3 37
Shishaldin Volcano, vol., Ak., U.S. E7 79
Shishmaref, Ak., U.S. B6 79
Shively, Ky., U.S. B4 94
Shivpuri, India H7 38
Shizuoka, Japan H11 30
Shkodër, Alb. G3 16
Shoal Creek, stm., U.S. B4 119
Shoal Harbour, Newf., Can. D4 72
Shoal Lake, Man., Can. D1 70
Shoals, In., U.S. G4 91
Shoals, Isles of, is., Me., U.S. E2 96
Shoalwater, Cape, c., Wa., U.S. C1 124
Shōdo-shima, i., Japan H7 30
Shoemakersville, Pa., U.S. F10 115
Sholāpur, India D3 37
Shongopovi, Az., U.S. B5 80
Shonto, Az., U.S. A5 80
Shoreham, Mi., U.S. F4 99
Shores Acres, R.I., U.S. E4 116
Shoreview, Mn., U.S. m12 100
Shorewood, Il., U.S. k8 90
Shorewood, Mn., U.S. n11 100
Shorewood, Wi., U.S. E6 126
Short Beach, Ct., U.S. D4 84
Shoshone, Id., U.S. G4 89
Shoshone, co., Id., U.S. B2 89
Shoshone, stm., Wy., U.S. B4 127
Shoshone Falls, wtfl., Id., U.S. G4 89
Shoshone Lake, l., Wy., U.S. B2 127
Shoshone Mountains, mts., Nv., U.S. E4 105
Shoshone Peak, mtn., Nv., U.S. G5 105
Shoshone Range, mts., Nv., U.S. C5 105
Shoshong, Bots. F5 44
Shoshoni, Wy., U.S. C4 127
Shoup, Id., U.S. D4 89
Shouxian, China C5 28
Show Low, Az., U.S. C5 80
Shreve, Oh., U.S. B3 112
Shreveport, La., U.S. B2 95
Shrewsbury, Eng., U.K. I10 7
Shrewsbury, Ma., U.S. B4 98
Shrewsbury, N.J., U.S. C4 107
Shrewsbury, Pa., U.S. G8 115
Shuajingsi, China E7 26
Shuangcheng, China B12 26
Shuangyashan, China B13 26
Shubenacadie, N.S., Can. D6 71
Shuksan, Mount, mtn., Wa., U.S. A4 124
Shullsburg, Wi., U.S. F3 126
Shumagin Islands, is., Ak., U.S. E7 79
Shunde, China M2 28
Shungnak, Ak., U.S. B8 79
Shuqrā', Yemen F4 46
Shūshtar, Iran B4 46
Shuswap Lake, l., B.C., Can. D8 69
Shwebo, Mya. C3 34
Siaksriinderapura, Indon. N7 34
Siālkot, Pak. D6 38
Siam, Gulf of see Thailand, Gulf of, b., Asia J6 34
Sian see Xi'an, China E8 26
Siargao Island, i., Phil. D8 32
Šiaškotan, Ostrov, i., Russia H24 24
Šiauliai, Lith. F6 18
Šibenik, Cro. F10 14
Siberia see Sibir', reg., Russia D16 24
Siberut, Pulau, i., Indon. F2 32
Sibi, Pak. F2 38
Sibir' (Siberia), reg., Russia D16 24
Sibir'akova, Ostrov, i., Russia C9 24
Sibiti, Congo B2 44
Sibiu, Rom. D8 16
Sibley, Ia., U.S. A2 92
Sibley, La., U.S. B2 95
Sibley, co., Mn., U.S. F4 100
Sibolga, Indon. E2 32
Sibsāgar, India G16 38
Sibu, Malay. E5 32
Sibutu Island, i., Phil. E6 32
Sibuyan Island, i., Phil. C7 32
Sibuyan Sea, Phil. C7 32
Sicamous, B.C., Can. D8 69
Sichote-Alin', mts., Russia H21 24
Sichuan, prov., China E7 26
Sicié, Cap, c., Fr. I12 10
Sicilia, i., Italy L9 14
Sicily, Strait of, strt. L7 14
Sicily see Sicilia, i., Italy L9 14
Sico, stm., Hond. G5 64
Sicuani, Peru F4 54
Siddipet, India C5 37
Siderno, Italy K11 14
Sidhpur, India I5 38
Sidi bel Abbès, Alg. A5 42
Sidi Ifni, Mor. C3 42
Sidmouth, Eng., U.K. K9 7
Sidney, B.C., Can. E6 69
Sidney, Il., U.S. C5 90
Sidney, Ia., U.S. D2 92
Sidney, Mt., U.S. C12 103
Sidney, Ne., U.S. C3 104
Sidney, N.Y., U.S. C5 109
Sidney, Oh., U.S. B1 112
Sidney Lanier, Lake, res., Ga., U.S. B2 87
Sidon see Şaydā, Leb. C4 40
Sidra, Gulf of see Surt, Khalīj, b., Libya B9 42
Siedlce, Pol. C22 8
Siegburg, Ger. E7 8
Siegen, Ger. E8 8
Siěmréab, Camb. H7 34
Siena, Italy F6 14
Sierra, co., Ca., U.S. C3 82
Sierra, co., N.M., U.S. D2 108
Sierra Blanca Peak, mtn., N.M., U.S. D4 108
Sierra Colorada, Arg. E3 56
Sierra Estrella, mts., Az., U.S. m8 80
Sierra Leone, ctry., Afr. G3 42
Sierra Madre, Ca., U.S. m12 82
Sierra Vista, Az., U.S. F5 80
Sierre, Switz. F14 10
Siesta Key, i., Fl., U.S. E4 86
Sighetul Marmației, Rom. B7 16
Sighișoara, Rom. C8 16
Siglufjördur, Ice. B4 4
Signal Mountain, Tn., U.S. D8 119
Signal Peak, mtn., Az., U.S. D1 80
Signal Peak, mtn., Ut., U.S. F2 121
Signy-l'Abbaye, Fr. C11 10
Sigourney, Ia., U.S. C5 92
Sigüenza, Spain D9 12
Sigües, Spain C10 12
Siguiri, Gui. F4 42
Siilinjärvi, Fin. E16 6
Si-Kacha, Thai. H6 34
Sīkar, India G6 38
Sikasso, Mali F4 42
Sikeston, Mo., U.S. E8 102
Sikiá, Grc. I7 16
Síkinos, Grc. M9 16
Sikkim, state, India G13 38
Šikotan, Ostrov (Shikotan-tō), i., Russia I23 24
Sikt'ach, Russia D19 24
Silandro, Italy C5 14
Silao, Mex. G9 62
Silay, Phil. C7 32
Silba, Cro. E9 14
Silchar, India H15 38
Siler City, N.C., U.S. B3 110
Silesia, hist. reg., Pol. E16 8
Siletz, Or., U.S. C3 114
Silifke, Tur. A3 40
Silīguri, India G13 38
Siling Co, l., China E13 38
Silistra, Bul. E11 16
Šilka, Russia G18 24
Šilka, stm., Russia G17 24
Silkeborg, Den. H7 6
Sillamäe, Est. B10 18
Sillé-le-Guillaume, Fr. D6 10
Sillery, Que., Can. n17 74
Sillon de Talbert, pen., Fr. D3 10
Siloam Springs, Ar., U.S. A1 81
Silsbee, Tx., U.S. D5 120
Silt, Co., U.S. B3 83
Silvânia, Braz. G9 54
Silvassa, India B2 37
Silver Bay, Mn., U.S. C7 100
Silver Bow, co., Mt., U.S. E4 103
Silver City, Nv., U.S. D2 105
Silver City, N.M., U.S. E1 108
Silver Creek, Ne., U.S. C8 104
Silver Creek, N.Y., U.S. C1 109
Silver Creek, stm., Or., U.S. D7 114
Silverdale, Wa., U.S. B3 124
Silver Grove, Ky., U.S. h14 94
Silver Hill, Md., U.S. f9 97
Silver Lake, Ks., U.S. C8 93
Silver Lake, Ma., U.S. f11 98
Silver Lake, Mn., U.S. F4 100
Silver Lake, Wi., U.S. F5 126
Silver Lake, l., De., U.S. D3 85
Silver Lake, l., Ia., U.S. A3 92
Silver Lake, l., Me., U.S. C3 96
Silver Lake, l., N.H., U.S. E2 106
Silver Lake, l., N.H., U.S. C4 106
Silver Lake, l., Or., U.S. D7 114
Silver Lake, l., Wa., U.S. g13 124
Silverpeak, Nv., U.S. F4 105
Silver Peak Range, mts., Nv., U.S. F4 105
Silver Spring, Md., U.S. C3 97
Silver Springs, Nv., U.S. D2 105
Silver Star Mountain, mtn., Wa., U.S. A5 124
Silverthrone Mountain, mtn., B.C., Can. D4 69
Silvertip Mountain, mtn., Mt., U.S. C3 103
Silverton, Co., U.S. D3 83
Silverton, Id., U.S. B3 89
Silverton, N.J., U.S. C4 107
Silverton, Oh., U.S. o13 112
Silverton, Or., U.S. C4 114
Silvi, Italy G9 14
Silvies, stm., Or., U.S. D7 114
Silview, De., U.S. B3 85
Silvis, Il., U.S. B3 90
Simanggang, Malay. E5 32
Šimanovsk, Russia G19 24
Simav, Tur. J12 16
Simcoe, Ont., Can. F4 73
Simcoe, Lake, l., Ont., Can. C5 73
Simeulue, Pulau, i., Indon. M3 34
Simferopol', Ukr. I4 22
Simi Valley, Ca., U.S. E4 82
Simla, India E7 38
Simmesport, La., U.S. D4 95
Simms Stream, stm., N.H., U.S. g7 100
Simojovel [de Allende], Mex. I13 62
Simonette, stm., Alta., Can. B1 68
Simplon Pass, Switz. F15 10
Simpson, Pa., U.S. C11 115
Simpson, co., Ky., U.S. D3 94
Simpson, co., Ms., U.S. D4 101
Simpson Creek, stm., W.V., U.S. k10 125
Simpson Desert, des., Austl. D7 50
Simpson Peninsula, pen., N.W. Ter., Can. C15 66
Simpsonville, Ky., U.S. B4 94
Simpsonville, S.C., U.S. B3 117
Simsboro, La., U.S. B3 95
Simsbury, Ct., U.S. B4 84
Simušir, Ostrov, i., Russia H24 24
Sīnā', Shibh Jazīrat (Sinai Peninsula), pen., Egypt C12 42
Sinabang, Indon. M4 34
Sinai Peninsula see Sīnā', Shibh Jazīrat, pen., Egypt C12 42
Sin'aja, stm., Russia E18 24

Name | Map Ref | Page

Sinaloa, stm., Mex. E5 62
Sīnāwan, Libya B8 42
Sincé, Col. C5 58
Sincé, Col. J10 64
Sincelejo, Col. C5 58
Sinclair, Wy., U.S. E5 127
Sindri, India I12 38
Sines, Port. H3 12
Sinfães, Port. D3 12
Singānallūr, India G4 37
Singapore, Sing. N7 34
Singapore, ctry., Asia E3 32
Singapore Strait, strt., Asia N7 34
Singen [Hohentwiel], Ger. H8 8
Singida, Tan. B6 44
Singkang, Indon. F7 32
Singkawang, Indon. E4 32
Siniscola, Italy I4 14
Sinj, Cro. F11 14
Sinjah, Sudan F12 42
Sinkāt, Sudan E13 42
Sinnamary, Fr. Gu. B8 54
Sinnemahoning Creek, stm., Pa., U.S. D5 115
Sinop, Tur. G15 4
Sinskoje, Russia E19 24
Sintang, Indon. E5 32
Sint Eustatius, i., Neth. Ant. F16 64
Sint Marten (Saint-Martin), i., N.A. E16 64
Sint-Niklaas, Bel. D4 8
Sinton, Tx., U.S. E4 120
Sintra, Port. G2 12
Sinŭiju, N. Kor. C11 26
Sion, Switz. F14 10
Sioux, co., Ia., U.S. A1 92
Sioux, co., Ne., U.S. B2 104
Sioux, co., N.D., U.S. C4 111
Sioux Center, Ia., U.S. A1 92
Sioux City, Ia., U.S. B1 92
Sioux Falls, S.D., U.S. D9 118
Sioux Lookout, Ont., Can. o17 73
Sioux Rapids, Ia., U.S. B2 92
Siping, China C11 26
Sipiwesk Lake, l., Man., Can. B3 70
Sipsey, stm., Al., U.S. B2 78
Sipsey Fork, stm., Al., U.S. A2 78
Siracusa, Italy L10 14
Sirājganj, Bngl. H13 38
Sir Douglas, Mount, mtn., Can. D3 68
Sir Edward Pellew Group, is., Austl. C7 50
Siren, Wi., U.S. C1 126
Siret, stm., Eur. C11 16
Sirevåg, Nor. G5 6
Sir James MacBrien, Mount, mtn., N.W. Ter., Can. D7 66
Sirohi, India H5 38
Sirsa, India F6 38
Sir Sandford, Mount, mtn., B.C., Can. D9 69
Sirsi, India E3 37
Sir Wilfrid Laurier, Mount, mtn., B.C., Can. C8 69
Sisak, Cro. D11 14
Siskiyou, co., Ca., U.S. B2 82
Siskiyou Mountains, mts., U.S. F3 114
Siskiyou Pass, Or., U.S. E4 114
Sisseton, S.D., U.S. B8 118
Sisseton Indian Reservation, U.S. B8 118
Sissiboo, stm., N.S., Can. E4 71
Sisson Branch Reservoir, res., N.B., Can. B2 71
Sissonville, W.V., U.S. C3 125
Sisteron, Fr. H12 10
Sisters, Or., U.S. C5 114
Sistersville, W.V., U.S. B4 125
Sītāpur, India G9 38
Sitka, Ak., U.S. D12 79
Sitka National Historical Park, Ak., U.S. m22 79
Sitka Sound, strt., Ak., U.S. m22 79
Sittard, Neth. D5 8
Sittoung, stm., Mya. E4 34
Sittwe (Akyab), Mya. D2 34
Situbondo, Indon. m16 33a
Sivas, Tur. H15 4
Sīwah, Egypt C11 42
Siwān, India G11 38
Sjælland, i., Den. I8 6
Skagen, Den. H8 6
Skagerrak, strt., Eur. H7 6
Skagit, co., Wa., U.S. A4 124
Skagway, Ak., U.S. D12 79
Skaidi, Nor. A15 6
Skamania, co., Wa., U.S. D3 124
Skaneateles, N.Y., U.S. C4 109
Skaneateles Lake, l., N.Y., U.S. C4 109
Skārdu, Pak. C6 38
Skarżysko-Kamienna, Pol. D20 8
Skeena Mountains, mts., B.C., Can. E7 66
Skegness, Eng., U.K. H13 7
Skeleton Lake, l., Ont., Can. B5 73
Skellefteå, Swe. D13 6
Skelleftehamn, Swe. D13 6
Skiatook, Ok., U.S. A5 113
Skiatook Reservoir, res., Ok., U.S. A5 113
Skibotn, Nor. B13 6
Skiddaw, mtn., Eng., U.K. G9 7
Skien, Nor. G7 6
Skierniewice, Pol. D20 8
Skihist Mountain, mtn., B.C., Can. D7 69
Skikda, Alg. A7 42
Skillet Fork, stm., Il., U.S. E5 90
Skillingaryd, Swe. H10 6
Śkład, Russia C18 24
Škofja Loka, Slo. C9 14
Skokie, Il., U.S. A6 90
Skokomish Indian Reservation, Wa., U.S. B2 124
Skopje, Mac. H5 16
Skövde, Swe. G9 6
Skovorodino, Russia G18 24
Skowhegan, Me., U.S. D3 96
Skull Valley, val., Ut., U.S. C3 121
Skull Valley Indian Reservation, Ut., U.S. C3 121
Skuna, stm., Ms., U.S. B4 101
Skunk, stm., Ia., U.S. D6 92
Skwentna, stm., Ak., U.S. g15 79
Skye, Island of, i., Scot., U.K. D6 7
Skykomish, stm., Wa., U.S. B4 124
Skyland, Nv., U.S. D2 105
Skyland, N.C., U.S. f10 110
Skyline, Al., U.S. A3 78
Slagnäs, Swe. D12 6
Slamet, Gunung, vol., Indon. m14 33a
Slancy, Russia B11 18
Slano, Cro. G12 14
Slater, Ia., U.S. C4 92
Slater, Mo., U.S. B4 102
Slater, S.C., U.S. A3 117
Slatersville, R.I., U.S. A3 116
Slatersville Reservoir, res., R.I., U.S. B3 116
Slatington, Pa., U.S. E10 115
Slaton, Tx., U.S. C2 120
Slaughter, La., U.S. D4 95
Slave, stm., Can. D10 66
Slave Lake, Alta., Can. B3 68
Slavonia see Slavonija, reg., Cro. D12 14
Slavonija, reg., Cro. D12 14
Slavonska Požega, Cro. D12 14
Slavonski Brod, Cro. D2 16
Slayton, Mn., U.S. G3 100
Sleeping Bear Dunes National Lakeshore, Mi., U.S. D4 99
Sleeping Bear Point, c., Mi., U.S. D4 99
Sleepy Eye, Mn., U.S. F4 100
Slickville, Pa., U.S. F2 115
Slidell, La., U.S. D6 95
Sliderock Mountain, mtn., Mt., U.S. D3 103
Sligo, Ire. G4 7
Slinger, Wi., U.S. E5 126
Slippery Rock, Pa., U.S. D1 115
Sliven, Bul. G10 16
Sloan, Ia., U.S. B1 92
Sloan, N.Y., U.S. C2 109
Slocomb, Al., U.S. D4 78
Slonim, Bela. H8 18
Slope, co., N.D., U.S. C2 111
Slovakia, ctry., Eur. G19 8
Slovenia, ctry., Eur. C9 14
Slovenjgradec, Slo. C10 14
Slovenska Bistrica, Slo. C10 14
Sluck, Bela. H10 18
Sl'ud'anka, Russia G14 24
Słupsk (Stolp), Pol. A17 8
Smackover, Ar., U.S. D3 81
Small Point, c., Me., U.S. g8 96
Smallwood Reservoir, res., Newf., Can. g8 72
Smederevo, Yugo. E4 16
Smethport, Pa., U.S. C5 115
Šmidovič, Russia H20 24
Šmidta, Ostrov, i., Russia A12 24
Smith, co., Ks., U.S. C5 93
Smith, co., Ms., U.S. C4 101
Smith, co., Tn., U.S. A5 119
Smith, co., Tx., U.S. C5 120
Smith, stm., U.S. D3 123
Smith, stm., Mt., U.S. D5 103
Smith and Sayles Reservoir, res., R.I., U.S. B2 116
Smith Bay, b., Ak., U.S. A9 79
Smith Canyon, val., Co., U.S. D7 83
Smith Center, Ks., U.S. C5 93
Smithers, B.C., Can. B4 69
Smithers, W.V., U.S. C3 125
Smithfield, N.C., U.S. B4 110
Smithfield, Pa., U.S. G2 115
Smithfield, Ut., U.S. B4 121
Smithfield, Va., U.S. D6 123
Smith Island, i., U.S. D5 97
Smith Island, i., Va., U.S. C7 123
Smith Mountain Lake, res., Va., U.S. C3 123
Smith Peak, mtn., Id., U.S. A2 89
Smith Point, c., Ma., U.S. D7 98
Smith Point, c., Va., U.S. C6 123
Smiths, Al., U.S. C4 78
Smithsburg, Md., U.S. A2 97
Smiths Falls, Ont., Can. C8 73
Smiths Grove, Ky., U.S. C3 94
Smithton, Austl. H9 50
Smithton, Il., U.S. E4 90
Smithtown, N.Y., U.S. n15 109
Smithville, Ga., U.S. E2 87
Smithville, Ms., U.S. A5 101
Smithville, Mo., U.S. B3 102
Smithville, Oh., U.S. B4 112
Smithville, Tn., U.S. D8 119
Smithville, Tx., U.S. D4 120
Smithville Lake, res., Mo., U.S. B3 102
Smoke Creek Desert, des., Nv., U.S. C2 105
Smokey, Cape, c., N.S., Can. C9 71
Smokey Dome, mtn., Id., U.S. F4 89
Smoky, stm., Alta., Can. B1 68
Smoky Hill, stm., U.S. D5 93
Smoky Lake, Alta., Can. B4 68
Smoky Mountains, mts., Id., U.S. F4 89
Smolensk, Russia G15 18
Smooth Rock Falls, Ont., Can. o19 73
Smoothstone Lake, l., Sask., Can. C2 75
Smyrna, De., U.S. C3 85
Smyrna, Ga., U.S. C2 87
Smyrna, Tn., U.S. B5 119
Smyrna, stm., De., U.S. C3 85
Smyth, co., Va., U.S. f10 123
Smythe, Mount, mtn., B.C., Can. E8 66
Snake, stm., U.S. D5 100
Snake, stm., Mn., U.S. B1 100
Snake, stm., Ne., U.S. B4 104
Snake Range, mts., Nv., U.S. E7 105
Snake River Plain, pl., Id., U.S. F2 89
Snake River Range, mts., U.S. C2 127
Sneads, Fl., U.S. B2 86
Sneedville, Tn., U.S. C10 119
Sneek, Neth. B5 8
Snipe Keys, is., Fl., U.S. H5 86
Snohomish, Wa., U.S. B3 124
Snohomish, co., Wa., U.S. A4 124
Snoqualmie, Wa., U.S. B4 124
Snoqualmie, stm., Wa., U.S. B4 124
Snoqualmie Pass, Wa., U.S. B4 124
Snowbank Lake, l., Mn., U.S. B7 100
Snowdon, mtn., Wales, U.K. H8 7
Snowdonia National Park, Wales, U.K. I9 7
Snowdrift, N.W. Ter., Can. D10 66
Snowflake, Az., U.S. C5 80
Snow Hill, Md., U.S. D7 97
Snow Hill, N.C., U.S. B5 110
Snowking Mountain, mtn., Wa., U.S. A4 124
Snow Lake, Man., Can. B1 70
Snowmass Mountain, mtn., Co., U.S. B3 83
Snow Peak, mtn., Wa., U.S. A7 124
Snowshoe Lake, l., Me., U.S. B4 96
Snowshoe Peak, mtn., Mt., U.S. B1 103
Snow Water Lake, l., Nv., U.S. C7 105
Snowyside Peak, mtn., Id., U.S. F4 89
Snyder, Ok., U.S. C3 113
Snyder, Tx., U.S. C2 120
Snyder, co., Pa., U.S. E7 115
Soacha, Col. E5 58
Soalala, Madag. E9 44
Soap Lake, Wa., U.S. B6 124
Sobat, stm., Sudan G12 42
Sobinka, Russia F23 18
Sobral, Braz. D10 54
Socastee, S.C., U.S. D9 117
Sochi see Soči, Russia I5 22
Soči, Russia I5 22
Social Circle, Ga., U.S. C3 87
Society Hill, S.C., U.S. B8 117
Socorro, Col. D6 58
Socorro, N.M., U.S. C3 108
Socorro, co., N.M., U.S. D2 108
Socorro, Isla, i., Mex. H4 62
Socotra see Suquṭrā, i., Yemen F5 46
Soc Trang, Viet. J8 34
Socuéllamos, Spain F9 12
Sodankylä, Fin. C16 6
Soda Springs, Id., U.S. G7 89
Soddy-Daisy, Tn., U.S. D8 119
Söderhamn, Swe. F11 6
Södertälje, Swe. G11 6
Sodo, Eth. G2 46
Sodus, N.Y., U.S. B3 109
Soest, Ger. D8 8
Sofia, stm., Madag. E9 44
Sofia see Sofija, Bul. G7 16
Sofija (Sofia), Bul. G7 16
Sogamoso, Col. E6 58
Sognafjorden, Nor. F5 6
Søgne, Nor. G6 6
Soignies, Bel. E4 8
Sointula, B.C., Can. D4 69
Soissons, Fr. C10 10
Sokal'skogo, Proliv, strt., Russia B14 24
Söke, Tur. L11 16
Sokodé, Togo G6 42
Sokol, Russia B23 18
Sokol, Russia C19 24
Sokoto, Nig. F7 42
Sol, Costa del, Spain I7 12
Solana, Fl., U.S. F5 86
Solano, Phil. p19 33b
Solano, co., Ca., U.S. C3 82
Solbad Hall in Tirol, Aus. H11 8
Soldier, stm., Ia., U.S. C2 92
Soldier Key, i., Fl., U.S. s3 86
Soldotna, Ak., U.S. g16 79
Soledad, Col. B5 58
Soledad, Ca., U.S. D3 82
Soledad, Ven. C11 58
Soleduck, stm., Wa., U.S. B1 124
Solingen, Ger. D7 8
Sollefteå, Swe. E11 6
Sollentuna, Swe. G11 6
Sóller, Spain F14 12
Solnečnogorsk, Russia E19 18
Sologoncy, Russia D16 24
Solok, Indon. O6 34
Solomon, Ks., U.S. D6 93
Solomon, stm., Ks., U.S. C6 93
Solomon Islands, ctry., Oc. G23 2
Solomons, Md., U.S. D5 97
Solomon Sea, Oc. A10 50
Solon, Ia., U.S. C6 92
Solon, Oh., U.S. A4 112
Solothurn, Switz. E14 10
Solsona, Spain D13 12
Soltau, Ger. C9 8
Solvay, N.Y., U.S. B4 109
Solwezi, Zam. D5 44
Soma, Tur. J11 16
Somalia, ctry., Afr. G4 46
Sombor, Yugo. D3 16
Sombrerete, Mex. F8 62
Somerdale, N.J., U.S. D2 107
Somers, Ct., U.S. B6 84
Somers, Mt., U.S. B2 103
Somerset, Man., Can. E2 70
Somerset, Ky., U.S. C5 94
Somerset, Ma., U.S. C5 98
Somerset, N.J., U.S. B3 107
Somerset, Oh., U.S. C3 112
Somerset, Pa., U.S. F3 115
Somerset, Tx., U.S. k7 120
Somerset, Wi., U.S. C1 126
Somerset, co., Me., U.S. C2 96
Somerset, co., Md., U.S. D6 97
Somerset, co., N.J., U.S. B3 107
Somerset, co., Pa., U.S. G3 115
Somerset Island, i., N.W. Ter., Can. B14 66
Somerset Reservoir, res., Vt., U.S. E3 122
Somers Point, N.J., U.S. E3 107
Somersville, Ct., U.S. B6 84
Somersworth, N.H., U.S. D5 106
Somerton, Az., U.S. E1 80
Somervell, co., Tx., U.S. C4 120
Somerville, Ma., U.S. B5 98
Somerville, N.J., U.S. B3 107
Somerville, Tn., U.S. B2 119
Somerville, Tx., U.S. D4 120
Somerville Lake, res., Tx., U.S. D4 120
Someș (Szamos), stm., Eur. B6 16
Sömmerda, Ger. D11 8
Somonauk, Il., U.S. B5 90
Somoto, Nic. H4 64
Son, stm., India H10 38
Sønderborg, Den. I7 6
Sondershausen, Ger. D10 8
Søndre Strømfjord, Grnld. C22 66
Sondrio, Italy C4 14
Song Cau, Viet. H10 34
Songea, Tan. D7 44
Songhua, stm., China B12 26
Songjiang, China D10 28
Songkhla, Thai. K6 34
Songnim, N. Kor. D12 26
Sonīpat, India F7 38
Son La, Viet. D7 34
Sonmiāni Bay, b., Pak. H2 38
Sonneberg, Ger. E11 8
Sonoita, Mex. B3 62
Sonoma, Ca., U.S. C2 82
Sonoma, co., Ca., U.S. C2 82
Sonoma Peak, mtn., Nv., U.S. C4 105
Sonoma Range, mts., Nv., U.S. C4 105
Sonora, Ca., U.S. D3 82
Sonora, Tx., U.S. D2 120
Sonora, state, Mex. C4 62
Sonseca, Spain F8 12
Sonsón, Col. E5 58
Sonsonate, El Sal. H3 64
Sonsorol Islands, is., Palau D9 32
Son Tay, Viet. D8 34
Sonthofen, Ger. H10 8
Soochow see Suzhou, China D9 28
Soperton, Ga., U.S. D4 87
Sophia, W.V., U.S. D3 125
Sopot, Pol. A18 8
Sopron, Hung. H16 8
Sopur, India C6 38
Sora, Italy H8 14
Sore, Fr. H6 10
Sorel, Que., Can. C4 74
Sorgono, Italy I4 14
Sorgues, Fr. H11 10
Soria, Spain D9 12
Sorocaba, Braz. G5 57
Sorong, Indon. F9 32
Soroti, Ug. H12 42
Sorrento, Italy I9 14
Sorrento, La., U.S. D5 95
Sorsele, Swe. D11 6
Sorsogon, Phil. C7 32
Sort, Spain C13 12
Sorūbī, Afg. C3 38
Sos del Rey Católico, Spain C10 12
Sosnovo-Oz'orskoje, Russia G16 24
Sosnowiec, Pol. E19 8
Šoštanj, Slo. C10 14
Sotkamo, Fin. D17 6
Soto la Marina, Mex. F10 62
Sotteville, Fr. C8 10
Soucook, stm., N.H., U.S. D4 106
Soudan, Mn., U.S. C6 100
Souderton, Pa., U.S. F11 115
Souhegan, stm., N.H., U.S. E3 106
Souillac, Fr. H8 10
Sŏul (Seoul), S. Kor. D12 26
Soulac-sur-Mer, Fr. G5 10
Souris, Man., Can. E1 70
Souris, P.E.I., Can. C7 71
Sousa, Braz. E11 54
Sousse, Tun. N5 14
South, stm., Ia., U.S. C4 92
South, stm., N.C., U.S. C4 110
South Acton, Ma., U.S. g10 98
South Africa, ctry., Afr. G5 44
South Amboy, N.J., U.S. C4 107
South America E4 53
South Amherst, Ma., U.S. B2 98
South Amherst, Oh., U.S. A3 112
Southampton, Ont., Can. C3 73
Southampton, Eng., U.K. K11 7
Southampton, N.Y., U.S. n16 109
Southampton, co., Va., U.S. D5 123
Southampton Island, i., N.W. Ter., Can. D16 66
South Andaman, i., India I2 34
South Anna, stm., Va., U.S. C5 123
South Aulatsivik Island, i., Newf., Can. E20 66
South Australia, state, Austl. F7 50
Southaven, Ms., U.S. A3 101
South Bald Mountain, mtn., Co., U.S. A5 83
South Baldy, mtn., N.M., U.S. D2 108
South Barre, Vt., U.S. C3 122
South Bay, Fl., U.S. F6 86
South Beloit, Il., U.S. A4 90
South Bend, In., U.S. A5 91
South Bend, Wa., U.S. C2 124
South Berwick, Me., U.S. E2 96
South Bloomfield, Oh., U.S. C3 112
South Boston, Va., U.S. D4 123
South Bound Brook, N.J., U.S. B3 107
South Branch Lake, l., Me., U.S. C4 96
Southbridge, Ma., U.S. B3 98
South Bristol, Me., U.S. E3 96
South Britain, Ct., U.S. D3 84
South Broadway, Wa., U.S. C5 124
South Bruny, i., Austl. H9 50
South Burlington, Vt., U.S. C2 122
Southbury, Ct., U.S. D3 84
South Carolina, state, U.S. D6 117
South Charleston, Oh., U.S. C2 112
South Charleston, W.V., U.S. C3 125
South Chicago Heights, Il., U.S. m9 90
South China Sea, Asia C5 32
South Coffeyville, Ok., U.S. A6 113
South Congaree, S.C., U.S. D5 117
South Connellsville, Pa., U.S. G2 115
South Dakota, state, U.S. C5 118
South Dartmouth, Ma., U.S. C6 98
South Daytona, Fl., U.S. C5 86
South Deerfield, Ma., U.S. B2 98
South Dennis, Ma., U.S. C7 98
South Duxbury, Ma., U.S. B6 98
South East Cape, c., Austl. H9 50
Southeast Cape, c., Ak., U.S. C6 79
South Easton, Ma., U.S. B5 98
Southeast Pass, strt., La., U.S. E7 95
Southeast Point, c., R.I., U.S. h7 116
South Elgin, Il., U.S. B5 90
Southend-on-Sea, Eng., U.K. J13 7
Southern Alps, mts., N.Z. E3 52
Southern Cross, Austl. F3 50
Southern Indian Lake, l., Man., Can. f8 70
Southern Pines, N.C., U.S. B3 110
Southern Ute Indian Reservation, Co., U.S. D2 83
South Euclid, Oh., U.S. g9 112
Southey, Sask., Can. G3 75
South Fabius, stm., Mo., U.S. A5 102
South Fallsburg, N.Y., U.S. D6 109
Southfield, Mi., U.S. o15 99
South Fork, Pa., U.S. F4 115
South Fox Island, i., Mi., U.S. C5 99
South Fulton, Tn., U.S. A3 119
South Gastonia, N.C., U.S. B1 110
South Gate, Ca., U.S. n12 82
Southgate, Ky., U.S. h14 94
Southgate, Mi., U.S. p15 99
South Georgia, i., Falk. Is. G9 56
South Glastonbury, Ct., U.S. C5 84
South Glens Falls, N.Y., U.S. B7 109
South Grafton, Ma., U.S. B4 98
South Grand, stm., Mo., U.S. C3 102
South Hadley, Ma., U.S. B2 98
South Hadley Falls, Ma., U.S. B2 98
South Hamilton, Ma., U.S. A6 98
South Haven, In., U.S. A3 91
South Haven, Mi., U.S. F4 99
South Henik Lake, l., N.W. Ter., Can. D13 66
South Hero Island, i., Vt., U.S. B2 122
South Hill, Va., U.S. D4 123
South Hingham, Ma., U.S. h12 98
South Holland, Il., U.S. k9 90
South Holston Lake, res., U.S. A9 119
South Hooksett, N.H., U.S. D4 106
South Hopkinton, R.I., U.S. F1 116
South Houston, Tx., U.S. r14 120
South Hutchinson, Ks., U.S. f11 93
South Indian Lake, Man., Can. A2 70
Southington, Ct., U.S. C4 84
South International Falls, Mn., U.S. B5 100
South Island, i., N.Z. E3 52
South Island, i., S.C., U.S. E9 117
South Jacksonville, Il., U.S. D3 90
South Jordan, Ut., U.S. C3 121
South Kenosha, Wi., U.S. F6 126
South Lake Tahoe, Ca., U.S.D. C4 82
South Lancaster, Ma., U.S. B4 98
South Laurel, Md., U.S. *B4 97
South Lebanon, Oh., U.S. C1 112
South Lyon, Mi., U.S. F7 99
South Magnetic Pole C26 47
South Manitou Island, i., Mi., U.S. C4 99
South Marsh Island, i., Md., U.S. D5 97
South Miami, Fl., U.S. G6 86
South Miami Heights, Fl., U.S. s13 86
South Mills, N.C., U.S. A6 110
South Milwaukee, Wi., U.S. F6 126
Southmont, N.C., U.S. B2 110
South Moose Lake, l., Man., Can. C1 70
South Mountain, mtn., Id., U.S. G2 89
South Mountain, mtn., N.M., U.S. k8 108
South Mountains, mts., Az., U.S. m8 80
South Mountains, mts., N.C., U.S. B1 110
South Nahanni, stm., N.W. Ter., Can. D7 66
South New River Canal, Fl., U.S. r3 86
South Ogden, Ut., U.S. B4 121
Southold, N.Y., U.S. m16 109
South Orange, N.J., U.S. B4 107
South Orkney Islands, is., B.A.T. C8 47
South Paris, Me., U.S. D2 96
South Park, val., Co., U.S. B5 83
South Pass, Wy., U.S. D4 127
South Pass, strt., La., U.S. F6 95
South Patrick Shores, Fl., U.S. D6 86
South Pekin, Il., U.S. C4 90
South Pittsburg, Tn., U.S. D8 119
South Plainfield, N.J., U.S. B4 107
South Platte, stm., U.S. C6 76
South Point, c., Mi., U.S. D7 99
South Pole, Ant. A12 47
Southport, Eng., U.K. H9 7
Southport, Fl., U.S. u16 86
Southport, In., U.S. E5 91
Southport, N.Y., U.S. C4 109
Southport, N.C., U.S. D4 110
South Portland, Me., U.S. E2 96
South Portsmouth, Ky., U.S. B6 94
South Range, Mi., U.S. A2 99
South River, Ont., Can. B5 73
South River, N.J., U.S. C4 107
South River, b., Md., U.S. C4 97
South Ronaldsay, i., Scot., U.K. C10 7
South Royalton, Vt., U.S. D3 122
South Saint Paul, Mn., U.S. n12 100
South Sandwich Islands, is., Falk. Is. D10 47
South San Francisco, Ca., U.S. h8 82
South Saskatchewan, stm., Can. F11 66
South Shetland Islands, is., B.A.T. C7 47
South Shields, Eng., U.K. F11 7
Southside, Al., U.S. B3 78
Southside Place, Tx., U.S. r14 120
South Sioux City, Ne., U.S. B9 104
South Skunk, stm., Ia., U.S. C4 92
South Stony Brook, N.Y., U.S. *n15 109

Name	Map Ref	Page
South Streator, Il., U.S.	B5	90
South Toms River, N.J., U.S.	D4	107
South Torrington, Wy., U.S.	D8	127
South Tucson, Az., U.S.	E5	80
South Valley Stream, N.Y., U.S.	*n15	109
South Venice, Fl., U.S.	E4	86
South Ventana Cone, vol., Ca., U.S.	D3	82
South Waverly, Pa., U.S.	C8	115
South Wellfleet, Ma., U.S.	C8	98
South Wellington, B.C., Can.	f12	69
South West Africa see Namibia, ctry., Afr.	F3	44
South Westbury, N.Y., U.S.	*n15	109
South West Cape, c., Austl.	H9	50
Southwest Channel, strt., Fl., U.S.	E4	86
South West City, Mo., U.S.	E3	102
Southwest Harbor, Me., U.S.	D4	96
Southwest Head, c., N.B., Can.	E3	71
Southwest Miramichi, stm., N.B., Can.	C3	71
Southwest Pass, strt., La., U.S.	E3	95
Southwest Pass, strt., La., U.S.	F6	95
Southwest Point, c., R.I., U.S.	h7	116
South Weymouth Naval Air Station, mil., Ma., U.S.	h12	98
South Whitley, In., U.S.	B6	91
South Williamson, Ky., U.S.	C7	94
South Williamsport, Pa., U.S.	D7	115
South Windham, Ct., U.S.	C7	84
South Windham, Me., U.S.	E2	96
South Windsor, Ct., U.S.	B5	84
Southwood, Co., U.S.	*B6	83
Southwood Acres, Ct., U.S.	A5	84
South Woodstock, Ct., U.S.	B8	84
South Yarmouth, Ma., U.S.	C7	98
South Zanesville, Oh., U.S.	C3	112
Sovetsk (Tilsit), Russia	F4	18
Sovetskaja Gavan', Russia	H22	24
Spa, Bel.	E5	8
Spain, ctry., Eur.	G7	4
Spalding, co., Ga., U.S.	C2	87
Spanaway, Wa., U.S.	B3	124
Spangler, Pa., U.S.	E4	115
Spaniard's Bay, Newf., Can.	E5	72
Spanish Fork, Ut., U.S.	C4	121
Spanish Fort, Al., U.S.	E2	78
Spanish Lake, Mo., U.S.	f13	102
Spanish North Africa, dep., Afr.	A4	42
Spanish Peak, mtn., Or., U.S.	C7	114
Spanish Sahara see Western Sahara, dep., Afr.	D3	42
Spanish Town, Jam.	E9	64
Sparks, Ga., U.S.	E3	87
Sparks, Nv., U.S.	D2	105
Sparta, Ga., U.S.	C4	87
Sparta, Il., U.S.	E4	90
Sparta, Mi., U.S.	E5	99
Sparta, Mo., U.S.	D4	102
Sparta (Lake Mohawk), N.J., U.S.	A3	107
Sparta, N.C., U.S.	A1	110
Sparta, Tn., U.S.	D8	119
Sparta, Wi., U.S.	E3	126
Spartanburg, S.C., U.S.	B4	117
Spartanburg, co., S.C., U.S.	B3	117
Sparta see Spárti, Grc.	L6	16
Spartel, Cap, c., Mor.	J6	12
Spárti (Sparta), Grc.	L6	16
Spartivento, Capo, c., Italy	K3	14
Sparwood, B.C., Can.	E10	69
Spassk-Dal'nij, Russia	I20	24
Spavinaw Creek, stm., Ok., U.S.	A7	113
Spear, Cape, c., Newf., Can.	E5	72
Spearfish, S.D., U.S.	C2	118
Spearman, Tx., U.S.	A2	120
Spearville, Ks., U.S.	E4	93
Speed, In., U.S.	H6	91
Speedway, In., U.S.	E5	91
Spence Bay, N.W. Ter., Can.	C14	66
Spencer, In., U.S.	F4	91
Spencer, Ia., U.S.	A2	92
Spencer, Ma., U.S.	B4	98
Spencer, N.C., U.S.	B2	110
Spencer, Tn., U.S.	D8	119
Spencer, W.V., U.S.	C3	125
Spencer, Wi., U.S.	D3	126
Spencer, co., In., U.S.	H4	91
Spencer, co., Ky., U.S.	B4	94
Spencer, Cape, c., Ak., U.S.	k21	79
Spencer Gulf, b., Austl.	F7	50
Spencer Lake, l., Me., U.S.	C2	96
Spencerport, N.Y., U.S.	B3	109
Spencerville, Md., U.S.	B4	97
Spencerville, Oh., U.S.	B1	112
Sperry, Ok., U.S.	A6	113
Spesutie Island, i., Md., U.S.	B5	97
Spey, stm., Scot., U.K.	D9	7
Speyer, Ger.	F8	8
Spiceland, In., U.S.	E7	91
Spicer, Mn., U.S.	E4	100
Spider Lake, l., Wi., U.S.	B2	126
Spindale, N.C., U.S.	B1	110
Spink, co., S.D., U.S.	C7	118
Spirit Lake, Id., U.S.	B2	89
Spirit Lake, Ia., U.S.	A2	92
Spirit Lake, l., Ia., U.S.	A2	92
Spirit Lake, l., Wa., U.S.	C3	124
Spirit River, Alta., Can.	B1	68
Spirit River Flowage, res., Wi., U.S.	C4	126
Spiro, Ok., U.S.	B7	113
Spittal an der Drau, Aus.	I13	8
Spitz, Aus.	G15	8
Split, Cro.	F11	14
Split, Cape, c., N.S., Can.	D5	71
Split Lake, l., Man., Can.	A4	70
Split Rock Creek, stm., U.S.	G2	100
Splügen, Switz.	F16	10
Spofford Lake, l., N.H., U.S.	E2	106
Spokane, Wa., U.S.	B8	124
Spokane, co., Wa., U.S.	B8	124
Spokane, stm., U.S.	B8	124
Spokane, Mount, mtn., Wa., U.S.	B8	124
Spokane Indian Reservation, Wa., U.S.	B8	124
Spoleto, Italy	G7	14
Spoon, stm., Il., U.S.	C3	90
Spooner, Wi., U.S.	C2	126
Spooner Lake, l., Wi., U.S.	C2	126
Spornoje, Russia	E24	24
Spotswood, N.J., U.S.	C4	107
Spotsylvania, co., Va., U.S.	B5	123
Sprague, W.V., U.S.	n13	125
Sprague, stm., Or., U.S.	E5	114
Sprague Lake, l., Wa., U.S.	B7	124
Spratly Island, i., Asia	D5	32
Spremberg, Ger.	D14	8
Spring, stm., Ar., U.S.	A4	81
Spring Arbor, Mi., U.S.	F6	99
Spring Bay, b., Ut., U.S.	B3	121
Springbok, S. Afr.	G3	44
Springboro, Oh., U.S.	C1	112
Spring Brook, stm., Pa., U.S.	n18	115
Spring City, Pa., U.S.	F10	115
Spring City, Tn., U.S.	D9	119
Spring City, Ut., U.S.	D4	121
Spring Creek, stm., U.S.	D4	104
Spring Creek, stm., Nv., U.S.	C4	105
Spring Creek, stm., N.D., U.S.	B3	111
Springdale, Newf., Can.	D3	72
Springdale, Ar., U.S.	A1	81
Springdale, Oh., U.S.	n13	112
Springdale, Pa., U.S.	E2	115
Springdale, S.C., U.S.	D5	117
Springer, N.M., U.S.	A5	108
Springerville, Az., U.S.	C6	80
Springfield, Co., U.S.	D8	83
Springfield, Fl., U.S.	u16	86
Springfield, Ga., U.S.	D5	87
Springfield, Il., U.S.	D4	90
Springfield, Ky., U.S.	C4	94
Springfield, Ma., U.S.	B2	98
Springfield, Mn., U.S.	F4	100
Springfield, Mo., U.S.	D4	102
Springfield, Ne., U.S.	C9	104
Springfield, N.J., U.S.	B4	107
Springfield, Oh., U.S.	C2	112
Springfield, Or., U.S.	C4	114
Springfield, Pa., U.S.	p20	115
Springfield, S.D., U.S.	E8	118
Springfield, Tn., U.S.	A5	119
Springfield, Vt., U.S.	E4	122
Springfield, Va., U.S.	g12	123
Springfield, Lake, res., Il., U.S.	D4	90
Springfontein, S. Afr.	H5	44
Spring Garden, Guy.	D13	58
Spring Glen, Ut., U.S.	D5	121
Spring Green, Wi., U.S.	E3	126
Spring Grove, Il., U.S.	h8	90
Spring Grove, Mn., U.S.	G7	100
Spring Grove, Pa., U.S.	G8	115
Spring Hill, Fl., U.S.	D4	86
Spring Hill, Ks., U.S.	D9	93
Springhill, La., U.S.	A2	95
Spring Hill, Tn., U.S.	B5	119
Spring Hope, N.C., U.S.	B4	110
Spring Island, i., S.C., U.S.	G6	117
Spring Lake, Mi., U.S.	E4	99
Spring Lake, N.J., U.S.	C4	107
Spring Lake, N.C., U.S.	B4	110
Spring Lake, l., Me., U.S.	C2	96
Spring Lake, res., U.S.	B3	90
Spring Lake Heights, N.J., U.S.	C4	107
Spring Mountains, mts., Nv., U.S.	G6	105
Springport, Mi., U.S.	F6	99
Springs, S. Afr.	G5	44
Springside, Sask., Can.	F4	75
Springvale, Me., U.S.	E2	96
Spring Valley, Ca., U.S.	o16	82
Spring Valley, Il., U.S.	B4	90
Spring Valley, Mn., U.S.	G6	100
Spring Valley, N.Y., U.S.	g12	109
Spring Valley, Wi., U.S.	D1	126
Springville, Al., U.S.	B3	78
Springville, Ia., U.S.	B6	92
Springville, N.Y., U.S.	C2	109
Springville, Ut., U.S.	C4	121
Spruce Fork, stm., W.V., U.S.	m12	125
Spruce Grove, Alta., Can.	C4	68
Spruce Knob, mtn., W.V., U.S.	C6	125
Spruce Knob-Seneca Rocks National Recreation Area, W.V., U.S.	C5	125
Spruce Mountain, mtn., Az., U.S.	C3	80
Spruce Mountain, mtn., Nv., U.S.	C7	105
Spruce Pine, N.C., U.S.	f10	110
Spruce Run Reservoir, res., N.J., U.S.	B3	107
Spur, Tx., U.S.	C2	120
Spurr, Mount, mtn., Ak., U.S.	g15	79
Squam Lake, l., N.H., U.S.	C4	106
Squapan Lake, l., Me., U.S.	B4	96
Square Lake, l., Me., U.S.	A4	96
Squatec, Que., Can.	B9	74
Squaw Cap Mountain, mtn., N.B., Can.	B3	71
Squaw Hill, mtn., Wy., U.S.	E7	127
Squaw Peak, mtn., Mt., U.S.	C2	103
Squibnocket Point, c., Ma., U.S.	D6	98
Squinzano, Italy	I13	14
Squire, W.V., U.S.	D3	125
Sragen, Indon.	m15	33a
Srednyj Chrebet, mts., Russia	F26	24
Srednekolymsk, Russia	D24	24
Srednerusskaja Vozvyšennost', plat., Russia	H20	18
Srednesibirskoje Ploskogorje, plat., Russia	D14	24
Sremska Mitrovica, Yugo.	E3	16
Sri Gangānagar, India	F5	38
Srīkākulam, India	C7	37
Sri Lanka, ctry., Asia	H5	36
Srīnagar, India	C6	38
Srīrampur, India	C3	37
Stack Reservoir, res., R.I., U.S.	C3	116
Stade, Ger.	B9	8
Stadthagen, Ger.	C9	8
Stafford, Eng., U.K.	I10	7
Stafford, Ks., U.S.	E5	93
Stafford, Va., U.S.	B5	123
Stafford, co., Ks., U.S.	D5	93
Stafford, co., Va., U.S.	B5	123
Stafford Pond, l., R.I., U.S.	D6	116
Stafford Springs, Ct., U.S.	B6	84
Staked Plain see Estacado, Llano, pl., U.S.	E6	76
Stalheim, Nor.	F6	6
Stalingrad see Volgograd, Russia	H6	22
Stalowa Wola, Pol.	E22	8
Stambaugh, Mi., U.S.	B2	99
Stamford, Ct., U.S.	E1	84
Stamford, Tx., U.S.	C3	120
Stamford, Vt., U.S.	F2	122
Stamford, Lake, res., Tx., U.S.	C3	120
Stamping Ground, Ky., U.S.	B5	94
Stamps, Ar., U.S.	D2	81
Stanaford, W.V., U.S.	D3	125
Stanberry, Mo., U.S.	A3	102
Standerton, S. Afr.	G5	44
Standing Rock Indian Reservation, U.S.	B4	118
Standish, Mi., U.S.	E7	99
Stanfield, Az., U.S.	E3	80
Stanfield, Or., U.S.	B7	114
Stanford, Ky., U.S.	C5	94
Stanhope, N.J., U.S.	B3	107
Stanislaus, co., Ca., U.S.	D3	82
Stanley, Falk. Is.	G5	56
Stanley, N.C., U.S.	B1	110
Stanley, N.D., U.S.	A3	111
Stanley, Va., U.S.	B4	123
Stanley, Wi., U.S.	D3	126
Stanley, co., S.D., U.S.	C5	118
Stanley Falls, wtfl, Zaire	A5	44
Stanleytown, Va., U.S.	D3	123
Stanleyville, N.C., U.S.	A2	110
Stanleyville see Kisangani, Zaire	A5	44
Stanly, co., N.C., U.S.	B2	110
Stann Creek, Belize	F3	64
Stanovoj Chrebet, mts., Russia	F19	24
Stanovoje Nagorje (Stanovoy Mountains), mts., Russia	F16	24
Stanstead, Que., Can.	D5	74
Stanton, Ia., U.S.	D2	92
Stanton, Ky., U.S.	C6	94
Stanton, Mi., U.S.	E5	99
Stanton, Ne., U.S.	C8	104
Stanton, Tx., U.S.	C2	120
Stanton, co., Ks., U.S.	E2	93
Stanton, co., Ne., U.S.	C8	104
Stantonsburg, N.C., U.S.	B5	110
Stanwood, Ia., U.S.	C6	92
Stanwood, Wa., U.S.	A3	124
Staples, Mn., U.S.	D4	100
Stapleton, Al., U.S.	E2	78
Star, Id., U.S.	F2	89
Star, N.C., U.S.	B3	110
Starachowice, Pol.	D21	8
Staraja Russa, Russia	C14	18
Stara Planina (Balkan Mountains), mts., Eur.	G8	16
Stara Zagora, Bul.	G9	16
Starbuck, Mn., U.S.	E3	100
Star City, Ar., U.S.	D4	81
Star City, W.V., U.S.	B5	125
Stargard Szczeciński (Stargard in Pommern), Pol.	B15	8
Stargo, Az., U.S.	D6	80
Stark, co., Il., U.S.	B4	90
Stark, co., N.D., U.S.	C3	111
Stark, co., Oh., U.S.	B4	112
Starke, Fl., U.S.	C4	86
Starke, co., In., U.S.	B4	91
Starks, La., U.S.	D2	95
Starkville, Ms., U.S.	B5	101
Star Lake, l., Mn., U.S.	D3	100
Starnberg, Ger.	G11	8
Starogard Gdański, Pol.	B18	8
Star Peak, mtn., Nv., U.S.	C3	105
Starr, co., Tx., U.S.	F3	120
Startex, S.C., U.S.	B3	117
Start Point, c., Eng., U.K.	K9	7
Startup, Wa., U.S.	B4	124
State Center, Ia., U.S.	B4	92
State College, Pa., U.S.	E6	115
Stateline, Nv., U.S.	E2	105
State Line, Pa., U.S.	G6	115
Staten Island, i., N.Y., U.S.	k12	109
Statenville, Ga., U.S.	F4	87
Statesboro, Ga., U.S.	D5	87
Statesville, N.C., U.S.	B2	110
Statham, Ga., U.S.	C3	87
Statue of Liberty National Monument, N.J., U.S.	k8	107
Staunton, Il., U.S.	D4	90
Staunton, Va., U.S.	B3	123
Stavanger, Nor.	G5	6
Stavropol', Russia	H6	22
Stayner, Ont., Can.	C4	73
Stayton, Or., U.S.	C4	114
Steamboat, Nv., U.S.	D2	105
Steamboat Mountain, mtn., Mt., U.S.	C4	103
Steamboat Mountain, mtn., Wy., U.S.	E4	127
Steamboat Springs, Co., U.S.	A4	83
Stearns, Ky., U.S.	D5	94
Stearns, co., Mn., U.S.	E4	100
Stearns Brook, stm., N.H., U.S.	A4	106
Stebbins, Ak., U.S.	C7	79
Steele, Al., U.S.	B3	78
Steele, Mo., U.S.	E8	102
Steele, N.D., U.S.	C6	111
Steele, co., Mn., U.S.	F5	100
Steele, co., N.D., U.S.	B8	111
Steele, Mount, mtn., Wy., U.S.	E6	127
Steeleville, Il., U.S.	E4	90
Steelton, Pa., U.S.	F8	115
Steelville, Mo., U.S.	D6	102
Steenkool, Indon.	F9	32
Steens Mountain, mts., Or., U.S.	E8	114
Stefansson Island, i., N.W. Ter., Can.	B11	66
Steger, Il., U.S.	B6	90
Steilacoom, Wa., U.S.	f10	124
Steinbach, Man., Can.	E3	70
Steinhatchee, stm., Fl., U.S.	C3	86
Steinkjer, Nor.	D8	6
Stellenbosch, S. Afr.	H3	44
Stenay, Fr.	C12	10
Stendal, Ger.	C11	8
Stephen, Mn., U.S.	B2	100
Stephens, Ar., U.S.	D2	81
Stephens, co., Ga., U.S.	B3	87
Stephens, co., Ok., U.S.	C4	113
Stephens, co., Tx., U.S.	C3	120
Stephens City, Va., U.S.	A4	123
Stephens Lake, res., Man., Can.	A4	70
Stephenson, Mi., U.S.	C3	99
Stephenson, co., Il., U.S.	A4	90
Stephens Passage, strt., Ak., U.S.	m23	79
Stephenville, Newf., Can.	D2	72
Stephenville, Tx., U.S.	C3	120
Stephenville Crossing, Newf., Can.	D2	72
Sterling, Ak., U.S.	g16	79
Sterling, Co., U.S.	A7	83
Sterling, Il., U.S.	B4	90
Sterling, Ks., U.S.	D5	93
Sterling, Ok., U.S.	C3	113
Sterling, Va., U.S.	A5	123
Sterling, co., Tx., U.S.	D2	120
Sterling City, Tx., U.S.	D2	120
Sterling Heights, Mi., U.S.	o15	99
Sterling Reservoir, res., Co., U.S.	A7	83
Sterlington, La., U.S.	B3	95
Sterlitamak, Russia	G9	22
Stettin see Szczecin, Pol.	B14	8
Stettler, Alta., Can.	C4	68
Steuben, co., In., U.S.	A7	91
Steuben, co., N.Y., U.S.	C3	109
Steubenville, Oh., U.S.	B5	112
Stevenage, Eng., U.K.	J12	7
Stevens, co., Ks., U.S.	E2	93
Stevens, co., Mn., U.S.	E3	100
Stevens, co., Wa., U.S.	A7	124
Stevens Creek Dam, U.S.	C4	87
Stevenson, Al., U.S.	A4	78
Stevenson, Ct., U.S.	D3	84
Stevenson, Wa., U.S.	D4	124
Stevenson Lake, l., Man., Can.	C4	70
Stevens Pass, Wa., U.S.	B4	124
Stevens Peak, mtn., Id., U.S.	B3	89
Stevens Point, Wi., U.S.	D4	126
Stevensville, Md., U.S.	C5	97
Stevensville, Mi., U.S.	F4	99
Stevensville, Mt., U.S.	D2	103
Stewart, co., Ga., U.S.	D2	87
Stewart, co., Tn., U.S.	A4	119
Stewart Island, i., N.Z.	G1	52
Stewart Mountain, mtn., Az., U.S.	k9	80
Stewartstown, Pa., U.S.	G8	115
Stewartsville, Mo., U.S.	B3	102
Stewartville, Mn., U.S.	G6	100
Stewiacke, N.S., Can.	D6	71
Steyr, Aus.	G14	8
Stigler, Ok., U.S.	B6	113
Stigliano, Italy	I11	14
Stikine, stm., B.C., Can.	E7	66
Stikine, stm., Ak., U.S.	D13	79
Stikine Ranges, mts., B.C., Can.	E6	66
Still, stm., Ct., U.S.	B3	84
Stillaguamish, North Fork, stm., Wa., U.S.	A4	124
Stillaguamish, South Fork, stm., Wa., U.S.	A4	124
Stillhouse Hollow Lake, res., Tx., U.S.	D4	120
Stillman Valley, Il., U.S.	A4	90
Stillmore, Ga., U.S.	D4	87
Stillwater, Mn., U.S.	E6	100
Stillwater, Ok., U.S.	A4	113
Stillwater, co., Mt., U.S.	E7	103
Stillwater Range, mts., Nv., U.S.	D3	105
Stillwater Reservoir, res., N.Y., U.S.	B5	109
Stillwater Reservoir, res., R.I., U.S.	B3	116
Stilwell, Ok., U.S.	B7	113
Stimson, Mount, mtn., Mt., U.S.	B3	103
Stine Mountain, mtn., Mt., U.S.	E3	103
Stinking Lake, l., N.M., U.S.	A3	108
Stinnett, Tx., U.S.	B2	120
Štip, Mac.	H6	16
Stirling, Alta., Can.	E4	68
Stirling, Ont., Can.	C7	73
Stirling, Scot., U.K.	E9	7
Stjørdalshalsen, Nor.	E8	6
Stockbridge, Ga., U.S.	C2	87
Stockbridge, Mi., U.S.	F6	99
Stockbridge-Munsee Indian Reservation, Wi., U.S.	D5	126
Stockdale, Tx., U.S.	E4	120
Stockerau, Aus.	G16	8
Stockholm, Swe.	G12	6
Stockton, Ca., U.S.	D3	82
Stockton, Il., U.S.	A3	90
Stockton, Ks., U.S.	C4	93
Stockton, Md., U.S.	D7	97
Stockton, Mo., U.S.	D4	102
Stockton Island, i., Wi., U.S.	B3	126
Stockton Lake, res., Mo., U.S.	D4	102
Stoddard, Wi., U.S.	E2	126
Stoddard, co., Mo., U.S.	E8	102
Stoke-on-Trent, Eng., U.K.	H10	7
Stokes, co., N.C., U.S.	A2	110
Stokesdale, N.C., U.S.	A3	110
Stolbovoj, Ostrov, i., Russia	C21	24
Stollings, W.V., U.S.	n12	125
Ston, Cro.	G12	14
Stone, co., Ar., U.S.	B3	81
Stone, co., Ms., U.S.	E4	101
Stone, co., Mo., U.S.	E4	102
Stoneboro, Pa., U.S.	D1	115
Stone Corral Lake, l., Or., U.S.	E7	114
Stoneham, Ma., U.S.	g11	98
Stonehaven, Scot., U.K.	E10	7
Stone Mountain, Ga., U.S.	C2	87
Stone Mountain, mtn., Ga., U.S.	C2	87
Stones River National Battlefield, hist., Tn., U.S.	B4	119
Stoneville, N.C., U.S.	A3	110
Stonewall, Man., Can.	D3	70
Stonewall, La., U.S.	B2	95
Stonewall, Ms., U.S.	C5	101
Stonewall, co., Tx., U.S.	C2	120
Stonewood, W.V., U.S.	k10	125
Stoney Creek, Ont., Can.	D5	73
Stonington, Ct., U.S.	D8	84
Stonington, Il., U.S.	D4	90
Stonington, Me., U.S.	D4	96
Stono, stm., S.C., U.S.	k11	117
Stono Inlet, b., S.C., U.S.	F8	117
Stony Brook, N.Y., U.S.	n15	109
Stony Brook, stm., N.J., U.S.	C3	107
Stony Creek, stm., Va., U.S.	C5	123
Stony Island, i., N.Y., U.S.	B4	109
Stony Plain, Alta., Can.	C3	68
Stony Point, N.C., U.S.	B1	110
Storby, Fin.	F12	6
Støren, Nor.	E8	6
Storey, co., Nv., U.S.	D2	105
Storfors, Swe.	G10	6
Storkerson Peninsula, pen., N.W. Ter., Can.	B11	66
Storlien, Swe.	E9	6
Storm Lake, Ia., U.S.	B2	92
Storm Lake, l., Ia., U.S.	B2	92
Storm Mountain, mtn., Ak., U.S.	h16	79
Stornoway, Scot., U.K.	C6	7
Storrs, Ct., U.S.	B7	84
Storuman, Swe.	D11	6
Storvreta, Swe.	G11	6
Story, Wy., U.S.	B6	127
Story, co., Ia., U.S.	B4	92
Story City, Ia., U.S.	B4	92
Stoughton, Sask., Can.	H4	75
Stoughton, Ma., U.S.	B5	98
Stoughton, Wi., U.S.	F4	126
Stover, Mo., U.S.	C5	102
Stow, Oh., U.S.	A4	112
Stow Creek, stm., N.J., U.S.	E2	107
Stowe, Pa., U.S.	F10	115
Stowe, Vt., U.S.	C3	122
Stoyoma Mountain, mtn., B.C., Can.	E7	69
Strabane, Pa., U.S.	F1	115
Strafford, Mo., U.S.	D4	102
Strafford, co., N.H., U.S.	D4	106
Straffordville, Ont., Can.	E4	73
Strahan, Austl.	H9	50
Strakonice, Czech.	F13	8
Stralsund, Ger.	A13	8
Stranraer, Scot., U.K.	G7	7
Strasbourg, Fr.	D14	10
Strasburg, Co., U.S.	B6	83
Strasburg, Oh., U.S.	B4	112
Strasburg, Pa., U.S.	G9	115
Strasburg, Va., U.S.	B4	123
Stratford, Ont., Can.	D3	73
Stratford, Ct., U.S.	E3	84
Stratford, Ia., U.S.	B4	92
Stratford, N.J., U.S.	D2	107
Stratford, Ok., U.S.	C5	113
Stratford, Tx., U.S.	A1	120
Stratford, Wi., U.S.	D3	126
Stratford Point, c., Ct., U.S.	E3	84
Stratford-upon-Avon, Eng., U.K.	I11	7
Stratham, N.H., U.S.	D5	106
Strathmore, Alta., Can.	D4	68
Strathmore, Ca., U.S.	D4	82
Strathroy, Ont., Can.	E3	73
Stratton, Co., U.S.	B8	83
Straubing, Ger.	G12	8
Strausberg, Ger.	C13	8
Strawberry, stm., Ar., U.S.	A4	81
Strawberry, stm., Ut., U.S.	C5	121
Strawberry Mountain, mtn., Or., U.S.	C8	114
Strawberry Point, Ia., U.S.	B6	92
Strawberry Point, c., Ma., U.S.	B6	98
Strawberry Range, mts., Or., U.S.	C8	114
Strawberry Reservoir, res., Ut., U.S.	C4	121
Streator, Il., U.S.	B5	90
Stretensk, Russia	G17	24
Strickland, stm., Pap. N. Gui.	m15	50a
Strimón (Struma), stm., Eur.	I7	16
Stromness, Scot., U.K.	C9	7
Stromsburg, Ne., U.S.	C8	104
Strömstad, Swe.	G8	6
Strömsund, Swe.	E10	6
Strong, Ar., U.S.	D3	81
Strong, Me., U.S.	D2	96
Strong, stm., Ms., U.S.	C4	101
Strong City, Ks., U.S.	D7	93
Stronghurst, Il., U.S.	C3	90
Strongsville, Oh., U.S.	A4	112
Stronsay, i., Scot., U.K.	B10	7
Stroud, Ok., U.S.	B5	113
Stroudsburg, Pa., U.S.	E11	115
Stroudwater, stm., Me., U.S.	g7	96
Strum, Wi., U.S.	D2	126
Struma (Strimón), stm., Eur.	H7	16
Strumble Head, c., Wales, U.K.	I7	7
Strumica, Mac.	H6	16
Strunino, Russia	E21	18
Struthers, Oh., U.S.	A5	112
Stryker, Oh., U.S.	A1	112
Stuart, Fl., U.S.	E6	86
Stuart, Ia., U.S.	C3	92
Stuart, Ne., U.S.	B6	104
Stuart, Va., U.S.	D2	123
Stuart, Mount, mtn., Wa., U.S.	B5	124
Stuart Lake, l., B.C., Can.	B5	69
Stuarts Draft, Va., U.S.	B3	123
Stull, stm., Can.	B5	70
Stump Lake, l., N.D., U.S.	B7	111
Stump Pond, res., R.I., U.S.	D2	116
Stung Treng, Camb.	H8	34
Stupino, Russia	G21	18
Sturbridge, Ma., U.S.	B3	98
Sturgeon, Mo., U.S.	B5	102
Sturgeon, stm., Mi., U.S.	B4	99
Sturgeon Bay, Wi., U.S.	D6	126
Sturgeon Bay, b., Man., Can.	C3	70
Sturgeon Falls, Ont., Can.	A5	73

Index

Name Map Ref Page
Sturgeon Lake, l., Ont., Can. C6 73
Sturgis, Sask., Can. F4 75
Sturgis, Ky., U.S. e10 94
Sturgis, Mi., U.S. G5 99
Sturgis, S.D., U.S. C2 118
Sturtevant, Wi., U.S. F6 126
Stutsman, co., N.D., U.S. B6 111
Stuttgart, Ger. G9 8
Stuttgart, Ar., U.S. C4 81
Suaita, Col. D6 58
Subang, Indon. m13 33a
Subansiri, stm., Asia G16 38
Subiaco, Italy H8 14
Sublette, Ks., U.S. E3 93
Sublette, co., Wy., U.S. D2 127
Sublett Range, mts., Id., U.S. G6 89
Sublimity, Or., U.S. C4 114
Subotica, Yugo. C3 16
Sučan, Russia I20 24
Sucarnoochee, stm., Al., U.S. C1 78
Succasunna, N.J., U.S. B3 107
Suceava, Rom. B10 16
Süchbaatar, Mong. A8 26
Suchumi, Geor. I6 22
Sucre, Bol. G5 54
Sucuaro, Col. E8 58
Sudan, ctry., Afr. F12 42
Sudan, reg., Afr. F7 42
Sudbury, Ont., Can. A4 73
Sudbury, Ma., U.S. B5 98
Sudbury, stm., Ma., U.S. B5 98
Sudbury Center, Ma., U.S. g10 98
Sudbury Reservoir, res., Ma., U.S. g10 98
Sudeten see Sudety, mts., Eur. E15 8
Sudety, mts., Eur. E15 8
Sue, stm., Sudan G11 42
Sueca, Spain F11 12
Suez see As-Suways, Egypt C12 42
Suez Canal see Suways, Qanāt as-, Egypt D3 40
Suffern, N.Y., U.S. D6 109
Suffield, Ct., U.S. B5 84
Suffolk, Va., U.S. D6 123
Suffolk, co., Ma., U.S. B5 98
Suffolk, co., N.Y., U.S. n15 109
Sugar, stm., U.S. F4 126
Sugar, stm., N.H., U.S. D2 106
Sugar City, Id., U.S. F7 89
Sugar Creek, Mo., U.S. h11 102
Sugarcreek, Pa., U.S. D2 115
Sugar Creek, stm., Oh., U.S. C2 112
Sugar Creek, stm., Pa., U.S. C8 115
Sugar Grove, Va., U.S. D1 123
Sugar Hill, Ga., U.S. B2 87
Sugar Island, i., Mi., U.S. B6 99
Sugar Land, Tx., U.S. E5 120
Sugarland Run, Va., U.S. *A5 123
Sugar Loaf, Va., U.S. C3 123
Sugarloaf Mountain, mtn., Mt., U.S. C4 103
Sugar Notch, Pa., U.S. n17 115
Suggi Lake, l., Sask., Can. C4 75
Sugoj, stm., Russia E25 24
Şuḩār, Oman D6 46
Suhl, Ger. E10 8
Suiattle, stm., Wa., U.S. A4 124
Suide, China D9 26
Suihua, China B12 26
Suining, China E8 26
Suiping, China B2 28
Suitland, Md., U.S. C4 97
Suizhong, China C11 26
Suja, Russia E24 18
Sukabumi, Indon. m13 32
Sukagawa, Japan E13 30
Sukhumi see Suchumi, Geor. I6 22
Sukkertoppen, Grnld. C22 66
Sukkur, Pak. G3 38
Sukumo, Japan J5 30
Sula, Kepulauan, is., Indon. F8 32
Sulaimān Range, mts., Pak. F3 38
Sulawesi (Celebes), i., Indon. F7 32
Sullana, Peru D2 54
Sulligent, Al., U.S. B1 78
Sullivan, Il., U.S. D5 90
Sullivan, In., U.S. F3 91
Sullivan, Mo., U.S. C6 102
Sullivan, co., In., U.S. F3 91
Sullivan, co., Mo., U.S. A4 102
Sullivan, co., N.H., U.S. D2 106
Sullivan, co., N.Y., U.S. D6 109
Sullivan, co., Pa., U.S. D9 115
Sullivan, co., Tn., U.S. C11 119
Sullivan Lake, l., Alta., Can. D5 68
Sullivans Island, S.C., U.S. k12 117
Sully, Fr. E9 10
Sully, Ia., U.S. C5 92
Sully, co., S.D., U.S. C5 118
Sulmona, Italy G8 14
Sulphur, La., U.S. D2 95
Sulphur, Ok., U.S. C5 113
Sulphur, stm., U.S. D2 81
Sulphur Spring Range, mts., Nv., U.S. C5 105
Sulphur Springs, Tx., U.S. C5 120
Sultan, Wa., U.S. B4 124
Sultānpur, India G10 38
Sulu Archipelago, is., Phil. D7 32
Sulu Sea, Asia D6 32
Sulzbach-Rosenberg, Ger. F11 8
Sumas, Wa., U.S. A3 124
Sumatera (Sumatra), i., Indon. F3 32
Sumatra see Sumatera, i., Indon. F3 32
Sumba, i., Indon. G7 32
Sumbawa, i., Indon. G6 32
Sumbawanga, Tan. C6 44
Sumedang, Indon. m13 33a
Šumen, Bul. F10 16
Sumenep, Indon. m16 33a
Sumiton, Al., U.S. B2 78
Summerfield, N.C., U.S. A3 110
Summerford, Newf., Can. D4 72
Summer Island, i., Mi., U.S. C4 99
Summer Lake, l., Or., U.S. E6 114
Summerland, B.C., Can. E8 69
Summers, co., W.V., U.S. D4 125
Summerside, P.E.I., Can. C6 71
Summersville, W.V., U.S. C4 125
Summersville Lake, res., W.V., U.S. C4 125
Summerton, S.C., U.S. D7 117
Summertown, Tn., U.S. B4 119
Summerville, Ga., U.S. B1 87
Summerville, S.C., U.S. E7 117
Summit, Il., U.S. k9 90
Summit, Ms., U.S. D3 101
Summit, N.J., U.S. B4 107
Summit, Tn., U.S. h11 119
Summit, co., Co., U.S. B4 83
Summit, co., Oh., U.S. A4 112
Summit, co., Ut., U.S. C5 121
Summit Hill, Pa., U.S. E10 115
Summit Lake, l., Ia., U.S. C3 92
Summit Lake Indian Reservation, Nv., U.S. B2 105
Summit Mountain, mtn., Nv., U.S. D5 105
Summit Peak, mtn., Co., U.S. D4 83
Summitville, In., U.S. D6 91
Sumner, Il., U.S. E6 90
Sumner, Ia., U.S. B5 92
Sumner, Wa., U.S. B3 124
Sumner, co., Ks., U.S. E6 93
Sumner, co., Tn., U.S. A5 119
Sumner, Lake, res., N.M., U.S. C5 108
Sumner Dam, N.M., U.S. C5 108
Sumner Strait, strt., Ak., U.S. m23 79
Sumoto, Japan H7 30
Šumperk, Czech. F16 8
Sumqayıt, Azer. I7 22
Sumrall, Ms., U.S. D4 101
Šumšu, Ostrov, i., Russia G25 24
Sumter, S.C., U.S. D7 117
Sumter, co., Al., U.S. C1 78
Sumter, co., Fl., U.S. D4 86
Sumter, co., Ga., U.S. D2 87
Sumter, co., S.C., U.S. D7 117
Sumy, Ukr. G4 22
Sun, stm., Mt., U.S. C4 103
Sunagawa, Japan p19 30a
Sunapee, N.H., U.S. D2 106
Sunapee Lake, l., N.H., U.S. D2 106
Sunbright, Tn., U.S. C9 119
Sunbury, Oh., U.S. B3 112
Sunbury, Pa., U.S. E8 115
Sunchales, Arg. C4 56
Sun City, Az., U.S. k8 80
Suncook, N.H., U.S. D4 106
Suncook, stm., N.H., U.S. D4 106
Suncook Lakes, l., N.H., U.S. D4 106
Sunda, Selat, strt., Indon. G4 32
Sundance, Wy., U.S. B8 127
Sundance Mountain, mtn., Wy., U.S. B8 127
Sundarbans, reg., Asia J13 38
Sunderland, Ont., Can. C5 73
Sunderland, Eng., U.K. G11 7
Sundown, Tx., U.S. C1 120
Sundre, Alta., Can. D3 68
Sundridge, Ont., Can. B5 73
Sundsvall, Swe. E11 6
Sunflower, Ms., U.S. B3 101
Sunflower, co., Ms., U.S. B3 101
Sunflower, Mount, mtn., Ks., U.S. C2 93
Sungaidareh, Indon. O6 34
Sungei Patani, Malay. L6 34
Suniteyouqi, China C9 26
Sunland Park, N.M., U.S. F3 108
Sunlight Creek, stm., Wy., U.S. B3 127
Sunman, In., U.S. F7 91
Sunndalsøra, Nor. E7 6
Sunnyside, Newf., Can. E5 72
Sunnyside, Wa., U.S. C5 124
Sunnyvale, Ca., U.S. k8 82
Sun Prairie, Wi., U.S. E4 126
Sunray, Tx., U.S. A2 120
Sunrise Manor, Nv., U.S. *G6 105
Sunset, La., U.S. D3 95
Sunset, Ut., U.S. B4 121
Sunset Beach, Hi., U.S. f9 88
Sunset Crater Volcano National Monument, Az., U.S. B4 80
Sunset Lake, l., Vt., U.S. D2 122
Suntar, Russia E17 24
Suntar-Chajata, Chrebet, mts., Russia E22 24
Suntaug Lake, l., Ma., U.S. f11 98
Sun Valley, Id., U.S. F4 89
Sun Valley, Nv., U.S. D2 105
Sunyani, Ghana G5 42
Suō-nada, Japan I4 30
Suonenjoki, Fin. E16 6
Suordach, Russia D20 24
Superior, Az., U.S. D4 80
Superior, Mt., U.S. C2 103
Superior, Ne., U.S. D7 104
Superior, Wi., U.S. B1 126
Superior, Wy., U.S. E4 127
Superior, Lake, l., N.A. B9 76
Superstition Mountains, mts., Az., U.S. m10 80
Supetar, Cro. F11 14
Suphan Buri, Thai. G6 34
Suqian, China B7 28
Suquamish, Wa., U.S. B3 124
Suquṭrā (Socotra), i., Yemen F5 46
Şūr (Tyre), Leb. C4 40
Şūr, Oman D6 46
Sur, Point, c., Ca., U.S. D3 82
Surabaya, Indon. m16 33a
Surakarta, Indon. m15 32
Şūrān, Syria B5 40
Surat, India B2 37
Surat Thani (Ban Don), Thai. J5 34
Surendranagar, India I4 38
Surfside, Fl., U.S. s13 86
Surfside Beach, S.C., U.S. D10 117
Surgoinsville, Tn., U.S. C11 119
Sūri, India I12 38
Surigao, Phil. D8 32
Surin, Thai. G7 34
Suriname, ctry., S.A. C7 54
Sūrmaq, Iran B5 46
Surprise, Az., U.S. k8 80
Surrey, N.D., U.S. A4 111
Surry, co., N.C., U.S. A2 110
Surry, co., Va., U.S. C6 123
Surry Mountain Lake, res., N.H., U.S. D2 106
Surt, Libya B9 42
Surt, Khalīj, b., Libya B9 42
Sürüç, Tur. A6 40
Suruga-wan, b., Japan H11 30
Susa, Italy D2 14
Susanville, Ca., U.S. B3 82
Susitna, stm., Ak., U.S. C10 79
Susquehanna, Pa., U.S. C10 115
Susquehanna, co., Pa., U.S. C10 115
Susquehanna, stm., U.S. A5 97
Susquehanna, West Branch, stm., Pa., U.S. D5 115
Sussex, N.B., Can. D4 71
Sussex, N.J., U.S. A3 107
Sussex, Wi., U.S. m11 126
Sussex, co., De., U.S. F4 85
Sussex, co., N.J., U.S. A3 107
Sussex, co., Va., U.S. D5 123
Susurluk, Tur. J12 16
Sutherland, S. Afr. H4 44
Sutherland, Ia., U.S. B2 92
Sutherland, Ne., U.S. C4 104
Sutherlin, Or., U.S. D3 114
Sutlej (Satluj) (Langqên), stm., Asia F4 38
Sutter, co., Ca., U.S. C3 82
Sutter Creek, Ca., U.S. C3 82
Sutton, Que., Can. D5 74
Sutton, Ne., U.S. D8 104
Sutton, W.V., U.S. C4 125
Sutton, co., Tx., U.S. D2 120
Sutton Lake, res., W.V., U.S. C4 125
Sutwik Island, i., Ak., U.S. D8 79
Suur Munamägi, hill, Est. D10 18
Suwa, Japan F11 30
Suwałki, Pol. A22 8
Suwanee, Ga., U.S. B2 87
Suwannee, co., Fl., U.S. B3 86
Suwannee, stm., U.S. C4 86
Suwannee Sound, strt., Fl., U.S. C3 86
Suways, Qanāt as- (Suez Canal), Egypt D3 40
Suwŏn, S. Kor. D12 26
Suxian, China B5 28
Suzaka, Japan F11 30
Suzhou (Soochow), China D9 28
Suzuka, Japan H9 30
Suzu-misaki, c., Japan E10 30
Suzzara, Italy D5 14
Svappavaara, Swe. C13 6
Svartenhuk, pen., Grnld. B22 66
Sv'atoj Nos, Mys, c., Russia C22 24
Sveg, Swe. E10 6
Svenljunga, Swe. H9 6
Svensen, Or., U.S. A3 114
Sverdlovsk see Jekaterinburg, Russia F10 22
Svetlaja, Russia H21 24
Svetlyj, Russia F17 24
Svištov, Bul. F9 16
Svobodnyj, Russia G19 24
Svolvær, Nor. B10 6
Swain, co., N.C., U.S. f9 110
Swainsboro, Ga., U.S. D4 87
Swakopmund, Nmb. F2 44
Swampscott, Ma., U.S. B6 98
Swan, stm., Can. C1 70
Swan Creek, stm., Oh., U.S. e6 112
Swan Falls, wtfl, Id., U.S. F2 89
Swan Hill, Austl. G8 50
Swan Hills, Alta., Can. B3 68
Swan Islands, is., Hond. F6 64
Swan Lake, l., Man., Can. C1 70
Swan Lake, l., Me., U.S. D4 96
Swan Lake, l., Ne., U.S. C3 104
Swannanoa, N.C., U.S. f10 110
Swan Peak, mtn., Mt., U.S. C3 103
Swan Range, mts., Mt., U.S. C3 103
Swan River, Man., Can. C1 70
Swansboro, N.C., U.S. C5 110
Swansea, Wales, U.K. J9 7
Swansea, Il., U.S. E4 90
Swanson Lake, res., Ne., U.S. D4 104
Swanton, Oh., U.S. A2 112
Swanton, Vt., U.S. B2 122
Swanzey Center, N.H., U.S. E2 106
Swarthmore, Pa., U.S. p20 115
Swartswood Lake, l., N.J., U.S. A3 107
Swartz Creek, Mi., U.S. F7 99
Swayzee, In., U.S. C6 91
Swaziland, ctry., Afr. G6 44
Swea City, Ia., U.S. A3 92
Sweden, ctry., Eur. C10 4
Sweeny, Tx., U.S. r14 120
Sweet Grass, co., Mt., U.S. E7 103
Sweet Home, Or., U.S. C4 114
Sweetser, In., U.S. C6 91
Sweet Springs, Mo., U.S. C4 102
Sweetwater, Tn., U.S. D9 119
Sweetwater, Tx., U.S. C2 120
Sweetwater, co., Wy., U.S. E3 127
Sweetwater, stm., Wy., U.S. D4 127
Sweetwater Creek, Fl., U.S. p10 86
Sweetwater Creek, stm., Ok., U.S. B1 113
Swellendam, S. Afr. H4 44
Swepsonville, N.C., U.S. A3 110
Świdnica (Schweidnitz), Pol. E16 8
Swift, co., Mn., U.S. E3 100
Swift, stm., N.H., U.S. B4 106
Swift Creek, stm., N.C., U.S. B5 110
Swift Creek, stm., Va., U.S. n17 123
Swift Creek Reservoir, res., Wa., U.S. C3 124
Swift Diamond, stm., N.H., U.S. g7 106
Swifton, Ar., U.S. B4 81
Swinburne, Cape, c., N.W. Ter., Can. B13 66
Swindon, Eng., U.K. J11 7
Swinford, Ire. H4 7
Swinomish Indian Reservation, Wa., U.S. A3 124
Świnoujście (Swinemünde), Pol. B14 8
Swisher, Ia., U.S. C6 92
Swisher, co., Tx., U.S. B2 120
Swissvale, Pa., U.S. k14 115
Switzer, W.V., U.S. D3 125
Switzerland, Fl., U.S. m8 86
Switzerland, co., In., U.S. G7 91
Switzerland, ctry., Eur. F9 4
Swoyerville, Pa., U.S. D10 115
Syalach, Russia D18 24
Sycamore, Al., U.S. B3 78
Sycamore, Il., U.S. B5 90
Sycamore, Oh., U.S. B2 112
Sycamore Creek, stm., W.V., U.S. m13 125
Sydenham, Ont., Can. C8 73
Sydney, Austl. F10 50
Syke, Ger. C8 8
Sykesville, Md., U.S. B4 97
Sykesville, Pa., U.S. D4 115
Sykkylven, Nor. E6 6
Syktyvkar, Russia E8 22
Sylacauga, Al., U.S. B3 78
Sylhet, Bngl. H14 38
Sylva, N.C., U.S. f9 110
Sylvania, Al., U.S. A4 78
Sylvania, Ga., U.S. D5 87
Sylvania, Oh., U.S. A2 112
Sylvan Lake, Alta., Can. C3 68
Sylvan Lake, Mi., U.S. o15 99
Sylvan Lake, l., In., U.S. B7 91
Sylvan Pass, Wy., U.S. B2 127
Sylvester, Ga., U.S. E3 87
Sym, Russia E11 24
Symmes Creek, stm., Oh., U.S. D3 112
Symsonia, Ky., U.S. f9 94
Syracuse, In., U.S. B6 91
Syracuse, Ks., U.S. E2 93
Syracuse, Ne., U.S. D9 104
Syracuse, N.Y., U.S. B4 109
Syracuse, Ut., U.S. B3 121
Syrdarja (Syr Darya), stm., Asia I11 22
Syria, ctry., Asia B5 40
Syriam, Mya. F4 34
Syrian Desert see Shām, Bādiyat ash-, des., Asia C6 40
Sysladobsis Lake, l., Me., U.S. C4 96
Syzran', Russia G7 22
Szamos (Someș), stm., Eur. B6 16
Szczecin (Stettin), Pol. B14 8
Szczecinek (Neustettin), Pol. B16 8
Szeged, Hung. I20 8
Székesfehérvár, Hung. H18 8
Szentes, Hung. I20 8
Szolnok, Hung. H20 8
Szombathely, Hung. H16 8

T

Taal, Lake, l., Phil. r19 33b
Tabaco, Phil. r20 33b
Tabarka, Tun. M3 14
Tabatinga, Serra da, hills, Braz. F10 54
Tabbys Peak, mtn., Ut., U.S. C3 121
Tabelbala, Alg. C5 42
Taber, Alta., Can. E4 68
Tabernes de Valldigna, Spain F11 12
Tablas Island, i., Phil. C7 32
Table Head, c., Newf., Can. B4 72
Table Mountain, mtn., Az., U.S. E5 80
Table Rock Lake, res., U.S. E4 102
Table Top, mtn., Az., U.S. E3 80
Tabor, Russia C24 24
Tabor, Ia., U.S. D2 92
Tabora, Tan. C6 44
Tabor City, N.C., U.S. C4 110
Tabou, C. Iv. H4 42
Tabrīz, Iran J7 22
Tabūk, Sau. Ar. C2 46
Tacámbaro de Codallos, Mex. H9 62
Tachikawa, Japan G12 30
Tacna, Peru G4 54
Tacoma, Wa., U.S. B3 124
Taconic Range, mts., U.S. A1 98
Tacuarembó, Ur. C5 56
Tacubaya, Mex. C7 62
Tadjerouine, Tun. N3 14
Tadoule Lake, l., Man., Can. E13 66
Tadoussac, Que., Can. A8 74
Tādpatri, India E5 37
Taegu, S. Kor. D12 26
Taejŏn, S. Kor. D12 26
Tafalla, Spain C10 12
Taft, Ca., U.S. E4 82
Taft, Tx., U.S. F4 120
Tagajō, Japan D13 30
Taganrog, Russia H5 22
Taglio di Po, Italy D7 14
Taguatinga, Braz. B5 57
Taguke, China D11 38
Tagula Island, i., Pap. N. Gui. B10 50
Tagus (Tejo) (Tajo), stm., Eur. F3 12
Tahan, Gunong, mtn., Malay. L7 34
Tahat, mtn., Alg. D7 42
Tahlequah, Ok., U.S. B7 113
Tahoe, Lake, l., U.S. E1 105
Tahoe City, Ca., U.S. C3 82
Tahoka, Tx., U.S. C2 120
Taholah, Wa., U.S. B1 124
Tahoua, Niger F7 42
Tahquamenon, stm., Mi., U.S. B5 99
Tahsis, B.C., Can. E4 69
Tahtsa Peak, mtn., B.C., Can. C4 69
T'aichung, Tai. K9 28
T'aichunghsien, Tai. K9 28
Taihape, N.Z. C5 52
Tai Hu, l., China D9 28
Tailai, China B11 26
Tain, Scot., U.K. D8 7
T'ainan, Tai. L9 28
T'aipei, Tai. J10 28
T'aipeihsien, Tai. J10 28
Taiping, Malay. L6 34
Taishun, China H8 28
Taitao, Península de, pen., Chile F2 56
T'aitung, Tai. M10 28
Taivalkoski, Fin. D17 6
Taiwan (T'aiwan), ctry., Asia G11 26
Taiwan Strait, strt., Asia K8 28
Taixian, China C9 28
Taixing, China C9 28
Taiyuan, China D9 26
Taizhou, China C8 28
Ta'izz, Yemen F3 46
Tajikistan, ctry., Asia J12 22
Tajitos, Mex. B3 62
Tajmyr, Ozero, l., Russia C14 24
Tajmyr, Poluostrov, pen., Russia B14 24
Tajšet, Russia F13 24
Tajumulco, Volcán, vol., Guat. G2 64
Tak, Thai. F5 34
Takada, Japan E11 30
Takalar, Indon. G6 32
Takamatsu, Japan H7 30
Takaoka, Japan F10 30
Takapuna, N.Z. B5 52
Takasaki, Japan F12 30
Takatsuki, Japan H8 30
Takawa, Japan I3 30
Takayama, Japan F10 30
Takefu, Japan G9 30
Takêv, Camb. I8 34
Takijuq Lake, l., N.W. Ter., Can. C10 66
Takikawa, Japan p19 30a
Takla Lake, l., B.C., Can. B5 69
Taklimakan Shamo, des., China D3 26
Takoma Park, Md., U.S. f8 97
Taku Glacier, Ak., U.S. k22 79
Tala, Mex. G8 62
Talagang, Pak. D5 38
Talaimannar, Sri L. H5 37
Talara, Peru D2 54
Talarrubias, Spain F6 12
Talasea, Pap. N. Gui. m17 50a
Talaud, Kepulauan, is., Indon. E8 32
Talavera de la Reina, Spain F7 12
Talawdī, Sudan F12 42
Talbot, co., Ga., U.S. D2 87
Talbot, co., Md., U.S. C5 97
Talbot Island, i., Fl., U.S. B5 86
Talbot Lake, l., Man., Can. B2 70
Talbotton, Ga., U.S. D2 87
Talca, Chile D2 56
Talcahuano, Chile D2 56
Talent, Or., U.S. E4 114
Taliabu, Pulau, i., Indon. F7 32
Taliaferro, co., Ga., U.S. C4 87
Talihina, Ok., U.S. C6 113
Talkeetna, Ak., U.S. C10 79
Talkeetna Mountains, mts., Ak., U.S. f17 79
Talladega, Al., U.S. B3 78
Talladega, co., Al., U.S. B3 78
Tallahassee, Fl., U.S. B2 86
Tallahatchie, co., Ms., U.S. B3 101
Tallahatchie, stm., Ms., U.S. B3 101
Tallapoosa, Ga., U.S. C1 87
Tallapoosa, co., Al., U.S. C4 78
Tallapoosa, stm., Al., U.S. C3 78
Tallassee, Al., U.S. C4 78
Talleyville, De., U.S. A3 85
Tallinn, Est. B7 18
Tall Kalakh, Syria B5 40
Tallmadge, Oh., U.S. A4 112
Tall Tamir, Syria A7 40
Tallulah, La., U.S. B4 95
Tal'menka, Russia G10 24
Talo, mtn., Eth. F2 46
Tāloqān, Afg. B3 38
Talquin, Lake, res., Fl., U.S. B2 86
Talu, Indon. N5 34
Taluk, Indon. O6 34
Tama, Ia., U.S. C5 92
Tama, co., Ia., U.S. B5 92
Tamale, Ghana G5 42
Tamalpais, Mount, mtn., Ca., U.S. h7 82
Tamana, Japan J3 30
Tamanrasset, Alg. D7 42
Tamaqua, Pa., U.S. E10 115
Tamaroa, Il., U.S. E4 90
Tamazula de Gordiano, Mex. H8 62
Tamazunchale, Mex. G10 62
Tambacounda, Sen. F3 42
Tambohorano, Madag. E8 44
Tambov, Russia I24 18
Tambura, Sudan G11 42
Tamchaket, Maur. E3 42
Tamel Aike, Arg. F2 56
Tamiahua, Laguna de, b., Mex. G11 62
Tamiami Canal, Fl., U.S. G6 86
Tamil Nadu, state, India G5 37
Tam Ky, Viet. G10 34
Tampa, Fl., U.S. E4 86
Tampa Bay, b., Fl., U.S. E4 86
Tampere, Fin. F14 6
Tampico, Mex. F11 62
Tampico, Il., U.S. B4 90
Tamrida, Yemen F5 46
Tamsagbulag, Mong. B10 26
Tamworth, Austl. F10 50
Tana, Nor. A17 6
Tana, stm., Eur. A16 6
Tana, stm., Kenya B7 44
Tana, Lake, l., Eth. F2 46
Tanabe, Japan I8 30
Tanaga Island, i., Ak., U.S. E4 79
Tanahjampea, Pulau, i., Indon. G7 32
Tanami Desert, des., Austl. C5 50
Tanana, Ak., U.S. B9 79
Tanana, stm., Ak., U.S. C10 79
Tananarive see Antananarivo, Madag. E9 44
Tānda, India G10 38
Tandil, Arg. D5 56
Tando Ādam, Pak. H3 38
Tando Muhammad Khān, Pak. H3 38

Name — Map Ref — Page
Tanega-shima, i., Japan u30 31b
Taney, co., Mo., U.S. E4 102
Taneycomo, Lake, res., Mo., U.S. E4 102
Taneytown, Md., U.S. A3 97
Tanezrouft, des., Afr. D5 42
Tanga, Tan. C7 44
Tangail, Bngl. H13 38
Tanganyika, Lake, l., Afr. C5 44
Tanger (Tangier), Mor. A4 42
Tangerang, Indon. m13 33a
Tangermünde, Ger. C11 8
Tanggula Shan, mts., China D13 38
Tangier, Va., U.S. C7 123
Tangier Island, i., Va., U.S. C6 123
Tangier Sound, strt., Md., U.S. D6 97
Tangier see Tanger, Mor. A4 42
Tangipahoa, co., La., U.S. D5 95
Tangipahoa, stm., La., U.S. D5 95
Tangra Yumco, l., China E12 38
Tangshan, China D10 26
Tanimbar, Kepulauan, is., Indon. G9 32
Tanjungbalai, Indon. M5 34
Tanjungkarang-Telukbetung, Indon. k12 32
Tanjungpinang, Indon. N8 34
Tanjungselor, Indon. E6 32
Tānk, Pak. D4 38
Tännäs, Swe. E9 6
Tanner, Al., U.S. A3 78
Tânout, Niger F7 42
Tanshui, Tai. J10 28
Ṭanṭā, Egypt B12 42
Tanuku, India D6 37
Tanzania, ctry., Afr. C6 44
Taos, Mo., U.S. C5 102
Taos, N.M., U.S. A4 108
Taos, co., N.M., U.S. A4 108
Taos Pueblo, N.M., U.S. A4 108
Taoudenni, Mali D5 42
Tapachula, Mex. J13 62
Tapah, Malay. L6 34
Tapajós, stm., Braz. E7 54
Taphan Hin, Thai. F6 34
Tāpi, stm., India B2 37
Tappahannock, Va., U.S. C6 123
Tappan, N.Y., U.S. g13 109
Tappan, Lake, res., N.J., U.S. g9 107
Tappan Lake, res., Oh., U.S. B4 112
Taqātu' Hayyā, Sudan E13 42
Taquaritinga, Braz. F4 57
Tar, stm., N.C., U.S. B5 110
Tara, Ont., Can. C3 73
Tarābulus (Tripoli), Leb. B4 40
Ṭarābulus (Tripoli), Libya B8 42
Ṭarābulus (Tripolitania), reg., Libya B8 42
Tarakan, Indon. E6 32
Tarancón, Spain E8 12
Taranto, Italy I12 14
Taranto, Golfo di, b., Italy I12 14
Tarapacá, Col. I8 58
Tarare, Fr. G11 10
Tarascon, Fr. J8 10
Tarata, Bol. G5 54
Tarazona, Spain D10 12
Tarazona de la Mancha, Spain F10 12
Tarbert, Scot., U.K. F7 7
Tarbert, Scot., U.K. D6 7
Tarbes, Fr. I7 10
Tarboro, N.C., U.S. B5 110
Tarcento, Italy C8 14
Taree, Austl. F10 50
Tareja, Russia C12 24
Tarentum, Pa., U.S. E2 115
Tarfaya, Mor. C3 42
Targhee Pass, U.S. E7 89
Tarifa, Punta de, c., Spain I6 12
Tariffville, Ct., U.S. B4 84
Tarija, Bol. H6 54
Tarim, stm., China C3 26
Tarīn Kowt, Afg. D1 38
Tarkio, Mo., U.S. A2 102
Tarkwa, Ghana G5 42
Tarlac, Phil. q19 32
Tarn, stm., Fr. I8 10
Tärnaby, Swe. D10 6
Tarnak, stm., Afg. D2 38
Tarnów, Pol. E20 8
Tarnowskie Góry, Pol. E18 8
Tarpey, Ca., U.S. D4 82
Tarpon, Lake, l., Fl., U.S. o10 86
Tarpon Springs, Fl., U.S. D4 86
Tarquinia, Italy G6 14
Tarragona, Spain D13 12
Tarrant, Al., U.S. B3 78
Tarrant, co., Tx., U.S. C4 120
Tarrasa, Spain D14 12
Tarryall Mountains, mts., Co., U.S. B5 83
Tarrytown, N.Y., U.S. D7 109
Tarsus, Tur. A4 40
Tartagal, Arg. A4 56
Tartas, Fr. I6 10
Tartu, Est. C9 18
Tarṭūs, Syria B4 40
Tarutung, Indon. M5 34
Tašauz, Turk. I9 22
Tasejeva, stm., Russia F12 24
Tasejevo, Russia F12 24
Taseko Mountain, mtn., B.C., Can. D6 69
Tashi Gang Dzong, Bhu. G14 38
Tashkent see Taškent, Uzb. I11 22
Tasikmalaya, Indon. m14 33a
Taškent, Uzb. I11 22
Tasmania, state, Austl. H9 50
Tasman Sea, Oc. G11 50
Tasso, Tn., U.S. D9 119
Taštagol, Russia G11 24
Tatabánya, Hung. H18 8
Tatarskij Proliv, strt., Russia H22 24
Tate, Ga., U.S. B2 87
Tate, co., Ms., U.S. A4 101
Tateville, Ky., U.S. D5 94
Tateyama, Japan H12 30
Tathlina Lake, l., N.W. Ter., Can. D9 66
Tatnam, Cape, c., Man., Can. f9 70
Tatta, Pak. H2 38
Tattnall, co., Ga., U.S. D4 87
Tatum, N.M., U.S. D6 108
Tatvan, Tur. H16 4
Tau, Nor. G5 6
Taubaté, Braz. G6 57
Tauberbischofsheim, Ger. F9 8
Taujskaja Guba, b., Russia F24 24
Taumarunui, N.Z. C5 52
Taum Sauk Mountain, mtn., Mo., U.S. D6 102
Taungdwingyi, Mya. D3 34
Taunggyi, Mya. D4 34
Taungup Pass, Mya. E3 34
Taunton, Eng., U.K. J9 7
Taunton, Ma., U.S. C5 98
Taunton, stm., Ma., U.S. C5 98
Taupo, Lake, l., N.Z. C5 52
Tauranga, N.Z. B6 52
Taureau, Réservoir, res., Que., Can. C4 74
Taurus Mountains see Toros Dağları, mts., Tur. H14 4
Tauste, Spain D10 12
Tavares, Fl., U.S. D5 86
Tavernier, Fl., U.S. G6 86
Tavira, Port. H4 12
Tavoy Point, c., Mya. H5 34
Tavşanlı, Tur. J13 16
Tawakoni, Lake, res., Tx., U.S. C4 120
Tawas City, Mi., U.S. D7 99
Tawas Lake, l., Mi., U.S. D7 99
Tawau, Malay. E6 32
Tawitawi Island, i., Phil. D6 32
Ṭawkar, Sudan E13 42
Taxco de Alarcón, Mex. H10 62
Tay, Loch, l., Scot., U.K. E8 7
Taylor, B.C., Can. A7 69
Taylor, Az., U.S. C5 80
Taylor, Ar., U.S. D2 81
Taylor, Mi., U.S. p15 99
Taylor, Pa., U.S. D10 115
Taylor, Tx., U.S. D4 120
Taylor, co., Fl., U.S. B3 86
Taylor, co., Ga., U.S. D2 87
Taylor, co., Ia., U.S. D3 92
Taylor, co., Ky., U.S. C4 94
Taylor, co., Tx., U.S. C3 120
Taylor, co., W.V., U.S. B4 125
Taylor, co., Wi., U.S. C3 126
Taylor, stm., Co., U.S. C4 83
Taylor, Mount, mtn., N.M., U.S. B2 108
Taylor Mill, Ky., U.S. k14 94
Taylor Mountain, mtn., Id., U.S. E4 89
Taylor Park Reservoir, res., Co., U.S. C4 83
Taylors, S.C., U.S. B3 117
Taylors Falls, Mn., U.S. E6 100
Taylors Island, i., Md., U.S. D5 97
Taylorsville, In., U.S. F6 91
Taylorsville, Ky., U.S. B4 94
Taylorsville, Ms., U.S. D4 101
Taylorsville, N.C., U.S. B1 110
Taylorville, Il., U.S. D4 90
Tayma', Sau. Ar. C2 46
Tay Ninh, Viet. I9 34
Tayoltita, Mex. E7 62
Taytay, Phil. C6 32
Taz, stm., Russia D10 24
Taza, Mor. B5 42
Tazewell, Tn., U.S. C10 119
Tazewell, Va., U.S. e10 123
Tazewell, co., Il., U.S. C4 90
Tazewell, co., Va., U.S. e10 123
Tazin Lake, l., Sask., Can. E11 66
Tbessa, Alg. A7 42
Tbilisi, Geor. I6 22
Tbong, Camb. H8 34
Tchefuncta, stm., La., U.S. D5 95
Tchibanga, Gabon B2 44
Tchien, Lib. G4 42
Tchula, Ms., U.S. B3 101
Tczew, Pol. A18 8
Tea, S.D., U.S. D9 118
Teacapán, Mex. F7 62
Teague, Tx., U.S. D4 120
Teakean Butte, mtn., Id., U.S. C2 89
Te Anau, Lake, l., N.Z. F1 52
Teaneck, N.J., U.S. h8 107
Teano, Italy H9 14
Teaticket, Ma., U.S. C6 98
Tebingtinggi, Indon. M5 34
Téboursouk, Tun. M4 14
Tecate, Mex. A1 62
Tecolotlan, Mex. G7 62
Tecomán, Mex. H8 62
Tecpan de Galeana, Mex. I9 62
Tecuala, Mex. F7 62
Tecuci, Rom. D11 16
Tecumseh, Ont., Can. E2 73
Tecumseh, Ks., U.S. k14 93
Tecumseh, Mi., U.S. G7 99
Tecumseh, Ne., U.S. D9 104
Tecumseh, Ok., U.S. B5 113
Tedžen (Harīrūd), stm., Asia J10 22
Teeswater, Ont., Can. C3 73
Tefé, Braz. D6 54
Tegal, Indon. m14 32
Tegucigalpa, Hond. G4 64
Tehachapi, Ca., U.S. E4 82
Tehachapi Mountains, mts., Ca., U.S. E4 82
Tehama, co., Ca., U.S. B2 82
Tehrān, Iran J8 22
Tehuacán, Mex. H11 62
Tehuantepec, Mex. I12 62
Tehuantepec, Golfo de, b., Mex. J12 62
Tehuantepec, Istmo de, Mex. I12 62
Teide, Pico de, mtn., Spain p24 13b
Tejamén, Mex. E7 62
Tejkovo, Russia E23 18
Tejupan, Punta, c., Mex. H8 62
Tekamah, Ne., U.S. C9 104
Tekirdağ, Tur. I11 16
Tekoa, Wa., U.S. B8 124
Tekonsha, Mi., U.S. F5 99
Tela, Hond. G4 64
Telavåg, Nor. F5 6
Tel Aviv-Yafo, Isr. C4 40
Teleckoje, Ozero, l., Russia G11 24
Telén, Arg. D3 56
Telescope Peak, mtn., Ca., U.S. D5 82
Teles Pires, stm., Braz. E7 54
Telfair, co., Ga., U.S. E4 87
Telford, Pa., U.S. F11 115
Telfs, Aus. H11 8
Teli, Russia G12 24
Telkwa, B.C., Can. B4 69
Tell City, In., U.S. I4 91
Teller, co., Co., U.S. C5 83
Tellicherry, India G3 37
Tellico Plains, Tn., U.S. D9 119
Telluride, Co., U.S. D3 83
Telok Anson, Malay. L6 34
Telos Lake, l., Me., U.S. B3 96
Temagami, Lake, l., Ont., Can. G16 66
Tembeling, stm., Malay. L7 34
Tembenči, stm., Russia D13 24
Temecula, Ca., U.S. F5 82
Temerloh, Malay. M7 34
Teminabuan, Indon. F9 32
Témiscouata, Lac, l., Que., Can. B9 74
Te-Moak Indian Reservation, Nv., U.S. C6 105
Temósachic, Mex. C6 62
Tempe, Az., U.S. D4 80
Temperance, Mi., U.S. G7 99
Temperance, stm., Mn., U.S. C8 100
Tempio Pausania, Italy I4 14
Temple, Ga., U.S. C1 87
Temple, Ok., U.S. C3 113
Temple, Pa., U.S. F10 115
Temple, Tx., U.S. D4 120
Temple Terrace, Fl., U.S. o11 86
Templin, Ger. B13 8
Temuco, Chile D2 56
Tena, Ec. H4 58
Tenafly, N.J., U.S. B5 107
Tenaha, Tx., U.S. D5 120
Tenāli, India D6 37
Tendaho, Eth. F3 46
Tende, Col de, Eur. H14 10
Ten Degree Channel, strt., India J2 34
Ténéré, des., Niger E8 42
Tenerife, i., Spain p24 13b
Tengchong, China B5 34
Tenino, Wa., U.S. C3 124
Tenkāsi, India H4 37
Tenkiller Ferry Lake, res., Ok., U.S. B6 113
Tenkodogo, Burkina F5 42
Tenmile, stm., U.S. B5 116
Tenmile Creek, stm., W.V., U.S. k10 125
Tenmile Lake, l., Mn., U.S. D4 100
Tennant Creek, Austl. C6 50
Tennessee, state, U.S. B5 119
Tennessee, stm., U.S. D9 76
Tennessee Pass, Co., U.S. B4 83
Tennessee Ridge, Tn., U.S. A4 119
Tennille, Ga., U.S. D4 87
Tenom, Malay. D6 32
Tenryū, stm., Japan G10 30
Tensas, co., La., U.S. B4 95
Tensas, stm., La., U.S. B4 95
Tensaw, stm., Al., U.S. E2 78
Ten Sleep, Wy., U.S. B5 127
Tenterfield, Austl. E10 50
Ten Thousand Islands, is., Fl., U.S. G5 86
Teocaltiche, Mex. G8 62
Teófilo Otoni, Braz. D8 57
Tepa, Indon. G8 32
Tepatitlán [de Morelos], Mex. G8 62
Tepic, Mex. G7 62
Teplice, Czech. E13 8
Teramo, Italy G8 14
Teresina, Braz. E10 54
Teresópolis, Braz. G7 57
Termez, Uzb. B2 38
Termini Imerese, Italy L8 14
Términos, Laguna de, b., Mex. H14 62
Termoli, Italy G9 14
Ternej, Russia H21 24
Terni, Italy G7 14
Ternopil', Ukr. H3 22
Terpenija, Mys, c., Russia H22 24
Terpenija, Zaliv, b., Russia H22 24
Terra Alta, W.V., U.S. B5 125
Terrace, B.C., Can. B3 69
Terracina, Italy H8 14
Terralba, Italy J3 14
Terra Nova National Park, Newf., Can. D4 72
Terrebonne, Que., Can. D4 74
Terrebonne, Or., U.S. C5 114
Terrebonne, co., La., U.S. E5 95
Terrebonne Bay, b., La., U.S. E5 95
Terre Haute, In., U.S. F3 91
Terre Hill, Pa., U.S. F9 115
Terrell, Tx., U.S. C4 120
Terrell, co., Ga., U.S. E2 87
Terrell, co., Tx., U.S. D1 120
Terrell Hills, Tx., U.S. k7 120
Terrenceville, Newf., Can. E4 72
Terry, Ms., U.S. C3 101
Terry, Mt., U.S. D11 103
Terry, co., Tx., U.S. C1 120
Terrytown, Ne., U.S. C2 104
Terryville, Ct., U.S. C3 84
Teruel, Spain E10 12
Tervola, Fin. C15 6
Teseney, Erit. E2 46
Teshekpuk Lake, l., Ak., U.S. A9 79
Teshio, Japan o19 30a
Teslin, Yukon, Can. D6 66
Teslin, stm., Can. D6 66
Tesouro, Braz. D2 57
Tessalit, Mali D6 42
Tesuque, N.M., U.S. B4 108
Tete, Moz. E6 44
Teterow, Ger. B12 8
Teton, co., Id., U.S. F7 89
Teton, co., Mt., U.S. C4 103
Teton, co., Wy., U.S. C2 127
Teton, stm., Mt., U.S. C5 103
Teton Pass, Wy., U.S. C2 127
Teton Range, mts., Wy., U.S. C2 127
Teton Village, Wy., U.S. C2 127
Tétouan, Mor. A4 42
Tetovo, Mac. G4 16
Tet'uche, Russia I21 24
Teulada, Italy K3 14
Teulon, Man., Can. D3 70
Teutopolis, Il., U.S. D5 90
Teuva, Fin. E13 6
Tevere (Tiber), stm., Italy G7 14
Teverya, Isr. C4 40
Tewksbury, Ma., U.S. A5 98
Texada Island, i., B.C., Can. E5 69
Texarkana, Ar., U.S. D1 81
Texarkana, Tx., U.S. C5 120
Texas, co., Mo., U.S. D5 102
Texas, co., Ok., U.S. e9 113
Texas, state, U.S. D3 120
Texas City, Tx., U.S. E5 120
Texhoma, Ok., U.S. e9 113
Texico, N.M., U.S. C6 108
Texoma, Lake, res., U.S. D5 113
Teyvareh, Afg. D1 38
Teziutlán, Mex. H11 62
Tezpur, India G15 38
Thabazimbi, S. Afr. F5 44
Thai Binh, Viet. D9 34
Thailand, ctry., Asia B3 32
Thailand, Gulf of, b., Asia J6 34
Thai Nguyen, Viet. D8 34
Thal, Pak. D4 38
Thames, stm., Ont., Can. E3 73
Thames, stm., Eng., U.K. J14 7
Thames, stm., Ct., U.S. D7 84
Thamesville, Ont., Can. E3 73
Thāna, India C2 37
Thanh Hoa, Viet. E8 34
Thanh Pho Ho Chi Minh (Saigon), Viet. I9 34
Thanjāvūr, India G5 37
Thar Desert (Great Indian Desert), des., Asia G3 38
Thargomindah, Austl. E8 50
Thatcher, Az., U.S. E6 80
Thaton, Mya. F4 34
Thayer, Mo., U.S. E6 102
Thayer, co., Ne., U.S. D8 104
Thayetmyo, Mya. E3 34
Thayne, Wy., U.S. D1 127
Thealka, Ky., U.S. C7 94
The Barrens, plat., Tn., U.S. B5 119
The Bight, Bah. B10 64
The Cheviot, mtn., Eng., U.K. F10 7
The Colony, Tx., U.S. *C4 120
The Dalles, Or., U.S. B5 114
The Dells, val., Wi., U.S. E4 126
Thedford, Ont., Can. D3 73
The English Company's Islands, is., Austl. B7 50
The Everglades, sw., Fl., U.S. G6 86
The Fens, sw., Eng., U.K. I12 7
The Flat Tops, mts., Co., U.S. B3 83
The Flume, wtfl, N.H., U.S. B3 106
The Graves, is., Ma., U.S. g12 98
The Hague see 's-Gravenhage, Neth. C4 8
The Heads, c., Or., U.S. E2 114
Thelon, stm., N.W. Ter., Can. D12 66
The Narrows, strt., Wa., U.S. f10 124
Theodore, Austl. D10 50
Theodore, Al., U.S. E1 78
Theodore Roosevelt Lake, res., Az., U.S. D4 80
Theodore Roosevelt National Park (South Unit), N.D., U.S. C2 111
Theodore Roosevelt National Park (North Unit), N.D., U.S. B2 111
The Pas, Man., Can. C1 70
The Plains, Oh., U.S. C3 112
Theresa, Wi., U.S. E5 126
Thermopolis, Wy., U.S. C4 127
The Rockies, mts., Wa., U.S. C3 124
Thessalon, Ont., Can. p19 73
Thessaloníki (Salonika), Grc. I6 16
Thetford Mines, Que., Can. C6 74
The Thimbles, is., Ct., U.S. E5 84
The Village, Ok., U.S. B4 113
The Warburton, stm., Austl. E7 50
The Wash, b., Eng., U.K. I13 7
The Weald, reg., Eng., U.K. J13 7
Thibodaux, La., U.S. E5 95
Thief, stm., Mn., U.S. B2 100
Thief Lake, l., Mn., U.S. B3 100
Thief River Falls, Mn., U.S. B2 100
Thielsen, Mount, mtn., Or., U.S. D4 114
Thiene, Italy D6 14
Thiensville, Wi., U.S. E6 126
Thiers, Fr. G10 10
Thiès, Sen. F2 42
Thika, Kenya B7 44
Thimphu, Bhu. G13 38
Thingangyun, Mya. F4 34
Thionville, Fr. C13 10
Thíra, i., Grc. M9 16
Third Lake, l., N.H., U.S. f7 106
Thirsk, Eng., U.K. G11 7
Thisted, Den. H7 6
Thívai (Thebes), Grc. K7 16
Thiviers, Fr. G7 10
Thomas, Ok., U.S. B3 113
Thomas, co., Ga., U.S. F3 87
Thomas, co., Ks., U.S. C2 93
Thomas, co., Ne., U.S. C5 104
Thomasboro, Il., U.S. C5 90
Thomaston, Ct., U.S. C3 84
Thomaston, Ga., U.S. D2 87
Thomaston, Me., U.S. D3 96
Thomaston Reservoir, res., Ct., U.S. C3 84
Thomastown, Ire. I5 7
Thomasville, Al., U.S. D2 78
Thomasville, Ga., U.S. F3 87
Thomasville, N.C., U.S. B2 110
Thompson, Man., Can. B3 70
Thompson, Ct., U.S. B8 84
Thompson, N.D., U.S. B8 111
Thompson, stm., U.S. A4 102
Thompson Falls, Mt., U.S. C1 103
Thompson Island, i., Ma., U.S. g11 98
Thompson Lake, l., U.S. D2 96
Thompson Peak, mtn., Ca., U.S. B2 82
Thompson Peak, mtn., N.M., U.S. h9 108
Thompson Reservoir, res., Or., U.S. E5 114
Thomsen, stm., N.W. Ter., Can. B9 66
Thomson, Ga., U.S. C4 87
Thon Buri, Thai. H6 34
Thongwa, Mya. F4 34
Thonon-les-Bains, Fr. F13 10
Thonotosassa, Fl., U.S. D4 86
Thonze, Mya. F3 34
Thorburn, N.S., Can. D7 71
Thoreau, N.M., U.S. B1 108
Thornbury, Ont., Can. C4 73
Thorndale, Tx., U.S. D4 120
Thornton, Ont., Can. C5 73
Thorntown, In., U.S. D4 91
Thorold, Ont., Can. D5 73
Thorp, Wi., U.S. D3 126
Thorsby, Al., U.S. C3 78
Thouars, Fr. F6 10
Thousand Islands, is., N.Y., U.S. A4 109
Thousand Lake Mountain, mtn., Ut., U.S. E4 121
Thousand Springs Creek, stm., U.S. B7 105
Thrace, hist. reg., Eur. G13 4
Thrakikón Pélagos, Grc. I8 16
Three Fingered Jack, mtn., Or., U.S. C5 114
Three Forks, Mt., U.S. E5 103
Three Hills, Alta., Can. D4 68
Three Lakes, Wi., U.S. C4 126
Three Mile Plains, N.S., Can. E5 71
Three Oaks, Mi., U.S. G4 99
Three Pagodas Pass, Asia G5 34
Three Points, Cape, c., Ghana H5 42
Three Rivers, Ma., U.S. B3 98
Three Rivers, Mi., U.S. G5 99
Three Rivers, Tx., U.S. E3 120
Three Sisters, mtn., Or., U.S. C5 114
Three Springs, Austl. E3 50
Throckmorton, co., Tx., U.S. C3 120
Throop, Pa., U.S. m18 115
Throssell Range, mts., Austl. D4 50
Thu Dao Mot, Viet. I9 34
Thule, Grnld. B19 128
Thun, Switz. F14 10
Thunder Bay, Ont., Can. o17 73
Thunder Bay, b., Mi., U.S. D7 99
Thunder Bay, stm., Mi., U.S. D6 99
Thunderbird, Lake, res., Ok., U.S. B4 113
Thunderbolt, Ga., U.S. D5 87
Thunder Butte Creek, stm., S.D., U.S. B3 118
Thunersee, l., Switz. F14 10
Thüringen, hist. reg., Ger. D11 8
Thurles, Ire. I5 7
Thurmont, Md., U.S. A3 97
Thurso, Que., Can. D2 74
Thurso, Scot., U.K. C9 7
Thurston, co., Ne., U.S. B9 104
Thurston, co., Wa., U.S. C2 124
Tiancang, China C7 26
Tiandong, China C9 34
Tianjin (Tientsin), China D10 26
Tianjun, China D6 26
Tianmen, China E2 28
Tianshui, China E8 26
Tiaret, Alg. A6 42
Tibagi, Braz. A6 56
Tibasti, Sarīr, des., Libya D9 42
Tiber see Tevere, stm., Italy G7 14
Tibesti, mts., Chad D9 42
Tibet, hist. reg., China E12 38
Tiburón, Isla, i., Mex. C3 62
Tice, Fl., U.S. F5 86
Tichît, Maur. E4 42
Tichvin, Russia B16 18
Tickfaw, stm., La., U.S. C5 95
Ticonderoga, N.Y., U.S. B7 109
Ticul, Mex. G15 62
Tide Head, N.B., Can. B3 71
Tidjikdja, Maur. E3 42
Tieling, China C11 26
Tienen, Bel. E4 8
Tien Shan, mts., Asia C2 26
Tientsin see Tianjin, China D10 26
Tierra Amarilla, N.M., U.S. A3 108
Tierra Blanca, Mex. H11 62
Tierra del Fuego, Isla Grande de, i., S.A. G3 56
Tierralta, Col. C4 58
Tietê, stm., Braz. F3 57
Tieton, Wa., U.S. C5 124
Tieton, stm., Wa., U.S. C4 124
Tieton Dam, Wa., U.S. C4 124
Tiffany Mountain, mtn., Wa., U.S. A6 124
Tiffin, Oh., U.S. A2 112
Tiffin, stm., Oh., U.S. A1 112
Tift, co., Ga., U.S. E3 87
Tifton, Ga., U.S. E3 87
Tigard, Or., U.S. h12 114
Tigerton, Wi., U.S. D4 126
Tigil', Russia F25 24
Tignall, Ga., U.S. C4 87
Tignish, P.E.I., Can. C5 71
Tigre, stm., Peru D3 54
Tigris (Dijlah), stm., Asia A3 46
Tiguentourine, Alg. C7 42
Tijesno, Cro. F10 14
Tijuana, Mex. A1 62
Tikamgarh, India H8 38
Tikrīt, Iraq B3 46
Tilburg, Neth. D5 8

Name	Map Ref	Page
Tilbury, Ont., Can.	E2	73
Tilden, Il., U.S.	E4	90
Tilden, Ne., U.S.	B8	104
Tilghman, Md., U.S.	C5	97
Tilghman Island, i., Md., U.S.	C5	97
Tilhar, India	G8	38
Tillabéry, Niger	F6	42
Tillamook, Or., U.S.	B3	114
Tillamook, co., Or., U.S.	B3	114
Tillanchong Island, i., India	J2	34
Tillery, Lake, res., N.C., U.S.	B2	110
Tillman, co., Ok., U.S.	C2	113
Tillmans Corner, Al., U.S.	E1	78
Tillsonburg, Ont., Can.	E4	73
Tilton, Il., U.S.	C6	90
Tilton, N.H., U.S.	D3	106
Tiltonsville, Oh., U.S.	B5	112
Timaru, N.Z.	F3	52
Timbalier Island, i., La., U.S.	E5	95
Timberlake, Va., U.S.	C3	123
Timberville, Va., U.S.	B4	123
Timbuktu see Tombouctou, Mali	E5	42
Timimoun, Alg.	C6	42
Timiris, Cap, c., Maur.	E2	42
Timişoara, Rom.	D5	16
Timmins, Ont., Can.	o19	73
Timmonsville, S.C., U.S.	C8	117
Timms Hill, hill, Wi., U.S.	C3	126
Timor, i., Indon.	G8	32
Timor Sea	B5	50
Timotes, Ven.	C7	58
Timpanogos Cave National Monument, Ut., U.S.	C4	121
Timpton, stm., Russia	F19	24
Tims Ford Lake, res., Tn., U.S.	B5	119
Tinaquillo, Ven.	C8	58
Tindivanam, India	F5	37
Tindouf, Alg.	C4	42
Tingmerkpuk Mountain, mtn., Ak., U.S.	B7	79
Tingo María, Peru	E3	54
Tingvoll, Nor.	E7	6
Tinharé, Ilha de, i., Braz.	F11	54
Tinker Air Force Base, mil., Ok., U.S.	B4	113
Tinley Park, Il., U.S.	k9	90
Tinniswood, Mount, mtn., B.C., Can.	D6	69
Tinogasta, Arg.	B3	56
Tinsukia, India	G16	38
Tinton Falls, N.J., U.S.	C4	107
Tioga, La., U.S.	C3	95
Tioga, N.D., U.S.	A3	111
Tioga, co., N.Y., U.S.	C4	109
Tioga, co., Pa., U.S.	C7	115
Tioga, stm., Pa., U.S.	B7	115
Tiogue Lake, res., R.I., U.S.	D3	116
Tioman, Pulau, i., Malay.	M8	34
Tionesta Creek, stm., Pa., U.S.	C3	115
Tionesta Lake, res., Pa., U.S.	D3	115
Tioughnioga, stm., N.Y., U.S.	C4	109
Tippah, co., Ms., U.S.	A5	101
Tippah, stm., Ms., U.S.	A4	101
Tipp City, Oh., U.S.	C1	112
Tippecanoe, co., In., U.S.	D4	91
Tippecanoe, stm., In., U.S.	C4	91
Tipperary, Ire.	I4	7
Tipton, Ca., U.S.	D4	82
Tipton, In., U.S.	D5	91
Tipton, Ia., U.S.	C6	92
Tipton, Mo., U.S.	C5	102
Tipton, Ok., U.S.	C2	113
Tipton, co., In., U.S.	D5	91
Tipton, co., Tn., U.S.	B2	119
Tipton, Mount, mtn., Az., U.S.	B1	80
Tiptonville, Tn., U.S.	A2	119
Tiquisate, Guat.	G2	64
Tiracambu, Serra do, plat., Braz.	D9	54
Tīrān, Maḍīq, strt.	F4	40
Tiran, Strait of see Tīrān, Maḍīq, strt.	F4	40
Tiranë, Alb.	H3	16
Tirano, Italy	C5	14
Tiraspol, Mol.	H3	22
Tirat Karmel, Isr.	C4	40
Tire, Tur.	K11	16
Tiree, i., Scot., U.K.	E6	7
Tîrgovişte, Rom.	E9	16
Tîrgu-Jiu, Rom.	D7	16
Tîrgu Mureş, Rom.	C8	16
Tîrgu-Ocna, Rom.	C10	16
Tírnavos, Grc.	J6	16
Tirschenreuth, Ger.	F12	8
Tiruchchirāppalli, India	G5	37
Tirunelveli, India	H4	37
Tirupati, India	F5	37
Tiruppattūr, India	F5	37
Tiruppur, India	G4	37
Tiruvannāmalai, India	F5	37
Tishomingo, Ok., U.S.	C5	113
Tishomingo, co., Ms., U.S.	A5	101
Tiskilwa, Il., U.S.	B4	90
Tisza (Tisa), stm., Eur.	C4	16
Tit-Ary, Russia	C19	24
Titicaca, Lago, l., S.A.	G5	54
Titonka, Ia., U.S.	A3	92
Titov Veles, Mac.	H5	16
Titule, Zaire	H11	42
Titus, co., Tx., U.S.	C5	120
Titusville, Fl., U.S.	D6	86
Titusville, Pa., U.S.	C2	115
Tiverton, Ont., Can.	C3	73
Tiverton, Eng., U.K.	K9	7
Tiverton, R.I., U.S.	D6	116
Tivoli, Italy	H7	14
Tizimín, Mex.	G15	62
Tizi-Ouzou, Alg.	A6	42
Tlahualilo de Zaragoza, Mex.	D8	62
Tlaltenango de Sánchez Román, Mex.	G8	62
Tlaxiaco, Mex.	I11	62
Tlemcen, Alg.	B5	42
Tlētē Ouāte Gharbī, Jabal, mtn., Syria	B6	40
Toamasina, Madag.	E9	44
Toano, Va., U.S.	C6	123
Toano Range, mts., Nv., U.S.	C7	105
Toast, N.C., U.S.	A2	110
Toba, Japan	H9	30
Toba, Danau, l., Indon.	M5	34
Tobacco Root Mountains, mts., Mt., U.S.	E5	103
Tobago, i., Trin.	I17	64
Toba Inlet, b., B.C., Can.	D5	69
Toba Kākar Range, mts., Pak.	E2	38
Tobarra, Spain	G10	12
Tobermory, Scot., U.K.	E6	7
Tobin, Mount, mtn., Nv., U.S.	C4	105
Tobin Lake, l., Sask., Can.	D4	75
Tobin Range, mts., Nv., U.S.	C4	105
Tobique, stm., N.B., Can.	B2	71
Tobruk see Ṭubruq, Libya	B10	42
Tobyhanna, Pa., U.S.	D11	115
Tocantínia, Braz.	E9	54
Tocantinópolis, Braz.	E9	54
Tocantins, stm., Braz.	D9	54
Toccoa, Ga., U.S.	B3	87
Toccoa, stm., Ga., U.S.	B2	87
Toccoa Falls, Ga., U.S.	B3	87
Tochigi, Japan	F12	30
Töcksfors, Swe.	G8	6
Toco, Chile	A3	56
Tocopilla, Chile	A2	56
Todd, co., Ky., U.S.	D2	94
Todd, co., Mn., U.S.	D4	100
Todd, co., S.D., U.S.	D5	118
Todi, Italy	G7	14
Todos Santos, Mex.	F4	62
Todtnau, Ger.	H7	8
Tofield, Alta., Can.	C4	68
Tofino, B.C., Can.	E5	69
Togiak, Ak., U.S.	D7	79
Togian, Kepulauan, is., Indon.	F7	32
Togo, ctry., Afr.	G6	42
Togwotee Pass, Wy., U.S.	C2	127
Tohakum Peak, mtn., Nv., U.S.	C2	105
Tohatchi, N.M., U.S.	B1	108
Tohopekaliga, Lake, l., Fl., U.S.	D5	86
Toiyabe Range, mts., Nv., U.S.	D4	105
Tok, Ak., U.S.	C11	79
Tōkamachi, Japan	E11	30
Tokara-kaikyō, strt., Japan	u30	31b
Tokara-rettō, is., Japan	v29	31b
Tokat, Tur.	G15	4
Tokelau Islands, dep., Oc.	G1	2
Toki, Japan	G10	30
Tokuno-shima, i., Japan	x28	31b
Tokushima, Japan	H7	30
Tokuyama, Japan	H4	30
Tōkyō, Japan	G12	30
Tokzār, Afg.	C2	38
Toleak Point, c., Wa., U.S.	B1	124
Toledo, Spain	F7	12
Toledo, Il., U.S.	D5	90
Toledo, Ia., U.S.	B5	92
Toledo, Oh., U.S.	A2	112
Toledo, Or., U.S.	C3	114
Toledo Bend Reservoir, res., U.S.	C2	95
Tolentino, Italy	F8	14
Toler, Ky., U.S.	C7	94
Toliara, Madag.	F8	44
Toljatti, Russia	G7	22
Tol'ka, Russia	E10	24
Tolland, Ct., U.S.	B6	84
Tolland, co., Ct., U.S.	B6	84
Tollesboro, Ky., U.S.	B6	94
Tolleson, Az., U.S.	m8	80
Tolmezzo, Italy	C8	14
Tolmin, Slo.	C8	14
Tolo, Teluk, b., Indon.	F7	32
Tolono, Il., U.S.	D5	90
Tolosa, Spain	B9	12
Tolstoj, Mys, c., Russia	F25	24
Tolt Reservoir, res., Wa., U.S.	B4	124
Toluca, Il., U.S.	C4	90
Toluca, Nevado de, vol., Mex.	H10	62
Toluca [de Lerdo], Mex.	H10	62
Tom', stm., Russia	F11	24
Tomah, Wi., U.S.	E3	126
Tomahawk, Wi., U.S.	C4	126
Tomahawk Lake, l., Wi., U.S.	C4	126
Tomakomai, Japan	q19	30a
Tomar, Port.	F3	12
Tomaszów Mazowiecki, Pol.	D20	8
Tomatlán, Mex.	H7	62
Tombador, Serra do, plat., Braz.	F7	54
Tomball, Tx., U.S.	D5	120
Tombigbee, stm., U.S.	D1	78
Tombouctou (Timbuktu), Mali	E5	42
Tombstone, Az., U.S.	F5	80
Tombua, Ang.	E2	44
Tomelloso, Spain	F9	12
Tom Green, co., Tx., U.S.	D2	120
Tomini, Teluk, b., Indon.	F7	32
Tommot, Russia	F19	24
Tom Nevers Head, c., Ma., U.S.	D8	98
Tomo, stm., Col.	E8	58
Tompkins, co., N.Y., U.S.	C4	109
Tompkinsville, Ky., U.S.	D4	94
Tomptokan, Russia	F20	24
Tomra, Nor.	E6	6
Toms, stm., N.J., U.S.	C4	107
Tomsk, Russia	F10	24
Toms River, N.J., U.S.	D4	107
Tonalá, Mex.	I13	62
Tonasket, Wa., U.S.	A6	124
Tonawanda Indian Reservation, N.Y., U.S.	B2	109
Tondabayashi, Japan	H8	30
Tone, stm., Japan	F12	30
Tonga, ctry., Oc.	H1	2
Tonganoxie, Ks., U.S.	C8	93
Tongbai, China	C2	28
Tongchuan, China	D8	26
Tongeren, Bel.	E5	8
Tongguan, China	E9	26
Tonghai, China	B7	34
Tonghua, China	C12	26
Tongliao, China	C11	26
Tongling, China	E6	28
Tongsa Dzong, Bhu.	G14	38
Tongtianheyan, China	D15	38
Tongue, Scot., U.K.	C8	7
Tongue, stm., Mt., U.S.	E10	103
Tongue, stm., Tx., U.S.	p13	120
Tongzi, China	F8	26
Tonk, India	G6	38
Tonkawa, Ok., U.S.	A4	113
Tonkin, Gulf of, b., Asia	E9	34
Tonle Sap see Sab, Tônlé, l., Camb.	H7	34
Tonneins, Fr.	H7	10
Tonnerre, Fr.	E10	10
Tonopah, Nv., U.S.	E4	105
Tønsberg, Nor.	G8	6
Tonstad, Nor.	G6	6
Tonto National Monument, Az., U.S.	D4	80
Tonto Natural Bridge, Az., U.S.	C4	80
Tooele, Ut., U.S.	C3	121
Tooele, co., Ut., U.S.	C2	121
Toole, co., Mt., U.S.	B5	103
Toombs, co., Ga., U.S.	D4	87
Toomsboro, Ga., U.S.	D3	87
Toowoomba, Austl.	E10	50
Topeka, In., U.S.	A6	91
Topeka, Ks., U.S.	C8	93
Topia, Mex.	E6	62
Topock, Az., U.S.	C1	80
Toppenish, Wa., U.S.	C5	124
Topsfield, Ma., U.S.	A6	98
Topsham, Me., U.S.	E3	96
Topton, Pa., U.S.	F10	115
Toquima Range, mts., Nv., U.S.	E5	105
Torbay, Newf., Can.	E5	72
Torbert, Mount, mtn., Ak., U.S.	g15	79
Torch Lake, l., Mi., U.S.	D5	99
Tordesillas, Spain	D6	12
Töre, Swe.	D14	6
Torgau, Ger.	D12	8
Torhout, Bel.	D3	8
Torino (Turin), Italy	D2	14
Torit, Sudan	H12	42
Torkestān, Band-e, mts., Afg.	C2	38
Torneälven, stm., Eur.	B12	4
Torngat Mountains, mts., Can.	f8	72
Toro, Spain	D6	12
Toronto, Ont., Can.	D5	73
Toronto, Oh., U.S.	B5	112
Toronto Lake, res., Ks., U.S.	E7	93
Toro Peak, mtn., Ca., U.S.	F5	82
Tororo, Ug.	A6	44
Toros Dağları, mts., Tur.	H14	4
Torquay (Torbay), Eng., U.K.	K9	7
Torquemada, Spain	C7	12
Torrance, Ca., U.S.	n12	82
Torrance, co., N.M., U.S.	C3	108
Torrão, Port.	G3	12
Torre Annunziata, Italy	I9	14
Torre Baja, Spain	E10	12
Torreblanca, Spain	E12	12
Torrecilla en Cameros, Spain	C9	12
Torre de Moncorvo, Port.	D4	12
Torredonjimeno, Spain	H8	12
Torrelaguna, Spain	E8	12
Torrelavega, Spain	B7	12
Torremaggiore, Italy	H10	14
Torremolinos, Spain	I7	12
Torrens, Lake, l., Austl.	F7	50
Torrente, Spain	F11	12
Torreón, Mex.	E8	62
Torres Novas, Port.	F3	12
Torres Strait, strt., Oc.	B8	50
Torres Vedras, Port.	F2	12
Torrevieja, Spain	H11	12
Torridon, Scot., U.K.	D7	7
Torriglia, Italy	E4	14
Torrijos, Spain	F7	12
Torrington, Ct., U.S.	B3	84
Torrington, Wy., U.S.	D8	127
Torrox, Spain	I8	12
Torsby, Swe.	F9	6
Tórshavn, Faer. Is.	C6	4
Tortola, i., Br. Vir. Is.	E15	64
Tortoli, Italy	J4	14
Tortona, Italy	E3	14
Tortosa, Spain	E12	12
Tortue, Île de la, i., Haiti	D11	64
Toruń, Pol.	B18	8
Toržok, Russia	D17	18
Tosa-shimizu, Japan	J5	30
Tosa-wan, b., Japan	I6	30
Tostado, Arg.	B4	56
Totagatic, stm., Wi., U.S.	B2	126
Totana, Spain	H10	12
Toteng, Bots.	F4	44
Tôtes, Fr.	C8	10
Tot'ma, Russia	B25	18
Totowa, N.J., U.S.	B4	107
Totson Mountain, mtn., Ak., U.S.	C8	79
Tottenham (part of Alliston Beeton Tecumseth and Tottenham), Ont., Can.	C5	73
Tottori, Japan	G7	30
Toubkal, Jbel, mtn., Mor.	B4	42
Touchet, stm., Wa., U.S.	C7	124
Touggourt, Alg.	B7	42
Touisset, Ma., U.S.	C5	98
Toul, Fr.	D12	10
Toulon, Fr.	I12	10
Toulon, Il., U.S.	B4	90
Toulouse, Fr.	I8	10
Tounan, Tai.	L9	28
Toungoo, Mya.	E4	34
Tourcoing, Fr.	B10	10
Tournai, Bel.	E3	8
Tournon, Fr.	G11	10
Tournus, Fr.	F11	10
Tours, Fr.	E7	10
Touside, Pic, mtn., Chad	D9	42
Toussaint Creek, stm., Oh., U.S.	f7	112
Toutle, North Fork, stm., Wa., U.S.	C3	124
Tovar, Ven.	C7	58
Towanda, Il., U.S.	C5	90
Towanda, Ks., U.S.	E7	93
Towanda, Pa., U.S.	C9	115
Towanda Creek, stm., Pa., U.S.	C8	115
Tower City, Pa., U.S.	E8	115
Town Creek, Al., U.S.	A2	78
Towner, N.D., U.S.	A5	111
Towner, co., N.D., U.S.	A6	111
Towns, co., Ga., U.S.	B3	87
Townsend, De., U.S.	C3	85
Townsend, Mt., U.S.	D5	103
Townshend Reservoir, res., Vt., U.S.	E3	122
Townsville, Austl.	C9	50
Towson, Md., U.S.	B4	97
Toyama, Japan	F10	30
Toyohashi, Japan	H10	30
Toyokawa, Japan	H10	30
Toyonaka, Japan	H8	30
Toyooka, Japan	G7	30
Toyota, Japan	G10	30
Tozeur, Tun.	B7	42
Trabzon, Tur.	G15	4
Tracadie, N.B., Can.	B5	71
Tracy, N.B., Can.	D3	71
Tracy, Que., Can.	C4	74
Tracy, Ca., U.S.	D3	82
Tracy, Mn., U.S.	F3	100
Tracy City, Tn., U.S.	D8	119
Tracyton, Wa., U.S.	e10	124
Tradewater, stm., Ky., U.S.	C2	94
Traer, Ia., U.S.	B5	92
Trafford, Pa., U.S.	k14	115
Trafford, Lake, l., Fl., U.S.	F5	86
Trail, B.C., Can.	E9	69
Trail Creek, In., U.S.	A4	91
Traill, co., N.D., U.S.	B8	111
Trail Ridge, mtn., U.S.	F4	87
Tralee, Ire.	I3	7
Tranås, Swe.	G10	6
Trancas, Arg.	B3	56
Trang, Thai.	K5	34
Trangan, Pulau, i., Indon.	G9	32
Trani, Italy	H11	14
Transylvania, co., N.C., U.S.	f10	110
Transylvania, hist. reg., Rom.	C7	16
Transylvanian Alps see Carpaţii Meridionali, mts., Rom.	D8	16
Trapani, Italy	K7	14
Trappe, Md., U.S.	C5	97
Trapper Peak, mtn., Mt., U.S.	E2	103
Traun, Aus.	G14	8
Traunstein, Ger.	H12	8
Travelers Rest, S.C., U.S.	B3	117
Traverse, co., Mn., U.S.	E2	100
Traverse, Lake, l., U.S.	B9	118
Traverse City, Mi., U.S.	D5	99
Tra Vinh, Viet.	J9	34
Travis, co., Tx., U.S.	D4	120
Travis Air Force Base, mil., Ca., U.S.	C2	82
Travnik, Bos.	E12	14
Tray Mountain, mtn., Ga., U.S.	B3	87
Treasure, co., Mt., U.S.	D9	103
Treasure Island Naval Station, mil., Ca., U.S.	h8	82
Trecate, Italy	D3	14
Trego, co., Ks., U.S.	D4	93
Tregosse Islets, is., Austl.	C10	50
Tréguier, Fr.	D3	10
Treherne, Man., Can.	E2	70
Treinta y Tres, Ur.	C6	56
Trélazé, Fr.	E6	10
Trelew, Arg.	E3	56
Trelleborg, Swe.	I9	6
Tremblant, Mont, mtn., Que., Can.	C3	74
Tremont, Il., U.S.	C4	90
Tremont, Pa., U.S.	E9	115
Tremonton, Ut., U.S.	B3	121
Tremp, Spain	C12	12
Trempealeau, Wi., U.S.	D2	126
Trempealeau, co., Wi., U.S.	D2	126
Trempealeau, stm., Wi., U.S.	D2	126
Trenche, stm., Que., Can.	B5	74
Trenčín, Slov.	G18	8
Trenque Lauquen, Arg.	D4	56
Trent, stm., N.C., U.S.	B5	110
Trente et un Milles, Lac des, l., Que., Can.	C2	74
Trento, Italy	C6	14
Trenton, Ont., Can.	C7	73
Trenton, Fl., U.S.	C4	86
Trenton, Ga., U.S.	B1	87
Trenton, Il., U.S.	E4	90
Trenton, Mi., U.S.	F7	99
Trenton, Mo., U.S.	A4	102
Trenton, Ne., U.S.	D4	104
Trenton, N.J., U.S.	C3	107
Trenton, Oh., U.S.	C1	112
Trenton, Tn., U.S.	B3	119
Trepassey, Newf., Can.	E5	72
Trepassey Bay, b., Newf., Can.	E5	72
Tres Arroyos, Arg.	D4	56
Tresckow, Pa., U.S.	E10	115
Três Corações, Braz.	F6	57
Tres Esquinas, Col.	G5	58
Três Lagoas, Braz.	F3	57
Três Marias, Represa, res., Braz.	E6	57
Tres Picos, Cerro, mtn., Arg.	D4	56
Três Pontas, Braz.	F6	57
Tres Puntas, Cabo, c., Arg.	F3	56
Três Rios, Braz.	G7	57
Treutlen, co., Ga., U.S.	D4	87
Treviglio, Italy	D4	14
Treviso, Italy	D7	14
Trevor, Wi., U.S.	n11	126
Trevorton, Pa., U.S.	E8	115
Treynor, Ia., U.S.	C2	92
Trezevant, Tn., U.S.	A3	119
Triadelphia, W.V., U.S.	A4	125
Triadelphia Reservoir, res., Md., U.S.	B3	97
Triangle, Va., U.S.	B5	123
Tribune, Ks., U.S.	D2	93
Trichūr, India	G4	37
Tri City, Or., U.S.	E3	114
Trident Peak, mtn., Nv., U.S.	B3	105
Trieben, Aus.	H14	8
Trier, Ger.	F6	8
Trieste, Italy	D8	14
Trigg, co., Ky., U.S.	D2	94
Triglav, mtn., Slo.	C8	14
Trigo Mountains, mts., Az., U.S.	D1	80
Tríkala, Grc.	J5	16
Trikora, Puncak, mtn., Indon.	F10	32
Tri Lakes, In., U.S.	B7	91
Trim, Ire.	H6	7
Trimble, Tn., U.S.	A2	119
Trimble, co., Ky., U.S.	B4	94
Trimont, Mn., U.S.	G4	100
Trincheras, Mex.	B4	62
Trincomalee, Sri L.	H6	37
Třinec, Czech.	F18	8
Tring Jonction, Que., Can.	C6	74
Trinidad, Bol.	F6	54
Trinidad, Col.	E7	58
Trinidad, Cuba	D8	64
Trinidad, Co., U.S.	D6	83
Trinidad, Tx., U.S.	C4	120
Trinidad, i., Trin.	I17	64
Trinidad and Tobago, ctry., N.A.	I17	64
Trinidad Head, c., Ca., U.S.	B1	82
Trinity, Al., U.S.	A2	78
Trinity, Tx., U.S.	D5	120
Trinity, co., Ca., U.S.	B2	82
Trinity, co., Tx., U.S.	D5	120
Trinity, stm., Ca., U.S.	B2	82
Trinity, stm., Tx., U.S.	D5	120
Trinity Bay, b., Newf., Can.	D5	72
Trinity Islands, is., Ak., U.S.	D9	79
Trinity Mountain, mtn., Id., U.S.	F3	89
Trinity Mountains, mts., Ca., U.S.	B2	82
Trinity Peak, mtn., Nv., U.S.	C3	105
Trinity Range, mts., Nv., U.S.	C3	105
Trion, Ga., U.S.	B1	87
Tripoli, Ia., U.S.	B5	92
Trípolis, Grc.	L6	16
Tripoli see Ṭarābulus, Leb.	B4	40
Tripoli see Ṭarābulus, Libya	B8	42
Tripp, S.D., U.S.	D8	118
Tripp, co., S.D., U.S.	D6	118
Triumph, La., U.S.	E6	95
Trivandrum, India	H4	37
Trnava, Slov.	G17	8
Troarn, Fr.	C6	10
Trobriand Islands, is., Pap. N. Gui.	A10	50
Trochu, Alta., Can.	D4	68
Trogir, Cro.	F11	14
Trois-Pistoles, Que., Can.	A8	74
Trois-Rivières, Que., Can.	C5	74
Trois-Rivières-Ouest, Que., Can.	C5	74
Trojan, Bul.	G8	16
Trollhättan, Swe.	G9	6
Trombetas, stm., Braz.	C7	54
Tromelin, i., Afr.	E10	44
Tromsø, Nor.	B12	6
Trona, Ca., U.S.	E5	82
Tronador, Monte, mtn., S.A.	E2	56
Trondheim, Nor.	E8	6
Trondheimsfjorden, Nor.	E8	6
Tropea, Italy	K10	14
Trophy Mountain, mtn., B.C., Can.	D8	69
Trotwood, Oh., U.S.	C1	112
Troup, co., Ga., U.S.	C1	87
Trousdale, co., Tn., U.S.	A5	119
Trout, stm., Fl., U.S.	m8	86
Trout, stm., Vt., U.S.	B3	122
Trout Creek, Ont., Can.	B5	73
Trout Creek Pass, Co., U.S.	C5	83
Trout Lake, Wa., U.S.	D4	124
Trout Lake, l., N.W. Ter., Can.	D8	66
Trout Lake, l., Ont., Can.	o16	73
Trout Lake, l., Mn., U.S.	B6	100
Trout Lake, l., Wi., U.S.	B4	126
Troutman, N.C., U.S.	B2	110
Trout Peak, mtn., Wy., U.S.	B3	127
Trout River, Newf., Can.	D2	72
Trouville [-sur-Mer], Fr.	C7	10
Troy, Al., U.S.	D4	78
Troy, Id., U.S.	C2	89
Troy, Il., U.S.	E4	90
Troy, Ks., U.S.	C8	93
Troy, Mi., U.S.	o15	99
Troy, Mo., U.S.	C7	102
Troy, Mt., U.S.	B1	103
Troy, N.H., U.S.	E2	106
Troy, N.Y., U.S.	C7	109
Troy, N.C., U.S.	B3	110
Troy, Oh., U.S.	B1	112
Troy, Pa., U.S.	C8	115
Troy, Tn., U.S.	A2	119
Troyes, Fr.	D11	10
Troy Peak, mtn., Nv., U.S.	E6	105
Truchas Peak, mtn., N.M., U.S.	B4	108
Trucial States see United Arab Emirates, ctry., Asia	D5	46
Truckee, Ca., U.S.	C3	82
Truckee, stm., U.S.	D2	105
Trujillo, Hond.	G4	64
Trujillo, Peru	E3	54
Trujillo, Spain	F6	12
Trujillo, Ven.	C7	58
Truman, Mn., U.S.	G4	100
Trumann, Ar., U.S.	B5	81
Trumansburg, N.Y., U.S.	C4	109
Trumbull, Ct., U.S.	E3	84
Trumbull, co., Oh., U.S.	A5	112
Trumbull, Mount, mtn., Az., U.S.	A2	80
Truro, Eng., U.K.	K7	7
Trussville, Al., U.S.	B3	78
Trustom Pond, l., R.I., U.S.	G3	116
Truth or Consequences (Hot Springs), N.M., U.S.	D2	108
Trutnov, Czech.	E15	8
Tryon, N.C., U.S.	f10	110
Tržič, Slo.	C9	14
Tsala Apopka Lake, l., Fl., U.S.	D4	86
Tsaratanana, Madag.	E9	44
Tsaratanana, Massif du, mts., Madag.	D9	44
Tschida, Lake, res., N.D., U.S.	C4	111
Tshabong, Bots.	G4	44

Name | Map Ref | Page
Tshangalele, Lac, l., Zaire D5 44
Tshikapa, Zaire C4 44
Tshofa, Zaire C5 44
Tshuapa, stm., Zaire B4 44
Tsoying, Tai. M9 28
Tsu, Japan H9 30
Tsubame, Japan E11 30
Tsuchiura, Japan F13 30
Tsugaru-kaikyō, strt., Japan A13 30
Tsukumi, Japan I4 30
Tsukushi-sanchi, mts., Japan I3 30
Tsumeb, Nmb. E3 44
Tsuruga, Japan G9 30
Tsuruoka, Japan D12 30
Tsushima, is., Japan H2 30
Tsushima-kaikyō, strt., Japan I2 30
Tsuyama, Japan G7 30
Tual, Indon. G9 32
Tualatin, stm., Or., U.S. h11 114
Tuba City, Az., U.S. A4 80
Tuban, Indon. m16 33a
Tubarão, Braz. B7 56
Tubruq, Libya B10 42
Tucannon, stm., Wa., U.S. C8 124
Tucano, Braz. F11 54
Tuckahoe, N.Y., U.S. h13 109
Tuckahoe, stm., N.J., U.S. E3 107
Tucker, Ga., U.S. h8 87
Tucker, co., W.V., U.S. B5 125
Tucker Island, i., N.J., U.S. E4 107
Tuckerman, Ar., U.S. B4 81
Tuckernuck Island, i., Ma., U.S. D7 98
Tuckerton, N.J., U.S. D4 107
Tucson, Az., U.S. E5 80
Tucumcari, N.M., U.S. B6 108
Tucumcari Mountain, mtn., N.M., U.S. B6 108
Tucupita, Ven. C11 58
Tucuruí, Braz. D9 54
Tudela, Spain C10 12
Tudmur (Palmyra), Syria B6 40
Tugaloo Lake, res., U.S. B1 117
Tug Fork, stm., U.S. C2 125
Tuguegarao, Phil. p19 32
Tugur, Russia G21 24
Tukangbesi, Kepulauan, is., Indon. G7 32
Tuktoyaktuk, N.W. Ter., Can. C6 66
Tukwila, Wa., U.S. f11 124
Tula, Mex. F10 62
Tula, Russia G20 18
Tulalip Indian Reservation, Wa., U.S. A3 124
Tulancingo, Mex. G10 62
Tulare, Ca., U.S. D4 82
Tulare, co., Ca., U.S. D4 82
Tulare Lake, l., Ca., U.S. D4 82
Tularosa, N.M., U.S. D3 108
Tularosa Mountains, mts., N.M., U.S. D1 108
Tularosa Valley, val., N.M., U.S. E3 108
Tulcán, Ec. G4 58
Tulcea, Rom. D12 16
Tule Lake, sw., Ca., U.S. B3 82
Tule River Indian Reservation, Ca., U.S. E4 82
Tule Valley, val., Ut., U.S. D2 121
Tulia, Tx., U.S. B2 120
Ṭūlkarm, W. Bank C4 40
Tullahoma, Tn., U.S. B5 119
Tullamore, Ire. H5 7
Tulle, Fr. G8 10
Tullins, Fr. G12 10
Tulsa, Ok., U.S. A6 113
Tulsa, co., Ok., U.S. B6 113
Tuluá, Col. E4 58
Tulum, Mex. G16 62
Tulun, Russia G14 24
Tulungagung, Indon. n15 33a
Tuma, stm., Nic. H5 64
Tumacacori National Monument, Az., U.S. F4 80
Tumaco, Col. G3 58
Tuman-gang, stm., Asia C12 26
Tumany, Russia E25 24
Tumatumari, Guy. E13 58
Tumba, Lac, l., Zaire B3 44
Tumbes, Peru D2 54
Tumble Mountain, mtn., Mt., U.S. E7 103
Tumbler Ridge, B.C., Can. B7 69
Tumen, China C12 26
Tumiritinga, Braz. E8 57
Tumkūr, India F4 37
Tummo, Libya D8 42
Tumsar, India B5 37
Tumuc-Humac Mountains, mts., S.A. C8 54
Tumwater, Wa., U.S. B3 124
Tunbridge Wells, Eng., U.K. J13 7
Tunduru, Tan. D7 44
Tundža, stm., Eur. G10 16
Tung, stm., Russia D17 24
Tungabhadra, stm., India E4 37
Tungabhadra Reservoir, res., India E4 37
Tungchiang, Tai. M9 28
Tungsha Tao (Pratas Islands), is., Tai. G10 26
Tungshih, Tai. K9 28
Tunica, Ms., U.S. A3 101
Tunica, co., Ms., U.S. A3 101
Tunis, Tun. M5 14
Tunisia, ctry., Afr. B7 42
Tunja, Col. E6 58
Tunkhannock, Pa., U.S. C10 115
Tunk Lake, l., Me., U.S. D4 96
Tunnel Hill, Ga., U.S. B1 87
Tunp Range, mts., Wy., U.S. D2 127
Tununak, Ak., U.S. C6 79
Tunxi, China F7 28
Tuobuja, Russia E18 24
Tuolumne, Ca., U.S. D3 82
Tuolumne, co., Ca., U.S. C4 82
Tuolumne, stm., Ca., U.S. D3 82
Tupã, Braz. F3 57
Tupaciguara, Braz. E4 57
Tupanciretã, Braz. B6 56
Tupelo, Ms., U.S. A5 101
Tupiza, Bol. H5 54
Tupper Lake, N.Y., U.S. A6 109
Tupper Lake, l., N.Y., U.S. A6 109
Túquerres, Col. G4 58
Tura, India H14 38
Tura, Russia E14 24
Turan, Russia G12 24
Turbat, Pak. D1 36
Turbeville, S.C., U.S. D7 117
Turbo, Col. C4 58
Turda, Rom. C7 16
Turgutlu, Tur. K11 16
Turimiquire, Cerro, mtn., Ven. B11 58
Turin see Torino, Italy D2 14
Turkey, ctry., Asia H14 4
Turkey, stm., Ia., U.S. B6 92
Turkey Creek, stm., Ok., U.S. A3 113
Turkey Point, c., Md., U.S. B5 97
Turkmenistan, ctry., Asia I9 22
Turks and Caicos Islands, dep., N.A. D12 64
Turks Islands, is., T./C. Is. D12 64
Turku (Åbo), Fin. F14 6
Turley, Ok., U.S. A6 113
Turlock, Ca., U.S. D3 82
Turnbull, Mount, mtn., Az., U.S. D5 80
Turneffe Islands, is., Belize F4 64
Turner, Or., U.S. C4 114
Turner, co., Ga., U.S. E3 87
Turner, co., S.D., U.S. D8 118
Turners Falls, Ma., U.S. A2 98
Turner Valley, Alta., Can. D3 68
Turnhout, Bel. D4 8
Turnor Lake, l., Sask., Can. m7 75
Turnu-Măgurele, Rom. F8 16
Turpan, China C4 26
Turquino, Pico, mtn., Cuba E9 64
Turrell, Ar., U.S. B5 81
Turret Peak, mtn., Az., U.S. C4 80
Turtle Creek, Pa., U.S. k14 115
Turtle Flambeau Flowage, res., Wi., U.S. B3 126
Turtle Lake, N.D., U.S. B5 111
Turtle Lake, Wi., U.S. C1 126
Turtle Lake, l., Sask., Can. D1 75
Turtle Mountain Indian Reservation, N.D., U.S. A6 111
Turu, stm., Russia D14 24
Turuchan, stm., Russia D11 24
Turuchansk, Russia D11 24
Tuscaloosa, Al., U.S. B2 78
Tuscaloosa, co., Al., U.S. B2 78
Tuscarawas, co., Oh., U.S. B4 112
Tuscarawas, stm., Oh., U.S. B4 112
Tuscarora Indian Reservation, N.Y., U.S. B2 109
Tuscarora Mountain, mtn., Pa., U.S. F6 115
Tuscarora Mountains, mts., Nv., U.S. B5 105
Tuscola, Il., U.S. D5 90
Tuscola, co., Mi., U.S. E7 99
Tuscumbia, Al., U.S. A2 78
Tuskegee, Al., U.S. C4 78
Tusket, stm., N.S., Can. E4 71
Tustumena Lake, l., Ak., U.S. g16 79
Tuticorin, India H5 37
Tutóia, Braz. D10 54
Tuttle, Ok., U.S. B4 113
Tuttle Creek Lake, res., Ks., U.S. C7 93
Tututalak Mountain, mtn., Ak., U.S. B7 79
Tutwiler, Ms., U.S. A3 101
Tuvalu, ctry., Oc. G24 2
Ṭuwayq, Jabal, mts., Sau. Ar. D4 46
Tuxedo, N.C., U.S. f10 110
Tuxedo Park, De., U.S. i7 85
Tuxpan, Mex. G7 62
Tuxpan de Rodríguez Cano, Mex. G11 62
Tuxtla Gutiérrez, Mex. I13 62
Túy, Spain C3 12
Tuy Hoa, Viet. H10 34
Tuz Gölü, l., Tur. H14 4
Tuzigoot National Monument, Az., U.S. C4 80
Tuzla, Bos. E2 16
Tveitsund, Nor. G7 6
Tver', Russia E18 18
Tweed, Ont., Can. C7 73
Tweedsmuir Provincial Park, B.C., Can. C4 69
Tweedy Mountain, mtn., Mt., U.S. E4 103
Twelvepole Creek, stm., W.V., U.S. C2 125
Twentymile Creek, stm., W.V., U.S. C3 125
Twentynine Palms, Ca., U.S. E5 82
Twentynine Palms Marine Corps Base, mil., Ca., U.S. E5 82
Twiggs, co., Ga., U.S. D3 87
Twillingate, Newf., Can. D4 72
Twin Buttes, mtn., Or., U.S. C4 114
Twin Buttes Reservoir, res., Tx., U.S. D2 120
Twin City, Ga., U.S. D4 87
Twin Creek, stm., Oh., U.S. C1 112
Twin Falls, Id., U.S. G4 89
Twin Falls, co., Id., U.S. G4 89
Twin Knolls, Az., U.S. m9 80
Twin Lakes, Ga., U.S. F3 87
Twin Lakes, Wi., U.S. F5 126
Twin Lakes, l., Ct., U.S. A2 84
Twin Lakes, l., Ia., U.S. B3 92
Twin Lakes, l., Me., U.S. C4 96
Twin Mountains, mtn., Wy., U.S. E7 127
Twin Peaks, mts., Id., U.S. E4 89
Twin Rivers, N.J., U.S. C4 107
Twinsburg, Oh., U.S. A4 112
Twin Valley, Mn., U.S. C2 100
Twisp, Wa., U.S. A5 124
Two Harbors, Mn., U.S. C7 100
Two Hills, Alta., Can. C5 68
Two Mile Beach, N.J., U.S. F3 107
Two Rivers, Wi., U.S. D6 126
Two Rivers, North Branch, stm., Mn., U.S. B2 100
Two Rivers, South Branch, stm., Mn., U.S. B2 100
Tybee Island, Ga., U.S. D6 87
Tychy, Pol. E18 8
Tygart Lake, res., W.V., U.S. B5 125
Tygart River, Falls of the, wtfl, W.V., U.S. k10 125
Tygart Valley, stm., W.V., U.S. B4 125
Tyger, stm., S.C., U.S. B4 117
Tyler, Mn., U.S. F2 100
Tyler, Tx., U.S. C5 120
Tyler, co., Tx., U.S. D5 120
Tyler, co., W.V., U.S. B4 125
Tyler, Lake, res., Tx., U.S. C5 120
Tyler Branch, stm., Vt., U.S. B3 122
Tyler Heights, W.V., U.S. C3 125
Tylertown, Ms., U.S. D3 101
Tymochtee Creek, stm., Oh., U.S. B2 112
Tyndall, S.D., U.S. E8 118
Tyndall Air Force Base, mil., Fl., U.S. u16 86
Tyonek, Ak., U.S. C9 79
Tyre see Ṣūr, Leb. C4 40
Tyrma, Russia G20 24
Tyrone, N.M., U.S. E1 108
Tyrone, Ok., U.S. e9 113
Tyrone, Pa., U.S. E5 115
Tyronza, Ar., U.S. B5 81
Tyrrell, co., N.C., U.S. B6 110
Tyrrhenian Sea (Mare Tirreno), Eur. I6 14
Tysse, Nor. F5 6
Tzaneen, S. Afr. F6 44

U

Uatumã, stm., Braz. D7 54
Uaupés, Braz. D5 54
Ubá, Braz. F7 57
Ubangi (Oubangui), stm., Afr. H9 42
Ube, Japan I4 30
Úbeda, Spain G8 12
Uberaba, Braz. E5 57
Uberlândia, Braz. E4 57
Ubly, Mi., U.S. E8 99
Ubon Ratchathani, Thai. G8 34
Ubundi, Zaire B5 44
Učami, Russia E13 24
Ucayali, stm., Peru E4 54
Uchiura-wan, b., Japan q18 30a
Ucluelet, B.C., Can. E5 69
Ucon, Id., U.S. F7 89
Uda, stm., Russia G13 24
Uda, stm., Russia G20 24
Udaipur, India H5 38
Udall, Ks., U.S. E6 93
Uddevalla, Swe. G8 6
Udgīr, India C4 37
Udine, Italy C8 14
Udipi, India F3 37
Udon Thani, Thai. F7 34
Udskaja Guba, b., Russia G21 24
Udža, Russia C17 24
Ueckermünde, Ger. B14 8
Ueda, Japan F11 30
Uele, stm., Zaire H10 42
Uelen, Russia D31 24
Uelzen, Ger. C10 8
Ueno, Japan H9 30
Uere, stm., Zaire H11 42
Ufa, Russia G9 22
Uganda, ctry., Afr. A6 44
Ugashik Lakes, l., Ak., U.S. D8 79
Ugine, Fr. G13 10
Uglegorsk, Russia H22 24
Uglič, Russia D21 18
Uhrichsville, Oh., U.S. B4 112
Uíge, Ang. C3 44
Uinta, co., Wy., U.S. E2 127
Uinta, stm., Ut., U.S. C5 121
Uintah, co., Ut., U.S. D6 121
Uintah and Ouray Indian Reservation, Ut., U.S. C5 121
Uinta Mountains, mts., Ut., U.S. C5 121
Uitenhage, S. Afr. H5 44
Uivak, Cape, c., Newf., Can. f9 72
Ujandina, stm., Russia D22 24
Uji, Japan H8 30
Ujiji, Tan. B5 44
Ujjain, India I6 38
Ujungpandang, Indon. G6 32
Uka, Russia F26 24
Ukiah, Ca., U.S. C2 82
Ukraine, ctry., Eur. H4 22
Ulaanbaatar (Ulan Bator), Mong. B8 26
Ulaangom, Mong. B5 26
Ulak Island, i., Ak., U.S. E4 79
Ulan Bator see Ulaanbaatar, Mong. B8 26
Ulan-Ude, Russia G15 24
Ulhāsnagar, India C2 37
Uliastaj, Mong. B6 26
Ulindi, stm., Zaire B5 44
Ulja, Russia F22 24
Uljanovsk, Russia G7 22
Ullapool, Scot., U.K. D7 7
Ullŭng-do, i., S. Kor. D13 26
Ulm, Ger. G10 8
Ulsan, S. Kor. D12 26
Ulster, co., N.Y., U.S. D6 109
Ulster, hist. reg., Eur. G5 7
Ulu, Russia E19 24
Ulubat Gölü, l., Tur. I12 16
Ulungur Hu, l., China B4 26
Ulysses, Ks., U.S. E2 93
Umag, Cro. D8 14
Uman', Ukr. H4 22
Umanak, Grnld. B22 66
Umanak Fjord, Grnld. B22 66
Umatilla, Fl., U.S. D5 86
Umatilla, Or., U.S. B7 114
Umatilla, co., Or., U.S. B8 114
Umatilla, stm., Or., U.S. B7 114
Umatilla Indian Reservation, Or., U.S. B8 114
Umbagog Lake, l., U.S. A4 106
Umcolcus Lake, l., Me., U.S. B4 96
Umeå, Swe. E13 6
Umm Durmān (Omdurman), Sudan E12 42
Umnak Island, i., Ak., U.S. E6 79
Umnäs, Swe. D11 6
Umpqua, stm., Or., U.S. D3 114
Umsaskis Lake, l., Me., U.S. B3 96
Umtata, S. Afr. H5 44
Umzinto, S. Afr. H6 44
Unadilla, Ga., U.S. D3 87
Unadilla, stm., N.Y., U.S. C5 109
Unalakleet, Ak., U.S. C7 79
Unalaska Island, i., Ak., U.S. E6 79
'Unayzah, Sau. Ar. C3 46
Uncasville, Ct., U.S. D7 84
Uncompahgre, stm., Co., U.S. C3 83
Uncompahgre Mountains, mts., Co., U.S. C3 83
Uncompahgre Peak, mtn., Co., U.S. C3 83
Underwood, Al., U.S. B3 78
Underwood, N.D., U.S. B4 111
Ungava, Péninsule d', pen., Que., Can. g12 74
Ungava Bay, b., Can. E19 66
União dos Palmares, Braz. E11 54
Unicoi, Tn., U.S. C11 119
Unicoi, co., Tn., U.S. C11 119
Unicoi Mountains, mts., U.S. D9 119
Unimak Island, i., Ak., U.S. D7 79
Unimak Pass, strt., Ak., U.S. E6 79
Union, Ky., U.S. k13 94
Union, Ms., U.S. C4 101
Union, Mo., U.S. C6 102
Union, Or., U.S. B9 114
Union, S.C., U.S. B4 117
Union, Wa., U.S. B2 124
Union, co., Ar., U.S. D3 81
Union, co., Fl., U.S. B4 86
Union, co., Ga., U.S. B2 87
Union, co., Il., U.S. F4 90
Union, co., In., U.S. E8 91
Union, co., Ia., U.S. C3 92
Union, co., Ky., U.S. C2 94
Union, co., La., U.S. B3 95
Union, co., Ms., U.S. A4 101
Union, co., N.J., U.S. B4 107
Union, co., N.M., U.S. A6 108
Union, co., N.C., U.S. B2 110
Union, co., Oh., U.S. B2 112
Union, co., Or., U.S. B8 114
Union, co., Pa., U.S. E7 115
Union, co., S.C., U.S. B4 117
Union, co., S.D., U.S. E9 118
Union, co., Tn., U.S. C10 119
Union, West Branch, stm., Me., U.S. D4 96
Union Beach, N.J., U.S. C4 107
Union Bridge, Md., U.S. A3 97
Union City, Ca., U.S. h8 82
Union City, Ga., U.S. C2 87
Union City, In., U.S. D8 91
Union City, Mi., U.S. F5 99
Union City, N.J., U.S. h8 107
Union City, Oh., U.S. B1 112
Union City, Ok., U.S. B4 113
Union City, Pa., U.S. C2 115
Union City, Tn., U.S. A2 119
Union Flat Creek, stm., Wa., U.S. C8 124
Union Gap, Wa., U.S. C5 124
Union Grove, Wi., U.S. F5 126
Union Lake, l., N.J., U.S. E2 107
Union Pier, Mi., U.S. G4 99
Union Point, Ga., U.S. C3 87
Union Springs, Al., U.S. C4 78
Uniontown, Al., U.S. C2 78
Uniontown, Ky., U.S. C2 94
Uniontown, Oh., U.S. B4 112
Uniontown, Pa., U.S. G2 115
Union Village, R.I., U.S. B3 116
Union Village Reservoir, res., Vt., U.S. D4 122
Unionville, Ct., U.S. B4 84
Unionville, Mo., U.S. A4 102
United Arab Emirates, ctry., Asia D5 46
United Kingdom, ctry., Eur. E7 4
United Nations Headquarters, N.Y., U.S. h12 109
United States, ctry., N.A. D7 76
United States Air Force Academy, mil., Co., U.S. B6 83
United States Military Academy, mil., N.Y., U.S. C6 109
United States Naval Academy, mil., Md., U.S. C4 97
Unity Reservoir, res., Or., U.S. C8 114
University City, Mo., U.S. C7 102
University Heights, Ia., U.S. C6 92
University Heights, Oh., U.S. h9 112
University Park, Ia., U.S. C5 92
University Park, N.M., U.S. E3 108
University Park, Tx., U.S. n10 120
University Place, Wa., U.S. f10 124
Unnão, India G9 38
Uozu, Japan F10 30
Upata, Ven. C11 58
Upemba, Lac, l., Zaire C5 44
Upernavik, Grnld. B21 66
Upington, S. Afr. G4 44
Upland, Ca., U.S. E5 82
Upland, In., U.S. D7 91
Upleta, India J4 38
Upolu Point, c., Hi., U.S. C6 88
Upper Ammonoosuc, stm., N.H., U.S. A4 106
Upper Arlington, Oh., U.S. B2 112
Upper Arrow Lake, l., B.C., Can. F9 66
Upper Arrow Lake, res., B.C., Can. D9 69
Upperco, Md., U.S. A4 97
Upper Darby, Pa., U.S. G11 115
Upper Greenwood Lake, N.J., U.S. A4 107
Upper Humber, stm., Newf., Can. D3 72
Upper Iowa, stm., Ia., U.S. A5 92
Upper Island Cove, Newf., Can. E5 72
Upper Kapuas Mountains, mts., Asia E5 32
Upper Klamath Lake, l., Or., U.S. E4 114
Upper Marlboro, Md., U.S. C4 97
Upper New York Bay, b., U.S. k8 107
Upper Red Lake, l., Mn., U.S. B4 100
Upper Saddle River, N.J., U.S. A4 107
Upper Sandusky, Oh., U.S. B2 112
Upper Sheila [Haut Sheila], N.B., Can. B5 71
Upper Volta see Burkina Faso, ctry., Afr. F5 42
Uppsala, Swe. G11 6
Upright, Cape, c., Ak., U.S. C5 79
Upshur, co., Tx., U.S. C5 120
Upshur, co., W.V., U.S. C4 125
Upson, co., Ga., U.S. D2 87
Upton, Que., Can. D5 74
Upton, Ky., U.S. C4 94
Upton, Ma., U.S. B4 98
Upton, Wy., U.S. B8 127
Upton, co., Tx., U.S. D2 120
Uquía, Cerro, mtn., Ven. E11 58
Urabá, Golfo de, b., Col. C4 58
Ural, stm., Asia H8 22
Ural Mountains see Ural'skije gory, mts., Russia F9 22
Ural'sk, Kaz. G8 22
Ural'skije gory (Ural Mountains), mts., Russia F9 22
Urania, La., U.S. C3 95
Urbana, Il., U.S. C5 90
Urbana, Oh., U.S. B2 112
Urbancrest, Oh., U.S. m10 112
Urbandale, Ia., U.S. C4 92
Urbino, Italy F7 14
Urgenč, Uzb. I10 22
Uribe, Col. F5 58
Uribia, Col. B6 58
Urla, Tur. K10 16
Uruaçu, Braz. C4 57
Uruapan [del Progreso], Mex. H8 62
Urubamba, stm., Peru F4 54
Urucuia, stm., Braz. D6 57
Uruguaiana, Braz. B5 56
Uruguay, ctry., S.A. C5 56
Uruguay (Uruguai), stm., S.A. C5 56
Ürümqi, China C4 26
Ur'ung-Chaja, Russia C16 24
Urun-Islāmpur, India D3 37
Urup, Ostrov, i., Russia H23 24
Usa, Japan I4 30
Uşak, Tur. K13 16
Usedom, i., Eur. B14 8
Ushibuka, Japan J3 30
Ushuaia, Arg. G3 56
Usolje-Sibirskoje, Russia G14 24
Usquepaug, R.I., U.S. F3 116
Ussel, Fr. G9 10
Ussuri (Wusuli), stm., Asia B14 26
Ussurijsk, Russia I20 24
Ust'-Barguzin, Russia G15 24
Ust'-Belaja, Russia D28 24
Ust'Čaun, Russia D28 24
Ústí nad Labem, Czech. E14 8
Ust'-Kamčatsk, Russia F26 24
Ust'-Kamenogorsk, Kaz. H10 24
Ust'-Kut, Russia F15 24
Ust'-Maja, Russia E20 24
Ust'-Nera, Russia E22 24
Usu, China C3 26
Usuki, Japan I4 30
Usulután, El Sal. H3 64
Usumacinta, stm., N.A. I14 62
Utah, co., Ut., U.S. C4 121
Utah, state, U.S. D4 121
Utah Lake, l., Ut., U.S. C4 121
Utashinai, Japan p20 30a
Ute Creek, stm., N.M., U.S. A6 108
Ute Mountain Indian Reservation, U.S. D2 83
Ute Reservoir, res., N.M., U.S. B6 108
Utete, Tan. C7 44
Uthai Thani, Thai. G6 34
Utiariti, Braz. F7 54
Utica, Il., U.S. B5 90
Utica, Mi., U.S. F7 99
Utica, Ms., U.S. C3 101
Utica, Ne., U.S. D8 104
Utica, N.Y., U.S. B5 109
Utica, Oh., U.S. B3 112
Utiel, Spain F10 12
Utikuma Lake, l., Alta., Can. B3 68
Utrecht, Neth. C5 8
Utrera, Spain H6 12
Utsunomiya, Japan F12 30
Uttar Pradesh, state, India G8 38
Uusikaupunki (Nystad), Fin. F13 6
Uvá, stm., Col. F8 58
Uvalde, Tx., U.S. E3 120
Uvalde, co., Tx., U.S. E3 120
Uvdal, Nor. F7 6
Uvinza, Tan. C6 44
Uvs Nuur, l., Asia A5 26
Uwajima, Japan I5 30
'Uwaynāt, Jabal al-, mtn., Afr. D10 42
Uwharrie, stm., N.C., U.S. B3 110
Uxbridge, Ma., U.S. B4 98
Uyuni, Bol. H5 54
Uyuni, Salar de, pl., Bol. H5 54
Uzbekistan, state, Asia I10 22
Uzerche, Fr. G8 10
Uzès, Fr. H11 10
Užice, Yugo. F3 16
Uzlovaja, Russia H21 18
Uzunköprü, Tur. H10 16

Name — Map Ref — Page

Užur, Russia F11 24

V

Vaala, Fin. D16 6
Vaasa (Vasa), Fin. E13 6
Vác, Hung. H19 8
Vaca Key, i., Fl., U.S. H5 86
Vacaville, Ca., U.S. C3 82
Vaccarès, Étang de, b., Fr. I11 10
Vach, stm., Russia E9 24
Vacherie, La., U.S. h10 95
Vadsø, Nor. A17 6
Vaduz, Liech. H9 8
Váh, stm., Slov. G18 8
Vaiden, Ms., U.S. B4 101
Vail, Co., U.S. B4 83
Vākhān, stm., Afg. B5 38
Vākhān, reg., Afg. B5 38
Vålådalen, Swe. E9 6
Val-Bélair, Que., Can. n17 74
Valcheta, Arg. E3 56
Valcourt, Que., Can. D5 74
Valdagno, Italy D6 14
Val-David, Que., Can. C3 74
Valdecañas, Embalse de, res., Spain F6 12
Valdemarsvik, Swe. G11 6
Valdepeñas, Spain G8 12
Valderrobres, Spain E12 12
Valders, Wi., U.S. D6 126
Valdés, Península, pen., Arg. E4 56
Valdese, N.C., U.S. B1 110
Valdez, Ak., U.S. C10 79
Val-d'Isère, Fr. G13 10
Valdivia, Chile D2 56
Valdivia, Col. D5 58
Val-d'Or, Que., Can. k11 74
Valdosta, Ga., U.S. F3 87
Vale, Or., U.S. D9 114
Valemount, B.C., Can. C8 69
Valença, Braz. B9 57
Valença, Port. C3 12
Valençay, Fr. E8 10
Valence, Fr. H11 10
Valencia, Spain F11 12
Valencia, Az., U.S. m7 80
Valencia, Ven. C8 58
Valencia, co., N.M., U.S. C3 108
Valencia, Golfo de, b., Spain F12 12
Valencia de Alcántata, Spain F4 12
Valencia de Don Juan, Spain C6 12
Valencia Heights, S.C., U.S. D6 117
Valenciennes, Fr. B10 10
Valentine, Ne., U.S. B5 104
Valenza, Italy D3 14
Valera, Ven. C7 58
Valga, Est. D9 18
Valhalla, N.Y., U.S. D7 109
Valhermoso Springs, Al., U.S. A3 78
Valjevo, Yugo. E3 16
Valkeakoski, Fin. F15 6
Valkenswaard, Neth. D5 8
Valladolid, Mex. G15 62
Valladolid, Spain D7 12
Vall de Uxó, Spain F11 12
Vallecito Reservoir, res., Co., U.S. D3 83
Valle de Guanape, Ven. C10 58
Valle de la Pascua, Ven. C9 58
Valle de Santiago, Mex. G9 62
Valle de Zaragoza, Mex. D7 62
Valledupar, Col. B6 58
Vallée-Jonction, Que., Can. C7 74
Valle Hermoso, Mex. E11 62
Vallejo, Ca., U.S. C2 82
Vallelunga Pratameno, Italy L8 14
Vallenar, Chile B2 56
Valletta, Malta N9 14
Valley, Ne., U.S. C9 104
Valley, co., Id., U.S. E3 89
Valley, co., Mt., U.S. B10 103
Valley, co., Ne., U.S. C6 104
Valley, stm., Man., Can. D1 70
Valley Center, Ks., U.S. E6 93
Valley City, N.D., U.S. C8 111
Valley Cottage, N.Y., U.S. g13 109
Valley East, Ont., Can. p19 73
Valley Falls, Ks., U.S. C8 93
Valley Falls, R.I., U.S. B4 116
Valley Forge, Pa., U.S. o20 115
Valley Mills, Tx., U.S. D4 120
Valley Park, Mo., U.S. f12 102
Valley Springs, S.D., U.S. D9 118
Valley Station, Ky., U.S. g11 94
Valley Stream, N.Y., U.S. n15 109
Valleyview, Alta., Can. B2 68
Valley View, Pa., U.S. E8 115
Valliant, Ok., U.S. D6 113
Vallo della Lucania, Italy I10 14
Valls, Spain D13 12
Vallscreek, W.V., U.S. D3 125
Valmeyer, Il., U.S. E3 90
Valognes, Fr. C5 10
Valparai, India G4 37
Valparaíso, Chile C2 56
Valparaíso, Mex. F8 62
Valparaiso, Fl., U.S. u15 86
Valparaiso, In., U.S. B3 91
Valréas, Fr. H11 10
Vals, Tanjung, c., Indon. G10 32
Valtimo, Fin. E17 6
Val Verda, Ut., U.S. C4 121
Valverde, Dom. Rep. E12 64
Val Verde, co., Tx., U.S. E2 120
Valverde del Camino, Spain H5 12
Van, Tur. H16 4
Van, Tx., U.S. C5 120
Van, W.V., U.S. n12 125
Van Alstyne, Tx., U.S. C4 120
Vanavara, Russia E14 24
Van Buren, Ar., U.S. B1 81
Van Buren, In., U.S. C6 91
Van Buren, Me., U.S. A5 96
Van Buren, Mo., U.S. E6 102
Van Buren, co., Ar., U.S. B3 81
Van Buren, co., Ia., U.S. D6 92
Van Buren, co., Mi., U.S. F4 99
Van Buren, co., Tn., U.S. D8 119
Vance, co., N.C., U.S. A4 110
Vance Air Force Base, mil., Ok., U.S. A3 113
Vanceboro, N.C., U.S. B5 110
Vanceburg, Ky., U.S. B6 94
Vancleave, Ms., U.S. E5 101
Vancouver, B.C., Can. E6 69
Vancouver, Wa., U.S. D3 124
Vancouver, Cape, c., Austl. G3 50
Vancouver Island, i., B.C., Can. E4 69
Vancouver Island Ranges, mts., B.C., Can. D4 69
Vandalia, Il., U.S. E4 90
Vandalia, Mo., U.S. B6 102
Vandenberg Air Force Base, mil., Ca., U.S. E3 82
Vander, N.C., U.S. B4 110
Vanderbilt Peak, mtn., N.M., U.S. E1 108
Vanderburgh, co., In., U.S. H2 91
Vandergrift, Pa., U.S. E2 115
Vanderhoof, B.C., Can. C5 69
Van Diemen Gulf, b., Austl. B6 50
Vänern, l., Swe. G9 6
Vänersborg, Swe. G9 6
Vangaindrano, Madag. F9 44
Van Gölü, l., Tur. H16 4
Vangunu, i., Sol.Is. A11 50
Van Horn, Tx., U.S. o12 120
Van Horne, Ia., U.S. B5 92
Vanier, Ont., Can. h12 73
Vāniyambādi, India F5 37
Vankarem, Russia D30 24
Vankleek Hill, Ont., Can. B10 73
Van Kull, Kill, stm., N.J., U.S. k8 107
Van Lear, Ky., U.S. C7 94
Van Meter, Ia., U.S. C4 92
Vännäs, Swe. E12 6
Vannes, Fr. E4 10
Van Rees, Pegunungan, mts., Indon. F10 32
Vanrhynsdorp, S. Afr. H3 44
Vansant, Va., U.S. e9 123
Vansbro, Swe. F10 6
Vansittart Island, i., N.W. Ter., Can. C16 66
Vanuatu, ctry., Oc. H24 2
Van Vleck, Tx., U.S. r14 120
Van Wert, Oh., U.S. B1 112
Van Wert, co., Oh., U.S. B1 112
Van Zandt, co., Tx., U.S. C5 120
Varades, Fr. E5 10
Vārānasi (Benares), India H10 38
Varaždin, Cro. C11 14
Varazze, Italy E3 14
Varberg, Swe. H9 6
Vardaman, Ms., U.S. B4 101
Vardar (Axiós), stm., Eur. H6 16
Vardø, Nor. A18 6
Varennes, Que., Can. D4 74
Varennes-sur-Allier, Fr. F10 10
Varese, Italy D3 14
Varginha, Braz. F6 57
Varina, Va., U.S. C5 123
Varkaus, Fin. E16 6
Varkhān, stm., Afg. D1 38
Varna, Bul. F11 16
Värnamo, Swe. H10 6
Varnville, S.C., U.S. F5 117
Varzy, Fr. E10 10
Vasai (Bassein), India C2 37
Vashon, Point, c., Wa., U.S. e11 124
Vashon Island, i., Wa., U.S. f11 124
Vass, N.C., U.S. B3 110
Vassar, Mi., U.S. E7 99
Västerås, Swe. G11 6
Västervik, Swe. H11 6
Vasto, Italy G9 14
Vas'ugan, stm., Russia F9 24
Vatican City (Città del Vaticano), ctry., Eur. H7 14
Vatnajökull, Ice. C4 4
Vättern, l., Swe. G10 6
Vaucouleurs, Fr. D12 10
Vaudreuil, Que., Can. D3 74
Vaughan, Ont., Can. D5 73
Vaughn, Mt., U.S. C5 103
Vaughn, N.M., U.S. C4 108
Vaupés (Uaupés), stm., S.A. G7 58
Vauxhall, Alta., Can. D4 68
Växjö, Swe. H10 6
Vazante, Braz. D5 57
V'azemskij, Russia H20 24
V'az'ma, Russia F17 18
V'azniki, Russia E25 18
Veazie, Me., U.S. D4 96
Vechta, Ger. C8 8
Veedersburg, In., U.S. D3 91
Veendam, Neth. B6 8
Vegreville, Alta., Can. C4 68
Vejer de la Frontera, Spain I6 12
Vejle, Den. I7 6
Vela Luka, Cro. G11 14
Velda Rose Estates, Az., U.S. *D4 80
Velenje, Slo. C10 14
Vélez-Málaga, Spain I7 12
Vélez Rubio, Spain H9 12
Velhas, Rio das, stm., Braz. D6 57
Velike Lašče, Slo. D9 14
Velikije Luki, Russia E13 18
Veliko Tărnovo, Bul. F9 16
Vella Lavella, i., Sol.Is. A11 50
Velletri, Italy H7 14
Vellore, India F5 37
Velma, Ok., U.S. C4 113
Velva, N.D., U.S. A5 111
Venado Tuerto, Arg. C4 56
Venango, co., Pa., U.S. D2 115
Venda Nova, Braz. E7 57
Vendeuvre-sur-Barse, Fr. D11 10
Vendôme, Fr. E8 10
Veneta, Or., U.S. C3 114
Venezia (Venice), Italy D7 14
Venezuela, ctry., S.A. B5 54
Venezuela, Golfo de, b., S.A. B7 58
Veniaminof, Mount, mtn., Ak., U.S. D8 79
Venice, Fl., U.S. E4 86
Venice, Il., U.S. E3 90
Venice, Gulf of, b., Eur. D7 14
Venice see Venezia, Italy D7 14
Vénissieux, Fr. G11 10
Venlo, Neth. D6 8
Venosa, Italy I10 14
Ventanas, Ec. H3 58
Ventnor City, N.J., U.S. E4 107
Ventspils, Lat. D4 18
Ventuari, stm., Ven. E9 58
Ventura (San Buenaventura), Ca., U.S. E4 82
Ventura, co., Ca., U.S. E4 82
Venustiano Carranza, Mex. I13 62
Vera, Spain H10 12
Veracruz [Llave], Mex. H11 62
Verāval, India J4 38
Verbania, Italy D3 14
Vercelli, Italy D3 14
Verchères, Que., Can. D4 74
Verchn'aja Amga, Russia F19 24
Verchneimbatskoje, Russia E11 24
Verchojansk, Russia D20 24
Verchojanskij Chrebet, mts., Russia D19 24
Verda, Ky., U.S. D6 94
Verde, stm., Az., U.S. C4 80
Verden, Ger. C9 8
Verdi, Nv., U.S. D2 105
Verdigre, Ne., U.S. B7 104
Verdigris, Ok., U.S. A6 113
Verdigris, stm., U.S. A6 113
Verdi Peak, mtn., Nv., U.S. C6 105
Verdun, Que., Can. q19 74
Verdun, Fr. C12 10
Vereeniging, S. Afr. G5 44
Vergara, Spain B9 12
Vergennes, Vt., U.S. C2 122
Verissimo, Braz. E4 57
Vermilion, Alta., Can. C5 68
Vermilion, Oh., U.S. A3 112
Vermilion, co., Il., U.S. C6 90
Vermilion, co., La., U.S. E3 95
Vermilion, stm., Alta., Can. C5 68
Vermilion, stm., Il., U.S. C5 90
Vermilion, stm., La., U.S. E3 95
Vermilion, stm., Mn., U.S. B6 100
Vermilion, stm., Oh., U.S. A3 112
Vermilion Bay, b., La., U.S. E3 95
Vermilion Lake, l., Mn., U.S. C6 100
Vermilion Pass, Can. D2 68
Vermillion, S.D., U.S. E9 118
Vermillion, co., In., U.S. E2 91
Vermillion, East Fork, stm., S.D., U.S. D8 118
Vermillion, stm., Que., Can. B4 74
Vermont, Il., U.S. C3 90
Vermont, state, U.S. D3 122
Vermontville, Mi., U.S. F5 99
Vernal, Ut., U.S. C6 121
Verneuil-sur-Avre, Fr. D7 10
Vernon, B.C., Can. D8 69
Vernon, Fr. C8 10
Vernon, Al., U.S. B1 78
Vernon, Tx., U.S. B3 120
Vernon, co., La., U.S. C2 95
Vernon, co., Mo., U.S. D3 102
Vernon, co., Wi., U.S. E3 126
Vernon Hills, Il., U.S. h9 90
Vernonia, Or., U.S. B3 114
Vero Beach, Fl., U.S. E6 86
Véroia, Grc. I6 16
Verona, Ont., Can. C8 73
Verona, Italy D6 14
Verona, Ms., U.S. A5 101
Verona, N.J., U.S. B4 107
Verona, Pa., U.S. k14 115
Verona, Wi., U.S. E4 126
Verret, Lake, l., La., U.S. E4 95
Versailles, Fr. D9 10
Versailles, In., U.S. F7 91
Versailles, Ky., U.S. B5 94
Versailles, Mo., U.S. C5 102
Versailles, Oh., U.S. B1 112
Vert, Cap, c., Sen. F2 42
Vertientes, Cuba D8 64
Vertou, Fr. E5 10
Verviers, Bel. E5 8
Vesoul, Fr. E13 10
Vestal, N.Y., U.S. C4 109
Vestavia Hills, Al., U.S. g7 78
Vestmannaeyjar, Ice. C3 4
Vesuvio, vol., Italy I9 14
Vesuvius see Vesuvio, vol., Italy I9 14
Veszprém, Hung. H17 8
Vetlanda, Swe. H10 6
Vevay, In., U.S. G7 91
Vevey, Switz. F13 10
Veynes, Fr. H12 10
Viadana, Italy E5 14
Vian, Ok., U.S. B7 113
Viana del Bollo, Spain C4 12
Viana do Alentejo, Port. G3 12
Viana do Castelo, Port. D3 12
Viangchan, Laos F7 34
Viareggio, Italy F5 14
Viborg, Den. H7 6
Viborg, S.D., U.S. D8 118
Vibo Valentia, Italy K11 14
Viburnum, Mo., U.S. D6 102
Vic-en-Bigorre, Fr. I7 10
Vicente, Point, c., Ca., U.S. n12 82
Vicenza, Italy D6 14
Vich, Spain D14 12
Vichada, stm., Col. E8 58
Vichy, Fr. F10 10
Vici, Ok., U.S. A2 113
Vicksburg, Mi., U.S. F5 99
Vicksburg, Ms., U.S. C3 101
Vicksburg National Military Park, Ms., U.S. C3 101
Viçosa, Braz. F7 57
Victor, Ia., U.S. C5 92
Victor, N.Y., U.S. C3 109
Victoria, B.C., Can. E6 69
Victoria, Newf., Can. E5 72
Victoria (Xianggang), H.K. M3 28
Victoria, Sey. B11 44
Victoria, Ks., U.S. D4 93
Victoria, Tx., U.S. E4 120
Victoria, Va., U.S. *C4 123
Victoria, state, Austl. G9 50
Victoria, co., Tx., U.S. E4 120
Victoria, Lake, l., Afr. B6 44
Victoria, Mount, mtn., Mya. D2 34
Victoria de las Tunas, Cuba D9 64
Victoria Falls, wtfl, Afr. E5 44
Victoria Harbour, Ont., Can. C5 73
Victoria Island, i., N.W. Ter., Can. B10 66
Victoria Lake, res., Newf., Can. D3 72
Victoria Land, reg., Ant. B28 47
Victoria Nile, stm., Ug. H12 42
Victoria Peak, mtn., Belize F3 64
Victoria Strait, strt., N.W. Ter., Can. C12 66
Victoriaville, Que., Can. C6 74
Victoria West, S. Afr. H4 44
Victorville, Ca., U.S. E5 82
Vičuga, Russia D24 18
Vidalia, Ga., U.S. D4 87
Vidalia, La., U.S. C4 95
Vidisha, India I7 38
Vidor, Tx., U.S. D5 120
Viechtach, Ger. F12 8
Viedma, Arg. E4 56
Viedma, Lago, l., Arg. F2 56
Viella, Spain C12 12
Vienna, Ga., U.S. D3 87
Vienna, Il., U.S. F5 90
Vienna, Mo., U.S. C6 102
Vienna, Va., U.S. B5 123
Vienna, W.V., U.S. B3 125
Vienna see Wien, Aus. G16 8
Vienne, Fr. G11 10
Vientiane see Viangchan, Laos F7 34
Vieques, Isla de, i., P.R. E15 64
Vieremä, Fin. E16 6
Vierwaldstätter See, l., Switz. F15 10
Vierzon, Fr. E9 10
Vieste, Italy H11 14
Vietnam, ctry., Asia B4 32
Vieux Desert, Lac, l., Wi., U.S. B4 126
Vigan, Phil. p19 33b
Vigevano, Italy D3 14
Vignola, Italy E5 14
Vigo, Spain C3 12
Vigo, co., In., U.S. F3 91
Vihti, Fin. F15 6
Vijayawāda, India D6 37
Vijosë (Aóös), stm., Eur. I3 16
Vikajärvi, Fin. C16 6
Viking, Alta., Can. C5 68
Vila Coutinho, Moz. D6 44
Vila do Conde, Port. D3 12
Vila Fontes, Moz. E7 44
Vilafranca del Panadés, Spain D13 12
Vila Franca de Xira, Port. G3 12
Vilanculos, Moz. F7 44
Vila Nova de Famalicão, Port. D3 12
Vila Nova de Foz Côa, Port. D4 12
Vila Nova de Gaia, Port. D3 12
Vila Pery, Moz. E6 44
Vila Real, Port. D4 12
Vilas, co., Wi., U.S. B4 126
Vila Velha, Braz. F8 57
Vila Velha de Ródão, Port. F4 12
Vilhelmina, Swe. D11 6
Vilhena, Braz. F6 54
Vil'kickogo, Proliv, strt., Russia B14 24
Villa Ahumada, Mex. B6 62
Villa Bella, Bol. F5 54
Villablino, Spain C5 12
Villa Bruzual, Ven. C8 58
Villacañas, Spain F8 12
Villacarriedo, Spain B8 12
Villacarrillo, Spain G8 12
Villach, Aus. I13 8
Villacidro, Italy J3 14
Villa Colón (Caucete), Arg. C3 56
Villa del Rosario, Ven. I11 64
Villa de Méndez, Mex. E10 62
Villadiego, Spain C7 12
Villafranca del Bierzo, Spain C5 12
Villafranca de los Barros, Spain G5 12
Villafranca di Verona, Italy D5 14
Villa Frontera, Mex. D9 62
Villagaracía, Spain C3 12
Villa Grove, Il., U.S. D5 90
Villaguay, Arg. C5 56
Villa Hayes, Para. B5 56
Villahermosa, Mex. I13 62
Villajoyosa, Spain G11 12
Villalón de Campos, Spain C6 12
Villalonga, Arg. D4 56
Villalpando, Spain D6 12
Villa María, Arg. C4 56
Villamartín, Spain I6 12
Villa Montes, Bol. H6 54
Villanova Monteleone, Italy I3 14
Villanueva, Col. B6 58
Villanueva de Córdoba, Spain G7 12
Villanueva de la Serena, Spain G6 12
Villanueva de los Infantes, Spain G9 12
Villanueva del Río y Minas, Spain H6 12
Villanueva y Geltrú, Spain D13 12
Villa Park, Il., U.S. k8 90
Villa Pedro Montoya, Mex. G10 62
Villarcayo, Spain C8 12
Villa Rica, Ga., U.S. C2 87
Villarreal, Spain F11 12
Villarrica, Chile D2 56
Villarrobledo, Spain F9 12
Villas, N.J., U.S. E3 107
Villa San Giovanni, Italy K10 14
Villasayas, Spain D9 12
Villa Unión, Arg. B4 56
Villavicencio, Col. E6 58
Villaviciosa de Córdoba, Spain G6 12
Villedieu, Fr. D5 10
Villefort, Fr. H10 10
Villefranche, Fr. G11 10
Villefranche-de-Rouergue, Fr. H9 10
Villena, Spain G11 12
Villeneuve-de-Berg, Fr. H11 10
Villeneuve-Saint-Georges, Fr. D9 10
Villeneuve-sur-Lot, Fr. H7 10
Ville Platte, La., U.S. D3 95
Villers-Bocage, Fr. C6 10
Villers-Cotterêts, Fr. C10 10
Ville Saint-Georges, Que., Can. C7 74
Villeurbanne, Fr. G11 10
Villingen-Schwenningen, Ger. G8 8
Villisca, Ia., U.S. D3 92
Villupuram, India G5 37
Vilnius, Lith. G8 18
Vilonia, Ar., U.S. B3 81
Vilsbiburg, Ger. G12 8
Vil'uj, stm., Russia E18 24
Vil'ujsk, Russia E18 24
Vimianzo, Spain B2 12
Vimoutiers, Fr. D7 10
Vina, stm., Cam. G8 42
Viña del Mar, Chile C2 56
Vinalhaven, Me., U.S. D4 96
Vinalhaven Island, i., Me., U.S. D4 96
Vinaroz, Spain E12 12
Vincennes, In., U.S. G2 91
Vincent, Al., U.S. B3 78
Vinces, Ec. H3 58
Vindeln, Swe. D12 6
Vindhya Range, mts., India I7 38
Vine Brook, stm., Ma., U.S. g11 98
Vinegar Hill, mtn., Or., U.S. C8 114
Vine Grove, Ky., U.S. C4 94
Vineland, N.J., U.S. E2 107
Vineyard Haven, Ma., U.S. D6 98
Vineyard Sound, strt., Ma., U.S. D6 98
Vinh, Viet. E8 34
Vinhais, Port. D4 12
Vinh Long, Viet. I8 34
Vinita, Ok., U.S. A6 113
Vinkovci, Cro. D2 16
Vinnytsya, Ukr. H3 22
Vinson Massif, mtn., Ant. B4 47
Vinton, Ia., U.S. B5 92
Vinton, La., U.S. D2 95
Vinton, Va., U.S. C3 123
Vinton, co., Oh., U.S. C3 112
Viola, Il., U.S. B3 90
Violet, La., U.S. k12 95
Vipava, Slo. D8 14
Vipiteno, Italy C6 14
Virac, Phil. C7 32
Viramgām, India I5 38
Viranşehir, Tur. A6 40
Virden, Man., Can. E1 70
Virden, Il., U.S. D4 90
Vire, Fr. D6 10
Virgin, stm., U.S. G8 105
Virginia, S. Afr. G5 44
Virginia, Al., U.S. g6 78
Virginia, Il., U.S. D3 90
Virginia, Mn., U.S. C6 100
Virginia, state, U.S. C4 123
Virginia Beach, Va., U.S. D7 123
Virginia City, Nv., U.S. D2 105
Virginia Peak, mtn., Nv., U.S. D2 105
Virgin Islands, dep., N.A. E15 64
Virje, Cro. C11 14
Virkie, Scot., U.K. B11 7
Viroqua, Wi., U.S. E3 126
Virovitica, Cro. D12 14
Virtaniemi, Fin. B17 6
Virudunagar, India H4 37
Vis, Cro. F11 14
Visalia, Ca., U.S. D4 82
Visby, Swe. H12 6
Viscount Melville Sound, strt., N.W. Ter., Can. B10 66
Viseu, Port. E4 12
Vishākhapatnam, India D7 37
Vislinskij Zaliv, b., Eur. A19 8
Visnagar, India I5 38
Vista, Ca., U.S. F5 82
Vistula see Wisła, stm., Pol. A18 8
Vitarte, Peru F3 54
Vitebsk, Bela. F13 18
Viterbo, Italy G7 14
Vitigudino, Spain D5 12
Vitim, Russia F16 24
Vitim, stm., Russia F16 24
Vitória, Braz. F8 57
Vitoria, Spain C9 12
Vitória da Conquista, Braz. C8 57
Vitré, Fr. D5 10
Vitry-le-François, Fr. D11 10
Vitteaux, Fr. E11 10
Vittel, Fr. D12 10
Vittoria, Italy M9 14
Vittorio Veneto, Italy D7 14
Viver, Spain F11 12
Vivero, Spain B4 12
Vivian, La., U.S. B2 95
Viviers, Fr. H11 10
Vivonne, Fr. F7 10
Vizcachas, Meseta de las, plat., Arg. G2 56
Vizcaíno, Desierto de, des., Mex. D3 62
Vizianagaram, India C7 37
Vizille, Fr. G12 10
Vlaardingen, Neth. D4 8
Vladikavkaz, Russia I6 22
Vladimir, Russia E23 18
Vladivostok, Russia E35 128
Vlissingen (Flushing), Neth. D3 8
Vlorë, Alb. I3 16
Vltava, stm., Czech. F14 8
Vöcklabruck, Aus. G13 8
Vodnjan, Cro. E8 14
Vogelsberg, mts., Ger. E9 8
Voghera, Italy E4 14

Name	Map Ref	Page
Vohenstrauss, Ger.	F12	8
Vohibinany, Madag.	E9	44
Vohimarina, Madag.	D10	44
Voi, Kenya	B7	44
Voinjama, Lib.	G4	42
Voiron, Fr.	G12	10
Voitsberg, Aus.	H15	8
Volcano, Hi., U.S.	D6	88
Volchov, Russia	B15	18
Volda, Nor.	E6	6
Volga, S.D., U.S.	C9	118
Volga, stm., Russia	H7	22
Volgograd (Stalingrad), Russia	H6	22
Volkovysk, Bela.	H7	18
Voločanka, Russia	C12	24
Vologda, Russia	B22	18
Volokolamsk, Russia	E18	18
Vólos, Grc.	J6	16
Volta, Lake, res., Ghana	G5	42
Volta Blanche (White Volta), stm., Afr.	F5	42
Volta Noire (Black Volta), stm., Afr.	F6	42
Volta Redonda, Braz.	G6	57
Volterra, Italy	F5	14
Volusia, co., Fl., U.S.	C5	86
Volžskij, Russia	H6	22
Von Frank Mountain, mtn., Ak., U.S.	C9	79
Vonore, Tn., U.S.	D9	119
Voríai Sporádhes, is., Grc.	J7	16
Voronež, Russia	G5	22
Voronezh see Voronež, Russia	G5	22
Vosges, mts., Fr.	D14	10
Voskresensk, Russia	F21	18
Voss, Nor.	F6	6
Vostočno-Sibirskoje More (East Siberian Sea), Russia	C25	24
Vostočnyj Sajan, mts., Russia	G13	24
Votkinsk, Russia	F8	22
Votuporanga, Braz.	F4	57
Vouziers, Fr.	C11	10
Voyageurs National Park, Mn., U.S.	B5	100
Vraca, Bul.	F7	16
Vrangel'a, Ostrov, i., Russia	C29	24
Vranje, Yugo.	G5	16
Vrhnika, Slo.	D9	14
Vryburg, S. Afr.	G4	44
Vryheid, S. Afr.	G6	44
Vsevidof, Mount, mtn., Ak., U.S.	E6	79
Vsevoložsk, Russia	A13	18
Vukovar, Cro.	D2	16
Vulcan, Alta., Can.	D4	68
Vung Tau (Cap-St.-Jacques), Viet.	I9	34
Vuoggatjålme, Swe.	C11	6
Vuoksenniska, Fin.	F17	6
Vyborg, Russia	A11	18
Vyška, Russia	D18	18
Vyšnij Voloček, Russia	D17	18
Vysokogornyj, Russia	G21	24

W

Name	Map Ref	Page
Wa, Ghana	F5	42
Waawaa, Puu, mtn., Hi., U.S.	D6	88
Wabana (Bell Island), Newf., Can.	E5	72
Wabasca, Alta., Can.	B4	68
Wabasca, stm., Alta., Can.	f1	68
Wabash, In., U.S.	C6	91
Wabash, co., Il., U.S.	E6	90
Wabash, co., In., U.S.	C6	91
Wabash, stm., U.S.	H2	91
Wabasha, Mn., U.S.	F6	100
Wabasha, co., Mn., U.S.	F6	100
Wabasso, Fl., U.S.	E6	86
Wabasso, Mn., U.S.	F3	100
Wabaunsee, co., Ks., U.S.	D7	93
Wabeno, Wi., U.S.	C5	126
Wabowden, Man., Can.	B2	70
Wabush, Newf., Can.	h8	72
Waccamaw, stm., U.S.	D9	117
Waccamaw, Lake, l., N.C., U.S.	C4	110
Waccasassa Bay, b., Fl., U.S.	C4	86
Wachusett Mountain, mtn., Ma., U.S.	B4	98
Wachusett Reservoir, res., Ma., U.S.	B4	98
Waco, Tx., U.S.	D4	120
Waco Lake, res., Tx., U.S.	D4	120
Waconda Lake, res., Ks., U.S.	C5	93
Waconia, Mn., U.S.	F5	100
Waddeneilanden, is., Neth.	B5	8
Waddenzee, Neth.	B5	8
Waddi, Chappal, mtn., Nig.	G8	42
Waddington, Mount, mtn., B.C., Can.	D5	69
Wadena, Mn., U.S.	D3	100
Wadena, co., Mn., U.S.	D4	100
Wädenswil, Switz.	E15	10
Wadesboro, N.C., U.S.	C2	110
Wādī Halfā', Sudan	D12	42
Wading, stm., N.J., U.S.	D3	107
Wadley, Ga., U.S.	D4	87
Wad Madanī, Sudan	F12	42
Wadmalaw Island, i., S.C., U.S.	F7	117
Wadsworth, Il., U.S.	h9	90
Wadsworth, Nv., U.S.	D2	105
Wadsworth, Oh., U.S.	A4	112
Wagener, S.C., U.S.	D5	117
Wageningen, Neth.	D5	8
Wager Bay, b., N.W. Ter., Can.	C15	66
Wagga Wagga, Austl.	G9	50
Wagin, Austl.	F3	50
Wagner, S.D., U.S.	D7	118
Wagoner, Ok., U.S.	B6	113
Wagoner, co., Ok., U.S.	B6	113
Wagontire Mountain, mtn., Or., U.S.	D7	114
Wągrowiec, Pol.	C17	8
Wah, Pak.	D5	38
Waha, Libya	C9	42
Wahiawa, Hi., U.S.	B3	88
Wahiawa Reservoir, res., Hi., U.S.	g9	88
Wahkiakum, co., Wa., U.S.	C2	124
Wahoo, Ne., U.S.	C9	104
Wahpeton, N.D., U.S.	C9	111
Wahweap Creek, stm., Ut., U.S.	F4	121
Waialua, Hi., U.S.	B3	88
Waialua Bay, b., Hi., U.S.	B3	88
Waianae, Hi., U.S.	B3	88
Waianae Range, mts., Hi., U.S.	f9	88
Waidhofen an der Ybbs, Aus.	H14	8
Waigeo, Pulau, i., Indon.	F9	32
Waihi, N.Z.	B5	52
Waikapu, Hi., U.S.	C5	88
Waikiki Beach, Hi., U.S.	g10	88
Wailua, Hi., U.S.	A2	88
Wailuku, Hi., U.S.	C5	88
Waimanalo, Hi., U.S.	B4	88
Waimanalo Bay, b., Hi., U.S.	g11	88
Waimea, Hi., U.S.	f9	88
Waimea, Hi., U.S.	B2	88
Wainwright, Alta., Can.	C5	68
Wainwright, Ak., U.S.	A8	79
Waipahu, Hi., U.S.	B3	88
Waipio Acres, Hi., U.S.	g9	88
Waipio Peninsula, pen., Hi., U.S.	g10	88
Waipukurau, N.Z.	D6	52
Waite Park, Mn., U.S.	E4	100
Waits, stm., Vt., U.S.	C4	122
Waitsburg, Wa., U.S.	C7	124
Wajir, Kenya	H3	46
Wakarusa, In., U.S.	A5	91
Wakarusa, stm., Ks., U.S.	D8	93
Wakasa-wan, b., Japan	G8	30
Wakatomika Creek, stm., Oh., U.S.	B3	112
Wakayama, Japan	H8	30
Wake, co., N.C., U.S.	B4	110
WaKeeney, Ks., U.S.	C4	93
Wakefield, Que., Can.	D2	74
Wakefield, Ks., U.S.	C6	93
Wakefield, Ma., U.S.	B5	98
Wakefield, Mi., U.S.	n12	99
Wakefield, Ne., U.S.	B9	104
Wakefield, R.I., U.S.	F3	116
Wakefield, Va., U.S.	D6	123
Wake Forest, N.C., U.S.	B4	110
Wake Island, dep., Oc.	E24	2
Wakema, Mya.	F3	34
Wakeman, Oh., U.S.	A3	112
Wakkanai, Japan	n19	30a
Wakulla, co., Fl., U.S.	B2	86
Walbridge, Oh., U.S.	e6	112
Wałbrzych (Waldenburg), Pol.	E16	8
Walcott, Ia., U.S.	C7	92
Walcott, Lake, res., Id., U.S.	G5	89
Walden, Ont., Can.	A3	73
Walden, Co., U.S.	A4	83
Walden, N.Y., U.S.	D6	109
Walden Ridge, mtn., Tn., U.S.	D8	119
Waldheim, Sask., Can.	E2	75
Waldo, Ar., U.S.	D2	81
Waldo, co., Me., U.S.	D3	96
Waldoboro, Me., U.S.	D3	96
Waldo Lake, l., Ma., U.S.	h11	98
Waldo Lake, l., Or., U.S.	D4	114
Waldport, Or., U.S.	C2	114
Waldron, Ar., U.S.	C1	81
Waldron, In., U.S.	F6	91
Waldshut, Ger.	H8	8
Waldwick, N.J., U.S.	A4	107
Wales, ter., U.K.	I9	7
Wales Island, i., N.W. Ter., Can.	C15	66
Waleska, Ga., U.S.	B2	87
Walgett, Austl.	E9	50
Walhalla, N.D., U.S.	A8	111
Walhalla, S.C., U.S.	B1	117
Walhonding, stm., Oh., U.S.	B3	112
Walker, Ia., U.S.	B6	92
Walker, La., U.S.	g10	95
Walker, Mi., U.S.	E5	99
Walker, Mn., U.S.	C4	100
Walker, co., Al., U.S.	B2	78
Walker, co., Ga., U.S.	B1	87
Walker, co., Tx., U.S.	D5	120
Walker, stm., Nv., U.S.	D3	105
Walker Lake, l., Nv., U.S.	E3	105
Walker River Indian Reservation, Nv., U.S.	D3	105
Walkersville, Md., U.S.	B3	97
Walkerton, Ont., Can.	C3	73
Walkerton, In., U.S.	B5	91
Walkertown, N.C., U.S.	A2	110
Walkerville, Mt., U.S.	D4	103
Wall, S.D., U.S.	D3	118
Wallace, Id., U.S.	B3	89
Wallace, N.C., U.S.	B4	110
Wallace, co., Ks., U.S.	D2	93
Wallaceburg, Ont., Can.	E2	73
Wallace Lake, res., La., U.S.	B2	95
Walla Walla, Wa., U.S.	C7	124
Walla Walla, co., Wa., U.S.	C7	124
Walla Walla, stm., U.S.	C7	124
Walled Lake, Mi., U.S.	o15	99
Wallen, In., U.S.	B7	91
Wallenpaupack, Lake, l., Pa., U.S.	D11	115
Waller, Tx., U.S.	q14	120
Waller, co., Tx., U.S.	E4	120
Wallingford, Ct., U.S.	D4	84
Wallingford, Vt., U.S.	E3	122
Wallington, N.J., U.S.	h8	107
Wallis and Futuna, dep., Oc.	G1	2
Wallkill, N.Y., U.S.	D6	109
Wallkill, stm., N.Y., U.S.	D6	109
Wall Lake, Ia., U.S.	B2	92
Wall Lake, l., Ia., U.S.	B2	92
Walloomsac, stm., U.S.	F2	122
Walloon Lake, l., Mi., U.S.	C6	99
Wallowa, Or., U.S.	B9	114
Wallowa, co., Or., U.S.	B9	114
Wallowa Mountains, mts., Or., U.S.	B9	114
Wallula, Lake, res., U.S.	C7	124
Wallum Lake, l., U.S.	A1	116
Walnut, Il., U.S.	B4	90
Walnut, Ia., U.S.	C2	92
Walnut, stm., Ks., U.S.	E6	93
Walnut Canyon National Monument, Az., U.S.	B4	80
Walnut Cove, N.C., U.S.	A2	110
Walnut Creek, Ca., U.S.	h8	82
Walnut Creek, stm., Ks., U.S.	D4	93
Walnut Grove, Al., U.S.	A3	78
Walnut Grove, Mn., U.S.	F3	100
Walnutport, Pa., U.S.	E10	115
Walnut Ridge, Ar., U.S.	A5	81
Walpole, Ma., U.S.	B5	98
Walpole, N.H., U.S.	D2	106
Walsall, Eng., U.K.	I11	7
Walsenburg, Co., U.S.	D6	83
Walsh, Co., U.S.	D8	83
Walsh, co., N.D., U.S.	A8	111
Walsrode, Ger.	C9	8
Walterboro, S.C., U.S.	F6	117
Walter F. George Dam, U.S.	D4	78
Walter F. George Lake, res., U.S.	D4	78
Walters, Ok., U.S.	C3	113
Walthall, co., Ms., U.S.	D3	101
Waltham, Ma., U.S.	B5	98
Walthill, Ne., U.S.	B9	104
Walthourville, Ga., U.S.	E5	87
Walton, In., U.S.	C5	91
Walton, Ky., U.S.	B5	94
Walton, N.Y., U.S.	C5	109
Walton, co., Fl., U.S.	u15	86
Walton, co., Ga., U.S.	C3	87
Walvis Bay, Nam.	F2	44
Walworth, Wi., U.S.	F5	126
Walworth, co., S.D., U.S.	B5	118
Walworth, co., Wi., U.S.	F5	126
Wamac, Il., U.S.	E4	90
Wamba, stm., Afr.	C3	44
Wamego, Ks., U.S.	C7	93
Wamesit, Ma., U.S.	A5	98
Wamsutter, Wy., U.S.	E5	127
Wanaka, N.Z.	F2	52
Wanamingo, Mn., U.S.	F6	100
Wanapum Dam, Wa., U.S.	C6	124
Wanapum Lake, res., Wa., U.S.	B6	124
Wanaque, N.J., U.S.	A4	107
Wanaque Reservoir, res., N.J., U.S.	A4	107
Wanatah, In., U.S.	B4	91
Wanchese, N.C., U.S.	B7	110
Wando, stm., S.C., U.S.	F8	117
Wando Woods, S.C., U.S.	k11	117
Wanganui, N.Z.	C5	52
Wanganui, stm., N.Z.	C5	52
Wangaratta, Austl.	G9	50
Wangen [im Allgäu], Ger.	H9	8
Wangpan Yang, b., China	E10	28
Wānkāner, India	I4	38
Wanxian, China	E8	26
Wapakoneta, Oh., U.S.	B1	112
Wapato, Wa., U.S.	C5	124
Wapawekka Lake, l., Sask., Can.	C3	75
Wapello, Ia., U.S.	C6	92
Wapello, co., Ia., U.S.	C5	92
Wapiti, stm., Can.	B1	68
Wappapello, Lake, res., Mo., U.S.	D7	102
Wappingers Falls, N.Y., U.S.	D7	109
Wapsipinicon, stm., Ia., U.S.	B6	92
War, W.V., U.S.	D3	125
Waramaug, Lake, l., Ct., U.S.	C2	84
Warangal, India	C5	37
Ward, Ar., U.S.	B4	81
Ward, co., N.D., U.S.	A4	111
Ward, co., Tx., U.S.	D1	120
Warden, Wa., U.S.	C6	124
Wardha, India	B5	37
Ward Mountain, mtn., Mt., U.S.	D2	103
Ware, Ma., U.S.	B3	98
Ware, co., Ga., U.S.	E4	87
Ware, stm., Ma., U.S.	B3	98
War Eagle Mountain, mtn., Id., U.S.	G2	89
Wareham, Ma., U.S.	C6	98
Warehouse Point, Ct., U.S.	B5	84
Waren, Ger.	B12	8
Warendorf, Ger.	D7	8
Ware Shoals, S.C., U.S.	C3	117
Warfield, B.C., Can.	E9	69
Warminster, Eng., U.K.	J10	7
Warminster, Pa., U.S.	F11	115
Warm Springs Indian Reservation, Or., U.S.	C5	114
Warm Springs Reservoir, res., Or., U.S.	D8	114
Warnemünde, Ger.	A12	8
Warner, N.H., U.S.	D3	106
Warner, Ok., U.S.	B6	113
Warner, stm., N.H., U.S.	D3	106
Warner Mountains, mts., Ca., U.S.	B3	82
Warner Peak, mtn., Or., U.S.	E7	114
Warner Robins, Ga., U.S.	D3	87
Warr Acres, Ok., U.S.	B4	113
Warren, Ar., U.S.	D3	81
Warren, Il., U.S.	A4	90
Warren, In., U.S.	C7	91
Warren, Ma., U.S.	B3	98
Warren, Mi., U.S.	F7	99
Warren, Mn., U.S.	B2	100
Warren, Oh., U.S.	A5	112
Warren, Or., U.S.	B4	114
Warren, Pa., U.S.	C3	115
Warren, R.I., U.S.	D5	116
Warren, Vt., U.S.	C3	122
Warren, co., Ga., U.S.	C4	87
Warren, co., Il., U.S.	C3	90
Warren, co., In., U.S.	D3	91
Warren, co., Ia., U.S.	C4	92
Warren, co., Ky., U.S.	C3	94
Warren, co., Ms., U.S.	C3	101
Warren, co., Mo., U.S.	C6	102
Warren, co., N.J., U.S.	B3	107
Warren, co., N.Y., U.S.	B7	109
Warren, co., N.C., U.S.	A4	110
Warren, co., Oh., U.S.	C1	112
Warren, co., Pa., U.S.	C3	115
Warren, co., Tn., U.S.	D8	119
Warren, co., Va., U.S.	B4	123
Warren, stm., U.S.	D5	116
Warren Park, In., U.S.	k10	91
Warren Peaks, mts., Wy., U.S.	B8	127
Warrensburg, Il., U.S.	D4	90
Warrensburg, Mo., U.S.	C4	102
Warrensburg, N.Y., U.S.	B7	109
Warrensville Heights, Oh., U.S.	h9	112
Warrenton, S. Afr.	G4	44
Warrenton, Ga., U.S.	C4	87
Warrenton, Mo., U.S.	C6	102
Warrenton, N.C., U.S.	A4	110
Warrenton, Or., U.S.	A3	114
Warrenton, Va., U.S.	B5	123
Warrenville, Il., U.S.	k8	90
Warrenville, S.C., U.S.	D4	117
Warri, Nig.	G7	42
Warrick, co., In., U.S.	H3	91
Warrina, Austl.	E7	50
Warrington, Eng., U.K.	H10	7
Warrington, Fl., U.S.	u14	86
Warrior, Al., U.S.	B3	78
Warrior Lake, res., Al., U.S.	C2	78
Warrnambool, Austl.	G8	50
Warroad, Mn., U.S.	B3	100
Warsaw, Il., U.S.	C2	90
Warsaw, In., U.S.	B6	91
Warsaw, Ky., U.S.	B5	94
Warsaw, Mo., U.S.	C4	102
Warsaw, N.Y., U.S.	C2	109
Warsaw, N.C., U.S.	B4	110
Warsaw, Va., U.S.	C6	123
Warsaw see Warszawa, Pol.	C21	8
Warszawa (Warsaw), Pol.	C21	8
Warta, stm., Pol.	C15	8
Wartburg, Tn., U.S.	C9	119
Warthe see Warta, stm., Pol.	C15	8
Warwick, Austl.	E10	50
Warwick, Que., Can.	D6	74
Warwick, Eng., U.K.	I11	7
Warwick, Md., U.S.	B6	97
Warwick, N.Y., U.S.	D6	109
Warwick, R.I., U.S.	D4	116
Wasaga Beach, Ont., Can.	C4	73
Wasatch, co., Ut., U.S.	C4	121
Wasco, Ca., U.S.	E4	82
Wasco, co., Or., U.S.	B5	114
Waseca, Mn., U.S.	F5	100
Waseca, co., Mn., U.S.	F5	100
Washakie, co., Wy., U.S.	C5	127
Washakie Needles, mts., Wy., U.S.	C3	127
Washburn, Il., U.S.	C4	90
Washburn, Ia., U.S.	B5	92
Washburn, Me., U.S.	B4	96
Washburn, N.D., U.S.	B5	111
Washburn, Wi., U.S.	B3	126
Washburn, co., Wi., U.S.	C2	126
Washburn, Mount, mtn., Wy., U.S.	B2	127
Washington, D.C., U.S.	C3	97
Washington, Ga., U.S.	C4	87
Washington, Il., U.S.	C4	90
Washington, In., U.S.	G3	91
Washington, Ia., U.S.	C6	92
Washington, Ks., U.S.	C6	93
Washington, Ky., U.S.	B6	94
Washington, La., U.S.	D3	95
Washington, Ms., U.S.	D2	101
Washington, Mo., U.S.	C6	102
Washington, N.J., U.S.	B3	107
Washington, N.C., U.S.	B5	110
Washington, Pa., U.S.	F1	115
Washington, Ut., U.S.	F2	121
Washington, co., Al., U.S.	D1	78
Washington, co., Ar., U.S.	A1	81
Washington, co., Co., U.S.	B7	83
Washington, co., Fl., U.S.	u16	86
Washington, co., Ga., U.S.	C4	87
Washington, co., Id., U.S.	E2	89
Washington, co., Il., U.S.	E4	90
Washington, co., In., U.S.	G5	91
Washington, co., Ia., U.S.	C6	92
Washington, co., Ks., U.S.	C6	93
Washington, co., Ky., U.S.	C4	94
Washington, co., La., U.S.	D5	95
Washington, co., Me., U.S.	D5	96
Washington, co., Md., U.S.	A2	97
Washington, co., Mn., U.S.	E6	100
Washington, co., Ms., U.S.	B3	101
Washington, co., Mo., U.S.	D7	102
Washington, co., Ne., U.S.	C9	104
Washington, co., N.Y., U.S.	B7	109
Washington, co., N.C., U.S.	B6	110
Washington, co., Oh., U.S.	C4	112
Washington, co., Ok., U.S.	A6	113
Washington, co., Or., U.S.	B3	114
Washington, co., Pa., U.S.	F1	115
Washington, co., R.I., U.S.	E2	116
Washington, co., Tn., U.S.	C11	119
Washington, co., Tx., U.S.	D4	120
Washington, co., Ut., U.S.	F2	121
Washington, co., Vt., U.S.	C3	122
Washington, co., Va., U.S.	f9	123
Washington, co., Wi., U.S.	E5	126
Washington, state, U.S.	B5	124
Washington, Lake, l., Fl., U.S.	D6	86
Washington, Lake, l., Mn., U.S.	E4	100
Washington, Lake, l., Ms., U.S.	B3	101
Washington, Lake, l., Wa., U.S.	e11	124
Washington, Mount, mtn., N.H., U.S.	B4	106
Washington Court House, Oh., U.S.	C2	112
Washington Island, i., Wi., U.S.	C7	126
Washington Park, Il., U.S.	E3	90
Washington Terrace, Ut., U.S.	B4	121
Washita, co., Ok., U.S.	B2	113
Washita, stm., Ok., U.S.	C4	113
Washoe, co., Nv., U.S.	C2	105
Washoe City, Nv., U.S.	D2	105
Washougal, Wa., U.S.	D3	124
Washow Bay, b., Man., Can.	D3	70
Washtenaw, co., Mi., U.S.	F7	99
Wasilla, Ak., U.S.	C10	79
Wasior, Indon.	F9	32
Waskom, Tx., U.S.	C5	120
Waspán, Nic.	G5	64
Wasque Point, c., Ma., U.S.	D7	98
Wassen, Switz.	F15	10
Wassookeag, Lake, l., Me., U.S.	C3	96
Wassuk Range, mts., Nv., U.S.	E3	105
Wataga, Il., U.S.	B3	90
Watauga, co., N.C., U.S.	A1	110
Watauga, stm., Tn., U.S.	C12	119
Watauga Lake, res., Tn., U.S.	C12	119
Watchaug Pond, l., R.I., U.S.	F2	116
Watch Hill Point, c., R.I., U.S.	G1	116
Watchung, N.J., U.S.	B4	107
Waterbury, Ct., U.S.	C3	84
Waterbury, Vt., U.S.	C3	122
Waterbury Center, Vt., U.S.	C3	122
Waterbury Reservoir, res., Vt., U.S.	C3	122
Wateree, stm., S.C., U.S.	D6	117
Wateree Lake, res., S.C., U.S.	C6	117
Waterford, Ire.	I5	7
Waterford, Ct., U.S.	D7	84
Waterford, N.Y., U.S.	C7	109
Waterford, Pa., U.S.	C2	115
Waterford, Wi., U.S.	F5	126
Waterhen Lake, l., Man., Can.	C2	70
Waterloo, Bel.	E4	8
Waterloo, Ont., Can.	D4	73
Waterloo, Que., Can.	D5	74
Waterloo, Il., U.S.	E3	90
Waterloo, In., U.S.	B7	91
Waterloo, Ia., U.S.	B5	92
Waterloo, N.Y., U.S.	C4	109
Waterloo, Wi., U.S.	E5	126
Waterman, Il., U.S.	B5	90
Waterman Reservoir, res., R.I., U.S.	B3	116
Waterproof, La., U.S.	C4	95
Watersmeet, Mi., U.S.	n12	99
Waterton Lakes National Park, Alta., Can.	E3	68
Watertown, Ct., U.S.	C3	84
Watertown, Ma., U.S.	g11	98
Watertown, N.Y., U.S.	B5	109
Watertown, S.D., U.S.	C8	118
Watertown, Tn., U.S.	A5	119
Watertown, Wi., U.S.	E5	126
Water Valley, Ms., U.S.	A4	101
Waterville, Ks., U.S.	C7	93
Waterville, Me., U.S.	D3	96
Waterville, Mn., U.S.	F5	100
Waterville, N.Y., U.S.	C5	109
Waterville, Oh., U.S.	A2	112
Waterville, Wa., U.S.	B5	124
Watervliet, Mi., U.S.	F4	99
Watervliet, N.Y., U.S.	C7	109
Watford, Ont., Can.	E3	73
Watford City, N.D., U.S.	B2	111
Wathena, Ks., U.S.	C9	93
Watkins, Mn., U.S.	E4	100
Watkins Glen, N.Y., U.S.	C4	109
Watkinsville, Ga., U.S.	C3	87
Watonga, Ok., U.S.	B3	113
Watonwan, co., Mn., U.S.	F4	100
Watonwan, stm., Mn., U.S.	G4	100
Watseka, Il., U.S.	C6	90
Watson Lake, Yukon, Can.	D7	66
Watsontown, Pa., U.S.	D8	115
Watsonville, Ca., U.S.	D3	82
Watts Bar Dam, Tn., U.S.	D9	119
Watts Bar Lake, res., Tn., U.S.	D9	119
Wattsville, S.C., U.S.	B4	117
Wattwil, Switz.	E16	10
Watubela, Kepulauan, is., Indon.	F9	32
Waubaushene, Ont., Can.	C5	73
Waubay, S.D., U.S.	B8	118
Waubay Lake, l., S.D., U.S.	B8	118
Wauchula, Fl., U.S.	E5	86
Wauconda, Il., U.S.	h8	90
Waugh Mountain, mtn., Id., U.S.	D4	89
Waukee, Ia., U.S.	C4	92
Waukegan, Il., U.S.	A6	90
Waukesha, Wi., U.S.	F5	126
Waukesha, co., Wi., U.S.	E5	126
Waukewan, Lake, l., N.H., U.S.	C3	106
Waukomis, Ok., U.S.	A4	113
Waukon, Ia., U.S.	A6	92
Waunakee, Wi., U.S.	E4	126
Wauneta, Ne., U.S.	D4	104
Waungumbaug Lake, l., Ct., U.S.	B6	84
Waupaca, Wi., U.S.	D4	126
Waupaca, co., Wi., U.S.	D5	126
Waupun, Wi., U.S.	E5	126
Wauregan, Ct., U.S.	C8	84
Waurika, Ok., U.S.	C4	113
Waurika Lake, res., Ok., U.S.	C3	113
Wausau, Wi., U.S.	D4	126
Wausau, Lake, res., Wi., U.S.	D4	126
Wauseon, Oh., U.S.	A1	112
Waushara, co., Wi., U.S.	D4	126
Wautoma, Wi., U.S.	D4	126
Wauwatosa, Wi., U.S.	m12	126
Wave Hill, Austl.	C6	50
Waveland, Ms., U.S.	E4	101
Waverley, N.S., Can.	E6	71
Waverly, Il., U.S.	D4	90
Waverly, Ia., U.S.	B5	92
Waverly, Ks., U.S.	D8	93
Waverly, Mn., U.S.	E5	100
Waverly, Mo., U.S.	B4	102
Waverly, Ne., U.S.	D9	104
Waverly, N.Y., U.S.	C4	109
Waverly, Oh., U.S.	C3	112
Waverly, Tn., U.S.	A4	119
Waverly, Va., U.S.	C5	123
Waverly, W.V., U.S.	B3	125
Waverly Hall, Ga., U.S.	D2	87
Wāw, Sudan	G11	42
Wawanesa, Man., Can.	E2	70
Wawasee, Lake, l., In., U.S.	B6	91
Wawayanda Lake, l., N.J., U.S.	A4	107
Wawota, Sask., Can.	H4	75
Waxahachie, Tx., U.S.	C4	120
Waxhaw, N.C., U.S.	C2	110
Waycross, Ga., U.S.	E4	87
Wayland, Ia., U.S.	C6	92
Wayland, Ma., U.S.	g10	98
Wayland, Mi., U.S.	F5	99
Wayland, N.Y., U.S.	C3	109

Name — Map Ref — Page

Waylyn, S.C., U.S. k12 117
Waymart, Pa., U.S. C11 115
Wayne, Mi., U.S. p15 99
Wayne, Ne., U.S. B8 104
Wayne, N.J., U.S. B4 107
Wayne, W.V., U.S. C2 125
Wayne, co., Ga., U.S. E5 87
Wayne, co., Il., U.S. E5 90
Wayne, co., In., U.S. E7 91
Wayne, co., Ia., U.S. D4 92
Wayne, co., Ky., U.S. D5 94
Wayne, co., Mi., U.S. F7 99
Wayne, co., Ms., U.S. D5 101
Wayne, co., Mo., U.S. D7 102
Wayne, co., Ne., U.S. B8 104
Wayne, co., N.Y., U.S. B3 109
Wayne, co., N.C., U.S. B4 110
Wayne, co., Oh., U.S. B4 112
Wayne, co., Pa., U.S. C11 115
Wayne, co., Tn., U.S. B4 119
Wayne, co., Ut., U.S. E4 121
Wayne, co., W.V., U.S. C2 125
Wayne City, Il., U.S. E5 90
Waynesboro, Ga., U.S. C4 87
Waynesboro, Ms., U.S. D5 101
Waynesboro, Pa., U.S. G6 115
Waynesboro, Tn., U.S. B4 119
Waynesboro, Va., U.S. B4 123
Waynesburg, Oh., U.S. B4 112
Waynesburg, Pa., U.S. G1 115
Waynesville, Mo., U.S. D5 102
Waynesville, N.C., U.S. f10 110
Waynesville, Oh., U.S. C1 112
Waynetown, In., U.S. D3 91
Waynewood, Va., U.S. g12 123
Waynoka, Ok., U.S. A3 113
Wayzata, Mn., U.S. n11 100
Wazīrābād, Pak. D6 38
Weakley, co., Tn., U.S. A3 119
Weatherford, Ok., U.S. B3 113
Weatherford, Tx., U.S. C4 120
Weatherly, Pa., U.S. E10 115
Weatogue, Ct., U.S. B4 84
Weaver, Al., U.S. B4 78
Weaver Mountains, mts., Az., U.S. C3 80
Weaverville, Ca., U.S. B2 82
Weaverville, N.C., U.S. f10 110
Webb, Al., U.S. D4 78
Webb, Ms., U.S. B3 101
Webb, co., Tx., U.S. F3 120
Webb City, Mo., U.S. D3 102
Webbers Falls, Ok., U.S. B6 113
Webberville, Mi., U.S. F6 99
Webb Lake, l., Me., U.S. D2 96
Weber, co., Ut., U.S. B4 121
Weber City, Va., U.S. f9 123
Webster, Ma., U.S. B4 98
Webster, N.Y., U.S. B3 109
Webster, Pa., U.S. F2 115
Webster, S.D., U.S. B8 118
Webster, co., Ga., U.S. D2 87
Webster, co., Ia., U.S. B3 92
Webster, co., Ky., U.S. C2 94
Webster, co., La., U.S. B2 95
Webster, co., Ms., U.S. B4 101
Webster, co., Mo., U.S. D5 102
Webster, co., Ne., U.S. D7 104
Webster, co., W.V., U.S. C4 125
Webster City, Ia., U.S. B4 92
Webster Groves, Mo., U.S. f13 102
Webster Reservoir, res., Ks., U.S. C4 93
Webster Springs, W.V., U.S. C4 125
Websterville, Vt., U.S. C4 122
Weddell Sea, Ant. B8 47
Wedgeport, N.S., Can. F4 71
Wedgewood, Mo., U.S. f13 102
Wedowee, Al., U.S. B4 78
Weed, Ca., U.S. B2 82
Weed Heights, Nv., U.S. E2 105
Weedon, Que., Can. D6 74
Weedsport, N.Y., U.S. B4 109
Weedville, Pa., U.S. D5 115
Weehawken, N.J., U.S. h8 107
Weeksbury, Ky., U.S. C7 94
Weeping Water, Ne., U.S. D9 104
Wegscheid, Ger. G13 8
Weiden in der Oberpfalz, Ger. F12 8
Weifang, China D10 26
Weihai, China D11 26
Weilburg, Ger. E8 8
Weilheim, Ger. H11 8
Weimar, Ger. E11 8
Weimar, Tx., U.S. E4 120
Weiner, Ar., U.S. B5 81
Weinheim, Ger. F8 8
Weipa, Austl. B8 50
Weippe, Id., U.S. C3 89
Weir, Ks., U.S. E9 93
Weir, Lake, l., Fl., U.S. C5 86
Weirsdale, Fl., U.S. D5 86
Weirton, W.V., U.S. A4 125
Weiser, Id., U.S. E2 89
Weiser, stm., Id., U.S. E2 89
Weishi, China A3 28
Weissenburg in Bayern, Ger. F10 8
Weissenfels, Ger. D11 8
Weiss Lake, res., U.S. A4 78
Weisswasser, Ger. D14 8
Weiz, Aus. H15 8
Wejherowo, Pol. A18 8
Welch, W.V., U.S. D3 125
Welcome, Mn., U.S. G4 100
Welcome, S.C., U.S. B3 117
Weld, co., Co., U.S. A6 83
Weldon, N.C., U.S. A5 110
Weldon Spring, Mo., U.S. f12 102
Weleetka, Ok., U.S. B5 113
Welkom, S. Afr. G5 44
Welland, Ont., Can. E5 73
Wellesley, Ont., Can. D4 73
Wellesley, Ma., U.S. B5 98
Wellesley Islands, is., Austl. C7 50
Wellford, S.C., U.S. B3 117
Wellington, Ont., Can. D7 73
Wellington, N.Z. D5 52
Wellington, Co., U.S. A5 83
Wellington, Ks., U.S. E6 93
Wellington, Mo., U.S. B4 102
Wellington, Nv., U.S. E2 105
Wellington, Oh., U.S. A3 112
Wellington, Tx., U.S. B2 120
Wellington, Ut., U.S. D5 121
Wellington, Isla, i., Chile F2 56
Wellington Channel, strt., N.W. Ter., Can. A14 66
Wellman, Ia., U.S. C6 92
Wells, Me., U.S. E2 96
Wells, Mi., U.S. C3 99
Wells, Mn., U.S. G5 100
Wells, Nv., U.S. B7 105
Wells, co., In., U.S. C7 91
Wells, co., N.D., U.S. B6 111
Wells, stm., Vt., U.S. C4 122
Wellsboro, Pa., U.S. C7 115
Wellsburg, Ia., U.S. B5 92
Wellsburg, W.V., U.S. A4 125
Wellston, Oh., U.S. C3 112
Wellston, Ok., U.S. B4 113
Wellsville, Ks., U.S. D8 93
Wellsville, Mo., U.S. B6 102
Wellsville, N.Y., U.S. C3 109
Wellsville, Oh., U.S. B5 112
Wellsville, Ut., U.S. B4 121
Wellton, Az., U.S. E1 80
Wels, Aus. G14 8
Welsh, La., U.S. D3 95
Welshpool, Wales, U.K. I9 7
Wembley, Alta., Can. B1 68
Wenatchee, Wa., U.S. B5 124
Wenatchee, stm., Wa., U.S. B5 124
Wenatchee Lake, l., Wa., U.S. B5 124
Wenatchee Mountains, mts., Wa., U.S. B5 124
Wendell, Id., U.S. G4 89
Wendell, N.C., U.S. B4 110
Wendover, Ut., U.S. C1 121
Wenham, Ma., U.S. A6 98
Wenham Lake, l., Ma., U.S. f12 98
Wenona, Il., U.S. B4 90
Wenshan, China C8 34
Wentworth, Lake, l., N.H., U.S. C4 106
Wentzville, Mo., U.S. C7 102
Wenzhou, China G9 28
Weohyakapka, Lake, l., Fl., U.S. E5 86
Wernigerode, Ger. D10 8
Wertheim, Ger. F9 8
Wesel, Ger. D6 8
Weser, stm., Ger. B8 8
Weslaco, Tx., U.S. F4 120
Wesleyville, Newf., Can. D5 72
Wesleyville, Pa., U.S. B2 115
Wessel Islands, is., Austl. B7 50
Wesserunsett Lake, l., Me., U.S. D3 96
Wessington Springs, S.D., U.S. C7 118
Wesson, Ms., U.S. D3 101
West, Tx., U.S. D4 120
West, stm., Ct., U.S. D5 84
West, stm., Ma., U.S. h9 98
West, stm., Vt., U.S. E3 122
West Acton, Ma., U.S. g10 98
West Alexandria, Oh., U.S. C1 112
West Allis, Wi., U.S. m11 126
West Alton, Mo., U.S. f13 102
West Andover, Ma., U.S. A5 98
West Baden Springs, In., U.S. G4 91
West Baton Rouge, co., La., U.S. D4 95
West Bay, b., Fl., U.S. u16 86
West Bay, b., N.C., U.S. B6 110
West Bay, b., Tx., U.S. r15 120
West Bend, Ia., U.S. B3 92
West Bend, Wi., U.S. E5 126
West Bengal, state, India I12 38
West Berlin, N.J., U.S. D3 107
West Billerica, Ma., U.S. f10 98
West Blocton, Al., U.S. B2 78
Westborough, Ma., U.S. B4 98
West Bountiful, Ut., U.S. C4 121
West Boylston, Ma., U.S. B4 98
West Branch, Ia., U.S. C6 92
West Branch, Mi., U.S. D6 99
West Branch Reservoir, res., Ct., U.S. B3 84
West Bridgewater, Ma., U.S. B5 98
Westbrook, Ct., U.S. D6 84
Westbrook, Me., U.S. E2 96
Westbrook, Mn., U.S. F3 100
West Burlington, Ia., U.S. D6 92
West Butte, mtn., Mt., U.S. B5 103
Westby, Wi., U.S. E3 126
West Cache Creek, stm., Ok., U.S. C3 113
West Caldwell, N.J., U.S. B4 107
West Canada Creek, stm., N.Y., U.S. B6 109
West Carroll, co., La., U.S. B4 95
West Carrollton, Oh., U.S. C1 112
West Carthage, N.Y., U.S. B5 109
Westchester, Il., U.S. k9 90
West Chester, Pa., U.S. G10 115
Westchester, co., N.Y., U.S. D7 109
West Chicago, Il., U.S. k8 90
West Chop, c., Ma., U.S. D6 98
West College Corner, In., U.S. E8 91
West Columbia, S.C., U.S. D5 117
West Columbia, Tx., U.S. E5 120
West Concord, Ma., U.S. B5 98
West Concord, Mn., U.S. F6 100
West Concord, N.C., U.S. B2 110
Westconnaug Reservoir, res., R.I., U.S. C2 116
West Cote Blanche Bay, b., La., U.S. E4 95
West Covina, Ca., U.S. m13 82
West Crossett, Ar., U.S. D4 81
West Cumberland, Me., U.S. E2 96
West Dennis, Ma., U.S. C7 98
West Des Moines, Ia., U.S. C4 92
West Elk Mountains, mts., Co., U.S. C3 83
West Elk Peak, mtn., Co., U.S. C3 83
Westerly, R.I., U.S. F1 116
Western Australia, state, Austl. D4 50
Western Desert see Gharbīyah, Aṣ-Ṣaḥrā' al-, des., Egypt C11 42
Western Ghāts, mts., India E3 37
Westernport, Md., U.S. m12 97
Western Sahara, dep., Afr. D3 42
Western Samoa, ctry., Oc. G1 2
Western Springs, Il., U.S. k9 90
Westerstede, Ger. B7 8
Westerville, Oh., U.S. B3 112
West Falkland, i., Falk. Is. G4 56
West Falmouth, Ma., U.S. C6 98
West Fargo, N.D., U.S. C9 111
West Feliciana, co., La., U.S. D4 95
Westfield, N.B., Can. D3 71
Westfield, In., U.S. D5 91
Westfield, Ma., U.S. B2 98
Westfield, N.J., U.S. B4 107
Westfield, N.Y., U.S. C1 109
Westfield, Pa., U.S. C6 115
Westfield, Wi., U.S. E4 126
Westfield, stm., Ma., U.S. B2 98
West Fork, Ar., U.S. B1 81
West Fork, stm., W.V., U.S. B4 125
West Frankfort, Il., U.S. F5 90
West Freehold, N.J., U.S. C4 107
West Friendship, Md., U.S. B4 97
Westgate, Fl., U.S. F6 86
West Grand Lake, l., Me., U.S. C5 96
West Grove, Pa., U.S. G10 115
West Hanover, Ma., U.S. h12 98
West Hartford, Ct., U.S. B4 84
West Haven, Ct., U.S. D4 84
West Hazleton, Pa., U.S. E9 115
West Helena, Ar., U.S. C5 81
West Hill Reservoir, res., Ma., U.S. B4 98
Westhope, N.D., U.S. A4 111
West Indies, is. E12 64
West Island, i., Ma., U.S. C6 98
West Jefferson, N.C., U.S. A1 110
West Jefferson, Oh., U.S. C2 112
West Jordan, Ut., U.S. C3 121
West Kingston, R.I., U.S. F3 116
West Lafayette, In., U.S. D4 91
West Lafayette, Oh., U.S. B4 112
Westlake, La., U.S. D2 95
Westlake, Oh., U.S. h9 112
West Lake, l., Me., U.S. C4 96
Westland, Mi., U.S. F7 99
West Laramie, Wy., U.S. E7 127
West Lawn, Pa., U.S. F10 115
West Lebanon, In., U.S. D3 91
West Liberty, Ia., U.S. C6 92
West Liberty, Ky., U.S. C6 94
West Liberty, Oh., U.S. B2 112
West Liberty, W.V., U.S. f8 125
West Linn, Or., U.S. B4 114
Westlock, Alta., Can. B4 68
West Long Branch, N.J., U.S. C4 107
West Lorne, Ont., Can. E3 73
West Marion, N.C., U.S. f10 110
West Medway, Ma., U.S. B5 98
West Memphis, Ar., U.S. B5 81
West Miami, Fl., U.S. s13 86
West Middlesex, Pa., U.S. D1 115
West Mifflin, Pa., U.S. F2 115
West Milton, Oh., U.S. C1 112
West Milwaukee, Wi., U.S. m12 126
Westminster, Ca., U.S. n12 82
Westminster, Co., U.S. B5 83
Westminster, Md., U.S. A4 97
Westminster, S.C., U.S. B1 117
West Monroe, La., U.S. B3 95
Westmont, Ca., U.S. *n12 82
Westmont, Il., U.S. k9 90
Westmont, N.J., U.S. D2 107
Westmont, Pa., U.S. F4 115
Westmoreland, Tn., U.S. A5 119
Westmoreland, co., Pa., U.S. F2 115
Westmoreland, co., Va., U.S. B6 123
Westmorland, Ca., U.S. F6 82
West Musquash Lake, l., Me., U.S. C5 96
West Mystic, Ct., U.S. D8 84
West Newton, Pa., U.S. F2 115
West New York, N.J., U.S. h8 107
West Nishnabotna, stm., Ia., U.S. C2 92
West Norriton, Pa., U.S. o20 115
Weston, Ct., U.S. E2 84
Weston, Ma., U.S. g10 98
Weston, Mo., U.S. B3 102
Weston, Oh., U.S. A2 112
Weston, Or., U.S. B8 114
Weston, W.V., U.S. B4 125
Weston, Wi., U.S. *D4 126
Weston, co., Wy., U.S. C8 127
Weston-super-Mare, Eng., U.K. J10 7
West Orange, N.J., U.S. B4 107
Westover, Md., U.S. D6 97
Westover, W.V., U.S. B5 125
Westover Air Force Base, mil., Ma., U.S. B2 98
West Palm Beach, Fl., U.S. F6 86
West Pawlet, Vt., U.S. E2 122
West Pearl, stm., La., U.S. D6 95
West Pelzer, S.C., U.S. B3 117
West Pensacola, Fl., U.S. u14 86
West Peoria, Il., U.S. C4 90
Westphalia, Mi., U.S. F6 99
West Pittsburg, Pa., U.S. E1 115
West Pittston, Pa., U.S. m17 115
West Plains, Mo., U.S. E6 102
West Point, Ca., U.S. C3 82
West Point, Ga., U.S. D1 87
West Point, Ia., U.S. D6 92
West Point, Ky., U.S. C4 94
West Point, Ms., U.S. B5 101
West Point, Ne., U.S. C9 104
West Point, N.Y., U.S. D7 109
West Point, Va., U.S. C6 123
West Point, mtn., Ak., U.S. C11 79
West Point Lake, res., U.S. C1 87
Westport, Ont., Can. C8 73
Westport, N.Z. D3 52
Westport, Ct., U.S. E2 84
Westport, In., U.S. F6 91
Westport, Wa., U.S. C1 124
West Portsmouth, Oh., U.S. D2 112
West Quoddy Head, c., Me., U.S. D6 96
Westray, i., Scot., U.K. B10 7
Westray Firth, strt., Scot., U.K. B9 7
West Reading, Pa., U.S. F10 115
West Rutland, Vt., U.S. D2 122
West Saint Paul, Mn., U.S. n12 100
West Salem, Il., U.S. E5 90
West Salem, Oh., U.S. B3 112
West Salem, Wi., U.S. E2 126
West Scarborough, Me., U.S. E2 96
West Seneca, N.Y., U.S. C2 109
West Simsbury, Ct., U.S. B4 84
West Slope, Or., U.S. g12 114
West Spanish Peak, mtn., Co., U.S. D6 83
West Springfield, Ma., U.S. B2 98
West Springfield, Va., U.S. g12 123
West Swanzey, N.H., U.S. E2 106
West Terre Haute, In., U.S. F3 91
West Thompson Lake, res., Ct., U.S. B8 84
West Union, Ia., U.S. B6 92
West Union, Oh., U.S. D2 112
West Union, W.V., U.S. B4 125
West Unity, Oh., U.S. A1 112
West University Place, Tx., U.S. r14 120
West Valley City, Ut., U.S. C4 121
West Vancouver, B.C., Can. f12 69
West Van Lear, Ky., U.S. C7 94
West View, Pa., U.S. h13 115
Westville, Il., U.S. C6 90
Westville, In., U.S. A4 91
Westville, N.H., U.S. E4 106
Westville, N.J., U.S. D2 107
Westville, Ok., U.S. A7 113
Westville Lake, res., Ma., U.S. B3 98
West Virginia, state, U.S. C4 125
West Walker, stm., U.S. E2 105
West Wareham, Ma., U.S. C6 98
West Warwick, R.I., U.S. D3 116
Westwego, La., U.S. k11 95
Westwood, Ca., U.S. B3 82
Westwood, Ks., U.S. k16 93
Westwood, Ky., U.S. B7 94
Westwood, Ma., U.S. B5 98
Westwood, N.J., U.S. B4 107
Westwood Lakes, Fl., U.S. s13 86
West Wyoming, Pa., U.S. n17 115
West Yarmouth, Ma., U.S. C7 98
West Yellowstone, Mt., U.S. F5 103
West York, Pa., U.S. G8 115
Wetar, Pulau, i., Indon. G8 32
Wetaskiwin, Alta., Can. C4 68
Wethersfield, Ct., U.S. C5 84
Wet Mountains, mts., Co., U.S. C5 83
Wetumka, Ok., U.S. B5 113
Wetumpka, Al., U.S. C3 78
Wetzel, co., W.V., U.S. B4 125
Wetzlar, Ger. E8 8
Wewahitchka, Fl., U.S. B1 86
Wewak, Pap. N. Gui. k15 50a
Wewoka, Ok., U.S. B5 113
Wexford, Ire. I6 7
Wexford, co., Mi., U.S. D5 99
Weyauwega, Wi., U.S. D5 126
Weymouth, Eng., U.K. K10 7
Weymouth, Ma., U.S. B6 98
Whaleysville, Md., U.S. D7 97
Whalsay, i., Scot., U.K. A12 7
Whangarei, N.Z. A5 52
Wharton, N.J., U.S. B3 107
Wharton, Tx., U.S. E4 120
Wharton, co., Tx., U.S. E4 120
What Cheer, Ia., U.S. C5 92
Whatcom, co., Wa., U.S. A4 124
Whatcom, Lake, l., Wa., U.S. A3 124
Wheatfield, In., U.S. B3 91
Wheatland, Ca., U.S. C3 82
Wheatland, Ia., U.S. C7 92
Wheatland, Wy., U.S. D8 127
Wheatland, co., Mt., U.S. D7 103
Wheatland Reservoir, res., Wy., U.S. E7 127
Wheatley, Ont., Can. E2 73
Wheaton, Il., U.S. B5 90
Wheaton, Md., U.S. B3 97
Wheaton, Mn., U.S. E2 100
Wheaton, Mo., U.S. E3 102
Wheat Ridge, Co., U.S. B5 83
Wheelbarrow Peak, mtn., Nv., U.S. F5 105
Wheeler, Ms., U.S. A5 101
Wheeler, Tx., U.S. B2 120
Wheeler, co., Ga., U.S. D4 87
Wheeler, co., Ne., U.S. C7 104
Wheeler, co., Or., U.S. C6 114
Wheeler, co., Tx., U.S. B2 120
Wheeler Air Force Base, mil., Hi., U.S. g9 88
Wheeler Lake, res., Al., U.S. A2 78
Wheeler Peak, mtn., Ca., U.S. C4 82
Wheeler Peak, mtn., Nv., U.S. E7 105
Wheeler Peak, mtn., N.M., U.S. A4 108
Wheelersburg, Oh., U.S. D3 112
Wheeling, Il., U.S. h9 90
Wheeling, W.V., U.S. A4 125
Wheeling Creek, stm., W.V., U.S. f8 125
Wheelwright, Ky., U.S. C7 94
Whetstone, stm., U.S. E2 100
Whidbey Island, i., Wa., U.S. A3 124
Whidbey Island Naval Air Station, mil., Wa., U.S. A3 124
Whigham, Ga., U.S. F2 87
Whiskey Peak, mtn., Wy., U.S. D5 127
Whiskeytown-Shasta Trinity National Recreation Area, Ca., U.S. B2 82
Whistler, B.C., Can. D6 69
Whitacres, Ct., U.S. A5 84
Whitakers, N.C., U.S. A5 110
Whitbourne, Newf., Can. E5 72
Whitby, Ont., Can. D6 73
Whitchurch-Stouffville, Ont., Can. D5 73
White, co., Ar., U.S. B4 81
White, co., Ga., U.S. B3 87
White, co., Il., U.S. E5 90
White, co., In., U.S. C4 91
White, co., Tn., U.S. D8 119
White, stm., N.A. D4 66
White, stm., U.S. C4 81
White, stm., U.S. D5 118
White, stm., U.S. C7 121
White, stm., Az., U.S. D5 80
White, stm., In., U.S. H2 91
White, stm., Mi., U.S. E4 99
White, stm., Nv., U.S. E6 105
White, stm., Tx., U.S. C2 120
White, stm., Vt., U.S. D4 122
White, stm., Wa., U.S. B4 124
White, stm., Wa., U.S. B5 124
White, Lake, l., Austl. D5 50
White Bay, b., Newf., Can. D3 72
White Bear, stm., Newf., Can. E3 72
White Bear Lake, Mn., U.S. E5 100
White Bluff, Tn., U.S. A4 119
White Butte, mtn., N.D., U.S. C2 111
White Castle, La., U.S. D4 95
White Center, Wa., U.S. e11 124
White City, Or., U.S. E4 114
White Clay Creek, stm., U.S. A3 104
White Cloud, Mi., U.S. E5 99
Whitecourt, Alta., Can. B3 68
White Creek, stm., U.S. E2 122
Whiteday, stm., W.V., U.S. h10 125
White Deer, Tx., U.S. B2 120
White Earth Indian Reservation, Mn., U.S. C3 100
White Earth Lake, l., Mn., U.S. C3 100
Whiteface, stm., Mn., U.S. C6 100
Whiteface Mountain, mtn., N.Y., U.S. f11 109
Whitefield, N.H., U.S. B3 106
Whitefish, Mt., U.S. B2 103
Whitefish Bay, Wi., U.S. m12 126
Whitefish Bay, b., Mi., U.S. B6 99
Whitefish Lake, l., Mn., U.S. D4 100
Whitefish Range, mts., Mt., U.S. B2 103
Whiteford, Md., U.S. A5 97
White Hall, Al., U.S. C3 78
White Hall, Ar., U.S. C3 81
White Hall, Il., U.S. D3 90
Whitehall, Mi., U.S. E4 99
Whitehall, Mt., U.S. E4 103
Whitehall, N.Y., U.S. B7 109
Whitehall, Oh., U.S. m11 112
Whitehall, Wi., U.S. D2 126
Whitehall Reservoir, res., Ma., U.S. h9 98
Whitehaven, Eng., U.K. G9 7
White Haven, Pa., U.S. D10 115
Whitehorn, Point, c., Wa., U.S. A3 124
Whitehorse, Yukon, Can. D5 66
White Horse, N.J., U.S. C3 107
Whitehouse, Oh., U.S. A2 112
White House, Tn., U.S. A5 119
White Island Shores, Ma., U.S. C6 98
White Knob Mountains, mts., Id., U.S. F5 89
White Lake, l., La., U.S. E3 95
Whiteman Air Force Base, mil., Mo., U.S. C4 102
White Meadow Lake, N.J., U.S. *B3 107
White Mesa Natural Bridge, Az., U.S. A4 80
White Mountain Peak, mtn., Ca., U.S. D4 82
White Mountains, mts., U.S. D4 82
White Mountains, mts., N.H., U.S. B3 106
Whitemouth, stm., Man., Can. E4 70
Whitemouth Lake, l., Man., Can. E4 70
White Nile (Al-Bahr al-Abyad), stm., Sudan F12 42
White Oak, Oh., U.S. o12 112
White Oak Creek, stm., Oh., U.S. D2 112
Whiteoak Creek, stm., Tn., U.S. A4 119
White Oak Lake, res., Ar., U.S. D2 81
White Pigeon, Mi., U.S. G5 99
White Pine, Mi., U.S. m12 99
White Pine, Tn., U.S. C10 119
White Pine, co., Nv., U.S. D6 105
White Plains, Md., U.S. C4 97
White Plains, N.Y., U.S. D7 109
Whiteriver, Az., U.S. D6 80
White River Junction, Vt., U.S. D4 122
White Rock, B.C., Can. E6 69
White Russia see Belarus, ctry., Eur. G3 18
White Salmon, Wa., U.S. D4 124
White Salmon, stm., Wa., U.S. D4 124
White Sands Missile Range, mil., N.M., U.S. E3 108
White Sands National Monument, N.M., U.S. E3 108
Whitesboro, N.Y., U.S. B5 109
Whitesboro, Tx., U.S. C4 120
Whitesburg, Ga., U.S. C2 87
Whitesburg, Ky., U.S. C7 94
Whites Creek, stm., Tn., U.S. g10 119
White Sea see Beloje more, Russia D5 22
Whiteside, co., Il., U.S. B3 90
White Sulphur Springs, Mt., U.S. D6 103
White Sulphur Springs, W.V., U.S. D4 125
Whitesville, Ky., U.S. C3 94
White Swan, Wa., U.S. C5 124
White Tank Mountains, mts., Az., U.S. k7 80
Whiteville, N.C., U.S. C4 110
Whiteville, Tn., U.S. B2 119
White Volta (Volta Blanche), stm., Afr. F5 42
Whitewater, Ks., U.S. E6 93
Whitewater, Wi., U.S. F5 126
Whitewater, stm., U.S. F7 91
Whitewater, stm., Ks., U.S. E6 93

Name	Map Ref	Page
Whitewater Baldy, mtn., N.M., U.S.	D1	108
Whitewater Bay, b., Fl., U.S.	G6	86
Whitewood, S.D., U.S.	C2	118
Whitewright, Tx., U.S.	C4	120
Whitfield, co., Ga., U.S.	B2	87
Whitfield Estates, Fl., U.S.	q10	86
Whiting, In., U.S.	A3	91
Whiting, Ia., U.S.	B1	92
Whiting, Wi., U.S.	D4	126
Whiting Field Naval Air Station, mil., Fl., U.S.	u14	86
Whitinsville, Ma., U.S.	B4	98
Whitley, co., In., U.S.	B6	91
Whitley, co., Ky., U.S.	D5	94
Whitley City, Ky., U.S.	D5	94
Whitman, Ma., U.S.	B6	98
Whitman, W.V., U.S.	D2	125
Whitman, co., Wa., U.S.	B8	124
Whitman Square, N.J., U.S.	D2	107
Whitmire, S.C., U.S.	B4	117
Whitmore Lake, Mi., U.S.	p14	99
Whitmore Village, Hi., U.S.	f9	88
Whitney, S.C., U.S.	B4	117
Whitney, Tx., U.S.	D4	120
Whitney, Lake, res., Tx., U.S.	D4	120
Whitney, Mount, mtn., Ca., U.S.	D4	82
Whitney Point Lake, res., N.Y., U.S.	C5	109
Whittier, Ak., U.S.	C10	79
Whittier, Ca., U.S.	F4	82
Whitwell, Tn., U.S.	D8	119
Wholdaia Lake, l., N.W. Ter., Can.	D12	66
Whyalla, Austl.	F7	50
Wiarton, Ont., Can.	C3	73
Wibaux, Mt., U.S.	D12	103
Wibaux, co., Mt., U.S.	D12	103
Wichita, Ks., U.S.	E6	93
Wichita, co., Ks., U.S.	D2	93
Wichita, co., Tx., U.S.	B3	120
Wichita Falls, Tx., U.S.	C3	120
Wichita Mountains, mts., Ok., U.S.	C3	113
Wick, Scot., U.K.	C9	7
Wickenburg, Az., U.S.	D3	80
Wickiup Reservoir, res., Or., U.S.	E5	114
Wickliffe, Ky., U.S.	f8	94
Wickliffe, Oh., U.S.	A4	112
Wicklow, Ire.	I6	7
Wicklow Head, c., Ire.	I6	7
Wicklow Mountains, mts., Ire.	H6	7
Wicomico, co., Md., U.S.	D6	97
Wicomico, stm., Md., U.S.	D6	97
Wiconisco, Pa., U.S.	E8	115
Widefield, Co., U.S.	C6	83
Wielkopolska, reg., Pol.	D17	8
Wien (Vienna), Aus.	G16	8
Wiener Neustadt, Aus.	H16	8
Wiesbaden, Ger.	E8	8
Wiesloch, Ger.	F8	8
Wiggins, Ms., U.S.	E4	101
Wiggins Peak, mtn., Wy., U.S.	C3	127
Wikwemikong, Ont., Can.	B3	73
Wilbarger, co., Tx., U.S.	B3	120
Wilber, Ne., U.S.	D9	104
Wilberforce, Oh., U.S.	C2	112
Wilbraham, Ma., U.S.	B3	98
Wilbur, Wa., U.S.	B7	124
Wilburton, Ok., U.S.	C6	113
Wilcannia, Austl.	F8	50
Wilcox, Pa., U.S.	C4	115
Wilcox, co., Al., U.S.	D2	78
Wilcox, co., Ga., U.S.	E3	87
Wild, stm., U.S.	B4	106
Wild Ammonoosuc, stm., N.H., U.S.	B3	106
Wild Branch, stm., Vt., U.S.	B4	122
Wilder, Id., U.S.	F2	89
Wilder, Vt., U.S.	D4	122
Wilder Dam, U.S.	C2	106
Wildhorse Creek, stm., Ok., U.S.	C4	113
Wild Horse Reservoir, res., Nv., U.S.	B6	105
Wildorado, Tx., U.S.	B1	120
Wild Rice, stm., Mn., U.S.	C2	100
Wild Rice, stm., N.D., U.S.	C8	111
Wildwood, Fl., U.S.	D4	86
Wildwood, N.J., U.S.	F3	107
Wildwood Crest, N.J., U.S.	F3	107
Wilhelm, Mount, mtn., Pap. N. Gui.	m16	50a
Wilhelmina Gebergte, mts., Sur.	C7	54
Wilhelmina Peak see Trikora, Puntjak, mtn., Indon.	F10	32
Wilhelmshaven, Ger.	B8	8
Wilkes, co., Ga., U.S.	C4	87
Wilkes, co., N.C., U.S.	A1	110
Wilkes-Barre, Pa., U.S.	D10	115
Wilkesboro, N.C., U.S.	A1	110
Wilkes Land, reg., Ant.	C24	47
Wilkin, co., Mn., U.S.	D2	100
Wilkinsburg, Pa., U.S.	F2	115
Wilkinson, W.V., U.S.	D3	125
Wilkinson, co., Ga., U.S.	D3	87
Wilkinson, co., Ms., U.S.	D2	101
Will, co., Il., U.S.	B6	90
Willacoochee, Ga., U.S.	E3	87
Willacy, co., Tx., U.S.	F4	120
Willamette, stm., Or., U.S.	C3	114
Willamette Pass, Or., U.S.	D4	114
Willamina, Or., U.S.	B3	114
Willapa Bay, b., Wa., U.S.	C1	124
Willard, Mo., U.S.	D4	102
Willard, Oh., U.S.	A3	112
Willard, Ut., U.S.	B3	121
Willard Bay, b., Ut., U.S.	B3	121
Willards, Md., U.S.	D7	97
Willard Stream, stm., Vt., U.S.	B5	122
Willcox, Az., U.S.	E6	80
Willcox Playa, l., Az., U.S.	E5	80
Willemstad, Neth. Ant.	H13	64
William Bill Dannelly Reservoir, res., Al., U.S.	C2	78
Williams, Az., U.S.	B3	80
Williams, Ca., U.S.	C2	82
Williams, co., N.D., U.S.	A2	111
Williams, co., Oh., U.S.	A1	112
Williams, stm., Vt., U.S.	E3	122
Williams, stm., W.V., U.S.	C4	125
Williams Air Force Base, mil., Az., U.S.	D4	80
Williams Bay, Wi., U.S.	F5	126
Williamsburg, In., U.S.	E8	91
Williamsburg, Ia., U.S.	C5	92
Williamsburg, Ky., U.S.	D5	94
Williamsburg, Oh., U.S.	C1	112
Williamsburg, Pa., U.S.	F5	115
Williamsburg, Va., U.S.	C6	123
Williamsburg, co., S.C., U.S.	D8	117
Williams Fork, stm., Co., U.S.	A3	83
Williams Lake, B.C., Can.	C6	69
Williamson, N.Y., U.S.	B3	109
Williamson, W.V., U.S.	D2	125
Williamson, co., Il., U.S.	F4	90
Williamson, co., Tn., U.S.	B5	119
Williamson, co., Tx., U.S.	D4	120
Williamsport, In., U.S.	D3	91
Williamsport, Md., U.S.	A2	97
Williamsport, Pa., U.S.	D7	115
Williamston, Mi., U.S.	F6	99
Williamston, N.C., U.S.	B5	110
Williamston, S.C., U.S.	B3	117
Williamstown, Ky., U.S.	B5	94
Williamstown, Ma., U.S.	A1	98
Williamstown, N.J., U.S.	D3	107
Williamstown, Pa., U.S.	E8	115
Williamstown, Vt., U.S.	C3	122
Williamstown, W.V., U.S.	B3	125
Williamsville, Il., U.S.	D4	90
Williamsville, N.Y., U.S.	C2	109
Willimantic, Ct., U.S.	C7	84
Willimantic, stm., Ct., U.S.	B6	84
Willimantic Reservoir, res., Ct., U.S.	C7	84
Willingboro, N.J., U.S.	C3	107
Willis, Tx., U.S.	D5	120
Willis Islets, is., Austl.	C9	50
Williston, Fl., U.S.	C4	86
Williston, N.D., U.S.	A2	111
Williston, S.C., U.S.	E5	117
Williston Lake, res., B.C., Can.	B6	69
Willits, Ca., U.S.	C2	82
Willmar, Mn., U.S.	E3	100
Willoughby, Oh., U.S.	A4	112
Willoughby, Lake, l., Vt., U.S.	B4	122
Willoughby Hills, Oh., U.S.	A4	112
Willow, Ak., U.S.	g17	79
Willow Creek, stm., Nv., U.S.	E5	105
Willow Creek, stm., Ut., U.S.	D6	121
Willow Creek, stm., Wy., U.S.	C6	127
Willow Grove Naval Air Station, mil., Pa., U.S.	F11	115
Willowick, Oh., U.S.	A4	112
Willowmore, S. Afr.	H4	44
Willow Reservoir, res., Wi., U.S.	C3	126
Willow Run, De., U.S.	i7	85
Willow Run, Mi., U.S.	p14	99
Willows, Ca., U.S.	C2	82
Willow Springs, Il., U.S.	k9	90
Willow Springs, Mo., U.S.	E6	102
Willston, Va., U.S.	*B5	123
Wilmar, Ar., U.S.	D4	81
Wilmerding, Pa., U.S.	k14	115
Wilmette, Il., U.S.	A6	90
Wilmington, De., U.S.	B3	85
Wilmington, Il., U.S.	B5	90
Wilmington, Ma., U.S.	A5	98
Wilmington, N.C., U.S.	C5	110
Wilmington, Oh., U.S.	C2	112
Wilmington, Vt., U.S.	F3	122
Wilmington Manor, De., U.S.	i7	85
Wilmore, Ky., U.S.	C5	94
Wilmot, Ar., U.S.	D4	81
Wilson, Ar., U.S.	B5	81
Wilson, Ks., U.S.	D5	93
Wilson, La., U.S.	D4	95
Wilson, N.C., U.S.	B5	110
Wilson, Ok., U.S.	C4	113
Wilson, Pa., U.S.	E11	115
Wilson, Wy., U.S.	C2	127
Wilson, co., Ks., U.S.	E8	93
Wilson, co., N.C., U.S.	B5	110
Wilson, co., Tn., U.S.	A5	119
Wilson, co., Tx., U.S.	E3	120
Wilson, Cape, c., N.W. Ter., Can.	C16	66
Wilson, Mount, mtn., Az., U.S.	B1	80
Wilson, Mount, mtn., Ca., U.S.	m12	82
Wilson, Mount, mtn., Co., U.S.	D2	83
Wilson, Mount, mtn., Nv., U.S.	E7	105
Wilson, Mount, mtn., Or., U.S.	B5	114
Wilson Creek, stm., Wa., U.S.	B6	124
Wilson Creek, stm., Wa., U.S.	B5	124
Wilson Lake, res., Al., U.S.	A2	78
Wilson Lake, res., Ks., U.S.	D4	93
Wilsons Beach, N.B., Can.	E3	71
Wilsonville, Al., U.S.	B3	78
Wilsonville, Or., U.S.	h12	114
Wilton, Al., U.S.	B3	78
Wilton, Ct., U.S.	E2	84
Wilton, Ia., U.S.	C6	92
Wilton, Me., U.S.	D2	96
Wilton, N.H., U.S.	E3	106
Wilton, N.D., U.S.	B5	111
Wiluna, Austl.	E4	50
Wimauma, Fl., U.S.	E4	86
Wimico, Lake, l., Fl., U.S.	C1	86
Winamac, In., U.S.	B4	91
Wincheck Pond, l., R.I., U.S.	E1	116
Winchendon, Ma., U.S.	A3	98
Winchester, Ont., Can.	B9	73
Winchester, Eng., U.K.	J11	7
Winchester, Il., U.S.	D3	90
Winchester, In., U.S.	D8	91
Winchester, Ks., U.S.	k15	93
Winchester, Ky., U.S.	C5	94
Winchester, Ma., U.S.	g11	98
Winchester, Nv., U.S.	G6	105
Winchester, N.H., U.S.	E2	106
Winchester, Oh., U.S.	D2	112
Winchester, Tn., U.S.	B5	119
Winchester, Va., U.S.	A4	123
Winchester Bay, Or., U.S.	D2	114
Wind, stm., Wa., U.S.	D4	124
Wind, stm., Wy., U.S.	C4	127
Windber, Pa., U.S.	F4	115
Wind Cave National Park, S.D., U.S.	D2	118
Winder, Ga., U.S.	C3	87
Windermere, Eng., U.K.	G10	7
Windfall, In., U.S.	D6	91
Windgap, Pa., U.S.	E11	115
Windham, Ct., U.S.	C7	84
Windham, Oh., U.S.	A4	112
Windham, co., Ct., U.S.	B7	84
Windham, co., Vt., U.S.	F3	122
Windhoek, Nmb.	F3	44
Wind Lake, Wi., U.S.	F5	126
Wind Lake, l., Wi., U.S.	n11	126
Windmill Point, c., Va., U.S.	C6	123
Windom, Mn., U.S.	G3	100
Windom Peak, mtn., Co., U.S.	D3	83
Windorah, Austl.	E8	50
Window Rock, Az., U.S.	B6	80
Wind Point, Wi., U.S.	n12	126
Wind River Indian Reservation, Wy., U.S.	C4	127
Wind River Peak, mtn., Wy., U.S.	D3	127
Wind River Range, mts., Wy., U.S.	C3	127
Windsor (part of Grand Falls-Windsor), Newf., Can.	D4	72
Windsor, Ont., Can.	E1	73
Windsor, Que., Can.	D5	74
Windsor, Eng., U.K.	J12	7
Windsor, Co., U.S.	A6	83
Windsor, Ct., U.S.	B5	84
Windsor, Il., U.S.	D5	90
Windsor, Mo., U.S.	C4	102
Windsor, N.C., U.S.	A6	110
Windsor, Pa., U.S.	G8	115
Windsor, Vt., U.S.	E4	122
Windsor, Va., U.S.	D6	123
Windsor, co., Vt., U.S.	D3	122
Windsor Heights, Ia., U.S.	e8	92
Windsor Locks, Ct., U.S.	B5	84
Windward Islands, is., N.A.	H17	64
Windward Passage, strt., N.A.	E10	64
Windy Hill, S.C., U.S.	C8	117
Windy Peak, mtn., Wa., U.S.	A6	124
Winefred Lake, l., Alta., Can.	B5	68
Winfield, Al., U.S.	B2	78
Winfield, Ia., U.S.	C6	92
Winfield, Ks., U.S.	E7	93
Winfield, Mo., U.S.	C7	102
Winfield, W.V., U.S.	C3	125
Wing, stm., Mn., U.S.	D3	100
Wingate, N.C., U.S.	C2	110
Wingham, Ont., Can.	D3	73
Winifrede, W.V., U.S.	m12	125
Winisk, stm., Ont., Can.	n18	73
Winisk Lake, l., Ont., Can.	F15	66
Wink, Tx., U.S.	D1	120
Winkelman, Az., U.S.	E5	80
Winkler, Man., Can.	E3	70
Winkler, co., Tx., U.S.	D1	120
Winlock, Wa., U.S.	C3	124
Winn, co., La., U.S.	C3	95
Winnebago, Il., U.S.	A4	90
Winnebago, Mn., U.S.	G4	100
Winnebago, Ne., U.S.	B9	104
Winnebago, Wi., U.S.	h8	126
Winnebago, co., Il., U.S.	A4	90
Winnebago, co., Ia., U.S.	A4	92
Winnebago, co., Wi., U.S.	D5	126
Winnebago, stm., Ia., U.S.	A4	92
Winnebago, Lake, l., Wi., U.S.	E5	126
Winnebago Indian Reservation, Ne., U.S.	B9	104
Winneconne, Wi., U.S.	D5	126
Winnemucca, Nv., U.S.	C4	105
Winnemucca Lake, l., Nv., U.S.	C2	105
Winner, S.D., U.S.	D6	118
Winneshiek, co., Ia., U.S.	A6	92
Winnetka, Il., U.S.	A6	90
Winnfield, La., U.S.	C3	95
Winnibigoshish, Lake, l., Mn., U.S.	C4	100
Winnipeg, Man., Can.	E3	70
Winnipeg, stm., Can.	D4	70
Winnipeg, Lake, l., Man., Can.	C3	70
Winnipeg Beach, Man., Can.	D3	70
Winnipegosis, Man., Can.	D2	70
Winnipegosis, Lake, l., Man., Can.	C2	70
Winnipesaukee, Lake, l., N.H., U.S.	C4	106
Winnisquam, N.H., U.S.	C3	106
Winnisquam Lake, l., N.H., U.S.	C3	106
Winnsboro, La., U.S.	B4	95
Winnsboro, S.C., U.S.	C5	117
Winnsboro, Tx., U.S.	C5	120
Winnsboro Mills, S.C., U.S.	C5	117
Winona, Mn., U.S.	F7	100
Winona, Ms., U.S.	B4	101
Winona, Mo., U.S.	D6	102
Winona, co., Mn., U.S.	F7	100
Winona Lake, In., U.S.	B6	91
Winona Lake, l., Vt., U.S.	C2	122
Winooski, Vt., U.S.	C2	122
Winooski, stm., Vt., U.S.	C3	122
Winslow, Az., U.S.	C5	80
Winslow, In., U.S.	H3	91
Winslow, Me., U.S.	D3	96
Winsted, Ct., U.S.	B3	84
Winsted, Mn., U.S.	F4	100
Winston, Fl., U.S.	D4	86
Winston, Or., U.S.	D3	114
Winston, co., Al., U.S.	A2	78
Winston, co., Ms., U.S.	B4	101
Winston-Salem, N.C., U.S.	A2	110
Winter Garden, Fl., U.S.	D5	86
Winter Harbor, Me., U.S.	D4	96
Winter Haven, Fl., U.S.	D5	86
Winter Park, Fl., U.S.	D5	86
Winter Park, N.C., U.S.	C5	110
Winterport, Me., U.S.	D4	96
Winter Ridge, mtn., Or., U.S.	E6	114
Winters, Ca., U.S.	C2	82
Winters, Tx., U.S.	D3	120
Winterset, Ia., U.S.	C4	92
Wintersville, Oh., U.S.	B5	112
Winterswijk, Neth.	D6	8
Winterthur, Switz.	E15	10
Winterton, Newf., Can.	E5	72
Winterville, Ga., U.S.	C3	87
Winterville, N.C., U.S.	B5	110
Winthrop, Ia., U.S.	B6	92
Winthrop, Me., U.S.	D3	96
Winthrop, Ma., U.S.	B6	98
Winthrop, Mn., U.S.	F4	100
Winthrop, Lake, l., Ma., U.S.	h10	98
Winthrop Harbor, Il., U.S.	A6	90
Winton, Austl.	D8	50
Winton, N.C., U.S.	A6	110
Winton Lake, res., Oh., U.S.	o12	113
Winyah Bay, b., S.C., U.S.	E9	117
Wirt, co., W.V., U.S.	B3	125
Wiscasset, Me., U.S.	D3	96
Wisconsin, state, U.S.	D4	126
Wisconsin, stm., Wi., U.S.	E3	126
Wisconsin, Lake, res., Wi., U.S.	E4	126
Wisconsin Dells, Wi., U.S.	E4	126
Wisconsin Rapids, Wi., U.S.	D4	126
Wise, Va., U.S.	f9	123
Wise, co., Tx., U.S.	C4	120
Wise, co., Va., U.S.	e9	123
Wishek, N.D., U.S.	C6	111
Wishram, Wa., U.S.	D4	124
Wisła, stm., Pol.	A18	8
Wismar, Ger.	B11	8
Wisner, La., U.S.	C4	95
Wisner, Ne., U.S.	C9	104
Wissota, Lake, res., Wi., U.S.	D2	126
Wister, Ok., U.S.	C7	113
Wister Lake, res., Ok., U.S.	C7	113
Witbank, S. Afr.	G5	44
Withamsville, Oh., U.S.	C1	112
Witherspoon, Mount, mtn., Ak., U.S.	g18	79
Withlacoochee, stm., U.S.	B3	86
Withlacoochee, stm., Fl., U.S.	C4	86
Witless Bay, Newf., Can.	E5	72
Witt, Il., U.S.	D4	90
Wittenberg, Ger.	D12	8
Wittenberg, Wi., U.S.	D4	126
Wittenberge, Ger.	B11	8
Wittlich, Ger.	F6	8
Wittman, Md., U.S.	C5	97
Wittmann, Az., U.S.	D3	80
Wittstock, Ger.	B12	8
Wixom, Mi., U.S.	o14	99
Wixom Lake, res., Mi., U.S.	E6	99
Włocławek, Pol.	C19	8
Woburn, Ma., U.S.	B5	98
Wokam, Pulau, i., Indon.	G9	32
Woking, Eng., U.K.	J12	7
Wolcott, Ct., U.S.	C4	84
Wolcott, In., U.S.	C3	91
Wolcottville, In., U.S.	A7	91
Wolf, stm., Ms., U.S.	E4	101
Wolf, stm., Tn., U.S.	e9	119
Wolf, stm., Wi., U.S.	C5	126
Wolf Creek, Or., U.S.	E3	114
Wolf Creek, stm., U.S.	A2	113
Wolf Creek, stm., W.V., U.S.	m13	125
Wolf Creek Pass, Co., U.S.	D3	83
Wolfe, co., Ky., U.S.	C6	94
Wolfeboro, N.H., U.S.	C4	106
Wolfeboro Falls, N.H., U.S.	C4	106
Wolfe City, Tx., U.S.	C4	120
Wolfen, Ger.	D12	8
Wolfenbüttel, Ger.	C10	8
Wolf Lake, Mi., U.S.	E4	99
Wolf Lake, l., Il., U.S.	k9	90
Wolf Mountain, mtn., Ak., U.S.	B9	79
Wolf Point, Mt., U.S.	B11	103
Wolfsberg, Aus.	I14	8
Wolfsburg, Ger.	C10	8
Wolf Swamp, sw., N.C., U.S.	C5	110
Wolgast, Ger.	A13	8
Wollaston, Cape, c., N.W. Ter., Can.	B9	66
Wollaston, Islas, is., Chile	H3	56
Wollaston Lake, l., Sask., Can.	m8	75
Wollaston Peninsula, pen., N.W. Ter., Can.	C10	66
Wollongong, Austl.	F10	50
Wolverhampton, Eng., U.K.	I10	7
Woman Lake, l., Mn., U.S.	D4	100
Womelsdorf, Pa., U.S.	F9	115
Wonder Lake, Il., U.S.	A5	90
Wonewoc, Wi., U.S.	E3	126
Wŏnsan, N. Kor.	D12	26
Wood, co., Oh., U.S.	A2	112
Wood, co., Tx., U.S.	C5	120
Wood, co., W.V., U.S.	B3	125
Wood, co., Wi., U.S.	D3	126
Wood, stm., Sask., Can.	H2	75
Wood, stm., R.I., U.S.	F2	116
Wood, stm., Wy., U.S.	C3	127
Wood, Mount, mtn., Mt., U.S.	E7	103
Woodall Mountain, mtn., Ms., U.S.	A5	101
Woodbine, Ga., U.S.	F5	87
Woodbine, Ia., U.S.	C2	92
Woodbine, Ky., U.S.	D5	94
Woodbine, N.J., U.S.	E3	107
Woodbridge, Ct., U.S.	D3	84
Woodbridge, Va., U.S.	B5	123
Woodbridge [Township], N.J., U.S.	B4	107
Woodburn, In., U.S.	B8	91
Woodburn, Or., U.S.	B4	114
Woodbury, Ct., U.S.	C3	84
Woodbury, Ga., U.S.	D2	87
Woodbury, Mn., U.S.	F6	100
Woodbury, N.J., U.S.	D2	107
Woodbury, Tn., U.S.	B5	119
Woodbury, co., Ia., U.S.	B1	92
Woodcliff Lake, N.J., U.S.	g8	107
Woodcliff Lake, l., N.J., U.S.	g8	107
Wood Dale, Il., U.S.	k9	90
Wood End, spit, Ma., U.S.	B7	98
Woodfield, S.C., U.S.	C6	117
Woodford, co., Il., U.S.	C4	90
Woodford, co., Ky., U.S.	B5	94
Woodhull, Il., U.S.	B3	90
Woodlake, Ca., U.S.	D4	82
Woodland, Ca., U.S.	C3	82
Woodland, Me., U.S.	C5	96
Woodland, N.C., U.S.	A5	110
Woodland, Wa., U.S.	D3	124
Woodland Acres, Co., U.S.	D6	83
Woodland Park, Co., U.S.	C5	83
Woodlark Island, i., Pap. N. Gui.	A10	50
Woodlawn, Ky., U.S.	e9	94
Woodlawn, Md., U.S.	g10	97
Woodlawn, Oh., U.S.	n13	112
Woodlawn, Va., U.S.	D2	123
Woodmont, Ct., U.S.	E4	84
Woodmoor, Md., U.S.	B4	97
Woodridge, Il., U.S.	k8	90
Wood-Ridge, N.J., U.S.	h8	107
Wood River, Il., U.S.	E3	90
Wood River, Ne., U.S.	D7	104
Woodroffe, Mount, mtn., Austl.	E6	50
Woodruff, S.C., U.S.	B3	117
Woodruff, Wi., U.S.	C4	126
Woodruff, co., Ar., U.S.	B4	81
Woods, co., Ok., U.S.	A3	113
Woods, Lake, res., Tn., U.S.	B5	119
Woods, Lake of the, l., N.A.	G14	66
Woodsboro, Tx., U.S.	E4	120
Woods Cross, Ut., U.S.	C4	121
Woodsfield, Oh., U.S.	C4	112
Woods Hole, Ma., U.S.	C6	98
Woodson, Ar., U.S.	C3	81
Woodson, co., Ks., U.S.	E8	93
Woodstock, N.B., Can.	C2	71
Woodstock, Ont., Can.	D4	73
Woodstock, Ga., U.S.	B2	87
Woodstock, Il., U.S.	A5	90
Woodstock, Md., U.S.	B4	97
Woodstock, N.Y., U.S.	C6	109
Woodstock, Vt., U.S.	D3	122
Woodstock, Va., U.S.	B4	123
Woodstown, N.J., U.S.	D2	107
Woodsville, N.H., U.S.	B2	106
Woodville, N.Z.	D5	52
Woodville, Fl., U.S.	B2	86
Woodville, Ms., U.S.	D2	101
Woodville, Oh., U.S.	A2	112
Woodville, Tx., U.S.	D5	120
Woodville, Wi., U.S.	D1	126
Woodward, Ia., U.S.	C4	92
Woodward, Ok., U.S.	A2	113
Woodward, co., Ok., U.S.	A2	113
Woodworth, La., U.S.	C3	95
Woolmarket, Ms., U.S.	E5	101
Woolrich, Pa., U.S.	D7	115
Woolsey Peak, mtn., Az., U.S.	D3	80
Woomera, Austl.	F7	50
Woonsocket, R.I., U.S.	A3	116
Woonsocket, S.D., U.S.	C7	118
Woonsocket Reservoir Number Three, res., R.I., U.S.	B3	116
Wooramel, Austl.	E2	50
Wooster, Oh., U.S.	B4	112
Worcester, S. Afr.	H3	44
Worcester, Eng., U.K.	I10	7
Worcester, Ma., U.S.	B4	98
Worcester, co., Md., U.S.	D7	97
Worcester, co., Ma., U.S.	A3	98
Worden, Il., U.S.	E4	90
Worden Pond, l., R.I., U.S.	F3	116
Workington, Eng., U.K.	G9	7
Worland, Wy., U.S.	B5	127
Worms, Ger.	F8	8
Worth, Il., U.S.	k9	90
Worth, co., Ga., U.S.	E3	87
Worth, co., Ia., U.S.	A4	92
Worth, co., Mo., U.S.	A3	102
Worthing, Eng., U.K.	K12	7
Worthington, In., U.S.	F4	91
Worthington, Ky., U.S.	B7	94
Worthington, Mn., U.S.	G3	100
Worthington, Oh., U.S.	B2	112
Worthington Peak, mtn., Nv., U.S.	F6	105
Wowoni, Pulau, i., Indon.	F7	32
Wrangell, Ak., U.S.	D13	79
Wrangell, Cape, c., Ak., U.S.	E2	79
Wrangell, Mount, mtn., Ak., U.S.	f19	79
Wrangell Island, i., Ak., U.S.	m24	79
Wrangell Mountains, mts., Ak., U.S.	C11	79
Wrangell-Saint Elias National Park, Ak., U.S.	C11	79
Wrath, Cape, c., Scot., U.K.	C7	7
Wray, Co., U.S.	A8	83
Wreck Reefs, rf., Austl.	D11	50
Wrens, Ga., U.S.	C4	87
Wrentham, Ma., U.S.	B5	98
Wrexham, Wales, U.K.	H9	7
Wright, co., Ia., U.S.	B4	92
Wright, co., Mn., U.S.	E4	100
Wright, co., Mo., U.S.	D5	102
Wright, Mount, mtn., Mt., U.S.	C4	103
Wright Brothers National Memorial, hist., N.C., U.S.	A7	110
Wright City, Mo., U.S.	C8	102
Wright City, Ok., U.S.	C6	113
Wright-Patterson Air Force Base, mil., Oh., U.S.	C1	112
Wrightson, Mount, mtn., Az., U.S.	F5	80
Wrightstown, N.J., U.S.	C3	107
Wrightstown, Wi., U.S.	D5	126
Wrightsville, Ar., U.S.	C3	81
Wrightsville, Ga., U.S.	D4	87
Wrightsville, Pa., U.S.	F8	115
Wrightsville Beach, N.C., U.S.	C5	110
Wrightsville Reservoir, res., Vt., U.S.	C3	122
Wrigley, N.W. Ter., Can.	D8	66
Wrocław (Breslau), Pol.	D17	8
Wuchuan, China	D11	34
Wudu, China	E7	26
Wugang, China	F9	26
Wuhan, China	E3	28
Wuhu, China	D7	28
Wunstorf, Ger.	C9	8

Name — Map Ref — Page

Wupatki National Monument, Az., U.S. B4 80
Wuppertal, Ger. D7 8
Wurtsmith Air Force Base, mil., Mi., U.S. D7 99
Würzburg, Ger. F9 8
Wurzen, Ger. D12 8
Wushan, China E8 26
Wushenqi, China D8 26
Wusong, China D10 28
Wutongqiao, China F7 26
Wuwei, China D7 26
Wuwei, China D6 28
Wuxi (Wuhsi), China D9 28
Wuyi Shan, mts., China I5 28
Wuyuan, China C8 26
Wuzhong, China D8 26
Wuzhou (Wuchow), China C11 34
Wyaconda, stm., Mo., U.S. A6 102
Wyandot, co., Oh., U.S. B2 112
Wyandotte, Mi., U.S. F7 99
Wyandotte, co., Ks., U.S. C9 93
Wyanet, Il., U.S. B4 90
Wyk, Ger. A8 8
Wylie, Lake, res., U.S. A5 117
Wyman Lake, res., Me., U.S. C3 96
Wymore, Ne., U.S. D9 104
Wyndham, Austl. C5 50
Wynndel, B.C., Can. E9 69
Wynne, Ar., U.S. B5 81
Wynnewood, Ok., U.S. C4 113
Wynoochee, stm., Wa., U.S. B2 124
Wyoming, Ont., Can. E2 73
Wyoming, De., U.S. D3 85
Wyoming, Il., U.S. B4 90
Wyoming, Ia., U.S. B6 92
Wyoming, Mi., U.S. F5 99
Wyoming, Mn., U.S. E6 100
Wyoming, Oh., U.S. o13 112
Wyoming, Pa., U.S. n17 115
Wyoming, R.I., U.S. E2 116
Wyoming, co., N.Y., U.S. C2 109
Wyoming, co., Pa., U.S. D9 115
Wyoming, co., W.V., U.S. D3 125
Wyoming, state, U.S. C5 127
Wyoming Peak, mtn., Wy., U.S. C2 127
Wyoming Range, mts., Wy., U.S. D2 127
Wyomissing, Pa., U.S. F10 115
Wysocking Bay, b., N.C., U.S. B7 110
Wythe, co., Va., U.S. D1 123
Wytheville, Va., U.S. D1 123

X

Xai-Xai, Moz. G6 44
Xangongo, Ang. E3 44
Xánthi, Grc. H8 16
Xapuri, Braz. F5 54
Xenia, Oh., U.S. C2 112
Xertigny, Fr. D13 10
Xi, stm., China G9 26
Xiaguan, China E9 26
Xiahe, China D7 26
Xiamen (Amoy), China K7 28
Xi'an (Sian), China E8 26
Xiangcheng, China B2 28
Xiangfan, China E9 26
Xiangkhoang, Laos E7 34
Xiangride, China D6 26
Xiangtan, China H1 28
Xianyou, China J7 28
Xiaogan, China E2 28
Xiaolan, China M2 28
Xiashi, China E9 28
Xichang, China F7 26
Xiegeer, China F12 38
Xigazê, China F13 38
Xihua, China B3 28
Xilinhaote, China C10 26
Xinavane, Moz. G6 44
Xingtai, China D9 26
Xingu, stm., Braz. D8 54
Xingyi, China B8 34
Xinhui, China M2 28
Xining, China D7 26
Xinjiang Uygur Zizhiqu, prov., China B9 38
Xinxiang, China D9 26
Xinyang, China C3 28
Xiping, China B3 28
Xique-Xique, Braz. F10 54
Xizang Zizhiqu, prov., China D12 38
Xuancheng, China E7 28
Xuanhua, China C10 26
Xuchang, China A2 28
Xuwen, China D11 34
Xuyong, China F8 26
Xuzhou (Süchow), China A6 28

Y

Yaan, China E7 26
Yacolt, Wa., U.S. D3 124
Yacuiba, Bol. H6 54
Yādgīr, India D4 37
Yadkin, co., N.C., U.S. A2 110
Yadkin, stm., N.C., U.S. B2 110
Yadkinville, N.C., U.S. A2 110
Yainax Butte, mtn., Or., U.S. E5 114
Yaizu, Japan H11 30
Yakima, Wa., U.S. C5 124
Yakima, co., Wa., U.S. C4 124
Yakima, stm., Wa., U.S. C6 124
Yakima Indian Reservation, Wa., U.S. C5 124
Yakobi Island, i., Ak., U.S. m21 79
Yakumo, Japan q18 30a
Yaku-shima, i., Japan u30 31b
Yakutat, Ak., U.S. D12 79
Yakutat Bay, b., Ak., U.S. D11 79
Yala, Thai. K6 34
Yale, Mi., U.S. E8 99
Yale, Ok., U.S. A5 113
Yale, Mount, mtn., Co., U.S. C5 83
Yale Lake, res., Wa., U.S. D3 124
Yalobusha, co., Ms., U.S. A4 101
Yalobusha, stm., Ms., U.S. B4 101
Yalta, Ukr. I4 22
Yalu (Amnok-kang), stm., Asia C12 26
Yamachiche, Que., Can. C5 74
Yamagata, Japan D13 30
Yamaguchi, Japan H4 30
Yamato-takada, Japan H8 30
Yambio, Sudan H11 42
Yamdena, Pulau, i., Indon. G9 32
Yamethin, Mya. D4 34
Yamhill, Or., U.S. h11 114
Yamhill, co., Or., U.S. B3 114
Yamoussoukro, C. Iv. G4 42
Yampa, stm., Co., U.S. A2 83
Yamsay Mountain, mtn., Or., U.S. E5 114
Yamuna, stm., India H9 38
Yanbu', Sau. Ar. D2 46
Yancey, co., N.C., U.S. f10 110
Yanceyville, N.C., U.S. A3 110
Yanchang, China D9 26
Yancheng, China B9 28
Yandoon, Mya. F3 34
Yangjiang, China G9 26
Yangon (Rangoon), Mya. B2 32
Yangquan, China D9 26
Yangtze see Chang, stm., China E10 26
Yangzhou, China C8 28
Yanji, China C12 26
Yankton, S.D., U.S. E8 118
Yankton, co., S.D., U.S. D8 118
Yanqi, China C4 26
Yantai (Chefoo), China D11 26
Yantic, stm., Ct., U.S. C7 84
Yaoundé, Cam. H8 42
Yapen, Pulau, i., Indon. F10 32
Yaqui, stm., Mex. C5 62
Yaraka, Austl. D8 50
Yardley, Pa., U.S. F12 115
Yardville, N.J., U.S. C3 107
Yaritagua, Ven. B8 58
Yarmouth, Me., U.S. E2 96
Yarnell, Az., U.S. C3 80
Yarumal, Col. D5 58
Yashiro-jima, i., Japan I5 30
Yates, co., N.Y., U.S. C3 109
Yates Center, Ks., U.S. E8 93
Yates City, Il., U.S. C3 90
Yathkyed Lake, l., N.W. Ter., Can. D13 66
Yatsushiro, Japan J3 30
Yatta Plateau, plat., Kenya B7 44
Yaupi, Ec. I4 58
Yavapai, co., Az., U.S. C3 80
Yavarí (Javari), stm., S.A. D4 54
Yavatmāl, India B5 37
Yaví, Cerro, mtn., Ven. E10 58
Yaviza, Pan. J9 64
Yawatahama, Japan I5 30
Yawgoog Pond, l., R.I., U.S. E1 116
Yaxian, China E10 34
Yazd, Iran B5 46
Yazoo, co., Ms., U.S. C3 101
Yazoo, stm., Ms., U.S. C3 101
Yazoo City, Ms., U.S. C3 101
Ye, Mya. G4 34
Yeadon, Pa., U.S. p21 115
Yeagertown, Pa., U.S. E6 115
Yecheng, China B7 38
Yecla, Spain G10 12
Yei, stm., Sudan G12 42
Yekaterinburg see Jekaterinburg, Russia F10 22
Yell, co., Ar., U.S. B2 81
Yell, i., Scot., U.K. A11 7
Yellow, stm., U.S. u15 86
Yellow, stm., In., U.S. B4 91
Yellow, stm., Wi., U.S. D3 126
Yellow, stm., Wi., U.S. C3 126
Yellow Creek, stm., Tn., U.S. A4 119
Yellowhead Pass, Can. C1 68
Yellow see Huang, stm., China D10 26
Yellowjacket Mountains, mts., Id., U.S. D4 89
Yellowknife, N.W. Ter., Can. D10 66
Yellow Lake, l., Wi., U.S. C1 126
Yellow Medicine, co., Mn., U.S. F2 100
Yellow Sea, Asia D11 26
Yellow Springs, Oh., U.S. C2 112
Yellowstone, co., Mt., U.S. D8 103
Yellowstone, stm., U.S. D10 103
Yellowstone Lake, l., Wy., U.S. B2 127
Yellowstone National Park, co., Mt., U.S. E6 103
Yellowstone National Park, U.S. B2 127
Yellville, Ar., U.S. A3 81
Yelm, Wa., U.S. C3 124
Yemassee, S.C., U.S. F6 117
Yemen, ctry., Asia E4 46
Yenangyaung, Mya. D3 34
Yen Bai, Viet. D8 34
Yendéré, Burkina F5 42
Yendi, Ghana G5 42
Yenisey see Jenisej, stm., Russia D11 24
Yenshui, Tai. L9 28
Yentna, stm., Ak., U.S. f16 79
Yeovil, Eng., U.K. K10 7
Yerevan see Jerevan, Arm. I6 22
Yerington, Nv., U.S. E2 105
Yerington Indian Reservation, Nv., U.S. D2 105
Yermasóyia, Cyp. B3 40
Yermo, Ca., U.S. E5 82
Yerupajá, Nevado, mtn., Peru F3 54
Yerushalayim (Jerusalem), Isr. D4 40
Yeste, Spain G9 12
Yevpatoriya, Ukr. H4 22
Yexian, China B2 28
Yiannitsá, Grc. I6 16
Yibin, China F7 26
Yichang, China E9 26
Yichun, China B12 26
Yichun, China H3 28
Yilan, China B12 26
Yiliang, China B7 34
Yinchuan, China D8 26
Yingde, China K2 28
Yingkou, China C11 26
Yining, China C3 26
Yirga Alem, Eth. G2 46
Yishan, China B10 34
Yíthion, Grc. M6 16
Yitulihe, China A11 26
Yiyang, China F9 26
Ylivieska, Fin. D15 6
Ynykčanskij, Russia E21 24
Yoakum, Tx., U.S. E4 120
Yoakum, co., Tx., U.S. C1 120
Yockanookany, stm., Ms., U.S. C4 101
Yocona, stm., Ms., U.S. A4 101
Yogyakarta, Indon. m15 32
Yoho National Park, B.C., Can. D9 69
Yokkaichi, Japan H9 30
Yokohama, Japan G12 30
Yokosuka, Japan G12 30
Yokote, Japan C13 30
Yola, Nig. G8 42
Yolo, co., Ca., U.S. C2 82
Yolombó, Col. D5 58
Yomba Indian Reservation, Nv., U.S. D4 105
Yonago, Japan G6 30
Yoncalla, Or., U.S. D3 114
Yonezawa, Japan E13 30
Yongdeng, China D7 26
Yongdingzhen, China A6 34
Yongfeng, China H4 28
Yonkers, N.Y., U.S. E7 109
Yopal, Col. E6 58
York, Ont., Can. D5 73
York, Eng., U.K. H11 7
York, Al., U.S. C1 78
York, Me., U.S. E2 96
York, Ne., U.S. D8 104
York, Pa., U.S. G8 115
York, S.C., U.S. B5 117
York, co., Me., U.S. E2 96
York, co., Ne., U.S. D8 104
York, co., Pa., U.S. G8 115
York, co., S.C., U.S. A5 117
York, co., Va., U.S. C6 123
York, stm., Ont., Can. B7 73
York, stm., Va., U.S. C6 123
York, Cape, c., Austl. B8 50
York Beach, Me., U.S. E2 96
York Harbor, Me., U.S. E2 96
Yorklyn, De., U.S. A3 85
Yorktown, In., U.S. D7 91
Yorktown, Tx., U.S. E4 120
Yorktown, Va., U.S. C6 123
Yorktown Manor, R.I., U.S. E4 116
Yorkville, Il., U.S. B5 90
Yorkville, N.Y., U.S. B5 109
Yorkville, Oh., U.S. B5 112
Yoro, Hond. G4 64
Yoron-jima, i., Japan x28 31b
Yosemite National Park, Ca., U.S. D4 82
Yŏsu, S. Kor. E12 26
Youbou, B.C., Can. g11 69
Youghal, Ire. J5 7
Youghiogheny, stm., U.S. F2 115
Youghiogheny River Lake, res., U.S. G3 115
Young, Az., U.S. C5 80
Young, co., Tx., U.S. C3 120
Young Harris, Ga., U.S. B3 87
Youngs, Lake, l., Wa., U.S. f11 124
Youngstown, N.Y., U.S. B1 109
Youngstown, Oh., U.S. A5 112
Youngsville, La., U.S. D3 95
Youngsville, Pa., U.S. C3 115
Youngtown, Az., U.S. k8 80
Youngwood, Pa., U.S. F2 115
Youyang, China F8 26
Ypres see Ieper, Bel. E2 8
Ypsilanti, Mi., U.S. F7 99
Yreka, Ca., U.S. B2 82
Yssingeaux, Fr. G11 10
Ystad, Swe. I9 6
Yu, stm., China C10 34
Yuanling, China F9 26
Yuba, co., Ca., U.S. C3 82
Yuba, stm., Ca., U.S. C3 82
Yuba City, Ca., U.S. C3 82
Yūbari, Japan p19 30a
Yucatan Channel, strt., N.A. C4 64
Yucatan Peninsula, pen., N.A. H15 62
Yucca Lake, l., Nv., U.S. F5 105
Yucca Mountain, mtn., Nv., U.S. G5 105
Yuci, China D9 26
Yueyang, China F2 28
Yugoslavia, ctry., Eur. G11 4
Yukon, Ok., U.S. B4 113
Yukon, prov., Can. D6 66
Yukon, stm., N.A. m19 76a
Yukuhashi, Japan I3 30
Yulee, Fl., U.S. B5 86
Yulin, China D8 26
Yulin, China C11 34
Yuma, Az., U.S. E1 80
Yuma, Co., U.S. A8 83
Yuma, co., Az., U.S. E1 80
Yuma, co., Co., U.S. A8 83
Yuma Marine Corps Air Station, mil., Az., U.S. E1 80
Yumen, China D6 26
Yuncheng, China D9 26
Yunnan, prov., China F7 26
Yurimaguas, Peru E3 54
Yuriria, Mex. G9 62
Yü Shan, mtn., Tai. L9 28
Yushu, China E6 26
Yutan, Ne., U.S. C9 104
Yutian, China B9 38
Yuty, Para. B5 56
Yuxian, China A2 28
Yuyao, China E10 28
Yverdon, Switz. F13 10
Yvetot, Fr. C7 10

Z

Zaandam, Neth. C4 8
Zabīd, Yemen F3 46
Zabrze, Pol. E18 8
Zacapa, Guat. G3 64
Zacapu, Mex. H9 62
Zacatecas, Mex. F8 62
Zachary, La., U.S. D4 95
Zacualtipán, Mex. G10 62
Zadar, Cro. E10 14
Zadetkyi Kyun, i., Mya. J5 34
Zafer Burnu, c., N. Cyp. B4 40
Zafra, Spain G5 12
Zagreb, Cro. D10 14
Zāgros, Kūhhā-ye, mts., Iran B5 46
Zāhedān, Iran C7 46
Zahlah, Leb. C4 40
Zaire, ctry., Afr. B4 44
Zajsan, Kaz. H10 24
Zajsan, Ozero, l., Kaz. H10 24
Zákinthos, i., Grc. L4 16
Zakopane, Pol. F19 8
Zalaegerszeg, Hung. I16 8
Zambezi (Zambeze), stm., Afr. E6 44
Zambia, ctry., Afr. D5 44
Zamboanga, Phil. D7 32
Zamfara, stm., Nig. F7 42
Zamora, Ec. J3 58
Zamora, Spain D6 12
Zamora de Hidalgo, Mex. H8 62
Zamość, Pol. E23 8
Zanesville, Oh., U.S. C4 112
Zanjān, Iran J7 22
Zanzibar, Tan. C7 44
Zanzibar, i., Tan. C7 44
Zaouia el Kahla, Alg. C7 42
Zaouiet el Mgaïz, Tun. M5 14
Zaoz'ornyj, Russia F12 24
Zapadnyj Sajan, mts., Russia G12 24
Zapala, Arg. D2 56
Zapata, Tx., U.S. F3 120
Zapata, co., Tx., U.S. F3 120
Zapata, Península de, pen., Cuba C7 64
Zaporizhzhya, Ukr. H5 22
Zaragoza, Spain D11 12
Zarajsk, Russia G21 18
Zárate, Arg. C5 56
Zaraza, Ven. C10 58
Zard Kūh, mtn., Iran B5 46
Zarembo Island, i., Ak., U.S. m23 79
Zarghūn Shahr, Afg. D3 38
Zaria, Nig. F7 42
Żary (Sorau), Pol. D15 8
Zarzal, Col. E4 58
Zāskār, stm., India D7 38
Zāskār Mountains, mts., Asia C4 36
Zavala, co., Tx., U.S. E3 120
Zavolžje, Russia E26 18
Zavolžsk, Russia D25 18
Zawiercie, Pol. E19 8
Zduńska Wola, Pol. D18 8
Zearing, Ia., U.S. B4 92
Zebulon, Ga., U.S. C2 87
Zebulon, N.C., U.S. B4 110
Zeehan, Austl. H9 50
Zeeland, Mi., U.S. F5 99
Zeerust, S. Afr. G5 44
Zehdenick, Ger. C13 8
Zeigler, Il., U.S. F4 90
Zeila, Som. F3 46
Zeitz, Ger. D12 8
Zeja, Russia G19 24
Zeja, stm., Russia G19 24
Železnogorsk-Ilimskij, Russia F14 24
Zelienople, Pa., U.S. E1 115
Zelina, Cro. D11 14
Zell, Ger. E7 8
Zell am See, Aus. H12 8
Zemio, Cen. Afr. Rep. G11 42
Zenica, Bos. E12 14
Zenith, Wa., U.S. f11 124
Zenobia Peak, mtn., Co., U.S. A2 83
Zephyr Cove, Nv., U.S. E2 105
Zephyrhills, Fl., U.S. D4 86
Zerbst, Ger. D12 8
Zereh, Gowd-e, l., Afg. D1 36
Zermatt, Switz. F14 10
Zeytindağ, Tur. K11 16
Zgierz, Pol. D19 8
Zhalutegi, China C11 26
Zhangjiakou (Kalgan), China C9 26
Zhangzhou (Longxi), China K6 28
Zhanjiang, China D11 34
Zhaoan, China L6 28
Zhaotong, China F7 26
Zhaxigang, China D8 38
Zhejiang, prov., China F10 26
Zhengzhou, China E9 26
Zhenjiang, China C8 28
Zhenyuan, China F8 26
Zhob, stm., Pak. E3 38
Zhongba, China F10 38
Zhongshan, China M2 28
Zhoushan Dao, i., China E11 28
Zhoushan Qundao, is., China E10 28
Zhujiangkou, stm., Asia M2 28
Zhumadian, China C3 28
Zhungeerqi, China D9 26
Zhuoxian, China D10 26
Zhuzhou, China H2 28
Zhytomyr, Ukr. G3 22
Zia Indian Reservation, N.M., U.S. h7 108
Zibo, China D10 26
Ziebach, co., S.D., U.S. C4 118
Ziel, Mount, mtn., Austl. D6 50
Zielona Góra (Grünberg), Pol. D15 8
Žigalovo, Russia G15 24
Žigansk, Russia D18 24
Zigong, China F7 26
Ziguinchor, Sen. F2 42
Zihuatanejo, Mex. I9 62
Žilina, Slov. F18 8
Zillah, Wa., U.S. C5 124
Zillertaler Alpen, mts., Eur. B6 14
Zilwaukee, Mi., U.S. E7 99
Zima, Russia G14 24
Zimbabwe, ctry., Afr. E5 44
Zimmerman, Mn., U.S. E5 100
Zinder, Niger F7 42
Zion, Il., U.S. A6 90
Zion National Park, Ut., U.S. F3 121
Zion Reservoir, res., Az., U.S. C6 80
Zionsville, In., U.S. E5 91
Zipaquirá, Col. E5 58
Zirkel, Mount, mtn., Co., U.S. A4 83
Ziro, India G15 38
Zitácuaro, Mex. H9 62
Zittau, Ger. E14 8
Ziway, Lake, l., Eth. G2 46
Žižickoje, Ozero, l., Russia E14 18
Zlarin, Cro. F10 14
Zlín, Czech. F17 8
Žlobin, Bela. I13 18
Zmeinogorsk, Russia G10 24
Znojmo, Czech. G16 8
Zolfo Springs, Fl., U.S. E5 86
Zomba, Mwi. E7 44
Zonguldak, Tur. G14 4
Zorita, Spain F6 12
Zouar, Chad D9 42
Zrenjanin, Yugo. D4 16
Zuckerhütl, mtn., Aus. I11 8
Zudañez, Bol. G6 54
Zuera, Spain D11 12
Zug, Switz. E15 10
Zugspitze, mtn., Eur. H10 8
Zuiderzee see IJsselmeer, Neth. C5 8
Zumba, Ec. J3 58
Zumbo, Moz. E6 44
Zumbro, stm., Mn., U.S. F6 100
Zumbrota, Mn., U.S. F6 100
Zuni (Zuni Pueblo), N.M., U.S. B1 108
Zuni, stm., U.S. C6 80
Zuni Indian Reservation, N.M., U.S. B1 108
Zuni Mountains, mts., N.M., U.S. B1 108
Zunyi, China F8 26
Zuqar, Jazīrat, i., Yemen F3 46
Zurich, Ont., Can. D3 73
Zürich, Switz. E15 10
Zürichsee, l., Switz. E15 10
Zutphen, Neth. C6 8
Zvishavane, Zimb. F6 44
Zvolen, Slov. G19 8
Zwettl, Aus. G15 8
Zwickau, Ger. E12 8
Zwolle, Neth. C6 8
Zwolle, La., U.S. C2 95
Zyr'anka, Russia D24 24
Żyrardów, Pol. C20 8

World Political Information

This table lists the area, population, population density, form of government, political status, and capital for every country in the world.

The populations are estimates for January 1, 1995 made by Rand McNally on the basis of official data, United Nations estimates, and other available information. Area figures include inland water.

The political units listed in the table are categorized by political status, as follows: A–independent countries; B–internally independent political entities which are under the protection of other countries in matters of defense and foreign affairs; C–colonies and other dependent political units; D–the major administrative subdivisions of Australia, Canada, China, the United Kingdom, and the United States. For comparison, the table also includes the continents and the world.

All footnotes to this table appear on page 196.

Country, Division or Region English (Conventional)	Area in sq. mi.	Area in sq. km.	Estimated Population 1/1/95	Pop. per sq. mi.	Pop. per sq. km.	Form of Government and Political Status	Capital
† Afghanistan	251,826	652,225	19,715,000	78	30	Islamic republic A	Kābol (Kabul)
Africa	11,700,000	30,300,000	697,600,000	60	23		
Alabama	52,423	135,775	4,254,000	81	31	State (U.S.) D	Montgomery
Alaska	656,424	1,700,139	614,000	0.9	0.4	State (U.S.) D	Juneau
† Albania	11,100	28,748	3,394,000	306	118	Republic A	Tiranë
Alberta	255,287	661,190	2,632,000	10	4.0	Province (Canada) D	Edmonton
† Algeria	919,595	2,381,741	27,965,000	30	12	Provisional military government A	Alger (Algiers)
American Samoa	77	199	56,000	727	281	Unincorporated territory (U.S.) C	Pago Pago
† Andorra	175	453	59,000	337	130	Parliamentary co-principality (Spanish and French protection) B	Andorra
† Angola	481,354	1,246,700	10,690,000	22	8.6	Republic A	Luanda
Anguilla	35	91	7,100	203	78	Dependent territory (U.K. protection) B	The Valley
Anhui	53,668	139,000	59,490,000	1,108	428	Province (China) D	Hefei
Antarctica	5,400,000	14,000,000	[1]	—	—		
† Antigua and Barbuda	171	442	67,000	392	152	Parliamentary state A	St. Johns
† Argentina	1,073,519	2,780,400	34,083,000	32	12	Republic A	Buenos Aires and Viedma [4]
Arizona	114,006	295,276	4,070,000	36	14	State (U.S.) D	Phoenix
Arkansas	53,182	137,742	2,468,000	46	18	State (U.S.) D	Little Rock
† Armenia	11,506	29,800	3,794,000	330	127	Republic A	Jerevan
Aruba	75	193	67,000	893	347	Self-governing territory (Netherlands protection) B	Oranjestad
Asia	17,300,000	44,900,000	3,422,700,000	198	76		
† Australia	2,966,155	7,682,300	18,205,000	6.1	2.4	Federal parliamentary state A	Canberra
Australian Capital Territory	927	2,400	309,000	333	129	Territory (Australia) D	Canberra
† Austria	32,377	83,856	7,932,000	245	95	Federal republic A	Wien (Vienna)
† Azerbaijan	33,436	86,600	7,491,000	224	87	Republic A	Baku
† Bahamas	5,382	13,939	275,000	51	20	Parliamentary state A	Nassau
† Bahrain	267	691	563,000	2,109	815	Monarchy A	Al-Manāmah
† Bangladesh	55,598	143,998	119,370,000	2,147	829	Republic A	Dhaka (Dacca)
† Barbados	166	430	261,000	1,572	607	Parliamentary state A	Bridgetown
Beijing Shi	6,487	16,800	11,490,000	1,771	684	Autonomous city (China) D	Beijing (Peking)
† Belarus	80,155	207,600	10,425,000	130	50	Republic A	Minsk
† Belgium	11,783	30,518	10,075,000	855	330	Constitutional monarchy A	Bruxelles (Brussels)
† Belize	8,866	22,963	212,000	24	9.2	Parliamentary state A	Belmopan
† Benin	43,475	112,600	5,433,000	125	48	Republic A	Porto-Novo and Cotonou
Bermuda	21	54	61,000	2,905	1,130	Dependent territory (U.K.) C	Hamilton
† Bhutan	17,954	46,500	1,758,000	98	38	Monarchy (Indian protection) B	Thimphu
† Bolivia	424,165	1,098,581	6,790,000	16	6.2	Republic A	La Paz and Sucre
† Bosnia and Herzegovina	19,741	51,129	4,481,000	227	88	Republic A	Sarajevo
† Botswana	224,711	582,000	1,438,000	6.4	2.5	Republic A	Gaborone
† Brazil	3,286,500	8,511,996	159,690,000	49	19	Federal republic A	Brasília
British Columbia	365,948	947,800	3,395,000	9.3	3.6	Province (Canada) D	Victoria
British Indian Ocean Territory	23	60	[1]	—	—	Dependent territory (U.K.) C	
† Brunei	2,226	5,765	289,000	130	50	Monarchy A	Bandar Seri Begawan
† Bulgaria	42,855	110,994	8,787,000	205	79	Republic A	Sofija (Sofia)
† Burkina Faso	105,792	274,000	10,275,000	97	38	Republic A	Ouagadougou
Burma, see Myanmar	—	—	—	—	—		
† Burundi	10,745	27,830	6,192,000	576	222	Republic A	Bujumbura
California	163,707	424,002	32,090,000	196	76	State (U.S.) D	Sacramento
† Cambodia	69,898	181,035	9,713,000	139	54	Constitutional monarchy A	Phnum Pénh (Phnom Penh)
† Cameroon	183,568	475,440	13,330,000	73	28	Republic A	Yaoundé
† Canada	3,849,674	9,970,610	28,285,000	7.3	2.8	Federal parliamentary state A	Ottawa
† Cape Verde	1,557	4,033	429,000	276	106	Republic A	Praia
Cayman Islands	100	259	33,000	330	127	Dependent territory (U.K.) C	Georgetown
† Central African Republic	240,535	622,984	3,177,000	13	5.1	Republic A	Bangui
† Chad	495,755	1,284,000	6,396,000	13	5.0	Republic A	N'Djamena
† Chile	292,135	756,626	14,050,000	48	19	Republic A	Santiago
† China (excl. Taiwan)	3,689,631	9,556,100	1,196,980,000	324	125	Socialist republic A	Beijing (Peking)
Christmas Island	52	135	1,000	19	7.4	External territory (Australia) C	
Cocos (Keeling) Islands	5.4	14	600	111	43	Territory (Australia) C	
† Colombia	440,831	1,141,748	34,870,000	79	31	Republic A	Santa Fe de Bogotá
Colorado	104,100	269,620	3,649,000	35	14	State (U.S.) D	Denver
† Comoros (excl. Mayotte)	863	2,235	540,000	626	242	Federal Islamic republic A	Moroni
† Congo	132,047	342,000	2,474,000	19	7.2	Republic A	Brazzaville
Connecticut	5,544	14,358	3,266,000	589	227	State (U.S.) D	Hartford
Cook Islands	91	236	19,000	209	81	Self-governing territory (New Zealand protection) B	Avarua
† Costa Rica	19,730	51,100	3,379,000	171	66	Republic A	San José
† Cote d'Ivoire	124,518	322,500	14,540,000	117	45	Republic A	Abidjan and Yamoussoukro [4]
† Croatia	21,829	56,538	4,801,000	220	85	Republic A	Zagreb
† Cuba	42,804	110,861	11,560,000	270	104	Socialist republic A	La Habana (Havana)
† Cyprus (excl. North Cyprus)	2,276	5,896	551,000	242	93	Republic A	Nicosia (Levkosia)
Cyprus, North [2]	1,295	3,355	182,000	141	54	Republic A	Nicosia (Lefkosa)
† Czech Republic	30,450	78,864	10,430,000	343	132	Republic A	Praha (Prague)
Delaware	2,489	6,447	709,000	285	110	State (U.S.) D	Dover
† Denmark	16,639	43,094	5,207,000	313	121	Constitutional monarchy A	København (Copenhagen)
District of Columbia	68	177	575,000	8,456	3,249	Federal district (U.S.) D	Washington
† Djibouti	8,958	23,200	557,000	62	24	Republic A	Djibouti
† Dominica	305	790	89,000	292	113	Republic A	Roseau
† Dominican Republic	18,704	48,442	7,896,000	422	163	Republic A	Santo Domingo
† Ecuador	105,037	272,045	11,015,000	105	40	Republic A	Quito
† Egypt	386,662	1,001,449	58,100,000	150	58	Socialist republic A	Al-Qāhirah (Cairo)
† El Salvador	8,124	21,041	5,280,000	650	251	Republic A	San Salvador
England	50,352	130,410	48,730,000	968	374	Administrative division (U.K.) D	London
† Equatorial Guinea	10,831	28,051	394,000	36	14	Republic A	Malabo
† Eritrea	36,170	93,679	3,458,000	96	37	Republic A	Asmera
† Estonia	17,413	45,100	1,515,000	87	34	Republic A	Tallinn
† Ethiopia	446,953	1,157,603	55,070,000	123	48	Provisional military government A	Adis Abeba
Europe	3,800,000	9,900,000	712,100,000	187	72		
Faeroe Islands	540	1,399	49,000	91	35	Self-governing territory (Danish protection) B	Tórshavn
Falkland Islands [3]	4,700	12,173	2,100	0.4	0.2	Dependent territory (U.K.) C	Stanley

Country, Division or Region English (Conventional)	Area in sq. mi.	Area in sq. km.	Estimated Population 1/1/95	Pop. per sq. mi.	Pop. per sq. km.	Form of Government and Political Status	Capital
† Fiji	7,056	*18,274*	775,000	110	*42*	Republic A	Suva
† Finland	130,559	*338,145*	5,098,000	39	*15*	Republic A	Helsinki (Helsingfors)
Florida	65,758	*170,313*	13,995,000	213	*82*	State (U.S.) D	Tallahassee
† France (excl. Overseas Departments)	211,208	*547,026*	58,000	275	*106*	Republic A	Paris
French Guiana	35,135	*91,000*	138,000	3.9	*1.5*	Overseas department (France) C	Cayenne
French Polynesia	1,359	*3,521*	217,000	160	*62*	Overseas territory (France) C	Papeete
Fujian	46,332	*120,000*	31,720,000	685	*264*	Province (China) D	Fuzhou
† Gabon	103,347	*267,667*	1,035,000	10	*3.9*	Republic A	Libreville
† Gambia	4,127	*10,689*	1,082,000	262	*101*	Provisional military government A	Banjul
Gansu	173,746	*450,000*	23,700,000	136	*53*	Province (China) D	Lanzhou
Gaza Strip	146	*378*	774,000	5,301	*2,048*	Israeli territory with limited self-government	...
Georgia	59,441	*153,953*	7,065,000	119	*46*	State (U.S.) D	Atlanta
† Georgia	26,911	*69,700*	5,704,000	212	*82*	Republic A	Tbilisi
† Germany	137,822	*356,955*	81,710,000	593	*229*	Federal republic A	Berlin and Bonn
† Ghana	92,098	*238,533*	17,210,000	187	*72*	Republic A	Accra
Gibraltar	2.3	*6.0*	32,000	13,913	*5,333*	Dependent territory (U.K.) C	Gibraltar
Golan Heights	454	*1,176*	29,000	64	*25*	Occupied by Israel	...
† Greece	50,949	*131,957*	10,475,000	206	*79*	Republic A	Athínai (Athens)
Greenland	840,004	*2,175,600*	57,000	0.1	*—*	Self-governing territory (Danish protection) B	Godthåb (Nuuk)
† Grenada	133	*344*	92,000	692	*267*	Parliamentary state A	St. George's
Guadeloupe (incl. Dependencies)	687	*1,780*	432,000	629	*243*	Overseas department (France) C	Basse-Terre
Guam	209	*541*	152,000	727	*281*	Unincorporated territory (U.S.) C	Agana
Guangdong	68,726	*178,000*	66,550,000	968	*374*	Province (China) D	Guangzhou (Canton)
† Guatemala	42,042	*108,889*	10,420,000	248	*96*	Republic A	Guatemala
Guernsey (incl. Dependencies)	30	*78*	64,000	2,133	*821*	Crown dependency (U.K. protection) B	St. Peter Port
† Guinea	94,926	*245,857*	6,469,000	68	*26*	Provisional military government A	Conakry
† Guinea-Bissau	13,948	*36,125*	1,111,000	80	*31*	Republic A	Bissau
Guizhou	65,637	*170,000*	34,355,000	523	*202*	Province (China) D	Guiyang
† Guyana	83,000	*214,969*	726,000	8.7	*3.4*	Republic A	Georgetown
Hainan	13,127	*34,000*	6,945,000	529	*204*	Province (China) D	Haikou
† Haiti	10,714	*27,750*	7,069,000	660	*255*	Provisional military government A	Port-au-Prince
Hawaii	10,932	*28,313*	1,181,000	108	*42*	State (U.S.) D	Honolulu
Hebei	73,359	*190,000*	64,640,000	881	*340*	Province (China) D	Shijiazhuang
Heilongjiang	181,082	*469,000*	37,345,000	206	*80*	Province (China) D	Harbin
Henan	64,479	*167,000*	90,495,000	1,403	*542*	Province (China) D	Zhengzhou
† Honduras	43,277	*112,088*	5,822,000	135	*52*	Republic A	Tegucigalpa
Hong Kong	414	*1,072*	5,927,000	14,316	*5,529*	Chinese territory under British administration C	Victoria (Xianggang)
Hubei	72,356	*187,400*	57,100,000	789	*305*	Province (China) D	Wuhan
Hunan	81,081	*210,000*	64,280,000	793	*306*	Province (China) D	Changsha
† Hungary	35,919	*93,030*	10,270,000	286	*110*	Republic A	Budapest
† Iceland	39,769	*103,000*	265,000	6.7	*2.6*	Republic A	Reykjavík
Idaho	83,574	*216,456*	1,129,000	14	*5.2*	State (U.S.) D	Boise
Illinois	57,918	*150,007*	11,870,000	205	*79*	State (U.S.) D	Springfield
† India (incl. part of Jammu and Kashmir)	1,237,062	*3,203,975*	909,150,000	735	*284*	Federal republic A	New Delhi
Indiana	36,420	*94,328*	5,805,000	159	*62*	State (U.S.) D	Indianapolis
† Indonesia	752,410	*1,948,732*	193,680,000	257	*99*	Republic A	Jakarta
Inner Mongolia (Nei Mongol Zizhiqu)	456,759	*1,183,000*	22,745,000	50	*19*	Autonomous region (China) D	Hohhot
Iowa	56,276	*145,754*	2,862,000	51	*20*	State (U.S.) D	Des Moines
† Iran	632,457	*1,638,057*	63,810,000	101	*39*	Islamic republic A	Tehrān
† Iraq	169,235	*438,317*	20,250,000	120	*46*	Republic A	Baghdād
† Ireland	27,137	*70,285*	3,546,000	131	*50*	Republic A	Dublin (Baile Átha Cliath)
Isle of Man	221	*572*	72,000	326	*126*	Crown dependency (U.K. protection) B	Douglas
† Israel	8,019	*20,770*	5,059,000	631	*244*	Republic A	Yerushalayim (Jerusalem)
† Italy	116,324	*301,277*	57,330,000	493	*190*	Republic A	Roma (Rome)
† Jamaica	4,244	*10,991*	2,568,000	605	*234*	Parliamentary state A	Kingston
† Japan	145,870	*377,801*	125,360,000	859	*332*	Constitutional monarchy A	Tōkyō
Jersey	45	*116*	86,000	1,911	*741*	Crown dependency (U.K. protection) B	St. Helier
Jiangsu	39,614	*102,600*	70,980,000	1,792	*692*	Province (China) D	Nanjing
Jiangxi	64,325	*166,600*	39,980,000	622	*240*	Province (China) D	Nanchang
Jilin	72,201	*187,000*	26,095,000	361	*140*	Province (China) D	Changchun
† Jordan	35,135	*91,000*	4,028,000	115	*44*	Constitutional monarchy A	ʻAmmān
Kansas	82,282	*213,110*	2,575,000	31	*12*	State (U.S.) D	Topeka
† Kazakhstan	1,049,156	*2,717,300*	17,025,000	16	*6.3*	Republic A	Alma-Ata and Akmola (4)
Kentucky	40,411	*104,665*	3,835,000	95	*37*	State (U.S.) D	Frankfort
† Kenya	224,961	*582,646*	28,380,000	126	*49*	Republic A	Nairobi
Kiribati	313	*811*	79,000	252	*97*	Republic A	Bairiki
† Korea, North	46,540	*120,538*	23,265,000	500	*193*	Socialist republic A	P'yŏngyang
† Korea, South	38,230	*99,016*	44,655,000	1,168	*451*	Republic A	Sŏul (Seoul)
† Kuwait	6,880	*17,818*	1,866,000	271	*105*	Constitutional monarchy A	Al-Kuwayt (Kuwait)
Kwangsi Chuang (Guangxi Zhuang Zizhiqu)	91,236	*236,300*	44,765,000	491	*189*	Autonomous region (China) D	Nanning
† Kyrgyzstan	76,641	*198,500*	4,541,000	59	*23*	Republic A	Biškek
† Laos	91,429	*236,800*	4,768,000	52	*20*	Socialist republic A	Viangchan (Vientiane)
† Latvia	24,595	*63,700*	2,532,000	103	*40*	Republic A	Rīga
† Lebanon	4,015	*10,400*	3,660,000	912	*352*	Republic A	Bayrūt (Beirut)
† Lesotho	11,720	*30,355*	1,967,000	168	*65*	Constitutional monarchy under military rule A	Maseru
Liaoning	56,255	*145,700*	41,775,000	743	*287*	Province (China) D	Shenyang (Mukden)
† Liberia	38,250	*99,067*	2,771,000	72	*28*	Republic A	Monrovia
† Libya	679,362	*1,759,540*	5,148,000	7.6	*2.9*	Socialist republic A	Ṭarābulus (Tripoli)
† Liechtenstein	62	*160*	30,000	484	*188*	Constitutional monarchy A	Vaduz
† Lithuania	25,212	*65,300*	3,757,000	149	*58*	Republic A	Vilnius
Louisiana	51,843	*134,275*	4,360,000	84	*32*	State (U.S.) D	Baton Rouge
† Luxembourg	998	*2,586*	396,000	397	*153*	Constitutional monarchy A	Luxembourg
Macau	7.0	*18*	396,000	56,571	*22,000*	Chinese territory under Portuguese administration C	Macau
† Macedonia	9,928	*25,713*	2,102,000	212	*82*	Republic A	Skopje
† Madagascar	226,658	*587,041*	13,645,000	60	*23*	Republic A	Antananarivo
Maine	35,387	*91,653*	1,260,000	36	*14*	State (U.S.) D	Augusta
† Malawi	45,747	*118,484*	8,984,000	196	*76*	Republic A	Lilongwe
† Malaysia	127,320	*329,758*	19,505,000	153	*59*	Federal constitutional monarchy A	Kuala Lumpur
† Maldives	115	*298*	251,000	2,183	*842*	Republic A	Male
† Mali	482,077	*1,248,574*	9,585,000	20	*7.7*	Republic A	Bamako
† Malta	122	*316*	368,000	3,016	*1,165*	Republic A	Valletta
Manitoba	250,947	*649,950*	1,131,000	4.5	*1.7*	Province (Canada) D	Winnipeg
† Marshall Islands	70	*181*	55,000	786	*304*	Republic (U.S. protection) A	Majuro (island)

Country, Division or Region English (Conventional)	Area in sq. mi.	Area in sq. km.	Estimated Population 1/1/95	Pop. per sq. mi.	Pop. per sq. km.	Form of Government and Political Status	Capital
Martinique	425	*1,100*	384,000	904	*349*	Overseas department (France) C	Fort-de-France
Maryland	12,407	*32,135*	5,045,000	407	*157*	State (U.S.) D	Annapolis
Massachusetts	10,555	*27,337*	6,117,000	580	*224*	State (U.S.) D	Boston
† Mauritania	395,956	*1,025,520*	2,228,000	5.6	*2.2*	Republic A	Nouakchott
† Mauritius (incl. Dependencies)	788	*2,040*	1,121,000	1,423	*550*	Republic A	Port Louis
Mayotte [5]	144	*374*	95,000	660	*254*	Territorial collectivity (France) C	Dzaoudzi and Mamoudzou [4]
† Mexico	759,534	*1,967,183*	93,860,000	124	*48*	Federal republic A	Ciudad de México (Mexico City)
Michigan	96,810	*250,738*	9,615,000	99	*38*	State (U.S.) D	Lansing
† Micronesia, Federated States of	271	*702*	122,000	450	*174*	Republic (U.S. protection) A	Kolonia and Paliker [4]
Midway Islands	2.0	*5.2*	500	250	*96*	Unincorporated territory (U.S.) C	
Minnesota	86,943	*225,182*	4,595,000	53	*20*	State (U.S.) D	St. Paul
Mississippi	48,434	*125,443*	2,678,000	55	*21*	State (U.S.) D	Jackson
Missouri	69,709	*180,546*	5,330,000	76	*30*	State (U.S.) D	Jefferson City
† Moldova	13,012	*33,700*	4,377,000	336	*130*	Republic A	Chişinău (Kishinev)
† Monaco	0.7	*1.9*	31,000	44,286	*16,316*	Constitutional monarchy A	Monaco
† Mongolia	604,829	*1,566,500*	2,462,000	4.1	*1.6*	Republic A	Ulaanbaatar (Ulan Bator)
Montana	147,046	*380,850*	840,000	5.7	*2.2*	State (U.S.) D	Helena
Montserrat	39	*102*	13,000	333	*127*	Dependent territory (U.K.) C	Plymouth
† Morocco (excl. Western Sahara)	172,414	*446,550*	26,890,000	156	*60*	Constitutional monarchy A	Rabat
† Mozambique	308,642	*799,380*	17,860,000	58	*22*	Republic A	Maputo
† Myanmar	261,228	*676,577*	44,675,000	171	*66*	Provisional military government A	Yangon (Rangoon)
† Namibia	318,253	*824,272*	1,623,000	5.1	*2.0*	Republic A	Windhoek
Nauru	8.1	*21*	10,000	1,235	*476*	Republic A	Yaren District
Nebraska	77,358	*200,358*	1,628,000	21	*8.1*	State (U.S.) D	Lincoln
† Nepal	56,827	*147,181*	21,295,000	375	*145*	Constitutional monarchy A	Kāṭmāṇḍau (Kathmandu)
† Netherlands	16,164	*41,864*	15,425,000	954	*368*	Constitutional monarchy A	Amsterdam and 's-Gravenhage (The Hague)
Netherlands Antilles	309	*800*	187,000	605	*234*	Self-governing territory (Netherlands protection) B	Willemstad
Nevada	110,567	*286,368*	1,444,000	13	*5.0*	State (U.S.) D	Carson City
New Brunswick	28,355	*73,440*	764,000	27	*10*	Province (Canada) D	Fredericton
New Caledonia	7,358	*19,058*	183,000	25	*9.6*	Overseas territory (France) C	Nouméa
Newfoundland	156,649	*405,720*	594,000	3.8	*1.5*	Province (Canada) D	St. John's
New Hampshire	9,351	*24,219*	1,100,000	118	*45*	State (U.S.) D	Concord
New Jersey	8,722	*22,590*	7,985,000	916	*353*	State (U.S.) D	Trenton
New Mexico	121,598	*314,939*	1,655,000	14	*5.3*	State (U.S.) D	Santa Fe
New South Wales	309,500	*801,600*	6,171,000	20	*7.7*	State (Australia) D	Sydney
New York	54,475	*141,089*	18,460,000	339	*131*	State (U.S.) D	Albany
† New Zealand	104,454	*270,534*	3,558,000	34	*13*	Parliamentary state A	Wellington
† Nicaragua	50,054	*129,640*	4,438,000	89	*34*	Republic A	Managua
† Niger	489,191	*1,267,000*	9,125,000	19	*7.2*	Provisional military government A	Niamey
† Nigeria	356,669	*923,768*	97,300,000	273	*105*	Provisional military government A	Lagos and Abuja
Ningsia Hui (Ningxia Huizu Zizhiqu)	25,637	*66,400*	4,908,000	191	*74*	Autonomous region (China) D	Yinchuan
Niue	100	*259*	1,900	19	*7.3*	Self-governing territory (New Zealand protection) B	Alofi
Norfolk Island	14	*36*	2,700	193	*75*	External territory (Australia) C	Kingston
North America	9,500,000	*24,700,000*	453,300,000	48	*18*		
North Carolina	53,821	*139,397*	7,065,000	131	*51*	State (U.S.) D	Raleigh
North Dakota	70,704	*183,123*	656,000	9.3	*3.6*	State (U.S.) D	Bismarck
Northern Ireland	5,461	*14,144*	1,636,000	300	*116*	Administrative division (U.K.) D	Belfast
Northern Mariana Islands	184	*477*	51,000	277	*107*	Commonwealth (U.S. protection) B	Saipan (island)
Northern Territory	519,771	*1,346,200*	182,000	0.4	*0.1*	Territory (Australia) D	Darwin
Northwest Territories	1,322,910	*3,426,320*	57,000	—	—	Territory (Canada) D	Yellowknife
† Norway (incl. Svalbard and Jan Mayen)	149,412	*386,975*	4,339,000	29	*11*	Constitutional monarchy A	Oslo
Nova Scotia	21,425	*55,490*	933,000	44	*17*	Province (Canada) D	Halifax
Oceania (incl. Australia)	3,300,000	*8,500,000*	28,400,000	8.6	*3.3*		
Ohio	44,828	*116,103*	11,270,000	251	*97*	State (U.S.) D	Columbus
Oklahoma	69,903	*181,049*	3,282,000	47	*18*	State (U.S.) D	Oklahoma City
† Oman	82,030	*212,457*	2,089,000	25	*9.8*	Monarchy A	Masqaṭ (Muscat)
Ontario	412,581	*1,068,580*	10,435,000	25	*9.8*	Province (Canada) D	Toronto
Oregon	98,386	*254,819*	3,098,000	31	*12*	State (U.S.) D	Salem
† Pakistan (incl. part of Jammu and Kashmir)	339,732	*879,902*	129,630,000	382	*147*	Federal Islamic republic A	Islāmābād
† Palau (Belau)	196	*508*	17,000	87	*33*	Republic A	Koror and Melekeok [4]
† Panama	29,157	*75,517*	2,654,000	91	*35*	Republic A	Panamá
† Papua New Guinea	178,704	*462,840*	4,057,000	23	*8.8*	Parliamentary state A	Port Moresby
† Paraguay	157,048	*406,752*	4,400,000	28	*11*	Republic A	Asunción
Pennsylvania	46,058	*119,291*	12,215,000	265	*102*	State (U.S.) D	Harrisburg
† Peru	496,225	*1,285,216*	23,095,000	47	*18*	Republic A	Lima
† Philippines	115,831	*300,000*	67,910,000	586	*226*	Republic A	Manila
Pitcairn (incl. Dependencies)	19	*49*	100	5.3	*2.0*	Dependent territory (U.K.) C	Adamstown
† Poland	121,196	*313,895*	38,730,000	320	*123*	Republic A	Warszawa (Warsaw)
† Portugal	35,516	*91,985*	9,907,000	279	*108*	Republic A	Lisboa (Lisbon)
Prince Edward Island	2,185	*5,660*	141,000	65	*25*	Province (Canada) D	Charlottetown
Puerto Rico	3,515	*9,104*	3,625,000	1,031	*398*	Commonwealth (U.S. protection) B	San Juan
† Qatar	4,412	*11,427*	519,000	118	*45*	Monarchy A	Ad-Dawḥah (Doha)
Qinghai	277,994	*720,000*	4,670,000	17	*6.5*	Province (China) D	Xining
Quebec	594,860	*1,540,680*	7,157,000	12	*4.6*	Province (Canada) D	Québec
Queensland	666,876	*1,727,200*	3,259,000	4.9	*1.9*	State (Australia) D	Brisbane
Reunion	969	*2,510*	660,000	681	*263*	Overseas department (France) C	Saint-Denis
Rhode Island	1,545	*4,002*	1,024,000	663	*256*	State (U.S.) D	Providence
† Romania	91,699	*237,500*	22,745,000	248	*96*	Republic A	Bucureşti (Bucharest)
† Russia	6,592,849	*17,075,400*	150,500,000	23	*8.8*	Federal republic A	Moskva (Moscow)
† Rwanda	10,169	*26,338*	7,343,000	722	*279*	Republic A	Kigali
St. Helena (incl. Dependencies)	121	*314*	7,000	58	*22*	Dependent territory (U.K.) C	Jamestown
† St. Kitts and Nevis	104	*269*	42,000	404	*156*	Parliamentary state A	Basseterre
† St. Lucia	238	*616*	138,000	580	*224*	Parliamentary state A	Castries
St. Pierre and Miquelon	93	*242*	6,700	72	*28*	Territorial collectivity (France) C	Saint-Pierre
† St. Vincent and the Grenadines	150	*388*	110,000	733	*284*	Parliamentary state A	Kingstown
† San Marino	24	*61*	24,000	1,000	*393*	Republic A	San Marino
† Sao Tome and Principe	372	*964*	127,000	341	*132*	Republic A	São Tomé
Saskatchewan	251,866	*652,330*	1,018,000	4.0	*1.6*	Province (Canada) D	Regina
† Saudi Arabia	830,000	*2,149,690*	18,190,000	22	*8.5*	Monarchy A	Ar-Riyāḍ (Riyadh)
Scotland	30,421	*78,789*	5,142,000	169	*65*	Administrative division (U.K.) D	Edinburgh
† Senegal	75,951	*196,712*	8,862,000	117	*45*	Republic A	Dakar
† Serbia	34,116	*88,361*	10,095,000	296	*114*	Republic (Yugoslavia) D	Beograd (Belgrade)
† Seychelles	175	*453*	75,000	429	*166*	Republic A	Victoria

World Political Information

Country, Division or Region English (Conventional)	Area in sq. mi.	Area in sq. km.	Estimated Population 1/1/95	Pop. per sq. mi.	Pop. per sq. km.	Form of Government and Political Status	Capital
Shandong	59,074	*153,000*	89,400,000	1,513	*584*	Province (China) D	Jinan
Shanghai Shi	2,394	*6,200*	14,125,000	5,900	*2,278*	Autonomous city (China) D	Shanghai
Shansi (Shānxī)	60,232	*156,000*	30,405,000	505	*195*	Province (China) D	Taiyuan
Shensi (Shǎnxī)	79,151	*205,000*	34,830,000	440	*170*	Province (China) D	Xi'an (Sian)
Sichuan	220,078	*570,000*	113,470,000	516	*199*	Province (China) D	Chengdu
† Sierra Leone	27,925	*72,325*	4,690,000	168	*65*	Transitional military government A	Freetown
† Singapore	246	*636*	2,921,000	11,874	*4,593*	Republic A	Singapore
Sinkiang (Xinjiang Uygur Zizhiqu)	617,764	*1,600,000*	16,040,000	26	*10*	Autonomous region (China) D	Ürümqi
† Slovakia	18,933	*49,035*	5,353,000	283	*109*	Republic A	Bratislava
† Slovenia	7,820	*20,253*	1,993,000	255	*98*	Republic A	Ljubljana
† Solomon Islands	10,954	*28,370*	393,000	36	*14*	Parliamentary state A	Honiara
† Somalia	246,201	*637,657*	7,187,000	29	*11*	None A	Muqdisho (Mogadishu)
† South Africa	471,010	*1,219,909*	44,500,000	94	*36*	Republic A	Pretoria, Cape Town, and Bloemfontein
South America	6,900,000	*17,800,000*	313,900,000	45	*18*		
South Australia	379,925	*984,000*	1,493,000	3.9	*1.5*	State (Australia) D	Adelaide
South Carolina	32,007	*82,898*	3,702,000	116	*45*	State (U.S.) D	Columbia
South Dakota	77,121	*199,745*	735,000	9.5	*3.7*	State (U.S.) D	Pierre
South Georgia (incl. Dependencies)	1,450	*3,755*	(1)	—	—	Dependent territory (U.K.) C	
† Spain	194,885	*504,750*	39,260,000	201	*78*	Constitutional monarchy A	Madrid
Spanish North Africa (6)	12	*32*	146,000	12,167	*4,563*	Five possessions (Spain) C	
† Sri Lanka	24,962	*64,652*	18,240,000	731	*282*	Socialist republic A	Colombo and Kotte
† Sudan	967,500	*2,505,813*	25,840,000	27	*10*	Provisional military government A	Al-Kharṭūm (Khartoum)
† Suriname	63,251	*163,820*	426,000	6.7	*2.6*	Republic A	Paramaribo
† Swaziland	6,704	*17,364*	889,000	133	*51*	Monarchy A	Mbabane and Lobamba
† Sweden	173,732	*449,964*	8,981,000	52	*20*	Constitutional monarchy A	Stockholm
Switzerland	15,943	*41,293*	7,244,000	454	*175*	Federal republic A	Bern (Berne)
† Syria	71,498	*185,180*	14,100,000	197	*76*	Socialist republic A	Dimashq (Damascus)
Taiwan	13,900	*36,002*	21,150,000	1,522	*587*	Republic A	T'aipei
† Tajikistan	55,251	*143,100*	6,073,000	110	*42*	Republic A	Dušanbe
† Tanzania	341,217	*883,749*	28,350,000	83	*32*	Republic A	Dar es Salaam and Dodoma
Tasmania	26,178	*67,800*	492,000	19	*7.3*	State (Australia) D	Hobart
Tennessee	42,146	*109,158*	5,175,000	123	*47*	State (U.S.) D	Nashville
Texas	268,601	*695,676*	18,330,000	68	*26*	State (U.S.) D	Austin
† Thailand	198,115	*513,115*	59,870,000	302	*117*	Constitutional monarchy A	Krung Thep (Bangkok)
Tianjin Shi	4,363	*11,300*	9,337,000	2,140	*826*	Autonomous city (China) D	Tianjin (Tientsin)
Tibet (Xizang Zizhiqu)	471,045	*1,220,000*	2,275,000	4.8	*1.9*	Autonomous region (China) D	Lhasa
† Togo	21,925	*56,785*	4,332,000	198	*76*	Provisional military government A	Lomé
Tokelau Islands	4.6	*12*	1,500	326	*125*	Island territory (New Zealand) C	
Tonga	288	*747*	110,000	382	*147*	Constitutional monarchy A	Nuku'alofa
† Trinidad and Tobago	1,980	*5,128*	1,281,000	647	*250*	Republic A	Port of Spain
† Tunisia	63,170	*163,610*	8,806,000	139	*54*	Republic A	Tunis
† Turkey	300,948	*779,452*	62,030,000	206	*80*	Republic A	Ankara
† Turkmenistan	188,456	*488,100*	4,035,000	21	*8.3*	Republic A	Aščhabad
Turks and Caicos Islands	193	*500*	14,000	73	*28*	Dependent territory (U.K.) C	Grand Turk
Tuvalu	10	*26*	10,000	1,000	*385*	Parliamentary state A	Funafuti
† Uganda	93,104	*241,139*	18,270,000	196	*76*	Republic A	Kampala
† Ukraine	233,090	*603,700*	52,140,000	224	*86*	Republic A	Kyyiv (Kiev)
† United Arab Emirates	32,278	*83,600*	2,855,000	88	*34*	Federation of monarchs A	Abū Ẓaby (Abu Dhabi)
† United Kingdom	94,249	*244,101*	58,430,000	620	*239*	Parliamentary monarchy A	London
† United States	3,787,425	*9,809,431*	262,530,000	69	*27*	Federal republic A	Washington
† Uruguay	68,500	*177,414*	3,317,000	48	*19*	Republic A	Montevideo
Utah	84,904	*219,902*	1,890,000	22	*8.6*	State (U.S.) D	Salt Lake City
† Uzbekistan	172,742	*447,400*	22,860,000	132	*51*	Republic A	Taškent
† Vanuatu	4,707	*12,190*	161,000	34	*13*	Republic A	Port Vila
Vatican City	0.2	*0.4*	1,000	5,000	*2,500*	Monarchical-sacerdotal state A	Città del Vaticano (Vatican City)
† Venezuela	352,145	*912,050*	21,395,000	61	*23*	Federal republic A	Caracas
Vermont	9,615	*24,903*	578,000	60	*23*	State (U.S.) D	Montpelier
Victoria	87,877	*227,600*	4,570,000	52	*20*	State (Australia) D	Melbourne
† Vietnam	127,428	*330,036*	73,760,000	579	*223*	Socialist republic A	Ha Noi
Virginia	42,769	*110,771*	6,595,000	154	*60*	State (U.S.) D	Richmond
Virgin Islands (U.S.)	133	*344*	97,000	729	*282*	Unincorporated territory (U.S.) C	Charlotte Amalie
Virgin Islands, British	59	*153*	13,000	220	*85*	Dependent territory (U.K.) C	Road Town
Wake Island	3.0	*7.8*	300	100	*38*	Unincorporated territory (U.S.) C	
Wales	8,015	*20,758*	2,922,000	365	*141*	Administrative division (U.K.) D	Cardiff
Wallis and Futuna	98	*255*	14,000	143	*55*	Overseas territory (France) C	Mata-Utu
Washington	71,303	*184,674*	5,360,000	75	*29*	State (U.S.) D	Olympia
West Bank (incl. East Jerusalem and Jericho)	2,347	*6,078*	1,717,000	732	*282*	Israeli territory with limited self-government	
Western Australia	975,101	*2,525,500*	1,729,000	1.8	*0.7*	State (Australia) D	Perth
Western Sahara	102,703	*266,000*	215,000	2.1	*0.8*	Occupied by Morocco C	
† Western Samoa	1,093	*2,831*	172,000	157	*61*	Constitutional monarchy A	Apia
West Virginia	24,231	*62,759*	1,838,000	76	*29*	State (U.S.) D	Charleston
Wisconsin	65,503	*169,653*	5,120,000	78	*30*	State (U.S.) D	Madison
Wyoming	97,818	*253,349*	473,000	4.8	*1.9*	State (U.S.) D	Cheyenne
† Yemen	203,850	*527,968*	12,910,000	63	*24*	Republic A	Ṣan'ā'
Yugoslavia	39,449	*102,173*	10,765,000	273	*105*	Republic A	Beograd (Belgrade)
Yukon Territory	186,661	*483,450*	28,000	0.2	*0.1*	Territory (Canada) D	Whitehorse
Yunnan	152,124	*394,000*	39,140,000	257	*99*	Province (China) D	Kunming
† Zaire	905,355	*2,344,858*	43,365,000	48	*18*	Republic A	Kinshasa
† Zambia	290,587	*752,618*	8,809,000	30	*12*	Republic A	Lusaka
Zhejiang	39,305	*101,800*	43,930,000	1,118	*432*	Province (China) D	Hangzhou
† Zimbabwe	150,872	*390,757*	11,075,000	73	*28*	Republic A	Harare
WORLD	57,900,000	*150,100,000*	5,628,000,000	97	*37*		

† Member of the United Nations (1993).
(1) No permanent population.
(2) North Cyprus unilaterally declared its independence from Cyprus in 1983.
(3) Claimed by Argentina.
(4) Future capital.
(5) Claimed by Comoros.
(6) Comprises Ceuta, Melilla, and several small islands.

World Geographical Information

General

MOVEMENTS OF THE EARTH

The earth makes one complete revolution around the sun every 365 days, 5 hours, 48 minutes, and 46 seconds.

The earth makes one complete rotation on its axis in 23 hours, 56 minutes and 4 seconds.

The earth revolves in its orbit around the sun at a speed of 66,700 miles per hour (107,343 kilometers per hour).

The earth rotates on its axis at an equatorial speed of more than 1,000 miles per hour (1,600 kilometers per hour).

MEASUREMENTS OF THE EARTH

Estimated age of the earth, at least 4.6 billion years.

Equatorial diameter of the earth, 7,926.38 miles *(12,756.27 kilometers).*

Polar diameter of the earth, 7,899.80 miles *(12,713.50 kilometers).*

Mean diameter of the earth, 7,917.52 miles *(12,742.01 kilometers).*

Equatorial circumference of the earth, 24,901.46 miles *(40,075.02 kilometers).*

Polar circumference of the earth, 24,855.34 miles *(40,000.79 kilometers).*

Difference between equatorial and polar circumferences of the earth, 46.12 miles *(74.23 kilometers).*

Weight of the earth, 6,600,000,000,000,000,000,000 tons, or 6,600 billion billion tons *(6,000 billion billion metric tons).*

THE EARTH'S SURFACE

Total area of the earth, 197,000,000 square miles *(510,000,000 square kilometers).*

Total land area of the earth (including inland water and Antarctica), 57,900,000 square miles *(150,100,000 square kilometers).*

Highest point on the earth's surface, Mt. Everest, Asia, 29,028 feet *(8,848 meters).*

Lowest point on the earth's land surface, shores of the Dead Sea, Asia, 1,299 feet *(396 meters)* below sea level.

Greatest known depth of the ocean, the Mariana Trench, southwest of Guam, Pacific Ocean, 35,810 feet *(10,915 meters).*

THE EARTH'S INHABITANTS

Population of the earth is estimated to be 5,477,000,000 *(January 1, 1993).*

Estimated population density of the earth, 95 per square mile *(36 per square kilometer).*

EXTREMES OF TEMPERATURE AND RAINFALL OF THE EARTH

Highest temperature ever recorded, 136° F. *(58° C.)* at Al-'Azīzīyah, Libya, Africa, on September 13, 1922.

Lowest temperature ever recorded, -129° F. *(-89° C.)* at Vostok, Antarctica on July 21, 1983.

Highest mean annual temperature, 94° F. *(34° C.)* at Dallol, Ethiopia.

Lowest mean annual temperature, -70° F. *(-50° C.)* at Plateau Station, Antarctica.

The greatest local average annual rainfall is at Mt. Waialeale, Kauai, Hawaii, 460 inches *(11,680 millimeters).*

The greatest 24-hour rainfall, 74 inches *(1,880 millimeters),* is at Cilaos, Reunion Island, March 15-16, 1952.

The lowest local average annual rainfall is at Arica, Chile, .03 inches *(8 millimeters).*

The longest dry period, over 14 years, is at Arica, Chile, October 1903 to January 1918.

The Continents

CONTINENT	Area (sq. mi.) *(sq. km.)*	Estimated Population Jan. 1, 1993	Population per sq. mi. *(sq. km.)*	Mean Elevation (feet) *(M.)*	Highest Elevation (feet) *(m.)*	Lowest Elevation (feet) *(m.)*	Highest Recorded Temperature	Lowest Recorded Temperature
North America	9,500,000 *(24,700,000)*	438,200,000	46 *(18)*	2,000 *(610)*	Mt. McKinley, Alaska, United States 20,320 *(6,194)*	Death Valley, California, United States 282 *(84)* below sea level	Death Valley, California 134° F *(57° C)*	Northice, Greenland -87° F *(-66° C)*
South America	6,900,000 *(17,800,000)*	310,700,000	45 *(17)*	1,800 *(550)*	Cerro Aconcagua, Argentina 22,831 *(6,959)*	Salinas Chicas, Argentina 138 *(42)* below sea level	Rivadavia, Argentina 120° F *(49° C)*	Sarmiento, Argentina -27° F *(-33° C)*
Europe	3,800,000 *(9,900,000)*	694,700,000	183 *(70)*	980 *(300)*	Gora El'brus, Russia 18,510 *(5,642)*	Caspian Sea, Asia-Europe 92 *(28) below sea level*	Sevilla, Spain 122° F *(50° C)*	Ust' Ščugor, Russia -67° F *(-55° C)*
Asia	17,300,000 *(44,900,000)*	3,337,800,000	193 *(74)*	3,000 *(910)*	Mt. Everest, China-Nepal 29,028 *(8,848)*	Dead Sea, Israel-Jordan 1,299 *(396)* below sea level	Tirat Zevi, Israel 129° F *(54° C)*	Ojm'akon and Verchojansk, Russia -90° F *(-68° C)*
Africa	11,700,000 *(30,300,000)*	668,700,000	57 *(22)*	1,900 *(580)*	Kilimanjaro, Tanzania 19,340 *(5,895)*	Lac Assal, Djibouti 502 *(153)* below sea level	Al-'Azīzīyah, Libya 136° F *(58° C)*	Ifrane, Morocco -11° F *(-24° C)*
Oceania, incl. Australia	3,300,000 *(8,500,000)*	26,700,000	8.1 *(3.1)*	....	Mt. Wilhelm, Papua New Guinea 14,793 *(4,509)*	Lake Eyre, South Australia, Australia 52 *(16)* below sea level	Cloncurry, Queensland, Australia 128° F *(53° C)*	Charlotte Pass, New South Wales, Australia -8° F *(-22° C)*
Australia	2,966,155 *(7,682,300)*	16,965,000	5.7 *(2.2)*	1,000 *(300)*	Mt. Kosciusko, New South Wales 7,316 *(2,230)*	Lake Eyre, South Australia 52 *(16)* below sea level	Cloncurry, Queensland 128° F *(53° C)*	Charlotte Pass, New South Wales -8° F *(-22° C)*
Antarctica	5,400,000 *(14,000,000)*	....	....	6,000 *(1830)*	Vinson Massif 16,066 *(4,897)*	sea level	Vanda Station 59° F *(15° C)*	Vostok -129° F *(-89° C)*
World	57,900,000 *(150,100,000)*	5,477,000,000	95 *(36)*	....	Mt. Everest, China-Nepal 29,028 *(8,848)*	Dead Sea, Israel-Jordan 1,299 *(396)* below sea level	Al-'Azīzīyah, Libya 136° F *(58° C)*	Vostok, Antarctica -129° F *(-89° C)*

Historical Populations *

AREA	1650	1750	1800	1850	1900	1920	1950	1970	1980	1990
North America	*5,000,000*	*5,000,000*	*13,000,000*	*39,000,000*	106,000,000	147,000,000	219,000,000	316,600,000	365,000,000	423,600,000
South America	*8,000,000*	*7,000,000*	*12,000,000*	*20,000,000*	38,000,000	61,000,000	111,000,000	187,400,000	239,000,000	293,700,000
Europe	*100,000,000*	*140,000,000*	*190,000,000*	265,000,000	400,000,000	453,000,000	530,000,000	623,700,000	660,300,000	688,000,000
Asia	*335,000,000*	*476,000,000*	*593,000,000*	*754,000,000*	*932,000,000*	*1,000,000,000*	*1,418,000,000*	2,086,200,000	2,581,000,000	3,156,100,000
Africa	*100,000,000*	*95,000,000*	*90,000,000*	*95,000,000*	*118,000,000*	*140,000,000*	*199,000,000*	346,900,000	463,800,000	648,300,000
Oceania, incl. Australia	*2,000,000*	*2,000,000*	*2,000,000*	*2,000,000*	6,000,000	9,000,000	13,000,000	19,200,000	22,700,000	26,300,000
Australia	*	*	*	*	4,000,000	6,000,000	8,000,000	12,460,000	14,510,000	16,950,000
World	*550,000,000*	*725,000,000*	*900,000,000*	*1,175,000,000*	*1,600,000,000*	*1,810,000,000*	*2,490,000,000*	3,580,000,000	4,332,000,000	5,236,000,000

** Figures prior to 1970 are rounded to the nearest million. Figures in italics represent very rough estimates.*

Largest Countries : Population

		Population 1/1/93			Population 1/1/93
1	China	1,179,030,000	16	Turkey	58,620,000
2	India	873,850,000	17	Thailand	58,030,000
3	United States	256,100,000	18	United Kingdom	57,890,000
4	Indonesia	186,180,000	19	France	57,570,000
5	Brazil	159,030,000	20	Egypt	57,050,000
6	Russia	150,500,000	21	Italy	56,550,000
7	Japan	124,710,000	22	Ukraine	51,990,000
8	Pakistan	123,490,000	23	Ethiopia	51,715,000
9	Bangladesh	120,850,000	24	South Korea	43,660,000
10	Nigeria	91,700,000	25	Myanmar	43,070,000
11	Mexico	86,170,000	26	Zaire	39,750,000
12	Germany	80,590,000	27	Spain	39,155,000
13	Vietnam	69,650,000	28	Poland	38,330,000
14	Philippines	65,500,000	29	Colombia	34,640,000
15	Iran	60,500,000	30	South Africa	33,017,000

Largest Countries : Area

		Area (sq. mi.)	Area (sq. km.)			Area (sq. mi.)	Area (sq. km.)
1	Russia	6,592,849	*17,075,400*	16	Indonesia	752,410	*1,948,732*
2	Canada	3,849,674	*9,970,610*	17	Libya	679,362	*1,759,540*
3	United States	3,787,425	*9,809,431*	18	Iran	632,457	*1,638,057*
4	China	3,680,601	*9,550,100*	19	Mongolia	604,829	*1,566,500*
5	Brazil	3,286,500	*8,511,996*	20	Peru	496,225	*1,285,216*
6	Australia	2,966,155	*7,682,300*	21	Chad	495,755	*1,284,000*
7	India	1,237,062	*3,203,975*	22	Niger	489,191	*1,267,000*
8	Argentina	1,073,519	*2,780,400*	23	Mali	482,077	*1,248,574*
9	Kazakhstan	1,049,156	*2,717,300*	24	Angola	481,354	*1,246,700*
10	Sudan	967,500	*2,505,813*	25	Ethiopia	446,953	*1,157,603*
11	Algeria	919,595	*2,381,741*	26	Colombia	440,831	*1,141,748*
12	Zaire	905,446	*2,345,095*	27	South Africa	433,246	*1,122,102*
13	Greenland	840,004	*2,175,600*	28	Bolivia	424,165	*1,098,581*
14	Saudi Arabia	830,000	*2,149,690*	29	Mauritania	395,956	*1,025,520*
15	Mexico	759,534	*1,967,183*	30	Egypt	386,662	*1,001,449*

Principal Mountains

NORTH AMERICA

	Height (feet)	Height (meters)
McKinley, Mt., ▲ Alaska (▲ United States; ▲ North America)	20,320	*6,194*
Logan, Mt., ▲ Canada (▲ Yukon; ▲ St. Elias Mts.)	19,524	*5,951*
Orizaba, Pico de, ▲ Mexico	18,406	*5,610*
St. Elias, Mt., Alaska-Canada	18,008	*5,489*
Popocatépetl, Volcán, Mexico	17,930	*5,465*
Foraker, Mt., Alaska	17,400	*5,304*
Ixtacihuatl, Mexico	17,159	*5,230*
Lucania, Mt., Canada	17,147	*5,226*
Fairweather, Mt., Alaska-Canada (▲ British Columbia)	15,300	*4,663*
Whitney, Mt., ▲ California,	14,494	*4,418*
Elbert, Mt., ▲ Colorado (▲ Rocky Mts.)	14,433	*4,399*
Massive, Mt., Colorado	14,421	*4,396*
Harvard, Mt., Colorado	14,420	*4,395*
Rainier, Mt., ▲ Washington (▲ Cascade Range)	14,410	*4,392*
Williamson, Mt., California	14,375	*4,382*
Blanca Pk., Colorado (▲ Sangre de Cristo Mts.)	14,345	*4,372*
La Plata Pk., Colorado	14,336	*4,370*
Uncompahgre Pk., Colorado (▲ San Juan Mts.)	14,309	*4,361*
Grays Pk., Colorado (▲ Front Range)	14,270	*4,349*
Evans, Mt., Colorado	14,264	*4,348*
Longs Pk., Colorado	14,255	*4,345*
Wrangell, Mt., Alaska	14,163	*4,317*
Shasta, Mt., California	14,162	*4,317*
Pikes Pk., Colorado	14,110	*4,301*
Colima, Nevado de, Mexico	13,993	*4,265*
Tajumulco, Volcán, ▲ Guatemala (▲ Central America)	13,845	*4,220*
Gannett Pk., ▲ Wyoming	13,804	*4,207*
Mauna Kea, ▲ Hawaii	13,796	*4,205*
Grand Teton, Wyoming	13,770	*4,197*
Mauna Loa, Hawaii	13,679	*4,169*
Kings Pk., ▲ Utah	13,528	*4,123*
Cloud Pk., Wyoming (▲ Bighorn Mts.)	13,167	*4,013*
Wheeler Pk., ▲ New Mexico	13,161	*4,011*
Boundary Pk., ▲ Nevada	13,143	*4,006*
Waddington, Mt., Canada (▲ Coast Mts.)	13,104	*3,994*
Robson, Mt., Canada (▲ Canadian Rockies)	12,972	*3,954*
Granite Pk., ▲ Montana	12,799	*3,901*
Borah Pk., ▲ Idaho	12,662	*3,859*
Humphreys Pk., ▲ Arizona	12,633	*3,851*
Chirripó, Cerro, ▲ Costa Rica	12,530	*3,819*
Columbia, Mt., Canada (▲ Alberta)	12,294	*3,747*
Adams, Mt., Washington	12,276	*3,742*
Gunnbjørn Mtn., ▲ Greenland	12,139	*3,700*
San Gorgonio Mtn., California	11,499	*3,505*
Barú, Volcán, ▲ Panama	11,411	*3,475*
Hood, Mt., ▲ Oregon	11,239	*3,426*
Lassen Pk., California	10,457	*3,187*
Duarte, Pico, ▲ Dominican Rep. (▲ West Indies)	10,417	*3,175*
Haleakala Crater, Hawaii (▲ Maui)	10,023	*3,055*
Paricutín, Mexico	9,213	*2,808*
El Pital, Cerro, ▲ El Salvador-Honduras	8,957	*2,730*
La Selle, Pic, ▲ Haiti	8,773	*2,674*
Guadalupe Pk., ▲ Texas	8,749	*2,667*
Olympus, Mt., Washington (▲ Olympic Mts.)	7,965	*2,428*
Blue Mountain Pk., ▲ Jamaica	7,402	*2,256*
Harney Pk., ▲ South Dakota (▲ Black Hills)	7,242	*2,207*
Mitchell, Mt., ▲ North Carolina (▲ Appalachian Mts.)	6,684	*2,037*
Clingmans Dome, North Carolina-▲ Tennessee (▲ Great Smoky Mts.)	6,643	*2,025*
Turquino, Pico, ▲ Cuba	6,470	*1,972*
Washington, Mt., ▲ New Hampshire (▲ White Mts.)	6,288	*1,917*
Rogers, Mt., ▲ Virginia	5,729	*1,746*
Marcy, Mt., ▲ New York (▲ Adirondack Mts.)	5,344	*1,629*
Katahdin, Mt., ▲ Maine	5,268	*1,606*
Kawaikini, Hawaii (▲ Kauai)	5,243	*1,598*
Spruce Knob, ▲ West Virginia	4,862	*1,482*
Pelée, Montagne, ▲ Martinique	4,583	*1,397*
Mansfield, Mt., ▲ Vermont (▲ Green Mts.)	4,393	*1,339*
Punta, Cerro de, ▲ Puerto Rico	4,389	*1,338*
Black Mtn., ▲ Kentucky-Virginia	4,145	*1,263*
Kaala, Hawaii (▲ Oahu)	4,040	*1,231*

SOUTH AMERICA

	Height (feet)	Height (meters)
Aconcagua, Cerro, ▲ Argentina; ▲ Andes; (▲ South America)	22,831	*6,959*
Ojos del Salado, Nevado, Argentina-▲ Chile	22,615	*6,893*
Illimani, Nevado, ▲ Bolivia	22,579	*6,882*
Bonete, Cerro, Argentina	22,546	*6,872*
Huascarán, Nevado, ▲ Peru	22,133	*6,746*
Llullaillaco, Volcán, Argentina-Chile	22,057	*6,723*
Yerupaja, Nevado, Peru	21,765	*6,634*
Tupungato, Cerro, Argentina-Chile	21,555	*6,570*
Sajama, Nevado, Bolivia	21,463	*6,542*
Illampu, Nevado, Bolivia	20,873	*6,362*
Chimborazo, ▲ Ecuador	20,702	*6,310*
Antofalla, Volcán, Argentina	20,013	*6,100*
Cotopaxi, Ecuador	19,347	*5,897*
Misti, Volcán, Peru	19,101	*5,822*
Huila, Nevado del, Colombia (▲ Cordillera Central)	16,896	*5,150*
Bolívar, Pico, ▲ Venezuela	16,427	*5,007*
Fitzroy, Monte (Cerro Chaltel), Argentina-Chile	11,073	*3,375*
Neblina, Pico da, ▲ Brazil-Venezuela	9,888	*3,014*

EUROPE

	Height (feet)	Height (meters)
El'brus, gora, ▲ Russia (▲ Caucasus; ▲ Europe)	18,510	*5,642*
Dykh-Tau, Mt., Russia	17,073	*5,204*
Shkhara, Mt., ▲ Georgia-Russia	16,627	*5,068*
Blanc, Mont (Monte Bianco), ▲ France-▲ Italy (▲ Alps)	15,771	*4,807*
Dufourspitze, Italy-▲ Switzerland	15,203	*4,634*
Weisshorn, Switzerland	14,783	*4,506*
Matterhorn, Italy-Switzerland	14,692	*4,478*
Finsteraarhorn, Switzerland	14,022	*4,274*
Jungfrau, Switzerland	13,642	*4,158*
Écrins, Barre des, France	13,458	*4,102*
Viso, Monte, Italy (▲ Alpes Cottiennes)	12,602	*3,841*
Grossglockner, ▲ Austria	12,457	*3,797*
Teide, Pico de, ▲ Spain (▲ Canary Is.)	12,188	*3,715*
Mulhacén, ▲ Spain (continental)	11,410	*3,478*
Aneto, Pico de, Spain (▲ Pyrenees)	11,168	*3,404*
Perdido, Monte, Spain	11,007	*3,355*
Etna, Monte, Italy (▲ Sicily)	10,902	*3,323*
Zugspitze, Austria-▲ Germany	9,721	*2,963*
Musala, ▲ Bulgaria	9,596	*2,925*
Olympus, Mount (Óros Ólimbos), ▲ Greece	9,570	*2,917*
Corno Grande, Italy (▲ Apennines)	9,554	*2,912*
Triglav, ▲ Slovenia	9,393	*2,863*
Korabit, Maja e ▲ Albania-Macedonia	9,035	*2,754*
Cinto, Monte, France (▲ Corsica)	8,878	*2,706*
Gerlachovský Štít, ▲ Slovakia (▲ Carpathian Mts.)	8,711	*2,655*
Moldoveanu, ▲ Romania	8,346	*2,544*
Rysy, Czechoslovakia-▲ Poland	8,199	*2,499*
Glittertinden, ▲ Norway (▲ Scandinavia)	8,110	*2,472*
Parnassos, Greece	8,061	*2,457*
Ídhi, Óros, Greece (▲ Crete)	8,057	*2,456*
Pico, Ponta do, ▲ Portugal (▲ Azores Is.)	7,713	*2,351*
Hvannadalshnúkur, ▲ Iceland	6,952	*2,119*
Kebnekaise, ▲ Sweden	6,926	*2,111*
Estrela, ▲ Portugal (continental)	6,539	*1,993*
Narodnaja, gora, Russia (▲ Ural Mts.)	6,217	*1,895*
Sancy, Puy de, France (▲ Massif Central)	6,184	*1,885*
Marmora, Punta la, Italy (▲ Sardinia)	6,017	*1,834*
Hekla, Iceland	4,892	*1,491*
Nevis, Ben, ▲ United Kingdom (▲ Scotland)	4,406	*1,343*
Haltiatunturi, ▲ Finland-Norway	4,357	*1,328*
Vesuvio, Italy	4,190	*1,277*
Snowdon, United Kingdom (▲ Wales)	3,560	*1,085*
Carrauntoohil, ▲ Ireland	3,406	*1,038*
Kékes, ▲ Hungary	3,330	*1,015*
Scafell Pikes, United Kingdom (▲ England)	3,210	*978*

ASIA

	Height (feet)	Height (meters)
Everest, Mount, ▲ China-▲ Nepal (▲ Tibet; ▲ Himalayas; ▲ Asia; ▲ World)	29,028	*8,848*
K2 (Qogir Feng), China-▲ Pakistan (▲ Kashmir; ▲ Karakoram Range)	28,250	*8,611*
Kānchenjunga, ▲ India-Nepal	28,208	*8,598*
Makālu, China-Nepal	27,825	*8,481*
Dhawlagiri, Nepal	26,810	*8,172*
Nānga Parbat, Pakistan	26,660	*8,126*
Annapurna, Nepal	26,504	*8,078*
Gasherbrum, China-Pakistan	26,470	*8,068*
Xixabangma Feng, China	26,286	*8,012*
Nanda Devi, India	25,645	*7,817*
Kamet, China-India	25,447	*7,756*
Namjagbarwa Feng, China	25,442	*7,755*
Muztag, China (▲ Kunlun Shan)	25,338	*7,723*
Tirich Mir, Pakistan (▲ Hindu Kush)	25,230	*7,690*
Gongga Shan, China	24,790	*7,556*
Kula Kangri, ▲ Bhutan	24,784	*7,554*
Kommunizma, pik, ▲ Tajikistan (▲ Pamir)	24,590	*7,495*
Nowshāk, ▲ Afghanistan-Pakistan	24,557	*7,485*
Pobedy, pik, China-Russia	24,406	*7,439*
Chomo Lhari, Bhutan-China	23,997	*7,314*
Muztag, China	23,891	*7,282*
Lenin, pik, ▲ Kyrgyzstan-Tajikistan	23,406	*7,134*
Api, Nepal	23,399	*7,132*
Kangrinboqê Feng, China	22,028	*6,714*
Hkakabo Razi, ▲ Myanmar	19,296	*5,881*
Damāvend, Qollah-ye, ▲ Iran	18,386	*5,604*
Ağrı Dağı, ▲ Turkey	16,804	*5,122*
Jaya, Puncak, ▲ Indonesia (▲ New Guinea)	16,503	*5,030*
Fūlādī, Kūh-e, Afghanistan	16,243	*4,951*
Kl'učevskaja Sopka, vulkan, Russia (▲ Puluostrov Kamčatka)	15,584	*4,750*
Trikora, Puncak, Indonesia	15,584	*4,750*
Belucha, gora, Russia-Kazakhstan	14,783	*4,506*
Munch Chajrchan Ula, Mongolia	14,311	*4,362*
Kinabalu, Gunong, ▲ Malaysia (▲ Borneo)	13,455	*4,101*
Yü Shan, ▲ Taiwan	13,114	*3,997*
Erciyes Dağı, Turkey	12,851	*3,917*
Kerinci, Gunung, Indonesia (▲ Sumatra)	12,467	*3,800*
Fuji-san, ▲ Japan (▲ Honshu)	12,388	*3,776*
Rinjani, Indonesia (▲ Lombok)	12,224	*3,726*
Semeru, Indonesia (▲ Java)	12,060	*3,676*
Nabī Shu'ayb, Jabal an-, ▲ Yemen (▲ Arabian Peninsula)	12,008	*3,660*
Rantekombola, Bulu, Indonesia (▲ Celebes)	11,335	*3,455*
Slamet, Indonesia	11,247	*3,428*
Phan Si Pan, ▲ Vietnam	10,312	*3,143*
Shām, Jabal ash-, ▲ Oman	9,957	*3,035*
Apo, Mount, ▲ Philippines (▲ Mindanao)	9,692	*2,954*
Pulog, Mount, Philippines (▲ Luzon)	9,626	*2,934*
Bia, Phou, ▲ Laos	9,249	*2,819*
Shaykh, Jabal ash-, Lebanon-▲ Syria	9,232	*2,814*
Paektu-san, ▲ North Korea-China	9,003	*2,744*
Inthanon, Doi, ▲ Thailand	8,530	*2,600*
Pidurutalagala, ▲ Sri Lanka	8,281	*2,524*
Mayon Volcano, Philippines	8,077	*2,462*
Asahi-dake, Japan (▲ Hokkaidō)	7,513	*2,290*
Tahan, Gunong, Malaysia (▲ Malaya)	7,174	*2,187*
Ólimbos, ▲ Cyprus	6,401	*1,951*
Halla-san, ▲ South Korea	6,398	*1,950*
Aôral, Phnum, ▲ Cambodia	5,948	*1,813*
Kujū-san, Japan (▲ Kyūshū)	5,863	*1,787*
Ramm, Jabal, ▲ Jordan	5,755	*1,754*
Meron, Hare, ▲ Israel	3,963	*1,208*
Carmel, Mt., Israel	1,791	*546*

AFRICA

	Height (feet)	Height (meters)
Kilimanjaro, ▲ Tanzania (▲ Africa)	19,340	*5,895*
Kirinyaga (Mount Kenya), ▲ Kenya	17,058	*5,199*
Margherita Peak, ▲ Uganda-▲ Zaire	16,763	*5,109*
Ras Dashen Terara, ▲ Ethiopia	15,158	*4,620*
Meru, Mount, Tanzania	14,978	*4,565*
Karisimbi, Volcan, ▲ Rwanda-Zaire	14,787	*4,507*
Elgon, Mount, Kenya-Uganda	14,178	*4,321*
Toubkal, Jbel, ▲ Morocco (▲ Atlas Mts.)	13,665	*4,165*
Cameroon Mountain, ▲ Cameroon	13,451	*4,100*
Ntlenyana, Thabana, ▲ Lesotho	11,425	*3,482*
eNjesuthi, ▲ South Africa	11,306	*3,446*
Koussi, Emi, ▲ Chad (▲ Tibesti)	11,204	*3,415*
Kinyeti, ▲ Sudan	10,456	*3,187*
Santa Isabel, Pico de, ▲ Equatorial Guinea (▲ Bioko)	9,869	*3,008*
Tahat, ▲ Algeria (▲ Ahaggar)	9,541	*2,908*
Maromokotro, ▲ Madagascar	9,436	*2,876*
Kātrīnā, Jabal, ▲ Egypt	8,668	*2,642*
Sao Tome, Pico de, ▲ Sao Tome	6,640	*2,024*

OCEANIA

	Height (feet)	Height (meters)
Wilhelm, Mount, ▲ Papua New Guinea	14,793	*4,509*
Giluwe, Mount, Papua New Guinea	14,330	*4,368*
Bangeta, Mt., Papua New Guinea	13,520	*4,121*
Victoria, Mount, Papua New Guinea (▲ Owen Stanley Range)	13,238	*4,035*
Cook, Mount, ▲ New Zealand (▲ South Island)	12,349	*3,764*
Ruapehu, New Zealand (▲ North Island)	9,177	*2,797*
Balbi, Papua New Guinea (▲ Solomon Is.)	9,000	*2,743*
Egmont, Mount, New Zealand	8,260	*2,518*
Orohena, Mont, ▲ French Polynesia (▲ Tahiti)	7,352	*2,241*
Kosciusko, Mount, ▲ Australia (▲ New South Wales)	7,316	*2,230*
Silisili, Mount, ▲ Western Samoa	6,096	*1,858*
Panié, Mont, ▲ New Caledonia	5,341	*1,628*
Bartle Frere, Australia (▲ Queensland)	5,322	*1,622*
Ossa, Mount, Australia (▲ Tasmania)	5,305	*1,617*
Woodroffe, Mount, Australia (▲ South Australia)	4,724	*1,440*
Sinewit, Mt., Papua New Guinea (▲ Bismarck Archipelago)	4,462	*1,360*
Tomanivi, ▲ Fiji (▲ Viti Levu)	4,341	*1,323*
Meharry, Mt., Australia (▲ Western Australia)	4,104	*1,251*
Ayers Rock, Australia	2,844	*867*

ANTARCTICA

	Height (feet)	Height (meters)
Vinson Massif, ▲ Antarctica	16,066	*4,897*
Kirkpatrick, Mount, Antarctica	14,856	*4,528*
Markham, Mount, Antarctica	14,049	*4,282*
Jackson, Mount, Antarctica	13,747	*4,190*
Sidley, Mount, Antarctica	13,717	*4,181*
Wade, Mount, Antarctica	13,399	*4,084*

▲ Highest mountain in state, country, range, or region named.

Oceans, Seas and Gulfs

	Area (sq. mi.)	Area (sq. km.)
Pacific Ocean	63,800,000	*165,200,000*
Atlantic Ocean	31,800,000	*82,400,000*
Indian Ocean	28,900,000	*74,900,000*
Arctic Ocean	5,400,000	*14,000,000*
Arabian Sea	1,492,000	*3,864,000*
South China Sea	1,331,000	*3,447,000*
Caribbean Sea	1,063,000	*2,753,000*
Mediterranean Sea	967,000	*2,505,000*
Bering Sea	876,000	*2,269,000*
Bengal, Bay of	839,000	*2,173,000*
Okhotsk, Sea of	619,000	*1,603,000*
Norwegian Sea	597,000	*1,546,000*
Mexico, Gulf of	596,000	*1,544,000*
Hudson Bay	475,000	*1,230,000*
Greenland Sea	465,000	*1,204,000*

Principal Lakes

	Area (sq. mi.)	Area (sq. km.)
Caspian Sea, Asia—Europe (Salt)	143,240	*370,990*
Superior, Lake, Canada—U.S.	31,700	*82,100*
Victoria, Lake, Kenya—Tanzania—Uganda	26,820	*69,463*
Aral Sea, Asia (Salt)	24,700	*64,100*
Huron, Lake, Canada—U.S.	23,000	*60,000*
Michigan, Lake, U.S.	22,300	*57,800*
Tanganyika, Lake, Africa	12,350	*31,986*
Bajkal, ozero, Russia	12,200	*31,500*
Great Bear Lake, Canada	12,095	*31,326*
Malawi, Lake (Lake Nyasa), Malawi—Mozambique—Tanzania	11,150	*28,878*
Great Slave Lake, Canada	11,030	*28,568*
Erie, Lake, Canada—U.S.	9,910	*25,667*
Winnipeg, Lake, Canada	9,416	*24,387*
Ontario, Lake, Canada—U.S.	7,540	*19,529*
Balchaš, ozero, Kazakhstan	Δ 7,100	*18,300*
Ladožskoje ozero, Russia	6,833	*17,700*
Chad, Lake (Lac Tchad), Cameroon—Chad—Nigeria	6,300	*16,300*
Onežskoje ozero, Russia	3,753	*9,720*
Eyre, Lake, Australia (Salt)	Δ 3,700	*9,500*
Titicaca, Lago, Bolivia—Peru	3,200	*8,300*
Nicaragua, Lago de, Nicaragua	3,150	*8,158*
Mai—Ndombe, Lac, Zaire	Δ 3,100	*8,000*
Athabasca, Lake, Canada	3,064	*7,935*
Reindeer Lake, Canada	2,568	*6,650*
Tônlé Sab, Cambodia	Δ 2,500	*6,500*
Rudolf, Lake, Ethiopia—Kenya (Salt)	2,473	*6,405*
Issyk-Kul', ozero, Kyrgyzstan (Salt)	2,425	*6,280*
Torrens, Lake, Australia (Salt)	2,300	*5,900*
Albert, Lake, Uganda—Zaire	2,160	*5,594*
Vänern, Sweden	2,156	*5,584*
Nettilling Lake, Canada	2,140	*5,542*
Winnipegosis, Lake, Canada	2,075	*5,374*
Bangweulu, Lake, Zambia	1,930	*4,999*
Nipigon, Lake, Canada	1,872	*4,848*
Orūmīyeh, Daryācheh-ye, Iran (Salt)	Δ 1,815	*4,701*
Manitoba, Lake, Canada	1,785	*4,624*
Woods, Lake of the, Canada—U.S.	1,727	*4,472*
Kyoga, Lake, Uganda	1,710	*4,429*
Gairdner, Lake, Australia (Salt)	Δ 1,700	*4,300*
Great Salt Lake, U.S. (Salt)	1,680	*4,351*

Δ *Due to seasonal fluctuations in water level, areas of these lakes vary considerably.*

Principal Rivers

	Length (miles)	Length (km.)
Nile, Africa	4,145	*6,671*
Amazon-Ucayali, South America	4,000	*6,400*
Yangtze (Chang), Asia	3,900	*6,300*
Mississippi-Missouri, North America	3,740	*6,019*
Huang (Yellow), Asia	3,395	*5,464*
Ob'-Irtyš, Asia	3,362	*5,410*
Río de la Plata-Paraná, South America	3,030	*4,876*
Congo (Zaïre), Africa	2,900	*4,700*
Paraná, South America	2,800	*4,500*
Amur-Argun', Asia	2,761	*4,444*
Amur (Heilong), Asia	2,744	*4,416*
Lena, Asia	2,700	*4,400*
Mackenzie, North America	2,635	*4,241*
Mekong, Asia	2,600	*4,200*
Niger, Africa	2,600	*4,200*
Jenisej, Asia	2,543	*4,092*
Missouri-Red Rock, North America	2,533	*4,076*
Mississippi, North America	2,348	*3,779*
Murray-Darling, Australia	2,330	*3,750*
Missouri, North America	2,315	*3,726*
Volga, Europe	2,194	*3,531*
Madeira, South America	2,013	*3,240*
São Francisco, South America	1,988	*3,199*
Grande, Rio (Río Bravo), North America	1,885	*3,034*
Purús, South America	1,860	*2,993*
Indus, Asia	1,800	*2,900*
Danube, Europe	1,776	*2,858*
Brahmaputra, Asia	1,770	*2,849*
Yukon, North America	1,770	*2,849*
Salween (Nu), Asia	1,750	*2,816*
Zambezi, Africa	1,700	*2,700*
Vil'uj, Asia	1,647	*2,650*
Tocantins, South America	1,640	*2,639*
Orinoco South America,	1,600	*2,600*
Paraguay, South America	1,610	*2,591*
Amu Darya, Asia	1,578	*2,540*
Murray, Australia	1,566	*2,520*
Ganges, Asia	1,560	*2,511*
Pilcomayo, South America	1,550	*2,494*
Euphrates, Asia	1,510	*2,430*
Ural, Asia	1,509	*2,428*
Arkansas, North America	1,459	*2,348*
Colorado, North America (U.S.-Mexico)	1,450	*2,334*
Aldan, Asia	1,412	*2,273*
Syrdarja, Asia	1,370	*2,205*
Dnieper, Europe	1,400	*2,200*
Araguaia, South America	1,400	*2,200*
Kasai (Cassai), Africa	1,338	*2,153*
Tarim, Asia	1,328	*2,137*
Kolyma, Asia	1,323	*2,129*
Orange, Africa	1,300	*2,100*
Negro, South America	1,300	*2,100*
Ayeyarwady, Asia	1,300	*2,100*
Red, North America	1,270	*2,044*
Juruá, South America	1,250	*2,012*
Columbia, North America	1,200	*2,000*
Xingu, South America	1,230	*1,979*
Ucayali, South America	1,220	*1,963*
Saskatchewan-Bow, North America	1,205	*1,939*
Peace North America,	1,195	*1,923*
Tigris, Asia	1,180	*1,899*
Don, Europe	1,162	*1,870*
Songhua, Asia	1,140	*1,835*
Pečora, Europe	1,124	*1,809*
Kama, Europe	1,122	*1,805*
Limpopo, Africa	1,100	*1,800*
Angara, Asia	1,105	*1,779*
Snake, North America	1,038	*1,670*
Uruguay, South America	1,025	*1,650*
Churchill, North America	1,000	*1,600*
Marañón, South America	1,000	*1,600*
Tobol, Asia	989	*1,591*
Ohio, North America	981	*1,579*
Magdalena, South America	950	*1,529*
Roosevelt, South America	950	*1,529*
Oka, Europe	900	*1,500*
Xiang, Asia	930	*1,497*
Godāvari, Asia	930	*1,497*
Canadian, North America	906	*1,458*
Brazos, North America	900	*1,400*
Salado, South America	900	*1,400*
Darling, Australia	864	*1,390*
Fraser, North America	851	*1,370*
Parnaíba, South America	850	*1,368*
Colorado, North America (Texas)	840	*1,352*
Dniester, Europe	840	*1,352*
Rhine, Europe	820	*1,320*
Narmada, Asia	800	*1,300*
St. Lawrence, North America	800	*1,300*
Ottawa, North America	790	*1,271*
Athabasca, North America	765	*1,231*
Pecos, North America	735	*1,183*
Severskij Donec, Europe	735	*1,183*
Green, North America	730	*1,175*
White, North America (Ar.-Mo.)	720	*1,159*
Cumberland, North America	720	*1,159*
Elbe (Labe), Europe	720	*1,159*
James, North America (N./S. Dakota)	710	*1,143*
Gambia, Africa	680	*1,094*
Yellowstone, North America	671	*1,080*
Tennessee, North America	652	*1,049*
Gila, North America	630	*1,014*
Wisła (Vistula), Europe	630	*1,014*
Tagus (Tejo) (Tajo), Europe	625	*1,006*
Loire, Europe	625	*1,006*
Cimarron, North America	600	*1,000*
North Platte, North America	618	*995*
Albany, North America	610	*982*
Tisza (Tisa), Europe	607	*977*
Back, North America	605	*974*
Ouachita, North America	605	*974*
Sava, Europe	585	*941*
Nemunas (Neman), Europe	582	*937*
Branco, South America	580	*933*
Meuse (Maas), Europe	575	*925*
Oder (Odra), Europe	565	*909*
Rhône, Europe	500	*800*

Principal Islands

	Area (sq. mi.)	Area (sq. km.)
Grønland (Greenland), North America	840,000	*2,175,600*
New Guinea, Asia—Oceania	309,000	*800,000*
Borneo (Kalimantan), Asia	287,300	*744,100*
Madagascar, Africa	226,500	*587,000*
Baffin Island, Canada	195,928	*507,451*
Sumatera (Sumatra), Indonesia	182,860	*473,606*
Honshū, Japan	89,176	*230,966*
Great Britain, United Kingdom	88,795	*229,978*
Victoria Island, Canada	83,897	*217,291*
Ellesmere Island, Canada	75,767	*196,236*
Sulawesi (Celebes), Indonesia	73,057	*189,216*
South Island, New Zealand	57,708	*149,463*
Jawa (Java), Indonesia	51,038	*132,187*
North Island, New Zealand	44,332	*114,821*
Cuba, North America	42,800	*110,800*
Newfoundland, Canada	42,031	*108,860*
Luzon, Philippines	40,420	*104,688*
Ísland (Iceland), Europe	39,800	*103,000*
Mindanao, Philippines	36,537	*94,630*
Ireland, Europe	32,600	*84,400*
Hokkaidō, Japan	32,245	*83,515*
Novaja Zeml'a (Novaya Zemlya), Russia	31,900	*82,600*
Sachalin, ostrov (Sakhalin), Russia	29,500	*76,400*
Hispaniola, North America	29,400	*76,200*
Banks Island, Canada	27,038	*70,028*
Tasmania, Australia	26,200	*67,800*
Sri Lanka, Asia	24,900	*64,600*
Devon Island, Canada	21,331	*55,247*
Tierra del Fuego, Isla Grande de, South America	18,600	*48,200*
Kyūshū, Japan	17,129	*44,363*
Melville Island, Canada	16,274	*42,149*
Southampton Island, Canada	15,913	*41,214*
Spitsbergen, Norway	15,260	*39,523*
New Britain, Papua New Guinea	14,093	*36,500*
T'aiwan, Asia	13,900	*36,000*
Hainan Dao, China	13,100	*34,000*
Prince of Wales Island, Canada	12,872	*33,339*
Vancouver Island, Canada	12,079	*31,285*
Sicilia (Sicily), Italy	9,926	*25,709*
Somerset Island, Canada	9,570	*24,786*
Sardegna (Sardinia), Italy	9,301	*24,090*
Shikoku, Japan	7,258	*18,799*
Seram (Ceram)	7,191	*18,625*
Nordaustlandet (North East Land), Norway	6,350	*16,446*
New Caledonia, Oceania	6,252	*16,192*
Timor, Indonesia	5,743	*14,874*
Flores, Indonesia	5,502	*14,250*
Samar, Philippines	5,100	*13,080*
Negros, Philippines	4,907	*12,710*
Palawan, Philippines	4,550	*11,785*
Panay, Philippines	4,446	*11,515*
Jamaica, North America	4,200	*11,000*
Hawaii, United States	4,034	*10,448*
Cape Breton Island, Canada	3,981	*10,311*
Mindoro, Philippines	3,759	*9,735*
Kodiak Island, United States	3,670	*9,505*
Bougainville, Papua New Guinea	3,600	*9,300*
Cyprus, Asia	3,572	*9,251*
Puerto Rico, North America	3,500	*9,100*
New Ireland, Papua New Guinea	3,500	*9,000*
Corse (Corsica), France	3,367	*8,720*
Kríti (Crete), Greece	3,189	*8,259*
Vrangel'a, ostrov (Wrangel Island), Russia	2,800	*7,300*
Leyte, Philippines	2,785	*7,214*
Guadalcanal, Solomon Islands	2,060	*5,336*
Long Island, United States	1,377	*3,566*

World Populations

This table includes every urban center of 50,000 or more population in the world, as well as many other important or well-known cities and towns.

The population figures are all from recent censuses (designated C) or official estimates (designated E), except for a few cities for which only unofficial estimates are available (designated U). The date of the census or estimate is specified for each country. Individual exceptions are dated in parentheses.

For many cities, a second population figure is given accompanied by a star (★). The starred population refers to the city's entire metropolitan area, including suburbs. These metropolitan areas have been defined by Rand McNally, following consistent rules to facilitate comparisons among the urban centers of various countries. Where a place is part of the metropolitan area of another city, that city's name is specified in parentheses preceded by a (★). Some important places that are considered to be secondary central cities of their areas are designated by (★ ★) preceding the name of the metropolitan area's main city. A population preceded by a triangle (▲) refers to an entire municipality, commune, or other district, which includes rural areas in addition to the urban center itself. The names of capital cities appear in CAPITALS; the largest city in each country is designated by the symbol (•).

For more recent population totals for countries, see the Rand McNally population estimates in the World Political Information table.

AFGHANISTAN / Afghānestān

1988 E 15,513,000

Cities and Towns

Herāt 177,300
Jalālābād (1982 E) 58,000
• KĀBOL 1,424,400
Mazār-e Sharīf 130,600
Qandahār 225,500
Qondūz (1982 E) 57,000

ALBANIA / Shqipëri

1987 E 3,084,000

Cities and Towns

Durrës 78,700
Elbasan 78,300
Korçë 61,500
Shkodër 76,300
• TIRANË 255,700
Vlorë 67,700

ALGERIA / Algérie / Djazaïr

1987 C 23,038,942

Cities and Towns

Aïn el Beïda 61,997
Aïn Oussera 44,270
Aïn Témouchent 47,479
• ALGER (ALGIERS) (★ 2,547,983) 1,507,241
Annaba (Bône) 305,526
Bab Ezzouar (★ Alger) 55,211
Barika 56,488
Batna 181,601
Béchar 107,311
Bejaïa (Bougie) 114,534
Biskra 128,281
Blida 170,935
Bordj Bou Arreridj 84,264
Bordj el Kiffan (★ Alger) 61,035
Bou Saada 66,688
Constantine 440,842
El Asnam 129,976
El Djelfa 84,207
El Eulma 67,933
El Wad 70,073
Ghardaïa 89,415
Ghilizane 80,091
Guelma 77,821
Jijel 62,793
Khemis 55,335
Khenchla 69,743
Laghouat 67,214
Lemdiyya 85,195
Maghniyya 52,275
Mostaganem 114,037
Mouaskar 64,691
M'Sila 65,805
Oran 628,558
Saïda 80,825
Sidi bel Abbès 152,778
Skikda 128,747
Souq Ahras 83,015
Stif 170,182
Tébessa 107,559
Tihert 95,821
Tizi-Ouzou 61,163
Tlemcen 126,882
Touggourt 70,645
Wargla 81,721

AMERICAN SAMOA / Amerika Samoa

1980 C 32,279

Cities and Towns

• PAGO PAGO 3,075

ANDORRA

1986 C 46,976

Cities and Towns

• ANDORRA 18,463

ANGOLA

1989 E 9,739,100

Cities and Towns

Benguela (1983 E) 155,000
Huambo (Nova Lisboa) (1983 E) 203,000
Lobito (1983 E) 150,000
• LUANDA 1,459,900
Lubango (1984 E) 95,915
Namibe (1981 E) 100,000

ANGUILLA

1984 C 6,680

Cities and Towns

• THE VALLEY 1,042

ANTIGUA AND BARBUDA

1977 E 72,000

Cities and Towns

• SAINT JOHNS 24,359

ARGENTINA

1980 C 27,947,446

Cities and Towns

Almirante Brown (★ Buenos Aires) 331,919
Avellaneda (★ Buenos Aires) 334,145
Bahía Blanca 223,818
Berazategui (★ Buenos Aires) 201,862
Berisso (★ Buenos Aires) 66,152
• BUENOS AIRES (★ 10,750,000) 2,922,829
Campana (★ Buenos Aires) 54,832
Caseros (Tres de Febrero) (★ Buenos Aires) 345,424
Catamarca (★ 90,000) 78,799
Comodoro Rivadavia 96,817
Concordia 94,222
Córdoba (★ 1,070,000) 993,055
Corrientes 180,612
Esteban Echeverría (★ Buenos Aires) 188,923
Florencio Varela (★ Buenos Aires) 173,452
Formosa 93,603
General San Martín (★ Buenos Aires) 385,625
General Sarmiento (San Miguel) (★ Buenos Aires) 502,926
Godoy Cruz (★ Mendoza) 142,408
Gualeguaychú 51,400
Junín 62,458
Lanús (★ Buenos Aires) 466,980
La Plata (★ ★ Buenos Aires) 477,175
La Rioja 67,043
Las Heras (★ Mendoza) 101,579
Lomas de Zamora (★ Buenos Aires) 510,130
Mar del Plata 414,696
Mendoza (★ 650,000) 119,088
Mercedes 50,992
Merlo (★ Buenos Aires) 292,587
Moreno (★ Buenos Aires) 194,440
Morón (★ Buenos Aires) 598,420
Necochea 51,069
Neuquén 90,089
Olavarría 64,097
Paraná 161,638
Pergamino 68,612
Pilar (★ Buenos Aires) 84,429
Posadas 143,889
Presidencia Roque Sáenz Peña 49,341
Punta Alta 56,620
Quilmes (★ Buenos Aires) 446,587
Rafaela 53,273
Resistencia 220,104
Río Cuarto 110,254
Rosario (★ 1,045,000) 938,120
Salta 260,744
San Carlos de Bariloche 48,980
San Fernando (★ Buenos Aires) 133,624
San Francisco (★ 58,536) 51,932
San Isidro (★ Buenos Aires) 289,170
San Juan (★ 300,000) 118,046
San Justo (★ Buenos Aires) 949,566
San Lorenzo (★ Rosario) 96,891
San Luis 70,999
San Miguel de Tucumán (★ 525,000) 392,888
San Nicolás de los Arroyos 98,495
San Rafael 70,959
San Salvador de Jujuy 124,950
Santa Fe 292,165
Santiago del Estero (★ 200,000) 148,758
San Vincente (★ Buenos Aires) 55,803
Tandil 79,429
Tigre (★ Buenos Aires) 206,349
Trelew 52,372
Vicente López (★ Buenos Aires) 291,072
Villa Krause (★ San Juan) 66,693
Villa María 67,560
Villa Nueva (★ Mendoza) 164,670
Zárate 67,143

ARMENIA / Hayastan

1989 C 3,283,000

Cities and Towns

Abovjan (1987 E) 53,000
Čardžou 161,000
Ečmiadzin (★ Jerevan) (1987 E) 53,000
• JEREVAN (★ 1,315,000) 1,199,000
Kirovakan (1987 E) 169,000
Kumajri 120,000
Razdan (1987 E) 56,000

ARUBA

1987 E 64,763

Cities and Towns

• ORANJESTAD 19,800

AUSTRALIA

1989 E 16,833,100

Cities and Towns

Adelaide (★ 1,036,747) 12,340
Albury (★ 66,530) 40,730
Auburn (★ Sydney) 49,950
Ballarat (★ 80,090) 36,680
Bankstown (★ Sydney) 158,750
Bendigo (★ 67,920) 32,050
Berwick (★ Melbourne) 64,100
Blacktown (★ Sydney) 210,900
Blue Mountains (★ Sydney) 70,800
Brisbane (★ 1,273,511) 744,828
Broadmeadows (★ Melbourne) 105,500
Cairns (★ 80,875) 42,839
Camberwell (★ Melbourne) 87,700
Campbelltown (★ Sydney) 139,500
CANBERRA (★ 271,362) (1986 C) 247,194
Canning (★ Perth) 69,104
Canterbury (★ Sydney) 135,200
Caulfield (★ Melbourne) 70,100
Coburg (★ Melbourne) 54,500
Cockburn (★ Perth) 49,802
Dandenong (★ Melbourne) 59,400
Darwin (★ 72,937) 63,900
Doncaster (★ Melbourne) 107,300
Enfield (★ Adelaide) 64,058
Essendon (★ Melbourne) 55,300
Fairfield (★ Sydney) 176,350
Footscray (★ Melbourne) 48,700
Frankston (★ Melbourne) 90,500
Geelong (★ 148,980) 13,190
Gosford 126,600
Gosnells (★ Perth) 71,862
Heidelberg (★ Melbourne) 63,500
Hobart (★ 181,210) 47,280
Holroyd (★ Sydney) 82,500
Hurstville (★ Sydney) 66,350
Ipswich (★ Brisbane) 75,283
Keilor (★ Melbourne) 103,700
Knox (★ Melbourne) 121,300
Lake Macquarie (★ Newcastle) 161,700
Launceston (★ 92,350) 32,150
Leichhardt (★ Sydney) 58,950
Liverpool (★ Sydney) 99,750
Logan (★ Brisbane) 142,222
Mackay (★ 50,885) 22,583
Marion (★ Adelaide) 74,631
Marrickville (★ Sydney) 84,650
Melbourne (★ 3,039,100) 55,300
Melville (★ Perth) 85,590
Mitcham (★ Adelaide) 63,301
Moorabbin (★ Melbourne) 98,900
Newcastle (★ 425,610) 130,940
Noarlunga (★ Adelaide) 77,352
Northcote (★ Melbourne) 49,100
North Sydney (★ Sydney) 53,400
Nunawading (★ Melbourne) 96,400
Oakleigh (★ Melbourne) 57,600
Parramatta (★ Sydney) 134,600
Penrith (★ Sydney) 152,650
Perth (★ 1,158,387) 82,413
Preston (★ Melbourne) 82,000
Randwick (★ Sydney) 119,200
Redcliffe (★ Brisbane) 48,123
Rockdale (★ Sydney) 88,200
Rockhampton (★ 61,694) 58,890
Ryde (★ Sydney) 94,400
Salisbury (★ Adelaide) 106,129
Shoalhaven 64,070
Southport (★ 254,861) 135,408
South Sydney (★ Sydney) 74,100
Springvale (★ Melbourne) 88,700
Stirling (★ Perth) 181,556
Sunshine (★ Melbourne) 97,700
• Sydney (★ 3,623,550) 9,800
Tea Tree Gully (★ Adelaide) 82,324
Toowoomba 81,071
Townsville (★ 111,972) 83,339
Wagga Wagga 52,180
Wanneroo (★ Perth) 163,324
Waverley (★ Melbourne) 126,300
Waverley (★ Sydney) 61,850
Willoughby (★ Sydney) 53,950
Wollongong (★ 236,690) 174,770
Woodville (★ Adelaide) 82,590
Woollahra (★ Sydney) 53,850

AUSTRIA / Österreich

1981 C 7,555,338

Cities and Towns

Graz (★ 325,000) 243,166
Innsbruck (★ 185,000) 117,287
Klagenfurt (★ 115,000) 87,321
Linz (★ 335,000) 199,910
Salzburg (★ 220,000) 139,426
Sankt Pölten (★ 67,000) 50,419
Villach (★ 65,000) 52,692
Wels (★ 76,000) 51,060
• WIEN (VIENNA) (★ 1,875,000) (1988 E) 1,482,800

AZERBAIJAN / Azärbayjan

1989 C 7,029,000

Cities and Towns

Ali-Bajramly (1987 E) 51,000
• BAKU (★ 2,020,000) 1,150,000
Chudžand 160,000
Gjandža 278,000
Kurgan-T'ube (1987 E) 55,000
Mingečaur (1987 E) 78,000
Nachičevan' (1987 E) 51,000
Šeki (Nucha) (1987 E) 54,000
Sumgait (★ Baku) 231,000

BAHAMAS

1982 E 218,000

Cities and Towns

• NASSAU 135,000

BAHRAIN / Al-Baḥrayn

1981 C 350,798

Cities and Towns

• AL-MANĀMAH (★ 224,643) 115,054
Al-Muḥarraq (★ Al-Manāmah) 57,688

BANGLADESH

1981 C 87,119,965

Cities and Towns

Barisāl 172,905
Begamganj 69,623
Bhairab Bāzār 63,563
Bogra 68,749
Brāhmanbāria 87,570
Chāndpur 85,656
Chittagong (★ 1,391,877) 980,000
Chuādanga 76,000
Comilla 184,132
• DHAKA (DACCA) (★ 3,430,312) 2,365,695
Dinājpur 96,718
Farīdpur 66,579
Gulshan (★ Dhaka) 215,444
Jamālpur 91,815
Jessore 148,927
Khulna 648,359
Kishorganj 52,302
Kushtia 74,892
Mādārīpur 63,917
Mīrpur (★ Dhaka) 349,031
Mymensingh 190,991
Naogaon 52,975
Nārāyanganj (★ ★ Dhaka) 405,562
Narsinghdi 76,841
Nawābganj 87,724
Noākhāli 59,065
Pābna 109,065
Patuākhāli 48,121
Rājshāhi 253,740
Rangpur 153,174
Saidpur 126,608
Sātkhira 52,156
Sherpur 48,214
Sirājganj 106,774
Sītākunda (★ Chittagong) 237,520
Sylhet 168,371
Tangail 77,518
Tongi (★ Dhaka) 94,580

BARBADOS

1980 C 244,228

Cities and Towns

• BRIDGETOWN (★ 115,000) 7,466

BELARUS / Byelarus'

1989 C 10,200,000

Cities and Towns

Baranoviči 159,000
Bobrujsk 223,000
Borisov 144,000
Brest 258,000
Gomel' 500,000
Grodno 270,000
Lida (1987 E) 81,000
• MINSK (★ 1,650,000) 1,589,000
Mogil'ov 356,000
Molodečno (1987 E) 87,000
Mozyr' 101,000
Novopolock (1987 E) 90,000
Orša 123,000
Pinsk 119,000
Polock (1987 E) 80,000
Rečica (1987 E) 71,000
Sluck (1987 E) 55,000
Soligorsk (1987 E) 92,000
Svetlogorsk (1987 E) 68,000
Vitebsk 350,000
Žlobin (1987 E) 52,000
Žodino (1987 E) 51,000

BELGIUM / België / Belgique

1987 E 9,864,751

Cities and Towns

Aalst (Alost) (★ Bruxelles) 77,113
Anderlecht (★ Bruxelles) 88,849
Antwerpen (★ 1,100,000) 479,748
Brugge (Bruges) (★ 223,000) 117,755
• BRUXELLES (BRUSSEL) (★ 2,385,000) 136,920
Charleroi (★ 480,000) 209,395
Forest (★ Bruxelles) 48,266
Genk (★ ★ Hasselt) 61,391
Gent (Gand) (★ 465,000) 233,856
Hasselt (★ 290,000) 65,563
Ixelles (★ Bruxelles) 76,241
Kortrijk (Courtrai) (★ 202,000) 76,216
La Louvière (★ 147,000) 76,340
Leuven (Louvain) (★ 173,000) 84,583
Liège (Luik) (★ 750,000) 200,891
Mechelen (Malines) (★ 121,000) 75,808
Molenbeek-St.-Jean (★ Bruxelles) 69,764
Mons (Bergen) (★ 242,000) 89,697
Mouscron (★ Lille, France) 53,713
Namur (★ 147,000) 102,670
Oostende (Ostende) (★ 122,000) 68,318

C Census. E Official estimate. U Unofficial estimate.
• Largest city in country.

★ Population or designation of metropolitan area, including suburbs (see headnote).
▲ Population of an entire municipality, commune, or district, including rural area.

Roeselare (Roulers) 51,963
Schaerbeek (★ Bruxelles) 104,919
Seraing (★ Liège) 61,731
Sint-Niklaas (Saint-Nicolas) 68,082
Tournai (Doornik) (▲ 66,998) 44,900
Uccle (★ Bruxelles) 75,876
Verviers (★ 101,000) 53,498

BELIZE

1985 E 166,400

Cities and Towns

• Belize City 47,000
BELMOPAN 4,500

BENIN / Bénin

1984 E 3,825,000

Cities and Towns

Abomey 53,000
• COTONOU 478,000
Natitingou (1975 E) 51,000
Ouidah (1979 E) 53,000
Parakou 92,000
PORTO-NOVO 164,000

BERMUDA

1985 E 56,000

Cities and Towns

• HAMILTON (★ 15,000) 1,676

BHUTAN / Druk-Yul

1982 E 1,333,000

Cities and Towns

• THIMPHU 12,000

BOLIVIA

1985 E 6,429,226

Cities and Towns

Cochabamba 317,251
• LA PAZ 992,592
Oruro 178,393
Potosí 113,380
Santa Cruz 441,717
SUCRE 86,609
Tarija 60,621

BOSNIA AND HERZEGOVINA / Bosna i Hercegovina

1987 E 4,400,464

Cities and Towns

Banja Luka (▲ 193,890) 130,900
• SARAJEVO (▲ 479,688) 341,200
Tuzla (▲ 129,967) 67,300
Zenica (▲ 144,869) 67,500

BOTSWANA

1987 E 1,169,000

Cities and Towns

Francistown (1986 E) 43,837
• GABORONE 107,677
Selebi Phikwe (1986 E) 41,382

BRAZIL / Brasil

1985 E 135,564,395

Cities and Towns

Alagoinhas (▲ 116,959) 87,500
Alegrete (▲ 71,898) 56,700
Alvorada 105,730
Americana 156,030
Anápolis 225,840
Apucarana (▲ 92,812) 73,700
Aracaju 360,013
Araçatuba 129,304
Araguari (▲ 96,035) 84,300
Arapiraca (▲ 147,879) 91,400
Araraquara (▲ 145,042) 07,500
Araras (▲ 71,652) 59,900
Araxá 61,418
Assis (▲ 74,238) 63,100
Bagé (▲ 106,155) 70,800
Barbacena (▲ 99,337) 80,200
Barra do Piraí (▲ 78,189) 55,700
Barra Mansa (★ Volta Redonda) 149,200
Barretos 80,202
Bauru 220,105
Bayeux (★ João Pessoa) 67,182
Belém (★ 1,200,000) 1,116,578
Belford Roxo (★ Rio de Janeiro) 340,700
Belo Horizonte (★ 2,950,000) 2,114,429
Betim (★ Belo Horizonte) 96,810
Blumenau 192,074
Boa Vista 66,028
Botucatu (▲ 71,139) 62,600
Bragança Paulista (▲ 105,099) 76,300
BRASÍLIA 1,567,709
Caçapava (▲ 64,213) 56,600
Cachoeira do Sul (▲ 91,492) 58,900
Cachoeirinha (★ Porto Alegre) 73,117
Cachoeiro de Itapemirim (▲ 138,156) 95,000
Campina Grande 279,929
Campinas (★ 1,125,000) 841,016
Campo Grande 384,398
Campos (▲ 366,716) 187,900
Campos Elyseos (★ Rio de Janeiro) 188,200
Canoas (★ Porto Alegre) 261,222
Carapicuíba (★ São Paulo) 265,856
Carazinho (▲ 62,108) 48,500
Cariacica (★ Vitória) 74,300
Caruaru (▲ 190,794) 152,100
Cascavel (▲ 200,485) 123,100
Castanhal (▲ 89,703) 71,200
Catanduva (▲ 80,309) 71,400
Caucaia (★ Fortaleza) 78,500
Cavaleiro (★ Recife) 106,600
Caxias (▲ 148,230) 66,300
Caxias do Sul 266,809
Chapecó (▲ 100,997) 64,200
Coelho da Rocha (★ Rio de Janeiro) 164,400
Colatina (▲ 106,260) 58,600
Colombo (★ Curitiba) 65,900
Conselheiro Lafaiete 77,958
Contagem (★ Belo Horizonte) 152,700
Corumbá (▲ 80,666) 65,800
Crato (▲ 86,371) 52,700
Criciúma (▲ 128,410) 85,900
Cruz Alta (▲ 71,817) 58,300
Cruzeiro 63,918
Cubatão (★ Santos) 98,322
Cuiabá (▲ 279,651) 220,400
Curitiba (★ 1,700,000) 1,279,205
Diadema (★ São Paulo) 320,187
Divinópolis 139,940
Dourados (▲ 123,757) 89,200
Duque de Caxias (★ Rio de Janeiro) 353,200
Embu (★ São Paulo) 119,791
Erechim (▲ 70,709) 54,300
Esteio (★ Porto Alegre) 58,964
Feira de Santana (▲ 355,201) 278,600
Ferraz de Vasconcelos (★ São Paulo) 68,831
Florianópolis (★ 365,000) 178,400
Fortaleza (★ 1,825,000) 1,582,414
Foz do Iguaçu (▲ 182,101) 124,900
Franca 182,820
Garanhuns 73,100
Goiânia (★ 990,000) 923,333
Governador Valadares (▲ 216,957) 192,300
Guaratinguetá (▲ 93,534) 80,400
Guarujá (★ Santos) 83,500
Guarulhos (★ São Paulo) 571,700
Ijuí (▲ 82,064) 64,400
Ilhéus (▲ 145,810) 79,400
Imperatriz (▲ 235,453) 119,500
Ipatinga (★ 270,000) 149,100
Ipiíba (★ Rio de Janeiro) 116,200
Itabira (▲ 81,771) 66,300
Itabuna (▲ 167,543) 142,200
Itajaí 104,232
Itajubá (▲ 69,675) 61,500
Itapecerica da Serra (★ São Paulo) 65,500
Itapetininga (▲ 105,512) 76,700
Itapevi (★ São Paulo) 66,825
Itaquaquecetuba (★ São Paulo) 91,366
Itaquari (★ Vitória) 163,900
Itaúna 61,446
Itu (▲ 92,786) 77,900
Ituiutaba (▲ 85,365) 74,900
Itumbiara (▲ 78,844) 57,200
Jaboatão (★ Recife) 82,900
Jacareí 149,061
Jaú (▲ 92,547) 74,500
Jequié (▲ 127,070) 82,100
João Pessoa (★ 550,000) 348,500
Joinvile 302,877
Juàzeiro (★ Petrolina) 78,600
Juàzeiro do Norte 159,806
Juiz de Fora 349,720
Jundiaí (▲ 313,652) 268,900
Lajes (▲ 143,246) 103,600
Lavras 52,100
Limeira 186,986
Linhares (▲ 122,453) 53,400
Londrina (▲ 346,676) 200,400
Lorena 63,230
Luziânia (▲ 98,408) 71,400
Macapá (▲ 168,839) 109,400
Maceió 482,195
Manaus 809,914
Marabá (▲ 133,559) 92,700
Marília (▲ 136,187) 116,100
Maringá 196,871
Mauá (★ São Paulo) 269,321
Mesquita (★ Rio de Janeiro) 161,300
Mogi das Cruzes (★ São Paulo) 144,800
Mogi-Guaçu (▲ 91,994) 81,800
Mogi-Mirim (▲ 63,313) 52,300
Monjolo (★ Rio de Janeiro) 113,900
Montes Claros (▲ 214,472) 183,500
Mossoró (▲ 158,723) 128,300
Muriaé (▲ 80,466) 57,600
Muribeca dos Guararapes (★ Recife) 171,200
Natal 510,106
Neves (★ Rio de Janeiro) 163,600
Nilópolis (★ Rio de Janeiro) 112,800
Niterói (★ Rio de Janeiro) 441,684
Nova Friburgo (▲ 143,529) 103,500
Nova Iguaçu (★ Rio de Janeiro) 592,800
Novo Hamburgo (★ Porto Alegre) 167,744
Olinda (★ Recife) 316,600
Osasco (★ São Paulo) 591,568
Ourinhos (▲ 65,841) 58,100
Paranaguá (▲ 94,809) 82,300
Paranavaí (▲ 75,511) 60,900
Parnaíba (▲ 116,206) 90,200
Parque Industrial (★ Belo Horizonte) 228,400
Passo Fundo (▲ 137,843) 117,500
Passos (▲ 79,393) 65,500
Patos 74,298
Patos de Minas (▲ 99,027) 69,000
Paulo Afonso (▲ 86,182) 75,300
Pelotas (▲ 277,730) 210,300
Petrolina (★ 225,000) 92,100
Petrópolis (★ Rio de Janeiro) 170,300
Pindamonhangaba (▲ 86,990) 64,100
Pinheirinho (★ Curitiba) 51,600
Piracicaba (▲ 252,079) 211,000
Poá (★ São Paulo) 66,006
Poços de Caldas 100,004
Ponta Grossa 223,154
Porto Alegre (★ 2,600,000) 1,272,121
Porto Velho (▲ 202,011) 152,700
Pouso Alegre (▲ 65,958) 58,300
Praia Grande (★ Santos) 67,800
Presidente Prudente 155,883
Queimados (★ Rio de Janeiro) 113,700
Recife (★ 2,625,000) 1,287,623
Ribeirão Prêto 383,125
Rio Branco (▲ 145,486) 109,800
Rio Claro 129,859
Rio de Janeiro (★ 10,150,000) 5,603,388
Rio Grande 164,221
Rio Verde (▲ 92,954) 59,400
Rondonópolis (▲ 101,642) 65,500
Salvador (★ 2,050,000) 1,804,438
Santa Bárbara d'Oeste 95,818
Santa Cruz do Sul (▲ 115,288) 60,300
Santa Maria (▲ 196,827) 163,900
Santana do Livramento (▲ 70,489) 60,100
Santarém (▲ 226,618) 120,800
Santa Rita (★ João Pessoa) 60,100
Santo André (★ São Paulo) 635,129
Santo Ângelo (▲ 107,559) 57,700
Santos (★ 1,065,000) 460,100
São Bernardo do Campo (★ São Paulo) 562,485
São Caetano do Sul (★ São Paulo) 171,005
São Carlos 140,383
São Gonçalo (★ Rio de Janeiro) 262,400
São João da Boa Vista (▲ 61,653) 50,400
São João del Rei (▲ 74,385) 61,400
São João de Meriti (★ Rio de Janeiro) 241,700
São José do Rio Prêto 229,221
São José dos Campos 372,578
São José dos Pinhais (★ Curitiba) 64,100
São Leopoldo (★ Porto Alegre) 114,065
São Lourenco da Mata (★ Recife) 65,936
São Luís (★ 600,000) 227,900
• São Paulo (★ 15,175,000) 10,063,110
São Vicente (★ Santos) 239,778
Sapucaia do Sul (★ Porto Alegre) 91,820
Sete Lagoas 121,418
Sete Pontes (★ Rio de Janeiro) 72,300
Sobral (▲ 112,275) 69,400
Sorocaba 327,468
Suzano (★ São Paulo) 128,924
Taboão da Serra (★ São Paulo) 122,112
Tatuí (▲ 69,358) 56,000
Taubaté 205,120
Teófilo Otoni (▲ 126,265) 82,700
Teresina (★ 525,000) 425,300
Teresópolis (▲ 115,859) 92,600
Timon (★ Teresina) 68,300
Tubarão (▲ 82,082) 70,400
Uberaba 244,875
Uberlândia 312,024
Uruguaiana (▲ 105,862) 91,500
Varginha 74,630
Vicente de Carvalho (★ Santos) 102,700
Vila Velha (★ Vitória) 91,900
Vitória (★ 735,000) 201,500
Vitória da Conquista (▲ 198,150) 145,800
Vitória de Santo Antão (▲ 100,450) 67,800
Volta Redonda (★ 375,000) 219,267

BRITISH VIRGIN ISLANDS

1980 C 12,034

Cities and Towns

• ROAD TOWN 2,479

BRUNEI

1981 C 192,832

Cities and Towns

• BANDAR SERI BEGAWAN (★ 64,000) 22,777

BULGARIA / Bâlgarija

1986 E 9,913,000

Cities and Towns

Blagoevgrad 67,766
Burgas 186,369
Dimitrovgrad 54,898
Dobrič 110,471
Gabrovo 81,688
Haskovo 89,273
Jambol 92,321
Kârdžali 56,906
Kazanlâk 61,780
Kjustendil 54,773
Loveč (1985 E) 48,862
Mihajlovgrad 53,529
Pazardžik 79,198
Pernik 96,277
Pleven 132,206
Plovdiv 349,148
Razgrad 51,277
Ruse 186,428
Silistra 54,627
Sliven 104,345
• SOFIJA (SOFIA) (★ 1,205,000) 1,119,152
Stara Zagora 153,538
Šumen 102,886
Varna 303,071
Veliko Târnovo 70,610
Vidin 63,813
Vraca 77,934

BURKINA FASO

1985 C 7,964,705

Cities and Towns

Bobo Dioulasso 228,668
Koudougou 51,926
• OUAGADOUGOU 441,514

BURUNDI

1986 E 4,782,000

Cities and Towns

• BUJUMBURA 273,000
Gitega 95,000

CAMBODIA / Kämpŭchéa

1986 E 7,492,000

Cities and Towns

Kâmpóng Saôm (1981 E) 53,000
• PHNUM PÉNH 700,000

CAMEROON / Cameroun

1986 E 10,446,409

Cities and Towns

Bafoussam (1985 E) 89,000
Bamenda (1985 E) 72,000
• Douala 1,029,731
Foumban (1985 E) 50,000
Garoua (1985 E) 96,000
Kumba (1985 E) 67,000
Maroua 103,653
Ngaoundéré (1985 E) 61,000
Nkongsamba 123,149
YAOUNDÉ 653,670

CANADA

1986 C 25,354,064

CANADA: ALBERTA

1986 C 2,375,278

Cities and Towns

Calgary (★ 671,326) 636,104
Edmonton (★ 785,465) 573,982
Fort McMurray (★ 48,497) 34,949
Lethbridge 58,841
Medicine Hat (★ 50,734) 41,804
Red Deer 54,425

CANADA: BRITISH COLUMBIA

1986 C 2,889,207

Cities and Towns

Burnaby (★ Vancouver) 145,161
Chilliwack (★ 50,288) 41,337
Kamloops 61,773
Kelowna (★ 89,730) 61,213
Matsqui (★ 88,420) 51,449
Nanaimo (★ 60,420) 49,029
Prince George 67,621
Richmond (★ Vancouver) 108,492
Vancouver (★ 1,380,729) 431,147
Victoria (★ 255,547) 66,303

CANADA: MANITOBA

1986 C 1,071,232

Cities and Towns

Brandon 38,708
Portage la Prairie 13,198
Winnipeg (★ 625,304) 594,551

CANADA: NEW BRUNSWICK

1986 C 710,422

Cities and Towns

Fredericton (★ 65,768) 44,352
Moncton (★ 102,084) 55,468
Saint John (★ 121,265) 76,381

CANADA: NEWFOUNDLAND

1986 C 568,349

Cities and Towns

Corner Brook (★ 33,730) 22,719
Gander 10,207
Saint John's (★ 161,901) 96,216

CANADA: NORTHWEST TERRITORIES

1986 C 52,238

Cities and Towns

Inuvik 3,389
Yellowknife 11,753

CANADA: NOVA SCOTIA

1986 C 873,199

Cities and Towns

Dartmouth (★ Halifax) 65,243
Halifax (★ 295,990) 113,577
Sydney (★ 119,470) 27,754

CANADA: ONTARIO

1986 C 9,113,515

Cities and Towns

Barrie (★ 67,703) 48,287
Brampton (★ Toronto) 188,498
Brantford (★ 90,521) 76,146
Burlington (★ Hamilton) 116,675
Cambridge (Galt) (★ ★ Kitchener) 79,920
East York (★ Toronto) 101,085
Etobicoke (★ Toronto) 302,973
Gloucester (★ Ottawa) 89,810
Guelph (★ 85,962) 78,235
Hamilton (★ 557,029) 306,728
Kingston (★ 122,350) 55,050
Kitchener (★ 311,195) 150,604
London (★ 342,302) 269,140
Markham (★ Toronto) 114,597
Mississauga (★ Toronto) 374,005
Nepean (★ Ottawa) 95,490
Niagara Falls (★ ★ Saint Catharines) 72,107
North Bay (★ 57,422) 50,623
North York (★ Toronto) 556,297
Oakville (★ Toronto) 87,107
Oshawa (★ 203,543) 123,651
OTTAWA (★ 819,263) 300,763
Peterborough (★ 87,083) 61,049
Saint Catharines (★ 343,258) 123,455
Sarnia (★ 85,700) 49,033
Sault Sainte Marie (★ 84,617) 80,905

C Census. E Official estimate.
• Largest city in country.

U Unofficial estimate.

★ Population or designation of metropolitan area, including suburbs (see headnote).
▲ Population of an entire municipality, commune, or district, including rural area.

Scarborough (★ Toronto) 484,676
Sudbury (★ 148,877) 88,717
Thunder Bay (★ 122,217) 112,272
• Toronto (★ 3,427,168) 612,289
Vaughan (★ Toronto) 65,058
Waterloo (★ Kitchener) 58,718
Windsor (★ 253,988) 193,111
York (★ Toronto) 135,401

CANADA: PRINCE EDWARD ISLAND

1986 C 126,646

Cities and Towns

Charlottetown (★ 53,868) 15,776
Summerside (★ 15,614) 8,020

CANADA: QUÉBEC

1986 C 6,540,276

Cities and Towns

Beauport (★ Québec) 62,869
Brossard (★ Montréal) 57,441
Charlesbourg (★ Québec) 68,996
Chicoutimi (★ 158,468) 61,083
Gatineau (★ Ottawa) 81,244
Hull (★ Ottawa) 58,722
Jonquière (★ ★ Chicoutimi) 58,467
LaSalle (★ Montréal) 75,621
Laval (★ Montréal) 284,164
Longueuil (★ Montréal) 125,441
Montréal (★ 2,921,357) 1,015,420
Montréal-Nord (★ Montréal) 90,303
Québec (★ 603,267) 164,580
Sainte-Foy (★ Québec) 69,615
Saint-Hubert (★ Montréal) 66,218
Saint-Laurent (★ Montréal) 67,002
Saint-Léonard (★ Montréal) 75,947
Sherbrooke (★ 129,960) 74,438
Trois-Rivières (★ 128,888) 50,122
Verdun (★ Montréal) 60,246

CANADA: SASKATCHEWAN

1986 C 1,010,198

Cities and Towns

Moose Jaw (★ 37,219) 35,073
Prince Albert (★ 40,841) 33,686
Regina (★ 186,521) 175,064
Saskatoon (★ 200,665) 177,641

CANADA: YUKON

1986 C 23,504

Cities and Towns

Dawson 896
Whitehorse 15,199

CAPE VERDE / Cabo Verde

1990 C 336,798

Cities and Towns

• PRAIA 61,797

CAYMAN ISLANDS

1988 E 25,900

Cities and Towns

• GEORGETOWN 13,700

CENTRAL AFRICAN REPUBLIC / République centrafricaine

1984 E 2,517,000

Cities and Towns

• BANGUI 473,817
Bouar (1982 E) 48,000

CHAD / Tchad

1979 E 4,405,000

Cities and Towns

Abéché 54,000
Moundou 66,000
• N'DJAMENA 303,000
Sarh 65,000

CHILE

1982 C 11,329,736

Cities and Towns

Antofagasta 185,486
Apoquindo (★ Santiago) 175,735
Arica 139,320
Calama 81,684
Cerrillos (★ Santiago) 67,013
Cerro Navia (★ Santiago) 137,777
Chillán 118,163
Concepción (★ 675,000) 267,891
Conchalí (★ Santiago) 157,884
Copiapó 69,045
Coquimbo 62,186
Coronel (★ Concepción) 65,918
Curicó 60,550
El Bosque (★ Santiago) 143,717
Huechuraba (★ Santiago) 56,313
Independencia (★ Santiago) 86,724
Iquique 110,153
La Cisterna (★ Santiago) 95,863
La Florida (★ Santiago) 191,883
La Granja (★ Santiago) 109,168
La Pintana (★ Santiago) 73,932
La Reina (★ Santiago) 80,452
La Serena 83,283
Las Rejas (★ Santiago) 147,918
Lo Espejo (★ Santiago) 124,462
Lo Prado (★ Santiago) 103,575
Los Ángeles 70,529
Macul (★ Santiago) 113,100
Maipú (★ Santiago) 114,117
Ñuñoa (★ Santiago) 168,919
Osorno 95,286
Pedro Aguirre Cerda (★ Santiago) 145,207
Peñalolén (★ Santiago) 137,298
Providencia (★ Santiago) 115,449
Pudahuel (★ Santiago) 97,578
Puente Alto (★ Santiago) 109,239
Puerto Montt 84,410
Punta Arenas 95,332
Quilpué (★ Valparaíso) 84,136
Quinta Normal (★ Santiago) 128,989
Rancagua 139,925
Recoleta (★ Santiago) 164,292
Renca (★ Santiago) 93,928
San Antonio 61,486
San Bernardo (★ Santiago) 117,132
San Joaquín (★ Santiago) 123,904
San Miguel (★ Santiago) 88,764
San Ramón (★ Santiago) 99,410
• SANTIAGO (★ 4,100,000) 232,667
Talca 128,544
Talcahuano (★ ★ Concepción) 202,368
Temuco 157,297
Valdivia 100,046
Valparaíso (★ 675,000) 265,355
Villa Alemana (★ Valparaíso) 55,766
Viña del Mar (★ Valparaíso) 244,899
Vitacura (★ Santiago) 72,038

CHINA / Zhongguo

1988 E 1,103,983,000

Cities and Towns

Abagnar Qi (▲ 100,700) (1986 E) 71,700
Acheng (1985 E) 100,304
Aihui (▲ 135,000) (1986 E) 76,700
Akesu (▲ 345,900) (1986 E) 143,100
Altay (▲ 141,700) (1986 E) 62,800
Anci (Langfang) (▲ 522,800) (1986 E) 122,100
Anda (▲ 425,500) (1986 E) 130,200
Andong (1986 E) 579,800
Ankang (1985 E) 89,188
Anqing (▲ 433,900) (1986 E) 213,200
Anshan 1,330,000
Anshun (▲ 214,700) (1986 E) 128,800
Anyang (▲ 541,900) (1986 E) 361,200
Baicheng (▲ 282,000) (1986 E) 198,600
Baiquan (1985 E) 50,996
Baiyin (▲ 301,900) (1986 E) 157,100
Baoding (▲ 535,100) (1986 E) 423,200
Baoji (▲ 359,500) (1986 E) 286,200
Baoshan (▲ 688,400) (1986 E) 52,300
Baotou (Paotow) 1,130,000
Baoying (1985 E) 50,479
Bei'an (▲ 440,500) (1986 E) 199,500
Beihai (▲ 175,900) (1986 E) 119,000
BEIJING (PEKING) (★ 6,450,000) 6,710,000
Beipiao (▲ 603,700) (1986 E) 180,900
Bengbu (▲ 612,600) (1986 E) 403,900
Benxi (Penhsi) 860,000
Bijie (1985 E) 54,871
Binxian (▲ 177,900) (1986 E) 86,700
Binxian (1982 C) 127,326
Boli (1985 E) 61,990
Bose (▲ 271,400) (1986 E) 82,000
Boshan (1975 U) 100,000
Boxian (1985 E) 63,222
Boxing (1982 C) 57,554
Boyang (1985 E) 60,688
Butha Qi (Zalantun) (▲ 389,500) (1986 E) 111,300
Cangshan (Bianzhuang) (1982 C) 79,334
Cangzhou (▲ 293,600) (1986 E) 196,700
Changchun (▲ 2,000,000) 1,822,000
Changde (▲ 220,800) (1986 E) 178,200
Changge (1982 C) 67,002
Changji (▲ 233,400) (1986 E) 110,500
Changqing (1982 C) 65,094
Changsha 1,230,000
Changshou (1985 E) 51,923
Changshu (▲ 998,000) (1986 E) 281,300
Changtu (1985 E) 49,937
Changyi (1982 C) 64,513
Changzhi (▲ 463,400) (1986 E) 273,000
Changzhou (Changchow) (1986 E) 522,700
Chaoan (▲ 1,214,500) (1986 E) 265,400
Chaoxian (▲ 739,500) (1986 E) 116,800
Chaoyang, Guangdong prov. (1985 E) 85,968
Chaoyang, Liaoning prov. (▲ 318,900) (1986 E) 180,300
Chengde (▲ 330,400) (1986 E) 226,600
Chengdu (Chengtu) (▲ 2,960,000) 1,884,000
Chenghai (1985 E) 50,631
Chenxian (▲ 191,900) (1986 E) 143,500
Chifeng (Ulanhad) (▲ 882,900) (1986 E) 299,000
Chongqing (Chungking) (▲ 2,890,000) 2,502,000
Chuxian (▲ 365,000) (1986 E) 113,300
Chuxiong (▲ 379,400) (1986 E) 67,700
Da'an (1985 E) 70,552
Dachangzhen (1975 U) 50,000
Dalian (Dairen) 2,280,000
Danyang (1985 E) 48,449
Daqing (▲ 880,000) 640,000
Dashiqiao (1985 E) 68,898
Datong (1985 E) 55,529
Datong (▲ 1,040,000) 810,000
Dawa (1985 E) 142,581
Daxian (▲ 209,400) (1986 E) 142,000
Dehui (1985 E) 60,247
Dengfeng (1982 C) 49,746
Deqing (1982 C) 48,726
Deyang (▲ 753,400) (1986 E) 184,800
Dezhou (▲ 276,200) (1986 E) 161,300
Didao (1975 U) 50,000
Dinghai (1985 E) 50,161
Dongchuan (Xincun) (▲ 275,100) (1986 E) 67,400
Dongguan (▲ 1,208,500) (1986 E) 254,900
Dongsheng (▲ 121,300) (1986 E) 57,500
Dongtai (1985 E) 65,788
Dongying (▲ 514,400) (1986 E) 178,100
Dukou (▲ 551,200) (1986 E) 380,200
Dunhua (▲ 448,000) (1986 E) 217,100
Duyun (▲ 386,600) (1986 E) 123,800
Echeng (▲ 938,000) (1986 E) 217,400
Enshi (▲ 679,000) (1986 E) 84,300
Ergun Zuoqi (1985 E) 55,970
Feixian (1982 C) 73,246
Fengcheng (1985 E) 66,745
Foshan (▲ 312,700) (1986 E) 243,500
Fujin (1985 E) 60,948
Fuling (▲ 973,500) (1986 E) 166,300
Fushun (Funan) 1,290,000
Fuxian (Wafangdian) (▲ 960,700) (1986 E) 246,200
Fuxinshi 700,000
Fuyang (▲ 195,200) (1986 E) 143,400
Fuyu, Heilongjiang prov. (1985 E) 48,670
Fuyu, Jilin prov. (1985 E) 98,373
Fuzhou, Fujian prov. (▲ 1,240,000) 910,000
Fuzhou, Jiangxi prov. (▲ 171,800) (1986 E) 106,700
Gaixian (1985 E) 67,587
Ganhe (1985 E) 48,128
Ganzhou (▲ 346,000) (1986 E) 191,600
Gaoqing (Tianzhen) (1982 C) 70,411
Gaoyou (1985 E) 57,844
Gejiu (Kokiu) (▲ 341,700) (1986 E) 193,600
Golmud (1986 E) 60,300
Gongchangling (1982 C) 49,281
Guanghua (▲ 420,000) (1986 E) 104,400
Guangyuan (▲ 805,500) (1986 E) 162,200
Guangzhou (Canton) (▲ 3,420,000) 3,100,000
Guanxian, Shandong prov. (1982 C) 49,782
Guanxian, Sichuan prov. (1985 E) 65,039
Guilin (Kweilin) (▲ 457,500) (1986 E) 324,200
Guixian (1985 E) 61,970
Guiyang (Kweiyang) (▲ 1,430,000) 1,030,000
Haicheng (▲ 984,800) (1986 E) 210,700
Haifeng (1985 E) 50,401
Haikou (▲ 289,600) (1986 E) 209,200
Hailaer (1986 E) 180,000
Hailin (1985 E) 58,909
Hailong (Meihekou) (▲ 534,200) (1986 E) 117,500
Hailun (1985 E) 83,448
Haiyang (Dongcun) (1982 C) 77,098
Hami (Kumul) (▲ 270,300) (1986 E) 146,400
Hancheng (▲ 304,200) (1986 E) 66,600
Handan (▲ 1,030,000) 870,000
Hangu (1975 U) 100,000
Hangzhou (Hangchow) 1,290,000
Hanzhong (▲ 415,000) (1986 E) 151,700
Harbin 2,710,000
Hebi (▲ 321,600) (1986 E) 158,500
Hechi (▲ 266,800) (1986 E) 74,400
Hechuan (1985 E) 65,237
Hefei (▲ 930,000) 740,000
Hegang (1986 E) 588,300
Helong (1985 E) 62,665
Hengshui (▲ 286,500) (1986 E) 83,100
Hengyang (▲ 601,300) (1986 E) 419,200
Heze (Caozhou) (▲ 1,001,500) (1986 E) 115,400
Hohhot (▲ 830,000) 670,000
Hongjiang (▲ 67,000) (1986 E) 54,300
Horqin Youyi Qianqi (Ulan Hot) (▲ 192,100) (1986 E) 129,100
Hotan (▲ 122,800) (1986 E) 71,700
Houma (▲ 158,500) (1986 E) 67,000
Huadian (1985 E) 75,183
Huaian (1985 E) 65,673
Huaibei (▲ 447,200) (1986 E) 252,100
Huaide (▲ 899,400) (1986 E) 187,600
Huaihua (▲ 427,100) (1986 E) 102,000
Huainan (▲ 1,110,000) 700,000
Huaiyin (Wangying) (▲ 382,500) (1986 E) 201,700
Huanan (1985 E) 66,596
Huanggang (1982 C) 65,961
Huangshi (1986 E) 451,900
Huayun (Huarong) (▲ 313,500) (1986 E) 81,000
Huinan (Chaoyang) (1985 E) 52,429
Huizhou (▲ 182,100) (1986 E) 117,000
Hulan (1985 E) 74,989
Hunjiang (Badaojiang) (▲ 687,700) (1986 E) 442,600
Huzhou (▲ 964,400) (1986 E) 208,500
Jiading (1985 E) 60,718
Jiamusi (Kiamusze) (▲ 557,700) (1986 E) 429,800
Jian (▲ 184,300) (1986 E) 132,200
Jiangling (1985 E) 77,887
Jiangmen (▲ 231,700) (1986 E) 168,800
Jiangyin (1985 E) 66,476
Jiangyou (1985 E) 72,663
Jianou (1985 E) 55,180
Jiaohe (1985 E) 51,504
Jiaojiang (▲ 385,200) (1986 E) 82,300
Jiaoxian (1985 E) 51,869
Jiaozuo (▲ 509,900) (1986 E) 335,400
Jiawang (1975 U) 50,000
Jiaxing (▲ 686,500) (1986 E) 210,200
Jiayuguan (▲ 102,100) (1986 E) 73,800
Jiexiu (1985 E) 51,300
Jieyang (1985 E) 98,531
Jilin (Kirin) 1,200,000
Jinan (Tsinan) (▲ 2,140,000) 1,546,000
Jinchang (Baijiazui) (▲ 136,000) (1986 E) 90,500
Jincheng (▲ 612,700) (1986 E) 99,900
Jingdezhen (Kingtechen) (▲ 569,700) (1986 E) 304,000
Jingmen (▲ 946,500) (1986 E) 227,000
Jinhua (▲ 799,900) (1986 E) 147,800
Jining, Nei Monggol prov. (1986 E) 163,300
Jining, Shandong prov. (▲ 765,700) (1986 E) 222,600
Jinshi (▲ 219,700) (1986 E) 73,700
Jinxi (▲ 634,300) (1986 E) 223,100
Jinxian (1985 E) 95,761
Jinzhou (Chinchou) (▲ 810,000) 710,000
Jishou (▲ 194,500) (1986 E) 59,500
Jishu (1985 E) 75,587
Jiujiang (▲ 382,300) (1986 E) 248,500
Jiuquan (Suzhou) (▲ 269,900) (1986 E) 56,300
Jiutai (1985 E) 63,021
Jixi (▲ 820,000) 700,000
Jixian (1985 E) 59,725
Juancheng (1982 C) 54,110
Junan (Shizilu) (1982 C) 90,222
Junxian (▲ 423,400) (1986 E) 97,000
Juxian (1982 C) 51,666
Kaifeng (▲ 629,100) (1986 E) 458,800
Kaili (▲ 342,100) (1986 E) 96,600
Kaiping (1985 E) 54,145
Kaiyuan (▲ 342,100) (1986 E) 96,600
Kaiyuan (1985 E) 85,762
Karamay (1986 E) 185,300
Kashi (▲ 194,500) (1986 E) 146,300
Keshan (1985 E) 65,088
Korla (▲ 219,000) (1986 E) 129,400
Kunming (▲ 1,550,000) 1,310,000
Kuqa (1985 E) 63,847
Kuytun (1986 E) 60,200
Laiwu (▲ 1,041,800) (1986 E) 143,500
Langxiang (1985 E) 64,658
Lanxi (1985 E) 53,236
Lanxi (▲ 606,800) (1986 E) 70,500
Lanzhou (Lanchow) (▲ 1,420,000) 1,297,000
Lechang (1986 E) 56,913
Lengshuijiang (▲ 277,600) (1986 E) 101,700
Lengshuitan (▲ 362,000) (1986 E) 60,900
Leshan (▲ 972,300) (1986 E) 307,300
Lhasa (▲ 107,700) (1986 E) 84,400
Lianyungang (Xinpu) (▲ 459,400) (1986 E) 288,000
Liaocheng (▲ 724,300) (1986 E) 119,000
Liaoyang (▲ 576,900) (1986 E) 442,600
Liaoyuan (1986 E) 370,400
Liling (▲ 856,300) (1986 E) 107,100
Linfen (▲ 530,100) (1986 E) 157,600
Lingling (▲ 515,300) (1986 E) 72,700
Lingyuan (1985 E) 66,825
Linhai (1985 E) 52,653
Linhe (▲ 365,900) (1986 E) 99,800
Linkou (1985 E) 52,936
Linqing (▲ 603,000) (1986 E) 87,000
Linqu (1982 C) 84,196
Linxia (▲ 150,200) (1986 E) 72,900
Linyi (▲ 1,365,000) (1986 E) 190,000
Liuzhou 680,000
Longjiang (1985 E) 51,156
Longyan (▲ 378,500) (1986 E) 114,500
Loudi (▲ 254,300) (1986 E) 84,200
Lu'an (▲ 163,400) (1986 E) 122,600
Lufeng (1985 E) 53,015
Luohe (▲ 159,100) (1986 E) 102,300
Luoyang (Loyang) (▲ 1,090,000) 760,000
Luzhou (▲ 360,300) (1986 E) 237,800

C Census. E Official estimate. U Unofficial estimate.
• Largest city in country.
★ Population or designation of metropolitan area, including suburbs (see headnote).
▲ Population of an entire municipality, commune, or district, including rural area.

Maanshan (▲ 367,000) (1986 E) 258,900
Manzhouli (1986 E) 116,600
Maoming (▲ 434,900) (1986 E) 118,600
Meixian (▲ 740,600) (1986 E) 169,100
Mengxian 55,000
Mengyin (1982 C) 70,602
Mianyang, Sichuan prov. (▲ 848,500) (1986 E) 233,900
Minhang (1975 U) 60,000
Mishan (1985 E) 54,919
Mixian (1982 C) 64,776
Mudanjiang 650,000
Nahe (1985 E) 49,725
N'aizishen (1985 E) 51,982
Nancha (1975 U) 50,000
Nanchang (▲ 1,260,000) 1,090,000
Nanchong (▲ 238,100) (1986 E) 158,000
Nanjing (Nanking) 2,390,000
Nanning (▲ 1,000,000) 720,000
Nanpiao (1982 C) 67,274
Nanping (▲ 420,800) (1986 E) 157,100
Nantong (▲ 411,000) (1986 E) 308,800
Nanyang (▲ 294,800) (1986 E) 199,400
Neihuang (1982 C) 56,039
Neijiang (▲ 298,500) (1986 E) 191,100
Ning'an (1985 E) 49,334
Ningbo (▲ 1,050,000) 570,000
Ningyang (1982 C) 55,424
Nong'an (1985 E) 55,966
Nunjiang (1985 E) 59,276
Orogen Zizhiqi (1985 E) 48,042
Panshan (▲ 343,100) (1986 E) 248,100
Panshi (1985 E) 59,270
Pingdingshan (▲ 819,900) (1986 E) 363,200
Pingliang (▲ 362,500) (1986 E) 85,400
Pingxiang (▲ 1,286,700) (1986 E) 368,700
Pingyi (1982 C) 89,373
Pingyin (1982 C) 62,827
Potou (▲ 456,100) (1986 E) 59,000
Puqi (1985 E) 65,239
Putian (▲ 265,400) (1986 E) 64,600
Putuo (1985 E) 50,962
Puyang (▲ 1,086,100) (1986 E) 131,000
Qian Gorlos (1985 E) 79,494
Qingdao (Tsingtao) 1,300,000
Qingjiang (▲ 246,617) (1982 C) 150,000
Qingyuan (1985 E) 51,756
Qinhuangdao (Chinwangtao) (★ 436,000) (1986 E) 307,500
Qinzhou (▲ 923,400) (1986 E) 97,100
Qiqihar (Tsitsihar) (▲ 1,330,000) 1,180,000
Qitaihe (▲ 309,900) (1986 E) 166,400
Qixia (1982 C) 54,158
Qixian (1982 C) 53,041
Quanzhou (Chuanchou) (▲ 436,000) (1986 E) 157,000
Qujing (▲ 758,000) (1986 E) 135,000
Quxian (▲ 704,800) (1986 E) 124,000
Raoping (1985 E) 54,831
Rizhao (▲ 970,300) (1986 E) 93,300
Rongcheng (1982 C) 52,878
Rugao (1985 E) 50,643
Ruian (1985 E) 57,993
Sanmenxia (Shanxian) (▲ 150,000) (1986 E) 79,000
Sanming (▲ 214,300) (1986 E) 144,900
• Shanghai (★ 9,300,000) 7,220,000
Shangqiu (Zhuji) (▲ 199,400) (1986 E) 125,400
Shangrao (▲ 142,500) (1986 E) 113,000
Shangshui (1982 C) 50,191
Shantou (Swatow) (▲ 790,000) 560,000
Shanwei (1985 E) 61,234
Shaoguan (1986 E) 363,100
Shaowu (▲ 266,700) (1986 E) 81,400
Shaoxing (▲ 250,900) (1986 E) 167,100
Shaoyang (▲ 465,900) (1986 E) 218,600
Shashi (1986 E) 253,700
Shenxian (1982 C) 50,208
Shenyang (Mukden) (▲ 4,370,000) 3,910,000
Shenzhen (▲ 231,900) (1986 E) 189,600
Shiguaigou (1975 U) 50,000
Shihezi (▲ 549,300) (1987 E) 304,700
Shijiazhuang 1,220,000
Shiyan (▲ 332,600) (1986 E) 227,300
Shizuishan (▲ 317,400) (1986 E) 225,500
Shouguang (1982 C) 83,400
Shuangcheng (1985 E) 91,163
Shuangliao (1985 E) 67,326
Shuangyashan (1986 E) 427,300
Shuicheng (▲ 2,216,500) (1986 E) 363,500
Shulan (1986 E) 50,582
Shunde (1985 E) 50,262
Siping (▲ 357,800) (1986 E) 280,100
Sishui (1982 C) 82,990
Songjiang (1985 E) 71,864
Songjianghe (1985 E) 53,023
Suihua (▲ 732,100) (1986 E) 200,400
Suileng (1985 E) 68,399
Suining (▲ 1,174,900) (1986 E) 118,500
Suixian (▲ 1,281,600) (1986 E) 187,700
Suqian (1985 E) 50,742
Suxian (▲ 218,600) (1986 E) 123,300
Suzhou (Soochow) 740,000
Tai'an (▲ 1,325,400) (1986 E) 215,900
Taiyuan (▲ 1,980,000) 1,700,000
Taizhou (▲ 210,800) (1987 E) 143,200
Tancheng (1982 C) 61,857
Tangshan (▲ 1,440,000) 1,080,000
Tao'an (1985 E) 76,269
Tengxian (1985 E) 53,254
Tianjin (Tientsin) (▲ 5,540,000) 4,950,000
Tianshui (▲ 953,200) (1986 E) 209,500
Tiefa (▲ 146,367) (1982 C) 60,000
Tieli (1985 E) 102,527
Tieling (▲ 454,100) (1986 E) 326,100
Tongchuan (▲ 393,200) (1986 E) 268,900
Tonghua (▲ 367,400) (1986 E) 290,200
Tongliao (▲ 253,100) (1986 E) 190,100
Tongling (▲ 216,400) (1986 E) 182,900
Tongren (1985 E) 50,307
Tongxian (1985 E) 97,168
Tumen (▲ 99,700) (1986 E) 77,600
Tunxi (▲ 104,500) (1986 E) 61,800
Turpan (▲ 196,800) (1986 E) 52,300
Ürümqi 1,060,000
Wangkui (1985 E) 52,021
Wangqing (1985 E) 61,237
Wanxian (▲ 280,800) (1986 E) 138,700
Weifang (▲ 1,042,200) (1986 E) 312,500
Weihai (▲ 220,800) (1986 E) 83,000
Weinan (▲ 699,400) (1986 E) 111,300
Weishan (Xiazhen) (1982 C) 57,932
Weixian (Hanting) (1982 C) 50,180
Wenzhou (▲ 530,600) (1986 E) 372,200
Wuchang (1985 E) 64,403
Wuhai (1986 E) 266,000
Wuhan 3,570,000
Wuhu (▲ 502,200) (1986 E) 396,000
Wulian (Hongning) (1982 C) 51,718
Wusong (1982 C) 64,017
Wuwei (Liangzhou) (▲ 804,000) (1986 E) 115,500
Wuxi (Wuhsi) 880,000
Wuzhong (▲ 402,400) (1986 E) 48,600
Wuzhou (Wuchow) (▲ 261,500) (1986 E) 194,800
Xiaguan (▲ [illegible]) (1986 E) 112,100
Xiamen (Amoy) (▲ 546,400) (1986 E) 343,700
Xi'an (Sian) (▲ 2,580,000) 2,210,000
Xiangfan (▲ 421,200) (1986 E) 314,900
Xiangtan (▲ 511,100) (1986 E) 389,500
Xianning (▲ 402,200) (1986 E) 122,200
Xianyang (▲ 641,000) (1986 E) 285,900
Xiaogan (▲ 1,204,400) (1986 E) 125,500
Xiaoshan (1985 E) 63,074
Xichang (▲ 161,000) (1986 E) 105,000
Xinghua (1985 E) 75,573
Xinglongzhen (1982 C) 52,961
Xingtai (▲ 350,800) (1986 E) 265,600
Xinhui (1985 E) 77,381
Xining (Sining) 620,000
Xinmin (1985 E) 47,900
Xintai (▲ 1,157,300) (1986 E) 171,400
Xinwen (Suncun) (1975 U) 50,000
Xinxian (▲ 398,600) (1986 E) 74,200
Xinxiang (▲ 540,500) (1986 E) 411,000
Xinyang (▲ 234,200) (1986 E) 169,100
Xinyu (▲ 610,600) (1986 E) 140,200
Xuancheng (1985 E) 52,387
Xuanhua (1975 U) 140,000
Xuanwei (1982 C) 70,081
Xuchang (▲ 247,200) (1986 E) 167,800
Xuguit Qi (Yakeshi) (1986 E) 390,000
Xuzhou (Süchow) 860,000
Yaan (▲ 277,600) (1986 E) 89,200
Yan'an (▲ 259,800) (1986 E) 86,700
Yancheng (▲ 1,251,400) (1986 E) 258,400
Yangcheng (1982 C) 57,255
Yangjiang (1986 E) 91,433
Yangquan (▲ 478,900) (1986 E) 295,100
Yangzhou (▲ 417,300) (1986 E) 321,500
Yanji (▲ 216,900) (1986 E) 175,000
Yanji (Longjing) (1985 E) 55,035
Yanling (1982 C) 52,679
Yantai (Chefoo) (▲ 717,300) (1986 E) 327,000
Yanzhou (1985 E) 48,972
Yaxian (Sanya) (▲ 321,700) (1986 E) 70,500
Yi'an (1986 E) 54,253
Yibin (Ipin) (▲ 636,500) (1986 E) 218,800
Yichang (Ichang) (1986 E) 410,500
Yichuan (1982 C) 58,914
Yichun, Heilongjiang prov. 840,000
Yichun, Jiangxi prov. (▲ 770,200) (1986 E) 132,600
Yidu (1985 E) 54,838
Yilan (1985 E) 50,436
Yima (▲ 84,800) (1986 E) 53,700
Yinan (Jiehu) (1982 C) 67,803
Yinchuan (▲ 396,900) (1986 E) 268,200
Yingchengzi (1985 E) 59,072
Yingkou (▲ 480,000) (1986 E) 366,900
Yingtan (▲ 116,200) (1986 E) 64,500
Yining (Kuldja) (▲ 232,000) (1986 E) 153,200
Yiyang (▲ 365,000) (1986 E) 155,300
Yiyuan (Nanma) (1982 C) 53,800
Yongan (▲ 269,000) (1986 E) 105,100
Yongchuan (1985 E) 70,444
Yuci (▲ 420,700) (1986 E) 171,000
Yueyang (▲ 411,300) (1986 E) 239,500
Yulin, Guangxi Zhuangzu prov. (▲ 1,228,800) (1986 E) 115,600
Yulin, Shaanxi prov. (1985 E) 51,610
Yumen (Laojunmiao) (▲ 160,100) (1986 E) 84,300
Yuncheng, Shandong prov. (1982 C) 54,262
Yuncheng, Shansi prov. (▲ 434,900) (1986 E) 87,000
Yunyang (1982 C) 54,903
Yushu (1985 E) 57,222
Yuyao (▲ 772,700) (1986 E) 109,700
Zaozhuang (▲ 1,602,000) (1986 E) 292,200
Zhangjiakou (Kalgan) (▲ 640,000) 500,000
Zhangye (▲ 394,200) (1986 E) 73,000
Zhangzhou (Longxi) (▲ 310,400) (1986 E) 159,400
Zhanhua (Fuguo) (1982 C) 48,193
Zhanjiang (▲ 920,900) (1986 E) 335,500
Zhaodong (1985 E) 99,836
Zhaoqing (Gaoyao) (▲ 187,600) (1986 E) 145,700
Zhaotong (▲ 546,600) (1986 E) 77,500
Zhaoyuan (1982 C) 56,389
Zhengzhou (Chengchow) (▲ 1,580,000) 1,150,000
Zhenjiang (1986 E) 412,400
Zhongshan (Shiqizhen) (▲ 1,059,700) (1986 E) 238,700
Zhoucun (1975 U) 50,000
Zhoukouzhen (▲ 220,400) (1986 E) 110,500
Zhuhai (▲ 155,000) (1986 E) 88,800
Zhumadian (▲ 149,500) (1986 E) 99,400
Zhuoxian (1985 E) 54,523
Zhuzhou (Chuchow) (▲ 499,600) (1986 E) 344,800
Zibo (Zhangdian) (▲ 2,370,000) 840,000
Zigong (Tzukung) (▲ 909,300) (1986 E) 361,700
Zixing (▲ 334,300) (1986 E) 97,100
Ziyang (1985 E) 57,349
Zouping (1982 C) 49,274
Zouxian (1985 E) 61,578
Zunyi (▲ 347,600) (1986 E) 236,600

COLOMBIA

1985 C 27,867,326

Cities and Towns

Armenia 187,130
Barrancabermeja 137,406
Barranquilla (★ 1,140,000) 899,781
Bello (★ Medellín) 212,861
Bucaramanga (★ 550,000) 352,326
Buenaventura 160,342
Buga 82,992
Cali (★ 1,400,000) 1,350,565
Cartagena 531,426
Cartago 97,791
Ciénaga 56,860
Cúcuta (★ 445,000) 379,478
Dos Quebradas (★ Pereira) 101,480
Duitama 56,390
Envigado (★ Medellín) 91,391
Florencia 66,430
Floridablanca (★ Bucaramanga) 143,824
Girardot 70,078
Ibagué 292,965
Itagüí (★ Medellín) 137,623
Magangué 49,160
Malambo (★ Barranquilla) 52,584
Manizales (★ 330,000) 299,352
Medellín (★ 2,095,000) 1,468,089
Montería 157,466
Neiva 194,556
Ocaña 51,443
Palmira 175,186
Pasto 197,407
Pereira (★ 390,000) 233,271
Popayán 141,964
• SANTA FE DE BOGOTÁ (★ 4,260,000) 3,982,941
Santa Marta 177,922
Sincelejo 120,537
Soacha (★ Santa Fe de Bogotá) 109,051
Sogamoso 64,437
Soledad (★ Barranquilla) 165,791
Tuluá 99,721
Tunja 93,792
Valledupar 142,771
Villa Rosario (★ Cúcuta) 63,615
Villavicencio 178,685

COMOROS / Al-Qumur / Comores

1990 E 452,742

Cities and Towns

• MORONI 23,432

CONGO

1984 C 1,912,429

Cities and Towns

• BRAZZAVILLE 585,812
Dolisie 40,104
Pointe-Noire 294,203

COOK ISLANDS

1986 C 18,155

Cities and Towns

• AVARUA 9,678

COSTA RICA

1988 E 2,851,000

Cities and Towns

Limón (▲ 62,600) 40,400
• SAN JOSÉ (★ 670,000) 278,600

COTE D'IVOIRE / Côte d' Ivoire

1983 E 9,300,000

Cities and Towns

• ABIDJAN 1,950,000
Bouaké 275,000
Daloa 70,000
Korhogo 125,000
Man 55,000
YAMOUSSOUKRO 80,000

CROATIA / Hrvatska

1987 E 4,673,517

Cities and Towns

Osijek (▲ 162,490) 106,800
Rijeka (▲ 199,282) 166,400
Split 197,074
• ZAGREB 697,925

CUBA

1987 E 10,288,000

Cities and Towns

Bayamo 108,716
Camagüey 265,588
Cárdenas (1981 C) 59,352
Cienfuegos 112,225
Guantánamo 179,091
Holguín 199,861
• LA HABANA (HAVANA) (★ 2,125,000) 2,036,800
Manzanillo (1981 C) 87,830
Matanzas 106,954
Palma Soriano (1981 C) 55,851
Pinar del Río 108,109
Santa Clara 182,349
Santiago de Cuba 364,554
Victoria de las Tunas (1985 E) 91,400

CYPRUS / Kıbrıs / Kípros

1982 C 512,097

Cities and Towns

Lemesós (Limassol) (★ 107,161) 74,782
• NICOSIA (LEVKOSÍA) (★ 185,000) 48,221

CYPRUS, NORTH / Kuzey Kıbrıs

1985 E 160,287

Cities and Towns

• NICOSIA (LEFKOŞA) 37,400

CZECH REPUBLIC / Česká Republika

1990 E 10,362,553

Cities and Towns

Brno (★ 450,000) 392,285
České Budějovice (★ 114,000) 99,428
Chomutov (★ 80,000) 55,735
Děčín (★ 72,000) 56,034
Frýdek-Místek (★ Ostrava) 66,791
Havířov (★ Ostrava) 92,037
Hradec Králové (★ 113,000) 101,302
Jihlava 54,855
Karlovy Vary (Carlsbad) 58,039
Karviná (★ ★ Ostrava) 69,521
Kladno (★ 88,500) 73,347
Liberec (★ 175,000) 104,256
Mladá Boleslav 49,195
Most (★ 135,000) 71,360
Olomouc (★ 126,000) 107,044
Opava (★ 77,500) 63,440
Ostrava (★ 760,000) 331,557
Pardubice 95,909
Plzeň (★ 210,000) 175,038
• PRAHA (PRAGUE) (★ 1,325,000) 1,215,656
Přerov 51,996
Prostějov 52,074
Teplice (★ 94,000) 55,287
Ústí nad Labem (★ 115,000) 106,499
Zlín (★ 124,000) 87,189

DENMARK / Danmark

1990 E 5,135,409

Cities and Towns

Ålborg (▲ 155,019) 114,000
Århus (▲ 261,437) 200,000
Esbjerg (▲ 81,504) 71,900
Frederiksberg (★ København) 85,611
Gentofte (★ København) 65,303
Gladsakse (★ København) 60,882
Helsingør (Elsinore) (★ København) 56,701
• KØBENHAVN (★ 1,685,000) 466,723
Kongens Lyngby (★ København) 49,317
Odense (▲ 176,133) 140,100
Randers 61,020

DJIBOUTI

1976 E 226,000

Cities and Towns

• DJIBOUTI 120,000

C Census. E Official estimate. U Unofficial estimate.
• Largest city in country.
★ Population or designation of metropolitan area, including suburbs (see headnote).
▲ Population of an entire municipality, commune, or district, including rural area.

DOMINICA
1984 E ... 77,000

Cities and Towns

• ROSEAU ... 9,348

DOMINICAN REPUBLIC / República Dominicana
1981 C ... 5,647,977

Cities and Towns

Barahona ... 49,334
La Romana ... 91,571
San Cristóbal ... 58,520
San Francisco de Macorís ... 64,906
San Juan [de la Maguana] ... 49,764
San Pedro de Macorís ... 78,562
Santiago [de los Caballeros] ... 278,638
• SANTO DOMINGO ... 1,313,172

ECUADOR
1987 E ... 9,923,000

Cities and Towns

Alfaro (★ Guayaquil) (1982 C) ... 51,023
Ambato ... 126,067
Cuenca ... 201,490
Esmeraldas ... 120,387
• Guayaquil (★ 1,580,000) ... 1,572,615
Ibarra (1982 C) ... 53,428
Loja (1982 C) ... 71,652
Machala ... 144,396
Manta ... 135,990
Milagro ... 102,884
Portoviejo ... 141,568
Quevedo (1982 C) ... 67,023
QUITO (★ 1,300,000) ... 1,137,705
Riobamba (1982 C) ... 75,455
Santo Domingo de los Colorados ... 104,059

EGYPT / Miṣr
1986 C ... 48,205,049

Cities and Towns

Abū Kabīr ... 69,509
Akhmīm ... 70,602
Al-'Arīsh ... 67,638
Al-Fayyūm ... 212,523
Al-Ḥawāmidīyah (★ Al-Qāhirah) ... 73,060
Al-Iskandarīyah (Alexandria) (★ 3,350,000) ... 2,917,327
Al-Ismā'īlīyah (★ 235,000) ... 212,567
Al-Jīzah (Giza) (★ Al-Qāhirah) ... 1,870,508
Al-Maḥallah al-Kubrā ... 358,844
Al-Manṣūrah (★ 375,000) ... 316,870
Al-Manzilah ... 55,090
Al-Maṭarīyah ... 74,554
Al-Minyā ... 179,136
• AL-QĀHIRAH (CAIRO) (★ 9,300,000) ... 6,052,836
Al-Uqṣur (Luxor) ... 125,404
Armant ... 54,650
Ashmūn ... 54,450
As-Sinbillāwayn ... 60,285
As-Suways (Suez) ... 326,820
Aswān ... 191,461
Asyūṭ ... 273,191
Az-Zaqāzīq ... 245,496
Bahtīm (★ Al-Qāhirah) ... 275,807
Banhā ... 115,571
Banī Suwayf ... 151,813
Bilbays ... 96,540
Bilqās Qism Awwal ... 73,162
Būlāq ad-Dakrūr (★ Al-Qāhirah) ... 148,787
Būr Sa'īd (Port Said) ... 399,793
Būsh ... 54,482
Damanhūr ... 190,840
Disūq ... 78,119
Dumyāṭ (Damietta) ... 89,498
Hawsh 'Īsā (1980 C) ... 53,619
Idkū ... 70,729
Jirjā ... 70,899
Kafr ad-Dawwār (★ Al-Iskandarīyah) ... 195,102
Kafr ash-Shaykh ... 102,910
Kafr az-Zayyāt ... 58,061
Kawm Umbū ... 52,131
Maghāghah ... 50,807
Mallawī ... 99,062
Manfalūṭ ... 52,644
Minūf ... 69,883
Mīt Ghamr (★ 100,000) ... 92,253
Qalyūb ... 86,684
Qinā ... 119,794
Rashīd (Rosetta) ... 52,014
Rummānah ... 50,014
Samālūṭ ... 62,404
Sāqiyat Makkī ... 51,062
Sawhāj ... 132,965
Shibīn al-Kawm ... 132,751
Shubrā al-Khaymah (★ Al-Qāhirah) ... 710,794
Sinnūris ... 55,323
Ṭahṭā ... 58,516
Ṭalkhā (★ Al-Manṣūrah) ... 55,757
Tantā ... 334,505
Warrāq al-'Arab (★ Al-Qāhirah) ... 127,108
Ziftā (★ ★ Mīt Ghamr) ... 69,050

EL SALVADOR
1985 E ... 5,337,896

Cities and Towns

Delgado (★ San Salvador) ... 67,684
Mejicanos (★ San Salvador) ... 91,465
Nueva San Salvador (★ San Salvador) ... 53,688
San Miguel ... 88,520
• SAN SALVADOR (★ 920,000) ... 462,652
Santa Ana ... 137,879
Soyapango (★ San Salvador) ... 60,000

EQUATORIAL GUINEA / Guinea Ecuatorial
1983 C ... 300,000

Cities and Towns

• MALABO ... 31,630

ERITREA
1987 E ... 2,951,100

Cities and Towns

• ASMERA (1988 E) ... 319,353
Mitsiwa (1984 C) ... 15,441

ESTONIA / Eesti
1989 C ... 1,573,000

Cities and Towns

Kohtla-Järve (1987 E) ... 78,000
Narva (1987 E) ... 81,000
Pärnu (1987 E) ... 53,000
• TALLINN ... 482,000
Tartu ... 114,000

ETHIOPIA / Ityopiya
1987 E ... 43,004,600

Cities and Towns

• ADIS ABEBA (★ 1,500,000) (1988 E) ... 1,686,300
Akaki Beseka (★ Adis Abeba) ... 54,146
Bahir Dar ... 54,800
Debre Zeyit ... 51,143
Dese ... 68,848
Dire Dawa (1988 E) ... 117,042
Gonder ... 68,958
Harer ... 62,160
Jima ... 60,992
Mekele ... 61,583
Nazret ... 76,284

FAEROE ISLANDS / Føroyar
1990 E ... 47,946

Cities and Towns

• TÓRSHAVN ... 14,767

FALKLAND ISLANDS
1986 C ... 1,916

Cities and Towns

• STANLEY ... 1,200

FIJI
1986 C ... 715,375

Cities and Towns

Lautoka (★ 39,057) ... 28,728
• SUVA (★ 141,273) ... 69,665

FINLAND / Suomi
1988 E ... 4,938,602

Cities and Towns

Espoo (Esbo) (★ Helsinki) ... 164,569
Hämeenlinna ... 42,486
• HELSINKI (HELSINGFORS) (★ 1,040,000) ... 490,034
Joensuu ... 47,099
Jyväskylä (★ 93,000) ... 65,719
Kotka ... 57,745
Kouvola (★ 53,821) ... 31,933
Kuopio ... 78,916
Lahti (★ 108,000) ... 74,300
Lappeenranta (▲ 53,780) ... 47,400
Oulu (★ 121,000) ... 98,582
Pori ... 77,395
Tampere (★ 241,000) ... 170,533
Turku (Åbo) (★ 228,000) ... 160,456
Vaasa (Vasa) ... 53,737
Vantaa (Vanda) (★ Helsinki) ... 149,063

FRANCE
1982 C ... 54,334,871

Cities and Towns

Aix-en-Provence (★ 126,552) ... 121,327
Ajaccio ... 54,089
Albi (★ 60,181) ... 45,947
Alès (★ 70,180) ... 43,268
Amiens (★ 154,498) ... 131,332
Angers (★ 195,859) ... 136,038
Angoulême (★ 103,552) ... 46,197
Annecy (★ 112,632) ... 49,965
Antibes (★ ★ Cannes) ... 62,859
Antony (★ Paris) ... 54,610
Argenteuil (★ Paris) ... 95,347
Arras (★ 80,477) ... 41,736
Asnières [-sur-Seine] (★ Paris) ... 71,077
Aubervilliers (★ Paris) ... 67,719
Aulnay-sous-Bois (★ Paris) ... 75,996
Avignon (★ 174,264) ... 89,132
Bayonne (★ 127,477) ... 41,381
Beauvais (★ 55,817) ... 52,365
Belfort (★ 76,221) ... 51,206
Besançon (★ 120,772) ... 113,283
Béthune (★ 258,383) ... 25,508
Béziers (★ 81,347) ... 76,647
Bordeaux (★ 640,012) ... 208,159
Boulogne-Billancourt (★ Paris) ... 102,582
Boulogne-sur-Mer (★ 98,566) ... 47,653
Bourges (★ 92,202) ... 76,432
Brest (★ 201,145) ... 156,060
Brive-la-Gaillarde (★ 64,301) ... 51,511
Caen (★ 183,526) ... 114,068
Calais (★ 100,823) ... 76,527
Cannes (★ 295,525) ... 72,259
Châlons-sur-Marne (★ 63,061) ... 51,137
Chalon-sur-Saône (★ 78,064) ... 56,194
Chambéry (★ 96,163) ... 53,427
Champigny-sur-Marne (★ Paris) ... 76,176
Charleville-Mézières (★ 67,694) ... 58,667
Châteauroux (★ 66,851) ... 51,942
Cherbourg (★ 85,485) ... 28,442
Cholet ... 55,524
Clermont-Ferrand (★ 256,189) ... 147,361
Colmar (★ 82,468) ... 62,483
Colombes (★ Paris) ... 78,777
Courbevoie (★ Paris) ... 59,830
Créteil (★ Paris) ... 71,693
Dieppe (★ 41,812) ... 35,957
Dijon (★ 215,865) ... 140,942
Douai (★ 202,366) ... 42,576
Drancy (★ Paris) ... 60,183
Dunkerque (★ 195,705) ... 73,120
Épinay-sur-Seine (★ Paris) ... 50,314
Fontenay-sous-Bois (★ Paris) ... 52,627
Forbach (★ 99,606) ... 27,187
Grenoble (★ 392,021) ... 156,637
Hagondange (★ 119,669) ... 9,091
Ivry-sur-Seine (★ Paris) ... 55,699
La Rochelle (★ 102,143) ... 75,840
La Seyne [-sur-Mer] (★ Toulon) ... 57,659
Laval (★ 55,984) ... 50,360
Le Havre (★ 254,595) ... 199,388
Le Mans (★ 191,080) ... 147,697
Levallois-Perret (★ Paris) ... 53,500
Lille (★ 1,020,000) ... 168,424
Limoges (★ 171,689) ... 140,400
Lorient (★ 104,025) ... 62,554
Lyon (★ 1,275,000) ... 413,095
Maisons-Alfort (★ Paris) ... 51,065
Mantes-la-Jolie (★ 170,265) ... 43,564
Marseille (★ 1,225,000) ... 874,436
Maubeuge (★ 105,714) ... 36,061
Melun (★ 82,479) ... 35,005
Mérignac (★ Bordeaux) ... 51,306
Metz (★ 186,437) ... 114,232
Montbéliard (★ 128,194) ... 31,836
Montluçon (★ 67,963) ... 49,912
Montpellier (★ 221,307) ... 197,231
Montreuil-sous-Bois (★ Paris) ... 93,368
Mulhouse (Mülhausen) (★ 220,613) ... 112,157
Nancy (★ 306,982) ... 96,317
Nanterre (★ Paris) ... 88,578
Nantes (★ 464,857) ... 240,539
Neuilly-sur-Seine (★ Paris) ... 64,170
Nice (★ 449,496) ... 337,085
Nîmes (★ 132,343) ... 124,220
Niort (★ 61,959) ... 58,203
Orléans (★ 220,478) ... 102,710
• PARIS (★ 9,775,000) (1987 E) ... 2,078,900
Pau (★ 131,265) ... 83,790
Perpignan (★ 137,915) ... 111,669
Pessac (★ Bordeaux) ... 50,267
Poitiers (★ 103,204) ... 79,350
Quimper ... 56,907
Reims (★ 199,388) ... 194,656
Rennes (★ 234,418) ... 117,234
Roanne (★ 81,786) ... 48,705
Roubaix (★ ★ Lille) ... 101,602
Rouen (★ 379,879) ... 101,945
Rueil-Malmaison (★ Paris) ... 63,412
Saint-Brieuc (★ 83,900) ... 48,563
Saint-Chamond (★ 82,059) ... 40,267
Saint-Denis (★ Paris) ... 90,829
Saint-Étienne (★ 317,228) ... 204,955
Saint-Maur-des-Fossés (★ Paris) ... 80,811
Saint-Nazaire (★ 130,271) ... 68,348
Saint-Quentin (★ 71,887) ... 63,567
Sarcelles (★ Paris) ... 53,630
Strasbourg (★ 400,000) ... 248,712
Tarbes (★ 78,056) ... 51,422
Thionville (★ 138,034) ... 40,573
Toulon (★ 410,393) ... 179,423
Toulouse (★ 541,271) ... 347,995
Tourcoing (★ ★ Lille) ... 96,908
Tours (★ 262,786) ... 132,209
Troyes (★ 125,240) ... 63,581
Valence (★ 106,041) ... 66,356
Valenciennes (★ 349,505) ... 40,275
Vénissieux (★ Lyon) ... 64,804
Versailles (★ Paris) ... 91,494
Villejuif (★ Paris) ... 52,448
Villeneuve-d'Ascq (★ Lille) ... 59,527
Villeurbanne (★ Lyon) ... 115,960
Vitry-sur-Seine (★ Paris) ... 85,263

FRENCH GUIANA / Guyane française
1982 C ... 73,022

Cities and Towns

• CAYENNE ... 38,091

FRENCH POLYNESIA / Polynésie française
1988 C ... 188,814

Cities and Towns

• PAPEETE (★ 80,000) ... 23,555

GABON
1985 E ... 1,312,000

Cities and Towns

Franceville ... 58,800
Lambaréné ... 49,500
• LIBREVILLE ... 235,700
Port Gentil ... 124,400

GAMBIA
1983 C ... 696,000

Cities and Towns

• BANJUL (★ 95,000) ... 44,536

GEORGIA / Sakartvelo
1989 C ... 5,449,000

Cities and Towns

Batumi ... 136,000
Gori (1987 E) ... 62,000
Kutaisi ... 235,000
Poti (1977 E) ... 54,000
Rustavi (★ Tbilisi) ... 159,000
Suchumi ... 121,000
• TBILISI (★ 1,460,000) ... 1,260,000

GERMANY / Deutschland
1989 E ... 78,389,735

Cities and Towns

Aachen (★ 535,000) ... 233,255
Aalen (★ 80,000) ... 62,812
Ahlen ... 52,836
Altenburg ... 53,288
Arnsberg ... 73,912
Aschaffenburg (★ 145,000) ... 62,048
Augsburg (★ 405,000) ... 247,731
Baden-Baden ... 50,761
Bad Homburg (★ Frankfurt am Main) ... 51,035
Bad Salzuflen (★ ★ Herford) ... 50,875
Bamberg (★ 120,000) ... 69,809
Bautzen ... 52,394
Bayreuth (★ 90,000) ... 70,933
Bergheim (★ Köln) ... 55,997
Bergisch Gladbach (★ Köln) ... 101,983
Bergkamen (★ Essen) ... 48,489
BERLIN (★ 3,825,000) ... 3,352,848
Bielefeld (★ 515,000) ... 311,946
Bitterfeld (★ 105,000) ... 20,513
Bocholt ... 67,565
Bochum (★ ★ Essen) ... 389,087
BONN (★ 570,000) ... 282,190
Bottrop (★ Essen) ... 116,363
Brandenburg ... 94,872
Braunschweig (★ 330,000) ... 253,794
Bremen (★ 800,000) ... 535,058
Bremerhaven (★ 190,000) ... 126,934
Castrop-Rauxel (★ Essen) ... 77,660
Celle ... 71,050
Chemnitz (★ 450,000) ... 311,765
Cottbus ... 128,639
Cuxhaven ... 55,249
Darmstadt (★ 305,000) ... 136,067
Delmenhorst (★ ★ Bremen) ... 72,901
Dessau (★ 140,000) ... 103,867
Detmold ... 66,809
Dinslaken (★ Essen) ... 63,246
Dormagen (★ Köln) ... 55,935
Dorsten (★ Essen) ... 75,518
Dortmund (★ ★ Essen) ... 587,328
Dresden (★ 670,000) ... 518,057
Duisburg (★ ★ Essen) ... 527,447
Düren (★ 110,000) ... 83,120
Düsseldorf (★ 1,190,000) ... 569,641
Eberswalde ... 54,822
Eisenhüttenstadt ... 53,048
Emden ... 49,803
Erfurt ... 220,016
Erlangen (★ ★ Nürnberg) ... 100,583
Eschweiler (★ ★ Aachen) ... 53,516
• Essen (★ 4,950,000) ... 620,594
Esslingen (★ Stuttgart) ... 90,537
Flensburg (★ 103,000) ... 85,830
Frankfurt am Main (★ 1,855,000) ... 625,258
Frankfurt an der Oder ... 87,863
Freiberg ... 51,341
Freiburg [im Breisgau] (★ 225,000) ... 183,979
Friedrichshafen ... 52,295
Fulda (★ 79,000) ... 54,320
Fürth (★ ★ Nürnberg) ... 98,832
Garbsen (★ Hannover) ... 59,225
Garmisch-Partenkirchen ... 25,908
Gelsenkirchen (★ ★ Essen) ... 287,255
Gera ... 134,834
Giessen (★ 160,000) ... 71,751
Gladbeck (★ Essen) ... 79,187
Göppingen (★ 155,000) ... 52,873
Görlitz ... 77,609
Goslar (★ 84,000) ... 45,614
Gotha ... 57,365
Göttingen ... 118,073
Greifswald ... 68,597
Grevenbroich (★ Düsseldorf) ... 59,204
Gummersbach ... 49,017
Gütersloh (★ ★ Bielefeld) ... 83,407
Hagen (★ ★ Essen) ... 210,640
Halle (★ 475,000) ... 236,044
Halle-Neustadt (★ Halle) ... 93,446
Hamburg (★ 2,225,000) ... 1,603,070
Hameln (★ 72,000) ... 57,642
Hamm ... 173,611
Hanau (★ ★ Frankfurt am Main) ... 84,300
Hannover (★ 1,000,000) ... 498,495
Hattingen (★ Essen) ... 56,242
Heidelberg (★ ★ Mannheim) ... 131,429
Heidenheim (★ 89,000) ... 48,497
Heilbronn (★ 230,000) ... 112,278
Herford (★ 120,000) ... 61,700
Herne (★ Essen) ... 174,664
Herten (★ Essen) ... 68,111
Hilden (★ Düsseldorf) ... 53,725
Hildesheim (★ 140,000) ... 103,512
Hof ... 50,938
Hoyerswerda ... 69,361
Hürth (★ Köln) ... 49,094
Ingolstadt (★ 138,000) ... 97,702
Iserlohn ... 93,337
Jena ... 108,010
Kaiserslautern (★ 138,000) ... 96,990
Karlsruhe (★ 485,000) ... 265,100
Kassel (★ 360,000) ... 189,156
Kempten (Allgäu) ... 60,052
Kerpen (★ Köln) ... 54,699
Kiel (★ 335,000) ... 240,675
Kleve ... 44,416
Koblenz (★ 180,000) ... 107,286
Köln (Cologne) (★ 1,760,000) ... 937,482
Konstanz ... 72,862
Krefeld (★ ★ Essen) ... 235,423
Landshut ... 57,194
Langenfeld (★ Düsseldorf) ... 50,777
Leipzig (★ 700,000) ... 545,307
Leverkusen (★ Köln) ... 157,358
Lippstadt ... 60,396
Lübeck (★ 260,000) ... 210,681
Lüdenscheid ... 76,118
Ludwigsburg (★ Stuttgart) ... 79,342
Ludwigshafen (★ ★ Mannheim) ... 158,478
Lüneburg ... 60,053
Lünen (★ Essen) ... 85,584
Magdeburg (★ 400,000) ... 290,579
Mainz (★ ★ Wiesbaden) ... 174,828
Mannheim (★ 1,400,000) ... 300,468
Marburg an der Lahn ... 70,905
Marl (★ Essen) ... 89,651

C Census. E Official estimate. U Unofficial estimate.
• Largest city in country.

★ Population or designation of metropolitan area, including suburbs (see headnote).
▲ Population of an entire municipality, commune, or district, including rural area.

Meerbusch (★ Düsseldorf) 50,452
Menden 54,899
Minden (★ 125,000) 75,169
Moers (★ Essen) 101,809
Mönchengladbach (★ 410,000) 252,910
Mülheim an der Ruhr (★ Essen) 175,454
München (Munich) (★ 1,955,000) 1,211,617
Münster 248,919
Neubrandenburg 90,471
Neumünster 79,574
Neunkirchen (★ 135,000) 50,784
Neuss (★ Düsseldorf) 143,976
Neustadt an der Weinstrasse...............50,453
Neuwied (★ 150,000) 60,665
Norderstedt (★ Hamburg) 66,747
Nürnberg (★ 1,030,000) 480,078
Oberhausen (★ ★ Essen)..............221,017
Offenbach (★ Frankfurt am Main)..............112,450
Offenburg 51,730
Oldenburg 140,785
Osnabrück (★ 270,000) 154,594
Paderborn 114,148
Passau 49,137
Pforzheim (★ 220,000) 108,887
Plauen 77,593
Potsdam (★ Berlin) 142,862
Ratingen (★ Düsseldorf) 89,880
Ravensburg (★ 75,000) 44,146
Recklinghausen (★ Essen) 121,666
Regensburg (★ 205,000) 119,078
Remscheid (★ ★ Wuppertal) 120,979
Reutlingen (★ 160,000) 100,400
Rheine 69,324
Rosenheim 54,304
Rostock 253,990
Rüsselsheim (★ ★ Wiesbaden)..........58,426
Saarbrücken (★ 385,000)..............188,467
Saarlouis (★ 115,000) 37,662
Salzgitter 111,674
Sankt Augustin (★ Bonn)..................50,230
Schwäbisch Gmünd 57,861
Schwedt 52,419
Schweinfurt (★ 110,000) 52,818
Schwerin 130,685
Schwerte (★ Essen) 49,017
Siegburg (★ 170,000).......34,402
Siegen (★ 200,000).........106,160
Sindelfingen (★ Stuttgart) 57,524
Solingen (★ ★ Wuppertal) 160,824
Stendal......................49,906
Stolberg (★ ★ Aachen) 56,182
Stralsund 75,498
Stuttgart (★ 1,925,000) 562,658
Suhl 56,345
Trier (★ 125,000) 95,692
Troisdorf (★ ★ Siegburg)............62,011
Tübingen 76,046
Ulm (★ 210,000)...........106,508
Unna (★ Essen) 61,989
Velbert (★ Essen) 88,058
Viersen (★ ★ Mönchengladbach)...76,163
Villingen-Schwenningen 76,258
Weimar 63,412
Wesel 57,986
Wetzlar (★ 105,000) 50,299
Wiesbaden (★ 795,000) 254,209
Wilhelmshaven (★ 135,000) 89,892
Wismar.......................58,058
Witten (★ Essen) 109,637
Wittenberg 53,358
Wolfenbüttel (★ ★ Braunschweig) 50,960
Wolfsburg 125,831
Worms (★ ★ Mannheim) 74,809
Wuppertal (★ 830,000) 371,283
Würzburg (★ 210,000) 125,589
Zweibrücken (★ 105,000)..............33,377
Zwickau (★ 165,000) 121,749

GHANA

1984 C 12,205,574

Cities and Towns

• ACCRA (★ 1,250,000) 859,640
Ashiaman (★ Accra) 49,427
Cape Coast 86,620
Koforidua 54,400
Kumasi (★ 600,000) 348,880
Obuasi 60,146
Sekondi-Takoradi (★ 175,352)...............93,882
Tafo (★ Kumasi)..............50,432
Tamale (★ 168,091) 136,828
Tema (★ ★ Accra) 99,608
Teshie (★ Accra) 62,954

GIBRALTAR

1988 E 30,077

Cities and Towns

• GIBRALTAR 30,077

GREECE / Ellás

1981 C...................9,740,417

Cities and Towns

Aiyáleo (★ Athínai)...........81,906
• ATHÍNAI (ATHENS) (★ 3,027,331) 885,737
Áyios Dhimítrios (★ Athínai) 51,421
Galátsion (★ Athínai).........50,096
Ilioúpolis (★ Athínai) 69,560
Iráklion (★ 110,958) 102,398
Kalamariá (★ Thessaloníki) 51,676
Kallithéa (★ Athínai).........117,319
Kavála 56,375
Keratsínion (★ Athínai) 74,179
Khalándrion (★ Athínai) 54,320
Khaniá (★ 61,976) 47,451
Khíos (★ 29,742) 24,070
Koridhallós (★ Athínai) 61,313
Lárisa 102,048
Néa Ionía (★ Athínai) 59,202
Néa Liósia (★ Athínai) 72,427
Néa Smírni (★ Athínai) 67,408
Níkaia (★ Athínai)............90,368
Palaión Fáliron (★ Athínai) 53,273
Pátrai (★ 154,596)..........142,163
Peristérion (★ Athínai) 140,858
Piraiévs (Piraeus) (★ ★ Athínai) 196,389
Spárti (Sparta) (★ 14,388) 12,975
Thessaloníki (Salonika) (★ 706,180) 406,413
Víron (★ Athínai).............57,880
Vólos (★ 107,407)...........71,378
Zográfos (★ Athínai).........84,548

GREENLAND / Grønland / Kalaallit Nunaat

1990 E 55,558

Cities and Towns

• GODTHÅB (NUUK) 12,217

GRENADA

1981 C 89,088

Cities and Towns

• SAINT GEORGE'S (★ 25,000) 4,788

GUADELOUPE

1982 C 328,400

Cities and Towns

BASSE-TERRE (★ 26,600) 13,656
Les Abymes (★ Pointe-à-Pitre)...................56,165
• Pointe-à-Pitre (★ 83,000) 25,310

GUAM

1980 C 105,979

Cities and Towns

• AGANA (★ 44,000) 896

GUATEMALA

1989 E...................8,935,395

Cities and Towns

Escuintla 60,673
• GUATEMALA (★ 1,400,000) 1,057,210
Quetzaltenango 88,769

GUERNSEY

1986 C.......................55,482

Cities and Towns

• SAINT PETER PORT (★ 36,000) 16,085

GUINEA / Guinée

1986 E....................6,225,000

Cities and Towns

• CONAKRY 800,000
Kankan......................100,000
Kindia 80,000
Labé 110,000
Nzérékoré (1983 C) 55,356

GUINEA-BISSAU / Guiné-Bissau

1988 E......................945,000

Cities and Towns

• BISSAU 125,000

GUYANA

1983 E......................918,000

Cities and Towns

• GEORGETOWN (★ 188,000) 78,500

HAITI / Haïti

1987 E...................5,531,802

Cities and Towns

Cap-Haïtien...................72,161
• PORT-AU-PRINCE (★ 880,000) 797,000

HONDURAS

1988 C...................4,376,839

Cities and Towns

Choluteca 53,799
El Progreso 55,523
La Ceiba 68,289
San Pedro Sula 279,356
• TEGUCIGALPA 551,606

HONG KONG

1986 C...................5,395,997

Cities and Towns

Kowloon (Jiulong) (★ ★ Victoria) 774,781
Kwai Chung (★ Victoria) 131,362
New Kowloon (Xinjiulong) (★ ★ Victoria) 1,526,910
Sha Tin (★ Victoria) 355,810
Sheung Shui 87,206
Tai Po.......................119,679
Tsuen Wan (Quanwan) (★ Victoria)...............514,241
Tuen Mun (★ Victoria) 262,458
• VICTORIA (★ 4,770,000) 1,175,860
Yuen Long 75,740

HUNGARY / Magyarország

1990 C................. 10,375,000

Cities and Towns

Békéscsaba (▲ 67,621) 58,800
• BUDAPEST (★ 2,565,000) 2,016,132
Debrecen...................212,247
Dunaújváros.................59,049
Eger 61,908
Győr 129,356
Kaposvár.....................71,793
Kecskemét (▲ 102,528) 81,200
Miskolc.....................196,449
Nagykanizsa 54,059
Nyíregyháza (▲ 114,166) 88,500
Pécs 170,119
Sopron 55,088
Szeged.....................175,338
Székesfehérvár.............108,990
Szolnok 78,333
Szombathely 85,418
Tatabánya....................74,271
Veszprém 63,902
Zalaegerszeg................62,221

ICELAND / Ísland

1987 E......................247,357

Cities and Towns

• REYKJAVÍK (★ 137,941)...............93,425

INDIA / Bharat

1981 C................685,184,692

Cities and Towns

Abohar 86,334
Achalpur 81,186
Ādilābād 53,482
Adītyapur (★ Jamshedpur)............53,421
Ādoni 108,939
Agartala....................132,186
Āgra (★ 747,318)...........694,191
Ahmadābād (★ 2,400,000) 2,059,725
Ahmadnagar (★ 181,210)...............143,937
Ajmer 375,593
Akola 225,412
Akot 51,936
Alandur (★ Madras)..........97,449
Alīgarh 320,861
Alijal 74,493
Allahābād (★ 650,070) 616,051
Alleppey....................169,940
Alwar 145,795
Amalner 67,516
Amarnāth (★ Bombay) 96,347
Ambāla (★ 233,110) 104,565
Ambāla Sadar (★ Ambāla)................80,741
Ambattur (★ Madras) 115,901
Āmbūr 66,042
Amrāvati 261,404
Amreli (★ 58,241) 56,598
Amritsar....................594,844
Amroha 112,682
Anakāpalle 73,179
Ānand........................83,936
Anantapur 119,531
Arcot (★ 94,363) 38,836
Arkonam 59,405
Arni 49,365
Arrah.......................125,111
Aruppukkottai 72,245
Asansol (★ 1,050,000) 183,375
Ashoknagar-Kalyangarh (★ Hābra) 55,176
Āttūr 50,517
Aurangābād (★ 316,421)..............284,607
Avadi (★ Madras)...........124,701
Azamgarh 66,523
Badagara 64,174
Bāgalkot 67,858
Baharampur (★ 102,311)...............92,889
Bahraich 99,889
Baidyabāti (★ Calcutta) 70,573
Bālāghāt (★ 53,183) 49,564
Balāngīr 54,943
Balasore 65,779
Ballālpur....................61,398
Ballia.......................61,704
Bālly (★ Calcutta)...........147,735
Bālly (★ Calcutta)...........54,859
Bālurghāt (★ 112,621) 104,646
Bānda.......................72,379
Bangalore (★ 2,950,000) 2,476,355
Bangaon 69,885
Bānkura 94,954
Bansberia (★ Calcutta) 77,020
Bāpatla......................55,347
Bārākpur (★ Calcutta) 115,253
Baranagar (★ Calcutta) 170,343
Bārāsat (★ Calcutta).........66,504
Bareilly (★ 449,425) 386,734
Barmer 55,554
Baroda (★ 744,881) 734,473
Bārsi 72,537
Bāruni......................56,366
Basīrhāt 81,040
Basti 69,357
Batala (★ 101,966) 87,135
Beāwar 89,998
Begusarai (★ 68,305).......56,633
Behāla (South Suburban) (★ Calcutta) 378,765
Bela........................49,932
Belgaum (★ 300,372).......274,430
Bellary 201,579
Berhampur 162,550
Bettiah 72,167
Bhadrakh 60,600
Bhadrāvati (★ 130,606) 53,551
Bhadrāvati New Town (★ ★ Bhadrāvati) 77,055
Bhadreswar (★ Calcutta) 58,858
Bhāgalpur 225,062
Bhandāra 56,025
Bharatpur 105,274
Bhathinda 124,453
Bhātpāra (★ Calcutta) 260,761
Bhaunagar (★ 308,642) 307,121
Bhilai (★ 490,214) 290,090
Bhīlwāra....................122,625
Bhīmavaram................101,894
Bhind 74,515
Bhiwandi (★ Bombay) 115,298
Bhiwāni 101,277
Bhopāl 671,018
Bhubaneswar 219,211
Bhuj (★ 70,211) 69,693
Bhusāwal (★ 132,142) 123,133
Bīdar 78,856
Bihār 151,343
Bijāpur 147,313
Bijnor 56,713
Bīkaner (★ 287,712)........253,174
Bilāspur (★ 187,104) 147,218
Bīr 80,287
Bodhan 50,807
Bodināyakkanūr 59,168
Bokāro Steel City (★ 264,480)..............224,099
Bombay (★ 9,950,000) ..8,243,405
Botād 50,274
Brajrajnagar 54,033
Broach (★ 120,524) 110,070
Budaun 93,004
Budge Budge (★ Calcutta) ....[illegible]
Bulandshahr...............103,436
Bulsār (★ Bombay) 54,017
Burdwān 167,364
Burhānpur.................140,896
• Calcutta (★ 11,100,000).........3,305,006
Calicut (★ 546,058).........394,447
Cambay 68,791
Cannanore (★ 157,797) 60,904
Chākdaha 59,308
Chakradharpur (★ 44,532)...............29,272
Chālisgaon 59,342
Champdāni (★ Calcutta) 76,138
Chandannagar (★ Calcutta) 101,925
Chandausi...................66,970
Chandīgarh (★ 422,841) 373,789
Chandrapur 115,777
Changanācheri 51,955
Channapatna 50,725
Chāpra 111,564
Chhatarpur..................51,959
Chhindwāra 75,178
Chidambaram (★ 62,543) 55,920
Chikmagalūr 60,582
Chilakalurupet 61,645
Chīrāla 72,040
Chitradurga 74,580
Chittaranjan (★ 61,045) 50,748
Chittoor 86,230
Churu (★ 62,070)............61,811
Cochin (★ 685,836).........513,249
Coimbatore (★ 965,000) 704,514
Cooch Behār (★ 80,101) 62,127
Coonoor (★ 92,242) 44,750
Cuddalore 127,625
Cuddapah 103,125
Cuttack (★ 327,412)........269,950
Dabgram 76,402
Dāhod (★ 82,256) 55,256
Dāltonganj 51,952
Damoh (★ 76,758)...........75,573
Dānāpur (★ Patna) 58,684
Darbhanga 176,301
Darjiling 57,603
Datia 49,386
Dāvangere 196,621
Dehra Dūn (★ 293,010) 211,416
Dehri 90,409
Delhi (★ 7,200,000).......4,884,234
Delhi Cantonment (★ Delhi) 85,166
Deoband 51,270
Deoghar (★ 59,120) 52,904
Deolāli (★ ★ Nāsik) 77,666
Deolāli Cantonment (★ Nāsik)...................57,745
Deoria.......................55,720
Dewās 83,465
Dhamtari 55,797
Dhānbād (★ 825,000).......120,221
Dharmapuri..................51,223
Dharmavaram 50,969
Dhorāji (★ 77,716)...........76,556
Dhrāngadhra 51,280
Dhule 210,759
Dibrugarh (1971 C)..........80,348
Dindigul 164,103
Dombivli (★ Bombay) 103,222
Durg (★ ★ Bhilai) 114,637
Durgāpur 311,798
Elūru 168,154
English Bāzār 79,010
Erode (★ 275,999)..........142,252
Etah 53,784
Etāwah.....................112,174
Faizābād (★ 143,167) 101,873
Farīdābād New Township (★ Delhi) 330,864
Farrukhābād (★ 160,796)...............145,793
Fatehpur, Rājasthān state.........................51,084
Fatehpur, Uttar Pradesh state 84,831
Fīrozābād 202,338
Fīrozpur (★ 105,840) 61,162
Gadag 117,368
Gāndhīdham (★ 61,489) 61,415
Gāndhinagar 62,443
Gangāwati 58,735
Garden Reach (★ Calcutta) 191,107
Gārulia (★ Calcutta) 57,061
Gauhāti (★ 200,377) (1971 C) 123,783
Gaya 247,075
Ghāziābād (★ 287,170) 271,730
Ghāzīpur 60,725
Giridih 65,444
Godhra (★ 86,228) 85,784
Gonda 70,847
Gondal (★ 66,818)............66,096
Gondia 100,423
Gorakhpur (★ 307,501) 290,814
Gudivāda 80,198
Gudiyāttam (★ 80,674) 75,044
Gulbarga 221,325
Guna (★ 64,659) 60,255
Guntakal 84,599
Guntūr 367,699
Gurgaon (★ 100,877).........89,115
Gwalior (★ 555,862).........539,015
Hābra (★ 129,610) 74,434
Hājīpur 62,520
Haldwāni 77,300
Hālisahar (★ Calcutta) 95,579
Hānsi 50,365
Hanumāngarh 60,071
Hāpur 102,837
Hardoi.......................67,259
Hardwār (★ 145,946) 114,180
Harihar 52,334
Hassan......................71,534
Hāthras 92,962
Hazāribāgh 80,155
Hindupur 55,901
Hinganghāt 59,075
Hisār (★ 137,369) 131,309
Hoshiārpur 85,648
Hospet (★ 115,351) 90,572
Howrah (★ Calcutta).........744,429
Hubli-Dhārwār 527,108
Hugli-Chinsurah (★ Calcutta)..............125,193
Hyderābād (★ 2,750,000) 2,187,262
Ichalkaranji 133,751
Imphāl......................156,622
Indore (★ 850,000) 829,327

C Census. E Official estimate. U Unofficial estimate.
• Largest city in country.
★ Population or designation of metropolitan area, including suburbs (see headnote).
▲ Population of an entire municipality, commune, or district, including rural area.

Itārsi (★ 69,619) 62,499
Jabalpur (★ 757,303) 614,162
Jabalpur Cantonment (★ Jabalpur) 61,026
Jādabpur (★ Calcutta) 251,968
Jagdalpur (★ 63,632) 51,286
Jagtiāl 53,213
Jaipur (★ 1,025,000) 977,165
Jālgaon 145,335
Jālna 122,276
Jalpaiguri 61,743
Jamālpur 78,356
Jammu (★ 223,361) 206,135
Jāmnagar (★ 317,362) 277,615
Jamshedpur (★ 669,580) 438,385
Jangoon 70,727
Jaridih (★ 101,946) 46,477
Jaunpur 105,140
Jetpur (★ 63,074) 62,806
Jeypore 53,981
Jhānsi (★ 284,141) 246,172
Jharia (★ ★ Dhānbād) 57,496
Jhārsuguda 54,859
Jīnd 56,748
Jodhpur 506,345
Jotacamund 78,277
Jullundur (★ 441,552) 408,186
Junāgadh (★ 120,416) 118,646
Kadaiyanallūr 60,306
Kadiri 52,774
Kaithal 58,385
Kākināda 226,409
Kālahasti 51,306
Kālol (★ Ahmadābād) 69,946
Kalyān (★ Bombay) 136,052
Kāmārhāti (★ Calcutta) 234,951
Kambam 50,340
Kāmthi (★ Nāgpur) 67,364
Kānchipuram (★ 145,254) 130,926
Kānchrāpāra (★ Calcutta) 88,798
Kānpur (★ 1,875,000) 1,481,789
Kānpur Cantonment (★ Kānpur) 90,311
Kapūrthala 50,300
Karād 54,364
Kāraikkudi (★ 100,141) 66,993
Karīmnagar 86,125
Karnāl 132,107
Karūr (★ 93,810) 72,692
Kāsganj 61,402
Kashīpur 51,773
Katihār (★ 122,005) 104,781
Kayankulam 61,327
Kerkend (★ Dhānbād) 75,186
Khadki Cantonment (★ Pune) 80,835
Khāmgaon 61,992
Khammam 98,757
Khandwa 114,725
Khanna 53,761
Kharagpur (★ 232,575) 150,475
Kharagpur Railway Settlement (★ Kharagpur) 82,100
Khargon 52,749
Khurja 67,119
Kishanganj 51,790
Kishangarh 62,032
Kolār 65,834
Kolār Gold Fields (★ 144,385) 77,679
Kolhāpur (★ 351,392) 340,625
Konnagar (★ Calcutta) 51,211
Korba 83,387
Kota 358,241
Kottagūdem 94,894
Kottayam 64,431
Kovilpatti 63,964
Krishnanagar 98,141
Kumbakonam (★ 141,794) 132,832
Kundla (★ 51,431) 49,740
Kurnool 206,362
Lakhīmpur 61,003
Lalitpur 55,756
Lātūr 111,986
Lucknow (★ 1,060,000) 895,721
Lucknow Cantonment (★ Lucknow) 59,614
Ludhiāna 607,052
Machilīpatnam (Bandar) 138,530
Madanapalle 54,938
Madgaon (Margao) (★ 64,858) 53,076
Madras (★ 4,475,000) 3,276,622
Madurai (★ 960,000) 820,891
Mahbūbnagar 87,503
Mahuva (★ 56,072) 53,625
Mainpuri 58,928
Mālegaon 245,883
Māler Kotla 65,756
Malkajgiri (★ Hyderābād) 65,776
Mandasor 77,603
Mandya 100,285
Mangalore (★ 306,078) 172,252
Mango (★ Jamshedpur) 67,284
Manjeri 53,959
Manmād 51,439
Mannārgudi 51,738
Mathura (★ 160,995) 147,493
Maunath Bhanjan 86,326
Māyūram 67,675
Meerut (★ 536,615) 417,395
Meerut Cantonment (★ Meerut) 94,210
Mehsāna (★ 73,024) 72,872
Melappālaiyam (★ Tirunelveli) 57,683
Mettuppālaiyam 59,537
Mhow (★ 76,037) 70,130
Midnapore 86,118
Miraj (★ ★ Sāngli) 105,455
Mirzāpur 127,787
Modinagar (★ 87,665) 78,243
Moga 80,272
Mokāma 51,047
Monghyr 129,260
Morādābād (★ 345,350) 330,051
Morena 69,864
Mormugao 69,684
Morvi 73,327
Motihāri (★ 63,212) 57,911
Muktsar 50,941
Murwāra (★ 123,017) 77,862
Muzaffarnagar 171,816
Muzaffarpur 190,416
Mysore (★ 479,081) 441,754
Nabadwip (★ 129,800) 109,108
Nadiād 142,689
Nāgappattinam (★ 90,650) 82,828
Nāgda 56,602
Nāgercoil 171,648
Nagīna 50,405
Nāgpur (★ 1,302,066) 1,219,461
Naihāti (★ Calcutta) 114,607
Najībābād 55,109
Nalgonda 62,458
Nānded 191,269
Nandurbār 65,394
Nandyāl 88,185
Nangi (★ Calcutta) 54,035
Narasaraopet 67,032
Nāsik (★ 429,034) 262,428
Navsāri (★ 129,266) 106,793
Nawābganj (★ 62,216) 51,518
Neemuch (★ 68,853) 65,860
Nellore 237,065
NEW DELHI (★ ★ Delhi) 273,036
Neyveli (★ 98,866) 88,000
Nizāmābād 183,061
North Bārākpur (★ Calcutta) 81,758
North Dum Dum (★ Calcutta) 96,418
Nowgong (1971 C) 56,537
Ongole 85,302
Orai 66,397
Outer Burnpur (★ Asansol) 86,803
Pālanpur 61,262
Pālayankottai (★ ★ Tirunelveli) 87,302
Pālghāt (★ 117,986) 111,245
Pāli 91,568
Pallavaram (★ Madras) 83,901
Palni (★ 68,389) 64,444
Pānchur (★ Calcutta) 51,223
Pandharpur 64,380
Pānihāti (★ Calcutta) 205,718
Pānīpat 137,927
Paramagudi 61,149
Parbhani 109,364
Pātan 79,196
Pathānkot 110,039
Patiāla (★ 206,254) 205,141
Patna (★ 1,025,000) 776,371
Pattukkottai 49,484
Phagwāra (★ 75,961) 72,499
Pīlibhīt 88,548
Pimpri-Chinchwad (★ Pune) 220,966
Pollāchi (★ 114,971) 82,354
Pondicherry (★ 251,420) 162,636
Ponmalai (★ Tiruchchirāppalli) 55,995
Ponnūru Nidubrolu 50,206
Porbandar (★ 133,307) 115,182
Port Blair 49,634
Proddatūr 107,070
Pudukkottai 87,952
Pune (Poona) (★ 1,775,000) 1,203,351
Pune Cantonment (★ Pune) 85,986
Puri 100,942
Purnea (★ 109,875) 91,144
Purūlia 73,904
Quilon (★ 167,598) 137,943
Rabkavi Banhatti 51,693
Rāe Bareli 89,697
Rāichūr 124,762
Raiganj (★ 66,705) 60,343
Raigarh (★ 69,791) 68,060
Raipur 338,245
Rājahmundry (★ 268,370) 203,358
Rājapālaiyam 101,640
Rajhara-Jharandalli 55,307
Rājkot 445,076
Rāj-Nāndgaon 86,367
Rājpura 58,645
Rāmpur 204,610
Rānāghāt (★ 83,744) 58,356
Rānchī (★ 502,771) 489,626
Rānībennur 58,118
Rānīganj (★ 119,101) 48,702
Ratlām (★ 155,578) 142,319
Raurkela (★ 322,610) 206,821
Raurkela Civil Township (★ Raurkela) 96,000
Rewa 100,641
Rewāri 51,562
Rishra (★ Calcutta) 81,001
Robertson Pet (★ Kolār Gold Fields) 61,099
Rohtak 166,767
Roorkee (★ 79,076) 61,851
Sāgar (★ 207,479) 160,392
Sahāranpur 295,355
Saharsa 57,580
Sahijpur Bogha (★ Ahmadābād) 65,327
Salem (★ 518,615) 361,394
Sambalpur (★ 162,214) 110,282
Sambhal 108,232
Sāngli (★ 268,988) 152,339
Sāntipur 82,980
Sardarnagar (★ Ahmadābād) 50,128
Sardārshahr (★ 56,388) 55,473
Sasarām 73,457
Sātāra 83,336
Satna (★ 96,667) 90,476
Saunda (★ 99,990) 70,780
Secunderābād Cantonment (★ Hyderābād) 135,994
Sehore 52,190
Seoni 54,017
Serampore (★ Calcutta) 127,304
Shāhjahānpur (★ 205,095) 185,396
Shāmli 51,850
Shillong (★ 174,703) 109,244
Shimoga 151,783
Shivpuri 75,738
Sholāpur (★ 514,860) 511,103
Shrirampur 55,491
Sidhpur (★ 52,706) 51,953
Sīkar 102,970
Silchar (1971 C) 52,596
Silīguri 154,378
Simla 70,604
Sindri (★ ★ Dhānbād) 70,645
Sirsa 89,068
Sītāpur 101,210
Sivakāsi (★ 83,072) 59,827
Siwān 51,284
Sonīpat 109,369
South Dum Dum (★ Calcutta) 230,266
Sri Gangānagar 123,692
Srīkākulam 68,145
Srīnagar (★ 606,002) 594,775
Srīrangam (★ Tiruchchirāppalli) 64,241
Srīvilliputtūr 61,458
Sujāngarh 55,546
Surat (★ 913,806) 776,583
Surendranagar (★ 130,602) 89,619
Tādepallegūdem 62,574
Tādpatri 53,920
Tāmbaram (★ Madras) 86,923
Tānda 54,474
Tanuku 53,618
Tellicherry (★ 98,704) 75,561
Tenāli 119,257
Tenkāsi 49,214
Thāna (★ Bombay) 309,897
Thānesar 49,052
Thanjāvūr 184,015
Theni-Allinagaram 53,018
Tindivanam 56,520
Tinsukia (1971 C) 54,911
Tiruchchirāppalli (★ 609,548) 362,045
Tiruchengodu 53,941
Tirunelveli (★ 323,344) 128,850
Tirupati 115,292
Tiruppattūr 52,422
Tiruppur (★ 215,859) 165,223
Tiruvannāmalai 89,462
Tiruvottiyūr (★ Madras) 134,014
Titāgarh (★ Calcutta) 104,534
Tonk 77,653
Trichūr (★ 170,122) 77,923
Trivandrum (★ 520,125) 483,086
Tumkūr 108,670
Tuticorin (★ 250,677) 192,949
Udaipur 232,588
Udamalpet 54,852
Udgīr 50,564
Ujjain (★ 282,203) 278,454
Ulhāsnagar (★ Bombay) 273,668
Unnāo 75,983
Upleta 54,907
Uttarpara-Kotrung (★ Calcutta) 79,598
Valparai 115,452
Vāniyambādi (★ 75,042) 59,107
Vārānasi (Benares) (★ 925,000) 708,647
Vellore (★ 274,041) 174,247
Verāval (★ 105,307) 85,048
Vidisha 65,521
Vijayawāda (★ 543,008) 454,577
Vikramasingapuram 49,319
Villupuram 77,091
Virudunagar 68,047
Vishākhapatnam (★ 603,630) 565,321
Vizianagaram 114,806
Warangal 335,150
Wardha 88,495
Yamunānagar (★ 160,424) 109,304
Yavatmāl 89,071
Yemmiganur 50,701

INDONESIA

1980 C 147,490,298

Cities and Towns

Ambon (▲ 207,702) 111,914
Balikpapan (▲ 279,852) 208,040
Banda Aceh (Kuturaja) 71,868
Bandung (★ 1,800,000) (1985 C) 1,633,000
Banjarmasin (1983 E) 424,000
Banyuwangi 90,378
Batang 49,328
Bekasi (★ Jakarta) 144,290
Binjai 71,444
Blitar (★ 100,000) 78,503
Bogor (★ 560,000) 246,946
Bojonegoro 57,483
Bukittinggi (▲ 70,691) 55,577
Cianjur 105,655
Cibinong 87,580
Cilacap 127,017
Cimahi (★ Bandung) (1971 C) 72,367
Ciparay 66,854
Cirebon (★ 275,000) 223,504
Denpasar 159,233
Depok (★ Jakarta) 126,693
Garut 145,624
Genteng 59,481
Gorontalo (▲ 97,610) 63,554
Gresik 86,418
• JAKARTA (★ 1,000,000) (1989 E) 9,200,000
Jambi (▲ 230,046) 155,761
Jayapura (Sukarnapura) 60,641
Jember 171,284
Jombang 58,800
Karawang 72,195
Kediri (▲ 221,830) 176,261
Kisaran 58,129
Klangenang 64,013
Klaten 117,560
Kudus 154,478
Kupang 84,587
Lumajang 58,495
Madiun (★ 180,000) 150,562
Magelang (★ 160,000) 123,358
Majalaya 87,474
Malang (1983 E) 547,000
Manado 217,091
Mataram 210,485
Medan (1985 E) 2,110,000
Mojokerto 68,849
Padang (▲ 657,000) (1983 E) 405,600
Padangsidempuan 56,984
Palangkaraya (▲ 60,447) 51,686
Palembang (1983 E) 874,000
Pangkalpinang 90,078
Parepare (▲ 86,360) 62,865
Pasuruan (★ 125,000) 95,864
Pati 50,159
Pekalongan (★ 260,000) 132,413
Pekanbaru 186,199
Pemalang 72,663
Pematangsiantar (★ 175,000) 150,296
Ponorogo 55,523
Pontianak (1983 E) 343,000
Pringsewu 56,115
Probolinggo 100,296
Purwakarta 61,995
Purwokerto 143,787
Salatiga 85,740
Samarinda (▲ 264,012) 182,473
Semarang (1983 E) 1,206,000
Serang 78,209
Sibolga 59,466
Sidoarjo 56,090
Singaraja 53,368
Singkawang 58,693
Situbondo 58,299
Sorong 52,041
Subang 52,041
Sukabumi (★ 225,000) 109,898
Surabaya (1985 E) 2,345,000
Surakarta (★ 575,000) (1983 E) 491,000
Taman 64,358
Tangerang 97,091
Tanjungkarang-Telukbetung (★ 375,000) 284,167
Tasikmalaya 192,267
Tebingtinggi (▲ 92,068) 69,596
Tegal (★ 340,000) 131,440
Tembilahan 52,140
Tulungagung 91,585
Ujungpandang (Makasar) (1983 E) 841,000
Yogyakarta (★ 510,000) (1983 E) 421,000

IRAN / Īrān

1986 C 49,445,010

Cities and Towns

Ābādān (1976 C) 296,081
Āghā Jārī (1982 E) 64,000
Ahar (1982 E) 52,000
Ahvāz 579,826
Āmol 118,242
Andīmeshk (1982 E) 53,000
Arāk 265,349
Ardabīl 281,973
Bābol 115,320
Bakhtarān (Kermānshāh) 560,514
Bandar-e 'Abbās 201,642
Bandar-e Anzalī (Bandar-e Pahlavī) (1982 E) 83,000
Bandar-e Būshehr 120,787
Bandar-e Māh Shahr (1982 E) 88,000
Behbahān (1982 E) 84,000
Bīrjand (1982 E) 68,000
Bojnūrd (1982 E) 82,000
Borāzjān (1982 E) 53,000
Borūjerd 183,879
Dezfūl 151,420
Do Rūd (1982 E) 52,000
Emāmshahr (Shāhrūd) (1982 E) 68,000
Eşfahān (★ 1,175,000) 986,753
Eslāmābād (1982 E) 71,000
Eslāmshahr (★ Tehrān) 215,129
Fasā (1982 E) 67,000
Gonbad-e Qābūs (1982 E) 75,000
Gorgān 139,430
Hamadān 272,499
Īlām (1982 E) 75,000
Jahrom (1982 E) 68,000
Karaj (★ Tehrān) 275,100
Kāshān 138,599
Kāzerūn (1982 E) 63,000
Kermān 257,284
Khomeynīshahr (★ Eşfahān) 104,647
Khorramābād 208,592
Khorramshahr (1976 C) 146,709
Khvoy 115,343
Mahābād (1982 E) 63,000
Malāyer 103,640
Marāgheh 100,679
Marand (1982 E) 59,000
Marv Dasht (1982 E) 72,000
Mashhad 1,463,508
Masjed Soleymān 104,787
Mīāndoāb (1982 E) 52,000
Mīāneh (1982 E) 57,000
Najafābād 129,058
Neyshābūr 109,258
Orūmīyeh (Reẓā'īyeh) 300,746
Qā'emshahr 109,288
Qazvīn 248,591
Qom 543,139
Qomsheh (1982 E) 67,000
Qūchān (1982 E) 61,000
Rafsanjān (1982 E) 61,000
Rāmhormoz (1982 E) 53,000
Rasht 290,897
Sabzevār 129,103
Sanandaj 204,537
Saqqez (1982 E) 76,000
Sārī 141,020
Semnān (1982 E) 54,000
Shahr-e Kord (1982 E) 63,000
Shīrāz 848,289
Sīrjān (1982 E) 67,000
Tabrīz 971,482
• TEHRĀN (★ 7,500,000) 6,042,584
Torbat-e Heydarīyeh (1982 E) 62,000
Varāmīn (1982 E) 51,000
Yazd 230,483
Zābol (1982 E) 58,000
Zāhedān 281,923
Zanjān 215,261
Zarrīn Shahr (1982 E) 69,000

IRAQ / Al 'Irāq

1985 E 15,584,987

Cities and Towns

Ad-Dīwānīyah (1970 E) 62,300
Al-'Amārah 131,758
Al-Başrah 616,700
Al-Hillah 215,249
Al-Kūt 73,022
Al-Mawşil 570,926
An-Najaf 242,603
An-Nāşirīyah 138,842
Ar-Ramādī 137,388
As-Samāwah 75,293
As-Sulaymānīyah 279,424
• BAGHDĀD (1987 C) 3,841,268
Ba'qūbah 114,516
Irbīl 333,903
Karbalā' 184,574
Kirkūk (1970 E) 207,900

IRELAND / Éire

1986 C 3,540,643

Cities and Towns

Cork (★ 173,694) 133,271
• DUBLIN (BAILE ÁTHA CLIATH) (★ 1,140,000) 502,749
Dún Laoghaire (★ Dublin) 54,715
Galway 47,104
Limerick (★ 76,557) 56,279
Waterford (★ 41,054) 39,529

ISLE OF MAN

1986 C 64,282

Cities and Towns

• DOUGLAS (★ 28,500) 20,368

C Census. E Official estimate.
• Largest city in country.
U Unofficial estimate.
★ Population or designation of metropolitan area, including suburbs (see headnote).
▲ Population of an entire municipality, commune, or district, including rural area.

ISRAEL / Isrā'īl / Yisra'el

1989 E	4,386,000

Cities and Towns

City	Population
Al-Khalīl (Hebron) (1971 E)	43,000
Ashdod	74,700
Ashqelon	56,300
Bat Yam (★ Tel Aviv-Yafo)	133,100
Bayt Lahm (Bethlehem) (1971 E)	25,000
Be'ér Sheva (Beersheba)	113,200
Bene Beraq (★ Tel Aviv-Yafo)	109,400
Elat	24,700
Giv'atayim (★ Tel Aviv-Yafo)	45,600
Hefa (★ 435,000)	222,600
Herzliyya (★ Tel Aviv-Yafo)	71,600
Holon (★ Tel Aviv-Yafo)	146,100
Kefar Sava (★ Tel Aviv-Yafo)	54,800
Lod (Lydda) (★ Tel Aviv-Yafo)	41,300
Nābulus (1971 E)	64,000
Nazerat (Nazareth) (★ 77,000)	50,600
Netanya (★ Tel Aviv-Yafo)	117,800
Petah Tiqwa (★ Tel Aviv-Yafo)	133,600
Ra'ananna (★ Tel Aviv-Yafo)	49,400
Ramat Gan (★ Tel Aviv-Yafo)	115,700
Rehovot (★ Tel Aviv-Yafo)	72,500
Rishon leZiyyon (★ Tel Aviv-Yafo)	123,800
• Tel Aviv-Yafo (★ 1,735,000)	317,800
YERUSHALAYIM (AL-QUDS) (JERUSALEM) (★ 530,000)	493,500

ITALY / Italia

1987 E	57,290,519

Cities and Towns

City	Population
Afragola (★ Napoli)	59,397
Alessandria (▲ 96,014)	76,100
Altamura	54,784
Ancona	104,409
Andria	88,348
Arezzo (▲ 91,681)	74,200
Asti (▲ 75,459)	63,600
Avellino	56,407
Aversa (★ Napoli)	57,827
Bari (★ 475,000)	362,524
Barletta	86,954
Benevento (▲ 65,661)	54,400
Bergamo (★ 345,000)	118,959
Biella	51,788
Bitonto	51,962
Bologna (★ 525,000)	432,406
Bolzano	101,515
Brescia	199,286
Brindisi	92,280
Busto Arsizio (★ Milano)	78,056
Cagliari (★ 305,000)	220,574
Caltanissetta	62,352
Carpi (▲ 60,614)	49,500
Carrara (★ ★ Massa)	69,229
Caserta	65,974
Casoria (★ Napoli)	54,100
Castellammare [di Stabia] (★ Napoli)	68,491
Catania (★ 550,000)	372,486
Catanzaro	102,558
Cava de'Tirreni (★ Salerno)	52,028
Cerignola	53,463
Cesena (▲ 90,012)	72,600
Chieti	55,827
Cinisello Balsamo (★ Milano)	78,917
Civitavecchia	50,806
Collegno (★ Torino)	49,334
Cologno Monzese (★ Milano)	52,554
Como (★ 165,000)	91,738
Cosenza (★ 150,000)	106,026
Cremona	76,070
Crotone (▲ 61,005)	53,600
Ercolano (★ Napoli)	62,783
Ferrara (▲ 143,950)	113,300
Firenze (★ 640,000)	425,835
Foggia	155,051
Forlì (▲ 110,482)	91,200
Gela	79,378
Genova (Genoa) (★ 805,000)	727,427
Giugliano in Campania (★ Napoli)	51,187
Grosseto (▲ 70,592)	56,400
La Spezia (★ 185,000)	108,937
Latina (▲ 98,479)	67,800
Lecce	100,981
Livorno	174,065
Lucca	88,024
Manfredonia	57,707
Mantova (▲ 56,817)	49,000
Marsala	80,468
Massa (★ 145,000)	66,872
Matera	52,819
Messina	268,896
Mestre (★ Venezia)	189,700
• Milano (Milan) (★ 3,750,000)	1,495,260
Modena	176,880
Molfetta	64,519
Moncalieri (★ Torino)	62,306
Monza (★ Milano)	122,064
Napoli (Naples) (★ 2,875,000)	1,204,211
Nicastro (▲ 67,562)	52,100
Novara	102,742
Padova (★ 270,000)	225,769
Palermo	723,732
Parma	175,842
Pavia	82,065
Perugia (▲ 146,713)	106,700
Pesaro (▲ 90,336)	78,700
Pescara	131,027
Piacenza	105,626
Pisa	104,384
Pistoia (▲ 90,689)	76,800
Pordenone	50,825
Portici (★ Napoli)	76,302
Potenza (▲ 67,114)	57,600
Pozzuoli (★ Napoli)	65,000
Prato (★ 215,000)	164,595
Quartu Sant'Elena	52,838
Ragusa	67,748
Ravenna (▲ 136,016)	86,500
Reggio di Calabria	178,821
Reggio nell'Emilia (▲ 130,086)	107,300
Rho (★ Milano)	50,876
Rimini (▲ 130,698)	114,600
Rivoli (★ Torino)	50,786
ROMA (ROME) (★ 3,175,000)	2,815,457
Salerno (★ 250,000)	154,848
San Giorgio a Cremano (★ Napoli)	63,656
San Remo	60,797
San Severo	55,239
Sassari	120,152
Savona (★ 112,000)	62,300
Scandicci (★ Firenze)	54,367
Sesto San Giovanni (★ Milano)	91,624
Siena	59,712
Siracusa	122,857
Taranto	244,997
Terni (▲ 111,157)	94,500
Torino (★ 1,550,000)	1,035,565
Torre Annunziata (★ Napoli)	57,508
Torre del Greco (★ Napoli)	105,066
Trapani (▲ 73,083)	63,000
Trento (▲ 100,202)	81,500
Treviso	85,083
Trieste (Triest)	239,031
Udine (★ 126,000)	100,211
Varese	88,353
Venezia (Venice) (★ 420,000)	88,700
Vercelli	51,008
Verona	259,151
Viareggio (▲ 59,146)	50,300
Vicenza	110,449
Vigevano	62,671
Vittoria	54,795

JAMAICA

1982 C	2,190,357

Cities and Towns

City	Population
• KINGSTON (★ 770,000) (1987 E)	646,400
Montego Bay	70,265
Portmore (★ Kingston)	73,426
Spanish Town (★ Kingston)	89,097

JAPAN / Nihon

1985 C	121,048,923

Cities and Towns

City	Population
Abiko (★ Tōkyō)	111,659
Ageo (★ Tōkyō)	170,507
Aizu-wakamatsu	118,140
Akashi (★ Ōsaka)	263,363
Akishima (★ Tōkyō)	97,543
Akita	296,400
Aioi	52,074
Amagasaki (★ Ōsaka)	509,115
Anjō	133,059
Aomori	294,045
Arao (★ Ōmuta)	62,570
Asahikawa	363,631
Asaka (★ Tōkyō)	94,431
Ashikaga	167,656
Ashiya (★ Ōsaka)	87,127
Atami	49,374
Atsugi (★ Tōkyō)	175,600
Ayase (★ Tōkyō)	71,152
Beppu	134,775
Bisai (★ Nagoya)	56,234
Chiba (★ Tōkyō)	788,930
Chichibu	61,013
Chigasaki (★ Tōkyō)	185,030
Chikushino (★ Fukuoka)	63,242
Chiryū (★ Nagoya)	50,506
Chita (★ Nagoya)	70,013
Chitose	73,610
Chōfu (★ Tōkyō)	191,071
Chōshi	87,883
Daitō (★ Ōsaka)	122,441
Dazaifu (★ Fukuoka)	57,737
Ebetsu (★ Sapporo)	90,328
Ebina (★ Tōkyō)	93,159
Fuchū (★ Tōkyō)	201,972
Fuji (★ 370,000)	214,448
Fujieda (★ Shizuoka)	111,985
Fujiidera (★ Ōsaka)	65,252
Fujimi (★ Tōkyō)	85,697
Fujinomiya (★ ★ Fuji)	112,642
Fujisawa (★ Tōkyō)	328,387
Fuji-yoshida	54,796
Fukaya (▲ 89,121)	71,600
Fukuchiyama (▲ 65,995)	56,200
Fukui	250,261
Fukuoka (★ 1,750,000)	1,160,440
Fukushima	270,762
Fukuyama	360,261
Funabashi (★ Tōkyō)	506,966
Fussa (★ Tōkyō)	51,478
Gamagōri	85,580
Gifu	411,743
Ginowan	69,206
Gotemba	74,882
Gushikawa	51,351
Gyōda	79,359
Habikino (★ Ōsaka)	111,394
Hachinohe	241,430
Hachiōji (★ Tōkyō)	426,654
Hadano (★ Tōkyō)	141,803
Hagi	52,740
Hakodate	319,194
Hamada	51,071
Hamakita	77,228
Hamamatsu	514,118
Hanamaki (▲ 69,886)	54,500
Handa (★ Nagoya)	92,883
Hannō (★ Tōkyō)	66,550
Hashima	59,760
Hasuda (★ Tōkyō)	53,991
Hatogaya (★ Tōkyō)	55,424
Hatsukaichi (★ Hiroshima)	52,020
Hekinan	63,778
Higashihiroshima (★ Hiroshima)	84,717
Higashikurume (★ Tōkyō)	110,079
Higashimatsuyama	70,426
Higashimurayama (★ Tōkyō)	123,798
Higashiōsaka (★ Ōsaka)	522,805
Higashiyamato (★ Tōkyō)	69,881
Hikari (★ Tokuyama)	49,246
Hikone	94,204
Himeji (★ 660,000)	452,917
Himi (▲ 62,112)	52,300
Hino (★ Tōkyō)	156,031
Hirakata (★ Ōsaka)	382,257
Hiratsuka (★ Tōkyō)	229,990
Hirosaki (▲ 176,082)	134,800
Hiroshima (★ 1,575,000)	1,044,118
Hita (▲ 65,730)	57,900
Hitachi	206,074
Hōfu	118,067
Honjō	56,495
Hōya (★ Tōkyō)	91,568
Hyūga	59,163
Ibaraki (★ Ōsaka)	250,463
Ichihara (★ Tōkyō)	237,617
Ichikawa (★ Tōkyō)	397,822
Ichinomiya (★ ★ Nagoya)	257,388
Ichinoseki (▲ 60,941)	49,200
Iida (▲ 92,401)	65,000
Iizuka (★ 110,000)	81,868
Ikeda (★ Ōsaka)	101,683
Ikoma (★ Ōsaka)	86,293
Imabari	125,115
Imari (▲ 62,044)	50,700
Inagi (★ Tōkyō)	50,766
Inazawa (★ Nagoya)	94,479
Inuyama (★ Nagoya)	68,723
Iruma (★ Tōkyō)	118,603
Isahaya	88,376
Ise (Uji-yamada)	105,455
Isesaki	112,459
Ishinomaki	122,674
Itami (★ Ōsaka)	182,731
Itō	70,197
Iwaki (Taira)	350,569
Iwakuni	111,833
Iwamizawa	81,664
Iwata	80,810
Iwatsuki (★ Tōkyō)	100,903
Izumi (★ Ōsaka)	137,641
Izumi (★ Sendai)	124,216
Izumi-ōtsu (★ Ōsaka)	67,755
Izumi-sano (★ Ōsaka)	91,563
Izumo (▲ 80,749)	68,000
Jōyō (★ Ōsaka)	81,850
Kadoma (★ Ōsaka)	140,590
Kaga	68,630
Kagoshima	530,502
Kainan (★ Wakayama)	50,779
Kaizuka (★ Ōsaka)	79,591
Kakamigahara	124,464
Kakegawa (▲ 68,724)	55,600
Kakogawa (★ Ōsaka)	227,311
Kamagaya (★ Tōkyō)	85,705
Kamaishi	60,007
Kamakura (★ Tōkyō)	175,495
Kameoka	76,207
Kamifukuoka (★ Tōkyō)	57,638
Kanazawa	430,481
Kani (★ Nagoya)	69,630
Kanoya (▲ 76,029)	60,200
Kanuma (▲ 88,078)	73,200
Karatsu (▲ 78,744)	70,100
Kariya (★ Nagoya)	112,403
Kasai	52,107
Kasaoka (▲ 60,598)	53,500
Kashihara (★ Ōsaka)	112,888
Kashiwa (★ Tōkyō)	273,128
Kashiwara (★ Ōsaka)	73,252
Kashiwazaki (▲ 86,020)	73,350
Kasuga (★ Fukuoka)	75,555
Kasugai (★ Nagoya)	256,990
Kasukabe (★ Tōkyō)	171,890
Katano (★ Ōsaka)	64,205
Katsuta	102,763
Kawachi-nagano (★ Ōsaka)	91,313
Kawagoe (★ Tōkyō)	285,437
Kawaguchi (★ Tōkyō)	403,015
Kawanishi (★ Ōsaka)	136,376
Kawasaki (★ Tōkyō)	1,088,624
Kesennuma	68,137
Kimitsu (▲ 84,310)	71,900
Kiryū	131,267
Kisarazu	120,201
Kishiwada (★ Ōsaka)	185,731
Kitaibaraki	51,035
Kitakyūshū (★ 1,525,000)	1,056,402
Kitami	107,281
Kitamoto (★ Tōkyō)	58,114
Kiyose (★ Tōkyō)	65,066
Kōbe (★ ★ Ōsaka)	1,410,834
Kōchi	312,241
Kodaira (★ Tōkyō)	158,673
Kōfu	202,405
Koga (★ Tōkyō)	57,541
Koganei (★ Tōkyō)	104,642
Kokubunji (★ Tōkyō)	95,467
Komae (★ Tōkyō)	73,784
Komaki (★ Nagoya)	113,284
Komatsu	106,041
Kōnan (★ Nagoya)	92,049
Kōnosu (★ Tōkyō)	60,565
Kōriyama	301,673
Koshigaya (★ Tōkyō)	253,479
Kudamatsu (★ ★ Tokuyama)	54,445
Kuki (★ Tōkyō)	58,636
Kumagaya	143,496
Kumamoto	555,719
Kunitachi (★ Tōkyō)	64,881
Kurashiki	413,632
Kure (★ ★ Hiroshima)	226,488
Kurume	222,847
Kusatsu (★ Ōsaka)	87,542
Kushiro	214,541
Kuwana (★ Nagoya)	94,731
Kyōto (★ ★ Ōsaka)	1,479,218
Machida (★ Tōkyō)	321,188
Maebashi	277,319
Maizuru	98,775
Marugame	74,272
Matsubara (★ Ōsaka)	136,455
Matsudo (★ Tōkyō)	427,473
Matsue	140,005
Matsumoto	197,340
Matsusaka	116,886
Matsuyama	426,658
Mihara	85,975
Miki (★ Ōsaka)	74,527
Minō (★ Ōsaka)	114,770
Misato (★ Tōkyō)	107,964
Mishima (★ ★ Numazu)	99,600
Mitaka (★ Tōkyō)	166,252
Mito	228,985
Miura (★ Tōkyō)	50,471
Miyako	61,654
Miyakonojō (▲ 132,098)	107,600
Miyazaki	279,114
Mobara	76,929
Moriguchi (★ Ōsaka)	159,400
Morioka	235,469
Moriyama	53,052
Mukō (★ Ōsaka)	52,216
Munakata	60,971
Muroran (★ 195,000)	136,208
Musashimurayama (★ Tōkyō)	60,930
Musashino (★ Tōkyō)	138,783
Mutsu	49,292
Nabari	56,474
Nagahama	55,631
Nagano	336,973
Nagaoka	183,756
Nagaokakyō (★ Ōsaka)	75,242
Nagareyama (★ Tōkyō)	124,682
Nagasaki	449,382
Nagoya (★ 4,800,000)	2,116,381
Naha	303,674
Nakama (★ Kitakyūshū)	50,294
Nakatsu	66,260
Nakatsugawa	53,277
Nanao	50,582
Nara (★ Ōsaka)	327,702
Narashino (★ Tōkyō)	136,365
Narita	77,181
Naruto	64,329
Naze	49,765
Neyagawa (★ Ōsaka)	258,228
Niigata	475,630
Niihama	132,184
Niitsu (▲ 63,846)	55,600
Niiza (★ Tōkyō)	129,287
Nishinomiya (★ Ōsaka)	421,267
Nishio	91,930
Nobeoka	136,381
Noboribetsu (★ Muroran)	58,370
Noda (★ Tōkyō)	105,937
Nōgata	64,479
Noshiro (▲ 59,170)	50,400
Numazu (★ 495,000)	210,490
Obihiro	162,932
Ōbu (★ Nagoya)	66,606
Ōdate (▲ 71,794)	60,900
Odawara	185,941
Ōgaki	145,910
Ōita	390,096
Okaya	61,747
Okayama	572,479
Okazaki	284,996
Okegawa (★ Tōkyō)	61,499
Okinawa	101,210
Ōme (★ Tōkyō)	110,828
Ōmi-hachiman (★ Ōsaka)	63,791
Ōmiya (★ Tōkyō)	373,022
Ōmura	69,472
Ōmuta (★ 225,000)	159,424
Ōnojō (★ Fukuoka)	69,435
Onomichi	100,640
Ōsaka (★ 16,450,000)	2,636,249
Ōta	133,670
Otaru (★ ★ Sapporo)	172,486
Ōtsu (★ Ōsaka)	234,551
Owariashi (★ Nagoya)	57,415
Oyama (▲ 134,242)	113,100
Sabae	61,452
Saeki	54,706
Saga	168,252
Sagamihara (★ Tōkyō)	482,778
Saijō	56,516
Sakado (★ Tōkyō)	87,586
Sakai (★ Ōsaka)	818,271
Sakaide	66,087
Sakata	101,392
Sakura (★ Tōkyō)	121,213
Sakurai	58,894
Sanjō	86,325
Sano	80,753
Sapporo (★ 1,900,000)	1,542,979
Sasebo	250,633
Satte	51,462
Sayama (★ Tōkyō)	144,366
Sayama (★ Ōsaka)	50,246
Seki	64,149
Sendai, Kagoshima pref. (▲ 71,444)	57,800
Sendai, Miyagi pref. (★ 1,175,000)	700,254
Sennan (★ Ōsaka)	60,059
Seto	124,623
Settsu (★ Ōsaka)	86,332
Shibata (▲ 77,219)	62,800
Shijōnawate (★ Ōsaka)	50,352
Shiki (★ Tōkyō)	58,935
Shimada (▲ 72,388)	63,200
Shimizu (★ ★ Shizuoka)	242,166
Shimodate (▲ 63,958)	52,400
Shimonoseki (★ ★ Kitakyūshū)	269,169
Shiogama (★ Sendai)	61,825
Shizuoka (★ 975,000)	468,362
Sōka (★ Tōkyō)	194,205
Suita (★ Ōsaka)	348,948
Suwa	52,329
Suzuka	164,936
Tachikawa (★ Tōkyō)	146,523
Tagajō (★ Sendai)	54,436
Tagawa	59,727
Tajimi (★ Nagoya)	84,829
Takada	130,659
Takaishi (★ Ōsaka)	66,974
Takamatsu	326,999
Takaoka (★ 220,000)	175,780
Takarazuka (★ Ōsaka)	194,273
Takasago (★ Ōsaka)	91,434
Takasaki	231,766
Takatsuki (★ Ōsaka)	348,784
Takayama	65,033
Takefu	69,148
Takikawa	52,004
Tama (★ Tōkyō)	122,135
Tamano	76,954
Tanabe (▲ 70,835)	59,800
Tanashi (★ Tōkyō)	71,331
Tatebayashi	75,141
Tenri	69,120
Tochigi	86,290
Toda (★ Tōkyō)	76,960
Tōkai (★ Nagoya)	95,278
Toki	65,308
Tokoname (★ Nagoya)	53,077
Tokorozawa (★ Tōkyō)	275,168
Tokushima	257,884
Tokuyama (★ 250,000)	112,638
• TŌKYŌ (★ 27,700,000)	8,354,615
Tomakomai	158,061
Tondabayashi (★ Ōsaka)	102,619
Toride (★ Tōkyō)	78,608
Tosu	55,791
Tottori	137,060
Toyama	314,111
Toyoake (★ Nagoya)	57,969
Toyohashi	322,142

C Census. E Official estimate. U Unofficial estimate.
• Largest city in country.

★ Population or designation of metropolitan area, including suburbs (see headnote).
▲ Population of an entire municipality, commune, or district, including rural area.

Toyokawa 107,430
Toyonaka (★ Ōsaka) 413,213
Toyota 308,111
Tsu 150,690
Tsuchiura 120,175
Tsuruga 65,670
Tsuruoka 100,200
Tsushima (★ Nagoya) 58,735
Tsuyama 86,837
Ube (★ 230,000) 174,855
Ueda 116,178
Ueno (▲ 60,812) 51,800
Uji (★ Ōsaka) 165,411
Uozu 49,825
Urasoe 81,611
Urawa (★ Tōkyō) 377,235
Urayasu (★ Tōkyō) 93,756
Ushiku 51,926
Utsunomiya 405,375
Uwajima 71,381
Wakayama (★ 495,000) 401,352
Wakkanai 51,854
Wakō (★ Tōkyō) 55,212
Warabi (★ Tōkyō) 70,408
Yachiyo (★ Tōkyō) 142,184
Yaizu (★ Shizuoka) 108,558
Yamagata 245,158
Yamaguchi 124,213
Yamato (★ Tōkyō) 177,669
Yamato-kōriyama (★ Ōsaka) 89,624
Yamato-takada (★ Ōsaka) 65,223
Yao (★ Ōsaka) 276,394
Yashio (★ Tōkyō) 67,635
Yatsushiro (▲ 108,790) 88,700
Yawata (★ Ōsaka) 72,356
Yokkaichi 263,001
Yokohama (★ ★ Tōkyō) 2,992,926
Yokosuka (★ Tōkyō) 427,116
Yonago 131,792
Yonezawa 93,721
Yono (★ Tōkyō) 71,597
Yotsukaidō (★ Tōkyō) 67,008
Yukuhashi 65,527
Zama (★ Tōkyō) 100,000
Zushi (★ Tōkyō) 57,656

JERSEY

1986 C 80,212

Cities and Towns

• SAINT HELIER (★ 46,500) 27,083

JORDAN / Al-Urdun

1989 E 3,111,000

Cities and Towns

Al-Baq'ah (★ 'Ammān) (1989 E) 63,985
• 'AMMĀN (★ 1,450,000) 936,300
Ar-Ruṣayfah (★ 'Ammān) 72,580
Az-Zarqā' (★ ★ 'Ammān) 318,055
Irbid 167,785

KAZAKHSTAN

1989 C 16,538,000

Cities and Towns

Aktau 159,000
Akt'ubinsk 253,000
• ALMA-ATA (★ 1,190,000) 1,128,000
Arkalyk (1987 E) 71,000
Aterau 149,000
Balchaš (1987 E) 84,000
Čelinograd 277,000
Čimkent 393,000
Džambul 307,000
Džezkazgan 109,000
Ekibastuz 135,000
Karaganda 614,000
Kentau (1987 E) 60,000
Kokčetav 137,000
Kustanaj 224,000
Kzyl-Orda 153,000
Leninogorsk (1987 E) 69,000
Pavlodar 331,000
Petropavlovsk 241,000
Rudnyj 124,000
Šachtinsk (1987 E) 62,000
Saptajev (1987 E) 64,000
Šaran' (1987 E) 64,000
Ščučinsk (1987 E) 53,000
Semipalatinsk 334,000
Taldy-Kurgan 119,000
Temirtau 212,000
Turkestan (1987 E) 77,000
Ural'sk 200,000
Ust'-Kamenogorsk 324,000
Žanatas (1987 E) 53,000
Zyr'anovsk (1987 E) 55,000

KENYA

1990 E 24,870,000

Cities and Towns

Eldoret (1979 C) 50,503
Kisumu (1984 E) 167,100
Machakos (1983 E) 92,300
Meru (1979 C) 72,049
Mombasa 537,000
• NAIROBI 1,505,000
Nakuru (1984 E) 101,700

KIRIBATI

1988 E 68,207

Cities and Towns

BAIRIKI 2,230
• Bikenibeu 4,580

KOREA, NORTH / Chosŏn-minjujuŭi-inmīn-konghwaguk

1981 E 18,317,000

Cities and Towns

Ch'ŏngjin 490,000
Haeju (1983 E) 213,000
Hamhŭng (1970 E) 150,000
Hŭngnam (1976 E) 260,000
Kaesŏng 259,000
Kanggye (1967 E) 130,000
Kimch'aek (Sŏngjin) (1967 E) 265,000
Namp'o 241,000
• P'YŎNGYANG (★ 1,600,000) 1,283,000
Sinŭiju 305,000
Songnim (1944 C) 53,035
Wŏnsan (1981 E) 398,000

KOREA, SOUTH / Taehan-min'guk

1985 C 40,448,486

Cities and Towns

Andong 114,216
Anyang (★ Sŏul) 361,577
Bucheon (★ Sŏul) 456,292
Changwŏn (★ Masan) 173,508
Chech'on 102,274
Cheju 202,911
Chinhae 121,341
Chinju 227,309
Ch'ŏnan 170,196
Ch'ŏngju 350,256
Chŏnju 79,323
Chŏnju, Chŏlla Pukdo prov. 426,473
Ch'unch'ŏn 162,988
Ch'ungju 113,331
Ch'ungmu 87,459
Inch'ŏn (★ ★ Sŏul) (1989 E) 1,628,000
Iri 192,269
Kangnŭng 132,897
Kimch'ŏn 77,254
Kimhae 77,903
Kumi 142,094
Kŭmsŏng 58,897
Kunsan 185,649
Kwangju (1989 E) 1,165,000
Kwangmyŏng (★ Sŏul) 219,611
Kyŏngju 127,544
Masan (★ 625,000) 448,746
Mokp'o 236,085
Namwŏn 61,447
P'ohang 260,691
Pusan (★ 3,800,000) (1989 E) 3,773,000
P'yŏngt'aek (▲ 180,513) 63,400
Samch'ŏnp'o 62,466
Sŏgwipo 82,311
Sŏkch'o 69,501
Sŏngnam (★ Sŏul) 447,692
Songtan 66,357
• SŎUL (★ 15,850,000) (1989 E) 10,522,000
Sunch'ŏn (▲ 116,323) 121,958
Suwŏn (★ Sŏul) 430,752
T'aebaek 113,997
Taegu (1989 C) 2,207,000
Taejŏn (1989 E) 1,041,000
Tongduchŏn 68,633
Tonghae 91,691
Ŭijŏngbu (★ Sŏul) 162,700
Ulsan 551,014
Wŏnju 151,165
Yŏngch'ŏn 52,811
Yŏngju 84,742
Yŏsu 171,933

KUWAIT / Al-Kuwayt

1985 C 1,697,301

Cities and Towns

Al-Aḥmadī (★ 285,000) 26,899
Al-Farwānīyah (★ Al-Kuwayt) 68,701
Al-Fuḥayḥīl (★ Al-Aḥmadī) 50,081
Al-Jahrah (★ Al-Kuwayt) 111,222
• AL-KUWAYT (★ 1,375,000) 44,335
As-Sālimīyah (★ Al-Kuwayt) 153,359
Aṣ-Ṣulaybīyah (★ Al-Kuwayt) 51,314
Ḥawallī (★ Al-Kuwayt) 145,126
Qalīb ash-Shuyūkh (★ Al-Kuwayt) 114,771
South Khīṭān (★ Al-Kuwayt) 69,256
Subahiya (★ Al-Aḥmadī) 60,787

KYRGYZSTAN

1989 C 4,291,000

Cities and Towns

• BIŠKEK 616,000
Džalal-Abad (1987 E) 74,000
Kara-Balta (1987 E) 55,000
Oš 213,000
Prževal'sk (1987 E) 64,000
Tokmak (1987 E) 71,000

LAOS / Lao

1985 C 3,584,803

Cities and Towns

Savannakhet (1975 E) 53,000
Viangchan (Vientiane) 377,409

LATVIA / Latvija

1989 C 2,681,000

Cities and Towns

Daugavpils 127,000
Jelgava (1987 E) 72,000
Jūrmala (★ Rīga) (1987 E) 65,000
Liepāja 114,000
• RĪGA (★ 1,005,000) 915,000
Ventspils (1987 E) 52,000

LEBANON / Lubnān

1982 U 2,637,000

Cities and Towns

• BAYRŪT (★ 1,675,000) 509,000
Ṣaydā 105,000
Ṭarābulus (Tripoli) 198,000

LESOTHO

1986 C 1,577,536

Cities and Towns

• MASERU 109,382

LIBERIA

1986 E 2,221,000

Cities and Towns

• MONROVIA 465,000

LIBYA / Lībiyā

1984 C 3,637,488

Cities and Towns

Banghāzī 435,886
Darnah 62,179
Misrātah 131,031
• ṬARĀBULUS (TRIPOLI) 990,697
Ṭubruq (Tobruk) 75,282
Zāwiyat al-Bayḍā' 67,120

LIECHTENSTEIN

1990 E 28,452

Cities and Towns

• VADUZ 4,874

LITHUANIA / Lietuva

1989 C 3,690,000

Cities and Towns

Alytus (1987 E) 71,000
Kaunas 423,000
Klaipėda (Memel) 204,000
Panevėžys 126,000
Šiauliai 145,000
• VILNIUS 582,000

LUXEMBOURG

1985 E 366,000

Cities and Towns

• LUXEMBOURG (★ 136,000) 76,130

MACAU

1987 E 429,000

Cities and Towns

• MACAU 429,000

MACEDONIA / Makedonija

1987 E 2,064,581

Cities and Towns

Bitola (▲ 143,090) 76,200
• SKOPJE (▲ 547,214) 444,900

MADAGASCAR / Madagasikara

1984 E 9,731,000

Cities and Towns

• ANTANANARIVO (1985 E) 663,000
Antsirabe (▲ 95,000) 50,100
Antsiranana 100,000
Fianarantsoa 130,000
Mahajanga 85,000
Toamasina 100,000
Toliara 55,000

MALAWI / Malaŵi

1987 C 7,982,607

Cities and Towns

• Blantyre 331,588
LILONGWE 233,973

MALAYSIA

1980 C 13,136,109

Cities and Towns

Alor Setar 69,435
Batu Pahat 64,727
Butterworth (★ ★ George Town) 77,982
George Town (Pinang) (★ 495,000) 248,241
Ipoh 293,849
Johor Baharu (★ Singapore, Sing.) 246,395
Kelang 192,080
Keluang 50,315
Kota Baharu 167,872
Kota Kinabalu (Jesselton) 55,997
• KUALA LUMPUR (★ 1,475,000) 919,610
Kuala Terengganu 180,296
Kuantan 131,547
Kuching 72,555
Melaka 87,494
Miri 52,125
Muar (Bandar Maharani) 65,151
Petaling Jaya (★ Kuala Lumpur) 207,805
Sandakan 70,420
Seremban 132,911
Sibu 85,231
Taiping 146,000
Telok Anson 49,148

MALDIVES

1985 C 181,453

Cities and Towns

• MALE 46,334

MALI

1987 C 7,620,225

Cities and Towns

• BAMAKO 646,163
Gao 54,874
Mopti 73,979
Ségou 88,877
Sikasso 73,050
Tombouctou (Timbuktu) 31,925

MALTA

1989 E 349,014

Cities and Towns

• VALLETTA (★ 215,000) 9,210

MARSHALL ISLANDS

1980 C 30,873

Cities and Towns

• Jarej-Uliga-Delap 8,583

MARTINIQUE

1982 C 328,566

Cities and Towns

• FORT-DE-FRANCE (★ 116,017) 99,844

MAURITANIA / Mauritanie / Mūrītāniyā

1987 E 2,007,000

Cities and Towns

• NOUAKCHOTT 285,000

MAURITIUS

1987 E 1,008,864

Cities and Towns

Beau Bassin-Rose Hill (★ Port Louis) 93,125
Curepipe (★ Port Louis) 64,243
• PORT LOUIS (★ 420,000) 139,730
Quatre Bornes (★ Port Louis) 65,480
Vacoas-Phoenix (★ Port Louis) 55,667

MAYOTTE

1985 E 67,205

Cities and Towns

• DZAOUDZI (★ 6,979) 5,865

MEXICO / México

1980 C 67,395,826

Cities and Towns

Acapulco [de Juárez] 301,902
Aguascalientes 293,152
Atlixco 53,207
Campeche 128,434
Cancún 33,273
Celaya 141,675
Chihuahua 385,603
Chilpancingo [de los Bravo] 67,498
Ciudad Chetumal 56,709
Ciudad del Carmen 72,489
• CIUDAD DE MÉXICO (MEXICO CITY) (★ 14,100,000) 8,831,079
Ciudad de Valles 65,609
Ciudad Guzmán 60,938
Ciudad Juárez 544,496
Ciudad Madero (★ Tampico) 132,444
Ciudad Mante 70,647
Ciudad Obregón 165,572
Ciudad Victoria 140,161
Coatzacoalcos 127,170
Colima 86,044
Córdoba 99,972
Cuernavaca 192,770
Culiacán 304,826
Delicias 65,504
Durango 257,915
Ecatepec (★ Ciudad de México) 741,821
Ensenada 120,483
Fresnillo 56,066
Garza García (★ Monterrey) 81,974
Gómez Palacio (★ ★ Torreón) 116,967
Guadalajara (★ 2,325,000) 1,626,152
Guadalupe (★ Monterrey) 370,524
Guaymas 54,826
Hermosillo 297,175
Hidalgo del Parral 75,590
Iguala 66,005
Irapuato 170,138
Jalapa Enríquez 204,594
La Paz 91,453
León [de los Aldamas] 593,002
Los Mochis 122,531
Matamoros 188,745
Mazatlán 199,830
Mérida 400,142
Mexicali (★ 365,000) 341,559
Minatitlán 106,765
Monclova 115,786
Monterrey (★ 2,015,000) 1,090,009
Morelia 297,544
Naucalpan de Juárez (★ Ciudad de México) 723,723
Navojoa 62,901
Nezahualcóyotl (★ Ciudad de México) 1,341,230
Nogales 65,603
Nuevo Laredo 201,731
Oaxaca [de Juárez] 154,223
Orizaba (★ 215,000) 114,848
Pachuca [de Soto] 110,351
Piedras Negras 67,455
Poza Rica de Hidalgo 166,799
Puebla [de Zaragoza] (★ 1,055,000) 835,759
Puerto Vallarta 38,645
Querétaro 215,976
Reynosa 194,693
Río Bravo 55,236
Salamanca 96,703
Saltillo 284,937
San Luis Potosí (★ 470,000) 362,371
San Luis Río Colorado 76,684
San Nicolás de los Garza (★ Monterrey) 280,696
Santa Catarina (★ Monterrey) 87,673
Soledad Díez Gutiérrez (★ San Luis Potosí) 49,173
Tampico (★ 435,000) 267,957
Tapachula 85,766
Tehuacán 79,547
Tepic 145,741
Tijuana 429,500
Tlalnepantla (★ Ciudad de México) 778,173
Tlaquepaque (★ Guadalajara) 133,500
Toluca [de Lerdo] 199,778
Torreón (★ 575,000) 328,086
Tulancingo 53,400
Tuxpan de Rodríguez Cano 56,037
Tuxtla Gutiérrez 131,096
Uruapan [del Progreso] 122,828
Veracruz [Llave] (★ 385,000) 284,822
Villahermosa 158,216
Zacatecas 80,088
Zamora de Hidalgo 86,998
Zapopan (★ Guadalajara) 345,390

MICRONESIA, FEDERATED STATES OF

C Census. E Official estimate. U Unofficial estimate.
• Largest city in country.
★ Population or designation of metropolitan area, including suburbs (see headnote).
▲ Population of an entire municipality, commune, or district, including rural area.

1985 E 94,534

Cities and Towns

• KOLONIA 6,306

MOLDOVA

1989 C 4,341,000

Cities and Towns

Bălţi 159,000
• CHIŞINĂU 665,000
Râbniţa (1987 E) 58,000
Tighina 130,000
Tiraspol 182,000

MONACO

1982 C 27,063

Cities and Towns

• MONACO (★ 87,000) 27,063

MONGOLIA / Mongol Ard Uls

1989 E 2,040,000

Cities and Towns

Darchan (1985 E) 69,800
• ULAANBAATAR 548,400

MONTSERRAT

1980 C 11,606

Cities and Towns

• PLYMOUTH 1,568

MOROCCO / Al-Magreb

1982 C 20,419,555

Cities and Towns

Agadir 110,479
Beni-Mellal 95,003
Berkane 60,490
• Casablanca (Dar-el-Beida) (★ 2,475,000) 2,139,204
El-Jadida (Mazagan) 81,455
Fès (★ 535,000) 448,823
Kenitra 188,194
Khemisset 58,925
Khouribga 127,181
Ksar-el-Kebir 73,541
Larache 63,893
Marrakech (★ 535,000) 439,728
Meknès (★ 375,000) 319,783
Mohammedia (Fedala) (★ Casablanca) 105,120
Nador 62,040
Oued-Zem 58,744
Oujda 260,082
RABAT (★ 980,000) 518,616
Safi 197,309
Salé (★ ★ Rabat) 289,391
Settat 65,203
Sidi Kacem 55,833
Sidi Slimane 50,457
Tanger (Tangier) (★ 370,000) 266,346
Taza 77,216
Tétouan 199,615

MOZAMBIQUE / Moçambique

1989 E 15,326,476

Cities and Towns

Beira 291,604
Chimoio (1986 E) 86,928
Inhambane (1986 E) 64,274
• MAPUTO 1,069,727
Nacala-Velha 101,615
Nampula 197,379
Pemba (1986 E) 50,215
Quelimane 78,520
Tete (1986 E) 56,178
Xai-Xai (1986 E) 51,620

MYANMAR

1983 C 34,124,908

Cities and Towns

Bago (Pegu) 150,528
Chauk 51,437
Dawei (Tavoy) 69,882
Henzada 82,005
Kale 52,028
Lashio 88,590
Magway 54,881
Mandalay 532,949
Mawlamyine (Moulmein) 219,961
Maymyo 63,782
Meiktila 96,496
Mergui (Myeik) 88,600
Mogok 49,392
Monywa 106,843
Myingyan 77,060
Myitkyinā 56,427
Pakokku 71,860
Pathein (Bassein) 144,096
Pyè (Prome) 83,332
Pyinmana 52,962
Shwebo 52,185
Sittwe (Akyab) 107,621
Taunggyi 108,231
Thaton 61,790
Toungoo 65,861
• YANGON (RANGOON) (★ 2,800,000) 2,705,039

Yenangyaung 62,582

NAMIBIA

1988 E 1,760,000

Cities and Towns

• WINDHOEK 114,500

NAURU / Naoero

1987 E 8,000

Cities and Towns

NEPAL / Nepāl

1981 C 15,022,839

Cities and Towns

Birātnagar 93,544
• KĀTHMĀNDAU (★ 320,000) 235,160

NETHERLANDS / Nederland

1989 E 14,880,000

Cities and Towns

Alkmaar (★ 121,000) (1987 E) 87,034
Almelo (1986 E) 62,421
Alphen aan den Rijn (1986 E) 55,812
Amersfoort (★ 130,158) (1986 E) 89,596
Amstelveen (★ Amsterdam) (1986 E) 68,090
• AMSTERDAM (★ 1,860,000) 696,500
Apeldoorn 147,300
Arnhem (★ 296,362) 129,000
Breda (★ 155,613) 121,400
Delft (★ ★ 's-Gravenhage) (1986 E) 87,440
Den Helder (1986 E) 63,231
Deventer (1986 E) 64,806
Dordrecht (★ 202,126) 108,300
Eindhoven (★ 379,377) 190,700
Enschede (★ 288,000) 145,200
Gouda (1986 E) 60,927
Groningen (★ 206,781) 167,800
Haarlem (★ Amsterdam) 149,200
Heerlen (★ 266,617) (1986 E) 93,871
Helmond (1987 E) 63,909
Hengelo (★ ★ Enschede) (1986 E) 76,694
Hilversum (★ Amsterdam) (1986 E) 86,125
Hoorn (1987 E) 53,788
IJmuiden (★ Amsterdam) (1986 E) 57,157
Kerkrade (★ Heerlen) (1986 E) 52,885
Leeuwarden (1986 E) 84,966
Leiden (★ 182,244) 109,200
Maastricht (★ 160,026) 116,400
Nieuwegein (★ Utrecht) (1987 E) 56,719
Nijmegen (★ 240,085) 145,400
Oss (1986 E) 50,343
Purmerend (★ Amsterdam) (1987 E) 52,257
Roosendaal (1986 E) 57,385
Rotterdam (★ 1,110,000) 576,300
Schiedam (★ Rotterdam) (1986 E) 69,078
'S-GRAVENHAGE (THE HAGUE) (★ 770,000) 443,900
's-Hertogenbosch (★ 189,067) (1986 E) 89,039
Spijkenisse (★ Rotterdam) (1987 E) 62,394
Tilburg (★ 224,934) 155,100
Utrecht (★ 518,779) 230,700
Venlo (★ 87,000) (1986 E) 63,475
Vlaardingen (★ Rotterdam) (1986 E) 75,536
Zaandam (★ Amsterdam) 129,600
Zeist (★ Utrecht) (1986 E) 59,743
Zoetermeer (★ 's-Gravenhage) (1987 E) 85,349
Zwolle (1986 E) 88,438

NETHERLANDS ANTILLES / Nederlandse Antillen

1990 E 189,687

Cities and Towns

• WILLEMSTAD (★ 130,000) (1981 C) 31,883

NEW CALEDONIA / Nouvelle-Calédonie

1989 C 164,173

Cities and Towns

• NOUMÉA (★ 88,000) 65,110

NEW ZEALAND

1986 C 3,307,084

Cities and Towns

• Auckland (★ 850,000) 149,046
Christchurch (★ 320,000) 168,200
Dunedin (★ 109,000) 76,964
Hamilton (★ 101,814) 94,511
Lower Hutt (★ Wellington) 63,862
Manukau (★ Auckland) 177,248
Napier (★ 107,060) 49,428
Palmerston North (★ 67,405) 60,503
Takapuna (★ Auckland) 69,419
Waitemata (★ Auckland) 96,365
WELLINGTON (★ 350,000) 137,495

NICARAGUA

1985 E 3,272,100

Cities and Towns

Chinandega 75,000
Granada (1981 E) 64,642
León 101,000
• MANAGUA 682,000
Masaya 75,000
Matagalpa 68,000

NIGER

1988 C 7,250,383

Cities and Towns

Agadez 50,164
Maradi 112,965
• NIAMEY 398,265
Tahoua 51,607
Zinder 120,892

NIGERIA

1987 E 101,907,000

Cities and Towns

Aba 239,800
Abakaliki 56,800
Abeokuta 341,300
ABUJA (1993 U) 250,000
Ado-Ekiti 287,000
Afikpo 65,790
Agege 83,810
Akure 129,600
Amaigbo 53,690
Apomu 49,570
Awka 88,800
Azare 50,020
Bauchi 68,840
Benin City 183,200
Bida 100,200
Calabar 139,800
Deba 110,600
Duku 52,880
Ede 245,200
Effon-Alaiye 122,300
Ejigbo 84,570
Emure-Ekiti 58,750
Enugu 252,500
Epe 80,560
Erin-Oshogbo 59,940
Eruwa 49,140
Fiditi 49,440
Gboko 49,390
Gbongan 53,990
Gombe 86,120
Gusau 126,200
Ibadan 1,144,000
Idah 50,550
Idanre 56,080
Ife 237,000
Ifon-Oshogbo 65,980
Igboho 85,230
Igbo-Ora 68,060
Igede-Ekiti 56,570
Ihiala 73,240
Ijebu-Igbo 78,680
Ijebu-Ode 124,900
Ijero-Ekiti 76,420
Ikare 112,500
Ikerre 195,400
Ikire 94,450
Ikirun 144,900
Ikole 71,860
Ikorodu 147,700
Ikot Ekpene 69,440
Ila 210,800
Ilawe-Ekiti 147,300
Ilesha 302,100
Illobu 159,000
Ilorin 380,000
Inisa 95,630
Ipoti-Ekiti 53,220
Ise-Ekiti 82,580
Iseyin 173,500
Iwo 289,100
Jimeta 66,130
Jos 164,700
Kaduna 273,200
Kano 538,300
Katsina 165,000
Kaura Namoda 52,910

Keffi 57,790
Kishi 77,210
Kumo 118,200
Lafia 97,810
Lafiagi 57,580
• LAGOS (★ 3,800,000) 1,213,000
Lalupon 56,130
Lere 49,670
Maiduguri 255,100
Makurdi 98,350
Minna 109,300
Mubi 51,190
Mushin (★ Lagos) 266,100
Nguru 78,770
Offa 157,500
Ogbomosho 582,900
Oka 114,400
Oke-Mesi 55,040
Okwe 52,550
Olupona 65,720
Ondo 135,300
Onitsha 298,200
Opobo 64,620
Oron 62,260
Oshogbo 380,800
Owo 146,600
Oyan 50,930
Oyo 204,700
Pindiga 64,130
Port Harcourt 327,300
Potiskum 56,490
Sapele 111,200
Shagamu 93,610
Shaki 139,000
Shomolu (★ Lagos) 120,700
Sokoto 163,700
Ugep 81,910
Umuahia 52,550
Uyo 60,500
Warri 100,700
Zaria 302,800

NIUE

1986 C 2,531

Cities and Towns

• ALOFI 811

NORTHERN MARIANA ISLANDS

1980 C 16,780

Cities and Towns

• Chalan Kanoa 2,678

NORWAY / Norge

1987 E 4,190,000

Cities and Towns

Bærum (★ Oslo) (1985 E) 83,000
Bergen (★ 239,000) 209,320
Drammen (★ 73,000) (1985 E) 50,700
Fredrikstad (★ 52,000) (1983 E) 27,618
Hammerfest (1983 E) 7,208
Kristiansand (1985 E) 62,200
• OSLO (★ 720,000) 452,415
Stavanger (★ 132,000) (1985 E) 94,200
Tromsø (1985 E) 47,800
Trondheim 135,010

OMAN / 'Umān

1981 E 919,000

Cities and Towns

• MASQAT (MUSCAT) 50,000
Şūr (1980 E) 30,000

PAKISTAN / Pākistān

1981 C 84,253,644

Cities and Towns

Ahmadpur East 56,979
Bahāwalnagar 74,533
Bahāwalpur (★ 180,263) 152,009
Chārsadda 62,530
Chīchāwatni 50,241
Chiniot 105,559
Chishtiān Mandi 01,959
Daska 55,555
Dera Ghāzi Khān 102,007
Dera Ismāīl Khān (★ 68,145) 64,358
Drigh Road Cantonment (★ Karāchi) 56,742
Faisalabad (Lyallpur) 1,104,209
Gojra 68,000
Gujrānwāla (★ 658,753) 600,993
Gujrānwāla Cantonment (★ Gujrānwāla) 57,700
Gujrāt 155,058
Hāfizābād 83,464
Hyderābād (★ 800,000) 702,539
ISLĀMĀBĀD (★ ★ Rāwalpindi) 204,364
Jacobābād 79,365
Jarānwāla 69,459
Jhang Maghiāna 195,558
Jhelum (★ 106,462) 92,646
Kamālia 61,107
Kāmoke 71,097
• Karāchi (★ 5,300,000) 4,901,627

Karāchi Cantonment (★ Karāchi) 181,981
Kasūr 155,523
Khairpur 61,447
Khānewāl 89,090
Khānpur 70,589
Khushāb 56,274
Kohāt (★ 77,604) 55,832
Lahore (★ 3,025,000) 2,707,215
Lahore Cantonment (★ Lahore) 245,474
Lārkāna 123,890
Leiah 51,482
Mandi Būrewāla 86,311
Mardān (★ 147,977) 141,842
Miānwāli 59,159
Mingāora 88,078
Mīrpur Khās 124,371
Multān (★ 732,070) 696,316
Muzaffargarh 53,000
Nawābshāh 102,139
Okāra (★ 153,483) 127,455
Pākpattan 69,820
Peshāwar (★ 566,248) 506,896
Peshāwar Cantonment (★ Peshāwar) 59,352
Quetta (★ 285,719) 244,842
Rahīmyār Khān (★ 132,635) 119,036
Rāwalpindi (★ 1,040,000) 457,091
Rāwalpindi Cantonment (★ Rāwalpindi) 337,752
Sādiqābād 63,935
Sāhīwal 150,954
Sargodha (★ 291,362) 231,895
Sargodha Cantonment (★ Sargodha) 59,467
Shekhūpura 141,168
Shikārpur 88,138
Siālkot (★ 302,009) 258,147
Sukkur 190,551
Tando Ādam 62,744
Turbat 52,337
Vihāri 53,799
Wāh 122,335
Wazīrābād 62,725

PALAU / Belau

1986 C 13,873

Cities and Towns

• KOROR 8,629

PANAMA / Panamá

1990 C 2,315,047

Cities and Towns

Colón (★ 96,000) 54,469
David 65,635
• PANAMÁ (★ 770,000) 411,549
San Miguelito (★ Panamá) 242,529

PAPUA NEW GUINEA

1987 E 3,479,400

Cities and Towns

Lae 79,600
• PORT MORESBY 152,100
Rabaul (1980 C) 14,954

PARAGUAY

1985 E 3,279,000

Cities and Towns

• ASUNCIÓN (★ 700,000) 477,100
Fernando de la Mora (★ Asunción) 80,000
Lambaré (★ Asunción) 84,000
Puerto Presidente Stroessner 64,000
San Lorenzo (★ Asunción) (1982 C) 74,632

PERU / Perú

1981 C 17,031,221

Cities and Towns

Arequipa (★ 446,942) 108,023
Ayacucho (★ 69,533) 57,432
Breña (★ Lima) 112,000
Cajamarca 62,259
Callao (★ ★ Lima) 264,133
Cerro de Pasco (★ 66,373) 55,597
Chiclayo (★ 279,527) 213,095
Chimbote 223,341
Chorrillos (★ Lima) 141,881
Chosica 65,139
Cuzco (★ 184,550) 89,563
Huancayo (★ 164,954) 64,045
Huánuco 61,812
Ica 114,786
Iquitos 178,738
Jesús María (★ Lima) 83,179
Juliaca 87,651
La Victoria (★ Lima) 270,778
• LIMA (★ 4,608,010) 371,122
Lince (★ Lima) 80,456
Magdalena (★ Lima) 55,535
Miraflores (★ Lima) 103,453
Pisco 55,604
Piura (★ 207,934) 144,609

C Census. E Official estimate. U Unofficial estimate.
• Largest city in country.

★ Population or designation of metropolitan area, including suburbs (see headnote).
▲ Population of an entire municipality, commune, or district, including rural area.

Pucallpa … 112,263
Pueblo Libre (★ Lima) … 83,985
Puno … 67,397
Rímac (★ Lima) … 184,484
San Isidro (★ Lima) … 71,203
San Martin de Porras (★ Lima) … 404,856
Santiago de Surco (★ Lima) … 146,636
Sullana … 89,037
Surquillo (★ Lima) … 134,158
Tacna … 97,173
Talara … 57,351
Trujillo (★ 354,301) … 202,469
Vitarte (★ Lima) … 145,504

PHILIPPINES / Pilipinas

1990 C … 60,477,000

Cities and Towns

Angeles … 236,000
Antipolo (▲ 68,912) (1980 C) … 54,117
Bacolod … 364,000
Bacoor (★ Manila) (1980 C) … 90,364
Baguio … 183,000
Baliuag (1980 C) … 70,555
Biñan (★ Manila) (1980 C) … 83,684
Binangonan (1980 C) … 80,980
Bocaue (1980 C) … 49,693
Butuan (▲ 228,000) … 99,000
Cabanatuan (▲ 173,000) … 75,700
Cagayan de Oro (▲ 340,000) … 255,000
Cainta (★ Manila) (1980 C) … 59,025
Calamba (▲ 121,175) (1980 C) … 72,359
Caloocan (★ Manila) … 746,000
Carmona (★ Manila) (1980 C) … 65,014
Cavite (★ 175,000) … 92,000
Cebu (★ 720,000) … 610,000
Cotabato … 127,000
Dagupan … 122,000
Davao (▲ 850,000) … 569,300
Dumaguete … 80,000
General Santos (Dadiangas) (▲ 250,000) … 157,600
Guagua (1980 C) … 72,609
Iloilo … 311,000
Isabela (Basilan) (▲ 49,891) (1980 C) … 11,491
Jolo (1980 C) … 52,429
Lapu-Lapu (Opon) … 146,000
Las Piñas (★ Manila) (1984 E) … 190,364
Legaspi (▲ 121,000) … 63,000
Lucena … 151,000
Mabalacat (▲ 80,966) (1980 C) … 54,988
Makati (★ Manila) (1984 E) … 408,991
Malabon (★ Manila) (1984 E) … 212,930
Malolos (1980 C) … 95,699
Mandaluyong (★ Manila) (1984 E) … 226,670
Mandaue (★ Cebu) … 180,000
Mangaldan (1980 C) … 50,434
• MANILA (★ 6,800,000) … 1,587,000
Marawi … 92,000
Marikina (★ Manila) (1984 E) … 248,183
Meycauayan (★ Manila) (1980 C) … 83,579
Muntinglupa (★ Manila) (1984 E) … 172,421
Naga … 115,000
Navotas (★ Manila) (1984 E) … 146,899
Olongapo … 192,000
Pagadian (▲ 107,000) … 52,400
Parañaque (★ Manila) (1984 E) … 252,791
Pasay (★ Manila) … 354,000
Pasig (★ Manila) (1984 E) … 318,853
Puerto Princesa (▲ 92,000) … 52,000
Quezon City (★ Manila) … 1,632,000
San Fernando (1980 C) … 110,891
San Juan del Monte (★ Manila) (1984 E) … 139,126
San Pablo (▲ 161,000) … 83,900
San Pedro (1980 C) … 74,556
Santa Cruz (1980 C) … 60,620
Santa Rosa (★ Manila) (1980 C) … 64,325
Tacloban … 138,000
Tagbilaran … 56,000
Tagig (★ Manila) (1984 E) … 130,719
Taytay (★ Manila) (1980 C) … 75,328
Valenzuela (★ Manila) (1984 E) … 275,725
Zamboanga (▲ 444,000) … 107,000

PITCAIRN

1988 C … 59

Cities and Towns

• ADAMSTOWN … 59

POLAND / Polska

1989 E … 37,775,100

Cities and Towns

Będzin (★ Katowice) … 77,300
Bełchatów … 53,600
Biała Podlaska … 50,900
Białystok … 263,900
Bielsko-Biała … 179,600
Bydgoszcz … 377,900
Bytom (Beuthen) (★ ★ Katowice) … 228,000
Chełm … 63,300
Chorzów (★ ★ Katowice) … 133,300
Częstochowa … 254,600
Dąbrowa Górnicza (★ Katowice) … 133,200
Elbląg (Elbing) … 124,600
Ełk … 49,600
Gdańsk (Danzig) (★ 909,000) … 461,500
Gdynia (★ ★ Gdańsk) … 250,200
Gliwice (Gleiwitz) (★ ★ Katowice) … 222,500
Głogów … 70,100
Gniezno … 68,900
Gorzów Wielkopolski (Landsberg an der Warthe) … 121,500
Grudziądz … 99,900
Inowrocław … 75,100
Jastrzębie-Zdrój … 102,200
Jaworzno (★ Katowice) … 97,400
Jelenia Góra (Hirschberg) … 92,700
Kalisz … 105,600
• Katowice (★ 2,778,000) … 365,800
Kędzierzyn Kozle … 71,600
Kielce … 211,100
Konin … 78,500
Koszalin (Köslin) … 105,600
Kraków (★ 828,000) … 743,700
Legionowo (★ Warszawa) … 50,000
Legnica (Liegnitz) … 102,800
Leszno … 56,700
Łódź (★ 1,061,000) … 851,500
Łomża … 56,300
Lubin … 78,800
Lublin (★ 389,000) … 339,500
Mielec … 58,600
Mysłowice (★ Katowice) … 91,200
Nowy Sącz … 75,100
Olsztyn (Allenstein) … 158,800
Opole (Oppeln) … 125,800
Ostrowiec Świętokrzyski … 76,300
Ostrów Wielkopolski … 71,200
Pabianice (★ Łódź) … 74,400
Piekary Śląskie (★ Katowice) … 68,200
Piła (Schneidemühl) (1988 E) … 70,000
Piotrków Trybunalski … 80,100
Płock … 119,300
Poznań (★ 672,000) … 586,500
Pruszków (★ Warszawa) … 52,700
Przemyśl … 67,300
Puławy … 52,200
Racibórz (Ratibor) … 61,700
Radom … 223,600
Radomsko … 49,700
Ruda Śląska (★ Katowice) … 167,700
Rybnik … 140,000
Rzeszów … 148,600
Siedlce … 69,200
Siemianowice Śląskie (★ Katowice) … 79,200
Skarżysko-Kamienna … 50,200
Słupsk (Stolp) … 98,500
Sosnowiec (★ ★ Katowice) … 258,700
Stalowa Wola … 67,600
Starachowice … 55,400
Stargard Szczeciński (Stargard in Pommern) … 68,400
Suwałki … 57,900
Świdnica (Schweidnitz) … 61,800
Świętochłowice (★ Katowice) … 58,700
Szczecin (Stettin) (★ 449,000) … 409,500
Tarnów … 119,100
Tarnowskie Góry (★ Katowice) … 72,700
Tczew … 58,400
Tomaszów Mazowiecki … 69,200
Toruń … 199,600
Tychy (★ Katowice) … 187,600
Wałbrzych (Waldenburg) (★ 207,000) … 141,400
WARSZAWA (★ 2,323,000) … 1,651,200
Włocławek … 119,500
Wodzisław Śląski … 109,800
Wrocław (Breslau) … 637,400
Zabrze (Hindenburg) (★ ★ Katowice) … 201,400
Zamość … 59,000
Zawiercie … 55,700
Zgierz (★ Łódź) … 58,500
Zielona Góra (Grünberg) … 111,800
Żory … 65,300

PORTUGAL

1981 C … 9,833,014

Cities and Towns

Amadora (★ Lisboa) … 95,518
Barreiro (★ Lisboa) … 50,863
Braga … 63,033
Coimbra … 74,616
• LISBOA (LISBON) (★ 2,250,000) … 807,167
Porto (★ 1,225,000) … 327,368
Setúbal … 77,885
Vila Nova de Gaia (★ Porto) … 62,469

PUERTO RICO

1980 C … 3,196,520

Cities and Towns

Aguadilla (★ 152,793) … 22,039
Arecibo (★ 160,336) … 48,779
Bayamón (★ San Juan) … 185,087
Caguas (★ San Juan) … 87,214
Carolina (★ San Juan) … 147,835
Guaynabo (★ San Juan) … 65,075
Mayagüez (★ 200,464) … 82,968
Ponce (★ 232,551) … 161,739
• SAN JUAN (★ 1,775,260) … 424,600

QATAR / Qaṭar

1986 C … 369,079

Cities and Towns

• AD-DAWHAH (DOHA) (★ 310,000) … 217,294
Ar-Rayyān (★ Ad-Dawḥah) … 91,996

REUNION / Réunion

1982 C … 515,814

Cities and Towns

• SAINT-DENIS (▲ 109,072) … 84,400

ROMANIA / România

1986 E … 22,823,479

Cities and Towns

Alba-Iulia … 66,100
Alexandria … 52,802
Arad … 187,744
Bacău … 179,877
Baia Mare … 139,704
Bârlad … 70,365
Bistrița … 77,267
Botoșani … 108,775
Brăila … 235,620
Brașov … 351,493
• BUCUREȘTI (BUCHAREST) (★ 2,275,000) … 1,989,823
Buzău … 136,080
Călărași … 69,350
Cluj-Napoca … 310,017
Constanța … 327,676
Craiova … 281,044
Deva … 77,976
Drobeta-Turnu Severin … 99,366
Focșani … 86,411
Galați … 295,372
Giurgiu … 68,002
Hunedoara … 88,514
Iași … 313,060
Lugoj … 53,665
Medgidia … 48,409
Mediaș … 72,816
Onești … 52,329
Oradea … 213,846
Petroșani (★ 76,000) … 49,131
Piatra-Neamț … 109,393
Pitești … 157,190
Ploiești (★ 310,000) … 234,886
Râmnicu Vâlcea … 96,051
Reșița … 105,914
Roman … 72,415
Satu Mare … 130,082
Sfântu Gheorghe … 67,587
Sibiu … 177,511
Slatina … 76,714
Suceava … 96,317
Târgoviște … 91,990
Târgu Jiu … 87,693
Târgu Mureș … 158,998
Timișoara … 325,272
Tulcea … 86,336
Turda … 61,594
Vaslui … 65,070
Zalău … 57,283

RUSSIA / Rossija

1989 C … 147,386,000

Cities and Towns

Abakan … 154,000
Achtubinsk (1987 E) … 53,000
Ačinsk … 122,000
Alapajevsk (1987 E) … 51,000
Aleksandrov (1987 E) … 66,000
Aleksin (1987 E) … 72,000
Al'metjevsk … 129,000
Amursk (1987 E) … 54,000
Angarsk … 266,000
Anžero-Sudžensk … 108,000
Apatity (1987 E) … 80,000
Archangel'sk … 416,000
Armavir … 161,000
Arsenjev (1987 E) … 67,000
Art'om (1987 E) … 73,000
Arzamas … 109,000
Asbest (1987 E) … 83,000
Astrachan' … 509,000
Azov (1987 E) … 81,000
Balakovo … 198,000
Balašicha (★ Moskva) … 136,000
Balašov (1987 E) … 99,000
Barnaul (★ 665,000) … 602,000
Batajsk (★ Rostov-na-Donu) (1987 E) … 98,000
Belebej (1987 E) … 51,000
Belgorod … 300,000
Belogorsk (1987 E) … 71,000
Beloreck (1987 E) … 75,000
Belovo (1987 E) … 118,000
Berdsk (★ Novosibirsk) (1987 E) … 77,000
Berezniki … 201,000
Ber'ozovskij (1987 E) … 51,000
Bijsk … 233,000
Birobidžan (1987 E) … 82,000
Blagoveščensk … 206,000
Bor (★ Nižnij Novgorod) (1987 E) … 65,000
Borisoglebsk (1987 E) … 69,000
Boroviči (1987 E) … 64,000
Br'ansk … 452,000
Bratsk … 255,000
Bud'onnovsk (1987 E) … 54,000
Bugul'ma (1987 E) … 88,000
Buguruslan (1987 E) … 53,000
Bujnaksk (1987 E) … 53,000
Buzuluk (1987 E) … 82,000
Čajkovskij (1987 E) … 83,000
Čapajevsk (1987 E) … 87,000
Čeboksary … 420,000
Čechov (1987 E) … 57,000
Čel'abinsk (★ 1,325,000) … 1,143,000
Čeremchovo (1987 E) … 73,000
Čerepovec … 310,000
Čerkessk … 113,000
Černogorsk (1987 E) … 80,000
Chabarovsk … 601,000
Chasav'urt (1987 E) … 74,000
Chimki (★ Moskva) … 133,000
Cholmsk (1987 E) … 50,000
Čistopol' (1987 E) … 65,000
Čita … 366,000
Čusovoj (1987 E) … 59,000
Derbent (1987 E) … 83,000
Dimitrovgrad … 124,000
Dmitrov (1987 E) … 64,000
Dolgoprudnyj (★ Moskva) (1987 E) … 71,000
Domodedovo (★ Moskva) (1987 E) … 51,000
Dubna (1987 E) … 64,000
Dzeržinsk (★ Nižnij Novgorod) … 285,000
Elektrostal' … 153,000
Elista (1987 E) … 85,000
Engel's (★ ★ Saratov) … 182,000
Fr'azino (★ Moskva) (1987 E) … 52,000
Gatčina (★ Sankt-Peterburg) (1987 E) … 81,000
Georgijevsk (1987 E) … 62,000
Glazov … 104,000
Groznyj … 401,000
Gubkin (1987 E) … 75,000
Gukovo (1987 E) … 72,000
Gus'-Chrustal'nyj (1987 E) … 75,000
Inta (1987 E) … 58,000
Irbit (1987 E) … 53,000
Irkutsk … 626,000
Išim (1987 E) … 65,000
Išimbaj (1987 E) … 67,000
Iskitim (1987 E) … 69,000
Ivanovo … 481,000
Ivantejevka (★ Moskva) (1987 E) … 53,000
Iževsk … 635,000
Jakutsk … 187,000
Jaroslavl' … 633,000
Jefremov (1987 E) … 58,000
Jegorjevsk (1987 E) … 73,000
Jejsk (1987 E) … 77,000
Jekaterinburg (Sverdlovsk) (★ 1,620,000) … 1,367,000
Jelec … 120,000
Jermolajevo (1987 E) … 62,000
Jessentuki (1987 E) … 84,000
Joškar-Ola … 242,000
Jurga (1987 E) … 92,000
Južno-Sachalinsk … 157,000
Kaliningrad (Königsberg) … 401,000
Kaliningrad (★ Moskva) … 160,000
Kaluga … 312,000
Kamensk-Šachtinskij (1987 E) … 75,000
Kamensk-Ural'skij … 209,000
Kamyšin … 122,000
Kanaš (1987 E) … 53,000
Kansk … 110,000
Kaspijsk (1987 E) … 61,000
Kazan' (★ 1,140,000) … 1,094,000
Kemerovo … 520,000
Kimry (1987 E) … 61,000
Kinel' (1979 C) … 40,873
Kinešma … 105,000
Kiriši (1987 E) … 51,000
Kirov … 441,000
Kirovo-Čepeck (1987 E) … 89,000
Kisel'ovsk (★ ★ Prokopjevsk) … 128,000
Kislovodsk … 114,000
Kizel (1979 C) … 40,157
Klimovsk (★ Moskva) (1987 E) … 57,000
Klin (1987 E) … 95,000
Klincy (1987 E) … 72,000
Kol'čugino (1979 C) … 43,686
Kolomna … 162,000
Kolpino (★ Sankt-Peterburg) … 142,000
Komsomol'sk-na-Amure … 315,000
Kopejsk (★ Čel'abinsk) (1987 E) … 99,000
Korkino (1981 E) … 63,000
Korsakov (1979 C) … 43,348
Kostroma … 278,000
Kotlas (1987 E) … 69,000
Kovrov … 160,000
Krasnodar … 620,000
Krasnogorsk (★ Moskva) (1987 E) … 89,000
Krasnojarsk … 912,000
Krasnokamensk (1987 E) … 70,000
Krasnokamsk (1987 E) … 58,000
Krasnoturjinsk (1987 E) … 66,000
Krasnoufimsk (1979 C) … 40,027
Krasnoural'sk (1979 C) … 38,212
Krasnyj Sulin (1979 C) … 42,281
Kropotkin (1987 E) … 73,000
Krymsk (1983 E) … 50,000
Kstovo (★ Nižnij Novgorod) (1987 E) … 64,000
Kujbyšev (1987 E) … 51,000
Kulebaki (1979 C) … 48,302
Kungur (1987 E) … 83,000
Kurgan … 356,000
Kursk … 424,000
Kušva (1979 C) … 43,089
Kuzneck (1987 E) … 98,000
Kyzyl (1987 E) … 80,000
Labinsk (1987 E) … 58,000
Leninogorsk (1987 E) … 61,000
Leninsk-Kuzneckij … 165,000
Lipeck … 450,000
Liski (1987 E) … 54,000
Livny (1987 E) … 51,000
Lobn'a (★ Moskva) (1987 E) … 59,000
L'ubercy (★ Moskva) … 165,000
Lys'va (1987 E) … 77,000
Lytkarino (★ Moskva) (1987 E) … 51,000
Machačkala … 315,000
Magadan … 152,000
Magnitogorsk … 440,000
Majkop … 149,000
Meždurečensk … 107,000
Miass … 168,000
Michajlovka (1987 E) … 58,000
Mičurinsk … 109,000
Mineral'nyje Vody (1987 E) … 75,000
Minusinsk (1987 E) … 72,000
Mončegorsk (1987 E) … 65,000
Moršansk (1987 E) … 51,000
• MOSKVA (MOSCOW) (★ 13,100,000) … 8,769,000
Murmansk … 468,000
Murom … 124,000
Mytišči (★ Moskva) … 154,000
Naberežnyje Čelny … 501,000
Nachodka … 165,000
Nal'čik … 235,000
Naro-Fominsk (1987 E) … 60,000
Nazarovo (1987 E) … 63,000
Neftejugansk (1987 E) … 86,000
Ner'ungri (1987 E) … 68,000
Nevinnomyssk … 121,000
Nikolo-Berjozovka … 107,000
Nižnekamsk … 191,000
Nižnevartovsk … 242,000
Nižnij Novgorod (★ 2,025,000) … 1,438,000
Nižnij Tagil … 440,000
Noginsk … 123,000
Nojabr'sk (1987 E) … 77,000
Noril'sk … 174,000
Novgorod … 229,000
Novoaltajsk (★ Barnaul) (1987 E) … 51,000
Novočeboksarsk … 115,000
Novočerkassk … 187,000
Novodvinsk (1987 E) … 50,000
Novokujbyševsk (★ Kujbyšev) … 113,000
Novokuzneck … 600,000
Novomoskovsk (★ 365,000) … 146,000
Novorossijsk … 186,000
Novošachtinsk … 106,000
Novosibirsk (★ 1,600,000) … 1,436,000
Novotroick … 106,000
Novyj Urengoj (1987 E) … 79,000
Obninsk … 100,000
Odincovo (★ Moskva) … 125,000
Okt'abr'skij … 105,000
Omsk (★ 1,175,000) … 1,148,000

C Census. E Official estimate. U Unofficial estimate.
• Largest city in country.
★ Population or designation of metropolitan area, including suburbs (see headnote).
▲ Population of an entire municipality, commune, or district, including rural area.

Orechovo-Zujevo (★ 205,000) ... 137,000
Orel ... 337,208
Orenburg ... 547,000
Orsk ... 271,000
Osinniki (1987 E) ... 63,000
Partizansk (1979 C) ... 45,628
P'atigorsk ... 129,000
Pavlovo (1987 E) ... 72,000
Pavlovskij Posad (1987 E) ... 71,000
Pečora (1987 E) ... 64,000
Penza ... 543,000
Perm' (★ 1,160,000) ... 1,091,000
Pervoural'sk ... 142,000
Petrodvorec (★ Sankt-Peterburg) (1987 E) ... 77,000
Petropavlovsk-Kamčatskij ... 269,000
Petrozavodsk ... 270,000
Podol'sk (★ Moskva) ... 210,000
Polevskoj (1987 E) ... 71,000
Prochladnyj (1987 E) ... 53,000
Prokopjevsk (★ 410,000) ... 274,000
Pskov ... 204,000
Puškin (★ Sankt-Peterburg) (1987 E) ... 97,000
Puškino (1987 E) ... 74,000
Ramenskoje (1987 E) ... 86,000
R'azan' ... 515,000
Reutov (★ Moskva) (1987 E) ... 68,000
Revda (1987 E) ... 66,000
Roslavl' (1987 E) ... 61,000
Rossoš' (1987 E) ... 55,000
Rostov-na-Donu (★ 1,165,000) ... 1,020,000
Rubcovsk ... 172,000
Ruzajevka (1987 E) ... 53,000
Rybinsk ... 252,000
Ržev (1987 E) ... 70,000
Šachty ... 224,000
Šadrinsk (1987 E) ... 87,000
Safonovo (1987 E) ... 56,000
Salavat ... 150,000
Sal'sk (1987 E) ... 62,000
Samara (★ 1,505,000) ... 1,257,000
Sankt-Peterburg (Saint Petersburg) (★ 5,825,000) ... 4,456,000
Saransk ... 312,000
Sarapul ... 111,000
Saratov (★ 1,155,000) ... 905,000
Ščelkovo (★ Moskva) ... 109,000
Ščokino (1987 E) ... 70,000
Sergijev Posad ... 115,000
Serov ... 104,000
Serpuchov ... 144,000
Severodvinsk ... 249,000
Severomorsk (1987 E) ... 55,000
Slav'ansk-Na-Kubani (1987 E) ... 57,000
Smolensk ... 341,000
Soči ... 337,000
Sokol (1979 C) ... 45,424
Solikamsk ... 110,000
Solncevo (★ Moskva) (1984 E) ... 62,000
Solnečnogorsk (★ Moskva) (1987 E) ... 53,000
Sosnovyj Bor (1987 E) ... 56,000
Spassk-Dal'nij (1987 E) ... 60,000
Staryj Oskol ... 174,000
Stavropol' ... 318,000
Sterlitamak ... 248,000
Stupino (1987 E) ... 73,000
Šuja (1987 E) ... 72,000
Surgut ... 248,000
Svobodnyj (1987 E) ... 78,000
Syktyvkar ... 233,000
Syzran' ... 174,000
Taganrog ... 291,000
Talnach (1987 E) ... 54,000
Tambov ... 305,000
Tichoreck (1987 E) ... 67,000
Tichvin (1987 E) ... 70,000
Tobol'sk (1987 E) ... 82,000
Toljatti ... 630,000
Tomsk ... 502,000
Toržok (1987 E) ... 51,000
Troick (1987 E) ... 91,000
Tuapse (1987 E) ... 64,000
Tujmazy (1987 E) ... 54,000
Tula (★ 640,000) ... 540,000
Tulun (1987 E) ... 56,000
T'umen' ... 477,000
Tver' ... 451,000
Tyndinskij (1987 E) ... 61,000
Uchta ... 111,000
Ufa (★ 1,100,000) ... 1,083,000
Uglič (1979 C) ... 39,872
Ulan-Ude ... 353,000
Uljanovsk ... 625,000
Usolje-Sibirskoje ... 107,000
Ussurijsk ... 162,000
Ust'-Ilimsk ... 109,000
Ust'-Kut (1987 E) ... 58,000
Uzlovaja (★ Novomoskovsk) (1987 E) ... 63,000
V'az'ma (1987 E) ... 57,000
Velikije Luki ... 114,000
Verchn'aja Salda (1987 E) ... 56,000
Vičuga (1987 E) ... 51,000
Vladikavkaz ... 300,000
Vladimir ... 350,000
Vladivostok ... 648,000
Volchov (1987 E) ... 51,000
Volgodonsk ... 176,000
Volgograd (Stalingrad) (★ 1,360,000) ... 999,000
Vologda ... 283,000
Vol'sk (1987 E) ... 66,000
Volžsk (1987 E) ... 60,000
Volžskij (★ Volgograd) ... 269,000
Vorkuta ... 116,000
Voronež ... 887,000
Voskresensk (1987 E) ... 80,000
Votkinsk ... 103,000
Vyborg (1987 E) ... 81,000
Vyksa (1987 E) ... 60,000
Vyšnij Voločok (1987 E) ... 70,000
Zelenograd (★ Moskva) ... 158,000
Železnodorožnyj (★ Moskva) (1987 E) ... 90,000
Železnogorsk (1987 E) ... 81,000
Zel'onodol'sk (1987 E) ... 93,000
Žigulevsk (1977 E) ... 50,000
Zima (1987 E) ... 51,000
Zlatoust ... 208,000
Žukovskij ... 101,000

RWANDA

1983 E ... 5,762,000

Cities and Towns

Butare ... 30,000
• KIGALI ... 181,600

SAINT HELENA

1987 C ... 5,644

Cities and Towns

• JAMESTOWN ... 1,413

SAINT KITTS AND NEVIS

1980 C ... 44,404

Cities and Towns

• BASSETERRE ... 14,725
Charlestown ... 1,771

SAINT LUCIA

1987 E ... 142,342

Cities and Towns

• CASTRIES ... 53,933

SAINT PIERRE AND MIQUELON / Saint-Pierre-et-Miquelon

1982 C ... 6,041

Cities and Towns

• SAINT-PIERRE ... 5,371

SAINT VINCENT AND THE GRENADINES

1987 E ... 112,589

Cities and Towns

• KINGSTOWN (★ 28,936) ... 19,028

SAN MARINO

1988 E ... 22,304

Cities and Towns

• SAN MARINO ... 2,777

SAO TOME AND PRINCIPE / São Tomé e Príncipe

1970 C ... 73,631

Cities and Towns

• SÃO TOMÉ ... 17,380

SAUDI ARABIA / Al-'Arabīyah as-Su'ūdīyah

1980 E ... 9,229,000

Cities and Towns

Abhā (1974 C) ... 30,150
Ad-Dammām ... 200,000
Al-Hufūf (1974 C) ... 101,271
Al-Khubar (1974 C) ... 48,817
Al-Madīnah (Medina) ... 290,000
Al-Mubarraz (1974 C) ... 54,325
AR-RIYĀḌ (RIYADH) ... 1,250,000
Aṭ-Ṭā'if ... 300,000
Buraydah (1974 C) ... 69,940
Hā'il (1974 C) ... 40,502
• Jiddah ... 1,300,000
Makkah (Mecca) ... 550,000
Najran (1974 C) ... 47,501
Tabūk (1974 C) ... 74,825

SENEGAL / Sénégal

1988 C ... 6,881,919

Cities and Towns

• DAKAR ... 1,447,642
Diourbel ... 77,548
Kaolack ... 152,007
Louga ... 52,763
Saint-Louis ... 160,689
Thiès ... 184,902
Ziguinchor ... 124,283

SEYCHELLES

1984 E ... 64,718

Cities and Towns

• VICTORIA ... 23,000

SIERRA LEONE

1985 C ... 3,515,812

Cities and Towns

Bo ... 59,768
• FREETOWN (★ 525,000) ... 469,776
Kenema ... 52,473
Koidu ... 82,474
Makeni ... 49,038

SINGAPORE

1989 E ... 2,685,400

Cities and Towns

• SINGAPORE (★ 3,025,000) ... 2,685,400

SLOVAKIA / Slovenská Republika

1990 E ... 5,287,000

Cities and Towns

Banská Bystrica ... 87,834
• BRATISLAVA ... 442,999
Košice ... 237,099
Martin ... 66,678
Nitra ... 91,297
Poprad ... 53,039
Prešov ... 90,121
Prievidza ... 52,624
Trenčín ... 57,813
Trnava ... 72,866
Žilina ... 97,508

SLOVENIA / Slovenija

1987 E ... 1,936,606

Cities and Towns

• LJUBLJANA (▲ 316,607) ... 233,200
Maribor (▲ 187,651) ... 107,400

SOLOMON ISLANDS

1986 C ... 285,176

Cities and Towns

• HONIARA ... 30,413

SOMALIA / Somaliya

1984 E ... 5,423,000

Cities and Towns

Berbera ... 65,000
Hargeysa ... 70,000
Kismayu ... 70,000
Marka ... 60,000
• MUQDISHO ... 600,000

SOUTH AFRICA / Suid-Afrika

1985 C ... 23,385,645

Cities and Towns

Alberton (★ Johannesburg) ... 66,155
Alexandra (★ Johannesburg) ... 67,276
Atteridgeville (★ Pretoria) ... 73,439
Bellville (★ Cape Town) ... 68,915
Benoni (★ Johannesburg) ... 94,926
Bloemfontein (★ 235,000) ... 104,381
Boksburg (★ Johannesburg) ... 110,832
Botshabelo (★ Bloemfontein) ... 95,625
CAPE TOWN (KAAPSTAD) (★ 1,790,000) ... 776,617
Carletonville (★ 120,499) ... 97,874
Daveyton (★ Johannesburg) ... 99,056
Diepmeadow (★ Johannesburg) ... 192,682
Durban (★ 1,550,000) ... 634,301
East London (Oos-Londen) (★ 320,000) ... 85,699
Elsies River (★ Cape Town) ... 70,067
Evaton (★ Vereeniging) ... 52,559
Galeshewe (★ Kimberley) ... 63,238
Germiston (★ ★ Johannesburg) ... 116,718
Grassy Park (★ Cape Town) ... 50,193
Guguletu (★ Cape Town) ... 63,893
• Johannesburg (★ 3,650,000) ... 632,369
Kagiso (★ Johannesburg) ... 50,647
Katlehong (★ Johannesburg) ... 137,745
Kayamnandi (★ Port Elizabeth) ... 220,548
Kempton Park (★ Johannesburg) ... 87,721
Kimberley (★ 145,000) ... 74,061
Klerksdorp (★ 205,000) ... 48,947
Kroonstad (★ 65,165) ... 22,886
Krugersdorp (★ Johannesburg) ... 73,767
Kwa Makuta (★ Durban) ... 71,378
Kwa Mashu (★ Durban) ... 111,593
Kwanobuhle (★ Port Elizabeth) ... 52,376
Kwa-Thema (★ Johannesburg) ... 78,640
Ladysmith (★ 31,670) ... 25,102
Lekoa (Shapeville) (★ Vereeniging) ... 218,392
Madadeni (★ Newcastle) ... 65,832
Mamelodi (★ Pretoria) ... 127,033
Mangaung (★ Bloemfontein) ... 79,851
Newcastle (★ 155,000) ... 34,931
Ntuzuma (★ Durban) ... 61,834
Nyanga (★ Cape Town) ... 148,882
Osizweni (★ Newcastle) ... 51,934
Paarl (★ ★ Cape Town) ... 63,671
Parow (★ Cape Town) ... 60,294
Pietermaritzburg (★ 230,000) ... 133,809
Pinetown (★ Durban) ... 55,770
Port Elizabeth (★ 690,000) ... 272,844
PRETORIA (★ 960,000) ... 443,059
Randburg (★ Johannesburg) ... 74,347
Roodepoort-Maraisburg (★ Johannesburg) ... 141,764
Sandton (★ Johannesburg) ... 86,089
Soshanguve (★ Pretoria) ... 68,598
Soweto (★ Johannesburg) ... 521,948
Springs (★ Johannesburg) ... 68,235
Tembisa (★ Johannesburg) ... 149,282
Uitenhage (★ ★ Port Elizabeth) ... 54,987
Umlazi (★ Durban) ... 194,933
Vanderbijlpark (★ ★ Vereeniging) ... 59,865
Vereeniging (★ 525,000) ... 60,584
Verwoerdburg (★ Pretoria) ... 49,891
Vosloosrus (★ Johannesburg) ... 52,061
Welkom (★ 215,000) ... 54,488
Witbank (★ 77,171) ... 41,784

SPAIN / España

1988 E ... 39,217,804

Cities and Towns

Albacete ... 125,997
Alcalá de Guadaira ... 50,935
Alcalá de Henares (★ Madrid) ... 150,021
Alcobendas (★ Madrid) ... 73,455
Alcorcón (★ Madrid) ... 139,796
Alcoy ... 66,074
Algeciras ... 99,528
Alicante ... 261,051
Almería ... 157,644
Avilés (★ 131,000) ... 87,811
Badajoz (▲ 122,407) ... 106,400
Badalona (★ Barcelona) ... 225,229
Baracaldo (★ Bilbao) ... 113,502
Barcelona (★ 4,040,000) ... 1,714,355
Bilbao (★ 985,000) ... 384,733
Burgos ... 160,561
Cáceres ... 71,598
Cádiz (★ 240,000) ... 156,591
Cartagena (▲ 172,710) ... 70,000
Castelló de la Plana ... 131,809
Ciudad Real ... 56,300
Córdoba ... 302,301
Cornella (★ Barcelona) ... 86,866
Coslada (★ Madrid) ... 88,705
Dos Hermanas (▲ 88,456) ... 00,000
Elche (▲ 180,256) ... 158,300
Elda ... 56,756
El Ferrol del Caudillo (★ 129,000) ... 86,503
El Puerto de Santa María (▲ 62,285) ... 49,900
Fuenlabrada (★ Madrid) ... 128,872
Getafe (★ Madrid) ... 135,367
Gijón ... 262,156
Granada ... 263,334
Granollers (★ Barcelona) ... 49,045
Guadalajara ... 61,309
Hospitalet (★ Barcelona) ... 278,449
Huelva ... 137,826
Irún ... 54,886
Jaén ... 106,435
Jerez de la Frontera (▲ 183,007) ... 156,200
La Coruña ... 248,862
La Línea ... 60,956
Las Palmas de Gran Canaria (▲ 366,347) ... 319,000
Leganés (★ Madrid) ... 168,403
León (★ 159,000) ... 136,558
Lérida (▲ 109,795) ... 91,500
Linares ... 58,622
Logroño ... 119,038
Lugo (▲ 78,795) ... 68,700
• MADRID (★ 4,650,000) ... 3,102,846
Málaga ... 574,456
Manresa ... 65,607
Mataró ... 100,817
Mérida ... 52,368
Móstoles (★ Madrid) ... 181,648
Murcia (▲ 314,124) ... 149,800
Orense ... 106,042
Oviedo (▲ 190,073) ... 168,900
Palencia ... 76,692
Palma [de Mallorca] (▲ 314,608) ... 249,000
Parla (★ Madrid) ... 66,253
Portugalete (★ Bilbao) ... 57,813
Prat del Llobregat (★ Barcelona) ... 64,193
Puertollano ... 52,284
Reus ... 83,800
Sabadell (★ Barcelona) ... 189,489
Salamanca ... 159,342
San Baudilio de Llobregat (★ Barcelona) ... 77,502
San Fernando (★ ★ Cádiz) ... 81,975
San Sebastián (★ 285,000) ... 177,622
San Sebastián de los Reyes (★ Madrid) ... 51,653
Santa Coloma de Gramanet (★ Barcelona) ... 136,042
Santa Cruz de Tenerife ... 215,228
Santander (▲ 190,795) ... 166,800
Santiago de Compostela (▲ 88,110) ... 68,800
Santurce-Antiguo (★ Bilbao) ... 52,334
Segovia ... 54,402
Sevilla (★ 945,000) ... 663,132
Talavera de la Reina ... 68,158
Tarragona (▲ 109,586) ... 63,500
Tarrasa (★ Barcelona) ... 161,410
Toledo ... 59,551
Torrejón de Ardoz (★ Madrid) ... 83,267
Torrente (★ València) ... 55,751
Valencia (★ 1,270,000) ... 743,933
Valladolid ... 331,461
Vigo (▲ 271,128) ... 179,500
Vitoria (Gasteiz) ... 204,264
Zamora ... 62,047
Zaragoza ... 582,239

SPANISH NORTH AFRICA / Plazas de Soberanía en el Norte de África

1988 E ... 122,905

Cities and Towns

• Ceuta ... 67,188
Melilla ... 55,717

SRI LANKA

1986 E ... 16,117,000

Cities and Towns

Battaramulla (★ Colombo) (1981 C) ... 56,535
• COLOMBO (★ 2,050,000) ... 683,000
Dehiwala-Mount Lavinia (★ Colombo) ... 191,000
Galle ... 109,000
Jaffna ... 143,000
Kandy ... 130,000
KOTTE (★ Colombo) ... 104,000
Maharagama (★ Colombo) (1981 C) ... 49,765
Matale (1985 E) ... 57,000
Matara (1985 E) ... 57,000
Moratuwa (★ Colombo) ... 138,000
Negombo (1986 E) ... 76,000
Ratnapura (1985 E) ... 51,000
Trincomalee (1985 E) ... 51,000

SUDAN / As-Sūdān

1983 C ... 20,564,364

Cities and Towns

Al-Fāshir (1973 C) ... 51,902
• AL-KHARṬŪM (★ 1,450,000) ... 476,218
Al-Kharṭūm Baḥrī (★ Al-Kharṭūm) ... 341,146
Al-Qaḍārif (1973 C) ... 66,465
Al-Ubayyiḍ ... 140,000
Atbarah ... 73,000
Būr Sūdān (Port Sudan) ... 206,727
Jūbā (1980 E) ... 116,000
Kassalā ... 143,000
Kūstī (1973 C) ... 65,257
Nyala (1973 C) ... 59,852

C Census. E Official estimate. U Unofficial estimate.
• Largest city in country.

★ Population or designation of metropolitan area, including suburbs (see headnote).
▲ Population of an entire municipality, commune, or district, including rural area.

Umm Durmān (Omdurman) (★ ★ Al-Kharṭūm) ... 526,287
Wad Madanī ... 141,000
Wāw (1980 E) ... 116,000

SURINAME

1988 E ... 392,000

Cities and Towns

• PARAMARIBO (★ 296,000) ... 241,000

SWAZILAND

1986 C ... 712,131

Cities and Towns

LOBAMBA ... 0
Manzini (★ 30,000) ... 18,084
• MBABANE ... 38,290

SWEDEN / Sverige

1990 E ... 8,527,036

Cities and Towns

Borås ... 101,231
Borlänge ... 46,424
Eskilstuna ... 89,460
Gävle (▲ 88,081) ... 67,500
Göteborg (★ 710,894) ... 431,840
Halmstad (▲ 79,362) ... 50,900
Helsingborg ... 108,359
Huddinge (★ Stockholm) ... 73,107
Järfälla (★ Stockholm) ... 56,386
Jönköping ... 110,860
Karlstad ... 76,120
Linköping ... 120,562
Luleå ... 67,903
Lund (★ ★ Malm320) ... 86,412
Malmö (★ 445,000) ... 232,908
Mölndal (★ Göteborg) ... 51,767
Nacka (★ Stockholm) ... 63,114
Norrköping ... 119,921
Örebro ... 120,353
Södertälje (★ Stockholm) ... 81,460
Sollentuna (★ Stockholm) ... 50,606
Solna (★ Stockholm) ... 51,427
• STOCKHOLM (★ 1,449,972) ... 672,187
Sundsvall (▲ 93,404) ... 50,600
Täby (★ Stockholm) ... 56,553
Trollhättan ... 50,602
Tumba (★ Stockholm) ... 68,255
Umeå (▲ 90,004) ... 58,700
Uppsala ... 164,754
Västerås ... 118,386
Växjö (▲ 68,849) ... 45,500

SWITZERLAND / Schweiz / Suisse / Svizzera

1990 E ... 6,673,850

Cities and Towns

Arbon (★ 41,100) ... 12,284
Baden (★ 70,700) ... 14,545
Basel (Bâle) (★ 575,000) ... 169,587
BERN (BERNE) (★ 298,800) ... 134,393
Biel (Bienne) (★ 81,900) ... 52,023
Fribourg (Freiburg) (★ 56,800) ... 33,962
Genève (Geneva) (★ 460,000) ... 165,404
Lausanne (★ 259,900) ... 122,600
Locarno (★ 42,350) ... 14,149
Lugano (★ 94,800) ... 26,055
Luzern (★ 159,500) ... 59,115
Sankt Gallen (★ 125,000) ... 73,191
Sankt Moritz (1987 E) ... 5,335
Solothurn (★ 56,800) ... 15,429
Thun (★ 77,200) ... 37,707
Winterthur (★ 107,400) ... 85,174
• Zürich (★ 860,000) ... 342,861

SYRIA / Sūrīyah

1988 E ... 11,338,000

Cities and Towns

Al-Ḥasakah (1981 C) ... 73,426
Al-Lādhiqīyah (Latakia) ... 249,000
Al-Qāmishlī ... 126,236
As-Suwaydā' ... 46,844
Dar'ā (1981 C) ... 49,534
Dārayyā ... 53,204
Dayr az-Zawr ... 112,000
• DIMASHQ (DAMASCUS) (★ 1,950,000) ... 1,326,000
Dūmā (★ Dimashq) ... 66,130
Halab (Aleppo) (★ 1,275,000) ... 1,261,000
Ḥamāh ... 222,000
Ḥimṣ ... 447,000
Idlib (1981 C) ... 51,682
Jaramānah (★ Dimashq) ... 96,681
Madīnat ath Thawrah ... 58,151
Ṭarṭūs (1981 C) ... 52,589

TAIWAN / T'aiwan

1988 E ... 19,672,612

Cities and Towns

Changhua (▲ 206,603) ... 158,400
Chiai ... 254,875
Chilung ... 348,541
Chungho (★ T'aipei) ... 343,389
Chungli ... 247,639
Chutung ... 104,797
Fangshan (★ Kaohsiung) ... 276,259
Fengyüan (▲ 144,434) ... 115,300
Hsichih (★ T'aipei) (1980 C) ... 70,031
Hsinchu ... 309,899
Hsinchuang (★ T'aipei) ... 259,001
Hsintien (★ T'aipei) ... 205,094
Hualien ... 106,658
Ilan (▲ 81,751) (1980 C) ... 70,900
Kangshan (1980 C) ... 78,049
Kaohsiung (★ 1,845,000) ... 1,342,797
Lotung (1980 C) ... 57,925
Lukang (1980 C) ... 72,019
Miaoli (1980 C) ... 81,500
Nant'ou (1980 C) ... 84,038
P'ingchen (★ T'aipei) ... 134,925
P'ingtung (▲ 204,990) ... 167,600
Sanchung (★ T'aipei) ... 362,171
Shulin (★ T'aipei) (1980 C) ... 75,700
Tach'i (1980 C) ... 67,209
T'aichung ... 715,107
T'ainan ... 656,927
• T'AIPEI (★ 6,130,000) ... 2,637,100
T'aipeihsien (★ T'aipei) ... 506,220
T'aitung (▲ 109,358) ... 79,800
Taoyüan ... 220,255
T'oufen (1980 C) ... 66,536
T'uch'eng (★ T'aipei) ... 70,500
Yangmei (1980 C) ... 84,353
Yüanlin (▲ 116,936) ... 51,300
Yungho (★ T'aipei) ... 242,252
Yungkang (▲ 114,904) ... 59,600

TAJIKISTAN

1989 C ... 5,112,000

Cities and Towns

Chudžand ... 160,000
• DUŠANBE ... 595,000
Kul'ab (1987 E) ... 71,000

TANZANIA

1984 E ... 21,062,000

Cities and Towns

Arusha ... 69,000
• DAR ES SALAAM ... 1,300,000
DODOMA ... 54,000
Iringa ... 67,000
Kigoma (1978 C) ... 50,044
Mbeya ... 93,000
Morogoro ... 72,000
Moshi ... 62,000
Mtwara (1978 C) ... 48,510
Mwanza (1978 C) ... 110,611
Tabora ... 87,000
Tanga ... 121,000
Zanzibar (1985 E) ... 133,000

THAILAND / Prathet Thai

1988 E ... 54,960,917

Cities and Towns

Chiang Mai ... 164,030
Hat Yai ... 138,046
Khon Kaen ... 131,340
• KRUNG THEP (BANGKOK) (★ 6,450,000) ... 5,716,779
Nakhon Ratchasima ... 204,982
Nakhon Sawan ... 105,220
Nakhon Si Thammarat ... 72,407
Nonthaburi (★ Krung Thep) ... 218,354
Pattaya ... 56,402
Phitsanulok ... 77,675
Phra Nakhon Si Ayutthaya ... 60,847
Samut Prakan (★ Krung Thep) ... 73,327
Samut Sakhon ... 53,984
Saraburi ... 61,206
Songkhla ... 84,433
Ubon Ratchathani ... 100,374
Udon Thani ... 81,202
Yala ... 67,383

TOGO

1981 C ... 2,702,945

Cities and Towns

• LOMÉ (1984 E) ... 400,000
Sokodé ... 48,098

TOKELAU

1986 C ... 1,690

TONGA

1986 C ... 94,535

Cities and Towns

• NUKU'ALOFA ... 21,265

TRINIDAD AND TOBAGO

1990 C ... 1,234,388

Cities and Towns

• PORT OF SPAIN (★ 370,000) ... 50,878
San Fernando (★ 75,000) ... 30,092

TUNISIA / Tunis / Tunisie

1984 C ... 6,975,450

Cities and Towns

Ariana (★ Tunis) ... 98,655
Bardo (★ Tunis) ... 65,669
Béja ... 46,708
Ben Arous (★ Tunis) ... 52,105
Binzert ... 94,509
Gabès ... 92,258
Gafsa ... 60,970
Hammam Lif (★ Tunis) ... 47,009
Houmt Essouk ... 92,269
Kairouan ... 72,254
Kasserine ... 47,606
La Goulette (★ Tunis) ... 61,609
Menzel Bourguiba ... 51,399
Nabeul (★ 75,000) ... 39,531
Sfax (★ 310,000) ... 231,911
Sousse (★ 160,000) ... 83,509
• TUNIS (★ 1,225,000) ... 596,654
Zarzis ... 49,063

TURKEY / Türkiye

1990 C ... 56,969,109

Cities and Towns

Adana ... 931,555
Adapazarı ... 174,353
Adıyaman ... 101,306
Afyon ... 98,618
Ağrı ... 57,837
Akhisar ... 74,002
Aksaray ... 92,038
Akşehir ... 51,669
Amasya ... 55,602
ANKARA (★ 2,650,000) ... 2,553,209
Antakya (Antioch) ... 124,443
Antalya ... 378,726
Aydın ... 106,603
Bafra ... 66,209
Balıkesir ... 171,967
Bandırma ... 77,211
Batman ... 148,121
Bolu ... 60,600
Burdur ... 56,095
Bursa ... 838,323
Çanakkale ... 53,887
Ceyhan ... 85,000
Çorlu ... 77,025
Çorum ... 116,260
Denizli ... 203,130
Diyarbakır ... 375,767
Dörtyol ... 48,030
Düzce ... 62,606
Edirne ... 102,325
Elazığ ... 211,720
Elbistan ... 55,114
Ereğli, Konya prov. ... 74,332
Ereğli, Zonguldak prov. ... 63,776
Erzincan ... 90,799
Erzurum ... 241,344
Eskişehir ... 413,305
Gaziantep ... 627,584
Gebze (★ İstanbul) ... 156,594
Gemlik ... 50,212
Giresun ... 67,536
Gölcük ... 65,000
İçel (Mersin) ... 420,750
İnegöl ... 71,095
İskenderun ... 156,198
Isparta ... 111,706
• İstanbul (★ 7,550,000) ... 6,748,435
İzmir (★ 1,900,000) ... 1,762,849
İzmit ... 254,768
Kadirli ... 55,193
Kahramanmaraş ... 229,066
Karabük ... 104,869
Karaman ... 76,682
Kars ... 79,496
Kastamonu ... 52,363
Kayseri ... 416,276
Kilis ... 81,469
Kırıkhan ... 69,323
Kırıkkale ... 203,666
Kırşehir ... 74,546
Kızıltepe ... 60,445
Konya ... 509,208
Kozan ... 54,934
Kütahya ... 131,286
Lüleburgaz ... 51,978
Malatya ... 276,666
Manisa ... 158,283
Mardin ... 52,994
Nazilli ... 80,209
Nevşehir ... 52,514
Niğde ... 54,822
Nizip ... 58,259
Nusaybin ... 50,605
Ödemiş ... 511,110
Ordu ... 101,306
Osmaniye ... 122,315
Polatlı ... 61,026
Rize ... 51,586
Salihli ... 71,035
Samsun ... 301,412
Şanlıurfa ... 276,528
Siirt ... 66,607
Silvan (Miyafarkin) ... 59,959
Sincan (★ Ankara) ... 92,262
Sivas ... 219,122
Siverek ... 63,366
Söke ... 50,598
Soma ... 50,165
Tarsus ... 191,333
Tatvan ... 52,404
Tekirdağ ... 80,207
Tokat ... 83,174
Trabzon ... 144,805
Turgutlu ... 73,734
Turhal ... 71,406
Uşak ... 104,980
Van ... 153,525
Viranşehir ... 58,394
Yalova ... 72,874
Yarımca (1985 C) ... 48,420
Yozgat ... 51,360
Zonguldak (★ 220,000) ... 120,300

TURKMENISTAN

1989 C ... 3,534,000

Cities and Towns

• AŠCHADAD ... 398,000
Krasnovodsk (1987 E) ... 59,000
Mary (1987 E) ... 89,000
Nebit-Dag (1987 E) ... 85,000
Tašauz ... 112,000

TURKS AND CAICOS ISLANDS

1990 C ... 12,350

Cities and Towns

• GRAND TURK ... 3,761

TUVALU

1979 C ... 7,349

Cities and Towns

• FUNAFUTI ... 2,191

UGANDA

1990 E ... 17,213,407

Cities and Towns

Jinja (1982 E) ... 55,000
• KAMPALA ... 1,008,707

UKRAINE / Ukrayina

1989 C ... 51,704,000

Cities and Towns

Alchevs'k (★ Stakhanov) ... 126,000
Antratsyt (★ ★ Krasnyy Luch) (1987 E) ... 70,000
Artemivs'k (1987 E) ... 91,000
Berdyans'k ... 132,000
Berdychiv (1987 E) ... 89,000
Bila Tserkva ... 197,000
Bilhorod-Dnistrovs'kyy (1987 E) ... 54,000
Brovary (★ Kyyiv) (1987 E) ... 73,000
Bryanka (Stakhanov) (1987 E) ... 65,000
Cherkasy ... 290,000
Chernihiv ... 296,000
Chernivtsi ... 257,000
Chervonohrad (1987 E) ... 71,000
Dniprodzerzhyns'k (★ ★ Dnipropetrovs'k) ... 282,000
Dnipropetrovs'k (★ 1,600,000) ... 1,179,000
Donets'k (★ 2,200,000) ... 1,110,000
Drohobych (1987 E) ... 76,000
Druzhkivka (★ Kramatorsk) (1987 E) ... 70,000
Dymytrov (★ ★ Krasnoarmiys'k) (1987 E) ... 62,000
Dzhankoy (1987 E) ... 51,000
Fastiv (1987 E) ... 55,000
Feodosiya (1987 E) ... 83,000
Horlivka (★ 710,000) ... 337,000
Illichivs'k (★ Odesa) (1987 E) ... 52,000
Ivano-Frankivs'k ... 214,000
Izmayil (1987 E) ... 90,000
Izyum (1987 E) ... 63,000
Kalush (1987 E) ... 67,000
Kam'yanets-Podil's'kyy ... 102,000
Kerch ... 174,000
Kharkiv (★ 1,940,000) ... 1,611,000
Khartsyz'k (★ Donets'k) (1987 E) ... 69,000
Kherson ... 355,000
Khmel'nyts'kyy ... 237,000
Kirovohrad ... 269,000
Kolymyya (1987 E) ... 63,000
Konotop (1987 E) ... 93,000
Korosten' (1987 E) ... 72,000
Kostyantynivka ... 108,000
Kovel' (1987 E) ... 66,000
Kramatorsk (★ 465,000) ... 198,000
Krasnoarmiys'k (★ 175,000) (1987 E) ... 70,000
Krasnodon (1987 E) ... 52,000
Krasnyy Luch (★ 250,000) ... 113,000
Kremenchuk ... 236,000
Kryvyy Rih ... 713,000
• KYYIV (KIEV) (★ 2,900,000) ... 2,587,000
Lozova (1987 E) ... 68,000
Lubny (1987 E) ... 58,000
Luhans'k ... 497,000
Luts'k ... 198,000
L'viv ... 790,000
Lysychans'k (★ 410,000) ... 127,000
Makiyivka (★ ★ Donets'k) ... 430,000
Marhanets' (1987 E) ... 55,000
Mariupol' (Ždanov) ... 517,000
Melitopol' ... 174,000
Mukacheve (1987 E) ... 88,000
Mykolayiv ... 503,000
Nizhyn (1987 E) ... 81,000
Nikopol' ... 158,000
Nova Kakhovka (1987 E) ... 53,000
Novohrad-Volyns'kyy (1987 E) ... 52,000
Novomoskovsk (1987 E) ... 76,000
Novovolynsk (1987 E) ... 54,000
Odesa (★ 1,185,000) ... 1,115,000
Oleksandriya ... 103,000
Pavlohrad ... 131,000
Pervomays'k (1987 E) ... 79,000
Poltava ... 315,000
Pryluky (1987 E) ... 73,000
Rivne ... 228,000
Romny (1987 E) ... 53,000
Roven'ky (1987 E) ... 68,000
Rubizhne (★ ★ Lysychans'k) (1987 E) ... 72,000
Sevastopol' ... 356,000
Severodonets'k (★ ★ Lysychans'k) ... 131,000
Shakhtars'k (★ ★ Torez) (1987 E) ... 73,000
Shostka (1987 E) ... 87,000
Simferopol' ... 344,000
Slov'yans'k (★ ★ Kramatorsk) ... 135,000
Smila (1987 E) ... 76,000
Snizhne (★ Torez) (1987 E) ... 68,000
Stakhanov (★ 610,000) ... 112,000
Stryy (1987 E) ... 63,000
Sumy ... 291,000
Sverdlovsk (1987 E) ... 84,000
Svitlovods'k (1987 E) ... 55,000
Ternopil ... 205,000
Torez (★ 290,000) (1987 E) ... 88,000
Uman' (1987 E) ... 89,000
Uzhhorod ... 117,000
Vinnytsya ... 374,000
Yalta (1987 E) ... 89,000
Yenakiyeve (★ ★ Horlivka) ... 121,000
Yevpatoriya ... 108,000
Zaporizhzhya ... 884,000
Zhovti Zody (1987 E) ... 61,000
Zhytomyr ... 292,000

UNITED ARAB EMIRATES / Al-Imārāt al-'Arabīyah al-Muttaḥidah

1980 C ... 980,000

Cities and Towns

ABŪ ZABY (ABU DHABI) ... 242,975
Al-'Ayn ... 101,663
Ash-Shāriqah ... 125,149
• Dubayy ... 265,702

UNITED KINGDOM

1981 C ... 55,678,079

UNITED KINGDOM: ENGLAND

1981 C ... 46,220,955

Cities and Towns

Aldershot (★ London) ... 53,665
Aylesbury ... 51,999
Barnsley ... 76,783
Barrow-in-Furness ... 50,174
Basildon (★ London) ... 94,800
Basingstoke ... 73,027
Bath ... 84,283
Bebington (★ Liverpool) ... 62,618
Bedford ... 75,632
Beeston and Stapleford (★ Nottingham) ... 64,785
Benfleet (★ London) ... 50,783
Birkenhead (★ Liverpool) ... 99,075
Birmingham (★ 2,675,000) ... 1,013,995
Blackburn (★ 221,900) ... 109,564
Blackpool (★ 280,000) ... 146,297
Bognor Regis ... 50,323
Bolton (★ ★ Manchester) ... 143,960
Bootle ... 70,860
Bournemouth (★ 315,000) ... 142,829
Bracknell (★ London) ... 52,257
Bradford (★ ★ Leeds) ... 293,336
Brentwood (★ London) ... 51,212
Brighton (★ 420,000) ... 134,581
Bristol (★ 630,000) ... 413,861
Burnley (★ 160,000) ... 76,365

C Census. E Official estimate. U Unofficial estimate.
• Largest city in country.
★ Population or designation of metropolitan area, including suburbs (see headnote).
▲ Population of an entire municipality, commune, or district, including rural area.

Burton [upon Trent] 59,040
Bury (★ Manchester) 61,785
Cambridge 87,111
Cannock (★ Birmingham) 54,503
Canterbury 34,546
Carlisle 72,206
Chatham (★ London) 65,835
Cheadle and Gatley (★ Manchester)............59,478
Chelmsford (★ London) 91,109
Cheltenham 87,188
Cheshunt (★ London)........49,616
Chester 80,154
Chesterfield (★ 127,000) 73,352
Colchester 87,476
Corby 48,704
Coventry (★ 645,000) 318,718
Crawley (★ London) 80,113
Crewe.......................59,097
Crosby (★ Liverpool) 54,103
Darlington 85,519
Dartford (★ London) 62,032
Derby (★ 275,000)...........218,026
Dewsbury (★ ★ Leeds) 49,612
Doncaster 74,727
Dover 33,461
Dudley (★ ★ Birmingham) 186,513
Eastbourne 86,715
Eastleigh (★ Southampton)..........58,585
Ellesmere Port (★ Liverpool) 65,829
Epsom and Ewell (★ London) 65,830
Exeter.......................88,235
Fareham / Portchester (★ Portsmouth)............55,563
Farnborough (★ London) 48,063
Gateshead (★ Newcastle upon Tyne) 91,429
Gillingham (★ London) 92,531
Gloucester (★ 115,000) 106,526
Gosport (★ Portsmouth) 69,664
Gravesend (★ London) 53,450
Greasby / Moreton (★ Liverpool) 56,410
Great Yarmouth 54,777
Grimsby (★ 145,000) 91,532
Guildford (★ London) 61,509
Halesowen (★ Birmingham) 57,533
Halifax 76,675
Harlow (★ London) 79,150
Harrogate 63,637
Hartlepool (★ ★ Teesside)............91,749
Hastings 74,979
Havant (★ Portsmouth) 50,098
Hemel Hempstead (★ London) 80,110
Hereford 48,277
High Wycombe (▲ 156,800) 69,575
Hove (★ Brighton) 65,587
Huddersfield (▲ 377,400) 147,825
Huyton-with-Roby (★ Liverpool) 62,011
Ipswich.....................129,661
Keighley (★ Leeds) 49,188
Kidderminster 50,385
Kingston upon Hull (★ 350,000) 322,144
Kingswood (★ Bristol) 54,736
Kirkby (★ Liverpool) 52,825
Leeds (★ 1,540,000)........445,242
Leicester (★ 495,000) 324,394
Lincoln 79,980
Littlehampton 46,028
Liverpool (★ 1,525,000) 538,809
• LONDON (★ 11,100,000).........6,574,009
Lowestoft 59,430
Luton (★ 220,000)...........163,209
Macclesfield 47,525
Maidenhead (★ London) 59,809
Maidstone 86,067
Manchester (★ 2,775,000)............437,612
Mansfield (★ 198,000) .....[illegible]
Margate 53,137
Middleton (★ Manchester)............51,373
Milton Keynes 36,886
Newcastle-under-Lyme (★ ★ Stoke-on-Trent) 73,208
Newcastle upon Tyne (★ 1,300,000) 199,064
Northampton 154,172
Norwich (★ 230,000) 169,814
Nottingham (★ 655,000) 273,300
Nuneaton (★ ★ Coventry)............60,337
Oldbury / Smethwick (★ Birmingham) 153,268
Oldham (★ ★ Manchester) 107,095
Oxford (★ 230,000)..........113,847
Penzance 18,501
Peterborough................113,404
Plymouth (★ 290,000) 238,583
Poole (★ ★ Bournemouth) 122,815
Portsmouth (★ 485,000) 174,218
Preston (★ 250,000)........166,675
Ramsgate 36,678
Reading (★ 200,000) 194,727
Redditch (★ Birmingham) 61,639
Rochdale (★ ★ Manchester) 97,292
Rotherham (★ ★ Sheffield) 122,374
Royal Leamington Spa (★ ★ Coventry)............56,552
Rugby.......................59,039
Runcorn (★ Liverpool) 63,995
Saint Albans (★ London)................76,709
Saint Helens 114,397
Sale (★ Manchester).........57,872
Salford (★ Manchester) 96,525
Scunthorpe 79,043
Sheffield (★ 710,000).......470,685
Shrewsbury 57,731
Slough (★ London) 106,341
Solihull (★ Birmingham) 93,940
Southampton (★ 415,000) 211,321
Southend-on-Sea (★ London)...............155,720
Southport (★ ★ Liverpool)............88,596
South Shields (★ ★ Newcastle upon Tyne) 86,488
Stafford 60,915
Staines (★ London)..........51,949
Stevenage...................74,757
Stockport (★ Manchester)...........135,489
Stoke-on-Trent (★ 440,000) 272,446
Stourbridge (★ Birmingham) 55,136
Stratford-upon-Avon 20,941
Stretford (★ Manchester)............47,522
Sunderland (★ ★ Newcastle upon Tyne) 195,064
Sutton Coldfield (★ Birmingham) 102,572
Swindon 127,348
Tanworth....................63,260
Taunton 47,793
Teesside (★ 580,000).......245,215
Torquay (★ 112,400) 54,430
Tunbridge Wells 57,699
Wakefield (★ ★ Leeds) 74,764
Wallasey (★ Liverpool) 62,465
Walsall (★ ★ Birmingham) 177,923
Walton and Weybridge (★ London)................50,031
Warrington 81,366
Waterlooville (★ Portsmouth)............57,296
Watford (★ London) 109,503
West Bromwich (★ Birmingham) 153,725
Weston-super-Mare 60,821
Widnes 55,973
Wigan (★ ★ Manchester) 88,725
Winchester 34,127
Windsor (★ London) 30,832
Woking (★ London)...........92,667
Wolverhampton (★ ★ Birmingham) 263,501
Worcester 75,466
Worthing (★ ★ Brighton) 90,687
York (★ 145,000)...........123,126

UNITED KINGDOM: NORTHERN IRELAND

1987 E...................1,575,200

Cities and Towns

Antrim (1981 C) 22,342
Ballymena (1981 C) 28,166
Bangor (★ Belfast) 70,700
Belfast (★ 685,000).........303,800
Castlereagh (★ Belfast) 57,900
Londonderry (★ 97,200) 97,500
Lurgan (★ 63,000) (1981 C) 20,991
Newtownabbey (★ Belfast) 72,300

UNITED KINGDOM: SCOTLAND

1989 E...................5,090,700

Cities and Towns

Aberdeen 210,700
Ayr (★ 100,000) (1981 C) 48,493
Clydebank (★ Glasgow) (1981 C)..................51,832
Coatbridge (1981 C).........50,831
Cumbernauld (★ Glasgow) 50,300
Dundee 172,540
Dunfermline (★ 125,817) (1981 C) 52,105
East Kilbride (★ Glasgow) 69,500
Edinburgh (★ 630,000) 433,200
Glasgow (★ 1,800,000) 695,630
Greenock (★ 101,000) (1981 C) 58,436
Hamilton (★ Glasgow) (1981 C) 51,666
Irvine (★ 94,000) 55,900
Kilmarnock (★ 84,000) (1981 C) 51,799
Kirkcaldy (★ 148,171) (1981 C) 46,356
Paisley (★ Glasgow) (1981 C) 84,330
Stirling (★ 61,000) (1981 C) 36,640

UNITED KINGDOM: WALES

1981 C...................2,790,462

Cities and Towns

Barry (★ Cardiff).............44,443
Cardiff (★ 625,000).........262,313
Cwmbran (★ Newport) 44,592
Llanelli 45,336
Neath (★ ★ Swansea) 48,687
Newport (★ 310,000).......115,896
Port Talbot (★ 130,000) 40,078
Rhondda (★ ★ Cardiff) 70,980
Swansea (★ 275,000) 172,433

UNITED STATES

1990 C................248,709,873

UNITED STATES: ALABAMA

1990 C...................4,040,587

Cities and Towns

Birmingham 265,968
Decatur 48,761
Dothan 53,589
Florence.....................36,426
Gadsden 42,523
Huntsville...................159,789
Mobile.......................196,278
Montgomery.................187,106
Tuscaloosa..................77,759

UNITED STATES: ALASKA

1990 C.....................550,043

Cities and Towns

Anchorage 226,338
Fairbanks 30,843
Juneau 26,751

UNITED STATES: ARIZONA

1990 C...................3,665,228

Cities and Towns

Chandler 90,533
Flagstaff 45,857
Glendale 148,134
Mesa........................288,091
Peoria 50,618
Phoenix 900,013
Scottsdale..................130,069
Sun City 57,000
Tempe 141,865
Tucson.....................405,390
Yuma 54,923

UNITED STATES: ARKANSAS

1990 C...................2,350,725

Cities and Towns

Fort Smith...................72,798
Little Rock 175,795
North Little Rock 61,741
Pine Bluff 57,140

UNITED STATES: CALIFORNIA

1990 C................. 29,760,021

Cities and Towns

Alameda 76,459
Alhambra....................82,106
Anaheim 266,406
Antioch......................62,195
Bakersfield 174,820
Baldwin Park 69,330
Bellflower 61,815
Berkeley 102,724
Beverly Hills 31,971
Buena Park 68,784
Burbank......................93,643
Camarillo 52,303
Carlsbad 63,126
Carson 83,995
Cerritos 53,240
Chino 59,682
Chula Vista.................135,163
Citrus Heights 107,439
Clovis 50,323
Compton 90,454
Concord 111,348
Corona 76,095
Costa Mesa 96,357
Cucamonga 101,409
Daly City 92,311
Diamond Bar 53,672
Downey 91,444
East Los Angeles 126,379
El Cajon.....................88,693
El Monte 106,209
Encinitas 55,386
Escondido..................108,635
Fairfield 77,211
Fontana 87,535
Fountain Valley 53,691
Fremont 173,339
Fresno 354,202
Fullerton 114,144
Gardena.....................49,847
Garden Grove 143,050
Glendale 180,038
Hacienda Heights............52,354
Hawthorne 71,349
Hayward 111,498
Hesperia 50,418
Huntington Beach 181,519
Huntington Park 56,065
Inglewood 109,602
Irvine.......................110,330
La Habra 51,266
Lakewood 73,557
La Mesa 52,931
Lancaster 97,291
Livermore 56,741
Lodi 51,874
Long Beach 429,433
Los Angeles 3,485,398
Lynwood 61,945
Merced 56,216
Milpitas 50,686
Mission Viejo 72,820
Modesto 164,730
Montebello 59,564
Monterey Park 60,738
Moreno Valley 118,779
Mountain View 67,460
Napa.........................61,842
National City 54,249
Newport Beach..............66,643
Norwalk 94,279
Oakland 372,242
Oceanside..................128,398
Ontario 133,179
Orange 110,658
Oxnard 142,216
Palmdale 68,842
Palm Springs 40,181
Palo Alto 55,900
Pasadena 131,591
Pico Rivera..................59,177
Pleasanton 50,553
Pomona 131,723
Redding 66,462
Redlands 60,394
Redondo Beach 60,167
Redwood City 66,072
Rialto 72,388
Richmond 87,425
Riverside 226,505
Rosemead 51,638
Sacramento 369,365
Salinas 108,777
San Bernardino.............164,164
San Diego 1,110,549
San Francisco 723,959
San Jose 782,248
San Leandro 68,223
San Mateo 85,486
Santa Ana..................293,742
Santa Barbara...............85,571
Santa Clara 93,613
Santa Clarita 110,642
Santa Cruz 49,040
Santa Maria 61,284
Santa Monica 86,905
Santa Rosa 113,313
Santee 52,902
Simi Valley 100,217
South Gate...................86,284
South San Francisco 54,312
Stockton 210,943
Sunnyvale 117,229
Thousand Oaks 104,352
Torrance 133,107
Tustin 50,689
Union City 53,762
Upland 63,374
Vacaville 71,479
Vallejo.....................109,199
Ventura (San Buenaventura) 92,575
Visalia.......................75,636
Vista 71,872
Walnut Creek 60,569
West Covina 96,086
Westminster.................78,118
Whittier 77,671
Yorba Linda 52,422

UNITED STATES: COLORADO

1990 C...................3,294,394

Cities and Towns

Arvada 89,235
Aurora 222,103
Boulder 83,312
Colorado Springs 281,140
Denver 467,610
Fort Collins..................87,758
Greeley 60,536
Lakewood 126,481
Longmont 51,555
Pueblo 98,640
Thornton 55,031
Westminster.................74,625

UNITED STATES: CONNECTICUT

1990 C...................3,287,116

Cities and Towns

Bridgeport..................141,686
Bristol 60,640
Danbury 65,585
East Hartford.................50,452
Fairfield 52,400
Greenwich...................58,000
Hamden 53,100
Hartford 139,739
Manchester 51,000
Meriden 59,479
Milford 48,168
New Britain 75,491
New Haven 130,474
Norwalk 78,331
Stamford 108,056
Stratford 50,400
Waterbury..................108,961
West Hartford 59,100
West Haven 54,021

UNITED STATES: DELAWARE

1990 C.....................666,168

Cities and Towns

Dover 27,630
Newark 25,098
Wilmington 71,529

UNITED STATES: DISTRICT OF COLUMBIA

1990 C.....................606,900

Cities and Towns

WASHINGTON 606,900

UNITED STATES: FLORIDA

1990 C................ 12,937,926

Cities and Towns

Boca Raton 61,492
Cape Coral 74,991
Carol City 52,800
City of Sunrise 64,407
Clearwater 98,784
Corol Springs 79,443
Daytona Beach 61,921
Delray Beach 47,181
Fort Lauderdale 149,377
Gainesville...................84,770
Hialeah 188,004
Hollywood..................121,697
Jacksonville 635,230
Kendall 53,100
Lakeland 70,576
Largo 65,674
Lauderhill....................49,708
Melbourne...................59,646
Miami 358,548
Miami Beach 92,639
North Miami 49,998
Orlando 164,693
Palm Bay....................62,632
Pembroke Pines 65,452
Pensacola 58,165
Plantation 66,692
Pompano Beach..............72,411
Port Saint Lucie 55,866
Saint Petersburg 238,629
Sarasota 50,961
Tallahassee 124,773
Tampa 280,015
West Palm Beach 67,643

UNITED STATES: GEORGIA

1990 C...................6,478,216

Cities and Towns

Albany 78,122
Athens 45,734
Atlanta 394,017
Columbus 178,681
Macon 106,612
Savannah 137,560

UNITED STATES: HAWAII

1990 C...................1,108,229

Cities and Towns

Hilo 37,808
Honolulu 365,272
Pearl City 30,993

UNITED STATES: IDAHO

1990 C...................1,006,749

Cities and Towns

Boise 125,738
Idaho Falls 43,929
Pocatello 46,080

UNITED STATES: ILLINOIS

1990 C................. 11,430,602

Cities and Towns

Arlington Heights 75,460
Aurora 99,581
Bloomington.................51,972
Champaign 63,502
Chicago 2,783,726
Cicero 67,436
Decatur 83,885
Des Plaines 53,223
Elgin 77,010
Evanston 73,233
Joliet 76,836

C Census. E Official estimate. U Unofficial estimate.
• Largest city in country.
★ Population or designation of metropolitan area, including suburbs (see headnote).
▲ Population of an entire municipality, commune, or district, including rural area.

- Mount Prospect 53,170
- Naperville 85,351
- Oak Lawn 56,182
- Oak Park 53,648
- Peoria 113,504
- Rockford 139,426
- Schaumburg 68,586
- Skokie 59,432
- Springfield 105,227
- Waukegan 69,392
- Wheaton 51,464

UNITED STATES: INDIANA

1990 C 5,544,159

Cities and Towns

- Anderson 59,459
- Bloomington 60,633
- Evansville 126,272
- Fort Wayne 173,072
- Gary 116,646
- Hammond 84,236
- Indianapolis 731,327
- Kokomo 44,962
- Lafayette 43,764
- Michigan City 33,822
- Muncie 71,035
- South Bend 105,511
- Terre Haute 57,483

UNITED STATES: IOWA

1990 C 2,776,755

Cities and Towns

- Ames 47,198
- Cedar Rapids 108,751
- Council Bluffs 54,315
- Davenport 95,333
- Des Moines 193,187
- Dubuque 57,546
- Iowa City 59,738
- Sioux City 80,505
- Waterloo 66,467

UNITED STATES: KANSAS

1990 C 2,477,574

Cities and Towns

- Kansas City 149,767
- Lawrence 65,608
- Olathe 63,352
- Overland Park 111,790
- Topeka 119,883
- Wichita 304,011

UNITED STATES: KENTUCKY

1990 C 3,685,296

Cities and Towns

- Frankfort 25,968
- Lexington 225,366
- Louisville 269,063
- Owensboro 53,549

UNITED STATES: LOUISIANA

1990 C 4,219,973

Cities and Towns

- Alexandria 49,188
- Baton Rouge 219,531
- Bossier City 52,721
- Houma 96,982
- Kenner 72,033
- Lafayette 94,440
- Lake Charles 70,580
- Metairie 149,428
- Monroe 54,909
- New Orleans 496,938
- Shreveport 198,525

UNITED STATES: MAINE

1990 C 1,227,928

Cities and Towns

- Augusta 21,325
- Bangor 33,181
- Lewiston 39,757
- Portland 64,358

UNITED STATES: MARYLAND

1990 C 4,781,468

Cities and Towns

- Annapolis 33,187
- Baltimore 736,014
- Bethesda 62,936
- Columbia 75,883
- Dundalk 65,800
- Rockville 44,835
- Silver Spring 76,200
- Towson 49,445
- Wheaton 58,300

UNITED STATES: MASSACHUSETTS

1990 C 6,016,425

Cities and Towns

- Boston 574,283
- Brockton 92,788
- Brookline 54,718
- Cambridge 95,802
- Chicopee 56,632
- Fall River 92,703
- Framingham 64,989
- Haverhill 51,418
- Holyoke 43,704
- Lawrence 70,207
- Lowell 103,439
- Lynn 81,245
- Malden 53,884
- Medford 57,407
- New Bedford 99,922
- Newton 82,585
- Peabody 47,039
- Pittsfield 48,622
- Quincy 84,985
- Salem 38,091
- Somerville 76,210
- Springfield 156,983
- Taunton 49,832
- Waltham 57,878
- Weymouth 54,063
- Worcester 169,759

UNITED STATES: MICHIGAN

1990 C 9,295,297

Cities and Towns

- Ann Arbor 109,592
- Battle Creek 53,540
- Clinton 85,866
- Dearborn 89,286
- Dearborn Heights 60,838
- Detroit 1,027,974
- East Lansing 50,677
- Farmington Hills 74,652
- Flint 140,761
- Grand Rapids 189,126
- Kalamazoo 80,277
- Lansing 127,321
- Livonia 100,850
- Pontiac 71,166
- Redford 54,387
- Rochester Hills 61,766
- Roseville 51,412
- Royal Oak 65,410
- Saginaw 69,512
- Saint Clair Shores 68,107
- Southfield 75,728
- Sterling Heights 117,810
- Taylor 70,811
- Troy 72,884
- Warren 144,864
- Westland 84,724
- Wyoming 63,891

UNITED STATES: MINNESOTA

1990 C 4,375,099

Cities and Towns

- Bloomington 86,335
- Brooklyn Park 56,381
- Burnsville 51,288
- Coon Rapids 52,978
- Duluth 85,493
- Minneapolis 368,383
- Minnetonka 48,370
- Plymouth 50,889
- Rochester 70,745
- Saint Cloud 48,812
- Saint Paul 272,235

UNITED STATES: MISSISSIPPI

1990 C 2,573,216

Cities and Towns

- Biloxi 46,319
- Hattiesburg 41,882
- Jackson 196,637

UNITED STATES: MISSOURI

1990 C 5,117,073

Cities and Towns

- Columbia 69,101
- Florissant 51,206
- Independence 112,301
- Jefferson City 35,481
- Kansas City 435,146
- Saint Charles 54,555
- Saint Joseph 71,852
- Saint Louis 396,685
- Springfield 140,494

UNITED STATES: MONTANA

1990 C 799,065

Cities and Towns

- Billings 81,151
- Great Falls 55,097
- Helena 24,569

UNITED STATES: NEBRASKA

1990 C 1,578,385

Cities and Towns

- Grand Island 39,386
- Lincoln 191,972
- Omaha 335,795

UNITED STATES: NEVADA

1990 C 1,201,833

Cities and Towns

- Carson City 40,443
- Henderson 64,942
- Las Vegas 258,295
- Paradise 124,682
- Reno 133,850
- Sparks 53,367
- Sunrise Manor 95,362

UNITED STATES: NEW HAMPSHIRE

1990 C 1,109,252

Cities and Towns

- Concord 36,006
- Manchester 99,567
- Nashua 79,662

UNITED STATES: NEW JERSEY

1990 C 7,730,188

Cities and Towns

- Atlantic City 37,986
- Bayonne 61,444
- Brick [Township] 64,800
- Camden 87,492
- Cherry Hill 69,319
- Clifton 71,742
- East Orange 73,552
- Edison 88,680
- Elizabeth 110,002
- Irvington 59,774
- Jersey City 228,537
- Newark 275,221
- Passaic 58,041
- Paterson 140,891
- Trenton 88,675
- Union 50,024
- Union City 58,012
- Vineland 54,780
- Woodbridge [Township] (1986 U) 95,100

UNITED STATES: NEW MEXICO

1990 C 1,515,069

Cities and Towns

- Albuquerque 384,736
- Las Cruces 62,126
- Roswell 44,654
- Santa Fe 55,859

UNITED STATES: NEW YORK

1990 C 17,990,455

Cities and Towns

- Albany 101,082
- Binghamton 53,008
- Buffalo 328,123
- Cheektowaga 84,387
- Greece 64,600
- Irondequoit 52,322
- Levittown 53,286
- Mount Vernon 67,153
- New Rochelle 67,265
- • New York 7,322,564
- Niagara Falls 61,840
- Rochester 231,636
- Schenectady 65,566
- Syracuse 163,860
- Tonawanda 65,284
- Troy 54,269
- Utica 68,637
- Yonkers 188,082

UNITED STATES: NORTH CAROLINA

1990 C 6,628,637

Cities and Towns

- Asheville 61,607
- Charlotte 395,934
- Durham 136,611
- Fayetteville 75,695
- Gastonia 54,732
- Greensboro 183,521
- High Point 69,496
- Raleigh 207,951
- Rocky Mount 48,997
- Wilmington 55,530
- Winston-Salem 143,485

UNITED STATES: NORTH DAKOTA

1990 C 638,800

Cities and Towns

- Bismarck 49,256
- Fargo 74,111
- Grand Forks 49,425

UNITED STATES: OHIO

1990 C 10,847,115

Cities and Towns

- Akron 223,019
- Canton 84,161
- Cincinnati 364,040
- Cleveland 505,616
- Cleveland Heights 54,052
- Columbus 632,910
- Dayton 182,044
- Elyria 56,746
- Euclid 54,875
- Hamilton 61,368
- Kettering 60,569
- Lakewood 59,718
- Lorain 71,245
- Mansfield 50,627
- Parma 87,876
- Springfield 70,487
- Toledo 332,943
- Warren 50,793
- Youngstown 95,732

UNITED STATES: OKLAHOMA

1990 C 3,145,585

Cities and Towns

- Broken Arrow 58,043
- Edmond 52,315
- Lawton 80,561
- Midwest City 52,267
- Norman 80,071
- Oklahoma City 444,719
- Tulsa 367,302

UNITED STATES: OREGON

1990 C 2,842,321

Cities and Towns

- Beaverton 53,310
- Eugene 112,669
- Gresham 68,235
- Portland 437,319
- Salem 107,786

UNITED STATES: PENNSYLVANIA

1990 C 11,881,643

Cities and Towns

- Abington Township 59,300
- Allentown 105,090
- Altoona 51,881
- Bensalem 56,788
- Bethlehem 71,428
- Bristol 57,129
- Erie 108,718
- Harrisburg 52,376
- Haverford Township 51,800
- Lancaster 55,551
- Lower Merion 58,003
- Penn Hills 51,430
- Philadelphia 1,585,577
- Pittsburgh 369,879
- Reading 78,380
- Scranton 81,805
- Upper Darby 86,100

UNITED STATES: RHODE ISLAND

1990 C 1,003,464

Cities and Towns

- Cranston 76,060
- East Providence 50,380
- Pawtucket 72,644
- Providence 160,728
- Warwick 85,427

UNITED STATES: SOUTH CAROLINA

1990 C 3,486,703

Cities and Towns

- Charleston 80,414
- Columbia 98,052
- Greenville 58,282
- North Charleston 70,218

UNITED STATES: SOUTH DAKOTA

1990 C 696,004

Cities and Towns

- Pierre 12,906
- Rapid City 54,523
- Sioux Falls 100,814

UNITED STATES: TENNESSEE

1990 C 4,877,185

Cities and Towns

- Chattanooga 152,466
- Clarksville 75,494
- Jackson 48,949
- Knoxville 165,121
- Memphis 610,337
- Nashville 487,969

UNITED STATES: TEXAS

1990 C 16,986,510

Cities and Towns

- Abilene 106,654
- Amarillo 157,615
- Arlington 261,721
- Austin 465,622
- Baytown 63,850
- Beaumont 114,323
- Brownsville 98,962
- Bryan 55,002
- Carrollton 82,169
- College Station 52,456
- Corpus Christi 257,453
- Dallas 1,006,877
- Denton 66,270
- El Paso 515,342
- Fort Worth 447,619
- Galveston 59,070
- Garland 180,650
- Grand Prairie 99,616
- Houston 1,630,553
- Irving 155,037
- Killeen 63,535
- Laredo 122,899
- Longview 70,311
- Lubbock 186,206
- McAllen 84,021
- Mesquite 101,484
- Midland 89,443
- Odessa 89,699
- Pasadena 119,363
- Plano 128,713
- Port Arthur 58,724
- Richardson 74,840
- San Angelo 84,474
- San Antonio 935,933
- Tyler 75,450
- Victoria 55,076
- Waco 103,590
- Wichita Falls 96,259

UNITED STATES: UTAH

1990 C 1,722,850

Cities and Towns

- Ogden 63,909
- Orem 67,561
- Provo 86,835
- Salt Lake City 159,936
- Sandy 75,058
- West Valley City 86,976

UNITED STATES: VERMONT

1990 C 562,758

Cities and Towns

- Burlington 39,127
- Montpelier 8,247
- Rutland 18,230

UNITED STATES: VIRGINIA

1990 C 6,187,358

Cities and Towns

- Alexandria 111,183
- Arlington 170,936
- Chesapeake 151,976
- Danville 53,056
- Hampton 133,793
- Lynchburg 66,049
- Newport News 170,045
- Norfolk 261,229
- Petersburg 38,386
- Portsmouth 103,907
- Richmond 203,056
- Roanoke 96,397
- Suffolk 52,141
- Virginia Beach 393,069

UNITED STATES: WASHINGTON

1990 C 4,866,692

Cities and Towns

- Bellevue 86,874
- Bellingham 52,179
- Everett 69,961
- Lakewood Center 62,000
- Olympia 33,840
- Seattle 516,259
- Spokane 177,196
- Tacoma 176,664
- Yakima 54,827

UNITED STATES: WEST VIRGINIA

1990 C 1,793,477

Cities and Towns

- Charleston 57,287
- Huntington 54,844
- Parkersburg 33,862
- Wheeling 34,882

UNITED STATES: WISCONSIN

1990 C 4,891,769

Cities and Towns

- Appleton 65,695
- Eau Claire 56,856
- Fond du Lac 37,757
- Green Bay 96,466
- Janesville 52,133
- Kenosha 80,352
- La Crosse 51,003
- Madison 191,262
- Milwaukee 628,088
- Oshkosh 55,006
- Racine 84,298
- Sheboygan 49,676
- Waukesha 56,958
- Wausau 37,060
- Wauwatosa 49,366
- West Allis 63,221

UNITED STATES: WYOMING

1990 C 453,588

Cities and Towns

- Casper 46,742
- Cheyenne 50,008
- Laramie 26,687

C Census. E Official estimate. U Unofficial estimate.
• Largest city in country.

★ Population or designation of metropolitan area, including suburbs (see headnote).
▲ Population of an entire municipality, commune, or district, including rural area.

URUGUAY

1985 C ... 2,955,241

Cities and Towns

- Las Piedras (★ Montevideo) ... 58,288
- • MONTEVIDEO (★ 1,550,000) ... 1,251,647
- Paysandú ... 76,191
- Rivera ... 57,316
- Salto ... 80,823

UZBEKISTAN / Ŭzbekiston

1989 C ... 19,906,000

Cities and Towns

- Almalyk ... 114,000
- Andižan ... 293,000
- Angren ... 131,000
- Bekabad (1987 E) ... 80,000
- Buchara ... 224,000
- Chodžejli (1987 E) ... 55,000
- Čirčik (★ Taškent) ... 156,000
- Denau (1987 E) ... 53,000
- Džizak ... 102,000
- Fergana ... 200,000
- Gulistan (1987 E) ... 51,000
- Jangijul' (1987 E) ... 71,000
- Karši ... 156,000
- Kattakurgan (1987 E) ... 63,000
- Kokand ... 182,000
- Margilan ... 125,000
- Namangan ... 308,000
- Navoi ... 107,000
- Nukus ... 169,000
- Samarkand ... 366,000
- • TAŠKENT (★ 2,325,000 ... 2,073,000
- Termez (1987 E) ... 72,000
- Urgenč ... 128,000

VANUATU

1989 C ... 142,419

Cities and Towns

- • PORT VILA (★ 23,000) ... 18,905

VATICAN CITY / Città del Vaticano

1988 E ... 766

VENEZUELA

1981 C ... 14,516,735

Cities and Towns

- Acarigua ... 91,662
- Barcelona ... 156,461
- Barinas ... 110,462
- Barquisimeto ... 497,635
- Baruta (★ Caracas) ... 200,063
- Cabimas ... 140,435
- Cagua ... 53,704
- Calabozo ... 61,995
- • CARACAS (★ 3,600,000) ... 1,816,901
- Carora ... 58,694
- Carúpano ... 64,579
- Catia La Mar (★ Caracas) ... 87,916
- Chacao (★ Caracas) ... 72,703
- Ciudad Bolívar ... 182,941
- Ciudad Guayana ... 314,497
- Ciudad Ojeda (Lagunillas) ... 83,565
- Coro ... 96,339
- Cumaná ... 179,814
- El Limón ... 65,122
- El Tigre ... 73,595
- Guacara ... 72,727
- Guanare ... 64,025
- Guarenas (★ Caracas) ... 101,742
- La Victoria ... 70,828
- Los Dos Caminos (★ Caracas) ... 63,346
- Los Teques (★ Caracas) ... 112,857
- Maiquetía (★ Caracas) ... 66,056
- Maracaibo ... 890,643
- Maracay ... 322,560
- Maturín ... 154,976
- Mérida ... 143,209
- Petare (★ Caracas) ... 395,715
- Porlamar ... 51,079
- Pozuelos ... 80,342
- Puerto Cabello ... 71,759
- Puerto la Cruz ... 53,881
- Punto Fijo ... 71,114
- San Cristóbal ... 198,793
- San Felipe ... 57,526
- San Fernando de Apure ... 57,308
- San Juan de los Morros ... 57,219
- Turmero ... 111,186
- Valencia ... 616,224
- Valera ... 102,068
- Valle de la Pascua ... 55,761

VIETNAM / Viet Nam

1979 C ... 52,741,766

Cities and Towns

- Bac Giang ... 54,506
- Bien Hoa ... 187,254
- Buon Me Thuot ... 71,815
- Ca Mau ... 67,484
- Cam Pha ... 76,697
- Cam Ranh (1973 E) ... 118,111
- Can Tho ... 182,856
- Da Lat ... 87,136
- Da Nang ... 318,653
- Hai Duong ... 54,579
- Hai Phong (▲ 1,279,067) (1989 C) ... 456,000
- HA NOI (★ 1,500,000) (1989 C) ... 1,089,000
- Hoa Binh ... 51,187
- Hon Gai ... 114,573
- Hue ... 165,710
- Long Xuyen ... 112,485
- Minh Hai ... 72,517
- My Tho ... 101,493
- Nam Dinh ... 160,179
- Nha Trang ... 172,663
- Phan Thiet ... 75,241
- Play Cu ... 58,088
- Qui Nhon ... 127,211
- Rach Gia ... 81,075
- Sa Dec ... 73,104
- Soc Trang ... 74,967
- Thai Binh ... 79,566
- Thai Nguyen ... 138,023
- Thanh Hoa ... 72,646
- • Thanh Pho Ho Chi Minh (Saigon) (★ 3,100,000) (1989 C) ... 3,169,000
- Tra Vinh ... 44,020
- Tuy Hoa ... 46,617
- Viet Tri ... 72,108
- Vinh ... 159,753
- Vinh Long ... 71,505
- Vung Tau ... 81,694

VIRGIN ISLANDS OF THE UNITED STATES

1980 C ... 96,569

Cities and Towns

- • CHARLOTTE AMALIE (★ 32,000) ... 11,842

WALLIS AND FUTUNA / Wallis et Futuna

1983 E ... 12,408

Cities and Towns

- • MATA-UTU ... 815

WESTERN SAHARA

1982 E ... 142,000

Cities and Towns

- • EL AAIÚN ... 93,875

WESTERN SAMOA / Samoa i Sisifo

1981 C ... 156,349

Cities and Towns

- • APIA ... 33,170

YEMEN / Al-Yaman

1990 E ... 11,282,000

Cities and Towns

- 'Adan (★ 318,000) (1984 E) ... 176,100
- Al-Hudaydah (1986 C) ... 155,110
- Al-Mukallā (1984 E) ... 58,000
- • SAN'Ā' (1986 C) ... 427,150
- Ta'izz (1986 C) ... 178,043

YUGOSLAVIA / Jugoslavija

1987 E ... 10,342,020

Cities and Towns

- • BEOGRAD (★ 1,400,000) ... 1,130,000
- Kragujevac (▲ 171,609) ... 94,800
- Niš (▲ 240,219) ... 168,400
- Novi Sad (▲ 266,772) ... 176,000
- Pančevo (★ Beograd) ... 62,700
- Podgorica (▲ 145,163) ... 82,500
- Priština (▲ 244,830) ... 125,400
- Subotica (▲ 153,306) ... 100,500
- Zrenjanin (▲ 140,009) ... 65,400

ZAIRE / Zaïre

1984 C ... 29,671,407

Cities and Towns

- Bandundu ... 63,189
- Beni ... 73,319
- Boma ... 88,556
- Bukavu ... 171,064
- Butembo ... 78,633
- Gandajika ... 60,263
- Gemena ... 62,641
- Goma ... 76,745
- Ilebo (Port-Francqui) ... 48,831
- Isiro ... 78,871
- Kabinda ... 81,752
- Kalemie (Albertville) ... 70,694
- Kananga (Luluabourg) ... 290,898
- Kikwit ... 146,784
- Kindu ... 68,044
- • KINSHASA (LÉOPOLDVILLE) (1986 E) ... 3,000,000
- Kisangani (Stanleyville) ... 282,650
- Kolwezi ... 201,382
- Likasi (Jadotville) ... 194,465
- Lubumbashi (Élisabethville) ... 543,268
- Manono ... 51,755
- Matadi ... 144,742
- Mbandaka (Coquilhatville) ... 125,263
- Mbuji-Mayi (Bakwanga) ... 423,363
- Mwene-Ditu ... 72,567
- Tshikapa ... 105,484
- Yangambi ... 53,726

ZAMBIA

1980 C ... 5,661,801

Cities and Towns

- Chililabombwe (Bancroft) (★ 56,582) ... 25,900
- Chingola ... 130,872
- Kabwe (Broken Hill) ... 127,420
- Kalulushi ... 53,383
- Kitwe (★ 283,962) ... 207,500
- Livingstone ... 61,296
- Luanshya (★ 113,422) ... 61,600
- • LUSAKA ... 535,830
- Mufulira (★ 138,824) ... 77,100
- Ndola ... 250,490

ZIMBABWE

1983 E ... 7,740,000

Cities and Towns

- Bulawayo ... 429,000
- Chitungwiza (★ Harare) ... 202,000
- Gweru (1982 C) ... 78,940
- • HARARE (★ 890,000) ... 681,000
- Kwekwe (1982 C) ... 47,976
- Mutare (1982 C) ... 75,358

C Census. E Official estimate. U Unofficial estimate.
• Largest city in country.

★ Population or designation of metropolitan area, including suburbs (see headnote).
▲ Population of an entire municipality, commune, or district, including rural area.

United States General Information

Geographical Facts

ELEVATION

The highest elevation in the United States is Mount McKinley, Alaska, 20,320 feet.

The lowest elevation in the United States is in Death Valley, California, 282 feet below sea level.

The average elevation of the United States is 2,500 feet.

EXTREMITIES

Direction	Location	Latitude	Longitude
North	Point Barrow, Ak.	71° 23'N.	156° 29'W.
South	Ka Lae (point) Hi.	18° 56'N.	155° 41'W.
East	West Quoddy Head, Me.	44° 49'N.	66° 57'W.
West	Cape Wrangell, Ak.	52° 55'N.	172° 27'E.

LENGTH OF BOUNDARIES

The total length of the Canadian boundary of the United States is 5,525 miles.

The total length of the Mexican boundary of the United States is 1,933 miles.

The total length of the Atlantic coastline of the United States is 2,069 miles.

The total length of the Pacific and Arctic coastline of the United States is 8,683 miles.

The total length of the Gulf of Mexico coastline of the United States is 1,631 miles.

The total length of all coastlines and land boundaries of the United States is 19,841 miles.

The total length of the tidal shoreline and land boundaries of the United States is 96,091 miles.

GEOGRAPHIC CENTERS

The geographic center of the United States (including Alaska and Hawaii) is in Butte County, South Dakota at 44° 58'N., 103° 46'W,

The geographic center of North America is in North Dakota, a few miles west of Devils Lake, at 48° 10'N., 100° 10'W.

EXTREMES OF TEMPERATURE

The highest temperature ever recorded in the United States was 134° F., at Greenland Ranch, Death Valley, California, on July 10, 1913.

The lowest temperature ever recorded in the United States was -80° F., at Prospect Creek, Alaska, on January 23, 1971.

Historical Facts

TERRITORIAL ACQUISITIONS

Accession	Date	Area (sq. mi.)	Cost in Dollars
Original territory of the Thirteen States	1790	888,685	
Purchase of Louisiana Territory, from France	1803	827,192	$11,250,000
By treaty with Spain: Florida	1819	58,560	5,000,000
Other areas	1819	13,443	
Annexation of Texas	1845	390,144	
Oregon Territory, by treaty with Great Britain	1846	285,580	
Mexican Cession	1848	529,017	$15,000,000
Gadsden Purchase, from Mexico	1853	29,640	$10,000,000
Purchase of Alaska, from Russia	1867	586,412	7,200,000
Annexation of Hawaiian Islands	1898	6,450	
Puerto Rico, by treaty with Spain	1899	3,435	
Guam, by treaty with Spain	1899	212	
American Samoa, by treaty with Great Britain and Germany	1900	76	
Virgin Islands, by purchase from Denmark	1917	133	$25,000,000

Note: The Philippines, ceded by Spain in 1898 for $20,000,000 were a territorial possession of the United States from 1898 to 1946. On July 4, 1946 they became the independent Republic of the Philippines.

Note: The Canal Zone, ceded by Panama in 1903 for $10,000,000 was a territory of the United States from 1903 to 1979. As a result of treaties signed in 1977, sovereignty over the Canal Zone reverted to Panama in 1979.

WESTWARD MOVEMENT OF CENTER OF POPULATION

Year	U.S.Population Total at Census	Approximate Location
1790	3,929,214	23 miles east of Baltimore, Md.
1800	5,308,483	18 miles west of Baltimore, Md.
1810	7,239,881	40 miles northwest of Washington, D.C.
1820	9,638,453	16 miles east of Moorefield, W. Va.
1830	12,866,020	19 miles southwest of Moorefield, W. Va.
1840	17,069,453	16 miles south of Clarksburg, W. Va.
1850	23,191,876	23 miles southeast of Parkersburg, W. Va.
1860	31,443,321	20 miles southeast of Chillicothe, Ohio
1870	39,818,449	48 miles northeast of Cincinnati, Ohio
1880	50,155,783	8 miles southwest of Cincinnati, Ohio
1890	62,947,714	20 miles east of Columbus, Ind.
1900	75,994,575	6 miles southeast of Columbus, Ind.
1910	91,972,266	Bloomington, Ind.
1920	105,710,620	8 miles southeast of Spencer, Ind.
1930	122,775,046	3 miles northeast of Linton, Ind.
1940	131,669,275	2 miles southeast of Carlisle, Ind.
1950	150,697,361	8 miles northwest of Olney, Ill.
1960	179,323,175	6 miles northwest of Centralia, Ill.
1970	204,816,296	5 miles southeast of Mascoutah, Ill.
1980	226,549,010	1/4 mile west of DeSoto, Mo.
1990	248,709,873	10 miles southeast of Steelville, Mo.

State Areas and Populations

STATE	Land Area* square miles	Water Area* square miles	Total Area* square miles	Area Rank land area	1990 Population	1990 Population per square mile	1980 Population	1970 Population	1960 Population	Population Rank 1990	1980	1970
Alabama	50,750	1,673	52,423	28	4,040,587	80	3,894,046	3,444,354	3,266,740	22	22	21
Alaska	570,374	86,051	656,424	1	550,043	1.0	401,851	302,583	226,167	49	50	50
Arizona	113,642	364	114,006	6	3,665,228	32	2,716,756	1,775,399	1,302,161	24	29	33
Arkansas	52,075	1,107	53,182	27	2,350,725	45	2,286,357	1,923,322	1,786,272	33	33	32
California	155,973	7,734	163,707	3	29,760,021	191	23,667,372	19,971,069	15,717,204	1	1	1
Colorado	103,730	371	104,100	8	3,294,394	32	2,889,735	2,209,596	1,753,947	26	28	30
Connecticut	4,845	698	5,544	48	3,287,116	678	3,107,576	3,032,217	2,535,234	27	25	24
Delaware	1,955	535	2,489	49	666,168	341	594,317	548,104	446,292	46	47	41
District of Columbia	61	7	68	.....	606,900	9,949	638,432	756,668	763,956	.....	.....	.....
Florida	53,997	11,761	65,758	26	12,937,926	240	9,747,015	6,791,418	4,951,560	4	7	9
Georgia	57,919	1,522	59,441	21	6,478,216	112	5,462,982	4,587,930	3,943,116	11	13	15
Hawaii	6,423	4,508	10,932	47	1,108,229	173	964,691	769,913	632,772	41	39	40
Idaho	82,751	823	83,574	11	1,006,749	12	944,127	713,015	667,191	42	41	43
Illinois	55,593	2,325	57,918	24	11,430,602	206	11,427,414	11,110,285	10,081,158	6	5	5
Indiana	35,870	550	36,420	38	5,544,159	155	5,490,212	5,195,392	4,662,498	14	12	11
Iowa	55,875	401	56,276	23	2,776,755	50	2,913,808	2,825,368	2,757,537	30	27	25
Kansas	81,823	459	82,282	13	2,477,574	30	2,364,236	2,249,071	2,178,611	32	32	28
Kentucky	39,732	679	40,411	36	3,685,296	93	3,660,324	3,220,711	3,038,156	23	23	23
Louisiana	43,566	8,277	51,843	33	4,219,973	97	4,206,098	3,644,637	3,257,022	21	19	20
Maine	30,865	4,523	35,387	39	1,227,928	40	1,125,043	993,722	969,265	38	38	38
Maryland	9,775	2,633	12,407	42	4,781,468	489	4,216,933	3,923,897	3,100,689	19	18	18
Massachusetts	7,838	2,717	10,555	45	6,016,425	768	5,737,093	5,689,170	5,148,578	13	11	10
Michigan	56,809	40,001	96,810	22	9,295,297	164	9,262,044	8,881,826	7,823,194	8	8	7
Minnesota	79,617	7,326	86,943	14	4,375,099	55	4,075,970	3,806,103	3,413,864	20	21	19
Mississippi	46,914	1,520	48,434	31	2,573,216	55	2,520,698	2,216,994	2,178,141	31	31	29
Missouri	68,898	811	69,709	18	5,117,073	74	4,916,759	4,677,623	4,319,813	15	15	13
Montana	145,556	1,490	147,046	4	799,065	5.5	786,690	694,409	674,767	44	44	44
Nebraska	76,878	481	77,358	15	1,578,385	21	1,569,825	1,485,333	1,411,330	36	35	35
Nevada	109,806	761	110,567	7	1,201,833	11	800,508	488,738	285,278	39	43	47
New Hampshire	8,969	382	9,351	44	1,109,252	124	920,610	737,681	606,921	40	42	42
New Jersey	7,419	1,303	8,722	46	7,730,188	1,042	7,365,011	7,171,112	6,066,782	9	9	8
New Mexico	121,365	234	121,598	5	1,515,069	12	1,303,542	1,017,055	951,023	37	37	37
New York	47,224	7,251	54,475	30	17,990,455	381	17,558,165	18,241,391	16,782,304	2	2	2
North Carolina	48,718	5,103	53,821	29	6,628,637	136	5,880,415	5,084,411	4,556,155	10	10	12
North Dakota	68,994	1,710	70,704	17	638,800	9.3	652,717	617,792	632,446	47	46	46
Ohio	40,953	3,875	44,828	35	10,847,115	265	10,797,603	10,657,423	9,706,397	7	6	6
Oklahoma	68,679	1,224	69,903	19	3,145,585	46	3,025,487	2,559,463	2,328,284	28	26	27
Oregon	96,003	2,383	98,386	10	2,842,321	30	2,633,156	2,091,533	1,768,687	29	30	31
Pennsylvania	44,820	1,239	46,058	32	11,881,643	265	11,864,751	11,800,766	11,319,366	5	4	3
Rhode Island	1,045	500	1,545	50	1,003,464	960	947,154	949,723	859,488	43	40	39
South Carolina	30,111	1,896	32,007	40	3,486,703	116	3,120,730	2,590,713	2,382,594	25	24	26
South Dakota	75,898	1,224	77,121	16	696,004	9.2	690,768	666,257	680,514	45	45	45
Tennessee	41,220	926	42,146	34	4,877,185	118	4,591,023	3,926,018	3,567,089	17	17	17
Texas	261,914	6,687	268,601	2	16,986,510	65	14,225,288	11,198,655	9,579,677	3	3	4
Utah	82,168	2,736	84,904	12	1,722,850	21	1,461,037	1,059,273	890,627	35	36	36
Vermont	9,249	366	9,615	43	562,758	61	511,456	444,732	389,881	48	48	48
Virginia	39,598	3,171	42,769	37	6,187,358	156	5,346,797	4,651,448	3,966,949	12	14	14
Washington	66,582	4,721	71,303	20	4,866,692	73	4,132,353	3,413,244	2,853,214	18	20	22
West Virginia	24,087	145	24,231	41	1,793,477	74	1,950,186	1,744,237	1,860,421	34	34	34
Wisconsin	54,314	11,190	65,503	25	4,891,769	90	4,705,642	4,417,821	3,951,777	16	16	16
Wyoming	97,105	714	97,818	9	453,588	4.7	469,557	332,416	330,066	50	49	49
United States	3,536,342	251,083	3,787,425	.....	248,709,873	70	226,542,360	203,302,031	179,323,175	.....	.....	.....

*Area figures for all states does not equal U.S. total due to rounding.

United States Populations and Zip Codes

The following alphabetical list shows populations for all counties and over 15,000 selected cities and towns in the United States. ZIP codes are shown for all of the cities listed in the table. The state abbreviation following each name is that used by the United States Postal Service.

ZIP codes are listed for cities and towns after the state abbreviations. For each city with more than one ZIP code, the range of numbers assigned to the city is shown: For example, the ZIP code range for Chicago is 60601–99, and this indicates that the numbers between 60601 and 60699 are valid Chicago ZIP codes. ZIP codes are not listed for counties.

Populations for cities and towns appear as *italics* after the ZIP codes, and populations for counties appear after the state abbreviations. These populations are either 1990 census figures or, where census data are not available, estimates created by Rand McNally. City populations are for central cities, not metropolitan areas. For New England, 1990 census populations are given for incorporated cities. Estimates are used for unincorporated places that are not treated separately by the census. 'Town' (or 'township') populations are not included unless the town is considered to be primarily urban and contains only one commonly used placename.

Counties are identified by a square symbol (□).

Abbreviations for State Names

AK	Alaska	IA	Iowa	MS	Mississippi	PA	Pennsylvania
AL	Alabama	**ID**	Idaho	**MT**	Montana	**RI**	Rhode Island
AR	Arkansas	**IL**	Illinois	**NC**	North Carolina	**SC**	South Carolina
AZ	Arizona	**IN**	Indiana	**ND**	North Dakota	**SD**	South Dakota
CA	California	**KS**	Kansas	**NE**	Nebraska	**TN**	Tennessee
CO	Colorado	**KY**	Kentucky	**NH**	New Hampshire	**TX**	Texas
CT	Connecticut	**LA**	Louisiana	**NJ**	New Jersey	**UT**	Utah
DC	District of Columbia	**MA**	Massachusetts	**NM**	New Mexico	**VA**	Virginia
		MD	Maryland	**NV**	Nevada	**VT**	Vermont
DE	Delaware	**ME**	Maine	**NY**	New York	**WA**	Washington
FL	Florida	**MI**	Michigan	**OH**	Ohio	**WI**	Wisconsin
GA	Georgia	**MN**	Minnesota	**OK**	Oklahoma	**WV**	West Virginia
HI	Hawaii	**MO**	Missouri	**OR**	Oregon	**WY**	Wyoming

A

Abbeville, AL 36310 • *3,173*
Abbeville, LA 70510–11 • *11,187*
Abbeville, SC 29620 • *5,778*
Abbeville □, SC • *23,862*
Abbotsford, WI 54405 • *1,916*
Abbott Run Valley, RI 02864 • *1,050*
Aberdeen, ID 83210 • *1,406*
Aberdeen, MD 21001 • *13,087*
Aberdeen, MS 39730 • *6,837*
Aberdeen, NC 28315 • *2,700*
Aberdeen, OH 45101 • *1,329*
Aberdeen, SD 57401–02 • *24,927*
Aberdeen, WA 98520 • *16,565*
Abernathy, TX 79311 • *2,720*
Abilene, KS 67410 • *6,242*
Abilene, TX 79601–08 • *106,654*
Abingdon, IL 61410 • *3,597*
Abingdon, VA 24210 • *7,003*
Abington, MA 02351 • *13,817*
Abington [Township], PA 19001 • *59,084*
Abita Springs, LA 70420 • *1,296*
Absarokee, MT 59001 • *1,067*
Absecon, NJ 08201 • *7,298*
Academia, OH 43050 • *1,447*
Acadia □, LA • *55,882*
Accomack □, VA • *31,703*
Ackerman, MS 39735 • *1,573*
Ackley, IA 50601 • *1,696*
Acton, CA 93510 • *1,471*
Acton, MA 01720 • *2,300*
Acushnet, MA 02743 • *6,030*
Acworth, GA 30101 • *4,519*
Ada, MN 56510 • *1,708*
Ada, OH 45810 • *5,413*
Ada, OK 74820–21 • *15,820*
Ada □, ID • *205,775*
Adair □, IA • *8,409*
Adair □, KY • *15,360*
Adair □, MO • *24,577*
Adair □, OK • *18,421*
Adairsville, GA 30103 • *2,131*
Adams, CO 80022 • *2,200*
Adams, MA 01220 • *6,356*
Adams, NY 13605 • *1,753*
Adams, WI 53910 • *1,715*
Adams □, CO • *265,038*
Adams □, ID • *3,254*
Adams □, IL • *66,090*
Adams □, IN • *31,095*
Adams □, IA • *4,866*
Adams □, MS • *35,356*
Adams □, NE • *29,625*
Adams □, ND • *3,174*
Adams □, OH • *25,371*
Adams □, PA • *78,274*
Adams □, WA • *13,603*
Adams □, WI • *15,682*
Adams Center, NY 13606 • *1,675*
Adamstown, PA 19501 • *1,108*
Adamsville, AL 35005 • *4,161*
Adamsville, RI 02801 • *600*
Adamsville, TN 38310 • *1,745*
Addis, LA 70710 • *1,222*
Addison, CT 06033 • *2,460*
Addison, IL 60101 • *32,058*
Addison, NY 14801 • *1,842*
Addison, TX 75001 • *8,783*
Addison □, VT • *32,953*
Addyston, OH 45001 • *1,198*
Adel, GA 31620 • *5,093*
Adel, IA 50003 • *3,304*
Adelanto, CA 92301 • *8,517*
Adelphi, MD 20783 • *13,524*
Adobe Acres, NM 87105 • *2,400*
Adrian, MI 49221 • *22,097*
Adrian, MN 56110 • *1,141*
Adrian, MO 64720 • *1,582*
Advance, MO 63730 • *1,139*
Affton, MO 63123 • *21,106*
Afton, DE 19810 • *1,200*
Afton, MN 55001 • *2,645*
Afton, WY 83110 • *1,394*
Agawam, MA 01001 • *10,190*
Agoura Hills, CA 91301 • *20,390*
Ahoskie, NC 27910 • *4,391*
Aiea, HI 96701 • *8,906*
Aiken, SC 29801–03 • *19,872*
Aiken □, SC • *120,940*
Ainsworth, NE 69210 • *1,870*
Air Park West, NE 68524 • *3,100*
Aitkin, MN 56431 • *1,698*
Aitkin □, MN • *12,425*
Ajo, AZ 85321 • *2,919*
Akiachak, AK 99551 • *400*
Akron, CO 80720 • *1,599*
Akron, IA 51001 • *1,450*
Akron, NY 14001 • *2,906*
Akron, OH 44301–98 • *223,019*
Akron, PA 17501 • *3,869*
Alabaster, AL 35007 • *14,732*
Alachua, FL 32615 • *4,529*
Alachua □, FL • *181,596*
Alakanuk, AK 99554 • *544*
Alamance □, NC • *108,213*
Alameda, CA 94501 • *76,459*
Alameda, NM 87114 • *5,900*
Alameda □, CA • *1,279,182*
Alamo, CA 94507 • *12,277*
Alamo, NV 89001 • *400*
Alamo, TN 38001 • *2,426*
Alamo, TX 78516 • *8,210*
Alamogordo, NM 88310–11 • *27,596*
Alamo Heights, TX 78208 • *6,502*
Alamosa, CO 81101–02 • *7,579*
Alamosa □, CO • *13,617*
Alamosa East, CO 81101 • *1,389*
Albany, CA 94706 • *16,327*
Albany, GA 31701–07 • *78,122*
Albany, IN 47320 • *2,357*
Albany, KY 42602 • *2,062*
Albany, MN 56307 • *1,548*
Albany, MO 64402 • *1,958*
Albany, NY 12201–60 • *101,082*
Albany, OR 97321 • *29,462*
Albany, TX 76430 • *1,962*
Albany, WI 53502 • *1,140*
Albany □, NY • *292,594*
Albany □, WY • *30,797*
Albemarle, NC 28001–02 • *14,939*
Albemarle □, VA • *68,040*
Albert Lea, MN 56007 • *18,310*
Albertson, NY 11507 • *5,166*
Albertville, AL 35950 • *14,507*
Albertville, MN 55301 • *1,251*
Albia, IA 52531 • *3,870*
Albion, IL 62806 • *2,116*
Albion, IN 46701 • *1,823*
Albion, MI 49224 • *10,066*
Albion, NE 68620 • *1,916*
Albion, NY 14411 • *5,863*
Albion, PA 16401 • *1,575*
Albion, RI 02802 • *1,600*
Albuquerque, NM 87101–99 • *384,736*
Alburtis, PA 18011 • *1,415*
Alcester, SD 57001 • *843*
Alcoa, TN 37701 • *6,400*
Alcona □, MI • *10,145*
Alcorn □, MS • *31,722*
Alden, NY 14004 • *2,457*
Alderson, WV 24910 • *1,152*
Alderwood Manor, WA 98011 • *16,524*
Aledo, IL 61231 • *3,681*
Alexander □, IL • *10,626*
Alexander □, NC • *27,544*
Alexander City, AL 35010 • *14,917*
Alexandria, IN 46001 • *5,709*
Alexandria, KY 41001 • *5,592*
Alexandria, LA 71301–15 • *49,188*
Alexandria, MN 56308 • *7,838*
Alexandria, VA 22301–20 • *111,183*
Alexandria Bay, NY 13607 • *1,194*
Alfalfa □, OK • *6,416*
Alfred, NY 14802 • *4,559*
Alger □, MI • *8,972*
Algoma, WI 54201 • *3,353*
Algona, IA 50511 • *6,015*
Algona, WA 98001 • *1,694*
Algonac, MI 48001 • *4,551*
Algonquin, IL 60102 • *11,663*
Algood, TN 38501 • *2,399*
Alhambra, CA 91801–99 • *82,106*
Alice, TX 78332–33 • *19,788*
Aliceville, AL 35442 • *3,009*
Aliquippa, PA 15001 • *13,374*
Allamakee □, IA • *13,855*
Allegan, MI 49010 • *4,547*
Allegan □, MI • *90,509*
Allegany, NY 14706 • *1,980*
Allegany □, MD • *74,946*
Allegany □, NY • *50,470*
Alleghany □, NC • *9,590*
Alleghany □, VA • *13,176*
Allegheny □, PA • *1,336,449*
Allen, TX 75002 • *18,309*
Allen, TX 75002 • *18,309*
Allen □, IN • *300,836*
Allen □, KS • *14,638*
Allen □, KY • *14,628*
Allen □, LA • *21,226*
Allen □, OH • *109,755*
Allendale, NJ 07401 • *5,900*
Allendale, SC 29810 • *4,410*
Allendale □, SC • *11,722*
Allen Park, MI 48101 • *31,092*
Allenton, RI 02852 • *600*
Allentown, NJ 08501 • *1,828*
Allentown, PA 18101–95 • *105,090*
Alliance, NE 69301 • *9,765*
Alliance, OH 44601 • *23,376*
Allison, IA 50602 • *1,000*
Allison Park, PA 15101 • *5,600*
Allouez, WI 54301 • *14,431*
Alloway, NJ 08001 • *1,371*
Allyn, WA 98524 • *1,100*
Alma, AR 72921 • *2,959*
Alma, GA 31510 • *3,663*
Alma, MI 48801 • *9,034*
Alma, NE 68920 • *1,226*
Almont, MI 48003 • *2,354*
Aloha, OR 97006 • *34,284*
Alondra Park, CA 90249 • *12,215*
Alpena, MI 49707 • *11,354*
Alpena □, MI • *30,605*
Alpha, NJ 08865 • *2,530*
Alpharetta, GA 30201–02 • *13,002*
Alpine, CA 91901 • *9,695*
Alpine, NJ 07620 • *1,716*
Alpine, TX 79830–31 • *5,637*
Alpine, UT 84003 • *3,492*
Alpine □, CA • *1,113*
Alsip, IL 60658 • *18,227*
Alta, IA 51002 • *1,820*
Altadena, CA 91001–02 • *42,658*
Altamont, IL 62411 • *2,296*
Altamont, KS 67330 • *1,048*
Altamont, NY 12009 • *1,519*
Altamont, OR 97601 • *18,591*
Altamonte Springs, FL 32701 • *34,879*
Alta Sierra, CA 95949 • *5,709*
Altavista, VA 24517 • *3,686*
Alto, TX 75925 • *1,027*
Alton, IL 62002 • *32,905*
Alton, IA 51003 • *1,063*
Alton, NH 03809 • *975*
Alton Bay, NH 03810 • *1,000*
Altoona, FL 32702 • *1,300*
Altoona, IA 50009 • *7,191*
Altoona, PA 16601–03 • *51,881*
Altoona, WI 54720 • *5,889*
Alturas, CA 96101 • *3,231*
Altus, OK 73521–23 • *21,910*
Alva, FL 33920 • *1,200*
Alva, OK 73717 • *5,495*
Alvarado, TX 76009 • *2,918*
Alvin, TX 77511–12 • *19,220*
Amador □, CA • *30,039*
Amagansett, NY 11930 • *2,188*
Amana, IA 52203 • *540*
Amarillo, TX 79101–76 • *157,615*
Ambler, PA 19002 • *6,609*
Amboy, IL 61310 • *2,377*
Ambridge, PA 15003 • *8,133*
Amelia, LA 70340 • *2,447*
Amelia, OH 45102 • *1,837*
Amelia □, VA • *8,787*
Amenia, NY 12501 • *1,057*
American Canyon, CA 94589 • *7,706*
American Falls, ID 83211 • *3,757*
American Fork, UT 84003–04 • *15,696*
Americus, GA 31709 • *16,512*
Amery, WI 54001 • *2,657*
Ames, IA 50010 • *47,198*
Amesbury, MA 01913 • *12,109*
Amherst, MA 01002–04 • *17,824*
Amherst, NH 03031 • *850*
Amherst, NY 14226 • *45,600*
Amherst, OH 44001 • *10,332*
Amherst, VA 24521 • *1,060*
Amherst □, VA • *28,578*
Amherstdale, WV 25607 • *1,200*
Amite, LA 70422 • *4,236*
Amite □, MS • *13,328*
Amity, OR 97101 • *1,175*
Amityville, NY 11701 • *9,286*
Ammon, ID 83401 • *5,002*
Amory, MS 38821 • *7,093*
Amsterdam, NY 12010 • *20,714*
Anaconda, MT 59711 • *10,278*
Anacortes, WA 98221 • *11,451*
Anadarko, OK 73005 • *6,586*
Anaheim, CA 92801–25 • *266,406*
Anahola, HI 96703 • *1,181*
Anahuac, TX 77514 • *1,993*
Anamosa, IA 52205 • *5,100*
Anandale, LA 71301 • *2,000*
Anchorage, AK 99501–40 • *226,338*
Anchorage, KY 40223 • *2,082*
Andalusia, AL 36420 • *9,269*
Anderson, AK 99744 • *628*
Anderson, CA 96007 • *8,299*
Anderson, IN 46011–18 • *59,459*
Anderson, MO 64831 • *1,432*
Anderson, SC 29621–25 • *26,184*
Anderson □, KS • *7,803*
Anderson □, KY • *14,571*
Anderson □, SC • *145,196*
Anderson □, TN • *68,250*
Anderson □, TX • *48,024*
Andover, KS 67002 • *4,047*
Andover, MA 01810 • *8,242*
Andover, MN 55304 • *15,216*
Andover, NY 14806 • *1,125*
Andover, OH 44003 • *1,216*
Andrew □, MO • *14,632*
Andrews, IN 46702 • *1,118*
Andrews, NC 28901 • *2,551*
Andrews, SC 29510 • *3,050*
Andrews, TX 79714 • *10,678*
Andrews □, TX • *14,338*
Androscoggin □, ME • *105,259*
Angelina □, TX • *69,884*
Angels Camp, CA 95222 • *2,409*
Angier, NC 27501 • *2,235*
Angle Lake, WA 98188 • *5,000*
Angleton, TX 77515–16 • *17,140*
Angola, IN 46703 • *5,824*
Angola, NY 14006 • *2,231*
Angoon, AK 99820 • *638*
Aniak, AK 99557 • *540*
Anita, IA 50020 • *1,068*
Ankeny, IA 50021 • *18,482*
Anna, IL 62906 • *4,805*
Anna, OH 45302 • *1,164*
Annalee Heights, VA 22042 • *1,750*
Anna Maria, FL 34216 • *1,744*
Annandale, MN 55302 • *2,054*
Annandale, VA 22003 • *50,975*
Annapolis, MD 21401–05 • *33,187*
Ann Arbor, MI 48103–08 • *109,592*
Anne Arundel □, MD • *427,239*
Anniston, AL 36201–06 • *26,623*
Annville, PA 17003 • *4,294*
Anoka, MN 55303–04 • *17,192*
Anoka □, MN • *243,641*
Anson, TX 79501 • *2,644*
Anson □, NC • *23,474*
Ansonia, CT 06401 • *18,403*
Ansonia, OH 45303 • *1,279*
Ansted, WV 25812 • *1,643*
Antelope □, NE • *7,965*
Anthony, FL 32617 • *1,200*
Anthony, KS 67003 • *2,516*
Anthony, NM 88021 • *5,160*
Anthony, RI 02816 • *2,980*
Anthony, TX 88021 • *3,328*
Antigo, WI 54409 • *8,276*
Antioch, CA 94509 • *62,195*
Antioch, IL 60002 • *6,105*
Antlers, OK 74523 • *2,524*
Anton, TX 79313 • *1,212*
Antrim, NH 03440 • *1,325*
Antrim □, MI • *18,185*
Antwerp, OH 45813 • *1,677*
Apache, OK 73006 • *1,591*
Apache □, AZ • *61,591*
Apache Junction, AZ 85217–20 • *18,100*
Apalachicola, FL 32320 • *2,602*
Apalachin, NY 13732 • *1,208*
Apex, NC 27502 • *4,968*
Aplington, IA 50604 • *1,034*
Apollo, PA 15613 • *1,895*
Apollo Beach, FL 33572 • *6,025*
Apopka, FL 32703–04 • *13,512*
Appalachia, VA 24216 • *1,994*
Appanoose □, IA • *13,743*
Appleton, MN 56208 • *1,552*
Appleton, WI 54911–15 • *65,695*
Appleton City, MO 64724 • *1,280*
Apple Valley, CA 92307–08 • *46,079*
Apple Valley, MN 55124 • *34,598*
Applewood, CO 80401 • *11,069*
Appleyard, WA 98801 • *1,207*
Appling □, GA • *15,744*
Appomattox, VA 24522 • *1,707*
Appomattox □, VA • *12,298*
Aptos, CA 95003 • *9,061*
Aquia Harbour, VA 22554 • *6,308*
Arab, AL 35016 • *6,321*
Arabi, LA 70032 • *8,787*
Aransas □, TX • *17,892*
Aransas Pass, TX 78336 • *7,180*
Arapahoe, NE 68922 • *1,001*
Arapahoe □, CO • *391,511*
Arbuckle, CA 95912 • *1,912*
Arcade, CA 95821 • *4,582*
Arcade, NY 14009 • *2,081*
Arcadia, CA 91006–07 • *48,290*
Arcadia, FL 33821 • *6,488*
Arcadia, IN 46030 • *1,468*
Arcadia, LA 71001 • *3,079*
Arcadia, SC 29320 • *2,088*
Arcadia, WI 54612 • *2,166*
Arcanum, OH 45304 • *1,953*
Arcata, CA 95521 • *15,197*
Archbald, PA 18403 • *6,291*
Archbold, OH 43502 • *3,440*
Archdale, NC 27263 • *6,913*
Archer, FL 32618 • *1,372*
Archer □, TX • *7,973*
Archer City, TX 76351 • *1,748*
Archuleta □, CO • *5,345*
Arco, ID 83213 • *1,016*
Arcola, IL 61910 • *2,678*
Arden, CA 95825 • *62,900*
Arden Hills, MN 55112 • *9,199*
Ardmore, AL 35739 • *1,090*
Ardmore, IN 46628 • *2,250*
Ardmore, OK 73401–03 • *23,079*
Ardsley, NY 10502 • *4,272*
Arenac □, MI • *14,931*
Argos, IN 46501 • *1,642*
Arizona Sunsites, AZ 85625 • *1,100*
Arkadelphia, AR 71923 • *10,014*
Arkansas □, AR • *21,653*
Arkansas City, KS 67005 • *12,762*
Arkoma, OK 74901 • *2,393*
Arlington, GA 31713 • *1,513*
Arlington, MA 02174 • *44,630*
Arlington, MN 55307 • *1,886*
Arlington, NE 68002 • *1,178*
Arlington, NY 12603 • *11,948*
Arlington, OH 45814 • *1,267*
Arlington, SD 57212 • *908*
Arlington, TN 38002 • *1,541*
Arlington, TX 76010–18 • *261,721*
Arlington, VT 05250 • *1,311*
Arlington, VA 22201–19 • *170,936*
Arlington, WA 98223 • *4,037*
Arlington □, VA • *170,936*
Arlington Heights, IL 60004–07 • *75,460*
Arma, KS 66712 • *1,542*
Armada, MI 48005 • *1,548*
Armijo, NM 87105 • *14,600*
Armonk, NY 10504 • *2,745*
Armour, SD 57313 • *854*
Armstrong, IA 50514 • *1,025*
Armstrong □, PA • *73,478*
Armstrong □, TX • *2,021*
Arnaudville, LA 70512 • *1,444*
Arnold, MD 21012 • *20,261*
Arnold, MN 55803 • *1,500*
Arnold, MO 63010 • *18,828*
Arnold, PA 15068 • *6,113*
Arnold Mills, RI 02864 • *600*
Aroostook □, ME • *86,936*
Arroyo Grande, CA 93420–21 • *14,378*
Artesia, CA 90701–03 • *15,464*
Artesia, NM 88210–11 • *10,610*
Arthur, IL 61911 • *2,112*
Arthur □, NE • *462*
Arundel Village, MD 21225 • *3,370*
Arvada, CO 80001–06 • *89,235*
Arvin, CA 93203 • *9,286*
Asbury Park, NJ 07712 • *16,799*
Ascension □, LA • *58,214*
Ashaway, RI 02804 • *1,584*
Ashburn, GA 31714 • *4,827*
Ashburnham, MA 01430 • *1,300*
Ashdown, AR 71822 • *5,150*
Ashe □, NC • *22,209*
Asheboro, NC 27203 • *16,362*
Asherton, TX 78827 • *1,608*
Asheville, NC 28801–16 • *61,607*
Ashford, AL 36312 • *1,926*
Ash Grove, MO 65604 • *1,128*
Ashland, AL 36251 • *2,034*
Ashland, CA 94541 • *16,590*
Ashland, IL 62612 • *1,257*
Ashland, KS 67831 • *1,032*
Ashland, KY 41101–05 • *23,622*
Ashland, MA 01721 • *9,165*
Ashland, MO 65010 • *1,252*
Ashland, NE 68003 • *2,136*
Ashland, NH 03217 • *1,915*
Ashland, OH 44805 • *20,079*
Ashland, OR 97520 • *16,234*
Ashland, PA 17921 • *3,859*
Ashland, VA 23005 • *5,864*
Ashland, WI 54806 • *8,695*
Ashland □, OH • *47,507*
Ashland □, WI • *16,307*
Ashland City, TN 37015 • *2,552*
Ashley, ND 58413 • *1,052*
Ashley, OH 43003 • *1,059*
Ashley, PA 18706 • *3,291*
Ashley □, AR • *24,319*
Ashtabula, OH 44004 • *21,633*
Ashtabula □, OH • *99,821*
Ashton, ID 83420 • *1,114*
Ashton, IL 61006 • *1,042*
Ashton, MD 20861 • *1,800*
Ashton, RI 02864 • *820*
Ashville, AL 35953 • *1,494*
Ashville, OH 43103 • *2,254*
Ashwaubenon, WI 54304 • *16,376*
Asotin □, WA • *17,605*
Aspen, CO 81611–15 • *5,049*
Aspen Hill, MD 20906 • *45,494*
Aspermont, TX 79502 • *1,214*
Aspinwall, PA 15215 • *2,880*
Assinippi, MA 02339 • *1,400*
Assonet, MA 02702 • *1,200*
Assumption, IL 62510 • *1,244*
Assumption □, LA • *22,753*
Astoria, IL 61501 • *1,205*
Astoria, OR 97103 • *10,069*
Atascadero, CA 93422–23 • *23,138*
Atascosa □, TX • *30,533*
Atchison, KS 66002 • *10,656*
Atchison □, KS • *16,932*
Atchison □, MO • *7,457*
Atco, NJ 08004 • *2,020*
Athens, AL 35611 • *16,901*
Athens, GA 30601–13 • *45,734*
Athens, IL 62613 • *1,404*
Athens, NY 12015 • *1,708*
Athens, OH 45701 • *21,265*
Athens, PA 18810 • *3,468*
Athens, TN 37303 • *12,054*
Athens, TX 75751 • *10,967*
Athens □, OH • *59,549*
Atherton, CA 94027 • *7,163*
Athol, MA 01331 • *8,732*
Atkins, AR 72823 • *2,834*
Atkins, VA 24311 • *1,130*
Atkinson, NE 68713 • *1,380*
Atkinson □, GA • *613*
Atlanta, GA 30301–83 • *394,017*
Atlanta, IL 61723 • *1,616*
Atlanta, TX 75551 • *6,118*
Atlantic, IA 50022 • *7,432*
Atlantic □, NJ • *224,327*
Atlantic Beach, FL 32233 • *11,636*
Atlantic City, NJ 08401–06 • *37,986*
Atlantic Highlands, NJ 07716 • *4,629*
Atmore, AL 36502 • *8,046*
Atoka, OK 74525 • *3,298*
Atoka □, OK • *12,778*
Attala □, MS • *18,481*
Attalla, AL 35954 • *6,859*
Attica, IN 47918 • *3,457*
Attica, NY 14011 • *2,630*
Attleboro, MA 02703 • *38,383*
Atwater, CA 95301 • *22,282*
Atwater, MN 56209 • *1,053*
Atwood, IL 61913 • *1,253*
Atwood, KS 67730 • *1,388*
Atwood, TN 38220 • *1,066*
Auberry, CA 93602 • *1,866*
Auburn, AL 36830–49 • *33,830*
Auburn, CA 95603–04 • *10,592*

Auburn, GA 30203 • 3,139
Auburn, IL 62615 • 3,724
Auburn, IN 46706 • 9,379
Auburn, KY 42206 • 1,273
Auburn, ME 04210-12 • 24,309
Auburn, MA 01501 • 14,845
Auburn, MI 48611 • 1,855
Auburn, NE 68305 • 3,443
Auburn, NY 13021-24 • 31,258
Auburn, WA 98001-02 • 33,102
Auburndale, FL 33823 • 8,858
Auburn Heights, MI 48321 • 17,076
Audrain □, MO • 23,599
Audubon, IA 50025 • 2,524
Audubon, NJ 08106 • 9,205
Audubon, PA 19407 • 6,328
Audubon □, IA • 7,334
Auglaize □, OH • 44,585
August, CA 95201 • 6,376
Augusta, AR 72006 • 2,759
Augusta, GA 30901-19 • 44,639
Augusta, KS 67010 • 7,876
Augusta, KY 41002 • 1,336
Augusta, ME 04330-38 • 21,325
Augusta, WI 54722 • 1,510
Augusta □, VA • 54,677
Aulander, NC 27805 • 1,209
Ault, CO 80610 • 1,107
Aumsville, OR 97325 • 1,650
Aurora, CO 80010-19 • 222,103
Aurora, IL 60504-07 • 99,581
Aurora, IN 47001 • 3,825
Aurora, MN 55705 • 1,965
Aurora, MO 65605 • 6,459
Aurora, NE 68818 • 3,810
Aurora, OH 44202 • 9,192
Aurora □, SD • 3,135
Au Sable, MI 48750 • 1,542
Au Sable Forks, NY 12912 • 2,100
Austell, GA 30001 • 4,173
Austin, IN 47102 • 4,310
Austin, MN 55912 • 21,907
Austin, NV 89310 • 370
Austin, TX 78701-89 • 465,622
Austin □, TX • 19,832
Austintown, OH 44512 • 32,371
Autauga □, AL • 34,222
Ava, MO 65608 • 2,938
Avalon, CA 90704 • 2,918
Avalon, NJ 08202 • 1,809
Avalon, PA 15202 • 5,784
Avella, PA 15312 • 1,200
Avenal, CA 93204 • 9,770
Avenel, MD • 5,600
Avenel, NJ 07001 • 15,504
Aventura, FL 33180 • 14,914
Averill Park, NY 12018 • 1,656
Avery □, NC • 14,867
Avilla, IN 46710 • 1,366
Avis, PA 17721 • 1,506
Avoca, IA 51521 • 1,497
Avoca, NY 14809 • 1,033
Avoca, PA 18641 • 2,897
Avocado Heights, CA 91746 • 14,232
Avon, CT 06001 • 13,937
Avon, MA 02322 • 5,026
Avon, NY 14414 • 2,995
Avon, OH 44011 • 7,337
Avon by the Sea, NJ 07717 • 2,165
Avondale, AZ 85323 • 16,169
Avondale, LA 70094 • 5,813
Avondale, OH 45404 • 5,000
Avondale Estates, GA 30002 • 2,209
Avon Lake, OH 44012 • 15,066
Avonmore, PA 15618 • 1,089
Avon Park, FL 33825 • 8,042
Avoyelles □, LA • 39,159
Ayden, NC 28513 • 4,740
Ayer, MA 01432 • 2,889
Azalea Park, FL 32807 • 8,926
Azle, TX 76020 • 8,868
Aztec, NM 87410 • 5,479
Azusa, CA 91702 • 41,333

B

Babbitt, MN 55706 • 1,562
Babbitt, NV • 1,800
Babylon, NY 11702-04 • 12,249
Baca □, CO • 4,556
Bacliff, TX 77518 • 5,549
Bacon □, GA • 9,566
Bad Axe, MI 48413 • 3,484
Baden, PA 15005 • 5,074
Badin, NC 28009 • 1,481
Bagdad, AZ 86321 • 1,858
Bagdad, FL 32530 • 1,457
Baggs, WY 82321 • 272
Bagley, MN 56621 • 1,388
Bailey □, TX • 7,064
Baileys Crossroads, VA 22041 • 19,507
Bainbridge, GA 31717 • 10,712
Bainbridge, NY 13733 • 1,550
Baird, TX 79504 • 1,658
Bairdford, PA 15006 • 1,200
Baker, LA 70714 • 13,233
Baker, MT 59313 • 1,818
Baker, OR 97814 • 9,140
Baker □, FL • 18,486
Baker □, GA • 3,615
Baker □, OR • 15,317
Bakersfield, CA 93301-89 • 174,820
Balch Springs, TX 75180 • 17,406
Bald Knob, AR 72010 • 2,653
Baldwin, FL 32234 • 1,450
Baldwin, GA 30511 • 1,439
Baldwin, LA 70514 • 2,379
Baldwin, NY 11510 • 22,719
Baldwin, PA 15234 • 21,923
Baldwin, WI 54002 • 2,022
Baldwin □, AL • 98,280
Baldwin □, GA • 39,530
Baldwin City, KS 66006 • 2,961
Baldwin Park, CA 91706 • 69,330
Baldwinsville, NY 13027 • 6,591
Baldwinville, MA 01436 • 1,795
Baldwyn, MS 38824 • 3,204
Balfour, NC 28706 • 1,118
Ball, LA 71405 • 3,305
Ballard □, KY • 7,902
Ballardvale, MA 01810 • 1,270
Ballinger, TX 76821 • 3,975
Ballston Spa, NY 12020 • 4,937
Ballwin, MO 63011 • 21,816
Balmville, NY 12550 • 2,963
Baltic, CT 06330 • 2,000
Baltimore, MD 21201-99 • 736,014
Baltimore, OH 43105 • 2,971
Baltimore □, MD • 692,134
Baltimore Highlands, MD 21227 • 7,300
Bamberg, SC 29003 • 3,843
Bamberg □, SC • 16,902
Bandera □, TX • 10,562
Bandon, OR 97411 • 2,215
Bangor, ME 04401-02 • 33,181
Bangor, MI 49013 • 1,922
Bangor, PA 18013 • 5,383
Bangor, WI 54614 • 1,076
Bangor Township, MI 48706 • 17,494
Bangs, TX 76823 • 1,555
Banks □, GA • 10,308
Banner □, NE • 852
Banning, CA 92220 • 20,570
Bannock □, ID • 66,026
Baraboo, WI 53913 • 9,203
Baraga, MI 49908 • 1,231
Baraga □, MI • 7,954
Barataria, LA 70036 • 1,160
Barber □, KS • 5,874
Barberton, OH 44203 • 27,623
Barbour □, AL • 25,417
Barbour □, WV • 15,699
Barboursville, WV 25504 • 2,774
Barbourville, KY 40906 • 3,658
Bardstown, KY 40004 • 6,801
Bargersville, IN 46106 • 1,681
Bar Harbor, ME 04609 • 2,768
Barker Heights, NC 28739 • 1,137
Barling, AR 72923 • 4,078
Barnegat, NJ 08005 • 1,160
Barnes □, ND • 12,545
Barnesboro, PA 15714 • 2,530
Barnesville, GA 30204 • 4,747
Barnesville, MN 56514 • 2,066
Barnesville, OH 43713 • 4,326
Barnsdall, OK 74002 • 1,316
Barnstable, MA 02630 • 2,790
Barnstable □, MA • 186,605
Barnwell, SC 29812 • 5,255
Barnwell □, SC • 20,293
Barrackville, WV 26559 • 1,443
Barre, MA 01005 • 1,094
Barre, VT 05641 • 9,482
Barren □, KY • 34,001
Barrington, IL 60010-11 • 9,504
Barrington, NJ 08007 • 6,774
Barrington, RI 02806 • 15,849
Barron, WI 54812 • 2,986
Barron □, WI • 40,750
Barron Lake, MI 49120 • 1,600
Barrow, AK 99723 • 3,469
Barrow □, GA • 29,721
Barry, IL 62312 • 1,391
Barry □, MI • 50,057
Barry □, MO • 27,547
Barstow, CA 92310-12 • 21,472
Bartholomew □, IN • 63,657
Bartlesville, OK 74003-06 • 34,256
Bartlett, IL 60103 • 19,373
Bartlett, TN 38134 • 26,989
Bartlett, TX 76511 • 1,439
Barton, OH 43905 • 1,039
Barton, VT 05822 • 908
Barton □, KS • 29,382
Barton □, MO • 11,312
Bartonville, IL 61607 • 5,643
Bartow, FL 33830 • 14,716
Bartow □, GA • 55,911
Barview, OR 97420 • 1,402
Basalt, CO 81621 • 1,128
Basehor, KS 66007 • 1,591
Basile, LA 70515 • 1,808
Basin, WY 82410 • 1,180
Basking Ridge, NJ 07920 • 3,060
Bassett, VA 24055 • 1,579
Bass Lake, IN 46534 • 1,500
Bastrop, LA 71220-21 • 13,916
Bastrop, TX 78602 • 4,044
Bastrop □, TX • 38,263
Batavia, IL 60510 • 17,076
Batavia, NY 14020-21 • 16,310
Batavia, OH 45103 • 1,700
Bates □, MO • 15,025
Batesburg, SC 29006 • 4,082
Batesville, AR 72501-03 • 9,187
Batesville, IN 47006 • 4,720
Batesville, MS 38606 • 6,403
Bath, ME 04530 • 9,799
Bath, NY 14810 • 5,801
Bath, PA 18014 • 2,358
Bath, SC 29816 • 2,242
Bath □, KY • 9,692
Bath □, VA • 4,799
Baton Rouge, LA 70801-98 • 219,531
Battle Creek, MI 49015-17 • 53,540
Battle Ground, WA 98604 • 3,758
Battle Mountain, NV 89820 • 3,542
Baudette, MN 56623 • 1,146
Bawcomville, LA 71291 • 2,250
Baxley, GA 31513 • 3,841
Baxter, MN 56425 • 3,695
Baxter, TN 38544 • 1,289
Baxter □, AR • 31,186
Baxter Springs, KS 66713 • 4,351
Bay, AR 72411 • 1,660
Bay □, FL • 126,994
Bay □, MI • 111,723
Bayard, NE 69334 • 1,196
Bayard, NM 88023 • 2,598
Bayberry, NY 13088 • 6,710
Bay City, MI 48706-08 • 38,936
Bay City, OR 97107 • 1,027
Bay City, TX 77414 • 18,170
Bayfield, CO 81122 • 1,090
Bayfield □, WI • 14,008
Bay Head, NJ 08742 • 1,226
Baylor □, TX • 4,385
Bay Minette, AL 36507 • 7,168
Bayonet Point, FL 34667 • 21,860
Bayonne, NJ 07002 • 61,444
Bayou Cane, LA 70359 • 15,876
Bayou George, FL 32401 • 1,500
Bayou La Batre, AL 36509 • 2,456
Bay Pines, FL 33504 • 4,171
Bayport, MN 55003 • 3,200
Bayport, NY 11705 • 7,702
Bay Ridge, MD 21403 • 1,989
Bay Saint Louis, MS 39520-21 • 8,063
Bay Shore, NY 11706 • 21,279
Bayshore Gardens, FL 34207 • 17,062
Bayside, WI 53217 • 4,789
Bay Springs, MS 39422 • 1,729
Baytown, TX 77520-22 • 63,850
Bay Village, OH 44140 • 17,000
Bayville, NY 11709 • 7,193
Beach, IL 60085 • 9,513
Beach, ND 58621 • 1,205
Beach Haven, NJ 08008 • 1,475
Beachwood, NJ 08722 • 9,324
Beachwood, OH 44122 • 10,677
Beacon, NY 12508 • 13,243
Beacon Falls, CT 06403 • 1,285
Beacon Square, FL 34652 • 6,265
Beadle □, SD • 18,253
Bear, DE 19701 • 1,200
Bearden, AR 71720 • 1,021
Beardstown, IL 62618 • 5,270
Bear Lake □, ID • 6,084
Bear Town, MS 39648 • 1,277
Beatrice, NE 68310 • 12,354
Beatty, NV 89003 • 1,623
Beattyville, KY 41311 • 1,131
Beaufort, NC 28516 • 3,808
Beaufort, SC 29901-03 • 9,576
Beaufort □, NC • 42,283
Beaufort □, SC • 86,425
Beaumont, CA 92223 • 9,685
Beaumont, MS 39423 • 1,054
Beaumont, TX 77701-26 • 114,323
Beauregard □, LA • 30,083
Beaver, OK 73932 • 1,584
Beaver, PA 15009 • 5,028
Beaver, UT 84713 • 1,998
Beaver, WV 25813 • 1,244
Beaver □, OK • 6,023
Beaver □, PA • 186,093
Beaver □, UT • 4,765
Beavercreek, OH 45385 • 33,626
Beaverdale, PA 15921 • 1,000
Beaver Dam, KY 42320 • 2,904
Beaver Dam, WI 53916 • 14,196
Beaver Falls, PA 15010 • 10,687
Beaverhead □, MT • 8,424
Beaverton, MI 48612 • 1,150
Beaverton, OR 97005-07 • 53,310
Beckemeyer, IL 62219 • 1,070
Becker □, MN • 27,881
Beckham □, OK • 18,812
Beckley, WV 25801-02 • 18,296
Bedford, IN 47421 • 13,817
Bedford, IA 50833 • 1,528
Bedford, MA 01730 • 13,067
Bedford, NH 03102 • 1,400
Bedford, OH 44146 • 14,822
Bedford, PA 15522 • 3,137
Bedford, TX 76021-22 • 43,762
Bedford, VA 24523 • 6,073
Bedford □, PA • 47,919
Bedford □, TN • 30,411
Bedford □, VA • 45,656
Bedford Heights, OH 44146 • 12,131
Bedford Hills, NY 10507 • 3,140
Bee □, TX • 25,135
Beebe, AR 72012 • 4,455
Beecher, IL 60401 • 2,032
Beecher, MI 48458 • 14,465
Beech Grove, IN 46107 • 13,383
Beech Island, SC 29842 • 1,500
Bee Ridge, FL 34233 • 6,406
Beeville, TX 78102-04 • 13,547
Beggs, OK 74421 • 1,150
Bel Air, MD 21014 • 8,860
Bel Aire, KS 67220 • 3,695
Belchertown, MA 01007 • 2,339
Belcourt, ND 58316 • 2,458
Belding, MI 48809 • 5,969
Belen, NM 87002 • 6,547
Belfast, ME 04915 • 6,355
Belfast, NY 14711 • 1,100
Belfield, ND 58622 • 887
Belford, NJ 07718 • 6,300
Belgrade, MT 59714 • 3,411
Belhaven, NC 27810 • 2,269
Belington, WV 26250 • 1,850
Belknap □, NH • 49,216
Bell, CA 90201 • 34,365
Bell □, KY • 31,506
Bell □, TX • 191,088
Bellair, FL 32073 • 5,200
Bellaire, MI 49615 • 1,104
Bellaire, OH 43906 • 6,028
Bellaire, TX 77401-02 • 13,842
Bella Vista, AR 72712 • 9,083
Bellbrook, OH 45305 • 6,511
Belle, MO 65013 • 1,218
Belle, WV 25015 • 1,421
Belleair, FL 34616 • 3,968
Belle Chasse, LA 70037 • 8,512
Bellefontaine, OH 43311 • 12,142
Bellefontaine Neighbors, MO 63137 • 10,922
Bellefonte, DE 19809 • 1,243
Bellefonte, PA 16823 • 6,358
Belle Fourche, SD 57717 • 4,335
Belle Glade, FL 33430 • 16,177
Belle Isle, FL 32809 • 5,272
Belle Meade, TN 37205 • 2,839
Bellemoor, DE 19802 • 1,040
Belle Plaine, IA 52208 • 2,834
Belle Plaine, KS 67013 • 1,649
Belle Plaine, MN 56011 • 3,149
Belle Vernon, PA 15012 • 1,213
Belleview, FL 32506 • 8,000
Belleview, FL 32620 • 2,666
Belle View, VA 22307 • 3,500
Belleville, IL 62220-25 • 42,785
Belleville, KS 66935 • 2,517
Belleville, MI 48111-12 • 3,270
Belleville, NJ 07109 • 34,213
Belleville, PA 17004 • 1,589
Belleville, WI 53508 • 1,456
Bellevue, ID 83313 • 1,275
Bellevue, IA 52031 • 2,239
Bellevue, KY 41073 • 6,997
Bellevue, MI 49021 • 1,401
Bellevue, NE 68005 • 30,982
Bellevue, OH 44811 • 8,146
Bellevue, PA 15202 • 9,126
Bellevue, WA 98004-09 • 86,874
Bellflower, CA 90706-07 • 61,815
Bell Gardens, CA 90201 • 42,355
Bellingham, MA 02019 • 4,535
Bellingham, WA 98225-27 • 52,179
Bellmawr, NJ 08031 • 12,603
Bellmead, TX 76705 • 8,336
Bellmore, NY 11710 • 16,438
Bellows Falls, VT 05101 • 3,313
Bellport, NY 11713 • 2,572
Bells, TN 38006 • 1,643
Bellville, OH 44813 • 1,568
Bellville, TX 77418 • 3,378
Bellwood, IL 60104 • 20,241
Bellwood, PA 16617 • 1,976
Bellwood, VA 23234 • 6,178
Belmar, NJ 07719 • 5,877
Belmond, IA 50421 • 2,500
Belmont, CA 94002 • 24,127
Belmont, MA 02178 • 24,720
Belmont, MS 38827 • 1,554
Belmont, NY 14813 • 1,006
Belmont, NC 28012 • 8,434
Belmont □, OH • 71,074
Bel-Nor, MO 63133 • 2,935
Beloit, KS 67420 • 4,066
Beloit, OH 44609 • 1,037
Beloit, WI 53511-12 • 35,573
Beloit North, WI 53511 • 5,457
Belpre, OH 45714 • 6,796
Belt, MT 59412 • 571
Belton, MO 64012 • 18,150
Belton, SC 29627 • 4,646
Belton, TX 76513 • 12,476
Beltrami □, MN • 34,384
Beltsville, MD 20705 • 14,476
Belvedere, GA 30032 • 6,100
Belvedere, SC 29841 • 6,133
Belvedere Park, GA 30032 • 18,089
Belvidere, IL 61008 • 15,958
Belvidere, NJ 07823 • 2,669
Belzoni, MS 39038 • 2,536
Bement, IL 61813 • 1,668
Bemidji, MN 56601-19 • 11,245
Benavides, TX 78341 • 1,788
Benbrook, TX 76126 • 19,564
Bend, OR 97701-09 • 20,469
Benewah □, ID • 7,937
Ben Hill □, GA • 16,245
Benicia, CA 94510 • 24,437
Benkelman, NE 69021 • 1,193
Benld, IL 62009 • 1,604
Ben Lomond, CA 95005 • 7,884
Bennett, CO 80102 • 1,757
Bennett □, SD • 3,206
Bennettsville, SC 29512 • 9,345
Bennington, VT 05201 • 9,532
Bennington □, VT • 35,845
Bennion, UT 84118 • 9,575
Bensalem, PA 19020-21 • 52,368
Bensenville, IL 60106 • 17,767
Bensley, VA 23234 • 5,093
Benson, AZ 85602 • 3,824
Benson, MN 56215 • 3,235
Benson, NC 27504 • 2,810
Benson □, ND • 7,198
Bent □, CO • 5,048
Bentleyville, PA 15314 • 2,673
Benton, AR 72015 • 18,177
Benton, IL 62812 • 7,216
Benton, KY 42025 • 3,899
Benton, LA 71006 • 2,047
Benton □, AR • 97,499
Benton □, IN • 9,441
Benton □, IA • 22,429
Benton □, MN • 30,185
Benton □, MS • 8,046
Benton □, MO • 13,859
Benton □, OR • 70,811
Benton □, TN • 14,524
Benton □, WA • 112,560
Benton City, WA 99320 • 1,806
Benton Harbor, MI 49022-23 • 12,818
Benton Heights, MI 49022 • 5,465
Bentonville, AR 72712-14 • 11,257
Benwood, WV 26031 • 1,669
Benzie □, MI • 12,200
Beowawe, NV 89821 • 250
Berea, KY 40403 • 9,126
Berea, OH 44017 • 19,051
Berea, SC 29611 • 13,535
Beresford, SD 57004 • 1,849
Bergen, NY 14416 • 1,103
Bergen □, NJ • 825,380
Bergenfield, NJ 07621 • 24,458
Berkeley, CA 94701-10 • 102,724
Berkeley, IL 60163 • 5,137
Berkeley, MO 63134 • 12,450
Berkeley, RI 02864 • 830
Berkeley □, SC • 128,776
Berkeley □, WV • 59,253
Berkeley Heights, NJ 07922 • 11,980
Berkley, MI 48072 • 16,960
Berks □, PA • 336,523
Berkshire □, MA • 139,352
Berlin, CT 06037 • 1,040
Berlin, MD 21811 • 2,616
Berlin, NH 03570 • 11,824
Berlin, NJ 08009 • 5,672
Berlin, NY 12022 • 1,200
Berlin, PA 15530 • 2,064
Berlin, WI 54923 • 5,371
Bernalillo, NM 87004 • 5,960
Bernalillo □, NM • 480,577
Bernardsville, NJ 07924 • 6,597
Berne, IN 46711 • 3,559
Bernice, LA 71222 • 1,543
Bernie, MO 63822 • 1,847
Berrien □, GA • 14,153
Berrien □, MI • 161,378
Berrien Springs, MI 49103 • 1,927
Berry, AL 35546 • 1,218
Berryville, AR 72616 • 3,212
Berryville, VA 22611 • 3,097
Berthoud, CO 80513 • 2,990
Bertie □, NC • 20,388
Bertrand, MI 49120 • 5,500
Berwick, LA 70342 • 4,375
Berwick, ME 03901 • 2,378
Berwick, PA 18603 • 10,976
Berwyn, IL 60402 • 45,426
Berwyn, PA 19312 • 8,150
Bessemer, AL 35020-23 • 33,497
Bessemer, MI 49911 • 2,272
Bessemer, PA 16112 • 1,196
Bessemer City, NC 28016 • 4,698
Bethalto, IL 62010 • 9,507
Bethany, CT 06525 • 1,170
Bethany, IL 61914 • 1,369
Bethany, MO 64424 • 3,005
Bethany, OK 73008 • 20,075
Bethany, WV 26032 • 1,139
Bethany Beach, DE 19930 • 326
Bethel, AK 99559 • 4,674
Bethel, CT 06801 • 8,835
Bethel, ME 04217 • 1,225
Bethel, NC 27812 • 1,842
Bethel, OH 45106 • 2,407
Bethel, VT 05032 • 1,866
Bethel Acres, OK 74801 • 2,505
Bethel Park, PA 15102 • 33,823
Bethesda, MD 20813-17 • 62,936
Bethesda, OH 43719 • 1,161
Bethlehem, CT 06751 • 1,976
Bethlehem, PA 18015-18 • 71,428
Bethpage, NY 11714 • 15,761
Bettendorf, IA 52722 • 28,132
Beulah, ND 58523 • 3,363
Beverly, MA 01915 • 38,195
Beverly, NJ 08010 • 2,973
Beverly, OH 45715 • 1,444
Beverly Hills, CA 90209-13 • 31,971
Beverly Hills, FL 32665 • 6,163
Beverly Hills, MI 48009 • 10,610
Bexar □, TX • 1,185,394
Bexley, OH 43209 • 13,088
Bibb □, AL • 16,576
Bibb □, GA • 149,967
Bicknell, IN 47512 • 3,357
Biddeford, ME 04005 • 20,710
Bienville □, LA • 15,979
Big Bear City, CA 92314 • 3,500
Big Bend, WI 53103 • 1,299
Big Delta, AK 99737 • 400
Big Flats, NY 14814 • 2,658
Bigfork, MT 59911 • 1,080
Biggs, CA 95917 • 1,581
Big Horn □, MT • 11,337
Big Horn □, WY • 10,525
Big Lake, MN 55309 • 3,113
Big Lake, TX 76932 • 3,672
Big Pine, CA 93513 • 1,158
Big Piney, WY 83113 • 454
Big Rapids, MI 49307 • 12,603
Big Sandy, MT 59520 • 740
Big Sandy, TX 75755 • 1,185
Big Spring, TX 79720-21 • 23,093
Big Stone □, MN • 6,285
Big Stone Gap, VA 24219 • 4,748
Big Timber, MT 59011 • 1,557
Billerica, MA 01821-22 • 6,840
Billings, MT 59101-08 • 81,151
Billings □, ND • 1,108
Billings Heights, MT 59105 • 8,480
Biloxi, MS 39530-35 • 46,319
Biltmore Forest, NC 28803 • 1,327
Bingham, ME 04920 • 1,071
Bingham □, ID • 37,583
Binghamton, NY 13901-05 • 53,008
Birchwood City, MD 20745 • 4,870
Birchwood Park, DE 19711 • 2,250
Bird Island, MN 55310 • 1,326
Birdsboro, PA 19508 • 4,222
Birmingham, AL 35201-61 • 265,968
Birmingham, MI 48009-12 • 19,997
Bisbee, AZ 85603 • 6,288
Biscayne Gardens, FL 33168 • 13,000
Biscayne Park, FL 33161 • 3,068
Biscoe, NC 27209 • 1,484
Bishop, CA 93514-15 • 3,475
Bishop, TX 78343 • 3,337
Bishopville, SC 29010 • 3,560
Bismarck, MO 63624 • 1,579
Bismarck, ND 58501-07 • 49,256
Biwabik, MN 55708 • 1,097
Bixby, OK 74008 • 9,502
Black Canyon City, AZ 85324 • 1,811
Black Creek, WI 54106 • 1,152
Black Diamond, WA 98010 • 1,422
Black Earth, WI 53515 • 1,248
Blackfoot, ID 83221 • 9,646
Blackford □, IN • 14,067
Black Forest, CO 80908 • 8,143
Black Hawk, SD 57718 • 1,955
Black Hawk □, IA • 123,798
Black Jack, MO 63031 • 6,128
Black Lick, PA 15716 • 1,100
Blacklick Estates, OH 43227 • 10,080
Black Mountain, NC 28711 • 5,418
Black Point Beach Club, CT 06357 • 1,200
Black River, NY 13612 • 1,349
Black River Falls, WI 54615 • 3,490
Blacksburg, SC 29702 • 1,907
Blacksburg, VA 24060-63 • 34,590
Blackshear, GA 31516 • 3,263
Blackstone, MA 01504 • 4,460
Blackstone, VA 23824 • 3,497
Blackville, SC 29817 • 2,688
Blackwell, OK 74631 • 7,538
Blackwood, NJ 08012 • 5,120
Bladen □, NC • 28,663
Bladenboro, NC 28320 • 1,821
Bladensburg, MD 20710 • 8,064
Blades, DE 19973 • 834
Blaine, MN 55433 • 38,975
Blaine, TN 37709 • 1,326
Blaine, WA 98230 • 2,489
Blaine □, ID • 13,552
Blaine □, MT • 6,728
Blaine □, NE • 675
Blaine □, OK • 11,470
Blair, NE 68008 • 6,860
Blair, WI 54616 • 1,126
Blair □, PA • 130,542
Blairsville, PA 15717 • 3,595
Blakely, GA 31723 • 5,595
Blakely, PA 18447 • 7,222
Blanchard, LA 71009 • 1,175
Blanchard, OK 73010 • 1,922
Blanchester, OH 45107 • 4,206
Blanco, TX 78606 • 1,238
Blanco □, TX • 5,972
Bland □, VA • 6,514
Blanding, UT 84511 • 3,162
Blasdell, NY 14219 • 2,900

Blauvelt, NY 10913 • 4,470
Blawnox, PA 15238 • 1,626
Bleckley □, GA • 10,430
Bledsoe □, TN • 9,669
Blende, CO 81006 • 1,330
Blennerhassett, WV 26101 • 2,924
Blissfield, MI 49228 • 3,172
Block Island, RI 02807 • 620
Bloomer, WI 54724 • 3,085
Bloomfield, CT 06002 • 7,120
Bloomfield, IN 47424 • 2,592
Bloomfield, IA 52537 • 2,580
Bloomfield, MO 63825 • 1,800
Bloomfield, NE 68718 • 1,181
Bloomfield, NJ 07003 • 45,061
Bloomfield, NM 87413 • 5,214
Bloomfield Hills, MI 48302–04 • 4,288
Bloomfield Township, MI 48302 • 42,137
Bloomingdale, GA 31302 • 2,271
Bloomingdale, IL 60108 • 16,614
Bloomingdale, NJ 07403 • 7,530
Bloomingdale, TN 37660 • 10,953
Blooming Prairie, MN 55917 • 2,043
Bloomington, CA 92316 • 15,116
Bloomington, IL 61701–04 • 51,972
Bloomington, IN 47401–08 • 60,633
Bloomington, MN 55420 • 86,335
Bloomington, TX 77951 • 1,888
Bloomsburg, PA 17815 • 12,439
Blossburg, PA 16912 • 1,571
Blossom, TX 75416 • 1,440
Blount □, AL • 39,248
Blount □, TN • 85,969
Blountstown, FL 32424 • 2,404
Blountsville, AL 35031 • 1,527
Blountville, TN 37617 • 2,605
Blowing Rock, NC 28605 • 1,257
Blue Ash, OH 45242 • 11,860
Blue Diamond, NV 89004 • 420
Blue Earth, MN 56013 • 3,745
Blue Earth □, MN • 54,044
Bluefield, VA 24605 • 5,363
Bluefield, WV 24701 • 12,756
Blue Grass, IA 52726 • 1,214
Blue Hills, CT 06002 • 3,206
Blue Island, IL 60406 • 21,203
Blue Lake, CA 95525 • 1,235
Blue Mound, IL 62513 • 1,161
Blue Rapids, KS 66411 • 1,131
Blue Ridge, GA 30513 • 1,336
Blue Ridge, VA 24064 • 2,840
Blue Ridge Summit, PA 17214 • 1,800
Blue Springs, MO 64014–15 • 40,153
Bluewell, WV 24701 • 2,752
Bluff City, TN 37618 • 1,390
Bluffdale, UT 84065 • 2,152
Bluff Park, AL 35226 • 8,000
Bluffton, IN 46714 • 9,020
Bluffton, OH 45817 • 3,367
Blythe, CA 92225–26 • 8,428
Blytheville, AR 72315–19 • 22,906
Boalsburg, PA 16827 • 2,206
Boardman, OH 44512 • 38,596
Boardman, OR 97818 • 1,387
Boaz, AL 35957 • 6,928
Boca Grande, FL 33921 • 1,200
Boca Raton, FL 33431–34 • 61,492
Boerne, TX 78006 • 4,274
Bogalusa, LA 70427–29 • 14,280
Bogart, GA 30622 • 1,018
Bogata, TX 75417 • 1,421
Boger City, NC 28092 • 1,373
Bogota, NJ 07603 • 7,824
Bohemia, NY 11716 • 9,556
Boiling Springs, NC 28017 • 2,445
Boiling Springs, PA 17007 • 1,978
Boise, ID 83701–15 • 125,738
Boise □, ID • 3,509
Boise City, OK 73933 • 1,509
Bolingbrook, IL 60440 • 40,843
Bolivar, MO 65613 • 6,845
Bolivar, NY 14715 • 1,261
Bolivar, TN 38008 • 5,969
Bolivar □, MS • 41,875
Bollinger □, MO • 10,619
Bolton Landing, NY 12814 • 1,600
Bon Air, VA 23235 • 16,413
Bonaventure, FL 33317 • 6,000
Bond □, IL • 14,991
Bondsville, MA 01009 • 1,992
Bonduel, WI 54107 • 1,210
Bondurant, IA 50035 • 1,584
Bonham, TX 75418 • 6,686
Bon Homme □, SD • 7,089
Bonifay, FL 32425 • 2,612
Bonita, CA 91903 • 12,542
Bonita Springs, FL 33923 • 13,600
Bonneauville, PA 17325 • 1,282
Bonner □, ID • 26,622
Bonners Ferry, ID 83805 • 2,193
Bonner Springs, KS 66012 • 6,413
Bonne Terre, MO 63628 • 3,871
Bonneville □, ID • 72,207
Bonney Lake, WA 98390 • 7,494
Bonnie Doone, NC 28303 • 3,893
Bono, AR 72416 • 1,220
Booker, TX 79005 • 1,236
Boomer, WV 25031 • 1,051
Boone, IA 50036 • 12,392
Boone, NC 28607 • 12,915
Boone □, AR • 28,297
Boone □, IL • 30,806
Boone □, IN • 38,147
Boone □, IA • 25,186
Boone □, KY • 57,589
Boone □, MO • 112,379
Boone □, NE • 6,667
Boone □, WV • 25,870
Booneville, AR 72927 • 3,804
Booneville, MS 38829 • 7,955
Boonsboro, MD 21713 • 2,445
Boonton, NJ 07005 • 8,343
Boonville, CA 95415 • 1,000
Boonville, IN 47601 • 6,724
Boonville, MO 65233 • 7,095
Boonville, NY 13309 • 2,220
Boonville, NC 27011 • 1,009
Boothbay Harbor, ME 04538 • 1,267
Borden □, TX • 799
Bordentown, NJ 08505 • 4,341
Borger, TX 79007–08 • 15,675
Boron, CA 93516 • 2,101
Borrego Springs, CA 92004 • 2,244

Boscobel, WI 53805 • 2,706
Bosque □, TX • 15,125
Bossert Estates, NJ 08505 • 1,830
Bossier □, LA • 86,088
Bossier City, LA 71111–13 • 52,721
Boston, GA 31626 • 1,395
Boston, MA 02101–99 • 574,283
Boswell, PA 15531 • 1,485
Botetourt □, VA • 24,992
Bothell, WA 98011–12 • 12,345
Botkins, OH 45306 • 1,340
Bottineau, ND 58318 • 2,598
Bottineau □, ND • 8,011
Boulder, CO 80301–08 • 83,312
Boulder, MT 59632 • 1,316
Boulder □, CO • 225,339
Boulder City, NV 89005–06 • 12,567
Boulder Creek, CA 95006 • 6,725
Boulder Hill, IL 60538 • 8,894
Boulevard Heights, MD 20743 • 1,820
Boundary □, ID • 8,332
Bound Brook, NJ 08805 • 9,487
Bountiful, UT 84010–11 • 36,659
Bourbon, IN 46504 • 1,672
Bourbon, MO 65441 • 1,188
Bourbon □, KS • 14,966
Bourbon □, KY • 19,236
Bourbonnais, IL 60914 • 13,934
Bourg, LA 70343 • 2,073
Bourne, MA 02532 • 1,284
Boutte, LA 70039 • 1,200
Bovina, TX 79009 • 1,549
Bowdon, GA 30108 • 1,981
Bowie, MD 20715–21 • 37,589
Bowie, TX 76230 • 4,990
Bowie □, TX • 81,665
Bowling Green, FL 33834 • 1,836
Bowling Green, KY 42101–04 • 40,641
Bowling Green, MO 63334 • 2,976
Bowling Green, OH 43402 • 28,176
Bowman, ND 58623 • 1,741
Bowman, SC 29018 • 1,063
Bowman □, ND • 3,596
Box Butte □, NE • 13,130
Box Elder, SD 57719 • 2,680
Box Elder □, UT • 36,485
Boxford, MA 01921 • 2,072
Boyce, LA 71409 • 1,361
Boyd □, KY • 51,150
Boyd □, NE • 2,835
Boyertown, PA 19512 • 3,759
Boyes Hot Springs, CA 95416 • 5,973
Boyle □, KY • 25,641
Boyne City, MI 49712 • 3,478
Boynton Beach, FL 33435–37 • 46,194
Bozeman, MT 59715 • 22,660
Bracken □, KY • 7,766
Brackenridge, PA 15014 • 3,784
Brackettville, TX 78832 • 1,740
Braddock, PA 15104 • 4,682
Braddock Heights, MD 21714 • 4,778
Bradenton, FL 34201–10 • 43,779
Bradenville, PA 15620 • 1,100
Bradford, OH 45308 • 2,005
Bradford, PA 16701 • 9,625
Bradford, RI 02808 • 1,604
Bradford, TN 38316 • 1,154
Bradford, VT 05033 • 672
Bradford □, FL • 22,515
Bradford □, PA • 60,967
Bradfordwoods, PA 15015 • 1,329
Bradley, FL 33835 • 1,108
Bradley, IL 60915 • 10,792
Bradley, WV 25818 • 2,144
Bradley □, AR • 11,793
Bradley □, TN • 73,712
Bradley Beach, NJ 07720 • 4,475
Bradner, OH 43406 • 1,093
Brady, TX 76825 • 5,946
Braham, MN 55006 • 1,139
Braidwood, IL 60408 • 3,584
Brainerd, MN 56401 • 12,353
Braintree, MA 02184 • 33,836
Branch □, MI • 41,502
Branch Village, RI 02895 • 400
Branchville, SC 29432 • 1,107
Brandenburg, KY 40108 • 1,857
Brandon, FL 33510 • 57,985
Brandon, MS 39042–43 • 11,077
Brandon, SC 29611 • 2,170
Brandon, SD 57005 • 3,543
Brandon, VT 05733 • 1,902
Brandywine, MD 20613 • 1,406
Branford, CT 06405 • 27,603
Branford Hills, CT 06405 • 3,460
Branson, MO 65616 • 3,706
Brantley, AL 36009 • 1,015
Brantley □, GA • 11,077
Brant Rock, MA 02020 • 1,850
Bratenahl, OH 44108 • 1,356
Brattleboro, VT 05301–04 • 8,612
Brawley, CA 92227 • 18,923
Braxton □, WV • 12,998
Brazil, IN 47834 • 7,640
Brazoria, TX 77422 • 2,717
Brazoria □, TX • 191,707
Brazos □, TX • 121,862
Brea, CA 92621–22 • 32,873
Breathitt □, KY • 15,703
Breaux Bridge, LA 70517 • 6,515
Breckenridge, CO 80424 • 1,285
Breckenridge, MI 48615 • 1,301
Breckenridge, MN 56520 • 3,708
Breckenridge, TX 76024 • 5,665
Breckenridge Hills, MO 63114 • 5,404
Breckinridge □, KY • 16,312
Brecksville, OH 44141 • 11,818
Breese, IL 62230 • 3,567
Bremen, GA 30110 • 4,356
Bremen, IN 46506 • 4,725
Bremen, OH 43107 • 1,386
Bremer □, IA • 22,813
Bremerton, WA 98310–15 • 38,142
Bremond, TX 76629 • 1,110
Brenham, TX 77833–34 • 11,952
Brent, AL 35034 • 2,776
Brent, FL 32503 • 21,624
Brentwood, CA 94513 • 7,563
Brentwood, MD 20722 • 3,005
Brentwood, MO 63144 • 8,150
Brentwood, NY 11717 • 45,218
Brentwood, NY • 45,218
Brentwood, OH 45231 • 3,568

Brentwood, PA 15227 • 10,823
Brentwood, SC 29405 • 2,000
Brentwood, TN 37027 • 16,392
Brevard, NC 28712 • 5,388
Brevard □, FL • 398,978
Brewer, ME 04412 • 9,021
Brewster, MA 02631 • 1,818
Brewster, NY 10509 • 1,566
Brewster, OH 44613 • 2,307
Brewster, WA 98812 • 1,633
Brewster □, TX • 8,681
Brewton, AL 36426–27 • 5,885
Briarcliff Manor, NY 10510 • 7,070
Brick [Township], NJ 08723 • 55,473
Bridge City, LA 70094 • 8,327
Bridge City, TX 77611 • 8,034
Bridgehampton, NY 11932 • 1,997
Bridgeport, AL 35740 • 2,936
Bridgeport, CT 06601–50 • 141,686
Bridgeport, IL 62417 • 2,118
Bridgeport, MI 48722 • 8,569
Bridgeport, NE 69336 • 1,581
Bridgeport, OH 43912 • 2,318
Bridgeport, PA 19405 • 4,292
Bridgeport, TX 76026 • 3,581
Bridgeport, WA 98813 • 1,498
Bridgeport, WV 26330 • 6,739
Bridger, MT 59014 • 692
Bridgeton, MO 63044 • 17,779
Bridgeton, NJ 08302 • 18,942
Bridgetown, OH 45211 • 11,460
Bridgeview, IL 60455 • 14,402
Bridgeville, DE 19933 • 1,210
Bridgeville, PA 15017 • 5,445
Bridgewater, MA 02324 • 7,242
Bridgewater, NJ 08807 • 5,630
Bridgewater, VA 22812 • 3,918
Bridgman, MI 49106 • 2,140
Bridgton, ME 04009 • 2,195
Brielle, NJ 08730 • 4,406
Brigantine, NJ 08203 • 11,354
Brigham City, UT 84302 • 15,644
Brighton, AL 35020 • 4,518
Brighton, CO 80601 • 14,203
Brighton, IL 62012 • 2,270
Brighton, MI 48116 • 5,686
Brighton, NY 14610 • 34,455
Brilliant, OH 43913 • 1,672
Brillion, WI 54110 • 2,840
Brinkley, AR 72021 • 4,234
Briscoe □, TX • 1,971
Bristol, CT 06010–11 • 60,640
Bristol, IN 46507 • 1,133
Bristol, NH 03222 • 1,483
Bristol, RI 02809 • 21,625
Bristol, TN 37620–25 • 23,421
Bristol, VT 05443 • 1,801
Bristol, VA 24201–03 • 18,426
Bristol □, MA • 506,325
Bristol □, RI • 48,859
Bristol [Township], PA 19007 • 58,773
Bristow, OK 74010 • 4,062
Britt, IA 50423 • 2,133
Britton, SD 57430 • 1,394
Broadalbin, NY 12025 • 1,397
Broad Brook, CT 06016 • 1,280
Broadkill Beach, DE 19968 • 390
Broadus, MT 59317 • 572
Broadview, IL 60153 • 8,713
Broadview Heights, OH 44141 • 12,219
Broadview Park, FL 33314 • 6,109
Broadwater □, MT • 3,318
Broadway, VA 22815 • 1,209
Brockport, NY 14420 • 8,749
Brockton, MA 02401–05 • 92,788
Brockway, PA 15824 • 2,207
Brocton, NY 14716 • 1,387
Brodhead, KY 40409 • 1,140
Brodhead, WI 53520 • 3,165
Brodheadsville, PA 18322 • 1,500
Broken Arrow, OK 74011–14 • 58,043
Broken Bow, NE 68822 • 3,778
Broken Bow, OK 74728 • 3,961
Bronson, MI 49028 • 2,342
Bronx □, NY • 1,203,789
Bronxville, NY 10708 • 6,028
Brooke □, WV • 26,992
Brookfield, CT 06804 • 1,500
Brookfield, IL 60513 • 18,876
Brookfield, MA 01506 • 2,968
Brookfield, MO 64628 • 4,888
Brookfield, VA 22021 • 2,100
Brookfield, WI 53005 • 35,184
Brookfield Center, CT 06804 • 1,400
Brookhaven, MS 39601 • 10,243
Brookhaven, PA 19015 • 8,567
Brookhaven, WV 26505 • 3,836
Brookings, OR 97415 • 4,400
Brookings, SD 57006 • 16,270
Brookings □, SD • 25,207
Brooklawn, NJ 08030 • 1,805
Brookline, MA 02146 • 54,718
Brooklyn, CT 06234 • 1,400
Brooklyn, IN 46111 • 1,162
Brooklyn, IA 52211 • 1,439
Brooklyn, OH 44144 • 11,706
Brooklyn, SC 29720 • 1,850
Brooklyn Center, MN 55429 • 28,887
Brooklyn Park, MD 21225 • 10,987
Brooklyn Park, MN 55443 • 56,381
Brookneal, VA 24528 • 1,344
Brook Park, OH 44142 • 22,865
Brookport, IL 62910 • 1,070
Brooks, KY 40109 • 2,464
Brooks □, GA • 15,398
Brooks □, TX • 8,204
Brookshire, TX 77423 • 2,922
Brookside, AL 35036 • 1,365
Brookside, DE 19713 • 15,307
Brookston, IN 47923 • 1,804
Brooksville, FL 34601–14 • 7,440
Brooksville, MS 39739 • 1,098
Brookville, IN 47012 • 2,529
Brookville, NY 11545 • 3,716
Brookville, OH 45309 • 4,621
Brookville, PA 15825 • 4,184
Brookwood, NJ 08527 • 5,500
Broomall, PA 19008 • 10,930
Broome □, NY • 212,160
Broomfield, CO 80020–21 • 24,638
Broussard, LA 70518 • 3,213
Broward □, FL • 1,255,488
Browardale, FL 33311 • 6,257

Brown □, IL • 5,836
Brown □, IN • 14,080
Brown □, KS • 11,128
Brown □, MN • 26,984
Brown □, NE • 3,657
Brown □, OH • 34,966
Brown □, SD • 35,580
Brown □, TX • 34,371
Brown □, WI • 194,594
Brown City, MI 48416 • 1,244
Brown Deer, WI 53209 • 12,236
Brownfield, TX 79316 • 9,560
Brownfields, LA 70811 • 5,229
Browning, MT 59417 • 1,170
Brownsburg, IN 46112 • 7,628
Browns Mills, NJ 08015 • 11,429
Brownstown, IN 47220 • 2,872
Brownsville, FL 33142 • 15,607
Brownsville, OR 97327 • 1,281
Brownsville, PA 15417 • 3,164
Brownsville, TN 38012 • 10,019
Brownsville, TX 78520–26 • 98,962
Brownville, LA 71291 • 1,700
Brownville, NY 13615 • 1,138
Brownwood, TX 76803–04 • 18,387
Broxton, GA 31519 • 1,211
Broyhill Park, VA 22042 • 3,600
Bruce, MS 38915 • 2,127
Bruceton, TN 38317 • 1,586
Brule □, SD • 5,485
Brundidge, AL 36010 • 2,472
Brunswick, GA 31520–22 • 16,433
Brunswick, ME 04011 • 14,683
Brunswick, MD 21716 • 5,117
Brunswick, MO 65236 • 1,074
Brunswick, OH 44212 • 28,230
Brunswick □, NC • 50,985
Brunswick □, VA • 15,987
Brush, CO 80723 • 4,165
Brusly, LA 70719 • 1,824
Bryan, OH 43506 • 8,348
Bryan, TX 77801–06 • 55,002
Bryan □, GA • 15,438
Bryan □, OK • 32,089
Bryans Road, MD 20616 • 3,809
Bryant, AR 72022 • 5,269
Bryantville, MA 02327 • 1,800
Bryn Mawr, WA 98178 • 1,500
Bryson City, NC 28713 • 1,145
Buchanan, GA 30113 • 1,009
Buchanan, MI 49107 • 4,992
Buchanan, VA 24066 • 1,222
Buchanan □, IA • 20,844
Buchanan □, MO • 83,083
Buchanan □, VA • 31,333
Buckeye, AZ 85326 • 5,038
Buckeye Lake, OH 43008 • 2,986
Buckhannon, WV 26201 • 5,909
Buckingham □, VA • 12,873
Buckley, WA 98321 • 3,516
Bucknell Manor, VA 22307 • 2,300
Buckner, MO 64016 • 2,873
Bucks □, PA • 541,174
Bucksport, ME 04416 • 2,989
Bucksport, SC 29527 • 1,022
Bucyrus, OH 44820 • 13,496
Buda, TX 78610 • 1,795
Budd Lake 0L, NJ • 7,272
Buechel, KY 40218 • 7,081
Buena, NJ 08310 • 4,441
Buena Park, CA 90620–24 • 68,784
Buena Vista, CO 81211 • 1,752
Buena Vista, FL 34691 • 3,000
Buena Vista, GA 31803 • 1,472
Buena Vista, VA 24416 • 6,406
Buena Vista □, IA • 19,965
Buffalo, IA 52728 • 1,260
Buffalo, MN 55313 • 6,856
Buffalo, MO 65622 • 2,414
Buffalo, NY 14201–40 • 328,123
Buffalo, OK 73834 • 1,312
Buffalo, SC 29321 • 1,569
Buffalo, TX 75831 • 1,555
Buffalo, WY 82834 • 3,302
Buffalo □, NE • 37,447
Buffalo □, SD • 1,759
Buffalo □, WI • 13,584
Buffalo Center, IA 50424 • 1,081
Buffalo Grove, IL 60089 • 36,427
Buford, GA 30518 • 8,771
Buhl, ID 83316 • 3,516
Buhler, KS 67522 • 1,277
Buies Creek, NC 27506 • 2,085
Bullhead City, AZ 86430 • 21,951
Bullitt □, KY • 47,567
Bulloch □, GA • 43,125
Bullock □, AL • 11,042
Bull Shoals, AR 72619 • 1,534
Buna, TX 77612 • 1,900
Bunche Park, FL 33054 • 4,000
Buncombe □, NC • 174,821
Bunker Hill, IL 62014 • 1,722
Bunker Hill, OR 97420 • 1,242
Bunkerville, NV 89007 • 300
Bunkie, LA 71322 • 5,044
Bunnell, FL 32110 • 1,873
Buras, LA 70041 • 1,600
Burbank, CA 91501–10 • 93,643
Burbank, IL 60459 • 27,600
Burdickville, RI 02808 • 500
Bureau □, IL • 35,688
Burgaw, NC 28425 • 1,807
Burgettstown, PA 15021 • 1,634
Burgin, KY 40310 • 1,009
Burien, WA 98062 • 25,089
Burkburnett, TX 76354 • 10,145
Burke, SD 57523 • 756
Burke, VA 22015 • 57,734
Burke □, GA • 20,579
Burke □, NC • 75,744
Burke □, ND • 3,002
Burkesville, KY 42717 • 1,815
Burleigh □, ND • 60,131
Burleson, TX 76028 • 16,113
Burleson □, TX • 13,625
Burley, ID 83318 • 8,702
Burlingame, CA 94010–11 • 26,801
Burlingame, KS 66413 • 1,074
Burlington, CO 80807 • 2,941
Burlington, IA 52601 • 27,208
Burlington, KS 66839 • 2,735
Burlington, KY 41005 • 6,070
Burlington, MA 01803 • 23,302

Burlington, NJ 08016 • 9,835
Burlington, NC 27215–17 • 39,498
Burlington, ND 58722 • 995
Burlington, VT 05401–04 • 39,127
Burlington, WA 98233 • 4,349
Burlington, WI 53105 • 8,855
Burlington □, NJ • 395,066
Burnet, TX 78611 • 3,423
Burnet □, TX • 22,677
Burnett □, WI • 13,084
Burney, CA 96013 • 3,423
Burnham, PA 17009 • 2,197
Burns, OR 97720 • 2,913
Burns, TN 37029 • 1,127
Burns, WY 82053 • 254
Burns Flat, OK 73624 • 1,027
Burnsville, MN 55337 • 51,288
Burnsville, NC 28714 • 1,482
Burnt Hills, NY 12027 • 1,550
Burr Ridge, IL 60521 • 7,669
Burt □, NE • 7,868
Burton, MI 48509 • 27,617
Burton, OH 44021 • 1,349
Burton, SC 29902 • 6,917
Burtonsville, MD 20866 • 5,853
Burwell, NE 68823 • 1,278
Bushnell, FL 33513 • 1,998
Bushnell, IL 61422 • 3,288
Butler, AL 36904 • 1,872
Butler, GA 31006 • 1,673
Butler, IN 46721 • 2,601
Butler, MO 64730 • 4,099
Butler, NJ 07405 • 7,392
Butler, PA 16001–03 • 15,714
Butler, WI 53007 • 2,079
Butler □, AL • 21,892
Butler □, IA • 15,731
Butler □, KS • 50,580
Butler □, KY • 11,245
Butler □, MO • 38,765
Butler □, NE • 8,601
Butler □, OH • 291,479
Butler □, PA • 152,013
Butner, NC 27509 • 4,679
Butte, MT 59701–03 • 33,336
Butte □, CA • 182,120
Butte □, ID • 2,918
Butte □, SD • 7,914
Buttonwillow, CA 93206 • 1,301
Butts □, GA • 15,326
Buxton, NC 27920 • 1,300
Buzzards Bay, MA 02532 • 3,250
Byers, CO 80103 • 1,065
Byesville, OH 43723 • 2,435
Byfield, MA 01922 • 1,200
Bylas, AZ 85530 • 1,219
Byron, GA 31008 • 2,276
Byron, IL 61010 • 2,284
Byron, MN 55920 • 2,441
Byron, WY 82412 • 470

C

Cabarrus □, NC • 98,935
Cabell □, WV • 96,827
Cabin Creek, WV 25035 • 1,300
Cabin John, MD 20818 • 1,690
Cabool, MO 65689 • 2,006
Cabot, AR 72023 • 8,319
Cache, OK 73527 • 2,251
Cache □, UT • 70,183
Caddo □, LA • 248,253
Caddo □, OK • 29,550
Cadillac, MI 49601 • 10,104
Cadiz, KY 42211 • 2,148
Cadiz, OH 43907 • 3,439
Cadott, WI 54727 • 1,328
Cahaba Heights, AL 35243 • 4,778
Cahokia, IL 62206 • 17,550
Cairnbrook, PA 15924 • 1,081
Cairo, GA 31728 • 9,035
Cairo, IL 62914 • 4,846
Cairo, NY 12413 • 1,273
Calais, ME 04619 • 3,963
Calaveras □, CA • 31,998
Calavo Gardens, CA 91941 • 6,100
Calcasieu □, LA • 168,134
Calcutta, OH 43920 • 1,212
Caldwell, ID 83605–06 • 18,400
Caldwell, KS 67022 • 1,351
Caldwell, NJ 07006 • 7,549
Caldwell, OH 43724 • 1,786
Caldwell, TX 77836 • 3,181
Caldwell □, KY • 13,232
Caldwell □, LA • 9,810
Caldwell □, MO • 8,380
Caldwell □, NC • 70,709
Caldwell □, TX • 26,392
Caledonia, MN 55921 • 2,846
Caledonia, NY 14423 • 2,262
Caledonia □, VT • 27,846
Calera, AL 35040 • 2,106
Calera, OK 74730 • 1,536
Calexico, CA 92231–32 • 18,633
Calhoun, GA 30701 • 7,135
Calhoun □, AL • 116,034
Calhoun □, AR • 5,826
Calhoun □, FL • 11,011
Calhoun □, GA • 5,013
Calhoun □, IL • 5,322
Calhoun □, IA • 11,508
Calhoun □, MI • 135,982
Calhoun □, MS • 14,908
Calhoun □, SC • 12,753
Calhoun □, TX • 19,053
Calhoun □, WV • 7,885
Calhoun City, MS 38916 • 1,838
Calhoun Falls, SC 29628 • 2,328
Caliente, NV 89008 • 1,111
Califon, NJ 07830 • 1,073
California, MD 20619 • 7,626
California, MO 65018 • 3,465
California, PA 15419 • 5,748
Calipatria, CA 92233 • 2,690
Calistoga, CA 94515 • 4,468
Callahan □, TX • 11,859
Callaway, FL 32401 • 12,253
Callaway □, MO • 32,809
Calloway □, KY • 30,735
Calmar, IA 52132 • 1,026
Calumet □, WI • 34,291

Calumet City, IL 60409 • 37,840
Calumet Park, IL 60643 • 8,418
Calvert, TX 77837 • 1,536
Calvert □, MD • 51,372
Calvert City, KY 42029 • 2,531
Calverton, MD 20705 • 12,046
Calverton Park, MO 63136 • 1,404
Camanche, IA 52730 • 4,436
Camarillo, CA 93010–11 • 52,303
Camas, WA 98607 • 6,442
Camas □, ID • 727
Cambria, CA 93428 • 5,382
Cambria □, PA • 163,029
Cambrian Park, CA 95124 • 2,998
Cambridge, IL 61238 • 2,124
Cambridge, MD 21613 • 11,514
Cambridge, MA 02138 • 95,802
Cambridge, MN 55008 • 5,094
Cambridge, NE 69022 • 1,107
Cambridge, NY 12816 • 1,906
Cambridge, OH 43725 • 11,748
Cambridge City, IN 47327 • 2,091
Cambridge Springs, PA 16403 • 1,837
Camden, AL 36726 • 2,414
Camden, AR 71701 • 14,380
Camden, DE 19934 • 1,899
Camden, ME 04843 • 4,022
Camden, NJ 08101–10 • 87,492
Camden, NY 13316 • 2,552
Camden, OH 45311 • 2,210
Camden, SC 29020 • 6,696
Camden, TN 38320 • 3,643
Camden □, GA • 30,167
Camden □, MO • 27,495
Camden □, NJ • 502,824
Camden □, NC • 5,904
Camdenton, MO 65020 • 2,561
Camelot, WA 98002 • 4,900
Cameron, LA 70631 • 2,041
Cameron, MO 64429 • 4,831
Cameron, TX 76520 • 5,580
Cameron, WV 26033 • 1,177
Cameron, WI 54822 • 1,273
Cameron □, LA • 9,260
Cameron □, PA • 5,913
Cameron □, TX • 260,120
Cameron Park, CA 95682 • 11,897
Camilla, GA 31730 • 5,008
Camino, CA 95709 • 1,500
Camp □, TX • 9,904
Campbell, CA 95008–09 • 36,048
Campbell, FL 34746 • 3,884
Campbell, MO 63933 • 2,165
Campbell, OH 44405 • 10,038
Campbell □, KY • 83,866
Campbell □, SD • 1,965
Campbell □, TN • 35,079
Campbell □, VA • 47,572
Campbell □, WY • 29,370
Campbellsport, WI 53010 • 1,732
Campbellsville, KY 42718–19 • 9,577
Camp Hill, AL 36850 • 1,415
Camp Hill, PA 17011 • 7,831
Camp Point, IL 62320 • 1,230
Camp Springs, MD 20748 • 16,392
Camp Verde, AZ 86322 • 6,243
Canaan, CT 06018 • 1,194
Canadensis, PA 18325 • 1,200
Canadian, TX 79014 • 2,417
Canadian □, OK • 74,409
Canajoharie, NY 13317 • 2,278
Canal Fulton, OH 44614 • 4,157
Canal Winchester, OH 43110 • 2,617
Canandaigua, NY 14424–25 • 10,725
Canastota, NY 13032 • 4,673
Canby, MN 56220 • 1,826
Canby, OR 97013 • 8,983
Candler □, GA • 7,744
Candlewood Isle, CT 06812 • 1,100
Candlewood Shores, CT 06804 • 1,620
Cando, ND 58324 • 1,564
Caney, KS 67333 • 2,062
Canfield, OH 44406 • 5,409
Canisteo, NY 14823 • 2,421
Cannelton, IN 47520 • 1,786
Cannon □, TN • 10,467
Cannon Beach, OR 97110 • 1,221
Cannondale, CT 06897 • 1,500
Cannon Falls, MN 55009 • 3,232
Canon City, CO 81212 • 12,687
Canonsburg, PA 15317 • 9,200
Canterbury, DE 19943 • 500
Canton, CT 06019 • 1,563
Canton, GA 30114 • 4,817
Canton, IL 61520 • 13,922
Canton, MA 02021 • 18,182
Canton, MI 48187 • 57,047
Canton, MS 39046 • 10,062
Canton, MO 63435 • 2,623
Canton, NY 13617 • 6,379
Canton, NC 28716 • 3,790
Canton, OH 44701–99 • 84,161
Canton, PA 17724 • 1,966
Canton, SD 57013 • 2,787
Canton, TX 75103 • 2,949
Cantonment, FL 32533 • 3,200
Canutillo, TX 79835 • 4,500
Canyon, TX 79015 • 11,365
Canyon □, ID • 90,076
Canyon Lake, CA 92380 • 7,938
Canyon Lake, TX 78130 • 9,975
Canyonville, OR 97417 • 1,219
Capac, MI 48014 • 1,583
Cape Canaveral, FL 32920 • 8,014
Cape Charles, VA 23310 • 1,398
Cape Coral, FL 33904 • 74,991
Cape Elizabeth, ME 04107 • 8,854
Cape Girardeau, MO 63701–02 • 34,438
Cape Girardeau □, MO • 61,633
Cape May, NJ 08204 • 4,668
Cape May □, NJ • 95,089
Cape May Court House, NJ 08210 • 4,426
Cape Saint Claire, MD 21401 • 7,878
Capitola, CA 95010 • 10,171
Capitol Heights, MD 20743 • 3,633
Capitol View, SC 29209 • 10,456
Captain Cook, HI 96704 • 2,595
Captiva, FL 33924 • 1,200
Caraway, AR 72419 • 1,178
Carbon □, MT • 8,080
Carbon □, PA • 56,846
Carbon □, UT • 20,228
Carbon □, WY • 16,659
Carbondale, CO 81623 • 3,004
Carbondale, IL 62901–03 • 27,033
Carbondale, KS 66414 • 1,526
Carbondale, PA 18407 • 10,664
Carbon Hill, AL 35549 • 2,115
Cardington, OH 43315 • 1,770
Carencro, LA 70520 • 5,429
Carey, OH 43316 • 3,684
Caribou, ME 04736 • 9,415
Caribou □, ID • 6,963
Carle Place, NY 11514 • 5,107
Carleton, MI 48117 • 2,770
Carlin, NV 89822 • 2,220
Carlinville, IL 62626 • 5,416
Carlisle, AR 72024 • 2,253
Carlisle, IA 50047 • 3,241
Carlisle, KY 40311 • 1,639
Carlisle, OH 45005 • 4,872
Carlisle, PA 17013 • 18,419
Carlisle □, KY • 5,238
Carl Junction, MO 64834 • 4,123
Carlsbad, CA 92008–09 • 63,126
Carlsbad, NM 88220–21 • 24,952
Carlstadt, NJ 07072 • 5,510
Carlton, OR 97111 • 1,289
Carlton □, MN • 29,259
Carlyle, IL 62231 • 3,474
Carmel, CA 93921–23 • 4,239
Carmel, IN 46032 • 25,380
Carmel, NY 10512 • 3,395
Carmi, IL 62821 • 5,564
Carmichael, CA 95608–09 • 48,702
Carnation, WA 98014 • 1,243
Carnegie, OK 73015 • 1,593
Carnegie, PA 15106 • 9,278
Carney, MD 21234 • 25,578
Carneys Point, NJ 08069 • 7,686
Carnot, PA 15108 • 4,750
Caro, MI 48723 • 4,054
Carol City, FL 33055 • 53,331
Caroleen, NC 28019 • 1,100
Carolina Beach, NC 28428 • 3,630
Caroline □, MD • 27,035
Caroline □, VA • 19,217
Carol Stream, IL 60188 • 31,716
Carpentersville, IL 60110 • 23,049
Carpinteria, CA 93013–14 • 13,747
Carrabelle, FL 32322 • 1,200
Carrboro, NC 27510 • 11,553
Carrier Mills, IL 62917 • 1,991
Carrington, ND 58421 • 2,267
Carrizo Springs, TX 78834 • 5,745
Carrizozo, NM 88301 • 1,075
Carroll, IA 51401 • 9,579
Carroll □, AR • 18,654
Carroll □, GA • 71,422
Carroll □, IL • 16,805
Carroll □, IN • 18,809
Carroll □, IA • 21,423
Carroll □, KY • 9,292
Carroll □, MD • 123,372
Carroll □, MS • 9,237
Carroll □, MO • 10,748
Carroll □, NH • 35,410
Carroll □, OH • 26,521
Carroll □, TN • 27,514
Carroll □, VA • 26,594
Carrollton, AL 35447 • 1,170
Carrollton, GA 30117 • 16,029
Carrollton, IL 62016 • 2,507
Carrollton, KY 41008 • 3,715
Carrollton, MI 48724 • 6,521
Carrollton, MO 64633 • 4,406
Carrollton, OH 44615 • 3,042
Carrollton, TX 75006–08 • 82,169
Carrolltown, PA 15722 • 1,286
Carrollwood, FL 33618 • 11,400
Carson, CA 90749 • 83,995
Carson □, TX • 6,576
Carson City, MI 48811 • 1,158
Carson City, NV 89701–21 • 40,443
Carter □, KY • 24,340
Carter □, MO • 5,515
Carter □, MT • 1,503
Carter □, OK • 42,919
Carter □, TN • 51,505
Carteret, NJ 07008 • 19,025
Carteret □, NC • 52,556
Carter Lake, IA 51510 • 3,200
Cartersville, GA 30120 • 12,035
Carterville, IL 62918 • 3,630
Carterville, MO 64835 • 2,013
Carthage, IL 62321 • 2,657
Carthage, MS 39051 • 3,819
Carthage, MO 64836 • 10,747
Carthage, NY 13619 • 4,344
Carthage, TN 37030 • 2,386
Carthage, TX 75633 • 6,496
Caruthersville, MO 63830 • 7,389
Carver, MA 02330 • 1,500
Carver □, MN • 47,915
Carver Ranch Estates, FL 33023 • 5,600
Carville, LA 70721 • 1,108
Cary, IL 60013 • 10,043
Cary, NC 27511 • 43,858
Caryville, TN 37714 • 1,751
Casa de Oro, CA 92077 • 9,500
Casa Grande, AZ 85222 • 19,082
Casas Adobes, AZ 85704 • 12,155
Cascade, CO 80809 • 1,000
Cascade, ID 83611 • 877
Cascade, IA 52033 • 1,812
Cascade, MT 59421 • 729
Cascade □, MT • 77,691
Cascade Vista, WA 98058 • 7,800
Casey, IL 62420 • 2,914
Casey □, KY • 14,211
Cashion, AZ 85329 • 3,014
Cashmere, WA 98815 • 2,544
Casper, WY 82601–15 • 46,742
Caspian, MI 49915 • 1,031
Cass □, IL • 13,437
Cass □, IN • 38,413
Cass □, IA • 15,128
Cass □, MI • 49,477
Cass □, MN • 21,791
Cass □, MO • 63,808
Cass □, NE • 21,318
Cass □, ND • 102,874
Cass □, TX • 29,982
Cass City, MI 48726 • 2,276
Casselberry, FL 32707–08 • 18,911
Casselton, ND 58012 • 1,601
Cassia □, ID • 19,532
Cassopolis, MI 49031 • 1,822
Cassville, MO 65625 • 2,371
Cassville, WI 53806 • 1,144
Castanea, PA 17726 • 1,123
Castile, NY 14427 • 1,078
Castle Dale, UT 84513 • 1,704
Castle Hayne, NC 28429 • 1,182
Castle Hills, DE 19720 • 1,475
Castle Park, CA 92011 • 6,300
Castle Point, MO 63136 • 7,800
Castle Rock, CO 80104 • 8,708
Castle Rock, WA 98611 • 2,067
Castle Shannon, PA 15234 • 9,135
Castleton, VT 05735 • 600
Castleton on Hudson, NY 12033 • 1,491
Castlewood, VA 24224 • 2,110
Castro □, TX • 9,070
Castro Valley, CA 94546 • 48,619
Castroville, TX 78009 • 2,159
Caswell □, NC • 20,693
Catahoula □, LA • 11,065
Catalina Foothills, AZ 85718 • 1,470
Catasauqua, PA 18032 • 6,662
Cataumet, MA 02534 • 1,500
Catawba □, NC • 118,412
Catawissa, PA 17820 • 1,683
Cathedral City, CA 92234–35 • 30,085
Catlettsburg, KY 41129 • 2,231
Catlin, IL 61817 • 2,173
Catonsville, MD 21228 • 35,233
Catoosa, OK 74015 • 2,954
Catoosa □, GA • 42,464
Catron □, NM • 2,563
Catskill, NY 12414 • 4,690
Cattaraugus, NY 14719 • 1,100
Cattaraugus □, NY • 84,234
Cavalier, ND 58220 • 1,508
Cavalier □, ND • 6,064
Cave City, AR 72521 • 1,503
Cave City, KY 42127 • 1,953
Cave Creek, AZ 85331 • 2,925
Cave Junction, OR 97523 • 1,126
Cave Spring, VA 24018 • 24,053
Cavetown, MD 21720 • 1,533
Cayce, SC 29033 • 11,163
Cayuga, IN 47928 • 1,083
Cayuga □, NY • 82,313
Cayuga Heights, NY 14850 • 3,457
Cazenovia, NY 13035 • 3,007
Cecil □, MD • 71,347
Cedar □, IA • 17,381
Cedar □, MO • 12,093
Cedar □, NE • 10,131
Cedar Bluff, AL 35959 • 1,174
Cedar Bluff Two, TN 37722 • 2,000
Cedarburg, WI 53012 • 9,895
Cedar City, UT 84720–22 • 13,443
Cedar Crest, NM 87008 • 1,200
Cedaredge, CO 81413 • 1,380
Cedar Falls, IA 50613 • 34,298
Cedar Grove, NJ 07009 • 12,053
Cedar Grove, WV 25039 • 1,213
Cedar Grove, WI 53013 • 1,521
Cedar Hill, MO 63016 • 1,966
Cedar Hill, TX 75104 • 19,976
Cedar Hills, OR 97005 • 9,294
Cedarhurst, NY 11516 • 5,716
Cedar Lake, IN 46303 • 8,885
Cedar Rapids, IA 52401–10 • 108,751
Cedar Springs, MI 49319 • 2,600
Cedartown, GA 30125 • 7,978
Cedarville, NJ 08311 • 1,100
Cedarville, OH 45314 • 3,210
Celina, OH 45822 • 9,650
Celina, TN 38551 • 1,493
Celina, TX 75009 • 1,737
Celoron, NY 14720 • 1,232
Cementon, PA 18052 • 1,050
Center, CO 81125 • 1,963
Center, ND 58530 • 826
Center, TX 75935 • 4,950
Centerburg, OH 43011 • 1,323
Centereach, NY 11720 • 26,720
Center Line, MI 48015 • 9,026
Center Moriches, NY 11934 • 5,987
Center Point, AL 35215 • 22,657
Center Point, IA 52213 • 1,693
Centerville, IN 47330 • 2,398
Centerville, IA 52544 • 5,936
Centerville, MA 02632 • 9,190
Centerville, OH 45459 • 21,082
Centerville, PA 15417 • 3,842
Centerville, SD 57014 • 887
Centerville, TN 37033 • 3,616
Centerville, UT 84014 • 11,500
Central, NM 88026 • 1,835
Central, SC 29630 • 2,438
Central City, CO 80427 • 335
Central City, IL 62801 • 1,390
Central City, IA 52214 • 1,063
Central City, KY 42330 • 4,979
Central City, NE 68826 • 2,868
Central City, PA 15926 • 1,246
Central Falls, RI 02863 • 17,637
Central Heights, AZ 85501 • 1,500
Centralia, IL 62801 • 14,274
Centralia, MO 65240 • 3,414
Centralia, WA 98531 • 12,101
Central Islip, NY 11722 • 26,028
Central Park, WA 98520 • 2,669
Central Point, OR 97502 • 7,509
Central Square, NY 13036 • 1,671
Central Valley, CA 96019 • 4,340
Central Valley, NY 10917 • 1,929
Central Village, CT 06332 • 1,600
Centre, AL 35960 • 2,893
Centre □, PA • 123,786
Centre City, NJ 08051 • 2,070
Centre Hall, PA 16828 • 1,203
Centreville, AL 35042 • 2,508
Centreville, IL 62207 • 7,489
Centreville, MD 21617 • 2,097
Centreville, MI 49032 • 1,516
Centreville, MS 39631 • 1,771
Centreville, VA 22020 • 26,585
Century, FL 32535 • 1,989
Century Village, FL 33409 • 8,363
Ceredo, WV 25507 • 1,916
Ceres, CA 95307 • 26,314
Cerritos, CA 90703 • 53,240
Cerro Gordo, IL 61818 • 1,436
Cerro Gordo □, IA • 46,733
Chadbourn, NC 28431 • 2,005
Chadds Ford, PA 19317 • 1,200
Chadron, NE 69337 • 5,588
Chadwicks, NY 13319 • 2,000
Chaffee, MO 63740 • 3,059
Chaffee □, CO • 12,684
Chaffin, MA 01520 • 3,980
Chagrin Falls, OH 44022 • 4,146
Chalfonte, DE 19810 • 1,740
Challis, ID 83226 • 1,073
Chalmette, LA 70043–44 • 31,860
Chama, NM 87520 • 1,048
Chamberlain, SD 57325 • 2,347
Chambers □, AL • 36,876
Chambers □, TX • 20,088
Chambersburg, PA 17201 • 16,647
Chamblee, GA 30341 • 7,668
Champaign, IL 61820–21 • 63,502
Champaign □, IL • 173,025
Champaign □, OH • 36,019
Champion, OH 44481 • 5,270
Champlain, NY 12919 • 1,273
Champlin, MN 55316 • 16,849
Chandler, AZ 85224–27 • 90,533
Chandler, IN 47610 • 3,099
Chandler, OK 74834 • 2,596
Chandler, TX 75758 • 1,630
Chandler Heights, AZ 85227 • 1,000
Chanhassen, MN 55317 • 11,732
Channahon, IL 60410 • 4,266
Channel Lake, IL 60002 • 1,660
Channelview, TX 77530 • 25,564
Chantilly, VA 22021–22 • 29,337
Chanute, KS 66720 • 9,488
Chapel Hill, NC 27514–16 • 38,719
Chapel Square, VA 22003 • 2,400
Chapman, KS 67431 • 1,264
Chapmanville, WV 25508 • 1,110
Chappaqua, NY 10514 • 6,380
Chardon, OH 44024 • 4,446
Chariton, IA 50049 • 4,616
Chariton □, MO • 9,202
Charleroi, PA 15022 • 5,014
Charles □, MD • 101,154
Charles City, IA 50616 • 7,878
Charles City □, VA • 6,282
Charles Mix □, SD • 9,131
Charleston, AR 72933 • 2,128
Charleston, IL 61920 • 20,398
Charleston, MS 38921 • 2,328
Charleston, MO 63834 • 5,085
Charleston, SC 29401–22 • 80,414
Charleston, WV 25301–75 • 57,287
Charleston □, SC • 295,039
Charlestown, IN 47111 • 5,889
Charlestown, NH 03603 • 1,173
Charlestown, RI 02813 • 1,500
Charles Town, WV 25414 • 3,122
Charlevoix, MI 49720 • 3,116
Charlevoix □, MI • 21,468
Charlotte, MI 48813 • 8,083
Charlotte, NC 28201–41 • 395,934
Charlotte, TX 78011 • 1,475
Charlotte □, FL • 110,975
Charlotte □, VA • 11,688
Charlotte Hall, MD 20622 • 1,992
Charlotte Harbor, FL 33980 • 3,327
Charlottesville, VA 22901–08 • 40,341
Charlton □, GA • 8,496
Charlton City, MA 01508 • 1,400
Charter Oak, CA 91724 • 8,858
Chase □, KS • 3,021
Chase □, NE • 4,381
Chase City, VA 23924 • 2,442
Chaska, MN 55318 • 11,339
Chatfield, MN 55923 • 2,226
Chatham, IL 62629 • 6,074
Chatham, MA 02633 • 1,916
Chatham, NJ 07928 • 8,007
Chatham, NY 12037 • 1,920
Chatham, VA 24531 • 1,354
Chatham □, GA • 216,935
Chatham □, NC • 38,759
Chatom, AL 36518 • 1,094
Chatsworth, GA 30705 • 2,865
Chatsworth, IL 60921 • 1,186
Chattahoochee, FL 32324 • 4,382
Chattahoochee □, GA • 16,934
Chattanooga, TN 37401–22 • 152,466
Chattaroy, WV 25667 • 1,182
Chattooga □, GA • 22,242
Chautauqua □, KS • 4,407
Chautauqua □, NY • 141,895
Chauvin, LA 70344 • 3,375
Chaves □, NM • 57,849
Chazy, NY 12921 • 1,000
Cheatham □, TN • 27,140
Cheboygan, MI 49721 • 4,999
Cheboygan □, MI • 21,398
Checotah, OK 74426 • 3,290
Cheektowaga, NY 14225 • 84,387
Chehalis, WA 98532 • 6,527
Chelan, WA 98816 • 2,969
Chelan □, WA • 52,250
Chelmsford, MA 01824 • 32,388
Chelsea, MA 02150 • 28,710
Chelsea, MI 48118 • 3,772
Chelsea, OK 74016 • 1,620
Chelsea Estates, DE 19720 • 1,320
Cheltenham Township, PA 19012 • 35,509
Chemung □, NY • 95,195
Chenango □, NY • 51,768
Chenango Bridge, NY 13745 • 2,890
Cheney, KS 67025 • 1,560
Cheney, WA 99004 • 7,723
Cheneyville, LA 71325 • 1,005
Chenoa, IL 61726 • 1,732
Chenoweth, OR 97058 • 3,246
Chepachet, RI 02814 • 900
Cheraw, SC 29520 • 5,505
Cherokee, AL 35616 • 1,479
Cherokee, IA 51012 • 6,026
Cherokee, OK 73728 • 1,787
Cherokee □, AL • 19,543
Cherokee □, GA • 90,204
Cherokee □, IA • 14,098
Cherokee □, KS • 21,374
Cherokee □, NC • 20,170
Cherokee □, OK • 34,049
Cherokee □, SC • 44,506
Cherokee □, TX • 41,049
Cherokee Village, AR 72525 • 3,200
Cherry □, NE • 6,307
Cherry Hill, NJ 08002–03 • 69,319
Cherry Hills Village, CO 80110 • 5,245
Cherryland, CA 94541 • 11,088
Cherryvale, KS 67335 • 2,464
Cherry Valley, CA 92223 • 5,945
Cherry Valley, IL 61016 • 1,615
Cherry Valley, MA 01611 • 1,120
Cherryville, NC 28021 • 4,756
Chesaning, MI 48616 • 2,567
Chesapeake, OH 45619 • 1,073
Chesapeake, VA 23320–28 • 151,976
Chesapeake, WV 25315 • 1,896
Chesapeake Beach, MD 20732 • 2,403
Cheshire, CT 06410 • 25,684
Cheshire, MA 01225 • 1,100
Cheshire □, NH • 70,121
Chesilhurst, NJ 08089 • 1,526
Chesnee, SC 29323 • 1,280
Chester, CA 96020 • 2,082
Chester, CT 06412 • 1,563
Chester, IL 62233 • 8,194
Chester, MT 59522 • 942
Chester, NJ 07930 • 1,214
Chester, NY 10918 • 3,270
Chester, PA 19013–16 • 41,856
Chester, SC 29706 • 7,158
Chester, VT 05143 • 550
Chester, VA 23831 • 14,896
Chester, WV 26034 • 2,905
Chester □, PA • 376,396
Chester □, SC • 32,170
Chester □, TN • 12,819
Chester Depot, VT 05144 • 500
Chesterfield, IN 46017 • 2,730
Chesterfield, SC 29709 • 1,373
Chesterfield □, SC • 38,577
Chesterfield □, VA • 209,274
Chesterton, IN 46304 • 9,124
Chestertown, MD 21620 • 4,005
Chester Township, PA 19013 • 5,399
Chestnut Hill Estates, DE 19713 • 1,730
Chestnut Ridge, NY 10952 • 7,517
Cheswick, PA 15024 • 1,971
Cheswold, DE 19936 • 321
Chetek, WI 54728 • 1,953
Chetopa, KS 67336 • 1,357
Chevak, AK 99563 • 598
Cheverly, MD 20785 • 6,023
Cheviot, OH 45211 • 9,616
Chevy Chase, MD 20815 • 8,559
Chewelah, WA 99109 • 1,945
Cheyenne, WY 82001–09 • 50,008
Cheyenne □, CO • 2,397
Cheyenne □, KS • 3,243
Cheyenne □, NE • 9,494
Cheyenne Wells, CO 80810 • 1,128
Chicago, IL 60601–66 • 2,783,726
Chicago Heights, IL 60411 • 33,072
Chicago Ridge, IL 60415 • 13,643
Chickamauga, GA 30707 • 2,149
Chickasaw, AL 36611 • 6,649
Chickasaw □, IA • 13,295
Chickasaw □, MS • 18,085
Chickasha, OK 73018 • 14,988
Chico, CA 95926–28 • 40,079
Chicopee, MA 01013–22 • 56,632
Chicora, PA 16025 • 1,058
Chiefland, FL 32626 • 1,917
Childersburg, AL 35044 • 4,579
Childress, TX 79201 • 5,055
Childress □, TX • 5,953
Chilhowie, VA 24319 • 1,971
Chili Center, NY 14624 • 4,360
Chillicothe, IL 61523 • 5,959
Chillicothe, MO 64601 • 8,804
Chillicothe, OH 45601 • 21,923
Chillum, MD 20783 • 31,309
Chilton, WI 53014 • 3,240
Chilton □, AL • 32,458
Chimayo, NM 87522 • 2,789
China Grove, NC 28023 • 2,732
Chincoteague, VA 23336 • 3,572
Chinle, AZ 86503 • 5,059
Chino, CA 91708–10 • 59,682
Chinook, MT 59523 • 1,512
Chino Valley, AZ 86323 • 4,837
Chipley, FL 32428 • 3,866
Chippewa □, MI • 34,604
Chippewa □, MN • 13,228
Chippewa □, WI • 52,360
Chippewa Falls, WI 54729 • 12,727
Chisago □, MN • 30,521
Chisago City, MN 55013 • 2,009
Chisholm, ME 04239 • 1,653
Chisholm, MN 55719 • 5,290
Chittenango, NY 13037 • 4,734
Chittenden □, VT • 131,761
Choctaw, OK 73020 • 8,545
Choctaw □, AL • 16,018
Choctaw □, MS • 9,071
Choctaw □, OK • 15,302
Choteau, MT 59422 • 1,741
Chouteau, OK 74337 • 1,771
Chouteau □, MT • 5,452
Chowan □, NC • 13,506
Chowchilla, CA 93610 • 5,930
Chrisman, IL 61924 • 1,136
Christian □, IL • 34,418
Christian □, KY • 68,941
Christian □, MO • 32,644
Christiana, DE 19702 • 500
Christiana, PA 17509 • 1,045
Christiansburg, VA 24073 • 15,004
Christmas, FL 32709 • 1,200
Christopher, IL 62822 • 2,774
Chubbuck, ID 83202 • 7,791
Chugwater, WY 82210 • 192
Chula Vista, CA 91909–15 • 135,163
Church Hill, TN 37642 • 4,834
Churchill, OH 44505 • 7,700
Churchill □, NV • 17,938
Church Point, LA 70525 • 4,677
Churchville, NY 14428 • 1,731
Churubusco, IN 46723 • 1,781
Cibola □, NM • 23,794
Cicero, IL 60650 • 67,436
Cicero, IN 46034 • 3,268
Cimarron, KS 67835 • 1,626
Cimarron □, OK • 3,301
Cimarron Hills, CO 80906 • 11,160
Cincinnati, OH 45201–75 • 364,040
Cinnaminson, NJ 08077 • 14,583
Circle, MT 59215 • 805

Circle Pines, MN 55014 • *4,704*
Circleville, OH 43113 • *11,666*
Cisco, TX 76437 • *3,813*
Citra, FL 32113 • *1,500*
Citronelle, AL 36522 • *3,671*
Citrus, CA 91702 • *9,481*
Citrus □, FL • *93,515*
Citrus Heights, CA 95610–11 • *107,439*
City Of Sunrise, FL 33313 • *64,407*
City View, SC 29611 • *1,490*
Clackamas, OR 97015 • *2,578*
Clackamas □, OR • *278,850*
Claiborne, LA 71291 • *8,300*
Claiborne □, LA • *17,405*
Claiborne □, MS • *11,370*
Claiborne □, TN • *26,137*
Clair-Mel City, FL 33619 • *7,000*
Clairton, PA 15025 • *9,656*
Clallam □, WA • *56,464*
Clanton, AL 35045 • *7,669*
Clara City, MN 56222 • *1,307*
Clare, MI 48617 • *3,021*
Clare □, MI • *24,952*
Claremont, CA 91711 • *32,503*
Claremont, NH 03743 • *13,902*
Claremore, OK 74017–18 • *13,280*
Clarence, MO 63437 • *1,026*
Clarendon, AR 72029 • *2,072*
Clarendon, TX 79226 • *2,067*
Clarendon □, SC • *28,450*
Clarendon Hills, IL 60514 • *6,994*
Claridge, PA 15623 • *1,200*
Clarinda, IA 51632 • *5,104*
Clarion, IA 50525 • *2,703*
Clarion, PA 16214 • *6,457*
Clarion □, PA • *41,699*
Clark, NJ 07066 • *14,629*
Clark, SD 57225 • *1,292*
Clark □, AR • *21,437*
Clark □, ID • *762*
Clark □, IL • *15,921*
Clark □, IN • *87,777*
Clark □, KS • *2,418*
Clark □, KY • *29,496*
Clark □, MO • *7,547*
Clark □, NV • *741,459*
Clark □, OH • *147,548*
Clark □, SD • *4,403*
Clark □, WA • *238,053*
Clark □, WI • *31,647*
Clarkdale, AZ 86324 • *2,144*
Clarke □, AL • *27,240*
Clarke □, GA • *87,594*
Clarke □, IA • *8,287*
Clarke □, MS • *17,313*
Clarke □, VA • *12,101*
Clarkesville, GA 30523 • *1,151*
Clarksburg, WV 26301–02 • *18,059*
Clarksdale, MS 38614 • *19,717*
Clarks Summit, PA 18411 • *5,433*
Clarkston, GA 30021 • *5,385*
Clarkston, MI 48346–48 • *1,005*
Clarkston, WA 99403 • *6,753*
Clarksville, AR 72830 • *5,833*
Clarksville, DE 19970 • *500*
Clarksville, IN 47129 • *19,833*
Clarksville, IA 50619 • *1,382*
Clarksville, TN 37040–43 • *75,494*
Clarksville, TX 75426 • *4,311*
Clarksville, VA 23927 • *1,243*
Clarkton, MO 63837 • *1,113*
Clatskanie, OR 97016 • *1,629*
Clatsop □, OR • *33,301*
Claude, TX 79019 • *1,199*
Clawson, MI 48017 • *13,874*
Claxton, GA 30417 • *2,464*
Clay, KY 42404 • *1,173*
Clay □, AL • *13,252*
Clay □, AR • *18,107*
Clay □, FL • *105,986*
Clay □, GA • *3,364*
Clay □, IL • *14,460*
Clay □, IN • *24,705*
Clay □, IA • *17,585*
Clay □, KS • *9,158*
Clay □, KY • *21,746*
Clay □, MN • *50,422*
Clay □, MS • *21,120*
Clay □, MO • *153,411*
Clay □, NE • *7,123*
Clay □, NC • *7,155*
Clay □, SD • *13,186*
Clay □, TN • *7,238*
Clay □, TX • *10,024*
Clay □, WV • *9,983*
Clay Center, KS 67432 • *4,613*
Clay City, KY 40312 • *1,258*
Claymont, DE 19702 • *9,800*
Claypool, AZ 85532 • *1,942*
Claysburg, PA 16625 • *1,399*
Clayton, AL 36016 • *1,564*
Clayton, DE 19938 • *1,163*
Clayton, GA 30525 • *1,613*
Clayton, MO 63105 • *10,074*
Clayton, NJ 08312 • *6,155*
Clayton, NM 88415 • *2,484*
Clayton, NY 13624 • *2,160*
Clayton, NC 27520 • *4,756*
Clayton □, GA • *182,052*
Clayton □, IA • *19,054*
Clear Creek □, CO • *7,619*
Clearfield, KY 40313 • *1,250*
Clearfield, PA 16830 • *6,633*
Clearfield, UT 84015 • *21,435*
Clearfield □, PA • *78,097*
Clearlake, CA 95422 • *11,804*
Clear Lake, IA 50428 • *8,183*
Clear Lake, SD 57226 • *1,247*
Clearlake, WA 98235 • *1,100*
Clear Lake Shores, TX 77565 • *1,096*
Clearwater, FL 34615–30 • *98,784*
Clearwater, KS 67026 • *1,875*
Clearwater, SC 29822 • *4,731*
Clearwater □, ID • *8,505*
Clearwater □, MN • *8,309*
Cleburne, TX 76031–33 • *22,205*
Cleburne □, AL • *12,730*
Cleburne □, AR • *19,411*
Cle Elum, WA 98922 • *1,778*
Cleland Heights, DE 19805 • *1,120*
Clementon, NJ 08021 • *5,601*
Clemmons, NC 27012 • *6,020*
Clemson, SC 29631–33 • *11,096*
Clendenin, WV 25045 • *1,203*
Cleona, PA 17042 • *2,322*
Clermont, FL 34711–12 • *6,910*
Clermont □, OH • *150,187*
Cleveland, GA 30528 • *1,653*
Cleveland, MS 38732–33 • *15,384*
Cleveland, OH 44101–99 • *505,616*
Cleveland, OK 74020 • *3,156*
Cleveland, TN 37311–12 • *30,354*
Cleveland, TX 77327–28 • *7,124*
Cleveland, WI 53015 • *1,398*
Cleveland □, AR • *7,781*
Cleveland □, NC • *84,714*
Cleveland □, OK • *174,253*
Cleveland Heights, OH 44118 • *54,052*
Cleves, OH 45002 • *2,208*
Clewiston, FL 33440 • *6,085*
Cliffside Park, NJ 07010 • *20,393*
Clifton, AZ 85533 • *2,840*
Clifton, CO 81520 • *12,671*
Clifton, IL 60927 • *1,347*
Clifton, NJ 07011–15 • *71,742*
Clifton, TX 76634 • *3,195*
Clifton Forge, VA 24422 • *4,679*
Clifton Heights, PA 19018 • *7,111*
Clifton Knolls, NY 12065 • *5,636*
Clifton Springs, NY 14432 • *2,175*
Clinch □, GA • *6,160*
Clint, TX 79836 • *1,035*
Clinton, AR 72031 • *2,213*
Clinton, CT 06413 • *3,439*
Clinton, IL 61727 • *7,437*
Clinton, IN 47842 • *5,040*
Clinton, IA 52732–33 • *29,201*
Clinton, KY 42031 • *1,547*
Clinton, LA 70722 • *1,904*
Clinton, ME 04927 • *1,485*
Clinton, MD 20735 • *19,987*
Clinton, MA 01510 • *7,943*
Clinton, MI 49236 • *2,475*
Clinton, MS 39056 • *21,847*
Clinton, MO 64735 • *8,703*
Clinton, NJ 08809 • *2,054*
Clinton, NY 13323 • *2,238*
Clinton, NC 28328 • *8,204*
Clinton, OK 73601 • *9,298*
Clinton, SC 29325 • *7,987*
Clinton, TN 37716 • *8,972*
Clinton, UT 84015 • *7,945*
Clinton, WA 98236 • *2,000*
Clinton, WI 53525 • *1,849*
Clinton □, IL • *33,944*
Clinton □, IN • *30,974*
Clinton □, IA • *51,040*
Clinton □, KY • *9,135*
Clinton □, MI • *57,883*
Clinton □, MO • *16,595*
Clinton □, NY • *85,969*
Clinton □, OH • *35,415*
Clinton □, PA • *37,182*
Clinton Township, MI 48043 • *85,866*
Clintonville, WI 54929 • *4,351*
Clintwood, VA 24228 • *1,542*
Clio, AL 36017 • *1,365*
Clio, MI 48420 • *2,629*
Clive, IA 50322 • *7,462*
Cloquet, MN 55720 • *10,885*
Closter, NJ 07624 • *8,094*
Cloud □, KS • *11,023*
Clover, SC 29710 • *3,422*
Cloverdale, CA 95425 • *4,924*
Cloverdale, IN 46120 • *1,681*
Cloverleaf, TX 77015 • *18,230*
Cloverport, KY 40111 • *1,207*
Clovis, CA 93612–13 • *50,323*
Clovis, NM 88101–03 • *30,954*
Clute, TX 77531 • *8,910*
Clyde, NY 14433 • *2,409*
Clyde, NC 28721 • *1,041*
Clyde, OH 43410 • *5,776*
Clyde, TX 79510 • *3,002*
Clymer, PA 15728 • *1,499*
Coachella, CA 92236 • *16,896*
Coahoma, TX 79511 • *1,133*
Coahoma □, MS • *31,665*
Coal □, OK • *5,780*
Coal City, IL 60416 • *3,907*
Coal Fork, WV 25306 • *2,100*
Coalgate, OK 74538 • *1,895*
Coal Grove, OH 45638 • *2,251*
Coalinga, CA 93210 • *8,212*
Coalville, UT 84017 • *1,065*
Coatesville, PA 19320 • *11,038*
Coats, NC 27521 • *1,493*
Cobb □, GA • *447,745*
Cobden, IL 62920 • *1,090*
Cobleskill, NY 12043 • *5,268*
Cochise □, AZ • *97,624*
Cochituate, MA 01778 • *6,046*
Cochran, GA 31014 • *4,390*
Cochran □, TX • *4,377*
Cochranton, PA 16314 • *1,174*
Cocke □, TN • *29,141*
Cockeysville, MD 21030 • *18,668*
Cockrell Hill, TX 75211 • *3,746*
Cocoa, FL 32922–27 • *17,722*
Cocoa Beach, FL 32931–32 • *12,123*
Coconino □, AZ • *96,591*
Coconut Creek, FL 33060 • *27,485*
Codington □, SD • *22,698*
Cody, WY 82414 • *7,897*
Coeburn, VA 24230 • *2,165*
Coeur d'Alene, ID 83814 • *24,563*
Coffee □, AL • *40,240*
Coffee □, GA • *29,592*
Coffee □, TN • *40,339*
Coffey □, KS • *8,404*
Coffeyville, KS 67337 • *12,917*
Cohasset, MA 02025 • *6,800*
Cohoes, NY 12047 • *16,825*
Cokato, MN 55321 • *2,180*
Coke □, TX • *3,424*
Cokeville, WY 83114 • *493*
Colbert, OK 74733 • *1,043*
Colbert □, AL • *51,666*
Colby, KS 67701 • *5,396*
Colby, WI 54421 • *1,532*
Colchester, CT 06415 • *3,212*
Colchester, IL 62326 • *1,645*
Cold Bay, AK 99571 • *148*
Cold Spring, KY 41076 • *2,880*
Cold Spring, MN 56320 • *2,459*
Cold Spring Harbor, NY 11724 • *4,789*
Coldwater, MI 49036 • *9,607*
Coldwater, MS 38618 • *1,502*
Coldwater, OH 45828 • *4,335*
Cole □, MO • *63,579*
Colebrook, NH 03576 • *2,444*
Cole Camp, MO 65325 • *1,054*
Coleman, MI 48618 • *1,237*
Coleman, TX 76834 • *5,410*
Coleman □, TX • *9,710*
Coleraine, MN 55722 • *1,041*
Coles □, IL • *51,644*
Colfax, CA 95713 • *1,306*
Colfax, IA 50054 • *2,462*
Colfax, LA 71417 • *1,696*
Colfax, WA 99111 • *2,713*
Colfax, WI 54730 • *1,110*
Colfax □, NE • *9,139*
Colfax □, NM • *12,925*
College, AK 99701 • *11,249*
Collegedale, TN 37315 • *5,048*
College Park, GA 30337 • *20,457*
College Park, MD 20740–41 • *21,927*
College Place, WA 99324 • *6,308*
College Station, AR 72053 • *3,800*
College Station, TX 77840–45 • *52,456*
Collegeville, PA 19426 • *4,227*
Colleton □, SC • *34,377*
Colleyville, TX 76034 • *12,724*
Collier □, FL • *152,099*
Collierville, TN 38017 • *14,427*
Collin □, TX • *264,036*
Collingdale, PA 19023 • *9,175*
Collingswood, NJ 08108 • *15,289*
Collingsworth □, TX • *3,573*
Collins, MS 39428 • *2,541*
Collins Park, DE 19720 • *2,100*
Collinsville, AL 35961 • *1,429*
Collinsville, CT 06022 • *2,591*
Collinsville, IL 62234 • *22,446*
Collinsville, OK 74021 • *3,612*
Collinsville, VA 24078 • *7,280*
Collinwood, TN 38450 • *1,014*
Colmar Manor, MD 20722 • *1,249*
Coloma, MI 49038 • *1,679*
Colon, MI 49040 • *1,224*
Colonia, NJ 07067 • *18,238*
Colonial Beach, VA 22443 • *3,132*
Colonial Heights, TN 37663 • *6,716*
Colonial Heights, VA 23834 • *16,064*
Colonial Park, PA 17109 • *13,777*
Colonie, NY 12212 • *8,019*
Colorado □, TX • *18,383*
Colorado City, AZ 86021 • *2,426*
Colorado City, CO 81019 • *1,149*
Colorado City, TX 79512 • *4,749*
Colorado Springs, CO 80901–99 • *281,140*
Colquitt, GA 31737 • *1,991*
Colquitt □, GA • *36,645*
Colstrip, MT 59323 • *3,035*
Colton, CA 92324 • *40,213*
Columbia, CA 95310 • *1,799*
Columbia, IL 62236 • *5,524*
Columbia, KY 42728 • *3,845*
Columbia, MD 21044–46 • *75,883*
Columbia, MS 39429 • *6,815*
Columbia, MO 65201–05 • *69,101*
Columbia, PA 17512 • *10,701*
Columbia, SC 29201–92 • *98,052*
Columbia, TN 38401–02 • *28,583*
Columbia □, AR • *25,691*
Columbia □, FL • *42,613*
Columbia □, GA • *66,031*
Columbia □, NY • *62,982*
Columbia □, OR • *37,557*
Columbia □, PA • *63,202*
Columbia □, WA • *4,024*
Columbia □, WI • *45,088*
Columbia City, IN 46725 • *5,706*
Columbia City, OR 97018 • *1,003*
Columbia Falls, MT 59912 • *2,942*
Columbia Heights, MN 55421 • *18,910*
Columbiana, AL 35051 • *2,968*
Columbiana, OH 44408 • *4,961*
Columbiana □, OH • *108,276*
Columbine, CO 80123 • *23,969*
Columbus, GA 31901–09 • *178,681*
Columbus, IN 47201–03 • *31,802*
Columbus, KS 66725 • *3,268*
Columbus, MS 39701–05 • *23,799*
Columbus, MT 59019 • *1,573*
Columbus, NE 68601 • *19,480*
Columbus, OH 43201–91 • *632,910*
Columbus, TX 78934 • *3,367*
Columbus, WI 53925 • *4,093*
Columbus □, NC • *49,587*
Columbus Grove, OH 45830 • *2,231*
Columbus Junction, IA 52738 • *1,616*
Colusa, CA 95932 • *4,934*
Colusa □, CA • *16,275*
Colver, PA 15927 • *1,024*
Colville, WA 99114 • *4,360*
Colwich, KS 67030 • *1,091*
Comal □, TX • *51,832*
Comanche, OK 73529 • *1,695*
Comanche, TX 76442 • *4,087*
Comanche □, KS • *2,313*
Comanche □, OK • *111,486*
Comanche □, TX • *13,381*
Combee Settlement, FL 33801 • *5,463*
Combined Locks, WI 54113 • *2,190*
Comfort, TX 78013 • *1,477*
Commack, NY 11725 • *36,124*
Commerce, CA 90040 • *12,135*
Commerce, GA 30529 • *4,108*
Commerce, OK 74339 • *2,426*
Commerce, TX 75428 • *6,825*
Commerce City, CO 80022 • *16,466*
Common Fence Point, RI 02871 • *860*
Como, MS 38619 • *1,387*
Compton, CA 90220–24 • *90,454*
Comstock, MI 49041 • *5,600*
Comstock Park, MI 49321 • *6,530*
Concho □, TX • *3,044*
Concord, CA 94518–24 • *111,348*
Concord, MA 01742 • *4,680*
Concord, MO 63128 • *19,859*
Concord, NH 03301–03 • *36,006*
Concord, NC 28025–27 • *27,347*
Concord, TN 37901 • *3,420*
Concordia, KS 66901 • *6,167*
Concordia, MO 64020 • *2,160*
Concordia □, LA • *20,828*
Conecuh □, AL • *14,054*
Conejos □, CO • *7,453*
Conemaugh, PA 15909 • *1,470*
Congers, NY 10920 • *8,003*
Conklin, NY 13748 • *1,800*
Conley, GA 30027 • *5,528*
Conneaut, OH 44030 • *13,241*
Connell, WA 99326 • *2,005*
Connellsville, PA 15425 • *9,229*
Connersville, IN 47331 • *15,550*
Conover, NC 28613 • *5,465*
Conrad, MT 59425 • *2,891*
Conroe, TX 77301–05 • *27,610*
Conshohocken, PA 19428 • *8,064*
Constantia, NY 13044 • *1,140*
Constantine, MI 49042 • *2,032*
Continental, OH 45831 • *1,214*
Contoocook, NH 03229 • *1,334*
Contra Costa □, CA • *803,732*
Converse, IN 46919 • *1,144*
Converse, SC 29329 • *1,173*
Converse, TX 78109 • *8,887*
Converse □, WY • *11,128*
Convoy, OH 45832 • *1,200*
Conway, AR 72032 • *26,481*
Conway, FL 32809 • *13,159*
Conway, NH 03818 • *1,604*
Conway, PA 15027 • *2,424*
Conway, SC 29526–27 • *9,819*
Conway □, AR • *19,151*
Conway Springs, KS 67031 • *1,384*
Conyers, GA 30207–08 • *7,380*
Cook □, GA • *13,456*
Cook □, IL • *5,105,067*
Cook □, MN • *3,868*
Cooke □, TX • *30,777*
Cookeville, TN 38501–02 • *21,744*
Coolidge, AZ 85228 • *6,927*
Coon Rapids, IA 50058 • *1,266*
Coon Rapids, MN 55433 • *52,978*
Cooper, TX 75432 • *2,153*
Cooper □, MO • *14,835*
Cooper City, FL 33328 • *20,791*
Cooper Road, LA 71107 • *11,050*
Coopersburg, PA 18036 • *2,599*
Cooperstown, NY 13326 • *2,180*
Cooperstown, ND 58425 • *1,247*
Coopersville, MI 49404 • *3,421*
Coos □, NH • *34,828*
Coos □, OR • *60,273*
Coosa □, AL • *11,063*
Coos Bay, OR 97420 • *15,076*
Copake, NY 12516 • *1,200*
Copiague, NY 11726 • *20,769*
Copiah □, MS • *27,592*
Coplay, PA 18037 • *3,267*
Copperas Cove, TX 76522 • *24,079*
Coquille, OR 97423 • *4,121*
Coral Gables, FL 33134 • *40,091*
Coral Hills, MD 20743 • *11,032*
Coral Springs, FL 33065 • *79,443*
Coral Terrace, FL 33157 • *23,255*
Coralville, IA 52241 • *10,347*
Coral Way Village, FL 33155 • *9,000*
Coram, NY 11727 • *30,111*
Coraopolis, PA 15108 • *6,747*
Corbin, KY 40701–02 • *7,419*
Corcoran, CA 93212 • *13,364*
Corcoran, MN 55340 • *5,199*
Cordaville, MA 01772 • *1,530*
Cordele, GA 31015 • *10,321*
Cordell, OK 73632 • *2,903*
Cordova, AL 35550 • *2,623*
Cordova, AK 99574 • *2,110*
Cordova, NC 28330 • *1,200*
Corinth, MS 38834 • *11,820*
Corinth, NY 12822 • *2,760*
Cornelia, GA 30531 • *3,219*
Cornelius, NC 28031 • *2,581*
Cornelius, OR 97113 • *6,148*
Cornell, WI 54732 • *1,541*
Corning, AR 72422 • *3,323*
Corning, CA 96021 • *5,870*
Corning, IA 50841 • *1,806*
Corning, NY 14830 • *11,938*
Cornville, AZ 86325 • *1,200*
Cornwall, PA 17016 • *3,231*
Cornwall on Hudson, NY 12520 • *3,093*
Corona, CA 91718–20 • *76,095*
Coronado, CA 92118 • *26,540*
Coronado, CO 80229 • *6,890*
Corpus Christi, TX 78401–82 • *257,453*
Corrigan, TX 75939 • *1,764*
Corriganville, MD 21524 • *1,020*
Corry, PA 16407 • *7,216*
Corsicana, TX 75110 • *22,911*
Corson □, SD • *4,195*
Corte Madera, CA 94925 • *8,272*
Cortez, CO 81321 • *7,284*
Cortez, FL 34215 • *4,509*
Cortland, NY 13045 • *19,801*
Cortland, OH 44410 • *5,666*
Cortland □, NY • *48,963*
Corunna, MI 48817 • *3,091*
Corvallis, OR 97330–33 • *44,757*
Corydon, IN 47112 • *2,661*
Corydon, IA 50060 • *1,675*
Coryell □, TX • *64,213*
Coshocton, OH 43812 • *12,193*
Coshocton □, OH • *35,427*
Cosmopolis, WA 98537 • *1,372*
Costa Mesa, CA 92626–28 • *96,357*
Costilla □, CO • *3,190*
Cottage Grove, MN 55016 • *22,935*
Cottage Grove, OR 97424 • *7,402*
Cottle □, TX • *2,247*
Cottleville, MO 63338 • *2,300*
Cotton □, OK • *6,651*
Cottondale, AL 35453 • *1,960*
Cotton Plant, AR 72036 • *1,150*
Cottonport, LA 71327 • *2,600*
Cotton Valley, LA 71018 • *1,130*
Cottonwood, AL 36320 • *1,385*
Cottonwood, AZ 86326 • *5,918*
Cottonwood, CA 96022 • *1,747*
Cottonwood, ID 83522 • *822*
Cottonwood, UT 84121 • *11,554*
Cottonwood □, MN • *12,694*
Cottonwood Heights, UT 84121 • *28,766*
Cotuit, MA 02635 • *1,750*
Cotulla, TX 78014 • *3,694*
Coudersport, PA 16915 • *2,854*
Coulee Dam, WA 99116 • *1,087*
Council, ID 83612 • *831*
Council Bluffs, IA 51501–03 • *54,315*
Council Grove, KS 66846 • *2,228*
Country Club Hills, IL 60478 • *15,431*
Country Homes, WA 99218 • *5,126*
Countryside, IL 60525 • *5,716*
Coupeville, WA 98239 • *1,377*
Coushatta, LA 71019 • *1,845*
Covedale, OH 45238 • *6,669*
Covelo, CA 95428 • *1,057*
Coventry, CT 06238 • *10,063*
Coventry, DE 19720 • *1,165*
Coventry, RI 02816 • *6,980*
Covina, CA 91722–24 • *43,207*
Covington, GA 30209 • *10,026*
Covington, IN 47932 • *2,747*
Covington, KY 41011–18 • *43,264*
Covington, LA 70433–34 • *7,691*
Covington, OH 45318 • *2,603*
Covington, TN 38019 • *7,487*
Covington, VA 24426 • *6,991*
Covington □, AL • *36,478*
Covington □, MS • *16,527*
Cowan, TN 37318 • *1,738*
Cowarts, AL 36321 • *1,400*
Coweta, OK 74429 • *6,159*
Coweta □, GA • *53,853*
Cowley, WY 82420 • *477*
Cowley □, KS • *36,915*
Cowlitz □, WA • *82,119*
Cowpens, SC 29330 • *2,176*
Coxsackie, NY 12051 • *2,789*
Cozad, NE 69130 • *3,823*
Crab Orchard, WV 25827 • *2,919*
Crabtree, PA 15624 • *1,000*
Crafton, PA 15205 • *7,188*
Craig, AK 99921 • *1,260*
Craig, CO 81625–26 • *8,091*
Craig □, OK • *14,104*
Craig □, VA • *4,372*
Craighead □, AR • *68,956*
Craigsville, WV 26205 • *1,955*
Cramerton, NC 28032 • *2,371*
Cranbury, NJ 08512 • *1,255*
Crandall, TX 75114 • *1,652*
Crandon, WI 54520 • *1,958*
Crane, AZ 85365 • *2,650*
Crane, MO 65633 • *1,218*
Crane, TX 79731 • *3,533*
Crane □, TX • *4,652*
Cranford, NJ 07016 • *22,624*
Cranston, RI 02910 • *76,060*
Craven □, NC • *81,613*
Crawford, NE 69339 • *1,115*
Crawford □, AR • *42,493*
Crawford □, GA • *8,991*
Crawford □, IL • *19,464*
Crawford □, IN • *9,914*
Crawford □, IA • *16,775*
Crawford □, KS • *35,568*
Crawford □, MI • *12,260*
Crawford □, MO • *19,173*
Crawford □, OH • *47,870*
Crawford □, PA • *86,169*
Crawford □, WI • *15,940*
Crawfordsville, IN 47933 • *13,584*
Crawfordville, FL 32327 • *1,110*
Creedmoor, NC 27522 • *1,504*
Creek □, OK • *60,915*
Creighton, NE 68729 • *1,223*
Creighton, PA 15030 • *1,658*
Crenshaw □, AL • *13,635*
Creola, AL 36525 • *1,896*
Cresaptown, MD 21502 • *4,645*
Crescent, OK 73028 • *1,236*
Crescent City, CA 95531 • *4,380*
Crescent City, FL 32112 • *1,859*
Crescent Springs, KY 41016 • *2,179*
Cresco, IA 52136 • *3,669*
Cresskill, NJ 07626 • *7,558*
Cresson, PA 16630 • *1,784*
Cressona, PA 17929 • *1,694*
Cresthaven, FL 33064 • *2,400*
Crest Hill, IL 60435 • *10,643*
Crestline, CA 92325 • *8,594*
Crestline, OH 44827 • *4,934*
Creston, IA 50801 • *7,911*
Creston, OH 44217 • *1,848*
Crestview, FL 32536 • *9,886*
Crestview, HI 96797 • *10,000*
Crestwood, IL 60445 • *10,823*
Crestwood, KY 40014 • *1,435*
Crestwood, MO 63126 • *11,234*
Crestwood Village, NJ 08759 • *8,030*
Creswell, OR 97426 • *2,431*
Crete, IL 60417 • *6,773*
Crete, NE 68333 • *4,841*
Creve Coeur, IL 61611 • *5,938*
Creve Coeur, MO 63141 • *12,304*
Crewe, VA 23930 • *2,276*
Cricket, NC 28659 • *2,015*
Cridersville, OH 45806 • *1,885*
Crisfield, MD 21817 • *2,880*
Crisp □, GA • *20,011*
Crittenden □, AR • *49,939*
Crittenden □, KY • *9,196*
Crocker, MO 65452 • *1,077*
Crockett, CA 94525 • *3,228*
Crockett, TX 75835 • *7,024*
Crockett □, TN • *13,378*
Crockett □, TX • *4,078*
Crofton, MD 21114 • *12,781*
Cromwell, CT 06416 • *1,100*
Crook □, OR • *14,111*
Crook □, WY • *5,294*
Crookston, MN 56716 • *8,119*
Crooksville, OH 43731 • *2,601*
Crosby, MN 56441 • *2,073*
Crosby, ND 58730 • *1,312*
Crosby, TX 77532 • *1,811*
Crosby □, TX • *7,304*
Crosbyton, TX 79322 • *2,026*
Cross □, AR • *19,225*
Cross City, FL 32628 • *2,041*
Crossett, AR 71635 • *6,282*
Crosslake, MN 56442 • *1,132*
Cross Lanes, WV 25313 • *10,878*
Cross Plains, TN 37049 • *1,025*
Cross Plains, TX 76443 • *1,063*
Cross Plains, WI 53528 • *2,098*
Crossville, AL 35962 • *1,350*
Crossville, TN 38555 • *6,930*
Croswell, MI 48422 • *2,174*

Crothersville, IN 47229 • *1,687*
Croton-on-Hudson, NY 10520 • *7,018*
Crow Agency, MT 59022 • *1,446*
Crowell, TX 79227 • *1,230*
Crowley, LA 70526–27 • *13,983*
Crowley, TX 76036 • *6,974*
Crowley □, CO • *3,946*
Crown Point, IN 46307 • *17,728*
Crownpoint, NM 87313 • *2,108*
Crow Wing □, MN • *44,249*
Crozet, VA 22932 • *2,256*
Crystal, MN 55428 • *23,788*
Crystal Bay, NV 89402 • *1,200*
Crystal Beach, FL 34681 • *1,450*
Crystal City, MO 63019 • *4,088*
Crystal City, TX 78839 • *8,263*
Crystal Falls, MI 49920 • *1,922*
Crystal Lake, CT 06029 • *1,200*
Crystal Lake, FL 33803 • *5,300*
Crystal Lake, IL 60014 • *24,512*
Crystal Lawns, IL 60435 • *1,660*
Crystal River, FL 32629 • *4,044*
Crystal Springs, MS 39059 • *5,643*
Cuba, IL 61427 • *1,440*
Cuba, MO 65453 • *2,537*
Cuba, NY 14727 • *1,690*
Cuba City, WI 53807 • *2,024*
Cucamonga, CA 91730 • *101,409*
Cudahy, CA 90201 • *22,817*
Cudahy, WI 53110 • *18,659*
Cuero, TX 77954 • *6,700*
Culberson □, TX • *3,407*
Culbertson, MT 59218 • *796*
Cullen, LA 71021 • *1,642*
Cullman, AL 35055–56 • *13,367*
Cullman □, AL • *67,613*
Culloden, WV 25510 • *2,907*
Cullowhee, NC 28723 • *1,200*
Culpeper, VA 22701 • *8,581*
Culpeper □, VA • *27,791*
Culver, IN 46511 • *1,404*
Culver City, CA 90230–33 • *38,793*
Cumberland, KY 40823 • *3,112*
Cumberland, MD 21501–05 • *23,706*
Cumberland, WI 54829 • *2,163*
Cumberland □, IL • *10,670*
Cumberland □, KY • *6,784*
Cumberland □, ME • *243,135*
Cumberland □, NJ • *138,053*
Cumberland □, NC • *274,566*
Cumberland □, PA • *195,257*
Cumberland □, TN • *34,736*
Cumberland □, VA • *7,825*
Cumberland Center, ME 04021 • *1,890*
Cumberland Foreside, ME 04110 • *1,000*
Cumberland Hill, RI 02864 • *6,379*
Cuming □, NE • *10,117*
Cumming, GA 30130 • *2,828*
Cupertino, CA 95014–16 • *40,263*
Currituck □, NC • *13,736*
Curry □, NM • *42,207*
Curry □, OR • *19,327*
Curtisville, PA 15032 • *1,285*
Curwensville, PA 16833 • *2,924*
Cushing, OK 74023 • *7,218*
Cusseta, GA 31805 • *1,107*
Custer, SD 57730 • *1,741*
Custer □, CO • *1,926*
Custer □, ID • *4,133*
Custer □, MT • *11,697*
Custer □, NE • *12,270*
Custer □, OK • *26,897*
Custer □, SD • *6,179*
Cut Bank, MT 59427 • *3,329*
Cutchogue, NY 11935 • *1,730*
Cuthbert, GA 31740 • *3,730*
Cutler, FL 33157 • *16,201*
Cutler Ridge, FL 33157 • *21,268*
Cutlerville, MI 49508 • *11,228*
Cut Off, LA 70345 • *5,325*
Cuyahoga □, OH • *1,412,140*
Cuyahoga Falls, OH 44221–24 • *48,950*
Cynthiana, KY 41031 • *6,497*
Cypress, CA 90630 • *42,655*
Cypress Lake, FL 33919 • *10,491*
Cypress Quarters, FL 34972 • *1,343*
Cyril, OK 73029 • *1,072*

D

Dacono, CO 80514 • *2,228*
Dacula, GA 30211 • *2,217*
Dade □, FL • *1,937,094*
Dade □, GA • *13,147*
Dade □, MO • *7,449*
Dade City, FL 33525–26 • *5,633*
Dadeville, AL 36853 • *3,276*
Daggett □, UT • *690*
Dagsboro, DE 19939 • *398*
Dahlonega, GA 30533 • *3,086*
Daingerfield, TX 75638 • *2,572*
Dakota □, MN • *275,227*
Dakota □, NE • *16,742*
Dakota City, IA 50529 • *1,024*
Dakota City, NE 68731 • *1,470*
Dale, IN 47523 • *1,553*
Dale □, AL • *49,633*
Dale City, VA 22193 • *47,170*
Daleville, AL 36322 • *5,117*
Daleville, IN 47334 • *1,681*
Dalhart, TX 79022 • *6,246*
Dallam □, TX • *5,461*
Dallas, GA 30132 • *2,810*
Dallas, NC 28034 • *3,012*
Dallas, OR 97338 • *9,422*
Dallas, PA 18612 • *2,567*
Dallas, TX 75201–99 • *1,006,877*
Dallas □, AL • *48,130*
Dallas □, AR • *9,614*
Dallas □, IA • *29,755*
Dallas □, MO • *12,646*
Dallas □, TX • *1,852,810*
Dallas Center, IA 50063 • *1,454*
Dallas City, IL 62330 • *1,037*
Dallastown, PA 17313 • *3,974*
Dalton, GA 30720–22 • *21,761*
Dalton, MA 01226–27 • *6,707*
Dalton, OH 44618 • *1,377*
Dalton, PA 18414 • *1,369*
Dalton Gardens, ID 83814 • *1,951*
Daly City, CA 94014–17 • *92,311*

Damascus, MD 20872 • *9,817*
Dana Point, CA 92629 • *31,896*
Danbury, CT 06810–13 • *65,585*
Danbury, TX 77534 • *1,447*
Dandridge, TN 37725 • *1,540*
Dane □, WI • *367,085*
Dania, FL 33004 • *13,024*
Daniels □, MT • *2,266*
Danielson, CT 06239 • *4,441*
Dannemora, NY 12929 • *4,005*
Dansville, NY 14437 • *5,002*
Dante, VA 24237 • *1,083*
Danvers, MA 01923 • *24,174*
Danville, AR 72833 • *1,585*
Danville, CA 94526 • *31,306*
Danville, IL 61832–34 • *33,828*
Danville, IN 46122 • *4,345*
Danville, KY 40422–23 • *12,420*
Danville, OH 43014 • *1,001*
Danville, PA 17821 • *5,165*
Danville, VA 24540–43 • *53,056*
Daphne, AL 36526 • *11,290*
Darby, PA 19023 • *11,140*
Darby Township, PA 19036 • *10,955*
Dardanelle, AR 72834 • *3,722*
Dare □, NC • *22,746*
Darien, CT 06820 • *18,130*
Darien, GA 31305 • *1,783*
Darien, IL 60559 • *18,341*
Darien, WI 53114 • *1,158*
Darke □, OH • *53,619*
Darley Woods, DE 19810 • *1,220*
Darlington, SC 29532 • *7,311*
Darlington, WI 53530 • *2,235*
Darlington □, SC • *61,851*
Darrington, WA 98241 • *1,042*
Dartmouth Woods, DE 19810 • *1,970*
Dassel, MN 55325 • *1,082*
Dauphin □, PA • *237,813*
Davenport, FL 33837 • *1,529*
Davenport, IA 52801–09 • *95,333*
Davenport, WA 99122 • *1,502*
David City, NE 68632 • *2,522*
Davidson, NC 28036 • *4,046*
Davidson □, NC • *126,677*
Davidson □, TN • *510,784*
Davidsville, PA 15928 • *1,167*
Davie, FL 33328 • *47,217*
Davie □, NC • *27,859*
Daviess □, IN • *27,533*
Daviess □, KY • *87,189*
Daviess □, MO • *7,865*
Davis, CA 95616–17 • *46,209*
Davis, OK 73030 • *2,543*
Davis □, IA • *8,312*
Davis □, UT • *187,941*
Davison, MI 48423 • *5,693*
Davison □, SD • *17,503*
Davisville, RI 02852 • *500*
Dawes □, NE • *9,021*
Dawson, GA 31742 • *5,295*
Dawson, MN 56232 • *1,626*
Dawson □, GA • *9,429*
Dawson □, MT • *9,505*
Dawson □, NE • *19,940*
Dawson □, TX • *14,349*
Dawson Springs, KY 42408 • *3,129*
Day □, SD • *6,978*
Dayton, KY 41074 • *6,576*
Dayton, MN 55327 • *4,443*
Dayton, NV 89403 • *2,217*
Dayton, NJ 08810 • *1,200*
Dayton, OH 45401–90 • *182,044*
Dayton, OR 97114 • *1,526*
Dayton, TN 37321 • *5,671*
Dayton, TX 77535 • *5,151*
Dayton, WA 99328 • *2,468*
Dayton, WY 82836 • *565*
Daytona Beach, FL 32114–25 • *61,921*
Dayville, CT 06241 • *1,500*
Deadwood, SD 57732 • *1,830*
Deaf Smith □, TX • *19,153*
Deal, NJ 07723 • *1,179*
Deale, MD 20751 • *4,151*
Dearborn, MI 48120–26 • *89,286*
Dearborn □, IN • *38,835*
Dearborn Heights, MI 48127 • *60,838*
De Baca □, NM • *2,252*
De Bary, FL 32713 • *7,176*
Decatur, AL 35601–03 • *48,761*
Decatur, GA 30030–37 • *17,336*
Decatur, IL 62521–26 • *83,885*
Decatur, IN 46733 • *8,644*
Decatur, MI 49045 • *1,760*
Decatur, MS 39327 • *1,248*
Decatur, TN 37322 • *1,361*
Decatur, TX 76234 • *4,252*
Decatur □, GA • *25,511*
Decatur □, IN • *23,645*
Decatur □, IA • *8,338*
Decatur □, KS • *4,021*
Decatur □, TN • *10,472*
Decherd, TN 37324 • *2,196*
Deckerville, MI 48427 • *1,015*
Decorah, IA 52101 • *8,063*
Dedham, MA 02026 • *23,782*
Deep River, CT 06417 • *2,520*
Deerfield, IL 60015 • *17,327*
Deerfield, WI 53531 • *1,617*
Deerfield Beach, FL 33441–43 • *46,325*
Deer Lodge, MT 59722 • *3,378*
Deer Lodge □, MT • *10,278*
Deer Park, NY 11729 • *28,840*
Deer Park, OH 45236 • *6,181*
Deer Park, TX 77536 • *27,652*
Deer Park, WA 99006 • *2,278*
Defiance, OH 43512 • *16,768*
Defiance □, OH • *39,350*
De Forest, WI 53532 • *4,882*
De Funiak Springs, FL 32433 • *5,120*
De Graff, OH 43318 • *1,331*
De Kalb, IL 60115 • *34,925*
De Kalb, MS 39328 • *1,073*
De Kalb, TX 75559 • *1,976*
De Kalb □, AL • *54,651*
De Kalb □, GA • *545,837*
De Kalb □, IL • *77,932*
De Kalb □, IN • *35,324*
De Kalb □, MO • *9,967*
De Kalb □, TN • *14,360*
Delafield, WI 53018 • *5,347*
Del Aire, CA 90250 • *8,040*
Delanco, NJ 08075 • *3,316*

De Land, FL 32720–24 • *16,491*
Delano, CA 93215–16 • *22,762*
Delano, MN 55328 • *2,709*
Delavan, IL 61734 • *1,642*
Delavan, WI 53115 • *6,073*
Delavan Lake, WI 53115 • *2,177*
Delaware, OH 43015 • *20,030*
Delaware □, IN • *119,659*
Delaware □, IA • *18,035*
Delaware □, NY • *47,225*
Delaware □, OH • *66,929*
Delaware □, OK • *28,070*
Delaware □, PA • *547,651*
Delaware City, DE 19706 • *1,682*
Delcambre, LA 70528 • *1,978*
Del City, OK 73115 • *23,928*
De Leon, TX 76444 • *2,190*
De Leon Springs, FL 32130 • *1,481*
Delevan, NY 14042 • *1,214*
Delhi, LA 71232 • *3,169*
Delhi, NY 13753 • *3,064*
Delhi Hills, OH 45238 • *27,647*
Dell Rapids, SD 57022 • *2,484*
Dellwood, MO 63136 • *5,245*
Del Mar, CA 92014 • *4,860*
Delmar, DE 19940 • *962*
Delmar, MD 21875 • *1,430*
Delmar, NY 12054 • *8,360*
Del Norte, CO 81132 • *1,674*
Del Norte □, CA • *23,460*
Del Park Manor, DE 19808 • *1,550*
Delphi, IN 46923 • *2,531*
Delphos, OH 45833 • *7,093*
Delran, NJ 08075 • *14,811*
Delray Beach, FL 33444–47 • *47,181*
Del Rio, FL 33617 • *8,248*
Del Rio, TX 78840–42 • *30,705*
Delta, CO 81416 • *3,789*
Delta, OH 43515 • *2,849*
Delta, UT 84624 • *2,998*
Delta □, CO • *20,980*
Delta □, MI • *37,780*
Delta □, TX • *4,857*
Delta Junction, AK 99737 • *652*
Deltaville, VA 23043 • *1,082*
Deltona, FL 32725 • *50,828*
Demarest, NJ 07627 • *4,800*
Deming, NM 88030–31 • *10,970*
Demopolis, AL 36732 • *7,512*
Demorest, GA 30535 • *1,088*
Demotte, IN 46310 • *2,482*
Denham Springs, LA 70726–27 • *8,381*
Denison, IA 51442 • *6,604*
Denison, TX 75020–21 • *21,505*
Denmark, SC 29042 • *3,762*
Denmark, WI 54208 • *1,612*
Dennis, MA 02638 • *2,500*
Dennison, OH 44621 • *3,282*
Dennis Port, MA 02639 • *2,775*
Denny Terrace, SC 29203 • *1,885*
Dent □, MO • *13,702*
Denton, MD 21629 • *2,977*
Denton, NC 27239 • *1,292*
Denton, TX 76201–06 • *66,270*
Denton □, TX • *273,525*
Dentsville, SC 29204 • *11,839*
Denver, CO 80201–95 • *467,610*
Denver, IA 50622 • *1,600*
Denver, PA 17517 • *2,861*
Denver □, CO • *467,610*
Denver City, TX 79323 • *5,145*
Denville, NJ 07834 • *14,380*
De Pere, WI 54115 • *16,569*
Depew, NY 14043 • *17,673*
Deposit, NY 13754 • *1,936*
Depue, IL 61322 • *1,729*
De Queen, AR 71832 • *4,633*
De Quincy, LA 70633 • *3,474*
Derby, CT 06418 • *12,199*
Derby, KS 67037 • *14,699*
Derby, NY 14047 • *1,200*
Derby Line, VT 05830 • *855*
De Ridder, LA 70634 • *9,868*
Dermott, AR 71638 • *4,715*
Derry, NH 03038 • *20,446*
Derry, PA 15627 • *2,950*
Derwood, MD 20855 • *1,500*
Des Allemands, LA 70030 • *2,504*
Des Arc, AR 72040 • *2,001*
Deschutes □, OR • *74,958*
Desert Hot Springs, CA 92240 • *11,668*
Desha □, AR • *16,798*
Deshler, OH 43516 • *1,876*
Desloge, MO 63601 • *4,150*
De Smet, SD 57231 • *1,172*
Des Moines, IA 50301–95 • *193,187*
Des Moines, WA 98188 • *17,283*
Des Moines □, IA • *42,614*
De Soto, IL 62924 • *1,500*
De Soto, IA 50069 • *1,033*
De Soto, KS 66018 • *2,291*
De Soto, MO 63020 • *5,993*
De Soto, TX 75115 • *30,544*
De Soto □, FL • *23,865*
De Soto □, LA • *25,346*
De Soto □, MS • *67,910*
Despard, WV 26301 • *1,018*
Des Peres, MO 63131 • *8,395*
Des Plaines, IL 60016–19 • *53,223*
Destin, FL 32540–41 • *8,080*
Destrehan, LA 70047 • *8,031*
Detroit, MI 48201–44 • *1,027,974*
Detroit Lakes, MN 56501–02 • *6,635*
Deuel □, NE • *2,237*
Deuel □, SD • *4,522*
Devils Lake, ND 58301 • *7,782*
Devine, TX 78016 • *3,928*
Devola, OH 45750 • *2,736*
Devon, PA 19333 • *6,620*
Devonshire, DE 19810 • *2,120*
Dewey, OK 74029 • *3,326*
Dewey □, OK • *5,551*
Dewey □, SD • *5,523*
Dewey Beach, DE 19971 • *204*
Deweyville, TX 77614 • *1,218*
De Witt, AR 72042 • *3,553*
De Witt, IA 52742 • *4,514*
De Witt, MI 48820 • *3,964*
De Witt, NY 13214 • *8,244*
De Witt □, IL • *16,516*
De Witt □, TX • *18,840*
Dexter, ME 04930 • *2,650*
Dexter, MI 48130 • *1,497*

Dexter, MO 63841 • *7,559*
Dexter, NY 13634 • *1,030*
Diamond Bar, CA 91765 • *53,672*
Diamond Hill, RI 02864 • *810*
Diamond Lake, IL 60060 • *1,500*
Diamond Springs, CA 95619 • *2,872*
Diamondville, WY 83116 • *864*
Diaz, AR 72043 • *1,363*
D'Iberville, MS 39532 • *6,566*
Diboll, TX 75941 • *4,341*
Dickens □, TX • *2,571*
Dickenson □, VA • *17,620*
Dickey □, ND • *6,107*
Dickinson, ND 58601–02 • *16,097*
Dickinson, TX 77539 • *9,497*
Dickinson □, IA • *14,909*
Dickinson □, KS • *18,958*
Dickinson □, MI • *26,831*
Dickson, TN 37055 • *8,791*
Dickson □, TN • *35,061*
Dickson City, PA 18519 • *6,276*
Dierks, AR 71833 • *1,263*
Dighton, KS 67839 • *1,361*
Dighton, MA 02715 • *1,100*
Dillard, OR 97432 • *1,000*
Dilley, TX 78017 • *2,632*
Dillingham, AK 99576 • *2,017*
Dillon, MT 59725 • *3,991*
Dillon, SC 29536 • *6,829*
Dillon □, SC • *29,114*
Dillsboro, IN 47018 • *1,200*
Dillsburg, PA 17019 • *1,925*
Dilworth, MN 56529 • *2,562*
Dimmit □, TX • *10,433*
Dimmitt, TX 79027 • *4,408*
Dimondale, MI 48821 • *1,247*
Dingmans Ferry, PA 18328 • *1,200*
Dinuba, CA 93618 • *12,743*
Dinwiddie □, VA • *20,960*
Dishman, WA 99213 • *9,671*
District Heights-Forestville, MD 20747 • *6,704*
District of Columbia 0T15, DC •
Divernon, IL 62530 • *1,178*
Divide □, ND • *2,899*
Dixfield, ME 04224 • *1,300*
Dix Hills, NY 11746 • *25,849*
Dixie □, FL • *10,585*
Dixon, CA 95620 • *10,401*
Dixon, IL 61021 • *15,144*
Dixon, MO 65459 • *1,585*
Dixon □, NE • *6,143*
Dixonville, PA 15734 • *1,000*
Dobbs Ferry, NY 10522 • *9,940*
Dobson, NC 27017 • *1,195*
Docena, AL 35060 • *1,000*
Dock Junction, GA 31520 • *7,094*
Doddridge □, WV • *6,994*
Dodge □, GA • *17,607*
Dodge □, MN • *15,731*
Dodge □, NE • *34,500*
Dodge □, WI • *76,559*
Dodge Center, MN 55927 • *1,954*
Dodge City, KS 67801 • *21,129*
Dodge Park, MD 20785 • *4,842*
Dodgeville, WI 53533 • *3,882*
Dolgeville, NY 13329 • *2,452*
Dolomite, AL 35061 • *2,590*
Dolores □, CO • *1,504*
Dolton, IL 60419 • *23,930*
Dona Ana, NM 88032 • *950*
Dona Ana □, NM • *135,510*
Donaldsonville, LA 70346 • *7,949*
Donalsonville, GA 31745 • *2,761*
Doneraile, SC 29532 • *1,276*
Doniphan, MO 63935 • *1,713*
Doniphan □, KS • *8,134*
Donley □, TX • *3,696*
Donna, TX 78537 • *12,652*
Donora, PA 15033 • *5,928*
Dooly □, GA • *9,901*
Door □, WI • *25,690*
Dora, AL 35062 • *2,214*
Doraville, GA 30340 • *7,626*
Dorchester □, MD • *30,236*
Dorchester □, SC • *83,060*
Dormont, PA 15216 • *9,772*
Dorothy Pond, MA 01527 • *1,670*
Dorr, MI 49323 • *1,450*
Dorset, VT 05251 • *550*
Dorsey, MD 21227 • *1,186*
Dothan, AL 36301–04 • *53,589*
Double Springs, AL 35553 • *1,138*
Dougherty □, GA • *96,311*
Douglas, AZ 85607–08 • *12,822*
Douglas, GA 31533 • *10,464*
Douglas, MI 49406 • *1,040*
Douglas, WY 82633 • *5,076*
Douglas □, CO • *60,391*
Douglas □, GA • *71,120*
Douglas □, IL • *19,464*
Douglas □, KS • *81,798*
Douglas □, MN • *28,674*
Douglas □, MO • *11,876*
Douglas □, NE • *416,444*
Douglas □, NV • *27,637*
Douglas □, OR • *94,649*
Douglas □, SD • *3,746*
Douglas □, WA • *26,205*
Douglas □, WI • *41,758*
Douglass, KS 67039 • *1,722*
Douglasville, GA 30133–35 • *11,635*
Dousman, WI 53118 • *1,277*
Dover, AR 72837 • *1,055*
Dover, DE 19901–03 • *27,630*
Dover, FL 33527 • *2,606*
Dover, MA 02030 • *2,163*
Dover, NH 03820 • *25,042*
Dover, NJ 07801 • *15,115*
Dover, OH 44622 • *11,329*
Dover, PA 17315 • *1,884*
Dover, TN 37058 • *1,341*
Dover-Foxcroft, ME 04426 • *3,077*
Dover Plains, NY 12522 • *1,847*
Dowagiac, MI 49047 • *6,409*
Downers Grove, IL 60515–17 • *46,858*
Downey, CA 90239–42 • *91,444*
Downingtown, PA 19335 • *7,749*
Downs, KS 67437 • *1,119*
Downsville, NY 13755 • *1,100*
Doylestown, OH 44230 • *2,668*
Doylestown, PA 18901 • *8,575*
Dracut, MA 01826 • *25,594*

Drain, OR 97435 • *1,011*
Draper, UT 84020 • *7,257*
Drayton, ND 58225 • *961*
Drayton, SC 29333 • *1,443*
Drayton Plains, MI 48330 • *18,000*
Dreamland Villa, AZ 85205 • *3,400*
Dresden, OH 43821 • *1,581*
Dresden, TN 38225 • *2,488*
Dresslerville, NV 89410 • *180*
Drew, MS 38737 • *2,349*
Drew □, AR • *17,369*
Drexel, NC 28619 • *1,746*
Drexel, OH 45427 • *5,143*
Drexel Hill, PA 19026 • *29,744*
Dripping Springs, TX 78620 • *1,033*
Druid Hills, GA 30333 • *12,174*
Drumright, OK 74030 • *2,799*
Dryden, NY 13053 • *1,908*
Dry Ridge, KY 41035 • *1,601*
Duarte, CA 91010 • *20,688*
Dublin, CA 94568 • *23,229*
Dublin, GA 31021 • *16,312*
Dublin, OH 43017 • *16,366*
Dublin, PA 18917 • *1,985*
Dublin, TX 76446 • *3,190*
Dublin, VA 24084 • *2,012*
Du Bois, PA 15801 • *8,286*
Dubois, WY 82513 • *895*
Dubois □, IN • *36,616*
Duboistown, PA 17701 • *1,201*
Dubuque, IA 52001–04 • *57,546*
Dubuque □, IA • *86,403*
Duchesne, UT 84021 • *1,308*
Duchesne □, UT • *12,645*
Dudley, MA 01570–71 • *3,700*
Due West, SC 29639 • *1,220*
Dukes □, MA • *11,639*
Dulce, NM 87528 • *2,438*
Duluth, GA 30136 • *9,029*
Duluth, MN 55801–16 • *85,493*
Dumas, AR 71639 • *5,520*
Dumas, TX 79029 • *12,871*
Dumfries, VA 22026 • *4,282*
Dumont, NJ 07628 • *17,187*
Dunaire, GA 30032 • *7,170*
Dunbar, PA 15431 • *1,213*
Dunbar, WV 25064 • *8,697*
Duncan, OK 73533–34 • *21,732*
Duncan, SC 29334 • *2,152*
Duncan Falls, OH 43734 • *1,200*
Duncannon, PA 17020 • *1,450*
Duncansville, PA 16635 • *1,309*
Duncanville, TX 75116 • *35,748*
Dundalk, MD 21222 • *65,800*
Dundee, FL 33838 • *2,335*
Dundee, IL 60118 • *3,728*
Dundee, MI 48131 • *2,664*
Dundee, NY 14837 • *1,588*
Dundee, OR 97115 • *1,663*
Dundy □, NE • *2,582*
Dunedin, FL 34697–98 • *34,012*
Dunellen, NJ 08812 • *6,528*
Dunkirk, IN 47336 • *2,739*
Dunkirk, NY 14048 • *13,989*
Dunklin □, MO • *33,112*
Dunlap, IN 46514 • *5,705*
Dunlap, IA 51529 • *1,251*
Dunlap, TN 37327 • *3,731*
Dunleith, DE 19801 • *2,600*
Dunmore, PA 18512 • *15,403*
Dunn, NC 28334–35 • *8,336*
Dunn □, ND • *4,005*
Dunn □, WI • *35,909*
Dunnellon, FL 32630 • *1,624*
Dunn Loring Woods, VA 22180 • *2,800*
Dunseith, ND 58329 • *723*
Dunsmuir, CA 96025 • *2,129*
Dunwoody, GA 30338 • *26,302*
Du Page □, IL • *781,666*
Duplin □, NC • *39,995*
Dupont, CO 80024 • *5,200*
Dupont, PA 18641 • *2,984*
Dupont Manor, DE 19901 • *1,059*
Duquesne, PA 15110 • *8,525*
Du Quoin, IL 62832 • *6,697*
Durand, IL 61024 • *1,100*
Durand, MI 48429 • *4,283*
Durand, WI 54736 • *2,003*
Durango, CO 81301–02 • *12,430*
Durant, IA 52747 • *1,549*
Durant, MS 39063 • *2,838*
Durant, OK 74701–02 • *12,823*
Durham, CA 95938 • *1,500*
Durham, CT 06422 • *2,650*
Durham, NH 03824 • *9,236*
Durham, NC 27701–22 • *136,611*
Durham □, NC • *181,835*
Duryea, PA 18642 • *4,869*
Duson, LA 70529 • *1,465*
Dutchess □, NY • *259,462*
Duval □, FL • *672,971*
Duval □, TX • *12,918*
Duxbury, MA 02331–32 • *1,637*
Dwight, IL 60420 • *4,230*
Dyer, IN 46311 • *10,923*
Dyer, TN 38330 • *2,204*
Dyer □, TN • *34,854*
Dyersburg, TN 38024–25 • *16,317*
Dyersville, IA 52040 • *3,703*
Dysart, IA 52224 • *1,230*

E

Eagan, MN 55121 • *47,409*
Eagar, AZ 85925 • *4,025*
Eagle, CO 81631 • *1,580*
Eagle, ID 83616 • *3,327*
Eagle, NE 68347 • *1,047*
Eagle, WI 53119 • *1,182*
Eagle □, CO • *21,928*
Eagle Grove, IA 50533 • *3,671*
Eagle Lake, MN 56024 • *1,703*
Eagle Lake, TX 77434 • *3,551*
Eagle Lake, WI 53139 • *1,000*
Eagle Pass, TX 78852–53 • *20,651*
Eagle Point, OR 97524 • *3,008*
Eagle River, WI 54521 • *1,374*
Eagleton Village, TN 37801 • *5,331*
Earle, AR 72331 • *3,393*
Earlham, IA 50072 • *1,157*
Earlimart, CA 93219 • *5,881*

Earlington, KY 42410 • *1,833*
Earlville, IL 60518 • *1,435*
Early □, GA • *11,854*
Earth, TX 79031 • *1,228*
Easley, SC 29640–42 • *15,195*
East Alton, IL 62024 • *7,063*
East Arlington, VT 05252 • *600*
East Aurora, NY 14052 • *6,647*
East Bangor, PA 18013 • *1,006*
East Barre, VT 05649 • *700*
East Baton Rouge □, LA • *380,105*
East Berlin, PA 17316 • *1,175*
East Bernard, TX 77435 • *1,544*
East Bethel, MN 55005 • *8,050*
East Billerica, MA 01821 • *3,830*
East Brady, PA 16028 • *1,047*
East Brewton, AL 36426 • *2,579*
East Bridgewater, MA 02333 • *3,270*
East Brookfield, MA 01515 • *1,396*
East Brooklyn, CT 06239 • *1,481*
East Brunswick, NJ 08816 • *43,548*
East Carbon, UT 84520 • *1,270*
East Carroll □, LA • *9,709*
Eastchester, NY 10709 • *18,537*
East Chicago, IN 46312 • *33,892*
East Cleveland, OH 44112 • *33,096*
East Compton, CA 90221 • *7,967*
East Dennis, MA 02641 • *1,500*
East Detroit, MI 48021 • *35,283*
East Douglas, MA 01516 • *1,945*
East Dubuque, IL 61025 • *1,914*
East Falmouth, MA 02536 • *5,577*
East Farmingdale, NY 11735 • *4,510*
East Feliciana □, LA • *19,211*
East Flat Rock, NC 28726 • *3,218*
East Gaffney, SC 29340 • *3,278*
Eastgate, WA 98007 • *4,434*
East Glenville, NY 12302 • *6,518*
East Granby, CT 06026 • *1,200*
East Grand Forks, MN 56721 • *8,658*
East Grand Rapids, MI 49506 • *10,807*
East Greenville, PA 18041 • *3,117*
East Greenwich, RI 02818 • *11,865*
East Half Hollow Hills, NY 11746 • *7,010*
Eastham, MA 02642 • *1,150*
East Hampton, CT 06424 • *2,167*
Easthampton, MA 01027 • *15,580*
East Hampton, NY 11937 • *1,402*
East Hanover, NJ • *9,926*
East Hartford, CT 06128 • *50,452*
East Haven, CT 06512 • *26,144*
East Helena, MT 59635 • *1,538*
East Hemet, CA 92343 • *17,611*
East Hills, NY 11576 • *6,746*
East Islip, NY 11730 • *14,325*
East Jordan, MI 49727 • *2,240*
Eastlake, OH 44094 • *21,161*
East La Mirada, CA 90638 • *9,367*
Eastland, TX 76448 • *3,690*
Eastland □, TX • *18,488*
East Lansing, MI 48823–26 • *50,677*
East Las Vegas, NV 89112 • *11,087*
East Liverpool, OH 43920 • *13,654*
East Longmeadow, MA 01028 • *12,905*
East Los Angeles, CA 90022 • *126,379*
East Lyme, CT 06333 • *1,200*
Eastman, GA 31023 • *5,153*
East Marietta, GA 30062 • *11,900*
East Marion, NY 11939 • *1,500*
East Matunuck, RI 02879 • *500*
East Meadow, NY 11554 • *36,609*
East Middlebury, VT 05740 • *500*
East Midvale, UT 84047 • *3,800*
East Millinocket, ME 04430 • *2,075*
East Moline, IL 61244 • *20,147*
East Montpelier, VT 05651 • *600*
East Naples, FL 33962 • *22,951*
East Newark, NJ 07029 • *2,157*
East Newnan, GA 30263 • *1,173*
East Norriton, PA 19401 • *13,324*
East Northport, NY 11731 • *20,411*
Easton, MD 21601 • *9,372*
Easton, PA 18042–44 • *26,276*
East Orange, NJ 07017–19 • *73,552*
East Orleans, MA 02643 • *1,850*
Eastover, SC 29044 • *1,044*
East Palatka, FL 32131 • *1,989*
East Palestine, OH 44413 • *5,168*
East Palo Alto, CA 94303 • *23,451*
East Patchogue, NY 11772 • *20,195*
East Pea Ridge, WV 25705 • *4,980*
East Peoria, IL 61611 • *21,378*
East Pepperell, MA 01463 • *2,296*
East Petersburg, PA 17520 • *4,197*
East Pittsburgh, PA 15112 • *2,160*
Eastpoint, FL 32328 • *1,577*
East Point, GA 30344 • *34,402*
Eastport, ME 04631 • *1,965*
Eastport, NY 11941 • *1,500*
East Porterville, CA 93257 • *5,790*
East Port Orchard, WA 98366 • *5,409*
East Prairie, MO 63845 • *3,416*
East Providence, RI 02914 • *50,380*
East Quogue, NY 11942 • *4,372*
East Richmond, CA 94805 • *5,100*
East Ridge, TN 37412 • *21,101*
East River, CT 06443 • *3,440*
East Rochester, NY 14445 • *6,932*
East Rockaway, NY 11518 • *10,152*
East Rockingham, NC 28379 • *4,158*
East Rutherford, NJ 07073 • *7,902*
East Saint Louis, IL 62201–08 • *40,944*
Eastsound, WA 98245 • *1,100*
East Spencer, NC 28039 • *2,055*
East Stroudsburg, PA 18301 • *8,781*
East Tawas, MI 48730 • *2,887*
East Templeton, MA 01438 • *1,300*
East Troy, WI 53120 • *2,664*
East Tustin, CA 92705 • *10,000*
East Vestal, NY 13902 • *6,310*
East View, WV 26301 • *1,222*
East Walpole, MA 02032 • *3,760*
East Wareham, MA 02538 • *1,500*
East Washington, PA 15301 • *2,126*
East Wenatchee, WA 98802 • *2,701*
East Windsor, NJ 08520 • *15,000*
Eastwood, MI 49001 • *6,340*
Eastwood Hills, UT 84106 • *1,200*
Eaton, CO 80615 • *1,959*
Eaton, IN 47338 • *1,614*
Eaton, OH 45320 • *7,396*
Eaton □, MI • *92,879*
Eaton Rapids, MI 48827 • *4,695*

Eatonton, GA 31024 • *4,737*
Eatontown, NJ 07724 • *13,800*
Eatonville, WA 98328 • *1,374*
Eau Claire, WI 54701–03 • *56,856*
Eau Claire □, WI • *85,183*
Ebensburg, PA 15931 • *3,872*
Eccles, WV 25836 • *1,162*
Echo Bay, NV 89040 • *120*
Echols □, GA • *2,334*
Eckhart Mines, MD 21528 • *1,333*
Eclectic, AL 36024 • *1,087*
Economy, PA 15005 • *9,519*
Ecorse, MI 48229 • *12,180*
Ector □, TX • *118,934*
Edcouch, TX 78538 • *2,878*
Eddy □, NM • *48,605*
Eddy □, ND • *2,951*
Eddystone, PA 19013 • *2,446*
Eddyville, IA 52553 • *1,010*
Eddyville, KY 42038 • *1,889*
Eden, NY 14057 • *3,088*
Eden, NC 27288 • *15,238*
Eden, TX 76837 • *1,567*
Eden Prairie, MN 55344 • *39,311*
Edenton, NC 27932 • *5,268*
Edgar, WI 54426 • *1,318*
Edgar □, IL • *19,595*
Edgartown, MA 02539 • *3,062*
Edgecombe □, NC • *56,558*
Edgefield, SC 29824 • *2,563*
Edgefield □, SC • *18,375*
Edgeley, ND 58433 • *680*
Edgemere, MD 21221 • *9,226*
Edgemont, SD 57735 • *906*
Edgemoor, DE 19802 • *5,853*
Edgerton, KS 66021 • *1,244*
Edgerton, MN 56128 • *1,106*
Edgerton, OH 43517 • *1,896*
Edgerton, WI 53534 • *4,254*
Edgerton, WY 82635 • *247*
Edgewater, AL 35224 • *1,120*
Edgewater, CO 80214 • *4,613*
Edgewater, FL 32132 • *15,337*
Edgewater, MD 21037 • *1,600*
Edgewater, NJ 07020 • *5,001*
Edgewater Park, NJ 08010 • *8,388*
Edgewood, IN 46011 • *2,057*
Edgewood, KY 41017 • *8,143*
Edgewood, MD • *3,470*
Edgewood, MD 21040 • *23,903*
Edgewood, OH 44004 • *5,189*
Edgewood, PA 15218 • *3,581*
Edgewood, WA 98372 • *2,650*
Edgeworth, PA 15143 • *1,670*
Edina, MN 55410 • *46,070*
Edina, MO 63537 • *1,283*
Edinboro, PA 16412 • *7,736*
Edinburg, TX 78539–40 • *29,885*
Edinburgh, IN 46124 • *4,536*
Edison, GA 31746 • *1,182*
Edison, NJ 08817–20 • *88,680*
Edmond, OK 73034 • *52,315*
Edmonds, WA 98020 • *30,744*
Edmondson Heights, MD 21207 • *4,750*
Edmonson □, KY • *10,357*
Edmonton, KY 42129 • *1,477*
Edmore, MI 48829 • *1,126*
Edmunds □, SD • *4,356*
Edna, TX 77957 • *5,343*
Edwards, MS 39066 • *1,279*
Edwards □, IL • *7,440*
Edwards □, KS • *3,787*
Edwards □, TX • *2,266*
Edwardsburg, MI 49112 • *1,142*
Edwardsville, IL 62025 • *14,579*
Edwardsville, KS 66113 • *3,979*
Edwardsville, PA 18704 • *5,399*
Effingham, IL 62401 • *11,851*
Effingham □, GA • *25,687*
Effingham □, IL • *31,704*
Egg Harbor City, NJ 08215 • *4,583*
Egypt, MA 02066 • *1,100*
Egypt Lake, FL 33614 • *14,580*
Ehrenberg, AZ 85334 • *1,500*
Elba, AL 36323 • *4,011*
Elbert □, CO • *9,646*
Elbert □, GA • *18,949*
Elberta, GA 31093 • *1,559*
Elberton, GA 30635 • *5,682*
Elbow Lake, MN 56531 • *1,186*
Elburn, IL 60119 • *1,275*
El Cajon, CA 92019–22 • *88,693*
El Campo, TX 77437 • *10,511*
El Centro, CA 92243–44 • *31,384*
El Cerrito, CA 94530 • *22,869*
Eldersburg, MD 21784 • *9,720*
Eldon, IA 52554 • *1,070*
Eldon, MO 65026 • *4,419*
Eldora, IA 50627 • *3,038*
El Dorado, AR 71730–31 • *23,146*
Eldorado, IL 62930 • *4,536*
El Dorado, KS 67042 • *11,504*
Eldorado, TX 76936 • *2,019*
El Dorado □, CA • *125,995*
El Dorado Hills, CA 95630 • *6,395*
El Dorado Springs, MO 64744 • *3,830*
Eldridge, IA 52748 • *3,378*
Eleanor, WV 25070 • *1,256*
Electra, TX 76360 • *3,113*
Eleele, HI 96705 • *1,489*
El Encanto Heights, CA 93117 • *7,700*
Elfers, FL 34680 • *12,356*
Elgin, IL 60120–23 • *77,010*
Elgin, ND 58533 • *765*
Elgin, OR 97827 • *1,586*
Elgin, TX 78621 • *4,846*
Elida, OH 45807 • *1,486*
Elizabeth, NJ 07201–08 • *110,002*
Elizabeth City, NC 27906–09 • *14,292*
Elizabethton, TN 37643–44 • *11,931*
Elizabethtown, KY 42701–02 • *18,167*
Elizabethtown, NC 28337 • *3,704*
Elizabethtown, PA 17022 • *9,952*
Elizabethville, PA 17023 • *1,467*
Elk □, KS • *3,327*
Elk □, PA • *34,878*
Elkader, IA 52043 • *1,510*
Elk City, OK 73644 • *10,428*
Elk Grove, CA 95624 • *17,483*
Elk Grove Village, IL 60009 • *33,429*
Elkhart, IN 46514–17 • *43,627*
Elkhart, KS 67950 • *2,318*
Elkhart, TX 75839 • *1,076*

Elkhart □, IN • *156,198*
Elkhart Lake, WI 53020 • *1,019*
Elkhorn, NE 68022 • *1,398*
Elkhorn, WI 53121 • *5,337*
Elkin, NC 28621 • *3,790*
Elkins, WV 26241 • *7,420*
Elkland, PA 16920 • *1,849*
Elk Mountain, WY 82324 • *174*
Elko, NV 89801–02 • *14,736*
Elko □, NV • *33,530*
Elk Point, SD 57025 • *1,423*
Elk Rapids, MI 49629 • *1,626*
Elkridge, MD 21227 • *12,953*
Elk River, MN 55330 • *11,143*
Elkton, KY 42220 • *1,789*
Elkton, MD 21921–22 • *9,073*
Elkton, VA 22827 • *1,935*
Elkview, WV 25071 • *1,047*
Ellaville, GA 31806 • *1,724*
Ellendale, DE 19941 • *313*
Ellendale, ND 58436 • *1,798*
Ellensburg, WA 98926 • *12,361*
Ellenton, FL 34222 • *2,573*
Ellenville, NY 12428 • *4,243*
Ellerbe, NC 28338 • *1,132*
Ellerslie, MD 21529 • *1,500*
Ellettsville, IN 47429 • *3,275*
Ellicott City, MD 21043 • *41,396*
Ellijay, GA 30540 • *1,178*
Ellington, CT 06029 • *1,500*
Ellinwood, KS 67526 • *2,329*
Elliott □, KY • *6,455*
Ellis, KS 67637 • *1,814*
Ellis □, KS • *26,004*
Ellis □, OK • *4,497*
Ellis □, TX • *85,167*
Ellisville, MS 39437 • *3,634*
Ellisville, MO 63011 • *7,545*
Ellport, PA 16117 • *1,243*
Ellsworth, KS 67439 • *2,294*
Ellsworth, ME 04605 • *5,975*
Ellsworth, PA 15331 • *1,048*
Ellsworth, WI 54011 • *2,706*
Ellsworth □, KS • *6,586*
Ellwood City, PA 16117 • *8,894*
Elma, WA 98541 • *3,011*
Elm City, NC 27822 • *1,624*
Elmer, NJ 08318 • *1,571*
Elm Grove, WI 53122 • *6,261*
Elmhurst, IL 60126 • *42,029*
Elmira, NY 14901–05 • *33,724*
El Mirage, AZ 85335 • *5,001*
Elmira Heights, NY 14903 • *4,359*
Elmont, NY 11003 • *28,612*
El Monte, CA 91731–34 • *106,209*
Elmora, PA 15737 • *1,500*
Elmore, OH 43416 • *1,334*
Elmore □, AL • *49,210*
Elmore □, ID • *21,205*
Elmwood, IL 61529 • *1,841*
Elmwood Park, IL 60635 • *23,206*
Elmwood Park, NJ 07407 • *17,623*
Elmwood Place, OH 45216 • *2,937*
Eloise, FL 33880 • *1,408*
Elon College, NC 27244 • *4,394*
Eloy, AZ 85231 • *7,211*
El Paso, IL 61738 • *2,499*
El Paso, TX 79901–99 • *515,342*
El Paso □, CO • *397,014*
El Paso □, TX • *591,610*
El Portal, FL 33138 • *2,457*
El Reno, OK 73036 • *15,414*
Elroy, WI 53929 • *1,533*
Elsa, TX 78543 • *5,242*
Elsberry, MO 63343 • *1,898*
El Segundo, CA 90245 • *15,223*
Elsmere, DE 19805 • *5,935*
Elsmere, KY 41018 • *6,847*
Elsmere, NY 12054 • *4,180*
El Sobrante, CA 94803 • *9,852*
Elton, LA 70532 • *1,277*
El Toro, CA 92630 • *62,685*
Elvins, MO 63601 • *1,391*
Elwood, IN 46036 • *9,494*
Elwood, KS 66024 • *1,079*
Elwood, NJ 08217 • *1,400*
Elwood, NY 11731 • *10,916*
Ely, MN 55731 • *3,968*
Ely, NV 89301 • *4,756*
Elyria, OH 44035–39 • *56,746*
Elysburg, PA 17824 • *1,890*
Emanuel □, GA • *20,546*
Emerson, GA 30137 • *1,201*
Emerson, NJ 07630 • *6,930*
Emery □, UT • *10,332*
Eminence, KY 40019 • *2,055*
Emmaus, PA 18049 • *11,157*
Emmet □, IA • *11,569*
Emmet □, MI • *25,040*
Emmetsburg, IA 50536 • *3,940*
Emmett, ID 83617 • *4,601*
Emmitsburg, MD 21727 • *1,688*
Emmonak, AK 99581 • *642*
Emmons □, ND • *4,830*
Empire, NV 89405 • *300*
Emporia, KS 66801 • *25,512*
Emporia, VA 23847 • *5,306*
Emporium, PA 15834 • *2,513*
Emsworth, PA 15202 • *2,892*
Encampment, WY 82325 • *490*
Encinitas, CA 92023–24 • *55,300*
Enderlin, ND 58027 • *997*
Endicott, NY 13760 • *13,531*
Endwell, NY 13760 • *12,602*
Enfield (Thompsonville), CT 06082–83 • *8,458*
Enfield, NH 03748 • *1,560*
Enfield, NC 27823 • *3,082*
England, AR 72046 • *3,351*
Engleside, VA 22309 • *24,058*
Englewood, CO 80110–12 • *29,387*
Englewood, FL 34223–24 • *15,025*
Englewood, NJ 07631–32 • *24,850*
Englewood, OH 45322 • *11,432*
Englewood, TN 37329 • *1,611*
Englewood Cliffs, NJ 07632 • *5,634*
Englishtown, NJ 07726 • *1,268*
Enid, OK 73701–06 • *45,309*
Enka, NC 28728 • *5,567*
Ennis, MT 59729 • *773*
Ennis, TX 75119–20 • *13,883*
Enoch, UT 84720 • *1,947*
Enola, PA 17025 • *5,961*

Enon, OH 45323 • *2,605*
Enoree, SC 29335 • *1,107*
Enosburg Falls, VT 05450 • *1,350*
Ensley, FL 32504 • *16,362*
Enterprise, AL 36330–31 • *20,123*
Enterprise, OR 97828 • *1,905*
Enterprise, WV 26568 • *1,058*
Enumclaw, WA 98022 • *7,227*
Ephraim, UT 84627 • *3,363*
Ephrata, PA 17522 • *12,133*
Ephrata, WA 98823 • *5,349*
Epping, NH 03042 • *1,384*
Epworth, IA 52045 • *1,297*
Erath, LA 70533 • *2,428*
Erath □, TX • *27,991*
Erial, NJ 08081 • *2,500*
Erick, OK 73645 • *1,083*
Erie, CO 80516 • *1,258*
Erie, IL 61250 • *1,572*
Erie, KS 66733 • *1,276*
Erie, PA 16501–65 • *108,718*
Erie □, NY • *968,532*
Erie □, OH • *76,779*
Erie □, PA • *275,572*
Erin, TN 37061 • *1,586*
Erlanger, KY 41018 • *15,979*
Erma, NJ 08204 • *2,045*
Errol Heights, OR 97266 • *10,487*
Erwin, NC 28339 • *4,061*
Erwin, TN 37650 • *5,015*
Escalon, CA 95320 • *4,437*
Escambia □, AL • *35,518*
Escambia □, FL • *262,798*
Escanaba, MI 49829 • *13,659*
Escatawpa, MS 39552 • *3,902*
Escondido, CA 92025–27 • *108,635*
Esmeralda □, NV • *1,344*
Esmond, RI 02917 • *4,320*
Espanola, NM 87532 • *8,389*
Esparto, CA 95627 • *1,487*
Esperance, WA 98043 • *11,236*
Espy, PA 17815 • *1,430*
Essex, CT 06426 • *2,500*
Essex, MD 21221 • *40,872*
Essex, MA 01929 • *1,507*
Essex, VT 05451 • *800*
Essex □, MA • *670,080*
Essex □, NJ • *778,206*
Essex □, NY • *37,152*
Essex □, VT • *6,405*
Essex □, VA • *8,689*
Essex Fells, NJ 07021 • *2,363*
Essex Junction, VT 05452–53 • *8,396*
Essexville, MI 48732 • *4,088*
Estacada, OR 97023 • *2,016*
Estelle, LA 70072 • *14,091*
Estell Manor, NJ 08319 • *1,404*
Estes Park, CO 80517 • *3,184*
Estherville, IA 51334 • *6,720*
Estill, SC 29918 • *2,387*
Estill □, KY • *14,614*
Estill Springs, TN 37330 • *1,408*
Etna, PA 15223 • *4,200*
Etowah, TN 37331 • *3,815*
Etowah □, AL • *99,840*
Ettrick, VA 23803 • *5,290*
Euclid, OH 44117 • *54,875*
Eudora, AR 71640 • *3,155*
Eudora, KS 66025 • *3,006*
Eufaula, AL 36027 • *13,220*
Eufaula, OK 74432 • *2,652*
Eugene, OR 97401–05 • *112,669*
Euless, TX 76039–40 • *38,149*
Eunice, LA 70535 • *11,162*
Eunice, NM 88231 • *2,676*
Eupora, MS 39744 • *2,145*
Eureka, CA 95501–02 • *27,025*
Eureka, IL 61530 • *4,435*
Eureka, KS 67045 • *2,974*
Eureka, MO 63025 • *4,683*
Eureka, MT 59917 • *1,043*
Eureka, NV 89316 • *650*
Eureka, SC 29706 • *1,738*
Eureka, SD 57437 • *1,197*
Eureka □, NV • *1,547*
Eureka Springs, AR 72632 • *1,900*
Eustis, FL 32726–27 • *12,967*
Eutaw, AL 35462 • *2,281*
Evangeline □, LA • *33,274*
Evans, CO 80620 • *5,877*
Evans, GA 30809 • *2,000*
Evans □, GA • *8,724*
Evans City, PA 16033 • *2,054*
Evansdale, IA 50707 • *4,638*
Evanston, IL 60201–04 • *73,233*
Evanston, WY 82930–31 • *10,903*
Evansville, IN 47701–37 • *126,272*
Evansville, WI 53536 • *3,174*
Evansville, WY 82636 • *1,403*
Evart, MI 49631 • *1,744*
Evarts, KY 40828 • *1,063*
Eveleth, MN 55734 • *4,064*
Everett, MA 02149 • *35,701*
Everett, PA 15537 • *1,777*
Everett, WA 98201–08 • *69,961*
Evergreen, AL 36401 • *3,911*
Evergreen, CO 80439 • *7,582*
Evergreen Park, IL 60642 • *20,874*
Everman, TX 76140 • *5,672*
Everson, WA 98247 • *1,490*
Ewa, HI 96706 • *3,780*
Ewa Beach, HI 96706–07 • *14,315*
Ewing Township, NJ 08618 • *34,185*
Excelsior Springs, MO 64024 • *10,354*
Exeter, CA 93221 • *7,276*
Exeter, NH 03833 • *9,556*
Exeter, PA 18643 • *5,691*
Exmore, VA 23350 • *1,115*
Experiment, GA 30223 • *3,762*
Eyota, MN 55934 • *1,448*

F

Fabens, TX 79838 • *5,599*
Factoryville, PA 18419 • *1,310*
Fairbank, IA 50629 • *1,018*
Fairbanks, AK 99701 • *30,843*
Fair Bluff, NC 28439 • *1,068*
Fairborn, OH 45324 • *31,300*
Fairburn, GA 30213 • *4,013*
Fairbury, IL 61739 • *3,643*

Fairbury, NE 68352 • *4,335*
Fairchance, PA 15436 • *1,918*
Fairdale, KY 40118 • *6,563*
Fairfax, CA 94930 • *6,931*
Fairfax, DE 19803 • *2,075*
Fairfax, MN 55332 • *1,276*
Fairfax, OK 74637 • *1,749*
Fairfax, SC 29827 • *2,317*
Fairfax, VA 22030–39 • *19,622*
Fairfax □, VA • *818,584*
Fairfield, AL 35064 • *12,200*
Fairfield, CA 94533 • *77,211*
Fairfield, CT 06430–32 • *53,418*
Fairfield, IL 62837 • *5,439*
Fairfield, IA 52556 • *9,768*
Fairfield, ME 04937 • *2,794*
Fairfield, NJ 07004 • *7,615*
Fairfield, OH 45014 • *39,729*
Fairfield, TX 75840 • *3,234*
Fairfield □, CT • *827,645*
Fairfield □, OH • *103,461*
Fairfield □, SC • *22,295*
Fairfield Bay, AR 72088 • *2,332*
Fair Grove, NC 27360 • *1,500*
Fairhaven, MA 02719 • *15,759*
Fair Haven, NJ 07704 • *5,270*
Fair Haven, VT 05743 • *2,432*
Fairhope, AL 36532–33 • *8,485*
Fair Lawn, NJ 07410 • *30,548*
Fairlawn, OH 44313 • *5,779*
Fairlawn, VA 24141 • *2,399*
Fairlea, WV 24902 • *1,743*
Fairless Hills, PA 19030 • *9,026*
Fairmont, IL 60441 • *2,260*
Fairmont, MN 56031 • *11,265*
Fairmont, NC 28340 • *2,489*
Fairmont, WV 26554–55 • *20,210*
Fairmount, IN 46928 • *3,130*
Fairmount, NY 13031 • *12,266*
Fairmount Heights, MD 20743 • *1,238*
Fair Oaks, CA 95628 • *26,867*
Fair Oaks, GA 30060 • *6,996*
Fairoaks, PA 15003 • *1,854*
Fair Plain, MI 49022 • *8,051*
Fairport, NY 14450 • *5,943*
Fairport Harbor, OH 44077 • *2,978*
Fairton, NJ 08320 • *1,359*
Fairview, MT 59221 • *869*
Fairview, NJ 07022 • *10,733*
Fairview, OK 73737 • *2,936*
Fairview, OR 97024 • *2,391*
Fairview, PA 16415 • *1,988*
Fairview, TN 37062 • *4,210*
Fairview Heights, IL 62208 • *14,351*
Fairview Park, IN 47842 • *1,446*
Fairview Park, OH 44126 • *18,028*
Fairview Shores, FL 32804 • *13,192*
Fairway, KS 66205 • *4,173*
Fairwood, WA 98058 • *2,000*
Fairwood, WA 99218 • *5,807*
Falconer, NY 14733 • *2,653*
Falcon Heights, MN 55113 • *5,380*
Falfurrias, TX 78355 • *5,788*
Falkville, AL 35622 • *1,337*
Fall Branch, TN 37656 • *1,203*
Fallbrook, CA 92028 • *22,095*
Fall City, WA 98024 • *1,582*
Fall Creek, WI 54742 • *1,034*
Fallon, NV 89406 • *6,438*
Fallon □, MT • *3,103*
Fall River, MA 02720–26 • *92,703*
Fall River □, SD • *7,353*
Falls □, TX • *17,712*
Falls Church, VA 22040–46 • *9,578*
Falls City, NE 68355 • *4,769*
Falls Creek, PA 15840 • *1,087*
Fallston, MD 21047 • *5,730*
Falls Township, PA 19054 • *36,083*
Falmouth, KY 41040 • *2,378*
Falmouth, ME 04105 • *7,610*
Falmouth, MA 02540 • *4,047*
Falmouth, VA 22405 • *3,541*
Fannin □, GA • *15,992*
Fannin □, TX • *24,804*
Fanwood, NJ 07023 • *7,115*
Fargo, ND 58102–09 • *74,111*
Faribault, MN 55021 • *17,085*
Faribault □, MN • *16,937*
Farley, IA 52046 • *1,354*
Farmer City, IL 61842 • *2,114*
Farmers Branch, TX 75234 • *24,250*
Farmersburg, IN 47850 • *1,159*
Farmersville, CA 93223 • *6,235*
Farmerville, LA 71241 • *3,334*
Farmingdale, ME 04345 • *2,070*
Farmingdale, NJ 07727 • *1,462*
Farmingdale, NY 11735 • *8,022*
Farmington, AR 72730 • *1,322*
Farmington, CT 06032 • *2,500*
Farmington, IL 61531 • *2,535*
Farmington, ME 04938 • *4,197*
Farmington, MI 48335–36 • *10,132*
Farmington, MN 55024 • *5,940*
Farmington, MO 63640 • *11,598*
Farmington, NH 03835 • *3,567*
Farmington, NM 87401–02 • *33,997*
Farmington, UT 84025 • *9,028*
Farmington Hills, MI 48331–34 • *74,652*
Farmingville, NY 11738 • *14,842*
Farmland, IN 47340 • *1,412*
Farmville, NC 27828 • *4,392*
Farmville, VA 23901 • *6,046*
Farragut, TN 37922 • *12,793*
Farrell, PA 16121 • *6,841*
Farwell, TX 79325 • *1,373*
Faulk □, SD • *2,744*
Faulkland Heights, DE 19808 • *1,300*
Faulkner □, AR • *60,006*
Faulkton, SD 57438 • *809*
Fauquier □, VA • *48,741*
Fayette, AL 35555 • *4,909*
Fayette, IA 52142 • *1,317*
Fayette, MS 39069 • *1,853*
Fayette, MO 65248 • *2,888*
Fayette, OH 43521 • *1,248*
Fayette □, AL • *17,962*
Fayette □, GA • *62,415*
Fayette □, IL • *20,893*
Fayette □, IN • *26,015*
Fayette □, IA • *21,843*
Fayette □, KY • *225,366*
Fayette □, OH • *27,466*
Fayette □, PA • *145,351*

Fayette □, TN • 25,559
Fayette □, TX • 20,095
Fayette □, WV • 47,952
Fayetteville, AR 72701–03 • 42,099
Fayetteville, GA 30214 • 5,827
Fayetteville, NC 28301–14 • 75,695
Fayetteville, PA 17222 • 3,033
Fayetteville, TN 37334 • 6,921
Fayetteville, WV 25840 • 2,182
Fayville, MA 01745 • 1,000
Federal Heights, CO 80221 • 9,342
Federalsburg, MD 21632 • 2,365
Federal Way, WA 98003 • 67,554
Feeding Hills, MA 01030 • 5,470
Fellowship, NJ 08057 • 4,250
Fellsmere, FL 32948 • 2,179
Felton, CA 95041 • 5,350
Felton, DE 19943 • 683
Fennimore, WI 53809 • 2,378
Fennville, MI 49408 • 1,023
Fenton, MI 48430 • 8,444
Fentress □, TN • 14,669
Ferdinand, IN 47532 • 2,318
Fergus □, MT • 12,083
Fergus Falls, MN 56537–38 • 12,362
Ferguson, MO 63135 • 22,286
Fernandina Beach, FL 32034 • 8,765
Fern Creek, KY 40291 • 16,406
Ferndale, CA 95536 • 1,331
Ferndale, MD 21061 • 16,355
Ferndale, MI 48220 • 25,084
Ferndale, PA 15905 • 2,020
Ferndale, WA 98248 • 5,398
Fernley, NV 89408 • 5,164
Fern Park, FL 32730 • 8,294
Fernway, PA 16063 • 9,072
Ferriday, LA 71334 • 4,111
Ferris, TX 75125 • 2,212
Ferron, UT 84523 • 1,606
Ferry □, WA • 6,295
Ferry Farms, VA 22405 • 1,600
Fessenden, ND 58438 • 655
Festus, MO 63028 • 8,105
Fieldale, VA 24089 • 1,018
Fig Garden, CA 93704 • 9,000
Filer, ID 83328 • 1,511
Fillmore, CA 93015–16 • 11,992
Fillmore, UT 84631 • 1,956
Fillmore □, MN • 20,777
Fillmore □, NE • 7,103
Findlay, OH 45839–40 • 35,703
Finley, TN 38030 • 1,014
Finney □, KS • 33,070
Fircrest, WA 98466 • 5,258
Firebaugh, CA 93622 • 4,429
Firestone, CO 80520 • 1,358
Fisher, IL 61843 • 1,526
Fisher □, TX • 4,842
Fishers, IN 46038 • 7,508
Fishkill, NY 12524 • 1,957
Fiskdale, MA 01518 • 2,189
Fitchburg, MA 01420 • 41,194
Fitzgerald, GA 31750 • 8,612
Five Points, NM 87105 • 4,200
Flagler □, FL • 28,701
Flagler Beach, FL 32136 • 3,820
Flagstaff, AZ 86001–16 • 45,857
Flanders, NJ 07836 • 3,040
Flandreau, SD 57028 • 2,311
Flathead □, MT • 59,218
Flatonia, TX 78941 • 1,295
Flat River, MO 63601 • 4,823
Flat Rock, MI 48134 • 7,290
Flat Rock, NC 28731 • 1,200
Flatwoods, KY 41139 • 7,799
Fleetwood, PA 19522 • 3,478
Fleming □, KY • 12,292
Flemingsburg, KY 41041 • 3,071
Flemington, NJ 08822 • 4,047
Flemington, PA 17745 • 1,321
Fletcher, NC 28732 • 2,787
Fletcher, OK 73541 • 1,002
Flint, MI 48501–32 • 140,761
Flint City, AL 35601 • 1,033
Flippin, AR 72634 • 1,006
Flomaton, AL 36441 • 1,811
Flora, IL 62839 • 5,054
Flora, IN 46929 • 2,179
Flora, MS 39071 • 1,482
Florala, AL 36442 • 2,075
Floral City, FL 32636 • 2,609
Floral Park, NY 11001–05 • 15,947
Florence, AL 35630–33 • 36,426
Florence, AZ 85232 • 7,510
Florence, CA 90001 • 43,900
Florence, CO 81226 • 2,990
Florence, KY 41042 • 18,624
Florence, MS 39073 • 1,831
Florence, NJ 08518 • 4,203
Florence, OR 97439 • 5,162
Florence, SC 29501–06 • 29,813
Florence □, SC • 114,344
Florence □, WI • 4,590
Floresville, TX 78114 • 5,247
Florham Park, NJ 07932 • 8,521
Florida, NY 10921 • 2,497
Florida City, FL 33034 • 5,806
Florida Ridge, FL 32960 • 12,218
Florin, CA 95828 • 24,330
Florissant, MO 63031–34 • 51,206
Flossmoor, IL 60422 • 8,651
Flower Hill, NY 11050 • 4,490
Flowery Branch, GA 30542 • 1,251
Flowood, MS 39208 • 2,860
Floyd □, GA • 81,251
Floyd □, IN • 64,404
Floyd □, IA • 17,058
Floyd □, KY • 43,586
Floyd □, TX • 8,497
Floyd □, VA • 12,005
Floydada, TX 79235 • 3,896
Flushing, MI 48433 • 8,542
Flushing, OH 43977 • 1,042
Fluvanna □, VA • 12,429
Foard □, TX • 1,794
Folcroft, PA 19032 • 7,506
Foley, AL 36535–36 • 4,937
Foley, MN 56329 • 1,854
Folkston, GA 31537 • 2,285
Follansbee, WV 26037 • 3,339
Folly Beach, SC 29439 • 1,398
Folsom, CA 95630 • 29,802
Folsom, NJ 08037 • 2,181
Fonda, NY 12068 • 1,007
Fond du Lac, WI 54935–36 • 37,757
Fond du Lac □, WI • 90,083
Fontana, CA 92334–36 • 87,535
Fontana, WI 53125 • 1,635
Foothill Farms, CA 95841 • 17,135
Ford □, IL • 14,275
Ford □, KS • 27,463
Ford City, CA 93268 • 3,781
Ford City, PA 16226 • 3,413
Ford Heights, IL 60411 • 4,259
Fords, NJ 08863 • 14,392
Fords Prairie, WA 98531 • 2,480
Fordyce, AR 71742 • 4,729
Foreman, AR 71836 • 1,267
Forest, MS 39074 • 5,060
Forest, OH 45843 • 1,594
Forest □, PA • 4,802
Forest □, WI • 8,776
Forest Acres, SC 29206 • 7,197
Forest City, IA 50436 • 4,430
Forest City, NC 28043 • 7,475
Forest City, PA 18421 • 1,846
Forestdale, AL 35214 • 10,395
Forestdale, RI 02824 • 530
Forest Dale, VT 05745 • 350
Forest Grove, OR 97116 • 13,559
Forest Hill, TX 76119 • 11,482
Forest Hills, PA 15221 • 7,335
Forest Knolls, CA 94933 • 2,000
Forest Lake, MN 55025 • 5,833
Forest Park, GA 30050–51 • 16,925
Forest Park, IL 60130 • 14,918
Forest Park, LA 71291 • 1,400
Forest Park, OH 45240 • 18,609
Forked River, NJ 08731 • 1,950
Forks, WA 98331 • 2,862
Forney, TX 75126 • 4,070
Forrest, IL 61741 • 1,124
Forrest □, MS • 68,314
Forrest City, AR 72335 • 13,364
Forreston, IL 61030 • 1,361
Forsyth, GA 31029 • 4,268
Forsyth, IL 62535 • 1,275
Forsyth, MO 65653 • 1,175
Forsyth, MT 59327 • 2,178
Forsyth □, GA • 44,083
Forsyth □, NC • 265,878
Fort Ashby, WV 26719 • 1,288
Fort Atkinson, WI 53538 • 10,227
Fort Bend □, TX • 225,421
Fort Benton, MT 59442 • 1,660
Fort Bragg, CA 95437 • 6,078
Fort Branch, IN 47648 • 2,447
Fort Collins, CO 80521–26 • 87,758
Fort Covington, NY 12937 • 1,200
Fort Davis, TX 79734 • 1,100
Fort Defiance, AZ 86504 • 4,489
Fort Deposit, AL 36032 • 1,240
Fort Dodge, IA 50501 • 25,894
Fort Edward, NY 12828 • 3,561
Fort Fairfield, ME 04742 • 1,729
Fort Gaines, GA 31751 • 1,248
Fort Gibson, OK 74434 • 3,359
Fort Hall, ID 83203 • 2,681
Fort Kent, ME 04743 • 2,123
Fort Laramie, WY 82212 • 243
Fort Lauderdale, FL 33301–51 • 149,377
Fort Lee, NJ 07024 • 31,997
Fort Loramie, OH 45845 • 1,042
Fort Loudon, PA 17224 • 1,200
Fort Lupton, CO 80621 • 5,159
Fort Madison, IA 52627 • 11,618
Fort McKinley, OH 45426 • 9,740
Fort Meade, FL 33841 • 4,976
Fort Mill, SC 29715 • 4,930
Fort Mitchell, KY 41017 • 7,438
Fort Morgan, CO 80701 • 9,068
Fort Myers, FL 33901–19 • 45,206
Fort Myers Beach, FL 33931–32 • 9,284
Fort Myers Shores, FL 33905 • 5,460
Fort Oglethorpe, GA 30742 • 5,880
Fort Payne, AL 35967 • 11,838
Fort Pierce, FL 34945–54 • 36,830
Fort Pierre, SD 57532 • 1,854
Fort Plain, NY 13339 • 2,416
Fort Recovery, OH 45846 • 1,313
Fort Scott, KS 66701 • 8,362
Fort Shawnee, OH 45806 • 4,128
Fort Smith, AR 72901–17 • 72,798
Fort Stockton, TX 79735 • 8,524
Fort Sumner, NM 88119 • 1,269
Fort Thomas, KY 41075 • 16,032
Fortuna, CA 95540 • 8,788
Fort Valley, GA 31030 • 8,198
Fortville, IN 46040 • 2,690
Fort Walton Beach, FL 32547–48 • 21,471
Fort Washington Forest, MD 20744 • 1,010
Fort Wayne, IN 46801–99 • 173,072
Fort Wingate, NM 87316 • 950
Fort Worth, TX 76101–85 • 447,619
Fort Wright, KY 41011 • 6,570
Forty Fort, PA 18704 • 5,049
Fort Yukon, AK 99740 • 580
Fosston, MN 56542 • 1,529
Foster □, ND • 3,983
Foster City, CA 94404 • 28,176
Foster Village, HI 96818 • 3,700
Fostoria, OH 44830 • 14,983
Fountain, CO 80817 • 9,984
Fountain □, IN • 17,808
Fountain Hill, PA 18015 • 4,637
Fountain Inn, SC 29644 • 4,388
Fountain Place, LA • 9,200
Fountain Valley, CA 92708 • 53,691
Four Corners, OR 97301 • 12,156
Four Oaks, NC 27524 • 1,308
Fowler, CA 93625 • 3,208
Fowler, CO 81039 • 1,154
Fowler, IN 47944 • 2,333
Fowlerville, MI 48836 • 2,648
Foxboro, MA 02035 • 5,706
Fox Chapel, PA 15238 • 5,319
Fox Lake, IL 60020 • 7,478
Fox Lake, WI 53933 • 1,269
Fox Point, WI 53217 • 7,238
Fox River Grove, IL 60021 • 3,551
Frackville, PA 17931 • 4,700
Framingham, MA 01701 • 64,994
Franconia, VA 22310 • 19,882
Frankenmuth, MI 48734 • 4,408
Frankford, DE 19945 • 591
Frankfort, IL 60423 • 7,180
Frankfort, IN 46041 • 14,754
Frankfort, KY 40601–22 • 25,968
Frankfort, MI 49635 • 1,546
Frankfort, NY 13340 • 2,693
Frankfort, OH 45628 • 1,065
Franklin, IN 46131 • 12,907
Franklin, KY 42134–35 • 7,607
Franklin, LA 70538 • 9,004
Franklin, MA 02038 • 9,965
Franklin, NE 68939 • 1,112
Franklin, NH 03235 • 8,304
Franklin, NJ 07416 • 4,977
Franklin, NC 28734 • 2,873
Franklin, OH 45005 • 11,026
Franklin, PA 16323 • 7,329
Franklin, TN 37064–65 • 20,098
Franklin, TX 77856 • 1,336
Franklin, VA 23851 • 7,864
Franklin, WI 53132 • 21,855
Franklin □, AL • 27,814
Franklin □, AR • 14,897
Franklin □, FL • 8,967
Franklin □, GA • 16,650
Franklin □, ID • 9,232
Franklin □, IL • 40,319
Franklin □, IN • 19,580
Franklin □, IA • 11,364
Franklin □, KS • 21,994
Franklin □, KY • 43,781
Franklin □, LA • 22,387
Franklin □, ME • 29,008
Franklin □, MA • 70,092
Franklin □, MS • 8,377
Franklin □, MO • 80,603
Franklin □, NE • 3,938
Franklin □, NY • 46,540
Franklin □, NC • 36,414
Franklin □, OH • 961,437
Franklin □, PA • 121,082
Franklin □, TN • 34,725
Franklin □, TX • 7,802
Franklin □, VT • 39,980
Franklin □, VA • 39,549
Franklin □, WA • 37,473
Franklin Lakes, NJ 07417 • 9,873
Franklin Park, IL 60131 • 18,485
Franklin Park, PA 15143 • 10,109
Franklin Square, NY 11010 • 28,205
Franklinton, LA 70438 • 4,007
Franklinton, NC 27525 • 1,615
Franklinville, NJ 08322 • 1,020
Franklinville, NY 14737 • 1,739
Frankston, TX 75763 • 1,127
Frankton, IN 46044 • 1,736
Fraser, MI 48026 • 13,899
Frazee, MN 56544 • 1,176
Frazeysburg, OH 43822 • 1,165
Frazier Park, CA 93225 • 2,201
Frederic, WI 54837 • 1,124
Frederica, DE 19946 • 761
Frederick, MD 21701–02 • 40,148
Frederick, OK 73542 • 5,221
Frederick □, MD • 150,208
Frederick □, VA • 45,723
Fredericksburg, IA 50630 • 1,011
Fredericksburg, TX 78624 • 6,934
Fredericksburg, VA 22401–08 • 19,027
Fredericktown, MO 63645 • 3,950
Fredericktown, OH 43019 • 2,443
Fredericktown, PA 15333 • 1,052
Fredonia, AZ 86022 • 1,207
Fredonia, KS 66736 • 2,599
Fredonia, NY 14063 • 10,436
Fredonia, WI 53021 • 1,558
Freeborn □, MN • 33,060
Freeburg, IL 62243 • 3,115
Freedom, CA 95019 • 8,361
Freedom, PA 15042 • 1,897
Freedom, WY 83120 • 450
Freehold, NJ 07728 • 10,742
Freeland, MI 48623 • 1,421
Freeland, PA 18224 • 3,909
Freeman, SD 57029 • 1,293
Freemansburg, PA 18017 • 1,946
Freeport, IL 61032 • 25,840
Freeport, ME 04032 • 1,829
Freeport, NY 11520 • 39,894
Freeport, PA 16229 • 1,983
Freeport, TX 77541 • 11,389
Freer, TX 78357 • 3,271
Freestone □, TX • 15,818
Fremont, CA 94536–39 • 173,339
Fremont, IN 46737 • 1,407
Fremont, MI 49412 • 3,875
Fremont, NE 68025 • 23,680
Fremont, NC 27830 • 1,710
Fremont, OH 43420 • 17,648
Fremont □, CO • 32,273
Fremont □, ID • 10,937
Fremont □, IA • 8,226
Fremont □, WY • 33,662
French Island, WI 54601 • 4,478
French Lick, IN 47432 • 2,087
Frenchtown, NJ 08825 • 1,528
Fresno, CA 93701–94 • 354,202
Fresno □, CA • 667,490
Frewsburg, NY 14738 • 1,817
Friars Point, MS 38631 • 1,334
Friday Harbor, WA 98250 • 1,492
Fridley, MN 55432 • 28,335
Friend, NE 68359 • 1,111
Friendship, NY 14739 • 1,423
Friendswood, TX 77546 • 22,814
Frio □, TX • 13,472
Friona, TX 79035 • 3,688
Frisco, CO 80443 • 1,601
Frisco City, AL 36445 • 1,581
Fritch, TX 79036 • 2,335
Frontenac, KS 66762 • 2,588
Frontier □, NE • 3,101
Front Royal, VA 22630 • 11,880
Frostburg, MD 21532 • 8,075
Frostproof, FL 33843 • 2,808
Fruita, CO 81521 • 4,045
Fruit Heights, UT 84037 • 3,900
Fruitland, ID 83619 • 2,400
Fruitland, MD 21826 • 3,511
Fruitland Park, FL 34731 • 2,754
Fruitport, MI 49415 • 1,090
Fruitvale, CO 81504 • 1,070
Fruitvale, WA 98902 • 4,125
Fruitville, FL 34232 • 9,808
Fryeburg, ME 04037 • 1,580
Fulda, MN 56131 • 1,212
Fullerton, CA 92631–35 • 114,144
Fullerton, NE 68638 • 1,452
Fulton, IL 61252 • 3,698
Fulton, KY 42041 • 3,078
Fulton, MS 38843 • 3,387
Fulton, MO 65251 • 10,033
Fulton, NY 13069 • 12,929
Fulton □, AR • 10,037
Fulton □, GA • 648,951
Fulton □, IL • 38,080
Fulton □, IN • 18,840
Fulton □, KY • 8,271
Fulton □, NY • 54,191
Fulton □, OH • 38,498
Fulton □, PA • 13,837
Fultondale, AL 35068 • 6,400
Funkstown, MD 21734 • 1,136
Fuquay-Varina, NC 27526 • 4,562
Furnas □, NE • 5,553
Fyffe, AL 35971 • 1,094

G

Gabbs, NV 89409 • 667
Gadsden, AL 35901–05 • 42,523
Gadsden □, FL • 41,105
Gaffney, SC 29340–42 • 13,145
Gage □, NE • 22,794
Gages Lake, IL 60030 • 8,349
Gahanna, OH 43230 • 27,791
Gaines □, TX • 14,123
Gainesboro, TN 38562 • 1,002
Gainesville, FL 32601–14 • 84,770
Gainesville, GA 30501–07 • 17,885
Gainesville, TX 76240 • 14,256
Gaithersburg, MD 20877–79 • 39,542
Galax, VA 24333 • 6,670
Galena, AK 99741 • 833
Galena, IL 61036 • 3,647
Galena, KS 66739 • 3,308
Galesburg, IL 61401–02 • 33,530
Galesburg, MI 49053 • 1,863
Gales Ferry, CT 06335 • 1,191
Galesville, WI 54630 • 1,278
Galeton, PA 16922 • 1,370
Galeville, NY 13088 • 4,695
Galion, OH 44833 • 11,859
Gallatin, MO 64640 • 1,864
Gallatin, TN 37066 • 18,794
Gallatin □, IL • 6,909
Gallatin □, KY • 5,393
Gallatin □, MT • 50,463
Gallia □, OH • 30,954
Galliano, LA 70354 • 4,294
Gallipolis, OH 45631 • 4,831
Gallitzin, PA 16641 • 2,003
Gallup, NM 87301–05 • 19,154
Galt, CA 95632 • 8,889
Galva, IL 61434 • 2,742
Galveston, IN 46932 • 1,609
Galveston, TX 77550–54 • 59,070
Galveston □, TX • 217,399
Gambell, AK 99742 • 525
Gambier, OH 43022 • 2,073
Gambrills, MD 21054 • 1,200
Ganado, AZ 86505 • 3,400
Ganado, TX 77962 • 1,701
Gang Mills, NY 14870 • 2,738
Gantt, SC 29605 • 13,891
Gap, PA 17527 • 1,200
Garberville, CA 95440 • 1,200
Garden □, NE • 2,460
Gardena, CA 90247–49 • 49,847
Garden City, GA 31408 • 7,410
Garden City, ID 83704 • 6,369
Garden City, KS 67846 • 24,097
Garden City, MI 48135–36 • 31,846
Garden City, MO 64747 • 1,225
Garden City, NY 11530 • 21,686
Garden City Park, NY 11040 • 7,437
Gardendale, AL 35071 • 9,251
Garden Grove, CA 92640–45 • 143,050
Garden Home, OR 97223 • 5,500
Gardiner, ME 04345 • 6,746
Gardner, IL 60424 • 1,237
Gardner, KS 66030 • 3,191
Gardner, MA 01440 • 20,125
Gardnerville, NV 89410 • 2,177
Gardnerville Ranchos, NV 89410 • 7,455
Garfield, NJ 07026 • 26,727
Garfield □, CO • 29,974
Garfield □, MT • 1,589
Garfield □, NE • 2,141
Garfield □, OK • 56,735
Garfield □, UT • 3,980
Garfield □, WA • 2,248
Garfield Heights, OH 44125 • 31,739
Garfield Park, DE 19720 • 1,415
Garland, TX 75040–48 • 180,650
Garland, UT 84312 • 1,637
Garland □, AR • 73,397
Garner, IA 50438 • 2,916
Garner, NC 27529 • 14,967
Garnett, KS 66032 • 3,210
Garrard □, KY • 11,579
Garretson, SD 57030 • 924
Garrett, IN 46738 • 5,349
Garrett □, MD • 28,138
Garrettsville, OH 44231 • 2,014
Garrison, MD 21055 • 5,045
Garrison, ND 58540 • 1,530
Garvin □, OK • 26,605
Garwood, NJ 07027 • 4,227
Gary, IN 46401–11 • 116,646
Gary, WV 24836 • 1,355
Garysburg, NC 27831 • 1,057
Garyville, LA 70051 • 3,181
Garza □, TX • 5,143
Gas City, IN 46933 • 6,296
Gasconade □, MO • 14,006
Gasport, NY 14067 • 1,336
Gassville, AR 72635 • 1,167
Gaston, NC 27832 • 1,003
Gaston □, NC • 175,093
Gastonia, NC 28051–56 • 54,732
Gate City, VA 24251 • 2,214
Gates, NY 14624 • 30,000
Gates □, NC • 9,305
Gatesville, TX 76528 • 11,492
Gatlinburg, TN 37738 • 3,417
Gautier, MS 39553 • 10,088
Gaylord, MI 49735 • 3,256
Gaylord, MN 55334 • 1,935
Gearhart, OR 97138 • 1,027
Geary, OK 73040 • 1,347
Geary □, KS • 30,453
Geauga □, OH • 81,129
Geistown, PA 15904 • 2,749
Gem □, ID • 11,844
Genesee, ID 83832 • 725
Genesee, MI 48437 • 1,400
Genesee □, MI • 430,459
Genesee □, NY • 60,060
Geneseo, IL 61254 • 5,990
Geneseo, NY 14454 • 7,187
Geneva, AL 36340 • 4,681
Geneva, IL 60134 • 12,617
Geneva, IN 46740 • 1,280
Geneva, NE 68361 • 2,310
Geneva, NY 14456 • 14,143
Geneva, OH 44041 • 6,597
Geneva □, AL • 23,647
Geneva-on-the-Lake, OH 44041 • 1,626
Genoa, IL 60135 • 3,083
Genoa, NE 68640 • 1,082
Genoa, NV 89411 • 190
Genoa, OH 43430 • 2,262
Genoa City, WI 53128 • 1,277
Gentry, AR 72734 • 1,726
Gentry □, MO • 6,848
George, IA 51237 • 1,066
George □, MS • 16,673
Georgetown, CA 95634 • 2,000
Georgetown, CT 06829 • 1,694
Georgetown, DE 19947 • 3,732
Georgetown, IL 61846 • 3,678
Georgetown, IN 47122 • 2,092
Georgetown, KY 40324 • 11,414
Georgetown, MA 01833 • 2,100
Georgetown, OH 45121 • 3,627
Georgetown, SC 29440–42 • 9,517
Georgetown, TX 78626–28 • 14,842
Georgetown □, SC • 46,302
George West, TX 78022 • 2,586
Georgiana, AL 36033 • 1,933
Gering, NE 69341 • 7,946
Gerlach, NV 89412 • 200
Germantown, IL 62245 • 1,167
Germantown, MD 20874 • 41,145
Germantown, OH 45327 • 4,916
Germantown, TN 38138 • 32,893
Germantown, WI 53022 • 13,658
Gettysburg, PA 17325 • 7,025
Gettysburg, SD 57442 • 1,510
Giants Neck, CT 06357 • 1,200
Gibbon, NE 68840 • 1,525
Gibbstown, NJ 08027 • 5,404
Gibsland, LA 71028 • 1,224
Gibson □, IN • 31,913
Gibson □, TN • 46,315
Gibsonburg, OH 43431 • 2,579
Gibson City, IL 60936 • 3,396
Gibsonia, FL 33805 • 5,168
Gibsonia, PA 15044 • 3,500
Gibsonton, FL 33534 • 7,706
Gibsonville, NC 27249 • 3,441
Giddings, TX 78942 • 4,093
Gideon, MO 63848 • 1,104
Gifford, FL 32960 • 6,278
Gig Harbor, WA 98335 • 3,236
Gila □, AZ • 40,216
Gila Bend, AZ 85337 • 1,747
Gilbert, AZ 85234 • 29,188
Gilbert, MN 55741 • 1,934
Gilbert, OR 97266 • 4,000
Gilbertsville, PA 19525 • 3,994
Gilbertville, MA 01031 • 1,029
Gilchrist □, FL • 9,667
Gilcrest, CO 80623 • 1,084
Giles □, TN • 25,741
Giles □, VA • 16,366
Gilford Park, NJ 08753 • 8,668
Gillespie, IL 62033 • 3,645
Gillespie □, TX • 17,204
Gillett, WI 54124 • 1,303
Gillette, WY 82716–17 • 17,635
Gilliam □, OR • 1,717
Gilman, IL 60938 • 1,816
Gilman, VT 05904 • 500
Gilmer, TX 75644 • 4,822
Gilmer □, GA • 13,368
Gilmer □, WV • 7,669
Gilpin □, CO • 3,070
Gilroy, CA 95020–21 • 31,487
Girard, IL 62640 • 2,164
Girard, KS 66743 • 2,794
Girard, OH 44420 • 11,304
Girard, PA 16417 • 2,879
Girardville, PA 17935 • 1,889
Glacier □, MT • 12,121
Glades □, FL • 7,591
Glade Spring, VA 24340 • 1,435
Gladeview, FL 33138 • 15,637
Gladewater, TX 75647 • 6,027
Gladstone, MI 49837 • 4,565
Gladstone, MO 64118 • 26,243
Gladstone, NJ 07934 • 2,111
Gladstone, OR 97027 • 10,152
Gladwin, MI 48624 • 2,682
Gladwin □, MI • 21,896
Glasco, NY 12432 • 1,538
Glascock □, GA • 2,357
Glasford, IL 61533 • 1,115
Glasgow, KY 42141–42 • 12,351
Glasgow, MO 65254 • 1,295
Glasgow, MT 59230 • 3,572
Glasgow, VA 24555 • 1,140
Glasgow Village, MO 63137 • 5,199
Glassboro, NJ 08028 • 15,614
Glasscock □, TX • 1,447
Glassport, PA 15045 • 5,582
Glastonbury, CT 06033 • 7,082
Gleason, TN 38229 • 1,402
Glen Allen, VA 23060 • 9,010
Glen Avon, CA • 12,663
Glenbrook, NV 89413 • 400
Glen Burnie, MD 21061 • 37,305
Glen Burnie Park, MD 21061 • 3,260
Glen Carbon, IL 62034 • 7,731
Glencoe, AL 35905 • 4,670
Glencoe, IL 60022 • 8,499
Glencoe, MN 55336 • 4,648
Glen Cove, NY 11542 • 24,149

Glendale, AZ 85301–12 • 148,134
Glendale, CA 91201–14 • 180,038
Glendale, CO 80222 • 2,453
Glendale, MS 39401 • 1,329
Glendale, MO 63122 • 5,945
Glendale, OH 45246 • 2,445
Glendale, RI 02826 • 700
Glendale, SC 29346 • 1,049
Glen Dale, WV 26038 • 1,612
Glendale, WI 53209 • 14,088
Glendale Heights, IL 60139 • 27,973
Glendive, MT 59330 • 4,802
Glendo, WY 82213 • 195
Glendola, NJ 07719 • 2,340
Glendora, CA 91740 • 47,828
Glendora, NJ 08029 • 5,201
Glen Ellyn, IL 60137–38 • 24,944
Glen Gardner, NJ 08826 • 1,665
Glenham, NY 12527 • 2,832
Glen Head, NY 11545 • 6,870
Glen Lyon, PA 18617 • 2,082
Glenmora, LA 71433 • 1,686
Glenn □, CA • 24,798
Glennallen, AK 99588 • 451
Glenn Dale, MD 20769 • 9,689
Glenns Ferry, ID 83623 • 1,304
Glennville, GA 30427 • 3,676
Glenolden, PA 19036 • 7,260
Glenpool, OK 74033 • 6,688
Glen Raven, NC 27215 • 2,616
Glen Ridge, NJ 07028 • 7,076
Glen Rock, NJ 07452 • 10,883
Glen Rock, PA 17327 • 1,688
Glenrock, WY 82637 • 2,153
Glen Rose, TX 76043 • 1,949
Glens Falls, NY 12801 • 15,023
Glenside, PA 19038 • 8,704
Glen Ullin, ND 58631 • 927
Glenview, IL 60025 • 37,093
Glenville, WV 26351 • 1,923
Glenwood, AR 71943 • 1,354
Glenwood, IL 60425 • 9,289
Glenwood, IA 51534 • 4,571
Glenwood, MN 56334 • 2,573
Glenwood, VA 24541 • 2,276
Glenwood City, WI 54013 • 1,026
Glenwood Farms, VA 23223 • 3,200
Glenwood Hills, GA 30032 • 5,240
Glenwood Springs, CO 81601–02 • 6,561
Glidden, IA 51443 • 1,099
Globe, AZ 85501–02 • 6,062
Gloster, MS 39638 • 1,323
Gloucester, MA 01930–31 • 28,716
Gloucester, VA 23061 • 1,200
Gloucester □, NJ • 230,082
Gloucester □, VA • 30,131
Gloucester City, NJ 08030 • 12,649
Gloucester Point, VA 23062 • 8,509
Glouster, OH 45732 • 2,001
Gloversville, NY 12078 • 16,656
Gloverville, SC 29828 • 2,753
Glynn □, GA • 62,496
Gnadenhutten, OH 44629 • 1,226
Goddard, KS 67052 • 1,804
Godfrey, IL 62035 • 5,436
Goffstown, NH 03045 • 2,700
Gogebic □, MI • 18,052
Golconda, NV 89414 • 200
Gold Bar, WA 98251 • 1,078
Gold Beach, OR 97444 • 1,546
Golden, CO 80401–03 • 13,116
Goldendale, WA 98620 • 3,319
Golden Gate, FL 33999 • 14,148
Golden Glades, FL 33055 • 25,474
Golden Meadow, LA 70357 • 2,049
Golden Valley, MN 55427 • 20,971
Golden Valley □, MT • 912
Golden Valley □, ND • 2,108
Goldfield, NV 89013 • 600
Goldsboro, NC 27530–34 • 40,709
Goldthwaite, TX 76844 • 1,658
Goleta, CA 93117 • 28,600
Golf Manor, OH 45237 • 4,154
Goliad, TX 77963 • 1,946
Goliad □, TX • 5,980
Gonzales, CA 93926 • 4,660
Gonzales, LA 70737 • 7,003
Gonzales, TX 78629 • 6,527
Gonzales □, TX • 17,205
Gonzalez, FL 32560 • 7,669
Goochland □, VA • 14,163
Goodhue □, MN • 40,690
Gooding, ID 83330 • 2,820
Gooding □, ID • 11,633
Goodland, FL 33933 • 1,000
Goodland, IN 47948 • 1,033
Goodland, KS 67735 • 4,983
Goodlettsville, TN 37072 • 11,219
Goodman, MS 39079 • 1,256
Goodman, MO 64843 • 1,094
Goodsprings, NV 89019 • 150
Goodview, MN 55987 • 2,878
Goodwater, AL 35072 • 1,040
Goodwell, OK 73939 • 1,065
Goodyear, AZ 85338 • 6,258
Goose Creek, SC 29445 • 24,692
Gordo, AL 35466 • 1,918
Gordon, GA 31031 • 2,468
Gordon, NE 69343 • 1,803
Gordon □, GA • 35,072
Gordonsville, VA 22942 • 1,351
Gorham, ME 04038 • 3,618
Gorham, NH 03581 • 1,910
Gorman, TX 76454 • 1,290
Goshen, IN 46526 • 23,797
Goshen, NY 10924 • 5,255
Goshen, OH 45122 • 1,400
Goshen □, WY • 12,373
Gosnell, AR 72319 • 3,783
Gosper □, NE • 1,928
Gothenburg, NE 69138 • 3,232
Gould, AR 71643 • 1,470
Goulding, FL 32503 • 4,159
Goulds, FL 33170 • 7,284
Gouverneur, NY 13642 • 4,604
Gove □, KS • 3,231
Gowanda, NY 14070 • 2,901
Gower, MO 64454 • 1,249
Gowrie, IA 50543 • 1,028
Grace, ID 83241 • 973
Graceville, FL 32440 • 2,675
Gracewood, GA 30812 • 1,000
Grady □, GA • 20,279
Grady □, OK • 41,747
Grafton, MA 01519 • 1,520
Grafton, ND 58237 • 4,840
Grafton, OH 44044 • 3,344
Grafton, WV 26354 • 5,524
Grafton, WI 53024 • 9,340
Grafton □, NH • 74,929
Graham, CA 90002 • 10,600
Graham, NC 27253 • 10,426
Graham, TX 76046 • 8,986
Graham □, AZ • 26,554
Graham □, KS • 3,543
Graham □, NC • 7,196
Grainger □, TN • 17,095
Grain Valley, MO 64029 • 1,898
Grambling, LA 71245 • 5,484
Gramercy, LA 70052 • 2,412
Granbury, TX 76048–49 • 4,045
Granby, CT 06035 • 9,369
Granby, MA 01033 • 1,327
Granby, MO 64844 • 1,945
Grand □, CO • 7,966
Grand □, UT • 6,620
Grand Bay, AL 36541 • 3,383
Grand Blanc, MI 48439 • 7,760
Grand Caillou, LA 70360 • 1,400
Grand Canyon, AZ 86023 • 1,499
Grand Coteau, LA 70541 • 1,118
Grandfield, OK 73546 • 1,224
Grand Forks, ND 58201–06 • 49,425
Grand Forks □, ND • 70,683
Grand Haven, MI 49417 • 11,951
Grand Island, NE 68801–03 • 39,386
Grand Isle, LA 70358 • 1,455
Grand Isle □, VT • 5,318
Grand Junction, CO 81501–06 • 29,034
Grand Ledge, MI 48837 • 7,579
Grand Marais, MN 55604 • 1,171
Grand Prairie, TX 75050–54 • 99,616
Grand Rapids, MI 49501–99 • 189,126
Grand Rapids, MN 55744 • 7,976
Grand Saline, TX 75140 • 2,630
Grand Terrace, CA 92324 • 10,946
Grand Traverse □, MI • 64,273
Grandview, MO 64030 • 24,967
Grandview, WA 98930 • 7,169
Grandview Heights, OH 43212 • 7,010
Grandville, MI 49418 • 15,624
Granger, IN 46530 • 20,241
Granger, TX 76530 • 1,190
Granger, WA 98932 • 2,053
Grangeville, ID 83530 • 3,226
Granite, OK 73547 • 1,844
Granite □, MT • 2,548
Granite City, IL 62040 • 32,862
Granite Falls, MN 56241 • 3,083
Granite Falls, NC 28630 • 3,253
Granite Falls, WA 98252 • 1,060
Granite Quarry, NC 28072 • 1,646
Graniteville, MA 01886 • 1,010
Graniteville, SC 29829 • 1,158
Graniteville, VT 05654 • 500
Grant, NE 69140 • 1,239
Grant □, AR • 13,948
Grant □, IN • 74,169
Grant □, KS • 7,159
Grant □, KY • 15,737
Grant □, LA • 17,526
Grant □, MN • 6,246
Grant □, NE • 769
Grant □, NM • 27,676
Grant □, ND • 3,549
Grant □, OK • 5,689
Grant □, OR • 7,853
Grant □, SD • 8,372
Grant □, WA • 54,758
Grant □, WV • 10,428
Grant □, WI • 49,264
Grant Park, IL 60940 • 1,024
Grants, NM 87020 • 8,626
Grantsburg, WI 54840 • 1,144
Grants Pass, OR 97526–27 • 17,488
Grantsville, UT 84029 • 4,500
Grantville, GA 30220 • 1,180
Granville, IL 61326 • 1,407
Granville, NY 12832 • 2,646
Granville, OH 43023 • 4,353
Granville □, NC • 38,345
Grapeland, TX 75844 • 1,450
Grapevine, TX 76051 • 29,202
Grasonville, MD 21638 • 2,439
Grass Lake, IL 60002 • 2,191
Grass Valley, CA 95945 • 9,048
Gratiot □, MI • 38,982
Graves □, KY • 33,550
Gravette, AR 72736 • 1,412
Gray, GA 31032 • 2,189
Gray, LA 70359 • 1,500
Gray □, KS • 5,396
Gray □, TX • 23,967
Grayling, MI 49738 • 1,944
Graylyn Crest, DE 19810 • 4,380
Grays Harbor □, WA • 64,175
Grayslake, IL 60030 • 7,388
Grayson, KY 41143 • 3,510
Grayson □, KY • 21,050
Grayson □, TX • 95,021
Grayson □, VA • 16,278
Graysville, AL 35073 • 2,241
Graysville, TN 37338 • 1,301
Grayville, IL 62844 • 2,043
Great Barrington, MA 01230 • 2,810
Great Bend, KS 67530 • 15,427
Great Falls, MT 59401–06 • 55,097
Great Falls, SC 29055 • 2,307
Great Falls, VA 22066 • 6,945
Great Neck, NY 11020–27 • 8,745
Great Neck Estates, NY 11021 • 2,790
Greece, NY 14626 • 15,632
Greece, NY • 15,632
Greeley, CO 80631–34 • 60,536
Greeley □, KS • 1,774
Greeley □, NE • 3,006
Green, OR 97470 • 5,076
Green □, KY • 10,371
Green □, WI • 30,339
Greenacres, CA 93308 • 7,379
Green Acres, DE 19803 • 1,140
Greenacres, WA 99016 • 4,250
Greenacres City, FL 33463 • 18,683
Green Bay, WI 54301–24 • 96,466
Greenbelt, MD 20770 • 21,096
Greenbriar, VA 22033 • 6,200
Greenbrier, AR 72058 • 2,130
Green Brier, TN 37073 • 2,873
Greenbrier □, WV • 34,693
Green Brook, NJ 08812 • 2,380
Greencastle, IN 46135 • 8,984
Greencastle, PA 17225 • 3,600
Green Cove Springs, FL 32043 • 4,497
Greendale, IN 47025 • 3,881
Greendale, WI 53129 • 15,128
Greene, IA 50636 • 1,142
Greene, NY 13778 • 1,812
Greene □, AL • 10,153
Greene □, AR • 31,804
Greene □, GA • 11,793
Greene □, IL • 15,317
Greene □, IN • 30,410
Greene □, IA • 10,045
Greene □, MS • 10,220
Greene □, MO • 207,949
Greene □, NY • 44,739
Greene □, NC • 15,384
Greene □, OH • 136,731
Greene □, PA • 39,550
Greene □, TN • 55,853
Greene □, VA • 10,297
Greeneville, TN 37743–44 • 13,532
Greenfield, CA 93927 • 7,464
Greenfield, IL 62044 • 1,162
Greenfield, IN 46140 • 11,657
Greenfield, IA 50849 • 2,074
Greenfield, MA 01301–02 • 14,016
Greenfield, MO 65661 • 1,416
Greenfield, OH 45123 • 5,172
Greenfield, TN 38230 • 2,105
Greenfield, WI 53220 • 33,403
Greenfield Plaza, IA 50315 • 2,200
Green Forest, AR 72638 • 2,050
Green Harbor, MA 02041 • 1,900
Greenhills, OH 45218 • 4,393
Green Island, NY 12183 • 2,490
Green Lake, WI 54941 • 1,064
Green Lake □, WI • 18,651
Greenlawn, NY 11740 • 13,208
Greenlee □, AZ • 8,008
Greenock, PA 15047 • 2,500
Greenport, NY 11944 • 2,070
Green River, WY 82935 • 12,711
Green Rock, IL 61241 • 2,615
Greensboro, AL 36744 • 3,047
Greensboro, GA 30642 • 2,860
Greensboro, MD 21639 • 1,441
Greensboro, NC 27401–95 • 183,521
Greensburg, IN 47240 • 9,286
Greensburg, KS 67054 • 1,792
Greensburg, KY 42743 • 1,990
Greensburg, PA 15601 • 16,318
Green Springs, OH 44836 • 1,446
Greensville □, VA • 8,853
Greentown, IN 46936 • 2,172
Green Tree, PA 15220 • 4,905
Greenup, IL 62428 • 1,616
Greenup, KY 41144 • 1,158
Greenup □, KY • 36,742
Green Valley, AZ 85614 • 13,231
Green Valley, MD 21771 • 9,424
Greenview, SC 29203 • 5,515
Greenville, AL 36037 • 7,492
Greenville, CA 95947 • 1,396
Greenville, DE 19807 • 800
Greenville, GA 30222 • 1,167
Greenville, IL 62246 • 4,806
Greenville, KY 42345 • 4,689
Greenville, ME 04441 • 1,601
Greenville, MI 48838 • 8,101
Greenville, MS 38701–04 • 45,226
Greenville, NH 03048 • 1,135
Greenville, NY 10583 • 9,528
Greenville, NC 27834–36 • 44,972
Greenville, OH 45331 • 12,863
Greenville, PA 16125 • 6,734
Greenville, RI 02828 • 8,303
Greenville, SC 29601–16 • 58,282
Greenville, TX 75401–03 • 23,071
Greenville □, SC • 320,167
Greenwich, CT 06830–36 • 58,441
Greenwich, NY 12834 • 1,961
Greenwich, OH 44837 • 1,442
Greenwood, AR 72936 • 3,984
Greenwood, DE 19950 • 578
Greenwood, IN 46142 • 26,265
Greenwood, LA 71033 • 2,092
Greenwood, MS 38930 • 18,906
Greenwood, MO 64034 • 1,505
Greenwood, PA 16601 • 1,650
Greenwood, SC 29646–49 • 20,807
Greenwood □, KS • 7,847
Greenwood □, SC • 59,567
Greenwood Lake, NY 10925 • 3,208
Greenwood Village, CO 80111 • 7,589
Greer, SC 29650–52 • 10,322
Greer □, OK • 6,559
Gregg □, TX • 104,948
Gregory, SD 57533 • 1,384
Gregory □, SD • 5,359
Greilickville, MI 49684 • 1,060
Grenada, MS 38901 • 10,864
Grenada □, MS • 21,555
Gresham, OR 97030 • 68,235
Gresham Park, GA 30316 • 9,000
Gretna, FL 32332 • 1,981
Gretna, LA 70053–54 • 17,208
Gretna, NE 68028 • 2,249
Gretna, VA 24557 • 1,339
Greybull, WY 82426 • 1,789
Gridley, CA 95948 • 4,631
Gridley, IL 61744 • 1,304
Griffin, GA 30223–24 • 21,347
Griffith, IN 46319 • 17,916
Grifton, NC 28530 • 2,393
Griggs □, ND • 3,303
Griggsville, IL 62340 • 1,218
Grimes, IA 50111 • 2,653
Grimes □, TX • 18,828
Grindall Creek, VA 23234 • 1,710
Grinnell, IA 50112 • 8,902
Griswold, IA 51535 • 1,049
Groesbeck, OH 45239 • 6,684
Groesbeck, TX 76642 • 3,185
Grosse Ile, MI 48138 • 9,781
Grosse Pointe, MI 48236 • 5,681
Grosse Pointe Farms, MI 48236 • 10,092
Grosse Pointe Park, MI 48230 • 12,857
Grosse Pointe Woods, MI 48225 • 17,715
Grossmont, CA 91941 • 2,600
Groton, CT 06340 • 9,837
Groton, MA 01450 • 1,044
Groton, NY 13073 • 2,398
Groton, SD 57445 • 1,196
Grottoes, VA 24441 • 1,455
Grove, OK 74344 • 4,020
Grove City, FL 34224 • 2,374
Grove City, OH 43123 • 19,661
Grove City, PA 16127 • 8,240
Grove Hill, AL 36451 • 1,551
Groveland, FL 34736 • 2,300
Groveland, MA 01834 • 3,780
Groveport, OH 43125 • 2,948
Grover City, CA 93433 • 11,656
Groves, TX 77619 • 16,513
Groveton, NH 03582 • 1,255
Groveton, TX 75845 • 1,071
Groveton, VA 22303 • 19,997
Groveton Gardens, VA 22303 • 2,600
Grovetown, GA 30813 • 3,596
Groveville, NJ 08620 • 2,900
Gruetli-Laager, TN 37339 • 1,810
Grulla, TX 78548 • 1,335
Grundy, VA 24614 • 1,305
Grundy □, IL • 32,337
Grundy □, IA • 12,029
Grundy □, MO • 10,536
Grundy □, TN • 13,362
Grundy Center, IA 50638 • 2,491
Gruver, TX 79040 • 1,172
Guadalupe, AZ 85283 • 5,458
Guadalupe, CA 93434 • 5,479
Guadalupe □, NM • 4,156
Guadalupe □, TX • 64,873
Guernsey, WY 82214 • 1,155
Guernsey □, OH • 39,024
Gueydan, LA 70542 • 1,611
Guilford, CT 06437 • 2,588
Guilford, ME 04443 • 1,082
Guilford □, NC • 347,420
Guin, AL 35563 • 2,464
Gulf □, FL • 11,504
Gulf Breeze, FL 32561 • 5,530
Gulf Gate Estates, FL 34231 • 11,622
Gulfport, FL 33707 • 11,727
Gulfport, MS 39501–07 • 40,775
Gulf Shores, AL 36542 • 3,261
Gumboro, DE 19945 • 200
Gunnison, CO 81230 • 4,636
Gunnison, UT 84634 • 1,298
Gunnison □, CO • 10,273
Guntersville, AL 35976 • 7,038
Gurdon, AR 71743 • 2,199
Gurley, AL 35748 • 1,007
Gurnee, IL 60031 • 13,701
Gustine, CA 95322 • 3,931
Guthrie, KY 42234 • 1,504
Guthrie, OK 73044 • 10,518
Guthrie □, IA • 10,935
Guthrie Center, IA 50115 • 1,614
Guttenberg, IA 52052 • 2,257
Guttenberg, NJ 07093 • 8,268
Guymon, OK 73942 • 7,803
Gwinhurst, DE 19809 • 1,340
Gwinn, MI 49841 • 2,370
Gwinner, ND 58040 • 585
Gwinnett □, GA • 352,910
Gypsum, CO 81637 • 1,750

H

Haakon □, SD • 2,624
Habersham □, GA • 27,621
Hacienda Heights, CA 91745 • 52,354
Hackensack, NJ 07601–08 • 37,049
Hackettstown, NJ 07840 • 8,120
Hackleburg, AL 35564 • 1,161
Haddam, CT 06438 • 1,200
Haddonfield, NJ 08033 • 11,628
Haddon Heights, NJ 08035 • 7,860
Hadlock, WA 98339 • 1,752
Hagerman, NM 88232 • 961
Hagerstown, IN 47346 • 1,835
Hagerstown, MD 21740 • 35,445
Hahira, GA 31632 • 1,353
Hahnville, LA 70057 • 2,599
Hailey, ID 83333 • 3,687
Haines, AK 99827 • 1,238
Haines City, FL 33844 • 11,683
Hainesport, NJ 08036 • 1,250
Halawa Heights, HI 96701 • 7,000
Hale □, AL • 15,498
Hale □, TX • 34,671
Hale Center, TX 79041 • 2,067
Haledon, NJ 07508 • 6,951
Haleiwa, HI 96712 • 2,442
Hales Corners, WI 53130 • 7,623
Halethorpe, MD 21227 • 19,750
Haleyville, AL 35565 • 4,452
Half Hollow Hills, NY 11746 • 5,110
Half Moon, NC 28540 • 6,306
Half Moon Bay, CA 94019 • 8,886
Halfway, MD 21740 • 8,873
Halifax □, NC • 55,516
Halifax □, VA • 29,033
Haliimaile, HI 96768 • 841
Hall □, GA • 95,428
Hall □, NE • 48,925
Hall □, TX • 3,905
Hallandale, FL 33009 • 30,996
Hallettsville, TX 77964 • 2,718
Hallie, WI 54729 • 1,300
Hallock, MN 56728 • 1,304
Hallowell, ME 04347 • 2,534
Halls, TN 37918 • 6,450
Halls, TN 38040 • 2,431
Halls Crossroads, TN 37918 • 1,900
Hallstead, PA 18822 • 1,274
Hallsville, TX 75650 • 2,288
Halstead, KS 67056 • 2,015
Haltom City, TX 76117 • 32,856
Hamblen □, TN • 50,480
Hamburg, AR 71646 • 3,098
Hamburg, IA 51640 • 1,248
Hamburg, NJ 07419 • 2,566
Hamburg, NY 14075 • 10,442
Hamburg, PA 19526 • 3,987
Hamden, CT 06514 • 52,434
Hamel, MN 55340 • 3,096
Hamilton, AL 35570 • 5,787
Hamilton, IL 62341 • 3,281
Hamilton, MA 01936 • 1,000
Hamilton, MI 49419 • 1,000
Hamilton, MO 64644 • 1,737
Hamilton, MT 59840 • 2,737
Hamilton, NY 13346 • 3,790
Hamilton, OH 45011–18 • 61,368
Hamilton, TX 76531 • 2,937
Hamilton □, FL • 10,930
Hamilton □, IL • 8,499
Hamilton □, IN • 108,936
Hamilton □, IA • 16,071
Hamilton □, KS • 2,388
Hamilton □, NE • 8,862
Hamilton □, NY • 5,279
Hamilton □, OH • 866,228
Hamilton □, TN • 285,536
Hamilton □, TX • 7,733
Hamilton City, CA 95951 • 1,811
Hamilton Square, NJ 08690 • 10,970
Ham Lake, MN 55304 • 8,924
Hamlet, NC 28345 • 6,196
Hamlin, TX 79520 • 2,791
Hamlin, WV 25523 • 1,030
Hamlin □, SD • 4,974
Hammond, IN 46320–27 • 84,236
Hammond, LA 70401–04 • 15,871
Hammond, WI 54015 • 1,097
Hammonton, NJ 08037 • 12,208
Hampden, ME 04444 • 3,895
Hampden □, MA • 456,310
Hampden Highlands, ME 04444 • 1,540
Hampshire, IL 60140 • 1,843
Hampshire □, MA • 146,568
Hampshire □, WV • 16,498
Hampstead, MD 21074 • 2,608
Hampton, AR 71744 • 1,562
Hampton, GA 30228 • 2,694
Hampton, IA 50441 • 4,133
Hampton, NH 03842 • 7,989
Hampton, NJ 08827 • 1,515
Hampton, SC 29924 • 2,997
Hampton, TN 37658 • 2,236
Hampton, VA 23651–70 • 133,793
Hampton □, SC • 18,191
Hampton Bays, NY 11946 • 7,893
Hamtramck, MI 48212 • 18,372
Hana, HI 96713 • 683
Hanahan, SC 29406 • 13,176
Hanamaulu, HI 96715 • 3,611
Hanapepe, HI 96716 • 1,395
Hanceville, AL 35077 • 2,246
Hancock, MD 21750 • 1,926
Hancock, MI 49930 • 4,547
Hancock, NY 13783 • 1,330
Hancock □, GA • 8,908
Hancock □, IL • 21,373
Hancock □, IN • 45,527
Hancock □, IA • 12,638
Hancock □, KY • 7,864
Hancock □, ME • 46,948
Hancock □, MS • 31,760
Hancock □, OH • 65,536
Hancock □, TN • 6,739
Hancock □, WV • 35,233
Hand □, SD • 4,272
Hanford, CA 93230–32 • 30,897
Hankinson, ND 58041 • 1,038
Hanna, WY 82327 • 1,076
Hanna City, IL 61536 • 1,205
Hannibal, MO 63401 • 18,004
Hanover, IN 47243 • 3,610
Hanover, MA 02339 • 2,500
Hanover, NH 03755 • 6,538
Hanover, PA 17331 • 14,399
Hanover □, VA • 63,306
Hanover Center, MA 02339 • 1,000
Hanover Park, IL 60103 • 32,895
Hanover Township, NJ 07981 • 11,538
Hansen, ID 83334 • 848
Hansford □, TX • 5,848
Hanson, MA 02341 • 2,188
Hanson □, SD • 2,994
Hapeville, GA 30354 • 5,483
Happy Valley, OR 97236 • 1,519
Harahan, LA 70123 • 9,927
Haralson □, GA • 21,966
Harbeson, DE 19951 • 500
Harbor, OR 97415 • 2,143
Harbor Beach, MI 48441 • 2,089
Harborcreek, PA 16421 • 1,500
Harbor Springs, MI 49740 • 1,540
Hardee □, FL • 19,499
Hardeeville, SC 29927 • 1,583
Hardeman □, TN • 23,377
Hardeman □, TX • 5,283
Hardin, IL 62047 • 1,071
Hardin, MT 59034 • 2,940
Hardin □, IL • 5,189
Hardin □, IA • 19,094
Hardin □, KY • 89,240
Hardin □, OH • 31,111
Hardin □, TN • 22,633
Hardin □, TX • 41,320
Harding □, NM • 987
Harding □, SD • 1,669
Hardinsburg, KY 40143 • 1,900
Hardwick, GA 31034 • 8,800
Hardwick, VT 05843 • 1,400
Hardy □, WV • 10,977
Harford □, MD • 182,132
Hargill, TX 78549 • 1,030
Harker Heights, TX 76543 • 12,841
Harkers Island, NC 28531 • 1,759
Harlan, IN 46743 • 1,200
Harlan, IA 51537 • 5,148
Harlan, KY 40831 • 2,686
Harlan □, KY • 36,574
Harlan □, NE • 3,810
Harlem, FL 33440 • 2,826
Harlem, GA 30814 • 2,199
Harlem, MT 59526 • 882
Harleysville, PA 19438 • 7,405
Harlingen, TX 78550–52 • 48,735
Harlowton, MT 59036 • 1,049
Harmon □, OK • 3,793
Harmony, MN 55939 • 1,081
Harmony, PA 16037 • 1,054
Harmony, RI 02829 • 820
Harnett □, NC • 67,822
Harney □, OR • 7,060
Harper, KS 67058 • 1,735
Harper □, KS • 7,124

Harper □, OK • *4,063*
Harpers Ferry, WV 25425 • *308*
Harper Woods, MI 48225 • *14,903*
Harrah, OK 73045 • *4,206*
Harriman, TN 37748 • *7,119*
Harrington, DE 19952 • *2,311*
Harrington Park, NJ 07640 • *4,623*
Harris, RI 02816 • *1,050*
Harris □, GA • *17,788*
Harris □, TX • *2,818,199*
Harrisburg, AR 72432 • *1,943*
Harrisburg, IL 62946 • *9,289*
Harrisburg, OR 97446 • *1,939*
Harrisburg, PA 17101–13 • *52,376*
Harris Hill, NY 14221 • *4,577*
Harrison, AR 72601–02 • *9,922*
Harrison, MI 48625 • *1,835*
Harrison, NJ 07029 • *13,425*
Harrison, NY 10528 • *23,308*
Harrison, OH 45030 • *7,518*
Harrison, TN 37341 • *7,191*
Harrison □, IN • *29,890*
Harrison □, IA • *14,730*
Harrison □, KY • *16,248*
Harrison □, MS • *165,365*
Harrison □, MO • *8,469*
Harrison □, OH • *16,085*
Harrison □, TX • *57,483*
Harrison □, WV • *69,371*
Harrisonburg, VA 22801 • *30,707*
Harrison Township, MI 48045 • *24,685*
Harrisonville, MO 64701 • *7,683*
Harristown, IL 62537 • *1,319*
Harrisville, RI 02830 • *1,654*
Harrisville, UT 84404 • *3,004*
Harrisville, WV 26362 • *1,839*
Harrodsburg, KY 40330 • *7,335*
Hart, MI 49420 • *1,942*
Hart, TX 79043 • *1,221*
Hart □, GA • *19,712*
Hart □, KY • *14,890*
Hartford, AL 36344 • *2,448*
Hartford, CT 06101–99 • *139,739*
Hartford, IL 62048 • *1,676*
Hartford, KY 42347 • *2,532*
Hartford, MI 49057 • *2,341*
Hartford, SD 57033 • *1,262*
Hartford, VT 05047 • *500*
Hartford, WI 53027 • *8,188*
Hartford □, CT • *851,783*
Hartford City, IN 47348 • *6,960*
Hartington, NE 68739 • *1,583*
Hartland, ME 04943 • *1,038*
Hartland, WI 53029 • *6,906*
Hartley, IA 51346 • *1,632*
Hartley □, TX • *3,634*
Hartsdale, NY 10530 • *9,587*
Hartselle, AL 35640 • *10,795*
Hartshorne, OK 74547 • *2,120*
Hartsville, SC 29550 • *8,372*
Hartsville, TN 37074 • *2,188*
Hartville, OH 44632 • *2,031*
Hartwell, GA 30643 • *4,555*
Harvard, IL 60033 • *5,975*
Harvard, MA 01451 • *1,200*
Harvey, IL 60426 • *29,771*
Harvey, LA 70058 • *21,222*
Harvey, MI 49855 • *1,377*
Harvey, ND 58341 • *2,263*
Harvey □, KS • *31,028*
Harwich, MA 02645 • *4,399*
Harwich Port, MA 02646 • *2,300*
Harwinton, CT 06791 • *5,228*
Harwood Heights, IL 60656 • *7,680*
Hasbrouck Heights, NJ 07604 • *11,488*
Haskell, AR 72015 • *1,342*
Haskell, OK 74436 • *2,143*
Haskell, TX 79521 • *3,362*
Haskell □, KS • *3,886*
Haskell □, OK • *10,940*
Haskell □, TX • *6,820*
Haslett, MI 48840 • *10,230*
Hastings, MI 49058 • *6,549*
Hastings, MN 55033 • *15,445*
Hastings, NE 68901–02 • *22,837*
Hastings, PA 16646 • *1,431*
Hastings-on-Hudson, NY 10706 • *8,000*
Hatboro, PA 19040 • *7,382*
Hatch, NM 87937 • *1,136*
Hatfield, MA 01038 • *1,234*
Hatfield, PA 19440 • *2,650*
Hatteras, NC 27943 • *1,660*
Hattiesburg, MS 39401–07 • *41,882*
Hatton, ND 58240 • *800*
Haubstadt, IN 47639 • *1,455*
Haughton, LA 71037 • *1,664*
Hauppauge, NY 11788 • *19,750*
Hauula, HI 96717 • *3,479*
Havana, FL 32333 • *1,654*
Havana, IL 62644 • *3,610*
Havelock, NC 28532 • *20,268*
Haven, KS 67543 • *1,198*
Haverford [Township], PA 19083 • *52,371*
Haverhill, MA 01830–35 • *51,418*
Haverstraw, NY 10927 • *9,438*
Havre, MT 59501 • *10,201*
Havre de Grace, MD 21078 • *8,952*
Havre North, MT 59501 • *1,110*
Hawaii □, HI • *120,317*
Hawaiian Gardens, CA 90716 • *13,639*
Hawarden, IA 51023 • *2,439*
Hawi, HI 96719 • *924*
Hawkins □, TN • *44,565*
Hawkinsville, GA 31036 • *3,527*
Hawley, MN 56549 • *1,655*
Hawley, PA 18428 • *1,244*
Haworth, NJ 07641 • *3,384*
Haw River, NC 27258 • *1,855*
Hawthorne, CA 90250–51 • *71,349*
Hawthorne, FL 32640 • *1,305*
Hawthorne, NV 89415–16 • *4,162*
Hawthorne, NJ 07506 • *17,084*
Hawthorne, NY 10532 • *4,764*
Hayden, CO 81639 • *1,444*
Hayden, ID 83835 • *3,744*
Hayes □, NE • *1,222*
Hayesville, OR 97303 • *14,318*
Hayfield, MN 55940 • *1,283*
Hayfield, VA 22310 • *2,300*
Hayfork, CA 96041 • *2,605*
Haynesville, LA 71038 • *2,854*
Hays, KS 67601 • *17,767*
Hays □, TX • *65,614*
Haysville, KS 67060 • *8,364*
Hayti, MO 63851 • *3,280*
Hayward, CA 94540–46 • *111,498*
Hayward, WI 54843 • *1,897*
Hayward Addition, SD 57106 • *1,000*
Haywood □, NC • *46,942*
Haywood □, TN • *19,437*
Hazard, KY 41701 • *5,416*
Hazardville, CT 06082 • *5,179*
Hazel Crest, IL 60429 • *13,334*
Hazel Dell, WA 98660 • *15,386*
Hazel Green, AL 35750 • *2,208*
Hazel Green, WI 53811 • *1,171*
Hazel Park, MI 48030 • *20,051*
Hazelwood, MO 63042–45 • *15,324*
Hazelwood, NC 28738 • *1,678*
Hazen, AR 72064 • *1,668*
Hazen, ND 58545 • *2,818*
Hazlehurst, GA 31539 • *4,202*
Hazlehurst, MS 39083 • *4,221*
Hazlet, NJ 07730 • *23,013*
Hazleton, PA 18201 • *24,730*
Headland, AL 36345 • *3,266*
Healdsburg, CA 95448 • *9,469*
Healdton, OK 73438 • *2,872*
Healy, AK 99743 • *487*
Heard □, GA • *8,628*
Hearne, TX 77859 • *5,132*
Heath, OH 43056 • *7,231*
Heavener, OK 74937 • *2,601*
Hebbronville, TX 78361 • *4,465*
Heber City, UT 84032 • *4,782*
Heber Springs, AR 72543 • *5,628*
Hebron, IN 46341 • *3,183*
Hebron, KY 41048 • *1,200*
Hebron, NE 68370 • *1,765*
Hebron, ND 58638 • *888*
Hebron, OH 43025 • *2,076*
Hector, MN 55342 • *1,145*
Heeia, HI 96744 • *5,010*
Heflin, AL 36264 • *2,906*
Hegins, PA 17938 • *1,200*
Helena, AL 35080 • *3,918*
Helena, AR 72342 • *7,491*
Helena, GA 31037 • *1,256*
Helena, MT 59601–26 • *24,569*
Helena, OK 73741 • *1,043*
Hellam, PA 17406 • *1,375*
Hellertown, PA 18055 • *5,662*
Helmetta, NJ 08828 • *1,211*
Helotes, TX 78023 • *1,535*
Helper, UT 84526 • *2,148*
Hemet, CA 92343–44 • *36,094*
Hemlock, MI 48626 • *1,601*
Hemphill, TX 75948 • *1,182*
Hemphill □, TX • *3,720*
Hempstead, NY 11550–54 • *49,453*
Hempstead, TX 77445 • *3,551*
Hempstead □, AR • *21,621*
Henagar, AL 35978 • *1,934*
Henderson, KY 42420 • *25,945*
Henderson, LA 70517 • *1,543*
Henderson, NV 89015–16 • *64,942*
Henderson, NC 27536 • *15,655*
Henderson, TN 38340 • *4,760*
Henderson, TX 75652–53 • *11,139*
Henderson □, IL • *8,096*
Henderson □, KY • *43,044*
Henderson □, NC • *69,285*
Henderson □, TN • *21,844*
Henderson □, TX • *58,543*
Henderson's Point, MS 39571 • *1,114*
Hendersonville, NC 28739 • *7,284*
Hendersonville, TN 37075 • *32,188*
Hendricks □, IN • *75,717*
Hendry □, FL • *25,773*
Hennepin □, MN • *1,032,431*
Hennessey, OK 73742 • *1,902*
Henniker, NH 03242 • *1,693*
Henrico □, VA • *217,881*
Henrietta, NY 14467 • *1,200*
Henrietta, NC 28076 • *1,412*
Henrietta, TX 76365 • *2,896*
Henry, IL 61537 • *2,591*
Henry □, AL • *15,374*
Henry □, GA • *58,741*
Henry □, IL • *51,159*
Henry □, IN • *48,139*
Henry □, IA • *19,226*
Henry □, KY • *12,823*
Henry □, MO • *20,044*
Henry □, OH • *29,108*
Henry □, TN • *27,888*
Henry □, VA • *56,942*
Henryetta, OK 74437 • *5,872*
Henryville, IN 47126 • *1,132*
Hephzibah, GA 30815 • *2,466*
Heppner, OR 97836 • *1,412*
Herculaneum, MO 63048 • *2,263*
Hercules, CA 94547 • *16,829*
Hereford, TX 79045 • *14,745*
Herington, KS 67449 • *2,685*
Heritage Village, CT 06488 • *9,700*
Herkimer, NY 13350 • *7,945*
Herkimer □, NY • *65,797*
Hermann, MO 65041 • *2,754*
Hermantown, MN 55811 • *6,761*
Herminie, PA 15637 • *2,000*
Hermiston, OR 97838 • *10,040*
Hermitage, PA 16148 • *15,300*
Hermosa Beach, CA 90254 • *18,219*
Hernando, FL 32642 • *2,103*
Hernando, MS 38632 • *3,125*
Hernando □, FL • *101,115*
Herndon, VA 22070–71 • *16,139*
Herrin, IL 62948 • *10,857*
Herscher, IL 60941 • *1,278*
Hershey, PA 17033 • *11,860*
Hertford, NC 27944 • *2,105*
Hertford □, NC • *22,523*
Hesperia, CA 92345 • *50,418*
Hesston, KS 67062 • *3,012*
Hettinger, ND 58639 • *1,574*
Hettinger □, ND • *3,445*
Hewitt, TX 76643 • *8,983*
Hewlett, NY 11557 • *6,620*
Heyburn, ID 83336 • *2,714*
Heyworth, IL 61745 • *1,627*
Hialeah, FL 33010–16 • *188,004*
Hiawatha, IA 52233 • *4,986*
Hiawatha, KS 66434 • *3,603*
Hibbing, MN 55746–47 • *18,046*
Hickman, KY 42050 • *2,689*
Hickman, NE 68372 • *1,081*
Hickman □, KY • *5,566*
Hickman □, TN • *16,754*
Hickory, NC 28601–03 • *28,301*
Hickory □, MO • *7,335*
Hickory Hills, IL 60457 • *13,021*
Hicksville, NY 11801–05 • *40,174*
Hicksville, OH 43526 • *3,664*
Hico, TX 76457 • *1,342*
Hidalgo, TX 78557 • *3,292*
Hidalgo □, NM • *5,958*
Hidalgo □, TX • *383,545*
Higganum, CT 06441 • *1,692*
Higginsville, MO 64037 • *4,693*
High Bridge, NJ 08829 • *3,886*
Highland, CA 92346 • *34,439*
Highland, IL 62249 • *7,525*
Highland, IN 46322 • *23,696*
Highland, MI 48356–57 • *750*
Highland, NY 12528 • *4,492*
Highland □, OH • *35,728*
Highland □, VA • *2,635*
Highland Falls, NY 10928 • *3,937*
Highland Heights, OH 44124 • *6,249*
Highland Lakes, NJ 07422 • *4,550*
Highland Park, IL 60035 • *30,575*
Highland Park, MI 48203 • *20,121*
Highland Park, NJ 08904 • *13,279*
Highland Park, TX 75205 • *8,739*
Highlands, NJ 07732 • *4,849*
Highlands, TX 77562 • *6,632*
Highlands □, FL • *68,432*
Highland Springs, VA 23075 • *13,823*
Highmore, SD 57345 • *835*
High Point, NC 27260–65 • *69,496*
High Ridge, MO 63049 • *2,380*
High Spire, PA 17034 • *2,668*
High Springs, FL 32643 • *3,144*
Hightstown, NJ 08520 • *5,126*
Highview, KY 40228 • *14,814*
Highwood, IL 60040 • *5,331*
Hilbert, WI 54129 • *1,211*
Hildale, UT 84784 • *1,325*
Hill □, MT • *17,654*
Hill □, TX • *27,146*
Hill City, KS 67642 • *1,835*
Hillcrest, NY 10977 • *6,447*
Hillcrest Center, CA 93306 • *26,900*
Hillcrest Heights, MD 20748 • *17,136*
Hilliard, FL 32046 • *1,751*
Hilliard, OH 43026 • *11,796*
Hillsboro, IL 62049 • *4,400*
Hillsboro, KS 67063 • *2,704*
Hillsboro, MO 63050 • *1,625*
Hillsboro, NH 03244 • *1,826*
Hillsboro, ND 58045 • *1,488*
Hillsboro, OH 45133 • *6,235*
Hillsboro, OR 97123–24 • *37,520*
Hillsboro, TX 76645 • *7,072*
Hillsboro, WI 54634 • *1,288*
Hillsborough, CA 94010 • *10,667*
Hillsborough, NC 27278 • *4,263*
Hillsborough □, FL • *834,054*
Hillsborough □, NH • *336,073*
Hillsdale, MI 49242 • *8,170*
Hillsdale, NJ 07642 • *9,750*
Hillsdale □, MI • *43,431*
Hillside, IL 60162 • *7,672*
Hillside, NJ 07205 • *21,044*
Hillside Heights, DE 19711 • *1,500*
Hillsville, VA 24343 • *2,008*
Hillview, KY 40229 • *6,119*
Hilo, HI 96720–21 • *37,808*
Hilton, NY 14468 • *5,216*
Hilton Head Island, SC 29928 • *23,694*
Hinckley, IL 60520 • *1,682*
Hinds □, MS • *254,441*
Hines, OR 97738 • *1,452*
Hinesville, GA 31313 • *21,603*
Hingham, MA 02043 • *5,454*
Hinsdale, IL 60521–22 • *16,029*
Hinsdale, NH 03451 • *1,718*
Hinsdale □, CO • *467*
Hinton, OK 73047 • *1,233*
Hinton, WV 25951 • *3,433*
Hiram, GA 30141 • *1,389*
Hiram, OH 44234 • *1,330*
Hitchcock, TX 77563 • *5,868*
Hitchcock □, NE • *3,750*
Hitchcock Lake, CT 06716 • *1,640*
Hobart, IN 46342 • *21,822*
Hobart, OK 73651 • *4,305*
Hobbs, NM 88240–41 • *29,115*
Hobe Sound, FL 33455 • *11,507*
Hoboken, NJ 07030 • *33,397*
Hockessin, DE 19707 • *2,430*
Hocking □, OH • *25,533*
Hockley □, TX • *24,199*
Hodgeman □, KS • *2,177*
Hodgenville, KY 42748 • *2,721*
Hoffman Estates, IL 60194–95 • *46,561*
Hogansville, GA 30230 • *2,976*
Hohenwald, TN 38462 • *3,760*
Ho-Ho-Kus, NJ 07423 • *3,935*
Hoisington, KS 67544 • *3,182*
Hoke □, NC • *22,856*
Hokes Bluff, AL 35903 • *3,739*
Holbrook, AZ 86025–29 • *4,686*
Holbrook, MA 02343 • *11,041*
Holbrook, NY 11741 • *25,273*
Holcomb, KS 67851 • *1,400*
Holden, MA 01520 • *4,040*
Holden, MO 64040 • *2,389*
Holden, WV 25625 • *1,246*
Holden Heights, FL 32805 • *4,387*
Holdenville, OK 74848 • *4,792*
Holdrege, NE 68949 • *5,671*
Holgate, OH 43527 • *1,290*
Holiday, FL 34690 • *19,360*
Holiday City at Berkeley, NJ 08757 • *5,750*
Holladay, UT 84117 • *22,189*
Holland, MI 49422–24 • *30,745*
Holland, NY 14080 • *1,288*
Holland, OH 43528 • *1,210*
Holland, PA 18966 • *5,250*
Holland, TX 76534 • *1,118*
Hollandale, MS 38748 • *3,576*
Holley, NY 14470 • *1,890*
Holliday, TX 76366 • *1,475*
Hollidaysburg, PA 16648 • *5,624*
Hollins, VA 24019 • *13,305*
Hollis, OK 73550 • *2,584*
Hollister, CA 95023–24 • *19,212*
Hollister, MO 65672 • *2,628*
Holliston, MA 01746 • *12,622*
Holly, MI 48442 • *5,595*
Holly Hill, FL 32117 • *11,141*
Holly Hill, SC 29059 • *1,478*
Holly Springs, GA 30142 • *2,406*
Holly Springs, MS 38634–35 • *7,261*
Hollywood, FL 33019–29 • *121,697*
Hollywood, SC 29449 • *2,094*
Holmen, WI 54636 • *3,220*
Holmes □, FL • *15,778*
Holmes □, MS • *21,604*
Holmes □, OH • *32,849*
Holstein, IA 51025 • *1,449*
Holt, AL 35404 • *4,125*
Holt, MI 48842 • *11,744*
Holt □, MO • *6,034*
Holt □, NE • *12,599*
Holton, KS 66436 • *3,196*
Holtsville, NY 11742 • *14,972*
Holtville, CA 92250 • *4,820*
Holualoa, HI 96725 • *3,834*
Holyoke, CO 80734 • *1,931*
Holyoke, MA 01040–41 • *43,704*
Homedale, ID 83628 • *1,963*
Home Gardens, CA 91720 • *7,780*
Homeland Park, SC 29621 • *6,569*
Home Place, IN 46240 • *1,300*
Homer, AK 99603 • *3,660*
Homer, IL 61849 • *1,264*
Homer, LA 71040 • *4,152*
Homer, MI 49245 • *1,758*
Homer, NY 13077 • *3,476*
Homer City, PA 15748 • *1,809*
Homerville, GA 31634 • *2,560*
Homestead, FL 33030–35 • *26,866*
Homestead, PA 15120 • *4,179*
Hometown, IL 60456 • *4,769*
Homewood, AL 35209 • *22,922*
Homewood, IL 60430 • *19,278*
Homewood, OH 45015 • *2,550*
Hominy, OK 74035 • *2,342*
Homosassa, FL 32646 • *2,113*
Hondo, TX 78861 • *6,018*
Honea Path, SC 29654 • *3,841*
Honeoye Falls, NY 14472 • *2,340*
Honesdale, PA 18431 • *4,972*
Honey Brook, PA 19344 • *1,184*
Honey Grove, TX 75446 • *1,681*
Honeypot Glen, CT 06410 • *1,200*
Honeyville, UT 84314 • *1,112*
Honokaa, HI 96727 • *2,186*
Honolulu, HI 96801–50 • *365,272*
Honolulu □, HI • *836,231*
Honomu, HI 96728 • *532*
Hood □, TX • *28,981*
Hood River, OR 97031 • *4,632*
Hood River □, OR • *16,903*
Hoodsport, WA 98548 • *1,100*
Hooker, OK 73945 • *1,551*
Hooker □, NE • *793*
Hooksett, NH 03106 • *2,573*
Hoonah, AK 99829 • *795*
Hooper Bay, AK 99604 • *845*
Hoopeston, IL 60942 • *5,871*
Hoosick Falls, NY 12090 • *3,490*
Hoover, AL 35216 • *39,788*
Hooverson Heights, WV 26037 • *3,056*
Hopatcong, NJ 07843 • *15,586*
Hope, AR 71801 • *9,643*
Hope, IN 47246 • *2,171*
Hope, RI 02831 • *270*
Hopedale, MA 01747 • *3,961*
Hope Mills, NC 28348 • *8,184*
Hope Valley, RI 02832 • *1,446*
Hopewell, NJ 08525 • *1,968*
Hopewell, VA 23860 • *23,101*
Hopewell Junction, NY 12533 • *1,786*
Hopkins, MN 55343–47 • *16,534*
Hopkins, SC 29061 • *1,600*
Hopkins □, KY • *46,126*
Hopkins □, TX • *28,833*
Hopkinsville, KY 42240–41 • *29,809*
Hopkinton, MA 01748 • *2,305*
Hopkinton, RI 02833 • *550*
Hopwood, PA 15445 • *2,021*
Hoquiam, WA 98550 • *8,972*
Horicon, WI 53032 • *3,873*
Hornell, NY 14843 • *9,877*
Horn Lake, MS 38637 • *9,069*
Horry □, SC • *144,053*
Horse Cave, KY 42749 • *2,284*
Horseheads, NY 14844–45 • *6,802*
Horsham, PA 19044 • *15,051*
Horton, KS 66439 • *1,885*
Hortonville, WI 54944 • *2,029*
Hot Spring □, AR • *26,115*
Hot Springs, SD 57747 • *4,325*
Hot Springs □, WY • *4,809*
Hot Springs National Park, AR 71901–14 • *32,462*
Hot Springs Village, AR 71901 • *6,361*
Houghton, MI 49931 • *7,498*
Houghton, NY 14744 • *1,740*
Houghton □, MI • *35,446*
Houghton Lake, MI 48629 • *3,353*
Houghton Lake Heights, MI 48630 • *2,449*
Houlton, ME 04730 • *5,627*
Houma, LA 70360–64 • *96,982*
Housatonic, MA 01236 • *1,184*
Houston, DE 19954 • *487*
Houston, MN 55943 • *1,013*
Houston, MS 38851 • *3,903*
Houston, MO 65483 • *2,118*
Houston, PA 15342 • *1,445*
Houston, TX 77001–99 • *1,630,553*
Houston □, AL • *81,331*
Houston □, GA • *89,208*
Houston □, MN • *18,497*
Houston □, TN • *7,018*
Houston □, TX • *21,375*
Houtzdale, PA 16651 • *1,204*
Howard, SD 57349 • *1,156*
Howard, WI 54303 • *9,874*
Howard □, AR • *13,569*
Howard □, IN • *80,827*
Howard □, IA • *9,809*
Howard □, MD • *187,328*
Howard □, MO • *9,631*
Howard □, NE • *6,055*
Howard □, TX • *32,343*
Howard City, MI 49329 • *1,351*
Howard Lake, MN 55349 • *1,343*
Howards Grove-Millersville, WI 53083 • *2,329*
Howell, MI 48843–44 • *8,184*
Howell □, MO • *31,447*
Howland, ME 04448 • *1,304*
Howland, OH 44484 • *6,732*
Hoxie, AR 72433 • *2,676*
Hoxie, KS 67740 • *1,342*
Hoyt Lakes, MN 55750 • *2,348*
Huachuca City, AZ 85616 • *1,782*
Hubbard, OH 44425 • *8,248*
Hubbard, OR 97032 • *1,881*
Hubbard, TX 76648 • *1,589*
Hubbard □, MN • *14,939*
Hubbell, MI 49934 • *1,174*
Huber Heights, OH 45424 • *38,696*
Huber Ridge, OH 43081 • *5,255*
Huber South, OH 45439 • *4,800*
Hudson, FL 34667 • *7,344*
Hudson, IL 61748 • *1,006*
Hudson, IA 50643 • *2,037*
Hudson, MA 01749 • *14,267*
Hudson, MI 49247 • *2,580*
Hudson, NH 03051 • *7,626*
Hudson, NY 12534 • *8,034*
Hudson, NC 28638 • *2,819*
Hudson, OH 44236 • *5,159*
Hudson, WI 54016 • *6,378*
Hudson, WY 82515 • *392*
Hudson □, NJ • *553,099*
Hudson Falls, NY 12839 • *7,651*
Hudson Lake, IN 46552 • *1,347*
Hudsonville, MI 49426 • *6,170*
Hudspeth □, TX • *2,915*
Huerfano □, CO • *6,009*
Hueytown, AL 35023 • *15,280*
Huffakers, NV 89501 • *150*
Hughes, AR 72348 • *1,810*
Hughes □, OK • *13,023*
Hughes □, SD • *14,817*
Hughesville, MD 20637 • *1,319*
Hughesville, PA 17737 • *2,049*
Hugo, MN 55038 • *4,417*
Hugo, OK 74743 • *5,978*
Hugoton, KS 67951 • *3,179*
Hulett, WY 82720 • *429*
Hull, IA 51239 • *1,724*
Hull, MA 02045 • *10,466*
Humansville, MO 65674 • *1,084*
Humble, TX 77338–39 • *12,060*
Humboldt, IA 50548 • *4,438*
Humboldt, KS 66748 • *2,178*
Humboldt, NE 68376 • *1,003*
Humboldt, TN 38343 • *9,651*
Humboldt □, CA • *119,118*
Humboldt □, IA • *10,756*
Humboldt □, NV • *12,844*
Hummels Wharf, PA 17831 • *1,069*
Humphreys □, MS • *12,134*
Humphreys □, TN • *15,795*
Hunt □, TX • *64,343*
Hunterdon □, NJ • *107,776*
Huntertown, IN 46748 • *1,330*
Huntingburg, IN 47542 • *5,242*
Huntingdon, PA 16652 • *6,843*
Huntingdon, TN 38344 • *4,180*
Huntingdon □, PA • *44,164*
Huntington, IN 46750 • *16,389*
Huntington, MA 01050 • *1,200*
Huntington, NY 11743 • *18,243*
Huntington, TX 75949 • *1,794*
Huntington, UT 84528 • *1,875*
Huntington, VA 22303 • *7,489*
Huntington, WV 25701–79 • *54,844*
Huntington □, IN • *35,427*
Huntington Bay, NY 11743 • *1,521*
Huntington Beach, CA 92646–49 • *181,519*
Huntington Park, CA 90255 • *56,065*
Huntington Station, NY 11746 • *28,247*
Huntington Woods, MI 48070 • *6,419*
Huntley, IL 60142 • *2,453*
Huntsville, AL 35801–24 • *159,789*
Huntsville, AR 72740 • *1,605*
Huntsville, MO 65259 • *1,567*
Huntsville, TX 77340–44 • *27,925*
Hurley, NM 88043 • *1,534*
Hurley, NY 12443 • *4,644*
Hurley, WI 54534 • *1,782*
Hurlock, MD 21643 • *1,706*
Huron, OH 44839 • *7,030*
Huron, SD 57350 • *12,448*
Huron □, MI • *34,951*
Huron □, OH • *56,240*
Hurricane, UT 84737 • *3,915*
Hurricane, WV 25526 • *4,461*
Hurst, TX 76053–54 • *33,574*
Hurt, VA 24563 • *1,294*
Hutchins, TX 75141 • *2,719*
Hutchinson, KS 67501–05 • *39,308*
Hutchinson, MN 55350 • *11,523*
Hutchinson □, SD • *8,262*
Hutchinson □, TX • *25,689*
Huxley, IA 50124 • *2,047*
Hyannis, MA 02601 • *14,120*
Hyannis Port, MA 02647 • *1,100*
Hyattsville, MD 20780–89 • *13,864*
Hybla Valley, VA 22306 • *15,491*
Hydaburg, AK 99922 • *384*
Hyde, PA 16843 • *1,643*
Hyde □, NC • *5,411*
Hyde □, SD • *1,696*
Hyde Park, NY 12538 • *2,550*
Hyde Park, UT 84318 • *2,190*
Hydeville, VT 05750 • *450*
Hyndman, PA 15545 • *1,019*
Hyrum, UT 84319 • *4,829*

I

Iberia □, LA • *68,297*
Iberville □, LA • *31,049*
Ida, MI 48140 • *1,000*
Ida □, IA • *8,365*
Idabel, OK 74745 • *6,957*
Ida Grove, IA 51445 • *2,357*
Idaho □, ID • *13,783*
Idaho Falls, ID 83401–15 • *43,929*
Idaho Springs, CO 80452 • *1,834*
Idalou, TX 79329 • *2,074*
Ilion, NY 13357 • *8,888*

Illmo, MO 63780 • *1,368*
Imlay, NV 89418 • *250*
Imlay City, MI 48444 • *2,921*
Immokalee, FL 33934 • *14,120*
Imperial, CA 92251 • *4,113*
Imperial, NE 69033 • *2,007*
Imperial, PA 15126 • *3,200*
Imperial □, CA • *109,303*
Imperial Beach, CA 91932–33 • *26,512*
Incline Village, NV 89450 • *4,500*
Independence, CA 93526 • *1,000*
Independence, IA 50644 • *5,972*
Independence, KS 67301 • *9,942*
Independence, KY 41051 • *10,444*
Independence, LA 70443 • *1,632*
Independence, MO 64050–58 • *112,301*
Independence, OH 44131 • *6,500*
Independence, OR 97351 • *4,425*
Independence, WI 54747 • *1,041*
Independence □, AR • *31,192*
Indiana, PA 15701 • *15,174*
Indiana □, PA • *89,994*
Indianapolis, IN 46201–90 • *731,327*
Indian Harbour Beach, FL 32937 • *6,933*
Indian Head, MD 20640 • *3,531*
Indian Heights, IN 46902 • *3,669*
Indian Hills, CO 80454 • *2,000*
Indian Neck, CT 06405 • *2,430*
Indianola, IA 50125 • *11,340*
Indianola, MS 38751 • *11,809*
Indian Ridge Estates, AZ 85715 • *1,260*
Indian River □, FL • *90,208*
Indian Rocks Beach, FL 34635 • *3,963*
Indian Springs, NV 89018 • *1,164*
Indiantown, FL 34956 • *4,794*
Indian Trail, NC 28079 • *1,942*
Indio, CA 92201–02 • *36,793*
Ingalls Park, IL 60431 • *2,730*
Ingham □, MI • *281,912*
Ingleside, TX 78362 • *5,696*
Inglewood, CA 90301–12 • *109,602*
Inglewood, TX 98011 • *6,500*
Ingram, PA 15205 • *3,901*
Inkom, ID 83245 • *769*
Inkster, MI 48141 • *30,772*
Inman, KS 67546 • *1,035*
Inman, SC 29349 • *1,742*
Inniswold, LA 70809 • *1,100*
Inola, OK 74036 • *1,444*
Institute, WV 25112 • *1,400*
Interlachen, FL 32148 • *1,160*
International Falls, MN 56649 • *8,325*
Inver Grove Heights, MN 55076–77 • *22,477*
Inverness, CA 94937 • *1,422*
Inverness, FL 32650–52 • *5,797*
Inverness, IL 60067 • *6,503*
Inverness, MS 38753 • *1,174*
Inwood, FL 33880 • *6,824*
Inwood, NY 11696 • *7,767*
Inwood, WV 25428 • *1,360*
Inyo □, CA • *18,281*
Iola, KS 66749 • *6,351*
Iola, WI 54945 • *1,125*
Iona, ID 83427 • *1,049*
Ione, CA 95640 • *6,516*
Ionia, MI 48846 • *5,935*
Ionia □, MI • *57,024*
Iosco □, MI • *30,209*
Iota, LA 70543 • *1,256*
Iowa, LA 70647 • *2,588*
Iowa □, IA • *14,630*
Iowa □, WI • *20,150*
Iowa City, IA 52240–46 • *59,738*
Iowa Falls, IA 50126 • *5,424*
Iowa Park, TX 76367 • *6,072*
Ipswich, MA 01938 • *4,132*
Ipswich, SD 57451 • *965*
Iraan, TX 79744 • *1,322*
Iredell □, NC • *92,931*
Irion □, TX • *1,629*
Irmo, SC 29063 • *11,280*
Iron □, MI • *13,175*
Iron □, MO • *10,726*
Iron □, UT • *20,789*
Iron □, WI • *6,153*
Irondale, AL 35210 • *9,454*
Irondequoit, NY 14617 • *52,322*
Ironia, NJ 07845 • *1,110*
Iron Mountain, MI 49801 • *8,525*
Iron River, MI 49935 • *2,095*
Ironton, MO 63650 • *1,539*
Ironton, OH 45638 • *12,751*
Ironwood, MI 49938 • *6,849*
Iroquois □, IL • *30,787*
Irvine, CA 92713–20 • *110,330*
Irvine, KY 40336 • *2,836*
Irving, TX 75060–63 • *155,037*
Irvington, KY 40146 • *1,180*
Irvington, NJ 07111 • *59,774*
Irvington, NY 10533 • *6,348*
Irwin, PA 15642 • *4,604*
Irwin □, GA • *8,649*
Isabella □, MI • *54,624*
Isanti, MN 55040 • *1,228*
Isanti □, MN • *25,921*
Iselin, NJ 08830 • *16,141*
Ishpeming, MI 49849 • *7,200*
Islamorada, FL 33036 • *1,220*
Island □, WA • *60,195*
Island Heights, NJ 08732 • *1,470*
Island Park, NY 11558 • *4,860*
Island Park, RI 02871 • *1,240*
Island Pond, VT 05846 • *1,222*
Isla Vista, CA 93117 • *20,395*
Isle of Palms, SC 29451 • *3,680*
Isle of Wight □, VA • *25,053*
Isleta, NM 87022 • *1,703*
Islington, MA 02090 • *4,920*
Islip, NY 11751 • *18,924*
Islip Terrace, NY 11752 • *5,530*
Issaquah, WA 98027 • *7,786*
Issaquena □, MS • *1,909*
Italy, TX 76651 • *1,699*
Itasca, IL 60143 • *6,947*
Itasca, TX 76055 • *1,523*
Itasca □, MN • *40,863*
Itawamba □, MS • *20,017*
Ithaca, MI 48847 • *3,009*
Ithaca, NY 14850–52 • *29,541*
Itta Bena, MS 38941 • *2,377*
Iuka, MS 38852 • *3,122*
Iva, SC 29655 • *1,174*

Ives Estates, FL 33162 • *13,531*
Ivins, UT 84738 • *1,630*
Ivoryton, CT 06442 • *2,200*
Izard □, AR • *11,364*

J

Jacinto City, TX 77029 • *9,343*
Jack □, TX • *6,981*
Jackpot, NV 89825 • *570*
Jacksboro, TN 37757 • *1,568*
Jacksboro, TX 76056 • *3,350*
Jackson, AL 36545 • *5,819*
Jackson, CA 95642 • *3,545*
Jackson, GA 30233 • *4,076*
Jackson, KY 41339 • *2,466*
Jackson, LA 70748 • *3,891*
Jackson, MI 49201–04 • *37,446*
Jackson, MN 56143 • *3,559*
Jackson, MS 39201–98 • *196,637*
Jackson, MO 63755 • *9,256*
Jackson, OH 45640 • *6,144*
Jackson, SC 29831 • *1,681*
Jackson, TN 38301–08 • *48,949*
Jackson, WI 53037 • *2,486*
Jackson, WY 83001–02 • *4,472*
Jackson □, AL • *47,796*
Jackson □, AR • *18,944*
Jackson □, CO • *1,605*
Jackson □, FL • *41,375*
Jackson □, GA • *30,005*
Jackson □, IL • *61,067*
Jackson □, IN • *37,730*
Jackson □, IA • *19,950*
Jackson □, KS • *11,525*
Jackson □, KY • *11,955*
Jackson □, LA • *15,705*
Jackson □, MI • *149,756*
Jackson □, MN • *11,677*
Jackson □, MS • *115,243*
Jackson □, MO • *633,232*
Jackson □, NC • *26,846*
Jackson □, OH • *30,230*
Jackson □, OK • *28,764*
Jackson □, OR • *146,389*
Jackson □, SD • *2,811*
Jackson □, TN • *9,297*
Jackson □, TX • *13,039*
Jackson □, WV • *25,938*
Jackson □, WI • *16,588*
Jackson Center, OH 45334 • *1,398*
Jacksonville, AL 36265 • *10,283*
Jacksonville, AR 72076 • *29,101*
Jacksonville, FL 32201–98 • *635,230*
Jacksonville, IL 62650–51 • *19,324*
Jacksonville, NC 28540–46 • *30,013*
Jacksonville, OR 97530 • *1,896*
Jacksonville, TX 75766 • *12,765*
Jacksonville Beach, FL 32250 • *17,839*
Jaffrey, NH 03452 • *2,558*
Jal, NM 88252 • *2,156*
Jamesburg, NJ 08831 • *5,294*
James City, NC 28560 • *4,279*
James City □, VA • *34,859*
James Island, SC 29412 • *24,124*
Jamestown, CA 95327 • *2,178*
Jamestown, KY 42629 • *1,641*
Jamestown, NY 14701–02 • *34,681*
Jamestown, NC 27282 • *2,600*
Jamestown, ND 58401–02 • *15,571*
Jamestown, OH 45335 • *1,794*
Jamestown, RI 02835 • *2,156*
Jamestown, TN 38556 • *1,862*
James Town, WY 82935 • *280*
Janesville, CA 96114 • *1,200*
Janesville, MN 56048 • *1,969*
Janesville, WI 53545–47 • *52,133*
Jarrettsville, MD 21084 • *2,148*
Jasmine Estates, FL 34668 • *17,136*
Jasonville, IN 47438 • *2,200*
Jasper, AL 35501–02 • *13,553*
Jasper, FL 32052 • *2,099*
Jasper, GA 30143 • *1,772*
Jasper, IN 47546–47 • *10,030*
Jasper, TN 37347 • *2,780*
Jasper, TX 75951 • *6,959*
Jasper □, GA • *8,453*
Jasper □, IL • *10,609*
Jasper □, IN • *24,960*
Jasper □, IA • *34,795*
Jasper □, MS • *17,114*
Jasper □, MO • *90,465*
Jasper □, SC • *15,487*
Jasper □, TX • *31,102*
Jay, OK 74346 • *2,220*
Jay □, IN • *21,512*
Jean, NV 89019 • *150*
Jeanerette, LA 70544 • *6,205*
Jeannette, PA 15644 • *11,221*
Jeff Davis □, GA • *12,032*
Jeff Davis □, TX • *1,946*
Jefferson, GA 30549 • *2,763*
Jefferson, IA 50129 • *4,292*
Jefferson, LA 70121 • *14,521*
Jefferson, NC 28640 • *1,300*
Jefferson, OH 44047 • *3,331*
Jefferson, OR 97352 • *1,805*
Jefferson, PA 15025 • *9,533*
Jefferson, TX 75657 • *2,199*
Jefferson, WI 53549 • *6,078*
Jefferson □, AL • *651,525*
Jefferson □, AR • *85,487*
Jefferson □, CO • *438,430*
Jefferson □, FL • *11,296*
Jefferson □, GA • *17,408*
Jefferson □, ID • *16,543*
Jefferson □, IL • *37,020*
Jefferson □, IN • *29,797*
Jefferson □, IA • *16,310*
Jefferson □, KS • *15,905*
Jefferson □, KY • *664,937*
Jefferson □, LA • *448,306*
Jefferson □, MS • *8,653*
Jefferson □, MO • *171,380*
Jefferson □, MT • *7,939*
Jefferson □, NE • *8,759*
Jefferson □, NY • *110,943*
Jefferson □, OH • *80,298*
Jefferson □, OK • *7,010*
Jefferson □, OR • *13,676*
Jefferson □, PA • *46,083*

Jefferson □, TN • *33,016*
Jefferson □, TX • *239,397*
Jefferson □, WA • *20,146*
Jefferson □, WV • *35,926*
Jefferson □, WI • *67,783*
Jefferson City, MO 65101–10 • *35,481*
Jefferson City, TN 37760 • *5,494*
Jefferson Davis □, LA • *30,722*
Jefferson Davis □, MS • *14,051*
Jefferson Farms, DE 19720 • *3,130*
Jefferson Manor, VA 22303 • *2,300*
Jeffersontown, KY 40299 • *23,221*
Jefferson Valley, NY 10535 • *6,420*
Jefferson Village, VA 22042 • *2,500*
Jeffersonville, GA 31044 • *1,545*
Jeffersonville, IN 47129–31 • *21,841*
Jeffersonville, KY 40337 • *1,854*
Jeffersonville, OH 43128 • *1,281*
Jeffrey City, WY 82310 • *1,882*
Jellico, TN 37762 • *2,447*
Jemez Pueblo, NM 87024 • *1,301*
Jemison, AL 35085 • *1,898*
Jena, LA 71342 • *2,626*
Jenison, MI 49428–29 • *17,882*
Jenkins, KY 41537 • *2,751*
Jenkins □, GA • *8,247*
Jenkintown, PA 19046 • *4,574*
Jenks, OK 74037 • *7,493*
Jennings, LA 70546 • *11,305*
Jennings, MO 63136 • *15,905*
Jennings □, IN • *23,661*
Jennings Lodge, OR 97222 • *11,480*
Jensen Beach, FL 34957–58 • *9,884*
Jerauld □, SD • *2,425*
Jericho, NY 11753 • *13,141*
Jericho, VT 05465 • *1,300*
Jermyn, PA 18433 • *2,263*
Jerome, ID 83338 • *6,529*
Jerome, PA 15937 • *1,074*
Jerome □, ID • *15,138*
Jersey □, IL • *20,539*
Jersey City, NJ 07301–11 • *228,537*
Jersey Shore, PA 17740 • *4,353*
Jerseyville, IL 62052 • *7,382*
Jessamine □, KY • *30,508*
Jessup, MD 20794 • *6,537*
Jessup, PA 18434 • *4,605*
Jesup, GA 31545 • *8,958*
Jesup, IA 50648 • *2,121*
Jewell, IA 50130 • *1,106*
Jewell □, KS • *4,251*
Jewett City, CT 06351 • *3,349*
Jim Hogg □, TX • *5,109*
Jim Thorpe, PA 18229 • *5,048*
Jim Wells □, TX • *37,679*
Joanna, SC 29351 • *1,735*
Jo Daviess □, IL • *21,821*
John Day, OR 97845 • *1,836*
Johnson, KS 67855 • *1,348*
Johnson, VT 05656 • *1,470*
Johnson □, AR • *18,221*
Johnson □, GA • *8,329*
Johnson □, IL • *11,347*
Johnson □, IN • *88,109*
Johnson □, IA • *96,119*
Johnson □, KS • *355,054*
Johnson □, KY • *23,248*
Johnson □, MO • *42,514*
Johnson □, NE • *4,673*
Johnson □, TN • *13,766*
Johnson □, TX • *97,165*
Johnson □, WY • *6,145*
Johnsonburg, PA 15845 • *3,350*
Johnson City, NY 13790 • *16,890*
Johnson City, TN 37601–15 • *49,381*
Johnson Creek, WI 53038 • *1,259*
Johnsonville, SC 29555 • *1,415*
Johnston, IA 50131 • *4,702*
Johnston, RI 02919 • *26,542*
Johnston, SC 29832 • *2,688*
Johnston □, NC • *81,306*
Johnston □, OK • *10,032*
Johnston City, IL 62951 • *3,706*
Johnstown, CO 80534 • *1,579*
Johnstown, NY 12095 • *9,058*
Johnstown, OH 43031 • *3,237*
Johnstown, PA 15901–09 • *28,134*
Joliet, IL 60431–36 • *76,836*
Jones, OK 73049 • *2,424*
Jones □, GA • *20,739*
Jones □, IA • *19,444*
Jones □, MS • *62,031*
Jones □, NC • *9,414*
Jones □, SD • *1,324*
Jones □, TX • *16,490*
Jonesboro, AR 72401–03 • *46,535*
Jonesboro, GA 30236–37 • *3,635*
Jonesboro, IL 62952 • *1,728*
Jonesboro, IN 46938 • *2,073*
Jonesboro, LA 71251 • *4,305*
Jonesborough, TN 37659 • *3,091*
Jones Creek, TX 77541 • *2,160*
Jonesport, ME 04649 • *1,525*
Jonestown, MS 38639 • *1,467*
Jonesville, LA 71040 • *2,720*
Jonesville, MI 49250 • *2,283*
Jonesville, NC 28642 • *1,549*
Jonesville, SC 29053 • *1,205*
Joplin, MO 64801–04 • *40,961*
Joppatowne, MD 21085 • *11,084*
Jordan, MN 55352 • *2,909*
Jordan, NY 13080 • *1,325*
Joseph, OR 97846 • *1,073*
Josephine □, OR • *62,649*
Joshua, TX 76058 • *3,828*
Joshua Tree, CA 92252 • *3,898*
Jourdanton, TX 78026 • *3,220*
Juab □, UT • *5,817*
Juanita, WA 98033 • *10,500*
Judith Basin □, MT • *2,282*
Judsonia, AR 72081 • *1,915*
Julesburg, CO 80737 • *1,295*
Julian, CA 92036 • *1,284*
Junction, TX 76849 • *2,654*
Junction City, KS 66441 • *20,604*
Junction City, KY 40440 • *1,983*
Junction City, OR 97448 • *3,670*
Juneau, AK 99801–03 • *26,751*
Juneau, WI 53039 • *2,157*
Juneau □, WI • *21,650*
Juniata □, PA • *20,625*
Jupiter, FL 33458 • *24,986*
Justice, IL 60458 • *11,137*

Justin, TX 76247 • *1,234*

K

Kaaawa, HI 96730 • *1,138*
Kadoka, SD 57543 • *736*
Kahaluu, HI 96725 • *380*
Kahaluu, HI 96744 • *3,068*
Kahoka, MO 63445 • *2,195*
Kahuku, HI 96731 • *2,063*
Kahului, HI 96732–33 • *16,889*
Kailua, HI 96734 • *36,818*
Kailua Kona, HI 96739–40 • *9,126*
Kake, AK 99830 • *700*
Kalaheo, HI 96741 • *3,592*
Kalama, WA 98625 • *1,210*
Kalamazoo, MI 49001–09 • *80,277*
Kalamazoo □, MI • *223,411*
Kalawao □, HI • *130*
Kalispell, MT 59901 • *11,917*
Kalkaska, MI 49646 • *1,952*
Kalkaska □, MI • *13,497*
Kalona, IA 52247 • *1,942*
Kamas, UT 84036 • *1,061*
Kamiah, ID 83536 • *1,157*
Kamuela (Waimea), HI 96743 • *5,972*
Kanab, UT 84741 • *3,289*
Kanabec □, MN • *12,802*
Kanawha □, WV • *207,619*
Kandiyohi □, MN • *38,761*
Kane, PA 16735 • *4,590*
Kane □, IL • *317,471*
Kane □, UT • *5,169*
Kaneohe, HI 96744 • *35,448*
Kankakee, IL 60901 • *27,575*
Kankakee □, IL • *96,255*
Kannapolis, NC 28081–83 • *29,696*
Kansas City, KS 66101–19 • *149,767*
Kansas City, MO 64101–99 • *435,146*
Kapaa, HI 96746 • *8,149*
Kapaau, HI 96755 • *1,083*
Kaplan, LA 70548 • *4,535*
Karnes □, TX • *12,455*
Karnes City, TX 78118 • *2,916*
Karns, TN 37921 • *1,458*
Kasson, MN 55944 • *3,514*
Kathleen, FL 33849 • *2,743*
Katy, TX 77449–50 • *8,005*
Kauai □, HI • *51,177*
Kaufman, TX 75142 • *5,238*
Kaufman □, TX • *52,220*
Kaukauna, WI 54130 • *11,982*
Kaumakani, HI 96747 • *803*
Kaunakakai, HI 96748 • *2,658*
Kay □, OK • *48,056*
Kaycee, WY 82639 • *256*
Kayenta, AZ 86033 • *4,372*
Kaysville, UT 84037 • *13,961*
Keaau, HI 96749 • *1,584*
Kealakekua, HI 96750 • *1,453*
Kealia, HI 96751 • *700*
Keansburg, NJ 07734 • *11,069*
Kearney, MO 64060 • *1,790*
Kearney, NE 68847–48 • *24,396*
Kearney □, NE • *6,629*
Kearns, UT 84118 • *28,374*
Kearny, AZ 85237 • *2,262*
Kearny, NJ 07031–32 • *34,874*
Kearny □, KS • *4,027*
Keego Harbor, MI 48320 • *2,932*
Keene, NH 03431 • *22,430*
Keene, TX 76059 • *3,944*
Keeseville, NY 12944 • *1,854*
Keewatin, MN 55753 • *1,118*
Keith □, NE • *8,584*
Keizer, OR 97303 • *21,884*
Kekaha, HI 96752 • *3,506*
Keller, TX 76248 • *13,683*
Kellogg, ID 83837 • *2,591*
Kelseyville, CA 95451 • *2,861*
Kelso, WA 98626 • *11,820*
Kemmerer, WY 83101 • *3,020*
Kemp, TX 75143 • *1,184*
Kemper □, MS • *10,356*
Kenai, AK 99611 • *6,327*
Kenbridge, VA 23944 • *1,264*
Ken Caryl, CO 80123 • *24,391*
Kendall, FL 33156 • *87,271*
Kendall □, IL • *39,413*
Kendall □, TX • *14,589*
Kendall Park, NJ 08824 • *7,127*
Kendallville, IN 46755 • *7,773*
Kenedy, TX 78119 • *3,763*
Kenedy □, TX • *460*
Kenilworth, IL 60043 • *2,402*
Kenilworth, NJ 07033 • *7,574*
Kenly, NC 27542 • *1,549*
Kenmare, ND 58746 • *1,214*
Kenmore, NY 14217 • *17,180*
Kenmore, WA 98028 • *8,917*
Kennebec □, ME • *115,904*
Kennebunk, ME 04043 • *4,206*
Kennebunkport, ME 04046 • *1,100*
Kennedy Heights, LA 70001 • *2,000*
Kennedy Township, PA 15108 • *7,152*
Kenner, LA 70062–65 • *72,033*
Kennesaw, GA 30144 • *8,936*
Kennett, MO 63857 • *10,941*
Kennett Square, PA 19348 • *5,218*
Kennewick, WA 99336–37 • *42,155*
Kennydale, WA 98056 • *2,000*
Kenosha, WI 53140–44 • *80,352*
Kenosha □, WI • *128,181*
Kenova, WV 25530 • *3,748*
Ken Rock, IL 61109 • *3,300*
Kensett, AR 72082 • *1,741*
Kensington, CA 94707 • *4,974*
Kensington, CT 06037 • *8,306*
Kensington, MD 20895 • *1,713*
Kent, OH 44240 • *28,835*
Kent, WA 98031–32 • *37,960*
Kent □, DE • *110,993*
Kent □, MD • *17,842*
Kent □, MI • *500,631*
Kent □, RI • *161,135*
Kent □, TX • *1,010*
Kentfield, CA 94904 • *6,030*
Kentland, IN 47951 • *1,798*
Kenton, DE 19955 • *232*
Kenton, OH 43326 • *8,356*
Kenton, TN 38233 • *1,366*

Kenton □, KY • *142,031*
Kentwood, LA 70444 • *2,468*
Kentwood, MI 49508 • *37,826*
Kenvil, NJ 07847 • *3,050*
Kenwood, OH 45236 • *7,469*
Kenyon, MN 55946 • *1,552*
Kenyon, RI 02836 • *400*
Keokea, HI 96790 • *900*
Keokuk, IA 52632 • *12,451*
Keokuk □, IA • *11,624*
Keosauqua, IA 52565 • *1,020*
Keota, IA 52248 • *1,000*
Kerens, TX 75144 • *1,702*
Kerhonkson, NY 12446 • *1,629*
Kermit, TX 79745 • *6,875*
Kern □, CA • *543,477*
Kernersville, NC 27284–85 • *10,836*
Kernville, CA 93238 • *1,656*
Kerr □, TX • *36,304*
Kerrville, TX 78028–29 • *17,384*
Kershaw, SC 29067 • *1,814*
Kershaw □, SC • *43,599*
Ketchikan, AK 99901 • *8,263*
Ketchum, ID 83340 • *2,523*
Kettering, MD 20772 • *9,901*
Kettering, OH 45429 • *60,569*
Kettle Falls, WA 99141 • *1,272*
Kewanee, IL 61443 • *12,969*
Kewaskum, WI 53040 • *2,515*
Kewaunee, WI 54216 • *2,750*
Kewaunee □, WI • *18,878*
Keweenaw □, MI • *1,701*
Keya Paha □, NE • *1,029*
Key Biscayne, FL 33149 • *8,854*
Key Largo, FL 33037 • *11,336*
Keyport, NJ 07735 • *7,586*
Keyser, WV 26726 • *5,870*
Keystone Heights, FL 32656 • *1,315*
Key West, FL 33040–41 • *24,832*
Kiana, AK 99749 • *385*
Kidder □, ND • *3,332*
Kiel, WI 53042 • *2,910*
Kihei, HI 96753 • *11,107*
Kilauea, HI 96754 • *1,685*
Kilgore, TX 75662–63 • *11,066*
Killdeer, ND 58640 • *722*
Killeen, TX 76540–47 • *63,535*
Killen, AL 35645 • *1,047*
Kilmarnock, VA 22482 • *1,109*
Kimball, NE 69145 • *2,574*
Kimball □, NE • *4,108*
Kimberly, AL 35091 • *1,096*
Kimberly, ID 83341 • *2,367*
Kimberly, WI 54136 • *5,406*
Kimble □, TX • *4,122*
Kincaid, IL 62540 • *1,353*
Kinder, LA 70648 • *2,246*
Kinderhook, NY 12106 • *1,293*
King, NC 27021 • *4,059*
King □, TX • *354*
King □, WA • *1,507,319*
King and Queen □, VA • *6,289*
King City, CA 93930 • *7,634*
King Cove, AK 99612 • *451*
Kingfisher, OK 73750 • *4,095*
Kingfisher □, OK • *13,212*
King George □, VA • *13,527*
Kingman, AZ 86401–02 • *12,722*
Kingman, KS 67068 • *3,196*
Kingman □, KS • *8,292*
King of Prussia, PA 19406 • *18,406*
Kings, MS 39180 • *1,165*
Kings □, CA • *101,469*
Kings □, NY • *2,300,664*
King Salmon, AK 99613 • *696*
Kingsburg, CA 93631 • *7,205*
Kingsbury □, SD • *5,925*
Kingsford, MI 49801 • *5,480*
Kingsgate, WA 98011 • *14,259*
Kingsland, GA 31548 • *4,699*
Kingsland, TX 78639 • *2,725*
Kingsley, IA 51028 • *1,129*
Kings Mountain, NC 28086 • *8,763*
Kings Park, NY 11754 • *17,773*
Kings Park, VA 22151 • *6,000*
Kings Park West, VA 22032 • *6,000*
Kings Point, FL 33484 • *12,422*
Kings Point, NY 11024 • *4,843*
Kingsport, TN 37660–65 • *36,365*
Kingston, ID 83839 • *1,000*
Kingston, MA 02364 • *4,774*
Kingston, NJ 08528 • *1,200*
Kingston, NY 12401 • *23,095*
Kingston, OH 45644 • *1,153*
Kingston, OK 73439 • *1,237*
Kingston, PA 18704 • *14,507*
Kingston, RI 02881 • *6,504*
Kingston, TN 37763 • *4,552*
Kingston Springs, TN 37082 • *1,529*
Kingstown, MD 21620 • *1,660*
Kingstree, SC 29556 • *3,858*
Kingsville, MD 21087 • *3,550*
Kingsville (North Kingsville), OH 44048 • *1,243*
Kingsville, TX 78363–64 • *25,276*
King William □, VA • *10,913*
Kingwood, TX 77339 • *37,397*
Kingwood, WV 26537 • *3,243*
Kinloch, MO 63140 • *2,702*
Kinnelon, NJ 07405 • *8,470*
Kinney □, TX • *3,119*
Kinsey, AL 36301 • *1,679*
Kinsley, KS 67547 • *1,875*
Kinston, NC 28501–03 • *25,295*
Kiowa, KS 67070 • *1,160*
Kiowa □, CO • *1,688*
Kiowa □, KS • *3,660*
Kiowa □, OK • *11,347*
Kipnuk, AK 99614 • *470*
Kirby, TX 78219 • *8,326*
Kirbyville, TX 75956 • *1,871*
Kirkland, IL 60146 • *1,011*
Kirkland, WA 98033–34 • *40,052*
Kirksville, MO 63501 • *17,152*
Kirkwood, DE 19708 • *350*
Kirkwood, MO 63122 • *27,291*
Kirtland, NM 87417 • *3,552*
Kirtland, OH 44094 • *5,881*
Kissimmee, FL 34741–46 • *30,050*
Kit Carson □, CO • *7,140*
Kitsap □, WA • *189,731*
Kittanning, PA 16201 • *5,120*
Kittery, ME 03904 • *5,151*

Kittery Point, ME 03905 • 1,093
Kittitas □, WA • 26,725
Kittson □, MN • 5,767
Kitty Hawk, NC 27949 • 1,937
Klamath □, OR • 57,702
Klamath Falls, OR 97601-03 • 17,737
Klawock, AK 99925 • 722
Kleberg □, TX • 30,274
Klein, TX 77379 • 12,000
Klickitat □, WA • 16,616
Knightdale, NC 27545 • 1,884
Knights Landing, CA 95645 • 1,000
Knightstown, IN 46148 • 2,048
Knob Noster, MO 65336 • 2,261
Knott □, KY • 17,906
Knox, IN 46534 • 3,705
Knox, PA 16232 • 1,182
Knox □, IL • 56,393
Knox □, IN • 39,884
Knox □, KY • 29,676
Knox □, ME • 36,310
Knox □, MO • 4,482
Knox □, NE • 9,534
Knox □, OH • 47,473
Knox □, TN • 335,749
Knox □, TX • 4,837
Knox City, TX 79529 • 1,440
Knoxville, IL 61448 • 3,243
Knoxville, IA 50138 • 8,232
Knoxville, TN 37901-50 • 165,121
Kodiak, AK 99615 • 6,365
Kohler, WI 53044 • 1,817
Kokomo, IN 46901-04 • 44,962
Koloa, HI 96756 • 1,791
Konawa, OK 74849 • 1,508
Koochiching □, MN • 16,299
Koontz Lake, IN 46574 • 1,615
Kootenai □, ID • 69,795
Koppel, PA 16136 • 1,024
Kosciusko, MS 39090 • 6,986
Kosciusko □, IN • 65,294
Kossuth □, IA • 18,591
Kotlik, AK 99620 • 461
Kotzebue, AK 99752 • 2,751
Kountze, TX 77625 • 2,056
Kouts, IN 46347 • 1,603
Krebs, OK 74554 • 1,955
Kremmling, CO 80459 • 1,166
Krotz Springs, LA 70750 • 1,285
Kula, HI 96790 • 1,300
Kulpmont, PA 17834 • 3,233
Kuna, ID 83634 • 1,955
Kurtistown, HI 96760 • 910
Kutztown, PA 19530 • 4,704
Kwethluk, AK 99621 • 558
Kwigillingok, AK 99622 • 278
Kyle, TX 78640 • 2,225

L

Labadieville, LA 70372 • 1,821
La Barge, WY 83123 • 493
La Belle, FL 33935 • 2,703
Labette □, KS • 23,693
La Canada Flintridge, CA 91011 • 19,378
Lac du Flambeau, WI 54538 • 1,180
La Center, KY 42056 • 1,040
Lacey, WA 98503 • 19,279
Lackawanna, NY 14218 • 20,585
Lackawanna □, PA • 219,039
Laclede □, MO • 27,158
Lacombe, LA 70445 • 6,523
Lacon, IL 61540 • 1,986
Laconia, NH 03246-47 • 15,743
Lacoochee, FL 33537 • 2,072
Lac qui Parle □, MN • 8,924
La Crescent, MN 55947 • 4,311
La Crescenta, CA 91214 • 12,500
La Crosse, KS 67548 • 1,427
La Crosse, WI 54601-03 • 51,003
La Crosse □, WI • 97,904
La Cygne, KS 66040 • 1,066
Ladd, IL 61329 • 1,283
Ladera Heights, CA 90045 • 6,316
Ladoga, IN 47954 • 1,124
Ladson, SC 29456 • 13,540
Ladue, MO 63124 • 8,847
Lady Lake, FL 32159 • 8,071
Ladysmith, WI 54848 • 3,938
Lafayette, AL 36862 • 3,151
Lafayette, CA 94549 • 23,501
Lafayette, CO 80026 • 14,548
Lafayette, GA 30728 • 6,313
Lafayette, IN 47901-06 • 43,764
Lafayette, LA 70501-09 • 94,440
Lafayette, NC 28304 • 3,200
Lafayette, OR 97127 • 1,292
La Fayette, RI 02852 • 640
Lafayette, TN 37083 • 3,641
Lafayette □, AR • 9,643
Lafayette □, FL • 5,578
Lafayette □, LA • 164,762
Lafayette □, MS • 31,826
Lafayette □, MO • 31,107
Lafayette □, WI • 16,076
Lafayette Southwest, LA • 5,500
La Feria, TX 78559 • 4,360
Lafitte, LA 70067 • 1,507
La Follette, TN 37766 • 7,192
Lafourche □, LA • 85,860
La Grande, OR 97850 • 11,766
La Grange, GA 30240-41 • 25,597
La Grange, IL 60525 • 15,362
Lagrange, IN 46761 • 2,382
La Grange, KY 40031 • 3,853
La Grange, MO 63448 • 1,102
La Grange, NC 28551 • 2,805
Lagrange, OH 44050 • 1,199
La Grange, TX 78945 • 3,951
Lagrange □, IN • 29,477
La Grange Highlands, IL 60525 • 3,660
La Grange Park, IL 60525 • 12,861
Laguna Beach, CA 92651-54 • 23,170
Laguna Hills, CA 92653 • 46,731
Laguna Niguel, CA 92677 • 44,400
La Habra, CA 90631-33 • 51,266
Lahaina, HI 96761 • 9,073
La Harpe, IL 61450 • 1,407
Laie, HI 96762 • 5,577
Laingsburg, MI 48848 • 1,148
La Junta, CO 81050 • 7,637

Lake □, CA • 50,631
Lake □, CO • 6,007
Lake □, FL • 152,104
Lake □, IL • 516,418
Lake □, IN • 475,594
Lake □, MI • 8,583
Lake □, MN • 10,415
Lake □, MT • 21,041
Lake □, OH • 215,499
Lake □, OR • 7,186
Lake □, SD • 10,550
Lake □, TN • 7,129
Lake Alfred, FL 33850 • 3,622
Lake Andes, SD 57356 • 846
Lake Arrowhead, CA 92317 • 6,539
Lake Arthur, LA 70549 • 3,194
Lake Barcroft, VA 22041 • 8,686
Lake Bluff, IL 60044 • 5,513
Lake Butler, FL 32054 • 2,116
Lake Carmel, NY 10512 • 8,489
Lake Charles, LA 70601-29 • 70,580
Lake City, AR 72437 • 1,833
Lake City, FL 32055-56 • 10,005
Lake City, IA 51449 • 1,841
Lake City, MN 55041 • 4,391
Lake City, PA 16423 • 2,519
Lake City, SC 29560 • 7,153
Lake City, TN 37769 • 2,166
Lake Crystal, MN 56055 • 2,084
Lake Delta, NY 13440 • 1,980
Lake Delton, WI 53940 • 1,470
Lake Elmo, MN 55042 • 5,903
Lake Elsinore, CA 92330-31 • 18,285
Lake Erie Beach, NY 14006 • 4,509
Lakefield, MN 56150 • 1,679
Lake Forest, FL 33023 • 5,400
Lake Forest, IL 60045 • 17,836
Lake Geneva, WI 53147 • 5,979
Lake Grove, NY 11755 • 9,612
Lake Hamilton, AR 71913 • 1,331
Lake Havasu City, AZ 86403-05 • 24,363
Lake Helen, FL 32744 • 2,344
Lakehurst, NJ 08733 • 3,078
Lake in the Hills, IL 60102 • 5,866
Lake Jackson, TX 77566 • 22,776
Lake Katrine, NY 12449 • 1,998
Lakeland, FL 33801-13 • 70,576
Lakeland, GA 31635 • 2,467
Lakeland Highlands, FL 33801 • 9,972
Lakeland Village, CA 92330 • 5,159
Lake Linden, MI 49945 • 1,203
Lake Lorraine, FL 32569 • 6,779
Lake Luzerne, NY 12846 • 1,160
Lake Magdalene, FL 33612 • 15,973
Lake Mary, FL 32746 • 5,929
Lake Mills, IA 50450 • 2,143
Lake Mills, WI 53551 • 4,143
Lakemore, OH 44250 • 2,684
Lake Odessa, MI 48849 • 2,256
Lake Of The Woods □, MN • 4,076
Lake Orion, MI 48360-62 • 3,057
Lake Oswego, OR 97034-35 • 30,576
Lake Park, FL 33403 • 6,704
Lake Placid, FL 33852 • 1,158
Lake Placid, NY 12946 • 2,485
Lakeport, CA 95453 • 4,390
Lake Preston, SD 57249 • 663
Lake Providence, LA 71254 • 5,380
Lake Ridge, VA 22192 • 23,862
Lake Ronkonkoma, NY 11779 • 18,997
Lake Shore, MD 21122 • 13,269
Lakeside, CA 92040 • 39,412
Lakeside, CT 06488 • 1,200
Lakeside, FL 32073 • 29,137
Lakeside, OR 97449 • 1,437
Lakeside, VA 23228 • 12,081
Lakeside Park, KY 41017 • 3,131
Lakeside-Pinetop, AZ 85935 • 2,422
Lake Station, IN 46405 • 13,899
Lake Stevens, WA 98258 • 3,380
Lake Telemark, NJ 07866 • 1,121
Lakeview, GA 30741 • 5,237
Lake View, IA 51450 • 1,303
Lakeview, MI 48850 • 1,108
Lake View, NY 14085 • 1,460
Lakeview, NY 11552 • 5,476
Lakeview, OH 43331 • 1,056
Lakeview, OR 97630 • 2,526
Lake Villa, IL 60046 • 2,857
Lake Village, AR 71653 • 2,791
Lakeville, CT 06039 • 1,800
Lakeville, MA 02346 • 1,948
Lakeville, MN 55044 • 24,854
Lakeville, NY 14480 • 1,000
Lake Wales, FL 33853 • 9,670
Lake Wissota, WI 54729 • 2,175
Lakewood, CA 90711-16 • 73,557
Lakewood, CO 80215 • 126,481
Lakewood, IL 60014 • 1,609
Lakewood, IA 50211 • 1,950
Lakewood, NJ 08701 • 26,095
Lakewood, NY 14750 • 3,564
Lakewood, OH 44107 • 59,718
Lakewood, WA 98259 • 58,412
Lakewood Center, WA 98499 • 58,412
Lakewood Park, FL 34951 • 7,211
Lake Worth, FL 33460-67 • 28,564
Lake Zurich, IL 60047 • 14,947
Lakin, KS 67860 • 2,060
Lakota, ND 58344 • 898
La Luz, NM 88337 • 1,625
Lamar, CO 81052 • 8,343
Lamar, MO 64759 • 4,168
Lamar, PA 16848 • 1,200
Lamar, SC 29069 • 1,125
Lamar □, AL • 15,715
Lamar □, GA • 13,038
Lamar □, MS • 30,424
Lamar □, TX • 43,949
La Marque, TX 77568 • 14,120
Lamb □, TX • 15,072
Lambert, MS 38643 • 1,131
Lambertville, MI 48144 • 7,860
Lambertville, NJ 08530 • 3,927
La Mesa, CA 91941-44 • 52,931
La Mesa, NM 88044 • 900
Lamesa, TX 79331 • 10,809
La Mirada, CA 90637-38 • 40,452
Lamoille, NV 89828 • 110
Lamoille □, VT • 19,735
Lamoni, IA 50140 • 2,319
Lamont, CA 93241 • 11,517
La Moure, ND 58458 • 970

La Moure □, ND • 5,383
Lampasas, TX 76550 • 6,382
Lampasas □, TX • 13,521
Lanai City, HI 96763 • 2,400
Lanark, IL 61046 • 1,382
Lancashire, DE 19810 • 1,175
Lancaster, CA 93534-39 • 97,291
Lancaster, KY 40444 • 3,421
Lancaster, NH 03584 • 1,859
Lancaster, NY 14086 • 11,940
Lancaster, OH 43130 • 34,507
Lancaster, PA 17601-05 • 55,551
Lancaster, SC 29720-21 • 8,914
Lancaster, TX 75146 • 22,117
Lancaster, WI 53813 • 4,192
Lancaster □, NE • 213,641
Lancaster □, PA • 422,822
Lancaster □, SC • 54,516
Lancaster □, VA • 10,896
Lancaster Village, DE 19805 • 1,100
Landen, OH 45040 • 9,263
Lander, WY 82520 • 7,023
Lander □, NV • 6,266
Landess, IN 46944 • 1,500
Landis, NC 28088 • 2,333
Land O' Lakes, FL 34639 • 7,892
Landover, MD 20784 • 5,052
Landrum, SC 29356 • 2,347
Lane □, KS • 2,375
Lane □, OR • 282,912
Lanesboro, MA 01237 • 1,000
Lanett, AL 36863 • 8,985
Langdon, ND 58249 • 2,241
Langeloth, PA 15054 • 1,112
Langhorne, PA 19047 • 1,361
Langlade □, WI • 19,505
Langley, SC 29834 • 1,714
Langley Park, MD 20783 • 17,474
Langston, OK 73050 • 1,471
Lanham, MD 20706 • 5,000
Lanier □, GA • 5,531
Lansdale, PA 19446 • 16,362
Lansdowne, MD 21227 • 9,430
Lansdowne, PA 19050 • 11,712
L'Anse, MI 49946 • 2,151
Lansford, PA 18232 • 4,583
Lansing, IL 60438 • 28,086
Lansing, IA 52151 • 1,007
Lansing, KS 66043 • 7,120
Lansing, MI 48901-33 • 127,321
Lantana, FL 33462 • 8,392
La Palma, CA 90623 • 15,392
La Paz □, AZ • 13,844
Lapeer, MI 48446 • 7,759
Lapeer □, MI • 74,768
Lapel, IN 46051 • 1,742
La Place, LA 70068-69 • 24,194
La Plata, MD 20646 • 5,841
La Plata, MO 63549 • 1,401
La Plata □, CO • 32,284
Laporte, CO 80535 • 1,300
La Porte, IN 46350 • 21,507
La Porte, TX 77571-72 • 27,910
La Porte □, IN • 107,066
La Porte City, IA 50651 • 2,128
La Pryor, TX 78872 • 1,343
La Puente, CA 91744-49 • 36,955
Lapwai, ID 83540 • 932
Laramie, WY 82063-71 • 26,687
Laramie □, WY • 73,142
Larchmont, NY 10538 • 6,181
Larchmont North, NY 10538 • 11,240
Laredo, TX 78040-44 • 122,899
Largo, FL 34640-49 • 65,674
Larimer □, CO • 186,136
Larimore, ND 58251 • 1,464
La Riviera, CA 95826 • 10,986
Larkspur, CA 94939 • 11,070
Larksville, PA 18704 • 4,700
Larned, KS 67550 • 4,490
Larose, LA 70373 • 5,772
Larue □, KY • 11,679
La Salle, CO 80645 • 1,783
La Salle, IL 61301 • 9,717
La Salle □, IL • 106,913
La Salle □, LA • 13,662
La Salle □, TX • 5,254
Las Animas, CO 81054 • 2,481
Las Animas □, CO • 13,765
Las Cruces, NM 88001-08 • 62,126
Lassen □, CA • 27,598
Las Vegas, NV 89101-99 • 258,295
Las Vegas, NM 87701 • 14,753
Latah □, ID • 30,617
Lathrop, MO 64465 • 1,794
Lathrop Wells, NV 89020 • 350
Latimer □, OK • 10,333
Laton, CA 93242 • 1,415
Latrobe, PA 15650 • 9,265
Latta, SC 29565 • 1,565
Lauderdale □, AL • 79,661
Lauderdale □, MS • 75,555
Lauderdale □, TN • 23,491
Lauderdale Lakes, FL 33313 • 27,341
Lauderhill, FL 33313 • 49,708
Laughlin, NV 89028-29 • 140
Laughlintown, PA 15655 • 1,000
Laurel, DE 19956 • 3,226
Laurel, FL 34272 • 8,245
Laurel, MD 20707-09 • 19,438
Laurel, MS 39440-42 • 18,827
Laurel, MT 59044 • 5,686
Laurel, VA 23060 • 13,011
Laurel □, KY • 43,438
Laurel Bay, SC 29902 • 4,972
Laureldale, PA 19605 • 3,726
Laurel Hill, NC 28351 • 2,314
Laurence Harbor, NJ 08879 • 6,361
Laurens, IA 50554 • 1,550
Laurens, SC 29360 • 9,694
Laurens □, GA • 39,988
Laurens □, SC • 58,092
Laurinburg, NC 28352-53 • 11,643
Laurium, MI 49913 • 2,268
Lavaca, AR 72941 • 1,253
Lavaca □, TX • 18,690
La Vale, MD 21502 • 5,000
Lavallette, NJ 08735 • 2,200
La Vergne, TN 37086 • 7,499
La Verkin, UT 84745 • 1,771
La Verne, CA 91750 • 30,897
Laverne, OK 73848 • 1,269
La Vista, GA 30329 • 4,900

La Vista, NE 68128 • 9,840
Lavonia, GA 30553 • 1,840
Lawai, HI 96765 • 1,787
Lawndale, CA 90260-61 • 27,331
Lawnside, NJ 08045 • 2,841
Lawrence, IN 46226 • 26,763
Lawrence, KS 66044-46 • 65,608
Lawrence, MA 01840-45 • 70,207
Lawrence, NY 11559 • 6,513
Lawrence □, AL • 31,513
Lawrence □, AR • 17,457
Lawrence □, IL • 15,972
Lawrence □, IN • 42,836
Lawrence □, KY • 13,998
Lawrence □, MS • 12,458
Lawrence □, MO • 30,236
Lawrence □, OH • 61,834
Lawrence □, PA • 96,246
Lawrence □, TN • 35,303
Lawrenceburg, IN 47025 • 4,375
Lawrenceburg, KY 40342 • 5,911
Lawrenceburg, TN 38464 • 10,412
Lawrence Park, PA 16511 • 4,310
Lawrenceville, GA 30243-46 • 16,848
Lawrenceville, IL 62439 • 4,897
Lawrenceville, NJ 08648 • 6,446
Lawrenceville, VA 23868 • 1,486
Lawson, MO 64062 • 1,876
Lawsonia, MD 21817 • 1,326
Lawtell, LA 70550 • 1,014
Lawton, MI 49065 • 1,685
Lawton, OK 73501-07 • 80,561
Layton, UT 84040-41 • 41,784
Laytonville, CA 95454 • 1,133
Lea □, NM • 55,765
Leachville, AR 72438 • 1,743
Lead, SD 57754 • 3,632
Leadville, CO 80461 • 2,629
Leadwood, MO 63653 • 1,247
League City, TX 77573-74 • 30,159
Leake □, MS • 18,436
Leakesville, MS 39451 • 1,129
Lealman, FL 33714 • 21,748
Leavenworth, KS 66048 • 38,495
Leavenworth, WA 98826 • 1,692
Leavenworth □, KS • 64,371
Leavittsburg, OH 44430 • 2,220
Leawood, KS 66206 • 19,693
Lebanon, DE 19901 • 130
Lebanon, IL 62254 • 3,688
Lebanon, IN 46052 • 12,059
Lebanon, KY 40033 • 5,695
Lebanon, MO 65536 • 9,983
Lebanon, NH 03766 • 12,183
Lebanon, NJ 08833 • 1,036
Lebanon, OH 45036 • 10,453
Lebanon, OR 97355 • 10,950
Lebanon, PA 17042 • 24,800
Lebanon, TN 37087-88 • 15,208
Lebanon, VA 24266 • 3,386
Lebanon □, PA • 113,744
Lebanon Junction, KY 40150 • 1,741
Le Center, MN 56057 • 2,006
Le Claire, IA 52753 • 2,734
Lecompte, LA 71346 • 1,592
Lee, MA 01238 • 2,020
Lee □, AL • 87,146
Lee □, AR • 13,053
Lee □, FL • 335,113
Lee □, GA • 16,250
Lee □, IL • 34,392
Lee □, IA • 38,687
Lee □, KY • 7,422
Lee □, MS • 65,581
Lee □, NC • 41,374
Lee □, SC • 18,437
Lee □, TX • 12,854
Lee □, VA • 24,496
Leechburg, PA 15656 • 2,504
Leedom Estates, DE 19720 • 1,100
Leeds, AL 35094 • 9,946
Leelanau □, MI • 16,527
Lee Park, PA 18702 • 3,800
Leesburg, FL 34748-49 • 14,903
Leesburg, GA 31763 • 1,452
Leesburg, OH 45135 • 1,063
Leesburg, VA 22075 • 16,202
Lees Summit, MO 64063-64 • 46,418
Leesville, LA 71446 • 7,638
Leesville, SC 29070 • 2,025
Leetonia, OH 44431 • 2,070
Leetsdale, PA 15056 • 1,387
Leflore □, MS • 37,341
Le Flore □, OK • 43,270
Le Grand, CA 95333 • 1,205
Lehi, UT 84043 • 8,475
Lehigh □, PA • 291,130
Lehigh Acres, FL 33936 • 13,611
Lehighton, PA 18235 • 5,914
Leicester, MA 01524 • 3,200
Leipsic, DE 19901 • 236
Leipsic, OH 45856 • 2,203
Leisure City, FL 33033 • 19,379
Leitchfield, KY 42754-55 • 4,965
Leland, MS 38756 • 6,366
Le Mars, IA 51031 • 8,454
Lemay, MO 63125 • 18,005
Lemhi □, ID • 6,899
Lemmon, SD 57638 • 1,614
Lemmon Valley, NV 89501 • 4,100
Lemon Grove, CA 91945-46 • 23,984
Lemont, IL 60439 • 7,348
Lemont, PA 16851 • 2,613
Lemoore, CA 93245 • 13,622
Lena, IL 61048 • 2,605
Lenawee □, MI • 91,476
Lenexa, KS 66215 • 34,034
Lennox, CA 90304 • 22,757
Lennox, SD 57039 • 1,767
Lenoir, NC 28645 • 14,192
Lenoir □, NC • 57,274
Lenoir City, TN 37771 • 6,147
Lenox, IA 50851 • 1,303
Lenox, MA 01240 • 1,687
Leo, IN 46765 • 1,200
Leominster, MA 01453 • 38,145
Leon, IA 50144 • 2,047
Leon □, FL • 192,493
Leon □, TX • 12,665
Leonard, TX 75452 • 1,744
Leonardo, NJ 07737 • 3,720
Leonardtown, MD 20650 • 1,475
Leonia, NJ 07605 • 8,365

Leon Valley, TX 78238 • 9,581
Leoti, KS 67861 • 1,738
Lepanto, AR 72354 • 2,033
Le Roy, IL 61752 • 2,777
Le Roy, NY 14482 • 4,974
Leslie, MI 49251 • 1,872
Leslie, SC 29730 • 1,102
Leslie □, KY • 13,642
Lester Prairie, MN 55354 • 1,180
Le Sueur, MN 56058 • 3,714
Le Sueur □, MN • 23,239
Letcher □, KY • 27,000
Levelland, TX 79336-38 • 13,986
Levittown, NY 11756 • 53,286
Levittown, PA 19058 • 55,362
Levy □, FL • 25,923
Lewes, DE 19958 • 2,295
Lewis □, ID • 3,516
Lewis □, KY • 13,029
Lewis □, MO • 10,233
Lewis □, NY • 26,796
Lewis □, TN • 9,247
Lewis □, WA • 59,358
Lewis □, WV • 17,223
Lewis and Clark □, MT • 47,495
Lewisburg, OH 45338 • 1,584
Lewisburg, PA 17837 • 5,785
Lewisburg, TN 37091 • 9,879
Lewisburg, WV 24901 • 3,598
Lewisport, KY 42351 • 1,778
Lewiston, ID 83501 • 28,082
Lewiston, ME 04240-43 • 39,757
Lewiston, MN 55952 • 1,298
Lewiston, NY 14092 • 3,048
Lewiston, UT 84320 • 1,532
Lewistown, IL 61542 • 2,572
Lewistown, MT 59457 • 6,051
Lewistown, PA 17044 • 9,341
Lewisville, AR 71845 • 1,424
Lewisville, TX 75067 • 46,521
Lexington, IL 61753 • 1,809
Lexington, KY 40501-96 • 225,366
Lexington, MA 02173 • 28,974
Lexington, MS 39095 • 2,227
Lexington, MO 64067 • 4,860
Lexington, NE 68850 • 6,601
Lexington, NC 27292-93 • 16,581
Lexington, OH 44904 • 4,124
Lexington, OK 73051 • 1,776
Lexington, SC 29071-73 • 3,289
Lexington, TN 38351 • 5,810
Lexington, VA 24450 • 6,959
Lexington □, SC • 167,611
Lexington Park, MD 20653 • 9,943
Libby, MT 59923 • 2,532
Liberal, KS 67901-05 • 16,573
Liberty, IN 47353 • 2,051
Liberty, KY 42539 • 1,937
Liberty, MO 64068 • 20,459
Liberty, NY 12754 • 4,128
Liberty, NC 27298 • 2,047
Liberty, SC 29657 • 3,228
Liberty, TX 77575 • 7,733
Liberty □, FL • 5,569
Liberty □, GA • 52,745
Liberty □, MT • 2,295
Liberty □, TX • 52,726
Liberty Acres, CA 90250 • 4,700
Liberty Center, OH 43532 • 1,084
Liberty Lake, WA 99019 • 2,015
Libertyville, IL 60048 • 19,174
Licking, MO 65542 • 1,328
Licking □, OH • 128,300
Lidgerwood, ND 58053 • 799
Lighthouse Point, FL 33064 • 10,378
Ligonier, IN 46767 • 3,443
Ligonier, PA 15658 • 1,638
Lihue, HI 96766 • 5,536
Lilbourn, MO 63862 • 1,378
Lilburn, GA 30247 • 9,301
Lillington, NC 27546 • 2,048
Lilly, PA 15938 • 1,162
Lima, NY 14485 • 2,165
Lima, OH 45801-09 • 45,549
Limestone, ME 04750-51 • 1,245
Limestone □, AL • 54,135
Limestone □, TX • 20,946
Limon, CO 80828 • 1,831
Lincoln, AL 35096 • 2,941
Lincoln, AR 72744 • 1,460
Lincoln, CA 95648 • 7,248
Lincoln, DE 19960 • 500
Lincoln, IL 62656 • 15,418
Lincoln, KS 67455 • 1,381
Lincoln, ME 04457 • 3,399
Lincoln, MA 01773 • 2,860
Lincoln, NE 68501-72 • 191,972
Lincoln □, AR • 13,690
Lincoln □, CO • 4,529
Lincoln □, GA • 7,442
Lincoln □, ID • 3,308
Lincoln □, KS • 3,653
Lincoln □, KY • 20,045
Lincoln □, LA • 41,745
Lincoln □, ME • 30,357
Lincoln □, MN • 6,890
Lincoln □, MS • 30,278
Lincoln □, MO • 28,892
Lincoln □, MT • 17,481
Lincoln □, NE • 32,508
Lincoln □, NV • 3,775
Lincoln □, NM • 12,219
Lincoln □, NC • 50,319
Lincoln □, OK • 29,216
Lincoln □, OR • 38,889
Lincoln □, SD • 15,427
Lincoln □, TN • 28,157
Lincoln □, WA • 8,864
Lincoln □, WV • 21,382
Lincoln □, WI • 26,993
Lincoln □, WY • 12,625
Lincoln Acres, CA 91947 • 1,800
Lincoln City, OR 97367 • 5,892
Lincoln Heights, OH 45215 • 4,805
Lincoln Park, CO 81212 • 3,728
Lincoln Park, GA 30286 • 1,755
Lincoln Park, MI 48146 • 41,832
Lincoln Park, NJ 07035 • 10,978
Lincolnshire, IL 60069 • 4,931
Lincolnton, GA 30817 • 1,476
Lincolnton, NC 28092 • 6,847
Lincoln Village, CA 95207 • 4,236
Lincoln Village, OH 43228 • 9,958

Lincolnwood, IL 60645 • *11,365*
Lincroft, NJ 07738 • *4,740*
Linda, CA 95901 • *13,033*
Lindale, GA 30147 • *4,187*
Lindale, TX 75771 • *2,428*
Linden, AL 36748 • *2,548*
Linden, MI 48451 • *2,415*
Linden, NJ 07036 • *36,701*
Linden, TN 37096 • *1,099*
Linden, TX 75563 • *2,375*
Lindenhurst, IL 60046 • *8,038*
Lindenhurst, NY 11757 • *26,879*
Lindenwold, NJ 08021 • *18,734*
Lindgren Acres, FL 33177 • *22,290*
Lindon, UT 84042 • *3,818*
Lindsay, CA 93247 • *8,338*
Lindsay, OK 73052 • *2,947*
Lindsborg, KS 67456 • *3,076*
Lindstrom, MN 55045 • *2,461*
Linesville, PA 16424 • *1,166*
Lineville, AL 36266 • *2,394*
Lingle, WY 82223 • *473*
Linglestown, PA 17112 • *3,700*
Linn, MO 65051 • *1,148*
Linn □, IA • *168,767*
Linn □, KS • *8,254*
Linn □, MO • *13,885*
Linn □, OR • *91,227*
Lino Lakes, MN 55014 • *8,807*
Linthicum Heights, MD • *2,950*
Linthicum Heights, MD 21090 • *7,547*
Linton, IN 47441 • *5,814*
Linton, ND 58552 • *1,410*
Linwood, NJ 08221 • *6,866*
Lipscomb, AL 35020 • *2,892*
Lipscomb □, TX • *3,143*
Lisbon, IA 52253 • *1,452*
Lisbon, ME 04250 • *1,240*
Lisbon, NH 03585 • *1,246*
Lisbon, ND 58054 • *2,177*
Lisbon, OH 44432 • *3,037*
Lisbon Falls, ME 04252 • *4,674*
Lisle, IL 60532 • *19,512*
Litchfield, CT 06759 • *1,378*
Litchfield, IL 62056 • *6,883*
Litchfield, MI 49252 • *1,317*
Litchfield, MN 55355 • *6,041*
Litchfield □, CT • *174,092*
Litchfield Park, AZ 85340 • *3,303*
Lithia Springs, GA 30057 • *11,403*
Lithonia, GA 30058 • *2,448*
Lititz, PA 17543 • *8,280*
Little Canada, MN 55110 • *8,971*
Little Chute, WI 54140 • *9,207*
Little Compton, RI 02837 • *500*
Little Creek, DE 19961 • *167*
Little Falls, MN 56345 • *7,232*
Little Falls, NJ 07424 • *11,294*
Little Falls, NY 13365 • *5,829*
Little Ferry, NJ 07643 • *9,989*
Littlefield, TX 79339 • *6,489*
Little River □, AR • *13,966*
Little Rock, AR 72201–31 • *175,795*
Little Silver, NJ 07739 • *5,721*
Littlestown, PA 17340 • *2,974*
Littleton, CO 80120–27 • *33,685*
Littleton, MA 01460 • *2,867*
Littleton, NH 03561 • *4,633*
Little Valley, NY 14755 • *1,188*
Live Oak, CA 95062 • *15,212*
Live Oak, CA 95953 • *4,320*
Live Oak, FL 32060 • *6,332*
Live Oak, TX 78233 • *10,023*
Live Oak □, TX • *9,556*
Live Oak Manor, LA 70094 • *2,150*
Livermore, CA 94550 • *56,741*
Livermore, KY 42352 • *1,534*
Livermore Falls, ME 04254 • *1,935*
Livingston, AL 35470 • *3,530*
Livingston, CA 95334 • *7,317*
Livingston, MT 59047 • *6,701*
Livingston, NJ 07039 • *26,609*
Livingston, TN 38570 • *3,809*
Livingston, TX 77351 • *5,019*
Livingston □, IL • *39,301*
Livingston □, KY • *9,062*
Livingston □, LA • *70,526*
Livingston □, MI • *115,645*
Livingston □, MO • *14,592*
Livingston □, NY • *62,372*
Livingston Manor, NY 12758 • *1,482*
Livonia, MI 48150–54 • *100,850*
Livonia, NY 14487 • *1,434*
Llangollen Estates, DE 19720 • *1,070*
Llano, TX 78643 • *2,962*
Llano □, TX • *11,631*
Lloyd Harbor, NY 11743 • *3,343*
Lochearn, MD 21207 • *25,240*
Loch Lomond, VA 22110 • *3,292*
Lockhart, FL 32810 • *11,636*
Lockhart, TX 78644 • *9,205*
Lock Haven, PA 17745 • *9,230*
Lockland, OH 45215 • *4,057*
Lockney, TX 79241 • *2,207*
Lockport, IL 60441 • *9,401*
Lockport, LA 70374 • *2,500*
Lockport, NY 14094 • *24,426*
Lockwood, MO 65682 • *1,041*
Lockwood, MT 59101 • *3,967*
Locust, NC 28097 • *1,940*
Locust Grove, GA 30248 • *1,681*
Locust Grove, OK 74352 • *1,326*
Lodi, CA 95240–42 • *51,874*
Lodi, NJ 07644 • *22,355*
Lodi, OH 44254 • *3,042*
Lodi, WI 53555 • *2,093*
Logan, IA 51546 • *1,401*
Logan, OH 43138 • *6,725*
Logan, UT 84321 • *32,762*
Logan, WV 25601 • *2,206*
Logan □, AR • *20,557*
Logan □, CO • *17,567*
Logan □, IL • *30,798*
Logan □, KS • *3,081*
Logan □, KY • *24,416*
Logan □, NE • *878*
Logan □, ND • *2,847*
Logan □, OH • *42,310*
Logan □, OK • *29,011*
Logan □, WV • *43,032*
Logandale, NV 89021 • *500*
Logansport, IN 46947 • *16,812*
Logansport, LA 71049 • *1,390*
Loganville, GA 30249 • *3,180*
Lolo, MT 59847 • *2,746*
Loma Linda, CA 92354 • *17,400*
Lombard, IL 60148 • *39,408*
Lomira, WI 53048 • *1,542*
Lomita, CA 90717 • *19,382*
Lompoc, CA 93436 • *37,649*
Lonaconing, MD 21539 • *1,122*
London, KY 40741 • *5,757*
London, OH 43140 • *7,807*
Londonderry, NH 03053 • *10,114*
Londontown, MD 21037 • *6,992*
Lone Grove, OK 73443 • *4,114*
Lone Pine, CA 93545 • *1,818*
Long □, GA • *6,202*
Long Beach, CA 90801–88 • *429,433*
Long Beach, IN 46360 • *2,044*
Long Beach, MS 39560 • *15,804*
Long Beach, NY 11561 • *33,510*
Long Beach, WA 98631 • *1,236*
Longboat Key, FL 34228 • *5,937*
Long Branch, NJ 07740 • *28,658*
Long Lake, IL 60041 • *2,888*
Longmeadow, MA 01106 • *15,467*
Longmont, CO 80501–02 • *51,555*
Longport, NJ 08403 • *1,224*
Long Prairie, MN 56347 • *2,786*
Long Valley, NJ 07853 • *1,744*
Long View, NC 28601 • *3,229*
Longview, TX 75601–15 • *70,311*
Longview, WA 98632 • *31,499*
Longwood, FL 32750 • *13,316*
Lonoke, AR 72086 • *4,022*
Lonoke □, AR • *39,268*
Lonsdale, MN 55046 • *1,252*
Lonsdale, RI 02865 • *3,850*
Loogootee, IN 47553 • *2,884*
Lookout Mountain, TN 37350 • *1,901*
Lorain, OH 44052–55 • *71,245*
Lorain □, OH • *271,126*
Lordsburg, NM 88045 • *2,951*
Lorenzo, TX 79343 • *1,208*
Loretto, PA 15940 • *1,072*
Loretto, TN 38469 • *1,515*
Loris, SC 29569 • *2,067*
Lorton, VA 22079 • *15,385*
Los Alamitos, CA 90720–21 • *11,676*
Los Alamos, NM 87544 • *11,455*
Los Alamos □, NM • *18,115*
Los Altos, CA 94022–24 • *26,303*
Los Altos Hills, CA 94022 • *7,514*
Los Angeles, CA 90001–99 • *3,485,398*
Los Angeles □, CA • *8,863,164*
Los Banos, CA 93635 • *14,519*
Los Fresnos, TX 78566 • *2,473*
Los Gatos, CA 95030–32 • *27,357*
Los Lunas, NM 87031 • *6,013*
Los Molinos, CA 96055 • *1,709*
Los Nietos, CA 90606 • *7,100*
Los Osos, CA 93402 • *8,000*
Los Padillas, NM 87105 • *2,400*
Los Ranchos de Albuquerque, NM 87107 • *3,955*
Los Serranos, CA 91709 • *7,099*
Lost Hills, CA 93249 • *1,212*
Loudon, TN 37774 • *4,026*
Loudon □, TN • *31,255*
Loudonville, NY 12211 • *10,822*
Loudonville, OH 44842 • *2,915*
Loudoun □, VA • *86,129*
Louisa, KY 41230 • *1,990*
Louisa, VA 23093 • *1,088*
Louisa □, IA • *11,592*
Louisa □, VA • *20,325*
Louisburg, KS 66053 • *1,964*
Louisburg, NC 27549 • *3,037*
Louisiana, MO 63353 • *3,967*
Louisville, CO 80027 • *12,361*
Louisville, GA 30434 • *2,429*
Louisville, IL 62858 • *1,098*
Louisville, KY 40201–99 • *269,063*
Louisville, MS 39339 • *7,169*
Louisville, OH 44641 • *8,087*
Loup □, NE • *683*
Loup City, NE 68853 • *1,104*
Love □, OK • *8,157*
Loveland, CO 80537–39 • *37,352*
Loveland, OH 45140 • *9,990*
Loveland Park, OH 45140 • *1,357*
Lovell, WY 82431 • *2,131*
Lovelock, NV 89419 • *2,069*
Loves Park, IL 61111 • *15,462*
Loving, NM 88256 • *1,243*
Loving □, TX • *107*
Lovington, IL 61937 • *1,143*
Lovington, NM 88260 • *9,322*
Lowell, AR 72745 • *1,224*
Lowell, IN 46356 • *6,430*
Lowell, MA 01850–54 • *103,439*
Lowell, MI 49331 • *3,983*
Lowell, NC 28098 • *2,704*
Lowellville, OH 44436 • *1,349*
Lower Burrell, PA 15068 • *12,251*
Lower Merion Township, PA 10003 • *59,620*
Lower Paia, HI 96779 • *1,500*
Lowndes □, AL • *12,658*
Lowndes □, GA • *75,981*
Lowndes □, MS • *59,308*
Lowville, NY 13367 • *3,632*
Loxley, AL 36551 • *1,161*
Loyal, WI 54446 • *1,244*
Loyall, KY 40854 • *1,100*
Lubbock, TX 79401–99 • *186,206*
Lubbock □, TX • *222,636*
Lucas □, IA • *9,070*
Lucas □, OH • *462,361*
Lucasville, OH 45648 • *1,575*
Luce □, MI • *5,763*
Lucedale, MS 39452 • *2,592*
Lucerne, CA 95458 • *2,011*
Lucernemines, PA 15754 • *1,074*
Lucerne Valley, CA 92356 • *1,300*
Luck, WI 54853 • *1,022*
Ludington, MI 49431 • *8,507*
Ludlow, KY 41016 • *4,736*
Ludlow, MA 01056 • *18,150*
Ludlow, VT 05149 • *1,123*
Ludowici, GA 31316 • *1,291*
Lufkin, TX 75901–03 • *30,206*
Lugoff, SC 29078 • *3,211*
Lula, GA 30554 • *1,018*
Luling, LA 70070 • *2,803*
Luling, TX 78648 • *4,661*
Lumber City, GA 31549 • *1,429*
Lumberport, WV 26386 • *1,014*
Lumberton, MS 39455 • *2,121*
Lumberton, NC 28358–59 • *18,601*
Lumpkin, GA 31815 • *1,250*
Lumpkin □, GA • *14,573*
Luna □, NM • *18,110*
Luna Pier, MI 48157 • *1,507*
Lund, NV 89317 • *330*
Lunenburg, MA 01462 • *1,694*
Lunenburg □, VA • *11,419*
Luray, VA 22835 • *4,587*
Lusk, WY 82225 • *1,504*
Lutcher, LA 70071 • *3,907*
Luther, OK 73054 • *1,560*
Lutherville-Timonium, MD 21093 • *16,442*
Lutz, FL 33549 • *10,552*
Luverne, AL 36049 • *2,555*
Luverne, MN 56156 • *4,382*
Luxemburg, WI 54217 • *1,151*
Luxora, AR 72358 • *1,338*
Luzerne, PA 18709 • *3,206*
Luzerne □, PA • *328,149*
Lycoming □, PA • *118,710*
Lyford, TX 78569 • *1,674*
Lykens, PA 17048 • *1,986*
Lyman, SC 29365 • *2,271*
Lyman, WY 82937 • *1,896*
Lyman □, SD • *3,638*
Lynbrook, NY 11563 • *19,208*
Lynch, KY 40855 • *1,166*
Lynchburg, OH 45142 • *1,212*
Lynchburg, TN 37352 • *4,721*
Lynchburg, VA 24501–06 • *66,049*
Lyncourt, NY 13208 • *4,516*
Lynden, WA 98264 • *5,709*
Lyndhurst, NJ 07071 • *18,262*
Lyndhurst, OH 44124 • *15,982*
Lyndon, KY 40222 • *8,037*
Lyndonville, VT 05851 • *1,255*
Lyndora, PA 16045 • *3,000*
Lynn, IN 47355 • *1,183*
Lynn, MA 01901–08 • *81,245*
Lynn □, TX • *6,758*
Lynne Acres, MD 21207 • *5,910*
Lynnfield, MA 01940 • *11,274*
Lynn Garden, TN 37665 • *7,213*
Lynn Garden, TN 37665 • *3,950*
Lynn Haven, FL 32444 • *9,298*
Lynnwood, WA 98036–37 • *28,695*
Lynwood, CA 90262 • *61,945*
Lyon □, IA • *11,952*
Lyon □, KS • *34,732*
Lyon □, KY • *6,624*
Lyon □, MN • *24,789*
Lyon □, NV • *20,001*
Lyon Mountain, NY 12952 • *1,000*
Lyons, CO 80540 • *1,227*
Lyons, GA 30436 • *4,502*
Lyons, IL 60534 • *9,828*
Lyons, KS 67554 • *3,688*
Lyons, NE 68038 • *1,144*
Lyons, NY 14489 • *4,280*
Lytle, TX 78052 • *2,255*

M

Mabank, TX 75147 • *1,739*
Mableton, GA 30059 • *25,725*
Mabscott, WV 25871 • *1,543*
Mabton, WA 98935 • *1,482*
MacClenny, FL 32063 • *3,966*
Macedon, NY 14502 • *1,400*
Macedonia, OH 44056 • *7,509*
Machesney Park, IL 61111 • *19,033*
Machias, ME 04654 • *1,773*
Mackinac □, MI • *10,674*
Mackinaw, IL 61755 • *1,331*
Mackinaw City, MI 49701 • *875*
Macomb, IL 61455 • *19,952*
Macomb □, MI • *717,400*
Macon, GA 31201–95 • *106,612*
Macon, IL 62544 • *1,282*
Macon, MS 39341 • *2,256*
Macon, MO 63552 • *5,571*
Macon □, AL • *24,928*
Macon □, GA • *13,114*
Macon □, IL • *117,206*
Macon □, MO • *15,345*
Macon □, NC • *23,499*
Macon □, TN • *15,906*
Macoupin □, IL • *47,679*
Macungie, PA 18062 • *2,597*
Madawaska, ME 04756 • *3,653*
Madeira, OH 45243 • *9,141*
Madelia, MN 56062 • *2,237*
Madera, CA 93637–39 • *29,281*
Madera □, CA • *88,090*
Madill, OK 73446 • *3,069*
Madison, AL 35758 • *14,904*
Madison, AR 72359 • *1,263*
Madison, CT 06443 • *2,139*
Madison, FL 32340 • *3,345*
Madison, GA 30650 • *3,483*
Madison, IL 62060 • *4,629*
Madison, IN 47250 • *12,006*
Madison, ME 04950 • *2,956*
Madison, MN 56256 • *1,951*
Madison, MS 39110 • *7,471*
Madison, NE 68748 • *2,135*
Madison, NJ 07940 • *15,850*
Madison, NC 27025 • *2,371*
Madison, OH 44057 • *2,477*
Madison, SD 57042 • *6,257*
Madison, WV 25130 • *3,051*
Madison, WI 53701–19 • *191,262*
Madison □, AL • *238,912*
Madison □, AR • *11,618*
Madison □, FL • *16,569*
Madison □, GA • *21,050*
Madison □, ID • *23,674*
Madison □, IL • *249,238*
Madison □, IN • *130,669*
Madison □, IA • *12,483*
Madison □, KY • *57,508*
Madison □, LA • *12,463*
Madison □, MS • *53,794*
Madison □, MO • *11,127*
Madison □, MT • *5,989*
Madison □, NE • *32,655*
Madison □, NY • *69,120*
Madison □, NC • *16,953*
Madison □, OH • *37,068*
Madison □, TN • *77,982*
Madison □, TX • *10,931*
Madison □, VA • *11,949*
Madison Heights, MI 48071 • *32,196*
Madison Heights, VA 24572 • *11,700*
Madisonville, KY 42431 • *16,200*
Madisonville, TN 37354 • *3,033*
Madisonville, TX 77864 • *3,569*
Madras, OR 97741 • *3,443*
Madrid, IA 50156 • *2,395*
Maeser, UT 84078 • *2,598*
Magalia, CA 95954 • *8,987*
Magdalena, NM 87825 • *861*
Magee, MS 39111 • *3,607*
Magna, UT 84044 • *17,829*
Magnolia, AR 71753 • *11,151*
Magnolia, MS 39652 • *2,245*
Magnolia, NJ 08049 • *4,861*
Magoffin □, KY • *13,077*
Mahanoy City, PA 17948 • *5,209*
Mahaska □, IA • *21,522*
Mahnomen, MN 56557 • *1,154*
Mahnomen □, MN • *5,044*
Mahomet, IL 61853 • *3,103*
Mahoning □, OH • *264,806*
Mahopac, NY 10541 • *7,755*
Mahwah, NJ 07430 • *7,500*
Maiden, NC 28650 • *2,574*
Maili, HI 96792 • *6,059*
Maine, NY 13802 • *1,110*
Maitland, FL 32751 • *9,110*
Maize, KS 67101 • *1,520*
Major □, OK • *8,055*
Makaha, HI 96792 • *7,990*
Makakilo City, HI 96706 • *9,828*
Makawao, HI 96768 • *5,405*
Makaweli, HI 96769 • *700*
Malabar, FL 32950 • *1,977*
Malad City, ID 83252 • *1,946*
Malaga, NJ 08328 • *2,140*
Malakoff, TX 75148 • *2,038*
Malden, MA 02148 • *53,884*
Malden, MO 63863 • *5,123*
Malheur □, OR • *26,038*
Malibu, CA 90264–65 • *10,000*
Malone, NY 12953 • *6,777*
Malta, MT 59538 • *2,340*
Malvern, AR 72104 • *9,256*
Malvern, IA 51551 • *1,210*
Malvern, OH 44644 • *1,112*
Malvern, PA 19355 • *2,944*
Malverne, NY 11565 • *9,054*
Mamaroneck, NY 10543 • *17,325*
Mammoth, AZ 85618 • *1,845*
Mammoth Lakes, CA 93546 • *4,785*
Mammoth Spring, AR 72554 • *1,097*
Mamou, LA 70554 • *3,483*
Manahawkin, NJ 08050 • *1,594*
Manasquan, NJ 08736 • *5,369*
Manassas, VA 22110–11 • *27,957*
Manassas Park, VA 22111 • *6,734*
Manatee □, FL • *211,707*
Manawa, WI 54949 • *1,169*
Mancelona, MI 49659 • *1,370*
Monchaug, MA 01526 • *1,000*
Manchester, CT 06040 • *51,618*
Manchester, GA 31816 • *4,104*
Manchester, IA 52057 • *5,137*
Manchester, KY 40962 • *1,634*
Manchester, MD 21102 • *2,810*
Manchester, MA 01944 • *5,424*
Manchester, MI 48158 • *1,753*
Manchester, MO 63011 • *6,542*
Manchester, NH 03101–10 • *99,567*
Manchester, NY 14504 • *1,598*
Manchester, OH 45144 • *2,223*
Manchester, PA 17345 • *1,830*
Manchester, TN 37355 • *7,709*
Manchester, VT 05254 • *561*
Manchester Center, VT 05255 • *1,574*
Mandan, ND 58554 • *15,177*
Mandeville, LA 70448 • *7,083*
Mangum, OK 73554 • *3,344*
Manhasset, NY 11030 • *7,718*
Manhattan, KS 66502 • *37,712*
Manhattan, MT 59741 • *1,034*
Manhattan Beach, CA 90266 • *32,063*
Manheim, PA 17545 • *5,011*
Manila, AR 72442 • *2,635*
Manistee, MI 49660 • *6,734*
Manistee □, MI • *21,265*
Manistique, MI 49854 • *3,456*
Manito, IL 61546 • *1,711*
Manitou Springs, CO 80829 • *4,535*
Manitowoc, WI 54220–21 • *32,520*
Manitowoc □, WI • *80,421*
Mankato, KS 66956 • *1,037*
Mankato, MN 56001–03 • *31,477*
Manlius, NY 13104 • *4,764*
Manly, IA 50456 • *1,349*
Mannford, OK 74044 • *1,826*
Manning, IA 51455 • *1,484*
Manning, SC 29102 • *4,428*
Mannington, WV 26582 • *2,184*
Manokotak, AK 99628 • *385*
Manomet, MA 02345 • *1,500*
Manor, TX 78653 • *1,041*
Manorhaven, NY 11050 • *5,672*
Mansfield, AR 72944 • *1,018*
Mansfield, LA 71052 • *5,389*
Mansfield, MA 02048 • *7,170*
Mansfield, MO 65704 • *1,429*
Mansfield, OH 44901–07 • *50,627*
Mansfield, PA 16933 • *3,538*
Mansfield, TX 76063 • *15,607*
Mansfield Center, CT 06250 • *1,043*
Manson, IA 50563 • *1,844*
Mansura, LA 71350 • *1,601*
Manteca, CA 95336 • *40,773*
Manteno, IL 60950 • *3,488*
Manti, UT 84642 • *2,268*
Manton, MI 49663 • *1,161*
Mantua, NJ 08051 • *1,350*
Mantua, OH 44255 • *1,178*
Mantua Hills, VA 22031 • *1,600*
Manvel, TX 77578 • *3,733*
Manville, NJ 08835 • *10,567*
Manville, RI 02838 • *3,030*
Many, LA 71449 • *3,112*
Many Farms, AZ 86538 • *1,294*
Maple Bluff, WI 53704 • *1,352*
Maple Grove, MN 55369 • *38,736*
Maple Heights, OH 44137 • *27,089*
Maple Lake, MN 55358 • *1,394*
Maple Plain, MN 55359 • *2,005*
Maple Shade, NJ 08052 • *19,211*
Mapleton, IA 51034 • *1,294*
Mapleton, MN 56065 • *1,526*
Mapleton, UT 84663 • *3,572*
Maple Valley, WA 98038 • *1,211*
Mapleville, RI 02839 • *1,300*
Maplewood, MN 55109 • *30,954*
Maplewood, MO 63143 • *9,962*
Maplewood, NJ 07040 • *21,756*
Maquoketa, IA 52060 • *6,111*
Marana, AZ 85653 • *2,187*
Marathon, FL 33050 • *8,857*
Marathon, NY 13803 • *1,107*
Marathon, WI 54448 • *1,606*
Marathon □, WI • *115,400*
Marble Falls, TX 78654 • *4,007*
Marblehead, MA 01945 • *19,971*
Marble Hill, MO 63764 • *1,447*
Marbleton, WY 83113 • *634*
Marbury, MD 20658 • *1,244*
Marceline, MO 64658 • *2,645*
Marcellus, MI 49067 • *1,193*
Marco, FL 33937 • *9,493*
Marcus, IA 51035 • *1,171*
Marcus Hook, PA 19061 • *2,546*
Marengo, IL 60152 • *4,768*
Marengo, IA 52301 • *2,270*
Marengo □, AL • *23,084*
Marfa, TX 79843 • *2,424*
Margate, FL 33063 • *42,985*
Margate, MD 21060 • *1,900*
Margate City, NJ 08402 • *8,431*
Marianna, AR 72360 • *5,910*
Marianna, FL 32446 • *6,292*
Maricopa, AZ 85239 • *1,600*
Maricopa, CA 93252 • *1,193*
Maricopa □, AZ • *2,122,101*
Mariemont, OH 45227 • *3,118*
Marienville, PA 16239 • *1,400*
Maries □, MO • *7,976*
Marietta, GA 30060–68 • *44,129*
Marietta, OH 45750 • *15,026*
Marietta, OK 73448 • *2,306*
Marin □, CA • *230,096*
Marina, CA 93933 • *26,436*
Marina del Rey, CA 90292 • *7,431*
Marine City, MI 48039 • *4,556*
Marinette, WI 54143 • *11,843*
Marinette □, WI • *40,548*
Maringouin, LA 70757 • *1,149*
Marion, AL 36756 • *4,211*
Marion, AR 72364 • *4,391*
Marion, IL 62959 • *14,545*
Marion, IN 46952–53 • *32,618*
Marion, IA 52302 • *20,403*
Marion, KS 66861 • *1,906*
Marion, KY 42064 • *3,320*
Marion, MA 02738 • *1,426*
Marion, MS 39342 • *1,359*
Marion, NY 14505 • *1,080*
Marion, NC 28752 • *4,765*
Marion, OH 43301–02 • *34,075*
Marion, PA 17235 • *1,000*
Marion, SC 29571 • *7,658*
Marion, SD 57043 • *831*
Marion, VA 24354 • *6,630*
Marion, WI 54950 • *1,242*
Marion □, AL • *29,830*
Marion □, AR • *12,001*
Marion □, FL • *194,833*
Marion □, GA • *5,590*
Marion □, IL • *41,561*
Marion □, IN • *797,159*
Marion □, IA • *30,001*
Marion □, KS • *12,888*
Marion □, KY • *16,499*
Marion □, MS • *25,544*
Marion □, MO • *27,682*
Marion □, OH • *64,274*
Marion □, OR • *228,483*
Marion □, SC • *33,899*
Marion □, TN • *24,860*
Marion □, TX • *9,984*
Marion □, WV • *57,249*
Marionville, MO 65705 • *1,920*
Mariposa, CA 95338 • *1,152*
Mariposa □, CA • *14,302*
Marissa, IL 62257 • *2,375*
Marked Tree, AR 72365 • *3,100*
Markesan, WI 53946 • *1,496*
Markham, IL 60426 • *13,136*
Markham, TX 77456 • *1,206*
Markle, IN 46770 • *1,208*
Marks, MS 38646 • *1,758*
Marksville, LA 71351 • *5,526*
Marlboro, NY 12542 • *2,200*
Marlboro □, SC • *29,361*
Marlborough, CT 06447 • *5,535*
Marlborough, MA 01752 • *31,813*
Marlborough, NH 03455 • *1,211*
Marlene Village, OR 97005 • *1,500*
Marlette, MI 48453 • *1,924*
Marley, MD 21060 • *7,100*
Marlin, TX 76661 • *6,386*
Marlinton, WV 24954 • *1,148*
Marlow, OK 73055 • *4,416*
Marlow Heights, MD 20748 • *5,885*
Marlton, NJ 08053 • *10,228*
Marmaduke, AR 72443 • *1,164*
Marmet, WV 25315 • *1,879*
Maroa, IL 61756 • *1,602*
Marquette, MI 49855 • *21,977*
Marquette □, MI • *70,887*
Marquette □, WI • *12,321*
Marquette Heights, IL 61554 • *3,077*
Marrero, LA 70072–73 • *36,671*
Mars, PA 16046 • *1,713*
Marseilles, IL 61341 • *4,811*
Marshall, AR 72650 • *1,318*
Marshall, IL 62441 • *3,555*
Marshall, MI 49068 • *6,891*
Marshall, MN 56258 • *12,023*
Marshall, MO 65340 • *12,711*
Marshall, TX 75670–71 • *23,682*
Marshall, WI 53559 • *2,329*
Marshall □, AL • *70,832*
Marshall □, IL • *12,846*
Marshall □, IN • *42,182*

Marshall □, IA • 38,276
Marshall □, KS • 11,705
Marshall □, KY • 27,205
Marshall □, MN • 10,993
Marshall □, MS • 30,361
Marshall □, OK • 10,829
Marshall □, SD • 4,844
Marshall □, TN • 21,539
Marshall □, WV • 37,356
Marshallton, DE 19808 • 1,765
Marshalltown, IA 50158 • 25,178
Marshallville, GA 31057 • 1,457
Marshfield, MA 02050 • 4,002
Marshfield, MO 65706 • 4,374
Marshfield, WI 54449 • 19,291
Marshfield Hills, MA 02051 • 2,201
Mars Hill, ME 04758 • 1,500
Mars Hill, NC 28754 • 1,611
Marshville, NC 28103 • 2,020
Marsing, ID 83639 • 798
Marstons Mills, MA 02648 • 8,017
Mart, TX 76664 • 2,004
Martha Lake, WA 98012 • 10,155
Martin, SD 57551 • 1,151
Martin, TN 38237 • 8,600
Martin □, FL • 100,900
Martin □, IN • 10,369
Martin □, KY • 12,526
Martin □, MN • 22,914
Martin □, NC • 25,078
Martin □, TX • 4,956
Martinez, CA 94553 • 31,808
Martinez, GA 30907 • 33,731
Martinsburg, PA 16662 • 2,119
Martinsburg, WV 25401 • 14,073
Martins Ferry, OH 43935 • 7,990
Martinsville, IL 62442 • 1,161
Martinsville, IN 46151 • 11,677
Martinsville, VA 24112–15 • 16,162
Marvell, AR 72366 • 1,545
Maryland City, MD 20724 • 6,813
Maryland Heights, MO 63043 • 25,407
Marysville, CA 95901 • 12,324
Marysville, KS 66508 • 3,359
Marysville, MI 48040 • 8,515
Marysville, OH 43040 • 9,656
Marysville, PA 17053 • 2,425
Marysville, WA 98270 • 10,328
Maryville, MO 64468 • 10,663
Maryville, TN 37801–04 • 19,208
Mascot, TN 37806 • 2,138
Mascoutah, IL 62258 • 5,511
Mason, MI 48854 • 6,768
Mason, NV 89447 • 400
Mason, OH 45040 • 11,452
Mason, TX 76856 • 2,041
Mason, WV 25260 • 1,053
Mason □, IL • 16,269
Mason □, KY • 16,666
Mason □, MI • 25,537
Mason □, TX • 3,423
Mason □, WA • 38,341
Mason □, WV • 25,178
Masonboro, NC 28403 • 7,010
Mason City, IL 62664 • 2,323
Mason City, IA 50401 • 29,040
Masontown, PA 15461 • 3,759
Massac □, IL • 14,752
Massapequa, NY 11758 • 22,018
Massapequa Park, NY 11762 • 18,044
Massena, NY 13662 • 11,719
Massillon, OH 44646–48 • 31,007
Mastic, NY 11950 • 13,778
Mastic Beach, NY 11951 • 10,293
Masury, OH 44438 • 1,836
Matagorda □, TX • 36,928
Matamoras, PA 18336 • 1,934
Matawan, NJ 07747 • 9,270
Mather, PA 15346 • 1,300
Mathews □, VA • 8,348
Mathis, TX 78368 • 5,423
Matoaca, VA 23803 • 1,967
Mattapoisett, MA 02739 • 2,949
Matteson, IL 60443 • 11,378
Matthews, NC 28105–06 • 13,651
Mattituck, NY 11952 • 3,902
Mattoon, IL 61938 • 18,441
Mattydale, NY 13211 • 6,418
Matunuck, RI 02879 • 550
Maud, OK 74854 • 1,204
Maugansville, MD 21767 • 1,707
Maui □, HI • 100,374
Mauldin, SC 29662 • 11,587
Maumee, OH 43537 • 15,561
Maunaloa, HI 96770 • 405
Maunawili, HI 96734 • 4,847
Maury □, TN • 54,812
Mauston, WI 53948 • 3,439
Maverick □, TX • 36,378
Maxton, NC 28364 • 2,373
Maxwell Acres, WV 26041 • 1,000
Mayer, AZ 86333 • 1,800
Mayes □, OK • 33,366
Mayfield, KY 42066 • 9,935
Mayfield, PA 18433 • 1,890
Mayfield Heights, OH 44124 • 19,847
Mayflower, AR 72106 • 1,415
Mayflower Village, CA 91016 • 4,978
Maynard, MA 01754 • 10,325
Maynardville, TN 37807 • 1,298
Mayo, MD 21106 • 2,537
Mayodan, NC 27027 • 2,471
Mays Landing, NJ 08330 • 2,090
Maysville, KY 41056 • 7,169
Maysville, MO 64469 • 1,176
Maysville, OK 73057 • 1,203
Mayville, MI 48744 • 1,010
Mayville, NY 14757 • 1,636
Mayville, ND 58257 • 2,092
Mayville, WI 53050 • 4,374
Maywood, CA 90270 • 27,850
Maywood, IL 60153–54 • 27,139
Maywood, NJ 07607 • 9,473
Mazomanie, WI 53560 • 1,377
McAdoo, PA 18237 • 2,459
McAlester, OK 74501–02 • 16,370
McAllen, TX 78501–04 • 84,021
McAlmont, AR 72117 • 1,800
McAlpine, MD 21043 • 2,230
McArthur, OH 45651 • 1,541
McCall, ID 83638 • 2,005
McCamey, TX 79752 • 2,493
McCandless, PA 15237 • 28,781

McCaysville, GA 30555 • 1,065
McClain □, OK • 22,795
McCleary, WA 98557 • 1,235
McCloud, CA 96057 • 1,555
McClure, PA 17841 • 1,070
McColl, SC 29570 • 2,685
McComb, MS 39648 • 11,591
McComb, OH 45858 • 1,544
McCone □, MT • 2,276
McConnellsburg, PA 17233 • 1,106
McConnelsville, OH 43756 • 1,804
McCook, NE 69001 • 8,112
McCook □, SD • 5,688
McCormick, SC 29835 • 1,659
McCormick □, SC • 8,868
McCracken □, KY • 62,879
McCreary □, KY • 15,603
McCrory, AR 72101 • 1,971
McCulloch □, TX • 8,778
McCurtain □, OK • 33,433
McDermitt, NV 89421 • 373
McDonald □, MO • 16,938
McDonough, GA 30253 • 2,929
McDonough □, IL • 35,244
McDowell □, NC • 35,681
McDowell □, WV • 35,233
McDuffie □, GA • 20,119
McEwen, TN 37101 • 1,442
McFarland, CA 93250 • 7,005
McFarland, WI 53558 • 5,232
McGehee, AR 71654 • 4,997
McGill, NV 89318 • 1,258
McGrath, AK 99627 • 528
McGraw, NY 13101 • 1,074
McGregor, TX 76657 • 4,683
McHenry, IL 60050–51 • 16,177
McHenry □, IL • 183,241
McHenry □, ND • 6,528
McIntosh □, GA • 8,634
McIntosh □, ND • 4,021
McIntosh □, OK • 16,779
McKean □, PA • 47,131
McKee City, NJ 08232 • 1,200
McKeesport, PA 15130–35 • 26,016
McKees Rocks, PA 15136 • 7,691
McKenzie, TN 38201 • 5,168
McKenzie □, ND • 6,383
McKinley □, NM • 60,686
McKinleyville, CA 95521 • 10,749
McKinney, TX 75069–70 • 21,283
McLaughlin, SD 57642 • 780
McLean, VA 22101 • 38,168
McLean □, IL • 129,180
McLean □, KY • 9,628
McLean □, ND • 10,457
McLeansboro, IL 62859 • 2,677
McLennan □, TX • 189,123
McLeod □, MN • 32,030
McLoud, OK 74851 • 2,493
McMechen, WV 26040 • 2,130
McMinn □, TN • 42,383
McMinnville, OR 97128 • 17,894
McMinnville, TN 37110 • 11,194
McMullen □, TX • 817
McNairy □, TN • 22,422
McPherson, KS 67460 • 12,422
McPherson □, KS • 27,268
McPherson □, NE • 546
McPherson □, SD • 3,228
McQueeney, TX 78123 • 2,063
McRae, GA 31055 • 3,007
McRoberts, KY 41835 • 1,101
McSherrystown, PA 17344 • 2,769
Mead, WA 99021 • 2,150
Meade, KS 67864 • 1,526
Meade □, KS • 4,247
Meade □, KY • 24,170
Meade □, SD • 21,878
Meadowbrook, FL 32808 • 5,200
Meadowood, DE 19711 • 2,100
Meadville, PA 16335 • 14,318
Meagher □, MT • 1,819
Mebane, NC 27302 • 4,754
Mecca, CA 92254 • 1,966
Mechanic Falls, ME 04256 • 2,388
Mechanicsburg, OH 43044 • 1,803
Mechanicsburg, PA 17055 • 9,452
Mechanicsville, IA 52306 • 1,012
Mechanicsville, VA 23111 • 22,027
Mechanicville, NY 12118 • 5,249
Mecklenburg □, NC • 511,433
Mecklenburg □, VA • 29,241
Mecosta □, MI • 37,308
Medfield, MA 02052 • 5,985
Medford, MA 02155 • 57,407
Medford, NJ 08055 • 1,800
Medford, NY 11763 • 21,274
Medford, OK 73759 • 1,172
Medford, OR 97501–04 • 46,951
Medford, WI 54451 • 4,283
Medford Lakes, NJ 08055 • 4,462
Media, PA 19063–65 • 5,957
Mediapolis, IA 52637 • 1,637
Medical Lake, WA 99022 • 3,664
Medicine Bow, WY 82329 • 389
Medicine Lodge, KS 67104 • 2,453
Medina, NY 14103 • 6,686
Medina, OH 44256 • 19,231
Medina, WA 98039 • 2,981
Medina □, OH • 122,354
Medina □, TX • 27,312
Medway, MA 02053 • 3,890
Meeker, CO 81641 • 2,098
Meeker, OK 74855 • 1,003
Meeker □, MN • 20,846
Meeteetse, WY 82433 • 368
Mehlville, MO 63129 • 27,557
Meigs, GA 31765 • 1,120
Meigs □, OH • 22,987
Meigs □, TN • 8,033
Meiners Oaks, CA 93023 • 3,329
Melbourne, AR 72556 • 1,562
Melbourne, FL 32901–10 • 59,646
Melbourne Beach, FL 32951 • 3,021
Melcher, IA 50163 • 1,302
Mellette □, SD • 2,137
Melrose, FL 32666 • 1,700
Melrose, MA 02176 • 28,150
Melrose, MN 56352 • 2,561
Melrose Park, FL 33312 • 6,477
Melrose Park, IL 60160–63 • 20,859
Melville, LA 71353 • 1,562
Melville, NY 11747 • 12,586

Melvindale, MI 48122 • 11,216
Memphis, FL 34221 • 6,760
Memphis, MI 48041 • 1,221
Memphis, MO 63555 • 2,094
Memphis, TN 38101–87 • 610,337
Memphis, TX 79245 • 2,465
Mena, AR 71953 • 5,475
Menahga, MN 56464 • 1,076
Menands, NY 12204 • 4,333
Menard, TX 76859 • 1,606
Menard □, IL • 11,164
Menard □, TX • 2,252
Menasha, WI 54952 • 14,711
Mendenhall, MS 39114 • 2,463
Mendham, NJ 07945 • 4,890
Mendocino, CA 95460 • 1,008
Mendocino □, CA • 80,345
Mendota, CA 93640 • 6,821
Mendota, IL 61342 • 7,018
Mendota Heights, MN 55118 • 9,431
Menifee □, KY • 5,092
Menlo Park, CA 94025–28 • 28,040
Menno, SD 57045 • 768
Menominee, MI 49858 • 9,398
Menominee □, MI • 24,920
Menominee □, WI • 3,890
Menomonee Falls, WI 53051–52 • 26,840
Menomonie, WI 54751 • 13,547
Mentor, OH 44060–61 • 47,358
Mentor-on-the-Lake, OH 44060 • 8,271
Mequon, WI 53092 • 18,885
Meraux, LA 70075 • 8,000
Merced, CA 95339–44 • 56,216
Merced □, CA • 178,403
Mercedes, TX 78570 • 12,694
Mercer, PA 16137 • 2,444
Mercer, WI 54547 • 1,300
Mercer □, IL • 17,290
Mercer □, KY • 19,148
Mercer □, MO • 3,723
Mercer □, NJ • 325,824
Mercer □, ND • 9,808
Mercer □, OH • 39,443
Mercer □, PA • 121,003
Mercer □, WV • 64,980
Mercer Island, WA 98040 • 20,816
Mercersburg, PA 17236 • 1,640
Mercerville, NJ 08619 • 15,600
Merchantville, NJ 08109 • 4,095
Meredith, NH 03253 • 1,654
Meredosia, IL 62665 • 1,134
Meriden, CT 06450 • 59,479
Meridian, ID 83642 • 9,596
Meridian, MS 39301–09 • 41,036
Meridian, PA 16001 • 3,473
Meridian, TX 76665 • 1,390
Meridian Hills, IN 46260 • 1,728
Meridianville, AL 35759 • 2,852
Meriwether □, GA • 22,411
Merkel, TX 79536 • 2,469
Merriam, KS 66203 • 11,821
Merrick, NY 11566 • 23,042
Merrick □, NE • 8,042
Merrifield, VA 22031 • 8,399
Merrill, WI 54452 • 9,860
Merrillville, IN 46410 • 27,257
Merrimac, MA 01860 • 2,050
Merrimack, NH 03054 • 1,300
Merrimack □, NH • 120,005
Merritt Island, FL 32952–54 • 32,886
Merryville, LA 70653 • 1,235
Merton, WI 53056 • 1,199
Mesa, AZ 85201–16 • 288,091
Mesa □, CO • 93,145
Mescalero, NM 88340 • 1,159
Mesilla, NM 88046 • 1,975
Mesquite, NV 89024 • 1,871
Mesquite, TX 75149–50 • 101,484
Metairie, LA 70001–11 • 149,428
Metamora, IL 61548 • 2,520
Metcalfe, MS 38760 • 1,092
Metcalfe □, KY • 8,963
Methuen, MA 01844 • 39,990
Metlakatla, AK 99926 • 1,407
Metropolis, IL 62960 • 6,734
Metter, GA 30439 • 3,707
Metuchen, NJ 08840 • 12,804
Metzger, OR 97223 • 3,149
Mexia, TX 76667 • 6,933
Mexico, ME 04257 • 2,302
Mexico, MO 65265 • 11,290
Mexico, NY 13114 • 1,555
Meyersdale, PA 15552 • 2,518
Miami, AZ 85539 • 2,018
Miami, FL 33101–99 • 358,548
Miami, OK 74354–55 • 13,142
Miami □, IN • 36,897
Miami □, KS • 23,466
Miami □, OH • 93,182
Miami Beach, FL 33139 • 92,639
Miami Lakes, FL 33014 • 12,750
Miamisburg, OH 45342–43 • 17,834
Miami Shores, FL 33138 • 10,084
Miami Springs, FL 33166 • 13,268
Micco, FL 32958 • 8,757
Michigan Center, MI 49254 • 4,863
Michigan City, IN 46360 • 33,822
Middleboro (Middleborough Center), MA 02346 • 6,837
Middleburg, FL 32068 • 6,223
Middleburg, PA 17842 • 1,422
Middleburgh, NY 12122 • 1,436
Middleburg Heights, OH 44130 • 14,702
Middlebury, CT 06762 • 4,140
Middlebury, IN 46540 • 2,004
Middlebury, VT 05753 • 6,007
Middlefield, CT 06455 • 1,200
Middlefield, OH 44062 • 1,898
Middle Island, NY 11953 • 7,848
Middleport, NY 14105 • 1,876
Middleport, OH 45760 • 2,725
Middle River, MD 21220 • 24,616
Middlesboro, KY 40965 • 11,328
Middlesex, NJ 08846 • 13,055
Middlesex □, CT • 143,196
Middlesex □, MA • 1,398,468
Middlesex □, NJ • 671,780
Middlesex □, VA • 8,653
Middleton, ID 83644 • 1,851
Middleton, MA 01949 • 4,135
Middleton, WI 53562 • 13,289
Middletown, CA 95461 • 2,000
Middletown, CT 06457 • 42,762

Middletown, DE 19709 • 3,834
Middletown, IN 47356 • 2,333
Middletown, KY 40243 • 5,016
Middletown, MD 21769 • 1,834
Middletown, NJ 07718 • 62,298
Middletown, NY 10940 • 24,160
Middletown, OH 45042–44 • 46,022
Middletown, PA 17057 • 9,254
Middletown, RI 02840 • 3,350
Middletown, VA 22645 • 1,061
Middletown Township, PA 19037 • 6,866
Middleville, MI 49333 • 1,966
Midfield, AL 35228 • 5,559
Midland, MI 48640–42 • 38,053
Midland, PA 15059 • 3,321
Midland, TX 79701–12 • 89,443
Midland □, MI • 75,651
Midland □, TX • 106,611
Midland City, AL 36350 • 1,819
Midland Park, KS 67216 • 1,200
Midland Park, NJ 07432 • 7,047
Midland Park, SC 29405 • 1,300
Midlothian, IL 60445 • 14,372
Midlothian, TX 76065 • 5,141
Midvale, UT 84047 • 11,886
Midway, DE 19971 • 500
Midway, KY 40347 • 1,290
Midway, OR 97233 • 19,000
Midway, PA 15060 • 1,043
Midway, UT 84049 • 1,554
Midwest, WY 82643 • 495
Midwest City, OK 73110 • 52,267
Mifflin □, PA • 46,197
Mifflinburg, PA 17844 • 3,480
Mifflinville, PA 18631 • 1,329
Milaca, MN 56353 • 2,182
Milam □, TX • 22,946
Milan, GA 31060 • 1,056
Milan, IL 61264 • 5,831
Milan, IN 47031 • 1,529
Milan, MI 48160 • 4,040
Milan, MO 63556 • 1,767
Milan, NM 87021 • 1,911
Milan, OH 44846 • 1,464
Milan, TN 38358 • 7,512
Milbank, SD 57252 • 3,879
Milesburg, PA 16853 • 1,144
Miles City, MT 59301 • 8,461
Milford, CT 06460 • 48,168
Milford, DE 19963 • 6,040
Milford, IL 60953 • 1,512
Milford, IN 46542 • 1,388
Milford, IA 51351 • 2,170
Milford, ME 04461 • 2,228
Milford, MA 01757 • 23,339
Milford, MI 48380–82 • 5,511
Milford, NE 68405 • 1,886
Milford, NH 03055 • 8,015
Milford, NJ 08848 • 1,273
Milford, OH 45150 • 5,660
Milford, PA 18337 • 1,064
Milford, UT 84751 • 1,107
Mililani Town, HI 96789 • 29,359
Millard □, UT • 11,333
Millbrae, CA 94030 • 20,412
Millbrook, AL 36054 • 6,050
Millbrook, NY 12545 • 1,339
Millburn, NJ 07041 • 18,630
Millbury, MA 01527 • 4,940
Millbury, OH 43447 • 1,081
Mill City, OR 97360 • 1,555
Millcreek, UT 84109 • 32,230
Millcreek Township, PA 16505 • 46,100
Milledgeville, GA 31061 • 17,727
Milledgeville, IL 61051 • 1,076
Mille Lacs □, MN • 18,670
Millen, GA 30442 • 3,808
Miller, SD 57362 • 1,678
Miller □, AR • 38,467
Miller □, GA • 6,280
Miller □, MO • 20,700
Miller Place, NY 11764 • 9,315
Millersburg, OH 44654 • 3,051
Millersburg, PA 17061 • 2,729
Millers Falls, MA 01349 • 1,084
Millersport, OH 43046 • 1,010
Millersville, PA 17551 • 8,099
Mill Hall, PA 17751 • 1,702
Milliken, CO 80543 • 1,605
Millington, MI 48746 • 1,114
Millington, TN 38053 • 17,866
Millinocket, ME 04462 • 6,922
Millis, MA 02054 • 3,777
Millport, AL 35576 • 1,203
Mills, WY 82644 • 1,574
Mills □, IA • 13,202
Mills □, TX • 4,531
Millsboro, DE 19966 • 1,643
Millstadt, IL 62260 • 2,566
Milltown, NJ 08850 • 6,968
Millvale, PA 15209 • 4,341
Mill Valley, CA 94941–42 • 13,038
Millville, MA 01529 • 1,693
Millville, NJ 08332 • 25,992
Millville, UT 84326 • 1,202
Millwood, WA 99212 • 1,559
Milnor, ND 58060 • 651
Milo, ME 04463 • 2,129
Milpitas, CA 95035–36 • 50,686
Milroy, PA 17063 • 1,456
Milstead, GA 30207 • 1,500
Milton, DE 19968 • 1,417
Milton, FL 32570–71 • 7,216
Milton, MA 02186 • 25,725
Milton, NH 03851 • 1,000
Milton, NY 12547 • 1,140
Milton, PA 17847 • 6,746
Milton, VT 05468 • 1,578
Milton, WA 98354 • 4,995
Milton, WV 25541 • 2,242
Milton, WI 53563 • 4,434
Milton-Freewater, OR 97862 • 5,533
Milwaukee, WI 53201–95 • 628,088
Milwaukee □, WI • 959,275
Milwaukie, OR 97222 • 18,692
Mimosa Park, LA 70070 • 4,516
Mims, FL 32754 • 9,412
Mina, NV 89422 • 400
Minco, OK 73059 • 1,411
Minden, LA 71055 • 13,661
Minden, NE 68959 • 2,749
Minden, NV 89423 • 1,441
Mine Hill, NJ 07801 • 3,250

Mineola, NY 11501 • 18,994
Mineola, TX 75773 • 4,321
Miner, MO 63801 • 1,218
Miner □, SD • 3,272
Mineral □, CO • 558
Mineral □, MT • 3,315
Mineral □, NV • 6,475
Mineral □, WV • 26,697
Mineral Point, WI 53565 • 2,428
Mineral Springs, AR 71851 • 1,004
Mineral Wells, TX 76067 • 14,870
Minersville, PA 17954 • 4,877
Minerva, OH 44657 • 4,318
Minetto, NY 13115 • 1,252
Mineville, NY 12956 • 1,000
Mingo □, WV • 33,739
Mingo Junction, OH 43938 • 4,297
Minidoka □, ID • 19,361
Minier, IL 61759 • 1,155
Minneapolis, KS 67467 • 1,983
Minneapolis, MN 55401–80 • 368,383
Minnehaha □, SD • 123,809
Minneota, MN 56264 • 1,417
Minnetonka, MN 55345 • 48,370
Minocqua, WI 54548 • 1,280
Minonk, IL 61760 • 1,982
Minooka, IL 60447 • 2,561
Minot, ND 58701–02 • 34,544
Minquadale, DE 19720 • 790
Minster, OH 45865 • 2,650
Mint Hill, NC 28212 • 11,567
Minturn, CO 81645 • 1,066
Mio, MI 48647 • 1,500
Mira Loma, CA 91752 • 15,786
Miramar, FL 33023 • 40,663
Misenheimer, NC 28109 • 1,000
Mishawaka, IN 46544–46 • 42,608
Mishicot, WI 54228 • 1,296
Missaukee □, MI • 12,147
Mission, KS 66205 • 9,504
Mission, TX 78572 • 28,653
Mission Hills, KS 66205 • 3,446
Mission Viejo, CA 92691 • 72,820
Mississippi □, AR • 57,525
Mississippi □, MO • 14,442
Mississippi State, MS 39762 • 12,400
Missoula, MT 59801–07 • 42,918
Missoula □, MT • 78,687
Missouri City, TX 77459 • 36,176
Missouri Valley, IA 51555 • 2,888
Mitchell, IL 62040 • 1,320
Mitchell, IN 47446 • 4,669
Mitchell, NE 69357 • 1,743
Mitchell, SD 57301 • 13,798
Mitchell □, GA • 20,275
Mitchell □, IA • 10,928
Mitchell □, KS • 7,203
Mitchell □, NC • 14,433
Mitchell □, TX • 8,016
Mitchellville, IA 50169 • 1,670
Mizpah, NJ 08342 • 1,000
Moab, UT 84532 • 3,971
Moberly, MO 65270 • 12,839
Mobile, AL 36601–95 • 196,278
Mobile □, AL • 378,643
Mobridge, SD 57601 • 3,768
Mocanaqua, PA 18655 • 1,100
Mocksville, NC 27028 • 3,399
Modesto, CA 95350–56 • 164,730
Modoc □, CA • 9,678
Moenkopi, AZ 86045 • 1,200
Moffat □, CO • 11,357
Mogadore, OH 44260 • 4,008
Mohall, ND 58761 • 931
Mohave □, AZ • 93,497
Mohawk, NY 13407 • 2,986
Mohnton, PA 19540 • 2,484
Mojave, CA 93501–02 • 3,763
Mokena, IL 60448 • 6,128
Molalla, OR 97038 • 3,651
Moline, IL 61265 • 43,202
Molino, FL 32577 • 1,207
Momence, IL 60954 • 2,968
Monaca, PA 15061 • 6,739
Monahans, TX 79756 • 8,101
Monarch Mills, SC 29379 • 2,214
Moncks Corner, SC 29461 • 5,607
Mondovi, WI 54755 • 2,491
Monee, IL 60449 • 1,044
Monessen, PA 15062 • 9,901
Monett, MO 65708 • 6,529
Monette, AR 72447 • 1,115
Monfort Heights, OH 45239 • 9,745
Moniteau □, MO • 12,298
Monmouth, IL 61462 • 9,489
Monmouth, OR 97361 • 6,288
Monmouth □, NJ • 553,124
Monmouth Beach, NJ 07750 • 3,303
Monmouth Junction, NJ 08852 • 1,570
Mono □, CA • 9,956
Monon, IN 47959 • 1,585
Monona, IA 52159 • 1,520
Monona, WI 53716 • 8,637
Monona □, IA • 10,034
Monongah, WV 26554 • 1,018
Monongahela, PA 15063 • 4,928
Monongalia □, WV • 75,509
Monroe, GA 30655 • 9,759
Monroe, IA 50170 • 1,739
Monroe, LA 71201–13 • 54,909
Monroe, MI 48161 • 22,902
Monroe, NY 10950 • 6,672
Monroe, NC 28110–12 • 16,127
Monroe, OH 45050 • 4,490
Monroe, UT 84754 • 1,472
Monroe, WA 98272 • 4,278
Monroe, WI 53566 • 10,241
Monroe □, AL • 23,968
Monroe □, AR • 11,333
Monroe □, FL • 78,024
Monroe □, GA • 17,113
Monroe □, IL • 22,422
Monroe □, IN • 108,978
Monroe □, IA • 8,114
Monroe □, KY • 11,401
Monroe □, MI • 133,600
Monroe □, MS • 36,582
Monroe □, MO • 9,104
Monroe □, NY • 713,968
Monroe □, OH • 15,497
Monroe □, PA • 95,709
Monroe □, TN • 30,541
Monroe □, WV • 12,406

Monroe □, WI • 36,633
Monroe Center, CT 06468 • 7,900
Monroe City, MO 63456 • 2,701
Monroe Park, DE 19807 • 1,000
Monroeville, AL 36460–61 • 6,993
Monroeville, IN 46773 • 1,232
Monroeville, OH 44847 • 1,381
Monroeville, PA 15146 • 29,169
Monrovia, CA 91016 • 35,761
Monsey, NY 10952 • 13,986
Monson, MA 01057 • 2,101
Montague, CA 96064 • 1,415
Montague, MI 49437 • 2,276
Montague □, TX • 17,274
Mont Alto, PA 17237 • 1,395
Montauk, NY 11954 • 3,001
Mont Belvieu, TX 77580 • 1,323
Montcalm □, MI • 53,059
Montchanin, DE 19710 • 500
Montclair, CA 91763 • 28,434
Montclair, NJ 07042–44 • 37,729
Mont Clare, PA 19453 • 1,800
Monteagle, TN 37356 • 1,138
Montebello, CA 90640 • 59,564
Montecito, CA 93108 • 9,300
Montello, NV 89830 • 200
Montello, WI 53949 • 1,329
Monterey, CA 93940 • 31,954
Monterey, TN 38574 • 2,559
Monterey □, CA • 355,660
Monterey Park, CA 91754 • 60,738
Montesano, WA 98563 • 3,064
Montevallo, AL 35115 • 4,239
Montevideo, MN 56265 • 5,499
Monte Vista, CO 81144 • 4,324
Montezuma, GA 31063 • 4,506
Montezuma, IN 47862 • 1,134
Montezuma, IA 50171 • 1,651
Montezuma □, CO • 18,672
Montgomery, AL 36101–99 • 187,106
Montgomery, IL 60538 • 4,267
Montgomery, MN 56069 • 2,399
Montgomery, NY 12549 • 2,696
Montgomery, OH 45242 • 9,753
Montgomery, PA 17752 • 1,631
Montgomery, WV 25136 • 2,449
Montgomery □, AL • 209,085
Montgomery □, AR • 7,841
Montgomery □, GA • 7,163
Montgomery □, IL • 30,728
Montgomery □, IN • 34,436
Montgomery □, IA • 12,076
Montgomery □, KS • 38,816
Montgomery □, KY • 19,561
Montgomery □, MD • 757,027
Montgomery □, MS • 12,388
Montgomery □, MO • 11,355
Montgomery □, NY • 51,981
Montgomery □, NC • 23,346
Montgomery □, OH • 573,809
Montgomery □, PA • 678,111
Montgomery □, TN • 100,498
Montgomery □, TX • 182,201
Montgomery □, VA • 73,913
Montgomery City, MO 63361 • 2,281
Montgomery Village, MD 20879 • 32,315
Monticello, AR 71655 • 8,116
Monticello, FL 32344 • 2,573
Monticello, GA 31064 • 2,289
Monticello, IL 61856 • 4,549
Monticello, IN 47960 • 5,237
Monticello, IA 52310 • 3,522
Monticello, KY 42633 • 5,357
Monticello, MN 55362 • 4,941
Monticello, MS 39654 • 1,755
Monticello, NY 12701 • 6,597
Monticello, UT 84535 • 1,806
Monticello, WI 53570 • 1,140
Montmorency □, MI • 8,936
Montour □, PA • 17,735
Montour Falls, NY 14865 • 1,845
Montoursville, PA 17754 • 4,983
Montpelier, ID 83254 • 2,656
Montpelier, IN 47359 • 1,880
Montpelier, OH 43543 • 4,299
Montpelier, VT 05601–02 • 8,247
Montrose, AL 36559 • 1,400
Montrose, CO 81401–02 • 8,854
Montrose, MI 48457 • 1,811
Montrose, PA 18801 • 1,982
Montrose, VA 23231 • 6,405
Montrose □, CO • 24,423
Montvale, NJ 07645 • 6,946
Montville, CT 06353 • 16,673
Montville, NJ 07045 • 2,600
Monument, CO 80132 • 1,020
Monument Beach, MA 02553 • 1,800
Monument Heights, VA 23226 • 2,500
Moodus, CT 06469 • 1,170
Moody, TX 76557 • 1,329
Moody □, SD • 6,507
Moonachie, NJ 07074 • 2,817
Moorcroft, WY 82721 • 768
Moore, OK 73160 • 40,318
Moore □, NC • 59,013
Moore □, TN • 4,721
Moore □, TX • 17,865
Moorefield, WV 26836 • 2,148
Moore Haven, FL 33471 • 1,432
Mooreland, OK 73852 • 1,157
Moorestown, NJ 08057 • 16,500
Mooresville, IN 46158 • 5,541
Mooresville, NC 28115 • 9,317
Moorhead, MN 56560–61 • 32,295
Moorhead, MS 38761 • 2,417
Moorpark, CA 93020–21 • 25,494
Moose Lake, MN 55767 • 1,206
Moosic, PA 18507 • 5,339
Moosup, CT 06354 • 3,289
Mora, MN 55051 • 2,905
Mora, NM 87732 • 1,200
Mora □, NM • 4,264
Moraga, CA 94556 • 15,852
Moraine, OH 45439 • 5,989
Moravia, NY 13118 • 1,559
Morehead, KY 40351 • 8,357
Morehead City, NC 28557 • 6,046
Morehouse, MO 63868 • 1,068
Morehouse □, LA • 31,938
Morenci, AZ 85540 • 1,799
Morenci, MI 49256 • 2,342
Moreno Valley, CA 92387–88 • 118,779
Morgan, UT 84050 • 2,023
Morgan □, AL • 100,043
Morgan □, CO • 21,939
Morgan □, GA • 12,883
Morgan □, IL • 36,397
Morgan □, IN • 55,920
Morgan □, KY • 11,648
Morgan □, MO • 15,574
Morgan □, OH • 14,194
Morgan □, TN • 17,300
Morgan □, UT • 5,528
Morgan □, WV • 12,128
Morgan City, LA 70380–81 • 14,531
Morganfield, KY 42437 • 3,776
Morgan Hill, CA 95037–38 • 23,928
Morganton, NC 28655 • 15,085
Morgantown, KY 42261 • 2,284
Morgantown, MS 39120 • 3,288
Morgantown, WV 26502–07 • 25,879
Moriarty, NM 87035 • 1,399
Morningdale, MA 01505 • 1,130
Morocco, IN 47963 • 1,044
Moroni, UT 84646 • 1,115
Morrill □, NE • 5,423
Morrilton, AR 72110 • 6,551
Morris, AL 35116 • 1,136
Morris, IL 60450 • 10,270
Morris, MN 56267 • 5,613
Morris, OK 74445 • 1,216
Morris □, KS • 6,198
Morris □, NJ • 421,353
Morris □, TX • 13,200
Morrison, IL 61270 • 4,363
Morrison □, MN • 29,604
Morrison City, TN 37660 • 2,032
Morrisonville, IL 62546 • 1,113
Morrisonville, NY 12962 • 1,742
Morris Plains, NJ 07950 • 5,219
Morristown, NJ 07960–63 • 16,189
Morristown, TN 37813–16 • 21,385
Morrisville, NY 13408 • 2,732
Morrisville, PA 19067 • 9,765
Morrisville, VT 05661 • 1,984
Morro Bay, CA 93442–43 • 9,664
Morrow, GA 30260 • 5,168
Morrow, OH 45152 • 1,206
Morrow □, OH • 27,749
Morrow □, OR • 7,625
Morton, IL 61550 • 13,799
Morton, MS 39117 • 3,212
Morton, TX 79346 • 2,597
Morton, WA 98356 • 1,130
Morton □, KS • 3,480
Morton □, ND • 23,700
Morton Grove, IL 60053 • 22,408
Moscow, ID 83843 • 18,519
Moscow, PA 18444 • 1,527
Moses Lake, WA 98837 • 11,235
Mosheim, TN 37818 • 1,451
Mosinee, WI 54455 • 3,820
Moss Bluff, LA 70611 • 8,039
Moss Point, MS 39563 • 17,837
Motley □, TX • 1,532
Mott, ND 58646 • 1,019
Moulton, AL 35650 • 3,248
Moultrie, GA 31768 • 14,865
Moultrie □, IL • 13,930
Mound, MN 55364 • 9,634
Mound Bayou, MS 38762 • 2,222
Mound City, MO 64470 • 1,273
Moundridge, KS 67107 • 1,531
Mounds, IL 62964 • 1,407
Mounds View, MN 55432 • 12,541
Moundsville, WV 26041 • 10,753
Moundville, AL 35474 • 1,348
Mountainair, NM 87036 • 926
Mountain Brook, AL 35223 • 19,810
Mountain City, NV 89831 • 110
Mountain City, TN 37683 • 2,169
Mountain Grove, MO 65711 • 4,182
Mountain Home, AR 72653 • 9,027
Mountain Home, ID 83647 • 7,913
Mountain Iron, MN 55768 • 3,362
Mountain Lake, MN 56159 • 1,906
Mountain Lake Park, MD 21550 • 1,938
Mountain Lakes, NJ 07046 • 3,847
Mountain Park, GA 30087 • 11,025
Mountainside, NJ 07092 • 6,657
Mountain View, AR 72560 • 2,439
Mountain View, CA 94039–43 • 67,460
Mountain View, CO 80521 • 2,100
Mountain View, MO 65548 • 2,036
Mountain View, NM 87105 • 2,300
Mountain View, OK 73062 • 1,086
Mountain View, WY 82604 • 1,200
Mountain View, WY 82939 • 1,189
Mountain Village, AK 99632 • 674
Mount Airy, MD 21771 • 3,730
Mount Airy, NC 27030 • 7,156
Mount Angel, OR 97362 • 2,778
Mount Arlington, NJ 07856 • 3,630
Mount Ayr, IA 50854 • 1,796
Mount Carmel, IL 62863 • 8,287
Mount Carmel, PA 17851 • 7,196
Mount Carroll, IL 61053 • 1,726
Mount Clemens, MI 48043–46 • 18,405
Mount Dora, FL 32757 • 7,196
Mount Ephraim, NJ 08059 • 4,517
Mount Freedom, NJ 07970 • 1,920
Mount Gay, WV 25637 • 1,200
Mount Gilead, NC 27306 • 1,336
Mount Gilead, OH 43338 • 2,846
Mount Healthy, OH 45231 • 7,580
Mount Holly, NJ 08060 • 10,639
Mount Holly, NC 28120 • 7,710
Mount Holly Springs, PA 17065 • 1,925
Mount Hope, WV 25880 • 1,573
Mount Horeb, WI 53572 • 4,182
Mount Jackson, VA 22842 • 1,583
Mount Jewett, PA 16740 • 1,029
Mount Joy, PA 17552 • 6,398
Mount Juliet, TN 37122 • 5,389
Mount Kisco, NY 10549 • 9,108
Mountlake Terrace, WA 98043 • 19,320
Mount Lebanon, PA 15228 • 33,362
Mount Morris, IL 61054 • 2,919
Mount Morris, MI 48458 • 3,292
Mount Morris, NY 14510 • 3,102
Mount Olive, AL 35117 • 2,270
Mount Olive, IL 62069 • 2,126
Mount Olive, NC 28365 • 4,582
Mount Olympus, UT 84117 • 7,413
Mount Orab, OH 45154 • 1,929
Mount Penn, PA 19606 • 2,883
Mount Pleasant, IA 52641 • 8,027
Mount Pleasant, MI 48858–59 • 23,285
Mount Pleasant, NC 28124 • 1,027
Mount Pleasant, PA 15666 • 4,787
Mount Pleasant, SC 29464–65 • 30,108
Mount Pleasant, TN 38474 • 4,278
Mount Pleasant, TX 75455 • 12,291
Mount Pleasant, UT 84647 • 2,092
Mount Pocono, PA 18344 • 1,795
Mount Prospect, IL 60056 • 53,170
Mount Pulaski, IL 62548 • 1,610
Mountrail □, ND • 7,021
Mount Rainier, MD 20712 • 7,954
Mount Savage, MD 21545 • 1,640
Mount Shasta, CA 96067 • 3,460
Mount Sinai, NY 11766 • 8,023
Mount Sterling, IL 62353 • 1,922
Mount Sterling, KY 40353 • 5,362
Mount Sterling, OH 43143 • 1,647
Mount Union, PA 17066 • 2,878
Mount Vernon, GA 30445 • 1,914
Mount Vernon, IL 62864 • 16,988
Mount Vernon, IN 47620 • 7,217
Mount Vernon, IA 52314 • 3,657
Mount Vernon, KY 40456 • 2,654
Mount Vernon, MO 65712 • 3,726
Mount Vernon, NY 10550–53 • 67,153
Mount Vernon, OH 43050 • 14,550
Mount Vernon, TX 75457 • 2,219
Mount Vernon, WA 98273 • 17,647
Mount View, RI 02852 • 610
Mount Washington, KY 40047 • 5,226
Mount Wolf, PA 17347 • 1,365
Mount Zion, IL 62549 • 4,522
Moville, IA 51039 • 1,306
Moweaqua, IL 62550 • 1,785
Mower □, MN • 37,385
Moyock, NC 27958 • 1,400
Muenster, TX 76252 • 1,387
Muhlenberg □, KY • 31,318
Mukilteo, WA 98275 • 7,007
Mukwonago, WI 53149 • 4,457
Mulberry, AR 72947 • 1,448
Mulberry, FL 33860 • 2,988
Mulberry, IN 46058 • 1,262
Mulberry, NC 28659 • 2,339
Muldraugh, KY 40155 • 1,376
Muldrow, OK 74948 • 2,889
Muleshoe, TX 79347 • 4,571
Mullan, ID 83846 • 821
Mullens, WV 25882 • 2,006
Mullica Hill, NJ 08062 • 1,117
Mullins, SC 29574 • 5,910
Multnomah □, OR • 583,887
Mulvane, KS 67110 • 4,674
Muncie, IN 47302–08 • 71,035
Muncy, PA 17756 • 2,702
Munday, TX 76371 • 1,600
Mundelein, IL 60060 • 21,215
Munford, TN 38058 • 2,326
Munfordville, KY 42765 • 1,556
Munhall, PA 15120 • 13,158
Munising, MI 49862 • 2,783
Munster, IN 46321 • 19,949
Murfreesboro, AR 71958 • 1,542
Murfreesboro, NC 27855 • 2,580
Murfreesboro, TN 37129–33 • 44,922
Murphy, MO 63026 • 9,342
Murphy, NC 28906 • 1,575
Murphys, CA 95247 • 1,517
Murphysboro, IL 62966 • 9,176
Murray, KY 42071 • 14,439
Murray, UT 84107 • 31,282
Murray □, GA • 26,147
Murray □, MN • 9,660
Murray □, OK • 12,042
Murrells Inlet, SC 29576 • 3,334
Murrysville, PA 15668 • 17,240
Muscatine, IA 52761 • 22,881
Muscatine □, IA • 39,907
Muscle Shoals, AL 35661 • 9,611
Muscoda, WI 53573 • 1,287
Muscogee □, GA • 179,278
Muscoy, CA 92405 • 7,541
Muse, PA 15350 • 1,250
Muskego, WI 53150 • 16,813
Muskegon, MI 49440–45 • 40,283
Muskegon □, MI • 158,983
Muskegon Heights, MI 49444 • 13,176
Muskingum □, OH • 82,068
Muskogee, OK 74401–03 • 37,708
Muskogee □, OK • 68,078
Musselshell □, MT • 4,106
Mustang, OK 73064 • 10,434
Myerstown, PA 17067 • 3,236
Myrtle Beach, SC 29577–78 • 24,848
Myrtle Grove, FL 32506 • 17,402
Myrtle Point, OR 97458 • 2,712
Mystic, CT 06355 • 2,618
Mystic Island, NJ 08087 • 7,400

N

Naalehu, HI 96772 • 1,027
Naamans Gardens, DE 19810 • 1,500
Nabnasset, MA 01886 • 3,600
Nacogdoches, TX 75961–63 • 30,872
Nacogdoches □, TX • 54,753
Nags Head, NC 27959 • 1,838
Nahant, MA 01908 • 3,828
Nahunta, GA 31553 • 1,049
Nampa, ID 83651–53 • 28,365
Nanakuli, HI 96792 • 9,575
Nance □, NE • 4,275
Nanticoke, PA 18634 • 12,267
Nantucket, MA 02554 • 3,069
Nantucket □, MA • 6,012
Nanty Glo, PA 15943 • 3,190
Nanuet, NY 10954 • 14,065
Napa, CA 94558–59 • 61,842
Napa □, CA • 110,765
Napanoch, NY 12458 • 1,068
Naperville, IL 60540 • 85,351
Naples, FL 33939–42 • 19,505
Naples, NY 14512 • 1,237
Naples, TX 75568 • 1,508
Naples, UT 84078 • 1,334
Naples Park, FL 33963 • 8,002
Napoleon, ND 58561 • 930
Napoleon, OH 43545 • 8,884
Nappanee, IN 46550 • 5,510
Naranja, FL 33032 • 5,790
Narberth, PA 19072 • 4,278
Narragansett, RI 02882 • 3,721
Narrows, VA 24124 • 2,082
Naselle, WA 98638 • 1,000
Nash, TX 75569 • 2,162
Nash □, NC • 76,677
Nashua, IA 50658 • 1,476
Nashua, NH 03060–63 • 79,662
Nashville, AR 71852 • 4,639
Nashville, GA 31639 • 4,782
Nashville, IL 62263 • 3,202
Nashville, MI 49073 • 1,654
Nashville, NC 27856 • 3,617
Nashville, TN 37201–35 • 487,969
Nashwauk, MN 55769 • 1,026
Nassau, NY 12123 • 1,254
Nassau □, FL • 43,941
Nassau □, NY • 1,287,348
Nassau Shores, NY 11758 • 5,110
Natalia, TX 78059 • 1,216
Natchez, MS 39120–22 • 19,460
Natchitoches, LA 71457–58 • 16,609
Natchitoches □, LA • 36,689
Natick, MA 01760 • 30,100
National City, CA 91950–51 • 54,249
National Park, NJ 08063 • 3,413
Natrona □, WY • 61,226
Natrona Heights, PA 15065 • 12,200
Naugatuck, CT 06770 • 30,625
Nautilus Park, CT 06340 • 6,500
Nauvoo, IL 62354 • 1,108
Navajo □, AZ • 77,658
Navarre, OH 44662 • 1,635
Navarro □, TX • 39,926
Navasota, TX 77868–69 • 6,296
Navesink, NJ 07752 • 1,420
Nazareth, PA 18064 • 5,713
Neah Bay, WA 98357 • 1,300
Nebraska City, NE 68410 • 6,547
Nederland, CO 80466 • 1,099
Nederland, TX 77627 • 16,192
Nedrow, NY 13120 • 2,980
Needham, MA 02192 • 27,557
Needles, CA 92363 • 5,191
Needville, TX 77461 • 2,199
Neenah, WI 54956–57 • 23,219
Neffs, OH 43940 • 1,213
Negaunee, MI 49866 • 4,741
Neillsville, WI 54456 • 2,680
Nekoosa, WI 54457 • 2,557
Neligh, NE 68756 • 1,742
Nelson □, KY • 29,710
Nelson □, ND • 4,410
Nelson □, VA • 12,778
Nelsonville, OH 45764 • 4,563
Nemacolin, PA 15351 • 1,097
Nemaha □, KS • 10,446
Nemaha □, NE • 7,980
Nenana, AK 99760 • 393
Neodesha, KS 66757 • 2,837
Neoga, IL 62447 • 1,678
Neosho, MO 64850 • 9,254
Neosho □, KS • 17,035
Nephi, UT 84648 • 3,515
Neptune, NJ 07753 • 28,366
Neptune Beach, FL 32233 • 6,816
Neptune City, NJ 07753 • 4,997
Nesconset, NY 11767 • 10,712
Nescopeck, PA 18635 • 1,651
Neshoba □, MS • 24,800
Nesquehoning, PA 18240 • 3,364
Ness □, KS • 4,033
Ness City, KS 67560 • 1,724
Netcong, NJ 07857 • 3,311
Nether Providence Township, PA 19013 • 13,229
Nettleton, MS 38858 • 2,462
Nevada, IA 50201 • 6,009
Nevada, MO 64772 • 8,597
Nevada □, AR • 10,101
Nevada □, CA • 78,510
Nevada City, CA 95959 • 2,855
New Albany, IN 47150–51 • 36,322
New Albany, MS 38652 • 6,775
New Albany, OH 43054 • 1,621
Newark, AR 72562 • 1,159
Newark, CA 94560 • 37,861
Newark, DE 19711–15 • 25,098
Newark, NJ 07101–75 • 275,221
Newark, NY 14513 • 9,849
Newark, OH 43055–58 • 44,389
Newark Valley, NY 13811 • 1,082
New Athens, IL 62264 • 2,010
Newaygo, MI 49337 • 1,336
Newaygo □, MI • 38,202
New Baden, IL 62265 • 2,602
New Baltimore, MI 48047 • 5,798
New Bedford, MA 02740–48 • 99,922
Newberg, OR 97132 • 10,086
New Berlin, NY 13411 • 1,220
New Berlin, WI 53151 • 33,592
New Bern, NC 28560–64 • 17,363
Newbern, TN 38059 • 2,515
Newberry, FL 32669 • 1,644
Newberry, MI 49868 • 1,873
Newberry, SC 29108 • 10,542
Newberry □, SC • 33,172
New Bethlehem, PA 16242 • 1,151
New Bloomfield, PA 17068 • 1,092
New Boston, MI 48164 • 1,200
New Boston, OH 45662 • 2,717
New Boston, TX 75570 • 5,057
New Braunfels, TX 78130–33 • 27,334
New Bremen, OH 45869 • 2,558
New Brighton, MN 55112 • 22,207
New Brighton, PA 15066 • 6,854
New Britain, CT 06050–53 • 75,491
New Brockton, AL 36351 • 1,184
New Brunswick, NJ 08901–06 • 41,711
New Buffalo, MI 49117 • 2,317
Newburg, KY 40218 • 21,647
Newburgh, IN 47629–30 • 2,880
Newburgh, NY 12550–53 • 26,454
Newburgh Heights, OH 44105 • 2,310
Newburyport, MA 01950–52 • 16,317
New Canaan, CT 06840 • 17,864
New Carlisle, IN 46552 • 1,446
New Carlisle, OH 45344 • 6,049
New Carrollton, MD 20784 • 12,002
New Cassel, NY 11590 • 10,257
New Castle, AL 35119 • 1,100
New Castle, DE 19720 • 4,837
New Castle, IN 47362 • 17,753
Newcastle, OK 73065 • 4,214
New Castle, PA 16101–08 • 28,334
Newcastle, WY 82701 • 3,003
New Castle □, DE • 441,946
New City, NY 10956 • 33,673
Newcomerstown, OH 43832 • 4,012
New Concord, OH 43762 • 2,086
New Cumberland, PA 17070 • 7,665
New Cumberland, WV 26047 • 1,363
New Egypt, NJ 08533 • 2,327
Newell, IA 50568 • 1,089
Newell, WV 26050 • 1,724
New Ellenton, SC 29809 • 2,515
Newellton, LA 71357 • 1,576
New England, ND 58647 • 663
New Fairfield, CT 06812 • 4,600
Newfane, NY 14108 • 3,001
Newfield, NJ 08344 • 1,592
New Franklin, MO 65274 • 1,107
New Freedom, PA 17349 • 2,920
New Glarus, WI 53574 • 1,899
New Hampton, IA 50659 • 3,660
New Hanover □, NC • 120,284
New Hartford, CT 06057 • 1,269
New Haven, CT 06501–36 • 130,474
New Haven, IN 46774 • 9,320
New Haven, MI 48048 • 2,331
New Haven, MO 63068 • 1,757
New Haven, WV 25265 • 1,632
New Haven □, CT • 804,219
New Holland, GA 30501 • 1,200
New Holland, PA 17557 • 4,484
New Holstein, WI 53061 • 3,342
New Hope, AL 35760 • 2,248
New Hope, MN 55428 • 21,853
New Hope, NC 27604 • 5,694
New Hope, PA 18938 • 1,400
New Hyde Park, NY 11040 • 9,728
New Iberia, LA 70560–62 • 31,828
Newington, CT 06131 • 29,208
Newington, VA 22122 • 17,965
New Johnsonville, TN 37134 • 1,643
New Kensington, PA 15068 • 15,894
New Kent □, VA • 10,445
Newkirk, OK 74647 • 2,168
New Lenox, IL 60451 • 9,627
New Lexington, OH 43764 • 5,117
New Lisbon, WI 53950 • 1,491
Newllano, LA 71461 • 2,660
New London, CT 06320 • 28,540
New London, IA 52645 • 1,922
New London, NH 03257 • 3,180
New London, OH 44851 • 2,642
New London, WI 54961 • 6,658
New London □, CT • 254,957
New Madrid, MO 63869 • 3,350
New Madrid □, MO • 20,928
Newman, CA 95360 • 4,151
Newmanstown, PA 17073 • 1,410
Newmarket, NH 03857 • 4,917
New Market, TN 37820 • 1,086
New Market, VA 22844 • 1,435
New Martinsville, WV 26155 • 6,705
New Matamoras, OH 45767 • 1,002
New Miami, OH 45011 • 2,555
New Milford, CT 06776 • 5,775
New Milford, NJ 07646 • 15,990
Newnan, GA 30263–65 • 12,497
New Orleans, LA 70101–95 • 496,938
New Oxford, PA 17350 • 1,617
New Paltz, NY 12561 • 5,463
New Paris, IN 46553 • 1,007
New Paris, OH 45347 • 1,801
New Philadelphia, OH 44663 • 15,698
New Philadelphia, PA 17959 • 1,283
New Plymouth, ID 83655 • 1,313
Newport, AR 72112 • 7,459
Newport, DE 19804 • 1,240
Newport, KY 41071–76 • 18,871
Newport, ME 04953 • 1,843
Newport, MI 48166 • 1,100
Newport, MN 55055 • 3,720
Newport, NH 03773 • 3,772
Newport, NC 28570 • 2,516
Newport, OR 97365 • 8,437
Newport, PA 17074 • 1,568
Newport, RI 02840 • 28,227
Newport, TN 37821 • 7,123
Newport, VT 05855 • 4,434
Newport, WA 99156 • 1,691
Newport □, RI • 87,194
Newport Beach, CA 92657–63 • 66,643
Newport East, RI 02840 • 11,080
Newport Hills, WA 98002 • 14,736
Newport News, VA 23601–09 • 170,045
New Port Richey, FL 34652–56 • 14,044
New Prague, MN 56071 • 3,569
New Preston, CT 06777 • 1,217
New Providence, NJ 07974 • 11,439
New Richland, MN 56072 • 1,237
New Richmond, OH 45157 • 2,408
New Richmond, WI 54017 • 5,106
New River Station, NC 28542 • 9,732
New Roads, LA 70760 • 5,303
New Rochelle, NY 10801–05 • 67,265
New Rockford, ND 58356 • 1,604
New Salem, ND 58563 • 909
New Sarpy, LA 70078 • 2,946
New Sharon, IA 50207 • 1,136
New Smyrna Beach, FL 32168–70 • 16,543
New Tazewell, TN 37825 • 1,864
Newton, AL 36352 • 1,580
Newton, IL 62448 • 3,154
Newton, IA 50208 • 14,789
Newton, KS 67114 • 16,700
Newton, MA 02158 • 82,585
Newton, MS 39345 • 3,701
Newton, NJ 07860 • 7,521
Newton, NC 28658 • 9,304
Newton, TX 75966 • 1,885
Newton □, AR • 7,666
Newton □, GA • 41,808
Newton □, IN • 13,551
Newton □, MS • 20,291
Newton □, MO • 44,445
Newton □, TX • 13,569
Newton Falls, OH 44444 • 4,866
Newtown, CT 06470 • 1,800
New Town, ND 58763 • 1,388
Newtown, OH 45244 • 1,589
Newtown Square, PA 19073 • 11,366

New Ulm, MN 56073 • *13,132*
Newville, PA 17241 • *1,349*
New Washington, OH 44854 • *1,057*
New Washoe City, NV 89701 • *2,875*
New Waterford, OH 44445 • *1,278*
New Whiteland, IN 46184 • *4,097*
New Wilmington, PA 16142 • *2,706*
New Windsor, NY 12553 • *8,898*
New York, NY 10001–99 • *7,322,564*
New York □, NY • *1,487,536*
Nez Perce □, ID • *33,754*
Niagara, WI 54151 • *1,999*
Niagara □, NY • *220,756*
Niagara Falls, NY 14301–05 • *61,840*
Niantic, CT 06357 • *3,048*
Nibley, UT 84321 • *1,167*
Niceville, FL 32578 • *10,507*
Nicholas □, KY • *6,725*
Nicholas □, WV • *26,775*
Nicholasville, KY 40356 • *13,603*
Nicholls, GA 31554 • *1,003*
Nichols Hills, OK 73116 • *4,020*
Nickerson, KS 67561 • *1,137*
Nicollet □, MN • *28,076*
Nicoma Park, OK 73066 • *2,353*
Nikishka, AK 99635 • *1,109*
Niland, CA 92257 • *1,183*
Niles, IL 60648 • *28,284*
Niles, MI 49120 • *12,458*
Niles, OH 44446 • *21,128*
Ninety Six, SC 29666 • *2,099*
Ninilchik, AK 99639 • *456*
Niobrara □, WY • *2,499*
Nipomo, CA 93444 • *7,109*
Niskayuna, NY 12309 • *4,942*
Nisswa, MN 56468 • *1,391*
Nitro, WV 25143 • *6,851*
Niwot, CO 80544 • *2,666*
Nixa, MO 65714 • *4,707*
Nixon, NV 89424 • *150*
Nixon, TX 78140 • *1,995*
Noank, CT 06340 • *1,406*
Noble, OK 73068 • *4,710*
Noble □, IN • *37,877*
Noble □, OH • *11,336*
Noble □, OK • *11,045*
Nobles □, MN • *20,098*
Noblesville, IN 46060 • *17,655*
Nocatee, FL 33864 • *1,300*
Nocona, TX 76255 • *2,870*
Nodaway □, MO • *21,709*
Noel, MO 64854 • *1,169*
Nogales, AZ 85621 • *19,489*
Nokomis, FL 34274–75 • *3,448*
Nokomis, IL 62075 • *2,534*
Nolan □, TX • *16,594*
Nome, AK 99762 • *3,500*
Noorvik, AK 99763 • *531*
Nora Springs, IA 50458 • *1,505*
Norco, CA 91760 • *23,302*
Norco, LA 70079 • *3,385*
Norcross, GA 30071 • *5,947*
Norfolk, CT 06058 • *1,500*
Norfolk, NE 68701 • *21,476*
Norfolk, NY 13667 • *1,412*
Norfolk, VA 23501–93 • *261,229*
Norfolk □, MA • *616,087*
Norland, FL 33169 • *22,109*
Normal, IL 61761 • *40,023*
Norman, OK 73069–72 • *80,071*
Norman □, MN • *7,975*
Normandy, MO 63121 • *4,480*
Norridge, IL 60656 • *14,459*
Norridgewock, ME 04957 • *1,496*
Norris, TN 37828 • *1,303*
Norris City, IL 62869 • *1,341*
Norristown, PA 19401–09 • *30,749*
North Adams, MA 01247 • *16,797*
North Albany, OR 97321 • *4,325*
North Amherst, MA 01059 • *6,239*
North Amityville, NY 11701 • *13,849*
Northampton, MA 01060–61 • *29,289*
Northampton, PA 18067 • *8,717*
Northampton □, NC • *20,798*
Northampton □, PA • *247,105*
Northampton □, VA • *13,061*
North Andover, MA 01845 • *20,129*
North Andrews Gardens, FL 33308 • *9,002*
North Apollo, PA 15673 • *1,391*
North Arlington, NJ 07032 • *13,790*
North Atlanta, GA 30319 • *27,812*
North Attleboro, MA 02760–63 • *16,178*
North Auburn, CA 95603 • *10,301*
North Augusta, SC 29841 • *15,351*
North Aurora, IL 60542 • *5,940*
North Babylon, NY 11703 • *18,081*
North Baltimore, OH 45872 • *3,139*
North Bay Shore, NY 11706 • *12,799*
North Beach, MD 20714 • *1,173*
North Bellmore, NY 11710 • *19,707*
North Bellport, NY 11713 • *8,182*
North Belmont, NC 28012 • *10,762*
North Bend, NE 68649 • *1,249*
North Bend, OR 97459 • *9,614*
North Bend, WA 98045 • *2,578*
North Bennington, VT 05257 • *1,520*
North Bergen, NJ 07047 • *48,414*
North Berwick, ME 03906 • *1,568*
North Billerica, MA 01862 • *5,400*
Northborough, MA 01532 • *5,761*
North Braddock, PA 15104 • *7,036*
North Branch, MI 48461 • *1,023*
North Branch, MN 55056 • *1,867*
North Branch, NJ 08876 • *2,620*
North Branford, CT 06471 • *6,600*
Northbridge, MA 01534 • *3,570*
Northbrook, IL 60062 • *32,308*
Northbrook, OH 45231 • *11,471*
North Brookfield, MA 01535 • *2,635*
North Brunswick, NJ 08902 • *31,287*
North Brunswick Township, NJ 08902 • *31,287*
North Caldwell, NJ 07006 • *5,832*
North Canton, OH 44720 • *14,748*
North Cape May, NJ 08204 • *3,574*
North Charleston, SC 29406 • *70,218*
North Chicago, IL 60064 • *34,978*
North City, WA 98155 • *8,200*
North Cohasset, MA 02025 • *1,045*
North College Hill, OH 45239 • *11,002*
North Collins, NY 14111 • *1,335*
North Conway, NH 03860 • *2,032*
North Corbin, KY 40701 • *1,601*
North Crossett, AR 71635 • *3,358*
North Dartmouth, MA 02747 • *8,080*
North Decatur, GA 30033 • *13,936*
North Dighton, MA 02764 • *1,174*
North Druid Hills, GA 30033 • *14,170*
North Eagle Butte, SD 57625 • *1,423*
North East, MD 21901 • *1,913*
North East, PA 16428 • *4,617*
North Eastham, MA 02651 • *1,570*
Northeast Henrietta, NY 14534 • *10,650*
North Easton, MA 02356 • *4,420*
North Fair Oaks, CA 94025 • *13,912*
North Falmouth, MA 02556 • *3,150*
Northfield, IL 60093 • *4,635*
Northfield, MA 01360 • *1,322*
Northfield, MN 55057 • *14,684*
Northfield, NH 03276 • *1,375*
Northfield, NJ 08225 • *7,305*
Northfield, OH 44067 • *3,624*
Northfield, VT 05663 • *1,889*
Northfield Falls, VT 05664 • *600*
North Fond du Lac, WI 54935 • *4,292*
Northford, CT 06472 • *3,180*
North Fort Myers, FL 33903 • *30,027*
Northglenn, CO 80233 • *27,195*
North Grafton, MA 01536 • *3,050*
North Great River, NY 11722 • *3,964*
North Grosvenordale, CT 06255 • *1,705*
North Gulfport, MS 39501 • *4,966*
North Haledon, NJ 07508 • *7,987*
North Hampton, NH 03862 • *1,000*
North Haven, CT 06473 • *22,249*
North Highlands, CA 95660 • *42,105*
North Hill, WA 98166 • *5,706*
North Houston, TX 77086 • *12,800*
North Hudson, WI 54016 • *3,101*
North Industry, OH 44707 • *3,250*
North Judson, IN 46366 • *1,582*
North Kansas City, MO 64116 • *4,130*
North Kingstown, RI 02852–54 • *2,750*
North Kingsville, OH 44068 • *2,672*
North La Junta, CO 81050 • *1,076*
Northlake, IL 60164 • *12,505*
North Las Vegas, NV 89030–31 • *47,707*
North Lauderdale, FL 33068 • *26,506*
North Lewisburg, OH 43060 • *1,160*
North Liberty, IN 46554 • *1,366*
North Liberty, IA 52317 • *2,926*
North Lindenhurst, NY 11757 • *10,563*
North Little Rock, AR 72114–20 • *61,741*
North Logan, UT 84321 • *3,768*
North Madison, OH 44057 • *8,699*
North Manchester, IN 46962 • *6,383*
North Mankato, MN 56001 • *10,164*
North Massapequa, NY 11758 • *19,365*
North Merrick, NY 11566 • *12,113*
North Merrydale, LA 70812 • *4,000*
North Miami, FL 33161 • *49,998*
North Miami Beach, FL 33162 • *35,359*
North Muskegon, MI 49445 • *3,919*
North Myrtle Beach, SC 29582 • *8,636*
North Naples, FL 33963 • *13,422*
North New Hyde Park, NY 11040 • *14,359*
North Ogden, UT 84404 • *11,668*
North Olmsted, OH 44070 • *34,204*
North Oxford, MA 01537 • *1,250*
North Palm Beach, FL 33408 • *11,343*
North Park, IL 61111 • *15,806*
North Patchogue, NY 11772 • *7,374*
North Pembroke, MA 02358 • *2,485*
North Plainfield, NJ 07060 • *18,820*
North Platte, NE 69101–03 • *22,605*
Northport, AL 35476 • *17,366*
North Port, FL 34287 • *11,973*
Northport, NY 11768 • *7,572*
North Prairie, WI 53153 • *1,322*
North Providence, RI 02911 • *32,090*
North Reading, MA 01864 • *11,455*
North Richland Hills, TX 76118 • *45,895*
Northridge, OH 45502 • *5,939*
Northridge, OH 45414 • *9,448*
North Ridgeville, OH 44039 • *21,564*
North Riverside, IL 60546 • *6,005*
North Royalton, OH 44133 • *23,197*
North Salt Lake, UT 84054 • *6,474*
North Sarasota, FL 34234 • *6,702*
North Scituate, MA 02060 • *4,891*
North Sioux City, SD 57049 • *2,019*
North Springfield, OR 97477 • *5,451*
North Springfield, VT 05150 • *750*
North Springfield, VA 22151 • *8,996*
North Star, DE 19711 • *1,030*
North St. Paul, MN 55109 • *12,376*
North Sudbury, MA 01776 • *2,630*
North Syracuse, NY 13212 • *7,363*
North Tarrytown, NY 10591 • *8,152*
North Terre Haute, IN 47805 • *2,000*
North Tewksbury, MA 01876 • *1,030*
North Tonawanda, NY 14120 • *34,989*
North Troy, VT 05859 • *723*
North Tunica, MS 38676 • *1,314*
Northumberland, PA 17857 • *3,860*
Northumberland □, PA • *96,771*
Northumberland □, VA • *10,524*
North Uxbridge, MA 01538 • *1,500*
Northvale, NJ 07647 • *4,563*
North Valley Stream, NY 11580 • *14,574*
North Vernon, IN 47265 • *5,311*
North Versailles, PA 15137 • *12,302*
Northview, MI 49505 • *13,712*
Northview, OH 45322 • *10,337*
Northville, MI 48167 • *6,226*
Northville, NY 12134 • *1,180*
North Wales, PA 19454 • *3,802*
North Wantagh, NY 11793 • *12,276*
North Warren, PA 16365 • *1,232*
North Wildwood, NJ 08260 • *5,017*
North Wilkesboro, NC 28659 • *3,384*
North Windham, ME 04062 • *4,077*
Northwood, IA 50459 • *1,940*
Northwood, ND 58267 • *1,166*
Northwood, OH 43619 • *5,506*
Northwoods, MO 63121 • *5,106*
North York, PA 17404 • *1,689*
Norton, KS 67654 • *3,017*
Norton, MA 02766 • *1,899*
Norton, OH 44203 • *11,477*
Norton, VA 24273 • *4,247*
Norton □, KS • *5,947*
Norton Shores, MI 49441 • *21,755*
Nortonville, KY 42442 • *1,209*
Norwalk, CA 90650–52 • *94,279*
Norwalk, CT 06850–56 • *78,331*
Norwalk, IA 50211 • *5,726*
Norwalk, OH 44857 • *14,731*
Norway, ME 04268 • *3,023*
Norway, MI 49870 • *2,910*
Norwell, MA 02061 • *1,200*
Norwich, CT 06360 • *37,391*
Norwich, NY 13815 • *7,613*
Norwich, VT 05055 • *1,000*
Norwood, MA 02062 • *28,700*
Norwood, MN 55368 • *1,351*
Norwood, NJ 07648 • *4,858*
Norwood, NY 13668 • *1,841*
Norwood, NC 28128 • *1,617*
Norwood, OH 45212 • *23,674*
Norwood, PA 19074 • *6,162*
Norwoodville, IA 50317 • *1,200*
Nottoway □, VA • *14,993*
Novato, CA 94947–49 • *47,585*
Novi, MI 48374–77 • *32,998*
Nowata, OK 74048 • *3,896*
Nowata □, OK • *9,992*
Noxubee □, MS • *12,604*
Nuckolls □, NE • *5,786*
Nueces □, TX • *291,145*
Nulato, AK 99765 • *359*
Nunda, NY 14517 • *1,347*
Nutley, NJ 07110 • *27,099*
Nutter Fort, WV 26301 • *1,819*
Nutting Lake, MA 01865 • *3,180*
Nyack, NY 10960 • *6,558*
Nye □, NV • *17,781*
Nyssa, OR 97913 • *2,629*

O

Oak Bluffs, MA 02557 • *1,124*
Oak Brook, IL 60521 • *9,178*
Oak Creek, WI 53154 • *19,513*
Oakdale, CA 95361 • *11,961*
Oakdale, GA 30080 • *1,080*
Oakdale, LA 71463 • *6,832*
Oakdale, MN 55128 • *18,374*
Oakdale, NY 11769 • *7,875*
Oakdale, PA 15071 • *1,752*
Oakes, ND 58474 • *1,775*
Oakfield, NY 14125 • *1,818*
Oakfield, WI 53065 • *1,003*
Oak Forest, IL 60452 • *26,203*
Oak Grove, KY 42262 • *2,863*
Oak Grove, LA 71263 • *2,126*
Oak Grove, OR 97267 • *12,576*
Oak Grove, SC 29073 • *7,173*
Oak Harbor, OH 43449 • *2,637*
Oak Harbor, WA 98277 • *17,176*
Oak Hill, MI 49660 • *1,000*
Oak Hill, OH 45656 • *1,831*
Oak Hill, WV 25901 • *6,812*
Oakhurst, OK 74050 • *2,200*
Oakland, CA 94601–62 • *372,242*
Oakland, IA 51560 • *1,496*
Oakland, ME 04963 • *3,510*
Oakland, MD 21550 • *2,078*
Oakland, NE 68045 • *1,279*
Oakland, NJ 07436 • *11,997*
Oakland, RI 02830 • *600*
Oakland □, MI • *1,083,592*
Oakland City, IN 47660 • *2,810*
Oakland Park, FL 33334 • *26,326*
Oak Lawn, IL 60453–59 • *56,182*
Oaklawn, KS 67216 • *4,200*
Oakley, CA 94561 • *18,374*
Oakley, KS 67748 • *2,045*
Oaklyn, NJ 08107 • *4,430*
Oakmont, PA 15139 • *6,961*
Oak Orchard, DE 19966 • *350*
Oak Park, CA 91301 • *5,000*
Oak Park, IL 60301–05 • *53,648*
Oak Park, MI 48237 • *30,462*
Oak Ridge, FL 32809 • *15,388*
Oakridge, OR 97463 • *3,063*
Oak Ridge, TN 37830 • *27,310*
Oakton, VA 22124 • *24,610*
Oak Valley, NJ 08090 • *5,400*
Oakville, CT 06779 • *8,741*
Oakville, MO 63129 • *31,750*
Oakwood, GA 30566 • *1,464*
Oakwood, IL 61858 • *1,533*
Oakwood, OH 45419 • *3,392*
Oberlin, KS 67749 • *2,197*
Oberlin, LA 70655 • *1,808*
Oberlin, OH 44074 • *8,191*
Obetz, OH 43207 • *3,167*
Obion, TN 38240 • *1,241*
Obion □, TN • *31,717*
Oblong, IL 62449 • *1,616*
O'Brien □, IA • *15,444*
Ocala, FL 32670–78 • *42,045*
Ocean □, NJ • *433,203*
Oceana, WV 24870 • *1,791*
Oceana □, MI • *22,454*
Ocean Bluff, MA 02065 • *2,500*
Ocean City, FL 32548 • *5,422*
Ocean City, MD 21842 • *5,146*
Ocean City, NJ 08226 • *15,512*
Ocean Gate, NJ 08740 • *2,078*
Ocean Grove, MA 02777 • *4,560*
Oceano, CA 93445 • *6,169*
Ocean Park, WA 98640 • *1,650*
Ocean Port, NJ 07757 • *6,146*
Oceanside, CA 92054–56 • *128,398*
Oceanside, NY 11572 • *32,423*
Ocean Springs, MS 39564–65 • *14,658*
Ocean [Township], NJ 07712 • *23,570*
Ocean View, DE 19970 • *606*
Oceanville, NJ 08231 • *1,000*
Ochiltree □, TX • *9,128*
Ocilla, GA 31774 • *3,182*
Ocoee, FL 34761 • *12,778*
Oconee □, GA • *17,618*
Oconee □, SC • *57,494*
Oconomowoc, WI 53066 • *10,993*
Oconto, WI 54153 • *4,474*
Oconto □, WI • *30,226*
Oconto Falls, WI 54154 • *2,584*
Odebolt, IA 51458 • *1,158*
Odell, IL 60460 • *1,030*
Odem, TX 78370 • *2,366*
Odenton, MD 21113 • *12,833*
Odessa, DE 19730 • *303*
Odessa, MO 64076 • *3,695*
Odessa, TX 79760–68 • *89,699*
Odin, IL 62870 • *1,150*
Odon, IN 47562 • *1,475*
O'Donnell, TX 79351 • *1,102*
Oelwein, IA 50662 • *6,493*
O'Fallon, IL 62269 • *16,073*
O'Fallon, MO 63366 • *18,698*
Ogallala, NE 69153 • *5,095*
Ogden, IA 50212 • *1,909*
Ogden, KS 66517 • *1,494*
Ogden, UT 84401–14 • *63,909*
Ogdensburg, NJ 07439 • *2,722*
Ogdensburg, NY 13669 • *13,521*
Ogemaw □, MI • *18,681*
Ogle □, IL • *45,957*
Oglesby, IL 61348 • *3,619*
Oglethorpe, GA 31068 • *1,302*
Oglethorpe □, GA • *9,763*
Ogunquit, ME 03907 • *1,492*
Ohatchee, AL 36271 • *1,042*
Ohio □, IN • *5,315*
Ohio □, KY • *21,105*
Ohio □, WV • *50,871*
Ohioville, PA 15059 • *3,865*
Oil City, LA 71061 • *1,282*
Oil City, PA 16301 • *11,949*
Oildale, CA 93308 • *26,553*
Oilton, OK 74052 • *1,060*
Ojai, CA 93023–24 • *7,613*
Okaloosa □, FL • *143,776*
Okanogan, WA 98840 • *2,370*
Okanogan □, WA • *33,350*
Okarche, OK 73762 • *1,160*
Okauchee, WI 53069 • *2,300*
Okauchee Lake, WI 53058 • *3,819*
Okawville, IL 62271 • *1,274*
Okeechobee, FL 34972–74 • *4,943*
Okeechobee □, FL • *29,627*
Okeene, OK 73763 • *1,343*
Okemah, OK 74859 • *3,085*
Okemos, MI 48864 • *20,216*
Okfuskee □, OK • *11,551*
Oklahoma □, OK • *599,611*
Oklahoma City, OK 73101–80 • *444,719*
Oklawaha, FL 32179 • *1,200*
Okmulgee, OK 74447 • *13,441*
Okmulgee □, OK • *36,490*
Okolona, KY 40219 • *18,902*
Okolona, MS 38860 • *3,267*
Oktibbeha □, MS • *38,375*
Ola, AR 72853 • *1,090*
Olathe, CO 81425 • *1,263*
Olathe, KS 66061–62 • *63,352*
Olcott, NY 14126 • *1,432*
Old Bethpage, NY 11804 • *5,610*
Old Bridge, NJ 08857 • *22,151*
Old Forge, NY 13420 • *1,061*
Old Forge, PA 18518 • *8,834*
Oldham □, KY • *33,263*
Oldham □, TX • *2,278*
Old Harbor, AK 99643 • *284*
Old Orchard Beach, ME 04064 • *7,789*
Old Saybrook, CT 06475 • *1,820*
Oldsmar, FL 34677 • *8,361*
Old Tappan, NJ 07675 • *4,254*
Old Town, ME 04468 • *8,317*
Olean, NY 14760 • *16,946*
Olive Branch, MS 38654 • *3,567*
Olive Hill, KY 41164 • *1,809*
Olivehurst, CA 95961 • *9,738*
Oliver, PA 15472 • *3,271*
Oliver □, ND • *2,381*
Oliver Springs, TN 37840 • *3,433*
Olivet, MI 49076 • *1,604*
Olivette, MO 63132 • *7,573*
Olivia, MN 56277 • *2,623*
Olla, LA 71465 • *1,410*
Olmito, TX 78575 • *1,400*
Olmos Park, TX 78212 • *2,161*
Olmsted □, MN • *106,470*
Olmsted Falls, OH 44138 • *6,741*
Olney, IL 62450 • *8,664*
Olney, MD 20832 • *23,019*
Olney, TX 76374 • *3,519*
Olton, TX 79064 • *2,116*
Olympia, WA 98501–07 • *33,840*
Olympia Heights, FL 33175 • *36,900*
Olyphant, PA 18447 • *5,222*
Omaha, NE 68101–72 • *335,795*
Omak, WA 98841 • *4,117*
Omro, WI 54963 • *2,836*
Onalaska, WI 54650 • *11,284*
Onancock, VA 23417 • *1,434*
Onarga, IL 60955 • *1,281*
Onawa, IA 51040 • *2,936*
Onaway, MI 49765 • *1,039*
Oneco, FL 34264 • *6,417*
Oneida, NY 13421 • *10,850*
Oneida, OH 45042 • *1,650*
Oneida, TN 37841 • *3,502*
Oneida □, ID • *3,492*
Oneida □, NY • *250,836*
Oneida □, WI • *31,679*
O'Neill, NE 68763 • *3,852*
Oneonta, AL 35121 • *4,844*
Oneonta, NY 13820 • *13,954*
Onida, SD 57564 • *761*
Onondaga □, NY • *468,973*
Onset, MA 02558 • *1,461*
Onslow □, NC • *149,838*
Ontario, CA 91761–62 • *133,179*
Ontario, OH 44862 • *4,026*
Ontario, OR 97914 • *9,392*
Ontario □, NY • *95,101*
Ontonagon, MI 49953 • *2,040*
Ontonagon □, MI • *8,854*
Oolitic, IN 47451 • *1,424*
Ooltewah, TN 37363 • *1,200*
Oostburg, WI 53070 • *1,931*
Opal Cliffs, CA 95062 • *5,940*
Opa-Locka, FL 33054–56 • *15,283*
Opelika, AL 36801–03 • *22,122*
Opelousas, LA 70570–71 • *18,151*
Opp, AL 36467 • *6,985*
Opportunity, WA 99206 • *22,326*
Oquawka, IL 61469 • *1,442*
Oracle, AZ 85623 • *3,043*
Oradell, NJ 07649 • *8,024*
Oran, MO 63771 • *1,164*
Orange, CA 92664–69 • *110,658*
Orange, CT 06477 • *12,830*
Orange, MA 01364 • *3,791*
Orange, NJ 07050–52 • *29,925*
Orange, TX 77630–31 • *19,381*
Orange, VA 22960 • *2,582*
Orange □, CA • *2,410,556*
Orange □, FL • *677,491*
Orange □, IN • *18,409*
Orange □, NY • *307,647*
Orange □, NC • *93,851*
Orange □, TX • *80,509*
Orange □, VT • *26,149*
Orange □, VA • *21,421*
Orange Beach, AL 36561 • *2,253*
Orangeburg, SC 29115–16 • *13,739*
Orangeburg □, SC • *84,803*
Orange City, FL 32763 • *5,347*
Orange City, IA 51041 • *4,940*
Orange Grove, MS 39503 • *15,676*
Orange Grove, TX 78372 • *1,175*
Orange Lake, FL 32681 • *1,000*
Orange Park, FL 32073 • *9,488*
Orangevale, CA 95662 • *26,266*
Orangeville, UT 84537 • *1,459*
Orchard City, CO 81410 • *2,218*
Orchard Homes, MT 59801 • *10,317*
Orchard Mesa, CO 81501 • *5,977*
Orchard Park, NY 14127 • *3,280*
Orchards, WA 98662 • *8,828*
Orchard Valley, WY 82007 • *3,321*
Orcutt, CA 93455 • *1,500*
Ord, NE 68862 • *2,481*
Ordway, CO 81063 • *1,025*
Oregon, IL 61061 • *3,891*
Oregon, OH 43616 • *18,334*
Oregon, WI 53575 • *4,519*
Oregon □, MO • *9,470*
Oregon City, OR 97045 • *14,698*
Orem, UT 84057–59 • *67,561*
Orfordville, WI 53576 • *1,219*
Orient, NY 11957 • *1,000*
Orinda, CA 94563 • *16,642*
Orion, IL 61273 • *1,821*
Oriskany, NY 13424 • *1,450*
Orland, CA 95963 • *5,052*
Orlando, FL 32801–72 • *164,693*
Orland Park, IL 60462 • *35,720*
Orleans, IN 47452 • *2,083*
Orleans, IN 47452 • *2,161*
Orleans, MA 02653 • *1,699*
Orleans, VT 05860 • *806*
Orleans □, LA • *496,938*
Orleans □, NY • *41,846*
Orleans □, VT • *24,053*
Orlovista, FL 32811 • *5,990*
Ormond Beach, FL 32174–76 • *29,721*
Ormond By The Sea, FL 32174 • *8,157*
Orofino, ID 83544 • *2,868*
Orono, ME 04473 • *9,789*
Orono, MN 55323 • *7,285*
Orosi, CA 93647 • *5,486*
Oroville, CA 95965–66 • *11,960*
Oroville, WA 98844 • *1,505*
Orrville, OH 44667 • *7,712*
Orting, WA 98360 • *2,106*
Ortonville, MI 48462 • *1,252*
Ortonville, MN 56278 • *2,205*
Orwell, OH 44076 • *1,258*
Orwigsburg, PA 17961 • *2,780*
Osage, IA 50461 • *3,439*
Osage, WY 82723 • *350*
Osage □, KS • *15,248*
Osage □, MO • *12,018*
Osage □, OK • *41,645*
Osage Beach, MO 65065 • *2,599*
Osage City, KS 66523 • *2,689*
Osakis, MN 56360 • *1,256*
Osawatomie, KS 66064 • *4,590*
Osborne, KS 67473 • *1,778*
Osborne □, KS • *4,867*
Osburn, ID 83849 • *1,579*
Osceola, AR 72370 • *8,930*
Osceola, IN 46561 • *1,999*
Osceola, IA 50213 • *4,164*
Osceola, WI 54020 • *2,075*
Osceola □, FL • *107,728*
Osceola □, IA • *7,267*
Osceola □, MI • *20,146*
Osceola Mills, PA 16666 • *1,310*
Oscoda, MI 48750 • *1,061*
Oscoda □, MI • *7,842*
Osgood, IN 47037 • *1,688*
Oshkosh, WI 54901–04 • *55,006*
Oskaloosa, IA 52577 • *10,632*
Oskaloosa, KS 66066 • *1,074*
Osprey, FL 34229 • *2,597*
Osseo, MN 55369 • *2,704*
Osseo, WI 54758 • *1,551*
Ossian, IN 46777 • *2,428*
Ossining, NY 10562 • *22,582*
Osterville, MA 02655 • *2,911*
Oswego, IL 60543 • *3,876*
Oswego, KS 67356 • *1,870*
Oswego, NY 13126 • *19,195*
Oswego □, NY • *121,771*
Otay, CA 92010 • *6,400*
Oteen, NC 28805 • *1,400*
Otego, NY 13825 • *1,068*
Otero □, CO • *20,185*
Otero □, NM • *51,928*
Othello, WA 99327 • *4,638*
Otis Orchards, WA 99027 • *3,200*
Otoe □, NE • *14,252*
Otsego, MI 49078 • *3,937*
Otsego □, MI • *17,957*
Otsego □, NY • *60,517*
Ottawa, IL 61350 • *17,451*
Ottawa, KS 66067 • *10,667*
Ottawa, OH 45875 • *3,999*
Ottawa □, KS • *5,634*
Ottawa □, MI • *187,768*
Ottawa □, OH • *40,029*
Ottawa □, OK • *30,561*
Ottawa Hills, OH 43606 • *4,543*
Otterbein, IN 47970 • *1,291*
Otter Tail □, MN • *50,714*
Ottumwa, IA 52501 • *24,488*
Ouachita □, AR • *30,574*
Ouachita □, LA • *142,191*
Ouray, CO 81427 • *644*
Ouray □, CO • *2,295*
Outagamie □, WI • *140,510*
Overland, MO 63114 • *17,987*
Overland Park, KS 66204 • *111,790*
Overlea, MD 21206 • *12,137*
Overlook, OH 45431 • *6,000*
Overton, NV 89040 • *1,111*

Overton, TX 75684 • *2,105*
Overton □, TN • *17,636*
Ovid, MI 48866 • *1,442*
Owasso, OK 74055 • *11,151*
Owatonna, MN 55060 • *19,386*
Owego, NY 13827 • *4,442*
Owen □, IN • *17,281*
Owen □, KY • *9,035*
Owensboro, KY 42301–03 • *53,549*
Owensville, IN 47665 • *1,053*
Owensville, MO 65066 • *2,325*
Owensville, OH 45160 • *1,019*
Owenton, KY 40359 • *1,306*
Owings Mills, MD 21117 • *9,474*
Owingsville, KY 40360 • *1,491*
Owosso, MI 48867 • *16,322*
Owsley □, KY • *5,036*
Owyhee, NV 89832 • *908*
Owyhee □, ID • *8,392*
Oxford, AL 36203 • *9,362*
Oxford, CT 06483 • *1,600*
Oxford, GA 30267 • *1,945*
Oxford, IN 47971 • *1,273*
Oxford, KS 67119 • *1,143*
Oxford, MA 01540 • *5,969*
Oxford, MI 48370–71 • *2,929*
Oxford, MS 38655 • *9,984*
Oxford, NJ 07863 • *1,767*
Oxford, NY 13830 • *1,738*
Oxford, NC 27565 • *7,913*
Oxford, OH 45056 • *18,937*
Oxford, PA 19363 • *3,769*
Oxford □, ME • *52,602*
Oxnard, CA 93030–35 • *142,216*
Oxon Hill, MD 20745 • *36,267*
Oyster Bay, NY 11771 • *6,687*
Ozark, AL 36360–61 • *12,922*
Ozark, AR 72949 • *3,330*
Ozark, MO 65721 • *4,243*
Ozark □, MO • *8,598*
Ozaukee □, WI • *72,831*
Ozona, FL 34660 • *1,500*
Ozona, TX 76943 • *3,181*

P

Paauilo, HI 96776 • *620*
Pace, FL 32571 • *6,277*
Pacific, MO 63069 • *4,350*
Pacific, WA 98047 • *4,622*
Pacific □, WA • *18,882*
Pacifica, CA 94044 • *37,670*
Pacific Beach, WA 98571 • *1,200*
Pacific City, OR 97135 • *1,500*
Pacific Grove, CA 93950 • *16,117*
Pacific Palisades, HI 96782 • *10,000*
Packwood, WA 98361 • *1,010*
Pacolet, SC 29372 • *1,736*
Paddock Lake, WI 53168 • *2,662*
Paden City, WV 26159 • *2,862*
Paducah, KY 42001–03 • *27,256*
Paducah, TX 79248 • *1,788*
Page, AZ 86040 • *6,598*
Page □, IA • *16,870*
Page □, VA • *21,690*
Pageland, SC 29728 • *2,666*
Page Manor, OH 45431 • *9,300*
Pagosa Springs, CO 81147 • *1,207*
Pahala, HI 96777 • *1,520*
Pahoa, HI 96778 • *1,027*
Pahokee, FL 33476 • *6,822*
Pahrump, NV 89041 • *7,424*
Paia, HI 96779 • *2,091*
Paincourtville, LA 70391 • *1,550*
Painesville, OH 44077 • *15,699*
Painted Post, NY 14870 • *1,950*
Paintsville, KY 41240 • *4,354*
Pajarito, NM 87105 • *1,400*
Palacios, TX 77465 • *4,418*
Palatine, IL 60067 • *39,253*
Palatka, FL 32177 • *10,201*
Palestine, IL 62451 • *1,619*
Palestine, TX 75801–02 • *18,042*
Palisade, CO 81526 • *1,871*
Palisades Park, NJ 07650 • *14,536*
Palm Bay, FL 32905 • *62,632*
Palm Beach, FL 33480 • *9,814*
Palm Beach □, FL • *863,518*
Palm Beach Gardens, FL 33410 • *22,965*
Palm Coast, FL 32135 • *14,287*
Palmdale, CA 93550–51 • *68,842*
Palm Desert, CA 92260–61 • *23,252*
Palmer, AK 99645 • *2,866*
Palmer, MA 01069 • *4,069*
Palmer, MS 39401 • *2,765*
Palmer, TX 75152 • *1,659*
Palmer Lake, CO 80133 • *1,480*
Palmer Park, MD 20785 • *7,019*
Palmerton, PA 18071 • *5,394*
Palmetto, FL 34220–21 • *9,268*
Palmetto, GA 30268 • *2,612*
Palmetto Estates, FL 33157 • *12,293*
Palm Harbor, FL 34682–85 • *50,256*
Palm Springs, CA 92262–64 • *40,181*
Palm Springs, FL 33460 • *9,763*
Palm Springs North, FL 33015 • *5,300*
Palm Valley, FL 32082 • *9,960*
Palmyra, MO 63461 • *3,371*
Palmyra, NJ 08065 • *7,056*
Palmyra, NY 14522 • *3,566*
Palmyra, PA 17078 • *6,910*
Palmyra, WI 53156 • *1,539*
Palo Alto, CA 94301–09 • *55,900*
Palo Alto □, IA • *10,669*
Palo Pinto □, TX • *25,055*
Palos Heights, IL 60463 • *11,478*
Palos Hills, IL 60465 • *17,803*
Palos Park, IL 60464 • *4,199*
Palos Verdes Estates, CA 90274 • *13,512*
Pamlico □, NC • *11,372*
Pampa, TX 79065–66 • *19,959*
Pamplico, SC 29583 • *1,314*
Pana, IL 62557 • *5,796*
Panaca, NV 89042 • *700*
Panama, OK 74951 • *1,528*
Panama City, FL 32401–13 • *34,378*
Panama City Beach, FL 32407–08 • *4,051*
Pandora, OH 45877 • *1,009*
Panguitch, UT 84759 • *1,444*
Panhandle, TX 79068 • *2,353*
Panola □, MS • *29,996*
Panola □, TX • *22,035*
Panora, IA 50216 • *1,100*
Panthersville, GA 30032 • *9,874*
Paola, KS 66071 • *4,698*
Paoli, IN 47454 • *3,542*
Paoli, PA 19301 • *5,603*
Paonia, CO 81428 • *1,403*
Papaikou, HI 96781 • *1,634*
Papillion, NE 68046 • *10,372*
Paradise, CA 95969 • *25,408*
Paradise, NV 89109 • *124,682*
Paradise Hills, NM 87114 • *5,513*
Paradise Valley, AZ 85253 • *11,671*
Paradise Valley, NV 89426 • *150*
Paragould, AR 72450–51 • *18,540*
Paramount, CA 90723 • *47,669*
Paramount, MD 21740 • *1,878*
Paramus, NJ 07652–53 • *25,067*
Parchment, MI 49004 • *1,958*
Pardeeville, WI 53954 • *1,630*
Paris, AR 72855 • *3,674*
Paris, IL 61944 • *8,987*
Paris, KY 40361–62 • *8,730*
Paris, MO 65275 • *1,486*
Paris, TN 38242 • *9,332*
Paris, TX 75460–61 • *24,699*
Park □, CO • *7,174*
Park □, MT • *14,562*
Park □, WY • *23,178*
Park City, KS 67219 • *5,050*
Park City, UT 84060 • *4,468*
Parke □, IN • *15,410*
Parker, AZ 85344 • *2,897*
Parker, CO 80134 • *5,450*
Parker, FL 32401 • *4,598*
Parker, SD 57053 • *984*
Parker □, TX • *64,785*
Parker City, IN 47368 • *1,323*
Parkersburg, IA 50665 • *1,804*
Parkersburg, WV 26101–06 • *33,862*
Parkesburg, PA 19365 • *2,981*
Park Falls, WI 54552 • *3,104*
Park Forest, IL 60466 • *24,656*
Park Hills, KY 41015 • *3,321*
Parkin, AR 72373 • *1,847*
Parkland, WA 98444 • *20,882*
Park Layne, OH 45344 • *4,895*
Park Rapids, MN 56470 • *2,863*
Park Ridge, IL 60068 • *36,175*
Park Ridge, NJ 07656 • *8,102*
Park River, ND 58270 • *1,725*
Parkrose, OR 97230 • *21,108*
Parkston, SD 57366 • *1,572*
Parkville, MD 21234 • *31,617*
Parkville, MO 64152 • *2,402*
Parkwater, WA 99211 • *4,300*
Parkway, CA 95823 • *12,000*
Parkwood, NC 27713 • *4,123*
Parkwood, WA 98366 • *6,853*
Parlier, CA 93648 • *7,938*
Parma, ID 83660 • *1,597*
Parma, OH 44129 • *87,876*
Parma Heights, OH 44130 • *21,448*
Parmer □, TX • *9,863*
Parole, MD 21401 • *10,054*
Parowan, UT 84761 • *1,873*
Parrish, AL 35580 • *1,433*
Parshall, ND 58770 • *943*
Parsons, KS 67357 • *11,924*
Parsons, TN 38363 • *2,033*
Parsons, WV 26287 • *1,453*
Pasadena, CA 91101–09 • *131,591*
Pasadena, MD 21122 • *10,012*
Pasadena, TX 77501–08 • *119,363*
Pascagoula, MS 39567–68 • *25,899*
Pasco, WA 99301–02 • *20,337*
Pasco □, FL • *281,131*
Pascoag, RI 02859 • *5,011*
Paso Robles, CA 93446–47 • *18,583*
Pasquotank □, NC • *31,298*
Passaic, NJ 07055 • *58,041*
Passaic □, NJ • *453,060*
Pass Christian, MS 39571 • *5,557*
Pataskala, OH 43062 • *3,046*
Patchogue, NY 11772 • *11,060*
Paterson, NJ 07501–44 • *140,891*
Patrick □, VA • *17,473*
Patten, ME 04765 • *1,256*
Patterson, LA 70392 • *4,736*
Patterson, NY 12563 • *1,200*
Patton, PA 16668 • *2,206*
Paul, ID 83347 • *901*
Paulding, OH 45879 • *2,605*
Paulding □, GA • *41,611*
Paulding □, OH • *20,488*
Paullina, IA 51046 • *1,134*
Paulsboro, NJ 08066 • *6,577*
Pauls Valley, OK 73075 • *6,150*
Pawcatuck, CT 06379 • *5,289*
Paw Creek, NC 28130 • *1,700*
Pawhuska, OK 74056 • *3,825*
Pawling, NY 12564 • *1,974*
Pawnee, IL 62558 • *2,384*
Pawnee, OK 74058 • *2,197*
Pawnee □, KS • *7,555*
Pawnee □, NE • *3,317*
Pawnee □, OK • *15,575*
Pawnee City, NE 68420 • *1,008*
Paw Paw, MI 49079 • *3,169*
Pawtucket, RI 02860–65 • *72,644*
Paxton, IL 60957 • *4,289*
Paxton, MA 01612 • *1,550*
Payette, ID 83661 • *5,592*
Payette □, ID • *16,434*
Payne, OH 45880 • *1,244*
Payne □, OK • *61,507*
Paynesville, MN 56362 • *2,275*
Payson, AZ 85541 • *8,377*
Payson, IL 62360 • *1,114*
Payson, UT 84651 • *9,510*
Peabody, KS 66866 • *1,349*
Peabody, MA 01960–61 • *47,039*
Peace Dale, RI 02883 • *3,100*
Peach □, GA • *21,189*
Peach Orchard, GA 30906 • *13,800*
Peachtree City, GA 30269 • *19,027*
Pea Ridge, AR 72751 • *1,620*
Pearisburg, VA 24134 • *2,064*
Pearl, MS 39208 • *19,588*
Pearland, TX 77581 • *18,697*
Pearl City, HI 96782 • *30,993*
Pearl River, LA 70452 • *1,507*
Pearl River, NY 10965 • *15,314*
Pearl River □, MS • *38,714*
Pearsall, TX 78061 • *6,924*
Pearson, GA 31642 • *1,714*
Pecatonica, IL 61063 • *1,760*
Pecos, NM 87552 • *1,012*
Pecos, TX 79772 • *12,069*
Pecos □, TX • *14,675*
Peculiar, MO 64078 • *1,777*
Pedricktown, NJ 08067 • *1,500*
Peebles, OH 45660 • *1,782*
Peekskill, NY 10566 • *19,536*
Pogram, TN 37143 • *1,371*
Pekin, IL 61554–55 • *32,254*
Pekin, IN 47165 • *1,095*
Pelahatchie, MS 39145 • *1,553*
Pelham, AL 35124 • *9,765*
Pelham, GA 31779 • *3,869*
Pelham, NY 10803 • *6,413*
Pelham Manor, NY 10803 • *5,443*
Pelican Rapids, MN 56572 • *1,886*
Pella, IA 50219 • *9,270*
Pell City, AL 35125 • *8,118*
Pell Lake, WI 53157 • *2,018*
Pemberton, NJ 08068 • *1,367*
Pemberville, OH 43450 • *1,279*
Pembina □, ND • *9,238*
Pembroke, GA 31321 • *1,503*
Pembroke, MA 02359 • *2,000*
Pembroke, NC 28372 • *2,241*
Pembroke, VA 24136 • *1,064*
Pembroke Park, FL 33009 • *4,933*
Pembroke Pines, FL 33024 • *65,452*
Pemiscot □, MO • *21,921*
Pen Argyl, PA 18072 • *3,492*
Penbrook, PA 17103 • *2,791*
Pender, NE 68047 • *1,208*
Pender □, NC • *28,855*
Pendleton, IN 46064 • *2,309*
Pendleton, OR 97801 • *15,126*
Pendleton, SC 29670 • *3,314*
Pendleton □, KY • *12,036*
Pendleton □, WV • *8,054*
Pendley Hills, GA 30032 • *5,400*
Pend Oreille □, WA • *8,915*
Penfield, NY 14526 • *6,260*
Penn Acres, DE 19720 • *2,430*
Penn Hills, PA 15235 • *51,430*
Pennington, NJ 08534 • *2,537*
Pennington □, MN • *13,306*
Pennington □, SD • *81,343*
Pennington Gap, VA 24277 • *1,922*
Pennsauken, NJ 08110 • *34,733*
Pennsboro, WV 26415 • *1,282*
Pennsburg, PA 18073 • *2,460*
Penns Grove, NJ 08069 • *5,228*
Pennsville, NJ 08070 • *12,218*
Penn Yan, NY 14527 • *5,248*
Penobscot □, ME • *146,601*
Pensacola, FL 32501–26 • *58,165*
Pentwater, MI 49449 • *1,050*
Peoria, AZ 85345 • *50,618*
Peoria, IL 61601–56 • *113,504*
Peoria □, IL • *182,827*
Peoria Heights, IL 61614 • *6,930*
Peotone, IL 60468 • *2,947*
Pepeekeo, HI 96783 • *1,813*
Pepin □, WI • *7,107*
Pepperell, MA 01463 • *2,350*
Pepper Pike, OH 44124 • *6,185*
Pequannock, NJ 07440 • *12,844*
Perdido, AL 36562 • *1,200*
Perham, MN 56573 • *2,075*
Perkasie, PA 18944 • *7,878*
Perkins, OK 74059 • *1,925*
Perkins □, NE • *3,367*
Perkins □, SD • *3,932*
Perquimans □, NC • *10,447*
Perrine, FL 33157 • *15,576*
Perris, CA 92370 • *21,460*
Perry, FL 32347 • *7,151*
Perry, GA 31069 • *9,452*
Perry, IA 50220 • *6,652*
Perry, MI 48872 • *2,163*
Perry, NY 14530 • *4,219*
Perry, OH 44081 • *1,012*
Perry, OK 73077 • *4,978*
Perry, UT 84302 • *1,211*
Perry □, AL • *12,759*
Perry □, AR • *7,969*
Perry □, IL • *21,412*
Perry □, IN • *19,107*
Perry □, KY • *30,283*
Perry □, MS • *10,865*
Perry □, MO • *16,648*
Perry □, OH • *31,557*
Perry □, PA • *41,172*
Perry □, TN • *6,612*
Perry Hall, MD 21128 • *22,723*
Perry Heights, OH 44646 • *9,055*
Perryman, MD 21130 • *2,160*
Perrysburg, OH 43551–52 • *12,551*
Perryton, TX 79070 • *7,607*
Perryville, AR 72126 • *1,141*
Perryville, MD 21903 • *2,456*
Perryville, MO 63775 • *6,933*
Pershing □, NV • *4,336*
Person □, NC • *30,180*
Perth Amboy, NJ 08861–63 • *41,967*
Peru, IL 61354 • *9,302*
Peru, IN 46970 • *12,843*
Peru, NE 68421 • *1,110*
Peru, NY 12972 • *1,565*
Peshtigo, WI 54157 • *3,154*
Petal, MS 39465 • *7,883*
Petaluma, CA 94952–55 • *43,184*
Peterborough, NH 03458 • *2,685*
Petersburg, AK 99833 • *3,207*
Petersburg, IL 62675 • *2,261*
Petersburg, IN 47567 • *2,449*
Petersburg, MI 49270 • *1,201*
Petersburg, TX 79250 • *1,292*
Petersburg, VA 23801–05 • *38,386*
Petersburg, WV 26847 • *2,360*
Petersville, AL 35633 • *1,730*
Petoskey, MI 49770 • *6,056*
Petroleum □, MT • *519*
Petros, TN 37845 • *1,286*
Pettis □, MO • *35,437*
Pevely, MO 63070 • *2,831*
Pewaukee, WI 53072 • *4,941*
Pewee Valley, KY 40056 • *1,283*
Pharr, TX 78577 • *32,921*
Phelps, KY 41553 • *1,120*
Phelps, NY 14532 • *1,978*
Phelps □, MO • *35,248*
Phelps □, NE • *9,715*
Phenix City, AL 36867–69 • *25,312*
Philadelphia, MS 39350 • *6,758*
Philadelphia, NY 13673 • *1,478*
Philadelphia, PA 19101–96 • *1,585,577*
Philadelphia □, PA • *1,585,577*
Phil Campbell, AL 35581 • *1,317*
Philip, SD 57567 • *1,077*
Philippi, WV 26416 • *3,132*
Philipsburg, MT 59858 • *925*
Philipsburg, PA 16866 • *3,048*
Phillips, TX 79007 • *1,729*
Phillips, WI 54555 • *1,592*
Phillips □, AR • *28,838*
Phillips □, CO • *4,189*
Phillips □, KS • *6,590*
Phillips □, MT • *5,163*
Phillipsburg, KS 67661 • *2,828*
Phillipsburg, NJ 08865 • *15,757*
Philmont, NY 12565 • *1,623*
Philo, IL 61864 • *1,028*
Philomath, OR 97370 • *2,983*
Phoenix, AZ 85001–82 • *983,403*
Phoenix, IL 60426 • *2,217*
Phoenix, NY 13135 • *2,435*
Phoenix, OR 97535 • *3,239*
Phoenixville, PA 19460 • *15,066*
Piatt □, IL • *15,548*
Picayune, MS 39466 • *10,633*
Picher, OK 74360 • *1,714*
Pickaway □, OH • *48,255*
Pickens, MS 39146 • *1,285*
Pickens, SC 29671 • *3,042*
Pickens □, AL • *20,699*
Pickens □, GA • *14,432*
Pickens □, SC • *93,894*
Pickerington, OH 43147 • *5,668*
Pickett □, TN • *4,548*
Pico Rivera, CA 90660–61 • *59,177*
Piedmont, AL 36272 • *5,288*
Piedmont, CA 94611 • *10,602*
Piedmont, MO 63957 • *2,166*
Piedmont, OK 73078 • *2,522*
Piedmont, SC 29673 • *4,143*
Piedmont, WV 26750 • *1,094*
Pierce, ID 83546 • *746*
Pierce, NE 68767 • *1,615*
Pierce □, GA • *13,328*
Pierce □, NE • *7,827*
Pierce □, ND • *5,052*
Pierce □, WA • *586,203*
Pierce □, WI • *32,765*
Pierce City, MO 65723 • *1,382*
Pierceton, IN 46562 • *1,030*
Pierre, SD 57501 • *12,906*
Pierre Part, LA 70339 • *3,053*
Pierson, FL 32180 • *2,988*
Pierz, MN 56364 • *1,014*
Pigeon, MI 48755 • *1,207*
Pigeon Cove, MA 01966 • *1,660*
Pigeon Forge, TN 37863 • *3,027*
Piggott, AR 72454 • *3,777*
Pike □, AL • *27,595*
Pike □, AR • *10,086*
Pike □, GA • *10,224*
Pike □, IL • *17,577*
Pike □, IN • *12,509*
Pike □, KY • *72,583*
Pike □, MS • *36,882*
Pike □, MO • *15,969*
Pike □, OH • *24,249*
Pike □, PA • *27,966*
Pike Lake, MN 55811 • *1,004*
Pikesville, MD 21208 • *24,815*
Piketon, OH 45661 • *1,717*
Pikeville, KY 41501–02 • *6,324*
Pikeville, TN 37367 • *1,771*
Pilot Mountain, NC 27041 • *1,181*
Pilot Point, TX 76258 • *2,538*
Pilot Rock, OR 97868 • *1,478*
Pilot Station, AK 99650 • *463*
Pima, AZ 85543 • *1,725*
Pima □, AZ • *666,880*
Pimmit Hills, VA 22043 • *6,019*
Pinal □, AZ • *116,379*
Pinardville, NH 03045 • *4,654*
Pinckney, MI 48169 • *1,603*
Pinckneyville, IL 62274 • *3,372*
Pinconning, MI 48650 • *1,291*
Pine □, MN • *21,264*
Pine Bluff, AR 71601–13 • *57,140*
Pine Bluffs, WY 82082 • *1,054*
Pine Bridge, CT 06403 • *1,160*
Pine Bush, NY 12566 • *1,445*
Pine Castle, FL 32809 • *8,276*
Pine City, MN 55063 • *2,613*
Pinedale, WY 82941 • *1,181*
Pine Grove, PA 17963 • *2,110*
Pine Grove Mills, PA 16868 • *1,129*
Pine Hill, NJ 08021 • *9,854*
Pine Hills, FL 32808 • *35,322*
Pinehurst, MA 01866 • *6,614*
Pinehurst, NJ 08201 • *1,850*
Pinehurst, NC 28374 • *5,103*
Pine Island, MN 55963 • *2,125*
Pine Island, NY 10969 • *1,200*
Pine Knot, KY 42635 • *1,549*
Pine Lawn, MO 63120 • *5,092*
Pine Level, NC 27568 • *1,217*
Pinellas □, FL • *851,659*
Pinellas Park, FL 34664–66 • *43,426*
Pine Plains, NY 12567 • *1,312*
Pine Ridge, SD 57770 • *2,596*
Pinetops, NC 27864 • *1,514*
Pine Valley, CA 91962 • *1,297*
Pineville, KY 40977 • *2,198*
Pineville, LA 71360–61 • *12,251*
Pineville, NC 28134 • *2,970*
Pinewald, NJ 08721 • *1,700*
Pinewood, FL 33168 • *15,518*
Pinewood Park, FL 33168 • *8,300*
Piney Point, MD 20674 • *1,200*
Piney View, WV 25906 • *1,085*
Pinole, CA 94564 • *17,460*
Pinson, AL 35126 • *1,430*
Pioche, NV 89043 • *830*
Pioneer, OH 43554 • *1,287*
Pipestone, MN 56164 • *4,554*
Pipestone □, MN • *10,491*
Piqua, OH 45356 • *20,612*
Pirtleville, AZ 85626 • *1,364*
Piscataquis □, ME • *18,653*
Piscataway, NJ 08854–55 • *42,223*
Pisgah, OH 45069 • *15,660*
Pisgah Forest, NC 28768 • *1,899*
Pismo Beach, CA 93448–49 • *7,669*
Pitcairn, PA 15140 • *4,087*
Pitkin □, CO • *12,661*
Pitman, NJ 08071 • *9,365*
Pitt □, NC • *107,924*
Pittsboro, NC 27312 • *1,436*
Pittsburg, CA 94565 • *47,564*
Pittsburg, KS 66762 • *17,775*
Pittsburg, TX 75686 • *4,007*
Pittsburg □, OK • *40,581*
Pittsburgh, PA 15201–90 • *369,879*
Pittsfield, IL 62363 • *4,231*
Pittsfield, ME 04967 • *3,222*
Pittsfield, MA 01201–03 • *48,622*
Pittsfield, NH 03263 • *1,717*
Pittsford, VT 05763 • *650*
Pittston, PA 18640–44 • *9,389*
Pittsylvania □, VA • *55,655*
Piute □, UT • *1,277*
Pixley, CA 93256 • *2,457*
Placentia, CA 92670 • *41,259*
Placer □, CA • *172,796*
Placerville, CA 95667 • *8,355*
Plain City, OH 43064 • *2,278*
Plain City, UT 84404 • *2,722*
Plain Dealing, LA 71064 • *1,074*
Plainedge, NY 11714 • *8,739*
Plainfield, CT 06374 • *2,856*
Plainfield, IL 60544 • *4,557*
Plainfield, IN 46168 • *10,433*
Plainfield, NJ 07059–63 • *46,567*
Plainfield, VT 05667 • *600*
Plainfield Heights, MI 49505 • *5,000*
Plains, MT 59859 • *992*
Plains, PA 18705 • *4,694*
Plains, TX 79355 • *1,422*
Plainsboro, NJ 08536 • *1,560*
Plainview, MN 55964 • *2,768*
Plainview, NE 68769 • *1,333*
Plainview, NY 11803 • *26,207*
Plainview, TX 79072–73 • *21,700*
Plainville, CT 06062 • *17,392*
Plainville, KS 67663 • *2,173*
Plainville, MA 02762 • *5,857*
Plainwell, MI 49080 • *4,057*
Plaistow, NH 03865 • *1,850*
Plano, IL 60545 • *5,104*
Plano, TX 75074–75 • *128,713*
Plantation, FL 33317 • *66,692*
Plant City, FL 33564–67 • *22,754*
Plantersville, MS 38862 • *1,046*
Plantsite, AZ 85540 • *1,500*
Plantsville, CT 06479 • *7,050*
Plaquemine, LA 70764–65 • *7,186*
Plaquemines □, LA • *25,575*
Platte, SD 57369 • *1,311*
Platte □, MO • *57,867*
Platte □, NE • *29,820*
Platte □, WY • *8,145*
Platte City, MO 64079 • *2,947*
Platteville, CO 80651 • *1,515*
Platteville, WI 53818 • *9,708*
Plattsburg, MO 64477 • *2,248*
Plattsburgh, NY 12901 • *21,255*
Plattsmouth, NE 68048 • *6,412*
Pleasant Gap, PA 16823 • *1,699*
Pleasant Garden, NC 27313 • *2,228*
Pleasant Grove, AL 35127 • *8,458*
Pleasant Grove, UT 84062 • *13,476*
Pleasant Hill, CA 94523 • *31,585*
Pleasant Hill, IL 62366 • *1,030*
Pleasant Hill, IA 50301 • *3,671*
Pleasant Hill, MO 64080 • *3,827*
Pleasant Hill, OH 45359 • *1,066*
Pleasant Hills, PA 15236 • *8,884*
Pleasanton, CA 94566 • *50,553*
Pleasanton, KS 66075 • *1,231*
Pleasanton, TX 78064 • *7,678*
Pleasant Prairie, WI 53158 • *11,961*
Pleasants □, WV • *7,546*
Pleasant Valley, MO 64068 • *2,731*
Pleasant Valley, NY 12569 • *1,688*
Pleasant View, CO 80401 • *3,460*
Pleasant View, UT 84404 • *3,603*
Pleasantville, IA 50225 • *1,536*
Pleasantville, NJ 08232 • *16,027*
Pleasantville, NY 10570–72 • *6,592*
Pleasure Beach, CT 06385 • *1,356*
Pleasure Ridge Park, KY 40258 • *25,131*
Plentywood, MT 59254 • *2,136*
Plover, WI 54467 • *8,176*
Plum, PA 15239 • *25,609*
Plumas □, CA • *19,739*
Plumsteadville, PA 18949 • *1,200*
Plymouth, CT 06782 • *1,070*
Plymouth, FL 32768 • *2,700*
Plymouth, IN 46563 • *8,303*
Plymouth, MA 02360–61 • *7,258*
Plymouth, MI 48170 • *9,560*
Plymouth, MN 55441 • *50,889*
Plymouth, NH 03264 • *3,967*
Plymouth, NC 27962 • *4,328*
Plymouth, OH 44865 • *1,942*
Plymouth, PA 18651 • *7,134*
Plymouth, WI 53073 • *6,769*
Plymouth □, IA • *23,388*
Plymouth □, MA • *435,276*
Plymouth Township, PA 19401 • *17,168*
Poca, WV 25159 • *1,124*
Pocahontas, AR 72455 • *6,151*
Pocahontas, IA 50574 • *2,085*
Pocahontas □, IA • *9,525*
Pocahontas □, WV • *9,008*
Pocasset, MA 02559 • *2,200*
Pocatalico, WV 25320 • *2,450*
Pocatello, ID 83201–06 • *46,080*
Pocola, OK 74902 • *3,664*
Pocomoke City, MD 21851 • *3,922*
Poinsett □, AR • *24,664*
Point Clear, AL 36564 • *2,125*
Pointe Coupee □, LA • *22,540*
Point Hope, AK 99766 • *639*
Point Marion, PA 15474 • *1,344*
Point Pleasant, NJ 08742 • *18,177*
Point Pleasant, WV 25550 • *4,996*
Point Pleasant Beach, NJ 08742 • *5,112*
Poipu, HI 96756 • *975*
Polk, PA 16342 • *1,267*
Polk □, AR • *17,347*

Polk □, FL • *405,382*
Polk □, GA • *33,815*
Polk □, IA • *327,140*
Polk □, MN • *32,498*
Polk □, MO • *21,826*
Polk □, NE • *5,675*
Polk □, NC • *14,416*
Polk □, OR • *49,541*
Polk □, TN • *13,643*
Polk □, TX • *30,687*
Polk □, WI • *34,773*
Polk City, FL 33868 • *1,439*
Polk City, IA 50226 • *1,908*
Polo, IL 61064 • *2,514*
Polson, MT 59860 • *3,283*
Pomeroy, OH 45769 • *2,259*
Pomeroy, WA 99347 • *1,393*
Pomona, CA 91765–69 • *131,723*
Pomona, NJ 08240 • *2,624*
Pompano Beach, FL 33060–69 • *72,411*
Pompano Beach Highlands, FL 33060 • *17,915*
Pompton Lakes, NJ 07442 • *10,539*
Ponca City, OK 74601–04 • *26,359*
Ponchatoula, LA 70454 • *5,425*
Pondera □, MT • *6,433*
Ponte Vedra Beach, FL 32082 • *1,700*
Pontiac, IL 61764 • *11,428*
Pontiac, MI 48340–43 • *71,166*
Pontotoc, MS 38863 • *4,570*
Pontotoc □, MS • *22,237*
Pontotoc □, OK • *34,119*
Pooler, GA 31322 • *4,453*
Poolesville, MD 20837 • *3,796*
Pope □, AR • *45,883*
Pope □, IL • *4,373*
Pope □, MN • *10,745*
Poplar, MT 59255 • *881*
Poplar Bluff, MO 63901 • *16,996*
Poplarville, MS 39470 • *2,561*
Poquonock Bridge, CT 06340 • *2,770*
Poquoson, VA 23662 • *11,005*
Portage, IN 46368 • *29,060*
Portage, MI 49081 • *41,042*
Portage, PA 15946 • *3,105*
Portage, WI 53901 • *8,640*
Portage □, OH • *142,585*
Portage □, WI • *61,405*
Portage Lakes, OH 44319 • *13,373*
Portageville, MO 63873 • *3,401*
Portales, NM 88130 • *10,690*
Port Allegany, PA 16743 • *2,391*
Port Allen, LA 70767 • *6,277*
Port Angeles, WA 98362 • *17,710*
Port Aransas, TX 78373 • *2,233*
Port Arthur, TX 77640–43 • *58,724*
Port Barre, LA 70577 • *2,144*
Port Bolivar, TX 77650 • *1,600*
Port Byron, IL 61275 • *1,002*
Port Byron, NY 13140 • *1,359*
Port Carbon, PA 17965 • *2,134*
Port Charlotte, FL 33952 • *41,535*
Port Chester, NY 10573 • *24,728*
Port Clinton, OH 43452 • *7,106*
Port Dickinson, NY 13901 • *1,785*
Port Edwards, WI 54469 • *1,848*
Porter, IN 46304 • *3,118*
Porter, TX 77365 • *7,000*
Porter □, IN • *128,932*
Porterdale, GA 30270 • *1,278*
Porterville, CA 93257–58 • *29,563*
Port Ewen, NY 12466 • *3,444*
Port Gibson, MS 39150 • *1,810*
Port Henry, NY 12974 • *1,263*
Port Hueneme, CA 93041–44 • *20,319*
Port Huron, MI 48060–61 • *33,694*
Port Isabel, TX 78578 • *4,467*
Port Jefferson, NY 11777 • *7,455*
Port Jefferson Station, NY 11776 • *7,232*
Port Jervis, NY 12771 • *9,060*
Portland, CT 06480 • *5,645*
Portland, IN 47371 • *6,483*
Portland, ME 04101–12 • *64,358*
Portland, MI 48875 • *3,889*
Portland, OR 97201–99 • *437,319*
Portland, TN 37148 • *5,165*
Portland, TX 78374 • *12,224*
Port Lavaca, TX 77979 • *10,886*
Port Monmouth, NJ 07758 • *3,800*
Port Neches, TX 77651 • *12,974*
Port Norris, NJ 08349 • *1,701*
Port O'Connor, TX 77982 • *1,031*
Portola, CA 96122 • *2,193*
Port Orange, FL 32127 • *35,317*
Port Orchard, WA 98366 • *4,984*
Port Orford, OR 97465 • *1,025*
Port Penn, DE 19731 • *300*
Port Richey, FL 34667–74 • *2,523*
Port Royal, SC 29935 • *2,985*
Port Saint Joe, FL 32456 • *4,044*
Port Saint Lucie, FL 34952 • *55,866*
Port Salerno, FL 34992 • *7,786*
Portsmouth, NH 03801–02 • *25,925*
Portsmouth, OH 45662 • *22,676*
Portsmouth, RI 02871 • *3,540*
Portsmouth, VA 23701–09 • *103,907*
Port St. John, FL 32922 • *8,933*
Port Sulphur, LA 70083 • *3,523*
Port Townsend, WA 98368 • *7,001*
Portville, NY 14770 • *1,040*
Port Vue, PA 15133 • *4,641*
Port Washington, NY 11050 • *15,387*
Port Washington, WI 53074 • *9,338*
Port Wentworth, GA 31407 • *4,012*
Posen, IL 60469 • *4,226*
Posey □, IN • *25,968*
Poseyville, IN 47633 • *1,089*
Post, TX 79356 • *3,768*
Post Falls, ID 83854 • *7,349*
Postville, IA 52162 • *1,472*
Poteau, OK 74953 • *7,210*
Poteet, TX 78065 • *3,206*
Poth, TX 78147 • *1,642*
Potlatch, ID 83855 • *790*
Potomac, MD 20851 • *45,634*
Potomac Heights, MD 20640 • *1,524*
Potomac Park, MD 21502 • *1,800*
Potosi, MO 63664 • *2,683*
Potsdam, NY 13676 • *10,251*
Pottawatomie □, KS • *16,128*
Pottawatomie □, OK • *58,760*
Pottawattamie □, IA • *82,628*
Potter □, PA • *16,717*
Potter □, SD • *3,190*
Potter □, TX • *97,874*
Potter Valley, CA 95469 • *1,500*
Pottstown, PA 19464 • *21,831*
Pottsville, PA 17901 • *16,603*
Poughkeepsie, NY 12601–03 • *28,844*
Poulsbo, WA 98370 • *4,848*
Poultney, VT 05764 • *1,731*
Poway, CA 92064 • *43,516*
Powder River □, MT • *2,090*
Powder Springs, GA 30073 • *6,893*
Powell, OH 43065 • *2,154*
Powell, TN 37849 • *7,534*
Powell, WY 82435 • *5,292*
Powell □, KY • *11,686*
Powell □, MT • *6,620*
Powellhurst, OR 97236 • *28,756*
Powellton, WV 25161 • *1,905*
Power □, ID • *7,086*
Poweshiek □, IA • *19,033*
Powhatan □, VA • *15,328*
Powhatan Point, OH 43942 • *1,807*
Poydras, LA 70085 • *4,029*
Poynette, WI 53955 • *1,662*
Prague, OK 74864 • *2,308*
Prairie □, AR • *9,518*
Prairie □, MT • *1,383*
Prairie City, IA 50228 • *1,360*
Prairie City, OR 97869 • *1,117*
Prairie du Chien, WI 53821 • *5,659*
Prairie du Sac, WI 53578 • *2,380*
Prairie Grove, AR 72753 • *1,761*
Prairie View, TX 77446 • *4,004*
Prairie Village, KS 66208 • *23,186*
Pratt, KS 67124 • *6,687*
Pratt □, KS • *9,702*
Prattville, AL 36066–67 • *19,587*
Preble □, OH • *40,113*
Premont, TX 78375 • *2,914*
Prentiss, MS 39474 • *1,487*
Prentiss □, MS • *23,278*
Prescott, AZ 86301–14 • *26,455*
Prescott, AR 71857 • *3,673*
Prescott, WI 54021 • *3,243*
Presho, SD 57568 • *654*
Presidio, TX 79845 • *3,072*
Presidio □, TX • *6,637*
Presque Isle, ME 04769 • *10,550*
Presque Isle □, MI • *13,743*
Preston, ID 83263 • *3,710*
Preston, IA 52069 • *1,025*
Preston, MN 55965 • *1,530*
Preston □, WV • *29,037*
Prestonsburg, KY 41653 • *3,558*
Price, UT 84501 • *8,712*
Price □, WI • *15,600*
Prichard, AL 36610 • *34,311*
Priest River, ID 83856 • *1,560*
Primrose, RI 02895 • *500*
Prince Edward □, VA • *17,320*
Prince Frederick, MD 20678 • *1,885*
Prince George □, VA • *27,394*
Prince Georges □, MD • *729,268*
Princes Lakes, IN 46164 • *1,055*
Princess Anne, MD 21853 • *1,666*
Princeton, FL 33032 • *7,073*
Princeton, IL 61356 • *7,197*
Princeton, IN 47670 • *8,127*
Princeton, KY 42445 • *6,940*
Princeton, MN 55371 • *3,719*
Princeton, MO 64673 • *1,021*
Princeton, NJ 08540–43 • *12,016*
Princeton, NC 27569 • *1,181*
Princeton, WV 24740 • *7,043*
Princeton, WI 54968 • *1,458*
Princeton Junction, NJ 08550 • *2,362*
Princeville, IL 61559 • *1,421*
Princeville, NC 27886 • *1,652*
Prince William □, VA • *215,686*
Prineville, OR 97754 • *5,355*
Prior Lake, MN 55372 • *11,482*
Proctor, MN 55810 • *2,974*
Proctor, VT 05765 • *1,979*
Proctorsville, VT 05153 • *480*
Prophetstown, IL 61277 • *1,749*
Prospect, CT 06712 • *6,807*
Prospect, KY 40059 • *2,788*
Prospect, OH 43342 • *1,148*
Prospect, OR 97536 • *1,200*
Prospect, PA 16052 • *1,122*
Prospect Heights, IL 60070 • *15,239*
Prospect Park, NJ 07508 • *5,053*
Prospect Park, PA 19076 • *6,764*
Prosperity, SC 29127 • *1,116*
Prosperity, WV 25909 • *1,322*
Prosser, WA 99350 • *4,476*
Providence, KY 42450 • *4,123*
Providence, RI 02901–40 • *160,728*
Providence, UT 84332 • *3,344*
Providence □, RI • *596,270*
Provincetown, MA 02657 • *3,374*
Provo, UT 84601–06 • *86,835*
Prowers □, CO • *13,347*
Prudenville, MI 48651 • *1,100*
Prudhoe Bay, AK 99734 • *47*
Pryor, OK 74361–62 • *8,327*
Pueblo, CO 81001–19 • *98,640*
Pueblo □, CO • *123,051*
Puhi, HI 96766 • *1,210*
Pukalani, HI 96788 • *5,879*
Pulaski, NY 13142 • *2,525*
Pulaski, TN 38478 • *7,895*
Pulaski, VA 24301 • *9,985*
Pulaski, WI 54162 • *2,200*
Pulaski □, AR • *349,660*
Pulaski □, GA • *8,108*
Pulaski □, IL • *7,523*
Pulaski □, IN • *12,643*
Pulaski □, KY • *49,489*
Pulaski □, MO • *41,307*
Pulaski □, VA • *34,496*
Pullman, WA 99163–65 • *23,478*
Pumphrey, MD 21227 • *5,483*
Punta Gorda, FL 33948–55 • *10,747*
Punxsutawney, PA 15767 • *6,782*
Purcell, OK 73080 • *4,784*
Purcellville, VA 22132 • *1,744*
Purvis, MS 39475 • *2,140*
Pushmataha □, OK • *10,997*
Putnam, CT 06260 • *6,835*
Putnam □, FL • *65,070*
Putnam □, GA • *14,137*
Putnam □, IL • *5,730*
Putnam □, IN • *30,315*
Putnam □, MO • *5,079*
Putnam □, NY • *83,941*
Putnam □, OH • *33,819*
Putnam □, TN • *51,373*
Putnam □, WV • *42,835*
Putney, VT 05346 • *1,100*
Puyallup, WA 98371–74 • *23,875*

Q

Quail Oaks, VA 23234 • *1,500*
Quaker Hill, CT 06375 • *2,052*
Quakertown, PA 18951 • *8,982*
Quanah, TX 79252 • *3,413*
Quarryville, PA 17566 • *1,642*
Quartz Hill, CA 93536 • *9,626*
Quartzsite, AZ 85346 • *1,876*
Quay □, NM • *10,823*
Quechee, VT 05059 • *550*
Queen Annes □, MD • *33,953*
Queen City, TX 75572 • *1,748*
Queen Creek, AZ 85242 • *2,667*
Queens □, NY • *1,951,598*
Queensborough, WA 98021 • *4,850*
Questa, NM 87556 • *1,707*
Quidnessett, RI 02852 • *3,300*
Quidnick, RI 02816 • *2,300*
Quilcene, WA 98376 • *1,200*
Quincy, CA 95971 • *2,700*
Quincy, FL 32351 • *7,444*
Quincy, IL 62301–06 • *39,681*
Quincy, MA 02169 • *84,985*
Quincy, MI 49082 • *1,680*
Quincy, WA 98848 • *3,738*
Quinebaug, CT 06262 • *1,031*
Quinhagak, AK 99655 • *501*
Quinlan, TX 75474 • *1,360*
Quinton, OK 74561 • *1,133*
Quitman, GA 31643 • *5,292*
Quitman, MS 39355 • *2,736*
Quitman, TX 75783 • *1,684*
Quitman □, GA • *2,209*
Quitman □, MS • *10,490*
Quonochontaug, RI 02813 • *1,500*

R

Rabun □, GA • *11,648*
Raceland, KY 41169 • *2,256*
Raceland, LA 70394 • *5,564*
Racine, WI 53401–08 • *84,298*
Racine □, WI • *175,034*
Radcliff, KY 40159–60 • *19,772*
Radford, VA 24141–43 • *15,940*
Radnor Township, PA 19087 • *28,705*
Raeford, NC 28376 • *3,469*
Ragland, AL 35131 • *1,807*
Rahway, NJ 07065–67 • *25,325*
Rainbow City, AL 35901 • *7,673*
Rainelle, WV 25962 • *1,681*
Rainier, OR 97048 • *1,674*
Rains □, TX • *6,715*
Rainsville, AL 35986 • *3,875*
Raleigh, MS 39153 • *1,291*
Raleigh, NC 27601–61 • *207,951*
Raleigh □, WV • *76,819*
Raleigh Hills, OR 97225 • *6,066*
Ralls, TX 79357 • *2,172*
Ralls □, MO • *8,476*
Ralston, NE 68127 • *6,236*
Rambleton Acres, DE 19720 • *1,700*
Ramblewood, NJ 08054 • *6,181*
Ramona, CA 92065 • *13,040*
Ramsay, MI 49959 • *1,075*
Ramseur, NC 27316 • *1,186*
Ramsey, MN 55303 • *12,408*
Ramsey, NJ 07446 • *13,228*
Ramsey □, MN • *485,765*
Ramsey □, ND • *12,681*
Ranchester, WY 82839 • *676*
Rancho Cordova, CA 95670 • *48,731*
Rancho Mirage, CA 92270 • *9,778*
Rancho Palos Verdes, CA 90274 • *41,659*
Rancho Rinconado, CA 95014 • *4,206*
Ranchos de Taos, NM 87557 • *1,779*
Rancocas Woods, NJ 08060 • *1,250*
Rand, WV 25306 • *2,400*
Randall □, TX • *89,673*
Randallstown, MD 21133 • *26,277*
Randleman, NC 27317 • *2,612*
Randolph, ME 04345 • *1,949*
Randolph, MA 02368 • *30,093*
Randolph, NY 14772 • *1,298*
Randolph, VT 05060 • *2,200*
Randolph, WI 53956 • *1,729*
Randolph □, AL • *19,881*
Randolph □, AR • *16,558*
Randolph □, GA • *8,023*
Randolph □, IL • *34,583*
Randolph □, IN • *27,148*
Randolph □, MO • *24,370*
Randolph □, NC • *106,546*
Randolph □, WV • *27,803*
Randolph Hills, MD 20852 • *4,180*
Random Lake, WI 53075 • *1,439*
Rangely, CO 81648 • *2,278*
Ranger, TX 76470 • *2,803*
Rankin, PA 15104 • *2,503*
Rankin, TX 79778 • *1,011*
Rankin □, MS • *87,161*
Ransom □, ND • *5,921*
Ransomville, NY 14131 • *1,542*
Ranson, WV 25438 • *2,890*
Rantoul, IL 61866 • *17,212*
Raoul, GA 30510 • *1,400*
Rapid City, SD 57701–09 • *54,523*
Rapides □, LA • *131,556*
Rapid Valley, SD 57701 • *5,968*
Rappahannock □, VA • *6,622*
Raritan, NJ 08869 • *5,798*
Rathdrum, ID 83858 • *2,000*
Raton, NM 87740 • *7,372*
Ravalli □, MT • *25,010*
Raven, VA 24639 • *2,640*
Ravena, NY 12143 • *3,547*
Ravenel, SC 29470 • *2,165*
Ravenna, NE 68869 • *1,317*
Ravenna, OH 44266 • *12,069*
Ravenswood, WV 26164 • *4,189*
Rawlins, WY 82301 • *9,380*
Rawlins □, KS • *3,404*
Ray, ND 58849 • *603*
Ray □, MO • *21,971*
Raymond, MS 39154 • *2,275*
Raymond, NH 03077 • *2,516*
Raymond, WA 98577 • *2,901*
Raymondville, TX 78580 • *8,880*
Raymore, MO 64083 • *5,592*
Rayne, LA 70578 • *8,502*
Raynham, MA 02767 • *3,709*
Raynham Center, MA 02768 • *3,709*
Raytown, MO 64133 • *30,601*
Rayville, LA 71269 • *4,411*
Reading, MA 01867 • *22,539*
Reading, MI 49274 • *1,127*
Reading, OH 45215 • *12,038*
Reading, PA 19601–12 • *78,380*
Reagan □, TX • *4,514*
Real □, TX • *2,412*
Reamstown, PA 17567 • *2,649*
Rector, AR 72461 • *2,268*
Red Bank, NJ 07701–04 • *10,636*
Red Bank, SC 29073 • *6,112*
Red Bank, TN 37415 • *12,322*
Red Bay, AL 35582 • *3,451*
Redbird, OH 44057 • *1,600*
Red Bluff, CA 96080 • *12,363*
Red Bud, IL 62278 • *2,918*
Red Cloud, NE 68970 • *1,204*
Redding, CA 96001–03 • *66,462*
Redding, CT 06875 • *1,000*
Redfield, AR 72132 • *1,082*
Redfield, SD 57469 • *2,770*
Redford, MI 48239 • *54,387*
Redgranite, WI 54970 • *1,009*
Red Hook, NY 12571 • *1,794*
Redkey, IN 47373 • *1,383*
Red Lake □, MN • *4,525*
Red Lake Falls, MN 56750 • *1,481*
Redlands, CA 92373–75 • *60,394*
Red Lion, PA 17356 • *6,130*
Red Lodge, MT 59068 • *1,958*
Redmond, OR 97756 • *7,163*
Redmond, WA 98052–53 • *35,800*
Red Oak, GA 30272 • *2,800*
Red Oak, IA 51566 • *6,264*
Red Oak, TX 75154 • *3,124*
Red Oaks, LA 70815 • *1,600*
Red Oaks Mill, NY 12603 • *4,906*
Redondo Beach, CA 90277–78 • *60,167*
Red River □, LA • *9,387*
Red River □, TX • *14,317*
Red Springs, NC 28377 • *3,799*
Red Willow □, NE • *11,705*
Red Wing, MN 55066 • *15,134*
Redwood, UT 84119 • *1,850*
Redwood □, MN • *17,254*
Redwood City, CA 94061–65 • *66,072*
Redwood Falls, MN 56283 • *4,859*
Redwood Valley, CA 95470 • *1,300*
Reed City, MI 49677 • *2,379*
Reedley, CA 93654 • *15,791*
Reedsburg, WI 53959 • *5,834*
Reedsport, OR 97467 • *4,796*
Reedsville, PA 17084 • *1,030*
Reedsville, WI 54230 • *1,182*
Reedurban, OH 44710 • *6,650*
Reese, MI 48757 • *1,414*
Reeves □, TX • *15,852*
Reform, AL 35481 • *2,105*
Refugio, TX 78377 • *3,158*
Refugio □, TX • *7,976*
Rehoboth Beach, DE 19971 • *1,234*
Reidland, KY 42001 • *4,054*
Reidsville, GA 30453 • *2,469*
Reidsville, NC 27320–23 • *12,183*
Reinbeck, IA 50669 • *1,605*
Reisterstown, MD 21136 • *19,314*
Reliance, WY 82943 • *500*
Remington, IN 47977 • *1,247*
Remsen, IA 51050 • *1,513*
Reno, NV 89501–70 • *133,850*
Reno □, KS • *62,389*
Renovo, PA 17764 • *1,526*
Rensselaer, IN 47978 • *5,045*
Rensselaer, NY 12144 • *8,255*
Rensselaer □, NY • *154,429*
Renton, WA 98055–59 • *41,688*
Renville, MN 56284 • *1,315*
Renville □, MN • *17,673*
Renville □, ND • *3,160*
Republic, MI 49879 • *1,100*
Republic, MO 65738 • *6,292*
Republic, PA 15475 • *1,400*
Republic □, KS • *6,482*
Reserve, LA 70084 • *8,847*
Reston, VA 22090 • *48,556*
Revere, MA 02151 • *42,786*
Rexburg, ID 83440 • *14,302*
Reynolds, GA 31076 • *1,166*
Reynolds □, MO • *6,661*
Reynoldsburg, OH 43068 • *25,748*
Reynoldsville, PA 15851 • *2,818*
Rhea □, TN • *24,344*
Rhinebeck, NY 12572 • *2,725*
Rhinelander, WI 54501 • *7,427*
Rialto, CA 92376–77 • *72,388*
Rice □, KS • *10,610*
Rice □, MN • *49,183*
Rice Lake, WI 54868 • *7,998*
Rich □, UT • *1,725*
Richardson, TX 75080–83 • *74,840*
Richardson □, NE • *9,937*
Richardson Park, DE 19804 • *1,100*
Richardton, ND 58652 • *625*
Richboro, PA 18954 • *5,332*
Richfield, MN 55423 • *35,710*
Richfield, UT 84701 • *5,593*
Richfield Springs, NY 13439 • *1,565*
Richford, VT 05476 • *1,425*
Rich Hill, MO 64779 • *1,317*
Richland, GA 31825 • *1,668*
Richland, MO 65556 • *2,029*
Richland, WA 99352 • *32,315*
Richland □, IL • *16,545*
Richland □, LA • *20,629*
Richland □, MT • *10,716*
Richland □, ND • *18,148*
Richland □, OH • *126,137*
Richland □, SC • *285,720*
Richland □, WI • *17,521*
Richland Center, WI 53581 • *5,018*
Richland Hills, TX 76118 • *7,978*
Richlands, VA 24641 • *4,456*
Richlandtown, PA 18955 • *1,195*
Richmond, CA 94801–08 • *87,425*
Richmond, IL 60071 • *1,016*
Richmond, IN 47374–75 • *38,705*
Richmond, KY 40475–76 • *21,155*
Richmond, ME 04357 • *1,775*
Richmond, MI 48062 • *4,141*
Richmond, MO 64085 • *5,738*
Richmond, TX 77469 • *9,801*
Richmond, UT 84333 • *1,955*
Richmond, VT 05477 • *650*
Richmond, VA 23201–94 • *203,056*
Richmond □, GA • *189,719*
Richmond □, NY • *378,977*
Richmond □, NC • *44,518*
Richmond □, VA • *7,273*
Richmond Beach, WA 98160 • *5,000*
Richmond Heights, FL 33156 • *8,583*
Richmond Heights, MO 63117 • *10,448*
Richmond Heights, OH 44143 • *9,611*
Richmond Highlands, WA 98133 • *26,037*
Richmond Hill, GA 31324 • *2,934*
Rich Square, NC 27869 • *1,058*
Richton, MS 39476 • *1,034*
Richton Park, IL 60471 • *10,523*
Richwood, OH 43344 • *2,186*
Richwood, WV 26261 • *2,808*
Riddle, OR 97469 • *1,143*
Ridge, NY 11961 • *11,734*
Ridgecrest, CA 93555 • *27,725*
Ridgecrest, WA 98155 • *5,500*
Ridgefield, CT 06877 • *6,363*
Ridgefield, NJ 07657 • *9,996*
Ridgefield, WA 98642 • *1,297*
Ridgefield Park, NJ 07660 • *12,454*
Ridgeland, MS 39157–58 • *11,714*
Ridgeland, SC 29936 • *1,071*
Ridgely, MD 21660 • *1,034*
Ridgely, TN 38080 • *1,775*
Ridgetop, TN 37152 • *1,132*
Ridgeville, SC 29472 • *1,625*
Ridgewood, NJ 07450–52 • *24,152*
Ridgway, IL 62979 • *1,103*
Ridgway, PA 15853 • *4,793*
Ridley Park, PA 19078 • *7,592*
Ridley Township, PA 19018 • *33,771*
Rifle, CO 81650 • *4,636*
Rigby, ID 83442 • *2,681*
Riley □, KS • *67,139*
Rimersburg, PA 16248 • *1,053*
Rincon, GA 31326 • *2,697*
Ringgold, GA 30736 • *1,675*
Ringgold, LA 71068 • *1,856*
Ringgold □, IA • *5,420*
Ringling, OK 73456 • *1,250*
Ringwood, NJ 07456 • *12,623*
Rio, FL 34957 • *1,054*
Rio Arriba □, NM • *34,365*
Rio Blanco □, CO • *5,972*
Rio Dell, CA 95562 • *3,012*
Rio Del Mar, CA 95003 • *8,919*
Rio Grande, NJ 08242 • *2,505*
Rio Grande □, CO • *10,770*
Rio Grande City, TX 78582 • *9,891*
Rio Hondo, TX 78583 • *1,793*
Rio Linda, CA 95673 • *9,481*
Rio Rancho, NM 87124 • *32,505*
Rio Vista, CA 94571 • *3,316*
Ripley, MS 38663 • *5,371*
Ripley, NY 14775 • *1,189*
Ripley, OH 45167 • *1,816*
Ripley, TN 38063 • *6,188*
Ripley, WV 25271 • *3,023*
Ripley □, IN • *24,616*
Ripley □, MO • *12,303*
Ripon, WI 54971 • *7,241*
Rising Sun, DE 19934 • *540*
Rising Sun, IN 47040 • *2,311*
Rising Sun, MD 21911 • *1,263*
Rison, AR 71665 • *1,258*
Ritchie □, WV • *10,233*
Rittman, OH 44270 • *6,147*
Ritzville, WA 99169 • *1,725*
Riverbank, CA 95367 • *8,547*
Riverdale, CA 93656 • *1,980*
Riverdale, GA 30274 • *9,359*
Riverdale, IL 60627 • *13,671*
Riverdale, MD 20737–38 • *5,185*
Riverdale, NJ 07457 • *2,370*
Riverdale, UT 84405 • *6,419*
River Edge, NJ 07661 • *10,603*
River Falls, WI 54022 • *10,610*
River Forest, IL 60305 • *11,669*
River Grove, IL 60171 • *9,961*
Riverhead, NY 11901 • *8,814*
River Heights, UT 84321 • *1,274*
River Hills, WI 53217 • *1,612*
River Oaks, TX 76114 • *6,580*
River Pines, MA 01821 • *3,620*
River Ridge, LA 70123 • *14,800*
River Road, OR 97404 • *9,443*
River Rouge, MI 48218 • *11,314*
Riverside, AL 35135 • *1,004*
Riverside, CA 92501–19 • *226,505*
Riverside, IL 60546 • *8,774*
Riverside, NJ 08075 • *7,974*
Riverside, PA 17868 • *1,991*
Riverside □, CA • *1,170,413*
Riverton, IL 62561 • *2,638*
Riverton, NJ 08077 • *2,775*
Riverton, UT 84065 • *11,261*
Riverton, VT 05663 • *150*
Riverton, WY 82501 • *9,202*
Riverton Heights, WA 98188 • *14,182*
River Vale, NJ 07675 • *9,410*
Riverview, FL 33569 • *6,478*
Riverview, MI 48192 • *13,894*
Rivesville, WV 26588 • *1,064*
Riviera Beach, FL 33404 • *27,639*
Riviera Beach, MD 21122 • *11,376*
Roane □, TN • *47,227*
Roane □, WV • *15,120*
Roan Mountain, TN 37687 • *1,220*
Roanoke, AL 36274 • *6,362*
Roanoke, IL 61561 • *1,910*
Roanoke, IN 46783 • *1,018*
Roanoke, TX 76262 • *1,616*
Roanoke, VA 24001–38 • *96,397*
Roanoke □, VA • *79,332*
Roanoke Rapids, NC 27870 • *15,722*
Roaring Spring, PA 16673 • *2,615*

Robbins, IL 60472 • *7,498*
Robbinsdale, MN 55422 • *14,396*
Robersonville, NC 27871 • *1,940*
Robert Lee, TX 76945 • *1,276*
Roberts, WI 54023 • *1,043*
Roberts □, SD • *9,914*
Roberts □, TX • *1,025*
Robertsdale, AL 36567 • *2,401*
Robertson □, KY • *2,124*
Robertson □, TN • *41,494*
Robertson □, TX • *15,511*
Robertsville, NJ 07746 • *9,841*
Robeson □, NC • *105,179*
Robinson, IL 62454 • *6,740*
Robinson, TX 76706 • *7,111*
Robstown, TX 78380 • *12,849*
Rochdale, MA 01542 • *1,105*
Rochelle, GA 31079 • *1,510*
Rochelle, IL 61068 • *8,769*
Rochelle Park, NJ 07662 • *5,587*
Rochester, IL 62563 • *2,676*
Rochester, IN 46975 • *5,969*
Rochester, MI 48306–09 • *7,130*
Rochester, MN 55901–06 • *70,745*
Rochester, NH 03867–68 • *26,630*
Rochester, NY 14601–92 • *231,636*
Rochester, PA 15074 • *4,156*
Rochester, VT 05767 • *500*
Rochester, WA 98579 • *1,150*
Rochester Hills, MI 48309 • *61,766*
Rock □, MN • *9,806*
Rock □, NE • *2,019*
Rock □, WI • *139,510*
Rockaway, NJ 07866 • *6,243*
Rockbridge □, VA • *18,350*
Rockcastle □, KY • *14,803*
Rock Creek, MN 55067 • *1,040*
Rock Creek 0M, OR • *8,282*
Rockdale, IL 60436 • *1,709*
Rockdale, MD 21207 • *5,885*
Rockdale, TX 76567 • *5,235*
Rockdale □, GA • *54,091*
Rock Falls, IL 61071 • *9,654*
Rockford, IL 61101–32 • *139,426*
Rockford, MI 49341 • *3,750*
Rockford, MN 55373 • *2,665*
Rockford, OH 45882 • *1,119*
Rock Hall, MD 21661 • *1,584*
Rock Hill, MO 63124 • *5,217*
Rock Hill, SC 29730–32 • *41,643*
Rockingham, NC 28379 • *9,399*
Rockingham □, NH • *245,845*
Rockingham □, NC • *86,064*
Rockingham □, VA • *57,482*
Rock Island, IL 61201–04 • *40,552*
Rock Island □, IL • *148,723*
Rockland, ME 04841 • *7,972*
Rockland, MA 02370 • *15,695*
Rockland □, NY • *265,475*
Rockledge, FL 32955–56 • *16,023*
Rockledge, PA 19111 • *2,679*
Rocklin, CA 95677 • *19,033*
Rockmart, GA 30153 • *3,356*
Rockport, IN 47635 • *2,315*
Rockport, ME 04856 • *1,100*
Rockport, MA 01966 • *4,690*
Rock Port, MO 64482 • *1,438*
Rockport, TX 78382 • *4,753*
Rock Rapids, IA 51246 • *2,601*
Rock River, WY 82083 • *190*
Rocksprings, TX 78880 • *1,339*
Rock Springs, WY 82901–02 • *19,050*
Rockton, IL 61072 • *2,928*
Rock Valley, IA 51247 • *2,540*
Rockville, IN 47872 • *2,706*
Rockville, MD 20847–59 • *44,835*
Rockville Centre, NY 11570–71 • *24,727*
Rockwall, TX 75087 • *10,486*
Rockwall □, TX • *25,604*
Rockwell, IA 50469 • *1,008*
Rockwell, NC 28138 • *1,598*
Rockwell City, IA 50579 • *1,981*
Rockwell Park, NC 28213 • *2,600*
Rockwood, MI 48173 • *3,141*
Rockwood, OR 97233 • *11,000*
Rockwood, PA 15557 • *1,014*
Rockwood, TN 37854 • *5,348*
Rocky Creek, FL 33615 • *7,800*
Rocky Ford, CO 81067 • *4,162*
Rocky Hill, CT 06067 • *14,559*
Rocky Mount, NC 27801–04 • *48,997*
Rocky Mount, VA 24151 • *4,098*
Rocky Point, NY 11778 • *8,596*
Rocky River, OH 44116 • *20,410*
Rodeo, CA 94572 • *7,589*
Roderfield, WV 24881 • *1,200*
Rodney Village, DE 19901 • *1,745*
Roebling, NJ 08554 • *2,415*
Roebuck, SC 29376 • *1,966*
Roeland Park, KS 66203 • *7,706*
Roessleville, NY 12205 • *10,753*
Roger Mills □, OK • *4,147*
Rogers, AR 72756–57 • *24,692*
Rogers, TX 76569 • *1,131*
Rogers □, OK • *55,170*
Rogers City, MI 49779 • *3,642*
Rogersville, AL 35652 • *1,125*
Rogersville, TN 37857 • *4,149*
Rogue River, OR 97537 • *1,759*
Rohnert Park, CA 94927–28 • *36,326*
Roland, IA 50236 • *1,035*
Roland, OK 74954 • *2,481*
Rolette □, ND • *12,772*
Rolla, MO 65401 • *14,090*
Rolla, ND 58367 • *1,286*
Rolling Fork, MS 39159 • *2,444*
Rolling Hills Estates, CA 90274 • *7,789*
Rolling Meadows, IL 60008 • *22,591*
Rollinsford, NH 03869 • *2,645*
Roma, TX 78584 • *8,059*
Rome, GA 30161–65 • *30,326*
Romo, IL 61562 • *1,902*
Rome, NY 13440 • *44,350*
Rome City, IN 46784 • *1,138*
Romeo, MI 48065 • *3,520*
Romeoville, IL 60441 • *14,074*
Romney, WV 26757 • *1,966*
Romulus, MI 48174 • *22,897*
Ronan, MT 59864 • *1,547*
Ronceverte, WV 24970 • *1,754*
Ronkonkoma, NY 11779 • *20,391*
Roodhouse, IL 62082 • *2,139*
Rooks □, KS • *6,039*
Roosevelt, NY 11575 • *15,030*
Roosevelt, UT 84066 • *3,915*
Roosevelt □, MT • *10,999*
Roosevelt □, NM • *16,702*
Roosevelt Park, MI 49441 • *3,885*
Rosamond, CA 93560 • *7,430*
Roscoe, IL 61073 • *2,079*
Roscoe, TX 79545 • *1,446*
Roscommon □, MI • *19,776*
Roseau, MN 56751 • *2,396*
Roseau □, MN • *15,026*
Roseboro, NC 28382 • *1,441*
Rosebud, TX 76570 • *1,638*
Rosebud □, MT • *10,505*
Roseburg, OR 97470 • *17,032*
Rosedale, MD 21237 • *18,703*
Rosedale, MS 38769 • *2,595*
Rose Hill, KS 67133 • *2,399*
Rose Hill, NC 28458 • *1,287*
Rose Hill, VA 22310 • *12,675*
Roseland, CA 95407 • *8,779*
Roseland, FL 32957 • *1,379*
Roseland, LA 70456 • *1,093*
Roseland, NJ 07068 • *4,847*
Roseland, OH 44906 • *3,000*
Roselle, IL 60172 • *20,819*
Roselle, NJ 07203 • *20,314*
Roselle Park, NJ 07204 • *12,805*
Rosemead, CA 91770 • *51,638*
Rosemont, CA 95826 • *22,851*
Rosemount, MN 55068 • *8,622*
Rosenberg, TX 77471 • *20,183*
Rosepine, LA 70659 • *1,135*
Roseto, PA 18013 • *1,555*
Roseville, CA 95678 • *44,685*
Roseville, IL 61473 • *1,151*
Roseville, MI 48066 • *51,412*
Roseville, MN 55113 • *33,485*
Roseville, OH 43777 • *1,847*
Rosewood Heights, IL 62024 • *4,821*
Rosiclare, IL 62982 • *1,378*
Roslyn Heights, NY 11577 • *6,405*
Ross, OH 45061 • *2,124*
Ross □, OH • *69,330*
Rossford, OH 43460 • *5,861*
Rossmoor, CA 90720 • *9,893*
Ross Township, PA 15237 • *33,482*
Rossville, GA 30741–42 • *3,601*
Rossville, IL 60963 • *1,334*
Rossville, IN 46065 • *1,175*
Rossville, KS 66533 • *1,052*
Roswell, GA 30075–77 • *47,923*
Roswell, NM 88201–02 • *44,654*
Rotan, TX 79546 • *1,913*
Rothschild, WI 54474 • *3,310*
Rothsville, PA 17543 • *2,097*
Rotterdam, NY 12303 • *21,228*
Roulette, PA 16746 • *1,500*
Round Lake, IL 60073 • *3,550*
Round Lake Beach, IL 60073 • *16,434*
Round Mountain, NV 89045 • *210*
Round Rock, TX 78664 • *30,923*
Roundup, MT 59072 • *1,808*
Rouses Point, NY 12979 • *2,377*
Routt □, CO • *14,088*
Rouzerville, PA 17250 • *1,188*
Rowan □, KY • *20,353*
Rowan □, NC • *110,605*
Rowland, NC 28383 • *1,139*
Rowland Heights, CA 91748 • *32,700*
Rowlett, TX 75088 • *23,260*
Rowley, MA 01969 • *1,144*
Roxboro, NC 27573 • *7,332*
Roy, UT 84067 • *24,603*
Royal Oak, MI 48067–73 • *65,410*
Royal Pines, NC 28704 • *1,600*
Royalton, IL 62983 • *1,191*
Royersford, PA 19468 • *4,458*
Royse City, TX 75089 • *2,206*
Royston, GA 30662 • *2,758*
Rubidoux, CA 92509 • *24,367*
Rugby, ND 58368 • *2,909*
Ruidoso, NM 88345 • *4,600*
Ruidoso Downs, NM 88346 • *920*
Ruleville, MS 38771 • *3,245*
Rumford, ME 04276 • *5,419*
Rumson, NJ 07760 • *6,701*
Runge, TX 78151 • *1,139*
Runnels □, TX • *11,294*
Runnemede, NJ 08078 • *9,042*
Rupert, ID 83350 • *5,455*
Rupert, WV 25984 • *1,104*
Rural Hall, NC 27045 • *1,652*
Rush □, IN • *18,129*
Rush □, KS • *3,842*
Rush City, MN 55069 • *1,497*
Rushford, MN 55971 • *1,485*
Rushmere, VA 23430 • *1,064*
Rush Springs, OK 73082 • *1,229*
Rushville, IL 62681 • *3,229*
Rushville, IN 46173 • *5,533*
Rushville, NE 69360 • *1,127*
Rusk, TX 75785 • *4,366*
Rusk □, TX • *43,735*
Rusk □, WI • *15,079*
Ruskin, FL 33570–70 • *6,046*
Russell, KS 67665 • *4,781*
Russell, KY 41169 • *4,014*
Russell, PA 16345 • *1,000*
Russell □, AL • *46,860*
Russell □, KS • *7,835*
Russell □, KY • *14,716*
Russell □, VA • *28,667*
Russell Springs, KY 42642 • *2,363*
Russellville, AL 35653 • *7,812*
Russellville, AR 72801 • *21,260*
Russellville, KY 42276 • *7,454*
Russellville, OR 97216 • *6,500*
Russellville, TN 37860 • *1,069*
Ruston, LA 71270–73 • *20,027*
Ruth, NV 89319 • *550*
Rutherford, NJ 07070–75 • *17,790*
Rutherford, TN 38369 • *1,303*
Rutherford □, NC • *56,918*
Rutherford □, TN • *118,570*
Rutherfordton, NC 28139 • *3,617*
Rutland, MA 01543 • *2,145*
Rutland, VT 05701–02 • *18,230*
Rutland □, VT • *62,142*
Rye, NH 03870 • *835*
Rye, NY 10580 • *14,936*
Rye Brook, NY 10573 • *7,765*

S

Sabattus, ME 04280 • *3,696*
Sabetha, KS 66534 • *2,341*
Sabina, OH 45169 • *2,662*
Sabinal, TX 78881 • *1,584*
Sabine □, LA • *22,646*
Sabine □, TX • *9,586*
Sac □, IA • *12,324*
Sacaton, AZ 85221 • *1,452*
Sac City, IA 50583 • *2,492*
Sachse, TX 75040 • *5,346*
Sackets Harbor, NY 13685 • *1,313*
Saco, ME 04072 • *15,181*
Sacramento, CA 95801–66 • *369,365*
Sacramento □, CA • *1,041,219*
Saddle Brook, NJ 07662 • *13,296*
Saddle River, NJ 07458 • *2,950*
Saegertown, PA 16433 • *1,066*
Safety Harbor, FL 34695 • *15,124*
Safford, AZ 85546 • *7,359*
Sagadahoc □, ME • *33,535*
Sagamore, MA 02561 • *2,589*
Sagamore Hills, OH 44067 • *4,700*
Sag Harbor, NY 11963 • *2,134*
Saginaw, MI 48601–08 • *69,512*
Saginaw, TX 76179 • *8,551*
Saginaw □, MI • *211,946*
Saguache □, CO • *4,619*
Saint Albans, VT 05478 • *7,339*
Saint Albans, WV 25177 • *11,194*
Saint Andrews, SC 29407 • *9,908*
Saint Andrews, SC 29210 • *25,692*
Saint Ann, MO 63074 • *14,489*
Saint Anne, IL 60964 • *1,153*
Saint Ansgar, IA 50472 • *1,063*
Saint Anthony, ID 83445 • *3,010*
Saint Anthony, MN 55418 • *7,727*
Saint Augustine, FL 32084–86 • *11,692*
Saint Bernard, OH 45217 • *5,344*
Saint Bernard □, LA • *66,631*
Saint Charles, IL 60174–75 • *22,501*
Saint Charles, MD 20601 • *28,717*
Saint Charles, MI 48655 • *2,144*
Saint Charles, MN 55972 • *2,642*
Saint Charles, MO 63301–03 • *54,555*
Saint Charles □, LA • *42,437*
Saint Charles □, MO • *212,907*
Saint Charles Mesa, CO 81006 • *7,050*
Saint Clair, MI 48079 • *5,116*
Saint Clair, MO 63077 • *3,917*
Saint Clair, PA 17970 • *3,524*
Saint Clair □, AL • *50,009*
Saint Clair □, IL • *262,852*
Saint Clair □, MI • *145,607*
Saint Clair □, MO • *8,457*
Saint Clair Shores, MI 48080–82 • *68,107*
Saint Clairsville, OH 43950 • *5,162*
Saint Cloud, FL 34769–73 • *12,453*
Saint Cloud, MN 56301–04 • *48,812*
Saint Croix □, WI • *50,251*
Saint Croix Falls, WI 54024 • *1,640*
Saint David, AZ 85630 • *1,500*
Saint Elmo, IL 62458 • *1,473*
Saint Francis, KS 67756 • *1,495*
Saint Francis, MN 55070 • *2,538*
Saint Francis, SD 57572 • *815*
Saint Francis, WI 53207 • *9,245*
Saint Francis □, AR • *28,497*
Saint Francisville, LA 70775 • *1,700*
Saint Francois □, MO • *48,904*
Sainte Genevieve, MO 63670 • *4,411*
Sainte Genevieve □, MO • *16,037*
Saint George, SC 29477 • *2,077*
Saint George, UT 84770–71 • *28,502*
Saint Georges, DE 19733 • *500*
Saint Helena, CA 94574 • *4,990*
Saint Helena □, LA • *9,874*
Saint Helens, OR 97051 • *7,535*
Saint Henry, OH 45883 • *1,907*
Saint Ignace, MI 49781 • *2,568*
Saint Ignatius, MT 59865 • *778*
Saint James, MN 56081 • *4,364*
Saint James, MO 65559 • *3,256*
Saint James, NY 11780 • *12,703*
Saint James □, LA • *20,879*
Saint James City, FL 33956 • *1,094*
Saint Jo, TX 76265 • *1,048*
Saint John, IN 46373 • *4,921*
Saint John, KS 67576 • *1,357*
Saint Johns, AZ 85936 • *3,294*
Saint Johns, MI 48879 • *7,284*
Saint Johns, MO 63114 • *7,466*
Saint Johns □, FL • *83,829*
Saint Johnsbury, VT 05819 • *6,424*
Saint Johnsville, NY 13452 • *1,825*
Saint John the Baptist □, LA • *39,996*
Saint Joseph, IL 61873 • *2,052*
Saint Joseph, LA 71366 • *1,517*
Saint Joseph, MI 49085 • *9,214*
Saint Joseph, MN 56374 • *3,294*
Saint Joseph, MO 64501–08 • *71,852*
Saint Joseph □, IN • *247,052*
Saint Joseph □, MI • *58,913*
Saint Landry □, LA • *80,331*
Saint Lawrence □, NY • *111,974*
Saint Leo, FL 33574 • *1,009*
Saint Louis, MI 48880 • *3,828*
Saint Louis, MO 63101–88 • *396,685*
Saint Louis □, MN • *198,213*
Saint Louis □, MO • *993,529*
Saint Louis Park, MN 55426 • *43,787*
Saint Lucie □, FL • *150,171*
Saint Maries, ID 83861 • *2,442*
Saint Martin □, LA • *43,978*
Saint Martinville, LA 70582 • *7,137*
Saint Mary □, LA • *58,086*
Saint Marys, AK 99658 • *441*
Saint Marys, GA 31558 • *8,187*
Saint Marys, IN 46556 • *1,800*
Saint Marys, KS 66536 • *1,791*
Saint Marys, OH 45885 • *8,441*
Saint Marys, PA 15857 • *5,511*
Saint Marys, WV 26170 • *2,148*
Saint Marys □, MD • *75,974*
Saint Marys City, MD 20686 • *3,200*
Saint Matthews, KY 40207 • *15,800*
Saint Matthews, SC 29135 • *2,345*
Saint Michael, MN 55376 • *2,506*
Saint Michaels, MD 21663 • *1,301*
Saint Paris, OH 43072 • *1,842*
Saint Paul, AK 99660 • *763*
Saint Paul, IN 47272 • *1,032*
Saint Paul, MN 55101–89 • *272,235*
Saint Paul, MO 63366 • *1,192*
Saint Paul, NE 68873 • *2,009*
Saint Paul, VA 24283 • *1,007*
Saint Paul Park, MN 55071 • *4,965*
Saint Pauls, NC 28384 • *1,992*
Saint Peter, MN 56082 • *9,421*
Saint Peters, MO 63376 • *45,779*
Saint Petersburg, FL 33701–84 • *238,629*
Saint Petersburg Beach, FL 33706 • *9,200*
Saint Rose, LA 70087 • *2,800*
Saint Simons Island, GA 31522 • *12,026*
Saint Stephen, SC 29479 • *1,697*
Saint Stephens, NC 28601 • *8,734*
Saint Tammany □, LA • *144,508*
Salamanca, NY 14779 • *6,566*
Sale Creek, TN 37373 • *1,050*
Salem, AR 72576 • *1,474*
Salem, IL 62881 • *7,470*
Salem, IN 47167 • *5,619*
Salem, MA 01970–71 • *38,091*
Salem, MO 65560 • *4,486*
Salem, NH 03079 • *12,000*
Salem, NJ 08079 • *6,883*
Salem, OH 44460 • *12,233*
Salem, OR 97301–14 • *107,786*
Salem, SD 57058 • *1,289*
Salem, UT 84653 • *2,284*
Salem, VA 24153 • *23,756*
Salem, WV 26426 • *2,063*
Salem, WI 53168 • *1,020*
Salem □, NJ • *65,294*
Salida, CO 81201 • *4,737*
Salina, KS 67401–02 • *42,303*
Salina, OK 74365 • *1,153*
Salina, UT 84654 • *1,943*
Salinas, CA 93901–15 • *108,777*
Saline, MI 48176 • *6,660*
Saline □, AR • *64,183*
Saline □, IL • *26,551*
Saline □, KS • *49,301*
Saline □, MO • *23,523*
Saline □, NE • *12,715*
Salineville, OH 43945 • *1,474*
Salisbury, CT 06068 • *1,600*
Salisbury, MD 21801–03 • *20,592*
Salisbury, MA 01952 • *3,729*
Salisbury, MO 65281 • *1,881*
Salisbury, NC 28144–46 • *23,087*
Sallisaw, OK 74955 • *7,122*
Salmon, ID 83467 • *2,941*
Salmon Creek, WA 98665 • *11,989*
Saltillo, MS 38866 • *1,782*
Salt Lake □, UT • *725,956*
Salt Lake City, UT 84101–90 • *159,936*
Salt Springs, FL 32113 • *1,500*
Saltville, VA 24370 • *2,300*
Saltwater, WA 98188 • *2,200*
Saluda, SC 29138 • *2,798*
Saluda □, SC • *16,357*
Salyersville, KY 41465 • *1,917*
Samoset, FL 34208 • *3,119*
Sampson □, NC • *47,297*
Samson, AL 36477 • *2,190*
Samtown, LA 71301 • *3,500*
San Andreas, CA 95249 • *2,115*
San Angelo, TX 76901–06 • *84,474*
San Anselmo, CA 94960 • *11,743*
San Antonio, TX 78201–99 • *935,933*
Sanatoga, PA 19464 • *5,534*
San Augustine, TX 75972 • *2,337*
San Augustine □, TX • *7,999*
San Benito, TX 78586 • *20,125*
San Benito □, CA • *36,697*
San Bernardino, CA 92401–27 • *164,164*
San Bernardino □, CA • *1,418,380*
Sanborn, IA 51248 • *1,345*
Sanborn □, SD • *2,833*
San Bruno, CA 94066 • *38,961*
San Carlos, AZ 85550 • *2,918*
San Carlos, CA 94070 • *26,167*
San Carlos Park, FL 33912 • *11,785*
San Clemente, CA 92672–74 • *41,100*
Sandalfoot Cove, FL 33433 • *14,214*
Sanders □, MT • *8,669*
Sanderson, TX 79848 • *1,128*
Sandersville, GA 31082 • *6,290*
Sand Hill, MA 02066 • *1,800*
Sandia, NM 87047 • *6,742*
San Diego, CA 92101–99 • *1,110,549*
San Diego, TX 78384 • *4,983*
San Diego □, CA • *2,498,016*
San Dimas, CA 91773 • *32,397*
Sandoval, IL 62882 • *1,535*
Sandoval □, NM • *63,319*
Sand Point, AK 99661 • *878*
Sandpoint, ID 83862–65 • *5,203*
Sand Springs, OK 74063 • *15,346*
Sandston, VA 23150 • *3,630*
Sandstone, MN 55072 • *2,057*
Sandusky, MI 48471 • *2,403*
Sandusky, OH 44870–71 • *29,764*
Sandusky □, OH • *61,963*
Sandwich, IL 60548 • *5,567*
Sandwich, MA 02563 • *2,998*
Sandy, OR 97055 • *4,152*
Sandy, UT 84070 • *75,058*
Sandy Hook, CT 06482 • *1,100*
Sandy Springs, GA 30328 • *67,842*
Sandy Springs, SC 29677 • *1,200*
San Felipe Pueblo, NM 87001 • *1,557*
San Fernando, CA 91340–46 • *22,580*
Sanford, FL 32771–73 • *32,387*
Sanford, ME 04073 • *10,296*
Sanford, NC 27330–31 • *14,475*
San Francisco, CA 94101–88 • *723,959*
San Francisco □, CA • *723,959*
Sangamon □, IL • *178,386*
Sanger, CA 93657 • *16,839*
Sanger, TX 76266 • *3,508*
Sanibel, FL 33957 • *5,468*
Sanilac □, MI • *39,928*
San Jacinto, CA 92383 • *16,210*
San Jacinto □, TX • *16,372*
San Joaquin □, CA • *480,628*
San Jose, CA 95101–96 • *782,248*
San Juan, TX 78589 • *10,815*
San Juan □, CO • *745*
San Juan □, NM • *91,605*
San Juan □, UT • *12,621*
San Juan □, WA • *10,035*
San Juan Capistrano, CA 92690–93 • *26,183*
San Leandro, CA 94577–79 • *68,223*
San Lorenzo, CA 94580 • *19,987*
San Luis, AZ 85634 • *4,212*
San Luis Obispo, CA 93401–12 • *41,958*
San Luis Obispo □, CA • *217,162*
San Manuel, AZ 85631 • *4,009*
San Marcos, CA 92069 • *38,974*
San Marcos, TX 78666–67 • *28,743*
San Marino, CA 91108 • *12,959*
San Mateo, CA 94401–04 • *85,486*
San Mateo □, CA • *649,623*
San Miguel □, CO • *3,653*
San Miguel □, NM • *25,743*
San Pablo, CA 94806 • *25,158*
San Patricio □, TX • *58,749*
Sanpete □, UT • *16,259*
San Rafael, CA 94901–15 • *48,404*
San Ramon, CA 94583 • *35,303*
San Remo, NY 11754 • *7,770*
San Saba, TX 76877 • *2,626*
San Saba □, TX • *5,401*
Sans Souci, SC 29609 • *7,612*
Santa Ana, CA 92701–08 • *293,742*
Santa Anna, TX 76878 • *1,249*
Santa Barbara, CA 93101–90 • *85,571*
Santa Barbara □, CA • *369,608*
Santa Clara, CA 95050–56 • *93,613*
Santa Clara, OR 97404 • *12,834*
Santa Clara, UT 84765 • *2,322*
Santa Clara □, CA • *1,497,577*
Santa Cruz, CA 95060–67 • *49,040*
Santa Cruz, NM 87567 • *975*
Santa Cruz □, AZ • *29,676*
Santa Cruz □, CA • *229,734*
Santa Fe, NM 87501–06 • *55,859*
Santa Fe, TX 77510 • *8,429*
Santa Fe □, NM • *98,928*
Santa Fe Springs, CA 90670–71 • *15,520*
Santa Margarita, CA 93453 • *1,200*
Santa Maria, CA 93454–56 • *61,284*
Santa Monica, CA 90401–11 • *86,905*
Santa Paula, CA 93060–61 • *25,062*
Santaquin, UT 84655 • *2,386*
Santa Rosa, CA 95401–09 • *113,313*
Santa Rosa, NM 88435 • *2,263*
Santa Rosa □, FL • *81,608*
Santa Venetia, CA 94901 • *6,000*
Santa Ynez, CA 93460 • *4,200*
Santee, CA 92071 • *52,902*
Santo Domingo Pueblo, NM 87052 • *2,866*
San Ygnacio, TX 78067 • *1,000*
Sappington, MO 63126 • *10,917*
Sapulpa, OK 74066–67 • *18,074*
Saraland, AL 36571 • *11,751*
Saranac, MI 48881 • *1,461*
Saranac Lake, NY 12983 • *5,377*
Sarasota, FL 34230–43 • *50,961*
Sarasota □, FL • *277,776*
Sarasota Springs, FL 34232 • *16,088*
Saratoga, CA 95070–71 • *28,061*
Saratoga, TX 77585 • *1,200*
Saratoga, WY 82331 • *1,969*
Saratoga □, NY • *181,276*
Saratoga Springs, NY 12866 • *25,001*
Sarcoxie, MO 64862 • *1,330*
Sardis, GA 30456 • *1,116*
Sardis, MS 38666 • *2,128*
Sargent □, ND • *4,549*
Sarpy □, NE • *102,583*
Sartell, MN 56377 • *5,393*
Satanta, KS 67870 • *1,073*
Satellite Beach, FL 32937 • *9,889*
Satsuma, AL 36572 • *5,194*
Saugerties, NY 12477 • *3,915*
Saugus, MA 01906 • *25,549*
Sauk □, WI • *46,975*
Sauk Centre, MN 56378 • *3,581*
Sauk City, WI 53583 • *3,019*
Sauk Rapids, MN 56379 • *7,825*
Sauk Village, IL 60411 • *9,926*
Saukville, WI 53080 • *3,695*
Sault Sainte Marie, MI 49783 • *14,689*
Saunders □, NE • *18,285*
Saunderstown, RI 02874 • *400*
Sausalito, CA 94965–66 • *7,152*
Savage, MD 20763 • *2,850*
Savage, MN 55378 • *9,906*
Savanna, IL 61074 • *3,819*
Savannah, GA 31401–20 • *137,560*
Savannah, MO 64485 • *4,352*
Savannah, TN 38372 • *6,547*
Savoonga, AK 99769 • *519*
Savoy, IL 61874 • *2,674*
Sawyer □, WI • *14,181*
Saxonburg, PA 16056 • *1,345*
Saxtons River, VT 05154 • *541*
Saybrook Manor, CT 06475 • *1,073*
Saydel, IA 50313 • *3,500*
Saylesville, RI 02865 • *3,510*
Saylorsburg, PA 18353 • *1,500*
Sayre, OK 73662 • *2,881*
Sayre, PA 18840 • *5,791*
Sayreville, NJ 08872 • *34,986*
Sayville, NY 11782 • *16,550*
Scalp Level, PA 15963 • *1,158*
Scappoose, OR 97056 • *3,529*
Scarborough, ME 04074 • *2,586*
Scarsdale, NY 10583 • *16,987*
Schaumburg, IL 60192–94 • *68,586*
Schenectady, NY 12301–09 • *65,566*
Schenectady □, NY • *149,285*
Schererville, IN 46375 • *19,926*
Schertz, TX 78154 • *10,555*
Schiller Park, IL 60176 • *11,189*
Schleicher □, TX • *2,990*
Schley □, GA • *3,588*
Schofield, WI 54476 • *2,415*
Schoharie, NY 12157 • *1,045*
Schoharie □, NY • *31,859*
Schoolcraft, MI 49087 • *1,517*
Schoolcraft □, MI • *8,302*
Schroon Lake, NY 12870 • *1,100*
Schulenburg, TX 78956 • *2,455*
Schurz, NV 89427 • *617*
Schuyler, NE 68661 • *4,052*
Schuyler □, IL • *7,498*
Schuyler □, MO • *4,236*
Schuyler □, NY • *18,662*
Schuylerville, NY 12871 • *1,364*
Schuylkill □, PA • *152,585*

Schuylkill Haven, PA 17972 • 5,610
Scioto □, OH • 80,327
Scituate, MA 02066 • 5,180
Scobey, MT 59263 • 1,154
Scotch Plains, NJ 07076 • 21,160
Scotchtown, NY 10940 • 8,765
Scotia, CA 95565 • 1,200
Scotia, NY 12302 • 7,359
Scotland, SD 57059 • 968
Scotland □, MO • 4,822
Scotland □, NC • 33,754
Scotland Neck, NC 27874 • 2,575
Scotlandville, LA 70807 • 15,113
Scott, LA 70583 • 4,912
Scott □, AR • 10,205
Scott □, IL • 5,644
Scott □, IN • 20,991
Scott □, IA • 150,979
Scott □, KS • 5,289
Scott □, KY • 23,867
Scott □, MN • 57,846
Scott □, MS • 24,137
Scott □, MO • 39,376
Scott □, TN • 18,358
Scott □, VA • 23,204
Scott City, KS 67871 • 3,785
Scott City, MO 63780 • 4,292
Scottdale, GA 30079 • 8,636
Scottdale, PA 15683 • 5,184
Scott Lake, FL 33055 • 14,588
Scottsbluff, NE 69361–63 • 13,711
Scotts Bluff □, NE • 36,025
Scottsboro, AL 35768 • 13,786
Scottsburg, IN 47170 • 5,334
Scottsdale, AZ 85250–71 • 130,069
Scotts Valley, CA 95066–67 • 8,615
Scottsville, KY 42164 • 4,278
Scottsville, NY 14546 • 1,912
Scott Township, PA 15106 • 17,118
Scottville, MI 49454 • 1,287
Scranton, PA 18501–19 • 81,805
Screven □, GA • 13,842
Scurry □, TX • 18,634
Seabreeze, DE 19971 • 350
Sea Bright, NJ 07760 • 1,693
Seabrook, MD 20706 • 7,660
Seabrook, NJ 08302 • 1,457
Seabrook, TX 77586 • 6,685
Sea Cliff, NY 11579 • 5,054
Seadrift, TX 77983 • 1,277
Seaford, DE 19973 • 5,689
Seaford, NY 11783 • 15,597
Seaford, VA 23696 • 2,340
Seagate, NC 28403 • 5,444
Sea Girt, NJ 08750 • 2,099
Seagoville, TX 75159 • 8,969
Seagraves, TX 79359 • 2,398
Sea Isle City, NJ 08243 • 2,692
Seal Beach, CA 90740 • 25,098
Sealy, TX 77474 • 4,541
Seaman, OH 45679 • 1,013
Searchlight, NV 89029 • 430
Searcy, AR 72143 • 15,180
Searcy □, AR • 7,841
Searsport, ME 04974 • 1,151
Seaside, CA 93955 • 38,901
Seaside, OR 97138 • 5,359
Seaside Heights, NJ 08751 • 2,366
Seaside Park, NJ 08752 • 1,871
Seat Pleasant, MD 20743 • 5,359
Seattle, WA 98101–99 • 516,259
Sebastian, FL 32958 • 10,205
Sebastian □, AR • 99,590
Sebewaing, MI 48759 • 1,923
Sebree, KY 42455 • 1,510
Sebring, FL 33870–72 • 8,900
Sebring, OH 44672 • 4,848
Secaucus, NJ 07094 • 14,061
Security, CO 80911 • 6,660
Sedalia, MO 65301–02 • 19,800
Sedan, KS 67361 • 1,306
Sedgwick, KS 67135 • 1,438
Sedgwick □, CO • 2,690
Sedgwick □, KS • 403,662
Sedona, AZ 86336 • 7,720
Sedro Woolley, WA 98284 • 6,031
Seekonk, MA 02771 • 12,269
Seeley, CA 92273 • 1,228
Seelyville, IN 47878 • 1,090
Seguin, TX 78155–56 • 18,853
Seiling, OK 73663 • 1,031
Selah, WA 98942 • 5,113
Selawik, AK 99770 • 596
Selby, SD 57472 • 707
Selbyville, DE 19975 • 1,335
Selden, NY 11784 • 20,608
Seldovia, AK 99663 • 316
Selinsgrove, PA 17870 • 5,384
Sellersburg, IN 47172 • 5,745
Sellersville, PA 18960 • 4,479
Sells, AZ 85634 • 2,750
Selma, AL 36701–02 • 23,755
Selma, CA 93662 • 14,757
Selma, NC 27576 • 4,600
Selmer, TN 38375 • 3,838
Seminole, OK 74868 • 7,071
Seminole, TX 79360 • 6,342
Seminole □, FL • 287,529
Seminole □, GA • 9,010
Seminole □, OK • 25,412
Seminole Park, FL 34647 • 8,000
Semmes, AL 36575 • 2,250
Senath, MO 63876 • 1,622
Senatobia, MS 38668 • 4,772
Seneca, IL 61360 • 1,878
Seneca, KS 66538 • 2,027
Seneca, MO 64865 • 1,885
Seneca, PA 16346 • 1,300
Seneca, SC 29678–79 • 7,726
Seneca □, NY • 33,683
Seneca □, OH • 59,733
Seneca Falls, NY 13148 • 7,370
Sequatchie □, TN • 8,863
Sequim, WA 98382 • 3,616
Sequoyah □, OK • 33,828
Sergeant Bluff, IA 51054 • 2,772
Sesser, IL 62884 • 2,087
Seven Hills, OH 44131 • 12,339
Seven Oaks, SC 29210 • 15,722
Severn, MD 21144 • 24,499
Severna Park, MD 21146 • 25,879
Sevier □, AR • 13,637
Sevier □, TN • 51,043
Sevier □, UT • 15,431
Sevierville, TN 37862 • 7,178
Seville, OH 44273 • 1,810
Sewanee, TN 37375 • 2,128
Seward, AK 99664 • 2,699
Seward, NE 68434 • 5,634
Seward □, KS • 18,743
Seward □, NE • 15,450
Sewell, NJ 08080 • 1,870
Sewickley, PA 15143 • 4,134
Seymour, CT 06483 • 14,288
Seymour, IN 47274 • 15,576
Seymour, MO 65746 • 1,636
Seymour, TN 37865 • 7,026
Seymour, TX 76380 • 3,185
Seymour, WI 54165 • 2,782
Seymourville, LA 70764 • 2,891
Shackelford □, TX • 3,316
Shady Cove, OR 97539 • 1,351
Shady Side, MD 20764 • 4,107
Shadyside, OH 43947 • 3,934
Shady Spring, WV 25918 • 1,929
Shafter, CA 93263 • 8,409
Shaftsbury, VT 05262 • 700
Shaker Heights, OH 44120 • 30,831
Shakopee, MN 55379 • 11,739
Shaler Township, PA 15116 • 30,533
Shallowater, TX 79363 • 1,708
Shamokin, PA 17872 • 9,184
Shamokin Dam, PA 17876 • 1,690
Shamrock, TX 79079 • 2,286
Shannock, RI 02875 • 950
Shannon, GA 30172 • 1,703
Shannon, MS 38868 • 1,419
Shannon □, MO • 7,613
Shannon □, SD • 9,902
Shannontown, SC 29150 • 7,900
Sharkey □, MS • 7,066
Sharon, MA 02067 • 5,893
Sharon, PA 16146 • 17,493
Sharon, TN 38255 • 1,047
Sharon, WI 53585 • 1,250
Sharon Hill, PA 19079 • 5,771
Sharonville, OH 45241 • 13,153
Sharp □, AR • 14,109
Sharpes, FL 32922 • 3,348
Sharpley, DE 19803 • 1,250
Sharpsburg, MD 21782 • 659
Sharpsburg, NC 27878 • 1,536
Sharpsburg, PA 15215 • 3,781
Sharpsville, PA 16150 • 4,729
Shasta □, CA • 147,036
Shattuck, OK 73858 • 1,454
Shaw, MS 38773 • 2,349
Shawano, WI 54166 • 7,598
Shawano □, WI • 37,157
Shawnee, KS 66203 • 37,993
Shawnee, OK 74801–02 • 26,017
Shawnee □, KS • 160,976
Shawneetown, IL 62984 • 1,575
Sheboygan, WI 53081–83 • 49,676
Sheboygan □, WI • 103,877
Sheboygan Falls, WI 53085 • 5,823
Sheffield, AL 35660–62 • 10,380
Sheffield, IA 50475 • 1,174
Sheffield, MA 01257 • 1,100
Sheffield, PA 16347 • 1,294
Sheffield Lake, OH 44054 • 9,825
Shelbina, MO 63468 • 2,172
Shelburn, IN 47879 • 1,147
Shelburne Falls, MA 01370 • 1,996
Shelby, MI 49455 • 48,655
Shelby, MS 38774 • 2,806
Shelby, MT 59474 • 2,763
Shelby, NC 28150–51 • 14,669
Shelby, OH 44875 • 9,564
Shelby □, AL • 99,358
Shelby □, IL • 22,261
Shelby □, IN • 40,307
Shelby □, IA • 13,230
Shelby □, KY • 24,824
Shelby □, MO • 6,942
Shelby □, OH • 44,915
Shelby □, TN • 826,330
Shelby □, TX • 22,034
Shelbyville, IL 62565 • 4,943
Shelbyville, IN 46176 • 15,336
Shelbyville, KY 40065 • 6,238
Shelbyville, TN 37160 • 14,049
Sheldon, IL 60966 • 1,109
Sheldon, IA 51201 • 4,937
Sheldon, TX 77028 • 1,653
Shelley, ID 83274 • 3,536
Shell Lake, WI 54871 • 1,161
Shellman, GA 31786 • 1,162
Shell Rock, IA 50670 • 1,385
Shelter Island, NY 11964 • 1,193
Shelton, CT 06484 • 35,418
Shelton, WA 98584 • 7,241
Shenandoah, IA 51601 • 5,572
Shenandoah, PA 17976 • 6,221
Shenandoah, VA 22849 • 2,213
Shenandoah □, VA • 31,636
Shepherd, MI 48883 • 1,413
Shepherd, TX 77371 • 1,812
Shepherdstown, WV 25443 • 1,287
Shepherdsville, KY 40165 • 4,805
Sherborn, MA 01770 • 1,490
Sherburn, MN 56171 • 1,105
Sherburne, NY 13460 • 1,531
Sherburne □, MN • 41,945
Sheridan, AR 72150 • 3,098
Sheridan, CO 80110 • 4,976
Sheridan, IL 60551 • 1,288
Sheridan, IN 46069 • 2,046
Sheridan, OR 97378 • 3,979
Sheridan, WY 82801 • 13,900
Sheridan □, KS • 3,043
Sheridan □, MT • 4,732
Sheridan □, NE • 6,750
Sheridan □, ND • 2,148
Sheridan □, WY • 23,562
Sheridan Beach, WA 98155 • 6,518
Sherman, TX 75090–91 • 31,601
Sherman □, KS • 6,926
Sherman □, NE • 3,718
Sherman □, OR • 1,918
Sherman □, TX • 2,858
Sherrelwood, CO 80221 • 16,636
Sherrill, NY 13461 • 2,864
Sherwood, AR 72116 • 18,893
Sherwood, OR 97140 • 3,093
Sherwood Manor, CT 06082 • 6,357
Sherwood Park, DE 19808 • 2,000
Shiawassee □, MI • 69,770
Shickshinny, PA 18655 • 1,108
Shillington, PA 19607 • 5,062
Shiloh, OH 44878 • 11,607
Shiloh, PA 17404 • 8,245
Shiner, TX 77984 • 2,074
Shinglehouse, PA 16748 • 1,243
Shinnston, WV 26431 • 2,543
Ship Bottom, NJ 08008 • 1,352
Shippensburg, PA 17257 • 5,331
Shiprock, NM 87420 • 7,687
Shirley, MA 01464 • 1,559
Shirley, NY 11967 • 22,936
Shishmaref, AK 99772 • 456
Shively, KY 40216 • 15,535
Shoemakersville, PA 19555 • 1,443
Shore Acres, MA 02066 • 1,200
Shores Acres, RI 02852 • 410
Shoreview, MN 55112 • 24,587
Shorewood, IL 60435 • 6,264
Shorewood, MN 55331 • 5,917
Shorewood, WI 53211 • 14,116
Shorewood Hills, WI 53705 • 1,680
Short Beach, CT 06405 • 2,500
Shortsville, NY 14548 • 1,485
Shoshone, ID 83352 • 1,249
Shoshone □, ID • 13,931
Shoshoni, WY 82649 • 497
Show Low, AZ 85901 • 5,019
Shreve, OH 44676 • 1,584
Shreveport, LA 71101–10 • 198,525
Shrewsbury, MA 01545 • 23,400
Shrewsbury, MO 63119 • 6,416
Shrewsbury, NJ 07702 • 3,096
Shrewsbury, PA 17361 • 2,672
Shullsburg, WI 53586 • 1,236
Shungnak, AK 99773 • 223
Sibley, IA 51249 • 2,815
Sibley □, MN • 14,366
Sicklerville, NJ 08081 • 1,750
Sidney, IL 61877 • 1,027
Sidney, IA 51652 • 1,253
Sidney, MT 59270 • 5,217
Sidney, NE 69162 • 5,959
Sidney, NY 13838 • 4,720
Sidney, OH 45365 • 18,710
Siegle, LA 71291 • 1,600
Sierra □, CA • 3,318
Sierra □, NM • 9,912
Sierra Madre, CA 91024 • 10,762
Sierra Vista, AZ 85635–36 • 32,983
Siesta Key, FL 34242 • 7,772
Signal Hill, CA 90806 • 8,371
Signal Mountain, TN 37377 • 7,034
Sigourney, IA 52591 • 2,111
Sikeston, MO 63801 • 17,641
Siler City, NC 27344 • 4,808
Siloam Springs, AR 72761 • 8,151
Silsbee, TX 77656 • 6,368
Silt, CO 81652 • 1,095
Silver Bay, MN 55614 • 1,894
Silver Bow □, MT • 33,941
Silver City, NV 89428 • 100
Silver City, NM 88061–62 • 10,683
Silver Creek, NY 14136 • 2,927
Silverdale, WA 98383 • 7,660
Silver Grove, KY 41085 • 1,102
Silver Hill, MD 20746 • 1,580
Silver Lake, KS 66539 • 1,390
Silver Lake, MA 01887 • 2,900
Silver Lake, WI 53170 • 1,801
Silverpeak, NV 89047 • 190
Silver Spring, MD 20901–12 • 76,046
Silver Springs, FL 32688 • 1,082
Silver Springs, NV 89429 • 2,253
Silver Springs Shores, FL 32672 • 6,421
Silverton, NJ 08753 • 9,175
Silverton, OH 45236 • 5,859
Silverton, OR 97381 • 5,635
Silview, DE 19804 • 1,500
Silvis, IL 61282 • 6,926
Simi Valley, CA 93062–65 • 100,217
Simmesport, LA 71369 • 2,092
Simpson, PA 18407 • 1,670
Simpson □, KY • 15,145
Simpson □, MS • 23,953
Simpsonville, SC 29681 • 11,708
Simsbury, CT 06070 • 5,577
Sinclair, WY 82334 • 500
Sinton, TX 78387 • 5,549
Sioux □, IA • 29,903
Sioux □, NE • 1,549
Sioux □, ND • 3,761
Sioux Center, IA 51250 • 5,074
Sioux City, IA 51101–11 • 80,505
Sioux Falls, SD 57101–18 • 100,814
Siskiyou □, CA • 43,531
Sisseton, SD 57262 • 2,181
Sistersville, WV 26175 • 1,797
Sitka, AK 99835 • 8,588
Skagit □, WA • 79,555
Skagway, AK 99840 • 692
Skamania □, WA • 8,289
Skaneateles, NY 13152 • 2,724
Skiatook, OK 74070 • 4,910
Skokie, IL 60076–77 • 59,432
Skowhegan, ME 04976 • 6,990
Sky Lake, FL 32809 • 6,202
Skyland, NV 89448 • 660
Skyland, NC 28776 • 1,100
Skyway, WA 98178 • 8,500
Slackwoods, NJ 08638 • 8,100
Slater, IA 50244 • 1,268
Slater, MO 65349 • 2,186
Slater, SC 29683 • 1,000
Slatersville, RI 02876 • 2,330
Slatington, PA 18080 • 4,678
Slaton, TX 79364 • 6,078
Slayton, MN 56172 • 2,147
Sleepy Eye, MN 56085 • 3,694
Slickville, PA 15684 • 1,178
Slidell, LA 70458–61 • 24,124
Slinger, WI 53086 • 2,340
Slippery Rock, PA 16057 • 3,008
Sloan, NY 14225 • 3,830
Sloatsburg, NY 10974 • 3,035
Slocomb, AL 36375 • 1,906
Slope □, ND • 907
Smackover, AR 71762 • 2,232
Smethport, PA 16749 • 1,734
Smith □, KS • 5,078
Smith □, MS • 14,798
Smith □, TN • 14,143
Smith □, TX • 151,309
Smith Center, KS 66967 • 2,016
Smithers, WV 25186 • 1,162
Smithfield, NC 27577 • 7,540
Smithfield, PA 15478 • 1,000
Smithfield, UT 84335 • 5,566
Smithfield, VA 23430 • 4,686
Smith River, CA 95567 • 1,000
Smiths, AL 36877 • 1,700
Smithsburg, MD 21783 • 1,221
Smithton, IL 62285 • 1,587
Smithtown, NY 11787 • 25,638
Smithville, MO 64089 • 2,525
Smithville, OH 44677 • 1,354
Smithville, TN 37166 • 3,791
Smithville, TX 78957 • 3,196
Smyrna, DE 19977 • 5,231
Smyrna, GA 30080–82 • 30,981
Smyrna, TN 37167 • 13,647
Smyth □, VA • 32,370
Sneads, FL 32460 • 1,746
Sneedville, TN 37869 • 1,446
Snellville, GA 30278 • 12,084
Snohomish, WA 98290 • 6,499
Snohomish □, WA • 465,642
Snoqualmie, WA 98065 • 1,546
Snowflake, AZ 85937 • 3,679
Snow Hill, MD 21863 • 2,217
Snow Hill, NC 28580 • 1,378
Snyder, OK 73566 • 1,619
Snyder, TX 79549 • 12,195
Snyder □, PA • 36,680
Soap Lake, WA 98851 • 1,149
Socastee, SC 29577 • 10,426
Social Circle, GA 30279 • 2,755
Socorro, NM 87801 • 8,159
Socorro □, NM • 14,764
Soda Springs, ID 83276 • 3,111
Soddy-Daisy, TN 37379 • 8,240
Sodus, NY 14551 • 1,904
Sodus Point, NY 14555 • 1,190
Solana, FL 33950 • 1,128
Solana Beach, CA 92075 • 12,962
Solano □, CA • 340,421
Soldotna, AK 99669 • 3,482
Soledad, CA 93960 • 7,146
Solomons, MD 20688 • 1,500
Solon, IA 52333 • 1,050
Solon, OH 44139 • 18,548
Solvay, NY 13209 • 6,717
Somerdale, NJ 08083 • 5,440
Somers, CT 06071 • 9,108
Somerset, KY 42501–02 • 10,733
Somerset, MA 02725 • 17,655
Somerset, NJ 08873–75 • 22,070
Somerset, OH 43783 • 1,390
Somerset, PA 15501 • 6,454
Somerset, TX 78069 • 1,144
Somerset, WI 54025 • 1,065
Somerset □, ME • 49,767
Somerset □, MD • 23,440
Somerset □, NJ • 240,279
Somerset □, PA • 78,218
Somers Point, NJ 08244 • 11,216
Somersville, CT 06072 • 1,200
Somersworth, NH 03878 • 11,249
Somerton, AZ 85350 • 5,282
Somervell □, TX • 5,360
Somerville, MA 02143 • 76,210
Somerville, NJ 08876–77 • 11,632
Somerville, TN 38068 • 2,047
Somerville, TX 77879 • 1,542
Somonauk, IL 60552 • 1,263
Sonoma, CA 95476 • 8,121
Sonoma □, CA • 388,222
Sonora, CA 95370 • 4,153
Sonora, TX 76950 • 2,751
Soperton, GA 30457 • 2,797
Sophia, WV 25921 • 1,182
Soquel, CA 95073 • 9,188
Sorrento, LA 70778 • 1,119
Souderton, PA 18964 • 5,957
Sound Beach, NY 11789 • 9,102
South Acton, MA 01720 • 3,220
South Amboy, NJ 08879 • 7,863
South Amherst, MA 01002 • 5,053
South Amherst, OH 44001 • 1,765
Southampton, NY 11968–69 • 3,980
Southampton □, VA • 17,550
South Ashburnham, MA 01466 • 1,110
Southaven, MS 38671 • 17,949
South Barre, VT 05670 • 1,314
South Bay, FL 33493 • 3,558
South Belmar, NJ 07719 • 1,482
South Beloit, IL 61080 • 4,072
South Bend, IN 46601–80 • 105,511
South Bend, WA 98586 • 1,551
South Berwick, ME 03908 • 5,877
Southborough, MA 01772 • 1,450
South Boston, VA 24592 • 6,997
South Bound Brook, NJ 08880 • 4,185
South Bradenton, FL 34205 • 20,398
Southbridge, MA 01550 • 13,631
South Broadway, WA 98902 • 2,735
South Burlington, VT 05403 • 12,809
Southbury, CT 06488 • 3,000
South Charleston, OH 45368 • 1,626
South Charleston, WV 25303 • 13,645
South Chicago Heights, IL 60411 • 3,597
South Congaree, SC 29169 • 2,406
South Connellsville, PA 15425 • 2,204
South Dartmouth, MA 02748 • 9,850
South Daytona, FL 32121 • 12,482
South Decatur, GA 30034 • 19,350
South Deerfield, MA 01373 • 1,906
South Dennis, MA 02660 • 2,500
South Duxbury, MA 02332 • 3,017
South Easton, MA 02375 • 1,530
South Elgin, IL 60177 • 7,474
South El Monte, CA 91733 • 20,850
Southern Pines, NC 28387–88 • 9,129
South Euclid, OH 44121 • 23,866
South Fallsburg, NY 12779 • 2,115
South Farmingdale, NY 11735 • 15,377
Southfield, MI 48034 • 75,728
South Fork, PA 15956 • 1,197
South Fulton, TN 38257 • 2,688
South Gastonia, NC 28052 • 5,487
South Gate, CA 90280 • 86,284
Southgate, FL 34239 • 7,324
Southgate, KY 41071 • 3,266
South Gate, MD 21061 • 27,564
Southgate, MI 48195 • 30,771
South Glastonbury, CT 06073 • 1,570
Southglenn, CO 80122 • 43,087
South Glens Falls, NY 12801 • 3,506
South Grafton, MA 01560 • 2,610
South Hackensack, NJ 07606 • 2,229
South Hadley, MA 01075 • 5,340
South Hadley Falls, MA 01075 • 5,100
South Hamilton, MA 01982 • 2,720
South Haven, IN 46383 • 6,112
South Haven, MI 49090 • 5,563
South Hill, NY 14850 • 5,423
South Hill, VA 23970 • 4,217
South Hingham, MA 02043 • 4,080
South Holland, IL 60473 • 22,105
South Hooksett, NH 03106 • 3,638
South Hopkinton, RI 02813 • 900
South Houston, TX 77587 • 14,207
South Huntington, NY 11746 • 9,624
South Hutchinson, KS 67505 • 2,444
Southington, CT 06489 • 38,518
South International Falls, MN 56679 • 2,806
South Jacksonville, IL 62650 • 3,187
South Jordan, UT 84065 • 12,220
South Lake Tahoe, CA 95702 • 21,586
South Lancaster, MA 01561 • 1,772
South Laramie, WY 82070 • 1,500
South Laurel, MD 20708 • 18,591
South Lebanon, OH 45065 • 2,696
South Lockport, NY 14094 • 7,112
South Lyon, MI 48178 • 5,857
South Miami, FL 33143 • 10,404
South Miami Heights, FL 33157 • 30,030
South Milwaukee, WI 53172 • 20,958
South Nyack, NY 10960 • 3,352
South Ogden, UT 84403 • 12,105
Southold, NY 11971 • 5,192
South Orange, NJ 07079 • 16,390
South Paris, ME 04281 • 2,320
South Pasadena, CA 91030 • 23,936
South Patrick Shores, FL 32937 • 10,249
South Pekin, IL 61564 • 1,184
South Pittsburg, TN 37380 • 3,295
South Plainfield, NJ 07080 • 20,489
Southport, FL 32409 • 1,992
Southport, IN 46227 • 1,969
Southport, NY 14904 • 7,753
Southport, NC 28461 • 2,369
South Portland, ME 04106 • 23,163
South River, NJ 08882 • 13,692
South Royalton, VT 05068 • 700
South Saint Paul, MN 55075–77 • 20,197
South Salt Lake, UT 84115 • 10,129
South San Francisco, CA 94080–83 • 54,312
South San Gabriel, CA 91770 • 7,700
South San Jose Hills, CA 91744 • 17,814
South Sarasota, FL 34239 • 5,298
South Setauket, NY 11733 • 5,990
Southside, AL 35901 • 5,580
Southside Place, TX 77005 • 1,392
South Sioux City, NE 68776 • 9,677
South Stony Brook, NY 11790 • 6,120
South Streator, IL 61364 • 2,334
South Sumter, SC 29150 • 4,371
South Toms River, NJ 08757 • 3,869
South Torrington, WY 82240 • 300
South Tucson, AZ 85713 • 5,093
South Valley Stream, NY 11581 • 5,328
South Venice, FL 34293 • 11,951
South Walpole, MA 02071 • 1,300
South Waverly, PA 14892 • 1,049
South Wellfleet, MA 02663 • 2,300
South Westbury, NY 11590 • 9,732
Southwest Harbor, ME 04679 • 1,952
South Whitley, IN 46787 • 1,482
South Whittier, CA 90605 • 51,100
Southwick, MA 01077 • 1,170
South Williamsport, PA 17701 • 6,496
South Windham, CT 06266 • 1,644
South Windham, ME 04082 • 1,350
South Windsor, CT 06074 • 10,800
Southwood, CO 80120 • 2,050
Southwood Acres, CT 06082 • 8,963
South Woodstock, CT 06267 • 1,112
South Yarmouth, MA 02664 • 10,358
South Yuba City, CA 95991 • 8,816
South Zanesville, OH 43701 • 1,969
Spalding □, GA • 54,457
Spanaway, WA 98387 • 15,001
Spangler, PA 15775 • 2,068
Spanish Fork, UT 84660 • 11,272
Spanish Fort, AL 36527 • 3,732
Spanish Lake, MO 63138 • 20,322
Sparks, GA 31647 • 1,205
Sparks, NV 89431–36 • 53,367
Sparr, FL 32192 • 1,100
Sparta, GA 31087 • 1,710
Sparta, IL 62286 • 4,853
Sparta, MI 49345 • 3,968
Sparta (Lake Mohawk), NJ 07871 • 8,930
Sparta, NC 28675 • 1,957
Sparta, TN 38583 • 4,681
Sparta, WI 54656 • 7,788
Spartanburg, SC 29301–18 • 43,467
Spartanburg □, SC • 226,800
Spearfish, SD 57783 • 6,966
Spearman, TX 79081 • 3,197
Speedway, IN 46224 • 13,092
Spencer, IN 47460 • 2,609
Spencer, IA 51301 • 11,066
Spencer, MA 01562 • 6,306
Spencer, NC 28159 • 3,219
Spencer, TN 38585 • 1,125
Spencer, WV 25276 • 2,279
Spencer, WI 54479 • 1,757
Spencer □, IN • 19,490
Spencer □, KY • 6,801
Spencerport, NY 14559 • 3,606
Spencerville, MD 20868 • 1,780
Spencerville, OH 45887 • 2,288
Spicer, MN 56288 • 1,020
Spindale, NC 28160 • 4,040
Spink □, SD • 7,981
Spirit Lake, ID 83869 • 790
Spirit Lake, IA 51360 • 3,871
Spiro, OK 74959 • 2,146
Spokane, WA 99201–28 • 177,196
Spokane □, WA • 361,364
Spooner, WI 54801 • 2,464
Spotswood, NJ 08884 • 7,983
Spotsylvania □, VA • 57,403
Sprague, WV 25926 • 2,090

Spring, TX 77373 • *33,111*
Spring Arbor, MI 49283 • *2,010*
Springboro, OH 45066 • *6,590*
Spring City, PA 19475 • *3,433*
Spring City, TN 37381 • *2,199*
Spring Creek 0M, NV • *5,866*
Springdale, AR 72764–66 • *29,941*
Springdale, OH 45246 • *10,621*
Springdale, PA 15144 • *3,992*
Springdale, SC 29169 • *3,226*
Springer, NM 87747 • *1,262*
Springerville, AZ 85938 • *1,802*
Springfield, CO 81073 • *1,475*
Springfield, FL 32401 • *8,715*
Springfield, GA 31329 • *1,415*
Springfield, IL 62701–94 • *105,227*
Springfield, KY 40069 • *2,875*
Springfield, MA 01101–05 • *156,983*
Springfield, MI 49015 • *5,582*
Springfield, MN 56087 • *2,173*
Springfield, MO 65801–99 • *140,494*
Springfield, NE 68059 • *1,426*
Springfield, NJ 07081 • *13,240*
Springfield, OH 45501–06 • *70,487*
Springfield, OR 97477–78 • *44,683*
Springfield, PA 19064 • *24,160*
Springfield, SD 57062 • *834*
Springfield, TN 37172 • *11,227*
Springfield, VT 05156 • *4,207*
Springfield, VA 22150 • *23,706*
Spring Garden, PA 17403 • *11,127*
Spring Green, WI 53588 • *1,283*
Spring Grove, IL 60081 • *1,066*
Spring Grove, MN 55974 • *1,153*
Spring Grove, PA 17362 • *1,863*
Spring Hill, FL 34606 • *31,117*
Spring Hill, KS 66083 • *2,191*
Springhill, LA 71075 • *5,668*
Spring Hill, TN 37174 • *1,464*
Spring Hope, NC 27882 • *1,221*
Spring Lake, MI 49456 • *2,537*
Spring Lake, NJ 07762 • *3,499*
Spring Lake, NC 28390 • *7,524*
Spring Lake Heights, NJ 07762 • *5,341*
Spring Lake Park, MN 55432 • *6,532*
Springvale, ME 04083 • *3,542*
Spring Valley, IL 61362 • *5,246*
Spring Valley, MN 55975 • *2,461*
Spring Valley, NY 10977 • *21,802*
Spring Valley, WI 54767 • *1,051*
Springville, AL 35146 • *1,910*
Springville, IA 52336 • *1,068*
Springville, NY 14141 • *4,310*
Springville, UT 84663–64 • *13,950*
Spruce Pine, NC 28777 • *2,010*
Spur, TX 79370 • *1,300*
Staatsburg, NY 12580 • *1,100*
Stafford, KS 67578 • *1,344*
Stafford □, KS • *5,365*
Stafford □, VA • *61,236*
Stafford Springs, CT 06076 • *4,100*
Stambaugh, MI 49964 • *1,281*
Stamford, CT 06901–12 • *108,056*
Stamford, NY 12167 • *1,211*
Stamford, TX 79553 • *3,817*
Stamford, VT 05352 • *400*
Stamps, AR 71860 • *2,478*
Stanaford, WV 25927 • *1,706*
Stanberry, MO 64489 • *1,310*
Standish, MI 48658 • *1,377*
Stanfield, AZ 85272 • *1,700*
Stanfield, OR 97875 • *1,568*
Stanford, CA 94305 • *18,097*
Stanford, KY 40484 • *2,686*
Stanhope, NJ 07874 • *3,393*
Stanislaus □, CA • *370,522*
Stanley, NC 28164 • *2,823*
Stanley, ND 58784 • *1,371*
Stanley, VA 22851 • *1,186*
Stanley, WI 54768 • *2,011*
Stanley □, SD • *2,453*
Stanleytown, VA 24168 • *1,563*
Stanleyville, NC 27045 • *4,779*
Stanly □, NC • *51,765*
Stanton, CA 90680 • *30,491*
Stanton, KY 40380 • *2,795*
Stanton, MI 48888 • *1,504*
Stanton, NE 68779 • *1,549*
Stanton, TX 79782 • *2,576*
Stanton □, KS • *2,333*
Stanton □, NE • *6,244*
Stanwood, WA 98292 • *1,961*
Staples, MN 56479 • *2,754*
Stapleton, AL 36578 • *1,300*
Starbuck, MN 56381 • *1,143*
Star City, AR 71667 • *2,138*
Star City, WV 26505 • *1,251*
Stargo, AZ 85540 • *1,038*
Stark □, IL • *6,534*
Stark □, ND • *22,832*
Stark □, OH • *367,585*
Starke, FL 32091 • *5,226*
Starke □, IN • *22,747*
Starkville, MS 39759 • *18,458*
Starr □, TX • *40,518*
Startex, SC 29377 • *1,162*
State Center, IA 50247 • *1,248*
State College, PA 16801–05 • *38,923*
Stateline, NV 89449 • *1,379*
State Line, PA 17263 • *1,253*
Statesboro, GA 30458 • *15,854*
Statesville, NC 28677 • *17,567*
Statham, GA 30666 • *1,360*
Staunton, IL 62088 • *4,806*
Staunton, VA 24401 • *24,461*
Stayton, OR 97383 • *5,011*
Steamboat, NV 89511 • *450*
Steamboat Springs, CO 80487 • *6,695*
Stearns, KY 42647 • *1,550*
Stearns □, MN • *118,791*
Stebbins, AK 99671 • *400*
Steele, AL 35987 • *1,046*
Steele, MO 63877 • *2,395*
Steele, ND 58482 • *762*
Steele □, MN • *30,729*
Steele □, ND • *2,420*
Steeleville, IL 62288 • *2,059*
Steelton, PA 17113 • *5,152*
Steelville, MO 65565 • *1,465*
Steger, IL 60475 • *8,584*
Steilacoom, WA 98388 • *5,728*
Stephens, AR 71764 • *1,137*
Stephens □, GA • *23,257*
Stephens □, OK • *42,299*
Stephens □, TX • *9,010*
Stephens City, VA 22655 • *1,186*
Stephenson □, IL • *48,052*
Stephenville, TX 76401 • *13,502*
Sterling, AK 99672 • *3,802*
Sterling, CO 80751 • *10,362*
Sterling, IL 61081 • *15,132*
Sterling, KS 67579 • *2,115*
Sterling, MA 01564 • *1,250*
Sterling, VA 22170 • *20,512*
Sterling □, TX • *1,438*
Sterling City, TX 76951 • *1,096*
Sterling Heights, MI 48310–14 • *117,810*
Sterlington, LA 71280 • *1,140*
Steuben □, IN • *27,446*
Steuben □, NY • *99,088*
Steubenville, OH 43952 • *22,125*
Stevens □, KS • *5,048*
Stevens □, MN • *10,634*
Stevens □, WA • *30,948*
Stevenson, AL 35772 • *2,046*
Stevenson, WA 98648 • *1,147*
Stevens Point, WI 54481 • *23,006*
Stevensville, MI 49127 • *1,230*
Stevensville, MT 59870 • *1,221*
Stewart □, GA • *5,654*
Stewart □, TN • *9,479*
Stewartstown, PA 17363 • *1,308*
Stewartville, MN 55976 • *4,520*
Stickney, IL 60402 • *5,678*
Stigler, OK 74462 • *2,574*
Stillwater, MN 55082–83 • *13,882*
Stillwater, NY 12170 • *1,531*
Stillwater, OK 74074–76 • *36,676*
Stillwater □, MT • *6,536*
Stilwell, OK 74960 • *2,663*
Stinnett, TX 79083 • *2,166*
Stirling, NJ 07980 • *1,800*
Stockbridge, GA 30281 • *3,359*
Stockbridge, MA 01262 • *2,408*
Stockbridge, MI 49285 • *1,202*
Stockdale, TX 78160 • *1,268*
Stockholm, NJ 07460 • *1,200*
Stockton, CA 95201–19 • *210,943*
Stockton, IL 61085 • *1,871*
Stockton, KS 67669 • *1,507*
Stockton, MO 65785 • *1,579*
Stoddard □, MO • *28,895*
Stokes □, NC • *37,223*
Stokesdale, NC 27357 • *2,134*
Stollings, WV 25646 • *1,200*
Stone □, AR • *9,775*
Stone □, MS • *10,750*
Stone □, MO • *19,078*
Stoneboro, PA 16153 • *1,091*
Stoneham, MA 02180 • *22,203*
Stone Harbor, NJ 08247 • *1,025*
Stone Mountain, GA 30083 • *6,494*
Stoneville, NC 27048 • *1,109*
Stonewall, LA 71078 • *1,266*
Stonewall, MS 39363 • *1,148*
Stonewall □, TX • *2,013*
Stonewood, WV 26301 • *1,996*
Stonington, CT 06378 • *1,100*
Stonington, IL 62567 • *1,006*
Stony Brook, NY 11790 • *13,726*
Stony Point, NY 10980 • *10,587*
Stony Point, NC 28678 • *1,286*
Storey □, NV • *2,526*
Storm Lake, IA 50588 • *8,769*
Storrs, CT 06268 • *12,198*
Story, WY 82842 • *700*
Story □, IA • *74,252*
Story City, IA 50248 • *2,959*
Stottville, NY 12172 • *1,369*
Stoughton, MA 02072 • *26,777*
Stoughton, WI 53589 • *8,786*
Stow, MA 01775 • *1,200*
Stow, OH 44224 • *27,702*
Stowe, PA 19464 • *3,598*
Stowe, VT 05672 • *450*
Stowe Township, PA 15136 • *7,681*
Strabane, PA 15363 • *1,200*
Strafford, MO 65757 • *1,166*
Strafford □, NH • *104,233*
Strasburg, CO 80136 • *1,005*
Strasburg, OH 44680 • *1,995*
Strasburg, PA 17579 • *2,568*
Strasburg, VA 22657 • *3,762*
Stratford, CT 06497 • *49,389*
Stratford, DE 19720 • *1,950*
Stratford, NJ 08084 • *7,614*
Stratford, OK 74872 • *1,404*
Stratford, TX 79084 • *1,781*
Stratford, WI 54484 • *1,515*
Stratford Landing, VA 22308 • *2,800*
Strathmore, CA 93267 • *2,353*
Strathmore, NJ 07747 • *7,060*
Strawberry Point, IA 52076 • *1,357*
Streamwood, IL 60103 • *30,987*
Streator, IL 61364 • *14,121*
Streetsboro, OH 44241 • *9,932*
Stromsburg, NE 68666 • *1,241*
Strongsville, OH 44136 • *35,308*
Stroud, OK 74079 • *2,666*
Stroudsburg, PA 18360 • *5,312*
Struthers, OH 44471 • *12,284*
Stryker, OH 43557 • *1,468*
Stuart, FL 34994–97 • *11,936*
Stuart, IA 50250 • *1,522*
Stuarts Draft, VA 24477 • *5,087*
Sturbridge, MA 01566 • *2,093*
Sturgeon Bay, WI 54235 • *9,176*
Sturgis, KY 42459 • *2,184*
Sturgis, MI 49091 • *10,130*
Sturgis, SD 57785 • *5,330*
Sturtevant, WI 53177 • *3,803*
Stutsman □, ND • *22,241*
Stuttgart, AR 72160 • *10,420*
Sublette, KS 67877 • *1,378*
Sublette □, WY • *4,843*
Sublimity, OR 97385 • *1,491*
Succasunna, NJ 07876 • *7,750*
Sudbury, MA 01776 • *1,860*
Sudbury Center, MA 01776 • *2,590*
Sudley, VA 22110 • *7,321*
Suffern, NY 10901 • *11,055*
Suffield, CT 06078 • *1,353*
Suffolk, VA 23432–38 • *52,141*
Suffolk □, MA • *663,906*
Suffolk □, NY • *1,321,864*
Sugar City, ID 83448 • *1,275*
Sugar Creek, MO 64054 • *3,982*
Sugarcreek, PA 16323 • *5,532*
Sugar Grove, VA 24375 • *1,027*
Sugar Hill, GA 30518 • *4,557*
Sugar Land, TX 77478–79 • *24,529*
Sugarland Run, VA 22170 • *9,357*
Sugar Loaf, VA 24018 • *2,000*
Sugar Notch, PA 18706 • *1,044*
Suisun City, CA 94585 • *22,686*
Suitland, MD 20746 • *35,400*
Sulligent, AL 35586 • *1,886*
Sullivan, IL 61951 • *4,354*
Sullivan, IN 47882 • *4,663*
Sullivan, MO 63080 • *5,661*
Sullivan □, IN • *18,993*
Sullivan □, MO • *6,326*
Sullivan □, NH • *38,592*
Sullivan □, NY • *69,277*
Sullivan □, PA • *6,104*
Sullivan □, TN • *143,596*
Sullivans Island, SC 29482 • *1,623*
Sully □, SD • *1,589*
Sulphur, LA 70663–64 • *20,125*
Sulphur, OK 73086 • *4,824*
Sulphur Springs, TX 75482 • *14,062*
Sultan, WA 98294 • *2,236*
Sumiton, AL 35148 • *2,604*
Summerfield, NC 27358 • *2,051*
Summers □, WV • *14,204*
Summersville, WV 26651 • *2,906*
Summerville, GA 30747 • *5,025*
Summerville, SC 29483–85 • *22,519*
Summit, IL 60501 • *9,971*
Summit, MS 39666 • *1,566*
Summit, NJ 07901 • *19,757*
Summit, TN 37363 • *8,307*
Summit □, CO • *12,881*
Summit □, OH • *514,990*
Summit □, UT • *15,518*
Summit Hill, PA 18250 • *3,332*
Sumner, IL 62466 • *1,083*
Sumner, IA 50674 • *2,078*
Sumner, WA 98390 • *6,281*
Sumner □, KS • *25,841*
Sumner □, TN • *103,281*
Sumter, SC 29150–54 • *41,943*
Sumter □, AL • *16,174*
Sumter □, FL • *31,577*
Sumter □, GA • *30,228*
Sumter □, SC • *102,637*
Sunbury, OH 43074 • *2,046*
Sunbury, PA 17801 • *11,591*
Sun City, AZ 85351 • *38,126*
Sun City, CA 92381 • *14,930*
Sun City Center, FL 33573 • *8,326*
Suncook, NH 03275 • *5,214*
Sundance, WY 82729 • *1,139*
Sundown, TX 79372 • *1,759*
Sunflower □, MS • *32,867*
Sunland Park, NM 88063 • *8,179*
Sunny Isles, FL 33160 • *11,772*
Sunnyside, CA 93727 • *5,000*
Sunnyside, WA 98944 • *11,238*
Sunnyvale, CA 94086–89 • *117,229*
Sun Prairie, WI 53590 • *15,333*
Sunray, TX 79086 • *1,729*
Sunrise Manor, NV 89110 • *95,362*
Sunset, FL 33143 • *15,810*
Sunset, LA 70584 • *2,201*
Sunset, UT 84015 • *5,128*
Sunset Beach, HI 96712 • *800*
Sun Valley, ID 83353–54 • *938*
Sun Valley, NV 89433 • *11,391*
Superior, AZ 85273 • *3,468*
Superior, MT 59872 • *881*
Superior, NE 68978 • *2,397*
Superior, WI 54880 • *27,134*
Superior, WY 82945 • *273*
Suquamish, WA 98392 • *3,105*
Surf City, NJ 08008 • *1,375*
Surfside, FL 33154 • *4,108*
Surfside Beach, SC 29575 • *3,845*
Surgoinsville, TN 37873 • *1,499*
Surprise, AZ 85374 • *7,122*
Surrey, ND 58785 • *856*
Surry □, NC • *61,704*
Surry □, VA • *6,145*
Susanville, CA 96130 • *7,279*
Susquehanna, PA 18847 • *1,760*
Susquehanna □, PA • *40,380*
Sussex, NJ 07461 • *2,201*
Sussex, WI 53089 • *5,039*
Sussex □, DE • *113,229*
Sussex □, NJ • *130,943*
Sussex □, VA • *10,248*
Sutherland, NE 69165 • *1,032*
Sutherlin, OR 97479 • *5,020*
Sutter □, CA • *64,415*
Sutter Creek, CA 95685 • *1,835*
Sutton, NE 68979 • *1,353*
Sutton □, TX • *4,135*
Suwanee, GA 30174 • *2,412*
Suwannee □, FL • *26,780*
Swain □, NC • *11,268*
Swainsboro, GA 30401 • *7,361*
Swampscott, MA 01907 • *13,650*
Swannanoa, NC 28778 • *3,538*
Swansboro, NC 28584 • *1,165*
Swansea, IL 62221 • *8,201*
Swanton, OH 43558 • *3,557*
Swanton, VT 05488 • *2,360*
Swanwyck Estates, DE 19720 • *1,320*
Swarthmore, PA 19081 • *6,157*
Swartz Creek, MI 48473 • *4,851*
Swatara Township, PA 17111 • *19,700*
Swayzee, IN 46986 • *1,059*
Swedesboro, NJ 08085 • *2,024*
Sweeny, TX 77480 • *3,297*
Sweet Grass □, MT • *3,154*
Sweet Home, OR 97386 • *6,850*
Sweet Springs, MO 65351 • *1,595*
Sweetwater, FL 33152 • *13,909*
Sweetwater, TN 37874 • *5,066*
Sweetwater, TX 79556 • *11,967*
Sweetwater □, WY • *38,823*
Sweetwater Creek, FL 33614 • *18,000*
Swift □, MN • *10,724*
Swisher □, TX • *8,133*
Swissvale, PA 15218 • *10,637*
Switzer, WV 25647 • *1,004*
Switzerland, FL 32043 • *2,400*
Switzerland □, IN • *7,738*
Swoyerville, PA • *5,630*
Sycamore, AL 35149 • *1,250*
Sycamore, IL 60178 • *9,708*
Sykesville, MD 21784 • *2,303*
Sykesville, PA 15865 • *1,387*
Sylacauga, AL 35150 • *12,520*
Sylva, NC 28779 • *1,809*
Sylvan Beach, NY 13157 • *1,119*
Sylvania, GA 30467 • *2,871*
Sylvania, OH 43560 • *17,301*
Sylvan Lake, MI 48320 • *1,884*
Sylvester, GA 31791 • *5,702*
Syosset, NY 11791 • *18,967*
Syracuse, IN 46567 • *2,729*
Syracuse, KS 67878 • *1,606*
Syracuse, NE 68446 • *1,646*
Syracuse, NY 13201–90 • *163,860*
Syracuse, UT 84075 • *4,658*

T

Tabor City, NC 28463 • *2,330*
Tacoma, WA 98401–99 • *176,664*
Taft, CA 93268 • *5,902*
Taft, TX 78390 • *3,222*
Tahlequah, OK 74464–65 • *10,398*
Tahoe City, CA 95730 • *1,300*
Tahoka, TX 79373 • *2,868*
Takoma Park, MD 20912 • *16,700*
Talbot □, GA • *6,524*
Talbot □, MD • *30,549*
Talbotton, GA 31827 • *1,046*
Talent, OR 97540 • *3,274*
Taliaferro □, GA • *1,915*
Talihina, OK 74571 • *1,297*
Talladega, AL 35160 • *18,175*
Talladega □, AL • *74,107*
Tallahassee, FL 32301–17 • *124,773*
Tallahatchie □, MS • *15,210*
Tallapoosa, GA 30176 • *2,805*
Tallapoosa □, AL • *38,826*
Tallassee, AL 36078 • *5,112*
Talleyville, DE 19803 • *6,346*
Tallmadge, OH 44278 • *14,870*
Tallulah, LA 71282–84 • *8,526*
Tama, IA 52339 • *2,697*
Tama □, IA • *17,419*
Tamalpais Valley, CA 94941 • *5,000*
Tamaqua, PA 18252 • *7,943*
Tamarac, FL 33321 • *44,822*
Tamiami, FL 33165 • *33,845*
Tampa, FL 33601–97 • *280,015*
Tanana, AK 99777 • *345*
Taney □, MO • *25,561*
Taneytown, MD 21787 • *3,695*
Tangipahoa □, LA • *85,709*
Taos, NM 87571 • *4,065*
Taos □, NM • *23,118*
Taos Pueblo, NM 87571 • *1,030*
Tappahannock, VA 22560 • *1,550*
Tappan, NY 10983 • *6,867*
Tara Hills, CA 94564 • *6,000*
Tarboro, NC 27886 • *11,037*
Tarentum, PA 15084 • *5,674*
Tariffville, CT 06081 • *1,477*
Tarkio, MO 64491 • *2,243*
Tarpey, CA 93727 • *4,000*
Tarpon Springs, FL 34688–91 • *17,906*
Tarrant, AL 35217 • *8,046*
Tarrant □, TX • *1,170,103*
Tarrytown, NY 10591 • *10,739*
Tate, GA 30177 • *1,000*
Tate □, MS • *21,432*
Tattnall □, GA • *17,722*
Taunton, MA 02780 • *49,832*
Tavares, FL 32778 • *7,383*
Tavernier, FL 33070 • *2,433*
Tawas City, MI 48763–64 • *2,009*
Taylor, AZ 85939 • *2,418*
Taylor, MI 48180 • *70,811*
Taylor, PA 18517 • *6,941*
Taylor, TX 76574 • *11,472*
Taylor □, FL • *17,111*
Taylor □, GA • *7,642*
Taylor □, IA • *7,114*
Taylor □, KY • *21,146*
Taylor □, TX • *119,655*
Taylor □, WV • *15,144*
Taylor □, WI • *18,901*
Taylor Mill, KY 41015 • *5,530*
Taylors, SC 29687 • *19,619*
Taylorsville, IN 47280 • *1,044*
Taylorsville, MS 39168 • *1,412*
Taylorsville, NC 28681 • *1,566*
Taylorville, IL 62568 • *11,133*
Tazewell, TN 37879 • *2,150*
Tazewell, VA 24651 • *4,176*
Tazewell □, IL • *123,692*
Tazewell □, VA • *45,960*
Tchula, MS 39169 • *2,186*
Teague, TX 75860 • *3,268*
Teaneck, NJ 07666 • *37,825*
Teaticket, MA 02536 • *2,600*
Tecumseh, MI 49286 • *7,462*
Tecumseh, NE 68450 • *1,702*
Tecumseh, OK 74873 • *5,750*
Tehachapi, CA 93561 • *5,791*
Tehama □, CA • *49,625*
Tekamah, NE 68061 • *1,852*
Telfair □, GA • *11,000*
Telford, PA 18969 • *4,238*
Tell City, IN 47586 • *8,088*
Teller □, CO • *12,468*
Telluride, CO 81435 • *1,309*
Temecula, CA 92390 • *27,099*
Tempe, AZ 85280–86 • *141,865*
Temperance, MI 48182 • *6,542*
Temple, GA 30179 • *1,870*
Temple, OK 73568 • *1,223*
Temple, PA 19560 • *1,491*
Temple, TX 76501–05 • *46,109*
Temple City, CA 91780 • *31,100*
Temple Terrace, FL 33617 • *16,444*
Templeton, MA 01468 • *1,000*
Tenafly, NJ 07670 • *13,326*
Tenaha, TX 75974 • *1,072*
Tenino, WA 98589 • *1,292*
Tennessee Ridge, TN 37178 • *1,271*
Tennille, GA 31089 • *1,552*
Tensas □, LA • *7,103*
Ten Sleep, WY 82442 • *311*
Terra Alta, WV 26764 • *1,713*
Terrebonne □, LA • *96,982*
Terre Haute, IN 47801–08 • *57,483*
Terre Hill, PA 17581 • *1,282*
Terrell, TX 75160 • *12,490*
Terrell □, GA • *10,653*
Terrell □, TX • *1,410*
Terrell Hills, TX 78209 • *4,592*
Terry, MT 59349 • *659*
Terry □, TX • *13,218*
Terrytown, LA 70053 • *23,787*
Terryville, CT 06786 • *5,426*
Terryville, NY 11776 • *7,380*
Tesuque, NM 87574 • *1,490*
Teton □, ID • *3,439*
Teton □, MT • *6,271*
Teton □, WY • *11,172*
Teton Village, WY 83025 • *250*
Teutopolis, IL 62467 • *1,417*
Tewksbury, MA 01876 • *10,540*
Texarkana, AR 75502 • *22,631*
Texarkana, TX 75501–05 • *31,656*
Texas □, MO • *21,476*
Texas □, OK • *16,419*
Texas City, TX 77590–92 • *40,822*
Texico, NM 88135 • *966*
Thatcher, AZ 85552 • *3,763*
Thayer, MO 65791 • *1,996*
Thayer □, NE • *6,635*
Thayne, WY 83127 • *267*
The Colony, TX 75056 • *22,113*
The Dalles, OR 97058 • *11,060*
Theodore, AL 36582 • *6,509*
The Plains, OH 45780 • *2,644*
Thermalito, CA 95965 • *5,646*
Thermopolis, WY 82443 • *3,247*
The Village, OK 73120 • *10,353*
The Village of Indian Hill, OH 45243 • *5,383*
The Woodlands, TX 77380 • *29,205*
Thibodaux, LA 70301–02 • *14,035*
Thief River Falls, MN 56701 • *8,010*
Thiensville, WI 53092 • *3,301*
Thomas, OK 73669 • *1,246*
Thomas □, GA • *38,986*
Thomas □, KS • *8,258*
Thomas □, NE • *851*
Thomasboro, IL 61878 • *1,250*
Thomaston, CT 06787 • *3,590*
Thomaston, GA 30286 • *9,127*
Thomaston, ME 04861 • *2,445*
Thomasville, AL 36784 • *4,301*
Thomasville, GA 31792 • *17,457*
Thomasville, NC 27360–61 • *15,915*
Thompson, ND 58278 • *930*
Thompson Falls, MT 59873 • *1,319*
Thomson, GA 30824 • *6,862*
Thonotosassa, FL 33592 • *1,500*
Thoreau, NM 87323 • *1,099*
Thorndale, TX 76577 • *1,092*
Thorndike, MA 01079 • *1,100*
Thornton, CO 80229 • *55,031*
Thorntown, IN 46071 • *1,506*
Thornwood, NY 10594 • *7,025*
Thorofare, NJ 08086 • *1,800*
Thorp, WI 54771 • *1,657*
Thorsby, AL 35171 • *1,465*
Thousand Oaks, CA 91359–62 • *104,352*
Three Forks, MT 59752 • *1,203*
Three Oaks, MI 49128 • *1,786*
Three Rivers, MA 01080 • *3,006*
Three Rivers, MI 49093 • *7,413*
Three Rivers, TX 78071 • *1,889*
Throckmorton, TX 76083 • *1,036*
Throckmorton □, TX • *1,880*
Throop, PA 18512 • *4,070*
Thunderbolt, GA 31404 • *2,786*
Thurmont, MD 21788 • *3,398*
Thurston □, NE • *6,936*
Thurston □, WA • *161,238*
Tiburon, CA 94920 • *7,532*
Tice, FL 33905 • *3,971*
Ticonderoga, NY 12883 • *2,770*
Tierra Amarilla, NM 87575 • *900*
Tiffin, OH 44883 • *18,604*
Tift □, GA • *34,998*
Tifton, GA 31793–94 • *14,215*
Tigard, OR 97223 • *29,344*
Tillamook, OR 97141 • *4,001*
Tillamook □, OR • *21,570*
Tillman □, OK • *10,384*
Tillmans Corner, AL 36619 • *17,988*
Tillson, NY 12486 • *1,688*
Tilton, IL 61833 • *2,729*
Tilton, NH 03276 • *1,380*
Tiltonsville, OH 43963 • *1,517*
Timberlake, VA 24502 • *10,314*
Timberville, VA 22853 • *1,596*
Timmonsville, SC 29161 • *2,182*
Timpson, TX 75975 • *1,029*
Tinley Park, IL 60477 • *37,121*
Tinton Falls, NJ 07724 • *12,361*
Tioga, LA 71477 • *1,200*
Tioga, ND 58852 • *1,278*
Tioga □, NY • *52,337*
Tioga □, PA • *41,126*
Tippah □, MS • *19,523*
Tipp City, OH 45371 • *6,027*
Tippecanoe □, IN • *130,598*
Tipton, CA 93272 • *1,383*
Tipton, IN 46072 • *4,751*
Tipton, IA 52772 • *2,998*
Tipton, MO 65081 • *2,026*
Tipton, OK 73570 • *1,043*
Tipton □, IN • *16,119*
Tipton □, TN • *37,568*
Tiptonville, TN 38079 • *2,149*
Tishomingo, OK 73460 • *3,116*
Tishomingo □, MS • *17,683*
Titus □, TX • *24,009*
Titusville, FL 32780–83 • *39,394*
Titusville, PA 16354 • *6,434*
Tiverton, RI 02878 • *7,259*
Tivoli, NY 12583 • *1,035*
Toast, NC 27049 • *2,125*
Tobyhanna, PA 18466 • *1,200*
Toccoa, GA 30577 • *8,266*
Todd □, KY • *10,940*
Todd □, MN • *23,363*
Todd □, SD • *8,352*
Todd Estates, DE 19713 • *2,000*
Togiak, AK 99678 • *613*
Tohatchi, NM 87325 • *661*
Tok, AK 99780 • *935*
Toledo, IL 62468 • *1,199*

Toledo, IA 52342 • 2,380
Toledo, OH 43601-99 • 332,943
Toledo, OR 97391 • 3,174
Tolland, CT 06084 • 1,200
Tolland □, CT • 128,699
Tolleson, AZ 85353 • 4,434
Tolono, IL 61880 • 2,605
Toluca, IL 61369 • 1,315
Tomah, WI 54660 • 7,570
Tomahawk, WI 54487 • 3,328
Tomball, TX 77375 • 6,370
Tombstone, AZ 85638 • 1,220
Tom Green □, TX • 98,458
Tompkins □, NY • 94,097
Tompkinsville, KY 42167 • 2,861
Toms River, NJ 08753-57 • 7,524
Tonawanda, NY 14150-51 • 17,284
Tonawanda, NY 14223 • 65,284
Tonganoxie, KS 66086 • 2,347
Tonkawa, OK 74653 • 3,127
Tonopah, NV 89049 • 3,616
Tooele, UT 84074 • 13,887
Tooele □, UT • 26,601
Toole □, MT • 5,046
Toombs □, GA • 24,072
Topeka, KS 66601-99 • 119,883
Toppenish, WA 98948 • 7,419
Topsfield, MA 01983 • 2,711
Topsham, ME 04086 • 6,147
Topton, PA 19562 • 1,987
Toronto, OH 43964 • 6,127
Torrance, CA 90501-10 • 133,107
Torrance □, NM • 10,285
Torrington, CT 06790 • 33,687
Torrington, WY 82240 • 5,651
Totowa, NJ 07512 • 10,177
Touisset, MA 02777 • 1,520
Toulon, IL 61483 • 1,328
Towaco, NJ 07082 • 1,020
Towanda, KS 67144 • 1,289
Towanda, PA 18848 • 3,242
Tower City, PA 17980 • 1,518
Town and Country, WA 99210 • 4,921
Town Creek, AL 35672 • 1,379
Towner, ND 58788 • 669
Towner □, ND • 3,627
Town 'n Country, FL 33615 • 60,946
Towns □, GA • 6,754
Townsend, DE 19734 • 322
Townsend, MA 01469 • 1,164
Townsend, MT 59644 • 1,635
Towson, MD 21204 • 49,445
Tracy, CA 95376-78 • 33,558
Tracy, MN 56175 • 2,059
Tracy City, TN 37387 • 1,556
Tracyton, WA 98393 • 2,621
Traer, IA 50675 • 1,552
Trafford, PA 15085 • 3,345
Trail Creek, IN 46360 • 2,463
Traill □, ND • 8,752
Transylvania □, NC • 25,520
Travelers Rest, SC 29690 • 3,069
Traverse □, MN • 4,463
Traverse City, MI 49684 • 15,155
Travis □, TX • 576,407
Treasure □, MT • 874
Treasure Island, FL 33706 • 7,266
Trego □, KS • 3,694
Tremont, IL 61568 • 2,088
Tremont, PA 17981 • 1,814
Tremonton, UT 84337 • 4,264
Trempealeau, WI 54661 • 1,039
Trempealeau □, WI • 25,263
Trenton, FL 32693 • 1,287
Trenton, GA 30752 • 1,994
Trenton, IL 62293 • 2,481
Trenton, MI 48183 • 20,586
Trenton, MO 64683 • 6,129
Trenton, NE 69044 • 10,000
Trenton, NJ 08601-91 • 88,675
Trenton, OH 45067 • 6,189
Trenton, TN 38382 • 4,836
Tresckow, PA 18254 • 1,033
Treutlen □, GA • 5,994
Trevorton, PA 17881 • 2,058
Triangle, VA 22172 • 4,740
Tri City, OR 97457 • 3,585
Trigg □, KY • 10,361
Tri Lakes, IN 46725 • 3,299
Trimble □, KY • 6,090
Trinidad, CO 81082 • 8,580
Trinidad, TX 75163 • 1,056
Trinity, AL 35673 • 1,380
Trinity, NC 27370 • 5,469
Trinity, TX 75862 • 2,648
Trinity □, CA • 13,063
Trinity □, TX • 11,445
Trion, GA 30753 • 1,661
Tripoli, IA 50676 • 1,188
Tripp □, SD • 6,924
Triumph, LA 70041 • 1,200
Trona, CA 93562 • 1,400
Trooper, PA 19401 • 5,137
Trotwood, OH 45426 • 8,816
Troup □, GA • 55,536
Trousdale □, TN • 5,920
Troutdale, OR 97060 • 7,852
Troutman, NC 28166 • 1,493
Troy, AL 36081 • 13,051
Troy, ID 83871 • 699
Troy, IL 62294 • 6,046
Troy, KS 66087 • 1,073
Troy, MI 48083-84 • 72,884
Troy, MO 63379 • 3,811
Troy, MT 59935 • 953
Troy, NH 03465 • 2,097
Troy, NY 12180-83 • 54,269
Troy, NC 27371 • 3,404
Troy, OH 45373 • 19,478
Troy, PA 16947 • 1,262
Troy, TN 38260 • 1,047
Truckee, CA 95734 • 3,484
Truman, MN 56088 • 1,292
Trumann, AR 72472 • 6,304
Trumansburg, NY 14886 • 1,611
Trumbull, CT 06611 • 32,000
Trumbull □, OH • 227,813
Trussville, AL 35173 • 8,266
Truth or Consequences (Hot Springs), NM 87901 • 6,221
Tryon, NC 28782 • 1,680
Tualatin, OR 97062 • 15,013
Tuba City, AZ 86045 • 7,323
Tuckahoe, NY 10707 • 6,302
Tucker, GA 30084 • 25,781
Tucker □, WV • 7,728
Tuckerman, AR 72473 • 2,020
Tuckerton, NJ 08087 • 3,048
Tucson, AZ 85701-51 • 405,390
Tucumcari, NM 88401 • 6,831
Tukwila, WA 98188 • 11,874
Tulare, CA 93274-75 • 33,249
Tulare □, CA • 311,921
Tularosa, NM 88352 • 2,615
Tulelake, CA 96134 • 1,010
Tulia, TX 79088 • 4,699
Tullahoma, TN 37388 • 16,761
Tulsa, OK 74101-94 • 367,302
Tulsa □, OK • 503,341
Tumwater, WA 98502 • 9,976
Tunica, MS 38676 • 1,175
Tunica □, MS • 8,164
Tunkhannock, PA 18657 • 2,251
Tununak, AK 99681 • 316
Tuolumne, CA 95379 • 1,686
Tuolumne □, CA • 48,456
Tupelo, MS 38801-03 • 30,685
Tupper Lake, NY 12986 • 4,087
Turley, OK 74156 • 2,930
Turlock, CA 95380-81 • 42,198
Turner, OR 97392 • 1,281
Turner □, GA • 8,703
Turner □, SD • 8,576
Turners Falls, MA 01376 • 4,731
Turtle Creek, PA 15145 • 6,556
Turtle Lake, ND 58575 • 681
Tuscaloosa, AL 35401-06 • 77,759
Tuscaloosa □, AL • 150,522
Tuscarawas □, OH • 84,090
Tuscola, IL 61953 • 4,155
Tuscola □, MI • 55,498
Tuscumbia, AL 35674 • 8,413
Tuskegee, AL 36083 • 12,257
Tustin, CA 92680-81 • 50,689
Tuttle, OK 73089 • 2,807
Tutwiler, MS 38963 • 1,391
Tuxedo Park, DE 19804 • 1,300
Twentynine Palms, CA 92277-78 • 11,821
Twiggs □, GA • 9,806
Twin City, GA 30471 • 1,466
Twin Falls, ID 83301-03 • 27,591
Twin Falls □, ID • 53,580
Twin Knolls, AZ 85207 • 5,210
Twin Lakes, CA 95060 • 5,379
Twin Lakes, WI 53181 • 3,989
Twin Rivers, NJ 08520 • 7,715
Twinsburg, OH 44087 • 9,606
Two Harbors, MN 55616 • 3,651
Two Rivers, WI 54241 • 13,030
Tybee Island, GA 31328 • 2,842
Tyler, MN 56178 • 1,257
Tyler, TX 75701-13 • 75,450
Tyler □, TX • 16,646
Tyler □, WV • 9,796
Tyler Heights, WV 25312 • 4,070
Tylertown, MS 39667 • 1,938
Tyndall, SD 57066 • 1,201
Tyrone, NM 88065 • 950
Tyrone, PA 16686 • 5,743
Tyrrell □, NC • 3,856
Tysons Corner, VA 22102 • 13,124

U

Ucon, ID 83454 • 895
Uhrichsville, OH 44683 • 5,604
Uinta □, WY • 18,705
Uintah □, UT • 22,211
Ukiah, CA 95482 • 14,599
Uleta, FL 33162 • 10,000
Ulster □, NY • 165,304
Ulysses, KS 67880 • 5,474
Umatilla, FL 32784 • 2,350
Umatilla, OR 97882 • 3,046
Umatilla □, OR • 59,249
Unadilla, GA 31091 • 1,620
Unadilla, NY 13849 • 1,265
Unalakleet, AK 99684 • 714
Unalaska, AK 99685 • 3,089
Uncasville, CT 06382 • 1,597
Underwood, AL 35630 • 1,950
Underwood, ND 58576 • 976
Unicoi □, TN • 16,549
Union, KY 41091 • 1,001
Union, MS 39365 • 1,875
Union, MO 63084 • 5,909
Union, NJ 07083 • 50,024
Union, OH 45322 • 5,501
Union, OR 97883 • 1,847
Union, SC 29379 • 9,836
Union, UT 84047 • 13,684
Union □, AR • 46,719
Union □, FL • 10,252
Union □, GA • 11,993
Union □, IL • 17,619
Union □, IN • 6,976
Union □, IA • 12,750
Union □, KY • 16,557
Union □, LA • 20,690
Union □, MS • 22,085
Union □, NJ • 493,819
Union □, NM • 4,124
Union □, NC • 84,211
Union □, OH • 31,969
Union □, OR • 23,598
Union □, PA • 36,176
Union □, SC • 30,337
Union □, SD • 10,189
Union □, TN • 13,694
Union Beach, NJ 07735 • 6,156
Union City, CA 94587 • 53,762
Union City, GA 30291 • 8,375
Union City, IN 47390 • 3,612
Union City, MI 49094 • 1,767
Union City, NJ 07087 • 58,012
Union City, OH 45390 • 1,984
Union City, OK 73090 • 1,000
Union City, PA 16438 • 3,537
Union City, TN 38261 • 10,513
Uniondale, NY 11553 • 20,328
Union Gap, WA 98903 • 3,120
Union Grove, WI 53182 • 3,669
Union Lake, MI 48386-87 • 8,500
Union Park, FL 32817 • 6,890
Union Pier, MI 49129 • 1,039
Union Point, GA 30669 • 1,753
Union Springs, AL 36089 • 3,975
Union Springs, NY 13160 • 1,142
Uniontown, AL 36786 • 1,730
Uniontown, KY 42461 • 1,008
Uniontown, OH 44685 • 1,500
Uniontown, PA 15401 • 12,034
Union Village, RI 02895 • 2,150
Unionville, CT 06085 • 3,500
Unionville, MO 63565 • 1,989
Universal City, TX 78148 • 13,057
University City, MO 63130 • 40,087
University Gardens, NY 11020 • 4,600
University Heights, IA 52240 • 1,042
University Heights, OH 44118 • 14,790
University Park, IL 60466 • 6,204
University Park, NM 88003 • 4,520
University Park, TX 75205 • 22,259
University Place, WA 98465 • 27,701
Upland, CA 91785-86 • 63,374
Upland, IN 46989 • 3,295
Upper Arlington, OH 43221 • 34,128
Upper Darby, PA 19082-83 • 84,054
Upper Dublin Township, PA 19002 • 22,348
Upper Greenwood Lake, NJ 07421 • 2,734
Upper Merion Township, PA 19406 • 26,138
Upper Moreland Township, PA 19090 • 25,874
Upper Providence Township, PA 19063 • 9,727
Upper Saddle River, NJ 07458 • 7,198
Upper Saint Clair, PA 15241 • 19,692
Upper Sandusky, OH 43351 • 5,906
Upshur □, TX • 31,370
Upshur □, WV • 22,867
Upson □, GA • 26,300
Upton, MA 01568 • 1,500
Upton, WY 82730 • 980
Upton □, TX • 4,447
Urbana, IL 61801 • 36,344
Urbana, OH 43078 • 11,353
Urbandale, IA 50322 • 23,500
Usquepaug, RI 02892 • 400
Utah □, UT • 263,590
Utica, MI 48315-18 • 5,081
Utica, MS 39175 • 1,033
Utica, NY 13501-05 • 68,637
Utica, OH 43080 • 1,997
Uvalde, TX 78801-02 • 14,729
Uvalde □, TX • 23,340
Uxbridge, MA 01569 • 3,340

V

Vacaville, CA 95687-88 • 71,479
Vacherie, LA 70090 • 2,169
Vadnais Heights, MN 55110 • 11,041
Vail, CO 81657-58 • 3,659
Valatie, NY 12184 • 1,487
Valdese, NC 28690 • 3,914
Valdez, AK 99686 • 4,068
Valdosta, GA 31601-04 • 39,806
Vale, OR 97918 • 1,491
Valencia, AZ 85326 • 1,200
Valencia □, NM • 45,235
Valencia Heights, SC 29205 • 4,122
Valentine, NE 69201 • 2,826
Valhalla, NY 10595 • 6,200
Valinda, CA 91744 • 18,735
Vallejo, CA 94589-92 • 109,199
Valle Vista, CA 92343 • 8,751
Valley, AL 36854 • 8,173
Valley, NE 68064 • 1,775
Valley □, ID • 6,109
Valley □, MT • 8,239
Valley □, NE • 5,169
Valley Center, KS 67147 • 3,624
Valley City, ND 58072 • 7,163
Valley Cottage, NY 10989 • 9,007
Valley Falls, KS 66088 • 1,253
Valley Falls, RI 02864 • 11,175
Valley Forge, PA 19481-82 • 1,500
Valley Mills, TX 76689 • 1,085
Valley Park, MO 63088 • 4,165
Valley Ridge, WA 98188 • 6,500
Valley Springs, SD 57068 • 739
Valley Station, KY 40272 • 22,840
Valley Stream, NY 11580-82 • 33,946
Valley View, PA 17983 • 1,749
Valparaiso, FL 32580 • 4,672
Valparaiso, IN 46383-84 • 24,414
Val Verda, UT 84010 • 3,712
Val Verde □, TX • 38,721
Van, TX 75790 • 1,854
Van Alstyne, TX 75095 • 2,090
Van Buren, AR 72956 • 14,979
Van Buren, ME 04785 • 2,759
Van Buren □, AR • 14,008
Van Buren □, IA • 7,676
Van Buren □, MI • 70,060
Van Buren □, TN • 4,846
Vance □, NC • 38,892
Vanceburg, KY 41179 • 1,713
Vancleave, MS 39564 • 3,214
Vancouver, WA 98660-68 • 46,380
Vandalia, IL 62471 • 6,114
Vandalia, MO 63382 • 2,683
Vandalia, OH 45377 • 13,882
Vandenberg Village, CA 93436 • 5,871
Vander, NC 28301 • 1,179
Vanderburgh □, IN • 165,058
Vandergrift, PA 15690 • 5,904
Van Horn, TX 79855 • 2,930
Van Lear, KY 41265 • 1,050
Vansant, VA 24656 • 1,187
Van Vleck, TX 77482 • 1,534
Van Wert, OH 45891 • 10,891
Van Wert □, OH • 30,464
Van Zandt □, TX • 37,944
Varina, VA 23231 • 2,500
Varnville, SC 29944 • 1,970
Vassar, MI 48768 • 2,559
Vaughn, MT 59487 • 2,270
Veazie, ME 04401 • 1,610
Veedersburg, IN 47987 • 2,192
Velda Rose Estates, AZ 85205 • 2,330
Velva, ND 58790 • 968
Venango □, PA • 59,381
Veneta, OR 97487 • 2,519
Venice, FL 34292-93 • 16,922
Venice, IL 62090 • 3,571
Venice Gardens, FL 34293 • 7,701
Ventnor City, NJ 08406 • 11,005
Ventura (San Buenaventura), CA 93001-07 • 92,575
Ventura □, CA • 669,016
Veradale, WA 99037 • 7,836
Verda, KY 40828 • 1,133
Verdi, NV 89439 • 1,140
Vergennes, VT 05491 • 2,578
Vermilion, OH 44089 • 11,127
Vermilion □, IL • 88,257
Vermilion □, LA • 50,055
Vermillion, SD 57069 • 10,034
Vermillion □, IN • 16,773
Vernal, UT 84078-79 • 6,644
Vernon, AL 35592 • 2,247
Vernon, CT 06066 • 30,200
Vernon, TX 76384 • 12,001
Vernon □, LA • 61,961
Vernon □, MO • 19,041
Vernon □, WI • 25,617
Vernon Hills, IL 60061 • 15,319
Vernonia, OR 97064 • 1,808
Vero Beach, FL 32960-68 • 17,350
Verona, MS 38879 • 2,893
Verona, NJ 07044 • 13,597
Verona, PA 15147 • 3,260
Verona, WI 53593 • 5,374
Versailles, IN 47042 • 1,791
Versailles, KY 40383 • 7,269
Versailles, MO 65084 • 2,365
Versailles, OH 45380 • 2,351
Vestal, NY 13850-51 • 5,530
Vestavia Hills, AL 35216 • 19,749
Vevay, IN 47043 • 1,393
Vian, OK 74962 • 1,414
Vicksburg, MI 49097 • 2,216
Vicksburg, MS 39180-82 • 20,908
Victor, NY 14564 • 2,308
Victoria, KS 67671 • 1,157
Victoria, TX 77901-05 • 55,076
Victoria, VA 23974 • 1,830
Victoria □, TX • 74,361
Victorville, CA 92392-93 • 40,674
Vidalia, GA 30474 • 11,078
Vidalia, LA 71373 • 4,953
Vidor, TX 77662 • 10,935
Vienna, GA 31092 • 2,708
Vienna, IL 62995 • 1,446
Vienna, VA 22180-83 • 14,852
Vienna, WV 26105 • 10,862
View Park, CA 90043 • 5,900
Vigo □, IN • 106,107
Vilas □, WI • 17,707
Villa Grove, IL 61956 • 2,734
Villa Hills, KY 41016 • 7,739
Villa Park, CA 92667 • 6,299
Villa Park, IL 60181 • 22,253
Villa Rica, GA 30180 • 6,542
Villas, NJ 08251 • 8,136
Ville Platte, LA 70586 • 9,037
Villisca, IA 50864 • 1,332
Vilonia, AR 72173 • 1,133
Vincennes, IN 47591 • 19,859
Vincent, AL 35178 • 1,767
Vine Grove, KY 40175 • 3,586
Vineland, NJ 08360 • 54,780
Vineyard Haven, MA 02568 • 1,762
Vinita, OK 74301 • 5,804
Vinton, IA 52349 • 5,103
Vinton, LA 70668 • 3,154
Vinton, VA 24179 • 7,665
Vinton □, OH • 11,098
Viola, NY 10952 • 4,504
Violet, LA 70092 • 8,574
Virden, IL 62690 • 3,635
Virginia, IL 62691 • 1,767
Virginia, MN 55792 • 9,410
Virginia Beach, VA 23450-67 • 393,069
Virginia City, NV 89440 • 920
Viroqua, WI 54665 • 3,922
Visalia, CA 93277-79 • 75,636
Vista, CA 92083-84 • 71,872
Vivian, LA 71082 • 4,156
Volcano, HI 96785 • 1,516
Volga, SD 57071 • 1,263
Volusia □, FL • 370,712

W

Wabash, IN 46992 • 12,127
Wabash □, IL • 13,111
Wabash □, IN • 35,069
Wabasha, MN 55981 • 2,384
Wabasha □, MN • 19,744
Wabasso, FL 32970 • 1,145
Wabaunsee □, KS • 6,603
Waco, TX 76701-16 • 103,590
Waconia, MN 55387 • 3,498
Wade Hampton, SC 29607 • 20,014
Wadena, MN 56482 • 4,131
Wadena □, MN • 13,154
Wadesboro, NC 28170 • 3,645
Wading River, NY 11792 • 5,317
Wadley, GA 30477 • 2,473
Wadsworth, IL 60083 • 1,826
Wadsworth, NV 89442 • 640
Wadsworth, OH 44281 • 15,718
Wagner, SD 57380 • 1,462
Wagoner, OK 74467 • 6,894
Wagoner □, OK • 47,883
Wahiawa, HI 96786 • 17,386
Wahkiakum □, WA • 3,327
Wahoo, NE 68066 • 3,681
Wahpeton, ND 58074-75 • 8,751
Waialua, HI 96791 • 3,943
Waianae, HI 96792 • 8,758
Waikapu, HI 96793 • 729
Wailua, HI 96746 • 2,018
Wailuku, HI 96793 • 10,688
Waimanalo, HI 96795 • 3,508
Waimea, HI 96712 • 600
Waimea, HI 96796 • 5,972
Wainwright, AK 99782 • 492
Waipahu, HI 96797 • 31,435
Waipio Acres, HI 96786 • 5,304
Waite Park, MN 56387 • 5,020
Wakarusa, IN 46573 • 1,667
Wake □, NC • 423,380
Wa Keeney, KS 67672 • 2,161
Wakefield, MA 01880 • 24,825
Wakefield, MI 49968 • 2,318
Wakefield, NE 68784 • 1,082
Wakefield, RI 02879-83 • 3,450
Wakefield, VA 23888 • 1,070
Wake Forest, NC 27587-88 • 5,769
Wakulla □, FL • 14,202
Walbridge, OH 43465 • 2,736
Walcott, IA 52773 • 1,356
Walden, NY 12586 • 5,836
Waldo, AR 71770 • 1,495
Waldo, FL 32694 • 1,017
Waldo □, ME • 33,018
Waldoboro, ME 04572 • 1,420
Waldport, OR 97394 • 1,595
Waldron, AR 72958 • 3,024
Waldwick, NJ 07463 • 9,757
Walhalla, ND 58282 • 1,131
Walhalla, SC 29691 • 3,755
Walker, LA 70785 • 3,727
Walker, MI 49504 • 17,279
Walker □, AL • 67,670
Walker □, GA • 58,340
Walker □, TX • 50,917
Walkersville, MD 21793 • 4,145
Walkerton, IN 46574 • 2,061
Walkertown, NC 27051 • 1,200
Walkerville, MT 59701 • 605
Wall, SD 57790 • 834
Wallace, ID 83873 • 1,010
Wallace, NC 28466 • 2,939
Wallace □, KS • 1,821
Walla Walla, WA 99362 • 26,478
Walla Walla □, WA • 48,439
Walled Lake, MI 48390 • 6,278
Wallen, IN 46806 • 1,000
Waller, TX 77484 • 1,493
Waller □, TX • 23,390
Wallingford, CT 06492 • 17,827
Wallingford, VT 05773 • 1,148
Wallington, NJ 07057 • 10,828
Wallis, TX 77485 • 1,001
Wallkill, NY 12589 • 2,125
Wallowa □, OR • 6,911
Walnut, CA 91789 • 29,105
Walnut, IL 61376 • 1,463
Walnut Cove, NC 27052 • 1,088
Walnut Creek, CA 94593-98 • 60,569
Walnut Park, CA 90255 • 14,722
Walnutport, PA 18088 • 2,055
Walnut Ridge, AR 72476 • 4,388
Walpole, MA 02081 • 5,495
Walsenburg, CO 81089 • 3,300
Walsh □, ND • 13,840
Walterboro, SC 29488 • 5,492
Walters, OK 73572 • 2,519
Walthall □, MS • 14,352
Waltham, MA 02154 • 57,878
Walthourville, GA 31333 • 2,024
Walton, IN 46994 • 1,053
Walton, KY 41094 • 2,034
Walton, NY 13856 • 3,326
Walton □, FL • 27,760
Walton □, GA • 38,586
Walworth, WI 53184 • 1,614
Walworth □, SD • 6,087
Walworth □, WI • 75,000
Wamac, IL 62801 • 1,501
Wamego, KS 66547 • 3,706
Wamesit, MA 01876 • 2,700
Wamsutter, WY 82336 • 240
Wanaque, NJ 07465 • 9,711
Wanchese, NC 27981 • 1,380
Wando Woods, SC 29405 • 5,253
Wantagh, NY 11793 • 18,567
Wapakoneta, OH 45895 • 9,214
Wapato, WA 98951 • 3,795
Wapello, IA 52653 • 2,013
Wapello □, IA • 35,687
Wappingers Falls, NY 12590 • 4,605
War, WV 24892 • 1,081
Ward, AR 72176 • 1,269
Ward □, ND • 57,921
Ward □, TX • 13,115
Warden, WA 98857 • 1,639
Ware, MA 01082 • 6,533
Ware □, GA • 35,471
Wareham, MA 02571 • 2,607
Warehouse Point, CT 06088 • 1,880
Ware Shoals, SC 29692 • 2,497
Waretown, NJ 08758 • 1,283
Warminster, PA 18974 • 35,463
Warner, OK 74469 • 1,479
Warner Robins, GA 31088 • 43,726
Warr Acres, OK 73132 • 9,288
Warren, AR 71671 • 6,455
Warren, IL 61087 • 1,550
Warren, IN 46792 • 1,185
Warren, MA 01083 • 1,516
Warren, MI 48089-93 • 144,864
Warren, MN 56762 • 1,813
Warren, OH 44481-85 • 50,793
Warren, PA 16365 • 11,122
Warren, RI 02885 • 11,385
Warren, VT 05674 • 350
Warren □, GA • 6,078
Warren □, IL • 19,181
Warren □, IN • 8,176
Warren □, IA • 36,033
Warren □, KY • 76,673
Warren □, MS • 47,880
Warren □, MO • 19,534
Warren □, NJ • 91,607
Warren □, NY • 59,209
Warren □, NC • 17,265
Warren □, OH • 113,909
Warren □, PA • 45,050
Warren □, TN • 32,992
Warren □, VA • 26,142
Warren Park, IN 46219 • 1,763
Warrensburg, IL 62573 • 1,274
Warrensburg, MO 64093 • 15,244
Warrensburg, NY 12885 • 3,204
Warrensville Heights, OH 44122 • 15,745
Warrenton, GA 30828 • 2,056
Warrenton, MO 63383 • 3,564
Warrenton, OR 97146 • 2,681
Warrenton, VA 22186 • 4,830
Warrenville, IL 60555 • 11,333
Warrenville, SC 29851 • 1,029
Warrick □, IN • 44,920
Warrington, FL 32507 • 16,040
Warrington, PA 18976 • 6,980

Warrior, AL 35180 • 3,280
Warroad, MN 56763 • 1,679
Warsaw, IL 62379 • 1,882
Warsaw, IN 46580–81 • 10,968
Warsaw, KY 41095 • 1,202
Warsaw, MO 65355 • 1,696
Warsaw, NY 14569 • 3,830
Warsaw, NC 28398 • 2,859
Warwick, NY 10990 • 5,984
Warwick, RI 02886–89 • 85,427
Wasatch □, UT • 10,089
Wasco, CA 93280 • 12,412
Wasco □, OR • 21,683
Waseca, MN 56093 • 8,385
Waseca □, MN • 18,079
Washakie □, WY • 8,388
Washburn, IL 61570 • 1,075
Washburn, IA 50706 • 1,400
Washburn, ME 04786 • 1,880
Washburn, ND 58577 • 1,506
Washburn, WI 54891 • 2,285
Washburn □, WI • 13,772
Washington, DC 20001–99 • 606,900
Washington, GA 30673 • 4,279
Washington, IL 61571 • 10,099
Washington, IN 47501 • 10,838
Washington, IA 52353 • 7,074
Washington, KS 66968 • 1,304
Washington, LA 70589 • 1,253
Washington, MO 63090 • 10,704
Washington, NJ 07882 • 6,474
Washington, NC 27889 • 9,075
Washington, PA 15301 • 15,864
Washington, UT 84780 • 4,198
Washington □, AL • 16,694
Washington □, AR • 113,409
Washington □, CO • 4,812
Washington □, FL • 16,919
Washington □, GA • 19,112
Washington □, ID • 8,550
Washington □, IL • 14,965
Washington □, IN • 23,717
Washington □, IA • 19,612
Washington □, KS • 7,073
Washington □, KY • 10,441
Washington □, LA • 43,185
Washington □, ME • 35,308
Washington □, MD • 121,393
Washington □, MN • 145,896
Washington □, MS • 67,935
Washington □, MO • 20,380
Washington □, NE • 16,607
Washington □, NY • 59,330
Washington □, NC • 13,997
Washington □, OH • 62,254
Washington □, OK • 48,066
Washington □, OR • 311,554
Washington □, PA • 204,584
Washington □, RI • 110,006
Washington □, TN • 92,315
Washington □, TX • 26,154
Washington □, UT • 48,560
Washington □, VT • 54,928
Washington □, VA • 45,887
Washington □, WI • 95,328
Washington Court House, OH 43160 • 12,983
Washington Park, FL 33314 • 6,930
Washington Park, IL 62204 • 7,431
Washington Terrace, UT 84403 • 8,189
Washington Township, NJ 07675 • 9,245
Washita □, OK • 11,441
Washoe □, NV • 254,667
Washoe City, NV 89701 • 400
Washougal, WA 98671 • 4,764
Washtenaw □, MI • 282,937
Wasilla, AK 99687 • 4,028
Waskom, TX 75692 • 1,812
Watauga, TX 76148 • 20,009
Watauga □, NC • 36,952
Watchung, NJ 07060 • 5,110
Waterbury, CT 06701–26 • 108,961
Waterbury, VT 05676 • 1,702
Waterbury Center, VT 05677 • 500
Waterford, CT 06385 • 17,930
Waterford, MI 48327–29 • 66,692
Waterford, NY 12188 • 2,370
Waterford, PA 16441 • 1,492
Waterford, WI 53185 • 2,431
Waterford Works, NJ 08089 • 1,200
Waterloo, IL 62298 • 5,072
Waterloo, IN 46793 • 2,040
Waterloo, IA 50701–07 • 66,467
Waterloo, NY 13165 • 5,116
Waterloo, WI 53594 • 2,712
Waterman, IL 60556 • 1,074
Waterproof, LA 71375 • 1,080
Watertown, CT 06795 • 20,456
Watertown, FL 32055 • 3,340
Watertown, MA 02172 • 33,284
Watertown, NY 13601–03 • 29,429
Watertown, SD 57201 • 17,592
Watertown, TN 37184 • 1,250
Watertown, WI 53094 • 19,142
Water Valley, MS 38965 • 3,610
Waterville, ME 04901–03 • 17,173
Waterville, MN 56096 • 1,771
Waterville, NY 13480 • 1,664
Waterville, OH 43566 • 4,517
Watervliet, MI 49098 • 1,867
Watervliet, NY 12189 • 11,061
Watford City, ND 58854 • 1,784
Wathena, KS 66090 • 1,160
Watkins Glen, NY 14891 • 2,207
Watkinsville, GA 30677 • 1,600
Watonga, OK 73772 • 3,408
Watonwan □, MN • 11,682
Watseka, IL 60970 • 5,424
Watsontown, PA 17777 • 2,310
Watsonville, CA 95076–77 • 31,099
Wattsville, SC 29360 • 1,324
Wauchula, FL 33873 • 3,253
Wauconda, IL 60084 • 6,294
Waukee, IA 50263 • 2,512
Waukegan, IL 60085–87 • 69,392
Waukesha, WI 53186–88 • 56,958
Waukesha □, WI • 304,715
Waukomis, OK 73773 • 1,322
Waukon, IA 52172 • 4,019
Waunakee, WI 53597 • 5,897
Waupaca, WI 54981 • 4,957
Waupaca □, WI • 46,104
Waupun, WI 53963 • 8,207

Wauregan, CT 06387 • 1,200
Waurika, OK 73573 • 2,088
Wausau, WI 54401–02 • 37,060
Wauseon, OH 43567 • 6,322
Waushara □, WI • 19,385
Wautoma, WI 54982 • 1,784
Wauwatosa, WI 53213 • 49,366
Waveland, MS 39576 • 5,369
Waverly, IL 62692 • 1,402
Waverly, IA 50677 • 8,539
Waverly, MI 48917 • 15,614
Waverly, NE 68462 • 1,869
Waverly, NY 14892 • 4,787
Waverly, OH 45690 • 4,477
Waverly, TN 37185 • 3,925
Waverly, VA 23890 • 2,223
Waxahachie, TX 75165 • 18,168
Waxhaw, NC 28173 • 1,294
Waycross, GA 31501 • 16,410
Wayland, MA 01778 • 2,550
Wayland, MI 49348 • 2,751
Wayland, NY 14572 • 1,976
Waylyn, SC 29405 • 2,400
Waymart, PA 18472 • 1,337
Wayne, MI 48184–88 • 19,899
Wayne, NE 68787 • 5,142
Wayne, NJ 07470–74 • 47,025
Wayne, WV 25570 • 1,128
Wayne □, GA • 22,356
Wayne □, IL • 17,241
Wayne □, IN • 71,951
Wayne □, IA • 7,067
Wayne □, KY • 17,468
Wayne □, MI • 2,111,687
Wayne □, MS • 19,517
Wayne □, MO • 11,543
Wayne □, NE • 9,364
Wayne □, NY • 89,123
Wayne □, NC • 104,666
Wayne □, OH • 101,461
Wayne □, PA • 39,944
Wayne □, TN • 13,935
Wayne □, UT • 2,177
Wayne □, WV • 41,636
Wayne City, IL 62895 • 1,099
Waynesboro, GA 30830 • 5,701
Waynesboro, MS 39367 • 5,143
Waynesboro, PA 17268 • 9,578
Waynesboro, TN 38485 • 1,824
Waynesboro, VA 22980 • 18,549
Waynesburg, OH 44688 • 1,068
Waynesburg, PA 15370 • 4,270
Waynesville, MO 65583 • 3,207
Waynesville, NC 28786 • 6,758
Waynesville, OH 45068 • 1,949
Waynewood, VA 22308 • 5,000
Wayzata, MN 55391 • 3,806
Weakley □, TN • 31,972
Weatherford, OK 73096 • 10,124
Weatherford, TX 76086–87 • 14,804
Weatherly, PA 18255 • 2,640
Weatogue, CT 06089 • 2,521
Weaver, AL 36277 • 2,715
Weaverville, CA 96093 • 3,370
Weaverville, NC 28787 • 2,107
Webb, AL 36376 • 1,039
Webb □, TX • 133,239
Webb City, MO 64870 • 7,449
Webberville, MI 48892 • 1,698
Weber □, UT • 158,330
Weber City, VA 24251 • 1,377
Webster, MA 01570 • 11,849
Webster, NY 14580 • 5,464
Webster, PA 15087 • 1,000
Webster, SD 57274 • 2,017
Webster □, GA • 2,263
Webster □, IA • 40,342
Webster □, KY • 13,955
Webster □, LA • 41,989
Webster □, MS • 10,222
Webster □, MO • 23,753
Webster □, NE • 4,279
Webster □, WV • 10,729
Webster City, IA 50595 • 7,894
Webster Groves, MO 63119 • 22,987
Websterville, VT 05678 • 600
Wedgewood, MO 63031 • 6,700
Weed, CA 96094 • 3,062
Weed Heights, NV 89447 • 230
Weedsport, NY 13166 • 1,996
Weehawken, NJ 07087 • 12,385
Weeping Water, NE 68463 • 1,008
Weigelstown, PA 17315 • 8,665
Weimar, TX 78962 • 2,052
Weippe, ID 83553 • 532
Weirsdale, FL 32195 • 1,500
Weirton, WV 26062 • 22,124
Weiser, ID 83672 • 4,571
Wekiva Springs, FL 32750 • 23,026
Welch, WV 24801 • 3,028
Welcome, SC 29611 • 6,560
Weld □, CO • 131,821
Weldon, NC 27890 • 1,392
Weleetka, OK 74880 • 1,112
Wellesley, MA 02181 • 26,615
Wellfleet, MA 02007 • 1,200
Wellford, SC 29385 • 2,511
Wellington, CO 80549 • 1,340
Wellington, FL 33414 • 20,670
Wellington, KS 67152 • 8,411
Wellington, NV 89444 • 280
Wellington, OH 44090 • 4,140
Wellington, TX 79095 • 2,456
Wellington, UT 84542 • 1,632
Wellman, IA 52356 • 1,085
Wells, ME 04090 • 1,200
Wells, MI 49894 • 1,150
Wells, MN 56097 • 2,465
Wells, NV 89835 • 1,256
Wells □, IN • 25,948
Wells □, ND • 5,864
Wellsboro, PA 16901 • 3,430
Wellsburg, WV 26070 • 3,385
Wellston, OH 45692 • 6,049
Wellsville, KS 66092 • 1,563
Wellsville, MO 63384 • 1,430
Wellsville, NY 14895 • 5,241
Wellsville, OH 43968 • 4,532
Wellsville, UT 84339 • 2,206
Wellton, AZ 85356 • 1,066
Welsh, LA 70591 • 3,299
Wenatchee, WA 98801–07 • 21,756
Wendell, ID 83355 • 1,963

Wendell, NC 27591 • 2,822
Wendover, UT 84083 • 1,127
Wenham, MA 01984 • 3,897
Wenonah, NJ 08090 • 2,331
Wentzville, MO 63385 • 5,088
Weslaco, TX 78596 • 21,877
Wesleyville, PA 16510 • 3,655
Wessington Springs, SD 57382 • 1,083
Wesson, MS 39191 • 1,510
West, TX 76691 • 2,515
West Acton, MA 01720 • 5,230
West Alexandria, OH 45381 • 1,460
West Allis, WI 53214 • 63,221
West Andover, MA 01810 • 1,970
West Athens, CA 90247 • 8,859
West Babylon, NY 11704 • 42,410
West Barnstable, MA 02668 • 1,000
West Baton Rouge □, LA • 19,419
West Bay Shore, NY 11706 • 4,907
West Bend, WI 53095 • 23,916
West Berlin, NJ 08091 • 2,970
West Billerica, MA 01862 • 1,920
West Blocton, AL 35184 • 1,468
Westborough, MA 01581 • 3,917
West Bountiful, UT 84087 • 4,477
West Boylston, MA 01583 • 3,130
West Bradenton, FL 34205 • 4,528
West Branch, IA 52358 • 1,908
West Branch, MI 48661 • 1,914
West Bridgewater, MA 02379 • 2,140
Westbrook, CT 06498 • 2,060
Westbrook, ME 04092 • 16,121
West Brookfield, MA 01585 • 1,419
West Burlington, IA 52655 • 3,083
Westbury, NY 11590 • 13,060
Westby, WI 54667 • 1,866
West Caldwell, NJ 07004 • 10,422
West Cape May, NJ 08204 • 1,026
West Carroll □, LA • 12,093
West Carrollton, OH 45449 • 14,403
West Carson, CA 90502 • 20,143
West Carthage, NY 13619 • 2,166
West Chatham, MA 02669 • 1,504
Westchester, FL 33136 • 29,883
Westchester, IL 60153 • 17,301
West Chester, PA 19380–82 • 18,041
Westchester □, NY • 874,866
West Chicago, IL 60185–86 • 14,796
West Columbia, SC 29169–72 • 10,588
West Columbia, TX 77486 • 4,372
West Compton, CA 90220 • 5,451
West Concord, MA 01742 • 5,761
West Concord, NC 28027 • 5,859
West Covina, CA 91790–93 • 96,086
West Crossett, AR 71635 • 2,019
West Dennis, MA 02670 • 2,307
West Des Moines, IA 50265 • 31,702
West Elmira, NY 14905 • 5,218
Westerly, RI 02891 • 16,477
Westernport, MD 21562 • 2,454
Western Springs, IL 60558 • 11,984
Westerville, OH 43081–82 • 30,269
West Fairview, PA 17025 • 1,403
West Falmouth, MA 02574 • 1,600
West Fargo, ND 58078 • 12,287
West Feliciana □, LA • 12,915
Westfield, IN 46074 • 3,304
Westfield, MA 01085–86 • 38,372
Westfield, NJ 07090–92 • 28,870
Westfield, NY 14787 • 3,451
Westfield, PA 16950 • 1,119
Westfield, WI 53964 • 1,125
Westford, MA 01886 • 1,200
West Fork, AR 72774 • 1,607
West Frankfort, IL 62896 • 8,526
West Freehold, NJ 07728 • 11,166
Westgate, FL 33401 • 2,100
West Gate, VA 22110 • 6,565
West Gate of Lomond, VA 22110 • 5,400
West Glens Falls, NY 12801 • 5,964
West Goshen, PA 19380 • 8,948
West Grove, PA 19390 • 2,128
Westham, VA 23229 • 3,200
West Hanover, MA 02339 • 1,700
West Hartford, CT 06127 • 60,110
West Haven, CT 06516 • 54,021
West Haven, OR 97225 • 3,400
West Haverstraw, NY 10993 • 9,183
West Hazleton, PA 18201 • 4,136
West Helena, AR 72390 • 9,695
West Hempstead, NY 11552 • 17,689
West Hollywood, CA 90069 • 36,118
Westhope, ND 58793 • 578
West Hyannisport, MA 02672 • 1,200
West Islip, NY 11795 • 28,419
West Jefferson, NC 28694 • 1,002
West Jefferson, OH 43162 • 4,504
West Jordan, UT 84084 • 42,892
West Kingston, RI 02892 • 1,150
West Lafayette, IN 47906–07 • 25,907
West Lafayette, OH 43845 • 2,129
Westlake, LA 70669 • 5,007
Westlake, OH 44145 • 27,018
Westlake Village, CA 91361 • 7,455
Westland, MI 48185 • 84,724
West Lawn, PA 19609 • 1,606
West Liberty, IA 52776 • 2,935
West Liberty, KY 41472 • 1,887
West Liberty, OH 43357 • 1,613
West Liberty, WV 26074 • 1,434
West Linn, OR 97068 • 16,367
West Long Branch, NJ 07764 • 7,690
West Marion, NC 28752 • 1,291
West Medway, MA 02053 • 1,940
West Melbourne, FL 32901 • 8,399
West Memphis, AR 72301 • 28,259
Westmere, NY 12203 • 6,750
West Miami, FL 33174 • 5,727
West Mifflin, PA 15122–23 • 23,644
West Milford, NJ 07480 • 25,430
West Milton, OH 45383 • 4,348
West Milwaukee, WI 53214 • 3,973
Westminster, CA 92683–84 • 78,118
Westminster, CO 80030–31 • 74,625
Westminster, MD 21157 • 13,068
Westminster, SC 29693 • 3,120
West Modesto, CA 95351 • 6,135
West Monroe, LA 71291–94 • 14,096
Westmont, CA 90044 • 31,100
Westmont, IL 60559 • 21,228
Westmont, NJ 08108 • 5,630
Westmont, PA 15905 • 5,789
Westmoreland, TN 37186 • 1,726

Westmoreland □, PA • 370,321
Westmoreland □, VA • 15,480
Westmorland, CA 92281 • 1,380
West Mystic, CT 06388 • 3,595
West Newton, PA 15089 • 3,152
West New York, NJ 07093 • 38,125
West Norriton, PA 19401 • 15,209
West Nyack, NY 10960 • 3,437
Weston, CT 06883 • 1,370
Weston, MA 02193 • 11,169
Weston, MO 64098 • 1,528
Weston, OH 43569 • 1,716
Weston, WV 26452 • 4,994
Weston, WI 54476 • 9,714
Weston □, WY • 6,518
West Orange, NJ 07052 • 39,103
Westover, WV 26505 • 4,201
West Palm Beach, FL 33401–20 • 67,643
West Pasco, WA 99301 • 7,312
West Paterson, NJ 07424 • 10,982
West Pawlet, VT 05775 • 350
West Pensacola, FL 32505 • 22,107
West Peoria, IL 61604 • 5,314
West Pittsburg, CA 94565 • 17,453
West Pittsburg, PA 16160 • 1,133
West Pittston, PA 18643 • 5,590
West Plains, MO 65775 • 8,913
West Point, CA 95255 • 1,500
West Point, GA 31833 • 3,571
West Point, IA 52656 • 1,079
West Point, KY 40177 • 1,216
West Point, MS 39773 • 8,489
West Point, NE 68788 • 3,250
West Point, NY 10996–97 • 8,024
West Point, UT 84015 • 4,258
West Point, VA 23181 • 2,938
Westport, CT 06880–83 • 24,407
Westport, IN 47283 • 1,478
Westport, WA 98595 • 1,892
West Portsmouth, OH 45662 • 3,551
West Puente Valley, CA 91744 • 20,254
West Reading, PA 19611 • 4,142
West Rutland, VT 05777 • 2,246
West Sacramento, CA 95691 • 28,898
West Saint Paul, MN 55118 • 19,248
West Salem, IL 62476 • 1,042
West Salem, OH 44287 • 1,534
West Salem, WI 54669 • 3,611
West Sayville, NY 11796 • 4,680
West Seneca, NY 14224 • 47,866
West Simsbury, CT 06092 • 2,149
West Slope, OR 97225 • 7,959
West Springfield, MA 01089–90 • 27,537
West Springfield, VA 22152 • 28,126
West Swanzey, NH 03469 • 1,055
West Terre Haute, IN 47885 • 2,495
West Union, IA 52175 • 2,490
West Union, OH 45693 • 3,096
West Unity, OH 43570 • 1,677
West University Place, TX 77005 • 12,920
West Upton, MA 01587 • 1,300
Westvale, NY 13219 • 5,952
West Valley City, UT 84120 • 86,976
Westview, FL 33168 • 9,668
West View, PA 15229 • 7,734
Westville, IL 61883 • 3,387
Westville, IN 46391 • 5,255
Westville, NJ 08093 • 4,573
Westville, OK 74965 • 1,374
West Wareham, MA 02576 • 2,059
West Warren, MA 01092 • 1,200
West Warwick, RI 02893 • 29,268
West Webster, NY 14580 • 8,690
Westwego, LA 70094–96 • 11,218
West Whittier, CA 90606 • 13,800
West Willow, MI 48198 • 4,300
Westwood, CA 96137 • 2,017
Westwood, KS 66205 • 1,772
Westwood, KY 41101 • 5,300
Westwood, MA 02090 • 6,500
Westwood, MI 49007 • 8,957
Westwood, NJ 07675 • 10,446
Westwood Lakes, FL 33165 • 11,522
West Wyoming, PA 18644 • 3,117
West Yarmouth, MA 02673 • 5,409
West Yellowstone, MT 59758 • 913
West York, PA 17404 • 4,283
Wethersfield, CT 06129 • 25,651
Wetumka, OK 74883 • 1,427
Wetumpka, AL 36092 • 4,670
Wetzel □, WV • 19,258
Wewahitchka, FL 32465 • 1,779
Wewoka, OK 74884 • 4,050
Wexford □, MI • 26,360
Weyauwega, WI 54983 • 1,665
Weymouth, MA 02188 • 54,063
Whalom, MA 01420 • 1,340
Wharton, NJ 07885 • 5,405
Wharton, TX 77488 • 9,011
Wharton □, TX • 39,955
Whatcom □, WA • 127,780
Wheatland, CA 95692 • 1,631
Wheatland, WY 82201 • 3,271
Wheatland □, MT • 2,246
Wheaton, IL 60187–89 • 51,464
Wheaton, MD 20902 • 58,300
Wheaton, MN 56296 • 1,615
Wheat Ridge, CO 80033–34 • 29,419
Wheeler, TX 79096 • 1,393
Wheeler □, GA • 4,903
Wheeler □, NE • 948
Wheeler □, OR • 1,396
Wheeler □, TX • 5,879
Wheelersburg, OH 45694 • 5,113
Wheeling, IL 60090 • 29,911
Wheeling, WV 26003 • 34,882
Whitacres, CT 00000 • 2,110
White □, AR • 54,676
White □, GA • 13,006
White □, IL • 16,522
White □, IN • 23,265
White □, TN • 20,090
White Bear Lake, MN 55110 • 24,704
White Bluff, TN 37187 • 1,988
White Castle, LA 70788 • 2,102
White Center, WA 98126 • 15,700
White City, OR 97503 • 5,891
White City, UT 84070 • 6,506
White Cloud, MI 49349 • 1,147
White Deer, TX 79097 • 1,125
Whitefield, NH 03598 • 1,041
Whitefish, MT 59937 • 4,368
Whitefish Bay, WI 53217 • 14,272

White Hall, AR 71602 • 3,849
White Hall, IL 62092 • 2,814
Whitehall, MI 49461 • 3,027
Whitehall, MT 59759 • 1,067
Whitehall, NY 12887 • 3,071
Whitehall, OH 43213 • 20,572
Whitehall, PA 15227 • 14,451
Whitehall, WI 54773 • 1,494
White Haven, PA 18661 • 1,132
White Horse, NJ 08610 • 9,397
White Horse Beach, MA 02381 • 1,200
Whitehouse, OH 43571 • 2,528
White House, TN 37188 • 2,987
White House Station, NJ 08889 • 1,400
White Island Shores, MA 02538 • 2,000
White Meadow Lake, NJ 07866 • 8,002
White Oak, MD 20901 • 18,671
White Oak, OH 45239 • 12,430
White Oak, PA 15131 • 8,761
White Pigeon, MI 49099 • 1,458
White Pine, MI 49971 • 1,142
White Pine, TN 37890 • 1,771
White Pine □, NV • 9,264
White Plains, MD 20695 • 3,560
White Plains, NY 10601–07 • 48,718
Whiteriver, AZ 85941 • 3,775
White River Junction, VT 05001 • 2,521
White Rock, NM 87544 • 6,192
White Salmon, WA 98672 • 1,861
Whitesboro, NY 13492 • 4,195
Whitesboro, TX 76273 • 3,209
Whitesburg, KY 41858 • 1,636
White Settlement, TX 76108 • 15,472
Whiteside □, IL • 60,186
White Sulphur Springs, MT 59645 • 963
White Sulphur Springs, WV 24986 • 2,779
Whiteville, NC 28472 • 5,078
Whiteville, TN 38075 • 1,050
Whitewater, WI 53190 • 12,636
Whitewood, SD 57793 • 891
Whitewright, TX 75491 • 1,713
Whitfield □, GA • 72,462
Whitfield Estates, FL 34243 • 3,152
Whiting, IN 46394 • 5,155
Whiting, WI 54481 • 1,838
Whitinsville, MA 01588 • 5,639
Whitley □, IN • 27,651
Whitley □, KY • 33,326
Whitley City, KY 42653 • 1,133
Whitman, MA 02382 • 13,534
Whitman, WV 25652 • 1,651
Whitman □, WA • 38,775
Whitman Square, NJ 08012 • 3,490
Whitmire, SC 29178 • 1,702
Whitmore Lake, MI 48189 • 3,251
Whitmore Village, HI 96786 • 3,373
Whitney, SC 29303 • 4,052
Whitney, TX 76692 • 1,626
Whitney Point, NY 13862 • 1,054
Whittier, AK 99693 • 243
Whittier, CA 90601–12 • 77,671
Whitwell, TN 37397 • 1,622
Wibaux, MT 59353 • 628
Wibaux □, MT • 1,191
Wichita, KS 67201–78 • 304,011
Wichita □, KS • 2,758
Wichita □, TX • 122,378
Wichita Falls, TX 76301–11 • 96,259
Wickenburg, AZ 85358 • 4,515
Wickliffe, OH 44092 • 14,558
Wickliffe, OH 44515 • 7,240
Wicomico □, MD • 74,339
Wiconisco, PA 17097 • 1,321
Widefield, CO 80911 • 12,112
Wiggins, MS 39577 • 3,185
Wilbarger □, TX • 15,121
Wilber, NE 68465 • 1,527
Wilberforce, OH 45384 • 2,639
Wilbraham, MA 01095 • 3,352
Wilburton, OK 74578 • 3,092
Wilcox, PA 15870 • 1,000
Wilcox □, AL • 13,568
Wilcox □, GA • 7,008
Wilder, ID 83676 • 1,232
Wilder, VT 05088 • 1,576
Wildorado, TX 79098 • 2,000
Wildwood, FL 34785 • 3,421
Wildwood, IL 60030 • 2,034
Wildwood, NJ 08260 • 4,484
Wildwood Crest, NJ 08260 • 3,631
Wilkes □, GA • 10,597
Wilkes □, NC • 59,393
Wilkes-Barre, PA 18701–73 • 47,523
Wilkesboro, NC 28697 • 2,573
Wilkin □, MN • 7,516
Wilkinsburg, PA 15221 • 21,080
Wilkinson □, GA • 10,228
Wilkinson □, MS • 9,678
Wilkins Township, PA 15145 • 7,487
Will □, IL • 357,313
Willacoochee, GA 31650 • 1,205
Willacy □, TX • 17,705
Willamina, OR 97396 • 1,717
Willard, MO 65781 • 2,177
Willard, NY 14588 • 1,339
Willard, OH 44890 • 6,210
Willard, UT 84340 • 1,298
Willcox, AZ 85643 • 3,122
Williams, AZ 86046 • 2,532
Williams, CA 95987 • 2,297
Williams □, ND • 21,129
Williams □, OH • 30,950
Williams Bay, WI 53191 • 2,108
Williamsburg, IA 52361 • 2,174
Williamsburg, KY 40769 • 5,493
Williamsburg, MA 01096 • 1,200
Williamsburg, OH 45176 • 2,322
Williamsburg, PA 16693 • 1,456
Williamsburg, VA 23185–88 • 11,530
Williamsburg □, SC • 36,815
Williamson, NY 14589 • 1,768
Williamson, WV 25661 • 4,154
Williamson □, IL • 57,733
Williamson □, TN • 81,021
Williamson □, TX • 139,551
Williamsport, IN 47993 • 1,798
Williamsport, MD 21795 • 2,103
Williamsport, PA 17701–03 • 31,933
Williamston, MI 48895 • 2,922
Williamston, NC 27892 • 5,503
Williamston, SC 29697 • 3,876
Williamstown, KY 41097 • 3,023
Williamstown, MA 01267 • 4,791

Williamstown, NJ 08094 • *10,891*
Williamstown, PA 17098 • *1,509*
Williamstown, VT 05679 • *650*
Williamstown, WV 26187 • *2,774*
Williamsville, IL 62693 • *1,140*
Williamsville, NY 14221 • *5,583*
Willimantic, CT 06226 • *14,746*
Willingboro, NJ 08046 • *36,291*
Willis, TX 77378 • *2,764*
Williston, FL 32696 • *2,179*
Williston, ND 58801–02 • *13,131*
Williston, SC 29853 • *3,099*
Williston Park, NY 11596 • *7,516*
Willits, CA 95490 • *5,027*
Willmar, MN 56201 • *17,531*
Willoughby, OH 44094–95 • *20,510*
Willoughby Hills, OH 44092 • *8,427*
Willow Brook, CA 90222 • *32,772*
Willowbrook, IL 60521 • *8,598*
Willow Grove, PA 19090 • *16,325*
Willowick, OH 44094 • *15,269*
Willow Run, DE 19805 • *1,600*
Willow Run, MI 48198 • *7,200*
Willows, CA 95988 • *5,988*
Willow Springs, IL 60480 • *4,509*
Willow Springs, MO 65793 • *2,038*
Willston, VA 22044 • *2,000*
Wilmerding, PA 15148 • *2,222*
Wilmette, IL 60091 • *26,690*
Wilmington, DE 19801–99 • *71,529*
Wilmington, IL 60481 • *4,743*
Wilmington, MA 01887 • *17,654*
Wilmington, NC 28401–12 • *55,530*
Wilmington, OH 45177 • *11,199*
Wilmington, VT 05363 • *550*
Wilmington Island, GA 31410 • *11,230*
Wilmington Manor, DE 19720 • *8,568*
Wilmington Manor Gardens, DE 19720 • *1,500*
Wilmore, KY 40390 • *4,215*
Wilmot, AR 71676 • *1,047*
Wilson, AR 72395 • *1,068*
Wilson, NY 14172 • *1,307*
Wilson, NC 27893–95 • *36,930*
Wilson, OK 73463 • *1,639*
Wilson, PA 18042 • *7,830*
Wilson, WY 83014 • *500*
Wilson □, KS • *10,289*
Wilson □, NC • *66,061*
Wilson □, TN • *67,675*
Wilson □, TX • *22,650*
Wilsonville, AL 35186 • *1,185*
Wilsonville, OR 97070 • *7,106*
Wilton, CT 06897 • *7,200*
Wilton, IA 52778 • *2,577*
Wilton, ME 04294 • *2,453*
Wilton, NH 03086 • *1,165*
Wilton, ND 58579 • *728*
Wilton Manors, FL 33334 • *11,804*
Wimauma, FL 33598 • *2,932*
Winamac, IN 46996 • *2,262*
Winchendon, MA 01475 • *4,316*
Winchester, IL 62694 • *1,769*
Winchester, IN 47394 • *5,095*
Winchester, KY 40391–92 • *15,799*
Winchester, MA 01890 • *20,267*
Winchester, NV 89101 • *23,365*
Winchester, NH 03470 • *1,735*
Winchester, TN 37398 • *6,305*
Winchester, VA 22601 • *21,947*
Windber, PA 15963 • *4,756*
Windcrest, TX 78239 • *5,331*
Winder, GA 30680 • *7,373*
Windgap, PA 18091 • *2,741*
Windham, CT 06280 • *1,100*
Windham, OH 44288 • *2,943*
Windham □, CT • *102,525*
Windham □, VT • *41,588*
Wind Lake, WI 53185 • *3,000*
Windom, MN 56101 • *4,283*
Window Rock, AZ 86515 • *3,306*
Wind Point, WI 53402 • *1,941*
Windsor, CO 80550 • *5,062*
Windsor, CT 06095 • *27,817*
Windsor, IL 61957 • *1,143*
Windsor, MO 65360 • *3,044*
Windsor, NC 27983 • *2,056*
Windsor, PA 17366 • *1,355*
Windsor, VT 05089 • *3,478*
Windsor, VA 23487 • *1,025*
Windsor □, VT • *54,055*
Windsor Heights, IA 50311 • *5,190*
Windsor Hills, CA 90052 • *6,200*
Windsor Locks, CT 06096 • *12,358*
Windy Hill, SC 29506 • *1,622*
Windy Hills, DE 19711 • *1,130*
Winfield, AL 35594 • *3,689*
Winfield, IA 52659 • *1,051*
Winfield, KS 67156 • *11,931*
Winfield, NJ 07036 • *1,785*
Winfield, WV 25213 • *1,164*
Wingate, NC 28174 • *2,821*
Wink, TX 79789 • *1,189*
Winkler □, TX • *8,626*
Winlock, WA 98596 • *1,027*
Winn □, LA • *16,269*
Winnebago, IL 61088 • *1,840*
Winnebago, MN 56098 • *1,565*
Winnebago, WI 54985 • *1,433*
Winnebago □, IL • *252,913*
Winnebago □, IA • *12,122*
Winnebago □, WI • *140,320*
Winneconne, WI 54986 • *2,059*
Winnemucca, NV 89445 • *6,134*
Winner, SD 57580 • *3,354*
Winneshiek □, IA • *20,847*
Winnetka, IL 60093 • *12,174*
Winnfield, LA 71483 • *6,138*
Winnsboro, LA 71295 • *5,755*
Winnsboro, SC 29180 • *3,475*
Winnsboro, TX 75494 • *2,904*
Winnsboro Mills, SC 29180 • *2,275*
Winona, MN 55987 • *25,399*
Winona, MS 38967 • *5,705*
Winona, MO 65588 • *1,081*
Winona □, MN • *47,828*
Winona Lake, IN 46590 • *4,053*
Winooski, VT 05404 • *6,649*
Winslow, AZ 86047 • *8,190*
Winslow, ME 04901 • *5,436*
Winsted, CT 06098 • *8,254*
Winsted, MN 55395 • *1,581*
Winston, FL 33801 • *9,118*
Winston, OR 97496 • *3,773*
Winston □, AL • *22,053*
Winston □, MS • *19,433*
Winston-Salem, NC 27101–27 • *143,485*
Winter Garden, FL 34787 • *9,745*
Winter Haven, FL 33880–84 • *24,725*
Winter Park, FL 32789–90 • *22,242*
Winter Park, NC 28403 • *4,504*
Winterport, ME 04496 • *1,274*
Winters, CA 95694 • *4,639*
Winters, TX 79567 • *2,905*
Winterset, IA 50273 • *4,196*
Winter Springs, FL 32708 • *22,151*
Wintersville, OH 43952 • *4,102*
Winterville, NC 28590 • *2,816*
Winthrop, ME 04364 • *2,819*
Winthrop, MA 02152 • *18,127*
Winthrop, MN 55396 • *1,279*
Winthrop Harbor, IL 60096 • *6,240*
Winton, CA 95388 • *7,559*
Wirt □, WV • *5,192*
Wiscasset, ME 04578 • *1,350*
Wisconsin Dells, WI 53965 • *2,393*
Wisconsin Rapids, WI 54494–95 • *18,245*
Wise, VA 24293 • *3,193*
Wise □, TX • *34,679*
Wise □, VA • *39,573*
Wishek, ND 58495 • *1,171*
Wisner, LA 71378 • *1,153*
Wisner, NE 68791 • *1,253*
Withamsville, OH 45245 • *5,000*
Witherbee, NY 12998 • *1,000*
Wittenberg, WI 54499 • *1,145*
Wixom, MI 48393 • *8,550*
Woburn, MA 01801 • *35,943*
Wolcott, CT 06716 • *6,070*
Wolcott, NY 14590 • *1,544*
Wolfe □, KY • *6,503*
Wolfeboro, NH 03894 • *2,783*
Wolfe City, TX 75496 • *1,505*
Wolf Lake, MI 49442 • *4,110*
Wolf Point, MT 59201 • *2,880*
Wolf Trap, VA 22182 • *13,133*
Womelsdorf, PA 19567 • *2,270*
Wonder Lake, IL 60097 • *6,664*
Wood □, OH • *113,269*
Wood □, TX • *29,380*
Wood □, WV • *86,915*
Wood □, WI • *73,605*
Woodbine, GA 31569 • *1,212*
Woodbine, IA 51579 • *1,500*
Woodbine, NJ 08270 • *2,678*
Woodbourne, NY 12788 • *1,155*
Woodbourne, OH 45459 • *6,000*
Woodbridge, CT 06525 • *7,924*
Woodbridge, NJ 07095 • *17,434*
Woodbridge, VA 22191–94 • *26,401*
Woodbridge [Township], NJ 07095 • *17,434*
Woodburn, IN 46797 • *1,321*
Woodburn, OR 97071 • *13,404*
Woodbury, CT 06798 • *1,212*
Woodbury, GA 30293 • *1,429*
Woodbury, MN 55125 • *20,075*
Woodbury, NJ 08096 • *10,904*
Woodbury, NY 11797 • *8,008*
Woodbury, TN 37190 • *2,287*
Woodbury □, IA • *98,276*
Woodcliff Lake, NJ 07675 • *5,303*
Wood Dale, IL 60191 • *12,425*
Woodfield, SC 29206 • *8,862*
Woodford □, IL • *32,653*
Woodford □, KY • *19,955*
Woodhaven, MI 48183 • *11,631*
Woodlake, CA 93286 • *5,678*
Woodland, CA 95695 • *39,802*
Woodland, ME 04694 • *1,287*
Woodland, WA 98674 • *2,500*
Woodland Park, CO 80863 • *4,610*
Woodlawn, KY 42001 • *1,600*
Woodlawn, MD 21207 • *5,329*
Woodlawn, MD 20784 • *5,329*
Woodlawn, OH 45215 • *2,674*
Woodlawn, VA 24381 • *1,689*
Woodlynne, NJ 08107 • *2,547*
Woodmere, NY 11598 • *15,578*
Woodmont, CT 06460 • *1,770*
Woodmoor, MD 21207 • *8,630*
Woodridge, IL 60517 • *26,256*
Wood-Ridge, NJ 07075 • *7,506*
Wood River, IL 62095 • *11,490*
Wood River, NE 68883 • *1,156*
Woodruff, SC 29388 • *4,365*
Woodruff, WI 54568 • *1,500*
Woodruff □, AR • *9,520*
Woods □, OK • *9,103*
Woodsboro, TX 78393 • *1,731*
Woods Cross, UT 84087 • *5,384*
Woodsfield, OH 43793 • *2,832*
Woods Hole, MA 02543 • *1,080*
Woodside, CA 94062 • *5,035*
Woodson □, KS • *4,116*
Woodstock, GA 30188 • *4,361*
Woodstock, IL 60098 • *14,353*
Woodstock, NY 12498 • *1,870*
Woodstock, VT 05091 • *1,037*
Woodstock, VA 22664 • *3,182*
Woodstown, NJ 08098 • *3,154*
Woodsville, NH 03785 • *1,122*
Woodville, FL 32362 • *2,760*
Woodville, MS 39669 • *1,393*
Woodville, OH 43469 • *1,953*
Woodville, TX 75979 • *2,636*
Woodward, IA 50276 • *1,197*
Woodward, OK 73801–02 • *12,340*
Woodward □, OK • *18,976*
Woodway, TX 76710 • *8,695*
Woonsocket, RI 02895 • *43,877*
Woonsocket, SD 57385 • *766*
Wooster, OH 44691 • *22,191*
Worcester, MA 01601–15 • *169,759*
Worcester □, MD • *35,028*
Worcester □, MA • *709,705*
Worland, WY 82401 • *5,742*
Worth, IL 60482 • *11,208*
Worth □, GA • *19,745*
Worth □, IA • *7,991*
Worth □, MO • *2,440*
Wortham, TX 76693 • *1,020*
Worthington, IN 47471 • *1,473*
Worthington, KY 41183 • *1,751*
Worthington, MN 56187 • *9,977*
Worthington, OH 43085 • *14,869*
Wrangell, AK 99929 • *2,479*
Wray, CO 80758 • *1,998*
Wrens, GA 30833 • *2,414*
Wrentham, MA 02093 • *2,110*
Wright, FL 32548 • *18,945*
Wright □, IA • *14,269*
Wright □, MN • *68,710*
Wright □, MO • *16,758*
Wright City, MO 63390 • *1,250*
Wrightstown, NJ 08562 • *3,843*
Wrightstown, WI 54180 • *1,262*
Wrightsville, AR 72183 • *1,062*
Wrightsville, GA 31096 • *2,331*
Wrightsville, PA 17368 • *2,396*
Wrightsville Beach, NC 28480 • *2,937*
Wrightwood, CA 92397 • *3,308*
Wurtsboro, NY 12790 • *1,048*
Wyandanch, NY 11798 • *8,950*
Wyandot □, OH • *22,254*
Wyandotte, MI 48192 • *30,938*
Wyandotte □, KS • *161,993*
Wyanet, IL 61379 • *1,017*
Wyckoff, NJ 07481 • *15,372*
Wymore, NE 68466 • *1,611*
Wynne, AR 72396–97 • *8,187*
Wynnewood, OK 73098 • *2,451*
Wyoming, DE 19934 • *977*
Wyoming, IL 61491 • *1,462*
Wyoming, MI 49509 • *63,891*
Wyoming, MN 55092 • *2,142*
Wyoming, OH 45215 • *8,128*
Wyoming, PA 18644 • *3,255*
Wyoming □, NY • *42,507*
Wyoming □, PA • *28,076*
Wyoming □, WV • *28,990*
Wyomissing, PA 19610 • *7,332*
Wythe □, VA • *25,466*
Wytheville, VA 24382 • *8,038*

X

Xenia, OH 45385 • *24,664*

Y

Yadkin □, NC • *30,488*
Yadkinville, NC 27055 • *2,525*
Yakima, WA 98901–09 • *54,827*
Yakima □, WA • *188,823*
Yakutat, AK 99689 • *534*
Yale, MI 48097 • *1,977*
Yale, OK 74085 • *1,392*
Yalobusha □, MS • *12,033*
Yamhill □, OR • *65,551*
Yancey □, NC • *15,419*
Yanceyville, NC 27379 • *1,973*
Yankton, SD 57078 • *12,703*
Yankton □, SD • *19,252*
Yaphank, NY 11980 • *5,000*
Yardley, PA 19067 • *2,288*
Yardville, NJ 08620 • *6,190*
Yarmouth, ME 04096 • *3,338*
Yarmouth, MA 02675 • *1,200*
Yarnell, AZ 85362 • *1,500*
Yates □, NY • *22,810*
Yates Center, KS 66783 • *1,815*
Yavapai □, AZ • *107,714*
Yazoo □, MS • *25,506*
Yazoo City, MS 39194 • *12,427*
Yeadon, PA 19050 • *11,980*
Yeagertown, PA 17099 • *1,150*
Yell □, AR • *17,759*
Yellow Medicine □, MN • *11,684*
Yellow Springs, OH 45387 • *3,973*
Yellowstone □, MT • *113,419*
Yellowstone National Park, WY 82190 • *400*
Yellowstone National Park □, MT • *52*
Yellville, AR 72687 • *1,181*
Yelm, WA 98597 • *1,337*
Yerington, NV 89447 • *2,367*
Yermo, CA 92398 • *1,092*
Yoakum, TX 77995 • *5,611*
Yoakum □, TX • *8,786*
Yolo □, CA • *141,092*
Yonkers, NY 10701–10 • *188,082*
Yorba Linda, CA 92686 • *52,422*
York, AL 36925 • *3,160*
York, ME 03909 • *3,130*
York, NE 68467 • *7,884*
York, PA 17401–07 • *42,192*
York, SC 29745 • *6,709*
York □, ME • *164,587*
York □, NE • *14,428*
York □, PA • *339,574*
York □, SC • *131,497*
York □, VA • *42,422*
Yorketown, NJ 07726 • *6,313*
York Harbor, ME 03911 • *2,555*
Yorklyn, DE 19736 • *600*
Yorkshire, NY 14173 • *1,340*
Yorktown, IN 47396 • *4,106*
Yorktown, NY 10598 • *5,270*
Yorktown, TX 78164 • *2,207*
Yorktown, VA 23690–93 • *270*
Yorktown Heights, NY 10598 • *7,690*
Yorktown Manor, RI 02852 • *2,520*
Yorkville, IL 60560 • *3,925*
Yorkville, NY 13495 • *2,972*
Yorkville, OH 43971 • *1,246*
Yosemite National Park, CA 95389 • *1,073*
Young □, TX • *18,126*
Youngstown, NY 14174 • *2,075*
Youngstown, OH 44501–15 • *95,732*
Youngsville, LA 70592 • *1,195*
Youngsville, PA 16371 • *1,775*
Youngtown, AZ 85363 • *2,542*
Youngwood, PA 15697 • *3,372*
Ypsilanti, MI 48197–98 • *24,846*
Yreka, CA 96097 • *6,948*
Yuba □, CA • *58,228*
Yuba City, CA 95991–92 • *27,437*
Yucaipa, CA 92399 • *20,000*
Yucca Valley, CA 92284–86 • *13,701*
Yukon, OK 73099 • *20,935*
Yulee, FL 32097 • *6,915*
Yuma, AZ 85364–69 • *54,923*
Yuma, CO 80759 • *2,719*
Yuma □, AZ • *106,895*
Yuma □, CO • *8,954*

Z

Zachary, LA 70791 • *9,036*
Zanesville, OH 43701–02 • *26,778*
Zapata, TX 78076 • *7,119*
Zapata □, TX • *9,279*
Zavala □, TX • *12,162*
Zebulon, GA 30295 • *1,035*
Zebulon, NC 27597 • *3,173*
Zeeland, MI 49464 • *5,417*
Zeigler, IL 62999 • *1,746*
Zelienople, PA 16063 • *4,158*
Zenith, WA 98188 • *1,100*
Zephyr Cove, NV 89448 • *1,700*
Zephyrhills, FL 33539–44 • *8,220*
Ziebach □, SD • *2,220*
Zillah, WA 98953 • *1,911*
Zilwaukee, MI 48604 • *1,850*
Zimmerman, MN 55398 • *1,350*
Zion, IL 60099 • *19,775*
Zionsville, IN 46077 • *5,281*
Zolfo Springs, FL 33890 • *1,219*
Zumbrota, MN 55992 • *2,312*
Zuni (Zuni Pueblo), NM 87327 • *5,857*
Zwolle, LA 71486 • *1,779*